BOOKS FOR COLLEGE LIBRARIES

BOOKS
FOR COLLEGE
LIBRARIES

A CORE COLLECTION OF 50,000 TITLES

Third edition

A project of the Association of College and Research Libraries

Volume 6
Index

American Library Association
Chicago and London 1988

Preliminary pages composed by Impressions, Inc.,
in Times Roman on a Penta-driven
Autologic APS-μ5
Phototypesetting system

Text pages composed by Logidec, Inc., in Times Roman on an
APS-5 digital typesetter

Printed on 50 lb. Glatfelter B-16, a pH neutral stock,
and bound in Roxite B-grade cloth by
Edwards Brothers.

The paper used in this publication meets the minimum
requirements of American National Standard for Information
Sciences—Permanence of Paper for Printed Library Materials,
ANSI Z39.48-1984.

Library of Congress Cataloging-in-Publication Data

Books for college libraries.

"A project of the Association of College and Research
Libraries."

Contents: v. 1. Humanities—v. 2. Language
and literature—v. 3. History—[etc.]
1. Libraries, University and college—Book
lists. 2. Bibliography—Best books. I. Association of
College and Research Libraries.
Z1039.C65B67 1988   025.2′1877   88-16714
ISBN 0-8389-3357-2 (v. 1)
ISBN 0-8389-3356-4 (v. 2)
ISBN 0-8389-3355-6 (v. 3)
ISBN 0-8389-3354-8 (v. 4)
ISBN 0-8389-3358-0 (v. 5)
ISBN 0-8389-3359-9 (v. 6)

BOOKS FOR COLLEGE LIBRARIES

Volumes 1–6   Contents

Vol. 1   HUMANITIES

A   General Works
B–BD, BH–BJ   Philosophy
BL–BX   Religion. Mythology
M–MT   Music
N–NX   Fine Arts

Vol. 2   LANGUAGE AND LITERATURE

P   Language and Literature: General
PA   Classical Languages and Literatures
PB–PH   Modern European Languages. Slavic Languages and Literatures
PJ–PL   Oriental Languages and Literatures
PN   Literature: General and Comparative
PQ   Romance Literatures: French, Italian, Spanish, Portuguese
PR   English Literature
PS   American Literature
PT   German, Dutch, and Scandinavian Literatures

Vol. 3   HISTORY

C   Auxiliary Sciences of History
CB   History of Civilization and Culture
CC–CN   Archaeology. Minor Historical Sciences
CR–CT   Heraldry. Genealogy. General Biography
D   History: General. Historiography
DA–DR   Europe
DS   Asia
DT   Africa
DU–DX   Australia. New Zealand. Oceania
E–F   The Americas

Vol. 4   SOCIAL SCIENCES

G–GF   Geography. Oceanography. Human Ecology
GN   Anthropology. Ethnology. Archaeology
GR–GT   Folklore. Customs. Costume
GV   Recreation. Physical Training. Sports. Dance
H–HA   Social Sciences: General. Statistics
HB–HJ   Economics. Population
HM–HV   Sociology. Social History. Social Pathology
HX   Socialism. Communism. Anarchism
J   Political Science
K   Law
L   Education

Vol. 5   PSYCHOLOGY. SCIENCE. TECHNOLOGY. BIBLIOGRAPHY

BF   Psychology
Q–QA   Science. Mathematics. Computer Science
QB–QE   Physical Sciences: Astronomy, Physics, Meteorology, Chemistry, Geology
QH–QR   Natural Sciences: Biology, Botany, Zoology, Anatomy, Physiology, Bacteriology
R   Medicine. Psychiatry. Nursing
S   Agriculture. Conservation
T   Technology. Engineering
TR   Photography
TS–TX   Manufactures. Crafts. Home Economics
U–V   Military Science. Naval Science
Z   Book Industries. Bibliography. Library Science

Vol. 6   INDEXES

Author
Title
Subject

Volume 6   Contents

Author Index

This computer-generated index lists all main entries except title and includes joint authors, editors, translators, etc. named in Roman-numbered tracings at the end of entries. The following Library of Congress MARC fields were selected to compile this index: 100, 110, 111, 700, 710, and 711. In a few cases duplicate index lines may appear for the same name, with or without variations, that the computer read as separate entries. The file has been sorted according to ALA filing rules as much as possible. File order is word by word. Any group of letters separated from another with a space are treated as a word. Acronyms and initials set without spaces or periods between letters are filed as words.

2 serious ladies. 2.11401

A. C. Bhaktivedanta Swami Prabhupāda, 1896-1977. 1.1728
A co-founder. 4.6643
A Lady. 4.5916
A. S. W. Rosenbach Fellowship in Bibliography Fund. 2.3592, 5.8282
Aagaard, Knut, 1939- joint author. 4.351
Aagaard-Mogensen, Lars, 1944-. 1.1353
Aandahl, Fredrick. 4.8973
Aarne, Antti Amatus, 1867-1925. 4.818
Aaron, Daniel, 1912-. 2.10244, 2.10431, 3.6283, 3.6329, 3.6334
Aaron, Henry J. 4.3459, 4.4690, 4.4698, 4.4704, 4.4718, 4.5806, 5.4708
Aaron, Richard Ithamar, 1901-. 1.678
Abadi, Jacob. 3.3744
Abadie, Ann J. 2.12670
Abadie, M. J. 1.1607
Abadinsky, Howard, 1941-. 4.6754
Abate, Frank R. 2.14, 2.3804
Abbondante, Paul J. joint author. 4.2448
Abbot, W. W. (William Wright), 1922-. 3.8256
Abbott, Claude Colleer, 1889-. 2.7827-2.7828
Abbott, David, 1937-. 5.1690, 5.1942
Abbott, Edith, 1876-1957. 4.3274
Abbott, Edwin Abbott, 1838-1926. 5.1638
Abbott, Frank Frost, 1860-1924. 4.8834
Abbott, Grace, 1878-1939. 4.6867
Abbott, Isabella Aiona. joint author. 5.3713
Abbott, Jack Henry, 1944-. 4.6905
Abbott, Nabia, 1897-. 1.2022
Abbott, R. Tucker (Robert Tucker), 1919-. 5.3845-5.3846
Abbott, Richard H. 3.7167
Abbott, Thomas Kingsmill. 1.878
Abbott, Walter M., ed. 1.3123
Abbotts, John. joint author. 5.6609
ABC-Clio Information Services. 4.5566, 5.7846, 5.8386, 5.8392, 5.8406
Abdel-Rahim, Muddathir, 1932-. 4.8814
Abdellah, Faye G. 5.5185
'Abdu'l-Bahá, 1844-1921. 1.2095
Abdullah I, King of Jordan, 1882-1951. 3.4035
Abdullah, Munshi, 1796-1854. 3.4541
Abe, Kōbō, 1924-. 2.2124-2.2126
Abegglen, James C. 4.4176
Abel, Andrew B., 1952-. 4.1450
Abel, Edward W. 5.2780
Abel, Elie. joint author. 3.934
Abel, Elizabeth. 2.2556, 2.5987
Abel, Ernest L., 1943-. 4.6658, 5.234
Abel, Reuben, 1911-. 1.104
Abel, Richard, 1941-. 2.2891
Abel-Smith, Brian. 5.4631
Abel-Vidor, Suzanne. 3.9078
Abelard, Peter, 1079-1142. 1.378, 1.2738
Abell, Aaron Ignatius. 1.2997
Abell, George O. (George Ogden), 1927-1983. 5.650, 5.1717
Abell, Walter. 3.4
Abella, Irving M., 1940-. 3.6417, 3.8796
Abelove, Henry. 3.408
Abelson, Harold. 5.1158
Abelson, Philip Hauge. 4.3676

Abelson, Robert P. 5.450
Abelson, Robert P. joint author. 5.289
Abensour, Emmanuel S., (jt. author) 4.5294
Aberbach, Joel D. 4.8367
Abercrombie, Lascelles, 1881-1938. 2.7782
Abercrombie, M. (Michael), 1912-1979. 5.3181
Abercrombie, Nicholas. 4.4966
Abernethy, Thomas Perkins, 1890-. 3.6915, 3.8135, 3.8183, 3.8343
Abian, Alexander, 1925-. 5.1363
Abler, Ronald. joint author. 4.160
Ablin, Fred, comp. 4.10133
Abraham, Claude. 2.4018
Abraham, Claude Kurt, 1931-. 2.4038, 2.4050
Abraham, Farid F., ed. 5.5771
Abraham, Gerald, 1904-. 1.3464-1.3465, 1.3631, 1.3662, 1.3726-1.3727, 1.3752, 1.3836, 1.3880, 1.3883, 1.3940, 1.3959, 1.3974, 1.3982
Abraham, Gerald Ernest Heal, 1904- ed. 1.3941
Abraham, Henry Julian, 1921-. 4.9375, 4.9662, 4.9787
Abraham, Hilda C. 5.4915
Abraham, Horst, 1941-. 4.996
Abraham, Karl, 1877-1925. 5.126, 5.192, 5.4915
Abraham Lincoln Association (Springfield, Ill.) 3.7299
Abraham, Max, 1875-1922. 5.2366
Abraham, Ralph. 5.1653
Abraham, Suzanne. 5.4937
Abrahamian, Ervand, 1940-. 3.4085
Abrahams, Cecil Anthony. 2.10086
Abrahams, Lionel. 2.10041
Abrahams, Peter, 1919-. 2.10057-2.10058, 3.5448
Abrahams, Roger D. 2.1047, 4.767, 4.781, 5.8195
Abrahams, William Miller, 1919- joint author. 2.9201-2.9202
Abrahamsen, Adele A. 5.8330
Abrahamsson, Bernhard J. 4.3957
Abramov, Fyodor. 2.1535
Abramov, S. Zalman, 1908-. 1.1933
Abramowitz, Alan. 4.7940
Abramowitz, Milton, 1915-1958. ed. 5.1123
Abrams, Charles, 1902-1970. 4.6199
Abrams, David M. 5.545
Abrams, Le Roy, 1874-1956. 5.3679
Abrams, M. H. (Meyer Howard), 1912-. 2.2356, 2.2614, 2.2668, 2.5815, 2.6072, 2.8318
Abrams, Natalie. 5.4565
Abramsky, Chimen, 1916-. 3.3985
Abramson, Doris E. 2.10518
Abramson, Joan. 4.9565
Abramson, Norman. 5.1021
Abramson, Victor, 1906- joint author. 4.1967
Abro, A. d'. 5.1893, 5.2043
Absar, Ilyas, joint author. 5.2824
Abse, Dannie. 2.8370
Abse, Joan, 1926-. 2.8032
Abu Izzeddin, Nejla M. 3.3794
Abu-Lughod, Janet. 4.6338
Abu-Lughod, Janet L. 3.5181
Abubaker, Sa'ad, 1939-. 3.5360
Abun-Nasr, Jamil M. 3.5193
Abzug, Robert H. 3.7268
Academy of American Poets. 2.10767

Academy of Motion Picture Arts and Sciences. 2.3074
Achebe, Chinua. 2.10037, 2.10101-2.10106
Achenbaum, W. Andrew. 4.5810, 5.8360
Acheson, Dean, 1893-1971. 3.7554, 3.7622, 4.8198
Achilles Tatius. 2.331
Achinstein, Peter. 1.1236, 5.861
Achinstein, Peter. ed. 1.513
Achtemeier, Paul J. 1.2506, 1.2901
Achtert, Walter S. 2.1041, 2.2518
Acinapuro, Philip J. 4.10464
Acker, William Reynolds Beal, 1907- ed. and tr. 1.6320
Ackerknecht, Erwin Heinz, 1906-. 5.4497-5.4498
Ackerman, Amy S. 4.10266
Ackerman, Bruce A. 4.7622
Ackerman, Edward Augustus, 1911-. 4.11
Ackerman, Eugene, 1920-. 5.3492
Ackerman, Evelyn Bernette. 3.2234
Ackerman, James S. 1.5123, 1.5441
Ackerman, John. 2.9414
Ackerman, Kenneth B. 4.4336
Ackerman, Phyllis, 1893-. 1.5045, 1.6588
Ackerman, Robert William, 1910-. 2.5599
Ackermann, Robert John, 1933-. 5.862
Ackermann, Wilhelm, 1896-. 1.1211
Ackery, Phillip Ronald. 5.3879
Ackley, Clifford S. 1.6464
Ackoff, Russell L. 5.863
Ackrill, J. L. 1.295
Ackroyd, Peter R. ed. 1.2509
Acomb, Frances Dorothy, 1907-. 3.2069
Acree, William E. (William Eugene) 5.2910
Acri, Michael James, 1932- joint author. 5.8123
Acton, John Emerich Edward Dalberg Acton, baron. 3.610, 4.7623
Actors' Equity Association. 2.3266
Adair, Douglass. 4.7828
Adair, John Eric, 1934-. 3.7944
Adalard, Saint, d. 826. 1.3237
Adam, Antoine. 2.3846, 2.3850, 2.3901, 2.4319
Adam, James, d. 1794. 1.5379, 2.535
Adam, Jan, 1920-. 4.3230
Adam, Karl, 1876-. 1.3198
Adam, Robert, 1728-1792. 1.5379
Adamany, David W. 4.8122-4.8123
Adamec, Ludwig W. 3.4114
Adami, Giuseppe, 1878-1946. ed. 1.3949
Adamic, Louis, 1899-1951. 4.3342
Adamov, Arthur. 2.4352
Adams, A. E. 5.3050
Adams, Abigail, 1744-1818. 3.7044, 3.7051-3.7052
Adams, Alexander B. 3.5839
Adams, Annie Elizabeth, d. 1926, tr. 3.2337
Adams, Ansel, 1902-. 5.6933, 5.6944, 5.6975, 5.6981
Adams, Bert N. 4.5607
Adams, Brooks, 1848-1927. 3.504
Adams, Bruce, 1947-. 4.7984
Adams, Carolyn Teich. 4.3246, 4.5184
Adams, Charles F., 1945- joint author. 4.4663
Adams, Charles Francis, 1807-1886. 3.7045, 3.7423

Adams, Charles J. 1.1525
Adams, Charles J. ed. 5.8449
Adams, David Michael. 5.2635, 5.2864
Adams, Ephraim Douglass, 1865-1930. 3.6272,
  3.7352
Adams family. 3.7050
Adams, Frank D. (Frank Dawson), 1859-1942.
  5.2947
Adams, Gary L. 4.10925
Adams, George Plimpton, 1882-1961. ed. 1.569
Adams, George Rollie. 4.5167
Adams, Hazard, 1926-. 1.1351, 2.7422, 2.8506
Adams, Henry, 1838-1918. 2.10887-2.10889,
  3.453, 3.1951, 3.6234-3.6236, 3.6335, 3.6978
Adams, Henry E., 1931- joint author. 5.4953
Adams, Henry Hitch, 1917-. 3.543
Adams, Herbert Baxter, 1850-1901. 3.6246
Adams, J. Stacy. joint author. 4.4917
Adams, James Truslow, 1878-1949.
  3.6068-3.6069, 3.6198, 3.6332, 3.6876
Adams, Jane. 4.4267
Adams, John, 1735-1826. 3.6966, 3.7043-3.7044,
  3.7051, 4.8795
Adams, John Clarke, 1910-. 4.8623
Adams, John Cranford, 1903-. 2.6706, 3.9152
Adams, John P. (John Phillip), 1932-. 3.7966
Adams, John Quincy, 1767-1848. 3.7045,
  3.7068, 3.7120-3.7121
Adams, John R., 1900-. 2.11232
Adams, John S., 1938-. 4.160, 4.6207, 4.6231
Adams, Joseph Quincy, 1881-1946. 2.3286,
  2.3296, 2.6201
Adams, Laura. 2.12103
Adams, Léonie, 1899-. 2.11291
Adams, M. J. 5.5938
Adams, Nina S. ed. 3.4456
Adams, Oscar Sherman, 1874-   . 4.212
Adams, P. F. (Peter F.) 5.6510
Adams, Paul. 5.4679
Adams, Percy G. 2.3451
Adams, Peter, 1947-. 3.5598
Adams, R. L. P. (Roger Lionel Poulter) 5.4417
Adams, Richard, 1920-. 2.9611
Adams, Richard Newbold, 1924-. 3.9028,
  4.5259
Adams, Richard Perrill, 1917-. 2.11684
Adams, Robert M., 1926-. 3.123
Adams, Robert Martin, 1915-. 2.4104, 2.4305,
  2.6588, 2.7937, 2.8884, 2.8902, 3.5, 4.7394
Adams, Robert McCormick, 1926-. 3.3766,
  4.598
Adams, Roger, 1889-1971. 5.2717, 5.2727,
  5.2738
Adams, Ruth, 1923-. 4.1652
Adams, Sam, 1916-. 5.1261
Adams, Sherman, 1899-1986. 3.7816
Adams-Smith, William N., 1929- joint author.
  5.4500
Adams, Stephen D. 2.12361
Adams, Walter, 1922 Aug. 27-. 4.1927, 4.2017
Adams, William Yewdale, 1927-. 3.5185, 3.5837
Adamson, Alan H. 4.2179
Adamson, Arthur W. 5.2896
Adamson, Madeleine, 1951-. 4.5230
Adas, Michael, 1943-. 4.2453
Adburgham, Alison. 2.3691
Adby, P. R. 5.1547, 5.6268
Adcock, Fleur. 2.10203
Adcock, Frank Ezra, Sir, 1886-1968. 3.2554
Addams, Jane. 4.5168, 4.6627
Addington, Larry H. 5.7317
Addis, Laird. 1.115
Addison, James Thayer, 1887-. 1.3314
Addison, John T. 4.3327, 4.3357
Addison, Joseph, 1672-1719. 2.6271-2.6272,
  2.6274-2.6275, 2.6887-2.6888, 3.1538
Addison, Max R. 4.6614
Addo, N. O. ed. 4.1712
Ade, George, 1866-1944. 2.10891-2.10893
Adedeji, Adebayo. 4.2606
Adeleye, R. A. 3.5369
Adelman, Alan, 1949-. 3.9149
Adelman, Bob. 4.5152
Adelman, Irma. 4.2563, 4.2755
Adelman, Irving. 5.7808, 5.8124
Adelman, Morris Albert. 4.3693, 4.3753,
  4.3756, 5.6145
Adelson, Joseph. 4.10090, 5.621

Aden, LeRoy. 1.1563
Adenauer, Konrad, 1876-1967. 3.2471
Ades, Dawn. 1.4895, 1.5857, 1.6289
Adey, Robert C.S. 2.3469
Adgar, Jean Claude. 4.8813
Adhémar, Jean. 1.6085, 1.6499, 1.6502
Adie, W. A. C. 3.4667
Adiyodi, K. G. 5.3875
Adjaye, Joseph K., 1940-. 3.5332
Adkins, A. W. H. (Arthur W. H.)
  1.1418-1.1419
Adkins, Bernard. 5.6316
Adkins, C. J. (Clement John) 5.2240
Adkins, Nelson Frederick, 1897-. 2.10871
Adlai Stevenson Institute of International
  Affairs. 3.7851
Adler, Alfred, 1870-1937. 5.127-5.128
Adler, Cyrus, 1863-1940. ed. 3.3810, 3.6561
Adler, Helmut E. tr. 5.242
Adler, Kurt Herbert, 1905-. 1.4483
Adler, Margot. 5.677
Adler, Mortimer Jerome, 1902-. 1.139, 1.574,
  2.2447, 2.3805, 4.6680, 4.10002, 4.10815,
  4.10829
Adler, Norman, 1942-. 4.8195
Adler, Richard. 4.5735
Adler, Ronald. 5.2098
Adler, Samuel, 1928-. 1.4487
Adler, Thomas P. 2.11316
Adlington, William, fl. 1566. tr. 2.649
Adloff, Richard. 4.8808
Adloff, Richard. 3.5375, 3.5386-3.5387, 3.5556
Adoff, Arnold. comp. 2.10747
Adorno, Gretel. 1.966
Adorno, Theodor W., 1903-1969. 1.966-1.968,
  1.4362, 4.5022
Adrian, Arthur A., 1906-. 2.7670
Adrian, Charles R. 4.8243
Adrian, James J. 5.6087
Adūnīs, 1930-. 2.1840
Advanced Seminar on Lower Central American
  Archaeology (1980: School of American
  Research) 3.9030
Advanced Transit Association (Washington,
  D.C.) 5.5935
Adzigian, Denise Allard. 4.7898
Aebi, Hugo. 5.2657
AEI National Energy Project. 4.3766, 4.3790
Aerospace Corporation. 5.5936
Aers, David. 2.5612
Aeschylus. 2.332, 2.406-2.407, 2.410,
  2.413-2.414
Afanas'ev, A. N. (Aleksandr Nikolaevich),
  1826-1871. 2.1292
Affleck, W. S. 5.6222
Affron, Charles. 2.2945, 2.4242
Afgan, Naim. 5.6155
Afgan, Naim. ed. 5.2261
Afigbo, A. E. (Adiele Eberechukwu) 3.5364
Afnan, Soheil Muhsin. 1.371
African Bibliographic Center. 3.8970
African Studies Association. 3.5062
Aft, Lawrence S. 5.5619
Aga Rossi, Elena. joint author. 3.921
Agar, Herbert, 1897-. 3.7555
Agar, Michael. 4.496
Agarwal, B. K. (Bipin Kumar), 1931-. 5.2325
Agate, Edward. tr. 1.4492
Agate, James, 1877-1947. 2.3314, 2.5845
Agee, James. 2.2875, 2.11292-2.11296, 3.8278
Agee, Philip. 4.7901
Agee, William C. 1.5921
Agehananda Bharati, Swami, 1923-. 1.1699,
  1.1780
Ageno, Franca, ed. 2.4977
Ager, D. V. (Derek Victor) 5.3003, 5.3129
Agerschou, Hans. 5.5972
Aggarwal, Narindar K. 5.8340
Aggarwal, Raj. 4.2640
Aggeler, Geoffrey, 1939-. 2.9648
Agmon, Tamir. 4.4491
Agnar Thortharson, 1917-. 2.13995
Agnew, Allen Francis, 1918-. 5.6727
Agnew, Brad, 1939-. 3.5741
Agnew, John A. 4.6193
Agnon, Shmuel Yosef, 1888-1970. 2.1779-2.1781
Agonito, Rosemary. 4.5917
Agree, George E., joint author. 4.8123

Agresti, Alan. 5.1405
Agresto, John. 4.9744
Agricola, Georg, 1494-1555. 5.6760
Agulhon, Maurice. 3.2150
Aharoni, Miriam. 3.3828
Aharoni, Yohanan, 1919-1976. 1.2549, 3.3828,
  4.179
Ahearn, Barry. 2.12833
Ahern, Emily M. 4.642, 4.6139
Ahl, Frederick M. 2.736
Ahlbrandt, Roger S. 4.5216
Ahlfors, Lars Valerian, 1907-. 5.1483, 5.1493
Ahlmann, Hans Wilhelmsson, 1889-. 4.316
Ahlstrom, Sydney E. 1.2370
Ahlstrom, Sydney E. comp. 1.2765
Ahmad, Eqbal. 3.7851
Ahmad, Feroz. 3.3589, 3.3592
Ahmad, Iftikhar. 4.6170
Ahmad, Imtiaz, 1940-. 1.2004
Ahmad, Jamil-ud-Din. comp. 3.4282
Ahmad, Nafis, 1911-. 4.64, 4.2520
Ahmed, Bashiruddin. joint author. 4.8716
Ahmed, H. 5.6537
Ahmed, Manzoor, 1940- joint author. 4.10970
Ahmed, Paul I. 5.4808
Ahmed-ud-Din, Feroz. 2.10120
Ahmed, Viqar. 4.2515
Åhnebrink, Lars. 2.10533
Ahnlund, Nils, 1889-1957. 3.3391
Aho, Alfred V. 5.1159, 5.1226, 5.1240
Ahrens, L. H. (Louis Herman), 1918-. 5.3105
Ahuja, Vijay. 5.6408
Aiba, Shuichi, 1923-. 5.6867
Aichinger, Ilse. 2.13671-2.13672
Aichinger, Peter, 1933-. 2.9914
Aichiniger, Ilse, 1921-. 2.13670
AIDS Project Los Angeles. 5.4983
Aigner, Martin, 1942-. 5.1273
Aijaz Ahmad, ed. 2.1899
Aiken, Conrad, 1889-1973. 2.5532,
  2.11299-2.11302
Aiken, Henry David, 1912-. 4.10072, 4.10160
Aiken, Wilford Merton, 1882-. 4.10607
Aikens, C. Melvin. 3.5769, 4.742
Aikin, Judith Popovich, 1946-. 2.13491
Ainslie, Tom. 4.1065
Ainsworth, Frank. 4.6549
Ainsworth, G. C. (Geoffrey Clough), 1905-.
  5.5395
Ainsworth, William Harrison, 1805-1882.
  2.7345
Ainsztein, Reuben. 3.1082
Aird, John Shields, 1919-. 4.1704
Aisiku, J. U. 4.10148
Aït Sabbah, Fatna. 4.5509
Aitchison, Leslie. 5.6756
Aitken, George Atherton, 1860-1917. 2.7274
Aitken, Hugh G. J. 4.4625
Aitken, Hugh G. J. 4.2115, 4.4249,
  5.6422-5.6423
Aitken, M. J. (Martin Jim) 3.226
Aitken, William Russell. 2.8780, 5.7997
Aïtmatov, Chingiz. 2.1619-2.1620
Ajami, Fouad. 3.3737, 4.7624
Ajayi, J. F. Ade. 3.5323, 4.189
Ajdukiewicz, Kazimierz. 1.1215
Akademie der Wissenschaften der DDR.
  Zentralinstitut für Literaturgeschichte. 5.8010
Akademischer Verein Hütte, Berlin. 5.6112
Akao, Nobutoshi. 4.2546
Ake, Claude. 2.2603
Akehurst, Michael Barton. 4.9004
Akenside, Mark, 1721-1770. 2.6890
Akenson, Donald H. 3.8830, 4.10123
Akeroyd, Joanne V. 5.8479
Akers, Charles W. 3.7053
Akers, Ronald L. 4.5053
Akert, Konrad. ed. 5.4346
Akhiezer, A. I. (Aleksandr Il'ich), 1911-.
  5.1979, 5.2373
Akhmatova, Anna Andreevna, 1889-1966.
  2.1536-2.1537
Akimushkin, O. F. 1.6420
Akin, John S. 5.4657
Akiner, Shirin. 3.3027
Akinsanya, Adeoye A. 4.3065
Akita, George. 4.8750
Akiyama, Terukazu, 1918-. 1.5066, 1.6333

Akrigg, G. P. V. 3.1463-3.1464
Aksakov, S. T. (Sergeĭ Timofeevich), 1791-1859. 3.3031
Aksenov, Vasiliĭ Pavlovich, 1932-. 2.1301, 2.1621-2.1623
Akurgal, Ekrem. 1.4708
Akutagawa, Ryūnosuke, 1892-1927. 2.2035, 2.2071
Āl Ahmad, Jalāl. 2.1976
al-Ashʿarī, ʿAlī ibn Ismāʿīl, 873?-935? 1.2044
al-Badrī, Hasan. 3.3937
Al-Faruqi, Isma'il R., 1921-. 1.1588
al-Ghazzali, 1058-1111. 1.373
Al-Hakim, Tawfiq. 2.1846
Al-Khatib al-Tibrizi, Muhammad ibn Abd Allah, fl. 1337. 1.2037
al-Lārī, ʿAbd al-Ghafūr, d. 1506. 1.2061
Al-Layla, Muhammad Anis H. 5.6013
al-Majdūb, Tāhā. 3.3937
Al-Tusi, Nasir al-Din Muhammad ibn Muhammad, 1201-1274. 1.1483
Alabama Symposium on English and American Literature. (6th: 1979: University of Alabama) 4.10753
Alabama Symposium on English and American Literature. (8th: 1981: University of Alabama) 2.10969
Alabama Writers' Project. 3.8282
Alabaster, John S. 5.3909
Alain-Fournier, 1886-1914. 2.4530-2.4531
Alajalov, Constantin, 1900- illus. 2.12486
Alanbrooke, Alan Francis Brooke, Viscount, 1883-. 3.899, 3.975
Aland, Kurt. 1.2280
Alarcón, Pedro Antonio de, 1833-1891. 2.5212
Alas, Leopoldo, 1852-1901. 2.5213
Alavi, Hamza, 1921-. 4.5482
Alba, Víctor. 4.8682
Albanese, Catherine L. 3.6908
Albany Institute of History and Art. 1.5325
Albee, Edward, 1928-. 2.12837-2.12847
Albérès, René-Marill, 1920-. 2.3867
Alberoni, Francesco. 5.440
Albers, Anni. 5.7080
Albers, Josef. 1.4878, 1.5805
Albers, Patricia. 3.5740
Albert, Adrien. 5.2915
Albert, Bill. 4.4180
Albert, Kenneth J., 1943-. 4.2639
Albert. Linette, joint author. 3.4110
Albert, Martin L., 1939-. 5.4795
Albert, Phyllis Cohen. 3.3959
Albert, Walter. 5.8171
Albert, Walter. ed. 2.4461
Alberti, Leon Battista, 1404-1472. 1.5098, 1.5466, 1.6338
Alberti, Rafael, 1902-. 2.5230
Albertini, Luigi, 1871-1941. 3.770
Albertini, Rudolf von. 3.3635, 4.8907
Alberts, Bruce. 5.3601
Alberts, Robert C. 1.5982
Albertson, F. W. (Frederick William) joint author. 5.3786
Alberty, Robert A. 5.2803
Albinski, Henry Stephen. 3.6157
Albion, Mark S., 1951-. 4.4425, 4.4435
Albion, Robert Greenhalgh, 1896-. 3.7641, 4.3952, 4.4218, 5.7496, 5.8301
Alborg, Juan Luis. 2.5084, 2.5133
Albrecht-Carrié, René, 1904-. 3.678, 3.709, 3.859, 3.2856
Albrecht, Robert C. 1.3418
Albright, David E. 3.5086, 4.7027
Albright, John Rupp, 1937- joint author. 5.2076
Albright, William Foxwell, 1891-1971. 1.1595, 1.2504
Albritton, Claude C., 1913-. 5.2948, 5.2977, 5.3082
Alcaeus. 2.315
Alchian, Armen Albert, 1914-. 5.1025
Alcina Franch, José. 3.5692
Alcock, Antony Evelyn. 4.3506, 4.7487
Alcock, John, 1942-. 5.3861, 5.4052
Alcock, Leslie. 3.1313
Alcock, R. M. joint author. 5.2893
Alcock, Rutherford, Sir, 1809-1897. 3.4879
Alcorn, John, 1923-. 2.5974

Alcott, Louisa May, 1832-1888. 2.10897-2.10901
Alden, John Doughty, 1921-. 5.7451
Alden, John Richard, 1908-. 3.6890, 3.6895, 3.8134, 3.8136-3.8137
Alderfer, E. Gordon (Everett Gordon), 1915- ed. 1.3347
Alderman, Geoffrey. 3.3946, 4.8506
Alderman, Richard B. 4.943
Alderson, Wroe. 4.4275
Aldington, Richard, 1892-1962. 2.4057, 2.7979, 2.8268, 2.8373-2.8376
Aldiss, Brian Wilson, 1925-. 1.5830, 2.5977, 2.9612-2.9613
Aldous, Joan. 4.5602
Aldred, Cyril. 1.6665
Aldrich Chemical Company. 5.2679, 5.2683
Aldrich, Keith. 2.420
Aldridge, Alfred Owen, 1915-. 1.3338, 3.6988
Aldridge, John W. 2.10611
Aldridge, John W. 2.3425, 2.10397
Alegría, Ciro, 1909-1967. 2.5423-2.5424
Alegría, Fernando, 1918-. 2.5311
Aleixandre, Vicente, 1898-. 2.5228-2.5229
Aleksander, Igor. 5.1001
Alekseeva, Liudmila, 1927-. 4.5376
Alembert, Jean Le Rond d', 1717-1783. 2.3104
Alex, William, fl. 1963-. 1.5451
Alexander, Alan, 1943-. 4.8875
Alexander, Alex E. 4.798
Alexander, Charles C. 3.7817
Alexander, Christopher. 1.5462
Alexander, Claudia B. 2.3734
Alexander, Edgar. 3.2507
Alexander, Franz, 1891-. 5.4802
Alexander, Harold Rupert Leofric George Alexander, 1st Earl, 1891-1969. 3.798
Alexander, Herbert E. 4.8124-4.8127
Alexander, J. J. G. (Jonathan James Graham) 1.6406
Alexander, Jeffrey C. 4.4780
Alexander, John J. 5.2703, 5.2846
Alexander, John T. 3.3089
Alexander, John W. (John Wesley), 1918-. 4.4117
Alexander, Kern. 4.9580, 4.10658
Alexander, Lewis M. 4.9309, 4.9311
Alexander, Lloyd. tr. 2.4525
Alexander, M. David. 4.9580
Alexander, Michael J. 2.12337
Alexander, Michael Van Cleave, 1937-. 3.1397
Alexander, R. McNeill. 5.3890, 5.3914, 5.4261, 5.4267
Alexander, Robert Jackson, 1918-. 3.8961, 3.9184, 3.9266, 3.9273, 3.9307, 4.3398, 4.8301
Alexander, Samuel, 1859-1938. 1.1339
Alexander, Shana. 4.9506
Alexander, Sidney, 1912-. 1.6280, 3.2853
Alexander, Stella. 1.2460
Alexander, Thomas Benjamin, 1918-. 3.8344, 4.8047
Alexander, Wilfrid Backhouse, 1885-. 5.3936
Alexander, William, 1938-. 2.2982
Alexander, William Marvin, 1912-. 4.10447, 4.10499, 4.10503
Alexander-Williams, John. 3.8224
Alexandersson, Gunnar. 4.1764, 4.1928, 4.3954
Alexandridis, Nikitas A., 1943-. 5.1141
Alexeieff, Alexandre, 1901-. 2.1292
Alexopoulos, Constantine John, 1907-. 5.3720, 5.3728, 5.3730
Alfieri, Vittorio, 1749-1803. 2.4985-2.4986
Alfin-Slater, Roslyn, 1916-. 5.4233
Alföldi, Andreas, 1895-1981. 3.2759, 3.2816
Alfonso, Robert J., 1928-. 4.10633
Alfred C. Kinsey Institute for Sex Research. 4.5526
Algar, Hamid. 1.2082, 2.1841, 3.4082, 3.4087
Algardi, Alessandro, 1598-1654. 1.5725
Algarin, Joanne P. 5.8067
Algie, Jimmy. 4.6532
Algren, Nelson, 1909-. 2.11306-2.11308
Ali, Ahmed, 1908-. 2.1905-2.1906
Ali, M. A. (Mohamed Ather), 1932-. 5.4375
Ali, Sheikh Rustum. 4.7792
Ali, Syed Ameer, 1849-1928. 1.2043
Aliber, Robert Z. 4.4561
Aliber, Robert Z. joint author. 4.4507

Alimba, Nan. joint author. 4.10889
Alinder, James. 3.5846
Alinsky, Saul David, 1909-1972. 4.5179
Alisjahbana, S. Takdir (Sutan Takdir), 1908-. 3.4556
Alisky, Marvin. 2.69
Alison, Archibald, 1757-1839. 1.4640
Alissi, Albert S. 4.6504
Alitto, Guy. 1.1139
Aljian, George W. 4.4324
Alkire, Leland G. 5.8317
Alkon, Paul K. (Paul Kent) 2.6982
Alker, Hayward R. 4.9243
Allaby, Michael. 5.3185
Allain, Marie-Françoise. 2.8765
Allan, Frank D. 5.4163
Allan, John, 1884-1955. 3.4220
Allan, Mea. 5.3194
Alland, Alexander, 1931-. 3.5384, 4.443, 4.477
Allard, Dean C., 1933- joint author. 3.4507
Allardice, Corbin. 4.3812
Allardt, Erik. 4.8671
Allchin, Bridget. 3.4188-3.4189
Allchin, Frank Raymond, 1923-. 3.4188-3.4189
Alldritt, Keith. 2.9189
Allee, Warder Clyde, 1885- ed. and tr. 5.3814
Allemand, Maurice, 1872- ed. 2.3930-2.3931, 2.4074
Allemann, Beda. 2.13724
Allen, Anne. 4.967
Allen, B. L. 5.4114
Allen, C. G. (Charles Geoffry) 2.210
Allen, C. W. (Clabon Walter) 5.1768
Allen, Charles, 1940-. 3.4199
Allen, Charles Albert, 1913-. 2.3580
Allen, Charles E. joint author. 4.9763
Allen, Christopher. 4.5467
Allen, Daniel. 1.3616
Allen, Diogenes. ed. 1.865
Allen, Don Cameron, 1904-. 2.2743, 2.5788
Allen, Donald Merriam, 1912-. 2.2729, 2.10778, 2.11575, 2.12263
Allen, Durward Leon, 1910-. 5.5496
Allen, Edgar, 1892-1943, ed. 5.4258
Allen, Ethan, 1738-1789. 1.1889
Allen, Everett S. 5.5487
Allen, Frederick Lewis, 1890-1954. 3.6070, 3.7506-3.7507
Allen, G. C. (George Cyril), 1900-. 4.2459
Allen, G. Freeman (Geoffrey Freeman) 5.6070
Allen, Gardner Weld, 1856-1944. 3.6952
Allen, Garland E. 5.3296
Allen, Gay Wilson, 1903-. 1.600, 2.10729, 2.11024, 2.11272-2.11273
Allen, Gerald. joint author. 1.5492
Allen, Harold, 1912-. 1.5517
Allen, Harold Byron, 1902-. 2.2, 2.206
Allen, Irving L., 1931-. 2.1145
Allen, J. W. (John William), 1865-1944. 4.7273
Allen, James. 5.1007
Allen, James Lane, 1849-1925. 2.10905
Allen, John Jay, 1932-. 1.5552
Allen, John Logan, 1941-. 3.8481
Allen, John M. (John Morgan), 1924- ed. 5.3585
Allen, John Scott, 1925- joint author. 5.6215
Allen, Joseph Henry, 1820-1898. 2.253
Allen, Joseph P. 5.6710
Allen Memorial Art Museum. 1.6483, 1.6488
Allen, Michael J. B. 3.5967
Allen, Michael J. B. comp. 2.701
Allen, Nick, 1950-. 4.2964
Allen, P. E. (Phillip E.) 5.6477
Allen, Pamela P., joint author. 4.5122
Allen, Paula Gunn. 2.10298
Allen, Percy Stafford, 1869-1933. 3.167
Allen, Polly Reynolds. 4.4562-4.4563
Allen, Prudence. 4.5844
Allen, R. G. D. (Roy George Douglas). 4.1288
Allen, Reginald E., 1931-. 1.244, 1.249
Allen, Richard, 1903-. 3.3859
Allen, Richard C. 5.3007
Allen, Richard F. 2.13984
Allen, Robert H., joint author. 4.987
Allen, Robert L., 1942-. 4.5122
Allen, Robert S. 5.7831
Allen, Roy F., 1937-. 2.13488
Allen, Roy George Douglas. 4.1289

Allen, Thomas B. 5.3952
Allen, Thomas William, 1862-, ed. 2.483
Allen, Vernon L., 1933-. 4.1857, 4.10371
Allen, W. E. D. (William Edward David), 1901-. 3.3301
Allen, W. Sidney (William Sidney), 1918-. 2.236
Allen, Walter Ernest, 1911-. 2.2517, 2.5940
Allen, Walter Recharde. 3.6748
Allen, Warren Dwight, 1885-. 1.4366
Allen, William Francis, 1830-1889, comp. 1.3438
Allen, William Richard, 1924- ed. 4.1270, 4.4103
Allen, William Sheridan. 3.2409, 3.2433
Aller, Lawrence H. (Lawrence Hugh), 1913- ed. 5.1773
Alles, Alfred. 5.5656
Alley, Rewi, 1897-. 1.6621
Alley, Robert S., 1932-. 2.2854
Alley, Ronald. 1.6022
Allgeier, Elizabeth R. 4.5829
Allibone, Samuel Austin, 1816-1889. 5.7925
Allin, Craig W. (Craig Willard) 5.3225
Allin, Janet. 5.7579
Allinger, Norman L. ed. 5.2875
Allingham, Margery, 1904-1966. 2.8378
Allinson, Francis Greeleaf, 1856-. 2.520
Allione, Tsultrim, 1947-. 1.2163
Allis, Jeannette B. 5.7900
Allison, Alexander W. (Alexander Ward) 2.6095
Allison, Franklin Elmer, 1892-1972. 5.5280
Allison, Graham T. 3.6480, 5.7236
Allison, Harrison C. 4.6808
Allison, Joel. 5.4844
Allison, Roy. 3.3293
Allison, Susan, 1845-1937. 3.8866
Allmand, C. T. 3.1379
Allmen, Jean-Jacques von, 1917-. 1.2980
Allodi, Mary. 1.6448
Allott, Kenneth. 2.8769
Allott, Kenneth. ed. 2.7059, 2.7346
Allott, Miriam Farris. joint author. 2.8769
Allott, Miriam Farris. comp. 2.7449
Allott, Miriam Farris. ed. 2.3408
Alloway, Lawrence, 1926-. 1.4867
Allport, Floyd Henry, 1890-. 5.256
Allport, Gordon W. (Gordon Willard), 1897-1967. 1.1561, 5.17, 5.117, 5.444, 5.502-5.505, 5.513, 5.6431
Allston, Washington, 1779-1843. 1.5916
Allswang, John M. 4.8838
Allworth, Edward. ed. 3.3321
Allworth, Edward. 3.3025, 3.3321-3.3322
Alm, Alvin L. 4.3748
Almansi, Guido, 1931-. 2.5040
Almond, Brenda. 4.10261
Almond, Gabriel Abraham, 1911-. 3.7556, 4.7235
Almroth, Bo O. joint author. 5.5862
Alnasrawi, Abbas. 4.3757
Alonso, Alicia. 4.1162
Alonso, Dámaso, 1898-. 2.5093, 2.5097, 2.5115, 2.5119
Alonso, Marcelo. 4.3810
Alper, Joel. 5.6396
Alpern, Hymen, 1895-1967. comp. 2.5148
Alperovitz, Gar. 3.7790, 4.2008
Alpers, Antony, 1919-. 2.9083-2.9084
Alpers, Edward A. 4.4245
Alpers, Paul J. 2.5790, 2,6526
Alpers, Svetlana. 1.6237
Alpert, Harry, 1912-. 4.4758
Alpert, Hollis. 2.3233
Alpher, Joseph. 3.3852
Alphonso-Karkala, John B., 1923- comp. 2.1928
Alred, Gerald J. 5.5504
Alschuler, Alfred S., 1939-. 4.10692
Alsop lectures, 1938. 1.3481
Alspaugh, William J. 5.8048
Alston, Philip. 4.9387
Alston, R. C. 2.934
Alt, Arthur Tilo, 1931-. 2.13661
Alt, James E. 4.1286, 4.7773, 4.8420
Altbach, Edith Hoshino. 4.6124
Altbach, Philip G. 4.9964, 4.10887, 5.7582, 5.8157
Altemeyer, Bob, 1940-. 4.5020

Alter, Dinsmore, 1888-1968. 5.1711
Alter, Robert. 1.2568, 1.2605, 2.1786, 2.3416, 2.4308
Alter, Steven. 4.2636
Alterman, Jack. joint author. 4.3705
Altheim, Franz, 1898-. 1.1658
Altholz, Josef Lewis, 1933-. 1.6715
Altick, Richard Daniel, 1915-. 2.5489-2.5490, 2.7575, 3.322, 3.1588, 5.5654, 5.7686, 5.7928
Altieri, Charles, 1942-. 2.10506-2.10507
Altizer, Thomas J. J. 1.2801-1.2802
Altman, Dennis. 4.5534
Altman, Edward I., 1941-. 4.4447
Altman, Irwin. 5.316
Altman, Janet Gurkin, 1945-. 2.3477
Altman, Philip L. 5.3595
Altman, Philip L. ed. 5.3303, 5.4227
Altman, Stuart H. 5.4621
Altmann, Alexander, 1906-. 1.376, 1.876
Altmeyer, Arthur Joseph, 1891-. 4.3457
Alton, Thad P. (Thad Paul) 4.2403
Altshuler, Alan A., 1936-. 4.3817, 4.3915
Altura, Burton M. 5.4228
Aluko, Olajide. 3.5098
Alvarado, Pedro de, 1485?-1541. 3.9054
Alvarez, A. (Alfred), 1929-. 2.6184
Alvarez-Péreyre, Jacques. 2.10048
Alvarez, Rodolfo, 1936-. 4.5182
Alvin, Juliette. 1.4408
Alvord, Clarence Walworth, 1868-1928. 3.8297, 3.8407
Alwitt, Linda F. 4.4431
Amado, Jorge, 1912-. 2.5468-2.5469
Amadou-Koumba. 4.811
Amann, Ronald, 1943-. 4.2408, 5.5543
Amato, Joseph Anthony. 1.1500
Amatruda, Catherine (Strunk) 1903- joint author. 5.601
Ambert, Alba N., 1946-. 4.10890
Ambler, Charles Henry, 1876-1957. 4.3968
Ambler, Eric, 1909-. 2.8379-2.8381
Ambler, John S. (John Steward) 4.7052
Ambrose, Alice, 1906-. 1.109, 1.753, 1.1065, 1.1079
Ambrose, Gordon. 5.4899
Ambrose, James E. 5.5878, 5.5886
Ambrose, Stephen E. 3.7833-3.7834, 5.7241
Ameri, Houshang, 1935-. 4.9262
American Abstract Artists. 1.4802
American Academic Association for Peace in the Middle East. 4.5401
American Academy of Arts and Sciences. 1.2409, 4.1652, 4.2098, 4.2106
American Academy of Arts and Sciences, Boston. Commission on the Year 2000. 3.6071
American Academy of Arts and Sciences, Boston. Midwest Center. 4.2883
American Academy of Orthopaedic Surgeons. 5.5025
American Anthropological Association. 3.217, 3.4390, 4.509, 4.5254
American Antiquarian Society. 3.6192, 5.7759
American Artist Group, New York. 1.5931
American Assembly. 4.1687, 4.3578, 4.3892, 4.7977
American Association for Chinese Studies. 3.4869
American Association for Health, Physical Education, and Recreation. Division of Safety Education. 4.906
American Association for Protecting Children. 4.6564
American Association for State and Local History. 1.6377, 3.267, 3.425, 3.441, 3.6190, 4.5167, 5.8388
American Association for the Advancement of Science. 1.4284, 4.293, 5.804, 5.3805, 5.3808, 5.6693
American Association for the Advancement of Science. Committee on Environmental Alterations. Power Study Group. 4.3718, 5.5999, 5.6871
American Association for the Advancement of Science. Office of International Science. 4.6181

American Association for the Advancement of Science. Office of Science Education. 5.8422
American Association for the Advancement of Science. Section D—Astronomy. 5.1687
American Association for the Advancement of Science. Section E—Geology and Geography. 5.6727
American Association for the Advancement of Science. Section H—Anthropology. 5.1687
American Association for the Advancement of Science. Section on Information and Communication. 5.336
American Association for the Advancement of Science. Section on Medical Sciences. 5.4290
American Association for the Advancement of Science. Section on Psychology. 5.336
American Association for the Advancement of Slavic Studies. Research and Development Committee. 3.3211
American Association for the History of Medicine. 5.4174
American Association of Advertising Agencies. 4.4429
American Association of Community and Junior Colleges. 4.9937
American Association of Engineering Societies. 5.5663
American Association of Junior Colleges. 4.10559
American Association of Museums. 1.47
American Association of Physics Teachers. 5.1894, 5.2290, 5.2296, 5.2328, 5.2380, 5.2409, 5.2469
American Association of Social Workers. 4.6473
American Association on Mental Deficiency. 5.4973
American Astronautical Society. 5.6691
American Bar Association. 4.9475
American Bar Association. Steering Committee on War, Foreign Affairs, and Constitutional Power. 4.9741
American Bible Society. 1.2501
American Bibliographical Center. 5.7824
American Board of Medical Specialties. 5.4549
American Catholic Historical Association. 1.3265
American Chemical Society. 5.2599, 5.2633, 5.2661, 5.2705, 5.5804, 5.6231
American Chemical Society. Chemical Abstracts Service. 5.2585, 5.2774, 5.8117
American Chemical Society. Committee on Professional Training. 5.2620
American Chemical Society. Division of Nuclear Chemistry and Technology. 5.6302, 5.6619
American Chemical Society. Meeting. (189th: 1985: Miami Beach, Fla.) 5.6302
American Civil Liberties Union. 4.9659-4.9660, 4.9725
American College of Neuropsychopharmacology. 5.4876
American College Personnel Association. 4.10279
American Comparative Literature Association. 2.2697
American Conference of Governmental Industrial Hygienists. 5.4726
American Conference of Governmental Industrial Hygienists. Committee on Industrial Ventilation. 5.6100
American Contract Bridge League. 4.1066
American Council for the Arts. 1.6746
American Council of Learned Societies. 1.949, 1.3445, 2.5113, 3.6288-3.6289, 3.6291, 5.808, 5.3343
American Council of Learned Societies. Committee on Latin American Studies. 5.7909
American Council of Learned Societies. Committee on Studies of Chinese Civilization. 1.160, 1.6725, 2.2152, 4.5416
American Council of Learned Societies Devoted to Humanistic Studies. Planning Group on Comparative Communist Studies. 4.7094
American Council of Learned Societies Devoted to Humanistic Studies. Russian Translation Project. 4.8643

American Council on Education. 4.9936-4.9937, 4.10056, 4.10087, 4.10089, 4.10588, 4.10624
American Council on Education. American Youth Commission. 3.6651, 3.6755
American Council on Public Affairs. 3.911
American Documentation Institute. 5.7638
American Economic Association. 4.1268, 4.1502, 4.1976, 4.4104, 4.4136, 4.4689, 5.8373
American Education Fellowship. 4.10607
American Educational Research Association. 4.10165, 4.10286, 4.10288, 4.10710
American Educational Theatre Association. 2.3137
American Electroplaters' Society. 5.7067
American Enterprise Institute for Public Policy Research. 4.3138, 4.3461, 4.3893, 4.4590, 4.7729, 4.7970, 4.8001, 4.8113, 4.8163, 4.8295, 4.8672, 4.8953
American Enterprise Institute for Public Policy Research. Center for Health Policy Research. 5.4638
American Federation of Arts. 1.4590, 1.4889, 1.5091, 1.6447, 1.6580, 3.5910
American Film Institute. 2.2933
American Football Coaches Association. 4.1030
American Geographical Society of New York. 4.156, 4.185
American Geological Institute. 5.6727
American Geological Institute. Conference (1959: Duluth, Minn.) 5.2988
American Geophysical Union. Meeting. (1980: Toronto, Ont.) 5.2527
American Heart Association. 5.4991
American Historical Association. 1.1797, 3.1976, 3.7178, 3.7308, 3.8300, 3.8374, 4.1375, 5.7829, 5.7988, 5.7990-5.7992, 5.8220
American Historical Association. Albert J. Beveridge Memorial Fund. 3.7180, 3.7232
American Historical Association. Committee on Graduate Education. 3.448
American Historical Association. Committee on Quantitative Data. 3.429
American Home Economics Association. Textiles and Clothing Section. 5.7078
American Horticultural Society. 5.5333, 5.5360
American Institute for Research in the Behavioral Sciences. 3.5393
American Institute of Architects. 4.6317
American Institute of Biological Sciences. 5.4006
American Institute of Indian Studies. 1.179
American Institute of Mining, Metallurgical, and Petroleum Engineers. 4.3722
American Institute of Physics. 5.1894, 5.1998, 5.2011, 5.2290, 5.2296, 5.2328, 5.2380, 5.2469
American Institute of Public Opinion. 4.5228
American Jewish Committee. 3.6561, 4.1670
American Jewish Historical Society. 3.6571
American Kennel Club. 5.5454
American Legislators' Association. 4.8242
American Library Association. 1.39, 1.5162, 5.7606, 5.7628, 5.7653-5.7654, 5.7692
American Library Association. Board on Resources of American Libraries. 5.7682
American Library Association. Collection Development Committee. 5.7619
American Library Association. Commission on Freedom and Equality of Access to Information. 5.7651
American Library Association. Committee on Resources of American Libraries. National Union Catalog Subcommittee. 5.7667
American Library Association. Filing Committee. 5.7634
American Library Association. Office for Intellectual Freedom. 5.7653
American Library Association. Reference and Subscription Books Review Committee. 5.7714
American Library Association. Resources and Technical Services Division. 5.7647
American Marketing Association. Comparative Marketing Committee. 4.4315
American Mathematical Society. 5.1027
American Medical Association. 5.4548, 5.4732, 5.4757
American Medical Association. Division of Drugs. 5.5135

American Meteorological Society. 5.2497
American Meteorological Society. Committee on the Compendium of Meteorology. 5.2495
American Museum of Natural History. 3.5717, 3.5746, 3.5873, 4.380, 4.493, 4.549, 4.560, 4.2078, 4.9351, 5.3994
American Musicological Society. 1.3853
American Name Society. 2.197
American National Standards Institute. 5.6249
American Nuclear Society. 5.5997, 5.6294
American Orthopsychiatric Association. 4.6573, 5.4881
American Pharmaceutical Association. 5.5149
American Pharmaceutical Association. Committee on National Formulary. 5.5149
American Pharmaceutical Association. National Formulary Board. 5.5149
American Philological Association. 2.477
American Philosophical Society. 3.8479-3.8480
American Physiological Society (1887-) 5.4170
American Political Science Association. 4.7381, 4.7635
American Political Science Association. Committee on Political Parties. 4.8172
American Production and Inventory Control Society. Handbook Editorial Board. 5.7021
American Psychiatric Association. Committee on Public Information. 5.4797
American Psychiatric Association. Joint Commission on Public Affairs. 5.4797
American Psychological Association. 4.10710, 5.1, 5.68-5.69, 5.414, 5.4818, 5.7633
American Psychological Association. Committee on Women. 4.5838
American Psychological Association. Standards for educational & psychological tests. 4.10710
American Public Health Association. 5.4672, 5.5984, 5.6020
American-Scandinavian Foundation. 1.2228, 2.13971, 3.3388
American School of Classical Studies at Athens. 3.2556
American Society for Clinical Pharmacology and Therapeutics. 5.5135
American Society for Horticultural Science. 5.5335
American Society for Information Science. 5.7638, 5.7640
American Society for Metals. 5.5712, 5.5807, 5.5819, 5.6754, 5.6769
American Society for Political and Legal Philosophy. 4.4732, 4.4918, 4.4969, 4.4979, 4.5028, 4.7516, 4.7610, 4.7619-4.7620, 4.7635, 4.7653, 4.7656, 4.7662, 4.7705, 4.7740, 4.7774, 4.9363
American Society for Testing and Materials. 5.5756, 5.5814
American Society for Training and Development. 4.4380
American Society for Training and Development. Media Division. 4.10289a
American Society of Agricultural Engineers. 5.5291
American Society of Cinematographers. 5.7002
American Society of Civil Engineers. Committee on Sampling and Testing. 5.5894
American Society of Civil Engineers. Urban Transportation Division. 5.5935
American Society of Civil Engineers. Urban Transportation Research Council. 4.4081
American Society of Composers, Authors and Publishers. 1.3540
American Society of Heating, Refrigerating and Air-Conditioning Engineers. 5.6099
American Society of International Law. 3.3860, 4.7653, 4.9080
American Society of Lubrication Engineers. 5.6245
American Society of Mammalogists. 5.3974
American Society of Mechanical Engineers. Applied Mechanics Division. 5.5730
American Society of Photogrammetry. 4.23-4.24, 5.5829
American Sociological Association. 4.5106
American Sociological Society. 5.7273
American Studies Association. 3.6073
American Teilhard de Chardin Association. 1.3062

American Universities Field Staff. 3.1154
American University at Cairo. 4.5462
American University. Foreign Area Studies. 3.4057
American University (Washington, D.C.) 3.9185
American University (Washington, D.C.). Foreign Area Studies. 3.1905, 3.1936, 3.2464, 3.2475, 3.2679, 3.2821, 3.2965, 3.3010, 3.3288, 3.3398, 3.3492, 3.3545, 3.3600, 3.3692, 3.3769, 3.3783, 3.3924, 3.4029, 3.4066, 3.4107-3.4108, 3.4143, 3.4157, 3.4362, 3.4421, 3.4441, 3.4458, 3.4478, 3.4552, 3.4557, 3.4613, 3.4866, 3.4875, 3.5131, 3.5204, 3.5239, 3.5285, 3.5301, 3.5304, 3.5311, 3.5337, 3.5371, 3.5380, 3.5383, 3.5388, 3.5390, 3.5396, 3.5403, 3.5491, 3.9059, 3.9066, 3.9077, 3.9091, 3.9110, 3.9114, 3.9121, 3.9136, 3.9172, 3.9178, 3.9187, 3.9232, 3.9237, 3.9257, 3.9272, 3.9311
American University (Washington, D.C.). Foreign Area Studies. 3.5268
American University (Washington, D.C.). Foreign Area Studies. 3.3328, 3.3547, 3.3569, 3.3604, 3.3792, 3.4046, 3.4061, 3.4121, 3.4518, 3.4533, 3.4587, 3.4992, 3.5039, 3.5170, 3.5199, 3.5203, 3.5209, 3.5255, 3.5292, 3.5305, 3.5350, 3.5411, 3.5417, 3.5445, 3.5509, 3.5518, 3.5533, 3.8874, 3.9080, 3.9228, 3.9281
American University (Washington, D.C.). Foreign Areas Studies Division. 3.4375, 3.4441, 3.4478, 3.4490, 3.5337, 3.5380, 3.5383, 3.5390, 3.9272
American Water Resources Association. 4.2928
American Water Works Association. 5.6020
Ameriks, Karl, 1947-. 1.918
Ameringer, Charles D., 1926-. 3.9079
Amerio, Luigi. 5.1555
Ames, Charles Edgar, 1895-. 4.4012
Ames, John G. (John Griffith), 1834-1910. 5.7774
Ames, Lois. 2.12459
Ames, Louise Bates. 4.5719
Ames Research Center. 5.1728
Ames, Roger T. 1.1803
Ames, William, 1576-1633. 1.2256
Ames, William E. 2.3672
Ames, William F. 5.1524, 5.5723
Ames, Winslow. 1.5819
Amherst College. 1.97
Amiet, Pierre. 1.4696
Amin, Samir. 3.5191, 4.1516, 4.2570, 4.2592
Amis, Kingsley. 2.5978, 2.6099, 2.8382-2.8384
Amjad, Rashid, 1947-. 4.2515
Amling, Frederick. 4.4451
Ammer, Christine. 1.3489
Ammerman, David, 1938-. 3.8107
Ammon, Harry. 3.7118
Ammons, A. R., 1926-. 2.11310
Ammons, Elizabeth. 2.11234
Amon Carter Museum of Western Art. 1.4904, 1.5919, 1.5965, 1.5998, 1.6382, 1.6450
Amory, Mark, 1941-. 2.9501
Amos, William. 2.2413
Ampalavanar, Rajeswary. 5.8064
Amrine, Renee. 4.7992
Amrita Pritam, 1919-. 2.1912-2.1914
Amrouche, Jean, 1906-. 2.4475
Amsalem, Michel A. 5.5629
Amsden, Alice Hoffenberg. 4.3241
Amsden, Charles Avery, 1899-1941. 3.5830
Amstutz, Walter. 1.5791
Amundsen, Roald, 1872-1928. 4.106
Amyot, Grant. 4.8629
Amyx, James W. 5.6800
Amyx, Raleigh DeGeer. 4.921
An, Tai Sung, 1931-. 3.5038, 3.5040
Anacreon. 2.330
Anaejionu, Paul. 4.3726
Anagnōstakēs, Manolēs. 2.614
Anagnostopoulos, Athan. 2.580
Anajionu, Paul. 5.6691
Analog Devices, Inc. 5.6577
Anand, Kewal Krishna. 1.1820
Anand, Mulk Raj, 1905-. 2.10124-2.10125
Anastaplo, George, 1925-. 4.9700
Anastas, Peter, 1937-. 3.5937
Anastasi, Anne, 1908-. 5.201

Anastasiow, Mary, 1952-. 4.5672
Anastasiow, Nicholas J. 4.5672
Anatoliĭ, A., 1929-1979. 2.1624
Anaya, Rudolfo A. 2.10812
Anchin, Jack C. (Jack Charles), 1951-. 5.4872
Andaya, Barbara Watson. 3.4537
Andaya, Leonard Y. 3.4537, 3.4550
Andemicael, Berhanykun. 4.9250
Anderer, Jeanne. 5.6130
Andersen, Charles J. joint author. 4.10087
Andersen, H. C. (Hans Christian), 1805-1875.
    2.14008
Andersen, Kristi. 4.8204
Andersen Nexø, Martin, 1869-1954.
    2.14027-2.14028
Andersen, Poul Gerhard. 1.4141
Andersen, Richard, 1946-. 2.12956
Andersen, Wayne V. 1.5659, 1.6107
Anderson, Alan Ross. 5.1036
Anderson, Albert, 1928-. 1.2914
Anderson, Annelise Graebner. 4.6775
Anderson, Arthur J. O. 3.8881, 3.8888
Anderson, B. W. (Basil William), 1901-. 5.3025
Anderson, Barbara Gallatin. joint author. 4.463
Anderson, Benedict R. O'G. (Benedict Richard
    O'Gorman), 1936-. 3.4569
Anderson, Bernhard W. 1.2580
Anderson, Bette Roda, 1945-. 5.2578
Anderson, Bruce, 1947-. 5.6101, 5.6106
Anderson, Charles Roberts, 1902-. 2.10996,
    2.11140-2.11141
Anderson, Courtney. 1.3026
Anderson, Dale A. (Dale Arden), 1936-. 5.1660
Anderson, David D. 2.11328
Anderson, David L. 5.2389
Anderson, David R. 4.4382
Anderson, Dennis, 1937- joint author. 4.3797
Anderson, Dole A., 1917-. 4.4292
Anderson, Donald F. 3.7709
Anderson, Donald K., 1922-. 2.6576
Anderson, Donald M. 5.7519
Anderson, Donald R. 3.8177
Anderson, E. Ruth, 1928-. 1.3753
Anderson, E. W. (Edward William), 1908-.
    5.4100
Anderson, Elaine. joint author. 5.3172
Anderson, Elijah. 4.4931
Anderson, Elliot. 2.1783
Anderson, Emily. 1.3794
Anderson, Emily Ann. 1.3934
Anderson, Eric, 1949-. 3.6802
Anderson, Eugene Newton. 3.675, 3.2479,
    4.862, 4.8357, 4.8618
Anderson, Evelyn. 4.3657
Anderson, Farris, 1938-. 2.5282
Anderson, Frederick, 1926-. 2.10937, 2.10939,
    2.10967
Anderson, Frederick R. 4.1841
Anderson, Fulton Henry, 1895-. 1.667, 1.669
Anderson, George Kumler, 1901-. 2.5525,
    2.5588
Anderson, George Wishart. 1.2576
Anderson, Gerald H. 1.2463, 1.2762
Anderson, Graham. 2.269
Anderson, Howard Peter, ed. 2.7912
Anderson, Hugh, 1920-. 1.2881
Anderson-Imbert, Enrique. 2.5297
Anderson Imbert, Enrique, 1910-. 2.5296,
    2.5319
Anderson, Irvine H., 1928-. 4.3787
Anderson, J. J. 2.6137, 2.6381
Anderson, J. K. (John Kinloch) 2.565
Anderson, J. M. 5.3509, 5.3771
Anderson, James D. 4.10832
Anderson, James L. 4.6806, 5.1895
Anderson, James Maxwell, 1933-. 2.145
Anderson, James Norman Dalrymple. 1.2039
Anderson, Jean, 1929-. 5.7132
Anderson, Jervis. 3.6848, 3.8043
Anderson, John Alvin. 3.5846
Anderson, John Edward. 4.3902, 4.3905, 5.5930
Anderson, John Q. ed. 3.7373
Anderson, Judith H. 2.5639
Anderson, Karen, 1947-. 4.6016
Anderson, Ken, 1949-. 4.1028
Anderson, L. R. (Loren Runar), 1941- joint
    author. 5.5896
Anderson, Lee G. 4.1898, 5.5482

Anderson, Lewis Edward, 1912- joint author.
    5.3705
Anderson, Lisa, 1950-. 4.5470
Anderson, M. G. 4.301
Anderson, M. S. (Matthew Smith) 3.647, 3.682,
    3.3098
Anderson, Margaret. 5.8039
Anderson, Margaret C. 2.10714
Anderson, Margaret Lavinia. 3.2299
Anderson, Marian, 1902-. 1.4086
Anderson, Martin. 5.7367
Anderson, Mary P. 5.5970
Anderson, Mary R., 1937-. 1.1384
Anderson, Maxwell, 1888-1959. 2.11311-2.11314
Anderson, Michael. 4.5619
Anderson, Michael John, 1937-. 2.2810
Anderson, Nels, 1889-. 4.6287
Anderson, Patrick, 1936-. 3.7615
Anderson, Paul M., 1926-. 5.6286
Anderson, Paul S. 4.10471
Anderson, Pauline Safford (Relyea) joint
    author. 4.8357
Anderson, Perry. 4.7015
Anderson, Poul, 1926-. 2.12850-2.12851
Anderson, Quentin, 1912-. 2.10371
Anderson, R. C. (Roger Charles), b. 1883. joint
    author. 5.7497
Anderson, Richard C. (Richard Chase), 1934-.
    4.10360
Anderson, Richmond K., 1907- joint author.
    4.5674
Anderson, Robert Henry, 1918- joint author.
    4.10716
Anderson, Romola. 5.7497
Anderson, Sherwood, 1876-1941.
    2.11317-2.11327
Anderson, Stanley H. 5.5497
Anderson, Sydney, 1927-. 5.3974
Anderson, Terry Lee, 1946-. 4.2932, 4.9759
Anderson, Thomas D. 3.9147
Anderson, Thornton, 1915-. 4.7300
Anderson, W. E. K., ed. 2.8052
Anderson, Wallace Ludwig, 1917-. 2.12404
Anderson, William. 2.4934, 3.8269
Anderson, William James, 1864-1900. 1.5218
Anderson, William Scovil, 1927-. 2.799
Andersson, Johan Gunnar, 1874-1960. 3.4624
Andersson, Theodore, 1903-. 4.10891
Andersson, Theodore Murdock, 1934-. 2.2689,
    2.13979
Andō, Hirofumi. 4.1702
Andō, Hiroshige, 1797-1858. 2.2069
Andolsen, Barbara Hilkert. 4.5953
Andrade, E. N. da C. (Edward Neville da
    Costa), 1887-1971. 5.1955, 5.1963
Andræ, Tor, 1885-1947. 1.2012
André, Louis, 1867-1948. 3.2032
André, Rae. 5.4663
Andreae, Bernard. 1.4726
Andreano, Ralph L., 1929- ed. 4.1868, 4.1919
Andreasen, Alan R., 1934-. 4.2055
Andreen, Brian. 5.2636
Andreski, Stanislav. ed. 1.819
Andrew, A. M. 5.5563
Andrew, Christopher M. 3.2194
Andrew, James Dudley, 1945-. 2.2946-2.2947
Andrew, of Wyntoun, 1350?-1420? 2.9843
Andrew, Warren. 5.4153-5.4154
Andrewartha, H. G. (Herbert George), 1907-.
    5.3512, 5.4053, 5.4070
Andrewes, A. 3.2596
Andrewes, Antony, 1910-. 2.562, 3.2544
Andrewes, Christopher Howard, Sir, 1896-.
    5.4474
Andrews, Alexander, 1824?-1873. 2.3682
Andrews, B. G. 2.10147, 5.8081
Andrews, Charles McLean, 1863-1943. 3.6009,
    3.6862-3.6863, 3.6916
Andrews, E. A. (Ethan Allen), 1787-1858. 2.258
Andrews, Edward Deming. 1.3412, 1.6560
Andrews, Emily S. 4.3455
Andrews, Faith. joint author. 1.6560
Andrews, George E., 1938-. 5.1281
Andrews, George F., 1918-. 3.9046
Andrews, Henry Nathaniel, 1910-.
    5.3173-5.3174
Andrews, Howard Lucius, 1906- joint author.
    5.2430

Andrews, J. Cutler, 1908-. 2.3668,
    3.7396-3.7397
Andrews, John, 1933- joint author. 1.5456
Andrews, John A. C., joint author. 5.7258
Andrews, Keith. 1.4991, 1.6160
Andrews, Kenneth R. 3.1274, 4.4225
Andrews, Kenneth William. 5.6770
Andrews, Lynn V. 3.5864-3.5865
Andrews, Oliver. 1.5778
Andrews, Robert C. 4.10932
Andrews, Theodora. 5.8288, 5.8381
Andrews, Wayne. 1.5281, 3.7448
Andrews, William L., 1946-. 2.10927
Andreyev, Leonid, 1871-1919. 2.1467-2.1468,
    2.1508
Andrić, Ivo, 1892-1975. 2.1207-2.1208, 2.1210
Andrien, Kenneth J., 1951-. 4.4667
Andriole, Stephen J. 5.1002
Andriot, John L. 4.1249, 5.7775-5.7776
Andronov, A. A. (Aleksandr Aleksandrovich),
    1901-1952. 5.1659
Andrus, James Russell, 1902-. 4.2452
Andrus, Lisa Fellows. 1.6357
Andrusz, Gregory D. 4.3499
Andrzejewski, Jerzy. 2.1698
Anesaki, Masaharu, 1873-1949. 1.1759
Angel, Marc. 3.3971
Angeles, Peter Adam, 1931-. 1.2827
Angelici, Robert J. 5.2704
Angelico, fra, ca. 1400-1455. 1.6202
Angell, James W. (James Waterhouse),
    1898-1986. 3.863
Angell, Robert Cooley, 1899-. 3.1157, 4.5633
Angelo, Anthony H. 4.9924
Angelov, Dimitŭr Simeonov. 3.3540
Anger, Vinzenz, joint author. 5.2671
Angier, Carole, 1943-. 2.9278
Angira, Jared. 2.10096
Angle, Paul M. (Paul McClelland), 1900-1975.
    ed. 3.7278
Anglemyer, Mary, 1909-. 5.8420-5.8421
Anglin, Donald L. joint author. 5.6624
Anglo-Palestinian Archives Committee. 5.8251
Anglo-Saxon chronicle. 3.1309
Angoff, Allan. ed. 2.10424
Angoff, Charles, 1902-. 2.10711, 2.12132,
    2.12236
Angress, Werner T. 3.2418
Angrist, Stanley W. 5.6322
Anguizola, G. A., 1927-. 5.5981
Angus-Butterworth, L. M. (Lionel Milner).
    3.416
Angus, H. T. (Harold T.) 5.5817
Anhalt, István. 1.4205
Anisfeld, Moshe. 2.115
Anker, Richard, 1943-. 4.1642
Anna, Timothy E., 1944-. 3.8930, 3.8999,
    3.9305
Annan, Noel Gilroy Annan, Baron, 1916-.
    2.8116
Annas, George J. 4.9544
Annas, Julia. 1.288, 4.7347
Annette Walters Memorial Conference on the
    Philosophy of Women's Liberation (1981:
    Milwaukee, Wis.) 4.5837
Annin, Suzette H. 4.679
Anouilh, Jean, 1910-. 2.4353-2.4361
Anozie, Sunday Ogbonna. 2.10311
Anrod, Charles W joint comp. 4.3343
Ansārī al-Harawī, 'Abd Allāh ibn Muhammad,
    1006-1089. 1.2086
Ansari, Javed A. 4.1799
Ansary, Adel I. joint author. 4.4296
Ansbacher, Heinz Ludwig, 1904-. 5.128
Ansbacher, Rowena R. 5.128
Anschel, Eugene. comp. 3.6482
Anschutz, Richard Paul, 1902-. 1.730
Anscombe, G. E. M. 1.259, 1.1067
Anscombe, G. E. M. (Gertrude Elizabeth
    Margaret) 1.1248
Anscombe, G. E. M. (Gertrude Elizabeth
    Margaret) ed. 1.1071
Anscombe, G. E. M. (Gertrude Elizabeth
    Margaret) 1.296, 5.632, 5.1035
Anscombe, Isabelle. 1.6533
Ansell, Martin F. (Martin Frederick) 5.2718
Anselm, Saint, Archbishop of Canterbury,
    1033-1109. 1.379-1.380, 1.2990

Anson, Barry Joseph, 1894-. 5.4143
Anson, Doris C., tr. 4.7642
Anson, William Reynell, Sir, 1843-1914. 4.9401
Anstaett, Herbert Bulow, 1902-. 5.7756
Anstey, Roger. 3.5425, 4.6449
Anstey, Sandra. 2.9427
Anstey, Vera Powell, 1889-. 4.2498
Antal, Frederick. 1.5007, 1.6033
Antell, Will. 4.10893
Antes, Richard L. 4.10713
Anthony, Edward, 1895-. 2.12116
Anthony, James R. 1.3704
Anthony, Kenneth R. M. 5.5254
Anthony, L. J. 5.5500
Anthony, Michael, 1932-. 2.9997-2.9998
Anthony, Rayford Gaines, 1935- joint author.
   5.6813
Anthony, Susan B. (Susan Brownell),
   1820-1906. 4.5999
Anthropological Survey of India. 3.4201
Antill, James M. 5.5705
Antin, Mary, 1881-1949. 3.6189
Antiques. 1.6517
Anton, Howard. 5.1356
Anton, Thomas Julius. 4.8881
Antoninus, Brother. 2.11332
Antoniou, Jim. 4.3923
Antonius, George. 3.3730
Anuman Rajadhon, Phrayā, 1888-1969. 3.4520
Anwar, Chairil, 1922-1949. 2.2287
Anweiler, Oskar. 3.3173
Anyon, Roger, 1952-. 3.5908
Anzaldúa, Gloria. 2.10702
Apachean Symposium, New Orleans, 1969.
   3.5837
Apel, Willi. 1.3425, 1.3504, 1.4117, 1.4155,
   1.4244
Aperture, Inc. 5.6924
Apes, William, b. 1798. 3.5788
Apfel, Roberta J., 1938-. 5.4730
Apollinaire, Guillaume, 1880-1918.
   2.4363-2.4366
Apollodorus. 2.333, 2.419
Apollodorus, of Athens. 2.333, 2.419-2.420
Apolloni, Tony. 4.6611
Apollonio, Umbro, 1911- comp. 1.6734
Apollonius, Rhodius. 2.334
Apostol, Tom M. 5.1318, 5.1435
Appadorai, A. (Angadipuram), 1902-. 3.4295
Appel, Alfred. 2.1296, 2.12668
Appel, Willa. 1.1868
Appelbaum, Stanley. ed. 1.6451
Appell, George N. 4.641
Appia, Adolphe, 1862-1928. 2.3096
Appianus, of Alexandria. 2.335
Appignanesi, Lisa. 2.3185
Apple, James MacGregor, 1915-. 5.7018
Apple, Lawrence B. 4.679
Apple, Max. 2.12852
Apple, Michael W. 4.10763, 4.10773-4.10774
Apple, R. W. (Raymond Walter), 1934-. 3.7914
Applebee, Arthur N. 4.10472
Appleby, Joyce Oldham. 4.7303
Applegath, John. 5.8371
Applegath, Vivian. 5.8371
Appleman, Philip, 1926-. 4.1587
Appleton, Augusta Isabella, b. 1841. 5.7748
Appleton, Charles Leonard, 1900-. 2.3106
Appleton, William Worthen. 2.3351, 2.3358
Applewhite, Thomas H. 5.6894
Appleyard, Donald. 4.3924
Applied Nucleonics Company. 5.6151
Apps, Jerold W., 1934-. 4.10981
ApRoberts, Ruth. 2.7356, 2.8238
Apsche, Jack. 5.308
Apter, David Ernest, 1924-. 4.2874, 4.7483
Apter, Steven J. (Steven Jeffrey), 1945-.
   4.10703, 4.10942
Apter, T. E. 2.9588
Aptheker, Bettina. 4.9458
Aptheker, Herbert, 1915-. 3.6605, 3.6824,
   3.6826-3.6827, 3.6829, 3.7228
Apuleius. 2.649, 2.704
Arad, Yitzhak, 1926-. 3.1087
Aragon, 1897-. 2.4369-2.4378
Arand, Louis A., 1892- ed. and tr. 1.2207
Arango, E. Ramón (Ergasto Ramón) 3.2976
Arasaratnam, Sinnappah. 3.4366

Arata, Esther Spring, joint author. 5.7800
Arato, Andrew. 4.4872
Arbeau, Thoinot, 1519-1595. 4.1090
Arber, Agnes Robertson, 1879-1960. 5.3635
Arberry, A. J. (Arthur John), 1905-1969.
   1.1784, 1.2026-1.2027, 1.2064, 1.2083, 2.1838,
   2.1968, 3.4069
Arberry, Arthur John, tr. 1.2078
Arbib, Michael A. 5.997
Arboleda, Amadio Antonio. 5.7582
Arbus, Diane, 1923-1971. 5.6958
Arbuthnot, John, 1667-1735. 2.7191
Archdeacon, Thomas J. 3.6503
Archer, Clive. 4.9263
Archer, Dane, 1946-. 4.6685
Archer-Hind, Laura, ed. 3.1374
Archer, J. S. (John S) 5.6801
Archer, John Clark, 1881-1957. 1.1828
Archer, Leonard Courtney, 1911-. 2.2779
Archer M. Huntington Art Gallery. 1.4985
Archer, Margaret Scotford. 4.5291
Archer, Robert R. 5.5734
Archer, Sarah Ellen. 5.5199
Archer, W. G. (William George), 1907-. 1.6307,
   2.1975
Archer, William, 1856-1924. 2.2794, 2.3115,
   2.7805
Archibald, Douglas N. 2.8346
Archibald, Marion. 1.4935
Archibald, Raymond Clare, 1875-1957. ed.
   5.1568
Architectural Iron Works (Firm) 1.5501
Architectural League of New York. 1.5459
Arciniegas, Germán, 1900-. 3.5987, 3.8965,
   3.9146
Arco Publishing. 4.1018
Arctic Institute of North America. 3.5725,
   4.743, 5.8207
Ardagh, John, 1928-. 4.2331-4.2332
Ardant, Gabriel. 4.8365
Arden, John. 2.8386
Arden of Feversham. 2.6679
Ardener, Shirley. 4.5891
Arditti, Rita, 1934-. 5.5066
Ardrey, Robert. 5.3376
Ardzrooni, Leon. 4.1271
Arendt, Hannah. 1.83, 2.13666, 3.454, 3.2380,
   4.4964, 4.7593, 4.7611
Arens, Alvin A. 4.4402
Arens, W., 1940-. 3.5302, 3.6062
Arensberg, Conrad Maynadier. 4.626-4.627
Aretino, Pietro, 1492-1556. 2.4955-2.4957
Arey, Leslie Brainerd, 1891-. 5.4121, 5.4155
Argan, Giulio Carlo. 1.5594, 1.5733
Argonne National Laboratory. 5.2447
Argonne National Laboratory. ZGS Users
   Group. 5.2447
Argonne Universities Association. 5.2447
Arguedas, José María. 2.5425-2.5426
Argüelles, José, 1939-. 1.1821
Argüelles, Miriam, 1943- joint author. 1.1821
Argyle, Barry. 2.10142
Argyll, George Douglas Campbell, 8th Duke of,
   1823-1900. 4.1433
Argyris, Chris, 1923-. 4.2693, 4.10977
Arias, Paolo Enrico. 1.6631
Ariès, Philippe. 1.1323, 4.5743
Arieti, Silvano. 5.342, 5.4796, 5.4839, 5.4923
Arima, Tatsuo. 3.4899
Ariosto, Lodovico, 1474-1533. 2.4958-2.4962
Ariotti, Piero E. 1.6682
Aris, Rutherford. 5.1938
Arishima, Takeo, 1878-1923. 2.2072
Aristophanes. 2.336, 2.423-2.430
Aristoteles. 2.344, 2.347
Aristotle. 1.282-1.286, 1.288-1.289, 1.291-1.292,
   2.328, 2.337-2.343, 2.345-2.352, 2.436-2.439,
   2.2530, 2.2727-2.2728, 2.2826, 2.7339-2.7340,
   5.832-5.834, 5.3797
Aristotle, Spurious and doubtful works.
   Movement of animals. 2.342
Ariyoshi, Sawako, 1931-. 2.2127-2.2128
Arjomand, Said Amir. 3.4079
Arkell, William Joscelyn, 1904-1958. 5.3139
Arkes, Hadley. 5.8111
Arksey, Laura. 5.8111
Arkush, Allan, 1949-. 1.1968
Arland, Marcel, 1899- ed. 2.4079

Arlen, Michael, 1895-1956. 2.8387
Arlen, Michael J. 2.2850
Arlinghaus, Bruce E. 5.7348
Arlow, Jacob A. 5.129
Armacost, D. L. (David L.), 1944-. 5.1536
Armand, D. L. (David L'vovich) ed. 4.2368
Armarego, W. L. F. joint author. 5.6848
Armbruster, David Alvin, 1890-. 4.987
Armens, Sven M. 2.7036
Armes, Roy. 2.2876, 2.2888, 2.2892
Armistead, Samuel G., 1927-. 2.906
Armitage, Merle, 1893-1975. ed. 4.1140
Armour, David A. ed. 3.8434
Armour, Philip K. 5.4697
Armour, Richard Willard, 1906-. 3.6330
Armour, Robert A. 2.2868
Arms, Suzanne. 5.5062
Armson, Kenneth Avery, 1927-. 5.5425
Armstead, H. Christopher H. 5.6208, 5.6291
Armstrong, A. H. (Arthur Hilary). 1.221
Armstrong, A. H. (Arthur Hilary). tr. 2.389
Armstrong, Anne, 1924-. 3.1142
Armstrong, Bruce. 2.13736
Armstrong, Christopher, 1942-. 4.8271
Armstrong, D. M. (David Malet), 1926-. 1.145,
   1.686, 1.1336
Armstrong, Elizabeth Howard, 1898-. 3.8679
Armstrong, Isobel. comp. 2.5823
Armstrong, J. D. (James David), 1945-. 4.9264
Armstrong, John Alexander, 1922-. 3.3303,
   4.8659
Armstrong, Judith. 2.3468
Armstrong, Katherine Fairlie, 1892-. 5.4144,
   5.4148
Armstrong, Louis, 1900-1971. 1.4078
Armstrong, Margaret E. 5.5177
Armstrong, Regis J. 1.3135
Armstrong, Terry R., 1946-. 4.6798
Armstrong, Tom, 1932-. 1.5657, 1.5891
Armstrong, William A. 1.668
Armstrong, William J. 5.7483
Armstrong, Willis C. 3.6413
Arnade, Charles W. 3.9275
Arnason, H. Harvard. 1.4803, 1.5663, 1.5958
Arnaud, Jacqueline. comp. 2.4847
Arndt, Johann, 1555-1621. 1.3056
Arndt, Walter, 1916- ed. and tr. 2.1412
Arndt, Walter W., 1916-. 2.1407-2.1408, 2.1536,
   2.13715
Arnett, Ross H. 5.3863
Arney, William Ray. 5.4591, 5.5065
Arngrímur Sigurðsson, 1933-. 2.915
Arnheim, Daniel D. 4.972
Arnheim, M. T. W. (Michael T. W.) 4.7353
Arnheim, Rudolf. 1.4604-1.4605, 1.4618,
   1.5111, 1.5490, 1.6127, 2.2934
Arnim, Ludwig Achim, Freiherr von,
   1781-1831. 2.13548
Arnold, Armin. ed. 2.10268
Arnold, Chester Arthur, 1901-. 5.3636
Arnold, Corliss Richard. 1.4146
Arnold, Darlene Baden, 1948-. 4.10347
Arnold, Denis. 1.3505, 1.3771, 1.3796, 1.3873,
   1.3931
Arnold, Donald Robert, 1935-. 5.2919
Arnold, Edward Vernon, 1857-1926. 1.326
Arnold, Edwin, Sir, 1832-1904. 2.1934, 2.1940
Arnold, Florence A. 5.8091
Arnold, Janet. 4.828
Arnold, June, 1926- Charles H. 4.3381, 4.11015
Arnold, Matthew, 1822-1888. 1.2531, 2.510,
   2.7346-2.7351, 2.7353, 4.5318
Arnold, R. Douglas, 1950-. 4.7969
Arnold, Thomas Walker, Sir, 1864-1930, ed.
   3.3653
Arnold, Thurman Wesley, 1891-1969. 4.1517,
   4.9489
Arnol'd, V. I. (Vladimir Igorevich), 1937-.
   5.1510, 5.1654
Arnold, Wilhelm, 1911-. 5.11
Arnon, Itzhak, 1909-. 4.2892
Arnopoulos, Sheila McLead. 3.8822
Arnopoulos, Sheila McLeod. joint author.
   3.8822
Arnott, Peter D. 2.301-2.302, 2.3364
Arnould, Eric J. 4.5485
Arnove, Robert F. 4.9964
Arnow, Harriette Louisa (Simpson) 2.11333

Arnow, Harriette Louisa Simpson, 1908-.
    3.8351
Arnson, Curtis. 2.1784
Arntzen, Etta. 5.8181
Arny, Rose, ed. 5.7764
Aron, Raymond, 1905-. 1.849, 3.455-3.456,
    3.746, 3.1158, 3.2213, 3.7557, 4.1781, 4.4737,
    4.4760, 4.7251, 4.9020, 5.7149
Aronian, Sona. 2.1524
Aronowitz, Frederick. 5.5944
Aronowitz, Stanley. 4.3562
Arons, Stephen. 4.10734
Aronsberg, Emanuel, tr. 3.3048
Aronson, Arnold. 2.3140
Aronson, Chaim, 1825-1888. 3.4001
Aronson, Elliot. 4.3717, 4.4980, 4.4986, 5.409
Aronson, J. Richard (Jay Richard), 1937-.
    4.4659
Aronson, Jerrold L., 1940-. 1.552
Aroskar, Mila A. joint author. 5.5195
Arp, Jean, 1887-1966. 1.5702
Arp, Thomas R. 2.2734
Arpaci, Vedat S., 1928-. 5.6195
Arpan, Jeffrey S. 4.3832
Arrabal, Fernando. 2.4379-2.4380
Arrian. 2.353, 3.545
Arrington, Leonard J. 1.3384, 4.2040
Arrington, Lewis R., 1919-. 5.5452
Arrivé, Michel. ed. 2.4590
Arrow, Kenneth Joseph, 1921-. 4.1290, 4.1575,
    4.3716, 4.5021
Arrowsmith, William, 1924-. 2.757, 2.2543,
    2.5052
Arrubla, Gerardo, 1872-1946. joint author.
    3.9174
Art Gallery of Greater Victoria. 3.5814
Art Gallery of Ontario. 1.4982, 1.6359, 1.6489
Art Institute of Chicago. 1.4831, 1.5186, 1.6053,
    1.6161, 1.6362, 1.6532, 3.5816, 5.6929, 5.6950
Art Museum of South Texas. 1.6008
Artaud, Antonin, 1896-1948. 2.3082, 2.4381
Arte no Brasil. 1.4923
Arter, David. 4.8670, 4.8673
Arthaud, Claude, 1927-. 1.4854
Arthaud, Jacques, joint author. 3.4445
Arthur, C. J. (Christopher John), 1940- ed.
    4.7071
Arthur D. Little, Inc. 4.4033
Arthur, John, 1939-. 1.5936a
Arthur, King. 2.3949
Arthur, Paul, 1945-. 4.8568
Arthur, William, 1796-1875. 3.302
Arthurs, H. W. (Harry William), 1935-. 4.3516
Artibise, Alan F. J. 4.5251, 4.6246, 5.7897
Artin, Emil, 1898-1962. 5.1271, 5.1292, 5.1357
Arts Council of Great Britain. 1.4934, 1.4978
Artsimovich, L. A. (Lev Andreevich),
    1909-1973. 5.2383
Artz, Frederick Binkerd, 1894-. 3.124, 3.692
Artzybasheff, Boris, 1899- illus. 2.11719
Arundell, Dennis Drew. 2.3330
Aruri, Naseer Hasan, 1934-. 3.3823
Arvey, Verna, 1910-. 1.3994
Arvin, Newton, 1900-1963. 2.11145
Arwas, Victor. 1.4839, 1.6643
Arya, Atam Parkash. 5.2048
Arzáns de Orsúa y Vela, Bartolomé, 1676-1736.
    3.9279
Arzeliès, Henri, 1913-. 5.1927
Asad, Talal. ed. 4.411
Asaf'ev, B. V. (Boris Vladimirovich),
    1884-1949. 1.3728
Asakawa, Kanichi, 1874-1945, ed. 3.4870
Asals, Frederick. 2.13212
Asante, Molefi K., 1942-. 4.5006
Asante, S. K. B. 4.2621
Asbell, Bernard. 4.8041
Asch, Sholem, 1880-1957. 2.1797-2.1800
Ascham, Roger, 1515-1568. 2.6429
Aschenbrenner, Karl. 1.1301
Ascher, Marcia, 1935-. 3.9290
Ascher, Robert, 1931- joint author. 3.9290
Ascherson, Neal. 3.3341
Aschner, Fritz. 5.6292
Ascoli, Max, 1888-. 3.2900
Asdell, S. A. (Sydney Arthur), 1897-. 5.4252
Ash, Douglas. 1.6554
Ash, Harrison Boyd, tr. 2.654

Ash, Lee. 5.7661
Ashbaugh, Carolyn. 4.3590
Ashbery, John. 2.11334-2.11337
Ashbrook, Joseph, d. 1980. 5.1721
Ashbrook, William, 1922-. 1.3854, 1.4515
Ashburner, M. 5.3479
Ashby, M. F. 5.5757
Ashdown, Paul, 1944-. 2.11293
Ashe, Dora Jean. ed. 2.6556
Ashe, Geoffrey. 1.2903
Ashelford, Jane. 4.845
Ashenfelter, Orley, 1942- ed. 4.3116
Asher, Frederick M. 1.5753
Asher, Robert E., 1910-. 4.4572, 4.9205
Ashford, Daisy. 2.8389
Ashford, Douglas Elliott. 4.8452
Ashford, Nicholas Askounes. 4.3502
Ashford, Norman. 5.5927, 5.6681, 5.6683
Ashk, Upendra Nath, 1910-. 2.1887
Ashley, L. F. joint author. 2.2703
Ashley, Maurice, 1907-. 3.1480, 3.1509
Ashley, Robert Paul, 1915- ed. 2.6252
Ashmole, Bernard, 1894-. 1.5632, 1.5634
Ashmore, Harry S. 3.8341
Ashton, Dore. 1.4894, 1.5660, 1.5958, 1.6065,
    1.6698
Ashton, E. H. (Edmund Hugh), 1911-. 3.5478
Ashton, E. T. (Elwyn Thomas) 3.6598
Ashton, George D. 4.317
Ashton, Indira. 5.5019
Ashton, Julia F. 5.8452
Ashton, Peter K. joint author. 4.3809
Ashton, Robert. 3.1420
Ashton, T. S. (Thomas Southcliffe) 4.2262,
    4.2271
Ashton-Warner, Sylvia. 2.10206-2.10208,
    4.10886
Ashtor, Eliyahu, 1914-. 3.4002, 4.2426
Ashwin, Cliv. 1.5835
Ashworth, Georgina. 4.6457
Ashworth, Mary Wells. 3.7028
Ashworth, Tony. 3.789
Ashworth, William. 1.5602
Asia House Gallery. 1.5752, 1.6337, 3.4278
Asia Society. 1.5752, 1.6334, 3.4845
Asia Society. Asian Literature Program. 2.1893
Asia Society. Galleries. 1.6371
Asian Development Bank. 4.2432, 4.2436,
    4.2982
Asian Studies Association of Australia. 3.4418,
    3.4568
Asiatic Society of Japan. 3.4942
Asiegbu, Johnson U. J. 3.5365
Asimov, Isaac, 1920-. 2.7292, 2.10828, 2.10831,
    2.12853-2.12855, 5.807, 5.1712, 5.1831,
    5.2433, 5.2604
Asimow, Robert M. 5.5766
Asiwaju, A. I., 1939-. 3.5344
Askeland, Donald R. 5.5758
Aslanian, Carol B. 4.10982
Aslin, Elizabeth. 1.6534
Aslund, Anders, 1952-. 4.3003
Asp, C. Elliott. 4.10014
Aspen Institute for Humanistic Studies. 2.60,
    4.1592
Aspen Institute for Humanistic Studies.
    Education Program. 1.6694
Asprey, Robert B. 5.7226
Asselineau, Roger. 2.11274
Assembly of Behavioral and Social Sciences
    (U.S.). Committee on Ability Testing.
    4.10709
Assembly of Behavioral and Social Sciences
    (U.S.). Committee on Aging. 4.5795
Assembly of Behavioral and Social Sciences
    (U.S.). Committee on Occupational
    Classification and Analysis. 4.3260
Assembly of Life Sciences (U.S.). Committee on
    Diet, Nutrition, and Cancer. 5.4772
Assembly of Mathematical and Physical
    Sciences (U.S.). Committee on Hazardous
    Substances in the Laboratory. 5.2637
Asser, John, d. ca. 909. 3.1320
Asso, Doreen. 5.4260
Associated Ideas, Inc. 5.5639
Association européenne océanique. 5.5632
Association for Asian Studies. 1.2169, 3.3640,
    3.4451, 5.8030

Association for Asian Studies. Meeting. (36th:
    1984: Washington, D.C.) 4.8719
Association for Asian Studies. Ming
    Biographical History Project Committee.
    3.4710
Association for Canadian Studies in the United
    States. 3.6417
Association for Consumer Research (U.S.)
    4.4328
Association for Educational Communications
    and Technology. 4.10289a
Association for Library Service to Children.
    5.7719
Association for Supervision and Curriculum
    Development. 4.10444, 4.10632
Association for the Advancement of
    Psychoanalysis. 4.5929
Association for the Study of Modern and
    Contemporary France (Great Britain) 4.5358
Association of American Geographers. 4.8,
    4.14, 4.44, 5.8165, 5.8202
Association of American Geographers.
    Commission on College Geography. Panel on
    Environmental Education. 5.3523
Association of American Geographers.
    Comparative Metropolitan Analysis Project.
    4.160, 4.6207, 4.6231
Association of American Geographers.
    Geography in Liberal Education Project. 4.39
Association of American Law Schools. 4.9363,
    4.9475
Association of American Painters and
    Sculptors, New York. 1.4669
Association of Assistant Librarians. 5.8168
Association of Casualty and Surety Companies.
    Accident Prevention Dept. 4.3943
Association of Governing Boards of Universities
    and Colleges. 4.10600
Association of Iron and Steel Engineers. 5.6787
Association of Life Insurance Medical Directors
    of America. 5.4629
Association of Professional Recording Studios.
    5.6561
Association of Social Anthropologists of the
    Commonwealth. 4.466, 4.625
Association of Theological Schools in the
    United States and Canada. 1.3002
Associazione elettrotecnica ed elettronica
    italiana. 5.5959
Astell, Mary, 1668-1731. 1.1514, 4.5916
Aster, Howard. 2.9944
Aster, Sidney, 1942-. 3.892, 5.8260
Astin, A. E. 3.2770-3.2771
Astin, Alexander W. 4.10073, 4.10587, 4.10748,
    4.10892
Astle, Melvin J. 5.2649
Astley, Thea, 1925-. 2.10153
Aston, Margaret. 3.604
Aston, T. H. (Trevor Henry) 4.11009
Aston, William George, 1841- tr. 3.4930
Astronomisches Rechen-Institut, Heidelberg.
    5.1679
Asturias, Miguel Angel. 2.5368-2.5369
Aśvaghosa. 1.1737, 1.1745, 2.1127
Aswell, Edward Campbell, 1900-1958. 2.12775
AT & T Bell Laboratories. Technical
    Publication Dept. 5.6417
Atget, Eugène, 1856-1927. 5.6973
Athanasius, Saint, Patriarch of Alexandria, d.
    373. 1.2183
Athanassakis, Apostolos N. 2.491
Athans, Michael. 5.6176
Athearn, Robert G. 3.8466, 4.4011
Athenagoras, 2d cent. 1.2190
Atherton, Alexine L. 5.8257
Atherton, James Stephen. 2.8869
Atherton, Lewis Eldon. 3.8307, 3.8489
Atherton, Wallace N. 4.3328
Athey, Isabella, ed. 1.5484
Athletic Institute. 4.973
Atiya, Aziz Suryal, 1898-. 3.595
Atiyah, Michael Francis, 1929-. 5.1358
Atiyeh, George Nicholas, 1923-. 5.8035
Atkin, Robert S., 1945-. 4.3156
Atkins, Anthony G., 1939-. 5.5775
Atkins, G. Pope, 1934-. 3.6441, 4.9017
Atkins, John Alfred, 1916-. 2.8770, 2.8825,
    2.9195, 2.9251

Atkins, John William Hey, 1874- .
  2.2502-2.2504
Atkins, P. W. (Peter William), 1940-. 5.2798,
  5.2825
Atkins, Warren H. 4.3949
Atkinson, Brooks, 1894-. 2.3221
Atkinson, Bruce Wilson. 5.2520
Atkinson, Charles Francis, 1880-. 3.17, 3.149,
  3.197
Atkinson, Clarissa W. 1.1611
Atkinson, Dick. 4.4781
Atkinson, James, 1914- ed. and tr. 1.2346
Atkinson, James B., 1934-. 2.4971
Atkinson, Keith, 1942-. 5.6736
Atkinson, Kendall E. 5.1425
Atkinson, Michael M. 4.8283, 4.8290
Atkinson, Richard C. 4.10348
Atkinson, Richard C. joint author. 5.107
Atkinson, Rita L. joint author. 5.107
Atkinson, Ronald F., 1928-. 3.457
Atlantic Council of the United States. Nuclear
  Fuels Policy Working Group. 4.9179
Atlantic Council Working Group on the United
  States and Canada. 3.6413
Atlantic Institute for International Affairs.
  4.1823
Atlas, James. 2.12454
Atlas, Ronald M., 1946-. 5.4458
Atmore, Anthony. joint author. 3.5075, 3.5079,
  3.5083
'Attār, Farīd al-Dīn, d. ca. 1230. 2.1966
Attebery, Brian, 1951-. 2.10550
Attenborough, David, 1926-. 5.3364
Attewell, P. B. 5.6093
Atticus, Titus Pomponius. 2.715
Attridge, Derek. 2.1043, 2.5795
Attwater, Donald, 1892-1977. 1.3246
Atwell, Donald. 3.4124
Atwood, Alice C. (Alice Cary), 1876-1947. joint
  author. 5.8116
Atwood, Elmer Bagby, 1906-. 2.1119, 2.1152
Atwood, Jim D., 1940-. 5.2877
Atwood, Margaret Eleanor, 1939-. 2.9881,
  2.9896, 2.9906-2.9910
Atwood, Thomas, d. 1793. 3.9131
Aubert de La Rüe, E. (Edgar), 1901-. 5.3242
Aubert, Marcel, 1884-1962. 1.5699
Aubert, Roger. 1.3158
Aubey, Robert T. 4.1556
Aubigné, Agrippa d', 1552-1630. 2.3977
Aubin, Jean Pierre. 5.1500
Auboyer, Jeannine. 3.117, 3.4190
Aubrey, Henry G. 4.4585
Auburn, Mark S. 2.6990, 2.7252
Auchard, John. 5.7792
Auchincloss, Louis. 2.3505, 2.11340-2.11342
Auden, W. H. (Wystan Hugh), 1907-1973.
  1.3442, 2.2405, 2.2562, 2.3739, 2.3802,
  2.4139, 2.6101, 2.8390-2.8399, 2.10771
Audouze, Jean. 5.1739
Audra, Ruth Ashley, 1888- tr. 1.827
Audrieth, L. F. (Ludwig Frederick), 1901-.
  5.6861
Audubon, John James. 5.3944, 5.3950
Audy, J. Ralph. 5.438
Auerbach, Doris. 2.10519
Auerbach, Erich, 1892-1957. 2.2401, 2.4935
Auerbach, Max, 1879-. 1.5823
Auerbach, Nina, 1943-. 2.5727, 2.5986
Augarten, Stan. 5.6522
Augelli, John P. joint author. 3.8963, 3.9144
Augstein, Rudolf, 1923-. 1.2884
August, Eugene R., 1935-. 1.731, 5.8380
Augusti, Giuliano. 5.5833
Augustine, Saint, Bishop of Hippo. 1.2182,
  1.2185, 1.2201-1.2207, 2.650
Augustus, Emperor of Rome, 63 B.C.-14 A.D.
  2.314
Augustus, John, 1785-1859. 4.6900
Aukerman, Robert C., 1910-. 4.10410, 4.10417
Aulard, F.-A. (François-Alphonse) 1849-1928.
  3.2094
Aulén, Gustaf, 1879-. 1.2772, 1.2874
Auletta, Ken. 4.6619
Ault, Norman, 1880-1950. 2.6151, 2.6154,
  2.7196
Aung-Thwin, Michael. 3.4425
Aunger, Edmund A. 4.7524

Aungerville, Richard, known as Richard de
  Bury, Bp. of Durham, 1287-1345. 5.7671
Aurand, Harold W. 4.3389
Aurenhammer, Hans. 1.5410
Auslander, Maurice. 5.1360
Aussieker, Bill, joint author. 4.10582
Austen, Jane, 1775-1817. 2.7364, 2.7366-2.7368
Austen-Leigh, James Edward, 1798-1874.
  2.7369
Austen-Leigh, Richard Arthur, 1872-1961.
  2.7370
Austen-Leigh, William. 2.7370
Austen, Roger. 2.10555
Auster, Paul, 1947-. 2.3927
Austin, Anne L., 1891- joint author. 5.5162
Austin, Anthony. 4.6857
Austin, C. R. (Colin Russell), 1914-. 5.4049
Austin, D. G. 5.6816
Austin, Dennis, 1922-. 3.5339
Austin, George A. 5.382
Austin, Gilbert R. 4.10400, 4.10715
Austin, Gregory A. 5.4956
Austin, J. L. (John Langshaw), 1911-1960.
  1.738-1.739
Austin, M. M. 3.2633, 4.1730
Austin, Mary C. 4.10456
Austin, Nancy. 4.2748
Austin, Norman. 2.511
Austin, Oliver Luther, 1903-. 5.3937
Austin, R. G. (Roland Gregory), 1901-1974.
  2.784-2.785, 2.787, 2.789
Austin, Timothy R., 1952-. 2.2427
Austin, William W. 1.3666, 1.3868
Australian Institute of International Affairs.
  3.3636, 3.4566, 3.5571
Australian National University. 2.5667
Authier, Jerry, joint author. 4.1224
Automobile Manufacturers Association. 4.4033
Auton, Graeme P. joint author. 3.2468
Auty, Phyllis. 3.3558
Auty, Robert. 1.5030, 2.1222, 3.3040
Avakumovic, Ivan. 4.7195, 4.8304
Avalon Arthur. 1.1691
Avedon, Elliott M. 4.1061
Aveling, Edward Bibbins, 1851-1898. tr. 4.7064
Aveling, Eleanor Marx, 1855-1898. 4.1509
Aveling, Harry. 2.2286, 3.4561
Aveni, Anthony F. 3.8902
Averbuch, Gloria, 1951-. 4.963
Averill, Deborah M. 2.9864
Averoff-Tossizza, Evangelos, 1910-. 3.2705
Averroës, 1126-1198. 1.368, 4.7348
Avery, Benedict Raymund, 1919-. 1.3256
Avery, Catherine B. 2.911, 2.2509
Avery, Emmett Langdon, 1903-. 2.6950
Avery, Eric. 5.4600
Avery, Evelyn Gross, 1940-. 2.10612
Avery, Laurence G. 2.11314
Avery Library. 1.5553
Avery, Mary Williamson, 1907-. 3.8640
Avery, Milton, 1885-1965. 1.5794
Avery, Thomas Eugene. 4.1765, 5.6993
Avez, A. (André) joint author. 5.1654
Avi-Yonah, Michael, 1904-1974. 3.2511, 3.3827,
  3.3851, 3.3901, 4.148
Avicenna, 980-1037. 1.369-1.370
Avila, Donald L. joint author. 5.466
Avineri, Shlomo. 3.4017, 4.6948
Avis, Walter S. 5.7894
Avis, Walter Spencer, 1919- ed. 2.1161
Avrett, Eugene H., 1933-. 5.1769
Avrich, Paul. 3.3050, 4.10024
Avril, François. 1.6411, 3.148
Avtgis, Alexander W., 1931- joint author.
  5.6482
Awolalu, J. Omosade. 1.1863
Awolowo, Obafemi, 1909-. 3.5361
Awoonor, Kofi, 1935-. 2.2295
Axelrad, Jacob. 2.10872
Axelrod, Alan, 1952-. 1.6707, 2.10913
Axelrod, Charles David. 5.343
Axelrod, Joseph, 1918-. 4.10088
Axelrod, Saul. 5.308
Axelrod, Steven Gould, 1944-. 2.12049
Axelsen, Jens. joint author. 2.920
Axelson, Eric, 1913- ed. 3.5436
Axen, Richard, joint author. 4.10988

Axline, Virginia Mae, 1911-. 4.10387
Axsom, Richard H., 1943-. 1.6447
Axtell, James. 3.5817, 4.10185
Ayala, Francisco José, 1934-. 5.3365
Ayckbourn, Alan, 1939-. 2.9614
Aycock, Marlyn. 3.7918
Aydelotte, William Osgood. 3.5435
Aydelotte, William Osgood. ed. 3.428
Ayensu, Edward S. 5.3647, 5.3792
Ayer, A. J. (Alfred Jules), 1910-. 1.105, 1.449,
  1.507, 1.742-1.743, 1.767-1.768, 1.1080,
  1.1293
Ayllon, Teodoro, 1929-. 5.4887
Aylward, G. H. 5.2646
Aymard, André. 3.117
Aymé, Marcel, 1902-1967. 2.4386
Ayoub, Mahmoud. 1.2030
Ayrer, Jacob, d. 1605. 2.6606
Ayres, Bill. joint author. 1.4279
Ayres, Robert U. 4.1221, 5.6626
Ayub Khan, Mohammad, 1907-1974. 3.4136
Ayusawa, Iwao Frederick, 1894-. 4.3422
Āzād, Abūlkalām, 1888-1958. 3.4283
Azbel, David. 5.6842
Azéma, Jean-Pierre. 3.1061
Azevedo, Fernando de, 1894-. 3.9189
Azevedo, Mario Joaquim. 5.4682
Azikiwe, Nnamdi, 1904-. 3.5100, 3.5362
Aziz Ahmad. 1.2003
Azrael, Jeremy R., 1935-. 3.1178
Azrin, Nathan H., 1930- joint author. 5.4887
Azuela, Mariano, 1873-1952. 2.5333-2.5335

Bâ, Mariama. 2.4866-2.4867
Baade, Eivind. 5.4208
Baaklini, Abdo I. 4.8776
Baal-Teshuva, Jacob. 3.1172
Baase, Sara. 5.1160
Baatz, Wilmer H. 5.7873
Babai, Don. joint author. 5.959
Babb, Howard S. 2.7377, 2.8708
Babb, Hugh Webster, 1887-. 4.8643
Babb, Lawrence. 2.6438
Babb, Lawrence A. 1.1696
Babbage, Charles, 1791-1871. 5.1126
Babbitt, Frank Cole, 1867-1935. 2.390
Babbitt, Irving, 1865-1933. 2.2360, 2.2615,
  2.10240, 2.11343
Babchuk, Nicholas. 4.6173
Babcock, Emily Atwater. 3.587
Babel', I. (Isaak), 1894-1941. 2.1540
Babelon, André. 2.4070
Babinger, Franz, 1891-1967. 3.3581
Babkin, Boris Petrovich, 1877-. 5.4175
Babuscio, Jack. 4.8356
Bacarisse, Salvador. 2.5314
Bacchelli, Riccardo, 1891-. 2.5001, 2.5020
Bacchylides. 2.441-2.442
Baccini, P. 4.315
Bach, Adolf, 1890-. 2.1174
Bach, Bob. 1.3458
Bach, Carl Philipp Emanuel, 1714-1788. 1.3785,
  1.4541
Bach, Hans I. (Hans Israel), 1902-. 3.3966
Bach, Kent. 2.67
Bacharach, A. L. (Alfred Louis), 1891-1966.
  joint ed. 5.4202
Bacharach, Jere L., 1938-. 3.3710
Bachelard, Gaston, 1884-1962. 1.825
Bachelard, H. S. 5.4328
Bachhofer, Ludwig, 1894-. 1.5748
Bachmaier, Helmut. 2.13590
Bachmann, Alberto Abraham, 1875- . 1.4161
Bachmann, Ingeborg. 2.13673-2.13674
Bachrach, Peter. 4.1667, 4.7563
Bachrack, Stanley D., 1927-. 4.9059
Back, Kurt W. 4.4932
Back, William, 1925-. 4.307, 4.309
Backer, John H., 1902-. 3.1145
Backhouse, Janet. 1.4935, 1.6424, 1.6426
Backman, Jules, 1910-. 4.4421
Backofen, Walter A. 5.7053
Backscheider, Paula. 2.5671
Backstrom, Charles Herbert, 1926-. 4.5014
Backus, John. 1.4372
Backus, Karen. 5.4482
Bacon, Corinne, 1865-1944. comp. 5.8170

Bacon, D. J. 5.2926
Bacon, Francis, 1561-1626. 1.665-1.668, 2.6430, 3.1398
Bacon, G. E. (George Edward), 1917-. 5.2811
Bacon, Gershon C. (Gershon Chaim) 5.8242
Bacon, Margaret Hope. 4.6004
Bacon, Roger, 1214?-1294. 1.382
Bacon, Tony. 1.4133
Bacou, Roseline. 1.4978, 1.6139
Bacovcin, Helen, 1934-. 1.3113
Bacow, Lawrence S. 4.3480
Badawy, Alexander. 1.5084, 1.5215
Baddeley, Alan D., 1934-. 5.322, 5.4350
Baden, John. 4.1903
Bader, Barbara. 1.5829
Badger, Daniel D. 1.5501
Badgley, John H., 1930-. 4.7107
Badian, E. 3.2736, 3.2753, 3.2777, 4.1737
Badrud-Din, Abdul-Amir. 4.4545
Badura-Skoda, Eva. 1.3935
Badura-Skoda, Paul. 1.3935
Baechler, Glenn. 5.6621
Baechtold, Jakob, 1848-1897. 2.13621
Baeck, Leo, 1873-1956. 1.1963
Baehr, P. R. (Peter R.) 4.9206
Baer, Adela S., 1931- comp. 5.3454
Baer, Curtis O. 1.5825
Baer, Eleanora A. 1.26
Baer, Eva. 1.6654
Baer, Gabriel. 4.5394, 4.5469
Baer, George W. 3.5249
Baer, Judith A. 4.9697
Baer, Michael A., joint author. 4.8260
Baer, Morley. 1.5562
Baer, Yitzhak, 1888-. 3.4003
Baerwald, Hans H. 3.4976, 4.8756
Baëta, C. G. 1.1854
Bagarozzi, Dennis A. joint author. 4.6542
Bagby, Philip. 3.458
Bagchi, Amiya Kumar. 4.1797
Bagdikian, Ben H. 2.57
Bagehot, Walter, 1826-1877. 2.5533, 4.7438, 4.8381, 4.8385
Bagger, Jonathan, 1955-. 5.2143
Bagley, Robert W. 1.6672
Bagnall, Austin Graham, 1912-. 5.8085
Bagnall, Nicholas. 2.960
Bagnara, Joseph T. (Joseph Thomas), 1929-. 5.4248
Bagnold, Enid. 2.8411
Bagnold, Ralph A. (Ralph Alger), 1896-. 5.3121
Bagrow, Leo. 4.224
Bagwell, William, 1923-. 4.10718
Bahāʾ Allāh, 1817-1892. 1.2095
Bahadur, Satya Prakash, ed. and tr. 2.1886
Bahl, Roy W. 4.8842
Bahm, Archie J. 1.427
Bahn, Anita K. 5.4684
Bahr, Howard M. 1.2416
Bahro, Rudolf, 1935-. 4.6980
Baier, Kurt. 1.1434
Baierlein, Ralph. 5.2172
Bailar, John Christian, 1904-. 5.2697, 5.2839
Bailbé, Jacques, ed. 2.3977
Bailey, Alfred Goldsworthy. 3.8663
Bailey, Alton Edward, 1907-1953. 5.6894
Bailey, Anthony. 3.2983
Bailey, Arthur W. 5.3264
Bailey, Charles W., joint author. 3.1013
Bailey, Cyril, 1871-1957. ed. and tr. 2.317, 2.451, 2.738
Bailey, D. K. (David Kenneth), 1931-. 5.3066
Bailey, D. R. Shackleton (David Roy Shackleton), 1917-. 2.722, 3.2782
Bailey, David Roy Shackleton. 2.715
Bailey, Elizabeth E. 4.4087
Bailey, Ethel Zoe. joint author. 5.5311
Bailey, F. G. (Frederick George) 3.4351
Bailey, Henry Christopher, 1878-1961. 2.8412
Bailey, James, 1932- ed. 4.6317
Bailey, James Edward, 1942-. 5.7034
Bailey, James Osler. 2.3486, 2.6175, 2.7774
Bailey, John A. 5.5404
Bailey, John W., 1934-. 3.5871
Bailey, L. H. (Liberty Hyde), 1858-1954. 5.3669, 5.5255, 5.5310-5.5311
Bailey, Mabel Driscoll, 1904-. 2.11315
Bailey, Martin J., ed. 4.4706

Bailey, Peter, 1937-. 4.884
Bailey, Richard W. 2.1109
Bailey, Ronald Albert, 1933-. 5.2627
Bailey, Ronald W., comp. 3.6730
Bailey, Stephen Kemp. 4.8007, 4.9550, 4.9587
Bailey, Sydney Dawson. 4.9204, 4.9207-4.9208, 4.9244, 4.9252
Bailey, Thomas Andrew, 1902-. 3.820, 3.846, 3.6306, 3.6328, 3.6340, 3.6394-3.6395, 4.9042
Baillie, Hugh, 1890-1966. 2.3603
Baillie, John, 1886-1960. 1.2839
Baillio, Joseph. 1.6155
Baily, Samuel L. 3.8960
Bailyn, Bernard. 2.3594, 3.7972, 4.9989
Bailyn, Bernard. joint author. 3.6110
Bailyn, Bernard. ed. 3.6883, 4.9480
Bain, David Haward. 3.4599
Bain, Henry M., 1926-. 4.7745
Bain, Iain. 1.4946
Bain, Joe Staten, 1912-. 4.1562
Bain, Kenneth Ray, 1942-. 3.6453
Bain, R. Nisbet (Robert Nisbet), 1854-1909. 3.3093
Bain, Richard C. 4.8141
Bain, Robert. 2.10461
Bainbridge, Beryl, 1933-. 2.9615-2.9616
Baines, Anthony. 1.4125, 1.4165
Baines, Anthony. 1.4126, 1.4163
Baines, Barbara J. (Barbara Joan) 2.6586
Baines, Jocelyn, 1924-. 2.8555
Baines, William Peter, 1878- tr. 2.4329
Bainton, Roland Herbert, 1894-. 1.414, 1.2288, 1.2336-1.2338, 1.2922, 1.3008, 1.3420, 3.467, 5.8447
Bair, Deirdre. 2.8426
Bair, Frank E. 5.2577
Baird, Albert Craig, 1883- ed. 2.3535, 2.10853, 2.10859
Baird, Donald, 1926-. 5.7959
Baird, James. 2.12544
Baird, Jo. 4.5991
Baird, John D. 2.6957
Baird, Joseph Armstrong. 1.5523
Baird, Pamela C. joint author. 4.2061
Baird, Robert, 1798-1863. 1.2371
Bairoch, Paul. 4.1798
Bajema, Carl Jay, 1937- comp. 4.457
Bajpai, Shiva G. 4.180
Bakal, Yitzhak. 4.6883
Bakalar, James B., 1943- joint author. 4.6660
Bakeless, John Edwin, 1894-. 2.6613, 3.8482
Baker, Alan, 1939-. 5.1346
Baker, Arthur Ernest, 1876-. 2.8165
Baker, Byron. 3.5619
Baker, Carlos, 1909-1987. 2.11138, 2.8107, 2.11852-2.11855
Baker, David, 1931-. 1.3754, 1.4484, 5.6716
Baker, Derek. 4.5857
Baker, Donald C. 2.6300
Baker, Donn, 1928-. 5.6479
Baker, Doran J. 5.2307
Baker, Dorothy Dodds, 1907-. 2.11344
Baker, Doyle C. 4.2990
Baker, E. H., 1937-. 5.5866
Baker, Elizabeth C 1934- ed. 1.5193
Baker, Ella, 1903-1986. 4.5993
Baker, Ernest Albert, 1869-1941. 2.5941, 2.6043, 2.6910
Baker, Frank, 1910-. 1.3371, 2.7336
Baker, George, 1941-. 1.1876
Baker, George A. (George Allen), 1932-. 5.1975
Baker, George Pierce, 1903-. 2.2795, 2.6815, 4.4003
Baker, Gladys, 1910-. 5.5216, 5.5260
Baker, Gladys L., 1910- joint author. 5.5219
Baker, Gordon E. 4.8119
Baker, Gordon P. 1.1074
Baker, Herbert G. 5.5312
Baker, Herschel Clay, 1914-. 1.1318, 2.3350, 2.7808
Baker, Holly Cutting, 1949-. 4.774
Baker, Houston A. 2.10304, 2.10307-2.10309, 2.10686
Baker, Houston A. comp. 2.12812
Baker, Hugh D. R. 5.5630, 4.6268
Baker, Jean H. 4.8199
Baker, Jeffrey, 1925-. 2.8327
Baker, John C., 1949-. 5.7322

Baker, John Norman Leonard. 4.45
Baker, John Randal, 1900-. 5.4160
Baker, Kenneth R., 1943-. 5.7035
Baker, Leonard. 4.9821
Baker, Lester. joint author. 5.4941
Baker, Lewis, 1953-. 3.334
Baker, Michael, 1948-. 2.3101
Baker, Michael A., ed. 4.7696
Baker, Oliver Edwin, 1883-1949. 4.153
Baker, Paul R. 1.5312
Baker, Ray Stannard, 1870-1946. 2.3604, 3.6658, 3.7719
Baker, Robert. 5.6944
Baker, Robert Fulton, 1917-. 4.4081
Baker, Robin, 1944-. 5.3970
Baker, Sheridan Warner, 1918-. 2.7023, 2.11856
Baker, T. Lindsay. 5.6235
Baker, Theodore, 1851-1934. 1.3529
Baker, Victor R. 5.1815
Baker, William A. joint author. 4.4218
Baker, William J. (William Joseph), 1938-. 4.929
Bakewell, P. J. (Peter John), 1943-. 4.3737
Bakhash, Shaul. 3.4091
Bakish, David. joint author. 5.7799
Bakke, Dennis. 5.6150
Bakke, E. Wight (Edward Wight), 1903- comp. 4.3343
Bakker, Dirk. 3.5733, 3.9078
Baklanoff, Eric N. 4.4627
Bakunin, Mikhail Aleksandrovich, 1814-1876. 4.7196-4.7197
Bakvis, Herman. 4.8272
Balabanian, Norman, 1922-. 5.6334
Balabanoff, Angelica, 1878-1965. 4.7084
Balachandran, M. 5.8433
Balachandran, Sarojini. 5.8162
Balakian, Anna Elizabeth, 1915-. 2.3877, 2.3881, 2.4428
Balakrishnan, Nagalingam. 3.4361
Balanchine, George. 1.4508
Balandier, Georges. 3.5224
Balanis, Constantine A., 1938-. 5.6491
Balassa, Bela A. 4.4132-4.4133, 4.4163, 4.4586
Balasuriya, Tissa. 1.3225
Balázs, Béla, 1884-1949. 2.2935
Balazs, Etienne, 1905-1963. 3.4629
Balbert, Peter, 1942-. 2.8971
Balbus, Isaac D. 4.7586
Balcomb, Kenneth C., 1940-. 5.4008
Bald, Marjory Amelia. 2.5721
Bald, R. C. (Robert Cecil), 1901-1965. 2.6217, 2.6460, 2.6635-2.6636
Baldanza, Frank. 2.8532, 2.9771
Baldass, Ludwig von, 1887-. 1.6264
Baldensperger, Fernand, 1871-1958. 5.8274
Balderston, Katharine Canby, 1895-. 2.7049
Baldi, Philip. 2.220
Baldick, Robert. 2.4248
Baldini, Umberto. 1.5734
Baldinucci, Filippo, 1625-1696. 1.5011
Baldovinetti, Alesso, ca. 1425-1499. 1.6190
Baldridge, J. Victor. 4.10596
Baldrige, Letitia. 1.1518
Baldry, H. C. 1.229
Baldung, Hans, d. 1545. 1.4986
Baldwin, Alfred Lee, 1914-. 5.559
Baldwin, Alice Mary, 1879-. 3.6917
Baldwin, Allen J. 5.5680
Baldwin, Barry. 2.576
Baldwin, Dane Lewis. 2.7852
Baldwin, Frank. ed. 3.5029
Baldwin H. Ward Publications, Inc. 4.4606
Baldwin, James, 1924-. 2.12856-2.12862, 3.6659-3.6661
Baldwin, James Mark, 1861-1934. ed. 1.99
Baldwin, John L. 4.145
Baldwin, Leland Dewitt, 1897-. 3.7041, 3.8093
Baldwin, Lewis M., joint comp. 2.10682
Baldwin, Marilyn Austin, ed. 2.10957
Baldwin, Robert E. 4.2535, 4.4169
Baldwin, Sidney, 1922-. 4.2951
Baldwin, Thomas F. 4.4068
Baldwin, Thomas Whitfield, 1890-. 2.6862
Baldwin, William, ca. 1518-1563? 2.6428
Baldwin, William Lee. 4.3741
Bales, Robert Freed, 1916-. 4.4933, 4.5054, 4.5654

Balfour, Edward, 1813-1889. 3.4152
Balfour, Michael Leonard Graham, 1908-.
  3.1132, 3.1159, 3.2344, 3.2410, 3.2461
Balfour, Ronald Edmond. 2.8598
Balibar, Etienne, 1942-. 4.1515
Balikci, Asen, 1929-. 3.5873
Balinsky, B. I. (Boris Ivan), 1905-. 5.4122
Balio, Tino. 2.2906, 2.3079
Balkin, Richard. 2.2523
Ball, A. Gordon. 4.2936
Ball, George W. 3.1160
Ball, Howard, 1937-. 4.9727, 4.9837
Ball, Hugo, 1886-1927. 1.6731
Ball, J. N. 4.4099
Ball, John Dudley, 1911-. 2.3474
Ball, Robert Hamilton, 1902- joint author.
  2.5869
Ball-Rokeach, Sandra. 4.5004
Ball, Samuel. 4.10370
Ball, Vic. 5.5345
Ball, Victoria Kloss. 1.5210
Balla, David A. 5.4977
Ballance, Robert H. 4.1799
Ballantine, Cecil. 2.7748
Ballard, Allen B. 4.10850
Ballard, Dana Harry. 5.5939
Ballard, Edward G. 1.1311
Ballard, J. G., 1930-. 2.9617-2.9618
Ballard, Jack S. 5.7350
Ballard, Joseph. 4.9600
Ballard, Stanley S. joint author. 5.2297
Ballet, Arthur H., comp. 2.10792
Ballet Caravan, Inc., New York. 4.1078
Balliett, Whitney. 1.4262, 1.4268
Ballinger, Rex Edward. 2.5356
Ballou, Glen. 5.6558
Ballou, Mary B., 1949-. 5.4890
Ballou, Patricia K. 5.8458
Ballou, Stephen V. 4.10618
Ballstadt, Carl, 1931-. 2.9886
Balma, Michael J., joint author. 4.4372
Balmain, Keith George, joint author. 5.6256
Balmori, Diana. 4.5609
Balmuth, Miriam. 2.1008
Baloyra, Enrique A., 1942-. 3.9068
Balsdon, J. P. V. D. (John Percy Vyvian
  Dacre), 1901-. 3.2739, 3.2799
Balthasar, Hans Urs von, 1905-. 1.2245
Baltimore, David. 5.3502, 5.3597
Baltimore Museum of Art. 1.6458
Baltzell, E. Digby (Edward Digby), 1915-.
  4.5124
Baltzer, Klaus, 1928-. 1.2615
Bālurāv, S. 2.1926
Baly, Denis. 1.2550
Balys, Jonas, 1909- jt. author. 4.805
Balzac, Honoré de. 2.76, 2.3818, 2.4110,
  2.4114-2.4120
Bal'zak, S.S. 4.2364
Balzer, Marjorie Mandelstam. 5.8017
Bambara, Toni Cade. 2.12865, 3.6753
Bamberg, Robert D., ed. 2.11109
Bamberger, Joan. 4.5939
Bambrick, S. (Susan) 4.3725
Bambrough, Renford. ed. 1.259
Bamford, C. G. (Colin Grahame) 4.2216
Bamford, James. 5.7361
Bamford, Paul Walden, 1921-. 5.7505
Banani, Amin. 2.1977
Bancquart, Marie Claire. 2.4203
Bancroft, George, 1800-1891. 3.6314
Bancroft, Hubert Howe, 1832-1918. 3.8567,
  3.8588, 3.8644
Bancroft-Hunt, Norman. 3.5748
Bandura, Albert, 1925-. 4.5040, 4.10374, 5.4888
Bandyopadhyay, Bibhutibhushan, 1894-. 2.1860
Bandyopadhyay, Manik, 1908-1956.
  2.1858-2.1859, 2.1876
Bandyopādhyāẏa, Bibhūtibhūshana, 1896?-1950.
  2.1861
Bandyopadhyaya, Jayantanuja. 3.4229
Bandyopādhyāẏa, Tārāśañkara, 1898-1971.
  2.1862-2.1863, 2.1876
Bane, Mary Jo. 4.5584, 4.5593, 4.10784
Banerjee, Anil Chandra. 1.1825
Banerji, Arun Kumar, 1944-. 3.4237
Banerji, Sures Chandra, 1917-. 2.1851
Banes, Sally. 4.1166

Banfield, Alexander William Francis, 1918-.
  5.3988
Banfield, Edward C. 4.5364, 4.8843
Bang, Herman, 1857-1912. 2.14011
Bangerter, Lowell A., 1941-. 2.13784
Bangs, Carl, 1922-. 1.3319
Banham, Reyner. 1.5261-1.5262
Bank, Stephen P., 1941-. 5.616
Bankier, Joanna. 2.3750
Banks, Ann. 3.6057
Banks, Arthur. 4.119-4.121, 4.177
Banks, Ferdinand E. 4.1766
Banks, Harlan Parker, 1913-. 5.3175
Banks, Michael. 4.9130
Banks, Olive. 4.5871
Banks, Paul, 1957-. 1.3919
Banks, Robert F., 1936-. 4.3438
Banks, Stuart. 5.5457
Banks, Theodore Howard, 1895- ed. 2.6983
Bankwitz, Philip Charles Farwell. 5.7201
Bann, Stephen. 3.415
Bann, Stephen. comp. 1.4840
Banner, James M., 1935-. 3.7112
Banning, Lance, 1942-. 3.6979
Bannister, Robert C. 4.4891
Banno, Masataka. 3.4735
Bannon, Joseph J. 4.890
Banowetz, Joseph. 1.4542
Banta, H. David (Henry David), 1938-. 5.4609
Banti, Luisa, 1894-. 3.2756
Banting, Keith G. 4.2131
Bantock, G. H. (Geoffrey Herman), 1914-.
  2.11630, 4.10239
Banville, Théodore Faullain de, 1823-1891.
  2.4130-2.4131
Banwart, George J. 5.4460
Bar-Tal, Daniel. 4.10762
Bar-Zohar, Michael, 1938-. 3.3910
Barabba, Vincent P., 1934-. 4.1248
Barac, Antun, 1894-1955. 2.1198
Baraka, Amina. 2.10693
Baraka, Imamu Amiri, 1934-. 2.10687, 2.10693,
  2.12868-2.12869, 4.6460
Barakat, Halim Isber. 3.5190
Baral, Robert. 1.4223
Baran, Paul A. 4.1518, 4.2757
Baranson, Jack. 4.3834
Barany, George, 1922-. 3.1940
Baras, Victor. 4.1670
Baras, Zvi. 3.3851
Barasch, Moshe. 1.5746
Baratta, Alessandro. 5.5833
Baratz, Morton S. 4.3390
Barbash, Jack. 4.3344, 4.3349, 4.3434, 4.3631
Barbash, Jack. ed. 4.3345
Barbeau, Arthur E. 3.841
Barber, Benjamin R., 1939-. 4.7564
Barber, Bernard. 4.5055, 4.5280, 4.6375, 5.4608
Barber, C. L. (Cesar Lombardi) 2.6758
Barber, Charles Laurence. 2.980, 2.5745
Barber, Elinor G. 4.6400
Barber, Elinor G. joint author. 4.5280
Barber, Eric Arthur, 1888- ed. 2.247, 2.317
Barber, H. 5.6342
Barber, James. 3.1646
Barber, James David. 4.5226, 4.7917, 4.8114
Barber, James P. 3.5465
Barber, Philip Willson, 1903-. 2.3092
Barber, Richard W. 3.290, 3.343, 3.1367
Barber, Stanley A. 5.5278
Barber, Theodore Xenophon, 1927-. 5.4900
Barbi, Michele, 1867-1941. 2.4933
Barbier, Jacques A., 1944-. 3.9259
Barbour, Hugh. comp. 1.3346
Barbour, Ian G. 5.5511
Barbour, James Murray, 1897-. 1.4379
Barbour, John, d. 1395. 2.9843
Barbour, Kenneth Michael. 3.5174, 4.191,
  4.1708
Barbour, Roger William, 1919- joint author.
  5.3925
Barchilon, Jacques. 2.4045
Barclay, Glen St. John, 1930-. 2.5983, 3.5542
Barclay, Harold B. 3.3702
Barclay, Alexander, 1475?-1552. 2.1010
Bard, Allen J. 5.2911
Bard, Rachel, 1921-. 3.3487
Bardach, John E. 5.3259, 5.5466

Bardhan, Pranab K. 4.2984
Bardwick, Judith M. 4.5918, 4.5925
Barea, Arturo, 1897-1957. 3.3455
Bareau, Juliet Wilson. 1.4975
Bareham, Tony. 2.7618
Barfield, Claude E. 4.4660
Barfield, Owen, 1898-. 1.4, 2.2713, 2.7598
Barford, Philip. 1.4527
Barger, Harold. 4.4212
Barghoorn, Frederick Charles, 1911-. 3.3240,
  4.8646
Bargon, Joachim. 5.6533
Bari, Shamsul. 3.4142
Barile, Paolo. joint author. 4.8623
Baring-Gould, Ceil. 2.14101
Baring-Gould, William Stuart, 1913-. 2.7680,
  2.14101
Baring, Maurice, Hon. 1874-1945, comp. 2.1309
Barish, Jonas A. 2.3102, 2.6605
Baritz, Loren, 1928-. 3.4498, 3.6074, 4.5231
Barja, César. 2.5098, 2.5109
Barkan, D. D. 5.5915
Barkan, Joel D. 4.8798
Barkenbus, Jack N. 4.3810
Barker, A. J. 3.812
Barker, Andrew, 1943-. 1.3644
Barker, Arthur Edward, 1911-. 2.7165
Barker-Benfield, G. J. 4.5493
Barker, Charles Albro, 1904-. 3.6075
Barker, Christine R. 2.13849
Barker, Dudley. 3.5527
Barker, Elisabeth. 3.3599
Barker, Ernest, Sir. 3.37, 3.77, 3.86, 3.1288,
  4.7212, 4.7275, 4.7288, 4.7339, 4.7354-4.7355,
  4.7372, 4.7468, 4.7475, 4.7525
Barker, Eugene Campbell, 1874-1956. 3.8322
Barker, George, 1913-. 2.8413
Barker, Judith. 4.2610
Barker, Lucius Jefferson, 1928-. 3.6662
Barker, Murl. 2.1531
Barker, Nancy Nichols. 3.1978
Barker, Richard Hindry, 1902-. 2.6637, 2.6937
Barker, Roger Garlock, 1903-. 4.6301, 5.315
Barker, Stephen Francis. ed. 1.513
Barker, Virgil, 1890-. 1.5884
Barkin, Solomon, 1907-. 4.3440
Barksdale, Richard. 2.11901
Barkun, Michael. 1.2949
Barlach, Ernst, 1870-1938. 2.13675
Barlett, Donald L. 5.6007
Barlow, Frank. 1.2435, 1.2437, 3.1321
Barlow, Frank. 3.1322, 3.1343
Barlow, Harold. 1.3569, 1.3596
Barlow, Judith E. 2.10791
Barlow, Nora. ed. 5.3190
Barlow, Shirley Ann. 2.473
Barltrop, J. A. 5.2920
Barna, Arpad. joint author. 5.6472
Barna, Ion. 2.3040
Barnaby, Frank. 4.9168
Barnaby, John M. 4.1040
Barnard, Chester Irving, 1886-1961. 4.2641
Barnard, D. J. 5.5315
Barnard, Harry, 1906-. 3.7484, 3.8409
Barnard, Noel. 3.4689
Barnard, T. C. (Toby Christopher) 3.1834
Barnard, William D. 4.8209
Barnave, Joseph, 1761-1793. 4.7426
Barnds, William J. 3.4131, 3.5011
Barner, Wilfried. 2.13630
Barnes, Albert C. (Albert Coombs), 1872-1951.
  1.5101
Barnes, Arthur Chapman, 1891-. 5.5330
Barnes, Barry. 5.744
Barnes, Burton Verne, 1930- joint author.
  5.3785
Barnes, Catherine A. 4.9683
Barnes, Christopher J. 2.1592
Barnes, Djuna. 2.11345
Barnes, Graham. 5.4897
Barnes, Harry Elmer, 1889-1968. 3.22, 3.376,
  4.4738, 4.5087-4.5088, 4.6841
Barnes, J. A. (John Arundel), 1918-. 4.574
Barnes, J. Wesley. joint author. 5.5597
Barnes, John, 1931-. 2.10149
Barnes, Jonathan. 1.230, 1.284, 1.292,
  1.297-1.298, 1.324
Barnes, Mildred, joint comp. 5.3029

Barnes, Milton. Warner, joint comp. 2.5508
Barnes, Norman. 4.921
Barnes, Peter, 1931-. 2.9619
Barnes, R. H. (Robert Harrison), 1944-. 3.5930
Barnes, Ralph Mosser, 1900-. 5.5620
Barnes, Robert D. joint author. 5.3802
Barnes, Robert D. 5.3831
Barnes, Timothy David. 1.2213, 3.2811
Barnes, Virgil E. (Virgil Everett), 1903- comp. 5.3029
Barnet, Richard J. 3.1204, 3.7558, 4.2730, 4.9062
Barnett, A. D, ed. 3.3638
Barnett, A. Doak. 3.4679, 3.4774, 3.4783, 4.2470, 4.2487, 4.9077
Barnett, Correlli. 3.781, 3.791, 3.1000, 3.1264, 3.1642
Barnett, George Leonard. 2.7903-2.7904
Barnett, Harold Joseph, 1917-. 4.1767
Barnett, Jonathan. 1.5582, 4.6307
Barnett, Louise K. 2.7308
Barnett, Richard David, 1909-. 1.5614-1.5615, 3.4006
Barnett, Rosalind C. 4.5919
Barnett, S. A. (Samuel Anthony), 1915-. 5.4041
Barnett, Zolo George, 1914- ed. 4.10160
Barney, Stephen A. 2.943
Barney, William L. 3.7185, 3.7336
Barnhart, Clarence Lewis, 1900-. 2.1081, 2.1089, 2.1094-2.1095, 2.5486
Barnhart, John Donald, 1895-. 3.8389, 3.8392
Barnhart, Robert K. 2.1094, 2.1095
Barnie, John. 3.1328
Barnlund, Dean C. comp. 4.5001
Barnouw, Adriaan Jacob, 1877-1968. 2.13943, 3.2987
Barnouw, Erik, 1908-. 2.2900
Barnstone, Aliki. 2.3748
Barnstone, Willis, 1927-. 2.575, 2.3748, 2.5143, 2.5195, 2.5273
Barnwell, John, 1947-. 3.8245
Baroff, George S. 5.4971
Baroja, Pío, 1872-1956. 2.5232
Baron, David P. 4.4550
Baron, Hans, 1900-. 3.2851
Baron, Salo Wittmayer, 1895-. 3.3832, 3.3838, 3.3902, 3.3992, 3.6562
Baron, Samuel Haskell, 1921-. 4.7087
Barone, Michael. 4.7851, 4.7995
Barr, Alfred Hamilton, 1902-. 1.4818-1.4819, 1.4841, 1.4874, 1.6119, 1.6130
Barr, Avron, 1949-. 5.1010
Barr, Donald. 4.10029
Barr, James. 1.2538, 1.2793
Barr, Marleen S. 2.10591
Barr, Paul C. 5.5696
Barra, Donald. 1.4495
Barraclough, E. M. C. 3.288
Barraclough, Geoffrey, 1908-. 1.3146, 1.3213, 3.377, 3.1330, 3.2249, 3.2263, 4.125
Barraga, Natalie. 4.6599
Barral, Robert. 2.3990
Barratt Brown, Michael. 4.1519, 4.4185
Barratt, Ernest S. 5.427
Barrault, Jean Louis. 2.3367, 2.3370
Barrell, John. 1.6015, 2.5690
Barrenechea, Ana María. 2.5377
Barreno, Maria Isabel, 1939-. 2.5460
Barret-Kriegel, Blandine. 4.6703
Barrett, Anthony, 1941-. 1.5351
Barrett, C. K. (Charles Kingsley), 1917-. 1.2712
Barrett, David B. 1.2285
Barrett, Douglas E. 1.6308
Barrett, E. C. (Eric Charles) 4.19, 5.6713
Barrett, Gerald R. comp. 2.8972
Barrett, James Wyman, 1885- ed. 2.3667
Barrett, Laurence I. 3.7937
Barrett, Leonard E. 3.6728
Barrett, Norman S. 3.3648
Barrett, Paul H. 5.3197
Barrett, Richard A. 4.480
Barrett, Stanley R. 4.5473
Barrett, William, 1913-. 1.450, 1.484, 3.8041
Barrett, William Spencer. 2.457
Barricelli, Jean Pierre. 2.1492, 2.2371
Barrie, J. M. (James Matthew), 1860-1937. 2.7389-2.7390
Barrie, James Matthew, bart., Sir. 2.7388

Barrier, N. Gerald (Norman Gerald) 3.4271
Barrington, Ernest James William. 5.4244
Barrios de Chungara, Domitila. 4.6087
Barrios, Eduardo, 1884-1963. 2.5404
Barroll, J. Leeds (John Leeds), 1928-. 2.5843, 2.6776
Barron, Caroline M. ed. 3.1369
Barron, Hal S. 4.5193
Barron, Jerome A. 4.9714-4.9715
Barron, John, 1930-. 4.6839-4.6840
Barron, Neil, 1934-. 2.3454
Barron, Samuel Landon, 1910- tr. 4.1467
Barron, Stephanie. 1.5715
Barron, W. R. J. (William Raymond Johnston) 2.6415
Barron's Educational Series, Inc. College Division. 4.9938
Barros, James. 3.732, 3.870, 3.2685, 3.2710
Barrow, G. W. S. 3.1788, 3.1791
Barrow, Gordon M. 5.2799
Barrow, Reginald Haynes, 1893-. 2.536
Barrow, Robin. 4.10183
Barrow, Terence, 1923-. 1.5096, 1.5770
Barrows, Susanna, 1944-. 4.5041
Barry, B. T. K. 5.6790
Barry, Brian M. 4.7657
Barry, Frederick, 1876-, ed. 5.2035
Barry, Jan, 1943- joint comp. 2.10755
Barry, Philip, 1896-. 2.11346
Barry, Roger Graham. 5.2581
Barry, Tom, 1950-. 4.4628
Barry, Vincent E. 5.4558
Barrymore, Ethel, 1879-1959. 2.3240
Barrymore, Lionel, 1878-1954. 2.3242
Barsacq, Léon, 1906-1969. 2.3007
Barsam, Richard Meran. 2.2983
Barsby, John A. 2.743
Barsom, John M., 1938-. 5.5785
Barston, R. P. (Ronald Peter) 4.9314
Bart, Benjamin F. 2.4197
Bart, Benjamin F. ed. 2.4188
Bart, Pauline. 4.6736
Bartee, Thomas C. 5.6572
Bartel, Nettie R. 4.10953
Bartels, Robert, 1913-. 4.4276, 4.4315
Bartenieff, Irmgard. 5.254
Barth, Alan. 4.8039
Barth, Fredrik, 1928-. 3.4064, 4.470
Barth, Gunther Paul. 4.6201
Barth, Herbert, 1910-. 1.4036
Barth, John. 2.12876-2.12882
Barth, Karl. 1.381, 1.1478-1.1479, 1.2258, 1.2453, 1.2708, 1.2753, 1.2763, 1.2773, 1.3017, 1.3049, 1.3285
Barth, Markus. ed. 1.2717
Barth, R. L. (Robert L.). 2.10705
Barth, Tom. F. W. (Tom. Fredrik Weiby), 1899-1971. 5.3031
Bartha, Richard. joint author. 5.4458
Barthelme, Donald. 2.12887-2.12894
Barthes, Roland. 1.7, 1.6681, 2.76, 2.146, 2.2339, 2.2536, 2.4052, 5.6953
Bartholet, Carolyn, joint author. 5.7791
Bartholomew, Augustus Theodore, 1882-1933. 2.7511, 2.7514, 2.7615
Bartholomew, David J. 4.1202
Bartke, Wolfgang. 3.4809, 4.8743
Bartle, Robert Gardner, 1927-. 5.1436
Bartlett, C. J. (Christopher John), 1931-. 3.1704 5.323, 5.378
Bartlett, Frederic Charles, Sir, 1887-1969. 5.323, 5.378
Bartlett, Irving H. 3.7095, 3.7257
Bartlett, John, 1820-1905. 2.3728, 2.6683
Bartlett, John R. (John Raymond) 1.2625
Bartlett, M. S. (Maurice Stevenson) 5.1409
Bartlett, Norman. 3.6411
Bartlett, Phyllis Brooks. 2.6562, 2.7939
Bartlett, Robert. 3.1353
Bartley, Numan V. 3.8267, 4.8097
Bartley, William Warren, 1934-. 5.924
Bartók, Béla, 1881-1945. 1.3787
Bartol'd, V. V. (Vasiliĭ Vladimirovich), 1869-1930. 3.4067
Bartollas, Clemens. 4.6869, 4.6893
Bartolozzi, Bruno. 1.4549
Barton, Allan F. M. 5.2036
Barton, Anne. 2.6597, 2.6719
Barton, Derek, Sir, 1918-. 5.2714

Barton, Frank. 2.3698
Barton, John H. 4.9163
Barton, Josef J. 3.8387
Barton, Len. 4.10777
Barton, Lucy, 1891-. 2.3126
Barton, Margaret, 1897-. 2.3340
Barton, Roger, 1903-. 4.4432
Barton, Roy Franklin, 1883-1947. 3.4590
Bartram, John, 1699-1777. 5.3189
Bartram, William, 1739-1823. (jt. author) 5.3189
Bartsch, Karl, 1832-1888. ed. 2.13534
Bartz, Patricia McBride, 1921-. 4.2558
Baruch, Bernard M. (Bernard Mannes), 1870-1965. 3.7624
Baruch, Grace K. joint author. 4.5919
Barut, A. O. (Asim Orhan), 1926-. 5.2161
Barzun, Jacques, 1907-. 1.3817, 2.1138, 2.2563, 2.2616, 3.51, 3.151, 3.378, 3.410, 3.497, 4.10057, 4.10570, 5.8172
Basch, Françoise. 2.6032
Basch, Norma. 4.9903
Bascom, Willard. 4.348
Bascom, William Russell, 1912-. 4.810
Baserga, Renato. 5.3614
Basevi, Giorgio, 1938-. 4.4189
Basham, A. L. (Arthur Llewellyn) 3.4179, 3.4191
Basham, Richard Dalton. 3.8810
Basheer, Vaikom Muhammad, 1910-. 2.2267
Bashevkin, Sylvia B. 4.5965
Basil, Saint, Bishop of Caesarea, ca. 329-379. 2.356
Baskervill, Charles Read, 1872-1935, ed. 2.6224-2.6225
Baskerville, Barnet. 2.3532, 2.10856
Baskette, Floyd K. 2.3563
Baskin, Bo. 4.3064
Baskin, Leonard, 1922-. 1.6437, 2.419, 2.9711, 2.9717
Basler, Roy P. (Roy Prentice), 1906-. 3.7301
Basler, Roy Prentice, 1906-. 3.7299-3.7300
Basolo, Fred, 1920-. 5.2708, 5.2840
Basore, John William, 1870- tr. 2.692
Bass, Alan R., joint ed. 4.4358
Bass, Allan D. ed. 5.4290
Bass, Bernard M. 4.4954
Bass, Ellen. joint comp. 2.10740
Bass, George Fletcher. 3.240
Bass, Herbert J. ed. 3.6221
Bass, Jack. 3.8170, 4.9849
Bass, Scott A. joint author. 4.10720
Bassan, Fernande. 5.8005
Bassan, Maurice, comp. 2.10982
Bassani, Giorgio. 2.5021-2.5023
Bassegoda Nonell, Juan. 1.5443
Bassett, John Earl, 1942-. 2.11707
Bassett, Samuel Eliot, 1873-1936. 2.492
Bassler, G. Clayton. joint author. 5.2747
Basso, Keith H., 1940-. 3.5837-3.5838, 3.5842
Bassoff, Bruce, 1941-. 2.8734
Bastable, Charles Francis, 1855-. 4.4195
Bastid, Marianne. 4.2469
Bastide, Roger, 1898-1974. 1.1879, 3.5688
Bastin, John Sturgus, 1927- comp. 3.4538
Basu, Asoke, 1938- joint author. 4.6520
Basu, Manoje. 2.1864
Bat Ye'or. 3.3657
Bataille, Gretchen M., 1944-. 3.5833
Batatu, Hanna, 1926-. 4.8774
Batchelder, Marjorie Hope, 1903-. 2.2837
Batchelor, G. K. (George Keith) 5.1662
Batchelor, John, 1942-. 5.7382
Bate, Philip. 1.4166, 1.4169, 1.4174
Bate, Walter Jackson, 1918-. 1.1386, 2.2460, 2.7083-2.7084, 2.7595, 2.7855, 2.7873
Bateman, Alan Mara, joint author. 5.6729
Bateman, Alan Mara. 5.6728-5.6729
Bateman, Wayne, 1951-. 1.4457
Bates, Daniel G. 3.3701
Bates, David, 1945-. 3.2224
Bates, M. Searle (Miner Searle), 1897-1978. 1.3009
Bates, Marston, 1906-1974. 4.109, 4.1609, 5.3302, 5.3377, 5.3513
Bates, Robert H. 4.2992
Bates, Robert Latimer, 1912-. 5.2939, 5.6792
Bates, Stephen, 1958-. 4.7789

Bates, Susannah, 1941-. 5.7726
Bates, Timothy Mason. 3.6735
Bateson, Frederick Wilse, 1901-. 2.5769, 2.5914, 2.6943, 5.7933, 5.7937
Bateson, Gregory. 3.5649
Bateson, Mary Catherine. 4.425
Bateson, P. P. G. (Paul Patrick Gordon), 1938-. 5.4106
Bath, Geoffrey. 5.1707
Báth, Markus. 5.3114
Bathe, Basil W. 5.7419
Bathe, Klaus-Jürgen. 5.5725
Bathie, William W. 5.6218
Batho, Edith Clara, 1895-. 2.5521
Bathurst, Robin G. C. 5.3062
Batschelet, Edward. 5.3309
Batshaw, Mark L., 1945-. 5.5082
Batson, Benjamin A. (Benjamin Arthur), 1942-. 3.4530
Batstone, Eric. 4.3341
Battaglia, Richard A. 5.5439
Battan, Louis J. 5.2553, 5.2559
Battcock, Gregory, 1937- ed. 1.4805, 1.4849, 1.6730, 2.2948
Batten, Charles. 2.5933
Batten, Donna. 4.7898
Batten, Roger Lyman. joint author. 5.2969
Battenhouse, Roy Wesley, 1912- ed. 1.2484
Battersby, Martin. 1.4838, 1.6540
Battestin, Martin C. 2.5677
Battigelli, Mario C. 5.5022
Battin, M. Pabst. 1.1325
Battis, Emery John, 1915-. 3.7971
Battiscombe, Georgina. 2.8010
Battison, Edwin A. 1.6667
Battisti, Eugenio. 1.5439, 1.6208
Baudelaire, Charles, 1821-1867. 1.4670, 1.4963, 2.3859, 2.4133-2.4139, 2.11201
Baudet, E. H. P. (Ernest Henri Philippe), 1919-. 3.98
Bauer, Arnold J. 4.5273
Bauer, Carlos. 2.5156
Bauer, Caroline Feller. 4.10316
Bauer, David L. 5.3880
Bauer, Edward L. 5.2647
Bauer, Erwin A. 5.5491
Bauer, Felice, 1887-1960. 2.13795
Bauer, Gerhard. 5.2682
Bauer, K. Jack (Karl Jack), 1926-. 3.7135
Bauer, P. T. (Péter Tamás) 4.2749, 4.2758-4.2761
Bauer, Raymond Augustine, 1916-. 3.3205, 3.3241, 4.2703, 4.4171, 4.4429
Bauer, Walter, 1877-1960. 1.2961
Bauer, Wolfgang. 2.2201
Bauer, Yehuda. 3.1083
Baugh, Albert Croll, 1891-. 2.967, 2.5511, 2.6311
Baugh, Edward. 2.9974
Baugh, John, 1949-. 2.1156
Baugher, Joseph F. 5.1725
Baughman, James P. 4.3896
Bauhaus. 1.4649
Baum, Andrew. 5.4584, 5.4845
Baum, Dale, 1943-. 4.8190
Baum, Lawrence. 4.9788
Baum, Martha. 4.5822
Baum, Paull F. (Paull Franklin), 1886-. 2.8015, 2.11140
Baum, Warren Charles. 4.2325
Baum, Willa K. 3.425, 3.441
Bauman, Lawrence, joint author. 5.2640
Bauman, Zygmunt. 1.1304, 4.4870
Baumbach, Jonathan. 2.10851-2.10852
Baumeister, Theodore, 1897-. 5.6112
Baumer, Franklin Le Van, ed. 3.87
Baumer, Rachel Van M., 1928-. 2.3393
Baumert, John H. joint author. 5.1799
Baumgart, Winfried. 4.8912
Baumgartel, Elise J., 1892-. 3.5137
Baumol, Daniel. 4.3089
Baumol, William J. 4.1385, 4.1478, 4.1837, 4.2089, 4.2998, 4.3009
Baumol, William J. joint ed. 4.1989
Baumont, Maurice, 1892-. 3.716
Baur-Heinhold, Margarete. 2.3173

Baur, John I. H. (John Ireland Howe), 1909-1987. 1.4869, 1.4882, 1.4891, 1.5679, 1.5900, 1.5908, 1.5937
Baur, Karla. 4.5499
Bautier, Robert Henri. 4.2184
Bavier, Richard. 5.8239
Bawcutt, Priscilla J. 2.6470
Bawden, Charles R. 3.4865
Bawden, Liz-Anne. 2.2873
Bax, Dirk. 1.6240
Baxandall, Michael. 1.5783, 1.6180
Baxandall, Rosalyn Fraad, 1939-. 4.3275
Baxby, Derrick. 5.4534
Baxter, Annette Kar. 2.12190
Baxter, Charles, 1848-1919. 2.8121
Baxter, Craig. 3.4141
Baxter, James K. 2.10209-2.10211
Baxter, James Phinney, 1893-. 5.788, 5.7433
Baxter, John. 2.3005, 2.3010
Baxter, John Walker. 2.6476
Baxter, Maurice G. (Maurice Glen), 1920-. 3.7096
Baxter, Sandra, 1945-. 4.5954
Baxter, Stephen Bartow, 1929-. 3.1514
Bay, Christian, 1921-. 4.7625-4.7626
Bay, Edna G. 4.6158
Bayfield, Matthew Albert, 1852-1922. ed. 2.481
Baykov, Alexander, 1899-. 4.2372
Bayle, Pierre, 1647-1706. 3.323
Bayles, Michael D. 4.1627
Bayless, Jon W., joint author. 5.6278
Bayless, Kathryn G. 4.973
Bayley, John, 1925-. 2.1419, 2.2421
Baylin, Frank. 5.6394
Baylis, John. 5.7300
Bayliss, Gwyn M. 5.8228
Baylor, Ann M. joint author. 5.5024
Baylor, Robert. comp. 2.6097
Baym, Max Isaac. 3.6237
Baym, Nina. 2.10287
Bayne, John M., joint author. 4.7868
Bayne, Pauline Shaw. 1.3546
Baynes, Cary F. tr. 2.2181
Baynes, Norman Hepburn, 1877-1961. ed. 3.2393
Baynham, Dorsey. 4.10495
Bayor, Ronald H., 1944-. 3.8046
Bazaraa, M. S., 1943-. 5.5586, 5.5594
Bazelon, David T., 1923-. 4.1978
Bazelon, Irwin. 1.4232
Bazin, André. 2.2893, 2.2936, 2.3063
Bazin, Maurice, joint author. 5.2098
Bazin, Nancy Topping, 1934-. 2.9589
Beach, D. N. 3.5510
Beach, David, 1938-. 1.4423
Beach, Frank Ambrose, 1911-. 4.5501, 4.5503, 5.4085, 5.4298
Beach, Joseph Warren, 1880-1957. 2.3523, 2.5525, 2.5814, 2.7783, 2.7951, 2.8400, 2.10482, 2.10613
Beach, Milo Cleveland. 1.6421
Beach, William W. joint author. 4.149
Beadle, L. C. (Leonard C.) 5.3280
Beadle, Muriel. 4.10398
Beadle, Richard. 2.6213-2.6214
Beagle, Peter S. 2.12898
Beaglehole, J. C. (John Cawte) 3.5535, 3.5594, 4.89
Beakley, George C. 5.5694
Beale, Howard K. (Howard Kennedy), 1899-1959. 3.6250, 3.7457, 3.7699, 4.10577
Beales, Derek Edward Dawson. 3.380
Beals, Alan R. 4.5424, 5.8354
Beals, Ralph Leon, 1901-. 4.4335
Beam, George D., joint author. 4.8072
Beam, Jacob D., 1908-. 3.7627
Bean, Lee L. 4.5674, 5.4833
Bean, Louis Hyman, 1896-. 4.8137
Bean, Lowell John. 3.5724, 3.5847
Bean, Philip. 5.4840
Bean, R. (Ron), 1938-. 4.3435
Beanblossom, Ronald E., 1941- ed. 1.713
Bear, Jacob. 4.295
Bearce, George Donham, 1922-. 3.4260
Beard, Charles Austin, 1874-1948. 3.38, 3.6076-3.6078, 3.6315, 3.7750-3.7751, 4.1948-4.1949, 4.7823, 4.7826, 4.7833, 4.9043, 4.9046, 4.9645

Beard, Charles Relly, 1891-1958. joint author. 4.839
Beard, Geoffrey W. 1.5502, 1.5504
Beard, James, 1903-. 5.7130
Beard, James Franklin, 1919-. 2.10972
Beard, Mary Ritter, 1876-1958. 3.6003, 3.6077-3.6078, 3.6315, 4.5841, 4.5845
Beard, Miriam, 1901-. 4.4252
Beard, Robert W., joint ed. 1.1228
Bearden, Romare, 1914-. 1.4890
Beardon, Alan F. 5.1494
Beardsell, Peter R., 1940- ed. 2.5389
Beardsley, Aubrey, 1872-1898. 1.5842, 2.8271
Beardsley, John. 1.4845, 1.4916
Beardsley, Monroe C. 1.1365
Beardsley, Monroe C. ed. 1.419
Beardsley, Richard King, 1918-. 3.4873, 4.5447
Beare, William. 2.641
Bearse, Ray, ed. 3.7960, 3.7968, 3.7990
Beasley, Jerry C. 2.7243, 5.7967
Beasley, Maurine Hoffman. 4.1959
Beasley-Murray, George Raymond, 1916-. 1.3015
Beasley, W. G. (William G.), 1919-. 3.4915, 3.4950
Beaton, James D., 1930-. 5.5294
Beaton, Roderick. 2.572
Beatson, Elizabeth Home, joint author. 1.6413
Beatson, Peter. 2.10187
Beattie, Ann. 2.12899-2.12900
Beattie, J. H. M. (John H. M.) 4.469
Beattie, John. 3.5284, 4.474
Beattie, Susan. 1.5688
Beatty, J. Kelly. 5.1790
Beatty, John C. 5.5653
Beatty, Richmond Croom, 1905-1961. 2.10665, 2.10942, 2.10978
Beaty, H. Wayne. 5.6259
Beaty, Jerome, 1924-. 2.7694
Beaubien, Anne K. 5.7648
Beauchamp, Dan E. 5.4958
Beauchamp, Henry King, 1866-1907, ed. and tr. 3.4167
Beauchamp, Tom L. 1.709, 1.1454, 4.4268
Beaufort, L. F. de (Lieven Ferdinand de), 1879-. 5.3812
Beaufre, André. 3.950
Beaujeu-Garnier, Jacqueline. 4.1651
Beauman, Sally. 2.3331
Beaumarchais, Jean-Pierre de. 2.3819
Beaumarchais, Pierre Augustin Caron de, 1732-1799. 2.4049, 2.4061
Beaumont, Cyril W. (Cyril William), 1891-1976. 4.1101, 4.1117, 4.1170, 4.1173
Beaumont de La Bonninière, Gustave Auguste de, 1802-1866. 3.7200
Beaumont, Francis, 1584-1616. 2.6554-2.6556
Beaumont, Jane, 1945-. 5.8259
Beaumont, Keith, 1944-. 2.4594
Beaumont, Peter. 3.3687, 4.2983
Beaurline, Lester A. 2.6598
Beaurline, Lester A. ed. 2.7286
Beauvoir, Simone de, 1908-. 1.1465, 2.4388-2.4401, 4.5950, 4.6588
Beaver, Frank Eugene. 5.6998
Beaver, Paul Chester, 1905-. 5.4759, 5.4761
Beaver, Stanley Henry. 4.2251
Beaverbrook, Max Aitken, Baron, 1879-1964. 3.1692
Beazley, Charles Raymond, Sir, 1868-1955. 4.60
Beazley, J. D. (John Davidson), 1885-1970. 1.6634-1.6635, 1.6638
Bebb, Phillip N., 1941-. 1.2326
Bebel, August, 1840-1913. 4.7056
Bebey, Francis. 1.3747
Becerra, Rosina M. 4.5812, 4.6570
Bechert, Heinz, 1932-. 1.2142
Bechet, Sidney, 1897-1959. 1.4080
Bechtel, Helmut. 5.5349
Beck, Brenda E. F. 2.2273, 4.5435
Beck, Carl, 1930-. 4.7587, 4.7752, 4.9868
Beck, Emily Morison. 2.3728
Beck, F. (Felix) 5.3596
Beck, Hans Georg, 1910-. 1.4694
Beck, J. Murray (James Murray), 1914-. 3.8803, 4.8317
Beck, Jacob. 5.280
Beck, L. J. (Leslie John) 1.786, 1.789

Beck, Lewis White. 1.861, 1.882
Beck, Lewis White. ed. and tr. 1.913
Beck, Lois, 1944-. 4.5910
Beck, Paul Allen. 4.7773
Beck, Richard, 1897- ed. 2.13994
Beck, Simone. 5.7135
Beck, Stanley M. 4.8274
Beckenbach, Edwin F. 5.1417
Becker, Abraham Samuel, 1927-. 4.9154
Becker, Beverly J., 1930-. 4.910
Becker, Carl Lotus, 1873-1945. 1.432, 3.61,
    3.379, 3.459, 3.6918, 4.7683, 4.7818
Becker, David. 1.6458
Becker, E. Lovell (Ernest Lovell), 1923-. 5.4486
Becker, Edwin D. 5.2681
Becker, Edwin D. joint author. 5.2314
Becker, Felix, 1864-1928. 1.4584
Becker, Gary Stanley, 1930-. 4.3115, 4.10543
Becker, George Joseph. 2.2402, 2.2661, 2.11587,
    2.12156
Becker, George Joseph. ed. 1.6720
Becker, Georges, 1916-. 2.3826
Becker, Howard Saul, 1928-. 4.6467, 4.6668
Becker, James. 4.10449
Becker, Laurence A. 4.10914
Becker, Lawrence C. 4.9374
Becker, Marion Rombauer. joint author. 5.7134
Becker, Marvin B. 3.2827
Becker, Otto, 1885-1955. 3.2309
Becker, Richard, 1887-1955. 5.2366
Becker, Robert A., 1943-. 4.7834
Becker, Robert O. 5.4207
Becker, Seymour. 3.3327
Becker, Stephen D., 1927-. 1.5847
Beckerman, Bernard. 2.6863
Beckett, I. F. W. (Ian Frederick William)
    5.7307
Beckett, J. C. (James Camlin), 1912-. 3.1814,
    3.1831, 3.1835
Beckett, Ronald Bryner. 1.6027
Beckett, Samuel, 1906-. 2.4403-2.4411,
    2.8416-2.8425
Beckford, George L. 4.1826
Beckford, William, 1760-1844. 2.7397
Beckingsale, B. W. 3.1406, 3.1434
Beckley, Robert E. 1.1870
Beckman, Theodore N., 1894-. 4.4383
Beckman, William A. 5.6102
Beckmann, George M. 3.4971, 4.8763
Beckson, Karl E., 1926-. 2.2357
Beckwith, Burnham P. (Burnham Putnam),
    1904-. 3.73
Beckwith, John, 1918-. 1.4743, 1.5168
Beckwith, T. G. (Thomas G.) 5.5682
Bécquer, Gustavo Adolfo, 1836-1870. 2.5214
Bečvář, Antonín, 1901-. 5.1737
Bedau, Hugo Adam. 4.7511, 4.9861
Beddington, J. R. 5.3980
Beddoes, Thomas Lovell, 1803-1849. 2.7399
Bédé, Jean Albert. 2.2670
Bede, the Venerable, Saint, 673-735. 1.2431,
    2.651
Bedell, Madelon. 2.10896, 2.10899
Bedford, Emmett G. 2.7194
Bedi, Mohinder S., joint author. 4.9236
Bedient, Calvin. 2.12649
Bedient, Phillip Edward, 1922- joint author.
    5.1507
Bédier, Joseph, 1864-1938. 2.3824, 2.3958,
    2.3967
Bedjaoui, Mohammed. 4.4137
Bedlington, Stanley J., 1928-. 3.4543
Bedouin, Jean Louis, ed. 2.4422
Bedworth, David D. 5.7034
Beech, John R. 4.10345
Beecher, Henry Ward, 1813-1887. 1.3335
Beecher, Jonathan. ed. 4.7165
Beede, Benjamin R. 4.9378
Beedle, Lynn S. 5.6088
Beeftink, W. G. 5.3780
Beegle, J. Allan (Joseph Allan), 1918- joint
    author. 4.6368
Beehr, Terry A. 4.4355
Beekman, E. M., 1939-. 2.13955
Beeler, John. 3.1263, 5.7186
Beeman, Donald, ed. 5.6330
Beeman, Richard R. 3.8205, 3.8216
Beenackers, A. A. C. M. 5.6855

Beer, Ferdinand Pierre, 1915-. 5.5732, 5.5772
Beer, George Louis, 1872-1920. 4.8909-4.8910
Beer, Gillian. 2.6026, 2.7945
Beer-Hofmann, Richard, 1866-1945. 2.13676
Beér, J. M. (János Miklós), 1923- ed. 5.2261
Beer, John B. 2.7423, 2.7436, 2.8323, 2.8660
Beer, John Bernard. 2.7596
Beer, Lawrence Ward, 1932-. 4.7680
Beer, Michael. 4.4362
Beer, Samuel Hutchison, 1911-. 3.1647, 4.4671,
    4.8069, 4.8424
Beerbohm, Max, Sir, 1872-1956. 2.3315,
    2.8435-2.8438
Beere, Carole A., 1944-. 4.5914
Beermann, W. 5.4135
Beers, Henry Putney, 1907-. 5.7825
Beers, Norman R., 1911- joint ed. 5.2500
Beers, Thomas W. 5.5431
Beeson, B. F., joint author. 5.1261
Beeson, Paul B. (Paul Bruce), 1908-. 5.4488
Beeston, A. F. L. (Alfred Felix Landon) 2.1833
Beethoven, Ludwig van, 1770-1827.
    1.3794-1.3795
Begab, Michael J. 4.6612, 5.4973
Begg, David K. H. 4.1460
Begin, Menachem, 1913-. 3.3915
Begleiter, Henri. joint author. 5.4959
Begon, Michael. 5.3337, 5.3514
Béguin, Albert, 1898-. 2.4221, 2.4415
Béhague, Gerard. 1.4285
Behan, Brendan. 2.8442-2.8443
Behler, Ernst, 1928- ed. 2.13655
Behler, John, joint author. 5.3921
Behlmer, Rudy. 2.2907
Behman, M. Reza, 1945-. 4.8770
Behn, Aphra, 1640-1689. 2.6899
Behney, Clyde J. joint author. 5.4609
Behnke, John A. 5.4215, 5.4574
Behr, Roy L., 1958-. 4.8165
Behrend, George. 5.6074
Behrend, Jeanne, 1911- ed. 1.3878
Behrendt, Stephen C., 1947-. 2.7120
Behrendt, Walter Curt, 1884-1945. 1.5263
Behrens, Catherine Betty Abigail. 3.2041
Behrens, Heinrich. 5.8423
Behrman, Jack N. 4.2731, 4.4167
Behrman, S. N. (Samuel Nathaniel), 1893-1973.
    2.8439, 2.11347
Beichman, Arnold. 2.12803, 4.9237
Beichman, Janine. 2.2076
Beidler, John, 1941-. 5.1220
Beidler, Philip D. 2.10433, 2.10969
Beidler, William, 1928-. 1.198
Beier, Ulli. 2.2308
Beiglböck, W., 1939-. 5.2142
Beisner, Robert L. 3.7498
Beisser, Arnold R. 4.5810
Beit-Hallahmi, Benjamin. 4.5744
Beitz, Charles R. 4.8985
Beizer, Boris, 1934-. 5.1161
Beja, Morris. 2.2974, 2.6052
Beker, Avi. 4.9169
Beker, Johan Christiaan, 1924-. 1.2703
Belanger, Terry. 5.7693
Belaúnde, Víctor Andrés, 1883-. 3.9164
Belch, Jean. 4.10304
Belcher, David W. 4.3125
Belden, Jack, 1910-. 3.4775
Belding, William G. 5.5712
Belfort, Georges. 5.6027
Belgian Environmental Mutagen Society. 5.4728
Belin, David W. 3.7878
Beling, Willard A. 4.3420, 4.3671
Belinsky, Vissarion Grigoryevich, 1811-1848.
    1.1109
Belitt, Ben, 1911-. 2.5230
Beljame, Alexandre, 1843?-1906. 2.5656
Belkaoui, Ahmed, 1943-. 4.4397
Belkin, Gary S. 4.10277
Belknap, Dorothy C. 1.6445
Belknap, Robert L. 2.1264
Bell, Alan P., 1932-. 4.5526, 4.5528
Bell, Aubrey F. G. (Aubrey Fitz Gerald),
    1882-1950. 2.5449-2.5450
Bell, C. Gordon. 5.1228
Bell, C. Ritchie. 5.5364
Bell, Cecil, 1935-. 4.2701

Bell, Christopher Richard Vincent, 1911-. 4.93
Bell, Clive, 1881-1964. 1.5124-1.5125, 2.8444
Bell, Colin. 4.6180
Bell, Coral. 5.7217
Bell, Corydon, 1894-. 5.2541
Bell, Daniel. 3.6178, 4.5101, 4.5125, 4.6986
Bell, Daniel. 3.6071, 3.7818, 4.4782
Bell, David A., 1930-. 5.6550
Bell, David Scott. 4.8594
Bell, Derrick, A. 4.10794
Bell, Eric Temple, 1883-1960. 5.1086
Bell, F. G. (Frederic Gladstone) 5.5889
Bell, Harold Idris, Sir, 1879-. 3.5155
Bell, Inglis Freeman, 1917-. 5.7890, 5.7934,
    5.7959, 5.7970
Bell, J. Bowyer, 1931-. 3.1857, 3.3861
Bell, Jack, 1904-. 3.7643
Bell, Jimmy. 4.6816
Bell, John. 2.9217
Bell, Marvin. 2.12901
Bell, Michael. comp. 1.6383
Bell, Michael Davitt. 2.10605, 2.11066
Bell, Michael J. (Michael Joseph), 1947-. 3.6749
Bell, Millicent. 2.12112
Bell, Peter D. 4.5345
Bell, Quentin. 2.9590, 4.833
Bell, R. C., Mrs., tr. 1.6212
Bell, R. P. (Ronald Percy) 5.2878
Bell, Richard, 1876-. 3.3651
Bell, Robert E. 1.1639
Bell, Roger J. (Roger John), 1947-. 3.5645
Bell, Ronald, 1931-. 3.4901
Bell, Susan G. 4.6091
Bell Telephone Laboratories, Inc. 5.6418,
    5.6479
Bell, Thomas L. joint author. 4.2783
Bell, William J. 5.3865, 5.3875
Bellack, Arno A. 4.10433
Bellah, Robert Neelly, 1927-. 1.1836, 1.2409,
    3.4889, 3.6079
Bellairs, Angus d'A. 5.3916-5.3917
Bellak, Leopold, 1916-. 5.545, 5.4847
Bellamy, David J. joint author. 4.284
Bellamy, Edward, 1850-1898. 2.10907, 4.7179
Bellamy, Joe David. 2.10833
Bellas, Ralph A. 2.8011
Belleau, Remy, 1527?-1577. 2.3997
Belli, Donna, joint author. 5.8476
Belli, Giuseppe Gioachino, 1791-1863. 2.4987
Bellman, Richard Ernest, 1920-. 5.1004, 5.1417
Bello, Ahmadu, Sir, 1909-. 3.5363
Bello, Andrés, 1781-1865. 2.890
Bello, José Maria, 1880-. 3.9213
Belloc, Hilaire, 1870-1953. 2.7564,
    2.8445-2.8447
Belloli, Andrea P. A. 1.4648, 1.6362
Bellone, Enrico. 5.1928
Bellot, Hugh Hale, 1890-. 3.6203
Bellow, Saul. 2.11348-2.11357
Bellwood, Peter S. 4.672, 4.748
Belmonte, Thomas, 1946-. 4.5365
Belnap, Nuel D., 1930-. 1.1255, 5.1036
Belo, Jane, comp. 3.4585
Belo, Jane. 4.535
Beloff, Max, 1913-. 3.733, 3.1195, 3.1205,
    3.1648-3.1649, 3.3057, 4.9010, 4.9069
Belote, James H. 3.1004
Belote, William M., joint author. 3.1004
Belous, Richard S. joint author. 4.3158
Belove, Charles. 5.6452, 5.6464
Belsey, Catherine. 2.2428
Belshaw, Cyril S. 4.2598, 4.5479
Belt, Lida M. 1.3754
Bely, Andrey, 1880-1934. 2.1474-2.1475
Belz, Carl. 1.4283
Belz, Herman. 3.7308, 4.9684
Bembo, Pietro, 1470-1547. 2.4963-2.4964
Bemelmans, Ludwig, 1898-1962. 2.11364
Bemis, Samuel Flagg, 1891-1973. 3.6396-3.6397,
    3.6934, 3.7037, 3.7039, 3.7122-3.7123, 3.9012,
    5.8263
Ben-Ami, Shlomo. 3.3456-3.3457
Ben-Amos, Paula. 1.5089
Ben-David, Joseph. 5.828
Ben-Dor, Gabriel. 3.3879
Ben-Ephraim, Gavriel, 1946-. 2.8980
Ben-Gurion, David, 1886-1973. 3.3926
Ben-Sasson, Haim Hillel, 1914-1977. 3.3850

Bénac, Henri, 1913- ed. 2.4069
Benade, Arthur H. 1.4373
Benardete, Jane. 2.10819
Benardete, M. J. (Maír José), 1895- ed. 2.5179
Benavente, Jacinto, 1866-1954. 2.5234
Benay, Jacques G., comp. 2.3935
Benchley, Nathaniel, 1915-. 2.11366
Benchley, Robert, 1889-1945. 2.11365
Benda, Julien, 1867-1956. 2.4024
Bendall, D. S. 5.3340
Bender, Arnold E. 5.7103
Bender, Barbara. 4.717
Bender, Gerald J. 3.5407
Bender, Gordon Lawrence, 1918-. 4.283
Bender, Harold Stauffer, 1897-1962. 1.3304
Bender, James F. (James Frederick), 1905-. 2.1021
Bender, Myron L., 1924-. 5.2879
Bender, Robert M. 2.6128, 2.6144
Bender, Thomas. 4.6202
Bendiner, Elmer. 4.9181
Bendiner, Robert. 4.10666
Bendix, Reinhard. 4.5446
Bendix, Reinhard. 4.4765, 4.4826, 4.6374, 4.7550
Bendix, Reinhard. joint author. 4.6382
Bendix, Reinhard. 4.6397, 4.7252
Bendixson, Terence. 4.4031
Benecke, Gerhard. 3.2274, 3.2280
Benedetti, Robert L. 2.3105, 2.3112
Benedict, Manson. 5.6617
Benedict, Michael Les. 3.7455, 3.7458
Benedict, Murray Reed, 1892-. 4.2937
Benedict, Robert P. 5.2232, 5.6239
Benedict, Ruth, 1887-1948. 3.4884, 4.397, 4.518
Benedict, Ruth Fulton. 4.426
Benedict, Saint, Abbot of Monte Cassino. 1.3239
Benedikt, Michael, 1935- ed. and tr. 2.3939
Benefield, Larry D. 5.6031
Benenson, Abram S., 1914-. 5.4672
Benería, Lourdes. 4.5484
Beneš, Edvard, 1884-1948. 3.1916, 3.1931
Benesch, Otto, 1896-1964. 1.4760, 1.6159
Benét, Mary Kathleen. 4.4344
Benét, Stephen Vincent, 1898-1943. 2.11367-2.11371
Benet, Sula, 1903-. 5.4214
Benét, William Rose, 1886-1950. 2.2345, 2.11374-2.11375, 2.12825
Benevolo, Leonardo. 1.5254, 1.5583
Bénézet, Louis Tomlinson, 1915-. 4.10588
Bénézit, Emmanuel, 1854-1920. 1.4581
Benfey, O. Theodor (Otto Theodor), 1925-. 5.2848
Bengtson, Hermann, 1909-. 5.8223
Bengtsson, Arvid. 4.912
Benítez, Fernando, 1911-. 3.8926
Benjamin, Anna S. 1.2206
Benjamin, Gerald. 4.7704
Benjamin, Gerald. joint author. 4.8264
Benjamin, Harold Raymond Wayne 1893-1969. 4.9958
Benjamin, Thomas, 1952-. 3.8938
Benjamin, Walter, 1892-1940. 2.2609
Benjaminson, Peter, 1945-. 2.3596
Benkovic, Stephen J., joint author. 5.4409
Benn, Gottfried, 1886-1956. 2.13678
Benn, Maurice B., 1914-. 2.13556
Benn, Tony, 1925-. 4.8426, 4.8543
Bennassar, Bartolomé. 3.3402
Bennett, Alan, 1934-. 2.9620
Bennett, Arnold, 1867-1931. 2.8452-2.8457
Bennett, Benjamin, 1939-. 2.13492
Bennett, Bruce Lanyon, 1917- joint author. 4.898
Bennett, Charles Edwin, 1858- tr. 2.671
Bennett, Daphne. 3.2330
Bennett, Edward L. 5.4351
Bennett, Edwin Keppel. 2.13501
Bennett, Geoffrey Martin. 3.1280
Bennett, George W. (George William), 1908-. 5.5471
Bennett, H. R. 5.1585
Bennett, H. S. (Henry Stanley), 1889-. 2.5600, 3.1373, 5.7546
Bennett, Hal. 2.12902
Bennett, Harry. 5.6822

Bennett, Henry Stanley. 4.2258
Bennett, J. A. W. (Jack Arthur Walter) 2.5601, 2.6331
Bennett, J. A. W. (Jack Arthur Walter) ed. 2.6383
Bennett, Joan (Frankau). 2.7700
Bennett, Joan Frankau. 2.6914, 2.9585
Bennett, John William, 1915-. 3.8860
Bennett, Jonathan Francis. 1.864, 1.906, 1.1098
Bennett, Lerone, 1928-. 3.6606-3.6607
Bennett, Neville. 4.10260
Bennett, Norman Robert, 1932-. 3.5065, 3.5289
Bennett, Ralph Francis. 3.960
Bennett, Randy Elliot, 1952-. 4.10935
Bennett, Richard Bedford Bennett, 1st Viscount, 1870-1947. 4.2133
Bennett, Scott. 2.3690
Bennett, Tom, 1944-. 4.1029
Bennett, Tony. 1.1363
Bennett, W. Lance. 4.5226
Bennett, Wendell Clark, 1905-1953. 3.9158, 3.9282
Bennett, William, 1941-. 5.5131
Bennett, William John, 1943-. 4.10827
Bennett, William R. (William Ralph), 1904-. 5.6343
Bennetts, R. G. 5.6475
Bennigsen, Alexandre. 3.3028
Benningfield, Lloyd M. joint author. 5.6273
Bennis, Warren G. ed. 4.4922
Benoit, Emile. 4.1979
Bensel, Richard Franklin, 1949-. 4.8048
Bensman, David, 1949-. 4.3383
Bensman, Joseph. joint author. 4.6373
Bensman, Marvin R., 1937-. 4.9536
Benson, Adolph Burnett, 1881- ed. 3.6594
Benson, Arthur Christopher, 1862-1925. 2.7982, 2.8168
Benson, C. David. 2.5610
Benson, C. T. (Clark T.) 5.1293
Benson, Charles Scott. 4.10653, 4.10728
Benson, Evelyn Rose. 5.5205
Benson, Ezra Taft. 4.2952
Benson, Gigi. 5.6994
Benson, Harry. 5.6994
Benson, Jackson J. 2.11864
Benson, John. 4.3536
Benson, K. Blair. 5.6439
Benson, Larry Dean, 1929-. 2.6312, 2.6409, 2.6413
Benson, Lee. 3.6268, 3.6273, 3.8031, 4.4005, 4.8103
Benson, Lyman David, 1909-. 5.3649, 5.3655, 5.3694
Benson, Mary. 4.8794
Benson, Robert Louis, 1925-. 3.5967
Benson, Rowland. 5.6220
Benson, Sidney William, 1918-. 5.2634
Benson, Susan Porter, 1943-. 4.4331
Benson, Thomas W. 2.64
Benstock, Bernard. 2.9152
Benstock, Bernard. joint author. 2.8903
Benstock, Shari, 1944-. 2.8903
Benston, George J. 4.3014
Benston, Kimberly W. 2.12871, 2.12874
Bent, Arthur Cleveland, 1866-1954. 5.3963
Benthall, Jonathan. 1.4806
Bentham, Frederick. 2.3141
Bentham, Jeremy, 1748-1832. 1.722-1.723, 4.1408, 4.7439, 4.7728
Bentinck, Morris. 2.4490
Bentley, Arthur Fisher, 1870-1957. 4.7217
Bentley College. Center for Business Ethics. 4.4101, 4.4269-4.4273, 4.4273a
Bentley, E. C. (Edmund Clerihew), 1875-1956. 2.8460-2.8461
Bentley, Eric, 1916-. 2.2806, 2.3175, 2.3205, 2.3760-2.3761, 2.4898-2.4899, 2.8080, 3.7539
Bentley, G. Carter. 5.8097
Bentley, G. E. (Gerald Eades), 1930-. 2.7403, 2.7419
Bentley, Gerald Eades, 1901-. 2.2521, 2.3287, 2.3297, 2.6691, 2.6715
Bentley, Joyce. 2.8273
Bentley, Michael, 1948-. 4.8409
Benton, Arthur Lester, 1909-. 5.5093
Benton, Charlotte, joint comp. 1.5264

Benton, Thomas Hart, 1889-1975. 1.5918, 2.12560
Benton, Tim. comp. 1.5264
Benvenisti, Meron, 1934-. 3.3818
Benvenuti, Antonia. 2.4901
Benz, Ernst, 1907-. 1.3107
Beranek, Leo Leroy, 1914-. 1.5494, 5.6344
Beranek, William, 1946-. 5.855
Berberian, Mimi. 5.6054
Bercovitch, Sacvan. 2.10262, 2.10392, 2.10527
Berdan, Frances. 3.8881
Berdecio, Roberto, ed. 1.6451
Berdiaev, Nikolaï, 1874-1948. 1.1110-1.1111, 3.186, 3.460, 3.3114
Berding, Andrew Henry Thomas. 3.7649
Berdoe, Edward, 1836-1916. 2.7477
Bereday, George Z. F. 4.9972
Berelson, Bernard, 1912-. 4.7953, 4.7958
Berend, T. Iván (Tibor Iván), 1930-. 4.2349-4.2350
Berendt, Joachim Ernst. 1.4316
Berenson, Bernard, 1865-1959. 1.4606, 1.5126, 1.5196-1.5197, 1.5839, 1.6178
Berent, Irwin M. 5.8247
Berent, Jerzy. 4.5299
Beres, Louis René. 4.9170
Beresford, M. W. (Maurice Warwick), 1920-. 3.1326, 3.1721
Berestetskiĭ, V. B. (Vladimir Borisovich) joint autho.ˑ 5.2373
Berg, A. Scott (Andrew Scott) 2.2520
Berg, Arne, 1917-. 5.6095
Berg, Barbara J. 4.6006
Berg, Fred Anderson, 1948-. 3.6940
Berg, Geri, 1946-. 5.4600
Berg, Ivar E. 4.3563, 4.4254, 4.10729
Berg, Joseph M. 5.4976
Berg, L. S. (Lev Semenovich), 1876-1950. 4.253
Berg, Larry L. joint author. 4.9846
Berg, Leo van den. 4.6315
Berg, Maxine, 1950-. 4.1316
Berg, Richard E. 5.2224
Berg, Robert J. 4.2612
Berg, Robert L. 5.4648
Berg, Stephen. 2.10776
Berg, William J. 2.790
Bergen, Arthur R. 5.6282
Bergen, Bernard J. joint author. 4.5072
Bergen, Bernard J. 5.4591
Berger, A. (André), 1942-. 5.2528
Berger, Arthur, 1912-. 1.3842
Berger, Arthur Asa, 1933-. 2.77
Berger, Bennett M. 4.5788, 4.6354
Berger, Brigitte. 4.5650
Berger, Carl. 3.8667
Berger, Carl Clinton, 1939-. 3.8737
Berger, Dorothea, 1907-. 2.13645
Berger, Fred R., 1937-. 1.733
Berger, Gaston. 1.1017
Berger, Gordon Mark, 1942-. 4.8760
Berger, Jennifer. 2.1074
Berger, John. 1.4619, 1.5116
Berger, Klaus, 1901-. 1.5843, 1.6108
Berger, Meyer, 1898-1959. 2.3663
Berger, Michael L., 1943-. 4.4037
Berger, Morroe. 2.4297, 4.9685
Berger, Peter L. 1.1289, 1.1572-1.1573, 1.2754, 4.4827, 4.5650
Berger, Raoul. 4.9639, 4.9734, 4.9745, 4.9860
Berger, Sidney E. 2.10946
Berger, Suzanne. 1.2254, 4.2913
Berger, Thomas, 1924-. 2.12903-2.12905
Berger, Wolfgang H. 5.2984
Bergeron, David Moore. 2.6793
Bergeron, Louis, 1929-. 3.2121
Bergey, D. H. (David Hendricks), 1860-1937. 5.4452
Bergfeld, Joachim, 1906-. 1.4046
Berggren, William A. 5.3154
Bergh, Simon van den, 1882-. 1.368
Berghahn, Volker Rolf. 3.2338, 5.7248
Berghorn, Forrest J., 1934-. 4.5813
Bergin, Allen E., 1934-. 5.4854
Bergin, Thomas Goddard, 1904-. 2.4880, 2.4912, 2.4936, 2.4945, 4.1031
Bergk, Theodor, 1812-1881. 2.321
Bergman, Andrew. 2.2908
Bergman, Anni, 1919-. 5.603

Bergman, Elihu. 4.1675
Bergman, Elihu. joint author. 4.1667
Bergman, Gösta Mauritz, 1905-1975. 2.3142
Bergman, Ingmar, 1918-. 2.3035, 2.14083
Bergman, Nils Gösta, 1894-. 2.922
Bergmann, Barbara R. 4.6031
Bergmann, Fredrick Louis, 1916-. 2.7031
Bergmann, Gustav, 1906-. 1.508-1.509, 5.864
Bergmann, Merrie. 1.1198
Bergmann, Peter Gabriel. 5.2084-5.2085
Bergmeyer, Hans Ulrich. 5.3316
Bergmeyer, Jürgen. 5.3316
Bergner, Michael. 4.9324
Bergonzi, Bernard. 2.8253
Bergquist, Charles W. 3.9175
Bergquist, G. William, ed. 5.7950
Bergquist, Patricia R. 5.3839
Bergreen, Laurence. 2.11297
Bergson, Abram, 1914-. 4.2373, 4.2392, 4.2402,
    4.2405, 4.2407
Bergson, Henri, 1859-1941. 1.827-1.829, 1.1273,
    2.3786
Bergsten, C. Fred, 1941-. 4.4161, 4.4560
Bergsträsser, Ludwig, 1883-1960. 4.8602
Beringause, Arthur F., 1919-. 3.419
Berk, Richard A. joint author. 4.6223, 4.6879
Berke, Beverly. joint author. 5.7088
Berke, Roberta Elzey. 2.10487
Berkeley, Anthony. 2.8586
Berkeley, Dorothy Smith. 5.3637
Berkeley, Edmund. 5.3637, 5.7522
Berkeley, George, 1685-1753. 1.686-1.689
Berkeley, George Fitz-Hardinge, 1870-. 3.2857
Berkeley, Joan (Weld) Mrs. 3.2857
Berkes, Ross N. 4.9236
Berkey, Martha Lou. 4.6752
Berkhofer, Robert F. 3.5824
Berki, R. N. 4.6929
Berkin, Carol. 3.6962, 4.5963, 4.5992
Berkouwer, G. C. (Gerrit Cornelis), 1903-.
    1.3012, 1.3283
Berkowitz, Leonard, 1926-. 5.419
Berkowitz, N. (Norbert), 1923-. 5.6873
Berlak, Ann. 4.10122
Berlak, Harold. 4.10122
Berlant, Anthony, joint author. 3.5918
Berlant, Anthony. 3.5913
Berle, Adolf Augustus, 1895-1971. 4.1929,
    4.3010, 4.3055
Berleant-Schiller, Riva. 4.4444, 4.6367
Berlekamp, Elwyn R. 5.1256
Berlin, Adele. 1.2534
Berlin, Charles, 1936-. 5.8233
Berlin, Edward A. 1.4277
Berlin, Graydon Lennis, 1943-. 5.6993
Berlin, Ira, 1941-. 3.6634, 3.7385
Berlin, Irving Norman, 1917-. 5.5079
Berlin, Isaiah. 1.457, 1.744, 1.1092, 2.1445,
    3.505, 4.6949, 4.7663
Berlin, Joyce E., joint author. 5.4630
Berliner, David C. 4.10919
Berliner, Joseph S. 4.2400, 4.2743
Berlioz, Hector, 1803-1869. 1.3808,
    1.3815-1.3816, 1.4488, 1.4498
Berlitz, Charles Frambach, 1913-. 2.1100
Berlyne, D. E. 5.214, 5.379
Berman, Harold Joseph, 1918-. 4.9349, 4.9916
Berman, Harry M, 1902-1944. 5.3012
Berman, Larry. joint author. 5.8407
Berman, Larry. 3.4499, 4.7888
Berman, Lawrence V. (Lawrence Victor) 5.8238
Berman, Louis Arthur. 4.5790
Berman, Louise M. 4.10269
Berman, M. (Marshall), 1939-. 3.187
Berman, Maureen R., 1948-. 4.9322
Berman, Milton. 3.6253
Berman, Neil David, 1947-. 2.10585
Berman, R. (Robert) 5.2211
Berman, Robert P., 1950-. 5.7322, 5.7470
Berman, Ronald. 2.6794, 3.6080, 4.4422
Bermel, Albert. 2.2827
Bermingham, Alan. 5.6440
Bernac, Pierre. 1.3946, 1.4570
Bernal, Ignacio. 3.8880
Bernal, J. D. (John Desmond), 1901-. 3.52,
    5.1929
Bernal, Joe, 1927- joint author. 3.8328
Bernanos, Georges, 1888-1948. 2.4412-2.4415

Bernard, Antoine, 1890-1969. 2.3965
Bernard, Bruce. 5.6967
Bernard, de Clairvaux, saint, 1090-91-1153.
    1.3067
Bernard, Jessie Shirley, 1903-. 4.5561, 4.5634,
    4.5921, 4.6017, 5.483
Bernard, of Clairvaux, Saint, 1090 or 91-1153.
    1.3143, 1.3257
Bernard, Paul P. 3.1885-3.1886, 4.86
Bernard, Richard M., 1948-. 4.6241
Bernard Silvestris, fl. 1136. 2.818
Bernard, Thomas J. 4.6687
Bernays, Paul. 5.1632
Bernbaum, Ernest, 1879-. 2.5682, 2.5913, 2.6069
Bernd, Clifford A. 2.13473, 2.13662
Berndt, Ronald Murray, 1916-. 4.599, 4.677
Berne, Eric. 4.4923, 5.4896
Berne, Michel. 4.2447
Berner, Robert A., 1935-. 5.3118
Bernet Kempers, August Johan, 1906-. 1.5056
Bernhard, Henry, ed. 3.2355
Bernhard, Thomas. 2.13880-2.13881
Bernhard, Winfred E. A., comp. 4.8153
Bernhardt, Sarah, 1844-1923. 2.3371-2.3372
Bernhardt, William F. 2.2707, 2.2709-2.2710
Bernheim, Alfred L., 1893-. 2.3266
Bernheim, Kayla F. 5.4924
Bernheimer, Richard. 1.4595
Bernier, Bernard A. 5.7771
Bernier, François, 1620-1688. 3.4256
Bernier, Ivan. 4.8274
Bernini, Gian Lorenzo, 1598-1680. 1.5010
Berns, Walter, 1919-. 4.6848, 4.7673, 4.9701
Bernstein, Barton J. ed. 3.7791, 3.7802
Bernstein, Barton J. 3.6204
Bernstein, Basil B. 2.24
Bernstein, Carl, 1944-. 3.7916, 3.7925
Bernstein, Eckhard. 2.13465
Bernstein, Eduard, 1850-1932. 4.7057
Bernstein, Gail Lee. 4.7124
Bernstein, Harry, 1909-. 3.9211
Bernstein, Irving, 1916-. 4.3564-4.3566
Bernstein, Jeremy, 1929-. 5.841, 5.952, 5.1945,
    5.2457
Bernstein, John Andrew, 1944-. 1.908
Bernstein, Marilyn. joint author. 4.10636
Bernstein, Marver H. 4.3079, 4.7980
Bernstein, Ralph, 1933-. 4.20
Bernstein, Richard J. 1.587, 4.1203
Bernstein, Richard J. ed. 1.626
Béroul, 12th cent. 2.3965
Berquist, Goodwin F. (Goodwin Fauntleroy),
    1930-. 2.2534
Berreman, Gerald Duane, 1930-. 3.4360, 4.568
Berridge, Geoff. 4.9213
Berrie, A. M. M. 5.5313
Berrigan, Daniel. 1.3263
Berrill, N. J. (Norman John), 1903-. 5.4123
Berrol, Selma Cantor. 4.10903
Berry, Brian Joe Lobley, 1934-. 4.196, 4.4119,
    4.6288, 4.6302
Berry, Chuck. 1.4087
Berry, Cicely. 2.3539
Berry, Donald Stilwell, 1911-. 4.4024
Berry, Dorothea M. 5.8148
Berry, Edward I. 2.6766
Berry, Eliot, 1949-. 2.13072
Berry, F. A. (Frederic Aroyce), 1906- ed.
    5.2500
Berry, Faith. 2.11902
Berry, Herbert. 2.7287
Berry, I. William. 4.997
Berry, Jean de France, duc de, 1340-1416.
    1.6428
Berry, Jeffrey M., 1948-. 4.8035
Berry, L. G. (Leonard Gascoigne), 1914-.
    5.3013
Berry, Leonard, 1930-. 4.1812
Berry, Mary Elizabeth, 1947-. 3.4939
Berry, Mary Frances. 3.6639, 4.9789
Berry, R. Albert. 4.2893, 4.8343
Berry, R. Stephen, 1931-. 5.2800
Berry, Ralph, 1931-. 2.6720, 2.6882
Berry, Richard W., 1933- joint author. 5.6798
Berry, Robert C. 4.931, 4.9578
Berry, Sara. 3.5354
Berry, Virginia (Gingerick) 3.593

Berry, Wallace. 1.4475
Berry, William B. N. 5.3083
Berryman, John, 1914-1972. 2.5624, 2.10983,
    2.11376-2.11380
Bers, Lipman. 5.1527
Bers, Melvin K. 4.3311
Berson, Lenora E. 4.3206
Berst, Charles A. 2.8081
Bertalanffy, Ludwig von, 1901-1972. 5.113
Bertault, Philippe. 2.4121
Bertelé, René. ed. 2.4633
Bertelson, David. 3.8116
Bertensson, Sergei, 1885-1962. 1.3953
Berthier, Alexandre, prince de Neuchâtel et de
    Wagram, 1753-1815. 3.6947
Berthoff, Rowland Tappan, 1921-. 3.6537,
    4.5126
Berthoff, Warner. 2.10382, 2.11160
Berthold, Margot, 1922-. 2.3167
Bertholf, Robert J. 2.7433
Bertholle, Louisette. 5.7135
Bertier de Sauvigny, Guillaume de, 1912-.
    3.1890, 3.2143
Bertin, John J., 1938-. 5.6661
Bertin, Léon, 1896-1956. 5.3804
Bertocci, Angelo Philip, 1907-. 2.4140
Bertocci, Peter Anthony. 1.571
Bertocci, Philip A., 1940-. 3.2142
Bertolotti, Mario. 5.6490
Berton, Pierre, 1920-. 3.7105, 3.8650, 3.8658,
    4.4016
Bertonasco, Marc F., 1934-. 2.6965
Bertram, James M. 2.10204
Bertrand Russell Peace Foundation. 4.9341
Bertsch, Gary Kenneth, 1944-. 4.6966
Berval, René de. 3.4452
Berve, Helmut, 1896-. 1.5220
Berwick, Robert C. 5.1007
Berztiss, A. T. 5.1162
Besançon, Robert M. (Robert Martin) 5.1890
Besant, Annie Wood, 1847-1933. 4.5677
Besant, C. B. 5.5695
Besant, Walter, Sir, 1836-1901. 2.7400
Beschloss, Michael R. 3.7777
Beschner, George M. 4.6667
Besford, Pat. 4.988
Beshers, James M. 4.6289
Beshir, Mohamed Omer, 1926-. 3.5169
Bessason, Haraldur, 1931-. 2.13980
Besser, Gretchen R. 2.4715
Bessette, Joseph M. 4.7930
Bessinger, Jess B. 2.6278
Bessom, Malcolm E. 1.4409
Best, Alan C. G. 5.5052
Best, Alan D. 2.13868, 2.13935
Best, Arthur. 4.2062
Best, Charles Herbert, 1899-. 5.4191
Best, Elsdon, 1856-1931. 3.5608
Best, Ernest. 1.2719
Best, Geoffrey Francis Andrew. 3.653
Best, John Hardin. 4.10165
Best, Judith. 4.7964
Best, Myron G. 5.3043
Best, Reba A. 5.8122
Bester, Alfred. 2.12906
Bestor, Arthur Eugene, 1908-. 4.10218
Besterman, Theodore. 1.5045, 2.4106, 5.7680
Bet ha-sefer la-talmide hu. l. 'a. sh. Sh.
    Rotberg. 5.8236
Betancourt, Philip P., 1936-. 3.2590
Béteille, André. 3.4172
Beth, H. L. 4.3964
Beth, Hans Ludwig. 4.3959
Bethe, Hans Albrecht, 1906-. 5.2049, 5.2126
Bethel, Elizabeth Rauh. 3.8253
Bethell, Leslie. 3.8975
Bethell, Samuel Leslie. 2.6721
Béthemont, Jacques. 3.2824
Bethurum, Dorothy, ed. 2.2627
Beti, Mongo, 1932-. 2.4868-2.4869
Betjeman, John, 1906-. 2.8462-2.8464, 2.9374
Bettelheim, Bruno. 4.819, 4.5708, 4.5745,
    4.10337, 5.149, 5.5097, 5.5110
Bettenson, Henry Scowcroft. tr. 1.2204
Bettenson, Henry Scowcroft. ed. 1.2272
Bettenson, Henry Scowcroft. 1.2199
Betteridge, Harold T. ed. 2.1189
Betteridge, W. (Walter), 1911-. 5.6791

Betti, Ugo, 1892-1953. 2.5024
Bettmann, Otto. joint author. 1.3494
Betts, Doris. 2.12907-2.12908
Betts, Emmett Albert, 1903-. 4.10457
Betts, John Rickards, 1917-1971. 4.932
Betts, Raymond F. 4.7531, 4.8896, 4.8928
Betts, Richard K., 1947-. 3.6498, 5.7220, 5.7261
Betts, Robert B. 3.8483
Betts, Robert Brenton. 1.2461
Betz, Frederick, 1915-. 5.5890
Betz, Hans Dieter. 1.2716
Beuchat, Henri, joint author. 3.5877
Beuf, Ann H., 1938-. 5.5086
Beurdeley, Jean Michel. joint author. 1.5756
Beuys, Joseph. 1.4988
Bevan, Clifford. 1.4177
Bevan, Edwyn Robert, 1870-1943. 3.3797,
  3.5156
Bevan, William, 1922- joint ed. 5.106
Bévenot, Maurice, ed. and tr. 1.2191
Beveridge, Albert Jeremiah, 1862-1927. 3.7004,
  3.7291
Beveridge, John, 1857-. 2.13987
Beveridge, W. I. B. (William Ian Beardmore),
  1908-. 5.972, 5.4741
Beveridge, William Henry Beveridge, Baron,
  1879-1963. 4.1505, 4.3192, 4.3229
Beverley, Robert, ca. 1673-ca. 1722. 3.8184
Beverton, R. J. H. 5.3980
Beville, Hugh Malcolm. 4.4063
Bevington, David Martin. 2.5859
Bevis, Richard W. 2.5911
Bew, Paul. 3.1872
Bewley, J. Derek, 1943-. 5.3736
Bewley, Marius. 2.10276, 2.10534
Beye, Charles Rowan. 2.274, 2.421, 2.493
Beyer, Edvard, 1920-. 2.14039
Beyer, Glenn H. ed. 4.6249
Beyer, Harald, 1891-. 2.14030
Beyer, Robert T. (Robert Thomas), 1920-.
  5.2050
Beyer, Stephan. 1.2150
Beyer, William H., comp. 5.1401
Beyer, William H. 5.1125, 5.2649
Beyme, Klaus von. 4.7780
Bez, H. E. 5.1248
Bèze, Théodore de, 1519-1605. 2.3938, 4.7552
Bézier, Pierre. 5.6247
Bezirgan, Basima Qattan, 1933-. 4.5908
Bezkorovainy, Anatoly. 5.4402
Bezucha, Robert J. 3.2230, 4.5293
Bhagat, Rabi S. 4.4355
Bhagwati, Jagdish N., 1934-. 4.1784, 4.2762,
  4.4105, 4.4134-4.4135, 4.4138, 4.4239
Bhardwaj, Surinder Mohan. 1.1720
Bhargava, Moti Lal. 4.8717
Bhargava, Vijay K., 1948-. 5.6390
Bharier, Julian. 4.2564
Bhartrhari. 2.1943, 2.1953
Bhaskaran, M. K., tr. 2.2270
Bhatnagar, P. L., 1912-. 5.1669
Bhatt, Siddheshwar Rameshwar, 1939-. 1.211
Bhattacharjea, Ajit. 3.4314
Bhattacharya, Deben. tr. 2.1877
Bhattacharya, Sachchidananda. 3.4212
Bhattacharya, Sibajiban. 1.179
Bhattacharyya, Narendra Nath, 1934-. 1.217,
  1.1733
Bhattacharyya, Rameswar. 5.7508
Bhavabhūti, 8th cent. 2.1955
Bhavnani, Enakshi. 4.1110
Biale, David, 1949-. 1.1990
Bialer, Irv, 1919-. 5.5115
Bialer, Seweryn. 3.3248, 4.8652, 4.8657
Bialer, Seweryn. comp. 3.984
Bialik, Hayyim Nahman, 1873-1934. 2.1782
Bialystok, Ellen. 5.406
Bianchi Bandinelli, Ranuccio, 1900-1975.
  1.4727, 1.4731
Bianco, Carla. 3.8096
Bianco, David. 1.3447
Bianco, Lucien. 3.4751
Biancolli, Louis Leopold. joint comp. 1.3803
Biancolli, Louis Leopold. 1.4090
Bibb, Henry, b. 1815. 3.7207, 3.7212
Bibby, Cyril. 5.3206
Bibby, Geoffrey. 4.723
Bibby, John F. 4.8001-4.8002

Biber, Barbara, 1903-. 4.10401
Bibliographical Society of America. 5.7730,
  5.7753
Biblograf, S.A. 2.904
Bicentennial Commission of Florida. 3.6943
Bichell, David. 5.4221
Bickart, Theodore A., 1935-. 5.6334
Bickel, Alexander M. 4.7512, 4.9447
Bickers, Bernard W. 1.3142
Bickerton, Derek, 1926-. 2.116, 2.2337
Bickham, George, d. 1769. 5.7523
Bickley, R. Bruce, 1942-. 2.11049, 2.11052
Bickman, Martin, 1945-. 2.11156
Bickmore, D. P. 4.169
Biddiss, Michael Denis. 3.183
Biddle, Francis, 1886-1968. 4.9490
Bidelman, Patrick Kay. 4.6114
Bidwell, Percy Wells, 1888-. 5.5232
Bidwell, R. G. S. (Roger Grafton Shelford),
  1927-. 5.3740
Bidwell, Robin. 4.7722
Bidwell, Robin Leonard. 3.4062, 4.8789
Bieber, Margarete, 1879-. 1.5621, 2.303
Biederman, Paul. 4.4085
Biegel, David E. 5.4701
Bieler, Ludwig. 1.3190
Bien, Peter. ed. 4.7165
Bien, Peter. 2.568
Bien, Peter. 2.600
Bienefeld, M. A. 4.3159
Bienen, Henry. 4.2588, 4.8799, 4.8809
Bienstock, Penny, joint author. 4.2685
Bienvenu, Richard. ed. 4.7165
Bier, Justus, 1899-. 1.5718
Bier, Robert A. 5.8217
Bierce, Ambrose, 1842-1914? 2.10909-2.10910
Bierhorst, John. 2.2334
Bierhorst, John. comp. 2.2324
Bierley, Paul E. 1.3993
Bierstedt, Robert, 1913-. 4.4771
Biesanz, Karen Zubris. 3.9076
Biesanz, Mavis Hiltunen. 3.9076
Biesanz, Richard. 3.9076
Bietenholz, Peter G. 2.822
Biggadike, E. Ralph, 1939-. 4.3033
Biggers, Earl Derr, 1884-1933. 2.11383
Bigsby, C. W. E. comp. 2.10310, 2.12848
Bigsby, C. W. E. 1.6732, 2.9818, 2.10520
Bijou, Sidney William, 1908-. 5.560
Bikle, Lucy Leffingwell (Cable) 2.10920
Biklen, Douglas. 4.5102
Bilbao, Jon. joint author. 3.5687
Bilderback, David E. 5.3680
Biles, Jack I., 1920-. 2.8709
Biles, Roger, 1950-. 3.8415
Bilhana, 11th cent. 2.1953
Billcliffe, Roger. 5.7072
Biller, Henry B. 5.611-5.612
Billeskov Jansen, F. J. (Frederik Julius), 1907-.
  2.14007
Billett, Michael. 5.6243
Billias, George Athan, 1919-. 3.6888, 3.6997
Billigmeier, Robert H. 4.4896
Billigmeier, Robert Henry. 3.6545
Billingham, John. 5.1728
Billings, Dwight B., 1948-. 4.2038
Billings, John Shaw, 1838-1913. 5.5031
Billings, Marland Pratt, 1902-. 5.3123
Billings, Warren M., 1940-. 3.8185-3.8186
Billingsley, Andrew. 3.6750, 4.6552
Billingsley, Hobert Sherwood. joint author.
  4.987
Billington, David P. 5.5834, 5.5867
Billington, James H. 3.3022, 4.5051
Billington, Monroe Lee. 3.8155
Billington, Ray Allen, 1903-. 1.3171, 3.6205,
  3.6265, 3.6343-3.6345, 3.8453, 3.8490
Billington, Sandra. 4.870
Billmeyer, Fred W. 5.2764, 5.5676
Billy, André, 1882-1971. 2.4122
Bilmanis, Alfreds, 1887-1948. 3.3313
Bilson, John F. O. 4.4465
Binder, Arnold. 4.6831
Binder, Gerhart. 3.2458
Binder, Leonard. 3.3787, 4.5471
Binder, Robert. 5.1163
Bindman, David. 1.4953-1.4954, 1.6453-1.6454
Bindman, Geoffrey. joint author. 4.9421
Bindoff, S. T. (Stanley Thomas), 1908-. 3.1386

Bindra, Dalbir. 5.215
Binford, Lewis Roberts, 1930-. 3.217, 3.227,
  3.262
Binford, Sally R. 3.217
Bingel, Werner A. 5.2301
Bingham, Hiram, 1875-1956. 3.9288
Bingham, Jane. 5.7716
Bingham, Madeleine, Baroness Clanmorris.
  1.5404, 2.3357
Bingham, Millicent (Todd) 1880-. 4.369
Bingham, Richard D. 4.7688
Binham, Philip. 2.1753
Binion, Rudolph, 1927-. 3.736, 3.2200, 3.2394
Binkley, Robert Cedric, 1897-1940. 3.710
Binkley, Wilfred Ellsworth, 1883-. 4.7922
Binkley, William Campbell, 1889- joint ed.
  3.8339
Binni, Walter, 1913-. 2.4876
Binns, Archie, 1899-. 2.3254
Binns, J. W. 2.634, 2.749
Binns, Ronald, 1948-. 2.9059
Binstock, Robert H. 4.5798
Binyon, Laurence, 1869-1943. 1.5043
Biological Sciences Curriculum Study. 5.3305
Biological Services Program (U.S.) 5.3263
Bion, of Phlossa near Smyrna. 2.555
BioSciences Information Service of Biological
  Abstracts. 5.3289
Bioy Casares, Adolfo. joint author. 2.5376
Birch, Anthony Harold. 4.7738, 4.8410, 4.8421
Birch, Carol L. 5.8355
Birch, Cyril, 1925- ed. 2.2152, 2.2185, 2.2200
Birch, G. G. (Gordon Gerard), 1934-. 5.6890
Birch, Herbert George, 1918-1973. joint author.
  4.5709
Birch, L. Charles, 1918-. 5.3512, 5.4053
Birch, Thomas William. 4.197
Birchfield, Mary Eva, 1909-. 5.8268
Bird, Alan. 2.8289
Bird, Charles S. (Charles Stephen), 1935-. 4.648
Bird, E. C. F. (Eric Charles Frederick), 1930-.
  4.272
Bird, Graham R. 4.4581, 4.4583
Bird, James Harold, 1923-. 4.3953
Bird, John. 1.3879
Bird, Junius Bouton, 1907-. 3.9282
Bird, Otto A., 1914-. 1.69
Bird, R. Byron (Robert Byron), 1924-. 5.2064,
  5.5749
Bird, Richard Miller, 1938-. 4.4694, 4.4707
Bird, S. J. Glenn. 5.5822
Birdsall, Charles K. 5.2388
Birdwhistell, Ray L., 1918-. 5.460
Bireley, Robert. 3.2279
Birenbaum, Arnold. 4.5056
Birge, Edward A. (Edward Asahel) 5.3448
Birgin, Haydee. 4.4157
Birkeland, Peter W. 5.5270
Birket-Smith, Kaj, 1893-. 3.49, 3.5874
Birkhead, Edith. 2.3456
Birkhead, T. R. 5.3942
Birkhoff, Garrett, 1911-. 5.1272, 5.1309, 5.1437,
  5.1511
Birkner, Michael J., 1950-. 3.7072
Birley, Anthony Richard. 3.2791
Birman, Joan S., 1927-. 5.1598
Birmingham, David. 3.5232, 3.5402
Birmingham, David. joint author. 4.4244
Birmingham, Stephen. 2.12113
Birn, Randi. 2.14051
Birnbaum, Alfred. 1.6313
Birnbaum, H. Jean. joint author. 4.6733
Birnbaum, Max. 4.9939
Birnberg, Thomas B. 4.8908
Birnes, William J. 5.1191
Birney, Earle, 1904-. 2.9054, 2.9913
Birney, James Gillespie, 1792-1857. 3.7232
Birnie, Patricia W. 4.9314
Birns, Peter M. 5.1164
Birrell, Derek. 4.8570
Birren, James E. 5.624, 5.5003
Bīrūnī, Muhammad ibn Ahmad, 973?-1048.
  3.4192
Birx, H. James. 4.446
Bishop, Elizabeth, 1911-1979. 2.5467,
  2.11384-2.11385
Bishop, Errett, 1928-1983. 5.1433
Bishop, Ferman. 2.12575

Bishop, James. 5.6150
Bishop, John Lyman. 2.2252
Bishop, John Peale, 1892-1944. 2.10712, 2.11388-2.11389
Bishop, Jonathan. 2.11032
Bishop, Lloyd, 1933-. 2.3861
Bishop, Maurice. 3.9134
Bishop, Morris, 1893-1973. 2.4000, 2.4951, 3.8710
Bishop, Olga Bernice. 5.7886
Bishop, Owen. 5.2003
Bishop, Richard C. 4.1575
Bishop, Robert Charles. 1.6541, 1.6581
Bishop, Thomas, 1929-. 2.3936
Bishop, Walter W. 5.3141
Biskup, Peter. 4.668
Bismarck, Otto, Fürst von, 1815-1898. 3.2308-3.2309
Bissell, Claude Thomas ed. 3.8652
Bissell, Richard E. 3.6491
Bissex, Glenda L. 4.10420
Bisson, G. E. 4.7682
Bista, Dor Bahadur. 3.4350, 3.4376
Bithell, Jethro, 1878-1962. 2.1179
Bitner, Harry, 1916- joint author. 4.9471
Bitterman, M. E. 5.4103
Bittlingmayer, George. 4.3036
Bittner, William Robert. 2.11202
Bixler, Norma. 3.4335
Bixley, Paul F. 5.6209
Bizarro Ujpán, Ignacio. 3.9063-3.9064
Bizer, Ernst. 3.2277
Bjerke, Lucie. 2.918
Bjork, Robert E., 1949-. 2.14084
Bjorken, James D. 5.2109, 5.2152
Björkman, Erik, 1872-1919. 2.956
Björkman, Stig, 1938-. 2.3035
Blaauw, Adriaan. ed. 5.1840
Black, Charles Lund, 1915-. 4.6849, 4.9640
Black, Clanton C. 5.3761
Black, Conrad. 3.8812
Black, Cyril Edwin, 1915- ed. 3.3033, 4.5370, 4.6976, 4.9275
Black, David St. Clair, joint author. 5.2741
Black, Donald J. 4.5079, 4.6815
Black, Edwin R. 4.8273
Black Elk, 1863-1950. 3.5789
Black, Henry Campbell, 1860-1927. 4.9443
Black, Homer A., 1923-. 4.4414
Black, Hugo LaFayette, 1886-1971. 4.9446
Black, Ian. 5.5929
Black, James, 1932- ed. 2.6680
Black, Jan Knippers, 1940-. 3.9136
Black, Jeremy. 3.1539
Black, John, 1783-1855. tr. 2.4994
Black, John Bennett, 1883-1964. 3.1421
Black, John D. (John Donald), 1883-1960. 4.2884
Black, John Reddie, 1827-1880. 3.4948
Black, Joseph, 1728-1799. 5.5665
Black, Mary C. 1.6567
Black, Mary E. 5.7096
Black, Matthew. ed. 1.2524
Black, Max, 1909-. 1.463-1.465, 1.537-1.538, 1.1209, 1.1227, 1.4624
Black, Michael. 5.3736
Black, Nancy B. 4.10272
Black, Peter E. 5.5994
Black, R. D. Collison. 4.2311
Black, R. D. Collison. ed. 4.1331
Black Sparrow Press, Los Angeles. 2.13405
Black, Stanley W. 4.4557
Black Women's Community Development Foundation. 3.6773
Blackall, Eric A. (Eric Albert) 2.13503, 2.13571
Blackbeard, Bill. 2.3817
Blackbourn, David, 1949-. 3.2296
Blackburn, Bonnie J. 1.3853
Blackburn, Graham, 1940-. 5.7415
Blackburn, Paul. 2.12909
Blackburn, Simon. 2.100
Blackburn, Thomas C. 3.5724, 3.5860
Blacker, Carmen. 1.1329, 3.4896
Blackett, R. J. M., 1943-. 3.1293
Blackham, H. J. (Harold John), 1903-. 1.485
Blackhurst, A. Edward. 4.10928
Blacking, John. 1.4389
Blackley, D. C. 5.7082

Blackman, Aylward M. (Aylward Manley), 1883-1956. tr. 2.1763
Blackman, Geoffrey Emett. 4.169
Blackman, John L. 4.3163
Blackman, Margaret B. 3.5886
Blackman, Philip, 1881- ed. and tr. 1.1938
Blackman, Sue Anne Batey. joint author. 4.1837
Blackmer, Donald L. M. 4.8630
Blackmore, David Richard, 1938-. 5.6222
Blackmore, R. D. (Richard Doddridge), 1825-1900. 2.7401
Blackmore, Ruth Matteson. 5.7923
Blackmore, Susan J., 1951-. 5.662
Blackmur, R. P. (Richard P.), 1904-1965. 2.2738, 2.3507, 2.5760, 2.10263, 2.10808, 2.11119
Blackmur, Richard P. 2.5736
Blacksell, Mark, 1942-. 4.2185
Blackstock, Nelson. 4.6829
Blackstock, Paul W., ed. 3.3065
Blackstone, Bernard, 1911-. 2.9591
Blackstone, William, Sir, 1723-1780. 4.9410
Blackwall, Eric Albert. 2.1176
Blackwelder, Julia Kirk, 1943-. 4.6078
Blackwell, David Harold, 1919-. 5.1377
Blackwell, Harold Richard, 1921-. 5.235
Blackwell, James Edward, 1925-. 4.4772, 4.10862
Blackwell, Kenneth. 1.759
Blackwell, William Leslie. 4.2365
Blackwood, Algernon, 1869-1951. 2.8465
Blackwood, William, 1836-1912. 2.8551
Blades, James. 1.4180, 1.4561
Blagden, Isa Jane, 1816-1873. 2.7479
Blahut, Richard E. 5.6365
Blaikie, Piers M. 4.2873
Blaine, Karen. 4.10694
Blainey, Ann, 1935-. 2.7845
Blainey, Geoffrey. 3.5566
Blair, Bruce G., 1947-. 5.7356
Blair, Claude. 5.7246
Blair, Clay, 1925-. 3.1040, 3.7871
Blair, Dorothy S. 2.4842, 2.4848
Blair, Hugh, 1718-1800. 2.7100
Blair, Joan, 1929-. 3.7871
Blair, John G. 2.3420
Blair, Karen J. 4.6172
Blair, Patricia Wohlgemuth. 5.5124
Blair, Peter D. 4.1402
Blair, Timothy R. 4.10460
Blair, W. Frank, 1912-. 5.3891
Blair, Walter, 1900-. 2.3791, 2.10650-2.10651, 2.10841, 2.10943
Blais, Marie Claire. 2.4809-2.4813
Blake, Cecil A. 4.5006
Blake, G. Noel, 1914-. 4.4123
Blake, Gerald Henry. 3.3679, 3.3724
Blake, Gerald Henry. joint author. 3.3687
Blake, John Ballard, 1922-. 5.8283
Blake, John William. 3.5325
Blake, Judith. 4.1614
Blake, Kathleen. 2.5728
Blake, Leslie Spencer, 1925-. 5.5667
Blake, N. F. (Norman Francis) 2.6316
Blake, Nicholas. 2.8595
Blake, Patricia. ed. 2.1297
Blake, Peter, 1920-. 1.5306, 1.5416
Blake, Ralph M. 5.865
Blake, Robert, 1916-. 3.1629, 3.1687, 3.5512, 4.8531
Blake, Robert Rogers, 1918-. 4.4325
Blake, Roland Patton, ed. 4.3477
Blake, S. F. (Sidney Fay), 1892-1959. 5.8116
Blake, Warren Barton, 1883-1918, ed. 3.6023
Blake, William, 1757-1827. 1.4947, 1.6386, 2.7117, 2.7403-2.7407, 2.7410
Blakemore, Colin. joint author. 5.4306
Blakemore, Colin. 5.246
Blakemore, Harold. 4.2135
Blakemore, J. S. (John Sydney), 1927-. 5.2191
Blaker, Alfred A., 1928-. 5.6989, 5.6991
Blalock, Hubert M. 4.1204, 4.4784
Blaman, Anna, 1905-1960. 2.13953
Blanchard, Alain, 1938-. 5.6520
Blanchard, Harold Hooper, 1891-. 2.3711
Blanchard, J. Richard. 5.8090
Blanchard, Kendall, 1942-. 4.541
Blanchard, Kenneth H. 4.2695

Blanchard, Rae. 2.6270, 2.7270-2.7273
Blanchot, Maurice. 2.2340, 2.2361, 2.4416
Blanco, Hugo. 4.2843
Bland, David. 1.5826
Bland, Randall Walton. 4.9738, 4.9823
Blandford, Linda A. 4.9442
Blandford, Percy W. 5.5295
Blane, Howard T., 1926-. 4.6639
Blank, Arthur S., 1936-. 5.4946
Blank, Blanche Davis, 1923- joint author. 4.8195
Blank, David Eugene. 4.8352
Blankert, Albert. 1.6256
Blanksten, George I. 4.8344
Blanning, T. C. W. 3.2500
Blanpain, R. (Roger), 1932-. 4.3515
Blanshard, Brand, 1892-1987. 1.510, 1.575, 4.10817, 5.380
Blasco Ibáñez, Vicente, 1867-1928. 2.5236-2.5238
Blase, Melvin G. ed. 4.2897
Blaser, Robin. 2.13331
Blashford-Snell, John. 5.7176
Blasi, Augusto, joint author. 5.199
Blasi, Joseph R. 4.7168
Blasi, Vincent, 1943-. 4.9838
Blasier, Cole, 1925-. 3.9011, 3.9013, 3.9107
Blasis, Carlo, 1803-1878. 4.1087
Blass, Friedrich Wilhelm, 1843-1907. 2.248
Blassingame, John W. 3.6602, 3.6639, 3.7201, 3.7213, 3.7236, 3.8318
Blasucci, Luigi, ed. 2.4914
Blatt, Burton, 1927-. 4.10522
Blatt, Harvey. 5.3035, 5.3051-5.3052
Blatt, John Markus. 5.2422
Blatt, Sidney J. (Sidney Jules). joint author. 5.4844
Blatter, Janet. 1.5097
Blau, Francine D. 4.6032
Blau, Joseph L. (Joseph Leon), 1909-1986. 1.554, 1.1916, 1.1926, 3.6562, 3.7073
Blau, Peter Michael. 4.2642, 4.3215, 4.3239, 4.4897, 4.7749-4.7750
Blau, Zena Smith, 1922-. 4.5814
Blaug, Mark. 4.1304, 4.1352, 4.1383
Blaukopf, Kurt. 1.3916
Blauner, Robert. 3.6505, 4.3430
Blaustein, Albert P., 1921-. 4.9377-4.9378, 4.9380, 4.9782
Blaustein, Eric B. 4.9380
Blaustein, Phyllis Jil. 4.9380
Blechman, Barry M. 5.7470
Blechschmidt, Erich, 1904-. 5.4164
Bleck, E. E. (Eugene Edmund), 1923-. 5.5083
Bledstein, Burton J. 4.10069
Blegen, Carl William, 1887-. 3.2595
Blegen, Theodore Christian, 1891-1969. 3.6004, 3.6592, 3.8496
Blehl, Vincent Ferrer. 1.3137
Bleiberg, Germán, 1915-. 2.5113, 3.3409
Bleich, David. 2.35
Bleier, Ruth, 1923-. 4.4192
Bleikasten, André. 2.11679
Bleiler, Everett Franklin, 1920-. 2.2408, 2.3462, 2.7911, 2.8001, 2.9447, 2.10573
Blenkinsopp, Joseph, 1927-. 1.2582
Bleser, Carol K. Rothrock. 3.8248
Blesh, Rudi, 1899-. 1.4317-1.4318, 1.4810
Blevins, Leon W., 1937-. 4.7863
Blevins, Robert D. 5.5743, 5.5748, 5.5854
Blewett, John P. (John Paul), 1910-. 5.2390, 5.2439
Bleyer, Willard Grosvenor, 1873-1935. 2.3583
Bleznick, Donald William, 1924-. 2.5196, 5.8029
Blickle, Peter. 3.2278
Bligh, J. 5.4203
Blinder, Alan S. 4.4655
Blinoff, Marthe. 3.3018
Blish, James. 2.11391-2.11392
Bliss, Alan Joseph. 2.1097
Bliss, Gilbert Ames, 1876-1951. 5.1465
Bliss, L. C. (Lawrence C.) 5.3570
Bliss, Michael. 5.4407
Bliss, Michael. joint comp. 4.2133
Blissett, Marlan. 4.7885
Blitsten, Dorothy Rubovits, 1907-. 4.5562
Blitzer, Charles. joint author. 3.173

Bliven, Bruce, 1916-. 3.8025
Blixen, Karen (Dinesen) baronesse. 2.14017
Blixen, Karen Dinesen, baronesse, 1885-1962.
    2.14018
Bloch, Abraham P. 3.3844
Bloch, Bernard, 1907-1965. 2.1988
Bloch, Chana, 1940-. 2.7063
Bloch, E. Maurice. 1.5920
Bloch, Ernst, 1885-1977. 1.1542
Bloch-Hoell, Nils. 1.3389
Bloch, Marc Léopold Benjamin, 1886-1944.
    3.381, 3.580, 3.844, 3.977, 4.2852, 4.6418,
    5.4778
Block, Adrienne Fried. 1.3604
Block, Alan A. 4.6686
Block, Alan W. 4.10281
Block, Andrew, 1892-. 5.7960
Block, Haskell M. ed. 2.3764
Block, Maxine, ed. 3.324
Block, Ned. 5.318
Block, Walter, 1941-. 4.3484
Blocker, Clyde E. 4.10557
Blocker, H. Gene. 4.4971
Blocker, Jack S. 4.6649
Blockley, D. I. 5.5860
Blockmans, Willem Pieter. 3.2958
Blockson, Charles L. 3.294
Blodgett, Harold William, 1900- ed. 2.11267
Blodgett, Harriet. 2.8481
Blofeld, John Eaton Calthorpe, 1913-. 1.1757,
    1.1800, 1.1805, 1.2125
Blok, Aleksandr Aleksandrovich, 1880-1921.
    2.1469
Blok, Anton. 4.6719
Blom, Eric, 1888-1959. 1.4531
Blon, Eric, 1888- , tr. 1.3978
Blong, R. J. (Russell J.) 5.3107
Blood, Robert O. 4.5585
Bloom, Alfred. 1.2169
Bloom, Allan David, 1930-. 3.6082, 4.7346
Bloom, Arthur L. (Arthur Leroy), 1928-. 4.260
Bloom, Benjamin Samuel, 1913-. 4.10170,
    4.10349, 5.609
Bloom, Edward Alan, 1914-. 2.5660, 2.6893,
    2.11474
Bloom, Floyd E. 5.4301
Bloom, Harold. 2.7404, 2.7424, 2.8024, 2.8108,
    2.8347
Bloom, Irene. 1.161
Bloom, Ken. 1.3574
Bloom, Lillian D. 2.5660
Bloom, Lillian D. joint author. 2.11474
Bloom, Lois. 4.10391
Bloom, Lynn Z., 1934-. 2.11661, 5.8110
Bloom, Martin, 1934-. 4.6486
Bloom, Robert, 1930-. 2.8507
Bloom, William, 1899-. 5.4157
Bloomfield, Arthur I. (Arthur Irving) 4.4494
Bloomfield, B. C. (Barry Cambray) 1.27
Bloomfield, G. T. (Gerald Taylor) 4.3816
Bloomfield, Leonard, 1887-1949. 2.131
Bloomfield, Maurice, 1855-1928. ed. 2.1931
Bloomfield, Maxwell H. 4.9487
Bloomfield, Morton W. (Morton Wilfred),
    1913-1987. 2.6397
Bloomfield, Paul, 1898-. 3.5607
Bloomfield, Victor A. 5.2795
Bloomster, Edgar L. 5.7509
Blos, Peter. 4.5750
Blotner, Joseph Leo, 1923-. 2.3479, 2.10564,
    2.11685, 2.12428
Blough, Glenn Orlando. 4.10490
Bloy, Léon, 1846-1917. 2.4147
Blu, Karen I. 3.5869
Bluck, Richard Stanley Harold, ed. 2.534
Blue, Frederick J. 4.8220
Bluemel, Carl, 1893-. 1.5622
Bluestone, Barry. 4.3205, 4.4330
Bluhm, William Theodore, 1923-. 4.7258,
    4.8572
Blum, Albert A. 4.3437
Blum, Daniel C. 2.2867, 2.3206
Blum, David, 1935-. 1.4077
Blum, Eleanor. 5.8110
Blum, Harold Francis, 1899-. 5.3324
Blum, Jerome, 1913-. 4.5281, 4.6366, 4.6410
Blum, John Morton, 1921-. 3.7520, 3.7690,
    3.7700, 3.7720, 3.7752

Blum, Paul Charles, 1898-. 4.2555
Blum, Richard H. 4.6655-4.6656
Blum, Robert M. 3.4415
Blum, Shirley Neilsen. 1.6259
Blum, Walter J., joint author. 4.4693
Blumberg, Arthur, 1923-. 4.4937, 4.10669
Blumberg, Paul. 4.4957
Blumberg, Phyllis, 1933-. 4.10669
Blume, Friedrich, 1893-. 1.3466, 1.3502, 1.3632,
    1.4245
Blume, Helmut, 1920-. 3.9085
Blumenfeld, Hans. 4.6308
Blumenson, Martin. 3.7613
Blumenstock, David I. (David Irving),
    1913-1963. 5.2504
Blumenthal, Monica D. 4.5245
Blumer, Herbert, 1900-1987. 4.5057
Blumin, Stuart M. 4.5212
Blumstein, Philip. 4.5651
Blundell, T. L. 5.2930
Blunden, Caroline. 3.4630
Blunden, Edmund, 1896-1974. 2.7328, 2.7784,
    2.7846, 2.7905, 2.8099
Blunden, John. 5.6726
Blunt, Anthony, 1907-. 1.4959, 1.5438,
    1.5803-1.5804, 1.6025
Blunt, Anthony Sir, 1907-. 1.5000, 1.5245,
    1.5434, 1.6137
Blunt, Wilfrid, 1901-. 1.3926
Blutstein, Howard I. 3.9066, 3.9172, 3.9178
Bly, Robert. comp. 2.14062
Bly, Robert. 2.3736, 2.12910
Blyden, Edward Wilmot, 1832-1912. 3.5415
Blyth, Reginald Horace. 2.2006
Blythe, Wilfred. 3.4535
B'nai B'rith. Anti-defamation League.
    5.8238-5.8239
Boahen, A. Adu. 3.5235
Boak, Arthur Edward Romilly, 1888-1962.
    3.2809
Boak, Denis. 2.4622
Board, K. 5.6539
Board of Governors of the Federal Reserve
    System (U.S.) 4.4533-4.4534, 4.4536
Boardman, Eugene Powers. 3.4727
Boardman, John, 1927-. 1.4717, 1.6636, 1.6639,
    3.2519, 3.2561, 3.2639
Boardman, Robert, 1945-. 3.1261, 4.9100
Boas, Franz, 1858-1942. 1.4683, 3.5901, 4.398,
    4.403, 4.426, 4.433, 4.536
Boas, Frederick S. (Frederick Samuel),
    1862-1957. 2.5860-2.5862, 2.5910, 2.6215,
    2.6478, 2.6606, 2.6614
Boas, George, 1891-. 1.6081, 3.24, 3.140
Boase, Alan Martin. 2.3921, 2.4011
Boase, T. S. R. (Thomas Sherrer Ross),
    1898-1974. 1.4930
Boateng, E. A. 3.5101, 3.5336
Boatner, Mark Mayo, 1921-. 3.5995, 3.7337,
    5.7239
Boatwright, Howard. 1.4424
Boaz, Martha Terosse, 1913-. 4.10554
Bobango, Gerald J. 3.3548
Bobbitt, Philip. 4.9641
Bobbitt, Richard, 1924-. 1.4463
Bober, Harry, 1915-. 5.1173
Bobrowski, Johannes, 1917-1965. 2.13680
Bobrowski, Tadeusz, 1829-1894. 2.8550
Boccaccio, Giovanni, 1313-1375. 2.4901-2.4911,
    2.6352
Bocheński, Innocentius Maria, 1902-. 1.1156
Bochenski, Joseph M., 1902-. 1.470, 1.1154
Bochner, Jay, 1940-. 2.4463
Bochner, S. (Salomon), 1899-. 5.1066
Bochner, Stephen. 4.619, 4.5008
Bociurkiw, Bohdan R. 4.7139
Bock, Hal. 4.994
Bock, Manfred. 1.5020
Bock, Philip K. 4.621
Bock, Richard Darrell, 1927-. 5.38
Bockoven, J. Sanbourne. 5.4860
Bockris, J. O'M. (John O'M.), 1923-. 5.2912
Bocock, Robert. 1.1622
Bodde, Derk. 1.152-1.153, 3.4692, 3.4784
Boddewyn, J. J. (Jean J.) 4.4436
Boddy, John. 5.4304
Bode, Boyd Henry, 1873-1953. 4.10219, 4.10350

Bode, Carl, 1911-. 2.10245, 2.12130, 2.12133,
    3.6083, 3.8101
Bodechtel, Johann. 5.1812
Bodelsen, Carl Adolf Gottlieb, 1894- joint
    author. 2.921
Bodelson, Carl Adolf Gottlieb, 1894-. 2.11631
Boden, Margaret A. 5.18, 5.285, 5.481, 5.1005
Bodian, Nat G., 1921-. 5.7575
Bodin, Jean, 1530-1596. 3.426, 4.7383
Bodinski, Lois H. 5.5129
Bodky, Erwin, 1896-1958. 1.4528
Bodley, John H. 4.502
Bodmer, Karl, 1809-1893. 1.6389
Bodmer, W. F. (Walter Fred), 1936- joint
    author. 5.3424
Bodnar, John E., 1944-. 3.6506, 3.8095, 4.3537,
    4.5217
Bodrova, Valentina. 4.1642
Boehm, Barry W. 5.1165
Boehner, Philotheus, Father, ed. and tr. 1.389
Boer, Tjitze J. de, 1866-. 1.364
Boersma, Anne. 5.3154
Boes, Duane C., joint author. 5.1394
Boesch, Bruno, 1911-. 2.13452
Boëthius, Axel, 1889-1969. 1.5224
Boethius, d. 524. 1.335-1.336
Boff, Clodovis. 1.2803
Boff, Kenneth R. 5.266
Boff, Leonardo. 1.2803, 1.2856
Bogan, Louise, 1897-1970. 2.2564, 2.2644,
    2.11393
Bogard, Travis. 2.6883, 2.12289
Bogart, Kenneth P. 5.1274
Bogdanor, Vernon, 1943-. 4.7726, 4.8364,
    4.8370, 4.8435
Boger, Louise Ade. 1.6553
Boggan, E. Carrington. 4.9679
Boggs, Carl. 4.7020, 4.7025, 4.7082
Boggs, Jean Sutherland. 1.6090
Bogin, Meg. 2.884
Bogle, Donald. 2.2996
Bogoliubov, N. N. (Nikolaĭ Nikolaevich), 1909-.
    5.2153
Bogucka, Maria. 3.3333
Bogue, Allan G. ed. 3.428
Bogue, Allan G. 3.7309, 4.2958, 4.8103
Bogue, Donald Joseph, 1918-. 4.1610, 4.1668,
    4.6182, 4.6203
Bogue, Margaret Beattie, 1924-. 3.8404
Bohannan, Laura. 4.604
Bohannan, Paul. 3.5066, 4.519
Bohannan, Paul. ed. 4.9351
Bohen, Halcyone H., 1937-. 4.5586
Bohi, Douglas R. 4.3702, 4.3713, 4.3772-4.3773
Bohle, Bruce. 1.3500
Bohlen, Charles E. (Charles Eustis), 1904-.
    3.7631
Böhm-Bawerk, Eugen von, 1851-1914. 4.1520
Bohm, David. 5.1896, 5.2110, 5.2127
Bohm, Robert A. 5.6117-5.6118
Böhme, Helmut. 3.2304, 4.2337
Böhme, Jakob, 1575-1624. 1.3083-1.3084
Bohn, Hinrich L., 1934-. 5.5275
Bohn, Mark. 5.2266
Bohne, Harald, ed. 5.7882
Bohner, Charles H. 2.12650
Böhner, Philotheus, Father. 1.1158
Bohr, Niels Hendrik David, 1885-. 5.2051
Bohr, Niels Henrik David, 1885-1962. 5.1884,
    5.1897-5.1898
Boiardo, Matteo Maria, 1440 or 41-1494.
    2.4965
Boileau Despréaux, Nicolas, 1636-1711. 2.4012
Boime, Albert. 1.4650, 1.6084
Boisdeffre, Pierre de. 2.3867-2.3868
Boisselier, Jean. 1.5187, 1.5756, 1.6311
Boissevain, Jeremy. 4.5058
Boissier, Gaston, 1823-1908. 3.2781
Boissonnade, P. (Prosper), 1862-1935. 4.3097
Boitani, Piero. 2.6347
Boje, R., 1934-. 5.3563
Bojer, Johan, 1872-1959. 2.14042
Bok, Bart Jan, 1906-. 5.1858
Bok, Derek Curtis. 4.3346, 4.10575
Bok, Edward William, 1863-1930. 2.3605
Bok, Priscilla Fairfield. joint author. 5.1858
Bok, Sissela. 1.1492-1.1493, 5.4574
Boklund, Gunnar. 2.6880

Boksenbaum, Howard. 4.3718, 5.5999, 5.6871
Bokser, Ben Zion, 1907-. 1.1894
Boland, Bridget. 3.1414
Bold, Alan Norman, 1943-. 2.8783, 2.8786,
2.9365
Bold, Harold Charles, 1909-. 5.3641, 5.3709,
5.3730
Boléat, Mark. 4.3483
Boles, Donald E. (Donald Edward), 1926-.
4.10745
Boles, Janet K., 1944-. 4.6033
Boles, John B. 1.3033, 3.7186
Boleslavsky, Richard, 1889-1937. 2.3113
Boley, Forrest I. 5.2384
Bolgar, R. R. 3.88
Bolingbroke, Henry St. John, Viscount,
1678-1751. 3.1233
Bolinger, Dwight Le Merton, 1907-. 2.101,
2.1030
Bolitho, Harold. 3.4946
Bolitho, Hector, 1898-. 3.4312
Bolívar, Simón, 1783-1830. 3.9166
Bolkhovitinov, N. N. (Nikolaĭ Nikolaevich)
3.6483
Boll, Eleanor Stoker. 4.5567
Böll, Heinrich. 2.13681-2.13696
Boll, Theophilus Ernest Martin, 1902-. 2.9323
Bollacher, Martin. 2.13610
Bollay, Eugene, 1912- joint ed. 5.2500
Boller, Paul F. 1.561, 1.564
Bollery, Joseph, 1890-. 2.4336
Bolles, Richard Nelson. 4.4265
Bolles, Robert C. 5.482
Bolognese, Don. 2.9685
Bolt, Bruce A., 1930-. 5.3087, 5.3115
Bolt, Robert. 2.8466-2.8467
Boltho, Andrea. 4.2195
Boltianskiĭ, V. G. (Vladimir Grigor'evich),
1925-. 5.1574
Boltin, Lee. 1.4943
Bolton, Brenda. 4.5859
Bolton, Herbert Eugene, 1870-1953. 3.8323,
3.8569, 3.8572, 3.8603-3.8604
Bolton, James R., 1937- joint author. 5.2413
Bolton, Phyllis L. 5.706
Bolton, W. F. (Whitney French), 1930-. 2.6289,
2.9190
Bolz, Ray E., 1918- ed. 5.5666
Bolz, Roger William. 5.7045
Bombardier, Gary, joint author. 4.7869
Bombay. University. Dept. of Sociology. 4.5481
Bommarito, James W., 1922-. jt. author. 5.582
Bon, J. 1.5790
Bonachea, Ramón L. 3.9096
Bonachea, Rolando E., ed. 3.9093
Bonadio, Felice A. 4.8153
Bonaparte, Louis-Lucien, prince, 1813-1891.
2.1010
Bonaventure, Saint, Cardinal, ca. 1217-1274.
1.3134, 1.3259
Bonavia, Duccio, 1935-. 3.9289
Bond, Beverley W. (Beverley Waugh), b. 1881.
3.8368
Bond, Beverley Waugh, 1881-. 3.8381
Bond, Brian. 3.714
Bond, Carl E. 5.3895
Bond, Courtney C. J. 4.141
Bond, David J. 2.4650
Bond, Donald Frederic, 1898-. 2.6272, 2.6276
Bond, Edward. 2.9621-2.9623
Bond, George C. 1.2466
Bond, George Doherty, 1903-. 1.2148
Bond, Harold L. 3.2803
Bond, Otto Ferdinand, 1885- ed. 2.902
Bond, R. Warwick (Richard Warwick),
1857-1943. ed. 2.6490
Bond, Richmond Pugh, 1899-. 2.6273
Bondada, Murthy V. A. 5.5935
Bondanella, Julia Conaway. 2.4874
Bondanella, Peter E., 1943-. 2.2901, 2.4874,
2.4905, 2.4907, 3.2931, 4.7389, 4.7395
Bondi, Hermann. 5.2014
Bondi, Richard, joint author. 1.1474
Bondurant, Joan Valérie, 1918-. 4.5035
Bondy, Jeffrey S. (Jeffrey Stefan), 1955-. 4.2684
Bone, Edith, tr. 2.1608
Bone, Robert A. 2.10314, 2.10577
Boneparth, Ellen, 1945-. 4.6072

Bonfante, Giuliano. 2.228
Bonfante, Larissa. 2.228, 2.820
Bonhoeffer, Dietrich, 1906-1945. 1.1480, 1.2799,
1.2892, 1.3287
Bonilla, Heraclio. 3.9018
Bonin, Gerhardt von, 1890-. 5.4151
Bonine, Michael E., 1942-. 4.5409
Bónis, Ferenc. 1.3792
Bonitz, Hermann, 1814-1888. 2.440
Bonjour, Edgar, 1898-. 3.3510
Bonnat, Yves. joint comp. 2.3149
Bonnefoy, Yves. 2.4417-2.4418
Bonnell, Victoria E. 4.3661
Bonner, David M. ed. 5.3586
Bonner, Jack W., 1940-. 5.595
Bonner, James Frederick, 1910-. 5.3751
Bonner, John Tyler. 5.3485-5.3486, 5.3729,
5.4090
Bonney, Richard. 4.8577
Bonnie, Richard J. 4.9576
Bonoma, Thomas V. 4.4277
Bonomi, Patricia U. 3.8027
Bonora, Ettore. 2.5009
Bonpland, Aimé, 1773-1858. 3.9150
Bonsal, Philip Wilson, 1903-. 3.6437
Bonsal, Stephen, 1865-1951. 3.853
Bonser, Wilfrid, 1887-1972. 5.7985
Bonta, Juan Pablo. 1.5487
Bontempo, Charles J. 1.106
Bontemps, Arna Wendell, 1902-1973. 1.3892,
2.3747, 2.10315, 2.10749, 2.11394-2.11395,
3.6648, 3.7208, 4.769
Bony, Jean. 1.5361, 1.5531
Bookchin, Murray. 4.7188
Booker, Henry G. 5.2406
Boole, George, 1815-1864. 1.1199
Boolootian, Richard A. 5.3798
Boom, B. K. (Boudewijn Karel), 1891- joint
author. 5.5357
Boon, Louis Paul. 2.13957
Boone, Edgar John, 1930-. 4.10983
Boone, William T., 1944-. 4.918
Boor, Helmut de, 1891-. 2.13453, 2.13534
Boorman, Howard L., ed. 3.4810
Boorman, Jane, joint ed. 3.8513
Boorsch, Suzanne. 1.6522
Boorstin, Daniel J. (Daniel Joseph), 1914-. 3.40,
3.6084-3.6086, 3.6864, 3.6963, 4.7304
Booser, E. Richard. 5.6245
Booth, Anne. 4.2533
Booth, Bradford Allen, comp. 2.7367, 2.8231
Booth, Charles, 1840-1916. 4.6624
Booth, Harold Simmons, 1891-. 5.2705
Booth, Heather, 1950-. 4.3632
Booth, Kellogg S. 5.5653
Booth, Larry, joint author. 5.6951
Booth, Mark W., 1943-. 1.3523, 2.5772
Booth, Michael R. ed. 2.6234, 2.6240
Booth, Michael R. comp. 2.6239
Booth, Michael R. 2.3308, 2.5843, 2.5919
Booth, Philip E. 2.11396
Booth, Stephen. 2.6672
Booth, Taylor L. 5.6573
Booth, Wayne C. 2.2429, 2.3501
Boothby, William M. (William Munger), 1918-.
5.1620
Boothroyd, Carl W. (Carl William), 1915-.
5.5399
Boraston, Ian, joint author. 4.3341
Borchard, Edwin Montefiore, 1884-1951.
4.9047, 4.9896
Borchardt, Knut. joint author. 4.2340
Borchert, James, 1941-. 3.6797
Borchert, Wolfgang, 1921-1947. 2.13698-2.13699
Bordeau, Sanford P. 5.2337
Borden, Henry, 1901-. 3.8738
Borden, Morton. 3.6563
Borden, Neil Hopper, 1895-. 4.4426
Borden, Robert Laird, Sir, 1854-1937. 3.8738
Bordicks, Katherine J. 5.4746
Bordin, Ruth Birgitta Anderson, 1917-. 4.6642
Bordley, James, 1900-. 5.4520
Bordman, Gerald Martin. 1.3907,
1.4215-1.4216, 2.3186
Bordo, Michael D. 4.4495
Bordwell, David. 2.2909, 2.3038
Bordwell, Sally, 1947-. 4.6740
Borel, Jacques, ed. 2.4317

Borenstein, Audrey, 1930-. 4.6034
Boretz, Benjamin. comp. 1.3461
Borevich, Z. I. (Zenon Ivanovich) 5.1319
Borg, Alan. 1.5503
Borg, Dorothy, 1902-. 3.4850, 3.6457
Borgatta, Edgar F., 1924-. 4.5811, 5.506
Borgerhoff, E. B. O. (Elbert Benton
Op'tEynde), 1908-1968. 2.3851
Borges, Jorge Luis, 1899-. 2.5374-2.5376
Borgese, Elisabeth Mann. 4.9313, 5.6750
Borgos, Seth, 1952-. 4.5230
Borgstrom, Georg, 1912-. 5.7111
Boring, Edwin Garrigues, 1886-1968. 5.77, 5.94,
5.236, 5.242, 5.258
Borjas, George J. 4.3612
Bork, Robert H. 4.9525
Borkenau, Franz, 1900-1957. 3.3464
Borklund, Elmer. 2.10239
Borman, Leonard D. joint author. 4.6535
Bormann, F. Herbert, 1922-. 5.3270
Bormann, Martin, 1900-1945. 3.2391
Bormann, Werner, 1915- ed. 4.174
Born, Ernest, 1898- joint author. 1.3237
Born, Lester Kruger, 1903- ed. and tr. 4.7400
Born, Max. 5.714, 5.1899, 5.2015-5.2016,
5.2044, 5.2277
Bornand, Odette. 2.8021
Bornecque, Jacques Henry. 2.4172
Borning, Bernard C. 3.6251
Bornkamm, Günther. 1.2666, 1.2879
Bornkamm, Heinrich, 1901-. 1.2344
Bornkamm, Karin, 1928-. 1.2344
Bornstein, Morris, 1927-. 4.1321, 4.2227
Boroush, Mark A. 5.5633
Borowiec, Andrew. 3.2687
Borowitz, Eugene B. 1.1917
Borowski, Tadeusz. 2.1699
Borrello, Alfred. 2.8415
Borroff, Edith, 1925-. 1.3633
Borroff, Marie. 2.6416, 2.6424, 2.10488
Borroff, Marie. ed. 2.12545
Borror, Donald Joyce, 1907-. 5.3856, 5.3860
Borrow, George Henry, 1803-1881. 3.3400
Borrowman, Merle L. 4.10517
Börsch-Supan, Helmut. 1.6170-1.6171
Borse, G. J. (Garold J.) 5.5720
Borsellino, Antonio. 5.4385
Börsenverein des Deutschen Buchhandels.
5.8007
Borsook, Eve. 1.6394
Bort, Barry D. joint author. 5.8068
Borthwick, R. L. 4.8411
Boruch, Robert F. 4.9604
Borum, Poul. 2.13999
Borus, Michael E. 4.3306
Borwick, John. 5.6561
Borysewicz, Edward, 1939-. 4.1046
Borza, Eugene N. 3.2629
Bos, H. J. M. 5.1070
Bos, Hendricus Cornelis, 1926- jt. author.
4.1284
Bosanquet, Bernard, 1848-1923. 1.1366, 4.7440
Bosch, Hieronymus, d. 1516. 1.6242
Boschot, Adolphe, 1871-1955. 2.4217, 2.4219
Boschung, Herbert T. 5.3908
Bosco, Umberto, 1900-. 2.4873, 2.4931
Bose, Ashish. 4.6195
Bose, Aurobindo. tr. 2.1869
Bose, Aurobindo. 2.1868
Bose, Bimal K. 5.6555
Bose, Christine E. 4.3251
Bose, Subhas Chandra, 1897-1945. 3.4284
Boserup, Ester. 4.1591, 4.3302
Bosi, Roberto, 1924-. 3.3396
Bosk, Charles L. 5.5032
Boskin, Michael J. 4.3462, 4.4690
Bosley, Keith. 2.1750, 2.4263
Bosmajian, Haig A. 4.7674, 4.9870
Bosquet, Alain, 1919- ed. 2.4806
Bossard, James Herbert Siward, 1888-1960.
4.5567, 4.5635
Bossert, William H., 1937- joint author. 5.3446
Bossing, Nelson Louis, 1893-. 4.10423
Bosson, Rex, 1943-. 4.3721
Bossuet, Jacques Bénigne, 1627-1704. 2.4014,
3.523
Bossy, John. 1.3189
Bost, Sophie, 1835-1922. 3.8497

Bost, Théodore, 1834-1920. 3.8497
Bostetter, Edward Everett, 1914-. 2.5816
Boston, Bruce O. 4.10918
Boston. Museum of Fine Arts. Dept. of Prints and Drawings. 1.6462, 1.6493
Boston, Penelope J. 5.6714
Boston Women's Health Book Collective. 5.4689
Boswell, James, 1740-1795. 2.6902-2.6904, 2.7085-2.7086, 3.1809
Boswell, John. 4.5532
Boswell, Thomas D. 3.6542
Bosworth, A. B. 3.2624
Bosworth, Barry, 1942-. 4.1503, 4.2076
Bosworth, Clifford Edmund. 1.2028, 3.4067, 3.4078, 3.4115
Bosworth, Clifford Edmund. joint author. 3.3653
Bosworth, Joseph, 1789-1876. 2.945
Bosworth, R. J. B. 3.2882
Botanical Society of America. Pacific Section. 5.3680
Botanical Society of the British Isles. 5.3645
Botero, Fernando, 1932-. 1.6008
Bothwell, Robert. 3.8774, 3.8787
Botkin, Benjamin Albert, 1901-. 3.7210, 3.7401
Botkin, Daniel B. 5.3782
Botstein, David. 5.3449
Bott, Elizabeth. 4.5636
Bott, Martin Harold Phillips, 1926-. 5.3088
Bott, Raoul, 1924-. 5.1615
Botticelli, Sandro, 1444 or 5-1510. 1.6191
Bottigheimer, Karl S. 3.1813
Bottiglia, William F., comp. 2.4107
Bottle, R. T. 5.3293
Bottle, R. T. ed. 5.2600
Bottomore, T. B. 4.1531, 4.4743, 4.4783, 4.7043
Bottoms, David. 2.10777
Boucé, Paul-Gabriel. 2.7259, 2.7264
Boucé, Paul-Gabriel. ed. 2.7267
Boucher, Anthony, 1911-1968. 2.3476
Boucher, Douglas H. 5.3584
Boucher, E. A. 5.2908
Boucher, François León Louis, 1885-. 4.829
Bouchier, David. 4.5232, 4.6102
Boucicault, Dion, 1820-1890. 2.7438
Boudaille, Georges. joint author. 1.6129
Boudreaux, H. Bruce, 1914-. 5.3850
Boughner, Daniel Cliness, 1909-. 2.2788
Bouglé, Célestin Charles Alfred, 1870-1940. 3.4173
Bouhdiba, Abdelwahab. 1.2087
Boulby, Mark. 2.13903
Boulding, Elise. ed. 3.68
Boulding, Kenneth Ewart, 1910-. 3.188, 4.1746, 4.1979, 4.2643, 4.4938, 4.9104
Boulenger, Jacques. 2.4003
Boulez, Pierre, 1925-. 1.3667
Boullée, Etienne Louis, 1728-1799. 1.5414
Bouloiseau, Marc. 3.2078
Boulton, James T. 1.1370, 2.6972
Boulton, James T. ed. 1.1370
Boulton, Mary Georgina. 4.5665
Boulton, Matthew, 1728-1809. 5.6213
Boulware, Marcus H. 3.6810
Boumann, Ludwig, 1801-1871. 1.930
Bourassa, Robert, 1933-. 4.3798
Bourdin, Henri Louis, ed. 3.6024
Bourdon, David. 1.5742
Bouret, Jean. 1.6059
Bourgeois, Joanne. 5.3054
Bourgeois, Louise, 1911-. 1.5661
Bourget, Paul, 1852-1935. 2.4148
Bourguignon, Erika, 1924-. 1.1562
Bourjaily, Vance Nye. 2.11397
Bourlière, François, 1913-. 5.3556
Bourne, Geoffrey H. (Geoffrey Howard), 1909- ed. 5.3587, 5.4220
Bourne, Kenneth. 3.1604, 3.1608
Bourne, Larry S. 4.6197
Bourne, Randolph Silliman, 1886-1918. 2.11398
Bourne, Richard. 4.5781
Bourns, Inc. 5.6521
Bouthilet, Lorraine. 4.5738
Boutilier, James A. 5.7454
Boutilier, Mary A. joint author. 4.5957
Boutilier, Mary A. 4.964
Bouyer, Louis, 1913-. 1.3215, 1.3251, 1.3274

Bova, Ben, 1932-. 2.3487
Bovini, Giuseppe. 1.5506
Bovis, H. Eugene, 1928-. 3.3817
Bowden, Edwin T. 2.10878
Bowden, Henry Warner. 1.1587, 1.2271
Bowden, Henry Warner. ed. 1.2371
Bowden, John Stephen. 1.2224
Bowden, K. F. (Kenneth F.), 1916-. 4.343
Bowden, Ken. joint author. 4.1034
Bowden, Mary Weatherspoon. 2.10873, 2.11098
Bowden, Muriel Amanda. 2.6319
Bowden, Roger J. (Roger John), 1943-. 4.1394
Bowder, Diana. 3.2812
Bowen, Catherine Drinker. 2.11400, 3.311, 3.6989, 4.9817
Bowen, E. G. (Emrys George), 1900-. 3.539
Bowen, Elizabeth, 1899-1973. 2.8468-2.8480
Bowen, Harold, joint author. 3.3665
Bowen, Harvey Kent, joint author. 5.6900
Bowen, Howard, 1908-. 4.2702
Bowen, Howard Rothmann, 1908-. 4.10074, 4.10576, 4.10597
Bowen, Humphrey John Moule. 5.2624
Bowen, James, 1928-. 4.9948
Bowen, Jesse Chester, 1865-1948. 4.3149
Bowen, Kurt Derek. 4.5344
Bowen, Merlin, 1910-. 2.11165
Bowen, Norman Levi, 1887-1956. 5.3044
Bowen, Ralph Henry, 1919-. 3.8497, 4.7595
Bowen, Roger W., 1947-. 3.4959
Bowen, William G. 4.3216, 4.4499
Bowen, Zack R. 1.3446, 2.8905, 2.8949
Bower, Ames S. 5.8477
Bower, Blair T. joint author. 4.1845
Bower, Eli Michael. 2.10827
Bower, Frank A. 5.2515
Bower, Gordon H. joint author. 4.10348, 4.10353
Bower, Gordon H. 5.295
Bower, Robert T. 4.4066
Bower, T. G. R., 1941-. 5.554
Bowering, Peter. 2.8826
Bowers, David Freick, 1906- ed. 3.6081
Bowers, Faubion, 1917-. 2.3396, 4.1109
Bowers, Fredson Thayer. ed. 2.6554
Bowers, Fredson Thayer. 1.596, 1.598, 1.1540, 2.5883, 2.6568, 2.6836, 5.108, 5.7676
Bowers, Fredson Thayer 1905-. 1.527, 2.11268
Bowers, Kenneth S. 5.658
Bowers, Malcolm B. 5.4921
Bowers, Neal, 1948-. 2.12980
Bowers, William J. 4.6850
Bowersock, G. W. (Glen Warren), 1936-. 3.2795, 3.4033
Bowersox, Donald J. 4.4312
Bowes, Anna De Planter. 5.7123
Bowes, Pratima. 1.1701
Bowie, Malcolm. 2.3857, 2.4264
Bowie, Norman E., 1942-. 4.4268
Bowie, Robert Richardson, 1909-. 3.7559
Bowie, Theodore Robert. 1.4885
Bowker, Albert Hosmer, 1919-. 5.5673
Bowker, Lee H. 4.6745, 4.6843, 4.6859
Bowker (R. R.) Company. Serials Bibliography Dept. 5.8313
Bowker, Richard Rogers, 1848-1933. 5.7748
Bowlby, John. 4.5715, 5.434
Bowle, John. 3.29, 3.1215, 4.7406
Bowler, M. G. 5.2214, 5.2423
Bowler, Peter J. 5.3341-5.3342
Bowles, Gloria. 4.5915
Bowles, Jane Auer, 1917-1973. 2.11401
Bowles, Joseph E. 5.5916
Bowles, Paul, 1910-. 2.12912-2.12914
Bowles, Roy Tyler. 4.6545
Bowles, Samuel. 4.2009, 4.10730
Bowles, Stephen E., 1943-. 5.8136
Bowley, A. L. (Arthur Lyon) Sir, 1869-1957. 4.1291
Bowley, Marian, 1911-. 4.1354
Bowlt, John E. 1.5035
Bowman, Albert Hall, 1921-. 3.6442
Bowman, Isaiah, 1878-1950. 3.9269, 4.12, 4.363, 4.378
Bowman, James S., 1945-. 5.8365
Bowman, M. J. 4.8966
Bowman, Mary Ann. 5.8446
Bowman, Sylvia E. 2.10908

Bownas, Geoffrey. joint comp. 2.2019
Bowne, Borden Parker, 1847-1910. 1.1264, 1.1312
Bowness, Alan. 1.5698
Bowness, Alan. ed. 1.5694
Bowra, C. M. (Cecil Maurice), 1898-1971. 2.267, 2.310, 2.317, 2.508, 2.2755, 2.2770
Bowra, Cecil Maurice, Sir. 2.403, 2.2766
Bowring, Richard John, 1947-. 2.2050, 2.2079
Bowser, Eileen. ed. 2.3076
Bowser, Frederick P. 4.6440
Bowsky, William M. 3.2850, 3.2953
Box, George E. P. 5.1415
Box, Paul C. 4.3943
Boxer, C. R. (Charles Ralph), 1904-. 1.2464, 3.3494, 3.9206-3.9207, 4.5867, 4.8934, 4.8937
Boxer, Marilyn J. 4.5868
Boxill, Bernard R. 3.6700
Boxshall, Geoffrey Allan. 5.3510
Boyanus, Semen Karlovich, 1871-1952. 2.1228
Boyce, Benjamin, 1903-. 2.5580, 2.6886
Boyce, David George, 1942-. 3.1840
Boyce, George Arthur, 1898-. 3.5914
Boyce, Gray Cowan, 1899-. 5.8225
Boyce, Mary. 1.1781
Boyce, Ronald R. 4.80
Boyce, William E. 5.1501
Boyd, Brian. 2.12225
Boyd, Doug. 1.1816
Boyd, Douglas A. 2.2843
Boyd, Ernest Augustus, 1887-1946. 2.4343
Boyd, Gavin. joint author. 3.3643
Boyd, James Dixon, 1907-1968. 5.4165
Boyd, John, 1935-. 4.10430
Boyd, John D. 2.2372
Boyd, Julian P. (Julian Parks), 1903-. 3.6973
Boyd, Malcolm. 1.3772
Boyd, Robert Neilson. 5.2722
Boyd, William, 1874-1962. 4.10186-4.10187
Boyd, William Kenneth, 1879-1938. ed. 3.8189
Boyde, Patrick. 2.4918, 2.4943
Boydston, Jo Ann, 1924-. 1.584, 4.10224, 4.10230
Boyer, Carl B. (Carl Benjamin), 1906-. 5.1067, 5.1447
Boyer, Ernest L. 4.10047, 4.10075, 4.10818
Boyer, Howard E. 5.5807
Boyer, Mildred, 1926-. 4.10891
Boyer, Paul D. ed. 5.4411
Boyer, Paul S. ed. 3.352
Boyer, Paul S. 1.2388, 4.6204, 4.9719
Boyer, Richard Owen, 1903-1973. 3.7272
Boyer, Robert H., 1937- joint author. 2.5969
Boyer, Robert S. 5.1231
Boyers, Robert. 2.10490
Boylan, Henry. 3.344
Boyle, Andrew. 1.6232
Boyle, Charles. 5.5515
Boyle, Kay, 1902-. 2.11402-2.11406
Boyle, Marie A. (Marie Ann) 5.4242
Boyle, Raymond A. 4.3949
Boyle, Robert, Hon. 1627-1691. 5.2621
Boyle, T. Coraghessan. 2.12915
Boylestad, Robert L. 5.6269, 5.6458
Boyne, Walter J., 1929-. 5.6675
Boynton, Percy Holmes, 1875-1946. 2.10346
Bozell, L. Brent, joint author. 3.7666
Bozeman, Adda Bruemmer, 1908-. 4.9002, 4.9276
Bozeman, Theodore Dwight, 1942-. 1.1596
Bozzola, Angelo, joint author. 1.4847
Braaten, Carl E., 1929-. 1.2758, 1.2883
Brabant, Frank Herbert, 1892-. 3.2171
Brabazon, James. 2.9309
Bracegirdle, Brian. 5.5541
Bracher, Karl Dietrich, 1922-. 3.2371, 3.2434-3.2435
Brachet, J. (Jean), 1909-. 5.3589, 5.4134
Brachin, Pierre. 2.1168
Brack, Gene M. 3.6472
Brack, M. comp. 2.5508
Brack, M. 2.7258
Brackbill, Yvonne. 5.600
Bracken, Harry McFarland, 1926-. 1.692
Brackenridge, H. H. (Hugh Henry), 1748-1816. 2.10862-2.10863
Bradbrook, Frank W. 2.7365

Bradbrook, M. C. (Muriel Clara), 1909-.
2.5637, 2.5871, 2.5876, 2.5884, 2.6502,
2.6692, 2.6722-2.6723, 2.6864, 2.7105, 2.8556,
2.9060
Bradburn, Norman M. 4.1230
Bradburn, Norman M. joint author. 4.1231
Bradbury, John M. 2.10443-2.10444
Bradbury, Katharine L. 4.6205
Bradbury, Malcolm, 1932-. 2.5942, 2.6181,
2.8656, 2.9625-2.9628, 2.10614, 2.11358
Bradbury, Ray, 1920-. 2.11407-2.11410
Braddock, Joseph, 1902-. 3.2689
Braddon, M. E. (Mary Elizabeth), 1837-1915.
2.7934
Braden, Charles Samuel, 1887-. 1.2389, 3.8920
Braden, Gordon, 1947-. 2.5774
Braden, Waldo Warder, 1911- ed. 2.3535,
2.10859
Bradford, Gamaliel, 1863-1932. 3.6286
Bradford, H. F. (Harry F.) 5.4300
Bradford, James C. 5.7421
Bradford, William, 1588-1657. 3.7987
Bradlee, Benjamin. 3.7872
Bradley, A. C. (Andrew Cecil), 1851-1935.
1.1432, 2.5535, 2.6777, 2.8162
Bradley, Anthony, 1942-. 2.9867
Bradley, David, 1950-. 2.12916-2.12917
Bradley, F. H. (Francis Herbert), 1846-1924.
1.1171, 1.1265
Bradley, Francis Herbert. 1.1431
Bradley, Harold Whitman. 3.5640
Bradley, Ian C. 4.8555
Bradley, J. F. N. (John Francis Nejez), 1930-.
3.1908, 3.3200
Bradley, J. L. 1.5153
Bradley, John Lewis. 2.8031, 2.8033
Bradley, Marion Zimmer. 2.12918
Bradley, Omar Nelson, 1893-1981. 3.952
Bradley, Philip D., ed. 4.3347
Bradley, Raymond S., 1948-. 5.2525
Bradley, Sculley, 1897-. 2.10665, 2.10942,
2.10978, 2.11060, 2.11267
Bradley, Stephen P., 1941-. 5.1548
Bradner, Leicester, 1899-. 2.6542
Bradshaw, Gillian, 1956-. 2.12919
Bradstreet, Anne, 1612?-1672. 2.10864-2.10865
Brady, Frank. 2.6905-2.6906
Brady, George Stuart, 1887-. 5.5759
Brady, Ignatius C. 1.3135
Brady, James E., 1938-. 5.2625
Brady, Michael, 1945-. 5.1007, 5.6170-5.6171
Brady, Nyle C. 5.5261
Braeman, John. 3.6945, 3.7629
Braeman, John. ed. 3.7508, 3.7605
Bragadin, Marc' Antonio, 1906-. 3.1036
Braham, Allan. 1.5413, 1.5419
Braham, Randolph L. 3.1114, 3.3972
Brahmananda, P. R. 4.3234
Braibanti, Ralph J. D. 3.4131
Braider, Donald, 1923-. 1.5917
Braidwood, Robert J. (Robert John), 1907-.
3.112
Braiker, Harriet B., 1948-. 4.6784
Brailsford, Henry Noel, 1873-1958. 3.1488
Brain, C. K. (Charles Kimberlin) 4.701
Brain, Peter J. 4.8962
Brain, Robert. 3.5397
Braine, John. 2.9629
Brainerd, George W. (George Walton),
1909-1956. 3.9040
Braisted, William Reynolds. 3.6375
Braithwaite, R. B. (Richard Bevan) 5.866
Braithwaite, William Stanley, 1878-1962.
2.11411
Bramah, Ernest. 2.9342-2.9343
Bramble, J. C. 2.754
Bramblett, Claud A. 5.4015
Brameld, Theodore Burghard Hurt, 1904-.
4.9963, 4.10177, 4.10220-4.10222
Brams, Steven J. 4.7965
Bramsted, Ernest Kohn. 3.2436
Bramwell, Martyn. 4.193
Branch, Alan E. 4.3950, 4.3956
Branch, Michael, 1940-. 2.1750
Branch, Watson Gailey, comp. 2.11166
Brancusi, Constantin, 1876-1957. 1.5743-1.5744
Brand, C. M. (Coenraad M.) 4.7252
Brand, Carl Fremont. 4.8535

Brand, J. C. D. (John Charles Drury) 5.2801
Brand, Louis, 1885-. 5.1502
Brand, Myles. 1.134
Brandeis, Louis Dembitz, 1856-1941. 3.7424,
4.1930, 4.9447
Brandeis University. Poses Institute of Fine
Arts. 3.6063
Brandel, Rose. 1.3463, 1.4346
Brandell, Gunnar. 2.14078
Brandenburg, Erich, 1868-1946. 3.2284, 3.2337
Brandenburg, Frank Ralph, 1926-. 3.8939
Brander, Laurence, 1903-. 2.7498, 2.7820,
2.9188
Brander, Michael. 5.5490
Brandes, Eric A. (Eric Adolph) 5.6765
Brandes, Georg Morris Cohen, 1842-1927.
2.5723
Brandes, Stanley H. 4.800
Brandon, Henry, 1916-. 3.7896
Brandon, James R. 2.2034, 2.3386, 2.3393,
2.3400
Brandon, James R. comp. 2.2838
Brandon, Robert N. 5.3403
Brandon, Ruth. 4.9429
Brandon, S. G. F. (Samuel George Frederick),
1907-1971. 1.1523, 1.2896, 1.4637
Brandrup, J., ed. 5.2773
Brandt, Allan M. 5.4769
Brandt, Bill. 5.6963, 5.6984
Brandt, Conrad. 3.4680, 4.7109
Brandt, Otto, 1892-1935. 3.2250
Brandt, Richard B. 1.1406, 1.1443
Brandt, Steven A. 4.744
Brandt, Willy, 1913-. 4.4143
Brandwein, Paul Franz, 1912- joint author.
5.3216
Brandwood, Leonard. 1.243
Brandys, Kazimierz. 2.1700
Brannen, Peter. 4.3183
Branner, H. C. (Hans Christian), 1903-1966.
2.14022
Brannigan, Augustine, 1949-. 5.956
Branscomb, Lewis M., 1926-. 4.1772
Brant, Irving, 1885-. 3.7099
Brant, Sebastian, 1458-1521. 2.13528
Brantley, Richard E. 2.8326
Brantlinger, Patrick, 1941-. 2.5724, 4.5002
Branyan, Robert L. comp. 3.7819
Brasch, Charles. 2.1914, 2.10213
Brasier, M. D. 5.3153
Brasil, Emanuel. joint comp. 2.5467
Brass, Paul R. 3.4357, 4.8705, 4.8715, 4.10142
Brass, William. 4.1710
Brass Workers History Project. 4.3738
Brassaï, 1899-. 5.6964
Brasseur, Guy. 5.2522
Brater, Ernest Fredrick, 1912-. 5.5965
Brathwaite, Edward. 2.9985-2.9988
Braton, Norman R. joint author. 5.7060
Brauch, Hans Günter, 1947-. 4.9157
Braude, Benjamin. 3.3709
Braude, William Gordon, 1907- tr. 1.1942,
1.1944
Braudel, Fernand. 3.359, 3.2525, 4.1744, 4.1747
Braudy, Leo. 2.10412
Braudy, Leo. comp. 2.12104
Brauer, Heinrich, ed. 1.5010
Brault, Gerard Joseph. 2.3960
Braun, Aurel. 3.3531
Braun-Blanquet, J. (Josias), 1884-. 5.3765
Braun, Dieter. 3.4099
Braun, Dietrich, 1928-. 1.1479
Braun, E. Lucy (Emma Lucy), 1889-. 5.3781
Braun, Ernest, 1925-. 5.5516
Braun, Molly. 3.5710
Braun, Samuel J., 1934-. 4.10402
Braun, Sidney David, 1912- ed. 2.3820
Braun, Susan. 4.1094
Braun, Thom. 2.7396
Braun, Volker, 1939-. 2.13882-2.13883
Brauner, Charles J. 4.10162, 4.10538
Braunfels, Wolfgang. 1.5521
Braunmuller, A. R., 1945-. 2.6645
Braunthal, Gerard, 1923-. 4.8613
Brautigam, Patsy Fowler. 5.7654
Brautigan, Richard. 2.11412-2.11414
Braverman, Harry. 4.2678
Bravmann, René A. 1.5086

Brawer, Florence B., 1922-. 4.10560
Brawley, Benjamin Griffith, 1982-1939. 2.10688,
2.11012-2.11013
Bray, Jean, 1932-. 5.5037
Bray, Olin H. 5.1234
Bray, Wayne D. 4.9041
Brazier, Phyllis. 4.3674
Brazier, Rodney. 4.9418
Break, George F. 4.3462, 4.4661, 4.9765
Bréal, Michel, 1832-1915. 2.223
Breasted, James Henry, 1865-1935. 3.5135,
3.5152
Brebner, John Alexander. 2.9238
Brebner, John Bartlet. 3.5966, 3.8668,
3.8800-3.8801
Brecher, Jeremy. 4.3738
Brecher, Michael. 3.3857
Brecht, Arnold, 1884-. 3.2361, 4.7221
Brecht, Bertolt, 1898-1956. 2.3083,
2.13700-2.13705
Brecht, Martin. 1.2339
Breckinridge, Scott D. 4.7902
Bredero, G. A. (Gerbrand Adriaenszoon),
1585-1618. 2.13947
Bredius, Abraham, 1855-1946. 1.6251
Bredsdorff, Elias. 2.13966, 2.14004, 2.14009,
5.8021
Bredvold, Louis I. 4.7417
Bredvold, Louis Ignatius, 1888-. 2.5525, 2.6087,
2.6259, 2.6995
Brée, Germaine. 2.3837, 2.3869, 2.3909, 2.4563,
2.4663
Brée, Germaine. ed. 2.4456
Brée, Germaine. comp. 2.3937
Breech, James. 2.2681, 2.2889
Breed, Paul Francis, 1916-. 1.3588, 5.8005,
5.8125
Breeden, Robert, ed. 3.6065
Breen, David. 3.8839, 4.3698
Breen, Jon L., 1943-. 2.3470
Breen, T. H. 3.8187, 3.8215, 4.7808
Breeskin, Adelyn Dohme, 1896-. 1.5922, 1.6438
Bregman, Alvan. 5.7884
Bréhier, Émile, 1876-1952. 1.127, 1.342
Breimyer, Harold F. 4.3680
Breisach, Ernst. 3.382
Breitmaier, E. 5.2682
Breitman, George. ed. 3.6675
Brekke, Milo. 1.3002
Bremer, Francis J. 3.7945
Bremner, John B., 1920-. 2.1004
Bremner, Robert Hamlett, 1917- ed. 3.7508,
3.7605, 4.6553
Brenan, Gerald. 1.3260, 2.5089, 3.3401, 3.3452
Brenchley, David L. 5.6049
Brende, Joel Osler. 5.7370
Brendel, Otto, 1901-1973. 1.4725
Breneman, David W. 4.10558
Brengle, K. G. 5.5316
Brennan, Christopher John, 1870-1932. 2.10154
Brennan, Maeve. 2.12920
Brenner, Charles, 1913-. 5.129, 5.410, 5.4902
Brenner, Louis. 3.5368
Brent, Edward E., 1949-. 4.6826
Brent, Linda, 1818-1896. 3.7211
Brentano, Clemens Maria, 1778-1842. 2.13552
Brentano, Franz Clemens, 1838-1917. 1.1466
Brentano, Robert, 1926-. 3.2937
Brereton, Cloudesley Shovell Henry, 1863- joint
tr. 1.827
Brereton, Geoffrey. 2.3829, 2.3874,
2.3892-2.3893
Brereton, Geoffrey. ed. 2.4726
Bresciani-Turroni, Costantino. 4.4520
Breslauer, George W. 4.8653
Bresler, Boris. 5.5875
Bresler, Jack Barry, 1923- comp. 5.3422
Breslin, James E. B., 1935-. 2.10489
Bresnick, David. 4.10894
Bressler, Barry. 4.1386
Bretall, Robert Walter, 1913-. 1.3294, 1.3297
Bretherick, L. 5.5556
Bretnor, Reginald. 2.3487
Breton, André,1896-1966. 1.1399, 1.5880,
2.4421-2.4427
Breton, Nicholas, 1545?-1626? 2.6432-2.6433
Brett, George Sidney, 1879-1944. 5.70
Brett-James, Antony, 1920-. 2.2611

Brett, R. L. 2.8308
Brett-Smith, Herbert Francis Brett, ed. 2.7992
Brettell, Richard R. 5.6950
Bretton, Henry L., 1916-. 4.8792
Breuer, Marcel, 1902-. 1.5305-1.5306, 1.6569
Breuer, Melvin A. 5.6468
Breuil, Henri, 1877-1961. 4.704
Breul, Karl, 1860-1932. 2.1189
Brewer, Anthony, 1942-. 4.1536
Brewer, Derek, 1923-. 2.6345, 2.6355-2.6356, 2.6358, 2.6373
Brewer, Ebenezer Cobham, 1810-1897. 2.2350-2.2351
Brewer, Elisabeth. comp. 2.6417
Brewer, James Gordon. 5.8200
Brewer, James W., 1942-. 5.1097
Brewer, John, 1947-. 3.1566, 4.2295
Brewer, Peter G. 4.320
Brewer, Thomas L., 1941-. 4.3026
Brewitt-Taylor, C. H. 2.2221
Brews, J. R. 5.6507
Brewster, David, Sir, 1781-1868. 5.4376
Brewster, Dorothy, 1883-. 2.9028, 2.9592-2.9593
Brewster, John Monroe, 1904- joint ed. 1.613
Brewton, John Edmund, 1898-. 2.2711
Brewton, Sara Westbrook. 2.2711
Breyer, Betty Jane. 2.8200
Breyer, Stephen G., 1938-. 4.3080, 4.3714
Breymeyer, A. I. (Alicja I.), 1932-. 5.3555
Breytenbach, Breyten. 2.13963
Breznitz, Shelomo. 5.447
Brian, P. L. Thibaut, 1930-. 5.6849
Brice, William Charles. 3.3678, 4.164
Brickell, Henry M. 4.10982
Bricker, Diane D. 4.10905, 4.10949
Brickman, William W. 4.9947, 4.10107, 4.10939, 5.8244
Brickner, Philip W., 1928-. 5.4686
Bridenbaugh, Carl. ed. 3.6015
Bridenbaugh, Carl. 1.3315, 1.5310, 3.1456, 3.6010, 3.6871, 3.8012, 3.8087, 3.8130, 3.8218, 3.8221
Bridenbaugh, Jessica, joint author. 3.8087
Bridenthal, Renate. 4.6123
Bridge, F. R. 3.679
Bridge, Raymond. 4.983
Bridges-Adams, William, 1889-1965. 2.3282
Bridges, D. S. (Douglas S.), 1945-. 5.1433
Bridges, Daisy Caroline. 5.5153
Bridges, Robert Seymour, 1844-1930. 2.7171, 2.7827
Bridges, Ronald. 1.2494
Bridgman, P. W. (Percy Williams), 1882-1961. 5.1900-5.1902, 5.2004, 5.2241
Bridgman, Richard. 2.10535, 2.11255, 2.12517
Brieger, Gert H., comp. 5.4521
Brière, O. 1.1138
Brierly, James Leslie, 1881-1955. 4.9284-4.9285
Briffault, Robert, 1876-1948. 2.883, 4.5552
Brigance, William Norwood, 1896-1960, ed. 2.10649
Brigard Silva, Camilo de, ed. 2.5415
Briggs, A. D. P. 2.1420
Briggs, Asa, 1921-. 3.1581, 3.1618, 4.4065, 5.6207
Briggs, D. (David), 1936-. 5.3790
Briggs, D. E. (Dennis Edward) 5.5323
Briggs, E. Donald. 4.8277
Briggs, Geoffrey. 3.289, 5.1809
Briggs, Harold Edward, 1896-. 3.8495
Briggs, John W., 1937-. 3.8062
Briggs, Julia. 2.8710
Briggs, Katharine Mary. 4.788
Briggs, Lawrence Palmer. 3.4443
Briggs, Leslie J. 4.10266
Briggs, Robin. 3.2006
Briggs, Thomas Henry, 1877-. 4.10500
Brigham, Clarence Saunders, 1877-1963. 2.3592, 5.8322
Brigham, James A. 2.8605
Brigham, John, 1945-. 4.9663
Bright, Charles, 1943-. 4.7507
Bright, James Wilson, 1852-1926. 2.939
Bright, John, 1908-. 1.2614, 3.3885
Bright, William, 1928-. 2.130
Brightman, Carol. joint author. 1.5797
Brightman, Edgar Sheffield, 1884-1953. 1.502

Brignano, Russell C. (Russell Carl), 1935-. 5.7866
Briley, Bruce E. (Bruce Edwin), 1936-. 5.6420
Brill, A. A. (Abraham Arden), 1874-1948. 5.130, 5.133, 5.4783
Brill, Alida. 4.7694
Brilliant, Richard. 1.4712
Brillouin, Léon, 1889-. 5.867, 5.1903
Briloff, Abraham J. 4.4388, 4.4407
Brimley, Vern. 4.10654
Brinch Hansen, Per, 1938-. 5.1142
Bring, Mitchell. 5.5372
Brink, André Philippus, 1935-. 2.13964
Brink, C. O. (Charles Oscar), 1907-. 2.719
Brink, Pamela J. 5.5186
Brinker, Russell C. (Russell Charles), 1908-. 5.5820
Brinkley, Alan. 3.7753
Brinkley, Roberta Florence. ed. 2.5648
Brinkley, Roberta Florence. 2.6255
Brinkmann, Roland, 1898-. 5.3004
Brinkmeyer, Robert H. 2.10294
Brinley, Thomas, 1906- ed. 4.8940
Brinnin, John Malcolm, 1916-. 2.9415-2.9416, 2.12518
Brinton, Crane, 1898-1968. 3.89, 3.659, 3.2109, 4.7289, 4.7612, 4.9107
Brisbin, Richard A. 4.10800
Briscoe, John, 1938-. 2.732-2.733
Briscoe, Mary Louise. 5.8110, 5.8466
Brisman, Shimeon. 5.8234
Brissenden, Paul Frederick, 1885-. 4.3554
Brissenden, R. F. ed. 2.5667
Brissenden, R. F. 2.5666, 2.5668-2.5669
Bristol, Roger Pattrell. 5.7752-5.7753, 5.7759
Bristow, Eugene Kerr, 1927-. 2.1404, 2.1485
Bristow, Geoff. 5.6568
Britan, Halbert Hains, 1874-. 1.796
British Academy. 3.3822, 4.448
British Architectural Library. 5.7086
British Association for the Advancement of Science. Research Committee. 4.74
British Broadcasting Corporation. 1.5206, 2.1096
British Committee of Historic Towns. 4.171
British Computer Society. PL/I Specialist Group. 5.1224
British Council. 2.9073
British Ecological Society. 5.3771-5.3772
British Film Academy. 2.3017
British Institute of International Affairs. 3.862
British Institute of Persian Studies. 3.4068
British Library. 1.4737, 1.4935, 1.6419, 1.6461, 2.6132, 2.6136-2.6137, 2.6143, 5.7670
British Library. Bibliographic Services Division. 5.7912
British Library. Board. 1.5184
British Museum. 1.4737, 1.4935, 1.5614, 2.441
British Museum. Department of Prints and Drawings. 1.6461
British Museum. Dept. of Printed Books. King's Library. 5.7541
British Museum. Dept. of Prints and Drawings. 1.6474
British Museum. Dept. of Western Asiatic Antiquities. 1.5615
British Museum. MSS (Sloane 2463) 5.5044
British Museum. Trustees. 1.5184
British Ornithologists' Union. 5.3935
British Politics Group. 4.8422
Britt, George, 1895-. 2.3621
Brittain, James E., 1931-. 5.6252
Brittain, Joan T., 1928- joint author. 2.13217
Brittain, W. Lambert. 1.4652
Brittan, Arthur. 4.5059, 4.5872
Brittan, Samuel. 4.7033
Britten, Benjamin, 1913-1976. 1.3455
Brittin, Burdick H. 4.9277
Brittin, Norman A. 2.12162
Britton, D. Guyver (Dorothy Guyver), 1922-. 2.2065
Britton, Nathaniel Lord, 1859-1934. 5.3673
Britton, Scott G., 1954-. 5.6796
Brizio, Anna Maria. joint author. 5.823
Broad, C. D. (Charlie Dunbar), 1887-1971. 1.746, 5.103, 5.638
Broad, David J. 5.4280
Broad, Lewis, 1900-. 2.8068

Broad, Violet M. joint author. 2.8068
Broad, William, 1951-. 5.857
Broadbent, Donald Eric. 5.19, 5.64
Broadbent, R. J. 2.2839
Broadhead, Philip. 4.7387
Broadhead, Robert S., 1947-. 5.4598
Broadus, Robert N. 5.7621
Broberg, Gunnar, 1942-. 5.3215
Broch, Hermann, 1886-1951. 2.13712-2.13713
Bröchner, Jessie, tr. 2.14065
Brock, Arthur John. tr. 2.368
Brock, Bernard L. 2.3533
Brock, Colin. 4.10104
Brock, Gerald W. 4.4050
Brock, Irving, tr. 3.4256
Brock, Michael. 4.8461
Brock, Peter, 1920-. 4.9108, 4.9112, 4.9118
Brock, Thomas D. 5.4435, 5.4442
Brock, Thomas D. ed. and tr. 5.4444
Brock, Van K. 2.12921
Brock, William Ranulf. 3.7459, 4.8251
Brockbank, Philip. 2.6648
Brockelmann, Carl, 1868-1956. 2.1834
Brockett, Oscar Gross, 1923-. 2.3161, 2.3176
Brockman, C. Frank (Christian Frank), 1902-. 4.893
Brockriede, Wayne. joint autho. 2.3537
Brockway, Wallace, 1905- ed. 2.3782
Brod, Craig. 5.1249
Brod, Max, 1884-1968. ed. 2.13788
Broda, Paul, 1939-. 5.4450
Brodbeck, May. 5.882
Brode, Patrick, 1950-. 4.9432
Broder, Nathan. joint tr. 1.3938
Broder, Nathan. ed. 1.3702
Broder, Nathan. 1.3786
Brodeur, Arthur Gilchrist, 1888-. 2.6294
Brodeur, Paul. 4.9775
Brodhead, Richard H., 1947-. 2.11067
Brodie, Bernard, 1910-. 5.7173, 5.7252, 5.7384
Brodie, Fawn McKay, 1915-. 3.7061, 5.7173
Brodie, Leo. 5.1215
Brodsky, Annette M. 5.4818
Brodsky, Joseph, 1940-. 2.1625
Brody, Baruch A. comp. 5.868
Brody, David. tr. 3.7605
Brody, David. 4.3167, 4.3348, 4.3530
Brody, Elaine. 1.4238
Brody, Elaine M. 5.4666
Brody, Erness Bright. 5.350
Brody, Howard. 5.4550
Brody, J. J. 3.5909-3.5910
Brody, Jane E. 5.5133
Brody, Linda. 4.10915
Brody, Nathan. joint author. 5.350
Brody, Saul Nathaniel. 5.4764
Broe, Mary Lynn. 2.13262
Broecker, Wallace S., 1931-. 4.342
Brøgger, A. W. (Anton Wilhelm), 1884-. 5.7501
Broek, David. 5.5786
Broek, Jan Otto Marius, 1904-1974. 4.37, 4.82
Brøndsted, Johannes, 1890-1965. 3.3358
Broer, Marion Ruth. 5.4263
Brogan, D. W. (Denis William), 1900-1974. 3.2172, 3.6088, 3.7754, 4.7850
Brogan, Denis William. 3.2207, 3.6087
Brogan, Marianne C. 5.2599
Brogan, T. V. F. (Terry V. F.) 5.7980
Broglie, Louis de, 1892-. 5.2052, 5.2144
Brohm, Jean Marie, 1940-. 4.954
Broker, Ignatia. 3.5855
Bromberg, J. Philip, 1936-. 5.2802
Bromberg, Joan Lisa. 5.2450
Brombert, Beth Archer. tr. 2.4656
Brombert, Victor H. 2.3834, 2.3899, 2.4243
Brombert, Victor H. ed. 2.4311
Brome, Alexander, 1620-1666. 2.6909
Brome, Richard, d. 1652? 2.6230, 2.6560
Bromfield, Louis, 1896-1956. 2.11416-2.11417
Bromhead, P. A. 4.8469
Bromiley, G. W., ed. and tr. 1.2354
Bromiley, Geoffrey William. 1.2711, 1.2773
Bromiley, Geoffrey William. ed. and tr. 2.249
Bromke, Adam. 3.3277
Bromley, Daniel W., 1940- joint author. 4.2885
Bromley, David G. 1.1869, 1.1875, 1.3410
Brommer, Frank. 1.5630
Bromwich, Rachel. 2.837

Brondfield, Jerry, 1913-. 4.1015
Broner, E. M. 2.2414
Bronfenbrenner, Martha Ornstein, 1879-1915. 5.746
Bronfenbrenner, Martin, 1914-. 4.1563, 4.2544
Bronfenbrenner, Urie, 1917-. 5.581
Bronowski, Jacob, 1908-1974. 1.420, 1.6682, 2.7411, 3.209, 5.842, 5.869-5.870
Bronowski, Rita. 1.6682
Bronson, Bertrand Harris, 1902-. 1.4344, 2.6357
Bronstein, Arthur J. 2.1018
Brontë, Anne, 1820-1849. 2.7439-2.7441, 2.7444
Brontë, Charlotte, 1816-1855. 2.7444-2.7447
Brontë, Emily, 1818-1848. 2.7444, 2.7457-2.7459
Brook, Barry S. 1.3547
Brook, G. L. (George Leslie), 1910-. 2.935, 2.6136, 2.6406
Brook, Peter. 2.2790
Brook, Richard J. 5.1396
Brook-Shepherd, Gordon, 1918-. 3.1897
Brooke, Christopher Nugent Lawrence. 3.130, 3.602
Brooke, Christopher Nugent Lawrence. joint author. 1.3232
Brooke, Christopher Nugent Lawrence. 4.2303
Brooke, Henry, 1703?-1783. 2.6910
Brooke, John. 3.1560, 3.1567, 4.8475
Brooke, Rupert, 1887-1915. 2.8485-2.8486
Brooke, Tucker, 1883-1946. 2.6700
Brooke, Zachary Nugent, 1883-. 1.2438
Brooker, Peter. 2.12338
Brookes, B. C. (Bertram Claude) ed. 2.2526
Brookes, Jean Ingram. 3.5550
Brookes, Stella Brewer, 1903-. 2.11053
Brookfield, H. C. 4.40
Brookings Institution. 4.1464, 4.1809, 4.1954, 4.1956, 4.1988, 4.2051, 4.2953, 4.3513, 4.3710, 4.3877, 4.3885, 4.4612, 4.4663, 4.4682, 4.4687, 4.4698, 4.4710, 4.4712, 4.4718, 4.5155, 4.6568, 4.7981, 4.8059, 4.9205, 5.4708, 5.7409, 5.7781
Brookings Institution, Washington, D.C. Transport Research Program. 4.3872, 4.3875, 4.4080
Brookins, Geraldine Kearse. 3.6748
Brooklyn, 1976 Symposium (1976: Brooklyn College) 3.8059
Brooklyn College. Institute for Studies in American Music. 1.3901
Brooklyn Museum. 1.4866, 1.4906, 1.5186, 1.6284
Brookner, Anita. 1.5149, 1.6087, 1.6110, 2.9630-2.9634
Brookner, Eli, 1931-. 5.6434
Brooks, Alexander D. 5.8377
Brooks, Brian S. 2.3563
Brooks, C. E. P. (Charles Ernest Pelham) 5.2526
Brooks, Cleanth, 1906-. 2.2465, 2.2762, 2.3426, 2.5746, 2.6071, 2.7181, 2.10663, 2.11686-2.11687, 2.12670
Brooks, D. R. (Daniel R.), 1951-. 5.3384
Brooks-Davies, Douglas. 2.6527
Brooks, Douglas. 2.7020
Brooks, Glenwood C., joint author. 4.10779
Brooks, Gwendolyn, 1917-. 2.10750, 2.11418-2.11421
Brooks, H. Allen (Harold Allen), 1925-. 1.5299
Brooks, John Langdon, 1920-. 5.3212
Brooks, Karen (Karen McConnell) 4.2977
Brooks, Lester. joint author. 3.6647
Brooks, Nicholas. 1.3310
Brooks, Penelope H. 5.4970
Brooks, Peter. 2.3443, 2.3904
Brooks, Richard A., 1931-. 5.7999
Brooks, Tilford. 1.4296
Brooks, Tim. 2.2847
Brooks, Van Wyck, 1886-1963. 2.10264, 2.10372, 2.10380, 2.10383, 2.10398, 2.10436-2.10437, 2.10719, 2.10950-2.10951, 2.11089, 2.11398, 2.11422, 3.6162
Brookshire, David S. 4.1575
Broome, Peter, 1937-. 2.4636
Broome, Richard, 1948-. 4.665
Broomfield, J. H. 3.4330
Brophy, Brigid, 1929-. 1.5800
Brophy, James D. 2.9327, 2.9859
Brophy, Jere E. 4.10313

Brose, David S. 3.5733
Brosnan, John. 2.3006
Brossard, E. B. 4.3758
Brosseau, Mathilde. 1.5344
Brotherston, Gordon. ed. 2.5443
Brotherston, Gordon. 2.5312, 2.5317
Brothwell, Don R. ed. 3.228
Broude, Norma. 1.4628
Broudy, Harry S. 4.10030
Broughton, Dorothy. 2.6984
Broughton, Leslie Nathan, 1877-1952. 2.7495, 5.7936
Broughton, Panthea Reid. 2.11688, 2.13244
Broughton, T. Alan (Thomas Alan), 1936-. 2.12922-2.12923
Broumas, Olga, 1949-. 2.12924
Broun, Heywood, 1888-1939. 4.6758
Broun, May Heywood, tr. 2.5292
Broven, John. 1.4273
Brower, David R. 5.5498
Brower, James E. 5.3537
Brower, Reuben Arthur, 1908-. 2.2544, 2.5496, 2.5782, 2.6811, 2.7201, 2.11752
Brower, Robert Hopkins, 1923-. 2.2008
Brown, A. Theodore (Andrew Theodore), 1923-. 3.8367, 4.6210
Brown, Alan. 2.4821
Brown, Alan R., comp. 5.613
Brown, Alec, 1900-1962. 2.1526
Brown, Alison, 1934-. 3.2929
Brown, Anne S. Kinsolving. joint comp. 3.6947
Brown, Anthony Cave. 3.1133
Brown, Archie, 1938-. 3.3005, 4.7590
Brown, Ashley, 1923-. 2.10505
Brown, Barbara E. 5.8395
Brown, Bertram S. ed. 5.4702
Brown, Bill, 1930-. 4.6825
Brown, C. C. (Charles Cuthbert) 4.806
Brown, Carleton Fairchild, 1869- ed. 2.6115, 2.6130-2.6131, 2.6346, 5.7941
Brown, Cecil H., 1944-. 4.495
Brown, Charles Brockden, 1771-1810. 2.10912
Brown, Charles Henry, 1910-. 2.10917
Brown, Christopher, 1948-. 1.6368
Brown, Christopher C. 5.7975
Brown, Christopher M. 5.5939
Brown, Clarence, 1929-. 2.1303, 2.1577
Brown, Clarence Fleetwood, ed.and tr. 2.1574
Brown, Claud L., 1925-. 5.3683
Brown, Claude, 1937-. 3.6818
Brown, D. Clayton (Deward Clayton), 1941-. 4.3806
Brown, David, 1929-. 1.3834
Brown, David Alexander. 5.3008
Brown, David (P. David C.) 1.6510
Brown, Dee Alexander. 3.5772, 3.8454
Brown, Delmer Myers, 1909-. 3.4916
Brown, Deming, 1919-. 2.1268, 2.10339
Brown, E. Cary (Edgar Cary) 4.1376
Brown, E. D. (Edward Duncan) joint author. 4.9292
Brown, E. Evan. 5.5467
Brown, E. K. 2.6175
Brown, E. K. (Edward Killoran), 1905-1951. 2.3447, 2.6175, 2.11475
Brown, E. Richard. 5.4525
Brown, Earle B. 5.2275
Brown, Edward James, 1909-. 2.1269, 2.1573
Brown, Emily Clara. 3.4300
Brown, Emily Clark, 1895-. 4.3418, 4.3507
Brown, Ernest Henry Phelps, 1906-. 4.3123
Brown, Esther Lucile, 1898-. 5.5182
Brown, Evan L. 5.4356
Brown, Francis, 1903-. 2.3630
Brown, Francis Andrew, 1915-. 2.13632
Brown, Frank Edward, 1908-. 1.5225, 3.2721
Brown, Fredric, 1906-1972. 2.11424
Brown, G. Baldwin. 1.5100
Brown, G. C. (Geoff C.) 5.3089
Brown, George Douglas, 1869-1902. 2.7462
Brown, Gerald Griffiths. 2.5110
Brown, Gerald Saxon, ed. 3.6337
Brown, Gerard Baldwin, 1849-1932. 1.5100
Brown, H. Rap, 1943-. 3.6819
Brown, Harold, 1927-. 5.7262
Brown, Harrison, 1917-1986. 4.362
Brown, Harry, 1917-1986. 2.11425
Brown, Harry James, ed. 3.7402

Brown, Henry Phelps, Sir, 1906-. 4.3411, 4.3442, 4.3642
Brown, Herbert Charles, 1912-. 5.2710, 5.2783
Brown, Herbert Ross, 1902-. 2.10606
Brown, Homer E., 1909-. 5.6335
Brown, Howard Mayer. 1.3570, 1.3647, 1.3705
Brown, Ian, 1947-. 5.8064
Brown, Ira Vernon, ed. 1.2
Brown, Ivor John Carnegie, 1891-. 2.8073
Brown, J. A. C. (James Alexander Campbell), 1911-1964. 5.150
Brown, J. F. (James F.), 1928-. 3.3544
Brown, J. Gordon. joint author. 4.8436
Brown, James Allison, 1934-. 3.5733
Brown, James H. 5.3237
Brown, James Russell, 1932-. 5.1604
Brown, James Seay, 1944-. 3.8282
Brown, James W. (James Wilson), 1913 Sept. 18-. 4.10324
Brown, Janet, 1952-. 2.10517
Brown, Jerry, 1936-. 5.3268
Brown, Jessica S. 3.8115
Brown, John, 1923-. 5.6426
Brown, John Arthur. 3.5747
Brown, John Howard, 1840-1917, ed. 3.6287
Brown, John Mason, 1900-1969. 2.3192, 2.3207, 2.7901, 2.12467
Brown, John Russell. 2.6852
Brown, John Russell. ed. 2.6879, 2.6881
Brown, Jonathan. 1.6287, 3.3445
Brown, Jonathan C., 1942-. 4.2165
Brown, Judith C. 1.3264, 4.2360
Brown, Judith K. 4.570
Brown, Judith M. (Judith Margaret), 1944-. 3.4272, 3.4307
Brown, Julia Prewitt, 1948-. 2.6006
Brown, June. 4.6546
Brown, Karl. 2.3047
Brown, Kendall W., 1949-. 4.4666
Brown, Kenneth Douglas. 4.8550
Brown, L. Carl (Leon Carl), 1928-. 3.3723
Brown, Lancelot, 1716-1783. 5.5378
Brown, Lawrence. 1.3439
Brown, Lawrence A., 1935-. 4.1860
Brown, Lawrence D. (Lawrence David), 1947-. 5.4463
Brown, Les, 1914-. 2.2848, 4.10782
Brown, Lester O. 5.6039
Brown, Lester Russell, 1934-. 4.1592, 4.1782, 4.2763
Brown, Letitia Woods. 3.6798
Brown, Lloyd Arnold, 1907-. 4.225
Brown, Lloyd Wellesley, 1938-. 2.7378, 2.9977, 2.10034
Brown, Lucy M. 5.7991
Brown, M. C. (Michael Charles) 5.4325
Brown, M. E. (Margaret Elizabeth) ed. 5.3913
Brown, MacAlister. 4.7120
Brown, Malcolm Johnston, 1910-. 2.7715, 3.1841
Brown, Marshall G., 1906-. 5.8443
Brown, Mary Louise, 1916-. 5.5017
Brown, Maurice F., 1928-. 2.11176
Brown, Maurice John Edwin. 1.3609, 1.3975-1.3976, 1.4521
Brown, Mervyn. 3.5313
Brown, Michael, 1947-. 5.4897
Brown, Michael K. 4.6801
Brown, Milton Wolf, 1911-. 1.4669, 1.5901, 1.6381
Brown, Murray, 1929- ed. 4.1953
Brown, Myrtle L. (Myrtle Laurestine), 1926-. 5.4240
Brown, Nancy Pollard, ed. 2.6520
Brown, Norman L. 5.6115
Brown, Norman Oliver, 1913-. 3.6, 5.193
Brown, Patrick B. 5.1164
Brown, Paula, 1925-. 4.678
Brown, Penelope Jane. 5.2924
Brown, Percy, 1872-1955. 1.5447
Brown, Peter Robert Lamont. 1.1574, 1.1663, 1.2485, 1.3226
Brown, Phil. 5.4698
Brown, R. Hanbury (Robert Hanbury) 5.1752
Brown, Ralph Hall, 1898-1948. 3.6346
Brown, Raymond Edward. 1.2643, 1.2726, 1.2901
Brown, Raymond Edward. ed. 1.2670, 1.2727

Brown, Raymond Edward. comp. 1.2525
Brown, Richard D. 3.7969, 3.7993
Brown, Richard Henry. 5.1003
Brown, Richard Maxwell. 3.8238
Brown, Robert Craig. 3.8740
Brown, Robert Eldon, 1907-. 3.7970, 4.7824
Brown, Robert Goodell. 5.5689, 5.7037
Brown, Robert K. 1.5857
Brown, Robert McAfee, 1920-. 1.2251, 1.3098
Brown, Roger Hamilton. 3.7107
Brown, Roger William. 2.32, 2.87, 4.4981, 5.381
Brown, Rosellen. 2.12925
Brown, S. J. (Samuel J.) 5.5712
Brown, Sanborn Conner, 1913-. 5.826, 5.2380
Brown, Seyom. 3.7560, 3.7897
Brown, Seyom. joint author. 4.8267
Brown, Stanley. 3.5632
Brown, Stanley Barber, 1919- ed. 5.699, 5.3308
Brown, Sterling Allen, 1901-. 2.10316, 2.10689, 2.11426
Brown, Stuart C. 1.866, 1.1558
Brown, Stuart Gerry, 1912-. 1.635, 3.8410
Brown, Thomas, 1663-1704. 2.6886
Brown, Thomas N., 1920-. 3.6550
Brown, Truesdell Sparhawk, 1906-. 3.2563, 3.2566
Brown, Virginia H. 4.1042
Brown, W. Norman (William Norman), 1892-1975. 3.4290
Brown, Wendy M. 5.3276
Brown, Wesley, 1945-. 2.12926
Brown, William A., 1930-. 3.4867
Brown, William Edward, 1904-. 2.1254-2.1255
Brown, William Wells, 1815-1884. 3.6811, 3.7212
Browne, Donald R. 4.4064
Browne, E. J. (E. Janet), 1950-. 5.724
Browne, Edgardo. 5.2832
Browne, Edward Granville, 1862-1926. 2.1962
Browne, Eric C. 4.7723
Browne, Margaret H. 4.3123
Browne, Nina Eliza, ed. 1.5162
Browne, Ray Broadus. ed. 2.10265
Browne, Susan E. 4.6597
Browne, Thomas, Sir, 1605-1682. 2.6911-2.6913
Browne, Turner. 5.6925
Brownell, Blaine A. 4.6245
Brownell, Charles E. 1.6380
Brownell, Morris R. 2.7205
Brownell, William Crary, 1851-1928. 2.10528
Brownfeld, Allan C., 1939- joint author. 4.6781
Browning, Christopher R. 3.1084
Browning, David Clayton, 1894- ed. 2.5482-2.5483, 2.6651
Browning, Elizabeth Barrett, 1806-1861. 2.7463-2.7469, 2.7480
Browning, Iain. 3.3826, 3.4037
Browning, Philip L. 4.10934
Browning, Preston M. 2.13213
Browning, Reed. 4.8558
Browning, Robert, 1812-1889. 2.7467, 2.7470-2.7474, 2.7478-2.7480,
Browning, Robert, 1914-. 3.2662, 3.2680, 3.2815
Browning, Robert Marcellus, 1911-. 2.13486-2.13487
Browning, Rufus P. 3.6795
Brownlie, Ian. comp. 4.9382
Brownlie, Ian. 4.9286
Brownlow, Kevin. 2.2910-2.2911
Brownlow, Louis, 1879-. 4.7887
Brownmiller, Susan. 4.6732
Brownson, Carleton Lewis, 1866- tr. 2.398
Brownson, Charles Bruce, 1914- ed. 4.7996
Brownson, Orestes Augustus, 1803-1876. 4.7847
Brownstein, Rachel M. 2.5970
Brownstone, David M. 5.7574
Brozen, Yale, 1917-. 4.3036
Brubacher, John Seiler, 1898-. 4.9949, 4.10058, 4.10552
Brubaker, Rogers. 4.4766
Bruccoli, Matthew Joseph, 1931-. 2.11522, 2.11726, 2.12275-2.12276
Bruce, F. F. (Frederick Fyvie), 1910-. 1.2512, 1.2657
Bruce-Gardyne, Jock. 3.1710, 4.8419
Bruce, George, 1909- comp. 2.9844
Bruce, George Ludgate, 1910-. 3.533
Bruce, J. W. (James William), 1952-. 5.1631

Bruce, Joseph Percy, 1861-. 1.163
Bruce, Philip Alexander, 1856-1933. 3.8188
Bruce, Phyllis. 2.9900
Bruce, Robert V. 3.7381
Bruce S., Roberto D. 3.8908
Bruch, Hilde, 1904-. 5.4939
Bruchac, Joseph, 1942-. 2.10744, 2.10746
Bruchey, Stuart Weems. 4.1748
Bruck, Peter. 2.10306
Bruck, Richard Hubert. 5.1369
Brucker, Gene A. 3.2921-3.2923, 4.5775
Bruckmann, Gerhart. 4.1790
Bruder, Mary Newton, 1939- joint author. 2.1006
Bruegel, Pieter, ca. 1525-1569. 1.6261
Brueggemann, Walter. 1.2583
Bruffee, Kenneth A. 2.3524
Bruford, Walter Horace. 3.2281, 3.2506
Brugger, Bill. 3.4785, 3.4806
Bruhn, Erik. 4.1178
Bruhn, John G., 1934-. 5.8294
Bruice, Thomas C. 5.4409
Bruininks, Robert H. 4.6613
Brumbaugh, Aaron John, 1890- ed. 4.10056
Brumberg, Abraham. comp. 3.3246
Brumberg, Abraham. 3.3345
Brumberg, Abraham. ed. 3.3257
Brumberg, Joan Jacobs. 1.3323
Brumble, H. David. 2.13947, 5.7733
Brumfitt, J. H. 3.424
Brun, Christian, joint author. 5.8215
Brun, Ellen. 4.2562
Brundage, James A. 4.5488
Brundenius, Claes, 1938-. 4.2152
Brune, Lester H. 3.6398
Bruneau, Thomas C. 1.3187, 3.3506
Brunelleschi, Filippo, 1377-1446. 1.5439
Bruner, Jerome S. (Jerome Seymour) 2.117, 4.10240-4.10241, 4.10351, 5.95, 5.259, 5.382
Bruner, M. C. (Marc C.) 5.3544
Brunhes, Jean, 1869-1930. 4.363
Brunhoff, Suzanne de. 4.1324
Brunhouse, Robert Levere, 1908-. 3.9032
Brunkow, Robert deV., 1947-. 5.8448
Brunn, Stanley D. 4.7494
Brunner, Emil, 1889-1966. 1.1481, 1.2906, 1.2941
Brunner, John, 1934-. 2.9635-2.9636
Brunner, Karl, 1887-. 2.950
Brunner-Traut, Emma. ed. 1.4700
Bruno, Giordano, 1548-1600. 1.412
Brunsden, Denys. joint author. 4.257
Brunschwig, Henri, 1904-. 4.8923
Brunskill, R. W. 1.5564
Brunt, P. A. 2.353
Brunvand, Jan Harold. 4.772-4.773, 5.8193
Brus, Włodzimierz. 4.7094
Brusaw, Charles T. 5.5504
Brush, Don Orr. 5.5862
Brush, Lorelei R., 1946-. 5.1062
Brush, Stephen B., 1943-. 4.2180
Brush, Stephen G. 5.1930, 5.1994, 5.2079, 5.2184
Brushwood, John Stubbs, 1920-. 2.5313, 2.5326
Brusianin, Vasiliĭ Vasil'evich, 1867-. 2.1467
Brustein, Robert Sanford, 1927-. 2.3177
Brutus, Dennis, 1924-. 2.9637
Brutzkus, David Anatol. 1.5608
Bruun, Bertel. 5.3956
Bruun, Geoffrey, 1898-. 3.660, 3.2073
Bruun, Per. 5.5973
Bruyn, J. 1.6252
Bryan, C. D. B. (Courtlandt Dixon Barnes) 3.4509
Bryan, Frank M. 4.8261
Bryan, M. Leonard. 5.8206
Bryan, William Frank, 1879- ed. 2.6346
Bryant, Arthur, Sir, 1899-. 3.899, 3.975
Bryant, Donald Cross, 1905- ed. 2.3780
Bryant, J. A. (Joseph Allen), 1919-. 2.6599
Bryant, Keith L. 3.8538
Bryant, Kenneth E. 2.1879
Bryant, Margaret M., 1900-. 2.962
Bryant, Peter, 1937-. 5.590
Bryant, Shasta M. 2.5155, 5.7902
Bryant, William Cullen, 1908-. 2.10915-2.10916
Bryce, James Bryce, Viscount, 1838-1922. 3.2252, 3.6089, 3.6336, 3.9154, 4.7558, 4.7848

Bryer, Jackson R. joint comp. 2.11726
Bryer, Jackson R. 2.11738
Bryer, Jackson R. ed. 2.10406
Brymer, Jack. 1.4170
Bryson, Thomas A., 1931-. 3.3753, 5.8040
Bryusov, Valery Yakovlevich, 1873-1924. 2.1473
Brzezinski, Zbigniew K., 1928-. 3.1177, 3.3213, 3.7840, 4.7599
Bskal-bzaṅ-rgya-mtsho, Dalai Lama VII, 1708-1757. 1.2139
Bstan-'dzin-rgya-mtsho, Dalai Lama XIV, 1935-. 1.1778, 1.2144, 1.2164
Bstan-'dzin-rgya-mtsho, XIV, Dalai Lama, 1935-. 1.2144
Bstan-pa'i-ñi-ma, 4th Panchen Lama of Tashilhunpo, 1781-1854. 1.2165
Bubenick, David V. 5.6005
Buber, Martin, 1878-1965. 1.969-1.970, 1.976, 1.1491, 1.1543, 1.1921-1.1922, 1.1954, 1.2556, 1.2814, 4.6930
Bubner, Rüdiger, 1941-. 1.964
Bucchioni, Eugene. 3.6556, 4.10849
Bucchioni, Eugene. joint comp. 3.6588
Bucer, Martin, 1491-1551. 1.2352
Buchan, Alastair. 4.4819, 4.9021, 5.7298
Buchan, David, 1939-. 2.6106, 2.9839
Buchan, John, 1875-1940. 2.8046, 2.8488-2.8489
Buchan, Joseph. 4.2680
Buchanan, Albert Russell, 1906-. 3.1022, 3.1126
Buchanan, Allen E., 1948-. 4.6950
Buchanan-Brown, John. ed. 2.2346
Buchanan, Bruce G. 5.1247
Buchanan, Constance H. 1.1611
Buchanan, George, 1506-1582. 2.3938
Buchanan, James M. 4.1423, 4.1479, 4.1514, 4.4644, 4.4723, 4.7565
Buchanan, Keith M. 4.4391
Buchanan, Robert Ogilvie, 1894-. 4.2688
Buchanan, William, 1918-. 4.5015
Bucher, Charles Augustus, 1912-. 4.900, 4.911
Bücher, Rolf. 2.13724
Bucher, Walter H. (Walter Herman), 1888-. 5.3090
Buchler, Justus, 1914-. 1.627, 2.2714
Buchner, Alexandr. 1.3514, 1.4286
Buchner, Edward Franklin, 1868-1929, tr. 4.10194
Büchner, Georg, 1813-1837. 2.13554-2.13555
Buchsbaum, David Alvin, joint author. 5.1360
Buchsbaum, Herbert J., 1934-. 5.5057
Buchsbaum, Ralph Morris, 1907-. 5.3832
Buchtel, Henry A. 5.4309
Buck, Carl Darling, 1866-1955. 2.224
Buck, David D., 1936-. 3.4864
Buck, Elizabeth Hawthorn, Mrs., joint author. 3.8071
Buck, Ellen F., joint author. 5.1448
Buck, James Harold. 5.7341
Buck, John Lossing, 1890-. 4.2863
Buck, N. Lewis (Nelson Lewis) joint author. 5.5682
Buck, Pearl S. (Pearl Sydenstricker), 1892-1973. 2.11427-2.11432, 4.6584
Buck, Peter Henry, 1880-1951. 3.5611, 3.5620
Buck, R. Creighton (Robert Creighton), 1920-. 5.1448
Buck, Solon J. (Solon Justus), 1884-1962. 3.8071, 4.2817
Buckingham, J. joint author. 5.2871
Buckland, Gail. 5.6931
Buckland, William R. 5.1400
Buckle, Henry Thomas. 3.33
Buckle, Richard. 4.1132, 4.1152, 4.1177
Buckler, John. 3.2616
Buckler, William Earl, 1924-. 2.5710, 2.6262, 2.7475, 2.8157
Buckley, Jerome Hamilton. joint author. 2.6182
Buckley, Jerome Hamilton. 2.6169
Buckley, Jerome Hamilton. comp. 2.5701, 2.5954, 2.7813, 2.8156, 2.8169, 5.7946
Buckley, John J. (John Jay), 1947-. 5.5116
Buckley, John W. 4.4394
Buckley, Kenneth. 4.4626
Buckley, Marlene H., 1938- joint author. 4.4394
Buckley, Peter. 2.11857, 5.200
Buckley, Roger, 1944-. 3.4977
Buckley, Roger Norman, 1937-. 4.6433
Buckley, Thomas E., 1939-. 1.2414

Buckley, William F. (William Frank), 1925-.
  1.5, 3.7541, 3.7666, 4.7852
Buckner, Michael D. 5.4565
Bucksbaum, Philip H. 5.2486
Buczacki, S. T. 5.5401
Budd, Louis J. 2.10952, 2.10954
Budd, Susan. 1.1888
Budden, Julian. 1.4022
Buddhaghosa. 1.1769, 1.2138
Budevsky, O. 5.2655
Budge, Bruce P., joint comp. 4.4393
Budge, E. A. Wallis (Ernest Alfred Wallis), Sir,
  1857-1934. 2.1764
Budge, Sir Ernest Alfred Wallis, 1857-1934.
  3.5241
Budgen, Frank Spencer Curtis, 1882-. 2.8885
Budiardjo, Carmel. 3.4584
Budinski, Kenneth G. 5.5760
Budnick, J. I., 1929- ed. 5.2175
Budoff, Milton, 1929-. 4.10294
Budrys, Algis, 1931-. 2.12927
Budson, Richard D. 5.4809
Budyko, M. I. (Mikhail Ivanovich) 5.2492,
  5.2530, 5.2572
Budzbon, Przemysław. 5.7435
Bueche, F. (Frederick), 1923-. 5.1990
Buechel, Eugene. 5.5846
Buehler, Calvin Adam, 1896-. 5.2731
Buehrig, Edward H. (Edward Henry), 1910-.
  3.7714
Buel, Jesse, 1778-1839. 5.5258
Buel, Joy Day. 3.336
Buel, Richard, 1933-. 3.336, 4.8146
Buel, Ronald A. 4.4038
Buell, Emmett H. 4.10800
Buell, Lawrence. 2.10395, 2.10438, 2.11227
Buell, Raymond Leslie, 1896-1946. 3.5102,
  3.5413
Buell, Thomas B. 5.7423
Buell, Victor P. 4.4283
Buenker, John D. 5.7837, 5.8185, 5.8405
Buero Vallejo, Antonio, 1916-. 2.5239
Buffa, Elwood Spencer, 1923-. 5.7026
Buffington, Robert. 2.12370
Buffum, Imbrie, 1915-. 2.3978
Bufkin, E. C. 2.9140
Bugelski, B. R. (Bergen Richard), 1913-.
  4.10352, 5.294
Buhl Foundation. 3.8093
Buhle, Mari Jo, 1943-. 4.6035, 4.8080, 5.8472
Buhle, Paul, 1944-. 4.8080
Buhler, Charlotte Malachowski, 1893-1974.
  4.5716
Bühler, Georg, 1837-1898. ed. 1.1685
Buhler, Kathryn C. 1.6655
Bühler, W. K. (Walter Kaufmann), 1944-.
  5.1093
Buhr, R. J. A. 5.1208
Buisseret, David. 3.2019
Buitenen, J. A. B. van (Johannes Adrianus
  Bernardus van) 1.1686, 1.1688, 2.1952, 4.803
Buitenen, J. A. B. van (Johannes Adrianus
  Bernardus van) tr. 2.1935
Buitenen, J. A. B. van (Johannes Adrianus
  Bernardus van) joint author. 1.199
Buitenhuis, Peter. comp. 2.11108
Bujra, Janet M. 4.5905
Bukalski, Peter J. 5.8137
Bukharin, Nikolaï Ivanovich, 1888-1938.
  4.1521, 4.7096-4.7097
Bukofzer, Manfred F., 1910-1955. 1.3655
Bulatao, Rodolfo A., 1944-. 4.1640
Bulatović, Miodrag, 1930-. 2.1211
Buley, R. Carlyle (Roscoe Carlyle), 1893-1968.
  3.8373
Bulgakov, Mikhail Afanas'evich, 1891-1940.
  2.1542-2.1543
Bulgakov, Sergeï Nikolaevich, 1871-1944.
  1.3106
Bulkin, Bernard J. 5.2685
Bull, George. 1.1513
Bull, Hedley. 3.3636, 4.9023, 4.9128
Bullard, Edgar John, 1942-. 1.5923
Bullard, Fred M. (Fred Mason), 1901-. 5.3108
Bullard, Roger Aubrey. 1.1522
Bullaty, Sonja. 5.3686
Bullen, K. E. (Keith Edward), 1906-. 5.1761
Bullen, R. J. joint author. 3.679

Bullett, Gerald William, 1893-1958. 2.6145
Bulliet, Richard W. 3.3668
Bullinger, Heinrich, 1504-1575. 1.2354
Bullins, Ed. 2.12928-2.12931
Bullion, John L., 1944-. 4.4669
Bullis, Glenna E. 4.5719
Bullitt, John Marshall, 1921- ed. 2.6087
Bullock, Alan, 1914-. 3.199, 3.2395
Bullock, Alan Louis Charles, ed. 3.1700, 4.8932
Bullock, Chris, 1945-. 5.7949
Bullock-Davies, Constance. 2.1019
Bullock, Henry Allen. 4.10863
Bullock, Theodore Holmes. 5.4116, 5.4316
Bullock, Wynn. 5.6939
Bullough, Bonnie. joint author. 5.5159
Bullough, Bonnie. 5.5181
Bullough, Edward, 1880-1934. 1.393, 1.1387
Bullough, Geoffrey, 1901-. 2.6160, 2.6434,
  2.6712
Bullough, R. K. (Robert Keith), 1929-. 5.2148
Bullough, Vern L. 4.5486, 4.5488, 4.5530,
  5.5159
Bullough, Vern L. joint author. 5.7218
Bulmer, Martin. 4.4822
Bulmer-Thomas, Ivor, 1905-. 2.329
Bülow, Bernhard Heinrich Martin Karl, Fürst
  von, 1849-1929. 3.2347
Bultitude, John. 5.5340
Bultmann, Rudolf Karl, 1884-1976. 1.1552,
  1.2267, 1.2651, 1.2654, 1.2674, 1.2728,
  1.2740-1.2741
Bumgardner, Georgia B. 3.6192
Bumpass, Larry L. 4.1577
Bunbury, Edward Herbert, Sir, bart.,
  1811-1895. 4.57
Bunce, David, 1948- tr. 2.2279
Bunce, M. F. 4.6372
Bunche, Ralph J. (Ralph Johnson), 1904-1971.
  3.6663
Bundy, Alan. 5.1253
Bundy, Carol. 2.2691
Bundy, McGeorge. 3.7687, 4.7853
Bungay, Henry R. (Henry Robert), 1928-.
  5.6881
Bunge, Frederica M. 3.3692, 3.4107, 3.4421,
  3.4518, 3.4533, 3.4557, 3.4587, 3.4613,
  3.4875, 3.4992, 3.5039, 3.5533
Bunge, Mario Augusto. 1.1334, 5.871, 5.1939
Bunge, William Wheeler, 1928-. 4.198
Bunin, Ivan Alekseevich, 1870-1953.
  2.1477-2.1480
Bunker, Gerald E. 3.4839
Bunkley, Allison Williams. 3.9245
Bunn, John William, 1898-. 4.979
Bunnell, Peter C. 5.6956
Bunsell, A. R. joint author. 5.5762
Bunting, Basil. 2.8490
Bunting, John R. 4.1980
Bunting, Josiah. 2.12932
Buñuel, Luis, 1900-. 2.3036
Bunyan, James, 1898-. 3.3175-3.3176
Bunyan, John, 1628-1688. 1.2214-1.2215,
  2.6915-2.6918
Bunzel, John H., 1924-. 4.1981
Bunzel, Ruth Leah, 1898-. 3.5940
Buol, S. W. 5.5262
Burack, Elmer H. 4.4375-4.4376
Burago, Alla, tr. 2.1576
Buranelli, Nan, 1917-. 5.7359
Buranelli, Vincent. 2.11205, 4.9456, 5.7359
Burbank, Rex J. 2.12720
Burbidge, E. Margaret. joint author. 5.1860
Burbidge, Geoffrey R. 5.1860
Burch, George Bosworth, 1902-. 1.3067
Burch, James M., joint author. 5.2279
Burch, John G. 5.5605
Burch, Noel, joint author. 4.10698
Burch, Philip H. 4.3935
Burch, William R., 1933- joint author. 4.876
Burcham, W. E. 5.2429
Burchard, John Ely, 1898-. 1.5282, 4.6304
Burchfield, Joe D. 5.3084
Burchfield, R. W. 2.963, 2.1059, 2.1085
Burckel, Nicholas C. joint author. 5.7837,
  5.8405
Burckhardt, Jacob, 1818-1897. 1.5430, 1.6274,
  3.461, 3.524, 3.2813, 3.2845
Burckhardt, Sigurd, 1916-1966. 2.6724

Burckhardt, Titus. 1.4747
Burden, Hamilton Twombly, 1937-. 3.2426
Burdick, Eugene, 1918-. 2.11434, 2.11994
Burdon, Randal Mathews, 1896-. 3.5591
Bureau of International Research of Harvard
  University and Radcliffe College. 3.5468
Buresch, Matthew. 5.6326
Burford, Alison. 4.3094
Burford, Ray. 1.4105
Burg, B. R. (Barry Richard), 1938-. 1.3342
Burg, David F. 5.5657
Burg, Steven L., 1950-. 4.8689
Burge, Edward James. 5.2424
Burger, Heinz Otto, 1903-. 2.13454, 2.13782
Bürger, Peter, 1936-. 1.1390
Burgess, Ann Wolbert. 4.6737
Burgess, Anthony, 1917-. 2.8875, 2.9638-2.9647
Burgess, C. (Christopher) joint author. 5.2893
Burgess, C. F. (Chester Francis) 2.7037
Burgess, Eric. joint author. 5.6705
Burgess, Eric. 5.1811, 5.7397
Burgess, Ernest Watson, 1886-1966. 4.4828,
  4.4836, 4.5637, 4.6182, 4.6298, 4.6882
Burgess, Gelett, 1866-1951. 2.11435
Burgess, James, 1832-1916. ed. 1.5446
Burgess, Robert Lewis, 1931-. 5.3544
Burgess, William A., 1924-. 5.5018
Burghardt, Walter J. 4.5900
Burghes, David N. 5.1642
Bürgin, Hans. 2.13836
Burgin, John Carroll. 1.4562
Burgin, Victor. 5.6936
Burgis, Nina. 2.8229
Burian, Richard M. 5.3403
Burk, Creighton A. 5.2981
Burk, Kathleen. 3.839
Burk, Robert Fredrick, 1955-. 3.6664
Burke, Doreen Bolger, 1949-. 1.5887
Burke, Edmund, 1729-1797. 1.1370, 3.2090,
  4.7417-4.7418
Burke, Gerald L. 1.5605
Burke, James, 1936-. 5.5527
Burke, Joseph. 1.6457
Burke, Kenneth, 1897-. 1.539, 1.576-1.577,
  1.1582, 2.2565-2.2567, 2.11436, 3.462
Burke, Peter. comp. 4.2186
Burke, Peter. 3.78
Burke, Robert E. (Robert Eugene), 1921-.
  3.8612
Burke, S. M. 3.4125
Burke, T. E. 1.757
Burke, William Jeremiah, 1902-. 5.7784
Burke, William T. joint author. 4.9315
Burkert, Walter, 1931-. 1.239, 1.1649
Burkhard, Marianne. 2.13637
Burkhardt, Christian C., 1924-. 5.5407
Burkhardt, Frederick, 1912-. 1.596, 1.598,
  1.1540, 5.108, 5.3192
Burkhardt, Richard Wellington, 1944-. 5.3207
Burkhart, Charles, comp. 2.8533
Burkhart, Charles (Charles L.) 1.4440
Burkhauser, Richard V. 4.3460, 4.3474-4.3475
Burkhead, Jesse. 4.4720
Burkholder, J. Peter (James Peter) 1.3900
Burkholder, Mark A., 1943-. 4.9908, 4.9910
Burkholder, Robert E. 2.11028
Burki, Shahid Javed. 3.4126
Burkill, T. Alec. 1.2744
Burkin, A. R. (Alfred Richard) 5.6789
Burks, Ardath W. 3.4872
Burks, Richard Voyles, 1913-. 4.7016
Burl, Aubrey. 4.730
Burleigh, John H. S. 1.2449
Burling, Robbins, 1926-. 3.4386
Burlingame, Roger, 1889-1967. 2.3612
Burlingham, Dorothy. 4.5717, 5.64, 5.5098
Burlingham, Dorothy. joint author. 4.5739
Burma Research Society. Text Publication
  Fund. 3.4426
Burman, Frans, 1628-1679. 1.791
Burman, Peter J. 5.5561
Burmeister, Edwin. 4.1522
Burn, A. R. (Andrew Robert), 1902-. 3.2597,
  3.2601, 3.2603
Burn, William Laurence. 3.1609, 3.9138
Burnaby, John. 1.2202
Burne, Glenn S. (Glenn Stephen), 1921-. 2.4577

Burne-Jones, Edward Coley, Sir, 1833-1898.
  2.6310
Burnell, A. C. (Arthur Coke), 1840-1882. joint
  author. 2.1162
Burner, David, 1937-. 3.7745, 4.8200
Burnet, Frank Macfarlane, Sir, 1899-. 5.3325,
  5.4467, 5.4475
Burnet, Gilbert, 1690-1726. 1.1428
Burnet, John, 1863-1928. 1.222, 1.231, 1.258,
  2.532
Burnett, Alan D. 4.7500
Burnett, Anne Pippin, 1925-. 2.286, 2.443,
  2.465
Burnett, Ben G., jt. author. 4.3400
Burnett, David G. 1.4918
Burnett, Edmund Cody, 1864-. 3.7014
Burnett, John, 1925-. 4.3497
Burnett, Whit, 1899- comp. 2.10843
Burney, Charles, 1726-1814. 1.3657-1.3658
Burney, Charles Allen. 3.4042
Burney, Fanny, 1752-1840. 2.6891-2.6894
Burney, James, 1750-1821. 4.90
Burney, William A. 2.12546
Burnham, Dorothy K. joint author. 5.7097
Burnham, Harold B. 5.7097
Burnham, Jack, 1931-. 1.4607, 1.4620, 1.5649
Burnham, James, 1905-1987. 4.7466
Burnham, Judith Benjamin, joint author. 1.4620
Burnham, Robert. 5.1732
Burnham, Walter Dean. ed. 4.8171
Burnham, Walter Dean. 4.8099, 4.8173
Burnier, Raymond. 1.5539
Burnim, Kalman A. joint author. 2.3333
Burnim, Kalman A. 2.3341
Burns, Alan Cuthbert, Sir, 1887-. 3.5633
Burns, Allan F. (Allan Frank), 1945-. 2.2332
Burns, E. Bradford. 3.9202
Burns, Edward McNall, 1897-. 3.6090
Burns, Eveline Mabel Richardson, 1900-. 4.3446
Burns, Grant, 1947-. 5.8256
Burns, Hobert W. 4.10162
Burns, James Alexander Scott, 1916-. 5.8088
Burns, James MacGregor. 3.6316, 3.6385,
  3.7778-3.7779, 3.7873, 4.4945
Burns, John P. 4.8734
Burns, Kenneth R. 5.5175
Burns, N. H. (Ned Hamilton), 1932- joint
  author. 5.5882
Burns, Noel M. 3.8429
Burns, Norman T., ed. 2.2396
Burns, Richard Dean. 3.7808, 5.8061, 5.8264
Burns, Robert, 1759-1796. 2.7497-2.7499,
  2.7502, 2.7506
Burns, Robert Ignatius. 3.3429, 3.3488-3.3490,
  4.2415
Burns, Ronald M. ed. 3.8686
Burns, Scott. 4.1997
Burns, Shannon. 5.7979
Burns, Wayne, 1918-. 2.8000
Burnside, Irene Mortenson, 1923-. 5.5006
Burnyeat, Myles. 1.324
Buros Institute of Mental Measurements. 5.8155
Buros, Oscar Krisen, 1905-. 5.540, 5.7978,
  5.8153, 5.8155
Burr, John Roy, 1933-. 1.448
Burr, Nelson Rollin, 1904-. 1.2384
Burr, Robert Nathan, 1906-. 3.9264
Burr, Wesley R., 1936-. 4.5638
Burrage, Henry Sweetser, 1837-1926. 3.5988
Burrell, David B. 1.2822
Burrell, David B. joint author. 1.1474
Burrello, Leonard C., 1942-. 4.10937
Burris-Meyer, Harold, 1902-. 1.5546, 2.3146,
  5.6563
Burris, Robert H. (Robert Harza), 1914-.
  5.3761, 5.4219
Burroughs, Alan, 1897-1965. 1.5885, 1.6376
Burroughs, Edgar Rice, 1875-1950. 2.11438
Burroughs, Nannie Helen, 1879-. 3.6786
Burroughs, Peter. 3.8718
Burroughs, William S., 1914-. 2.12933-2.12935
Burrow, J. A. (John Anthony) 2.5602, 2.5613
Burrow, J. W. (John Wyon), 1935-. 4.7274
Burrow, James Gordon, 1922-. 5.4526
Burrows, Graham D. 5.4934
Burrows, Paul. 4.1387, 4.1855
Burrows, William, 1908-. 5.4439
Burrup, Percy E., 1910-. 4.10654

Bursk, Edward Collins, 1907- ed. 4.4250, 4.4326
Burstall, M. L. joint author. 5.6814
Burstein, Albert H., joint author. 5.4273
Bursten, Ben. 4.9509
Burstyn, Varda. 4.5550
Bursztajn, Harold. 5.4554
Burt, Alfred LeRoy, 1888-. 3.8719
Burt, Forrest D. 2.9105
Burt, Larry W., 1950-. 3.5798
Burt, T. P. 4.301
Burt, William Henry, 1903-. 5.3983
Burtchaell, James Tunstead. 1.2522
Burtless, Gary T., 1950-. 4.5806
Burton, Andrew. 5.282
Burton, Andrew. joint author. 5.388
Burton, Dwight L. 2.2422
Burton, Ernest De Witt, 1856-1925. 1.2682
Burton, Ian. 4.319
Burton, John, 1945-. 4.3327
Burton, John W. (John Wear), 1915-. 4.9022,
  4.9130
Burton, Margaret Ernestine, 1885-. 4.9182
Burton, Maurice, 1898-. 5.3804
Burton, Richard Francis, Sir, 1821-1890.
  2.1842, 3.4048, 3.4139, 3.5172
Burton, Robert, 1577-1640. 2.6437
Burton, Sarah K. 1.72
Burton, William Henry, 1890-. 4.10257
Burtt, Edwin A. (Edwin Arthur), 1892-. 1.120,
  1.1544
Buruma, Ian. 3.4885
Bury, J. B. (John Bagnell), 1861-1927. 3.38,
  3.572, 3.582, 3.2567, 3.2669, 3.2801
Bury, J. P. T. (John Patrick Tuer), 1908-.
  3.2184-3.2185
Bury, John Bagnell. 3.2574, 3.2802
Busch, Eberhard, 1937-. 1.3284
Busch, Francis X. (Francis Xavier), b. 1879.
  4.9454
Busch, Frederick, 1941-. 2.12937-2.12939,
  2.13073
Busch, G. K. 4.3323
Busch, Hans, 1914-. 1.4029
Busch, Harris. ed. 5.4743
Busch, Moritz, 1821-1899. 3.2310, 3.6044
Busch, Noel Fairchild, 1906-. 2.3676
Busch-Reisinger Museum. 1.6304
Busch, Wilhelm, 1832-1908. 2.13714-2.13715
Buse, Rueben C. 4.2885
Bush-Brown, Albert. joint author. 1.5282
Bush-Brown, James. 5.5366
Bush-Brown, Louise Carter, 1897- joint author.
  5.5366
Bush, Clifford L., 1915-. 4.10932
Bush, Clive. 3.6091
Bush, Douglas, 1896-. 1.405, 2.5644, 2.5747,
  2.5777-2.5778, 2.7111, 2.7168, 2.7371, 2.7856
Bush, Eric Wheler. 3.807
Bush, M. L. 3.1415
Bush, Patricia J. 5.5138
Bush, Richard Clarence, 1923-. 1.1788
Bush, Robert, 1917-. 2.11139
Bush, Robert R. joint ed. 5.51
Bush, Robert R. 5.53
Bush, Rod. 3.6712
Bush, Susan. 1.6321, 1.6372, 1.6725
Bush, Vannevar, 1890-1974. 5.7205
Busha, Charles H. 5.7600, 5.7604
Bushman, Richard L. 1.3383, 3.8021
Bushnell, Amy. 4.4673
Bushnell, D. (David), 1938-. 5.5868
Bushnell, David S. 4.10559
Bushnell, Geoffrey Hext Sutherland. 3.9283
Bushnell, Howard. 1.4094
Businger, Joost Alois. joint author. 5.2518
Busoni, Ferruccio, 1866-1924. 1.3497
Buss, Arnold H., 1924-. 5.420
Buss, Claude Albert. 3.6469
Buss, Fran Leeper, 1942-. 4.6040
Bussabarger, Robert F. 1.6527
Bussink, Willem C. F., 1929- joint author.
  4.2529
Bussmann, Georg. 1.4994
Bussy, Dorothy. 2.4557
Butcher, David. 5.7922
Butcher, Margaret Just, 1913-. 1.6712
Butcher, Philip, 1918-. 2.10703
Butera, Federico, 1940-. 5.5622

Buthlay, Kenneth. 2.8787
Butler, Alban, 1711-1773. 1.3246
Butler, Anne M., 1938-. 4.5540
Butler, Christopher. 1.6703
Butler, David, 1924-. 4.7725, 4.7735, 4.8362,
  4.8370, 4.8412, 4.8483, 4.8494-4.8501
Butler, David E. 4.2223, 4.8481-4.8482
Butler, David E. 1924-. 4.8484
Butler, Edward Cuthbert, 1858-1934. 1.3080,
  1.3121, 1.3238
Butler, Francine. 5.8416
Butler, George D. (George Daniel), 1893-.
  4.886
Butler, Guy, 1918-. 2.10049
Butler, Harold Edgeworth, 1878-. 2.688, 2.690
Butler, James Ramsay Montagu, 1889-. 4.8407
Butler, Jeffrey. 3.5475, 4.8795
Butler, Johnnella E. 3.6603
Butler, Jon, 1940-. 3.6548
Butler, Joseph, 1692-1752. 1.2958
Butler, Joseph H. 4.4118
Butler, Marilyn. 2.7687, 2.7993
Butler, Martin. 2.5890
Butler, Michael. 2.13748-2.13749
Butler, Pamela. 4.5922
Butler, Pierce, 1886-1953. 5.7601
Butler, Rohan d'Olier. 3.2049
Butler, Ronnie, 1931-. 2.4128
Butler, Ruth, 1931-. 1.5611
Butler, Samuel, 1612-1680. 2.6923-2.6926,
  2.7511-2.7516
Butler, Thomas, 1929-. 2.1217
Butler, William Jack, 1919-. 4.7682
Butler, William Vivian, 1927-. 2.5956
Butlin, J. A. 4.1839
Butlin, Martin. 1.4947, 1.6038
Butor, Michel. 2.4433-2.4436
Butow, Robert Joseph Charles, 1924-. 3.1146,
  3.4986
Butt, John Everett. 2.5520, 2.5657, 2.7186,
  2.7649
Butt, John Everett. ed. 2.7187
Buttel, Frederick H. 4.6369, 5.8167
Buttel, Robert. 2.9705
Butter, Peter H. 2.9128
Butterfield, Herbert, 1900-. 1.2246, 3.383-3.384,
  3.1207, 3.1554, 3.2135, 4.9023-4.9024, 5.715
Butterfield, L. H. (Lyman Henry), 1909-.
  3.7043, 3.7050-3.7051
Butterfield, R. W. 2.10494, 2.11526
Butterick, George F. 2.10778, 2.12281
Butters, J. Keith (John Keith), 1915-. 4.3015
Butterworth, Bernard B., 1923-. 5.3998
Butterworth, Charles E. 2.4091
Butterworth, D. (David) 5.5752
Butterworth, George William, 1879-. 1.2487
Buttinger, Joseph. 3.4471-3.4472
Buttlar, Lois, 1934-. 3.6534, 5.7857
Button, James W., 1942-. 4.6724
Button, Kenneth John. 4.4043
Buttrick, George Arthur, 1892- ed. 1.2508,
  1.2526
Butts, Hugh F., joint author. 2.1159
Butts, R. Freeman (Robert Freeman), 1910-.
  4.9981
Butwell, Richard A., 1929-. 3.4341
Butwin, Frances. joint author. 2.1814
Butwin, Frances. 2.1811
Butwin, Joseph, 1943-. 2.1814
Butzer, Karl W. 3.250, 4.699
Buvinić, Mayra. 4.6181
Buxton, David Roden, 1910-. 1.5525
Buxton, Jean Carlile, 1921-. 1.1859
Buxton, John. ed. 2.6510, 2.6952
Byatt, A. S. (Antonia Susan), 1936-. 2.9772
Bybee, Rodger W. 4.10693
Byerly, Greg, 1949-. 4.5521, 5.8387
Byers, Douglas S., 1903- ed. 3.8894
Byers, T. J. 5.6592
Bykaŭ, Vasil', 1924-. 2.1626
Bylander, E. G. 5.6564
Bylanski, P. 5.6398
Bylebyl, Jerome J. 5.4174
Byler, Mary Gloyne. 5.7738
Bynner, Witter, 1881-1968. 2.8981,
  2.11439-2.11441
Bynon, Theodora. 2.157
Bynum, Caroline Walker. 1.3052

Bynum, David E. 4.763
Bynum, R. Cary. 4.3832
Bynum, W. F. (William F.), 1943-. 5.724
Byrd, Max. 2.5691-2.5692
Byrd, William, 1674-1744. 3.8189-3.8192
Byrde, Robert Jocelyn Walter. 5.5415
Byrer, Thomas G. 5.7056
Byrne, C. Judith (Claire Judith), 1944-. 5.4738
Byrne, F. J. (Francis John), 1934-. 3.1815
Byrne, M. St. Clare (Muriel St. Clare), 1895-.
    3.1414
Byrnes, James Francis, 1879-1972. 3.1143,
    3.7632
Byrnes, Robert Francis. 3.3132, 3.3960
Byron, George Gordon Byron, Baron,
    1788-1824. 2.7519, 2.7521-2.7523, 2.7530,
    2.7534
Byron, George Gordon Noël Byron, 6th baron,
    1788-1824. 2.7518
Byron, William. 2.5175
Bysiewicz, Shirley R. joint author. 4.9471
Bythell, Duncan. 4.3001, 4.3543
Bywater, Ingram, 1840-1914. 2.2727

C. Bertelsmann Verlag. 4.174
C.S. Hammond & Company. 4.124
Cabaniss, Allen, 1911-. 3.1985
Cabanne, Pierre. 1.6099
Cabell, James Branch, 1879-1958.
    2.11442-2.11447
Cable, George Washington, 1844-1925.
    2.10918-2.10919
Cabrera Infante, G. (Guillermo), 1929-. 2.5358
Cachin, Françoise. 1.4975
Cadenhead, Ivie Edward, 1923-. 3.8935
Cadet, J. M., 1935-. 2.9650
Cadogan, Peter H. 5.1797
Cadwalader, Sandra L. 3.5797
Cady, Edwin Harrison. 2.10567, 2.10984,
    2.11087, 2.11092
Cady, Edwin Harrison. ed. 2.10666
Cady, John Frank, 1901-. 3.4338, 3.4392,
    3.4405, 3.4410
Cady, Norma W. 2.11092
Cadzow, James A. 5.6366
Caelleigh, Addeane S. 5.8041
Caesar, Julius. 2.652-2.653
Caesar, Michael. 2.4883
Cagan, Phillip. 4.4500
Cage, John. 1.3467, 1.3831, 2.12940-2.12941
Caglioti, Luciano. 5.6817
Cagnac, Bernard, 1931-. 5.2128
Cahalane, Victor Harrison, 1901-. 5.3984
Cahen, Claude. 3.3577
Cahill, Fred V. 4.9746
Cahill, James Francis, 1926-. 1.6322-1.6325,
    1.6328-1.6329, 1.6337
Cahill, Marion Cotter, 1901-. 4.3157
Cahn, Edmond Nathaniel, 1906-1964. 4.7566
Cahn, R. S. (Robert Sidney), 1899-. 5.2597
Cahn, R. W. (Robert W.), 1924-. 5.6777
Cahn, Walter. 1.6425
Cahoon, Nelson Corey. 5.6324
Caiden, Gerald E. 4.3514, 5.8357
Caiger-Smith, Alan. 1.6629
Caillet Bois, Julio, comp. 2.5321
Cailliet, Émile, 1894-. 1.806
Caillois, Roger, 1913-. 2.4081, 3.53
Cain, Glen George. ed. 4.2084
Cain, James M. (James Mallahan), 1892-1977.
    2.11450
Cain, P.J. 4.2272
Cain, T. G. S. (Thomas Grant Steven) 2.1440
Caine, Lynn. 5.435
Caird, Edward, 1835-1908. 1.942
Caird, G. B. (George Bradford), 1917-. 1.2536,
    1.2702, 1.2732
Cairncross, Alec, Sir, 1911-. 4.2286, 4.4612
Cairncross, Alexander Kirkland. 4.4455
Cairncross, John. 2.4016
Cairns, David. ed. 1.3816
Cairns, Francis. 2.781
Cairns, H. Alan C. 3.5487
Cairns, Huntington, 1904- ed. 2.12125
Cairns, John. 5.4770
Cairns, John Campbell, 1924-. 3.2195
Cajori, Florian, 1859-1930. 5.1068
Calabrese, Edward J., 1946-. 5.4669

Calabresi, Guido, 1932-. 4.9514
Calder, Alexander, 1898-1976. 1.4892,
    1.5662-1.5663
Calder, Angus. 2.1287, 3.1216, 3.1703
Calder, Daniel Gillmore. 2.5591, 2.6306
Calder, Daniel Gillmore. joint comp. 2.701
Calder, Grace J. 2.7559
Calder, Jenni. 2.9191
Calder, Kenneth J. 3.827
Calder, Kent E. 4.2540
Calder-Marshall, Arthur. 2.3043, 2.8491,
    2.12019, 2.12030
Calder, Nigel. 5.2086, 5.2434, 5.2573
Calder, Robert Lorin. 2.9106
Calder, William Moir, 1881-. 3.2351
Calderío, Francisco, 1908-. 3.9100
Calderón de la Barca, Pedro, 1600-1681.
    2.5163-2.5164
Caldwell, Bruce J. 4.1384
Caldwell, Colin. 1.6457
Caldwell, Erskine, 1903-. 2.11451-2.11457
Caldwell, Helen. 2.5477, 4.1149
Caldwell, John, 1938-. 1.3648, 1.4159, 1.6378
Caldwell, John Charles. ed. 4.1712
Caldwell, John H., 1928-. 4.999
Caldwell, Malcolm. 3.4487
Caldwell, Mark. 2.6096
Calef, George W. (George Waller), 1944-.
    5.4045
Calendar, Richard. joint author. 5.3419
Calhoon, Robert M. (Robert McCluer) 3.6956
Calhoun, Arthur Wallace, 1885-. 4.5568
Calhoun, Craig J., 1952-. 4.3655
Calhoun, Frederick S. 4.10501
Calhoun, John C. (John Caldwell), 1782-1850.
    3.7069, 4.7840
Calhoun, Mary Lynne. 4.10943
Calhoun, Richard James. 2.12981
Calhoun, Thomas O. 2.7326
Cali, François. 1.4854
Califano, Joseph A., 1931-. 4.5157
California Academy of Sciences, San Francisco.
    3.5889
California Institute of Technology, Pasadena.
    Hixon Fund. 5.181
California Palace of the Legion of Honor.
    1.5088, 1.6056, 3.8900
California. University. Center for Slavic and
    East European Studies. 3.3518, 4.2974
California. University. Center for the Study of
    Law and Society. 4.6726
California. University. Research Program on
    Unemployment. 4.3222
California. University, Santa Barbara. Dept. of
    Political Science. 4.5902
California. University. Survey Research Center.
    3.6708
Calin, William, 1936-. 2.3842
Calina, Josephine. 2.6714
Calingaert, Peter. 5.1166
Calisher, Hortense. 2.12942-2.12946
Calkins, Fay. 4.3596
Calkins, Robert G. 1.4735, 1.6400
Callaghan, Morley, 1903-. 2.9916-2.9918
Callaghy, Thomas M. 3.5443, 4.7130
Callaham, Ludmilla Ignatiev. 5.2589
Callahan, Daniel, 1930-. 4.5696, 4.5700
Callahan, James J. 5.4678
Callahan, James Morton, 1864-1956. 4.9064
Callahan, Sidney Cornelia. 4.5700
Callahan, William James, 1937-. 1.3194
Callan, Edward, 1917-. 2.8401, 2.10090
Callan, Richard J., 1932-. 2.5370
Callcott, George H., 1929-. 3.6206
Callcott, Wilfrid Hardy, 1895-. 3.8931, 3.9014
Callen, Herbert B. 5.2242
Calleo, David P., 1934-. 3.2321
Callimachus. 2.357
Callistratus, Sophista. 2.384
Callow, Alexander B. 4.6200
Calmette, Joseph, 1873-1952. 3.1986
Calvert, James. 5.7781
Calvert, Peter. 3.8929, 3.8940
Calvin, Jack. 5.3823
Calvin, Jean, 1509-1564. 1.2523, 1.3404-1.3405,
    4.7385
Calvin, Melvin, 1911-. 5.3318
Calvino, Italo. 2.5025-2.5028, 2.5030

Calvino, Italo. comp. 4.795
Calvino, Italo. 2.5029-2.5030
Calvocoressi, Michel D., 1877-1944. 1.3941
Calvocoressi, Peter, 1921-. 3.900
Cam, Helen Maud, 1885-1968. 3.1327
Camargo Foundation. 5.8002
Camarillo, Albert. 3.8631
Cambon, Glauco. 2.4968, 2.5041
Cambridge, Eng. University. Corpus Christi
    College. Library. 3.1311
Cambridge Group for the History of Population
    and Social Structure. 4.5789
Cambridge. University. Constituciones
    Vniuersitatis Cantebrigiensis. 4.11007
Cambridge University Library. 1.2133
Cambridge Women's Peace Collective. 4.9147
Cambron-McCabe, Nelda H. 4.9585, 4.10656,
    4.10664
Camden, Archie, 1888-1979. 1.4557
Cameron, A. (Alastair), 1917-. 5.6244
Cameron, Averil. ed. 3.2667
Cameron, Averil. 3.2656
Cameron, Christina. 1.5343
Cameron, Deborah, 1958-. 2.126
Cameron, Eugene N. (Eugene Nathan), 1910-.
    5.6722
Cameron, George Glenn, 1905- ed. 3.3764
Cameron, I. R. 5.6611
Cameron, James, 1911-. 3.725
Cameron, John, 1914-. 4.10169
Cameron, John R. 5.4614
Cameron, Judy. 4.1167
Cameron, Keith. 2.3979
Cameron, Kenneth Neill. 2.8100, 2.8106
Cameron, Mary Owen. 4.6753
Cameron, Meribeth Elliott, 1905-. 3.4736
Cameron, Rondo E. 4.2188
Cameron, Sharon. 2.11248
Camhi, Jeffrey M., 1941-. 5.4305
Camic, Charles. 4.5334
Cammett, John McKay, 1927-. 4.7078
Camões, Luís de, 1524?-1580. 2.5452-2.5454
Camp, Dennis. 2.12015
Camp, Walter Mason, 1867-1925. 3.5781
Campaign for Political Rights (U.S.) 4.7916
Campana, Dino, 1885-1932. 2.5031
Campanella, Tommaso, 1568-1639. 4.7177
Campbell, A. (Alistair), 1907-. 3.1312
Campbell, Alan K. 4.8842
Campbell, Angus. 4.8076, 4.8115, 4.8117
Campbell, Arthur A. joint author. 4.1643
Campbell, Ballard C., 1940-. 4.8254
Campbell, Bernard Grant. 4.447
Campbell-Boross, Laszlo Ferenc. 4.4164
Campbell, Bruce, 1912-. 5.3935
Campbell, Bruce F. 1.2097
Campbell, C. L. (C. Lee) 5.5397
Campbell, Charles Arthur. 1.1444
Campbell, Charles Soutter, 1911-. 3.7417
Campbell, Christiana McFadyen, 1915-. 4.2938
Campbell, Clarice T. 4.10882
Campbell, Colin Dearborn, 1917-. 4.3461
Campbell, David A. 2.288, 2.316
Campbell, Doak Sheridan, 1888-. 4.10432
Campbell, Douglas M., 1943-. 5.1030
Campbell, Edward D. C., 1946-. 2.3009
Campbell, Edward Fay. joint comp. 1.2544
Campbell, Eila M. J., joint ed. 3.1726
Campbell, Gordon, 1886-1953. 3.286
Campbell, Hilbert H. 2.7319
Campbell, Iain D. 5.3317
Campbell, Ian M. (Ian McIntyre), 1941-. 5.2506
Campbell, J. B. 3.2793
Campbell, Jacquelyn. 5.4967
Campbell, James, 1935-. 3.1314
Campbell, James B., 1944-. 5.5264
Campbell, Jane, 1934-. 3.5288
Campbell, Jeremy, 1931-. 5.1022
Campbell, Joan, 1929-. 1.6526
Campbell, John B., joint author. 4.4595
Campbell, John Coert, 1911-. 3.3563
Campbell, John Hardin, 1946- joint author.
    5.7038
Campbell, John Wood, 1910-1971. 2.12947
Campbell, Joseph, 1904-. 1.1606-1.1607, 1.1819,
    2.8870, 5.168

Campbell, K. S. W. (Kenton Stewart Wall)
  5.3008
Campbell, Leon G. 3.9301
Campbell, Lily Bess, 1883-1967. 2.3294, 2.5633,
  2.6428, 2.6767, 2.6778
Campbell, Marjorie Wilkins, 1902-. 3.8835,
  3.8862
Campbell, N. J. M. 5.7434
Campbell, Oscar James, 1879-1970.
  2.6170-2.6171, 2.6684, 2.6814
Campbell, Patrick, Mrs., 1865-1940. 2.8070
Campbell, Paul J. joint author. 5.8281
Campbell, R. H. (Roy Hutcheson) 4.1355,
  4.2296-4.2297
Campbell, Rex R. 3.6765
Campbell, Roald Fay, 1905-. 4.10634
Campbell, Robert, 1922-. 4.10880
Campbell, Robert Jean. 5.4798
Campbell, Robert Wellington. 4.2374, 4.3781,
  5.6141
Campbell, Roy, 1901-1957. 2.5456,
  2.10059-2.10061
Campbell, Stuart L., 1938-. 3.2155
Campbell, William Giles, 1902-. 4.10618
Campenhausen, Hans, Freiherr von, 1903-.
  1.2482-1.2483, 1.2514, 1.2813
Campion, Dan, 1949-. 2.11281
Campion, Frank D., 1921-. 5.4477
Campion, Thomas, 1567-1620. 2.6441
Camps, William Anthony. 2.765, 2.800
Camus, Albert, 1913-1960. 2.4439-2.4455,
  4.5042
Camus, Raoul F. 1.4203
Canada. 4.8276
Canada. Dominion Bureau of Statistics. 4.1252
Canada. Geographical Branch. 4.139
Canada. Geography Division. 4.139
Canada. Parliament, 1865. 4.8282
Canada. Royal Commission on Newspapers.
  2.3678
Canaday, John, 1907-. 1.4780, 1.5936a
Canadian Arctic Resources Committee. 5.4045
Canadian Association of Geographers. 3.8661
Canadian Books in Print Committee. 5.7882
Canadian Institute of Internatonal Affairs.
  3.8696
Canadian Library Association. 5.7885
Canadian Music Council. 1.3700
Canadian Social Science Research Council.
  3.447
Canaletto, 1697-1768. 1.6195
Canary, Robert H. 3.413, 3.6248
Canavan, Francis, 1917-. 4.9702
Canby, Henry Seidel, 1878-1961. 2.3441,
  2.10246
Cancian, Frank. 4.2149
Candea, Dan. 5.7027
Candee, Marjorie Dent, 1904- ed. 3.324
Candolle, Alphonse de, 1806-1893. 5.5314
Canestrari, Guido. 3.287
Canetti, Elias, 1905-. 2.13717-2.13722
Canfield, Arthur Graves, 1859-1947. 2.4111
Canfield, D. Lincoln (Delos Lincoln), 1903- ed.
  2.902
Canfield, Gae Whitney, 1931-. 3.5934
Canfield, J. Douglas (John Douglas), 1941-.
  2.11676
Canham, Erwin D. 2.3658
Cannan, Edwin, 1861-1935. 4.1345
Cannan, Gilbert, 1884-1955. tr. 2.4699
Cannistraro, Philip V., 1942-. 3.2884
Cannon, Garland Hampton, 1924-. 2.1849
Cannon, John Ashton. 3.414, 4.8459
Cannon, Lou. 3.7940
Cannon, R. D. (Roderick David), 1938-. 5.2880
Cannon, Susan Faye. 5.776
Cannon, Walter B. (Walter Bradford),
  1871-1945. 5.4187, 5.4347
Cannon, William Ragsdale, 1916-. 1.2289
Canny, Nicholas P. 3.1830, 3.1833
Cantacuzino, Sherban. 1.5385
Cantarow, Ellen. 4.5993
Canter, Larry W. 5.5995, 5.6023
Cantillon, Richard, d. 1734. 4.1406
Cantor, Arthur, 1920- joint author. 2.3227
Cantor, Harold, 1926-. 2.12260
Cantor, Jay. 2.12948
Cantor, Norman F. 3.125

Cantor, Sheila, 1939-. 5.5119
Cantril, Hadley, 1906-1969. 3.193, 4.5015,
  4.5060, 5.535, 5.6431
Cantwell, Robert, 1945-. 1.4272
Canzona, Nicholas A. 3.5026
Capaldi, Nicholas. joint comp. 5.868
Čapek, Josef, 1887-1945. 2.1664
Čapek, Karel, 1890-1938. 2.1662-2.1667
Capek, Thomas, 1861-1950. 3.6536
Capel, Lee M. ed. and tr. 1.1394
Capers, Gerald Mortimer. 3.7088, 3.7151,
  3.8352
Capie, Forrest. 4.4513
Caplan, Jane. 3.35
Caplan, Lionel. 4.8885
Caplan, Nathan S. 4.9866
Caplan, Neil. 3.3862
Caplan, Patricia. 4.5905
Caplovitz, David. 1.3060, 4.4551
Caplow, Theodore. 1.2416, 4.2644, 4.4965,
  4.5569
Capobianco, Michael. 5.1283
Caponigri, Aloysius Robert, 1913- tr. 1.661
Capote, Truman, 1924-. 2.11463-2.11467
Capouya, Emile, ed. 4.7182
Capp, B. S. 3.1489
Cappel, Dorothy Hagberg. 3.7019
Cappon, Lester Jesse, 1900-. 3.7044, 4.158
Cappuccilli, Joanna. 4.6611
Capra, Fritjof. 4.8612, 5.872
Caputi, Anthony Francis, 1924-. 2.6625
Caracciolo Trejo, Enrique, comp. 2.5324
Carano, Paul. 3.5646
Caras, Roger A. 5.3810
Carathéodory, Constantin, 1873-1950. 5.1466
Carballido, Emilio. 2.5337
Carberry, James J. 5.6853
Carbone, Peter F. 4.10254
Carcopino, Jérôme, 1881-1970. 3.2729
Cardano, Girolamo, 1501-1576. 5.817
Cardé, Ring T. 5.3865
Carden, Patricia. 2.1541
Cardenal, Ernesto. 2.5371
Carder, Michael, joint author. 4.5682
Cardinal, Roger. 1.4626
Cardinale, Susan. 4.5839
Cardona, Rodolfo, 1924-. 2.5294
Cardoso, Fernando Henrique. 4.2136, 4.8329
Cardoza, Anthony L., 1947-. 3.2947
Cardozo, Benjamin N. (Benjamin Nathan),
  1870-1938. 4.9359
Cardozo-Freeman, Inez. 4.6917
Cardozo, Jacob Lopes. 2.5878
Cardozo, Jacob N. (Jacob Newton), 1786-1873.
  4.1409
Cardozo, Richard N. 4.4301
Cardwell, Kenneth H., 1920-. 1.5318
Careless, J. M. S. (James Maurice Stockford),
  1919-. 3.8669, 3.8717, 3.8720-3.8721, 3.8823
Carell, Paul. 3.991
Carens, James F. (James Francis), 1927-.
  2.8905, 2.9502
Caretti, Lanfranco. 2.4984
Carew, Jean V., 1936-. 4.10697
Carew, Thomas, 1595?-1639? 2.6443
Carey, Frances. 1.6461
Carey, Francis A., 1937-. 5.2719
Carey, Henry, 1687?-1743. 2.6928
Carey, Henry Charles, 1793-1879. 4.1410-4.1411
Carey, Iskandar, 1924-. 4.638
Carey, John. 2.6461
Carey, John. ed. 2.7112, 2.7815
Carey, P. B. R. 3.4561
Cargill, Jack. 3.2617
Cargill, Oscar, 1898-. 2.10247, 2.12290
Cargill Thompson, W. D. J. (William David
  James) 1930-1978. 4.7387
Carin, Arthur A. 4.10485
Cariola Sutter, Carmen. 5.8402
Cariou, Mavis. 5.7884
Carkhuff, Robert R. joint author. 5.4859
Carleton University. Institute of Canadian
  Studies. 4.2127
Carleton, William, 1794-1869. 2.7540
Carlgren, W. M. 3.3395
Carling, Christine. 2.160
Carlisle, Rodney P. 4.3970
Carls, Carl Dietrich, 1905-. 1.5716

Carlson, A. Bruce, 1937-. 5.6367
Carlson, Carl Lennart. 2.3693
Carlson, Delbert G. 5.5464-5.5465
Carlson, Elof Axel. 5.3413, 5.3423
Carlson, Eric W. 2.2341
Carlson, George, 1940- ill. 3.6535
Carlson, Marvin A., 1935-. 2.3097, 2.3366
Carlson, Victor I. 1.6458
Carlsson, Anni. 2.13778
Carlton, David, 1938-. 3.1665, 4.9172
Carlton, David L. (David Lee), 1948-. 4.3846
Carlton, Eric. 4.5083
Carlton, Peter Lynn, 1931-. 5.232
Carlton, Richard K., ed. 4.3101
Carlyle, A. J. (Alexander James), 1861-1943.
  4.7267, 4.7664
Carlyle, Jane Welsh, 1801-1866. 2.7542, 2.7549
Carlyle, Margaret. 4.2353
Carlyle, Robert Warrand, Sir, 1859-1934.
  4.7267
Carlyle, Thomas, 1795-1881. 2.7544-2.7547,
  2.7549, 2.11023, 4.5317
Carman, Harry James, 1884-1964. 5.5231,
  5.5258
Carman, W. Y. 5.7383
Carmichael, Douglas, 1923- tr. 1.418
Carmichael, Joel. 3.3195
Carmichael, Leonard, 1898-. 4.10387, 5.561,
  5.4874
Carmichael, Stokely. 3.6701
Carmo, Manfredo Perdigão do. 5.1627
Carnall, Geoffrey. 2.5657
Carnap, Rudolf, 1891-1970. 1.511, 1.540, 1.578,
  1.1200-1.1203, 1.1230, 5.1037, 5.1384
Carne, E. Bryan, 1928-. 5.6345
Carnegie, Andrew, 1835-1919. 4.1573
Carnegie Commission on Higher Education.
  4.10076, 4.10081, 4.10550, 4.10582, 4.10589,
  4.10598, 4.10842
Carnegie Council on Policy Studies in Higher
  Education. 4.10074, 4.10093, 4.10609,
  4.10612, 4.10616, 4.10749, 4.10758
Carnegie Dunfermline Trust. 4.6335
Carnegie Endowment for International Peace.
  4.9207, 4.9306, 4.9328
Carnegie Endowment for International Peace.
  Division of International Law. 4.9188, 4.9308
Carnegie Forum on Education and the
  Economy. Task Force on Teaching as a
  Profession. 4.10527
Carnegie Foundation for the Advancement of
  Teaching. 4.10047, 4.10075, 4.10077, 4.10613,
  4.10759, 4.10819, 5.4603
Carnegie Institute. Museum of Art. 1.4883
Carnegie Institution of Washington. Division of
  Historical Research. 4.156
Carneiro, Robert L. (Robert Leonard), 1927-
  ed. 4.4845
Carnell, Hilary. 2.5561
Carner, Mosco. 1.3950
Carnesale, Albert. 5.7236
Carnevali, Doris L. joint author. 5.5170
Carnevali, Doris L. 5.5166
Carnochan, W. B. 2.5689
Carnot, Sadi, 1796-1832. 5.2243
Carnoy, Martin. 4.1287, 4.9998, 4.10012,
  4.10834
Carnoy, Martin. comp. 4.10764
Caro, Anthony, 1924-. 1.5690-1.5691
Caro, Robert A. 1.5589, 3.7886
Caroe, G. M. 5.694
Carolan, Jacqueline M. 5.4747
Caron, François. 4.2320
Carossa, Hans, 1878-1956. 2.13723
Carosso, Vincent P. 4.4623
Carpenter, C. Ray (Clarence Ray), 1905- ed.
  5.4014
Carpenter, Carole Henderson, 1944-. 5.8196
Carpenter, Frederic Ives, 1903-. 2.11931
Carpenter, Humphrey. 2.2702, 2.8402
Carpenter, Michael, 1940-. 5.7626
Carpenter, Philip L. (Philip Lee), 1933-. 5.5381
Carpenter, Rhys, 1889-. 1.4713, 1.5123
Carpentier, Alejo, 1904-. 2.5359-2.5362
Carr, Archie Fairly. 5.3924
Carr, Brian. 1.760
Carr, David William, 1936-. 4.4633
Carr, Donald Eaton, 1903-. 5.4357, 5.6121

Carr, Dorothy. 1.2356
Carr, Edward Hallett. 3.463, 3.668, 3.3206, 4.7198, 4.7484, 4.9011, 4.9274
Carr, Emily, 1871-1945. 1.5997
Carr, Ian. 1.4083
Carr, Jean Ferguson. 2.11017
Carr, John Dickson, 1906-1977. 2.11470
Carr, John Laurence. 3.2070
Carr, Lois Green. 3.8103
Carr, M. H. (Michael H.) 5.1816
Carr, Raymond. 3.3448, 3.3453, 3.3460, 3.3473, 3.6479
Carr, Robert Kenneth, 1908-. 3.7542, 4.9642
Carr-Saunders, A. M. (Alexander Morris), Sir, 1886-1966. 4.1611
Carr, Virginia Spencer. 2.12077
Carr, William, 1921-. 3.2285, 3.2396
Carrà, Massimo, 1922- comp. 1.4852
Carras, Mary C. 3.4301
Carré, Jean Jacques. 4.2333
Carrell, Norman. 1.3773
Carrère d'Encausse, Hélène. 3.3321
Carrillo de Albornoz, Angel Francisco, 1905-. 1.3010
Carrillo, Elisa A. 3.2898
Carringer, Robert L. 2.3026
Carrington, Charles Edmund, 1897-. 2.7892, 3.1218
Carrington, David K., 1938-. 4.221
Carrington, Henry Beebee, 1824-1912. 3.6930
Carrington, Patricia. 1.1635
Carrithers, Michael. 5.493
Carritt, E. F. (Edgar Frederick), 1876-1964. 1.1345
Carroll, Charles F., 1936-. 4.3841
Carroll, David. comp. 2.1098, 2.7706
Carroll, Eber Malcolm, 1893-1959. 3.1976
Carroll, Holbert N. 4.8051
Carroll, J. Douglas. 5.1407
Carroll, John, Abp., 1735-1815. 1.3265
Carroll, John Alexander. 3.7028
Carroll, John E. (John Edward), 1944-. 3.6415
Carroll, John J. 2.7213
Carroll, John M. (John Melvin), 1928-. 3.5782
Carroll, Joseph T. 3.944
Carroll, Lewis, 1832-1898. 2.7673, 2.7675-2.7677, 5.1257
Carroll-Najder, Halina. 2.8559
Carroll, Paul Vincent, 1900-1968. 2.8492
Carroll, Peter N. 3.6179
Carroll, Stephen J., 1940-. 4.10655
Carroll, Susan J., 1950-. 4.5968
Carroll, W. E. (William Ernest), 1882- joint author. 5.5450
Carruth, Gorton. 2.10282, 3.6201
Carruth, Hayden, 1921- comp. 2.10764
Carruthers, Mary. 2.6398
Carse, Adam von Ahn, 1878-1958. 1.4122, 1.4137, 1.4164, 1.4198
Carson, Ada Lou. 2.10881
Carson, Clayborne, 1944-. 3.6790
Carson, Herbert L. joint author. 2.10881
Carson, Rachel, 1907-1964. 4.328, 5.3245, 5.5416
Carson, Ralph S. 5.6485
Carson, Robert Barry, 1934-. 4.4006
Carstairs, Andrew McLaren. 4.8369
Carstairs, G. M. (G. Morris) 3.4165
Carsten, F. L. (Francis Ludwig) 3.867, 3.1895, 3.1901, 3.2366, 3.2482, 4.8598
Carstensen, Vernon Rosco, 1907- ed. 4.2821
Carswell, Catherine MacFarlane, 1879-1946. 2.8982
Carte, Elaine H., joint author. 4.6797
Carte, Gene E. 4.6797
Cartellieri, Otto, 1872-1930. 3.2219
Carter, Angela, 1940-. 2.9651-2.9653
Carter, Ashton B. 5.7409
Carter, Bernard. 4.2422
Carter, Charles H. 5.4972
Carter, Dan T. 3.7460, 4.9463
Carter, E. Eugene. joint author. 4.4576
Carter, Edward Carlos, 1928-. 1.6380
Carter, Elliott, 1908-. 1.3468, 1.3832
Carter, Everett. 2.11090
Carter, Genevieve W. 4.6592
Carter, Gwendolen Margaret, 1906-. 3.5096, 3.5442, 3.5451, 3.5469

Carter, Harley. 5.6446
Carter, Hodding, 1907-1972. 2.3608
Carter, Howard, 1873-1939. 3.5154
Carter, Hugh. 4.1648
Carter, Jared. 2.2523
Carter, Jeri. 4.10934
Carter, Jimmy, 1924-. 3.7931
Carter, John, 1905-1975. 5.7694
Carter, John Ross. 1.2148
Carter, Paul Allen, 1926-. 1.2405, 3.6092
Carter, Robert Melvin, 1929-. 4.6868
Carter, Ronald. 2.30
Carter, Thomas Francis, 1882-1925. 5.7550
Carter, William Douglas, 1926-. 5.2974
Carter, William Horsfall, 1900- joint tr. 1.827
Carterette, Edward C. 5.260
Cartier-Bresson, Henri, 1908-. 5.6976
Cartledge, Paul. 3.2647
Cartledge, T. M. 1.3431
Cartlidge, David R. 1.2679
Cartmell, Edward. 5.2835
Cartmell, Van H., joint comp. 2.3765
Cartmell, Van Henry, 1896-. 2.3766, 2.10796
Cartter, Allan Murray. 4.3126
Cartwright, Dorwin, ed. 4.4934
Cartwright, Frederick Fox. 5.4544
Cartwright, William H. (William Holman), 1915-. 3.6207
Carty, R. Kenneth. 4.8564
Carus-Wilson, E. M. (Eleanora Mary), 1897-1977. 4.1723, 4.3850
Caruthers, Clifford M., 1935-. 2.11983
Carver, Michael, 1915-. 5.7198
Carver, Raymond. 2.12949
Carver, Robert E., 1931-. 5.3053
Carvill, James. 5.5662
Carvounis, Chris C. 4.4728
Carwardine, Richard. 1.3034
Cary, Earnest, 1879-. 2.358, 2.364
Cary, Elisabeth Luther, 1867-1936. 1.5985
Cary, Joyce, 1888-1957. 2.8493-2.8505
Cary, M. (Max), 1881-1958. 3.2517, 3.2521, 3.2530, 3.2754, 4.56
Cary, Patrick, fl. 1651. 2.6929
Cary, Richard, 1909-. 2.11134
Cary, William Lucius, 1910- joint author. 4.3015
Casalduero, Joaquín. 2.5183, 2.5224
Casale, Ottavio M. 2.4999
Casalis, Georges. 1.3285
Casals, Pablo, 1876-1973. 1.4076
Casarett, Louis J. 5.4720
Casas, Bartolomé de las, 1474-1566. 3.8990-3.8991
Casciati, Fabio. 5.5833
Casciato, Arthur D. 2.13347
Case, Arthur Ellicott, 1894-1946. 2.6228, 2.7293
Case, James H., 1940-. 4.1404
Case, Lynn Marshall, 1903-. 3.269, 3.711
Case, Margaret H. 5.8047
Case, R. Maynard (Richard Maynard) 5.4206
Case, Ted J. 5.3273, 5.3515
Caserio, Marjorie C., joint author. 5.2723
Casey, Daniel J., 1937-. 2.9736
Casey, Jay. 4.5839
Casey, Michael, 1947-. 2.12950
Cash, Arthur H. (Arthur Hill), 1922-. 2.7281-2.7282
Cash, Wilbur Joseph, 1901-1941. 3.8117
Cashman, Sean Dennis. 3.7405
Casino, Eric. 3.4594
Caskey, Helen, joint author. 4.10461
Caso, Alfonso, 1896-1970. 3.8903
Casona, Alejandro, 1903-1965. 2.5279-2.5280
Caspari, Carl Paul, 1819-1892. 2.1831
Caspari, Fritz, 1914-. 1.406
Casper, Barry M. 5.2029
Casper, Jonathan D. 4.9476, 4.9664, 4.9858
Cass, James. 4.9939
Cassanelli, Lee V., 1946-. 3.5256
Cassar, George H. 3.803
Cassata, Mary B., 1930-. 5.8436
Cassel, Christine K. 5.5002
Cassel, Gustav, 1866-1945. 4.1467, 4.1549
Cassell, Douglas A. 5.6177
Cassell, Richard A., 1921-. 2.8634
Cassels, Alan, 1929-. 3.2839

Cassels, J. W. S. (John William Scott) ed. 5.1317
Cassen, Robert. 4.1706, 4.4162
Casserly, Michael D. 4.10720
Cassidy, Frederic Gomes, 1907-. 2.939, 2.973, 2.1144
Cassill, R. V. (Ronald Verlin), 1919-. 2.3776
Cassirer, Ernst, 1874-1945. 1.399, 1.409, 1.433, 1.816, 1.899, 1.977-1.981, 1.1286, 2.88, 3.479, 4.7458
Cassirer, H. W. (Heinrich Walter), 1903-. 1.884
Cassius Dio Cocceianus. 2.358
Cassola, Carlo, 1917-. 2.5032
Casson, Lionel, 1914-. 3.558, 5.7498
Casson, Mark, 1945-. 4.3019
Casson, Stanley, 1889-1944. 1.5623
Castañeda de Nágera, Pedro de,$. 3.5981
Castañeda, Jorge. 4.9209
Castel, Albert E. 3.7456
Castellanos, Rosario. 2.5338
Castells, Manuel. 4.6192, 4.6290
Castelot, André. 3.2128
Castex, Pierre, 1915-. 2.4336
Castex, Pierre Georges, 1915-. 2.3826, 2.3907, 2.4110, 2.4333
Castiglione, Baldassare. 1.1513
Castillo, Carlos, 1890- ed. 2.902
Castle, Barbara, 1911-. 3.1713
Castle, Gray. 4.4638
Castle, Terry. 2.7215
Castleman, Harry. 1.3626
Castleman, Riva. joint author. 1.4976
Castleman, Riva. 1.6433-1.6434
Castles, Stephen. 4.3632-4.3633
Castro, Américo, 1885-1972. 2.5099, 2.5180, 3.3403
Castro, Ernesto Manuel de Melo e. 2.5451
Castro, Fidel, 1927-. 3.9093, 3.9101
Castro, José I. (José Ignacio), 1948-. 5.3912
Castronovo, David. 2.12768
Caswell, Hollis Leland, 1901-. 4.10432
Català Roca, Francesc. 1.6511, 1.6616
Cataldo, Christine Z. 4.5722
Catalogue of colour reproductions prior to 1860. 1.6486
Catanzariti, John, 1942-. 3.6977
Cate, Curtis, 1924-. 5.6654
Cate, James Lea, 1899- ed. 3.1054
Cater, Douglass, 1923-. 2.3553
Cater, Harold Dean, 1908- ed. 3.6235
Catford, John Cunnison, 1917-. 2.179
Cathedral of St. John the Divine (New York, N.Y.) 1.1976
Cather, Willa, 1873-1947. 2.11471-2.11473
Catherine II, Empress of Russia, 1729-1796. 3.3102
Catherine, of Cleves, Duchess, consort of Arnold, van Egmond, Duke of Gelderland, 1417-1476. 1.6429
Cathey, W. Thomas, 1937-. 5.5937
Catholic Church. 1.6428
Catholic Church. National Conference of Catholic Bishops. Committee on Evangelization. 1.3179
Catholic Church. Pope. 1.3132
Catholic Church. Pope (1073-1085: Gregory VII) 1.3150
Catholic Library Association. 1.29
Catholic Theological Society of America. 4.5513
Catholic University of America. 1.3131
Catledge, Turner, 1901-. 2.3609
Catlin, George E. G. 4.7470
Catlin, George Edward Gordon, 1896-. 4.7469
Catlin, Stanton Loomis. 1.4855
Cato, Marcus Porcius, 234-149 B.C. 2.654
Caton, Charles Edwin, 1928- ed. 2.198
Catt, Carrie Chapman, 1859-1947. 4.8079
Cattan, Henry. 3.3814
Cattell, Jaques, 1904-1960. 4.10154, 5.806
Cattell, Raymond B. (Raymond Bernard), 1905-. 5.39, 5.508-5.509, 5.520
Catton, Bruce, 1899-. 3.7303, 3.7338-3.7340, 3.7360-3.7362, 3.7477-3.7479, 3.8430, 4.1972
Catton, William Bruce, 1926-. 3.7303
Catudal, Honoré Marc, 1944-. 4.9305
Catullus, Gaius Valerius. 2.645, 2.655, 2.706-2.709
Caudet, Francisco, 1942-. 2.5220

Caudill, Harry M., 1922-. 4.2032
Caudrey, P. J., 1943-. 5.2148
Caughey, John L., 1941-. 4.4924
Caughey, John Walton, 1902-. 3.6249, 3.8599, 3.8606
Caughley, Graeme. 5.3338
Caute, David. 4.7054
Cauvin, Jean Pierre. 2.4421
Cavafy, Constantine, 1863-1933. 2.581-2.583
Cavaignac, Jacques Marie Eug8ene Godefroy, 1853-1905, jt. author. 2.4260
Cavalcanti, Guido, d. 1300. 2.4913
Cavaliero, Glen, 1927-. 2.9239, 2.9530
Cavalli-Sforza, Luigi Luca, 1922-. 5.3424
Cavallo, Adolph S. 1.4658
Cavan, Sherri. 4.5751
Cave, Roderick. 5.7554
Cave, Terence. 2.4001
Cavell, Stanley, 1926-. 1.1276
Cavendish, George, 1500-1561? 3.1413
Cavendish, Henry, 1731-1810. 5.2339
Caves, Richard E. 4.2120, 4.2739, 4.3020
Caves, Richard E. comp. 4.4136
Caviness, Madeline Harrison, 1938-. 1.6646, 1.6648
Cawelti, John G. 2.3427
Cawker, Ruth, 1953- joint author. 5.7891
Cawkwell, George. 3.2620
Cawley, A. C. (Arthur C.) ed. 2.6205, 2.6209
Cawley, A. C. (Arthur C.) 2.6137
Caws, Mary Ann. 2.3882-2.3883, 2.4419, 2.4421, 2.4465, 2.4467-2.4468, 2.4506, 2.4686
Cawson, Alan. 4.5312
Caxton, William, ca. 1422-1491. tr. 1.3247
Cayton, Andrew R. L. 3.8382
Cayton, Horace Roscoe, 1903-. 3.6732, 3.8423
Cazamian, Louis François, 1877-1965. 2.5530, 2.6014, 2.6061
Cazelles, Raymond. ed. 1.6428
CBE Style Manual Committee. 5.3295
CBS News. 3.1180
Ceaser, James W. 4.7941, 4.7947
Cebeci, Tuncer. 5.1665
Cecchetti, Giovanni, 1922-. 2.5000, 2.5017
Cecchi, Emilio, 1884-1966. 2.4877
Cech, Joseph J. 5.3899
Cecil, David, Lord, 1902-. 1.6019, 2.5534, 2.6021, 2.6185, 2.7785, 2.7983, 3.1603
Cecil, Joe S. 4.9604
Cecil, Robert, 1913-. 3.964
Cecil, Russell L. (Russell La Fayette), 1881-1965. 5.4754
Cedoline, Anthony J. 4.10679
Cela, Camilo Jose. 2.5242
Cela, Camilo José, 1916-. 2.5241, 2.5243
Celan, Paul. 2.13724-2.13726
Céline, Louis-Ferdinand, 1894-1961. 2.4507-2.4512
Cellina, Arrigo, 1941-. 5.1500
Cellini, Benvenuto, 1500-1571. 1.5728
Cendrars, Blaise, 1887-1961. 2.4460-2.4462
Cennini, Cennino, 15th cent. 1.6339
Censer, Jane Turner, 1951-. 4.5570
Centennial Symposium on the Future of History, Vanderbilt University, 1975. 3.357
Center for Advanced Study in the Behavioral Sciences (Stanford, Calif.) 5.4017
Center for Inter-American Relations. 1.5347, 5.7911
Center for Population Research (National Institute of Child Health and Human Development) 4.1577
Center for the Study of Democratic Institutions. 4.5902
Center for the Study of Ethics in the Professions (U.S.) 5.8161
Center of Military History. 3.4468
Centers, Richard. 4.6376
Centlivre, Susanna, 1667?-1723. 2.6930-2.6931
Central Institute of Indian Languages. 5.8338
Central Midwestern Regional Educational Laboratory. 1.6694
Central Renaissance Conference. University of Nebraska, 1962. 2.2561
Central States Anthropological Society (U.S.) 4.5490

Centre for Housing, Building, and Planning (United Nations) 4.1850
Centre Georges Pompidou. 5.6960
Centre national d'art contemporain. 1.4970
Centro de Estudios Económicos y Sociales del Tercer Mundo. 4.4157
Centro de Mejora y Demostracion de las Tecnicas Oleicolas. 5.5341
Centro Pedro Fabro de Montevideo. 1.3200
Cépède, Michel. 4.5294
Ceplair, Larry. 2.2912
Ceram, C. W., 1915-1972. 2.2881, 3.255
Cercle de la librairie (France) 5.7998
Cerf, Bennett, 1898-1971. 2.1842, 2.3765-2.3766, 2.10794-2.10796, 2.13524
Cermak, Laird S. 5.326
Cernuda, Luis. 2.5245
Cerny, Karl H. 4.8610, 4.8672
Cerny, Philip G., 1946-. 4.5358
Ceruzzi, Paul E. 5.1143
Cervantes Saavedra, Miguel de, 1547-1616. 2.5169, 2.5171-2.5174
Cervetto, L. 5.4385
Césaire, Aimé. 2.4835-2.4837
Cesari, Lamberto. 5.1470
Československá akademie věd. 5.955
Československá komise pro spolupráci s Unesco. 5.955
Cézanne, Paul. 1.6069-1.6070, 1.6074-1.6075
Chabal, Patrick, 1951-. 3.5410
Chabod, Federico. 3.2885, 4.7397
Chabot, Brian F. 5.3670
Chabot, Leon. joint author. 5.5951
Chabot, Victorin. 3.8709
Chabrol, Claude, 1930- joint author. 2.3053
Chace, James. 3.9057
Chadbourne, Richard McClain. 2.4284
Chadourne, Marc, 1895-. 2.4086
Chadwick, Bruce A. 1.2416
Chadwick, Henry, 1920-. 1.337, 1.2209, 1.2211, 1.2293
Chadwick, John, 1920-. 2.227, 3.284, 3.2579, 5.4494
Chadwick, Nora K. (Nora Kershaw), 1891-1972. 1.1671, 2.1311, 3.3078
Chadwick, Owen. ed. 1.3076, 1.3307
Chadwick, Owen. 1.1887, 1.2321, 1.3156, 1.3275
Chadwick, William Rowley. 2.7342
Chafe, William Henry. 3.8233, 4.6038-4.6039
Chafee, Zechariah, 1885-1957. 4.9505
Chafetz, Janet Saltzman. 4.5498, 4.5842
Chafetz, Morris E. 4.6639
Chaffee, Zechariah, 1885-. 4.7675
Chagnon, Napoleon A., 1938-. 4.509
Chai, Ch'u. 1.1794-1.1795
Chai, Winberg. 1.1794-1.1795, 3.3631
Chai'anan Samutwanit. 4.8768
Chaikin, Andrew, 1956-. 5.1790
Chaikin, Joseph, 1935-. 2.13317
Chaison, Gary N. 4.3337
Chaisson, Eric. 5.1700
Chaisson-Stewart, G. Maureen (Grace Maureen) 5.4931
Chakravarty, Amiya Chandra. 2.1870
Chalfant, H. Paul, 1929-. 1.1870, 5.8359
Chaliand, Gérard, 1934-. 3.3690, 3.4044
Chalk, Laurence. 5.3691
Chall, Jeanne Sternlicht, 1921-. 4.10458
Challener, Richard D. 3.7561, 5.7309
Challinor, John. 5.2940
Chalmers, A. F. (Alan Francis), 1939-. 5.873
Chalmers, David Mark. 3.7521
Chalmers, Robert Alexander. 5.2655
Chalpin, Lila K. 2.9302
Chamberlain, Basil Hall, 1850-1935. 3.4886
Chamberlain, Charles Joseph, 1863-. 5.3697
Chamberlain, Houston Stewart, 1855-1927. 3.43
Chamberlain, John, 1903-. 3.7522, 4.1931
Chamberlain, Joseph W. (Joseph Wyan), 1928-. 5.1803
Chamberlain, Martin Nichols, 1914-. 4.10979
Chamberlain, Neil W. 4.2707-4.2709, 4.3164, 4.3178, 4.4255
Chamberlain, Neville, 1869-1940. 3.871
Chamberlin, Edward, 1899-1967. 4.1488
Chamberlin, Hal. 1.4458
Chamberlin, J. Edward, 1943-. 2.5702

Chamberlin, Judi. 5.4694
Chamberlin, Waldo, 1905-. 4.9210
Chamberlin, William Henry, 1897-. 3.3177
Chambers, Clarke A. 4.6507
Chambers, E. K. (Edmund Kerchever), 1866-1954. 2.2636, 2.3170, 2.3288, 2.5611, 2.5849, 2.6148, 2.6689, 2.6693-2.6694, 2.6725, 2.7909
Chambers, Frank Pentland, 1900-. 3.782
Chambers, Fred B. 5.1244
Chambers, John M. 5.1402
Chambers, Jonathan David, 1898-1970. 5.5247
Chambers, R. J. (Raymond J.), 1917-. 4.4392
Chambers, R. W. (Raymond Wilson), 1874-1942. 2.1115, 2.5513, 2.5931, 2.6295, 2.6496
Chambers, Robert H. 2.12635
Chambers, Robert W. (Robert William), 1865-1933. 2.10924
Chambers-Schiller, Lee Virginia, 1948-. 4.5770
Chambers, Sir Edmund Kerchever, 1866-. 2.6695
Chambers, Whittaker. 3.7543
Chambers, William Nisbet, 1916-. 3.7087, 4.8171
Chambliss, William J. 4.6702
Chambliss, William J. joint author. 4.6686
Chambre, Tim. 1.3622
Chamisso, Adelbert von, 1781-1838. 2.13559
Champa, Kate H. 1.6161
Champa, Kermit Swiler. 1.6060, 1.6161
Champion, Larry S. 2.5663, 2.6779
Champlain, Samuel de, 1567-1635. 3.8711
Chan, Anita. 4.5457
Chan, Betty. 5.8424
Chan, E. C. S. (Eddie Chin Sun). 5.4438
Chan, Heng Chee. 4.8729
Chan, Wing-tsit, 1901-. 1.149-1.150, 1.164, 1.174, 1.1789, 1.1799, 1.1801, 5.8346-5.8347
Chance, Michael Robin Alexander, 1915-. 5.4091
Chancellor, John, 1927 July 1-. 5.3795
Chand, Malini. 4.6141
Chand, Phul. 4.8711
Chandar, Krishan. 2.1903
Chander, M. joint author. 5.6321
Chandler, Alfred Dupont. comp. and ed. 4.3819
Chandler, Alfred Dupont. 3.7517, 4.2746, 4.3792, 4.4256
Chandler, Alfred Dupont. ed. 4.3991
Chandler, D. S. (Dewitt Samuel), 1938- joint author. 4.9908
Chandler, Daniel. 4.10756
Chandler, David G. 3.2091, 5.7189, 5.7212
Chandler, David P. 3.4444
Chandler, Frank Wadleigh, 1873-1947. 2.3450
Chandler, Lester Vernon, 1905-. 4.4501, 4.4537
Chandler, Margaret K. 4.3431
Chandler, Marsha A., 1945-. 4.8283
Chandler, Ralph C., 1934-. 4.7215, 4.9626
Chandler, Raymond, 1888-1959. 2.11479
Chandler, William U., 1950- joint author. 5.6147
Chandna, K. 5.7698
Chandos, John. 4.10837
Chandra, Bipan. 4.2499
Chandra, Moti. joint author. 1.6422
Chandra, Pramod. 1.5046, 1.5749
Chandrasekhar, S. (Sripati), 1918-. 3.4178, 4.5677
Chandrasekhar, S. (Subrahmanyan), 1910-. 5.1663
Chaney, Margaret Stella, 1892-. 5.4234
Chang, Chen Chung, 1927-. 5.1055
Chang, Ch'eng-ch'i. 1.1779
Chang, Ch'eng-ch'i. ed. and tr. 2.2256
Chang, Chin-Liang, 1937-. 5.1038
Chang, Chün-mai, 1886-1969. 1.159, 1.1796
Chang, Chung-li, 1919-. 4.2493, 4.5411
Chang, Chung-yüan. 1.1771
Chang, Dae H. 4.6678
Chang, Hsin-pao, 1922-. 3.4723
Chang, K. C. (Kwang-chih) 5.4687
Chang, Kuo-t'ao, 1897-. 4.8744
Chang, Kwang-chih. 3.241, 3.4625, 3.4648, 3.4688, 3.4690, 4.862
Chang, Maria Hsia. 5.7270
Chang, Sheldon S. L. 5.6260

Chang, Te-i, 1847-1918. 3.4676
Chanin, Paul. 5.4003
Chanlett, Emil T. 5.5990
Channing, Edward, 1856-1931. 3.6317
Channing, Steven A. 3.8246, 3.8355
Channing, William Ellery, 1780-1842. 1.3413,
  1.3417
Chanoff, David. 3.4470
Chanson de Roland. 2.3958
Chao, Jing. joint author. 5.2041
Chao, Kang, 1929-. 4.1660, 4.2460
Chao, Yuen Ren, 1892-. 2.2141
Chapelle, Howard Irving. 5.7449, 5.7503,
  5.7507
Chapin, Bradley. 4.9856
Chaplin, Charlie, 1889-1977. 2.3247
Chaplin, Thomas Benjamin, 1822-1890. 3.8249
Chapman, Abraham. comp. 2.10691-2.10692
Chapman, Alan J. (Alan Jesse), 1925-. 5.2262
Chapman and Hall. 5.2781
Chapman, Bob. 3.230
Chapman, Brian. 4.7751, 4.8878
Chapman, Carleton B. 5.4559
Chapman, Charles Edward, 1880-1941. 3.8976
Chapman, Charles Frederic, 1881-. 5.7511
Chapman, Clark R. 5.1810
Chapman, D. R. (Dennis Raymond), 1926-
  joint author. 5.710
Chapman, David J. 5.3711
Chapman, George, 1559?-1634. 2.484,
  2.6561-2.6562
Chapman, Guy. 2.5521, 3.2173, 3.2190, 4.9911
Chapman, Janet G. 4.3443
Chapman, John, 1822-1894. 2.7705
Chapman, John, Father, 1865-1933. 1.3255,
  4.152
Chapman, John Stewart. 2.7531
Chapman, John William, 1923-. 4.4918, 4.5028,
  4.6958, 4.7186, 4.7247, 4.7249, 4.7255-4.7256,
  4.7516, 4.7572, 4.7635, 4.7653, 4.7656,
  4.7699, 4.7705, 4.7740, 4.7774, 4.9363,
  4.9370, 4.9381, 4.9699
Chapman, Joseph A. 5.3987
Chapman, Keith. 4.3780
Chapman, Kenneth. 5.6823
Chapman, Malcolm (Malcolm Kenneth) 2.829
Chapman, Maria Weston, 1806-1885. 2.7928
Chapman, P. F. (Peter F.) 4.3703
Chapman, R. W. (Robert William), 1881-1960.
  2.7086, 2.7369, 2.7372, 3.1809, 5.7932
Chapman, Raymond. 2.2537
Chapman, Richard A. 4.8453
Chapman, Robert L. 2.1146
Chapman, V. J. (Valentine Jackson), 1910-.
  5.3560, 5.3711, 5.3788
Chappell, Leslie H. 5.4079
Chappell, Warren, 1904-. 2.168
Chappelow, Allan. 2.8074, 2.8088
Chapple, J. A. V. (John Alfred Victor), 1928-.
  2.7724
Chapple, Richard L., 1944-. 2.1362
Chapple, Steve. 1.4354
Chaput, Marcel, 1918-. 3.8681
Char, René, 1907-. 2.4464-2.4466
Charalambous, George, 1922-. 5.7122
Charbonneaux, Jean, 1895-1969. 1.4714-1.4716,
  1.5640
Chardin, Jean Baptiste Siméon, 1699-1779.
  1.6076
Chargaff, Erwin. 5.4393
Charles, Amy Marie. 2.7064
Charles, C. M. 4.10694
Charles, David (David Owain Maurice) 1.310
Charles, d'Orléans, 1394-1465. 2.3969
Charles, Edna Kotin, 1921-. 2.8012
Charles-Edwards, Thomas Charles comp.
  3.1516
Charles Ives Centennial Festival-Conference,
  New York and New Haven, 1974. 1.3901
Charles, Joseph, 1906-1952. 3.7018
Charles-Picard, Colette. joint author. 3.5187
Charles-Picard, Gilbert. 3.2796, 3.5187
Charles River Associates. 3.3809, 4.3870
Charles Scribner's Sons. 5.6641
Charles V, Holy Roman Emperor, 1500-1558.
  3.8921
Charleston, R. J. (Robert Jesse), 1916-. 1.6642
Charlesworth, J. K. (John Kaye), 1889-. 5.3142

Charlesworth, M. J. (Maxwell John), 1925-.
  1.850
Charley, Helen. 5.7112
Charlier, Roger Henri. 5.5963
Charlot, Jean. 3.2214
Charlton, D. G. (Donald Geoffrey) 3.1965
Charlton, H. B. (Henry Buckley), 1890-. 2.6612,
  2.6759, 2.6780
Charlton, Sue Ellen M. 4.6166
Charlton, W., tr. 5.833
Charney, Maurice. 2.6768, 2.6795
Charniak, Eugene. 5.1006, 5.1019
Charnley, Blair. joint author. 2.3565
Charnley, Mitchell Vaughn, 1898-. 2.3565
Charpentier, Françoise. 2.3928
Charrière, Isabelle de, 1740-1805. 2.4064
Charters, Alexander N. 4.10975
Charters, Ann. 2.11956
Charters, Samuel Barclay. 1.4312, 1.4319
Chartier, Alain, 15th cent. 2.3971
Chartier, Armand B. 2.4132
Chartier, P. (Pierre) 5.6883
Chartkoff, Joseph L. 3.8602
Chartkoff, Kerry Kona. 3.8602
Charvat, William, 1905-1966. 2.11214
Chasdai ben Abraham Crescas, 1340-1410.
  1.301
Chase, Agnes, 1869-1963. 5.3696
Chase, Allan, 1913-. 4.6452, 5.4673
Chase, Chris. joint author. 3.7930
Chase, George Henry, 1874-1952. 1.5612
Chase, Gilbert, 1906-. 1.3495, 1.3683, 1.3732,
  1.4856, 3.8968
Chase, Harold William, 1922-. 4.9628
Chase, James S. 4.8142
Chase, Mary Ellen, 1887-1973. 2.7786,
  2.11482-2.11485
Chase, Richard Volney, 1914-1962. 2.10536,
  2.11167, 2.11275, 3.6094
Chase, Salmon P. (Salmon Portland),
  1808-1873. 3.7148
Chase, Stuart, 1888-. 3.195, 4.1234, 4.1973
Chasin, Barbara H. joint author. 4.2595
Chasin, Helen. 2.12951
Chaska, Norma S. 5.5190
Chastel, André, 1912-. 3.2829
Chastellux, François Jean, marquis de,
  1734-1788. 3.6021
Chateaubriand, François-René, vicomte de,
  1768-1848. 2.4149-2.4151
Châtelet, Albert. 1.6236
Chatfield, Charles, 1934-. 4.9141
Chatman, Seymour Benjamin, 1928- ed. 2.2541
Chatterjee, Anil, 1925- joint author. 4.2522
Chatterjee, Atul Chandra, Sir 1874-1955, joint
  author. 3.4160
Chatterjee, Suhrid K., tr. 2.1863
Chatterji, Suniti Kumar, 1890-1977. 2.1853
Chatterton, Thomas, 1752-1770. 2.6933
Chatterton, Wayne. joint author. 2.11309
Chattopadhyaya, Gautam, 1924- comp. 3.4327
Chatwin, G. A. F. M., ed. 2.7047
Chatzopoulos, Miltiadēs V. 3.2623
Chaucer, Geoffrey. 2.6310-2.6318,
  2.6321-2.6322, 2.6332-2.6335
Chaudhary, Anju Grover, 1945-. 4.5003
Chaudhuri, K. N. 4.4098
Chaudhuri, Nirad C., 1897-. 3.4166
Chaudhuri, Pramit. 4.2503
Chauhan, R. S., 1934-. 4.8777
Chaunu, Pierre. 3.176
Chauvin, Rémy. 5.647, 5.4092
Chaves, John F., joint author. 5.4900
Chávez, Carlos, 1899-. 1.4184
Chavez, Cesar, 1927-. 4.3375
Chávez, John R., 1949-. 3.8563
Chavira, Juan Antonio. 4.782
Chavkin, Wendy. 5.4667
Chawaf, Chantal. 2.4776-2.4777
Chawla, Krishan Kumar, 1942-. 5.5813
Chawla, Sudershan, 1924-. 3.3639
Chayefsky, Paddy, 1923-. 2.11487-2.11488
Chayes, Abram, 1922-. 3.7861
Chazan, Robert. 3.3956
Cheape, Charles W., 1945-. 4.3922
Checkland, Olive. 3.1806
Checkland, S. G. 3.1806
Checkoway, Barry. 4.6239

Chedid, Andrée, 1920-. 2.4469-2.4470
Cheek, Donald B. 5.4210
Cheek, Neil H. 4.876
Cheeney, R. F. 5.2975
Cheetham, Nicolas, Sir, 1910-. 3.2663
Cheetham, Russell J. 4.2534
Cheever, John. 2.11490-2.11495
Cheever, Susan. 2.11496
Cheffins, Ronald I. 4.9434
Cheit, Earl Frank. 4.10833
Chejne, Anwar G. 3.3432
Chekhov, Anton Pavlovich, 1860-1904.
  2.1483-2.1485, 2.1487-2.1488
Chekhov, Michael, 1891-1955. 2.3106, 2.3114
Chelkowski, Peter J. 2.1965
Chellas, Brian F. 1.1249
Chemical Industry Institute of Toxicology.
  Conference. 5.4731
Chemical Rubber Company. 5.1125, 5.1401,
  5.2639, 5.2649, 5.2725, 5.3332, 5.4400,
  5.5666, 5.5770
Chemical Technician Curriculum Project.
  Writing Team. 5.6823
Chen, Ching-chih, 1937-. 4.8939, 5.8417
Chen, Heyi. 3.4627
Ch'ên, Jerome, 1919-. 3.4767, 3.4825,
  3.4830-3.4831
Ch'en, Jo-hsi. 2.2250
Chen, Kan, 1928-. 5.5633
Ch'ên, Kenneth Kuan Shêng, 1907-. 1.1748,
  1.2114
Ch'en, Ku-ying. 1.1803
Chen, Kuan-I, 1926- comp. 4.2504
Ch'en, Kung-po, 1892-1946. 3.4769
Ch'en, Li-li. 2.2219
Chen, Lung-chu, 1935- joint author. 4.9383
Chen, Peter S. J. 4.2530
Chen, Theodore Hsi-en, 1902-. 4.10137
Chen, Wai-Kai, 1936-. 5.6275
Chenery, Hollis Burnley. 4.1819
Chenevix Trench, Charles, 1914-. 3.1266
Cheney, C. R. (Christopher Robert), 1906-.
  1.2439, 1.2442
Cheney, E. W. (Elliott Ward), 1929-. 5.1314
Cheney, Frances Neel, 1906-. 2.10505, 5.7712
Cheney, Sheldon. 1.1626, 1.6345, 2.3162,
  2.3178, 2.3213, 4.1119
Cheng, Chu-yüan. 4.2471-4.2472, 4.3711
Cheng, I-li. 2.2147
Cheng, Joseph K. H. 3.4810
Cheng, Thomas C. (Thomas Clement) 5.4080
Chénier, André, 1762-1794. 2.4065-2.4066
Chenu, Marie-Dominique, 1895-. 1.2751
Cheremisinoff, Nicholas P. 5.2038, 5.6196
Cherlin, Andrew J., 1948-. 4.5571
Chernetsov, Valeriĭ Nikolaevich, 1905-1970.
  4.743
Chernick, S. E. 4.2155
Chernin, Kim. 5.5132
Cherniss, Harold F. (Harold Fredrik),
  1904-1987. 1.276, 1.299-1.300
Cherniss, Michael D. 2.5596
Chernoff, John Miller. 1.4348
Chernov, V. M. (Viktor Mikhaĭlovich),
  1873-1952. 3.3178
Chernow, Burt. 1.5794
Chernyshevsky, Nikolay Gavrilovich,
  1828-1889. 1.1113, 2.1338
Cheronis, Nicholas Dimitrius, 1896-1962.
  5.2686
Cherry, Colin. 2.49
Cherry, Gordon Emanuel. 4.6331
Cherry, John A. joint author. 4.306
Cherry, John F. 3.262
Chertoff, Mordecai S., 1922- ed. 4.5401
Cheshire, David F. 2.2833
Cheska, Alyce Taylor. 4.541
Chesler, Phyllis. 5.4816
Chesneau, Roger. 5.7430, 5.7434
Chesneaux, Jean. 3.4669
Chesnut, Mary Boykin Miller, 1823-1886.
  3.7367-3.7368
Chesnutt, Charles Waddell, 1858-1932.
  2.10925-2.10926
Chess, Stella. joint author. 5.634
Chess, Stella. 4.5709
Chessman, G. Wallace. 3.7701

Chesterfield, Philip Dormer Stanhope, Earl of, 1694-1773. 3.1548
Chesterton, G. K. (Gilbert Keith), 1874-1936. 1.1527, 1.2259, 2.2568, 2.5703, 2.7481, 2.7560-2.7563, 2.7651, 2.8082
Chestnut Street Theatre (Philadelphia, Pa.) 2.3232
Chettle, Henry, d. 1607? 2.6491
Cheung, Y. K. 5.5849
Chevalier, Jacques, 1882-1962, ed. 1.802
Chevalier, Louis, 1911-. 4.6792
Chevalier, Michel, 1806-1879. 3.6029
Chevalier-Skolnikoff, Suzanne. 5.4022
Chevalley, Abel, 1868-1934. 2.880
Chevalley, Marguerite, 1880-. 2.880
Chevallier, Raymond, 1929-. 3.2713
Chevigny, Paul, 1935-. 3.6754
Chew, Allen F. 3.3296, 4.176
Chew, Geoffrey Foucar, 1924-. 5.2149
Chew, Samuel Peaco, 1910-. 5.7947
Cheyney, Arnold B. ed. 4.10972
Cheyney, Edward Potts, 1861-1947. 3.573
Chi, Hsi-sheng. 3.4770
Chi, Wen-shun. 2.2148
Chiang, Ch'ing, 1910-. 4.9923
Chiang, Gregory Kuei-Ke. 2.2146
Chiang, Kai-shek, 1887-1975. 3.4671
Chiang, Siang-tseh. 3.4733
Chiang, Yee, 1903-. 1.6606
Chiappelli, Fredi, 1921-. 3.5967
Chiappetta, Eugene L. 5.987
Chiari, Maria Agnese. 1.5792
Chibbett, David G. 1.6466
Chibnall, Marjorie. 3.566, 3.1340
Chicago, Judy, 1939-. 1.4893, 1.5927
Chicago Tribune, The. 2.12126
Chicago. University. Committee for the Comparative Study of New Nations. 4.7548
Chicago. University. Norman Wait Harris Memorial Foundation. 30th Institute, 1954. 4.1612
Chick, Victoria. 4.1461
Chickering, Arthur W., 1927-. 4.10082, 4.10546
Chickering, Howell D. 2.6290
Chicorel, Marietta. 5.8126
Chief Justice Earl Warren Conference on Advocacy in the United States. Cambridge, Mass., 1974. 4.9517
Chielens, Edward E. 5.8323
Ch'ien, Chung-shu, 1911-. 2.2237
Ch'ien, Tuan-shêng. 4.8732
Chien, Yu-wen, 1896-. 3.4728
Chiera, Edward, 1885-1933. 3.3764
Chikamatsu, Monzaemon, 1653-1725. 2.2060-2.2061
Chilcote, Ronald H. 3.5122
Child, Francis James, 1825-1896. 1.4344, 2.1010, 2.6107
Child, Irvin Long, 1915-. 4.5707, 4.5714, 5.229
Child, Julia. 5.7135
Child Welfare League of America. 4.6546
Childe, V. Gordon (Vere Gordon), 1892-1957. 3.118, 3.554, 3.3615, 3.693, 4.724
Childe, Vere Gordon. 3.119, 3.264
Childers, Erskine, 1870-1922. 2.8513
Childers, Thomas, 1946-. 4.8600
Childress, James F. 1.2995, 5.4573
Childs, Barney. joint comp. 1.3679
Childs, Brevard S. 1.2565, 1.2593
Childs, David, 1933-. 4.8608
Childs, John Lawrence, 1889-. 4.10223
Childs, Marquis William, 1903-. 3.7835, 4.3077
Chill, Emanuel, 1924- ed. 4.7426
Chilton, Ernest G., joint author. 5.5694
Chilton, John, 1931 or 2-. 1.3541, 1.4079
Chilton, Paul A. (Paul Anthony) 2.3986
Chilver, Guy Edward Farquhar. 3.2714
Ch'in Shih-huang ping ma yung po wu kuan. 3.4694
China House Gallery. 1.6622
China (People's Republic of China, 1949-) 4.2458
Chinard, Gilbert, 1881-1972. 3.7046
Chindahl, George Leonard. 4.1189
Ching, Julia. 1.1140
Chinn, Philip C., 1937-. 4.10481
Chinnock, Edward James, tr. 3.545
Chinoy, Ely. 4.3521

Chinoy, Helen Krich. joint ed. 2.3122
Chinoy, Helen Krich. 2.3109, 2.3200
Chiodi, Pietro. 1.851
Chipman, Ralph. 5.1786
Chipp, Hershel Browning, comp. 1.4788
Chippendale, Thomas, 1718-1779. 1.6577-1.6578
Chirgwin, Brian H. 5.2367
Chirlian, Paul M. 5.6523
Chironis, Nicholas P. 5.6795
Chisholm, Michael, 1931-. 4.360, 4.2811
Chisholm, Roderick M. 1.1277
Chisholm, Roderick M. ed. 1.534
Chisholm, Shirley, 1924-. 3.7856
Chisick, Harvey, 1946-. 4.10124
Chissell, Joan. 1.4074
Chiswick, Barry R. 4.8953
Chitty, Susan, Lady. 2.9517
Ch'iu, P'ing. 4.3610
Chodorow, Nancy. 4.5666
Chodorow, Stanley. 1.3152
Chögyam Trungpa, Trungpa Tulku, 1939-. 1.2149
Choi, Frederick D. S., 1942-. 4.4416
Choksy, Lois. 1.4410, 1.4416
Chomsky, Carol. 4.10473
Chomsky, Noam. 2.102-2.103, 2.132, 2.147, 2.190-2.191, 2.1009, 3.7846
Chonez, Claudine, 1912-. 2.4567
Chopey, Nicholas P. 5.6818
Chopin, Kate, 1851-1904. 2.10931-2.10932
Choppin, Gregory R. 5.2916
Chopra, Kasturi L., 1933-. 5.6327
Chopra, Pran Nath. 4.8717
Chorafas, Dimitris N. 5.1167, 5.6346, 5.6409
Chorley, Edward Clowes, 1865-1949. 1.3317
Chorley, Katharine Campbell Hopkinson Chorley, Baroness, 1897-. 2.7580
Chorley, Richard J. 4.32, 4.199, 4.261
Chorover, Stephan L. 4.4866
Chou, Chin-sheng, 1907-. 4.2466
Chou, Eric, 1915- joint author. 3.4815
Chou, Jung-tê, 1915-. 4.5413
Chou, Shun-hsin, 1915-. 4.4521
Chou, Ts'ê-tsung, 1916-. 3.4752, 3.4753
Chou, Wushow. 5.6410
Choudhury, G. W. (Golam Wahed), 1926-. 3.4100, 3.4127
Chow, Ven Te, 1919- ed. 4.288
Choy, Bong Youn, 1914-. 3.4994
Chrétien, de Troyes, 12th cent. 2.3945
Chrétien, de Troyes, 12th cent. 2.3946-2.3949, 2.3952
Chrimes, S. B. (Stanley Bertram), 1907-. 4.7555, 4.8387, 4.8394
Chrislock, Carl Henry. 3.8498
Chrisman, Miriam Usher. 3.2239
Christ, Carl F. 4.1292
Christ, Carol P. 1.1609, 1.1616
Christ, Charles L. (Charles Louis) joint author. 5.3102
Christakis, Alexander N. 5.5633
Christensen, Carl C., 1935-. 1.5176
Christensen, Daphne, joint author. 4.3920
Christensen, Erwin Ottomar, 1890-. 1.6542
Christenson, Carroll Lawrence, 1902-. 4.3744
Christenson, Charles O. 5.1586
Christenson, Reo Millard, 1918-. 4.2939
Christgau, Robert. 1.3627
Christian, Barbara. 2.10317, 2.10559
Christian, Reginald Frank. 2.1428, 2.1432, 2.1441
Christian, William A., 1905-. 1.776
Christiansen, Carla E. 5.8297
Christiansen, Donald. 5.6451
Christiansen, Keith. 1.6205
Christiansen, Reidar Thoralf, 1886- ed. 4.799
Christianson, Gale E. 5.1683, 5.1956
Christie, Agatha, 1890-1976. 2.8514-2.8517
Christie, Archibald H. 1.6545
Christie, Ian R. joint author. 5.7991
Christie, Ian R. 3.1555, 3.1568
Christie, John D., ed. 2.497
Christie, Richard, 1918-. 4.5023, 4.9978

Christine, de Pisan, ca. 1364-ca. 1431. 1.1515, 2.3973
Christman, Albert B. 5.7480
Christman, Donald A. 5.5703
Christman, Henry M. ed. 3.1147
Christman, Margaret C. S. joint author. 5.7089
Christo, 1935-. 1.5041, 1.5742
Christoffel, Tom. 4.9573
Christopher, A. J. 3.5103, 3.5444
Christopher, Georgia B., 1932-. 2.7166
Christopher, Milbourne. 4.1077
Christopher, Robert C., 1924-. 3.4887
Christy, Francis T. 4.4130
Christy, Robert W. joint author. 5.2371
Christy, Van Ambrose, 1900-. 1.4566
Chroust, Anton-Hermann, 1907-. 1.293-1.294
Chryssostomidis, Marjorie. 5.8329
Chrystal, K. Alec, 1946-. 4.1286
Chu, Donald. 4.910
Chu, Hsi, 1130-1200. 1.150, 1.162
Chu, Mamerto L. 5.5712
Ch'ü, T'ung-tsu. 4.5410, 4.8886, 4.9921
Chu Văn Tân. 3.4469
Chua, Leon O., 1936-. 5.6459
Chuang-tzu. 1.1798
Chubb, Basil. 4.8565
Chudoba, Bohdan. 3.623
Chuǐkov, V. I. (Vasiliǐ Ivanovich), 1900-. 3.985-3.986
Chujoy, Anatole, 1894- ed. 4.1080
Chukovskaia, Lidiia Korneevna. 2.1545
Chula, Prince, 1908-. 3.4526
Chun, Ki-Taek. 5.541
Chung, Catherine. 5.7643
Chung-kuo k'o hsüeh yüan. Tzu jan k'o hsüeh shih yen chiu so. 5.770
Chung-kuo kung ch'an tang. 3.4769
Chung-kuo wen hsüeh i shu kung tso che tai piao ta hui (4th: 1979: Peking, China) 1.6723
Chǔng, Kyǔng Cho. 3.5008, 3.5036
Chung, Ling, 1945-. 2.2216
Chung, Norman H., 1949-. 4.10100
Chunkath, A. 4.8711
Chunn, Jay C., 1938-. 5.4820
Chuo Kikuu cha Dar es Salaam. 1.1844
Chupack, Henry. 2.12362
Church, Alonzo, 1903-. 1.1204
Church, Benjamin, 1639-1718. 3.5775
Church, Charles Frederick, 1902-. 5.7123
Church, Helen Nichols. 5.7123
Church Historical Society (Great Britain) 3.2095
Church, Horace K. 5.5914
Church of Jesus Christ of Latter-Day Saints. 1.3379-1.3380
Church, R. J. Harrison (Ronald James Harrison) 3.5051, 3.5321, 4.2189
Church, Roy A. 4.2273, 4.4258
Church, William Farr, 1912-. 3.2024
Churchill, Allen, 1911-. 2.3660
Churchill, Caryl. 2.9654
Churchill, Charles, 1731-1764. 2.6934
Churchill, Creighton. 1.3440
Churchill, Reginald Charles. 2.5528
Churchill, Winston, Sir, 1874-1965. 3.783, 3.805, 3.872, 3.896, 3.901, 3.1161, 3.1219, 3.1515, 3.1637, 3.1655, 3.1695, 3.7776
Churchman, C. West (Charles West), 1913-. 5.874
Chusid, Martin. 1.4028
Chute, Marchette. 2.6338
Chute, Marchette Gaylord, 1909-. 2.6595, 2.6703
Chvátal, Vašek, 1946-. 5.5587
Ciano, Edda Mussolini, Contessa. 3.2895
Ciano, Galeazzo, conte. 3.2896-3.2897
Ciardi, John, 1916-. 2.2744, 2.4925-2.4927, 2.10734, 2.10772, 2.11498-2.11502
Ciarlet, Philippe G. 5.1528
Ciba Foundation. 5.604
Ciba Pharmaceutical Products, Inc. 5.4737
Cibber, Colley, 1671-1757. 2.6936, 2.7323
Ciborowski, Thomas J. 4.624
Cicero, Marcus Tullius. 2.656-2.670, 2.714-2.715
Cicourel, Aaron Victor, 1928-. 4.5061
El Cid Campeador. 2.5184
Ciechanowski, Jan M. 3.997
Cienciala, Anna M. 3.3285

Cieza de León, Pedro de, 1518-1554. 3.9294
Cigman, Gloria. 2.6321
Cikovsky, Nicolai. 1.5947
Ciment, Michel, 1938-. 2.3059
Cincinnati Art Museum. 1.6359
Cinel, Dino. 3.8629
Çinlar, E. (Erhan), 1941-. 5.1385
Cinnamon, Kenneth M. 4.6798
Ciochon, Russell L. 5.4023
Cioran, Samuel D. (Samuel David), 1941-.
   2.1355, 2.1422, 2.1531
Cipolla, Carlo M. comp. 4.1738
Cipolla, Carlo M. 4.1761, 4.2190, 4.2196,
   4.10751, 5.4652, 5.4766
Ciriacy-Wantrup, S. V. (Siegfried V.),
   1906-1980. 4.1897
Cirillo, Renato. 4.1364
Cirlot, Juan Eduardo. 6.1128
Cismaru, Alfred, 1929-. 2.4523
Cistone, Peter J. 4.10667
Citizens Conference on State Legislatures.
   4.8256
Citrine, Walter McLennan Citrine, baron,
   1887-. 3.1661
City Art Museum of St. Louis. 1.5952
Cixous, Hélène, 1937-. 2.4778-2.4779
Claar, Paul. 5.6248
Claerbout, Jon F. 5.6743
Clagett, Marshall, 1916-. 3.146, 5.716, 5.737
Claghorn, Charles Eugene, 1911-. 1.3530
Clague, Ewan, 1896-1987. 4.3546
Claiborne, Craig. 5.7138, 5.7141-5.7142
Clancy, Michael, 1950-. 5.1221
Clapeyron, E. (Emile), 1799-1864. 5.2243
Clapham, John. 1.3858
Clapham, John Harold, Sir, 1873-. 4.2245,
   4.2274, 4.2321, 4.4541
Clapp, Jane. 1.5609
Clapp, Priscilla, ed. 3.6458, 4.9095
Clapp, William Warland, 1826-1891. 2.3217
Clarac, Pierre, 1894-. 2.4029
Clare, John, 1793-1864. 2.7568-2.7570
Clare, Lilian Ada (Long) Mrs. 1865- tr. 4.538
Clare, of Assisi, Saint, 1194-1253. 1.3135
Clarence-Smith, W. G., 1948-. 4.8936
Clarendon, Edward Hyde, Earl of, 1609-1674.
   3.1472
Clarens, Carlos. 2.2992
Clareson, Thomas D. 2.3497, 2.10571, 5.7814
Clarfield, Gerard H. 3.7008, 5.7263
Claridge, Amanda. joint author. 3.2724
Clark, Andrew Hill, 1911-1975. 3.5596, 3.8807
Clark, Anne B., joint author. 3.2724
Clark, Audrey N. 4.5, 4.74, 4.4123
Clark, Barrett Harper, 1890-1953. 2.2796,
   2.2809
Clark, Beverly Lyon. 2.13215
Clark, Burton R. 4.10547, 4.11001
Clark, C. M. H. (Charles Manning Hope),
   1915-. 3.5558, 3.5567
Clark, Carol, 1947-. 1.6382
Clark, Cecily. ed. 3.1750
Clark, Champ, 1850-1921. 3.7430
Clark, Charles E., 1929-. 3.7959
Clark, Charles Manning Hope, 1915- ed. 3.5557
Clark, Colin, 1905-. 4.1768
Clark, Colin Whitcomb, 1931-. 5.1449
Clark, Dennis, 1927-. 3.8090
Clark, Dora Mae. 3.6939
Clark, Edward W., 1943-. 3.5784
Clark, Elizabeth A. (Elizabeth Ann), 1938-.
   1.2909
Clark, Ella Elizabeth, 1896-. 3.8486
Clark, Fiona. 4.855
Clark, Floyd Barzilia, 1886-. 4.9627
Clark, G. N. (George Norman), Sir, 1890-.
   3.170, 3.1240, 3.1493
Clark, Garth, 1947-. 1.6614
Clark, George L. (George Lindenberg), 1892-
   ed. 5.2322
Clark, George Norman, 1890-. 3.171, 4.2253
Clark, Gertrude M. 1.897
Clark, Gilbert. 4.10917
Clark, Grahame, 1907-. 3.113, 3.116, 4.594,
   4.695, 4.706
Clark, Grenville. 4.9211
Clark, Harry Hayden, 1901-1971.
   2.2511-2.2512, 5.7794

Clark, Henry, 1930-. 3.6783
Clark, Herbert M., joint author. 5.2437
Clark, J. Desmond (John Desmond), 1916-.
   4.186, 4.705, 4.744, 4.747
Clark, J. P., 1935-. 2.10108
Clark, James Midgley, 1888-1961. ed. and tr.
   1.3088
Clark, Jay. 1.1516
Clark, John, 1946-. 4.1862
Clark, John Bates, 1847-1938. 4.1424-4.1425,
   4.1564, 4.3056
Clark, John Maurice, 1884-. 4.1480, 4.1565,
   4.3056, 4.3330
Clark, John R., 1927-. 4.2928
Clark, John William. 5.4611, 5.6014
Clark, Joseph S. 4.8045
Clark, Judith E. 4.2928
Clark, K. L. (Keith L.) 5.1219
Clark, Katerina. 2.1290
Clark, Kenneth, 1903-. 1.5158, 1.5250, 1.5786,
   1.5841, 1.6356, 1.6736, 2.8025, 3.39
Clark, Kenneth Bancroft, 1914-. 3.6650, 4.5181,
   5.614
Clark, Kenneth McKenzie, Sir, 1903-. 1.6203,
   1.6213
Clark, Marjorie Ruth, 1899-. 4.3399
Clark, Martin. 4.7079
Clark, Mary Jo Dummer. 5.5206
Clark, Norman A. 3.8641
Clark, P. F. 5.3510
Clark, Paul, 1949-. 1.6724
Clark, Peter. 3.1737, 4.6253, 4.6255
Clark, Ramsey, 1927-. 4.6833
Clark, Reginald. 4.10864
Clark, Robert Judson. 1.4648, 1.6532
Clark, Robert Louis, 1949-. 4.5796
Clark, Robert P. 3.3481-3.3482
Clark, Ronald William. 1.770, 3.6990, 5.2452,
   5.3196, 5.3203, 5.5528
Clark, Rose Bertha. 4.12
Clark, S. D. (Samuel Delbert), 1910-. 3.8670,
   4.5246-4.5247
Clark, T. J. (Timothy J.) 1.4964, 1.6064, 1.6082
Clark, Terry N. 4.1232
Clark, Thomas A., 1944-. 3.6784
Clark, Thomas Dionysius, 1903-. 3.6347,
   3.8156, 5.5420
Clark, Tom, 1941-. 2.11957
Clark, Virginia P. 2.34
Clark, Walter Van Tilburg, 1909-1971.
   2.11503-2.11506
Clark, William, 1770-1838. 3.8477,
   3.8479-3.8480
Clark, William Bedford. 2.10652, 2.12651
Clark, William Bell, 1889-1968. ed. 3.6954
Clark, William C., 1948-. 4.2890
Clark, William R., 1938-. 5.4462
Clark, William Smith, 1900-. 2.3359
Clarke, A. D. B. (Alan Douglas Benson) 5.562,
   5.4976
Clarke, Ann M. (Ann Margaret). 5.562, 5.4976
Clarke, Arthur Charles, 1917-. 2.8518-2.8519
Clarke, Austin, 1850-1974. 2.8520-2.8521
Clarke, Avis Gertrude, 1902-. 5.8318
Clarke, C. 5.2099
Clarke, Carl Dame, 1904-. 1.5779
Clarke, Colin G. 4.4874
Clarke, David D. 5.449
Clarke, David L. 3.229-3.230, 3.238
Clarke, Desmond F. 5.875
Clarke, Duncan L. 4.9157
Clarke, Edwin. 5.4317, 5.4507
Clarke, Ernest G. (Ernest George) 1.2623
Clarke, Erskine, 1941-. 1.2418
Clarke, Frank H. 5.5152
Clarke, G. W. (Graeme Wilber), 1934- ed.
   1.2193
Clarke, Gordon R. 5.1224
Clarke, Grahame, 1907-. 3.263
Clarke, Hans Thacher, 1887-1972. joint ed.
   5.2738
Clarke, Harold D. 4.8277, 4.8294, 4.8313
Clarke, Helen Archibald, d. 1926. ed. 2.7463
Clarke, I. F. (Ignatius Frederick) 3.74
Clarke, John Henrik, 1915-. 2.10813, 2.13339,
   3.6834
Clarke, John Innes. 4.1661, 5.7204, 5.7211
Clarke, M. L. (Martin Lowther) 1.318

Clarke, Mary Cowden, 1809-1898. 2.7576
Clarke, Paul F. 5.2997
Clarke, Prescott. 3.4729
Clarke, R. H. (Richard Henry) 5.6426
Clarke-Stewart, Alison, 1943-. 4.5746, 4.6572
Clarke, Thomas Curtis, 1827-1901. 4.3990
Clarke, Thurston. 3.5219
Clarkson, E. N. K. (Euan Neilson Kerr), 1937-.
   5.3165
Clarkson, Jesse Dunsmore, 1897-. 3.3044
Clary, Jack T. 4.1028
Clasen, Claus Peter. 1.3303
Claude, Inis L. 4.9026, 4.9129
Claudel, Paul, 1868-1955. 2.4471-2.4475
Claudín, Fernando. 4.6965
Clausen, Chris A., 1940-. 5.6812
Clausen, Wendell Vernon, 1923- ed. 2.646
Clauser, Henry R. 5.5759
Clausewitz, Karl von, 1780-1831. 5.7206
Clausius, R. (Rudolf), 1822-1888. 5.2243
Clawson, Marion, 1905-. 4.2815, 4.2822-4.2824,
   5.5432
Clay, C. G. A., 1940-. 4.2259
Clay, Diskin. 1.332
Clay, Henry, 1777-1852. 3.7070
Clay, Lucius D. (Lucius DuBignon), 1897-1978.
   3.2454-3.2455
Clay, Marie M. 4.10418
Clayton, Anthony, 1928-. 3.5290
Clayton, Bruce. 2.11399
Clayton, C. R. I. 5.6086
Clayton, Florence E. 5.5022
Clayton, G. B. (George Burbridge) 5.6578
Clayton, George D. 5.5022
Clayton, John Powell. ed. 1.2857
Clayton, Keith M. 4.263, 4.313
Clayton, Keith M. ed. 4.168
Clayton, Thomas, 1932-. 2.6155, 2.7286
Clayton, Thompson. 4.1060
Cleage, Albert B. 3.6729
Clear, Todd R. 4.6894
Cleary, Edward L. 1.3183
Cleary, Thomas R. (Thomas Raymond), 1940-.
   2.7028
Cleaver, Eldridge, 1935-. 3.6699
Clebsch, William A. 1.2372
Clecak, Peter. 4.5158, 4.5233
Cleghorn, Reese, joint author. 4.8095
Cleland, John, 1709-1789. 2.6938
Cleland, Robert Glass, 1885-. 3.8600, 3.8614
Clemen, Wolfgang. 2.6842
Clemence, Richard Vernon, 1910-. 4.1377
Clemens, C. Herbert (Charles Herbert), 1939-.
   5.1581
Clemens, Paul G. E., 1947-. 4.2035
Clemens, Titus Ilavius, Alexandrinus. 1.2487
Clement I, Pope. 1.2208, 2.327
Clement I, Pope. supposed author. 2.327
Clement, Meredith O. 4.4139
Clement, of Alexandria, Saint, ca. 150-ca. 215.
   1.2209
Clement, Wallace. 4.5249, 5.8396
Clemente, Carmine D. 5.4141
Clementi, Muzio, 1752-1832. 1.4538
Clements, Barbara Evans, 1945-. 4.6128
Clements, Patricia. 2.9609
Clements, Robert John, 1912-. 2.4879, 2.4969,
   3.162
Clements, William M., 1945-. 5.7734
Cleminshaw, Clarence H. (Clarence Higbee),
   1902-. 5.1711
Clemmow, P. C. 5.2368
Clendening, Logan, 1884-1945. ed. 5.4499
Clepper, Henry Edward, 1901-1987. 5.5419
Clerc, Charles, 1926-. 2.13279
Clerk, Nathalie. 1.5342
Clermont-Crèvecœur, Jean François Louis,
   comte de, 1752-ca. 1824. 3.6947
Cleveland, Grover, 1837-1908. 3.7491
Cleveland Museum of Art. 1.4659, 1.4917,
   1.4965, 1.4968, 1.5064, 1.5073, 1.5076,
   1.5765, 1.6066, 1.6076, 1.6161, 1.6327,
   1.6382, 1.6622
Cleveland, William L. 3.3712
Cleverdon, Catherine Lyle. 4.8293
Clews, Hetty, 1929-. 2.3445
Cliff, Andrew David. joint author. 4.377
Cliff, Michelle. 2.12490

Clifford, Anne (Anne Marie) 5.7650
Clifford, Deborah Pickman. 2.11083
Clifford, Derek Plint. 1.6030
Clifford, James Lowry, 1901-. 2.5664-2.5665,
   2.7087, 2.7185, 2.7262
Clifford, Timothy. joint author. 1.6030
Clift, Dominique. 3.8811
Clift, R. (Roland) 5.1668, 5.6843
Clift, Virgil A. 3.6614
Clifton, N. Roy, 1909-. 2.2950
Clifton, Thomas, 1935-1978. 1.4406
Clinard, Lillian A. 5.6117-5.6118
Clinard, Marshall Barron, 1911-. 4.5062,
   4.6762, 4.6795
Clinard, Ruth Blackburn. joint author. 4.6762
Cline, Clarence Lee. ed. 2.7940
Cline, Howard Francis. 3.8873, 3.8916
Cline, Marjorie W. 5.8297
Cline, William R. joint author. 4.2893
Cline, William R. 4.1803, 4.4155, 4.4524
Clinton, Alan. 4.3403
Clinton-Baddeley, V. C. (Victor Clinton),
   1900-1970. 2.2828, 2.5847
Clinton, Catherine, 1952-. 4.5980, 4.6073
Clippinger, Marni. 4.4086
Clissold, Stephen. 3.3555, 3.3607, 3.9263
Clive, H. P. 2.3984
Clive, John Leonard, 1924-. 3.1212
Clocksin, W. F. (William F.), 1955-. 5.1225
Clogg, Richard, 1939-. 3.2681, 3.2691, 3.2706
Cloisters (Museum) 1.6592
Cloonan, William J. 4.2794
Clor, Harry M., 1929-. 4.9871
Closs, August, 1898-. 2.13489
Closs, Hannah Priebsch. joint author. 2.13463
Clouard, Henri. 2.3866
Cloudsley-Thompson, J. L. 5.4203, 5.4211
Clough, Arthur Hugh, 1819-1861.
   2.7577-2.7579, 3.2512
Clough, Cecil H. 4.7390
Clough, Ralph N., 1916-. 3.3632
Clough, Ray W., 1920-. 5.5855
Clough, Shepard Bancroft, 1901-. 3.208, 4.2191,
   4.2354
Clout, Hugh D. 4.1658, 4.2971, 4.5313, 4.6364
Cloutier, Nicole. joint author. 1.6000
Clover, Carol J., 1940-. 2.13975
Cloward, Richard A. joint author. 4.3600,
   4.6525
Clowes, Royston C., 1921-. 5.4447
Club of Rome. 4.1788, 4.1791, 4.9036
Clubb, Louise George. 2.4976
Clubb, O. Edmund (Oliver Edmund), 1901-.
   3.4681
Clubbe, John. 2.5818, 2.7552
Clum, John M. 2.11489
Clurman, Harold, 1901-. 2.3107, 2.3273
Clutterbuck, Richard L. 4.5343
Cnossen, Sijbren. 4.4716
Coaching Association of Canada. Sport
   Information Resource Centre. 5.8425
Coachman, Lawrence K., 1926-. 4.351
Coad, J. G. 5.7465
Coad, Oral Sumner, 1887-1976. 2.3187
Coale, Ansley J. 4.1628
Coan, Richard W. 5.510, 5.4695
Coate, Godfrey T. 5.6436
Coates, Austin. 3.5479
Coates, David. 4.8546-4.8547
Coates, Donald Robert, 1922- comp. 4.262
Coates, Harper Havelock, 1865- tr. 1.1774
Coates, Henry, 1880-. 1.3944
Coates, Willson Havelock. ed. 3.1471
Coats, A. W. (Alfred William), 1924- ed. 4.1331
Coats, Alice M. 5.5344
Cobb, Boughton. 5.3702
Cobb, Buell E. 1.4246
Cobb, Carl W. 2.5120, 2.5255
Cobb, David A., 1945-. 4.220, 5.8214
Cobb, Earle H. 4.2049
Cobb, J. Stanley. 5.3851
Cobb, James C. (James Charles), 1947-. 4.2022
Cobb, John B. 1.2858
Cobb, John B. joint ed. 1.1005, 1.2519
Cobb, John B. 1.2809
Cobb, Richard, 1917- joint ed. 3.2062
Cobb, Sidney, 1916- joint author. 5.541
Cobban, Alfred. ed. 3.1246

Cobban, Alfred. 3.177, 3.2007, 3.2096, 4.7290,
   4.9302
Cobban, Helena. 3.3784, 3.3863
Cobbett, Walter Willson, 1847-1937, ed. 1.4185
Cobbett, William, 1763-1835. 3.1729, 3.6030
Cobbs, John L. 2.11289
Cobbs, Price M., joint author. 3.6717
Cobden, Richard, 1804-1865. 3.6045
Coben, Stanley. 3.7678
Cobley, Leslie S. 5.5317
Coburn, Kathleen, 1905-. 2.7593
Cochran, Janis, 1947-. 3.4758
Cochran, Sherman, 1940-. 3.4758
Cochran, Thomas Childs, 1902-. 3.8072, 4.1870,
   4.1906, 4.1932-4.1933, 4.3694, 4.4213
Cochran, William, F.R.S. 5.2208
Cochran, William Gemmell, 1909-. 5.1398,
   5.1404
Cochrane, Charles Norris, 1889-1945. 1.2303
Cochrane, Eric W. 3.2832, 3.2918
Cochrane, Willard Wesley, 1914-. 4.2894,
   4.2940, 4.2955
Cockburn, Andrew, 1954-. 5.4013
Cockburn, J. S. 4.6787
Cockcroft, James D. 4.2146
Cockrum, Richard H. 5.6539
Cockshut, A. O. J. 2.5973, 2.7652, 2.8055,
   2.8232
Cocteau, Jean, 1889-1963. 2.4476-2.4484
Codere, Helen, ed. 3.5901
Codman, Ogden. joint author. 1.6550
Cody, Martin L., 1941-. 5.3273
Coe, Michael D. 3.8883, 3.8896, 3.8904, 3.9034
Coe, Richard N. 2.4584, 2.8427
Cœdès, George. 3.4393, 3.4420
Coelho, V. H., 1917-. 3.4355
Coenen, Frans, 1866-1936. 2.13948
Cofer, Charles Norval. 5.336
Coffey, Michael. 2.638
Coffey, S. (Samuel) 5.2718
Coffey, Thomas M. 3.974
Coffin, Berton. 1.3456, 1.3597
Coffin, David R. 1.5570, 1.5577
Coffin, Robert Peter Tristram, 1892-1955.
   2.11507
Coffin, Tristram Potter, 1922-. 2.10660, 4.777
Coffman, E. G. (Edward Grady), 1934-. 5.1169
Coffman, Edward M. 3.813
Coffman, Stanley K. 2.10479
Cogan, Robert, 1930-. 1.4425
Coggins, Clemency. 3.9045
Coggins, R. J., 1929-. 1.2602-1.2603, 1.2622
Coggle, J. E. 5.3627
Coghill, Annie Louisa Walker, d. 1907, ed.
   2.7977
Coghill, Nevill. 2.6322, 2.6332, 2.6339, 2.6392
Coghlan, Brian. 2.13785
Cognac Courvoisier (Firm) 1.4973
Cohen, Aaron, 1935-. 5.7616
Cohen, Aaron I. 1.3531, 1.3625
Cohen, Abner. ed. 4.625
Cohen, Albert Kircidel. 4.5063
Cohen, Albert Kircidel. ed. 4.6684
Cohen, Amnon, 1936-. 3.3816, 4.8775
Cohen, Arthur Allen, 1928-. 1.1892, 1.1914,
   1.1955, 1.1967
Cohen, Arthur M. 4.10560
Cohen, Bernard, 1937-. 4.5541
Cohen, Bernard C. 3.7792
Cohen, Bernard Cecil, 1926-. 2.3557
Cohen, Bernard Leonard, 1924-. 5.6598
Cohen, Daniel. 5.7102
Cohen, David K., 1934-. 4.10509
Cohen, David William. ed. 4.6425
Cohen, Dorothy M. 4.10411
Cohen, Edwin, 1934-. 5.6283
Cohen, Elaine, 1938- joint author. 5.7616
Cohen, Felix S., 1907-1953. 4.9360, 4.9772
Cohen, Gail A. 4.10540
Cohen, Gerald Allan, 1941-. 3.506
Cohen, Gillian. 5.261
Cohen, Gustave, 1879-. 2.3999, 2.4002, 2.4765
Cohen, Habiba S. 4.10126
Cohen, Hennig. ed. 2.10726
Cohen, Hennig. 4.777
Cohen, Henry, 1921 Sept. 29-. 5.6219

Cohen, Howard, 1944-. 4.5741
Cohen, I. Bernard, 1914-. 5.717-5.718,
   5.1640-5.1641, 5.1931, 5.2026, 5.2338
Cohen, Irvin Sol, 1917- joint author. 5.1362
Cohen, J. M. (John Michael), 1903-. 2.5171
Cohen, Jack S. joint author. 5.4420
Cohen, Jerome Alan. 4.6267, 4.9922
Cohen, Jerome Bernard, 1915-. 4.2542
Cohen, John Michael, 1903-, ed. 2.5144
Cohen, Joseph, 1926-. 2.8371
Cohen, L. Jonathan (Laurence Jonathan) 1.1182
Cohen, Leonard A. 5.4776
Cohen, Lester H., 1944-. 3.6909
Cohen, Marcel Samuel Raphaël, 1884-. 2.862
Cohen, Mark Nathan. 4.721
Cohen, Marshall. 2.2941
Cohen, Michael A., 1944-. 4.8805
Cohen, Michael D. 4.10589
Cohen, Michael Joseph, 1940-. 3.3922
Cohen, Morris L., 1927-. 4.9470
Cohen, Morris Raphael, 1880-1947. 1.555,
   1.579-1.581, 1.1190
Cohen, Myron L., 1937-. 4.643
Cohen, Myron S. 5.4712
Cohen, Naomi Wiener, 1927-. 3.6565
Cohen, Norm. 1.3436, 1.4289
Cohen, Paul A. 3.4739, 4.8735
Cohen, Philip K., 1943-. 2.8290
Cohen, Richard M. 3.7855
Cohen, Robert, 1938-. 2.3108, 2.4572
Cohen, Robert Carl. 3.6857
Cohen, Robin. 4.3670, 4.3674
Cohen, Ronald. joint author. 4.493
Cohen, Ronald. 4.610
Cohen, Sarah Blacher. 2.10657, 2.11359
Cohen, Saul Bernard. 4.7495
Cohen, Saul G., ed. 5.2858
Cohen, Selma Jeanne, 1920-. 4.1100, 4.1118,
   4.1147
Cohen, Sidney, 1910-. 4.6632, 4.6659
Cohen, Simon, 1894-. 3.3811
Cohen, Stephen D. 4.4217
Cohen, Stephen F. 3.3009, 3.3204, 3.3225
Cohen, Stephen P., 1936-. 5.7339
Cohen-Stratyner, Barbara Naomi. 4.1125
Cohen, Ted. 1.905
Cohen, Vered. 1.4422a
Cohen, Warren I. 3.7726
Cohen, Wilbur J. (Wilbur Joseph), 1913-1987.
   4.1669
Cohen, William B., 1941-. 3.5121, 4.8804,
   4.8926
Cohen, Yehudi A. 5.438
Cohen, Yehudi A. comp. 5.3378
Cohn, Alan M., 1926-. 2.8923
Cohn, Alfred E. (Alfred Einstein), 1879-1957.
   ed. 5.746
Cohn-Bendit, Daniel. 3.2215
Cohn-Bendit, Gabriel. joint author. 3.2215
Cohn, Bernard S., ed. 4.6408
Cohn, Dorrit Claire. 2.3481
Cohn, Haim Hermann, 1911- comp. 3.3833
Cohn, Harvey. 5.1340
Cohn, Louis F. (Louis Franklin), 1948-. 5.6002
Cohn, Marjorie B. 1.6111
Cohn, Norman Rufus Colin. 1.2314, 5.681
Cohn, P. M. (Paul Moritz) 5.1359
Cohn, Victor. 5.5163
Coit, Margaret L. 3.7625
Coke, Thomas, 1674-1727. 2.3322, 3.9086
Coke, Van Deren, 1921-. 1.4634
Coker, Francis William, 1878-. 4.7526
Coker, Jerry. 1.4485
Coker, Robert Ervin, 1876-. 5.3254
Colacurcio, Michael J. 2.11074
Colaianni, James F., 1922-. 1.3172
Colangelo, Vito J. 5.5809
Colbeck, Samuel C. 4.317
Colbert, Edwin Harris, 1905-. 5.3168, 5.3170
Colbert, Evelyn Speyer, 1918-. 3.4406
Colburn, David R. 3.6793
Colby College. Library. 2.1971
Colby, Merle Estes, 1902-1969. 3.8648
Colby, Robert Alan, 1920-. 2.8192
Colby, Vineta. 2.2547
Colby, William Egan, 1920-. 4.7903
Colchie, Thomas. 2.5323
Colclaser, Roy A. 5.6453

Cold Spring Harbor Laboratory. 5.3449, 5.3464
Coldstream, J. N. (John Nicolas), 1927-. 3.2580
Coldwell, David F. C. 2.6469
Cole, Arthur Charles, 1886-. 3.7141, 4.8217
Cole, Arthur Harrison, 1889- joint author.
    4.1915
Cole, Bill, 1937-. 1.4082
Cole, Charles Woolsey, 1906-. 4.1360
Cole, David, 1941-. 2.3098
Cole, David Chamberlin, 1928-. 4.2559
Cole, Donald Powell. 3.4050
Cole, Douglas. 2.6620
Cole, Edward Cyrus. joint author. 1.5546,
    2.3146
Cole, Fay Cooper, 1881-. 3.4554
Cole, G. D. H. (George Douglas Howard),
    1889-1959. 2.7962, 3.1517, 4.6377, 4.6931,
    4.7035, 4.7162, 4.8536
Cole, H. H. (Harold Harrison), 1897- ed.
    5.4253
Cole, Herbert M. ed. 1.5085
Cole, J. P. (John Peter), 1928-. 4.2137, 4.2393,
    4.2401, 4.2764
Cole, Jonathan R. 5.967
Cole, Juan Ricardo. 1.2089
Cole, Leonard A., 1933-. 5.968
Cole, Margaret, 1893-1980. 4.7029
Cole, Michael, 1938-. 5.65, 5.100, 5.291, 5.569
Cole, Monica M. 3.5440
Cole, Robert Hartzell. 4.4549
Cole, Sam. 4.2750
Cole, Sheila. 5.100
Cole, Stephen, 1941- joint author. 5.967
Cole, Toby, 1916-. 2.2797, 2.3109, 2.3122
Cole, W. Owen (William Owen) 1.1827
Cole, Wayne S. 3.7677, 3.7755
Cole, William Alan, joint author. 4.2247
Colegate, Isabel. 2.9655
Coleman, Alexander. 2.5457
Coleman, Arthur. 5.7801
Coleman, D. C. (Donald Cuthbert), 1920-.
    4.2260, 4.2275, 4.3857
Coleman, Earle Jerome. 1.6332
Coleman, Francis X. J. 1.903
Coleman, Henry, 1888-1965. 1.3431
Coleman, James Samuel, 1926-. 4.4806, 4.4898,
    4.5752, 4.10048-4.10049, 4.10783
Coleman, James Smoot. 3.5348
Coleman, Janet. 2.5609
Coleman, Kenneth. 3.8257, 3.8260
Coleman, Kenneth M. 3.9051
Coleman, Lee, 1938-. 4.9850
Coleman, R. (Roger), 1938-. 5.3609
Coleman, William, 1934-. 5.3297
Coleman, William D. (William Donald), 1950-.
    3.8817
Coleman, William E. 2.2534
Coleman, William Emmet, 1942-. 1.73
Coleridge, Ernest Hartley, 1846-1920. 2.7587
Coleridge, Samuel Taylor, 1772-1834. 2.5648,
    2.6726, 2.7586-2.7589, 2.7593-2.7594, 2.8308
Coleridge, Sara Coleridge, 1802-1852. 2.7604
Coles, Harry L. 3.7103
Coles, J. M. (John M.) 3.231-3.232, 4.713
Coles, Jane Hallowell. joint author.
    4.5994-4.5995
Coles, Michael G. H. 5.4312
Coles, Robert. 1.3263, 2.13214, 3.8171, 4.2091a,
    4.2092-4.2095, 4.11017, 5.6972
Coles, Robert. 2.13245, 4.5757, 4.5994-4.5995,
    4.6578
Coletta, Paolo Enrico, 1916-. 3.7428, 3.7710,
    5.7450, 5.7473, 5.7844
Colette, 1873-1954. 2.4486-2.4500
Colette, Sidonie Gabrielle, 1873-1954. 2.4496
Coletti, Luigi, 1886-. 1.6206
Colgan, Patrick W. 5.4069
Colgrave, Bertram. ed. 1.2431
Colie, Rosalie Littell. 2.6662
Colledge, Edmund. comp. 2.13942, 2.13944
Colledge, Edmund. 1.3072, 1.3087
College Entrance Examination Board. 4.10078,
    4.10608, 4.10893
College Entrance Examination Board. College
    Scholarship Service. 4.10599
Collender, Stanley E. 4.4680
Collester, J. Bryan. 5.8399
Collet, Pierre, 1948-. 5.1623

Collette, Alfred T. 5.987
Colletti, Lucio. 4.7142
Colley, John Scott. 2.6626
Colley, Linda. 4.8557
Collias, Elsie C. 5.4078
Collias, Nicholas E. (Nicholas Elias), 1914-.
    5.4078
Collie, C. H. 5.2173
Collie, Michael. 2.4251-2.4253, 2.7437, 2.7743
Collier, David, 1942-. 4.8329
Collier, Eugenia W. 2.10685
Collier, James Lincoln, 1928-. 1.4320
Collier, John, 1913-. 4.498, 4.5144
Collier, Malcolm, 1948-. 4.498
Collier, Paul. 4.3235
Collier, Peter. 3.7616
Collier, Richard, 1924-. 5.4763
Collier, Simon. 3.8977, 3.9262
Collin, Françoise, 1928-. 4.4102
Collin, P. H. 5.708
Collin, P. H. (Peter Hodgson) 4.4102
Collin, Robert E. 5.6492
Collinder, Björn, 1894-. 3.3397
Collingridge, David. 5.5517, 5.5630
Collings, E. W. 5.6784
Collingwood, R. G. (Robin George), 1889-1943.
    1.747-1.748, 1.1266, 1.1305, 1.4608, 3.385,
    3.1305, 4.7471
Collini, Stefan, 1947-. 4.7274
Collins, Adela Yarbro. 1.2730
Collins, Douglas, 1945-. 2.4738
Collins, Emily C. joint author. 5.8154
Collins, Fletcher. 1.3654
Collins, George Roseborough, 1917-. 1.5443
Collins, Henry Bascom, 1899-. 3.5876
Collins, Henry Hill, 1905-1961. 5.3826
Collins, J. Lawton (Joseph Lawton). 3.5016
Collins, James Daniel. 1.421, 1.486, 1.1122,
    1.1335, 1.1545
Collins, James J., 1936-. 4.6635
Collins, John Churton, 1848-1908. ed. 2.6582
Collins, John Joseph, 1946-. 1.2554
Collins, Joseph, 1945-. 4.2964
Collins, Larry. 3.3935, 3.4291
Collins, Marva. 4.10156
Collins, Michael, 1930-. 5.6706
Collins, Peter. 1.5242
Collins, Philip Arthur William. 2.7626, 2.7630,
    2.7667-2.7668
Collins, Randall, 1941-. 4.4785
Collins, Raymond F., 1935-. 1.2633
Collins, Robert M. 4.1338
Collins, Roger. 3.3480
Collins, Steven, 1951-. 5.493
Collins, Wilkie, 1824-1889. 2.7605-2.7609
Collins, William, 1721-1759. 2.6939
Collinson, J. D. (John David) 5.3064
Collinson, Patrick. 3.1429
Collinson, William Edward, 1889- joint author.
    2.1177
Collis, John Stewart, 1900-. 2.8623
Collis, Maurice, 1889-. 2.9351
Collison, Robert Lewis. 3.372
Collman, James P. (James Paddock) 1932-.
    5.2779
Collmer, Candace Whitmer. 5.4966
Collon-Gevaert, Suzanne. 1.5027
Collons, Rodger D. 4.2630
Collop, John, fl. 1640-1660. 2.6941
Colloquium on Common Learning (1981:
    University of Chicago) 4.10819
Colloquy on Early South East Asia (1973:
    London, England) 3.4383
Colman, David. 4.1800
Colman, Ernest Adrian Mackenzie. 2.6727
Colman, George, 1732-1794. 2.6236
Colman, William G. 4.8847
Colmer, John. 2.8657
Colombe, Jean, d. 1529. illus. 1.6428
Colón, Fernando, 1488-1539. 3.5972
Colonne, Guido delle, 13th century. 2.819
Colorado Springs Fine Arts Center. 1.6450
Colorado. University. 5.6694
Colorado. Writers' Program. 3.8555
Colowick, Sidney P. ed. 5.4410
Colson, Elizabeth, 1917-. 4.600
Colson, Francis Henry, 1857-1943. 2.383
Colston Research Society. 5.2108

Colton, Harold Sellers, 1881-. 3.5887
Colton, Joel G., 1918-. 3.609, 3.2201
Colton, Timothy J., 1947-. 4.8644
Colucci, Joseph M. 5.6877
Colum, Mary (Maguire) 2.8904, 2.11508
Colum, Padraic, 1881-1972. 2.8523-2.8525,
    2.8904
Columbia College (Columbia University)
    1.1798, 2.1936, 3.1, 3.90, 5.8337
Columbia University. 1.21, 1.97, 3.525, 4.9925
Columbia University. East Asian Institute.
    3.4769, 3.4808
Columbia University. Institute of War and
    Peace Studies. 4.9052, 4.9248
Columbia University. Legislative Drafting
    Research Fund. 4.9608
Columbia University. Press. 4.69
Columbia University. Research Institute on
    Communist Affairs. 3.4808, 3.7840, 4.7050
Columbia University. Russian Institute. 3.3211,
    4.8880
Columbia University. Teachers College.
    Institute of Psychological Research. 4.10363
Columbus, Christopher. 3.5976
Colver, A. Wayne (Anthony Wayne) 1.1551
Colvin, Geoffrey. 5.7586
Colvin, Howard Montagu. 1.5358, 1.5378
Colvin, Sidney, Sir, 1845-1927. ed. 2.8122
Colwell, Robert N. 4.23
Comber, L. C. 5.982
Comblin, Joseph, 1923-. 1.2804
Combs, Arthur Wright. 4.10242, 4.10262,
    4.10632, 5.466
Combs, Homer Carroll. 2.6459
Combs, James E. 3.6180
Combs, Jerald A. 3.6399, 3.7040
Comenius, Johann Amos, 1592-1670. 4.10184
Comer, James P. 4.10967
Comerchero, Victor. 2.12683
Comfort, Alex, 1920-. 1.1267, 2.8526
Comini, Alessandra. 1.6045
Comisso, Ellen Turkish. 4.3188
Comitas, Lambros. 5.7901
Comitas, Lambros. joint author. 4.5260
Comitas, Lambros. comp. 4.6429
Comité national français de géographie. 4.173
Commager, Henry Steele, ed. 1.3414, 2.723,
    2.11085, 3.6022, 3.6095-3.6096,
    3.6193-3.6194, 3.6318, 3.6324, 3.6884, 3.7311,
    4.5169, 4.7685
Commins, Dorothy. 2.2519
Commins, Eugene D. 5.2486
Commins, Saxe. comp. 2.4269
Commire, Anne. 2.2549
Commission of Inquiry into the Black Panthers
    and the Police. 4.6833
Commission of the European Communities.
    4.2217, 5.5037, 5.6883
Commission on Biochemical Nomenclature.
    5.4414
Commission on College Physics. 5.2384
Commission on Financing Higher Education.
    4.10062
Commission on Freedom of the Press. 2.3548
Commission on Non-traditional Study. 4.10548
Commission on Race and Housing. 3.6785
Committee for Economic Development. 4.2089,
    4.2710
Committee for Public Justice (U.S.) 4.6820
Committee for Rational Development (Sri
    Lanka) 3.4364
Committee for the World Atlas of Agriculture.
    4.136
Committee of Concerned Asian Scholars. 3.4456
Committee on African Development Strategies
    (U.S.) 4.2612
Committee on Basic Research in Education.
    4.10651
Committee on Institutional Cooperation. 1.6721
Commodity Research Bureau (New York,
    N.Y.) 4.4128
Common, Thomas, tr. 1.1045
Commoner, Barry, 1917-. 4.3704, 4.3718,
    5.5999, 5.6871
Commons, John Rogers, 1862-1945. 4.1305,
    4.1370, 4.1426, 4.1499, 4.1566, 4.1872, 4.3557
Commonwealth Fund. Legal Research
    Committee. 4.9905

Communications Trends, Inc. 5.7577
Communist International. 4.6926
Community for Creative Non-violence (Washington, D.C.) 4.6629
Comnena, Anna, b. 1083. 3.2671
Compaine, Benjamin M. 2.73
Companion, Audrey L. 5.2812
Comparato, Frank E. 5.7565
Comparetti, Domenico Pietro Antonio, 1835-1927. 2.807
Compayré, Gabriel, 1843-1913. 4.9974
Compcon. 20th, San Francisco, 1980. 5.6543
Compton, Arthur Holly, 1892-1962. 5.2017, 5.2416
Compton, Beulah Roberts. 4.6474
Compton, Boyd, ed. and tr. 4.8747
Compton-Burnett, I. (Ivy), 1884-1969. 2.8527-2.8531
Compton-Hall, Richard. 5.7440
Compton, Robert R. 5.2989
Compton, Susan P. 1.5038
Comrie, Bernard, 1947-. 2.1223
Comstock, George A. 4.4073
Comstock, Helen. 1.6562
Comstock, Helen. ed. 1.6512
Comstock, Jim F. 3.8225
Comstock, John Henry, 1849-1931. 5.3854
Comstock, Mary. 1.5620, 1.6668
Comte, Auguste, 1798-1857. 1.819-1.821, 4.4851
Conacher, D. J. 2.411, 2.466
Conant, James Bryant, 1893-1978. 4.9995, 4.10050-4.10051, 4.10200, 4.10492, 4.10518, 4.10732, 5.719, 5.843, 5.876, 5.983, 5.2738
Conant, Kenneth John, 1894-. 1.5232
Conant, Michael. 4.4001
Conant, Miriam Bernheim. 3.456
Conant, Roger, 1909-. 5.3920
Conard, Henry Shoemaker, 1874-. 5.3703, 5.3765
Conard, Robert C., 1933-. 2.13697
Conati, Marcello. 1.4023
Condit, Carl W. 1.5301, 4.4007
Condivi, Ascanio, b. ca. 1520. 1.5013
Condominas, Georges. 3.4430
Condon, Edward Uhler, 1902-1974. 5.1977, 5.2313, 5.6694
Condon, Gregg A., 1947-. 2.1028
Condon, Patricia. 1.6111
Condon, Richard G. (Richard Guy) 3.5875
Condorcet, Jean-Antoine-Nicolas de Caritat, marquis de, 1743-1794. 3.7
Cone, Carl B. 3.1561
Cone, Edward T. 1.3469, 1.3478, 1.4476
Cone, Edward T. joint comp. 1.3461
Cone, James H. 1.2786, 1.2796-1.2798, 1.2916
Confederate States of America. 4.9906
Conference Board. 4.1995
Conference of Heads of State or Government of Non-aligned Countries. 3.1147
Conference on a Century of Russian Foreign Policy, Yale University, 1961. 3.3056
Conference on Advertising and Consumer Psychology. (2nd: 1983: Chicago, Ill.) 4.4431
Conference on American Economic Institutional Change, 1850-1873, and the Impact of the Civil War, Greenville, Del., 1964. 4.1920
Conference on Bureaucracy and Political Development (1962: Center for Advanced Study in the Behavioral Sciences) 4.7752
Conference on Changes in the Status of Women in Eastern Europe (1981: George Washington University) 4.5964
Conference on Discrimination in Labor Markets, Princeton University, 1971. 4.3116
Conference on Education and Income, University of Wisconsin, 1968. 4.1955
Conference on Estuaries, Jekyll Island, 1964. 4.338
Conference on Ethical Issues and Moral Principles in United States Refugee Policy (1983: Washington, D.C.) 4.6538
Conference on Future, Technology, and Woman (1981: San Diego State University) 4.5898
Conference on Hope and the Future of Man, New York, 1971. 1.3062
Conference on Life in the Universe (1979: Ames Research Center) 5.1728

Conference on Ming Thought, Champaign, Ill., 1966. 3.4645
Conference on Modern Chinese Economic History, T'ai-pei, 1977. 4.2457
Conference on Modern Japan. 3.4889, 3.4896, 3.4971, 4.2544, 4.5446
Conference on New Communities, Washington, D.C., 1971. 4.6317
Conference on Oriental Classics in General Education, Columbia University, 1958. 2.1758
Conference on Population and Intergroup Relations, New York, N.Y., 1975. 4.1670
Conference on Production Relations, New York, 1965. 4.1953
Conference on Representation and Reapportionment Issues of the 1980s (1980: San Diego, Calif.) 4.9730
Conference on Research in Income and Wealth. 4.1950-4.1952, 4.1955
Conference on Research in National Income and Wealth. 4.1950
Conference on Seventeenth-Century Chinese Thought, Bellagio, Italy, 1970. 1.160
Conference on Sex and Behavior, Berkeley, Calif. 5.4085
Conference on Soviet Agricultural and Peasant Affairs, Santa Barbara, Calif., 1965. 4.2974
Conference on the Comparative Reception of Darwinism, Austin, Tex., 1972. 5.3343
Conference on the Industrial Composition of Income and Product, Brookings Institute, 1966. 4.1954
Conference on the Long-Term Worldwide Biological Consequences of Nuclear War (1983: Washington, D.C.) 5.3578
Conference on the Marine Transportation, Handling, and Storage of Bulk Chemicals. (6th: 1985: London, England) 5.6859
Conference on the Measurement of Labor Cost (1981: Williamsburg, Va.) 4.3147
Conference on the Modern History of Egypt, University of London, 1965. 3.5130
Conference on the Russian Revolution, Harvard University, 1967. 3.3173
Confucius. 1.165
Congar, Marie Joseph, 1904-. 1.3212
Congar, Yves Marie Joseph, 1904-. 1.3105
Conger, Amy, 1942-. 5.6932
Congrat-Butlar, Stefan. 2.193
Congress of African Peoples, Atlanta, 1970. 4.6460
Congressional Information Service. 5.7782
Congressional Quarterly, Inc. 3.3739, 3.6420, 3.7912, 3.7918, 3.8109, 4.7992, 4.7997, 4.8015, 4.8067, 4.8107, 4.9438, 4.9657, 4.9754, 5.7264
Congreve, William, 1670-1729. 2.6943-2.6946
Conisbee, Philip. 1.6049
Conkin, Paul Keith. 3.7756
Conklin, Groff, 1904-1968. ed. 2.10829
Conklin, Harold C. 4.185
Conklin, Henry, 1832-1915. 3.8032
Conkling, Philip W. 5.3269
Conley, Ronald W. 4.6608
Conley, Verena Andermatt, 1943-. 2.4780
Conlin, Joseph Robert. ed. 4.6924
Conn, Eric E. 5.3750, 5.4395
Connecticut Academy of Arts and Sciences. 2.5607
Connell, Evan S., 1924-. 2.12952-2.12953
Connell, Joseph H., joint author. 5.4073
Connell, K. H. (Kenneth Hugh), 1917-1973. 4.1696
Connell-Smith, Gordon. 3.9015
Connell, William Fraser. 4.10192
Connelley, William Elsey, 1855-1930. 2.11213
Connelly, Joseph Alvin, 1942-. 5.6524
Connelly, Marc, 1890-. 2.11509
Connelly, Thomas Lawrence. 3.7369
Connery, Robert Howe, 1907-. 3.7641, 4.8264
Connoisseur (The) 1.6505
Connolly, Cyril, 1903-1974. 2.5730, 2.8537-2.8539
Connolly, Joseph. 2.9559
Connolly, Julian W. 2.1481
Connolly, Michael B. (Michael Bahaamonde), 1941-. 4.4700
Connolly, Michael J. 4.9443

Connolly, Peter. 5.7178
Connolly, Terence Leo, 1888- ed. 2.2597
Connolly, Terry. 5.829
Connolly, Thomas Edmund, 1918-. 2.8139, 2.8879
Connor, Anthony, 1946-. 1.4295
Connor, Billie M., 1934-. 5.8130
Connor, Denis, 1934-. 5.5606
Connor, John M. 4.3679, 5.8130
Connor, Seymour V. 3.7136
Connor, Tony. 2.8540
Connor, W. Robert (Walter Robert), 1934-. 2.561, 3.2653
Connor, Walter D. 4.5296, 4.6794
Connors, Debra. 4.6597
Connors, Joseph. 1.5534
Connotillo, Barbara Cahn. 4.10540
Conolly, Brian. 5.5564
Conolly, L. W. (Leonard W.) 2.3100, 5.7951
Conolly, Violet. 4.2566
Conot, Robert E. 4.9334
Conover, Helen Field. 5.7679, 5.8074
Conquest, Robert. 2.6186, 3.3214, 3.3247, 3.3273, 4.8645
Conrad, Alfred H. 4.1756
Conrad, Clifton. 4.10590
Conrad, David Eugene. 4.2908
Conrad, David R., 1937-. 4.10251
Conrad, Geoffrey W. 3.8905
Conrad, Jessie (George). 2.8558
Conrad, Jessie George, d. 1936. 2.8557
Conrad, John Phillips, 1913-. 4.6853
Conrad, Joseph, 1857-1924. 2.8541-2.8547, 2.8549-2.8554
Conran, Anthony, 1931-. 2.848
Conron, Brandon. 2.9919
Conroy, Hilary, 1919-. 3.4957, 3.5002, 3.6559
Conroy, Patricia L. 2.14008
Consejo Latinoamericano de Ciencias Sociales. 5.8402
Conservation Foundation. 5.5992
Considine, Douglas Maxwell. ed. 5.6808
Considine, Douglas Maxwell. 5.705, 5.2596, 5.7033, 5.7104
Considine, Glenn D. 5.2596, 5.7033
Consortium for the Study of Intelligence. 5.7363
Consortium of University Film Centers. 4.10330
Constable, Archibald, 3.4256
Constable, John, 1776-1837. 1.6027
Constable, W. G. (William George), 1887-. 1.6043, 1.6194
Constant, Benjamin, 1767-1830. 2.4154-2.4155
Constant, Edward W. 5.6677
Constantelos, Demetrios J. 1.3108
Constantin, James A. 4.4127
Constantine, Joan M., joint author. 4.5785
Constantine, Larry L. 4.5785
Constantine, Mildred. 1.4795, 1.4834
Constantine, Stephen. 4.2305
Constantinescu, F. (Florin), 1938-. 5.2222
Contamine, Philippe. 5.7187
Contat, Michel. 2.4718, 2.4739
Conte, Frank P., 1929-. 5.3915
Contenau, G. (Georges), b. 1877. 3.3774
Contento, William. 5.7809
Contini, Gianfranco. comp. 2.4887
Contini, Gianfranco. 2.4889-2.4892, 2.5047
Contini, Gianfranco. ed. 2.4919
Convention of National Societies of Electrical Engineers of Western Europe. 5.5959
Converse, Philip E., 1928-. 4.5180
Conway, Alan. 3.6599
Conway, H. McKinley (Hobart McKinley), 1920- ed. 5.2574
Conway, Jill K., 1934-. 4.5981
Conway, John Horton. 5.1256, 5.1320
Conway, Lynn. joint author. 5.6536
Conway, Moncure Daniel, 1832-1907. 4.7424
Conwell, Chic, d. 1933. 4.6701
Conybeare, F. C. (Frederick Cornwallis), 1856-1924. 2.385
Conyers, James E., 1932-. 4.8091
Conze, Edward, 1904-. 1.1738-1.1739, 1.1766, 1.1769, 1.2107, 1.2130-1.2132
Conzelmann, Hans. 1.2294, 1.2655, 1.2713, 1.2720, 1.2859
Cook, Adrian. 3.8037

Cook, Albert S. (Albert Stanburrough),
  1853-1927. 2.6074, 2.6280-2.6281, 2.7057
Cook, Albert Spaulding. 2.2672
Cook, Alice Hanson. 4.3269, 4.3301, 4.3423
Cook, Arthur Bernard, 1868-1952. 1.1666
Cook, Blanche Wiesen. 3.7820
Cook, Bruce, 1932-. 4.5765
Cook, Chris, 1945-. 3.1709, 4.8358-4.8359,
  4.8485
Cook, David, 1929-. 2.10046, 2.10097
Cook, David A. 2.2877
Cook, Davidson, 1874-1941. ed. 2.8053
Cook, Dorothy Elizabeth, 1890-1959. 5.8170,
  5.8178
Cook, Edward Tyas, Sir, 1857-1919. 2.8023
Cook, Elizabeth Christine, 1876-. 2.3593
Cook, Francis Dojun, 1930-. 1.2166
Cook, J. M. (John Manuel) 3.2640, 3.4075
Cook, Joanne Valiant. 4.6545
Cook, John Wesley, 1933-. 1.5474
Cook, Olive. 1.5572
Cook, Ramsay. joint author. 3.8740
Cook, Ramsay. 3.8682, 3.8722, 3.8744
Cook, Reginald Lansing, 1903-. 2.11018,
  2.11753
Cook, Richard I. 2.7102
Cook, Robert Davis. 5.5850
Cook, Robert Manuel. 1.6632
Cook, Sherburne Friend, 1896-1974. 3.5720,
  4.1686
Cook, Sylvia Jenkins, 1943-. 2.10445
Cook, Walter Wheeler, 1873-1943. 4.9358
Cook, Warren L. 3.8592
Cooke, Alan, 1933-. 3.8867
Cooke, Alistair, 1908-. 3.6055, 3.7547
Cooke, D. J. (Derek John), 1947-. 5.1248
Cooke, Deryck. 1.4506
Cooke, Edward Ingram. 5.6810
Cooke, Harold Percy, 1882- tr. 2.347
Cooke, Jacob Ernest, 1924-. 3.6969, 3.6998,
  4.7827
Cooke, James J. 3.5117
Cooke, Melinda W. 3.5533
Cooke, Richard W. I. 5.6810
Cooke, Robert, 1935-. 5.3113
Cooke, Roger. 5.1438
Cooke, Ronald U. 4.281
Cooke, Thomas P. 4.6611
Cooke, William Bridge. 5.3724
Cooley, Charles Horton, 1864-1929.
  4.4982-4.4983
Cooley, Thomas, 1942-. 2.10942
Cooley, Thomas McIntyre, 1824-1898. 4.9646
Coolidge, Archibald Cary, 1866-1928. 2.11048,
  3.3582
Coolidge, Julian Lowell, 1873-1954. 5.1069
Cooling, B. Franklin. 3.7452
Coolman, Jacqueline, 1945-. 5.8268
Coomaraswamy, Ananda Kentish, 1877-1947.
  1.1813, 1.5044, 1.5127
Coomaraswamy, Radhika. 4.9919
Coombes, H. 2.9425
Coombs, Clyde Hamilton, 1912-. 5.41-5.43
Coombs, Orde. comp. 3.9139
Coombs, Philip Hall, 1915-. 4.9965, 4.10970
Coon, Carleton Stevens, 1904-. 3.3680, 4.702
Cooney, John. 2.3602
Coons, John E. 4.10635
Coontz, Sydney H. 4.1629
Cooper, A. M. 5.8437
Cooper, Arthur D., comp. 2.2212
Cooper, Cary L. 5.446
Cooper, Chester L. 3.4484
Cooper, David Edward. 1.466
Cooper, David Edwin, 1944-. 1.3548
Cooper, Doug. 5.1221
Cooper, Douglas, 1911-. 1.4842
Cooper, Emmanuel. 1.6609
Cooper, Frederick, 1947-. 4.6450
Cooper, Gayle. 5.7750
Cooper, George R. 5.6368
Cooper, Grosvenor. 1.4461
Cooper, Harris M. 4.10375
Cooper, Helen. 2.6323
Cooper, Helen A. 1.5979
Cooper-Hewitt Museum. 1.6544, 1.6597, 1.6629
Cooper, Homer Choppell, 1923-, jt. author.
  4.8076

Cooper, J. P. (John Phillips), 1920-1978. joint
  comp. 4.2268
Cooper, Jack R., 1924-. 5.4301
Cooper, Jackie. 5.1393
Cooper, James Fenimore, 1789-1851.
  2.10972-2.10973
Cooper, James William, 1943-. 5.2746
Cooper, John Charles. 1.2755
Cooper, John L., 1936-. 4.6817
Cooper, John M. (John Madison), 1939-. 1.311
Cooper, John Milton. 3.6307
Cooper, John Rex, 1912-. 2.7333
Cooper, Joshua, tr. 2.1317
Cooper, Julian, 1945-. 4.2408, 5.5543
Cooper, Kenneth H. 5.4693
Cooper, Kent, 1880-. 2.3611
Cooper, Lane, 1875-1959. 2.2530, 2.2825
Cooper, Lynn A. 5.321
Cooper, Martin, 1910-. 1.3706, 1.3798
Cooper, Michael, 1930- ed. 3.4878
Cooper, Patricia A. 5.4690
Cooper, Richard N. 4.4570
Cooper, S. Kerry. 4.4532
Cooper, Wendy A. 1.6519
Cooper, William J. (William James), 1940-.
  3.8138-3.8139
Cooper, William W. (William Wager), 1914-.
  4.4391
Cooperative Assessment of Experiential
  Learning (Project) 4.10626
Cooperative Research Project on Agricultural
  Technology in Latin America. 5.5256
Cooperman, Stanley. 2.10399
Coopersmith, Stanley, 1926-. 5.615
Coote, Stephen. 2.3755
Coover, James, 1925-. 1.3615
Coover, Robert. 2.12954-2.12955
Cope, Jack. 2.10050, 2.10063, 2.13962
Copeland, J. Isaac (James Isaac), 1910-. 5.7853
Copeland, Lewis. 2.3779
Copeland, Richard W. 5.1262
Cophen, Barry. 4.9057
Copi, Irving M. 1.1147, 1.1165, 1.1191, 1.1205,
  1.1256
Copi, Irving M. ed. 1.1228
Copland, Aaron, 1900-. 1.3483, 1.3668, 1.3841,
  1.4403, 1.4426
Copleston, Frederick Charles. 1.122, 1.348
Copley, Frank Olin. 2.624, 2.739
Coppa, Frank J. 3.2854
Copperud, Roy H., 1915-. 2.1040
Copson, E. T. (Edward Thomas), 1901-. 5.1529
Coptic Gnostic Library Project. 1.2968
Copway, George, Chippewa chief, 1818?-1863.
  3.5790
Corbally, John E. (John Edward), 1924-.
  4.10634
Corbet, G. B. (Gordon Barclay) 5.3978
Corbet, Richard, Bp. of Norwich, 1582-1635.
  2.6951
Corbett, Edward P. J. comp. 2.5481
Corbett, Julian Stafford, Sir, 1854-1922. 3.1275,
  3.1279
Corbett, Percy Ellwood, 1892-. 4.9003, 4.9278,
  5.7384
Corbière, Tristan, 1845-1875. 2.4156, 2.4158
Corbin, Arthur L. (Arthur Linton), 1874-1967.
  4.9513
Corbin, David. 4.3538
Corbin, Peter B., joint author. 4.4126
Corcoran Gallery of Art. 1.4916, 1.6284
Corcoran, John. 1.1223
Corcoran, Neil. 2.8853
Corcoran, Paul E., 1944-. 4.7046
Cordasco, Francesco, 1920-. 3.6556, 3.6588,
  4.10849, 4.10895, 5.7862
Cordell, Linda S. 3.5756
Cordell, Richard Albert. 2.9107
Corden, W. M. (Warner Max) 4.4564
Corder, Colin R. joint author. 4.4349
Cordesman, Anthony H. 5.7347
Cordié, Carlo. 2.4955
Cordilia, Ann. 4.6907
Cordingley, Reginald Annandale, 1896-. 1.5498
Cordner, Michael. 2.7009
Córdova, Efrén. 4.3627
Cordovero, Moses ben Jacob, 1522-1570. 1.1482
Core, George. 2.12369

Core, H. A. 5.5430
Corea, Gena. 5.4254
Coren, Stanley. 5.237, 5.4387
Corey, Albert Bickmore. 3.8723
Corey, Peter L. 3.5751
Corlew, Robert Ewing. 3.8346
Corley, Nora T. 5.7737
Corley, Robert Neil. joint author. 4.4396
Corley, T. A. B. (Thomas Anthony Buchanan),
  1923-. 3.2158
Corliss, Clark Edward. 5.4166
Corliss, Richard. 2.3033
Corliss, William R. 5.2507, 5.2556, 5.2557
Corliss, William R. joint author. 5.6604
Cormier, Frank. 4.3594
Cormier, Raymond J., 1938-. 2.3950
Corn, Alfred, 1943-. 2.12957-2.12958
Cornebise, Alfred E. 3.2419
Corneille, Pierre, 1606-1684. 2.4015-2.4017
Cornell, A. D. joint author. 5.670
Cornell, James. 5.1751, 5.1788
Cornell, Tim. 3.2725
Cornell University. 4.6249
Cornell University. Libraries. 5.8060
Cornell University. Modern Indonesia Project.
  3.4569
Cornell University. Peace Studies Program.
  4.9009
Cornell University. Program on Science,
  Technology, and Society. 4.2895
Cornell University. Southeast Asia Program.
  3.4519
Cornell University. Western Societies Program.
  3.1716
Cornell University Workshop on Food,
  Population, and Employment: the Social
  Impact of Modernizing Agriculture, Ithaca,
  N.Y., 1971. 4.2895
Cornell, William Kenneth. 2.3878
Cornelsen, Doris. 4.2346
Corner, Paul. 3.2949
Cornes, Paul. joint author. 4.6920
Cornet, Joseph. 1.5087
Cornevin, Marianne. 3.5449
Corney, Alan. 5.2378
Cornfeld, Gaalyahu, 1902-. 1.2543
Cornford, Frances Darwin, 1886-1960. 2.8580
Cornford, Francis Macdonald, 1874-1943.
  1.223-1.224, 1.232, 1.248, 1.253, 1.255, 2.348
Cornforth, John, 1937-. 1.5565, 1.5573, 1.6543
Corning, Howard McKinley, 1896-. 3.8638,
  3.8642
Corning Museum of Glass. 1.6642
Cornish, Dudley Taylor. 3.7388
Cornish, Edward, 1927-. 3.66
Cornish, Roger, 1934-. 2.6246
Cornsweet, Tom N. 5.4382
Cornwall, Ian Wolfram. 3.247
Cornwall, John. 4.1783
Corominas, Joan. 2.893
Corot, Jean-Baptiste-Camille, 1796-1875. 1.6078
Corpus Christi College (University of
  Cambridge) 3.1372
Corr, Michael. 4.3718, 5.5999, 5.6871
Correa, Gustavo. 2.5147
Corrigan, Robert Willoughby, 1927-. 2.4900,
  2.5157, 2.10800, 2.12176
Corrigan, Timothy. 2.2895
Corsi, Pietro. 5.736
Corsini, Raymond J. 5.12, 5.512
Corson, James Clarkson. 2.8054
Corson, Richard. 2.3129
Corson, William R. 4.7904
Cort, Louise Allison, 1944-. 1.6623
Cortada, James W. 3.3454, 3.3466, 3.6496
Cortázar, Julio. 2.5378-2.5385
Cortés Conde, Roberto. 5.8402
Cortés, Hernán, 1485-1547. 3.8921
Cortés, Juan B. 4.6677
Cortner, Richard C. 4.9665
Corvisier, André. 5.7294
Corwin, Edward Samuel, 1878-1963. 3.6935,
  4.7686, 4.7798-4.7799, 4.9618, 4.9628, 4.9738
Corwin, Harold G. joint author. 5.1857
Cory, Daniel, 1904-. 1.650
Corya, William L. 5.8288
Coser, Lewis A., 1913-. 3.6566, 4.4739, 4.4829,
  4.4939-4.4940, 4.8235, 5.7584

Ćosić, Dobrica, 1921-. 2.1212
Cosman, Carol. joint author. 2.4308
Cosman, Carol. 2.3749
Cosmas, Graham A. 3.7505
Costa, Charles Desmond Nuttall. 2.772
Costa, Joseph J. 4.6590
Costa, Maria Velho da. 2.5460
Costa, Paul T. joint author. 5.526
Costa, Richard Hauer. 2.9061
Costakis, Georgi. 1.5036
Costello, D.P. 2.1309
Costello, Elaine. 4.6606
Costello, John. joint author. 3.962
Costello, John. 3.819
Costello, Lawrence, joint comp. 4.3605
Costello, Peter. 2.4326, 2.9858
Costeloe, Michael P. 1.3186
Coster, Charles de, 1827-1879. 2.4157
Costich, Julia F. 2.4382
Costin, Lela B. 4.6547
Costonis, John J. 4.6340
Côté, Wilfred A. joint author. 5.5430
Cotes, Peter, 1912- joint author. 4.1184
Cotgrave, Randle, d. 1634? 2.878
Cotler, Julio. ed. 3.9018
Cotnam, Jacques. comp. 2.4807
Cott, Nancy F. 4.6007
Cott, Nancy F. comp. 4.5982
Cotter, Charles H. 5.7491
Cotter, Cornelius P. 4.8162
Cotter, Michael. 5.8062
Cotterill, Rodney, 1933-. 5.2080
Cottle, Basil. 3.308
Cottle, Thomas J. 4.5572, 4.6870, 4.10936,
    5.402
Cottom, Daniel. 2.5936
Cotton, Charles, 1630-1687. 2.6952, 5.5489
Cotton, Charles Andrew, 1885-. 5.3109
Cotton, F. Albert (Frank Albert), 1930-. 5.2698,
    5.2813
Cottrell, Leonard. ed. 3.218
Cottrell, Leonard Slater, 1899-. 3.7562
Cottrell, P. L. 4.3061
Cottrell, Robert D. 2.4501
Cottrell, William Frederick, 1903-. 4.3540
Cottrol, Robert J. 3.8019
Couch, William, comp. 2.10797
Coughlan, Margaret N., 1925-. 5.7717
Coughtry, Jay. 3.7218
Coulborn, Rushton, comp. 4.7374
Coulon, Virginia. 2.2691
Coulson, Andrew. 4.2619
Coulson, C. A. (Charles Alfred), 1910-1974.
    5.2836
Coulson, J. M. (John Metcalfe) 5.6829
Coulson, Jessie Senior, 1903- joint author.
    2.1083
Coulson, John, 1919-. 1.3248
Coulson, Noel J. (Noel James) 1.2040
Coulson, Robert N. (Robert Norris), 1943-.
    5.5405
Coulthard, G.R. 2.2694-2.2695
Coulton, G. G. (George Gordon), 1858-1947.
    3.1329
Coulton, J. J. 1.5217
Council for Exceptional Children. 4.10931
Council for Exceptional Children Division on
    Mental Retardation. 4.10949
Council, Norman. 2.6833
Council of Educational Facility Planners.
    4.10719
Council of Educational Facility Planners,
    International. 4.10719
Council of Europe. 3.1195
Council of Foreign Relations. 5.5540
Council of National Library Associations.
    5.7659
Council of State Governments. 4.8242
Council of the British National Bibliography.
    5.7912-5.7913
Council of Trent (1545-1563) 1.3130
Council on Economic Priorities. 5.6057
Council on Environmental Quality (U.S.) 5.5991
Council on Foreign Relations. 2.3558, 3.754,
    3.3563, 3.3726, 3.4414, 3.5099, 3.7577,
    4.2476, 4.2576, 4.2612, 4.7709, 4.8971,
    4.9021, 5.7338, 5.8253, 5.8255
Council on Postsecondary Accreditation. 4.9936

Council on Tall Buildings and Urban Habitat.
    5.6088-5.6089
Council on Undergraduate Research (U.S.)
    5.2636
Council on Wage and Price Stability (U.S.)
    4.2002
Counsilman, James E. 4.989
Countryman, Edward. 3.6944
Countryman, Vern. 4.9448, 4.9809
Counts, George S. (George Sylvester),
    1889-1974. 4.10003, 4.10243
Couper, A. D. 4.194
Couperie, Pierre. 1.5846
Couperus, Louis, 1863-1923. 2.13949
Coupland, R. T. 5.3554
Coupland, Reginald, 1884-. 3.8724
Courant, Richard, 1888-1972. 5.1105, 5.1450,
    5.1540
Courcelle, Pierre Paul, 1912-. 2.284
Courlander, Harold, 1908-. 1.4297, 4.785
Cournes, John, 1881- tr. 2.1525
Cournos, John, 1881-1966. 2.1530
Cournot, A. A. (Antoine Augustin), 1801-1877.
    4.1293
Court, William Henry Bassano. 4.2246
Courtenay, P. P. (Percy Philip) 4.2875
Courtés, Joseph, 1936-. 2.81
Courthéoux, Jean Paul. joint author. 4.2326
Courthion, Pierre. 1.6144, 1.6148
Courtine, Robert J. 5.7105
Courtney, E. (Edward), 1932-. 2.730
Courtney, John C. 4.8303
Courtney, Winifred F., 1918-. 2.7906
Courtwright, David T., 1952-. 4.6661
Cousin, John William, 1849-1910. 2.5482-2.5483
Cousins, Ewert H. 1.3134
Cousins, Ewert H. ed. 1.3062
Cousins, Paul M. 2.11050
Cousteau, Jacques Yves. 5.3251, 5.7514
Coustillas, Pierre. 2.7730, 2.7732, 2.7740
Coustillas, Pierre. comp. 2.7744
Coutinho, Afrânio. 2.5461
Couton, Georges. ed. 2.4039
Couton, Georges. 2.4015
Couturier, Jean J., joint author. 4.3512
Couturier, Maurice, 1939-. 2.12895
Couty, Daniel. 2.3819
Covarrubias, Miguel, 1904-1957. 3.8899
Covell, Charles V. 5.3883
Covell, Jon Etta Hastings Carter, 1910-. 1.2153
Covell, Ralph R. 1.3029
Covello, Vincent T. 5.5635
Coverdale, John F., 1940-. 3.3451, 4.8680
Covici, Pascal, 1885-1964, comp. 2.12524
Cowan, C. F. N. (Colin F. N.) 5.6510
Cowan, Edward A. 3.1801
Cowan, Ian Borthwick. 1.2359
Cowan, J. Milton. 2.1832
Cowan, James, 1870-1943. 3.5599
Cowan, John Charles, 1911- joint author.
    5.7129
Cowan, Louise, 1916-. 2.10446
Cowan, Ruth Schwartz, 1941-. 5.7100
Cowan, Sam, 1943-. 5.6469
Cowan, Samuel Tertius. 5.4429
Coward, Barry. 3.1441
Coward, Joan Wells, 1936-. 3.8356
Coward, Noel, 1899-1973. 2.8581-2.8582,
    2.8584-2.8585
Coward, Noel Pierce, 1899-. 2.8583
Cowardin, Lewis M. 5.3263
Cowart, David, 1947-. 2.13033, 2.13283
Cowart, Georgia. 1.4407
Coward, Bartlett. 1.5959
Cowdry, E. V. (Edmund Vincent), 1888-1975.
    5.4156
Cowell, Edward Byles, 1826-1903, ed. and tr.
    1.1737
Cowell, Frank Richard, 1897-. 3.2760
Cowell, Henry, 1897-1965. 1.3695, 1.3902
Cowell, Pattie. 2.10866
Cowell, Sidney Robertson, Mrs., joint author.
    1.3902
Cowen, Roy C., 1930-. 2.13588
Cowhey, Peter F., 1948-. 4.3765
Cowie, Alexander, 1896-. 2.10537
Cowie, Anthony Paul. 2.1105
Cowie, Leonard W. 3.624

Cowles, Virginia. 3.298
Cowley, Abraham, 1618-1667. 2.6953-2.6955
Cowley, Malcolm, 1898-. 2.4552, 2.10379,
    2.10400-2.10402, 2.10615, 2.11057,
    2.11510-2.11511, 2.11689
Cowley, W. H. (William Harold), 1899-.
    4.10591
Cowper, William, 1731-1800. 2.6957-2.6960
Cox, Allan, 1926-1987. comp. 5.3091
Cox, Annette. 1.5909
Cox, C. B. 2.5971
Cox, C. Barry (Christopher Barry), 1931-.
    5.3238, 5.3916
Cox, Clyde H. C. B. 2.8560
Cox, D. R. (David Roxbee) 5.877
Cox, Dianne L. 2.11660
Cox, Donald D. 5.3306
Cox, Edward Franklin, 1925-. 4.8100
Cox, Edward Godfrey, 1876-1963. 5.8208
Cox, Edwin Burk, 1930-. 4.4418
Cox, Harvey Gallagher. 1.2776
Cox, Henry Bartholomew. 4.9741
Cox, Hyde. ed. 2.11749
Cox, J. Halley, 1910-. 1.5784
Cox, J. Robert. 1.1237
Cox, James Melville, 1925-. 2.10953, 2.11754
Cox, John Stuart. 5.5674
Cox, June, 1919-. 4.10918
Cox, Kevin R., 1939-. 4.383, 4.2882, 4.6351
Cox, LaWanda C. Fenlason. 3.7287
Cox, Martha Heasley. 2.11309
Cox, Oliver C. (Oliver Cromwell), 1901-1974.
    3.6702, 4.6378
Cox, Peter R. 4.1613
Cox, Ralph Merritt, 1939-. 2.5216
Cox, Robert W., 1926-. 4.9265
Cox, Sandra J. 5.7884
Cox, Sidney, 1889-1952. 2.11755
Cox, Sue. 4.5924
Cox, Thomas S., 1944-. 3.5374
Cox, Warren Earle, 1895-. 1.6610
Cox, William Edwin, 1930-1978. 4.4302
Coxe, A. Cleveland (Arthur Cleveland),
    1818-1896. ed. 1.2194
Coxe, Louis Osborne, 1918-. 2.12405
Coxeter, H. S. M. (Harold Scott Macdonald),
    1907-. 5.1564, 5.1634, 5.1636
Coxhead, Elizabeth, 1909-. 2.7752, 2.7756
Coyle, J. D. (John D.) joint author. 5.2920
Coyle, Lee. 2.10894
Coyne, James C., 1947-. 5.4932
Cozens, Frederick Warren, 1890-. 4.933
Cozzens, James Gould. 2.11512-2.11521
Crabb, Cecil Van Meter, 1924-. 3.6400, 4.8112
Crabbe, George, 1754-1832. 2.7614-2.7616
Crabbs, Jack A., 1938-. 3.5158
Crabtree, Adam. 5.4968
Cracknell, Arthur P. 5.2508
Craddock, Patricia B. 3.2744
Craft, Robert. 1.4003-1.4006, 1.4008
Craft, Robert. joint author. 1.4010
Craft, Robert. jt. author. 1.4007
Crafts, Alden Springer, 1897-. 5.5391
Crafts, N. F. R. 4.2263
Cragg, Gerald R. (Gerald Robertson) 1.2364
Cragg, Kenneth. 1.2029, 1.2031, 1.2048-1.2049,
    1.2053, 1.2069
Crago, Hugh, 1946-. 5.7718
Crago, Maureen, 1939-. 5.7718
Craig, Albert M. 3.110, 3.4989
Craig, Allen Thornton, 1905- joint author.
    5.1389
Craig, C. Samuel. 4.4328
Craig, Charles Franklin, 1872-1950. 5.4759
Craig, D. H. 2.6484
Craig, David, 1932-. 2.9833
Craig, Edward Gordon, 1872-1966.
    2.3090-2.3091
Craig, Gerald M. 3.8726, 3.8824
Craig, Gordon Alexander, 1913-. 3.749, 3.873,
    3.2293, 3.2322, 3.2326, 3.2463, 5.7214
Craig, Hardin. 2.5525, 2.5634, 2.5850
Craig, James R., 1940-. 5.3022
Craig, Lois A. 1.5514
Craig, Maurice James. 1.5376
Craig, Robert D., 1934-. 3.5531
Craig, Robert L. 4.4380
Craig, William, 1929-. 3.996

Craigie, J. S. 5.3708
Craigie, William A. (William Alexander), Sir, 1867-1957. 2.1117, 2.1122, 2.1135
Craik, T. W. (Thomas Wallace) 2.3289, 2.5843
Crain, Robert L. 4.10787
Cralley, Lester V. 5.5020
Cralley, Lewis J., 1911-. 5.5020
Cram, Elizabeth S. 1.3106
Cram, Ralph Adams, 1863-1942. ed. 3.1951
Cramb lectures, 1936. 1.3481
Cramér, Harald, 1893-. 5.1386
Crampton, C. Gregory (Charles Gregory), 1911-. 3.5963
Crampton, R. J. 3.3542
Crampton, W. G. (William G.) 3.288
Cranach, Hans, d. 1537. 1.6167
Cranach, Lucas, 1472-1553. 1.6167-1.6168
Cranch, Mary (Smith), 1741-1811. 3.7052
Crandall, Rick. joint author. 4.1223
Crandall, Robert W. 4.2051, 4.3827, 5.4659
Crane, Eva. 5.5459
Crane, Hart, 1899-1932. 2.11523, 2.11525
Crane, Jocelyn. 5.3852
Crane, John Kenny, 1942-. 2.13346
Crane, Milton, 1917-. 2.6851
Crane. Robert I. 3.4217, 3.4271
Crane, Ronald Salmon, 1886-. 2.2430, 2.7046, 5.7935
Crane, Stephen, 1871-1900. 2.10978-2.10981
Crane, Verner Winslow, 1889-. 3.6991, 3.8240
Cranfield, C. E. B. 1.2710
Crankshaw, Edward. 3.1876, 3.1884, 3.1894, 3.2311, 3.3107, 3.3270
Cranston, Maurice William, 1920-. 1.672, 2.4092
Cranston, S. L. 1.1619
Crary, Catherine S., comp. 3.6957
Crashaw, Richard, 1613?-1649. 2.6964
Craton, Michael. 4.6441
Cratty, Bryant J. 4.951, 4.968, 4.10305, 4.10950
Cravalho, Ernest G. 5.4633
Craven, Avery Odelle, 1886-. 3.7074, 3.7083, 3.7399, 3.8140, 3.8209, 5.5246
Craven, Wayne. 1.5655
Craven, Wesley Frank, 1905-. 3.1054, 3.6208, 3.8131, 3.8194
Cravens, Richard H. 5.6978
Craver, Clara D. 5.2319
Crawford, Donald R. 5.6668
Crawford, Donald W., 1938-. 1.904
Crawford, James, 1948-. 4.9300
Crawford, Michael H. (Michael Hewson), 1939-. 3.2516, 3.2531, 4.458
Crawford, Michael J. 3.7114
Crawford, Phyllis, 1899-. 1.3593
Crawford, Richard, 1935- joint author. 1.3819
Crawford, Thomas. 2.7508, 2.8056
Crawford, Thomas. ed. 2.8043
Crawford, Walter Byron. 2.7603
Crawford, William, 1948-. 5.6947
Crawford, William Rex, 1898-. 3.8966
Crawfurd, John, 1783-1868. 3.4553
Crawley, Eduardo. 3.9247
Crawley, Richard, 1840-1893. 3.2607
Crawshaw, Nancy. 3.3695
Craypo, Charles, 1936-. 4.3350
Creagh, Patrick. ed. 2.5076
Creamer, Daniel Barnett, 1909-. 4.2083, 4.3835
Creasey, John. 2.8587
Creasy, Sir Edward Shepherd, 1812-1878. 3.3571
Crede, Charles E., joint ed. 5.5745
Cree, Edward H. (Edward Hodges), 1814-1901. 5.7484
Creel, George, 1876-1953. 3.7633
Creel, Herrlee Glessner, 1905-. 1.151, 3.4649, 4.7331
Creeley, Robert, 1922-. 2.11533-2.11534
Creeth, Edmund, ed. 2.6216
Crehan, A. S. 1.6026
Creigh, Dorothy Weyer. 3.8517
Creighton, Anthony. 2.9208
Creighton, Donald, 1902-1979. 3.8722
Creighton, Donald Grant. 3.8671-3.8673, 3.8725, 3.8743, 3.8756
Creighton, James Edwin, 1861-1924. 1.582
Creighton, James Lesley, 1934-. 1.3623
Creighton, Joanne V., 1942-. 2.9666

Creighton, Lucy Black. 4.2064
Creighton, Roger. 5.5931
Crelin, Edmund S., 1923-. 5.4145, 5.5088
Cremer, Lothar, 1905-. 1.5495
Cremin, Lawrence Arthur, 1925-. 4.9981-4.9982, 4.9992, 4.10013, 4.10020-4.10022
Cremins, James J. 4.9601
Cremlyn, Richard James William Campbell-Davys. 5.5412
Crenson, Matthew A., 1943-. 4.7976
Cresap, Dean Russell, 1912-. 4.8188
Crespi, Irving. joint author. 4.7858
Crespi, Juan. 3.8604
Cressey, Donald Ray, 1919-. 4.6756, 4.9882
Cressey, George Babcock, 1896-1963. 3.3609, 3.4621
Cresswell, M. J. joint author. 1.1251
Creswell, John. 5.7233, 5.7427
Creswell, K. A. C. (Keppel Archibald Cameron), Sir, b. 1879. 1.5236
Creswell, Keppel Archibald Cameron, 1879-. 1.5455
Crew, Michael A. 4.3039, 4.3041
Crewe, Ivor. 4.8505
Crews, Frederick C. 2.2399, 2.8658, 2.9112, 2.10664, 2.11062
Crews, Harry, 1935-. 2.12959-2.12960
Cribb, Phillip. 5.5349
Crichton, Elsie Robertson, 1885- joint author. 1.5736
Crichton, George Henderson, 1885-. 1.5720, 1.5736
Crichton, Michael, 1942-. 1.4898
Crichton Smith, Iain. 2.8588, 2.9847
Crick, Bernard R. ed. 4.7392
Crick, Bernard R. 2.9185, 2.9192, 4.7222-4.7223, 4.7305, 4.8463
Crickmer, Douglas F. 5.6746
Criddle, Byron. 4.8594
Crim, Keith R. 1.1522
Crimmins, James C. 4.2722
Cripps, Thomas. 2.2997-2.2998
Crisp, Olga. 4.2370
Crispino, Robert. 5.8060
Crist, Gary K. 5.7858
Cristofer, Michael. 2.12962
Critchfield, Charles Louis, 1910-. 5.2059
Crites, John Orr. joint author. 5.365
Crites, Laura L. 4.6689
Crittenden, Harriet, joint author. 1.3345
Croce, Arlene. 4.1106, 4.1129
Croce, Benedetto, 1866-1952. 1.1382, 1.4603, 2.2667, 2.2726, 2.4881, 2.4937, 3.386-3.387, 3.2878
Crocker, Lester G. 1.809, 1.814, 2.4093
Crocker, Richard L. 1.4114
Crockett, Davy, 1786-1836. 3.8347
Crockett, James Underwood. 5.5367
Crockett, Lawrence J. 5.5392
Crockett, Norman L. 3.6649
Croft-Cooke, Rupert, 1903-. 4.1184
Croft, Doreen J. 4.10404
Crofts, Freeman Wills, 1879-1957. 2.8589
Crofts, J. 2.7054
Croizier, Ralph C. comp. 3.4651
Croll, Elisabeth J. 4.5685
Croly, Herbert David, 1869-1930. 3.7500, 4.5170
Crombie, A. C. (Alistair Cameron), 1915-. 5.720
Crombie, I. M. 1.260-1.261
Crompton, Don. 2.8710
Cromwell, Florence S. 5.5142
Cronan, D. S. (David Spencer) 5.6735
Cronan-Hillix, W. A. (William Allen), 1927-. 5.28
Cronbach, Lee J. (Lee Joseph), 1916-. 5.44, 5.202
Crone, Donald K. 4.2525
Crone, G. R. (Gerald Roe) ed. 4.88
Crone, G. R. (Gerald Roe) 4.226
Crone, Patricia, 1940-. 1.2065
Cronin, A. J. (Archibald Joseph), 1896-1981. 2.8590
Cronin, Thomas E. 4.7923
Cronin, Vincent. 3.2050, 3.2129
Cronon, Edmund David. 3.6835

Cronon, William. 4.386
Cronquist, Arthur. 5.3672, 5.3678, 5.3690, 5.3692
Crook, D. P. (David Paul) 3.7353
Crook, J. Mordaunt (Joseph Mordaunt), 1937-. 1.4950, 1.5370, 1.5377
Crook, K. A. W. 5.3008
Crooke, William, 1848-1923. ed. 2.1162
Crooks, J. E. 5.2674
Crooks, Robert, 1941-. 4.5499
Croome, Derek J. 5.6096
Cropper, William H. 5.2111
Cropsey, Joseph. joint ed. 4.7264
Cros, Charles, 1842-1888. 2.4158
Crosby, Donald A. 2.86
Crosby, Elizabeth Caroline, 1888-. 5.4150
Crosland, Anthony, 1918-. 4.7037
Crosland, Margaret, 1920-. 2.3838
Crosman, Inge Karalus. 2.2450
Crosman, Robert, 1940-. 2.7121
Cross, Anthony Glenn. 2.1332
Cross, Charles A., 1920- joint author. 5.1817
Cross, Colin. 3.1681
Cross, F. L. (Frank Leslie), 1900-1968. ed. 1.2221
Cross, Frank Moore. 1.1905, 1.2615
Cross, Hardy, 1885-. 5.5874
Cross, Ian, 1925-. 2.10215-2.10216
Cross, K. Patricia (Kathryn Patricia), 1926-. 4.10078, 4.10978
Cross, Marion E. 3.8298
Cross, Mercer. 3.7918
Cross, Robert D., ed. 1.2998
Cross, Robert D. 1.3180
Cross, Samuel Hazzard, 1891-1946. 3.3080
Cross, Theodore L., 1924-. 3.6733
Cross, Whitney R. 1.2413
Cross, Wilbur Lucius, 1862-1948. 2.7024, 2.7823
Crossan, John Dominic. 1.2736, 1.2885
Crosskey, William Winslow. 4.9611
Crossley-Holland, Kevin. 2.6279
Crossley, John N. 5.1052
Crossman, R. H. S. (Richard Howard Stafford), 1907-1974. 3.1714, 4.6982, 4.7036, 4.8447
Crothers, Donald M. joint author. 5.2795
Crothers, Edward J., jt. author. 4.10348
Crotty, Kevin, 1948-. 2.530
Crotty, William J. 4.7942
Crouch, James Ensign, 1908-. 5.3997
Crouch, Milton, 1937-. 5.7850
Crouch, Tom D. 5.6647
Croucher, Trevor. 1.3617
Crouse, Nellis Maynard, 1884-. 3.8843
Crouse, William Harry, 1907-. 5.6624
Crouzet, François, 1922-. 4.2276
Crouzet, Maurice. 3.189
Crow, Charles L. 2.10587
Crow, Christine M. 2.4766
Crow, David Richard. 5.2913
Crow, James F. 5.3414, 5.3425, 5.3471
Crow, John Armstrong. 3.3404
Crow, Martin Michael, 1901- ed. 2.6340
Crowder, Michael, 1934-. 3.5045, 3.5323, 3.5328, 3.5358, 3.5366, 4.189
Crowder, Richard. 2.12433
Crowder, Robert George. 5.324a
Crowe, Barry. 2.1239
Crowe, Keith J. 3.5725
Crowell, Richard H. 5.1621
Crowley, F. K. (Francis Keble) 3.5568
Crowley, J. Donald (Joseph Donald) comp. 2.11068
Crowley, J. Donald (Joseph Donald) ed. 2.6970
Crowley, J. Donald (Joseph Donald) 2.11111
Crowley, James B. 3.4970
Crowley, John. 2.12963
Crowley, John William, 1945-. 2.10587
Crowley, Joseph M. 5.2345
Crown, Mr. (John), 1640?-1712. 2.6967
Crowson, P. S. (Paul Spiller) 3.1387
Crowther, Bosley. 2.2913
Crowther, J. G. (James Gerald), 1899-. 5.721, 5.777, 5.2010
Crowther, Richard L. 5.6225
Croyden, Margaret. 2.3179
Crozier, Alice C. 2.11235
Crozier, Brian. 3.1162, 3.2204, 3.4815

Crozier, Michel. 4.2663, 4.7559
Cruden, Robert. 3.6263
Crueger, Anneliese. 5.4442
Crueger, Wulf. 5.4442
Cruickshank, Charles Greig. 3.914, 3.1005,
   5.7304
Cruickshank, Helen Gere. 5.3189
Cruickshank, John. 2.4457
Cruickshank, John. ed. 2.3910
Cruickshank, William M. 4.10952
Cruickshank, William M. joint author. 4.10951
Cruikshank, Bruce. 3.4596
Cruikshank, Margaret. 4.5522
Crum, Howard Alvin, 1922-. 5.3705
Crum, Margaret. 2.7093
Crump, Gail Bruce, 1942-. 2.12219
Crump, Galbraith M. (Galbraith Miller), 1929-.
   2.7122
Crump, J. I. (James Irving), 1921-. 2.3390
Crump, R. W. (Rebecca W.), 1944-. 2.8007
Crunden, Robert Morse. 3.6097, 3.7406
Cruse, Harold. 3.6609, 3.6744
Cruse, Larry, 1944-. 4.219
Crutchfield, James Arthur. 5.5484
Cruxent, José María. jt. author. 3.9179
Cruz Costa, João. 1.663
Crystal, David, 1941-. 2.924
Csikós Nagy, Béla. 4.2229
Cua, A. S. (Antonio S.), 1932-. 1.1445
Cuadra, Carlos A., ed. 5.7638
Cuban, Larry. 4.10025, 4.10289
Cubberley, Ellwood Patterson, 1868-1941.
   4.9952, 4.9983
Cuca, Roberto, 1940-. 4.5678
Cudahy, Brian J. 5.6075
Cuddon, John A. 2.2347
Cudworth, Charles. 1.3884
Cuénin, Micheline. 2.4021
Cuervo, Rufino José, 1844-1911. ed. 2.890
Cuff, David J. 5.6143
Cuff, Robert D., 1941-. 3.6414, 4.1943
Culbert, T. Patrick, ed. 3.9033
Culbert, T. Patrick. 3.9035
Culhane, Paul J. 4.2825
Cullen, Charles T., 1940-. 3.6973
Cullen, Countee, 1903-1946. 2.10751,
   2.11535-2.11536
Cullen, Francis T. 4.5064
Cullen, John B. 2.11691
Cullen, L. M. (Louis M.) 4.2312
Cullen, Patrick, 1940-. 2.6540
Cullen, Rosemary. 2.10990
Culler, A. Dwight. 2.7348
Culler, A. Dwight (Arthur Dwight), 1917-.
   2.7357, 2.8176, 4.10196
Culler, Jonathan D. 2.43, 2.48, 2.2481, 2.2488,
   2.2491
Culley, Margaret. 2.10931
Cullinan, Bernice E. ed. 4.10854
Cullingford, Cecil Howard Dunstan. 4.280
Cullis, C. F. 5.2771
Cullmann, Oscar. 1.2247, 1.2669, 1.2693,
   1.2787, 1.2846, 1.2976, 1.3016
Culp, Gordon L. 5.6010
Culp/Wesner/Culp. 5.6010
Culpepper, R. Alan. 1.2694
Culshaw, John. 1.3954
Culverwell, Geoffrey. 1.6499
Cumberland, Charles Curtis. 3.8941-3.8942
Cumberland, Kenneth Brailey. 3.5538, 3.5597
Cumbler, John T. 4.3619
Cumings, Bruce, 1943-. 3.5014, 3.6470
Cumming, Robert Denoon, 1916-. 1.848, 4.7627
Cumming, Valerie. 4.857
Cumming, William Patterson, 1900-. 3.5977
Cummings, Abbott Lowell, 1923-. 1.5300
Cummings, E. E. (Edward Estlin), 1894-1962.
   2.11537-2.11541, 3.817
Cummings, Mary. 1.6743
Cummings, Milton C. 4.7952
Cummings, Paul. 1.4888
Cummings, Ronald G. 4.1575
Cummings, Scott, 1944-. 4.3603
Cummings, William K. 4.10144
Cummins, Arthur B. 5.6725
Cummins, Geraldine Dorothy, 1890-. 2.9353
Cummins, Robert. 5.34
Cunha, Burke A. 5.4707

Cunha, Celso Ferreira da. 2.909
Cunha, Dorothy Grant. joint author. 5.7645
Cunha, Dorothy Grant. 5.7646
Cunha, Euclydes da, 1866-1909. 3.9214
Cunha, George Daniel Martin. 5.7645-5.7646
Cunliffe, John William, 1865-1946. ed. 2.6480
Cunliffe-Jones, Hubert. 1.2745
Cunliffe, Marcus. 2.10261, 3.6228, 3.7027,
   4.7918
Cunliffe, Richard John. 2.515
Cunningham, Don R. 4.4438
Cunningham, Gail. 2.6033
Cunningham, Gilbert Farm, tr. 2.5191
Cunningham, J. V. (James Vincent), 1911-.
   2.11546
Cunningham, Lawrence. 1.3249
Cunningham, Marion. 5.7133
Cunningham, Michael R. 1.5076
Cunningham, Noble E., 1926-. 3.7019, 4.7836
Cunningham, Ruth, 1907-. 4.10376
Cunningham, Stephen. 4.3699
Cunningham, Valentine. 2.6025
Cunningham, Walker. 1.3829
Cunninghame Graham, R. B. (Robert Bontine),
   1852-1936. 2.8552, 2.8715, 3.9241, 3.9261
Cunnington, C. Willett (Cecil Willett),
   1878-1961. 4.839-4.840, 4.842, 4.846-4.847,
   4.849
Cunnington, Phillis Emily, 1887-. 4.839-4.840,
   4.842-4.844, 4.846-4.847, 4.849
Cupp, Eddie Wayne. 5.4759
Cupps, P. T. joint ed. 5.4253
Cureton, Thomas Kirk, 1901-. 4.926
Cureton, William, 1808-1864. 1.2305
Curhan, Joan P. 4.3748
Curl, James Stevens, 1937-. 1.5398
Curle, Adam. 4.10846
Curley, Daniel. 2.12964
Curley, Dorothy Nyren. comp. 2.10404
Curley, E. M. (Edwin M.), 1937-. 1.798, 1.1095
Curley, Richard T. 4.554
Curme, George Oliver, 1880-. 2.990-2.991
Curnow, Allen, 1911-. 2.10202
Curnow, Wystan, 1939- comp. 2.10196
Curran, Brian Dean. 3.5393
Curran, Charles E. 1.1470, 1.3203
Curran, H. Allen (Harold Allen), 1940-. 4.128
Curran, James. 2.3683
Curran, Joseph Maroney, 1932-. 3.1861
Curran, Stuart. 2.8109
Curran, William J. 5.4560
Currell, Melville. 4.6092
Current-García, Eugene. 2.11212
Current, Richard Nelson. 3.7159, 3.7279,
   3.7341, 3.8129, 3.8441
Currey, L. W. joint author. 2.3485
Currie, Archibald William. 4.4019
Currie, Harold W. 4.6996
Currie, J. M. 4.2917
Currie, Robert. 4.3404
Curry, Alan. 5.3287
Curry, David Park. 1.4907
Curry, Jane Leftwich, 1948-. 2.3551
Curry, Walter Clyde, 1887-. 2.6374, 2.6822
Curti, Merle. 3.6100
Curti, Merle Eugene, 1897-. 3.6099,
   3.6101-3.6103, 4.5201, 4.9142
Curtice, John. 4.8503
Curtin, Jeremiah, 1835-1906. tr. 2.1728-2.1729
Curtin, Philip D. joint author. 3.5066
Curtin, Philip D. 3.5064, 3.5322, 4.2581, 4.5263
Curtis, Brian. 5.3901
Curtis, Doris M. (Doris Malkin) Natalie. 3.5819
Curtis, George William, 1824-1892. 2.10989
Curtis, James L., 1922-. 5.4543
Curtis, James R., 1947-. 3.6542
Curtis, Kenneth M., 1931-. 3.6415
Curtis, L. F. (Leonard Frank) joint author. 4.19
Curtis, L. Perry (Lewis Perry), 1932-. 3.427
Curtis, Laura Ann. 2.6968
Curtis, Lewis Perry, 1900- ed. 2.7280
Curtis, Lynn A. 4.6774, 4.6776
Curtis, Michael, 1923-. 3.2175, 3.3858, 4.5401,
   4.7596
Curtis, William, 1948- joint author. 1.5418
Curtis, William J. R. 1.5266
Curtiss, Charles F. (Charles Francis) joint
   author. 5.2064

Curtiss, John Shelton. 1.3115, 3.3054
Curtius, Ernst Robert, 1886-1956. 2.2626
Curwen, Samuel, 1715-1802. 3.6961
Curzon of Kedleston, George Nathaniel
   Curzon, 1st Marquis, 1859-1925. 4.7502
Cusack, Odean. 5.5144
Cushing, D. H. 5.3561, 5.3904, 5.5476
Cushing, Frank Hamilton, 1857-1900. 3.5964
Cushing, Helen Grant, 1896-. 1.40
Cushman, Robert Frank, 1931-. 4.4638
Cushner, Nicholas P. 4.2866
Cussler, E. L. 5.6840
Cust, Robert Henry Hobart, 1861-. 1.5728
Custer, Benjamin Allen, 1912-. 5.7635
Custer, Jay F., 1955-. 3.5732
Cutcliffe, Stephen H. 5.8118
Cutileiro, José. 4.5388
Cutler, Anthony, 1934-. 1.5863
Cutler, Carl C., 1878-1966. 5.7488
Cutler, John. 5.6670
Cutler, John L, jt. comp. 5.7941
Cutler, Norman, 1949-. 1.1707
Cutler, Stephen J. 4.5106
Cutler, Wayne, 1938-. 3.7071
Cutright, Paul Russell, 1897-. 3.8478
Cutter, Charles. 5.8235
Cuttino, George Peddy. 4.9098
Cuttler, Charles D. 1.6010
Cuvillier, Rolande. 4.3151
Cuyás, Arturo, 1845-1925. 2.900
Cvitanović, Predrag. 5.2170
Cyert, Richard Michael, 1921-. 4.2664
Cynewulf. 2.6305
Cyprian, Saint, Bishop of Carthage. 1.2191
Cyr, Arthur I., 1945-. 4.8551
Cyrano de Bergerac, 1619-1655. 2.4020
Cyrillus, Saint, Bp. of Jerusalem, 315 (ca.)-396.
   1.2210
Cytryn, Leon. 5.5112
Czerniak, Robert J. 5.8358
Czerniaków, Adam, 1880-1942. 3.3990
Czerniawski, Adam, 1934-. 2.1732
Czigány, Lóránt. 2.1754
Czitrom, Daniel J., 1951-. 4.5223

Daalder, Hans. 4.8443
Dabney, Dick. 3.7639
Dabney, Virginius, 1901-. 3.8118, 3.8181
Dabydeen, Cyril, 1945-. 2.9921
Dacey, Philip. 2.12965
Dadié, Bernard Binlin, 1916-. 2.4851-2.4853
Daedalus. 3.6650
Daemmrich, Horst S., 1930-. 2.13618, 2.13642
Daffā', 'Alī 'Abd Allāh. 5.1081
Dafoe, John Wesley, 1866-1944. 3.8753
Dafydd ap Gwilym, 14th cent. 2.836
Dagg, Anne Innis. 5.4046
Daghistany, Ann, 1942-. 2.3446
Dahl, Linda, 1949-. 1.3490
Dahl, Ole-Johan, 1931-. 5.1170
Dahl, Robert Alan, 1915-. 4.7306, 4.7522,
   4.7567, 4.7597, 4.7731-4.7732, 4.7800, 4.8028,
   4.8868
Dahlberg, Charles, 1919- tr. 2.3964
Dahlberg, Edward, 1900-1977. 2.11547-2.11551
Dahlerup, Drude. 4.5887
Dahlgren Laboratory. 4.214
Dahlhaus, Carl, 1928-. 1.4047, 1.4359, 1.4391
Dahlie, Hallvard. 2.9951
Dahmen-Dallapiccola, Anna Liberia. 1.6744
Dahmus, Joseph Henry, 1909-. 3.126, 3.568
Dahrendorf, Ralf. 4.4830, 4.5360, 4.6379
Daiber, Franklin C. 5.3818
Daiches, David, 1912-. 2.2432-2.2433, 2.2515,
   2.5514, 2.5522, 2.5731, 2.5836, 2.6035,
   2.7503, 2.8123, 2.8128, 2.9594, 3.1803
Dailey, Timothy. 4.6750
Daily, Jay Elwood. ed. 5.7695
Daix, Pierre. 1.5876, 1.6129
Dakin, Arthur Hazard, 1905-. 2.11179
Dakin, Douglas. 3.2056, 3.2690, 3.2695
Dakyns, Henry Graham, tr. 3.545
Dal Co, Francesco, 1945- joint author. 1.5275
Dalal-Clayton, D. B. (D. Barry) 5.5221
Dale, Alzina Stone, 1931-. 2.7565
Dale, Amy Marjorie. ed. 2.463
Dale, Amy Marjorie. 2.455

Dale, Delbert A. 1.4560
Dale, Edward Everett, 1879-1972. 3.8491, 3.8529
Dales, John Harkness, 1920-. 4.2132, 4.4205
Dales, Richard C. 3.127
Daleski, H. M. (Hillel Matthew), 1926-. 2.8561
D'Alessio, Gregory J. 5.6230
Daley, Arthur. joint author. 4.880
Daley, Robert. 5.6655
Dalfiume, Richard M. 3.6724
Dalí, Salvador, 1904-. 1.6290
Dallas Museum of Art. 1.4851
Dallas Museum of Fine Arts. 1.6475
Dallek, Robert. 3.7757
Dällenbach, Lucien. 2.4750
Dallimore, Arnold A. 1.3395
Dallimore, William. 5.3695
Dallin, Alexander. 3.1071, 4.8656, 4.9156
Dallin, David J., 1889-1962. 4.8665
Dallmayr, Fred R. (Fred Reinhard), 1928-. 4.4795
Dallos, Peter. 5.4367
Dally, Ann G. 4.5667
Dally, James William. 5.5782
Daloz, Laurent A. 4.10980
Dalton, Dennis. 3.4101
Dalton, Margaret. 2.1427
Dalton, Melville. 4.2646
Dalton, Russell J. 4.7773
Dalven, Rae. 2.617
Dalven, Richard. 5.2192
Dalvi, M. Q. (M. Quasim) joint author. 4.3899
Daly, Augustin, 1838-1899. 2.10990
Daly, Herman E. 4.2765
Daly, M. W. 3.5167
Daly, Mary. 4.5873-4.5875, 4.5975
Daly, Mary E. 4.2317
Daly, Robert. 2.10485
Dalzell, Robert F. 3.7097
Dam, Kenneth W. 4.4565
Dam, Nikolaos van. 3.3801
Damask, A. C. 5.4615
D'Amato, Anthony A. joint author. 4.9691
Damaz, Paul F. 1.5278
Damien, Yvonne M. 5.8094
Damis, John James. 3.5218
Damon, Albert, 1918-1973. 4.441
Damon, Phillip, ed. 2.2426
Damon, S. Foster (Samuel Foster), 1893-1971. 2.7412, 2.12039
Dampier, William Cecil Dampier, Sir, 1867-1952. 5.722
Damrosch, Leopold. 2.6003
Dan Golenpaul Associates. 1.64
Dana, Doris, ed. 2.5408
Dana, Edward Salisbury, 1849-1935. 5.3012, 5.3020
Dana, James Dwight, 1813-1895. 5.3012, 5.3021
Dana, Richard Henry, 1815-1882. 3.7149
Dana, Samuel Trask, 1883-. 5.5433
Danby, Herbert, 1889-1953. 1.1940
Danby, John Francis. 2.5794, 2.6663
Dance Film Association. 4.1094
Dance, Stanley. 1.3749, 1.4321
Dancy, John Christopher. 1.2620
Dandin, 7th cent. 2.1944
D'Andrade, Kendall. 4.4274
D'Andrade, Roy G. 5.486
Danelski, David Joseph, 1930-. 3.7437, 4.9807
Daner, Francine Jeanne. 1.1710
Danet, Brenda, joint comp. 4.7766
Danforth, Loring M., 1949-. 4.869
Dangerfield, George, 1904-1986. 3.1688, 3.1862, 3.7075, 3.7116
Dangerfield, Stanley, 1911-. 5.5453
Danhof, Clarence H., 1911-. 5.5233
Daniel, Donald C. (Donald Charles), 1944-. 5.7221
Daniel, E. Valentine. 3.4211
Daniel, Glyn, 1914-. 4.698
Daniel, Glyn Edmund. 3.252-3.253, 4.691, 4.725
Daniel', IUlii, 1925- defendant. 4.9918
Daniel, Neil, 1932-. 4.10918
Daniel, Norman. 1.2070, 3.141, 3.3731
Daniel, Pete. 4.3686
Daniel, Samuel, 1562-1619. 2.6444, 2.6564
Daniel, Walter C. 2.3642
Daniell, Jere R. 3.7963

Daniells, Lorna M. 4.3046, 5.8368
Daniélou, Alain. 1.1708
Daniélou, Jean. 1.2290, 1.2521, 1.2984
Daniélou, Jean. ed. 1.3089
Daniels, Arlene Kaplan, 1930-. 4.3269
Daniels, Arthur Simpson. 4.915
Daniels, Barry V. 2.2789
Daniels, Belinda S. 5.8430
Daniels, Bruce Colin. 4.8840
Daniels, David, 1933-. 1.3578
Daniels, Douglas Henry. 3.8630
Daniels, Farrington, 1889-1972. 5.2808
Daniels, George H. 5.789
Daniels, Harvey A. 2.1123
Daniels, Jonathan, 1902-. 3.7758, 3.7809, 3.8157
Daniels, Norman, 1942-. 1.714, 4.7661
Daniels, Pamela, 1937-. 4.5659
Daniels, Richard W., 1942-. 5.6511
Daniels, Robert Vincent. 3.3037, 3.3179, 4.7085
Daniels, Roger. 3.1026, 3.8634
Daniels, William J. 4.8263
Danielson, Dennis Richard, 1949-. 2.7123
Danielson, Michael N. 4.7868
Danielsson, Bror, 1905- ed. 2.1026
Dankert, Clyde Edward, 1901- ed. 4.3152
Dankoff, Robert. 2.1979
Danks, Susan M. 5.3757
Danky, James Philip, 1947-. 5.8478
Danly, Robert Lyons, 1947-. 2.2074
Danner, Victor, 1926-. 1.2086
Dannhaeuser, Norbert, 1943-. 4.4297
D'Annunzio, Gabriele, 1863-1938. 2.5018
Danopoulos, Constantine P. (Constantine Panos) 3.2709
Danske selskab (Copenhagen, Denmark) 4.8671
Dante Alighieri, 1265-1321. 2.4914-2.4920, 2.4923-2.4928, 2.4944
Dante Society of America. 2.4945
Danto, Arthur Coleman, 1924-. 1.1278, 1.1354, 3.464
Dantzig, George Bernard, 1914-. 5.1368
Darbandi, Afkham, 1948-. 2.1966
Darbelnet, Jean, 1904- jt. author. 2.871
Darbishire, Helen. 2.7113, 2.8298
Darby, H. C. (Henry Clifford), 1909-. 3.1719, 3.1722-3.1727, 3.1733
D'Arcy, Martin Cyril, 1888-1976. 3.465
D'Arcy McNickle Center for the History of the American Indian. 3.5896
Darío, Rubén, 1867-1916. 2.5372
Darius, Jon. 5.6988
Dark, Harris, 1922-. 5.6627
Dark, Philip John Crosskey. 1.4924
Darke, Hubert, ed. and tr. 4.7324
Darling, Arthur B. (Arthur Burr), 1892-1971. 3.6964
Darling, Frank C. 4.8691
Darlington, C. D. (Cyril Dean), 1903-. 5.3789
Darlington, Philip Jackson, 1904-. 5.3813
Darlington, William Aubrey, 1890-. 2.7248
Darmstadter, Joel, 1928-. 4.3705
Darnell, Donald G. 2.11215
Darnell, James E. 5.3597
Darnton, Robert. 3.2046
Darrah, William Culp, 1909-. 5.6985, 5.6992
Darroch, Sandra Jobson. 3.1676
Darrow, Clarence, 1857-1938. 1.1882
Darst, David H. 2.5161
Darst, David M., 1947-. 4.4611
Dart, John, 1936-. 1.2965
Dart, Thurston, 1921-1971. 1.4115
Dartmouth College. 3.7072, 4.2780, 4.5072
Darty, Trudy, d. 1983. 4.5525
Darwin, Charles. 5.3117, 5.3180, 5.3190-5.3193, 5.3195, 5.3197, 5.3351-5.3354, 5.4348
Darwin, Charles Galton, Sir, 1887-. 3.71
Darwin College. 5.3340
Darwin, Erasmus, 1731-1802. 5.4176
Darwin, Francis, Sir, 1848-1925. ed. 5.3191
Darwīsh, Mahmūd. 2.1840, 2.1844
Das, Braja M., 1941-. 5.5895, 5.5917
Das, G. K. 2.8659-2.8660
Das, J. P. (Jagannath Prasad) 5.262
Das, Suhit Ranjan, 1931-. 5.6327
Dasbach, Joseph M. 5.8422
Dasgupta, Alokeranjan. ed. 2.1888
Dasgupta, Partha. 4.1769
Dasgupta, Ranajit, 1932- joint author. 4.2522

Dasgupta, Shashi Bhushan, 1912-1964. 1.2170, 2.1857
Dasgupta, Surama. 1.178
Dasgupta, Surendranath, 1885-1952. 1.178, 1.202, 2.1919
Dashiell, Alfred, 1901- joint author. 2.3441
Dashtī, 'Alī, 1895-. 2.1973
Dasmann, Raymond Fredric, 1919-. 5.5306
Dassin, Joan. 2.3551
Date, C. J. 5.1235
Dathorne, O. R., 1934-. 2.2296, 2.2696, 2.9980-2.9981
Daube, David. 1.2639
Dauben, Joseph Warren, 1944-. 5.1347
Daubenmire, Rexford F., 1904-. 5.3663
Daudet, Alphonse, 1840-1897. 2.4159-2.4167
Dauenhauer, Richard. 2.1753
Dauer, Sheila. 4.813
Dauer, Victor Paul, 1909-. 4.914
Daugherty, F. Mark, 1951-. 1.3598
Daum, E. (Edmund) 2.1230
Daum, Susan M., 1941- joint author. 5.5015
Daumas, Maurice. ed. 5.5529
Daumas, Maurice. 5.991
Daumier, Honoré, 1808-1879. 1.6086, 1.6501
Daunt, Marjorie, joint ed. 2.1115
Daunton, M. J. (Martin J.) 4.3495
D'Avenant, William, Sir, 1606-1668. 2.6566
Davenport, Arnold. 2.6482, 2.6621
Davenport, Basil, 1905- . 2.3495, 2.9380
Davenport, F. Garvin (Francis Garvin), 1905-. 3.8358
Davenport, Harold, 1907-. 5.1321
Davenport, Harold Alvin, 1895-. 5.4159
Davenport, Horace Willard, 1912-. 5.4223
Davenport, Millia. 4.832
Davenport, Paul. 4.9433
Davenport, W. G. (William George) joint author. 5.6786
Davenport, William H., 1922- joint author. 1.5784
Davenport, William Henry, 1908- joint comp. 5.5531
Daves, Charles W. ed. 2.6924
Davey, Frank, 1940-. 2.9915
Davey, Peter. 1.5367
David, Alfred, 1929-. 2.6359
David, F. W. 5.5699
David, Hans Theodore, 1902- ed. 1.3774
David, Henry Philip, 1923- ed. 5.5101
David, Jack, 1946-. 2.9878, 5.7887
David, Jacques Louis, 1748-1825. 1.6087
David Nichol Smith Memorial Seminar. 2nd, Canberra, 1970. 2.5668
David Nichol Smith Memorial Seminar. 3d, Canberra, 1973. 2.5669
David Nichol Smith Memorial Seminar. 4th, Canberra, 1976. 2.5666
David Nichol Smith Memorial Seminar. Canberra, 1966. 2.5667
David, Ottilie, b. 1892. 2.13796
David, Paul A. 3.7246, 4.2107
David, Pedro R. 4.6699
David, Zdeněk V. 3.2994
Davidovits, Paul. 5.3493
Davidow, Jeffrey. 3.5513
Davids, Jules. 3.7563
Davids, T. W. Rhys (Thomas William Rhys), 1843-1922. 1.1742-1.1743, 3.4193
Davidson, Arnold E., 1936-. 2.9911, 2.9967
Davidson, Avram. 2.12966
Davidson, Basil, 1914-. 3.5068-3.5069, 3.5085, 3.5226, 3.5228, 3.5326, 3.5343, 3.5408, 3.5432
Davidson, Bruce, 1933-. 3.6063
Davidson, Caroline. 5.974
Davidson, Cathy N., 1949-. 2.2414, 2.9911, 2.11218
Davidson, Chandler. 3.8334
Davidson, Colin William. 5.6370
Davidson, Donald, 1917-. 1.135, 1.632, 2.104, 2.6176, 2.11553, 3.6104
Davidson, Edward Hutchins. 2.11206
Davidson, Emily S., 1948-. 4.5736
Davidson, Florence Edenshaw, 1896-. 3.5886
Davidson, Frank Paul, 1918-. 5.5674
Davidson, Hilda Roderick Ellis. 2.6292, 3.3359
Davidson, Hugh McCullough, 1918-. 1.803, 1.807

Davidson, J. F. (John Frank) 5.6843
Davidson, J. Leroy. 1.5067
Davidson, James West. 1.2398, 3.6209
Davidson, James Wightman, 1915-1973. 3.5543, 3.5675
Davidson, John, 1947-. 2.7620, 4.3613
Davidson, John Wells. 3.7713
Davidson, Kenneth S. 4.10522
Davidson, Marshall. 3.6333
Davidson, Marshall B. ed. 5.3944
Davidson, Marshall B. 1.6513
Davidson, Philip Grant, 1902-. 3.6919
Davidson, Richard L. ed. 5.3469
Davidson, Roger H. 4.8009, 4.8063
Davidson, Roger H. joint author. 4.8002
Davidson, Sidney, 1919-. 4.4398
Davidson, Sue, 1925-. 4.3265
Davie, Donald. 2.5748, 2.8057, 2.8591, 2.8593, 2.12339
Davie, Donald. 2.5808, 2.6120, 2.6168, 2.8592, 2.12340
Davie, Michael. 2.9499
Davies, A. C. (Arthur Cyril) 5.7057
Davies, Alan J. 5.5726
Davies, Barbara S., 1938- joint author. 4.2074
Davies, Bronwyn, 1945-. 4.10765
Davies, Christie. 5.7597
Davies, Christie. joint author. 4.9429
Davies, Christopher S. (Christopher Shane) 3.1187
Davies, D. Hywel. 4.8560
Davies, David William, 1908-. 4.4097
Davies, Elwyn, ed. 4.5336
Davies, Eric H. 5.6862
Davies, Evelyn A., joint author. 4.915
Davies, Glyn A. O. 5.5709
Davies, Godfrey, 1892-1957. 3.1457, 3.1474, 5.7988
Davies, Howell. 3.8958
Davies, Hunter, 1936-. 2.8311
Davies, J. Clarence. 4.2074
Davies, John Booth. 1.4383
Davies, John Kenyon. 2.6145, 2.6445, 3.301, 3.2573
Davies, Keith A. 4.2844
Davies, Kenneth Gordon, ed. 3.6885
Davies, Kenneth Gordon. 4.8900
Davies, Laurence. 1.3870, 2.8547, 2.8716
Davies, Margaret Gay. 4.3107
Davies, Margery W. 4.3276
Davies, Martin. 1.1172, 1.6277
Davies, N. B. (Nicholas B.), 1952-. 5.3393, 5.4054
Davies, Nigel, 1920-. 3.8884
Davies, Norman. 3.3329-3.3330
Davies, P. C. W. 5.1762, 5.1904, 5.2094-5.2095, 5.2470
Davies, Peter, 1940-. 2.1053
Davies, Peter J., 1940- joint author. 5.3741
Davies, Phil, 1950-. 5.4961
Davies, R. G. (Richard Garfield), 1947-. 4.8457
Davies, R. R. 3.1758, 3.1760
Davies, R. W. (Robert William), 1925-. 4.2914, 5.5543
Davies, Reginald Thorne. ed. 2.6212
Davies, Reginald Thorne. 2.6133
Davies, Richard Gareth. 5.3857
Davies, Robertson, 1913-. 2.9922-2.9927, 2.9929
Davies, Stevie. 2.7124
Davies, Wallace Evan. 3.6191
Davies, Wendy. 3.1761
Davies, William David, 1911-. 1.1899, 1.2672, 1.2893
Davin, Dan, 1913-. 2.10199
Davin, Delia. 4.5685
Davis, A. C., fl. 1980-. 2.8785
Davis, A. R. (Albert Richard), 1924-. 2.2032
Davis, Allen Freeman, 1931-. 3.8089, 4.6469
Davis, Allison. 3.6755, 4.5198
Davis, Angela Yvonne, 1944-. 3.6756, 3.6821, 4.6909
Davis, Anne J., 1931-. 5.5195
Davis, Arthur Paul, 1904-. 2.10319, 2.10689, 2.10694-2.10695
Davis, Audrey B. 5.4610
Davis, Bernard David, 1916-. 5.4440
Davis, Calvin DeArmond. 4.9106

Davis, Charles T. (Charles Twitchell), 1918-1981. 2.10358
Davis, Charles T. (Charles Twitchell), 1918-1981, comp. 2.10696
Davis, Colin, 1927-. 1.4518
Davis, Daniel S. 3.6849
Davis, David Brion. 3.7187, 4.6412, 4.6419
Davis, David W., joint author. 4.7878
Davis, Dennis. joint author. 4.7253
Davis, Dick, 1945-. 2.1966
Davis, Douglas, 1933-. 1.6704
Davis, Ewart Arthur, joint author. 5.2206
Davis, Flora. 5.4095
Davis, Fred, 1925-. 5.443
Davis, Frederick G. 4.4404
Davis, Gary A., 1938-. 4.10913, 5.374
Davis, George, 1939-. 4.4339
Davis, Gwenda L. 5.3739
Davis, H. Ted (Howard Ted) 5.1938
Davis, Harold E., 1927-. 3.8258
Davis, Harold Eugene, 1902-. 1.658, 3.9008, 4.4770
Davis, Henry, 1866-. 1.2184
Davis, Herbert John, 1893-1967. 2.6944, 2.7289, 2.7305-2.7306
Davis, James C. (James Cushman) 3.2913
Davis, James C. (James Cushman) comp. 3.622
Davis, James Herbert. 2.4023
Davis, James W., 1920-. 4.7945, 4.8143
Davis, Jefferson, 1808-1889. 3.7321, 3.7370
Davis, Joan E., 1945-. 5.4786
Davis, Joe Lee. 2.11448
Davis, John C. 5.2991
Davis, John D., 1854-1926. 1.2505
Davis, John P., 1905- ed. 3.6610
Davis, Joseph Stancliffe, 1885-. 4.1775
Davis, Karen, 1942-. 5.4651
Davis, Kenneth C. 5.7595
Davis, Kenneth Culp. 4.9752-4.9753, 4.9755
Davis, Kenneth Sydney, 1912-. 3.8521
Davis, Lance Edwin. 4.1871
Davis, Lary V., joint author. 5.3306
Davis, Lenwood G. 5.7840-5.7841, 5.7867-5.7869, 5.8189, 5.8430
Davis, Madeleine. 5.5114
Davis, Merrell Rees, 1912-. 2.11159
Davis, Morton D., 1930-. 5.1378
Davis, Moshe. 1.1919
Davis, Natalie Zemon, 1928-. 3.1953
Davis, Nathaniel. 3.9267, 5.7870
Davis, Norman, 1913-. 2.6376, 2.6414
Davis, Nuel Pharr, 1915-. 2.7610
Davis, Peter B. 5.5126
Davis, Philip J., 1923-. 5.1032, 5.1432
Davis, R. G. 2.3276
Davis, R. H. C. (Ralph Henry Carless), 1918-. 3.1344
Davis, R. (Russ E.) 4.347
Davis, Ralph, 1915-. 4.2192
Davis, Rebecca Harding, 1831-1910. 2.10991
Davis, Richard, 1945-. 5.4815
Davis, Richard A. (Richard Albert), 1937-. 5.3120
Davis, Richard Beale. 2.6504, 2.10466, 3.8132, 3.8206, 5.7690
Davis, Robert Murray. 2.9503
Davis, Ronald L. F. 4.2909
Davis, Ronald W. (Ronald Wayne), 1941-. 5.3449
Davis, Sara deSaussure, 1943-. 2.10969
Davis, Stanley N. (Stanley Nelson), 1924-. 4.310
Davis, Stuart, 1894-1964. 1.5932
Davis, Susan Schaefer. 4.6159
Davis, Thadious M., 1944-. 2.11692
Davis, Thomas W., 1946-. 5.1144
Davis, Tracy. 5.7608
Davis, W. Alan. 5.6547
Davis, Walter R. 2.5992
Davis-Weyer, Caecilia, comp. 1.4739
Davis, William C., 1946-. 3.6982, 3.7364
Davis, William Morris, 1850-1934. 4.3
Davison, Archibald T. (Archibald Thompson), 1883-1961. 1.3425, 1.4499
Davison, Kenneth B. 4.7485, 5.7847
Davison, Roderic H. 3.3586
Davisson, Lee D. 5.6369
Davitz, Joel Robert. 5.5196
Davitz, Lois Jean. joint author. 5.5196

Davson, Hugh, 1909-. 5.4377
Davy, A. J. 5.3772
Davy, John, 1790-1868. 3.9140
Davydov, A. S. (Aleksandr Sergeevich), 1912-. 5.2129
Dawes, Clinton J. 5.3776
Dawes, Robyn M., 1936- joint author. 5.41
Dawidoff, Robert. 3.7011
Dawidowicz, Lucy S. 3.1086, 3.1095, 3.3952
Dawisha, A. I. 3.3738, 3.3752
Dawisha, Karen. 3.1928, 3.3752
Dawkins, Richard, 1941-. 5.3402, 5.3451
Dawley, Alan, 1943-. 4.3522
Dawood, N. J. ed. 3.452
Daws, Gavan. 3.5638
Dawson, Carl. 2.5704, 2.7361
Dawson, Carl. comp. 2.7358
Dawson, Christopher, 1889-1970. 1.1571, 1.2240-1.2241, 3.91, 3.142, 3.466, 3.3611
Dawson, Elmer Yale, 1918-1966. 5.3713
Dawson, John, 1946-. 5.4567
Dawson, John A. 4.4278
Dawson, John Philip. 4.9416
Dawson, Joseph G., 1945-. 5.7199
Dawson, Lawrence Hawkins. ed. 2.1049
Dawson, Nelson L. 4.9796
Dawson, Philip. 4.9913
Dawson, R. J. C. 5.7058
Dawson, Robert MacGregor, 1895-1958. 3.8745, 4.8269
Day, A. C. joint author. 5.5430
Day, A. Grove. 5.3639
Day, A. Grove (Arthur Grove), 1904-. 2.10155-2.10156, 3.5639, 5.8078
Day, Alan J. (Alan John) 4.7781, 4.9299
Day, Arthur Grove. 3.5639
Day, Clarence, 1874-1935. 2.11555
Day, Clive, 1871-1951. 3.4580
Day, Cyrus Lawrence, 1900-1968. 1.3485
Day, Donald, 1899-. 2.3263, 3.8324
Day, Dorothy, 1897-1980. 4.5117
Day, Douglas. ed. 2.9055
Day, Douglas. 2.8727, 2.9062
Day, James. 1.4394
Day, Joanne S. 5.2447
Day, John, 1948-. 1.2551
Day, John A. joint author. 5.2505
Day, John W. 5.3534
Day Lewis, C. (Cecil), 1904-1972. 2.797, 2.2742, 2.8594
Day, Lewis Foreman, 1845-1910. 5.7524
Day, Lucille. 5.989
Day, Malcolm M. 2.7321
Day, Marion Clyde, 1927-. 5.2845
Day, Michael. tr. 1.3218
Day, Michael H. 4.453
Day, Peter R., 1928- joint author. 5.3719
Day, Robert A., 1924-. 5.5505
Day, Robert Adams. 2.5943
Dayal, Deen. 3.4281
Dayan, Joan, 1949-. 2.4839
Dayan, Moshe, 1915-1981. 3.3824, 3.3933
Dayananda Sarasvati, Swami, 1824-1883. 1.1730
Daydí-Tolson, Santiago. 2.5121
Dayton, Deane K. 4.10325
Dazai, Osamu. 2.2093-2.2095
D'Azevedo, Warren L. ed. 1.6728
De Antonio, Emile. 1.4878
De Armond, Anna Janney, 1910-. 2.3607
De Bary, William Theodore, 1918-. 1.160-1.161, 1.2126, 2.1758, 3.107, 3.4180, 3.4610, 3.4645, 5.8337
De Beer, Gavin, Sir, 1899-1972. 5.3195
De Blij, Harm J. joint author. 3.5052
De Bray, R. G. A. (Reginald George Arthur) 2.1195
De Camp, L. Sprague (Lyon Sprague), 1907-. 2.5963
De Carlo, Nicola. 5.449
De Charms, Desiree. 1.3588
De Chasca, Edmund, 1903-. 2.5187
De Chazeau, Melvin Gardner. 4.3768
De Chiara, Joseph, 1929-. 1.5584
De Chickera, Ernst, joint ed. 2.2505
De Conde, Alexander. 3.6401, 3.7026, 3.7055, 3.7066, 3.7564
De Coppens, Peter Roche, 1938-. 4.4786

De Courtivron, Isabelle. 4.6120
De Duve, Christian. 5.3598
De Felice, Renzo, 1929-. 3.3980
De Forest, John William, 1826-1906. 2.10992
De Forest, Lee, 1873-1961. 5.6424
De Francia, Peter. 1.6115
De Gamez, Tana, 1920- ed. 2.901
De George, Richard T. 5.8342
De Grand, Alexander J., 1938-. 3.2883
De Grazia, Sebastian. comp. 4.7281
De Grazia, Sebastian. 4.7503
De Gruchy, John W. 3.5450
De Hart-Mathews, Jane. 2.3209
De Janvry, Alain. 2.2962
De Jesus, Ed. C. 4.5443
De Jong, Gordon F. joint comp. 4.1630
De Kiewiet, C. W. (Cornelius William), 1902-.
   3.5467
De Kooning, Willem, 1904-. 1.5795, 1.5933
De Kruif, Paul, 1890-1971. 5.4431
De la Croix, Horst. 1.4673
De La Cruz, Felix F. 5.4750
De La Cruz, Felix F. ed. 5.3469
De La Cruz, Jessie Lopez, 1919-. 4.5993
De la Garza, Rodolfo O. 3.6582
De la Mare, Walter, 1873-1956. 2.2569,
   2.8596-2.8597
De La Roche, Mazo, 1885-1961. 2.9930-2.9931
De La Torre, Lillian, 1902-. 2.11556
De Laguna, Frederica, 1906-. 3.5957
De Laubenfels, David J., 1925-. 5.3643
De León, Arnoldo, 1945-. 3.8336-3.8337
De Lerma, Dominique-René. 1.3565
De Long, Dwight Moore, 1892- joint author.
   5.3856
De Madariaga, Isabel, 1919-. 3.3106
De Marly, Diana. 5.7090
De Mendelssohn, Peter, 1908-. 2.13837
De Meyer, Adolf, Baron, 1868-1949. 4.1182
De Mille, Agnes. 4.1131
De Mille, Anna Angela (George) 1877-. 4.1373
De Morgan, Augustus, 1806-1871. 1.1206
De Morsier, Francoise, joint author. 4.2582
De Neufville, Richard, 1939-. 5.6684
De Onís, Harriet, 1899- tr. 2.5424, 3.9146,
   3.9294
De Onís, José. 3.9016
De Pauw, Linda Grant. 4.7202-4.7203, 4.9479
De Pury, Marianne. 2.13353
De Quincey, Thomas, 1785-1859. 2.5817
De Robertis, E. M. F. 5.3602
De Robertis, Eduardo D. P., 1913-. 5.3602
De Roberto, Federico, 1861-1927. 2.5063
De Sanctis, Francesco, 1817-1883. 2.4878
De Sanctis, G.B. 2.4956
De Santillana, Giorgio, 1902-. 5.723, 5.1692
De Santis, Vincent P. 4.8186
De Schweinitz, Karl, 1920-. 4.7532
De Sélincourt, Aubrey, 1894-1962. 2.5770
De Selincourt, Ernest, 1870-1943.
   2.6523-2.6524, 2.7848, 2.8296, 2.8298
De Seversky, Alexander Procofieff, 1894-.
   5.7398
De Silva, Anil. 1.5758
De Silva, K. M. 3.4363, 3.4372
De Smith, Stanley Alexander. 4.9418
De Sola, Ralph, 1908-. 2.1108
De Souza, Anthony R. 4.1801
De Ste. Croix, G. E. M. (Geoffrey Ernest
   Maurice) 3.2560, 3.2612
De, Sushil Kumar. 2.1852
De Terra, Helmut, 1900-. 5.820
De Tolnay, Charles, 1899-. 1.5014, 1.5840,
   1.6241
De Vane, William Clyde, 1898-. 2.7478, 2.7482
De Vitis, A. A. 2.8771, 2.9649
De Vos, George A. 4.5453, 4.6889
De Voto, Bernard Augustine, 1897-1955.
   2.3412, 2.10405, 2.10938, 2.10955, 2.10966,
   2.11559, 3.6348, 3.8471
De Vries, Jan, 1943-. 4.2194
De Vries, Louis, 1885-. 5.706
De Vries, Marten W. 5.4468
De Vries, Peter. 2.11561-2.11565
De Vries, Walter. joint author. 3.8170
De Waal Malefijt, Annemarie, 1914-. 4.542
De Weydenthal, Jan B. 3.3346, 4.8669
De Wiest, Roger J. M. ed. 4.295

De Wiest, Roger J. M. joint author. 4.310
De Witt, Benjamin Parke. 4.7855
De Witt, Norman Wentworth. 1.330, 2.447
Deacon, George Edward Raven, Sir, 1906- ed.
   4.329
Deacon, Margaret. 4.331
Deák, Francis, 1898-1972. 4.9331
Deák, István. 3.1941
Deakin, Alfred, 1856-1919. 4.8815
Deakin, F. W. (Frederick William), 1913-.
   3.1072, 3.2894
Deakin, Motley F. 2.9514
Dean, Alfred, 1933-. 5.4837
Dean-Baar, Susan. 4.4774
Dean, David M. 1.3318
Dean, Donald Stewart, 1916- joint author.
   5.4470
Dean, Edwin. 4.2754
Dean, James, 1943-. 2.6334
Dean, John Aurie, 1921-. 5.2650
Dean, John W. (John Wesley), 1938-. 3.7919
Dean, Leonard Fellows, 1909- ed. 2.6728
Dean, Nathan W. 5.2485
Dean, Vera Micheles, 1903-1972. 3.108, 3.4292
Dean, Warren. 4.2174
Dean, Winton. 1.3820, 1.3885-1.3886
Deane, Phyllis. 4.2247, 4.2264
Deane, Seamus, 1940-. 2.9656
Deanesly, Margaret. 1.2306, 1.2436
Deanne, Sidney Norton, 1878-1943, tr. 1.379
Dearden, C. W. 2.431
Dearing, Charles Lee, 1903-. 4.3885
Dearing, Vinton A. (Vinton Adams), 1920-.
   2.7033
Deasey, Denison. 4.10399
Deatherage, Fred E., 1913-. 5.7108
Deathridge, John. 1.4049
DeBakey, Michael E. (Michael Ellis), 1908-.
   5.4992
DeBenedetti, Charles. 4.9143
Debenham, Frank, 1883-1965. 4.46
DeBerry, Stephen. 5.4944
Debo, Angie, 1890-. 3.5858
Debo, Richard K., 1938-. 3.3180
Debreczeny, Paul. 2.1421
Debreu, Gerard. 4.1504
Debrix, Jean R., 1906- joint author. 2.3002
Debrunner, Albert, 1884- joint author. 2.248
Debs, Eugene V. (Eugene Victor), 1855-1926.
   4.6995
Debus, Allen G. 5.764
Debus, Allen G. ed. 5.816
Debussy, Claude, 1862-1918. 1.3497, 1.3846
DeCanio, Stephen J. 4.2959
Decavalles, Andonis. 2.615
Deckard, Barbara Sinclair. 4.5876, 4.8052,
   4.8062
Decker, Harold A., comp. 1.4500
DeConde, Alexander. 3.6456
DeCoster, Cyrus Cole, 1914-. 2.5226
Decter, Moshe. 3.7670
DeDecker, H. K., 1915-. 5.2221
Dedijer, Vladimir. 3.1898, 3.3553, 3.3559
Deegan, William L. 4.10561
Deely, John N. 2.78
Deer, W. A. (William Alexander) 5.3015,
   5.3026-5.3027
Deetz, Charles Henry, 1864-. 4.206, 4.212
Deetz, James. 3.7943
Deferrari, Roy Joseph, 1890-. 2.356
Deffenbacher, Kenneth. joint author. 5.4356
DeFilipps, Robert A. joint author. 5.3647
DeFleur, Melvin L. (Melvin Lawrence), 1923-.
   4.5004, 4.5007
Defoe, Daniel, 1661?-1731. 2.6968-2.6975,
   3.1728, 4.101
Defourneaux, Marcelin. 3.3405
DeFrain, John D. 4.5578
DeFrancis, John, 1911-. 2.2144
Degas, Edgar, 1834-1917. 1.5704, 1.6092
Degenhardt, Henry W. 4.7781, 4.9299
Degering, Hermann, 1866-1942. 1.6598
Degge, Rogena M. joint author. 1.4646
Dégh, Linda. 4.792
Degler, Carl N. 3.6319, 3.7193, 3.7371, 3.9225,
   4.6008
Degras, Jane Tabrisky, 1905-. 4.2375, 4.6926,
   4.9071

DeGrazia, Diane, 1943-. 1.5812
DeGregorio, William A., 1946-. 3.6308
Deguy, Michel. 2.4781
DeHaven, James Charles, 1912- joint author.
   4.2930
Dehio, Ludwig, 1888-. 4.9008
Dehmel, Richard, 1863-1920. 2.13727
Deichmann, William B. 5.4721
Deighton, K. 2.6271
Deissmann, Gustav Adolf, 1866-1937. 1.2664
Deitel, Harvey M., 1945-. 5.1171, 5.1188
Deiters, Hermann, 1833-1907, ed. 1.3806
Deitz, Samuel M. 4.10695
Déjeux, Jean. joint comp. 2.4847
Dejnozka, Edward L. 4.10164
Dejours, Pierre. 5.4229
Dekker, George. 2.12327
Dekker, George. comp. 2.10974
Dekker, Thomas, ca. 1572-1632. 2.6230,
   2.6447-2.6448, 2.6568-2.6571
Dekmejian, R. Hrair, 1933-. 1.2000
Del Aguila, Juan M. 3.9102
Del Mar, Donald. 4.2630
Del Mar, Norman, 1919-. 1.3999, 1.4193
Del Mar, William Arthur, 1880- joint ed.
   5.6262
Del Sesto, Steven L. 4.3813
Del Vecchio, John M., 1948-. 2.12967
Delacour, Jean, 1890-. 5.3962
Delacourcelle, Doris Winifred (Hill) 2.3997
Delacroix, Eugène, 1798-1863. 1.6093
Delaisement, Gérard, ed. 2.4270
Delaissé, L. M. J. 1.6417
Deland, Margaret Wade Campbell, 1857-1945.
   2.10993
Delaney, Frank, 1942-. 2.8886
Delanglez, Jean, 1896-1949. ed. 3.433
Delany, Martin Robison, 1812-1885. 3.6611
Delany, Samuel R. 2.12968-2.12972
Delany, Veronica. 2.6929
Delarue, Allison. 4.1137
Delattre, Pierre. 1.3456
Delaunay, Robert, 1885-1941. 1.6097
DeLaura, David J., ed. 1.3273
DeLaura, David J. 2.5938
Delavenay, Emile. 2.8983
Delavignette, Robert Louis, 1897-. 4.8926
Delaware Federal Writers' Project. 3.8097
Delaware. University, Newark. Dept. of
   History. 4.1869
Delbrück, Hans, 1848-1929. 5.7174
Delehaye, Hippolyte, 1859-1941. 1.3250
DeLeon, Peter. 5.6607
Deleuze, Gilles. 1.1056
Delevoryas, Theodore, 1929-. 5.3730
Delevoy, Robert L. 1.4799
Delgado, Christopher L. 4.2623
Delibes, Miguel. 2.5247
Delisle, Françoise Roussel. tr. 2.4531
Dell, David J. 5.8450
Dell, Floyd. 2.6437, 2.12483
Dellinger, David T., 1915-. 4.5234
DeLoach, Charlene. 5.5038
Deloffre, Frédéric. 2.4103
Deloney, Thomas, 1543?-1600. 2.6449-2.6450
DeLong, Fred. 5.6638
Deloria, Vine. 3.5797, 3.5799, 3.5832
Delorme, Eugene P. 4.6917
Delpar, Helen. ed. 3.8959
Delpuech, Jean Jacques, joint author. 5.2410
DeLuca, Sam. 4.1024-4.1025
Delury, George E. 4.7777
Delworth, Ursula. 5.4699
Delzell, Charles F. 3.357
DeMallie, Raymond J., 1946-. 3.5929
Demaray, John G. 2.7125
DeMarco, Tom. 5.1172, 5.5565
Demarest, Arthur Andrew. 3.8905
Demarquez, Suzanne. 1.3865
DeMause, Lloyd. 3.435
Dember, William N. (William Norton), 1928-.
   5.245
Demel, John T. 5.5645
Dement, William Charles, 1928-. 5.4353
Démény, János. ed. 1.3787
Demerath, Nicholas J., 1913-. 4.5679
Demeter, Karl, 1889-. 5.7372

Demetrius, of Phaleron, b. 350 B.C. 2.349, 2.446
Demetz, Peter, 1922-. 2.13481, 2.13564, 2.13706
D'Emilio, John. 4.5537
Demin, Mikhail. 2.1627
Deming, W. Edwards (William Edwards), 1900-. 4.1245
Demko, George J., 1933- comp. 4.2397
DeMolen, Richard L. 2.825
Demos, George D. joint ed. 4.10907
Demos, John. 4.5608, 5.678
Demos, John. comp. 3.6011
Demosthenes. 2.359-2.362, 2.447
Dempsey, Arthur D. 5.5187
Dempsey, Hugh Aylmer, 1929-. 3.5951, 4.4017
Dempsey, Michael W. 3.3648
Dempsey, Patricia Ann. 5.5187
Dempster, Derek D. joint author. 3.1048
Dempster, Germaine (Collette) 2.6375
Dempster, Germaine (Collette) joint ed. 2.6346
Dempster, M. A. H. (Michael Alan Howarth), 1938- joint author. 5.1547
Demske, James M. 1.997
Demtröder, W. 5.2315
Demus, Otto. 1.5507-1.5508, 1.6393
DeMuth, James, 1943-. 2.10653
Demuth, Norman, 1898-. 1.3956
Den Hartog, J. P. (Jacob Pieter), 1901-. 5.5744, 5.5773
DenBoer, Gordon, 1933-. 4.7834
Denby, Edwin, 1903-. 4.1171-4.1172
Deneke, Frederick J., 1942-. 5.5363
Dénes, József. 5.1282
Denham, John, Sir, 1615-1669. 2.6983
Denholm-Young, Noël, ed. and tr. 3.1364
Denieul-Cormier, Anne. 3.1970
Denis, Armand. 5.3990
Denisoff, R. Serge. 1.4356
Denison, Cara D. 1.5799
Denison, Edward Fulton, 1915-. 4.1934, 4.1956, 4.2193
Denison, George T. (George Taylor), 1839-1925. 5.7381
Denison, Harold, 1887- illus. 2.11369
Denmark. 4.3664
Denmark, Florence. 4.5838, 4.5947
Dennery, Philippe. 5.2174
Dennett, Tyler, 1883-. 3.4416, 3.7435
Denney, Reuel, 1913-. 4.881
Denney, Ronald C. 5.1892
Denning, Peter J., 1942-. 5.1169, 5.1370
Dennis, Alfred Lewis Pinneo, 1874-. 3.4923, 4.9044
Dennis, Arnett S. 5.2538
Dennis, Everette E. 4.9711
Dennis, Jack B. (Jack Bonnell) joint author. 5.1370
Dennis, James M. 1.5989
Dennis, Lawrence J. 4.10243
Dennis, Stephen N. 3.5992
Dennis, William Herbert, 1904-. 5.6757, 5.6785, 5.6788
Dennison, George, 1925-. 4.11005
Dennison, George M. 4.8262
Dennison, John Dewar, ed. 2.335
Dennison, Sam. 1.4254
Denniston, J. D. (John Dewar), 1887-1949. 2.239, 2.241, 2.454
Denniston, Lyle W. 4.9534
Denno, Robert F. 5.3872
Denny, Margaret. 2.10336
DeNovo, John A. 3.3754
Densmore, Frances, 1867-1957. 1.4306-1.4307
Denson, Alan. 2.9292
Dent, Alan. 2.8070
Dent, Edward Joseph, 1876-1957. 1.3936, 1.3965, 1.4207, 1.4213, 1.4228
Dent, H. C. (Harold Collett), 1894-. 4.10110
Dentan, Robert Claude, 1907- ed. 3.467
Dentler, Robert A., 1928-. 4.6345
Denton, Derek A. 5.4403
Denton, Jeffrey Howard. 4.8457
Denton L., Carlos F. 4.8328
Denton, Robert E., Jr. 4.7854
Deo, Narsingh, 1936- joint author. 5.1277
Dépestre, René. 2.4839
DeQuincey, Thomas, 1785-1859. 2.7622
Der Nister, 1884-1950. 2.1806

Derber, Milton. 4.3184
Derber, Milton. ed. 4.3351
Derleth, August William, 1909-1971. 2.11557
Dermer, Otis C. (Otis Clifford), 1909- joint author. 5.2597
Derrick, Ronald Albert, 1892-. 3.5634
Derrida, Jacques. 1.8, 1.1018, 2.89
Derry, Charles, 1951- joint author. 5.8138
Derry, John Wesley. 3.1563, 3.1577
Derry, T. K. (Thomas Kingston), 1905-. 3.3356, 3.3378, 3.3381, 3.3383, 5.5530, 5.5537
Derthick, Martha. 4.3463, 4.7869
Dertouzos, Michael L. 5.1232
Des Périers, Bonaventure, 1500?-1544? 2.3980
Desai, Akshayakumar Ramanlal. 4.5481
Desai, Meghnad. 4.4484
DeSalvo, Louise A., 1942-. 2.9296
Desan, Wilfrid. 1.494
Desborough, Vincent Robin d'Arba. 3.2581-3.2582
Descartes, René, 1596-1650. 1.787-1.788, 1.791-1.792, 5.835, 5.4177
Descharnes, Robert. 1.6290
Descombes, Vincent. 1.823
Deshen, Shlomo A. 3.3842
Deshpande, L. K. 4.3234
Desjardins, Marie Catherine Hortense, known as Mme de Villedieu, d.1683. 2.4021
Desmond, Adrian J., 1947-. 5.3171
Desmond, John F. 2.12673
Desmond, Robert William, 1900-. 2.3570-2.3571, 2.3574, 2.3576
Desoer, Charles A. 5.1543
Desomogyi, Joseph, ed. and tr. 2.1835
Despland, Michel. 1.919
Desportes, Georges, 1921-. 2.4841
Desrosiers, André. 3.8709
Dessauer, John P. 5.7569
Dessen, Alan C., 1935-. 2.5863-2.5864, 2.6600
Dessen, Cynthia S. 2.755
Desser, David. 2.3004
Destler, I. M. 4.4177
Dethier, V. G. (Vincent Gaston), 1915-. 5.3866
Detienne, Marcel. 1.1656, 3.2545
Detmers, Fred H. 5.7002
Detmold, Christian Edward, 1810-1887. tr. 4.7393
Detroit Institute of Arts. 1.4648, 1.4851, 1.6054, 1.6475, 1.6504, 3.5733, 3.9078
Detter Delupis, Ingrid, 1936-. 5.8252
Detterman, Douglas K. 5.356
Detweiler, Frederick German, 1881-1960. 2.3648
Detzer, Karl William, 1891-. 2.12434
Deuchler, Florens, 1931-. 1.4752, 1.6302
Deuchler, Martina, 1935-. 3.5003
Deutsch, Babette, 1895-. 2.1316, 2.5829, 2.11558
Deutsch, Charles, 1947-. 4.6637
Deutsch, Diana. 1.4387
Deutsch, Eliot. 1.199, 1.1368
Deutsch, Harold C. (Harold Charles) 3.2122, 3.2397, 3.2429
Deutsch, Helen. 2.3274
Deutsch, Helene, 1884-. 4.5923
Deutsch, Karl Wolfgang, 1912-. 4.7381, 4.7485, 4.7546, 4.9131
Deutsch, Lawrence J. 5.4368
Deutsch, Morton, 1920-. 4.4941, 4.4984
Deutsch, Otto Erich, 1883-1967. 1.3614, 1.3887, 1.3937, 1.3973, 1.3978
Deutsche Gesellschaft für Answärtige Politik. 3.1705
Deutscher, Isaac, 1907-1967. 3.3155-3.3157, 3.3233, 4.6974
Deutscher, Thomas Brian, 1949-. 2.822
Deutsches Archäologisches Institut. 1.5223
Deutsches Institut für Wirtschaftsforschung. 4.2346
Deva, Bigamudre Chaitanya, 1922-. 1.3735
DeVall, William B. joint author. 4.5529
Devaney, Kathleen. 4.10307
Devaney, Robert L., 1948-. 5.1624
Devanna, Mary Anne. 4.4359
Devaraja, N. K. (Nand Kishore), 1917-. 1.1137
Dever, William G. joint author. 1.2546
Deverall, Brian J. 5.5404

Devereux, Owen F. (Owen Francis), 1937-. 5.6771
Devèze, Michel. 3.650
Devine, Mary Elizabeth, joint ed. 5.7958
Devine, Michael D. 5.6149
Devine, T. M. (Thomas Martin) 4.2314
Devine, Thomas G., 1928-. 4.10336
Devkota, Laxmi Prasad, 1908-1959. 2.1910
Devlin, Albert J. 2.12669
Devlin, Christopher. 2.6521, 2.7824
Devlin, James E., 1938-. 2.11459
Devlin, John F., 1926-. 3.3793
Devlin, Keith J. 5.1348
Devlin, Kevin. 3.3346
Devol, Kenneth S. 4.9531
DeVore, Irven. 3.5484
DeVore, Irven. ed. 4.531, 5.4017
Devore, Wynetta. 4.6615
DeVorkin, David H., 1944-. 5.8103
DeVoto, Bernard Augustine, 1897-1955. 3.8472
Devoto, Giacomo. 2.851
DeVoto, Mark. 1.4467
DeVries, Duane. 2.7653
DeVries, Raymond G. 4.9545
DeWalt, Kathleen Musante. 5.7119
Dewan, S. B. 5.6509
Dewar, A. J., joint author. 5.4341
Dewart, Edward Hartley, 1828-1903, ed. 2.9894
Dewdney, A. K. 5.1639
Dewdney, John C. 3.3568, 3.3679, 4.175
D'Ewes, Simonds, Sir, 1602-1650. 3.1471
Dewey, John. 1.116, 1.583-1.586, 1.1161, 1.1279, 1.1528, 1.4596, 1.5101, 4.10224-4.10225, 4.10227-4.10229, 4.10384
Dewey, Melvil, 1851-1931. 5.7635
Dewhurst, C. Kurt. 1.6514
Dewing, H. B. (Henry Bronson), 1882-. 2.392
DeWitt, David P., 1934- joint author. 5.2265
DeWitt, Howard A. 1.4088
Dewoskin, Kenneth Joel. 2.2170
Dex, Shirley. 4.3277
Dexter, Byron Vinson, 1900- ed. 5.8253
Dexter, D. L. (David Lawrence), 1924- joint author. 5.2324
Dexter, Lewis Anthony. 4.8058
Dey, Nundo Lal. 3.4153
Deyermond, A. D. 2.5101
DeYoung, Carol D. 5.4696
Dharmakīrti, 7th cent. 1.1180
Dharmottara. 1.1180
D'Harnoncourt, Anne, 1943-. 1.4972
Dhavan, Rajeev. 5.7597
Dhillon, B. S. 5.7042
Di Castri, Francesco. ed. 5.3572
Di Castri, Francesco. 5.3565
Di Cesare, Mario A. 2.6156
Di Donato, Pietro, 1911-. 2.11566
Di Piero, W. S. 2.4998
Di Pietro, Robert J. 2.2690
Diagram Group. 4.961, 5.2005, 5.4692
Dialectics of Biology Group. 5.3327
Diamond, Arlyn, 1941-. 2.5585
Diamond, Edwin. 4.7789
Diamond, Harold J., 1934-. 1.3549
Diamond, Irene, 1947-. 4.5969
Diamond, Jared M. 5.3515
Diamond Lead Company. 4.2541
Diamond, Malcolm Luria. 1.971
Diamond, Milton. 4.5503
Diamond, Robert E. 2.936
Diamond, Solomon, 1906- comp. 5.71
Diamond, Stanley, 1922-. 4.484, 4.10181
Diamonstein, Barbaralee. 1.5958
Diaper, William, d. 1717. 2.6984
Diaz, Albert James. ed. 5.7675, 5.7703
Diaz, Albert James. 5.7704
Diaz-Briquets, Sergio. 4.1650
Díaz del Castillo, Bernal, 1496-1584. 3.8922
Diaz, Juan. 3.8603
Díaz-Plaja, Fernando. 3.3407
Díaz-Plaja, Guillermo, 1909-. 2.5085
Dibble, Charles E. 3.8888
Dibelius, Martin, 1883-1947. 1.2627, 1.2675, 1.2720, 1.2723
Dibner, Bern. joint author. 5.5547
Dice, Lee Raymond, 1887-. 5.3261
Dicey, Albert Venn, 1835-1922. 4.7724, 4.9402
Dichter, Harry, 1899-. 1.3544

Dick, Bernard F. 2.8711, 2.9269, 2.12625
Dick, Everett Newfon, 1898-. 3.8338, 3.8455
Dick, George, 1914-. 5.4671
Dick, Philip K. 2.12973-2.12974
Dick-Read, Grantly, 1890-1959. 5.5073
Dick, Robert C. 3.7235
Dick, Susan. 2.9568
Dick, Susan. ed. 2.7955
Dick, Trevor J. O. 5.8397
Dicken, Peter. joint author. 4.4120
Dickens, A. G. (Arthur Geoffrey), 1910-.
　1.2322, 1.2355-1.2356, 3.625
Dickens, Charles, 1812-1870. 2.7624-2.7628,
　2.7631-2.7633, 2.7635, 2.7651, 3.2823, 3.6032
Dickerson, Richard Earl. 5.2626
Dickes, E. W. (Ernest Walter), b. 1876. tr.
　3.2422, 3.3216
Dickey, James. 2.12975-2.12978
Dickey, John W., 1941-. 4.3903
Dickey, William. 2.12979
Dickhut, Harold W., 1911-. 4.4266
Dickie, George, 1926-. 1.1355-1.1356
Dickie, Kenneth J. joint author. 5.4612
Dickie, Margaret, 1935-. 2.11532, 2.13265
Dickinson, C. H. 5.5396
Dickinson, Emily, 1830-1886. 2.10994-2.10996
Dickinson, Fidelia. 5.8333
Dickinson, Goldsworthy Lowes. 4.9119
Dickinson, Gordon Cawood. 4.211
Dickinson, H. T. 4.7291
Dickinson, John, 1732-1808. 3.6927, 4.7376
Dickinson, Robert Eric, 1905-. 3.2242, 4.47,
　4.6250
Dickinson, Thomas Herbert, 1877-.
　2.3767-2.3769, 2.10521
Dickinson, William B. ed. 3.7912
Dickinson, William Croft, 1897-. 3.1773, 3.1786
Dickson, David. 4.2314, 5.790, 5.5519
Dickson, Gary W. 5.5607
Dickson, Leonard E. (Leonard Eugene), 1874-.
　5.1322
Dickson-Simpson, John Marmaduke, ed. 5.6224
Dickson, William John, 1904- joint author.
　5.5603
Diderot, Denis, 1713-1784. 1.813, 2.3115,
　2.4068-2.4071
Didion, Joan. 2.12983-2.12986
Dieckmann, Liselotte. 2.13580
Diehl, Charles, 1859-1944. 3.2657, 3.2659,
　3.2668
Diehl, Gaston. 1.5879
Diehl, Joanne Feit, 1947-. 2.10997
Diehl-Nagle, Sherra. 5.6453
Diehl, Richard A. joint author. 3.8896
Diejomaoh, Victor P. 4.2588
Diels, Hermann, 1848-1922. 1.218, 1.220, 2.322
Diem, Hermann, 1900-. 1.3289
Diener, Edward, 1946-. 4.1223
Diener, Thomas. 4.10556
Dienes, C. Thomas. joint author. 4.9715
Dienes, Leslie. 4.3712, 5.6142
Dies, Martin, 1901-. 3.7544
Diesendorf, Mark. 5.6124
Dieter, George Ellwood. 5.5774
Dieter, Melvin Easterday. 1.3357
Dieth, Eugen, 1893-1956, ed. 2.1114
Dietrich, Craig. 3.4787
Dietrich, Richard Vincent, 1924-. 5.3013,
　5.3034
Dieudonné, Jean Alexandre, 1906-. 5.1106,
　5.1439, 5.1576
Díez Echarri, Emiliano. 2.5086
Difco Laboratories. 5.4446
Diffie, Bailey W. (Bailey Wallys), 1902-1983.
　3.8978
DiGaetani, John Louis, 1943-. 1.4052
Digby, Anne. 4.10116
Digges, Mary Laurentia, 1910-. 1.2540
Diggins, John P. 3.2841, 4.6987, 4.7307
Diggle, James, ed. 2.7838
Diggory, Terence, 1951-. 2.10499
Dijksterhuis, E. J. (Eduard Jan), 1892-1965.
　5.725, 5.727
Dijkstra, Edsger Wybe. 5.1173
Dijkstra, Edsger Wybe. joint author. 5.1170
Dike, Kenneth Onwuka. 4.2587
Dilke, Charles Wentworth, 1789-1864. 2.7819
Dilke, Maria Dover (Walker) d. 1850. 2.7819

Dilke, Oswald Ashton Wentworth. 4.231
Dill, Samuel, Sir, 1844-. 3.2730
Dillard, Annie. 2.3525
Dillard, Heath, 1933-. 4.5860
Dillard, J. L. (Joey Lee), 1924-. 2.1126,
　2.1129-2.1130, 2.1153, 2.1155, 2.1160
Dillenberger, Jane. 1.4906
Dillenberger, John. 1.3280
Dilley, Arthur Urbane, 1873-. 1.6584
Dilliard, Irving, 1904- ed. 4.9446
Dilligan, Robert J. joint author. 2.7194
Dillingham, Harry C. 4.5194
Dillingham, William B. 2.10726,
　2.11168-2.11170
Dillon, Bert. 2.6410
Dillon, Francis. 3.7988
Dillon, George, 1906-. 2.4047, 2.4135
Dillon, John M. 1.322
Dillon, Katherine V. 3.1035
Dillon, Merton Lynn, 1924-. 3.7222, 3.7253
Dilthey, Wilhelm, 1833-1911. 1.982, 3.468
Dimbleby, Jonathan. 3.3864
DiMeglio, John E. 2.2834
Dimock, Edward C. 2.1875, 2.1921
Dimock, Edward C. ed.and tr. 4.804
Dimock, Marshall Edward, 1903- joint author.
　4.7889
Dimond, Paul R. 4.9589
Dimsdale, Joel E., 1947-. 3.1120
Din, Gilbert C. 3.5933
Dine, Jim, 1935-. 1.6439
Diner, Hasia R. 3.6551
Dinerstein, Herbert Samuel, 1919-. 3.7862,
　5.7323
Dinesen, Isak, 1885-1962. 2.14019-2.14020,
　3.5269
Dingle, Herbert, 1890-. 5.878
Dingman, Roger. 4.9158
Dinitz, Simon. joint author. 4.6864, 4.6869
Dinkin, Robert J. 4.8101
Dinnage, Rosemary. 4.6580
Dinnerstein, Leonard. 4.8957
Dinsmoor, William Bell, 1886-. 1.5218
Diogenes Laertius. 2.363
Dion, Léon, 1923-. 4.8314
Dionisotti, Carlo. 2.4963
Dionysius, of Halicarnassus. 2.364-2.365,
　2.449-2.450
Diop, Birago. 4.811
Diop, David. 2.4870
Dipple, Elizabeth. 2.9773
DiPrima, Richard C. 5.1501
Dirac, P. A. M. (Paul Adrien Maurice), 1902-.
　5.2018, 5.2150
Diraviam, K. 2.2274
Dircks, Phyllis T. 2.7032
Director, Stephen W., 1943-. 5.6276
Diringer, David, 1900-. 2.169-2.170, 2.173
Dirks, John Edward, 1919-. 1.3419
Dirksen, Herbert von, 1882-. 3.886
Dirlam, Joel B. joint author. 4.4313
Dirr, Michael A. 5.3684
Dirzo, Rodolfo. 5.3769
Disch, Thomas M. 2.12987
Discovery ('83-　　　) (1984: Chicago, Ill.)
　4.6596
Disher, Maurice Willson, 1893-. 2.2821
Dishman, Rod K. joint author. 5.5024
Disque, Robert O. 5.5884
Disraeli, Benjamin, Earl of Beaconsfield,
　1804-1881. 2.7393-2.7395
District of Columbia Historical Records Survey.
　1.3542
Ditchburn, R. W. 5.2278
Ditfurth, Hoimar von. 5.1713
Dittman, Richard. joint author. 5.2231
Dittmer, Lowell. 3.4823
Ditton, Jason. 4.4816
Ditzen, Rudolph, 1893-1947. 2.13728
Ditzion, Sidney Herbert, 1908-. 4.5573
Diubaldo, Richard J. 3.8868
Divine, Robert A. comp. 3.931
Divine, Robert A. 3.932, 3.7760, 3.7780, 3.7821,
　4.8948
Divine, Robert Alexander, 1929-. 3.7759
Dix, Gregory. 1.2986

Dixit, Avinash K. 4.1388, 4.2767
Dixit, Prabha. 3.4285
Dixon, A. F. G. (Anthony Frederick George)
　5.3877
Dixon, Bernard. 5.4443
Dixon, Peter, 1932-. 3.1574
Dixon, Robert C. (Robert Clyde), 1932-. 5.6371
Dixon, Robert Galloway, 1920-. 4.9731
Dixon, Robert L. joint author. 4.4401
Dixon, Robert S. 5.1738
Dixon, Roger, 1935-. 1.5371
Dixon, Samuel L., 1934- joint author. 4.6827
Dixon, Wilfrid Joseph, 1915-. 5.1395
Dixson, Miriam. 4.6163
Djambatan (Firm: Amsterdam, Netherlands)
　4.178
Djerassi, Carl. 5.5052
Djilas, Milovan, 1911-. 3.3556-3.3557, 3.3606,
　4.7105
Djwa, Sandra, 1939-. 2.9960
Dkon-mchog-'jigs-med-dhaṅ-po, Jam-dbyaṅs-
　bźad-pa II, 1728-1791. 1.2165
Dmytryshyn, Basil, 1925-. 3.3000-3.3001
Doan, Van Toai, 1946-. 3.4470
Doane, Alger Nicolaus, 1938-. 2.6304
Doane, Gilbert Harry, 1897-. 3.293
Dobash, R. Emerson. 4.6746
Dobash, Russell. joint author. 4.6746
Dobb, Maurice Herbert, 1900-. 4.1427, 4.1749,
　4.2376, 4.2768, 4.3127
Dobbie, Elliott Van Kirk, 1907- ed. 2.6277
Dobbs, Brian. 2.8018
Dobbs, Judy. joint author. 2.8018
Dobby, Ernest Henry George. 3.3614, 3.4381
Dobell, Clifford, 1886-1949. 5.3208
Dobell, Peter C. 3.8776
Dobelstein, Andrew W. 4.6477
Dobkin de Rios, Marlene. 4.553
Dobkowski, Michael N. 3.4016
Doblhofer, Ernst. 2.225
Döblin, Alfred, 1878-1957. 2.13729
Dobrée, Bonamy, 1891-. 2.5521, 2.5678, 2.5892,
　2.5909, 2.6231-2.6232, 2.6945-2.6946, 2.7322,
　2.7897, 2.7997, 3.1548
Dobrin, Bogoslav. 4.2418
Dobrin, Milton Burnett. 5.6738
Dobroszycki, Lucjan. 3.3983, 3.3989
Dobson, Austin, 1840-1921. 2.7042
Dobson, E. J. (Eric John) 2.1020, 2.6309
Dobson, F. 4.347
Dobson, James C., 1936- joint author. 4.6583
Dobson, John M. 3.7418
Dobson, Narda. 3.9058
Dobson, R. B. (Richard Barrie) 2.6427
Dobson, William Arthur Charles Harvey, 1913-.
　1.170
Dobyns, Henry F. 3.9292
Dobzhansky, Theodosius Grigorievich,
　1900-1975. 4.4892, 5.3356, 5.3379, 5.3628
Dock, Lavinia L., 1858-1956. joint author.
　5.5161
Dockrill, M. L. (Michael L.) joint author.
　5.7165
Dockstader, Frederick J. 3.5812, 3.5831, 3.5888
Doctorow, E. L., 1931-. 2.12988-2.12991
Dodd, A. E. (Arthur Edward) 5.6897
Dodd, Arthur Herbert. 4.2301
Dodd, C. H. (Clement Henry) 3.3576, 3.3597
Dodd, Charles Harold, 1884-1973. 1.2698,
　1.2887
Dodd, J. E. (James Edmund), 1952-. 5.2458
Dodd, J. Robert (James Robert), 1934-. 5.3155
Dodd, Janet S., 1944-. 5.2599
Dodd, Kurt. 5.2997
Dodd, Lawrence C., 1946-. 4.8008
Dodd, William Edward, 1869-1940. 3.7322,
　3.8141
Dodder, Laura. 4.6878
Dodds, Eric Robertson, 1893-. 2.452, 5.667
Dodds, Gordon B. (Gordon Barlow), 1932-.
　3.8636
Doder, Dusko. 3.3564
Dodge, Ernest Stanley. 3.5585
Dodge, Guy Howard. 4.7443
Dodge, Norton T. joint author. 4.3294
Dodge, Norton T. 1.5034
Dodge, Richard Elwood, 1868-. 4.363
Dodge, Robert K. 2.10742

Dodgson, Campbell, 1867-1948. 1.6474
Dodsley, Robert, 1703-1764. comp. 2.6218
Dodwell, C. R. (Charles Reginald) 1.4933,
  1.5862
Dodwell, Charles Reginald. 1.5099
Dodwell, Henry, 1879-1946. 3.4220
Dodwell, Peter C. 1930- ed. 5.5
Doe, Paula. 2.2040
Doebelin, Ernest O. 5.5690
Doenecke, Justus D. 3.7486
Doering, Mildred. 4.3312
Doeringer, Peter B. 4.3218
Doern, G. Bruce. joint author. 4.2123
Doern, G. Bruce. 4.3086, 5.769
Doernberg, Erwin. 1.3825
Doerner, Max, 1870-1939. 1.6343
Dōgen, 1200-1253. 1.2177
Doggett, JoElla, joint author. 5.7796
Doherty, R. D., joint author. 5.6775
Doherty, Robert W. 1.3351
Doherty, Terence. 5.4112
Dohmann, Barbara, 1936- joint author. 2.5302
Doi, Takeo. 2.2087, 5.431
Doi, Yoshiko, 1935-. 1.6313
Dolan, J. R. 3.309
Dolan, Jay P., 1936-. 1.3173, 1.3182
Dolan, John Patrick. 1.2281, 5.4500
Dolan, Josephine A. 5.5160
Dolbeare, Kenneth M. 4.9594
Dolby, A. W. E. 2.2197
Dolby, William. 2.2169
Dole, George F. 1.3385
Doleželová-Velingerová, Milena, 1932-. 2.2175
Dolge, Alfred, 1848-. 1.4152
Dolin, Arnold. 5.7568
Doll, Don, 1937-. 3.5846
Doll, Ronald C. 4.10435, 4.10525
Doll, Susan, 1954-. 2.3032
Dollard, John, 1900-. 3.6755, 3.8158, 4.4787,
  4.5065, 4.10373, 5.7163
Dollarhide, Louis D. 2.12670
Dolley, Michael. 3.280, 3.1822
Dolman, Antony J. 4.9036, 4.9132
Dolmen Press, Dublin. 2.7969, 2.8521
Dolmetsch, Arnold, 1858-1940. 1.4136
Dolnick, Sandy. 5.7617
Dolphin, David. 5.2777
Dolphin, Warren D. 5.3386
Domar, Evsey D. 4.2769
Dombrovskiĭ, IUriĭ Osipovich. 2.1546
Domenico, P. A. (Patrick A.) 5.5969
Domes, Jürgen. 3.4807
Domhoff, G. William. 3.6579, 4.5150-4.5151,
  4.5221, 4.5241, 4.6178, 4.8206
Domínguez, Jorge I., 1945-. 3.9000, 4.2138
Domínguez Ortiz, Antonio. 3.3437
Dominick, Joseph R. 2.2856
Dömling, Wolfgang, 1938-. 1.3779
Dommel, Paul R., 1933-. 4.4662
Dommen, Arthur J. 3.4453
Don-Yihya, Eli'ezer. 3.3835
Donachie, Matthew J. 5.5819
Donadoni, Eugenio, 1870-1924. 2.4879
Donagan, Alan. 1.1446
Donahue, John R. 1.2688
Donahue, Roy Luther, 1908- joint author.
  5.5292
Donahue, Thomas John, 1943-. 2.5231
Donald, David Herbert, 1920-. 3.7076,
  3.7161-3.7162, 3.7298, 3.7341, 3.7347-3.7348
Donaldson, E. T., comp. 2.6314
Donaldson, E. Talbot (Ethelbert Talbot) 2.6291,
  2.6396, 2.6399
Donaldson, Frances Lonsdale, Lady. 2.3332,
  3.1697
Donaldson, Gordon. 1.2360, 3.1776, 3.1779,
  3.1784, 3.1793-3.1794
Donaldson, Gordon. comp. 3.1774
Donaldson, Gordon. jt. ed. 3.1773
Donaldson, Ian G. 5.6209
Donaldson, James, Sir, 1831-1915, joint ed.
  1.2194
Donaldson, Margaret C. 4.10377
Donaldson, Robert H. 3.3074
Donaldson, Scott. 2.11722, 2.11727, 2.11858
Donaldson, Stephen. 2.12993
Donaldson, Thomas, 1945-. 4.2704
Donat, Alexander. 3.1078

Donatello, 1386?-1466. 1.5729
Donati Barcellona, Maria. 1.4666
Donato, Anthony. 1.4442
Dondore, Dorothy Anne, 1894-1946. 3.8295
Donegan, Jane B. (Jan Bauer), 1933-. 5.5060
Doney, Willis. 1.799
Donfried, Karl P. ed. 1.2670
Doni, Anton Francesco, 1513-1574. 2.4955
Donin, Hayim. 1.1982
Donington, Robert. 1.4050, 1.4123,
  1.4127-1.4128, 1.4208-1.4209
Donitz, Karl, 1892-. 3.1038
Donlan, Walter. 3.2546
Donleavy, J. P. (James Patrick), 1926-. 2.8599
Donn, Clifford B. 4.3652
Donnan, Elizabeth, 1883-1955, ed. 3.7188
Donne, John, 1572-1631. 1.3071, 1.3309,
  2.6452-2.6458
Donnelly, Jack. 4.7628
Donnelly, Murray S. 4.8323
Donnelly, Thomas C. (Thomas Claude), 1905-
  joint author. 4.7957
Donner, Frank J. 4.7905
Donner, Fred McGraw, 1945-. 3.3667
Donner, Henry Wolfgang. 2.7399
Donner, Wolf. 3.4517
Donnerstein, Edward I. 4.5547, 5.418
Donnithorne, Audrey. 4.2473
Donnithorne, Audrey. joint author. 4.2459
Donno, Daniel J. 2.4911
Donno, Daniel John, 1920-. 4.7177
Donno, Elizabeth Story, 1921-. 2.6152, 2.6483,
  2.7104
Donoghue, Denis. 2.5921, 2.10486
Donohue, James John, 1906-. 2.6333
Donohue, Jerry, 1920-. 5.2829
Donohue, John W., 1917-. 4.10810
Donohue, William A., 1947-. 4.7687
Donoso, José, 1924-. 2.5405-2.5406
Donovan, Josephine, 1941-. 2.2493
Donovan, Margaret. 5.6967
Donovan, Marilee Ivers. 5.4774
Donovan, Robert J. 5.3027, 3.7672,
  3.7793-3.7794, 3.7822
Donovan, Timothy Paul. 3.6238
Donovan, Timothy P., 1945-. 4.10474
Doob, Heather S. 4.10501
Doob, Leonard William, 1909-. 4.4946, 4.5065
Doody, Francis S 1917-. 4.1377
Doody, Margaret Anne. 2.7223
Dooley, D. J. (David Joseph), 1921-. 2.12012
Doolittle, Hilda, 1866-1961. 2.11567
Doolittle, James. 2.4334
Doorn, Jacobus Adrianus Antonius van, 1925-.
  5.7157
Dopp, Joseph. 1.1250
Doppler, Alfred, 1921-. 2.13656
Dopsch, Alfons, 1896-1953. 3.577
Doran, Charles F. 3.6416
Doran, J. E. 3.233
Doran, Madeleine, 1905-. 2.5865, 2.6843
Dordević, Mihailo. 2.1218
Dore, Ronald Philip. ed. 4.5446
Dore, Ronald Philip. 4.6273, 4.10623
Doremus, R. H. 5.6903
Dorey, T. A. (Thomas Alan) 3.2767
Dorf, Richard C. 5.6122, 5.6181
Dorfman, Gerald Allen, 1939-. 4.3634-4.3636
Dorfman, Joseph, 1905-. 4.1368-4.1369, 4.1379
Dorfman, Robert. 4.1276
Dorian, A. F. (Angelo Francis), 1908-. 5.707
Dorian, Frederick, 1902-. 1.4116
Dorian, Max. 4.3793
Döring, Herbert. 4.8611
Dorland, William Alexander Newman,
  1864-1956. 5.4485
Dorling, Alison Rosemary. 5.1117
Dormael, Armand van, 1916-. 4.4462
Dormon, James H. 3.6612
Dorn, Edward. 2.11575-2.11576
Dorn, Walter Louis. 3.641
Dornbusch, C. E. (Charles Emil), 1907-. 5.7836
Dorner, Peter, 1925-. 4.1773
Dorpalen, Andreas. 3.577
Dorr, Darwin, 1940-. 5.595
Dorr, Rheta Louise Childe, 1872-1948. 4.8085
Dörries, Hermann, 1895-1977. 3.2814
Dorris, Jonathan Truman, 1883-1972. 3.7461

Dorris, Michael A. 5.7738
Dorsen, Norman. 4.9659
Dorsen, Norman. joint author. 4.9655
Dorsen, Norman. ed. 4.9660
Dorsett, Lyle W. 3.8366, 4.8841
Dorsett, Lyle W. joint author. 3.8367
Dorsky, Susan, 1946-. 4.6136
Dorson, Richard Mercer, 1916-. 2.10840, 4.751,
  4.759, 4.761, 4.775-4.776
Dorst, Jean, 1924-. 5.3939
Dorsten, J. A. van. ed. 2.6507
Dorwart, Reinhold August, 1911-. 4.8616
Dos Passos, John, 1896-1970. 2.11577-2.11586
Dose, Klaus. joint author. 5.3319
Doshi, Saryu. 3.4346
Doskow, Minna. 2.7408
Doss, Martha Merrill. 4.3252, 4.6171
Dostoyevsky, Fyodor, 1821-1881. 2.1339,
  2.1341-2.1344, 2.1346-2.1361, 2.1363
Doten, Alfred, 1829-1903. 3.8607
Dothan, Trude Krakauer. 3.3791
Dotson, Lillian Ota, joint author. 5.8032
Dott, Robert H., 1929-. 5.2969
Doty, Robert M. 1.4908, 5.6965
Doubleday, Neal Frank. 2.11069
Dougall, John. 5.2366
Dougan, Alice Maria, 1876- ed. 5.8183
Dougherty, James E. 4.9027
Doughty, Charles Montagu, 1843-1926. 3.4049
Doughty, Harold. 4.9940
Doughty, Howard, 1904-. 3.6257
Doughty, Oswald. ed. 2.8017
Doughty, Oswald. 2.7597, 2.8019
Doughty, Paul L. joint author. 3.9292
Douglas, Alfred Bruce, Lord, 1870-1945.
  2.8274, 2.8600
Douglas, Althea. 2.6894
Douglas, Ann, 1942-. 2.10291
Douglas, Bodie Eugene, 1924-. 5.2703, 5.2846
Douglas, David Charles, 1898-. 3.1210, 3.1232,
  3.1342
Douglas, Edna. 4.4279
Douglas, Gawin, Bishop of Dunkeld,
  1474?-1522. 2.6469
Douglas, George H., 1934-. 2.12769
Douglas, George W. (George Warren), 1938-.
  4.4088
Douglas, George William, 1863-1945. 4.873
Douglas-Hamilton, Iain. 5.4039
Douglas-Hamilton, Oria. joint author. 5.4039
Douglas, Ian. 4.267
Douglas, Jack D. ed. 4.5071
Douglas, Jack D. 4.6730
Douglas, Jack D. joint author. 4.5075
Douglas, Keith Castellain, 1920-1944. 2.8601
Douglas, Kenneth. 2.5173
Douglas, Mary. 1.1529, 4.534, 4.613, 4.864
Douglas, Mary. comp. 1.1290
Douglas, Paul Howard, 1892-. 3.7636, 4.3128,
  4.3143, 4.3458
Douglas, Ronald G. 5.1480
Douglas, Roy, 1924-. 3.917-3.918, 3.951, 3.1702
Douglas, Stephen Arnold, 1813-1861. 3.7150,
  3.7295
Douglas, William A. B., 1929-. 3.1019
Douglas, William O. (William Orville), 1898-.
  4.9448, 4.9666, 4.9808
Douglass, Fenner. 1.4145
Douglass, Frederick. 3.7236-3.7238, 4.6041
Douglass, John. 5.3906
Douglass, William A. 3.2945, 3.3479, 3.5687,
  5.7855
Douhet, Giulio, 1869-1930. 5.7393
Doulis, Thomas. 2.569, 2.613
Doull, John, 1923- joint author. 5.4720
Doumas, Christos. 3.2594
Dover, Cedric. 1.4909
Dover, Kenneth James. 1.1420, 2.240, 2.432,
  2.522, 2.560, 2.562, 4.5533
Dover, Kenneth James. ed. 2.559
Dover, S. D. (Stanley David) joint author.
  5.2768
Dovring, Folke. 4.2846
Dow, James B. A., joint author. 4.2297
Dow Jones & Co. 4.4619
Dow Jones-Irwin. 4.4248, 4.4619
Dow, Miroslava Wein. 2.7465
Dowd, David Lloyd. 1.6088

Dowd, Douglas Fitzgerald, 1919-. 4.1873
Dowd, Laurence Phillips, 1914-. 4.3969
Dower, John W. 3.4987
Dowling, A. P. (Ann P.), 1952-. 5.2225
Dowling, Brendan B. (Brendan Robert), joint author. 4.2315
Dowling, William C. 2.6907
Downer, Alan Seymour, 1912-. 2.3180, 2.3352, 2.5839, 2.10522
Downes, Alfred Howard Campbell, 1882- tr. 1.349
Downes, Edward, 1911-. 1.4523
Downes, Kerry. 1.5368, 1.5388, 1.5405, 1.5407, 1.6275
Downey, Fairfax Davis, 1893-. 3.5774
Downey, Glanville, 1908-. 3.3803
Downie, J. A. (James Alan), 1951-. 2.7309
Downie, Patricia A. 5.5203
Downing, A. J. (Andrew Jackson), 1815-1852. 1.5567, 1.6552
Downing, Antoinette Forrester. 1.5303
Downing, Christine, 1931-. 1.1653
Downing, John A. 4.10338
Downs, Angela M., joint author. 5.1642
Downs, Anthony. 4.5218, 4.6205, 4.7753-4.7754
Downs, Donald Alexander. 4.9706
Downs, Elizabeth C. (Elizabeth Crooks) 5.7665
Downs, Joseph. 1.6563
Downs, Marion P. 5.5041
Downs, Michael. 4.7403
Downs, Robert Bingham, 1903-. 4.10189, 4.10191, 5.7598, 5.7665, 5.7682-5.7683
Downton, James V. 1.2100
Dowson, D. 5.6242
Dowson, Ernest Christopher, 1867-1900. 2.7679
Dowson, John, 1820-1881. 3.4251
Doyle, Arthur Conan, Sir, 1859-1930. 2.7680-2.7682
Doyle, Charles, 1928-. 2.10212
Doyle, Don Harrison, 1946-. 3.8354, 3.8428
Doyle, Jack, 1947-. 4.3681
Doyle, Kenneth O. joint author. 4.10347
Doyle, Mary Ellen, 1932-. 2.7711
Doyle, Paul A. 2.11433, 5.7929
Doyle, William, 1942-. 3.2076
Dozier, Robert R., 1932-. 3.1572
Draayer, I. (Ingrid), 1950-. 5.8425
Drabble, Margaret, 1939-. 2.5485, 2.5582, 2.8458, 2.9657-2.9665, 1.1589
Drabkin, I. E. (Israel Edward), 1905-1965. ed. and tr. 5.2027
Drache, Daniel, 1941- joint author. 5.8396
Drachman, Virginia G., 1948-. 5.4539
Dragadze, Tamara. 4.628
Draine, Betsy, 1945-. 2.9029
Drake, Charles L., 1924- joint author. 5.2981
Drake, Frank R. 5.1349
Drake, Frederick C., 1937-. 3.6381
Drake, Robert, 1930-. 2.13216
Drake, Robert M., 1920- joint author. 5.2263
Drake, St. Clair. 3.8423
Drake, Stillman. 5.1691, 5.2039
Drake, Stillman. ed. and tr. 5.2027
Drake, Stillman. tr. 5.2028
Drake, William. 2.12583-2.12584
Drake, William A, 1899-, ed. 2.4994
Draper, Alan B., joint author. 5.7039
Draper, Ronald P., 1928- comp. 2.8984
Draper, Theodore, 1912-. 3.4485, 3.6665, 4.6988-4.6989
Dray, William H. 3.469, 3.470, 3.507
Dray, William H. ed. 3.471
Drayton, Michael, 1563-1631. 2.6471
Dražić, Dragutin M., joint author. 5.2912
Drazin, P. G. 5.1670
Dreeben, Robert. 4.10766
Dreger, Ralph Mason. 5.520
Dreher, S. 5.8000
Dreijmanis, John. 4.7723
Dreisbach, Robert H. (Robert Hastings), 1916-. 5.4724
Dreisbach, Robert Rickert. 5.2810
Dreiser, Theodore, 1871-1945. 2.11590-2.11598
Drekmeier, Charles. 3.4194
Drell, Sidney D. (Sidney David), 1926- joint author. 5.2109, 5.2152
Drescher, Seymour. 4.6434, 4.7447
Dresner, Samuel H. 1.1988

Dresner, Stephen. 5.2022
Dressel, Paul Leroy, 1910-. 4.10571, 4.10592
Drevet, Marguerite L. 5.8001
Drew, Clifford J., 1943-. 5.978
Drew, Donald R. 4.3925
Drew, Elizabeth. 3.7920
Drew, Philip, 1943-. 1.5512
Drew University. Library. 1.3375
Drewal, Henry John. 3.5355
Drewal, Margaret Thompson. 3.5355
Drewery, Benjamin. 1.2745
Drewnowski, Jan F. 4.2228
Drewry, John Eldridge, 1902-. 2.2477
Drews, Robert. 3.3713
Drexler, Arthur. 1.5321, 1.5452
Dreyer, J. L. E. (John Louis Emil), 1852-1926. 5.1852
Dreyer, John Louis Emil, 1852-1926. 5.1684
Dreyer, June Teufel, 1939-. 3.4652
Dreyer, Sharon Spredemann. 5.8361
Dreyfus, Hubert L. 5.1008
Dreyfuss, Henry, 1904-. 5.7016
Drimmer, Melvin, comp. 3.6613
Drinker, Henry Sandwith, 1880-1965. 4.9477
Drinkwater, J. F. 3.1979
Drinnon, Richard. 3.5825
Driscoll, John Paul. 1.4899
Driscoll, Laura A. joint author. 4.10378
Driscoll, Richard. 5.4850
Driskell, David C. 1.4910
Driskell, Leon V., 1932-. 2.13217
Driver, Edwin D. 3.6758, 4.1671, 5.8287
Driver, Harold Edson, 1907-. 3.5691
Driver, Sam N., 1929-. 2.1538
Droms, William G., 1944-. 4.4451
Drone, Jeanette Marie, 1940-. 1.3576
Dronke, Peter. 2.2551, 2.2642
Dross, F. 2.13675
Droste-Hülshoff, Annette von, 1797-1848. 2.13560
Droz, Jacques. 3.693, 3.2498
Drucker, H. M. (Henry Matthew) 1.506, 4.8436, 4.8524, 4.8548
Drucker, Peter Ferdinand, 1909-. 4.2631, 4.2647, 4.2747, 4.3004
Drucker, Philip, 1911-. 3.5749
Drucker, Trudy. 2.7096
Drug Abuse Council (Washington, D.C.) 4.6670, 5.4428
Drummond, Ian M. 3.8774, 4.2306
Drummond, William, 1585-1649. 2.6473
Drury, Allen. 2.11608, 3.7898
Drvota, Mojmír. 2.1694
Dry, Murray. 4.7829
Dryden, John, 1631-1700. 2.6985-2.6992, 2.6994, 3.2512
Dryfhout, John, 1940-. 1.5672
Drysdale, Alasdair. 3.3724
Du Bellay, Joachim, 1525 (ca.)-1560. 2.3998
Du Bois, Cora Alice, 1903-. 4.632, 4.4988
Du Bois, W. E. B. (William Edward Burghardt), 1868-1963. 3.6641-3.6643, 3.6758, 3.6823-3.6829, 3.7189, 3.7462, 4.10865
Du Boulay, F. R. H. 3.2273
Du Boulay, F. R. H. ed. 3.1369
Du Boulay, Juliet. 4.5390
Du Guillet, Pernette, 1520?-1545. 2.3928
Du Maurier, George, 1834-1896. 2.7684
Du Pont de Nemours, Pierre Samuel, 1739-1817. 3.2043
Du Pont, Henry Francis, 1880-. 1.6563-1.6564
Du Preez, Wilhelmus Petrus. 4.7245
Du Prey, Pierre de la Ruffinière. 1.5401
Du Val, Miles Percy, 1896-. 4.3948
Dubbey, John Michael, 1934-. 5.1084
Dubé, Marcel, 1930-. 2.4827-2.4829
Dube, S. C. (Shyama Charan), 1922-. 4.5432
Dube, Wolf Dieter. 1.4984
Duberman, Martin B. ed. 3.7242
Duberman, Martin B. 2.11147, 2.12994, 3.7318
Dubinski, Roman R. (Roman Rudolph), 1936-. 2.6909
Dublin Institute for Advanced Studies. 2.835
Dublin, Thomas, 1946-. 4.3268
Dubnow, Simon, 1860-1941. 3.3849, 3.3993
Dubofsky, Melvyn, 1934-. 4.3555, 4.3567
DuBois, Ellen Carol, 1947-. 4.5999, 4.6026
DuBois, J. Harry (John Harry), 1903-. 5.6908

Dubois, Jean, grammarian. 2.882, 3.4167
Dubois, Paul, joint author. 4.2333
Dubos, René J. (René Jules), 1901-. 4.374, 4.434, 4.4963, 5.824, 5.844, 5.3491, 5.4432, 5.4551
DuBose, Francis M. 1.3021
Dubs, Homer Hasenpflug, 1892-. 1.168
Dubuffet, Jean, 1901-. 1.4970
Duby, Georges. 1.4736, 3.1354, 4.2967, 4.5084, 4.5346, 4.5622
Ducas, fl. 1455. 3.2673
Ducat, Craig R. 4.9628
Duce, David A. 5.1244
Duchamp, Marcel, 1887-1968. 1.4971, 1.6099, 1.6102
Duchen, Claire. 4.6115
Duchêne, François. 2.8403
Duck, Steve. 5.433
Duckett, Alfred. 4.1003
Duckett, Eleanor Shipley. 3.2268
Duckett, Kenneth W. 3.267
Duckworth, George Eckel, 1903-. 2.642, 2.703
Ducrot, Oswald. 2.11
Ducsik, Dennis W., 1946-. 4.9760
Dudden, Arthur Power, 1921-. 3.6105
Dudden, Faye E. 4.3264
Duddington, Natalia Aleksandrovna (Ertel'), Mrs. tr. 2.1423
Duddington, Nataliia Aleksandrovna Ėrtel'. tr. 1.1110
Dudenredaktion (Bibliographisches Institut) 2.1188
Duderstadt, James J., 1942-. 5.6296, 5.6614
Dudgeon, Dan E. 5.6372
Dudintsev, Vladimir Dmitrievich, 1918-. 2.1547
Dudley, Billy J. 4.8801
Dudley, Brian A. C. 5.3310
Dudley, Darle W. 5.6163
Dudley, Donald Reynolds. 1.321
Dudley, Donald Reynolds. joint author. 3.2767
Dudley, Edward J. 2.2416
Dudley, William S. 3.7114
Due, John Fitzgerald. jt. author. 4.4029
Due, John Fitzgerald. 4.4695, 4.4719
Duelli-Klein, Renate. 4.5915, 5.5066
Duellman, William Edward, 1930-. 5.3930
Duerden, Dennis. joint comp. 2.10043
Duerksen, Christopher J., 1948-. 4.2068
Duerr, Edwin, 1906-. 2.3116
Duesenberry, James Stemble, 1918-. 4.1570, 4.4507
Dufey, Gunter. 4.4589
Duff, A. M. (Arnold Mackay), 1900-. 2.633
Duff, J. D. (James Duff), 1860-1940. 2.675, 2.728, 2.1429
Duff, J. Wight (John Wight), 1866-1944. 2.625, 2.633, 2.644
Duff, M. J. B. 5.1374
Duff, Raymond S., 1923-. 5.4644
Duff, Wilson, 1925-. 3.5814
Duffett, John. ed. 4.9341
Duffey, Bernard I., 1917-. 2.10472
Duffie, John A. joint author. 5.6102
Duffy, Christopher, 1936-. 3.2137, 3.3053, 5.7320
Duffy, James, 1923-. 3.5123
Duffy, Maureen. 2.6900
Dufrenne, Mikel. 1.1393
Dufy, Raoul, 1877-1953. 1.4973
Dugan, Alan. 2.12995-2.12998
Dugard, John, 1936-. 4.9232
Duggal, Kartar Singh, 1917-. 2.1917, 2.1959
Duggan, Francis X. 2.11180
Dugger, Ronnie. 3.7887
Duhamel, Georges, 1884-1966. 2.4517
Duignan, Peter. joint author. 3.5104, 3.5423
Duignan, Peter. joint comp. 3.5105
Duignan, Peter. 5.8074
Duiker, William J., 1932-. 3.4462, 3.4465-3.4466, 3.4514
Duis, Perry, 1943-. 4.6641
Duke, Benjamin C. 4.10145
Duke, Charles R. 2.3405
Duke, Daniel Linden. 4.10680
Duke, James A., 1929-. 5.5332
Duke University. 3.8176
Duke University. Center for International Studies. 4.6157

Duke University. Center for the Study of Aging and Human Development. 5.4218
Duke University. Commonwealth-Studies Center. 3.8697
Duke University, Durham, N.C. Center for Southern Studies in the Social Sciences and the Humanities. 4.5195
Dukert, Joseph M. 4.3719
Dukes, Paul, 1934-. 3.3038, 3.3092
Dukore, Bernard Frank, 1931-. 2.2780
Duling, Dennis C. 1.2632
Dull, Jonathan R., 1942-. 3.6936
Dulles, Allen Welsh, 1893-1969. 2.3724, 3.2430, 5.7364
Dulles, Foster Rhea, 1900-1970. 3.6005, 3.6320, 3.6402, 3.6421-3.6422, 3.7419, 3.7565
Dumas, Alexandre, 1802-1870. 2.4172-2.4178, 2.4181-2.4182, 2.4723
Dumas, Charles, 1949-. 1.6239
Dumas, Marcelle, ed. 2.4524
DuMaurier, Daphne, Dame, 1907-. 2.8603
Dumbauld, Edward, 1905-. 4.9667
Dumenil, Lynn, 1950-. 4.6175
Dumézil, Georges, 1898-. 1.1637, 1.1660, 1.1670, 1.1817
Dummett, Michael A. E. 1.84
Dumond, Dwight Lowell, 1895-. 3.7178, 3.7190, 3.7232, 5.7849
Dumont d'Urville, Jules-Sébastien-César, 1790-1842. 3.5595
Dumont, Louis, 1911-. 4.633, 4.6405
Dumont, René, 1904-. 4.2575, 4.7014
Dumoulin, Heinrich. 1.1761, 1.2143, 1.2173
Dumville, D. N. 3.1310
Dun & Bradstreet Credit Services. 4.4410
Dun and Bradstreet, Inc. Marketing Services Division. 4.4251
Dunar, Andrew J. 3.7810
Dunaway, David King. 1.4098
Dunbabin, Thomas James. 3.2583, 3.2715
Dunbar, Carl Owen, 1891-. 5.3131
Dunbar, Henry, d. 1883, comp. 2.516
Dunbar-Nelson, Alice Moore, 1875-1935. 2.11610
Dunbar, Pamela. 1.6385
Dunbar, Paul Laurence, 1872-1906. 2.11011-2.11012
Dunbar, R. I. M. (Robin Ian MacDonald), 1947-. 5.4032
Dunbar, William, 1460?-1520? 2.6475
Dunbar, Willis Frederick, 1902-. 3.8431
Duncan, A. A. M. (Archibald Alexander McBeth) 3.1777, 3.1786
Duncan, Acheson J. (Acheson Johnston), 1904-. 5.7029
Duncan, Alastair, 1942-. 1.6579, 1.6652
Duncan-Clark, Samuel John, 1875-1938. 4.8233
Duncan, Delbert J. 4.4318
Duncan, Isadora, 1878-1927. 4.1119, 4.1133-4.1134
Duncan, J. Ann. 2.5327
Duncan, James S. (James Stuart), 1945-. 4.3482
Duncan-Jones, Katherine. ed. 2.6507
Duncan, Otis Dudley. joint author. 4.3215
Duncan, Otis Dudley. joint ed. 4.1595, 4.1623
Duncan, Otis Dudley. 4.6208
Duncan, Robert Edward. 2.11611-2.11615
Duncan, Ronald Frederick Henry, 1914-. 3.4305, 5.836, 5.4552
Duncker, Karl, 1903-. 5.383
Duncombe, Herbert Sydney. 4.8856
Dundes, Alan. 1.1602, 2.3806, 4.758, 4.765, 4.766, 4.793
Dundes, Alan. comp. 4.768
Dunford, Nelson. 5.1482
Dungan, David L. 1.2679, 1.2886
Dunham, Albert Millard, 1906- joint ed. 1.613
Dunham, Arthur Louis. 4.2322
Dunham, Katherine. 4.1136
Dunham, Vera Sadomirsky, 1912-. 2.1283
Dunitz, Jack D. 5.2931
Duniway, Abigail Scott, 1834-1915. 4.8081
Dunkerley, Harold B., 1921-. 4.2813
Dunkerley, Joy. joint author. 4.3705
Dunkling, Leslie, 1935-. 3.303
Dunlap, George Arthur, 1893-. 2.10544
Dunlap, Thomas R., 1943-. 5.3579

Dunlap, W. Crawford (William Crawford), 1918-. 5.2347
Dunlap, William, 1766-1839. 1.4859, 2.3188
Dunlay, Thomas W., 1944-. 3.5778, 3.8479
Dunleavy, Janet Egleson. 2.7959
Dunleavy, Patrick. 4.8502
Dunlop, Ian, 1940-. 1.4781, 1.6098
Dunlop, John B. comp. 2.1637
Dunlop, John B. 2.1641
Dunlop, John Thomas, 1914-. 4.3100, 4.3129, 4.3131, 4.3346, 4.3432, 4.3436, 4.3580, 4.3678
Dunmore, John, 1923-. 3.5536
Dunn, Dorothy, 1903-. 3.5813
Dunn, Douglas. 2.9672
Dunn, Frederick Sherwood, 1893-1962. 3.1141, 5.7384
Dunn, I. S. (Irving S.), 1923-. 5.5896
Dunn, James D. G., 1939-. 1.2236
Dunn, John, 1940-. 1.679
Dunn, Malcolm Harry, joint author. 5.2299
Dunn, Marvin, 1940-. 3.8277
Dunn, Mary Maples. ed. 3.8879
Dunn, Mary Maples. 3.8081, 4.7414
Dunn, Michael R. 4.3699
Dunn, Peter N. 2.5141, 2.5198
Dunn, Richard Minta. 4.8356
Dunn, Richard S. 3.7985, 3.8081, 3.9141
Dunn, Thomas Alexander. 2.6631
Dunn, William N. 4.1205
Dunne, Finley Peter, 1867-1936. 2.3792, 2.11616, 2.11618
Dunne, Gerald T. 4.9801, 4.9828
Dunne, Thomas, 1943-. 5.5989
Dunnell, Robert C., 1942-. 3.243
Dunnette, Marvin D. 4.4350
Dunning, James Morse, 1904-. 5.5125
Dunning, John, 1942-. 2.2845
Dunning, John H. 4.3021
Dunning, William Archibald, 1857-1922. 3.7463
Dun's Marketing Services. 4.4251
Duns Scotus, John, ca. 1266-1308. 1.384
Dunsany, Edward John Moreton Drax Plunkett, 18th Baron, 1878-1957. 2.8604
Dunseath, T. K. 2.6528
Dunsire, Andrew. 4.7755
Dunstan, Elizabeth. 4.189
Dunston, Patricia J., 1947-. 5.4820
Dupee, F. W. (Frederick Wilcox), 1904-. 2.11113, 2.11116, 2.11541
Dupeux, Georges. 4.5347
DuPlessis, Rachel Blau. 2.10435
Duplessis, Yvonne, 1912-. 1.6739
DuPont, Robert L., 1936-. 4.6669
DuPraw, Ernest J., 1931-. 5.3607
Dupré, Catherine. 2.8682
Dupré, Louis K., 1925-. 1.1033, 1.3093
Dupree, A. Hunter. 5.3638
Dupree, Louis, 1925-. 3.4109-3.4110
Dupuy, R. Ernest (Richard Ernest), 1887-1975. 3.532
Dupuy, Trevor Nevitt, 1916-. 3.532, 3.4866, 5.7258
Duram, James C., 1939-. 4.9810
Durán, Manuel, 1925-. 2.5176, 2.5258
Durán, Richard P. 4.10848
Durand, John, 1822-1908. 1.4616
Durand, Maurice M. 2.2260
Durand, Régis. 2.12895
Durant, David N. 3.8231
Durant, Will, 1885- ed. 1.958
Duras, Marguerite. 2.4518-2.4522
Durbin, Elizabeth F. 4.2284
Durbin, Paul T. 5.958
Durbin, Thomas M. 4.9732
Durcan, J. W. 4.3173
Durden, Robert Franklin. 3.7157, 4.8227
Dürer, Albrecht, 1471-1528. 1.4989, 1.5806, 1.6388, 1.6462-1.6463, 1.6604
Durfee, Harold Allen, 1920-. 1.462
D'Urfey, Thomas, 1653-1723. 1.3485, 2.7008
Durga Das Pvt. Ltd. 3.347
Durgnat, Raymond. 2.3052, 2.3064
Durgy, Robert G. 2.1361
Durham, Frank, 1935-. 5.1864
Durham, John George Lambton, 1st Earl of. 3.8726
Durham, Philip, 1912-. 2.11480
Düring, Ingemar, 1903-. 1.302

Durkheim, Emile. 1.1539, 4.543, 4.601, 4.2679, 4.4750, 4.4756-4.4757, 4.4788, 4.4852-4.4854, 4.4968, 4.6731, 4.7429, 4.9369, 4.10767, 4.10805
Durkin, Dolores. 4.10419
Durkin, Mary Brian. 2.9310
Durling, Robert M. 2.4948
Duroselle, Jean Baptiste, 1917-. 3.6443
Dürr, Volker. 3.2323
Durrani, Tariq S. 5.6739
Durrans, Thomas H. (Thomas Harold) 5.6862
Durrant, John D. 5.4369
Durrell, Lawrence. 2.8605-2.8606, 2.8608-2.8611, 3.3696, 5.6964
Dürrenmatt, Friedrich. 2.12621, 2.13731-2.13734
Durst, F. 5.6240
Dury, G. H. (George Harry), 1916-. 3.1732
Dushman, Saul, 1883-. 5.2042
Dusinberre, Juliet. 2.6808
Dutch, Robert A., ed. 2.1069
Dutt, C. P., ed. 4.7072
Dutt, Kalyan, 1924-. 4.2522
Dutt, Nalinaksha. 1.2154
Dutt, Romesh Chunder, 1848-1909. tr. 2.1937
Dutt, Srikant, 1954-1981. 4.4191
Dutton, Benjamin, 1883-1937. 5.7494
Dutton, Bertha Pauline, 1903-. 3.5758
Dutton, Denis. 1.1392, 1.5201
Dutton, John A. 5.2517
Dutton, Richard, 1948-. 2.6596
Dutton, Robert R. 2.11360
Duus, Peter, 1933-. 3.4969
Duveen, James Henry, 1873-. 1.5200
Duverger, Maurice, 1917-. 4.7220, 4.7782
Duyvendak, J. J. L. (Jan Julius Lodewijk), 1889- tr. 4.7330
Dvornik, Francis, 1893-. 3.585
Dvosin, Andrew J. 2.2653
Dwek, Raymond A. 5.3317
Dwight, Herbert Bristol, b. 1885. 5.1458
Dwivedi, Ram Awadh. 2.1882
Dworkin, Andrea. 4.5545
Dworkin, Anthony Gary. 4.5842
Dworkin, R. M. 4.9495
Dworkin, Rita, joint author. 5.7808
Dworkin, Rita. 5.8124
Dwoyer, Douglas L. 5.1667
Dwyer, Carlota Cárdenas de. 2.10681
Dwyer, Daisy Hilse. 4.812
Dwyer, Edward Bridgman, joint author. 3.8900
Dwyer, Jane Powell. 3.8900
Dyce, Alexander, 1798-1869. 2.6874, 2.6890, 2.8005
Dyck, Arthur J., 1932-. 5.4560
Dyck, Perry Rand, 1943-. 4.8312
Dydon, James, ed. 3.1817
Dye, Nancy Schrom, 1947-. 4.3273
Dye, Thomas R. 4.5222, 4.8244
Dyer, Colin L. 4.1698
Dyer, K. F. (Kenneth F.), 1939-. 4.965
Dyer, K. R. (Keith R.) 4.340
Dyer, Ruth. 3.5920
Dyk, Walter. 3.5793, 3.5920
Dykeman, Wilma. 3.8154, 3.8349
Dyker, David A. 4.2377
Dykhuizen, George, 1899-. 1.588
Dyos, H. J. (Harold James), 1921-1978. 4.6254
Dyson, A. E. 2.5749
Dyson, Anne Jane, 1912- joint author. 5.7970
Dyson, Freeman J. 5.7238
Dyson, H. V. D. (Henry Victor Dyson) 2.5520
Dyson, Hope. ed. 3.1613
Dyson, Kenneth H. F. 4.7284
Dyson, Lowell K., 1929-. 4.7151
Dyson, Robert D. 5.3599
Dyson, Stephen L. 3.2716
D'Zamko, Mary Elizabeth, 1927-. 4.10906
Dziech, Billie Wright, 1941-. 4.10841
Dziewanowski, M. K. 3.3336
Dziewicki, Michael Henry. 2.1723
Dziewoński, Kazimierz. 4.6197

Eacker, Jay N. 5.20-5.21
Eade, J. C. (John Christopher) 2.5666, 2.5669
Eades, J. S. (Jeremy Seymour), 1945-. 3.5345
Eadie, Donald. 5.6575
Eadmer, d. 1124? 1.3252

Eads, George C., 1942-. 4.4079
Eagle, Dorothy. 2.5561
Eagle, Morris N. 5.131
Eagleman, Joe R. 5.2544
Eagleson, John. 1.3227
Eagleson, Robert D. 2.6685
Eagleton, Clyde, 1891-1958. ed. 4.9198
Eagleton Institute of Politics. 4.6051
Eagleton, Terry, 1943-. 2.2461, 2.2468,
   2.2478-2.2479, 2.5515, 2.7216
Eagon, Angelo. 1.3559
Eakins, Thomas, 1844-1916. 1.4896, 1.5934
Ealy, Lawrence O., 1915-. 3.6476
Eames, Arthur Johnson, 1881-. 5.3731, 5.3733
Eames, John Douglas. 2.3078
Eames, Samuel Morris, 1916-. 1.573
Eames, Wilberforce, 1855-1937. 5.7730
Eardley, A. J. (Armand John), 1901-. 5.2993
Earl, David Magarey, 1911-. 3.4940
Earl, Donald C. 2.768, 3.2731
Earle, Alice Morse. 3.6012
Earle, Edward Mead, 1894-. 3.762
Earle, John, 1824-1903. 3.1311
Earle, Peter, 1937-. 3.1508
Earle, Ralph B., joint author. 5.542
Earle, Timothy K. 4.719
Earle, William, 1919-. 1.504
Early English Text Society. 2.1010
Earnshaw, A. (Alan) 5.2830
Earnshaw, Doris. 2.3750
Easlea, Brian. 3.54, 4.5489, 5.964
Easley, J. A. 5.589
East, Robert Abraham, 1909-. 4.1907
East-West Center. Culture Learning Institute.
   5.467
East-West Environment and Policy Institute
   (Honolulu, Hawaii) 4.1840
East-West Philosophers' Conference. 1.1141
Easterbrook, W. T. 4.2115
Easterlin, Richard Ainley, 1926-. 4.1672
Easterling, P. E. 2.275
Eastern Michigan University. Center of
   Educational Resources. 5.7798
Eastern Regional Remote Sensing Applications
   Center (U.S.) 4.26
Eastin, Roy B. joint author. 5.7781
Eastlake, Charles L. (Charles Locke),
   1836-1906. 1.5377, 1.6551
Eastlake, William. 2.11620
Eastman, Byron D. 4.1389
Eastman, Charles Alexander, 1858-1939. 3.5945
Eastman, John. 3.5996
Eastman Kodak Company. Ergonomics Group.
   5.5616
Eastman Kodak Company. Human Factors
   Section. 5.5616
Eastman, Lloyd E. 3.4433, 3.4771, 3.4773
Eastman, Mary Huse, 1878-1963. 5.8194
Eastman, Max, 1883-1969. 2.2673, 2.3784
Eastman, Susan Tyler. 2.2857
Easton, David, 1917-. 4.7224, 4.7236
Easton, Freda. 4.10704
Easum, Chester Verne. 3.2485
Easwaran, Eknath. 1.1625
Eaton, Clement. 3.7090, 3.7323, 3.7372,
   3.8142-3.8143
Eaton, J. Robert (James Robert), 1902-. 5.6283
Eaton, Leonard K. 1.5293
Eaton, Quaintance. 1.4572
Eaton, Walter Prichard, 1878-1957. 2.3271
Eaton, William Edward, 1943-. 4.10243
Eaton, William J., joint author. 4.3594
Eaves, T. C. Duncan (Thomas Cary Duncan),
   1918-. 2.7222, 2.11224
Eayrs, James George, 1926-. 3.8767, 4.9012
Eban, Abba Solomon, 1915-. 3.3934
Ebato, Akira, 1932-. 4.183
Ebel, Gerhard, joint author. 5.8423
Ebeling, Gerhard, 1912-. 1.2350, 1.2742
Ebeling, Walter, 1907-. 5.5234
Eberhard, Wolfram, 1909-. 3.4653, 3.4664,
   4.807, 4.5403, 4.5412
Eberhart, Richard, 1904-. 2.11621-2.11622
Eberhart, Sylvia, joint author. 3.7562
Eberts, Randall W. 4.10686
Eberwein, Jane Donahue, 1943-. 2.10762,
   2.10998
Eberwein, Robert T., 1940-. 2.2951

Eble, Kenneth Eugene. 2.11093, 2.11728,
   4.10263, 4.10572
Ebon, Martin. 5.663
Ebrey, Patricia Buckley, 1947-. 1.1510
Eby, Frederick, 1874-1968, ed. 4.10161
Eccles, John C. (John Carew), Sir, 1903-.
   5.4286, 5.4330-5.4331
Eccles, Mark. 2.6489
Eccles, W. J. (William John) 3.5684,
   3.8702-3.8704
Eccleshall, Robert. 4.7551
Echard, William E., 1931-. 3.2156
Echeruo, Michael J. C. 2.8508
Echeverria, Durand. 3.6106
Eck, Diana L. 1.1697, 1.1705
Eckard, Joseph D., 1942-. 5.5677
Ecke Tseng, Yu-ho, 1923-. 1.6607
Eckelberry, Don Richard, 1921-. 5.3959
Ecker, Tom. 4.1050
Eckermann, Johann Peter, 1792-1854. 2.13577
Eckert, E. R. G. (Ernst Rudolf Georg), 1904-.
   5.2263
Eckert, Roger. 5.4180
Eckhardt, Celia Morris, 1935-. 4.6001
Eckhart, Meister, d. 1327. 1.3086-1.3088
Eckley, Grace. 2.9787, 2.11617
Eckman, Fern Marja. 2.12863
Eckmann, Jean Pierre. joint author. 5.1623
Eckroth, David. 5.1009, 5.6809
Eckstein, Alexander, 1915-. 4.2474-4.2476,
   4.2478
Eckstein, Harry. 3.3380
Eckstein, Max A. joint author. 4.9967
Eckstein, Otto. 4.2010
Eco, Umberto. 2.79-2.80, 2.5079-2.5080
Ecological Society of America. Western Section.
   5.3680
Economic Council of Canada. 4.2128
Economic History Association. 4.1951-4.1952
Economic History Society. 4.1693, 4.1723,
   4.2272-4.2273, 4.2275, 4.4180
Economist Intelligence Unit (Great Britain)
   4.135
Economist (London, England) 4.1247
Eddington, Arthur Stanley, Sir, 1882-1944.
   5.879, 5.1865, 5.1905-5.1907
Eddins, Dwight, 1939-. 2.8348
Eddison, Eric Rucker, 1882-1945. 2.8613
Eddleman, Floyd Eugene. 5.7804
Eddy, Mary Baker, 1821-1910. 1.3328-1.3329
Eddy, Samuel Kennedy, 1926-. 3.3714
Ede, Carol Moore, 1944-. 1.5346
Ede, David. 5.8453
Edel, Abraham, 1908-. 1.303
Edel, Leon, 1907-. 2.3520, 2.5627, 2.10266,
   2.11103, 2.11114-2.11115, 2.11117, 2.11120,
   2.12764, 2.12766, 3.315
Edel, Leon Joseph, 1907- ed. 2.11101
Edelheit, Abraham J. 5.8248
Edelheit, Hershel. 5.8248
Edelson, Marshall. 5.194
Edelstein, Debra. 1.6111
Edelstein, Ludwig, 1902-1965. 3.62
Edelstein, Stuart J. 5.4988
Eden, Anthony, Earl of Avon, 1897-.
   3.1662-3.1664
Eden, Robert. 4.7629
Edey, Maitland Armstrong, 1910- joint author.
   4.455
Edgar, Neal L., 1927-. 5.8031
Edgar, Robert S., joint author. 5.3441
Edge, Hoyt L. 5.639
Edgell, Zee. 2.10026
Edgerton, Franklin, 1885-1963. 2.1934, 2.1942
Edgerton, Harold Eugene, 1903-. 5.6952
Edgerton, Robert B., 1931-. 4.6582
Edgerton, William Benbow, 1914-. 2.1399,
   2.2670
Edgeworth, Francis Ysidro, 1845-1926. 4.1261,
   4.1294
Edgeworth, Maria, 1767-1849. 2.7685-2.7686
Edgington, John Anthony. 5.1981
Edholm, O. G. (Otto Gustaf) 5.4202
Edições Melhoramentos. Seção Lexicográfica.
   2.912
Edie, James M. ed. 1.1103
Edinger, Edward F. 5.195
Edington, Jeffrey William. 5.2923

Edman, Irwin, 1896-1954. 1.643
Edmonds, A. R. 5.2468
Edmonds, J.M. (John Maxwell) 2.394
Edmonds, John Maxwell. 2.321, 2.330, 2.378
Edmonds, Margot. joint author. 3.8486
Edmonds, Robert L. 5.3677
Edmonds, Robin. 3.3249
Edmonds, Ronald R., 1935-. 4.10855
Edmonds, Walter Dumaux, 1903-.
   2.11624-2.11625
Edmondson, Linda Harriet. 4.6132
Edmondson, Walles Thomas, 1916- ed. 5.3255
Edmunds, John, 1913-. 1.4448
Edmunds, Lowell. 3.2609, 4.766
Edmunds, R. David (Russell David), 1939-.
   3.5785, 3.5939, 3.5949
Edmunds, Robert A. 5.1133
Edrozo, Arnora. 3.4591
Edsall, Marian S. 5.7655
Edson, Lee. 5.6656
Educational Fund for Individual Rights. 4.2713
Educational Policies Commission. 4.10052
Educational Research Information Center (U.S.)
   5.7632
Educational Research Service (Arlington, Va.)
   4.10281, 4.10501
Educational Resources Information Center
   (U.S.) 5.8151
Educational Testing Service. 4.10078, 4.10893
Educators' Progress Service. 1.25, 4.10326,
   4.10329
Educators' Progress Service, Randolph, Wis.
   4.10328
Edwardes, S. M. (Stephen Meredyth),
   1873-1927. 3.4252
Edwards, A. S. G. (Anthony Stockwell
   Garfield), 1942-. 2.5606
Edwards, A. W. F. (Anthony William
   Fairbank), 1935-. 5.3452
Edwards, Allen, 1944-. 1.3832
Edwards, Allen Louis. 5.45-5.46
Edwards, Anna Camp. 4.11004
Edwards, C. A. (Clive Arthur), 1925-. 5.3840
Edwards, C. H. (Charles Henry), 1937-. 5.1451
Edwards, Clifford D. 2.12394
Edwards, Corwin D., 1901-. 4.1982
Edwards, David Lawrence. 1.2432
Edwards, Edgar O. 4.3200
Edwards, Esther P., joint author. 4.10402
Edwards, Evangeline Dora, tr. 3.4628
Edwards, G. Thomas. 3.8589
Edwards, George C. 4.7924, 4.7934, 4.7939
Edwards, Gerry. 5.3758
Edwards, Gwynne. 2.5130, 2.5166
Edwards, H. L. R. 2.6517
Edwards, Harold M. 5.1323
Edwards, Harry, 1942-. 3.6831, 4.882, 4.944
Edwards, Henry John, 1869-1923, tr. 2.653
Edwards, I. E. S. (Iorwerth Eiddon Stephen),
   1909-. 3.5146
Edwards, James Don. 4.4414
Edwards, John, 1947-. 2.125
Edwards, Jonathan, 1703-1758. 1.562, 1.1506,
   1.3332
Edwards, L. M. 5.6210
Edwards, Lee R. 2.5585
Edwards, Mark U. 1.2340, 1.2345
Edwards, Maurice. 2.13587
Edwards, Newton, 1889-. 4.9583
Edwards, P. G. 3.5581
Edwards, Paul, 1923-. 1.101, 1.1435
Edwards, Paul Geoffrey, 1926-.
   2.13981-2.13982, 2.13989
Edwards, Peter David. 2.8239
Edwards, Philip. 2.6503, 2.6607, 2.6629
Edwards, R. Dudley (Robert Dudley), 1909- ed.
   3.1849
Edwards, R. E. (Robert E.), 1926-. 5.1556
Edwards, Ralph, 1894- ed. 1.6524
Edwards, Richard, 1940-. 4.3372, 4.3429,
   4.3558, 4.6736
Edwards, Richard Alan. 1.2677
Edwards, Ruth Dudley. 4.172
Edwards, Stewart, 1937-. 3.2165-3.2166
Edwards, Willie M. 5.8382
Eeden, Frederik van, 1860-1932. 2.13951
Eekman, Thomas. 2.1199, 2.1489
Eells, George. joint author. 1.4095

Eells, Richard Sedric Fox, 1917- joint author.
  4.6760
Efrat, Elisha. 4.6272
Efron, K. M., ed. 4.2368
Egan, E. W. 3.563
Egan, Ferol. 3.7153
Egan, Gerard. 4.4935
Egan, Michael. 2.10944
Egan, Ronald C., 1948-. 2.2217
Egan, Thomas P. joint author. 4.3809
Egan, William F. 5.6516
Egerton, Clement, tr. 2.2228
Eggeling, Julius, 1842-1918. 1.1690
Eggenberger, David. 3.534
Eggenschwiler, David, 1936-. 2.13218
Eggert, Gerald G. 4.3169
Eggleston, Edward, 1837-1902. 2.11015-2.11016,
  3.6013
Eglese, R. W. 5.5566
Egoff, Sheila A. 2.2703
Egret, Jean. 3.2057
Ehlers, Ernest G. 5.3035
Ehninger, Douglas. 2.3537
Ehre, Milton, 1933-. 2.1381, 2.1392
Ehrenberg, Ronald G. 4.3155
Ehrenberg, Victor, 1891-. 2.314, 2.433, 3.553,
  3.2533, 3.2547, 4.7356
Ehrenfeld, David W. 1.499
Ehrenhalt, Alan, 1947-. 4.7992
Ehrenpreis, Anne Henry, ed. 2.7257
Ehrenpreis, Irvin, 1920-. 2.5670, 2.7289,
  2.7299-2.7300
Ehrenreich, Barbara. 4.6042
Ehrenreich, John, 1943-. 4.6510
Ehrenwald, Jan, 1900-. 5.4863
Ehrenzweig, Anton, 1908-1966. 1.4621
Ehresmann, Donald L., 1937-. 5.8182, 5.8184
Ehrich, Robert W., ed. 3.546
Ehrismann, Gustav, 1855-. 2.13459
Ehrlich, Anne H. joint author. 4.1593
Ehrlich, Cyril. 1.3711, 1.4153
Ehrlich, Eugene H. 2.1021, 2.1140, 2.10282
Ehrlich, Paul R. 4.1593, 4.1607, 5.3578
Ehrlich, Walter, 1921-. 4.9619
Ehrman, Edith. joint author. 5.8033
Ehrman, John. 3.1578, 4.8444
Ehrmann, Henry Walter, 1908-. 4.8587
Eibl-Eibesfeldt, Irenäus. 5.421
Eiby, G. A. 5.3116
Eichelberger, Clark Mell, 1896-. 4.9214
Eichenbaum, Luise. 5.4891
Eichenberg, Fritz, 1901-. 1.6430, 2.9406
Eichendorff, Joseph, Freiherr von, 1788-1857.
  2.13561
Eicher, Carl K. 4.2990
Eichhorn, Donald H. 4.10502
Eichhorn, Heinrich K. (Heinrich Karl), 1927-.
  5.1834
Eichhorn, Susan E. 5.3642
Eichner, Alfred S. 4.3687
Eichner, Hans. 2.2367
Eichrodt, Walther, 1890-. 1.2577
Eickelman, Dale F., 1942-. 1.2011, 4.639
Eidelberg, Paul. 4.7819
Eidson, Bettye K., joint author. 4.6223
Eidsvik, Charles, 1943-. 2.2952
Eigen, M. (Manfred), 1927-. 5.880, 5.3387
Eigerman, Hyman, ed. 2.8295
Eigner, Edwin M. 2.8124
Eĭkhenbaum, Boris Mikhaĭlovich, 1886-1959.
  2.1442-2.1444
Eiland, Howard. 2.13384
Einar Ólafur Sveinsson, 1899-. 2.13985
Einarsson, Benedict. 2.396
Einarsson, Stefán, 1897-. 2.13993
Einaudi, Luigi R., 1936- ed. 3.9007
Einhard, 770(ca.)-840. 3.1989
Einspruch, Norman G. 5.6546
Einstein, Albert, 1879-1955. 5.1908, 5.1914,
  5.1932, 5.1946, 5.1948, 5.2087, 5.2146, 5.2219
Einstein, Alfred, 1880-1952. 1.3470, 1.3663,
  1.3876, 1.3938, 1.3977, 1.4235, 1.4396
Einzig, Paul, 1897-1973. 4.4555, 4.4559
Eisberg, Robert Martin. 5.2053
Eisdorfer, Carl. 5.4209
Eisele, Albert, 1936-. 3.7651
Eiseley, Loren C., 1907-1977. 5.3344
Eisen, Arnold M., 1951-. 1.1973

Eisenberg, Arthur. joint author. 4.9725
Eisenberg, Nancy. 4.5729
Eisenhower, David, 1948-. 3.7836
Eisenhower, Dwight D. (Dwight David),
  1890-1969. 3.902, 3.7517, 3.7832
Eisenhower, John S. D., 1922-. 3.919, 3.957
Eisenson, Harry E. 5.5548
Eisenson, Jon, 1907-. 5.5094
Eisenstadt, S. N. (Shmuel Noah), 1923-. 4.5400,
  4.7225
Eisenstaedt, Alfred. 5.6986
Eisenstein, Elizabeth L. 5.7542-5.7543
Eisenstein, Hester. 4.6043
Eisenstein, Sarah. 4.3278
Eisenstein, Sergei, 1898-1948. 2.2953-2.2954,
  2.3039
Eisenstein, Zillah R. 4.5878, 4.6037, 4.6044
Eisinger, Chester E. 2.10616
Eisler, Richard M. 5.456
Eisner, Elliot W. comp. 4.10436
Eisner, Elliot W. 4.10437
Eisner, Joel, 1959-. 2.2862
Eisner, Julian. 5.1598
Eisner, Lotte H. 2.3061-2.3062
Eisner, Thomas, 1929- comp. 5.4055
Eissfeldt, Otto, 1887-. 1.2564
Eitner, Lorenz. 1.6109
Eitner, Lorenz. comp. 1.4777
Eixarch, Thomas. 3.8603
Ekeh, Peter P. 4.4789
Ekelöf, Gunnar, 1907-1968. 2.14062
Ekirch, A. Roger, 1950-. 4.2039
Ekirch, Arthur Alphonse, 1915-. 3.6107, 3.6386
Ekman, Paul. 5.461
Ekwall, Eilert, 1877-1964. 3.1734
Ekwensi, Cyprian. 2.10110
El-Khawas, Mohamed A. 4.9057
El Saffar, Ruth S., 1941-. 2.5170
El-Shakhs, Salah. comp. 4.6278
El-Swaify, S. A. (Samir Aly) 5.5288
El-Wakil, M. M. (Mohamed Mohamed), 1921-
  5.6612
Elath, Eliahu, 1903-. 3.4025
Elazar, Daniel Judah. 3.6567, 4.8863
Elcock, H. J. (Howard James) 3.850
Elder, Dean. 1.4542
Elder, Earl Edgar, 1887-. 1.2046
Elder, John, 1933-. 5.3079
Elder, Joseph Walter. 3.4181
Elder, Lonne. 2.12999
Elder, Neil. 4.8670
Elder, Robert Ellsworth, 1915-. 3.7610
Elderfield, John. 1.4846, 1.4976, 1.4999
Eldersveld, Samuel James. 4.8716
Eldredge, Niles. 5.3388
Eleazu, Uma O. 4.8803
Elections Research Center (Governmental
  Affairs Institute) 4.7948
Electric Power Research Institute. 5.6151
Eleutherian Mills-Hagley Foundation. 4.1869,
  4.1920
Eley, Geoff, 1949-. 3.2296, 3.2305, 3.2332
Elia, Pasquale M. d', 1890- tr. 3.4760
Eliade, Mircea, 1907-. 1.203, 1.1344, 1.1525,
  1.1530-1.1531, 1.1842
Elias, Norbert. 3.44, 4.6390
Elias, Robert, 1950-. 4.6706
Elias, Robert Henry, 1914-. 2.11600
Elias, T. O. (Taslim Olawale) 4.9926
Elias, Thomas S. 5.3685
Eli'av, Ya'akov, 1917-. 3.3912
Eliel, Ernest Ludwig, 1921-. 5.2868-5.2869,
  5.2875
Eliot, Charles Norton Edgecumbe, Sir,
  1862-1931. 1.1675, 1.2121, 3.3573
Eliot, George, 1819-1880. 2.7690-2.7693,
  2.7698-2.7699
Eliot, T. S. (Thomas Stearns), 1888-1965.
  2.2452, 2.2745, 2.5761, 2.5872, 2.7888,
  2.8863, 2.11626-2.11629, 3.8
Elisofon, Eliot. 1.5764
Elisseeff, Danielle. 3.4626
Elisseeff, Vadime. 3.4626
Elitzur, Yuval. joint author. 4.8782
Elkin, A. P. (Adolphus Peter), 1891-1979.
  3.5583, 3.5618, 4.669
Elkin, Frederick. 4.5718
Elkin, Judith Laikin, 1928-. 3.9027

Elkin, Stanley, 1930- comp. 2.10844
Elkind, David, 1931-. 4.10213, 5.563, 5.5099
Elkins, Aubrey Christian, 1939- ed. 5.8276
Elkins, Stanley M. 3.7202
Elkouri, Edna Asper. 4.9558
Elkouri, Frank. 4.9558
Elledge, Scott. ed. 2.2499, 2.5505
Elledge, Scott. 2.7119
Ellekilde, Hans Lavrida, 1891-. 3.3355
Eller, Ronald D., 1948-. 4.2020
Eller, Vernard. 3.3290
Elliff, John T. 4.6818
Ellin, Stanley, 1916-. 2.13000
Ellinger, Herbert E. 5.6637
Ellington, Duke, 1899-1974. 1.3863
Ellinwood, Leonard Webster, 1905-. 1.3542,
  1.3684
Elliot, Alison J. 4.10392
Elliot, Henry Miers, Sir, 1808-1853. 3.4251
Elliot, James, 1943-. 5.1808
Elliot, Jeffrey M. 4.7792
Elliot, Jonathan, 1784-1846, ed. 4.7822
Elliott, Brian A. 4.6256
Elliott, Brig. 5.1210
Elliott, Charles, 1939-. 4.2582
Elliott, Charles Burke, 1861-1935. 3.4601
Elliott, Clark A. 5.809
Elliott, David, 1949-. 1.6003
Elliott, David W. P. 3.4451
Elliott, Delbert S. 4.6871
Elliott, Douglas B. 5.3661
Elliott, Emory, 1942-. 2.10343, 2.10368
Elliott, Glen R. 5.4209, 5.4585
Elliott, J. F. (James Franklin), 1924- joint
  author. 4.6800
Elliott, Jean Leonard. 3.8794
Elliott, John Hall. 1.2725
Elliott, John Huxtable. 3.172, 3.626, 3.3438,
  3.3486
Elliott, John Huxtable. joint author. 3.3445
Elliott, Lawrence. 3.7658
Elliott, Philip Ross Courtney. 4.6398
Elliott, Ralph Warren Victor. 2.7802
Elliott, Roy, Ph. D. 5.6772
Elliott, Ward E. Y. 4.9726
Ellis, Albert. 5.4895
Ellis, Alexander John, 1814-1890. 1.4382,
  2.1010
Ellis, B. D. (Brian David), 1929-. 1.1297
Ellis, Barbara W. 5.5333
Ellis, David Maldwyn. 3.8026, 4.2820
Ellis-Fermor, Una Mary, 1894-1958. 2.2781,
  2.5866, 2.6646, 2.6701
Ellis, Frank H. (Frank Hale), 1916- ed. 4.7422
Ellis, Havelock, 1859-1939. 2.6574,
  2.8620-2.8622, 4.5500
Ellis, Howard Sylvester, 1898-. 4.4104, 4.4556,
  4.4593
Ellis, Jack C., 1922-. 5.8138
Ellis, Jack D. 3.2182
Ellis, John R. 3.2621
Ellis, John Tracy, 1905-. 1.3170, 1.3174-1.3175
Ellis, L.F. (Lionel Frederic), 1885-. 3.954
Ellis, Leslie, joint author. 5.1261
Ellis, Lewis Ethan, 1898-. 3.7732
Ellis, Lionel Frederic, 1885-. 3.953
Ellis, Lynda B. M. joint author. 5.3492
Ellis, Norman R. ed. 5.4974
Ellis, Richard, 1938-. 5.4004
Ellis, Richard E. 4.9747
Ellis, Steven G., 1950-. 3.1828
Ellis, Willis Davis. 5.225
Ellison, Arthur E. 5.5025
Ellison, David L. 5.4650
Ellison, Gordon N. 5.6484
Ellison, Harlan. 2.10830, 2.13001-2.13002
Ellison, Herbert J. 3.4685
Ellison, John W. (John William), 1920-. 1.2502
Ellison, Norman. 5.6686
Ellison, Ralph. 2.10320, 2.13003-2.13004
Elliston, Frederick. 1.1011, 4.6046, 5.8365
Ellman, Michael. 4.2770
Ellmann, Mary. 2.2406
Ellmann, Richard, 1918-. 2.959, 2.8284,
  2.8342-2.8343, 2.8887, 2.8900, 2.8906, 2.8910,
  2.10732, 2.10766
Ellrodt, Robert. 2.6546
Ellsberg, Robert, 1955-. 4.5117

Ellsworth, Lucius F. ed. 4.1869
Ellsworth, P. T. (Paul Theodore), 1897-. 4.2176
Ellsworth, Scott. 3.8539
Ellul, Jacques. 1.1884, 1.2558, 1.2731, 1.2919, 4.4978, 4.5019, 5.5512
Ellwood, Robert S., 1933-. 1.2099
Elmaghraby, Salah Eldin, 1927-. 5.5568, 5.5596
Elman, Richard M. ed. 4.6624
Elman, Robert. 5.3187, 5.3986, 5.5492
Elmasry, Mohamed I., 1943-. 5.6527
Elmendorf, Mary L. (Mary Lindsay) 4.6085
Elon, Amos. 3.3927, 3.4026
Elpers, J. Richard, 1938- joint author. 5.4981
Elphick, Richard. 3.5447
Elrington, G. Aidan, ed. 1.393
Elrod, John W., 1940-. 1.1125
Elsasser, Albert B. joint author. 3.5721
Elsasser, Walter M., 1904-. 5.1949
Elsen, Albert Edward, 1927-. 1.4680, 1.5646, 1.5681, 1.5710
Elsheimer, Adam, 1578-1610. 1.4991
Elshtain, Jean Bethke, 1941-. 4.5955
Elson, Benjamin Franklin, 1921-. 2.187
Elson, Robert T. 5.7586
Elsschot, Willem, 1882-1960. 2.13960
Elster, Jon, 1940-. 4.6951
Elstun, Esther N., 1935-. 2.13677
Elsworth, J. D. (John David) 2.1476
Elting, John Robert. joint author. 4.166
Eltis, W. A. (Walter Alfred) 4.4517
Elton, Charles S. (Charles Sutherland), 1900-. 5.3516, 5.4056, 5.4071
Elton, G. R. (Geoffrey Rudolph) 3.627, 3.1388, 3.1399-3.1400, 3.1407, 5.7981
Elton, G. R. (Geoffrey Rudolph) ed. 4.8395
Elton, G. R. (Geoffrey Rudolph) 4.8397
Elton, L. R. B. (Lewis Richard Benjamin) 5.2425
Elton, Oliver, 1861-1945. 2.5683, 2.5696, 2.6472
Eltringham, S. K. (Stewart Keith) 5.3564
Eluard, Paul, 1895-1952. 2.4524-2.4525
Elvin-Lewis, Memory P. F., 1933- joint author. 5.5151
Elvin, Mark. ed. 4.6266
Elvin, Mark. 3.4630, 3.4665
Elving, Philip Juliber, 1913-. 5.2656
Elvot, Thomas, Sir 1490?-1546. 4.7556
Elwell-Sutton, L. P. (Laurence Paul) 5.8072
Elwes, Henry John, 1846-1922. 5.5351
Elwin, Malcolm, 1902-. 2.7532
Ely, John Hart, 1938-. 4.9643
Elytēs, Odysseas, 1911-. 2.577-2.580
Emanuel, James A. comp. 2.10697
Emanuel, James A. 2.11903
Emanuel, Muriel. 1.4807, 1.5265
Emanuels, H. W., jt. author. 5.8341
Embleton, Clifford. 4.277, 4.278
Embleton, Clifford. comp. 5.3119
Embree, Ainslie Thomas. ed. 3.4192
Embree, Ainslie Thomas. joint ed. 3.107
Embree, Ainslie Thomas. 3.4276, 3.4278, 5.8337
Embree, Ainslie Thomas. comp. 1.1695
Embree, John Fee, 1908-. 4.637, 5.8032
Embrey, Peter G. 5.3010
Emde, Robert N. 5.5105
Emden, Alfred Brotherston, 1888- ed. 4.9975
Emecheta, Buchi. 2.10109
Emeléus, H. J. (Harry Julius) ed. 5.2695, 5.2700
Emeneau, M. B. (Murray Barnson), 1904- tr. 2.1949
Emerick, Lon L. 5.4792
Emerson, Barbara. 3.2974
Emerson, Everett H., 1925-. 2.10367, 2.10956, 3.7975
Emerson, Ralph Waldo, 1803-1882. 2.2341, 2.11017-2.11023
Emerson, Rupert, 1899-. 3.5087, 4.7486, 4.9303
Emerson, Thomas Irwin, 1907-. 4.9655
Emerton, Ephraim, 1851-1935, ed. & tr. 1.3150
Emery, Edwin. joint comp. 3.6195
Emery, Edwin. 2.3584
Emery, Irene. 5.7079
Emery, Lynne Fauley. 4.1107
Emery, Michael C. comp. 3.6195
Emery, Michael C. 2.3584
Emery, Walter Byron, 1907-. 4.9539
Emery, William J. 4.345
Emlyn-Jones, C. J. 3.4039

Emme, Eugene Morlock. ed. 5.7394
Emmel, Hildegard, 1907-. 2.13497
Emmerich, Werner. joint author. 5.2046
Emmet, Boris, 1885-. 4.4333
Emmons, Chester Wilson, 1900-. 5.3725
Emmons, Glenroy. 5.8027
Emmons, Marilyn C. 5.8027
Emmons, Terence. 4.6391
Empey, LaMar Taylor, 1923-. 4.6860, 4.6872
Empringham, Toni. 2.10745
Empson, William, 1906-. 2.1065, 2.2715, 2.5583, 2.7167, 2.8624
Emrich, Duncan, 1908- comp. 2.10756
Emrich, Wilhelm. 2.13786
Emsley, J. (John) 5.2711
Emswiler, Sharon Neufer, 1944-. 1.2987
Emswiler, Thomas Neufer, 1941-. 1.2987
Enarson, Elaine Pitt, 1949-. 5.5434
Encel, Sol. 4.8819
Enchi, Fumiko, 1905-. 2.2096
Encyclopædia Britannica. 1.1, 2.204, 4.111
Endacott, G. B. 3.4863, 4.8725
Endean, R. 5.3281
Endelman, Todd M. 3.3947
Enderle, G. (Günter), 1944-. 5.5646
Enderton, Herbert B. 5.1039
Endicott, Stephen Lyon, 1928-. 3.1260
Endō, Shūsaku, 1923-. 2.2129-2.2131
Endy, Melvin B. 3.8080
Enge, Harald A. 5.2054
Engel, Barbara Alpern. 4.6133
Engel, Bernard F. 2.12201
Engel, Edwin A, 1907-. 2.12292
Engel, J. Ronald. 3.8401
Engel, James F. 4.4280
Engel, Lehman, 1910-. 1.4217, 1.4482
Engel, S. Morris, 1931-. 1.1069
Engelhard, Hermann, ed. 2.13660
Engelhard, Hermann. 2.13635
Engelhardt, Heinz, 1936-. 5.2692
Engelmann, Bernt, 1921-. 3.3967
Engelmann, Frederick C. 4.8299
Engemann, Joseph G. 5.3833
Engerman, Stanley L. joint comp. 4.1884
Engerman, Stanley L. joint author. 3.7245
Engineering Foundation (U.S.) 4.3931
Engineers Joint Council. 5.5663
England, J. B. A. 5.2438
England, Paula. 4.5588
Engle, Paul, 1908-. 2.11646
Englekirk, John Eugene, 1905-. 2.5303, 2.5320
Engler, Robert. 4.3769
English, Ava Champney, joint author. 5.14
English, Deirdre. 4.6042
English, Earl, 1905-. 4.10724
English, Horace Bidwell, 1892-. 5.14
English Institute. 2.2426, 2.2446, 2.2617, 2.2627, 2.3409, 2.5480, 2.5492, 2.5782
English Institute, Columbia University. 2.2424
English, Jane, 1947-. 4.6046
English, John, 1945-. 3.8739, 3.8750, 3.8774, 3.8831, 4.8309
English, Margaret. joint author. 4.9455
English, Mary R. 5.6117-5.6118
Englund, Steven. joint author. 2.2912
Engram, Eleanor. 3.6759
Enkvist, Nils Erik. 2.192
Enloe, Cynthia H., 1938-. 5.7162, 5.7373
Ennin, 794-864. 3.4616
Ennius, Quintus. 2.716-2.717
Enright, D. J. (Dennis Joseph), 1920-. 2.2505, 2.2570, 2.3715, 2.6190
Enríquez, Evangelina. joint author. 3.6583
Enscoe, Gerald E. joint ed. 2.5578
Enslen, Richard A., 1931-. 4.9626
Ensminger, M. Eugene. 5.5445, 5.5447
Ensor, Robert Charles Kirkwood, 1877-. 3.1619
Enthoven, Alain C., 1930-. 5.4634, 5.7265
Entrikin, John Bennett, 1899- joint author. 5.2686
Entwisle, Doris R. 4.10415
Entwistle, William J. (William James), 1895-1952. 2.886, 2.1193

Environment Information Center. Toxic Substances Reference Dept. 5.5558
Environmental Law Institute. 4.9571
Environmental Research Laboratories (U.S.) 5.2552
Enzensberger, Hans Magnus. 2.13736-2.13738
Eoff, Sherman Hinkle, 1900-. 2.5134
Eogan, George. joint author. 4.735
Eősze, László. 1.3909
Ephrussi, Boris, 1901-. 5.3426
Epictetus. 2.366
Epicurus. 2.451
EPIE Institute. 4.10298
Epps, Edgar G., 1929- joint author. 4.10856
Epstein, A. L. (Arnold Leonard) 4.615
Epstein, Barbara Leslie, 1944-. 4.6027
Epstein, Cynthia Fuchs. 4.3279
Epstein, David. 1.4477
Epstein, David F. 4.7830
Epstein, Dena J. 1.4298
Epstein, Edmund L. 2.8923
Epstein, Edward Jay, 1935-. 3.7879
Epstein, Emanuel. 5.3753
Epstein, Irwin. 4.6484
Epstein, Isidore, 1894-1962. 1.1897
Epstein, Jacob, Sir, 1880-1959. 1.5692
Epstein, Jerome S. 1.3435
Epstein, Joseph, 1937-. 4.5782
Epstein, Julius J., 1909-. 2.3024
Epstein, Klaus. 3.2244, 3.2349
Epstein, Leon D. 4.7783, 4.10574
Epstein, Lewis C. 5.1999
Epstein, Lewis Carroll. 5.2093
Epstein, Lillian. 4.1963
Epstein, Mortimer, 1880-1946. ed. 4.1543, 4.7214
Epstein, Samuel S. 5.6039
Equal Employment Advisory Council. 4.3257
Equal Rights Amendment Project. 4.9693
er-Rashid, Haroun. 3.4145
Erades, P. A, jt. author. 2.998
Erasmus, David A. 5.3844
Erasmus, Desiderius, d. 1536. 1.1496, 1.2937, 1.3058, 2.822-2.823, 4.7400
Erb, Peter C., 1943-. 1.3084
Erdélyi, Arthur. 5.1563
Erdelyi, Matthew Hugh. 5.132
Erdman, David V. 2.7404, 2.7407, 2.7425
Erdman, David V. ed. 2.5492
Erdmann, Carl, 1898-1945. 3.588
Erdoes, Richard. joint author. 3.5952
Erdrich, Louise. 2.13008
Erenberg, Lewis A., 1944-. 3.8039
Érenburg, Il'ia, 1891-1967. 2.1548-2.1553, 3.3996
Ergang, Robert Reinhold, 1898-. 3.2246, 3.2484
Erhard, Ludwig. 4.4233
Erhardt, Carl L. 5.4630
ERIC Clearinghouse for Junior Colleges. 4.10561
ERIC Clearinghouse on Handicapped and Gifted Children. 4.10911, 4.10916, 4.10931
ERIC Clearinghouse on Reading and Communication Skills. 4.10470
ERIC Processing and Reference Facility (U.S.) 4.10282
Erickson, Arthur, 1924-. 1.5347
Erickson, Arvel B. joint author. 3.1610
Erickson, Carolly, 1943-. 3.128
Erickson, Charlotte. 3.6538, 4.3604
Erickson, Edgar L. 3.1904
Erickson, Edwin E. 1.4284, 3.9311
Erickson, John. 3.987-3.988, 5.7330
Erickson, John D. 2.4843
Erickson, Kenneth Paul. 4.8339
Ericson, Eston Everett, 1890-1964. 5.7942
Ericson, Jonathon E. 4.719
Eriksen, Svend. 1.4961
Erikson, Erik H. (Erik Homburger), 1902-. 1.2341, 4.5727, 4.5803, 5.96, 5.196
Erikson, Kai T. 4.6536
Eriksson, Gunnar, 1931-. 5.3215
Eriksson, Torsten, 1906-1977. 4.6858
Erixon, Sigurd Emanuel, 1888-1968. 4.471
Erkenwald, Saint. 2.6132
Erlich, Alexander. 4.2378
Erlich, John. joint author. 4.1228

Erlich, Victor, 1914-. 2.1243, 2.1276, 2.1387, 2.1598
Erlikh, Hagai. 3.5254
Erman, Adolf, 1854-1937. 2.1763, 2.1765
Ermarth, Michael. 1.983
Ermatinger, Emil, 1873-1953. 2.13621
Ermolaev, Herman. 2.1246, 2.1604
Ernle, Rowland Edmund Prothero, Baron, 1851-1937. 5.5248
Ernst, Bruno. 1.5022
Ernst, Carl H. 5.3925
Ernst, Earle. 2.3397
Ernst, Earle. ed. 2.2028
Ernst, Jimmy, 1920-. 1.5936
Ernst, Joseph Albert. 4.4498
Ernst, Max, 1891-1976. 1.4992
Ernst, Morris L. 2.8881
Ernst, Morris Leopold, 1888-. 4.6759, 4.9872, 4.9875
Ernst, Robert, 1915-. 3.7002
Ernst, Robert T. 3.6608
Ernst, W. G. (Wallace Gary), 1931-. 5.3036
Erny, Pierre. 4.647
Eron, Leonard D. jt. author. 5.544
Ershkowitz, Miriam, comp. 3.8091
Erskine-Hill, Howard. 2.5679, 2.6257
Erskine, Thomas L. joint comp. 2.8972
Ervin, Sam J. (Sam James), 1896-1985. 3.7921
Ervine, St. John G. (St. John Greer), b. 1883. 2.8075
Erwin, Edward, 1937-. 5.4889
Esau, Katherine, 1898-. 5.3738
Escal, François. 2.4012
Eschholz, Paul A. 2.34
Eschmeyer, William N. 5.3907
Escot, Pozzi. joint author. 1.4425
Esdaile, Arundell James Kennedy, 1880-1956. 5.7677
Esenin, Sergeĭ Aleksandrovich, 1895-1925. 2.1555
Eshag, Eprime. 4.4461
Eshbach, Ovid Wallace, 1893-1958, ed. 5.5668
Eshleman, Clayton. 2.4781, 2.4835
Esler, Anthony. comp. 4.5113
Eslinger, Gary S., 1953-. 1.3598
Esmein, Jean, 1923-. 3.4788
Esmonin, Edmond, 1877-. 3.2016
Espejel, Carlos. 1.6616
Espenshade, Edward Bowman, 1910-. 4.112
Espenshade, Thomas J. 4.1673
Espina, Noni. 1.3589
Espinosa, Aurelio Macedonio, 1880-1958. 4.783
Espinosa, J. Manuel (José Manuel), 1909-. 4.783
Esposito, John L. 1.1997, 1.2001
Esposito, Vincent Joseph, 1900- ed. 4.157, 4.166
Essex Institute. 1.5315
Essick, Robert N. 1.4949, 1.6455
Essien-Udom, Essien Udosen. 3.6666
Essig, James D. 1.2477
Esslin, Martin. 2.2811, 2.3087, 2.4383, 2.9792
Esslin, Martin. ed. 2.8428
Esslinger, Dean R. 3.8402
Estall, R. C. 4.2018
Estall, Robert C. 4.2688
Estes, John E. 4.13
Estes, Richard, 1932-. 1.5936a
Estes, Richard J. 4.5103
Estes, William Kaye. 5.265
Estess, Sybil P., 1942-. 2.11386
Estève, Michel. ed. 2.4412
Estle, Thomas Leo, 1931- joint author. 5.2135
Estren, Mark James. 2.3814
Estrin, Saul. 4.3189
Estroff, Sue E. 5.4810
États-Unis. Bureau of Mines. 5.6723
Etcheson, Craig, 1955-. 3.4446
Eterovich, Francis H. ed. 3.1932
Ethel Percy Andrus Gerontology Center. 5.5003
Ethelwerd, d. 998. 3.1312
Etherege, George, Sir, 1635?-1691. 2.7009-2.7011
Etherton, Michael. 2.10040
Ethiopia. Relief and Rehabilitation Commission. 4.2617
Étiemble, René, 1909- ed. 2.3894
Etkin, Bernard. 5.6662
Ettinger, Jan van, 1902-. 4.9036
Ettinghausen, Richard. 1.5108, 1.5882

Ettles, C. M. Mc. 5.6244
Ettling, John, 1944-. 5.4674
Etulain, Richard W. 5.7855
Etzioni, Amitai. 4.2011, 4.4900, 4.9159, 4.9248, 5.3457
Etzioni, Amitai. joint comp. 4.4873
Etzioni, Amitai. 4.5183
Etzioni-Halevy, Eva. 4.7765
Etzioni-Halevy, Eva. comp. 4.4873
Etzold, Thomas H. 5.7266
Eubank, Keith. 3.874, 3.923
Euclid. 5.1102
Eudes, Dominique. 3.1067
Eudin, Xenia Joukoff. 3.3058, 3.3066, 3.3071
Eulau, Heinz, 1915-. 4.7237
Eunapius. 2.386
Euripides. 2.452, 2.454-2.455, 2.457-2.460, 2.462-2.464
Euromonitor Publications Limited. 4.2230
Europa Publications Limited. 3.328, 3.3608, 3.3685, 3.5220, 4.8355
European Centre for Political Studies. 4.8364, 4.8374, 4.8681
European Coordination Centre for Research and Documentation in Social Sciences. 4.2756, 4.6315
European Ecological Symposium. 1st, Norwich, Eng., 1977. 5.3772
Eusebius, of Caesarea, Bishop of Caesarea, ca. 260-ca. 340. 1.2488, 2.367, 2.385
Evans, Arthur, Sir, 1851-1941. 3.2591
Evans, B. Ifor (Benjamin Ifor), 1899-. 2.6844
Evans, Bergen, 1904-. 2.1137, 2.3729
Evans, Bertrand, 1912-. 2.6760
Evans, C. H. 1.5411
Evans, C. Stephen. 1.1126
Evans, Chad, 1951-. 2.3277
Evans, Charles, 1850-1935. 5.7751-5.7753
Evans, Charles Arthur Lovatt, Sir, 1884-. 5.4190
Evans, Christopher Francis. ed. 1.2509
Evans, Cornelia, joint author. 2.1137
Evans, D. A., joint author. 5.1873
Evans, D. E. 5.4206
Evans, David, fl. 1971-. 1.4274
Evans, David Stanley. 5.1733
Evans, E. Hilary. 5.3757
Evans, Eli N. 3.8180
Evans, Elizabeth, 1935-. 2.11984, 2.12672, 2.12789
Evans, Ellis D. 4.10403
Evans, Evan David. 3.1764
Evans, G. Blakemore (Gwynne Blakemore), 1912- ed. 2.6649
Evans, G. R. (Gillian Rosemary) 1.1486, 1.2821
Evans Gareth, of Australia. 4.8818
Evans, Grant, 1948-. 3.4434
Evans, Grose. 1.5983
Evans, Idrisyn Oliver, 1894- joint author. 3.286
Evans, Ivor H. ed. 2.2350
Evans, Jean, 1912-. 5.223
Evans, Joan, 1893-. 1.3236, 1.5136, 1.6535, 2.8028, 2.8034, 3.130
Evans, Joel R. 4.2063
Evans, John S. 3.251, 4.731
Evans, Jonathan St. B. T., 1948-. 5.384
Evans, Lawrence, 1935- ed. 2.7981
Evans, Linda. 4.5824
Evans, Mari, 1923-. 2.10312
Evans, Maurice. 2.5786
Evans, Michael, 1936-. 4.6952
Evans, Michael K. 4.1983
Evans, Nigel, 1954-. 5.6599
Evans, Oliver Wendell, 1915-. 2.12255
Evans, Owen, 1953-. 4.4512
Evans, Patricia Russell. 4.9442
Evans, Patrick David, 1944-. 2.10225
Evans, Peter Angus, 1929-. 1.3823
Evans, Philip A., 1935- joint author. 1.4081
Evans-Pritchard, E. E. (Edward Evan), 1902-1973. 3.5175-3.5177, 3.5183, 3.5202, 4.469, 4.520, 4.544, 4.562, 4.575, 4.602, 4.658
Evans-Pritchard, Edward Evan. 1.1861
Evans, Ralph Merrill. 5.2332
Evans, Richard Isadore, 1922-. 2.12177, 5.96, 5.99, 5.101-5.102, 5.157, 5.169, 5.513, 5.591, 5.4781
Evans, Richard J. 4.5879

Evans, Robert C. (Robert Church) 5.3718
Evans, Robert F. 1.2973
Evans, Robert John Weston. 3.1880
Evans, Robert Owen, 1919- ed. 2.8772
Evans, Robley Dunglison, 1907-. 5.2426
Evans, Rowland, 1921-. 3.7888, 3.7899
Evans, Sara A. (Sara Margaret), 1943-. 4.6045
Evans, Sebastian, 1830-1909. 3.1302
Evans, Tricia. 4.10475
Evans, Ulick Richardson. 5.5815
Evans, Walker, 1903-1975. 3.8278, 5.6959
Evans-Wentz, W. Y. (Walter Yeeling), 1878-1965. 1.1741, 1.2104
Evans, William Howard, 1924-. 4.10510
Evarts, Jeremiah, 1781-1831. 3.5849
Eveland, Wilbur. 3.3755
Evelyn, John, 1620-1706. 3.1502
Evelyn-White, Hugh Gerard, 1924-. 2.371
Evenson, Norma. 4.6330
Everdell, M. H. 5.2806
Everdell, William R. 4.7560
Everett, Dorothy, 1894-1953. 2.5603
Everett, James L., joint author. 5.5639
Everett, Peter B. (Peter Ben), 1943-. 5.316
Everett, Thomas H. 5.5334
Evergood, Philip, 1901-1973. 1.5937
Everhart, W. Harry (Watson Harry), 1918-. 5.5480
Everhart, William C. 5.5388
Evers, Hans-Dieter. ed. 4.5406
Evers, Larry. 2.2328, 2.2335
Eversley, David Edward Charles. 4.1614, 4.1637
Everson Museum of Art. 1.6614
Everson, William, 1912-. 2.11331-2.11332
Everson, William K. 2.2914
Everson, William K. joint author. 2.3012
Evert, Ray Franklin. 5.3642
Eves, Charles Kenneth, 1888-. 2.7207
Evrard, Louis, 1926-. 2.4292
Ewan, Joseph Andorfer, 1909-. 5.3636
Ewans, Michael, 1946-. 1.4051
Ewart, Gavin. 2.9673
Ewell, Judith, 1943-. 3.9183
Ewen, David, 1907-. 1.3532, 1.4218
Ewer, R. F. 5.3991
Ewers, John Canfield. 3.5950
Ewert, Alfred, 1891-. 2.860, 2.3965
Ewing, A.C. (Alfred Cyril), 1899-. 1.503, 1.1257
Ewing, Cortez Arthur Milton, 1896-1962. 4.8140
Ewing, Elizabeth. 4.853-4.854
Ewing, Galen Wood, 1914-. 5.2668
Ewing, John A. 4.6650
Experimental Psychology Society. 5.4376
Exquemelin, A. O. (Alexandre Olivier) 3.9142
Eyck, Erich, 1878-. 3.2312, 3.2333, 3.2362
Eyck, F. Gunther. 3.2956
Eyck, Frank. 3.2301
Eyck, Frank. comp. 3.700
Eyo, Ekpo. 1.5088
Eyre, S. R. 5.3664
Eyre-Todd, George, 1862-1937. ed. 2.9843
Eyring, Edward M., joint author. 5.2881
Eyring, Henry, 1901-. 5.2797, 5.2881
Eysenck, H. J. (Hans Jurgen), 1916-. 4.5338, 5.11, 5.351, 5.372, 5.514-5.516, 5.546, 5.4828, 5.4927
Eysenck, Michael W. 5.325, 5.514
Ezekiel, Raphael S., 1931-. 3.8437
Ezell, John Samuel. 4.4637

F.A. Brockhaus Wiesbaden (Firm) 1.18
Fa-hsien, ca. 337-ca. 422. 3.3612
Faber, Geoffrey Cust, Sir, 1889-1961, ed. 2.7034
Faber, Leonard C. 3.7043
Faber, Rodney B. 5.6486
Faberzhe (Firm) 1.6666
Fabian, B. C. 5.4122
Fabozzi, Frank J. 4.4603
Fabre, Geneviève. 2.3214, 5.7797
Fabre, Michel. 2.12817
Fabricant, Carole. 2.7311
Fabrycky, W. J. (Wolter J.), 1932-. 4.2726, 5.5702
Fabun, Don. 3.196
Fabunmi, L. A. 3.5165
Fackenheim, Emil L. 1.954, 1.1970
Fackler, Herbert V. 2.9290

Fackre, Gabriel J. 1.2766, 1.3293
Facts on File, Inc. 1.52, 1.1526, 1.2142, 3.219, 3.7854, 4.3795, 5.1680
Fadeev, Aleksandr, 1901-1956. 2.1560
Faderman, Lillian. 4.5523
Fadiman, Clifton, 1904-. 1.1045, 2.10909
Faerstein, Paul H., joint author. 4.2685
Fafunwa, A. Babs, 1923-. 4.10148
Fagan, Brian M. 3.254, 3.611
Fagan, Brian M. joint author. 4.716
Fage, J. D. 3.5067, 3.5070, 3.5324, 4.188
Fage, J. D. joint author. 3.5076
Fagen, M. D. 5.6418
Fagen, Richard R. ed. 3.9018
Fager, Charles (Charles Eugene), 1942-. 3.8286
Fagg, William Buller. 1.5764-1.5765, 1.5767
Fagles, Robert. tr. 2.442
Fahim, Hussein M., 1934-. 3.5178
Fahl, Ronald J., 1942-. 5.8198
Fain, Tyrus G. 4.7906
Fainsod, Merle, 1907-1972. 4.5377, 4.8647-4.8648
Fair, Ronald L. 2.13009
Fairbank, Alfred J. 5.7520
Fairbank, John King, 1907-. 1.3028, 3.110, 3.4631, 3.4660, 3.4663, 3.4666, 3.4675, 3.6423, 4.4238, 4.7109
Fairbank, Wilma. 1.5448
Fairbanks, Carol, 1935-. 2.10469, 4.6074, 5.7800
Fairbanks, Charles Herron, 1913- joint author. 3.5734
Fairbridge, Rhodes Whitmore, 1914-. 4.238, 4.321, 5.2496, 5.2942, 5.3054, 5.3101, 5.3147, 5.5267
Fairchild, B. H. 2.7434
Fairchild, Hoxie Neale, 1894-. 2.5577, 2.5699
Fairchild, Wilma B. 5.8165
Fairchilds, Cissie C. 4.3525
Fairclough, Henry Rushton, 1862-1936, tr. 2.700
Faires, R. A. (Ronald Arthur), 1910-. 5.2918
Fairfax, Edward, d. 1635. 2.4982
Fairfax, Sally K. 5.5433
Fairfield, Sheila. joint author. 1.6696
Fairgrieve, James, 1870-1953. 4.370
Fairhall, David. 5.7468
Fairley, Barker. 2.13581, 2.13608, 2.13643
Fairlie, Alison. 2.3857
Fairlie, Henry, 1924-. 3.7863, 4.8154
Fairman, Charles, 1897-. 4.9824
Fairservis, Walter Ashlin, 1921-. 3.4164, 4.850
Fairweather, Eugene Rathbone. ed. and tr. 1.360
Faith, Nicholas, 1933-. 4.4613
Faiz, Faiz Ahmad, 1911-. 2.1900
Fakhouri, Hani. 4.5472
Fakhry, Ahmed. 3.5147
Fakhry, Majid. 1.365
Falb, Peter L. 5.6176
Falconer, D. S. (Douglas Scott) 5.3470
Falconer, John Ironside, 1888-. 5.5232
Falconer, William Armistead, tr. 2.657
Faler, Paul G. (Paul Gustaf), 1940-. 4.3523
Fales, Dean A. 1.6568
Fales, Martha Gandy. 1.6656
Faletto, Enzo. joint author. 4.2136
Falk, Byron A. 5.8108
Falk, Doris V. 2.12293
Falk, Hjalmar, 1859-1928. 3.3353
Falk, Nancy Auer. 1.1613
Falk, Richard A. comp. 4.9080, 4.9339
Falk, Richard A. ed. 4.9029, 4.9275
Falk, Richard A. 4.7630, 4.9028, 4.9133, 4.9318
Falk, Signi Lenea. 2.12737
Falk, Valerie R. joint author. 5.8108
Falkener, Edward, 1814-1896. 4.878
Falkner, Thomas, 1707-1784. 3.9255
Falkowski, Paul G. 5.3252
Falkus, Malcolm E. 4.170
Fall, Aminata Sow. 2.4872
Fall, Bernard B., 1926-1967. 3.4435, 3.4473, 3.4489
Falla, P. S. (Paul Stephen), 1913-. 2.1235
Fallaci, Oriana. 2.5081
Fallers, Lloyd A. 4.9929
Fallico, Arturo B., comp. 1.397
Fallis, Richard. 2.9855
Fallois, Bernard de. 2.4749

Fallon, Gabriel. 2.9153
Fallows, David. 1.3857
Fallows, James M. 5.7267
Fallows, Marjorie R., 1926-. 3.6552
Falls, Cyril Bentham, 1888-. 3.715, 3.784, 5.7190
Falls, Harold B. 5.5024
Falnes, Oscar Julius, 1898-. 3.3377
Famularo, Joseph J. 4.4357
Fancher, Raymond E. 5.4903
Fancher, Robert T. 4.10816
Fang, Chao-ying, 1908-. 3.4710
Fang, Hsai-Yang. joint author. 5.5921
Fang, Josephine R. 5.7605
Fanger, Donald. 2.1373, 2.1388
Fann, K. T., 1937- comp. 1.740
Fanning, Charles. 2.11618
Fanning, Clara Elizabeth, 1878-1938, ed. 5.7763
Fano, L. joint author. 5.2055
Fano, Ugo. 5.2055
Fanon, Frantz, 1925-1961. 3.5118
Fanshawe, Anne Harrison, Lady, 1625-1680. 3.1499
Fanshawe, Richard, Sir, 1608-1666. 2.4970
Fanshel, David. 4.6579
Fant, Maureen B. 4.5847
Fantini, Mario D. 4.10031, 4.10646, 4.10802
FAO World Fishing Gear Congress (2nd: 1963: London, England) 5.5483
Far Eastern economic review. 4.2428
Fārābī. 1.372
Faraday, Michael, 1791-1867. 5.2336
Faragher, John Mack, 1945-. 3.8411, 4.5603
Farah, Madelain. 4.5565
Fararo, T. J. 4.4790
Farb, Peter. 2.26
Farber, Donald C. 2.3267
Farber, Eduard, 1892-. 5.2605, 5.2614-5.2616
Farber, Marvin, 1901-. 1.522
Farber, Samuel, 1939-. 3.9097
Fardo, Stephen W. 5.7032
Farella, John R. 3.5915
Farish, Margaret K. 1.3579, 1.3594-1.3595
Farkas, George, 1946-. 4.5588
Farkas, Hershel M. 5.1495
Farkas, Philip. 1.4547
Farley-Hills, David. 2.7229
Farley, James Aloysius, 1888-. 3.7640
Farley, Jennie. 4.10580
Farley, John, 1936-. 5.3480
Farley, Lawrence T., 1947-. 4.9266
Farley, Rawle, 1922-. 4.2139
Farley, Reynolds, 1938-. 3.6734
Farlow, Lesley. 4.1179
Farmer, David John, 1935-. 4.6830
Farmer, Fannie Merritt, 1857-1915. 5.7133
Farmer, Henry George, 1882-. 1.4201
Farmer, James, 1920-. 3.6832
Farmer, Paul, 1918-. 3.2077
Farmer, Philip José. 2.13010
Farmer, William Reuben. 1.2179
Farmer, William Reuben. ed. 3.3896
Farnell, Lewis Richard, 1856-1934. 1.1643
Farner, Donald Sankey, 1915- ed. 5.3938
Farnham, Willard. 2.6781
Farnie, Douglas Antony. 4.3853
Farnsworth, Beatrice. 3.3229
Farnsworth, Edith, tr. 2.5061
Farnsworth, Martha, 1867-1924. 3.8525
Farnsworth, Paul Randolph, 1899-. 1.4384
Farnsworth, Robert M. 2.12593, 2.12596
Faron, Louis C., 1923- joint author. 3.9156
Farooq, Ghazi Mumtaz. 4.1647
Farquhar, George. 2.7014-2.7016
Farquhar, J. N. (John Nicol), 1861-1929. 1.1811-1.1812
Farr, Dorothy Mary. 2.6580
Farr, Finis. 2.3625
Farr, James L. 4.4379
Farr, Marie Leonore, 1927-. 5.3728
Farrand, John. 5.3951
Farrand, Max, 1869-1945. 4.9612
Farrar, Clarissa Palmer. 5.8277
Farrar, Eleanor. 4.10509
Farrar, Thomas Clark, 1933-. 5.2314
Farrell, Brian. ed. 4.8566
Farrell, James T. (James Thomas), 1904-1979. 1.591, 2.11647-2.11655

Farrell, John Philip, 1939-. 2.5725
Farrell, Kate. joint author. 2.2732
Farrell, Kate. 2.3752
Farrell, Lois. 5.8090
Farrell, Michael P., 1942-. 4.5794
Farrell, Paul V. 4.4324
Farrell, R. B. (Ralph Barstow), 1908-. 2.1184
Farrer, Austin Marsden. 1.2768
Farrington, Benjamin, 1891-. 5.726, 5.781
Farris, Donald E. 4.3696
Farris, Martin T. 4.3894
Farris, Martin T. comp. 4.3880
Farris, Paul. joint author. 4.4435
Farriss, Nancy M. (Nancy Marguerite), 1938-. 3.9036
Farrukhzād, Furūgh. 2.1977
Farwell, Byron. 5.7346
Fasel, George W. 4.7419
Fasholé-Luke, Edward W. 1.2467
Fāsī, 'Allāl, 1910-1974. 3.5197
Fasman, Gerald D. 5.3332
Fasold, Ralph W. joint author. 2.1128
Fassett, Norman Carter, 1900-. 5.3668
Fast, Howard, 1914-. 2.11656
FAST (Program) 4.2217
Fasteau, Marc Feigen. 4.5834
Fastenrath, Fritz. 5.6073
Fastnedge, Ralph, 1913-. 1.6571-1.6572
Fate, Terry. 5.8375
Faucon, Louis, 1913- ed. 2.4440
Faugeras, O. D. 5.6166
Faul, Carol. 5.2949
Faul, Henry. 5.2949
Faulconer, Estelle, joint author. 3.8530
Faulk, Odie B. joint author. 3.7136
Faulkes, Anthony. 2.13992
Faulkner, Edwin J. 4.1038
Faulkner, Harold Underwood, 1890-1968. 3.7407, 4.1879, 4.1883
Faulkner, Larry R., 1944-. 5.2911
Faulkner, Peter. 2.7968, 2.7969, 2.9545
Faulkner, Peter. comp. 2.7972
Faulkner, Robert Kenneth. 4.9822
Faulkner, Virginia, 1913-. 2.10277
Faulkner, William, 1897-1962. 2.11657-2.11659, 2.11661-2.11675, 2.11677-2.11678, 2.11680-2.11683, 2.11689
Faunce, Roland Cleo, 1905-. 4.10423
Faure, Gunter. 5.3081
Faure, Robert. joint author. 4.2628
Faurot, Jeannette L. 2.2253
Fauset, Jessie Redmon. 2.11708
Fausold, Martin L., 1921-. 3.7740
Faust, d. ca. 1540. 2.13511, 2.13513
Faust, Albert Bernhardt, 1870-1951. 3.6546
Faust, David, 1952-. 5.881
Faust, Drew Gilpin. 3.8247
Faust, Ernest Carroll, 1890-. 5.4761
Faust, Patricia L. 3.7343
Fausto-Sterling, Anne, 1944-. 5.4201
Faux, Geoffrey P. 4.2008
Fava, Sylvia Fleis, 1927-. 4.3481
Favati, Guido. 2.4913
Faverty, Frederic Everett, 1902-. 2.5824, 2.7359
Fawcett, Don Wayne, 1917-. 5.3590, 5.4157
Fawcett, J. E. S. (James Edmund Sandford), 1913-. 4.9338
Fawtier, Robert, 1885-. 3.1990
Fax, Elton C. 1.4911-1.4912
Faxon, Charles Edward, 1846-1918. illus. 5.3688
Fay, C. R. (Charles Ryle), 1884-. 4.2277
Fay, John. 5.6678
Fay, Peter Ward, 1924-. 3.4724
Fay, Sidney Bradshaw, 1876-. 3.771, 3.2497
Fayed, M. E. (Muhammad E.) 5.6847
Fayerweather, John. 4.2729
Fayol, Henri, 1841-1925. 4.2648
Feagin, Joe R. 4.6511, 4.10793
Fearing, Kenneth, 1902-1961. 2.11709-2.11711
Feather, Leonard G. 1.3517, 1.3533-1.3534, 1.4322-1.4323
Featherman, David L. joint author. 4.5242
Featherstone, David. 5.6946
Featherstone, Joseph. 4.10431
Febvre, Lucien Paul Victor, 1878-1956. 2.4007, 3.1957, 5.7518
Fechner, Gustav Theodor, 1801-1887. 5.242

Feder, Bernard. joint author. 5.4886
Feder, Elaine. 5.4886
Feder, Judith M. 4.3450, 4.3452
Feder, Lillian. 2.229
Federal Architecture Project (U.S.) 1.5514
Federal Art Project. 1.5203
Federal Document Retrieval, Inc. 5.7643
Federal Reserve Bank of New York. 4.4494
Federal Writers' Project. 3.6057, 3.7210, 3.7958,
    3.8036, 3.8635, 3.8648
Federal writers' project. 3.8068, 3.8112
Federal Writers' Project (California) 3.8613
Federal writers' project. Connecticut. 3.8023
Federal writers' project. Florida. 3.8274
Federal Writer's Project. Illinois. 3.8405
Federal Writers' Project. Iowa. 3.8503
Federal Writers' Project. Kentucky. 3.8359
Federal Writers' Project. Maine. 3.7960
Federal Writers' Project. Massachusetts. 3.7990
Federal Writers' Project. Mississippi. 3.8287
Federal writers' project. New Hampshire.
    3.7965
Federal Writers' Project. North Carolina.
    3.8229
Federal Writers' Project. North Dakota. 3.8507
Federal writers' project. Rhode Island. 3.8010
Federal Writers' Project. South Dakota. 3.8514
Federal Writers' Project. Tennessee. 3.8350
Federal Writers' Project. Vermont. 3.7968
Federation of American Societies for
    Experimental Biology. 5.3595
Federer, Walter Theodore, 1915-. 4.1239
Federman, Daniel D. 5.4496
Federman, Raymond. 2.8434
Federn, Karl, 1868-1942. 3.482
Fedin, Konstantin, 1892-. 2.1561
Fedo, David A. 4.4273, 4.4273a
Fedor, Kenneth J. 4.3678
Fedorowicz, J. K., 1949-. 3.3333
Fedotov, G. P. (Georgiĭ Petrovich), 1886-1951.
    1.3114
Feduccia, J. Alan. 5.3947
Fee, Margery, 1948-. 5.7891
Feeley, Kathleen. 2.13219
Feeney, William R. 3.3634
Feenstra, Robert C. 4.4138
Feffer, Melvin. 5.517
Feher, Kamilo. 5.6391
Fehrenbach, T. R. 3.5017
Fehrenbacher, Don Edward. 3.7292, 3.7310,
    4.9620-4.9621
Fehrman, Carl Abraham Daniel, 1915-. 2.2760
Fei, Hsiao-t'ung. 4.2492, 4.5413
Feibleman, James Kern, 1904-. 1.628
Feierman, Steven, 1940-. 3.5294
Feifel, Herman. 1.1324
Feiffer, Jules. ed. 2.3568
Feiffer, Jules. 2.13011
Feig, Konnilyn G. 3.1088
Feigelman, William. 4.6577
Feigenbaum, Edward A. ed. 5.1018
Feigenbaum, Edward A. 5.1010
Feigl, Fritz, 1891-. 5.2652, 5.2671
Feigl, Herbert. 5.882
Feigon, Lee, 1945-. 3.4766
Feiling, Keith Grahame, Sir, 1884-. 3.1701
Fein, David A. 2.3970
Fein, Edith. 4.6561
Fein, Helen, 1934-. 3.1089
Feinberg, Gerald, 1933-. 5.2466
Feinberg, Walter, 1937-. 4.9954, 4.10019,
    4.10283
Feine, Paul, 1859-1933. 1.2628
Feiner, Benjamin. 5.5557
Feingold, Henry L., 1931-. 3.6568
Feingold, Richard. 2.5812
Feininger, Andreas, 1906-. 1.5790
Feininger, Lyonel, 1871-1956. 1.6440
Feinstein, C. H. 4.2282
Feinstein, Elaine. tr. 2.1610
Feinstein, Gerry. 4.1835
Feis, Herbert, 1893-1972. 3.883, 3.920, 3.933,
    3.1008, 3.1163, 3.6424, 4.4446
Feise, Ernst, 1884-. 2.13605
Feit, Walter, 1930-. 5.1294
Feiwel, George R. 4.1366, 4.2398, 4.2404
Fejes Tóth, L. 5.1584
Fejtö, François, 1909-. 3.701, 3.3532

Felbeck, David K. 5.5775
Feld, Steven. 3.5658
Feld, Werner J. 4.3022, 4.9267, 5.7268
Feldberg, Michael, 1943-. 4.6725
Feldhamer, George A. 5.3987
Feldhaus, Anne. 1.1700
Feldman, Arnold S. joint ed. 4.3112
Feldman, Arnold S. joint author. 4.5265
Feldman, Edmund Burke. 1.4622-1.4623
Feldman, Elaine B., 1926-. 5.5004
Feldman, Elliot J. 4.8275
Feldman, Gerald D. 4.2342, 4.3736
Feldman, Herbert. 3.4128-3.4129
Feldman, James M. 5.6503
Feldman, Julian. joint ed. 5.1018
Feldman, Kenneth A., 1937-. 4.10060
Feldman, Lily Gardner. 3.2462
Feldman, Louis H. 2.376
Feldman, Renata. 5.1827
Feldman, Saul D. 4.10842
Feldman, Seymour. 1.1097
Feldstein, Martin S. 4.1977, 4.3451
Feldstein, Stanley, 1937- comp. 4.3605
Felheim, Marvin, 1914-. 2.3253
Feliciano, Florentino P. 4.9325
Felknor, Bruce L. 4.8182
Fell, John L., 1927-. 2.2878-2.2879, 2.2915
Fellerer, Karl Gustav, 1902-. 1.4241
Fellini, Federico. 3.2041
Fellman, David, 1907- ed. 4.9581
Fellman, Michael. 3.7231
Fellmann, Jerome Donald, 1926- joint author.
    5.8204
Fellmeth, Robert C. 4.3891
Fellner, William John, 1905-. 4.3011
Fellowes, Edmund Horace, 1870-1951. 1.3830,
    1.3875, 1.4233, 1.4247, 2.6124
Fellows, Otis Edward, 1908-. 2.3919, 2.4072
Felner, Mira, 1947-. 2.2829
Felsenstein, Walter. 1.4110
Felstiner, John. 2.8440
Felton, Craig. 1.6220
Felzenberg, Alvin S. joint author. 5.8407
Fenby, Eric, 1906-. 1.3851
Fénelon, François de Salignac de La Mothe-,
    1651-1715. 2.4022
Feng, Meng-lung, 1574-1646. comp. 2.2200
Feng, Yu-lan, 1895-. 1.152-1.154
Fenichel, Carol. 5.4540
Fenichel, Carol H. 5.7639
Fenin, George N. 2.3012
Fenn, Dan Huntington, 1923- joint author.
    4.2703
Fenn, John, Sir, 1739-1794. 3.1374
Fennell, John Lister Illingworth. 2.1256, 3.3086
Fenneman, Nevin Melanchthon, 1865-.
    4.249-4.250
Fenner, Terrence W. 5.5639
Fennimore, Keith J. 2.11242
Fenno, Richard F., 1926-. 4.7973, 4.7998,
    4.8027, 4.8057
Fenollosa, Ernest Francisco, 1853-1908. 2.2682
Fenster, Saul K., 1933- joint author. 5.5781
Fenton, Charles A. 2.11371-2.11372
Fenton, Edward. 2.9674
Fenton, Edwin. 4.8956
Fenton, John H. 4.8077
Fenton, Mildred Adams, 1899-. 3.3416
Fenton, Steve, 1942-. 4.4751
Ferber, Edna, 1887-1968. 2.11712-2.11714
Ferber, Ellen, 1939-. 5.7572
Ferber, Marianne A., 1923-. 4.6032
Ferber, Robert, 1922-. 4.2003, 4.4303
Ferdon, Edwin N., 1913-. 3.9270
Ferencz, Benjamin B. 1920-. 4.8983, 4.9317
Ferguson, Alfred Riggs. 2.11017
Ferguson, Alfred Riggs. joint comp. 2.11019
Ferguson, Allen Richmond. 4.3972
Ferguson, Arthur B. 3.1385
Ferguson, Barbara J. 5.5368
Ferguson, C. E. (Charles E.) 4.1332
Ferguson, Charles Albert, 1921-. 2.4, 2.124,
    2.209
Ferguson, Charles Wright, 1901-. 3.1411
Ferguson, E. James (Elmer James), 1917-.
    3.6977
Ferguson, Eugene S. 5.8457

Ferguson, George Andrew. 5.1397
Ferguson, Howard, 1908-. 1.4140
Ferguson, J. De Lancey (John De Lancey),
    1888-. 2.7502, 2.7504, 2.8121
Ferguson, James Milton. ed. 4.4724
Ferguson, John, 1921-. 1.304, 1.1661, 2.289,
    4.7170
Ferguson, Lloyd N. 5.2850
Ferguson, Marilyn. 5.459
Ferguson, Mary Anne. 2.3725, 5.8277
Ferguson, Moira. 2.6073, 2.8292
Ferguson, Oliver Watkins, 1924-. 2.7307
Ferguson, Phil Moss, 1899-. 5.5876
Ferguson, Robert A., 1942-. 2.10389
Ferguson, Suzanne, 1939-. 2.11928
Ferguson, Wallace Klippert, 1902-. 3.155-3.156
Ferguson, William, 1924-. 3.1780
Ferguson, William Scott, 1875-1954. 3.2654
Fergusson, Francis. 2.4942, 2.6730
Fergusson, James, 1808-1886. 1.5446
Fergusson, Peter, 1934-. 1.5528
Ferlazzo, Paul J. 2.11000
Ferlinghetti, Lawrence. 2.11715-2.11717
Ferm, Deane William, 1927-. 1.2767
Ferm, Robert L. 1.2632
Ferman, Barbara. 4.8853
Ferman, Louis A. 4.3204
Ferman, Louis A. ed. 4.2096
Fermi, Enrico, 1901-1954. 5.1885, 5.2071
Fermi, Laura. 3.2901, 3.6508, 5.2421, 5.6597
Fermigier, André. 1.6121
Fern, Alan Maxwell, 1930-. 1.6437
Fernald, L. Dodge (Lloyd Dodge), 1929-. 5.84
Fernald, Merritt Lyndon, 1873-. 5.3674
Fernand Nathan (Firm) 4.129
Fernandes, Florestan. 3.9226
Fernández-Armesto, Felipe. 3.3484
Fernández de Oviedo y Valdés, Gonzalo,
    1478-1557. 3.9084
Fernandez, James W. 3.5322
Fernandez, John P., 1941-. 4.4340
Fernández Moreno, César. 2.5298
Fernandez, Ramon, 1894-1944. 2.4671
Fernández-Santamaría, J. A., 1936-. 4.7302
Fernando, Tissa. 3.4361
Fernea, Elizabeth Warnock. 3.5215, 4.5908,
    4.6151
Fernea, Robert A. (Robert Alan), 1932-. 3.5179
Fernie, E. C. 1.5362
Fernier, Robert. 1.6083
Ferns, H. S. (Henry Stanley), 1913-. 3.8746,
    3.9240, 4.2166
Ferrante, Joan M., 1936-. 2.2632, 2.3955
Ferrar, Harold. 2.8850
Ferrara, Peter J., 1956-. 4.3464
Ferrari, Domenico, 1940-. 5.1245
Ferrari, Ezio. 5.2440
Ferrari, R. L. (Ronald L.) 5.6265
Ferrarotti, Franco. 4.4861
Ferrater Mora, José, 1912-. 1.1129, 1.1135
Ferree, Myra Marx. 4.6048
Ferreira, Eduardo de Sousa, 1936-. 3.5124
Ferreiro, Emilia. 4.10408
Ferrell, Robert H. comp. 3.6404, 3.7566-3.7567
Ferrell, Robert H. 3.6396, 3.6403, 3.7806,
    3.7832, 4.9261
Ferrero, Guglielmo, 1871-1942. 3.508
Ferres, John H. 2.9877
Ferres, John H. comp. 2.12168
Ferrier, Janet Mackay. 2.3843
Ferris, Elizabeth G. 4.6537
Ferris, Ina. 2.8193
Ferris, Paul, 1929-. 2.9412, 2.9417
Ferris, Roxana S. (Roxana Stinchfield), 1895-.
    5.3679
Ferris, Sharon Paugh. 1.3552
Ferris, William R. 1.6523
Ferro, Marc. 3.785, 3.3181
Ferro, Robert. 2.13012
Ferron, Jacques. 2.4830
Ferry, Anne. 2.7126
Fersht, Alan, 1943-. 5.4412
Ferster, Charles B., 1922-. 5.299
Ferziger, Joel H. 5.5714
Fesenmaier, Daniel R. 4.889
Feshbach, Herman. joint author. 5.1968, 5.2414
Fest, Joachim C., 1926-. 3.2398
Fest, Wilfried, 1943-. 3.2286

Festinger, Leon, 1919-. 4.4985, 4.4993, 5.302, 5.313, 5.688
Festival of American Folklife. Family Folklore Program. 4.774
Festugière, A. J. (André Jean), 1898-1982. 1.1654
Fetler, Andrew. 2.13013
Fetrow, Fred M. 2.11821
Fetter, C. W. (Charles Willard), 1942-. 4.305
Fetterley, Judith, 1938-. 2.10596, 2.10821
Fetzer, John F. 2.13553
Feuchtwanger, E. J. 3.1620, 3.1625
Feuchtwanger, Lion, 1884-1958. 2.3466, 2.13739
Feudel, Werner. 2.13559
Feuer, Lewis Samuel, 1912-. 4.9977
Feuerbach, Ludwig, 1804-1872. 1.955-1.956
Feuerwerker, Albert. 4.2467
Feuerwerker, Albert. ed. 3.4659
Feuerwerker, Yi-tsi Mei, 1928-. 2.2236
Feuillerat, Albert, 1874-1953. 2.6505
Feuillet, Raoul-Auger, 1659 or 60-1710. 4.1088
Fey, Harold Edward, 1898- ed. 1.3099
Feydeau, Georges, 1862-1921. 2.4527-2.4528
Feyerabend, Paul K., 1924-. 5.883
Feynman, Richard Phillips. 5.1950, 5.1991, 5.1997
Feys, Robert, 1889-. 1.1250
Ffowcs Williams, John E. 5.2225
Fichte, Johann Gottlieb, 1762-1814. 1.921, 3.2283
Fichtenau, Heinrich. 3.1982
Fichter, George S. joint author. 5.3898
Fichtner, Paula S. 3.1882
Ficino, Marsilio, 1433-1499. 5.687
Fiction Collective (U.S.) 2.10852
Fidell, Estelle A. ed. 5.8132
Fidler, J. K. (John Kelvin) 5.6460
Fido, Martin. 2.8275
Fiedler, Hermann Georg, 1862-1945. ed. 2.13522
Fiedler, Leslie A. 2.2571, 2.10557, 2.10593, 2.13014, 3.6108
Field, Andrew, 1938-. 2.1585
Field, Daniel, 1938-. 4.2856
Field, Geoffrey G. 3.2348
Field, George B., 1929-. 5.1700
Field, George Wallis, 1914-. 2.13475
Field, Hazel Elizabeth, 1891-. 5.3998
Field, James A. 3.3756
Field, John, 1902- ed. 5.4170
Field, Joyce W., joint comp. 2.13163
Field, Leslie A. comp. 2.13163
Field, Leslie A. 2.12788
Field, Marilyn Jane. 4.5680
Field, Phyllis F. 3.6801
Field, Rachel, 1894-1942. 2.11718
Field, Richard S. 1.6443, 1.6472
Fieldhouse, D. K. (David Kenneth), 1925-. 4.8897-4.8899, 4.9424
Fielding, Gabriel, 1916-. 2.8414
Fielding, Henry, 1707-1754. 2.7018-2.7023
Fielding, K. J. 2.7555
Fielding, Kenneth Joshua. 2.7636
Fielding, Raymond. 2.3646-2.3647
Fielding, Raymond. comp. 5.6999
Fielding, Sarah, 1710-1768. 2.7030
Fields, Barbara Jeanne. 3.7215
Fields, Gary S. 4.2771
Fields, Rona M. 4.5316
Fields, Wayne. 2.10975
Fieser, Louis Frederick, 1899-. 5.2598, 5.2728, 5.2732, 5.2778
Fieser, Mary, 1909-. 5.2598, 5.2732, 5.2778
Fifer, Charles N., 1922-. 2.7015
Fifield, William, 1916-. 5.6892
Fifoot, C. H. S. (Cecil Herbert Stuart), 1899-. 4.9411
Figes, Eva. 2.9675-2.9676
Figgis, B. N. 5.2841
Figgis, John Neville, 1866-1919. 4.7554
Figley, Charles R., 1944-. 4.5657, 5.4945
Figlio, Robert M., joint author. 4.6886
Figueira, Thomas J. 4.1731
Figueiredo, Antonio de, 1929-. 3.3504
Figueroa, John J. comp. 2.9982
Filarete, ca. 1400-ca. 1469. 1.5467
Filby, P. William, 1911-. 5.7528, 5.7851, 5.8113, 5.8376

Filedt Kok, J. P. 1.4996
Filesi, Teobaldo. 3.5128
Filler, John. 4.10949
Filler, Louis, 1912-. 2.10713, 3.7243, 5.8391
Filson, Floyd Vivian, 1896- joint author. 1.2552
Filstead, William J. 4.6647
Finberg, Alexander Joseph, 1866-1939. 1.6039
Finberg, Herbert P.R., 1900-. 4.2847
Finch, Caleb Ellicott. 5.4215-5.4216
Finch, Christopher. 1.5855
Finch, Janet. 4.5668
Finch, M. H. J. (Martin Henry John) 4.2181, 4.3675
Fincham, J. R. S. 5.3427, 5.3719
Findlater, Richard, 1921-. 2.3329
Findlay, J. N. (John Niemeyer), 1903-. 1.914, 1.932, 1.945
Findlay, James F., 1930-. 1.3044
Findlay, Paul, tr. 1.4813
Findlay, Robert R., 1932-. 2.3176, 2.3385
Findlay, T. J. V. (Triston John Victor) joint author. 5.2646
Findley, Carter V., 1941-. 4.8773
Findling, John E. 3.6405
Fine, Elsa Honig. 1.4587, 1.4913
Fine, Lawrence. 1.1948
Fine, Reuben, 1914-. 5.151
Fine, Richard. 2.3034
Fine, Ruth, 1941-. 1.6441
Fine, Sidney, 1920-. 4.3166, 4.5128, 4.9825
Fine, Sidney A., 1920- ed. 3.6337
Finean, J. B. 5.3609
Finegan, Edward, 1940-. 2.982
Finegan, Jack, 1908-. 1.2553, 1.2645-1.2646
Finegan, Thomas Aldrich, 1929- joint author. 4.3216
Finer, Herman, 1898-1969. 4.7710
Finer, S. E. (Samuel Edward), 1915-. 4.4862, 4.7719, 4.8521-4.8522
Finerty, John C. 5.4156
Finestone, Harold. 4.6873
Finger, Seymour Maxwell, 1915-. 4.9238
Fink, Arthur E. (Arthur Emil), 1903-. 4.6477
Fink, Donald G. 5.6251, 5.6259, 5.6451
Fink, Leon, 1948-. 4.3556
Fink, Richard H. 4.1319
Finke, Ulrich. 1.6162
Finke, Wayne. 2.5322
Finkel, Asher J. 5.4727
Finkelhor, David. 4.5776, 5.4954
Finkelman, Paul, 1949-. 4.9622
Finkelpearl, Philip J. 2.6627
Finkelstein, Louis, 1895-. 1.1899, 3.3806
Finkl, Charles W., 1941-. 5.2941, 5.5267
Finlay, John L., 1939-. 3.8683
Finlay, Robert, 1940-. 3.2914
Finlayson, Roderick. 2.10214
Finley, Blanche, 1906-. 4.9203
Finley, John Huston, 1904-. 3.2610
Finley, M. I. (Moses I.), 1912-. 2.494, 3.82, 3.2513, 3.2534-3.2535, 3.2943, 4.1727, 4.1732, 4.6413, 4.7332, 4.7364
Finn, Chester E., 1944-. 4.10601, 4.10816
Finn, David, 1921-. 1.5696, 1.5727, 1.5786
Finn, Jeremy D. 5.1406
Finn, R. Welldon (Rex Welldon) 3.1338, 3.1727
Finnegan, Ruth H. comp. 4.816
Finnegan, Ruth H. 2.2297
Finneran, Richard J. 2.8330, 2.9853-2.9854
Finney, Charles G. (Charles Grandison), 1905-. 2.11719
Finney, Charles Grandison, 1792-1875. 1.3032
Finocchiaro, Maurice A., 1942-. 1.416
Finston, H. L. 5.2860
Fintel, Mark. 5.5873
Fioravanzo, Giuseppe, 1891-. 5.7425
Fiore, Peter Amadeus, 1927-. 2.6462, 2.7127
Fiore, Robert L. 2.5194
Fiorenza, Elisabeth Schüssler, 1938-. 1.2270
Fiorenza, Francis Schüssler. 1.2777
Fioretti di San Francesco. 1.3259
Fiori, Giuseppe, 1923-. 3.2899
Fiorina, Morris P. 4.8025
Firbank, Ronald, 1886-1926. 2.8625-2.8626
Firchow, Evelyn Scherabon. 2.13934
Firchow, Evelyn Scherabon. ed. 3.1989
Firchow, Peter Edgerly, 1937-. 2.8818, 2.8827, 2.13934

Firdawsī. 2.1967
Fire, John. 3.5952
Firebaugh, Morris W. 5.6133
Firestone, William A. 4.10645
Firkins, Ina Ten Eyck, 1866-1937, comp. 5.8127
Firmage, D. Allan (David Allan), 1918- joint author. 5.6080
First, Ruth. 2.10056
Firth, C. H. (Charles Harding), 1857-1936. 5.7305
Firth, Frank E. 5.5473
Firth, Gerald R. joint author. 4.10633
Firth, J. R. (John Rupert), 1890-1960. 2.5, 2.90
Firth, Raymond William, 1901-. 1.1623, 4.404, 4.427, 4.521, 4.555, 4.576
Firth, Stewart. 3.5666
Fisch, Max Harold, 1900-. 1.619
Fischbeck, Helmut J., 1928-. 5.2012
Fischbeck, Kurt, 1898-. 5.2012
Fischel, Oskar, 1870-1939. 1.6219
Fischer, Alfred G. 5.3167
Fischer, Claude S., 1948-. 4.6183, 4.6292
Fischer, David Hackett, 1935-. 3.431, 3.7058
Fischer-Dieskau, Dietrich, 1925-. 1.4053, 2.13518
Fischer, Fritz, 1908-. 3.778, 3.2334
Fischer-Galati, Stephen A. 3.3511, 3.3549-3.3550
Fischer, George, 1923-. 4.8636
Fischer, Joel. 4.6487
Fischer, Louis, 1924-. 3.729, 3.3146, 3.4304, 3.4308, 4.9598
Fischer, Michael, 1949-. 2.2434
Fischer von Erlach, Johann Bernhard, 1656-1723. 1.5410
Fischhoff, Baruch, 1946-. 4.2714
Fischler, Ingrid. 5.2784
Fischler, Shirley. 4.992
Fischler, Stan, 1932-. 4.992
Fischman, Arthur M. joint author. 4.6744
Fischman, Leonard L. 4.3727
Fish, Carl Russell, 1876-1932. 3.6033
Fish, John Hall, 1932-. 4.5207
Fish, Richard G. illus. 5.3559
Fish, Stanley Eugene. 2.2435, 2.2658, 2.6518, 2.7062, 2.7128
Fish, Stanley Eugene. comp. 2.5934
Fishbane, Michael A. 1.2569
Fishbein, Martin. joint ed. 4.4999
Fishbein, Morris, 1889-. 5.4483
Fishburn, Katherine, 1944-. 2.12818, 4.6049
Fishel, Andrew. 4.10780
Fisher, Alden L., 1928- ed. 1.840
Fisher, Angela. 4.852
Fisher, Anthony C. joint author. 4.1902
Fisher, Anthony C. 4.1785
Fisher, Barbara. 2.8509
Fisher, Barbara R. 4.1847
Fisher, Bart S. 4.4116
Fisher, Charles. 2.3645
Fisher, Charles Alfred. 3.4382
Fisher, Dexter. 2.10305
Fisher, Dorothea Frances (Canfield), Mrs. 1879-. 2.14019
Fisher, Franklin M. 4.3808, 4.9468
Fisher, Frederick Jack, ed. 4.2266
Fisher, George Park, 1827-1909. 1.2745
Fisher, Godfrey, (Sir) 1885-. 3.5196
Fisher, Harold A. joint author. 2.3544
Fisher, Harold Henry, 1890-. 3.3066, 3.3175
Fisher, Herbert Albert Laurens, 1865-1940. 4.8382
Fisher, Irving, 1867-1947. 4.1293, 4.1295, 4.1550
Fisher, Joan E. 1.6642
Fisher, John H. 2.6385
Fisher, John Robert. 4.4236, 4.8347, 5.6752
Fisher, John W., 1931-. 5.6083
Fisher, Katherine H., joint author. 5.4243
Fisher, Lawrence. 4.4281
Fisher, Lois H., 1936-. 2.5562
Fisher, Louis. 4.4656, 4.7864, 4.9636
Fisher, M. H., ed. 3.2317
Fisher, Margaret Welpley, 1903- joint author. 4.8778
Fisher, Nigel, Sir. 3.1674
Fisher, Philip, 1941-. 2.10607
Fisher, Raymond Henry, 1907-. 4.95

Fisher, Rhoda L. (Rhoda Lee), 1924- joint author. 2.3134
Fisher, Richard B. 5.4535
Fisher, Richard F. 5.5426
Fisher, Richard V. (Richard Virgil), 1928-. 5.3045
Fisher, Robin, 1946-. 3.5718, 4.91
Fisher, Roger, 1922-. 5.473
Fisher, Ronald Aylmer, Sir, 1890-1962. 5.3315, 5.3357
Fisher, Seymour. 2.3134, 5.152, 5.494
Fisher, Susan M., 1937-. 5.4730
Fisher, Sydney Nettleton, 1906-. 3.3715
Fisher, W. B. (William Bayne) 3.3684, 3.4070
Fisher, Walter R. joint comp. 2.6267
Fisher, Wesley A. joint comp. 4.5380
Fishkin, James S. 4.7230
Fishlow, Albert. 4.3992
Fishman, H. Charles (Herman Charles), 1946- joint author. 5.4883
Fishman, Joshua A. 2.1787
Fishman, Robert, 1946-. 4.6305
Fishman, William J. 3.3948
Fishwick, Marshall William. 3.6109, 3.6181, 3.6292
Fisk, E. K. (Ernest Kelvin) ed. 3.5651
Fisk, Elizabeth C. 4.10617
Fisk, Margaret. ed. 1.54
Fisk, Milton. 1.1485
Fiske, John, 1842-1901. 3.6284, 3.7016
Fiske, Richard S. 5.3112
Fiske, Roger. 1.4229
Fiszman, Joseph R. 4.10673
Fitch, Frederic B. (Frederic Brenton), 1908-1987. 1.1207
Fitch, James Marston. 1.5283
Fitch, Jennifer M. 5.2987
Fitch, Lyle C. (Lyle Craig) 4.4028
Fitchen, John. 1.5238
Fite, Emerson David, 1874-1953. 4.1921
Fite, Gilbert Courtland, 1918-. 3.8515, 4.2941, 4.2960, 4.3528
Fitoussi, Jean Paul. 4.3202
Fitt, Mary, 1897-1959. 1.219
Fitting, James Edward. 3.5713
Fitts, Dudley, 1903- tr. 2.741
Fitz, Earl E. 2.5471
Fitzgerald, A. E. (Arthur Eugene), 1909-. 5.6308
FitzGerald, Ann. 4.5881
Fitzgerald, C. P. (Charles Patrick), 1902-. 3.4632, 3.4686, 3.4700
FitzGerald, Edward. 2.1971-2.1972
Fitzgerald, F. Scott (Francis Scott), 1896-1940. 2.11720-2.11721, 2.11723-2.11725
FitzGerald, Frances, 1940-. 3.4480, 3.6271
Fitzgerald, L. S., joint author. 5.8169
Fitzgerald, Mike, 1951-. 4.6919
Fitzgerald, Oscar P. 1.6561
Fitzgerald, Oscar P. joint author. 3.4507
Fitzgerald, Penelope. 1.3268, 2.9677-2.9679
Fitzgerald, Robert, 1910-. 2.485, 2.490, 2.796
Fitzgerald, Sally. 2.13211
Fitzgerald, Stephen. 3.4656
Fitzgerald, Thomas K. 4.529
FitzGibbon, Constantine, 1919-. 2.9418
Fitzgibbon, Russell Humke, 1902-. 3.9123, 3.9231
Fitzhugh, George, 1806-1881. 3.7244
Fitzmaurice, John. 4.8635, 4.8674
Fitzmyer, Joseph A. 1.2649, 1.2692, 5.8240
Fitzmyer, Joseph A. joint comp. 1.2525
Fitzpatrick, Brian. 3.5579
Fitzpatrick, Catherine A. 4.6135
Fitzpatrick, John Clement, 1876-1940. 3.7035, 3.7129
Fitzpatrick, Joseph P. 3.6589
Fitzpatrick, Kathleen, 1905-. 3.5561
Fitzpatrick, M. Louise. 5.5160
Fitzpatrick, Sheila. 3.3182, 3.3211, 4.10131
Fitzsimons, M. A. (Matthew Anthony), 1912-. 3.417, 4.9087
Five Civilized Tribes Heritage Foundation. 2.11213
Fixx, James F. 4.1051
Fjelde, Rolf. 2.14035
Flacelière, Robert, 1904-. 3.2548
Fladeland, Betty, 1919-. 4.6443

Flagstad, Kirsten, 1895-1962. 1.4090
Flaherty, David H. comp. 4.9486
Flahiff, Frederick T., joint author. 2.6662
Flamini, Roland. 2.3027
Flanagan, Hallie, 1890-1969. 2.3208
Flanagan, Harley. Ronald G., joint author. 5.6316
Flanagan, John Clemans, 1906-. 4.10309
Flanagan, John Theodore, 1906- ed. 2.10725
Flanagan, Owen J. 5.23
Flanagan, Robert J. joint author. 4.2214
Flanagan, Scott C. 4.7773, 4.8891
Flanagan, Thomas. 3.8854
Flanagan, William G. joint author. 4.6285
Flanders, Allan D. 4.3645
Flanders, Harley. 5.1535
Flanders, Ned A. 4.10271
Flandrin, Jean Louis. 4.5623
Flanigan, William H. 4.8103
Flanner, Janet, 1892-. 3.2232
Flanz, Gisbert H. 4.8360, 4.9377
Flapan, Simha. 3.3865
Flath, Arnold William. 4.978
Flaubert, Gustave. 2.4183-2.4187, 2.4189-2.4196
Flavell, John H. 5.592
Flawn, Peter Tyrell. 5.2972
Flaxman, John, 1755-1826. 1.4953
Fleagle, John G. 5.4023
Fleagle, Robert Guthrie, 1918-. 5.2518
Fleckenstein, Josef. 3.2264
Flecker, James Elroy, 1884-1915. 2.8627
Fleet, Michael. 4.8342
Fleischer, David V. 3.9219
Fleischmann, Fritz, 1950-. 2.10595
Fleischner, Eva, 1925-. 1.1976
Fleisher, Wilfrid, 1897-. 4.5383
Fleishman, Avrom. 2.8562, 2.9595
Fleishman, Edwin A. ed. 4.4358
Fleming, David G., 1926-. 5.4288
Fleming, David L., 1934-. 1.3219
Fleming, Denna Frank, 1893-. 3.3060, 4.9183, 4.9194
Fleming, Donald, 1923-. 3.6110, 4.9480
Fleming, George. 4.294
Fleming, Gerald. 3.1090
Fleming, Ian, 1935-. 2.9680, 5.2733
Fleming, John. 1.4675, 1.5380, 1.6506
Fleming, Richard Howell, 1909- joint author. 4.326
Fleming, Robben Wright, 1916-. 4.9559
Fleming, Stuart James. 3.244
Fleming, Thomas J. 3.8063
Fleming, Walter Lynwood, 1874-1932, ed. 3.7464
Flemings, Merton C., 1929-. 5.6773
Flemming, Ernst Richard, b. 1866. 1.6674
Flemming, John Stanton, 1941-. 4.4485
Fleron, Frederic J., 1937- comp. 4.7141
Fles, Barthold, 1902-. 1.3673
Flesch, Rudolf Franz, 1911-. 4.10459
Fletcher, A. (Alan), 1903-. 5.1124
Fletcher, Angus John Stewart, 1930-. 2.2389, 2.7117
Fletcher, Anthony. 3.1740
Fletcher, Banister, Sir, 1866-1953. 1.5211
Fletcher, Colin. 4.895
Fletcher, Giles, 1588?-1623. 2.6478
Fletcher, Harris Francis, 1892-. 2.7169
Fletcher, Harvey, 1884-. 5.4278
Fletcher, Ian. 2.7946
Fletcher, James E. 2.2856
Fletcher, John, 1931-. 2.3518, 2.6554-2.6556, 2.8429, 4.1278
Fletcher, John Gould, 1886-1950. 2.11742
Fletcher, Joseph Francis, 1905-. 5.4561
Fletcher, Marilyn P., 1940-. 5.8175
Fletcher, Phineas, 1582-1650. 2.6478
Fletcher School of Law and Diplomacy. International Security Studies Program. 5.7251
Fletcher, Sheila. 4.10845
Fletcher, Willard Allen. 3.1105
Fletcher, William Isaac, 1844-1917. 1.36
Fleure, H. J. (Herbert John), 1877-1969. 4.390
Flew, Antony, 1923-. 1.100, 1.699, 1.1148-1.1150, 1.2216, 1.2769
Flexner, Abraham, 1866-1959. 5.4603
Flexner, Eleanor, 1908-. 4.5983, 4.6096

Flexner, James Thomas. 1.5892-1.5894, 1.5929, 1.5975, 3.7030, 3.7033, 4.5996
Flexner, Stuart Berg. joint author. 2.1148
Flexner, Stuart Berg. 2.1068
Flick, Alexander Clarence, 1869-1942. 3.7163
Flieger, Wilhelm. joint author. 4.1618
Fliess, Wilhelm, 1858-1928. 5.136, 5.147
Fligstein, Neil. 4.6357
Flinders, Peter. 2.4045
Fling, Robert Michael, 1941-. 1.3546
Flink, Salomon J., 1906-. 4.2443
Flinn, Glenys W. joint ed. 5.3072
Flinn, Michael W. (Michael Walter), 1917-. 4.1690, 4.1695, 4.3751
Flint, Harrison L. (Harrison Leigh), 1929-. 5.5361
Flint, John E. 3.5359
Flint, R. W., ed. 1.6735
Flint, Rachael Heyhoe. 4.1043
Flint, Richard Foster, 1902-. 5.3143-5.3144
Fløistad, Guttorm. 1.451
Flora, Francesco, 1891-. 2.4978
Flora, Joseph M. 2.10461
Flora, Peter, 1944-. 4.6468
Florence, P. Sargant (Philip Sargant), 1890-. 4.3120
Flores, Angel, 1900-. 2.5179, 2.13516
Flores, Ivan. 5.1145
Flores, John. 2.13931
Florida State University. 5.427, 5.4364
Florida State University. Center for Professional Development and Public Service. 5.3539
Florida State University. Dept. of Biological Science. 5.3539
Florida State University. Graduate Research Council. 5.3539
Florinsky, Michael T., 1894-. 3.3039, 3.3183
Florio, Allen. 5.7093
Florit, Eugenio, 1903-. 2.5319
Florkin, Marcel. ed. 5.3330
Florkin, Marcel. 5.2791
Florman, Samuel C. 5.5513
Florovsky, Georges, 1893-1979. 1.3101
Flory, Paul J. 5.2751
Flory, Thomas, 1947-. 4.9909
Flory, Wendy Stallard. 2.12332
Floud, Roderick. 4.2265
Flower, Desmond, 1907- ed. 2.7679
Flower, Elizabeth. 1.556
Flower, J. E. (John Ernest) 2.3500
Flower, Milton Embick. 3.6261
Flower, Newman, Sir, 1879-. 1.4016
Flowers, Brian Hilton. 5.2056
Flowers, Ronald B. (Ronald Bruce), 1935-. 4.9722
Floyd, Phylis. 1.6447
Floyd, Samuel A. 1.3566
Fluegel, Jane. 1.4979
Flügel, Siegfried. 5.1978
Flügge, Wilhelm, 1904-. 5.5869
Fluharty, Vernon Lee. 3.9176
Flurry, Robert L. 5.2826
Flye, James Harold. 2.11296
Flygare, W. H., 1936-. 5.2814
Flynn, Charles. 2.2920
Flynn, Charles L. 3.8268
Flynn, Frances. 5.8382
Flynn, James Robert, 1934-. 5.373
Flynn, Peter, 1936-. 3.9216
Flynt, J. Wayne, 1940-. 4.2023
Foakes, R. A. 2.3290, 2.5813
Focillon, Henri, 1881-1943. 1.4750
Fodor, Jerry A. 5.24, 5.263
Fodor, Jerry A. ed. 2.133
Foerster, Norman, 1887-. 2.10241, 2.10248, 2.10341
Foerster, Werner, 1897- comp. 1.2966
Fogarty, Robert S. 4.7154
Fogazzaro, Antonio, 1842-1911. 2.4988
Fogel, Aaron, 1947-. 2.8563
Fogel, Ephim Gregory, 1920- joint ed. 2.5492
Fogel, Robert William. ed. 3.428
Fogel, Robert William. 3.7245, 3.4993, 4.4013
Fogel, Robert William. comp. 4.1884
Fogel, Walter A. 4.3614, 4.9566
Fogelin, Robert J. 1.541, 1.1081, 1.1162
Fogelquist, Donald F. 2.5269
Fogelson, Robert M. 3.8620, 4.5243, 4.6819

Fogg Art Museum. 1.5024, 1.5077, 1.5325, 1.5648, 1.5902
Fogg, G. E. (Gordon Elliott), 1919-. 5.3707
Fogle, French Rowe. 2.6474
Fogle, Richard Harter. 2.7599, 2.11070
Fokine, Michel, 1880-1942. 4.1138
Folb, Edith A. 2.1158
Folb, Peter I., 1938-. 5.5137
Foley, Helene P., 1942-. 2.467, 4.5849
Foley, James D., 1942-. 5.5647
Foley, John Miles. 4.757, 4.762
Foley, Martha. comp. 2.10834
Foley, Martha. 2.10809
Foley, Suzanne. 1.6615
Foley, William E., 1938-. 3.8360
Folger Shakespeare Library. 2.6494, 2.6710, 2.6869
Folk, G. Edgar (George Edgar), 1914-. 5.4204
Folkenflik, Robert, 1939-. 2.7092
Folkman, David I. 4.3947
Follain, Jean, 1903-1971. 2.4529
Follett, Roy H. 5.5292
Follett, Wilson, 1887-1963. 2.1138
Folmsbee, Stanley John, 1899-. 3.8346-3.8347
Folsom, Ed, 1947-. 2.11281
Folsom, James K. 2.10594
Foltz, William J. joint ed. 4.7381
Folz, Robert. 3.1987, 4.7533
Fombrun, Charles J. 4.4359
Fomin, S. V. (Sergeĭ Vasil'evich) joint author. 5.1467, 5.1485
Fomin, S. V. (Sergeĭ Vasil'evich) 5.1605
Fondation nationale des sciences politiques. 5.8374
Foner, Eric. 3.6172, 3.7175, 3.7599, 4.6424, 4.10023
Foner, Jack D. 3.6725
Foner, Philip Sheldon, 1910-. 1.3443, 2.5366, 2.12031, 3.6601, 3.6731, 3.7020, 3.7237, 3.7247, 3.7357, 3.9095, 4.3270-4.3271, 4.3298, 4.3340, 4.3352, 4.6041, 4.7140, 4.7423, 4.10866
Fong, Wen. 1.6672
Fong, Wen C. 1.6370
Font, Pedro. 3.8603
Fontaine, Judith M. 5.8297
Fontana, Andrea. 4.5797
Fontane, Theodor, 1819-1898. 2.13563-2.13566
Fontein, Jan. 1.5063, 1.5881
Fontenrose, Joseph Eddy, 1903-. 3.2643, 4.822
Fontgalland, Bernard de. 4.3979
Food and Agriculture Organization of the United Nations. 4.2902-4.2903, 5.3909, 5.5220, 5.5341, 5.5483, 5.6021
Food and Agriculture Organization of the United Nations. Development Research and Training Service. Policy Analysis Division. 4.1594
Foord, Archibald S. 3.1520
Foot, M. R. D. (Michael Richard Daniel), 1919-. 3.1628, 5.7253
Foot, Michael, 1913-. 3.1699
Foot, Philippa. 1.1403, 1.1447
Foote, Henry Wilder, 1875-1964. 1.5938
Foote, Peter Godfrey. 3.3360
Foote, Shelby. 2.11743
Footman, David, 1895-. 3.3184
Forbath, Peter, joint author. 4.7903
Forbes, Christopher. 1.6666
Forbes, Elliot. ed. 1.3806
Forbes, Ernest R. 3.8798
Forbes, Esther. 2.11745-2.11746
Forbes, Fred R., 1949-. 5.8427
Forbes, Jennifer, 1941- joint author. 5.7934
Forbes, R. J. (Robert James), 1900-. 5.727
Force, Peter, 1790-1868. 3.6860
Force, Robert, 1934-. 5.4876
Forché, Carolyn. 2.13015
Forcucci, Samuel L. joint author. 1.4409
Forczek, Deborah. 3.6836
Ford, Betty, 1918-. 3.7930
Ford, Boris. 2.5523
Ford, Brian J. 5.3286
Ford, Cathy. 2.9902
Ford, Clellan Stearns, 1909-. 4.5501
Ford, Donald Herbert, 1921- joint author. 5.4323
Ford, E. B. (Edmund Briscoe), 1901-. 5.3879

Ford, Ford Madox, 1873-1939. 2.2610, 2.5737, 2.8541, 2.8546, 2.8564, 2.8628-2.8633
Ford Foundation. 3.7999, 4.3200, 4.3502, 4.3716, 4.5758, 4.5785, 4.7868, 4.10582
Ford Foundation. Energy Policy Project. 4.3811
Ford, Franklin L. (Franklin Lewis), 1920-. 3.661, 3.1962, 3.2505
Ford, George Harry, 1914-. 2.6019, 2.7628, 2.7654-2.7655, 2.7861
Ford, Gerald R., 1913-. 3.7931
Ford, Grace. joint author. 5.7921
Ford, Guy Stanton, 1873-1962. 3.2491, 3.6196
Ford, Hugh D., 1925- comp. 3.2228
Ford, James, 1884-1944, ed. 3.6786
Ford, Jesse Hill. 2.13016
Ford, John, 1586-ca. 1640. 2.6574-2.6575
Ford, Kenneth William, 1926-. 5.1992
Ford, Lewis S. 1.2810
Ford, P. R. J. 1.6585
Ford, Patrick Joseph, 1941- joint author. 4.10615
Ford, Percy, 1894-. 5.7921
Ford, Richard A., joint author. 5.2648
Ford, Thomas R., comp. 4.1630, 4.2842
Ford, Thomas W. 2.11804
Ford, Trevor David. 4.280
Ford, W. E. (William Ebenezer), 1878-. 5.3020
Ford, Wendy W. joint author. 5.1060
Ford, Worthington Chauncey, 1858-1941. ed. 3.6236, 3.7068
Forde, Cyril Daryll, 1902-. 3.5059, 4.523, 4.582, 4.595
Forde-Johnston, James L. 4.732
Fordin, Hugh, 1935-. 1.4109
Fordyce, C. J. (Christian James), 1901-. 2.707
Forehand, Walter. 2.779
Foreign Policy Association. 1.2050
Forell, George Wolfgang. 1.3364
Foreman-Peck, James. 4.1762
Forer, Lois G., 1914-. 4.9500
Forest History Society. 5.8198
Forester, C. S. (Cecil Scott), 1899-1966. 2.8640
Forester, John, 1929-. 4.4044
Forge, Andrew. 1.6123
Forisha-Kovach, Barbara. 4.3288
Forkel, Johann Nikolaus, 1749-1818. 1.3775
Forkner, Ben. 2.9869
Forman, James, 1928-. 3.6833
Forman, Martin. 4.4384
Forman, Richard T. T. 5.3517
Forman, Shepard, 1938-. 4.2839
Forman, W. (Werner) illus. 1.5615
Forman, W. (Werner) 3.5748
Formisano, Ronald P., 1939-. 4.8191-4.8192
Formo, Marvin W. 5.6894
Fornara, Charles W. 2.475, 3.2514
Fornatale, Peter. joint author. 1.4279
Fornell, Earl Wesley. 5.660
Forrest, Alan I. 3.2117, 4.6533
Forrest, James F. 2.6917
Forrest-Thomson, Veronica. 2.10491
Forrest, William George Grieve. 3.2575, 3.2648
Forster, Brenda, joint author. 4.6879
Forster, Donald F., joint author. 3.8751
Forster, E. M. (Edward Morgan), 1879-1970. 2.3421, 2.8598, 2.8641-2.8645, 2.8647-2.8655, 2.8661
Forster, Edward Seymour, 1879-1950, tr. 2.340, 2.347
Forster, Elborg, 1931-. 3.2039, 4.5282, 5.7118
Forster, John, 1812-1876. 2.7637, 2.7917
Forster, Margaret. 2.9681
Forster, Richard A., joint author. 5.3945
Forster, Robert, 1926-. 3.300, 3.345, 4.5282, 4.6392, 5.7118
Forstner, Lorne J., ed. 5.8276
Forsyth, Adrian. 5.3481
Forsyth, Ilene H. 1.5782
Forsyth, John Bruce, joint author. 5.2924
Forsyth, Michael. 1.4398
Forsythe, Charles E. (Charles Edward), 1899-. 4.974
Forsythe, David P., 1941-. 4.7631
Forte, Allen. 1.3669, 1.4380, 1.4427, 1.4464
Fortes, Meyer. ed. 4.577, 4.602
Fortescue, William, 1945-. 3.4257
Fortman, Edmund J., 1901-. 1.2833
Fortune, Nigel. joint author. 1.3796

Fortune, Reo Franklin, 1903-. 3.5631
Foscolo, Ugo, 1778-1827. 2.4989-2.4990
Foshay, Arthur Wellesley, 1912-. 4.10381
Foskett, A. C. (Antony Charles) 5.7629
Foss, Brian M. 1921- ed. 5.5
Foss, Brian M. 5.604
Foss, Hubert James, 1899-. 1.3481, 1.3807, 1.4186
Foss, Phillip O. 4.2827
Fossey, Dian. 5.4033
Foster, Adriance Sherwood, 1901-1973. 5.3732
Foster, Arthur R. 5.6600
Foster, Augustus John, Sir, bart, 1780-1848. 3.6027
Foster, Caxton C., 1929-. 5.1174
Foster, Charles Robert, 1927-. 3.1198
Foster, David William. 2.5123, 2.5299, 2.5310, 2.5373, 5.7881, 5.8023
Foster, E., tr. 1.3145
Foster, Edward Halsey. 2.11415
Foster, Frances Smith. 2.10530
Foster, George, 1948-. 4.4408, 4.4412
Foster, George McClelland, 1913-. 3.210, 3.8912, 3.8967, 4.428, 4.463, 4.5257
Foster, H. Lincoln. 5.5374
Foster, H. Schuyler (Harry Schuyler), 1905-. 3.7568
Foster, Hal. 1.1395
Foster, Herbert Baldwin, 1874-1906. 2.358
Foster, Herbert L. 4.10969
Foster, J. 5.2100
Foster, J. Bristol. joint author. 5.4046
Foster, James Ralph, 1890-. 2.6004
Foster, Kenelm. ed. 2.4918
Foster, Kenelm. 2.4954
Foster, Larry, 1934-. 5.4008
Foster, Michael Beresford. 4.7349
Foster, Norman G., joint author. 5.2743
Foster, Richard Jackson, 1928- joint ed. 2.2445
Foster, Robert, 1949-. 2.9434
Foster, Ronald S., joint author. 4.4383
Foster, Shirley. 2.6034
Foster, Stephen. 5.1892
Foster, Vanda. 4.858
Foster, Virginia Ramos. joint author. 2.5299, 5.8023
Foster, William S. 5.5988
Foster, William Z., 1881-1961. 4.8234
Foth, H. D. 5.5263
Foti, G. 5.6768
Fouad, Abdel-Aziz A., joint author. 5.6286
Foucault, Michel. ed. 4.6703
Foucault, Michel. 1.70, 4.6846, 5.4508
Foucher, A. (Alfred), 1865-1952. 1.1772
Fought, Sharon Gavin. 5.5210
Foulds, L. R., 1948-. 5.1275
Foulet, Lucien. 2.3976
Foulkes, Fred K. 4.4368
Foulkes, William David, 1935-. 5.651
Foundation Center. 1.59-1.61, 4.10583
Foundation Library Center. 1.60
Founders Society. 1.6050, 1.6054
Fouraker, Lawrence E. 4.1567
Fourastié, Jean, 1907-. 4.1984, 4.2326
Fourcade, Marie Madeleine. 3.1062
Fourier, Charles, 1772-1837. 4.7165
Fourier, Jean Baptiste Joseph, baron, 1768-1830. 5.1092
Fournier, Lionel. 1.6399
Fourquin, Guy. 4.1741
Fout, John C., 1937-. 4.6125
Fowke, Edith Fulton, 1913-. 5.8196
Fowkes, Robert Allen, 1913- joint author. 1.4238
Fowler, Alastair. ed. 2.7112
Fowler, Albert Vann, 1904-. 5.7147
Fowler, David C., 1921-. 1.2537, 2.5608, 2.6405
Fowler, Douglas. 2.12232
Fowler, Gene, 1890-1960. 2.3241
Fowler, H. W. (Henry Watson), 1858-1933, joint author. 2.1083
Fowler, Henry Watson, 1858-1933. 2.1082, 2.1090
Fowler, Ira. 5.4140
Fowler, John, 1906-. 1.6543
Fowler, John Stuart. 4.917
Fowler, Kenneth Alan. 3.1998
Fowler, Loretta, 1944-. 3.5843

Fowler, Marian, 1929-. 3.355
Fowler, R.H. (Ralph Howard), 1889-. 5.2176
Fowler, William, 1921-. 5.584
Fowler, William M., 1944-. 3.6953
Fowles, Gerald Wilfred Albert, joint author.
  5.2835
Fowles, Grant R. 5.1646, 5.2294
Fowles, John, 1926-. 1.749, 2.9682-2.9690
Fowlie, Wallace, 1908-. 1.1400, 2.2497, 2.3888,
  2.4171, 2.4265, 2.4278, 2.4280, 2.4309
Fowlkes, Martha R., 1940-. 4.5669
Fox, Annette Baker, 1912-. 4.9058
Fox, Anthony. 2.1181
Fox, Charles, 1921-. 1.3618
Fox, Charles Philip, 1913-. 4.4441
Fox, Cyril, Sir, 1882-1967. 4.391
Fox, Daniel M. 4.1375
Fox, Denton. tr. 2.13983
Fox, Denton. 2.6386
Fox, Dixon Ryan, 1887-1945. 3.6274
Fox, E. Inman (Edward Inman), 1933-. 2.5113
Fox, George, 1624-1691. 1.3355
Fox, Harrison W. 4.8029
Fox, Hugh, 1932-. 2.2327
Fox, John Howard. 2.3839
Fox, Karl August, 1917-. 4.1296
Fox-Lockert, Lucía, 1928-. 2.5096
Fox, Lynn H., 1944-. 4.10915
Fox, Mary Frank. 4.3280
Fox, Matthew, 1940-. 1.3086
Fox, Michael W., 1937-. 5.3992-5.3993
Fox, Ralph H. (Ralph Hartzler), 1913- joint
  author. 5.1621
Fox, Richard Gabriel, 1939-. 4.8707
Fox, Robin, 1934-. 4.578
Fox, Ruth A. 2.6439
Fox, Seymour. 4.9969
Fox, Sidney W. 5.3319
Fox, Stephen R. 3.6852, 5.3226
Fox, Vernon Brittain, 1916-. 4.6890
Fox, William T. R. (William Thornton
  Rickert), 1912-. 5.7384
Foxall, G. R. 4.4308
Foxe, John, 1516-1587. 1.2475
Foxley, Alejandro. 4.2162
Foxon, David Fairweather. 4.5544
Foxwell, Herbert Somerton, 1849-1936. 4.4472
Foyer, Christine H. 5.3759
Fraas, Arthur P. 5.6200
Fractor, David T. 4.1903
Frados, Joel. 5.6911
Frady, Marshall. 1.3041
Fraenger, Wilhelm, 1890-1964. 1.6242
Fraenkel, Eduard, 1888-1970. 2.410, 2.724
Fraenkel, Ernst, 1898-. 4.9328
Fraenkel, Heinrich, 1897-. 3.2385, 3.2389
Fraenkel, Osmond Kessler, 1888-. 4.9678
Fraga, Serafin. 5.2081
Fragnoli, Raymond R., 1948-. 3.8435
Fraiberg, Louis, 1913-. 2.10242
Fraisse, Paul. 5.403
Fraistat, Rose Ann C., 1952-. 2.11793
Frame, Donald Murdoch, 1911-. 2.3991,
  2.3993-2.3994, 2.4040
Frame, Janet. 2.10217-2.10224
Frame, Robin. 3.1826
Frampton, Kenneth. 1.5243, 1.5255
France, Anatole, 1844-1924. 2.3832,
  2.4203-2.4215
France. Bibliothèque nationale. 2.3947
France, Rachel, 1936-. 2.10789
Franceschini, Guido, conte, 1657-1698.
  defendant. 2.7476
Franchere, Ruth. 2.12032
Franchini, Patrizia Noémi, 1953-. 2.13904
Francis, Daniel. 4.3860
Francis, David. 2.3250
Francis, de Sales, Saint, 1567-1622.
  1.3217-1.3218
Francis, Dick. 2.9696
Francis, Doris, 1940-. 4.6593
Francis, Emerich K., 1906-. 4.620
Francis, Hywel. 4.3535
Francis, of Assisi, Saint, 1182-1226. 1.3135
Francis, W. Nelson (Winthrop Nelson), 1910-.
  2.207, 2.1131, 2.1141
Francis, Wayne L. 4.8257

Franciscans. Province of the most holy name of
  Jesus. 1.66
Franck, Irene M. 5.7574
Franck, Thomas M. 4.7968, 4.9215
Franco, Jean. 2.5300
François, Michel. 2.3987, 3.446
François-Poncet, André, 1887-. 3.2437
Francome, Colin. 4.5697
Franda, Marcus F. 3.4148, 4.2985, 4.7119
Franda, Marcus F. tr. 2.1863
Franda, Marcus F. joint author. 4.8715
Franey, Pierre. 5.7131
Frangi, Abdallah. 3.3906
Frängsmyr, Tore, 1938-. 5.3215
Frank, Andre Gunder, 1929-. 4.1750, 4.2168
Frank, Anne, 1929-1945. 3.1091
Frank, Charles P. 2.12770
Frank, Charles Raphael. 4.1808
Frank, Frederick S. 2.3457
Frank, Isaiah, 1917-. 4.3023
Frank, Jerome, 1889-1957. 4.9371, 4.9449,
  4.9453
Frank, Jerome David, 1909-. 4.8989, 5.4851
Frank, Joseph, 1916-. 2.1364-2.1366, 2.2675,
  2.3685
Frank-Kamenetskiĭ, D. A. (David Al'bertovich)
  5.2385
Frank L. Weil Institute for Studies in Religion
  and the Humanities. 4.7881
Frank, Lawrence Phillip. 3.5941
Frank, Peter, Apr. 7, 1924-. 2.13589
Frank, Philipp, 1884-1966. 5.885
Frank, Robert Gregg, 1943-. 5.4171
Frank, Robert Worth, 1914-. 2.6400
Frank, Robyn C. 5.7109
Frank, Ronald Edward, 1933-. 4.4067
Frank, Shirley. 4.5991
Frank, Tenney, 1876-1939. 2.630, 2.710, 3.2734,
  4.1739
Frank W. Pierce Memorial Conference, Cornell
  University, 1973. 4.9554
Frank, Waldo David, 1889-1967. 3.6111
Franke, Herbert, 1914-. 2.2201, 3.4705
Franke, Herbert W., 1927-. 1.5821
Franke, Richard W. 4.2595
Franke, Walter Henry, 1928- joint author.
  4.3223
Franke, Wolfgang, 1912-. 4.8739
Frankel, Ernst G. 4.3973-4.3974
Frankel, Francine R. 4.2505, 4.2986
Frankel, Haskel. joint author. 2.3118
Fränkel, Hermann Ferdinand, 1888-. 2.750
Frankel, Jonathan. 3.3998
Frankel, Joseph. 3.1706
Frankel, Marvin E., 1920-. 4.9889
Frankel, Max. 5.2754
Frankel, O. H. (Otto Herzberg), 1900-. 5.3219
Frankel, Philip H. 5.7349
Frankel, Theodore, 1929-. 5.2088
Frankel, Victor H. 5.4273
Frankel, Walter A., 1938-. 1.3580
Frankena, William K. 1.1448
Frankena, William K. joint author. 1.1321
Frankenstein, Alfred Victor, 1906-. 1.5940
Frankfort, Henri, 1897-1954. 1.1591, 1.1608,
  1.1852, 1.4697, 4.740
Frankfort, Henriette Antonia (Groenewegen)
  1896-. 1.4698
Frankfort, Henriette Antonia (Groenewegen)
  1896- joint author. 1.1591
Frankfurter, Felix, 1882-1965. 4.8065, 4.9450,
  4.9813-4.9814, 4.9839
Frankie, G. W. 5.5408
Frankiel, Sandra Sizer, 1946-. 1.2991
Frankl, Paul, 1878-1962. 1.5239-1.5240
Frankland, Noble, 1922- joint author. 3.1047
Franklin, Alexander, ed. 2.6206
Franklin, Benjamin. 3.6967, 3.6985-3.6987,
  4.10188, 5.2338
Franklin, Gene F. 5.6182
Franklin, H. Bruce (Howard Bruce), 1934-.
  2.10335, 3.3232
Franklin, Jerome L. 5.8384
Franklin, John Hope, 1915-. 3.6615-3.6616,
  3.6809, 3.7276, 3.7465, 3.8144-3.8145
Franklin, Julian H. 4.7384, 4.7552
Franklin, Kenneth L. 5.1689
Franklin, Philip, 1898-. 5.1440

Franklin, Vincent P. 4.10876
Franklyn, Julian. 3.285
Franks, Kenny Arthur, 1945-. 3.5852
Franks, Martha Ross. 5.4757
Franks, Roger G. E. 5.6830
Fransman, Martin. 4.1827
Frantz, Alison. 1.5632
Frantz, Charles. 4.439
Frantz, Joe Bertram, 1917-. 3.6266, 3.8319,
  3.8492
Franz, Anselm. 5.6675
Franz, Marie-Luise von, 1915-. 5.518
Franzini, Joseph B. joint author. 5.5962
Frappier, Jean. 2.3950
Frappier, Jean. ed. 2.3985
Frascina, Francis. 1.4784, 1.4879
Fraser, Allan. 5.5448
Fraser, Antonia, 1932-. 3.1491, 3.1795, 4.6093
Fraser/Associates. 4.7896
Fraser, Blair, 1909-1968. 3.8777
Fraser, Clarence M. 5.5462
Fraser, Colin. 2.20
Fraser, D. A. 5.2348
Fraser, David, 1920-. 3.976, 3.1268
Fraser, Derek. 4.9417
Fraser, Donald R. 4.4532
Fraser, Douglas. ed. 1.5085
Fraser, Douglas. comp. 1.4684
Fraser, G. S. (George Sutherland), 1915-.
  2.5732
Fraser, J. T. (Julius Thomas), 1923-. 5.1756
Fraser, Nicholas, 1948-. 3.9252
Fraser, P. M. (Peter Marshall) 3.5150
Fraser, Robert, 1947-. 2.10095
Fraser, Ronald, 1930-. 3.3465
Fraser, Stewart. 4.10203
Fraser-Tytler, William Kerr, Sir, 1886-. 3.4112
Fraser, W. Hamish. 4.2307
Frate, Dennis A., 1948-. 3.6760
Frauenfelder, Hans, 1922-. 5.2330, 5.2459
Fraunces Tavern Museum. 4.871
Frayne, John P., ed. 2.8334
Frayser, Suzanne G. 4.587
Frazer, James George, Sir, 1854-1941. 1.1603,
  1.2548, 2.679
Frazier, Edward Franklin, 1894-1962. 1.2419,
  3.6617, 3.6651, 3.6667, 3.6761
Frazier, Nancy. 4.10838
Frears, J. R., 1936-. 4.8592
Freccero, John. ed. 2.4930
Fréchet, Alec. 2.8683
Frechtman, Bernard, tr. 1.1465
Frederic, Harold, 1856-1898. 2.11033
Frederick II, King of Prussia, 1712-1786.
  3.2486, 5.7207, 5.7211
Frederick, Ralph H. joint author. 4.162
Frederick, Richard G. joint author. 5.3292
Frederick S. Wight Art Gallery. 1.6727
Fredericksen, Hazel, 1897-. 4.6555
Fredland, Roger. 3.543
Fredrickson, David A. (David Allen) 3.5723
Fredrickson, George M., 1934-. 3.6618, 3.7351
Fredriksen, John C. 5.7834
Fredro, Aleksander, hrabia, 1793-1876. 2.1701
Free Europe Committee. Mid-European Studies
  Center. 3.1935
Freebairn, Donald K. 4.2895
Freeborn, Richard. 2.1284, 2.1465
Freed, Donald. 4.9464
Freedberg, S. J. (Sydney Joseph), 1914-.
  1.6181-1.6182, 1.6218, 1.6221
Freedley, George, 1904- joint ed. 2.2809
Freedman, David Noel, 1922- comp. 1.2544
Freedman, Estelle B., 1947-. 4.6902
Freedman, Lawrence. 5.7362
Freedman, Marcia K. joint author. 4.3563
Freedman, Maurice. 4.5456
Freedman, Robert L., 1941-. 5.8098
Freedman, Robert Owen. 3.3748
Freedman, Samuel S., 1927-. 4.9634
Freehling, William W., 1935-. 3.7127, 3.7195
Freehof, Solomon Bennett, 1892-. 1.1947
Freeland, Richard M., 1941-. 3.7795
Freeley, Austin J. 2.3538
Freeman, A. Myrick, 1936-. 4.1842-4.1843,
  4.2073
Freeman, Bob A. 5.4439
Freeman, Christopher. 4.1862

Freeman, Derek. 4.685
Freeman, Donald E. 5.1236
Freeman, Douglas Southall, 1886-1953. 3.7028,
    3.7328, 3.7363
Freeman-Grenville, G. S. P. (Greville Stewart
    Parker) 3.272, 3.368
Freeman-Grenville, G. S. P. (Greville Stewart
    Parker) comp. 3.5237
Freeman, Harvey A. joint author. 5.1234
Freeman, Howard E. 4.4825
Freeman, Jennie, joint author. 4.8412
Freeman, Jo. 4.6050, 4.6071
Freeman, John. 1.4511
Freeman, John Crosby, comp. 1.6552
Freeman, Kathleen, 1897-1959. 1.220
Freeman, Lucy. 2.3473
Freeman, Margaret Beam, 1899-. 1.6592
Freeman, Margaret C. 4.3724
Freeman, Mary Eleanor Wilkins, 1852-1930.
    2.11034
Freeman, Michael, joint author. 4.3563
Freeman, Phyllis. 1.5647
Freeman, R. Austin (Richard Austin),
    1862-1943. 2.8670
Freeman, Richard B. (Richard Barry), 1943-.
    4.3307-4.3308, 4.3353
Freeman, Robert J. 4.4730
Freeman, Roger L. 5.6347, 5.6384
Freeman, Rosemary. 2.5792, 2.6529
Freeman, Ruth B. 5.5207
Freeman, Thomas Walter. 3.1869, 4.68, 4.1663
Freemon, Frank R. 5.4354
Freer Gallery of Art. 1.6354, 1.6421, 1.6481,
    1.6528
Freese, John Henry. 2.352
Freeth, Zahra Dickson. 3.4047
Freeze, R. Allan. 4.306-4.307, 4.309
Frege, Gottlob, 1848-1925. 1.1208-1.1209,
    5.1023, 5.1040
Freiberg, J. W. 2.3694, 4.4861
Freibert, Lucy M., 1922-. 2.10820
Freidel, Frank Burt. 3.7781, 5.7826
Freies Deutsches Hochstift. 2.13782
Freifelder, David, 1935-. 5.3331, 5.3418
Freifelder, Morris, 1907-. 5.2749
Freilich, Morris, 1928-. 4.488
Freimarck, Vincent, comp. 2.10837
Freire, Paulo, 1921-. 4.10236, 4.10752, 4.10768
Fremantle, Anne. 2.7923
Fremantle, Anne Jackson, 1909-. 1.344, 1.3132
Fremantle, Francesca. 1.2149
Fremantle, Richard. 1.6187
Frémont, John Charles, 1813-1890. 3.8473
Frenaye, Frances. 3.2900
French, A. (Alfred), 1916-. 2.1657-2.1658,
    2.1661, 4.1733
French, A. P. (Anthony Philip), 1920-. 5.1909,
    5.2030, 5.2057, 5.2130
French, Daniel Chester, 1850-1931. 1.5665
French, Hannah Dustin, 1907-. 5.7567
French Institute-Alliance Française de New
    York. 5.8002
French, John R. P. joint author. 5.541
French, Joseph Milton, 1895- ed. 2.7148
French, P. M. (Peter Michael), 1935-. 5.6769
French, Peter A. 1.467, 4.2705
French, Richard Anthony. 4.6264
French, Robert Dudley, 1888-. 2.6341
French, Warren G., 1922-. 2.10407-2.10410,
    2.11186, 2.12427, 2.12536
French, Wendell L., 1923-. 4.2701
French, William P. 5.7797
Frend, W. H. C. 1.2291, 1.2474, 1.2964, 1.2972
Frenkel', IA. I. (IAkov Il'ich), 1894-1952.
    5.2188
Frenkel, Jacob A. 4.4464, 4.4552
Frenkel, Stephen. joint author. 4.3341
Frerking, Marvin E. 5.6518
Freud, Anna, 1895-. 4.5717, 4.5739, 4.6548,
    4.9511, 5.134, 5.140, 5.564, 5.4917, 5.5100
Freud, Sigmund, 1856-1939. 1.1564, 1.2542,
    2.3787-2.3788, 4.5502, 5.133-5.148, 5.153,
    5.652, 5.4783, 5.4911
Freund, Bill. 3.5081
Freund, John E. 5.1387
Freund, Julien. 4.4767
Freund, Robert. 1.5889
Freund, Rudolf. 5.3906

Freund, William, 1806-1894. 2.258
Freundlich, Irwin, ed. 1.3582
Frey, Alexander H. 5.1575
Frey, Allan E. joint author. 4.377
Frey, Bruno S. 4.4140
Frey, David G. (David Grover), 1915-. 5.3146,
    5.3256
Frey, Donald E., 1941-. 4.4714
Frey, Richard L. ed. 4.1066
Frey, Robert W. 5.3158
Frey, Stephen L. (Stephen Louis), 1939-. 4.4337
Freyer, Tony Allan. 4.9897
Freyre, Gilberto, 1900-. 3.9190-3.9193
Friar, Kimon. 2.607, 2.614, 2.615, 2.620
Friar, Kimon. comp. 2.573
Friar, Kimon. tr. 2.592, 2.577
Frick Collection. 1.4661
Frick, Elizabeth. 3.432
Frick, John W. 2.3203
Fricke, Gerhard, 1901-. 2.13458, 2.13598,
    2.13646
Fridegård, Jan, 1897-1968. 2.14084
Friebert, Stuart, 1931-. 2.10769
Fried, Albert. ed. 4.6624
Fried, Albert. comp. 4.7003
Fried, Barbara, 1951-. 5.4199
Fried, Charles, 1935-. 1.1449
Fried, Erich. 2.13704
Fried, Jerome. ed. 4.753
Fried, Marc. 4.3618
Fried, Martha Nemes. 4.556
Fried, Michael. 1.5902, 1.5952, 1.6051
Fried, Morton H. (Morton Herbert), 1923-1986.
    4.556, 4.5417
Fried, Richard M., 1941-. 3.7667
Fried, Robert C. 4.8879
Friedan, Betty. 4.6018
Friedberg, Joan Brest, 1927-. 5.7724
Friedell, Egon, 1878-1938. 3.149
Frieden, Bernard J. 4.6318
Friedenberg, Edgar Zodiag, 1921-. 4.5753,
    4.10493
Friedenberg, Robert V. 4.7737
Friederich, Werner P. (Werner Paul), 1905-.
    2.2698
Friederich, Werner Paul, 1905-. 5.8274
Friedgut, Theodore H. 4.8654
Friedheim, Robert L. 4.334
Friedjung, Heinrich, 1851-1920. 3.2496
Friedl, Alfred E. 4.10486-4.10487
Friedl, Ernestine, 1920-. 4.5391
Friedlaender, Ann Fetter. 4.3877, 4.3989
Friedlaender, Israel, 1876-1920. tr. 3.3993
Friedlaender, Ludwig, 1824-1909. 3.2732
Friedlaender, Marc, 1905-. 3.7051
Friedlaender, Walter F., 1873-1966. 1.6055,
    1.6138, 1.6183, 1.6196
Friedland, William H. ed. 4.7131
Friedlander, Judith. 3.8910, 4.5951
Friedlander, Mark P. 5.6644
Friedländer, Max J., 1867-1958. 1.5102, 1.6168,
    1.6230-1.6231
Friedländer, Saul, 1932-. 3.443
Friedländer, Alan Warren. 2.5438, 2.6045, 2.8607
Friedman, Albert B. ed. 2.6108
Friedman, Alfred S. 4.6667
Friedman, Arthur, 1906-. 2.7041, 2.7338
Friedman, Arthur D. joint author. 5.6468
Friedman, Bruce Jay. ed. 2.13017-2.13020
Friedman, Ellen G., 1944-. 2.12986
Friedman, Gerald M. 5.3055
Friedman, Isaiah. 3.3914
Friedman, James W. 4.3038
Friedman, Jean E. 4.6022
Friedman, Joseph, 1944-. 4.3489
Friedman, Kathi V., 1943-. 4.5098
Friedman, Kenneth Michael. 5.4640
Friedman, Lawrence Jacob, 1940-. 3.7248
Friedman, Lawrence Meir, 1930-. 4.9483
Friedman, Leon. comp. 4.9638, 4.9797
Friedman, Leon. ed. 4.9682
Friedman, Leon. 4.9739
Friedman, Lucy Norman. 4.9978
Friedman, Maurice S. 1.972-1.975
Friedman, Maurice S. joint author. 1.976
Friedman, Melvin J. ed. 2.8433, 2.13220
Friedman, Melvin J. 2.3482, 2.13215
Friedman, Mildred S. 1.5020, 1.5857

Friedman, Milton, 1912-. 4.1262, 4.1457,
    4.1523, 4.1571, 4.3484, 4.4466, 4.4475,
    4.4497, 4.4502-4.4505
Friedman, Morton P. joint author. 5.260
Friedman, Norman. comp. 2.11542
Friedman, Norman. 2.11543, 5.7431, 5.7443,
    5.7513
Friedman, Saul S., 1937-. 3.1092
Friedman, Terry. 1.5387
Friedmann, Georges, 1902-. 4.3118
Friedmann, Herbert, 1900-1987. 1.6367
Friedmann, Wolfgang, 1907-. 4.9279
Friedrich, Carl J. (Carl Joachim), 1901-. 1.926,
    3.173, 3.633, 4.4732, 4.4969, 4.4979, 4.7218,
    4.7231, 4.7568, 4.7599, 4.7610, 4.7619-4.7620,
    4.7656, 4.7662, 4.7711-4.7713
Friedrich, Caspar David, 1774-1840.
    1.6170-1.6171
Friedrich, Gerhard, 1908- ed. 2.249
Friedrich, Johannes, 1893-1972. 2.226
Friedrich, Otto, 1929-. 3.2501
Friedrich, Paul, 1927-. 1.1669
Friedrich, Peter. 5.4413
Friedrichen, George Washington Salisbury.
    2.1059
Friedrichs, Robert Winslow, 1923-. 4.4791
Friedrichsen, George Washington Salisbury.
    2.1083
Friel, Brian. 2.9697
Friend, Joseph H. 2.1075
Friend, Robert. 2.1783
Friend, Theodore. 3.4602
Friendly, Fred W. 4.9467
Friendly, Henry J. 4.9451
Frier, John P. 5.6341
Frier, Mary E. Gazley. joint author. 5.6341
Frierson, William Coleman. 2.6036
Fries, Charles Carpenter, 1887-. 2.1032, 2.1132
Fries, Heinrich. 1.3100
Friesen, Abraham. 1.2329
Friesen, Gerald. 3.8857
Friess, Horace Leland. 1.957
Friis, Henning Kristian, 1911-. 4.3446
Friis, Herman Ralph, 1905-. 3.5540
Frings, Manfred S. ed. 1.999
Frisbie, Charlotte Johnson. 1.4308, 3.5765,
    3.5916
Frisby, Julian, joint author. 3.2410
Frisch, David H. 5.2391
Frisch, Helmut. 4.4486
Frisch, Hillel. 3.3883
Frisch, Karl von, 1886-. 5.3884
Frisch, Max, 1911-. 2.13740-2.13747
Frisch, Michael H. 3.8007
Frisch, Otto Robert, 1904-. 5.2058
Frisch, Teresa Grace. 1.4753
Frison, George C. 3.5739
Fritsch, E. F. 5.3462
Fritschler, A. Lee, 1937-. 4.4440
Fritz, George J. (George John), 1919- joint
    author. 5.3742
Fritz, Jack J. 5.6098
Fritz, James S. (James Sherwood), 1924-. 5.2687
Fritz, Kurt von, 1900-. 1.286, 4.7366
Fritzsch, Harald, 1943-. 5.1866, 5.2475
Frodin, D. G. 5.8115
Frodsham, J. D. comp. 3.4676
Froentjes, W. joint author. 1.6255
Fröhlich, A. (Albrecht), 1916- ed. 5.1317
Frohock, W. M. (Wilbur Merrill), 1908-.
    2.3911, 2.4281, 2.10411, 2.10617
Froissart, Jean, 1338?-1410? 3.564-3.565
Frolic, B. Michael, 1937-. 4.5459
Froman, Lewis Acrelius, 1935-. 4.8031
Frome, Michael. 5.5435
Fromentin, Eugène, 1820-1876. 1.6232
Fromhold, A. T. 5.2131
Fromm, Erich, 1900-. 1.1412, 1.2570,
    4.5024-4.5025, 4.6953, 5.653
Fromm, Erika. 5.659
Fromm, Gary. ed. 4.3875
Fromm, Gloria G., 1931-. 2.9284
Fromm-Reichmann, Frieda. 5.4852
Frondel, Clifford, 1907-. 5.3012
Frosch, John. 5.4922
Frost, A. B. (Arthur Burdett), 1851-1928.
    2.11048
Frost, Arthur Atwater, 1909-. 5.2890

Frost, Elinor, 1873-1938. 2.11751
Frost, Frank J., 1929-. 3.2536
Frost, J. William (Jerry William) 1.3349
Frost, Mervyn. 4.8995
Frost, Richard Aylmer, 1905-. 3.5270
Frost, Robert, 1874-1963. 2.11747-2.11751
Frost, William, 1917-. 2.5709
Frothingham, Octavius Brooks, 1822-1895.
    1.565
Froude, James Anthony, 1818-1894.
    2.7550-2.7552
Froula, Christine, 1950-. 2.12342
Fruehling, James A. 4.5828
Frühwald, Wolfgang. 2.13656
Fruman, Norman. 2.7600
Frushell, Richard C. 2.6930
Frutkin, Susan. 2.4838
Fruton, Joseph Stewart, 1912-. 5.4391
Fry, Christine L. 4.589
Fry, Christopher. 2.4355, 2.8671-2.8674
Fry, Dennis Butler. 5.4279
Fry, Donald K. 5.8019
Fry, Earl H. 3.1199
Fry, Edward F. 1.4905, 1.6346
Fry, Geoffrey Kingdon. 4.8454-4.8455
Fry, Gladys-Marie, 1931-. 3.7204
Fry, John R. 3.8424
Fry, Margery, 1874-1958 ed. 4.5715
Fry, Roger Eliot, 1866-1934. 1.5128, 1.6071,
    1.6149, 2.4262
Fry, Ron, joint author. 3.294
Frýd, Norbert. 2.1668
Fryde, E. B. 3.1245
Frye, Hardy T. 4.8096
Frye, Keith, 1935-. 5.3009
Frye, Marilyn. 4.5882
Frye, Northrop. ed. 2.2617, 2.7413
Frye, Northrop. 2.958, 2.2391, 2.2404, 2.2436,
    2.2538, 2.2561, 2.5684, 2.5762, 2.6761,
    2.7426, 2.9959, 2.11632, 3.8666
Frye, Nothrop, 1912-. 2.2424
Frye, Richard Nelson, 1920-. 3.3732, 3.4074,
    3.4077
Frye, Roland Mushat. 2.6653, 2.6828, 2.7161
Fryer, Donald W., 1920-. 4.2431
Fryer, Judith, 1939-. 2.10597
Fu, Charles Wei-hsün. 5.8347
Fu, K. S. (King Sun), 1930-. 5.6173, 5.6567
Fu, Lo-shu, 1920- ed. 3.4715
Fu, Marilyn. 1.6330
Fu, Shen, 1937-. 1.6330, 1.6369
Fuchs, Daniel, 1934-. 2.11361
Fuchs, Estelle. 3.5811, 4.10968
Fuchs, H. O. (Henry Otten), 1907-. 5.5697,
    5.5810
Fuchs, László. 5.1295-5.1296
Fuchs, Lawrence H. 4.5478, 4.5590
Fuchs, Roland J. joint author. 4.2397
Fuchs, Victor R. 4.2069, 4.3863, 5.4632, 5.4635
Fuchs, Wolfgang J., 1945-. 1.5844
Fuegi, John. 2.13707
Fuentes, Carlos. 2.5339-2.5345
Fuentes, Patricia de, ed. and tr. 3.8923
Fuerst, Wesley J., 1930-. 1.2620
Fuess, Claude Moore, 1855-1963. 3.7098,
    3.7449, 3.7737
Fugard, Athol. 2.10064-2.10069
Fuglestad, Finn, 1942-. 3.5389
Fuhrmann, Horst. 3.2269
Fujimura, Thomas Hikaru, 1919-. 2.5906
Fujisawa, Chikao, 1893-. 1.212
Fujiwara, Tamenari, 12th cent. 3.4934
Fujiwara, Yoshinobu, 995-1065. 3.4934
Fuks, Alexander, 1917-. 3.2549
Fukuda, Naomi. 5.8066
Fukui, Haruhiro, 1935-. 4.8694
Fulbright, J. William (James William), 1905-.
    3.7523, 3.7569, 5.7269
Fulcher, Leon C. 4.6549
Fuld, James J., 1916-. 1.3550
Fulenwider, Claire Knoche. 4.6051
Fullard, Harold. ed. 4.122, 4.181
Fuller, Arthur Buckminster, 1822-1862, ed.
    4.5890
Fuller, Benjamin Apthorp Gould, 1879-1956.
    1.123
Fuller, C. J. (Christopher John), 1949-. 3.4207
Fuller, Dudley D. 5.6246

Fuller, Edmund, 1914-. 2.12523
Fuller, George D. (George Damon), 1869- ed.
    and tr. 5.3765
Fuller, H. Kit. 5.2997
Fuller, J. F. C. (John Frederick Charles),
    1878-1966. 3.535, 3.903, 3.7342, 5.7191,
    5.7200, 5.7389
Fuller, John. 2.2773, 2.7035, 2.8404
Fuller, John P. 5.3010
Fuller, Lon L., 1902-. 4.9350, 4.9361, 4.9367
Fuller, Margaret, 1810-1850. 2.11189-2.11190,
    4.5890
Fuller, Reginald Horace. 1.2630, 1.2847
Fuller, Roy Broadbent, 1912-. 2.8676
Fuller, Wayne Edison, 1919-. 4.4045, 4.4047,
    4.10971
Fullerton, Brian. 3.3351
Fullerton, Iris J. 5.6066
Fullinwider, Robert K., 1942-. 4.9562, 5.7366
Fulmer, William E. 4.3339
Fulton, Chandler, 1934-. 5.3487
Fulton, John Farquhar, 1899-1960. 5.8282
Fulton, Len. 5.7572, 5.7702
Fulton, Robin. 2.8588, 2.9698
Fulton, William, 1939-. 5.1582
Fund for Assistance to Private Education. 4.184
Fund for Public Policy Research. 4.4710
Fung, Adrian K. 4.29
Fung, K. K. 4.2488
Fung, Y. C. (Yuan-cheng), 1919-. 5.1647
Funk, Charles Earle, 1881-1957. 2.1054
Funk, Rainer. 1.594
Funk, Robert Walter, 1926- ed. and tr. 2.248
Funston, Richard. 4.9840
Fuoss, Donald E. 4.907
Furbank, Philip Nicholas. 2.5069, 2.7517,
    2.8655
Furber, Holden, 1903-. 4.2497
Furci, Carmelo. 4.8341
Fürer-Haimendorf, Christoph von, 1909-.
    3.4204, 3.4347, 4.634
Fürer-Haimendorf, Elizabeth von. 5.8095
Furet, François, 1927-. 3.2058
Furia, Philip, 1943-. 2.12328
Furley, D. J., ed. and tr. 2.340
Furley, Peter A. (Peter Anthony), 1935-. 5.3239
Furlong, Margaret, ed. 5.8183
Furman, N. Howell (Nathaniel Howell),
    1892-1965. ed. 5.2693
Furman, Necah Stewart. 3.6267
Furmanov, Dm. (Dmitriĭ), 1891-1926. 2.1562
Furnas, J. C. (Joseph Chamberlain), 1905-.
    2.3349, 2.8125, 4.662
Furneaux, Henry, 1829-1900, ed. 2.774
Furneaux, Robin. 4.6423
Furness, Horace Howard, 1833-1912. 2.6647
Furnish, Victor Paul. 1.2671, 1.2706, 1.2714
Furniss, Brian Stanley. 5.2730
Furniss, Edgar Stephenson, 1890-. 4.3108
Furniss, Norman, 1944-. 4.6488
Furnivall, J. S. (John Sydenham) 3.4340, 3.4562
Furon, Raymond, 1898-. 5.3006
Furphy, Joseph, 1843-1912. 2.10148-2.10149
Furst, Charles. 5.4332
Furst, Lilian R. 2.2618
Furst, Peter T. 4.6662
Furtado, Celso. 4.2140, 4.2169
Furth, Montgomery. ed. and tr. 1.1208
Fürth, Reinhold, 1893- . 5.2219
Furttenbach, Joseph, 1591-1667. 2.3158
Fusfeld, Daniel Roland, 1922-. 3.6735
Fusi Aizpurúa, Juan Pablo, 1945- joint author.
    3.3473
Fuss, Peter Lawrence, 1932-. 1.639
Fussell, Edwin S. 2.10352, 2.12406
Fussell, G. E. (George Edwin), 1889-. 5.5248,
    5.5259
Fussell, K. R. jt. author. 5.5259
Fussell, Paul, 1924-. 2.1044, 2.5741, 2.6089
Fussner, F. Smith. 3.449
Fustel de Coulanges, 1830-1889. 4.7333-4.7334
Futabatei, Shimei, 1864-1909. 2.2073
Futagawa, Yukio, 1932-. 1.5255
Futrell, May DiPietro. 5.5007
Futrell, Robert Frank. 5.7399
Futrelle, Jacques, 1875-1912. 2.11763
Future Directions for a Learning Society.
    4.10982

Futuyma, Douglas J., 1942-. 5.3368, 5.3385
Fux, Johann Joseph, 1660-1741. 1.4448
Fyfe, Christopher. 3.5372
Fyfe, William Hamilton, 1878-. 2.349, 2.2727
Fynn, G. W. 5.5957
Fyzee, Asaf Ali Asghar. 1.2090

G.K. Hall & Company. 4.5978
Gabalac, Nancy W. 5.4890
Gabay, Sabit. 5.4782
Gabba, Emilio. 3.2516, 3.2772
Gabel, Robert A. 5.6277
Gabler, Hans Walter, 1938-. 2.8880, 2.8897
Gabler, Raymond. 5.4396
Gablik, Suzi. 1.6266
Gabo, Naum, 1890-. 1.5129
Gabor, Dennis, 1900-. 5.2287, 5.5626
Gaboriau, Emile, 1832-1873. 2.4216
Gabriel, Ralph Henry, 1890-1987. 3.6024,
    3.6112
Gabriel, Richard A. 5.7283
Gadamer, Hans Georg, 1900-. 1.85, 1.1306
Gadd, Cyril John. 1.5616
Gadd, David. 3.1748
Gadd, William Laurence, 1862- joint author.
    2.7634
Gadda, Carlo Emilio, 1893-1973. 2.5033
Gaddis, John Lewis. 3.6484, 3.7570-3.7571
Gaddis, William, 1922-. 2.13022
Gadow, Kenneth D. 5.5115
Gaeffke, Peter, 1927-. 2.1884
Gaff, Jerry G. joint author. 4.10573
Gaffney, Matthew P. 5.8281
Gage, John. 1.6040
Gage, N. L. (Nathaniel Lees), 1917-. 4.10264
Gager, John G. 1.1956, 1.2301
Gagey, Edmond McAdoo, 1901-. 2.10523
Gagliardi, Robert M., 1934-. 5.6395
Gagnebin, Bernard. ed. 2.4087
Gagnon, François Marc, 1935-. 1.5996
Gaige, Frederick H. 3.4379
Gailey, Harry A. 3.5335
Gaines, David P. 1.3097
Gaines, Ernest J., 1933-. 2.13024-2.13026
Gainsborough, Thomas, 1727-1788. 1.5801,
    1.6031, 1.6490
Gair, W. Reavley. 2.6623
Gaisford, John, 1949-. 4.512
Gakenheimer, Ralph A. 4.3906
Gal, Susan. 2.114
Galambos, Louis. 4.3045
Galambos, T. V. (Theodore V.) joint author.
    5.5885
Galantay, Ervin Y. 4.6310
Galanter, Eugene. joint ed. 5.51
Galanter, Eugene. 5.53
Galanter, Marc, 1931-. 4.9920
Galantière, Lewis, 1893- tr. 1.489
Galarza, Ernesto, 1905-. 4.3377
Galassi, Jonathan. 1.6683, 2.5039
Galassi, Peter. 1.4789
Galaway, Burt. 4.6474
Galbraith, John Kenneth, 1908-. 4.1306, 4.1372,
    4.1524, 4.1716, 4.1858, 4.1935, 4.1985-4.1986,
    4.1998
Galbraith, John S. 3.5463, 3.8847
Galbraith, V. H. (Vivian Hunter), 1889-. 3.1339
Galbraith, W. O. 3.9171
Galdon, Joseph A. 2.10134
Gale, Douglas. 4.4467-4.4468
Gale Research Company. 1.54-1.55, 1.6497,
    2.205, 2.2549, 2.2664, 2.2676, 2.3234, 4.2725,
    4.7898, 4.9445, 4.9944, 5.827, 5.971, 5.2577,
    5.6164, 5.7592, 5.7607, 5.7674, 5.7706,
    5.7785, 5.8112, 5.8312, 5.8317
Gale, Robert L., 1919-. 3.6258
Gale, Zona, 1874-1938. 2.11764-2.11765
Galeano, Eduardo H., 1940-. 4.2141
Galen. 2.368
Galenson, Walter, 1914-. 4.2478, 4.3098, 4.3100,
    4.3329, 4.3354, 4.3380, 4.3401, 4.3664
Galeries nationales du Grand Palais (France)
    1.4970, 1.4975, 1.4980-1.4981, 1.6053-1.6054,
    1.6076, 1.6146
Galey, John. 1.5182, 1.5541
Gálik, Marián. 2.2153
Galilei, Galileo, 1564-1642. 5.2027-5.2028,
    5.2039

Galilei, Galileo, 1564-1642. 5.2035
Galíndez, Jesús de, 1915-. 3.9123
Galishoff, Stuart. 5.4529
Gall, Eric P. (Eric Papineau), 1940-. 5.5001
Gall, Meredith D., 1942-. 4.10438
Gall, Sally M. 2.5834, 2.11805-2.11806
Gall, Timothy L. 5.5807
Gallagher, David Patrick. 2.5301
Gallagher, Donat. 2.9482
Gallagher, Edward Joseph, 1940-. 5.7795
Gallagher, Helen Mar (Pierce) d. 1942. 1.5320
Gallagher, James John, 1926-. 4.10904, 4.10920
Gallagher, Jeanette McCarthy, 1932-. 5.589
Gallagher, John, 1919-. 3.1220, 3.5115, 4.8904
Gallagher, John F. 2.7803
Gallagher, John S. (John Scott), 1933-. 5.6206
Gallagher, Marsha V. 1.6389
Gallagher, Matthew P. 3.3244
Gallagher, Michael, 4.8567
Gallagher, Richard H. 5.5852
Gallagher, Richard H. joint author. 5.5837
Gallagher, Richard H. ed. 5.5863
Gallagher, Tom, 1954-. 3.3500
Gallaher, Art, 1925-. 4.4899, 4.5129
Gallant, Donald M., 1929-. 5.4876
Gallegos, Rómulo, 1884-1969. 2.5445, 2.5447
Galli, Giorgio, 4.8628
Gallie, W. B., 1912-. 1.629, 3.472
Gallissaires, Pierre, ed. 2.4259
Gallistel, C. R., 1941- joint author. 5.1263
Gallois, Lucien Louis Joseph, 1857- joint
    author. 4.79
Gallop, David. 1.250
Gallop, Rodney, 1901-1948. 3.2218
Gallopoulos, Nicholas E. 5.6877
Galloway, David D. 2.3719, 2.10618
Galloway, George Barnes, 1898-. 4.8010-4.8011,
    4.8049
Gallup, Donald Clifford, 1913-. 2.12719
Gallup, George, 1930-. 1.1866
Gallup, George Horace, 1901-. 4.5227-4.5228
Gallup Organization. 1.1866
Galnoor, Itzhak. 4.8781
Galpin, Charles Josiah, 1864- joint editor.
    4.6371
Galpin, Francis William, 1858-1945. 1.4129,
    1.4138
Galpin, Francis Williams, 1858-1945. 1.3641
Galpin Society. 1.4126
Galston, Arthur William, 1920-. 5.3741
Galston, James Austin, 1881- tr. 1.6501
Galsworthy, John, 1867-1933. 2.8677-2.8681
Galt, John, 1779-1839. 2.7716-2.7717
Galtsoff, Paul Simon, 1887-. 5.3805
Galtung, Johan. 4.9173
Gálvez, Manuel, 1882-1962. 2.5387
Gambino, Richard. 3.6557
Gamble, Andrew. 4.2289
Gambs, John Saké, 1899-. 4.1337
Gammond, Peter. joint author. 1.3618
Gamow, George, 1904-1968. 5.838, 5.1698,
    5.1792, 5.1867, 5.2045, 5.2059
Gamson, William A. 4.5171
Gamson, Zelda F. 4.10272
Gandhi, Mahatma, 1869-1948. 1.207,
    3.4304-3.4306, 4.5036
Gandhi, Om P., 1935-. 5.6548
Gandy, Daniel Ross, 1935-. 3.8943
Ganiage, Jean. 4.8901
Ganin, Zvi. 3.4018
Gann, Lewis H., 1924-. 3.5104-3.5105, 3.5423,
    3.5508, 3.5516, 3.5524
Gannon, Linda. 5.5056
Gans, Carl, 1923-. 5.3918, 5.4274
Gans, Herbert J. 3.6182, 4.5203, 4.5213, 4.6319
Gans, M. H. (Mozes Heiman) 3.3981
Ganschow, Thomas W. 4.6966
Ganshof, François Louis, 1895-. 3.1988
Gantenbein, James Watson, 1900- ed. 3.9017
Gantmakher, F. R. (Feliks Ruvimovich) 5.1366
Ganz, Arthur F., 1928- comp. 2.2357, 2.9793
Ganz, Rudolph, 1877- ed. 1.4526
Gaposchkin, Cecilia Helena Payne, 1900-.
    5.1718, 5.1826
Gara, Larry. 3.7269
Gāragī, Balawanta, 1916-. 2.3392
Garaudy, Roger. 1.471, 4.6977

Garbarino, James. 4.6482, 4.6550, 4.6556,
    4.10014
Garbarino, Joseph William, 1919-. 4.10582
Garbarino, Merwyn S. 3.5946
Garber, Frederick. 2.11256
Garber, Herbert. 4.10715
Garber, Lee Orville, 1900-. 4.9579, 4.9583
Garber, Marjorie B. 2.6800, 2.6832
Garbuny, Max, 1912- joint author. 5.2046
Garcés, Francisco Tomás Hermenegildo,
    1738-1781. 3.8603
García de Diego, Carmen. 2.894
García de Diego, Vicente, 1878-. 2.894
Garcia de la Santa, Tomás, ed. 2.5207
Garcia, F. L. (Ferdinand Lawrence), 1909-.
    4.4443
García González de Nora, Eugenio, 1923-.
    2.5138
García Lorca, Federico, 1898-1936.
    2.5248-2.5257
Garcia Máiquez, Gabriel, 1928-. 2.5419
Garcia, Manuel, 1805-1906. 1.4568
García, Mario T. 3.8333
García Márquez, Gabriel, 1928-. 2.5416-2.5418,
    2.5420-2.5421
Garcia, Pilar A. joint author. 5.4243
Garcia, Russell. 1.4449
Garcilaso de la Vega, 1503-1536. 2.5189, 2.5190
Gard, Roger, comp. 2.11121
Garden Club of America. 5.5362
Gardezi, Hassan Nawaz. 4.2518
Gardiner, Alan Henderson, Sir, 1879-1963.
    3.5153
Gardiner, Patrick, ed. 3.473
Gardiner, Patrick L. 3.509
Gardiner, Robert, 1949-. 5.7431, 5.7435
Gardiner, Samuel Rawson, 1829-1902.
    3.1458-3.1460, 3.1473, 3.1499
Gårding, Lars, 1919-. 5.1107
Gardner, Albert Ten Eyck. 1.5658, 1.5943
Gardner, Alexander, 1821-1882. 3.7349
Gardner, Arthur, 1878-. 1.5682
Gardner, Averil. 2.9546
Gardner, Burleigh B. (Burleigh Bradford),
    1902- joint author. 4.5198
Gardner, Charles Sidney, 1900-. 3.4658
Gardner, Colin Oxenham. 2.10088
Gardner, Erle Stanley, 1889-1970. 2.11766
Gardner, Ernest Dean, 1915-. 5.4318
Gardner, Gerald Brosseau, 1884-. 5.675
Gardner, Helen. 1.4673, 2.2453
Gardner, Helen Louise, ed. 2.6094, 2.6116,
    2.6146, 2.6453-2.6454, 2.11633
Gardner, Howard. 5.352
Gardner, James B., 1950-. 4.5167
Gardner, Jane F. 4.5852
Gardner, John, 1933-. 2.1767, 2.5592, 2.6132,
    2.13027-2.13032, 4.7591
Gardner, John William, 1912-. 4.4958
Gardner, Joseph Lawrence, 1933-. 3.7702
Gardner, Lloyd C., 1934-. 3.7572, 3.7796
Gardner, Martin, 1914-. 1.86, 2.7675, 2.7677,
    5.1258, 5.2060
Gardner, Mary R., joint author. 4.5198
Gardner, Paul, 1930-. 4.1016
Gardner, Philip. comp. 2.8662
Gardner, Philip. 2.8385
Gardner, Rob. 5.5364
Gardner, Robert, 1890- tr. 2.661
Gardner, Sheldon. 5.80
Gardner, Stanley. 2.7427
Gardner, W. H. 2.7833
Gardner, W. H. (William Henry), 1902-. 2.7825
Gardner, W. J. (William James), 1825-1874.
    3.9111
Gardner, William, d. 1943. 5.6810
Gardner, William Bradford. 2.6986
Garey, Michael R. 5.1176
Garfield, Evelyn Picon. 2.5386
Garfield, James A. (James Abram), 1831-1881.
    3.7402
Garfield, Sol L. (Sol Louis), 1918-. 5.4854
Garfield, Sydney, 1915-. 5.5123
Garfinkel, Harold. 4.4792
Garfinkel, Paul E., 1946-. 5.4940
Garforth, F. W. (Francis William), 1917- ed.
    4.10195
Gargan, Edward T., 1922-. 3.36

Garin, Eugenio, 1909-. 3.2846, 5.686
Garioch, Robert. 2.9698
Garis, Robert. 2.7656
Garlan, Yvon. 5.7179
Garland, Hamlin, 1860-1940. 2.11035-2.11039
Garland, Henry B. (Henry Burnand) 2.13448
Garland, Henry Burnand. 2.13567, 2.13633,
    2.13650
Garland, Mary. 2.13448, 2.13601
Garlick, Kenneth, 1916-. 1.6035
Garlick, Raymond. 2.9872
Garmonsway, George Norman. 2.6292, 3.1308
Garner, Barry J., 1937- joint author. 4.6198
Garner, David M., 1947-. 5.4940
Garner, H. F. 4.258
Garner, John Leslie. tr. 3.2934
Garner, John S., 1945-. 4.6236
Garner, Les. 4.8508
Garner, Wendell R. 4.10709, 5.25
Garnett, Constance Black, 1862-1946.
    2.1346-2.1347, 2.1351-2.1352, 2.1354, 2.1379,
    3.3118
Garnett, David, 1892-. 2.8684
Garnett, Edward, 1868-1937. 2.1423, 2.8545,
    2.8549
Garnett, William. 5.6982
Garnsey, Peter. 4.4094
Garnsey, Wanda. 1.6621
Garofalo, James. joint author. 4.6707
Garofalo, Reebee, joint author. 1.4354
Garoian, Leon. jt. author. 4.3692
Garonna, P., 1948-. 4.3372
Garraghan, Gilbert J. (Gilbert Joseph),
    1871-1942. 3.433
Garrard, John Gordon. 2.1289, 2.1397, 3.3096
Garrard, Mary D. 1.4628
Garratt, Geoffrey Theodore, 1888-1942, jt.
    author. 3.4269
Garraty, John Arthur, 1920-. 3.312, 3.331,
    3.525, 3.6290, 3.6338, 3.7408, 3.7441, 3.7721,
    4.3193, 4.9785
Garraway, Michael O. (Michael Oliver) 5.3718
Garrels, Robert Minard, 1916-. 5.3102
Garrett, Clarke, 1935-. 1.2452
Garrett, George P., 1929-. 2.13036-2.13039,
    2.13104
Garrett, H. L. O. (Herbert Leonard Offley),
    1881-1941. 3.4252
Garrett, John, fl. 1845-1873. 3.4154
Garrett, John R. joint author. 4.10720
Garrett, Randall. 2.13040
Garrett, Richard. 4.9329
Garrett, Wendell D. 3.7043
Garrettson, Freeborn, 1752-1827. 1.3375
Garrick, David, 1717-1779. 2.6236, 2.7031
Garrigan, Kristine Ottesen, 1939-. 1.5251
Garrigue, Jean, 1912-1972. 2.11767
Garrison, Dee. 5.7663
Garrison, Fielding H. (Fielding Hudson),
    1870-1935. 5.4501, 5.8284
Garrison, Lucy McKim, joint comp. 1.3438
Garrison, Robert H. 5.4235
Garrod, Heathcote William. 2.2572, 2.6455,
    2.7849, 2.7862
Garrow, David J., 1953-. 3.6839, 4.8092
Garry, Stephen. 2.1603
Garshin, V. M. (Vsevolod Mikhaĭlovich),
    1855-1888. 2.1496
Garson, Robert A. 4.8197
Garthoff, Raymond L. 3.6493, 5.7197
Gartner, Lloyd P., 1927- comp. 4.10813
Gartner, Rosemary, 1952-. 4.6685
Garvey, Gerald, 1935-. 4.3814
Garvey, Marcus, 1887-1940. 3.6640, 3.6836
Garvey, Terence. 3.1183
Garvy, George. 4.4457
Gary, Lawrence E. 3.6752
Garza, Roberto J., 1934-. 2.10784
Gascoigne, Bamber. 3.4253
Gascoigne, Christina, 1938 or 9- illus. 3.4253
Gascoigne, George, 1542?-1577. 2.6480
Gaselee, Stephen, 1882-1943. 2.378
Gash, Norman. 3.1576, 3.1598, 3.1605-3.1606,
    3.1617, 4.8408
Gashus, O. K., ed. 5.5964
Gasiorowicz, Stephen. 5.2061, 5.2392
Gaskell, Elizabeth Cleghorn, 1810-1865. 2.7450,
    2.7719-2.7724

Gaskell, Philip. 2.2527, 3.1811, 5.7535
Gaskin, D. E. (David Edward), 1939-. 5.4005
Gass, Saul I. 5.5588
Gass, William H., 1924-. 2.13041-2.13042
Gassan, Arnold. 5.6917
Gassier, Pierre. 1.5817, 1.6291
Gassner, John, 1903-1967. 2.2782, 2.2784, 2.2802, 2.3092, 2.3181, 2.3770-2.3771, 2.10782, 2.12294
Gassner, Mollie, joint comp. 2.10782
Gasster, Michael, 1930-. 3.4745
Gaster, Theodor Herze, 1906-. 1.2548
Gaster, Theodor Herzl, 1906-. 1.1981
Gaston, Edwin W. 2.12395
Gaston, Georg, 1938-. 2.8773
Gaston, Paul M., 1928-. 3.8119
Gatchel, Robert J., 1947-. 5.4584, 5.4845
Gatell, Frank Otto. joint comp. 3.7198
Gates, Charles Marvin. 3.8596
Gates, David Murray, 1921-. 5.3576
Gates, Henry Louis. 2.10311, 2.10358
Gates, Hill. 4.642
Gates, Lillian F. 4.2834
Gates, Norman T. 2.8376
Gates, Paul Wallace, 1901-. 4.1875, 4.1922, 4.2819, 4.4010
Gatewood, Willard B. 3.8403
Gathercole, P. W. 1.5092
Gathorne-Hardy, Robert, 1902-. 2.7312
Gati, Charles. 4.3629
Gati, Toby Trister. 4.9229
Gatland, Howard Bruce. 5.6454
Gatland, Kenneth William, 1924-. 5.6692
Gatrell, V. A. C., 1941-. 4.6785
Gattegno, Caleb. 4.10335
Gatti, Florence M. 4.6677
Gatzke, Hans Wilhelm, 1915-. 3.875, 3.2339, 3.2356
Gau, George W. 4.3485
Gauba, Khalid Latif, 1899-. 3.4293
Gaudefroy-Demombynes, Maurice, 1862-1957. 3.3664
Gaudet, Hazel. joint author. 4.7953
Gaudry, Eric. 5.428
Gauguin, Paul, 1848-1903. 1.6104-1.6106
Gauld, Alan. 5.670
Gauldie, Enid. 4.3496
Gaulle, Charles de, 1890-1970. 3.978, 3.1164, 5.7310
Gaus, John Merriman, 1894-. 4.7889
Gaustad, Edwin Scott. 1.690, 1.1871, 1.2394, 1.2399, 4.148
Gaustad, Edwin Scott. ed. 1.2407
Gauthreaux, Sidney A. 5.4076
Gautier, Émile Felix, 1864-. 3.5217
Gautier, Théophile, 1811-1872. 2.4137, 2.4217-2.4219, 4.1173
Gautier-van Berchem, Marguerite. 1.5236
Gauvreau, Emile Henry, 1891-. 2.3614
Gauze, René. 3.5387
Gaventa, John, 1949-. 4.2021
Gaver, Jack. ed. 2.10798
Gavins, Raymond. 3.8219
Gavronsky, Serge. 2.3926
Gavronsky, Serge. comp. 2.3932
Gawalt, Gerard W. 4.9898
Gaworski, Michael, 1950- joint author. 5.7076
Gaxotte, Pierre. 3.2045
Gay, John, 1685-1732. 2.7033-2.7035, 2.7037
Gay, John Dennis. 1.2225
Gay, L. R. 4.10711
Gay, Peter, 1923-. 1.434-1.435, 3.358, 3.525, 3.6229, 4.7067, 5.484
Gay, Robert M. (Robert Malcolm), 1879-1961. joint author. 2.2524
Gay, Zhenya, illus. 2.4206
Gayle, Addison, 1932-. 1.6713, 2.12819
Gaylin, Willard. 4.9507
Gaylord, Charles N. 5.5832
Gaylord, Edwin Henry. 5.5832
Gaylord, Susan A. 5.4665
Gaythwaite, John. 5.5982
Gazzaniga, Michael S. 5.4306
Geach, P. T. (Peter Thomas), 1916-. 1.296, 1.1173, 1.1209, 1.3061
Geanakoplos, Deno John. 3.2655, 3.2677
Geankoplis, Christie J. 5.6852

Gear, C. William (Charles William), 1935-. 5.1512
Gearing, Fred O., 1922-. 4.10181
Geary, Dick. 4.3628
Gébelin, François, 1884-. 1.5575
Gebhard, David. 1.5327
Gebhardt, Bruno, 1858-1905. 3.2253
Gebhardt, Eike. 4.4872
Gedalge, André, 1856-1926. 1.4480
Geddes, Gary. 2.8565, 2.9900
Geddes, Patrick, Sir, 1854-1932. 1.5579, 4.6335
Geddes, W. R. (William Robert) 3.4522
Gedney, William J. ed. and tr. 3.4520
Geduld, Harry M. comp. 2.2937
Geduld, Harry M. 2.2976, 2.8119
Gee, E. Gordon (Elwood Gordon), 1944-. 4.10693
Gee, Emma. 3.6585
Gee, John Archer. 2.8553
Gee, Sherman. 5.5628
Geelhoed, E. Bruce, 1948-. 5.7282
Geen, Russell G., 1932-. 5.418
Geering, R. G. 2.10171, 2.10174
Geerlings, Gerald K. (Gerald Kenneth), 1897-. 1.5510
Geertz, Clifford. 1.2010, 4.475
Geertz, Clifford. ed. 4.7548
Geertz, Clifford. 1.1831, 4.5442
Geertz, Hildred. 4.579
Gehani, Narain, 1947-. 5.1209
Gehde, J. E. 1.6404
Geherin, David, 1943-. 2.10545
Gehl, Jürgen. 3.1878
Gehman, Henry Snyder, 1888-. 1.2505
Gehrels, Tom, 1925-. 5.1820
Geib, M. Margaret. 1.5280
Geiger, George Raymond, 1903-. 1.589
Geiger, H. Kent. 4.5626
Geiger, Roger L., 1943-. 5.976
Geiger, Rudolf, 1894-. 5.2501
Geijer, Agnes. 1.6677
Geikie, Archibald, Sir, 1835-1924. 5.2950
Geiogamah, Hanay, 1945-. 2.13043
Geipel, John, 1937-. 2.1063
Geiringer, Irene. 1.3777
Geiringer, Karl, 1899-. 1.3776-1.3777, 1.3821, 1.4130
Geis, Gilbert. comp. 4.6749
Geis, Gilbert. 4.6751
Geiser, Elizabeth A. 5.7568
Geisler, Charles C. 5.8167
Geisler, Rolf. 2.2352
Geismar, Maxwell David, 1909-. 2.10619-2.10622, 2.11985
Geiss, Imanuel. 3.2328
Geiss, Imanuel. ed. 3.767
Geiss, Imanuel. 3.5106
Geisst, Charles R. 4.4610
Geist, Alison. 4.9866
Geist, Anthony L., 1945-. 2.5266
Geist, Johann Friedrich, 1936-. 1.5542
Geist, Sidney. 1.5743
Geist, Valerius. 5.4043
Gelb, Arthur, 1924-. 2.12295
Gelb, Barbara. joint author. 2.12295
Gelb, Ignace J., 1907-. 2.171
Gelb, Joyce, 1940-. 4.6052
Gelb, Leslie H. 3.6498
Gelbaum, Bernard R. 5.1441
Geldard, Frank Arthur. 5.238
Geldzahler, Henry. 1.5903
Gelfand, Donald E. 4.5815
Gel'fand, I. M. (Izrail' Moiseevich). 5.1467
Gelfand, Stanley A., 1948-. 5.4370
Gélinas, Gratien, 1909-. 2.4814
Gellar, Sheldon. 4.8806
Geller, Evelyn. 5.7652
Geller, Mikhail, 1922-. 3.3207
Gellerman, Saul W. 4.4430
Gellermann, William, 1897-. 3.7545
Gellert, Walter. 5.1116
Gelles, Richard J. joint author. 4.5780
Gelles, Richard J. 4.5591, 4.5777
Gellhorn, Walter, 1906-. 4.7884, 4.9721
Gellman, Irwin F. 3.6438
Gellner, Ernest. ed. 3.5210
Gellner, Ernest. 1.2074, 3.5192
Gelman, Rochel. 5.1263

Gelpi, Albert. 2.10474, 2.11001, 2.12384
Gelpi, Barbara Charlesworth. 2.12384, 4.6047
Gelven, Michael. 1.995
Gelzer, Matthias, 1886-1974. 3.2737, 3.2787
Gemäldegalerie (Berlin, Germany: West) 1.6368
Gemmett, Robert J. 2.7398
Genauer, Emily, 1910-. 1.6007
Gendrop, Paul. 3.8897
General Motors Corporation. Research Laboratories. 5.6877
Genet, Anna M. 5.1724
Genet, Jean, 1910-. 2.4532-2.4540
Genet, Russell. 5.1724
Genette, Gérard, 1930-. 2.4664
Geneva Conference (1954) 3.5034
Geneva. Conference, 1954. 3.5034
Geneva Conference (1954) 3.4437
Gennaro, Alfonso R. 5.4484
Gennep, Arnold van, 1873-1957. 4.557
Genoud, François, ed. 3.2391
Genovese, Eugene D., 1930-. 3.7199, 3.7205
Gentilcore, R. Louis, 1924-. 4.142
Gentile, da Fabriano, ca. 1370-1427. 1.6205
Gentle, Ernest J. 5.6666
Gentry, Francis G. 2.13526
Gentry, Linnell. 1.3685
Gentz, William H., 1918-. 1.2220
Geoffrey, of Monmouth, Bishop of St. Asaph, 1100?-1154. 3.1302
Geological Association of Canada. 5.3132
Geological Society of America. 5.2977, 5.3002
Geological Society of London. 5.3141
Geological Survey (U.S.) 4.143, 4.311, 5.2997, 5.5991, 5.8213
Geological Survey (U.S.). Office of the Data Administrator. 5.2996
Geological Survey (U.S.). Office of the Data Base Administrator. 5.2996
Geophysics Research Forum (U.S.). Geophysics Study Committee. 5.3110, 5.6008
Georgano, G. N. 4.3867, 5.6621
George, Abraham M. 4.4569
George, Alexander L. 3.749, 4.9025, 5.7337
George C. Marshall Research Foundation. 3.2456
George Eliot Centennial Conference (1980: University of Puget Sound) 2.7701
George, Emily. 3.7645
George, Gerald S. 4.922
George, Henry, 1839-1897. 4.1374, 4.1428-4.1429, 4.1431, 4.1433, 4.4202
George, J. David (John David) 5.3820
George, Jennifer J. joint author. 5.3820
George, Julia B. 5.5192
George, K. M. 2.2265
George, M. Dorothy (Mary Dorothy) 1.5851-1.5852, 4.5332
George, Margaret. 3.1696
George, Mary W., 1948-. 5.7648
George, Paul S. joint author. 4.10499
George, Peter, 1924-1966. 2.9699
George Philip & Son. 4.181
George, Stefan Anton, 1868-1933. 2.13750-2.13751
George Washington Bicentennial Commission (U.S.) 3.7035
George Washington University. 4.9479
George Washington University. Institute for Sino-Soviet Studies. 3.3271
Georgetown University. Center for Contemporary Arab Studies. 3.5190
Georgetown University. Center for Strategic and International Studies. 3.4036, 4.2977
Georgi, Charlotte. 5.8375
Georgia. Dept. of Archives and History. 3.8255
Georgia State University. College of Business Administration. Business Publishing Division. 4.3832, 4.4294
Georgia Writers' Project. 3.8270
Georgiady, Nicholas Peter, 1921-. 4.10504
Gephart, Ronald M. 5.7832
Geraghty, James J. 4.144
Gérard, Albert S. 2.2298-2.2299
Gerard, Alexander, 1728-1795. 1.4641
Gérard-Gailly, Émile. 2.4058
Gerarde, Horace W. joint author. 5.4721
Geras, Norman, 1943-. 4.7060

Gerasimov, I. P. (Innokentiĭ Petrovich), 1905-
    ed. 4.2368
Gerber, David A., 1944-. 3.6804
Gerber, Douglas E. 2.525
Gerber, Ellen W. 4.962
Gerber, Haim. 4.5395
Gerber, John C. 2.10969
Gerber, John C. comp. 2.11061
Gerber, Richard, 1924-. 2.6057
Gerbi, Antonello, 1904-. 3.5686
Gerboth, Walter. 1.3575
Gerbrands, A. A. (Adrianus Alexander), 1917-.
    1.4629
Gerdes, Dick. 2.5437
Gerdts, William H. 1.5159, 1.5898, 1.5916,
    1.6366
Gere, James M. 5.5776, 5.5846
Geretsegger, Heinz. 1.5412
Gergely, Peter. joint author. 5.5831
Gerhard, Dietrich, 1896-. 3.80
Gerhart, Gail M. 3.5459
Gerig, Reginald, 1919-. 1.4156
Gérin-Lajoie, Paul, 1920-. 4.8276
Gérin, Winifred, 2.6895, 2.7442, 2.7451,
    2.7460-2.7461, 2.7725, 2.8002
Gerking, Shelby Delos, 1918-. 5.3905
Gerlach, Arch C. ed. 4.143
Gerlach, John C. 2.10578, 5.8140
Gerlach, Lana, joint author. 5.8140
Germain, Carel B. 4.6495, 4.6540
German, Frank Clifford, joint author. 4.2393
German, Mikhail IUr'evich. 1.5032
Germann, Georg. 1.5252
Germany. Auswärtiges Amt. 3.886, 3.2337,
    4.8978
Germany. Wehrmacht. Oberkommando. 3.963
Germany (West) 4.8607
Germino, Dante L. 4.7226, 4.8634
Gernet, Jacques. 3.4633
Gernet, Louis, 1882-. 3.2550
Gernsheim, Alison. joint author. 5.6918, 5.6928
Gernsheim, Helmut, 1913-. 5.6918, 5.6928
Geroch, Robert. 5.2101
Gerold-Tucholsky, Mary. joint ed. 2.13866
Gerontological Society. 5.4246
Gerould, Daniel Charles, 1928-. 2.1736, 2.1739,
    2.1748, 5.8018
Gerould, Gordon Hall, 1877- ed. 2.6075
Gerould, James Thayer, 1872- joint author.
    2.8228
Gerould, Winifred Gregory, 1885-. 2.8228,
    5.8318
Gerra, Ferdinando. ed. 2.5018
Gerrard, Anthony. 5.2279
Gerrish, B. A. (Brian Albert), 1931-. 1.2334,
    1.3407
Gerschenkron, Alexander. 4.2197
Gershator, David. 2.5257
Gershman, Herbert S. 2.3908
Gershoy, Leo, 1897-. 3.651, 3.2065
Gerson, H. (Horst) 1.5025, 1.6232, 1.6251
Gerson, Kathleen. 4.6019
Gerson, M. Sue. joint author. 4.3924
Gerson, Menachem, 1908-. 4.7166
Gerson, Noel Bertram, 1914-. 3.9073
Gerstel, David U., 1945-. 4.6654
Gerstenberger, Donna Lorine. 2.9774, 5.7810
Gerster, Georg, 1928- illus. 3.5179
Gerstinger, Heinz, 1919-. 2.5125
Gerstle, Kurt H. 5.5838
Gerteiny, Alfred G. 3.5394
Gerth, Hans Heinrich, 1908-. 4.1197, 4.5426
Gertrude Clarke Whittall Poetry and Literature
    Fund. 2.12435
Gertsch, Willis John, 1906-. 5.3855
Gertzog, Irwin N., 1933-. 4.8053
Gerutis, Albertas, 1905-. 3.3314
Gerver, Israel, ed. 4.4779
Geschwind, Norman. 5.4105
Gesell, Arnold, 1880-1961. 4.5719-4.5720,
    4.5754, 5.565, 5.580, 5.601-5.602
Gessner, Robert, 1907-. 2.2938
Gest, John Marshall, 1859-1934. ed. 2.7476
Getreu, Ian E. 5.6506
Getscher, Robert H. 1.6488
Gettleman, Marvin E. 3.8017
Getto, Giovanni. ed. 2.4997
Getty, Ian A. L., 1947-. 3.5731

Getzels, Jacob W. 5.348, 5.597
Geva, Tamara. 4.1139
Gevitz, Norman. 5.5212
Gewehr, Wesley Marsh, 1888-. 1.2415
Gewertz, Deborah B., 1948-. 3.5659
Gewirth, Alan. 1.1450, 4.7377
Gewirtz, Mindy L. 4.6777
Geyelin, Philip L. 3.7884
Geyl, Pieter, 1887-. 3.411, 3.474-3.475, 3.2131,
    3.2984, 3.2989-3.2990
Ghai, Dharam P. 4.2993
Ghalib, Mirza Asadullah Khan, 1797-1869.
    2.1899
Ghana. 3.5339
Gharāybah, Fawzī. 4.2445
Ghassemlou, Abdul Rahman. 3.3690
Ghazzālī, 1058-1111. 1.374, 1.2025, 4.5565
Ghelderode, Michel de, 1898-1962.
    2.4543-2.4544
Ghirshman, Roman. 1.4709
Ghosal, A. 5.5567
Ghose, Ajit Kumar, 1947-. 4.2876
Ghose, Aurobindo, 1872-1950. 1.1732
Ghose, Sankar, 1925-. 4.7114
Ghose, Sukumar, 1935- comp. 2.1876
Ghosh, Jyotish Chandra. 2.1854, 2.7176, 5.7932
Ghosh, Pradip K. 5.2684
Ghosh, Sachindralal. tr. 2.1859
Ghosh, Sucheta, 1949-. 3.4238
Ghoshal, Upendra Nath, 1886-1969. 4.7327
Ghurye, G. S. (Govind Sadashiv), 1893-. 3.4174
Giacquinta, Joseph B., 1937- joint author.
    4.10636
Giallombardo, Rose. 4.6863
Gialourēs, Nikolaos, 1917-. 1.5632-1.5633
Giamatti, A. Bartlett. 2.6530
Gianakos, Larry James. 2.2851
Gianaris, Nicholas V. 4.2348
Giancoli, Douglas C. 5.1993
Giannone, Richard. 2.13399
Gibaldi, Joseph, 1942-. 2.1041, 2.2371, 2.2518
Gibb, Hamilton Alexander Rosskeen. 1.1995,
    2.1982, 3.597, 3.3658-3.3659, 3.3665
Gibb, Terence Charles. 5.2331
Gibber, Beth. 4.3046
Gibbon, Edward, 1737-1794. 2.7039-2.7040,
    3.2802
Gibbon, Guy E., 1939-. 3.223
Gibbon, Peter. joint author. 3.1872
Gibbons, Don C. 4.6676
Gibbons, G. W. 5.1862
Gibbons, Gerard. 5.6519
Gibbons, John H., 1929-. 5.6147
Gibbons, Reginald. 2.5266
Gibbons, Stella, 1902-. 2.8685
Gibbs, A. M. (Anthony Matthews), 1933-.
    2.8083
Gibbs, J. Willard (Josiah Willard), 1839-1903.
    5.700, 5.2177
Gibbs, James L., ed. 3.5058
Gibbs, Lee W. 1.2256
Gibbs-Smith, Charles Harvard, 1909-.
    5.6645-5.6646
Gibellini, Rosino. 1.2806
Gibert, Stephen P. 3.7573
Gibian, George, 1.1265, 2.1382
Gibian, George. comp. 2.1298
Gibian, George. 2.1680
Gibian, George. ed. 3.3019
Giblin, P. J. 5.1607, 5.1631
Gibney, Frank, 1924-. 3.4888
Gibson, A. Boyce (Alexander Boyce),
    1900-1972. 2.1378
Gibson, Arthur C. 5.3237
Gibson, Charles, 1920-. 3.5685, 3.8892, 3.8979,
    4.8346
Gibson, Colin A. 2.6629
Gibson, D. Parke. 4.2056
Gibson, David, 1926-. 5.4980
Gibson, David W., 1944- joint author. 5.6065
Gibson, Donald B. 2.10480
Gibson, Eleanor Jack. 5.264, 5.395
Gibson, Gerald D., 1938-. 1.3616
Gibson, J. (Joseph) 5.6875
Gibson, James E., 1941-. 5.4731
Gibson, James Jerome, 1904-. 5.239
Gibson, James L. 4.7688
Gibson, James R. 3.8646

Gibson, Lay James. joint author. 4.4117
Gibson, Mary. 4.3581
Gibson, Robert L. (Robert Lewis), 1927-. 5.468
Gibson, Roger F. 1.633
Gibson, Ronald. 5.7827
Gibson, W. M. 5.2478
Gibson, W. Walker. 2.1037
Gibson, Walter S. 1.6260
Gibson, William. 2.11768
Gibson, William Carleton. 5.728
Gibson, William Merriam, 1912-. 2.10949,
    2.10968
Gicovate, Bernard, 1922-. 2.5190
Giddens, Anthony. 3.510, 4.4740-4.4741,
    4.4752, 4.4793-4.4796, 4.6380
Giddings, Paula. 3.6762
Giddins, Gary. 1.4263-1.4264
Giddy, Ian H. 4.4569
Giddy, Ian H. joint author. 4.4589
Gide, André, 1869-1951. 2.1367, 2.4545-2.4562,
    2.8276
Gidwitz, Betsy. 4.4076
Giedion, S. (Sigfried), 1888-1968. 1.4692,
    1.5130, 1.5213
Giedion-Welcker, Carola. 1.5650, 1.5702, 1.5744
Giegling, Franz, 1921- ed. 1.3611
Giele, Janet Zollinger. 4.5903
Gielgud, John, Sir, 1904-. 2.3344
Gienapp, William E. 3.7142
Giere, Ronald N. ed. 5.884
Gierke, Otto Friedrich von, 1841-1921. 4.7268,
    4.7275, 4.7415
Gierloff-Emden, Hans Günter. joint author.
    5.1812
Gies, Frances. 3.2001, 4.5856
Gies, Joseph. joint author. 4.3092, 4.5856
Giese, Arthur Charles, 1904-. 5.3622
Gieseking, John Eldon, 1905-. 5.5276
Gieseking, Walter, 1895-1956. 1.4539
Giesey, Ralph E. 4.8576
Gieske, Millard L. 4.8239
Gieysztor, Aleksander. 3.3332
Giffin, James M. 5.5464
Giffin, James M. joint author. 5.5465
Gifford, Barry, 1946-. 2.11958
Gifford, Don. 2.8888, 2.8907
Gifford, Douglas. 2.7816, 2.8792
Gifford, Ernest M. joint author. 5.3732
Gifford, Henry. 2.1433
Gifford, John A., 1947-. 3.242
Gifford, Prosser. ed. 3.5114, 3.5119
Gifford, Prosser. 3.5094
Giger, W. (Walter) 5.6024
Giggord, William, 1756-1826, ed. 2.6874
Gigli, Giuseppe, 1863-1921. 2.4902
Gijsen, Marnix, 1899-. 2.13958
Gil, Federico Guillermo. 4.8340
Gilbert, Alan, 1944-. 4.6248
Gilbert, Alan D. 1.2443
Gilbert, Allan H., 1888- ed. and tr. 4.7388
Gilbert, Charles, 1913- joint author. 4.4214
Gilbert, Charles M., 1910-. 5.3041
Gilbert, Christopher. 1.6578
Gilbert, Creighton. 1.4761, 1.5002, 2.4966
Gilbert, Dennis. 4.5237
Gilbert, Doris C. 5.507
Gilbert, Douglas, 1889-1948. 2.2830
Gilbert, Douglas L. 5.3982
Gilbert, Elliot L. ed. 2.7893
Gilbert, Felix, 1905-. 3.393, 3.873, 3.963,
    3.2916, 3.2930, 3.7025, 5.7214
Gilbert, Gorman, 1943-. 4.4039
Gilbert, Jack Glenn. 2.7330
Gilbert, James Burkhart. 3.6183
Gilbert, John, 1946- joint author. 4.4384
Gilbert, Katharine (Everett) 1886-1952. 1.1367
Gilbert, Martin, 1936-. 3.1254, 3.1656, 4.120,
    4.167, 4.177
Gilbert, Melvin Ballou. 4.1079
Gilbert, Michael Francis. 2.3444, 2.8686
Gilbert, Pamela. 5.8164
Gilbert, Sandra M. 2.5563, 2.10484, 2.10701,
    2.13044
Gilbert, Stephen G. 5.3999
Gilbert, Steven E. 1.4427
Gilbert, Stuart. 2.8889
Gilbert, Stuart. ed. 2.8900
Gilbert, Stuart. tr. 2.4446, 2.4724

Gilbert, W. S. (William Schwenck), 1836-1911.
1.4015, 2.7727-2.7728
Gilboa, Jehoshua A. 3.3997
Gilbreth, Frank Bunker, 1868-1924. 5.5601
Gilbreth, Lillian Moller, 1878-1972. 5.5602
Gilby, Thomas. 1.390, 4.7380
Gilchrist, Agnes Eleanor (Addison) 1907-.
1.5328
Gilchrist, David T., ed. 4.1920
Gilchrist, James Duncan. 5.6212, 5.6761
Gilchrist, John Thomas. 3.2063
Gilchrist, T. L. (Thomas Lonsdale) 5.2851
Gilder, George F., 1939-. 4.1525, 4.6743
Gildersleeve, Basil L. (Basil Lanneau),
1831-1924. ed. 2.313
Gildin, Hilail. 4.7435
Giles, Donna, 1949-. 5.458
Giles, Edward. 1.3144
Giles, Herbert Allen, 1845-1935. tr. 2.2232
Giles, James Richard, 1937-. 2.13105
Giles, Lionel, 1875-1958. tr. 5.7211
Giles, Mary E. 4.5974
Giles-Sims, Jean. 4.6747
Gilfillan, George, 1813-1878. 2.7240
Gili Gaya, Samuel. 2.892, 2.898
Giliomee, Hermann Buhr, 1938-. 3.5447
Gilkes, Michael. 2.9978
Gilkes, Patrick. 3.5246
Gilkey, Langdon Brown, 1919-. 1.1583, 1.2904
Gill, Brendan, 1914-. 2.11769
Gill, Dominic. 1.4147
Gill, Eric, 1882-1940. 1.5693
Gill, F. S. (Frank S.) 5.5019
Gill, K. F. 5.6186
Gill, Kay. 5.4482
Gill, Mary (Wright) illus. 5.3688
Gill, Merton Max, 1914-. 5.180, 5.4848
Gill, Michael D. 4.4624
Gill, Norman Thorpe. 5.5315
Gill, Philip E. 5.1549
Gill, Richard, 1922-. 2.6009
Gill, Sam D., 1943-. 4.545
Gill, Stephen Charles. 2.8304
Gillan, Garth, 1939-. 1.831
Gillard, David, 1929-. 3.686
Gille, Bertrand, 1920-. 4.2323
Gillers, Stephen, 1943- ed. 4.6820
Gillespie, Alan R. 5.2976
Gillespie, Dizzy, 1917-. 1.4084
Gillespie, Gerald Ernest Paul, 1933- ed. 2.13664
Gillespie, Lori, 1956-. 4.10299
Gillespie, Neal C., 1933-. 5.3198
Gillespie, Patricia H. 4.10946
Gillespie, Ronald J. (Ronald James) 5.2870
Gillett, Michael Cavenagh, Sir, 1907-. 3.4112
Gillette, A. S. (Arnold S.), 1904-. 2.3147
Gillette, J. Michael. 2.3147
Gillette, William. 3.7466, 4.9729
Gillham, Bill. 4.10705
Gilliam, Gwen. joint author. 4.6556
Gilliam, Reginald Earl. 3.6703
Gillie, Christopher. 2.8663
Gillie, Darsie Rutherford. 3.3287
Gillies, Eva. 3.5183
Gilligan, Carol, 1936-. 4.5927
Gillin, Donald G. 3.4840, 5.8033
Gillingham, John. 3.1348, 3.1376, 4.170
Gillings, Richard J. 5.1083
Gillion, Kenneth L. 4.2512
Gillis, John R. 4.5617, 4.5755
Gillispie, Charles Coulston. 5.729, 5.775, 5.808
Gillman, Leonard. 5.1587
Gillmor, C. Stewart, 1938-. 5.818
Gillmor, Desmond. 4.2313
Gillmor, Donald M. 4.9711
Gillon, Adam. 2.1733, 2.1744
Gilman, Alfred, 1908-. 5.5128
Gilman, Antonio. 4.738
Gilman, Arthur, 1837-1909. 3.3430
Gilman, Charlotte Perkins, 1860-1935.
2.11041-2.11042, 4.5653, 4.6053
Gilman, Lawrence, 1878-1939. 1.3915
Gilman, Stephen. 2.5199-2.5200
Gilman, William Henry, 1911-. 2.10336,
2.11021, 2.11159
Gilmartin, Gregory. 1.5302
Gilmore, Al-Tony. 4.1055
Gilmore, David D., 1943-. 4.5385

Gilmore, Grant. 4.9481
Gilmore, Michael T. 2.10393, 2.11158
Gilmore, Myron Piper, 1910-. 3.628
Gilmore, Robert, 1941-. 5.1537
Gilmore, Robert K. (Robert Karl), 1927-.
3.8365
Gilmour, David, 1952-. 3.3475
Gilmour, Robert S. (Robert Scott), 1940-.
4.7894
Gilmour, Robin. 2.6024
Giloi, Wolfgang. 5.5648
Gilpin, Robert. 4.4172
Gilpin, W. Clark. 1.3326
Gilroy, John, 1946-. 2.8305
Gilsenan, Michael. 1.1999
Gilson, Etienne, 1884-1978. 1.124, 1.333,
1.349-1.350, 1.383, 1.392-1.394, 1.422, 1.438,
1.1313, 1.1373, 1.2825, 1.3262, 1.5112,
1.6342, 2.4941
Gimbel, John. 3.2457, 3.2504
Gimmestad, Victor E. 2.10879
Gimpel, Jean. 1.5519
Gindin, James Jack, 1926-. 2.6007, 2.6037
Giner, Salvador. 4.5291
Ginger, Ray. 3.6049, 3.8414, 4.6997
Gingerich, Martin E. 5.7820
Gingerich, Owen. 5.1722, 5.1863
Ginsberg, Allen, 1926-. 2.11770
Ginsberg, Benjamin. 4.7517
Ginsberg, Leon H. 4.6512
Ginsberg, Morris, 1889-1970. 4.5319
Ginsborg, Paul. 3.2917
Ginsburg, Herbert. 4.10940
Ginsburg, Norton Sydney. 4.134, 4.4119
Ginsburg, Norton Sydney. ed. 4.182
Ginsburg, Soloman Wiener, 1899-1960, jt.
author. 5.7414
Ginsburgs, George. 4.8980, 4.9074
Gintis, Herbert. joint author. 4.10730
Ginzberg, Eli, 1911-. 4.2671, 4.5747, 5.7414
Ginzberg, Louis, 1873-1953. 1.1952, 3.3837
Ginzburg, Carlo. 1.2456
Ginzburg, Evgeniia Semenovna. 3.3227, 3.3242
Ginzburg, Natalia. 2.5034
Gioello, Debbie Ann. 5.7088
Gioia, Dana. 2.11947
Giono, Jean, 1895-1970. 2.4566-2.4567
Giordana, Carlo. 3.287
Giordano, Joseph. 5.4819
Giorgione, 1477-1511. 1.6206
Giovanni, da Pian del Carpine, Archbishop of
Antivari, d. 1252. 3.3611
Giovanni, Nikki. 2.13045-2.13046
Giovannoni, Jeanne M. joint author. 4.6552
Giovannoni, Jeanne M. 4.6570
Gippius, Vasilii Vasil'evich, 1890-. 2.1384
Gippius, Z. N. (Zinaida Nikolaevna),
1869-1945. 2.1498
Gipson, Lawrence Henry, 1880-. 3.1542, 3.6910
Giraldus, Cambrensis, 1146?-1223? 3.1818
Giralt, Georges. 5.6166
Girard, Denis. ed. 2.879
Girard, René, 1923-. 2.2373, 2.3506, 2.4672
Girardi, Enzo Noè. ed. 2.4989
Giraud, Jean, Agrégé des lettres. 2.3862
Giraud, Marcel, 1900-. 3.8311
Giraud, Raymond Dorner, ed. 2.4202
Giraudoux, Jean, 1882-1944. 2.4568-2.4571
Girdlestone, Cuthbert Morton, 1895-. 1.3955
Girgus, Joan R., 1942- joint author. 5.4387
Girgus, Sam B., 1941-. 2.10556, 3.6072
Girling, J. L. S. 3.4532
Gironella, José María. 2.5260-2.5261
Girouard, Mark, 1931-. 1.5253, 1.5400, 1.5568,
4.6393
Giroux, Henry A. 4.10015, 4.10809
Giroux, Robert. 2.11385
Girshick, Meyer A., joint author. 5.1377
Girton, Sandra Erdene. 5.4774
Giry, Marcel. 1.6063
Gisevius, Hans Bernd, 1904-. 3.2438
Gish, Nancy K., 1942-. 2.8789
Gismonti, Pedro Manuel. 1.4923
Gissing, Algernon, 1860-1937, ed. 2.7741
Gissing, Ellen, 1867- ed. 2.7741
Gissing, George, 1857-1903. 2.7657,
2.7730-2.7742
Gist, Noel Pitts, 1899-. 4.6458

Giteau, Madeleine. 1.5755
Gitelson, Susan Aurelia. 3.3858
Githens, Marianne. 4.5972
Gitler, Ira. joint author. 1.3534
Gitler, Ira. 1.3760
Gitlin, Todd. 2.70
Gitman, Leo. ed. 5.4246
Gittell, Marilyn. joint author. 4.10646, 4.10802
Gittell, Marilyn. comp. 4.10960
Gitterman, Alex, 1938- joint author. 4.6495
Gittinger, Mattiebelle. 4.635
Gittings, John. 3.4682
Gittings, Robert. 2.7760, 2.7775-2.7776, 2.7857,
2.8297
Gittins, Diana. 4.1646
Giuliani, Alfredo. 2.4979
Given, Ivan A., ed. 5.6725
Givens, R. Dale, 1928-. 5.7154-5.7155
Givner, Joan, 1936-. 2.12318
Gjelsvik, Tore, 1916-. 3.1069
Gjerde, Jon, 1953-. 3.8308
Gjerset, Knut, 1865-1936. 3.3374, 3.3379
Gjerstad, Einar, 1897-. 3.2718
Gjertsen, Derek. 5.730
Glaab, Charles Nelson, 1927-. 4.6210
Glacken, Clarence J. 4.364
Glackens, Ira, 1907-. 1.5939
Glad, Betty. 3.7935
Glad, John. 2.1315
Glad, Paul W., 1926-. 3.7429
Gladden, Edgar Norman. 4.7747
Gladkov, Fedor, 1883-1958. 2.1563
Gladstone, Alan. 4.3425
Gladwin, Thomas N. 4.2732, 4.2738
Glaessner, Martin F. (Martin Fritz), 1906-.
5.3166
Glahn, Elsé. 3.4646
Glaister, Geoffrey Ashall. 5.7540
Glaister, John, 1892-. 5.4715
Glaister, Stephen. 4.3868
Glansdorff, P. 5.2244
Glantz, Leonard H. 4.9544
Glanville, Stephen Ranulph Kingdon,
1900-1956, ed. 3.5138
Glanz, David. 4.5399
Glanz, Rudolf. 3.6569
Glare, P. G. W. 2.259
Glasby, G. P. 5.3024
Glaser, Arthur B. 5.6528
Glaser, Milton. 1.5837
Glaser-Wöhrer, Evelyn. 2.12884
Glasgow, Douglas G. 3.6763
Glasgow, Ellen Anderson Gholson, 1873-1945.
2.11772-2.11777
Glasheen, Adaline. 2.8871
Glasner, David. 4.3788
Glasner, Peter E. 1.1885
Glaspell, Susan, 1882-1948. 2.11784
Glasrud, Bruce A. 3.6524
Glass, Bentley, 1906-. 5.886, 5.3626
Glass, Billy P. 5.1804
Glass, D. V. (David Victor), 1911-. 4.1614,
4.5299
Glass, Gene V., 1940-. 4.10702
Glass, I. I., 1918-. 5.5754
Glassburner, Bruce, comp. 4.2531
Glasscote, Raymond M. 5.4981
Glasse, Robert M. 4.860
Glassie, Henry H. 2.9862
Glassman, Elizabeth. 1.6504
Glassman, Irvin. 5.2902
Glasstone, Samuel, 1897-. 5.2427, 5.2448,
5.5997, 5.6139
Glatstein, Jacob, 1896-1971. 2.1802-2.1804
Glatzer, Nahum Norbert, 1903-. 1.1902, 1.1989,
2.1781, 2.13789, 2.13793, 2.13796
Glatzer, Richard. 2.3037
Glaysher, Frederick, 1954-. 2.11820
Glaze, Anita J., 1940-. 3.5385
Glazebrook, G. P. de T. (George Parkin de
Twenebroker), 1899-. 3.8698, 3.8833
Glazer, Nathan. 1.1927, 3.8045, 4.8952
Glazier, Richard, 1851-1918. 1.6536
Gleason, Harold, 1892- joint editor. 1.3426
Gleason, Henry A. (Henry Allan), 1882-.
5.3672-5.3673
Gleason, Henry Allan, 1917-. 2.1014
Gleason, Philip. comp. 1.3176

Gleason, Ralph J. 1.4324
Gleason, Sarell Everett, 1905- joint author. 3.7582
Gleazer, Edmund J. 4.10562
Gleckner, Robert F. ed. 2.5578
Gleckner, Robert Francis, 1925-. 2.7428
Gleitman, Henry. 5.104
Gleitman, Lila R. 2.120
Glen, Duncan, 1933- comp. 2.8788
Glendale Adventist Medical Center. 5.8291
Glendening, Parris N. 4.7870
Glendinning, Nigel, 1929-. 1.6292
Glendinning, Robert James, 1931-. 2.13980
Glendinning, Victoria. 2.9297, 2.9328
Glendon, Mary Ann, 1938-. 4.9373
Glenn, Jules, 1921-. 5.153
Glenn, Kathleen Mary. 2.5275
Glenn, Robert W., 1944-. 5.7872
Gleser, Goldine C. joint author. 5.44
Gless, Darryl J., 1945-. 2.6669
Glessing, Robert J. 2.3654
Glick, David, 1908-. 5.3619
Glick, Leslie Alan. 4.9393
Glick, Paul C. joint author. 4.1648
Glick, Thomas F. ed. 5.3343
Glick, Thomas F. 3.3421
Glickman, Carl D. 4.10647, 4.10701
Glickman, Rose L. 4.3262
Glie, Rowen, comp. 5.5755
Gligorić, Svetozar. 4.1072-4.1073
Glikson, Paul. 3.4009
Glimcher, Arnold B. 1.5669
Gloag, John, 1896-. 1.4772
Glob, Peter Vilhelm, 1911-. 4.714
Global Interdependence Center. 4.4463, 4.4601
Global Tomorrow Coalition. 5.8420
Gloeckner, André, ed. 1.5709
Gloss, David S. 5.5552
Glotz, Gustave, 1862-1935. 4.3095
Glover, Arnold, 1865-1905. 2.7804
Glover, John Desmond. 4.1936
Glover, Michael, 1922-. 3.2125
Glover, Robert Hall, 1871-1947. 1.3023
Glubb, John Bagot, Sir, 1897-. 3.3745, 3.5157
Glück, Louise, 1943-. 2.13047
Gluckman, Max, 1911-1975. 4.523, 4.612, 4.649-4.650, 4.9352
Gluckstein, Ygael. 4.2462
Glueck, Nelson, 1900-. 3.3825
Glueck, Sheldon, 1896-. 4.9340
Glusker, Jenny Pickworth. 5.2932
Gluski, Jerzy. 2.3807
Gobineau, Arthur, comte de, 1816-1882. 3.2088
Goble, Danney, 1946-. 3.8533, 3.8536
Goble, Warwick. illus. 2.6315
Gochros, Harvey L. joint author. 4.6487
Godard, Jean Luc, 1930-. 2.3046
Godbold, E. Stanly. 3.6995
Goddard, Harold Clarke, 1878-1950. 1.566, 2.6731
Goddard, Pliny Earle, 1869-1928. 3.5750
Goddard Space Flight Center. 4.26, 5.6711
Godden, Rumer, 1907-. 2.8687-2.8689
Godechot, Jacques Léon, 1907-. 3.2059, 3.2080-3.2081, 4.8582
Godefroy, Vincent. 1.4024
Godley, A. D. (Alfred Denis), 1856-1925. 2.370
Godolphin, Francis Richard Borroum, ed. 2.402, 3.545
Godoy, Horacio H. joint author. 4.9136
Godron, Michel. 5.3517
Godwin, Gail. 2.13048
Godwin, R. Kenneth. joint author. 4.1634
Godwin, William, 1756-1836. 2.7747, 4.1559, 4.7420
Goebbels, Joseph, 1897-1945. 3.2381-3.2384
Goebel, Julius, 1892-1973. 4.9905
Goedertier, Joseph M. 3.4903
Goehlert, Robert, 1948-. 5.7848, 5.8352
Goehner, Patricia A. 5.5199
Goehring, Eleanor, 1904-. 4.780
Goeje, M. J. de (Michael Jan de), 1836-1909. 2.1831
Goelman, Hillel, 1951-. 5.7722
Goen, C. C. 1.2400
Goerke, Heinz. 5.3214
Goethe, Johann Wolfgang von, 1749-1832. 2.13568, 2.13572-2.13579

Goetz, Judith Preissle. 4.10284
Goetz-Stankiewicz, Marketa. 2.1659
Goetzmann, William H. 3.8456
Goff, Frederick Richmond, 1916- ed. 5.7557
Goffart, Walter A. 3.2817, 4.4650
Goffman, Erving. 2.63, 4.4901, 4.5066-4.5067
Gofman, John W. 5.4729
Gogarten, Friedrich, 1887-1967. 1.2935
Gogarty, Oliver St. John, 1878-1957. 2.8690-2.8691
Gogh, Vincent van, 1853-1890. 1.6243, 1.6247
Gogol', Nikolaĭ Vasil'evich, 1809-1852. 2.1379-2.1383, 2.3106
Gogos, Costas G. joint author. 5.6907
Goguel, François, 1909-. 4.8591
Gohberg, I. (Israel), 1928-. 5.1481
Gohdes, Clarence Louis Frank, 1901-. 2.10338, 2.11140, 5.7787
Gohlman, William E., ed. 1.370
Goist, Park Dixon. 4.6211
Goitein, S. D., 1900-. 3.598, 3.3854, 3.4008
Gökalp, Ziya, 1876-1924. 3.3570
Golab, Caroline. 4.8943
Golan, Galia. 3.1923, 3.1929, 3.3866
Golan, Naomi. 5.4870-5.4871
Golant, Stephen M. 4.5825
Golay, Frank H. 4.2536
Golay, John Ford. 4.8607
Golberg, Michael A. 4.3485
Golby, Michael. 4.10421
Gold, Alice Ross. 4.9978
Gold, Bela. 5.2511
Gold, Herbert, 1924-. 2.13049-2.13052
Gold, Martin, 1931-. 4.10726
Gold, Michael Evan. 4.3258
Gold, Penny Schine. 4.5863
Gold, Victor. ed. 5.2847
Goldberg, Alfred, 1918- ed. 5.7400
Goldberg, Anatol, d. 1982. 2.1554
Goldberg, Arthur J. 4.3547
Goldberg, Edward D. ed. 5.6021
Goldberg, Gerald Jay. 2.2469
Goldberg, Harvey, 1923-. 3.2186
Goldberg, Isaac, 1887-1938. 2.1808, 2.12134
Goldberg, Joe. 1.3757
Goldberg, Joseph Philip, 1918-. 4.3392
Goldberg, Kathy E. (Kathy Ellen), 1953-. 5.4149
Goldberg, Nancy Marmer. 2.2469
Goldberg, Richard J. 4.6539
Goldberg, Rita, 1949-. 2.7217
Goldberg, Roberta. 4.3266
Goldberg, Seymour, 1928- joint author. 5.1481
Goldberg, Steven S. (Steven Selig), 1950-. 4.9602
Goldberger, Arthur Stanley, 1930- joint author. 4.1962
Goldberger, Leo. 5.447
Goldberger, Marvin L. 5.2479
Goldberger, Robert F. 5.3624
Goldblat, Jozef. 4.9164
Goldblatt, Howard, 1939-. 1.6723
Golden, James L. 2.2534
Goldenberg, Edie N. 4.8116
Goldenberg, Naomi R. 1.1610
Goldenson, Robert M. 5.15
Golder, Frank Alfred, 1877-1929. 3.3048, 3.3141, 3.3175, 3.3318
Goldfarb, Jeffrey C. 3.3344
Goldfarb, Ronald L. 4.6910, 4.9869
Goldfeld, Stephen M. 4.1297
Goldfield, David R., 1944-. 4.6238, 4.6245
Goldgar, Bertrand A., 1927-. 2.5688, 2.7188
Goldiamond, Israel, 1919- joint author. 4.6502
Goldin, Edwin, 1933-. 5.2298
Goldin, Grace. joint author. 5.4706
Golding, John. 1.5877, 1.6133
Golding, William, 1911-. 2.8693-2.8707, 2.8709, 3.5132
Goldman, Aaron. 5.2511
Goldman, Albert Harry, 1927-. 1.4096
Goldman, Barbara H. 4.3288
Goldman, Charles Remington, 1930-. 5.5977
Goldman, Emma, 1869-1940. 4.7192
Goldman, Eric Frederick, 1915-. 3.6197, 3.7409, 3.7797, 3.7889
Goldman, Irving, 1911-. 3.5621
Goldman, Juliette. 4.5734

Goldman, Marshall I. 4.2379, 4.3783
Goldman, Martin. 5.1952
Goldman, Merle. 2.2151, 3.4789, 3.4805
Goldman, Nancy L. 5.7374
Goldman, Nathan C. 4.3831, 5.6691
Goldman, Perry M., ed. 4.7994
Goldman, Peter Louis, 1933-. 3.6845
Goldman, Richard Franko, 1910-. 1.4202
Goldman, Robert P., 1942-. 1.1693
Goldman, Ronald. 4.5734
Goldmann, Lucien. 2.3417, 2.3953
Goldmark, Josephine Clara, 1877-1950. 4.5134
Goldner, Nancy. 1.4009
Goldoni, Carlo, 1707-1793. 2.4991-2.4994
Goldron, Romain. 1.3639
Goldscheider, Calvin. joint author. 4.5592
Goldscheider, Calvin. 4.1631
Goldscheider, Ludwig, 1896-. 1.5637, 1.5735
Goldschmidt, Arthur, 1938-. 3.3716
Goldschmidt, Lucien. 5.7011
Goldschmidt, Richard Benedict, 1878-1958. 5.3358
Goldschmidt, Victor Moritz, 1888-1947. 5.3103
Goldsmith, Anthony, tr. 2.4186
Goldsmith, Arnold L. joint author. 2.2511
Goldsmith, Donald. 5.1727, 5.1880
Goldsmith, Emanuel S., 1935-. 2.1788-2.1789
Goldsmith, Harold F. 4.1581
Goldsmith, Lisa A. 5.4847
Goldsmith, Maurice. 5.2446
Goldsmith, Oliver, 1728-1774. 2.7041-2.7047, 2.7049, 2.7054
Goldsmith, Raymond William, 1904-. 4.1852, 4.2053
Goldsmith, William M. 4.7919
Goldspink, G. 5.4267
Goldstein, Amy J. 4.10627
Goldstein, Arnold P. 4.6813, 4.10703, 5.417, 5.454, 5.4829, 5.4969
Goldstein, Bernard, 1925-. 4.5740
Goldstein, Donald M. 3.1035
Goldstein, Herbert, 1922-. 5.1643
Goldstein, Howard, 1922-. 4.6478
Goldstein, Janice L., ed. 3.7912
Goldstein, Jeffrey H. 5.436
Goldstein, Joel K. (Joel Kramer), 1953-. 4.7971
Goldstein, Jonathan. 4.4220
Goldstein, Joseph. 3.4497, 4.6548, 4.9511
Goldstein, Kenneth S. 4.755
Goldstein, Larry Joel. 5.1341
Goldstein, Leon J. 3.476
Goldstein, Malcolm. 2.10516, 2.12721
Goldstein, Michael J. (Michael Joseph), 1930-. 4.5546
Goldstein, Richard (Richard N.) 5.3450
Goldstein, Sanford. 2.2075
Goldstein, Sidney, 1927-. 4.6195
Goldstein, Thomas. 5.765
Goldstine, Herman Heine, 1913-. 5.1468, 5.6571
Goldstrom, J. M. 4.10957
Goldstucker, Jac L. 4.4294
Goldthorpe, J. E. 4.5096
Goldthorpe, John H. 4.5340
Goldthwaite, Richard A. 1.5435
Goldwater, Barry M. (Barry Morris), 1909-. 3.7574, 4.7856
Goldwater, Robert John. 1.4643, 1.4800, 1.5706, 1.6105
Goldwhite, Harold. 5.2712
Goldwin, Robert A. 1922-. 4.7797, 4.7865, 4.8163, 4.9670
Goldziher, Ignác, 1850-1921. 1.1992, 1.2045, 2.1835
Golembiewski, Robert T. joint author. 4.4937
Golembiewski, Robert T. 4.4902
Golenpaul, Dan. 1.64
Golffing, Francis. 1.4601
Golledge, Reginald G., 1937-. 4.383
Gollerbakh, É. F. (Érikh Fedorovich), 1895-. 2.1528
Golley, Frank B. 5.3557
Gollin, A. M. (Alfred M.) 3.1675
Gollnick, Donna M. 4.10481
Gollwitzer, Helmut. 1.2268
Golomb, Michael, 1909-. 5.1503
Golombek, Harry, 1911-. 4.1070
Golovnin, Vasiliĭ Mikhaĭlovich, 1776-1831. 4.98
Golson, Jack. ed. 3.5622

Golub, Edward S., 1934-. 5.4463
Golub, Spencer. 2.3382
Golzé, Alfred R., 1905-. 5.5980
Gomberg, Irene L. 4.10602
Gombin, Richard, 1939-. 4.7092
Gombrich, E. H. (Ernst Hans), 1909-. 1.4609,
    1.4624, 1.4674, 1.4762, 5.246
Gombrich, Ernst Hans Josef, 1909-. 1.5131,
    1.5139
Gombrich, Richard Francis. 1.2142
Gombrowicz, Witold. 2.1703
Gomersall, Alan. 5.8104
Gomery, Douglas. 2.2917
Gomery, J. Douglas. 2.2977
Gómez-Ibáñez, José A., 1948-. 4.3917
Gomme, A. W. (Arnold Wycombe) 3.2568
Gomme, Arnold Wycombe, 1886-1959. 2.562
Gömöri, George, 1934-. 2.1721
Gompers, Samuel, 1850-1924. 4.3583-4.3584
Goncharov, Ivan Aleksandrovich, 1812-1891.
    2.1390-2.1391
Goncourt, Edmond de, 1822-1896. 1.6052,
    1.6720, 2.4227-2.4228, 2.4230-2.4231
Goncourt, Jules de, 1830-1870. 1.6052, 1.6720,
    2.4227-2.4228
Gonda, J. (Jan), 1905-. 1.1681
Gondran, Michel. 5.1284
Gonen, Jay Y., 1934-. 3.4019
Gönen, Turan. 5.6331
Góngora, Mario. 3.8980
Góngora y Argote, Luis de, 1561-1627. 2.5191
Gonnet, G. H. (Gaston H.) 5.1177
González, Justo L. 1.2273-1.2274
Gonzalez, Rafael C. 5.6173
González Vicen, Felipe. 2.5107
Gooch, G. P. (George Peabody), 1873-1968.
    3.388, 3.717, 3.1250, 3.2047, 3.2486, 3.3104,
    4.8398
Gooch, John. 5.7295
Good, Carter Victor, 1897-. 4.10166, 4.10285
Good, Dorothy. 5.6804
Good, Edwin M. (Edwin Marshall), 1928-.
    1.4154
Good, Ralph E. 5.3549
Good, Robert C. 3.5514
Good, Ronald, 1896-. 5.3665
Good, Thomas L., 1943-. 4.10313, 4.10375
Goodale, Jane Carter, 1926-. 4.586
Goodall, David W., 1914-. 5.3565
Goodall, David William. 5.3541
Goodall, Jane, 1934-. 5.4034
Goodchild, Peter. 5.1959
Goode, J. Paul, 1862-1932. 4.112
Goode, John Allen. 2.7745
Goode, Patrick. 4.7043
Goode, Richard B. 4.3018, 4.4676, 4.4711
Goode, Stephen H., 1925-. 1.32-1.33
Goode, William Josiah. 4.4948, 4.5640
Goodell, Gregory. 2.3000
Goodell, Helen, ed. 5.4349, 5.4935
Goodenough, Erwin Ramsdell, 1893-1965.
    1.2304
Goodenough, Ward Hunt. 3.5630
Goodenow, Ronald K. 4.10964
Goodfellow, Sally W. 1.6076
Goodfield, June, 1927-. 1.1343, 5.4468
Goodfriend, Lewis S. joint author. 5.6563
Goodhart, Arthur Lehman, Sir, 1891- ed.
    4.9407
Goodhart, C. A. E. (Charles Albert Eric).
    4.4469
Goodier, J. N. (James Norman), 1905- joint
    author. 5.1673
Goodison, Nicholas. 5.7014
Goodlad, John I. 1.6695, 4.10004, 4.10032,
    4.10171, 4.10434, 4.10716
Goodman, Alvin S. 5.5974
Goodman, David S. G. 4.8741
Goodman, Elliot Raymond, 1923-. 4.7545
Goodman, George J. W. 5.105
Goodman, Henry, 1893- ed. 2.11076
Goodman, Kenneth S. 4.10480, 5.396
Goodman, Lenn Evan, 1944-. 1.377
Goodman, Louis Sanford, 1906-. 5.5128
Goodman, Martin, 1953-. 3.3819
Goodman, Nelson. 1.87, 1.517, 1.1183, 1.1314,
    1.1402

Goodman, Paul, 1911-1972. 1.5580, 4.7518,
    4.10258, 5.115
Goodman, Paul S. 4.3156
Goodman, Percival. 1.5580
Goodman, Richard M. (Richard Merle), 1932-.
    5.5076
Goodman, Seymour E. 5.1178
Goodnow, Frank Johnson, 1859-1939. 4.8178
Goodnow, Jacqueline J. 5.382
Goodrich, Carter, 1897-1971. 4.3944, 4.3981
Goodrich, Edwin S. (Edwin Stephen),
    1868-1946. 5.3892
Goodrich, L. Carrington (Luther Carrington),
    1894-. 3.4667, 3.4710, 3.4931
Goodrich, Leland Matthew. 4.9134, 4.9217
Goodrich, Lloyd, 1897-. 1.4882, 1.4896, 1.5904,
    1.5944, 1.5966
Goodridge, Gerald William Frank Radcliffe.
    2.880
Goodridge, Jonathan Francis, 1924-   . 2.6393
Goodsell, Charles T. 4.7890
Goodsell, James Nelson, comp. 3.9103
Goodspeed, Edgar Johnson, 1871-1962. 1.2500,
    1.2515, 1.2682
Goodwin, Albert. 3.1573
Goodwin, Cardinal Leonidas, 1880- joint ed.
    3.8339
Goodwin, Craufurd D. W. 4.2110
Goodwin, Craufurd D. W. ed. 4.1331
Goodwin, Craufurd David Wycliffe, 1934-.
    4.1381-4.1382
Goodwin, Dennis W. 4.4294
Goodwin, Doris Kearns. 3.7890
Goodwin, Geoffrey L. 1.2239
Goodwin, Grenville, 1907-1940. 3.5842
Goodwin, H. Eugene, 1922-. 2.3561
Goodwin, K. L. 2.10039
Goodwin, Philip Lippincott, 1885-. 1.5353
Goodwin, William Lawrence, 1935-. 4.10378
Goodwyn, Lawrence. 3.7410
Goody, Richard M. 5.2510
Goodyear, Colin Crosland. 5.6373
Goodyear, Francis Richard David. ed. 2.7838
Goodyear, Frank Henry, 1944-. 1.4884
Googe, Barnabe, 1540-1594. 2.6481
Goold, G. P. 2.678, 2.709
Gooneratne, Wilbert, 1938-. 4.2455
Goossens, Leon, 1897-. 1.4553
Gopal, Sarvepalli. 3.4316, 3.4320
Göpfert, Herbert Georg. ed. 2.13646
Gopinathan, Saravanan. 5.7582
Gorbman, Aubrey, 1914-. 5.4245
Gordenker, Leon, 1923-. 4.9206, 4.9245
Gordimer, Nadine. 2.10041, 2.10070-2.10078
Gordon, Arnold J. 5.2648
Gordon, Arthur. 5.6643
Gordon, Bernard L. comp. 4.330
Gordon, Bertram M., 1945-. 3.1063
Gordon, Caroline, 1895-. 2.11786-2.11792
Gordon, David C. 3.3782
Gordon, David G., joint author. 5.1379
Gordon, David M. 4.2009, 4.3558
Gordon, E. V. (Eric Valentine), 1896-1938.
    2.6414, 2.6425
Gordon, Edmund I., ed. 2.1770
Gordon, Edmund W. 4.6573
Gordon, Edwin, 1927-. 1.4411
Gordon, Eleanor L., ed. 4.10008
Gordon, Giles, 1940-. 2.9848
Gordon, Harold J. 3.2372, 3.2399
Gordon, I. R. F. 2.7197
Gordon, Ian Alistair, 1908-. 2.5929
Gordon, J. E. (James Edward), 1913-. 5.5839
Gordon, John E., 1931-. 5.2720
Gordon, Leonard A. 3.4182
Gordon, Linda. 4.3275, 4.5689
Gordon, Lois G. 2.12896
Gordon, Lyndall. 2.9596
Gordon, M. K. (Marilyn Kay) joint author.
    5.1522
Gordon, M. (Michael) 5.1135
Gordon, Malcolm S. 5.4185, 5.4189
Gordon, Maria Matilda (Ogilvie) Dame, d.
    1939, tr. 5.2953
Gordon, Michael, 1940- comp. 4.5574
Gordon, Milton Myron, 1918-. 4.5130
Gordon, R. L. (Raymond L.) 1.1656
Gordon, Richard L., 1934-. 4.3706

Gordon, Robert, 1946-. 1.6123
Gordon, Robert Aaron. ed. 4.3222
Gordon, Robert J. (Robert James), 1940-.
    4.4475
Gordon, Suzanne, 1945-. 4.4925
Gordon, Thomas, 1918-. 4.10698
Gordon, Virginia N. 4.10605
Gordon Walker, Patrick Chrestien. 4.8448
Gordon, William A. 2.12191
Gordone, Charles. 2.13053
Gordus, Jeanne P. 4.3204
Gore, A. J. P. (Anthony John Poynter) 5.3550
Goreau, Angeline. 2.6901
Goreau, Laurraine. 1.4091
Gorelick, Sherry. 4.10814
Gorelick, Sherry. joint author. 4.10729
Goren, Charles Henry, 1901-. 4.1067
Gorenstein, Daniel. 5.1297
Gorenstein, Paul. 5.1751
Gorer, Geoffrey, 1905-. 3.4206
Gorgoni, Gianfranco. illus. 1.4872
Göring, Hermann, 1893-1946. defendant. 3.1073
Gorky, Maksim, 1868-1936. 2.1266,
    2.1501-2.1508
Görlach, Manfred. 2.1109
Gorlin, Robert J., 1923-. 5.5076
Görlitz, Walter, 1913-. 3.2254
Gorman, Alfred H. 4.10314
Gorman, G. E. 5.8444
Gorman, Herbert Sherman, 1893-1954. 2.8908
Gorman, Joseph Bruce. 3.7654
Gorman, Lyn. 5.8444
Gorman, Michael, 1941-. 5.7628
Gorman, Robert A. 4.6984
Gormley, William T., 1950-. 4.3042
Gornick, Vivian. 4.6990
Gornick, Vivian. comp. 4.5883
Gorovitz, Samuel. ed., comp. 1.719
Gorshkov, Sergeĭ Georgievich, 1910-. 5.7469
Gort, Michael, 1923-. 4.2072
Gorz, André. 4.3099
Gorzny, Willi. 5.690
Goscilo, Helena, 1945-. 2.1324
Gosden, P. H. J. H. 4.6177
Gosling, J. C. B. (Justin Cyril Bertrand) 1.251,
    1.262, 1.1503
Gosling, William. 3.303
Gosnell, Harold Foote, 1896-. 4.7734, 4.8120,
    4.8175
Gosner, Kenneth L., 1925-. 5.3835
Goss, R. O. 4.3958, 4.3960
Gosse, Edmund, 1849-1928. 2.2645, 2.6463,
    2.7748, 2.7990
Gossen, Gary H. 3.8913
Gossett, Thomas F. 2.11230, 3.6509
Gosudarstvennaia Tret'iakovskaia galereia.
    1.6278
Gosvāmī, Satsvarūpa Dāsa, 1939-. 1.1734
Goswami, Amit. 5.839
Goswami, Maggie. 5.839
Goswami, Shrivatsa. 2.1878
Gottcent, John H. 5.8445
Gottesman, Ronald. 2.10669
Gottfredson, Michael R. joint author. 4.6707
Gottfried, Kurt. 5.2460
Gottfried, von Strassburg, 13th cent. 2.13529
Gotthelf, Jeremias, 1797-1854. 2.13550
Gottlieb, Benjamin M., 1912-. 5.6744
Gottlieb, Gilbert, 1929-. 5.478
Gottlieb, Irving M. 5.6504
Gottlieb, Milton. 5.2046
Gottlieb, Richard. 5.6232
Gottlieb, Robert. 2.3659, 4.2027
Gottlieb, Wolfram Wilhelm. 3.824
Gottman, John Mordechai. 5.4861
Gottmann, Jean. 3.1185, 4.6237, 4.7496
Gotto, Antonio M. joint author. 5.4992
Gottschalk, Louis Moreau, 1829-1869. 1.3878
Gottschalk, Louis Reichenthal, 1899-. 3.389,
    3.2042, 3.2068
Gottschalk, Stephen. 1.3330
Gottschalk, Walter, 1894- joint author. 2.1182
Gottschalk, Walter Helbig, 1918-. 5.1589
Gottwald, Norman K. (Norman Karol), 1926-.
    1.2587
Götz, Rainer E., 1943- joint author. 5.5934
Goubert, Pierre. 3.2036
Goudeket, Maurice, 1889-1977. 2.4502

Goudie, Andrew. 4.237, 4.381
Goudriaan, Teun. 1.1727
Goudsblom, Johan. 4.5368
Goudsmit, Samuel Abraham, 1902-. 5.2305
Goudy, Frederic W. (Frederic William),
   1865-1947. 1.6599
Gough, Barry M. 3.5719, 3.8593
Gough, Ian. 4.2287
Gough, J. W. (John Wiedhofft) 4.7401, 4.7413,
   4.7527
Gough, Kathleen, 1925-. 4.585
Gough, Michael. 1.5169
Gould, Carol C. 4.5837, 4.5901
Gould, Edwin S. 5.2622, 5.2716
Gould, Eric, 1943-. 2.4587
Gould, George M. (George Milbry), 1848-1922.
   5.4484
Gould, Glenn. 1.3471
Gould, James A., 1922-. 1.1165
Gould, James Adams, 1922-. 1.1147
Gould, Jay Reid. joint author. 5.5508
Gould, Jean, 1909-. 2.12163
Gould, John, 1927-. 1.272, 2.304
Gould, Karen L. 2.4751
Gould, Leroy C. 4.6672
Gould, Lewis L. 3.7495, 3.7696
Gould, Peter R. 4.31
Gould, Richard A. 3.245
Gould, Robert, d. 1709? 2.3304
Gould, S. J. (Samuel Julius) 3.4009
Gould, Samuel B. 4.10548
Gould, Stephen Jay. 5.353, 5.3086, 5.3229,
   5.3345-5.3346, 5.3369, 5.3389
Gould, Thomas. 2.295
Gould, William B. 4.931, 4.9563
Goulden, I. P. 5.1280
Goulden, Joseph C. 3.5018, 4.3589
Goulden, Steven L. 5.5664
Gouldner, Alvin Ward, 1920-. 4.2649, 4.4797,
   4.4949, 4.7143
Gouré, Leon. 3.990
Gourevitch, Peter Alexis. 4.3413
Gourou, Pierre, 1900-. 3.4492, 4.110, 4.2861
Gourvitch, Alexander. 4.3194
Gove, Philip Babcock, 1902-1972. 2.1088,
   2.3452
Gove, Samuel Kimball. 3.8417
Gove, Walter R. 4.5080
Goveia, Elsa V. 4.6438
Governmental Affairs Institute (U.S.) 4.8106
Govindjee, 1933-. 5.3762
Gow, Andrew Sydenham Farrar, 1886-. 2.320,
   2.552-2.553
Gowa, Joanne S. 4.4592
Gowan, John Curtis. ed. 4.10907
Gowans, Alan. 1.5522
Gowar, John, 1945-. 5.6388
Gower, D. Michael, joint author. 5.4096
Gower, John, 1325?-1408. 2.6383-2.6384
Gowers, Ernest, Sir, 1880-1966. ed. 2.1090
Gowing, Lawrence. 1.4574
Gowing, Peter G. 3.4593
Goya, Francisco, 1746-1828. 1.5817, 1.6293,
   1.6465, 1.6493, 1.6495
Goyder, D. G. joint author. 4.9527
Goyen, William. 2.11794
Goytisolo, Juan. 2.5262-2.5264
Gozzano, Guido, 1883-1916. 2.5035
Gozzi, Carlo, conte, 1722-1806. 2.4996
Graaff, J. de V. 4.1432
Grabar, Oleg. 1.4748
Grabau, Amadeus William, 1870-. 5.2958,
   5.3164
Grabbe, Christian Dietrich, 1801-1836.
   2.13586-2.13587
Graber, Doris A. (Doris Appel), 1923-. 4.5016,
   4.5224, 4.6778
Grabill, Wilson H., joint author. 4.1643
Grabiner, Judith V. 5.1452
Graboïs, Aryeh, 1930-. 3.143
Grabowicz, George G. 2.1652
Graburn, Nelson H. H. 1.4691, 4.689
Grace, Gerald Rupert. 4.10678, 4.10959
Grace, Helen K. 5.5179
Grace, John R. joint author. 5.1668
Grace, Sherrill, 1944-. 2.9063
Gracie, David McI., 1932-. 4.3206
Gracie, Gordon, 1930- joint author. 5.5827

Gracq, Julien, 1910-. 2.4574
Grade, Arnold E., ed. 2.11751
Grade, Chaim, 1910-. 2.1805
Gradman, Barry, 1944-. 2.7871
Graebner, Norman A. 3.6349
Graebner, Norman A. ed. 3.7575
Graf, Alfred Byrd. 5.5347-5.5348
Graf, Rudolf F. 5.6447
Graf, Walter Hans, 1936-. 5.5968
Graff, Henry F. (Henry Franklin), 1921-. 3.378,
   3.6311
Graglia, Lino A. 4.9588
Graham, A. C. (Angus Charles) tr. 1.1804
Graham, A. C. (Angus Charles) ed. and tr.
   2.2190
Graham, Alexander John. 4.8895
Graham, Alexander Steel. Robert E. 4.2082
Graham, Bessie, 1883- comp. 5.7707
Graham, Clarence Henry, 1906- ed. 5.4378
Graham, David R. 4.4087
Graham, Desmond, 1940-. 2.8601-2.8602
Graham, Don, 1940-. 2.11185
Graham, Frank Dunstone, 1890-1949. 4.1489
Graham, Gerald Sandford, 1903-. 4.4186-4.4187
Graham, Hugh Davis. joint author. 4.8097
Graham, Hugh Davis. 4.5131
Graham, Ian Charles Cargill, 1919-. 3.6596
Graham, James Walter, 1906-. 1.5222
Graham, John, 1936-. 5.6361
Graham, Keith. 1.741
Graham, Lawrence S. 3.3503, 3.3505
Graham, Loren R. 5.786, 5.957
Graham Luján, James, joint tr. 2.5251
Graham, Otis L. 3.7524-3.7525
Graham, Philip, 1898-. 2.3270, 2.11140
Graham, Richard. 3.9194
Graham, Roger. 3.8769
Graham, Ronald L., 1935-. 5.1285
Graham, Sheilah. 2.11729
Graham, W. Fred, 1930-. 1.3400
Graham, Walter James, 1885-. 2.6888
Grahame, Kenneth, 1859-1932. 2.7750, 2.9110
Grainger, Leslie. 5.6875
Gram, Harvey, 1946- joint author. 4.1405
Gram, Moltke S. 1.916
Gramling, Oliver. 2.3581
Gramsci, Antonio, 1891-1937. 4.7075-4.7077,
   4.7083
Gran, Guy. 4.1829, 4.2594
Granatstein, J. L. 3.8747, 3.8768, 3.8778,
   4.8310, 5.7895
Granatstein, J. L. joint author. 3.6414
Grand Palais (Paris, France) 1.6120
Grandbois, Alain, 1900-1975. 2.4806
Grandgent, C. H. (Charles Hall), 1862-1939.
   2.4917, 2.4944
Grandison, Alice Georgie Cruickshank. 5.3928
Grandjean, E. (Etienne) 5.4264
Grandy, Richard E. 1.1210
Grandy, Walter T., 1933-. 5.2356
Granet, Marcel, 1884-1940. 1.1787, 3.4628,
   3.4634
Granger, Bill. 4.10912
Granger, Bruce Ingham, 1920-. 2.10869
Granger, Edith. 2.2707-2.2710
Granger, Frank Stephen, 1864- tr. 2.699
Granger, John Van Nuys, 1918-. 4.8990
Granger, Lori. 4.10912
Granick, David. 4.2380, 4.2740, 4.2744
Granit, Ragnar, 1900-. 5.4265, 5.4333
Gransden, Antonia. 3.1208
Grant, Alexander. 3.1790
Grant, Aline. 2.7998
Grant, Campbell, 1909-. 3.5823
Grant, Carl A. 4.10786
Grant, Carolyn. 4.5416
Grant, Claire. 5.2591
Grant, Donald Lee, 1919-. 4.6723
Grant, Douglas, 1921-, comp. 2.6987
Grant, Edward, 1926-. 5.731
Grant, Elliott Mansfield, 1895-1969. 2.4342
Grant, Eugene Lodewick, 1897-. 5.5700
Grant, Frederick C. (Frederick Clifton),
   1891-1974. 1.1659, 1.2507, 1.2637, 1.2680
Grant, Gail. 4.1174
Grant, Gerald. 4.10071, 4.10828
Grant, H. Roger, 1943-. 4.1908
Grant, John Ernest. 2.7405

Grant, John Webster, 1919-. 3.5726
Grant, Malcolm A. 5.6209
Grant, Mary McNierney. 4.4444
Grant, Michael, 1914-. 1.1640, 1.1662, 2.230,
   2.626, 2.11642, 3.277, 3.2515, 3.2527, 3.2804,
   3.3888
Grant, Peter M. 5.6510
Grant, Richard B. 2.4229, 2.4345
Grant, Robert McQueen, 1917-. 1.2195, 1.2287,
   1.2295, 1.2820, 1.2967
Grant, Roger L. 5.2591
Grant, Ulysses S. (Ulysses Simpson), 1822-1885.
   3.7403, 3.7476
Grant, Verne. 5.3370, 5.3382
Grant, W. L. (William Lawson), 1872-1935.
   3.8711
Grant, William, 1925-. 5.6445
Grant, William F. 5.3653
Grant, Wyn. 4.3073
Grantham, Dewey W. 3.8168
Granville-Barker, Harley, 1877-1946. 2.6696,
   2.6732-2.6733, 2.8071
Graphische Sammlung Albertina. 1.5806, 1.5811
Gras, Ann, 1926-. 4.10294
Gras, Norman Scott Brien, 1884-1956. 4.4253,
   5.5227
Grass, Günter, 1927-. 2.13752-2.13764
Grasselli, Jeanette G. 5.2659, 5.2685, 5.2725
Grasselli, Margaret Morgan, 1951-. 1.4981
Grassl, Marianne. 5.3316
Gratch, Bonnie. 5.8424
Grattan, Clinton Hartley, 1902-. 3.5544-3.5545,
   3.5552
Grattan-Guinness, I. 5.1070, 5.1092
Grätzer, George, 1936-. 5.1310
Grau, Shirley Ann. 2.13054-2.13059
Graubard, Allen, 1938-. 4.10302
Graubard, Paul S. 4.10908
Grauer, Bill, 1922-1963. joint author. 1.4330
Grauer, Robert T., 1945-. 5.1213
Graustein, Jeannette E. 5.3210
Gravagnuolo, Benedetto. 1.5411
Graver, Lawrence, 1931-. 2.8434
Graver, Suzanne. 2.7713
Graves, Carol. joint author. 5.8100
Graves, Edgar B. 5.7984
Graves, Harvey W. 5.6618
Graves, John Cowperthwaite. 5.1910
Graves, Morris, 1910-. 1.4897
Graves, Norman John. 4.36
Graves, Philip Perceval, 1876-, ed. 3.4035
Graves, Richard, 1715-1804. 2.7052
Graves, Robert, 1895-. 2.2716, 2.2768, 2.5750,
   2.5763-2.5765, 2.8717-2.8726, 3.1643
Grawe, Paul H. 2.2823
Gray, Andrew. 1.4038, 4.8433
Gray, Asa, 1810-1888. 5.3674
Gray, Basil, 1904-. 1.6306, 1.6308, 1.6420
Gray, C. H. (Charles Horace) ed. 5.4722
Gray, Camilla. 1.5033
Gray, Cleve. ed. 1.5674
Gray, D. M. (Donald Maurice), 1929-. 5.2542
Gray, Donald H. 5.5897
Gray, Douglas. 2.5601, 2.6079, 2.6387
Gray, Dwight E., 1903- ed. 5.2011
Gray, Edward, 1849-1920. 2.903
Gray, George E., 1927-. 4.3908
Gray, Henry, 1825-1861. 5.4141
Gray, Hugh, 1900-. 2.2936
Gray, Irwin. 4.2648
Gray, J. A. C. (John Alexander Clinton) 3.5674
Gray, J. Glenn (Jesse Glenn), 1913-1977. 1.927,
   5.7146
Gray, Jack, 1926-. 4.7590
Gray, James Henry, 1906-. 3.342, 3.8851,
   5.4275
Gray, John, 1913-. 1.2601, 4.1344
Gray, John Chipman, 1839-1915. 4.9502
Gray, John Milner, Sir, 1889-. 3.5287
Gray, Lawrence. 4.8632
Gray, Lewis Cecil, 1881-. 5.5242
Gray, Louis Herbert, 1875-1955, joint editor.
   1.1524
Gray, Melvin. 5.4928
Gray, Michael H., 1946-. 1.3616
Gray, Nicolete, 1911-. 1.6600
Gray, Nigel. 2.6053
Gray, Oscar S., 1926-. 4.9515

Gray, Paul E. 5.6497
Gray, Paul R., 1942-. 5.6529
Gray, Peter, 1908-. 5.3182-5.3183, 5.3285
Gray, Piers. 2.11634
Gray, Randal. 5.7435
Gray, Richard, 1929-. 3.5166, 4.4244
Gray, Richard A. 5.7684
Gray, Richard J. 2.10447, 2.12654
Gray, Robert M., 1943-. 5.6369
Gray, Ronald D. 2.13483
Gray, Simon, 1936-. 2.9700
Gray, Stephen, 1941-. 2.10045
Gray, Thomas, 1716-1771. 1.6386,
  2.7053-2.7055
Gray, Thomas James, 1917- ed. 5.5964
Gray, Virginia. 4.8247
Gray, William G. (William Gurin), 1948- joint
  author. 4.287
Graybill, Franklin A. joint author. 5.1394
Grayling, A. C. 1.1174
Graymont, Barbara. 3.5894
Grayson, Benson Lee, 1932-. 3.6481
Grayson, Cecil, ed. 1.5098
Grayson, Donald K. 4.692
Grayson, L. M., comp. 4.2133
Grayson, Leslie E. 4.3778
Grayson, Martin. 5.6809
Grayson, Robin F. 5.3287
Graziano, Anthony M., 1932-. 5.5108
Great Britain. 4.9421
Great Britain. Admiralty. 5.1679
Great Britain. Central Advisory Council for
  Education (England) 4.10120
Great Britain. Central Criminal Court. 2.8968
Great Britain. Central Office of Information.
  3.1730
Great Britain. Colonial Office. 3.6885, 4.8793
Great Britain. Committee of Inquiry into
  Shipping. 4.3977
Great Britain. Her Majesty's Stationery Office.
  5.7923
Great Britain. Inter-departmental Committee on
  Social Insurance and Allied Services. Social
  Insurance and Allied Services. 4.3229
Great Britain. Laws, statutes, etc. 4.8276
Great Britain. Ministry of Public Building and
  Works. 1.5358
Great Britain. Nautical Almanac Office.
  5.1678-5.1679
Great Britain. Office of Commonwealth
  Relations. 4.8793
Great Britain. Office of the Revels. 2.3296
Great Britain. Parliament. 3.1473, 3.6859
Great Britain. Parliament. House of Commons.
  4.8476
Great Britain. Public Record Office. 3.6885
Great Britain. United Kingdom National
  Commission for U.N.E.S.C.O. 4.296
Greaves, C. Desmond. 3.1866
Greaves, Harold Richard Goring, 1907-. 4.9184
Greaves, Richard L. 1.2215
Grebanier, Bernard D. N., 1903-. 2.6872
Grebene, Alan B., 1939-. 5.6530
Grebinger, Paul. 3.5757
Greeley, Andrew M., 1928-. 1.2373,
  3.6510-3.6511, 3.6553
Green, A. E. (Arthur Eric) 5.6297
Green, Adwin Wigfall, 1900-. 3.7630
Green, Anne, 1899- tr. 2.4645
Green, Archie. 1.4353
Green, Bert F. 5.60
Green, Carol Hurd. 3.353
Green, Constance McLaughlin, 1897-. 3.8110
Green, Dan S. 3.6758
Green, Daniel W. E. 5.1823
Green, David Marvin, 1932-. 5.243
Green, Don W. 5.6827
Green, Elizabeth A. H. 1.4501
Green, Elizabeth Alden, 1908-. 4.11002
Green, Fletcher Melvin, 1895-. 3.8114, 5.7853
Green, Frederick Charles, 1891-1964. 2.4041
Green, Graham, 1904-. 2.8751
Green, Henry, 1905-1974. 2.8730-2.8733, 2.8735
Green, J. (James), 1928-. 5.3824
Green, James R., 1944-. 4.8240
Green, Jesse. 3.5964
Green, Jonathan. 5.6923
Green, Julien, 1900-. 2.4575-2.4576, 2.4645

Green, Lewis, 1925-. 3.8649
Green, Martin A. 5.6328
Green, Martin Burgess, 1927-. 2.2380
Green, Matthew, 1696-1737. 2.7058
Green, Maurice B. (Maurice Berkeley) 5.6887
Green, Melvin M. joint author. 5.3409
Green, Michael D., 1941-. 3.5867
Green, Michael E. 5.2638
Green, Otis Howard, 1898-. 2.5100, 2.5102
Green, Paul, 1894-1981. 2.11796-2.11798
Green, Paul E. 4.4304, 5.1407
Green, Paul E. joint author. 4.4275
Green, Paul Eliot, 1924-. 5.6411
Green, Paul Michael. 4.8866
Green, Peter, 1924-. 2.729, 2.747, 2.7751,
  3.2625
Green, Philip, 1932-. 4.7569
Green, Robert, 1940-. 2.8635
Green, Roger Lancelyn. ed. 2.7676
Green, Roger Lancelyn. 2.7391
Green, Sue. 5.1224
Green, Thomas Hill, 1836-1882. 1.1432, 4.7632
Green, Vivian Hubert Howard. 3.1357
Green, Walter L., 1934- joint author. 5.5719
Green, William. 5.6672
Green, William A., 1935-. 4.2158
Greenberg, Blu, 1936-. 1.1986
Greenberg, Brian. 3.617
Greenberg, Cara. 5.7073
Greenberg, Clement, 1909-. 1.6699
Greenberg, David F. 4.6895
Greenberg, Dolores. 4.3988
Greenberg, Eliezer, 1896-. 2.1826, 2.1828
Greenberg, Hazel. 4.9693
Greenberg, Herbert J. 2.8405
Greenberg, Ira A., 1924- comp. 5.4894
Greenberg, Janelle Renfrow. 4.8441
Greenberg, Jay R., 1942-. 5.158
Greenberg, Joseph Harold, 1915-. 2.6, 2.2294
Greenberg, Louis M., 1933-. 3.2168
Greenberg, Mark. 1.5024
Greenberg, Marshall G., 1935-. 4.4067
Greenberg, Martin Harry. 2.10831, 2.10838,
  2.13088
Greenberg, Marvin J. 5.1588
Greenberg, Michael. 4.4231
Greenberg, Michael R. 5.5589
Greenberg, Milton, 1927-. 4.7793
Greenberg, Noah. ed. 1.3442
Greenberg, Roger P. joint author. 5.152
Greenberger, Evelyn Barish. 2.7581
Greenberger, Howard. 2.3222
Greenberger, Martin, 1931-. 5.7578
Greenblatt, Susan L. joint author. 4.10796
Greene, David Herbert, 1913-. 2.8148
Greene, Gayle, 1943-. 2.6809
Greene, Donald Johnson. 2.7079
Greene, Ellin, 1927-. 5.7719
Greene, Evarts Boutell, 1870-1947. 3.6965
Greene, Graham, 1904-. 2.2956, 2.5536, 2.8629,
  2.8737-2.8750, 2.8752-2.8768, 3.5412, 4.6791
Greene, Harlan. 2.13061
Greene, Harry Andrew, 1889-. 4.10476
Greene, Jack P. 3.6387
Greene, Jack P. ed. 4.6425
Greene, James H. (James Harnsberger), 1915-.
  5.7021
Greene, Jerome A. 3.5783
Greene, John C. 5.791, 5.3347
Greene, Lorenzo Johnston, 1899-. 3.7217
Greene, Maxine. 4.10016, 4.10178, 4.10244
Greene, Mott T., 1945-. 5.2951
Greene, Nathanael, 1935-. 3.6968, 4.8595
Greene, Richard Leighton. ed. 2.6118-2.6119
Greene, Robert, 1558?-1592. 2.6491, 2.6582
Greene, Theodora Marvin, 1931-. 5.2734
Greene, Theodore P., 1921-. 3.6113
Greene, Thomas McLernon, 1926-. 2.2771
Greene, Victor R. 3.6586
Greene, Walter H. 4.10491
Greenfield, Gerald Michael. joint author. 5.8185
Greenfield, Jeff. 4.4070
Greenfield, Kent Roberts, 1893-1967. 3.904,
  3.910, 3.2910
Greenfield, Norman S. 5.4307
Greenfield, Sidney M. 4.1556
Greenfield, Sidney M. ed. 4.5254
Greenfield, Stanley B. 2.5589, 2.6293, 5.7942

Greenfield, Sumner. 2.5294
Greengarten, I. M., 1949-. 4.7441
Greenhalgh, P. A. L. 5.7180
Greenhill, Basil. 5.7499
Greenhous, Brereton, 1929- joint author. 3.1019
Greenidge, A. H. J. (Abel Hendy Jones),
  1865-1906. 4.7357
Greenland, D. J. 5.5283
Greenlaw, Edwin Almiron, 1874-1931. ed.
  2.6522
Greenleaf, Richard E. comp. 1.3184
Greenleaf, W. H. 4.7292
Greenler, Robert, 1929-. 5.2555
Greeno, James G. joint author. 5.54
Greenough, Chester Noyes, 1874-1938. 2.5580
Greenough, Horatio, 1805-1852. 1.5666
Greenough, J. B. (James Bradstreet), 1833-1901.
  2.253, 2.1055
Greenough, Sarah, 1951-. 5.6961
Greenshields, Rod, 1933-. 5.6878
Greenslade, S. L. (Stanley Lawrence), 1905- ed.
  1.2197, 1.2509
Greenspan, Nancy Thorndike. joint author.
  5.5106
Greenspan, Stanley I. 5.511, 5.5106
Greenspoon, Leonard Jay. 1.2615
Greenstein, Carol Horn. 5.1041
Greenstein, Fred I. 3.7837, 4.5732, 5.8407
Greenstein, Jesse Leonard, 1909- ed. 5.1837
Greenstone, J. David. 4.3597
Greenwald, Douglas. 4.1273-4.1274
Greenwald, Jane. 4.10421
Greenwald, Maurine Weiner, 1944-. 4.3281
Greenway, John. 3.8921
Greenway, John L. 2.13965
Greenwood, Davydd J. 4.432
Greenwood, Edward Baker, 1933-. 2.1446
Greenwood, Gordon, 1913-, ed. 3.5570
Greenwood, Joen E. 4.9468
Greenwood, John, 1943-. 5.7856
Greenwood, N. N. (Norman Neill) 5.2830
Greenwood, Norman Neil. 5.2311
Greenwood, Peter Humphry. 5.3900
Greenwood, Val D. 3.295
Greep, Roy Orval, 1905-. 5.4158
Greer, Bobby G. joint author. 5.5038
Greer, David Clive, 1937-. 2.6124
Greer, Germaine, 1939-. 1.5859
Greer, Harold E. joint author. 3.8220
Greer, R. Douglas, 1942- joint comp. 1.4413
Greer, Scott A. 4.6293
Greer, Thomas H. 4.5132
Greeson, Phillip E. 4.2928
Greet, Anne Hyde. 2.4365-2.4366
Greeven, Heinrich, 1906-. 1.2723
Greever, Garland, 1883-. 2.11140
Greever, William S. 3.8457
Greevy, David U. 4.8136
Greg, W. W. (Walter Wilson), 1875-1959.
  2.5785, 2.6837-2.6838
Greg, Walter Wilson, 1875-. 5.7953
Gregg, Edward. 3.1536
Gregg, Josiah, 1806-1850. 3.8575
Gregg, Pauline. 3.1481, 4.2261, 4.2288, 4.5300
Gregg, Robert W., comp. 3.7847
Gregor, A. James (Anthony James), 1929-.
  3.6684, 4.7600, 5.7270
Gregor, Ian. 2.6023
Gregor, Ian. joint author. 2.8712
Gregorian, Vartan. 3.4116
Gregorovius, Ferdinand, 1821-1891. 3.2934
Gregory, Cedric Errol. 5.6721
Gregory, Charles Oscar, 1902-. 4.9552
Gregory, Derek. 4.356
Gregory, Dick. 2.3256, 3.6388
Gregory, Francis E. C. (Francis Edward
  Coulton) 4.2224
Gregory, Hollingsworth Franklin, 1906-. 5.6679
Gregory, Horace, 1898-. 2.11799, 2.12040
Gregory I, Pope, ca. 540-604. 1.2184, 1.3256
Gregory, J. (John), 1938-. 5.6851
Gregory, James Stothert, 1912-. 3.3007, 3.4729
Gregory, Lady, 1852-1932. 2.3360,
  2.7752-2.7755
Gregory, Michael J. 2.192
Gregory, of Nyssa, Saint, ca. 335-ca. 394.
  1.3089
Gregory, Paul R. 4.2381

Gregory, Philip Herries. 5.4459
Gregory, R. L. (Richard Langton). 5.26, 5.246
Gregory, Richard Paul Fitzgerald, 1938-.
    5.3760
Gregory, Robin. 1.4173, 1.4176
Gregory, Ross. 3.831
Gregory, Ruth W. (Ruth Wilhelme), 1910-.
    4.872
Gregory, S. (Stanley) 4.41
Gregory, Sinda, 1947-. 2.11812
Gregory, Theodor Emanuel Gugenheim. 4.4195
Gregory, Thomas West. 2.10822
Greider, William. 4.2012
Greiff, Constance M. 3.5997-3.5998
Greimas, Algirdas Julien. 2.81
Greiner, Donald J. 2.13074, 2.13381-2.13382
Greisen, Kenneth. 5.2494
Gremillion, Joseph. 4.5118
Grenander, M. E. (Mary Elizabeth), 1918-.
    2.10911
Grene, David. ed. 2.545
Grene, Marjorie Glicksman, 1910-. 1.487,
    1.1280
Grene, Nicholas. 2.8151
Grenell, Robert G. (Robert Gordon), 1916-.
    5.4782
Grenier, Roger, 1919-. 2.4439
Grennen, Joseph E. 2.6797
Grennes, Thomas. 4.3682
Grente, Georges, 1872-. 2.3822
Grenville, J. A. S. (John Ashley Soames),
    1928-. 3.737, 4.8968
Gresswell, R. Kay. ed. 4.312
Greub, Werner Hildbert, 1925-. 5.1311
Greve, Tim, 1926-. 3.3383
Grevels, Friedrich-Wilhelm. 5.2784
Greven, Philip J. 1.2374, 3.8001
Greville, Charles, 1794-1865. 3.1602
Greville, Fulke, Baron Brooke, 1554-1628.
    2.6144, 2.6434
Grevisse, Maurice. 2.866
Grew, Joseph C. (Joseph Clark), 1880-1965.
    3.4927
Grew, Raymond. 3.2863
Grey, David A. 4.9711
Grey, Gene W., 1931-. 5.5363
Grey, Ian, 1918-. 3.3088
Grey, Jerry. 5.6707
Grey, Zane, 1872-1939. 2.11800
Greyfié de Bellecombe, Louis. joint author.
    4.3424
Greyser, Stephen A. joint author. 4.4429
Greyser, Stephen A. 4.4437
Greyser, Stephen A. joint author. 4.4306
Griaule, Marcel, 1898-1956. 1.1857
Gribbin, John R. 5.1714, 5.1868, 5.2106
Gridley, Mark C., 1947-. 1.4325
Gridley, Roy E. 2.7488
Grieder, Jerome B. 3.4713
Grieder, Terence. joint author. 1.4855
Grieder, Terence. 3.5693
Grieger, Russell. 4.4895
Grier, William H. 3.6717
Grierson, Edward, 1914-1975. 3.1221
Grierson, Herbert John Clifford, Sir, 1866-1960.
    2.5537, 2.5645, 2.5751, 2.6157, 2.6452,
    2.8047, 2.8053-2.8054
Grierson, John, 1898-1972. 2.2984, 5.6650
Grierson, Sir Herbert John Clifford, 1866-1960.
    ed. 2.6160
Gries, John Matthew, 1877- ed. 3.6786
Griesbach, Heinz. 2.1178
Grieve, Alexander James, 1874-, ed. 2.7921
Grieve, M. J., joint author. 4.9015
Grieve, Michael. 2.8780-2.8781
Griffen, Clyde, 1929-. 4.3623
Griffen, Dana T., 1943- joint author. 5.3019
Griffen, Sally, 1936- joint author. 4.3623
Griffin, Brenda S. 4.6861
Griffin, Charles Carroll, 1902-. 5.7906
Griffin, Charles T., joint author. 4.6861
Griffin, David, 1939-. 1.1331, 1.2809, 1.2843
Griffin, Donald Redfield, 1915-. 5.3971, 5.4087,
    5.4101, 5.4188
Griffin, Dustin H. 2.7230
Griffin, Edward M., 1937-. 1.3337
Griffin, Grace Gardner. 5.8263
Griffin, Ivan H. 5.7061

Griffin, James. 3.5666
Griffin, James M. 4.3753
Griffin, Jasper. 3.2519
Griffin, Jonathan. 2.4465
Griffin, Keith B. ed. 4.2523
Griffin, Keith B. 4.2489, 4.2896
Griffin, Miriam T. (Miriam Tamara) 4.7371
Griffin, Susan. 2.13062
Griffin, W. Hall. 2.7483
Griffis, William Elliot, 1843-1928. 3.4995
Griffith, Belver C. 5.7640
Griffith, Cyril E. 3.6822
Griffith, Elisabeth. 4.6005
Griffith, Grace Kellogg. 2.12700
Griffith, Guy Thompson. 3.2559, 3.2630
Griffith, J. A. G. (John Aneurin Grey) 4.9423
Griffith, J. S. (John Stanley) 5.4319
Griffith-Jones, Stephany. 4.4725
Griffith, Paddy. 5.7222
Griffith, Ralph T. H. (Ralph Thomas
    Hotchkin), 1826-1906. 1.1678, 2.1938
Griffith, Robert, 1940-. 3.7668
Griffith, Samuel B. 5.7203, 5.7338
Griffith, T. Gwynfor (Thomas Gwynfor), 1926-.
    2.852
Griffith, William E. 4.7022
Griffiths, Antony. 1.6461
Griffiths, Brian. 4.4170
Griffiths, Bruce, 1938-. 2.843
Griffiths, David J. (David Jeffrey), 1942-. 5.2374
Griffiths, John Charles. 3.4111
Griffiths, Keith M. 2.2989
Griffiths, Mary Rose Millie, 1898-. 3.3044
Griffiths, Naomi Elizabeth Saundaus. 3.8802
Griffiths, Paul. 1.3788, 1.3928, 1.4192
Griffiths, Percival Joseph, Sir, 1899-. 3.4223
Griffiths, Phillip, 1938-. 5.1577
Griffiths, Richard M. 3.2188
Griffiths, Trevor. 2.9701
Grigg, David B. 5.5230, 5.5257
Grigg, John, 1924-. 3.1668-3.1670
Grigg, Neil S. 5.5978
Grigorenko, P. G. (Petr Grigor'evich), 1907-.
    3.3228, 3.3250
Grigsby, William G., 1927-. 4.3486
Grigson, Geoffrey, 1905-. 2.3756, 2.6127, 2.8790
Grillmeier, Alois, 1910-. 1.2848
Grillo, R. D. 4.517
Grillparzer, Franz, 1791-1872. 2.13589-2.13590
Grim, Ronald E. 5.7839
Grimal, Henri, 1910-. 3.755
Grimal, Pierre, 1912-. 3.2726
Grimald, Nicholas, 1519-1562. 2.6150
Grimaldi, John V., 1916-. 4.3478
Grimes, Alan Pendleton, 1919-. 4.7689, 4.8082,
    4.9635
Grimes, Ronald L., 1943-. 5.8099
Grimké, Sarah Moore, 1792-1873. 4.6028
Grimm, Harold John, 1901-. 1.2323, 1.2326
Grimm, Jacob, 1785-1863. 2.1185,
    2.13509-2.13510
Grimm, Reinhold. 2.13736
Grimm, Wilhelm, 1786-1859. 2.1185, 2.13510
Grimmelshausen, Hans Jakob Christoph von,
    1625-1676. 2.13543-2.13545
Grimshaw, James A. 2.13221
Grimshaw, Rex W. 5.6902
Grimsley, Ronald. 1.817-1.818
Grimstad, Kirsten. ed. 4.6066
Grimsted, David. 2.2822
Grimsted, Patricia Kennedy. 3.3117
Grimwood-Jones, Diana. joint author. 5.8037
Grindrod, Muriel. 3.2905
Grinker, Roy R. (Roy Richard), 1900-. 5.4936
Grinnell, Alan, 1936- joint author. 5.4316
Grinnell, George Bird. 3.5853
Grinspoon, Lester, 1928-. 4.6660
Grisewood, Harman, 1906-. 2.8851
Griswold, Alexander B. 1.5050
Griswold, Alfred Whitney, 1906-. 3.4417,
    4.2812
Griswold del Castillo, Richard. 3.8564
Griswold, Erwin N. (Erwin Nathaniel), 1904-.
    4.9885
Gritsch, Eric W. joint author. 5.8447
Gritsch, Eric W. 1.2349, 1.3305, 1.3361
Grob, Alan. 2.8324
Grob, Gerald N., 1931-. 4.3355, 5.4811-5.4812

Grobstein, Clifford, 1916-. 5.5049
Grodecki, Louis, 1910-. 1.5241
Groden, Michael. 2.8890
Grodzins, Morton. 4.7871
Grodzins, Morton Melvin. 4.7513
Grønbech, Bo. 2.14010
Grofman, Bernard. 4.7739, 4.9730
Grogan, Denis Joseph. 5.993
Grogg, Sam L. 2.2933
Grogg, Tom M., ed. 4.903
Grohmann, Will, 1887-1968. 1.6177
Grolier Club. 5.7011
Grolier Incorporated. 1.10
Grollman, Sigmund. 5.4193
Groner, Alex. 4.1885
Gröning, Karl. 2.3087
Gronlund, Norman Edward, 1920-. 4.10712
Groom, A. J. R. joint author. 4.9100
Groos, Rene, 1898-. 2.4029
Groover, Mikell P., 1939-. 5.7025, 5.7048
Gropius, Walter, 1883-1969. 1.5267-1.5268,
    1.5454
Gropman, Alan L., 1938-. 3.6726
Gropp, Arthur E., 1902-. 5.7903-5.7904
Grosart, Alexander Balloch, 1827-1899. 2.6569,
    2.7208
Groslier, Bernard Philippe. 1.5054, 3.4445
Gross, A. H., tr. 2.1799
Gross, Barry R., 1936-. 4.7700
Gross, Beatrice. 4.10033
Gross, Beatrice. comp. 4.10172
Gross, Bertram Myron, 1912-. 4.8032
Gross, Charles, 1857-1909. 5.7982, 5.7984
Gross, Charles A. 5.6287
Gross, Daniel R., comp. 3.9155
Gross, Donald. 5.5599
Gross, Harvey Seymour, 1922- ed. 2.2730
Gross, James A., 1933-. 4.9553
Gross, Jan Tomasz. 3.3340, 3.3348
Gross, John J. comp. 2.7894
Gross, John J. 2.3803, 2.5493, 2.7658, 2.12114
Gross, M. Grant (Meredith Grant), 1933-.
    4.327
Gross, Martin L. (Martin Louis), 1925-. 5.4799
Gross, Mason W., comp. 1.774
Gross, Michael, 1948-. 5.5051
Gross, Neal Crasilneck, 1920-. 4.10636, 4.10670
Gross, Miriam, ed. 2.9205
Gross, Rita M. 1.1613
Gross, Robert A., 1945-. 3.8002
Gross, Ronald. comp. 2.3741
Gross, Ronald. joint comp. 4.10172
Gross, Seymour Lee. 2.10359, 2.11058-2.11059
Gross, Stanley J. 5.4628
Gross, Theodore L. joint comp. 2.10697
Gross, Theodore L. 2.10348
Gross, Theodore L. comp. 2.10679
Gross, Theodore L. 2.11194
Grosse-Jütte, Annemarie, 1948-. 4.9216
Grossenheider, Richard Philip. 5.3983
Grosser, Alfred, 1925-. 3.2459, 3.2467
Grosser, Morton. 5.6688
Grosskurth, Phyllis. 2.8142-2.8143
Grossman, Gene M. 4.2762
Grossman, Herbert J., 1923-. 5.4973
Grossman, Joel B. 4.8066
Grossman, Jonathan, 1915-. 4.3091, 4.3595
Grossman, Lawrence, 1945-. 4.8203
Grossman, Lawrence S., 1948-. 4.2926
Grossman, Michael Baruch. 4.7935
Grossman, Ruth H. joint author. 4.10443
Grossman, Vasiliĭ Semenovich. 2.1564, 3.3996
Grossmann, Atina. 4.6123
Grossvogel, David I., 1925-. 2.2812, 2.3890
Grosz, George, 1893-1959. 1.4994
Grote, George, 1794-1871. 3.2576
Groth, A. Nicholas. 4.6733
Groth, Catherine Daae, 1888-. 3.4311
Grothendieck, A. (Alexandre) 5.1476
Grotowski, Jerzy, 1933-. 2.3117
Grouchy, Jean de. 5.4739
Group of Thirty. 4.4463, 4.4601
Grousset, René, 1885-1952. 3.42, 3.99, 3.4668,
    3.4851
Grout, Donald Jay. 1.3634, 1.4210
Groux, Guy. 4.3414
Grove, George, Sir, 1820-1900. 1.3503, 1.4524

Grove, Larry C. joint author. 5.1293
Grover, Harry Greenwood, 1881- ed. 5.4431
Grover, Ray, 1931-. 5.8086
Grover, Sonja C. 5.369
Groves, Charles Pelham. 1.2468
Groves, Leslie R., 1896-1970. 5.2417
Groves, Paul A. 3.5690
Grubb, Philip W. 5.5638
Grubb, W. Norton. joint comp. 4.10831
Grubbs, Henry Alexander, 1904-. 2.4767
Grube, Ernst J. 1.5234, 1.6611
Grube, G. M. A. (George Maximilian Anthony)
  1.263, 2.263, 2.468, 4.7345
Grube, Georges Maximilien Antoine, ed. and tr.
  2.446
Gruben, Gottfried. 1.5220
Gruber, Frank, 1904-1969. 2.11801
Gruber, Howard E. 5.593, 5.3197
Gruber, Ira D. 3.6948
Grubin, Harold L. joint author. 5.6517
Grubwieser, Victor, tr. 1.1963
Grudnitski, Gary. 5.5605
Gruelle, Johnny, 1880?-1938. ill. 2.13510
Gruen, Erich S. 2.2766
Grun, Bernard, 1901-1972. 3.369
Grünbaum, Adolf. 1.1340, 5.159
Grunberger, Richard. 3.2439
Grund, Francis Joseph, 1805-1863. 3.6034
Grundmann, Herbert, 1902-1970. 3.2253
Grundy, Isobel. 2.7172, 2.9609
Grundy, Joan. 2.7787
Grundy, Kenneth W. 4.7520, 5.7379
Gruneberg, Michael M. 4.4374, 5.5618
Grünewald, Matthias, 16th cent. 1.6172-1.6173
Grunfeld, Frederic V. 3.3968
Grunwald, Joseph, 1920-. 4.4179
Gruša, Jiří. 2.1685
Gruson, Edward S. 5.3945
Gruzalski, Bart. 5.4572
Gryphius, Andreas, 1616-1664. 2.13547
Grzimek, Bernhard. 5.3150, 5.3518, 5.3791,
  5.4057
Guardini, Romano, 1885-1968. 1.2226
Guarini, Battista, 1538-1612. 2.4970
Gubar, Susan, 1944-. 2.5563, 2.10484, 2.10701
Gubernick, David J. 5.4051
Gubert, Betty Kaplan, 1934-. 5.7871
Gubrium, Jaber F. 5.4713
Gubser, Peter. 3.4030
Gudelunas, William A. 3.8084
Gudeman, Jon E., 1936- joint author. 5.4981
Gudeman, Stephen. 4.2965
Guderian, Heinz, 1888-1954. 3.965
Gudiol, José. 1.6293
Gudorf, Christine E. 4.5953
Gudziǐ, N. K. (Nikolaǐ Kallinikovich),
  1887-1965. 2.1253
Guecioueur, Adda. 4.2572
Guéhenno, Jean, 1890-. 2.4094
Guelff, Richard, 1950-. 4.9323
Guenther, Herbert V. 1.2147, 1.2162,
  1.2171-1.2172
Guenther, Nancy Anderman, 1949-. 4.9441
Guenthner, Franz. 2.195
Guenthner-Reutter, M. 2.195
Guérard, Albert J. (Albert Joseph), 1914-.
  2.3508, 2.7788-2.7789, 2.8566
Guérard, Albert Léon, 1880-1959. 3.2008
Guercio, Francis Michael. 2.856
Guérin, Daniel, 1904-. 3.2106, 4.7180
Guerin, Philip J. 5.4881
Guerin, Wilfred L. 2.2437
Guerlac, Henry. 5.1957
Guerney, Bernard Guilbert, tr. 2.1518
Guerney, Bernard Guilbert. tr. 2.1299, 2.1515,
  2.1520
Guernsey, Otis L., 1918-. 2.3763
Guéroult, Martial. 1.793
Guerra, Francisco. 5.8286
Guerreiro, Miriam. 4.3859
Guess, Doug. 4.10944
Guest, Ann Hutchinson. 4.1083-4.1084
Guest, Harry. comp. 2.2031
Guest, John. 5.1805
Guest, Lynn, 1939- joint comp. 2.2031
Guest, Stephen Haden 1902-. 3.3165
Guevara, Ernesto, 1928-1967. 3.9098, 3.9277,
  4.7013, 5.7227

Guggenheim, E. A. (Edward Armand), 1901-.
  5.2176, 5.2245
Guggisberg, C. A. W. (Charles Albert Walter),
  1913-. 5.4000
Gugler, Josef. 4.6285
Guha, Ashok S. 4.2772
Guha, Ranajit. 3.4261
Guibert, Joseph de. 1.3242
Guibert, Rita. 2.5308
Guicciardini, Francesco, 1483-1540. 3.2853,
  3.2926
Guiccioli, Teresa (Gamba) contessa, afterwards
  Boissy, 1800?-1873. 2.7530
Guice, John D. W. 4.9780
Guichard, Léon, 1899-. 2.4685
Guicharnaud, Jacques, 1924-. 2.3889
Guicharnaud, June. 2.3889, 3.2222
Guiette, Robert, 1895-. 2.4801
Guiguet, Jean. 2.9597
Guilbeau, Phillip. 1.1117
Guilbert, John M. 5.3023
Guilford, C. joint author. 5.3028
Guilford, C. 5.3050
Guilford, J. P. (Joy Paul), 1897-. 5.47, 5.354
Guiliano, Edward. 2.7673
Guillain, Robert, 1908-. 4.2551
Guillaume, Alfred. 1.2014, 1.2038
Guillaume, de Lorris, fl. 1230. 2.3963-2.3964
Guillaume, Jeanne, 1943-. 3.5905
Guillebaud, Claude William, 1890- ed. 4.1448
Guillemin, Henri, 1903-. 2.4233, 2.4258, 3.2002
Guillemin, Jeanne, 1943-. 3.5905
Guillemin, V., 1937-. 5.1616
Guillén, Jorge, 1893-. 2.5116, 2.5265-2.5266
Guillén, Nicolás, 1902-. 2.5364
Guillet, Edwin Clarence, 1898-. 3.8728, 3.8826
Guinagh, Kevin, 1897-. 2.1099
Guiney, Louise Imogen, 1861-1920. 2.11044
Guinier, André. 5.2324
Güiraldes, Ricardo, 1886-1927. 2.5389-2.5390
Guirand, Félix, ed. 1.1605
Guiton, Jacques. 1.5482
Guiton, Margaret, joint author. 2.3909
Gulati, Basia. 2.4215
Gulick, John, 1924-. 3.3703
Gulick, Luther Halsey, 1892- ed. 4.7756
Gulik, Robert Hans van, 1910-1967. 1.6314,
  2.2229
Gullace, Giovanni. 2.2726
Gulland, J. A. 5.5475, 5.5478
Gullason, Thomas A. 2.10981
Gulley, Norman. 1.278
Gullick, J. M. 3.4539
Gulliver, P. H. 4.533
Gumerman, George J. 3.5715
Gummere, Richard M. (Richard Mott), 1883-.
  3.6014
Gump, Margaret. 2.13658
Gumperz, John Joseph, 1922-. 2.23, 2.27, 2.65
Gundersheimer, Werner L. 3.2948
Gunderson, Robert Gray. 3.7179
Gundry, Robert Horton. 1.2685
Gunn, Edward M. 2.2198, 2.2254
Gunn, James E., 1923-. 2.3488
Gunn, Neil Miller. 2.8791-2.8792
Gunn, Thom. 2.8793-2.8796
Gunnerson, Dolores A. 3.5898
Gunnis, Rupert. 1.5689
Gunsalus, I. C. (Irwin Clyde), 1912-. 5.4434
Gunsburg, Jeffery A. 3.979
Günter, Werner, 1898-. 2.13939
Gunther, Frances A. 5.5414
Gunther, Jane Davies. 5.5414
Gunther, John, 1901-1970. 3.6058
Guppy, Michael. 5.3507
Gupta, Amar. 5.1140
Gupta, Brijen Kishore, 1929-. 5.8054
Gupta, Ramesh, 1947-. 5.2038
Gupta, Sanjukta. 1.1727
Gupta, Satyadev. 4.3743
Gupta, Shanti Nath, 1929-. 1.180
Gupta, Shekhar. 3.4326
Gupta, Someshwar Chander. 5.6278
Gura, Philip F., 1950-. 2.10396, 3.7946
Guralnik, David Bernard, 1920-. 2.1091
Gurevich, Inge. 5.4707
Gurin, Joel, 1953-. 5.5131
Gurin, Patricia. 4.10856
Gurko, Miriam. 2.12164

Gurko, Vladimir Iosifovich, 1863-1927. 3.3161
Gurney, Edmund, 1847-1888. 1.4392
Gurney, Gene. joint author. 5.6644
Gurney, O. R. (Oliver Robert), 1911-. 3.3760
Gurock, Jeffrey S., 1949-. 5.8245
Gurr, Andrew. 2.3298, 2.9086
Gurr, M. I. (Michael Ian) 5.4423, 5.7128
Gurr, Ted Robert, 1936-. 4.5044, 4.5131, 4.6711
Gurtov, Melvin. 3.1184, 3.4474
Gurwitsch, Aron. 1.518
Gurwitz, Aaron S. 4.10657
Gusfield, Joseph R., 1923-. 4.4035, 4.6651
Guss, David M. 2.5409
Gussow, Joan Dye. 5.7115
Gustafson, Alrik, 1903-. 2.13971, 2.14061
Gustafson, James M. 1.1472
Gustafson, Ralph, 1909-. 2.9933
Gustafson, Thane. 4.8657
Gustave E. von Grunebaum Center for Near
  Eastern Studies. 3.598, 3.4082
Gustavus Adolphus College. 5.2455, 5.3491
Gutek, Gerald Lee. 4.1201, 4.10190
Guterbock, Thomas M. 4.8212
Guterman, Norbert, 1900-. 1.4699, 2.1292
Guth, DeLloyd J., 1938-. 3.7880, 5.7986
Guth, Dorothy Lobrano. 2.12706
Guth, James L. 1.2478
Gutheim, Frederick Albert, ed. 1.5473, 4.6329
Guthkelch, Adolph Charles Louis, d. 1916, ed.
  2.7294
Guthrie, A. B. (Alfred Bertram), 1901-.
  2.11802-2.11803
Guthrie, Anna Lorraine, ed. 1.39
Guthrie, D. M. (David Maltby) 5.4308
Guthrie, Helen Andrews. 5.7113
Guthrie, James W. 4.10660
Guthrie, Ramon, 1896-. 2.11805
Guthrie, Robert V. 5.85
Guthrie-Smith, Herbert, 1861-1940. 5.3282
Guthrie, Tyrone, Sir, 1900-1971. 2.3219, 2.3345
Guthrie, W. K. C. (William Keith Chambers),
  1906-. 1.224-1.227, 1.1644, 1.1667, 2.343
Guthrie, Woody, 1912-1967. 1.3433
Gutiérrez, Carlos María, 1926-. 3.9124
Gutiérrez, Gustavo, 1928-. 1.2924, 4.5119
Gutkind, Erwin Anton, 1886-. 4.372, 4.6184
Gutkind, Peter Claus Wolfgang. 4.2608, 4.3674,
  4.6336
Gutman, Herbert George, 1928-. 3.6764, 4.3568
Gutman, Israel. 3.1085, 3.1087, 3.1124, 3.3991
Gutman, Robert W. 1.4037
Gutnikov, George, 1938-. 5.2692
Gutteridge, William Frank, 1919-. 3.5088
Gutting, Gary. 5.954
Guttman, Irwin. 5.5715
Guttmann, Allen. 2.10299, 3.6114, 4.955, 4.975
Guttridge, Leonard F. joint author. 4.3168
Gutwirth, Madelyn. 2.4299
Guy, Albert G. 5.5761, 5.6774
Guy, Bp. of Amiens, d. 1075? 2.821
Guy, Patricia A. 2.2712
Guy, Richard K. 5.1118, 5.1256
Guyard, Marius François. 2.4254
Guyer, Melvin. joint author. 5.1379
Guyer, Paul, 1948-. 1.905
Guyton, Arthur C. 5.4194
Guzmán, Daniel de. 2.5346
Guzzo, Richard A. 4.2684
Gwaltney, John Langston. 3.6757
Gwinup, Thomas. 5.8333
Gwyn, Richard J., 1934-. 3.8792
Gwyn, Sandra. 3.8792, 3.8832
Gwyn, William B. 4.8422
Gwynn, Denis Rolleston, 1893-. 3.1848
Gwynn, Frederick Landis, 1916-. 2.12428
Gyorgy, Andrew, 1917-. 4.7021

H. D. (Hilda Doolittle), 1886-1961.
  2.11568-2.11573, 2.12341
H.W. Wilson Company. 3.324, 5.7681,
  5.7762-5.7763, 5.7765, 5.8106, 5.8150, 5.8170,
  5.8356, 5.8366, 5.8418, 5.8455
Haac, Oscar A. 2.4080
Haack, Susan. 1.1166, 1.1175
Haak, B. 1.6238
Haan, C. T. (Charles Thomas), 1941-. 4.276
Haar, D. ter. 5.2178
Haar, Jerry, 1947- joint author. 4.10105

Haar, Lester. 5.6206
Haarhoff, T. J. (Theodore Johannes), 1892-. 3.2521-3.2522
Haas, Ernst, 1921-. 3.6064
Haas, Ernst B. 4.3324, 4.9239, 5.959
Haas, George C. O. 1.1683
Haas, Marilyn L. 5.7735
Haas, R. C. G. (Ralph C. G.) 5.6068
Haas, Robert Bartlett. ed. 2.12509
Haas, Ruth B. 4.1898
Haas, Violet B., 1921-. 5.805
Haasen, P. (Peter) 5.6777
Habakkuk, H. J. ed. 4.2187
Habasque, Guy. 1.6347
Habegger, Alfred. 2.10568
Habel, Norman C. 1.2606
Habenstein, Robert W., joint author. 4.5555
Haber, Barbara. 4.5978
Haber, David. joint author. 4.9655
Haber, Ralph Norman. 5.247
Haber, William, 1899-. 4.3448
Haberman, Donald. 2.12722
Habermas, Jürgen. 1.986, 1.1287, 4.1763, 4.4893, 4.10549
Habib, Irfan, 1931-. 4.2496
Habig, Marion Alphonse, 1901- comp. 1.3258
Habington, William, 1605-1654. 2.7059
Hach, Clarence, 1917-. 4.10724
Hachmann, Rolf. 1.4734
Hachten, William A. 4.9716
Hacker, Louis Morton, 1899-. 3.6321, 4.1886-4.1887, 4.1957
Hacker, Marilyn, 1942-. 2.13063-2.13064
Hacker, P. M. S. (Peter Michael Stephan) joint author. 1.1074
Hacker, Seymour. 1.6069
Hackett, Charles Wilson, 1888- ed. 3.8339
Hackett, M. B. 4.11007
Hackett, Roger F. 3.4963
Hackh, Ingo W. D. (Ingo Waldemar Dagobert), 1890-1938. 5.2591
Hacking, Ian. 2.105, 5.888
Hackleman, Michael A. 5.6304
Hackman, Martha L., 1912-. 5.7685
Hackney, Sheldon. 3.8279
Hackstaff, L. H. 1.2206
Hadamard, Jacques, 1865-1963. 5.1042
Hadas, Moses, 1900-1966. 1.407, 2.262, 2.276, 2.629, 3.2537, 3.2747
Hadcock, R. Neville (Richard Neville) joint author. 1.3233
Haddad, Robert M., 1930-. 1.2462
Haddad, S. D. (Sam David), 1939-. 5.6223
Haddakin, Lilian. 2.7617
Haddon, Alfred C. (Alfred Cort), 1855-1940. 4.688
Hader, Arnulf. 4.3959
Hadfield, Charles, 1909-. 4.3946
Hadingham, Evan. 5.1688
Hadley, Charles D. joint author. 4.8158
Hadley, Jack. 4.3450
Hadley, Mac E. 5.4247
Hadley, Michael L. 3.1039
Hadlock, Richard. 1.3758
Hadow, Grace Eleanor, 1875- ed. 2.7044
Hadwiger, Don Frank, 1930-. 4.3684
Hady, Maureen E., 1952-. 5.8478
Haehling von Lanzenauer, Christoph. 4.2627
Haenchen, Ernst, 1894-. 1.2699
Haesaerts, Paul, 1901-. 1.6262
Häfele, Wolf. 5.6130
Hafen, Le Roy Reuben, 1893-. 3.8458, 4.4046
Hafez, E. S. E. (Elsayed Saad Eldin), 1922- ed. 5.4016, 5.5463
Haffenden, John. 2.11381-2.11382
Haffenden, Philip S. 3.7947
Haffner, Sebastian. 3.2400, 3.2416
Ḥāfiz, 14th cent. 2.1968
Hafkin, Nancy J. 4.6158
Haftmann, Werner. 1.5868
Hagan, William Thomas. 3.5862
Hagedorn, Hermann, 1882-1964. 3.6374
Hagen, Everett Einar, 1906-. 4.2773
Hagen, John W. 5.606
Hagen, Toni, 1917-. 3.4348
Hagen, Uta, 1919-. 2.3118
Hagen, Waltraud, Dr. 5.8010
Hagerty, D. Joseph. joint author. 5.6035

Hägg, Tomas. 2.270
Haggard, H. Rider (Henry Rider), Sir, 1856-1925. 2.7758
Haggard, Thomas R. 4.9560
Haggerty, Brian A. 4.8125
Haggett, Peter. joint ed. 4.32
Haggett, Peter. 4.83, 4.377
Haggett, Peter. joint author. 4.199
Haggh, Raymond H., 1920-. 1.4540
Hagihara, Yūsuke, 1897-. 5.1763
Hagler, M. O. 5.2451
Hagstrum, Jean H. 2.5629, 2.5680
Hagtvet, Bernt. 4.7609
Hague, Angela. 2.9775
Hague, René. 2.8854, 2.8858-2.8859
Hahlo, H. R. ed. 4.2734
Hahn, Ferdinand, 1926-. 1.2977
Hahn, Frank. joint author. 4.1290
Hahn, Lewis Edwin, 1908-. 1.836
Hahn, Robert O. 4.10494
Hahn, Roger, 1932-. 5.698
Hahn, Steven, 1951-. 3.8262
Haider, Donald H. 4.7872
Haig, Alexander Meigs, 1924-. 3.7938
Haig, Sir Wolseley, 1865-1938, jt. author. 3.4220
Haig, Stirling. 2.4028
Haigh, Christopher. 3.1244
Haigh, R. H. 3.2440
Haigh, Robert William, 1926-. 4.3771
Haight, Amanda. 2.1539
Haight, Gordon Sherman. 2.7699, 2.7701-2.7702, 2.7705
Haight, Gordon Sherman. ed. 2.7698
Haight, Gordon Sherman. comp. 2.6249
Haight, Timothy R. joint author. 2.60
Haile, Berard, 1874-1961. 3.5927
Haile, Harry Gerald, 1931-. 1.2342, 2.13513
Haile Selassie I, Emperor of Ethiopia, 1892-1975. 3.5247
Hailey, William Malcolm Hailey, Baron, 1872-1969. 3.5046, 4.8793
Haim, Sylvia G. ed. 3.3733
Haiman, Franklyn Saul. 4.9707
Haimson, Leopold H. 4.8665
Haimson, Leopold Henri. 4.7093
Hainaux, René. 2.3148
Hainaux, René. ed. 2.3150-2.3151
Hainaux, René. comp. 2.3149
Haines, Charles Grove, 1879-1948. 4.9644
Haines, Charles Reginald, tr. 2.354
Haines, David W. 3.6525
Haining, Peter. 2.8254
Hainstock, Elizabeth G. 4.10209
Hainsworth, Peter. 2.4883
Hair, William Ivy. 3.8316
Hájek, Otomar. 5.1606
Haken, H. 5.2280
Hakīm, Tawfīq. 2.1845
Hakkila, E. Arnold, 1931-. 5.6619
Hakluyt, Richard, 1552?-1616. 3.5988
Hakluyt Society. 4.87
Hakeda, Yoshito S. tr. 1.1745
Hakuin, 1686-1769. 1.1762
Halasz, Nicholas, 1895-. 3.2191
Halberstadt, Victor. 3.3475
Halberstam, David. 2.3651, 3.7864
Halbert, Michael. 4.4282
Haldane, J. B. S. (John Burdon Sanderson), 1892-1964. 5.845, 5.3359
Haldane, R. B. Haldane (Richard Burdon Haldane), Viscount, 1856-1928. tr. 1.958
Hale-Benson, Janice E., 1948-. 4.10851
Hale, Frederick. joint author. 5.8442
Hale, J. R. (John Rigby), 1923-. 3.629, 3.2828, 3.2915, 3.2925, 5.7194
Hale, Mason E. 5.3714, 5.3717
Hale, Oron J. (Oron James) 3.750
Hale, William M. 4.2568
Halecki, Oskar, 1891-1973. 3.527, 3.3331
Halem, Lynne Carol. 4.5783
Hales, Edward Elton Young, 1908-. 1.3157, 1.3163, 3.2875
Halevi, Gideon, 1928-. 5.7046
Halévy, Daniel, 1872-1962. 3.2176
Halévy, Elie, 1870-1937. 1.718, 3.1582
Haley, Alex. 3.6837, 3.6844

Haley, James L. 3.5840
Haley, Jay. 5.4853
Haley, Kenneth Harold Dobson. 3.2959
Haley, Russell I. 4.4293
Halfpenny, Peter. 4.4742
Haliburton, Gordon MacKay. 1.3043
Haliczer, Stephen, 1942-. 3.3441
Halio, Jay L. 2.9544
Halkett, Anne Murray, Lady, 1622-1699. 3.1499
Halkett, Samuel, 1814-1871. 5.7728
Halkias, Christos C., joint author. 5.6538
Halkin, Simon, 1898-. 2.1774
Hall, A. Rupert (Alfred Rupert), 1920-. 5.732
Hall, Calvin S. (Calvin Springer), 1909-. 5.92, 5.154, 5.519
Hall, Charles A. S. 5.3534
Hall, D. G. E. (Daniel George Edward), 1891-. 3.4394
Hall, D. J. (David John), 1943-. 3.8761
Hall, Daniel, Sir, 1864-1942. 5.5248
Hall, David D. 1.2401, 3.7955
Hall, Dennis. joint author. 5.2711
Hall, Donald, 1928-. 2.5488, 2.10738, 2.10768, 2.11807-2.11808, 2.12202
Hall, Douglas T., 1940-. 4.4371
Hall, E. Raymond (Eugene Raymond), 1902-. 5.3985
Hall, Edward Twitchell, 1914-. 4.5005, 5.404-5.405
Hall, Fred S. (Fred Smith), 1870-1946. ed. 4.6473
Hall, G. F. 5.5265
Hall, Gayle C. 4.10676
Hall, George R. 4.3040
Hall, Gwendolyn Midlo. 4.6432
Hall, Henry Edgar, 1928-. 5.2193
Hall, Jacquelyn Dowd. 4.6721
Hall, James, 1917-. 1.5156, 2.6038, 2.8349
Hall, James Norman, 1887-1951. joint author. 2.12256
Hall, James W. 4.10614
Hall, Jerome, 1901-. 4.9394, 4.9867
Hall, John. 5.5197
Hall, John Richard Clark, 1855-. 2.946
Hall, John Whitney, 1916-. 3.4873, 3.4941, 4.8893
Hall, Joseph, 1574-1656. 2.6482
Hall, Kenneth R. 4.4241, 4.8695
Hall, Kermit. 4.9613
Hall, Laurence. 4.10079
Hall, Linda B. (Linda Biesele), 1939-. 3.8947
Hall, Lowell H., 1937-. 5.2815
Hall, M. J. 5.5976
Hall, Marie Boas, 1919-. 5.695, 5.733
Hall, Marshall, 1910-. 5.1298
Hall, N. John. 2.8215, 2.8229
Hall, Peter Geoffrey. ed. 4.2887
Hall, Richard P. (Richard Pinkham), 1900-. 5.3837
Hall, Richard Seymour, 1925-. 3.5222, 3.5517
Hall, Robert Anderson, 1911-. 2.854
Hall, Robert Ernest, 1943-. 4.4488
Hall, Robert William. 4.7350
Hall, Thomas Steele, 1909-. 5.4172, 5.4177
Hallahan, Daniel P., 1944-. 4.10909, 4.10951
Hallam, A. (Anthony), 1933-. 5.2952, 5.3092, 5.3133, 5.3140, 5.3159
Hallam, Arthur Henry, 1811-1833. 2.7759
Hallberg, Peter. 2.13976, 2.13978, 2.13998
Halle, Louis Joseph, 1910-. 3.1165, 5.3284
Halle, Morris. 2.181
Halle, Morris. joint author. 2.1009
Hallenbeck, Cleve. 3.5983
Haller, John S. 4.5225, 5.4527
Haller, Mark H., 1928- ed. 3.8089
Haller, Robin M. joint author. 4.5225
Haller, William, 1885- ed. 3.1474
Halleran, Michael R. 2.469
Hallett, Garth. 1.1075
Hallett, Judith P., 1944-. 4.5853
Hallett, Robin. 3.5047
Halliburton, R. 3.5850
Halliday, David, 1916-. 5.1982
Halliday, F. E. (Frank Ernest), 1903-. 2.6850
Halliday, Fred. 3.5251
Halliday, Jon. 4.2547
Halliday, M. A. K. (Michael Alexander Kirkwood), 1925-. 2.21, 2.119, 2.159

Halliday, William Reginald, 1886-. 4.7335
Hallinan, Maureen T. 4.10312
Halline, Allan Gates. 2.10779, 2.10805
Hallion, Richard. 5.6658, 5.7410
Halliwell, Leslie. 2.2869-2.2870
Hallmark, Clayton L. 5.5946
Hallmundsson, Hallberg. 2.13970
Hallo, William W. 3.3719
Hallowell, A. Irving (Alfred Irving), 1892-1974.
    4.399
Hallowell, John H. (John Hamilton), 1913-.
    4.7570
Hallstein, Walter, 1901-. 3.1201
Halm, Hans, 1887- ed. 1.3606
Halman, Talât Sait. 2.1983
Halmos, Paul R. (Paul Richard), 1916-. 5.1364,
    5.1461
Halmos, Paul Richard, 1914-. 5.1350, 5.1590,
    5.1637
Halperin, Charles J. 3.3083
Halperín Donghi, Tulio. 3.9002, 3.9242
Halperin, John, 1941-. 2.6015, 2.7373
Halperin, Maurice. 3.9104
Halperin, Morton H. 4.9095, 5.7254
Halperin, Morton H. ed. 3.6458
Halperin, Samuel, 1930-. 3.4020
Halperin, Samuel William. 1.3192, 3.2363,
    3.2936
Halpern, Joseph. 2.4740
Halpern, Manfred. 4.5402
Halpern, Martin. 2.11177
Halpern, Siegmund, 1918-. 5.7030
Halpern, Stephen C. 4.9668, 4.9786
Halphen, Louis, 1880-1950. 3.1983
Halpin, Anne Moyer. 5.5355
Halporn, James W. 2.233
Halsband, Robert, 1914-. 2.7172, 2.7193,
    3.1550-3.1552
Halsey, A. H. 4.10771
Halsey, A. H. ed. 4.5322
Halsey, Martha T. 2.5240
Halson, Geoffrey. 2.9820
Halstead, Bruce W. 5.3811
Halstead, John P. 4.8918, 5.8226
Halstead, Linda G. 5.3811
Halsted, George Bruce, 1853-1922. 5.921
Haltiner, George J. 5.2582
Halttunen, Karen, 1951-. 4.6403
Halzen, F. (Francis) 5.2476
Ham, Roswell Gray, 1891-. 2.7178
Hamada, Shōji, 1894-1978. 1.6624
Hamada, Takashi, 1941-. 4.3934
Hamalian, Leo. 2.1760
Hamblen, Abigail Ann. 2.12565
Hambleton, Ronald, 1917-. 2.9932
Hamblin, Dora Jane, 1920-. 2.3674
Hamblin, W. Kenneth (William Kenneth),
    1928-. 5.2965
Hambourg, Maria Morris. 5.6973
Hambrick-Stowe, Charles E. 1.3054
Hamburg, David A., 1925-. 5.4035, 5.4585
Hamburg, Gary M. 3.3130
Hamburger, Joseph, 1922-. 3.1213, 4.7514
Hamburger, Michael. comp. 2.13933
Hamburger, Michael. 2.4783, 2.13517, 2.13726
Hamburger, Michael. tr. 2.13613,
    2.13857-2.13858
Hamburger, Viktor, 1900-. 5.4126
Hamby, Alonzo L. 3.7798
Hamel, Réginald. 2.4805
Hamer, David Allan. 4.8552
Hamer, Douglas. 2.6486
Hamermesh, Daniel S. 4.3449
Hamerow, Theodore S. 3.2306, 4.2198, 4.2338
Hames, Raymond B. 3.9161
Hamil, Frederick Coyne, 1903-. 3.8829
Hamill, Hugh M. ed. 3.8981
Hamill, Hugh M. 3.8932
Hamill, Ian. 5.7464
Hamilton, A. C. 2.6531
Hamilton, A. C. (Albert Charles), 1921-.
    2.6525, 2.6839
Hamilton, Alexander, 1712-1756. 3.6015,
    3.6969, 4.1909
Hamilton, Alice. 2.13383, 5.4530-5.4531, 5.4727
Hamilton, Charles Daniel, 1940-. 3.2618
Hamilton, Charles V. 4.9728
Hamilton, Charles V. joint author. 3.6701

Hamilton, Chris J. 5.8164
Hamilton, Dagmar S. 4.7983
Hamilton, Daniel Corning, 1918-. 4.3770
Hamilton, Earl J. (Earl Jefferson), 1899-.
    4.1506-4.1507
Hamilton, Eva May Nunnelley. 5.4236, 5.4242
Hamilton, F. E. Ian. 4.2424, 4.2691, 4.6264
Hamilton, George Heard. 1.4928, 1.5029,
    1.6116
Hamilton. Gordon. 4.6496
Hamilton, Henry, 1896-. 4.2298
Hamilton, Holman. 3.7171-3.7172
Hamilton, Ian, 1938-. 2.12051
Hamilton, J. R. 3.2626
Hamilton, Jean. 1.6595
Hamilton, Juan. 5.6961
Hamilton, K. G. (Kenneth Gordon), 1921-.
    2.10140
Hamilton, Kenneth. 2.13383
Hamilton, Michael Pollock, 1927-. 5.4587
Hamilton, Nigel. 2.13819, 3.1271-3.1272
Hamilton, Peter, 1949-. 4.339
Hamilton, R. W. 1.2551
Hamilton, Richard F. 4.3656, 4.8601
Hamilton, Rita. 2.5184
Hamilton, Russell G. 2.5479
Hamilton, Virginia Van der Veer. 3.8280,
    4.9658, 4.9802
Hamilton, William, 1924-. 1.2801
Hamilton, William James, 1903-. 5.4165
Hamlet, Desmond M. 2.7129
Hamlin, Alfred Dwight Foster, 1855-1926.
    1.6537
Hamlin, David, 1945-. 4.9708
Hamlin, Sarah Hull Jenkins Simpson,
    1887-1930. 1.5291
Hamlin, Talbot, 1889-1956. 1.5314
Hamlin, Talbot Faulkner, 1889-, ed. 1.5269,
    1.5291
Hamm, Charles. 1.3686, 1.4255
Hamm, Michael F. 4.6262
Hammacher, Abraham Marie. 1.5707-1.5708,
    1.5713, 1.6244
Hammacher-Van den Brande, Renilde. 1.6244
Hammack, David C. 3.8038
Hammarskjöld, Dag, 1905-1961. 3.1148, 4.9218
Hammel, Eugene A. 4.603
Hammer, Ellen J. (Ellen Joy), 1921-. 3.4436
Hammer, Kenneth, 1918-. 3.5781
Hammer, Lawrence H. 4.4415
Hammer, Louis, 1931-. 2.5153
Hammer, Mark J., 1931- joint author. 5.6014
Hammer, R. J. (Raymond J.) 1.2620
Hammer, Willie. 5.5553, 5.7044
Hammerman, Gay M. 5.7258
Hammersmith, Sue Kiefer. 4.5526
Hammett, Dashiell, 1894-1961. 2.11809-2.11811
Hammett, Jenny Yates. 1.2910
Hammett, Louis Plack, 1894-. 5.2852
Hammill, Donald D., 1934-. 4.10953, 4.10955
Hamming, Mynard C. 5.2743
Hamming, R. W. (Richard Wesley), 1915-.
    5.1375, 5.1426
Hammond, Allen L. 5.813
Hammond, Bray. 4.4531
Hammond, Eleanor Prescott, 1866-1933. 2.6135
Hammond, George Peter, 1896- joint ed.
    3.5985, 3.8339, 3.8570
Hammond, J. R. (John R.), 1933-. 2.9194
Hammond, John Lawrence Le Breton,
    1872-1949. 3.1628
Hammond, Kenneth A. 5.8165
Hammond, Mason. 2.251, 4.6191, 4.7336
Hammond, N. G. L. (Nicholas Geoffrey
    Lemprière), 1907-. 3.2510, 3.2577, 3.3598,
    4.126
Hammond, Norman. 3.9037
Hammond, Paul Y. 5.7351
Hammond, Phillip E., joint author. 4.9594
Hammond, Richard James, 1911-. 3.5125
Hammond, Robert. 4.18
Hammond, Susan Webb, joint author. 4.8029
Hammond, Thomas Taylor. 3.4119
Hampe, Karl, 1869-1936. 3.2265
Hampel, Clifford A. 5.2592, 5.2831
Hampel, Robert L. 4.10053
Hampshire, Stuart, 1914-. 1.1099
Hampson, Norman. 3.178, 3.662, 3.2066, 3.2082

Hampstead Nurseries, London. 4.5717
Hampton, Bill R., 1934-. 4.10648
Hamrin, Robert D. 4.1899
Hamsun, Knut, 1859-1952. 2.14043-2.14048
Han, Fei, d. 233 B.C. 1.167
Han, U-gŭn. 3.4996
Hanafusa, Hideo, 1923-. 5.6165
Hanan, Patrick. 2.2173
Hanau, Stella, joint author. 2.3274
Hanawalt, Barbara. 4.3253
Hanawalt, Philip C., 1931- comp. 5.3490
Hanbury, Harold Greville, 1898- ed. 4.9407
Hance, William Adams, 1916-. 3.5053, 4.1709,
    4.2576
Hancock, Graham. 4.2618
Hancock, Harold Bell, 1913-. 3.6958
Hancock, W. K. (William Keith), 1898-.
    3.1229, 3.5473
Hand, Learned, 1872-1961. 4.9452, 4.9669
Hand, Raymond. 2.1021
Hand, Wayland Debs, 1907-. 4.823
Handel, Charles William 1890-. 4.7458
Handel, George Frideric, 1685-1759. 1.3882,
    2.12832
Handford, Stanley Alexander, 1898- tr. 3.2749
Handke, Peter. 2.13885-2.13895
Handler, Edward. 4.7895
Handler, Jerome S. 4.6437
Handler, Joel F. 4.9501
Handler, Milton, 1903-. 4.1947
Handler, Philip, 1917- joint author. 5.4399
Handley, Eric Walter, ed. 2.523
Handlin, David P. 1.5558
Handlin, Lilian. 3.7086
Handlin, Mary Flug, 1913- joint author. 4.5756
Handlin, Oscar. 3.6006, 3.6116, 3.6275, 3.6322,
    3.6512-3.6514, 3.6668, 3.7239, 3.7427, 3.7680,
    3.7996, 4.5756, 4.6304, 4.9806, 5.7826
Handy, Richard Lincoln, 1929-. 5.5907
Handy, Robert T. 1.2375
Handy, Robert T. ed. 1.2925
Handy, W. C. (William Christopher),
    1873-1958. 1.3892
Handyside, John, 1883-1916. 1.895
Hane, Mikiso. 3.4908, 3.4972, 4.5448
Haney, Robert W. 4.9873
Hanf, Theodor. 5.5476
Hanfling, Oswald. 1.512
Hanfmann, George Maxim Anossov, 1911-.
    1.4732
Hanford, James Holly, 1882-. 2.7149, 2.7155
Hangen, Eva Catherine. 2.6550
Hanham, H. J. 3.1807, 4.8486, 5.7992
Hanhardt, John G. 1.6708
Hankamer School of Business. Center for
    Private Enterprise and Entrepreneurship.
    4.1557
Hanke, Lewis. 3.8992
Hankey, Maurice Pascal Alers Hankey, Baron,
    1877-1963. 3.799
Hankins, John Erskine, 1905-. 2.6532
Hankins, Thomas L. 5.734, 5.1094
Hanley, Alfred, 1942-. 2.11524
Hanley, Miles Lawrence, comp. 2.8883
Hanley, Thomas O'Brien. 1.3265
Hanley, William, 1931-. 2.13065
Hanlon, Joseph F. 5.7052
Hanna, A. J. (Alexander John) 3.5488, 3.5490
Hanna, Alfred Jackson, 1893-. 3.8934
Hanna, D. C. (David C.), 1941-. 5.2379
Hanna, J. Ray. 5.1532
Hanna, Judith Lynne. joint author. 4.6279
Hanna, Judith Lynne. 4.6283
Hanna, Kathryn Trimmer (Abbey) 1895- joint
    author. 3.8934
Hanna, William John, 1931-. 4.6279, 4.6283
Hanna, William S. 3.8074
Hannaway, Owen. 5.2606
Hannay, Alastair. 5.317
Hannay, Margaret P., 1944-. 2.9308
Hannay, N. B. (Norman Bruce), 1921-. 5.2865
Hanneman, William M. joint author. 5.6012
Hannerz, Ulf. 4.514
Hannesson, Jóhann S. 2.13973
Hanning, Robert W. 2.2631, 2.3955
Hannum, Hunter G. 2.13521
Hanrahan, Kathleen J. joint author. 4.9895
Hanrieder, Wolfram F. 3.2468

Hans, Nicholas A., 1888-. 4.10130
Hansberry, Lorraine, 1930-1965.
  2.11813-2.11814
Hanscombe, Gillian E. 2.9285
Hanse, Joseph. ed. 2.4157
Hansen, Allen Oscar, 1881-1944. 4.9990
Hansen, Alma, jt. ed. 3.1368
Hansen, Alvin Harvey, 1887-. 4.1958
Hansen, Bent, 1920-. 4.1298
Hansen, Esther Violet, 1898-. 3.4040
Hansen, Hans Jürgen, 1921-. 5.6095
Hansen, Harry, 1884- ed. 3.8309, 3.8330
Hansen, Klaus J. 1.3382
Hansen, Marcus Lee, 1892-1938. 4.8946-4.8947
Hansen, Martin Alfred, 1909-1955.
  2.14023-2.14024
Hansen, Niles M. 4.2114, 4.6212
Hansen, Peter S. 1.3670
Hansen, W. Lee. ed. 4.1955
Hansen, William F., 1941-. 2.6652
Hanslick, Eduard, 1825-1904. 1.3472, 1.4397
Hanson, Anne Coffin. 1.6117
Hanson, Bill. 4.6664
Hanson, Clare. 2.9086
Hanson, Donald W. 4.7293
Hanson, Earl D. 5.3405
Hanson, Earl Parker, 1899-. 3.9151
Hanson, Elizabeth. 2.2039
Hanson, Elizabeth M. 2.7543
Hanson, Judith. 1.2161
Hanson, Lawrence. 2.7543
Hanson, Norwood Russell. 1.88, 5.889-5.890
Hanson, Patricia King. joint author. 5.8270
Hanson, Patricia King. 2.2872, 2.2978
Hanson, Richard R. 5.5214
Hanson, Royce. 4.2054, 4.6222
Hanson, Stephen L. joint author. 5.8270
Hanson, Stephen L. 2.2872, 2.2978
Hanson, Walter Edmund, 1916- joint author.
  5.5919
Hansot, Elisabeth. 4.10640, 4.10738
Hapgood, Isabel Florence, 1850-1928. tr. 2.1478
Happé, Peter. 2.6204
Happold, F. Crossfield (Frederick Crossfield),
  1893-. 1.1627
Haq, Bilal U. 5.3154
Haq, Mahbub ul, 1934-. 4.1804, 4.2516
Harada, Kumao, 1888-1946. 3.4962
Haralambos, Michael. 1.4299
Haramundanis, Katherine, 1937- joint author.
  5.1718
Harap, Louis. 2.10355
Harari, Josué V. 2.2475
Harary, Frank. 5.1286
Harbage, Alfred, 1901-. 2.5889, 2.6567, 2.6734,
  2.6824, 2.6854-2.6855, 5.7954
Harbaugh, William Henry, 1920-. 3.7703
Harben, P. W. 5.6792
Harberger, Arnold C. ed. 4.2057, 4.4706
Harbert, Earl N., 1934-. 2.10376, 2.10890
Harbison, Frederick Harris. 4.3201
Harbison, Samuel P. 5.1211
Harborne, J. B. (Jeffrey B.) 5.3650
Harbottle, Michael. 4.9253
Harbottle, Thomas Benfield, d. 1904. 3.533
Harbour, William R. 4.7308
Harbridge House, Inc. 4.3822
Harbron, John D. 4.3962
Harcave, Sidney Samuel, 1916-. 3.3108
Harcleroad, Fred F. 4.10324, 4.10760
Harcourt, Geoffrey Colin. 4.1526
Hardach, Gerd, 1941-. 4.1774
Hardach, Karl. 4.2341
Hardacre, Helen, 1949-. 1.2167
Harden, Evelyn J. 2.1353
Harden, O. Elizabeth McWhorter (Oleta
  Elizabeth McWhorter), 1935-. 2.7689
Hardenberg, Friedrich, Freiher von, 1772-1801.
  2.13594
Harder, Edwin L. (Edwin Leland), 1905-.
  5.6158
Harder, Kelsie B. 2.197, 3.5993
Hardesty, Von, 1939-. 3.1056
Hardgrave, Robert L. 4.8704
Hardie, Martin, 1875-1952. 1.6384
Hardie, William Francis Ross. 1.312
Hardin, Charles Meyer. 5.5290
Harding, A. F. joint author. 4.713

Harding, Davis Philoon, 1914- joint editor.
  3.1413
Harding, Harold Friend, 1903- ed. 3.2608
Harding, Harry, 1946-. 3.4845, 4.8738
Harding, James. 1.3708, 1.3964
Harding, Sandra G. 4.5877
Harding, Susan Friend. 4.2880, 4.7507
Harding, T. Swann (Thomas Swann), 1890.
  5.5217
Harding, Thomas G. 4.528
Harding, Vincent. 3.6704
Harding, Walter Roy, 1917-. 2.11246,
  2.11249-2.11250
Hardison, O. B. 1.3216, 2.2728, 3.200
Hardison, O. B. comp. 2.2558
Hardison, O. B. 2.2706
Hardison, O. B. ed. 1.1380
Hardison, Osborne Bennett, 1928-. 2.5501
Hardman, J. B. S. (Jacob Benjamin Salutsky),
  1882-1968. ed. 4.3356
Hardoy, Jorge Enrique. 4.6248
Hardwick, Elizabeth. 2.2552, 2.11815-2.11816
Hardwick, Michael, 1924-. 2.7683
Hardwick, Mollie. joint author. 2.7683
Hardy, Barbara Nathan. 2.7379, 2.7659, 2.7695,
  2.7707
Hardy, C. De Witt. 4.10062
Hardy, E.G. (Ernest George), 1852-1925.
  3.2780
Hardy, Edward Rochie, 1908- ed. 1.2855
Hardy, Emma Lavinia Gifford, 1840-1912.
  2.7773
Hardy, Evelyn, 1902-. 2.7771, 2.7777
Hardy, Florence Emily, 1881-1937. 2.7770,
  2.7778
Hardy, Forsyth. ed. 2.2984
Hardy, G. H. 5.1454
Hardy, Godfrey Harold, 1877-1947. 5.1028,
  5.1324, 5.1418, 5.1453
Hardy, Harriet Louise, 1906-. 5.4727
Hardy, Henry. 1.744
Hardy, J. P. (John P.), 1933-. 2.7090
Hardy, James Daniel, 1904-. 5.4349
Hardy, James K. 5.6385
Hardy, John Edward. joint ed. 2.10359
Hardy, Neil O. 5.3598
Hardy, Peter. 3.4216, 3.4262, 4.7295
Hardy, Ralph Wilbur Frederick. 5.4457
Hardy, Stephen, 1948-. 4.940
Hardy, Thomas, 1840-1928. 2.7761-2.7763,
  2.7765-2.7766, 2.7770-2.7773, 2.7791
Hare, Denise Browne. 1.6065
Hare, F. Kenneth (Frederick Kenneth) 5.2579
Hare, John Ellis, 1933- joint author. 2.4805
Hare, Maud (Cuney), Mrs., 1874-1936. 1.4300
Hare-Mustin, Rachel T., 1928-. 5.4818
Hare, P. G. 4.2351
Hare, R. M. (Richard Mervyn) 1.1451, 1.1462
Hare, Richard. 2.1509, 4.5369
Hare, William F. 4.10173
Haren, Michael. 1.351
Haresign, William. 5.5449
Haresnape, Geoffrey, 1939-. 2.10093
Hareven, Tamara K. 4.3544
Hareven, Tamara K. ed. 4.5123
Harewood, George Lascelles, Earl of, 1923-.
  1.4509
Harget, Alan John, joint author. 5.2821
Hargreaves, John D. 3.5316, 3.5329-3.5330,
  3.5376
Hargreaves, Mary Wilma M. 5.5235
Hargrove, Erwin C. 4.7925
Harihārānanda Āranya, Swami. 1.205
Häring, Bernhard. 1.1471, 1.3205
Haring, Clarence Henry, 1885-1960. 3.8982,
  3.9210
Haring, Douglas Gilbert, 1894-. 4.393
Harington, John, Sir, 1560-1612. 2.4960, 2.6483
Harkabi, Yehoshafat, 1921-. 3.3867-3.3869
Harkess, Shirley. 4.3244
Harkins, Craig. 5.5506
Harkins, Paul Donal, 1904-. 3.897
Harkins, William Edward. 2.1410, 2.1653,
  2.1656
Harkness, Kenneth. 4.1071
Harlan, Louis R. 3.6853, 3.6855-3.6856
Harland, W. B. (Walter Brian), 1917-. 5.3085
Harle, James C. 1.5048, 1.5750

Harley, J. B. (John Brian) 4.235
Harley, Sharon. 3.6746
Harlow, Francis Harvey, 1928- joint author.
  3.5941
Harlow, George. 5.3016
Harlow, Harry Frederick, 1905-. 5.477
Harlow, Neal. 3.8605
Harlow, Nora. 4.10721
Harlow, Vincent Todd, 1898-. 3.1556, 4.8932
Harman, Avraham. ed. 3.3812
Harman, Gilbert. 1.1452
Harman, Gilbert. comp. 2.46
Harman, P. M. (Peter Michael), 1943-. 5.1933
Harman, Thomas L., 1942-. 4.9763
Harman, Willis W. 4.1719
Harmel, Robert, 1950-. 4.8155
Harmer, Bertha. 5.5167
Harmin, Merrill. joint author. 4.10315
Harmon, Austin Morris. ed. and tr. 2.380
Harmon, Maurice. 2.8936, 2.9779, 2.9852
Harmon, William, 1938-. 2.2348, 2.10735
Harms, Kathy. 3.2323
Harms, Robert W., 1946-. 4.4246
Harnack, Adolf von, 1851-1930. 1.2260, 1.2296,
  1.2743
Harned, Frederic T., ed. 3.3024
Harner, James L. 5.7962
Harnish, Robert M. joint author. 2.67
Harold, Charles Frederick, ed. 1897-1948.
  2.6264
Harootunian, Berj. 4.10703
Harootunian, Harry D., 1929-. 3.4951
Haroutunian, Joseph, 1904-. 1.2523, 1.2764
Harper & Row. 1.2506
Harper & Row, Publishers. 2.1101
Harper, Charles. joint author. 1.4620
Harper, Charles A. 5.6910
Harper, Donald Victor, 1927-. 4.3881
Harper, Douglas A. 4.6628
Harper, Fowler V. (Fowler Vincent), 1897-1965.
  4.9515
Harper, George McLean, 1863-1947. 2.8312
Harper, George Mills. 2.8350, 5.666
Harper, Howard M. 2.10623
Harper, Ida Husted, 1851-1931. 4.8086
Harper, J. Russell. 1.4919, 1.5993, 1.5999
Harper, J. Russell. ed. 1.5998, 3.8660
Harper, John L. 5.3514, 5.3773
Harper, Lawrence Averell, 1901-. 4.3965
Harper, Michael J. K. 5.5054
Harper, Michael S. 2.10690, 2.11426, 2.13066
Harper, Paula. joint author. 1.6136
Harper, Ralph, 1915-. 2.3471
Harper, Wilhelmina. comp. 2.11054
Harpsfield, Nicholas, 1519-1575. 2.6496
Harré, Rom. 5.13, 5.449, 5.495, 5.768, 5.887,
  5.891-5.893, 5.985
Harrell, David Edwin. 1.2479, 1.3035
Harrell, Jean G. (Jean Gabbert), 1921- comp.
  1.1389
Harrier, Richard C., ed. 2.6220
Harries, Karsten. 1.5533
Harrigan, John J. 4.8858
Harriman, W. Averell (William Averell),
  1891-1986. 3.934
Harrington, Fred H. 5.3995
Harrington, James, 1611-1677. 4.7402
Harrington, John Peabody. 3.5859
Harrington, John Wilbur, 1918-. 5.837
Harrington, Michael, 1928-. 3.190, 4.1805,
  4.2097, 4.5152, 4.6513, 4.6932, 4.6954
Harris, Alan Edward, 1936-. 4.10270
Harris, Albert Josiah. 4.10346
Harris, Ann Sutherland. 1.4757
Harris, Ben M. 4.10668
Harris, Brice, ed. 2.6233
Harris, Bryan, 1936-. 5.5762
Harris, Carl M., 1940-. 5.5599
Harris, Carl Vernon, 1937-. 4.8864
Harris, Charles B. 2.10624, 2.12885
Harris, Chauncy D. 5.8201
Harris, Chauncy Dennison, 1914-. 4.2364,
  4.6263, 5.8202-5.8204
Harris, Curtis C. 4.2070
Harris, Cyril M., 1917-. 5.5745, 5.6051
Harris, D. J. (David John) 4.8966
Harris, Diana K. 5.8383
Harris, Edward G. 5.2154

Harris, Eileen. 1.6575
Harris, Enriqueta. 1.6300
Harris, Ernest E. 1.3450
Harris, Errol E. 1.953, 1.1100, 1.1268
Harris, Frank, 1855-1931. 2.7803, 2.8277
Harris, George Lawrence, 1910-. 3.3768, 3.4375
Harris, George Washington, 1814-1869. 2.11045
Harris, Grace Gredys, 1926-. 1.1862
Harris, H. S. (Henry Silton), 1926-. 1.943-1.944
Harris, Harold Arthur. 4.879, 4.930
Harris, Harry. 5.3428
Harris, Henry, 1925-. 5.3429
Harris, James E. 3.5144
Harris, Jane Gary. 2.1575
Harris, Janie Miller. 5.7867
Harris, Jesse W., 1900-. 2.6431
Harris, Joel Chandler, 1848-1908.
   2.11047-2.11048
Harris, John, 1931-. 1.5384, 1.5389
Harris, John Noel. 5.7054
Harris, John Richard. 3.5138
Harris, Joseph, 1951- joint author. 5.1577
Harris, Joseph Pratt, 1896-. 4.8046
Harris, Julia Florida (Collier) 1875-. 2.11051
Harris, Kenneth E., 1943-. 3.7015
Harris, Larry D. 5.3221
Harris, Laurie Lanzen. 2.2664
Harris, Leon A. 2.12484
Harris, Leonard, 1948-. 3.6627
Harris, Marshall Dees, 1903-. 4.2816
Harris, Marvin, 1927-. 3.9024, 3.9222,
   4.485-4.486, 4.503, 4.5159
Harris, Neil, 1938-. 4.1192
Harris, R. W. (Ronald Walter) 3.1500
Harris, Richard Colebrook. 4.2121, 4.2831
Harris, Richard Jackson. 5.297
Harris, Robert D. 4.4672
Harris, Robin Sutton, 1919-. 4.10101
Harris, Roy, 1931-. 2.99
Harris, Sara. 1.3345
Harris Semiconductor (Firm) 5.6524
Harris, Seymour Edwin, 1897-. 4.1378, 4.1888,
   4.1987, 4.4519
Harris, Sheldon. 1.3511
Harris, Sheldon H. 3.6820
Harris, Townsend, 1804-1878. 3.6460
Harris, Walter Edgar, 1915- joint author.
   5.2688
Harris, Wendell V. 2.6008, 2.7582
Harris, William Charles, 1933-. 3.8288-3.8289
Harris, William H., 1927- ed. 1.21
Harris, William Hamilton, 1944-. 4.3391, 4.3608
Harris, William J., 1942-. 2.12872
Harris, William Vernon. 3.2764
Harris, Wilson. 2.10027-2.10032
Harris, Zellig Sabbettai, 1909-. 2.134
Harrison, Ada M. 2.7443
Harrison, Barbara J. 5.8055
Harrison, Bennett. 4.3205, 4.6213
Harrison, Beverly Wildung, 1932-. 4.5698,
   4.5952
Harrison, Brian. 3.4395
Harrison, Brian Howard. 3.1583, 4.8509
Harrison, Charles. 1.4784, 1.4941
Harrison, D. (David). 3.5501, 5.6843
Harrison, Deborah Sears. 2.1157
Harrison, Dick, 1937-. 2.9887
Harrison, Frank Llewellyn, 1905-. 1.3509,
   1.3715
Harrison, Fraser. comp. 2.6091
Harrison, G. B. (George Bagshawe), 1894-.
   2.5867, 2.6081, 2.6696-2.6697, 2.6704, 2.6915
Harrison, George Russell, 1898-. 5.2312
Harrison, Gordon A. 5.4676
Harrison, Ian T. 5.2735
Harrison, J. F. C. (John Fletcher Clews)
   4.5326, 4.7163
Harrison, James P. 4.8745
Harrison, Jane Ellen, 1850-1928. 1.1369, 1.1655
Harrison, John A., joint ed. 3.5001
Harrison, Jonathan. 1.710
Harrison, Joseph, 1944-. 4.2413
Harrison, Martin, 1930- joint author. 3.2216
Harrison, Max. 1.4326
Harrison, Michael A. 5.1373
Harrison, Paul Mansfield. 3.3320
Harrison, Peter, 1946 Oct. 16-. 5.3941
Harrison, Richard John, 1920-. 5.3979

Harrison, Ross. 1.724
Harrison, Roy M., 1948-. 5.6050
Harrison, Selig S. 3.3633
Harrison, Shuyen, joint author. 5.2735
Harrison, Sydney Gerald. 5.3658, 5.3695
Harrison, Thomas Perrin, 1897-. 2.3753
Harriss, G. L. 4.4668
Harriss, John. 4.2766
Harrisson, John A. C. 4.3304
Harrod, Leonard Montague, 1905-. 5.7696
Harrod, Roy Forbes, Sir, 1900-. 1.1184, 4.1349
Harrold, Charles Frederick, 1897-1948. 1.2231,
   1.3204, 2.7547, 2.7556
Harrop, John, 1932-. 2.3108
Harry, John E., 1940-. 5.5947
Harry, Joseph. 4.5529
Harry S. Truman Library. Institute for
   National and International Affairs. 3.5028,
   3.7808
Harry Steenbock Symposium. 5th, Madison,
   Wis., 1975. 5.3761
Harss, Luis, 1936-. 2.5302
Hart, Clive. 2.8872, 2.8891
Hart-Davis, Rupert. 2.7958, 2.8272, 2.9462
Hart, Donn Vorhis, 1918-. 3.4596, 4.684
Hart, Francis Russell. 2.9840
Hart, George L. 2.2281
Hart, H. L. A. (Herbert Lionel Adolphus),
   1907-. 4.9366, 4.9368
Hart, Hastings Hornell, 1851-1932. 4.6867
Hart, Ivor Blashka, 1889-. 5.822
Hart, James David, 1911-. 2.10233, 3.8598,
   5.7687
Hart, John, 1948-. 2.1026, 4.896
Hart, John M. (John Mason), 1935-. 4.7193
Hart, Joseph Truman, 1937-. 5.4862
Hart, Michael H. 5.1726
Hart, Moss, 1904-1961. joint author. 2.11944
Hart, Philip, 1914-. 1.3767, 1.4196
Hart, Robert A. 4.3141
Hart, Thomas R. 2.5211
Hart, Wilson R. 4.3510
Harte, Bret, 1836-1902. 2.11054
Harte, Kathleen M. 4.4116
Harte, N. B. 4.3850
Härtel, Herbert. 1.5185
Harter, Stephen P. joint author. 5.7604
Hartford, Robert. 1.4054
Harth, Dorothy E., comp. 2.10682
Harth, Erich. 5.4352
Harth, Phillip, 1926-. 2.7295
Harthan, John P. 1.6427
Hartigan, Richard Shelly. 5.7164
Hartjen, Clayton A 1943-. 4.6901
Hartl, Daniel L. 3.3418, 5.3472
Hartley, F. R. 5.2893
Hartley, L. P. (Leslie Poles), 1895-1972. 2.8797
Hartley, Marsden, 1877-1943. 1.5941
Hartman, Ann. 4.6543, 4.6557
Hartman, Chester W. 4.3487
Hartman, Geoffrey H. 2.2470, 2.2646, 2.2662,
   2.7829, 2.8319
Hartman, Robert W. 4.7986
Hartman, Robert W. joint author. 4.10652
Hartman, Tom, 1935-. 4.119, 4.121
Hartmann, Cyril Hughes, 1896-. 2.7098
Hartmann, Ernest. 5.657
Hartmann, Heidi I. 4.3260
Hartmann, Heinz, 1894-. 5.160, 5.197
Hartmann, Hudson Thomas, 1914-. 5.5318
Hartmann, R. R. K. 2.12
Hartmann, Susan M. 4.6020
Hartmann, von Aue, 12th cent. 2.13531-2.13533
Hartmann, William K. 5.1787
Hartness-Kane, Ann. 5.7905
Hartnett, J. P. (James P.) joint author. 5.2267
Hartnoll, Phyllis. 2.3088
Hartog, Howard, 1913-. 1.3671
Hartog, Joseph. 5.438
Hartree, Douglas R. (Douglas Rayner),
   1897-1958. 5.2162
Hartshorn, J.E. 4.3759
Hartshorne, Charles, 1897-. 1.1592-1.1593,
   1.2828
Hartshorne, Richard, 1899-. 4.14-4.15
Hartshorne, Thomas S. 3.6117
Hartsock, Nancy C. M. 4.4903
Hartt, Frederick. 1.5001, 1.5535, 1.6211

Hartwig, Gerald W. 5.4682
Hartwig, Joan. 2.6735
Hartz, Louis, 1919-. 3.6276
Harvard College Library. Dept. of Printing and
   Graphic Arts. 1.5325
Harvard Law Review Association. 4.9472
Harvard Law School. International Tax
   Program. 4.4707
Harvard University. 4.10898
Harvard University. Center for Criminal
   Justice. 4.6884
Harvard University. Center for European
   Studies. 4.3413
Harvard University. Center for International
   Affairs. 3.2196, 3.3787, 3.5000, 3.5513,
   3.9000, 4.1770, 4.2519, 4.7219, 4.8275,
   4.8799, 4.9052, 4.9249, 4.9321, 5.7160
Harvard University. Center for the Study of
   World Religions. 1.1717
Harvard University. Committee on Regional
   Studies. 3.4611
Harvard university. Committee on the
   objectives of a general education in a free
   society. 4.10005
Harvard University. Council on East Asian
   Studies. 3.4987, 4.2560
Harvard University. Dept. of Romance
   Languages andLiteratures. 2.3938
Harvard University. East Asian Research
   Center. 2.2151, 3.4611
Harvard University. Graduate School of
   Business Administration. 4.3715
Harvard University. Graduate School of
   Business Administration. Division of
   Research. 4.3015, 4.3033, 4.4429
Harvard University. Harvard Economic
   Research Project. 4.1937
Harvard University. Library. Dept. of Graphic
   Arts. 1.5827, 1.5828
Harvard University. Russian Research Center.
   3.3173
Harvard-Yenching Institute. 2.2030
Harvey, A. D. (Arnold D.) 2.5811
Harvey, A. E. (Anthony Ernest) 1.2882
Harvey, A. McGehee (Abner McGehee), 1911-.
   5.4520, 5.4753
Harvey, Barbara F. 3.1372
Harvey, Daniel Cobb, 1886-. 3.8808
Harvey, David, 1935-. 4.1527, 4.6294
Harvey, Godfrey Eric, 1889-. 3.4339
Harvey, Joan M. 5.7715, 5.8432
Harvey, John F. 5.6616
Harvey, John G. 4.332
Harvey, John Hooper. 1.5231, 1.5529, 5.7085
Harvey, Milton. 4.17
Harvey, Nigel, 1916-. 5.5299
Harvey, Paul, Sir, 1869-1948. 2.3823, 2.5485,
   3.2508
Harvey, Van Austin. 1.2249
Harvey, W. J. (William John), 1925-1967.
   2.7708
Harvey, William, 1578-1657. 5.4139, 5.4226
Harvie, Christopher, 1944-. 3.1808
Harvie, Christopher T. 3.1782
Harwell, Mark A. 5.7235
Harwell, Richard Barksdale. 2.12198
Harwin, Judith. 4.6636
Harwitz, Martin, 1931-. 5.1770
Harwitz, Mitchell, jt. author. 4.3932
Harwood, Alan. 5.4661
Harwood, John L. 5.3764
Harwood, John T. 2.5907
Hasan, Parvez. 4.2561
Hasan, Parvez. joint author. 4.2529
Hasbrouck, Paul De Witt, 1896-. 4.8050
Haschemeyer, Audrey E. V., 1936- joint author.
   5.4404
Haschemeyer, Rudy Harm, 1930-. 5.4404
Hasebroek, Johannes, 1893-. 4.4093
Hašek, Jaroslav, 1883-1923. 2.1669-2.1670
Hasel, Gerhard F. 1.2578
Haselkorn, Avigdor. 3.3251
Hashman, Judy Devlin. 4.1041
Haskell, Ann S. (Ann Sullivan) comp. 2.6076
Haskell, Barbara. 1.5941, 1.6708
Haskell, Francis, 1928-. 1.4671, 1.5005, 1.5198
Haskell, Molly. 2.3014
Haskins, Charles Homer, 1870-1937. 2.809

Haskins, George Lee, 1915-. 4.9899
Haskins, James, 1941-. 2.1159
Haslam, Gerald W. 2.10676
Haslam, Gerald W. comp. 2.10468
Haslam, Robert H. A., 1936-. 5.5078
Hass, Hans-Egon, 1916-1969, ed. 2.13767
Hass, Robert. 2.2767, 2.13067-2.13068
Hassall, Christopher, 1912-1963. 2.8487
Hassan, Ihab Habib, 1925-. 2.2677, 2.10413,
    2.10625
Hasse, John Edward, 1948-. 1.4278
Hasse, L. 4.347
Hassell, Ulrich von, 1881-1944. 3.2388
Hassenstein, Bernhard. 5.998
Hassinger, Edward Wesley. 5.4687
Hassler, Warren W. 3.7329
Hassrick, Peter H. 1.4904
Hast, Adele. 3.5735
Håstad, Elis Wilhelm, 1900-1959. 4.8678
Hastie, W. (William), 1842-1903. tr. 5.1871
Hastings, Adrian. 1.2469
Hastings, James, 1852-1922. 1.1524, 1.2507
Hastings, Paul, 1933-. 5.6071
Hatch, Elvin. 4.476
Hatch, Evelyn Marcussen. 2.18
Hatch, F. H. (Frederick Henry), 1864-1932.
    5.3046
Hatch, James Vernon, 1928- comp. 2.10785
Hatch, Jane M. 4.873
Hatch, John Charles. 3.5089, 3.5526
Hatch, Stephan L., 1945-. 5.5328
Hatcher, Harlan Henthorne, 1898-. 2.7496,
    2.10626
Hatcher, John. joint author. 4.5305
Hatcher, John. 4.1693
Hatcher, William S. 1.2096
Hatfield, Charles William. 2.7439, 2.7457
Hatfield, Henry Caraway, 1912-. 2.13468,
    2.13583
Hatfield, Michael. 4.2290
Hathaway, Richard B., 1947- joint author.
    5.6637
Hathcock, John N. 5.4986
Hathorn, Richmond Yancey, 1917-. 2.268
Hathway, D. E. (David Ernest), 1919-. 5.708
Hatsopoulos, G. N. (George N.) 5.2246
Hatto, A. T. (Arthur Thomas) tr. 2.13535
Hatton, Ragnhild Marie. 3.174, 3.1544, 3.2033,
    3.3394, 4.8580
Hatzfeld, Helmut Anthony, 1892-. 2.5206
Hauberg, Clifford A. 3.9127
Hauck, Richard Boyd, 1936-. 2.10654
Hauerwas, Stanley, 1940-. 1.1469, 1.1473-1.1474
Hauff, Wilhelm, 1802-1827. 2.13597
Haugen, Einar Ingvald, 1906-. 2.28, 2.917,
    2.919
Haugh, Richard S. (Richard Stanley), 1942-.
    2.1637, 2.1641
Haugh, Robert F. 2.10079
Haughton, Rosemary. 4.820
Hau'ofa, Epeli. 4.5676
Hauptman, Laurence M. 3.5895
Hauptmann, Gerhart, 1862-1946. 2.13767
Haury, Emil W. (Emil Walter), 1904-. 3.5716
Hause, Steven C., 1942-. 4.8590
Hauser, Arnold, 1892-1978. 1.4630, 1.4763,
    1.5148, 1.6690
Hauser, John R. joint author. 4.4300
Häuser, Karl, joint author. 4.2340
Hauser, Philip Morris, 1909-. 4.1595, 4.1605,
    4.1612, 4.6194
Hauser, Robert Mason. 4.5242
Hauser, Ronald. 2.13557
Hauser, Stuart T. 5.599
Hausman, E. 4.132
Hausman, Jerome J. 1.6695
Haussman, Fay, 1922-. 4.10105
Hautala, Richard R. 5.6231
Havard, William C. 3.8120, 4.8245
Havelock, Eric Alfred. 2.56, 2.238, 2.708
Havely, N. R. 2.6317, 2.6352
Haveman, Robert H. 4.2104, 4.3220,
    4.3474-4.3475
Havens, George Remington, 1890-. 3.1963
Havens, Raymond Dexter, 1880-1954. 2.7156,
    2.8313
Havens, Thomas R. H. 1.6745, 3.1009, 4.2988
Haver, Ronald. 2.3067

Haverkamp Begemann, Egbert. 1.6250
Havers, John Alan, 1925- ed. 5.5669
Havick, John J. 4.4052
Havighurst, Robert James, 1900-. 3.5811,
    4.10769, 4.10775
Havighurst, Walter, 1901-. 3.8379
Haviland, Virginia, 1911-. 5.7717
Havlice, Patricia Pate. 1.3590, 1.4582, 5.8221,
    5.8269
Hawaii. University, Honolulu. Dept. of Ocean
    Engineering. 5.5973
Hawes, Donald. joint author. 2.8196
Hawisher, Margaret F. joint author. 4.10943
Hawke, David Freeman. 4.7425
Hawkes, Charles Francis Christopher, 1905-.
    3.114
Hawkes, David. 2.2154, 2.2184, 2.2233
Hawkes, Glenn Rogers, 1919- joint author.
    4.2061
Hawkes, J. F. B., 1942-. 5.2372
Hawkes, Jacquetta Hopkins, 1910-. 3.120,
    3.261, 3.3704, 4.694
Hawkes, John, 1925-. 2.11817-2.11818,
    2.13069-2.13071
Hawkes, Terence. 2.158
Hawkesworth, Celia, 1942-. 2.1209
Hawking, S. W. (Stephen W.) 5.1862
Hawkins, David, 1913-. 4.10174
Hawkins, Desmond, 1908- ed. 2.8959
Hawkins, Edward Kenneth. 4.2534
Hawkins, Frederick William, 1849-1900. 2.3362,
    2.3368
Hawkins, Gordon, 1919- joint author. 4.6845
Hawkins, Hugh. 4.10997
Hawkins, Joellen Watson. 5.485
Hawkins, John, Sir, 1719-1789. 1.3630
Hawkins, R. A. J. 3.1843
Hawkins, Robert G. 4.4566
Hawks, Francis L. (Francis Lister), 1798-1866.
    comp. 3.4880
Hawksworth, D. L. 5.3715
Hawley, Amos Henry. 4.4831, 4.6295
Hawley, Gessner Goodrich, 1905-. 5.2590,
    5.2592
Hawley, John Stratton, 1941-. 1.1717, 2.1878,
    2.1880
Hawley, Mones E. 5.6874
Hawley, Willis D. 4.10799
Haworth-Booth, Mark. 5.6924
Haworth, Mary (Robbins) 1911- joint editor.
    5.576
Haws, Duncan. 5.7500
Hawthorn, Audrey. 3.5902
Hawthorne, Don. 1.5673
Hawthorne, Nathaniel. 2.11056-2.11060,
    2.12048
Hawtrey, R. G. (Ralph George), 1879-. 4.4470
Hax, Arnoldo C. joint author. 5.1548
Hax, Arnoldo C. 5.7027
Haxthausen, August, Freiherr von, 1792-1866.
    3.3011
Hay, Alex. 4.1033
Hay, Denys. 3.390, 3.560, 3.603, 3.2847
Hay, Douglas. 4.6786
Hay, Eloise Knapp. 2.8567
Hay, James G., 1936-. 4.1050, 5.4276
Hay, John, 1838-1905. 3.7435
Hay, Malcolm. 2.9624
Hay, Margaret Jean. 4.6154, 4.9925
Hay, Richard. 4.6338
Hay, William Walter, 1908-. 5.5923, 5.6072
Haya de la Torre, Víctor Raúl, 1895-. 3.9307
Hayakawa, S. I. (Samuel Ichiyé), 1906-. 1.496,
    2.1066, 2.11080
Hayami, Yūjirō, 1932-. 4.2889
Hayashi, Hiroko, 1943- joint author. 4.3301
Haycraft, Howard. ed. 2.2681, 2.5559, 2.5697,
    2.10234
Haydar Mīrzā, 1499 or 1500-1551. 3.3620
Hayden, Dolores. 4.6054, 4.7155
Hayden, John O. comp. 2.5819, 2.8058
Hayden, Robert Earl. 2.11819, 2.11820
Hayden, Robert Earl. comp. 2.10752
Haydn, Hiram Collins, 1907-1973. 2.3712, 3.168
Haydn, Joseph, 1732-1809. 1.3893
Haydon, Benjamin Robert, 1786-1846. 2.7468
Haydon, Glen, 1896-1966. tr. 1.4471
Hayduk, Leslie Alec. 4.10415

Hayek, Friedrich A. von (Friedrich August),
    1899-. 1.729, 4.1269, 4.2774, 4.3484, 4.4471,
    4.4487, 4.7665
Hayek, Friedrich A. von (Friedrich August
    von), 1899-. 4.7666
Hayes, Carlton Joseph Huntley, 1882-1964.
    3.92, 3.712
Hayes, Cheryl D. 4.5652
Hayes, Eugene Nelson, 1920-. 4.10924, 5.1788
Hayes, Francis C., 1904-. 2.5208
Hayes, Grace P. joint author. 5.7258
Hayes, John T. 1.5801, 1.6031-1.6032, 1.6387,
    1.6490
Hayes, M. Vincent. 4.8451
Hayes, Michael T., 1949-. 4.7733
Hayes, Paul M. 3.1584, 3.3382
Hayes, Peter, 1946-. 3.2323
Hayes-Roth, Frederick. 5.1246
Hayes, Wayland J., 1917-. 5.4733
Hayes, William. joint author. 5.4447
Hayes, William. 5.4448
Hayford, Harrison. 2.11148, 2.11150, 2.11155
Hayhurst, George. 5.5579
Hayim, Gila J., 1938-. 1.852
Haykal, Muhammad Hasanayn. 3.5163
Haykal, Muhammad Husayn, 1888-1956. 1.2013
Haykin, Simon S., 1931-. 5.6348, 5.6364, 5.6512
Hayman, David. joint author. 2.8891
Hayman, Ronald, 1932-. 1.1052, 2.3182, 2.4384,
    2.12178, 2.13708-2.13709
Hayne, Paul Hamilton, 1830-1886. 2.11075
Haynes, Frederick Emory, 1868-. 4.8156
Haynes, John Earl. 3.8500
Haynes, R. Brian. 5.4583
Haynes, Robert H., 1931- joint comp. 5.3490
Haynes, Robert V. 3.8335
Haynes, Williams, 1886-1960. 5.6811
Hays, H. R. (Hoffman Reynolds), 1904-. 4.472
Hays, Samuel P. 4.1900, 4.1910
Hayt, William Hart, 1920-. 5.6270
Hayter, Earl W. 5.5236
Hayward, Arthur Lawrence, 1885-1967. 2.856
Hayward, Charles Harold, 1898-. 1.6573
Hayward Gallery. 1.4934, 1.4973, 1.4978,
    1.5946, 1.6460
Hayward, Helena. 5.7071
Hayward, Helena. ed. 1.6554
Hayward, John, 1905-1965. ed. 2.6172, 2.7072
Hayward, Max. joint ed. 2.1297
Hayward, Max. 2.1270, 4.9918
Hayward, Philip Henry Cecil. 5.7171
Haywood, Big Bill, 1869-1928. 4.3586
Haywood, Charles, 1904-. 5.8197
Haywood, Harry, 1898-. 4.6999
Haywood, R. W. (Richard Wilson) 5.2260
Hazan, Marcella. 5.7137
Hazard, John N. (John Newbold), 1909-. 4.8651
Hazard, Lucy Lockwood, 1890-. 2.10347
Hazard, Paul, 1878-1944. 1.436, 3.644
Hazel, Joseph E., 1933-. 5.3130
Hazen, Margaret Hindle. joint author. 5.8219
Hazen, Robert M., 1948-. 5.2995, 5.8219
Hazlehurst, Cameron, 1941-. 3.5582
Hazlitt, William, 1778-1830. 2.5526, 2.5538,
    2.5766, 2.6801, 2.7804-2.7807
Hazlitt, William Carew, 1834-1913. ed. 2.6218
Hazon, Mario, 1885-. 2.859
H'Doubler, Margaret Newell, 1889-. 4.1091
Head, Bessie, 1937-. 2.10080-2.10081
Head, C. Grant, 1939-. 4.142
Head, Joseph. 1.1619
Head, K. H. 5.5910
Head, Sydney W. 2.2857, 4.4055, 4.4059
Headey, Bruce W. 4.8449
Headlam, Walter George, 1866-1908. 2.407
Headrick, Daniel R. 4.7534
Heady, Earl Orel, 1916- joint author. 4.2936
Heady, Ferrel. 4.7757
Heal, G. M. joint author. 4.1769
Heal, O. W. joint author. 5.3509
Heal, O. W. 5.3276, 5.3570
Heald, James E. 4.10504
Heald, Morrell. 4.2711
Heale, M. J. 4.7949
Healey, F. G. 2.865
Healey, George Harris, ed. 2.6975
Health Education Foundation (Washington,
    D.C.) 4.6639

Healy, Charles C. 4.4264
Healy, Paul F. 3.7693
Healy, Raymond J., ed. 2.3723
Healy, Timothy J. 5.6284
Heaney, Seamus. 2.9702-2.9704
Heard, Alexander. 3.8160, 4.8108, 4.8128
Heard-Bey, Frauke, 1941-. 3.4059
Hearder, Harry. 3.2834
Hearn, Charles R. 3.6118
Hearn, Lafcadio, 1850-1904. 2.4206,
   2.11076-2.11077, 3.4881
Hearn, M. F. (Millard Fillmore), 1938-. 1.5643
Hearn, Maxwell K. 1.6672
Hearn, Michael Patrick. 2.7631, 2.10941
Hearne, John, 1925-. 2.9994-2.9995
Hearne, Samuel, 1745-1792. 3.8842
Hearst, Eliot Sanford, 1932-. 5.204
Heath, A. F. (Anthony Francis) 4.8503
Heath-Brown, D. R. 5.1339
Heath, Douglas H. 4.10034, 4.10723
Heath, Dwight B. 5.8437
Heath, Dwight B. ed. 4.5252
Heath, G. Louis. 3.6699
Heath, Jeffrey. 2.9505
Heath, Jim F. 3.7841
Heath, Peter Lauchlan, 1922-. 1.923, 1.1206
Heath, Shirley Brice. 2.209, 4.10393
Heath, Stephen. 2.2339
Heath-Stubbs, John Francis Alexander, 1918-.
   2.5828, 2.6188
Heath, Thomas Little, Sir, 1861-1940. 5.1078,
   5.1102
Heath, William Webster, 1929-. 2.6092, 2.8482
Heather, Nick. 4.6644, 5.4961
Heaton, Herbert, 1890-. 3.497
Heaviside, Oliver, 1850-1925. 5.2369
Hebb, D. O. (Donald Olding) 5.205, 5.4309
Hebbel, Friedrich, 1813-1863. 2.13598-2.13599
Hebblethwaite, Peter. 1.3161
Hebel, Johann Peter, 1760-1826. 2.13602
Hebel, John William, 1891-1934, ed. 2.6082,
   2.6471
Heber, Reginald, 1783-1826. 3.4163
Heberle, Rudolf, 1896-. 4.5089
Hébert, Anne. 2.4815-2.4816
Hébert, Arthur Gabriel, 1886- tr. 1.2874
Hébert, Ernest. 2.13076
Hébert, Robert F. 4.1558
Hébert-Stevens, François, 1922-. 1.4854
Hechinger, Fred M. 4.10035
Hechinger, Grace. joint author. 4.10035
Hecht, Anthony, 1923-. 2.13077-2.13079
Hecht, Ben, 1893-1964. 2.11822-2.11825
Hecht, Hans, 1876-. 2.7505
Hecht, Jeff. 5.5948, 5.7392
Hecht, Marie B. 3.7000
Hecht, N. L. (Norman L.) 5.6037
Hechter, Michael. 3.1248
Heck, Shirley F. 4.10528
Heckert, J. Brooks (Josiah Brooks), 1893-.
   4.4595
Heckman, Richard A. 5.6055
Heckscher, August, 1913-. 3.8040
Heckscher, Eli F. (Eli Filip), 1879-1952. 4.1323,
   4.2411
Heclo, Hugh. 4.4722, 4.5184, 4.5301, 4.7926,
   4.7981
Hecock, Donald Sumner, 1906- joint author.
   4.7774
Hector, L. C. (Leonard Charles) 3.1372
Hedberg, Hollis Dow, 1903-. 5.3134
Hedetniemi, S. T., joint author. 5.1178
Hedges, William D. 4.10906
Hedges, William L. 2.11096
Hedgpeth, Joel Walker, 1911-. 5.3823
Hedin, Naboth, 1884- joint ed. 3.6594
Hedlund, Gustav Arnold, 1904-. 5.1589
Hedlund, Stefan, 1953-. 4.2981
Hedrick, Basil Calvin, 1932- comp. 3.5759
Hedrick, Earle Raymond, 1876-1943, tr. 5.1111
Heemskerck, Martin van, 1498-1574. 1.5023
Heer, Friedrich, 1916-. 1.128, 3.601, 3.2251
Heer, John E. joint author. 5.6035
Heer, Nicholas. 1.2061
Heermance, J. Noel. 2.10928
Heertje, Arnold, 1934-. 4.1541
Hees-Stauthamer, Jellemieke C. (Jellemieke
   Christine), 1950-. 5.5067

Heezen, Bruce C. 4.337
Hefferlin, J. B. Lon. 4.10080
Heffernan, Barbara Duffy. 5.3130
Heffner, Roe-Merrill Secrist, 1892-. 2.180
Heflebower, Richard Brooks, 1903- ed. 4.1976
Heftmann, Erich. 5.2663
Hegedus, Louis S. joint author. 5.2779
Hegel, Georg Wilhelm Friedrich, 1770-1831.
   1.925-1.930, 1.932, 1.939-1.941, 1.992, 1.1546,
   1.4592, 3.477, 4.9362
Hegel, Robert E., 1943-. 2.2174
Hegel Society of America. 1.952, 4.7454
Hegemann, Werner, 1881-1936. 1.5581
Hegener, Karen C. 4.10627
Heggen, Thomas, 1919-1949. 2.11826
Heggie, Ian Graeme. 5.5924
Heginbotham, Stanley J. 4.8882
Hegner, Robert William, 1880-1942. joint
   author. 5.3833
Heiber, Helmut, 1924-. 3.2381
Heicklen, Julian. 5.2512
Heidbreder, Edna Francis, 1890-. 5.78
Heidcamp, William H., 1944-. 5.3491
Heidegger, Martin, 1889-1976. 1.915,
   1.988-1.994, 1.996, 1.1057, 1.1262, 1.1315,
   2.106, 2.2717
Heidel, Alexander, 1907-. 2.1768
Heiden, Konrad. 3.2373, 3.2401
Heidenheimer, Arnold J. 4.5184, 4.6468
Heider, Fritz, 1896-. 5.161, 5.452
Heighton, Elizabeth J. 4.4438
Heilbron, J. L. 5.1962
Heilbroner, Robert L. 3.201, 3.7576, 4.1315,
   4.1528-4.1529, 4.1751, 4.2775-4.2776
Heilbrun, Carolyn G., 1926-. 2.2407, 2.3448,
   4.5928
Heilbrunn, Otto. 5.7223
Heiler, Friedrich, 1892-1967. 1.2989
Heilig, Peggy, 1942-. 4.8854
Heilman, Arthur W. 4.10460, 4.10465
Heilman, Robert Bechtold, 1906-. 2.6664,
   2.6670
Heilmann, Klaus. 5.475
Heim, Karl, 1874-1958. 1.2774
Heim, Michael Henry. 1.2402
Heimert, Alan. joint author. 3.6278
Heimert, Alan. 1.2402
Heims, Steve J. 5.1088
Heimsath, Charles Herman, 1928-. 4.5422
Heine, Carl. 4.8829
Heine-Geldern, Robert, 1885-1968. 3.4577
Heine, Heinrich, 1797-1856. 2.13603-2.13605
Heineman, Benjamin W. 3.1289
Heineman, Helen, 1936-. 2.8243
Heineman, William R. 5.2691
Heinemann, Margot. 2.6640
Heinich, Robert. 4.10290
Heinl, Robert Debs, 1916-. 5.7478
Heinlein, Robert A. (Robert Anson), 1907-.
   2.11827-2.11829
Heinrich, E. William (Eberhardt William),
   1918-. 5.3040
Heinrich, Janet. joint author. 5.5207
Heins, Conrad P. 5.6079-5.6080
Heinz, Anne M. 4.6769
Heise, George William. 5.6324
Heisenberg, Werner. 5.894, 5.1911-5.1912,
   5.2019, 5.2062-5.2063, 5.2112
Heiser, F. A. (Francis A.) 5.5809
Heiserman, Arthur Ray, 1929-. 2.6519
Heisig, James W., 1944-. 1.1565
Heiskanen, Piltti. 4.7095
Heisler, Sanford I. 5.5670
Heiss, Jerold. comp. 4.5641
Heisserer, A. J. 3.2619
Heitland, William Emerton, 1847-1935. 3.2761
Heitler, Walter, 1904-. 5.2145, 5.2375
Heitner, Robert R. ed. 2.13506
Heitzmann, William Ray. comp. 4.10535
Heizer, Robert Fleming, 1915-. 3.5721, 3.5960,
   5.8100
Helbling, Robert E. 2.13625
Held, David. 4.4798
Held, Gilbert, 1943-. 5.1239
Held, Julius Samuel, 1905-. 1.4775, 1.5028,
   1.6272
Held, Michael. 5.6926
Helfer, Ray E. 4.6558

Hélias, Pierre Jakez. 3.2222
Hélin, Maurice. 2.810
Heliodorus, of Emesa. 2.474
Hell, Henri. 1.3947
Hellebust, Johan A. 5.3708
Heller, Agnes. 3.391
Heller, Celia Stopnicka. 3.3984
Heller, Francis Howard. 3.5028
Heller, Joseph. 2.13080-2.13082
Heller, Jules. 1.6467
Heller, Mark. 3.3870
Heller, Reinhold. 1.5717, 1.6285
Heller, Robert L. (Robert Leo), 1919- ed.
   5.2988
Heller, Walter W. 4.1999
Hellie, Richard. 3.3087, 4.6444
Hellman, Caroline J. C. 4.3802
Hellman, Geoffrey Theodore, 1907-. 5.691
Hellman, Lillian, 1905-. 2.11830-2.11833
Hellman, Peter. 3.1077
Hellman, Richard, 1913-. 4.3802
Hellman, Ronald G. 4.8343
Hellmann, Donald C., 1933-. 3.4413, 3.4981
Helm, Ernest Eugene. 1.3709
Helm, Lewis M., 1931-. 4.7987
Helm, MacKinley, 1896-. 1.5954, 1.6004
Helman, Edith. tr. 2.5118
Helmer, John. 4.6671
Helmer, Olaf, 1910-. 3.67
Helmholtz, Hermann Ludwig Ferdinand von,
   1821-1894. 1.4382, 5.4379
Helmholz, A. Carl, ed. 5.2031
Helmreich, Ernst Christian. 1.2454, 3.3527
Helmreich, Ernst Christian. ed. 3.1935
Helmreich, Jonathan E. 3.2970
Helmreich, Paul C. 3.861
Helmreich, Robert, joint author. 5.492
Helms, Christine Moss. 3.3778, 3.4054
Helms, Ronald N. 5.6338
Helper, Hinton Rowan, 1829-1909. 3.7251
Helson, Harry, 1898- ed. 5.106
Helterman, Jeffrey. 2.5858
Helton, Tinsley. ed. 3.163
Heltzel, Virgil B. (Virgil Barney), 1896- joint
   comp. 2.6225
Heltzel, Virgil Barney, 1896- joint comp. 2.6224
Hemenway, Robert E., 1941-. 2.11912
Hemingway, Ernest, 1899-1961. 2.3710,
   2.11835-2.11852, 4.1053
Hemingway, Gregory H., 1931-. 2.11859
Hemingway, Mary Welsh, 1908-. 2.11860
Hemleben, Sylvester John. 4.9109
Hemlow, Joyce. 2.6894, 2.6896
Hemmer, Joseph J. 4.9532-4.9533
Hemming, John, 1935-. 3.9198, 3.9284, 3.9296
Hemmings, F. W. J. (Frederick William John),
   1920-. 2.4141, 2.4347-2.4348
Hemmings, Ray. 4.11010
Hempel, Carl Gustav, 1905-. 5.896
Hempel, Eberhard, 1886-. 1.4927
Hempel, Rose. 1.6726
Hemphill, William Edwin, 1912-. 3.7069
Hempleman, H. V. 5.5023
Henao, Jesús María, 1870-. 3.9174
Henbest, Nigel. 5.1701
Hench, John B. 2.3594
Hendee, Clare W. (Clare Worden), 1908-.
   5.5423
Hendel, Charles William, 1890-. 1.702
Henderson, Alexander Morell, 1914-, tr. 4.1473
Henderson, Algo Donmyer, 1897-. 4.10542
Henderson, Bill, 1941-. 2.10662, 5.7576
Henderson, Gail, 1949-. 5.4712
Henderson, George, 1931-. 1.4740, 1.4754,
   5.4662
Henderson, Gregory. 3.5000
Henderson, Harold Gould. ed. and tr. 2.2027
Henderson, Harry B. 2.10553
Henderson, Hazel. 4.1786
Henderson, James Mitchell, 1929-. 4.1434
Henderson, Jeff, 1943-. 2.13035
Henderson, Jeffrey. 2.300
Henderson, John Cleaves. 4.10735
Henderson, John S. 3.9038
Henderson, John William, 1910-. 3.4518
Henderson, Lawrence W., 1921-. 3.5405
Henderson, Lenneal J. comp. 3.6669
Henderson, Lenneal J. 3.6711

Henderson, Mary C., 1928-. 2.3223
Henderson, Nevile, Sir, 1882-1942. 3.925
Henderson, Peter, 1944-. 5.1180
Henderson, Philip, 1906-. 2.7966, 2.8138
Henderson, Robert M. 2.3048
Henderson, Stephen Evangelist, 1925- comp. 2.10753
Henderson, Suzanne Elizabeth. 5.7646
Henderson, Virginia. 5.5167, 5.5172, 5.8292
Henderson, W. O. (William Otto), 1904-. 4.1362, 4.2339, 4.8931
Hendley, Brian Patrick, 1939-. 4.9960
Hendrick, Burton Jesse, 1870-1949. 3.7277
Hendrick, George. joint author. 5.7810
Hendricks, Evan. 4.7916
Hendricks, Gordon. 1.5919, 1.5934, 1.5945, 5.7001
Hendricks, King, 1900-. 2.12029
Hendricks, Rhoda A. 1.1599
Hendrickson, John Raymond, ed. 2.7053
Hendriksen, Eldon S. comp. 4.4393
Hendry, John, 1952-. 5.2009
Heneman, Herbert Gerhard, 1944-. 4.4364
Hengel, Martin. 1.2849, 1.2920
Henifin, Mary Sue, 1953-. 5.4199, 5.5016
Henig, Jeffrey R., 1951-. 4.7873
Henig, Ruth B. (Ruth Beatrice) 4.9185
Henig, Stanley. 4.8374
Henige, David P. 3.442, 3.5060
Henin, R. A. 4.1711
Heninger, S. K. 5.7976
Henke, Frederick Goodrich, 1876-. 1.175
Henkenius, Mary Catherine. 2.2022
Henker, Barbara A. 5.5113
Henkin, Louis. 4.7633, 4.9030, 4.9388
Henkle, Roger B. 2.5716
Henle, Mary, 1913-. 5.72
Henle, Paul, ed. 2.32
Henley, Ernest J. 5.7043
Henley, Ernest M. joint author. 5.2459
Henley, John Reese. joint author. 5.3011
Henley, Nancy. 2.128
Henley, William Ernest, 1849-1903. 2.7812
Henn, T. R. 2.8145
Hennecke, Edgar, 1865-1951, ed. 1.2735
Hennepin, Louis, 17th cent. 3.8298
Hennesey, James J. 1.3122, 1.3177
Hennessey, Timothy M. 4.334
Hennessy, Alistair. 3.8983
Hennig, Ingo. 5.6825
Henning, Charles N. 4.4567
Henri, Florette. joint author. 3.841
Henrici, Arthur Trautwein, 1889-1943. 5.3725
Henriksen, Soren W. 5.5829
Henriksen, Thomas H. 3.5306-3.5307
Henríquez Ureña, Pedro, 1884-1946. 3.8968
Henry, Alexander, 1739-1824. 3.8434
Henry Art Gallery. 3.5882
Henry, Desmond Paul. 1.1159
Henry, DeWitt. 2.10848
Henry E. Huntington Library and Art Gallery. 2.7192
Henry Francis du Pont Winterthur Museum. 1.6563-1.6564, 1.6630, 1.6707
Henry, Françoise. 1.4945
Henry, George William, 1889-. 5.4806
Henry, Joseph, 1797-1878. 5.701
Henry, Jules, 1904-1969. 4.5153, 4.5642, 4.10175, 4.10245
Henry-Labordère, A. 5.5580
Henry, Laurin L. 3.7526
Henry, Louis, writer on demography. 4.1615
Henry, Merton G. 5.7144
Henry, O., 1862-1910. 2.11211
Henry, Patrick, 1939-. 1.2635
Henry, Robert E. 1.4504
Henry, the Minstrel, fl. 1470-1492. 2.9843
Henryson, Robert, 1430?-1506? 2.6386
Henshaw, Edmund Lee, ed. 3.6302
Henshaw, Richard, 1945-. 4.1017
Henshaw, Richard A. (Richard Aurel), 1921-. 2.1767
Hensher, David A., 1947-. 4.3913
Hensley, Jeannine, ed. 2.10864
Henson, Hilary. 2.15
Henthorn, William E. 3.4997
Hentoff, Nat. comp. 1.4327
Heper, Metin. 4.8771

Hepler, Susan Ingrid. 4.10469
Heppenheimer, T. A., 1947-. 5.6615
Hepple, Alexander, 1904-. 3.5474
Hepple, B. A. 4.3518
Hepworth, Barbara, Dame, 1903-1975. 1.5694
Heraclitus, of Ephesus. 1.236-1.237, 2.372
Herald, Earl Stannard. 5.3907
Héraucourt, Will. joint author. 2.1191
Herberg, Will. 1.1867, 1.1964
Herbert, Arthur Sumner. 1.2612
Herbert, David. 1.3455
Herbert, Eugenia W. 1.4631, 4.651
Herbert, Eugenia W. joint author. 3.6992
Herbert F. Johnson Museum of Art. 1.5910
Herbert, Frank. 2.13084
Herbert, George, 1593-1633. 2.6156, 2.7060-2.7061, 2.7069
Herbert, Gilbert. 5.6094
Herbert, Henry, Sir, 1595-1673. 2.3296
Herbert, Jean, 1897-. 1.1837
Herbert, Miranda C. 5.8112
Herbert, Nick. 5.2132
Herbert of Cherbury, Edward Herbert, Baron, 1583-1648. 2.6485
Herbert, Robert L., 1929-. 1.4808, 1.4978, 1.5135, 1.6056
Herbert, Sandra. 5.3193
Herbert, T. Walter (Thomas Walter), 1938-. 2.11157
Herbert, Zbigniew. 2.1740
Herberts, Kurt. 1.6344
Herbig, Katherine L. (Katherine Lydigsen) 5.7221
Herbst, Josephine, 1897-1969. 2.11867
Herd, Harold, 1893-. 2.3681
Herdeck, Donald E., 1924-. 2.2300, 2.2693
Herdeck, Margaret, 1949-. 2.2693
Herder, Johann Gottfried, 1744-1803. 2.13610, 3.478
Herdt, Gilbert H., 1949-. 4.671, 4.679, 4.682
Heredia, José-Maria de, 1842-1905. 2.4232
Herf, Jeffrey, 1947-. 3.2367
Herford, C.H. 2.6587
Herford, Julius, joint comp. 1.4500
Hering, Ewald, 1834-1918. 5.4383
Herington, C. J. 2.295, 2.297
Heriot, Angus, 1927-. 1.3762
Héritier, Jean, 1892-. 3.2015
Herity, Michael. 4.735
Herken, Gregg, 1947-. 3.1166, 5.7271
Herlihy, David. 3.2951-3.2952, 4.2359
Herlihy, David. comp. 3.131
Herling, John. 4.3384
Herma, John Leonard, 1911-, jt. author. 5.7414
Herman, Donald L. 4.8354
Herman, Herbert. ed. 5.5767
Herman, Judith Lewis, 1942-. 4.5515
Herman, Kali. 4.5997
Herman, Lewis Helmar, 1905-. 2.1142, 2.3130
Herman, Marguerite Shalett, joint author. 2.1142, 2.3130
Herman, Valentine. 4.7727, 4.8363
Hermand, Jost. 2.13604
Hermann, Charles F., 1938-. 4.8996
Hermann, Dan. joint author. 4.149
Hermann, Henry R. 5.3870
Hermann, Janet Sharp. 3.8293
Hermannsson, Halldór, 1878-. 2.13972-2.13973
Hermassi, Elbaki. 4.1806
Hermens, Ferdinand Aloys, 1906-. 4.7744
Hermet, Guy. 4.8683
Hermey, Carl. 2.3923
Hermon Dunlap Smith Center for the History of Cartography. 4.222
Hernandez, Donald J. 4.5686
Hernández, José, 1834-1886. 2.5391
Hernmarck, Carl, 1901-. 1.6659
Hernton, Calvin C. 3.6670
Hero, Alfred O. 4.9058
Herodian. 2.369
Herodotus. 2.370, 3.545
Herold, J. Christopher. 3.2075
Heron, Robert, 1764-1807. 2.7505
Herp, Anthony. 5.2762
Herpy, Miklós. 5.6532
Herr, Richard. 3.2061, 3.3447
Herrick, Allison Butler. 3.5285, 3.5292, 3.5403
Herrick, Francis Herkomer, 1900-. 4.9066

Herrick, Marvin Theodore, 1899-. 2.2819, 2.4884
Herrick, Robert, 1591-1674. 2.7070-2.7072
Herrick, Samuel, 1911-. 5.6717
Herrick, Virgil E., ed. 4.10477
Herrick, Virgil E. 4.10439
Herring, Edward Pendleton, 1903-. 4.7816, 4.7892, 4.8174
Herring, George C., 1936-. 3.4494, 3.4500, 3.9051
Herring, Harriet Laura. 4.5199
Herring, Helen Baldwin, joint author. 3.8984
Herring, Hubert Clinton, 1889-. 3.8984
Herring, Jack W., 1925-. 2.7471
Herring, Richard. 4.4463, 4.4601
Herrmann, Albert, 1886-1945. 4.182
Herrmann, Claudine, 1926-. 2.4298
Herrmann, Eleanor Krohn. 5.5160
Herrmann, Luke. 1.6041, 1.6360
Herrmann, Siegfried, 1926-. 1.2581
Herron, R. E. 5.553
Hersch, Paul. 5.6329
Hersen, Michel. 5.456
Hersey, John, 1914-. 2.11868-2.11869, 2.13006, 3.1011, 3.7799
Hersey, Paul. 4.2695
Hersh, Blanche Glassman, 1928-. 4.6029
Hersh, Jacques. joint author. 4.2562
Hersh, Reuben, 1927- joint author. 5.1032
Hersh, Richard H., 1942-. 4.10273
Hershbell, Jackson P., 1935-. 2.56
Hershberg, Theodore. 4.5215
Hershenson, Maurice. joint author. 5.247
Hershey, Alan M. joint author. 4.7868
Herskovits, Frances (Shapiro), 1897- joint author. 4.815
Herskovits, Melville J. (Melville Jean), 1895-1963. 3.6782, 4.419, 4.524, 4.530, 4.815
Herstein, I. N. 5.1112, 5.1269
Herstein, Sheila R. 5.7899
Hertz, Heinrich Rudolph, 1857-1894. 5.2358
Hertz, Joseph H. (Joseph Herman), 1872-1946. 1.1979
Hertzberg, Arthur. 3.3957
Hertzberg, Hans Wilhelm, 1895-. 1.2600
Hertzberg, Richard W., 1937-. 5.5789
Hertzberg, Steven. 3.8271
Herubin, Charles A., 1931-. 5.5821
Hervey of Ickworth, John Hervey, Baron, 1696-1743. 3.1545
Herwig, Holger H. 3.769, 3.2258, 5.7476
Herz, Gerhard, 1911-. 1.3778
Herz, Judith Scherer. 2.8661
Herzberg, Gerhard, 1904-. 5.2302-5.2303
Herzen, Aleksandr, 1812-1870. 3.702, 3.3118-3.3119
Herzfeld, Michael, 1947-. 4.794, 4.5835
Herzog, Chaim, 1918-. 3.3856, 3.3938
Heschel, Abraham Joshua, 1907-1972. 1.1547, 1.1966, 1.1980, 1.1988, 1.2610
Heschel, Susannah. 1.1987
Heselhaus, Clemens, ed. 2.13560
Heseltine, Janet E., ed. 2.3823
Heseltine, Michael, tr. 2.683
Heseltine, Nigel. 3.5310
Hesiod. 2.311, 2.371, 2.478-2.480
Heskett, Louise. 5.692
Hess, Andrew C. 3.5195
Hess, Beth B., 1928-. 4.6048
Hess, Kären M., 1939- joint author. 5.5680
Hess, Linda. 2.1885
Hess, Robert D. 4.5733, 4.10404
Hess, Thomas B. 1.5869, 5.6930
Hess, Thomas B. ed. 1.5193
Hess, Thomas B. 1.5795, 1.5933
Hess, Wilmot N. 5.2539
Hesse-Biber, Sharlene Janice. 4.3280
Hesse, Everett Wesley, 1908-. 2.5165
Hesse, Hermann, 1877-1962. 2.13769-2.13778
Hesse, M. G. (Marta Gudrun) 2.4825
Hesse, Mary B. 1.1182, 5.895
Hesse, Richard, 1868-1944. 5.3814
Hesseltine, William Best, 1902-1963. 3.7312-3.7313, 3.7398
Hester, Thomas R. joint author. 5.8100
Heston, Alan W. 4.1401
Hetherington, John Aikman, 1907-. 2.10157
Hetrick, David L., 1927-. 5.2445

Hett, Walter Stanley, tr. 2.337, 2.339, 2.351
Heurgon, Jacques. 3.2762
Heusch, Luc de. 4.563
Heuser, Alan. 2.7830
Heuss, Alfred, 1909-. 3.522
Heuvel, Jacques van den. ed. 2.4101
Heuvel, Jacques van den. 2.4103
Hevener, Fillmer. 4.10536
Hewing, Geoffrey J. D. 4.6361
Hewison, Robert, 1943-. 2.5742
Hewitt, Barnard Wolcott, 1906-. 2.3158, 2.3189
Hewitt, Cecil Rolph. 2.8968
Hewitt, Edwin, 1920-. 5.1552
Hewitt, Emily C. 1.3005
Hewitt, Eric John. 5.3754
Hewitt, G. F. (Geoffrey Frederick) 5.5752
Hewitt, George R. 3.1797
Hewitt, James Robert. 2.4665
Hewitt, Nancy A., 1951-. 4.6077
Hexter, J. H. (Jack H.), 1910-. 3.392, 3.412, 3.1469
Hey, Donald Holroyde. ed. 5.2593
Hey, J. S. 5.1782
Heyck, Thomas William, 1938-. 3.1590
Heyden, A. A. M. van der. ed. 3.2518
Heyden, Doris. 3.8897
Heydenreich, Ludwig Heinrich, 1903-. 1.5431, 1.6214, 5.5547
Heydenryk, Henry. 1.5199
Heyel, Carl, 1908-. 4.2635
Heyen, William, 1940-. 2.10773
Heyer, Anna Harriet, 1909-. 1.3551
Heyerdahl, Thor. 3.5623, 3.9270
Heyman, Neil M. 3.769
Heyman, R. P. (Robert Pieter), 1952-. 5.3822
Heymann, C. David (Clemens David), 1945-. 2.12343
Heymann, Frederick Gotthold, 1900-. 3.1910-3.1911, 3.1913
Heymann, Hans, 1920-. 4.2405
Heyward, Du Bose, 1885-1940. 2.11870-2.11871
Heywood, John, 1497?-1580? 2.6584
Heywood, Thomas, d. 1641. 2.6585
Heyworth, Peter, 1921-. 1.4101
Hezel, Francis X. 3.5629
Hiatt, Suzanne R., joint author. 1.3005
Hibbard, G. R. (George Richard), 1915-. 2.6497
Hibbard, Howard, 1928-. 1.5442, 1.5641, 1.5726, 1.6197
Hibbeler, R. C. 5.5736, 5.5740, 5.5840
Hibbert, Christopher, 1924-. 3.1630, 3.4277
Hibbett, Howard. 2.2010, 2.2029
Hick, John. 1.1548
Hick, John Harwood, 1922-. 1.2844
Hickerson, Harold, 1923-. 3.5856
Hickey, Gerald Cannon, 1925-. 3.4387, 3.4460-3.4461, 3.4475
Hickey, John T. 5.8060
Hickey, Joseph E. 4.6896
Hickling, Charles Frederick. 5.5470
Hickman, C. J. joint author. 5.3181
Hickman, Cleveland P. joint author. 5.3801
Hickman, Cleveland Pendleton, 1895-. 5.3801, 5.4153
Hickman, Janet. 4.10469
Hickman, Money L., joint author. 1.5881
Hickok, Lorena A. 4.1959
Hicks, Anthony. 1.3888
Hicks, David, 1939-. 3.4559
Hicks, David V. 4.10820
Hicks, James O. 5.5608
Hicks, John Donald, 1890-. 3.7733, 4.1960, 4.8228
Hicks, John Richard, Sir, 1904-. 4.1435-4.1437, 4.1490, 4.1530, 4.1724, 4.3130
Hicks, Joseph Junior. 5.6700
Hicks, Robert Drew, 1850-1929, tr. 2.363
Hicks, Russell G. 5.6059
Hicks, Tyler Gregory, 1921-. 5.5713
Hicks, Ursula Kathleen (Webb), 1896-. 4.4670
Hiden, John W. 3.2364
Hidore, John J. 5.2564
Hiernaux, Jean. 4.652
Hiers, John T. 2.12648
Hiesinger, Kathryn B., 1943-. 5.5636
Higashi, Chikara. 4.4193

Higdon, Archie, 1905-. 5.5777
Higginbotham, A. Leon, 1928-. 4.9686
Higginbotham, Don. 3.6887, 3.6920, 4.159
Higgins, Benjamin Howard, 1912-. 4.1807
Higgins, David H. 2.4924
Higgins, Dick, 1938-. 2.13595
Higgins, Donald J. H., 1943-. 4.8872
Higgins, George V., 1939-. 2.13085
Higgins, Ian. 2.4657
Higgins, Jean. joint author. 4.1807
Higgins, John C., 1935-. 5.1030
Higgins, Loretta Pierfedeici. 5.485
Higgins, Paul C. 4.6602
Higgins, Raymond L. 5.471
Higgins, Rosalyn. 4.9254
Higgins, Trumbull. 3.915
Higginson, G. R. joint author. 5.6242
Higginson, Thomas Wentworth, 1823-1911. 3.7386
Higgs, Eric S. joint ed. 3.228
Higgs, Henry, 1864-1940. 4.1275, 4.1406
Higgs, Robert. 3.6736, 4.1923
Higgs, Robert J., 1932-. 2.10429
Higham, John. 3.393, 3.6211, 3.6516-3.6517, 4.4947
Higham, John. ed. 3.6210
Higham, Robin D. S. 5.7395, 5.7407, 5.7842, 5.7993, 5.8296
Higham, Thomas Farrant, 1890- ed. 2.317, 2.403
Highet, Gilbert, 1906-1978. 2.731, 2.801, 2.2573-2.2574, 2.2700, 2.3789, 3.2538, 4.10259, 4.10265
Highfill, Philip H. 2.3333, 2.6749
Highsaw, Robert Baker, 1917-. 4.9836
Highsmith, Patricia, 1921-. 2.13086
Highsmith, Richard Morgan, 1920-. 4.1901
Highwater, Jamake. 1.5992
Higman, B. W., 1943-. 4.6435
Higman, Charles. 3.2602
Higonnet, Margaret R. 2.3448
Higuchi, Ichiyō, 1872-1896. 2.2074
Higuchi, Takayasu. 4.742
Hilberg, Raul, 1926-. 3.1093-3.1094, 3.3990
Hilberry, Conrad. 2.6941
Hilbert, David. 1.1211, 5.1540, 5.1632, 5.1635
Hildebrand, George C. 4.5437
Hildebrand, George Herbert. 4.2355
Hildebrand, Joel Henry, 1881-. 5.2906, 5.2909
Hildebrand, Milton, 1918-. 5.4109
Hildebrandt, Darlene Myers. 5.8121
Hildreth, Gertrude Howell, 1898-. 4.10339, 4.10468
Hileman, Sam. 2.5341
Hilferding, Rudolf, 1877-1941. 4.1531
Hilgard, Ernest Ropiequet, 1904-. 4.10353, 5.107, 5.181, 5.295, 5.300
Hilgard, Henry R. joint author. 5.4195
Hill, Archibald A. 2.1, 2.992
Hill, Brian. ed. 2.7513
Hill, Brian E. 2.2972
Hill, Brian W. 4.7418, 4.8519-4.8520
Hill, Charles C. 1.5995
Hill, Charles G., 1937-. 5.2887
Hill, Christopher, 1912-. 2.7162, 3.1442-3.1443, 3.1452, 3.1477, 3.1492, 4.2254
Hill, Claude. 2.13710
Hill, Danny, joint author. 4.980
Hill, David J., D. Phil. 5.3715
Hill, Donald L. 1.6697, 2.12712
Hill, Donald Routledge. 5.5659
Hill, Edward E. 5.7741
Hill, Errol. 2.3215, 2.6868
Hill, Forest Garrett, 1919-. 5.7387
Hill, Fredrick J. 5.6478
Hill, Geoffrey. 2.8800
Hill, George Birkbeck Norman, 1835-1903. 2.5807, 2.7085
Hill, George Francis, Sir, 1867-1948. 3.281, 3.2564, 3.3693
Hill, George H. 5.7841, 5.7867
Hill, Hamlin Lewis, 1931-. 2.10650, 2.10964
Hill, Helen, 1915-. 2.5968
Hill, Herbert. 2.10321, 2.10698, 3.2738
Hill, Holly. 3.3225
Hill, Jim Dan, 1897-. 5.7290
Hill, John. 1.754

Hill, John Edward Christopher, 1912-. 3.1449-3.1451, 3.1453
Hill, John Edwards. 5.4011
Hill, John Edwards. joint author. 5.3978
Hill, John Spencer, 1943-. 2.7589
Hill, Larry B. 4.8826
Hill, Lawrence F. (Lawrence Francis), 1890-. 3.6412
Hill, Leslie Rowland, 1935-. 5.4429
Hill, M. N. (Maurice Neville), 1919-. 4.325
Hill, Mary Armfield. 4.6003
Hill, Oliver. 1.5565, 1.5573
Hill, Patricia Ruth. 1.3025
Hill, Philip G. 5.6674
Hill, Philip G. (Philip George), 1934-. 2.3759
Hill, Philip Graham, 1910-. 5.6285
Hill, Polly, 1914-. 3.5351
Hill, Reuben, 1912-. 4.5643, 4.5648
Hill, Robert A., 1943-. 3.6836
Hill, Robert F. joint author. 3.6530
Hill, Robert L. 1928- joint ed. 5.2794
Hill, Robert W., 1941-. 2.12981
Hill, Ronald J., 1943-. 4.7301
Hill, Rosalind M. T. 4.5857
Hill, Samuel S. 1.2395, 3.7932
Hill, Stephen. joint author. 4.4966
Hill, Susan, 1942-. 2.9706-2.9707
Hill, W. Speed, ed. 1.3311
Hill, W. Speed (William Speed), 1935- ed. 1.3311
Hill, W. W. (Willard Williams), 1902-1974. 3.5953
Hill, Winfield. joint author. 5.6449
Hill, Winfred F. 4.10354
Hillas, A. M. 5.2326
Hille, Einar, 1894-. 5.1513-5.1514
Hillebrand, Harold Newcomb, 1887-. 2.3347
Hillegas, Mark Robert, 1926-. 2.8257
Hillel, Daniel. 5.5272-5.5274
Hiller, James K. 3.8870
Hiller, Marc D. 5.4566
Hillerbrand, Hans Joachim. ed. 1.2324
Hillerbrand, Hans Joachim. 1.2325
Hillerman, Tony. 2.13087
Hillery, D. 2.4318
Hilles, Frederick Whiley, 1900-. 2.5674-2.5675, 2.7045
Hillesum, Etty, 1914-1943. 3.3982
Hilley, John L. 4.4659
Hillgarth, J. N. 3.3422
Hillhouse, James Theodore, 1890-1956. 2.7022, 2.8059
Hilliard, Sam Bowers. 4.161
Hillier, Bevis, 1940-. 1.6613, 1.6691
Hillier, Frederick S. 5.5569
Hillier, Jack Ronald. 1.5079, 1.6478, 1.6485
Hillier, Jim. 2.2949
Hillier, Susan. 3.5969
Hillis, Newell Dwight, 1858-1929. 1.3335
Hillman, James. 5.198
Hillmer, Norman. 4.9065
Hillocks, George. 2.929
Hills, E. Sherbon (Edwin Sherbon) ed. 4.282
Hills, E. Sherbon (Edwin Sherbon) 5.3125
Hills, Jill. 4.5959
Hills, Michael Turner. 5.6386
Hills, Philip James. 5.7570
Hillway, Tyrus. 2.11161
Hillyer, Robert, 1895-1961. 2.11872
Hilsman, Roger. 3.7848, 4.7769
Hilson, J. C. 2.5662
Hiltebeitel, Alf. 1.1711
Hiltner, William Albert, 1914- ed. 5.1746
Hilton, Alison. 1.5034
Hilton, George Woodman. 4.4029
Hilton, Ian. 2.13921
Hilton, James, 1900-1954. 2.8801-2.8803
Hilton, R. H. (Rodney Howard), 1916-. 4.2849
Hilton, Ruth B. 1.3555
Hilton, Timothy, 1941-. 2.7858
Hilts, Philip J. 5.1964
Himelick, Raymond, ed. and tr. 1.3058
Himelstein, Morgan Yale. 2.3224
Himes, Chester B., 1909-. 2.11873-2.11874
Himmelblau, David Mautner, 1923-. 5.5595, 5.6824
Himmelfarb, Gertrude. 3.1591, 4.6623, 5.3199
Himmelfarb, Milton. 4.1670

Himmelstein, Jerome L. 4.6665
Himmelweit, Hilde T. 4.8504
Hinchen, John D. 5.6819
Hinchliffe, Arnold P., 1930-. 2.9794
Hind, Arthur Mayger, 1880-1957. 1.6431,
  1.6473
Hinde, Robert A. 4.4927, 5.4058
Hinde, Robert A. ed. 5.465, 5.3968
Hindelang, Michael J. comp. 4.6766
Hindelang, Michael J. 4.6707
Hindemith, Paul, 1895-1963. 1.4367, 1.4443,
  1.4450, 1.4465
Hinderer, Walter, 1934-. 2.13623, 2.13648
Hindess, Barry. 4.3650
Hinding, Andrea. 5.8477
Hindle, Brooke. 1.5961
Hindley, Donald. 4.8730
Hindley, J. Roger. 5.1053
Hindman, Darwin Alexander. 4.1062, 4.1076
Hinds, Martin. 1.2065
Hindson, Theodore T., 1942-. 4.9738
Hindus, Milton. 2.4673, 2.11730
Hindus, Milton. comp. 2.11278
Hine, Daryl. 2.10770
Hine, Jack Sylvester, 1923-. 5.2853
Hine, R. C. 4.4184
Hine, Robert V., 1921-. 3.8459
Hines, Jerome, 1921-. 1.4206
Hines, Thomas S. 1.5308, 1.5321-1.5322
Hingley, Ronald. 2.1278, 2.1368, 2.1490
Hingley, Ronald. ed. and tr. 2.1483
Hingley, Ronald. 2.1258, 2.1271
Hingorani, Anand T. 3.4306
Hingorani, Ganga A. (Ganga Anand), 1917-.
  3.4306
Hinks, Peter. 1.6664
Hinnebusch, William A. 1.3240
Hinnells, John R. 1.1526
Hinsie, Leland Earl, 1895-. 5.4798
Hinsley, F. H. (Francis Harry), 1918-. 3.1134,
  4.9113
Hinson, Maurice. 1.3567, 1.3582-1.3585
Hintikka, Jaakko, 1929-. 1.632, 1.1163, 1.1169,
  5.1043
Hintikka, Merrill B., 1939-. 4.5877
Hinton, E. (Ernest) 5.5711
Hinton, Frances. 3.350
Hinton, Harold C. 3.4614, 3.4677, 3.4790,
  3.4798, 3.5037, 4.8692
Hinton, James. 4.3412
Hinton, Leanne. 2.2330
Hinton, William. 3.4791, 4.2862, 4.2877
Hintz, Constance B., joint author. 3.563
Hintz, Howard William, 1903-. 2.10342
Hintze, Otto, 1861-1940. 3.2480
Hintzman, Douglas L. 5.296
Hinz, Evelyn J. 2.12249
Hipel, Keith W. 5.5971
Hipkiss, Robert A., 1935-. 2.11959
Hippisley Coxe, Antony. 4.1185
Hippocrates. 2.372, 5.4494
Hirano-Nakanishi, Marsha. 4.10883
Hiriyanna, Mysore, 1871-1950. 1.181
Hirmer, M. illus. 1.5631
Hirmer, Max. 1.4703, 1.4707, 1.4717, 1.4723,
  1.5172, 1.5220, 1.5624, 1.5700, 1.6631, 3.274
Hiro, Dilip. 3.1290, 4.8701
Hiroshima-shi Nagasaki-shi Genbaku Saigaishi
  Henshū Iinkai. 3.1012
Hirsch, Barry T., 1949-. 4.3357
Hirsch, E. D. (Eric Donald), 1928-. 2.2438
Hirsch, Foster. 2.3138
Hirsch, Fred. 4.2777
Hirsch, H. N. 4.9815
Hirsch, Jerrold, 1948-. 4.5197
Hirsch, Kathie S., 1954-. 5.5328
Hirsch, Marianne. 2.3526, 2.5987
Hirsch, Morris W., 1933-. 5.1515
Hirsch, Samson Raphael, 1808-1888. 1.1893
Hirsch, Susan E. 4.3621
Hirsch, Werner Zvi, 1920-. 4.2003
Hirschberger, Johannes. 1.129
Hirschfelder, Arlene B. 5.7738
Hirschfelder, Joseph Oakland, 1911-. 5.2064
Hirschfield, Robert S. 4.9631
Hirschhorn, Jeremy. 5.6162
Hirschler, M. M. 5.2771
Hirschman, Albert O. 4.2778

Hirschman, Lisa. 4.5515
Hirschon, Renee. 4.9372
Hirsh, Harold L. 5.4714
Hirsh, Sharon L. 1.6303
Hirshfeld, Alan. 5.1676
Hirshhorn Museum and Sculpture Garden.
  1.4905, 1.5715, 1.6008
Hirshleifer, Jack. 4.2930
Hirshson, Stanley P., 1928-. 3.7411
Hirst, Derek. 3.1461
Hirszowicz, Maria. 4.3426
Hisamatsu, Sen'ichi, 1894-1976. 2.1997
Hiscocks, Richard. 3.2472
Hiscox, Gardner Dexter, 1822?-1908. ed. 5.5548
Hispanic institute in the United States. 2.5330
Hispanic Society of America. 2.5113
Hiss, Alger. 3.7546
Historic American Buildings Survey. 1.5284,
  1.5516
Historic American Engineering Record. 1.5284
Historical Association (Great Britain) 3.1330
Historical Association of Kenya. 3.5261
Historical Evaluation and Research
  Organization. 3.4866
Historical Records Survey (New York, N.Y.)
  4.151
Hitch, Charles Johnston. 4.1772
Hitchcock, A. S. (Albert Spear), 1865-1935.
  5.3696
Hitchcock, Alfred, 1899-. 2.3056
Hitchcock, Elsie Vaughan. 2.5931, 2.6496
Hitchcock, H. Wiley (Hugh Wiley), 1923-.
  1.3510, 1.3687, 1.3901, 1.3903
Hitchcock, Henry Russell, 1903-. 1.5256,
  1.5258, 1.5270, 1.5279, 1.5296, 1.5324,
  1.5340, 1.5372, 1.5422
Hitchcock, James. 3.1178
Hitchins, Keith. 3.1933
Hite, Molly, 1947-. 2.13284
Hitiris, Theodore, joint author. 4.1387
Hitler, Adolf, 1889-1945. 3.963, 3.2390-3.2393,
  3.2405
Hitti, Philip Khûri, 1886-. 3.3661, 3.3669,
  3.3717, 3.3785, 3.3795, 3.4052
Hittle, James Donald, 1915-. 5.7357
Hixon, Thomas J., 1940- joint author. 5.4280
Hjelmslev, Louis, 1899-1965. 2.91
Hla Myint, U. 4.2432
Hłasko, Marek. 2.1705
Hlophe, Stephen S. 4.5476
Hnatek, Eugene R. 5.6579
Hnizdovsky, Jacques, 1915- ill. 2.3751
Ho, Chí Minh, 1890-1969. 3.4489
Ho, Mae-Wan. 5.3366
Ho, Mian Lian. 2.1118
Ho, Ping-ti, ed. 3.4786
Ho, Ping-ti. 4.1705, 4.5414
Ho, Sam P. S. 4.2494, 4.4634
Ho, Tse-Lok. 5.2861
Ho, Wai-kam. 1.5064, 1.6327
Hoag, John D. 1.5235
Hoagland, Mahlon B. 5.3410
Hoar, William Stewart, 1913-. 5.3915, 5.4186
Hoare, C. A. R. (Charles Antony Richard),
  1934-. 5.1170, 5.1181
Hoare, Quintin. 4.7075, 4.7077
Hoare, Quintin. ed. 4.7076
Hobbes, Thomas, 1588-1679. 1.670-1.671,
  3.1475, 4.7404-4.7405
Hobbs, Bruce E. 5.3126
Hobbs, Edward Henry. 4.7936
Hobbs, F. D. (Frederick Derek) 4.3926
Hobbs, Michael John. 5.4050
Hobbs, Richard. 1.6140
Hobbs, Robert Carleton, 1946-. 1.5676, 1.5910
Hoberman, J. 2.2957
Hoberman, Louisa Schell, 1942-. 4.5255
Hobhouse, L. T. (Leonard Trelawney),
  1864-1929. 4.5031, 4.7504
Hoboken, Anthony van, 1887-. 1.3610
Hobsbaum, Philip. 2.5752
Hobsbawm, E. J. (Eric J.), 1917-. 3.654, 3.667,
  4.824, 4.1534, 4.2248, 4.5302, 4.6933, 4.8631
Hobson, Fred C., 1943-. 2.10449
Hobson, Geary. 2.10677
Hobson, George Douglas. ed. 5.6802

Hobson, J. A. (John Atkinson), 1858-1940.
  4.2997, 4.8428
Hobson, Laura Keane Zametkin, 1900-. 2.11875
Hobson, Wilder, 1906-1964. 1.4328
Hobson, William. 5.4653
Hoch, Edward D., 1930-. 2.13088
Hoch-Smith, Judith. 1.1615
Hochachka, Peter W. 5.3507, 5.4205
Hochberg, Julian E. 1.4624
Hochhuth, Rolf. 2.13898
Hochman, Jiří. 3.3215
Hochman, Joel Simon. 4.6666
Hochman, Stanley. 2.2785, 3.7839
Hochmuth, Marie, joint ed. 2.3781
Hochschild, Jennifer L., 1950-. 4.10789
Hochstadt, Harry. 5.1561
Hocke, Gustav René, 1908-. 1.4764, 2.2619
Hockett, Charles Francis. 2.7, 2.135
Hockin, Thomas A., 1938-. 4.8285
Hocking, William Ernest. 1.1258, 1.1549
Hocks, Richard A., 1936-. 2.11111
Hodapp, Robert M. 5.4979
Hodder, Ian. 3.246
Hodder-Williams, Richard. 4.8790
Hoddinott, R. F. (Ralph F.), 1913-. 3.3539
Hodeir, André, 1921-. 1.3672, 4.4329
Hodgart, Matthew John Caldwell. 2.6109
Hodgart, Patricia. 2.8101
Hodge, Alan, 1915- (joint author) 3.1643
Hodge, Francis. 2.3110, 2.3202
Hodge, Frederick Webb, 1864-1956. ed. 3.5981
Hodge, Merle, 1944-. 2.9999
Hodge, Paul W. 5.1851, 5.1856
Hodge, W. H. (Walter Henricks), 1912-. 5.3700
Hodges, Andrew. 5.1098
Hodges, C. Walter (Cyril Walter), 1909-.
  1.5551, 2.6707
Hodges, David A., 1937-. 5.6470
Hodges, Donald Clark, 1923-. 3.8943, 3.9004
Hodges, Fletcher, Jr. 1.3869
Hodges, Herbert Arthur, 1905-. 1.984
Hodges, Margaret B., ed. 4.6473
Hodgett, Gerald Augustus John. 4.2199
Hodgetts, J. E., 1917-. 4.8288-4.8289
Hodgkin, Alan Lloyd. 5.4324
Hodgkin, Thomas Lionel, 1910-. 3.4463, 3.5107,
  3.5347
Hodgkins, Jordan Atwood, 1920-. 4.3752
Hodgkinson, Harold L. joint author. 4.10728
Hodgkinson, John, ca. 1767-1805. 2.3188
Hodgkiss, A. G. 5.8209
Hodgson, Geoff. 4.8537
Hodgson, Godfrey. 4.5160
Hodgson, Leonard, 1889-. 1.2836
Hodgson, Marshall G. S. 3.3650
Hodgson, Moira. 4.1120
Hodgson, Peter Crafts, 1934-. 1.2789, 1.3286
Hodgson, William Hope, 1875-1918.
  2.8804-2.8805
Hodler, Ferdinand, 1853-1918. 1.6303
Hodne, Fritz. 4.2410
Hodnett, Ernest Matelle, 1914- joint author.
  5.2686
Hodson, F. R. 3.233
Hodson, H. V. (Henry Vincent), 1906-. 4.6461
Hoebel, E. Adamson (Edward Adamson),
  1906-. 3.5854, 4.9353
Høffding, Harald, 1843-1931. 1.426
Hoeh, James A. 4.10672
Hoehling, A. A. (Adolph A.) 3.7365
Hoel, Lester A. 4.3908
Hoel, Paul Gerhard, 1905-. 4.1240, 5.1388
Hoenigswald, Henry M., 1915-. 2.150
Hoerder, Dirk. 4.3611
Hoermann, Roland. 2.13549
Hofacker, Erich, 1898-. 2.13841
Hofer, Philip. 1.5828
Hoff-Wilson, Joan, 1937-. 3.6485, 3.7746
Hoffecker, Carol E. 3.8098
Hoffer, Eric. 4.5045
Hoffer, Peter C. 4.9735
Hoffer, Thomas. 4.10048-4.10049
Hoffleit, Dorrit. 5.1847
Hoffman, Daniel, 1923-. 2.10412, 2.10608,
  2.10985, 2.11208
Hoffman, Daniel Gerard, 1923-. 2.10659

Hoffman, Frederick John. 2.2375, 2.3580, 2.10414, 2.10628, 2.11303, 2.11693
Hoffman, Frederick John. ed. 2.5738
Hoffman, George Walter. 3.1187, 3.3565, 4.2417, 4.3712
Hoffman, Harold M., 1903-. 4.9453
Hoffman, Hester Rosalyn Jacoby, 1895- comp. 5.7707
Hoffman, Malvina, 1887-. 1.5668, 1.5773
Hoffman, Michael A., 1944-. 4.746
Hoffman, Nancy. 4.10675
Hoffman, Richard Lester. joint comp. 2.6112
Hoffman, Robert Louis, 1937-. 3.2192
Hoffman, Ronald, 1941-. 4.2033
Hoffman, W. Michael. 4.4269-4.4273, 4.4273a
Hoffman, William M., 1939-. 2.10800
Hoffmann, Charles, 1921-. 4.1911
Hoffmann, Donald. 1.5326
Hoffmann, E. T. A. (Ernst Theodor Amadeus), 1776-1822. 2.13615-2.13617
Hoffmann, Frank W., 1949-. 1.3587
Hoffmann, Fritz L. (Fritz Leo), 1907-. 3.9256
Hoffmann, Helmut, 1912-. 1.2160
Hoffmann, Konrad, 1938-. 1.4752
Hoffmann, Léon-François. 2.4834
Hoffmann, Olga Mingo. 3.9256
Hoffmann, Peter, 1930-. 3.2431, 5.6879
Hoffmann, Roald, joint author. 5.2819
Hoffmann, Stanley. ed. 4.9013
Hoffmann, Stanley. 3.2196-3.2197, 3.7577, 4.8991, 4.9031
Hoffmeister, C. (Cuno), 1892-. 5.1842
Hofheinz, Roy, 1935-. 4.2540
Hofmann, Hans, 1880-1966. 1.5942
Hofmann, Werner, 1928-. 1.5719
Hofmannsthal, Hugo Hofmann, Elder von, 1874-1929, comp. 2.13523
Hofmannsthal, Hugo von, 1874-1929. 2.13782-2.13783
Hofstadter, Albert, 1910-. 1.1346, 1.1374
Hofstadter, Douglas R., 1945-. 5.1056
Hofstadter, Richard, 1916-1970. 3.6119, 3.6230, 3.6329, 3.6341, 3.6350, 3.7527-3.7528, 4.4773, 4.8147, 4.9984, 4.10061-4.10062
Hogan, Charles Beecher, 1906-. 2.6866
Hogan, James C. 2.414
Hogan, John C. (John Charles) 4.9590
Hogan, Robert Goode, 1930-. 2.7243, 2.9850, 2.9860
Hogan, Sharon A. 5.7648
Hogan, Thomas H. 5.7639
Hogan, W. P. (Warren Pat), 1929-. 4.4591
Hogan, William Thomas, 1919-. 4.3731
Hogarth, Paul, 1917-. 2.8968
Hogarth Press. 2.9127, 2.9577
Hogarth, William, 1697-1764. 1.4610, 1.6034, 1.6456-1.6457
Hogbin, Herbert Ian, 1904-. 3.5652
Hoge, Dean R., 1937-. 1.3179
Hoge, James O. 2.8174
Hogg, Ian V. 5.7382, 5.7388
Hogg, James, 1770-1835. 2.7814-2.7815
Hogg, Robert V. 4.4640, 5.1389
Hogg, Thomas Jefferson, 1792-1862. 2.8102
Hoggart, Richard, 1918-. 2.8406
Hogger, Christopher John. 5.1182
Hogrefe, Pearl. 4.6095, 4.6097
Hogwood, Christopher. 1.3888
Hohenberg, John. 2.3549, 2.3597
Hohenberg, Paul M. 4.6251
Hohfeld, Wesley Newcomb, 1879-1918. 4.9358
Hohl, Reinhold. 1.5705
Höhmann, Hans-Hermann. 4.2234
Höhne, Heinz, 1926-. 3.2427
Hoijer, Harry, 1904- ed. 2.92
Hoisington, William A., 1941-. 3.5213
Holahan, John. 4.3450, 4.3452
Holberg, Ludvig, baron. 2.14006
Holborn, Hajo, 1902-1969. 3.360, 3.497, 3.613, 3.741, 3.1057, 3.2276
Holbrook, David. 2.5830, 2.9419, 2.13263
Holcomb, Adele M. 1.4586
Holcombe, Arthur Norman, 1884-. 4.7801
Holcroft, Thomas, 1745-1809. 2.7076
Holdcroft, David. 2.68
Holden, Alan. 5.2925
Holden, Anthony, 1947- tr. 2.555
Holden, David. 3.2684, 3.4056

Holden, Karen C. 4.3460
Holden, Willis Sprague, 1909-. 2.3700
Hölderlin, Friedrich, 1770-1843. 2.13612-2.13613
Holderness, B. A. 4.2249
Holderness, Graham. 2.6769
Holdstock, Robert. 2.9708
Holdsworth, William Searle, Sir, 1871-1944. 4.9407
Hole, Francis Doan, 1913-. 5.5262, 5.5264
Hole, Judith. 4.6055
Holford, Ingrid. 5.2560
Holifield, E. Brooks. 1.2410, 1.3013
Holinshed, Raphael, d. 1580? 2.6714, 3.1368
Holl, Karl, 1866-1926. 1.2351
Hollaman, Keith. 2.3717
Holland, Barron. 5.8451
Holland, C. H. (Charles Hepworth) 5.3136
Holland, Charles Donald. 5.6813
Holland, Clive. joint author. 3.8867
Holland, Daniel M. (Daniel Mark), 1920-. 4.1554
Holland, DeWitte Talmadge, 1923- ed. 1.3047
Holland, F. Ross (Francis Ross), 1927-. 5.7495
Holland, Heinrich D. 5.2513
Holland, James, 1933-. 1.4181
Holland, John H. (John Henry), 1929-. 5.375
Holland, Norman Norwood, 1927-. 2.2376, 2.2400, 2.7012
Holland, R. F. (Roy Fraser), 1932-. 4.8902
Holland, Stuart. 4.7039
Holland, Tristram. 1.4934
Holland, Vyvyan Beresford, 1886-1967. 2.8266, 2.8278-2.8279
Hollander, Anne. 1.5190
Hollander, Gayle Durham. 4.5379
Hollander, John. 1.4399, 2.6070, 2.11876-2.11879
Hollander, Joyce P. 5.2957
Hollander, Myles. 5.1411
Hollander, Paul, 1932-. 4.4967, 4.5185
Hollander, Samuel. 4.1353, 4.1356, 4.1412
Hollander, Stanley C., 1919-. 4.4318
Hollander, Steven. 2.7289
Hollander, Zander. 4.994, 4.1011, 4.1014, 4.1022
Hollenbeck, Peter. 2.10705
Hollenweger, Walter J., 1927-. 1.3386
Holler, Frederick L. 5.8353
Holley, Donald, 1940-. 4.2818
Holley, I. B. (Irving Brinton), 1919-. 5.7401
Holli, Melvin G. 3.8421, 4.8866
Holliday, J. S. 3.8608
Hollingdale, R. J. 1.1051, 1.1053
Hollingdale, R. J. tr. 1.1050
Hollingshead, August de Belmont. joint author. 5.4644
Hollingshead, August de Belmont. 5.4831, 5.4833
Hollingsworth, Ellen Jane. joint author. 4.6214
Hollingsworth, J. Rogers (Joseph Rogers), 1932-. 3.7412, 4.6214
Hollingsworth, Thomas Henry. 4.1616
Hollington, Michael. 2.13765
Hollis, A. S. (Adrian Swayne) 2.744
Hollis, C. Carroll (Charles Carroll), 1911-. 2.11282
Hollis, Christopher, 1902-1977. 2.9196
Hollis, David. 5.8480
Hollis, Florence. 4.6498
Hollis, James R., 1930-. 2.9795
Hollister, C. Warren (Charles Warren), 1930-. 3.1315
Hollister, Charles D., 1936- joint author. 4.337
Hollister, Robert M. 4.6206
Hollon, W. Eugene (William Eugene), 1913-. 3.8475
Holloway, David, 1943-. 5.7324
Holloway, Dennis Glyn. 5.5802
Holloway, John. 2.5711, 2.5753, 2.6782
Holloway, Marcella Marie, Sister, 1913-. 2.7831
Holly, Brian P. 4.17
Holly, Michael Ann. 1.5152
Holm, Bernard J., joint author. 3.406
Holm, Bill, 1925-. 3.5751, 5.7000
Holm, Jeanne, 1921-. 5.7377

Holman, C. Hugh (Clarence Hugh), 1914-. 2.2348, 2.10450-2.10451, 2.10460, 2.12791, 5.7811
Holman, J. P. (Jack Philip) 5.2264
Holmberg, Börje. 4.10986
Holmes, Arthur, 1890-1965. 5.2966
Holmes, Brian. 4.9973
Holmes, Charles S. ed. 2.5497
Holmes, Charles Shively. 2.12588
Holmes, Clive. 3.1482
Holmes, Colin, 1938-. 4.2208, 4.8960
Holmes, Doris L., 1899-. 5.2966
Holmes, Dwight Oliver Wendell, 1877-. 4.10867
Holmes, Geoffrey S., 1928-. 4.8405
Holmes Group (U.S.) 4.10539
Holmes, Helen B. 5.5051
Holmes, J. Derek. 1.3142, 1.3164
Holmes, James S. 2.13945
Holmes, John Clellon, 1926-. 2.13089
Holmes, John Wendell, 1910-. 3.8779
Holmes, Karen A. joint author. 4.6741
Holmes, Martin. 4.2291
Holmes, Oliver W., 1938-. 1.1130
Holmes, Oliver Wendell, 1809-1894. 2.11079-2.11080, 3.7393, 4.9412, 4.9819-4.9820
Holmes, Pauline. 4.11003
Holmes, Richard, 1951-. 4.5202
Holmes, Sandra, 1945-. 5.3291
Holmes, Sarah Katherine (Stone) 1841-1907. 3.7373
Holmes, Stephen, 1948-. 4.7444
Holmes, Urban Tigner, 1900-. 2.3951, 4.825
Holmes-Walker, W. A., 1926-. 5.6906
Holmgren, Arthur H. 5.3678
Holmgren, Noel H. 5.3678
Holmquist, June Drenning. 3.8502
Holmstrom, Lynda Lytle. 4.5575
Holmyard, Eric John, 1891-1959. 5.2612
Holoman, D. Kern, 1947-. 1.3818
Holroyd, Michael. 2.9388, 2.9390
Holst, Gustav, 1874-1934. 1.4019
Holst, Imogen, 1907-. 1.3897, 1.4019
Holstein, Friedrich von, 1837-1909. 3.2317
Holsti, K. J. (Kalevi Jaakko), 1935-. 3.1167
Holsti, Ole R. 4.9025
Holt, Alix. 4.6129
Holt, Charles C. 4.2650
Holt, Elizabeth Basye Gilmore. 1.4787, 1.4793
Holt, Elizabeth Basye Gilmore. ed. 1.4681
Holt, James Clarke. comp. 4.8393
Holt, James Clarke. 3.1349
Holt, Janet. 1.4934
Holt, John, 1948- joint author. 5.8454
Holt, John Caldwell, 1923-. 4.10036, 4.10246, 4.10365, 4.10424
Holt, John G. 5.4452
Holt, Marion Peter. 2.5131
Holt, Marion Peter. comp. 2.5158
Holt, Michael F. (Michael Fitzgibbon) 3.7143
Holt, Nancy, 1938-. 1.5142
Holt, P. M. (Peter Malcolm) ed. 3.3644, 3.5130
Holt, P. M. (Peter Malcolm) 3.3734, 3.5167
Holt, R. C. (Richard C.), 1941-. 5.1198
Holt, Rackham. 5.5223
Holt, Robert R. ed. 5.4848
Holt, Robert R. comp. 5.162
Holt, Ted, 1943-. 2.8305
Holt, Thomas, 1942-. 3.6805
Holthaus, Gary H., 1932-. 2.13090
Holtje, Bert. 5.5703
Holtman, Robert B. 3.2126
Holton, Gerald James. 5.735, 5.1894, 5.1994
Holton, James R. 5.2519
Holton, Milne. 2.13937
Holton, Richard Henry, 1926- joint author. 4.2120
Holtz, Barry W. 1.1937
Holtz, R. D. (Robert D.) 5.5898
Holtzman, Eric, 1939-. 5.3600
Holub, Miroslav, 1923-. 2.1672
Holub, Robert C. 2.13451, 2.13604
Holum, Kenneth G. 3.2820
Holyoake, Sydney John. 2.872
Holz, Anita. 2.13786
Holz, Arno, 1863-1929. 2.13786
Holz, Robert K., 1930-. 4.28
Holzman, Albert George. 5.5572

Holzman, Franklyn D. 4.4182, 4.4235, 4.4703
Holzman, Philip S., 1922-. 5.180
Holzman, Red. 4.1012
Holzman, Richard S. 3.7320
Homans, George Caspar, 1910-. 3.1331, 4.580, 4.4987, 4.5068
Homans, Peter. ed. 1.1563
Homberger, Eric. comp. 2.12344
Homberger, Eric. 2.3500
Hombs, Mary Ellen. 4.6629
Homburger, Wolfgang S. 4.3929
Homburger, Wolfgang S. ed. 4.4030
Homel, Michael W. (Michael Wallace), 1944-. 4.10878
Homer. 2.371, 2.373-2.374, 2.481-2.486, 2.488-2.491, 2.495, 2.592, 2.7186
Homer, Sidney, 1902-. 4.4528
Homer, Thomas Johnston, 1858-. 4.6867
Homer, William Innes. 5.6955
Homo, Léon Pol, 1872-1957. 4.7367
Homze, Edward L. 4.3829
Honan, Park. joint author. 2.7484
Honan, Park. 2.7354, 2.7489
Hondros, John Louis. 3.1068
Hone, Ralph E. 2.9311
Honegger, Arthur, 1892-1955. 1.3898
Honegger, Barbara. 5.7367
Honeycombe, R. W. K. (Robert William Kerr) 5.5811
Honeyman, Steve. 2.3567
Hong, Edna Hatlestad, 1913-. 1.1118, 1.1553, 2.14015
Hong, Howard Vincent, 1912-. 1.1118, 1.1553, 2.14015
Honig, Edwin. 2.2390, 2.5163-2.5164, 2.5259
Honig, Werner K. ed. 5.301
Honigmann, E. A. J. 2.6783
Honigmann, John Joseph. 4.477-4.478
Honigsblum, Bonnie Birtwistle. 4.10619
Honjō, Shigeru, 1876-1945. 3.4972
Honolulu Academy of Arts. 3.8900
Honomichl, Jack J. 4.4305
Honour, Hugh. 1.4675, 1.4778, 1.6506, 1.6737
Honourable Society of Cymmrodorion (London, England) 3.1751
Honsberger, Ross, 1929-. 5.1325
Hont, Istvan, 1947-. 4.1346
Hood, D. W. (Donald Wilbur), 1918-. 4.355
Hood, Robert, 1797-1821. 4.105
Hood, Stuart. 3.2897
Hood, Thomas, 1799-1845. 2.7818-2.7819
Hood, Walter Kelly. 5.666
Hoog, Michel. 1.6097
Hoogenboom, Ari Arthur, 1927-. 3.8073
Hoogendoorn, C. J. 5.6155
Hook, Andrew. comp. 2.11588
Hook, Brian. 3.4612
Hook, J. N. (Julius Nicholas), 1913-. 3.307, 4.10510
Hook, Judith. 3.2954
Hook, Sidney, 1902-. 1.590, 1.595, 1.1034, 3.487, 3.511, 4.6967, 4.7571, 4.7634, 4.10231, 4.10427, 4.10578, 5.178
Hooker, Edward Niles. 2.6985
Hooker, Hyacinth Symonds, Lady. 5.3639
Hooker, J. T. 3.2584
Hooker, Joseph Dalton, Sir, 1817-1911. 5.3639
Hooker, M. B. 1.2002
Hooker, Michael. 1.867
Hooker, Richard James, 1913- ed. 3.8244
Hooker, Saralinda. 5.6091
Hookers, Joseph Datton, Sir, 1817-1916. 5.3633
Hooks, Bell. 4.5984, 4.6056
Hoole, Francis W. 4.334
Hooper, Alfred Gifford, comp. 2.10053
Hooper, Beverley. 4.90
Hooper, Edwin Bickford. 3.4507
Hooper, Franklin Henry, 1862-1940, ed. 1.14
Hooper, Walter. 2.9038
Hooper, Walter. ed. 2.2628
Hooper, William Davis, 1868-1945, tr. 2.654
Hoopes, Donelson F. 1.6379
Hoopes, Townsend J. 3.4486
Hoover, Benjamin Beard, 1921- ed. 2.6933
Hoover, Calvin Bryce, 1897-. 4.1787
Hoover, Dwight W., 1926-. 5.8394
Hoover, Edgar Malone, 1907-. 4.2045

Hoover, Herbert, 1874-1964. 3.7722, 3.7741, 3.7747, 4.1961, 4.7974, 5.6760
Hoover Institution on War, Revolution, and Peace. 2.1512, 3.4673, 3.4834
Hopcroft, John E., 1939-. 5.1159, 5.1240, 5.1371
Hope, A. D. (Alec Derwent), 1907-. 2.2731
Hope, Alec Derwent, 1907-. 2.8806
Hope, Chris. 5.6599
Hope, Richard, 1895-1955, tr. 1.289
Hope, T. E. 2.874
Hopkins, A. G. (Anthony G.) 4.2589
Hopkins, Arthur. 2.3094
Hopkins, Bill. ed. 1.3996
Hopkins, Charles D. 4.10713
Hopkins, Charles Howard, 1905- joint author. 1.2928
Hopkins, Donald R. 5.4767
Hopkins, Edward Washburn, 1857-1932. 1.1687
Hopkins, Gerard Manley, 1844-1889. 2.7823-2.7828
Hopkins, James F. 3.7070
Hopkins, Jasper. 1.3253
Hopkins, Jasper. ed. 1.380
Hopkins, Jeanne. 5.1681
Hopkins, Jeffrey. 1.2164
Hopkins, Joseph G. E. ed. 3.6332
Hopkins, Joseph G. E. 3.6291
Hopkins, Keith. 4.4094, 4.6415, 4.7368
Hopkins, Kenneth. 2.5771, 2.9240
Hopkins, Nicholas S. 4.5462
Hopkins, Phillip. 5.6452
Hopkins, Raymond F. 4.2888
Hopkins, Sheila V. 4.3442
Hopkins, Thomas J. 1.1702
Hopkins, W. G. 5.4325
Hopp, Vollrath. 5.6825
Hoppen, K. Theodore, 1941-. 3.1842
Hopper, Edward, 1882-1967. 1.5946, 1.6442
Hopper, R. J. (Robert John), 1910-. 4.1734
Hopper, Robert. 2.156
Hopper, Stanley Romaine, 1907- ed. 2.2377
Hopper, Vincent Foster, 1906-. 5.685
Hoppin, Richard H. 1.3649
Hopwood, Derek. ed. 5.8037
Hora, Bayard. 5.3682
Horace. 2.671-2.672, 2.702, 2.718, 2.721
Horace Mann-Lincoln Institute of School Experimentation. 4.10003, 4.10376
Horak, Stephan M., 1920-. 5.8015, 5.8017
Horcasitas, Fernando. ed. 3.8955
Hord, R. Michael, 1940-. 5.5940
Horden, John. 5.7728
Hordeski, Michael F. 5.6570, 5.6593
Horgan, Paul, 1903-. 2.11881-2.11883, 3.8332, 3.8574
Hori, Ichirō, 1910-1974. 1.1832
Horkenbach, Cuno, ed. 3.2360
Horkheimer, Mary Foley, 1905-. 4.10328
Horkheimer, Max, 1895-1973. 1.1007
Horlick, Allan Stanley, 1941-. 4.4219
Hörmander, Lars. 5.1484, 5.1530
Horn, Berthold. 5.1218, 5.6175
Horn, Daniel. 3.840
Horn, David, 1942-. 1.3560
Horn, David Bayne, 1901-1969. 3.1252
Horn, Lyle H., joint author. 5.2568
Horn, Maurice. 1.5845, 2.3812
Horn, Michiel, 1939-. 4.7007
Horn, Pamela. 4.2924
Horn, Pierre L. 2.2415
Horn, Walter William, 1908-. 1.3237
Hornback, Bert G., 1935-. 2.7693
Hornblow, Arthur, 1865-. 2.3190
Hornblower, Jane. 3.548
Hornblower, Simon. 3.2604
Hornbostel, Caleb. 5.5763
Horne, Alistair. 3.797, 3.980, 3.2163, 3.5207, 5.7313
Horne, Douglas F. (Douglas Favel), 1915-. 5.6945, 5.7065
Horne, Herman Harrell, 1874-. 4.10226
Horne, Peter. 4.6804
Horne, Ralph Albert, 1929-. 5.2628
Horney, Karen, 1885-1952. 4.5929, 5.163-5.164, 5.4784
Horngren, Charles T., 1926-. 4.4412
Hornstein, Harvey A., 1938-. 5.422

Hornung, Clarence Pearson. 1.6515
Hornung, E. W. (Ernest William), 1866-1921. 2.8807
Hornyak, William F. (William Frank), 1922- ed. 5.2000
Horonjeff, Robert. 5.6685
Horovitz, Israel. 2.13091
Horowitz, Dan. 5.7344
Horowitz, Daniel, 1938-. 4.2058
Horowitz, Daniel L. 4.3416
Horowitz, David, 1939- joint author. 3.7616
Horowitz, Ellis. 5.1205, 5.1241
Horowitz, Gad. 4.3626
Horowitz, Helen Lefkowitz. 4.10843
Horowitz, Irving Louis. 1.1291, 4.2779, 4.4775, 4.5253
Horowitz, Joseph, 1948-. 1.4104
Horowitz, Mardi Jon, 1934-. 5.4930
Horowitz, Morris Aaron. 4.3529, 4.3986
Horowitz, Paul, 1942-. 5.6449
Horridge, G. Adrian. 5.4287
Horridge, G. Adrian. joint author. 5.4116
Horrobin, David F. 5.4646
Horsfield, John. 5.7474
Horsfield, Peter G. 1.3001
Horsman, E. A. (Ernest Alan), 1918- ed. 2.6589
Horsman, Reginald. 3.7108
Horst, R. Kenneth (Ralph Kenneth), 1935-. 5.5400
Hörstadius, Sven Otto, 1898-. 5.4127
Horster, Marita. 1.6198
Hort, Arthur, Sir, 1864-1935. ed. 2.395
Horta, Maria Teresa. 2.5460
Horthy, Miklós, nagybányai, 1868-1957. 3.1942
Horton, Arthur MacNeill, 1947-. 5.4813
Horton, Derek, 1932-. 5.2762
Horton, Donald, 1910-. 5.7163
Horton, Homer L. Russell M. 2.3636
Horton, James Oliver. 3.8000
Horton, Lois E. joint author. 3.8000
Horton, Philip C. 2.3552
Horton, Rod William, 1910-. 2.10249
Horvat, Branko. 4.1325, 4.6979
Horváth, Csaba, 1930- joint author. 5.2644
Horwich, Paul. 5.897
Horwitz, Richard P., 1949-. 3.7961
Hösch, Edgar, 1935-. 3.3515
Hoselitz, Berthold Frank, 1913-. 3.3065, 4.1830, 4.2780
Hosey, Geoffrey R. 5.3287
Hosford, David H. 3.1510
Hosford, Ray E., 1933-. 4.6899
Hoskin, Marilyn B., 1945- joint author. 4.5763
Hosking, Geoffrey A. 2.1291
Hoskins, Betty B. 5.5051
Hoskins, W. G. (William George), 1908-. 3.1720
Hoskyns, Edwyn Clement, Sir, 1884-1937. tr. 1.2708
Hosny, A. N. 5.6216
Hosokawa, Bill. 3.6560
Hostetler, John Andrew, 1918-. 1.3367, 1.3369, 3.6581
Hostetter, G. H., 1939-. 5.6183, 5.6279
Hostetter, Richard. 4.7081
Hostrop, Richard W. joint comp. 4.10604
Hotman, François, sieur de Villiers Saint Paul, 1524-1590. 4.7552, 4.8576
Hotson, Leslie, 1897-. 2.3299, 2.6615, 2.6708, 2.6810
Hottel, Hoyt C. (Hoyt Clarke), 1903-. 5.6111
Hottenstein, Caroline. 5.3952
Hottinger, Arnold. 3.3718
Hou, Chi-ming, 1924-. 4.2457, 4.4631
Houaiss, Antônio. ed. 2.911
Hough, Emerson, 1857-1923. 2.11884
Hough, Graham Goulden, 1908-. 2.5698, 2.5820, 2.6533, 2.7938, 2.8985
Hough, Jerry F., 1935-. 3.3252, 4.8648
Hough, Richard Alexander, 1922-. 3.818, 3.1287
Houghton, David D. 5.5706
Houghton, Henry G. 5.2503
Houghton Library. 2.7859
Houghton, Richard Monckton Milnes, 1st baron, 1809-1885. 2.7854
Houghton, Walter Edwards, 1904-. 2.6177, 2.7584, 3.1592, 5.7919

Houldcroft, Peter Thomas. 5.7059
Houlden, J. L. (James Leslie) 1.2721
Houle, Cyril Orvin, 1913-. 4.10625
Houle, Peter J. 2.5854
Hounshell, David A. 5.7017
Hounsome, Terry. 1.3622
Hountondji, Paulin J., 1942-. 1.1145
Houpis, Constantine H. 5.6189
Houppert, Joseph W. 2.6492
Hourani, Albert Habib. 3.3721, 3.3798, 4.7283
Hours, Madeleine, 1913-. 1.6078
House, Herbert O. 5.2736
House, Humphrey, 1908-1955. 2.7645
House, Madeline. 2.7635
House, Robert William, 1920- joint author. 1.4412
Houseman, John. 2.3257-2.3259
Housman, A. E. (Alfred Edward), 1859-1936. 2.7837-2.7838
Houston, Charles S. 4.105
Houston, David Franklin, 1866-1940. 3.7715
Houston, J. M. (James Macintosh), 1922-. 4.251, 4.5283
Houston, James E. 5.7632
Houston, Jean. joint author. 5.233
Houston, John Porter. 2.3906, 2.4239
Houston, Sam, 1793-1863. 3.8324
Houtchens, Lawrence Huston, 1898-. 2.5539
Houthakker, Hendrik S. 4.2059
Houtsma, M. Th. (Martijn Theodoor), 1851-1943. 3.3660
Houwink, R. (Roelof), 1897-. 5.2221
Hovanessian, Shahen A., 1931-. 5.6435
Hovannisian, Richard G. 3.4045
Hovdenakk, Per. 1.5042
Hovdhaugen, Even. 2.39
Hovet, Erica. joint author. 4.9210
Hovet, Thomas. 4.9231
Hovet, Thomas. joint author. 4.9210
Hoving, Thomas, 1931-. 1.5990
Hovland, Carl Iver, 1912-. 2.50, 4.5018
Hovland, Michael A. 1.3599
How, Walter Wybergh, 1861-. 2.476
Howard, Christopher H. D. (Christopher Henry Durham), 1913-. 3.1621
Howard, Dick, 1943-. 4.7019
Howard, Donald Roy, 1927-. 2.6324, 2.6334
Howard, Ebenezer, Sir, 1850-1928. 4.6306
Howard, Gene L., 1940-. 3.8285
Howard, George, 1935-. 1.2715
Howard, Harry N. (Harry Nicholas), 1902-1987. 3.3590
Howard-Hill, T. H. (Trevor Howard) 5.7930
Howard, J. B. (Jack Benny), 1937- joint author. 5.6111
Howard, J. Woodford. 4.9826
Howard, James Henri, 1925-. 3.5948
Howard, John T. 5.8146
Howard, John Tasker, 1890-. 1.3688, 1.3869
Howard, Joseph Kinsey. 3.8543, 3.8852
Howard, Leon. 2.10369, 2.11162
Howard, Lillie P. 2.11913
Howard, Maureen, 1930-. 2.10861
Howard, Michael Charles, 1945-. 4.1326
Howard, Michael Eliot, 1922-. 3.676, 3.2162, 4.9114, 4.9326, 5.7195, 5.7206, 5.7249
Howard, Neale E. 5.1730
Howard, Richard. 2.4136, 2.10492, 2.13092-2.13094, 5.3946
Howard, Richard C. ed. 3.4810
Howard, Robert Ervin, 1906-1936. 2.11885
Howard, Robert P. 3.8406
Howard, Ronnalie Roper. 2.8020
Howard, Thomas. 2.9531
Howard University. Institute for the Study of Educational Policy. 4.10857, 4.10889
Howard, William James. 2.7571
Howarth, Oliver. 5.2304
Howarth, Osbert John Radcliffe, 1877-. 4.47
Howarth, Patrick. 2.9375
Howarth, Robert Guy, 1906-. 2.6158
Howarth, Stephen. 5.7471
Howarth, Thomas, 1914-. 1.5394
Howarth, W. D. (William Driver). 2.4042
Howarth, W. D. (William Driver). ed. 2.4043
Howarth, William L., 1940- comp. 2.11209
Howat, G. M. D. (Gerald Malcolm David), 1928-. 3.367, 3.1444

Howat, John K. 1.4899
Howe, Christopher. 4.2479
Howe, Daniel Walker. 4.8218
Howe, Florence. 4.10839
Howe, Florence. comp. 2.10740
Howe, George Frederick, ed. 5.8220
Howe, Harold, 1918-. 4.10008
Howe, Hubert S. 1.4459
Howe, Ilana Wiener. 2.3777
Howe, Irving. 2.1828, 4.8235
Howe, Irving. ed. 3.3154
Howe, Irving. 1.1963, 2.2559, 2.3480, 2.3777, 2.11329, 3.8048, 4.7090
Howe, Irving. comp. 2.1826
Howe, Irving. 2.1824, 2.2678, 2.11694, 3.8049
Howe, Jeanne. 5.5177
Howe, Joseph, 1804-1873. 2.9904
Howe, Julia Ward, 1819-1910. 2.11082
Howe, K. R. 3.5546
Howe, Katherine S. 1.6521
Howe, Leland W. 4.10806
Howe, Mark De Wolfe, 1906-. 3.7393, 4.7881, 4.9818-4.9820
Howe, Mary Martha, joint author. 4.10806
Howe, Michael W., joint author. 4.6502
Howe, P. P. (Percival Presland), 1886-1944. 2.7804
Howe, Robin. joint author. 5.7107
Howe, Will David, 1873-1946, joint author. 5.7784
Howe, William H. 5.3880
Howell, David, 1945-. 4.8534
Howell, Elsworth S. joint author. 5.5453
Howell, John R. joint author. 5.2270
Howell, Joseph T. 4.2050
Howell, Nancy. 3.5483
Howell, Peter. 2.742
Howell, Wilbur Samuel, 1904-. 1.1160
Howells, Coral Ann. 2.6002
Howells, Mildred, 1872- ed. 2.11088
Howells, William Dean, 1837-1920. 2.3502, 2.10949, 2.10957, 2.11084-2.11088
Howells, William White, 1908-. 4.546, 4.663
Hower, Ralph Merle, 1903-. 4.4332
Howes, Alan B. 2.7284-2.7285
Howes, Davis H., ed. 5.242
Howes, Frank Stewart, 1891-. 1.3716, 1.4507
Howes, Wright. 5.7754
Howie, R. A. (Robert Andrew) joint author. 5.3015
Howie, R. A. (Robert Andrew) 5.3027
Howie, Sherry Hill, 1941-. 4.10478
Howie-Willis, Ian, 1937-. 3.5668
Howkins, John, 1945-. 2.54
Howley, Aimee. 4.10921
Howley, Craig B. 4.10921
Howorth, Henry Hoyle, Sir, 1842-1923. 3.3621
Howorth, Jolyon. 4.5358
Howse, Derek. 5.1758
Howson, Susan, 1945-. 4.4516
Hoxie, Frederick E., 1947-. 3.5818
Hoy, Helen. 5.7892
Hoy, Suellen M. 5.8388
Hoyer, William J. 4.6813
Hoyle, Fred. 5.1702, 5.1869-5.1870, 5.6608
Hoyt, Edwin C. (Edwin Chase), 1916-. 4.9050
Hoyt, Edwin Palmer. 2.12422, 3.6889
Hoyt, Nancy, 1902-. 2.12829
Hoyt, Robert S. (Robert Stuart) 3.2807
Hoyt, Ronald E. 4.4141
Hrabak, Diane E. 4.7708
Hrabal, Bohumil, 1914-. 2.1686-2.1687
Hren, John J. joint author. 5.6774
Hrotsvitha, ca. 935-ca. 975. 2.820
Hrushevs'kyĭ, Mykhaĭlo, 1866-1934. 3.3302
Hsia, Chih-tsing, 1921-. 2.2172, 2.2176, 2.2202, 2.2204
Hsia, Tao-tai, 1921-. 2.2145
Hsia, Tsi-an, 1916-1965. 2.2159
Hsiao, Chün, 1908-. 2.2251
Hsiao, David K., 1933-. 5.1233
Hsiao, Gene T. 3.6433
Hsiao, Katharine H. Y. Huang (Katharine Huei-Ying Huang), 1923-. 4.4522
Hsiao, Kung-ch'üan, 1897-. 3.4741, 4.7282, 4.8736
Hsiao, Tso-liang, 1910-. 4.7110
Hsiao, Yü, 1894-. 3.4832

Hsieh, Andrew C. K., 1941-. 3.4758
Hsieh, Chiao-min. 3.4868
Hsieh, Winston, ed. 5.8398
Hsiung, James Chieh, 1935-. 3.3631, 3.4869
Hsiung, Shih-i, 1902- tr. 2.2223
Hsü, Cho-yün, 1930-. 4.5415
Hsu, Francis L. K., 1909-. 3.4635, 3.6540, 4.442
Hsü, Immanuel Chung-yueh, 1923-. 3.4711, 4.9078
Hsu, Kai-yu, 1922-. 2.2186, 2.2191, 3.4816
Hsu, T. C. (Tao-Chiuh), 1917-. 5.3430
Hsüeh, Chün-tu, 1922-. 3.4820
Hsün-tzu, 340-245 B.C. 1.168-1.169
Htin Aung, U, 1909-. 2.2257
Hu, Cheng-yen, ca. 1582-ca. 1672. 1.6477
Hu, S. David. 5.6295
Hu, S. T. (Sze-Tsen), 1914-. 5.1591-5.1592
Hu, Shi Ming, 1927-. 4.10138
Hu, Shih, 1891-1962. 1.156
Huang, Kerson, 1928-. 5.2179, 5.2477
Huang, Philip C., 1940-. 3.4742, 4.2868
Hubbard, Frank. 1.4150
Hubbard, Margaret, 1924-. 2.725-2.726, 2.766
Hubbard, Ruth, 1924-. 4.5949, 5.4199
Hubbard, Stuart W. 5.5649
Hubbard, William B. 5.1806
Hubbart, Henry Clyde, 1882-. 3.8374
Hubbell, Harry Mortimer, 1881-. 2.658
Hubbell, Jay B. (Jay Broadus), 1885-1979. 2.10373, 2.10377, 2.10452
Huber, Thomas M. 3.4988
Huberman, Leo, 1903-1968. 2.2425, 3.9105
Hubert, Jean. 1.4741, 1.5170
Hubin, Allen J. 5.7963
Hubler, Edward. 2.6673-2.6674
Hübner, Kurt, 1921-. 5.898
Huch, Ricarda Octavia, 1864-1947. 2.13474
Huck, Charlotte S. 4.10469
Hucker, Charles O. 3.4636, 3.4707-3.4708, 4.8740
Huder, Walther. 2.13801
Hudlicky, Milos, 1919-. 5.2753
Hudson, Charles M. 3.5753
Hudson, Derek. ed. 2.2506
Hudson, Derek. 2.7678
Hudson, Geoffrey Francis, 1903-. 3.100, 3.4407
Hudson, Herman. 1.3754
Hudson Institute. 3.72, 4.2784
Hudson, John C. 4.6243
Hudson, Kenneth. 5.5542, 5.5545
Hudson, Manley Ottmer, 1886-. 4.9148
Hudson, Michael C. 3.3722, 3.3787, 4.5094
Hudson, Raymond. 4.2218
Hudson, Robert P. 5.4502
Hudson, Ronald. 2.7480
Hudson, Ronald. ed. 2.7466
Hudson, Theodore R. 2.12873
Hudson, Travis. 3.5859-3.5860
Hudson, W. H. (William Henry), 1841-1922. 2.8808-2.8809
Hudson, W. J. 4.8827
Hudson, W. Ronald. joint author. 5.6068
Hudson-Williams, Thomas, 1873-. 2.221
Hudson, Winthrop Still, 1911-. 1.2376-1.2377
Hudspeth, Robert N. 2.11190
Huebener, Theodore, 1895-. 2.13930
Huebner, Kenneth H., 1942-. 5.5727
Huelsenbeck, Richard, 1892-1974. 1.6733
Huenemann, Ralph William, 1939-. 4.4634
Huet, Michel, 1917-. 4.1111
Huettich, H. G., 1946-. 2.13932
Huf, Linda. 2.10598
Huff, Archie Vernon, 1937-. 3.7102
Huff, Douglas, 1944-. 5.2455
Huffaker, C. B., 1914-. 5.5409
Huffaker, Robert, 1936-. 2.9691
Huffschmidt, Maynard M. 4.1840
Huftel, Sheila. 2.12179
Hufton, Olwen H. 4.2335, 4.6626
Hügel, Friedrich, Freiherr von, 1852-1925. 1.1550
Hugenholtz, F. W. N. comp. 3.2984
Hugg, Lawrence, 1949-. 3.6608
Huggett, Frank Edward. 4.5284
Huggett, Richard J. 4.16
Huggins, Nathan Irvin, 1927-. 1.6714, 2.10704, 3.7191, 3.7239
Hugh, of Saint-Victor, 1096?-1141. 1.3221

Hughes, A. E. (Antony Elwyn) 5.2194
Hughes, Charles Evans, 1862-1948. 3.7437
Hughes, Christopher. 3.3507
Hughes, Colin A. 4.8822
Hughes, Connie O. 4.1678
Hughes, David, 1930-. 2.9252
Hughes, Derek, 1944-. 2.7005
Hughes, E. R. (Ernest Richard), 1883-1956. 1.155
Hughes, Emmet John, 1920-. 3.7823
Hughes, Everett Cherrington, 1897-. 3.8819
Hughes, G. E. (George Edward), 1918-. 1.1251
Hughes, Glenn, 1894-1964. 2.3191
Hughes, Glyn Tegai. 2.839
Hughes, Gwilym Rees. 2.832
Hughes, H. Stuart (Henry Stuart), 1916-. 3.434, 3.742, 3.2907
Hughes, Helen MacGill, 1903-. 2.3541
Hughes, James J. 4.3227
Hughes, James Quentin. 5.7391
Hughes, James W. 4.1678, 4.3488, 4.6353
Hughes, John, 1930-. 3.4574
Hughes, Kathleen. 3.1812
Hughes, Langston, 1902-1967. 2.3747, 2.10814, 2.11395, 2.11864-2.11900, 4.769
Hughes, Leo, 1908-. 2.3316
Hughes, Marija Matich. 4.9694
Hughes, Merritt Yerkes, 1893-. 2.7116, 2.7118, 2.7144, 2.7168
Hughes, Olga Raevsky. 2.1596
Hughes, Philip, 1895-. 1.2275
Hughes, Richard Arthur Warren, 1900-1976. 2.2342, 2.8810, 2.9709, 2.9709a
Hughes, Robert, 1936-. 1.4782, 3.5575
Hughes, Russell Meriwether, 1898-. 4.1146
Hughes, Sally Smith. 5.4473
Hughes, Ted, 1930-. 2.9710-2.9717, 2.13254, 2.13260
Hughes, Terry. joint author. 3.819, 3.962
Hughes, Thomas, 1822-1896. 2.7840-2.7841
Hughes, Thomas Parke. 5.6288
Hughes, Thomas Patrick, 1838-1911. 1.1994
Hughes, Trevor Jones. 4.2480
Hughes, Vernon W. 5.2065
Hughes, Winifred, 1948-. 2.6031
Hughston, George A. 4.5799
Hugnet, Georges, 1906-1974. 1.4818
Hugo Black Symposium in American History. 1st, University of Alabama, 1976. 4.9658
Hugo Black Symposium in American History. (4th: 1979: University of Alabama in Birmingham) 1.2479
Hugo, Richard F. 2.11904-2.11905
Hugo, Victor, 1802-1885. 2.4233-2.4238
Huheey, James E. 5.2699
Huidobro, Vicente, 1893-1948. 2.5409
Huijzen, Chr. van. joint author. 5.4152
Huisken, Ronald. joint author. 4.9168
Huiskes, A. H. L. 5.3780
Huisman, Philippe. 3.2053
Huitt, Ralph K. 4.8012
Huizinga, Johan, 1872-1945. 3.55, 3.361, 3.1955, 3.2984
Hujvīrī, 'Alī ibn 'Usmān, d. ca. 1072. 1.2084
Huke, Robert E. 4.2537
Hulbert, Homer Bezaleel, 1863-1949. 3.4998
Hulbert, James Root, 1884- joint ed. 2.1135
Hulet, Claude L. (Claude Lyle), 1920- comp. 2.5466
Hull, Clark Leonard. 4.10369, 5.217-5.219
Hull, Cordell, 1871-1955. 3.7649
Hull, David L. comp. 5.3355
Hull, David L. 5.3326
Hull, Derek. 5.2926, 5.5794
Hull, Galen. 4.2594
Hull, Gloria T. 2.11610, 3.6747
Hull, N. E. H., 1949-. 4.9735
Hull, R. F. C. (Richard Francis Carrington), 1913-1974. 3.45
Hull, Richard W., 1940-. 3.5229, 4.6284
Hullfish, Henry Gordon, 1894-. 4.10366
Hulme, Keri. 2.10226
Hulme, T. E. (Thomas Ernest), 1883-1917. 1.1273
Hulse, Clark, 1947-. 2.5796
Hulst, Roger Adolf d'. 1.6265
Hulteng, John L., 1921-. 2.3562
Hultgren, Thor, 1902-. 4.3994

Hultkrantz, Åke. 4.471
Human Relations Area Files, Inc. 3.4387, 3.4454
Human Rights Internet. 4.7637
Humason, Gretchen L. 5.4161
Humayun Kabir, 1906-1969. comp. 2.1874
Humboldt, Alexander von, 1769-1859. 3.8879, 3.9150
Humboldt, Wilhelm, Freiherr von, 1767-1835. 3.403
Hume, David, 1711-1776. 1.697-1.698, 1.700, 1.1551, 3.1241, 4.1413
Hume, Robert D. 2.3301, 2.3322, 2.5893, 2.5897, 2.5912
Hume, Robert Ernest, 1877-1948. 1.1683
Humiston, Gerard E., 1939-. 5.2625
Humm, Harold Judson. 5.3712
Hummel, Arthur William, 1884-. 3.4657
Hummel, John H. joint author. 4.10695
Hümmelchen, Gerhard, 1927-. 3.1028
Hummer, T. R. 2.12982
Hummert, Paul A., 1918-. 2.8089
Humpherson, Roy. 2.2118
Humpherys, Anne. 2.7935
Humpherys, DeVerl S. 5.6513
Humphrey, Arthur Earl, joint author. 5.6867
Humphrey, Caroline. 4.2916
Humphrey, David C., 1937-. 4.10991
Humphrey, Doris, 1895-1958. 4.1121, 4.1147
Humphrey, Hubert H. (Hubert Horatio), 1911-1978. 3.7650
Humphrey, James Harry, 1911-. 5.617
Humphrey, John P. 4.7682
Humphrey, Robert, fl. 1954-. 2.3442
Humphreys, A. R. (Arthur Raleigh), 1911-. 2.5662, 2.7242, 3.1530
Humphreys, Janice. 5.4967
Humphreys, Patrick. 4.8504
Humphreys, R. A. (Robert Arthur), 1907-. 3.946
Humphreys, Sheila M. 5.804
Humphreys, W. J. (William Jackson), 1862-1949. 5.2502
Humphries, Charles W. (Charles Walter), 1932-. 3.8828
Humphries, Christopher John. 5.3232
Humphries, Colin M. (Colin Michael), 1938-. 5.1747
Humphries, Rolfe, 1894-1969. 2.11906
Hundert, Gershon David, 1946-. 5.8242
Hunerberg, Catherine. 4.10785
Hung, William, 1893-. 2.2214
Hungerford, Thomas W. 5.1270
Hungerland, Isabel Payson Creed, 1907-. 2.2718
Hungler, Bernadette P. 5.5188
Hunnigher, Benjamin. 2.2804
Hunt, Annie Mae, 1909-. 3.6808
Hunt, Barry D. (Barry Dennis), 1937-. 3.774
Hunt, Charles Butler, 1906-. 4.248
Hunt, David C., 1935-. 1.6389
Hunt, Edgar, 1909-. 1.4167
Hunt, Edward E. 4.464
Hunt, G. N. S. 1.2551
Hunt, G. W. 5.5861
Hunt, Gaillard, 1862-1924. ed. 4.7821
Hunt, Garry E. 5.1789
Hunt, George W., 1937-. 2.11497
Hunt, H. Allan. 4.3322
Hunt, Herbert James. 2.4112, 2.4123
Hunt, John Dixon. 2.7106
Hunt, Leigh, 1784-1859. 2.5539, 2.7842-2.7844
Hunt, Lynn Avery. 3.2097, 3.2120
Hunt, Marion Edith (Waugh) Holman, ed. 1.6016
Hunt, Mary Alice. 5.7719
Hunt, Michael H. 3.6426
Hunt, Morton M., 1920-. 4.6755, 5.267
Hunt, Richard N. 4.7452
Hunt, Robert Nigel Carew. 4.6934
Hunt, Roy E. 5.5891
Hunt, Stanley Ernest. 5.6602
Hunt, Timothy L. 4.3322
Hunt, V. Daniel. 5.1000, 5.6305
Hunt, William, 1944-. 3.1242, 3.1736
Hunt, William Holman, 1827-1910. 1.6016
Hunt, William R. 3.8645
Hunten, Donald M. 5.1803
Hunter, Albert. 4.5208

Hunter Blair, Peter, 1912-1982. 2.6287, 3.1319
Hunter, Dard, 1883-1966. 5.7074
Hunter, David E. 4.408
Hunter, Donald, 1898-. 5.5014
Hunter, Floyd. 4.4950
Hunter, G. K. ed. 2.5852
Hunter, G. K. 2.6493, 2.7130
Hunter, G. K. comp. 2.6884
Hunter, Geoffrey. 1.1197
Hunter, George Kirkpatrick. 2.6624
Hunter, Guy. 4.5468
Hunter, Holland. 4.3900
Hunter, J. A. 3.8958
Hunter, J. Paul, 1934-. 2.3744, 2.7025
Hunter, J. Stuart, 1923- joint author. 5.5715
Hunter, Janet. 3.4956
Hunter, Michael Cyril William. 5.696, 5.778
Hunter, Richard Alfred. ed. 5.4803
Hunter, Robert Grams. 2.6784
Hunter, S. K., joint comp. 2.6884
Hunter, Sam, 1923-. 1.4662, 1.4870, 1.5670, 1.5673, 1.5942
Hunter, Walter Samuel, 1889-1954, ed. 5.1
Hunter, William Bridges, 1915-. 2.6155a, 2.6593, 2.7147
Hunting, Warren Belknap, 1888-1918. 4.9651
Huntington, David C. 1.5928
Huntington, Ellsworth, 1876-1947. 4.365
Huntington, John C. 1.5047
Huntington, Richard. 4.590
Huntington, Samuel P. ed. 4.7594
Huntington, Samuel P. 4.7219, 5.7255, 5.7272
Huntington, Samuel P. joint author. 4.7559
Huntington, Susan L. 1.5047
Hupman, Richard D. comp. 4.8139
Huppé, Bernard Felix, 1911-. 2.5598, 2.6296
Hupping, Carol. 5.6113
Hurd, C. M. (Colin Michael), 1937-. 5.2204
Hurd, Charles, 1903-1968, ed. 2.10854
Hurd, Frank Kenneth, 1912- joint author. 5.2360
Hurd, Paul DeHart, 1905-. 5.3307
Hurd, Richard, Bp. of Worcester, 1720-1808. 2.7077
Hurewicz, Witold, 1904-1956. 5.1516
Hurewitz, J. C., 1914-. 3.3676, 3.3726, 3.3916
Hurlbut, Cornelius Searle, 1906-. 5.3021
Hurley, Alfred F. 5.7403
Hurley, F. Jack (Forrest Jack) 5.6996
Hursh-César, Gerald. 4.5014
Hurst, Jack. 1.3484
Hurst, James Willard, 1910-. 4.9484
Hurst, John G., 1927- joint author. 3.1326
Hurst, Marsha. 4.3247
Hurst, Michael. comp. 4.8965
Hurston, Zora Neale. 2.11908-2.11911, 4.770
Hurt, James, 1934-. 2.6286
Hurt, R. Douglas. 5.5237
Hurtado, Osvaldo. 4.5275
Hurvich, Leo Maurice, 1910-. 5.4384
Hurvitz, Leon, 1923-. 1.2134
Hurwitz, Leon. 4.9267
Husaini, M. A., tr. 2.1902
Husband, Margaret Fair Anderson. 2.8045
Husband, Timothy. 1.6646
Husbands, Christopher T. 3.1715, 4.8502
Husch, Bertram, 1923-. 5.5431
Huschke, R. E. (Ralph E.), 1925-. 5.2497, 5.2540
Husén, Torsten, 1916-. 4.9966, 4.10167
Hussain, Asaf. 4.5436
Hussain, Donna. 4.4346
Hussain, Khateeb M., 1924-. 4.4346
Hussaini, M. Yousuff. 5.1667
Husserl, Edmund, 1859-1938. 1.1008-1.1014, 1.1016
Hussey, Christopher, 1899-. 1.5573, 5.5382
Hussey, Edward. 5.834
Hussey, Maurice. 2.6202
Hussey, S. S., 1925-. 2.6360
Huston, James A. (James Alvin), 1918-. 5.7224
Huston, Perdita, 1936-. 4.6168
Hutcheon, Wallace, 1933-. 5.7506
Hutcheson, Ernest, 1871-1951. 1.4526
Hutcheson, Francis, 1694-1746. 1.1427-1.1429
Hutchings, Arthur, 1906-. 1.4199, 1.4525
Hutchings, Edward. 5.1950
Hutchings, R. T. joint author. 5.4146

Hutchins, Francis G. 3.4263, 3.8004
Hutchins, John Greenwood Brown, 1909-.
　5.7504
Hutchins, Robert Maynard, 1899-. 1.1, 4.9969,
　4.9996, 4.10232, 4.10544, 4.10821
Hutchinson, B. G. 4.3901
Hutchinson, Francis Ernest, 1871-1947. 2.7061,
　2.7327
Hutchinson, G. Evelyn (George Evelyn), 1903-.
　5.3260, 5.3520
Hutchinson, J. (John), 1884-1972. 5.3656
Hutchinson, John, 1793-1865, comp. 3.7973
Hutchinson, Lester, 1904-. 3.4259
Hutchinson, Lois Irene. 4.4343
Hutchinson, Richard Wyatt, 1894-. 3.2592
Hutchinson, Thomas, 1711-1780. 3.7973
Hutchinson, William Thomas, 1895-. 3.6254,
　3.6975
Hutchison, Bruce. 3.8659, 3.8748, 3.8864
Hutchison, Charles S. (Charles Strachan),
　1933-. 5.3039, 5.6733
Hutchison, D. 5.3042
Hutchison, George Scott, joint comp. 4.4326
Hutchison, Jane C. 1.6432
Hutchison, Keith. 4.2281
Hutchison, T. W. (Terence Wilmot) 4.1277,
　4.1307
Hutchison, Terence Wilmot. 4.1308
Hutchison, William R. 1.2792
Huters, Ted. 2.2187
Huters, Theodore. 2.2238
Huth, Hans, 1892-. 5.3228
Hutner, Frances Cornwall. 4.3259
Hutner, S. H. (Seymour Herbert), 1911-. 5.3838
Hutson, James H. 3.6897, 3.6937, 3.8075,
　4.7201
Hutten, Ernest H. (Ernest Hirschlaff), 1908-.
　5.899
Huttenback, Robert A. 3.5461, 4.8917
Hutterer, Karl L. 4.640
Hüttermann, H. 5.8008
Huttman, Elizabeth D., 1929-. 4.3481, 4.6591
Hutton, J. H. (John Henry), 1885-1968. 3.4175
Huxley, Aldous, 1894-1963. 2.2388, 2.2575,
　2.8812-2.8823, 4.4970, 4.5099, 5.671, 5.5140
Huxley, Anthony Julian, 1920- ed. 4.274-4.275,
　4.312
Huxley, Elspeth Joscelin Grant, 1907-. 5.5164
Huxley, Julian, 1887-1975. 1.1484, 1.1532,
　5.3204, 5.3431
Huxley, Leonard, 1860-1933. 5.3205, 5.3639
Huxley, Thomas Henry, 1825-1895. 1.1484,
　5.846, 5.3195, 5.3205, 5.3380
Huxtable, Ada Louise. 1.5485, 1.5543
Huyghe, René. 1.6095
Huỳnh, Kim Khánh. 4.7122
Huỳnh, Sanh Thông, 1926-. 2.2262
Huyser, Earl S., 1927-. 5.2726
Huysmans, J.-K. (Joris-Karl), 1848-1907.
　2.4244-2.4248
Hvorslev, Mikael Juul, 1895-. 5.5894
Hwang, David. 2.209
Hwang, Kai. 5.1155, 5.6580
Hyam, Ronald. 3.1222, 4.8913
Hyams, Edward, 1912-1975. 4.7051
Hyams, Paul R. 4.6409
Hyde, G. M. (George M.), 1941-. 2.1586
Hyde, George E., 1882-1968. 3.5936
Hyde, H. Montgomery (Harford Montgomery),
　1907-. 2.8280-2.8281
Hyde, Janet Shibley. 4.5487
Hyde, John Kenneth. 3.2843
Hyde, Lewis, 1945-. 2.5228
Hyde, Mary Morley Crapo. 2.7184
Hyde, Richard M. 5.4464
Hydén, Göran, 1938-. 4.2881
Hyder, Clyde Kenneth, 1902- joint ed. 2.7048
Hyer, Paul. joint author. 3.4860
Hyink, Bernard L. 4.8267
Hyman, Arthur, 1921-. 1.345
Hyman, Drew. joint author. 4.6875
Hyman, Harold Melvin, 1924-. 3.7306, 3.7332,
　4.7843
Hyman, Herbert Harvey. joint author. 5.4619
Hyman, Herbert Hiram, 1918-. 4.5792
Hyman, Irwin. 4.10707
Hyman, Larry M. 2.175
Hyman, Louis, 1912-. 3.3974

Hyman, Paula, 1946-. 3.3961
Hyman, Ronald T. joint author. 3.8960
Hyman, Sidney. 3.7628
Hyman, Stanley Edgar, 1919-1970. 2.2462,
　2.2471, 2.2507, 2.2576, 2.2679
Hymes, Dell H. joint author. 2.27
Hymes, Dell H. 2.22, 2.2329
Hymes, James L., 1913-. 4.10691
Hynd, George W. 4.10706
Hyndman, Donald W. 5.3047
Hynek, J. Allen (Joseph Allen), 1910-. 5.6695
Hyneman, Charles Shang, 1900-. 4.7813
Hynes, Hugh Bernard Noel, 1917-. 5.3566
Hynes, Samuel Lynn. 2.5743, 2.7762, 2.7790,
　3.1682
Hynes, Samuel Lynn. ed. 2.5506
Hynes, Samuel Lynn. comp. 2.8774, 2.9183
Hyppolite, Jean. 1.933, 1.1035
Hyslop, Lois Boe, 1908-. 2.4142
Hyslop, Marjorie R. 5.6766
Hytier, Jean. 2.4564, 2.4761, 2.4768

IAglom, A. M. joint author. 5.1664
IAkubaĭtis, Éduard Aleksandrovich. 5.6412
IAkubovich, V. A. (Vladimir Andreevich)
　5.1517
Ianni, Francis A. J. 4.6779
Iatrides, John O. 3.2703
IAU Colloquium. (67th: 1981: Zelenchukskaia,
　R.S.F.S.R.) 5.1747
Iberall, Arthur S. 5.994
Ibn 'Aṭā' Allāh, Ahmad ibn Muhammad, d.
　1309. 1.2086
Ibn Bābūyah, Abu Ja'far Muhammad ibn 'Ali
　al-Qummi al-Sadūq, d. 991. 1.2090
Ibn Hishām, 'Abd al-Malik, d. 834. 1.2014
Ibn Isbāk, Muhammad, d. ca. 768. 1.2014
Ibn Khaldūn, 1332-1406. 3.451-3.452
Ibn Taymīyah, Ahmad ibn 'Abd al-Halīm,
　1263-1328. 1.2067
Ibrahim, Saad Eddin. 4.2571, 4.5462
Ibsen, Henrik, 1828-1906. 2.14034-2.14035
Ibuse, Masuji, 1898-. 2.2097
Icaza, Jorge, 1906-. 2.5422
Ichimura, Shin'ichi, 1925- ed. 4.2433
Ickes, Harold L. (Harold LeClair), 1874-1952.
　3.7653
Idaho. Federal Writers' Project. 3.8549
Idaho State University. Dept. of History. 2.9887
Idelsohn, Abraham Zebi, 1882-1938. 1.4351
Idowu, E. Bolaji. 1.1845, 1.1864
Idyll, C. P. (Clarence P.) 5.3246
Idzerda, Stanley J. 3.6893
Idzikowski, Stanislas, joint author. 4.1117
IEEE Computer Society. 5.1140, 5.5653, 5.6543
Ifkovic, Edward, 1943-. 2.2690
Ifrah, Georges. 5.1264
Iggers, Georg G. 3.394, 3.2248
Iglauer, Edith. 1.5348
Iglitzin, Lynne B., 1931-. 4.5902
Ignatieff, Michael. 4.1346, 4.6918
Ignatius, of Loyola, Saint, 1491-1556. 1.3219
Ignatius, Saint, Bishop of Antioch, d. ca. 110.
　2.327
Ignatow, David, 1914-. 2.11914
Igoe, James. 5.8190
Igoe, Lynn, 1937-. 5.8190
Ihara, Saikaku, 1642-1693. 2.2062-2.2063
Ihde, Aaron John, 1909-. 5.2607
Ihde, Don, 1934-. 1.525, 1.846
Ihimaera, Witi Tame, 1944-. 2.10227
Ijiri, Yuji. 4.4391
IJsseling, Samuel, 1932-. 2.2533
Ike, Nobutaka. 4.8753
Ike, Nobutaka. ed. 3.945
Ikels, Charlotte. 3.7998
Ikime, Obaro. 3.5082
Iklé, Fred Charles. 4.9321
Iklé, Max. 4.4544
Ikram, Sheikh Mohamad, 1908-. 3.4123, 3.4196
Ilchman, Warren Frederick. joint comp. 4.7716
Ilg, Frances Lillian, 1902- joint author. 4.5719,
　5.565
Iliffe, John. 3.5300, 4.2605
Illich, Ivan, 1926-. 4.10006, 5.4645
Illick, Joseph E. 3.8076
Illingworth, Valerie. 5.1680

Illinois. Centennial Commission. 3.8407
Illinois Humanities Council. 2.929
Illinois Labor History Society. 4.3590
Illinois. University at Urbana-Champaign.
　Center for International Comparative Studies.
　4.5374
Illinois. University at Urbana-Champaign.
　Russian and East European Center. 2.1737,
　4.5374
Illuminating Engineering Society. 5.6337
Illuminating Engineering Society of North
　America. 5.6337
Ilogu, Edmund. 1.1858
Imlah, Albert Henry, 1901-. 4.4228
Immergut, E. H. joint ed. 5.2773
Immerwahr, Henry R. 2.477
Imms, A. D. (Augustus Daniel), 1880-1949.
　5.3857
Imperato, Pascal James. 5.4655
Impey, O. R. (Oliver R.) 1.5109
Inada, Kenneth K. 1.214, 5.8343
Inalcik, Halil, 1916-. 3.3579
Inbau, Fred Edward. joint author. 5.4716
Incropera, Frank P. 5.2265
Inden, Ronald B. 3.4328, 4.631
Independent Commission on International
　Development Issues. 4.4142-4.4143
Index of American Design. 1.6515
Index Society, New York. 5.7941
India. Ministry of Information and
　Broadcasting. 3.4155
India Office Library. 3.4289
India Office Records. 3.4289
India (Republic). Central Gazetteers Unit.
　3.4156
Indian Council of Social Science Research.
　5.5253
Indian Economic Association. 4.3234
Indiana University. 2.2697, 3.3618, 4.1652
Indiana. University. Afro-American Arts
　Institute. 1.3754
Indiana University, Bloomington. 3.3323
Indiana University, Bloomington. African
　Studies Program. 4.648
Indiana. University. Dept. of History and
　Philosophy of Science. 5.884
Indiana University. International Affairs Center.
　2.1759
Indiana University. Libraries. 5.7873
Indianapolis Museum of Art. 1.6622
Industrial Democracy in Europe. International
　Research Group. 4.3630
Industrial Relations Research Association.
　4.3349
Indy, Vincent d', 1851-1931. 1.3871
Infante, Mary Sue, 1939-. 5.5191
Infantry journal. 5.7163
Infeld, Leopold, 1898-1968. 5.1932, 5.1951
Infomap, Inc. 4.147
Information Access Corporation. 1.31, 5.8367
Ingalls, Jeremy, 1911- ed. and tr. 3.4722
Ingalls, Robert P., 1941-. 3.8033
Ingarden, Roman, 1893-. 1.1494, 2.2362
Inge, M. Thomas. joint author. 2.11554
Inge, M. Thomas. 2.11778, 3.6115
Inge, M. Thomas. ed. 2.11045
Inge, William. 2.11915-2.11916
Inge, William Ralph. 1.3092
Ingelhart, Louis E. (Louis Edward) 4.9597
Ingham, Keith P. D. 4.2300
Ingholt, Harald, 1896-. 1.5051
Ingle, Dwight Joyce, 1907- ed. 5.4479
Ingle, John Ide, 1919-. 5.5124
Ingles, O. G. 5.5900
Ingleson, John. 3.4568
Inglis, David Rittenhouse, 1905-. 5.2453
Inglis, Kenneth Stanley. 1.2445, 3.5576
Inglis, R. M. G. 5.1740
Ingold, Christopher, Sir, 1893-. 5.2854
Ingraham, John L. 5.4455
Ingraham, Larry H. 5.7243
Ingram, Derek George Woodward. 5.6398
Ingram, James C. 4.2528
Ingram, Vernon M. 5.4224
Ingram, William. 2.7170
Ingrams, Doreen. 3.3917

Ingres, Jean-Auguste-Dominique, 1780-1867.
  1.6111-1.6114
Ingstad, Anne Stine, 1918-. 3.8871
Ingstad, Helge, 1899-. 3.3361
Ingwersen, Faith. 2.14025, 2.14029
Ingwersen, Niels. joint author. 2.14025
Ingwersen, Niels. 2.14003, 2.14029
Inhaber, Herbert, 1941-. 5.6000
Inhelder, Bärbel. 5.567
Inhelder, Bärbel. joint author. 5.334, 5.574,
  5.588, 5.596
Innaurato, Albert, 1948-. 2.13095
Innes, C. D. 2.3339, 2.13494
Innes, Catherine Lynette. 2.10107
Innes, Mary M. 2.748
Innes, Michael, 1906-. 2.9386
Innes, Stephen. joint author. 3.8215
Inness, George, 1825-1894. 1.5947-1.5948
Innis, Harold A., 1894-1952. 4.2118
Innis, Harold Adams, 1894-1952. 2.3577,
  3.8836, 4.2116, 4.2122
Innocent III, Pope, 1160 or 61-1216. 1.2905
Inoguchi, Rikihei. 3.1055
Inose, Hiroshi, 1927-. 4.3934
Inoue, Hirochika, 1942-. 5.6165
Inoura, Yoshinobu, 1914-. 2.3398
Insdorf, Annette. 2.3069
Insingel, Mark. 2.13961
Inson, Graeme, joint author. 3.5564
Institut für Asienkunde (Hamburg, Germany)
  4.8743
Institut für Seeverkehrswirtschaft Bremen.
  4.3964
Institut geografii (Akademiia nauk SSSR)
  4.2368
Institut géographique national (France) 4.129
Institut Lenina. 3.3145
Institute for Advanced Studies of World
  Religions. 1.2166
Institute for Annual Review of United Nations
  Affairs. 4.9198
Institute for Computer Sciences and
  Technology. 5.4613
Institute for Cross-Cultural Research (U.S.)
  3.3288
Institute for Development of Educational
  Activities. 4.10449
Institute for International Economics (U.S.)
  4.4582
Institute for Policy Studies. 4.3487
Institute for Research on Public Policy.
  4.8274-4.8275, 4.8291
Institute for Sex Research. 4.5510, 4.5528
Institute for Strategic Studies (London,
  England) 5.7216
Institute for the Future. 5.6566
Institute for the History of Science, University
  of Wisconsin, 1957. 5.737
Institute for the Study of Human Issues. 4.2439
Institute for World Order. 4.7624
Institute in Hydrology for College Teachers,
  Princeton University, 1965. 4.295
Institute of Early American History and
  Culture (Williamsburg, Va.) 1.3054, 1.5310,
  3.6015, 3.6018, 3.6619, 3.6897, 3.6925,
  3.7002, 3.7009, 3.7019, 3.7048, 3.7971,
  3.8107, 3.8184, 3.8200, 3.8210, 3.8242,
  3.8258, 3.8357, 3.9141, 4.3106, 4.4498,
  4.7319, 4.7828, 4.8073, 4.8211, 4.9486
Institute of Economic Affairs (Great Britain)
  4.2394
Institute of Electrical and Electronics
  Engineers. 5.6249
Institute of International Education (New York,
  N.Y.) 4.10540, 4.10621-4.10622
Institute of Jewish Affairs. 3.3994, 3.4009
Institute of Labour and Industrial Relations
  (University of Michigan-Wayne State
  University) 4.3514
Institute of Medicine (U.S.) 5.4209, 5.4680,
  5.5124
Institute of Medicine (U.S.). Division of Health
  Care Services. 5.5184
Institute of Pacific Relations. 3.5006, 4.5440
Institute of Pacific Relations. American
  Council. 3.4949
Institute of Petroleum (Great Britain) 5.6802

Institute of Psycho-analysis (London, England)
  5.140
Institute of Race Relations. 3.5288
Institute of Southeast Asian Studies. 3.4576,
  4.3785, 4.5406, 4.5441, 5.8059
Institute of Transportation and Traffic
  Engineering. 4.4030
Institute of Transportation Engineers. 4.3929,
  4.3943, 5.6066
Institute of Women Today. 4.5837
Institute on the Structure of the Labor Market,
  American University, Washington, D.C.,
  1950. 4.3330
Institution of Electrical Engineers. 5.6398
Institution of Electrical Engineers. Electronics
  Division. 5.5959
Institution of Mechanical Engineers (Great
  Britain). Automobile Division. 5.6623
Institution of Mechanical Engineers (Great
  Britain). Combustion Engines Group. 5.6623
Instituto de Estudios Peruanos. 3.9018
Instituto Nacional de Investigaciones Agrarias.
  5.5341
Instituttet for sammenlignende kulturforskning,
  Oslo. 1.5191
Inter-American Development Bank. 4.2143
Inter-parliamentary Union. 4.7727
Inter-union Institute for Labor and Democracy.
  4.3356
Inter-university committee for African studies.
  3.5460
Inter-university Project on the History of the
  Menshevik movement. 4.8665
Inter-university Seminar on Armed Forces and
  Society. 5.7208
Intergovernmental Committee on Refugees.
  3.1101
International Advertising Association (1938-)
  4.4436
International African Institute. 3.5059, 3.5478
International Association for Quaternary
  Research. 5.3146
International Association of Agricultural
  Economists. 4.136
International Association of Music Libraries.
  1.3445
International Association of Universities.
  4.9934-4.9935
International Astronomical Union. 5.1679
International Atomic Energy Agency. 5.6298
International Automobile Program. 4.3817
International Bank for Reconstruction and
  Development. 4.1401, 4.1794, 4.2534, 4.2601,
  4.2607, 4.2613, 4.3233, 4.4053, 4.4568
International Biological Programme. 5.3541,
  5.3570
International Botanical Congress. (13th: 1981:
  Sydney, N.S.W.) 5.3654
International Cartographic Association.
  Commission II: Definition, Classification and
  Standardization of Technical Terms in
  Cartography. 4.75
International Center for Heat and Mass
  Transfer. 5.2261, 5.6155
International Center for Integrated and
  Biological Control. 5.5409
International Center of Photography. 5.6915
International City Management Association.
  4.8837, 4.8850
International City Managers' Association.
  4.8850
International Colloquium in the Philosophy of
  Science (1965: Bedford College) 5.900
International Colloquium of the Corpus
  Vitrearum. (11th: 1982: New York) 1.6646
International Commission for a History of the
  Scientific and Cultural Development of
  Mankind. 3.519
International Commission for the History of
  Towns. 4.171
International Commission of Folk Arts and
  Folklore. 4.471
International Commission of Jurists (1952-)
  4.7682
International Committee for Social Sciences
  Documentation. 5.8374
International Conference Group on Modern
  Portugal. 3.3505

International Conference of Building Officials.
  4.9762
International Conference on Behavioral Travel
  Demand (1975: Asheville, N.C.) 4.3931
International Conference on Biomass. (2nd:
  1982: Berlin, Germany: West) 5.6883
International Conference on Computers and the
  Humanities. (6th: 1983: North Carolina State
  University) 1.72
International Conference on Conrad,
  Canterbury, Eng., 1974. 2.8548
International Conference on Economic
  Development of Southeast Asia, Kyoto, 1972.
  4.2433
International Conference on Energy Options.
  (4th: 1984: London) 5.6129
International Conference on Optical Fibre
  Sensors. (1st: 1983: London, England) 5.5959
International Conference on Personal Rapid
  Transit, 2d, University of Minnesota, 1973.
  4.3902
International Conference on Polish-Jewish
  Studies (1984: Oxford, Oxfordshire) 3.3985
International Conference on Robotics and
  Intelligent Machines in Agriculture. (1st:
  1983: Tampa, Fla.) 5.5297
International Conference on Soil Conservation
  (1980: National College of Agricultural
  Engineering) 5.5286
International Conference on Soil Erosion and
  Conservation (1983: Honolulu, Hawaii)
  5.5288
International Conference on Soviet and East
  European Agricultural Affairs. (6th: 1981:
  Schloss Rauisch-Holzhausen) 4.2975
International Conference on Technology
  Assessment, Monaco, 1975. 5.5632
International Conference on the History of
  Urban and Regional Planning. 1st, London,
  1977. 4.6311
International Conference on the Utilization of
  Tidal Power, Nova Scotia Technical College,
  1970. 5.5964
International Congress for Modern
  Architecture. 4th, Athens, 1933. 1.5578
International Congress of Anthropological and
  Ethnological Sciences. 8th, Tokyo and Kyoto,
  1968. 5.4014
International Congress of Anthropological and
  Ethnological Sciences. 9th, Chicago, 1973.
  3.6760, 4.516, 4.571, 4.718, 4.5836, 5.7154
International Congress of Philosophy, 13th,
  Mexico, 1963. 1.661
International Congress of Primatology. (2nd:
  1968: Atlanta, Ga.) 5.4014
International Congress of Sport Psychology, 2d,
  Washington, D.C., 1968. 4.903
International Congress on Ericksonian
  Approaches to Hypnosis and Psychotherapy
  (1980: Phoenix, Ariz.) 5.4898
International Congress on Technology
  Assessment. 2d, University of Michigan,
  1976. 5.5633
International Council for Computers in
  Education. 4.10934
International Council for Educational
  Development. 4.10102, 4.10970
International Council for Science Policy Studies.
  5.962
International Council of Religious Education.
  American Standard Bible Committee. 1.2683
International Council of Scientific Unions. 5.992
International Council on the Future of the
  University. 4.10534
International Crisis Behavior Project. 3.2502
International Economic Association. 4.1484,
  4.2523, 4.2756, 4.2781-4.2782, 4.3131, 4.3202,
  4.3234, 4.8940, 5.8374
International Ecumenical Congress of Theology.
  (4th: 1980: São Paulo, Brazil) 1.3227
International Energy Agency. 4.3709
International Energy Symposium. (1st: 1980:
  Knoxville, Tenn.) 5.6117
International Energy Symposium. (2nd: 1981:
  Knoxville, Tenn.) 5.6118
International Exhibitions Foundation. 1.6475
International Federation of Gynecology and
  Obstetrics. 5.4255

International Federation of Teachers of French.
2.4798
International Football Association Board.
4.1019
International Geographical Union. Commission
on Geographical Education. 4.36
International Geographical Union. Commission
on National Settlement Systems. 4.6197
International Institute for Applied Systems
Analysis. 4.3912, 5.6017, 5.6299
International Institute for Applied Systems
Analysis. Energy Systems Program Group.
5.6130
International Institute for Labour Studies.
4.3424
International Institute for Strategic Studies.
3.4138, 5.7216
International Institute for the Study of Human
Reproduction. Center for Population and
Family Health. 4.1579
International Institute of Ibero-American
Literature. 2.5303, 2.5320, 2.5466
International Institute of Philosophy. 1.451
International Institute of Refrigeration. 5.6891
International Institute of Welding. 5.7062
International Josquin Festival-Conference, New
York, 1971. 1.3853
International Labor Office. World Employment
Programme. 4.6170
International Labour Office. 4.2876, 4.3199,
4.5484, 4.6155, 5.5622
International Labour Organisation. 5.5012
International League for the Rights of Man and
the New Democracy, Inc. 4.3101
International Lecture Course, 4th, Wageningen,
1965. 5.4135
International Machine Intelligence Workshop.
5.1012
International Mathematical Union. 5.1317
International Metallographic Society. 5.6769
International Military Tribunal. 3.1074
International Musicological Society. 1.3445,
1.3853
International Organization of Plant
Biosystematists. 5.3653
International Peace Academy. 4.9257
International Phonetic Association. 2.186
International Press Institute. 2.3572
International Printing Machinery and Allied
Trades Exhibition (1963: London, England)
5.7541
International Productivity Symposium. (1st:
1983: Tokyo, Japan) 4.2088
International Reading Association. 4.10410,
4.10455
International Repertory of Music Literature
(Organization) 1.3445
International Review Group of Social Science
Research on Population and Development.
4.1626
International Scholars' Conference. 1st, Wayne
State University, 1970. 1.2455
International security. 3.775
International Sedimentological Congress. 8th,
Heidelberg, 1971. 4.350
International Seminar on the Ramayana
Tradition in Asia (1975: New Delhi, India)
1.1694
International Sheep Breeding Congress, Muresk
and Perth, Australia, 1976. 5.5449
International Society for Technology
Assessment. 5.5632-5.5633
International Society of Soil Mechanics and
Foundation Engineering. 5.5893
International Society of Soil Science.
International Conference. (1981: Jerusalem)
5.5269
International Sociological Association. Research
Committee on Deviance and Social Control.
4.6750
International Statistical Institute. 5.1400
International Studies Association. Meeting.
(1980: Los Angeles, Calif.) 3.3631
International Study Workshop on Termite Caste
Differentiation (1982: International Centre of
Insect Physiology and Ecology) 5.3878
International Symposium in Economic History
(1979: University of East Anglia) 4.3061

International Symposium on Anthropology
(1952: New York). 4.395
International Symposium on Anthropology,
New York, 1952. 4.394
International Symposium on Autism. (1976:
Saint Gall, Switzerland) 5.5109
International Symposium on Biochemistry of
Exercise. (5th: 1982: Boston, Mass.) 5.4266
International Symposium on Cetacean
Research. (1st: 1963: Washington, D.C.)
5.4006
International Symposium on Herbicides and
Defoliants in War (1983: Ho Chi Minh City,
Vietnam) 5.3580
International Symposium on Humidity and
Moisture. (1963: Washington, D.C.) 5.2532
International Symposium on Man's Role in
Changing the Face of the Earth, Princeton,
N.J., 1955. 4.2
International Symposium on Methods and
Materials in Microelectronic Technology
(1982: Bad Neuenahr-Ahrweiler, Germany)
5.6533
International Symposium on Regulated Streams.
1st, Erie, Pa., 1979. 5.3567
International Symposium on Risk and
Reliability in Water Resources (1978:
University of Waterloo) 5.5971
International Symposium on Robotics Research.
(1st: 1983: Bretton Woods, N.H.) 5.6171
International Symposium on Robotics Research.
(2nd: 1984: Kyoto, Japan) 5.6165
International Symposium on Robotics Research.
(3rd: 1985: Gouvieux, France) 5.6166
International Symposium on Skin Senses. 1st,
Florida State University, 1966. 5.4364
International Symposium on the Holocaust,
Cathedral of St. John the Divine, 1974.
1.1976
International Theatre Institute. 2.3089,
2.3149-2.3151
International Theatre Institute of the United
States. 2.3081
International Typeface Corporation. 5.7525
International Union for Conservation of Nature
and Natural Resources. 5.5384
International Union for the Scientific Study of
Population. 4.6195
International Union of Biochemistry. 5.4414
International Union of Biochemistry.
Nomenclature Committee. 5.4414
International Union of Building Societies and
Savings Associations. 4.3483
International Union of Geological Sciences.
International Subcommission on Stratigraphic
Classification. 5.3134
International War Crimes Tribunal (1st: 1967:
Stockholm, Sweden and Roskilde, Denmark)
4.9341
Inverarity, Robert Bruce, 1909-. 3.5815
Investigative Reporters and Editors, Inc. 2.3567
Inwards, Richard, 1840-1937. 5.2584
Ionesco, Eugène. 2.4578-2.4583
Ionescu, Ghita. 3.3533, 3.3551
Iowa Center for Textual Studies. 2.10936
Ippolito, Dennis S. 4.4685, 4.8157
Ippolito, Richard A. 4.3465
Iqbal, Muhammad, Sir, 1877-1938. 2.1901,
3.4286
Ireland, Alleyne, 1871-. 2.3626
Ireland, Gordon, 1880-1950. 3.9055
Ireland, Kenneth F. 5.1326-5.1327
Ireland, Norma Olin, 1907-. 5.7828
Ireland, Timothy P., 1948-. 4.9018
Irele, Abiola. 2.4862
Irenaeus, Saint, Bishop of Lyon. 1.2187
Ireson, William Grant, 1914-. 5.5700
Iribas, Juan L. 2.903
Irish, William, 1903-1968. 2.11880
Iriye, Akira. 3.4402, 3.6459, 3.6461
Irokawa, Daikichi, 1925-. 3.4897
Irons, Edward D. 4.4527
Irons, Peter H., 1940-. 4.9769
Irons, William. 4.509
Irschick, Eugene F. 3.4324
Irvine, John. 4.5081, 5.975
Irvine, John Maxwell. 5.2066

Irvine, William, 1840-1911. 2.7484, 3.4258,
5.3200
Irvine, William P. 4.7743
Irving, David John Cawdell, 1938-. 3.966
Irving, Edward Burroughs, 1923-. 2.6297
Irving, Jack H., 1920-. 5.5936
Irving, John, 1942-. 2.13096
Irving, Laurence, 1897-. 2.3346
Irving, Robert Grant, 1940-. 1.5392
Irving, Washington, 1783-1859. 2.11094
Irwin, David G. 1.4938
Irwin, David G. ed. 1.5143
Irwin, Graham W. 3.605, 4.6411
Irwin, Leonard Bertram, 1904-. 4.4014
Irwin, M. C. (Michael Charles), 1934-. 5.1625
Irwin, Manley Rutherford. 4.9537
Irwin, Michael. 2.6011
Irwin, Peter George. joint author. 3.5653
Irwin, Terence. 1.247, 1.273
Irwin, William Andrew, 1884-. 1.1591
Irwin, William Robert, 1915-. 2.5964
Isaac, Rael Jean. 3.3928, 4.8785
Isaac, Rhys. 3.8195
Isaacman, Allen F. 3.5309, 4.2872
Isaacman, Barbara. joint author. 3.5309
Isaacs, Alan, 1925-. 5.710
Isaacs, Arnold R. 3.4493
Isaacs, Harold R. 3.4176
Isaacs, Harold Robert, 1910-. 2.2203, 3.4637,
3.4747
Isaacs, Jorge, 1837-1895. 2.5412
Isaacs, Nathan, 1895-1966. 4.10385
Isaacs, Neil David, 1931-. 4.1009
Isaacs, Neil S., 1934-. 5.2855
Isaacs, Norman E., 1908-. 2.3598
Isaacs, Susan Sutherland Fairhurst, 1885-1948.
4.10385
Isaacson, Joel. 1.6124
Isaacson, Robert Lee, 1928-. 5.4291
Isacco, Enrico. 1.6744
Isailović, Jordan, 1945-. 5.6590
Isaksson, Hans, 1942-. 2.14085
Isard, Walter. 4.2689-4.2690
Ise, John, 1885-. 5.5389
Isella, Dante. 2.5011
Iseminger, Gary. comp. 1.1151
Isenberg, Arnold. 1.1357
Isenberg, Artur, ed. 2.1859
Iser, Wolfgang. 2.2448, 2.3509
Isherwood, Christopher. 1.201, 2.8392-2.8393,
2.8398, 2.8832-2.8840
Isherwood, Robert M., 1935-. 3.2229
Ishiguro, Hidé. 1.874
Ishikawa, Sara, joint author. 1.5462
Ishikawa, Takuboku, 1885-1912. 2.2075
Ishimoto, Yasuhiro, 1921-. 5.5454
Isichei, Elizabeth Allo. 3.5352
ISIS (Organization) 4.5904
Iskander, Fazil'. 2.1628
Islam, M. Rafiqul. 3.4149
Islam, Nurul. 4.4192
Islamic University (Islāmābād, Pakistan).
Institute of Islamic History, Culture, and
Civilization. 5.8052
Ismael, Jacqueline S. 4.5407, 4.8788
Ismael, Tareq Y. 3.4073, 3.8775, 4.8788
Ismail, Amin R. 5.1151
Isocrates. 2.375
Israel, Fred L. joint author. 3.6392
Israel, Fred L. joint comp. 4.9797
Israel, Fred L. comp. 4.8964
Israël, Gérard, 1928-. 3.3895
Israël, Gerhard W., joint author. 5.2523
Israël, Guy. 5.1739
Israël, H. (Hans), 1902-. 5.2523
Israel, John. 3.4673, 3.4792
Israel, Jonathan Irvine. 3.2960, 3.8927
Israel. Miśrad ha-penim. 1.5608
Israel. Va'adah la-hakirat ha-eru'im be-mahanot
ha-pelitim be-Beirut. 3.3790
Israeli, Isaac, ca. 832-ca. 932. 1.376
Issawi, Charles Philip. comp. 4.2565
Issawi, Charles Philip. 3.3662, 4.2430, 4.2441,
4.2567
Isserman, Maurice. 4.8236
Istituto Carlo Cattaneo. 4.8628
Istituto geografico De Agostini. 4.113, 4.136
Istituto geografico DeAgostini, Novara. 4.111

Italy. 3.2890
Italy. Galleria nazionale (Parma, Italy) 1.5812
Itaya, Kikuo, 1898-. 2.2098
Itō, Kiyoshi, 1915-. 5.1382
Itō, Teiji, 1922-. 5.5373
Ittelson, William H. 5.4386
Itten, Johannes, 1888-1967. 1.4649, 1.6352
Ittmann, John W. 1.6458
Itzkoff, Seymour W. 4.451
Itzkowitz, Norman. 3.3575
Itzykson, Claude. 5.2155
Ivan IV, Czar of Russia, 1530-1584. 3.3085
Ivancevich, John M. 4.2654
Ivanov, V. I. (Viacheslav Ivanovich), 1866-1949.
  2.1374
Ivanov, Vsevolod Viacheslavovich, 1895-1963.
  2.1615
Ivanow, Wladimir. 1.2093-1.2094
Ivask, George, 1910- ed. 2.1517
Ivchenko, Valerian IAkovlevich, 1860-1935.
  4.1154
Iversen, Edwin S. 5.5469
Iverson, Peter. 3.5962
Ives, Charles, 1874-1954. 1.3497, 1.3899
Ives, Peter B. 5.8214
Ivey, Allen E. 4.1224
Ivison, J. M. 5.6271
Ivry, Alfred L., 1935- ed. 1.375
Iwao, Seiichi, 1900-. 3.4905
Iyanaga, Shōkichi, 1906-. 5.1026
Iyer, Raghavan Narasimhan. 4.7482
Izard, Carroll E. 5.414
Izard, Carroll E. (Carroll Ellis), 1923-. 5.412,
  5.429, 5.549
Izenour, George C. 1.5547
Izutsu, Toshihiko, 1914-. 1.2034-1.2035, 1.2080

J.B. Speed Art Museum. 1.6111
J. Whitaker & Sons. 5.7914, 5.7920
Jabavu, Noni. 3.5446
Jabès, Edmond. 2.4585-2.4586
Jablonski, David, 1953-. 5.3147
Jablonski, Stanley. 5.4487
Jaccottet, Philippe. 2.4782-2.4783
Jachimczyk, Maciej. 3.3985
Jack, Ian Robert James. 2.5700, 2.7474, 2.7490
Jack, Ian Robert James. ed. 2.7276
Jack, Jane. 2.6974
Jack-Roller. 4.6885
Jack, Ronald D. S. 2.9837
Jackall, Robert. 4.3067
Jackel, Susan. 4.6079
Jackendoff, Ray S. 1.4429
Jackiw, Roman W. 5.2126
Jacklin, Carol Nagy, joint author. 5.487
Jackman, Barry. 2.2066
Jackman, Mary R. 4.5238
Jackman, Robert W., 1946-. 4.5238
Jackman, S. W. (Sydney Wayne), 1925-. 2.7927
Jackowitz, Paul, 1955-. 5.1220
Jackson, A. J. (Aubrey Joseph) 5.6649
Jackson, Albert Bruce, 1876-. 5.3695
Jackson, Andrew, 1767-1845. 3.6970
Jackson, Arlene M., 1938-. 2.7767
Jackson, Benjamin Daydon, 1846-1927. 5.3630,
  5.3633
Jackson, Blyden. 2.10322
Jackson, Bruce. comp. 2.10661
Jackson, D. M. 5.1280
Jackson, Daphne F. 5.2480
Jackson, Donald, 1938-. 5.7533
Jackson, Donald Dean, 1919-. 3.7036, 3.7064,
  3.8473, 3.8484
Jackson, Emilie, tr. 2.4213
Jackson, Frank, 1943-. 5.268
Jackson, Gabriel. 3.3423, 3.3458, 3.3467
Jackson, Gabriel. comp. 3.3468
Jackson, Gabriele Bernhard, ed. 2.6590
Jackson, George, 1941-1971. 3.6705
Jackson, George Pullen, 1874-1953. 1.3444,
  1.4290
Jackson, Gregory, 1948-. 4.2005
Jackson, Herbert W. 5.6272
Jackson, Holbrook. 2.5706, 2.5722, 2.7910,
  2.7965, 5.7672
Jackson, Horace G. 5.6470
Jackson, J. Hampden (John Hampden), 1907-.
  3.3311

Jackson, J. R. de J. (James Robert de Jager)
  2.5758
Jackson, John, 1881-. 2.697
Jackson, John Brinckerhoff, 1909-. 4.382
Jackson, John David, 1925-. 5.2357
Jackson, John S., 1940-. 4.7942
Jackson, Joseph Hollister. 5.1799
Jackson, Joy J. 3.8317
Jackson, Julia A., 1939-. 5.2939
Jackson, Kenneth Hurlstone, 1909- ed. and tr.
  2.827
Jackson, Kenneth T. 4.6358
Jackson, Laura (Riding), 1901-. 2.2768,
  2.11917-2.11918
Jackson, Leland B. 5.6514
Jackson, MacDonald P. (MacDonald Pairman)
  2.10200
Jackson, Margaret, ed. 5.7763
Jackson, P. M. (Peter McLeod) 4.2672
Jackson, Percival E., 1891-. 4.9841
Jackson, Peter, 1955-. 4.384
Jackson, Philip L. 4.163
Jackson, Philip W. (Philip Wesley), 1928-.
  4.10310, 5.597
Jackson, R. M. (Richard Meredith), 1903-.
  4.9425
Jackson, Richard, 1936-. 1.3561, 2.10508
Jackson, Robert H. 3.5097
Jackson, Robert Houghwout, 1892-1954. 3.1074
Jackson, Robert J., 1936-. 4.8290, 4.8523
Jackson, Robert Louis. comp. 2.1345, 2.1486
Jackson, Robert Louis. 2.1259
Jackson, Robert Victor. 3.4138
Jackson, Rosemary. 2.3458
Jackson, Russell, 1949-. 2.7847
Jackson, Samuel Macauley, 1851-1912. ed.
  1.2223
Jackson, Shirley, 1920-. 2.11919-2.11922
Jackson, Sidney L. (Sidney Louis), 1914-1979.
  5.7656
Jackson, W. A. Douglas (William Arthur
  Douglas), 1923-. 4.7497, 5.5305
Jackson, W. T. H. (William Thomas Hobdell),
  1915-. 2.2557, 2.13530
Jackson, Wallace, 1930-. 2.7202
Jackson, William Godfrey Fothergill, 1917-.
  3.982
Jacob, Ellen. 4.1095
Jacob, Ernest Fraser, 1894-. 3.1375
Jacob, François, 1920-. 5.3390, 5.3411, 5.4449
Jacob, Heinrich Eduard, 1889-1967. 3.56
Jacob, Herbert, 1933-. 4.6769, 4.8247
Jacob, Louis A. 5.8050
Jacob, Lucy M., 1925-. 3.4371
Jacob, Margaret C., 1943-. 3.179
Jacob, Max, 1876-1944. 2.4588-2.4589
Jacobi, Hermann Georg, 1850-1937, tr. 1.1735
Jacobs, Arthur. 1.4014
Jacobs, Clyde Edward, 1925-. 4.9520
Jacobs, Dan N. (Daniel Norman), 1925-. 3.6575
Jacobs, David Michael, 1942-. 5.6696
Jacobs, Everett M. 4.2970
Jacobs, Harold R. 5.1254
Jacobs, J. A. (John Arthur), 1916-. 5.2963,
  5.3074
Jacobs, James Ripley, 1886-. 3.6366
Jacobs, Jane, 1916-. 1.5597, 4.6346
Jacobs, John, 1950-. 1.2101
Jacobs, Leland B. (Leland Blair), 1907- joint ed.
  4.10477
Jacobs, Lewis. comp. 2.2985
Jacobs, Lewis. 2.2918
Jacobs, Louis. comp. 1.2575
Jacobs, Louis. 1.1895, 1.1978, 1.1984
Jacobs, Melville, 1902-. 3.5861
Jacobs, Noah Jonathan, 1907-. 2.196
Jacobs, Norman, 1924-. 4.2434
Jacobs, Robert D., 1918-. 2.10457-2.10458
Jacobs, Sue-Ellen. 5.8461
Jacobs, Wilbur R. 3.5795
Jacobsen, Grethe. 5.8022
Jacobsen, Hans Adolf. ed. 3.905
Jacobsen, Hans Adolf. 3.888
Jacobsen, J. P. (Jens Peter), 1847-1885.
  2.14012-2.14013
Jacobsen, Jacques Noel. 3.5774
Jacobsen, Thorkild, 1904-. 1.1591, 1.1841
Jacobson, Arthur, 1929- joint comp. 1.550

Jacobson, D. C. 5.6768
Jacobson, Dan. 2.10082-2.10083
Jacobson, Gary C. 4.8022, 4.8129
Jacobson, Harold Karan. 4.9265, 4.9268
Jacobson, Howard, 1940-. 2.745
Jacobson, Lenore. joint author. 4.10386
Jacobson, Nathan, 1910-. 5.1268
Jacobson, Nolan Pliny. 1.214
Jacobus, de Voragine, ca. 1229-1298. 1.3247
Jacobus, Lee A. 2.10783
Jacobus, Mary. 2.8309
Jacoby, Annalee, 1916- joint author. 3.4772
Jacoby, Ed. 4.1049
Jacoby, Felix, 1876-. 3.2569
Jacoby, Henry. 4.7748
Jacoby, Jacob. 4.4307, 4.4328
Jacoby, Neil H. (Neil Herman), 1909-1979.
  4.3051, 4.3760, 4.6760
Jacoby, Russell. 4.6935
Jacoby, Susan. 4.10134
Jacolev, Leon. 5.706
Jacoway, Elizabeth, 1944-. 3.6793
Jacquot, Raymond G., 1938-. 5.6184
Jaeger, Edmund Carroll, 1887-. 5.3184, 5.3244
Jaeger, J. C. (John Conrad), 1907-. 5.1108
Jaeger, Marianne. 4.8504
Jaeger, Werner Wilhelm, 1888-1961. 1.305,
  1.2269, 1.3258, 3.2622
Jaenen, Cornelius J. 3.5796
Jaffa, Harry V. 3.7294, 4.7690
Jaffa, Herbert C. 5.8084
Jaffe, Bernard, 1896-. 5.793, 5.2617
Jaffe, Eliezer David, 1933-. 4.6571
Jaffe, Frederick S. 4.5701
Jaffé, Hans H. 5.2675
Jaffe, Irma B. 1.5974, 1.5980
Jaffe, Lorna S. 5.7301
Jaffe, Louis Leventhal. 4.9748
Jaffé, William. 4.1367
Jafri, Syed Husain M. 1.2088
Jagchid, Sechin, 1914-. 3.4860
Jaggar, Alison M. 4.5930, 4.6057
Jahan, Rounaq. 3.4130
Jāhiz, d. 868 or 9. 2.1843
Jahn, Karl, 1906- ed. 2.1963
Jahn, Otto, 1813-1869. 1.3939
Jahoda, Gloria. 3.5800, 3.8272
Jahoda, Gustav. 4.623
Jahoda, Marie. 4.5023
Jai Ratan, 1920-. 2.1889
Jain, Devaki, 1933-. 4.6141
Jain, Harish C. 4.3114
Jain, Lakshmi Chandra, 1909-. 2.1888
Jain, Rajendra Kumar. 3.4103-3.4104, 3.4106,
  3.4672
Jaini, Padmanabh S. 1.1736
Jakes, William C. 5.6432
Jaki, Stanley L. 5.1800
Jakle, John A. 3.8390
Jakobson, Max. 3.3292
Jakobson, Roman, 1896-. 2.33, 2.176, 2.181,
  2.1292
Jalāl al-Dīmī, Mawlānā, 1207-1283. 2.1969
Jalāl al-Dīn Rūmī, Maulana, 1207-1273. 2.1970
Jallut, Marguerite, joint author. 3.2053
Jamālzādah, Muhammad 'Alī. 2.1978
James, A. 5.6019
James, A. T. 5.4423
James, Alice, 1848-1892. 3.337
James, Bill, 1949-. 4.1000
James, Bruno Scott. tr. 1.3257
James, Burnett. 1.3822, 1.4034
James, C. L. R. (Cyril Lionel Robert), 1901-.
  3.9119
James, D. Clayton. 3.7611
James, Daniel, comp. 3.9277
James, David Gwilym, 1905-1968. 2.6823
James, Edward, 1947-. 3.1980, 3.3420
James, Edward T. ed. 3.352
James, Ellen, 1940-. 1.5350
James, Estelle. joint author. 4.3394
James, Fleming, 1904-. 4.9515
James, Glenn, 1882- ed. 5.1025
James, Henry, 1843-1916. 1.599, 1.5677, 2.2647,
  2.2663, 2.3084, 2.3413, 2.3424, 2.3519-2.3521,
  2.3860, 2.10266, 2.11100-2.11105, 2.11107,
  2.11109-2.11115, 4.10995
James I, King of England, 1566-1625. 3.1464

James, I. M. (Ioan Mackenzie), 1928-. 5.1593
James, James Alton, 1864-1962. 3.8647
James, Janet Wilson, 1918-. 1.2388, 3.352, 4.6009
James, Joseph B. (Joseph Bliss), 1912-. 4.7832, 4.9687
James Joyce Society. 2.8913-2.8914
James, Louis. 2.9279, 2.9975
James, M. R. (Montague Rhodes), 1862-1936. 2.8843
James, Marquis, 1891-1955. 3.8325
James, Mertice May, 1893- ed. 5.7763
James, Mr. Francis Godwin. 3.1836
James, Mr. Sydney V. 3.8013
James, P. D. 2.9721-2.9724
James, Patricia D. 4.1588
James, Philip Brutton, 1901- ed. 1.5695
James, Preston Everett, 1899-. 3.8962, 4.38, 4.48
James, Ralph C., 1929-. 4.3394
James, Reese Davis, 1889- ed. 2.3232
James, Reginald William, 1891-. 5.2323
James, Robert C. (Robert Clarke) joint author. 5.1025
James, Simon R. 4.5830
James, T. G. H. (Thomas Garnet Henry) 3.5133, 3.5139
James, William, 1842-1910. 1.452, 1.526-1.527, 1.596-1.599, 1.1540, 1.2237, 4.10355, 5.108, 5.411
Jameson, Dorothea, 1920- joint author. 5.4384
Jameson, Frederic. 2.151
Jameson, Fredric. 2.2480, 2.9045
Jameson, J. Franklin (John Franklin), 1859-1937. 3.6212, 3.6911
Jameson, Storm, 1891-. 2.8844
Jāmī, 1414-1492. 1.2061
Jamieson, G. A. (Graham A.), 1929-. 5.4047
Jamieson, Kathleen Hall. 4.7950
Jamieson, Stuart Marshall. 4.3397
Jamison, A. Leland (Albert Leland), 1911-. 1.2384
Jammer, Max. 5.2021, 5.2067, 5.2107, 5.2113
Jancovici, Bernard. 5.2247
Janda, Judy. 4.6086
Janda, Kenneth. 4.8155
Jane, Fred T., 1865-1916. 5.6640
Jane, Fred T. (Frederick Thomas), 1865-1916. ed. 5.7446
Jane Voorhees Zimmerli Art Museum. 1.5298
Janeway, Eliot. 4.1974
Janick, Jules, 1931-. 5.5336
Janik, Allan. 1.1241
Janis, Harriet Grossman. 1.4810
Janis, Harriet Grossman. joint author. 1.4318
Janis, Irving Lester, 1918-. 2.50, 3.7578, 5.376, 5.448, 5.474, 5.7396
Janis, Sidney, 1897-. 1.5905
Janko, Richard, 1955-. 2.2826
Janos, Andrew C. 3.1939
Janosik, Ellen Hastings. 5.4877
Janota, M. S. 6.6629
Janowitz, Morris. 2.3569, 4.4772, 4.5133, 5.7158, 5.7273, 5.7355
Janowitz, Morris. ed. 4.4812, 4.7239
Jans, Adrien. 2.4799
Jansen, Frederik Julius Billeskov, 1907-. 2.14001, 2.14004
Jansen, Marius B. 3.4762, 3.4889, 3.4952
Jansen, Marius B. joint comp. 3.4941
Janson, Anthony F. 1.4676
Janson, H. W. (Horst Woldemar), 1913-. 1.4676, 1.4679, 1.4779, 1.5140, 1.5647, 1.5729
Jantz, Harold Stein, 1907-. 2.13569
Janus, fl. 1972-. 5.6977
Japan. 3.4918
Japan. Bunkachō. 1.5076, 1.5881, 1.6334, 1.6391
Japan House Gallery. 1.5760, 1.6371
Japan. Mombushō. Nihon Yunesuko Kokunai Iinkai. 3.4874
Japan. Monbushō. 3.4883
Japan. Tsūshō Sangyōshō. 4.4242
Jaques Cattell Press. 1.82, 1.3540, 4.10154, 5.6144, 5.7660
Jaques-Dalcroze, Emile, 1865-1950. 1.4441
Jaques, Elliott. 4.3132
Jaques, Francis Lee, 1887-1969. illus. 5.3984

Jarausch, Konrad Hugo. 3.2346, 4.10127
Jardin, André, 1912-. 3.2144
Jarley, Paul. 4.3204
Jarman, A. O. H. (Alfred Owen Hughes) 2.832
Jarman, Douglas. 1.3812, 1.4060
Jarman, Ronald F. joint author. 5.262
Jarnow, Jeannette A. 4.3859
Jarolimek, John. ed. 4.10482
Jarolimek, John. 4.10483
Jarrard, Leonard E., 1930- ed. 5.4105
Jarrell, Hampton McNeely, 1904-. 3.7326
Jarrell, Randall, 1914-1965. 2.2769, 2.11923-2.11927
Jarrett, Bede, 1881-1934. 3.132
Jarrett, Derek. 3.1531
Jarry, Alfred, 1873-1907. 2.4590-2.4593
Jarry, Madeleine. 1.6589
Jarvella, R. J. 2.118
Jarvi, Edith T., 1921-. 5.7884
Jarvis, Caroline, ed. 5.3806
Jarvis, John J., joint author. 5.5586
Jasbir Singh, 1932-. 5.5253
Jaschek, Carlos. 5.1847
Jashemski, Wilhelmina Mary Feemster, 1910-. 3.2723
Jasik, Henry. 5.6430
Jasny, Naum, 1883-1967. 4.2375, 4.2382, 4.2976
Jasper, Tony. 1.3528
Jaspers, Karl. 1.130, 1.1024-1.1030, 1.1054, 1.1298, 1.1552, 3.191, 3.395, 3.1169
Jastram, Roy W., 1915-. 4.4496
Jastrow, Robert, 1925-. 5.1715, 5.4334
Jastrzebski, Zbigniew D. 5.5764
Jaszi, George. 4.2081
Jászi, Oszkár, 1875-1957. 4.7616
Jauch, Josef Maria, 1914-1974. 5.2114, 5.2376
Jauss, Hans Robert. 2.2485
Jaworski, Leon. 4.9469
Jay, Douglas, 1907-. 4.7040
Jay, Frank. 5.6249
Jay, John, 1745-1829. 3.6971
Jay, Martin, 1944-. 4.1225
Jay, Richard. 3.1636
Jayadeva, 12th cent. 2.1945
Jayant, Nuggehally S., 1946-. 5.6374
Jayanta Bhatta, fl. 850-910. 1.196
Jaycock, M. J. 5.2897
Jaycox, Elbert R. 5.5458
Jayne, Arthur Garland, 1882-. 2.14042
Jaynes, Julian, joint comp. 5.72
Jaynes, Julian. 5.269
Jayson, Lester S. ed. 4.9607
Jeal, Tim. 3.5438
Jean-Aubry, G. (Georges), 1882-1950. 2.8554
Jean, de Meun, d. 1305? 2.3963-2.3964
Jean, Marcel. 1.6348, 1.6738
Jean Paul, 1763-1825. 2.13644
Jeans, James Hopwood, Sir, 1877-1946. 1.4374, 5.738, 5.2171
Jeanson, Francis, 1922- ed. 2.4741
Jebb, Richard Claverhouse, Sir, 1841-1905. 2.308, 2.441, 2.542
Jech, Thomas J. 5.1351-5.1352
Jedin, Hubert, 1900-. 1.2281, 1.3118, 1.3120
Jedruch, Jacek. 4.8668
Jeffares, A. Norman (Alexander Norman), 1920-. 2.6196, 2.8344, 2.8351, 2.8362-2.8363, 2.9851
Jefferies, R. L. 5.3772
Jeffers, Robinson, 1887-1962. 2.11929-2.11930
Jefferson, Alan. 1.4015
Jefferson, Thomas, 1743-1826. 3.6972-3.6973, 3.7044, 3.8207, 4.10199
Jeffery, George Barker, 1891-. 5.1914
Jeffery, Lilian Hamilton. 3.2599
Jeffery, P. G. (Paul Geoffrey) 5.3042
Jeffrey, Charles. 5.3233, 5.3651
Jeffrey, David K., 1942-. 2.12961
Jeffrey, Julie Roy. 4.6076
Jeffrey, Lloyd N. 2.7822
Jeffrey, Richard C. 1.1176, 5.1384
Jeffrey, Robin. 3.4273
Jeffrey, William, 1921-. 4.9611
Jeffreys, Harold, Sir, 1891-. 5.902, 5.3075
Jeffreys-Jones, Rhodri. 4.5244
Jeffreys, Sheila. 4.6106
Jeffries, John. 5.8400
Jeffries, John W., 1942-. 3.8024

Jeffries, Theodore W. 5.739
Jehlen, Myra. 2.10392
Jelavich, Barbara, 1923-. 3.684, 3.3064, 3.3516-3.3518, 3.3525
Jelavich, Charles. 3.3517
Jelavich, Charles. ed. 3.3518
Jelavich, Charles. 3.3069, 3.3525
Jelinek, Estelle C. 3.321
Jelliffe, Derrick Brian. 5.4985
Jelliffe, E. F. Patrice. 5.4985
Jellinck, P. H. 5.3620
Jember, Gregory K. 2.947
Jencks, Charles. joint author. 5.5369
Jencks, Charles. 1.5271, 1.6686
Jencks, Christopher. 4.10063, 4.10778
Jencks, William P., 1927-. 5.2882
Jenkins, Adelbert H. 3.6718
Jenkins, Annibel. 2.7235
Jenkins, Brian, ed. 2.7081
Jenkins, Brian (Brian A.) 3.7358
Jenkins, D. T. 4.3856
Jenkins, Dafydd. 2.845
Jenkins, David Clay, 1926-. 4.5336
Jenkins, Elizabeth, 1907-. 2.7374
Jenkins, Frances B. (Frances Briggs), 1905- joint author. 5.7683
Jenkins, Francis Arthur, 1899-1960. 5.2281
Jenkins, Frank. 1.5365
Jenkins, Gwilym M., joint author. 5.1415
Jenkins, John J. 1.675
Jenkins, Linda Walsh. 2.3200
Jenkins, Peter George James, 1934-. 4.3646
Jenkins, Richard, 1952-. 4.5762
Jenkins, Robin, 1912-. 2.9725
Jenkins, Shirley. 4.6616
Jenkins, Shirley. ed. 4.3446
Jenkins, Thomas Atkinson, 1868-1935, ed. 2.3959
Jenkins, W. I. (William Ieuan) 4.8433
Jenkins, William M., joint author. 3.4331
Jenkinson, Edward B. 4.10708
Jenks, C. Wilfred (Clarence Wilfred), 1909-1973. 4.9149, 4.9287
Jenks, Elizabeth. 4.1963
Jenks, Leland Hamilton, 1892-. 3.6439, 4.4456
Jenks, William Alexander, 1918-. 3.2402
Jenks, William Furness, 1909-. 5.3002
Jenne, Frank H., 1920- joint author. 4.10491
Jenner, Philip N. 5.8058
Jenness, Diamond, 1886-1969. 3.5727
Jennewein, John Leonard, 1910- ed. 3.8513
Jennings, Anthony, MA. 4.9213
Jennings, Elizabeth, tr. 2.4967
Jennings, Francis, 1918-. 3.5801, 3.5896, 3.7948
Jennings, Ivor, Sir, 1903-1965. 4.8516, 4.9403
Jennings, J. N. (Joseph Newell) 4.279
Jennings, Jesse David, 1909-. 3.5707, 3.5714, 4.674
Jennings, Lawrence C. 3.2153
Jennings, M. Kent. joint author. 4.10642
Jennings, Walter, 1922-. 5.2665
Jenny, Hans, 1899-. 5.5271
Jens, Walter, 1923-. 2.13478
Jensen, Arthur Robert. 5.357, 5.368-5.369
Jensen, Clayne R. 4.892
Jensen, Donald N. 4.9582
Jensen, Gerard Edward, 1884-. 2.7019
Jensen, Hans, 1884-. 2.172
Jensen, Joan M. 4.3265, 4.6013
Jensen, Jørgen, 1936 July 30-. 4.737
Jensen, Kathleen, 1949-. 5.1222
Jensen, Line. 2.14002
Jensen, Lyle H., joint author. 5.2936
Jensen, Mead LeRoy, 1925-. 5.6728-5.6729
Jensen, Merrill. 3.6877, 3.7017, 4.7820, 4.7834, 4.9606
Jensen, Niels Lyhne. 2.14014
Jensen, Paul A., 1936-. 5.5597
Jensen, Randall W. 5.6461
Jensen, Richard J. 3.8303, 3.8408
Jensen, Robert G. 4.2369
Jensen, Ronald J., 1939-. 3.7475
Jensen, Vernon H. 4.3386
Jensen, William A. 5.3591, 5.3752
Jensen, William B. 5.2862
Jenson, Robert W. joint author. 1.3361
Jenson, Robert W. 1.2837, 1.3014
Jentschura, Hansgeorg. 5.7472

Jeppesen, Knud, 1892-. 1.4471
Jéquier, Nicolas, 1941-. 4.4584
Jeremias, Joachim, 1900-. 1.2860, 1.2888, 1.3018
Jeremy, David John, 1939-. 4.3844
Jerger, James. ed. 5.4371
Jerison, Meyer, 1922- joint author. 5.1587
Jerlov, Nils Gunnar. 4.346
Jernegan, Marcus Wilson, 1872-1949. 4.5239
Jernudd, Björn H. ed. 2.25
Jerome, Judson. 4.10064
Jerrard, H. G. 5.2023
Jerri, Abdul J., 1932-. 5.1562
Jerrold, Walter, 1865-1929. 2.6067, 2.7818, 2.7821
Jersild, Arthur Thomas, 1902-. 4.10382
Jerusalem. 1.5608
Jervis, Robert, 1940-. 4.8997
Jespersen, Otto, 1860-1943. 2.93, 2.165, 2.986, 2.993
Jesperson, Otto, 1860-1943. 2.968
Jess, 1923-. 2.11612
Jessen, Raymond James, 1910-. 4.1243
Jessop, Bob. 4.8418
Jessup, Bertram Emil, 1899- joint author. 1.1381
Jessup, Josephine Lurie. 2.10363
Jessup, Philip C. (Philip Caryl), 1897-. 3.7446, 4.9280, 4.9331
Jesuits. 3.8714
Jesus, Carolina Maria de. 4.5272
Jet Propulsion Laboratory (U.S.) 5.6719
Jett, Stephen C., 1938-. 3.5917
Jetzinger, Franz. 3.2403
Jeuck, John E., joint author. 4.4333
Jevons, F. R. (Frederick Raphael), 1929-. 5.960
Jevons, Herbert Stanley, 1875-, ed. 4.1438
Jevons, William Stanley, 1835-1882. 4.1348, 4.1438, 4.4472, 5.903
Jewell, Derek. 1.3864
Jewell, Helen M. 4.8873
Jewell, Malcolm Edwin, 1928-. 4.8258
Jewett, Paul King. 1.3006
Jewett, Robert. 1.2722, 3.6184
Jewett, Sarah Orne, 1849-1909. 2.11133
Jewish letters. 3.3855
Jewish Museum (New York, N.Y.) 3.3983
Jewish Publication Society. 1.2562
Jewish Publication Society of America. 1.2588, 1.2599, 3.3837, 3.4004, 3.6561
Jewish Theological Seminary of America. Institute for Religious and Social Studies. 2.2377
Jewkes, John, 1902-. 5.5640
Jeyakāntan, 1934-. 2.2274
Jha, Prem Shankar. 4.2507
Jhabvala, Ruth Prawer, 1927-. 2.9726-2.9728
Jhaveri, Sharad, joint author. 1.5313
Jia, Guanyan. 1.6587
Jick, Leon A. 1.1928
Jiménez Fajardo, Salvador. 2.4752, 2.5246
Jiménez, Francisco, 1943-. 2.10674
Jiménez, Juan Ramón, 1881-1958. 2.5268
Jiménez, Luz, d. 1965. 3.8955
Jinks, John L. 5.3453
Jippensha, Ikku, 1765-1831. 2.2069
Jirásek, Alois, 1851-1930. 2.1673
Jo, Yung-hwan, 1932- comp. 3.4993
Joachain, C. J. (Charles Jean) 5.2449
Joachim, Harold H. (Harold Henry), 1868-1938. 1.790
Joachimides, Christos M. 1.4801
Joad, Cyril Edwin Mitchinson, 1891-1953. 1.2227
Joannides, Paul. 1.5815
Jobes, Gertrude. 4.754
Jobs and Skills Programme for Africa. 4.2624, 4.2995
Jocano, F. Landa. 3.4591
Jocelyn, H.D. 2.716
Jōchi Daigaku. 1.1144
Jochim, Michael A. 4.720
Jockin-La Bastide, J. A. 2.1171
Jodelle, Etienne, 1532-1573. 2.3938
Joel, Amos E. 5.6418
Johannes, John R., 1943-. 4.8026
Johannesson, Eric O. 2.14080

Johannsen, Robert Walter, 1925-. 3.7137, 3.7150, 3.7152, 3.8595
Johansen, Dorothy O. 3.8596
Johanson, Donald C. 4.455
Johanssen, Terje, 1942-. 2.14032
Johansson, Eve. 5.7583
Johany, Ali D. 4.2447
John, Anna. 4.8371
John, Arthur Henry. 4.2302
John Bartholomew and Son. 4.116
John, Brian Stephen. joint author. 4.318
John, David T. 5.4760
John, Elizabeth Ann Harper, 1928-. 3.5760
John, Eric. 3.1314
John, Frederick W. joint author. 5.6908
John, Fritz, 1910-. 5.1450, 5.1527
John, J. A. 5.986
John, of Damascus, Saint. 2.355
John, of Salisbury, Bishop of Chartres, d. 1180. 1.387, 4.7375-4.7376
John of the Cross, Saint, 1542-1591. 1.3136, 1.3260
John Wiley & Sons. 5.5670
John XXIII, Pope, 1881-1963. 1.3160
Johnk, Carl Theodore Adolf, 1919-. 5.6255
Johnpoll, Bernard K. 4.7002
Johns, Anthony H. (Anthony Hearle) 2.2285
Johns, Edward Alistair. 4.5314
Johns Hopkins University. Center for Metropolitan Planning and Research. 4.6223
Johns Hopkins University. History of Ideas Club. 1.608
Johns, Jasper, 1930-. 1.5796
Johns, Jeannie S. joint author. 4.10952
Johns, Richard. 3.4056
Johns, Roe Lyell, 1900-. 4.10638, 4.10658
Johns, Stephanie Bernardo. 3.6504
Johns, William Henry. ed. 4.171
Johnsen, Arne Odd, 1909-. 5.5486
Johnson, Abby Arthur. 2.10323
Johnson, Allan Chester, 1881-. 4.1739, 4.8834
Johnson, Allen, 1870-1931. 3.6288
Johnson, Alvin Saunders, 1874- ed. 4.1199
Johnson, Arthur Menzies, 1921-. 4.3789, 4.3995
Johnson, B. L. C. (Basil Leonard Clyde), 1919-. 3.4144, 4.2454
Johnson, Barbara, 1947-. 2.2439
Johnson, Bernard. comp. 2.1200
Johnson, Carl R., 1937- joint author. 5.2857
Johnson, Chalmers A. ed. 3.1178, 3.4792
Johnson, Chalmers A. 3.4776, 4.3075, 4.5046
Johnson, Charles, fl. 1724-1736. 4.101
Johnson, Charles Albert, 1916-. 1.3374
Johnson, Charles Richard, 1948-. 2.13097-2.13098
Johnson, Charles Spurgeon, 1893-1956. 3.6652, 3.6786
Johnson. Christopher H. 4.7164
Johnson. Claude R., joint author. 4.4349
Johnson, Colin D. 5.2888
Johnson, Curtis D., 1939-. 5.7031
Johnson, D. Gale (David Gale), 1916-. 4.2977
Johnson, Dallas E., 1938-. 5.1412
Johnson, Daniel M. 3.6765
Johnson, David G. (David George), 1938-. 4.5419
Johnson, David S., 1945- joint author. 5.1176
Johnson-Davies, Denys. 2.1848
Johnson, Donald B. (Donald Barton), 1933-. 2.1587
Johnson, Donald Bruce, 1921-. 3.7694, 4.8144
Johnson, Douglas Porter. 1.3799
Johnson, Douglas W. J. ed. 3.606
Johnson, Douglas Wilson, 1878-1944. 4.270
Johnson, E. D. H. (Edward Dudley Hume) 2.5825
Johnson, E. Pauline, 1861-1913. 2.8845
Johnson, Edgar. 2.7638, 2.8048
Johnson, Elizabeth S. 4.1339, 4.5816
Johnson, Ellen H. 1.4868
Johnson, Eyvind, 1900-. 2.14086
Johnson Foundation (Racine, Wis.) 1.949
Johnson, Francis, 1796?-1876. 2.1964
Johnson, G. Wesley. 3.5392
Johnson, Gary L. 5.6306
Johnson, Gerald White, 1890-. 2.3624
Johnson, Glenn L. 2.2954
Johnson, Harold Earle. 1.3699

Johnson, Harold Edgar, 1915-. 1.3989
Johnson, Harry Alleyn. 3.6518, 3.6625
Johnson, Harry G. (Harry Gordon), 1923-1977. 4.1339, 4.1809, 4.4106, 4.4136, 4.4196-4.4198, 4.4207, 4.4473-4.4474, 4.4552
Johnson, Haynes Bonner, 1931-. 3.7933
Johnson, Hugh. 5.6893
Johnson, J. Rosamond (John Rosamond), 1873-1954. 1.3439
Johnson, James Allen, 1932-. 4.10537
Johnson, James B. 5.6589
Johnson, James Rosser. 1.6650
Johnson, James Turner. 5.7150
Johnson, James Weldon, 1871-1938. 1.3439, 2.10754, 2.11935-2.11937, 3.6838, 3.8055
Johnson, Jeffrey. joint author. 4.8608
Johnson, John Edwin, 1931- joint author. 5.5887
Johnson, John J., 1912-. 3.8985, 4.8325, 5.7159
Johnson, John Raven, 1900- joint author. 5.2727
Johnson, Karl F., joint author. 4.10663
Johnson, Kenneth F. 4.8942
Johnson, L. N., joint author. 5.2930
Johnson-Laird, P. N. (Philip Nicholas), 1936- joint author. 5.386
Johnson, Lee, art historian. 1.6094
Johnson, Lemuel A. 2.2412
Johnson, Lesley. 4.4876
Johnson, Lionel Pigot, 1867-1902. 2.7791
Johnson, Loch K., 1942-. 4.7907
Johnson. Lowell E., joint author. 4.10946
Johnson, Lyndon B. (Lyndon Baines), 1908-1973. 3.7885
Johnson, Lynwood A. 5.7020
Johnson, M. Bruce. 4.9523
Johnson, M. L. joint author. 5.3181
Johnson, Marilynn. 1.6522
Johnson, Mark, 1949- joint author. 2.107
Johnson, Martin W. (Martin Wiggo), 1893- joint author. 4.326
Johnson, Mary Lynn, 1937-. 2.7405
Johnson, Michael P., 1941-. 3.8252, 3.8263
Johnson, Norman Lloyd. 5.1399
Johnson, Orval G., 1917-. 5.582-5.583
Johnson, Pamela Hansford, 1912-. 2.8534, 2.8846-2.8848, 2.12790
Johnson, Patricia A. 4.9434
Johnson, Patricia J. joint author. 5.5175
Johnson, Paul, 1928-. 3.738
Johnson, Paul E., 1942-. 1.3040
Johnson, Paul R. (Paul Reynold), 1929- joint author. 4.3682
Johnson, Philip, 1906-. 1.5270, 1.5272, 1.5425, 1.5474
Johnson, R. Brimley (Reginald Brimley), 1867-1932. 2.5564
Johnson, Randal, 1948-. 2.2885
Johnson Research Associates. 3.9185
Johnson, Richard. 2.1013, 2.8407
Johnson, Richard Arnold. 5.1408
Johnson, Richard C. 5.6430
Johnson, Richard E., 1949-. 4.6862
Johnson, Robert, 1948-. 4.6695
Johnson, J. Robert Sherlaw. 1.3929
Johnson, Roger Orville. 1.3424
Johnson, Ronald C. joint author. 5.2840
Johnson, Ronald Maberry. joint author. 2.10323
Johnson, Rossiter, 1840-1931. ed. 3.6287
Johnson, Samuel, 1709-1784. 2.1079, 2.5807, 2.6717, 2.7054, 2.7078-2.7082, 2.7085, 3.1809
Johnson, Samuel A. 3.8524
Johnson, Susan Moore. 4.10683
Johnson, Thomas H. 2.10994
Johnson, Thomas Herbert. 2.10995, 2.11002
Johnson, Thomas Herbert. joint ed. 2.10708
Johnson, U. Alexis (Ural Alexis), 1908-. 3.7858
Johnson, Una E. 1.6436
Johnson, Uwe, 1934-. 2.13899-2.13902
Johnson, Virginia E. 4.5504, 5.4838
Johnson, Virginia E. joint author. 5.4257, 5.4952
Johnson, W. (William), 1922-. 5.5790, 5.6625, 5.7055
Johnson, Walter, 1867- ed. 3.7519, 5.3277
Johnson, Walter Gilbert, 1905-. 2.14073
Johnson, Walton R. 1.2466
Johnson, Wayne, 1946-. 5.6680

Johnson, Wendell Stacy, 1927-. 2.7360, 2.7650
Johnson, Willard L. joint author. 1.2141
Johnson, William, 1940-. 5.6997
Johnston, Bruce F., 1919-. 4.2890-4.2891, 4.2898, 4.2991
Johnston, Bruce Gilbert, 1905-. 5.5885
Johnston, Denis, 1901-. 2.8849
Johnston, E. H. (Edward Hamilton), 1885-1942. ed. and tr. 1.2127
Johnston, E. Russell (Elwood Russell), 1925-. 5.5732, 5.5772
Johnston, Edith Mary. 3.1837
Johnston, Edward, 1872-1944. 5.7526
Johnston, Grahame. 5.8082
Johnston, Hugh J. M., 1939-. 4.91
Johnston, J. (John), 1923-. 4.1299
Johnston, Jennifer, 1930-. 2.9730-2.9735
Johnston, Norman Bruce, 1921-. 4.6770, 4.6821
Johnston, O.R. 1.1497
Johnston, Ollie, 1912-. 1.5856
Johnston, R. J. (Ronald John) 4.356, 4.359, 4.2882, 4.9761
Johnston, Rory. 5.1013
Johnston, T. L. 4.3419
Johnston, W. Ross. 4.8911
Johnston, Walter Henry, 1895- tr. 5.1918, 5.2052
Johnston, William, 1925-. 1.1636
Johnston, William M., 1936-. 3.1874
Johnstone, John Keith, 1923-. 2.5733
Johnstone, P. T. 5.1057
Johnstone, R. A. W. (Robert Alexander Walker) 5.2680
Johnstone, Ronald C. B., joint author. 5.4040
Johnstone, Ronald L. 1.1575
Johnstone, William Crane, 1901-. 3.4342
Joiner, Jasper N. 5.5358
Joint Center for Political Studies (U.S.) 3.6710
Joint Center for Urban Studies. 4.6304
Joint Commission on Mental Health of Children. 5.5101
Joint Commission on Mental Illness and Health. 5.4832
Joint Committee on Contemporary China. 4.642
Joint Committee on Contemporary China. Subcommittee on Chinese Government and Politics. 3.4792
Joint Committee on Contemporary China. Subcommittee on Chinese Society. 5.8398
Joint Committee on Eastern Europe. 4.2231, 4.5279
Joint Committee on Japanese Studies. 4.8891, 4.8939, 4.9081
Joint Committee on Latin American Studies. 4.5610, 4.8329, 5.7909, 5.8402
Joint Committee on Slavic Studies. 3.3173, 4.5370
Joint Committee on the New Translation of the Bible. 1.2498
Joint Committee on the Union List of Serials. 5.8319-5.8320
Joint Information Service of the American Psychiatric Association and the National Association for Mental Health. 5.4981
Joinville, Jean, sire de, 1224?-1317? 3.586, 3.594, 3.1994
Jolas, Eugène, 1894-1952. 2.8917
Joll, Evelyn, 1925-. 1.6038
Joll, James. 3.726, 4.6927, 4.7181
Jolliffe, John Edward Austin, 1891-. 3.565, 4.8440
Jolly, Clifford J., 1939-. 5.4091
Jolly, William L. ed. 5.2707
Jolly, William L. 5.2706
Jomini, Henri, baron, 1779-1869. 5.7209
Jonas, Florence. 1.3948
Jonas, Gerald, 1935-. 5.4793
Jonas, Hans, 1903-. 1.1319, 1.1495
Jonas, Klaus W. ed. 2.9109
Jonas, Klaus Werner. 2.9108
Jonas, Manfred. ed. 3.7776
Jonas, Manfred. 3.6445
Jones, A. H. M. (Arnold Hugh Martin), 1904-1970. 3.2557-3.2558, 3.2750, 3.2805-3.2806, 3.5242, 4.1740, 4.7365
Jones, A.M. 1.4349
Jones, A. Philip (Arthur Philip), 1947-. 5.8251
Jones, Abeodu Bowen, ed. 3.5416

Jones, Alexander, 1906- ed. 1.2499
Jones, Alice Hanson, 1904-. 4.1904
Jones, Alun R. (Alun Richard) ed. 2.842
Jones, Ann, 1937-. 4.6690, 4.10858
Jones, Anne Goodwyn. 2.10599
Jones, Archer, 1926- joint author. 3.7369
Jones, Aubrey. 5.1719
Jones, Augustus J. 4.9688
Jones, Barry O. 4.3320
Jones, Bessie, 1902-. 1.4092
Jones, C. Eugene. joint author. 5.3631
Jones, Cecil Knight, 1872-1945. 5.7903
Jones, Charles, 1939-. 2.951
Jones, Charles A., 1949-. 4.4144
Jones, Charles Colcock, 1804-1863. 3.8265
Jones, Charles Edwin, 1932-. 1.3358
Jones, Charles O. 4.8013, 4.8059
Jones, Charles Williams, 1905- ed. 2.2621
Jones, Cheslyn. 1.2985
Jones, Chris, 1939-. 4.894
Jones, Christopher D. 3.2995
Jones, Christopher Prestige. 2.448, 2.537
Jones, Clarence Fielden, 1893-. 3.6357, 4.38
Jones, Clarence Medlycott, 1912- joint author. 4.1041
Jones, Claude Edward, 1907-. 2.7265
Jones, Clifford Ernest, ed. 2.7992
Jones, D. S. (Douglas Samuel) 5.3311
Jones, Daniel. ed. 2.1015, 2.1022, 2.1227, 2.9401
Jones, David Brian, ed. 4.135
Jones, David E., 1942-. 3.5863
Jones, David J. V. 4.3175
Jones, David Michael, 1895-1974. 2.8851-2.8852, 2.8856-2.8858
Jones, David Rayner Hunkin, 1945- joint author. 5.5757
Jones, Deborah. 2.6489
Jones, Dennis P. 4.10603
Jones, Derek C. 4.3179
Jones, Dorothy V. 3.5802
Jones, E. L. (Eric Lionel). 4.2200, 4.2968
Jones, Edmund David, ed. 2.5498
Jones, Edward Ellsworth, 1926-. 4.4921
Jones, Edward Trostle. 2.8798
Jones, Eldred D. 2.10115
Jones, Elvin W. 1.2155
Jones, Emrys, 1931-. 2.6820
Jones, Emrys Maldwyn, ed. 2.6547
Jones, Ernest, 1879-1958. 2.6654, 5.126, 5.155
Jones, Frank, 1915- tr. 2.4870
Jones, Frederic Joseph. 2.5077
Jones, Frederick Lafayette, 1901-. 2.8093-2.8094, 2.8098
Jones, G. A. (Grenville Arthur) 5.2473
Jones, Gareth Elwyn. 3.1755
Jones, Gareth Stedman. 4.6975
Jones, Gayl. 2.13099
Jones, Genesius. 2.11635
Jones, George, 1800-1870. 3.4880
Jones, Gillian P. 5.1244
Jones, Gwyn, 1907-. 2.847, 2.8861, 3.3354
Jones, H. (Harry), 1905-. 5.2205
Jones, Harry Stuart Vedder, 1878-1942. 2.6543
Jones, Henry Arthur, 1851-1929. 2.7847
Jones, Henry Festing, 1851-1928. ed. 2.7511
Jones, Henry Stuart, 1867-1939, ed. 2.247
Jones, Horace Leonard, 1879- tr. 2.393
Jones, Howard, 1918-. 3.7133, 4.6920
Jones, Howard Mumford, 1892-. 2.10236, 2.10267, 2.11080, 2.11327, 3.6120-3.6121, 4.10247, 5.7788
Jones, Huw Roland. 4.1653
Jones, Ian Shore. 4.3916
Jones, Inigo, 1573-1652. 1.5389, 1.5802
Jones, J. Knox. 5.3974
Jones, J. R. (James Rees), 1925-. 3.1445, 3.1494, 3.1505, 3.1511
Jones, Jacqueline, 1948-. 4.3250, 4.10868
Jones, James, 1921-1977. 2.13100-2.13103, 3.906
Jones, James H. (James Howard), 1943-. 5.4606
Jones, James William, 1943-. 3.7949
Jones, Johanna. 2.10143, 2.10198
Jones, John, 1924-. 2.8320
Jones, John Paul, 1747-1792. 3.6892
Jones, Joseph Jay, 1908-. 2.10143, 2.10198
Jones, Joseph M. (Joseph Marion), 1908-. 3.7800

Jones, Joseph Ramon, 1935-. 2.5173
Jones, Judith P. 2.13305
Jones, Kenneth Lyons. 5.5070
Jones, Kenneth W. 1.1729
Jones, Landon Y., 1943-. 4.5154
Jones, Leon, 1936-. 5.8152
Jones, LeRoi. 1.4301, 2.10717, 2.12866-2.12867, 2.12870
Jones, Lois Swan. 1.4645
Jones, Louise S., 1949-. 4.10699
Jones, Lyle V. joint author. 5.38
Jones, Lynds Eugene, 1853-1902. 5.7748
Jones, M. Monica B. 2.5662
Jones, Malcolm V. 2.1376
Jones, Margaret E. W., 1938-. 2.5135
Jones, Margo. 2.3139
Jones, Martin Hartley, 1942-. 5.6462
Jones, Max. 1.4079
Jones, Neville. 3.822
Jones, Oakah L. 3.8571
Jones, Percy Mansell. 2.3833
Jones, Peter d'Alroy. 3.8421
Jones Pierce, Thomas, 1905-1964. 4.5337
Jones, Phyllis Maud. 2.5499
Jones, R. Merfyn. 4.3441
Jones, R. V. (Reginald Victor), 1911-. 3.1079
Jones, Reginald Lanier, 1931-. 4.10931
Jones, Richard, 1790-1855. 4.1512, 4.1582
Jones, Richard E. (Richard Evan), 1940-. 5.4256
Jones, Richard Foster, ed. 1.665, 2.966
Jones, Richard Matthew, 1925-. 4.10372
Jones, Robert Edmond, 1887-1954. 2.3095, 2.3279
Jones, Robert Emmet, 1928-. 2.4224
Jones, Robert Francis, 1935-. 3.7029
Jones, Robert Leslie, 1907-. 4.2961
Jones, Robert M., 1939-. 5.5795
Jones, Robert Rivers, 1934- joint author. 3.6612
Jones, Robert W. (Robert William), 1940-. 5.6103
Jones, Rodney W. 4.8883
Jones-Roe, Charlotte A. 5.5364
Jones, Roger, 1947-. 1.5018
Jones, Royston Oscar, 1925-. 2.5103
Jones, Russell T., 1950-. 5.4822
Jones, Samuel B., 1933-. 5.3652
Jones, Stephen Barr, 1903-. 4.9308
Jones, Steven Swann, 1949-. 5.7789
Jones, Terry. 2.6325
Jones, Thomas, 1870- tr. 2.847
Jones, Thomas H., 1926-. 5.6480
Jones, Tom Bard, 1909-. 3.2807
Jones, Ulysses S. 5.5293
Jones, Vernon F., 1945-. 4.10699
Jones, W. Gareth, 1936-. 2.1335
Jones, W. Glyn. 3.3366
Jones, W. H. S. (William Henry Samuel), 1876-1963. 2.372, 2.382, 2.686
Jones, Warren H. joint author. 5.649
Jones, Whitney R. D. (Whitney Richard David), 1924-. 3.1389
Jones, Wilbur Devereux. 3.1610
Jones, William Frank. 1.654
Jones, William Ronald. 1.2915
Jones, Willis Knapp, 1895-. 2.3278
Jongman, A. J. 4.6714
Jonson, Ben, 1573?-1637. 2.6587-2.6595
Joos, Georg, 1894-1959. 5.1965
Joos, Martin. 2.1029, 2.1038
Jope, E. M. (Edward Martyn) 4.448
Jopling, Carol F., comp. 1.4693
Joramo, Marjorie K. 3.6527
Joravsky, David. 4.2980, 5.904
Jordaens, Jacob, 1593-1678. 1.6265
Jordan, A. C. 2.10085
Jordan, A. G. joint author. 4.8438
Jordan, Charlotte Brewster, Mrs. 2.5238
Jordan, D. W. (Dominic William) 5.1518
Jordan, David K. 1.1810
Jordan, David M., 1935-. 3.7431
Jordan, David P., 1939-. 3.2051, 3.2071
Jordan, David William, joint author. 3.8103
Jordan, Edward C. (Edward Conrad) 5.6256
Jordan, Elijah. 1.1436
Jordan, Frank, 1937-. 2.5818
Jordan, Jim M. 1.4995
Jordan, John Clark, 1883-. 2.6583

Jordan, John Emory, 1919-. 2.8310
Jordan, June, 1936-. 2.13106-2.13107
Jordan, K. Forbis (Kenneth Forbis) 1930-.
  4.10664
Jordan, Pat. joint author. 4.880
Jordan, Peter C. 5.2883
Jordan, Philip D., 1940-. 1.3096
Jordan, Philip Dillon, 1903-. 3.8381, 4.3942
Jordan, Robert S., 1929-. 4.9200, 4.9267
Jordan, Terry G. 4.375
Jordan, Thomas Edward. 5.4975
Jordan, Thomas F., 1936-. 5.2133
Jordan, Walter H. joint author. 5.5997
Jordan, Wilbur Kitchener, 1902-. 3.1416-3.1417
Jordan, William A. 4.4089
Jordan, William B., 1940-. 1.6220
Jordan, William C., 1948-. 3.1995
Jordan, Winthrop D. 3.6619, 3.7223
Jordan, Zbigniew A. ed. 4.6945
Jordon, Pascual, 1902-. 5.905
Jordy, William H. 1.5287, 3.6239
Jorgens, Elise Bickford. 1.4400
Jorgensen-Dahl, Arnfinn, 1939-. 4.6363
Jorgensen, Paul A. 2.6668, 2.6834
Jorgensen, Paul Alfred, 1916-. 2.6846
Jorgensen, William L. 5.2816
Jorns, Auguste. 1.3354
Jorrín, Miguel. 4.7297
Jose, Nicholas, 1952-. 2.5650
Josef-Haubrich-Kunsthalle Köln. 1.5715
Joseph, Alexander. joint author. 5.3216
Joseph, Bea, 1899- ed. 5.8106
Joseph, Bertram Leon. 2.3119, 2.3334
Joseph, Gloria I. 4.6058
Joseph, M. K. ed. 2.8091
Joseph, Richard A. 4.8812
Josephson, Hannah (Geffen) joint author.
  3.7681
Josephson, Matthew, 1899-1978. 2.10415,
  3.7413, 3.7529, 3.7681
Josephus, Flavius. 2.376, 3.3896-3.3897
Joshi, A. W. 5.2140
Josiah Macy, Jr. Foundation. 5.4541
Josipovici, Gabriel, 1940-. 2.2340
Joskow, Paul L. 4.3803, 5.4709
Josselin, Ralph, 1617-1683. 1.3312
Jost, Wilhelm, 1903-. 5.2220
Jouett, Matthew Harris, 1788-1827. 1.5976
Joughin, Louis. 4.9855
Joukowsky, Martha. 3.239
Jourard, Sidney M. 5.521
Jourda, Pierre, 1898- ed. 2.3942
Jouvenel, Bertrand de, 1903-. 4.7505, 4.7508
Jowell, Roger. 4.8503
Jowett, Benjamin, 1817-1893. tr. 3.545
Jowett, Garth. 2.2919
Jowitt, Kenneth. 4.8687
Joy, Charles Rhind, 1885- ed. 1.1061
Joyce, Bruce R. 4.10273, 4.10425
Joyce, Donald F. 5.7585
Joyce, James, 1882-1941. 2.8862-2.8868,
  2.8875-2.8878, 2.8880-2.8881, 2.8888, 2.8897,
  2.8900-2.8901, 2.8907, 2.8909, 2.8923
Joyce, James Avery. 4.7638, 4.9186
Joyce, Patrick. 4.2278
Joyce, Stanislaus. 2.8910
Joyner, Charles W. 3.8251
Juan, Jorge, 1713-1773. 3.9302
Juan y Santacilla, Jorge, 1713-1773. 3.9152
Juana Inés de la Cruz, Sister, 1651-1695. 2.5332
Judah, J. Stillson. 1.2390
Judd, Charles Hubbard, 1873-1946, tr. 5.111
Judd, Deane Brewster, 1900-1972. 5.2333
Judd, William R. 5.3038
Judelle, Beatrice, 1908-. 4.3859
Judge, Anne. 2.865
Judge, Harry George. 4.10119
Judson, C. Fred. 3.9099
Judson, Horace Freeland. 5.4418
Judson, Margaret Atwood, 1899-. 4.8400
Judy, Stephen N. 4.10479
Juergens, George. 2.3627
Jugenheimer, Robert W. 5.5324
Juhasz, Suzanne, 1942-. 2.10290, 2.10999,
  2.11003
Juilliard School of Music. 1.4422
Jukes, Geoffrey. 3.3317

Jul, Mogens. 5.6889
Jules-Rosette, Bennetta. 1.1847
Julian, Emperor of Rome, 331-363. 2.377
Julian, of Norwich, b. 1343. 1.3072
Julien, Charles André, 1891-. 3.5194
Jullian, Philippe. 1.6700, 1.6719, 2.5019
Jullien, Marc Antoine, 1775-1848. 4.10203
July, Robert William. 3.5073, 3.5317, 4.653
Jump, John Davies, 1913- comp. 2.8158
Jumper, Sidney R. 4.2783
Jung, C. G. (Carl Gustav), 1875-1961. 1.1566,
  1.2104, 3.5959, 5.9, 5.98, 5.165-5.169, 5.4911
Jung, Dieter. joint author. 5.7472
Jung Foundation for Analytical Psychology,
  New York. 5.195
Jung, Rodney Clifton, 1920-. 5.4759, 5.4761
Junge, Ewald. 3.273
Jünger, Ernst, 1895-. 2.13787
Jungk, Robert, 1913-. 5.2418
Junkins, Donald, 1931-. 2.3740
Jupp, James. 4.8724
Jupp, Peter. 4.8480
Jureidini, Paul A. 3.4036
Jusatz, Helmut J. (Helmut Joachim), 1907-
  joint ed. 4.131
Jusserand, J. J. (Jean Jules), 1855-1932. 2.5529,
  3.1332
Jussim, Estelle. 5.6979
Just, Leo, 1901-1964. ed. 3.2250
Justice, Donald Rodney, 1925-. 2.11939-2.11940
Justice, James H., 1941-. 5.6364
Justus, James H. 2.12652
Jutikkala, Eino, 1907-. 3.3289
Jütte, Rüdiger, 1944-. 4.9216
Juvenal. 2.673, 2.728-2.729
Juvenalis, Decimus Junius. Satirae. 2.646
Juviler, Peter H. 4.9917
Jūzajānī, 'Abd al-Wāhid ibn Muhammad, 11th
  cent. 1.370

Kaba, Lansiné. 1.2009
Kabir, 15th cent. 2.1885
Kadish, Sanford H. 4.6675
Kadish, Sanford H. joint author. 1.1321
Kadushin, Alfred. 4.6489, 4.6499, 4.6559
Kadushin, Charles. 5.4864, 5.7584
Kaegi, Walter Emil. 3.2818
Kael, Pauline. 2.3025
Kaelin, Eugene Francis, 1926-. 1.1375
Kaempfer, Engelbert, 1651-1716. 3.4909
Kaeppler, Adrienne Lois. 1.5092, 4.664
Kaestle, Carl F. 4.10023
Kafka, Franz, 1883-1924. 2.13788-2.13796
Kafrissen, Edward. 5.7050
Kafry, Ditsa. 5.409
Kagan, Donald. 3.2613-3.2615, 4.7358
Kagan, Jerome. 4.5757, 5.549, 5.568
Kagan, Jerome. joint author. 4.5705
Kagan, Richard L., 1943-. 3.3434
Kagen, Sergius. 1.3600
Kahin, George McTurnan. ed. 4.8692, 4.8696
Kahin, George McTurnan. 3.4570
Kahl, Joseph Alan, 1923-. 4.5237
Kahlefeld, Heinrich. 1.2936
Kahlenberg, Mary Hunt. 3.5918
Kahlenberg, Mary Hunt. joint author. 3.5913
Kähler, Martin, 1835-1912. 1.2883
Kahn, Albert Eugene, 1912-1979. 1.4076
Kahn, Alfred E. (Alfred Edward) 4.3082
Kahn, Alfred E. (Alfred Edward) joint author.
  4.3768
Kahn, Alfred J., 1919-. 4.3261, 4.5616, 4.6514,
  4.6523
Kahn, Brian. 5.990
Kahn, Charles H. 1.236
Kahn, Coppélia. 2.6745
Kahn, David, 1930-. 3.1135
Kahn, E. J. (Ely Jacques), 1916-. 3.5019,
  4.1674, 4.9060
Kahn, F. D. (Franz Daniel) 5.1861
Kahn, Frank J. 4.9538
Kahn, Harold L. 3.4716
Kahn, Herman, 1922-. 3.72, 4.2013, 4.2784,
  5.7237, 5.7256, 5.7385
Kahn, Melvin, 1930-. 4.8865
Kahn, Michael D., 1936-. 5.616
Kahn, Robert Louis, 1918- joint author. 4.4904,
  4.4917

Kahn, Roger. 2.11977, 4.1006
Kahn, Si. 4.4951
Kahneman, Daniel, 1934-. 5.309
Kahnweiler, Daniel Henry, 1884-. 1.6349
Kahrl, George Morrow, 1904- joint author.
  2.3343
Kaikō, Takeshi, 1930-. 2.2132
Kail, Robert V. 5.324, 5.606
Kain, John F. 4.3493
Kain, John F. joint author. 4.3937
Kain, Richard Morgan, 1908-. 2.8892, 2.8916
Kainz, Howard P. 1.934
Kaiser, David E., 1947-. 4.4234
Kaiser, Georg, 1878-1945. 2.13801-2.13804
Kaiser, Karl, 1934- ed. 3.1705
Kaiser, Marjorie M., 1933-. 4.10830
Kaiser, Robert G., 1943-. 3.3014
Kaiser, Walter Jacob. 2.824
Kajima, Shōzō, 1923- joint comp. 2.2031
Kalābādhī, Muhammad ibn Ibrāhīm, 10th cent.
  1.2078
Kalb, Bernard. joint author. 3.7860
Kalb, Marvin L. 3.7860
Kalbfleisch, J. G. 5.1383
Kaldor, Nicholas, 1908-1986. 4.1439-4.1440,
  4.2785, 4.4709
Kalecki, Michał. 4.1300, 4.1810
Kaledin, Eugenia. 4.6021
Kalevala. 2.1752
Kaley, Gabor. 5.4228
Kālidāsa. 2.1946-2.1947, 2.1949, 2.1955
Kalisch, Beatrice J., 1943-. 5.5154-5.5155
Kalisch, Philip Arthur. 5.5154-5.5155
Kalish, Donald. 1.1212
Kalken, Frans van, 1881-. 3.2967
Källén, Gunnar, 1926-1968. 5.2393
Kallen, Horace Meyer, 1882-. 1.89
Kallenbach, Jessamine S., 1915-. 5.7798
Kallir, Otto, 1894-. 1.5957
Kallman, Chester, 1921- ed. 1.3442
Kallmann, Helmut. 1.3538
Kalnein, Wend von, 1914-. 1.4960
Kalnins, Mara. 1.2729
Kalstone, David. 2.6511, 2.10509
Kalt, Joseph P. 4.3767
Kaltchas, Nicholas Stavrou, 1895-1937. 4.8619
Kalupahana, David J., 1933-. 1.2146
Kalven, Harry. 4.4693, 4.9692, 4.9888
Kalymon, Basil, 1944-. 4.3484
Kamali, Sabih Ahmad. 1.374
Kamarck, Andrew M. 4.2577, 4.2599
Kamen, Henry Arthur Francis. 3.3411, 3.3435,
  3.3446, 4.5285
Kamenka, Eugene. 1.1036
Kamerman, Sheila B. 4.3261, 4.5616, 4.5652,
  4.5725, 4.6523
Kamien, Morton I. 4.1863
Kamien, Roger. 1.3422
Kamin, Leon J. joint author. 5.351
Kamin, Leon J. 5.314, 5.358
Kaminkow, Marion J. 5.7852
Kaminsky, Alice R. 2.2454
Kaminsky, Howard, 1924-. 3.1912
Kamisar, Yale. 4.9883
Kamm, Oliver, b. 1888. joint ed. 5.2738
Kammen, Michael G. ed. 3.8029
Kammen, Michael G. 3.6016, 3.6878, 3.8028
Kampar, 9th cent. 2.2275
Kampelman, Max M., 1920-. 4.3552
Kamrany, Nake M., 1934-. 5.8042
Kamuf, Peggy, 1947-. 2.3902
Kanafani, Adib K. 4.3873
Kanamori, H. (Hiroo), 1936- joint author.
  5.3077
Kandel, Eric R. 5.4310
Kandinsky, Wassily, 1866-1944. 1.4601, 1.4811,
  1.5144
Kane, George. 2.5604, 2.6361, 2.6394-2.6396,
  2.6401
Kane, Hamidou. 2.4871
Kane, J. Herbert. ed. 1.3023
Kane, Joseph Nathan, 1899-. 1.22, 3.6309,
  3.6364
Kane, Patricia E. 1.6583, 1.6667
Kane, Paul, 1810-1871. 1.5998
Kane, Penny. 4.5685
Kane, Robert M. 4.4083
Kane, Thomas R. 5.5741

Kaneko, Hiroshi, 1933- illus. 2.2836
Kanes, Martin. 2.4129
Kanfer, Frederick H., 1925-. 5.454
K'ang-hsi, Emperor of China, 1654-1722. 3.4717
Kangle, R.P. 4.7328
Kani, John, joint author. 2.10068
Kani, John. 2.10069
Kanin, Garson, 1912-. 2.11941
Kanitkar, Helen A. 5.8095
Kann, Robert A., 1906-. 3.1875, 3.1881, 3.1896, 3.2994
Kannappan, Subbiah. joint author. 4.3666
Kanner, Barbara, 1925-. 4.6111
Kansai Keizai Kenkyū Sentā. 4.2433
Kansas. Federal Writers' Project. 3.8526
Kansas. University. Midwest Psychological Field Station. 5.315
Kansy, K. (Klaus), 1945-. 5.5646
Kant, Harold Sanford, joint author. 4.5546
Kant, Immanuel, 1724-1804. 1.878-1.879, 1.881, 1.883, 1.890-1.898, 1.912-1.913, 1.919, 1.1170, 1.1371, 4.7437, 4.9115, 4.10194, 5.1871
Kanter, Arnold. joint author. 4.9095
Kanter, Donald Lucky, 1925-. 4.4429
Kanter, Rosabeth Moss. 4.2696, 4.5576, 4.7156
Kantner, Claude Edgar, joint author. 2.1017
Kantor, Harry. 4.7714, 4.8349
Kantor, Harvey. 4.10832
Kantor, MacKinlay, 1904-. 2.11942-2.11943
Kantorowicz, Ernst Hartwig, 1895-1963. 3.2271, 4.7553
Kantra, Robert A. 2.6062
Kanury, A. Murty. 5.2903
Kany, Charles Emil, 1895-. 2.907
Kanya-Forstner, A. S. 3.2194
Kanzer, Mark, 1908-. 5.153
Kao, George, 1912-. 2.2250
Kao, Karl S. Y. 2.2199
Kapel, David E. 4.10164
Kaplan, A. D. H. (Abraham David Hannath), 1893-. 4.1988, 4.4313
Kaplan, Abraham, 1918-. 3.6122, 4.1206
Kaplan, Bernard. 5.3, 5.399
Kaplan, Berton H., 1930- ed. 5.4835
Kaplan, Charles, 1919-. 2.2431
Kaplan, Cora. 2.7464
Kaplan, Daniel P. 4.4087
Kaplan, David, 1929- joint comp. 4.396
Kaplan, E. Ann. 2.3015
Kaplan, Edward H., 1936-. 4.2466
Kaplan, Eugene J. 4.3076
Kaplan, Fred, 1937-. 2.7553, 2.7632, 2.7639
Kaplan, Harold, 1916-. 2.10388
Kaplan, Harold I., 1927-. 5.4878
Kaplan, Helen Singer, 1929-. 5.4950-5.4951
Kaplan, Herbert H. 3.3280
Kaplan, Irving, 1912-. 3.5239, 3.5268, 3.5292, 3.5337, 3.5371, 3.5403, 3.5417, 3.5518, 3.9110, 5.2068
Kaplan, John. 4.6663
Kaplan, Jonathan. 5.8236
Kaplan, Justin. 2.10958-2.10959, 2.11276
Kaplan, Lawrence S. 4.9019
Kaplan, Marion A. 4.6123
Kaplan, Marshall. joint author. 4.6318
Kaplan, Mike, 1918-. 2.2775
Kaplan, Milton, 1918- ed. 3.7348
Kaplan, Mordecai Menahem, 1881-. 1.1967
Kaplan, Morton A. 4.9005, 4.9281
Kaplan, Nathan Oram, 1917- ed. 5.4410
Kaplan, Oscar J. 5.4814
Kaplan, S. A. (Samuil Aronovich) 5.1827
Kaplan, Sidney, 1913-. 3.6813
Kaplan, Stephen S. 5.7325
Kaplan, Sydney Janet, 1939-. 2.6058
Kaplan, Wilfred, 1915-. 5.5708
Kaplansky, Irving, 1917-. 5.1112, 5.1299
Kapleau, Philip, 1912- ed. 1.2175
Kaplin, William A. 4.9603
Kaplinsky, Raphael. 5.6457
Kaplow, Jeffry. 3.2235
Kapp, Ernst, 1863-   tr. 1.286
Kappel, Robert. 4.3959
Kappen, Sebastian. 1.2862
Kappler, Charles Joseph, 1868-1946. 4.9771
Kapteyn, P. J. G. (Paul Joan George) 4.8969
Kapuściński, Ryszard. 3.4086

Karabel, Jerome. 4.10771
Karamanski, Theodore J., 1953-. 4.3861
Karamzin, Nikolaĭ Mikhaĭlovich, 1766-1826. 2.1331, 3.3081
Karan, Pradyumna P. (Pradyumna Prasad) 3.4331, 3.4349
Karcz, George, ed. 4.2979
Karcz, Jerzy F, ed. 4.2974
Kardiner, Abram, 1891-. 4.487, 4.525, 4.4988
Kardon, Randy H., 1954-. 5.4113
Karen, Robert. joint author. 5.7010
Karetzky, Stephen, 1946-. 5.7688
Karger, Barry L., 1939-. 5.2644
Kargon, Robert Hugh. 5.1953
Karier, Clarence J. 4.9985, 4.10218
Karis, Thomas, 1919- ed. 3.5451
Kark, Sidney L. 5.4654
Karkavitsas, Andreas, 1866-1923. 2.586
Karkoschka, Erhard. 1.4444
Karl, Barry Dean. 3.7509, 4.7978
Karl, Frederick Robert, 1927-. 2.6039-2.6040, 2.8542, 2.8547, 2.8568-2.8569, 2.9347, 2.10629
Karlen, Delmar. 4.9779
Karlesky, Joseph J., 1943-. 4.10553
Karlgren, Bernhard, 1889-. 2.2142-2.2143
Karlinsky, Simon. 2.1296, 2.1488, 2.1500
Karlinsky, Simon. comp. 2.1487
Karlstadt, Andreas Rudolff-Bodenstein von, ca. 1480-1541. 1.2317
Karma-gliṅ-pa, 14th cent. 1.2149
Karnes, Frances A. 5.8154
Karnow, Stanley. 3.4501
Karo, Wolf, 1924- joint author. 5.2752
Karol, K. S. 3.4793
Karolevitz, Robert F. 2.3656
Karolik, Martha Catherine Codman. 1.5883
Karolik, Maxim. 1.5883
Karp, Abraham J. 3.6570
Karp, Abraham J. comp. 3.6571
Karp, Gerald. joint author. 5.4123
Karp, Ivan. 3.5271, 4.648
Karpat, Kemal H. comp. 4.7298
Karpat, Kemal H. 4.7299
Karpinski, Leszek M. 5.8439
Karpov, Anatoly, 1951-. 4.1074
Karpovich, Michael, 1888-1959. 3.3047
Karrer, Wolfgang, 1941-. 2.10306
Karrow, Paul Frederick, 1930-. 5.5892
Karsavina, Tamara. 4.1150
Karski, Jan, 1914-. 3.3339
Karson, Marc. 4.3598
Karta (Firm) 4.132, 4.179
Kartini, Raden Adjeng, 1879-1904. 3.4579
Kartodirdjo, Sartono, 1921-. 4.5441
Karugire, Samwiri Rubaraza. 3.5286
Karve, Irawati Karmarkar, 1905-1970. 4.6406
Karwowski, Jacek. joint author. 5.2081
Käsemann, Ernst. 1.2652, 1.2711
Kaser, Michael Charles. 4.2232, 4.2234
Kashima, Tetsuden. 1.2168
Kasparov, G. K. (Garri Kimovich) 4.1074
Kasper, Walter. 1.2863
Kasperson, Roger E. 5.6054
Kasprzyk, Krystyna. 2.3980
Kass, Leon. 5.4563
Kass, Ray. 1.4897
Kassel, Steve. 5.6589
Kassis, Hanna E. 1.2033
Kassler, Jeanne. 5.4768
Kasson, John F., 1944-. 3.8061, 5.5520
Kast, Fremont Ellsworth, 1926-. 4.2651
Kastenbaum, Robert. 5.5008
Kastner, Joseph. 5.3188
Kastner, Leon Emile. ed. 2.6473
Kaszubski, Marek. 4.9445
Kataev, Valentin, 1897-. 2.1566-2.1568
Kataoka, Tetsuya. 3.4983
Katchadourian, Herant A. 5.490
Kateb, George. 4.7171
Kater, Michael H., 1937-. 4.8604
Kates, Gary, 1952-. 3.2098
Kates, Robert William. joint author. 4.319
Kates, Robert William. 4.1812
Katkin, Daniel. 4.6875
Katkov, George. 3.3198
Katō, Shizue, 1897-. 3.4900
Katō, Shūichi, 1919-. 1.5072

Katona, George, 1901-. 4.2060
Katrēs, Giannēs. 3.2707
Katritzky, Alan R. 5.2775
Katsh, Abraham Isaac, 1908- joint comp. 3.3930
Katsimpalēs, Geōrgios Kōnstantinou, 1899-. 2.605
Katz, Abraham, 1926-. 4.2399
Katz, Alfred H. (Alfred Hyman), 1916-. 4.6594
Katz, Barbara F. 4.9544
Katz, Bernard, 1911-. 5.4303
Katz, Daniel, 1903-. 4.4904, 4.4917
Katz, Dorothy Dittmer. 5.3595
Katz, Dorothy Dittmer. joint ed. 5.3303
Katz, Dorothy Dittmer. ed. 5.4227
Katz, Dovid. 2.1790
Katz, Elihu, 1926-. 4.4062, 4.7766
Katz, Ephraim. 2.2871
Katz, Harold Ambrose, 1921- joint author. 4.9552
Katz, Harry Charles, 1951-. 4.3185
Katz, Jacob, 1904-. 1.1957, 3.3834, 3.4010
Katz, James Everett. 5.794
Katz, Jay, 1922-. 5.4592
Katz, Jerrold J. joint ed. 2.133
Katz, Joel, 1943- joint author. 4.891
Katz, Jonathan. 3.7270, 4.5535, 4.5538
Katz, Joseph. ed. 2.10980, 4.10092, 4.10588
Katz, Linda Sternberg. 5.8311
Katz, Michael B. 4.6515-4.6516, 4.10096, 4.10961
Katz, Sedelle, 1923-. 4.6734
Katz, Silas, joint author. 5.6161, 5.6238
Katz, Stanley Nider. 4.5127
Katz, Steven T., 1944-. 1.1628-1.1629, 1.1971
Katz, William A., 1924-. 5.7622, 5.7649-5.7650, 5.8311
Katz, William Loren. 3.6653
Katz, Zev, ed. 3.3024
Katzan, Harry. 5.1146, 5.1207
Katzell, Raymond A., 1919-. 4.2685
Katzenbach, Nicholas de Belleville, 1922- joint author. 4.9281
Katzenellenbogen, Adolf Edmund Max, 1901-. 1.5532
Katzenstein, Peter J. 4.9070
Katzman, David M. 3.8438
Katzman, David M. (David Manners), 1941-. 4.3263
Katzman, Martin T. 5.6226
Katznelson, Ira. 4.8870
Katznelson, Yitzhak. 5.1553
Katzner, Kenneth. 2.1233
Kau, Michael Y. M., ed. 3.4822
Kauffman, Erle Galen, 1933-. 5.3130
Kauffman, James M. 4.10909
Kauffman, Louis H., 1945-. 5.1611
Kauffmann, C. M. (Claus Michael), 1931-. 1.6408
Kaufman, Art. 4.7865
Kaufman, Burton Ira. 4.4173
Kaufman, Edy. 3.9236
Kaufman, George S. (George Simon), 1889-1961. 2.11944
Kaufman, Gordon D. 1.2778, 1.2829
Kaufman, Herbert, 1922-. 4.7982, 5.5436
Kaufman, John E. 5.6337
Kaufman, Lloyd. 5.248, 5.266
Kaufman, Martin, 1940-. 5.4529
Kaufman, Perry J. 4.4636
Kaufman, Polly Welts, 1929-. 4.10674
Kaufman, A. (Arnold), 1911-. 4.2628, 5.5580
Kaufmann, Edgar, 1910- ed. 1.5296, 1.5339
Kaufmann, Emil, 1891-1953. 1.5246
Kaufmann, Felix. 4.1207
Kaufmann, Ralph James, 1924- ed. 2.5873, 2.8076
Kaufmann, Walter Arnold. ed. 1.488, 1.970
Kaufmann, Walter Arnold. tr. 1.1046, 1.1050
Kaufmann, Walter Arnold. 1.946, 1.1055
Kaufmann, Walter Arnold. comp. 4.7449
Kaufmann, Walter H. 3.2374
Kaufmann, William J. 5.1703, 5.1720, 5.1843, 5.1854, 5.1872, 5.2467
Kaufmann, William W. 3.9010, 5.7247
Kaufmann, Yehezkel, 1889-1963. 1.1898
Kaul, A. N. 2.10582

Kaul, A. N. ed. 2.11063
Kaunda, Kenneth D. (Kenneth David), 1924-. 4.5474
Kautalya. 4.7328-4.7329
Kautsky, Karl, 1854-1938. 1.417, 4.1538, 4.7068
Kauvar, Gerald B. comp. 2.6241
Kavan, Anna, 1904-1968. 2.8614-2.8619
Kavanagh, Barry F. 5.5822
Kavanagh, David, joint author. 4.8496
Kavanagh, Dennis. 4.8494, 4.8497, 4.8500, 4.8549
Kavanagh, Michael. 5.4018
Kavanagh, Patrick, 1904-1967. 2.8924-2.8926
Kavanagh, Peter. 2.3361
Kavass, Igor I. 4.8976
Kavenagh, W. Keith. 4.7807
Kaverin, V. (Veniamin), 1902-. 2.1569
Kavuma, Paulo, 1901-. 3.5264
Kawabata, Yasunari, 1899-1972. 2.2099-2.2103
Kawada, Yukiyosi, 1916-. 5.1026
Kawai, Kazuo, 1904-. 3.4978
Kawatake, Toshio, 1924- joint author. 2.3398
Kawatra, M. P., 1935- ed. 5.2175
Kay, David A., 1940- joint comp. 4.9134
Kay, Donald. 2.5672
Kay, George R. 2.4896, 2.5037
Kay, Karyn. 2.3016
Kay, Neil M. 4.2652
Kay, Norman Forber. 1.3988
Kay, Richard S. joint author. 4.3310
Kay-Robinson, Denys. 2.7800
Kaye, Frederick Benjamin, 1892-1930, ed. 1.1507
Kaye, Harvey J. 4.1725
Kaye, Hilary. 5.3646
Kaye, Joseph, 1912- joint author. 5.2041
Kaye, Kenneth. 5.558
Kaye, Seymour P. 4.3508
Kaye, Sidney. 5.4723
Kaynak, Erdener. 4.4111
Kaysen, Carl. 4.3057
Kazamias, Andreas M. ed. 4.10198
Kazamias, Andreas M. 4.9962
Kazan, Elia. 2.3059
Kazancigil, Ali. 3.3595
Kazantzakē, Galateia. 2.598
Kazantzakēs, Nikos, 1885-1957. 2.589, 2.591
Kazantzakis, Nikos, 1883-1957. 2.587-2.588, 2.590, 2.592-2.599
Kazarinoff, Nicholas D. 5.1419, 5.1572
Kazin, Alfred, 1915-. 2.2577, 2.10235, 2.10630-2.10631, 2.11601, 2.11731, 2.11945
Kazmer, Daniel R. 5.8404
Kazmer, Vera, joint author. 5.8404
Keach, William, 1942-. 2.8113
Kealey, Edward J. 3.1346, 5.4513
Kealey, Linda, 1947-. 4.5981
Kean, Beverly Whitney. 1.4672
Kean, P. M. (Patricia Margaret) 2.6362-2.6363, 2.6426
Keane, David. 1.4460
Keane, Molly, 1904-. 2.8928-2.8929
Kearney, E. I. 5.8169
Kearney, Nolan Charles, 1903-. 4.10426
Kearney, Richard. 1.453
Kearney, Robert N. 3.4361, 4.8723
Kearns, George. 2.12333
Kearns, James. 2.11548
Keates, J. S. 4.203
Keates, Jonathan, 1946-. 1.3889
Keating, H. R. F. (Henry Reymond Fitzwalter), 1926-. 2.5957, 2.5961
Keatley, Anne G. 5.5540
Keats, John, 1795-1821. 2.7848-2.7851, 2.7853-2.7854, 2.7869
Keble, John, 1792-1866. 2.7874
Keck, Caroline (Kohn) 1.6377
Keck, Leander E. 1.2704
Keddie, Nikki R. 1.2020, 1.2089, 3.4084, 4.5409, 4.5910
Kedourie, Elie. 3.3591
Kedward, H. R. (Harry Roderick) 3.1064
Kee, Howard Clark. 1.2658, 1.2686
Kee, James Edwin. 4.7875
Keech, William R. 4.7943, 4.8093
Keedwell, A. D., joint author. 5.1282

Keefe, Eugene K. 3.1905, 3.1936, 3.2475, 3.2679, 3.3010, 3.3398, 3.3492, 3.3545, 3.3547, 3.3600, 3.3692
Keefe, Joan. 2.3749
Keefe, Terry. 2.4402
Keefer, Louis E. 4.3929
Keegan, Desmond. 4.10986
Keegan, John, 1934-. 3.536, 3.889
Keegan, Warren J. 4.4112
Keele, Harold M. 4.6506
Keeler, Mary Frear. 5.7988
Keeler, Theodore E. 4.4002
Keeley, Edmund. 2.570, 2.574, 2.578, 2.584, 2.610, 2.618
Keeley, Edmund. tr. 2.579, 2.581
Keeley, Edmund. ed. 2.568, 2.608
Keen, Benjamin, 1913-. 3.5972, 3.8885
Keen, Ernest, 1937-. 5.270
Keen, Maurice Hugh. 3.291, 3.1358
Keen, Peter G. W. 4.2637
Keenan, Jeremy, 1945-. 3.5205
Keenan, Jerry. 3.5780
Keenan, Joseph Henry, 1900-. 5.2041, 5.2246
Keene, Donald. joint ed. 2.2185
Keene, Donald. ed. 2.2017, 2.2061
Keene, Donald. 2.1995, 2.2000, 2.2001, 2.2005, 2.2018, 2.2036, 2.2836
Keene, Donald. tr. 2.2060
Keene, James A., 1932-. 1.4418
Keene, Raymond D. 4.1075
Keeney, Ralph L., 1944-. 5.5600
Keenleyside, Hugh Llewellyn, 1898-. 3.8697
Keep, John L. H. 4.8664
Keepnews, Orrin. 1.4330
Keer, Dhananjay. 3.4299
Kees, Weldon, 1914-1955? 2.11946-2.11947
Keesing, Felix Maxwell, 1902-1961. 3.5539, 3.5624, 3.5672, 3.5904
Keesing, Marie M. (Marie Margaret) joint author. 3.5672
Keesing, Roger M., 1935-. 1.1881
Keeton, Morris T. 4.10626
Keeves, John P. joint author. 5.982
Kegan, Robert. 5.551
Kegley, Charles W. joint comp. 3.7847
Kegley, Charles W. ed. 1.3294
Kegley, Charles William, 1912-. 1.3297
Kehoe, Alice B., 1936-. 3.5702
Kehr, Eckart, 1902-1933. 3.2256
Kehr, Helen. 5.8014
Keig, Robert Joseph Brook, ed. 5.6224
Keiger, John F. V. 3.2180
Keightley, David N. 3.4689, 3.4691
Keikai, 8th/9th cent. comp. 1.2152
Keil, Charles. 1.4302
Keim, Albert N. 4.10747
Keir, Gillian. joint author. 4.2303
Keisler, H. Jerome. joint author. 5.1055
Keitel, Walter. 2.13563
Keith, Arthur Berriedale, 1879-1944. 1.197, 1.215, 1.1698, 2.1920, 2.1927, 3.1230, 3.4228
Keith, Jennie. 4.588
Keith-Lucas, Bryan. 4.8876
Keith, Robert. 4.4683
Keith, Robert G. 3.8993
Keith-Smith, Brian, 1934-. 2.13680
Kekes, John. 1.107
Kelber, Harry. 5.7558
Kelber, Werner H. 1.2687-1.2688
Kele, Max H. 3.2424
Keleman, Pál. 1.4857
Kell, George S., d. 1983. 5.6206
Kell, James H. 5.6066
Kellam, Sheppard G. 4.10278
Kellas, James G. 3.1775, 4.8562
Keller, Charles L. 5.7482
Keller, David (David Mathias) 1.73
Keller, Dean H. 5.8128
Keller, Evelyn Fox, 1936-. 5.906, 5.3412
Keller, Frances Richardson, 1917-. 2.10929
Keller, Franklin Jefferson, 1887-. 4.10498
Keller, Gary D. 2.10674
Keller, Gottfried, 1819-1890. 2.13619-2.13620
Keller, Hans, 1919- ed. 1.3824
Keller, Hermann, 1885-1967. 1.4462, 1.4496
Keller, Irvin A. 4.974
Keller, John Esten. 2.5160
Keller, Karl, 1933-. 2.10876

Keller, Mark, 1907-. 4.6647
Keller, Morton. 3.7414
Keller, Rosemary Skinner. 1.2387
Keller, Suzanne Infeld, 1927-. 4.4952
Kelletat, Alfred. 2.13543
Kelley, Alice van Buren. 2.9598
Kelley, David. 5.4890
Kelley, David H. 3.9049
Kelley, Donald R. 3.1958, 3.2012, 4.8579
Kelley, Edith Summers. 2.11949
Kelley, Harold H. 2.50
Kelley, J. Charles, 1913- joint comp. 3.5759
Kelley, Michael R., 1940-. 2.5855
Kelley, Philip. 2.7480
Kelley, Philip. ed. 2.7466
Kelley, Richard N., 1940- joint author. 5.5676
Kelley, Robert Lloyd, 1925-. 4.8148
Kelley, Stanley. 4.7951
Kellman, Martin C. 5.3666
Kellner, Bruce. 1.6709
Kellner, Douglas, 1943-. 1.611, 4.7055
Kellogg, Louise Phelps, ed. 1942 3.8370, 3.8444-3.8445
Kellogg, Robert. joint author. 2.3504
Kellogg, William W. 5.2516
Kelly, A. A. (Angeline A.) 2.8950, 2.9167
Kelly, Amy Ruth, 1878-. 3.1352
Kelly, Charles, 1889-. 3.8582
Kelly, Douglas. 2.3841
Kelly, Errol G. 5.6753
Kelly, Francis Michael, 1879-1945. 4.841
Kelly, Fred C. (Fred Charters), 1882-1959. 2.10895
Kelly, Gail Paradise. 3.4512, 4.9964, 4.10887
Kelly, Gary. 2.5994
Kelly, George Alexander, 1905-1967. 5.522
Kelly, J. N. D. (John Norman Davidson) 1.2489, 1.2748, 1.2956
Kelly, James, 1829-1907. 5.7747
Kelly, James J. 1.5651
Kelly, Joan, 1928-1982. 4.5884
Kelly, John R., 1944- joint author. 5.1189
Kelly, Marjorie. 1.2050
Kelly, Michael P. 4.7049
Kelly, Richard Michael, 1937-. 2.8775
Kelly, Rita Mae. 4.5957
Kelly, Thomas, 1929-. 3.2589
Kelman, Herbert C. ed. 4.8992
Kelsall, M. M. (Malcolm Miles), 1938-. 2.7030
Kelsay, Isabel Thompson, 1905-. 3.5893
Kelsen, Hans, 1881-1973. 4.9219, 4.9295-4.9296
Kelsey, Benjamin S., d. 1981. 5.7402
Kelsey, Lella B. 2.11765
Kelsey, W. Michael, 1945-. 2.2043
Keltie, Sir John Scott, 1840-1927, ed. 4.7214
Kelvin, Norman. 2.7967
Kemball, Robin. 2.1536
Kemble, Fanny, 1809-1893. 3.8264
Kemeny, John G. 4.4417, 5.907, 5.1210
Kemmer, Elizabeth Jane. 5.8362
Kemmerly, Jack E., 1924-. 5.6270
Kemp, Betty. 4.8439
Kemp, Friedhelm, 1914-. 2.13552
Kemp, Jerrold E. 4.10325
Kemp, John, joint tr. 1.958
Kemp, Lysander, 1920- tr. 3.8924
Kemp, Peter. 2.8260
Kemp, Peter Kemp. 5.7418, 5.7455
Kemp-Pritchard, Philip. 5.6842
Kemp, Robert, 1908-. 2.6608
Kempe, C. Henry. joint author. 4.6558, 4.6560
Kempe, C. Henry. 4.5518
Kempe, Margery, b. ca. 1373. 2.6389
Kempe, Ruth S. 4.6560
Kendall, Alan. 1.4107
Kendall, Lane C., 1912-. 4.3961
Kendall, Maurice G. (Maurice George), 1907-. 5.1390-5.1391, 5.1400
Kendall, Patricia L. 4.4800
Kendler, Howard Harvard, 1919- ed. 5.216
Kendrew, W. G. (Wilfrid George) 5.2561
Kendrick, Alexander. 2.3622
Kendrick, John W. ed. 4.1954
Kendrick, John W. 4.2091, 4.2683
Kendrick, T. D. (Thomas Downing) 1.4936
Kendrick, Walter M. 2.6096
Kenen, Peter B., 1932-. 4.4562-4.4563
Kenett, F. L. 1.5633, 1.5771

Kenez, Peter. 3.3199
Keniston, Hayward, b. 1883. 2.5237
Keniston, Kenneth. 4.5766-4.5767
Kenjō, Takashi. 5.6314
Kennan, George, 1845-1924. 3.3319
Kennan, George Frost, 1904-. 3.772, 3.1152,
  3.3059, 3.3061, 3.3070, 6.6486, 3.7579,
  3.7655, 3.7824, 3.7926, 4.9075
Kennan, Kent Wheeler, 1913-. 1.4472, 1.4489
Kennard, Earle Hesse, 1885- . 5.2180
Kennard, Jean E., 1936-. 2.10632
Kennebeck, Edwin. 4.9457
Kennedy, Arthur G., 1880-1954. 2.6377
Kennedy, Charles William, 1882-. 2.6282,
  2.6305
Kennedy, David M. 3.816
Kennedy, Ellen Conroy. 2.4844
Kennedy, Gail, 1900- joint ed. 1.528
Kennedy, Gavin. 4.1390
Kennedy, George Alexander, 1928-. 1.2647,
  2.309, 2.643, 2.767
Kennedy, Hugh (Hugh N.) 3.3673
Kennedy, James R. (James Randolph), 1928-.
  4.10287
Kennedy, John F. (John Fitzgerald), 1917-1963.
  3.6293, 3.7872
Kennedy, John G. 3.5186
Kennedy, John McFarland. tr. 1.1045
Kennedy, John Miller, 1942-. 5.249
Kennedy, John Pendleton, 1795-1870.
  2.11136-2.11137
Kennedy, Kieran Anthony. 4.2315
Kennedy, Lawrence F., comp. 4.7991
Kennedy, Liam, 1946-. 4.2318
Kennedy, Michael, 1926-. 1.3501, 1.3860,
  1.4020
Kennedy, Michael L. 3.2110
Kennedy, Pat. 5.5203
Kennedy, Paul M., 1945-. 3.1255, 3.1622,
  3.6446
Kennedy, Peter, 1943-. 4.1395
Kennedy, Richard S. ed. 2.12784
Kennedy, Richard S. 2.12780, 2.12783, 2.12792
Kennedy, Robert Emmet, 1937-. 4.1697
Kennedy, Robert F., 1925-1968. 3.6487
Kennedy, Ruth Wedgwood. 1.6190
Kennedy, Susan Estabrook. 4.5985, 5.8467
Kennelly, Brendan. 2.9866
Kenner, Hugh. 2.8430, 2.8893, 2.8894, 2.8911,
  2.9046, 2.9856, 2.10416, 2.12345, 2.12346,
  5.5864
Kenner, Hugh. ed. 2.11636
Kennett, James P. 5.2982
Kennett, Jiyu, 1924-. 1.2176
Kennett, Lee B. 4.6806, 5.7311, 5.7408
Kenney, Anne R., 1950-. 4.8590
Kenney, E. J. 2.627
Kenney, Edwin J. 2.8483
Kenney, William Howland. 2.10706
Kennington, Alice E. 3.6507
Kennington, Donald. 1.3572
Kennon, Noel F. 5.2927
Kenny, Anthony John Patrick. ed. 1.792
Kenny, Anthony John Patrick. 1.313-1.314,
  1.347, 1.794, 1.1082, 1.2823, 3.1409
Kenny, Maurice. 3.13108
Kenny, Michael, 1923-. 4.6252
Kenny, Shirley Strum. ed. 2.7269
Kenny, Shirley Strum. 2.7014
Kenny, Vincent S. 2.11153
Kenny, Virginia C. 2.5686
Kenrick, Donald. 3.5681
Kenshalo, Dan R. ed. 5.4364
Kensicki, Peter R. 4.4638
Kent, Allen. ed. 5.7695
Kent, Calvin A. 4.1555, 4.1557
Kent, D. V. (Dale V.) 3.2927
Kent, Earle Lewis, 1910-. 1.4375
Kent, George E. 2.10324
Kent, James, 1763-1847. 4.9503
Kent, James Albert, 1922-. 5.6815
Kent, Kate Peck. 3.5761, 3.5942
Kent, Leonard J., 1927-. 2.1379-2.1380, 2.13616
Kent, Marian. 3.765
Kent, Raymond K. 3.5314
Kent, Robert Thurston. 5.5601
Kent, Sherman. 4.7770
Kenton, Edna. 3.8714

Kenworthy, Leonard Stout, 1912-. 4.1226
Kenyatta, Jomo. 3.5280-3.5281
Kenyon, Cecelia M. ed. 4.7814
Kenyon, Frederic G. (Frederic George), Sir,
  1863-1952. 1.2510, 2.7470
Kenyon, Gerald S. ed. 4.903
Kenyon, Gerald S. joint author. 4.956
Kenyon, Gerald S. 4.960
Kenyon, J.P. (John Philipps), 1927-. 3.1506,
  4.8518
Kenyon, John Samuel, 1874-. 2.1016, 2.1023
Kenyon, Kathleen Mary. 1.2545, 3.3813,
  3.3829-3.3830
Kenyon review. 2.2680
Keohane, Nannerl O., 1940-. 4.6047, 4.7285
Keohane, Robert O. (Robert Owen), 1941-.
  4.4145, 4.9032
Keough, Jane S. 5.5333
Keown, R. 5.1300
Kepars, I. 5.8079
Kepes, Gyorgy, 1906- ed. 1.4642, 1.4812,
  1.5106, 1.5113
Kepler, Johannes, 1571-1630. 5.1696
Kepner, Charles Higgins, 1922-. 4.2665
Keppel, Francis 1916-. 4.9997
Keppler, Ann, 1946-. 5.5064
Ker, I. T. (Ian Turnbull) 4.10545
Ker, W. P. (William Paton), 1855-1923. 2.2624,
  2.5540, 2.5605
Ker, Walter Charles Alan, 1853-1929. 2.662,
  2.677
Kerber, Linda K. 4.6010
Kerblay, Basile H. 4.5373
Kerby-Miller, Charles ed. 2.7191
Kerensky, Aleksandr Fyodorovich, 1881-1970.
  3.3185
Kerensky, Oleg, 1930-. 2.5922
Kerényi, Karl, 1897-1973. 2.13835, 3.5959
Kerferd, G. B. 1.240
Kerkvliet, Benedict J. 3.4607
Kerman, Joseph, 1924-. 1.4234, 1.4360, 1.4404,
  1.4533
Kermish, Joseph. 3.3990
Kermode, Frank, 1919-. 2.2363, 2.2756, 2.5739,
  2.6070, 2.6126, 2.12547
Kern, Edith, 1912- ed. 2.4742
Kern, Fritz, 1884-1950. 4.7555
Kern, H. (Hendrik), 1833-1917. 1.2133
Kern, Jean B. 2.5916
Kern, Robert, 1934-. 4.7145
Kern, Sharon. joint author. 5.8138
Kernan, Alvin B. 2.6066, 2.6736, 2.6829
Kernberg, Otto F., 1928-. 5.4904, 5.4925
Kernell, Samuel, 1945-. 4.8022
Kerner, Robert Joseph, 1887-1956. 3.1915,
  3.3051, 3.3560
Kernighan, Brian W. 5.1183-5.1184, 5.1212
Kernodle, George Riley, 1907-. 2.3163
Kerns, Virginia, 1948-. 4.570
Kerouac, Jack. 2.11950-2.11955
Kerr, Clark, 1911-. 4.2632, 4.3343, 4.10555
Kerr, Donald Gordon Grady, 1913-. 4.141
Kerr, Elizabeth Margaret, 1905-. 2.11695
Kerr, Howard. 2.10587
Kerr, James Lennox, 1899-. 3.8872
Kerr, K. Austin (Kathel Austin) 4.3996, 4.6646
Kerr, Malcolm H. 4.2573
Kerr, Mary Margaret. 4.10700
Kerr, Richard. 5.1808
Kerr, Robert Malcolm, 1821-1902. ed. 4.9410
Kerr, Walter, 1913-. 2.2979
Kerrebrock, Jack L. 5.6676
Kerridge, Eric. 5.5249
Kerridge, Roy. 3.1291
Kerrigan, Anthony. 1.2261
Kerrigan, Anthony. tr. 2.5410
Kersaudy, François, 1948-. 3.926
Kersey, Harry A., 1935-. 4.3862
Kershaw, Alister. 2.8372
Kershaw, Diana R. 5.3799
Kershaw, Ian. 3.2441, 4.5362
Kertész, André. 5.6971
Kertész, Louise, 1939-. 2.12419
Kertesz, Stephen Denis, 1904- ed. 4.9087
Kertzer, David I., 1948-. 4.588, 4.5624, 4.6252
Kervasdoué, Jean de. 5.4618
Kery, Patricia Frantz. 1.5831
Kesey, Ken. 2.13109-2.13110

Kessel, Joseph, 1898-. 2.4596
Kessel, Richard G., 1931-. 5.4113
Kesselman, Mark. 4.3414, 4.8877
Kesselring, Joseph. 2.11961
Kessler, Edwin. 5.2552
Kessler-Harris, Alice. 4.3282-4.3283
Kessler, Harry, Graf, 1868-1937. 3.2353
Kessler, Jascha Frederick, 1929-. 2.1977
Kessler, Lauren. 2.3655
Kessler, Lawrence D. 3.4718
Kessler, Seymour. 5.4751
Kessner, Thomas. 3.8047
Kesteloot, Lilyan. ed. 2.4836
Kesteloot, Lilyan. 2.3714, 2.4802-2.4803
Kesten, Hermann, 1900-. 2.13833
Kester, Dale E. 5.5318
Kester, Dana R. 4.354
Kesterton, Wilfred H. 2.3677
Kestin, Joseph. 5.2248, 5.2256
Keswick, Maggie. 5.5369
Ketcham, Michael G. 2.6060
Ketcham, Ralph Louis, 1927-. 3.6123, 3.7100
Ketchum, Bostwick H., 1912-. 5.3542
Ketels, Henry. 4.991
Ketels, Violet. 2.6246
Kett, Joseph F. 5.4522
Kettell, Brian. 4.4600
Kettenacker, Lothar. 3.893
Ketterer, David. 2.10572
Kettl, Donald F. 4.5219
Kettle, Arnold. 2.5944
Kettle, Michael. 3.3203
Kettle, S. F. A. (Sidney Francis Alan) joint
  author. 5.2820
Kettle, S. F. A. (Sidney Francis Alan) 5.2842
Kettler, David. 4.4879
Kettner, James H. 4.8073
Ketton-Cremer, Robert Wyndham, 1906-.
  2.7056, 3.1529
Ketz, Louise Bilebof. 3.6198
Keve, Paul W. 4.6911
Kevles, Barbara L. 4.10614
Key, Mary Ritchie. 2.85, 5.462
Key, V. O. (Valdimer Orlando), 1908-1963.
  3.8160, 4.7240, 4.7784, 4.7952, 4.8246
Keyder, Çağlar. joint author. 4.2279
Keyes, Charles F. 4.616
Keyes, Clinton Walker, 1888-. 2.667
Keyes, Daniel. 2.13114
Keyes, Roger, 1919-. 3.2977
Keyes, Roger S. 1.6483
Keyfitz, Nathan, 1913-. 4.1617-4.1618, 4.1632,
  4.1649
Keyishian, Harry. 2.8388
Keynes, Geoffrey, ed. 2.7513
Keynes, Geoffrey, Sir, 1887-. 1.4948, 1.6386,
  2.6911, 2.7410, 2.8485-2.8486, 3.1685
Keynes, John Maynard, 1883-1946. 1.1078,
  1.1231, 3.1685, 4.1441, 4.1447, 4.1776
Keynes, R. D. 5.3179
Keynes, Simon. 3.1310, 3.1320
Keys, Thomas E. (Thomas Edward), 1908-.
  5.4994
Keyser, Daniel J., 1935-. 5.203
Keyssar, Helene. 2.5928
Kgositsile, Keorapetse. comp. 2.2307
Khadduri, Majid, 1908-. 1.2041, 1.2077, 3.3776,
  3.3779-3.3780
Khaïkin, S. È. (Semen Èmmanuilovich) joint
  author. 5.1659
Khalidi, Tarif, 1938-. 3.3652
Khalidi, Walid. 3.3788
Khalil, Muhammad, ed. 3.3647
Khambata, Adi J. 5.1147
Khan, Azizur Rahman. 4.2524
Khan, Shahamat U. 5.5281
Khandalavala, Karl J. 1.6422
Khantipālo, Phikkhu, 1933 or 4-. 1.1767
Kharbas, Datta Shankarrao. 5.8054
Kharms, Daniil, 1905-1942. 2.1298
Khera, Inder. joint author. 4.2640
Khinchin, Aleksandr IAkovlevich, 1894-1959.
  5.1420, 5.2181
Khomeini, Ruhollah. 3.4087
Khouri, Fred J. (Fred John) 3.3872
Khouri, Mounah Abdallah. comp. 2.1841
Khoury, Philip S. (Philip Shukry), 1949-.
  3.3799

Khrushchev, Nikita Sergeevich, 1894-1971.
3.3234, 3.3238, 3.3269
Ki, Tsurayuki, d. 945 or 6. 2.2022, 2.2046
Kiang, Kang-hu, 1883-. 2.2192
Kiang, Yen-Hsiung, 1947-. 5.6040
Kidd, B. J. (Beresford James), 1863-1948.
1.2286, 1.2297, 1.2318, 1.2362
Kidder, Alfred Vincent. 3.5762
Kidder, J. Edward (Jonathan Edward)
3.4932-3.4933
Kidder, Tracy. 5.6574
Kidney, Walter C. 3.326
Kidwell, Claudia B. 5.7089
Kidwell, Walter. 5.6266
Kieckhefer, Richard. 5.682
Kiefer, F. W. (Fred William), 1925- joint
author. 5.5896
Kiefer, Frederick, 1945-. 2.5885
Kiefer, Ralph W. 4.22
Kieffer, George H., 1930-. 5.3329
Kieft, David Owen. 3.2978
Kiely, Benedict. 2.8930-2.8931, 2.9871
Kiely, Robert. 2.6005
Kieniewicz, Stefan. 4.2857
Kieran, J. A., joint author. 3.5261
Kieran, John, 1892-. 1.64, 4.880
Kierkegaard, Søren, 1813-1855. 1.1118-1.1121,
1.1394, 1.1553, 1.2217-1.2219, 1.2228, 1.2230,
1.2914, 1.3057, 1.3288, 2.14015-2.14016
Kiernan, Ben. 3.4447
Kiernan, Brian. 2.10188
Kiernan, Kevin S., 1945-. 2.6298
Kiernan, Robert F. 2.10427, 2.12626
Kiernan, V. G. (Victor Gordon), 1913-. 2.1900,
3.677, 4.6936, 4.8905
Kiesler, Donald J. 5.4872
Kiesler, Sara B., 1940-. 4.5795
Kiesling, Stephen. 4.985
Kiger, Joseph Charles. 4.6506
Kihara, Tarō. 5.2817
Kihl, Young W., 1932-. 3.5013
Kihlström, Björn. joint author. 5.6748
Kiker, B. F. comp. 4.1547
Kikkawa, Jiro. 5.4059
Kikuchi, Chihiro, 1914- joint author. 5.6296
Kilbourn, William. 3.8730
Kilbride-Jones, H. E. 1.6669
Kilburn, K. 2.380
Kilby, Peter. joint author. 4.2898
Kilby, Peter. comp. 4.1552
Kilcup, Quincy. 2.3218
Kilcup, Rodney W. 3.1241
Kilgore, Sally. 4.10048
Kiljunen, Marja-Liisa. 4.2215
Killam, G. D. comp. 2.2301
Killam, G. D. 2.10038, 2.10098
Killanin, Michael Morris, Baron, 1914-. 4.982
Killham, John, comp. 2.8177
Killham, John. 2.8164
Killian, James Rhyne, 1904-. 5.821, 5.6952
Killian, Johnny H. ed. 4.9607
Killick, Tony. 4.2585, 4.4581, 4.4583
Killing, J. Peter. 4.2721
Killingsworth, Mark R., 1946-. 4.3195
Killorin, Joseph, 1926-. 2.11302
Killy, Walther. 2.13864
Kilminster, Richard. 4.4799
Kilmister, C. W. (Clive William) joint author.
5.2367
Kilmister, C. W. (Clive William) 5.2102
Kilpatrick, Sarah. 2.6897
Kilpatrick, William Heard, 1871-1965. 4.10274
Kilroy, James. 2.9863
Kilroy, James. joint author. 2.9860
Kilson, Martin. 4.646
Kilson, Martin. joint ed. 3.5087
Kim, C. I. Eugene (Chong Ik Eugene), 1930-.
3.3625, 3.3627
Kim, Chewŏn, 1909-. 1.5080, 1.6529
Kim, Chonghan. 3.5012
Kim, Elaine H. 2.10293
Kim, Han-Kyo, 1928-. 5.8071
Kim, Hong Nack. 3.5012
Kim, Hyung-chan. 3.6580
Kim, Illsoo, 1944-. 3.8054
Kim, Richard E., 1932-. 2.13116
Kim, Samuel S., 1935-. 3.4844, 4.9135
Kim, Sung Kyu 1939-. 5.1983

Kim, Wonyong, 1922- joint author. 1.6529
Kimambo, Isaria N. ed. 1.1844
Kimball, Arthur G. 2.2015
Kimball, Bruce A., 1951-. 4.10822
Kimball, Fiske, 1888-1955. 1.4962, 1.5315
Kimball, Solon Toothaker. comp. 4.10179
Kimball, Solon Toothaker. joint author. 4.626
Kimball, Warren F. 3.935
Kimbell Art Museum. 1.4846, 1.5760, 1.6111,
1.6155, 1.6220
Kimber, Richard, comp. 4.8437
Kimberly, John. 5.4618
Kimble, David. 3.5340
Kimble, George Herbert Tinley, 1908-. 3.5227,
4.61
Kimbrough, Emily, 1899- joint author. 2.12486
Kimbrough, Robert. 2.8544
Kimbrough, Robert. ed. 2.11110
Kimerling, A. Jon. 4.163
Kimmel, Douglas C. 5.623
Kimpel, Ben D., joint author. 2.7222
Kimura, Motoo, 1924-. 5.3391, 5.3425
Kincaid, James R. (James Russell) 2.7660
Kince, Eli, 1953-. 1.5836
Kindahl, James Keith, 1931- joint author.
4.1508
Kindall, Jerry. 4.1005
Kinderlehrer, David. 5.1421
Kindī, d. ca. 873. 1.375
Kindleberger, Charles Poor, 1910-. 4.1715,
4.1717, 4.2327, 4.4134, 4.4453
Kindred, Michael. 4.9508
King, Andrew J., 1941-. 3.7072
King, Anita, 1931-. 2.3732
King, Anthony D. 1.5476, 1.5569, 4.6337
King, Anthony Stephen. 4.2225, 4.7970, 4.8069,
4.8446, 4.8482
King, Anthony Stephen. joint author. 4.8483
King, Anthony Stuart. 5.3966
King, Bolton, 1860-. 3.2859
King, Bruce Alvin. ed. 2.10099
King, Bruce Alvin. 2.5646, 2.9875-2.9876,
2.9976
King, Charles, 1919-. 2.9845, 2.9847
King, Charles L. 2.5284
King, Cuchlaine A. M. 4.271
King, Cuchlaine A. M. joint author.
4.277-4.278
King, Cuchlaine A. M. 4.241
King, E. J. (Earl Judson), 1901-1962. 1.3444
King, Edith W. 4.10896
King, Ernest Joseph, 1878-1956. 3.6376
King, F. P. 3.5531, 3.5551
King, Grace Elizabeth, 1852-1932. 2.11138
King, H. G. R. ed. 4.108
King, Harry. 4.6702
King-Hele, Desmond, 1927-. 2.8110
King, Henry, 1592-1669. 2.7093
King, Homer W. 2.3610
King, Horace Williams, 1874-1951. joint author.
5.5965
King, J. E. (John Edward) 4.1326
King, J. Marin. 2.1611
King, James. 2.6960
King, James Roger, 1927- ed. 5.3938
King, James T. 1.703
King, Jere Clemens. 3.857, 3.2206
King, John, 1909-. 1.1066
King, John Edward, 1858-1939, tr. 2.651
King, Leslie J. joint comp. 4.4122
King, Lester Charles. 5.3094
King, Lester Snow, 1908-. 5.4503,
5.4516-5.4517, 5.4748
King, Martin Luther. 1.3322, 3.6671, 3.6706
King, Michael. 3.5565, 3.5610, 3.5614
King, Michael John. 2.12341
King, Pamela M. 2.6214
King, Philip Burke, 1903-. 5.2994
King, Philip J. 3.3699
King, R. Bruce. 5.6231
King, R. (Richard) 4.5235
King, Richard G., 1922-. 4.10102
King, Richard H. 2.10453
King, Robert C. 5.3408
King, Robert Harlen, 1935-. 1.2789
King, Robert R. 4.8688
King, Roma A. (Roma Alvah), 1914- ed.
2.7471

King, Russell. 3.2824, 4.2814
King, Stephen, 1947-. 2.75, 2.13115
King, Thomas James, 1925-. 2.3295
King, Wayne. 5.3921
King, William Francis Henry, 1843-1909. ed.
and tr. 2.3726
King, William Lyon Mackenzie, 1874-1950.
3.8750
King, Woodie. comp. 2.10786, 2.10815
Kingdon, Robert McCune, 1927-. 1.2332,
1.3408, 3.2010
Kingery, W. D. 5.6900
Kinghorn, Alexander Manson. 2.7209
Kinglsey, Charles, 1819-1875. 2.7877
Kingman, Russ. 2.12033
King's College (University of Cambridge) 4.508
Kingsbury, Jack Dean. 1.2684
Kingsbury, John Merriam, 1928-. 5.5394
Kingsford, Anthony. 1.5030
Kingslake, Rudolf. 5.2293
Kingsland, Sharon E. 5.3339
Kingsley, Charles. 2.6910, 2.7875-2.7876,
2.7878-2.7879, 5.6308
Kingsley, Henry, 1830-1876. 2.7882-2.7884
Kingsley Trust Association. 2.7978
Kingston, Paul W. 4.3261
Kingzett, Charles Thomas, 1852-1935. 5.2593
Kinkead, Eugene, 1906-. 3.5033
Kinkead-Weekes, Mark. 2.7224, 2.8712
Kinkle, Roger D., 1916-. 1.3524
Kinkley, Jeffrey C., 1948-. 2.2161
Kinloch, A. Murray. 5.7894
Kinnaird, John, 1924-. 2.7809
Kinnamon, Keneth. 2.12820, 2.12864
Kinne, Otto. 5.3562
Kinne, Wisner Payne. 2.3239
Kinnear, Thomas C., 1943-. 4.4280
Kinnell, Galway, 1927-. 2.11962-2.11964
Kinney, Arthur F., 1933-. 2.11661, 2.11690
Kinoshita, Junji, 1914-. 2.2104
Kinross, Patrick Balfour, Baron, 1904-. 3.3580,
3.3596
Kinsella, Thomas. 2.8932-2.8935
Kinsey, Alfred Charles, 1894-1956. 4.5494,
4.5510
Kinsky, Georg, 1882-1951. 1.3493, 1.3606
Kinsler, Lawrence E. 5.2228
Kinsley, David R. 1.1712-1.1713
Kinsley, James. comp. 2.6110
Kinsley, James. ed. 2.7497
Kinsley, James. 2.6475, 2.7717, 2.9838
Kinsman, Robert S. 3.154
Kipling, Rudyard, 1865-1936. 2.7886-2.7890
Kipnis, Claude. 2.3131
Kipp, Jacob W. 5.7407
Kippenhahn, Rudolf, 1926-. 5.1832
Kipping, Ernst. 3.6949
Kirby, Andrew. 4.1481
Kirby, D. G. 3.3294
Kirby, David K. 5.7812
Kirby, John B., 1938-. 3.6654
Kirby, John R. joint author. 5.262
Kirby, Percival Robson. 1.4139
Kirby, Ronald F. 4.3919
Kirby, Rosina Greene. 5.5383
Kirby, Stuart. 4.2552
Kirby, W. F. (William Forsell), 1844-1912.
2.1751
Kirch, Patrick Vinton. 4.673
Kirchenhahn, Otto. 4.7250
Kirchhoff, Frederick, 1942-. 2.8039
Kirchner, Walther. 3.3357
Kirilov, Nikolaï, 1922- comp. 2.1205
Kirk, Elizabeth D. 2.6402
Kirk, Frank, joint comp. 2.1205
Kirk, G. S. (Geoffrey Stephen), 1921-. 1.233,
1.237, 1.1650, 2.495-2.496, 2.513
Kirk, George Eden, 1911-. 3.3628
Kirk-Greene, A. H. M. (Anthony Hamilton
Millard) 4.2625
Kirk, Raymond E. (Raymond Eller),
1890-1957. 5.6809
Kirk, Russell. 2.11637, 3.6124, 4.7259
Kirk, Samuel Alexander, 1904-. 4.10926
Kirkbright, G. F. 5.2676
Kirkby, R. J. R. (Richard J. R.) 4.6269
Kirkendall, Richard Stewart, 1928-. 4.2942
Kirkham, Michael. 2.8728

Kirkham, Pat. 5.7071
Kirkland, Edward Chase, 1894-. 4.1878, 4.1889, 4.1912, 4.3895
Kirkland, J. J. (Joseph Jack), 1925- joint author. 5.2667
Kirkpatrick, C. H. (Colin H.), 1944-. 4.3069
Kirkpatrick, D. L. 2.2612, 2.5835, 2.5926, 2.6044
Kirkpatrick, Frederick Alexander, 1861-1953. 3.8994
Kirkpatrick, Ivone, Sir. 3.2902
Kirkpatrick, Jeane J. 4.5970
Kirkpatrick, John, 1905- ed. 1.3899
Kirkpatrick, Martha. 4.5920
Kirkpatrick, Ralph. 1.3966, 1.4529
Kirkpatrick, Robert George, 1943- joint author. 4.5551
Kirkup, James, 1918-. 2.2032, 2.8937-2.8938
Kirkwood, Gordon MacDonald, 1916-. 2.546
Kirp, David L. 4.9582, 4.10790
Kirsch, Edith W. 1.6415
Kirsch, Leonard Joel, 1934-. 4.3150
Kirsch-Volders, Micheline. 5.4728
Kirshbaum, Leo, 1907-. 2.6802
Kirshenblatt-Gimblett, Barbara, joint author. 3.3983
Kirshner, Joseph M. 5.6238
Kirshner, Julius. 4.5862
Kirst, Michael W. 4.10037, 4.10740
Kirstein, Lincoln, 1907-. 4.1168-4.1169, 4.1175-4.1176
Kirwan, Albert Dennis. 3.7092, 3.8290
Kirzner, Israel M. 4.1330, 4.1491
Kiš, Danilo, 1935-. 2.1213
Kisch, Guido, 1889-. 3.3964
Kiser, Clyde Vernon, 1904-. 4.1643
Kish, George, 1914-. 4.53
Kishibe, Shigeo. 1.3741
Kispert, Robert J. 2.937
Kisselgoff, Anna. 4.1153
Kissen, Morton. 5.4920
Kissin, Benjamin, 1917-. 5.4959
Kissinger, Henry, 1923-. 3.694, 3.1176, 3.7825, 3.7859, 3.7900
Kissinger, Peter T., 1944-. 5.2691
Kissinger, Warren S., 1922-. 1.2890
Kister, Kenneth F., 1935-. 5.8211
Kistler, Mark Oliver, 1918-. 2.13493
Kitagawa, Joseph Mitsuo, 1915-. 1.1832-1.1833, 4.6538
Kitagawa, Utamaro, 1753?-1806. 1.6485
Kitchen, Martin. 3.2255, 3.2340
Kitcher, Philip, 1947-. 4.510, 5.3392
Kitchin, C. R. (Christopher R.) 5.1740, 5.1771
Kitching, G. N. 4.2786
Kitching, Jessie Beatrice, 1919-. 4.1094
Kitching, R. L. (Roger Laurence), 1945-. 5.3535
Kitson Clark, G. S. R. (George Sidney Roberts), 1900-1975. 3.1593
Kitson, Frank. 5.7228
Kittel, Charles. 5.1976, 5.2031, 5.2115, 5.2195, 5.2257
Kittel, Gerhard, 1888-1948. ed. 2.249
Kittelson, David J. 5.8089
Kitto, Humphrey Davy Findley. 2.279, 2.290-2.291, 2.547
Kittredge, George Lyman, 1860-1941. 2.1055, 2.6364, 2.6418
Kittrie, Nicholas N., 1928-. 5.4714
Kittross, John M., 1929- joint author. 4.4058
Kitzinger, Ernst. 1.4737, 1.4744-1.4745
Kitzinger, Uwe W. joint author. 4.2223
Kitzinger, Uwe W. 4.2226
Kivisto, Peter, 1948-. 4.6991
Kivy, Peter. ed. 1.1427
Kivy, Peter. 1.712, 1.715, 1.4393
Kiwanuka, M. S. M. Semakula. 3.5279
Kiyota, Minoru, 1923-. 1.2155
Kjaerulff Nielsen, Bernhard, 1901-. 2.920
Klaeber, Friedrich, 1863- ed. 2.6288
Klafs, Carl E. 4.972
Klaits, Joseph. 3.2035
Klamer, Arjo. 4.1462
Klapisch-Zuber, Christiane. 4.2359
Klapp, Otto. 5.8003
Klare, Karl E. 4.7019
Klarén, Peter F., 1938-. 4.8350

Klarwill, Victor, 1873- ed. 3.620
Klass, Morton, 1927-. 4.5431
Klass, Philip, 1920-. 2.13117
Klass, Philip J. 5.6697
Klatzky, Roberta L. 5.327
Klauber, Laurence Monroe, 1883-1968. 5.3926
Klausner, Joseph, 1874-1958. 1.1974, 2.1775
Klaw, Spencer, 1920-. 5.830
Kleban, Morton H. 5.4666
Klee, Paul, 1879-1940. 1.4813, 1.4995, 1.5818, 1.6176
Kleene, Stephen Cole, 1909-. 5.1044
Klehr, Harvey. 4.6992
Kleiber, Max, 1893-. 5.4238
Klein, A. M. (Abraham Moses), 1909-1972. 2.9934
Klein, Attila O., 1930-. 5.3487
Klein, Barbara. 1.6107
Klein, Barry T. 3.5700
Klein, Burton H. 4.2343
Klein, Cornelis, 1937-. 5.3021
Klein, David Ballin, 1897-. 5.271
Klein, Donald W. 3.4811
Klein, Edward J. 1.3070
Klein, Ernest. 2.1057
Klein, Ethel, 1952-. 4.6059
Klein, Fannie J. 4.9777
Klein, Felix, 1849-1925. 5.1111, 5.1568
Klein, George Stuart, 1917-. 5.170, 5.180
Klein, H. Arthur. 5.2024
Klein, Herbert S. 3.9274, 3.9276, 4.4666, 4.6421
Klein, Holger Michael, 1938-. 2.3499-2.3500
Klein, Isaac. 1.1983
Klein, Joe, 1946-. 1.4111
Klein, Lawrence Robert. 4.1962
Klein, Leonard S. 2.2674, 2.5304
Klein, Lewis, 1927-. 2.2857
Klein, M. Frances. joint author. 4.10004
Klein, Malcolm W. 4.6868, 4.6874, 4.6876
Klein, Marcus. 2.10633
Klein, Martin A. 4.6448
Klein, Melanie. 5.171, 5.5107
Klein, Philip Shriver, 1909-. 3.7177, 3.8073
Klein, Richard G. 5.3163
Klein, Sanford A., 1950- joint author. 5.6102
Klein, Viola. joint author. 4.3242
Kleinbauer, W. Eugene, 1937- comp. 1.5122
Kleinbaum, Abby Wettan. 4.5855
Kleinberg, Jacob, 1914-. 5.6861
Kleinberg, Seymour, 1933-. 2.3718
Kleindorfer, Paul R. joint author. 4.3039
Kleinman, David S., 1920-. 4.1596
Kleist, Heinrich von, 1777-1811. 2.13622-2.13624
Kleist, James A. (James Aloysius), 1873-. 1.2208
Kleist, James Aloysius, 1873- ed. and tr. 1.2181
Kleitman, Nathaniel, 1895-. 5.4355
Klement, Frank L. 3.7307
Klemke, E. D., 1926- comp. 1.550, 1.755
Klemperer, Otto, 1885-1973. 1.4101
Kleppner, Otto, 1899-. 4.4433
Kleppner, Paul. 3.8304, 3.8420, 4.8102, 4.8104-4.8105
Klett, Mark, 1952-. 5.6983
Klevebring, Bjorn-Ivar, 1943- joint author. 4.1764
Klibansky, Raymond, 1905- ed. 3.479
Klibbe, Lawrence Hadfield, 1923-. 2.5217
Klickstein, Herbert S. joint author. 5.2587
Kliebard, Herbert M. 4.10433, 4.10440
Klimoff, Alexis, joint comp. 1.1637
Klimt, Gustav, 1862-1918. 1.6045
Klinck, Carl Frederick, 1908- ed. 2.9882
Klindt-Jensen, Ole. 3.3352, 3.3362
Kline, Draza. 4.6576
Kline, John M. 4.9392
Kline, Mary-Jo. 3.7051
Kline, Morris, 1908-. 5.1063, 5.1071-5.1072
Kline, Paul. 5.538
Kline, Paul. joint author. 5.509
Klineberg, Stephen L., 1940-. 5.402
Klingelhofer, Herbert E. 5.7522
Klingender, Francis Donald. 1.5164
Klinger, Eric, 1933-. 5.631
Klinghoffer, Arthur Jay, 1941-. 4.3782
Klingman, Peter D., 1945-. 3.7453

Klinkowitz, Jerome. 2.10634-2.10635, 2.13400-2.13401, 2.13403, 2.13896
Kliot, Nurit. 4.7499
Kliuchevskiĭ, V. O. (Vasiliĭ Osipovich), 1841-1911. 3.3041, 3.3094
Klockars, Carl B. 4.6705
Kloosterboer, Willemina. 4.3102
Klopfer, Peter H. 5.4051, 5.4060
Klöpffer, Walter, 1938-. 5.2320
Klopstock, Friedrich Gottlieb, 1724-1803. 2.13627
Klossowski, Pierre. 2.4597
Klotman, Phyllis Rauch. 2.2999, 2.10360, 5.7873
Klotman, Robert H. 1.4419
Klots, Alexander Barrett, 1903-. 5.3881
Klotz, Heinrich. joint author. 1.5474
Klotz, Irving M. (Irving Myron), 1916-. 5.2884, 5.2894
Klotz, Lynn C. 5.6868
Kluchkhohn, Paul, 1886-1957, ed. 2.13593
Kluckhohn, Clyde, 1905-1960. 3.11, 3.5919, 4.435, 4.489, 4.4877
Kluge, Eike-Henner W. 5.4576
Kluge, Friedrich, 1856-1926. 2.1183
Kluger, Richard. 4.9591
Klugman, Stuart A., 1949-. 4.4640
Klyne, M. A. 5.4375
Klyne, William. 5.2871
Knaack, Marcelle Size, 1921-. 5.7411
Knab, Eckhart. 1.5811
Knaplund, Paul, 1885-1964. 3.1223
Knapp, Bettina Liebowitz, 1926-. 2.3373, 2.4225, 2.4350
Knapp, Brian J. 4.290
Knapp, John Merrill. 1.3886
Knapp, Lewis M. (Lewis Mansfield) 2.7267
Knapp, Lewis Mansfield, 1894-. 2.7261, 2.7263
Knapp, Mark L. 5.463
Knapp, Mona. 2.9030
Knauss, John A. 4.344
Kneafsey, James T. 4.3869
Kneale, Martha. 1.1155
Kneale, W. C. (William Calvert) 1.1155
Knebel, Fletcher. 3.1013
Knecht, R. J. (Robert Jean) 3.2013
Kneese, Allen V. 4.1845-4.1846, 4.2076-4.2077, 4.3707, 5.6022
Knelles, Richard, 1550?-1610. 4.7383
Knibb, Michael A. (Michael Anthony), 1938-. 1.2622
Knickerbocker, K. L. (Kenneth Leslie) joint author. 2.7485
Knickerbocker, Kenneth Leslie, 1905-. 2.7478
Knief, Ronald Allen, 1944-. 5.6603
Knies, Earl A. 2.7455
Knight, Alan E. 2.3884
Knight, Austin Melvin, 1854-1927. 5.7490
Knight, C. Gregory. 3.5225, 4.5475
Knight, David M. 5.740
Knight, Douglas A. 1.2567
Knight, Edgar Wallace, 1885-1953. 4.9991, 4.9993
Knight, Elizabeth C., ed. 2.13616
Knight, Frank Hyneman, 1885-. 4.1309, 4.1553
Knight, George Wilson. 2.2378, 2.5754, 2.5840, 2.6675, 2.6737-2.6740, 2.6785-2.6787, 2.6856, 2.7524
Knight, Grant Cochran, 1893-1956. 2.10906
Knight, Karl F. 2.12371
Knight, Oliver. 3.3633
Knight, R. C. (Roy Clement), 1907- tr. 2.4048
Knight, Roger. 2.9129
Knight, Stephen Thomas. 2.2417
Knight, Thomas Stanley, 1921-. 1.620
Knight, W. F. Jackson (William Francis Jackson), 1895-1964. 2.497
Knight, Walter D. joint author. 5.2031
Knightley, Phillip. 2.3578
Knights, L. C. (Lionel Charles), 1906-. 2.5541, 2.5649, 2.6655, 2.6741
Knights, Peter R. 4.1683
Knoche, Ulrich, 1902-1968. 2.639
Knoepflmacher, U. C. 2.7703, 2.8092
Knoles, George Harmon. 3.6125
Knoll, Glenn F. 5.2442

Knoll, Paul W. 3.3279
Knollenberg, Bernhard, 1892-. 3.7031
Knopp, Konrad. 5.1422
Knorr, Klaus Eugen, 1911-. 4.1989, 4.4146,
  4.4166
Knott, J. F. (John Frederick) 5.5787
Knott, Thomas Albert, 1880-1945. 2.938,
  2.1023
Knowland, A. S. joint author. 2.8363
Knowland, A. S. 2.6221
Knowler, John T., 1942-. 5.4417
Knowles, Asa S. (Asa Smallidge), 1909-.
  4.10168, 4.10301
Knowles, David, 1896-. 1.352, 1.2307, 1.2441,
  1.3081, 1.3232-1.3234
Knowles, Horace. ed. 2.10667
Knowles, John, 1926-. 2.11965
Knowles, Malcolm Shepherd, 1913-. 4.10974,
  4.10976
Knowles, Roy. 5.6588
Knowlton, Charles, 1800-1850. 4.5677
Knowlton, James, 1943-. 2.11638
Knox, Bernard MacGregor Walker. 2.275,
  2.544, 2.548
Knox, D. Edward, 1940-. 3.1262
Knox, Donald, 1936-. 2.3022
Knox, Edward C. 2.4026
Knox, George. 1.5016, 1.5816
Knox, George L., 1841-1927. 3.8403
Knox, Israel, 1904-. 1.907
Knox, John, 1900-. 1.2179, 1.2361
Knox, John H. 5.2666
Knox, Paul L. 4.5292
Knox, Robert C. 5.6023
Knox, Ronald Arbuthnott, 1888-1957. 1.2238
Knox, T. M. (Thomas Malcolm), 1900-. 3.385,
  4.9362
Knudsen, Vern Oliver, 1893-1974. joint author.
  1.5547
Knuth, Donald Ervin, 1938-. 5.1185
Knutson, Jeanne Nickell, ed. 4.7246
Knuttgen, Howard G. 5.4266
Kobayashi, Hisashi. 5.1148
Kobayashi, Kōji, 1907-. 5.6392
Kobayashi, Shoshichi, 1932-. 5.1628
Kobbé, Gustave. 1.4509
Kobler, Franz, 1882-1965. ed. 3.3855
Koblick, Ian G., 1939-. 4.336
Koblitz, Ann Hibner. 5.1096
Koblitz, Neal, 1948-. 5.1328, 5.1583
Kobrin, Frances E. 4.5592
Kobrin, Solomon. 4.6876
Kobylańska, Krystyna. 1.3608
Kocańda, Stanisław. 5.5812
Koch, Adrienne, 1912-1971. 3.6277
Koch, Howard. comp. 2.3024
Koch, Kenneth, 1925-. 2.2732, 2.3752,
  2.10672-2.10673, 2.11966
Koch, Klaus, 1926-. 1.2532, 1.2584
Koch, Richard, 1921-. 4.6583
Koch, Robert, 1918-. 1.6645
Koch, Robert A., 1919-. 1.6270
Koch, Sigmund. 5.114
Koch, Sigmund. ed. 5.31
Koch, Stephen. 2.3073
Koch, Vivienne. 2.8352, 2.12751
Kochan, Lionel. 3.3845
Kochan, Lionel. ed. 3.3994
Kochan, Thomas A. 4.3185, 4.3579
Kochanek, Stanley A. 4.8704, 4.8708
Kochanowski, Jan, 1530-1584. 2.1706
Köchel, Ludwig von, Ritter, 1800-1877. 1.3611
Kocher, David C. 5.2488
Kocher, Paul Harold, 1907-. 2.6616
Kochetkova, N. D. 2.1334
Kochman, Thomas. 3.6707
Kochman, Thomas. comp. 3.6719
Kock, Theodor, 1820-1901. 2.321
Kocka, Jürgen. 4.5363
Kocsis, Jeanne. 5.8371
Kodály, Zoltán, 1882-1967. 1.4342, 1.4410
Kōdansha. 3.4871
Koebner, Richard, 1885-1958. 4.7535
Kœchlin, Charles, 1867-1950. 1.3866
Koechner, Walter, 1937-. 5.5956
Koegler, Horst. 4.1081
Koehl, Robert Lewis, 1922-. 3.2428
Koehler, Carlton S. 5.5408

Koehler, Ludmilla, 1917-. 1.1114
Koen, Ross Y., 1918-. 3.6427
Koenig, Constance R. 4.911
Koenig, Louis William, 1916-. 3.6294, 3.7804
Koenigsberg, Ernest. joint author. 4.2680
Koenigsberger, Dorothy. 1.400
Koenigsberger, H. G. (Helmut Georg) 3.621
Koeper, Frederick. joint author. 1.5290
Koerner, Robert M., 1933-. 5.5872
Koerner von Gustorf, Ernst A., 1932-1975.
  5.2784
Koestenbaum, Peter, 1928-. 1.1008
Koester, Helmut, 1926-. 1.2659
Koestler, Arthur, 1905-. 1.1597, 2.8939, 4.6982,
  5.344
Koettig, Margrit. 4.750
Kofele-Kale, Ndiva. 3.5401
Koffka, Kurt, 1886-1941. 5.227
Kogan, David. 4.8538
Kogan, Maurice. 4.8538
Kogan, Nathan. joint author. 5.579
Kogan, Norman. 3.2840, 3.2908, 4.8622
Kogon, Eugen, 1903-. 3.2442
Koh, Byung Chul. 3.5042
Kohák, Erazim V. 1.1115, 1.1337
Kohfeldt, Mary Lou. 2.7757
Kohl, Benjamin G. 5.8344
Kohl, Herbert R. 4.10157, 4.10267, 4.10340,
  4.10879
Kohl, Wilfrid L. 4.4189
Kohlberg, Lawrence, 1927-. 5.607
Kohler, Dayton, 1907-1972, ed. 2.2354, 2.2548
Kohler, Eric Louis, 1892-1976. 4.4391
Kohler-Koch, Beate, 1941-. 4.8681
Kohler, Max Adam, 1915-. 4.291
Köhler, Peter A. 4.3444
Köhler, Wolfgang, 1887-1967. 1.1302, 5.226
Kohli, Suresh. 2.1960
Kohli, Surindar Singh, 1920-. 1.1824
Kohlmeier, Albert Ludwig. 3.8375
Kohlstedt, Sally Gregory, 1943-. 5.792
Kohn, George C. 3.326
Kohn, Hans, 1891-1971. 3.192, 3.362, 3.690,
  3.756, 3.763, 3.864, 3.3216, 3.6126,
  4.7488-4.7490
Kohn, Lynette. 2.8776
Kohn, Robert Rothenberg, 1925-. 5.4217
Kohn, Walter S. G. 4.8597
Kohout, Pavel. 2.1674
Koht, Halvdan, 1873-1965. 2.14036
Kohut, Heinz. 5.496, 5.4912
Koine, Yoshio. 2.1990
Koistinen, Paul A. C. 4.2066
Kojecký, Roger. 2.11638
Kojève, Alexandre, 1902-1968. 1.935
Kojima Hōshi, d. 1374. supposed author.
  3.4937
Kokaska, Charles J. joint ed. 4.10907
Kökeritz, Helge, 1902-. 2.6378, 2.6847-2.6848
Kokoschka, Oskar, 1886-. 1.6046
Kokusai Bunka Shinkōkai. 1.213, 2.1996,
  2.2013, 2.2016
Kokusai Kirisutokyō Daigaku, Tokyo. Shakai
  Kagaku Kenkyūjo. 4.6265
Kokusai Kōryū Kikin. 1.5076
Kokusai Kyōiku Jōhō Sentā. 4.183
Kołakowski, Leszek. 1.1019, 4.6937
Kolar, Carol Koehmstedt, 1931-. 5.8275
Kolarz, Walter. 3.3320
Kolb, Albert, 1906-. 3.4384
Kolb, Gwin J. 2.1078
Kolb, Jack, 1946-. 2.7759
Kolb, Philip. 2.4670
Kolbe, A. Lawrence. 4.3040
Kolde, Endel Jakob, 1917-. 4.2733
Kolenda, Konstantin. 5.390
Koleśnik, Eugène M. 5.7434
Koliopoulos, Giannēs. 3.2686
Koljević, Svetozar. 2.1215-2.1216
Kolkey, Jonathan Martin. 4.7309
Kolko, Gabriel. joint comp. 4.9339
Kolko, Gabriel. 3.7580-3.7581, 4.1938, 4.2085
Kolko, Joyce. 3.7580
Kolkowicz, Roman. 5.7326
Koller, John M. 1.147
Koller, Marvin R. 4.5577
Kollontaï, A. (Aleksandra), 1872-1952. 4.6129
Kollwitz, Käthe, 1867-1945. 1.5808

Kolmogorov, A. N. (Andreĭ Nikolaevich),
  1903-. 5.1485
Kolneder, Walter. 1.4031, 1.4057
Kolodin, Irving, 1908-. 1.4224
Kolodny, Annette, 1941-. 2.10250, 3.6351
Kolodny, Robert C. 4.5504, 5.4838
Koltay, Emery, ed. 5.8310
Kolthoff, I. M. (Izaak Maurits), 1894-. 5.2656
Koltun, Elizabeth. 4.5911
Kolve, V. A. 2.5853, 2.6330
Komarov, Boris. 5.5993
Komarovsky, Mirra, 1906-. 4.5644, 4.10844
Kommers, Donald P. 4.7636
Kommunisticheskaia partiia Sovetskogo Soiuza.
  Sʹezd. (26th: 1981: Moscow, R.S.F.S.R.)
  4.8657
Komunistická strana Československa. Ústřední
  výbor. Komise pro vyřizování stranických
  rehabilitací. 3.1924
Kondratʹev, N. D. (Nikolaĭ Dmitrievich), 1892-.
  4.1713
Konefsky, Alfred S. 3.7072
Kong, F. K. 5.5798
Kong, Jin Au, 1942-. 5.6264
Kongtrul, Jamgon. 1.2161
Konheim, Alan G., 1934-. 5.7529
Konig, David Thomas, 1947-. 4.9902
Koninklijke Nederlandse Akademie van
  Wetenschappen. 3.3658
Konkordienbuch. 1.3363
Konorski, Jerzy. 5.4326, 5.4335
Konovalov, Serge, comp. 2.1241
Konparu, Kunio, 1926-. 2.3402
Konvitz, Milton Ridvas, 1908-. 1.528, 2.11025,
  4.8068, 4.9656, 4.9671
Konwicki, Tadeusz. 2.1707
Konyndyk, Kenneth. 1.1252
Koocher, Gerald P. 5.4777
Kook, Abraham Isaac, 1865-1935. 1.1894
Koon, Helene, 1925-. 2.12170
Koonin, Steven E. 5.1966
Koopmans, Tjalling Charles, 1910-. 4.1443
Koopowitz, Harold. 5.3646
Koosis, Paul. 5.1486
Kooten, G. van. 2.1171
Kopan, Andrew T., ed. 4.10963
Kopelev, Lev, 1912-. 4.6857
Kopf, David. 3.4198, 3.4329
Kopff, E. Christian. 2.415
Kopit, Arthur L. 2.13118
Kopp, Claire B. 4.5920
Kopp, Jane. 2.10728, 2.10825
Kopp, Karl, 1934-. 2.10728, 2.10825
Koppelman, Lee. joint author. 1.5584
Koppes, Clayton R., 1945-. 5.6660
Kopytoff, Igor. 4.6451
Korb, Lawrence J., 1939-. 5.7358
Korea (South) 3.5015, 3.5036
Koren, Yoram. 5.6168
Koreshoff, Deborah R. 5.5359
Koretz, Robert F., 1912- comp. 4.9549
Korff, Hermann August, 1882-. 2.13466
Korg, Jacob, 1922-. 2.7746
Kormondy, Edward John, 1926-. 5.3519
Kormoss, I. B. F. ed. 4.168
Korn, Granino Arthur, 1922-. 5.1115, 5.6261
Korn, Harold A., joint author. 4.9979
Korn, Harold Allen. 4.10092
Korn, Theresa M. joint author. 5.1115
Kornberg, Allan. 4.8277, 4.8333
Kornberg, Arthur, 1918-. 5.4405, 5.4419
Kornberg, H. L. joint author. 5.4200
Kornbluh, Joyce L. joint ed. 4.2096
Kornblum, William. 4.3531
Kornbluth, C. M. (Cyril M.), 1924-1958.
  2.13267
Körner, Stephan, 1913-. 1.900, 5.2108
Kornfelʹd, I. P. (Isaak Pavlovich) 5.1605
Kornhauser, Arthur William, 1896- ed. 4.3162
Kornhauser, William. 5.7601
Kornilov, A. A. (Aleksandr Aleksandrovich),
  1862-1925. 3.3109
Kornreich, Melvin, joint author. 5.4856
Korolenko, Vladimir Galaktionovich,
  1853-1921. 2.1513-2.1514
Korovkin, P. P. (Pavel Petrovich) 5.1423
Korr, Charles P. 3.1253
Korsch, Karl, 1886-1961. 4.7055

Kort, Michael. 3.3135
Kort, Wesley A. 2.10569
Kort, Wolfgang, 1939-. 2.13730
Korte, Friedhelm. 5.2657
Korth, Eugene H. 3.9260
Korwin, Yala H., 1923-. 1.5154
Kosack, Godula. 4.3633
Koschatzky, Walter. 1.5806, 1.5811, 1.6388
Koser, Reinhold, 1852-1914. 3.2487
Kosev, Dimitŭr Konstantinov, 1903-. 3.3540
Kosevich, Arnol'd Markovich. 5.1671
Kosicka, Jadwiga. 2.1736
Kosinski, Jerzy N., 1933-. 2.13119-2.13123
Kosiński, Leszek A. 4.1654, 4.1661
Koskoff, David E., 1939-. 3.7656
Kosnik, Anthony. 4.5513
Kosolapoff, G. M. (Gennady M.) 5.2787
Kosow, Irving L. 5.6309, 5.6319
Koss, Stephen E. 3.1667, 3.1677
Kosslyn, Stephen Michael, 1948-. 5.319-5.320
Kossmann, E. H. (Ernst Heinrich), 1922-.
  3.2028, 3.2972
Kostelanetz, Richard. 2.2669
Kostelanetz, Richard. comp. 1.3831, 2.3703
Kostelanetz, Richard. 2.10417, 2.10757, 2.12510
Kostof, Spiro. 1.5212, 1.5457
Kostrubala, Thaddeus, 1930-. 5.5026
Koszarski, Richard. 2.3001
Kot, Stanislaw, 1885-. 1.2975
Kothari, Rajni. 4.8699
Kotkin, Amy. 4.774
Kotre, John N. 1.3266
Kotsilibas-Davis, James. 2.3235, 2.3243
Kottak, Conrad Phillip. 3.5312
Köttelwesch, Clemens. 5.8008
Kotz, John C. joint author. 5.2702
Kotz, Samuel. 5.1399
Kotzwinkle, William. 2.13125
Kousoulas, D. George (Dimitrios George),
  1923-. 3.2693
Kousser, J. Morgan. 3.8164, 4.8098
Kouwenhoven, John Atlee, 1909-. 1.6705
Kovach, Joseph K., joint author. 5.79
Kovacs, William D. joint author. 5.5898
Kovalevsky, L., 1916- joint author. 5.5866
Kovel, Ralph M. 1.6657
Kovel, Terry H. joint author. 1.6657
Kovic, Ron. 3.4510
Kovrig, Bennett. 4.7045
Kowalke, Kim H., 1948-. 1.4061
Koyré, Alexandre, 1892-1964. 1.1330, 5.1640,
  5.1693
Koziara, Edward Clifford. joint author. 4.3511
Kozicki, Henry, 1924-. 3.413
Kozintsev, Grigoriĭ Mikhaĭlovich. 2.3029
Koziorowski, B. 5.6053
Kozloff, Max. 1.4843
Kozlowski, T. T. (Theodore Thomas), 1917-.
  5.3737, 5.3755
Kozlowski, Theodore Thomas. 5.3756
Kozmetsky, George. 4.4624
Kozol, Jonathan. 4.10038, 4.10103, 4.10303,
  4.10757
Kozulin, Alex. 5.87
Kra, Irwin. 5.1633
Kra, Irwin. joint author. 5.1495
Kraay, Colin M. 3.274, 3.276
Kracauer, Siegfried, 1889-1966. 2.2939
Krader, Lawrence. 3.3323
Kraditor, Aileen S. 3.7252, 4.8083
Kraditor, Aileen S. comp. 4.5986
Kraehe, Enno E. 3.1891
Kraeling, Carl Hermann, 1897-. 3.123
Kraenzel, Carl Frederick, 1906-. 3.8461
Krafft-Ebing, R. von (Richard von), 1840-1902.
  4.5516
Kraft, Alan M., 1925- joint author. 5.4837
Kraft, George D., 1937-. 5.6581
Kraft, Gerald. 4.3870
Kraft, James. 2.11439
Kraft, Robert A. ed. 1.2961
Krailsheimer, A. J. 2.3852
Krajewski, Robert J. 4.10650
Krakowski, Shmuel. 3.1115
Kramarae, Cheris. 2.127-2.128
Kramer, Bernard M., ed. 5.4702
Kramer, Dale. 2.3675, 2.7792, 2.10418
Kramer, Elaine Fialka, joint comp. 2.10404

Kramer, Hilton. 1.4783
Kramer, Jack. 1.5824
Kramer, John, 1943- joint author. 4.6875
Kramer, John E. 2.10546
Kramer, Lawrence, 1946-. 1.4401
Kramer, Leonie Judith Gibson. 2.10138,
  2.10145
Kramer, Maurice, joint comp. 2.10404
Kramer, Rita. 4.10210
Kramer, Samuel Noah, 1897-. 1.1785, 2.1769,
  3.3772-3.3773
Kramer, Shira. 5.4684
Kramer, Sylvia. 4.10785
Kramer, Victor A. 2.11298, 2.13239, 4.5196
Kramers, H. 5.6855
Kramers, Jacob, 1802-1869. 2.1171
Kramers, Johannes Hendrik, 1891-1951. 3.3658
Krammer, Arnold, 1941-. 3.3075
Kramnick, Isaac. 3.1546, 3.1716
Krampitz, Sydney Diane. 5.5189
Kramrisch, Stella, 1898-. 1.5189, 1.5539, 1.5754
Krane, Dale. 4.9727
Krantz, David H., 1938- ed. 5.40
Kranzberg, Melvin. 3.2164, 4.3092
Kranzberg, Melvin. comp. 5.5531
Kranzberg, Melvin. ed. 5.5534
Kranzler, David, 1930-. 3.3942
Krapp, George Philip, 1872-1934. 2.1124,
  2.1133, 2.5932
Krapp, George Phillip, 1872-1934, ed. 2.6277
Krappe, Alexander Haggerty, 1894-1947. tr.
  1.4235
Krasilovsky, M. William. 1.4355
Krasiński, Zygmunt, hrabia, 1812-1859. 2.1747
Krasner, Lee, 1908-. 1.5950
Krasnow, Erwin G. 4.9541
Kraus, Carl von, 1868-1952. ed. 2.13527
Kraus, John Daniel, 1910-. 5.1778
Kraus, Karl, 1874-1936. 2.13806
Kraus, Michael, 1901-. 2.11214, 3.180, 3.6127,
  3.6213
Kraus, Philip E., 1908-. 4.10379
Kraus, Richard G. 5.5143
Kraus, Sidney. 3.7931, 4.7253
Krause, David, 1917-. 2.9154
Krause, Lawrence B. 4.4161, 4.4175, 4.4491
Krause, Marie V. 5.5130
Krause, Paul C. 5.6310
Kraushaar, Otto F. 4.10727
Krauskopf, Konrad Bates, 1910-. 5.3104
Krausnick, Helmut. 3.2443
Krauss, André. 1.6245
Krauss, Ellis S. 4.8891
Krauss, Robert M., joint author. 4.4984
Krauss, Rosalind E. 1.4814, 1.5652
Krausz, Ernest. 4.5599
Krausz, Michael. 1.1392
Kraut, Alan M. 3.7234, 4.8944
Kraut, George P. 5.5737
Kraut, Richard, 1944-. 4.7352
Krautheimer, Richard, 1897-. 1.5518, 1.5730,
  3.2719, 3.2938
Krautheimer, Trude Hess. 1.5730
Kravis, Irving B. 4.1401
Krawiec, T. S. (Theophile Stanley), 1913-. 5.90
Krebs, Albert, 1899-. 3.2409
Krebs, Charles J. 5.3538
Krebs, Hans Adolf, Sir. 5.4200
Krebs, J. R. (John R.) 5.3393, 5.4054
Krebs, Robert D., 1931-. 5.6064
Krech, Shepard, 1944-. 3.8108
Krehbiel, Henry Edward, 1854-1923. ed. 1.3806
Kreidberg, Marvin, A. 5.7144
Kreider, Barbara A. 2.2787
Kreider, Jan F., 1942-. 5.6104, 5.6227, 5.6233
Kreimer, Evered. joint author. 5.1850
Kreissman, Bernard. 2.6997, 2.7220
Kreith, Frank. 5.2266, 5.6227, 5.6233
Kreith, Frank. joint author. 5.6104
Kreitler, Hans. 5.272
Kreitler, Shulamith, joint author. 5.272
Kreitlow, Burton W. 4.10984
Krell, David Farrell. 1.1057
Kren, George M., 1926-. 3.439
Krenek, Ernst, 1900-. 1.3673
Krenkel, Peter A. 5.6016
Krentz, Edgar. 1.2517
Krepon, Michael, 1946-. 5.7274

Kreps, Gary L. 5.4481
Kresge, David T. 4.3872
Kress, Gunther R. 2.159
Kress, Jack M. 4.9890
Kress, Robert. 1.3278
Kress, Stephen W. 5.3948
Kretzmann, Norman. 1.347, 1.1316
Krey, August C. (August Charles), 1887-1961.
  3.587, 3.592
Kreymborg, Alfred, 1883-1966. 2.11967
Kreyszig, Erwin. 5.1471, 5.1541
Kribbs, Jayne K. 2.11286
Krichbaum, Rollyn O. 1.5088
Krichmar, Albert. 5.8462, 5.8473
Krider, J. L. (Jake Luther), 1913-. 5.5450
Kriedemann, Paul E., joint author. 5.3745
Krieg, Noel R. 5.4438, 5.4452
Kriegel, Annie. 4.8593
Krieger, Leonard. 3.393, 3.422, 3.2259
Krieger, Leonard. ed. 3.613
Krieger, Murray, 1923-. 1.1349, 2.2424, 2.10251
Krieghbaum, Hillier. 2.3564
Krieghoff, Cornelius, 1815-1872. 1.5999
Kriegsman, Sali Ann. 4.1163
Krige, Eileen Jensen, 1904-. 3.5498
Krige, John. 5.860
Krige, Uys, 1910- joint author. 2.10050
Krinsky, David, 1959-. 2.2862
Kripalani, Krishna. 2.1872
Kripke, Saul A., 1940-. 1.1083
Krippner, Stanley, 1932-. 5.656, 5.5213
Kris, Ernst, 1900-1957. 1.4611
Krisch, A. D. 5.2447
Krishna Chaitanya, 1918-. 2.2266
Krishna Murari, 1944-. 3.4423
Krishna, Valerie. 2.6420-2.6421
Krishnaswamy, Subrahmanyam. joint author.
  2.2900
Krisnācāryapāda. 1.1744
Krispyn, Egbert. comp. 2.13946
Kristein, Barbara (Frank) ed. 4.9449
Kristein, Barbara Frank, joint author. 4.9453
Kristeller, Paul Oskar, 1905-. 1.401, 1.403,
  1.409, 1.415, 3.157-3.158
Kristensen, Tom, 1893-1974. 2.14026
Kristiansen, M. (Magne), 1932- joint author.
  5.2451
Kristjonsson, Hilmar. 5.5483
Kristof, Ladis K. D., ed. 3.3137
Kristol, Irving. 4.3052
Kristov, Khristo Angelov. 3.3540
Kritchevsky, David, 1920-. 5.4233
Kritz, Mary M. 4.8949
Kritzeck, James. 1.2068
Krleža, Miroslav, 1893-. 2.1219-2.1221
Krochmal, Arnold, 1919-. 5.5146
Krochmal, Connie. joint author. 5.5146
Krock, Arthur, 1886-. 3.7530
Krodel, Gerhard, 1926- ed. 1.2961
Kroeber, A. L. (Alfred Louis), 1876-1960.
  3.9-3.11, 3.5703, 3.5722, 4.394, 4.400, 4.421,
  4.429
Kroeber, Alfred Louis, 1876-. 3.23, 3.30, 4.4877
Kroeber, Donald W. 5.5609
Kroeber, Karl, 1926-. 2.2316, 2.5821
Kroeber, Theodora. 3.5792, 3.5960
Kroemer, Herbert, 1928- joint author. 5.2257
Kroemer, K. H. E., 1933- joint author. 5.5688
Kroenke, David. 5.1237
Kroetsch, Robert, 1927-. 2.9935
Kroff, Alexander Yale, 1912- joint comp.
  2.3937
Krogh, August, 1874-1949. 5.4230
Kroll, Judith, 1943-. 2.13264
Kroll, Oskar. 1.4171
Kronenberger, Louis, 1904-. 2.3802, 3.1570
Kronick, David A. (David Abraham), 1917-.
  2.3573
Kroodsma, Donald E. 5.3967
Krook, Dorothea. 2.11122
Krooss, Herman Edward, 1912-1975. 4.4214
Kropotkin, P. A. 4.7194
Kropotkin, Petr Alekseevich, kniaz', 1842-1921.
  3.2083, 4.4905, 4.7182
Kroschwitz, Jacqueline I. 5.6905
Krsnālīlāśukamuni, 1193-1293. 2.1950
Krueckeberg, Donald A. 4.6316, 4.6320
Krueger, Anne O. 4.3237, 4.4558

Krueger, David W. 5.4942
Krueger, Myron W. 1.6692
Krug, Edward August, 1911-. 4.10054
Krug, Mark M., 1915-. 4.10897
Kruger, Paul, 1925- ed. 5.6294
Kruger, Rayne, 1922-. 3.5504
Kruglak, Theodore Eduard. 2.3695
Kruisinga, Etsko, 1875-1944. 2.998
Krumbein, William Christian, 1902-. 5.3135
Krummel, Donald William, 1929-. 1.3562,
  5.7678
Krupat, Arnold. 2.10297, 3.5787
Krupp, E. C. (Edwin C.), 1944-. 5.1687
Kruse, Robert Leroy, 1941-. 5.1186
Krüssmann, Gerd. 5.5360
Krutch, Joseph Wood. 1.454-1.455, 2.3503,
  2.5894, 2.10524, 2.11210, 2.11251, 5.3267,
  5.4061
Krutilla, John V. 4.1902
Krutz, Gary. 5.6248
Krutz, Ronald L., 1938-. 5.1149
Kruuk, H. (Hans) 5.4002
Kruzas, Anthony Thomas. 4.6508, 5.4482
Krylov, Ivan Andreevich, 1768-1844.
  2.1394-2.1395
Krynski, Magnus J., 1922-. 2.1726, 2.1743
Kryter, Karl D. 5.4688, 5.6648
Krzyżanowski, Jerzy Ryszard. 2.1724
Krzyżanowski, Ludwik. 2.1735, 2.1744
KTO Press. 4.7207
Ku kung po wu yüan (China) 1.4668
Ku, Min-chuan. 4.9212
Kuan, Han-ch'ing, ca. 1210-ca. 1298. 2.2220,
  2.2223
Kubach, Hans Erich, 1909-. 1.5237
Kubie, Lawrence Schlesinger, 1896-. 5.181
Kubizek, August. 3.2404
Kubler, George, 1912-. 1.4597, 1.5040, 1.5352,
  3.5694, 3.9291
Kübler-Ross, Elisabeth. 5.633
Kublin, Hyman. 4.7123
Kubo, Ryōgo, 1920-. 5.6201
Kubrick, Stanley. 2.9699
Kučera, Henry. 2.1141
Kucharski, Józef, joint author. 5.6053
Küchemann, Dietrich, 1911-1976. 5.6663
Kuczaj, Stan A. 2.121
Kuczynski, Marguerite (Steinfeld), ed. 4.1407
Kuecken, John A. 5.6419
Kuehl, John Richard, 1928-. 2.13023
Kuehl, Warren F., 1924-. 4.9117
Kuehn, Robert E., 1932- comp. 2.8828
Kuehn, Thomas J., 1948-. 5.5539
Kuenne, Robert E. 4.1444
Kuerti, Gustav. 5.6665
Kugel, Robert B. 4.6609
Kuhn, A. T. 5.6869
Kuhn, Annette. 4.5880
Kuhn, Helmut, 1899- joint author. 1.1367
Kühn, Ludwig. 5.1859
Kuhn, Philip A. 3.4721
Kuhn, Reinhard Clifford. joint comp. 2.3935
Kuhn, Ryan A. 4.5840
Kuhn, Sherman M. (Sherman McAllister),
  1907-. 2.957
Kuhn, Thomas S. 5.908-5.909, 5.1695
Kühnel, Ernst, 1882-1964. 1.6548
Kuhner, Herbert, 1935-. 2.13937
Kuhns, Eileen Pease, 1923- joint author.
  4.10593
Kuhns, Richard Francis, 1924-. 1.1346, 1.4636
Kuile, Engelbert Hendrik ter, joint author.
  1.5025
Kuiper, Gerard Peter, 1905- ed. 5.1748
Kuisel, Richard F. 4.2328
Kuklick, Henrika. 4.8800
Kuleshov, L. V. (Lev Vladimirovich) 2.2940
Kulik, Gary. 4.3845
Kulkarni, V. B. 3.4250
Kultermann, Udo. 1.4850, 1.5653, 1.5870
Kumamoto, Hiromitsu. joint author. 5.7043
Kumar, Krishan. 4.5105
Kumar, Martha Joynt. joint author. 4.7935
Kumar, R. P. (Ramesh Pal), 1948-. 2.3696
Kumar, Shiv Kumar, 1921-. 2.3483
Kumar, Vinay. 5.4740
Kumarappa, Bharatan, 1896-1957. 4.5036
Kumin, Maxine, 1925-. 2.11968-2.11971

Kümmel, Werner Georg, 1905-. 1.2628, 1.2636
Kuna, Franz, 1933-. 2.13797
Kundera, Milan. 2.1688-2.1692
Kunene, Daniel P. 2.2313
Kunert, Günter, 1929-. 2.13808
Küng, Hans, 1928-. 1.1621, 1.2830, 1.2932,
  1.2959, 1.2994, 1.3011, 1.3169, 1.3196
K'ung, Shang-jen, 1648-1718. 2.2230
Kungl. Svenska vetenskapsakademien. 5.2566
Kuniholm, Bruce Robellet, 1942-. 3.3735,
  3.3873, 3.4092
Kunisch, Hermann, 1901-. 2.13656
Kunitz, Joshua, 1896-. 2.1304
Kunitz, Stanley, 1905-. 2.2547, 2.2550, 2.5559,
  2.5697, 2.10234, 2.11972
Kunitz, Stanley Jasspon, ed. 2.2681
Kunitz, Stephen J. 5.4663
Kunkel, Francis Leo, 1921-. 2.8777
Kunkel, Wolfgang, 1902-. 4.9398
Kunst, Jaap, 1891-. 1.4361
Kunst, Sabine. 5.6032
Kunstadter, Peter, ed. 3.4390
Kuntz, John Kenneth. 1.2566
Kuntz, Joseph Marshall, 1911-. 5.7972
Kuntz, Paul Grimley, 1915-. 1.777
Kunz, Jeffrey R. M. 5.4756
Kunz, Thomas H. 5.4010
Kunz, William J. 2.7289
Kunzle, David. 2.3811
Kuo, Benjamin C., 1930-. 5.6178, 5.6185
Kuo, Jo-hsü, fl. 1070-1075. 1.6315
Kuo, Kenneth K. 5.2904
Kuo, Sung-t'ao, 1818-1891. 3.4676
Kuo, Zing-Yang, 1898-1970. 5.478
Kup, Alexander Peter. 3.5373
Kuper, Adam. 4.473, 4.659
Kuper, Hilda. 3.5497, 3.5528-3.5529, 4.614,
  4.9927
Kuper, Leo. 3.5452, 4.6453, 4.9332, 4.9927
Küpper, Heinz. 2.1186
Kupperman, Karen Ordahl, 1939-. 3.8196
Kupperman, Robert H., 1935-. 4.6712
Kuprin, A. I. (Aleksandr Ivanovich),
  1870-1938. 2.1515
Kurath, Hans, 1891-. 2.957, 2.1120-2.1121,
  2.1143
Kuratowski, Kazimierz, 1896-. 5.1353
Kurbskiĭ, Andreĭ Mikhaĭlovich, kniaz', d. 1583.
  3.3085
Kurian, George. 2.3550
Kurian, George Thomas. 4.1246
Kurian, K. Mathew. 4.8706
Kurland, Philip B. 4.9637, 4.9842
Kurosh, A. G. 5.1301
Kurtén, Björn. 5.3172
Kurtz, Donna C. 3.2561
Kurtz, Edwin Bernard, 1894-. 5.6333
Kurtz, Ernest. 4.6645
Kurtz, Henry I. 4.2713
Kurtz, Katherine. 3.13126
Kurtz, Max, 1920-. 5.5701
Kurtz, Paul W. 1.553, 1.570, 4.10427
Kurtz, Russell Harold, 1890- ed. 4.6473
Kurtz, Ruth I. 5.5701
Kurtz, Stephen G., ed. 3.6897
Kurtz, Stephen G. 3.7042
Kurtz, Thomas E. 5.1210
Kushma, John J. (John James), 1949-. 3.7142
Kusic, George L., 1935-. 5.6289
Kusin, Vladimir V. 3.1925
Kusko, Alexander, 1921-. 5.6320
Kuslan, Louis I. 4.10488
Kusmer, Kenneth L., 1945-. 3.8388
Kusnitz, Leonard A. 3.6428
Kuspira, John, 1928-. 5.3432
Kussi, Peter. 2.1695
Kutal, Charles. 5.6231
Kutcher, Arthur. 1.5607
Kutler, Stanley I. 4.9758, 4.9790
Kutner, Marc Leslie. joint author. 5.1705
Kutsch, K. J. 1.3763
Kutzbach, Gisela. 5.2545
Kuusi, Matti, 1914-. 2.1750
Kuwana, Theodore. 5.2658
Kuwayama, George. 1.6391, 1.6671
Kuykendall, Ralph Simpson. 3.5639, 3.5641
Kuypers, Joseph A., joint author. 4.5818

Kuzmin, Mikhail Alekseevich, 1875-1936.
  2.1516
Kuznets, Simon. 4.1233
Kuznets, Simon Smith, 1901-. 4.1233, 4.1656,
  4.1752-4.1753, 4.1890, 4.1963, 4.2373,
  4.2787-4.2789
Kwak, Tae-Hwan, 1938-. 3.5012
Kwamena-Poh, M. A. 4.187
Kwan, Kian Moon, 1929-, jt. author. 4.4896
Kwanten, Luc. 3.4854
Kwavnick, David. 4.3624
Kwitny, Jonathan. 4.6717
Kyburg, Henry Ely, 1928-. 1.1185
Kyd, Thomas, 1558-1594. 2.6606-2.6607
Kynaston, Trent P. 1.4486
Kyōto Daigaku. Tōnan Ajia Kenkyū Sentā.
  4.2433

La Barre, Weston, 1911-. 1.1533, 3.5826
La Brie, Henry G. 2.3649
La Bruyère, Jean de, 1645-1696. 2.4024-2.4025
La Charité, Virginia A. 2.4637
La Claire, John W., 1951-. 5.3641
La Farge, Oliver, 1901-1963. 2.11975-2.11976
La Fayette, Madame de (Marie-Madeleine
  Pioche de La Vergne), 1634-1693. 2.4027
La Follette, Belle Case, 1859-1931. 3.7438
La Follette, Fola. 3.7438
La Follette, Robert M. (Robert Marion),
  1855-1925. 3.7439
La Fontaine, Jean de, 1621-1695. 2.4029, 2.4031
La Forest, G. V. (Gerard V.) 4.9435
La Gory, Mark, 1947-. 4.6303
La Guardia, Fiorello H. (Fiorello Henry),
  1882-1947. 3.7657
La Londe, William S. 5.5681
La Nauze, John Andrew, 1911-. 3.5573, 4.8816
La Palombara, Joseph G. ed. 4.7752
La Palombara, Joseph G. 4.8624
La Palombara, Joseph G. ed. 4.7786
La Piana, George, 1879-. 3.497
La Rochefoucauld, François, duc de, 1613-1680.
  2.4027, 2.4033-2.4034
La Salle College. 3.7727
La Taille, Jean de, 1533?-1611 or 12. 2.3938,
  2.3983-2.3984
Laban, Rudolf von, 1879-1958. 2.3133, 4.1085
Labaree, Benjamin Woods. 3.7974
Labaree, Benjamin Woods. joint author. 4.4218
Labaree, Leonard W. 3.6985
Labaree, Leonard Woods, 1897-. 3.6865, 3.6967,
  3.6985
Labarge, Margaret Wade. 3.1362, 3.2223
Labé, Louise, 1526?-1566. 2.3928, 2.3981-2.3982
Labedz, Leopold. 2.1270
LaBelle, Maurice Marc, 1939-. 2.4595
Laber, Jeri. 5.7133
Labh, Kapileshwar, 1938-. 3.4233
Laboratory of Viral Carcinogenesis (National
  Cancer Institute) 5.3464
Labour Research Department. 4.2580
Labov, William. 2.29, 2.1151, 2.1154
Labovitz, John R., 1943-. 4.9742
Labrousse, Elisabeth. 1.785
Labys, Walter C., 1937-. 4.3723
LaCapra, Dominick, 1939-. 1.853, 3.396, 4.4753
Lacey, A. R. (Alan Robert) 1.102, 1.108
Lacey, Robert. 3.1277
Lacey, W. K. (Walter Kirkpatrick) 3.2783,
  4.5560
Lach, Donald Frederick, 1917-. 3.81
Lachica, Eduardo. 3.4608
Lachman, Seymour. joint author. 4.10894
Lachmann, Karl Konrad Friedrich Wilhelm,
  1793-1851, ed. Des Minnesangs Frühling.
  2.13527
Lack, David Lambert. 5.3949, 5.3961, 5.3965,
  5.4072
Lack, Elizabeth. 5.3935
Lackey, Robert T. 5.5477
Lackie, J. M. 5.3625
Lackner, Bede K. 3.129
Lackner, Stephan. 1.6165
Laclos, Pierre Ambroise François Choderlos de,
  1741-1803. 2.4074-2.4075
Laclotte, Michel. joint author. 1.4978
Lacocque, André. 1.2616
Lacouture, Jean. 2.4623, 3.2202, 3.2205, 3.2211

Lacy, Allen. 2.5286
Lacy, Dan Mabry, 1914-. 5.7651
Lacy, Edward A., 1935-. 5.6455
Lacy, Gerald M. 2.8979
Lacy, W. C. (Willard C.) 5.6731
Lacy, Willard C. 5.6742
Lada, Josef, 1887-1957. 2.1669-2.1670
Ladd, Everett Carll. 4.5200, 4.8158, 4.10081
Ladd, George Eldon, 1911-. 1.2656
Ladd, M. F. C. (Marcus Frederick Charles) 5.2933
Ladefoged, Peter. 2.182
Ladenson, Robert F. 4.9703, 5.8161
Ladner, Joyce A. 3.6766-3.6767
Laet, Sigfried J. de. 3.234
LaFave, Wayne R. 4.9879
Lafaye, Jacques. 3.8875
Lafayette, Marie Joseph Paul Yves Roch Gilbert Du Motier, marquis de, 1757-1834. 3.6893
LaFeber, Walter. 3.7420, 3.9052
Lafferty, R. A. 2.13127
Lafferty, William M., 1939-. 4.8677
Lafleur, Laurence Julien, 1907-1966, ed. 1.722
LaFleur, William R. 2.1999, 2.2051
LaFond, Richard E. 5.4775
Lafore, Laurence Davis. 3.773
Laforet, Carmen. 2.5270
Laforgue, Jules, 1860-1887. 2.4249-2.4252
Lafuente Ferrari, Enrique. 1.6465
Lagadec, Patrick. 4.3479
Lagane, René. jt. author. 2.882
Lagarde, André. 2.3917, 2.3920
Lage, William Potter. joint author. 4.9047
Lagemann, Ellen Condliffe, 1945-. 4.9930
Lagercrantz, Olof Gustaf Hugo, 1911-. 2.14079
Lagerkvist, Pär, 1891-1974. 2.14087-2.14094
Lagerlöf, Selma, 1858-1940. 2.14065
Lagerlof, Selma Ottiliana Lovisa, 1858-1940. 2.14064
Lagler, Karl Frank, 1912-. 5.3896
Lago, Gladwyn Vaile, 1917-. 5.6273
Lago, Mary. 2.8655
Lagos Matus, Gustavo. 4.9136
Lagowski, J. J. ed. 5.6863
Lahav, Pnina, 1945-. 4.9389
LaHaye, Tim F. 4.10039
Lahee, Frederic Henry, 1884-. 5.2964
Lahey, Margaret, 1932- joint author. 4.10391
Lahr, John, 1941-. 2.3260, 2.9790
Lai, Whalen. 1.2174
Laidlaw, J. C., ed. 2.3971
Laidler, David E. W. 4.4489, 4.4493
Laidler, Harry Wellington, 1884-1970. 4.6928
Laidler, Keith James, 1916-. 5.2885
Laing, John, 1809-1880. 5.7728
Laing, Lloyd Robert. 3.1304
Laing, Margaret Irene. 3.4088
Laing, R. D. (Ronald David), 1927-. 5.4781
Laing, Ronald David. 4.5645, 5.413
Laird, Carobeth, 1895-. 3.5848
Laird, Charlton Grant, 1901-. 2.1125
Laird, Joan. 4.6543, 4.6557
Laistner, Max Ludwig Wolfram, 1890-. 3.133, 3.2743
Laitinen, Herbert August, 1915-. 5.2688
Lajpat Rai, Lala, 1865-1928. 3.4230
Lakatos, Imre. ed. 5.900
Lakatos, Imre. 5.1033
Lake, Dale G. 5.542
Lake, Elizabeth E. 5.6012
Lake, Kirsopp, 1872-. 2.327, 2.367
Lakey, George. 4.5037
Lakoff, George. 2.107
Lakos, Amos, 1946-. 5.8393
Lal, Deepak. 4.3235
Lal, Lakshmi Narain, 1925-. 3.4315
Lal, P. 1.1823
Lal, P. comp. 2.10122
Lal, R. 5.5283
Lala, Parag K., 1948-. 5.6582
Laleuf, André. 4.1984
Lalicker, Cecil G. 5.3167
Lall, Sanjaya. 4.4614
Lam, T. Y. (Tsit-Yuen), 1942-. 5.1335
Lamar, Howard Roberts. 3.8465, 3.8512, 3.8559
Lamar, René, 1889-. 2.6923

Lamartine, Alphonse de, 1790-1869. 2.4255-2.4256
Lamartine, Alphonse Marie Louis de, 1790-1869. 2.4254
Lamartine Yates, Paul. 4.2963, 4.3677
Lamb, Alastair, 1930-. 3.3629, 3.4345, 3.4852
Lamb, Beatrice (Pitney), 1904-. 3.4158
Lamb, Charles, 1775-1834. 2.5542, 2.7899-2.7902
Lamb, Charles M. 4.9786
Lamb, H. H. 5.2562
Lamb, Helen Boyden. 3.4476
Lamb, Horace, Sir, 1849-1934. 5.1651
Lamb, Mary, 1764-1847. 2.7899, 2.7902
Lamb, Michael E., 1953-. 4.5660
Lamb, Robert. 4.4729
Lamb, Roger. 5.13
Lamb, Sydney M. 2.152
Lamb, W. Kaye (William Kaye), 1904-. 3.8747, 4.4018
Lamb, Walter Rangeley Maitland, Sir 1882-, tr. 2.379
Lambe, T. William. 5.5899
Lamberg-Karlovsky, C. C., 1937-. 4.499
Lambert, Byron Cecil, 1923- ed. 2.11178
Lambert, Gavin. 2.3472
Lambert, Johann Heinrich, 1728-1777. 5.1697
Lambert, Malcolm (Malcolm D.) 1.2963
Lambert, Phyllis. 1.5517
Lambert Publications, Inc. 4.7708
Lambert, Richard D. 4.2513
Lambert, William Wilson, 1919- joint author. 5.506
Lamberton, D. M. (Donald McLean), 1927-. 5.5637
Lamberts, J. J. (Jacob Justin), 1910-. 2.997
Lambourne, Lionel. 1.6530
Lambright, W. Henry, 1939-. 5.795
Lambton, Ann Katharine Swynford. ed. 3.3644
Lambton, Ann Katharine Swynford. 4.7323
Laming-Emperaire, Annette, 1917-1977. 1.4685
Lamis, Alexander P. 3.8172
Lamm, Lawrence W. 2.3779
Lamm, Martin, 1880-1950. 2.14081
Lammers, William W. 4.5817
Lamming, George, 1927-. 2.9989-2.9991
Lamon, Lester C., 1942-. 3.6807
Lamont, Claire. 2.8044
Lamont, Corliss, 1902-. 1.501, 1.591, 1.2951
Lamont, Gary B. 5.6189
Lamontgne, Léopold. 3.8680
Lamoreaux, Naomi R. 4.3047
Lampe, G. W. H. (Geoffrey William Hugo), 1912-1980. ed. 1.2509
Lampe, Kenneth F. 5.4732
Lamphear, John. 3.5263
Lamphere, Louise. joint author. 4.5939
Lampl, Paul. 1.5606
Lampman, Archibald, 1861-1899. 2.9936
Lamson, Peggy. 4.7691
Lamson, Roy, 1908- ed. 2.6083
Lancashire, Anne Begor. 2.6553
Lancaster, Carol. 4.4727
Lancaster, Donald. 3.4431
Lancaster, F. Wilfrid (Frederick Wilfrid), 1933-. 5.7611
Lancaster, J. F. (John Frederick) 5.7062
Lancaster, Lewis R. 1.2174
Lancaster, Thomas D. 3.3477
Lancaster, William, 1938-. 3.4051
Lance, Eugene Mitchell. 5.4465
Lancour, Harold, 1908-. 5.7695, 5.8113
Lanczos, Cornelius, 1893-. 5.1073, 5.1644
Land, Aubrey C. 3.8104-3.8105
Land, Stephen K. 3.1418
Landa, Diego de, 1524-1579. 3.9039
Landa, Louis A., 1901-. 2.5661, 2.5665, 2.7301
Landau, Edmund, 1877-1938. 5.1329
Landau, L. D. (Lev Davidovich), 1908-1968. 5.1645, 5.1661, 5.1671, 5.1979-5.1980, 5.2069, 5.2134, 5.2166, 5.2340, 5.2359, 5.2362
Landau, Sidney I. 2.203, 5.4486
Landeira, Ricardo, 1944-. 2.5136
Lander, J. R. (Jack Robert), 1921-. 3.1377
Lander, Louise. 5.4594
Landes, David S. 4.2201, 4.4548, 5.7066
Landes, Kenneth Knight, 1899-. 5.6803
Landesman, Charles. 2.108

Landesman, Charles. comp. 1.146
Landgrebe, Ludwig, ed. 1.1013
Landgrebe, Ludwig. 1.439
Landheer, Bartholomeus, 1904- ed. 3.2982
Landis, James McCauley, 1899-1964. 4.9757, 4.9839
Landis, Joseph C. ed. and tr. 2.1827
Landman, Isaac, 1880-. 3.3811
Landolt, Hanspeter. 1.6158
Landon, Fred, 1880-. 3.8827
Landon, Grelun. 1.3513
Landon, Howard Chandler Robbins, 1926-. 1.3800, 1.3893-1.3896, 1.3940
Landon, Kenneth Perry, 1903-. 3.4531
Landor, Walter Savage, 1775-1864. 2.7909
Landow, George P. 2.5939, 2.8040
Landowska, Wanda. 1.4067
Landsberg, Hans H. 4.1994, 4.3716, 4.3719, 4.3745
Landsberg, Helmut Erich, 1906-. 4.131, 5.2558, 5.2571
Landsberg, Peter Theodore. 5.1755, 5.1873
Landsman, Ned C., 1951-. 3.8070
Landy, Frank J. 4.4379
Lane, Ann J., 1931-. 2.11041, 3.7203
Lane, Arthur, 1909-1963. 1.6612
Lane, Barbara G. 1.6233
Lane, Barbara Miller. 1.5423
Lane, Christel. 1.2458
Lane, David Stuart. 4.2391, 4.6968, 4.7588
Lane, Edward William, 1801-1876. 3.5149
Lane, Frederic Chapin, 1900-. 3.2912
Lane, Harlan L. 4.6607
Lane, Jack C., 1932-. 5.7843
Lane, John R., 1944-. 1.4883
Lane, Lauriat, joint ed. 2.7655
Lane, Neal F., 1938- joint author. 5.2135
Lane-Poole, Stanley, 1854-1931. 3.3430
Lane, Richard Douglas, 1926-. 1.6484
Lane, Robert Edwards. 4.5026, 4.7241
Lane, William Coolidge, 1859-1931, ed. 1.5162
Lane, William L., 1931-. 1.2689
Laney, Al, 1896-. 2.3661
Lang, Albert Scheffer. 4.4025
Lang, Andrew, 1844-1912. 2.636, 2.8042
Lang, Berel. comp. 4.7135
Lang, Cecil Y. 2.8137, 2.8167
Lang, Cecil Y. ed. 2.8134
Lang, David Marshall. 3.3312, 3.4041
Lang, David Marshall. joint author. 3.4042
Lang, Douglas Wallace. 5.7036
Lang, Gerald S. 5.4612
Lang, Gladys Engel. 3.7922
Lang, James. 4.2170
Lang, Kenneth R. 5.1722, 5.1772
Lang, Kurt, 1924-. 3.7922
Lang, Olga. 2.2246
Lang, Paul Henry. 1.3494
Láng, Paul Henry, 1900-. 1.3635
Lang, Paul Henry, 1901-. 1.3674, 1.3702, 1.3890
Lang, Serge, 1927-. 5.1029, 5.1267, 5.1442-5.1443, 5.1497, 5.1578
Langacker, Ronald W. 2.136
Langan, Thomas. 1.1000
Langan, Thomas. joint author. 1.422, 1.438
Langbaum, Robert Woodrow, 1924-. 2.5783
Langbort, Carol. 5.989
Langdon, A. Bruce. 5.2388
Langdon, Frank, 1919-. 3.4984
Langdon, George D. 3.7989
Lange, Ann E. 4.4273a
Lange, Carl Georg, 1834-1900. 5.411
Lange, Charles H. 3.5953
Lange, Dorothea. 5.6972
Lange, Ernest K. 4.916
Lange, Frederick W., 1944-. 3.9030, 4.6437
Lange, Kurt. 1.4703
Lange, Norbert Adolph, 1892-1970. 5.2650
Lange, Oskar, 1904-1965. 4.3068
Lange, Peter Michael. 4.8372
Lange, Victor, 1908-. 2.13467, 2.13477, 2.13524
Langefors, U. 5.6748
Langenbach, Randolph, 1945- joint author. 4.3544
Langenfelt, Gösta, 1888-. 4.3160
Langer, Ellen J., 1947-. 5.450
Langer, Paul Fritz, 1915-. 3.4455, 4.8764

Langer, Susanne Katherina Knauth, 1895-.
  1.605, 1.4612, 1.4644, 5.122
Langer, William L. (William Leonard),
  1896-1977. 3.526, 3.699, 3.718-3.720, 3.936,
  3.7582, 4.10994
Langeraar, W., 1915-. 4.233
Langevin, André, 1927-. 2.4831
Langford, Cooper Harold, 1895-. 1.1214
Langford, Michael John, 1933-. 5.6940
Langford, Walter M. 2.5328
Langguth, A. J., 1933-. 2.9134
Langhans, Edward A. joint author. 2.3333
Langkavel, Bernhard August, 1825-1902. 2.440
Langland, Elizabeth. 2.5987
Langland, William, 1330?-1400? 2.6390-2.6394,
  2.6396
Langley, Harold D. ed. 3.7776
Langley, J. Ayodele. 3.5331
Langley, Lester D. 3.9148
Langley, Stephen. 2.3236, 2.3268
Langlois, Pierre, of Paris. 5.8004
Langlotz, Ernst, 1895-. 1.5631
Langmaid, Janet. 5.8014
Langone, John, 1950-. 4.10947
Langs, Robert, 1928-. 5.4916
Languet, Hubert, 1518-1581. 4.7386, 4.7552
Langui, Emile. 1.5732
Langwill, Lyndesay Graham, 1897-. 1.3770,
  1.4172
Lanham, Richard A. 2.2466
Lanier, Sidney, 1842-1881. 2.11140-2.11141
Lanir, Zvi. 5.7343
Lankford, William T. 5.6787
Lankheit, Klaus. joint ed. 1.4811
Lanning, Edward P. 3.9285
Lanning, George, 1925- joint author. 2.3429
Lanning, John Tate, 1902-. 4.11006
Lannom, Laurence. 5.7641
Lannoy, Richard. 3.4183
LaNoue, George R. comp. 4.10659
Lanoux, Armand. 2.4344
Lanphear, Frederick O., joint author. 5.5381
Lansbury, Coral. 2.7726
Lansing, John Stephen. 3.4586
Lansing, Marjorie, 1916-. 4.5954
Lansing, Robert, 1864-1928. 3.832
Lansland, William, 1330?-1400? 2.6395
Lanson, Gustave, 1857-1934. 2.3825, 2.3827
Lantier, Raymond, 1886-, joint author. 4.704
Lantz, Herman R. 4.5135
Lantz, K. A. 2.1400, 2.1402
Lányi, Jenő. 1.5729
Lanyon, Wesley E. ed. 5.4088
Lanzillotti, Robert Franklin, 1921- joint author.
  4.4313
Lao, She, 1899-1966. 2.2249-2.2250
Lao-tzu. 1.1799, 1.1801-1.1802
Lapati, Americo D. 4.9584
Lapedes, Daniel N. 5.1891, 5.2943
Lapesa, Rafael. 2.887
Lapidge, Michael. 3.1320
Lapidus, Edith J. 4.9886
Lapidus, Gail Warshofsky. 4.6131, 4.6134
Lapidus, Ira M. (Ira Marvin) 4.6276
Lapidus, Leon. 5.1519
Lapierre, Dominique. joint author. 3.3935,
  3.4291
Lapiner, Alan C. 3.9159
Lapinski, Michael. 5.6063
Laporte, Léo F. 5.3157
Lapp, Diane. joint author. 4.10471
Lapp, John C., 1917-. 2.4030, 2.4054
Lapp, Ralph Eugene, 1917-. 5.2430
Lapp, Rudolph M. 3.6796
Lappé, Frances Moore. 4.2964, 5.7121
Lappé, Marc. 5.3458, 5.5134
Laprade, Jacques de. 2.4639
Laqueur, Walter, 1921-. 3.734, 3.1116, 3.1200,
  3.2370, 3.3871, 3.4021, 4.5114, 4.6713,
  4.7598, 4.7771, 5.7229
Larbaud, Valéry, 1881-1957. 2.4598
Larcher, W. (Walter), 1929-. 5.3767
Lardner, Dionysius, 1793-1859. 4.3980
Lardner, John, 1912-1960. 2.11977
Lardner, Ring, 1915-. 2.3793, 2.11978-2.11983,
  2.13128
Lardner, Thomas J., ed. 5.5734
Lardy, Nicholas R. 4.2481, 4.2989

Large, Brian. 1.3992
Larkin, Emmet J., 1927-. 4.3649
Larkin, John A. 4.5445
Larkin, Oliver W. 1.4860, 1.5956
Larkin, Philip. 2.8940-2.8943
Larkin, Philip. comp. 2.6189
Larkin, Philip. 2.8944
Larkin, Robert P. 4.357
Laroche, Maximilien. 2.4829
LaRoche, Nancy. 2.1106
Laroque, Robert. 2.4818
Larrabee, Eric. 1.6559, 3.6073
Larrabee, Harold Atkins, 1894- ed. 4.7728
Larrick, Nancy. 4.10409
Larrowe, Charles P. 4.3533
Larsen, Henrietta Melia. 4.1891
Larsen, Jakob Aall Ottesen. 4.7359
Larsen, Jens Peter, 1902-. 1.3891
Larsen, Lawrence Harold, 1931- joint comp.
  3.7819
Larsen, Nella. 2.11988-2.11989
Larsen, Stein Ugelvik. 4.7609
Larsen, Stephen C., 1943-. 4.10927
Larsen, Susan C. 1.4883
Larsgaard, Mary Lynette, 1946-. 4.216
Larson, Arthur. 3.7826, 3.7838
Larson, Boyd, 1934-. 5.6556
Larson, Cedric, 1908- joint author. 3.838
Larson, Charles R. 2.10295
Larson, Donald R., 1935-. 2.5210
Larson, Donna Rae. 5.7767
Larson, Harold J., 1934-. 5.5716
Larson, Laurence Marcellus, 1868-1938. 3.3371
Larson, Loren C., 1937-. 5.1119
Larson, Mildred L. 2.194
Larson, Roy A. 5.5346
Larson, T. A. (Taft Alfred), 1910-.
  3.8552-3.8553
LaRue, Jan. ed. 1.3462
LaRue, Jan. 1.4428
Larwood, Laurie. 4.4341
Lasagna, Louis, 1923- joint author. 5.5148
Lascelles, Mary. 2.7375
Lasch, Christopher. 4.5095, 4.5136, 4.5172,
  4.5186, 4.5564
Lash, Joseph P., 1909-. 3.937, 3.7788-3.7789,
  4.9813
Lashgari, Deirdre. 2.3750
Lashley, Karl Spencer, 1890-1958. 5.206, 5.224
Laska, Vera, 1923-. 5.8250
Lasker, Bruno, 1880-1965. 4.3105
Lasker, Henry. 1.4420
Laski, Harold Joseph, 1893-1950. 3.57, 3.6128,
  4.5032, 4.7294, 4.7472, 4.7509-4.7510, 4.7667,
  4.7927, 4.8472, 4.9820
Laski, Marghanita, 1915-. 2.7704
Laskin, Allen I., 1928- joint author. 5.4436
Lasko, Peter. 1.4742
Lasky, Melvin J., ed. 3.1948
Laslett, John H. M. 4.3358
Laslett, Peter. 4.5298, 4.5553, 4.5789, 4.7213,
  4.7227, 4.7230, 4.7254, 4.7276, 4.7411
Lass, Abraham Harold, 1907-. 2.1024
Lass, Betty, joint author. 2.1024
Lass, William E. 3.8501
Lassaigne, Jacques, 1910-. 1.6006, 1.6258
Lasser, J. K. (Jacob Kay), 1896-1954. 4.4399,
  4.4403, 4.4413
Lasson, Frans. 2.14020
Lasswell, Harold Dwight, 1902-. 4.5010, 4.7210,
  4.7228, 4.7232-4.7233, 4.7242, 4.7692, 4.9383,
  5.173, 5.472
Last, Rex William. joint author. 2.13849
Laszlo, Ervin, 1932- ed. 4.4889
Latham, A. J. H. 4.1811
Latham, Earl. 3.7548
Latham, Richard Thomas Edwin. 3.1229
Latham, Robert, 1912-. 3.1503-3.1504
Lathem, Edward Connery. ed. 2.11748
Lathem, Edward Connery. 2.11762
Lathem, Edward Connery. ed. 2.11749
Lathen, Emma, pseud. 2.13129
Lathi, B. P. (Bhagwandas Pannalal) 5.6349
Lathrap, Donald Ward, 1927-. 3.9199
Lathrop, John W. 5.6299
Latin American Studies Association. 5.8378
Latouche, Robert, 1881-. 4.1742

Latourette, Kenneth Scott. 1.2276-1.2277,
  1.2283, 1.2365, 1.3027
Latrobe, Benjamin Henry, 1764-1820. 1.6380
Latta, Geoffrey W., 1947-. 4.3066
Latta, Robert, 1865- ed. and tr. 1.862
Lattimore, Owen, 1900-. 3.4615, 3.4846, 3.7549
Lattimore, Richmond Alexander, 1906-. 2.296,
  2.323, 2.404, 2.413, 2.464, 2.479, 2.486, 2.489,
  2.526
Lātūkefu, Sione. 1.2473
Lau, Franz. 3.2277
Lau, Joseph S. M., 1934-. 2.2204, 2.2207-2.2208
Laudan, Larry. 5.741, 5.953
Lauderdale, James Maitland, 8th earl of,
  1759-1839. 4.1414
Lauer, Quentin. 1.936, 1.940, 1.947
Lauer, Robert H., editor. 4.5100, 4.10648
Lauf, Detlef Ingo. 1.5188
Lauff, George H., ed. 4.338
Laughlin, James, 1914-. 2.10715
Laughton, M. A. 5.6254
Launert, Edmund. 5.5349
Lauren, Paul Gordon. 4.9086
Laurence, Anya. 1.3535
Laurence, Dan H. ed. 2.8065, 2.8069
Laurence, Frank M. 2.11862
Laurence, Margaret. 2.9937-2.9940
Laurenson, Diana T. 2.2383
Laurenti, Luigi. 3.6785
Laurentin, René. 1.3124
Laurie, Bruce. 4.3622
Laurie, Peter. 4.6657
Laurie, Simon Somerville, 1829-1909. 4.9959
Laurila, Simo H. (Simo Heikki), 1920-. 5.5830
Lauring, Palle. 3.3367-3.3368
Lauter, Estella, 1940-. 1.6689
Lauterpacht, Hersch, Sir, 1897-1960. 4.8984,
  4.9150, 4.9288, 4.9290, 4.9301
Lauth, Thomas P. 4.9727
Lautréamont, comte de, 1846-1870.
  2.4169-2.4170
Laux, Jean K. 4.7139
LaValley, Albert J. 2.7557
Lave, Charles A. 4.4027
Lave, Lester B. 5.4659
Lavedan, Pierre, 1885-. 1.5591
Lavender, Abraham D. 3.6564
Lavender, David Sievert, 1910-. 3.8601
Laver, F. J. M. 5.6413
Laver, James, 1899-. 1.5986, 4.830
Lavers, Annette. 2.44
Lavers, Norman. 2.13124
Lavery, Brian. 5.7432
Lavigne, D. M. 5.3980
Lavigne, Marie, 1935-. 4.2233
Lavin, Irving, 1927-. 1.5012
Lavin, Mary, 1912-. 2.8947-2.8948, 2.11990
LaVine, W. Robert. 5.7093
Lavisse, Ernest, 1842-1922. 3.1975, 3.2488
Lavrin, Asunción. 4.6082
Lavrin, Janko, 1887-. 2.1248, 2.1393
Law, Alexander. 2.7209
Law of the Sea Institute. 4.9309
Law, Robin. 3.5346
Law School Admission Council. 4.9475
Law School Admission Services (U.S.) 4.9475
Law, William, 1686-1761. 1.3055
Lawden, Derek F. 5.2407
Lawhorne, Clifton O. 4.9519
Lawler, Donald L. 2.13403
Lawler, Eugene L. S. 1.1278
Lawless, Edward W. 5.5634
Lawless, Paul. 4.6622
Lawless, Ray McKinley, 1896-. 1.4288
Lawlis, Merritt E., 1918-. 2.6253,
  2.6450-2.6451, 2.6571
Lawlor, Hugh. 4.10104
Lawlor, Hugh Jackson, 1860-1938. 2.367
Lawlor, John. 2.6403, 2.6788
Lawlor, Sheila. 3.1863
Lawn, Martin. 4.10270
Lawrence, A. W. (Arnold Walter), 1900-.
  1.5219, 1.5617
Lawrence, D. H. (David Herbert) 1.2729,
  2.5014, 2.8952-2.8967, 2.8969-2.8970,
  2.8972-2.8979, 2.9001, 2.10268-2.10269
Lawrence, Douglas H. 5.302

Lawrence, Elwood Parsons. 4.1430
Lawrence, Frieda von Richthofen, 1879-1956. 2.9001-2.9002
Lawrence, Jacob, 1917-. 1.6381
Lawrence, John Shelton. joint author. 3.6184
Lawrence, Karen, 1949-. 2.8895
Lawrence, Paul R. 4.2666
Lawrence, Peter. 4.599
Lawrence, Preston Lee, joint author. 4.8328
Lawrence, Robert Gilford, 1923-. 2.6230, 2.9929
Lawrence, Robert Z., 1949-. 4.1503
Lawrence, T. E. (Thomas Edward), 1888-1935. 3.809
Lawrence, Thomas, Sir, 1769-1830. 1.6035
Lawrence, Vera Brodsky. 1.4291
Lawrence, William John, 1862-1940. 2.3291
Lawrey, James D., 1949-. 5.3716
Lawrie, R. A. (Ralston Andrew) 5.7120
Lawrie, Richard A. 5.6079
Laws, Kenneth. 5.4282
Laws, Richard M. 5.4040
Laws, Sophie. 1.2724
Lawshe, Charles Hubert, 1908-. 4.4372
Lawson, Alan. joint author. 5.8080
Lawson, Edwin D., 1923-. 5.8298
Lawson, Henry, 1867-1922. 2.10150-2.10151
Lawson, Joan. 4.1108
Lawson, Lewis A. joint ed. 2.13220
Lawson, Lewis A. 2.13239
Lawson, Nigel. 4.8419
Lawson, R. P., ed. and tr. 1.2192
Lawson, Rowena M. 4.3700
Lawson, Steven F., 1945-. 3.6791, 4.8094
Lawton, Thomas, 1931-. 1.6354, 1.6528
Lawyers Co-operative Publishing Company. 4.9440
Lax, Roger. 1.3591
Laxalt, Robert, 1923-. 3.3478, 3.6535, 3.8586
Laxness, Halldór, 1902-. 2.13996-2.13997
Layamon, fl. 1200. 2.6406
Laybourne, Kit. 5.7007
Layman, R. D., 1928-. 5.7481
Laymon, Charles M. ed. 1.2527
Layson, June. joint author. 4.920
Layton, Edwin T., 1928-. 5.5678
Layton-Henry, Zig. 3.1292, 4.8373, 4.8533
Layton, Irving, 1912-. 2.9943-2.9944
Layton, Robert. 1.3990, 1.4638
Lazar, Joyce B. 4.5738
Lazard, Madeleine. 2.3885
Lazarowicz, K. 2.13675
Lazarsfeld, Paul Felix. 5.7169
Lazarsfeld, Paul Felix. ed. 4.1208
Lazarsfeld, Paul Felix. 4.4800, 4.4806, 4.7953
Lazarus, Edward H., 1959-. 4.8165
Lazarus, Harold. 5.1128
Lazenby, Walter. 2.7996
Lazerowitz, Morris, 1909-. 1.109, 1.753, 1.1079, 1.1269
Lazerson, Marvin. comp. 4.10831
Lazerson, Marvin. 4.10097
Lazzarini, John. 4.1155
Lazzarini, Roberta. joint author. 4.1155
Lazzaro, Ralph. 1.2385
Le Bon, Gustave, 1841-1931. 4.5047
Le Brun, Jacques. 2.4022
Le Carré, John, 1931-. 2.9737
Le Clézio, J.-M. G. (Jean-Marie Gustave), 1940-. 2.4784
Le Corbusier, 1887-1965. 1.5471, 1.5482, 1.5578, 1.5590
Le Cren, E. D. 5.3545
Le Dantec, Y.-G. (Yves-Gérard), 1898-1958. ed. 2.4133, 2.4317
Lê, Duẩn, 1907-. 4.7121
Le Fanu, Joseph Sheridan, 1814-1873. 2.7911
Le Fanu, W. R. (William Richard), 1904- ed. 2.7249
Le Fort, Gertrud, Freün von, 1876-. 2.13809
Le Goff, Jacques, 1924-. 1.2946
Le Grand, Yves, 1908-. 5.4380
Le Guin, Ursula K., 1929-. 2.3459, 2.13130-2.13132
Le Hardouin, Maria. 2.4503
Le Huray, Peter. 1.4394
Le May, Iain. 5.5818
Le May, Reginald Stuart, 1885-. 1.5055
Le Patourel, John. 3.2225

Le Play, Frédéric, 1806-1882. 4.4759
Le Roy Ladurie, Emmanuel. 3.1972-3.1973, 3.2236-3.2237, 4.2855
Le Sage, Laurent, 1913-. 2.2498, 2.4573
Le Strange, G. (Guy), 1854-1933. 3.3683, 3.3688
Le Strange, Richard. 5.3660
Le Vine, Victor T. 3.3742, 3.5398, 4.8811
Lea, David A. M. (David Alexander Maclure) 3.5653
Lea, Frank Alfred, 1915-. 2.9137
Lea, Henry Charles, 1825-1909. 1.3050
Lea, James F. 2.601
Lea, Kathleen Marguerite. 2.4885
Lea, Tom, 1907-. 2.11992-2.11993
Leach, Arthur Francis, 1851-1915. 4.10111
Leach, Bernard, 1887-. 1.6624
Leach, Edmund Ronald. 4.401, 4.423, 4.481, 4.505, 4.597
Leach, Edmund Ronald. ed. 4.5421
Leach, Joseph. 2.3252
Leach, MacEdward, 1896-1967. 2.10660
Leach, Maria. ed. 4.753
Leach, Penelope. 5.5080
Leach, Richard H. 4.9433
Leach, William, 1944-. 4.6014
Leacock, Eleanor Burke, 1922-. 3.5705, 4.513, 4.572, 4.5557
Leacock, Stephen, 1869-1944. 2.9946-2.9947
Leacroft, Richard. 1.5550
Leacy, F. H. 4.1253
Leader, David P., 1943-. 5.4417
Leader, Isabel, joint author. 5.4742
Leader, Robert W., 1919-. 5.4742
Leadley Brown, Alison. 5.3546
Leaf, Murray J. 3.4209
Leaf, Walter, 1852-1927, ed. 2.481
League of Arab States. 3.3647
League of nations. Secretariat. Economic, Financial and Transit dept. 4.1700
Leahey, Thomas Hardy. 5.297
Leakey, Mary D. (Mary Douglas), 1913-. 4.422
Leal, Luis, 1907-. 2.5305, 2.5336, 2.5355
Leape, Jonathan. 4.3064
Lear, Edward, 1812-1888. 2.7910
Lear, Jonathan. 1.316
Learmonth, A. T. A., joint author. 3.4161
Lears, T. J. Jackson, 1947-. 3.6129
Leary, David E. 5.114
Leary, Lewis Gaston, 1906-. 2.5509, 2.10863, 5.7790-5.7792
Leary, William Gordon. 2.6742
Leaska, Mitchell Alexander. 2.9296, 2.9599
Leathart, Scott. 5.3681
Leatherbarrow, David. 1.5488
Leatherbarrow, William J. 2.1375
Leatherman, Le Roy. 4.1141
Leavenworth, Richard S. 5.5700
Leavis, F. R. (Frank Raymond), 1895-. 1.78, 2.2440, 2.5500, 2.5543, 2.5767, 2.5831, 2.7661, 2.8986
Leavis, Q. D. (Queenie Dorothy) joint author. 2.7661
Leavis, Q. D. (Queenie Dorothy) 2.5945
Leavitt, Harold J. ed. 4.4351
Leavitt, Helen, 1932-. 4.3936
Leavitt, Judith A. 5.8468
Leavitt, Judith Walzer. 5.4660, 5.4691, 5.5061
Leavitt, Richard F. 2.12738
Leavitt, Ruth. 1.5118
Leavitt, Sturgis Elleno, 1888-. 2.5126
LeBar, Frank M. 3.4387, 4.641
LeBar, Frank M. ed. 3.4454
Lebar, Jacques, 1911- joint author. 3.3895
Lebeau, Charles Nathan, 1913- joint author. 4.6522
Lebeaux, Richard, 1946-. 2.11252-2.11253
Lebeck, Anne. 2.408
Lebel, Robert. 1.6100
Lebens, Ralph M. 5.6105
Lebergott, Stanley. 4.2086
Lebhar, Godfrey Montague, 1882-. 4.4334
Leblanc, Hugues, 1924-. 1.1177, 1.1232
LeBlanc, Leslie. 4.9460
Leblanc, Maurice, 1864-1941. 2.4599
LeBlanc, Steven A. 3.222, 3.5908, 3.5910
Lebovich, William L. 1.5516
Lebovics, Herman. 3.2368

Lebra-Chapman, Joyce, 1925-. 3.4403, 4.6146, 5.7334
Lebra, Takie Sugiyama, 1930-. 3.4890, 4.6147
Lebsock, Suzanne. 4.6030
Leca, Ange Pierre. 3.5145
Lecaillon, Jacques. 4.1853
Lechevalier, Hubert A. joint author. 5.4436
Lecker, Robert, 1951-. 2.9878, 5.7887
Leckie, George Gaines. 1.2824, 3.8270
Leckie, Robert. 3.5020
Lecky, Prescott, 1892-1941. 5.523
LeClair, Tom, 1944-. 2.10280
Lecler, Joseph. 1.2476
Leclerc, Ivor. ed. 1.778
Leclerc, Ivor. 1.778-1.779
Leclercq, Jean, 1911-. 1.3053, 1.3231
Lecompte, Irvill Charles, 1872-. 4.363
LeCompte, Margaret Diane. 4.10284
Leconte de Lisle, 1818-1894. 2.4259
Leddy, Susan. 5.5169
Ledeen, Michael Arthur, 1941-. 3.2886
Lederer, Charles Michael. 5.2832
Lederer, Herbert, 1921-. 2.1178
Lederer, Ivo J. joint author. 3.3522
Lederer, Ivo J. ed. 3.3056
Lederer, Laura. 4.5548
Lederer, William Julius, 1912-. 2.11994
Ledermann, Walter, 1911-. 5.1104
Ledésert, Margaret. ed. 2.881
Ledésert, R. P. L. (René Pierre Louis) ed. 2.881
Ledet, David. 1.4554
Leduc, Joanne. 3.8848
Leduc, Violette, 1907-1972. 2.4600
Ledvinka, James. 4.9561
Ledwidge, Bernard, 1915-. 3.2217
Lee, A.H.E. 2.6117
Lee, Alan J. 2.3687
Lee, Alfred McClung, 1906-. 2.3585
Lee, Anthony K. (Anthony Kingston), 1933-. 5.4013
Lee, Asher. 5.7406
Lee, C. S. G. (C. S. George) 5.6173
Lee, Chae-Jin, 1936-. 3.4920, 3.6462
Lee, Charles Robert. 4.9906
Lee, Chong-Sik, 1931-. 3.5005, 4.7125
Lee, Dwight Erwin, 1898-. 3.761
Lee, Everett Spurgeon. 4.1581
Lee, Francis Graham. 4.9673
Lee, Frank A. 5.7114
Lee, Harper, 1926-. 2.11995
Lee, Henry Desmond Pritchard, Sir, 1908-. 1.1066
Lee, Hermione. 2.8484, 2.13306
Lee, I. K. (Ian Kenneth) 5.5900
Lee, J. T. (Jean Theodore), 1922-. 5.6659
Lee, John Doyle, 1812-1877. 3.8582
Lee, K. H. 2.462
Lee, Ki-Suk. 4.160
Lee, L. L. (Lawrence L.) 2.10353
Lee, Lawrence, 1941-. 2.11958
Lee, Lena Kim, joint author. 1.5080
Lee, Leo Ou-fan. 2.2157, 2.2160, 2.2204, 2.2241
Lee, Mabel, 1886-. 4.899
Lee, Marshall, 1921-. 5.7536
Lee, Maurice. 3.1497, 3.1796, 3.1798, 3.1800
Lee, Nathaniel, 1653?-1692. 2.7094
Lee, Norman, 1936-. 4.3069
Lee, Peter H., 1929-. 2.2138-2.2140
Lee, Philip R. joint author. 4.5701
Lee, R. Alton. 4.3570
Lee, Rex E., 1935-. 4.9695
Lee, Richard. 4.299
Lee, Richard B. 3.5484-3.5485, 4.513
Lee, Richard B. ed. 4.531
Lee, Richard C., 1952-. 4.10938
Lee, Richard Char-tung, 1939- joint author. 5.1038
Lee, Richard Henry, 1732-1794. 3.6927
Lee, Robert D. 4.7985
Lee, Robert Edward, 1942-. 5.3710
Lee, Ronald Demos, 1941-. 4.1640
Lee, Roy F. 3.6737
Lee, Sherman E. 1.5058, 1.5064, 1.5073, 1.5076
Lee, Sidney, Sir, 1859-1926. 2.5572
Lee, (Sir) Sidney, 1859-1926, ed. 3.1235
Lee, Sonia. 2.4850
Lee, Stan. 2.3815
Lee, Tanith. 2.9738-2.9739

Lee, Tanya H. 2.1102
Lee, Ulysses Grant, joint ed. 2.10689
Lee, Virginia, fl. 1972- joint author. 5.7138
Lee, W. Robert. 4.1689
Lee, Walt. 2.2990
Leech, A. R. 5.5027
Leech, Clifford. 2.5843, 2.5846, 2.6573, 2.6577, 2.6885
Leech, Geoffrey N. 2.199, 2.1007
Leech, John, 1817-1864. 2.8131
Leech, Kenneth. 1.3078
Leech, Margaret. 3.7387, 3.7496, 4.6758
Leed, Eric J. 3.790
Leeds, Anthony, 1925- ed. 5.3808
Leeds, Barry H. 2.13111
Leeds, Eng. University. Dept. of English Language and Medieval English Literature. 2.1114
Leedy, Paul D. 5.979
Leeming, Frank. 4.5460
Leemon, Thomas A. 4.11014
Leeper, Alexander Wigram Allen, 1887-1935. 3.1879
Lees, Gene. 2.1048
Lees, Lynn Hollen. 4.6251
Lees-Milne, James. 1.5381, 1.5390, 1.5574, 2.9141
Lees, Stephen. 4.8470
Leeson, Kenneth. joint author. 5.7581
Leeuw, G. van der (Gerardus), 1890-1950. 1.4632
Leeuw, Ronald de. 1.6239
Leeuwenhoek, Antoni van, 1632-1723. 5.3208
Lefebvre, Georges, 1874-1959. 3.2084, 3.2104-3.2105, 3.2123-3.2124, 4.2853, 4.8384
Lefebvre, Henri, 1901-. 1.472
Lefever, Ernest W. 4.9234
Lefevere, André. 2.2545
Lefevre, Carl A. 2.928
Leff, Gordon. 1.353, 1.2962
Lefkowitz, Jerome. 4.3519
Lefkowitz, Mary R., 1935-. 2.282, 4.5847
Lefkowitz, Monroe M., 1922-. 5.585
Lefler, Hugh Talmage, 1901-. 3.8226, 3.8228
Lefort, Claude. ed. 1.843
Lefort, René. 3.5252
Lefranc, Georges, 1904-. 4.3415
LeFree, Betty. 3.5954
Lefschetz, Solomon, 1884-1972. 5.1504, 5.1594
Left Handed, 1868-. 3.5793, 3.5920
Leftwich, A. W. 5.3793
Leftwich, Joseph, 1892- comp. 2.1825, 3.3807
Legal and Behavioral Institute. 4.5546
Légaré, Joseph, 1795-1855. 1.6000
Legarreta, Dorothy, 1926-. 3.3471
Léger, Alexis Saint-Léger, 1889-. 2.4603
Léger, Fernand, 1881-1955. 1.4613
Legg, Alicia. 1.4900
Legg, Keith R., 1935-. 4.8620
Legge, James, 1815-1897. 1.1795, 2.2178
Legge, James Granville, 1861-1940. 3.2302
Legget, Robert Ferguson. 3.8820, 5.5892
Legman, G. (Gershon), 1917-. 2.3799, 2.3801
Legon, Ronald P., 1941-. 3.2646
Legos, Patricia M., joint author. 4.10491
Legouis, Émile Hyacinthe, 1861-1937. 2.5530, 2.8316
Legouis, Pierre, 1891-. 2.7107
Legters, Lyman Howard, 1928-. 3.2476
Lehan, Richard Daniel, 1930-. 2.11602, 2.11732
Leheny, James. 3.1538
Lehman, David, 1948-. 2.11338
Lehman, Lois A. 4.6606
Lehman, Peter. joint author. 2.2959
Lehmann, David. 4.5480
Lehmann-Haupt, Hellmut, 1903-. 5.7567, 5.7587
Lehmann, John, 1907-. 2.9004
Lehmann, Lotte. 1.4571
Lehmann, Rosamond, 1901-. 2.9005-2.9007
Lehmann, Walter J., 1926-. 5.2818
Lehmann, Werner R. 2.13554
Lehmann, Winfred Philipp, 1916-. 2.137, 2.148, 2.218, 2.222, 2.914
Lehmberg, Stanford E. 4.8460
Lehmbruck, Wilhelm, 1881-1919. 1.5717, 1.5719

Lehninger, Albert L. 5.3333, 5.3506, 5.3612, 5.4397
Lehrer, Keith. ed. 1.713
Lehrer, Stanley. joint author. 4.10939
Lehrer, Steven. 5.4504
Lehrman, Philip Raphael, 1895-. 5.130
Leibbrand, Kurt. 4.3927
Leibenstein, Harvey. 4.1633, 4.2790
Leiber, Fritz, 1910-. 2.11996-2.11997
Leiber, Justin. 2.47
Leiblum, Sandra Risa. joint author. 5.4861
Leibniz, Gottfried Wilhelm, Freiherr von, 1646-1716. 1.862-1.865
Leibowitz, Herbert A. 2.11528
Leibowitz, René, 1913-1972. 1.3755
Leiby, James. 4.6517
Leicester, Henry Marshall, 1906-. 5.2587-5.2588, 5.2608, 5.2833, 5.4392
Leichtentritt, Hugo, 1874-1951. 1.4478
Leiden, Carl. 4.7613
Leidy, W. Philip (William Philip) 5.7778
Leifer, Michael. 3.4571
Leigh, Michael B. 3.4549
Leighly, John, 1895- ed. 4.324, 4.373
Leighton, Albert C. 4.3874
Leighton, Dorothea Cross, 1908- joint author. 3.5919
Leighton, Isabel, ed. 3.6130
Leighton, Philip D. 5.7615
Leighton, Ralph. 5.1950
Leighton, Robert B., joint author. 5.1991
Leijonhufvud, Axel. 4.1341
Leimer, Karl, 1858-1944. 1.4539
Leinsdorf, Erich, 1912-. 1.4102, 1.4497
Leiris, Michel, 1901-. 2.4604
Leis, Philip E. 3.5353
Leiser, Andrew T. 5.5897
Leiserson, William Morris, 1883-1957. 4.3359
Leishman, J. B. (James Blair), 1902-1962. 2.5800, 2.6465, 2.6676
Leisy, Ernest Erwin, 1887-. 2.10554, 2.11136
Leitch, Vincent B., 1944-. 2.2482
Leite, José Roberto Teixeira. 1.4923
Leitenberg, Milton. 5.8061
Leiter, Robert David, 1922-. 4.3393
Leiter, Samuel L. 2.3225, 2.3399
Leites, Nathan Constantin, 1912-. 3.3217, 4.7242, 4.8584
Leith, Dick, 1947-. 2.969
Leith, J. Clark. 4.1340
Leith, John H. 1.2954
Leith-Ross, Sylvia. 3.5366
Leitzmann, Hans, 1875-1942. 1.2298
Lejeune, Jean, joint author. 1.5027
Leki, Ilona. 2.4694
Lelchuk, Alan. 2.1785
Lellinger, David B. 5.3701
Lély, Gilbert. 2.4099
Lem, Stanisław. 2.1708-2.1713, 2.3455
Lemaire de Belges, Jean, b. 1473. 2.3985
LeMaistre, Catherine C. joint author. 5.8421
Lemaître, Georges Édouard. 2.3870
Lemaître, Jules, 1853-1914. 2.4260
Lemann, Bernard. 1.6501
Lemarchand, René. 3.5231, 3.5426
LeMaster, J. R., 1934-. 2.12561
LeMasters, E. E. 4.5578
Lemay, J. A. Leo (Joseph A. Leo), 1935-. 2.10870, 3.6986-3.6987, 5.7793
Lembcke, Jerry, 1943-. 4.3395
Lemert, Charles C., 1937-. 1.831, 4.4801
Lemire, Maurice. 2.4804
Lemisch, Jesse, 1936-. 3.6226
Lemkau, Paul, 1909-. 5.187
Lemoine, Maurice. 4.3103
Lemons, J. Stanley. 4.6060
Lemos, Carlos Alberto Cerqueira. 1.4923
Lenat, Douglas B. 5.1246
Lenau, Nicolaus, 1802-1850. 2.13628
Lenchek, Allen M., ed. 5.1779
Lenczowski, George. 3.3727, 3.4083
Lenczowski, John. 3.7849
Lender, Mark E., 1947-. 4.6652
Lendvai, Paul, 1929-. 3.3534
Leng, Shao Chuan, 1921-. 3.4763
Lengle, James I., 1949-. 4.7946
Lengyel, Bela A. (Bela Adalbert), 1910-. 5.6487
Lengyel, Frau Ilse (Schneider) 1.5637

Lengyel, Ilse (Schneider) 1.5735
Lenihan, J. M. A. 5.1944
Lenin, Vladimir Il'ich, 1870-1924. 3.3143-3.3145, 4.1532-4.1533, 4.7072, 4.7098-4.7099, 4.7101, 4.7146, 4.9304
Lenk, John D. 5.6534, 5.6554
Lenman, Bruce. 3.1802, 3.1804, 4.6785
Lenneberg, Eric H. 2.155
Lenneberg, Eric H. ed. 4.10394
Lennon, Thomas M. 1.800
Lennox, Charlotte, ca. 1729-1804. 2.7095
Lens, Sidney. 3.7850, 4.6969, 4.7001
Lensen, George Alexander, 1923-. 3.4925-3.4926, 3.5004
Lenski, Branko, 1928-. 2.1202
Lenski, Gerhard Emmanuel, 1924-. 1.1576, 4.6381
Lent, John A. 4.4060
Lentricchia, Frank. 2.2472
Lentz, Kendrick W. 5.6179
Lenz, Carolyn Ruth Swift, 1928-. 2.6809
Lenz, John W. 1.698
Lenz, Siegfried, 1926-. 2.13810-2.13815
Lenz, William E. 2.10588
Leo, Brother, d. 1271. 1.3259
Leo, Christopher. 4.2871
Leon, Derrick, 1908-1944. 2.8035
Léon. Harry Joshua. 3.3977
Leon, Harry Joshua. 2.3753
León, Luis de, 1528?-1591. 2.5195
Leon, Melvin, 1936-. 5.2461
León Portilla, Miguel. 1.661, 2.2333, 3.8924
Leonard, David K. 4.5104
Leonard, George Burr, 1923-. 4.10007
Leonard, H. Jeffrey. 4.1838
Leonard, Ira M., 1937-. 3.7144
Leonard, Irving Albert. 3.5991, 3.8876, 3.8995
Leonard, John William, 1849-. 3.6301
Leonard, Richard Anthony. 1.3729
Leonard, Sterling Andrus, 1888-1931. 2.981
Leonard, Thomas C., 1944-. 3.6367
Leonardo, da Vinci, 1452-1519. 1.5841, 1.6212, 1.6340
Leonards, G. A. 5.5918
Leondar, Barbara. 1.6685
Leone, Mark P. 1.2396, 4.696
Leonhard, Charles, 1915-. 1.4412
Leonhard, Wolfgang. 3.3253, 4.6978, 4.7026
Leoninus Magister, fl. 1160-1170. 1.3653
Leonov, Leonid, 1899-. 2.1570-2.1571
Leont'ev, Konstantin Nikolaevich, 1831-1891. 2.1261, 2.1517
Leontiades, James C. 4.2718
Leontief, Wassily W., 1906-. 4.1832, 4.1937, 4.1964, 4.1990
Leopardi, Giacomo, 1798-1837. 2.4997-2.5000
Leopold, A. Carl (Aldo Carl), 1919-. 5.3745
Leopold, Aldo, 1886-1948. 5.3230
Leopold, Luna Bergere, 1915-. 4.244, 4.298, 5.5989
Leopold, Richard William. 3.7447
Leppmann, Wolfgang. 2.13854
Leprohon, Pierre. 2.2902
Lepschy, Giulio C. joint author. 2.853
Leptin, Gert, 1929-. 4.2347
Lerdahl, Fred, 1943-. 1.4429
Lermack, Paul. 4.9854
Lerman, Abraham. 4.315
Lerman, Paul, 1926-. 4.6524, 4.6881
Lermontov, Mikhail IUr'evich, 1814-1841. 2.1396
Lerner, Abba Ptachya, 1903-. 4.1334
Lerner, Daniel. 4.5010
Lerner, Gerda, 1920-. 3.6768, 3.7250
Lerner, Janet W. 4.10954
Lerner, Max, 1902-. 3.6131, 4.1454, 4.7393, 4.7842, 4.10248
Lerner, Melvin J., 1929-. 4.4972
Lerner, Michael G. 2.4431
Lerner, Ralph. ed. 4.7269, 4.7348
Lerner, Richard M. 5.552
Lerner, Rita G. 5.1889, 5.2190
Lerner, Sally C., 1931-. 4.4972
Lerner, Warren. 4.7088
Lerond, Alain, jt. author. 2.882
LeRoy, L. W. (Leslie Walter), 1909-. 5.6807
Leroy, Macime, 1873-. 2.4283
Lesch, Ann Mosely. 3.3918

Lescott-Leszczynski, John, 1937-. 3.6544
Lesgold, Alan M. 5.397
LeShan, Lawrence L., 1920-. 5.641
Lesher, Stephan. 4.9792
Leskes, Theodore. 4.8068
Leskov, N. S. (Nikolaĭ Semenovich), 1831-1895. 2.1398-2.1401
Lesky, Albin, 1896-. 2.281, 2.292
Leslie, Charles M., 1923- ed. 4.547
Leslie, Charles Robert, 1794-1859. 1.6028
Leslie, Donald, 1922-. 3.3943
Leslie, Louis A., 1900-. 2.1028
Leslie, R. F. 3.3283-3.3284, 3.3337
Leslie, William C., 1920-. 5.6783
Lesnoff-Caravaglia, Gari. 4.5805
Lesser, Charles H., joint author. 5.7833
Lesser, Charles H. 3.6942
Lesser, Simon O. 2.2578
Lessing, Doris May. 2.9009-2.9027
Lessing, Gotthold Ephraim, 1729-1781. 1.4593, 2.13630-2.13631
Lester, Anthony. 4.9421
Lester, Henry M. 6.6941
LeStourgeon, Diana E. 2.9008
Lesznai, Lajos. 1.3789
Lethbridge, Roper, Sir, 1840-1919. 3.4275
Lettis, Richard. 3.1949
Letwin, William. ed. 4.1892
Letwin, William. 4.9526
Leuchtenburg, William Edward, 1922-. 3.6324, 3.7531, 3.7761, 4.1965
Leuilliot, Bernard. 2.4235
Leuschner, William A. 5.5422
Leusse, Hubert de. 2.4864
Leuzinger, Elsy. 1.5082
Lev, Baruch. 4.4409
Levaillant, Maurice, 1883- ed. 2.4151
Levandowsky, Michael. 5.3838
Levant, Howard. 2.12537
Levant, Lorna. 3.162
Levarie, Siegmund, 1914-. 1.3881
Levelt, W. J. M. (Willem J. M.), 1938-. 2.118
Levene, Ricardo, 1885-1959. 3.9239
Levenson, J. C. (Jacob Claver), 1922-. 3.6240
Levenson, Joseph Richmond, 1920-1969. 3.4638, 3.4821
Levenspiel, Octave. 5.6854
Levenston, Edward A. 2.1771
Levenston, Edward A. joint author. 2.1771
Lever, J. W. (Julius Walter) comp. 2.6129
Lever, Jill. 5.7086
Leverenz, David. 2.13285
Levering, Ralph B. 3.7583
Levernier, James. 2.10364
Leverson, Ada, 1865-1936. 2.9036
Levertov, Denise, 1923-. 2.13133-2.13135
Leveson, David, 1934-. 5.2986
Levesque, Jacques Henry, ed. 2.4593
Lévesque, René, 1922-. 3.8818
Levey, Judith S., 1936- ed. 1.21
Levey, Michael. joint author. 1.4960
Levey, Michael. 1.5865, 1.6189, 2.7984
Levey, Santina M. 1.6679
Levi, Albert William, 1911-. 1.125, 1.440
Levi, Carlo, 1902-1975. 3.2946
Levi, Edward Hirsch, 1911-. 4.9496
Levi, Hans Wolfgang. joint author. 5.6617
Levi, Isaac, 1930-. 5.910
Levi, Leo, 1926-. 5.2292
Levi, Mario Attilio, 1902-. 3.2526
Levi, Mark, 1951-. 5.1510
Levi, Peter. 2.1216, 3.2539
Lévi-Provençal, Évariste, 1894-1956. 3.3424
Lévi-Strauss, Claude. 3.5752, 3.9200-3.9201, 4.506, 4.537, 4.581
Levich, Richard M. 4.4566
Levien, Michael, 1927-. 5.7484
Levin, Dan. 2.1510
Levin, David, 1924-. 3.6231, 3.7978
Levin, Gail, 1948-. 1.5910, 1.5913, 1.5946, 1.6442
Levin, Harry. 2.2579, 2.2648, 2.3510, 2.3900, 2.4124, 2.6617, 2.6656, 2.8912, 5.395
Levin, Harvey Joshua, 1924-. 4.4071
Levin, Henry M. 4.3067, 4.9998, 4.10834
Levin, Joel R. 4.10371
Levin, Meyer, 1905-. 2.11998-2.11999
Levin, Nora. 3.1117, 4.3315

Levin, Norman Gordon. 3.7728
Levin, Richard Louis, 1922-. 2.5868, 2.5882
Levin, Simon A. joint comp. 5.3533
Lévinas, Emmanuel. 1.1020
Levine, Arthur. 4.10093, 4.10612, 4.10818
Levine, Daniel H. 1.2426, 1.3188, 4.8353
Levine, Daniel U., 1935-. 4.10775
Levine, David, 1946-. 4.3638
Levine, David O., 1955-. 4.10070
Levine, Donald M. 4.10784
Levine, Donald Nathan, 1931-. 4.5477
Levine, Edna Simon, 1910-. 4.6603
Levine, Edwin Burton, 1920-. 5.4495
Levine, Ellen, joint author. 4.6055
Levine, Erwin L. 4.9599
Levine, Eugene. 5.5185
Levine, George Lewis. 2.5937, 2.6013, 2.8092, 2.13285
Levine, Herbert Samuel, 1928-. 4.2402
Levine, Ira N., 1937-. 5.2804, 5.2827
Levine, Joel S. 2.2514
Levine, Lawrence W. 4.771
Levine, Madeline G. 2.1697
Levine, Martin D., 1938-. 5.5941
Levine, Melvin D. 5.5075
Levine, Michael K. 4.3734
Levine, Michael L. 3.7854
Levine, Mortimer. 3.1390
Levine, Murray, 1928-. 5.4700
Levine, Paul. 2.12992
Levine, Paula L. 5.8294
Levine, Philip, 1928-. 2.13136-2.13139
Levine, Richard A. ed. 2.5712
Levine, Richard A. 2.5826
Levine, Robert M. 3.9025
Levine, Seymour. 5.4208
Levine, Stephen, 1937-. 2.10700
Levine, Stephen I. 4.8823-4.8824
Levine, Sumner N. 4.4248, 4.4609
Levins, Hoag. 3.3874
Levins, Lynn Gartrell. 2.11696
Levinson, Daniel J. 5.625
Levinson, David, 1947-. 4.495
Levinson, David A. 5.5741
Levinson, Harry. 4.1867
Levinson, Henry S. 1.601
Levinson, Horace C. (Horace Clifford) 4.1068
Levinson, Louis. 5.4629
Levinson, Ronald Bartlett, 1896- . 1.264
Levitan, Sar A. 4.3158, 4.3476, 4.3509
Levitas, Gloria B. comp. 2.2320
Levitchi, Leon. 2.850
Levitine, George. 1.4967
Leviton, Alan E. 5.3922
Levitt, Annette S., 1938-. 2.7433
Levitt, J. (Jacob), 1911-. 5.3749
Levitt, John. 2.6406
Levitt, Morton. 2.602
Levitt, Theodore, 1925-. 4.4284
Levorsen, Arville Irving, 1894-1965. 5.2978
Levtzion, Nehemia. 3.5378
Levy, Alan. 2.12347, 4.891
Levy, Babette May, 1907-. 2.10874
Levy, Barry S. 5.5010
Lévy-Bruhl, Lucien, 1857-1939. 4.538
Levy, Daniel C. 3.8945
Levy, Eugene D. 2.11938
Levy, Florence Nightingale, 1870-1947, ed. 1.4590
Levy, Fred Jacob, ed. 3.1398
Levy, Jacques E. 4.3375
Levy, John M. 4.6215
Levy, Leonard Williams, 1923-. 4.7676, 4.7693, 4.9488, 4.9614, 4.9712, 4.9717, 4.9877
Levy, Matthys. joint author. 5.6090
Levy, Michael H. 4.4639
Levy, Paul, 1941-. 2.9388
Levy, Reuben. tr. 2.1762
Levy, Reuben. 4.5121
Levy, Richard S. 4.8603
Levy, Samuel, 1912-. 5.5856
Lewald, H. Ernest (Herald Ernest) 2.5396
Lewanski, Richard Casimir, 1918-. 5.8336
Lewellen, Ted C., 1940-. 4.609
Lewes, George Henry, 1817-1878. 2.2454, 2.3174
Lewin, Benjamin. 5.3416, 5.3466
Lewin, Bertram David, 1896-. 5.192

Lewin, Gertrud (Weiss) 4.4989
Lewin, Kurt, 1890-1947. 4.4989, 5.524
Lewin, Leonard, 1919-. 4.1012, 4.4048
Lewin, Miriam, 1931-. 5.66
Lewin, Ronald. 3.1080, 3.1273
Lewin, Thomas J., 1944-. 3.5333
Lewine, Richard. 1.3592
Lewine, Richard R. J. joint author. 5.4924
Lewinski, Jorge. 2.5582, 2.8886
Lewinson, Edwin R. 3.8056
Lewis, Anthony, 1927-. 3.6672, 4.9881
Lewis, Arnold. 1.5571
Lewis, Arthur J., 1919- joint author. 4.10447
Lewis, Bernard. ed. 3.3644
Lewis, Bernard. 1.2045, 1.2073, 3.397, 3.3588, 3.3709, 3.3736, 3.3743, 3.4053
Lewis, Bernard. comp. 3.3655
Lewis, C. D. (Colin David) 4.2681
Lewis, C. S. (Clive Staples), 1898-1963. 1.1487, 1.2263-1.2264, 1.3063, 1.3075, 2.2625, 2.2628, 2.2640, 2.5544, 2.5630, 2.7131, 2.9037-2.9042
Lewis, Charles Lee, 1886-. 3.7325
Lewis, Charlton Thomas, 1834-1904. 2.258
Lewis, Clarence Irving, 1883-1964. 1.606-1.607, 1.1213-1.1214, 1.1294
Lewis, D. Brian. 5.4096, 5.4366
Lewis, Daniel. 4.1179
Lewis, David K. 1.469, 1.1245
Lewis, David L. 1.6710, 3.6840, 3.8111
Lewis, David Malcolm. 2.304, 3.283
Lewis, Don, 1901-. 5.48
Lewis, Dori. 5.254
Lewis, E. Glyn. 2.113, 2.216
Lewis, Eleanor, 1938-. 5.6939
Lewis, Eugene. 4.7767
Lewis, G. J. 4.1655
Lewis, Geoffrey L. ed. 2.1984
Lewis, Geoffrey L. 2.1980-2.1981, 3.3574
Lewis, Gilbert Newton, 1875-1946. 5.2249
Lewis, Gordon K. 3.9125, 3.9145
Lewis, Harold Gregg, 1914-. 4.3144
Lewis, Harry R. 5.1372
Lewis, Helen Block. 5.4824
Lewis, Henry T. 5.5444
Lewis, Howard R. 5.4717
Lewis, Hywel David. 1.735
Lewis, I. M. 1.1634, 3.5257
Lewis, Ioan M. 4.482
Lewis, J. G. E. (John Gordon Elkan) 5.3853
Lewis, Jane (Jane E.) 4.6107
Lewis, Jerry M., 1924-. 3.6769
Lewis, Jill. joint author. 4.6058
Lewis, John Donald, 1905- joint author. 4.7616
Lewis, John Noel Claude, 1912-. 5.7544
Lewis, John Wilson, 1930-. 4.6267, 4.7107, 4.8746
Lewis, Kenneth E. 3.6352
Lewis, Lloyd, 1891-1949. 3.7330, 3.7477, 3.7480
Lewis, M. G. (Matthew Gregory), 1775-1818. 2.7912
Lewis, Mark F. ed. 5.4427
Lewis, Martha E. joint author. 5.4717
Lewis, Meriwether, 1774-1809. 3.8477, 3.8479-3.8480
Lewis, Merrill. 2.10353
Lewis, Naphtali. ed. 3.2711
Lewis, Oscar. 3.8058, 4.5262, 4.5423, 4.5611-4.5612
Lewis, P. S. (Peter Shervey) 4.5348
Lewis, Paula Gilbert. 2.4826
Lewis, R. W. B. (Richard Warrington Baldwin). 2.10243, 2.10374, 2.11529, 2.12699
Lewis, R. W. B. (Richard Warrington Baldwin). joint comp. 2.10663
Lewis, R. W. B. (Richard Warrington Baldwin). ed. 2.4624, 2.12689
Lewis, R. W. (Roland Wynne) 5.5711
Lewis, Richard Byrd, 1908-. 4.10324
Lewis, Richard J., Sr. 5.2590
Lewis, Robert E. 1.2905
Lewis, Ronald L., 1940-. 3.6731, 3.7216
Lewis, Roy, 1922-. 2.873
Lewis, Ruth M., 1916- joint author. 4.5262
Lewis, Samella S. 1.4914-1.4915
Lewis, Saunders, 1893-. 2.842
Lewis, Sinclair. 2.12000-2.12011, 2.12029
Lewis, Stephen R. 4.2517, 4.4691
Lewis, T. G. (Theodore Gyle), 1941-. 5.1187

Lewis, Theodore H., ed. 3.5981
Lewis, Thomas P. 1.3553
Lewis, W. Arthur (William Arthur), 1915-. 4.1757, 4.2791, 4.4107
Lewis, W. David (Walter David), 1931- ed. 4.1920
Lewis, W. H. (Warren Hamilton), 1895-. 3.2034
Lewis, W. S. (Wilmarth Sheldon), 1895-1979. 3.1528, 3.1565
Lewis, Walker. ed. 3.7094
Lewis, Walter Hepworth. 5.5151
Lewis, William Hubert, 1928- ed. 3.5090
Lewis, Wilmarth Sheldon, 1895-. 2.7331
Lewis, Wyndham, 1882-1957. 1.4815, 2.2522, 2.2649-2.2650, 2.6803, 2.9043-2.9044
Lewisohn, Ludwig, 1882-1955. tr. 2.13870
Lewitt, Sol, 1928-. 1.4900
Lewontin, Richard C., 1929-. 5.314, 5.3473
Lewy, Guenter, 1923-. 1.1585, 1.3191
Lewytzkyj, Borys. comp. 3.3218
Lexer, Matthias, 1830-1892. 2.1192
Lexicographical Centre for Canadian English. 2.1161
Ley, David. 4.376, 4.4874
Ley, P. 5.4705
Ley, Willy, 1906-1969. ed. 5.1871
Leyburn, James Graham. 3.6597, 3.9116
Leyda, Jay, 1910-. 1.3953, 2.2886, 2.2905, 2.2953-2.2954
Leyden, W. von (Wolfgang von), 1911-. 1.431, 4.7639
Leymarie, Jean. 1.6067, 1.6079, 1.6235, 1.6459
Leypoldt, Frederick, 1835-1884. 5.7748, 5.7755
Leys, Colin. 4.2586, 4.8414
Leyser, Karl. 3.2266
Lezama Lima, José. 2.5365
Lhamon, W. T. 2.10655
L'Heureux, J.M. 2.4252
Li, Chi, 1896-. 3.4650, 3.4654, 3.4862
Li, Chien-nung. 3.4722
Li Chih-ch'ang. 3.4617
Li, Ch'ing-chao, 1081-ca. 1141. 2.2216
Li, Choh-Ming, 1912-. 4.2482
Li, Jerome C. R. (Jerome Ching-ren), 1914-. 5.1392
Li, Ju-chen, ca. 1763-ca. 1830. 2.2231
Li, Lincoln. 3.4777
Li, Peter, 1935- joint author. 5.8046
Li, Po, 701-762. 2.2212
Li, Tze-chung, 1927-. 5.8350
Li, Yu-ning. 3.4693
Liang, Ch'i-ch'ao, 1873-1929. 3.4639
Liang, Ssu-ch'eng, 1901-. 1.5448
Lias, Godfrey. 3.1916
Liashchenko, Petr I. (Petr Ivanovich), 1876-1955. 4.2366
Liben, Lynn S. 4.6601
Liberia. Dept. of Information and Cultural Affairs. 3.5416
Liberman, Anatoly. 4.797
Liberty Hyde Bailey Hortorium. 5.5311
Liberty, Margot. 3.5738
Libo, Kenneth. 3.8048-3.8049
Library-Anthropology Resource Group (Chicago, Ill.) 5.8094
Library Association. 1.28
Library Information and Research Service. 3.3675
Library of Congress. 1.5284, 1.6450, 4.138, 5.7667-5.7669, 5.7783, 5.7829, 5.7832, 5.7852, 5.7909, 5.8263, 5.8319-5.8320
Library of Congress. Aerospace Technology Division. 2.1240
Library of Congress. American Revolution Bicentennial Office. 4.7201
Library of Congress. Catalog Publication Division. 5.7666, 5.7669, 5.8326
Library of Congress. Children's Book Section. 5.7717
Library of Congress. Congressional Research Service. 4.3368, 4.4683, 4.9607
Library of Congress. Descriptive Cataloging Division. 5.8280
Library of Congress. Economics Division. 4.3238
Library of Congress. General Reference and Bibliography Division. 5.7679, 5.7761

Library of Congress. Geography and Map Division. 5.8212
Library of Congress. Hispanic Division. 5.7909, 5.8378
Library of Congress. Hispanic Foundation. 5.7909
Library of Congress. Latin American, Portuguese, and Spanish Division. 5.7909
Library of Congress. Legislative Reference Service. 4.8139
Library of Congress. Manuscript Division. 3.6894
Library of Congress. Map Division. 5.8212
Library of Congress. National Preservation Program Office. 5.7647
Library of Congress. Orientalia Division. 3.4657
Library of Congress. Reference Dept. 2.12435
Library of Congress. Serial & Government Publications Division. 5.7771
Library of Congress. Subject Cataloging Division. 5.7630
Licata, Salvatore J. 4.5527
Lichine, Alexis, 1913-. 5.6892
Licht, Fred, 1928-. 1.5727, 1.6294-1.6295
Licht, Walter, 1946-. 4.3541
Lichtblau, Myron I., 1925-. 2.5388
Lichtenberg, D. B. (Don Bernett), 1928-. 5.2472
Lichtenberg, Joseph D. 5.556
Lichtenstein, Nelson. 3.7854, 4.3553
Lichtheim, George, 1912-. 1.473, 3.743, 3.1191, 4.6938, 4.6942, 4.7050, 4.7536
Lickona, Thomas. 1.1404
Lida de Malkiel, María Rosa. 2.5202
Liddell Hart, Basil Henry, 1895-. 3.537, 3.786, 3.810, 3.907, 3.967, 3.1001, 5.7145, 5.7308, 5.7331
Liddell, Henry George, 1811-1898. 2.247
Liddell, Robert, 1908-. 2.585, 2.3415, 2.3422, 2.7380
Lidoff, Joan. 2.10175
Lidtke, Vernon L. 4.8605
Lidz, Charles W. 4.6672
Lie, Trygve, 1896-. 4.9220
Lieb, Michael, 1940-. 2.7132, 2.7150
Lieb, Sandra R. 1.4097
Liebau, Friedrich, 1926-. 5.2713
Lieber, Stanley R. 4.889
Lieberman, Arthur S. 5.3223
Lieberman, E. James, 1934-. 4.5514
Lieberman, Gerald J. joint author. 5.5673
Lieberman, Gerald J. 5.5569
Lieberman, Jethro Koller. 4.9497
Lieberman, Laurence. 2.10510
Lieberman, Morton A., 1931-. 4.6535
Lieberman, Myron, 1919-. 4.10026, 4.10529
Lieberman, Ralph. 1.5436
Lieberman, Sima, 1927-. 4.2414
Lieberman, William Slattery, 1924- joint author. 1.4976
Lieberson, Stanley, 1933-. 3.6519
Liebert, Robert M., 1942-. 4.5736
Liebert, Roland J. 4.8844
Liebesny, Herbert, 1911-. 1.2041
Lieblich, Amia, 1939-. 4.7167
Liebling, A. J. (Abbott Joseph), 1904-1963. 2.3599
Liebman, Charles S. 3.3835
Liebman, Lance. 4.10792
Liebman, Robert C. 1.2478
Liebmann, M. J. (Michael J.), 1920-. 1.5714
Lief, Ruth Ann. 2.9197
Lieh-tzŭ, 4th cent. B.C. 1.1804
Liehm, Antonín J., 1924-. 2.1695, 2.2887, 2.2889
Liehm, Mira. 2.2889
Liem, Soei Liong. 3.4584
Lienhardt, Godfrey. 4.469
Lientz, Bennet P. 5.5570
Liess, Andreas, 1903-. 1.3943
Lieuwen, Edwin, 1923-. 3.9005, 4.3777
Lieven, D. C. B. 3.3163
Lievsay, John Leon. 1.3073
Liew, K. S. 3.4838
Life (Chicago) 5.4381
Lifshits, E. M. (Evgeniĭ Mikhaĭlovich) 5.1671, 5.2359

Lifshits, E. M. (Evgeniĭ Mikhaĭlovich) joint author. 5.1645, 5.1661, 5.1979, 5.2134, 5.2166, 5.2362
Lifshits, Evegeniĭ Mikhaĭlovich, joint author. 5.2340
Lifson, David S. 2.3403
Lifton, Robert Jay. 3.430, 3.4794, 4.9339, 5.451
Light, Ivan Hubert. 4.6185
Light, James F. 2.12684
Light, Martin. joint ed. 2.10265
Light, Paul Charles. 4.7937, 4.7972
Lightbown, R. W. 1.6191
Lightfoot, David. 2.122
Lightfoot, R. J. 5.5449
Lightfoot, Sara Lawrence. joint author. 4.10697
Lightfoot, Sara Lawrence. 4.10803
Lighthill, M. J., Sir. 5.2040
Lijphart, Arend. 4.7739
Likens, Gene E., 1935-. 5.3270-5.3271
Likert, Rensis, 1903-. 4.2653
Lilienthal, David Eli, 1899-1981. 3.7662, 5.6303
Lilienthal, Helen M. 3.7662
Lillard, Paula Polk. 4.10211
Liller, William, 1927-. 5.1731
Lilley, Sam. 5.2089
Lillich, Meredith P., 1932-. 1.6651
Lillich, Richard B. 4.9335, 4.9390
Lillie, Frank Rattray, 1870-1947. 5.4128
Lillo, George, 1693-1739. 2.7096
Lim, Patricia Pui Huen. 5.8059
Limbacher, James L. 2.3075
Limbourg, Pol de, ca. 1385-ca. 1416. 1.6428
Lin, E. C. C. 5.3450
Lin, Fung-Jen. joint author. 5.5885
Lin, Pen-Min, 1928- joint author. 5.6459
Lin, Piao, 1908-1971. 4.9923
Lin, T. Y. (Tung Yen), 1911-. 5.5882
Lin, Tai-yi, 1926-. 2.2231
Lin, Yü-sheng, 1934-. 3.4640
Lin, Yutang, 1895-1976. 2.1929, 3.4641
Lincoln, Abraham, 1809-1865. 3.7295, 3.7299-3.7302
Lincoln, C. Eric (Charles Eric), 1924-. 3.6673-3.6674
Lincoln, Kenneth. 2.10296
Lincoln, Mary (Todd) 1818-1882. 3.7290
Lincoln, Roger J. 5.3510
Lincoln, W. Bruce. 3.3120, 3.3133, 3.3164
Lind, Andrew William, 1901-. 4.1680
Lind, Levi Robert, 1906-. 2.4065, 2.4893
Lindbeck, George A. 1.3125
Lindberg, Carter, 1937-. 1.3362
Lindberg, David C. 5.713
Lindberg, Gary H., 1941-. 2.10532
Lindberg, James B. joint author. 4.4121
Lindberg, Roy A. 5.7060
Lindberg-Seyersted, Brita. 2.11004
Lindbergh, Anne Morrow, 1906-. 5.6652
Lindblom, Charles Edward, 1917-. 4.2792, 4.7857
Lindegren, Carl C. (Carl Clarence), 1896-. 5.3433
Lindemann, Albert S. 4.7017
Linden, Carl A. 3.3271
Linden, David. 5.6323
Linder, Cynthia A., 1923-. 2.7456
Lindert, Peter H. 4.1644, 4.4147
Lindesmith, Alfred Ray, 1905-. 4.9575
Lindey, Alexander, 1896- joint author. 4.9872
Lindfors, Bernth. 2.10084, 2.10107, 2.10119, 5.8077
Lindgren, Ernest. 2.2958
Lindheim, Barbara L. joint author. 4.5701
Lindley, Harlow, 1875-. 3.8381
Lindop, Grevel, 1948-. 2.5837, 2.7623
Lindow, John. 2.13975
Lindquist-Cock, Elizabeth. 5.6979
Lindquist, Everet Franklin. 5.49
Lindroth, Sten. 5.3215
Lindsay, Beverly. 4.6167
Lindsay, David, 1876-1945. 2.6486, 2.6608, 2.9050
Lindsay, Jack, 1900-. 1.6057, 1.6072, 1.6080, 2.7941
Lindsay, James F. 5.6161
Lindsay, Jennifer. 1.4197
Lindsay, Kenneth Clement, 1919-. 1.5144

Lindsay, Maurice, 1918-. 2.7500, 2.9049, 2.9835
Lindsay, Michael, 1909-. 3.4778
Lindsay, Robert Bruce. 3.58, 5.1913, 5.2223, 5.2227
Lindsay, Vachel, 1879-1931. 2.12015
Lindsay, W. M. (Wallace Martin), 1858-1937. 2.255
Lindsey, Almont, 1906-. 4.3170
Lindstrom, Thaïs S. 2.1385
Lindzey, Gardner. 4.4986
Lindzey, Gardner. joint author. 5.370, 5.519
Line, Maurice Bernard. 5.7602
Linebarger, Paul Myron Anthony, 1913-1966. 2.12017
Lineberry, Robert L. 4.6769
Linell, Per, 1944-. 2.177
Ling, Dwight L. 3.5212
Ling, Gilbert N., 1919-. 5.3623
Ling, Roger. 1.5224
Ling, Trevor Oswald. 1.1589
Lingard, Charles Cecil, 1901-. 4.8321
Linge, G. J. R. 4.2691
Lingenfelter, Judith. 5.8424
Lings, Martin. 1.2015
Link, Albert N. 4.1558
Link, Arthur Stanley. 3.7510, 3.7532, 3.7716, 3.7723, 3.7729
Link, Arthur Stanley. ed. 3.8114
Link, E. Perry (Eugene Perry), 1944-. 2.2177, 2.2188, 2.2205
Link, Eugene P., 1907-. 4.5120
Link, Eugene Perry, 1908-. 3.7021
Link, Frederick M. 5.7955
Link, George Konrad Karl. 2.396
Linke, Lilo. 3.9310
Linke, William F., 1924-. 5.2651
Linklater, Eric, 1899-1974. 2.9051
Linklater, Kristin. 2.3536
Links, J. G. 1.6194-1.6195
Linn, Michael D. 2.2, 2.206
Linnean Society of London. 5.3645, 5.3916
Linscott, Robert Newton, 1886-. 2.4966
Linsky, Leonard. 1.142, 1.1253
Linsley, Ray K. 4.291, 5.5962
Linstrum, Derek. 1.5409
Lintell, Mark. joint author. 4.3924
Lintner, John Virgil, 1916- joint author. 4.3015
Linton, Ralph, 1893-1953. 4.436, 4.487, 4.4895, 4.4988
Lion, Elizabeth M. 5.5201
Lion, Joanna. 4.4621
Lipchitz, Jacques, 1891-. 1.5707
Lipham, James M. 4.10672
Lipkin, Mack. 5.4648
Lipking, Lawrence I., 1934- comp. 2.2473
Lipman, Jean, 1909-. 1.4892, 1.5899, 1.6516, 1.6520
Lipman, Jean (Herzberg) 1909-. 1.5891
Lippard, Lucy R. 1.4900, 1.5146
Lippard, Lucy R. comp. 1.6740
Lippe, Aschwin. 1.5751
Lippincott, Benjamin Evans, 1902-. 4.3068, 4.7573
Lippit, Noriko Mizuta. 2.2038
Lippitt, Gordon L. joint author. 4.4381
Lippitt, Ronald. joint author. 4.4920
Lippmann, Walter, 1889-. 1.1413, 3.7584, 3.7617, 3.7717, 4.5017, 4.5173-4.5174, 4.7459-4.7460
Lipschutz, Mark R. 3.5233
Lipschutz, Ronnie D. 5.6056
Lipscomb, David M. 5.6052
Lipset, Seymour Martin. joint ed. 4.3329, 4.6374, 4.6384
Lipset, Seymour Martin. joint author. 4.10081
Lipset, Seymour Martin. 3.6132, 3.6389, 4.6382, 4.7574, 4.8305
Lipset, Seymour Martin. joint comp. 3.6350
Lipsey, Robert E. joint author. 4.4500
Lipsitz, Joan. 4.5758, 4.10505
Lipsky, David B., 1939- ed. 4.9554
Lipsky, Michael. 4.6490
Lipson, Henry Solomon, 1920-. 5.2934
Lipták, Béla G. ed. 5.5986
Lipton, Lenny, 1940-. 5.7003, 5.7005
Lipton, Michael. 4.1859, 4.2510
Liptzin, Solomon, 1901-. 2.1791, 2.10356
Lisca, Peter. 2.12538

Liscombe, R. W., 1946-. 1.5347, 1.5351, 1.5406
Liska, George. 3.1170, 4.9034-4.9035, 4.9298
Lispector, Clarice. 2.5470
Liss, Peggy K. 4.4221
Liss, Sheldon B. 4.7010
Lissitzyn, Oliver James, 1912-. 4.9151
Lister, David G. 5.2872
Lister, Florence Cline. 3.5745
Lister, Paul F. 5.1153
Lister, Robert Hill, 1915-. 3.5745
Liston, Linda L. joint author. 5.2574
Liszt, Franz, 1811-1886. 1.3837, 1.4035
Litan, Robert E., 1950-. 4.9522
Litman, Jacob, 1920-. 3.3986
Littell, Franklin Hamlin. 1.3302, 4.132
Littell, Franklin Hamlin. ed. 1.2455
Little Compton Historical Society. 3.5775
Little, Dolores E. 5.5166, 5.5170
Little, Elbert Luther. 4.154, 5.3686
Little, Ian Malcolm David. 4.1445, 4.2677, 4.2793
Little, Judy, 1941-. 2.7863
Little, Lester K. 1.3068
Little, Nina Fletcher, 1903-. 1.4865
Little, R. John. 5.3631
Little, Roger. ed. 2.4603
Little, Roger William, 1922- ed. 5.7208
Little, Stuart W. 2.3226-2.3227
Little, T. E. 2.5965
Little, William, 1848-1922. 2.1083
Littlefield, Daniel F. 3.5868, 5.7742
Littlefield, David W., 1940-. 5.8036
Littlefield, Larry J. 5.5403
Littleton, A. C. (Ananias Charles), 1886-. 4.4385-4.4386, 4.4395, 4.4400
Litto, Fredric M., 1939- comp. 2.10047
Litton, Glenn. 1.4220
Littré, Emile, 1801-1881. 2.875
Litvinov, Pavel Mikhaĭlovich, 1940-. 3.3259
Litwack, Leon F. 3.6635, 3.6788
Litwak, Eugene, 1925-. 4.10801
Litweiler, John. 1.4257
Litz, A. Walton. 2.7381, 2.8896, 2.12335
Litz, A. Walton. joint comp. 2.2473
Litzinger, Boyd. 2.7485
Litzinger, Boyd. comp. 2.7486
Liu, Chih-pu. 3.4670
Liu, Hsi-hung. 3.4676
Liu, Hsieh, ca. 465-ca. 522. 2.2155
Liu, James J. Y. 2.2163-2.2164, 2.2167, 2.2496
Liu, James T.C. 1.173
Liu, James Tzŭ-chien, 1919-. 4.8733
Liu, Ta-chung. ed. 4.2478
Liu, Ta-chung. 4.2483
Liu, Wu-chi, 1907-. 2.1759, 2.2156, 2.2194
Liublinskaia, Aleksandra Dmitrievna. 3.2021
Livermore, H. V., 1914-. 3.3417, 3.3495-3.3496, 3.9295
Livermore, Mary Ashton Rice, 1820-1905. joint ed. 3.354
Livermore, Seward W. 3.7731
Livermore, Shaw, 1926-. 3.7077
Livernash, E. Robert (Edward Robert) 4.3257, 4.3385
Liverpool Geological Society. 5.3072
Livesay, Harold C., joint author. 4.4291
Livesey, Derek L. (Derek Leonard), 1923-. 5.2070
Livesey, Herbert B. 4.10531
Livesley, R. K. 5.5728
Livezey, William Edmund, 1903-. 3.6378
Livingston, Arthur, 1883-. 4.7479
Livingston, Donald W. 1.703-1.704
Livingston, James C., 1930- ed. 1.2531
Livingston, Jane. 1.4916
Livingston, Judy. 5.5003
Livingston, M. Stanley (Milton Stanley) 5.2439
Livingston, Philip A., 1901-. 5.5353
Livingston, Robert J. 5.3539
Livingston, William S. 3.5578
Livingstone, David, 1813-1873. 3.5437
Livingstone, Elizabeth A. ed. 1.2221
Livingstone, Ian. 4.2995
Livy. 2.674, 3.2768
Ljungmark, Lars. 3.6595
Llewellyn, Catriona. joint author. 4.5340
Llewellyn-Jones, Derek. 4.1608, 5.4937

Llewellyn, Karl N. (Karl Nickerson), 1893-1962. 4.9473, 4.9852
Llewellyn, Richard. 2.9052
Lloyd, A. L. (Albert Lancaster), 1908-. 2.5250
Lloyd, Christopher, 1906-. 3.1281, 3.2134, 4.137, 5.7489
Lloyd, Cynthia B., 1943-. 4.3284-4.3285
Lloyd, David Myrddin. 2.841
Lloyd, David Wharton. 4.6257
Lloyd Evans, Barbara. 2.6743, 2.7452
Lloyd Evans, Barbara. joint author. 2.6729
Lloyd Evans, Gareth. 2.6729, 2.6743, 2.7452
Lloyd, G. E. R. (Geoffrey Ernest Richard), 1933-. 5.782-5.783, 5.4494
Lloyd, Genevieve. 1.1238
Lloyd George, David, 1863-1945. 3.800
Lloyd, Henry Demarest, 1847-1903. 4.3043
Lloyd, Herbert Marshall, 1862-. 3.5897
Lloyd, Howell A. 4.7286
Lloyd, John Benjamin. 5.3596
Lloyd, John Edward, Sir, 1861-1947. 3.1762
Lloyd-Jones, H., ed. 2.312
Lloyd, Margaret. 4.1126
Lloyd, Noel Glynne, 1946-. 5.1608
Lloyd, Peter Cutt. 5.4465
Lloyd, Peter E. 4.4120
Lloyd, R. (Richard), 1930-. 5.3909
Lloyd, Seton. 3.3762, 3.3767
Lloyd, Susan M. 2.1070
Lloyd, Thomas Cox. 5.6312
Lloyd Thomas, Mary Gwyneth. 2.7105
Lloyd, Trevor Owen. 3.1383, 3.1650
Lo, Andrew. 5.5288
Lo, Chung-min. 3.4694
Lo, Irving Yucheng, 1922-. 2.2194
Lo, Kuan-chung, ca. 1330-ca. 1400. 2.2221-2.2222, 2.2224
Loader, Colin, 1941-. 4.4762
Loades, D. M. 3.1419
Lobeck, A. K. (Armin Kohl), 1886-1958. 4.217, 4.246
Lobel, Arnold. ill. 2.10739
Lobel, Edgar, 1888- ed. 2.315
Lobel, Mary Doreen, 1900- ed. 4.171
Lobo, Susan. 4.5277
Lobrano, Gustav Stubbs, jt. author. 3.7163
Lochnan, Katharine Jordan. 1.6489
Lochner, Louis Paul, 1887-1975. ed. and tr. 3.2382
Lock, Clara Beatrice Muriel, 1914-. 4.6, 4.232
Lock, F. P. 2.6932, 2.7310
Lock, Fred. 5.8080
Lock, M. A. 5.3568
Lockard, Duane, 1921-. 4.8185
Locke, Alain LeRoy, 1886-1954. 1.4303, 1.6711, 3.6745
Locke, Harvey James, 1900- joint author. 4.5637
Locke, Hubert G. ed. 1.2455
Locke, John, 1632-1704. 1.673-1.674, 1.677, 1.2257, 4.7411-4.7413, 4.10185
Locke, Miriam Austin. 2.5672
Locke, Robert R., 1932-. 3.2177
Lockert, Lacy, ed. and tr. 2.4017
Lockhart, J. G. (John Gibson), 1794-1854. 2.7506
Lockhart, James. 3.8881, 3.8996-3.8997, 3.9297, 3.9303
Lockhart, Paula. 5.8365
Lockley, R. M. (Ronald Mathias), 1903-. 5.4007
Locklin, David Philip, 1897-. 4.3886
Lockridge, Kenneth A. 3.8003
Locksley, Gareth. 4.1320
Lockspeiser, Edward, 1905-1973. 1.3847-1.3848
Lockwood, A. P. M. (Antony Peter Murray), 1931- joint author. 5.5023
Lockwood, E. H. (Edward Harrington) 5.1573
Lockwood, W. B. (William Burley) 2.213
Lockwood, William Wirt, 1906-. 4.2543-4.2544
Lockyer, Roger. 3.1466
Lodder, Christina, 1948-. 1.5037
Lodge, David, 1935-. 2.6046, 2.8778
Lodge, Henry Cabot, 1902-. 3.6234, 3.7423, 3.7708, 3.7827
Lodge, Juliet. joint author. 4.8363
Lodge, Thomas, 1558?-1625. 2.6487
Lodish, Harvey F. 5.3597
Loeb, Catherine. 5.8464

Loeb, Edwin Meyer, 1894-. 3.4577
Loeb, Laurence D., 1942-. 3.3973
Loeb, Leonard B. (Leonard Benedict), 1891-.
  5.2182, 5.2381
Loebbecke, James K. joint author. 4.4402
Loehlin, John C. 5.370
Loehr, Max. 1.6316
Loehr, William. 4.1802, 4.4148
Loemker, Leroy E. ed. 1.863
Loemker, Leroy E. 1.868
Loescher, Gil. 4.7636, 4.8955
Loesser, Arthur, 1894-1969. 1.4148
Loetscher, Lefferts Augustine, 1904- ed. 1.2223
Loevinger, Jane. 5.199
Loewe, Herbert Martin James, 1882-1940, joint
  ed. and tr. 1.1941
Loewe, Michael. 1.1329, 3.4695
Loewen, James W. 3.8294
Loewenberg, Alfred. 1.3518
Loewenberg, Bert James, 1905-. 3.6214
Loewenberg, J   Joseph. joint author. 4.3511
Loewenberg, Jacob. 1.937
Loewenberg, Peter. 3.444
Loewenheim, Francis L. ed. 3.7776
Loewenthal, Erich, 1895?-1944. 2.13469
Loewy, Raymond, 1893-1986. 5.7015
Lofland, John. 1.1567, 4.4928
Löfstedt, Jan-Ingvar. 4.10743
Loftis, Anne, joint author. 4.3376
Loftis, John Clyde, 1919-. 2.5901, 2.5904,
  2.5915, 2.5917, 2.7253, 3.1499
Loftness, Robert L. 5.6140
Lofton, John. 4.9718
Loftus, Elizabeth F., 1944-. 4.9887, 5.328
Loftus, Geoffrey R. 5.328
Lofty, J. R., joint author. 5.3840
Logan, Eugenia. 2.7592
Logan, F. Donald. 3.3363
Logan, Frank Anderson. 5.303
Logan, George M., 1941-. 4.7176
Logan, James Venable, 1901-. 2.8321
Logan, Michael H. 4.464
Logan, Rayford Whittingham, 1897-. 3.6676,
  3.6812
Logasa, Hannah, 1879-1967. 5.8129
Loggins, Vernon, 1893-. 2.10325
Logsdon, Joseph. 3.7166
Logsdon, Tom, 1937-. 5.1150
Logue, Christopher, 1926-. 2.488
Logue, Dennis E. 4.4590
Logue, John, 1947-. 4.8675
Logue, William, 1934-. 3.2203
Loh, Philip Fook Seng. 4.10689
Lohafer, Susan. 2.3435
Lohner, Edgar. 2.13521
Lohse, Bernhard, 1928-. 1.2746
Lohse, Eduard, 1924-. 1.2660, 1.2718
Lohwater, A. J. 5.1027
Loisy, Alfred Firmin, 1857-1940. 1.2299
Lomask, Milton. 3.6983
Lomax, Alan, 1915-. 1.3432-1.3434, 1.3933,
  1.4284, 2.10758
Lomax, Derek W. 3.3425
Lomax, Elizabeth M. R. 4.5705
Lomax, John Avery, 1867-1948. comp. 2.10758
Lomax, Louis E., 1922-1970. 3.6677
Lomax, William. 3.1950
Lombardi, Jerry. 4.3738
Lombardi, John V. 3.9181, 4.1688
Lombardi, Vince. 4.1026
Lombroso, Cesare, 1835-1909. 4.6688
Lombroso-Ferrero, Gina, 1872-1944. 4.6688
Lomelí, Francisco A. 2.10301
Lomeo, Angelo. 5.3686
Lomnitz, Larissa Adler de. 4.5256
London and Cambridge Economic Service.
  3.751
London, Barbara, 1936-. 5.6913
London, Bruce. 4.6342
London, Ephraim, ed. 2.3720
London, Howard B. 4.10564
London, Jack, 1876-1916. 2.12019-2.12029
London, Julius, 1917-. 5.7234
London Mathematical Society. 5.1317
London School of Economics and Political
  Science. 3.1690
London, Vera C. M. joint author. 1.3232
Londré, Felicia Hardison, 1941-. 2.9819

Lonergan, Bernard J. F. 1.2834
Loney, Glenn Meredith, 1928- ed. 2.2782
Long, A. A. 1.325
Long, Clarence Dickinson, 1908-. 4.3145,
  4.3196
Long, David E. 3.3725
Long, David Foster, 1917-. 3.7101
Long, Dorothy R., joint author. 2.1000
Long, E. Hudson (Eugene Hudson), 1908-.
  2.10665, 2.10942, 2.10978, 5.7802
Long, Edward Le Roy. 1.1467
Long, Franklin A., 1910-. 4.9167, 5.5514
Long, Iris L. M. 4.33
Long, John Hamilton. 4.158
Long, Kenneth R. 1.4248
Long, Michael (Michael Dudley) 2.6789
Long, Nicholas James, 1929- ed. 4.10948
Long, Norman. 4.5483
Long, Ralph Bernard, 1906-. 2.994, 2.1000
Long, Richard A., 1927-. 2.10685
Long, Robert Emmet. 2.11123
Long, Rose-Carol Washton. 1.6282
Long, T. H. 2.1104
Long, Theodore Dixon, 1933-. 5.750
Longabaugh, Richard. joint author. 4.5731
Longair, M. S., 1941-. 5.1967, 5.2327
Longaker, Richard P. 4.9768
Longenecker, Richard N. 1.2667
Longfellow, Henry Wadsworth, 1807-1882.
  2.11144
Longford, Elizabeth Harman Pakenham,
  Countess of, 1906-. 2.7525, 3.1265, 3.1614,
  3.1712
Longford, Frank Pakenham, Earl of, 1905-.
  3.727, 3.1867
Longhurst, R. S. (Richard Samuel) 5.2282
Longinus, Cassius, ca. 213-273. 2.349, 2.518
Longley, Dennis. 5.7697
Longley, Edna. 2.9424
Longley, John Lewis, ed. 2.12653
Longley, Lawrence D. 4.9541
Longman Group Ltd. 4.187
Longnon, Auguste, 1844-1911. 2.3976
Longnon, Jean, 1887- ed. 1.6428
Longo, Michael J., 1935-. 5.2394
Longrigg, Stephen Hemsley. 4.3784
Longus. 2.378
Longworth, Philip, 1933-. 3.3095
Longyear, Rey M. (Rey Morgan), 1930-. 1.3664
Lönnrot, Elias, 1802-1884. 2.1752
Lönnroth, Lars. 2.13986
Lonsdale, Richard E. 4.2071
Lonsdale, Roger H. 2.6164
Lonsdale, Roger H. ed. 2.7397
Loo, Sonny G., joint author. 5.5567
Loome, Thomas Michael, 1935-. 1.3166
Loomis, Charles Price, 1905-. 4.6368
Loomis, Laura Alandis (Hibbard) 1883-1960.
  2.2633, 2.5619
Loomis, Louise Ropes, 1874-1958. 1.3119
Loomis, Richard Morgan, 1926-. 2.836
Loomis, Roger Sherman, 1887-1966. 2.2418,
  2.2633-2.2634, 2.2638, 2.6077
Loomis, Stanley. 3.2055
Looney, John G., 1941-. 3.6769
Loos, Anita, 1894-1981. 2.12036
Lopata, Helena Znaniecka, 1925-. 3.6587,
  4.5791, 4.5793
Lopate, Carol. 5.4541
Lopez, Claude Anne. 3.6992
Lopez, Donald S., 1923-. 5.6675
Lopez, Enrique Hank. 2.12320
Lopez, Felix M. 4.4373
López-Rey, José. 1.6492
Lopez, Robert Sabatino, 1910-. 3.93, 3.2848,
  4.4095
LoPiccolo, Joseph. 5.4948
LoPiccolo, Leslie. 5.4948
Lopreato, Joseph. 3.6558
Lora, Ronald. 4.7310
Loran, Erle, 1905-. 1.6073
L'Orange, Hans Peter, 1903-. 1.4728, 1.5160,
  1.5191
Lord, Albert Bates. 4.762
Lord, Carnes. 2.4981, 4.7340
Lord, Clifford Lee, 1912-. 4.151
Lord, Frederic, M., 1912-. 5.359
Lord, George de Forest, 1919-. 2.509, 2.6122

Lord, George deForest, 1919- ed. 2.6121
Lord, Mary. 2.10161
Lord, Robert Howard, 1885-1954. 3.3281
Lord, Walter, 1917-. 3.1014
Lorde, Audre. 2.13140-2.13141
Lorentz, H. A. (Hendrik Antoon), 1853-1928.
  5.1914, 5.2146, 5.2395
Lorentzatos, Zēsimos. 2.567
Lorenz, Clarissa M. 2.11304
Lorenz, Konrad, 1903-. 5.99, 5.4062
Lorenzen, David N. 1.1724
Lorenzine, Amleto. 1.5614
Lorimer, Douglas A. 3.1294
Lorimer, Emily (Overend) tr. 3.2729
Lorimer, Frank, 1894-. 4.1638, 4.1700
Lorimer, James, 1942-. 4.2833
Lorin, Harold. 5.1188
Lorr, Maurice, 1911-. 4.1244
Lorrain, Claude, 1600-1682. 1.4974
Lorsch, Jay William. joint author. 4.2666
Lorsch, Jay William. 4.2667
Lortie, Dan Clement, 1926-. 4.10530
Lorwin, Lewis Levitzki, 1883-1970. 4.3326,
  4.3548
Lorwin, Val R. (Val Rogin), 1907-. 3.429,
  4.3269
Los Alamos National Laboratory. 5.6106
Los Alamos Scientific Laboratory. 5.6106
Los Angeles County Museum. 1.4831, 1.6125
Los Angeles County Museum of Art. 1.4757,
  1.4842, 1.4899, 1.4910, 1.5069, 1.5186,
  1.5715, 1.5747, 1.5947, 1.5952, 1.6362,
  1.6391, 1.6671, 3.5918, 4.835
Loss, Richard. 4.7798-4.7799
Losskiĭ, N. O. (Nikolaĭ Onufrievich), 1870-1965.
  1.1104
Lot, Ferdinand, 1866-1952. 3.2808
Lotchin, Roger W. 3.8625, 4.6219
Loti, Pierre, 1850-1923. 2.4327-2.4330
Lotka, Alfred J. (Alfred James), 1880-1949.
  5.3299
Lotman, L. M. (Lidiia Mikhaĭlovna), 1917-.
  2.1424
Lott, Eric J. 1.200
Lotte, Fernand. 2.4113
Lottman, Herbert R. 2.4458, 3.2189, 3.2233
Lotz, Wolfgang, 1912-. 1.5431
Lotze, Dieter P. 2.13716
Loubère, J. A. E. 2.4753
Loubère, Leo A. 4.7047
Loucks, James F. 2.7473
Louder, Dean R., 1943-. 4.146
Loudon, J. C. (John Claudius), 1783-1843.
  1.6552
Loudon, Joseph Buist. 4.466
Loudon, T. V. 5.2992
Lougee, Carolyn C., 1942-. 4.6118
Lough, John. 1.16, 1.813, 2.3365, 2.3836,
  3.2018, 3.2048, 4.7287
Loughman, Michael, 1938-. 4.897
Louis-Frédéric, 1923-. 3.4891
Louis, Morris, 1912-1962. 1.5952
Louis, Paul, 1872-1948. 4.3096
Louis, René. ed. 2.3945
Louis, William Roger. 3.5094, 3.5114, 3.5119,
  3.5303, 3.5578, 4.8904
Louisiana Historical Association. 3.8317
Loukopoulou, Louiza D. 3.2623
Lounsbury, John H. joint author. 4.10508
Lounsbury, John H. 4.10507
Lounsbury, Thomas Raynesford, 1838-1915.
  2.1027
Lovaas, O. Ivar (Ole Ivar), 1927-. 5.5111
Lovberg, Ralph H. (Ralph Harvey) 5.2448
Love, Harold, 1937-. 2.5651, 2.6948
Love, J. D. (John D.) 5.5960
Love, James, 1948-. 4.2300
Love, Jean O., 1920-. 2.9600-2.9601
Lovecraft, H. P. (Howard Phillips), 1890-1937.
  2.3460
Lovecraft, Howard Phillips. 2.12037
Loveday, Simon, 1949-. 2.9692
Lovejoy, Arthur O. (Arthur Oncken),
  1873-1962. 1.136, 1.480, 1.529, 1.608, 3.24
Lovejoy, David S. (David Sherman), 1919-.
  1.2403, 3.6872
Lovejoy, Paul E. 4.6446
Lovelace, Earl, 1935-. 2.10000-2.10002

Lovelace, Richard, 1618-1658. 2.7097
Lovell, Bernard, Sir, 1913-. 5.1784, 5.6708
Lovell, Ernest James, 1918- ed. 2.7534
Lovell, John P., 1932-. 5.7240
Lovell, Reginald Ivan. 3.5468
Lovelock, Julian. joint author. 2.5749
Loveman, Brian. 3.9258, 4.2840
Lovenduski, Joni. 4.5959
Lover, Stanley F. 4.1019
Lovett, Clara Maria, 1939-. 3.2861, 3.2865,
   3.2870, 4.5963
Lovett, Gabriel H. 3.3450
Lovett, Harrington Verney, Sir, 1864-1945.
   3.4231
Lovett, Robert Woodberry. 5.8409
Lovoll, Odd Sverre. 3.6593
Lovrinic, Jean H. 5.4369
Low, Alfred D. 3.1902, 3.3969
Low, D. A. (Donald Anthony), 1927-. 3.4264,
   4.8919
Low, Donald A. 2.7509
Low, Julian William, 1904-. 5.2990
Low, Rachael. 2.2896-2.2898
Low, Victor. 4.10884
Low, W. Augustus. 3.6614
Lowance, Mason I., 1938-. 2.10439
Lowbury, Edward Joseph Lister. 2.6442
Lowe, Benjamin. 4.945
Lowe, C. J. (Cedric James), 1930-1975. 3.2879
Lowe, John P. 5.2828
Lowe, Marian. 4.5949
Lowe-McConnell, R. H. 5.3545, 5.3910
Lowe, Peter. 3.4411
Lowe-Porter, H. T. (Helen Tracy), 1876-1963.
   2.13821, 2.13827-2.13828, 2.13830-2.13831
Lowe, Robert, 1947-. 4.10738
Lowe, Robert William, 1853-1902. 2.7805
Lowe, Victor, 1907-. 1.780-1.781
Lowell, Amy, 1874-1925. 2.10500, 2.12038
Lowell, C. Stanley. 1.2391
Lowell Institute lectures, 1925. 5.854
Lowell, James Russell, 1819-1891. 2.11146
Lowell, Robert, 1917-1977. 2.4049,
   2.12041-2.12048
Lowenfeld, Berthold. 4.6600
Lowenfeld, Viktor. 1.4652
Lowenheim, Frederick Adolph, 1909-. 5.7067
Lowens, Irving, 1916-. 1.3689
Lowenstein, Tom. tr. 2.2314
Lowenthal, Abraham F. 3.9006, 3.9309
Lowenthal, Anne W. 1.5028
Lowenthal, David. comp. 4.5260
Lowenthal, David. joint comp. 4.6429
Lowenthal, David. 3.9090
Lowenthal, Leo. 2.2381
Lowenthal, Richard, 1908-. 4.7134
Lower, A. R. M., ed. 4.2122
Lower, Arthur Reginald Marsden, 1889-.
   3.8664, 4.3842
Lower, J. Arthur, 1907-. 3.4397
Lowery, Shearon. 4.5007
Lowes, John Livingston. 2.6342, 2.7601
Lowi, Theodore J. 4.5033
Lowie, Robert Harry, 1883-1957. 3.5870, 4.412,
   4.548, 4.592
Lowinsky, Edward E. (Edward Elias),
   1908-1985. 1.3853
Löwith, Karl, 1897-1973. 1.441, 3.512
Lowitt, Richard, 1922-. 3.7676, 4.1959, 4.2028
Lowman, Charles E., 1918-. 5.6562
Lowndes, Marie Adelaide Belloc, 1868-1947.
   2.9053
Lowrance, William W., 1943-. 5.961
Lowrie, Donald Alexander. 1.1112, 1.3106
Lowrie, Walter, 1868-1959. 1.1120,
   1.2217-1.2218, 1.2228, 1.3288
Lowry, Howard Foster, 1901-1967. joint author.
   2.7363
Lowry, Malcolm, 1909-1957. 2.9054-2.9058
Lowry, Margerie Bonner. ed. 2.9055
Lowry, Thomas H. 5.2856
Lowry, William P., 1927-. 5.3571
Loy, John W. 4.956, 4.960
Loyer, François. 1.5595
Loyn, H. R. (Henry Royston) 3.1324, 3.1984,
   4.2255, 4.8386
Lozoya, Jorge Alberto. 4.4157
Lu, Hsün, 1881-1936. 2.2171, 2.2239-2.2240

Lu, K'uan Yü, 1898- tr. 1.2135
Lü, Tsu-ch'ien, 1137-1181. 1.150
Lu, Yung-Chen, 1938-. 5.1617
Luard, Evan, 1926-. 4.2480, 4.9221, 4.9269
Lubac, Henri de, 1896-. 1.3199
Lubalin, Herb, 1918-. 1.5838
Lubbock, Percy, 1879-. 2.3428, 2.11100
Lubeck, Steven G., joint author. 4.6860
Lubell, Samuel. 3.7533, 3.7828, 3.7843
Lubin, George. 5.5793
Lubin, Maurice Alcibiade, 1917-. 2.2693
Luborsky, Lester, 1920-. 5.4905
Lubove, Roy. 3.8094, 4.3466, 4.3492, 4.6321,
   4.6327, 4.6518
Lubrano, Linda L. 5.966
Lubs, Herbert Augustus, 1929-. 5.4750
Luby, Barry J. 2.5322
Lucan, 39-65. 2.675
Lucas, Angela M. 4.5864
Lucas, Catherine. joint author. 4.843-4.844
Lucas, Colin. 3.2118
Lucas, E. V. (Edward Verrall), 1868-1938.
   2.7899, 2.7902, 2.7907
Lucas, F. L. (Frank Laurence), 1894-1967.
   2.470, 2.2539, 2.2807, 2.2816, 2.6878
Lucas, G. B. 5.5397
Lucas, Henry C. 5.5610
Lucas, Henry Stephen, 1889-1961. 3.6543
Lucas, James Sidney. 3.1002
Lucas, John, 1937-. 2.8459
Lucas, John Alexander. 5.5396
Lucas, L. T. 5.5397
Lucas, Noah. 3.3929
Lucas, Robert E. 4.1714
Lucas, St. John Welles Lucas, 1879-. 2.3922,
   2.4888
Lucas, William F., 1933-. 5.1109
Luce, John Victor, 1920-. 1.6742, 2.498
Luce, R. Duncan (Robert Duncan) ed.
   5.50-5.51
Luce, R. Duncan (Robert Duncan) 5.52-5.53
Luce, T. James (Torrey James), 1932-. 3.2748
Luchsinger, Arlene E. 5.3652
Luchsinger, Arlene E. joint author. 5.3294
Lucian, of Samosata. 2.380
Luciano, Dorothy S. 5.4198
Lucid, Robert Francis, ed. 3.7149
Lucie-Smith, Edward. 1.6509, 1.6555, 3.2003,
   5.7040
Lucius Root Eastman Arbitration Library, New
   York. 4.9853
Luck, Georg, 1926-. 2.640
Luck, James Murray, ed. 5.4389
Luckenbill, Daniel David, 1881-1927. 3.3763
Luckiesh, Matthew, 1883-. 5.4388
Luckmann, Thomas. joint author. 1.1289
Luckmann, William Henry, 1926-. 5.5406
Lucow, Ben. 2.6875
Lucretius Carus, Titus. 2.676, 2.738-2.739
Lüdemann, Gerd. 1.2668
Ludendorff, Erich, 1865-1937. 3.793
Ludewig, Walter. 2.1187
Ludlam, F. H. 5.2534
Ludlum, David McWilliams, 1910-.
   5.2498-5.2499, 5.2548
Ludmerer, Kenneth M. 5.4604
Ludwig, Allan I. 1.5789
Ludwig, Coy, 1939-. 1.5833
Ludwig, Ed, 1920- comp. 2.10683
Ludwig, Richard M., joint author. 5.7788
Ludz, Peter Christian, 1931-. 4.8614
Luebke, Frederick C., 1927-. 2.10277, 3.8493
Luecking, D. H. (Daniel H.) 5.1487
Luenberger, David G., 1937-. 5.1544, 5.5581
Luening, Otto, 1900-. 1.3913
Luft, David S. 2.13846
Lugard, Frederick John Dealtry, Baron,
   1858-1945. 3.5116
Luh, Bor Shiun, 1916-. 5.5326
Luhr, William. 2.2959
Luhrs, Kathleen, 1941-. 1.5887
Lui, C. W. K., 1955-. 5.5695
Luijpen, W. (Wilhelmus), 1922-. 1.1554
Lukács, György, 1885-1971. 2.2403, 2.3467,
   7044
Lukacs, John, 1924-. 3.3528, 3.6133
Lukacs, John A. 3.1196
Lukas, J. Anthony, 1933-. 3.7923, 3.7997

Lukashevich, Stephen. 1.1116
Łukasiewicz, Jan. 1.317
Łukasiewicz, Stanisław, doc. dr. hab. inż.
   5.5870
Luke, Helen M., 1904-. 4.5931
Luke, Timothy W. joint author. 3.3742
Lukehart, Charles M., 1946-. 5.2782
Luker, Kristin. 4.5690, 4.5702
Luker, Nicholas J. L. 2.1325
Lukes, Steven. 4.4754, 4.9369, 5.493
Lullies, Reinhard, 1907-. 1.5624
Lumb, R. D. 4.8832
Lumbreras, Luis Guillermo. 3.9286
Lumby, Esmond Walter Rawson. ed. 3.4289
Lumiansky, R. M. (Robert Mayer), 1913- ed.
   2.6411
Lumley, John L. (John Leask), 1930- joint
   author. 5.1666
Lumpkin, Grace. 2.12056
Lumumba, Patrice, 1925-1961. 3.5427, 3.5430
Luna, Juan de, b. ca. 1585. 2.5193
Lund, David H. 5.661
Lund, Roger D., 1949-. 5.7943
Lundahl, Mats, 1946-. 4.2154
Lundahl, Vera. 4.1086
Lundberg, Erik, 1907-. 4.1476, 4.1789
Lundberg, George Andrew, 1895-1966. 4.4821
Lundberg, Margaret J. 5.525
Lunden, Walter Albin, 1899- joint author.
   4.4977
Lundgren, Helge, 1914-. 5.5972
Lundin, Robert W. (Robert William), 1920-.
   1.4385
Lundquist, James. 2.12429
Lundsteen, Sara W. 4.10470
Lundwall, Sam J., 1941-. 2.3489
Lunn, Arnold Henry Moore, Sir, 1888-1974.
   1.5481, 3.3508
Lunn, Eugene. 1.474
Lunt, Paul Sanborn, jt. author. 4.6387-4.6388
Lupăih, Puggŭwon. 4.185
Lupton, Tom. comp. 4.3140
Luria, Maxwell, 1932- comp. 2.6112
Luria, S. E. (Salvador Edward), 1912-. 5.3300,
   5.4433
Lurie, Adolph G. 4.4602
Lurié, David. 5.2396
Lurie, Harry Lawrence, 1892-1973, ed. 4.6473
Lurie, Nancy Oestreich. ed. 3.5705
Lurier, Harold E., tr. 3.2672
Luriia, A. R. (Aleksandr Romanovich), 1902-.
   5.100, 5.207, 5.273, 5.339, 5.569, 5.4311,
   5.4336, 5.4344
Luschei, Martin. 2.13246
Luscomb, Florence, 1887-. 4.5993
Luscombe, David Edward, ed. 1.378
Lustgarten, Edgar, 1907-1978. 2.9065
Lustick, Ian, 1949-. 3.3841
Lustig, Arnošt. 2.1675-2.1677
Lütge, Friedrich Karl, 1901-. 4.2336
Luther, Martin, 1483-1546. 1.1496-1.1497,
   1.2317, 1.2346-1.2348, 1.2709, 1.2937,
   4.10161
Lüthi, Max, 1909-. 2.3465, 4.787
Luthin, Reinhard Henry, 1905-. 3.7618
Luthuli, Albert John, 1898-. 3.5472
Lüthy, Hans, joint author. 1.6302
Lutterman, Kenneth G. 4.5182
Luttgens, Kathryn, 1926-. 5.4277
Luttwak, Edward. 5.7183, 5.7213, 5.7344
Lutyens, Mary, 1908- ed. 2.8036
Lutz, Alma. 4.8087, 4.10158
Lutz, Donald S. 4.7813
Lutz, E. Russell, 1902-1970, joint author.
   4.9896
Lutz, Frank Eugene, 1879-1943. 5.3805
Lutz, Friedrich A. (Friedrich August), 1901-.
   4.1551
Lutz, Paul E. 5.3834
Lutz, Ralph Haswell, 1886-1968. 3.2341, 3.2417
Lutz, Vera C. 4.2356
Lutz, Wulf-Rüdiger. 4.8612
Luvaas, Jay. ed. and tr. 5.7207
Luxemburg, Rosa, 1871-1919. 3.3186, 4.7059
Luxemburg, W. A. J., 1929-. 5.1434, 5.1477
Luxenberg, Stan. 4.4321
Luxon, James T. 5.6541
Luxton, Meg. 4.6080

Luy, Jack A., joint author. 5.5796
Luyben, William L. 5.6833
Luža, Radomír. 3.1903
Luža, Radomír. ed. 3.1917
Luzi, Mario. 2.5036
Luzzatto, Gino, 1878-1964. 4.2352
Lwoff, André, 1902- ed. 5.3838
Lyall, Gavin. 3.1049
Lyas, Colin, comp. 1.542
Lybyer, Albert Howe, 1876-. 3.3583
Lyday, Leon F., 1939-. 2.5309
Lydolph, Paul E. 3.3015
Lydon, James F. 3.1823
Lydon, Mary. 2.4437
Lyell, Charles, Sir, 1797-1875. 3.6035
Lyell, Ruth Granetz. 2.3721
Lyell, William A. 2.2242
Lykes, Ira B. 5.5385
Lykken, David Thoreson. 4.6811
Lyle, John Tillman. 4.2810
Lyly, John, 1554?-1606. 2.6219, 2.6490-2.6491
Lyman, Princeton N., joint author. 4.2559
Lyman, Stanford M. 1.2397, 3.6539
Lyman, Warren J. 5.2744
Lynch, Charles T. 5.5770
Lynch, David, 1902-. 4.1966
Lynch, Hollis Ralph. comp. 3.6620
Lynch, Hollis Ralph. 3.5415
Lynch, John, 1927-. 3.3439, 3.9001, 3.9246, 4.8324
Lynch, Katherine A. 4.1580
Lynch, Kathleen Martha. 2.5895
Lynch, Kevin, 1918-. 1.5598, 3.63, 4.6312
Lynch, Lawrence M., 1927-. 4.6799
Lynch, Lawrence W. 2.4100
Lynch, Richard Chigley, 1932-. 1.3451
Lynd, Helen Merrell, 1896-. 4.5138, 4.5303
Lynd, Robert Staughton, 1892-. 4.5137-4.5138
Lynd, Staughton. 3.6980
Lynd, Staughton. ed. 4.5038
Lyne, R. O. A. M. 2.631
Lynen, John F. 2.10350
Lynes, Russell, 1910-. 3.6134
Lynn, Catherine. 1.6597
Lynn, Edward S. 4.4730
Lynn, John A. (John Albert), 1943-. 5.7314
Lynn, Kenneth Schuyler. 2.11091
Lynn, Paul A. 5.6375
Lynton, Norbert. 1.4816
Lyon, Bryce Dale, 1920-. 4.8388
Lyon, Christopher, 1949-. 2.3032
Lyon, Eugene, 1929-. 3.8273
Lyon, James K. 2.13711
Lyon, Jeff. 5.5089
Lyon, Leverett Samuel, 1885-. 4.1967
Lyon, Peter, 1915-. 2.3620
Lyon, Peyton V., 1921-. 3.8775, 3.8780
Lyons, Albert S. 5.4505
Lyons, Bridget Gellert. 2.5631
Lyons, David, 1935-. 1.1415
Lyons, Eugene, 1898-. 3.730
Lyons, F. S. L. (Francis Steward Leland), 1923-. 3.1843
Lyons, F. S. L. (Francis Stewart Lelend), 1923-. 3.1851
Lyons, Francis Stewart Leland, 1923-. 3.1855, 4.8563
Lyons, Gene Martin. 5.7275
Lyons, Islay, 1922-. 1.5051
Lyons, John, 1932-. 2.110
Lyons, John Ormsby, 1927-. 2.10590
Lyons, Louis Martin, 1897-. 2.3657
Lyons, Martyn. 3.2113
Lyons, Nathan. 5.6930
Lyons, Nathan. ed. 2.11262
Lyons, Phyllis I., 1942-. 2.2095
Lyse, Inge, 1898-. 5.6089
Lystad, Robert A., ed. 3.5062
Lythe, S. G. E. 4.2299
Lytle, Andrew Nelson, 1902-. 2.12057-2.12059
Lytle, Clifford M. 3.5832
Lytle, Guy Fitch, 1944-. 3.161
Lytle, Mark H. 3.6209
Lyttelton, Adrian, 1937-. 3.2887
Lyttelton, Humphrey, 1921-. 1.4269
Lytton, Edward Bulwer Lytton, Baron, 1803-1873. 2.7915-2.7917, 4.7178

Lytton, Edward George Earl Lytton Bulwer-Lytton: 1st baron, 1803-1873. 2.7914
Lyverse, Jenny M. 5.5361

M. Madeleva (Mary Madeleva), Sister, 1887-1964. 2.6365
Ma, Shang-keng, 1940-1983. 5.2167
Ma, Wendy Yu. 5.8031
Ma, Y. W. (Yau-Woon), 1940-. 2.2207
Maaløe, Ole. 5.4455
Maarleveld, A., joint author. 5.6841
Maas, Henry S. 4.5818
Maas, Paul, 1880-. 2.244
Maass, Arthur. ed. 4.8833
Maass, John, 1918-. 1.5294
Mabbett, Ian W. 4.8693
Mabbott, Thomas Ollive, 1898-1968. 2.11196
Mabogunje, Akin L. 4.6281
Mabro, Robert. 4.2590-4.2591
Mabry, Donald J., 1941-. 4.8334
Mac Lane, Saunders, 1909-. 5.1272, 5.1289
Mac Philibín, Liam. 2.405
MacAfee, Norman. 2.5048
MacAllister, Archibald T. 2.4926
Macalpine, Ida. joint ed. 5.4803
Macan, T. T. (Thomas Townley) 5.3547, 5.3553
MacAndrew, Elizabeth, 1924-. 2.3461
MacArdle, Donald W. ed. 1.3804
MacArthur, Robert H. 5.3240, 5.3243, 5.4073
Macartney, C. A. (Carlile Aylmer), 1895-1978. 3.1888, 3.1937, 3.3529
Macartney, Carlile Aylmer, 1895-. 3.1879, 3.1943
Macartney, George Macartney, Earl, 1737-1806. 3.4619
Macaulay, James. 1.5369
Macaulay, Rose, Dame. 2.9066-2.9067
Macaulay, Thomas Babington Macaulay, Baron, 1800-1859. 2.7044, 2.7918-2.7921, 3.1211, 3.1495
Macauley, Robie. 2.3429
MacAvoy, Paul W. joint author. 4.3714
MacAvoy, Paul W. 4.3790-4.3791, 4.3987, 4.4040
MacBean, Alasdair I. 4.4149
MacBeth, George. 2.9740
MacCaffrey, Isabel Gamble. 2.6534, 2.7133
MacCaffrey, Wallace T. 3.1422-3.1423
MacCaig, Norman, 1910-. 2.9068, 2.9846
MacCallum, Hugh Reid, ed. 2.7160
MacCallum, Mungo William, Sir, 1854-1942. 2.6770
MacCann, Richard Dyer. 5.8141
MacCarthy, Desmond, 1878-1952. 2.8084, 2.9069
Macchi, Vladimiro. 2.858
MacClintock, Carol, 1910-. 1.3430, 1.4124
Maccoby, Eleanor E., 1917-. 5.486-5.487
Maccoby, Michael, 1933-. 4.2687
Maccoby, Simon. 3.1519
MacCormack, Sabine. 3.2741
MacCracken, John Henry, 1875-1948, ed. 4.10056
MacCurdy, Raymond R. 2.5204
MacCurtain, Margaret. ed. 3.1817
MacCurtain, Margaret. 3.1829, 4.6113
MacDermott, Charles P., 1920-. 5.5803
Macdermott, Mercia. 3.3541
MacDiarmid, Hugh, 1892-. 2.8780-2.8785, 2.9834
MacDonagh, Oliver. 3.1844-3.1845, 4.8406
Macdonald, A. G. (Alister Gordon) 5.4203
Macdonald, Alexander W. 1.5052
Macdonald, C. 2.659
MacDonald, Charles Brown, 1922-. 3.955
MacDonald, David Keith Chalmers, 1920-. 5.1943
Macdonald, David W. (David Whyte) 5.3972
MacDonald, Dick, 1923-. 2.3679
Macdonald, Duncan Black, 1863-1943. 1.2055
Macdonald, Dwight. 2.13143, 3.3119, 3.6135
Macdonald, Dwight. ed. 2.3800
Macdonald, George, 1824-1905. 2.7922-2.7923
Macdonald, Gordon Andrew, 1911-. 5.3111
Macdonald, I. G. (Ian Grant) joint author. 5.1358
MacDonald, J. Fred. 2.2846

MacDonald, John D. (John Dann), 1916-1986. 2.13144
Macdonald, John N. joint author. 5.2872
Macdonald, Keith B. 4.339
Macdonald, Margaret. 1.1065
MacDonald, Margaret F. 1.5984
MacDonald, Margaret Read. 4.764
MacDonald, Michael, 1945-. 5.4804
Macdonald, Michael C. D. 4.6218
MacDonald, Norman. 4.2832
Macdonald, R. (Robert) 5.3066
MacDonald, Ross, 1915-. 2.12158
MacDonald Ross, G. (George) 1.869
MacDonald, Scott, 1942-. 2.11458
Macdonald, Stuart. 5.5637
MacDonald, William Lloyd. 1.5226, 3.2520
Macdonell, Archibald Gordon, 1895-1941. 2.9070
Macdonell, Arthur Anthony, 1854-1930. 2.1850, 2.1922-2.1923
Macdougall, Allan Ross, 1893-. 2.12161
MacDougall, Curtis Daniel, 1903-. 2.3566
MacDougall, E. Bruce (Edward Bruce), 1939-. 4.201
MacDougall, Hugh A. 3.1301
MacDowell, Betty. joint author. 1.6514
MacDowell, Douglas M. (Douglas Maurice) 4.9397
MacDowell, Marsha. joint author. 1.6514
Macedo, Helder. 2.5451
MacEwan, Arthur. 4.2966
Macey, Samuel L. 2.9929
Macfadyen, A. (Amyan) 5.3771, 5.4074
MacFadyen, J. Tevere. 4.2907
Macfarlane, Alan. 1.3312, 4.5620
Macfarlane, L. J. (Leslie John), 1924-. 4.5339, 4.7640
MacFarquhar, Roderick. 3.4803, 3.4808
MacFarquhar, Roderick. comp. 3.6429
MacGill, Caroline Elizabeth. 4.3882
MacGimsey, Robert. 1.3440
MacGinitie, George Eber, 1889-. 5.3821
MacGinitie, Nettie, joint author. 5.3821
Macgowan, Kenneth, 1888-1963. 2.2880, 2.3279
Macgregor, Frances M. Cooke, 1906-. 4.5742
MacGregor, Geddes. 1.2513
MacGregor, Heather Elise. 1.1117
MacGregor, James Grierson, 1934-. 5.6089
MacGregor, Morris J., 1931-. 3.6723, 5.7375-5.7376
Mach, Ernst, 1838-1916. 5.4361
Machado, Antonio, 1875-1939. 2.5271-2.5274
Machado de Assis, 1839-1908. 2.5472-2.5476
MacHale, Carlos F. 2.904
Machan, Tibor R. comp. 4.7641
Machan, Tibor R. 4.7668, 4.9523
Machen, Arthur, 1863-1947. 2.9071
Macherey, Pierre. 2.2364
Machiavelli, Niccolò, 1469-1527. 2.4971, 3.2920, 4.7388-4.7396, 5.7202
Machin, G. I. T. 1.2446
Machine Intelligence Workshop. 5.1012
Machlis, Joseph, 1906-. 1.3675, 1.4430
Machlup, Fritz, 1902-. 1.80, 4.1492, 5.7581
Machovec, Milan. 1.2864
Machwe, Prabhakar Balvant, 1917- tr. 2.1912
Macinko, George. 4.2829, 5.8165
MacIntosh, Anita R. joint author. 4.5596
MacIntyre, Alasdair C. 1.1453
MacIntyre, Alasdair C. comp. 1.948
MacIntyre, Alasdair C. 1.2769
MacIntyre, Carlyle Ferren, 1890-1967. 2.4156, 2.4316
MacIver, Robert M. (Robert Morrison), 1882-1970. 4.7461, 4.10579
Mack, Dietrich. joint author. 1.4036
Mack, Douglas S. ed. 2.7814
Mack, Heinz. 1.4837
Mack, John E., 1929-. 3.811
Mack, Mary Peter, 1927-. 1.725
Mack, Maynard, 1909-. 2.3704, 2.7186, 2.7189, 2.7198-2.7199
Mack Smith, Denis, 1920-. 3.2835, 3.2860, 3.2862, 3.2866, 3.2871, 3.2877, 3.2888, 3.2903, 3.2943
Mackail, J. W. (John William), 1859-1945. 2.655, 2.7970
Mackay, Agnes Ethel. 2.4769

MacKay, Angus, 1939-. 3.3426
MacKay, Robert Alexander, 1894- ed. 4.2125
Mackay, Ruddock F. 3.1286
MacKaye, Percy, 1875-1956. 2.6315
Macken, Bob. 1.4279
MacKendrick, Louis King, 1941-. 2.9955
MacKendrick, Paul Lachlan, 1914-. 3.2540
Mackenna, Stephen, 1872-1934. tr. 1.340-1.341
Mackenzie, Alexander, Sir, 1763-1820. 3.8844
Mackenzie, Charles, F.R.S. 3.9117
Mackenzie, Compton, Sir, 1883-1972. 2.9072
Mackenzie, Henry, 1745-1831. 2.7099
Mackenzie, Hettie Millicent (Hughes)
  1863-1942. 4.10193
MacKenzie, Jeanne. 4.7034
MacKenzie, Jeanne. joint author. 2.8255, 4.6925
Mackenzie, Mary Margaret. 1.274
MacKenzie, N. H., ed. 2.7825
MacKenzie, Norman H. 2.7834
MacKenzie, Norman Ian. 2.8255, 3.2138,
  4.6925, 4.7034
Mackenzie, Thomas. illus. 2.9382
MacKenzie, W. C. (William Cook), 1862-1952.
  3.1810
MacKenzie, W. S. 5.3028, 5.3050
Mackerness, Eric David. 1.3717
Mackerras, Colin. 2.3388-2.3389, 2.3391, 3.4655
Mackesy, Piers. 3.1579, 3.2133, 3.6898
MacKethan, Lucinda Hardwick. 2.10454,
  2.11137
Mackey, Benedict, 1846-1906, tr. 1.3217
Mackey, George Whitelaw, 1916-. 5.1302,
  5.1488, 5.2163
Mackey, Louis. 1.1123
Mackey, Wade C. 5.5661
Mackie, J. A. C. 3.4560, 3.4566
Mackie, J. L. (John Leslie) 1.676, 1.711, 1.1234,
  1.1407
Mackie, John Duncan, 1887-   . 3.1396
Mackin, Ronald. 2.1105
MacKinnon, Catharine A. 4.9567
Mackinnon, Doris Livingston. tr. 1.3802
MacKinnon, Frank. 4.8320
Mackintosh, Charles Rennie, 1868-1928. 1.5393
Mackintosh, H. R. (Hugh Ross), 1870-1936.
  1.2757
Mackintosh, N. J. (Nicholas John), 1935-.
  5.4102
Mackintosh, William Archibald, 1895-. 3.8837
Macklin, Ruth, 1938-. 4.9507
Macksey, Richard, 1931-. 2.12822
Mackworth, Cecily. 2.4367
MacLachlan, Colin M. 3.8928
MacLean, Douglas, 1947-. 5.7219
Maclean, Norman, 1932-. 5.3617
Maclehose, Louisa S. 1.5100
MacLeish, Archibald, 1892-. 2.12087-2.12091,
  4.8065
MacLennan, Beryce W. 5.4834
Macleod, David I. 4.6179
Macleod, M. D. 2.380
MacLeod, Malcolm, 1901-. 2.7073
MacLeod, Murdo J. 4.2150
MacLeod, Robert Brodie, 1907-1972. 5.73
MacLure, Millar, ed. 2.6609
Maclure, Stuart. 4.10112
Macmahon, Arthur Whittier, 1890-. 4.7879
MacMillan, Donald L. 4.6610
Macmillan, Duncan. 1.6296
MacMillan, Ernest, 1893- ed. 1.3701
MacMillan, Harold, 1894-. 3.1673
MacMillan, William Duncan, 1871-1948. 5.1652
Macmillan, William M. (William Miller),
  1885-1974. 3.5453
MacMullen, Ramsay, 1928-. 3.2800
Macnab, Roy Martin, 1923- ed. 2.10051
Macnaughton, William R., 1939-. 2.10965,
  2.13380
MacNeice, Louis, 1907-1963. 2.2746, 2.8353,
  2.8397, 2.9074-2.9076
MacNeil, Neil, 1923-. 3.7857, 4.8060
MacNiocaill, G. 3.1821
MacNutt, Francis Augustus, 1863-1927. 3.8921
MacNutt, W. S. 3.8806
MacNutt, William Stewart, 1908-. 3.8799
Macomber, James D., 1939-. 5.2317
Macomber, William B. 1.1001
Maconie, Robin. 1.3995

Macpherson, C. B. (Crawford Brough), 1911-
  4.7575-4.7576
MacPherson, J. C. (James C.), 1950-. 4.8291
Macpherson, James, 1942-. 2.7100, 4.10153
Macquarrie, John. 1.456, 1.1002, 1.2779
Macqueen, J. G. (James G.) 3.3761
MacQueen, James, 1778-1870. 3.5172
MacQueen, John. ed. 2.9842
MacRae, Duncan. 4.8055, 4.8585
Macrae, Norman, 1923-. 3.7901
Macray, William Dunn, 1826-1916. ed. 3.1472
Macready, William Charles,1793-1873. 2.7917
Macridis, Roy C. 4.7106
MacShane, Denis. 3.2212
MacShane, Frank. comp. 2.8636
MacShane, Frank. 2.11481
Macurdy, Grace Harriet, d. 1946. 3.2635
MacWilliams, Florence Jessie, 1917-. 5.1376
Macy, John W., 1917-. 4.7984
Madariaga, Constance Helen Margaret
  Archibald de, tr. 2.5181
Madariaga, Salvador de, 1886-. 2.5181, 3.3399,
  3.5973, 3.8986-3.8987
Madaule, Jacques, 1895-. 2.4474
Maday, Bela C. 3.4552
Maddala, G. S. 4.1396
Madden, A. F. 4.8920, 4.9424
Madden, David, 1933-. 2.10419, 2.10636,
  2.12220
Madden, Edward H. 1.656-1.657, 5.62, 5.911
Madden, John Thomas, 1882-1948. 4.4448
Madden, William Anthony, 1923- joint author.
  2.5937
Maddex, Jack P., 1941-. 3.8211
Maddi, Salvatore R. 5.526-5.527
Maddison, Angus. 4.1754
Maddow, Ben, 1909-. 5.6974
Maddox, Margaret. joint author. 3.2068
Madeja, Stanley S. 1.6694
Mades, Leonard. ed. 2.5148
Madhubuti, Haki R. 3.6644
Madigan, Michael T., 1949-. 5.4435
Madison, Charles Allan. 2.1792, 3.6296, 5.7588
Madison, Gary Brent. 1.838
Madison, James, 1751-1836. 3.6974-3.6975,
  4.7821-4.7822
Madison, James H. 3.8395-3.8396
Madsen, Charles H., 1933- joint comp. 1.4413
Madsen, Clifford K. comp. 1.4413
Madsen, Richard, 1941-. 1.1425, 4.5457
Maeder, Edward. 4.835
Maes-Jelinek, Hena. 2.10033
Maestro, Marcello T., 1907-. 4.6842
Maeterlinck, Maurice, 1862-1949. 2.4605,
  5.3887
Maffei, Anthony C. 4.10295
Magalaner, Marvin, 1920-. 2.6040,
  2.8913-2.8916, 2.9087
Magat, Richard. joint author. 4.10802
Magee, Bryan. 1.457, 1.963
Magee, Doug, 1947-. 4.6852
Magee, James J. 4.9803
Mager, Robert Frank, 1923-. 4.10296, 4.10309
Maghroori, Ray. 3.1184
Magie, William Francis, 1858-1943. 5.1886
Magill, Frank Northen. 2.2353-2.2355, 2.2394,
  2.2548, 2.2866, 2.2872, 2.2978, 2.5838, 5.8270
Magleby, David B. 4.9724
Magliocca, Larry A. 4.10928
Maglischo, Ernest W. 4.990
Magnanti, Thomas L., joint author. 5.1548
Magnarella, Paul J. 3.3691
Magner, Thomas F. 2.1206
Magnus, Philip Montefiore, Sir, bart., 1906-.
  3.1267, 3.1278, 3.1562, 3.1679
Magnusson, Frances W. 4.10588
Magny, Claude Edmonde. 2.3912
Magoulias, Harry J. 3.2673
Magoun, Francis Peabody, 1895- tr. 2.922,
  2.1752
Magoun, Horace Winchell, 1907-. 5.4337
Magrath, C. Peter. 4.9831
Magriel, Paul David, 1906-. 5.8429
Maguire, Daniel C. 4.4973, 5.4577
Maguire, John M. 4.6957
Maguire, Robert A. 2.1272, 2.1389, 2.1726,
  2.1743
Magyari, E., joint author. 5.2222

Mahābhārata. Sāvitryupākhyāna. 2.2581
Mahaffy, John Pentland, Sir, 1839-1919. 3.5156
Mahajan, Vijay. 4.4301
Mahan, A. T. (Alfred Thayer), 1840-1914.
  3.540, 3.1282, 3.2093, 3.6377, 3.7104, 5.7447
Mahan, L. Kathleen. 5.5085, 5.5130
Mahar, J. Michael. 3.4178, 5.8053
Mahard, Rita E. 4.10787
Mahdi, Muhsin. 3.571
Mahdi, Muhsin. joint ed. 4.7269
Mahdi, Muhsin. ed. and tr. 1.372
Maher, Charles A., 1944-. 4.10935
Maher, Gerry. 5.4564
Maher, Vanessa. 4.6160
Mahfūz, Najīb, 1912-. 2.1847
Mahler, Alma, 1879-1964. 1.3921
Mahler, Kurt. 5.1330
Mahler, Margaret S. 5.603, 5.5102
Mahler, Raphael, 1899-. 3.3907
Mahon, Denis. 1.6184
Mahon, John K. 5.7291
Mahoney, Dorothy. 5.7527
Mahoney, E. R. (E. Richard) 5.488
Mahoney, Gene, 1923-. 5.5967
Mahoney, Michael J. 5.455
Mahoney, Michael Sean. 5.1091
MaHood, James. 4.5511
Mahood, M. M. (Molly Maureen) 2.6050,
  2.6819, 2.8510
Mahowald, Mary Briody. 4.5938
Mahrer, Alvin R. 5.231, 5.4855
Maier, Barbara M., joint author. 5.4063
Maier, Bruno. 2.4973
Maier, Charles S. 3.876
Maier, Henry William. 5.570
Maier, John R. 2.1767
Maier, L., joint author. 5.2787
Maier, Paul L. 3.3897
Maier, Pauline, 1938-. 3.6921, 3.6981
Maier, Richard A., 1933-. 5.4063
Maihofer, C. 5.8008
Mail, Patricia D. 5.7739
Mailer, Norman. 2.12093-2.12102, 2.12182,
  3.7865, 4.8221
Maillard, Robert. ed. 1.5610
Mailloux, Steven. 2.2486
Maimonides, Moses, 1135-1204. 1.377, 1.1945,
  1.1961-1.1962
Main, Gloria L. (Gloria Lund), 1933-. 4.2034
Main, Iain G., 1932-. 5.2033
Main, Jackson Turner. 3.6899, 4.2031, 4.5139,
  4.7815, 4.7831
Maine, Henry Sumner, Sir, 1822-1888. 4.7321,
  4.7577, 4.9354
Mainga, Mutumba. 3.5519
Mainiero, Lina. 2.10283
Mainstone, R. J. (Rowland J.), 1923-. 5.6085
Mair, Lucy Philip, 1901-. 4.491, 4.654-4.655,
  4.660, 4.8828
Mairet, Philip, 1886- tr. 1.492
Mais, Roger. 2.9996
Maison, K. E. 1.6086
Maistre, Joseph Marie, comte de, 1753-1821.
  1.119
Maitland, Arthur. 5.2299
Maitland, Frederic William, 1850-1906. 3.1234,
  4.8382, 4.8391, 4.9408
Maitland, Leslie. 1.5345
Maitreyanātha. 1.2131
Maixner, Paul. 2.8129
Maizell, Robert E. (Robert Edward), 1924-.
  5.2601
Maizels, Alfred. 4.4100, 4.4164
Maizlish, Stephen E., 1945-. 3.7142, 3.8383
Majno, Guido. 5.4511
Majone, Giandomenico. 4.1236
Major, Clarence. 2.1167
Major, David C. 5.5974
Major, J. Russell (James Russell), 1921-. 4.8581
Major, John, 1936-. 5.1960
Major, Mabel, 1894-. 2.10471
Major, Ralph Hermon, 1884-. 5.4735
Majors, Frances J. 4.4885
Majors, William R., 1929-. 3.8345
Majumdar, Dhirendra Nath. 3.4202
Majumdar, Ramesh Chandra. 3.4240
Majumdar, Ramesh Chandra. ed. 3.4162
Makārim, Sāmī Nasīb. 1.1786

Maker, C. June. 4.10919, 4.10922
Makey, Walter. 1.3392
Makgetla, Neva. 4.4635
Makin, John H. 4.4588, 4.4590
Makino, Sajirō, 1906-. 5.3615
Makinson, Randell L., 1932-. 1.5309
Makler, Harry M., 1935-. 3.3503
Makridakis, Spyros G. 4.1242
Makrygiannēs, Iōoannēs, 1797-1864. 3.2694
Maksimov, Grigoriĭ Petrovich, 1893-1950.
    4.7197
Malacara, Daniel, 1937-. 5.2291
Malamat, Abraham. 3.3850
Malamud, Bernard. 2.13153-2.13162
Malamuth, Neil M. 4.5547
Maland, David. 3.634
Malantschuk, Gregor. 1.1118, 1.1124
Malbin, Michael J. 4.8030, 4.8130
Malcolm, Norman, 1911-. 1.1089, 5.27, 5.330
Malcolmson, Robert W. 3.1532
Maldonado-Denis, Manuel, 1933-. 3.9129
Male, D. H. (David Harold), 1939-. 5.2542
Mâle, Emile, 1862-1954. 1.5173-1.5175
Malebranche, Nicolas, 1638-1715. 1.799-1.800
Malenbaum, Wilfred. 4.2508
Malevich, Kazimir Severinovich, 1878-1935.
    1.5871
Malgrange, Pierre. 4.1400
Malherbe, François de, 1555-1628. 2.4037
Malik, Keshav. 2.1961
Malin, David. 5.1839
Malin, Irving. ed. 2.10680
Malin, Irving. comp. 2.10300
Malin, Irving. 2.10637, 2.12685, 2.13345
Malin, James Claude, 1893-. 3.7173, 3.8463,
    3.8523, 4.387, 5.5244
Malina, Bruce J. 1.2640
Malino, Frances. 3.3963
Malinowski, Bronislaw, 1884-1942. 4.405, 4.437,
    4.566, 4.611, 4.680, 4.4878, 4.5558-4.5559
Malinowsky, H. Robert (Harold Robert), 1933-.
    5.8419
Malins, Edward Greenway. 2.8345
Malinvaud, Edmond. joint author. 4.2333
Malinvaud, Edmond. 4.1301, 4.2782, 4.3202
Malkevitch, Joseph, 1942-. 5.1113
Malkiel, Yakov, 1914- ed. 2.148
Malko, Nicolai, 1883-1961. 1.4501
Malkoff, Karl. 2.12412
Malla, Kamal Prakash, 1936- ed. 3.4376
Mallac, Guy de, 1936-. 2.1597
Mallan, Lloyd. 5.6718
Mallarmé, Stéphane. 2.4261-2.4263
Mallas, John H. 5.1850
Mallea, Eduardo, 1903-. 2.5393-2.5395
Mallen, Bruce E. comp. 4.4285
Mallen, Bruce E. 4.4295
Mallet-Joris, Françoise, 1930-. 2.4606-2.4610
Mallett, Michael Edward. 3.2852
Malley, Elaine. 2.5297
Mallin, Samuel B. 1.844
Mallinson, Vernon. 2.4800, 3.2966
Mallion, Jean. ed. 2.4290
Mallock, William Hurrell, 1849-1923. 2.7924
Mallon, Florencia E., 1951-. 4.2845
Mallory, Vincent. joint author. 5.6563
Mallow, Alex. 5.5951
Malloy, James M. 3.9278, 4.8327
Malloy, Robert. 2.5447
Malm, William P. 1.3734, 1.3742-1.3743
Malmström, Vincent Herschel, 1926-. 3.3373
Malone, Bill C. 4.1256, 1.4276
Malone, Dumas, 1892-. 3.497, 3.6288, 3.6984,
    3.7062
Malone, Kemp, 1889-1971. 2.6366, 2.11140
Malone, Martin J. 4.495
Malone, Michael P. 3.8460, 3.8544, 3.8550,
    4.3729
Malone, Thomas F. ed. 5.2495
Maloney, Clarence. 4.561
Maloney, Dennis. 2.5271
Maloney, Elbert S. 5.7494
Maloney, George A., 1924-. 1.3109
Maloney, James O. 5.6827
Maloney, Linda M. 5.7422
Malory, Thomas, Sir, 15th cent. 2.6407-2.6408
Malouf, David, 1934-. 2.10158
Malpezzi, Frances M., 1946-. 5.7734

Malraux, André, 1901-1976. 1.4614, 1.4633,
    2.4076, 2.4611-2.4621, 3.102
Maltby, Arthur. 5.7636
Maltby, William S., 1940-. 3.3444
Malthus, T. R. (Thomas Robert), 1766-1834.
    4.1415-4.1416, 4.1493, 4.1513, 4.1586-4.1587
Maltin, Leonard. 2.2921, 2.2930, 2.3031, 2.3077
Maluccio, Anthony N. 4.6472, 4.6544, 4.6561
Malveaux, Julianne. 4.6024
Malvern, Lawrence E., 1916-. 5.1649, 5.5733
Malvino, Albert Paul. 5.6450
Malzberg, Barry N. 2.13165
Mamalakis, Markos. 4.2177
Mamalis, A. G. joint author. 5.6625
Mamatey, Victor S. ed. 3.1917
Mamber, Stephen. 2.2922
Mamet, David. 2.13166-2.13168
Mamonova, Tatyana, 1943-. 4.6135
Manassah, Jamal T. 5.6116
Mancall, Mark. 3.4714
Mänchen-Helfen, Otto. 3.584
Manchester, Alden Coe, 1922-. 4.3691
Manchester, Ellen. 5.6983
Manchester, Frederick Alexander, 1882-.
    2.11343
Manchester, Phyllis Winifred, joint ed. 4.1080
Manchester, Richard N. 5.1848
Manchester Symposium on Theatre, 2d, 1971.
    2.3306
Manchester, William Raymond, 1922-. 2.12135,
    3.1657, 3.7762, 3.7874
Mancini, Janet K. 3.8005
Mancke, Richard B., 1943-. 4.3808
Mandel, Bernard, 1920-. 4.3585
Mandel, Eli, 1922- comp. 2.9883
Mandel, Neville J. 3.3875
Mandel, Ruth B. 4.5971
Mandel, Siegfried. 2.13482
Mandela, Nelson, 1918-. 3.5454
Mandelbaum, Allen, 1926-. 2.798, 2.4923,
    2.5075
Mandelbaum, David Goodman, 1911-. 2.9,
    3.6727, 4.5427
Mandelbaum, Maurice, 1908-. 3.480, 3.513
Mandelbrot, Benoit B. 5.1566-5.1567
Mandelkern, Leo. 5.2765
Mandelkow, Karl Robert. 2.13572-2.13573
Mandell, Leon. joint author. 5.2889
Mandell, Richard D. 4.957, 4.977
Mandel'shtam, Nadezhda, 1899-. 2.1578-2.1579
Mandel'shtam, Osip, 1891-1938. 2.1574-2.1576
Mander, Carel van, 1548-1606. 1.6229
Mander, Raymond. 1.4048, 2.2840, 2.3317,
    2.8090
Mandeville, Bernard, 1670-1733. 1.1507
Mandeville, T. D. 5.5637
Mandl, F. (Franz), 1923-. 5.2116, 5.2156
Mandle, Jay R. 3.6792
Mandler, George. 5.274
Mandler, George. joint ed. 5.385
Mandler, Jean Matter. ed. 5.385
Mandrou, Robert. 3.175, 3.1959, 3.1964
Manet, Edouard, 1832-1883. 1.4975, 1.6118
Manetti, Antonio, 1423-1497. 1.5440
Mang, Karl, 1922-. 1.6558
Mangan, J. A. 4.908
Mangat, J. S. 3.5259
Manger, Itzik, 1900-1969. 2.1807
Mangione, Jerre Gerlando, 1909-. 3.6227
Mango, Cyril A. comp. 1.4746
Mango, Cyril A. 1.5233, 3.2658
Mangone, Gerard J. 4.9110, 4.9137
Mangum, Garth L. 4.3382
Manheim, Marvin L. 4.3878
Manheim, Ralph, 1907-. 2.4512, 2.13702,
    2.13704, 3.2390
Manhire, Bill, 1946-. 2.10205
Mani, Vettam, 1921-. 1.1689
Maniatis, Tom. 5.3462
Manifold, Gay, 1943-. 2.4295
Manin, IU. I. 5.1045
Mankiewicz, Frank, 1924-. 4.4072
Mankiewicz, Herman J. (Herman Jacob),
    1897-1953. 2.3025
Manko, Howard H. 5.7087
Manley, John F. 4.8064
Manley, Norman Washington, 1893-1969.
    3.9112

Manley, Seon. comp. 2.8917
Manlove, C. N. (Colin Nicholas), 1942-.
    2.5966-2.5967
Manly, John Matthews, 1865-1940. 2.6340,
    2.6343, 2.10420
Mann, Alfred, 1917-. 1.4448
Mann, Arthur. 3.7659
Mann, Cameron, bp., 1851-1932, comp. 2.7066
Mann, Cecil, ed. 2.10151
Mann, Coramae Richey, 1931-. 4.6691
Mann, David W. 4.10726
Mann, Erika, 1905-1969. 2.13834
Mann, Floyd Christopher, 1917-. 4.3152
Mann, Francis Oscar, ed. 2.6449
Mann, Golo, 1909-. 3.522, 3.2287
Mann, Heinrich, 1871-1950. 2.13817-2.13818
Mann, Horace, 1796-1859. 4.10201
Mann, Jill. 2.6320
Mann, John. 4.4607
Mann, K. H. (Kenneth Henry), 1923-. 5.3540
Mann, Lawrence. 5.7051
Mann, Leon, joint author. 5.376
Mann, Michael, 1942-. 4.4735
Mann, Nicholas. 2.4953
Mann, Otto, 1898-. 2.13634
Mann, Ralph. 3.8619
Mann, Ronald A. 5.1658
Mann, Thomas, 1875-1955. 2.1346, 2.13471,
    2.13778, 2.13820-2.13835
Mann, Thomas E. 4.8000, 4.8113
Mann, William, 1924-. 1.4514, 1.4516
Mann, William Neville. 4.4494
Manna, Zohar. 5.1190
Mannerheim, Carl Gustaf Emil, friherre,
    1867-1951. 3.3299
Manners, Gerald. 4.3732
Manners, Ian R. ed. 5.3523
Manners, Robert Alan, 1913- comp. 4.396
Manners, William, 1907-. 3.7660
Mannheim, Hermann, 1889- ed. 4.6679
Mannheim, Karl, 1893-1947. 4.4802, 4.4815,
    4.4832, 4.4879, 4.5090
Manning, Brian Stuart. 3.1483
Manning, Frederic. 2.10159
Manning, Frederick B. 5.7243
Manning, Helen (Taft), 1891-. 3.8813
Manning, Margaret J. 5.4466
Manning, Olivia. 2.9742-2.9743
Manning, Peter K. 4.6812
Manning, William Ray, 1871-. 3.9019
Manning, Winton Howard, 1930-. 4.10609
Mannino, Fortune V. (Fortune Vincent), 1928-.
    5.4834
Mannon, James M., 1942-. 5.5035
Manns, Peter. 1.2343
Manns, Torsten, 1923-. 2.3035
Mano, M. Morris, 1927-. 5.1229, 5.6584
Manor, James. 3.4374
Mansbridge, Jane J. 4.5966
Manser, Anthony Richards. 1.745
Manser, W. A. P. (William Arthur Peete)
    4.4594
Mansergh, Nicholas. 3.1225, 3.1231, 3.1852,
    4.8429
Mansergh, Nicholas. ed. 3.1226, 3.4289
Mansfield, Edwin. 4.2108
Mansfield, Harvey Claflin, 1932-. 4.7391, 4.7396
Mansfield, Katherine, 1888-1923. 2.6041,
    2.9079-2.9082, 2.9085
Mansfield, Peter, 1928-. 3.3663, 3.3682, 3.3728
Mansfield, Sue. 5.7151
Mansion, J. E. (Jean Edmond), 1870-1942.
    2.868, 2.881
Manso, Peter. 2.12105
Manson, Gary. 4.35
Manstein, Erich von, 1887-1973. 3.968
Mantegna, Andrea, 1431-1506. 1.6215
Mantell, Martin E., 1936-. 3.7468
Mantle, Robert Burns, 1873-1948, comp. 2.3770
Manton, Jo, 1919-. 2.7760, 2.8297
Mantoux, Paul, 1877-1956. 4.2267
Manu. 1.1685
Manuel, Frank Edward. 1.810
Manuel, Frank Edward. ed. 4.7172
Manuel, Ron C. 4.5819
Manuila, Alexandre. 5.4486
Manuscript Society (U.S.) 5.7522
Manuud, Antonio G., ed. 2.2290

Manvell, Roger, 1909-. 2.2896, 2.3249, 2.3354, 2.3356, 2.6861, 3.2385, 3.2389
Manwaring, David Roger, 1933-. 4.9595
Manzoni, Alessandro, 1785-1873. 2.5001-2.5004
Manzù, Giacomo, 1908-. 1.5731
Mao, Nathan K. joint author. 5.8045
Mao, Nathan Kwok-kuen, 1940-. 5.8046
Mao, Tse-tung, 1893-1976. 3.4795, 3.4824-3.4829, 3.4831, 5.7230
Mao, Tun, 1896-. 2.2248
Ma'oz, Moshe. 4.8780
Maple, Terry. 5.4036
Mappen, Marc. 5.679
Marable, Manning, 1950-. 3.6679
Marais, Johannes Stephanus. 3.5502
Maraldo, John C., joint author. 1.2143
Maramba, Asuncion David. comp. 2.2292
Marangoni, Roy D. joint author. 5.5682
Maraniss, James E., 1945-. 2.5167
Marantz, Paul. 3.3880
Marble, Duane Francis, 1931- joint comp. 4.196
Marc, David. 2.2852
Marc, Franz, 1880-1916. joint ed. 1.4811
Marcel, Gabriel, 1889-1973. 1.490, 1.640, 1.832-1.836, 1.1555
Marcell, David W. 5.7830
March, James G. joint author. 4.2664
March, James G. ed. 4.4906
March, James G. 4.2655, 4.10589, 4.10643
March, Jerry, 1929-. 5.2721
March, Ray A., 1934-. 4.6914
March, Robert H., 1937-. 5.1984
March, William, 1893-1954. 2.11460-2.11461
Marc'hadour, Germain. 3.1408
Marchaj, Czesław S. 5.7510
Marcham, Frederick George, 1898- joint ed. and tr. 4.8380
Marchand, C. Roland, 1933-. 4.9144
Marchand, Donald A. 4.6803
Marchand, Jean. ed. 2.4033
Marchand, Leslie Alexis, 1900-. 2.7521, 2.7523, 2.7526-2.7527
Marchand, Roland. 4.4423
Marchant, Alexander Nelson de Armond, 1912-. 3.9205
Marchant, Edgar Cardew, tr. 2.398-2.399
Marckwardt, Albert Henry, 1903-1975. 2.930, 2.1126
Marco, Guy A. 1.3552, 1.3577
Marcu, Eva Dorothea, 1907-. 3.632
Marcum, John A. 3.5409
Marcus Aurelius, Emperor of Rome, 121-180. 2.354
Marcus, Bruce, 1949-. 3.9134
Marcus, Geoffrey Jules, 1906-. 5.7456-5.7457
Marcus, George E. 4.4820
Marcus, George H. 5.5636
Marcus, Harold G. 3.5245, 3.5250
Marcus, Jacob Rader, 1896-. 3.3903, 3.6572, 4.5912-4.5913, 5.8241
Marcus, Jane. 2.9608
Marcus, Laurence R. 4.10737
Marcus, Maeva, 1941-. 4.9740
Marcus, R. B. (Robert B.) 5.6535
Marcus, Ralph, 1900-1956. 2.376
Marcus, Robert D., 1936-. 4.8216
Marcus, Stanley E., 1926-. 1.5675
Marcus, Stephen. 4.10756
Marcus, Y. 5.2907
Marcuse, Herbert, 1898-. 1.610, 1.1038, 4.4761, 4.4880, 4.6981, 5.174
Marcuse, Sibyl. 1.3515
Marczenko, Zygmunt. 5.2690
Marder, Arthur Jacob. 3.1003, 5.7458-5.7460
Marder, Daniel. ed. 2.10862
Marder, Leslie. 5.1915
Marder, Louis, 1915-. 2.6716
Marder, Tod A. 1.5298
Marek, George Richard, 1902-. 1.3801
Marenbon, John. 1.354
Marer, Paul. 4.2231
Mares, E. A., 1938-. 3.8577
Mareuil, André. 5.8004
Margaliot, Abraham, 1920-. 3.1087
Margaret Woodbury Strong Museum. 1.6538
Margenau, Henry, 1901- joint author. 5.1913
Margolies, Edward. 2.10326, 2.12821, 5.7799
Margolin, Judith B. 1.74

Margoliouth, Herschel Maurice, 1887-. 1.3074, 2.7103, 2.7414, 2.8317
Margolis, Carolyn. 4.99
Margolis, Joseph Zalman, 1924-. 1.90, 1.1347, 1.4615
Marguerite, Queen, consort of Henry II, King of Navarre, 1492-1549. 2.3986-2.3987
Margulies, Herbert F. 3.8447
Margulis, Lynn, 1938-. 5.3234, 5.3320, 5.3371, 5.3394, 5.3482
MARHO (Organization) 3.408
Marías, Julián, 1914-. 1.132, 2.5290
Mariátegui, José Carlos, 1894-1930. 3.9280
Marichal, Juan. 2.5094
Marie, de France, 12th cent. 2.3954-2.3955
Marien, Michael. 5.8119, 5.8371
Marietta, Jack D. 1.3350
Marijnissen, Roger H. 1.6261
Marill, René. 2.3913
Marín, Diego. 2.5087
Marín, Diego. comp. 2.5142
Marin, John, 1870-1953. 1.5953
Marinatos, Spyridon, 1901-. 1.4723
Marinetti, Filippo Tommaso, 1876-1944. 1.6735
Marini, Marino, 1904-. 1.5732
Marini, Stephen A., 1946-. 1.2404
Marino, Andrew A. 5.4207
Marinoni, Augusto. joint author. 5.823
Maritain, Jacques, 1882-1973. 1.489, 1.837, 1.1284, 1.1417, 1.2845, 2.4147, 3.481, 4.7476-4.7477, 4.7642, 4.10204
Maritain, Raïssa. comp. 2.4147
Marius, Richard. 3.1410
Marivaux, Pierre Carlet de Chamblain de, 1688-1763. 2.4078-2.4079
Mark, Bernard, 1908-1966. 3.998
Mark, H. F. (Herman Francis), 1895-. 5.2769, 5.6905
Mark, James E., 1934-. 5.5804
Markandaya, Kamala, 1924-. 2.10127
Markel, Michael H. 2.8448
Markell, Edward K. 5.4760
Marker, Frederick J. 2.13969
Marker, Lise-Lone, 1934-. 2.3244, 2.13969
Markham, James Walter, 1910-. 2.3606
Markham, Jesse William, 1916-. 4.1008
Markides, Kyriacos C. 3.3697
Markland, Murray F. 4.7375
Markle, Joyce B. 2.13385
Markov, Vladimir. comp. 2.1312
Markov, Vladimir. 2.1280
Marković, Mihailo, 1923-. 1.117, 4.6979
Markovitz, Irving Leonard, 1934-. 3.5108
Markowitz, Norman D. 3.7692
Marks, Alfred H. 5.8068
Marks, Claude. 1.5793
Marks, Elaine. 2.4504, 4.6120
Marks, Frederick W. 3.7697
Marks, John. 5.742
Marks, Joseph E. 4.1103
Marks, Lawrence E. 5.240, 5.244
Marks, Lionel S. (Lionel Simeon), 1871-. 5.6112
Marks, Richard, 1945- joint author. 1.6410
Marks, Sally. 3.851
Marle, Raimond van, 1888-1936. 1.6179
Marlowe, Christopher, 1564-1593. 2.6606, 2.6609-2.6612
Marmier, Pierre, 1922-. 5.2428
Marmor, Judd. 4.5531
Marmor, Theodore R. 4.3452
Marmullaku, Ramadan, 1939-. 3.3601
Maroger, Dominique, ed. 3.3102
Maroon, Fred J. 3.7898
Marot, Clément, 1495?-1544. 2.3989
Marotz-Baden, Ramona. 4.5730
Marovitz, Sanford E. 5.7787
Marquand, Allan, 1853-1924. 1.5738
Marquand, David. 3.1672, 4.8362
Marquand, John P. (John Phillips), 1893-1960. 2.12107, 2.12109-2.12111
Marquand, John Phillips. 2.12108
Marques, António Henrique R. de Oliveira. 3.3493, 3.3497
Marquette Hegel Symposium, 1970. 1.949
Marquette University. Dept. of Philosophy. 1.949
Márquez, Antonio, 1940-. 2.10812
Marquina, Ignacio. 3.8894

Marquis Academic Media. 4.5823
Marquis, Albert Nelson, d. 1943. 3.6301
Marquis, Don, 1878-1937. 2.12115, 2.12117
Marquis, Donald George, joint author. 5.300
Marquis, G. Welton. 1.4431
Marquis Who's Who, Inc. 5.816
Marr, David G. 3.4418, 3.4467
Marr, Phebe. 3.3781
Marr, William L., 1944-. 4.2117
Marriage, Ellen. 2.4120
Marriott, Alice Lee, 1910- joint author. 3.8530
Marriott, J. A. R. (John Arthur Ransome), Sir, 1859-1945. 3.683, 3.2481
Marriott, McKim, ed. 4.5424
Marris, Peter. 4.5187, 4.6341
Marrocco, W. Thomas (William Thomas), 1909- ed. 1.3426
Marrone, Steven P., 1947-. 1.386
Marrou, Henri Irénée. 1.2290
Marrow, James H. 1.4986
Marrus, Michael Robert. 3.3962
Marryat, Frederick, 1792-1848. 2.7925-2.7927
Marschall, Richard. 1.5845
Marsden, Cyril. 5.6864
Marsden, George M., 1939-. 1.2794
Marsden, Jerrold E. 5.1489
Marsden, Kenneth. 2.7793
Marsden, Norman. 3.4001
Marsella, Anthony J. 4.624, 5.467
Marsh, Arthur Ivor. joint author. 4.3508
Marsh, Clarence Stephen, 1882- ed. 4.10056
Marsh, David C. (David Charles) 4.5304
Marsh, David C. (David Charles) joint author. 4.3073
Marsh, Derick R. C. (Derick Rupert Clement), 1928-. 2.6790
Marsh, Earle. 2.2847
Marsh, Edward Howard, Sir, 1872-1953. 2.6187
Marsh, Frank Burr, 1880-1940. 3.2773-3.2774, 3.2798
Marsh, George Perkins, 1801-1882. 4.366
Marsh, James H. 1.20
Marsh, Jeanne C., 1948-. 4.9866
Marsh, Ngaio, 1899-. 2.9088
Marsh, R. W. 5.5415
Marsh, Reginald, 1898-1954. 1.6444
Marsh, Robert Mortimer. 3.4712
Marshak, Robert Eugene, 1916-. 5.2397
Marshall, Alan G., 1944-. 5.3334
Marshall, Alfred. 4.1333, 4.1446-4.1448, 4.2999, 4.4108, 4.4492
Marshall, Burke, 1922-. 3.4497
Marshall, Dale Rogers. 3.6795, 4.5104
Marshall, Donald Stanley, 1919- ed. 4.5490
Marshall, Dorothy. 1.3521
Marshall, F. Ray. comp. 4.3110
Marshall, F. Ray. 3.6738, 4.3396
Marshall, Geoffrey. 2.5896, 4.9419
Marshall, George O. 2.8178
Marshall, Herbert, 1906-. 2.3039, 2.3336, 2.3380
Marshall, I. Howard. 1.2650
Marshall, J. Lawrence, 1913-. 5.6107
Marshall, James M., 1924-. 3.8448
Marshall, Judi. 4.4338
Marshall, Lorna. 3.5434
Marshall, Mac. 5.8096
Marshall, Norman Bertram. 5.3247, 5.3897, 5.3903
Marshall, Paule, 1929-. 2.13169
Marshall, Richard, 1947-. 1.6615
Marshall, Richard H., 1897- ed. 1.1673
Marshall, Robert Lewis. 3.1780
Marshall, Rosalind Kay. 4.6112
Marshall, S. L. A. (Samuel Lyman Atwood), 1900-1977. 3.890, 3.5025
Marshall, Sybil. 4.789
Marshall, Tom, 1938-. 2.9890
Marshall, William Harvey. 2.7535, 2.7611
Marsilius, of Padua, d. 1342? 4.7377
Marston, F. S. (Frank Swain) 3.854
Marston, John, 1575?-1634. 2.6621-2.6624
Marston, Richard C. 4.4465
Marston, Robert Q., 1923-. 5.4680
Martel, José, 1883- joint comp. 2.5148
Martel, Leon. 3.942
Martell, Arthur Earl, 1916- ed. 5.2844
Martellotti, Guido, 1905- ed. 2.4947
Marten, Michael. 5.1701

Martens, Rainer, 1942-. 4.904
Martha Upton lectures, 1926. 1.186
Martí, José, 1853-1895. 2.5366-2.5367, 3.5683
Martial. 2.677, 2.741-2.742
Martin, Alan D. (Alan Douglas) 5.2476
Martin, Albro. 4.3982, 4.4000
Martin, Ben R. 5.975
Martin, Benjamin F., 1947-. 3.2187, 4.9912
Martin, Bernard, 1928-. 1.1900, 1.1929
Martin, Bradford G. 1.2081
Martin, Brian V. joint author. 4.3930
Martin, Burns. 2.7209-2.7210
Martin, Calvin. 3.5728
Martin, Charles H., 1945-. 4.9459
Martin-Chauffier, Louis, 1894- ed. 2.4033
Martin, Chester Bailey, 1882-1958. 3.8675,
   4.8270
Martin, Claude, 1933-. 2.4565
Martin, Clyde Eugene, joint author. 4.5494
Martin, Colin. 3.1439
Martin, Daniel, 1948-. 5.6301
Martin, David L. 4.8845
Martin du Gard, Roger, 1881-. 2.4625
Martin du Gard, Roger, 1881-1958. 2.4626
Martin, E. A. (Elizabeth A.) 4.9405, 5.3290
Martin, Edwin M. 3.4979
Martin, Elmer P. 3.6771
Martin, Ernest Walter, 1914-. 4.5325
Martin, Esmond Bradley. 3.5291
Martin, F. David, 1920-. 1.5772
Martin, F. X. (Francis X.) 3.1815-3.1816
Martin, Fenton S. 5.7848, 5.8352
Martin, Frederick, 1830-1883, ed. 4.7214
Martin, Frederick N. 5.5039
Martin, G. W. (George Willard), 1886-1971.
   5.3728
Martin, Ged. joint author. 3.1222
Martin, Geoffrey J. joint author. 4.48
Martin, George R. R. 2.13170
Martin, George Whitney. 1.3750, 1.4025,
   1.4510, 4.3591
Martin, Gérard J. joint author. 5.2410
Martin, Gottfried, 1901-. 1.870
Martin-Gropius-Bau (Berlin, Germany) 1.4801
Martin, Graham Dunstan. tr. 2.3982
Martin, Harold H. 3.8254
Martin, Henri Jean, 1924- joint author. 5.7518
Martin, Henry Desmond, 1908-. 3.3624
Martin, Hugh Robert. joint author. 5.6237
Martin, J. Douglas (James Douglas) 1.2096
Martin, J. W. (John Wilson), 1926-. 5.6775
Martin, James, 1933-. 4.4347, 5.1157, 5.5571,
   5.6350, 5.6397
Martin, James Harold, 1938- joint author.
   5.4162
Martin, James Kirby, 1943-. 4.6652
Martin, Jay. 2.10385, 2.11305, 2.12192, 2.12686
Martin, Joanne Mitchell. joint author. 3.6771
Martin, John Bartlow, 1915-1987. 3.7684-3.7685
Martin, John Frederick. 4.8201
Martin, John Joseph, 1893-. 4.1092, 4.1113,
   4.1140
Martin, John Rupert. 1.4776
Martin, John S. (John Stokes), 1929-. 4.10650
Martin, Joseph E. 5.6313
Martin, Joseph William, 1884-1968. 3.7672
Martin, Judith A., 1945-. 4.6562
Martin, Julia Augusta, 1810-1893. 2.7771
Martin, Kingsley, 1897-1969. 4.8442
Martin, Knute. 4.6594
Martin, L. John (Leslie John), 1921-. 4.5003
Martin, Laurence W. 3.828, 5.7217
Martin, Leonard Cyril, 1886-. 2.6912, 2.7325
Martin, Lionel. 3.9108
Martín, Luis. 4.6088
Martin, M. Kay, 1942-. 4.460
Martin, Mary Lou. 2.3954
Martin, Maryvonne L. 5.2410
Martin, Murray S. 3.6741
Martin, Paul S. (Paul Schultz), 1928-. 5.3163
Martin, Paul Sidney, 1899-. 3.5717
Martin, Philip L., 1949-. 4.3207
Martin, Philip W. 2.7536
Martin, Phyllis. 3.5044, 3.5232
Martin, Priscilla Clark. 2.913
Martin, Ralph G., 1920-. 3.6390
Martin, Ralph P. 1.2631, 1.2978
Martin, Rex. 3.514

Martin, Richard, M.A. 2.8665
Martin, Robert A. 2.12175
Martin, Robert Bernard. 2.5707, 2.6178, 2.7880,
   2.8170
Martin, Robert K., 1941-. 2.8661, 2.10478
Martin, Roland, 1912-. 1.4714-1.4716
Martin, Ronald H. 2.776, 2.778
Martin, Roscoe Coleman, 1903-1972. 4.7874
Martin, Russell. 5.6710
Martin, Ruth Marion Somers, 1914-. 5.7106
Martin, S. J. (Samuel John), 1936-. 5.4476
Martin, Samuel Elmo, 1924-. 2.1989
Martín-Santos, Luis, 1924-1964. 2.5295
Martin, Sarah S., 1945-. 5.8101
Martin, Susan Ehrlich. 4.6805
Martin, Terence. 2.11071
Martin, Thomas. 1.5726
Martin, Tyrone G. 5.7452
Martin, Violet Florence, 1865-1915.
   2.9349-2.9350
Martin, W. 2.11172-2.1173
Martin, Waldo E., 1951-. 3.7240
Martin, Wendy. 2.10477
Martin, William Edwin. 4.3088
Martin, Yves, 1929- joint ed. 3.8688
Martindale, Don. 4.4744
Martine, James J. 2.12291
Martineau, Harriet, 1802-1876. 1.820, 2.7928,
   3.6036
Martineau, Henri, 1882-1958. 2.4272, 2.4301,
   2.4312
Martinell, César, 1888-1973. 1.5444
Martinengo, Luciano. 2.5048
Martines, Lauro. 3.2838, 3.2928
Martines, Lauro. ed. 4.5367
Martinet, André. 2.138, 2.869
Martinez Alier, Verena. 4.5613
Martínez, Julio A. 2.10301
Martinez, Nancy C. (Nancy Conrad) 5.7972
Martinez Ruiz, Jos, 1873-1967. 2.5105
Martini, Arturo, 1889-1947. 1.5733
Martini, Fritz, 1909-. 2.13455, 2.13476
Martino, Pierre, 1880-1953. 2.3864
Martins, Wilson. 2.5464
Martinson, Harry, 1904-. 2.14062, 2.14095
Martis, Kenneth C. 4.151
Martna, Maret. 5.8207
Marton, Katherin. joint author. 4.4436
Marton, L. (Ladislaus), 1901- ed. 5.2000
Martonne, Emmanuel de, 1873-1955. 4.252,
   4.369
Martorana, S. V. 4.10593
Martos, Joseph, 1943-. 1.3222
Marty, Martin E., 1928-. 1.2284, 1.2378-1.2380,
   1.2756, 1.3365
Martyn, Edward. 2.9089
Martyn, J. Louis (James Louis), 1925-. 1.2695
Martz, John D. 4.7297, 4.8345
Martz, Linda. 4.6534
Martz, Louis Lohr. comp. 2.6159
Martz, Louis Lohr. 2.5801, 2.5805, 2.7157,
   2.7266, 2.11568
Maruyama, Masao, 1914-. 3.4980, 4.7296
Marvell, Andrew, 1621-1678. 2.7103-2.7104
Marvick, Elizabeth Wirth. 3.2025
Marvin, Ursula B. 5.3095
Marwick, Arthur, 1936-. 3.1644, 3.1693, 4.5240,
   4.5315
Marwick, Max, comp. 5.672
Marx. Daniel. 4.3963
Marx, Emanuel. 3.3840
Marx, Gary T. 3.6708
Marx, Jean L., joint author. 5.4771
Marx, Karl, 1818-1883. 1.471, 1.931, 1.1032,
   1.1890, 2.2385, 3.680, 3.3065, 3.3449, 4.1422,
   4.1500-4.1501, 4.1509, 4.1534-4.1536, 4.1589,
   4.4855, 4.5948, 4.6944-4.6947, 4.6953, 4.6956,
   4.7069-4.7074, 4.7101
Marx, Leo, 1919-. 3.6136
Marx, Melvin Herman. ed. 5.4
Marx, Melvin Herman. 5.28
Marx, Olga, 1894- tr. 1.1921, 2.13751
Marx, Siegfried, 1934-. 5.1745
Mary, André, 1880-. 2.3963
Mary Baldwin College, Staunton, Va. 2.11778
Maryland Historical Society. 1.6380
Maryland. State Planning Commission. 4.1944
März, Eduard. 4.4543

Marzan, Betty. joint author. 1.4653
Marzani, Carl. 4.7023
Marzari, F., 1938-1971, joint author. 3.2879
Marzials, Frank Thomas, Sir, 1840-1912, tr.
   3.594
Marzio, Peter C. 1.6503
Marzolf, Marion. 3.3601
Marzubān ibn Rustam, 11th cent. 2.1762
Marzullo, Benedetto, 1923-. 2.516-2.517
Mas 'ūd ibn 'Umar, Sa'd al-Dīn, al-Taftāzānī,
   1322-1389. 1.2046
Masaccio, 1401-1428? 1.6216
Masaryk, T. G. (Tomáš Garrigue), 1850-1937.
   3.3019
Masefield, G. B. (Geoffrey Bussell) 5.3658
Masefield, John, 1878-1967. 2.9090-2.9091,
   4.102
Maser, Edward Andrew, 1923-. 1.5165
Maser, Werner, 1922-. 3.2405
Masi, Dale A. 4.3503
Maskaleris, Thanasis. 2.606
Masling, Joseph M. 5.4910
Maslow, Abraham H. (Abraham Harold)
   5.528-5.529
Maslowski, Peter, 1944-. 3.6368
Masnick, George S., 1942-. 4.5593
Masolino, 1383-1447? 1.6217
Mason, A. E. W. (Alfred Edward Woodley),
   1865-1948. 2.9092
Mason, Alpheus Thomas, 1899-. 4.9827, 4.9830,
   4.9843
Mason, B. J. (Basil John) 5.2535-5.2536
Mason, Brian Harold, 1917-. 5.3013
Mason, C. M. (Colin M.) ed. 1.4185
Mason, Celestine B. joint author. 5.4786
Mason, Daniel Gregory, 1873-1953. 1.3923
Mason, Edward Sagendorph, 1899-. 3.2167,
   4.2560, 4.3048-4.3049, 4.4572
Mason, Ellsworth. 5.7614
Mason, Francis, joint author. 1.4508
Mason, Francis K. 3.958
Mason, George, 1725-1792. 3.6976
Mason, H. A. (Harold Andrew) 2.487
Mason, Haydn Trevor. 2.3855, 2.4108-2.4109
Mason, Howard S. joint ed. 5.3330
Mason, John Alden, 1885-1967. 3.9287
Mason, Julian Dewey, 1931- ed. 2.10883
Mason, Michael, 1924-. 3.4199
Mason, Philip. 3.4265, 3.5507, 5.7340
Mason, R. Hal (Robert Hal), 1929-. 4.2719,
   4.4247
Mason, Richard O. 4.1248
Mason, Roger, 1941-. 5.3067
Mason, Ronald J. 3.5736
Masonson, Leslie N. 4.4603
Masotti, Louis H. 3.8417
Maspero, Henri, 1883-1945. 1.1790
Mass, Jeffrey P. 3.4935
Massachusetts. Board of Education. 4.10201
Massachusetts Institute of Technology. 4.3817,
   5.2566, 5.3164, 5.4285, 5.7409
Massachusetts Institute of Technology. Center
   for International Studies. 3.4176, 4.2773
Massachusetts Institute of Technology. Dept. of
   Mechanical Engineering. 5.5734
Massachusetts Institute of Technology. Radar
   School. 5.6436
Massachusetts Institute of Technology.
   Spectroscopy Laboratory. 5.2312
Massenet, Jules, 1842-1912. 1.3924
Massengale, John Montague. 1.5302
Massey, Frank Jones. 5.1395
Massey, Harrie Stewart Wilson, Sir. 5.2399,
   5.2482
Massey, Mary Elizabeth. 4.1925
Massey, William S. 5.1609
Massialas, Byron G. 4.9962, 4.10367
Massie, Henry N. 5.5118
Massie, Robert K., 1929-. 3.3099, 3.3160
Massignon, Louis, 1883-1962. 1.2023
Massinger, Philip, 1583-1640. 2.6629-2.6630
Masson, Bernard. 2.4183
Masson, David, 1822-1907. 2.7622
Masson, J. Moussaieff (Jeffrey Moussaieff),
   1941-. 5.147
Masson, L. R. (Louis Rodrigue), 1833-1903.
   3.8845
Masson, M. R. (Mary R.) 5.2655

Masson, V. M. (Vadim Mikhaĭlovich), 1929-. 4.741
Massy, William F. joint author. 4.4306
Mast, Gerald, 1940-. 2.2882, 2.2941, 2.2980
Masterman, Sylvia. 3.5673
Masters, Donald C., 1908-. 3.8668
Masters, Donald Campbell, 1908-. 3.8668
Masters, Edgar Lee, 1868-1950. 2.12016, 2.12118-2.12119
Masters, Judith R., tr. 2.4090
Masters, Judith R. 4.7434
Masters, K. (Keith) 5.6884
Masters, Lowell F. 4.916
Masters, Robert E. L. 5.233
Masters, Roger D. ed. and tr. 2.4090
Masters, Roger D. 4.7434
Masters, William H. 4.5504, 5.4257, 5.4838, 5.4952
Masterson, Jenny (Gove) pseud. 5.117
Masterton, William L., 1927-. 5.2629
Mastin, B. A., ed. 1.2696
Mastny, Vojtech, 1936-. 3.1922
Masuda, Kō, 1890- ed. 2.1991
Masumi, Junnosuke, 1926- joint author. 4.8762
Masur, Gerhard, 1901-. 3.184, 3.9167
Matejka, Ladislav, 1919- comp. 2.1242
Matejko, Alexander J. 4.5381
Matematicheskiĭ institut im. V.A. Steklova. 5.1027
Materer, Timothy, 1940-. 2.9047
Mates, Benson, 1919-. 1.1157, 1.1216
Mates, Julian, 1927-. 1.4219
Mathaf al-Miṣrī. 3.5144
Matheopoulos, Helena. 1.3768
Mather, Cotton. 1.3045, 1.3333, 3.7950, 3.7976-3.7977
Mather, Frank Jewett, 1868-1953. 1.5895
Mather, John Russell, 1923-. 5.2563, 5.5975
Mather, Kenneth. 5.3453
Mather, Kirtley F. (Kirtley Fletcher), 1888- comp. 5.2938
Matheson, Richard, 1926-. 2.13171
Matheson, Scott. 4.7875
Matheson, William H., tr. 2.528
Mathews, Donald G. 1.2411
Mathews, Donald K. 4.913
Mathews, John Joseph, 1895-. 2.12120
Mathews, Joseph James, 1908-. 2.3579
Mathews, Mitford McLeod, 1891- ed. 2.1136
Mathews, R. H. (Robert Henry). 2.2149
Mathews, Thomas F. 1.5536-1.5537
Mathewson, Rufus W. 2.1252
Mathias, Harry. 5.7006
Mathias, Roland. 2.9872
Mathieson, Margaret. 4.10511
Mathieu, Pierre-Louis. 1.6126
Mathiez, Albert, 1874-1932. 3.2089
Mathis, Dovie C., joint comp. 2.10700
Mathisen, Trygve. 4.8998
Mathurin, Owen Charles. 3.5109
Mathys, Nicholas J. joint author. 4.4375-4.4376
Matilsky, Sarah. 4.6135
Matisse, Henri, 1869-1954. 1.4976, 1.5710, 1.6120
Matlaw, Myron, 1924-. 2.2808
Matlaw, Ralph E. 2.1352
Matlaw, Ralph E. comp. 2.1439
Matloff, Maurice, 1915-. 3.6365
Matson, Wallace I. 1.516
Matsuba, Shelley M., 1953-. 4.3710
Matsumura, Hideyuki, 1930-. 5.1361
Matsuno, Kōichirō. 5.3321
Matsuo, Bashō, 1644-1694. 2.2064-2.2065
Matt, Daniel Chanan. 1.1949
Matt, Leonard von. 1.4724
Matteson, David Maydole, 1871-1949. 3.7035
Matteson, Michael T. 4.2654
Mattfeld, Julius, 1893-1968. 1.3601
Matthaei, Julie A. 4.5987
Matthews, Brander, 1852-1929. 2.2798, 2.3120, 5.846
Matthews, David, 1943-. 1.3919
Matthews, Denis. 1.4105
Matthews, Denis. comp. 1.4149
Matthews, Donald R. joint author. 4.7943
Matthews, Donald R. 4.7966, 4.8042
Matthews, Douglas. joint author. 4.7851
Matthews, Douglas. 4.7995

Matthews, Fred H. 4.4777
Matthews, G. M., comp. 2.7864
Matthews, J. H. 2.4429, 2.4647
Matthews, J. Les (James Les), 1926-. 5.4162
Matthews, J. W. 2.8316
Matthews, Janice R., 1943- joint author. 5.3871
Matthews, Jill Julius. 4.6164
Matthews, John Frederick. 3.2725, 3.2819
Matthews, Joseph R. 5.7612
Matthews, M. C. 5.6086
Matthews, Mervyn. 4.5378, 4.10132
Matthews, Mildred Shapley. 5.1766, 5.1820, 5.1822
Matthews, P. H. (Peter Hugoe) 2.188
Matthews, R. C. O. (Robert Charles Oliver), 1927-. 4.2282
Matthews, Robert W., 1942-. 5.3871
Matthews, Washington, 1843-1905. 3.5922
Matthews, William, 1905-. 2.6078, 2.6412, 2.6422, 3.1503, 5.7944, 5.7994, 5.8111
Matthews, William Kleesmann, 1901-1958. 2.217, 2.1224
Matthias, Erich, ed. 3.2420
Matthias, John, 1941-. 2.14063
Matthiessen, F. O. (Francis Otto), 1902-1950. 2.5641, 2.10270, 2.10375, 2.10730, 2.11124, 2.11135, 2.11603, 2.11639
Matthiessen, Peter. 3.5669
Mattil, Edward L. 1.4653
Mattingly, Garrett, 1900-1962. 3.1404, 3.1440, 4.9085
Mattingly, Harold, 1884-1964. 2.355, 3.278, 3.2727
Mattingly, Paul H. 4.10520
Mattione, Richard P. 4.4615
Mattson, Guy. joint author. 5.6812
Maturin, Charles Robert, 1780-1824. 2.7932
Matusow, Allen J. 4.2943
Matusow, Allen J. joint ed. 3.7791
Matusow, Barbara. 2.3652
Matute, Ana María, 1926-. 2.5276
Matyas, Stephen M. 5.7530
Matz, Adolph, 1905-. 4.4415
Matz, Friedrich, 1890-1974. 1.4718
Matza, David. 4.5069
Matzner, Dorothe. 4.9455
Mau, Hermann. 3.2443
Maude, Aylmer, 1858-1938. 1.4617, 2.1429, 2.1434
Maude, George. 4.9076
Maude, H. E. (Henry Evans), 1906-. 3.5547
Maude, Louise Shanks, 1855-1939. 2.1429
Maugh, Thomas H. 5.4771
Maugham, Frederic Herbert Maugham, 1st Viscount, 1866-1958. 4.9342
Maugham, W. Somerset (William Somerset), 1874-1965. 2.2580, 2.3511, 2.9093-2.9104, 2.14100
Mauk, Charlotte E. 3.8617
Maul, George A. 4.323
Mauldin, Bill, 1921-. 3.916
Mauldin, R. Daniel, 1943-. 5.1121
Mauldon, Elizabeth. 4.920
Maung Maung Gyi. 4.8720
Maunier, René, 1887-. 4.8906
Maupassant, Guy de, 1850-1893. 2.4267-2.4270
Maurer, Armand A. (Armand Augustine), 1915-. 1.355, 1.438
Maurer, Christopher. 2.5253
Maurer, Evan M. 3.5816
Maurer, Harry. 4.3024
Maurer, Walter H. 1.1679
Maurer, Warren R. 2.13768
Mauriac, Claude, 1914-. 2.4430, 2.4627
Mauriac, François, 1885-1970. 2.4628-2.4632
Mauritshuis (Hague, Netherlands) 1.5024
Maurois, André, 1885-1967. 2.3522, 2.4125, 2.4152, 2.4179, 2.4240, 2.4293, 2.7528, 2.7640, 2.8103
Mauron, Charles. ed. 2.4262
Maurras, Charles, 1868-1952. 2.4294
Maury, F. 5.5122
Maury, Matthew Fontaine, 1806-1873. 4.324
Mauser, Gary A. 4.7790
Mauskopf, Seymour H. 5.636, 5.747
Mausner, Judith S. 4.4684
Mauss, Marcel, 1872-1950. 3.5877, 4.601, 4.866, 5.684

Mauzi, Robert. 2.4083
Mauzy, Diane K., 1942- joint author. 4.8728
Mavor, James, 1854-1925. 4.2367
Mawson, C. O. Sylvester (Christopher Orlando Sylvester), 1870-1938. 2.1100
Max-Planck-Institut für Ausländisches und Internationales Sozialrecht. 4.3444
Max-Planck-Institut für Bildungsforschung. 4.10741
Maximilian, prince of Baden, 1867-. 3.2351
Maxmen, Jerrold S. 5.4553
Maxon, Yale Candee, 1906-. 3.4973
Maxtone-Graham, John. 4.3955
Maxwell, Baldwin, 1893-. 2.5874
Maxwell, Constantia Elizabeth, ed. 3.1868, 3.1952
Maxwell, D. E. S. (Desmond Ernest Stewart), 1925-. 2.9861, 2.10538
Maxwell, Ian Stanley. 3.1725
Maxwell, James Ackley, 1897-1975. 4.4659
Maxwell, James Clerk, 1831-1879. 5.2339, 5.2341, 5.2363
Maxwell, Kenneth, 1941-. 3.9208
Maxwell, Mary. 1.481
Maxwell, Moreau S. 3.5878
Maxwell Museum of Anthropology. 3.5908
Maxwell, Neville George Anthony. 3.4298
Maxwell, Robert, 1923-. 3.3006
Maxwell, Robert S. 3.7440
Maxwell, Thomas R., 1911-. 3.8834
Maxwell, William. 2.12121-2.12122
May, Arthur James, 1899-1968. 3.695
May, Brian. 3.4575
May, Charles Edward, 1941-. 2.3439
May, Earl Chapin, 1873-1960. 4.1186
May, Elizabeth, writer on music. 1.4363
May, Ernest R. 3.833, 3.7117, 3.7421, 3.7585, 5.7360
May, Frederick, tr. 2.5056
May, Gary, 1944-. 3.7691
May, George Smith, 1924-. 3.8431, 4.3823
May, Gerald G. 5.29
May, Glenn Anthony. 3.4603
May, Henry Farnham, 1915-. 2.11229, 3.6025, 3.6138
May, Herbert Gordon, 1904-. 1.2497, 1.2551
May, John R. 2.10549
May, Keith M. 2.8829
May, Robert M. 5.3527
May, Rollo. 5.345, 5.430
May, Rollo. ed. 5.63
May, Timothy C. 4.3405
Mayakovsky, Vladimir, 1893-1930. 2.1572
Maybury-Lewis, David. 3.9197
Mayer, Adrian C. 3.4177, 3.5635
Mayer, Arno J. 3.825, 3.847
Mayer, Ben. 5.1731
Mayer, Claude Albert. 2.3989
Mayer, David. 2.2841
Mayer, Fanny Hagin, 1899-. 4.808
Mayer, Franziska (von Reicher) 1885- ed. 1.1466
Mayer, Frederick, 1921-. 4.9950
Mayer, George H. 4.8222
Mayer, Gustav, 1871-1948. 4.7066
Mayer, Hans Otto, 1903- joint author. 2.13836
Mayer, Harold M. (Harold Melvin), 1916-. 3.8412
Mayer, J. P. (Jacob Peter), 1903- ed. 4.7842
Mayer, Joseph Edward, 1904-. 5.2168
Mayer, Maria Goeppert, 1906-1972, joint author. 5.2168
Mayer-Oakes, Thomas Francis, 1912- ed. 3.4962
Mayer, Ralph, 1895-. 1.6373-1.6374
Mayer, Thomas, 1927-. 4.4507
Mayer, William V. 5.3305
Mayfield, Chris. 3.8159
Mayhall, Pamela D. (Pamela Douglass), 1939-. 4.6563
Mayhew, David R. 4.8003, 4.8023
Mayhew, Dorothy Ford, tr. 3.5217
Mayhew, Henry, 1812-1887. 4.6625
Mayhew, Katherine Camp. 4.11004
Mayhew, Lewis B. 4.10594, 4.10615
Mayhew, Lewis B. joint author. 4.10571
Maylam, Paul. 3.5480
Maynard, John, Sir, 1865-1943. 3.3165
Maynard, Mary. 4.5872

Maynard Smith, John, 1920-. 5.3372, 5.3483
Mayne, Jonathan. 1.4670
Mayne, Jonathan. ed. 1.4963
Mayne, Richard J. 3.1192
Mayne, Seymour, 1944-. 2.9945
Maynial, Édouard, 1879- ed. 2.4191, 2.4193
Mayo Clinic. Section of Clinical Microbiology.
 5.4445
Mayo, David J. 1.1325
Mayo, Elton, 1880-1949. 4.3316
Mayo, Henry Bertram, 1911-. 4.7004, 4.7578
Mayo, Lawrence Shaw, 1888-1947, ed. 3.7973
Mayo, Robert S., 1939-. 2.13611
Mayr, Ernst, 1904-. 5.3298, 5.3367, 5.3373,
 5.3395-5.3396, 5.3829
Mayr-Harting, Henry. 1.2434
Mayr, Otto. 5.6180
Mayrose, Vernon B. 5.5439
Mays, David John, 1896-. 3.8208
Mays, James Luther. 1.2619
Maza, Sarah C., 1953-. 4.3526
Mazar, Benjamin, 1906-. 3.3897
Mazia, Daniel, 1912- ed. 5.3588
Mazlish, Bruce, 1923-. 1.420, 3.483
Mazmanian, Daniel A., 1945-. 4.8160
Mazo, Joseph H. 4.1124
Mazour, Anatole Gregory, 1900-.
 3.3034-3.3035, 3.3123, 3.3290
Mazrui, Ali Al'Amin. 3.5078, 3.5091, 3.5110,
 4.5466
Mazrui, Ali Al'Amin. joint author. 3.5234
Mazur, Mary Ann, 1946- joint author. 4.6734
Mazur, Michael P. 4.2446
Mazurs, Edward G. 5.2834
Mazzali, Ettore. 2.4879
Mazzali, Ettore. ed. 2.4980
Mazzaro, Jerome. 2.4921, 2.12052
Mazzeo, Joseph Anthony, 1923-. 3.159, 3.181
Mazzini, Giuseppe, 1805-1872. 3.2874
Mazzolani, Federico M. 5.5888
Mazzotta, Giuseppe, 1942-. 2.4938
Mbiti, John S. 1.1594, 1.1846
Mboya, Tom. 3.5282
McAdam, Edward Lippincott, jr., joint ed.
 2.7080
McAdoo, William Gibbs, 1863-1941. 3.7665
McAleer, Edward C. ed. 2.7479
McAleese, Ray. joint author. 4.10321
McAlester, A. Lee (Arcie Lee), 1933-. 5.5557
McAlester, Virginia, 1943-. 1.5557
McAlister, John T., 1936-. 3.4477
McAlister, Lyle N. 3.5980
McAllester, David Park, 1916-. 1.4309
McAllister, Ian. 4.8416
McAllister, Jef Olivarius. 3.7858
McAllister, Marian Holland. 3.2520
McAlmon, Robert, 1895-1956. 2.12060
McAmis, Robert D. 3.4593
McAndrew, John. 1.5437, 1.5524
McArthur, Benjamin. 2.3204
McArthur, John H. 4.2334
McAuley, Alastair, 1938-. 4.2406, 4.3300
McAuley, James Phillip, 1917-. 2.10141
McAuley, Mary. 4.3662
McAuliffe, Kevin. 2.3666
McAvoy, Thomas Timothy, 1903-1969. 1.3181
McBain, Ed. 2.11907
McBath, James H. comp. 2.6267
McBean, Edward A. 5.5971
McBride, George McCutchen, 1876-. 4.2837,
 4.2841
McBride, R. Bruce. 4.6799
McBride, S. Dean (Samuel Dean), 1937-. 1.2618
McBride, Simon. 2.7800
McBrien, Richard P. 1.3201
McBryde, F. Webster (Felix Webster), 1908-.
 4.389
McBurney, William Harlin. 2.6260
McCabe, Cynthia Jaffee. 1.6008
McCabe, F. G. (Frank G.), 1953-. 5.1219
McCabe, John, 1920-. 2.3248
McCafferty, James A., comp. 4.6851
McCaffery, Larry, 1946-. 2.10280
McCaffery, Margo. 5.4744
McCaffrey, Anne. 2.13142
McCaghy, M. Dawn. 5.8469
McCahill, Thomas W. 4.6744
McCaig, I. R. (Isabel R.) 2.1105

McCall, James L. 5.6769
McCall, Storrs. comp. 1.1215
McCalla, Douglas, 1942-. 4.4222
McCallum, James Ramsay, ed. and tr. 1.2738
McCandless, Judith. 1.6296
McCandless, Perry, 1917-. 3.8360
McCandless, Stanley Russell. 2.3143
McCann, Brian M. 4.6614
McCann, Frank D. 3.943
McCann, Franklin Thresher, 1903-. 3.5989
McCann, Garth. 2.12836
McCann, Mary Ann. 5.4732
McCann, Michael, 1943-. 5.5013
McCarthy, Albert J. 1.4195
McCarthy, Albert J. joint comp. 1.4327
McCarthy, B. Eugene, 1934-. 2.7340
McCarthy, Eugene J., 1916-. 3.7893
McCarthy, John A. (John Aloysius), 1942-.
 2.13668
McCarthy, Martha M. 4.9585, 4.10746
McCarthy, Mary, 1912-. 2.3228,
 2.12061-2.12068
McCarthy, Richard Joseph. 1.2025, 1.2044
McCarthy, Thomas A. 1.987
McCarthy. Todd. 2.2920
McCarthy, W. E. J. (William Edward John)
 4.3173
McCarty, Donald James, 1921-. 4.10519
McCarty, Harold Hull, 1901-. 4.4121
McCarty, Perry L. 5.6024
McCash, William B., 1931-. 3.8261
McCaughey, Elizabeth P., 1948-. 3.7001
McCauley, Charley. 5.4970
McCauley, Martin. 3.2477, 3.3174, 3.3208
McCausland, Elizabeth, 1899-1966. 1.5949
McCawley, Peter. 4.2533
McClane, A. J. (Albert Jules), 1922- ed. 5.5488
McClatchy, J. D., 1945-. 2.12460
McCleary, John. 5.1614
McClellan, B. Edward (Bernard Edward),
 1939-. 2.11016
McClellan, Edwin, 1925-. 2.2088, 3.348
McClellan, Elisabeth, 1851-1920. 4.836
McClellan, James E. (James Edward), 1946-.
 5.689
McClellan, James H., 1947-. 5.6376
McClelland, B. J. 5.2258
McClelland, Ben W., 1943-. 4.10474
McClelland, Charles E. 4.10128
McClelland, David Clarence. 4.2794, 4.10825,
 5.116, 5.366
McClelland, Nancy Vincent, 1876-. 1.6570
McClelland, Peter D. 4.1251
McClenon, James. 5.648
McClintic, Miranda. 1.4905
McClintick, David, 1940-. 4.6757
McClintock, Cynthia. 3.9309
McClintock, Marsha Hamilton. 3.3681
McClintock, P. V. E. 5.2234
McCloskey, Donald N. 4.2265, 4.3735
McCloskey, Joanne Comi. 5.5179
McCloskey, Robert Green. 4.7311
McClosky, Herbert. 4.5229, 4.7694
McCloughry, Roy. 4.4471
McCloy, D. 5.6237
McCloy, Shelby Thomas, 1898-. 4.5349
McClung, Patricia A. 5.7623
McClure, Carma L. 5.5571
McClure, Mark S. 3.5872
McClure, Norman Egbert, 1893-. 2.6147
McClure, Samuel Sidney, 1857-1949. 2.3619
McCluskey, Neil Gerard. 4.5811
McClymont, William Graham. 3.5600
McColley, Diane Kelsey, 1934-. 2.7134
McCollum, John I. 2.3302
McComas, J. Francis, joint ed. 2.3723
McComb, Arthur Kilgore, 1895-. 1.5197
McComb, Ernest Hacket Kemper 1873-   ed.
 2.11039
McComb, Samuel, 1864-. 1.2989
McCombie, Sharon L. 4.6735
McConnaughey, Bayard Harlow, 1916-. 5.3248
McConnell, Allen, 1923-. 2.1336
McConnell, Frank D., 1942-. 2.2975, 2.8258,
 2.8306
McConnell, Winder. 2.13536
McCool, Gerald A. ed. 1.3140
McCord, Joan, joint author. 4.6696

McCord Museum. 1.5349-1.5350, 1.6448
McCord, William Maxwell, 1930-. 4.6696
McCorduck, Pamela, 1940-. 5.1011
McCorkle, Donald. 1.3607
McCorkle, Margit L. 1.3607
McCormac, Jack C. 5.5823
McCormack, Andrew Ross, 1943-. 4.7009
McCormack, Gavan. 3.4813
McCormack, W. J. 2.8210
McCormick, Arthur David. 3.4120
McCormick, E. H. (Eric Hall), 1906-. 2.10194
McCormick, Ernest J. (Ernest James) 4.4352,
 5.5687
McCormick, J. Frank, 1935-. 5.3519
McCormick, Michael E., 1936-. 5.6300
McCormick, Naomi B. 4.5829
McCormick, Peter (Peter J.) 1.1011
McCormick, Richard L. 3.7532, 3.8034
McCormick, Richard Patrick, 1916-. 3.8064,
 4.8159
McCormmach, Russell. 5.1934
McCorry, Jesse J., 1935- joint author. 3.6662
McCosh, Andrew M. joint author. 4.4382
McCown, Elizabeth R. 5.4035
McCoy, Alfred W. ed. 3.4456
McCoy, Alfred W. 4.5443
McCoy, Charles Allan, 1920- comp. 4.7312
McCoy, Clyde B., 1941-. 4.5194
McCoy, Donald R. 3.7811, 3.8527
McCoy, Horace, 1897-1955. 2.12069
McCoy, Neal Henry, 1905-. 5.1342
McCoy, Ralph E. (Ralph Edward), 1915-.
 5.7598, 5.8309
McCracken, Daniel D. 5.5721
McCracken, David. ed. 2.7747
McCracken, George Englert, 1904- ed. 1.2180
McCracken, Harold, 1894-. 1.5925
McCracken, R. J. joint author. 5.5262
McCrady, Barbara S. 5.4882
McCrary, Peyton, 1943-. 3.8312
McCraw, Thomas K. 4.3078
McCrea, Brian. 2.7029
McCrea, William Hunter. 5.2007
McCreadie, Marsha, 1943-. 2.2960
McCrie, Thomas, 1797-1875, tr. 1.805
McCrone, David. 4.6256
McCrum, Blanche Prichard, 1887-. 5.7761
McCubbin, Hamilton I. 4.5657
McCue, George. 1.3692
McCue, James F. 1.3364
McCuen, Richard H., 1941-. 5.5717
McCullagh, C. Behan. 3.398
McCullagh, Patrick. joint author. 4.18
McCullers, Carson, 1917-1967. 2.12070-2.12076,
 2.12840
McCullin, Don, 1935-. 3.3864
McCulloch, A. M. (Ann M.), 1949-. 2.10189
McCulloh, William E. 2.519
McCullough, Constance Mary, 1912- joint
 author. 4.10463
McCullough, David G. 3.9083, 5.6078
McCullough, David W. 2.10823
McCullough, Frances Monson, 1939-. 2.13260
McCullough, Helen Craig. tr. 2.2041
McCullough, Helen Craig. 3.4494
McCullough, Helen Craig. ed. and tr. 3.4937
McCullough, Joseph B. 2.10742, 2.11040
McCune, George McAfee, 1908-1948. 3.5001,
 3.5006
McCune, Shannon Boyd-Bailey, 1913-.
 3.4990-3.4991
McCutcheon, John Tinney, 1870-1949. 2.10893
McDaniel, Darl Hamilton, 1928-. 5.2703,
 5.2846
McDaniel, Gary L. 5.5343
McDaniel, George W. 3.8102
McDannald, Alexander Hopkins, 1877- ed. 1.11
McDavid, Raven Ioor. 2.10841
McDavid, Raven Ioor. joint author. 2.1121
McDermott, Drew V. joint author. 5.1019
McDermott, Drew V. 5.1006
McDermott, John, 1951-. 4.4700
McDermott, John Francis, 1902-. 3.6215
McDevitt, Joan Quinn. joint author. 5.5205
McDiarmid, Matthew P. 2.6608
McDonagh, Don. 4.1122-4.1123, 4.1142
McDonald, Alan T. 5.6130
McDonald, David R. 5.7739

McDonald, Forrest. 3.6999, 3.7059
McDonald, Gordon C. 3.5301, 3.5417
McDonald, James Harold, ed. 2.6520
McDonald, William A. (William Andrew),
  1913-. 3.2585
McDonnell, Kilian. 1.2480
McDonnell, Porter W., 1929-. 4.213
McDonnell, Thomas P. 2.12146
McDougal, Myres Smith, 1906-. 4.8986, 4.9315,
  4.9325, 4.9336, 4.9383
McDougall, Bonnie S., 1941-. 1.6724
McDougall, Richard. 2.12455
McDougall, Walter A., 1946-. 3.2198, 3.9133,
  5.6702
McDowell, Frederick P. W. 2.8664, 2.12400
McDowell, Frederick Peter Woll, 1915-.
  2.11779
McDowell, Jack. joint author. 4.991
McDowell, John Henry. 1.254
McDowell, Judith H., ed. 2.4089
McDowell, Margaret B. 2.12078
McDowell, R. B. (Robert Brendan), 1913-.
  3.1838
McDowell, W., joint ed. 5.2773
McElhiney, Paul T. joint comp. 4.3880
McElrath, Joseph R. 2.10865
McElroy, Frank E. 5.5554
McElroy, William David, 1917- ed. 5.3626
McElvaine, Robert S., 1947-. 3.6056, 3.7763
McElwee, William Lloyd, 1907- tr. 3.2496
McEvedy, Colin. 4.1582
McEvoy, J. J. 1.385
McEvoy, James, 1940- joint author. 5.5977
McEwen, Craig A. 4.6884
McEwen, Freeman Lester, 1926-. 5.5413
McEwen, William J. 4.5268
McFadden, David Revere. 1.6544
McFadden, George, 1916-. 1.1391, 2.7006
McFague, Sallie. 1.2252
McFarlan, F. Warren (Franklin Warren) 5.5611
McFarland, Andrew S., 1940-. 4.8036
McFarland, Horace Neill, 1923-. 1.1834
McFarland, M. Carter. 4.6325
McFarland, Robert D. 5.6103
McFarlane, Brian. 4.995
McFarlane, I. D. (Ian Dalrymple) 2.3845,
  2.4008
McFarlane, James Walter. 2.14031,
  2.14033-2.14034
McFarlane, K. B. (Kenneth Bruce) 1.6269,
  4.6394
McFee, June King. 1.4646
McFeely, Mary Drake. 5.8470
McFeely, William S. 3.7481
McFie, John, M.D. 5.4789
McGann, Jerome J. 2.31, 2.7519, 2.8140
McGann, Thomas Francis, 1920-. 3.9248
McGarry, Daniel D. 1.387
McGean, Thomas. 5.5932
McGeary, M. Nelson (Martin Nelson), 1906-.
  3.7444
McGee, John Seneca, 1927-. 4.3053
McGhee, Paul E. 5.436, 5.598
McGhehey, M. A. 4.10630
McGill, Ralph, 1898-1969. 3.8161
McGill, William J. (William James), 1922-.
  4.10989
McGillem, Clare D. 5.6368
McGinley, Phyllis, 1905-. 2.12079
McGinn, Bernard, 1937-. 1.2947-1.2948, 1.3053,
  1.3087
McGinniss, Joe. 3.7894
McGlynn, Daniel R. 5.6583
McGoldrick, Monica. 5.4819
McGovern, George S. (George Stanley), 1922-.
  4.3168
McGovern, John P. 5.4602
McGowan, Christopher. 5.3397
McGowan, Clement L., 1942-. 5.1189
McGowan, John J. 4.9468
McGrade, Arthur S. 4.7378
McGrath, Patrick. 3.1430
McGrath, William R. (William Restore), 1922-.
  4.3929
McGraw-Hill Book Company. 5.810, 5.1191,
  5.2944, 5.3511
McGraw-Hill, Inc. 2.2785
McGraw, James R. joint author. 2.3256

McGregor, Douglas. 4.4361
McGregor, F. A. 3.8749
McGregor, John C. (John Charles), 1905-.
  3.5763
McGregor, Malcolm Francis, 1910-. 3.2556
McGregor, O. R. (Oliver Ross), 1921-. 5.5248
McGregor, Ronald Stuart. 2.1883
McGrew, William Clement, 1944-. 4.10405
McGuane, Thomas. 2.13145
McGuigan, F. J. (Frank J.), 1924-. 5.208
McGuinness, Brian. 1.1087, 5.1023
McGuire, Christine H. 5.4597
McGuire, Joseph William. 4.4257
McGuire, Kenneth. 1.3179
McGuire, Martin Rawson Patrick, 1897-. 2.356
McGuire, Phillip, 1944-. 3.1128
McGuire, William, 1920-. 5.4911, 5.5837
McHale, John. 3.75
McHale, Vincent E., 1939-. 4.7775
McHarg, Ian L. 4.2078
McHenry, Dean Eugene, 1910-. 4.8306
McHenry, Donald F. 4.9306
McHugh, Heather, 1948-. 2.4529
McHugh, J. L. 5.5479
McHugh, Roger Joseph. 2.9852
McHugh, Roland. 2.8873-2.8874
McIlvaine, B., joint author. 5.8479
McIlwain, Charles Howard, 1871-1968. 4.7260,
  4.7706-4.7707, 4.8464
McIlwaine, Shields, 1902-. 2.10362
McIlwraith, A. K. (Archibald Kennedy) comp.
  2.6223
McIlwraith, A. K. (Archibald Kennedy) ed.
  2.6222
McInerny, Ralph M. 1.395
McInnis, Edgar, 1899-. 3.8674
McInnis, Raymond G. 5.8351, 5.8413
McIntire, C. T. 1.2248
McIntosh, C. Alison. 4.1691
McIntosh, John L. 5.8434
McIntosh, Robert P. (Robert Patrick) 5.3521
McIntyre, W. David (William David), 1932-.
  3.1224
McKane, William. 1.2609
McKay, Charles W., 1943-. 5.6591
McKay, Claude, 1890-1948. 2.12081-2.12085,
  3.6770, 3.8044
McKay, David Phares. 1.3819
McKay, Derek. 3.645
McKay, Douglas R. 2.5277
McKay, John P. 4.4023
McKay, John William, 1941-. 1.2607
McKay, Nellie Y. 2.12599
McKay, William Angus. 3.341
McKearin, George Skinner, 1874-. 1.6644
McKearin, Helen, joint author. 1.6644
McKee, Bob. 1.5647
McKee, C. S. joint author. 5.2899
McKee, Christopher. 3.7067
McKee, Kathleen Burke. 5.8479
McKee, Samuel. 4.1909
McKee, Thomas Hudson. 4.8145
McKelvey, Blake, 1903-. 4.6216-4.6217, 4.6903
McKelvey, Francis X. 5.6685
McKendrick, Neil. 4.2295
McKenna, Brian. 5.7995
McKenna, Richard. 2.13146
McKenna, Richard P., joint author. 5.6626
McKenna, Wayne. 2.7908
McKenney, James L. 5.5611
McKenney, Ruth, 1911-. 2.12086
McKennon, Joe. 4.1195
McKenny, Margaret. joint author. 5.3676
McKenzie, John L. 1.3210
McKenzie, Richard B. 4.3208
McKenzie, Robert Trelford. 4.3651, 4.8527
McKenzie, Roderick, 1887-1937, ed. 2.247
McKenzie, Roderick Duncan, 1885-1940. joint
  author. 4.6298
McKeon, Richard Peter. 1.282, 1.609
McKeown, Thomas. 5.4545
McKerrow, Ronald Brunlees, 1872-1940.
  2.6447, 2.6641, 2.6840-2.6841
McKerrow, W. S. 5.3156
McKibbin, Michael. 4.10273
McKibbin, Ross. 4.8545
McKie, Douglas. joint comp. 5.5665
McKie, James W. 4.3808

McKillip, Patricia A. 2.13147
McKillop, A. B. 3.8665
McKillop, Alan Dugald, 1892-. 2.5625, 2.5995,
  2.6087, 2.7225, 2.7317
McKillop, Susan Regan. 1.6204
McKim, Donald K. joint author. 1.2529
McKim, Margaret Grace, 1914-. 4.10461
McKim, Mead & White. 1.5316
McKinley, Edward H. 1.3409, 3.5127
McKinnell, Robert Gilmore. 5.3463
McKinney, Francis F   1891-. 3.7334
McKinney, John C., 1920- ed. 4.5195
McKinney, Mary Jane. 4.4447
McKinnon, John. 4.644
McKinnon, Ronald I. 4.4571
McKinnon, William T. 2.9077
McKinzie, Richard D. 1.5202
McKisack, May. 3.1365, 3.1369, 4.8466
McKissick, Floyd, 1922-. 3.6621
McKitrick, Eric L. 3.7254, 3.7467
McKivigan, John R., 1949-. 3.7256
McKnew, Donald H. 5.5112
McKnight, Brian E. 4.8887
McKnight, Edgar V. 1.2634
McKnight, Tom L. (Tom Lee), 1928-. 3.5563
McKusick, Leon. 5.4984
McLachlan, Alexander, 1820-1896. 2.9905
McLachlan, K. S. (Keith Stanley) 4.2983,
  5.8043
McLane, Charles B. 3.3072
McLaren, Angus. 4.859
McLaren, Ian A. 4.10690
McLaren, Norman, 1914-. 1.5798
McLarney, William O. joint author. 5.5466
McLauchlan, Gordon. 3.5593
McLaughlin, Andrew Cunningham, 1861-1947.
  4.7809
McLaughlin, Eleanor. 1.3000
McLaughlin, Glenn Everett. 4.1893
McLaughlin, Kenneth, 1943-. 3.8831
McLaughlin, T. G. 5.1585
McLaurin, R. D. (Ronald De), 1944-. 3.4036
McLean, Hugh, 1925- ed. 2.1300
McLean, Iain. 4.3648
McLean, Janice W. 4.2725
McLean, John Godfrey, 1917-. 4.3771
McLean, Ridley, 1872-1933, comp. 5.7424
McLean, Ruari. 5.7547
McLean, Sheila. 5.4564
McLeish, Kenneth, 1940-. 2.434
McLellan, David. 1.1037, 4.6939, 4.6946,
  4.6955-4.6956
McLellan, David S. 3.7623
McLelland, J. (John) 5.3966
McLemore, S. Dale. 3.6520
McLennan, Kenneth. 4.2089
McLeod, A. L. (Alan Lindsey), 1928-. 3.5456,
  3.6770
McLeod, Hugh. 1.1638, 1.2448
McLeod, Marian B. 3.5456
McLeod, Marion. 2.10205
McLeod, Raymond. 5.5612
McLeod, W. H. 1.1826, 3.4210
McLintock, Alexander H., ed. 3.5592
McLoughlin, Denis. 3.8462
McLoughlin, William Gerald. 1.2409,
  1.3036-1.3037, 1.3321, 1.3324, 1.3336, 3.8011
McLuhan, Marshall, 1911-. 2.51
McLure, Charles E. 4.4710
McLusky, Donald Samuel. 5.3543
McMahan, Jeff. 3.7939
McMahon, A. Michal (Adrian Michal), 1937-.
  5.6250
McMahon, Amos Philip, 1890-1947. 1.6340
McMahon, Joseph H. 2.4541
McMahon, Patrick Joseph. 5.6673
McMahon, Robert J., 1949-. 3.6452
McManis, Douglas R. 4.2019
McManners, John. 3.655, 3.2095, 4.5827
McManus, Edgar J. 3.7192
McMaster, Carolyn. 3.5495
McMath, Robert C., 1944-. 4.2911
McMenamin, Michael. 4.3690
McMichael, George L., 1927-. 2.10664
McMicking, Thomas, 1829-1866. 3.8848
McMillan Browse, P. D. A. 5.5356
McMillan, Carol, 1954-. 4.5932
McMillan, Claude. 5.5582

McMillan, James B., 1907-. 2.964
McMillan, James F., 1948-. 4.6119
McMillan, John, of Australia. 4.8818
McMillen, Donald H. 3.4861
McMillin, Scott. comp. 2.6197
McMinn, R. M. H. (Robert Matthew Hay)
  5.4146
McMinn, W. G., 1930-. 4.8817
McMullan, J. T. (John T.) 5.6114, 5.6132
McMullen, Roy. 1.6089
McMullin, Neil, 1940-. 1.2122
McMullin, Thomas A. 3.6295
McMurray, Foster. 4.10218
McMurray, George R., 1925-. 2.5306, 2.5407
McMurrin, Sterling M. 1.123
McMurry, Linda O. 5.5224
McNab, Robert, 1864-1917. 3.5589
McNair, Arnold D. (Arnold Duncan), baron,
  1885-. 4.9312
McNairn, Barbara. 3.258
McNally, Dennis. 2.11960
McNally, Terrence. 2.13149-2.13150
McNamara, Brooks. 1.5549, 2.3153, 4.1190
McNamara, Jo Ann, 1931-. 4.5769
McNamara, John E. 5.6399
McNamara, Walter (Walter J.) joint author.
  4.3690
McNamee, Lawrence P., 1934-. 5.6461
McNaugher, Thomas L. 5.7276
McNaught, Kenneth William Kirkpatrick,
  1918-. 3.8773
McNaughton, Howard Douglas. 2.10197,
  2.10210
McNeal, Brian Lester, 1938-. 5.5275
McNeal, Robert Hatch, 1930-. 3.3142, 3.3223,
  4.8661
McNeely, Jeffrey A. 5.5384
McNeil, Barbara. 5.8112
McNeil, Barbara J., 1941-. 5.4633
McNeil, Helen, 1942-. 2.11005
McNeil, John D. 4.10441
McNeile, Alan Hugh, 1871-1933. 1.2629
McNeill, D. B. (Donald Burgess), 1911-. 5.2023
McNeill, John Thomas, 1885-. 1.2433, 1.3406,
  4.7385
McNeill, William Hardy, 1917-. 3.31, 3.41,
  3.528, 3.2911, 3.3524, 4.1652, 4.5393, 5.4681
McNelis, James Ignatius, ed. 2.14006
McNellie, William, 1949-. 3.8938
McNickle, D'Arcy, 1904-1977. 2.12092
McNitt, Frank. 3.5921
McNitt, J. I. (James I.) 5.5440
McNulty, Paul J. 4.3109
McNutt, Dan J. 5.7968
McPartland, Brian J. 5.6336
McPartland, Joseph F. 5.6336
McPeck, John E. 4.10249
McPharlin, Paul, 1903-1948. 2.2837
McPhee, Carol. 4.5881
McPhee, Colin, 1901-1964. 1.3745
McPhee, John A. 5.2999-5.3001
McPheeters, D. W. 2.5244
McPherson, Barry D. joint author. 4.956
McPherson, Barry D. 4.960
McPherson, Edward, 1830-1895. 4.7846
McPherson, James Alan, 1943-. 2.13151-2.13152
McPherson, James M. 3.6678, 3.7255, 3.7344,
  3.8164
McPherson, William Heston, 1902-. 4.3517
McPhillips, Martin. 5.6232
McQuitty, Barbara J. 5.7661
McRae, Kenneth D. (Kenneth Douglas) 4.7383
McRae, Robert F. 1.873
McReynolds, Edwin C. 3.8361, 3.8530
McRoberts, Kenneth. 4.5250
McShane, Mark. 2.9741
McShine, Kynaston. 1.4809, 1.4895
McShine, Kynaston. joint author. 1.4972
McSwain, Eldridge Tracy, 1898- joint author.
  4.10428
McSwain, Romola. 3.5667
McSweeney, Kerry, 1941-. 2.3516, 2.7696
McVan, Alice Jane. 2.5274
McVaugh, Michael R. joint author. 5.636
McVaugh, Rogers, 1909-. 5.3671
McVay, Gordon. 2.1556
McVeigh, J. C. 5.6228
McVey, Ruth Thomas. ed. 3.4558

McVoy, D. Stevens. 4.4068
McVoy, Gary R. (Gary Richard), 1951-. 5.6002
McWeeny, R. 5.2836
McWhinney, Edward. 4.8286, 4.9297, 4.9337
McWhirter, Norris, 1925-. 1.24
McWhirter, Ross. 1.24
McWhorter, Lucullus Virgil, 1860-1944.
  2.12223
McWilliam, George Henry, tr. 2.4904
McWilliams, Carey, 1905-. 3.6521, 3.8560
McWilliams, John P. joint comp. 2.10974
McWilliams, John P. 2.10391
Meacham, Standish. 4.3637
Mead, Carver. 5.6536
Mead, Chris, 1959-. 4.1056
Mead, Frank Spencer, 1898-. 1.2395
Mead, George Herbert. 1.442, 1.612-1.615,
  4.4990-4.4991
Mead, Margaret, 1901-1978. 1.4686, 3.5627,
  3.5654, 3.5671, 3.6139, 4.397, 4.417, 4.424,
  4.681, 4.4881, 4.5505, 4.5706, 4.5742, 4.10770
Mead, Matthew, 1924- tr. 2.13858
Mead, Rita H. 1.3695
Mead, Ruth. tr. 2.13858
Mead, Sidney Earl, 1904-. 1.2381-1.2382
Mead, Sidney M. 1.5091, 1.5093
Meade, J. E. (James Edward), 1907-. 4.1449,
  4.4114, 4.4150, 4.4183, 4.4209
Meade, James E. (James Edward). 4.3209
Meader, Clarence Linton, 1868-. 2.1467
Meadows, Donella H. 4.1788, 4.1790
Meadows, Thomas Taylor. 3.4730
Meagher, Sylvia. 3.7881
Means, Barbara, 1949- joint author. 5.65
Means, Gardiner Coit, 1896-. 4.3055, 4.4286
Means, Gardiner Colt, 1896-. 4.1946
Means, Gordon Paul. 3.4544
Means, Philip Ainsworth, 1892-1944. 3.9304
Means, Spencer. 5.8273
Means, Winthrop Dickinson, joint author.
  5.3126
Mears, Clara. joint author. 5.477
Mech, L. David. 5.3994
Mecham, J. Lloyd (John Lloyd), 1893-. 3.9020
Mecham, John Lloyd, joint ed. 3.8339
Mechanic, David, 1936-. 5.4622, 5.4624
Meckier, Jerome. 2.8830
Mecklenburger, James. comp. 4.10604
Meckler, Alan M., 1945-. 5.7580
Meckler, Milton. 5.6156
Medawar, P. B. (Peter Brian), 1915-. 5.847,
  5.912, 5.3304, 5.4461, 5.4465
Meder, Joseph, 1857-1934. 1.5819
Mediaeval Academy of America. 5.8224
Medici, Lorenzo de', 1449-1492. 2.4972
Medicine, Beatrice. 3.5740
Medieval Academy of America. 5.8225
Medley, Dudley Julius, 1861- joint author.
  5.7989
Medley, Margaret. 1.6617
Medlicott, W. N. (William Norton), 1900-.
  3.685, 3.721, 3.1651
Medoff, James L., 1947-. 4.3353
Medsker, Leland L. joint author. 4.10516
Medsker, Leland L. 4.10565-4.10566
Medvedev, Roy Aleksandrovich, 1925-. 3.3187,
  3.3219-3.3220, 3.3224, 3.3226, 3.3254,
  3.3263-3.3264, 3.3272, 4.8637
Medvedev, Zhores A., 1925-. 3.3272, 5.3434
Meech, Sanford Brown. 2.6337
Meehan, Edward J. 5.2656
Meehan, Elizabeth M. 4.3254
Meehan, Eugene J. 4.3494
Meek, Margaret. 4.10341
Meek, Ronald L. ed. and tr. 4.1589
Meek, Ronald L. ed. 4.1407
Meek, Theophile James, 1881-1966, ed. 1.2500
Meeker, Richard Kilburn, 1925-. 2.11773
Meeks, Phillip J. 5.6691
Meeks, Wayne A. 1.2302
Meer, Frederik van der, 1904-. 4.133
Meeús, Adrien de, 1900-. 3.2968
Meeuse, Bastiaan. 3.3775
Meffen, John. 1.4535
Meggers, Betty Jane. 3.9312
Meggitt, Mervyn J., 1924-. 3.5660, 4.860
Meggs, Philip B. 5.7559
Megill, Allan. 1.1396

Megow, William F., 1936- joint author. 5.6482
Megson, T. H. G. (Thomas Henry Gordon)
  5.6671
Mehan, Hugh, 1941-. 4.4803, 4.10275
Mehlinger, Howard D. 3.3159
Mehlman, Felice. 1.6641
Mehmet, Ozay. 4.1813
Mehnert, Klaus, 1906-. 5.7691
Mehra, Parshotam. 3.4213, 3.4234
Mehring, Franz, 1846-1919. 4.6959
Mehta, J. L. (Jaswant Lal), 1931-. 1.91
Mehta, Ved, 1934-. 1.664, 3.4159, 3.4310
Mei, I-pao, 1900-. 1.172
Meid, Werner Volker, 1940-. 2.13485
Meier, August, 1923-. 3.6622-3.6623, 3.6655,
  3.6680, 3.6809, 3.8439
Meier, Gerald M. 4.2749, 4.2751, 4.2795,
  4.4151
Meier-Graefe, Julius, 1867-1935. 1.6246
Meier, John P. 1.2643
Meier, Lili, 1926-. 3.1077
Meier, Matt S. 5.7863
Meier, Richard, 1934-. 1.5319
Meier, Robert F. (Robert Frank), 1944-. 4.5062,
  4.6749
Meiggs, Russell. 3.283, 3.2574, 3.2605, 3.2722
Meighan, Clement Woodward, 1925-. 3.5695
Meigs, Cornelia Lynde, 1884- ed. 2.2704
Meijer, Reinder P. 2.13940
Meiklejohn, Alexander, 1872-1964.
  4.7677-4.7678, 4.10233
Meiksin, Z. H. 5.6595
Meiland, Jack W. 3.484
Meili, Richard. 5.11
Meine, Franklin Julius, 1896-1968. ed. 2.10727
Meinecke, Friedrich, 1862-1954. 3.485, 3.2282,
  3.2444, 4.7382, 4.8599
Meineke, August, 1790-1870. 2.321
Meiners, R. K. 2.12576
Meiners, Roger E. 4.6847
Meinhart, Noreen E. 5.4744
Meinig, D. W. (Donald William), 1924-. 3.6323,
  3.8320, 3.8597, 4.382, 4.2996
Meisel, James Hans, 1900-. 4.7480
Meisel, John. 4.8297
Meisel, Martin. 1.6716, 2.8085
Meiselman, David, ed. 4.4483
Meisner, Maurice J., 1931-. 3.4796, 4.7111
Meiss, Millard. 1.5864, 1.6188, 1.6412-1.6413,
  1.6415
Meister, Alton. 5.4424
Meister, Dick. 4.3376
Meja, Volker. 4.4879
Mekas, Jonas. 2.2923
Mekhon Shiloaḥ le-ḥeker ha-Mizraḥ ha-tikhon
  ve-Afrikah. 3.3677
Melady, Margaret Badum. joint author. 3.5265
Melady, Thomas Patrick. 3.5265
Melanchthon, Philipp, 1497-1560. 1.2352
Meland, Sam. 5.6267
Melanson, Richard A. 3.9132
Melcher, James R. joint author. 5.2408
Melchior, Claus. 2.8880
Melchior, Paul J. 5.2491
Melder, Keith. 4.6061
Melendez, Sarah E., 1941-. 4.10890
Melhorn, Charles M. 5.7444
Mell, Donald Charles. 5.7973
Mellaart, James. 3.115, 3.4038, 4.711-4.712
Mellaarts, Alan. 1.6586
Mellaarts, Arlette. 1.6586
Mellafe R., Rolando. 4.6427
Mellanby, Kenneth. 5.4012
Mellen, Joan. 2.3060
Mellenthin, F. W. von (Friedrich Wilhelm),
  1904-. 3.969
Meller, Helen Elizabeth. 4.5324
Mellers, Wilfrid Howard, 1914-. 1.3690, 1.3764,
  1.3844, 1.4089, 1.4099, 1.4357
Melling, A. 5.6240
Mellish, C. S. (Christopher S.), 1954-. 5.1225
Mello, Nancy K. 4.6653
Mellon, M. G. (Melvin Guy), 1893-. 5.2602
Mellor, John Williams, 1928-. 4.2500
Mellor, Joseph William, 1873-1938. 5.2623
Mellor, P. B. (Peter Bassindale), 1929-. 5.5790
Mellor, Roy E. H. 4.2383
Mellow, James R. 2.11733

Mellown, Elgin W. 5.7931
Melly, Diana. 2.9277
Melman, Seymour. 4.1991, 4.2656
Melmon, Kenneth L., 1934-. 5.5136
Melnechuk, Theodore. ed. 5.4321
Melnick, R. Shep, 1951-. 4.9572
Mel'nik, B. D. (Boris Davydovich) 5.6826
Mel'nikov, E. B. (Evgenĭ Borisovich) joint
    author. 5.6826
Mel'nikov, Nikolaĭ Nikolaevich. 5.5414
Melo, Welington de. 5.1618
Melosi, Martin V., 1947-. 3.898
Melossi, Dario, 1948-. 4.6888
Melot, Michel. 1.4975, 1.6459
Melton, J. Gordon. 1.1872-1.1873
Melton, Reginald F., 1934-. 4.10442
Meltsner, Michael, 1937-. 4.9862
Meltzer, Herbert L., 1921-. 5.4338
Meltzoff, Julian. 5.4856
Melville, Herman, 1819-1891. 2.11148-2.11150,
    2.11152, 2.11154-2.11155, 2.11159, 2.12048
Melville, Keith. 4.7157
Melzack, Ronald. 5.4365
Melzer, Manfred. 4.2347
Memmi, Albert. ed. 2.4847
Menaker, Esther. 5.182
Menander, of Athens. 2.312, 2.381, 2.523-2.524,
    2.558
Menard, Henry W. (Henry William),
    1920-1986. 5.743
Mencher, Samuel, 1918-1967. 4.6530
Mencius. 1.170
Mencken, H. L. (Henry Louis), 1880-1956.
    1.1534, 2.1127, 2.12123-2.12131, 3.7516
Mendel, Arthur, 1905- tr. 1.3774, 1.3938
Mendel, Arthur P. 4.7086
Mendel, Françoise, joint author. 4.7727
Mendel, Gregor, 1822-1884. 5.3407
Mendele Mokher Sefarim, 1835-1917. 2.1778,
    2.1794-2.1796
Mendeloff, John M. 4.3504
Mendelsohn, Ezra. 3.3953
Mendelsohn, Harold A. 4.7858
Mendelsohn, Jack, 1918-. 1.3417
Mendelsohn, John, 1928-. 3.1096, 3.1098,
    3.1102-3.1103, 3.1108, 3.1112-3.1113
Mendelson, Edward. 2.8390-2.8391, 2.8408,
    2.13286
Mendelson, Elliott. 5.1046
Mendelson, Jack H. (Jack Harold), 1929-.
    4.6653
Mendel'son, Lev Abramovich, ed. 4.1533
Mendelson, Wallace. 4.9844
Mendelssohn-Bartholdy, Albrecht, 1874-1936.
    3.2342
Mendelssohn-Bartholdy, Felix, 1809-1847.
    1.3925
Mendelssohn, K. (Kurt), 1906-. 3.5148
Mendelssohn, Moses, 1729-1786. 1.875, 1.1968
Mendes-Flohr, Paul R. 3.3805
Méndez Plancarte, Alfonso, 1909, ed. 2.5372
Mendilow, Adam Abraham, 1909-. 2.3498
Mendl, Wolf. 5.7296
Mendlovitz, Saul H. joint ed. 4.9029
Mendoza, Eric, joint author. 5.2056
Mendras, Henri. 4.5352
Menendez, Albert J. 5.8159
Menéndez Pidal, Ramón, 1869-1968. 2.889,
    2.5122, 3.3408, 3.3427
Mêng, S.M. 4.9102
Menger, Carl, 1840-1921. 4.1468-4.1469
Menger, Fredric M., 1937-. 5.2889
Menke, Frank Grant, 1885-1954. 4.927
Menkes, Joshua. 5.5635
Menn, Lise. 2.149
Mennel, Robert M. 4.6877
Mennell, Stephen. 4.7446
Menninger Foundation. Psychotherapy
    Research Project. 5.4843
Menninger, Karl, 1893-. 5.4825, 5.4906
Menninger, Karl Augustus, 1893-. 5.175
Menninger, Karl W., 1898-. 5.1265
Menon, Kumara Padmanabha Sivasankara,
    1898-. 3.4313
Menon, V. P. (Vapal Pangunni), 1894-1966.
    4.8697, 4.8718
Menzel, Donald Howard, 1901-. 5.1734, 5.6698
Menzel, Paul T., 1942-. 5.4636

Menzies, Allan, 1845-1916, ed. 1.2194
Meranto, Philip J., joint author. 4.8855
Mercer, Anne V., 1953-. 2.9888
Mercer, Ginger. 1.3458
Mercer, John, 1934-. 4.6193
Mercer, Johnny, 1909-. 1.3458
Merchant, Carolyn. 5.802
Mercier, Vivian, 1919-. 2.8431, 2.9870
Merck & Co. 5.4755, 5.5145
Meredith, D. J. 5.2234
Meredith, George, 1828-1909. 2.2824,
    2.7936-2.7940
Meredith, James Creed. 1.890
Meredith, Martin. 3.5092
Meredith, William, 1919-. 2.12137
Merezhkovsky, Dmitry Sergeyevich, 1865-.
    2.1518-2.1520
Mergen, Bernard. 4.5728
Meriam, J. L. (James L.) 5.5738, 5.5742
Mérimée, Ernest, 1846-1924. 2.5090
Mérimée, Prosper, 1803-1870. 2.4272
Merino, Barbara Dubis. joint author. 4.4389
Meritt, Benjamin Dean, 1899-. 3.2556
Meritt, Herbert Dean, 1904-. 2.944, 2.946
Meriwether, James B. ed. 2.11658
Meriwether, Robert Lee, 1890-1958. 3.7069
Merk, Frederick, 1887-. 3.6353, 3.7134, 3.7168,
    3.8326, 3.8637, 3.8850
Merkaz le-mehkarim estrategiyim 'al shem
    Yafeh. 5.7343
Merkelbach, Reinhold, 1918-. 2.311
Merker, Paul, 1881-, ed. 2.13450
Merkin, Donald H. 5.5055
Merkl, Peter H. 4.8379, 4.8609
Merleau-Ponty, Maurice, 1908-1961. 1.475,
    1.519, 1.839-1.843, 4.6970
Merli, Frank J., 1929-. 3.6406
Merman, Ethel. 1.4095
Mermin, N. David. 5.1916
Mernissi, Fatima. 4.5907
Merrell, David J. 5.3478
Merrens, Harry Roy. 3.8239
Merriam, Alan P., 1923-. 1.3573, 3.5428
Merriam, Charles Edward, 1874-1953. 4.7313,
    4.7462-4.7463, 4.7467, 4.8120, 4.8175
Merriam, Lawrence C. joint author. 4.893
Merriam-Webster, Inc. 2.1092, 3.325, 4.71
Merrifield, Ralph. 3.1742
Merrill, Andrea T. 3.9257
Merrill, Annabel Laura, 1905- joint author.
    5.7126
Merrill, Elmer Truesdell, 1860-1936, ed. 2.706
Merrill, George P. (George Perkins), 1854-1929.
    5.2955
Merrill, Harwood Ferry, 1904- ed. 4.2634
Merrill, Horace Samuel. 3.8305
Merrill, James Ingram. 2.12138-2.12144
Merrill, James M. 3.7331
Merrill, John Calhoun, 1924-. 2.3542-2.3544
Merrill-Oldham, Jan, 1947-. 5.7647
Merrill, Thomas F. 2.11771
Merrimack Valley Textile Museum. 4.3844
Merriman, Arthur Douglas. 5.6755
Merriman, John M. 3.2147, 3.2152, 4.5297,
    4.6260
Merriman, Lyle. 1.3603
Merriman, Roger Bigelow, 1876-. 3.635, 3.3412,
    3.3582
Merritt, Abrahm, 1882-1943. 2.12145
Merritt, Frederick S. 5.5672
Merry, Bruce. joint author. 2.5040
Mersereau, John, 1925-. 2.1288
Mersereau, Russell M. 5.6372
Mershon Center for Education in National
    Security. 4.9235
Mersky, Roy M. joint author. 4.9782
Mersky, Roy M. 4.9436
Merton, Robert King, 1910-. 4.4804, 4.4806,
    4.4833, 4.5111, 4.7746, 5.7169
Merton, Thomas, 1915-1968. 1.2917, 1.2921,
    1.3228-1.3229, 1.3245, 1.3270, 2.12146
Merwin, W. S. (William Stanley), 1927-. 2.3742,
    2.12147-2.12150
Merz, John Theodore, 1840-1922. 1.443
Merz, Timothy. joint author. 5.3421
Merzbacher, Eugen. 5.2117
Merzkirch, Wolfgang. 5.5750

Mesa-Lago, Carmelo, 1934-. 3.9107, 4.2153,
    4.2159, 4.3473, 4.7587
Mesarović, Mihajlo D. 4.1791
Meserole, Harrison T. joint author. 5.7933
Meserole, Harrison T. comp. 2.10760
Meserve, Walter J. 2.10512, 5.7803
Meskill, John Thomas, ed. 3.4662
Messenger, Christian K., 1943-. 2.10586
Messent, Peter B. 2.5975
Messerli, Jonathan, 1926-. 4.10202
Messiaen, Olivier, 1908-. 1.4432
Messick, Hank. 4.6796
Messing, Gordon M. 2.234
Meštrović, Ivan, 1883-1962. 1.5745
Metallurgical Society of A.I.M.E. 5.6754
Metastasio, Pietro, 1698-1782. 2.5005
Metcalf & Eddy. 5.6028
Metcalf, George R., 1914-. 4.10791
Metcalf, Harold J. 5.3494
Metcalf, Henry Clayton, 1867-. 5.5559
Metcalf, Keyes DeWitt, 1889-. 5.7615
Metcalf, Michael. 5.1216
Metcalf, Peter. joint author. 4.590
Metcalf, Priscilla. 5.1526
Metcalf, Robert Lee, 1916-. 5.5406
Metcalf, Thomas R., 1934-. 3.4279
Metcalfe, C. R. (Charles Russell) 5.3691, 5.3735
Metge, Alice Joan. 3.5609
Metrailer, Rosemary, 1944- joint author. 4.9691
Metress, Seamus P. 5.7861
Metropolitan Museum of Art (New York,
    N.Y.) 1.4648, 1.4694-1.4695, 1.4752, 1.4842,
    1.4899, 1.4943, 1.4975, 1.4982, 1.5088,
    1.5185, 1.5658, 1.5665, 1.5769, 1.5810,
    1.5887, 1.5947, 1.5990, 1.6050, 1.6053-1.6054,
    1.6122, 1.6489, 1.6496, 1.6522, 1.6618,
    1.6646, 1.6672, 2.3752, 3.160, 5.6929
Metropolitan Opera (New York, N.Y.) 1.4511
Metry, Amir. 5.6040
Metsys, Quentin, 1465 or 6-1530. 1.6268
Metz, Charles B. 5.3484
Metz, Christian. 2.2961
Metz, Johannes Baptist, 1928-. 1.3169
Metzger, Bruce Manning. ed. 1.2497
Metzger, Bruce Manning. 1.2621
Metzger, Walter P. 4.9984
Metzler, David E. 5.3335
Meulendyke, Eve. 1.6520
Mews, Siegfried. 2.13873
Mexico (City). Universidad Nacional. Consejo
    Técnico de Humanidades. 1.661
Meyburg, Arnim H. 4.3931
Meyburg, Arnim Hans. 4.3911
Meyendorff, John, 1926-. 1.2850, 1.3053,
    1.3102, 1.3110
Meyer, Alfred G. 4.5964, 4.6971, 4.7005,
    4.7102, 4.8649
Meyer-Arendt, Jurgen R. 5.2283
Meyer, Arnold Oskar, 1877-1944. ed. 3.2250
Meyer, Balthasar Henry, 1866- ed. 4.3882
Meyer, Beat. 5.6046
Meyer, Carl F. 5.6065
Meyer, Carl H. 5.7530
Meyer, Carol H., 1924-. 4.6479, 4.6493
Meyer, Conrad Ferdinand, 1825-1898.
    2.13635-2.13636
Meyer, Donald B. 5.88
Meyer, Donald Harvey, 1935-. 1.1422
Meyer, Erwin, 1899-. 5.2229
Meyer, Eugene, 1938-. 5.6110
Meyer, Franz Sales, 1849-. 1.6281, 1.6546
Meyer, Frederick Robert. 1.5774
Meyer, Hans Georg. 2.14037
Meyer, Henry Cord, 1913-. 3.759
Meyer, Henry Joseph, 1913- joint author.
    4.10801
Meyer, John Robert. 4.3887, 4.3917, 4.4051,
    4.4082, 4.4086
Meyer, John Robert. joint author. 4.1756,
    4.3870
Meyer, John Robert. ed. 4.3872
Meyer, John Robert. 4.3937
Meyer, John W. 4.4907
Meyer, Jürgen Bona, 1839-1897. 2.440
Meyer, Karl Ernest. 3.9106
Meyer, Leonard B. 1.4368-1.4369
Meyer, Leonard B. joint author. 1.4461
Meyer, Linda C. joint author. 4.6744

Meyer, Manfred. 5.8158
Meyer, Marshall W. joint author. 4.7749
Meyer, Marshall W. 4.4908
Meyer, Marshall W. comp. 4.4909
Meyer, Michael, 1945- joint author. 2.11250
Meyer, Michael A. comp. 3.3846
Meyer, Michael A. 1.1931
Meyer, Michael C. joint author. 5.8261
Meyer, Michael C. 3.8917, 3.8944
Meyer, Michael D. 4.3904
Meyer, Michael Leverson. 2.14038
Meyer, Priscilla. 2.1372
Meyer, Richard Hemmig. 4.4540
Meyer, Robert G., 1942-. 5.6529
Meyer, Robert T., 1911-1987. ed. and tr. 1.2183
Meyer, Roy Willard, 1925-. 2.10551, 3.5903
Meyer, Stuart L., 1937-. 5.1393
Meyer, Walter J. (Walter Joseph), 1943-. 5.1113
Meyerhoff, Hans. 2.2410
Meyers, Jeffrey. 2.8987, 2.9048, 2.9193, 2.11861, 2.11863
Meyers, Marc A. 5.5813
Meyers, Marvin. 3.7078
Meyers, Marvin. ed. 3.6974
Meyers, Robert A. (Robert Allen), 1936-. 5.6128, 5.6882
Meyers, Walter Earl, 1939-. 2.3490
Meyerson, Emile, 1859-1933. 1.1285
Meynell, Alice Christiana Thompson, 1847-1922. 2.7952
Meynell, Viola, 1886-1956. 2.7390, 2.7953
Meyrowitz, Joshua. 4.5009
Mezey, Robert. 2.10776
Mezu, Sebastian Okechukwu. 2.4865
Mezzanotte, Riccardo. 1.3520
M'Gonigle, R. Michael. 4.9391
Mi-la-ras-pa, 1040-1123. 2.2256
Mi Mi Khaing, 1916-. 3.4424
Miall, Andrew D. 5.3056
Miall, Bernard, 1876- tr. 3.2094, 5.3887
Micaud, Charles Antoine, 1910- ed. 3.5210
Michael, Franz H. 3.4709, 3.4731
Michael, Ian. 2.983, 2.5184
Michael, Jerome, 1890-1953. 4.6680
Michael, Richard Phillip, ed. 5.4302
Michael, Wolfgang, 1862-1945. 3.1522
Michaelis, Arnd. joint author. 3.3409
Michaelis, H. (Henriette), b. 1849. 2.912
Michaelis, John Udell, 1912-. 4.10443, 4.10484
Michaelis, Meir. 3.3975
Michaels, Barbara, 1927-. 3.5140
Michal, Jan M. 4.2319
Michałowski, Kazimierz. 1.4699
Michard, Laurent. joint author. 2.3917, 2.3920
Michaud, Guy. 2.3863, 2.3879
Michaux, Henri, 1899-. 2.4633-2.4635
Michel, Aloys Arthur. 4.2451
Michel, Henri, 1907-. 3.908
Michel, Laurence Anthony. 2.2817
Michel. Laurence Anthony, ed. 2.6564
Michel, Paul-Henri. 1.411
Michel, Thomas F., 1941-. 1.2067
Michelangelo Buonarroti, 1475-1564. 1.5441, 1.5734-1.5735, 2.4966-2.4967
Michelet, Jules, 1798-1874. 3.2102
Michell, George. 1.5234
Michell, H. (Humfrey), 1883-. 3.2649, 4.1735
Michell, R. H. 5.3609
Michels, Robert, 1876-1936. 4.7778
Michels, Volker. 2.13778
Michels, Walter C. (Walter Christian), 1906-1975. 5.2343
Michelson, A. M. 5.4426
Michelson, Albert Abraham, 1852-1931. 5.2276
Michener, Charles Duncan, 1918-. 5.3885
Michener, James A. (James Albert), 1907-. 1.6479, 2.12151-2.12155, 4.935
Michie, Donald. 5.1013
Michigan Business Executives Research Conference. 4.3969
Michigan State University. African Studies Center. 3.5063
Michigan. University Engineering Research Institute. 5.235
Michitsuna no Haha, ca. 935-995. 2.2053
Michotte, Albert Edouard, 1881-. 5.401
Mickel, Andrew B. 5.1222
Mickel, Emanuel J., 1937-. 2.3956

Mickel, Peter, joint author. 5.7472
Mickelsen, William C. 1.4113
Mickelson, Randolph. 4.4572
Mickens, Ronald E., 1943-. 5.1520
Mickiewicz, Adam, 1798-1855. 2.1714-2.1716, 2.1747
Mid-century Committee on Outcomes in Elementary Education. 4.10426
Middle East Libraries Committee. 5.8037
Middlebrook, Diane Wood. 2.10289
Middlebrook, Martin, 1932-. 3.796
Middlebrooks, E. Joe. joint author. 5.6013
Middlehurst, Barbara M. ed. 5.1748, 5.1773
Middlekauff, Robert. 3.6900, 3.7981
Middlemas, Keith, 1935-. 4.3643, 4.8375
Middleton, Alex L. A. 5.3940
Middleton, Drew, 1913-. 3.1052
Middleton, Gerard V. joint author. 5.3051
Middleton, John. 3.5288, 4.549-4.550, 4.560, 4.604
Middleton, Lucy. 4.6105
Middleton, Robert Gordon, 1908-. 5.6471, 5.6483
Middleton, Robin. 1.5460
Middleton, Roger. 4.2285
Middleton, Thomas. 2.6230, 2.6494, 2.6553, 2.6632-2.6636
Middleton, W. E. Knowles (William Edgar Knowles), 1902-. 5.2509
Midgley, Graham. 1.2214
Midgley, Mary, 1919-. 1.1455-1.1456, 1.1488
Midrash. Tehillim. 1.1944
Midwest Conference on Asian Affairs. 26th, Northern Illinois University, 1977. 3.4596
Midwest Modern Language Association. 2.2561
Midwinter, John E., joint author. 5.2300
Mieder, Wolfgang. 2.3806, 5.8412
Mielke, James H. 4.458
Miernyk, William H. 4.1279
Mierow, Charles Christopher, 1883-. 3.2270
Miers, Suzanne. 4.6442, 4.6451
Mies, Paul, 1889-. 1.3802
Mies van der Rohe Archive. 1.5426
Mieszkowski, Peter M. 4.6291
Migdalski, Edward C. 5.3898
Migge, Walther. 2.13548
Migliorini, Bruno. 2.852
Mignot, Claude. 1.5357
Míguez Bonino, José. 1.2805, 1.2861
Mihailovich, Vasa D. joint comp. 2.1201
Mihailovich, Vasa D. ed. 2.1197
Mikami, Yoshio. 5.1082
Mikasinovich, Branko. comp. 2.1201
Mikasinovich, Branko. 2.3798
Mikdashi, Zuhayr M. 4.1770
Mikesell, John L. 4.4719
Mikesell, Marvin W. ed. 4.40, 5.3523
Mikesell, Marvin W. 4.358
Mikesell, Raymond Frech. 4.3739
Mikhail, E. H. 2.8282, 5.7956, 5.7996
Mikhail, Edward M. 5.5827
Mikhail, Raouf Shaker. 2.5898
Milanich, Jerald T. 3.5734
Milanović, Petar T. 4.300
Milbrath, Lester W. 4.1847
Mileck, Joseph, 1922-. 2.13779
Milenkovitch, Deborah D. 4.2425
Miles, Gary B. 2.793
Miles, Hamish, 1894-1937, tr. 2.7640
Miles, Ian. 4.2750, 4.5081
Miles, Josephine, 1911-. 2.3743, 2.5719, 2.5755, 2.5802, 2.6269, 2.12157
Miles, Margaret Ruth. 1.1611, 1.2930
Miles, Matthew B. joint author. 5.542
Miles, Michael W., 1945-. 4.7314
Miles, Patrick. 2.1484
Miles, Peter. 2.8211
Miles, Rufus E. 5.4616
Mileur, Jean-Pierre. 2.7602
Milford, Frederick J., joint author. 5.2371
Milford, Humphrey Sumner, Sir, 1877-1952. 2.6173, 2.6958, 2.7842
Milford, Nancy. 2.11741
Milgate, Wesley, 1916-. 2.6456
Milgram, Arthur N. (Arthur Norton), 1912-. 5.1292
Milgram, Gail Gleason. 5.8438
Milgram, Stanley. 4.5027

Milhaud, Darius, 1892-1974. 1.3930
Milhollen, Hirst Dillon, 1906- ed. 3.7348
Milhous, Judith. 2.3322, 2.5897
Miliband, Ralph. 4.7473, 4.7589, 4.8425
Milisauskas, Sarunas. 4.726
Military History Symposium (Canada) 3d, Royal Military College, 1976. 3.774
Miliukov, P. N. (Pavel Nikolaevich), 1859-1943. 3.3020, 3.3166, 3.3188
Milius, Pauline H., joint author. 4.6568
Milivojević, Dragan Dennis. joint comp. 2.1201
Milkman, Harvey. 5.4955
Milkman, Ruth, 1954-. 4.3272
Mill, Harriet Hardy Taylor, 1807-1858. 1.729, 4.5893
Mill, John Stuart, 1806-1873. 1.719, 1.726, 1.728-1.729, 1.1186, 1.1556-1.1557, 4.5893, 4.7579, 4.7669-4.7670, 4.10195
Mill, P. J. (Peter John) 5.3841
Millais, Euphemia Chalmers Gray, Lady, 1828-1897. 2.8036
Millais, John Everett, Sir, 1829-1896. 2.8036
Millar, Fergus. 2.444, 3.2516, 3.3891
Millar, Gavin, joint author. 2.3017
Millar, Ian T. 5.2786
Millar, James R., 1936- ed. 4.5374
Millar, John Fitzhugh. 5.7502
Millar, Ronald William, 1928-. 4.454
Millar, T. B. (Thomas Bruce) 3.5580, 4.8967
Millard, Charles W. 1.5704
Millay, Edna St. Vincent, 1892-1950. 2.4135, 2.12160-2.12161
Miller, Alan L., ed. 1.1832
Miller, Albert Jay. 5.8123, 5.8410
Miller, Alfred Jacob, 1810-1874. 3.8472
Miller, Anita, 1928-. 4.9693
Miller, Arnold V. 1.930
Miller, Arthur, 1915-. 2.12166-2.12167, 2.12169, 2.12171-2.12175, 2.12177
Miller, Arthur I. 5.2083
Miller, Augustus Taylor, 1910- joint author. 5.4268
Miller, Barbara Stoler. 1.5189, 2.1943, 2.1945, 2.1946, 2.1953
Miller, Barbara Stoler. joint author. 3.4182
Miller, Betty Bergson Spiro, 1910-. 2.7469, 2.7487
Miller, Carman, 1940-. 3.8758
Miller, Charles I. 5.5431
Miller, Clem, 1916-1962. 4.8054
Miller, David Hewitt, 1918-. 4.292
Miller, David Hunter, 1875-. 4.9187
Miller, David L., 1903-. 1.613, 1.616, 4.4991
Miller, David M. 1.1718, 2.7158
Miller, David William, 1929-. 4.144
Miller, Dayton Clarence, 1866-1941. 1.4378
Miller, Delbert Charles, 1913-. 4.1227
Miller, Don, 1927-. 2.2924
Miller, Dorothy Canning, 1904-. 1.4874-1.4877
Miller, Douglas T. 3.6037, 3.6066
Miller, E. Eugene. 4.6908
Miller, Edmund Morris, 1881-1964. 5.8083
Miller, Edward, 1915-. 4.5305
Miller, Edward H. 5.3967
Miller, Edwin Haviland. comp. 2.11279
Miller, Edwin Haviland. 2.11163
Miller, Elizabeth Williams. 3.7950
Miller, Eric J. 4.3904
Miller, F. Leonard, joint author. 4.4320
Miller, Floyd John, 1940-. 3.7229
Miller, Frank Justus, 1858-. 2.681, 2.694
Miller, G. Tyler (George Tyler), 1931-. 5.2886
Miller, George Armitage, 1920-. 2.52, 4.10395, 5.35, 5.386, 5.464
Miller, George Bertram, 1926-. 5.7620
Miller, George Hall, 1919-. 4.9529
Miller, Harold Gladstone, 1898-. 3.5613
Miller, Henry. 2.8611, 2.8988, 2.12181-2.12189
Miller, Henry Knight, 1920-. 2.5661, 2.7026
Miller, Howard, 1941-. 4.10812
Miller, Irwin. 5.4637
Miller, J. C. (Jane Charlotte) 5.2660
Miller, J. Hillis (Joseph Hillis), 1928-. 2.3409, 2.5726, 2.5780, 2.5832, 2.7662, 2.7794, 2.12550, 2.12752
Miller, J. N. (James N.), 1943-. 5.2660
Miller, J. R. (James Rodger), 1943-. 3.8684
Miller, James Andrew. 3.5214

Miller, James Clifford. 4.2002
Miller, James Clifford. joint author. 4.4088
Miller, James Clifford. 4.3893
Miller, James Edwin, 1920-. 2.3413-2.3414, 2.10493, 2.11734
Miller, James Monroe. 5.2643
Miller, James Woodell, 1927-. 4.336
Miller, Jane, 1932-. 4.10888
Miller, Jane Kathryn. 3.2975
Miller, Jason. 2.13172
Miller, Jean Baker. comp. 4.5933
Miller, Jeffrey G. joint author. 5.7026
Miller, Jeffrey H. 5.3456, 5.3467
Miller, Jim, 1947-. 1.4282
Miller, John Chester, 1907-. 3.6901, 3.7022, 3.7056
Miller, John E., 1945-. 3.8446
Miller, John Frederick, 1928-. 4.162
Miller, John. 3.1507, 3.5601
Miller, John William. 1.92
Miller, Jonathan, 1934-. 5.125, 5.3201
Miller, Joseph, 1899-. 3.8566, 3.8578
Miller, Joseph Calder. 3.5404
Miller, Kenneth Hayes, 1876-1952, illus. 1.5955
Miller, Kenton. 5.5384
Miller, Lee Graham, 1902-1961. 2.3629
Miller, Lillian B. 1.5961
Miller, Loren. 4.9689
Miller, Lynn F. 1.4871
Miller, Lynn H. 3.1181
Miller, Lynn H. ed. 3.7597
Miller, Margaret Stevenson. 4.2394
Miller, Mark J. 4.8951
Miller, Merle, 1919-. 3.7812, 3.7891
Miller, Michael J. 5.5645
Miller, Nathan, 1927-. 5.7448
Miller, Neal E. (Neal Elgar), 1909-. 4.10373
Miller, Neal Elgar, 1909- joint author. 4.5065
Miller, Norbert. 2.13644
Miller, Norman N., 1933-. 3.5278
Miller, Orson K. 5.3726
Miller, P. McC. 4.1200
Miller, Paul J. W., tr. 1.418
Miller, Perry, 1905-1963. 1.567, 1.3332, 1.3340, 2.10238, 2.10707-2.10708, 2.10720, 2.10860, 2.11189, 3.6140-3.6142, 3.6334, 3.7951-3.7952, 3.8014
Miller, Peter M. 5.456
Miller, Peter M. (Peter Michael), 1942-. 4.6634
Miller, Philip Lieson, 1906- comp. and tr. 1.3459
Miller, Randall M. 2.2993, 3.7209
Miller, Raymond Curtis. ed. 3.6143
Miller, Reese P., 1934-. 1.787
Miller, Richard, 1926-. 1.4565
Miller, Richard B. 4.4529
Miller, Richard Bradford, 1927-. 4.4529
Miller, Richard I. 4.9324
Miller, Richard W., 1945-. 1.1039
Miller, Rita Seiden. 3.8059
Miller, Robert Keith, 1949-. 2.8285
Miller, Robert Lee, 1920-. 5.4107
Miller, Robert Moats. 1.3325
Miller, Robert Parsons, 1923-. 2.6348
Miller, Robert R., 1929- joint author. 4.2719
Miller, Robert Thomas, 1920-. 4.9722
Miller, Roberta Balstad. 4.6220
Miller, Ronald E. 4.1402
Miller, Rosalind S., 1923-. 4.6541
Miller, Roy Andrew. ed. 2.1988
Miller, Roy Andrew. 2.1985-2.1987
Miller, Russell E. 1.3421
Miller, S. M. (Seymour Michael), 1922-. 4.2014
Miller, Sally M., 1937-. 4.5236
Miller, Steven E. 3.775
Miller, Stuart Creighton, 1927-. 3.4600
Miller, Stuart J., 1938- joint author. 4.6869
Miller, Theodore K. 4.10279
Miller, Valentine Rodger, 1939-. 1.787
Miller, Walter, 1864-. 2.400, 2.665
Miller, Walter James, 1918-. 2.4321
Miller, Walter M., 1923-. 2.12195
Miller, Warren B., 1935-. 4.1634
Miller, Wayne Charles. 5.7858-5.7859
Miller, William, 1912- ed. 3.3584, 3.6329, 4.1870, 4.4215
Miller, William D. 3.8353
Miller, William G. (William Gerald) 5.7661

Miller, Wright Watts. 3.3274
Millerson, Gerald. 2.2859, 5.6442, 5.7009
Millet, Jean François, 1814-1875. 1.4978, 1.6121
Millett, Allan Reed. 3.6368, 5.7479
Millett, Fred Benjamin, 1890-. 2.10420
Millett, John David, 1912-. 4.10595, 4.10760
Millett, Kate. 4.5885
Millett, Stephen M., 1947-. 4.9625
Millgate, Jane. 2.8060
Millgate, Michael. 2.7770, 2.7772, 2.7779, 2.7795, 2.10638
Millgram, Abraham Ezra, 1901-. 1.1977
Milligan, Alice. 2.9089
Milligan, Burton Alviere, 1903-. 2.6584
Milligan, Ian. 2.5946
Milligan, Thomas A. 5.6495
Millikan, Robert Andrews, 1868-1953. 5.2398
Milliken, George A., 1943-. 5.1412
Milliman, Jerome W. joint author. 4.2930
Milling, Bryan E. 4.4598
Millington, Barry. 1.4039, 1.4048
Millis, Harry Alvin, 1873-1948. 4.3507
Millis, John S., 1903-. 5.4605
Millis, Nancy F., joint author. 5.6867
Millis, Walter, 1899-1968. 3.6369, 3.7501, 3.7586, 4.9160, 5.7277
Millman, Jacob, 1911-. 5.6481, 5.6538
Millman, Marcia. 5.4943
Millon, René, 1921-. 3.8895
Milloy, Ross. 4.7906
Mills, C. Wright (Charles Wright), 1916-1962. 3.6144, 4.1197, 4.1210, 4.3360, 4.4817, 4.4882, 4.6404
Mills, Clark, 1913-. 2.1715, 2.1735
Mills, D. E. 2.2057
Mills, Daniel Quinn. 4.3524
Mills, Dick. 5.5456
Mills, Elizabeth. ed. 1.4437
Mills, Gordon. 4.1403
Mills, John W. 1.5780
Mills, Olive, ed. 4.10089
Mills, Ralph J. 2.2747, 2.10501
Mills, Ralph J. ed. 2.12411
Mills, Richard Charles, 1886-1952. 3.5577
Millward, G. R. 5.6793
Milne, A. A. (Alan Alexander), 1882-1956. 2.9110-2.9111, 2.9113-2.9114
Milne, Alexander Taylor. 5.7983
Milne, Hamish. 1.3790
Milne, Isabel A, jt. ed. 3.1773
Milne, Lorus Johnson, 1912-. 5.3862
Milne, Margery Joan Greene, 1914- joint author. 5.3862
Milne, P. H. 5.5828
Milne, R. S. (Robert Stephen), 1919-. 4.8726, 4.8728
Milner, Andrew. 2.7163
Milner, Marc. 3.1037
Milner, Peter M. 5.4295
Milner, Ron, joint comp. 2.10786
Milnor, John Willard, 1931-. 5.1595
Miłosz, Czesław. 2.1696, 2.1718-2.1720, 2.1734, 2.1746
Miłosz, Czesław. tr. 2.1740
Miłosz, Czesław. 2.2754
Milsom, S. F. C. (Stroud Francis Charles), 1923-. 4.9413
Milton, John. 2.7110-2.7116, 2.7118-2.7119, 2.7142, 2.7144-2.7146, 2.7170
Milton, John R. comp. 2.2321
Milton, John R. 3.8510
Milton, Joyce. 4.9461
Milton, Sybil. 1.5097
Milward, Alan S. 4.1779, 4.2202-4.2204
Milwaukee Curriculum Theory Conference, University of Wisconsin-Milwaukee, 1976. 4.10444
Mims, Amy, tr. 2.619
Mims, Cedric A. 5.4749
Mims, Charles W. joint author. 5.3720
Mims, Edwin, 1872-1959. 2.3187, 2.11142
Mims, Stewart Lea, 1880-. 3.6028
Minasian, Stanley M., 1948-. 5.4008
Minault, Gail, 1939-. 4.5956
Minc, Henryk, 1919-. 5.1313
Minco, Marga. 3.1118
Minden, Shelley. 5.5066

Mindess, Sidney. 5.5799
Minear, Richard H. 4.9343
Miner, Dwight Carroll, 1904-. 4.9039
Miner, Earl Roy. joint author. 2.2008
Miner, Earl Roy. 2.1998, 2.2007, 2.5798, 2.7001, 2.7002
Miner, Earl Roy. ed. 2.5902, 2.6989
Miner, H. Craig. 3.8528
Miner, Horace Mitchell, 1912-. 3.8821
Miner, James F. 5.1222
Miner, Jerry, 1929- joint author. 4.4720
Miner, John B. 4.4363
Miner, Mary Green. 4.4363
Mines, Mattison, 1941-. 3.4205
Minford, John. 2.2183
Mingay, G. E. joint author. 5.5247
Mingay, G. E. 4.5306, 4.5327, 4.6395, 5.5226
Mingione, Enzo. 4.6186
Minichino, Camille. 5.6055
Minifie, Fred D. 5.4280
Minkin, Lewis. 4.8539
Minkowski, H. (Hermann), 1864-1909. 5.1914
Minnaert, M. G. J. (Marcel Gilles Jozef), 1893-. 5.2554
Minneapolis Institute of Arts. 1.6284, 1.6458
Minnesota Federal Writers' Project. 3.8499
Minnesota Museum of Art. 1.6544
Minnesota. University. Office for Advanced Drama Research. 2.10792
Mino, Yutaka. 1.6622
Minogue, Kenneth R. 4.7243
Minogue, Valerie. 2.4716
Minot, Stephen. 2.13173
Minoux, Michel. 5.1284
Mins, Leonard E., ed. and tr. 4.1537
Minshull, G. N. 4.2219
Minter, David L. 2.10529, 2.11697
Minton, Madge Rutherford. joint author. 5.3927
Minton, Sherman A. 5.3927
Mintz, Alan L. 2.7697
Mintz, Jerome R. 1.1923, 4.7199
Mintz, Sidney Wilfred, 1922-. 4.3542, 4.6430
Mintzberg, Henry. 4.2668
Minuchin, Salvador. 5.4880, 5.4883, 5.4941
Minucius Felix, Marcus. 1.2193
Minus, Paul M. 3.3207
Miracle, Andrew W. 2.112
Miranda, Francisco de, 1750-1816. 3.9182
Miranda, José Porfirio. 1.2533, 4.7137
Mirandé, Alfredo. 3.6583
Miriam Joseph, Sister, 1898-. 2.6845
Miró, Carmen A. 4.1626
Miró, Joan, 1893-. 1.6296
Miroff, Bruce. 3.7866
Mirollo, James V. 2.2620
Mirow, Kurt Rudolf. 4.3024
Mirrlees, James A., joint author. 4.2677
Mirror of perfection. 1.3259
Mirsky, Alfred E. joint ed. 5.3589
Mirsky, D. S., Prince, 1890-1939. 2.1249
Mish, Charles Carroll, 1913-. 2.6256, 2.6258, 5.7964
Mishal, Shaul, 1945-. 3.4031
Mishan, E. J. (Edward J.), 1917-. 4.1335, 4.2796
Mishima, Yukio, 1925-1970. 1.1426, 2.2019, 2.2023, 2.2106-2.2114
Mishler, William, 1947-. 4.8313
Misiunas, Romuald J. 3.3305
Miskimin, Harry A. 4.2205, 4.4518
Mislow, Kurt. 5.2873
Misner, Charles W. 5.2215
Mistichelli, Judith. joint author. 5.8118
Mistral, Gabriela, 1889-1957. 2.5408
Mitcalfe, Barry. 1.4350
Mitchell, Adrian Christopher William. 2.10138, 2.10145
Mitchell, Allan. 3.2178, 5.7315
Mitchell, Andrew A., 1939-. 4.4431
Mitchell, Arthur, 1872- tr. 1.828
Mitchell, Austin Vernon, 1934-. 4.8559
Mitchell, B. R. (Brian R.) 4.1254, 4.1260
Mitchell Beazley Ltd. 4.113
Mitchell, Broadus, 1892-. 4.1881
Mitchell, Bruce, 1920-. 2.931
Mitchell, Charity. joint author. 1.42
Mitchell, D. C. (Don C.) 4.10342
Mitchell, Daniel J. B. 4.3146

Mitchell, David J. 1.3243
Mitchell, Donald, 1925-. 1.3824, 1.3918-1.3920,
    1.3940
Mitchell, Donald W. (Donald William), 1911-.
    3.3055
Mitchell, Edgar D. 5.644
Mitchell, Edward B., comp. 2.12193
Mitchell, Edward John, 1937-. 4.3766
Mitchell, Elmer Dayton, 1889- joint author.
    4.10389
Mitchell, Enoch L., 1903-. 3.8346
Mitchell, Frank, 1881-1967. 3.5923
Mitchell, Franklin D. 3.8362
Mitchell, George Sinclair, 1902-1962. joint
    author. 3.6732
Mitchell, Greg. 5.4655
Mitchell, Henry H. 1.3046
Mitchell, Herschel K. joint author. 5.3443
Mitchell, Ian R. 3.2313
Mitchell, Jack N. 4.4867
Mitchell, James E. (James Edward), 1947-.
    5.4938
Mitchell, James Kenneth, 1930-. 5.5901
Mitchell, James Leslie, 1901-1935. 2.9115
Mitchell, John, 1711-1768. 4.121, 5.5231
Mitchell, John Hanson. 5.3265
Mitchell, Jonathan, 1959-. 3.3679
Mitchell, Juliet, 1940-. 4.5886, 4.5899
Mitchell, Larry D. 5.6192
Mitchell, Lee Clark, 1957-. 5.3227
Mitchell, Loften. 2.3238, 2.10515
Mitchell, Margaret, 1900-1949. 2.12196, 2.12198
Mitchell, Marianne. 5.468
Mitchell, P. M. (Phillip Marshall), 1916-.
    2.14001, 2.14005, 5.8020
Mitchell, R. J. (Robert J.) 5.5913
Mitchell, Richard H. 3.4914
Mitchell, Richard Scott, 1929-. 5.3011, 5.3030
Mitchell, Robert D., 1940-. 3.5690
Mitchell, S. Weir (Silas Weir), 1829-1914.
    2.11174
Mitchell, Stephen. 2.13853
Mitchell, Stephen A., 1946-. 5.158
Mitchell, Stewart, 1892- ed. 3.7052
Mitchell, Sydney Knox. 4.4701
Mitchell, Thomas N., 1939-. 3.2785
Mitchell, W. J. Thomas, 1942-. 1.6680
Mitchell, Wesley Clair, 1874-1948. 4.4508
Mitchell, William Burton. 3.9185
Mitchell, William E. 3.8050
Mitchell, William John, 1906- ed. and tr.
    1.4541
Mitchenson, Joe. joint author. 1.4048, 2.2840,
    2.3317
Mitchenson, Joe. jt. comp. 2.8090
Mitchison, Rosalind. 3.1781, 3.1799
Mitford, Jessica, 1917-. 4.867, 4.6912, 4.9465
Mitford, John, 1781-1859. 2.7344
Mitford, Mary Russell, 1787-1855. 2.7469
Mitford, Nancy, 1904-1973. 2.9116-2.9120
Mitgang, Herbert. ed. 2.12432
Mitgang, Herbert. 3.7286
Mitra, Premendra. 2.1876
Mitrany, David. 4.7547, 4.9138, 4.9289
Mitroff, Ian I. 4.1248, 4.2697
Mittal, Kewal Krishan, 1931-. 1.193
Mittelhölzer, Edgar. 2.9121-2.9122
Mitterand, Henri. 2.4344
Mitterauer, Michael. 4.5554
Mitton, Simon, 1946-. 5.1699, 5.1745, 5.1794,
    5.1853, 5.1855
Mitzel, Harold E. 4.10165
Mitzka, Walther. 2.1183
Mitzman, Arthur, 1931-. 4.4763
Miuller, V. K. (Vladimir Karlovich), 1880-.
    2.1234
Miura, Akira, 1927-. 2.1992
Mixon, J. Wilson. 4.2447
Miyagawa, Torao, 1908-. 1.6313
Miyajima, Shin'ichi. 1.6391
Miyakawa, Tetsuo Scott, joint author. 3.6559
Miyakawa, Tetsuo Scott. 1.2412
Miyashiro, Akiho. 5.3068
Miyoshi, Masao. 2.2011, 3.6463
Mizener, Arthur ed. 2.11735
Mizener, Arthur. 2.8637, 2.11736
Mizrahi, Andrée. 5.4642
Mizrahi, Arié. 5.4642

Mo, Ti, fl. 400 B.C. 1.171-1.172
Moayyad, Heshmat. 2.1978
Moberg, Vilhelm. 2.14096-2.14098, 3.3386
Mochul'skiĭ, K. (Konstantin), 1892-1948.
    2.1369, 2.1470
Mock, James Robert. 3.838
Mócsy, András. 3.2717
Modell, John. 3.8622
Modell, Judith Schachter, 1941-. 4.418
Modelski, Andrew M., 1929-. 4.138
Moder, Joseph J. 5.5562, 5.5568
Modern Greek Studies Association. 2.568
Modern Humanities Research Association.
    5.7936
Modern Language Association of America.
    2.1041, 2.2518, 2.3690, 2.5671, 2.6346,
    2.6647, 5.8271, 5.8332, 5.8345
Modern Language Association of America.
    American Literature Group. 2.10248
Modern Language Association of America.
    Commission on the Literatures and
    Languages of America. 2.10305
Modern Language Association of America.
    Committee on Research Activities. 2.2365
Modern Language Association of America.
    Comparative Literature Section. 2.2697
Modern Language Association of America.
    Spanish V. Bibliography Committee. 5.8028
Modern Language Association of America.
    Victorian Literature Group. 5.7945
Modiano, Patrick, 1945-. 2.4785
Modigliani, Franco. 4.1450
Moe, Phyllis. 2.10819
Moeller, Bernd, 1931-. 1.2330
Moeller, Therald. 5.2673, 5.2701
Moerk, Ernst L. 4.10396
Moers, Ellen, 1928-. 2.2553, 2.11604
Moeser, John V., 1942-. 4.8265
Moffat, Abbot Low, 1901-. 3.4528
Moffat, Riley Moore, 1947-. 4.234
Moffatt, Betty Clare. 5.4983
Moffatt, James, 1870-1944. tr. 1.2296
Moffatt, Michael, 1944-. 3.4325
Moffett, Charles S. 1.4975
Moffitt, Michael, 1951-. 4.4573
Moger, Allen Wesley, 1905-. 3.8212
Moggridge, D. E. (Donald Edward), 1943-.
    4.1350, 4.4514-4.4515
Mogulof, Melvin B. 4.8859
Mohammed Reza Pahlavi, Shah of Iran, 1919-.
    3.4089-3.4090
Mohan Ram, 1933-. 3.4235, 4.7115-4.7116
Mohanti, Prafulla. 4.5428
Mohanty, Jitindra Mohan, 1932-. 5.8338
Mohanty, Jitendranath, 1928-. 1.1021
Mohd. Taib Osman, 1934-. 2.2288
Mohl, Raymond A. 4.6221, 4.6620
Mohl, Ruth, 1891-. 2.2382
Mohlenbrock, Robert H., 1931-. 5.3648
Moholy-Nagy, László, 1895-1946.
    1.5114-1.5115, 5.6966
Moholy-Nagy, Sibyl, 1905-. 1.5592
Mohr, James C. 4.9864
Mohr, Lawrence B. 4.2698
Mohr, Lillian Holmen, 1926-. 4.3592
Mohraz, Judy Jolley. 4.10869
Mohring, Herbert. 4.3932
Mohrmann, Christine. joint author. 4.133
Mohs, Mayo. comp. 2.10832
Moik, Johannes G. 5.5942
Moir, Duncan W., joint author. 2.5127
Moise, Edwin E. 4.2878, 5.1565
Mojares, Resil B. 2.2291
Mojtabai, A. G., 1937-. 2.13174
Mojzes, Paul. 4.7138
Mokyr, Joel. 4.2316, 4.2362
Moldenhauer, Hans. 1.4058
Moldenhauer, Hans. comp. 1.4059
Moldenhauer, Rosaleen. 1.4058
Moldenhauer, W. C. 5.5288
Molenda, Michael. 4.10290
Molesworth, Charles, 1941-. 2.10495, 2.12897,
    2.13329
Molesworth, William, Sir, 1810-1855. 1.670
Moley, Raymond, 1886-. 3.7764-3.7765
Molière, 1622-1673. 2.4039-2.4041
Molina, Felipe S. 2.2335
Molina, Tirso de, 1571?-1648. 2.5204, 2.10022

Molinari, Cesare, 1935-. 2.3168
Molinaro, Ursule. 2.13902
Moline, Jon, 1937-. 1.279
Moliner, María. 2.897
Moliver, Donald M. 4.2448
Moll, John L. 5.2352
Mollenkott, Virginia R. 1.2539
Möller, Herbert. ed. 4.1692
Moller, Richard Jay. 4.9577
Mollett, J. A., 1923-. 4.2899
Molluzzo, John C. joint author. 5.1283
Molnar, Alex. 4.10444
Molnar, Donald J. 5.5386
Molnar, John Edgar. 5.7731
Molnar, Stephen, 1931-. 4.440
Molony, John N. (John Neylon), 1927-. 3.2889
Moltmann, Jürgen, ed. 1.2800
Moltmann, Jürgen. 1.2838, 1.2865, 1.2942,
    1.2993
Moltz, Howard. ed. 5.4106
Molyneux, Maxine. 3.5251
Momaday, Al, illus. 3.5899
Momaday, N. Scott, 1934-. 2.13175, 2.13177,
    3.5899
Momaday, Natachee Scott. 2.11261, 2.13176
Momen, Moojan. 1.2091
Momeni, Jamshid A., 1938-. 5.7874
Moment, Gairdner Bostwick, 1905-. 5.4215
Momigliano, Arnaldo. 2.272, 3.399-3.400,
    3.2551
Momigliano Lepschy, Anna Laura. 2.853
Mommsen, Theodor Ernst, 1905-1958. 3.363
Mommsen, Theodore, 1817-1903. 3.2751
Mommsen, Wilhelm 1892-. 4.8602
Mommsen, Wolfgang J., 1930-. 3.893, 4.7537
Monaco, James. 2.2894, 2.2942
Monaco, Paul. 2.3008
Monaco, Richard. 2.10775, 2.13179
Monaghan, Jay, 1891-. 3.7354
Monahan, William G. 4.10637
Monas, Sidney. 2.1576
Moncrieff, R. W. 5.4358
Mondolfo, L. F. (Lucio F.) 5.6782
Mondor, Henri, 1885-1962. 2.4266
Mondrian, Piet, 1872-1944. 1.4817
Monet, Claude, 1840-1926. 1.6122-1.6124
Monet, Jacques. 3.8685
Money, John, 1921-. 5.491
Money, Lloyd J., 1920-. 5.5925
Mongaït, Aleksandr L'vovich. 3.257
Mongan, Agnes. 1.6111
Monglond, André. Journal intime d'Oberman.
    2.4296
Mongrédien, Georges, 1901-. 3.2031
Monière, Denis, 1947-. 4.7279
Monin, A. S. (Andreĭ Sergeevich), 1921-. 5.1664
Monjian, Mercedes Cunningham. 2.11932
Monk of Malmesbury. 3.1364
Monk, Samuel Holt. 2.6971, 2.7313
Monkhouse, Francis John. 3.1188, 4.77, 4.204
Monkkonen, Eric H., 1942-. 4.6822
Monmonier, Mark S. 4.202
Monnet, Jean, 1888-. 3.731
Monod, Sylvère, 1921-. 2.7628
Monro, Isabel Stevenson, comp. 5.8170
Monro, Isabel Stevenson. 5.5861, 5.5886, 5.8178
Monro, Kate M., joint author. 5.5861, 5.5886
Monroe, Charles R. 4.10567
Monroe, Elizabeth. 3.3746
Monroe, Elizabeth. joint author. 3.5242
Monroe, John A., 1914-. 3.8100
Monroe, Kristen R., 1946-. 4.7954
Monroy, Alberto. 5.3484
Montagne, Robert, 1893-1954. 3.5211
Montagu, Ashley, 1905-. 4.430, 4.444, 4.479,
    4.567, 4.670, 4.4894, 4.5934, 4.10250, 5.423
Montagu, Ewen, 1901-. 3.1081
Montagu, Jennifer. 1.5725
Montagu, Jeremy. 1.4131, 1.4135
Montagu, Lady Mary (Pierrepont) Wortley,
    1689-1762. 3.1551
Montagu, Mary Wortley, Lady, 1689-1762.
    2.7172
Montague, Francis Charles, 1858-1935. 4.7439
Montague, John. comp. 2.9865
Montague, Richard, joint author. 1.1212
Montague, Susan P., 1942-. 3.6062
Montague, William Edward, 1931-. 4.10360

Montague, William Pepperell, 1873-1953, ed. 1.569
Montaigne, Michel de, 1533-1592. 2.3990-2.3992
Montale, Eugenio, 1896-. 1.6683, 2.5037-2.5039
Montana. Federal Writers' Project. 3.8542
Montefiore, Alan. 1.93, 1.734
Montefiore, C. G. (Claude Goldsmid), 1858-1938. ed. and tr. 1.1941
Monter, E. William. 1.2427, 5.680
Montesinos, José Fernández. 2.5137
Montesquieu, Charles de Secondat, baron de, 1689-1755. 2.4081-2.4082, 4.7427-4.7428
Montessori, Maria, 1870-1952. 4.10205-4.10208
Montgomery, Bruce, 1921-1978. 2.9123
Montgomery, Charles F. 1.6564, 1.6673
Montgomery, David, 1927-. 4.3571, 4.3599
Montgomery, Deane, 1909-. 5.1303
Montgomery, Douglas C. joint author. 5.7020
Montgomery, Florence M. 5.7081
Montgomery, Guy, comp. 2.6993
Montgomery, Hugh L. 5.1321
Montgomery, Robert Langford. 2.6512
Montgomery, Tommie Sue. 3.9069
Montgomery, W. David (William David), 1944-. 4.3773
Montgomery, W. (William), 1871-1930. tr. 1.2880
Montherlant, Henry de, 1896-1972. 2.4638-2.4640
Monti, Phillip J. 4.6813
Monti, Vincenzo, 1754-1828. 2.5006
Montias, John Michael, 1928-. 4.2231, 4.2420
Montilla, M. Robert. 4.6908
Montross, Lynn, 1895-1961. 3.5026, 5.7175
Mood, Alexander McFarlane, 1913-. 4.10550, 5.1394
Moodie, Carol Gayle, joint comp. 4.2191
Moodie, Thomas, joint comp. 4.2191
Moody, Anne, 1940-. 3.6846
Moody, Ernest A. (Ernest Addison), 1903-. 1.1235
Moody, John, 1868-1958. 4.3050
Moody, Joseph Nestor, 1904- ed. 1.3159
Moody, Peter R. 3.4842
Moody, Richard, 1911-. 2.3197, 2.3255, 2.10780
Moody, T. W. (Theodore William), 1907-. 3.1815-3.1816, 3.1843, 3.1854
Moody, William Vaughn, 1869-1910. 2.11175
Moody's Investors Service. 4.4622
Moog, Clodomir Vianna, 1906-. 3.9195
Mookerjee, Satkari. 1.216
Mookerji, Radhakumud, 1884-1964. 3.4241, 3.4247, 3.4249
Moon, Harold K., 1934-. 2.5281
Moon, Henry Lee, 1901-. 4.8180
Moon, Jeremy, 1955-. 4.3228
Moon, Penderel, 1905-. 3.4270, 3.4289
Moon, R. O. (Robert Oswald), 1865-1953. ed. and tr. 2.13576
Moon, Samuel, ed. 2.3772
Mooney, Harold A. 5.3401, 5.3670
Mooney, Harold A. ed. 5.3572
Mooney, James, 1861-1921. 3.5827
Mooney, James E., joint author. 5.7759
Mooney, Kevin C., 1955-. 5.5108
Moonitz, Maurice. ed. 4.4395
Moor, James, 1942- joint author. 1.1198
Moorcock, Michael, 1939-. 2.9744-2.9745
Moore, Alick. joint author. 5.3946
Moore, Arthur Dearth, 1895-. 5.2346
Moore, Barrington, 1913-. 3.3245, 4.3658, 4.5091
Moore, Brian, 1921-. 2.9948-2.9950
Moore, Brian C. J. 5.251
Moore, C. L. 2.13181
Moore, C. L. (Catherine Lucile), 1911-. 2.13180
Moore, Carl Allphin, 1911-. 5.2973
Moore, Charles Alexander, ed. 1.1141
Moore, Charles Alexander. 1.176
Moore, Charles Willard, 1925-. 1.5492
Moore, Charlotte Emma, 1898-. 5.2436
Moore, Clement Henry. ed. 4.7594
Moore, Clifford H. (Clifford Herschel), 1866-1931. 2.697
Moore, Clifton A. 5.6681
Moore, D. M. (David Moresby) 5.3766
Moore, David Cresap, 1925-. 4.8487

Moore, Deborah Dash, 1946-. 3.8051
Moore, Donald K. 2.7407
Moore, Doris Langley-Levy, 1903-. 2.7529, 2.7533
Moore, Edward C. (Edward Carter), 1917-. 1.530, 1.602, 1.630
Moore, Elizabeth A., joint author. 5.2630
Moore, Ernest G. 5.5218
Moore, Eva G. 3.6317
Moore, Francis D. (Francis Daniels), 1913-. 5.4222
Moore, Frank J. (Frank John), 1922-. 3.4519
Moore, Frank Ledlie. 1.3519
Moore, Frederick, 1870-. 3.4928
Moore, G. E. (George Edward), 1873-1958. 1.750-1.752, 1.756, 1.1078, 1.1408, 1.1437
Moore, George, 1852-1933. 2.7954-2.7958
Moore, George Foot, 1851-1931. 1.1909
Moore, Gerald. 1.3983, 2.2302, 2.2308, 2.10116
Moore, Gilbert W. 4.4527
Moore, Glover, 1911-. 3.7119
Moore, Gregory H. 5.1354
Moore, Harry Estill. 3.6354
Moore, Harry T. 2.8612
Moore, Harry Thornton. 2.8990, 2.12539
Moore, Harry Thornton. ed. 2.8989
Moore, Henry, 1898-. 1.5695-1.5696, 1.5698
Moore, Honor, 1945-. 2.10790
Moore, J. J. (John J.) 5.3570
Moore, J. M. (John Michael) 4.7338
Moore, J. Strother, 1947- joint author. 5.1231
Moore, Jack B. 3.6830
Moore, Jennifer Mills. 4.4272-4.4273
Moore, Jesse Thomas, 1936-. 3.6681
Moore, John, 1907-1967. 2.9426
Moore, John Aiken, 1920-. 2.5215
Moore, John Hampton, 1935-. 4.2419
Moore, John Hebron. 5.5245
Moore, John Leo, 1927-. 5.7264
Moore, John Norton, 1937-. 3.3860
Moore, John Robert, 1890-. 2.6976
Moore, John W. 5.2630, 5.2890
Moore, Ken. 5.5364
Moore, Kenneth, 1930-. 3.4007
Moore-Landecker, Elizabeth. 5.3721
Moore, Lillian. joint author. 4.1178
Moore, Lillian. 4.1096
Moore, Lynda J., 1948-. 5.4555
Moore, Lynda L. 4.3287
Moore, Madeline. 2.9602
Moore, Marianne, 1887-1972. 2.4031, 2.12199-2.12200
Moore, Marsha L. 5.7840
Moore, Merritt Hadden. 1.442
Moore, Michael C., 1947-. 5.4555
Moore, Mick. 4.2766
Moore, O. Ernest. 4.2160
Moore, Patrick. 5.1709, 5.1716, 5.1740, 5.1789, 5.1817, 5.1844
Moore, Patrick. joint author. 5.1821
Moore, Patrick. 5.1685, 5.1708
Moore, Peter D. joint author. 5.3238
Moore, Peter D. 4.284
Moore, Rayburn S., 1920-. 2.11075
Moore, Raymond Cecil, 1892-. 5.3167
Moore, Richard K. 4.29
Moore, Robert L. 1.1872
Moore, Ruth E. 5.3381
Moore, Sally Falk, 1924-. 4.558
Moore, Samuel, 1877-. 2.938, 2.1011
Moore, Steven, 1951-. 2.13023
Moore, T. Inglis (Tom Inglis), 1901-1978. 2.10139
Moore, T. Sturge (Thomas Sturge), 1870-1944. 2.9124
Moore, Terence. 2.160
Moore, Thomas, 1779-1852. 2.7250
Moore, Thomas C. 5.3746
Moore, Thomas Gale. 2.3269
Moore, Walter John, 1918-. 5.2805
Moore, Wilbert Ellis. 4.3111, 4.3433, 4.6399
Moore, Wilbert Ellis. ed. 4.3112
Moore, Will Grayburn. 2.3830, 2.3847, 2.3886, 2.4035, 2.4043-2.4044
Moorehead, Alan. 3.5171, 3.5173, 3.5562, 4.92
Moorer, Frank E. 2.12822
Moores, Donald F. 4.6604

Moorey, P. R. S. (Peter Roger Stuart), 1937-. 3.3831
Moorhead, James H. 1.2406
Moorhouse, Geoffrey, 1931-. 3.4266, 3.4358
Moorhouse, W. W. (Walter Wilson), 1913-1969. 5.3032
Moorman, Charles. 2.2635, 2.6143, 2.9532
Moorman, John R. H. (John Richard Humpidge), 1905-. 1.3258
Moorman, John R.H. (John Richard Humpidge), Bishop of Ripon, 1905-. 1.2429
Moorman, John Richard Humpidge. 1.2440
Moorman, Mary Trevelyan, 1905-. 2.8314
Moorman, Ruth. joint author. 2.2635
Moortgat, Anton, 1897-. 1.4704
Moos, Malcolm Charles, 1916-. 4.8118
Moos, Stanislaus von. 1.5417
Moote, Alanson Lloyd. 3.2029
Mora, Carl J. 2.2904
Mora, Gabriela. 2.2495
Moraes, Dom F., 1938-. 2.9125, 3.4302
Moraga, Cherríe. 2.10702
Moraga, José Joaquin, 1741-1785. 3.8603
Morakis, James C., joint author. 5.6407
Moramarco, Fred S., 1938-. 2.11552
Moran, Barbara K., joint comp. 4.5883
Moran, Emilio F. 4.379
Moran, James. 5.7560
Moran, Mary Hurley, 1947-. 2.9669
Moran, Richard. 4.9428
Moran, Ronald. 2.12476
Moran, Thomas, 1837-1926. 1.6382
Morand, Kathleen. 1.6415
Morante, Elsa, 1916-. 2.5043
Morantz-Sanchez, Regina Markell. 5.4540, 5.4542
Morantz, Toby Elaine, 1943-. 4.3860
Morassi, Antonio, 1892-. 1.6224
Moratto, Michael J. 3.5723
Moravcsik, J. M. E. comp. 1.306
Moravcsik, J. M. E. 1.270
Moravcsik, Michael J. 5.914
Moravia, Alberto, 1907-. 2.5044-2.5046
Morawetz, David. 4.1814
Morawetz, Herbert. 5.2766
Morawska, Ewa T. 3.8092
Morawski, Stefan. 1.1358
Morazé, Charles, 1913-. 4.1758
Mordden, Ethan, 1947-. 1.4211, 1.4214
Mordecai, Pamela. 2.9993
Mordell, L. J. (Louis Joel), 1888-. 5.1334
More, Paul Elmer, 1864-1937. 2.2581, 2.11178
More, Thomas, Sir, Saint, 1478-1535. 2.6495, 4.7175
Moreau de Saint-Méry, M. L. E. (Médéric Louis Elie), 1750-1819. 3.6028
Moreau, Gustave, 1826-1898. 1.6126
Morehead, Joe, 1931-. 5.7779
Morehouse, Laurence Englemohr, 1913-. 5.4268
Morehouse, Ward, 1898-. 2.3229, 2.3251, 5.8033
Moreland, W. H. (William Harrison), 1868-1938. 3.4160
Morell, David. 4.8768
Moreno Galván, José María. 1.6288
Moreton, N. Edwina. 3.1203
Moretti, Daniel S. 4.9876
Morf, Gustav. 2.8570
Morford, Mark P. O., 1929-. 2.737, 2.756
Morgan, Alun, 1928- joint author. 1.3618
Morgan, Ann Haven, 1882-. 5.4075
Morgan, Anne Hodges, 1940-. 3.8531, 3.8534
Morgan, Barbara Brooks, 1900-. 4.1143
Morgan, Bayard Quincy, 1883-. 5.8011
Morgan, D. V. 5.6539
Morgan, Dale Lowell, 1914-1971. 3.8584
Morgan, David, 1937-. 4.8084, 4.8510
Morgan, Derec Llwyd. 2.844
Morgan, Edmund Morris, 1878-1966. 4.9855
Morgan, Edmund Sears. 1.3398, 3.6902, 3.6925, 3.7047, 3.7220, 3.7953, 3.7986, 3.8015, 3.8223
Morgan, H. Wayne (Howard Wayne) 3.7404, 3.7502
Morgan, H. Wayne (Howard Wayne) ed. 3.6050
Morgan, H. Wayne (Howard Wayne) 3.7497, 3.8531, 3.8534
Morgan, Helen M. 3.6925
Morgan, James J., 1932- joint author. 4.302
Morgan, James N. 4.2087, 4.5795

Morgan, John Hartman, 1876- ed. 4.7321
Morgan, John Hill, 1870-1945. 1.5976
Morgan, Kenneth O. 3.1689, 3.1707, 3.1768
Morgan, Kenneth William. 1.2145
Morgan, Lewis Henry, 1818-1881. 3.5897, 4.564, 4.7322
Morgan, Millett Granger, 1941-. 5.6123
Morgan, Morris Hicky, 1859-1910, tr. 1.5469
Morgan, Newlin Dolbey, 1888-. 5.5874
Morgan, Nigel J. 1.6409-1.6410
Morgan, Prys. 2.838, 3.1752, 3.1756
Morgan, R. joint author. 5.6114, 5.6132
Morgan, R. P. C. (Royston Philip Charles), 1942-. 5.5286, 5.5289
Morgan, Robert J. 3.7132
Morgan, Robin. 4.5896, 4.6063
Morgan, Robin. comp. 4.6064
Morgan, Roger, 1932-. 3.1705, 4.8376
Morgan, W. B. (William Basil) 4.2900
Morgan, W. T. W. (William Thomas Wilson), 1927-. 3.5054, 3.5258, 4.2583
Morgan, William James. ed. 3.6954
Morgenbesser, Sidney, 1921- ed. 5.913
Morgenstern, Christian, 1871-1914. 2.13840
Morgenstern, Oskar, 1902-. 4.1302, 5.1380
Morgenstern, Sam. comp. 1.3496
Morgenstern, Sam. joint author. 1.3569, 1.3596
Morgenthaler, Walter, 1882-. 5.187
Morgenthau, Hans Joachim, 1904-. 3.7588, 4.7257, 4.9014
Morgenthau, Hans Jonchim, 1904-. 3.7587
Morgenthau, Ruth Schachter. 3.5377
Morgner, Irmtraud. 2.13904
Morholt, Evelyn. 5.3216
Mori, Allen A. 4.916
Mori, Ōgai, 1862-1922. 2.2077-2.2078, 3.348
Mörike, Eduard Friedrich, 1804-1875. 2.13638-2.13639
Morin, Edgar. 4.5356
Morin, Lucien. 4.6854
Morinis, E. Alan. 1.1721
Morisawa, Marie. 4.313
Morishima, James K. 5.4821
Morison, Elizabeth Forbes. 3.7962
Morison, Elting Elmore. 3.7688, 5.5538
Morison, Elting Elmore. joint author. 3.7962
Morison, Samuel Eliot, 1887-1976. 3.909, 3.1032-3.1033, 3.5968, 3.5974-3.5975, 3.6324-3.6325, 3.6886, 3.7954, 3.7982, 3.7987, 3.8712, 4.10996
Morison, Stanley, 1889-1967. 2.3684, 5.7562
Morison, Walker Angus, joint author. 2.1193
Morison, Walter Angus. 2.1540
Moriyasu, K. 5.2471
Morlan, Robert Loren, 1920-. 4.2912
Morley, Christopher, 1890-1957. 2.12205-2.12208
Morley, Edith Julia, 1875-, ed. 2.7077
Morley, James William, 1921-. 3.4917, 3.4919, 3.4922, 3.4965, 3.4971, 3.4981
Morley, John, 1838-1923. 3.1626
Morley, Patricia A. 2.9941
Morley, Peter. 4.462
Morley, Sylvanus Griswold, 1878- tr. 2.5459, 3.9040
Morley, Thomas, 1557-1603? 1.4433
Morlok, Edward K. 5.5926
Morn, Frank, 1937-. 4.6814
Mornay, Philippe de, seigneur du Plessis-Marly, 1549-1623. 4.7386
Mornet, Daniel, 1878-. 1.815, 2.3853, 3.2060
Morony, Michael G., 1939-. 3.3775
Morpeth, Robert S., joint author. 3.1776
Morphet, Edgar Leroy, 1895-. 4.10638, 4.10658
Morrall, John B. 3.576, 4.7270
Morrell, Albert M. 5.6441
Morrell, Jack. 5.693
Morrell, Robert E. joint author. 5.8070
Morrell, Robert E. 2.1998
Morrell, William Parker, 1899-. 3.5553, 5.6751
Morrelli, Howard F., 1935-. 5.5136
Morrill, J. S. (John Stephen) 3.1484
Morrill, Terence C. joint author. 5.2747
Morris, A. E. J. (Anthony Edwin James) 4.6313
Morris, Adah Vivian, 1895-1944. 1.40
Morris, Aldon D. 3.6682
Morris, C. B. (Cyril Brian) 2.5114

Morris, C. J. O. R. (Colin John Owen Rhonabwy) 5.2645
Morris, Charles William, 1901-. 1.543, 1.613, 4.4990
Morris, Clarence, 1903- ed. 3.6145
Morris, Colin M. 4.5474
Morris, Cynthia Taft, joint author. 4.2755, 4.3124
Morris, D. S. 3.2440
Morris, David B. 5.7203
Morris, David Joseph. 5.6377
Morris, Desmond. ed. 5.3806
Morris, Desmond. 4.445, 5.3973
Morris, Donald R. 3.7704
Morris, Edmund. 3.7704
Morris, Edwin T. 5.5370
Morris, Gregory L. 2.13034
Morris, Henry Madison, 1918-. 5.5966
Morris, Ivan I. 3.4902, 3.4907
Morris, Ivan I. ed. 2.2037, 2.2052, 3.4980
Morris, James A., 1938-. 3.9056, 3.9070
Morris, James Oliver, 1923-. 4.3549
Morris, Jan, 1926-. 3.1182
Morris, Jeffrey Brandon, 1941-. 3.6202
Morris, Joe Alex. ed. 2.3582, 3.7805
Morris, John. 3.1336
Morris-Jones, W. H. (Wyndraeth Humphreys) 3.4101, 3.4294
Morris, Leslie R. 5.7654
Morris, Mary, 1913-. 2.1058, 2.1101
Morris, Mervyn. 2.9993
Morris, Milton D. 4.8954
Morris, Monica B., 1928-. 1.1292
Morris, Morris David. 4.1815
Morris, P., joint author. 5.2645
Morris, Pamela. tr. 2.4413
Morris, Percy A., 1899-. 5.3847-5.3848
Morris, R. J. (Robert John) 4.4762
Morris, Richard, 1939-. 2.6218, 5.915, 5.1874, 5.2289
Morris, Richard Brandon, 1904-. 2.3540, 3.605, 3.6202, 3.6884, 3.6903, 3.6938, 4.3560, 4.3569
Morris, Robert, 1734-1806. 3.6977
Morris, Robert Charles, 1942-. 4.10870
Morris, Robert K. 2.6056, 2.9234, 2.13345
Morris, Roger. 3.7902
Morris, Rosemary. 2.2637
Morris, Sean. 5.3775
Morris, Thomas D., 1938-. 4.9623
Morris, Van Cleve. 4.10733
Morris, William, 1913-. 2.1058, 2.1080, 2.1101, 2.7960-2.7967
Morris, William E. 3.1949
Morris, Willie. 2.13182
Morris, Wright, 1910-. 2.3527, 2.12210-2.12218
Morrison, Andrew P., 1937-. 5.4947
Morrison, Blake, 1950-. 2.6192
Morrison, Coleman, joint author. 4.10456
Morrison, David, 1940-. 5.1717, 5.1766, 5.1818-5.1819
Morrison, Herbert Stanley, 1888-. 4.8434
Morrison, Hugh Sinclair, 1905-. 1.5292, 1.5330
Morrison, Kenneth M. 3.5835
Morrison, Michael A., 1949-. 5.2135
Morrison, Paul Guerrant, 1896-. 5.7915
Morrison, Philip. joint author. 5.2049
Morrison, Phylis, 1927-. 5.2925
Morrison, Ralph. 5.5683
Morrison, Robert Thornton, 1918-. 5.2722
Morrison, Rodney J., 1934-. 4.8684
Morrison, Theodore, 1901-. 2.12221-2.12222, 4.10987
Morrison, Toni. 2.13183-2.13185
Morrissette, Bruce, 1911-. 2.4695
Morrissey, Charles T. 3.7967
Morrow, Glenn R. (Glenn Raymond), 1895-1973. ed. and tr. 1.256
Morrow, John Howard, 1944-. 3.823
Morsberger, Robert Eustis, 1929-. 2.12589
Morse, Chandler, 1906-. 4.1767
Morse, Dan F. 3.5742
Morse, Dean. 4.3607
Morse, Douglass H., 1938-. 5.4064
Morse, Flo. 1.3411
Morse, Hosea Ballou, 1855-1934. 3.4678, 4.2464
Morse, John J., joint author. 4.2667
Morse, Josiah Mitchell, 1912-. 2.927
Morse, Marston, 1892-. 5.1469

Morse, Philip McCord, 1903-. 5.1954, 5.1968
Morse, Phyllis A. 3.5742
Morse, Richard M. (Richard McGee), 1922-. 3.9223
Morse, Ruth, ed. 2.6382
Morse, Samuel Crowell. 1.5763
Morse, Samuel French, 1916-. 2.12548
Morse, William Charles. 4.10948
Morse, William Charles. joint author. 4.10952
Morsey, Rudolf. jt. ed. 3.2420
Morstein Marx, Fritz, 1900-. 4.7758
Mortensen, Brita M. E., joint author. 2.13966
Mortenson, F. Joseph. 5.4065
Mortimer, Martin. 5.3337
Mortimer, Penelope, 1918-. 2.9746-2.9747
Mortimer, Rex Alfred. 4.8731
Mortimer, Robert G. 5.2807
Morton, Arthur Silver, 1870-1945. 3.8838
Morton, Catherine, ed. 2.821
Morton, David, 1920-. 1.3746
Morton, Desmond. 3.8695, 4.9431
Morton, Jacqueline. 2.984
Morton, John Bingham, 1893-. 2.8449
Morton, Leslie T. (Leslie Thomas), 1907- ed. 5.8284
Morton, Louis. 3.8193, 5.7275
Morton, Marian J., 1937-. 3.6216
Morton, Philip. 5.7068
Morton, Richard Lee, 1889-. 3.8197
Morton, W. L. (William Lewis), 1908-. 3.8676, 3.8699, 3.8731, 3.8770, 3.8858
Morton, William Fitch. 3.4921
Morwitz, Ernst, 1887-1971, tr. 2.13751
Mosbacher, Eric, 1903-. 2.5070
Mosca, Gaetano, 1858-1941. 4.7479
Moscati, Sabatino. 3.3700, 3.3786
Moscato, Michael. 4.9460
Moschovakis, Yiannis N. 5.1355
Moschus, of Syracuse. 2.555
Mosco, Vincent. 5.6400
Moscotti, Albert D. 3.4427
Moscow. Institut Marksa-Engel'sa-Lenina. 4.7072
Moscow, Warren. 4.8213
Mosel, James Norman, 1918-. 2.2258
Moseley, Edwin M., 1916- joint ed. 2.6252
Moseley, F. 5.2979
Moseley, William S. 5.8027
Mosely, Philip Edward, 1905-. 3.3178, 3.3255
Moser, Charles A. 2.1203, 2.1462
Moser, Hans Joachim, 1889-1967. 1.3980
Moser, Harold D. 3.6970
Moser, Thomas C. 2.8638
Moser, Thomas Colborn, 1923-. 2.8571
Moses, Alfred James, 1921-. 5.2082
Moses, Claire Goldberg, 1941-. 4.6117
Moses, Grandma, 1860-1961. 1.5957
Moses, Gregory A. 5.6614
Moses, Joel. 5.1232
Moses, Montrose Jonas, 1878-1934. ed. 2.3192, 2.10781
Moses, Wilson Jeremiah, 1942-. 3.6683, 3.6720
Mosher, Clelia Duel, 1863-1940. 4.5511
Mosher, Edith K., joint author. 4.9587
Mosher, Frederick C. 4.4731, 4.7882, 4.7979
Mosher, Steven W. 4.5458
Mosier, Richard David, 1917-. 2.1005
Moskoff, William. 4.3231
Moskos, Charles C. 4.9255
Moskow, Michael H. 4.3511
Mosley, Charlotte. 2.9120
Mosley, Derek J., joint author. 3.2554
Mosley, Hugh G. 4.2067
Mosley, Leonard, 1913-. 3.2387, 3.7638
Moss, Alfred A., 1943-. 3.6637
Moss, Claude Scott, 1924- joint author. 4.6899
Moss, Leonard, 1931-. 2.12180
Moss, Richard J. 2.926
Moss, Rowland Percy. joint author. 3.5321
Moss, Scott J. 4.1463
Moss, Sidney Phil, 1917-. 2.7665
Moss, Theodore Crandall, 1922-. 4.10506
Mossé, Claude, docteur ès lettres. 3.2652
Mossé, Fernand. 2.953
Mosse, George L. 3.4014
Mosse, George L. (George Lachmann), 1918-. 3.621, 3.681, 3.2358, 4.5491
Mosse, Werner Eugen. 3.2297, 3.3127

Mossman, Harland W. (Harland Winfield), 1898- joint author. 5.4165
Mossner, Ernest Campbell, 1907-. 1.701
Mosteller, Frederick, 1916-. 4.7959, 4.10898
Mostowski, Andrzej. 1.1217
Mostowski, Andrzej. joint author. 5.1353
Moszyńska, W., joint author. 4.743
Motherwell, Robert. 1.5958
Motil, John M. 5.5691
Motion, Andrew. 2.6192, 2.8945
Motley, John Lothrop, 1814-1877. 3.2961
Motley, Mary Penick, 1920-. 3.1127
Motley, Willard, 1909-1965. 2.13186-2.13187
Motolinía, Toribio, d. 1568. 3.8886
Motor Vehicle Manufacturers Association of the United States. 4.3815
Mott, Frank Luther, 1886-1964. 2.3586-2.3587, 2.3639, 5.7701
Mott, Michael. 1.3271
Mott, N. F. (Nevill Francis), Sir, 1905-. 5.2189, 5.2206, 5.2399
Mott, Nevill Francis, 1905- . 5.2118
Mottana, Annibale. 5.3016
Mottram, Ron. 2.13320
Motulsky, Arno G., 1923-. 5.3442
Moulder, Frances V. 4.2463
Moule, C. F. D. (Charles Francis Digby), 1908-. 1.2179, 1.2851
Moulton, Gary E. 3.8479-3.8480
Moulton, Richard Green, 1849-1924. 2.6816
Mounce, H. O. 1.1077
Mounce, Robert H. 1.2733
Mounsey, Helen. 4.2218
Mount, Ellis. 5.5501, 5.7610
Mount Zion Psychotherapy Research Group. 5.4908
Mountfield, David, 1938-. 3.5048
Mourelatos, Alexander P. D., 1936- comp. 1.234
Mourgues, Odette de. 2.4036, 2.4055
Mourning Dove, 1888-1936. 2.12223
Mousnier, Roland. 3.636, 3.2020, 4.5350
Moussinac, Léon, 1890-1964. 2.3154
Moutafakis, Nicholas J., 1941-. 1.1244
Mouton, Jane Srygley. joint author. 4.4325
Mowat, Robert Balmain, 1883-1941. 3.2127
Mower, A. Glenn (Alfred Glenn) 4.9384
Mower, Nancy R. 3.185
Mowrer, Orval Hobart, 1907-. 4.5065, 4.10356-4.10357
Mowry, George Edwin, 1909-. 3.7511, 3.7698, 3.8610
Moyer, Burton J., ed. 5.2031
Moyer, Reed. 4.3750
Moyle, Peter B. 3.3899
Moyles, R. G. 5.7888
Moynahan, Julian, 1925-. 2.8991
Moynihan, Daniel P. (Daniel Patrick), 1927-. 3.8045, 4.2098, 4.2105, 4.10898
Moynihan, M. 5.4030
Moynihan, Ruth Barnes. 4.6002
Moynihan, William T. 2.9420
Mozart, Leopold, 1719-1787. 1.4546
Mozart, Wolfgang Amadeus, 1756-1791. 1.3934
Mozley, J.H. 2.678
Mozley, James Frederic, 1887-. 1.2492
Mozley, John Henry, tr. 2.695
Mphahlele, Ezekiel. 2.2303
Mphahlele, Ezekiel. ed. 2.2309
Mpondo, Simon, tr. 2.4870
Mr. Sponge's sporting tour, Author of. 2.8131
Mrazek, Patricia Beezley. 4.5518
Mrázková, Daniela. 3.989
Mrosovsky, Kitty. 2.4192
Mrozek, Donald J. 4.936
Mrožek, Sławomir. 2.1741
Mu'assasat al-Kuwayt lil-Taqaddum al-'Ilmī. 5.6116
Mucha, Alphonse Marie, 1860-1939. 1.5858
Muchnic, Helen. 2.1273
Mudd, Stuart, 1893- ed. 4.1635
Mudge, Eugene Tenbroeck. 3.7012
Mudge, Isadore Gilbert, 1875-1957. 2.7714, 2.8185
Mudge, Lewis Seymour. 1.2518
Mudrack, K. (Klaus), 1924-. 5.6032
Mudrick, Marvin. 2.7382
Muehlbauer, Gene. 4.6878

Muehrcke, Juliana O. joint author. 4.208
Muehrcke, Phillip. 4.208
Muehsam, Gerd, 1913-. 1.5103
Mueller, Charles F. (Charles Francis) 4.3212
Mueller, Conrad George, 1920-. 5.252, 5.4381
Mueller, Dennis C. 4.3017, 4.7736
Mueller, Eva, 1920- joint author. 4.2060
Mueller, Frederick A. 1.4558
Mueller, Ivan Istran, 1930-. 5.1753
Mueller, John E. 4.1097
Mueller, John Henry, 1895-. 1.3691
Mueller, Martin, 1939-. 2.499
Mueller, Willard Fritz. 4.3692
Muenscher, Walter Conrad Leopold, 1891-1963. 5.5393
Muensterberger, Warner, 1913- ed. 4.666
Muet, Pierre-Alain. 4.1400
Mufti, Aftab A. 5.5650
Muggeridge, Malcolm, ed. 3.2896
Muggeridge, Malcolm, 1903-. 3.2897
Mugridge, Donald Henry. 5.7761
Muhammad 'Abduh, 1849-1905. 1.2057
Muhlenfeld, Elisabeth, 1944-. 3.335, 3.7368
Muir, Bernice L. 5.4752
Muir, Edwin, 1887-1959. 2.3423, 2.5522, 2.9126-2.9127
Muir, John, 1838-1914. 3.8617
Muir, Kenneth. 2.5638, 2.6677, 2.6682, 2.6711, 2.6744, 2.6762
Muir, Ramsay, 1872-1941. 4.122
Muir, Willa, 1890-. 2.13713
Muir, William Ker. 1.2016, 4.9596
Muirden, James. 5.1735
Muirden, James. joint author. 5.1736
Muirden, James. 5.1749
Muirhead, H. (Hugh) 5.1917
Muirhead, John H. (John Henry), 1855-1940. 1.185, 1.735
Muise, D. A. (Delphin Andrew), 1941-. 5.7895
Mukařovský, Jan. 2.2343
Mukerjea, Devavrata, tr. 2.1888
Mukerjee, Hirendranath, 1907-. 2.1858
Mukerjee, Tapan, joint comp. 4.1746
Mukerji, Chandra. 4.1755
Mukerji, Paresh Nath, 1882-. 1.205
Mukhamedzhanov, Kaltaĭ, joint author. 2.1620
Mukherjee, Pranab, 1935-. 4.2509
Mukherjee, S. N. 4.5421
Mukhopādhyāya, Suśīla, 1911-. 2.3395
Mulas, Ugo. 1.5663
Mulder, John M., 1946-. 3.7724
Muldoon, Maureen. 5.8289
Mules, Helen B., 1948-. 1.5799
Mulhauser, Frederick, ed. 2.7577
Mulhauser, Ruth E., 1913-. 2.4009
Mulisch, Harry, 1927-. 2.13952
Mulkay, M. J. (Michael Joseph), 1936-. 4.4834
Mulkeen, Anne, 1927-. 2.8799
Mulkern, John R. 4.7895
Mull, Richard F. 4.973
Mullahy, Patrick. 5.176, 5.4841
Mullally, Susan. 3.6803
Mullaney, Marie Marmo. 4.7147
Mullen, Edward J., 1942-. 2.11889
Mullen, Richard. 3.6042
Muller, Alexander V., ed. 4.9915
Müller, F. Max (Friedrich Max), 1823-1900. 1.1737, 2.1930, 2.1932
Muller, Gilbert H., 1941-. 2.13222, 2.13429
Müller, Grégoire. 1.4872
Müller, Heiner, 1929-. 2.13905-2.13906
Muller, Helmut A. 1.5495
Müller, Herbert Joseph, 1905-. 2.12794, 3.28, 3.94, 3.202-3.203
Muller, Jean M. 5.6082
Muller, Peter O. 4.6355
Müller, Ronald E. joint author. 4.2730
Muller, Siegfried Hermann, 1902-. 2.166
Müller, Theodor, 1905-. 1.5645
Mulligan, Raymond A., 1915- joint author. 4.6555
Mulliken, Ruth K. 5.5116
Mullin, Chris. 4.8426, 4.8543
Mullin, Donald C. 1.5548
Mullin, Gerald W. 3.7221
Mullin, Michael, 1938-. 3.7184
Mullinger, James Bass, 1834-1917. 4.11008
Mullins, Carolyn J. 4.1235

Mullins, June B., 1927-. 5.7724
Multatuli. 2.13950
Multhauf, Robert P. 5.2613, 5.8456
Mulvaney, Derek John. 4.749
Mulvey, Charles. 4.3331
Mulvihill, Edward R., ed. 2.5223
Mumford, Lewis, 1895-. 1.5285-1.5286, 1.5295, 1.5483, 2.11164, 3.2, 3.25-3.26, 3.211, 3.339, 3.6146, 4.6187, 4.6296, 4.7173
Mumpower, Jeryl, 1949-. 5.5635
Munck, Johannes, 1904-1965. 1.2665
Muncy, Raymond Lee. 4.5579
Mundo Lo, Sara de. 5.7910
Mundt, Robert J. 4.8854
Mundy, John Hine, 1917-. 1.3119, 4.5862
Municipal Art Society of New York. 1.5544
Munley, Anne. 5.4589
Munn, Geoffrey C. 1.6661
Munn, Glenn G. (Glenn Gaywaine), 1890-. 4.4443
Munnell, Alicia Haydock. 4.3456, 4.3467
Munro, Alice. 2.9952-2.9954
Munro, Donald James. 5.7983
Munro, Eleanor C. 1.4873
Munro, J. Forbes. 3.5272, 4.2578
Munro, Robert J. 4.9437
Munro, Thomas, 1897-. 1.1359, 1.5104
Munroe, John A., 1914-. 3.8099
Munroe, Robert L. 5.566
Munroe, Ruth H. 5.566
Munroe, Ruth Learned, 1903-. 5.177
Munrow, David. 1.4132
Munsell, A. E. O. (Alexander Ector Orr) ed. 1.6353
Munsell, Albert Henry, 1858-1918. 1.6353
Munsey, Brenda. 5.608
Munslow, Barry. 4.3675
Munson, Ronald, 1939-. 5.4562
Münsterberg, Hugo, 1863-1916. 2.2962
Munsterberg, Hugo, 1916-. 1.5059, 1.6363
Munting, Roger, 1945-. 4.2384
Muntz, Hope. ed. 2.821
Munz, Lucile Thompson. 5.8481
Munz, Peter, 1921-. 3.486
Murakami, Shigeyoshi, 1928-. 1.1835
Murali Manohar, K. 4.6142
Muraro, Michelangelo. joint author. 1.6475
Murasaki Shikibu, b. 978? 2.2047, 2.2049-2.2050
Murase, Miyeko. 1.6334-1.6335
Muraskin, William A. 4.6176
Murata, Kiyoaki, 1922-. 1.1760
Murck, Christian F. 1.6312, 1.6725
Murcott, Anne. 4.863
Murcray, D. G. 5.2511
Murdin, Lesley. 5.1849
Murdin, Paul. 5.1839, 5.1849
Murdoch, Brian, 1944-. 2.2630, 2.13462, 2.13816
Murdoch, Iris. 1.269, 1.854, 1.1457, 2.9748-2.9770
Murdoch, James, 1856-1921. 3.4910
Murdoch, John, 1945-. 1.6392
Murdoch, John Emery, 1927-. 5.763
Murdoch, Joseph B., 1927-. 5.6339
Murdoch, Tessa. 1.6305
Murdock, Bennet Bronson. 5.332
Murdock, Eugene Converse. 2.11244, 3.7382, 5.7368
Murdock, George Peter, 1897-. 3.4388, 3.5056, 4.438, 4.465, 4.526-4.527, 5.7740
Murdock, Kenneth B. 3.7950
Murdock, Kenneth Ballard, 1895-1975. 2.10370, 3.7980
Mure, G. R. G. (Geoffrey Reginald Gilchrist), 1893-. 1.307, 1.950
Muret, Eduard, 1833-1904. 2.1190
Murfree, Mary Noailles, 1850-1922. 2.11181-2.11182
Murie, Alan. 4.8570
Murie, Olaus Johan, 1889-1963. 5.4089
Murillo, Bartolomé Esteban, 1617-1682. 1.6298
Murin, William J. joint author. 5.8185
Muriuki, Godfrey. 3.5273
Muroga, Saburo. 5.6540
Murphey, Murray G., joint author. 1.556
Murphey, Rhoads, 1919-. 3.4267, 4.84, 4.2491
Murphree, Marshall W. 1.1860
Murphy, Agnes, 1912-. 4.8924

Murphy, Arthur E. 1.614
Murphy, Bruce Allen. 4.9798
Murphy, Charles Royier, 1884-. 2.4314
Murphy, E. Jefferson. 3.5074
Murphy, Francis Xavier, 1914-. 1.3165
Murphy, Gardner, 1895-. 4.10364, 5.74-5.75,
    5.79, 5.530, 5.642
Murphy, James Frederick, 1943-. 1.1505
Murphy, James Jerome. 2.1033, 2.2531
Murphy, James Jerome. comp. 2.2535
Murphy, Jeffrie G. 1.909, 1.1458
Murphy, John A. 3.1858
Murphy, John Francis, 1937-. 4.9222
Murphy, John J. (John Joseph), 1933-. 2.11476
Murphy, Larry S. joint author. 5.5292
Murphy, Lois Barclay, 1902-. 5.75, 5.5178
Murphy, Orville Theodore. 3.2044
Murphy, Paul L., 1923-. 4.7695, 4.8153, 4.9615
Murphy, Richard, 1927-. 2.9135, 2.9778-2.9779
Murphy, Robert William, 1902-. 5.5308
Murphy, Roland Edmund, 1917- joint comp.
    1.2525
Murphy, Rosalie. 2.11058
Murphy, Therese Cecile, ed. 1.4437
Murphy, Thomas P., 1931-. 4.8861, 4.10804
Murphy, Walter F., 1929-. 4.9778
Murr, Lawrence Eugene. 5.6776
Murray, Albert. 1.4314, 2.2397, 2.13188,
    3.6624, 3.8173
Murray, Augustus Taber, 1866-. 2.360,
    2.373-2.374
Murray-Brown, Jeremy, 1932-. 3.5277
Murray, Bruce C. 5.6705
Murray, David R. 4.6431
Murray, Edward. 2.12261
Murray, Francis X., 1937-. 4.3749
Murray, Gilbert, 1866-1957. 1.1645, 2.287,
    2.317, 2.471, 2.2761, 3.64
Murray, Henry Alexander, 1893-. 5.118
Murray, Isobel. 2.9841
Murray, J. D. (James Dickson) 5.1430
Murray, James Augustus Henry, Sir, 1837-1915.
    ed. 2.1084
Murray, Jocelyn. 3.5057
Murray, John Courtney. ed. 1.3011
Murray, John Tucker. 2.3292
Murray, Joseph James, 1930-. 5.3404
Murray, Katharine Maud Elisabeth. 2.925
Murray, Les A., 1938-. 2.2692
Murray, Linda. 1.4576
Murray, Margaret Alice. 1.5613
Murray, Martin J. 4.2527
Murray, Merrill Garver, 1900- jt. author.
    4.3448
Murray, Michael, 1932-. 5.6443
Murray, Mimi. 4.923
Murray, Oswyn. 3.2519, 3.2541
Murray, Pauli, 1910-. 3.6847
Murray, Peter. 1.4576, 1.5244, 1.5430, 1.5432
Murray, R. B. joint author. 5.6114, 5.6132
Murray, Raymond C. joint author. 5.3051
Murray, Raymond LeRoy, 1920-. 5.6605
Murray, Richard, 1942-. 1.4906
Murray, Robert K. 3.7550, 3.7734-3.7735
Murray, Ruth Lovell. 4.1183
Murray-Smith, Stephen. 2.10146
Murray, Tracy. 4.2717, 4.4200
Murray, W. J. (William J.) joint comp. 3.2063
Murray, Walter. 5.1549
Murray, Williamson. 3.877, 3.1053
Murrell, J. N. (John Norman) 5.2820-5.2821,
    5.2908
Murrin, John M. 3.7955, 4.5127
Murry, John Middleton, 1889-1957. 2.2540,
    2.2582, 2.5545, 2.6041, 2.7302, 2.7430,
    2.7865, 2.8993, 2.9081-2.9082, 2.9116
Mursell, James Lockhart, 1893-. 1.4386
Murstein, Bernard I. ed. 5.543
Murtagh, Bruce A. 5.5590
Murti, T. R. V. (Tirupattur Ramaseshayyer
    Venkatachala) 1.2159
Musa, Mark. 2.4905, 2.4907, 2.4928, 4.7389
Musa, Mark. tr. 2.4920
Musaeus, Grammaticus. 2.357
Muscatine, Charles. 2.5616, 2.6349
Muschg, Walter, 1898-1965. 2.13729
Muse, Benjamin. 3.6709
Musée du Louvre. 1.6053

Musées royaux des beaux-arts de Belgique.
    1.6257
Museo del Prado. 1.6298
Muser, Curt. 3.8887
Museum für Indische Kunst (Germany) 1.5185
Museum of Fine Arts, Boston. 1.4658, 1.5063,
    1.5620, 1.5690, 1.5827, 1.5881, 1.5883,
    1.5916, 1.5952, 1.5963-1.5964, 1.5991, 1.6076,
    1.6458, 1.6460, 1.6462, 1.6464, 1.6488,
    1.6493, 1.6496, 1.6655, 1.6668
Museum of Fine Arts, Houston. 1.5921, 1.6070,
    1.6296, 1.6504, 1.6521, 3.5733, 5.6950
Museum of London. 1.6305
Museum of Modern Art (New York, N.Y.)
    1.4662, 1.4789, 1.4809, 1.4818-1.4819, 1.4846,
    1.4851, 1.4874-1.4877, 1.4895, 1.4900, 1.4903,
    1.4972, 1.4976, 1.4979, 1.4999, 1.5157,
    1.5321, 1.5353, 1.5425, 1.5491, 1.5661,
    1.5664, 1.5690, 1.5711, 1.5873, 1.5906,
    1.5914-1.5915, 1.5921, 1.5933, 1.5950, 1.6070,
    1.6125, 1.6130, 1.6145-1.6146, 1.6433-1.6434,
    1.6569, 1.6675, 2.3076, 5.6959, 5.6964, 5.6973
Museum of Modern Art (Oxford, Oxfordshire)
    1.6003
Musgrave, Alan. ed. 5.900
Musgrave, Clifford. 1.6576
Musgrave, John K. 3.4387
Musgrave, Richard Abel, 1910-. 4.4643,
    4.4646-4.4647, 4.4689
Mushkat, Jerome. 4.8214
Music Library Association. 1.3628
Music Library Association. Committee on Basic
    Music Collection. 1.3546
Musil, Robert, 1880-1942. 2.13842-2.13845
Musruliio, Herbert Anthony, ed. and tr. 1.3089
Mussen, Paul Henry. ed. 5.561
Mussen, Paul Henry. 4.5729
Musset, Alfred de, 1810-1857. 2.4274, 2.4292
Musset, Lucien. 3.583
Mussett, A. E. (Alan E.) 5.3089
Mussolini, Benito, 1883-1945. 3.2890, 3.2900
Mussolini, Rachele Guidi, 1892-. 3.2904
Mussulman, Joseph A. 1.3694
Mustard, Helen Meredith, 1906- tr. 2.13540
Muster, John C. C. 5.1164
Muth, Eginhard J., 1928-. 5.5731
Mütherich, Florentine. 1.6404
Muthesius, Hermann, 1861-1927. 1.5566
Muthesius, Stefan. 1.5371, 1.5373
Mutibwa, Phares M. 3.5315
Mutswairo, Solomon M. 2.2312
Muzzy, Adrienne Florence, 1885-. 5.8314
Myant, M. R. (Martin R.) 3.1926
Mydans, Carl. 2.3623
Myer, Valerie Grosvenor. 2.7278, 2.9670
Myerhoff, Barbara G. 3.8633, 4.558, 4.5801
Myers, A. R. (Alec Reginald), 1912-1980.
    3.1298, 3.1743
Myers, Alan L., 1932-. 5.6831
Myers, Andrew B. 2.11095
Myers, Bernard Samuel, 1908-. 1.4575, 1.4578,
    1.6001
Myers, Charles Andrew, 1913-. 4.3201, 4.3221,
    4.3666, 4.4365
Myers, Denys Peter, 1884-. 3.849
Myers, Frederic William Henry, 1843-1901.
    5.643
Myers, Glenford J., 1946-. 5.6585
Myers, Gustavus, 1872-1942. 4.1894
Myers, Helen, 1946-. 1.4292
Myers, Jack. 2.10731
Myers, Jay, 1949-. 3.8656
Myers, Jerome K. (Jerome Keeley), 1921-.
    5.4833
Myers, Jerome L. 5.1413
Myers, John G. 4.4306
Myers, Kurtz. 1.3628-1.3629
Myers, Margaret G. (Margaret Good), 1899-.
    4.4651
Myers, Norman. 5.3222
Myers, O. M., ed. 2.6887
Myers, Patricia I., 1929-. 4.10955
Myers, Ramon Hawley, 1929-. 4.8939
Myers, Robert Manson, 1921-. 3.8265
Myers, Robin, fl. 1967-. 5.7926-5.7927
Myers, Rollo H. 1.3707, 1.3833, 1.3957
Myers, Shirley D. ed. 1.4578
Myers, William Starr, 1877-1956. 3.7741

Myerson, Joel. 2.10396, 2.11028, 2.11192,
    5.8345
Mykkeltvedt, Roald Y., 1929-. 4.9672
Myklebust, Jan Petter. 4.7609
Mylne, Vivienne. 2.3905
Mylonas, George E. (George Emmanuel),
    1898-. 3.2645
Mynors, R. A. B. (Roger Aubrey Baskerville),
    Sir, 1903- ed. 1.2431
Mynors, Roger Aubrey Baskerville, ed. 2.645
Myrdal, Alva Reimer, 1902-. 4.1701, 4.3242
Myrdal, Gunnar, 1898-. 3.6656, 4.1310, 4.1816,
    4.1992, 4.2435, 4.2797, 4.4152, 4.4476
Myrdal, Jan. 3.4797
Myres, J. N. L. (John Nowell Linton) 3.1316
Myres, John Linton, Sir, 1869-1954. 3.2532
Myres, Sandra L. 4.5988
Myrick, Kenneth Orne, 1897-. 2.6513
Myrivēlēs, Stratēs, 1892-. 2.603-2.604

Naamani, Israel T. comp. 3.3930
Nabī Bakhshu Khānu Balocu, 1917-. 5.8052
Nabokov, Vladimir. 2.1583
Nabokov, Vladimir Vladimirovich, 1899-1977.
    2.1330, 2.1386, 2.1413, 2.1580-2.1582, 2.1584,
    2.12224, 2.12226-2.12231, 2.12233
Nabors, Eugene. 4.9439
Nabseth, Lars, ed. 4.1861
Nachmansohn, David, 1899-. 5.2618
Nachtigall, Werner. 5.3874
Naddor, Eliezer. 4.2682
Nadeau, Maurice. 1.1401, 2.3873, 2.3914,
    2.4198
Nadel, Constance Gwen, joint comp. 4.1098
Nadel, Ira Bruce. 3.313
Nadel, Myron Howard, comp. 4.1098
Nadelhaft, Jerome J. 3.6946
Nadelson, Carol C. 5.5045
Nader, Helen, 1936-. 3.3410
Nader, Laura. 4.9376
Nader, Laura. ed. 4.9355
Nader, Ralph. 4.3891, 4.10714, 5.5021, 5.6609,
    5.6635
Nadler, Marcus, 1895- joint author. 4.4448
Nadworny, Milton J. 4.3572
Naef, Weston J., 1942-. 5.6929, 5.6957, 5.7011
Næss, Arne. 1.1003
Næss, Harald. 2.14049
Nafziger, E. Wayne. 4.1817, 4.2514, 4.2626
Nagami, Keiō, 1925-. 5.1596
Nagamori, Shigenobu, 1944-. 5.6314
Nāgārjuna, 2nd cent. 1.2139
Nagel, Donald A. 5.5083
Nagel, Ernest, 1901-. 1.1164, 1.1190,
    5.916-5.917, 5.1047
Nagel, James. 2.10986, 2.13083
Nagel, Otto, 1894-1967. 1.5809
Nagel, Paul C. 3.6147, 3.8363, 4.7866
Nagle, H. Troy, 1942-. 5.6190
Nagler, A. M. (Alois Maria), 1907-. 2.3164,
    2.6857
Nagy, Joseph Falaky. 2.828
Nagy, Steven. 5.5342
Nagy-Talavera, Nicholas M., 1929-. 3.1944
Naha, Ed. 1.3525
Nahal, Chaman Lal, 1927-. 2.10128
Nahm, Milton Charles, 1903-. 1.1376
Naik, J. A. 3.4096
Naill, Roger F. 5.6150
Naipaul, Shiva, 1945-. 2.10003-2.10005
Naipaul, V. S. (Vidiadhar Surajprasad), 1932-.
    2.10006-2.10011
Naipaul, Vidiadhar Surajprasad, 1932-. 2.10012
Nairn, A. E. M. 5.2983
Nairn, Allan. 4.10714
Nairn, Tom. 4.8430
Naish, George Prideaux Brabant. 5.7419
Naison, Mark, 1946-. 4.8238
Najder, Zdzisław. 2.8543, 2.8550, 2.8559,
    2.8572
Najita, Tetsuo. 3.4960
Najm al-Dīn Rāzī, 'Abd Allāh ibn Muhammad,
    d. 1256 or 7. 1.2082
Nakajima, Tadashi. joint author. 3.1055
Nakamoto, Kazuo, 1922-. 5.2678
Nakamura, Hajime, 1912-. 1.213, 3.109
Nakamura, Kyōko, 1932- tr. 1.2152
Nakamura, Mitsuo, pseud. 2.2013, 2.2016

Nakane, Chie, 1926-. 4.5449
Nakanishi, Don T. 4.10883
Nakanishi, Kōji, 1925-. 5.2792
Nakanoin Masatada no Musume, b. 1258. 2.2059
Nakhleh, Khalil. 4.5398
Nakicenovic, Nebojsa. 5.6130
Nalivkin, D. V. (Dmitriĭ Vasil'evich), 1889-. 5.3005
Nalty, Bernard C. 3.6723, 5.7375
Nam, Koon Woo. 3.5043
Namier, Julia, Lady. 3.421
Namier, Lewis Bernstein, 1888-. 3.612, 3.669, 3.703, 3.760, 3.865, 3.1523, 3.1557, 4.8402, 4.8475
Nammālvār. 2.2276
Nānak, Guru, 1469-1538. 1.1829
Nānamoli, Bhikkhu. 1.2123, 1.2138
Nance, Guinevera A. 2.13305
Nance, John J. 4.4090
Nance, William L. 2.11468
Nandan, Yash. 4.4852
Nandy, Pritish. tr. 2.1866
Nandy, Pritish. comp. 2.1958
Nandy, Pritish. 2.10129
Nandy, Pritish. ed. 2.1913
Nania, Georges. 5.1136
Naparstek, Arthur. 5.4701
Napoleon I, Emperor of the French, 1769-1821. 3.2132, 5.7211
Napoleon III, Emperor of the French, 1808-1873. 3.2154
Napolitano, Giorgio. 4.8631
Napper, Elizabeth. 1.2164
Narain, A. K. 3.4242
Narasimhaiah, C. D. 2.9874
Narasimhan, Chakravarthi V. 2.1936
Naravane, Vishwanath S. 2.1891
Narayana Rao, Nannapaneni. 5.2370
Narayanan, Vasudha. 1.1707
Narazaki, Muneshige, 1904-. 1.6480
Nardin, Terry, 1942-. 4.8993
Nardone, Nancy K. 1.3580, 1.3602
Nardone, Thomas R. 1.3581, 1.3602
Naremore, James. 2.9603
Naremore, Rita C. joint author. 2.156
Narins, Dorice. 5.4402
Narkiewicz, Olga A. 4.6972
Narlikar, Jayant Vishnu, 1938-. 5.1759, 5.1828, 5.1875
Naroll, Frada, joint author. 5.7218
Naroll, Raoul. 4.493, 5.7218
Narot, Ruth E. 4.10787
Narrow, Barbara W. 5.5204
Nasatir, Abraham Phineas, 1904-. 3.5933
Nasaw, David. 4.10040
Nasgaard, Roald. 1.6359
Nash, C. A. (Christopher Alfred), 1947-. 4.3898
Nash, Edward L. 4.4327
Nash, Ernest. 1.5227
Nash, Gary B. 3.6866-3.6867, 3.8078
Nash, George H., 1945-. 3.7534
Nash, Gerald D. 4.2029
Nash, Jay Bryan, 1886-. 4.877
Nash, June C., 1927-. 4.3539, 4.6083-4.6084
Nash, Manning. 3.4337
Nash, Mary, 1925-. 2.3338
Nash, Michael, 1946-. 4.3602
Nash, Ogden, 1902-1971. 2.12234-2.12235
Nash, Paul, 1924-. 4.10237
Nash, Roderick. comp. 5.5300
Nash, Roderick. 3.6148
Nash, Ronald H. 1.334
Nash, Thomas, 1567-1601. 2.6641-2.6643
Nash, Walter. 1.6118, 2.965
Nash, William P. 5.6659
Nashe, Thomas. 2.6643
Nashelsky, Louis. 5.6458
Nason, James D., joint author. 5.8096
Nasr, Seyyed Hossein. 1.2056
Nasri, William Z. ed. 5.7695
Nassaar, Christopher S. 2.8286
Nassau, Kurt. 5.2334
Nasution, Anwar. 4.4460
NASW Conference on Social Work Practice with Women (1st: 1980: Washington, D.C.) 4.6065
Natanson, Maurice Alexander, 1924-. 1.520

Natemeyer, Walter E. 4.2694
Nathan, George Jean, 1882-1958. 2.3085, 2.3210, 2.12236
Nathan, Leonard, 1924-. 2.1894, 2.1948
Nathan, Peter Wilfred. 5.4320
Nathan, Richard P. 4.4663
Nathan, Robert, 1894-. 2.12237-2.12241
Nathans, Elizabeth Studley. 4.8226
Nathanson, Jerome. 1.592
National Academy of Engineering. 5.5540, 5.5631
National Academy of Engineering. Committee on Technology and International Economic and Trade Issues. Automobile Panel. 4.3820
National Academy of Public Administration. 4.7926
National Academy of Sciences (U.S.) 5.811, 5.855, 5.992, 5.1027, 5.2988, 5.5540
National Academy of Sciences (U.S.). Committee on International Security and Arms Control. 4.9174
National Agricultural Library (U.S.) 5.8090, 5.8092
National Air and Space Museum. 5.6675
National Analysts, Inc. 4.1639
National Association for Retarded Citizens. Research and Demonstration Institute. 4.6614
National Association for Retarded Citizens. Residential Services and Facilities Committee. 4.6614
National Association of College and University Business Officers. 4.10600
National Association of Counties. 4.8837
National Association of Independent Schools. Commission on Educational Issues. 4.10053, 4.10509
National Association of Purchasing Management. 4.4324
National Association of Secondary-School Principals. Commission on the Experimental Study of the Utilization of the Staff in the Secondary School. 4.10495
National Association of Secondary School Principals (U.S.) 4.10053, 4.10509
National Association of Social Workers. 4.6065, 4.6473, 4.6509
National Audubon Society. 5.3284, 5.3686, 5.3906, 5.3921, 5.3923, 5.3948, 5.3950-5.3951, 5.3957, 5.3959, 5.3986
National Basketball Association. 4.1014
National Book League. 2.9073
National Book League (Great Britain) 5.7926
National Book Trust. 2.1858
National Broadcasting Company, Inc. 2.1021
National Bureau for Co-operation in Child Care. 4.6580
National Bureau of Economic Research. 4.1571, 4.1950-4.1954, 4.1977, 4.2072, 4.2083, 4.3145, 4.3237, 4.4464-4.4465, 4.4495, 4.4500, 4.5639
National Center for Education Statistics. 4.9931, 4.9941, 4.10783
National Center for Ground Water Research (U.S.) 5.6024
National Center for Higher Education Management Systems. 4.10603
National Coal Policy Project. 4.3749
National Collection of Fine Arts (U.S.) 1.4906, 1.5970
National College of Agricultural Engineering. 5.5286
National Commission on Resources for Youth. 4.5759
National Committee for Citizens in Education. 4.10688
National Conference for Family Violence Researchers (1981: Durham, N.H.) 4.5776
National Conference on Black Sociologists, University of Chicago, 1972. 4.4772
National Conference on Business Ethics. 1st, Bentley College, 1977. 4.4269
National Conference on Business Ethics. 2d, Bentley College, 1978. 4.4270
National Conference on Business Ethics. 3d, Bentley College, 1979. 4.4271
National Conference on Business Ethics (4th: 1981: Bentley College) 4.4272
National Conference on Business Ethics. (5th: 1983: Bentley College) 4.4273

National Conference on Business Ethics. (6th: 1985: Waltham, Mass.) 4.4101
National Conference on Personal Rapid Transit, 1st, University of Minnesota, 1971. 4.3905
National Conference on Soil Erosion, Purdue University, 1976. 5.5287
National Council for the Social Studies. 4.1222
National Council of Teachers of English. 4.10470
National Council of Teachers of English. Committee on Literary Scholarship and the Teaching of English. 2.5509
National Council of Teachers of English. Comparative Literature Committee. 2.2697
National Council of Teachers of English. Project on Career Education. 4.10830
National Council of the Churches of Christ in the United States of America. Office of Research, Evaluation and Planning. 1.2368
National Council on Family Relations. 4.5594
National Council on Measurement in Education. 4.10710
National Dance Association. 4.1086
National Education Association of the United States. Committee of Ten on Secondary School Studies. 4.10497
National Endowment for the Arts. 1.5946, 1.6447
National Endowment for the Humanities. 2.2161, 4.10827
National Fire Protection Association. 4.9763, 5.6108-5.6109
National Football League Properties, Inc. Creative Services Division. 4.1029
National Foreign Assessment Center (U.S.) 4.81
National Fund for Medical Education. Board of Directors. 5.4605
National Gallery of Art (U.S.) 1.4896, 1.4974, 1.4981, 1.4986, 1.5016, 1.5092, 1.5717, 1.5749, 1.5812, 1.5930, 1.5973, 1.6441, 1.6452, 1.6463, 1.6472, 1.6475, 1.6727, 3.5733, 3.5876, 5.6961
National Gallery of Canada. 1.5995, 1.6000, 1.6449
National Geographic Book Service. 5.7485
National Geographic Society (U.S.) 3.121, 5.3952, 5.8202
National Geographic Society (U.S.). Cartographic Division. 4.114
National Geographic Society (U.S.). Special Publications Division. 3.6065
National Historical Society. 3.7350
National Industrial Conference Board. 4.1866
National Information Center for Educational Media. 4.10322, 4.10331-4.10334
National Institute for Occupational Safety and Health. 5.4725, 5.5617
National Institute of Allergy and Infectious Diseases (U.S.) 5.4982
National Institute of Child Health and Human Development (U.S.) 4.6612, 5.3469, 5.4970
National Institute of Economic and Social Research. 4.1861
National Institute of Education (U.S.) 4.10282, 4.10832, 5.4351, 5.8151
National Institute of Education (U.S.). Study Group on the Conditions of Excellence in American Higher Education. 4.10083
National Institute of Mental Health Conference on Dyslexia, Rockville, Md., 1977. 5.5093
National Institute of Mental Health (U.S.) 4.1581, 4.5738, 4.5838, 5.4818, 5.5093
National Institute of Mental Health (U.S.). Mental Health Study Center. 5.511
National Institute of Public Affairs (U.S.) 4.7984
National Institute on Aging. 4.5795
National interracial conference, Washington, 1928. 3.6652
National Jewish Resource Center (U.S.) 5.8249
National Lawyers Guild. 1977 Middle East Delegation. 3.3876
National Library of Canada. 5.7883
National Library of Canada. Resources Survey Division. 5.7737
National Library of Medicine (U.S.) 5.8283
National Longitudinal Surveys of Labor Market Experience (U.S.) 4.3249, 4.3306

National Manpower Institute. 4.10835
National Middle School Association. 4.10507
National Municipal League. Advisory committee on the Revision of the Model City Charter. 4.8852
National Municipal League. Committee on State Government. 4.8250
National Municipal League. State Constitutional Studies Project. 4.8250
National Museum of History and Technology. 5.7089
National Museum of Ireland. 1.4943
National Museum of Natural Sciences (Canada) 5.3988
National Nursing Council. 5.5182
National Organization on Legal Problems of Education. 4.9579, 4.10630
National Portrait Gallery (Great Britain). 1.4665
National Recreation and Park Association. 4.886
National Research Council. Ad Hoc Committee on Geography. 4.34
National Research Council. Committee for Research in Problems of Sex. 5.4085
National Research Council. Committee on Dietary Allowances. 5.7125
National Research Council. Food and Nutrition Board. 5.7125
National Research Council of Canada. 1.53
National Research Council. Office of Scientific Personnel. Board on Human Resources. Panel on the Benefits of Higher Education. 4.10731
National Research Council (U.S.) 1.53, 4.2054, 5.992
National Research Council (U.S.). Astronomy Survey Committee. 5.1704
National Research Council (U.S.). Board on Agriculture. 5.5319
National Research Council (U.S.). Commission on Behavioral and Social Sciences and Education. Committee on National Urban Policy. 4.6222
National Research Council (U.S.). Commission on Engineering and Technical Systems. 4.3820
National Research Council (U.S.). Committee on Atmospheric Transport and Chemical Transformation in Acid Precipitation. 5.6003
National Research Council (U.S.). Committee on Behavioral and Social Aspects of Energy Consumption and Production. 4.3717
National Research Council (U.S.). Committee on Nuclear and Alternative Energy Systems. 5.6148
National Research Council (U.S.). Committee on Population and Demography. Panel on Fertility Determinants. 4.1640
National Research Council (U.S.). Committee on the Atmospheric Effects of Nuclear Explosions. 5.2531
National Research Council (U.S.). Committee on the Education and Employment of Women in Science and Engineering. 5.801
National Research Council (U.S.). Committee on the Scientific Basis of the Nation's Meat and Poultry Inspection Program. 5.7083
National Research Council (U.S.). Committee on Women's Employment and Related Social Issues. 4.3256
National Research Council (U.S.). Geophysics Study Committee. 5.2527
National Research Council (U.S.). Panel on Work, Family, and Community. 4.5652
National Research Council (U.S.). Steering Committee on Identification of Toxic and Potentially Toxic Chemicals for Consideration by the National Toxicology Program. 5.4719
National Safety Council. 5.5554
National School Boards Association. 4.10667
National Science Foundation (U.S.) 4.9604
National Society for the Study of Education. 4.10159
National Society of Film Critics. 2.2864
National Society of the Colonial Dames of America. Minnesota. 3.8298

National Standard Reference Data System (U.S.) 5.6206
National Strategy Information Center. 5.7363
National Symposia on Patient Education. 5.4593
National Symposium on Erosion and Soil Productivity (1984: New Orleans, La.) 5.5291
National Symposium on Wetlands, Disneyworld Village, Lake Buena Vista, Florida, 1978. 4.2928
National Textbook Company. 2.904
National Trust for Historic Preservation in the United States. 1.5665, 3.5992
National Video Clearinghouse. 2.2863
National Wildlife Federation. 5.3906, 5.3923
Natkiel, Richard. 4.127
NATO Advanced Research Workshop on Milankovitch and Climate (1982: Palisades, N.Y.) 5.2528
Nato Advanced Study Institute on Animal Learning, Reisensburg, Ger., 1976. 5.4103
NATO Advanced Study Institute on Photoreceptors (1981: Erice, Sicily) 5.4385
NATO Advanced Study Institute on Surface Modification and Alloying (1981: Trevi, Italy) 5.6768
Natsume, Sōseki, 1867-1916. 2.2082-2.2086
Nattrass, Jill. 4.2620
Natwar-Singh, K. ed. 2.1956
Naughton, John T. 2.4420
Naughton, Pamela J., 1954- joint author. 4.9634
Naughton, Thomas Raymond, 1908- joint author. 4.9905
Naval Historical Center (U.S.) 3.7114
Navarre, Yves, 1940-. 2.4786
Navarro, Marysa. joint author. 3.9252
Navarro Tomás, Tomás, 1884-. 2.891
Navarro y Ledesma, Francisco, 1869-1905. 2.5177
Navasky, Victor S. 2.2925, 4.9743
Nave, Gary. 4.10934
Naveh, Zeev. 5.3223
Navon, David H. 5.6498
Nayar, Baldev Raj. 5.5544
Nayfeh, Ali Hasan, 1933-. 5.1505
Naylor, Colin. 5.6926
Naylor, Gillian. 1.6531
Naylor, Gloria. 2.13189-2.13190
Neal, Ernest G. 5.3783
Neal, Fred Warner. joint author. 3.3565
Neal, Larry, 1937- joint comp. 2.10687
Neal, Steve, 1949-. 3.7695
Neale, A. D. (Alan Derrett) 4.9527
Neale, Caroline. 3.5061
Neale, John Ernest, Sir, 1890-. 3.1424, 3.1431, 3.2011
Neale, R. S. 4.5341
Neale, Walter C. 4.2865
Near Eastern History Group, Oxford. 4.4237
Neary, Peter. 3.8870
Neatby, H. Blair. 3.8745, 3.8771
Neatby, Hilda, 1904-1975. 3.8732
Neave, Edwin H. 4.4596
Neave, Sheffield Airey, 1879-1961. ed. 5.3830
Nebeker, Helen. 2.9280
Nebel, Henry M. 2.1333
Nebenzahl, Kenneth, 1927-. 4.159
Neblette, Carroll Bernard. 5.6934
Nebraska. Federal Writers' Project. 3.8518
Necheles, Ruth F., 1936-. 3.2067
Nederlands Instituut voor Buitenlandse Culturele Betrekkingen. 5.8341
Nee, Brett de Bary, 1943- joint author. 3.8626
Nee, Victor, 1945-. 3.8626
Needham, Dorothy (Moyle) 1896-. 5.4284
Needham, James George, 1868-. 5.3805
Needham, Joseph, 1900-. 3.4642-3.4643, 5.767, 5.771-5.772, 5.4119, 5.4136
Needham, Rodney. comp. 4.551
Needleman, Jacob. 1.1876
Needler, Martin C. 4.8333
Neel, Ann, 1927-. 5.30
Neely, Carol Thomas, 1939-. 2.6809
Neely, Mark E. 3.7280
Neely, Richard, 1941-. 4.9749
Neenan, William B., 1929-. 4.6348
Neergaard, Ejler B., joint author. 5.1986

Nef, John Ulric, 1899-. 3.12, 3.213, 3.216, 4.2206, 4.3071
Neff, Donald, 1930-. 3.5164
Neff, Emery Edward, 1892-. 2.2757, 2.7554, 2.12407, 3.401
Neff, Robert, 1930-. 1.4295
Neff, Thomas L. 4.3742
Neff, Walter Scott, 1910-. 5.408
Negandhi, Anant R. 4.2716, 4.2741
Nehemkis, Peter Raymond. joint author. 4.6760
Neher, Clark D. joint author. 3.4519
Nehls, Edward, ed. 2.8992
Nehru, Jawaharlal, 1889-1964. 3.4316-3.4319
Nei, Masatoshi. 5.3417
Neidhardt, Frederick C. 5.4455
Neidhardt, Hans Joachim. 1.6170
Neier, Aryeh, 1937-. 4.7697, 4.9709
Neĭgauz, Genrikh Gustavovich, 1888-1964. 1.4543
Neihardt, John Gneisenau, 1881-1973. 2.12242, 3.5789
Neill, Alexander Sutherland, 1883-1973. 4.11011-4.11012
Neill, Stephen, 1900-. 1.3022, 1.3024, 1.3099
Neilson, Katharine Bishop. 1.4660
Neilson, William A. W. 4.8291
Neiman, Fraser. 2.7349
Neisser, Ulric. 5.277-5.278
Neisworth, John T. 4.10930
Neitzke, Frederic William. 4.9547
Nekrasov, Nikolaĭ Alekseevich, 1821-1877. 2.1403
Nekrasov, Viktor, 1911-. 2.1588
Nekrich, A. M. (Aleksandr Moiseevich) 3.3207
Nelkin, Dorothy. 5.977, 5.988, 5.5518
Nelles, H. V. 4.2126
Nelli, Humbert S., 1930-. 3.8422
Nelsen, Olin Everett, 1898-. 5.4129
Nelson, Alan H. 2.5851
Nelson, Andrew Nathaniel. 2.1993
Nelson, Barbara J., 1949-. 4.6565, 5.8474
Nelson, Benjamin. 1.3288
Nelson, C. Michael (Charles Michael), 1941-. 4.10700
Nelson, Carl William, 1943-. 5.4572
Nelson, Daniel, 1941-. 4.3006
Nelson, Daniel N., 1948-. 3.3552
Nelson, E. Clifford, 1911-. 1.3359
Nelson, Gareth J. 5.3235
Nelson, George, 1908-. 1.5489
Nelson, George R., ed. 4.5382
Nelson, Hank. 3.5666
Nelson, Harold D. 3.3328, 3.5170, 3.5199, 3.5203-3.5204, 3.5209, 3.5239, 3.5255, 3.5268, 3.5305, 3.5311, 3.5350, 3.5380, 3.5388, 3.5390, 3.5396, 3.5411, 3.5445, 3.5491, 3.5509, 3.9077
Nelson, Harold L. ed. 4.9713
Nelson, Howard, 1947-. 2.12911
Nelson, Jack, 1944- joint author. 1.1198
Nelson, James Cecil, 1908-. 4.3983
Nelson, John Charles, joint ed. 2.3712
Nelson, Joseph S. 5.3902
Nelson, Keith L. 3.858
Nelson, Lowry, 1893-. 4.5261, 4.6365
Nelson, Paul David, 1941-. 3.6891
Nelson, Richard K. 3.5900
Nelson, Richard R. 4.1280
Nelson, Robert James, 1925-. 1.808, 2.4019
Nelson, Susan C. 4.10558
Nelson, Werner L. 5.5294
Nelson, William, 1908-. 2.6545
Nelson, William E., 1941-. 4.8855
Nelson, William Edward, 1940-. 4.7841, 4.9900
Němcová, Božena, 1820-1862. 2.1678
Nemerov, Howard. 2.2733, 2.12243-2.12246
Nemerov, Howard. ed. 2.10502
Nemerow, Nelson Leonard. 5.6029
Nemesius, Bp. of Emesa. 1.2210
Nemeyer, Carol A., 1929-. 5.7596
Nemhauser, George L. 5.1367
Nemo, John. 2.8927
Nemytskiĭ, Viktor Vladimirovich, 1900-. 5.1506
Nene, Vilas D. 5.6076
Nerbovig, Marcella Hannah, 1919-. 4.10445
Neri, Ferdinando, 1880-1954. ed. 2.4946
Nero, Anthony V. 5.6613
Neruda, Jan, 1834-1891. 2.1679

Neruda, Pablo, 1904-1973. 2.5410
Nerval, Gérard de, 1808-1855. 2.4221-2.4223
Nesbit, Robert Carrington, 1917-. 3.8443
Ness, Gayl D. 4.1702
Nessen, Ron, 1934-. 3.7927
Nest'ev, I. V. (Izrail' Vladimirovich), 1911-.
    1.3948
Nestor, annalist, d. 1115? 3.3080
Nestroy, Johann, 1801-1862. 2.9813
Netaji Research Bureau. 3.4284
Netboy, Anthony. 5.3911
Nethercot, Arthur Hobart, 1895-.
    2.6224-2.6225, 2.6956, 2.7590
Netschert, Bruce Carlton. 4.3720
Nettels, Curtis Putnam. 3.7032, 4.1874
Netter, Frank Henry, 1906-. 5.4737
Netting, Robert McC. 4.5485
Nettl, Bruno, 1930-. 1.4285, 1.4287, 1.4292,
    1.4364
Nettl, J. P. 4.7061
Nettleford, Rex M., 1933- ed. 3.9112
Nettleship, Anderson. 5.7154
Nettleship, Martin A., 1936-. 5.7154-5.7155
Nettleton, George Henry, 1874-1959. ed. 2.6228
Netton, Ian Richard. 1.367
Netzer, Dick, 1928-. 4.4708
Neu, Charles E. 3.6464
Neubauer, John, 1933-. 2.13596
Neuborne, Burt, 1941-. 4.9725, 4.9739
Neuenschwander, Ulrich. ed. 1.2819
Neuer Berliner Kunstverein. 1.4801
Neufeld, Edward Peter. 4.4452, 4.4539
Neufeld, Maurice F. joint ed. 4.3356
Neufeld, Maurice F. 4.3660
Neufeldt, Victor A. 2.7445
Neugarten, Bernice Levin, 1916- joint author.
    4.10769
Neugebauer, Friedrich. 1.6601
Neugebauer, O. (Otto), 1899-. 5.1079
Neugroschel, Joachim. 2.1829
Neuls-Bates, Carol. 1.3491, 1.3604
Neuman, Abraham A. (Abraham Aaron),
    1890-. 3.4004
Neuman, Daniel M., 1944-. 1.3736
Neumann, Bonnie Rayford. 2.8095
Neumann, Edward S. 5.5935
Neumann, Erich. 1.5697, 2.704
Neumann, Ernst-Georg, 1929- joint author.
    5.2229
Neumann, Franz. 3.6098
Neumann, Franz L. (Franz Leopold),
    1900-1954. 3.2421
Neumann, Sigmund, 1904-. 4.7602
Neumann, William Louis, 1915-. 3.6465
Neuner, Josef. 1.3124
Neurath, Hans, 1909- ed. 5.2794
Neurath, Otto, 1882-1945. 5.901
Neurosciences Research Program. 5.4321
Neusner, Jacob, 1932-. 1.1910-1.1911, 1.1913,
    1.1930, 3.3941
Neustadt, Richard E. 3.6447, 4.7928
Neutra, Richard Joseph, 1892-1970. 1.4598,
    1.5321, 1.5554
Nevakivi, Jukka. 3.3297
Nevill, Dorothy D. 5.230
Neville, Adam M. 5.5800
Neville, Richard F., 1931- joint author. 4.10633
Nevins, Allan. 2.3662, 3.402, 3.6220, 3.6318,
    3.6331, 3.7145-3.7146, 3.7169, 3.7345,
    3.7433, 3.7491-3.7492, 3.7589-3.7590, 4.1924
Nevins, Deborah, 1947-. 1.5544
Nevins, Francis M. 2.13088
Nevins, Francis M. comp. 2.10547
Nevitte, Neil. 4.8275
Nevius, Blake. 2.8535, 5.7813
New American Foundation. 5.8355
New Directions in the Study of Alcohol Group
    (Great Britain) 5.4961
New Family and New Woman Research
    Planning Group. 4.5951
New Hampshire Bicentennial Conference on the
    History of Geology, University of New
    Hampshire, 1976. 5.2956
New, Joan. 2.7275
New, Melvyn. 2.7275
New Mexico. Writers' Program. 3.8566
New Music Society of California. 1.3695
New, William H. comp. 2.9893

New York Botanical Garden. 5.3671, 5.3673,
    5.5334, 5.5366
New York City Ballet. 1.4009
New York (City). French Institute in the
    United States. 5.8002
New York (City). Knapp Commission. 4.6835
New York (City). Metropotitan Museum of
    Art. 5.6957
New York (City). Public Library. Slavonic
    Division. 5.8336
New York (City). Public School 61. 2.10673
New York (Colony). Supreme Court of
    Judicature. 4.9456
New York Drama Critics' Circle. 2.10798
New York Graphic Society. 1.6310, 1.6336
New York. Metropolitan Museum of Art.
    1.5296, 1.5625, 1.5903, 1.6633
New York. Museum of Modern Art. 1.4841,
    1.5452, 1.5703, 3.9158
New York. Museum of Modern Art. 1.4831
New York. Museum of Modern Art. 1.5279,
    1.6066, 1.6141, 1.6150
New York Public Library. 4.1096, 5.7664
New York (State). Laws, statutes, etc. 4.6867
New York State School of Industrial and Labor
    Relations. 4.9554
New York (State). Special Commission on
    Attica. 4.6916
New York. State University, Albany. Center for
    Inter-American Studies. 2.5391
New York Times. 5.7142
New York University. 3.487
New York University. Burma Research Project.
    5.8057
New York University. Graduate Program of
    Studies in United Nations and World Affairs.
    4.9198
New York University Institute of Philosophy.
    2d, 1958. 5.178
New York University Institute of Philosophy.
    5th, 1962. 3.487
New York University. Institute of Retail
    Management. 4.4328
New York University. Language and Reading
    Commission. 4.10854
New Zealand. Census and Statistics Dept.
    3.5588
New Zealand. Census and Statistics Office.
    3.5588
New Zealand. Dept. of Lands and Survey.
    4.195
New Zealand. Dept. of Statistics. 3.5588
New Zealand. Registrar-General's Office. 3.5588
Newald, Richard, 1894-1954. 2.13453
Newark Museum. 2.2932
Newberger, Eli H. 4.5781
Newberry Library. Center for the History of
    the American Indian. 3.5704
Newbery, David M. G. 4.4168
Newbold, George, joint author. 5.4899
Newbrun, Ernest. 5.5127
Newbury, C. W. (Colin Walter), 1929-. 3.5318,
    3.5678
Newby, Eric. 4.49
Newby, Hayes A. 5.5040
Newby, Howard. joint author. 4.6180
Newby, Howard. 4.2925, 4.2973, 4.6369
Newby, Idus A. 3.6684-3.6685
Newby, P. H. (Percy Howard), 1918-. 2.7688,
    2.9138-2.9139
Newcomb, Franc Johnson. 3.5924
Newcomb, Lawrence. 3.5675
Newcomb, Richard T. 4.3722
Newcomb, Theodore Mead, 1903- joint author.
    4.10060
Newcombe, Hanna, 1922-. 4.9247
Newcomer, James. 3.2981
Newell, Allen. 5.1228
Newell, Leonard E. 2.152
Newell, R. C. (Richard Charles) 5.3819
Newell, Richard S., 1933-. 3.4118
Newell, Virginia K. 5.1087
Newell, William Hare. 3.4536
Newey, Vincent. 2.6919, 2.6963
Newey, Walter W. 5.3239
Newfarmer, Richard S. 4.3060
Newhall, Beaumont, 1908-. 5.6919, 5.6932,
    5.6943, 5.6949

Newhaus, Richard John. 1.2816
Newitt, M. D. D. 3.5126, 3.5308
Newman, Alick. 4.189
Newman, Arnold, 1918-. 5.6987
Newman, Barnett, 1905-1970. 1.4901
Newman, Charles Hamilton, 1938-. 2.10639
Newman, Donald J. 4.6777, 4.9891
Newman, Ernest, 1868-1959. 1.3877,
    1.4040-1.4041, 1.4064, 1.4517
Newman, Evelyn S. 4.6777
Newman, Frank, 1927-. 4.9932, 4.10084
Newman, James L. 3.5225
Newman, James Roy, 1907-1966. 5.745, 5.1024,
    5.1047
Newman, John Henry, 1801-1890. 1.2231,
    1.3137, 1.3204, 1.3273, 2.7974, 4.10545
Newman, Katherine. 4.9356
Newman, Lindsay Mary. comp. 5.8013
Newman, Louis Israel, 1893-. 1.1924
Newman, Louise Michele. 4.6062
Newman, Melvin Spencer. 5.2729
Newman, Michael, 1939-. 4.10985
Newman, Oscar. 4.6698
Newman, Peter Charles. 3.8766
Newman, Richard. 5.7875
Newman, Robert B., joint author. 1.5547
Newman, Ruth G. 4.10948
Newman, Stephen L. 4.7643
Newman, Thelma R. 1.5785
Newman, William M., 1939-. 5.5651
Newman, William S. 1.3785, 1.4188-1.4190,
    1.4537
Newmark, Eileen. 4.5006
Newmark, N. M. (Nathan Mortimore),
    1910-1981. 5.5859
Newmeyer, Frederick J. 2.163
Newmyer, R. Kent. 4.9829
Newsholme, E. A. 5.5027
Newsom, Robert, 1944-. 2.7629
Newsome, Albert Ray, 1894-1951. joint author.
    3.8226
Newton, Arthur Percival, 1873-1942. 3.9087,
    4.62
Newton, Douglas. 1.5092, 1.5095
Newton, Gerald. 3.2985
Newton, Huey P. 3.6699, 3.6713
Newton, Isaac, Sir, 1642-1727. 5.1103, 5.1640,
    5.2273-5.2274
Newton, Judith Lowder. 2.5988, 2.10292
Newton, Norman T., 1898-. 5.5380
Newton, Robert R. 5.1694, 5.1796, 5.1798
Newton, Roger G. 5.2400
Newton, Walter Hughes, 1880-1941, joint
    author. 3.7741
Ng, Larry K. Y., ed. 4.1635
Ngô Vĩnh Long. 4.5438
Ngoc Huu. 2.2261
Ngũgĩ wa Thiong'o, 1938-. 2.10035
Nguyễn, Khac Viên. 2.2261, 3.4516
Nguyễn, Ngoc Bích. comp. 2.2263
Nguyễn, Ngoc Ngan. 3.4515
Nguyễn, Tràn Huân. 2.2260
Nhât Hanh, Thích. 3.4481
Nias, D. K. B. joint author. 4.5338
Niatum, Duane, 1938- comp. 2.10743
Niccols, Richard, 1584-1616. 2.6499
Nice, David C., 1952-. 4.7876
Nichiren, 1222-1282. 1.2120
Nichol, John Thomas. 3.3387
Nicholas, H. G. (Herbert George), 1911-.
    3.6448, 4.8488, 4.9223
Nicholas, James. 2.846
Nicholas, Marta R. 3.4142
Nicholas, of Cusa, Cardinal, 1401-1464. 1.388
Nicholas of Dunstable. 1.3267
Nicholas, Ralph W., joint author. 4.631
Nicholas, Warwick L. 5.3842
Nicholi, Armand M., 1928-. 5.4823
Nicholl, Charles. 2.6498
Nicholls, Anthony James, 1934- joint author.
    3.922
Nicholls, C. S. (Christine Stephanie) 3.5262
Nicholls, David. 3.9118
Nicholls, K. W. (Kenneth W.) 3.1824
Nicholls, Peter, 1939-. 2.3494
Nichols, Albert L. 4.1848
Nichols, Bill. 2.2943
Nichols, Charles Harold. 2.11395

Nichols, David, 1940-. 4.8131
Nichols, Fred J., 1939-. 2.816
Nichols, Geraldine Cleary. 2.5267
Nichols, J. Alden, 1919-. 3.2329
Nichols, J. G. (John Gordon), 1930-. 2.6514
Nichols, John Alden, 1919-. 3.2335
Nichols, John Gough, 1806-1873. 3.1499
Nichols, John Treadwell, 1940-. 2.13191
Nichols, Lee. 2.10042
Nichols, Mary Pickering. 1.4417
Nichols, Michael P. 5.4884
Nichols, Peter, 1927-. 2.9780-2.9783
Nichols, Roy F. (Roy Franklin), 1896-1973.
    3.7176, 4.8149
Nicholson, Barbara. 5.3658
Nicholson, Daniel Howard. 2.6117
Nicholson, Dwight R. (Dwight Roy) 5.2386
Nicholson, Lynda, tr. 1.3260
Nicholson, Margaret. 2.1139
Nicholson, Michael (Michael A.) 2.1641
Nicholson, N. L. (Norman Leon) 4.236
Nicholson, Norman, 1914-. 2.6961
Nicholson, Norman L. 3.8694
Nicholson, Ranald. 3.1778
Nicholson, Reynold Alleyne, 1868-1945. 1.2084,
    2.1836, 2.1969-2.1970
Nicholson, T. A. J. 5.5583
Nickell, Louis G., 1921-. 5.5322
Nickerson, H. K. (Helen Kelsall), 1918-. 5.1455
Nicklaus, Jack. 4.1034
Nicks, Oran W. 5.1814
Nicol, Donald MacGillivray. 3.2660,
    3.2675-3.2676
Nicolaevsky, Boris I., 1887-1966. 3.3137, 4.8660
Nicoll, Allardyce, 1894-. 2.2803, 2.3165-2.3166,
    2.3281, 2.3307, 2.4886, 2.5841-2.5842, 2.5880,
    2.5918, 2.6681, 2.6714, 2.6876
Nicollian, E. H. 5.6507
Nicoloff, Assen. 4.802
Nicolson, Benedict. 1.6044
Nicolson, Harold George, Hon., 1886-. 3.852,
    3.1684, 3.2139, 4.9083, 4.9088
Nicolson, Iain. 5.1793, 5.1844, 5.2216
Nicolson, Marjorie Hope, 1894-. 2.5546, 2.5779,
    2.5804, 2.5810, 2.7239
Nicolson, Nigel. 2.9298, 2.9586
Nida, Eugene Albert, 1914-. 2.8, 2.189
Nidditch, P. H. 1.674, 1.697, 1.700
Nie, Norman H. joint author. 4.8179
Niebel, Benjamin W. 5.5621, 5.7039
Niebuhr, H. Richard (Helmut Richard),
    1894-1962. 1.1476, 1.2242, 1.2255, 1.2815,
    1.2840, 1.3003
Niebuhr, Reinhold, 1892-1971. 1.1475, 1.2232,
    1.2253, 1.2907-1.2908, 1.3292, 3.515, 3.6149,
    3.6278, 3.7591-3.7592, 4.4974, 4.7211, 4.7506,
    4.7580
Niebuhr, Richard R. 1.2179, 1.3295
Nieh, Hua-ling, 1926-. 2.2162, 2.2247
Niehans, Jürg. 4.4477, 4.4553
Nielsen, George R. 3.6591
Nielsen, Kai. 1.1459, 4.7652
Nielsen, Larry A. 5.5477
Nieman, Donald G. 4.9690
Niemeyer, E. Victor (Eberhardt Victor), 1919-.
    4.8331
Niemi, Beth T., 1942- joint author. 4.3284
Nienhauser, William H. 5.8044
Niepoth, E. William, 1928-. 4.887
Niesel, Wilhelm. 1.3401
Niethammer, Carolyn J. 3.5834
Nietz, John Alfred, 1888-. 4.11016
Nietzsche, Friedrich Wilhelm, 1844-1900.
    1.1044-1.1051
Nieuwenhuys, R., 1927-. 5.4152
Nieuwenhuys, Robert, 1908-. 2.13955-2.13956
Nievergelt, Jurg. joint author. 5.1277
Nievo, Ippolito, 1831-1861. 2.5007-2.5008
Nightingale, Benedict, 1939-. 2.5923
Nightingale, C. joint author. 5.6460
Nightingale, Florence, 1820-1910. 5.5165,
    5.5180
Nightingale, J. D. 5.2100
Nigro, August J., 1934-. 2.10349
Nihon Bōeki Shinkōkai. 4.4242
Nihon Ginkō. Tōkeikyoku. 4.1258
Nihon Kokusai Seiji Gakkai. Taiheiyō Sensō
    Gen'in Kenkyūbu. 3.4917, 3.4922

Nihon Seisansei Honbu. 4.2088
Nihon Sūgakkai. 5.1026
Nijenhuis, Albert. 5.1276
Nijenhuis, Emmie te. 1.3737
Nijinska, Bronislava, 1891-1972. 4.1153
Nijinska, Irina. 4.1153
Nijinsky, Romola de Pulszky. ed. 4.1151
Nijinsky, Waslaw, 1890-1950. 4.1151
Nijmegen, Netherlands. Hoger Katechetisch
    Instituut. 1.3214
Nilakanta Sastri, K. A. (Kallidaikurichi Aiyah),
    1892-1975. 3.4219
Niles, John D. 2.5590, 2.6299
Nilon, Charles H. 5.7786
Nilson, Arthur H. 5.5880, 5.5883
Nilsson, Martin Persson, 1874-1967.
    1.1646-1.1647, 1.1657, 2.500
Nilsson, Nils J., 1933-. 5.1014
Nimer, Benjamin. 3.5383
Nimkoff, Meyer Francis, 1904- joint author.
    4.5580
Nimmo, Dan D. 4.7238
Nimmo, Harry. 3.4595
Nims, John Frederick, 1913-. 2.6098, 2.12247
Nin, Anaïs, 1903-1977. 2.12248-2.12254
Ninkovich, Frank A., 1944-. 3.7766
Nipperdey, Thomas. 3.2288
Nippon Gakujustu Shink1-okai. Dai 17 Sh1-o
    (Nihon Koten Hon'yaku) Iinkai. 2.2024
Nippon Gakujutsu Shinkōkai. Dai 17 Shō
    (Nihon Koten Hon'yaku) Iinkai. 2.2021
Nirenberg, Ted D., 1952-. 4.6634
Nisa. 3.5486
Nisbet, Ada. 2.7643
Nisbet, R. G. M. (Robin George Murdoch)
    2.725-2.726
Nisbet, Robert A. joint ed. 4.5111
Nisbet, Robert A., 4.4743, 4.4745-4.4746,
    4.4755, 4.4883, 4.7261, 4.10065
Nisbett, Alec. 5.6559
Nisetich, Frank J. 2.527
Nish, Ian Hill. 4.4958
Nishida, Kitarō, 1870-1945. 1.1144, 1.4627
Nishijima, K. (Kazuhiko), 1926-. 5.2157
Nishikawa, Kyōtarō. 1.5760
Nissen, Henrik S. 3.948
Nissen, Ursula. joint author. 5.8158
Nist, John A. 2.970, 2.5465
Nitchie, George Wilson, 1921-. 2.12203
Nite, Gladys, joint author. 5.5167
Nite, Norm N. 1.3536
Nitschke, August, 1926-. 3.522
Nivedita, Sister, 1867-1911. 1.1813
Niven, John. 3.7130, 3.7335
Niven, Larry. 2.13192-2.13193
Nixon, Edgar Burkhardt, 1902- ed. 3.7518,
    5.5301
Nixon, Paul, 1882- tr. 2.684
Nixon, Raymond Blalock, 1903-. 3.7434
Nixon, Richard M. (Richard Milhous), 1913-.
    3.7674, 3.7911, 3.7917
Nixon, W. C. 5.6537
Nixson, F. I. joint author. 4.1800
Nixson, F. I. 4.3069
Nizām al-Mulk, 1018-1092. 4.7324
Nketia, J. H. Kwabena. 1.3748
Nkosi, Lewis. 2.2304
Nkrumah, Kwame, 1909-1972. 3.5093, 3.5338,
    3.5341-3.5342, 4.2579, 4.7128
Noah, Harold J. 4.9967
Noakes, Jeremy. 3.2445
Noakes, Vivien, 1937-. 1.6036
Nobbs, Percy E. (Percy Erskine), 1875-1966.
    1.5349
Nobel Conference. 12th, Gustavus Adolphus
    College, 1976. 5.2455
Nobel Conference. 13th, Gustavus Adolphus
    College, 1977. 5.3491
Nobelstiftelsen. 1.62
Noble, Allen George, 1930-. 1.5280
Noble, Ben. 5.5710
Noble, C. A. (Charles Albert), b. 1867. joint tr.
    5.1111
Noble, David F. 5.5522
Noble, David W. 3.6150, 3.6279
Noble, Elmer Ray, 1909-. 5.4081
Noble, Gladwyn Kingsley, 1894-1940. 5.3933
Noble, Glenn Arthur, 1909-. 5.4081

Noble, Harold Joyce, 1903-1953. 3.5029
Noble, Joseph Veach, 1920-. 1.6633
Nochlin, Linda, ed. 1.6350
Nochlin, Linda. 1.4757, 1.4790, 1.4797
Noda, Yoshiyuki, 1912-. 4.9924
Noddings, Nel. 1.1502, 5.279
Noden, Alexandra B. 4.3509
Nodier, Charles, 1780-1844. 2.4275
Noe, Lee. ed. 1.61
Noel-Baker, Philip John, Baron, 1889-. 4.9155
Noël, Bernard, 1930-. 1.6267
Noël Hume, Ivor. 3.225
Noel, John Vavasour, 1912-. 5.7417, 5.7490
Noer, Deliar. 1.2005
Noer, Richard J., 1937- joint author. 5.2029
Noether, Emiliana Pasca, joint author. 3.2858
Noether, Emiliana Pasca. 3.2855
Noether, Emmy, 1882-1935. 5.1097, 5.1271
Nof, Shimon Y., 1946-. 5.7049
Nogee, Joseph L. joint author. 4.9162
Noggle, Burl. 3.7718
Noggle, Glen Ray, 1914-. 5.3742
Noirot, Ch. 5.3878
Nolan, David. 2.4929
Nolan, Joseph R. 4.9443
Noland, Aaron. 4.8596
Noll, Mark A., 1946-. 3.6912
Noll, Peter, 1936-. 5.6374
Noll, Roger G. ed. 4.934
Nolle, H. 5.5699
Nolot, Pierre. 1.6596
Nolte, Ernst, 1923-. 3.869
Nolte, William Henry, 1928-. 2.12124, 2.12136
Nolting, Orin Frederyc, 1903- ed. 4.8850
Noma, Hiroshi, 1915-. 2.2115
Noma, Seiroku. 1.5074, 1.6678
Nomizu, Katsumi, 1924-. 5.1312, 5.1628
Nonesuch Press. 2.7962
Noonan, Barry Christopher. 5.8478
Noonan, John Thomas, 1926-. 3.7224, 4.5684
Noor, Ahmed Khairy, 1938-. 5.5730
Nooteboom, Cees, 1933-. 2.13954
Norberg-Schulz, Christian. 1.5214,
    1.5247-1.5248
Norbye, Jan P. 5.6631
Nord, Friedrich Franz, 1889-. 5.4408
Nordby, Vernon J. 5.92
Nordenfalk, Carl Adam Johan, 1907-. 1.6403
Nordenskiöld, A. E. (Adolf Erik), 1832-1901.
    4.118
Nordhaus, William D. 4.1458, 4.9522
Nordhoff, Charles, 1887-1947. 2.12256
Nordlinger, Eric A. 4.7772, 4.8489
Nordyke, Eleanor C. 4.1681
Nore, Ellen, 1942-. 3.6252
Noreña, Carlos G. 1.404
Norgard, Katherine Eastlack, 1941-. 4.6563
Norlin, George, 1871-1942. 2.375
Norman, Aaron. 3.821
Norman, Adrian R. D. 4.4348
Norman, Arthur Geoffrey, 1905-. 5.5329
Norman, Charles, 1904-. 2.11544, 2.12348
Norman, Donald A. 5.333, 5.387
Norman, Dorothy, 1905-. 1.5953, 3.4319
Norman, E. Herbert, 1909-1957. 3.4942, 3.4949
Norman, Edward R. 1.2430, 3.1853
Norman, Geraldine. 1.5866
Norman, J. R. (John Roxborough), 1898-1944.
    5.3900
Norman, R. O. C. (Richard Oswald Chandler)
    5.2737
Normand, Charles Pierre Joseph, 1765-1840.
    1.5498
Norris, Bryan. 5.6526
Norris, Charles Head, 1910-. 5.5841
Norris, Christopher. 2.2483
Norris, Frank, 1870-1902. 2.2510, 2.3410,
    2.11184
Norris, George W. (George William),
    1861-1944. 3.7675
Norris, Kenneth S. (Kenneth Stafford) ed.
    5.4006
Norström, Göran. 4.3954
North American Commission on Stratigraphic
    Nomenclature. 5.2946
North Atlantic Treaty Organization. 5.4103
North Atlantic Treaty Organization. Scientific
    Affairs Division. 5.2449, 5.4385, 5.6768

North Carolina. America's Four Hundredth
  Anniversary Committee. 3.8198, 3.8232
North Carolina Botanical Garden. 5.5364
North Carolina. University. Dept. of English.
  2.10460
North Central Land Economics Research
  Committee. International Rural Institutions
  Subcommittee. 4.2897
North, Douglass Cecil. 4.1895, 4.1913, 4.2207
North, Douglass Cecil. joint author. 4.1871
North, James. 3.5455
North, Robert Carver. 3.3071, 3.4683
Northam, John, 1922-. 2.14041
Northeast-Midwest Institute (U.S.) 4.4680
Northedge, F. S. 3.1690, 4.9015, 4.9067
Northen, Helen. 4.6471, 4.6505
Northern, Jerry L. 5.5041
Northrop, F. S. C. (Filmer Stuart Cuckow),
  1893-. 1.774, 3.13-3.14
Northrup, Herbert Roof, 1918-. 3.6739, 4.3152
Northup, George Tyler, 1874-. 2.5091
Northup, Solomon, b. 1808. 3.7212
Northwestern University (Evanston, Ill.) 3.2323,
  3.5055
Northwestern University (Evanston, Ill.).
  Transportation Center. 4.3972
Northwood, Thomas D. 1.5493
Norton, Arthur P. (Arthur Philip) 5.1740
Norton, Charles A. 2.10945
Norton, Daniel Silas, 1908-1951. 1.1642
Norton, David L. 1.1499
Norton, Donna E. 5.7720
Norton, F. J. 4.788
Norton-Griffiths, M. 5.3828
Norton, Harry N. 5.5684
Norton, Hugh Stanton, 1921-. 4.1968, 4.3883
Norton, Lucy. ed. 3.2040
Norton, Mary Beth. 4.5992, 4.6011
Norton, Philip. 4.8415, 4.8476-4.8478
Norton-Taylor, Duncan. 5.7586
Norton, Thomas W. 5.6229
Norvell, George Whitefield, 1885-1970. 5.7689
Norwegian Archaeological Expedition to Easter
  Island and the East Pacific. 3.9270
Norwood, Frederick Abbott. 1.3370
Norwood, Gilbert, 1880-. 2.531, 2.761
Noshpitz, Joseph D. 5.5096
Nossal, Kim Richard. 4.9097
Nossiter, Bernard D. 4.2292
Nossiter, T. J. (Thomas Johnson) 4.7118
Notehelfer, F. G. 3.4961
Notes (Music Library Association) 1.3629
Notestein, Wallace, 1878-1969. 3.1454, 4.8474
Noth, Martin, 1902-1968. 1.2589,
  1.2594-1.2595, 3.3853
Notman, Malkah T. 5.5045
Notman, William. 3.8660
Nottingham, John Cato, 1928- joint author.
  3.5283
Nousiainen, Jaakko. 4.8666
Novák, Arne, 1880-1939. 2.1653
Novak, Barbara. 1.5896, 1.6358
Novak, Joseph Donald. 4.10358
Novak, Maximillian E. 2.5659, 2.6981, 2.7268
Novak, Maximillian E. joint author. 2.2416
Novak, Michael. 4.937
Novak, Robert D. joint author. 3.7888, 3.7899
Novak, Steven J., 1947-. 4.10094
Novalis, 1772-1801. 2.13593-2.13595
Novarr, David. 3.314
Nove, Alec. comp. 4.2235
Nove, Alec. 4.2375, 4.2385, 4.2386, 4.2395,
  4.6985
Noverre, Jean Georges, 1727-1810. 4.1101
Novick, David. 4.1771, 4.4677
Novick, Julius, 1939-. 2.3211
Novick, Melvin R., joint author. 5.359
Novikoff, Alex Benjamin, 1913-1987. 5.3600
Novitski, Edward. 5.3479
Novotny, Eva. 5.1838
Novotny, Fritz, 1902-. 1.4926, 1.6152
Novotny, Vladimir, 1938- joint author. 5.6016
Nowak, Marion, 1948- joint author. 3.6066
Nowak, Ronald M. 5.3976
Nowakowski, Marek. 2.1742
Nowell, Charles E. 3.3498-3.3499
Nowell, Elizabeth. 2.12783, 2.12793
Nowell-Smith, Geoffrey. 2.3071

Nowell-Smith, Geoffrey. ed. 4.7076
Nowell-Smith, Patrick Horace, 1914-. 1.1438
Noxon, James H. 1.705
Noyes, Alfred, 1880-1958. 2.9142
Noyes, Charles Reinold, 1884-. 4.1482
Noyes, George Rapall, 1873-1952. 2.1405,
  2.1706
Noyes, Gertrude Elizabeth, 1905- joint author.
  2.1077
Nozick, Martin. 1.2261, 2.5286
Nozick, Robert. 1.110, 4.7644-4.7645
Ntshona, Winston, joint author. 2.10068
Ntshona, Winston. 2.10069
Nuclear Control Institute (Washington, D.C.)
  5.6620
Nugent, Jeffrey B. 4.2450
Nugent, Robert. 2.4010, 2.4526
Nugent, Walter T. K. 4.8232
Núñez, Benjamín, 1912-. 3.8970
Núñez Cabeza de Vaca, Alvar, 16th cent.
  3.5981, 3.5983
Nunn, Frederick M., 1937-. 5.7292
Nunn, Godfrey Raymond, 1918-. 5.8034, 5.8328
Nunney, Malcolm James. 5.6628
Nurmi, Martin K. 2.7415
Nurmi, Ruth. 1.4544
Nürnberger, Helmuth. 2.13563
Nurse, Peter H. 2.3848
Nursing Theories Conference Group. 5.5192
Nussbaum, Allen. 5.2284
Nussbaum, Felicity. 2.5695
Nussbaum, Frederick Louis, 1885-. 3.642
Nussbaum, Martha Craven, 1947-. 5.3797
Nussbaumer, Henri J., 1931-. 5.1554
Nuti, D. M., joint comp. 4.2235
Nutt, Merle Caro. 5.6762
Nuttall, Zelia, 1858-1933. 3.8882
Nutter, G. Warren. 4.2387
Nutting, M. Adelaide (Mary Adelaide),
  1858-1948. 5.5161
Nutting, Wallace, 1861-1941. 1.6565
Nwabueze, B. O. (Benjamin Obi) 4.9928
Nwulia, Moses D. E., 1932-. 4.6445
Nybakken, James Willard. 5.3249
Nybakken, Oscar Edward, 1904-. 5.970
Nyberg, David, 1943-. 4.10308
Nyberg, Peter. 4.4512
Nye, Bill, 1850-1896. 2.3794
Nye, Joseph S. 4.9058, 4.9063, 5.7236
Nye, Joseph S. comp. 4.9249
Nye, Joseph S. joint author. 4.9032
Nye, Mary Jo. 5.1961
Nye, Peter Hague. 5.5279
Nye, Robert. 1.3308
Nye, Robert A. 4.5359
Nye, Russel Blaine, 1913-. 2.10271, 3.6046,
  3.6151, 3.6247, 3.6298
Nyer, Evan K. 5.6025
Nyerere, Julius K. (Julius Kambarage), 1922-.
  3.5298, 4.7133
Nygren, Anders, 1890-. 1.3064
Nyman, Heikki. 1.1068
Nyrop, Richard F. 3.1905, 3.2464, 3.3569,
  3.3604, 3.3769, 3.3792, 3.3924, 3.4029,
  3.4046, 3.4057, 3.4061, 3.4066, 3.4108,
  3.4121, 3.4143, 3.4157, 3.4362, 3.5131,
  3.5199, 3.5304, 3.9059, 3.9080, 3.9187, 3.9281
Nystrand, Raphael O. 4.10634
Nystrom, Paul C. 4.2633
Nyvall, Robert F. 5.5398

Ó Corráin, Donnchadh. 3.1819, 4.6113
Ó Tuathaigh, Gearóid. 3.1847
Ōae, Shigeru. 5.2788
Oak, Henry Lebbeus, 1844-1905. 3.8567
Oakes, Jeannie. 4.10717
Oakeshott, Michael Joseph, 1901-. 1.1511,
  4.7229, 4.7405, 4.7407
Oakeshott, R. Ewart. 5.7244
Oakeshott, Walter Fraser, 1903-. 1.5509, 1.6011
Oakley, Ann. 4.5888, 4.5899, 4.6103, 5.5059,
  5.5068
Oakley, Francis. 1.2308
Oakley, Helen McKelvey. 2.12209
Oakley, Kenneth Page, 1911-. 4.448
Oakley, Stewart. 3.3369
Oakman, Robert L., 1941-. 2.2423

Oates, Joyce Carol, 1938-. 2.10279,
  2.13194-2.13203, 4.1057
Oates, Stephen B. 3.6841, 3.7273, 3.7281-3.7282
Oates, Wallace E. joint author. 4.1837
Oates, Wallace E. 4.4649
Oates, Whitney Jennings, 1904- ed. 1.319
Oathout, John D. 4.9548
Obaldia, René de. 2.4641
O'Ballance, Edgar. 3.3936
O'Bannon, Loran S., 1910-. 5.6898
O'Barr, Jean F. 4.6157
O'Barr, Jean Fox, 1942-. 4.5889
Obbo, Christine. 4.6156
Ober, Kenneth H. 2.14005
Oberg, Antoinette A. 5.7722
Oberg, James E., 1944-. 5.6701, 5.6703, 5.6715
Oberg, Kalervo, 1901-1973. 3.5958
Oberholzer, Emil, 1883-. 5.187
Oberhuber, Konrad. 1.5811
Oberman, Heiko Augustinus. 1.1958, 1.2739,
  1.2752
Obeyesekere, Gananath. 1.2108
Obiechina, Emmanuel N., 1933-. 2.10100
Obler, Loraine K. joint author. 5.4795
Obler, Loraine K. 2.149
Obolensky, Dimitri, 1918-. 1.2307, 1.5030,
  2.1222, 2.1313, 2.2664, 3.3040
Oboler, Eli M. 4.9704
Oboler, Regina Smith, 1947-. 3.5275
Oborne, David J. 5.1250, 5.5618
Obregón, Mauricio. 3.5975
O'Brian, Patrick. 1.6131
O'Brien, Conor Cruise, 1917-. 3.1856, 3.1859,
  3.5431
O'Brien, D. P. (Denis Patrick), 1939-. 4.1317,
  4.1347
O'Brien, David M. 4.9518, 4.9764
O'Brien, Edna. 2.9784-2.9786
O'Brien, Edward Joseph Harrington, 1890-1941.
  2.10809
O'Brien, Flann, 1911-1966. 2.9169-2.9171
O'Brien, Grace, joint tr. 1.3849
O'Brien, Jacqueline Wasserman. 2.3265
O'Brien, John. 2.10327
O'Brien, Justin, 1906-1968. 2.4444, 2.4547,
  2.4558-2.4559
O'Brien, Kate, 1897-1974. 2.9143
O'Brien, Marie, tr. 1.3849
O'Brien, Mary. 4.5935
O'Brien, Mary-Win, joint author. 5.5021
O'Brien, Patricia H. (Patricia Helen), 1949-.
  4.6736
O'Brien, Patrick Karl. 4.2279
O'Brien, Philip J. joint author. 3.9268
O'Brien, Robert, 1932-. 4.6659
O'Brien, Tim. 2.13204
Obudho, Constance E. 3.6751, 5.7876
Obudho, Robert A. joint comp. 4.6278
O'Callaghan, Joseph F. 3.3418
O'Casey, Sean, 1880-1964. 2.9144-2.9151
Ochs, Carol. 1.3059
Ochs, Michael, 1943-. 1.4280
Ochse, Orpha Caroline, 1925-. 1.4144
Ochshorn, Judith, 1928-. 1.1612
Ochsner, Jeffrey Karl. 1.5323
O'Clair, Robert, joint comp. 2.10766
O'Connell, Agnes N. 5.91
O'Connell, David. 2.4513
O'Connell, James F. 4.750
O'Connell, Marvin Richard. 3.630
O'Connell, Richard L., tr. 2.5251
O'Connor, Anthony M. (Anthony Michael)
  4.2584, 4.6280
O'Connor, Edwin. 2.13205-2.13206
O'Connor, Flannery. 2.13208-2.13211
O'Connor, Francis V. comp. 1.5203
O'Connor, Francis V. 1.4902
O'Connor, Frank, 1903-1966. 2.3436, 2.3512,
  2.9156-2.9158
O'Connor, George A., 1944-. 5.5275
O'Connor, J. D. (Joseph Desmond) 2.183
O'Connor, James (James R.) 4.4657
O'Connor, John, 1870- tr. 2.4473
O'Connor, John E. 3.7007
O'Connor, Patrick J. (Patrick Joseph), 1947-.
  5.6586

O'Connor, Philip F. 2.13225
O'Connor, Raymond Gish. 3.1144
O'Connor, Richard, 1915-1975. 2.11423,
   2.12034
O'Connor, Rod, 1934- joint author. 5.2673
O'Connor, Ulick. 2.8692
O'Connor, William Van, 1915-1966. 2.2516,
   2.3430, 2.10482, 2.10503
Ocran, Emanuel Benjamin. 5.6642
O'Curry, Eugene, 1796-1862. 3.1820
Odagiri, Hiroko. 2.1998
Odden, Allan. 4.10656
Oddo, Sandra. 5.6232
O'Dea, Thomas F. 1.1577
Odelberg, Wilhelm. ed. 1.62
Odell, Alfred Taylor. 2.11224
Odell, George Clinton Densmore, 1866-1949.
   2.3230, 2.6858
Odell, John S., 1945-. 4.4574
Odell, Peter R. 4.2144, 4.3761-4.3762
Odell, Rice. 5.3224
Odell, S. Jack, 1933-. 1.106, 2.3543
O'Dell, Sterg. 5.7969
O'Dell, T. H. (Thomas Henry). 5.2405
Oden, J. Tinsley (John Tinsley), 1936-. 5.1533,
   5.5842
Odets, Clifford, 1906-1963. 2.12257-2.12259
Odishaw, Hugh. joint author. 5.1977
Odling-Smee, J. C. (John C.) 4.2282
Odložilík, Otakar, 1899-. 3.1914
Odo de Deuil, Abbot of Saint Denis, d.ca.1162.
   3.593
O'Doherty, Brian. ed. 1.4657
Odom, Keith C. 2.8735
O'Donnell, Charles Peter, 1904-. 3.4146
O'Donnell, James Joseph, 1950-. 1.2486
O'Donnell, Patrick, 1948-. 2.13075
O'Donnell, Thomas J., 1938-. 2.9003
O'Donoghue, Bernard. 2.2623
O'Donovan, Leo J. 1.3279
O'Donovan, Oliver. 5.5048
O'Driscoll, Robert. 2.8366, 3.85
Odum, Eugene Pleasants, 1913-. 5.3522
Odum, Howard Washington, 1884-1954. 3.6354,
   3.8162
Ōe, Kenzaburō, 1935-. 2.2133-2.2134
Oehser, Paul Henry, 1904-. 5.692
Oenslager, Donald, 1902-1975. 2.3160
Oesterley, W. O. E. (William Oscar Emil),
   1866-1950. 1.1624
O'Fahey, R. S. (Rex S.) 3.5168
O'Faolain, Julia. 2.9788
O'Faoláin, Seán, 1900-. 2.3437, 2.9160-2.9165
O'Farrell, Patrick James. 3.1832, 3.1846
Offen, Karen M. 4.6091
Offenbach, Jacques, 1819-1880. 3.6051
Offler, H. S. 3.3510
Offner, Arnold A. 3.7593
O'Flaherty, Liam, 1896-. 2.9166
O'Flaherty, Wendy Doniger. 1.1489, 1.1709,
   5.655
O'Gara, Gordon Carpenter, 1920-. 3.6380
Ogata, Sadako N. 3.4847
Ogburn, William Fielding, 1886-1959. 4.4884,
   4.5580
Ogden, August Raymond. 3.7552
Ogden, Charles Kay, 1880-. 1.723
Ogden, Dunbar H. 2.3152
Ogden, Jack. 1.6663
Ogden, Schubert Miles, 1928-. 1.2651, 1.2790,
   1.2866
Ogg, David, 1887-1965. 3.1498
Ogg, Frederic Austin, 1878-1951. 3.8369
Ogilvie, Marilyn Bailey. 5.812
Ogilvie, R. M. (Robert Maxwell), 1932-. 2.734,
   2.775, 2.2765
Ogilvy, Charles Stanley, 1913-. 5.1259
Ogilvy, David, 1911-. 4.4419, 4.4434
Ogilvy, J. D. A. (Jack David Angus), 1903-.
   2.6300
Ogle, Peggy Ahrenhold, 1952-. 4.6585
Oglesby, Clarkson Hill, 1908-. 5.5704, 5.6059
Ogorkiewicz, Richard M. 5.7390
O'Gorman, Frank. 4.8517
O'Gorman, James F. 1.5325
Ogot, Bethwell A. joint author. 1.2472
Ogot, Bethwell A. 3.5261
O'Grady, Joseph P., ed. 3.7727

Oh, John Kie-chiang, 1930-. 3.5010
Ohanian, Hans C. 5.2217
O'Hara, Charles E. 4.6810
O'Hara, Frank. 1.4886, 2.12263-2.12264
O'Hara, Frederick M. 4.2015
O'Hara, John, 1905-1970. 2.12266-2.12275,
   2.12277
O'Hehir, Diana, 1929-. 2.13226
O'Higgins, Paul. joint author. 4.3518
Ohio State Archaeological and Historical
   Society. 3.8381
Ohio State Center for Textual Studies. 2.11056
Ohio State University. 3.152
Ohio State University. East Asian Studies
   Program. 4.2549
Ohio State University. Research Foundation.
   4.6864
Ohl, John F., joint ed. 1.3427
Ohlin, Bertil Gotthard, 1899-. 4.4092
Ohlin, Göran, 1925-. 4.1619
Ohmann, Richard Malin. 2.8077
Ohring, George. 5.1807
Oinas, Felix J. 2.2392
Oinas, Felix J. comp. 4.796
Oka, Yoshitake, 1902-. 3.4968
Okakura, Kakuzo. 4.865
Okamoto, Shumpei. 3.4401
Okamoto, Shumpei. joint author. 3.6457
Ōkawa, Kazushi, 1908-. 4.2553
Oke, T. R. 5.2570
O'Keeffe, Georgia, 1887-. 1.5960
O'Keeffe, John, 1747-1833. 2.7173
Okenimkpe, Michael. 2.10097
Okey, Thomas, 1852-1935, ed. and tr. 1.3259
Okin, Susan Moller. 4.5936
Okita, Hajime. 2.2118
Ōkita, Saburō, 1914-. 4.2550
Oklahoma. University. Press. 3.8532
Okmulgee Cultural Foundation. 2.11213
Okot-Kotber, B. M. 5.3878
Okubo, Genji, joint author. 4.8763
Okun, Arthur M. 4.1322, 4.1464, 4.2001
Okun', L. B. (Lev Borisovich) 5.2462
Okun, Morris A. 4.10617
Olah, George A. (George Andrew), 1927-.
   5.2748
Olby, Robert C. (Robert Cecil) 5.3503
Old, R. W. 5.3459
Oldenberg, Hermann, 1854-1920. 2.1930
Oldenburg, Philip, joint author. 3.4142
Ol'denburg, S. S. (Sergeĭ Sergeevich) 3.3167
Oldenburg, Veena Talwar. 3.4359
Olderman, Raymond M. 2.10640
Oldfather, William Abbott, 1880-1945. 2.366
Oldham, Jack, 1947- joint author. 4.5740
Oldham, John. 2.7174
Oldham, K. Michael (Kenneth Michael) 4.4387
Oldham, Keith B. 5.1456, 5.1490
Oldman, Oliver Sanford. joint comp. 4.4694
Oldroyd, George. 1.4121
Oldsey, Bernard Stanley, 1923-. 2.8713
Oldshue, James Y. 5.6846
O'Leary, Brian, 1940-. 5.1790
O'Leary, Daniel Florencio, 1800-1854. 3.9165
O'Leary, De Lacy Evans, 1872-. 1.366
O'Leary, Greg. 4.9079
O'Leary, Timothy J., joint author. 5.7740
O'Leary, Vincent. 4.6894
O'Leary, Virginia E., 1943-. 4.5832, 4.5937
Olesha, IUriĭ Karlovich, 1899-1960. 2.1566,
   2.1589
Oleson, Alexandra, 1939-. 1.81, 5.5514
Oleszek, Walter J. joint author. 4.8063
Oleszek, Walter J. 4.8009, 4.8033
Olin, Spencer C. 3.8611
Oliphant, Mary C. Simms (Mary Chevillette
   Simms), 1891-. 2.11224
Oliphant, Mrs. (Margaret), 1828-1897.
   2.7975-2.7977
Oliphant, Pat, 1935- illus. 3.7904
Oliu, Walter E. 5.5504
Olivas, Michael A. 4.10889
Oliveira, Avelino Ignacio de, 1891-. 5.3002
Oliver, Andrew, 1906- ed. 3.6961
Oliver, Caroline. joint ed. 3.5050
Oliver, Caroline. 4.6153
Oliver, Clinton F., comp. 2.10787
Oliver, Derek. 1.3528

Oliver, Douglas L. 3.5534, 3.5676-3.5677,
   3.5679, 4.687
Oliver, Edward James, 1911-. 2.7987
Oliver, H. J. (Harold James) 2.6578
Oliver, John E. 5.2496, 5.2564
Oliver, Paul, 1927-. 4.826
Oliver, Peter, 1939-. 3.8825
Oliver, Revilo P. (Revilo Pendleton), 1910- ed.
   2.1951
Oliver, Robert W. 4.4575
Oliver, Roger W., 1945-. 2.5058
Oliver, Roland Anthony. ed. 3.5050, 3.5260
Oliver, Roland Anthony. 3.5045, 3.5067,
   3.5075, 3.5076, 3.5079, 3.5083, 4.716
Oliver, Thomas W. 4.9233
Oliver, W. H. (William Hosking), 1925-. 3.5602
Oliver, William Irvin, 1926- comp. 2.5325
Ollard, Richard Lawrence. 2.7180
Ollerenshaw, Philip, 1953-. 4.2318
Ollier, Cliff. 4.263
Ollis, W. David. 5.2714
Ollman, Bertell. 4.5070
Olmstead, Albert Ten Eyck, 1880-1945. 3.3770,
   3.4076
Olmstead, Kathleen A. 4.6561
Olmsted, Frederick Law, 1822-1903. 3.8146,
   3.8327, 4.6322
Olmsted, Gideon, 1749-1845. 3.6894
Olmsted, John Meigs Hubbell, 1911- joint
   author. 5.1441
Olney, James. 2.8365, 3.316-3.317
Olrik, Axel, 1864-1917. 2.14000, 3.3355
Olschak, Blanche Christine. 1.5070
Olschki, Leonardo, 1885-. 3.2825, 3.3613
Olsen, Donald J. 4.6334
Olsen, Edgar O. 4.3484
Olsen, Frederick L. 5.7099
Olsen, Johan P. joint author. 4.10643
Olsen, Johan P. 4.8676
Olsen, O. Wilford (Oliver Wilford), 1901-.
   5.4082
Olsen, Tillie. 2.10991
Olshen, Barry N. 2.9693
Olson, Carl. 1.1617
Olson, Charles, 1910-1970. 2.12278-2.12281
Olson, Clair Colby, 1901- joint ed. 2.6340
Olson, David H. L. 4.5589
Olson, David R. 5.406
Olson, Elder, 1909-. 2.9421, 2.12282
Olson, Eric, ed. 3.430
Olson, Everett Claire, 1910-. 5.4107
Olson, Gerald W. 5.5268
Olson, Glending. 2.2374
Olson, Harry Ferdinand, 1901-. 5.6560
Olson, James C. 3.5928, 3.8519
Olson, James Stuart, 1946-. 3.6523
Olson, Jerry C. (Jerry Corrie), 1944-. 4.4307
Olson, Laura Katz, 1945-. 4.5820
Olson, Mancur. 4.2798, 5.4638
Olson, Sherry H. 4.2042
Olson, William J., 1947-. 5.8041
Olsson, Gunnar, 1935-. 4.1483
Olszer, Krystyna. 2.1744
Olszewski, Ann G. 1.3552
Olton, Roy, 1922-. 4.8981
Olver, Peter J. 5.1521
O'Malley, Charles Donald. joint author. 5.4317
O'Malley, Charles Donald. tr. 5.4139
O'Malley, John E. joint author. 5.4777
O'Malley, Joseph J. ed. 1.931, 1.949
O'Malley, L. S. S. (Lewis Sydney Steward),
   1874-1941. 4.8710
O'Malley, Padraig. 3.1860
O'Malley, Susan Gushee, 1942-. 4.5993
Oman, Charles Chichele, 1901-. 1.6595
Oman, Charles William Chadwick, Sir,
   1860-1946. 5.7188
Omar Khayyam. 2.1971-2.1972
O'Meally, Robert G., 1948-. 2.13007
O'Meara, Dominic J. 1.309
O'Meara, John J. (John Joseph), 1919-. 3.1818
O'Meara, John Joseph. ed. and tr. 1.2185,
   1.2188
O'Meara, Patrick. 3.5044, 3.5442
Ominde, Simeon Hongo. 4.1711
Omnès, Roland. 5.2401
Omond, Thomas Stewart, 1846-1923. 2.1042
Omoyajowo, J. Akinyele. 1.3327

Omrčanin, Margaret Stewart. 2.12566
Omu, Fred I. A. 2.3699
Onasch, Konrad. 1.5177
Ondaatje, Michael, 1943-. 2.9956-2.9957
O'Neal, Hank. 4.5144
O'Neil, Maria Joan, 1937-. 4.6462
O'Neill, Bard E. 3.3877
O'Neill, Daniel J., comp. 2.10857
O'Neill, Eugene, 1888-1953. 2.12283-2.12288
O'Neill, John, 1933-. 4.468, 4.1211
O'Neill, Lois Decker. 3.351
O'Neill, Patrick, 1945-. 5.8012
O'Neill, Robert John. 5.7318
O'Neill, Thomas P., joint author. 3.1867
O'Neill, Timothy J. 4.9592
O'Neill, William F. 4.10268
O'Neill, William L. 3.7842, 4.5989
Onetti, Juan Carlos, 1909-. 2.5439-2.5440
Ong, DeWitt G. 5.6508
Ong, Walter J. 2.16, 2.2583
Ongka. 3.349
Ongkili, James P. 3.4545
Onions, C. T. (Charles Talbut), 1873-1965.
   2.1059, 2.1083, 2.6685
Ono, Motonori, 1904-. 1.1838
Onon, Urgungge. 3.4867
Ontario. Ministry of Citizenship and Culture.
   5.7884
Onwuanibe, Richard C. 4.7481
Ooi, Jin-Bee. 3.4534
Ōoka, Shōhei, 1909-. 2.2116
Ooms, Herman. 3.4947
Oosterbaan, John. 4.1657
Oosterveen, Karla, 1905-. 4.5789
Oparin, Aleksandr Ivanovich, 1894-1980. 5.3322
Opatoshu, Joseph, 1886-1954. 2.1808
Opdahl, Keith Michael. 2.11362
Open University. Curriculum Design and
   Development Course Team. 4.10270
Opfell, Olga S. 1.63, 1.2495
Opie, Iona Archibald. 2.6125, 4.817, 4.1063,
   4.1064
Opie, Iona Archibald. ed. 2.14102
Opie, Peter. 2.6125, 4.1063, 4.1064
Opie, Peter. joint author. 4.817
Opie, Peter. joint ed. 2.14102
Opland, Jeff, 1943-. 2.5594
Opler, Morris Edward, 1907- ed. 3.5837
Oppen, George. 2.12299
Oppenheim, A. Leo, 1904-1974. 3.3765, 3.3771
Oppenheim, Alan V., 1937-. 5.6363, 5.6378
Oppenheim, L. (Lassa), 1858-1919. 4.9290
Oppenheim, Micha Falk. 5.8235
Oppenheimer, Bruce Ian. 4.3774, 4.8008
Oppenheimer, Franz, 1864-1943. 4.7528
Oppenheimer, J. Robert. 5.848, 5.2435
Oppenheimer, Jane M. (Jane Marion), 1911-.
   5.4120, 5.4133
Oppenheimer, Martin. 4.7614
Oppenheimer, Paul, ed. 2.13514
Oppenheimer, Valerie Kincade. 4.5795
Oppenlander, Joseph C. 4.3943
Optical Society of America. Committee on
   Colorimetry. 5.2335
Orans, Martin. 3.4208
Orbach, Susie, 1946-. 5.4891
Orchin, Milton, 1914- joint author. 5.2675
Orczy, Emmuska Orczy, Baroness, 1865-1947.
   2.9172
Ord, Margery G. 5.3489
Ordericus Vitalis, 1075-1143? 3.566
Ordway, Frederick Ira, 1927- joint author.
   5.6689
Ore, Øystein, 1899-1968. 5.817
Orear, Jay. 5.2071
Oregon State University. 4.163, 5.3588
Orel, Harold, 1926-. 2.5507, 2.9515
Orel, Vítězslav. 3.3209
Orem, Dorothea E. (Dorothea Elizabeth),
   1914-. 5.5193
Oren, Nissan. 3.3543, 4.8685
Orenstein, Arbie. 1.3958
Orenstein, Henry. 4.5433
Orenstein, Sylvia. 5.8243
Orfield, Gary. 4.8004, 4.10798
Orford, Jim. 4.6636
Organ, Troy Wilson. 1.183

Organisation for Economic Co-operation and
   Development. 4.3906
Organisation for Economic Co-operation and
   Development. Development Centre. 4.4608
Organization of American Historians. 3.6221,
   3.7668, 3.7767
Orgel, Leslie E. 5.3323
Orgel, Stephen. joint author. 1.5389
Orgel, Stephen. 1.5802, 2.3303, 3.161
Orians, Gordon H. 5.3266, 5.3301
Oriard, Michael, 1948-. 2.13227
Oriensu Shūkyō Kenkyūjo. 3.4903
Origen. 1.2188, 1.2192, 1.2209, 1.2211
Origo, Iris, 1902-. 2.7530
Oriol, William E. 5.4666
O'Riordan, John. 2.9155
Orkand, Richard, joint author. 5.4316
Orkin, Mark. 3.5476
Orlans, Harold, 1921-. 4.5335
Orléans, Charlotte-Elisabeth, duchesse d',
   1652-1722. 3.2039
Orleans, Leo A. 5.974
Orlicky, Joseph. 5.7028
Orlob, Gerald T. 5.6017
Orlow, Dietrich. 3.2425
Orme, Nicholas. 4.10114
Ormerod, Beverley, 1937-. 2.4833
Ormerod, Henry Arderne, 1886-1964. 2.382
Ormond, Richard. 1.5967
Ormsby, Eric L. (Eric Linn), 1941-. 1.2062
Ormsby, Hilda Rodwell (Jones). 4.2329
Ormsby, John, 1829-1895. 2.5173
Ormsby, Margaret Anchoretta, 1909-. 3.8863,
   3.8866
Ornstein, Allan C. 4.10958
Ornstein, Donald, 1934-. 5.1462
Ornstein, Norman J. 4.7729, 4.8000-4.8001,
   4.8034, 4.8113
Ornstein, Robert. 2.5886
Ornstein, Robert Evans. ed. 2.6226
Ornstein, Robert Evans. 2.6227, 5.281, 5.4339
Ornston, L. Nicholas. 5.4434
Orozco, José Clemente, 1883-1949.
   1.6002-1.6003
Orpen, Goddard Henry, 1852-1932. 3.1825
Orrell, John. 2.6709
Orren, Gary R. 4.7654
Orrery, Roger Boyle, Earl of, 1621-1679. 2.7177
Orrey, Leslie. 1.4212
Ortega, James M., 1932-. 5.1427
Ortega, Julio. 2.5298, 2.5315
Ortega y Gasset, José, 1883-1955.
   1.1127-1.1128, 1.1383, 1.6301, 3.47-3.48,
   3.488, 3.3416
Ortego y Gasca, Philip D. comp. 2.10684
Orth, Samuel Peter, 1873-1922. 4.8161
Ortho Books. 5.5368
Ortiz, Alfonso, 1939-. 3.5943, 3.5955
Ortiz, Roxanne Dunbar. 4.9776
Ortiz, Simon J., 1941-. 2.10675,
   2.13228-2.13229
Ortner, Sherry B., 1941-. 1.1830, 4.569
Orton, Harold, 1898-1975. 2.1111, 2.1114,
   2.5518
Orton, Joe. 2.9789
Orwell, George, 1903-1950. 2.9173-2.9182,
   2.9185, 2.9187, 3.3472
Orwig, Gary W., 1945-. 4.10297
Orwin, Charles Stewart, 1876-. 4.2848
Orwin, Christabel Susan (Lowry). 4.2848
Orzel, Nick, ed. 2.10803
Orzeszkowa, Eliza, 1842-1910. 2.1722
Osaragi, Jirō, 1897-1973. 2.2117
Osborn, Andrew Delbridge, 1902-. 5.7625
Osborn, Carolyn, 1934-. 2.13230
Osborn, Fairfield, 1887-1969. ed. 4.1583
Osborn, Frederic J. 4.6306
Osborn, Frederic James, Sir, 1885-. 4.6332
Osborn, James Marshall. 2.6996
Osborn, James Marshall. ed. 2.2529
Osborn, Robert J. 4.8641
Osborne, Charles, 1927-. 1.4518, 3.5532
Osborne, Harold, 1905-. 1.4579, 1.4820, 1.6507,
   3.9271
Osborne, John, 1907-. 2.9207-2.9214,
   3.7903-3.7906, 3.7928
Osborne, Martha Lee, 1928-. 4.5843
Osborne, Milton E. 3.4419, 3.4440, 3.4448

Osborne, Richard Horsley. 3.3512, 4.2236
Osborne, Robert A. 2.2926
Osburn, Charles B. 5.8006
Osen, Lynn M. 5.1089
Osers, Ewald, 1917-. 2.1680
Oseth, John M., 1944-. 4.7908
Osgood, Charles Egerton. 1.544, 3.7594
Osgood, Charles Egerton. joint comp. 5.400
Osgood, Charles Grosvenor, 1871-1964. 2.6522,
   2.6541
Osgood, Herbert Levi, 1855-1918. 3.6873,
   3.6879
Osgood, Robert Endicott. 4.9319, 5.7297
Osgood, William F. (William Fogg), 1864-1943.
   5.1648
Osgoode Society. 4.9432
O'Shaughnessy, Arthur William Edgar,
   1844-1881. 2.7978
O'Shaughnessy, Peter. 3.5564
Osiński, Zbigniew. 2.3385
Osipow, Samuel H. 4.4263
Oskison, John Milton, 1874-. 2.12300
Osler, William, Sir, 1849-1919. 5.4478, 5.4536,
   5.4602, 5.4753
Osmańczyk, Edmund Jan, 1913-. 4.9224
Osmond, Humphry. joint author. 5.4800
Osmond, Nick. 2.4279
Osofsky, Gilbert, 1935-. 3.7212, 3.8057
Osofsky, Joy D. 5.555
Ospovat, Dov. 5.3202
Oss, Jacob Frederik van, 1875-. 5.6857
Ostaijen, Paul van, 1896-1928. 2.13959
Ostellino, Piero. 3.3254
Osten, Gert von der. 1.5019
Ostendorf, Berndt. 2.10328
Oster, Clinton V. 4.4082, 4.4086
Oster, Sharon. joint author. 5.6012
Osterburg, James W. joint author. 4.6810
Osterman, Paul. 4.3305
Osterweis, Rollin G. (Rollin Gustav), 1907-.
   3.8147
Osthaus, Carl R. 4.4538
Östör, Ákos. 1.1716
Ostrander, Gilman Marston, 1923-. 4.7802
Ostriker, Alicia. 2.7406, 2.10284
Ostrofsky, Benjamin, 1925-. 5.5698
Ostrogorski, Georgije. 3.2666
Ostrogorski, M. (Moisei), 1854-1919. 4.7785
Ostrom, Alan B., 1925-. 2.12753
Ostrom, John Ward, 1903- ed. 2.11200
Ostrom, Vincent, 1919-. 4.7315
Ostrovsky, Aleksandr Nikolaevich, 1823-1886.
   2.1404-2.1405
Ostrovsky, Erika. 2.4514
Ostrovsky, Nikolay, 1904-1936. 2.1590
Ostry, Bernard, 1927-. 3.8746
Ostwald, Martin, 1922-. 2.246
O'Sullivan, Judith. 1.6437
O'Sullivan, Vincent. 2.10200
O'Sullivan, Vincent James. 2.9080
Osur, Alan M., 1941-. 3.1129
Oswalt, Wendell H. 3.5706, 3.5879
Osyczka, Andrzej. 5.5718
Othmer, Donald F. (Donald Frederick), 1904-.
   5.6809
Otis, Brooks. 2.415, 2.751, 2.802
Ōtomo, Yakamochi, 718?-785. 2.2040
O'Toole, L. M. (Lawrence Michael), 1934-.
   2.1286
Ōtsuka, Ryūtarō. 3.5661
Ott, David H. 3.3878
Ott, Sandra. 3.2238
Ott, William E., 1945- joint author. 5.6467
Ottawa. National Gallery of Canada. 1.5998,
   1.6493
Ottaway, David. 4.7129
Ottaway, Marina. 4.7129
Otte, Carel, 1922- ed. 5.6294
Otte, Daniel. 5.3876
Otte, Enrique. 3.8996
Ottemiller, John H. (John Henry), 1916-1968.
   5.8130
Otten, Anna, comp. 2.13780
Otten, Karl, 1889-1963. 2.13525
Otten, L. (Lambert) 5.6847
Ottenberg, Phoebe, joint ed. 4.656
Ottenberg, Simon. ed. 4.656
Otterbein, Keith F. 5.7152

Ottman, Robert W. 1.4569
Otto, Christian F. 1.5428
Otto I, Bishop of Freising, d. 1158. 3.2270
Otto, Max Carl, 1876-. 1.617-1.618
Otto, Rudolf, 1869-1937. 1.1535, 1.1630
Ottoson, David, 1918-. 5.4322
Otway-Ruthven, Annette Jocelyn, 1909-. 3.1827
Otway, Thomas, 1652-1685. 2.7176-2.7177
Ouchi, William G. 4.2742
Ouden, P. den (Pieter den), 1874-1964. 5.5357
Oudshoorn, J. van, 1876-1951. 2.13948
Ouellet, Fernand. 4.2127
Ouellet, Henri. 5.3967
Ouellette, Fernand. 1.4018
Ouimette, Victor. 1.1131
Oulton, John Ernest Leonard, 1886-. 1.2209, 2.367
Ousby, Ian, 1947-. 2.6012
Outhwaite, William. 4.1212
Outka, Gene H. 1.3065
Outler, Albert Cook, 1908-. 1.2203
Overacker, Louise, 1891-. 4.8132
Overbury, Thomas, (Sir) 1581-1613. 2.6500
Overholt, Catherine, 1942-. 4.5833
Overholt, William H. 3.3637
Overman, Ralph T. 5.2437
Overmyer, Daniel L., 1935-. 1.2116
Overmyer, Grace. 2.11195
Overseas Development Council. 4.1592, 4.1815, 4.2612, 4.4155, 4.6168
Overstreet, Helen Mary, joint author. 4.6576
Overton, Richard Cleghorn, 1907-. 4.4008-4.4009
Overy, R. J. 3.1041
Ovid, 43 B.C.-17 or 18 A.D. 2.678-2.682, 2.743-2.745, 2.747-2.748
Ovington, Mary White, 1865-1951. 3.6645
Owen, A. E. 5.7047
Owen, Arthur Synge, ed. 2.458
Owen, Charles Abraham, 1914-. 2.6326-2.6327
Owen, David, 1955-. 4.10611
Owen, David R. 5.2250
Owen, Dennis E. (Dennis Edward), 1944-. 3.7932
Owen, Douglas David Roy. 2.2398
Owen, Edward Roger John. 4.2442
Owen, Eric Trevor, 1882-. 2.501
Owen, Frank F. E. 5.6401
Owen, John Beresford. 3.1543
Owen, Noel L. joint author. 5.2872
Owen, Norman G. 4.2538, 4.3689
Owen, Octavius Freire, 1816?-1873, tr. 1.291
Owen, Ray David, 1915- joint author. 5.3441
Owen, Robert, 1771-1858. 4.7161
Owen, S. G. (Samuel Griffith) 5.4488
Owen Smith, E. 4.3336
Owen, Stephen. 2.2165-2.2166
Owen, Tobias C. joint author. 5.1727
Owen, W. J. B. (Warwick Jack Burgoyne) ed. 2.8300
Owen, Wilfred. 2.9216-2.9217, 4.3885, 4.3907, 4.3918, 4.3938
Owen, William Harold, 1897-. 2.9217-2.9218
Owens, Charles E. 4.6816
Owens, Gary, 1939- joint author. 3.7881
Owens, Harry P. 3.7193
Owens, Joseph. 1.290
Owens, Leslie Howard. 3.7206
Owens, Peter H., joint author. 5.2823
Owram, Doug, 1947-. 3.8853
Owsley, Frank Lawrence, 1928-. 3.7106, 3.7380, 3.8148
Owsley, Harriet Fason Chappell. 3.6970
Oxenfeldt, Alfred Richard, 1917-. 4.4314
Oxenford, John, 1812-1877. tr. 2.13577
Oxford Centre for Postgraduate Hebrew Studies. 3.3819, 3.4001
Oxford, Eng. University. Bodleian Library. 3.1311
Oxford University Press. 4.135, 4.152, 4.168-4.169, 4.9405
Oxford University Press. Dictionary Dept. German Section. 2.1188
Oxtoby, John C. 5.1459
Oyono, Ferdinand, 1929-. 2.4642, 2.4854-2.4856
Ozaki, Bonnie D. (Bonnie Davis) 5.12
Ozanne, Robert W. 4.3701
Özbudun, Ergun. 3.3595

Ozenfant, Amédée, 1886-1966. 1.5121
Ozick, Cynthia. 2.13231
Ozima, Minoru. 5.2970
Özişik, M. Necati. joint author. 5.6200
Ozment, Steven E. 1.2315, 1.2327, 4.5615
Ozment, Steven E. comp. 1.2333

P.E.N. 2.1825
PSaratiÿsar, 1882-1921. 2.2279
Pa, Chin, 1905-. 2.2244-2.2245
Pacey, Arnold. 5.5549
Pach, Walter, 1883-1958. 1.6112, 1.6142
Pachai, B. 3.5493
Pachai, Bridglal. 3.5462
Pachauri, R. K. 4.3763
Pacheco, Josephine F. 4.10866
Pachmuss, Temira, 1927-. 2.1302, 2.1307, 2.1499
Pacholczyk, A. G., 1935-. 5.1775
Pachter, Henry Maximilian, 1907-. 3.2331
Pachter, Marc. 3.315
Pacific Institute for Public Policy Research. 4.9759
Pacifici, Sergio. 2.4882
Pack, Robert, 1929-. 2.12549
Packard, Randall M., 1945-. 3.5419
Packard, Sidney Raymond, 1893-. 3.147
Packard, Vance Oakley, 1914-. 4.4430, 4.6383
Packer, J.I. 1.1497
Packer, Nancy Huddleston. 2.13232
Paddison, Ronan. 4.7498
Padelford, Frederick Morgan, 1875-1942. ed. 2.6522
Paden, John N. ed. 3.5055
Paden, William Doremus, 1903- ed. 2.7048
Padfield, Harland. 4.4899
Padfield, Peter. 3.541, 5.7461
Padilla, Victoria. 5.5350
Padma Sambhava, ca. 717-ca. 762. 1.2104
Padmore, George, 1903-1959. 3.5111
Padover, Saul Kussiel, 1905-. 3.1954, 4.7561
Paetow, Louis John, 1880-1928. 5.8224-5.8225
Pagan, Frank G. 5.1206
Page, B. S. (Bertram Samuel) tr. 1.341
Page-Barbour Foundation. 4.10732
Page, Benjamin I. 4.7955
Page, Charles Hunt, 1909- joint comp. 4.947
Page, Denys Lionel, ed. 2.320
Page, Denys Lionel. 2.315, 2.318-2.319, 2.326, 2.406, 2.460, 2.502, 2.512, 2.540
Page, Donald Murray, 1939-. 5.8259
Page, Edward. 4.7768
Page, Eugene Richard, 1903-. 2.6942
Page, Frederick, 1879-. 2.7986
Page, Joseph A. 3.9217, 3.9253, 5.5021
Page, Lou Williams. joint comp. 5.1833, 5.1841
Page, Lou Williams. ed. 5.1710, 5.1750, 5.1791
Page, Lou Williams. 5.1723
Page, Lou Williams. joint author. 5.1829
Page, Norman. 2.7663, 2.7796, 2.7799, 2.7839
Page, Norman. comp. 2.7613
Page, Stanley W. 3.3306
Page, Talbot. 4.4131
Page, Thomas Nelson, 1853-1922. 2.11193
Page, Thornton. comp. 5.1833, 5.1841
Page, Thornton. ed. 5.1710, 5.1750, 5.1791, 5.6693
Page, Thornton. 5.1723, 5.1829
Page, Tim. 1.3471
Pagels, Elaine H., 1943-. 1.2700, 1.2969
Pagels, Heinz R., 1939-. 2.2139
Pagès, Georges, 1867-1939. 3.637
Paget, Paul, 1918-. 4.4874
Paget, Richard Arthur Surtees, Sir, bart., 1869-. 5.4281
Pagliaro, Harold E. comp. 2.6088
Paglin, Morton. ed. 4.1414
Pagna, Tom, joint author. 4.1027
Pagnol, Marcel, 1895-1974. 2.4643
Pahel, Kenneth, comp. 1.1405
Pai, Chih-ang. 2.2187
Paideia Group. 4.10829
Paige, Glenn D. 3.5030
Paine, Albert Bigelow, 1861-1937. 2.10948, 2.10960
Paine, Leslie. 5.4620
Paine, Robert Treat, 1900-. 1.5075

Paine, Thomas, 1737-1809. 1.1883, 3.6923, 4.7423
Paine, Whiton Stewart. 5.407
Painter, George Duncan, 1914-. 2.4153, 2.4674, 5.7555
Painter, James Allan. 2.8354
Painter, Nell Irvin. 3.6799, 4.7000
Painter, Sidney, 1902-1960. 3.134, 3.292, 3.575, 3.1350, 3.1355
Pais, Abraham, 1918-. 5.1947, 5.1985
Paisey, David. 1.6461
Pakeman, Sidney Arnold, 1891-. 3.4367
Pakenham, Thomas, 1933-. 3.1839, 3.5505
Pakistan Institute of Development Economics. 4.2517
Pakistan Philosophical Congress. 1.374
Pal, Pratapaditya. 1.5053, 1.5069, 1.5186, 1.5747, 1.5752, 1.6331, 1.6399
Pal, R. N. 4.8709
Palache, Charles, 1869-. 5.3012
Palamas, Köstes, 1859-1943. 2.605
Palda, Kristian S. 4.4287
Palen, J. John. 4.6297, 4.6342
Paléologue, Maurice, 1859-1944. 3.3189
Palermo, David Stuart, 1929- joint author. 5.292
Paley, Grace. 2.13233-2.13234
Paley, Vivian Gussin, 1929-. 4.10412, 4.10852
Palgrave, Francis Turner, 1824-1897. comp. 2.6102
Palgrave, Robert Harry Inglis, Sir, 1827-1919. 4.1275
Palik, Edward D. 5.2209
Palis Júnior, Jacob. 5.1618
Palisca, Claude V. 1.3656
Palisca, Claude V. joint author. 1.3634
Palisca, Claude V. 1.3725, 1.4422a
Palisca, Claude Victor. 1.3423
Palladio, Andrea, 1508-1580. 1.5468
Palley, Marian Lief, 1939-. 4.6052
Pallister, Janis L. 5.4168
Pallottino, Massimo. 3.2757
Palma, Michael, 1945-. 2.5035
Palmade, Guy P. 4.2324
Palmer, Alan Warwick. 3.656, 3.670, 3.3115
Palmer, Alan Warwick. joint author. 3.3529
Palmer, Alan Warwick. 3.735, 3.3519, 3.3554
Palmer, Arlene M. 1.6630
Palmer, Bruce, 1913-. 3.4502, 4.8229
Palmer, C. Eddie. 1.1870
Palmer, Colin A., 1942-. 4.6428
Palmer, D. J. (David John), 1935-. 2.8179
Palmer, David, ed. 2.6181
Palmer, Edgar M. joint author. 5.1286
Palmer, Eileen C. 2.2787
Palmer, Eustace. 2.10044
Palmer, Frank Robert, ed. 2.5
Palmer, Frederick, 1873-1958. 3.814, 3.6370
Palmer, Gregory. 3.6959
Palmer, H. P. (Henry Procter) joint author. 5.1861
Palmer, Helen H. 5.7804, 5.7970, 5.8131
Palmer, J. M. (John Michael), 1936-. 3.3763
Palmer, John, 1885-1944. 2.5898, 2.6804
Palmer, John Logan. 4.3217, 4.3220
Palmer, Joseph, Commander. 5.7416
Palmer, Leonard Robert. 2.252, 3.2586
Palmer, Norman Dunbar. 3.4094, 3.6450, 4.8700, 4.8713
Palmer, Norman Dunbar. joint author. 3.4763
Palmer, Pete. 4.927
Palmer, R. A. (Rex Alfred), 1936-. 5.2933
Palmer, R. R. (Robert Roswell), 1909-. 3.609, 3.652, 3.663, 3.2108, 4.123, 4.10125
Palmer, Ralph S. (Ralph Simon), 1914- ed. 5.3953
Palmer, Robert. 1.4275
Palmer, Robert C., 1947-. 4.9415
Palmer, Robin H. 4.5463
Palmer, Roy. 1.3441, 4.790
Palmer, Ted. 4.6891
Palmer, William J. 2.9694
Palmer, William Scott, pseud., ed. 1.3083
Palmes, J. C. (James C.) 1.5211, 1.5430
Palmore, Erdman Ballagh, 1930-. 4.5800, 4.5821, 5.4218
Palomo, María del Pilar. 2.5088
Palóu, Francisco, 1723-1789. 3.8603

Pálsson, Hermann. 2.13981-2.13983, 2.13989
Paltock, Robert, 1697-1767. 2.7179
Paludan, Phillip S., 1938-. 4.9616
Pan-American Assembly on Population, Cali,
   Colombia, 1965. 4.1687
Pan American Health Organization. 5.5124
Pan, Ku, 32-92. 4.2465
Panassié, Hugues. 1.4331
Pande, Govind Chandra, 1923-. 1.2106
Pandey, B. N. (Bishwa Nath), 1929-. 3.4321,
   4.8703
Pandit, Sneh. 1.1388
Panek, LeRoy. 2.5958, 2.6055
Panel on Environmental Education. 5.3523
Panem, Sandra, 1946-. 5.4471
Pangborn, Cyrus R. 1.1782
Pangborn, Edgar. 2.13235-2.13236
Pange, Pauline Laure Marie de Broglie,
   comtesse de, 1888-. 3.2241
Pangle, Thomas L. 4.7343, 4.7430
Pangrazi, Robert P. 4.914
Panikkar, K. M. (Kavalam Madhava),
   1896-1963. 4.5425
Panitch, Leo. 2.2310
Pankhurst, E. Sylvia (Estelle Sylvia), 1882-1960.
   3.5243, 4.8512
Pankhurst, Emmeline, 1858-1928. 4.8511
Pankhurst, Richard Keir Pethick, 1927-. 4.2593
Pannenberg, Wolfhart, 1928-. 1.2791, 1.2816,
   1.2867, 1.2957
Panneton, Phillippe, 1895-. 2.4819
Panofsky, Erwin, 1892-1968. 1.4594,
   1.4765-1.4766, 1.5132, 1.6169, 1.6234
Panofsky, Wolfgang Kurt Hermann, 1919-.
   5.2342
Panova, Vera Fedorovna, 1905-1973. 2.1591
Pansini, Anthony J. 5.6332
Pant, Sumitra Nandan, 1900-. 2.1888
Pantaleoni, Maffeo, 1857-1924. 4.1474
Panyella, Augusto. 1.6511
Panzar, John C., 1947-. 4.2998
Paolino, Thomas J., 1940-. 5.4882
Paolucci, Anne. 2.12849
Pap, Arthur, 1921-1959. 1.1281, 5.918
Papacosma, S. Victor, 1942-. 3.2700
Papadaki, Stamo. 1.5354
Papademetriou, Demetrios G. 4.8951
Papadimitriou, Christos H. 5.1550
Papadimitriou, Christos H. joint author. 5.1372
Papadopoulo, Alexandre. 1.4749
Papagiannis, Michael D., 1932-. 5.1785
Papandreou, Andreas George. 3.2708
Papanek, Gustav Fritz. 4.2519, 4.2532
Papashvily, Helen Waite. 2.10288
Papastephanou, Emmanuel. 2.598
Papen, Franz von, 1879-1969. 3.2411
Papenfuse, Edward C. 3.8100a
Paper, Lewis J. 3.7867, 4.9804
Papert, Seymour. 5.1064
Papias, Saint, Bp. of Hierapolis, 2d cent. v.
   Epistle to Diognetus. 1.2181
Papoulis, Athanasios, 1921-. 5.6379
Papp, Peggy. 5.4885
Pappas, Paul Constantine. 3.2696
Paquet, Basil T., 1944- joint comp. 2.10755
Paquet, Paul C. 5.3995
Paquet, Sandra Pouchet. 2.9992
Paquette, Leo A. 5.2776
Paquette, Radnor Joseph. 5.5927, 5.6062
Paradis, James G., 1942-. 5.965
Paradise, Nathaniel Burton, 1895-1942. 2.6488
Paradiso, John L. 5.3976
Pãratiyãr, 1882-1921. 2.2278
Paré, Ambroise, 1510?-1590. 5.4168
Pare, Richard. 1.5517
Paredes, Américo. comp. 4.784
Parenti, Lynne R. 5.3232
Pares, Bernard, Sir, 1867-1949. 2.1394, 3.3042,
   3.3136, 3.3162, 3.3168
Pares, Richard, 1902-1958. 3.1558
Paret, Peter. 1.4983, 3.2493-3.2494, 5.7206,
   5.7214, 5.7312
Pareto, Vilfredo, 1848-1923. 4.1475,
   4.4862-4.4863
Parfitt, G. D. 5.2897
Parfitt, George A. E. 2.6592, 2.6601
Parfitt, George A. E. comp. 2.6161
Parfitt, Rebecca Rowe, 1942-. 5.5063

Pargellis, Stanley McCrory, 1898-. 5.7989
Parini, Giuseppe, 1729-1799. 2.5009
Parins, James W. 5.7742
Paris, Arthur E., 1945-. 1.3388
Paris, Demetrius T., 1928-. 5.2360
Paris, Matthew, 1200-1259. 1.3230
Parise, Frank. 3.271
Parish, James Robert. 2.2855
Parish, Jewell. 2.1714
Parish, Peter J. 3.7346
Parish, Richard Vernon, 1934-. 5.2709
Parish, William L. 4.5631, 4.6271
Parisi, Joseph, 1944-. 2.10770
Park, Charles Frederick, 1903-. 4.3724, 5.3023
Park, Clara Claiborne. 5.4830
Park, George K., 1925-. 4.605
Park, Hong Kyoo, 1944-. 5.8071
Park, John Edgar, 1879-. 1.2989
Park, R. (Robert), 1933-. 5.5877
Park, Rebecca. 4.6135
Park, Robert Ezra, 1864-1944. 2.3643,
   4.4835-4.4837, 4.5048, 4.6298
Park, Roderic B., joint author. 5.3591
Park, Rolla Edward. 4.10655
Park, Roy. 2.7810, 2.7900
Parke, H. W. (Herbert William), 1903-. 3.2562,
   3.2644
Parke, Ross D. 5.4966
Parker, Albert. 5.6042
Parker, Albert D. 5.5911
Parker, Alexander Augustine. 2.3449, 2.5162
Parker, David. Henry W. 5.5704
Parker, David L. 4.1112
Parker, David. Mary S. 4.6028
Parker, De Witt Henry, 1885-. 1.1377
Parker, Donn B. 4.6764
Parker, Dorothy, 1893-1967. 2.12301-2.12303
Parker, Douglass. 2.428
Parker, Frank S., 1921-. 5.4401
Parker, Franklin, 1921-. 4.6470
Parker, Gail Thain, 1943-. 5.476
Parker, Geoffrey, 1933-. 3.2962-3.2963, 3.3442,
   4.2220, 4.6785, 4.8361
Parker, Glenn R. 4.8016
Parker, Hampton Wildman, 1897-1968. 5.3928
Parker, Harry, 1887-. 5.5878, 5.5886
Parker, Hershel. 2.11148, 2.11155
Parker, I. S. C. (Ian S. C.), 1936- joint author.
   5.4040
Parker, J. A., 1936-. 4.6781
Parker, J. A. (James Gordon), 1927-. 5.6758
Parker, K. J. (Kenneth John), 1926-. 5.6890
Parker, Pauline. 2.6535
Parker, Richard Bordeaux, 1923-. 3.5198
Parker, Robert Alexander Clarke, 1927-. 4.2904
Parker, Robert Stewart. 4.8821
Parker, Rozsika. 1.5194
Parker, Sybil P. 5.709, 5.2944, 5.3236, 5.3511,
   5.6131
Parker, T. H. L. (Thomas Henry Louis), ed.
   1.2357
Parker, T. H. L. (Thomas Henry Louis) 1.3402
Parker, Theodore, 1810-1860. 1.3414
Parker, Thomas, 1947-. 3.7853
Parker, W. Oren (Wilford Oren) 2.3155
Parker, William, 1921-. 5.8389
Parker, William E. (William Edward), 1932-.
   5.6922
Parker, William Mathie, 1891- ed. 2.8053
Parker, William Nelson. 4.2968
Parker, William Riley, 1906-1968. 2.7151,
   2.7154
Parkes, Henry Bamford, 1904-. 3.6152, 3.8918
Parkes, James William, 1896-. 1.1959, 3.3899
Parkes, Oscar. 5.7462
Parkinson, C. Northcote (Cyril Northcote),
   1909-. 3.32, 4.3008
Parkinson, G. H. R. (George Henry Radcliffe)
   1.1136
Parkinson, Richard N. 3.2745
Parkinson, Roger. 3.927-3.928, 3.8953
Parkinson, Thomas Francis, 1920- comp.
   2.12053
Parkinson, Tom. 4.4441
Parkman, Ebenezer, 1703-1782. 3.8009
Parkman, Francis. 3.5776, 3.6255-3.6256,
   3.6881, 3.8474, 3.8705-3.8707, 3.8713
Parks, Aileen Wells. ed. 2.11258

Parks, Bertram Hasloch, 1913- joint author.
   5.2918
Parks, Edd Winfield, 1906-1968. 2.11183,
   2.11258-2.11260
Parks, George Bruner, 1890-. 4.9, 5.8334-5.8335
Parks, Joseph Howard. 3.7426
Parks, Robert J. 4.4004
Parks, Roger N. 4.3845
Parmantier, Nicole. 1.4981
Parmeggiani, Luigi. 5.5012
Parmenides. 1.238, 1.248
Parmet, Herbert S. 3.7829, 3.7875, 4.8207
Parmet, Robert D., 1938-. 3.7144, 4.3606
Parnall, Peter. 5.3981
Parnes, Herbert S., 1919-. 4.3211
Paroissien, David. ed. 3.2823
Parr, J. Gordon (James Gordon), 1927-. 5.6758
Parra, Nicanor, 1914-. 2.5411
Parrinder, Edward Geoffrey. 1.1843, 1.1853,
   1.2071
Parrinder, Patrick. comp. 2.8259
Parrinder, Patrick. 2.3493, 2.5979, 2.7739
Parrington, Vernon Louis, 1871-1929. 2.10253
Parris, Guichard. 3.6647
Parris, Judith H. joint author. 4.8141
Parrish, Carl, ed. 1.3427
Parrish, Carl. 1.3428, 1.4118
Parrish, Lydia (Austin), Mrs., d1953, comp.
   1.3440
Parrish, Michael E. 4.9816
Parrish, Paul A., 1944-. 2.6966
Parrish, Stephen. 2.8299
Parrish, Stephen Maxfield. 2.7352, 2.8354
Parrish, Thomas (Thomas D.) 3.890
Parrish, Wayland Maxfield, 1887- ed. 2.3781
Parrish, William Earl, 1931- ed. 3.8360
Parron, Delores L. 5.4585
Parrot, André, 1901-. 1.4705-1.4706
Parrott, Bruce, 1945-. 4.2409
Parrott, Cecil, Sir, 1909-. 2.1671
Parrott, Ian. 1.3861
Parrott, Thomas Marc, 1866-1960. 2.5707,
   2.5869, 2.6561
Parry, Adam. ed. 2.514
Parry, Albert, 1901-. 2.10281
Parry, Benita. 2.5972
Parry, J. H. (John Horace), 1914-. 3.5978,
   3.8988, 3.9088, 4.50-4.51, 4.8330, 4.8894,
   4.8903, 4.8935, 5.7485
Parry, John H. (John Horace), 1914-. 3.8993
Parry, Linda. 1.6676
Parry, Milman. 2.514
Parry, Pamela Jeffcott. 1.4821
Parry, Thomas, 1904-. 2.833
Parry, William, 1934-. 5.1463
Parseghian, Ara, 1923-. 4.1027
Parsloe, Phyllida. 4.9396
Parson, Erwin Randolph. 5.7370
Parsonage, N. G. (Neville George) 5.2928
Parsons, Denys. 1.3571
Parsons, George. 4.3474
Parsons, Howard L. ed. 1.479
Parsons, I. M. (Ian Macnaghten) 2.9288
Parsons, Jeffrey R., jt. author. 3.8893
Parsons. Kenneth H., ed. 4.1426
Parsons, Neil. 5.463
Parsons, Stanley B. 4.149
Parsons, Talcott, 1902-. 3.6650, 4.1281, 4.1473,
   4.4733-4.4734, 4.4838-4.4839, 4.4865, 4.4910,
   4.4961-4.4962, 4.5654, 4.10085, 5.531
Parsons, Thomas Sturges, 1930-. 5.4110
Partch, Harry, 1901-. 1.4204
Parten, Mildred Bernice, 1902-. 4.5115
Parthasarathy, R. 2.10123
Parthenius, of Nicaea. 2.378
Partington, J. R. (James Riddick), 1886-1965.
   5.2609
Partington, James Riddick. 5.2610
Partington, Martin. 4.3444
Partner, Nancy F. 3.1297
Partner, Peter. 3.2933, 3.2939
Partnow, Elaine. 2.3733-2.3734, 5.6925
Partridge, A. C. (Astley Cooper) 2.942, 2.5776
Partridge, C. J. joint comp. 2.7744
Partridge, Colin. 4.500
Partridge, Edward Bellamy, 1916-. 2.6602
Partridge, Elinore Hughes. 5.7823

Partridge, Eric, 1894-. 2.924, 2.1001, 2.1056,
   2.1060, 2.1064, 2.1076, 2.1163-2.1164, 2.1166,
   2.6686
Pasachoff, Jay M. 5.1705, 5.1734
Pasadena Art Museum. 1.5902
Pascal, Blaise, 1623-1662. 1.802, 1.804-1.805,
   5.2035
Pascal, Roy, 1904-. 2.13463, 2.13470, 2.13498,
   3.318
Pascarella, Perry. 4.3121
Paschke, Donald V. tr. 1.4568
Pascoli, Giovanni, 1855-1912. 2.5047
Pasek, Jan Chryzostom. 3.3334
Paskar, Joanne. 5.8431
Paskins, Barrie. 5.7165
Pasmantier, Jeanne, joint ed. 2.5149
Pasolini, Pier Paolo, 1922-1975. 2.5048
Pasqualetti, Martin J., 1945-. 5.6610
Pasquill, F. 5.2521
Passage, Charles E. 2.13541, 2.13647, 2.13652
Passage, Charles E. tr. 2.13540
Passerin d'Entrèves, Alessandro, 1902-. 4.7271
Passin, Herbert. 3.6459
Passingham, R. E., 1943-. 5.479
Passmore, John Arthur. 1.736, 1.1239
Pasternak, Boris Leonidovich, 1890-1960.
   2.1592-2.1595
Pasternak, Burton. 4.5420
Pasto, Daniel J., 1936-. 5.2857
Paston letters. 3.1374
Pastor, Robert A. 4.4174
Pastore, José, 1935-. 4.5270
Pasztory, Esther. 3.8906
Patai, Raphael, 1910-. 1.1953
Patai, Saul. 5.2755, 5.2758-5.2761, 5.2849
Patañjali. 1.204-1.205
Patch, Howard Rollin, 1889-1963. 2.6367
Patchen, Kenneth, 1911-1972. 2.12304-2.12307
Pate, Michael. 2.2965
Patel, Sharad A. joint author. 5.5845
Pateman, Carole. 4.7515
Pater, Alan Frederick. 2.3737
Pater, Walter, 1839-1894. 1.6697, 2.7979-2.7981
Paterson, Donald G., 1942- joint author. 4.2117
Paterson, John, 1887-. 2.7764
Paterson, Thomas G., 1941-. 3.7595
Paterson, William E. 3.2469, 4.8378
Patey, Douglas Lane. 2.5504
Pathelin. 2.3972
Patinkin, Don. 4.1340, 4.1342-4.1343,
   4.4478-4.4479
Patitucci, Frank M., joint author. 4.8846
Patmanāpan, Nīla, 1938-. 2.2277
Patmore, Coventry Kersey Dighton, 1823-1896.
   2.7828, 2.7986
Patmore, Derek, 1908-. 2.7988-2.7989
Patnode, Robert A. joint author. 5.4464
Paton, Alan. 2.10087-2.10089
Paton, Herbert James, 1887-. 1.879, 1.885,
   1.910, 3.479
Paton, William Andrew, 1889-. 4.4401
Paton, William R., tr. 2.325
Paton, William Roger, 1921-. 2.391
Patrick, Alison. 3.2107
Patrick, Dale R. 5.7032
Patrick, Hugh T. 4.2548
Patrick, John Max, 1911-. 2.7071, 2.7075,
   2.7924
Patrick, Rembert Wallace, 1909-. 3.7374, 3.8114
Patrick, Robert, 1937-. 2.13237
Patrick, Walton R. 2.11986
Patrides, C. A. 1.2250, 2.5643, 2.7065, 2.7145
Patt, Beatrice P. (Shapiro) 1919-. 2.5233
Patte, Daniel. 1.2641
Pattee, Fred Lewis, 1863-1950. 2.10579
Patten, Bradley Merrill, 1889-1971.
   5.4130-5.4131, 5.4166
Patten, Robert L. 2.7646
Patterson, Annabel M. 2.7108
Patterson, Austin M. (Austin McDowell),
   1876-1956. 5.2594-5.2595
Patterson, Daniel W. (Daniel Watkins) 1.4251
Patterson, David S., 1937-. 4.9145
Patterson, Donald J. joint author. 5.6048
Patterson, Frank Allen, 1878-1944. 2.7110
Patterson, Gardner. 4.4153
Patterson, Henry, 1947- joint author. 3.1872
Patterson, Homer L., ed. 4.9945

Patterson, James Deane, 1934-. 5.2196
Patterson, James T. 3.7689, 3.7767, 4.5161,
   4.7877
Patterson, James William, 1940-. 5.6030
Patterson, Jerry E. 1.6629
Patterson, K. David (Karl David), 1941-.
   5.4682
Patterson, Lindsay. comp. 2.10788
Patterson, Margaret C. 5.8271
Patterson, Maureen L. P. 5.8048
Patterson, Michael. 2.3375-2.3376
Patterson, Nancy-Lou. 2.9958
Patterson, Orlando, 1940-. 4.617, 4.6420
Patterson, Richard. 5.7006
Patterson, Stephen E., 1937-. 4.7812
Patterson, Thomas E. 4.7961
Patterson, Walter C., 1936-. 5.6620
Pattison, Bruce. 1.3718
Pattison, E. Mansell, 1933-. 5.4590
Pattison, Robert. 4.10754
Pattison, Walter Thomas, 1903-. 2.5225
Patton, Carl V. 4.6239
Patton, George S. (George Smith), 1885-1945.
   3.897
Patton, George Smith, 1885-1945. 3.7613
Patty, F. A. (Frank Arthur), 1897-. 5.5022
Pauck, Marion. joint author. 1.3298
Pauck, Wilhelm, 1901-. 1.2352, 1.2709, 1.3281,
   1.3298
Paudler, William W., 1932-. 5.2411-5.2412
Paudrat, Jean Louis. 4.1111
Paues, Anna Carolina, 1867- ed. 5.7936
Paul, A. (Amal) 5.2694
Paul, Cedar. tr. 3.2294
Paul, Deirdre. 1.4784
Paul, Eden, tr. 3.2294
Paul, Ellen Frankel. 3.6575
Paul, Gordon L. 5.4865
Paul, James C. N. 4.9530
Paul, Jeffrey. 4.7645
Paul, John, 1922-. 5.4390
Paul Mellon Centre for Studies in British Art.
   1.4947, 1.4951, 1.5399, 1.5515, 1.5688,
   1.5984, 1.6038, 1.6490, 1.6549
Paul Mellon Foundation for British Art. 1.6044
Paul, Peter V. 4.6605
Paul, R. E. 5.5826
Paul, Richard P. 5.6171
Paul, Rodman Wilson. 3.8464, 3.8609
Paul, Shalom M. 1.2546
Paul, Sherman. 2.11530, 2.12754, 2.12771
Paul, Sherman. ed. 2.11029, 2.11254
Paul Wilhelm, Duke of Württemberg,
   1797-1860. 3.8302
Paulay, T., 1923- joint author. 5.5877
Paulhus, Joseph L. H. 4.291
Pauling, Linus, 1901-. 5.2136, 5.2305, 5.2631,
   5.2837
Pauling, Peter, joint author. 5.2631
Paullin, Charles Oscar, 1868 or 9-1944. 4.156
Paulsen, Kathryn. 4.5840
Paulson, Arvid. tr. 2.14071, 2.14075
Paulson, Joy. 4.6146
Paulson, Ronald. 1.4939, 1.6034, 1.6456, 2.7296
Paulston, Christina Bratt, 1932-. 2.1006
Paulu, Burton, 1910-. 4.4061
Pauly, Mark V., 1941-. 5.4639
Pauly, Reinhard G. 1.3659
Pauphilet, Albert. 2.3943-2.3944
Pausanias. 2.382
Paustovsky, Konstantin, 1893-1968. 2.1599
Pavarini, Massimo, 1947-. 4.6888
Pavelka, Ed. 4.1046
Pavese, Cesare. 2.5050-2.5054
Pavlidis, Theodosios. 5.5652
Pavlov, Ivan Petrovich, 1849-1936. 5.4343
Pavlovich, Natalie, 1940-. 5.5189
Pavoni, Joseph L. 5.6011, 5.6035
Pawel, Ernst. 2.13798
Pawley, Martin. 3.204
Pawlikowski, John. 1.2873
Paxson, Diana L. 2.13238
Paxton, John. joint author. 4.8358
Paxton, John. 1.6696, 3.370, 4.7214, 4.8359
Paxton, Robert O. 3.2208-3.2209, 3.3962
Payen, Jean Charles. 2.3840
Paykel, Eugene S. 5.4933
Paylor, Wilfrid, James, ed. 2.6500

Payne, Anthony, 1952-. 4.2151, 4.2156
Payne, Charles. 4.1162
Payne, Charles M. 4.10962
Payne, Clive, joint author. 4.5340
Payne, Darwin. 2.11290
Payne, F. William, 1924-. 4.3801, 5.6293
Payne, Humfry, 1902-1936. 1.5619
Payne, John, 1842-1916. 2.4906
Payne, Karen. 4.5664
Payne, Robert, 1911-. 2.2193
Payne, Robert O. 2.6368
Payne, Stanley G. 1.3193, 3.3413,
   3.3461-3.3462, 3.3483, 4.7603, 5.7333
Payton, Charles E. 5.6740
Paz, Mario. 5.5857
Paz, Octavio, 1914-. 1.6006, 2.5347-2.5348,
   3.8877
Pazos, Felipe. 4.4510
p'Bitek, Okot. 2.2310-2.2311
Peabody Institute, Baltimore. Library. 5.7528
Peabody Museum of Archaeology and
   Ethnology. 3.8882, 3.9045
Peabody, Robert L. joint author. 4.8012
Peabody, Robert L. ed. 4.8061
Peabody, Robert L. 4.8135
Peace Research Institute-Dundas. 4.9247
Peace, Richard Arthur. 2.1493
Peaceman, Donald W. 5.6806
Peacey, J. G. 5.6786
Peach, Bernard, 1918- ed. 1.1428
Peach, Ceri. 4.4874
Peach, William Nelson. 4.4127
Peacock, Alan T., 1922-. 4.4643, 4.4645, 4.4688
Peacock, Ronald, 1907-. 2.13570
Peacock, Thomas Love, 1785-1866. 2.7992
Peak, G. Wayne, joint author. 4.10642
Peake, Arthur Samuel, 1865-1929, ed. 1.2524
Peake, Dorothy Margaret, ed. 5.8132
Peake, Mervyn Laurence, 1911-1968. 2.8705,
   2.9220
Peale, Charles Willson, 1741-1827. 1.5961
Pearce, Frank. 4.6782
Pearce, I. F. (Ivor F.) 4.4591
Pearce, John K., 1935-. 5.4819
Pearce, Richard, 1932-. 2.10641
Pearce, Roy Harvey. 2.10475, 2.12550, 3.5804
Pearce, Roy Harvey. ed. 2.11280
Pearce, T. M. (Thomas Matthews), 1902-.
   2.10471
Pearcy, George Etzel, 1905-. 3.1156
Peardon, Lloyd G. 5.6739
Pearl, Anita May. 2.1147
Pearl, David, 1921-. 4.5738, 5.5093
Pearlman, Michael, 1944-. 5.7369
Pearlman, Moshe, 1911-. 3.3887
Pearman, A. D. joint author. 4.4043
Pearman, Richard A. 5.6557
Pearman, William A., 1940-. 5.8293
Pears, David Francis. ed. 1.769, 1.1270
Pearsall, Derek Albert. 2.5593, 2.5756, 2.6328,
   2.6390
Pearse, Andrew Chernocke. 4.2901
Pearse, Padraic, 1879-1916. 2.9221
Pearson, Alfred Chilton, 1861- ed. 2.541
Pearson, Carl E. 5.1114, 5.1672
Pearson, Charles S. 4.1818
Pearson, Donald Emanual, 1914- joint author.
   5.2731
Pearson, Frederick, 1936-. 4.214
Pearson, Gabriel. 2.7658
Pearson, H. 3.3659
Pearson, Hesketh, 1887-1964. 2.3335, 2.7729,
   2.8049, 2.8078, 2.8283
Pearson, J. D. 3.3659
Pearson, J. D. (James Douglas), 1911-. 5.8049,
   5.8452
Pearson, Karl 1857-1936. 5.919
Pearson, Lester B. 3.8786, 4.9089
Pearson, Lionel Ignacius Cusack. 3.2570,
   3.2572, 3.2631
Pearson, Norman Holmes, 1909-1975. 2.3739,
   2.12341
Pearson, Paul David, 1936-. 1.5445
Pearson, Ralph G. comp. 5.2863
Pearson, Ralph G. 5.2890
Pearson, Ralph G. joint author. 5.2708
Pearson, Roger, 1927-. 4.409
Peary, Gerald. 2.3016

Pease, Otis A. 3.6259
Peaslee, Amos Jenkins, 1887-. 4.9270, 4.9379
Peate, Iorwerth Cyfeiliog, 1901-. 3.1753
Peatross, C. Ford. 1.5284
Peattie, Lisa Redfield. 4.2809, 4.5278
Peattie, Mark R., 1930-. 3.4966, 4.8939
Peavy, Charles D. 2.13148
Peavy, Howard S. 5.5987
Pebay-Peyroula, Jean Claude, 1930- joint
    author. 5.2128
Pebworth, Ted-Larry. joint author. 2.6603
Peccei, Aurelio. 3.76, 3.214
Pechman, Joseph A., 1918-. 4.4658, 4.4692,
    4.4698, 4.4712, 4.9765
Peck, Arthur Leslie, 1902-. 2.328, 2.341
Peck, David R. joint author. 5.7949
Peck, Ellen, 1942- joint author. 4.5514
Peck, H. Daniel. 2.10976
Peck, Louis Francis, 1904-. 2.7913
Peck, Merton J. 4.3838
Peck, Ralph B. (Ralph Brazelton) 5.5919
Peck, Ralph Brazleton, joint author. 5.5908
Peckham, Howard Henry, 1910-. 3.6931-3.6932,
    3.8397
Peckham, Morse. 1.444
Peckolick, Alan. 1.5838
Pecsok, Robert L. 5.6823
Pede, William Harwood, 1913- ed. 3.8207
Peden, Margaret Sayers. 2.5318
Peden, William Harwood, 1913-. 2.10580
Pedersen, Holger, 1867-1953. 2.40
Pedersen, Paul, 1936-. 5.467, 5.469
Pedicord, Harry William. 2.7031
Pedicord, Harry William. ed. 2.7234
Pedlosky, Joseph. 5.2493
Pedretti, Erica. 2.13904
Peebles, P. J. E. (Phillip James Edwin) 5.1876
Peebles, Patrick. 4.1259
Peek, Walter W., joint comp. 2.2322
Peel, Edwin Arthur. 5.622
Peel, J. D. Y. (John David Yeadon), 1941-.
    3.5356, 4.4841
Peel, Roy Victor, 1896-. 4.7957, 4.8194-4.8195
Peele, George, 1556-1596. 2.6644
Peele, Gillian, 1949-. 4.7316
Peele, Stanton. 5.4957
Peerman, Dean G. 1.2756
Peers, E. Allison (Edgar Allison), 1891-1952.
    1.3082, 2.899, 2.5106, 2.5145
Peers, William R. (William Raymond), 1914-.
    3.4497
Peets, Elbert, 1886-1968, joint author. 1.5581
Pegis, Anton Charles, 1905- ed. 1.3133, 1.3139
Pegrum, Dudley Frank, 1898-. 4.3888
Péguy, Charles, 1873-1914. 2.4644-2.4645
Pehlke, Robert D. 5.6763
Pei, Mario, 1901-. 2.13, 2.139
Peierls, Rudolf Ernst, Sir, 1907-. 5.2119
Peikari, Behrouz. joint author. 5.6278
Peil, Margaret. 4.6286
Peintner, Max. joint author. 1.5412
Peirats, José. 4.3665
Peirce, Charles S. (Charles Sanders), 1839-1914.
    1.619, 1.621-1.625, 2.82
Peirce, Neal R. 3.7844, 3.8540, 3.8590
Pelczar, Michael J. (Michael Joseph), 1916-.
    4.10620, 5.4438
Pelczynski, Z. A. 4.7450-4.7451
Pelikan, Jaroslav Jan, 1923-. 1.71, 1.2749,
    1.2852, 1.2940, 1.3206
Pelinka, Anton, 1941-. 4.7024
Pélissier, René. 3.5406
Pellat, Charles, 1914- tr. 2.1843
Pellauer, Mary D. 4.5953
Pellegrino, Charles R. 5.1877
Pellegrino, Edmund D., 1920-. 5.4556-5.4557
Pelletier, Jean, 1926-. 3.2824
Pelletier, Kenneth R. 4.4356
Pelletier, Paul A., 1944-. 5.814
Pellico, Silvio, 1789-1854. 2.5010
Pelling, Henry. 3.1639, 3.1658, 3.1708, 4.3408,
    4.8490, 4.8528, 4.8540-4.8541
Pellowski, Anne. 4.10317
Pells, Richard H. 3.6153, 3.6185
Pelotte, Donald E. 1.3272
Peltason, J. W. (Jack Walter), 1923-. 4.9738,
    4.10631
Pelton, Joseph N. 5.6396

Pember, Don R., 1939-. 4.9535
Pemberton, William E., 1940-. 4.7893
Pempel, T. J., 1942-. 4.2554
Pemsel, Helmut, 1928-. 3.542
Pen, J. (Jan), 1921-. 4.3137
Peña, Albert. joint author. 3.8328
Pendarvis, Edwina D. 4.10921
Pender, Harold, 1879- ed. 5.6262
Pendergast, James F. 3.5892
Penders, C. L. M. (Christian Lambert Maria),
    1928-. 3.4567, 3.4573
Pendle, George. 3.9229
Pendse, Shripad Narayan, 1913-. 2.1908
Penelhum, Terence, 1929-. 1.535
Penfield, Wilder, 1891-. 5.4340, 5.4345
Peng, Syd S., 1939-. 5.6749
Peng, Tsung-hung. 4.342
Penguin (Firm) defendant. 2.8968
Penlington, Norman. 3.8759
Penman, Bruce. 2.5004
Penman, Bruce. 2.4897
Penn, Theodore Z. 4.3845
Penn, William, 1644-1718. 1.3347, 3.8081
Pennak, Robert W. (Robert William) 5.3794,
    5.3825
Pennell, Joseph Stanley, 1908-1963. 2.12308
Penner, Norman. 4.7008
Penney, David W. 3.5733
Penney, Norman, 1858-, ed. 1.3355
Penniman, Clara. 4.4715
Penniman, Howard Rae, 1916-. 4.7735,
    4.8295-4.8296, 4.8492, 4.8621, 4.8625-4.8626
Penniman, T. K. (Thomas Kenneth), 1895-.
    4.413
Penninger, Frieda Elaine. 5.7957
Pennington, Anne Elizabeth. 2.1216
Pennington, Campbell W. 3.8911
Pennington, Jean A. Thompson. 5.7123
Pennington, Kenneth. 1.3153
Pennock, J. Roland (James Roland), 1906-.
    4.4918, 4.5028, 4.6958, 4.7247, 4.7249,
    4.7255-4.7256, 4.7516, 4.7572, 4.7581, 4.7635,
    4.7653, 4.7699, 4.7740, 4.7774, 4.9363,
    4.9370, 4.9381, 4.9699
Pennock, James Roland. 4.7705
Pennock, James Roland, 1906-. 4.7186
Pennsylvania Academy of the Fine Arts.
    1.4884, 1.5916
Pennsylvania State University. 5.4346
Pennsylvania. University. Dept. of
    Anthropology. 4.1576
Penny, D. (David), 1938-. 5.3398
Penny, Nicholas, 1949-. 1.5018
Pennycuick, John. 5.283
Penrose, Boies. 4.65
Penrose, Edith Tilton. 4.3764
Penrose, Roland, Sir. 1.5711, 1.6133
Penton, M. James, 1932-. 1.3377
Pentony, DeVere Edwin, 1924-. 4.10988
Peñuelas, Marcelino C., 1916-. 2.5235
Penzien, Joseph. joint author. 5.5855
Penzler, Otto. 2.71
Penzoldt, Peter. 2.5953
Pepitone-Rockwell, Fran. 4.5587
Peplau, Hildegard E. 5.5198
Peplau, Letitia Anne. 5.439
Peplow, Michael W. 2.12450
Peplow, Michael W. joint comp. 2.10695
Pepper, Bert, 1932- joint author. 5.4837
Pepper, J. Mae. 5.5169
Pepper, Max P., joint author. 5.4833
Pepper, Stephen Coburn, 1891-. 1.1378-1.1379,
    1.5147
Pepper, Suzanne. 3.4782
Pepys, Samuel, 1633-1703. 3.1503-3.1504,
    5.7463
Peradotto, John, 1933-. 4.5851
Percival, Ian, 1931-. 5.1626
Percival, John, 1937-. 3.1984
Percy, Thomas, 1729-1811. 2.6111, 2.7181
Percy, Walker, 1916-. 2.13239-2.13243
Percy, William Alexander, 1885-1942. ed.
    2.7978
Perdue, Theda, 1949-. 3.5851
Perec, Georges, 1936-1982. 2.4787-2.4788
Pereira, H. G. 5.4474
Pereira, Luiz Carlos Bresser. 4.2171

Perelman, S. J. (Sidney Joseph), 1904-. 2.3795,
    2.12309
Perera, Victor, 1934-. 3.8908
Péret, Benjamin, 1899-1959. 2.4646
Peretz, Don, 1922-. 3.3729
Peretz, Isaac Leib, 1851 or 2-1915.
    2.1809-2.1810
Pérez Galdós, Benito, 1843-1920. 2.5218-2.5223
Pérez Gómez, Alberto, 1949-. 1.5356
Pérez, Louis A., 1943-. 3.9094
Perez-Venero, Alex. 3.9082
Perfetti, Charles A. 5.397
Perham, Margery Freda, 1895-. 3.1671, 3.5049,
    3.5112, 4.8920
Perisic, Zoran. 5.7008
Perit-Dutaillis, Charles Edmond 1868-1947.
    3.1991
Perkin, H. R. (Harold Robert), 1924-. 5.4451
Perkin, Harold James. 4.5328
Perkins, Bradford, 1925-. 3.7109, 3.7113
Perkins, D. N., 1942-. 5.346
Perkins, David. 1.6685, 2.6090, 2.8325, 5.7619
Perkins, Dexter, 1889-. 3.448, 3.6407-3.6408,
    3.7646, 4.9053-4.9056
Perkins, Donald Francis, 1935-. 5.3276
Perkins, Donald H. 5.2463
Perkins, Dwight Heald. 4.2460
Perkins, Edwin J. 4.1905
Perkins, Eric John. 5.3253
Perkins, Frances, 1882-1965. 3.7681
Perkins, Henry C. (Henry Crawford) 5.6202
Perkins, Howard Cecil, ed. 3.7180
Perkins, Moreland, 1927-. 5.241
Perkins, Pheme. 1.2673, 1.2970
Perkins, Robert L., 1930-. 1.2229
Perkins, V. F., 1936-. 2.2966
Perkins, Van L. 4.2950
Perkinson, Henry J. 4.9968, 4.9986, 4.9994
Perl, Teri. 5.1090
Perl, William R. 3.1119
Perle, George, 1915-. 1.3813, 1.4451-1.4452
Perlin, George C. 4.8311
Perlis, Vivian. 1.3841, 1.3901, 1.3904
Perlman, Bennard B. 1.5897
Perlman, Daniel. 5.439
Perlman, Helen Harris. 4.6500
Perlman, Janice E. 4.5271
Perlman, Jim, 1951-. 2.11281
Perlman, Mark. 4.3361, 4.3387
Perlman, Richard. joint comp. 4.3110
Perlman, Richard. 4.3227
Perlman, Selig, 1888-. 4.3093, 4.3362
Perlmutter, Amos. 3.3931, 5.7160
Perlmutter, Daniel D. 5.6833a
Perlo, Victor. 3.6740
Perloff, Marjorie. 2.12054, 2.12265
Perls, Frederick S. 5.179, 5.4866, 5.4892
Perman, Michael. 3.7469, 3.8169
Permanent International Altaistic Conference.
    5th, Bloomington, Ind., 1962. 3.3618
Pernick, Martin S. 5.5034
Pernoud, Régine, 1909-. 3.1996
Perón, Eva, 1919-1952. 3.9251
Perosa, Alessandro, 1910-. 2.815
Perret, Yvonne M., 1946-. 5.5082
Perrett, W. 5.1914
Perrin, D. D. (Douglas Dalzell), 1922-. 5.6848
Perrin, Dawn R. joint author. 5.6848
Perrin, Noel. 3.4938, 5.7699
Perrin, Norman. 1.2632, 1.2662, 1.2817, 1.2853
Perrine, Laurence. 2.2734
Perrins, Christopher M. 5.3940, 5.3942
Perrone, Gail. 5.8358
Perrow, Charles. 4.4911-4.4912, 5.5551
Perroy, Édouard. 3.1999
Perrucci, Carolyn Cummings. 5.805
Perry, B. E. (Ben Edwin), 1892-1968. 2.271
Perry, Bliss, 1860-1954. 2.10254
Perry, Charles R. 4.3219, 4.3388
Perry, David C. 4.6240
Perry, Edward S., joint author. 5.8141
Perry, Elizabeth J. 3.4674
Perry, Gillian. 1.4997
Perry, James W. (James Whitney), 1907-.
    2.1225
Perry, Janet. 2.5184
Perry, John R. 3.4081
Perry, Lewis, 1938-. 3.6154, 3.7231

Perry, Margaret, 1933-. 5.8191
Perry, Marvin. 3.3
Perry, Matthew Calbraith, 1794-1858. 3.4880
Perry, Michael J. 4.9674
Perry, Olney R., joint author. 5.1236
Perry, R. A. 5.3541
Perry, Ralph Barton, 1876-1957. 1.458, 1.603, 1.1303, 3.6155
Perry, Regenia. 1.4916
Perry, Robert H., 1924-. 5.6827
Perry, Roger, 1940-. 5.6050
Perry, Tilden Wayne. 5.5444
Perry, William E. 4.4406
Pers, Jessica S., joint author. 4.10728
Perse, Saint-John, 1889-1975. 2.4601-2.4602
Pershing, John J. (John Joseph), 1860-1948. 3.815
Persichetti, Vincent, 1915-. 1.4466
Persico, Enrico, 1900-. 5.2440
Persius. 2.646, 2.673, 2.702
Person, Henry Axel, 1903- ed. 2.6138
Perugi, Liberto. 1.5734
Pescatello, Ann M. 4.5906
Peschel, Enid Rhodes. 2.3924
Peshkin, Alan. 4.10811
Peskett, Arthur George, tr. 2.652
Peskin, Allan. 3.7488
Peskin, Henry M. 4.2076
Pessen, Edward, 1920-. 3.7079, 4.2112
Pessoa, Fernando, 1888-1935. 2.5458
Pestel, Eduard C. joint author. 4.1791
Petch, Simon. 2.8946
Petchenik, Barbara Bartz. 4.158, 4.209, 4.235
Peter, John Desmond, 1921-. 2.10049
Peterkiewicz, Jerzy, 1916-. 2.1745
Peterkin, Julia Mood, 1880-1961. 2.12310-2.12312
Peters, A. R. 3.2440
Peters, Edward, 1936-. 4.9555, 5.683
Peters, Erskine. 2.11698
Peters, F. E. (Francis E.) 1.1903, 1.1996, 3.3706
Peters, Gary L. 4.357
Peters, Gordon B. 1.4182
Peters, Guy. joint author. 4.4648
Peters, Helen. 2.6458
Peters, James Arthur, 1922- ed. 5.3435
Peters, Jean, 1935-. 5.7539
Peters, Joseph, 1951-. 5.3016
Peters, Lawrence J. 5.1192
Peters, Margot. 2.3337, 2.7453, 2.8079
Peters, R. S. (Richard Stanley), 1919-. 1.672, 4.10238, 5.70
Peters, Robert Anthony, 1926-. 2.971
Peters, Thomas J. 4.2748
Peters, William C. 5.6732
Petersen, Barbara A., 1945-. 1.4000
Petersen, Dan. 5.5555
Petersen, Karen, 1943-. 1.4583
Petersen, Norman R., 1933-. 1.2642
Petersen, Robert P. 4.5527
Petersen, Svend, 1911-. 4.8109
Petersen, William. 4.1584, 4.1590
Peterson, Carl R., joint author. 5.6674
Peterson, Charles S. 3.8583
Peterson, Edward Norman. 3.2406, 3.2460
Peterson, Frank Ross. 3.8551
Peterson, George E. 4.4705
Peterson, George L. 4.2826
Peterson, Gerald R. joint author. 5.6478
Peterson, James Lyle. 5.1193
Peterson, Jean Treloggen, 1942-. 3.4588
Peterson, John, 1947-. 3.4058
Peterson, Joseph L., 1945-. 4.6809
Peterson, Lee. 5.3659
Peterson, Linda Kauffman. 5.7721
Peterson, Mark A., 1944-. 4.6784
Peterson, Merrill D. 3.7063, 3.7065
Peterson, Merrill D. ed. 3.6972
Peterson, Nancy L. 4.5772
Peterson, Owen, 1924- ed. 2.10859
Peterson, Paul E. 4.8848, 4.10662
Peterson, Penelope L. 4.10312
Peterson, Rein, 1937-. 4.2673
Peterson, Richard E. 4.10973
Peterson, Richard F. 2.8923, 2.8951
Peterson, Roger L. 5.6393

Peterson, Roger Tory. 5.3659, 5.3676, 5.3950, 5.3954, 5.3960
Peterson, Susan (Susan Harnly) 3.5944
Peterson, Theodore Bernard, 1918-. 2.3546, 2.3640
Peterson, Trudy Huskamp, 1945-. 4.2944
Peterson, Virginia Marie, 1925-. 5.3950
Peterson, William S. 2.8245
Petesch, Natalie L. M., 1924-. 2.13249
Pethick, Derek, 1920-. 3.8594, 3.8865
Pethybridge, Roger William, 1934-. 3.3535, 4.5371
Petit-Dutaillis, Charles Edmond, 1868-1947. 4.8384
Petit, Jacques, 1928-. 2.4628
Petit, Paul. 3.2794
Petley, B. W. (Brian William) 5.2025
Petr z Mladenovic, d.1451. 1.3299
Petrarca, Francesco, 1304-1374. 1.409, 2.4946-2.4950, 2.6350
Petras, James F., 1937-. 3.9170
Pétrement, Simone. 1.860
Petrides, George A. 5.3689
Petrie, Charles, Sir, 1895-. 3.618-3.619
Petro, Sylvester, 1917-. 4.3363
Petronio, Giuseppe. ed. 2.4996
Petronius Arbiter. 2.683, 2.757
Petropulos, John Anthony. 3.2699
Petrov, Evgeniĭ, 1903-1942. joint author. 2.1565
Petrovich, Michael Boro. 3.691
Petrow, Richard. 3.1058
Petrowski, Dorothy D. 5.5208
Petrucelli, R. Joseph. joint author. 5.4505
Petry, Ann Lane, 1911-. 2.12313
Petry, Michael John. tr. 1.929
Petry, Ray C, 1903- ed. 1.3079
Petter, Henri. 2.10603
Pettet, E. C. 2.6763
Pettet, Ernest Charles. 2.7866
Petteys, Chris. 1.4588
Pettigrew, Thomas F. 3.6721
Pettijohn, F. J. (Francis John), 1904-. 5.3057-5.3058, 5.3063, 5.3065
Pettit, Arthur G. 2.10971
Pettit, Florence Harvey. 5.6904
Pettit, Henry, 1906-. 2.6261
Pettit, Norman. 1.3332
Pettman, Mary. 1.4665
Petty, Walter Thomas, 1918- joint author. 4.10476
Petulla, Joseph M. 4.2079
Petyt, K. M. 2.208
Petzoldt, Richard, 1907-. 1.4017
Peursen, Cornelis Anthonie van, 1920-. 1.521
Pevsner, Lucille W. 3.3593
Pevsner, Nikolaus. 1.4647, 1.4758, 1.4791, 1.4931, 1.5204-1.5205, 1.5355, 1.5513, 1.5526, 1.6508
Pey, Santiago. 2.895
Peyer, Bernd. 3.5712
Peyre, Henri, 1901-. 2.2699, 2.3880, 2.4143, 3.6158
Peyser, Joan. 1.3676
Pezeu-Massabuau, Jacques. 4.2555
Pfadt, Robert E. ed. 5.5407
Pfaff, Françoise. 2.3068
Pfaff, G. (Günther), 1951-. 5.5646
Pfaff, William, 1928-. 3.752
Pfafflin, J. R. (James R.) 5.5983
Pfaltzgraff, Robert L. joint author. 4.9027
Pfaltzgraff, Robert L. 5.7251
Pfandl, Ludwig, 1881-. 2.5104
Pfau, Werner. 5.1745
Pfeffer, Arthur. 1.73
Pfeffer, Leo, 1910-. 4.9720
Pfeffer, Richard M., ed. 3.7851
Pfeiffer, Bruce Brooks. 1.5334
Pfeiffer, John E., 1915-. 4.450, 4.700
Pfeiffer, Rudolf. 1.75-1.76
Pfister, Oskar, 1873-1956. 5.148
Pfister, Richard L. joint author. 4.4139
Pflanze, Otto. 3.2314
Pflieger, Pat. 2.5968
Pfordresher, John. 2.7361
Pfouts, Jane H. (Jane Hoyer), 1921-1982. 4.6477
Phadampa Sangay, fl. 1100. 1.2104
Phadke, Narayan Sitaram. 2.1909

Phadnis, Urmila, 1931-. 3.4368
Pharr, Susan J. 4.5958
Phelan, John Leddy, 1924-. 3.4597, 3.9314
Phelan, Josephine. 3.8729
Phelps, Edmund S. 4.1510
Phelps, Edmund S. ed. 4.4652
Phelps, Frederick M. 5.2312
Phelps, Robert, 1922-. 2.4483, 2.4488, 2.4499
Phelps, Steven. 1.4690
Phelps-Stokes Fund. 3.6610
Phelps, William Lyon, 1865-1943. 2.7212
Phi Delta Kappa. 4.10166
Phi Delta Kappa. Center on Evaluation, Development, and Research. 4.10676
Phidd, Richard W. 4.2123
Philadelphia Museum of Art. 1.4972, 1.5038, 1.5712, 1.5970, 1.6368, 1.6460, 1.6488, 1.6607, 5.5636, 5.6924
Philadelphia Social History Project. 4.5215
Philadelphia. Temple University. Committee for Urban Studies. 3.8089
Philbrick, Francis Samuel, 1876-. 3.6355
Philbrick, Thomas. 2.10868
Philbrook Art Center. 1.6366
Philip, Alan Butt. 3.1769
Philip, Alexander John, 1879-. 2.7634
Philip Hamilton McMillan Memorial Publication Fund. 3.6024
Philip, Lotte Brand. 1.6263
Philip Morris Incorporated. 1.5946
Philippi, Donald L. 3.4929
Philippides, Marios, 1950-. 3.2678
Philippines (Republic). National Economic Council. 4.1256
Philips, Ambrose, 1674-1749. 2.7182
Philips, Billy U., 1947-. 5.8294
Philips, Cyril Henry, 1912- ed. 3.4214, 3.4280, 3.4287
Philips, Edith, ed. 1.6720
Philliber, William W., 1943-. 4.5194
Phillips, Bruce F. 5.3851
Phillips, C. S. G. (Courtenay Stanley Goss) 5.2696
Phillips, Cabell B. H. 3.7801
Phillips, Cecil R. joint author. 5.5562
Phillips, Charles L. 6.6190
Phillips, Clifton Jackson. 3.8394
Phillips Collection. 1.4897
Phillips, David Graham, 1867-1911. 2.12314-2.12315
Phillips, David W. 5.3823
Phillips, Derek L. 1.1084, 4.4975
Phillips, Frank Coles, 1902-. 5.2921
Phillips, Harlan Buddington, 1920-. 4.9814
Phillips, Harry R. 5.5364
Phillips, Harry T., 1915-. 5.4665
Phillips, John G. (John Gardner), 1917-. 5.1711
Phillips, Kevin P. 4.8225
Phillips, Mark, 1946-. 3.2833
Phillips, Melanie, 1951-. 5.4567
Phillips, Melba, 1907- joint author. 5.2342
Phillips, Merton Ogden, 1900-. 4.1865
Phillips, Michael Curtis. 2.7429
Phillips, Michael Joseph. 2.9130
Phillips, Norman R. 4.10252
Phillips, P. C. B. 4.1397
Phillips, Patricia (Ann Patricia) 4.727
Phillips, Richard A., joint author. 5.2284
Phillips, Robert L. (Robert Lester), 1938-. 5.7153
Phillips, Robert S. comp. 2.7674
Phillips, Robert S. 2.11795
Phillips, Sandra S., 1945-. 5.6929
Phillips, Thomas Raphael, 1892-. 5.7204, 5.7211
Phillips, Ulrich Bonnell, 1877-1934. 3.7194, 3.8122
Phillips, William, 1907 Nov. 14-. 2.1347, 2.2560, 2.3705-2.3706
Phillips, William Revell, 1929-. 5.3019
Phillipson, D. W. 4.745
Philmus, Robert M. 2.5980
Philo, of Alexandria. 1.338, 2.383
Philological quarterly. 5.7935
Philological Society (Great Britain) 2.1084
Philostratus, the Athenian, 2nd/3rd cent. 2.384-2.386
Philostratus, the Lemnian, 3rd cent. 2.384
Philostratus, the Younger, 3rd cent. 2.384

Philp, Kenneth R., 1941-. 3.129, 3.6266
Philpott, Thomas Lee. 3.8425
Phipps, Lenore Bolling. 5.4877
Phipps, Ramsay Weston, 1838-1923. 3.2092
Phra Thĕpwisutthimĕthĭ (Ngŭam), 1906-.
  1.1746
Phrantzĕs, Geōrgios, b. 1401. 3.2678
Phycological Society of America. 5.3708
Physiological Society (Great Britain) 5.4202
Piaget, Jean, 1896-. 4.10212, 4.10383, 4.10390,
  4.10397, 5.284, 5.334, 5.361, 5.548, 5.567,
  5.571-5.575, 5.588, 5.591, 5.593-5.594, 5.596,
  5.610
Pialorsi, Frank. comp. 4.10899
Pianka, Eric R. 5.3524
Piazzetta, Giovanni Battista. 1.5016
Picasso, Pablo, 1881-1973. 1.4979, 1.5145
Piccioni, Leon, ed. 2.5073
Pichanick, Valerie Kossew, 1936-. 2.7929
Pichler, Walter, 1936- joint author. 1.5412
Pichois, Claude. 2.4486
Pichois, Claude. ed. 2.4133, 2.4137
Pick, Bernhard, 1842-1917. 1.2194
Pick, F.W. (Frederick Walter) 1912-. 3.3307
Pick, John. 2.7826, 2.7835
Pickard-Cambridge, Arthur Wallace, Sir,
  1873-1952. 2.293, 2.304
Pickard, George L. 4.345
Picken, Stuart D. B. 1.2465
Pickering, Andrew. 5.2456
Pickering, James S. (James Sayre) 5.1709
Pickering, W. S. F. 1.1539
Pickersgill, J. W., 1905-. 3.8751, 3.8789
Pickett, S. T. A. 5.3577
Pickett, Velma Bernice. 2.187
Pickus, Robert. 5.8258
Pico della Mirandola, Giovanni, 1463-1494.
  1.418
Picó, Rafael. 3.9126, 4.2161
Picon, Gaëtan. 2.3871, 2.4611
Picón-Salas, Mariano, 1901-1965. 3.8971
Picquenard, Armel. 5.6427
Picquet, D. Cheryn. 5.8122
Piehl, Mel. 1.3117
Piene, Otto. 1.4837
Pieper, Josef, 1904-. 1.361
Piepkorn, Arthur Carl. 1.1874
Pierce, Bessie Louise, 1890-. 3.8413
Pierce, Catherine S., 1942-. 4.5678
Pierce, Frank, 1915- ed. 2.5452
Pierce, John Robinson, 1910-. 5.6351
Pierce, Phyllis S. 4.4619
Piercy, Marge. 2.13250-2.13251
Piercy, Nigel. 4.4113
Pierpont Morgan Library. 1.4594, 1.5012,
  1.5799
Pierre, Andrew J. 4.3839
Pierson, Frank Cook, 1911- joint editor. 4.3135
Pierson, George Wilson, 1904-. 3.6040, 3.6159,
  4.10999-4.11000
Pierson, Peter. 3.3443
Pierson, William Harvey, 1911-. 1.5287
Pieterse, Cosmo, 1930- comp. 2.10043
Pietzschke, Fritz. 2.912
Pieyre de Mandiargues, André, 1909-.
  2.4648-2.4650
Pigford, Thomas H. joint author. 5.6617
Piggott, Derek. 5.6687
Piggott, Stuart. 1.1672, 3.4243, 3.555, 4.707,
  4.728
Piggott, Stuart. ed. 3.116, 4.734
Pigman, William Ward, 1910-. 5.2762
Pignatti, Terisio, 1920-. 1.5792, 1.6207
Pigors, Paul John William, 1900-. 4.4365
Pigott, William, 1927- joint author. 4.4567
Pigou, A. C. (Arthur Cecil), 1877-1959. 4.1442,
  4.1446, 4.1451, 4.1568, 4.1777, 4.3197
Pijawka, K. D. (K. David) 5.6610
Pikarsky, Milton. 4.3920
Pike, Douglas Eugene, 1924-. 3.4482-3.4483
Pike, Douglas Henry, 1908-. 3.5559, 3.5586
Pike, Fredrick B. 3.6418, 3.9293, 4.7592
Pike, John G. 3.5492
Pike, Kenneth Lee, 1912-. 2.162, 2.184-2.185,
  2.1134
Pike, Rob. 5.1184
Pike, Ruth, 1931-. 4.5386
Pike, Ruth L. 5.4240

Pilbrow, Richard. 2.3144
Pilcher, George William. 1.3394
Pilgrim Trust (Great Britain) 4.9427
Pilkey, Walter D. 5.5730
Pilkington, William T. 2.10592
Pillai, K. G. J. 4.4078
Pillar, Paul R., 1947-. 4.9330
Pilling, John. 2.3746
Pil'niak, Boris, 1894-1937. 2.1612-2.1613
Piłsudski, Józef, 1867-1935. 3.3287
Pinar, William. 4.10422
Pinborg, Jan. 1.347
Pincherle, Marc, 1888-1974. 1.3843, 1.4032
Pinchot, Gifford, 1865-1946. 3.7443, 5.5307
Pinckney, Elise, ed. 3.8241
Pinckney, Eliza Lucas, 1723-1793. 3.8241
Pindar. 2.313, 2.387, 2.525-2.529
Pindas, Pablo. 4.5730
Pinder, David. 4.2363
Pinder, George Francis, 1942-. 4.287
Pinder-Wilson, Ralph H. 1.6612
Pindyck, Robert S. 4.1720, 4.3754
Pindyck, Robert S. joint author. 4.3790
Pine, Fred, 1931-. 5.603
Pine, Vanderlyn R. 4.868
Piñeiro, Martín. 5.5256
Pinero, Arthur Wing, Sir, 1855-1934.
  2.7994-2.7995
Pines, Ayala M. 5.409
Pines, David, 1924-. 5.2207
Pines, Herman, 1902-. 5.2757
Pines, Shlomo, 1908- ed. and tr. 1.1962
Pinget, Robert. 2.4651-2.4655
Pinion, F. B. 2.7376, 2.7769, 2.7797-2.7798,
  2.8171
Pinkava, Jan. 5.6856
Pinkney, Alphonso. 3.6741
Pinkney, David H. 3.2146, 3.2231
Pinkus, Benjamin, 1933-. 3.3998
Pinney, Thomas. ed. 2.7692, 3.1211
Pinsent, John, 1922-. 1.1651
Pinsky, Robert. 2.13252-2.13253
Pinson, Koppel Shub, 1904-1961. 3.2289
Pinter, Harold, 1930-. 2.9791
Pinther, Miklos. 4.185
Pinto-Duschinsky, Michael, 1943-. 4.8499,
  4.8515
Pinto, Vivian de Sola, 1895-. 2.5519, 2.5833,
  2.6163, 2.7226, 2.7231, 2.7238, 2.7431, 2.8956
Piore, Michael J. 4.3000, 4.3314
Piore, Michael J. joint author. 4.3218
Piotrow, Phyllis Tilson. 4.5691
Pious, Richard M., 1944-. 4.7929
Piovesana, Gino K. 1.1142
Piozzi, Hester Lynch, 1741-1821. 2.7082,
  2.7088, 2.7183-2.7184
Piper, Henry Dan. 2.11737
Piper, Henry Dan. ed. 2.10379
Pipes, Richard. ed. and tr. 3.3081
Pipes, Richard. ed. 3.3173
Pipes, Richard. 3.3043, 3.3153, 3.3209, 3.3256,
  4.9016
Pipkin, John. joint author. 4.6303
Pippard, A. B. 5.2034, 5.2251
Pirandello, Luigi, 1867-1936. 2.5055-2.5057
Piranesi, Giovanni Battista, 1720-1778, illus.
  3.2802
Pirazzoli-t'Serstevens, Michèle. 1.5449, 3.4697
Pirenne, Henri, 1862-1935. 3.578, 3.2969,
  4.1743, 4.8835
Pirenne, Jacques, 1891-. 3.521
Pirie, Gordon. 2.11118
Pirinen, Kauko. joint author. 3.3289
Pirone, Pascal Pompey, 1907-. 5.5390
Pirsig, Robert M. 3.340
Pisani, Donald J. 4.2933
Pisar, Samuel. 4.4154
Pisarev, D. I. (Dmitriĭ Ivanovich), 1840-1868.
  1.9
Piscatori, James P. 1.2076, 4.7325
Pisemskiĭ, Alekseĭ Feofilaktovich, 1820-1881.
  2.1406
Pissarro, Camille, 1830-1903. 1.6134-1.6135
Pissarro, Lucien, 1863-1944. 1.6134
Piston, Walter, 1894-1976. 1.4467, 1.4473,
  1.4490
Pitaevskiĭ, L. P. (Lev Petrovich) 5.1671, 5.2166,
  5.2359

Pitcher, George. 1.694, 1.1085
Pitcher, George. comp. 1.1086
Pitcher, Harvey J. 2.1484, 2.1494
Pitcher, Wallace S. ed. 5.3072
Pitkin, Hanna Fenichel. 4.7398, 4.7741
Pitt, David C. 4.516
Pitt, David G. (David George), 1921-. 2.9961
Pitt, G. J. 5.6793
Pitt-Rivers, Julian Alfred. ed. 4.5295
Pitt-Rivers, Julian Alfred. 3.3491
Pittau, Joseph. 4.8751
Pitts, Robert E. 4.4310
Piven, Frances Fox. 4.3600, 4.6525
Pizarro, Pedro, 16th cent. 3.9298
Pizer, Donald. comp. 2.10842
Pizer, Donald. ed. 2.2510
Pizer, Donald. 2.10386, 2.10558, 2.10609,
  2.10978, 2.11187, 2.11599
Pizey, J. S. 5.2740
Place, Charles Alpheus, 1866-. 1.5307
Place, Janey Ann, 1946-. 2.3045
Placher, William C. (William Carl), 1948-.
  1.2747
Placksin, Sally. 1.4270
Placzek, Adolf K. 1.5208
Plaine, Henry L. 3.152
Plaks, Andrew Henry, 1945-. 2.2170
Plamenatz, J. P. 1.720
Plamenatz, John Petrov. 1.1040, 4.7062, 4.7277
Planck, Max, 1858-1947. 5.920, 5.1918, 5.2146
Plano, Jack C. 4.7215, 4.7793, 4.8981, 4.9271
Plant, Katharine C. 4.7906
Plant, Marjorie. 5.7549
Plantinga, Alvin. 1.1254, 1.2831
Plantinga, Leon. 1.3665, 1.3840, 1.3984
Plantinga, Theodore, 1947-. 1.985
Plascov, Avi. 3.4032
Plaskin, Glenn. 1.4066
Plaskow, Judith. 1.1616, 1.2911
Plath, Aurelia Schober. 2.13261
Plath, Sylvia. 2.13254-2.13261
Platnauer, Maurice. 2.257, 2.261, 2.459
Platnick, Norman I. joint author. 5.3235
Plato. 1.244, 1.247-1.257, 2.388, 2.532-2.535,
  4.7342-4.7346, 4.7351
Platonov, Andreĭ Platonovich, 1899-1951.
  2.1600-2.1602
Platonov, S. F. (Sergeĭ Fedorovich), 1860-1933.
  3.3048, 3.3067, 3.3087, 3.3089-3.3090
Platt, Anthony M. comp. 4.6726
Platt, Colin. 4.6258
Platt, D. C. M. (Desmond Christopher Martin),
  1934-. 4.4188, 4.4629
Platt, Elizabeth T. (Elizabeth Tower),
  1900-1943. 5.8199
Platt, Gerald M. joint author. 4.10085
Platt, John Rader, 1918-. 1.1326
Platt, John Talbot. 2.1118
Platt, Robert S. (Robert Swanton), 1891-.
  3.8973
Platt, Rutherford H. 4.2829
Platts, John Thompson, 1830-1904. 2.1881
Plauger, P. J., 1944- joint author. 5.1183
Plaut, W. Gunther, 1912- ed. 1.1918
Plautus, Titus Maccius. 2.684, 2.703, 2.760
Playford, John. joint comp. 4.7312
Pleasants, Henry. 1.3472, 1.3765
Pleck, Joseph H. 4.5594
Plekhanov, Georgiĭ Valentinovich. 3.516
Plekhanov, Georgiĭ Valentinovich, 1856-1918.
  3.516
Plenzdorf, Ulrich, 1934-. 2.13907-2.13908
Plesur, Milton. 3.7422
Pletcher, David M. 3.6356, 3.7487, 4.4020
Pletcher, Derek. 5.6870
Pletcher, Richard H. 5.1660
Pliny, the Elder. 1.4711, 2.686-2.687
Pliny, the Younger. 2.685
Plischke, Elmer, 1914-. 5.8265
Ploeg, Frederick van der, 1956-. 4.1391
Plog, Fred. 3.5717, 3.5764
Plog, Stanley C. 5.4808
Plomer, William, 1903-1973. 2.9223-2.9224
Plonsey, Robert. 5.4288
Ploski, Harry A. 3.6626
Ploss, Sidney I. comp. 4.8639
Plotinus. 1.340-1.341, 2.389
Plotke, David. 4.7025

Plotnicov, Leonard, ed. 4.5464
Plotnik, Arthur. 2.2528
Plotz, Helen. 2.10759
Plucknett, Donald L., 1931-. 5.5321
Plucknett, Theodore Frank Thomas, 1897-1965. 4.9414
Plumb, J. H. (John Harold), 1911-. 3.1524, 3.1553, 4.2295, 4.8403
Plumley, J. Martin. 1.1329
Plumly, Stanley. 2.13266
Plummer, Charles, 1851-1927. 3.1311
Plummer, David T. 5.2793
Plummer, Gail. 2.3111
Plummer, John, 1919-. 1.6429
Plummer, Kenneth. 4.4805, 4.5517
Plummer, Robert H., joint author. 4.10557
Plumpton, C. (Charles) joint author. 5.2367
Plung, Daniel L. 5.5506
Plutarch. 2.390, 3.2512
Pluvier, Jan M. 3.4404
Poague, Leland A., 1948-. 2.3050
Poate, J. M. 5.6768
Poblete Troncoso, Moisés, 1893-. 4.3400
Pochman, Henry A. 2.11094
Pochmann, Henry A. (Henry August), 1901-1973. 3.6160
Pocock, David Francis. 4.483
Pocock, Gordon. 2.4013
Pocock, J. G. A. (John Greville Agard), 1924-. 4.7399
Podlecki, Anthony J. 2.416, 3.2606
Podolny, Walter. 5.6082, 5.6084
Podrazik, Walter J. 1.3626
Podro, Michael. 1.4655
Poe, Edgar Allan, 1809-1849. 2.11196-2.11197, 2.11199-2.11200
Poen, Monte M., 1930-. 3.7807
Poesse, Walter. 2.5203
Poggi, Jack, 1928-. 2.3198
Poggioli, Renato, 1907-1963. 1.6701, 2.1260, 2.1279, 2.2772
Pogorelov, A. V. (Alekseĭ Vasil'evich), 1919-. 5.1633
Pogrow, Stanley. 4.10293
Pogue, Forest C. 3.7612
Pohl, Frederik. 2.13267
Pohl, Reinhard, Dr. 4.2346
Poincaré, Henri, 1854-1912. 5.921
Poincelot, Raymond P., 1944-. 5.5337, 5.5354
Pointon, G. E. (Graham E.) 2.1096
Poirier, Frank E., 1940-. 5.4020, 5.4022
Poirier, Richard. joint ed. 2.5496
Poirier, Richard. 2.10255, 2.10421, 2.11125, 2.11756, 2.12106
Poirion, Daniel. 2.3840
Pois, Robert A. 1.4998
Pokagon, Simon, 1830-1899. 3.5794
Pokrovskiĭ, M. N. (Mikhail Nikolaevich), 1868-1932. 3.3004, 3.3044
Poláčková-Henley, Káča. 2.1681
Polak, Fred. 3.50, 3.68
Polak, Frederik Lodewijk. 3.50
Polakoff, Keith Ian. 3.7482
Polan, A. J. 4.7100
Polansky, Norman Alburt, 1918-. 4.6463, 4.6554
Polanyi, Karl, 1886-1964. 4.1311, 4.1728, 4.1759
Polanyi, Michael, 1891-. 1.140, 4.5029, 5.849, 5.922
Pole, J. R. (Jack Richon) 3.6880, 4.7742, 4.9698
Poleman, Thomas T. 4.2895
Polenberg, Richard. 4.5140
Polhemus, Robert M. 2.6010
Poliakov, Léon, 1910-. 3.4011
Police Foundation (U.S.) 4.6818
Polich, Suzanne M., 1943-. 4.6784
Policy Studies Institute. 4.8376
Polišenský, Josef V. 3.638
Polit, Denise F. 5.5188
Politès, Linos, 1906-. 2.566
Political and Economic Planning. 4.1598
Political Geography Working Party. 4.7500
Politzer, Heinrich, 1910-. 2.13799
Poliziano, Angelo, 1454-1494. 2.4973-2.4975
Polk, Dora. 2.9478
Polk, James. 3.8666

Polk, James K. (James Knox), 1795-1849. 3.7071, 3.7169
Polk, William Roe, 1929-. 3.3674
Polkinghorne, J. C., 1930-. 5.2072
Pollack, Alan, joint author. 5.1616
Pollack, Herman W. 5.5765
Pollack, Jack Harrison. 4.9833
Pollack, Jonathan D. 3.6430
Pollack, Norman. 4.8230
Pollack, Peter. 5.6920
Pollak, Michael, 1918-. 3.3944
Pollak, Otto, 1908-. 4.6692
Pollak, Richard. 2.3560
Pollard, A. F. (Albert Frederick), 1869-1948. 3.1401, 3.1412, 4.8456
Pollard, Alfred W. (Alfred William), 1859-1944. 2.6207, 5.7915-5.7916
Pollard, Arthur. 2.8240
Pollard, Arthur. comp. 2.7619
Pollard, David E. 2.2243
Pollard, Ernest C. (Ernest Charles), 1906- joint author. 5.3496
Pollard, J. Graham (John Graham), 1929-. 3.281
Pollard, J. H. 4.1585
Pollard, James Edward, 1894-. 3.6310
Pollard, Sidney. 4.2209, 4.2283
Pollard, Sidney. comp. 4.2208
Pollitt, J. J. (Jerome Jordan), 1934-. 1.4719
Pollock, Bruce. 1.4281
Pollock, Frederick, Sir, 1845-1937. 4.9364, 4.9408
Pollock, George H. 5.511
Pollock, Gisella Linder. 5.2633
Pollock, Griselda. 1.5194
Pollock, Jackson, 1912-1956. 1.4902-1.4903
Pollock, John Charles. 1.3042, 3.1580
Pollock, Linda A. 4.5704
Pollock, Thomas Clark, 1902-. 2.3231
Polloway, Edward A. 4.10945
Polmar, Norman. 5.7442
Polner, Murray. joint author. 4.10894
Polonsky, Antony. 3.3286, 3.3331, 3.3985
Polsby, Nelson W. joint author. 4.8423
Polsby, Nelson W. 4.7944, 4.7967, 4.8869
Polsby, Nelson W. comp. 4.7920, 4.8014
Polsky, Howard W., joint author. 4.6883
Polsky, Ned. 4.5141
Polt, John Herman Richard, 1929-. 2.5392
Poltrack, David. 4.4439
Polya, George, 1887-. 5.1048, 5.1059, 5.1120, 5.1424
Polybius. 2.391
Polycarp, Saint, Bishop of Smyrna. 2.327
Polycarpus, Saint, Bp. of Smyrna. Epistola ad Philippenses. 1.2181
Polynesian Society, Wellington. 3.5622
Polytechnic Institute of Brooklyn. 4.4030
Polyviou, Polyvios G., 1949-. 3.3698, 4.9395
Pomerance, Bernard. 2.9796
Pomerleau, Cynthia S. 4.4540
Pomeroy, Earl Spencer, 1915-. 3.8488, 3.8591
Pomeroy, Lawrence R., 1925-. 5.3558
Pomeroy, Sarah B. 4.5848, 4.5854
Pomeroy, Wardell Baxter. 4.5497
Pomeroy, Wardell Baxter. joint author. 4.5494
Pomfret, John Edwin, 1898-. 3.6205, 3.6874, 3.8066-3.8067
Pommier, Jean, 1893-1973. 2.4051
Pomorska, Krystyna. ed. 2.1327
Pomorska, Krystyna. joint comp. 2.1242
Pomorska, Krystyna. 2.33
Pompa, Leon. 1.1090-1.1091
Pomper, Gerald M. 4.7859, 4.7960, 4.7962-4.7963
Pomper, Philip. 3.3126
Ponchaud, François, 1939-. 3.4449
Ponchie, Jean-Pierre. 1.43
Ponder, Wade H. 5.6823
Pondy, Louis R. joint ed. 4.4351
Ponge, Francis. 2.4656-2.4657
Ponsonby-Fane, Richard Arthur Brabazon, 1878-1937. 1.1839
Pontaut, Alain, 1925-. 2.4832
Pontecorvo, G. 5.3436
Pontecorvo, Giulio, 1923- joint author. 5.5484
Pontell, Henry N., 1950-. 4.6913

Pontin, A. J. 5.3583
Ponting, Herbert George. 4.107
Ponting, Kenneth G. 4.3850, 4.3856
Pontriagin, L. S. (Lev Semenovich), 1908-. 5.1597
Pool, Ithiel de Sola, 1917-. 4.4074, 4.7582
Poole, Austin Lane, 1889-1963. 3.1299, 3.1325, 4.8389
Poole, Reginald Lane, 1857-1939. ed. 3.1242
Poole, Richard, 1945-. 2.2342
Poole, Robert W., 1944-. 4.3081
Poole, Stafford. ed. 3.8990
Poole, William Frederick, 1821-1894. 1.36
Pooley, D. (Derek) joint author. 5.2194
Pooley, Robert Cecil, 1898-. 2.961
Poor, Janet Meakin. 5.5362
Poore, Benjamin Perley, 1820-1887. 5.7772
Poortmans, J. R. 5.4266
Poovey, Mary. 2.5729
Pope, Alexander, 1688-1744. 2.7186-2.7189, 2.7191-2.7192, 2.7194-2.7195
Pope, Arthur Upham, 1881-1969. ed. 1.5045
Pope, Carl. 5.6039
Pope, Daniel, 1946-. 4.4427
Pope-Hennessy, James. 2.8126, 2.8233
Pope-Hennessy, John, 1913-. 1.6223
Pope-Hennessy, John Wyndham, 1913-. 1.5721-1.5723, 1.5739, 1.6202, 1.6228
Pope-Hennessy, Una Birch, Dame, 1876-1949. 2.7881, 2.8050
Pope, Kenneth S. 5.441
Pope, Mildred Katharine, 1872-. 2.863
Pope, Norris, 1945-. 2.7671
Pope, Robert G. 1.3399
Pope, Willard Bissell. ed. 2.7468
Popelka, Gerald R. 5.5040
Popenoe, Cris. 4.7153
Popenoe, David, 1932-. 4.6352
Popenoe, Oliver. 4.7153
Popham, Janet, 1948-. 2.9808
Popkewitz, Thomas S. 4.10446
Popkin, Henry. ed. 2.6247
Popkin, Richard Henry, 1923-. 1.398, 1.408
Popkin, Samuel L. 4.2921
Poplin, Mary S., 1951-. 4.10927
Popov, E. P. (Egor Paul), 1913-. 5.5778
Popova, L. P. (Lucy P.) 2.1238
Popovics, Sandor, 1921-. 5.5801
Popper, Karl Raimund, Sir, 1902-. 1.118, 1.758, 1.1307, 3.489, 5.923-5.924
Popperwell, Ronald G. joint author. 2.13966
Popperwell, Ronald G. 3.3376
Poppino, Rollie E. 3.9203
Population Council. 4.1712, 4.5639, 5.4255
Porac, Clare. 5.237
Porada, Edith, 1912-. 1.4710
Porat, Dan I. 5.6472
Porath, Yehoshua. 3.3919-3.3920
Porcari, Serafino, joint author. 5.8226
Porcher, Jean. joint author. 1.4741
Porcher, Jean. 1.5170, 1.6414
Pore, Renate, 1943-. 4.6126
Porges, Stephen W. 5.4312
Porizek, Radoslav. joint author. 5.6414
Pörnbacher, Karl. 2.13589
Porphyry, ca. 234-ca. 305. 1.291, 1.340
Port, Michael Harry. 1.5515
Port of Oakland. Maritime Division. 4.3949
Porta, Carlo Antonio Melchiore Filippo, 1775-1821. 2.5011
Porta, Giambattista della, 1535?-1615. 2.4976
Portal, Roger. 3.3514
Porte, Joel. 2.11022, 2.11026
Porte, Michael Harry. 1.5515
Porter, Alan L. 5.5539
Porter, Arabel J. 2.2653
Porter, Bernard. 3.1227, 4.8914
Porter, Bruce D. 3.3346, 3.8277, 5.7327
Porter, Charlotte Endymion, 1859-1942. ed. 2.7463
Porter, David D. (David Dixon), 1813-1891. 3.7391
Porter, David T. 2.11006
Porter, Dorothy Burnett, 1905- comp. 2.10699
Porter, Eliot, 1901-. 5.6980
Porter, Fairfield. 1.5935
Porter, Gareth, 1942- joint author. 4.5437
Porter, Glenn. 4.1882, 4.4291
Porter, Hal. 2.10161-2.10162

Porter, John A. 4.5248
Porter, John R. 1.6000
Porter, Katherine Anne, 1890-1980.
  2.12316-2.12317, 2.12320
Porter, Kenneth R. 5.3919
Porter, Keyes, 1887- ed. 1.3542
Porter, Kirk Harold, 1891-. 4.8074
Porter, M. Gilbert. 2.11363, 2.13112
Porter, Maurice M. 1.4548
Porter, Michael E., 1947-. 4.2674-4.2675, 4.2739
Porter, Peter. 2.6193, 2.9797
Porter, Raymond J. 2.9222, 2.9859
Porter, Robert. 1.6746
Porter, Roger B. 4.2004
Porter, Roy, 1946-. 3.79, 5.724, 5.2954
Porter, Stephen C. 5.3145
Porter, Timothy. 4.3818
Porter, William Earl. 2.53
Porterfield, Amanda, 1947-. 4.6067
Portis, Alan M., 1926-. 5.2364
Portland International Wolf Symposium (1979)
  5.3995
Portmann, Adolf, 1897-. 5.3581
Portney, Paul R. 4.1898, 4.2073, 4.2076
Portoghesi, Paolo. 1.5277
Portugal, Franklin H. 5.4420
Porzio, Domenico, 1921-. 1.6499
Posada, José Guadalupe, 1852-1913. 1.6451
Pöschl, Viktor. 2.803
Posey, Alexander Lawrence, 1873-1908. 2.11213
Posey, Minnie (Harris) ed. 2.11213
Posgate, Dale. joint author. 4.5250
Poslusny, Elsa. 5.5202
Posner, Donald. 1.4775, 1.6157
Posner, Edward C., 1933- joint author. 5.6351
Posner, Ernst. 3.268
Posner, Michael I. 5.286
Posner, Richard A. 4.7658, 4.9504
Pospielovsky, Dimitry, 1935-. 1.3116
Post, Chandler Rathfon, 1881-1959. 1.5612,
  1.6286
Post, D. E. (Douglass Edmund), 1945-. 5.2449
Post, Elizabeth L. 1.1517
Post, Emily, 1873-1960. 1.1517
Post, James E., joint author. 4.2706
Post, Ken, 1935-. 4.8802
Post, Melville Davisson, 1871-1930. 2.12322
Postan, M. M. (Michael Moïssey), 1899-1981.
  4.2187, 4.2256, 4.4226, 4.5858
Poster, Mark. 1.824
Postgate, John Percival, 1853-1926, tr. 2.647,
  2.655
Postgate, Raymond William, 1896-1971. 2.9798,
  3.665, 3.1517
Postlethwaite, T. Neville. 4.10136, 4.10141,
  4.10167
Postlewait, Thomas. 5.965
Postman, Neil. 4.10041
Poston, Carol H. 4.6101
Poston, T. 5.1622
Postow, Betsy C., 1945-. 4.966
Potash, Robert A., 1921-. 5.7293
Potholm, Christian P., 1940-. 4.8796
Pottage, John, 1924-. 5.1034
Potter, David, 1915- comp. 2.10855
Potter, David Morris. 3.6161, 3.6217, 3.7181,
  3.7310, 3.8152, 3.8163
Potter, E. B. (Elmer Belmont), 1908-. 3.543
Potter, George Reuben, 1895-1954. 1.3309
Potter, George Richard, 1900-. 1.2353
Potter, George W. 3.6554
Potter, Jack M. 4.645
Potter, Joseph E. 4.1626
Potter, Karl H. comp. 1.179
Potter, Karl H. 1.184, 1.195
Potter, Kenneth Reginald. 3.1344
Potter, Neal. 4.4130
Potter, Norman N. 5.6885
Potter, Paul Edwin. joint author. 5.3057
Potter, Paul Edwin. 5.3063, 5.3065
Potter, Sandee. 4.5525
Pottinger, George. 3.1638
Pottker, Janice. 4.10780
Pottle, Frederick Albert, 1897-. 2.2739, 2.6908
Potts, Abbie Findlay, 1884-1964. 2.8307
Potts, Louis M., 1944-. 3.7003
Potts, Timothy C. 1.363
Potts, Willard, 1929-. 2.8918

Potvin, Gilles, 1923-. 1.3538
Pouchert, Charles J. 5.2679, 5.2683
Pough, Frederick H. 5.3018
Pough, Richard Hooper, 1904-. 5.3955, 5.3959
Poulantzas, Nicos Ar. 4.7455-4.7456
Poulet, Georges. 2.3835, 2.3858, 2.3875, 2.4675
Poulet, Robert, 1893-. 2.4507
Poulin, A. 2.10765
Poullada, Leon B., 1913-. 3.4117, 5.8042
Poulton, Diana. 1.3856
Poulton, Helen J. 5.8222
Pouncey, Peter R. 3.2611
Pound, Dorothy. 2.12335
Pound, Ezra, 1885-1972. 2.2420, 2.2449,
  2.2584-2.2586, 2.2682, 2.3713,
  2.12323-2.12326, 2.12329, 2.12333,
  2.12335-2.12336, 2.12338, 2.12341
Pound, Omar S. 2.12335
Pound, Roscoe, 1870-1964. 4.7698, 4.9345,
  4.9365, 4.9404, 4.9482
Pounds, Norman John Greville. 3.529-3.530,
  4.2237
Povey, John. 2.10062
Powderly, Terence Vincent, 1849-1924. 4.3593
Powdermaker, Hortense, 1903-1970. 2.2931
Powell, Adam Clayton, 1908-1972. 3.7679
Powell, Alan, 1936-. 3.5587
Powell, Anthony, 1905-. 2.9225-2.9232
Powell, Arthur G., 1937-. 4.10509
Powell, David, 1925-. 2.7569
Powell, Helen. 1.5488
Powell, J. David, 1938- joint author. 5.6182
Powell, James M. 3.569
Powell, Jocelyn, 1938-. 2.5899
Powell, John T. 4.1023
Powell, John Wesley, 1834-1902. 3.8562
Powell, Judy. 5.5333
Powell, Lawrence Clark, 1906-. 2.11933, 3.8579
Powell, Lawrence Fitzroy, 1881- ed. 2.7085
Powell, Lawrence N. 4.2905
Powell, M. J. D. (Michael James David), 1936-.
  5.1315
Powell, Ralph L. 3.4737
Powell, Ronald R. 5.7644
Powell, Sumner Chilton, 1924-. 3.8008
Powell, T. G. E. (Thomas George Eyre), 1916-.
  3.556
Powell, Thomas F. 1.641
Powell, Thomas H. 4.6585
Powell, Thomas Reed, 1880-1955. 4.9647
Powell, W. J. A. joint author. 5.5957
Powell, Walter W. 5.7584
Powell, William Stevens, 1919-. 3.8227-3.8228
Powelson, John P., 1920-. 4.1802, 4.4148
Power, Eileen Edna, 1889-1940. 3.579, 4.2244,
  4.4226, 4.5858
Power, Jonathan, 1941-. 4.7646
Power, Paul F., ed. 3.4309
Power, Richard Lyle, 1896-. 3.8376
Power, Thomas Francis, 1916-. 4.8925
Powers, D. B. 2.1229
Powers, Edwin. 4.9857
Powers, Elizabeth, 1944-. 4.6146
Powers, Gary J., 1945- joint author. 5.6835
Powers, J. F. (James Farl), 1917-.
  2.13268-2.13271
Powers, Jonathan. 5.1919
Powers, Lyall Harris, 1924-. 2.11114
Powers, Richard Gid, 1944-. 4.6823
Powers, Richard H. 4.10736
Powers, Sharon B. 2.8097
Powers, Thomas, 1940 Dec. 12-. 4.7909
Powicke, F. M. (Frederick Maurice), 1879-1963.
  3.1245, 4.9975
Powicke, Frederick Maurice, 1879-. 3.1360
Powicke, Maurice, Sir. 3.1359
Powley, Edward Barzillai, 1887-1968. 3.646
Pownall, David E., 1925-. 5.8278
Powys, John Cowper, 1872-1963. 2.9235-2.9237,
  4.10725
Prache, Anne. joint author. 1.5241
Prados, John. 4.7910-4.7911
Prager, Dennis, 1948-. 3.4012
Prager, Willy, 1903-. 5.6665
Prain, Ronald, Sir, 1907-. 4.3740
Prais, S. J. 4.3836
Prall, Stuart E. 3.1496
Prandi, Alfonso, 1920- joint author. 4.8628

Prang, M. E. 4.9430
Prange, Gordon William, 1910-. 3.1035
Prasad, Dhirendra Mohan, 1935-. 3.4370
Prasad, S. Benjamin. joint author. 4.2741
Prasow, Paul. 4.9555
Prasse, Leona E. 1.6440
Prater, Donald A., 1918-. 2.13879
Prather, H. Leon, 1921-. 3.8234
Pratolini, Vasco, 1913-. 2.5060
Pratt, Annis. 2.5989
Pratt, Cranford. 4.7132
Pratt, E. J. (Edwin John), 1882-1964. 2.9959
Pratt, Fletcher, 1897-1956. 2.12354, 3.1023
Pratt, George C. 2.2883
Pratt, Jane. 4.4102
Pratt, John Clark. ed. 2.13109
Pratt, Julius William, 1888-. 3.7110, 3.7499
Pratt, Norman T. (Norman Twombly), 1911-.
  2.773
Pratt, Orson, 1811-1881. 1.3380
Pratt, Wallace Everett, 1885-. 5.6804
Prausnitz, J. M. joint author. 5.6860
Prawdin, Michael, 1894-. 3.3619
Prawer, Joshua. 3.596
Prawer, Siegbert Salomon, 1925- comp. 1.3460,
  2.13520
Praz, Mario, 1896-. 1.4773, 2.2386, 2.2660,
  2.5018, 2.5575, 2.6016
Pre-congress Conference on War, Its Causes
  and Correlates, University of Notre Dame,
  1973. 5.7154-5.7155
Préaud, Tamara. 1.6120
Prebish, Charles S. 1.2140
Prebish, Charles S. ed. 1.2137
Preble, Edward, 1922- joint author. 4.525
Pred, Allan Richard, 1936-. 4.1914
Predmore, Richard Lionel. 2.5178
Prelutsky, Jack. 2.10739
Premacanda, 1881-1936. 2.1890
Premack, David. 5.362
Preminger, Alex. 2.2706
Premo, Steven. ill. 3.5855
Prendergast, Christopher. 2.4127
Prendergast, Curtis. 5.7586
Prendergast, Guy Lushington. 2.517
Prendergast, Karen A. 5.999
Prendergast, Michael L., 1946-. 5.4956
Prenis, John. 5.6127
Prenshaw, Peggy Whitman. 2.10464, 2.12671
Prentice, Ann E. 5.8435
Prentis, Steve. 5.6865
Prentiss, Stan. 5.6433
Preobrazhenskiĭ, Aleksandr Grigor'evich, d.
  1918. 2.1232
Preobrazhenskiĭ, E. A. (Evgeniĭ Alekseevich),
  1886-1937. joint author. 4.7096
Presbrey, Frank, 1855-1936. 4.4420
Presch, William, joint author. 5.4111
Prescott, David M., 1926-. 5.3616
Prescott, Frederick Clarke, 1871-1957. 2.11199
Prescott, J. R. V. (John Robert Victor) 4.9310
Prescott, Kenneth Wade, 1920-. 1.6446
Prescott, Peter S. 2.10428
Prescott, William, 1939-. 4.10270
Prescott, William Hickling, 1796-1859. 2.11214,
  3.3436, 3.8925, 3.9299
President's Conference on Home Building and
  Home Ownership, Washington, D.C., 1931.
  3.6786
Presiding Bishop's Fund for World Relief
  (Episcopal Church) 4.6538
Presley, John R. 1.1347
Presniakov, A. E. (Aleksandr Evgen'evich),
  1870-1929. 3.3084, 3.3121
Press, Frank. 5.2967
Press, Gerald A. (Gerald Alan), 1945-. 3.490
Press, John. comp. 2.6102
Press, John. 2.9078, 2.9241
Pressat, Roland. 4.1620
Presser, Stanley, 1950-. 4.1229
Pressman, Jeffrey L. 4.3225
Pressnell, L. S. ed. 4.2250
Prest, John M. 3.1632, 5.3644
Prest, Wilfrid R. 4.9348
Prestage, Jewel Limar, 1931-. 4.5972
Presthus, Robert Vance. 4.8292
Preston, Adrian W. 3.774
Preston, Antony, 1938-. 5.7438-5.7439

Preston, David A. joint author. 4.2144
Preston, Dickson J., 1914-. 3.7241
Preston, Howard L. 4.2041
Preston, Kendall, 1927-. 5.1374
Preston, Lee E. 4.2706
Preston, Michael B. 3.6711
Preston, Paul, 1946-. 3.3459, 3.3463, 3.3474
Preston, Richard Arthur. ed. 3.6417
Preston, Richard Arthur. 3.538, 3.6157, 3.8657, 4.8277, 5.7302
Preston, Samuel H. 4.1649
Preston, William, 1924-. 3.7551
Prestwich, Michael. 3.1363
Pretzel, Ulrich. 2.1192
Preusch, Deb. 4.4628
Prevenier, Walter. 3.2958
Prévert, Jacques, 1900-. 2.4659-2.4660
Previté-Orton, Charles William, 1877-1947. 3.559, 3.574
Previts, Gary John. 4.4389
Prévost, abbé, 1697-1763. 2.4083
Prévost, Antoine François, called Prévost d'Exiles, 1697-1763. 2.4084
Prevost, Gary. 3.3477
Prewett, Omer, 1939-. 5.2455
Price, Alan Frederick. 2.8152
Price, Cecil John Layton. ed. 2.7245
Price, Cecil John Layton. 2.3342, 2.7247
Price, Charles C. (Charles Coale), 1913-. 5.2767
Price, Curtis Alexander, 1945-. 1.3951
Price, David C. 1.3719
Price, David Eugene. 4.8164, 4.9737
Price, Derek J. de Solla (Derek John de Solla), 1922-1983. 5.850, 5.962
Price, Derek John de Solla. 5.851
Price, Don C. 3.4746
Price, George R. 2.6572
Price, Glanville. 2.214
Price, H. H. (Henry Habberley), 1899-. 1.1299
Price, Henry Habberley, 1899-. 1.1295
Price, Hugh Douglas. 4.7862
Price, Jacob M. ed. 3.429
Price, John Valdimir. 1.1551
Price, Lucien, 1883-. 1.775
Price-Mars, Jean, 1876-1969. 4.786
Price, Miles Oscar, 1890-1968. 4.9471
Price, Percival, 1901-. 3.266
Price, Peter W. 5.3858
Price, Reynolds, 1933-. 2.13272-2.13275
Price, Richard, 1941-. 3.6924, 3.9186, 4.6426
Price, Roger. 3.2151
Price, S. R. F. 3.2742
Price, Steven D. 1.4311
Price, Thomas, 1907- joint author. 3.5494
Price, William J. (William James), 1918-. 5.2443
Prichard, Edward Fretwell. 4.8065
Prichard, Mari. 2.2702
Prickett, Stephen. 2.5717
Pridham, B. R., 1934-. 3.4063, 4.2449
Pridham, Geoffrey, 1942-. 3.2445, 3.3476
Priebsch, Robert, 1866-1935. 2.1177
Pries, Nancy. 5.8111
Priest, Harold Martin, ed. 2.3738
Priestley, F. E. L. (Francis Ethelbert Louis), 1905- ed. 4.7420
Priestley, J. B. (John Boynton), 1894-. 2.6063, 2.7641, 2.7942, 2.9242-2.9250, 2.9946, 3.1731
Priestley, Joseph. 1.2, 5.702
Prieto, Antonio. 2.5088
Prigogine, I. (Ilya) 5.925
Prigogine, I. (Ilya) joint author. 5.2244
Primeaux, Martha, 1930-. 5.4662
Primrose, S. B. joint author. 5.3459
Prince, Hal. 2.3262
Prince, Judith Sosebee, joint author. 4.10279
Prince, Melvin. 4.4311
Princeton Conference on Chinese Narrative Theory, Princeton University, 1974. 2.2170
Princeton University. Art Museum. 1.6312, 1.6330, 1.6370, 1.6390, 1.6416, 1.6532
Princeton University. Center for Environmental Studies. 5.6157
Princeton University. Industrial Relations Section. 3.3116, 4.4499
Princeton University. Office of Population Research. 4.1639, 4.1700, 4.1710

Princeton University. Program of Study in American Civilization. 3.6081
Princeton University. Water Resources Program. 5.6009
Prindl, Andreas R. 4.4546
Pring, J. T. (Julian Talbot) 2.250
Pringle, Henry. 3.7712
Pringle, Henry Fowles, 1897-1958. 3.7705
Pringle, Mary Beth, 1943-. 2.2415
Pringle, Peter. 5.2454
Pringsheim, Ernst Georg, 1881-. 5.3706
Prins, Gwyn. 3.5520
Print Council of America. 5.8188
Printz-Påhlson, Göran, 1931-. 2.14063
Prinz, Martin. 5.3016
Prior, Arthur N. 1.1192, 1.1218-1.1219
Prior, Mary. 4.6110
Prior, Matthew, 1664-1721. 2.7206
Prior, Moody Erasmus, 1901-   . 2.6771
Prishvin, Mikhail Mikhaĭlovich, 1873-1954. 2.1523, 5.3231
Prisk, Berneice. 2.3127
Pritam, Amrita. 2.1915-2.1916
Pritchard, Allan, ed. 2.6955
Pritchard, Colin. 4.6531
Pritchard, James Bennett, 1909-. 1.2572-1.2574
Pritchard, John. 3.900
Pritchard, William H. 2.10496, 2.11757
Pritchett, C. Herman (Charles Herman), 1907-. 4.9629, 4.9632, 4.9675-4.9676, 4.9778
Pritchett, John Perry, 1902-. 3.8859
Pritchett, V. S. (Victor Sawdon), 1900-. 2.2651, 2.2665, 2.4126, 2.6265, 2.7947, 2.8118, 2.9253-2.9255
Pritchett, W. Kendrick (William Kendrick), 1909-. 2.450, 5.7181
Pritchett, William L. 5.5426
Prittie, Terence, 1913-. 3.2465, 3.2473-3.2474
Private Planning Association of Canada. 4.4207
Priyadarsini, S., 1943-. 4.6901
Probst, Emil Heinrich, 1877-1950. ed. 5.5667
Procacci, Ugo. 1.6216
Procházka, Theodor. 3.1918
Procopiow, Norma. 2.12055
Procopius. 2.392, 3.2667
Procter, Evelyn Emma Stefanos, 1897-. 3.3433
Professional Ski Instructors of America. 4.996
Professors World Peace Academy. Middle East Chapter. 4.6274
Proffer, Carl R. 2.1294, 2.1306, 2.1310, 2.1322, 2.1326, 2.1383, 2.1536
Proffer, Ellendea. 2.1294, 2.1306, 2.1310, 2.1322, 2.1326, 2.1544
Profio, A. Edward, 1931-. 5.2441
Project on Computer Databanks (National Academy of Sciences) 4.7696
Project to Improve College Teaching. 4.10572
Prokasy, William F. (William Frederick), 1930-. 5.304
Prokosch, Frederic, 1908-. 2.12355
Pronin, Barbara. 4.10682
Pronko, Leonard Cabell. 2.3891, 2.4362, 5.8069
Pronzini, Bill. 2.10548, 2.10838
Propertius, Sextus. 2.688, 2.764-2.765
Propp, V. IA. (Vladimir IAkovlevich), 1895-1970. 2.1293, 4.797, 4.821
Prosch, Harry, 1917- joint author. 1.140
Proshansky, Harold M., 1920- ed. 4.4992
Prosser, C. Ladd (Clifford Ladd), 1907-. 5.4181
Prosser, Franklin P. 5.6587
Prosser, William Lloyd, 1898-. 4.9516
Prothero, R. Mansell. joint ed. 4.1708
Prothero, R. Mansell. comp. 4.2870
Prothero, R. Mansell. 4.1654
Proudhon, P.-J. (Pierre-Joseph), 1809-1865. 4.1560
Prouse, Giovanni, joint author. 5.1555
Proust, Marcel, 1871-1922. 2.4661-2.4662, 2.4666-2.4670
Prouty, Charles Tyler, 1909-. 2.3318, 2.6581
Provencher, Ronald. 3.4385
Provine, William B. 5.3348, 5.3367
Provine, William B. comp. 5.3437
Prown, Jules David. 1.5888, 1.5930
Prpic, George J. 3.6541
Prucha, Francis Paul. comp. 3.5805, 4.9773
Prucha, Francis Paul. 3.5806-3.5807, 3.5849, 3.6371, 5.7743-5.7744

Prude, Jonathan. 4.2036
Prudentius, b. 348. 2.689
Prueitt, Melvin L. 1.5119
Pruessen, Ronald W. 3.7637
Pruessen, Ronald W. ed. 3.7597
Prus, Bolesław, 1847-1912. 2.1702
Průšek, Jaroslav. 2.1757, 2.2160
Prutton, M. 5.2210
Pruyser, Paul W., 1916-. 5.629
Prybyla, Jan S. 4.1327, 4.2484
Pryce-Jones, David, 1936-. 2.9506, 3.1066
Pryde, Duncan, 1937-. 3.5880
Pryde, George Smith, 1899-1961. 4.8561
Pryde, Philip R. 5.5304
Pryke, Kenneth G., 1932-. 3.8804
Pryor, Anthony, 1951- joint author. 4.1818
Pryor, Ruth. 2.9476
Pryse, Marjorie, 1948-. 2.10318, 2.11034
Prytherch, Raymond John. 5.7696
Przebienda, Edward, joint author. 2.1107
Przibram, Karl, 1878- comp. 5.2146
P'u, Sung-ling, 1640-1715. 2.2232
Public Affairs Conference Center. 4.8163
Public Affairs Information Service. 5.8356
Public Archives Canada. 1.6448
Public Education Association of the City of New York. 1.4823
Public Management Institute. 4.6527
Public Works Historical Society. 5.8388
Pucci, Pietro. 2.461
Puccini, Giacomo, 1858-1924. 1.3949
Puchala, Donald James, 1939-. 4.2888
Pucher, John R. joint author. 4.3915
Pudovkin, Vsevolod Illarionovich, 1893-1953. 2.2967
Puette, William J. 2.2048
Puff, C. Richard. 5.331
Pugh, A. (Alan) 5.1015
Pugh, Anthony. 5.5865
Pugh, Derek Salman. 4.2657
Pugh, Martin. 3.1623
Puhvel, Jaan. 1.1637
Puig, Manuel. 2.5400-2.5403
Pulci, Luigi, 1432-1484. 2.4977
Puligandla, R., 1930-. 1.182
Pullan, Brian S. 3.2844, 3.3978
Pulleyblank, Edwin G. (Edwin George), 1922-. 3.4701
Pullin, Faith. 2.11171
Pulos, Arthur J. 5.7013
Pulzer, Peter G. J. 3.4015, 4.8491
Pumpian-Mindlin, Eugene, 1908-1976, ed. 5.181
Punnett, R. M. (Robert Malcolm) 4.8445
Punter, David. 2.5626
Purcell, Gary R. 5.7603
Purcell, John Francis, 1916-. 5.6159
Purcell, Keith F., 1932-. 5.2702
Purcell, Sally, 1944- ed. 2.3969
Purcell, Victor, 1896-1965. 3.4389, 3.4738
Purdie, Edna, 1894-. 2.13600
Purdom, C. B. 2.8071
Purdom, C. B. (Charles Benjamin), 1883-. 2.8086
Purdy, James. 2.12356-2.12360, 2.12844
Purdy, James Malcolm. 2.12358
Purdy, Richard Little. 2.7772
Purkey, William Watson. joint author. 5.466
Purkis, John Arthur, 1933-. 2.8315
Purnal, Roland. 2.4234
Purpel, David E. 4.10807, 4.10809
Purrington, Robert D. 5.1864
Purseglove, J. W. (John William), 1921-. 5.5331
Pursell, Carroll W. ed. 5.5534
Purser, Louis Claude, 1854-1932, ed. 2.714
Purtle, Carol J., 1939-. 1.6263a
Purver, Margery. 5.697
Purves, William K. (William Kirkwood), 1934-. 5.3301
Purvis, J. S. (John Stanley), 1890-. 2.6211
Puryear, Paul Lionel, 1930-. 3.6711
Puschmann, Th. (Theodor), 1844-1899. 5.4599
Pusey, Merlo John, 1905-. 3.7647
Pushkarev, Boris. joint author. 1.5600
Pushkarev, Boris. 4.3909
Pushkarev, Sergeĭ Germanovich, 1888-. 3.3002, 3.3030, 3.3036
Pushkin, Aleksandr Sergeevich, 1799-1837. 2.1407-2.1415, 3.3585

Putnam, Donald F., 1903-1977. 3.8662
Putnam, Hilary. 1.1167
Putnam, Michael C. J. 2.782, 2.791, 2.794, 2.804
Putnam, Robert D. 4.7523, 4.8367
Putnam, Samuel, 1892-1950. 2.5172, 2.5174, 2.5462, 3.9214
Putney, Gail J. joint author. 5.627
Putney, Snell. 5.627
Putt, Arlene M. 5.5183
Puttenham, George, d. 1590. supposed author. 2.2719
Puttenham, Richard, 1520?-1601? supposed author. 2.2719
Puxon, Grattan. joint author. 3.5681
Puyana de Palacios, Alicia, 1941-. 4.2163
Pužman, Josef. 5.6414
Pye, David, 1932- joint author. 5.4097
Pye, David W., 1914-. 5.7041
Pye, Lucian W., 1921-. 3.4540, 3.4754, 3.4833, 3.4843, 4.7776
Pyenson, Lewis. 5.1940
Pyke, Magnus. 5.6886
Pyle, Gerald F. 5.4704
Pyle, Hilary. 2.9385
Pyle, Kenneth B. 3.4898
Pyle, Robert Michael. 5.3882
Pylee, M. V. (Moolamattom Varkey), 1922-. 4.8702
Pyles, Thomas, 1905-. 2.972
Pym, Barbara. 2.9799-2.9802
Pyman, Avril. 2.1471
Pyman, Avril. ed. 2.1469
Pynchon, Thomas. 2.13277-2.13278, 2.13281-2.13282
Pyne, Stephen J., 1949-. 5.5428-5.5429
Pyre, James Francis Augustin, 1871-1934. joint ed. 2.6170
Pyre, James Francis Augustine, 1871-1934, joint ed. 2.6171
Pyron, Darden Asbury. 2.12197

Qāsim, Samīḥ. 2.1840
Qian, Hao. 3.4627
Quade, E. S. (Edward S.) 4.1236
Quah, Jon S. T. 4.8729
Qualitz, Joseph E., 1948- joint author. 5.1370
Qualls, Barry V. 2.6027
Quance, C. Leroy, joint author. 4.2954
Quandt, Richard E. joint author. 4.1297, 4.1434
Quandt, William B. 3.3939
Quantz, Johann Joachim, 1697-1773. 1.4552
Quarles, Benjamin. comp. 3.7274
Quarles, Benjamin. 3.6951, 3.7258, 3.7288, 3.7389
Quarles, Francis, 1592-1644. 2.7208
Quarmby, David. 5.6380
Quarton, Gardner C., ed. 5.4321
Quasha, George. joint comp. 2.3741
Quasimodo, Salvatore, 1901-1968. 2.5061-2.5062
Quataert, Jean H. 4.5868, 4.6127
Queen, Ellery. ed. 2.3716
Queen, Ellery. 2.12363-2.12364, 5.8173
Queen, Stuart Alfred, 1890-. 4.5555
Quehen, Hugh de. 2.6926
Queirós, Eça de, 1845-1900. 2.5455-2.5456
Queneau, Raymond, 1903-1976. 1.935, 2.4676-2.4681
Quennell, Peter, 1905-. 2.7522, 2.8037, 2.9256
Quenouille, M. H. joint author. 5.986
Quental, Antero de, 1842-1891. 2.5459
Quesnay, François, 1694-1774. 4.1407
Quester, George H. 4.9009, 4.9175
Quezon, Philippines. Ateneo de Manila. Institute of Philippine Literature. 2.2290
Quhistani, Abu Ashaq. 1.2094
Quick, Michael. 1.5947
Quigley, Austin E., 1942-. 2.3280
Quigley, Ellen, 1955-. 2.9878
Quigley, John M. joint author. 4.3493
Quigley, Stephen Patrick, 1927-. 4.6605
Quiller-Couch, Arthur Thomas, Sir, 1863-1944. 2.2587, 2.2652, 2.5547-2.5550, 2.6100, 2.6179, 2.6250, 2.6801, 2.6817
Quilligan, Maureen, 1944-. 2.5579
Quilliot, Roger. 2.4440, 2.4442, 2.4459
Quimby, George Irving, 1913-. 3.227, 3.5737, 5.7000

Quimby, Robert S. 5.7316
Quine, W. V. (Willard Van Orman) 1.121, 1.545-1.546, 1.631-1.632, 1.1168, 1.1179, 1.1220
Quine, Willard Van Orman, 1908-. 1.1178
Quiney, Anthony, 1935-. 1.5396
Quinn, Alison M. 3.5969
Quinn, Arthur Hobson, 1875-1960. 2.10256, 2.10513-2.10514, 2.11203
Quinn, David B. 3.5969-3.5970, 3.8198
Quinn, David Beers, 1909-   . 3.5990
Quinn, Edward. 1.4992
Quinn, Edward G., 1932-. 2.2784, 2.6684, 2.6797
Quinn, Herbert Furlong, 1910-. 3.8687, 4.8316
Quinn, Kenneth. 2.711-2.712, 2.805
Quinn, Mary Bernetta. 2.12349
Quinn, Peter J. 5.3610
Quinn, Seabury. 2.12365
Quinn, T. J. (Terry J.) 5.2233
Quinn, Vincent Gerard, 1926-. 2.11574
Quinn, William H. 4.5799
Quinnam, Barbara. 5.7717
Quiney, Richard. 4.4807, 4.6697
Quint, Howard H. 4.6993
Quintana, Ricardo. 2.6235, 2.7303
Quintana, Ricardo. ed. 2.6166
Quintilian. 2.690
Quirk, Randolph. 2.140, 2.932, 2.995-2.996
Quirk, Robert E. 3.8948
Quiroga, Horacio, 1878-1937. 2.5441-2.5442
Qureshi, Ishtiaq Husain. 3.4197

R.R. Bowker Company. 1.4591, 4.10330, 5.7539, 5.7660, 5.7705, 5.7749, 5.7755-5.7757, 5.8107
R.R. Bowker Company. Book Division. 5.7594
R.R. Bowker Company. Dept. of Bibliography. 5.7593, 5.7764
R.R. Bowker Company, New York. 5.7659
R.R. Bowker Company. Publications Systems Dept. 5.7593
Raab, Earl. joint author. 3.6389
Raabe, Paul. 5.8009
Raabe, Wilhelm, 1831-1910. 2.13640
Raabe, Wilhelm Karl, 1831-1910. 2.13641
Ra'anan, Uri, 1926-. 5.7251
Raat, W. Dirk (William Dirk), 1939-. 5.7898
Rabb, Theodore K. 3.1155
Rabbat, Guy. 5.6531
Rabchevsky, George A., 1936-. 4.24
Rabe, David. 2.13289-2.13290
Rabearivelo, Jean Joseph, 1901-1937. 2.4857
Rabelais, François, ca. 1490-1553? 2.4003-2.4004
Rabin, Albert I. ed. 5.576
Rabin, Albert I. 4.5744
Rabiner, Lawrence R., 1943-. 5.6569
Rabinovich, Itamar, 1942-. 3.3789
Rabinovitz, Rubin. 2.6042, 2.8432
Rabinowitch, Alexander. 3.3009, 3.3202
Rabinowitch, Alexander. ed. 3.3137
Rabinowitch, Janet, ed. 3.3137
Rabinowitz, Howard N., 1942-. 3.6636
Rabinowitz, Philip. joint author. 5.1432
Rabinowitz, William. 4.10165
Rabkin, Eric S. 2.2393
Rabkin, Eric S. joint author. 2.3491
Rabon, Israel, b. 1900. 2.1815
Raboteau, Albert J. 1.2420
Raboy, Isaac. 2.1816
Raby, Frederic James Edward, 1888-. 2.811-2.813
Race, Jeffrey. 3.4491
Race, Robert Russell. 5.4225
Rachal, Patricia, ed. 4.6673
Rachal, William M. E., ed. 3.6975
Rachewiltz, Igor de. 4.96
Rachlin, Robert, 1937-. 4.4599
Rachman, Stanley. joint author. 5.4927
Racine, Jean, 1639-1699. 2.4046-2.4049
Rackham, Arthur, 1867-1939. 2.7750
Rackham, Harris, 1868-. 2.338, 2.344, 2.350-2.351, 2.656, 2.664, 2.666, 2.686-2.687
Rackin, Phyllis. 2.6791
Rad, Gerhard von, 1901-1971. 1.2579, 1.2596, 1.2608
Radcliffe, Ann Ward, 1764-1823. 2.7997

Radcliffe-Brown, A. R. (Alfred Reginald), 1881-1955. 4.490, 4.582, 4.606
Radcliffe College. 3.352
Radcliffe, Philip, 1905-. 1.3927
Raddatz, Fritz Joachim. joint ed. 2.13866
Radelet, Louis A. 4.6802
Rademacher, Hans, 1892-1969. 5.1260, 5.1331
Rademaker, C. S. M. 2.232
Rademaker, O. 5.6841
Rader, Benjamin G. 4.981, 4.1371
Rader, Charles M. joint author. 5.6376
Rader, Melvin Miller, 1903-. 1.1041, 1.1347a, 1.1381
Rader, Ralph Wilson, 1930-. 2.8163
Radfield, Robert, 1897-. 3.8956
Radford, Albert E. joint author. 5.3719
Radford, Andrew. 2.164
Radford, John. 5.388
Radhakrishnan, S. (Sarvepalli), 1888-1975. 1.126, 1.185-1.187, 1.1682, 1.1818
Radhakrishnan, S. (Sarvepalli), 1888-1975. 1.176
Radice, Betty. tr. 2.685
Radice, H. K. (Hugo K.) 4.2351
Radiguet, Raymond, 1903-1923. 2.4683-2.4684
Radin, Dorothea Prall. 2.1706
Radin, Paul, 1883-1959. 3.5959, 4.552
Radine, Lawrence B. 5.7161
Radio Telefís Éireann. 3.1816
Radishchev, Aleksandr Nikolaevich, 1749-1802. 4.5375
Radisson, Pierre Esprit, ca. 1636-1710. 3.8846
Radkey, Oliver Henry. 3.3190
Radler, Rudolf, 1934-. 2.2352
Radner, Daisie. 1.801
Radner, Daisie. 1.801
Radosh, Ronald. 3.7596, 4.9461
Radwan, Samir Muhammad. 4.2993
Radwān, Samīr Muhammad. 4.2591
Radwanski, George. 3.8793
Radway, Janice A., 1949-. 5.7725
Radzinowicz, Leon. 4.6681, 4.9427
Radzinowicz, Mary Ann. 2.7143, 2.10839
Rae, Catherine M., 1914-. 2.12695
Rae, Douglas W. 4.4959
Rae, John Bell, 1911-. 4.3824-4.3826, 4.3939
Rae, Kenneth, ed. 2.3089
Raeburn, John. 3.2037
Raeburn, Michael. 1.5209
Raeder, Erich, 1876-1960. 3.2352
Raeff, Marc. ed. 3.3023, 3.3103
Raeff, Marc. 3.3091
Raeside, Ian. tr. 2.1908
Raffel, Burton. 2.2287
Raffel, Burton. tr. 2.1576, 2.6284
Rafferty, Max Lewis, 1917-. 4.10253
Rafferty, S. S. 2.13291
Raffles, Thomas Stamford, Sir, 1781-1826. 3.4578
Rafiquzzaman, Mohamed. 5.1251
Rafter, Nicole Hahn, 1939-. 4.6780
Raghavan, V. (Venkatarama), 1908-. 1.1694
Raghunadha Rao, P. 3.4356
Raguin, Virginia Chieffo, 1941-. 1.6649
Ragus, Christopher. 5.6091
Ragusa, Olga. 2.5059
Rahbar, Daud, 1927-. 2.1904
Rahewin, d. 1177. 3.2270
Rahill, Frank. 2.2820
Rahman, Fazlur. 1.2032, 1.2051, 1.2063
Rahman, Mizanur. 3.4150
Rahn, Frank J. 5.5601
Rahner, Karl, 1904-. 1.2222, 1.2233, 1.2780, 1.2902, 1.2943, 1.3004, 1.3007, 1.3100, 1.3140-1.3141, 1.3202, 1.3223
Rahul, Ram. 3.4332, 3.4343
Rāhula, Walpola. 1.1768
Rahv, Philip, 1908-1973. 2.1323, 2.2588, 2.2653, 2.2666, 2.3705-2.3706
Rai, Gangeshwar. 2.8779
Rai, Sudha. 3.4168
Raibert, Marc H. 5.6169
Raiffa, Howard, 1924- joint author. 5.5600
Raimo, John, 1946-. 3.6285, 3.6861
Raina, Peter K., 1935-. 3.3347
Raine, Craig. 2.9803-2.9804
Raine, Kathleen, 1908-. 2.7416, 2.9257
Raine, Kathleen J. 2.7431

Raines, Howell. 3.6686
Raines, John C. 4.3206
Rainville, Earl David, 1907-. 5.1507-5.1508
Rainwater, Lee. 3.6772, 3.6779, 4.5692
Rainwater, Robert. joint author. 5.8181
Raisz, Erwin Josephus, 1893-. 4.205
Raitt, A. W. (Alan William) 2.4339
Raja Rao. 2.10130-2.10131
Rajagopalachari, C. (Chakravarti), 1878-1972. 2.2275
Raju, P. T. (Poolla Tirupati), 1904-. 1.188, 1.429
Rākeśa, Mohana, 1925-1972. 2.1889
Rakoff, Stuart H. 5.4640
Rakove, Milton L. 3.8418
Rakowska-Harmstone, Teresa. 4.7021
Raleigh, John Henry, 1920-. 2.7362, 2.12296
Raleigh, Walter, Sir, 1552?-1618. 2.6144-2.6145, 2.6501, 2.6717, 3.550
Ralston, Anthony. 5.1134
Ralston, Bruce A. joint author. 4.2783
Ralston, Jackson Harvey, 1857-1945. 4.9116
Ram Gopal, 1912-. 4.8717
Rama Rao Pappu, S. S. 1.182
Rama Rau, Santha, 1923-. 2.10132
Ramage, Janet, 1932-. 5.6134
Ramakrishna, 1836-1886. 1.210
Ramakrishna Rao, K. 5.637
Ramamoorthy, C. V. (Chittoor V.), 1926-. 5.1179
Ramanujan, A. K., 1929-. 2.2264, 2.2268, 2.2276, 2.2280
Ramaswamy, G. S., 1923-. 5.6097
Ramazani, Rouhollan K., 1928-. 3.3747
Ramazanoglu, Huseyin, 1947-. 4.2569
Rambert, Marie. 4.1156
Ramchand, Kenneth. 2.9979
Rameau, Pierre. 4.1089
Ramet, Pedro, 1949-. 1.1584
Ramirez, Bruce A. 4.9600
Ramirez, Bruno. 4.3573
Ramírez, Ronaldo. 4.6248
Rammelkamp, Julian S. 2.3669
Ramón y Cajal, Santiago, 1852-1934. 5.4118
Ramond, Pierre, 1943-. 5.2158
Ramos, Graciliano, 1892-1953. 2.5478
Rampersad, Arnold. 2.11609
Ramraj, Victor J. 2.9968
Ramsaur, Ernest Edmondson. 3.3587
Ramsay, Allan, 1685-1758. 2.7209
Ramsay, David, 1749-1815. 3.8235
Ramsay, George Gilbert, 1839-1921. 2.673
Ramsay, James Arthur. 5.4178
Ramsay, O. Bertrand (Ogden Bertrand), 1932-. 5.2874
Ramsaye, Terry, 1885-1954. 2.2927
Ramsdell, Charles William, 1877-1942. 3.7375
Ramsden, John, 1947-. 4.8530
Ramsey, Frederic, 1915- ed. 1.4332
Ramsey, Ian T. 1.2257
Ramsey, Jarold, 1937-. 2.2315
Ramsey, L. G. G. ed. 1.6505, 1.6524
Ramsey, Lee C., 1935-. 2.5620
Ramsey, Norman, 1915-. 5.2073
Ramsey, Paul. 1.1468, 2.7003, 5.4568-5.4569, 5.4607
Ramthun, Herta. 2.13701, 2.13705
Ramusack, Barbara N. 3.4288
Rana, A. P. 3.4232
Rana, Pashupati Shumshere J. B., 1941-. 3.4376
Rand, Ayn. 2.12366-2.12367
Rand Corporation. 3.6430, 3.9007, 4.2405, 4.2483, 4.6784, 4.7754, 5.7159, 5.7197, 5.7252
Rand, Edward Kennard, 1871-1945. 2.752, 3.135
Rand, G. K. (Graham K.) 5.5566
Rand McNally and Company. 4.113, 4.115, 4.123, 4.155, 4.159
Rand, Paul, 1914-. 1.5834
Randall, Alan, 1944-. 4.2826
Randall, Carrie L., 1947-. 5.4960
Randall, Clifford W. joint author. 5.6031
Randall, D. J. 5.3915
Randall, David J., 1938-. 5.4180
Randall, Elinor. 2.5366
Randall, Gerald. 1.5527
Randall, J. G. (James Garfield), 1881-1953. 3.7283, 3.7347, 4.7838

Randall, John Herman, 1899-. 1.409, 1.423, 1.445, 1.634, 2.11477
Randall, Laura Regina Rosenbaum. 4.2134, 4.2167
Randall, Margaret, 1936-. 4.6086
Randall, Merle, 1888-1950, joint author. 5.2249
Randall, Richard S. 4.9605
Randall, Ruth (Painter) 3.7289
Randall, Stephen J., 1944-. 4.3775
Randall, Vicky. 4.5960
Randel, Don Michael. 1.3504, 1.3506
Randel, William Peirce, 1909-. 2.11015
Randle, Robert F. 3.4437
Randles, Jenny. 5.6699
Randolph, Vance, 1892-. 1.3436, 2.1149, 2.10723, 4.778-4.779
Random House (Firm) 2.1068
Randsborg, Klavs. 3.3370
Ranelagh, John. 4.7912
Range, Willard, 1910-. 5.5243
Rangel Guerra, Alfonso. 4.10102
Ranger, T. O. (Terence O.) 3.5238, 3.5511, 4.824
Ranger, T. O. (Terence O.) ed. 1.1844
Ranis, Gustav. 5.855
Rank, Hugh. 2.13207
Ranke, Friedrich. 2.13529
Ranke, Leopold von, 1795-1886. 1.3145, 3.403, 3.491
Ránki, György, 1930-. 4.2238, 4.2349-4.2350
Rankin, H. D. 2.422
Rankin, Robb. 4.10672
Rankin, Robert A. (Robert Alexander), 1915-. 5.1336
Ranney, Austin. 3.7936, 4.7725, 4.7735, 4.7956, 4.8465, 4.8493
Ranney, Edward. 3.9284
Ransel, David L. 4.5625
Ransford, Oliver, 1914-. 5.4546
Ranshofen-Wertheimer, Egon Ferdinand, 1894-. 4.9188
Ransom, Charles, 1911-. 4.2221
Ransom, Harry Huntt, 1908-. 3.8321
Ransom, Hazel H. 3.8321
Ransom, Jay Ellis, 1914-. 5.3827
Ransom, John Crowe, ed. 2.2680, 2.2720, 2.2763, 2.12368-2.12369
Ransom, Roger L., 1938-. 4.2024
Ransom, Will, 1878-1955. 5.7548
Ransone, Coleman Bernard, 1920-. 4.8252
Ranum, Orest A. ed. 3.617
Ranum, Orest A. 3.2023
Rao, Dileep. 4.4442
Rao, V. K. R. V. (Vijendra Kasturi Ranga Varadaraja), 1908- ed. 4.2521
Rapaport, David. 5.162, 5.183, 5.184, 5.4848
Rapaport, David. ed. and tr. 5.4901
Raper, Julius Rowan, 1938-. 2.11780
Raphael, 1483-1520. 1.5815
Raphael, Bertram. 5.1127
Raphael, Chaim. 3.4005
Raphael, D. D. (David Daiches), 1916-. 4.1357, 4.7408
Raphael, Dana, 1926-. 4.571
Raphael, Elaine. 2.9685
Raphael, Ray. 4.10155
Raphael, Sylvia. 2.3818
Rapoport, Anatol, 1911-. 1.497-1.498, 3.6488, 5.1379
Rapp, Brian W. 4.8846
Rapp, George Robert, 1930-. 3.242
Rapp, Richard T. 4.2361
Rappaport, Roy A. 3.5655
Rappaport, Stephen P. joint author. 4.4729
Rappoport, Leon. 3.439
Rappoport, Zvi. 5.2754
Rapport, Samuel Berder, 1903-. 5.852
Rapson, E. J. (Edward James), 1861-1937. 3.4221
Rarey, Kanute P. 5.4996
Rashdall, Hastings, 1858-1924. 1.1439, 4.9975
Rashevsky, Nicolas, 1899-. 5.3495
Rashīd al-Dīn Ṭabīb, 1247?-1318. 3.517
Rashid, Jamil. 4.2518
Raskin, Eugene. 1.5477
Rasmo, Nicolò. 1.4957
Rasmussen, Knud, 1879-1933. 2.2314
Rasmussen, R. Kent. 3.5233

Rasmussen, Steen Eiler, 1898-. 1.5479, 3.1741
Rasmussen, Tom. 1.5224
Rasmussen, Wayne David, 1915-. 5.5219, 5.5238
Rasputin, Valentin Grigor'evich. 2.1629-2.1630
Rassam, Amal. 3.3701
Rastall, Richard. 1.4119
Ratchford, Fannie Elizabeth, 1888-. 2.7454
Rath, Reuben John, 1910-. 3.1893
Rathbone, Charles H., comp. 4.10118
Rathbun, John Wilbert, 1924-. 2.2511
Rathjen, Frederick W., 1929-. 3.8331
Rathjens, George W. 4.9167
Rathke, Ewald. 1.4852
Raths, Louis Edward. 4.10315
Ratliff, William E. 4.7011
Ratnam, K. J. joint author. 4.8726
Ratner, Joseph, 1901- ed. 1.586, 4.10227
Ratner, Lazarus G. 5.2447
Ratner, Leonard G. 1.3660, 1.4434
Ratner, Marc L. 2.13348
Ratté, John, 1936-. 1.3167
Rattigan, Terence, 1911-. 2.9258
Ratzel, Friedrich, 1844-1904. 4.367
Ratzinger, Joseph. 1.3004
Rauch, Basil, 1908-. 3.7768
Rauch, Georg von. 3.3305, 3.3308
Raum, Hans, 1940- joint author. 5.7850
Raup, David M. 5.3151
Rauschenbusch, Walter, 1861-1918. 1.2926
Rauschning, Hermann, 1887-. 3.2422
Raushenbush, Winifred. 4.4778
Raven, Alan. 5.7436
Raven, Charles E. (Charles Earle), 1885-1964. 5.3211
Raven, D. S. 2.245, 2.256
Raven, J. E. 1.265
Raven, J. E. (John Earle) 1.233
Raven, Peter H. 5.3642
Ravenhill, John. 4.2602
Ravenholt, Albert. 3.4609
Ravindranath, B. 5.6321
Ravitch, Diane. 4.9999-4.10000, 4.10017, 4.10099, 4.10816, 4.10964
Rawley, James A. 3.7174, 3.7400, 4.6422
Rawlings, Marjorie Kinnan, 1896-1953. 2.12375
Rawlins, Jack P. 2.8194
Rawlinson, George, 1812-1902. tr. 3.545
Rawlinson, H. G. (Hugh George), 1880-. 3.4169, 3.4244
Rawlinson, Jean. 4.1153
Rawls, John, 1921-. 4.7659
Rawls, Walton H. 1.6498
Rawlyk, George A. 3.8805
Rawson, Beryl. 3.2779
Rawson, Claude Julien. 2.7027, 2.7304
Rawson, Elizabeth. 3.95, 3.2784
Rawson, Jessica. 1.5068, 1.6670
Rawson, Philip S. 1.6625
Ray, Arthur J. 3.5729
Ray, Benjamin Caleb. 1.1848
Ray, Dorothy Jean. 3.5881-3.5883
Ray, Dvijendra Lala, 1863-1913. 2.1865
Ray, G. Carleton. 5.3906
Ray, G. F. (George Frank), 1915- ed. 4.1861
Ray, Gordon Norton, 1915-. 2.8186-2.8188
Ray, Lila. tr. 2.1862
Ray, Man, 1890-1976. 5.6960, 5.6977
Ray, Rajat Kanta. 4.4632
Rayback, Joseph G. 4.3559
Raychaudhuri, Tapan. 4.2496
Rayfield, Donald, 1942-. 3.4853
Rayleigh, John William Strutt, Baron, 1842-1919. 5.2223
Rayment, Paul Bernard Walter. 4.4164
Raymond, André. 4.6277
Raymond, Gregory A. joint author. 3.1199
Raymond, Jack, 1923-. 1.3619
Raymond, James C., 1940-. 2.964, 4.10753
Raymond, Marcel, 1897-. 2.3876, 2.4087
Raymond, William Ober, 1880-. 2.7491
Raynal, abbé, 1713-1796. 3.531
Raynor, Henry. 1.4358
Raynor, John Barrie. 5.2635
Raysor, Thomas Middleton, 1895- ed. 2.6726
Read, Benedict. 1.5687
Read, Campbell B. 5.1399

Read, Christopher, 1946-. 1.1674
Read, Clark P., 1921-. 5.4083
Read, Colin, 1943-. 3.8733
Read, Conyers, 1881-. 3.1435-3.1436, 3.1438, 5.7990
Read, Danny L., 1946- joint author. 1.3572
Read, Donald. 3.1594, 3.1601
Read, Frank Henry. 5.2361
Read, Gardner, 1913-. 1.4445-1.4446, 1.4491, 1.4536
Read, Herbert Edward, Sir, 1893-1968. 1.4577, 1.4599, 1.4639, 1.4755, 1.4824-1.4825, 1.5105, 1.5654, 1.5775, 1.5872, 2.1039, 2.2455, 2.2589-2.2591, 2.2721, 2.9259-2.9260, 2.11548, 4.7189, 4.10214
Read, James A. 4.3040
Read, Jan. 3.3431, 3.3485
Read, Jean B. 2.10164
Read, John. 1.6582
Read, John Lloyd, 1898-. 2.5330
Read, Malcolm. 2.13816
Read, Oliver. 5.7084
Reade, Brian. 1.5842
Reade, Charles, 1814-1884. 2.7999
Reading, England. University. Centre for the Advanced Study of Italian Society. 3.2906
Reading, H. G. 5.3060
Reading, Reid, 1937-. 3.9149
Ready, John F., 1932-. 5.5952
Reagan, Charles E. 1.847
Reagan, Christopher J., ed. 2.2396
Reagan, Michael D. 4.1993
Real Academia Española. 2.896
Real, James, joint author. 4.9160
Real, Michael R., 1940-. 4.5011
Reamer, Frederic G., 1953-. 4.6491
Reamy, Tom. 2.13292
Reaney, Percy Hide. 3.310
Reardon, Bernard M. G. 3.1966
Reardon, Betty. 4.9105
Reasons, Charles E., 1945-. 4.2129
Reavey, George, 1907- ed. 2.1314, 2.1593
Rebholz, Ronald A. 2.6435, 2.6549
Rébora, Piero, 1889-. 2.856
Rechcígl, Miloslav. 5.7124
Rechowicz, M. 5.6290
Recht, Roland. joint author. 1.5241
Reck, Andrew J. 1.563, 1.572
Reckless, Walter Cade. 4.6864
Record, Frank. 5.6005
Record, Wilson, 1916-. 3.6687
Reddaway, Peter. comp. 3.3258
Reddaway, William Fiddian, 1872-1949. 3.3276, 3.3309
Redden, John D. 4.10234
Reddick, John. 2.13766
Redding, J. Saunders (Jay Saunders), 1906-. 2.10329, 2.10694, 3.6628
Reddish, Vincent C. 5.1836
Reddy, Bandaru S. 5.4776
Reddy, J. N. (Junuthula Narasimha), 1945-. 5.1533, 5.5729
Reddy, William M. 4.3849
Redfearn, Paul L. 5.3703
Redfield, James M., 1935-. 2.503
Redfield, Margaret Park. 4.5413
Redfield, Robert. 3.59, 3.9043-3.9044, 4.402, 4.875, 4.4913
Redford, Emmette Shelburn, 1904-. 4.7885
Redgrave, G. R. (Gilbert Richard), b. 1844. joint author. 5.7915
Redgrave, Michael. 2.3121, 2.3353
Redgrave, Richard, 1804-1888. 1.6013
Redgrave, Samuel, 1802-1876. joint author. 1.6013
Redgrove, Peter. 2.9261
Redig de Campos, D. (Deoclecio) 1.4666
Redl, Fritz. 4.5721
Redlich, Frederick Carl, 1910- joint author. 5.4831
Redlich, Hans Ferdinand, 1903-1968. 1.3814, 1.3826
Redman, Ben Ray, 1896-1961. 2.1842, 2.4102
Redman, Charles L. 3.222, 3.237, 3.3707
Redman, Eric. 4.9736
Redman, G. P. 4.3173
Redmond, Walter Bernard. 5.8348
Redwood, Christopher, 1939-. 1.3850

Reed, Charles A. 4.718
Reed, Henry Hope. jt. author. 4.6230
Reed-Hill, Robert E. 5.6778
Reed, Hoyt Coe. 4.6802
Reed, Ishmael, 1938-. 2.13293-2.13295
Reed, James, 1944-. 4.5693
Reed, John, 1909-. 1.3979, 2.4845, 3.3191
Reed, John Robert, 1938-. 2.5720, 2.8261
Reed, Joseph W., 1932-. 2.11699
Reed, Marcia. 5.8111
Reed, Mark L. 2.8299
Reed, Michael, 1942-. 5.1974
Reed, Michael A. 3.1535
Reed, Phillip D. 4.9571
Reed, Roger. 1.5832
Reed, Ruddell. 5.7022
Reed, Stephen K. 5.389
Reed, Sue Welsh. 1.6460
Reed, T. J. (Terence James), 1937-. 2.13838
Reed, Terry, 1937-. 2.11469
Reed, Walt. 1.5832
Reed, Walter L. 2.3513
Reeder, Roberta. 2.1293
Reedy, George E., 1917-. 4.7931
Reefe, Thomas Q. 3.5420
Reehl, William F. 5.2744
Reely, Mary Katharine, 1881- ed. 5.7763
Rees, Albert, 1921-. 4.2752, 4.3116, 4.3148, 4.3224, 4.3364
Rees, Alwyn D. 3.1771, 4.5336
Rees, Charles W. (Charles Wayne) 5.2775
Rees, David, 1928-. 4.4653
Rees, Ennis. 2.6563
Rees, Jane Mitchell. 5.5085
Rees, Joan. 2.6565
Rees, Martin J., 1942-. 5.2007
Rees, Richard. ed. 1.857
Rees, Robert A. 2.10376
Rees, Samuel, 1936-. 2.8860
Rees, Terence. 2.3145
Reese, Gustave, 1899-1977. 1.3462-1.3463, 1.3650-1.3651
Reese, M. Lisle. 3.8514
Reese, Raymond C. 5.6089
Reeve, Clara, 1729-1807. 2.7211
Reeve, F. D. (Franklin D.), 1928-. 2.1285, 2.1318-2.1319, 2.1472, 2.1648
Reeve, W. D. 3.5015
Reeves, James. ed. 2.6113-2.6114
Reeves, James. 2.9262
Reeves, Mavis Mann. joint author. 4.7870
Reeves, Paschal, 1917- ed. 2.12784
Reeves, Richard. 3.7929
Reeves, Thomas C., 1936-. 3.7490
Reff, Morten. 1.4088
Reff, Theodore. 1.6070, 1.6091
Regan, David E. joint author. 4.6299
Regan, Robert, ed. 2.11204
Regan, Tom. 1.1454, 4.6630-4.6631
Regard, Maurice. 2.4149
Regelski, Thomas A., 1941-. 1.4421, 1.4435
Regensburger, Reinhold. 2.169
Regensteiner, Else, 1906-. 5.7098
Reghbati, Hassan K., 1949-. 5.6542
Regier, Cornelius C., 1884-. 3.7512
Regin, Deric. 3.185
Reginald, R. 2.3484
Regional Plan Association (New York, N.Y.) 4.3909
Rehder, Alfred, 1863-1949. 5.3687
Rehfuss, John, joint author. 4.8861
Rehr, Helen. 4.6541
Rehrauer, George. 5.8142-5.8143
Reich, Bernard. 3.3725, 3.6454
Reich, Charles A. 4.5162
Reich, Dorothy, ed. 2.13456
Reich, Michael. 4.3558
Reich, Nancy B. 1.4075
Reich, Peter A., 1940-. 2.123
Reich, Warren T. 5.3328
Reich, Wilhelm, 1897-1957. 5.185, 5.4907
Reich, Willi, 1898-. 1.3968, 1.4513
Reichard, Gary W., 1943-. 4.8224
Reichel-Dolmatoff, Gerardo. 3.9173
Reichenbach, Hans, 1891-1953. 1.111, 1.1246, 1.1288, 1.1341, 5.927, 5.1920, 5.2120
Reichert, Stefan. 2.13724
Reichl, L. E. 5.2169

Reichler, Joe. 4.1007
Reichley, James. 3.7907
Reid, Alastair, 1926-. 2.5375, 2.9263
Reid, Anthony. 3.4418, 3.4572
Reid, C. N. 5.5783
Reid, Constance. 5.1095
Reid, Dennis R. 5.5994
Reid, Helen F. 5.4587
Reid, Inez Smith. 3.6773
Reid, J. B. 2.7510
Reid, J. Gavin. 4.925, 5.4276
Reid, James Macarthur, 1901-1970. 2.9849
Reid, John Cowie. 2.7991, 2.10195
Reid, John Phillip. 4.9901
Reid, Joyce M. H. 2.3821
Reid, Malcolm, 1941-. 3.8814
Reid, P. R. (Patrick Robert), 1910-. 3.1076
Reid, Randall. 2.12687
Reid, Robert C. 5.6860
Reid, Robert D. (Robert Delaware), 1940-. 2.3566
Reid, Robert William. 5.748, 5.4441
Reid, S. R. 5.7055
Reid, T. R. 4.8024
Reid, Thomas, 1710-1796. 1.713, 1.715
Reid, W. Malcolm, 1910- joint author. 5.3294
Reid, William James, 1928-. 4.6501
Reidy, Joseph P. (Joseph Patrick), 1948-. 3.7385
Reif, F. (Frederick), 1927-. 5.2183
Reigstad, Paul. 2.14060
Reik, Theodor, 1888-1969. 5.186
Reilly, Bernard. 1.6497
Reilly, Edward R. 1.4552
Reilly, Edwin D. 5.1134
Reilly, John C. 5.7437
Reilly, John M. 2.6051, 2.12823
Reilly, John M. comp. 2.13005
Reilly, Mary. 4.10388
Reilly, Thomas W. 4.10415
Reiman, Donald H. 2.8097
Reiman, Jeffrey H. 4.6824
Reimer, Everett W. 4.10042
Rein, Martin. joint author. 4.5187
Rein, Mildred. 4.6526
Reinberg, Alain. 5.4213
Reineck, Hans-Erich. 5.3059
Reinecke, John E. 2.215
Reiner, Erica, 1926-. 3.3765
Reiner, Robert, 1946-. 4.6836
Reingold, Edward M., 1945-. 5.1277
Reingold, Ida H. 5.755
Reingold, Nathan, 1927-. 5.701, 5.755
Reinhard, David W., 1952-. 4.8223
Reinharz, Jehuda. 3.3805, 3.3913
Reinhold, Meyer, 1909- joint ed. 3.2711
Reintjes, J. Francis. 5.6436
Reischauer, August Karl, 1879-. 1.1758
Reischauer, Edwin O. (Edwin Oldfather), 1910-. 2.2030, 3.110, 3.4616, 3.4618, 3.4876, 3.4911, 3.6466
Reischauer, Robert D. (Robert Danton), 1941-. 4.10672
Reiser, Stanley Joel. 5.4515, 5.4560
Reisler, Mark. 4.3615
Reisman, John M. 5.4846
Reisner, Robert George. 1.4085
Reiss, David, 1937-. 4.5647
Reiss, Edmund. 2.5621
Reiss, Hans Siegbert. ed. 4.7437
Reiss, Howard. 5.2252
Reiss, Ira L. 4.5495
Reisser, Marsha J. 1.3566
Reissman, Leonard. joint author. 4.10106
Reisz, Karel. 2.3017
Reitberger, Reinhold C., 1946- joint author. 1.5844
Reiter, Elmar R. 5.2543
Reiter, Rayna R. 4.461
Reiterman, Tim. 1.2101
Reith, Herman R. 1.396
Reithmaier, Lawrence W. 5.6666
Reitlinger, Gerald, 1900-. 3.1070, 3.2446, 3.3954
Reitz, John R. 5.2371
Reklaitis, G. V., 1942-. 5.6820
Relaçam verdadeira dos trabalhos. 3.5981
Religious Advisory Committee on Refugee and Migration Affairs (U.S.) 4.6538
Reller, Theodore Lee. 4.10638

Remak, Joachim, 1920-. 3.1899
Remarque, Erich Maria, 1898-1970.
    2.13847-2.13848
Rembar, Charles. 4.9874
Rembrandt Harmenszoon van Rijn, 1606-1669.
    1.6251-1.6252
Remeš, Vladimír. 3.989
Remington, Frederic, 1861-1909. 1.4904
Remington, Joseph Price, 1847-1918. 5.5147
Remington, Robin Alison. 3.1179
Remini, Robert Vincent, 1921-. 3.7125
Remizov, Alekseĭ, 1877-1957. 2.1524-2.1527
Remnant, Peter. 1.864
Rempe, Melissa. 3.5859
Remy, Dorothy, 1943-. 4.3286
Renaissance Society of America. 1.3853
Renan, Ernest, 1823-1892. 1.2875, 2.4276
Renan, Sheldon, 1941-. 2.2987
Renard, Jules, 1864-1910. 2.4685
Renault, Mary. 2.9264-2.9268
Rendall, Jane, 1945-. 1.696
Rendell, Kenneth W. 5.7522
Rendell, Ruth, 1930-. 2.9805
Render, Sylvia Lyons. 2.10925, 2.10930
Rendra, W. S. 2.2286
Renfrew, Colin. 3.221, 3.224, 4.690, 4.698,
    4.729, 4.733
Renfrew, Jane M. 4.722
Renier, Gustaaf Johannes, 1892-. 3.492
Renn, Derek Frank. 1.5576
Renner, Frederic Gordon, 1897-. 1.5965
Rennert, Hugo Albert, 1858-1927. 2.3383,
    2.5124, 2.5209
Rennert, Jack. 1.5858
Rennie, Susan, ed. 4.6066
Rennie, Ysabel (Fisk) 1918-. 3.9243
Renoir, Alain. 2.6293
Renoir, Auguste, 1841-1919. 1.6142-1.6143
Renoir, Jean, 1894-. 2.3065
Renou, Louis, 1896-1966. 1.1677, 1.1815,
    3.4195
Renouard, Yves. 1.3154
Renouvin, Pierre, 1893-1974. 3.739-3.740
Rensch, Bernhard, 1900-. 5.3360
Renshon, Stanley Allen. 4.7248
Renstrom, Peter G., 1943-. 4.9626
Rentoul, Edgar, joint author. 5.4715
Renwick Gallery. 1.5325, 1.6532, 1.6544
Renwick, Isaac Parker Anderson, ed. 4.7214
Renwick, W. L. (William Lindsay), 1889-.
    2.5518, 2.5685
Reproductive Biology Research Foundation.
    5.4257
Reproductive Biology Research Foundation
    (U.S.) 5.4838
Reps, John William. 1.5596, 4.6242, 4.6326
Rescher, Nicholas. 1.871, 1.1196, 4.1574, 5.926
Research & Forecasts, Inc. 4.883
Research in international law. 4.9331
Research Institute for the Study of Man.
    4.5268, 5.7901
Research Seminar in Archaeology and Related
    Subjects. University of Sheffield, 1971. 4.690
Reshetar, John Stephen. 4.8640
Reskin, Barbara F. 4.3256
Resler, Henrietta, joint author. 4.5342
Resnick, Lauren B. 5.360, 5.1060
Resnick, Robert, 1923-. 5.1982, 5.2090
Resnick, Seymour. ed. 2.5149
Resnick, Stephen A. joint author. 4.8908
Resnick, William, 1922-. 5.6834
Resnikoff, Marvin. 5.6057
Resources for the Future. 4.1772, 4.1841,
    4.1843, 4.1845, 4.1898, 4.1902, 4.1994,
    4.2073, 4.2076, 4.2823, 4.2825, 4.2954,
    4.3702, 4.3705, 4.3713, 4.3716, 4.3720,
    4.3727, 4.3739, 4.3772, 4.3781, 4.4130-4.4131,
    4.6208, 4.6229, 5.5419, 5.5432, 5.5437,
    5.5484, 5.6022, 5.6626
Restif de La Bretonne, 1734-1806. 2.4086
Restle, Frank. 5.54, 5.377
Restle, Marcell, 1932-. 1.6396
Reston, James, 1909-. 1.2102, 2.3558
Restout, Denise. 1.4067
Reti, Ladislao. joint author. 5.5547
Reti, Ladislao. 5.823, 5.5547
Reti, Rudolph Richard, 1885-1957. 1.4453
Reuben, B. G. 5.6814

Reubens, Beatrice G. 4.3226, 4.3304
Reuber, Grant L. 4.4608
Reumann, John Henry Paul. ed. 1.2670
Réunion des musées nationaux (France)
    1.4978-1.4979, 1.6050, 1.6053-1.6054, 1.6070,
    1.6076, 1.6120, 1.6362
Reuss-Ianni, Elizabeth, 1944-. 4.6834
Reuter, Peter. 4.6718
Reutlinger, Shlomo. 5.7117
Reutter, E. Edmund, 1924-. 4.9586
Revard, Stella Purce. 2.7135
Reve, Karel van het. comp. 3.3259
Reveal, James L. 5.3678
Revel, Jean François. 4.7604
Reveley, W. Taylor. 4.7880
Revell, Peter. 2.11014
Reventlow, Henning, Graf. 1.2528
Reverby, Susan. 4.3275, 5.5157
Reverdy, Pierre, 1889-1960. 2.4686
Reves, Emery. 3.2423, 4.9121
Révész, Géza, 1878-1955. 2.154
Rew, Alan, 1942-. 4.517
Rewald, John, 1912-. 1.4796, 1.5709, 1.5731,
    1.6066, 1.6069, 1.6134-1.6135, 1.6351
Rex, John. 4.6459
Rexroth, Kenneth, 1905-. 2.2033, 2.2216,
    2.8957, 2.10497, 2.11332, 2.12376-2.12380
Rey, Agapito, joint ed. and tr. 3.5985, 3.8570
Rey, Alain. 2.876, 2.3819
Rey-Debove, Josette. 2.876-2.877
Rey, R. F. 5.6417
Reyes, Caroline. 5.7631
Reymont, Władysław Stanisław, 1867-1925.
    2.1723
Reyna, Ruth. 1.148
Reynolds, A. J. 5.5751
Reynolds, Barbara. 2.855, 2.4961
Reynolds, Beatrice, 1891- ed. and tr. 3.426
Reynolds, C. S. 5.3779
Reynolds, Charles. 4.7538
Reynolds, David, 1952-. 3.929
Reynolds, David K. 5.4867
Reynolds, David S., 1949-. 2.10570
Reynolds, Frank, 1930-. 1.2108, 5.8454
Reynolds, George Stanley, 1936-. 5.306
Reynolds, George W. M. (George William
    MacArthur), 1814-1879. 2.8001
Reynolds, Graham. 1.4951, 1.6020, 1.6029,
    1.6042
Reynolds, James H., 1930-. 5.61
Reynolds, Joshua, Sir, 1723-1792. 1.5133,
    1.6037, 2.5675
Reynolds, Leighton Durham. 2.770, 5.7521
Reynolds, Lloyd George, 1910-. 4.1820, 4.2802,
    4.3124, 4.3133
Reynolds, M. Lance. 5.55
Reynolds, Nancy, 1938-. 4.1093, 4.1175
Reynolds, Roger, 1934-. 1.3677
Reynolds, Vernon. 5.4024
Reynolds, William Craig, 1933-. 5.6202
Reznikoff, William S. 5.3467
Rhees, Rush. 5.1035
Rheingold, Harriet L. (Harriet Lange) ed.
    5.4086
Rhenisch, Madelyn B. joint author. 3.6533
Rhind, David. 4.2218
Rhine, J. B. (Joseph Banks), 1895-1980. 5.645
Rhine, Louisa E., 1891-. 5.646
Rhode, Eric, 1934-. 2.2884
Rhode Island Historical Society. 3.6968
Rhodes, Carolyn H. 5.8466
Rhodes, Daniel, 1911-. 1.6626
Rhodes, Ernest L. 5.8466
Rhodes, James Ford, 1848-1927. 3.7147
Rhodes James, Robert, 1933-. 3.808, 3.1631,
    3.1717
Rhodes, P. J. (Peter John) 4.7341
Rhodes, Philip. 5.4488
Rhodes, R. Crompton (Raymond Crompton)
    2.7251
Rhodes, R. Crompton (Raymond Crompton)
    ed. 2.7246
Rhodes, Susan R. 4.3312
Rhys, Hedley Howell. 1.5963
Rhys, Jean. 2.9271-2.9277
Riasanovsky, Nicholas Valentine, 1923-. 3.3045,
    3.3101, 3.3121-3.3122
Riaz Hassan. 4.5439

Ribeiro, Aileen. 4.848
Ribenboim, Paulo. 5.1338
Ribera, José de, 1588?-1652. 1.6220
Ribner, Irving. ed. 2.5877, 2.5887, 2.6610
Ricard, Robert. 1.3185
Ricardo-Campbell, Rita. 4.3469
Ricardo, David, 1772-1823. 4.1417
Ricatte, Robert. 2.4227, 2.4566
Ricchio, Paul P. 2.4605
Ricci, Luigi, 1842-1915, tr. 4.7393
Ricci, Matteo, 1552-1610. 1.3244
Ricci, Robert, joint author. 1.4486
Riccioni, Paolo. 3.287
Rice, Bradley Robert, 1948-. 4.6241
Rice, Cedric Bertram Fitzsimons, joint author.
    5.2664
Rice, David Gerard, 1945-. 1.1652
Rice, David Talbot, 1903-1972. 1.5181
Rice, Edward E. (Edward Earl), 1909-. 3.4799
Rice, Elmer L., 1892-1967. 2.12381-2.12382
Rice, Eugene F. 1.410
Rice, Howard Crosby, 1904- comp. 3.6947
Rice, Kym S. 4.871
Rice, Martin P. 1.2457
Rice, Paul F., 1921-. 5.5881
Rice, Rex. 5.6543
Rice, Stuart Alan, 1932- joint author. 5.2800
Rice, Stuart Arthur, 1889-. 4.8070
Rice, Tamara Abelson Talbot. joint author.
    1.5181
Rice University. 5.2
Rice, Victor Arthur, 1890-1964. 5.5441
Rice, Wallace, 1859-1939. 1.1882
Rich, Adrienne Cecile. 2.12383-2.12387, 4.5671
Rich, Bennett Milton, 1909-. 4.5822
Rich, Daniel Catton, 1904-. 1.6092
Rich, Jack C., 1914-. 1.5781
Rich, John Martin. comp. 4.10276
Rich, John Martin. 4.10696
Rich, Maria F. 1.3522
Rich, Norman. 3.671, 3.2318, 3.2447, 3.3124
Rich, Norman. ed. 3.2317
Richard, Alison F. 5.4025
Richard, Dorothy Elizabeth, 1909-. 4.8830
Richard, Naomi Noble. 1.4696
Richard, of St. Victor, d. 1173. 1.3090
Richard, Stephen. 5.7924
Richard, Yann. 3.4084
Richards, Alan, 1946-. 4.2994
Richards, Alan M. joint author. 5.4368
Richards, Alun. 2.9873
Richards, Angela. 5.134
Richards, Brian, 1928-. 4.3910
Richards, David, 1933- joint comp. 2.1241
Richards, David Gleyre, 1935-. 2.13558
Richards, Denis. 3.1050
Richards, Derek. 5.1626
Richards, Donald Sidney, ed. 4.4237
Richards, E. G. (Edward Graham). 5.2768
Richards, Eric. 4.2918
Richards, Glyn. 1.208
Richards, I. A. 2.2451
Richards, I. A. (Ivor Armstrong), 1893-.
    2.2441, 2.2532, 2.2722, 2.9282
Richards, Jack W., 1933-. 4.970, 4.980
Richards, James Maude. 1.5545
Richards, Janet Radcliffe. 4.6104
Richards, Jeffrey. 1.3149
Richards, K. S. 4.314
Richards, Kenneth Roland, ed. 2.3306
Richards, Martin. Emil. 1.4183
Richards, Owain Westmacott, 1901-. 5.3857
Richards, P. J. (Peter J.) 4.2455
Richards, Pamela. 4.6879
Richards, Paul. 4.189
Richards, Paul Westmacott. 5.3784
Richards, Peter G. joint author. 4.8876
Richards, Peter G. 4.8473, 4.8874
Richards, Stanley, 1918-. 1.3453-1.3454,
    2.6198-2.6199, 2.6245, 2.10799, 2.10804
Richards, T. H. 5.5735
Richardson, Alan, 1905-1975. 1.2224
Richardson, Beverley B. 5.1986
Richardson, Bonham C., 1939-. 4.8958
Richardson, Boyce. 3.5866
Richardson, Bradley M. 4.2549, 4.8757
Richardson, Brian. jt. comp. 3.1516

Richardson, Cyril Charles, 1909- ed. and tr.
1.2198
Richardson, D. H. S. (David H. S.) 5.3704
Richardson, Dorothy Miller, 1873-1957. 2.9283
Richardson, Edgar Preston, 1902-.
1.5889-1.5890, 1.5961
Richardson, Elmo R. 3.7830
Richardson, Emeline Hill. 3.2758
Richardson, Ernest Cushing, 1860-1939. 1.2194
Richardson, Frank M. 5.7166
Richardson, Geoffrey. 2.826
Richardson, H. G. (Henry Gerald), 1884-.
3.3949, 4.8392
Richardson, H. H. (Henry Hobson), 1838-1886.
1.5325
Richardson, Harry Van Buren. 1.3372
Richardson, Herbert Warren. ed. 1.380
Richardson, Herbert Warren. joint author.
1.2909
Richardson, Hugh Edward, 1905-. 1.5069,
3.4855
Richardson, I. W., 1934-. 5.1986
Richardson, J. F. (John Francis) 5.6829
Richardson, J. J. (Jeremy John) 4.3228, 4.8368,
4.8438
Richardson, J. J. (Jeremy John) joint comp.
4.8437
Richardson, Jacques. 4.352
Richardson, James F., 1931- joint author.
4.6221
Richardson, James T., 1941-. 1.3051
Richardson, Jeanne M., 1951- joint author.
5.8419
Richardson, Joanna. 2.4220, 2.4241, 2.4310
Richardson, Joe Martin. 4.10881
Richardson, John, 1924-. 1.6068
Richardson, John M. (John Martin), 1938-.
4.1790
Richardson, John T. E. 5.335
Richardson, Kathleen Schueller. 5.2856
Richardson, Lawrence. 2.764
Richardson, Lewis Fry, 1881-1953. 5.2583
Richardson, Lyon Norman, 1898-. 2.3641
Richardson, R. C. 3.1476
Richardson, Richard C. 4.10617
Richardson, Richard C. joint author. 4.10557
Richardson, Robert D., 1934-. 2.10390
Richardson, Samuel, 1689-1761. 2.7212-2.7214,
2.7219, 2.7221
Richardson, Stephen A. 4.6612
Richardson, Tony, 1941-1969. 1.4826
Richardson, William J. 1.1004
Richason, Benjamin F. 4.21
Riché, Pierre. 3.1956
Richelson, Jeffrey. 4.7913
Richer, Jean, 1915-. 2.4221
Richerson, Peter J. joint author. 5.5977
Richetti, John J. 2.5996, 2.6978
Richey, E. E. 3.4515
Richie, Donald, 1924-. 2.2903, 2.3060
Richler, Mordecai, 1931-. 2.9895, 2.9962-2.9966
Richman, Irving B. 3.8504
Richman, Michael. 1.5665
Richman, Sidney. 2.13164
Richmond, Douglas W., 1946-. 3.8949
Richmond, Ian Archibald, Sir, 1902-1965.
2.775, 3.1305
Richmond Independence Bicentennial
Commission. 3.8220
Richmond, Mary Ellen, 1861-1928. 4.6480
Richter, Conrad, 1890-1968. 2.12388-2.12393
Richter, Donald C., 1934-. 4.6727
Richter, Gerold. 5.1842
Richter, Gisela Marie Augusta, 1882-1972.
1.4720, 1.5161, 1.5625-1.5626, 1.5635-1.5636,
1.5788, 1.6557
Richter, Irma Anne. 1.5636
Richter, Irving. 4.3652
Richter, Jean Paul, 1847-1937, ed. 1.6212
Richter, Melvin, 1921-. 4.7427
Richter, Werner, 1888-1969. 3.2315
Rickards, C. (Clarence) 5.1135
Rickards, Teresa. 5.1892
Rickels, Milton. 2.11046
Rickert, Edith, 1871-1938. 2.10420
Rickert, Margaret Josephine, 1888-. 1.6012
Rickett, Harold William, 1896-. 5.3671
Ricketts, Edward Flanders, 1896-1948. 5.3823

Ricketts, Martin J. joint author. 4.3708
Rickey, George. 1.4827, 1.5671
Ricklefs, M. C. 3.4581
Ricklefs, M. C. (Merle Calvin) 3.4563
Ricklefs, Robert E. 5.3525
Rickman, H. P. (Hans Peter). 1.982
Rickover, Hyman George. 4.10001, 4.10009
Ricks, Christopher B. 2.7136, 2.8153, 2.8172
Ricks, David A. 4.3832
Ricœur, Paul. 1.453, 1.1022, 1.1308, 1.2518,
1.2913
Ricoeur, Paul, 1913-. 3.493
Ridd, Merrill K. 4.35
Riddel, Joseph N. 2.12551
Riddell, Peter. 4.2293
Riddell, Walter Alexander, 1881-. 3.8772
Ridenour, George M. 2.7520
Rideout, Walter Bates, joint ed. 2.10729
Rideout, Walter Bates. 2.10642, 2.11320,
2.11327
Rider, Don K., 1918-. 5.6135
Rider, Hope S. 3.6955
Ridge, John Rollin, 1827-1867. 2.11216
Ridge, Martin. 3.6345, 3.7432
Ridgely, Joseph Vincent. 2.10455, 2.11222,
2.11225
Ridgeway, Ann N., ed. 2.11930
Ridgway, William, Sir, 1853-1926. 2.3169
Ridgway, Brunilde Sismondo, 1929-.
1.5627-1.5629
Ridgway, Matthew B. (Matthew Bunker),
1895-. 3.5021
Ridgway, Sam H. 5.3979
Ridler, Anne, 1912-. 2.6746-2.6747, 2.8197,
2.9287, 2.9521-2.9522
Ridley, B. K. 5.1996
Ridley, Clarence Eugene, 1891- ed. 4.8850
Ridley, F. F. (Frederick F.) 4.8366
Ridley, Jasper Godwin. 1.3393, 3.1394, 3.1405
Ridolfi, Roberto, 1895-. 3.2932
Rie, Ellen D. 5.5095
Rie, Herbert E., 1931-. 5.5095
Riede, David G. 1.6718, 2.8141
Rieder, Jonathan. 3.8042
Riedt, Heinz, 1919-. 2.4995
Rieff, Philip, 1922-. 5.156
Riegel, Emil Raymond, 1882-1963. 5.6815
Riegel, Jay Arthur. 5.4249
Riegel, Robert Edgar, 1897-. 3.8466
Rieger, Rigomar. 5.3409
Riehl, Herbert, 1915-. 5.2580
Riehl-Sisca, Joan. 5.5194
Riehm, Diethard. 1.4171
Rieke, Richard D. 1.1241
Riel, Louis, 1844-1885. defendant. 4.9431
Riemann, Hugo, 1849-1919. 1.3806, 1.4113
Riemens, Leo. joint author. 1.3763
Riemenschneider, Tilman, d. 1531. 1.5718
Riemer, Donald N. 5.3777
Riepe, Dale Maurice, 1918-. 1.194, 1.522
Riesbeck, Christopher K. joint author. 5.1019
Riesbeck, Christopher K. 5.1020
Rieselbach, Leroy N. 4.7999
Riesman, David, 1909-. 4.1380, 4.10063,
4.10071, 4.10086, 5.628, 5.635
Riesman, Paul. 3.5395
Riesner, Dieter, joint author. 5.7938
Riess, Steven A. 4.938, 4.1001
Riewald, Jacobus Gerhardus. comp. 2.8441
Rifaat, Alifa. 2.1848
Rigby, T. H. (Thomas Henry), 1925-. 4.8662
Rigdon, Susan M., 1943- joint author. 4.5262
Rigdon, Walter, ed. 2.3237
Riggs, Fred Warren. 4.7759
Riggs, Gail Kershner. 5.5001
Riggs, Margaret M. 5.507
Riggs, Robert Edwon, 1927-. 4.9240, 4.9271
Riggs, Timothy A., 1942-. 5.8188
Rigney, Barbara Hill, 1938-. 2.5990
Riha, Thomas, ed. 3.3003
Riis, Jacob A. (Jacob August), 1849-1914.
4.6621
Rijksmuseum (Netherlands).
Rijksprentenkabinet. 1.4996
Rijksuniversiteit te Leiden. Centrum voor
Onderzoek van Maatschappelijke
Tegenstellingen. 4.6714
Rijnsdorp, John E. joint author. 5.6841

Riker, Dorothy Lois, 1904- joint author. 3.8392
Rikhye, Indar Jit, 1920-. 4.9257
Riley, Carolyn. 2.2671
Riley, Carroll L. joint comp. 3.5759
Riley, J. P. (John Price) 4.341
Riley, William Franklin. 5.5782
Rilke-Archiv (Weimar, Germany) 2.13850
Rilke, Rainer Maria, 1875-1926.
2.13850-2.13853
Rilla, Wolf Peter. 2.3018
Rimbaud, Arthur, 1854-1891. 2.4277-2.4280
Rimer, Alan E. joint author. 5.6038
Rimer, J. Thomas. 2.2012, 2.2080, 2.2105,
5.8070
Rimlinger, Gaston V., 1926-. 4.3445
Rimm, Sylvia B., 1935-. 4.10913
Rimmer, Douglas. 4.2622, 4.2625
Rimmington, Gerald T., joint author. 3.5492
Rimsky-Korsakov, Nikolay, 1844-1908. 1.4492
Rindfuss, Ronald R., 1946-. 4.1645
Rindler, Wolfgang, 1924-. 5.2091, 5.2105
Ring, Grete. 1.6048
Ring, Malvin E. 5.5121
Ring, Peter, 1941-. 5.2142
Ringe, Donald A. 2.10977
Ringelblum, Emanuel, 1900-1944. 3.3987
Ringer, Benjamin B. (Benjamin Bernard), 1920-.
3.6526
Ringer, Fritz K., 1934-. 4.9961, 4.10129
Ringler, Richard N., ed. 2.939
Ringler, William A., 1912-. 2.6506
Ringrose, David R. 4.2416
Rings, Werner. 3.1059
Rinsler, Norma, ed. 2.4223
Rinsler, Norma. 2.4226
Río, Angel del, 1900-1962. 2.5087, 2.5092
Riordan, James, 1936-. 4.941
Riordan, Michael. joint author. 5.6101
Riordan, Robert V., joint author. 4.6437
Riordon, William L., 1861-1909. 4.8215
Rioux, J. William. ed. 4.10688
Rioux, Marcel. ed. 3.8688
Ripa, Cesare, fl. 1600. 1.5165
Ripka, Hubert, 1895-. 3.1927
Ripley, C. Peter, 1941-. 3.7233
Ripley, Gordon, 1946-. 2.9888
Ripley, John, 1936-. 2.6660
Ripley, Randall B. 4.8043
Ripperger, E. A. joint author. 5.5842
Rippy, James Fred, 1892- ed. 3.8339, 3.9174
Riquer, Martín de, conde de Casa Dávalos,
1914- ed. 2.5169
Rischbieter, Henning. comp. 1.4828
Rischin, Moses, 1925-. 3.8052
Risebero, Bill, 1938-. 1.5257
Rish, F. L., 1929- joint author. 5.5866
Risjord, Norman K. 3.7080, 4.8189
Riskin, Carl. 4.2485
Risley, George, 1910-. 4.4288
Rist, John M. 1.328, 1.331, 1.343
Rist, Ray C. 4.10788, 4.10853
Ristelhueber, René, 1881-1960. 3.3526
Rister, Carl Coke, 1899-. 3.8458, 3.8535
Ristow, Walter William, 1908-. 5.8212
Ritcheson, Charles R. 3.1569, 3.7038
Ritchey, William M., joint author. 5.2725
Ritchie, Andrew Carnduff. 1.5906
Ritchie, Dennis M., 1941- joint author. 5.1212
Ritchie, G. J. (Gordon James) 5.6505
Ritchie, J. M. (James MacPherson), 1927-.
2.13480, 2.13495
Ritchie, James McPherson, 1927-. 2.13679
Ritchie, Maureen. 5.8459
Ritchie, Robert C., 1938-. 4.7811
Ritchie, Robert Lindsay Graeme, 1880-. 3.1789
Ritchie, William Augustus, 1903-. 3.5746
Ritsos, Giannēs, 1909-. 2.616-2.621
Ritt, Joseph Fels, 1893-. 5.1345, 5.1457, 5.1509
Ritter, Alan, 1937-. 4.7190, 4.7445
Ritter, E. A., 1890-. 3.5500
Ritter, Gerhard, 1888-1967. 3.2260, 3.2386,
3.2489, 3.2492
Ritter, Harry. 3.404
Ritzer, George. 4.4808
Riva, Joseph P. 5.6805
Rivera, José Eustasio, 1889-1928. 2.5413-2.5414
Rivers, Elias L. 2.5189
Rivers, Elias L. ed. and tr. 2.5146

Rivers, Isabel. 2.5789
Rivers, Larry, 1923-. 1.5797
Rivers, W. H. R. (William Halse Rivers),
    1864-1922. ed. 3.5617
Rivers, Wilga M. 2.36
Rivers, William L. 2.3554
Rivett, Patrick. 5.5573
Rivière, Claude, fl. 1969-. 3.5382
Riviere, Joan, 1883-. 5.141
Rivkin, Ellis, 1918-. 1.2895
Rivkin, Steven R. 4.9543
Rivlin, Harry Nathaniel, 1904-. 4.10496
Rivlin, Theodore J., 1926-. 5.1559
Rix, Sara E. joint author. 4.3313
Rizal, José, 1861-1896. 2.5448
Rizzi, Aldo. comp. 1.6491
Rizzo, Joseph V., 1942-. 4.10910
Roach, John, 1920-. 5.8227
Roach, William, 1907-. 2.3947
Roache, Joel, 1941-. 2.11623
Roadarmel, Gordon C., 1932- comp. 2.1896
Roark, James L. 3.7470, 3.8252
Roback, A. A. (Abraham Aaron), 1890-1965.
    5.89
Robb, Allan P. 2.10865
Robb, Carol S. 4.5952
Robb, John Donald, 1892-. 1.3437
Robbe-Grillet, Alain, 1922-. 2.3528,
    2.4687-2.4693
Robbins, Albert. 4.2713
Robbins, Caroline. 4.8404
Robbins, Ceila Dame. 2.3804
Robbins, Chandler S. 5.3956
Robbins, Fred P. 5.4913
Robbins, Herbert. joint author. 5.1105
Robbins, Ira A. 1.3620
Robbins, Keith. 3.878, 3.1633, 4.9140
Robbins, Lionel Charles, 1898-. 4.1359, 4.1452,
    4.1456
Robbins, Lionel Charles Robbins, Baron, 1898-.
    4.1778
Robbins, Robin Hugh A. 2.6913
Robbins, Rossell Hope, 1912- tr. 2.3968,
    2.6139-2.6140, 5.7941
Robbins, Sidney M. 4.4597
Robbins, Stanley L. (Stanley Leonard), 1915-.
    5.4740
Robbins, Trina. 2.3813
Robbins, Wilfred William, 1884-1952. 5.5391
Robe, Stanley Linn, 1915-. 2.5335
Robens, Erich. 5.2898
Robequain, Charles, 1897-. 3.4555
Roberge, James K., 1938- joint author. 5.6551
Robert, Alain. 5.1538
Robert de Basevorn, fl. 1322. 2.2535
Robert (Firm) 2.877
Robert, Guy. 2.4351
Robert, Henry M. (Henry Martyn), 1837-1923.
    4.7730
Robert Herrick Memorial Conference,
    University of Michigan, Dearborn, 1974.
    2.7075
Robert, Paul, 1910-. 2.876-2.877
Robert S. Peabody Foundation for Archaeology.
    3.8894
Robert, Sarah Corbin. 4.7730
Roberts, A. Wayne (Arthur Wayne), 1934-.
    5.1491
Roberts, Adam. 4.9323
Roberts, Albert R. 4.5764
Roberts, Alexander, 1826-1901, ed. 1.2194
Roberts, Andrew. 3.5521, 3.5525
Roberts, Anna S. (Mosser) joint ed. and tr.
    3.6028
Roberts, Arthur O. joint comp. 1.3346
Roberts, B. C. (Benjamin Charles), 1917-.
    4.3409, 4.3424
Roberts, Bryan R., 1939-. 4.6247
Roberts, Chalmers McGeagh, 1910-. 2.3671
Roberts, Charles George Douglas, Sir,
    1860-1943. 2.8003
Roberts, Clayton. 3.1446
Roberts, Daniel A. (Daniel Altman), 1922-.
    5.5399
Roberts, David, 1923-. 4.5307-4.5308
Roberts, David S., 1943-. 4.3417
Roberts, Elizabeth Madox, 1886-.
    2.12396-2.12399

Roberts, F. 4.3703
Roberts, Frank C. 3.329
Roberts, Harry V. joint author. 4.1241
Roberts, Henry L. 4.2859
Roberts, Howard C. 1.5496
Roberts, J. Deotis (James Deotis), 1927-. 1.2781
Roberts, J. M. (John Morris), 1928-. 3.648,
    3.2062, 3.2099
Roberts, J. W. 3.2651
Roberts, John Arthur, 1945-. 5.7436
Roberts, John D., 1918-. 5.2723
Roberts, John L. (John Leonard), 1936-. 5.2980
Roberts, John S. 1.4253
Roberts, JR. 4.5524
Roberts, Julian L., joint author. 5.2914
Roberts, Keith, 1935-. 2.9806
Roberts, Kenneth H. 5.7004
Roberts, Kenneth Lewis, 1885-1957. 2.12401,
    3.6028
Roberts, Lamar. 5.4345
Roberts, Laurance P. 1.5078
Roberts, M. Hugh P. 4.6275
Roberts, M. W. (Meirion Wynn) 5.2899
Roberts, Mary Lou. 4.4309
Roberts, Mary M. 5.5158
Roberts, Michael. 2.6123, 2.6193, 3.3384,
    3.3387, 3.3389-3.3390, 3.3392-3.3393
Roberts, Moss, 1937-. 2.2222
Roberts, Neil. 2.7709
Roberts, Paul Craig, 1939-. 4.2016
Roberts, Paul O. 4.3872
Roberts, Penfield, 1892-1944. 3.649
Roberts, Philip, 1942- joint author. 2.9624
Roberts, Richard A., 1935-. 5.6277
Roberts, Robert, 1905-1974. 4.5333
Roberts, Robert W. 4.6476, 4.6505
Roberts, Sheila, 1942-. 2.10084
Roberts, Simon. 4.9357
Roberts, Spencer E. comp. 2.1261
Roberts, Thomas Duval, 1903-. 3.4458, 3.5383,
    3.9121
Roberts, Tom Aerwyn. 1.1501
Roberts, W. Rhys (William Rhys), 1858-1929.
    tr. 2.349, 2.449
Roberts, Walter R., 1916-. 3.949
Roberts, Warren, 1916-. 2.8956
Robertshaw, D. 5.4232
Robertson, A. F. 4.661
Robertson, A. H. (Arthur Henry), 1913-.
    4.9385
Robertson, A. J. (Agnes Jane) ed. and tr.
    4.9409
Robertson, Alec. 1.3859
Robertson, Charles Grant, Sir, 1869-1948.
    3.2481
Robertson, Claire C., 1944-. 4.6161, 4.6448
Robertson, Constance Noyes. comp. 4.7160
Robertson, D. E. 5.5449
Robertson, D. W. (Durant Waite), 1914-.
    1.2205, 2.2629
Robertson, David Allan. 1.4952, 4.10056
Robertson, Dennis Holme, 1890-. 4.1264,
    4.4480-4.4481
Robertson, Donald, 1919-. 1.6405
Robertson, George Scott, Sir, 1852-1916. 3.4120
Robertson, Ian, 1951-. 4.6644, 5.4961
Robertson, J. Logie (James Logie), 1846-1922.
    ed. 2.7314
Robertson, J. M. (John Mackinnon), 1856-1933.
    ed. 1.695
Robertson, Jack C. 4.4404
Robertson, Jean, ed. 2.6508
Robertson, John George, 1867-1933. 2.13456
Robertson, Martin. 1.4721
Robertson, N. (Norman) 4.3639
Robertson, Priscilla Smith. 3.704, 4.6090
Robertson, R. N. 5.3611
Robertson, Stuart, 1892-1940. 2.973
Robertson, T. W. (Thomas William),
    1829-1871. 2.8004
Robertson, William Spence, 1872-. 3.8933,
    3.9009, 3.9182, 3.9239
Robey, Bryant. 4.1676
Robey, David. ed. 1.551
Robin, Martin. 4.8302
Robin, Richard S., ed. 1.630
Robins, Betty Dashew, joint author. 1.6527
Robins, C. Richard. 5.3906

Robins, Carolyn G. 5.7641
Robins, Elizabeth, 1862-1952. 2.11217
Robins-Mowry, Dorothy, 1921-. 4.6145
Robins, R. H. (Robert Henry) 2.38, 2.161
Robinson, Arthur Howard, 1915-. 4.207, 4.209,
    4.227
Robinson, Austin, 1897-. 4.3234
Robinson, Blackwell P. (Blackwell Pierce), ed.
    3.8229
Robinson, Charles Alexander, 1900-1965.
    3.2627
Robinson, Christopher. 2.521
Robinson, D. J. (David James), 1939-. 4.388
Robinson, Daniel N., 1937-. 5.82
Robinson, David, 1938-. 1.3415, 3.5084
Robinson, David Mason, 1932-. 5.4047
Robinson, Douglas Hill, 1918-. 5.7482
Robinson, E. A. G. (Edward Austin Gossage)
    4.2523, 4.2756, 4.2781
Robinson, Edwin Arlington, 1869-1935.
    2.12402-2.12403
Robinson, Elwyn B. 3.8508
Robinson, Enders A. 5.6739
Robinson, Eric, 1924-. 2.7569, 5.5665
Robinson, Francis. 3.3645
Robinson, Fred C. 2.6303
Robinson, Fred C. joint author. 5.7942
Robinson, Fred C. 2.931
Robinson, George, 1931-. 1.5786
Robinson, Geroid Tanquary, 1892-. 3.3169
Robinson, Glen O. 5.5437
Robinson, Gloria. 5.3438
Robinson, H. Alan, 1921-. 4.10512
Robinson, H. (Harry), 1915-. 4.2216
Robinson, H. Wheeler (Henry Wheeler),
    1872-1945. ed. 1.2511
Robinson, Halbert B. joint author. 5.5117
Robinson, Henry Morton, 1898-1961. 2.8870
Robinson, Hilary. 2.9352
Robinson, I. S. (Ian Stuart), 1947 Feb. 11-.
    1.3151
Robinson, J. Hedley. 5.1736
Robinson, Jackie, 1919-1972. 4.1003
Robinson, James K. joint ed. 2.10729
Robinson, James K. 2.7766
Robinson, James McConkey, 1924-. 1.1005,
    1.2519, 1.2800, 1.2880
Robinson, Jeffrey Cane, 1943-. 2.7870
Robinson, Jerry. 2.3816
Robinson, Joan, 1903-. 4.1263, 4.1282, 4.1494,
    4.1821
Robinson, John, 1909-. 4.3940
Robinson, John A. T. (John Arthur Thomas),
    1919-. 1.2626, 1.2771
Robinson, John Martin. 3.1238
Robinson, John P. 4.4994
Robinson, Judith Schiek, 1947-. 5.7780
Robinson, Kenneth, 1911-. 2.7612, 4.8920
Robinson, Kenneth W. 3.5541
Robinson, Kim Stanley. 2.13296
Robinson, Leif J. 5.1721
Robinson, Lennox, 1886-1958. 2.7754
Robinson, Lillian S. 4.6068
Robinson, Mairi. 2.1116
Robinson, Marguerite S. 4.8884
Robinson, Michael C. 5.8388
Robinson, Nancy M. 5.5117
Robinson, Patricia A., 1948-. 5.5507
Robinson, Paul A., 1940-. 1.4226, 4.5496
Robinson, Philip S. 4.2851
Robinson, Richard, 1902-. 1.280, 1.305, 1.1247
Robinson, Richard Alan Hodgson. 3.3501
Robinson, Richard D., 1921-. 3.3594
Robinson, Richard H., 1926-. 1.1776, 1.2141
Robinson, Ronald. 3.5115
Robinson, Ronald Edward, 1920-. 3.1220,
    4.8904
Robinson, Sherman. joint author. 4.2563
Robinson, Theodore Henry, 1881-. 1.2604
Robinson, Vester. 5.6463
Robinson, Walter Stitt. 3.8133
Robinson, William Alexander, 1884-. 3.7445
Robinson, William Henry, 1922-.
    2.10884-2.10886
Robinson, William Morrison, 1891-. 4.9907
Robison, Mary Louis (Clark) 5.7426
Robison, Samuel Shelburne, 1867-. 5.7426

Roblès, Emmanuel. 2.4696
Robock, Stefan Hyman, 1915-. 4.2172
Robson, Edgar Iliff, ed. 2.335
Robson, Eric, 1918-1954. 3.6904
Robson, James, 1890-, ed. 1.2037
Robson, L. L. (Leslie Lloyd), 1931-. 3.5616
Robson-Scott, W. D. (William Douglas) 1.1564
Robson, William Alexander, 1895- ed. 4.6299
Roca Franquesa, José María. joint author. 2.5086
Rochdale, John Durival Kemp, Viscount, 1906-. 4.3977
Roche, Elizabeth. 1.3507
Roche, Jerome. 1.3507
Roche, Maurice. 2.4789
Rochefort, Christiane. 2.4697
Rochester, John Wilmot, Earl of, 1647-1680. 2.7226-2.7228
Rochester, Stuart I., 1945-. 3.834
Rochlin, Fred, 1923-. 3.8494
Rochlin, Gene I. comp. 5.5523
Rochlin, Harriet, 1924-. 3.8494
Rock, David, 1945-. 3.9249
Rock, Howard B., 1944-. 4.3005
Rock, Irvin. 5.250, 5.253, 5.287
Rock, William R. 3.1256
Rockefeller Foundation. 3.5094
Rockey, K. C. (Kenneth Charles) 5.5851
Rockman, Bert A. 4.8367
Rockoff, Hugh. 4.2111
Rockwell, John. 3.1696
Rockwood, D. Stephen. 5.8385
Rodd, E. H. ed. 5.2718
Rodd, Laurel Rasplica. 2.2022
Roddick, Alan. 2.10213
Roddick, Jacqueline. joint author. 3.9268
Roden, Donald, 1944-. 4.10143
Roden, Martin S. 5.6402
Rodenwaldt, E. (Ernst), 1878- ed. 4.131
Roderick, Arthur James, ed. 3.1757
Roderick, Colin Arthur. 2.10152
Rodes, David Stuart. 2.7268
Rodes, David Stuart. ed. 2.7239
Rodgers, Bernard F., 1947-. 2.13307
Rodgers, Daniel T. 4.3574
Rodgers, Denny, 1900-. 5.3640
Rodgers, Harrell R. 4.2099
Rodgers, John, 1914- joint author. 5.3131
Rodgers, Richard, 1902-. 1.3960
Rodin, Auguste, 1840-1917. 1.5134
Rodin Museum, Philadelphia. 1.5712
Rodino, Peter W. 4.9733
Rodinson, Maxime. 1.2019, 3.3649
Rodman, Selden, 1909-. 1.4759, 1.5969
Rodney, Walter. 4.609
Rodó, José Enrique, 1872-1917. 2.5443
Rodríguez Fernández, Mario, 1933-. 2.5441
Rodríguez Monegal, Emir. 2.5323, 2.5375, 2.5440
Rodríguez O., Jaime E., 1940- joint author. 3.8928
Rodriguez, Raymond L. 5.3460
Rodriguez, Rita M., 1944-. 4.4576
Rodwin, Lloyd. 4.6206, 4.6339
Rodwin, Victor. 5.4618
Rodzinski, Halina. 1.4103
Roe, Anne, 1904-. 5.815
Roe, Daphne A., 1923-. 5.4987
Roe, Keith E. 5.3292
Roebuck, Janet. 4.5309
Roebuck, John Arthur, 1929-. 5.5688
Roeder, Edward. 4.8133
Roeder, Kenneth D. (Kenneth David), 1908-. 5.3867
Roeder, Richard B. joint author. 3.8544
Roehrig, Karla L. 5.4422
Rølvaag, O. E. (Ole Edvart), 1876-1931. 2.14054-2.14058
Rølvaag Symposium, St. Olaf College, Northfield, Minn., 1974. 2.14059
Roemer, John E. 4.1328
Roethke, Theodore, 1908-1963. 2.2747, 2.12410-2.12411
Roethlisberger, Fritz Jules, 1898-1974. 5.5603
Roethlisberger, Marcel, 1929- joint author. 1.6302
Roett, Riordan, 1938-. 3.9218
Roetter, Charles. 3.842

Roff, W. J. (William John) 5.6909
Roff, William R. 3.4542, 3.4551
Rogan, Helen. 5.7378
Rogers, Alan, 1933-. 3.6882
Rogers, Barbara, 1945-. 4.6169
Rogers, Benjamin Bickley, 1828-1919. tr. 2.336
Rogers, Carl R. (Carl Ransom), 1902-. 4.5655, 4.10359, 5.4868, 5.4873-5.4875
Rogers, David, 1930-. 4.10100
Rogers, Deborah Webster. 2.9435
Rogers, Eric M. 5.1995
Rogers, Everett M. 4.4885, 4.5673
Rogers, G. F. C. (Gordon Frederick Crichton) 5.6219
Rogers, H. (Hartley), 1926-. 5.1054
Rogers, H. J. 5.4451
Rogers, Ivor A. joint author. 2.9435
Rogers, Jack Bartlett. 1.2529
Rogers, James Edwin Thorold, 1823-1890. 4.3640
Rogers, Joseph William, 1906-. 5.7567
Rogers, Katharine M. 2.2411, 2.7337, 2.7343, 4.6108
Rogers, Martha E. 5.5173
Rogers, Mary F. (Mary Frances), 1944-. 4.4809
Rogers, Michael, 1935-. 3.3656
Rogers, Neville. ed. 2.8096
Rogers, Oscar A., joint author. 4.10882
Rogers, Pat. 2.5658, 2.5693, 2.7290
Rogers, Rosemarie, 1936- ed. 3.3024
Rogers, Samuel, 1763-1855. 2.8005
Rogers, Will, 1879-1935. 2.3263
Rogers, William Warren. 3.8281
Rogerson, J. W. (John William), 1935-. 1.2607
Roget, Peter Mark, 1779-1869. 2.1069-2.1070
Rogger, Hans. 3.3097, 3.3134
Rogin, Leo 1893-. 5.5298
Rogin, Michael Paul. 3.7669
Rogosin, Elinor. 4.1127
Rogow, Arnold A. 3.7642
Rohde, David W. 4.9791
Rohde, Peter Preisler, 1902-. 4.8667
Róheim, Géza, 1891-1953. 4.666
Rohen, Johannes W. (Johannes Wilhelm) 5.4147
Rohl, J. S. (Jeffrey Soden), 1938-. 5.1223
Röhl, John C. G. 3.2336
Rohlf, F. James, 1936-. 5.3312-5.3313
Rohlfs, Gerhard, 1892-. 2.864
Rohlfs, K. (Kristen), 1930-. 5.1780
Rohlich, Thomas H., 1946-. 2.2054
Rohmer, Eric, 1920-. 2.3053
Rohmer, Sax, 1883-1959. 2.9463
Rohn, Matthew. 1.6447
Rohn, Peter H. 4.8970
Rohr, John A. (John Anthony), 1934-. 4.7900
Rohrbough, Malcolm J. 3.8377
Rohrlich, F. joint author. 5.2376
Rohrlich, Ruby. 4.5836
Rohsenow, Warren M. 5.2267
Rohwer, Jürgen. 3.1028
Rohwer, Jürgen. joint ed. 3.905
Ro'i, Yaacov. 3.3076, 3.3324
Roider, Karl A. 3.1883
Rojas, Fernando de, d. 1541. 2.5197
Rojas, Ricardo, 1882-1957. 3.9168
Rojo, Jerry. 2.3153
Rokeach, Milton. 5.340
Rokes, Willis Park. 4.4642
Roland, Charles G. joint author. 5.4602
Roland, Charles Pierce, 1918-. 3.7376, 3.8174
Rolfe, John Carew, 1859-1943. tr. 2.691, 2.696
Rolfe, S. T. (Stanley Theodore), 1934-. 5.5785
Rolfsen, Dale. 5.1612
Rolland, Romain, 1866-1944. 2.4698-2.4699, 3.4311
Rolle, Richard, of Hampole, 1290?-1349. 1.3220
Rollefson, Gerhard Krohn, 1900- ed. 5.2586
Roller, David C., 1937-. 3.8113
Rolli, M. joint author. 5.8000
Rollin, Roger B. 2.7075
Rollins, Hyder Edward, 1889-1958. 2.6150, 2.6153, 2.7853, 2.7859
Rollyson, Carl E. (Carl Edmund) 2.11700
Rolo, Charles James, 1916-. 2.9481
Rolt, L. T. C., 1910-1974. 5.6215
Rom, William N. 5.5009
Romains, Jules, 1885-1972. 3.194

Roman, Charles Victor, 1864-. 3.6688
Roman de la Rose. 2.3963
Roman, Paul M. joint author. 4.4370
Romani, George T. 3.2942
Romano, Clare. joint author. 1.6468
Romano, Louis G. 4.10504
Romanoff, Alexis Lawrence, 1892-. 5.4132
Romanofsky, Peter. 4.6507
Romanucci-Ross, Lola. 3.5628
Romasco, Albert U. 3.7742
Rombauer, Irma von Starkloff, 1877-1962. 5.7134
Rome, Church of. Pope, 1878-1903 (Leo XIII) 4.1433
Romein, Jan Marius, 1893-. 3.614, 3.3641
Romer, Alfred, 1906-. 5.2419
Romer, Alfred Sherwood, 1894-. 5.3169, 5.3934, 5.4110
Romer, John. 3.5141-3.5142
Romero, José Luis, 1909-. 4.8337
Romig, Sherry H. 4.3902
Romilly, Jacqueline de. 2.266, 2.280, 2.563, 4.7337
Rommel, Erwin, 1891-1944. 3.1001, 5.7242
Romo, Ricardo. 3.8618
Rona, Peter A. 5.3100
Ronan, Colin A. 3.4643, 5.749, 5.1781, 5.1878
Ronart, Nandy. joint author. 3.5188
Ronart, Stephan. 3.5188
Ronda, James P., 1943-. 3.8485
Ronen, Simcha, 1935-. 4.3153-4.3154
Ronner, Heinz. 1.5313
Ronsard, Pierre de, 1524-1585. 2.3999
Rooke, Constance, 1942-. 2.13276
Roolvink, Roelof. 4.165
Room, Adrian. 5.7727
Rooney, John F. 4.146, 4.939
Rooney, John W. 3.2973
Rooney, Victor M. 5.1151
Roorbach, Orville A. (Orville Augustus), 1803-1861. 5.7746
Roos, Bernard W. 5.1969
Roos, Charles. joint author. 5.8283
Roos, Philip. 4.6614
Roose-Evans, James. 2.3183
Roose, Kenneth D. 4.10087
Roosevelt, Eleanor. 3.7786-3.7787
Roosevelt, Elliott, 1910-. 3.7782-3.7783
Roosevelt, Franklin D. (Franklin Delano), 1882-1945. 3.7518, 3.7769, 3.7776, 3.7783, 5.5301
Roosevelt, James, 1907- ed. 3.7598
Roosevelt, Nicholas, 1893-. 3.4604
Roosevelt, Theodore, 1858-1919. 3.7115, 3.7706-3.7708, 3.8296
Root, Robert Kilburn, 1877-. 2.6259, 2.6335, 2.6369, 2.6827
Roper, Derek. 2.6575
Roper, Elmo Burns, 1900-. 3.7535
Roper, John Herbert. 3.6262
Roper, Laura Wood. 5.5379
Roper, William, 1496-1578. 3.1413
Ropp, Steve C. 3.9056, 4.8336
Ropp, Theodore, 1911-. 5.7192
Rorabaugh, W. J. 4.6648
Rorschach, Hermann, 1884-1922. 5.187
Rorty, Amélie. 1.287, 5.415
Rorty, James, 1890-1973. 3.7670
Rorty, Richard. ed. 1.547
Rorty, Richard. 1.112
Rosa, Alfred F. 2.34
Rosaldo, Michelle Zimbalist. 4.5939, 4.6047
Rosaldo, Renato. 3.4592
Rosand, David. 1.5028, 1.6226, 1.6475
Rosberg, Carl Gustav. joint ed. 4.7131
Rosberg, Carl Gustav. 3.5283, 4.7130
Rosberg, Carl Gustav. joint author. 3.5097
Rosbottom, Ronald C., 1942-. 2.4077
Roscoe, Adrian A. 2.10036
Roscoe Pound-American Trial Lawyers Foundation. 4.9517
Rose, Albert, 1910-. 5.6596
Rose, Anne C., 1950-. 1.568
Rose, Anthony H. 5.4453
Rose, Arnold. 1.4563
Rose, Arnold Marshall, ed. 4.5092
Rose Art Museum. 3.6063

Rose, Barbara. 1.4880, 1.5888, 1.5907, 1.5950, 1.6296
Rose, Barbara. joint author. 1.5921
Rose, Barbara. comp. 1.4881
Rose, Bernice. 1.4900, 1.4903
Rose, Brian Geoffrey. 2.2854
Rose, Ellen Cronan, 1938-. 2.9667, 2.9671
Rose, Ernst, 1899-. 2.13457
Rose F. Kennedy Center for Research in Mental Retardation and Human Development. 4.6612
Rose, H. J. (Herbert Jennings), 1883-1961. 1.1641, 1.1648, 2.277, 2.628
Rose, Harold M. 3.6787
Rose-Innes, Alistair Christopher. 5.2235
Rose, J. (John Holland) Holland, 1855-1942. 3.2528
Rose, Jerry D., 1933-. 4.4995
Rose, Leo E. joint author. 3.3643
Rose, Leo E. 3.4377-3.4378, 4.8778
Rose, Lisle Abbott, 1936-. 3.7770, 3.8149
Rose, M. E. 5.2680
Rose, Mark. 2.3492, 2.6515, 2.6536
Rose, Mark H., 1942-. 4.3941
Rose, Martial. ed. 2.6210
Rose, Michael, 1937-. 4.3122
Rose. N. A. 3.3921
Rose, Phyllis, 1942-. 2.9604, 4.5618
Rose, R. B. 3.2114
Rose, Richard, 1933-. 4.4648, 4.7715, 4.8416-4.8417, 4.8420, 4.8422, 4.8431, 4.8498, 4.8507, 4.8525-4.8526, 4.8571
Rose, Saul. 4.7108
Rose, Sheldon D. 5.4879
Rose, Steven Peter Russell, 1938-. 5.314, 5.3327
Rose, Wendy. 2.13297
Rose, William, 1894-. 2.13512, 2.13606
Rose, William K., ed. 2.9044, 5.1774
Rose, Willie Lee Nichols, 1927-. 3.7195, 3.8250
Roseberry, William, 1950-. 4.2182
Roseboom, Eugene Holloway, 1892-. 3.8380-3.8381
Rosecrance, Richard N. 3.5572
Rosefielde, Steven. 5.7328
Rosemont, Franklin. 4.1133
Rosemont, Henry, 1934-. 4.10019
Rosen, Andrew. 4.8513
Rosen, Charles, 1927-. 1.3661, 1.3969, 1.4191
Rosen, Edward, 1906-. 5.1696
Rosen, Elliot A., 1928-. 3.7743
Rosen, George, 1910-. 4.2495, 4.2501, 4.5429, 5.4528, 5.4647, 5.4658
Rosen, Joe. 5.858-5.859
Rosen, Kenneth, comp. 2.10811
Rosen, Lawrence, 1941-. 3.5216
Rosen, Michael I. 5.1326
Rosen, Michael I. joint author. 5.1327
Rosen, Paul L. 4.9498
Rosen, Ruth. 4.5539
Rosen, Sherwin. 4.3090
Rosen, Stanley, 1942-. 4.8734
Rosen, Stephen I., 1943-. 5.4026
Rosenau, Helen. 1.5593
Rosenau, Helen. ed. 1.5414
Rosenau, James N. ed. 4.9033
Rosenau, James N. 4.9037
Rosenbaum, James E., 1943-. 4.3213
Rosenbaum, Jonathan. 2.2957
Rosenbaum, Marsha, 1948-. 5.4964
Rosenbaum, Robert J., 1943-. 3.8565
Rosenbaum, S. P. (Stanford Patrick), 1929-. 2.11105, 3.1747
Rosenberg, Alexander, 1946- joint author. 1.709
Rosenberg, Arthur, 1889-1943. 3.2365, 3.3192
Rosenberg, Bernard, 1923-. 3.6186, 4.4829
Rosenberg, Betty. 2.10565
Rosenberg, Charles E. 5.796, 5.4528
Rosenberg, David, 1914-. 5.699
Rosenberg, Edgar. 2.5584
Rosenberg, Emily S., 1944-. 3.7599
Rosenberg, H. M. (Harold Max) 5.2197
Rosenberg, Hans, 1904-. 4.8615
Rosenberg, Harold. 1.4829-1.4830, 1.4901, 1.5141, 2.12415
Rosenberg, Harry Ewing, 1932- joint author. 4.10908
Rosenberg, Isaac, 1890-1918. 2.9288
Rosenberg, Jakob, 1893- joint author. 1.6168

Rosenberg, Jay F. 1.1309
Rosenberg, Jerome H. 2.9912
Rosenberg, Jerry Martin. 4.4618, 5.1137
Rosenberg, John D. 2.8026, 2.8038
Rosenberg, M. Michael. 4.5076
Rosenberg, Marvin. 2.6665, 2.6671
Rosenberg, Morris. 5.497
Rosenberg, Morris. joint ed. 4.1208
Rosenberg, Nathan, 1927-. 4.1864, 4.2109
Rosenberg, Pierre. 1.4981, 1.6053, 1.6076
Rosenberg, Robert M., 1926-. 5.2894
Rosenberg, Rosalind, 1946-. 4.5990
Rosenberg, Samuel N. 2.867
Rosenberg, Sheldon. 2.17
Rosenberg, Stanley D. 4.5072, 4.5794
Rosenberry, Edward H. 2.11172
Rosenblatt, Aaron. 4.6497
Rosenblatt, David Hirsch. 5.2744
Rosenblatt, Louise M. (Louise Michelle) 2.2366
Rosenblatt, Paul C. 4.2715
Rosenblatt, Roger. 2.10560
Rosenblith, Walter A., ed. 5.4363
Rosenbloom, Jerry S. 4.3142
Rosenbloom, Paul C. 1.1221
Rosenblueth, Emilio, 1926- joint author. 5.5859
Rosenblum, Leonard A. ed. 5.4021
Rosenblum, Naomi. 5.6921
Rosenblum, Ralph. 5.7010
Rosenblum, Robert. 1.4774, 1.4779, 1.4844, 1.4900, 1.5867, 1.6113
Rosenfeld, Arthur H., 1926- joint author. 5.2071
Rosenfeld, Charles. 5.3113
Rosenfeld, Isaac, 1918-1956. 2.2654
Rosenfeld, L. (Leon), 1904-1974. 5.1884
Rosenfeld, Morris, 1862-1923. 2.1817
Rosenfeld, Myra Nan. 1.5553
Rosenfeld, Sybil, 1903-. 2.3017
Rosenfeld, Sybil Marion, 1903-. 2.3156, 2.3307, 2.3319
Rosenfelt, Deborah Silverton. 2.10292
Rosenfield, John M. 1.4733, 1.5077, 1.6371
Rosengarten, Theodore. 3.8249, 4.2910
Rosenheim, Margaret Keeney. 4.9893
Rosenkrantz, Barbara Gutmann, joint author. 4.5705
Rosenmeier, Henrik, 1931-. 1.1121
Rosenne, Shabtai. 4.9152
Rosenne, Shabtai. 4.9153
Rosenstone, Steven J. 4.8138, 4.8165
Rosenstone, Steven J. joint author. 4.8111
Rosenthal, Bernard, 1934-. 2.10394, 2.10837, 2.10914
Rosenthal, Daniel M. 5.5766
Rosenthal, Erwin Isak Jakob, 1904-. 4.7272
Rosenthal, Franz, 1914- ed. 3.451-3.452
Rosenthal, Harold D. 1.3521
Rosenthal, Judith. 5.5118
Rosenthal, M. L. (Macha Louis), 1917-. 2.5834, 2.10511
Rosenthal, Marilyn, 1934-. 2.2752
Rosenthal, Nan. 1.5671
Rosenthal, Norman. 1.4801
Rosenthal, Robert, 1933-. 4.10386, 5.67
Rosenthal, Robert Alan. 3.7999
Rosenthal, Stuart. 2.3042, 4.1867
Rosenthal, Ted L. 5.298
Rosenwaike, Ira, 1936-. 4.1684
Rosenwald, Lessing J. (Lessing Julius), 1891-1979. 1.6452, 1.6472
Rosenzweig, Adelle. 4.8926
Rosenzweig, Franz, 1886-1929. 1.1969, 1.1989
Rosenzweig, James Erwin, 1929- joint author. 4.2651
Rosenzweig, Mark R. 5.4351
Rosenzweig, Roy. 4.3501
Rosett, Arthur I., 1934-. 4.9882
Rosewater, Victor, 1871-1940. 2.3588
Rosier, James L. joint author. 2.930
Rosillo Callé, Francisco, 1945-. 5.6878
Rosing, Kenneth Earl. 4.3761
Rosinsky, Natalie M. (Natalie Myra) 2.10552
Roskell, John Smith. 3.1380
Roskill, Mark W., 1933-. 1.4656, 1.6061-1.6062
Roskill, Stephen Wentworth. 3.1030, 3.1285
Rosman, Bernice L. joint author. 5.4941
Rosnay, Joël de. 4.1213
Rosner, David 1947-. 5.4711

Rosner, Fred. 5.4512
Rosner, Gabriella. 4.9258
Rosner, Roy D., 1943-. 5.6403
Rosovsky, Henry. 4.2548
Rosovsky, Henry. joint author. 4.2553
Rosow, Jerome M. 4.2090, 4.3203
Rosow, Jerome M. ed. 4.3578
Ross, Alan O. 4.10956, 5.5103
Ross, Alan Strode Campbell. 2.1012
Ross, Alexander Milton, 1832-1897. 3.7271
Ross, Angus. 2.7214
Ross, Arthur Max. 4.3332
Ross, Barbara Joyce. 3.6646
Ross, Charles Alexander. 5.3859
Ross, Charles Derek. 3.1378, 3.1381-3.1382
Ross, Cleon W., 1934-. 5.3743
Ross, Craig M., 1952-. 4.973
Ross, David A., 1936-. 4.353
Ross, David O. 2.713
Ross, Earle Dudley, 1885-. 4.10066
Ross, Edyth L., 1916-. 4.6617
Ross, Elizabeth Dale. 4.10414
Ross, Euan James Ferguson, 1941- joint author. 5.2311
Ross, Graham, 1933-. 3.744
Ross, Graham G. 5.2483
Ross, Heather L. 4.5596
Ross, Herbert Holdsworth, 1908-. 5.3859
Ross, Ian K. 5.3722
Ross, Irwin. 3.7814
Ross, John, 1921-. 1.6468, 5.2800
Ross, John A., 1934-. 4.1579
Ross, John Dawson, 1853-1939. 2.7501
Ross, John F. 5.6428
Ross, John M. 4.1032
Ross, Joseph A. 5.6108
Ross, June R. P. 5.3859
Ross, Kenneth A. joint author. 5.1552
Ross, Margaret Louise. joint author. 5.4234
Ross, Martha. 3.373
Ross, Mary. comp. 3.8339
Ross, Monte ed. 5.5944
Ross, Philip. 4.3333
Ross, Ralph Gilbert. 4.7417
Ross, Ramon Royal. 4.10318
Ross, Robert Baldwin, 1869-1918. ed. 2.8267
Ross, Robert H. ed. 2.8160
Ross, Ruth A., 1933-. 4.5902
Ross-Sheriff, Fariyal, 1940-. 5.4820
Ross, Sinclair. 2.9969-2.9970
Ross, Stanley Robert, 1921-. 3.8946, 3.8950
Ross, Stephen David. 1.1352
Ross, Steven Joseph. 4.2043
Ross, Steven T. 5.7380
Ross, Thomasina, ed. 3.9150
Ross, W. D. (William David), 1877-. 1.277, 1.283, 1.308, 1.880, 1.1440, 1.1490, 2.437-2.439
Ross, William T. 2.11948
Rossabi, Morris. 3.4093
Rossel, Sven Hakon. 2.13968, 2.14008
Rosselli, John. 1.4230
Rosser, J. Barkley (John Barkley), 1907-. 1.1222
Rossetti, Christina Georgina, 1830-1894. 2.8006-2.8009
Rossetti, Dante Gabriel, 1828-1882. 2.8006, 2.8013-2.8017
Rossetti, William Michael, 1829-1919. 2.8006, 2.8008-2.8009, 2.8013, 2.8021-2.8022
Rossi, Alice S., 1922-. 4.5893-4.5894, 4.5973
Rossi, Ferdinando. 1.5505
Rossi, Jean J. 4.6647
Rossi, Paolo, 1923-. 3.494
Rossi, Peter Henry, 1921-. 4.4806, 4.6223, 4.6345
Rossiter, Arthur Percival. 2.6748
Rossiter, Clinton Lawrence, 1917-1970. 3.6017, 3.6391, 4.7721, 4.7803-4.7804, 4.7932, 4.9768
Rossiter, Frank R. 1.3905
Rossiter, Margaret W. 5.792, 5.803, 5.5239
Rossman, Charles. 2.5438
Rossman, Parker. 4.5536
Rostand, Edmond, 1868-1918. 2.4700, 2.9640
Rosten, Leo Calvin, 1908-. 2.3670, 2.3735, 2.12416
Roston, Murray. 2.5632, 2.7137
Rostov, Charles I. 1.6587
Rostovtsev, M. I. (Mikhail Ivanovich) 3.2752

Rostovzeff, Michael Ivanovitch, 1870-1952.
  3.122, 3.551, 3.2636, 3.2789, 3.3686, 3.3804
Rostow, Eugene V. (Eugene Victor), 1913-.
  4.9845
Rostow, W. W. (Walt Whitman), 1916-. 3.7513,
  4.1484-4.1485, 4.2280
Roszak, Theodore, 1933-. 3.205, 4.5097,
  4.10823
Rota, Gian Carlo, 1932- joint author. 5.1511
Rotberg, Robert I. joint author. 4.8795
Rotberg, Robert I. 3.1155, 3.5234, 4.646
Rotenstreich, Nathan, 1914-. 1.1915, 3.495
Roth, Cecil, 1899-1970. 3.3904, 3.3950, 3.3976
Roth, David Morris, 1935-. 3.8020
Roth, Guenther. 4.7063
Roth, H. Mark. 3.5417
Roth, Hans-Georg. Catharine, joint author.
  5.7791
Roth, Henry. 2.12417
Roth, John K. ed. 1.636
Roth, John R., 1939-. 5.3449
Roth, Joseph, 1894-1939. 2.13855-2.13856
Roth, Julius A. 5.5214
Roth, Leland M. 1.5317
Roth-Loly, Arlette, joint comp. 2.4847
Roth, Martin, 1934-. 2.11099
Roth, Philip. 2.13298-2.13304
Roth, Robert H., 1939-. 5.4301
Rotha, Paul, 1907-. 2.2986, 2.3043-2.3044
Rothbard, Murray Newton, 1926-. 4.7701
Rothbart, Harold A. 5.6191
Rothe, Anna Herthe, ed. 3.324
Rothenberg, Gunther Erich, 1923-. 5.7193,
  5.7345
Rothenberg, Jerome, 1931- comp. 2.2325
Rothenberg, Joshua. 1.1932
Rothenberg, Michael B. 5.5077
Rothenberg, Paula S., 1943-. 4.6057
Rothenberg, Robert E. 5.5058
Rothenstein, John, Sir, 1901-. 1.4942, 1.6021
Rothfels, Hans, 1891-1976. 3.2432
Rothman, Beatrice Katz. 5.5074
Rothman, David J. 4.6519, 4.8040
Rothman, Ellen K., 1950-. 4.5774
Rothman, Harry. 5.6878
Rothman, Jack. 4.1228
Rothman, Milton A. 5.2006
Rothmüller, Aron Marko. 1.3642
Rothschild, Brian J., 1934- ed. 5.5474
Rothschild, Bruce L., 1941- joint author. 5.1285
Rothschild, Henry, 1932-. 5.4683
Rothschild, Joan. 5.5521
Rothschild, Joseph. 3.2997, 4.8686
Rothschild, Kurt Wilhelm. 4.3134
Rothschild, Lincoln, 1902-. 1.5955
Rothschild, Miriam. 5.3796
Rothstein, Eric. ed. 2.5661
Rothstein, Eric. 2.5757, 2.5997, 2.7017
Rothstein, Frances. 4.2148
Rothstein, Marian, 1944-. 3.1957
Rothstein, William G. 5.4523
Rothwell, Kenneth J. joint author. 4.4139
Rothwell, Victor. 3.779, 3.1258
Rotkirchen, Livia. 3.1085
Rotman, Joseph J., 1934-. 5.1290, 5.1304
Rottenberg, Simon. 4.3138
Rottensteiner, Franz. 2.3455
Rottensteiner, Franz. comp. 2.3722
Rottmann, Larry, 1942- comp. 2.10755
Rotunda, Ronald D. 4.9661
Rotwein, Eugene. 4.1413
Rouault, Georges, 1871-1958. 1.6144
Roubaud, Jacques, 1932-. 2.4790
Roubaud, Noelle. 2.4291
Roudaut, Jean. 2.4464
Roudiez, Leon Samuel, 1917-. 2.3915
Rougé, Jean. 5.7486
Rougemont, Denis de, 1906-. 3.15, 3.1197,
  4.5507
Roughead, William Nicol. 2.8447
Roughgarden, Jonathan. 5.3474
Roumain, Jacques, 1907-1944. 2.4840
Round, John Horace, 1854-1928. 3.1341
Rourke, Constance, 1885-1941. 1.5971, 2.10655,
  3.6162
Rouse, Beatrice A. 4.6650
Rouse, Blair. 2.11781
Rouse, Irving. 3.5762, 3.9179

Rouse, Ruth, ed. 1.3099
Rouse, W. H. D. (William Henry Denham),
  1863-1950. 2.510, 2.650, 2.676
Rouse, William Henry Denham, tr. 2.683
Rousseau, Ann Marie, 1946-. 4.6586
Rousseau, G. S. (George Sebastian) ed. 2.5661,
  2.7267
Rousseau, Henri Julien Félix, 1844-1910. 1.6146
Rousseau, Jean-Jacques, 1712-1778. 2.3104,
  2.4087-2.4091, 4.7432-4.7434, 4.10186
Rout, Leslie B., 1936-. 3.9026
Routh, C. R. N. (Charles Richard Nairne)
  3.1384
Routh, Jane. 2.2384
Routley, Erik. 1.4239, 1.4249, 2.5959
Roux, Edward. 3.5457
Rover, Constance. 4.8514
Rovere, Richard Halworth, 1915-. 3.7536,
  3.7644, 3.7671, 3.7831
Rovin, Jeff. 2.74
Rovinsky, Robert T., 1940-. 2.13967
Rovira, Carmen. 5.7631
Rowan, Andrew T., 1962-. 4.10627
Rowan, Ford. 4.9540
Rowan-Robinson, Michael. 5.1879, 5.1883
Rowe, Colin. 1.5555
Rowe, Donald R. 5.5987
Rowe, George E., 1947-. 2.6638
Rowe, Mary Budd. 5.984
Rowe, Mike. 1.4304
Rowe, Nicholas, 1674-1718. 2.7233-2.7234
Rowe, William, ed. 2.5425
Rowe, William T. 4.4243
Rowell, George. comp. 2.6242
Rowell, George. ed. 2.6243
Rowell, George. 2.2799, 2.3309-2.3310, 2.7727
Rowell, Henry T., ed. 3.2729
Rowell, Henry Thompson, 1904-. 3.2797
Rowell, Thelma. 5.4027
Rowen, Herbert Harvey. 4.8578
Rowen, Herbert Harvey. comp. 3.2957
Rowland, Beatrice L. 5.5171
Rowland, Benjamin, 1904-1972. 1.4682, 1.5048,
  1.5107
Rowland, Beryl. 2.6370, 5.5044
Rowland, Christopher, 1947-. 1.2555
Rowland, Howard S. 5.5171
Rowland-Jones, Anthony. 1.4551
Rowland, K. T. 5.7516
Rowland, Leslie S. 3.7385
Rowland, Willard D. 2.2858
Rowlands, John, 1931-. 1.6175
Rowlands, M. J. 3.221
Rowlandson, Thomas, 1756-1827. 1.6387
Rowles, Ruth Anderson. 4.151
Rowley, C. D. (Charles Dunford) 3.5656
Rowley, Harold Henry, 1890-. 1.2507, 1.2524,
  1.2563
Rowley, Kelvin, 1948-. 3.4434
Rowley, William, 1585?-1642? joint author.
  2.6634
Rowntree, Lester, 1938-. 4.375
Rowse, A. L. (Alfred Leslie), 1903-. 2.6705,
  3.1425, 3.1735, 3.6868, 4.5310
Rowson, Mrs., 1762-1824. 2.11218
Rowton, Frederic, 1818-1854. 2.6105
Roxborough, Ian. 3.9268
Roxburgh, Edwin. joint author. 1.4553
Roxon, Lillian. 1.3525
Roy, Callista. 5.5168, 5.5194
Roy Chowdhury, Subrata. 3.4151
Roy, Claude, 1915-. 2.4369, 2.4701
Roy, G. Ross (George Ross), 1924-. 2.4808,
  2.7502
Roy, Gabrielle, 1909-. 2.4820-2.4824
Roy, Manisha, 1936-. 4.6143
Roy, Robert F. 5.3038
Royal Academy of Arts (Great Britain) 1.4953,
  1.5038, 1.6239, 1.6298, 1.6368
Royal Astronomical Society. 5.1789, 5.1793
Royal Botanic Gardens, Kew. 5.3633
Royal Commission on the Economic Union and
  Development Prospects for Canada. 4.2124
Royal Economic Society (Great Britain) 4.1268,
  4.1441, 4.1447-4.1448
Royal Entomological Society of London. 5.3879
Royal Historical Society (Great Britain) 5.7983,
  5.7988, 5.7990-5.7992

Royal Horticultural Society (Great Britain)
  5.5351
Royal Horticultural Society (Great Britain).
  Lily Committee. 5.5351
Royal Institute of Chemistry. 5.4722
Royal Institute of International Affairs. 1.2076,
  3.34, 3.747-3.748, 3.854, 3.1705, 3.1907,
  3.2905, 3.3588, 3.3592, 3.3752, 3.4389,
  3.4535, 3.4682, 3.4808, 3.7606, 3.9171,
  3.9229, 4.2232, 4.2510, 4.3784, 4.6926,
  4.7118, 4.7325, 4.9254, 4.9269
Royal Institute of International Affairs.
  Information Dept. 3.751, 3.3310
Royal Institute of Philosophy, London. 1.1558
Royal Irish Academy. 1.4943-1.4944
Royal Ontario Museum. 1.5065, 1.6448, 1.6640,
  5.7097
Royal Shakespeare Company. 2.7173
Royal Society for the Prevention of Accidents.
  5.5019
Royal Society (Great Britain) 4.448, 5.2189
Royal Society (Great Britain). Discussion
  Meeting. (1983 May 25-26: London, England)
  5.2007
Royal Society of Canada. 3.8680
Royal Society of London. Study Group on
  Non-Verbal Communication. 5.465
Royce, Anya Peterson. 4.618
Royce, James E. 4.6633
Royce, Josiah, 1855-1916. 1.424, 1.635-1.638,
  1.642, 1.877, 1.1509, 1.1620, 1.2826
Royce, William F. 5.5481
Royden, H. L. 5.1492
Royle, Trevor. 2.9832
Roysdon, Christine. joint author. 5.8118
Royster, Charles. 3.6941
Royston, Robert. comp. 2.10052
Rozanov, V. V. (Vasiliĭ Vasil'evich), 1856-1919.
  2.1261, 2.1528
Rozema, J. 5.3780
Rozenblit, Marsha L., 1950-. 3.3940
Różewicz, Tadeusz. 2.1725-2.1726
Rozman, Gilbert. 4.6270
Ru, Suichu. 3.4627
Rubadiri, David, joint comp. 2.10046
Rubel, Lee A. 5.1487
Rubens, Alfred, 1903-. 4.834
Rubens, Peter Paul, Sir, 1577-1640.
  1.6272-1.6273
Rubenstein, Edward, 1924-. 5.4496
Rubenstein, Roberta, 1944-. 2.9032
Rubin, Barry M. 3.3871, 3.3881
Rubin, David, 1924-. 2.1893, 2.1910
Rubin, Jay, 1941-. 2.2004
Rubin, Joan, 1932- ed. 2.25
Rubin, Lillian B. 4.5597
Rubin, Louis Decimus, 1923-. 2.10448,
  2.10456-2.10458, 2.10460-2.10461, 2.10656,
  2.10722, 2.10922, 2.12795-2.12796, 3.8128,
  3.8182, 5.7793
Rubin, Neville N. 3.5400
Rubin, Richard L. 3.7845
Rubin, Rick, 1949-. 4.5521, 5.8387
Rubin, Ruth. 1.4352
Rubin, Sol. 4.9859
Rubin, Theodore Isaac. 4.4929
Rubin, William Stanley. 1.4831, 1.4851, 1.4853,
  1.4979, 1.5690, 1.6070
Rubin, Zick. 4.5711
Rubinfeld, Daniel L. joint author. 4.1720
Rubins, Jack L. 5.4780
Rubinstein, Alvin Z. ed. 3.3062
Rubinstein, Alvin Z. 3.3077, 3.3221, 3.3260,
  3.3562, 3.3749, 4.9074, 4.9272
Rubinstein, Anton, 1829-1894. 1.3963
Rubinstein, Artur, 1887-. 1.4069-1.4070
Rubinstein, Charlotte Streifer. 1.4861
Rubió i Balaguer, Jordi, 1887-1982. tr. 2.5104
Rubner, Alex. 4.2444
Rubner, Michael. 3.3873
Rubulis, Aleksis, 1922-. 2.1749
Ruby, Jay. 2.3044, 4.492
Ruby, Robert H. 3.5747
Ruchames, Louis, 1917-. 4.3117
Ruck, Carl A. P. tr. 2.528
Rucker, Bryce W. 2.58
Rucker, Darnell, 1921-. 1.531
Rudavsky, David. joint comp. 3.3930

Rudd, Dale F. 5.6835
Rudd, Margaret, 1925-. 2.7432
Rudd, Niall. 2.720
Rudd, Niall. tr. 2.702
Rudder, Robert S. 2.5095
Rudé, George F. E. 3.664, 3.1571, 3.1745, 3.2072, 3.2100, 4.5049, 4.5286, 4.5355, 4.6856
Rudenstine, Angelica Zander. 1.4663, 1.5036
Ruderman, Malvin A. joint author. 5.2031
Rudge, A. W. (Alan W.) 5.6493-5.6494
Rudich, Norman. 2.2643
Rudin, Harry Rudolph, 1898-. 3.5399
Rudin, Walter, 1921-. 5.1444-5.1445, 5.1472
Rudinger, Hugo, illus. 5.5523
Rudman, Harry William, 1908-. 3.2864
Rudofsky, Bernard, 1905-. 1.5461, 1.5587
Rudolf, Max. 1.4502
Rudolph, Frederick. 4.10067, 4.10616
Rudolph, James D., 1947-. 3.8874, 3.9071, 3.9091, 3.9237
Rudolph, Kurt. 1.2971
Rudolph, Lloyd I. joint author. 4.10142
Rudolph, Lloyd I. 3.4105, 4.6407
Rudolph, Mae. joint author. 5.4381
Rudolph, Marguerita. 4.10411
Rudolph, Richard C. 1.5757
Rudolph, Susanne Hoeber. 4.10142
Rudolph, Susanne Hoeber. joint author. 3.4105, 4.6407
Rudolph, Wolfgang, 1923-. 4.3951
Rudow, Edward H., joint author. 5.4699
Rudwick, Elliott M. joint author. 3.6622, 3.6680, 3.8439
Rudwick, Elliott M. joint comp. 3.6623
Rudwick, M. J. S. 5.3138, 5.3148
Rudy, Stephen. 2.33, 2.1372
Rudy, Willis, 1920- joint author. 4.10058
Rue, John E. 3.4834
Rueckert, William H. (William Howe), 1926-. 2.11437, 2.12679
Ruedisili, Lon C. 5.6133
Ruellan, André. 4.8892
Ruether, Rosemary Radford. 1.1614, 1.1960, 1.2387, 1.2912, 1.2929, 1.2938, 1.2999-1.3000, 4.5895
Rufer, Josef, 1893-. 1.3613
Ruff, Marcel A, 1896-, ed. 2.4134
Ruffinelli, Jorge. 2.5350
Ruffle, John. 3.5134
Ruffner, Frederick G. ed. 1.54
Ruffner, James A. 2.1074, 5.2575, 5.2577
Rufinus Tyrannius, Aquileiensis, 345 (ca.)-410. 1.2189
Ruge, Friedrich. 3.1029
Rugg, Evelyn. joint comp. 2.5142
Rugg, Harold Ordway, 1886-1960. 4.10521, 5.347
Ruggiero, Guido, 1944-. 4.5520
Ruggiers, Paul G. 2.6329
Ruggles, Eleanor, 1916-. 2.3246, 2.12016a
Rugman, Alan M. 4.3027, 4.4616
Ruhmer, Eberhard. 1.6172
Ruisdael, Jacob van, 1628 or 9-1682. 1.5024
Ruiz i Calonja, Juan. 2.895
Ruiz, Juan, fl. 1343. 2.5201
Ruiz, Ramón Eduardo. 3.8951
Rukeyser, Muriel, 1913-. 2.5348, 2.12418
Ruland, Richard, 1932- comp. 2.11247
Rule, John C. ed. 3.2037
Rulfo, Juan. 2.5350-2.5354
Rumbelow, Donald. 4.6838
Rumberger, Russell W. 4.3309
Rumiantsev, Pavel Ivanovich. 1.4112
Rump, Ariane. 1.1799
Runciman, Steven, Sir. 1.2311, 1.3104, 1.3112, 3.589, 3.2944, 3.4583
Runciman, W. G. (Walter Garrison), 1934-. 4.1214, 4.7227, 4.7254, 4.7276
Runcorn, S. K. ed. 5.2489
Rundle, Bede. 5.288
Runfola, Ross. joint author. 4.953
Runyan, William McKinley. 5.36
Runyon, Damon, 1880-1946. 2.12420-2.12421
Ruoff, James E. 2.5487, 2.6797
Rupley, William H. 4.10460
Rupp, E. Gordon (Ernest Gordon), 1910-. 1.1496, 1.2335
Rupp, Kalman. 4.3304

Rupp, Leila J., 1950-. 3.1137
Rupprich, Hans, 1898-. 2.13453
Rus, Teodor. 5.1194
Rusch, William G. 1.2835
Ruse, Michael. 5.3349, 5.3399
Rush, Theressa Gunnels, 1945-. 5.7800
Rushdie, Salman. 2.10133
Rushton, Peters, 1915-1949. 1.1642
Rusk, Ralph Leslie, 1888-. 2.10470, 2.11020
Rusk, Robert R. (Robert Robertson), 1879-1972. 4.9953
Ruskin, John, 1819-1900. 1.5135-1.5136, 1.5480-1.5481, 2.8023-2.8031, 2.8036, 4.1418
Russ, Charles V. J. 2.1180
Russ, Joanna, 1937-. 2.2554, 2.13308
Russ, William Adam, 1903-. 3.5642-3.5643
Russell, Bertrand, 1872-1970. 1.759-1.766, 1.872, 1.1078, 1.1260, 1.1282, 1.1441, 1.1504, 1.1598, 3.1175, 4.7474, 4.9176, 4.10215-4.10216, 5.882, 5.928, 5.1049, 5.1921 1.771
Russell, Bertrand Russell, 3rd Earl, 1872-. 1.771
Russell, Conrad. 3.1391, 3.1485
Russell, D. A. (Donald Andrew) comp. 2.264
Russell, D. A. (Donald Andrew) 2.518
Russell, Delbert W. 2.4817
Russell, Diana E. H. 4.6738, 4.6742
Russell, Douglas A. 2.13938
Russell, Edward J. (Edward John), Sir, 1872-1965. 5.5266
Russell, Francis, 1910-. 4.9462
Russell, Frank, 1949-. 1.5259, 1.6582
Russell, Frank D., 1923-. 1.4839
Russell, Frederick H. 1.2923
Russell, George William, 1867-1935. 2.9289-2.9292
Russell, George William Erskine, 1853-1919. ed. 2.7353
Russell, Graeme, 1947-. 4.5662
Russell, H. Diane (Helen Diane) 1.4974
Russell, Howard S. 4.2957
Russell, I. Willis, 1903-. 2.964
Russell, James D. 4.10290
Russell, Jeffrey Burton. 1.1618, 1.2952-1.2953, 5.674
Russell, John, 1919-. 1.4785, 1.4993, 1.6023, 1.6156
Russell, John David. 2.9233
Russell, Letty M. 1.2560, 1.2939
Russell, Mariann, 1935-. 2.12595
Russell, Milton, 1933- joint author. 4.3713, 4.3772
Russell, Nelson Vance, 1895-. 3.8432
Russell, Nicholas J. 5.3764
Russell, Olive Ruth. 5.4578
Russell, R. D. (Richard Doncaster), 1929- joint author. 5.3074
Russell, Ross. 1.4333
Russell, Ruth B. 4.9196
Russell Sage Foundation. 1.60, 4.6473
Russell, Thomas. 4.4433
Russell, William Howard, Sir, 1820-1907. 3.6047
Russell, William Ritchie. 5.4341
Russell-Wood, A. J. R., 1939-. 3.9209, 3.9227
Russett, Bruce M. 5.4094, 4.9251
Russett, Bruce M. joint author. 4.9243
Russia. 4.9915
Russian S.F.S.R. Verkhovnyĭ Sud. 4.9918
Russo, David J. 3.6218
Russo, Luigi, 1892-1961. 2.5012
Russo, Nancy Felipe, 1943-. 5.91
Russo, Vito. 2.2991
Russo, William. 1.4454
Rust, James H. 5.6606
Rustin, Bayard, 1910-. 3.6689
Rustomji, Nari, 1919-. 3.4333
Rüstow, Alexander, 1885-1963. 3.46
Rustow, Dankwart A. 3.46, 4.3776, 4.8679
Rustow, Dankwart A. comp. 4.4953
Ruswa, Mirza Mohammad Hadi, 1857-1931. 2.1902
Rutgers Center of Alcohol Studies. 5.8438
Rutgers University. Art Gallery. 1.4965
Rutgers University. Center for Urban Policy Research. 4.6353
Ruth, Kent. ed. 3.8532
Rutherfoord, Peggy. ed. 2.3708

Rutherford, Andrew. comp. 2.7537
Rutherford, Andrew. ed. 2.7898
Rutherford Centennial Symposium, University of Canterbury, 1971. 5.2074
Rutherford, Ernest, 1871-1937. 5.2074, 5.2402
Rutherford, John David. 2.5331
Rutherford, Noel. 3.5680
Ruthven, Douglas M. (Douglas Morris), 1938-. 5.6838
Ruthven, K. K. 2.5510
Rutland, Robert Allen, 1922-. 2.3589, 3.6975, 3.7005, 4.7831
Rutledge, Albert J. 5.5386
Rutledge Books, Inc. 4.1029
Rutman, Anita H. 3.8217
Rutman, Darrett Bruce. 3.7994, 3.8217
Rutstein, David D. 5.4617
Ruttan, Vernon W. joint author. 4.2889
Rutter, Michael. 4.10121, 5.5109
Ruttkowski, W. V. (Wolfgang Victor), 1935-. 2.2358
Ruymgaart, P. A. (Peter Arnold), 1925-. 5.1546
Ruzek, Sheryl Burt. 5.5042
Ryals, Clyde de L., 1928-. 2.7492-2.7493, 2.8244
Ryan, Alan. 4.1561
Ryan, Cornelius. 3.961, 3.983
Ryan, Francis Aloysius, 1887-. 4.10234
Ryan, Francis J. (Francis Joseph), 1916- joint author. 5.3439
Ryan, Halford Ross. 2.10858
Ryan, John Morris. 3.9071
Ryan, Judith, 1943-. 2.13507
Ryan, Kevin. 4.10807
Ryan, Marleigh Grayer. 2.2073, 2.2092
Ryan, Mary Ellen, 1928- joint author. 4.2955
Ryan, Mary P. 4.5605
Ryan, Michael J. (Michael Joseph), 1953-. 5.3932
Ryan, Paul B. joint author. 3.820
Ryan, Peter, 1923- ed. 3.5650
Ryan, William, 1923-. 4.5188
Ryan, William J. 5.5120
Rybáček-Mlýnková, Jiřina. 5.8402
Rybalka, Michel. 2.4718
Rybalka, Michel. joint author. 2.4739
Rychlak, Joseph F. 5.533
Rychtman, Allen C. 5.2860
Rydberg, Jan, joint author. 5.2916
Rydel, Christine. 2.1295
Rydell, Robert W. 5.5655
Ryder, A. J. 3.2359
Ryder, Alan Frederick Charles. 3.2941
Ryder, Arthur William, 1877-1938. 2.1941, 2.1944, 2.1947
Ryder, Dorothy E. 5.7885
Ryder, Frank Glessner, 1916-. 2.13620
Ryder, John Douglas, 1907-. 5.6251
Ryder, Lewis H., 1941-. 5.2474
Rye, Owen S. 3.248
Ryerson, Richard Alan, 1942-. 3.8088
Ryken, Leland. 1.2535
Rykwert, Anne. 1.5382
Rykwert, Joseph, 1926-. 1.5249, 1.5382, 4.6314
Ryle, Anne. 2.1102
Ryle, Gilbert, 1900-1976. 1.773, 1.1243, 5.390
Ryle, Michael. 4.8471
Ryley, Robert M. 2.7334
Rymer, Thomas, 1641-1713. 2.7236
Rynne, Xavier. 1.3126-1.3129
Ryōkan, 1758-1831. 2.2070
Rypka, Jan, 1886-1968. 2.1963
Ryskamp, Charles. 2.6939, 2.6957, 2.6960, 2.6962
Ryther, John H. joint author. 5.5466
Rywkin, Michael. 3.3326
Rzepnicki, Tina L. 4.6567
Saarinen, Thomas F. (Thomas Frederick) 4.30
Saaty, Thomas L. 4.9161
Saba, Umberto, 1883-1957. 2.5064
Sabaliūnas, Leonas, 1934-. 3.3315
Sábato, Ernesto R. 2.5397-2.5399
Sabato, Larry. 4.8134, 4.8183
Sabbattini, Nicola, ca. 1575-1654. 2.3158
Sabel, Charles F. 4.3000
Sabin, Joseph, 1821-1881. 5.7730-5.7732
Sabine, George Holland, 1880-1961. 4.7262

Sabine, Lorenzo, 1803-1877. 3.6959
Sabine, Wallace Clement, 1868-1919. 1.5497
Sabins, Floyd F. 4.25
Sabisch, Christian. 2.3719
Sable, Martin Howard. 5.8403
Sabloff, Jeremy A. joint author. 3.5697, 4.499
Sabloff, Paula L. W. 3.5908
Sabnis, Gajanan M. 5.5871
Sabo, Donald F. 4.953
Saccio, Peter. 2.6772
Sacco, Nicola, 1891-1927. 4.6704
Sachar, Howard Morley, 1928-. 3.3908
Sachdev, Paul. 4.5703
Sachedina, Abdulaziz Abdulhussein, 1952-.
    1.2066
Sachs, Carolyn E., 1950-. 5.5240
Sachs, Curt, 1881-1959. 1.3640, 1.4120, 1.4134,
    4.1102
Sachs, Murray, 1924-. 2.4168
Sachs, Nelly. 2.13857-2.13858
Sachs, Paul Joseph, 1878-1965. 1.6470
Sachtouřes, Miltos, 1919-. 2.607
Sacilotto, Deli. joint author. 1.6469
Sack, Albert. 1.6566
Sackstein, David L. 5.4583
Sacks, Karen. 4.3286
Sacks, Michael Paul. 4.3232
Sacks, Peter M. 2.5781
Sacks, Stephen R. 4.3190
Sackville-West, V. (Victoria), 1892-1962.
    2.9294-2.9296
Sacramento Union. 3.5637
Saddhatissa, H. 1.2124
Saddlemyer, Ann. 2.8147
Sade, marquis de, 1740-1814. 2.4095-2.4098
Sadek, Konrad. 5.1128
Sader, Marion. 5.8316
Sa'dī. 2.1974
Sa'di, 1184-1292. 2.1975
Sadie, Stanley. 1.3503, 1.3510, 1.3516
Sadiq, Muhammad. 2.1897
Sadker, Myra. joint author. 4.10838
Sadleir, Michael, 1888-1957. 1.4601, 2.8230,
    2.8234, 5.7965
Sadock, Benjamin J., 1933- joint author. 5.4878
Sáenz de Santa María, Carmelo. 2.5188
Saerchinger, César, 1889- tr. 3.2423
Saf, Avital. 3.1124
Safa, Helen Icken. 4.6083-4.6084
Saff, Donald, 1937-. 1.6469
Saffady, William, 1944-. 5.7613, 5.7624
Safford, Frank, 1935-. 5.5623
Safire, William, 1929-. 3.7908, 4.7794
Safrai, Shemuel, 1919-. 3.3889-3.3890
Safran, Nadav. 3.3882, 3.3932, 3.5160
Šafránek, Miloš, 1894-. 1.3922
Sagan, Carl, 1934-. 5.363-5.364, 5.1729, 5.6693
Sagan, Dorion, 1959-. 5.3394, 5.3482
Sagan, Françoise. 2.4682
Sagan, Leonard A. 5.5998
Sagar, Keith M. 2.8994, 2.9719-2.9720
Sagarin, Edward, 1913- joint author. 4.5056
Sagarra, Eda. 4.5361
Sage, Daniel D. 4.10937
Sage, George Harvey. comp. 4.958
Sage, Leland L. (Leland Livingston), 1899-.
    3.8505
Sage, Lorna. 2.9033
Sager, Ruth. 5.3439-5.3440
Sager, Samuel. 4.8784
Sagi, Abraham. 4.5660
Sahagún, Bernardino de, d. 1590. 3.8888-3.8889
Sahal, Devendra. 5.5627
Saher, P. J. 1.430
Sahgal, Nayantara, 1927-. 3.4303
Sahitya Akademi. 2.1924
Sahli, Nancy Ann. 5.8475
Sahlins, Marshall David, 1930-. 3.5625, 4.494,
    4.528
Sahni, Sartaj. 5.1241
Said, Edward W. 2.2442, 3.3617
Saigyō, 1118-1190. 2.2051
Sailor, Wayne. 4.10944
Sainsbury, Diana. joint author. 5.4430
Sainsbury, Keith. 3.924
Saint, Andrew. 1.5399, 1.5458
Saint-Denis, Michel, 1897-. 2.3135, 2.3374
Saint-Denis, Suria. 2.3135

Saint-Exupéry, Antoine de, 1900-1944.
    2.4702-2.4703
Saint-Gaudens, Augustus, 1848-1907. 1.5672
Saint-Simon, Henri, comte de, 1760-1825.
    4.7053
Saint-Simon, Louis de Rouvroy, duc de,
    1675-1755. 3.2040
Saint Véran, Robert. 4.8808
Sainte-Beuve, Charles Augustin, 1804-1869.
    2.4283
Saintsbury, George, 1845-1933. 2.1045, 2.1051,
    2.2463, 2.2655, 2.5494, 2.5527, 2.5947, 2.6162
Sáinz de Robles, Federico Carlos, 1898-. 2.5218
Saito, Shiro. 5.8065
Sakanishi, Shio, 1896- tr. 2.2026
Sakata, Hiromi Lorraine. 1.3744
Sakharov, Andreĭ, 1921-. 3.198, 3.3261-3.3262
Saki, 1870-1916. 2.9132-2.9134
Sakiya, Tetsuo, 1926-. 4.3818
Salamanca, J. R. 2.13309-2.13310
Salamon, George. 2.13876
Salamon, Lester M. 4.7926
Salanave, Leon E., 1917-. 5.2550
Salant, Walter S. 4.4491
Salbstein, M. C. N. 3.3951
Sale, Kirkpatrick. 4.10722
Sale, Roger. 2.5551, 2.6537
Sale, William Merritt, 1899- ed. 2.7459
Salem, James M. 5.8133
Salem, Lionel. joint author. 5.2816
Salerno, Henry Frank, 1919- comp. 2.6244
Sales, Gillian. 5.4097
Salesbury, William, 1520?-1600? 2.1010
Salgādo, Gāmini, 1929-. 2.5844, 2.6666, 2.6853,
    4.6789
Salibi, Kamal S. (Kamal Suleiman), 1929-.
    3.3796
Salih, Halil Ibrahim. 3.3694
Salinas, Pedro, 1892-1951. 2.5094, 2.5111,
    2.5118
Salinger, J. D. (Jerome David), 1919-. 2.12423,
    2.12426
Salinger, Jerome David, 1919-. 2.12424-2.12426
Salinger, Pierre. 3.7868
Salisbury, Frank B. 5.3743, 5.6700
Salisbury, Harrison Evans, 1908-. 2.3664, 3.198,
    3.995
Salisbury, Neal. 3.5743
Salisbury, Stephan. 4.9551
Salk, Jonas, 1914-. 5.929
Salkey, Andrew. comp. 2.9983
Salkey, Andrew. ed. 2.9984
Salkin, Harvey M. 5.5591
Saller, Richard P. 4.1732
Sallis, John, 1938-. 1.523
Sallnow, John. 4.8371
Sallust, 86-34 B.C. 2.691, 3.2749
Sallustius, Neoplatonist. 1.1645
Salmon, Charles G. 5.5879, 5.5887
Salmon, Edward Togo. 3.2755, 3.2792
Salmon, J. B. 3.2641
Salmon, J. H. M. (John Hearsey McMillan),
    1925-. 3.2014, 4.8576
Salmon, Lucy Maynard, 1853-1927. 2.3545
Salmon, Merrilee H. 3.220
Salmon, Paul. 2.13460
Salmon, Wesley C. 1.1193, 5.930-5.931, 5.2096
Salomon, Bernard, 16th cent., illus. 1.2493
Salomon, Ernst von, 1902-1972. 3.2412
Salomon, Isidore Lawrence, 1899- tr. 2.5036
Salomon, Pierre. ed. 2.4290
Salomone, A. William (Arcangelo William),
    1915-. 3.2881
Saloutos, Theodore. 3.6547, 4.2945
Salpeter, Eliahu. 4.8782
Salsbury, Stephen. joint author. 4.3792
Salt, Henry Stephens, 1851-1939. ed. 4.1559
Salt, John. 4.1658
Salter, Elizabeth. 2.6404
Salter, Frederick Millet, 1895-1962. 2.5856
Salter, John Thomas, ed. 3.7619
Salter, Timothy, 1942- joint author. 2.6442
Salter, W. E. G. 4.2686
Salthe, Stanley N. 5.3374
Saltman, David. 5.7075
Saltykov, Mikhail Evgrafovich, 1826-1889.
    2.1422-2.1423

Saltzman, Barry. 5.2569
Salu, M. B., tr. 2.6308
Salu, M. B. 2.6336
Salvadori, Mario George, 1907-. 5.5853,
    5.6090-5.6091
Salvadori, Massimo L. 4.7058
Salvato, Joseph A. 5.4668
Salvatore, Nick, 1943-. 4.3584, 4.6998
Salvatorelli, Luigi, 1886-1974. 3.2836
Salvemini, Gaetano, 1873-1957. 3.405, 3.879,
    3.2876, 3.2891
Salvendy, Gavriel, 1938-. 5.5560, 5.5686
Salvini, Roberto. 1.5642
Salwak, Dale. 2.9458
Salway, Peter. 3.1306
Salzer, Felix. 1.4455
Salzman, Eric. 1.3678
Salzman, Jack. comp. 2.10716, 2.10850, 2.11605
Salzman, Paul. 2.5993
Sambhi, Piara Singh, joint author. 1.1827
Sambrook, James. 1.6717, 2.7315-2.7316
Sambrook, Joseph. 5.3462
Sambursky, Samuel, 1900-. 5.1935
Samiuddin, Abida. 3.4353
Sammons, Jeffrey L. 2.2490, 2.13607
Samora, Julian, 1920-. 3.8328
Samples, Gordon. 5.8134
Sampson, Anthony. 3.1711, 4.4077
Sampson, Edward C. 2.12707
Sampson, Edward E. 4.9979
Sampson, Geoffrey. 2.41
Sampson, George, 1873-1950. 2.5528
Sampson, Harold. 5.4908
Sampson, Roy J. 4.3894
Sams, Eric. 1.4522
Sams, K. I. joint author. 4.3639
Samsonowicz, Henryk. 3.3333
Samuel, Horace Barnett, 1883- tr. 1.1045
Samuel, Howard D. 4.8007
Samuel, Maurice, 1895-1972. 1.2541, 2.1782,
    3.4028
Samuel, Pierre, 1921- joint author. 5.1362
Samuel, R. H. (Richard H.), 1900- jt. ed.
    2.13593
Samuels, Charles Thomas, 1936-1974. 2.11126
Samuels, Ernest. 1.5150, 3.6241-3.6243, 3.6978
Samuels, M. L. (Michael Louis) 2.153
Samuels, Marwyn S. 4.376, 4.9307
Samuels, Robert E., 1913-. 4.4039
Samuels, Wilfred D. 3.6690
Samuelson, Paul Anthony, 1915-. 4.1265,
    4.1393, 4.1458
Samz, Jane. 5.1818
San Antonio Museum of Art. 1.4905
San Francisco. Institute for Philosophical
    Research. 1.139
San Francisco Museum of Modern Art. 1.4846,
    1.5912, 1.6615
San Juan, E. (Epifanio), 1938-. 2.8287
San Martín, Marta, joint author. 3.9096
Sánchez-Albornoz, Nicolás. 4.1685
Sánchez, Florencio, 1875-1910. 2.5444
Sánchez, Marta Ester. 2.10303
Sánchez, Pedro A., 1940-. 5.5282
Sanchez, Pedro C., joint author. 3.5646
Sánchez, Roberto G., ed. 2.5223
Sánchez-Sinencio, Edgar. 5.6477
Sanchez, Sonia, 1935-. 2.13311
Sand, George, 1804-1876. 2.4285-2.4292
Sandars, N. K. (Nancy K.) 1.4687, 3.2524
Sanday, Peggy Reeves. 4.5831
Sanday, W. (William), 1843-1920. 1.2710
Sandbach, F. H. 1.327, 2.299
Sandberg, Larry. 1.3452
Sandberg, Lars G. 4.3854
Sandblad, Nils Gosta. 1.6118
Sandbrook, Richard. 4.2610, 4.2614, 4.3670
Sandburg, Carl, 1878-1967. 2.12430-2.12432,
    3.7293, 3.7296
Sandeen, Ernest Robert, 1931-. 1.2795, 5.8442
Sandelowski, Margarete. 5.5072
Sandemose, Aksel, 1899-1965. 2.14050
Sander, David M. 5.6476
Sander, Volkmar. 2.13641
Sanderlin, George William, 1915- ed. 3.8991
Sanders, Charles Richard, 1904-. 2.7549
Sanders, Donald A. 4.10368
Sanders, E. P. 1.1912, 1.2707, 1.2899

Sanders, Herbert H. 5.6899
Sanders, I. J. (Ivor John) 3.299
Sanders, Irwin Taylor, 1909-. 3.3546, 4.5392, 4.6370
Sanders, John Essington, 1926- joint author. 5.3055
Sanders, Joseph Newbould. 1.2696
Sanders, Judith A. 4.10368
Sanders, Keith R. 4.7238
Sanders, Mark S. 5.5687
Sanders, Michael, 1945-. 3.843
Sanders, Ronald. 1.4062
Sanders, Scott R. (Scott Russell), 1945-. 2.8995
Sanders, Thomas Edward, 1926- comp. 2.2322
Sanders, William B., 1944-. 4.6865
Sanders, William T. 3.8893
Sanderson, James L. 2.6446
Sanderson, Miss J. Burdon, joint tr. 1.1546
Sanderson, R. T. (Robert Thomas), 1912-. 5.2822
Sanderson, Stewart. 2.1111
Sandier, S. 5.4642
Sandison, Alan. 2.9199
Sandler, Irving, 1925-. 1.5911
Sandler, Shmuel. 3.3883
Sandler, Stanley R., 1935-. 5.2752
Sandmaier, Marian. 4.6640
Sandmel, Samuel. 1.1907, 1.2638
Sandor, Bela Imre. 5.5779, 5.5784
Sandoval, Judith Hancock de. 1.4921
Sandow, Stuart A. ed. 4.10688
Sandoz, Ellis, 1931-. 1.1064, 4.8112
Sandoz, Mari, 1907-. 3.8520
Sandreuter, William O. 4.984
Sandrow, Nahma. 2.3404
Sands, Kathleen M. 3.5833
Sands, Matthew Linzee, joint author. 5.1991
Sandys, John Edwin, Sir, 1844-1922. 2.231, 2.387, 3.2728
Saner, Hans, 1934-. 1.917
Sanford, Charles L., 1920-. 3.6038
Sanford, Jonathan E. 4.4577
Sanford, Nevitt. ed. 4.10090
Sanger, Clyde. 3.8791
Sanger, Margaret, 1879-1966. 4.5675
Sanger, Ruth, joint author. 5.4225
SanGiovanni, Lucinda. 4.964
Sanguin, André-Louis, 1945-. 5.8205
Sanguineti, Edoardo. ed. 2.4997
Sanguineti, Edoardo. 2.4895
Saniel, Josefa M. 3.4924
Şanjur, Diva. 5.7116
Śaṅkarācārya. 1.1680
Śaṅkarakkuruppā, Ji., 1901-1978. 2.2268
Sankey, Benjamin. 2.12746
Sano, Emily J. 1.5760
Sansom, Clive, 1910-. 2.2759
Sansom, George Bailey, Sir, 1883-1965. 3.4892-3.4893, 3.4912
Sansom, William, 1912-. 2.9301
Sant, Roger W. 5.6150
Santa Celoria, Rita, ed. 2.4056
Santamaría, Francisco Javier, 1889-. 2.908
Santaniello, A. E. 1.5470
Santas, Gerasimos Xenophon. 1.242
Santas, Joan Foster. 2.11782
Santayana, George, 1863-1952. 1.643-1.649, 1.4600, 2.2592, 2.2749-2.2750, 2.11219, 4.7464
Santer, Mark. 1.2200
Santeusanio, Richard P., 1942-. 4.10515
Santibañez, James, 1931- joint comp. 2.10683
Santley, Robert S., jt. author. 3.8893
Sapegno, Natalino, 1901-. 2.4876-2.4877, 2.4975, 2.5002
Sapir, Edward, 1884-1939. 2.9, 2.94
Sapiro, Virginia. 4.5961, 4.6023
Sapolsky, Harvey M. 5.7445
Sapora, Allen Victor Heimback, 1912-. 4.10389
Saposs, David Joseph, 1886-. 4.3365
Sappho. 2.315
Saqqaf, Abdulaziz Y., 1951-. 4.6274
Saracho, Olivia N. 4.10938
Sarasohn, David. joint comp. 3.7198
Sarason, Seymour Bernard, 1919-. 4.6529, 4.10010, 4.10522, 5.32, 5.586
Sarasvati Amma, T. A. 5.1085
Saravanamuttoo, H. I. H. 5.6219

Sarbin, Theodore R. 5.189
Sard, R. D., 1915-. 5.1650
Sardar, Ziauddin. 5.784-5.785
SarDesai, D. R. 3.3639
Sargeant, Winthrop, 1903-. 1.4334
Sargeaunt, John, 1857- ed. and tr. 2.698
Sargent, Charles Sprague, 1841-1927. 5.3688
Sargent, Lydia. 4.7150
Sargent, Lyman Tower, 1940-. 5.7977
Sargent, M., joint author. 5.2676
Sargent, Porter. 4.10924
Sargent, Porter Edward, 1872-1951. 4.9942
Sargious, Michel. 5.6067
Sarianidi, V. I. (Viktor Ivanovich) joint author. 4.741
Sario, Leo. joint author. 5.1493
Sarkar, Badal. 2.1873
Sarkar, Jadunath, Sir, 1870-1958. 3.4257, 3.4258
Sarkar, Ranadhir Sarma, 1908-. 2.3559
Sarkisyanz, Manuel. 1.1764
Sarlós, Robert Károly, 1931-. 2.3275
Särlvik, Bo. 4.8455
Sarmiento, Domingo Faustino, 1811-1888. 3.9244
Sarmiento, Guillermo. 5.3274
Sarna, Jonathan D. 3.8053
Saroyan, William, 1908-. 2.12436-2.12440
Sarratt, Reed. 4.10871
Sarraute, Nathalie. 2.3529, 2.4704-2.4714
Sarrazin, Albertine. 2.4791
Sarris, Andrew. 2.2928, 2.2968
Sarti, Roland, 1937-. 3.2892, 4.3074
Sarton, George, 1884-1956. 5.751-5.753
Sarton, May, 1912-. 2.12441-2.12446
Sartori, Giovanni. 4.7583, 4.7787
Sartre, Jean Paul, 1905-. 1.476, 1.491-1.493, 1.495, 1.848, 2.2607-2.2608, 2.4144, 2.4199, 2.4532, 2.4542, 2.4718-2.4737, 2.4739, 2.4741
Sarukhán, José. 5.3769
Saso, Mary. 4.2552
Saso, Michael R. 1.1807
Sasowsky, Norman. 1.6444
Sassoon, Anne Showstack. 4.7478
Sassoon, Don. 4.8633
Sassoon, Siegfried, 1886-1967. 2.7943, 3.845
Sastri, P. S. 1.192
Satchell, William. 2.10229
Satchler, G. R. (George Raymond) 5.2481
Satina, Sophie, 1879-. 1.3953
Sato, Hideo, 1942-. 3.6462, 4.4177
Satō, Ryūzō, 1931-. 4.2550
Sato, Yasuhiro. 1.6391
Satow, Ernest Mason, Sir, 1843-1929. 3.4953, 4.9084
Satter, Ruth L. joint author. 5.3741
Satterfield, Charles N. 5.6839
Satterthwaite, Gilbert Elliott. 5.1740
Sattler, D. E. (Dietrich E.), 1939-. 2.13612
Satz, Ronald N. 3.5808
Saucier, Gene Allen. 4.4550
Sauer, Carl Ortwin, 1889-. 3.5979, 3.8573, 3.9143, 4.52, 4.240, 4.373, 5.5228
Sauer, Kenneth, 1931- joint author. 5.3336
Sauerländer, Willibald. 1.5700
Saul, S. B. joint author. 4.2202-4.2203
Saul, S. B. 4.4229
Saulnier, Verdun Louis. 2.3854
Saunders, Christopher Thomas. 4.2801
Saunders, Edward Manning, 1829-1916. 3.8764
Saunders, George, 1936-. 3.3546
Saunders, Hilary Aidan St. George, 1898-1951, joint author. 3.1050
Saunders, J. J. (John Joseph), 1910-1972. 3.3622
Saunders, John Warren, 1919-. 5.4124, 5.4137
Saunders, Laurance James. 4.5323
Saunders, P. T. (Peter Timothy), 1939-. 5.3366
Saunders, Robert J. 4.4053
Saunders, Thomas Bailey, 1860-1928. 1.958, 1.960-1.961, 2.7101
Saur, Karl Otto. 3.2470
Saur, Klaus Gerhard, comp. 5.7573
Saussure, Ferdinand de, 1857-1913. 2.141
Sauter, Marc Rodolphe, 1914-. 4.739
Sauvaget, Jean, 1901-1950. 5.8038
Sauvy, Alfred, 1898-. 4.1599, 4.2330
Savage, Andrea. 4.6484
Savage, Henry Lyttleton, 1892-. 2.6419
Savage, Paul L. joint author. 5.7283

Savage, Richard, d. 1743. 2.7237
Savage, William Sherman. 3.6794
Savant, C. J. 5.6183
Savas, Emanuel S. 4.3089
Savelle, Max, 1896-. 3.6163, 3.8708
Saveth, Edward Norman. 3.6219
Savitch, H. V. 4.5189
Savitt, Ronald. 4.4318
Savitt, Todd L., 1942-. 5.4529
Savitz, Leonard D. 4.6770, 4.6821
Savory, Roger. 3.4080
Savory, Teo. 2.4676
Savours, Ann. 4.107
Savvides, Geōrgios P. 2.579, 2.581
Sawa, Nagayo. 4.2874
Sawatzky, Harry Leonard, 1931-. 1.3366
Sawers, David. joint author. 5.5640
Sawers, Larry, 1942-. 4.6347
Sawhill, Isabel V. joint author. 4.5596
Sawhill, John C., 1936-. 5.6117
Sawkins, Frederick J. 5.6734
Sawyer, Donald T. 5.2914
Sawyer, P. H. 3.1337, 3.3364-3.3365
Sawyer, Ralph Alanson, 1895-. 5.2306
Sawyer, Ruth, 1880-1970. 4.10319
Sawyer, Thomas E. 3.3999
Sawyer, W. W. (Walter Warwick), 1911-. 5.1473
Sax, Joseph L. 3.6000
Sax, Karl, 1892-. 4.1621
Sax, N. Irving (Newton Irving) 5.2590, 5.5557
Saxe, Leonard. 4.10762
Saxe, Maurice, comte de, 1696-1750. 5.7211
Saxelby, F. Outwin. 2.7768
Saxén, Lauri. 5.4138
Saxena, K. M. S. joint author. 5.2081
Saxl, Fritz, 1890-1948. 1.4932
Saxo, Grammaticus, d. ca. 1204. 2.6652, 2.9443
Saxon, A. H. 4.1187, 4.1193
Saxton, Martha. 2.10903
Say, M. G. (Maurice George), 1902-. 5.6254, 5.6315
Sayce, Richard Anthony. 2.870
Sayeed, Khalid B. 3.4132
Sayer, Chloë. 4.837
Sayers, Dorothy L. (Dorothy Leigh), 1893-1957. 1.2234, 2.9303-2.9307
Sayers, Janet. 4.5846
Sayers, R. S. (Richard Sidney), 1908-. 4.4542
Sayers, Raymond S. 2.5463
Sayers, W. C. Berwick (William Charles Berwick), 1881-1960. 5.7636
Sayles, G. O. (George Osborne), 1901-. 3.1300, 4.8392, 4.8458
Sayles, Leonard R. 4.3366
Saylor, J. Galen (John Galen), 1902-. 4.10447
Sayre, Anne. 5.4173
Sayre, Eleanor. 1.6493
Sayre, Kenneth M., 1928-. 1.271, 5.123
Sayre, Wallace Stanley, 1905-1972. 4.7977
Saywell, John T., 1929-. 3.8651, 3.8815, 4.8315
Sayyid-Marsot, Afaf Lutfi. 3.5159, 3.5162
Scagel, Robert Francis, 1921-. 5.3698
Scalapino, Robert A. 3.3630, 3.3642, 4.7125, 4.8761, 4.8762, 4.8765, 4.9081
Scalapino, Robert A. ed. 3.5041
Scales, James R. (James Ralph), 1918-. 3.8533
Scales, L. E. 5.1551
Scalzi, John B. 5.6084
Scammell, Michael. comp. 2.1328
Scammell, Michael. 2.1640
Scammell, W. M. 4.4156
Scammon, Richard M. ed. 4.7948, 4.8106
Scanlan, James P. (James Patrick), 1927-. 1.1103, 1.1106
Scanlan, John A. 4.8955
Scanlan, Robert H. 5.5858
Scanzoni, John H., 1935-. 4.5598-4.5600
Scarborough, Dorothy, 1878-1935. 2.12447
Scarf, Maggie, 1932-. 5.4817
Scarisbrick, J. J. 3.1402
Scarr, Deryck. 3.5554, 3.5636
Scarr, Deryck. joint author. 3.5543
Scarr, Sandra. 5.371
Scarre, Christopher. 4.710
Scarrow, Howard A. 4.8193, 4.8298
Scates, Allen E. 4.1044
Scattergood, V. J. 2.6516

Šćepanović, Branimir, 1937-. 2.1214
Scève, Maurice, 16th cent. 2.4008
Schaaf, Barbara C. 2.11619
Schaar, John H. 4.8071
Schach, Paul. ed. 2.13985
Schachner, Nathan, 1895-. 3.7023
Schacht, Hjalmar Horace Greeley, 1877-1970.
    3.2413
Schacht, Joseph. 1.2042, 1.2054, 3.3653
Schacht, Richard, 1941-. 1.446
Schachter, Frances Fuchs, 1930-. 4.5723
Schadé, J. P. 5.4323
Schade, Werner. 1.6167
Schaefer, Vincent J. 5.2505
Schaeffer, Neil, 1940-. 2.3785
Schaerf, Carlo. 4.9172
Schafer, Donna E. joint author. 4.5813
Schafer, Edward H. 3.4702, 3.4858, 4.4096
Schäfer, Heinrich, 1868-1957. 1.4700
Schafer, John W. joint author. 5.5263
Schafer, R. Murray. 1.4376, 1.4414
Schafer, Ronald W., 1938- joint author. 5.6378,
    5.6569
Schafer, Roy. 5.4918
Schafer, Roy. joint author. 5.4848
Schafer, Roy. 5.188, 5.190, 5.4919
Schaff, Adam. 1.477
Schaff, David Schley, 1852-. 1.2278, 1.2955
Schaff-Herzog encyclopedia. 1.2223
Schaff, Philip, 1819-1893. 1.2278, 1.2383, 1.2955
Schaffer, Benjamin Bernard. 4.2215
Schaffer, Ronald. 5.8229
Schaffner, Kenneth F. 5.2212
Schaffner, Nicholas, 1953-. 1.4100
Schaie, K. Warner (Klaus Warner), 1928-.
    5.624
Schallenberg, Richard H., 1943-1980. 5.6325
Schaller, Elmer O. (Elmer Otto) joint author.
    4.4320
Schaller, George B. 5.4001, 5.4044
Schaller, Michael, 1947-. 3.6431, 3.6467
Schambra, William A. 4.7797, 4.9670
Schandler, Herbert Y., 1928-. 3.4503
Schank, Roger C., 1946-. 4.10343, 5.289, 5.1020
Schanzer, Ernest. 2.6661
Schapera, Isaac, 1905-. 3.5460, 4.565
Schapiro, Leonard Bertram, 1908-. 2.1463,
    3.3193, 3.3212, 4.7605, 4.8638, 4.8663
Schapiro, Meyer. 1.4786, 1.5171, 1.5178, 1.5644,
    1.6074, 1.6247
Schappes, Morris U. (Morris Urman), 1907- ed.
    3.6573
Schaps, David M. 4.5850
Schapsmeier, Edward L. 3.7635, 4.8150, 5.5241
Schapsmeier, Frederick H. 3.7635
Schapsmeier, Frederick H. joint author. 4.8150,
    5.5241
Scharf, Aaron, 1922-. 1.4635
Scharf, Lois. 4.3289
Scharf, Peter, 1945-. 4.6831, 4.6896
Scharff, Robert. comp. 4.998
Scharfstein, Ben-Ami, 1919-. 1.428
Scharnhorst, Gary. 2.11043
Schatt, Stanley. 2.13402
Schattschneider, Elmer Eric, 1892-1971. 4.4203,
    4.8176
Schatz, Ronald W., 1949-. 4.3527
Schatzberg, Michael G. 4.8810
Schaub, Thomas H., 1947-. 2.13287
Schauble, Paul G. 5.4815
Schauer, Frederick F. 4.7679
Schave, Barbara. 4.10454
Schawlow, A. L., 1921- ed. 5.2271, 5.2316
Schechner, Richard, 1934-. 2.3099, 2.3103,
    2.3153
Schechter, Martin. jt. author. 5.1527
Schechter, Solomon, 1847-1915. 1.1904
Schechter, Susan. 4.6708
Schecter, Jerrold L. 1.1770
Scheer, Bradley T. (Bradley Titus), 1914- comp.
    5.4179
Scheerenberger, R. C. 5.4978
Scheff, Peter A. 5.6047
Scheffer, Victor B. 5.3981, 5.4009
Scheffler, Israel. 1.1300, 4.9970, 4.9971,
    4.10255, 5.932
Scheffler, Israel. ed. 4.10163
Scheffler, Walter P. H. 2.13665

Scheflen, Albert E. 5.4926
Scheiber, Harry N. 4.1883, 4.3945
Scheick, William J. 1.3339, 5.7796
Scheidemann, Philipp, 1865-1939. 3.2354
Schein, Edgar H. 4.2699, 4.4378
Scheina, Robert L. joint author. 5.7437
Scheingold, Stuart A. 4.9499
Scheja, Georg. 1.6174
Scheler, Lucien. ed. 2.4524
Scheler, Lucien. 2.4003
Scheler, Max, 1874-1928. 1.1059-1.1060, 1.1320,
    1.1559
Schell, Herbert Samuel, 1899-. 3.8511
Schell, Jonathan, 1943-. 3.4488, 3.7909
Schell, Orville. 3.4622
Schellenberg, James A., 1932-. 4.4942
Schelling, Corinne Saposs. 4.10792
Schelling, Felix Emmanuel, 1858-1945. 2.5870
Schelling, Friedrich Wilhelm Joseph von,
    1775-1854. 1.922-1.923
Schelling, Thomas C., 1921-. 4.1844
Schellmann, Jörg. 1.5042
Schenk, George H. joint author. 5.2687
Schenk, Margaret T., 1919-. 5.5502
Schenk, Werner. joint author. 2.1230
Schenker, Heinrich, 1868-1935. 1.4456
Scheper-Hughes, Nancy. 5.4836
Scherchen, Hermann, 1891-1966. 1.4503
Scherer, F. M. (Frederic M.) 4.3054
Scherer, F. M. (Frederic M.) joint author.
    4.3838
Schérer, Jacques. 2.3933, 2.4062
Scherer, John L. ed. 3.4841
Scherer, Klaus Rainer. 2.20, 5.461
Scherman, Thomas, comp. 1.3803
Schermerhorn, R. A. (Richard Alonzo), 1903-.
    3.4203
Scherrei, Rita A. joint author. 4.10587
Schetky, L. McDonald. 5.5818
Scheub, Harold. 4.814
Scheuchzer, John Gaspar, 1702-1729, tr. 3.4909
Scheuerle, William H. 2.7884-2.7885
Scheven, Yvette. 5.8073
Schevill, Ferdinand, 1868-1954. 3.2483, 3.2919,
    3.2955
Schey, Harry Moritz, 1930-. 5.1365
Schick, Allen. 4.4681, 4.4683, 4.4687
Schick, Marvin. 4.9848
Schick, Richard P. 4.3512
Schicke, Walter, joint author. 5.2905
Schickel, Richard. 2.3261
Schider, Fritz, 1846-1907. 1.5823
Schieder, Theodor. 3.2490
Schieffelin, Edward L. 3.5662
Schier, Donald Stephen, 1914- joint ed. 2.2499
Schier, Peter, 1950-. 4.8743
Schiff, Gary S., 1947-. 4.8786
Schiff, Gert. 1.6132
Schiff, Leonard I. (Leonard Isaac), 1915-.
    5.2121
Schiff, Marilyn, 1939-. 1.4918
Schiffer, Menahem, joint author. 5.2098
Schiffer, Michael B. 3.249
Schiffer, Stephen R. 1.141
Schiffman, Susan S. 5.55
Schiffman, Yale M. 5.6230
Schiffrin, Harold Z. 3.4764
Schiffrin, Jacques. 2.4029
Schillebeeckx, Edward, 1914-. 1.2811, 1.2841,
    1.2868-1.2870, 1.3224
Schiller, Bradley R., 1943-. 4.2100
Schiller, Friedrich, 1759-1805. 1.1372,
    2.13646-2.13649
Schiller, Gertrud. 1.5167
Schiller, Herbert I., 1919-. 2.59
Schiller, Marvin, 1940- joint comp. 1.1405
Schilling, Bernard Nicholas. 2.6991
Schilling, Donald L. joint author. 5.6474
Schilling, Donald L. 5.6359, 5.6464
Schilling, Edmund, 1888-. 1.5804
Schilling, Jane Metzger, jt. author. 4.3164
Schilpp, Paul Arthur, 1897-. 1.209, 1.575,
    1.578, 1.593, 1.607, 1.651, 1.756, 1.758, 1.771,
    1.784, 1.836, 1.911, 1.976, 1.981, 1.1030
Schimmel, Annemarie. 1.2085, 1.6608, 2.1761,
    2.1898, 2.1918, 2.1925
Schimmel, David. joint author. 4.9598
Schindler, Anton Felix, 1795-1864. 1.3804

Schindler, G. E. 5.6418
Schiøtz, Aksel, 1906-. 1.4564
Schirmer, R. Heiner, 1942- joint author. 5.4406
Schiro, Michael. 4.10448
Schisgal, Murray, 1929-. 2.13312
Schlachter, Gail A. 4.10584, 5.7603, 5.8476
Schlagel, Richard H., 1925-. 5.712
Schlaifer, Robert. 4.2669, 4.2727
Schlauch, Margaret. 2.95, 2.974, 2.5991,
    2.13991
Schlebecker, John T. 5.8093
Schlee, Susan. 4.333
Schlegel, Alice. 4.573, 4.584
Schlegel, Friedrich von, 1772-1829. 2.2367,
    2.13655
Schlegel, Richard, 1913-. 5.933
Schleiermacher, Friedrich, 1768-1834. 1.957,
    1.1536, 1.2775, 1.2876
Schlereth, Thomas J. 1.437, 3.5999, 3.6137
Schleser, G. 5.6883
Schlesinger, Arthur Meier, 1917-. 2.3595,
    3.6007, 3.6200, 3.6280, 3.6392, 3.7124,
    3.7771, 3.7869, 4.6224, 4.7606, 4.7921,
    4.8166, 4.8946-4.8947
Schlesinger, Benjamin. 4.5519
Schlesinger, Carl, joint author. 5.7558
Schlesinger, Elfriede G. joint author. 4.6615
Schlesinger, Joseph A. 4.8253
Schlesinger, Rudolf. 4.5287
Schlesinger, Stephen C. 4.8170
Schlessinger, Nathan. 5.4913
Schlick, Moritz, 1882-1936. 1.1087
Schlobin, Roger C. 5.7966
Schlobin, Roger C. joint author. 2.3485
Schlosberg, Harold, 1904- joint author. 5.212
Schloss Charlottenburg. 1.4981
Schlossman, Steven L. 4.9894
Schlote, Werner. 4.4230
Schlueter, June. 2.13897
Schlueter, Paul, 1933-. 2.9034, 2.13060
Schluter, R. A., joint author. 5.2071
Schmalensee, Richard. 4.3803, 4.4428
Schmeckebier, Laurence Eli, 1906-. 1.4922,
    1.5745, 1.5931
Schmeckebier, Laurence Frederick, 1877-1959.
    5.7781
Schmeling, Gareth L. 2.445
Schmeller, Johann Andreas, 1785-1852. 2.1010
Schmelz, U. O. (Usiel Oskar) 3.4009
Schmemann, Alexander, 1921-. 1.3103
Schmid, Alex Peter. 4.6714
Schmid, Andrea Bodó. 4.924
Schmid, Calvin Fisher, 1901-. 5.1403
Schmid, Carol L. 4.5389
Schmidgall, Gary, 1945-. 1.4405
Schmidhauser, John R. (John Richard), 1922-.
    4.9648, 4.9846
Schmidt, A. V. C. 2.6318
Schmidt, A. V. C. (Aubrey Vincent Carlyle)
    2.6391
Schmidt, Albert-Marie. comp. 2.3929
Schmidt, Alvin J. 4.6173
Schmidt, Dorey. 2.9668
Schmidt-Görg, Joseph, 1897-. 1.3810
Schmidt, Hans, 1938-. 1.3810, 3.9120
Schmidt, Helmut Dan, joint author. 4.7535
Schmidt, Henry C., 1937-. 3.8878
Schmidt, Hugo, 1929-. 2.13629
Schmidt, Janet. 4.6897
Schmidt, John L., 1943-. 5.3982
Schmidt, Leo Anton, joint author. 4.4382
Schmidt, Maarten. joint ed. 5.1840
Schmidt, Martin, 1909-. 1.3376
Schmidt, Michael, 1947-. 2.5837, 2.6195
Schmidt, Milton O. (Milton Otto), 1910-.
    5.5824
Schmidt-Nielsen, Knut, 1915-. 5.4108,
    5.4182-5.4184
Schmidt, Peter R. (Peter Ridgway), 1942-.
    3.5295
Schmidt, Richard A. 5.6797
Schmiechen, James A., 1940-. 4.3858
Schmieder, Wolfgang. 1.3605
Schmincke, Hans-Ulrich. 5.3045
Schmithals, Walter. 1.2701
Schmitt, Bernadotte Everly, 1886-1969. 3.364,
    3.418, 3.722, 3.766, 3.776, 3.787
Schmitt, Francis Otto, 1903- ed. 5.4321

Schmitt, Fritz, 1904-. 2.13458
Schmitt, Hans A. joint author. 3.2291
Schmitt, Hans A. 3.2456
Schmitt, Karl Michael, 1922-. 3.6473, 4.7613
Schmitt, Peter J. 3.6164
Schmitt, Robert C. 4.1682
Schmitz, Carl August. 1.5771
Schmitz, E. Robert (Elie Robert), 1889-1949.
  1.4534
Schmitz, Hermann, 1882-. 1.6556
Schmitz, Kenneth L. 1.952
Schmokel, Wolfe W. 4.8933
Schmuck, Patricia A. 4.10311
Schmuck, Richard A. 4.10311
Schmutzler, Robert. 1.4794, 1.4832
Schnabel, Artur, 1882-1951. 1.4071-1.4072
Schnabel, Franz, 1887-. 3.2290
Schnabel, W. 5.2772
Schnackenburg, Rudolf, 1914-. 1.2697, 1.2818
Schnädelbach, Herbert, 1936-. 1.965
Schnaiberg, Allan. 4.1849
Schnall, David J. 4.8787
Schnapp, John B. 4.3822
Schnapper, Antoine. 1.4969
Schnapper, Morris Bartel, 1912- ed. 3.911
Schneede-Sczesny, Marina. 1.4994
Schneede, Uwe M. 1.4994
Schneemelcher, Wilhelm, 1914- ed. 1.2735
Schneer, Cecil J., 1923-. 5.2956
Schneewind, Elizabeth Hughes, ed. 1.1466
Schneewind, J. B. (Jerome B.), 1930-. 1.1424
Schneider, Ben Ross, 1920-. 2.3300
Schneider, Daniel R. 5.6820
Schneider, David Moses, 1899- joint author.
  4.580
Schneider, David Murray, 1918-. 4.585, 4.591,
  4.5581
Schneider, Edward L. 5.3508, 5.4216
Schneider, Elisabeth Wintersteen, 1897-. 2.7591
Schneider, Harold K. 4.596, 4.657
Schneider, Helen. 4.3360
Schneider, Herbert W. 1.557
Schneider, Herbert Wallace, 1892-. 1.2408,
  1.3396
Schneider, Jane. 4.2358
Schneider, Jerrold E. 4.8005
Schneider, Laurie, comp. 1.6209
Schneider, Peter, 1933- joint author. 4.2358
Schneider, Pierre. 1.4977, 1.6120
Schneider, Richard J. 2.11257
Schneiderman, Neil. 5.4582
Schneier, Edward V. joint author. 4.8177
Schneirla, T. C. (Theodore Christian),
  1902-1968. 5.480, 5.3888
Schnell, Donald E., 1936-. 5.3774
Schnitzer, M. 5.5281
Schnitzler, Arthur, 1862-1931. 2.13859-2.13861
Schnore, Leo Francis, 1927- joint ed. 4.6194
Schodek, Daniel L., 1941-. 5.5661
Schoen, Cathy. joint author. 5.4651
Schoen, Robert. joint author. 4.1649
Schoenbaum, David. 3.2448
Schoenbaum, S. (Samuel), 1927-. 2.6639, 2.6682,
  2.6690, 2.6698, 2.6710, 5.7954
Schoenberg, Arnold, 1874-1951. 1.3473-1.3474,
  1.3967, 1.3972, 1.4468-1.4469
Schoenberger, Robert A., comp. 4.7860
Schoenebaum, Eleanora W. 3.7854
Schoenfeld, Maxwell Philip, 1936-. 3.1659
Schoenhals, Kai P. 3.9132
Schoenherr, Richard A., joint author. 4.3239
Schoenung, Georgia. 2.1074
Schoff, Gretchen H., 1931-. 5.5507
Schofield, A. N. (Andrew Noel), 1930-. 5.5902
Schofield, Malcolm. 1.233, 1.235, 1.297, 1.324
Schofield, R. S. 4.1694
Schofield, W. (Wilfred) 5.5825
Schofield, William Henry, 1870-1920. 2.5581
Schoggen, Phil, joint author. 4.6301
Scholem, Gershom Gerhard, 1897-. 1.1925,
  1.1950-1.1951, 1.1975, 1.1985, 3.3970
Scholes, Marie V., joint author. 3.7711
Scholes, Percy Alfred, 1877-1958. 1.3505,
  1.3657-1.3658, 1.3712
Scholes, Robert E. 2.2474, 2.2489, 2.2492,
  2.3491, 2.3504, 2.3530, 2.5981
Scholes, Walter Vinton, 1916-. 3.7711
Scholz, John T. joint author. 3.4377

Schomburgk, Robert H. (Robert Hermann), Sir,
  1804-1865. 3.9130
Schönberg, Bessie, tr. 4.1102
Schonberg, Harold C. 1.3761, 1.3769
Schonberger, Howard B. 4.3884
Schonewald-Cox, Christine M. 5.3220
Schonhorn, Manuel, ed. 4.101
Schönzeler, Hans Hubert. 1.3827
School of American Research (Santa Fe, N.M.)
  3.5756, 3.5942, 3.5954, 3.9030, 4.5254
Schoolcraft, Henry Rowe, 1793-1864. 3.5820,
  3.8378
Schoolfield, George C. ed. 2.13519
Schoolman, Morton. 4.1209
Schopen, Lynn. 4.9246
Schopenhauer, Arthur, 1785-1860. 1.958-1.962,
  1.1498
Schopf, J. William, 1941-. 5.3162
Schopf, Thomas J. M. 5.3160
Schöpflin, George. 3.3008, 4.7591
Schopler, Eric. 5.5109
Schor, Ilya. 1.1980
Schor, Joel. 3.7259
Schorer, Mark, 1908-. 2.2443, 2.7417, 2.7695,
  2.12013-2.12014
Schorr, Alvin Louis, 1921-. 4.6566
Schorsch, Ismar. 3.3965
Schorske, Carl E. 3.1934, 4.8606
Schott, Grayce. 5.7716
Schott, Richard L. 4.7983
Schowengerdt, Robert A. 5.5943
Schrade, Leo, 1903-1964. 1.3932
Schrag, Calvin O. 1.1327
Schrag, Peter. 4.10966
Schram, Stuart R. ed. 3.4829, 4.2469
Schram, Stuart R. ed. and tr. 5.7230
Schram, Stuart R. 3.4835-3.4836
Schramm, Carl J. 4.4369
Schramm, Jacob Richard, 1885- ed. 5.3289
Schramm, Wilbur Lang, 1907-. 2.53, 2.3546
Schreiber, Flora Rheta. 5.4949
Schreiber, Mordecai. 3.3912
Schreiner, Olive, 1855-1920. 2.10055
Schreuder, D. M. (Deryck Marshall) 3.5441
Schreyer, Alice D. 5.7700
Schrieffer, J. R. (John Robert), 1931-. 5.2353
Schrock, Joann L. joint author. 3.5393
Schrödinger, Erwin. 5.1922, 5.2146-5.2147,
  5.2253
Schroeder, Carol L. 5.8022
Schroeder, Edward D. 5.6018
Schroeder, Eric, 1904-. 3.599
Schroeder, Henry Joseph, 1875-, tr. 1.3130
Schroeder, John H., 1943-. 3.7140
Schroeder, M. R. (Manfred Robert), 1926-.
  5.1332
Schroeder, Paul W. 3.1892, 3.3125
Schroeder, W. L. (Warren Lee), 1939-. 5.5903
Schroeer, Dietrich. 5.754
Schroeter, Leonard. 3.4000
Schubert, David, 1943-. 5.3488
Schubert, Franz, 1797-1828. 1.3973
Schubert, Glendon A. 4.7621
Schubert, Holger J. 2.13882
Schubnell, Matthias, 1953-. 2.13178
Schuck, Peter. joint author. 5.2142
Schücking, Levin Ludwig, 1878-1964. 2.6805
Schudson, Michael. 2.3590, 4.4424
Schueller, Wolfgang. 5.6092
Schug, Willis E. 4.9770
Schuhmann, Karl. 1.524
Schuker, Stephen A., 1939-. 4.4454
Schulberg, Budd. 2.12449
Schulberg, Budd Wilson, 1914-. 2.12448
Schull, Joseph. 3.8754
Schuller, David S. 1.3002
Schuller, Gunther. 1.4335, 1.4559
Schulman, Iván A. 2.5298
Schulman, L. S. (Lawrence S.), 1941-. 5.2141
Schulte, Janet E., 1958-. 4.5981
Schulte Nordholt, J. W. (Jan Willem), 1920-.
  3.6474, 3.6950
Schulte, Rainer, 1937-. 2.3702
Schultz, Arthur R. 5.7860
Schultz, Duane P. 5.534
Schultz, Henry, 1893-1938. 4.1495
Schultz, Howard Louis, joint author. 5.2065
Schultz, Randall L. 4.4299

Schultz, Stanley K. 4.10098
Schultz, Theodore William, 1902-. 4.1548,
  4.2883, 4.2886, 4.5639, 4.10651
Schultze, Charles L. 4.2953, 4.4682, 4.4686
Schultze, Charles L. joint author. 4.2077
Schultze, Jürgen. 1.4792
Schulz, Ann. 5.8262
Schulz, Bruno, 1892-1942. 2.1727
Schulz, Georg E., 1939-. 5.4406
Schulz, James H. 4.3454
Schulz, Max F. 2.13021
Schulze, Franz, 1927-. 1.5426
Schulze, Suzanne. 5.8370
Schulze, William D. 4.1575
Schulzinger, Robert D., 1945-. 3.7600-3.7601
Schumacher, E. F. (Ernst Friedrich), 1911-1977.
  4.1453
Schumacher, John N. 1.3195, 3.4598
Schumaker, Larry L., 1939-. 5.1316
Schuman, Frederick Lewis, 1904-. 3.561,
  3.2179, 4.8650, 4.9111
Schuman, Howard. 4.1229
Schuman, Mady, 1950-. 2.3103
Schumann, Paul L., 1955-. 4.3155
Schumann, Robert, 1810-1856. 1.3981
Schumer, Florence. jt. author. 5.544
Schumm, Stanley Alfred, 1927-. 4.261
Schumpeter, Elizabeth Boody. 4.4224
Schumpeter, Joseph Alois, 1883-1950. 4.1312,
  4.1318, 4.1378, 4.1470, 4.6983, 4.7539
Schunemann, R. Smith. joint comp. 3.6195
Schur, Edwin M. ed. 4.5582
Schur, Edwin M. 4.5073-4.5074, 4.5940, 4.7628
Schürer, Emil, 1844-1910. 3.3891
Schürer, Ernst. 2.13805
Schurmann, Franz, 1924-. 3.4800
Schurr, Sam H. 4.3720, 4.3745
Schurz, Carl, 1829-1906. 3.7448
Schurz, William Lyttle, 1886-1962. 3.8972
Schuster, Max Lincoln, 1897- ed. 2.3783
Schuster, Mel. 2.2899, 5.8144
Schuster, Michael H. 4.3338
Schuster, Michael R. 4.3312
Schuster, P. (Peter), 1941- joint author. 5.3387
Schutz, Alfred, 1899-1959. 4.1215, 4.4856
Schutz, Bernard F. 5.2103
Schutz, Howard G. 4.2061
Schütz, John Howard. 1.2705
Schuyers, Gerard P. joint author. 4.8962
Schuyler, George Samuel, 1895-. 2.3632
Schuyler, Montgomery, 1843-1914. 1.5297
Schuyler, Robert Livingstone, 1883-. 3.6288
Schwaab, Eugene Lincoln, 1909- comp. 3.8150
Schwab, Peter, 1940-. 3.5253
Schwab, Raymond. 3.111
Schwabe, Calvin W. 5.5461
Schwabe, Klaus. 3.848
Schwabe, Randolph, 1885-1948. joint author.
  4.841
Schwantes, Carlos A., 1945-. 3.8589
Schware, Robert, 1952-. 5.2516
Schwartz, Alan U., joint author. 4.9875
Schwartz, Anna Jacobson. joint author.
  4.4502-4.4503
Schwartz, Anna Jacobson. 4.4495, 4.4497
Schwartz, Arthur. 4.6502
Schwartz, Barry, 1938-. 4.4868
Schwartz, Benjamin Isadore, 1916-. 3.4748,
  4.7109, 4.7112
Schwartz, Bernard, 1923-. 4.9485, 4.9617,
  4.9653-4.9654, 4.9792, 4.9834
Schwartz, Charles. 1.3874, 1.3945
Schwartz, Charles F. 4.2081-4.2082
Schwartz, David N., 1956-. 5.7299, 5.7409
Schwartz, Delmore, 1913-1966. 2.12451-2.12453
Schwartz, Elliott, 1936-. 1.3679, 1.4436
Schwartz, Gary, 1940-. 1.6253
Schwartz, Harry, 1919-. 3.1930
Schwartz, Jack, 1946-. 3.4497
Schwartz, Jacob T. joint author. 5.1482
Schwartz, Jo Metcalf, ed. 1.3475
Schwartz, Julius, 1907-. 4.10490
Schwartz, Karlene V., 1936-. 5.3234
Schwartz, Kessel. 2.5112, 2.5150, 2.5307
Schwartz, Lloyd, 1941-. 2.11386
Schwartz, Marvin D. 1.6522
Schwartz, Maurice L. 4.269
Schwartz, Mel M. 5.7063

Schwartz, Mildred A. 3.8782, 4.8278, 4.8299
Schwartz, Mischa. 5.6352, 5.6405
Schwartz, Morris S., joint author. 5.4807
Schwartz, Murray L. joint author. 4.9530
Schwartz, Murray M. 2.6745
Schwartz, Nancy Lou. 4.1863
Schwartz, Pepper. 4.5651
Schwartz, Richard B. 3.1746
Schwartz, Ronald, 1937-. 2.5139
Schwartz, Sanford, 1948-. 2.10504
Schwartz, Stuart B. 3.8997, 4.3688, 4.8938
Schwàrtz, Tony. 4.5012
Schwartz, William B. 5.4708
Schwartzberg, Joseph E. 4.180
Schwarz, Arturo, 1924-. 1.6101-1.6102
Schwarz-Bart, André, 1928-. 2.4745-2.4746
Schwarz, Boris, 1906-. 1.3731
Schwarz, Egon, 1922-. 2.13562, 2.13860
Schwarz, Heinrich, 1894-1974. 5.6922
Schwarz, John E. 4.7861
Schwarz, Jordan A., 1937-. 3.7626, 3.7744
Schwarz, Leo Walder, 1906-. 3.3838
Schwarzbach, F. S., 1949-. 2.7648
Schwarzenbach, J. 5.6186
Schwarzenberger, Georg, 1908-. 4.9006, 4.9189,
    4.9291-4.9293
Schwarzfuchs, Simon. 3.3958
Schwebel, Stephen Myron, 1929-. 4.9225
Schweber, S. S. (Silvan S.) 5.2159
Schweik, Robert C. 5.7938
Schweitzer, Albert, 1875-1965. 1.1061-1.1062,
    1.2819, 1.2880, 1.3048, 1.3781, 3.16
Schweitzer, Bernhard, 1892-1966. 1.4722
Schweitzer, Carl Christoph. 4.9914
Schweitzer, Philip A. 5.5792, 5.6850
Schweizer, Eduard, 1913-. 1.2690
Schwendinger, Herman. 4.6739
Schwendinger, Julia R. 4.6739
Schwendowius, Barbara. 1.3779
Schweninger, Loren. 3.6850, 3.7214
Schwimmer, Sigmund. 5.7127
Schwinger, Julian Seymour, 1918- ed. 5.2377
Schwitters, Kurt, 1887-1948. 1.4999
Schwoerer, Lois G. 3.1512
Schyfter, Sara E. 2.5153
Sciascia, Leonardo. 2.5082
Science Museum (Great Britain) 5.6645
Science Museum of Minnesota. 3.9045
Science Research Council (Great Britain)
    5.1678
Scientific American, Inc. 5.4496
Scientific Foresight, Inc. 4.3804
Scientists' Institute for Public Information.
    Electric Power Task Force. 4.3718, 5.5999,
    5.6871
Scitovsky, Tibor. 4.1336, 4.2210
Scobbie, Irene. 3.3385
Scobie, Edward. 3.1295
Scobie, James R., 1929-. 3.9238, 4.5267
Scobie, James R., 1929-. 5.5252
Scobie, Stephen. 2.9920
Scorer, R. S. (Richard Segar), 1919-. 5.2533
Scott, A. C. (Adolphe Clarence), 1909-. 2.3387,
    2.3401, 3.4644
Scott, Alexander. 2.8781, 2.8792, 2.9846
Scott, Ann, 1950- joint author. 2.10056
Scott, Anne Firor, 1921-. 4.5998, 4.6012
Scott, Arthur Finley, 1907-. 2.2359
Scott, Beatrice, tr. 2.1527
Scott, Bob. 4.1035
Scott, Bruce R. joint author. 4.2334
Scott, Catherine J., 1950-. 3.5910
Scott, Eugene L., 1937-. 4.1037
Scott, Franklin Daniel, 1901-. 3.3349, 3.3388
Scott, Fred Newton, 1860-1931. 2.1467
Scott, George, 1925-. 4.9190
Scott, George M. 5.5613
Scott, George Walton. 2.7074
Scott, H. M. (Hamish M.), 1946-. 3.645
Scott, Harold. 2.2832
Scott, Helen G. 2.3056
Scott, Hilda, 1915-. 4.3255, 4.5384, 4.6089
Scott, James Brown, 1866-1943. joint ed. 4.7821
Scott, James C. 2.2920
Scott, James George, Sir, 1851-1935. 3.4336
Scott, James William, 1925- joint author. 5.8351
Scott, Joan Wallach. joint author. 4.3299
Scott, John, 1949-. 4.1542

Scott, John Adams, 1867-1947. 2.504
Scott, John Anthony, 1916- ed. 3.8264
Scott, John Paul, 1909-. 5.424
Scott, John Richard, joint author. 5.6909
Scott, John S., 1915-. 5.5658, 5.5985
Scott, Kenneth John, 1912-1961. 4.8825
Scott, Lloyd F., joint author. 4.10443
Scott, Margaret, 1928-. 2.9080
Scott, Mel, 1906-. 4.6324
Scott, Michael, 1949-. 2.6628
Scott-Moncrieff, C. K. (Charles Kenneth),
    1889-1930. tr. 2.3961, 2.4302
Scott Morton, Michael S. joint author. 4.2637
Scott, P. H. 2.8785
Scott, P. H. (Paul Henderson), 1920-. 2.7718
Scott, Patricia Bell. 3.6747
Scott, Paul, 1920-. 2.9807, 2.9810
Scott, Peter Dale. tr. 2.1740
Scott, Rachel. 4.10885
Scott, Richard A. (Richard Albert), 1921- joint
    author. 5.3178
Scott, Robert, 1811-1887, joint author. 2.247
Scott, Robert A., 1935-. 4.5075
Scott, Robert Edwin. 4.8332
Scott, Robert Haney. joint author. 4.4567
Scott, Robert Lane. 5.2906, 5.2909
Scott, Robert Lee, 1928- comp. 2.3533
Scott, Ronald Bodley. 5.4488
Scott, Ronald F. 5.5904
Scott, Tom, 1918-. 2.6477, 2.9842
Scott, W. Richard. joint author. 4.2642
Scott, W. Richard. 4.4907, 4.4914
Scott, Walter, Sir, 1771-1832. 2.5950, 2.6997,
    2.7044, 2.8041-2.8044, 2.8047, 2.8052-2.8054
Scott, Wilfred Welday, 1876-1932, ed. 5.2693
Scott, William, 1940-. 3.2119
Scott, William C. (William Clyde), 1937-.
    1.3645
Scott, Winfield Townley, 1910-1968. 2.12456
Scottish Book Conference (1979: North Texas
    State University) 5.1121
Scouten, Arthur Hawley, 1910-. 2.3301
Scoville, James G., 1940- joint author. 4.3335
Scragg, D. G. 2.1025
Scranton, Philip. 4.3847
Screech, M. A. (Michael Andrew) 2.4005
Scriblerus Club, London. 2.7191
Scripps, Edward Wyllis, 1854-1926. 2.3633
Scrivenor, M. LeM. 4.2454
Scruton, Roger. 1.425, 1.5463, 4.7216
Scudéry, Madeleine de, 1607-1701. 2.4056
Scull, Andrew T. 4.9369
Scullard, H. H. (Howard Hayes), 1903-. 3.2510,
    3.2518, 3.2754, 3.2763, 3.2769, 3.2775, 4.874
Scully, J. C. 5.5816
Scully, Vincent Joseph, 1920-. 1.5221, 1.5273,
    1.5288, 1.5303, 1.5341, 1.5559
Seaborg, Glenn Theodore, 1912-. 5.6604
Seabury, Paul. 3.9133, 4.9101
Seager, Allan, 1906-1968. 2.12413
Seager, Frederic H. 3.2181
Seager, Robert, 1924-. 3.6379, 3.7070
Seager, Robin. comp. 3.2778
Seagle, William, 1898- joint author. 4.6759
Seagraves, Eleanor R. 5.8420
Seagraves, Eleanor R. joint author. 5.8421
Seah, Chee Meow. 4.8729
Seal, Anil. 3.1220, 3.4274
Seal, Robert A. 5.8101-5.8102
Sealander, Judith. 4.3290
Seale, Bobby, 1936-. 3.6699
Seale, David. 2.549
Seale, Jan. 2.9668
Seale, Patrick. 3.3802
Sealey, Raphael. 3.2578
Sealock, Richard Burl, 1907-. 5.8299
Sealts, Merton M. 2.11150
Sealts, Merton M. comp. 2.11019
Seaman, Gerald R. 1.3730
Seaman, L. C. B. (Lewis Charles Bernard)
    3.1640
Seamon, David. 4.30
Searby, Peter. 4.10116
Search Institute. 1.3002
Searing, Susan E. 5.8463
Searle, Alfred Broadhead, 1877-1967. 5.6902
Searle, Campbell L., joint author. 5.6497
Searle, G. R. (Geoffrey Russell) 3.1683

Searle, John R. 1.138, 1.549, 2.66, 5.124
Searle, John R. comp. 1.548
Searles, George J. (George John), 1944-.
    2.10643
Sears, Francis Weston, 1898-. 5.1987
Sears, Minnie Earl, 1873-1933. 1.3593, 2.7714,
    2.8185, 5.7631
Sears, Paul Bigelow, 1891-. 4.385
Sears, Robert Richardson, 1908-. 4.5065, 4.5712
Sears, Sallie. 2.11127
Sears, Stephen W. 3.7366
Seashore, Carl Emil, 1866-. 1.4388, 1.4395
Seaton, Albert, 1921-. 3.992
Seaton, Ethel, joint ed. 5.7936
Seaton, Jean. 2.3683
Seaton, Robert Cooper, 1853-1915. 2.334
Seattle Art Museum. 3.5751, 3.8900
Seay, Albert. 1.3652
Sebeok, Thomas Albert, 1920- ed. 2.3, 2.42
Sebert, L. M. 4.236
Sebesky, Don. 1.4493
Seckel, Dietrich, 1910-. 1.5183
Seckinger, Ron. 3.9212
Secord, James A. 5.3137
Secord, Paul F. 5.22
Sedgewick, Robert, 1946-. 5.1195
Sedgwick, Romney, 1894- ed. 3.1545
Sedlacek, William E. 4.10779
Sedley, Charles, Sir, 1639?-1701. 2.7238
Sedra, Adel S. 5.6465
Sée, Henri Eugène, 1864-1936. 3.496
Seebach, J. Arthur, joint author. 5.1603
Seeger, Karlheinz. 5.2349
Seeger, Pete, 1919-. 1.3433, 1.3475
Seekins, Donald M. 3.4108
Seeley, John R. 4.6356
Seeley, John Robert, Sir, 1834-1895. 3.1228
Seelig, Sharon Cadman. 2.5803
Seely, Pauline Augusta, 1905-. 5.8299
Seers, Dudley. 4.2215, 4.2749
Seferis, George, 1900-1971. 2.608-2.609
Sefler, George F. 2.111
Sefton, James E. 3.7471
Segal, Aaron. 3.9115
Segal, Charles, 1936-. 2.453, 2.550
Segal, David. 4.6209
Segal, Erich, 1937-. 2.762
Segal, George, 1924-. 1.5673
Segal, Gerald, 1953-. 3.1203, 5.7335
Segal, Hanna. 5.172
Segall, Marshall H. 5.417
Segalman, Ralph. 4.6520
Segar, Mary Gertrude, ed. 2.7182
Segebrecht, Wulf. 2.13615
Segel, Harold B., 1930-. 2.1281, 2.1305, 2.1701,
    2.1747, 2.2765
Segel, Irwin H., 1935-. 5.4415
Segel, Lee A. 5.3504
Segrais, Jean Regnauld de, 1624-1701. 2.4027
Segrave, Jeffrey. 4.910
Segraves, Barbara Abbott. 3.221
Segre, Cesare. 2.4901, 2.4959
Segrè, Claudio G. 3.5200
Segre Consigli, Maria. 2.4901
Segre, Dan V. 3.3925
Segrè, Emilio. ed. 5.2075
Segrè, Emilio. 5.1936-5.1937, 5.2403
Segre, Sergio E. 5.2440
Segundo, Juan Luis. 1.2807, 1.3200
Sei Shōnagon, b. ca. 967. 2.2052
Seibold, Eugen. 5.2984
Seide, Katharine, comp. 4.9853
Seidel, Max, 1904-. 1.6261
Seidell, Atherton, 1878-. 5.2651
Seidenberg, A. (Abraham), 1916-. 5.1569
Seidenberg, Bernard, joint ed. 4.4992
Seidensticker, Edward, 1921-. 2.2081, 3.4877
Seider, Warren D. joint author. 5.6831
Seidlin, Oskar, 1911-. 2.13472
Seidman, Ann Willcox, 1926- joint author.
    4.4635
Seidman, Arthur H. 5.1145
Seidman, Harold. 4.7894
Seidman, Joel Isaac, 1906-. 4.3367
Seidman, Steven. 4.4748
Seifert, H. (Herbert), 1907-. 5.1598
Seifert, Jaroslav, 1901-. 2.1680
Seiffert, Ulrich. 5.6633

Seifman, Eli. 4.10138
Seigel, J. P. (Jules Paul) comp. 2.7558
Seigel, Jerrold E. 4.6960
Seiler, R. M. (Robert Morris) 2.7985
Seilhamer, George Overcash, 1839-1916. 2.3193
Seinfeld, John H. 5.6043
Seinfeld, John H. joint author. 5.1519
Seip, Terry L. 4.1926
Seippel, Robert G. 5.5958
Seitel, Peter. 4.813
Seitz, Frederick, 1911-. 5.2198, 5.5808
Seitz, William Chapin. 1.4833, 1.6125
Seixas, Judith S. 4.6638
Seki, Keigo, 1899- ed. 4.809
Sekler, Eduard F. (Eduard Franz) 1.5418
Selbie, John Alexander, 1856-1931, joint editor.
     1.1524
Selbin, Joel, 1931- joint author. 5.2845
Selby-Bigge, L. A. (Lewis Amherst), Sir,
     1860-1951. 1.697, 1.700
Selby, Hubert. 2.13313
Selby, John E. 3.8185
Selby, Michael John. 4.268
Selcraig, James Truett. 3.8306
Selden, David. 4.10684
Selden-Goth, Gisella, 1884- ed. 1.3925
Selden, Kyoko. 2.2038
Selden, Mark. 4.7113
Seldes, Gilbert Vivian, 1893-. 2.3194, 2.11979
Seldes, Marian. 2.3264
Seldin, J. P. 5.1053
Seldin, Maury, 1931-. 4.2828
Selesnick, Sheldon T., joint author. 5.4802
Self, Peter. 4.7760
Seliger, M. 1.505
Seligman, Edwin Robert Anderson, 1861-1939.
     ed. 4.1199
Sell, James L., 1947-. 4.30
Sella, Amnon. 3.3750
Sellar, William Young, 1825-1890. 2.635-2.636
Sellars, Roy Wood, 1880-. 1.1283
Sellars, Wilfrid. 1.94
Seller, Maxine, 1935-. 2.3196
Sellers, Charles Coleman, 1903-. 1.48, 1.5962
Sellers, Charles Grier. 3.7170
Sellers, Charles Grier. ed. 3.8123
Sellers (Robert C.) & Associates, Washington.
     5.7259
Sellers, William D. 5.2565
Selley, Richard C., 1939-. 5.3061
Sellin, Eric, 1933-. 2.4385, 4.1020
Sellin, Johan Thorsten, 1896-. 4.6886
Sells, A. Lytton (Arthur Lytton), 1895-. 2.5576
Selowsky, Marcelo. joint author. 5.7117
Seltman, Charles Theodore, 1886-1957. 3.275
Seltsam, William H., comp. 1.4225
Seltzer, Adele Szold, 1876-. 2.8979
Seltzer, Leon E. ed. 4.69
Seltzer, Robert M. 1.1901
Seltzer, Thomas. 2.8979
Selucký, Radoslav. 4.2239
Selvon, Samuel. 2.10016-2.10018
Selye, Hans, 1907-. 5.4299
Selz, Peter Howard, 1919-. 1.4795, 1.4823,
     1.4834, 1.5157, 1.6164, 1.6166, 1.6304
Selznick, David O., 1902-1965. 2.3066
Selznick, Philip, 1919-. 4.2658, 4.3805
Semat, Henry, 1900-. 5.2076
Sembdner, Helmut. ed. 2.13622
Sembène, Ousmane, 1923-. 2.4858-2.4861
Semel, Vicki Granet. 4.8210
Semenko, Irina Mikhailovna. 2.1466
Semiatin, S. L. 5.7056
Seminar for Science Writers on Weather
     Modification, 2d, New York, 1968. 5.2540
Seminar on Canadian-United States Relations.
     4.8275
Seminar on Methods of Detection,
     Measurement and Monitoring of Pollutants in
     the Marine Environment, Rome, 1970. 5.6021
Semmel, Bernard. 1.732, 4.4208
Semmel, Bernard. ed. 4.1415
Semmler, Clement. 2.10176
Semonche, John E., 1933-. 4.9793
Semple, Ellen Churchill, 1863-1932. 3.1189,
     3.6357, 4.367
Sen, Chanakya, 1921-. 4.7117
Sen, Gertrude (Emerson) 3.4170

Sen Gupta, Jyoti, 1915-. 3.4147
Sen, Samar Ranjan, 1916-. 2.1866
Sen, Sukumar. 2.1855
Sena, Cānakya, 1921-. 4.9073
Sénac, Jean. 2.4846
Senancour, Etienne Pivert de, 1770-1846. 2.4296
Sender, John. 4.2611
Sender, Ramón José, 1901-. 2.5283
Sendrey, Alfred, 1884-. 1.3554
Seneca, Lucius Annaeus, ca. 4 B.C.-65 A.D.
     2.683, 2.692-2.694, 2.703, 2.770-2.771
Senelick, Laurence. 2.1320, 2.2800
Seneviratne, H. L., 1934-. 1.2151
Seng, Peter J. 1.3487
Senger, Leslie W., joint author. 4.13
Senghor, Léopold Sédar, 1906-. 2.4862-2.4863
Sengle, Friedrich. 2.13669
Seni Pramoj, M. R., 1905-. 2.2259
Senior, Nassau William, 1790-1864. 4.1419,
     4.1511
Senkewicz, Robert M., 1947-. 3.8628
Senn, Alfred Erich. 3.3316
Sennett, Richard, 1943-. 2.13314-2.13315,
     4.5030, 4.5606
Sennett, Ted. 2.2994
Sensibar, Judith L. (Judith Levin), 1941-.
     2.11701
Serafimovich, A., 1863-1949. 2.1521-2.1522
Serafini-Sauli, Judith Powers. 2.4909
Serageldin, Ismail, 1944-. 4.3233
Serfaty, Simon. 4.8632
Sergeant, Elizabeth Shepley, 1881-. 2.11478,
     2.11758
Sergeĭchuk, S. 3.6432
Sergiovanni, Thomas J. 4.10639, 4.10649
Serjeant, E. P. joint author. 5.2915
Serjeantson, Mary Sidney, ed. 5.7936
Serle, Geoffrey. 1.6729
Serlio, Sebastiano. 1.5470, 1.5553, 2.3158
Serman, Il'ia Zakharovich. 2.1337
Sernett, Milton C., 1942-. 1.2417, 1.2421
Seroff, Victor Ilyitch, 1902-. 1.3756, 4.1135
Serow, William J. 4.1673
Serre, Jean Pierre. 5.1337, 5.1343
Servan-Schreiber, Jean Jacques. 3.1206
Service, Elman Rogers, 1915-. 4.528, 4.607,
     4.610
Seshadri, S. R., 1925-. 5.2387
Sesonske, Alexander. ed. 1.1348
Sessions, Kyle C. 1.2326
Sessions, Roger, 1896-. 1.3476-1.3478, 1.4235,
     1.4470
Sethi, Ravi. 5.1226
Setiloane, Gabriel M. 1.1856
Setlow, Richard B. (Richard Burton) 5.3496
Seton-Watson, Christopher. 2.2880
Seton-Watson, Hugh. 3.544, 3.1153, 3.3110,
     3.3131, 3.3523, 3.3530, 3.3536, 4.6973
Seton-Watson, R. W. (Robert William),
     1879-1951. 3.445, 3.687, 3.1585, 3.1879
Setright, L. J. K. 5.6632
Setton, Kenneth Meyer, 1914-. 3.590
Seurat, Georges, 1859-1891. 1.6149
Seventh-Day Adventist Hospital Association.
     5.8291
Severs, Jonathan Burke. 2.6350
Sévigné, Marie de Rabutin-Chantal, marquise
     de, 1626-1696. 2.4057-2.4058
Sewall, Richard Benson. ed. 2.11007
Sewall, Richard Benson. 2.2817, 2.11008
Sewall, Samuel, 1652-1730. 3.7983
Seward, A. C. (Albert Charles), 1863-1941.
     5.3176
Seward, Desmond, 1935-. 3.1971, 3.2000, 3.2054
Seward, Rudy Ray. 4.5583
Sewart, David. 4.10986
Sewell, Arthur. 2.6806
Sewell, Elizabeth, 1919-. 2.6065
Sewell, James Patrick. 4.1834
Sewell, Richard H. 3.7156, 3.7260
Sewell, William Hamilton, 1940-. 4.5354
Sewny, Kathryn W. 2.2707
Sewter, A. C. 1.6647
Sexsmith, Robert G. joint author. 5.5831
Sexton, Anne. 2.12457-2.12459
Sexton, Donald L. 4.1555
Sexton, James D. 3.9063-3.9064
Sexton, Linda Gray, 1953-. 2.12458-2.12459

Sexton, Patricia Cayo. 4.10011
Seybolt, Peter J. 2.2146
Seyer, Martin D. 5.6576
Seyersted, Per, 1921-. 2.10932-2.10933
Seyfert, Carl K., 1938-. 5.3124
Seyferth, Dietmar, 1929-. 5.2789
Seyler, H. L. 4.2071
Seymer, Lucy Ridgely (Buckler). 5.5180
Seymour, A. J. (Arthur J.) 2.3701
Seymour, Charles, 1912-. 1.5724, 1.5737,
     1.5740, 1.6192-1.6193, 3.835-3.836
Seymour-Smith, Charlotte. 4.407
Seymour-Smith, Martin. 1.3308, 2.8729
Seymour-Ure, Colin, 1938-. 4.7938
Seyssel, Claude de, 1450?-1520. 4.8579
Sforza, Carlo, conte, 1872-1952. 3.2826
Shaaber, M. A. (Matthias Adam), 1897-. 2.3686
Shabad, Theodore. 3.4801
Shabad, Theodore. joint author. 5.6142
Shabad, Theodore. 4.2369
Shaban, M. A. 3.3671
Shackelford, Laurel, 1946-. 3.8177
Shackford, James Atkins. 3.8348
Shackford, James Atkins. ed. 3.8347
Shackleton, J. R. 4.1320
Shackleton, Robert. 4.7431
Shackley, Theodore. 5.7232
Shadbolt, Doris. 1.5997
Shadbolt, Maurice. 2.10231
Shade, William G. joint author. 3.8084
Shade, William G. 4.6022
Shadowitz, Albert. 5.1923
Shadwell, Thomas, 1642?-1692. 2.7239
Shafarevich, I. R. (Igor' Rostislavovich), 1923-.
     5.1319
Shafer, Boyd C. 3.446
Shafer, Byron E. 4.8208
Shafer, Robert Eugene, 1925- joint author.
     4.10513
Shafer, Robert Jones, 1915-. 4.2412
Shaffer, Arthur H. 3.6913
Shaffer, Howard, 1948-. 5.4955
Shaffer, Peter, 1926-. 2.9312
Shafie, Mahmoud A. 4.1773
Shafritz, Jay M. 4.2645
Shaftesbury, Anthony Ashley Cooper, Earl of,
     1671-1713. 1.695
Shaha, Rishikesh. 4.8779
Shahane, Vasant Anant, 1923-. 2.9729
Shahn, Ben, 1898-1969. 1.5137, 1.5969, 1.6446,
     2.11379
Shaiken, Harley. 4.3318
Shain, Michael. 5.7697
Shaked, Gershon. 2.1785
Shakespeare, William, 1564-1616. 2.6646-2.6651,
     2.6672-2.6673, 2.6680, 2.6860, 2.13905
Shalamov, Varlam Tikhonovich. 2.1631
Shale, Richard, 1947-. 2.2929
Shalit, Amos de-, 1926-1969. 5.2414
Shalom, Stephen Rosskamm, 1948-. 3.6477
Shames, George H., 1926-. 5.4790
Shamim, Ahmad. joint author. 5.6013
Shampine, Lawrence F. 5.1522
Shan-hsi Shih-huang ling Ch'in yung k'eng k'ao
     ku fa chüeh tui. 3.4694
Shan-hsi Yün-kang shih k'u wen wu pao kuan
     so. 1.5759
Shanahan, William Oswald, 1913-. 5.7321
Shanas, Ethel. 4.5798
Shand, S. James (Samuel James), b. 1882.
     5.3048
Shane, Alex M. 2.1616
Shane, Harold Gray, 1914-. 4.10428
Shane, Orrin C., 1939-. 3.9045
Shang, Yang, d. 338 B.C. 4.7330
Shange, Ntozake. 2.13316
Shanin, Teodor. 4.5482
Shank, Theodore J. ed. 2.3774
Shankar, Ramamurti. 5.2137
Shankar, Ravi. 1.3738
Shankle, George Earlie. 3.6342
Shanklin, Eugenia, 1939-. 4.6367
Shanks, Merrill E., 1911- joint author. 5.1503
Shanks, Michael, 1927-. 4.2294
Shanmugam, K. Sam. 5.6353
Shanner, William Maurice, 1915-. 4.10309
Shannon, Claude E., 1916-. 5.6354
Shannon, David A. 4.8241

Shannon, Edgar Finley, 1918-. 2.6351, 2.8167, 2.8180
Shannon, Fred A. 4.1877
Shannon, Fred A. (Fred Albert), 1893-1963. 4.2949
Shannon, Richard. 3.1627
Shannon, Robert E., 1932-. 5.5578
Shannon, W. Wayne. 4.8056
Shannon, William Vincent. 3.6555
Shansi, China. Wen wu kung tso wei yüan hui. 1.5759
Shapero, Albert. 4.3520
Shapin, Steven. 5.744
Shapira, Anita. 3.4027
Shapira, Morris. ed. 2.2647
Shapiro, Alan E. (Alan Elihu), 1942-. 5.2273
Shapiro, Barbara E. 1.5347
Shapiro, Barbara J. 3.1455
Shapiro, Barbara Stern. 1.6460
Shapiro, Benson P. 4.4277
Shapiro, Beth J. 3.6527
Shapiro, Charles. ed. 2.6047
Shapiro, Charles, 1926-. 2.5951, 2.11601
Shapiro, David, 1926-. 1.5796, 2.11339, 5.4929
Shapiro, Deane H. 5.4893
Shapiro, Elliott, 1895-. 1.3544
Shapiro, Fred C. 5.6058
Shapiro, Harry Lionel, 1902-. 3.5670, 4.406
Shapiro, Henry D. 3.8178
Shapiro, Herman, 1922- ed. 1.346, 1.397
Shapiro, Howard I. 5.5053
Shapiro, June. 4.10785
Shapiro, Karl Jay, 1913-. 2.12461-2.12462, 5.7974
Shapiro, Lamed, 1878-1948. 2.1818
Shapiro, Leon N., joint author. 5.4830
Shapiro, Max S. 1.1599
Shapiro, Michael Steven. 4.10413
Shapiro, Sidney. 2.2224
Shapiro, Stuart Charles. 5.1009
Shapiro, Stuart L. (Stuart Louis), 1947-. 5.1845
Shapley, Harlow, 1885-1972. 5.852, 5.1675, 5.1851
Sharer, Robert J. 3.9040
Sharf, Andrew. 3.3905
Sharif, Omar, 1932-. 4.1067
Sharkansky, Ira. 4.8248-4.8249
Sharkey, Brian J. 5.5028
Sharkey, William W. 4.3037
Sharlet, Robert S. 3.3009
Sharma, B. N. Krishnamurti, 1909-. 1.191
Sharma, Chandradhar. 1.189
Sharma, Maha Nand. 2.9560
Sharma, P. Vallabh. 5.3080
Sharma, Ram Chandra, 1917-. 2.6667
Sharman, Lyon, 1872-1957. 3.4765
Sharon, Aryeh, 1900-. 1.5608
Sharon, Eldar. 1.5608
Sharp, Andrew. 3.5537, 3.5626
Sharp, Archibald, 1862-1934. 5.6639
Sharp, Cecil James, 1859-1924. comp. 2.6114
Sharp, Corona. 2.11131
Sharp, Dennis. 1.5264-1.5265, 1.5274, 1.5566
Sharp, Harold S. comp. 2.2774
Sharp, James Roger, 1936-. 3.7128
Sharp, Marjorie Z., joint comp. 2.2774
Sharp, Ronald A. 2.7872
Sharpe, A. G. ed. 5.2695
Sharpe, Charles Farquharson Stewart, 1907-. 5.3122
Sharpe, David M. 5.3544
Sharpe, Grant William. 5.5423
Sharpe, Myron E. ed. 4.2745
Sharpe, Wenonah. 5.5423
Sharples, Winston, joint author. 5.7004
Sharps, John Geoffrey. 2.7724
Sharratt, Peter. 2.3982
Sharrock, Roger. 2.6917, 2.6920, 2.7851
Shastri, Hari Prasad, 1882-1956. tr. 2.1939
Shastri, Jagdish Lal. 1.1678
Shatto, Susan. 2.8161
Shattock, Joanne. 2.3689
Shattuck, Charles Harlen, 1910-. 2.6869, 2.6873, 2.7917
Shattuck, Roger. joint ed. 2.2543
Shattuck, Roger. 1.6146, 2.4591, 3.2174
Shattuck, Roger. ed. 2.4364
Shatz, Marshall. comp. 4.7183

Shatzman, Israel. joint author. 3.2511
Shaughnessy, Mina P. 2.1034
Shaver, Phillip R. 4.4994
Shaw, A. G. L. (Alan George Lewers), 1916-. 4.2596
Shaw, Alan B. 5.3149
Shaw, Anna Moore. 3.5938
Shaw, Archer Hayes, 1876- ed. 3.7302
Shaw, Arnold. 1.3526
Shaw, Barton C., 1947-. 4.8231
Shaw, Bernard, 1856-1950. 1.3721-1.3724, 1.4519, 2.2840, 2.3086, 2.3320-2.3321, 2.3355, 2.5552, 2.6750, 2.8063-2.8067, 2.8069-2.8072, 2.8277, 2.14040, 4.7038, 4.7041
Shaw, Bob. 2.9811
Shaw, Bradley A., 1945-. 5.7911
Shaw, Brent D. 4.1732
Shaw, Christopher D. 5.1653
Shaw, Clifford Robe, 1896- ed. 4.6882
Shaw, David, M.A. 4.5812
Shaw, Dennis F. 5.8349
Shaw, Donald Leslie, 1930-. 2.5108, 2.5363, 2.5446
Shaw, Edward Stone. 4.4449
Shaw, Edwin. joint author. 5.2446
Shaw, Ezel Kural, joint author. 3.3572
Shaw, G. (Graham), 1942-. 5.2156
Shaw, G. K. (Graham Keith), 1938- joint author. 4.4645
Shaw, Herbert Kenneth Airy. 5.3634
Shaw, James H. 5.5495
Shaw, Joseph Thompson, 1874-. 2.10824
Shaw, Lois Banfill. 4.3249
Shaw, Margaret Renée Bryers, ed. and tr. 3.586
Shaw, Marion. 2.8161
Shaw, Martin Fallas, 1875-1958. 1.3431
Shaw, Marvin E. 5.341
Shaw, Mary Alison, 1932-. 4.169
Shaw, Melvin P. 5.6517
Shaw, Nate. 4.2910
Shaw, Peter, 1936-. 3.7048
Shaw, Philip E. 5.5342
Shaw, Ralph R. (Ralph Robert), 1907-1972. 5.7758
Shaw, Stanford Jay. 3.3572
Shaw, Susan, 1946-. 5.6946
Shaw, Thurstan. 3.5349
Shaw, Timothy M. 3.5098
Shaw, Valerie, 1941-. 2.3438
Shaw, William, 1749-1831. 2.7088
Shaw, William Harlan. 2.3128
Shawcross, John T. joint author. 2.7150
Shawcross, John T. 2.7138
Shawcross, John Thomas. 2.7114
Shawcross, William. 3.4496
Shawn, William, ed. 3.2232
Shay, Robert Paul, 1947-. 5.7303
Shcherbatskoĭ, Fedor Ippolitovich, 1866-1942. 1.1180
Shchutskiĭ, IUlian Konstantinovich, 1897-. 2.2179
Shea, William R. 5.1939
Sheaffer, Louis. 2.12297-2.12298
Sheahan, Eileen. 5.8145
Sheard, Kevin. 4.10629
Shearer, Barbara Smith. 5.8186
Shearer, Benjamin F. 5.8186
Shearer, Derek. 4.1287
Shearman, John K. G. 1.4767, 1.6222
Shearon, Ronald W. joint author. 4.10983
Sheats, Paul D. 2.8322
Shedd, Robert Gordon, 1921- joint ed. 2.3764
Shedlock, Marie L., 1854-1935. 4.10320
Sheean, Vincent, 1899-. 2.12165, 2.12585
Sheed, F. J. (Francis Joseph), 1897- tr. 1.383
Sheed, Wilfrid. 2.3778, 2.9812
Sheehan, Bernard W. 3.5770
Sheehan, Donald Henry, 1917- ed. 3.6220
Sheehan, Helena. 1.478
Sheehan, James J. 3.2298, 4.5293
Sheehan, Neil. 3.6500
Sheehan, Thomas F. 1.998
Sheehan, Thomas J., joint author. 4.942
Sheehy, Eugene P. (Eugene Paul), 1922-. 5.7713
Sheeler, Charles, 1883-1965. 1.5970
Sheffield, James R. 4.10152
Sheffield, John Holroyd, Earl of, 1735-1821. 2.7040

Sheffrin, Steven M. 4.1465
Sheingold, Daniel H. 5.6577
Shelby Cullom Davis Center for Historical Studies. 4.9976
Sheldon, Eric, 1930-. 5.2428
Sheldon, George William, 1843-1914. 1.5571
Shelford, Victor Ernest, 1877-. 5.3262
Shellabarger, Samuel, 1888-1954. 3.1549
Shelley, Louise I. 4.6682
Shelley, Mack C., 1950-. 4.8006
Shelley, Mary Wollstonecraft, 1797-1851. 2.8091, 2.8093-2.8094
Shelley, Percy Bysshe, 1792-1822. 2.8096-2.8098
Shelton, John S. 5.2959
Shelton, Suzanne. 4.1158
Shemel, Sidney. 1.4355
Shemu'eli, Avshalom. 3.3840
Shen, Liang Chi. 5.6264
Shen, Pu-hai, 400-337 B.C. 4.7331
Sheng, T. T. (Tai Tsu) 5.6535
Shenstone, William, 1714-1763. 2.7240-2.7241
Shepard, Ernest H. (Ernest Howard), 1879-1976. 2.9111
Shepard, Francis Parker, 1897-. 5.2985
Shepard, Irving. 2.12029
Shepard, Leslie. 2.5773
Shepard, Roger N. 5.321
Shepard, Sam, 1943-. 2.13317-2.13319
Shepard, Thomas, 1605-1649. 1.3343
Shephard, Bruce D., 1944-. 5.5046
Shephard, Carroll A., 1944-. 5.5046
Shephard, Charles. 3.9135
Shephard, Roy J. 5.4269-5.4271
Shepher, Israel. 4.7168
Shepherd, George W. 3.5458
Shepherd, Gordon M., 1933-. 5.4296
Shepherd, James F. 4.4216
Shepherd, Ray. 5.5114
Shepherd, Simon. 2.5891, 2.6251
Shepherd, W. G. (William Guy), 1935-. 2.721
Shepherd, William R. (William Robert), 1871-1934. 4.124
Sheppard, F. H. W. (Francis Henry Wollaston), 1921-. 4.2304
Sheppard, Harold L. 4.3313
Sheppard, Mubin, Tan Sri Datuk, 1905-. 1.6722
Sheppe, Walter. 3.8844
Shepperson, George. 3.5494
Sherbiny, Naiem A. 4.3233
Sherbo, Arthur, 1918-. 2.7091, 2.7255
Sherbowitz-Wetzor, Olgerd P. 3.3080
Sherburn, George Wiley, 1884-. 2.6259, 2.7200
Sherburne, Donald W. 1.782, 1.1331
Sherf, Zeev. 3.3923
Sherfey, Mary Jane, 1933-. 5.4259
Shergold, N. D. 2.3384
Sheridan, Betsy, 1758-1837. 2.7249
Sheridan, Eugene R. 3.8065
Sheridan, Frances Chamberlaine, 1724-1766. 2.7243
Sheridan, James E. 3.4749, 3.4819
Sheridan, Richard Brinsley, 1751-1816. 2.7244-2.7247
Sherif, Carolyn W. 4.4915
Sherif, Carolyn W. joint author. 4.4996, 4.5761
Sherif, Muzafer, 1905-. 4.4915, 4.4996-4.4997, 4.5018, 4.5761, 5.535
Sherlock, Philip Manderson, Sir. joint author. 3.9088
Sherman, A. J. (Ari Joshua) 4.8961
Sherman, A. Robert. 5.457
Sherman, Charles Lawton, 1894-. 4.7412
Sherman, Claire Richter. 1.4586
Sherman, Howard Jefferson, joint author. 5.1981
Sherman, James H., 1936-. 5.4198
Sherman, Jane, 1908-. 4.1160, 4.1164-4.1165
Sherman, Joan R. 2.10330
Sherman, John Clinton. ed. 4.152
Sherman, Julia Ann, 1934-. 4.5838, 4.5941
Sherman, Stuart Pratt, 1881-1926. 2.2593
Sherman, William L. joint author. 3.8917
Sherover, Charles M. 1.901
Sherr, Sol. 5.6565
Sherrard, Owen Aubrey, 1887-1962. 3.1525-3.1526
Sherrard, Philip. tr. 2.581
Sherrard, Philip. ed. 2.608

Sherrard, Philip. 2.571, 2.574, 2.578, 2.610
Sherratt, Andrew. 3.263
Sherrill, Robert. 3.8175, 4.6807
Sherrington, Charles Scott, Sir, 1857-1952. 5.4292
Sherrow, Fred, joint author. 1.3060
Sherry, Michael S., 1945-. 5.7278
Sherry, Norman. 2.8548, 2.8573-2.8574
Sherwin, Martin J. 3.938
Sherwin-White, A. N. (Adrian Nicholas) 4.7369
Sherwood, Dennis. 5.2935
Sherwood, Eva R., joint ed. 5.3406
Sherwood, Michael. 5.311
Sherwood, Robert E. (Robert Emmet), 1896-1955. 2.12463-2.12466
Sherwood, Roger. 1.5556
Sherwood, Thomas Kilgore, 1903-1976. 5.6832, 5.6860
Shestack, Alan. 1.4986, 1.6452
Shestov, Lev, 1866-1938. 2.1261
Shetelig, Haakon, 1877-1955. 3.3353, 5.7501
Shetter, William Z. 2.1170, 3.2986
Shetty, C. M., 1929- joint author. 5.5594
Shevell, Richard Shepherd. 5.6664
Shevky, Eshref. 4.5214
Shewan, Rodney. 2.8288
Shewmaker, Kenneth E., 1936-. 3.7072
Shewmon, Paul G. 5.6767
Shi, David E. 3.6165
Shibata, Hirofumi, 1929-. 4.4207
Shibutani, Tamotsu, 1920-. 4.4896
Shick, Tom W. 3.5414
Shideler, James H. 4.2946
Shields, Cornelius, 1895-. 4.986
Shiga, Naoya, 1883-1971. 2.2089-2.2090
Shigemitsu, Mamoru, 1887-1957. 3.4985
Shigley, Joseph Edward. 5.6192-5.6193
Shih, Ch'êng-chih. 4.8888
Shih, Chung-wen. 2.2168
Shih, Hsio-yen, 1933-. 1.6372
Shih, Nai-an, ca. 1290-ca. 1365. 2.2224
Shih, Yu-chung, 1902-. 2.2155, 3.4732
Shikes, Ralph E. 1.6136
Shillony, Ben-Ami. 3.4974, 4.8754
Shilov, G. E. (Georgiĭ Evgen'evich) 5.1474
Shils, Edward Albert, 1911-. 1.6, 1.144, 4.1216, 4.4802, 4.4961, 4.5090, 4.10534
Shils, Maurice E. (Maurice Edward), 1914-. 5.4239
Shimada, Shūjirō, 1907- joint author. 1.5077
Shimazaki, Tōson, 1872-1943. 2.2091
Shimer, Hervey Woodburn, 1872-. 5.3164
Shimer, Neltje Marie (Tannehill) 5.8091
Shimer, Neltje Marie Tannehill, ed. 1.39
Shimizu, Yoshiaki. 1.6371, 1.6390
Shimkin, Demitri Boris, 1916-. 3.6760
Shimkin, Edith M. 3.6760
Shimura, Gorō, 1930-. 5.1498
Shinagel, Michael. 2.6979
Shindul, Judith A. 4.5824
Shine, Ted. 2.10785
Shineberg, Dorothy Lois. 4.3843
Shinn, Eugene B., joint author. 4.6579
Shinn, Larry D., 1942-. 1.1522
Shinn, Rinn-Sup. 3.2679, 3.2821, 3.4613
Shinn, Roger Lincoln. 4.4976
Shinnie, Margaret. 3.5080
Shinoda, Minoru. 3.4936
Shinoda, Seishi, 1906-. 2.2075
Shinohara, Miyohei, 1919-. 4.2556
Shipler, David K., 1942-. 3.3016
Shipley, Joseph Twadell, 1893-. 2.1052, 2.2349, 2.3775
Shipman, Harry L. 5.1846
Shipman, Pat, 1949-. 5.4221
Shipp, Cameron. 3.3242
Shippey, T. A. 2.6283
Shipps, Jan, 1929-. 1.3378
Shipton, Clifford Kenyon, 1902-. 3.7941, 5.7759
Shirai, Taishirō. 4.3668
Shirakawa, Yoshikazu, 1935-. 3.4344
Shire, Helena Mennie. 2.6544
Shirêndêv, B., 1912-. 3.4867
Shirer, William L. (William Lawrence), 1904-. 2.12468, 3.1140, 3.2449
Shires, Henry M. 1.2648
Shirin Tahir-Kheli. 3.6475
Shirkov, D. V. (Dmitriĭ Vasil'evich) 5.2153

Shirley, James, 1596-1666. 2.6874
Shirley, John William, 1908-. 5.819
Shirley, Samuel, 1912-. 1.1097
Shirley, Virginia S. 5.2832
Shishido, Toshio, 1921-. 4.2550
Shister, Joseph. 4.3113
Shive, John N. (John Northrup), 1913-. 5.1988
Shively, Donald Howard, 1921- ed. 3.4896
Shivers, Alfred S. 2.12681
Shivers, Jay Sanford, 1930-. 4.888
Shklar, Judith N. 4.7436
Shlaim, Avi. 3.2502
Shloss, Carol. 2.13223
Shneiderman, Ben. 5.1196
Shneidman, Edwin S. 5.118
Sho-pow-tan. 2.12223
Shoaf, Jane V. 1.5799
Shoemaker, David P. 5.2809
Shoemaker, Richard H. 5.7750, 5.7758, 5.7760
Shoemaker, Thomas M., 1921-. 5.6333
Shoenberg, D. (David) 5.2350
Shofner, Jerrell H., 1929-. 3.8275
Shogan, Robert. 4.9812
Shokeid, Moshe. 3.3843
Shokeid, Moshe. joint author. 3.3842
Sholem Aleichem, 1859-1916. 2.1811-2.1813
Sholokhov, Mikhail Aleksandrovich, 1905-. 2.1603
Shonfield, Andrew, 1917-. 4.1792
Shooman, Martin L. 5.1252
Shopen, Timothy. 2.109
Shor, Ira, 1945-. 4.10776
Shor, Ronald E. 5.659
Shore, Barry. 4.2659
Shore, Bradd, 1945-. 4.686
Shore, Milton F. 5.4834
Shore, Paul J., 1956-. 5.279
Shore, W. Teignmouth (William Teignmouth), 1865-1932. ed. 2.8224
Shorey, Harry H. 5.4098
Shorey, Paul, 1857-1934. 1.266
Short, Anthony. 3.4546
Short, Charles, 1821-1886. 2.258
Short, Douglas D. 1.72
Short, James F. 4.5043
Short, K. R. M. (Kenneth R. M.) 3.1131
Short, Kenneth L. 5.1152
Short, Nicholas M. 4.26, 5.1813
Short, Roger Valentine, 1930-. 5.4049
Shorter, Aylward. 1.1849
Shorter, Clement K. 2.7719
Shorter, Clement King, 1857-1926. 2.7439
Shorter, Edward. 4.3177, 4.5656, 5.5043
Shortley, George, 1910-. 5.2313
Shortliffe, Edward Hance. 5.1247
Shostak, Marjorie, 1945-. 3.5486
Shostakovich, Dmitriĭ Dmitrievich, 1906-1975. 1.3987
Shotwell, James Thomson, 1874-1965. 4.9122
Shoup, Paul. 4.1255, 4.8690
Shoup, Terry E., 1944-. 5.5722
Shover, John L. 4.2947
Showalter, Dennis E. 3.2257
Showalter, Elaine. 2.2494, 2.5565
Showalter, English. 2.3903
Showell, Jak P. Mallmann. 5.7441, 5.7466
Showerman, Grant, 1870-1935. 2.680
Showman, Richard K. joint author. 5.7826
Showman, Richard K. 3.6968
Shrader, Stephen R., 1942-. 5.2318
Shrivastava, B. K. joint author. 3.6451
Shrock, David L. 4.3894
Shrock, Robert Rakes, 1904-. 5.3037, 5.3164
Shryock, Henry S. 4.1622
Shryock, John Knight, 1890-. 1.1797
Shryock, Richard Harrison. 3.8266, 5.4518
Shteĭnberg, Maksimilian Oseevich, 1883-1946. 1.4492
Shteppa, Konstantin Feodos'evich, 1896-1958. 3.450
Shu, Frank H. 5.1706
Shub, David, 1887-. 3.3147
Shubert, Bruno O. joint author. 5.5716
Shubik, Martin. 4.1220, 4.1569
Shugar, Gershon J., 1918-. 5.2640
Shugar, Ronald A., joint author. 5.2640
Shugart, H. H. 5.3782
Shugg, Roger W. (Roger Wallace) 3.8313

Shugrue, Michael Francis. 2.7016
Shukshin, Vasiliĭ Makarovich. 2.1632-2.1633
Shuler, Nettie Rogers, 1865-1939, joint author. 4.8079
Shulman, David Dean, 1949-. 1.1725
Shulman, Lawrence. 4.6464
Shulman, Marshall Darrow. 3.3063
Shulman, Max. 2.12469
Shultz, George Pratt. 4.3221, 4.3224, 4.3695
Shultz, Richard D. 5.6257
Shulvass, Moses A. (Moses Avigdor), 1909-. 3.3839
Shumaker, Wayne. 5.668
Shuman, R. Baird (Robert Baird), 1929-. 2.12262
Shumway, Floyd Mallory. jt. author. 3.6874
Shunami, Shlomo. 5.8237
Shunshō, 1255-1335. 1.1774
Shupe, Anson D. joint author. 1.3410
Shupe, Anson D. 1.1869, 1.1875, 4.5778
Shur, Shimon, 1921-. 5.8401
Shurcliff, William A. 5.2297
Shurkin, Joel N., 1938-. 5.1139
Shurr, William. 2.11173
Shuster, George Nauman, 1894-. 2.5784
Shusterich, Kurt Michael. 4.3728
Shusterman, David. 2.9348
Shute, Nevil, 1899-1960. 5.6653
Shuter-Dyson, Rosamund. 1.4390
Shy, John W. 3.6922
Sibley, David. 4.4943
Sibley, William F. 2.2090
Sices, David. 2.4971
Sichel, Walter Sydney, 1855-1933. 2.7395
Sicherman, Barbara. 3.353, 5.4531
Sicignano, Robert. 4.2015
Siciliano, Enzo, 1934-. 2.5049
Sickels, Robert J. 4.9680
Sicker, Philip. 2.11132
Sickert, Oswald. 2.2025
Sickman, L. C. S. (Laurence C. S.) 1.5060
Sid W. Richardson Foundation. 1.4904
Siddayao, Corazon M. 4.3785
Siddique, Sharon. 3.4576
Siddur. 1.1979
Sidel, Mark. 5.4664
Sidel, Ruth. joint author. 5.4626
Sidel, Ruth. 4.6574, 5.4625, 5.4664
Sidel, Victor W. 5.4625-5.4626, 5.4664
Sider, Ronald J. 1.2317
Sidey, Hugh. 3.7876
Sidgwick, Frank. ed. 2.6548
Sidgwick, Henry, 1838-1900. 1.1416, 1.1433
Sidgwick, Nevil Vincent, 1873-1952. 5.2786
Sidney, Philip, Sir, 1554-1586. 2.6144-2.6145, 2.6505-2.6508
Sidowski, Joseph B., 1925- ed. 5.37
Sieber, Roy, 1923-. 1.6580, 1.6675
Sieber, Ruth Rilke, 1901-. 2.13850
Sieber, Sam D. 4.5142
Siebert, Fredrick Seaton, 1902-. 2.3546
Siebert, William McC. 5.6274
Siedensticker, Edward, tr. 2.2053
Sieder, Reinhard. 4.5554
Siefert, Fritz, ed. 2.13586
Siegal, Barry S., 1947-. 2.2976
Siegbahn, Kai, 1918- ed. 5.2415
Siegel, Ben, 1925-. 2.1801
Siegel, Esther. joint author. 4.1112
Siegel, Frederick F., 1945-. 3.7514
Siegel, Irving Herbert. 4.3582
Siegel, Jacob S. 4.1622
Siegel, Marcia B. 4.1104-4.1105
Siegel, Mark Richard. 2.13280
Siegel, Robert, 1927-. 5.2270
Siegel, Sidney, 1916-1961. joint author. 4.1567
Siegfried, André, 1875-1959. 3.6166-3.6167, 3.8760, 4.8583
Sieghart, Paul. 4.9386
Siegler, Miriam. 5.4800
Siegman, A. E. 5.6488
Siegman, Gita. 1.51, 4.2065
Siemens Aktiengesellschaft. 5.6263, 5.6387
Siemon, Frederick, 1935-. 5.8175
Sienkiewicz, Henryk, 1846-1916. 2.1728-2.1730, 3.6052
Sierra Club. 4.896, 5.6980
Sieveking, Ann. 1.4688

Siever, Raymond. 5.2967, 5.3063
Sievers, Allen Morris, 1918-. 3.4564
Sievers, Gerd, ed. 1.3611
Sievers, Harry Joseph, 1920-. 3.7494
Sievers, Rodney M., 1943-. 3.7686
Sievers, Sharon L. 4.6148
Siewiorek, Daniel P. 5.1228
Sifakis, Carl. 4.6771
Siffin, William J. 4.8767
Sifneos, Peter E. (Peter Emanuel), 1920-. 5.4857
Sigaux, Gilbert, 1918- ed. 2.4174
Sigel, Roberta S. 4.5763
Siggia, Sidney. 5.2745
Sigler, Jay A. 4.9378
Sigmann, Jean, 1912-. 3.705
Sigmund, Paul E. ed. 3.1171
Sigmund, Paul E. 1.3277, 4.3028
Sigurdson, Jon. 5.773
Sigurdur A. Magnússon. 3.3375
Siirola, Jeffrey J., 1945- joint author. 5.6835
Sikelianos, Angelos, 1884-1951. 2.610
Siklos, S. T. C. 5.1862
Siks, Geraldine Brain. 2.3406
Silbergeld, Jerome. 1.6317
Silberger, Julius. 1.3331
Silberman, Charles E., 1925-. 4.6772, 4.10043
Silberman, Neil Asher, 1950-. 3.256
Silberschatz, Abraham. 5.1193
Silberschlag, Eisig, 1903-. 2.1776
Silbert, Irene A. 4.4311
Silbey, Joel H. 3.7081, 4.8103, 4.8151, 4.8202
Silk, M. G. (Maurice G.) 5.5788
Silke, James R. 2.3080
Silkin, Jon. 2.9313-2.9315
Silko, Leslie, 1948-. 2.13321-2.13322
Sill, Webster H., 1916-. 5.5410-5.5411
Sillery, A. 3.5481
Sillevis, John. 1.6239
Sillitoe, Alan. 2.9316-2.9319
Sillitoe, Paul. 3.5663
Sills, David L. ed. 4.1198
Sills, Stephanie, ed. 2.10787
Silone, Ignazio, 1900-1978. 2.5070-2.5071
Silva, Fred, comp. 2.3023
Silva, John M. 4.952
Silva, José Asunción, 1865-1896. 2.5415
Silver, A. I. 3.8689
Silver, Alain, 1947-. 2.2916
Silver, Allan, joint author. 4.3651
Silver, Brenda R., 1942-. 2.9605
Silver, Carole G. 2.7973
Silver, Christopher, 1951-. 4.6328
Silver, Daniel Jeremy. 1.1900
Silver, Edward A. (Edward Allen), 1937-. 4.2673
Silver, Harold. 4.10117, 4.10772
Silver, James W. (James Wesley), 1907-. 3.6264, 3.8292
Silver, Larry. 1.6268
Silver, Nathan, 1936-. 1.6686
Silver, Philip. 1.1132
Silver, Rollo Gabriel, 1909-. 5.7552
Silver, W. S. 5.4457
Silverberg, Robert. 2.13323-2.13324, 3.5699
Silverman, Arnold R., 1940-. 4.6577
Silverman, Corinne. 4.7897
Silverman, Eliane Leslau. 4.6081
Silverman, Joseph H. joint author. 2.906
Silverman, Kaja. 2.83
Silverman, Kenneth. comp. 2.10761
Silverman, Kenneth. 1.6706, 3.7977, 3.7979
Silverman, Maida. illus. 2.1782
Silverman, Richard A. ed. 5.1474
Silverman, Sydel. 4.415
Silverstein, Arthur M. 5.4675
Silverstein, Josef. 3.4428-3.4429
Silverstein, Mark, 1947-. 4.9799
Silverstein, Murray, joint author. 1.5462
Silverstein, Robert M. (Robert Milton), 1916-. 5.2747
Silvert, Kalman H. 3.8989, 4.10106
Silvert, Kalman H. ed. 3.1154
Silvertown, Jonathan W. 5.3770
Silvester, John R. 5.1291
Silvester, P. (Peet) 5.6265
Silvestri, Stefano. 4.8376
Silz, Walter, 1894-. 2.13504, 2.13626
Sim, Joe. 4.6919

Sima, Jonas, 1937-. 2.3035
Simak, Clifford D., 1904-. 2.12470
Simenon, Georges, 1903-. 2.4747-2.4748
Simeon, Richard. 3.8781, 4.8279
Simeone, Angela. 4.10581
Simeons, Charles. 5.6794
Simić, Andrei. 4.5801
Simioni, Attilio, ed. 2.4972
Simirenko, Alex. 3.3265
Simiu, Emil. 5.5858
Simkin, Penny, 1938-. 5.5064
Simkin, Tom. 5.3112
Simkins, Francis Butler, 1898-. 3.7451, 3.8124
Simmel, Georg, 1858-1918. 4.4857, 4.4944
Simmonds, George W. 4.8655
Simmonds, Robert B., 1945- joint author. 1.3051
Simmonds, Roy S. 2.11462
Simmons, Edwin H., 1921-. 5.7477
Simmons, Ernest Joseph, 1903-1972. 2.1416, 2.1435-2.1436, 2.1491
Simmons, George B., 1940-. 4.1647
Simmons, George Finlay, 1925-. 5.1599
Simmons, I. G. (Ian Gordon), 1937-. 5.3241
Simmons, Jack, 1915-. 3.5049
Simmons, James, 1933- comp. 2.9868
Simmons, John, 1938-. 4.10847
Simmons, John Stephen. 4.10513
Simmons, Marc. 3.8568
Simmons, R. C. (Richard C.), 1937-. 3.6859
Simms, D. Harper (Denton Harper), 1912-. 5.5285
Simms, Margaret C. 4.6024
Simms, William Gilmore, 1806-1870. 2.11220-2.11224
Simon, Alfred, 1907-. 1.3592
Simon, André Louis, 1877-1970. 5.7107
Simon, Barry. joint author. 5.1974
Simon, Bennett, 1933-. 5.4805
Simon, Claude. 2.4750
Simón Díaz, José. 5.8025-5.8026
Simon, Franz Eugen Simon, baron, 1893-. 5.2002
Simon, George Thomas. 1.4271
Simon, Gerhard. 1.2459
Simon, Henry William, 1901- ed. 1.4512
Simon, Herbert Alexander, 1916-. 4.2655, 4.2660, 4.2728, 4.7761, 5.391, 5.934
Simon, John K. 2.2500
Simon, John Y. ed. 3.7403
Simon, Julian Lincoln, 1932-. 4.1600-4.1601
Simon, Leonard, 1936-. 1.4910
Simon, Louis, 1908-. 4.10217
Simon, Neil. 2.12471-2.12472
Simon, Pierre Henri, 1903-1972. 2.3872
Simon, Reeva S. 3.3777
Simon, Rita James. 4.6783
Simon, Robert L., 1941-. 4.959
Simon, Roger D. 3.8095
Simon, Sidney B. 1.1516
Simon, Sidney B. joint author. 4.10315
Simon, Walter Michael, 1922-. 4.8617
Simonds, Rollin H. 4.3478
Simonov, Konstantin Mikhaĭlovich, 1915-. 2.1605
Simons, A. M., tr. 4.7068
Simons, Henry Calvert, 1899-1946. 4.4713
Simons, John D. 2.13653
Simons, N. E. 5.6086
Simonson, Lee, 1888-. 2.3093
Simpson, Alan. 1.3397
Simpson, B. Mitchell (Benjamin Mitchell), 1932-. 5.7156
Simpson, Charles R. 1.4887
Simpson, D. P. ed. 2.260
Simpson, David, 1951-. 1.1385
Simpson, Dick W. 4.8072, 4.8184
Simpson, Edmond. 5.4465
Simpson, Eileen B. 2.13325
Simpson, Evelyn. 2.6587
Simpson, Evelyn Mary Spearing, 1885-1963. 1.3309, 2.6466
Simpson, Eyler Newton. 4.2838
Simpson, George Eaton, 1904-. 1.1865
Simpson, George Gaylord, 1902-. 3.8850, 5.3152, 5.3361-5.3362, 5.3815, 5.3989
Simpson, Jacqueline. tr. 2.6292
Simpson, James R. 4.3696

Simpson, James W. 2.11086
Simpson, Jeffrey, 1949-. 3.8783
Simpson, Keith, 1949-. 5.7307
Simpson, Lesley Byrd, 1891-. 2.5186, 3.8919, 3.8998, 4.1686
Simpson, Lewis P. 2.10440
Simpson, Louis Aston Marantz, 1923-. 2.7817, 2.12350, 2.12473-2.12475
Simpson, Michael, 1934-. 2.419
Simpson, N. F. (Norman Frederick), 1919-. 2.9320-2.9321
Simpson, Percy. 2.5875, 2.6587
Simpson, Robert Drew. 1.3375
Simpson, Robert L. (Robert Lee), 1942-. 5.3549
Simpson, Robert Wilfred Levick, 1921-. 1.3828, 1.3942
Simpson, William Kelly. joint author. 3.3719
Simpson, William Kelly. comp. 2.1766
Sims, R. W. (Reginald William), 1926-. 5.8480
Sims-Wood, Janet L., 1945-. 5.7840, 5.7877, 5.8189
Simson, Otto Georg von, 1912-. 1.5520
Sinaĭ, IAkov Grigor'evich, 1935-. 5.1605
Sinclair, A. (Anne) 2.118
Sinclair, A. R. E. (Anthony Ronald Entrican) 5.3828
Sinclair, Andrew. 2.12035, 3.7736
Sinclair, Keith. 3.5603-3.5606
Sinclair, May. 2.9322
Sinclair, P. J. N. 4.4517
Sinclair, Robert, 1930-. 4.6197
Sinclair, T. A. (Thomas Alan), 1899-1961. 2.808, 4.7360
Sinclair, Upton, 1878-1968. 1.1891, 2.12477-2.12482, 4.5082
Sindermann, Carl J. 5.935, 5.5472
Sindler, Allan P. ed. 3.8176
Sindler, Allan P. 3.8314
Singelmann, Peter, 1942-. 4.2835
Singer, Anne, joint author. 5.577
Singer, Barnett. 4.6401
Singer, Barry. 5.650
Singer, Burns. joint comp. 2.1745
Singer, Charles, 1876-. 5.5533
Singer, Charles Joseph, 1876-1960. 5.756-5.758
Singer, Dorothea (Waley) 1884-. 1.412
Singer, Dorothy G. joint author. 4.5737
Singer, Godfrey Frank, 1905-. 2.3478
Singer, Hans Wolfgang, 1910-. 4.1799
Singer, I. M. (Isadore Manuel), 1924-. 5.1600
Singer, Irving. 1.1322
Singer, Isaac Bashevis, 1904-. 2.1819-2.1820
Singer, Isidore, 1859-1939. ed. 3.3810
Singer, Israel Joshua, 1893-1944. 2.1821-2.1823
Singer, Jerome E. 5.4845
Singer, Jerome L. 4.5737
Singer, Jerry A. 5.6682
Singer, Marcus George, 1926-. 1.1442
Singer, Milton B. 1.1715, 3.4218, 4.540
Singer, Milton B. ed. 3.4185, 4.6408
Singer, Peter. 1.951, 1.1414, 1.1460, 4.5039, 5.5050
Singer, Richard B. 5.4629
Singer, Robert D., 1931-. 5.577
Singer, Robert N. 4.969
Singer, S. Fred (Siegfried Fred), 1924-. 5.6126
Singer, Sam, 1944-. 5.4195
Singer, Stanley, 1925-. 5.2551
Singer, Werner, joint author. 1.3597
Singer, Werner. 1.3456
Singerman, Robert. 5.8246
Singh, Alam, 1927-. 5.5905
Singh, Amritjit. 2.10561
Singh, Avtar, 1947-. 5.1227
Singh, Balbir. 1.177
Singh, Baljit, 1929-. 4.8712
Singh, Chanan. joint author. 5.7042
Singh, G. 2.5042
Singh, I. B. (Indra Bir) joint author. 5.3059
Singh, Khushwant, tr. 2.1902
Singh, Khushwant. 1.1829, 2.1913, 3.4354
Singh, Madanjeet. 1.6397-1.6398
Singh, Nagendra. 3.4334
Singh, Nalini. 4.6141
Singh, Nau Nihal, 1923- joint author. 5.5567
Singh, Sarup. 2.5848
Singh, Shuk Deo, 1933-. 2.1885
Singh, V. B. ed. 4.2502

Singhal, Kishore. 5.6466
Singletary, Otis A. 3.7138, 3.7472
Singleton, Alan. 5.1135
Singleton, Charles Southward, 1909-. 2.4903,
  2.4906, 2.4916-2.4917, 2.4922, 2.4944
Singleton, Frederick Bernard. 3.3605, 4.2422
Singleton, Loy A. 5.6355
Singleton, Marvin Kenneth. 2.3673
Singleton, Mary Ann. 2.9035
Singleton, Paul. 5.4430
Singleton, W. T. (William Thomas) 5.4262
Singmaster, David. 5.1575
Sinha, Ramesh P. 4.3421
Sinjavskij, Andrej Donat'evič, 1925-. 2.1606
Sinkankas, John. 5.7069
Sinkin, Richard N. 3.8936
Sinnott, Roger W. 5.1676
Sinnreich, Masha. 4.2047
Sinopoulos, Takēs. 2.622
Sinor, Denis. ed. 3.3618
Sinor, Denis. 3.1938
Sipay, Edward R. 4.10346
Siporin, Max. 4.6481
Sippl, Charles J. 5.1138, 5.6404
Siracusa, Carl. 4.3616
Siracusa, Joseph M. 3.7602
Sirageldin, Ismail Abdel-Hamid. 4.3233
Sircello, Guy. 1.1360
Sirén, Osvald, 1879-. 1.6318-1.6319
Sirett, Hazel. 4.7637
Sirica, John J. 4.9466
Sirich, John Black, 1910-. 3.2112
Sirmans, Marion Eugene, 1934-1965. 3.8242
Sisam, Celia, comp. 2.6141
Sisam, Kenneth. joint comp. 2.6141
Sisam, Kenneth. 2.6080, 2.6301
Siskind, Aaron. 5.6930
Sisson, C. H. (Charles Hubert), 1914-. 1.3308,
  2.4924, 2.9325
Sisson, Charles Jasper, 1885-1966. 2.6489,
  2.6825
Sisson, Richard. 4.8722
Sissors, Jack Zanville, 1919-. 2.3563
Sithole, Ndabaningi, 1920-. 3.5113
Sitkoff, Harvard. 3.6691
Sitte, Camillo, 1843-1903. 1.5586
Sitter, John E. 2.5687
Sitter, L. U. de (Lamoraal Ulbo), 1902-. 5.3076
Sittig, Marshall. 5.6895
Sitwell, Dame Edith, 1887-1964. 2.10059
Sitwell, Edith, Dame, 1887-1964. 2.6702, 2.9326
Sitwell, Osbert, 1892-1969. 2.9329-2.9336
Sitwell, Sacheverell, 1897-. 1.3910,
  2.9338-2.9340
Sivan, Reuven. 2.1771
Sivaramamurti, C. 1.6309
Sivaraman, Krishna. 1.1726
Sivard, Ruth Leger. 4.4721
Sivaśaṅkarapilla, Takali, 1914-. 2.2269-2.2270
Sive, Mary Robinson, 1928-. 5.8160
Siverson, Randolph M. 4.9025
Sivirine, Alexis. 5.7514
Sizer, Frances Sienkiewicz. 5.4236
Sizer, Theodore, 1892-. 1.5978, 1.5981
Sizer, Theodore R. 4.10044, 4.10055, 4.10497
Sjoberg, Gideon. 4.6189
Skaggs, Merrill Maguire. 2.10459
Skaggs, Peggy. 2.10934
Skates, John Ray. 3.8291
Skeat, Walter W. (Walter William), 1835-1912.
  2.1061
Sked, Alan, 1947-. 3.1709
Skees, William D., 1939-. 5.1197
Skelley, Jeffrey. 4.3174
Skelton, Geoffrey. 1.4055
Skelton, John, 1460?-1529. 2.6516
Skelton, Oscar Douglas. 3.8727, 3.8755
Skelton, R. A. (Raleigh Ashlin), 1906-1970.
  4.224, 4.230
Skelton, Raleigh Ashlin. 4.222
Skelton, Robin. 2.2723, 2.8146, 2.8149, 2.9341
Skemp, Joseph Bright. 4.7344
Skendi, Stavro. 2.211, 3.3602
Skerl, Jennie. 2.12936
Skidelsky, Robert Jacob Alexander, 1939-.
  3.1686, 4.1351
Skidmore, Felicity. 4.3470
Skidmore, Thomas E. 3.9003, 3.9215, 3.9224

Skill, Thomas. 5.8436
Skillin, Marjorie E. 2.2524
Skilling, H. Gordon (Harold Gordon), 1912-.
  4.7018
Skilling, Hugh Hildreth, 1905-. 5.6280
Skilton, David. 2.7934, 2.8211
Skinner, Andrew S. 4.1355, 4.1358
Skinner, B. F. (Burrhus Frederic), 1904-.
  2.12485, 5.6, 5.299, 5.392, 5.547, 5.4293
Skinner, Brian J., 1928- joint author. 5.3034
Skinner, Charles Edward, 1897-. 5.3725
Skinner, Cornelia Otis, 1901-. 2.12486
Skinner, G. William (George William), 1925-.
  3.4521, 4.5456, 4.6266, 4.6268, 5.8398
Skinner, Gordon. 5.2891
Skinner, Henry Alan. 5.4492
Skinner, M. L. (Mary Louisa), 1876-1955. joint
  author. 2.8963
Skinner, Quentin. 4.7227, 4.7263
Skinner, Wickham. 5.7023
Skirrow, G. (Geoffrey) 4.341
Sklar, Kathryn Kish. 4.6000
Sklar, Lawrence. 5.2097
Sklar, Richard L. 5.367, 4.3730
Sklare, Marshall, 1921-. 1.1920, 3.6574
Skocpol, Theda. 4.5052
Skofronick, James G. joint author. 5.4614
Skolnick, Arlene S., 1933-. 4.5563
Skolnick, Jerome H. 4.5163, 4.5563
Skolnick, Joan. 5.989
Skolnikoff, Eugene B. 3.7603
Skomal, Edward N. 4.4032
Skoog, Douglas A. 5.2689
Skotheim, Robert Allen. 3.6232
Skovholt, Thomas M. 5.4815
Skowronek, Stephen. 4.7844
Skowronski, Sharon. 4.7775
Skrupskelis, Ignas K., 1938-. 1.527, 1.596,
  1.598, 1.1540, 5.108
Skully, Michael T. 4.4458
Skura, Meredith Anne, 1944-. 2.2484
Skurnik, W. A. E. 3.5391
Skutsch, Otto. 2.717
Škvorecký, Josef. 2.1681-2.1684
Skyrms, Brian. 1.1187
Slaby, Andrew Edmund. 4.6539
Slack, Paul. joint author. 4.6253
Slack, Paul. 5.4677
Slack, Robert C., ed. 5.7945
Slade, Carole. 4.10618
Slade, Ruth M. 3.5424
Slama, Chester C. 5.5829
Slater, George W. 4.7140
Slater, John Clarke, 1900-1976. 5.2122, 5.2138
Slater, Joseph, 1916-. 2.11017
Slater, Joseph Locke. 2.11023
Slater, Michael. 2.7627, 2.7644
Slater, Niall W., 1954-. 2.763
Slater, Phil. 4.4810
Slater, Philip Elliot. 3.6187
Slater, Philip N. 4.27
Slatkin, Montgomery. 5.3385
Slatkin, Wendy. 1.4589
Slatta, Richard W., 1947-. 3.9254
Slaughter, Jane, 1941-. 4.7145
Slauson, Nedra G. 5.8481
Slavens, Thomas P., 1928-. 1.103
Slavin, Arthur Joseph. 3.1392
Slavin, Morris, 1913-. 3.2116
Slaymaker, Thomas. 4.1042
Slayton, Robert A. 4.5209
Sledd, James H. 2.999, 2.1078
Sleeman, B. D. 5.3311
Sleeter, Christine E., 1948-. 4.10786
Slesser, Malcolm. 5.6120
Slessor, John Cotesworth, 1897-. 5.7405
Slessor, Kenneth, 1901-1971. 2.10163
Slicher van Bath, B. H. 4.2969
Slichter, Sumner H. (Sumner Huber),
  1892-1959. 4.3369, 4.3575
Slide, Anthony. joint author. 2.3049
Slide, Anthony. 2.2969
Sliker, Alan, 1936-. 5.5770
Sliney, David. 5.5953
Slingerland, Aårt. 5.5632
Slive, Seymour, 1920-. 1.5024, 1.6248, 1.6254
Sloan, Douglas. 4.10291
Sloan, Douglas. comp. 4.9987

Sloan, John, 1871-1951. 1.5972-1.5973
Sloane, David E. E., 1943-. 2.10718, 2.10970
Sloane, Ethel. 5.5047
Sloane, Eugene A. 4.1045
Sloane, Joseph C. 1.6058, 1.6077
Sloane, N. J. A. (Neil James Alexander), 1939-
  joint author. 5.1376
Sloane, Neil James Alexander, 1939-. 5.1416
Sloane, Peter J. 4.3114
Sloane, T. O'Conor (Thomas O'Conor),
  1851-1940. 5.5548
Slobin, Mark. 1.4347
Slocum, Robert B. 5.8109
Slonim, Marc, 1894-1976. 2.1250, 2.1262,
  2.1274, 2.3381
Slonim, Solomon. 4.9082
Slonimsky, Nicolas, 1894-. 1.3529, 1.3680
Slote, Bernice. 2.2561
Slotkin, James Sydney, 1913-1958, comp. 4.414
Slotkin, Richard, 1942-. 3.6358
Slout, William L. (William Lawrence) 4.1191
Słowacki, Juliusz, 1809-1849. 2.1731, 2.1747
Slowinski, Emil J. 5.2629
Sloyan, Gerard Stephen, 1919-. 1.2897
Slusser, Robert M. 4.8979-4.8980
Slusser, Robert M. joint author. 3.3058, 4.9072
Sly, David. 4.1711, 4.6195
Smagula, Howard J., 1942-. 1.4835
Smail, R. C. 3.591
Smailes, Arthur E. 4.6259
Smale, Stephen, 1930-. 5.1515, 5.1619
Small Area Estimation Conference (1978:
  Annapolis, Md.) 4.1581
Small, Kenneth A. 4.6205
Small, Melvin. 3.6372
Small, Miriam Rossiter. 2.11081
Small, R. J. (Ronald John) 4.259
Small, William J. 2.3555, 2.3653
Smalley, Beryl. 1.2530, 3.570, 3.1356
Smalley, Donald Arthur, 1907- ed. 2.7486,
  2.8241, 3.6041
Smallman, R. E. 5.6779
Smallwood, E. Mary. 3.3892
Smart, Barry. 1.830, 4.4811
Smart, Carol. 4.6693
Smart, Christopher, 1722-1771. 2.7254
Smart, Ninian, 1927-. 1.1537, 1.1590, 1.2981
Smeaton, Robert W. 5.6318
Smeck, N. E. 5.5265
Smedley, Agnes, 1890-1950. 3.4818, 4.6138
Smeets, Albert. 1.5026
Smelser, Marshall. 3.7082
Smelser, Neil J. joint author. 4.1281
Smelser, Neil J. ed. 4.6384
Smelser, Neil J. 4.4998, 4.5803
Smerk, George M. comp. 4.3889
Smerk, George M. 4.3921
Smernoff, Richard A. 2.4067, 2.4085
Smiley, Donald V. 4.8284
Smilor, Raymond W. 4.4624
Smith, A. J. (Albert James), 1924-. 2.5797,
  2.6464
Smith, A. J. M. (Arthur James Marshall), 1902-
  ed. 2.9897-2.9899
Smith, Abbot Emerson, 1906-. 4.3106
Smith, Adam. 1.3, 1.1430, 2.1035, 4.1266,
  4.1420
Smith, Alan A. 5.5711
Smith, Alan H. 4.2240
Smith, Alan M. 3.6524
Smith, Alexander Hanchett, 1904-. 5.3727
Smith, Alfred Emanuel, 1873-1944. 3.7682,
  3.7739
Smith, Alison. 3.5114
Smith, Annette (Annette J.) 2.4835
Smith, Anthony, 1938-. 2.3547, 2.3575
Smith, Anthony D. 4.7491
Smith, Apollo Milton Olin, joint author. 5.1665
Smith, Arnold, 1915-. 3.8791
Smith, Arthur Lee, 1927-. 3.888
Smith, Arthur Robert, 1925-. 3.7673
Smith, Arthur Whitmore, 1874-. 5.2344
Smith, B. Othanel (Bunnie Othanel), 1903-.
  4.10450
Smith, Barbara. 3.6747

Smith, Barbara Herrnstein. 2.2387, 2.2735
Smith, Bardwell L., 1925-. 1.1706,
    1.2108-1.2109, 1.2111, 3.4239
Smith, Bernard William. 1.5094
Smith, Betty, 1904-. 2.12487
Smith, Bonnie G., 1940-. 4.6116
Smith, Bradley F. 3.921, 3.1075
Smith, Bruce D. 3.5907
Smith, Bruce James, 1946-. 4.7562
Smith, Bruce L. R. 4.10553
Smith, Carl S. 2.10473
Smith, Carol A. 4.6362
Smith, Cecil Michener, 1906-. 1.4220
Smith, Chard Powers, 1894-. 2.12408
Smith, Charles Edward. joint ed. 1.4332
Smith, Charles Forster, 1852-. 2.397
Smith, Charlotte Turner, 1749-1806. 2.7257
Smith, Charlotte (Turner) Mrs. 1749-1806.
    2.7256
Smith, Christopher. 4.6596
Smith, Clarence Jay. 3.3172
Smith, Clark Ashton. 2.12488
Smith, Clifford T. (Clifford Thorpe), 1924- joint
    author. 4.2135
Smith, Colin, 1927- ed. 2.5185
Smith, Cordwainer, 1913-1966. 2.12018
Smith, Craig B. 5.6151-5.6152
Smith, Culver H. 2.3556
Smith, Cyril Stanley, 1903-. 5.6754
Smith, D. Howard (David Howard), b. 1900.
    1.166, 1.1791
Smith-Dampier, E. M., tr. 2.14000
Smith, Daniel Blake. 4.5604
Smith, Daniel Malloy, 1922-. 3.7730
Smith, Dave, 1942-. 2.10777
Smith, David, 1945-. 1.4905, 1.5674, 3.1765,
    4.3535
Smith, David E., 1936-. 4.8318
Smith, David Eugene, 1860-1944. 5.1074
Smith, David G. (David Graham) 5.2960
Smith, David K. 5.5598
Smith, David M. 4.356
Smith, David Marshall, 1936-. 4.361, 4.5112,
    4.6282
Smith, David Nichol, 1875-1962. 2.6165,
    2.6998, 2.7080, 2.7181, 2.7294
Smith, David W., 1948-. 5.4169, 5.4435, 5.5070
Smith, DeVerne Reed, 1936-. 4.676
Smith, Donald B. 3.5731
Smith, Donald Eugene, 1927-. 1.1586
Smith, Douglas, 1949 May 27-. 3.5084
Smith, Dwight La Vern, 1918-. 5.7854
Smith, E. Baldwin (Earl Baldwin), 1888-1956.
    1.5216, 1.5228, 1.5499
Smith, E. Brooks, 1917-. 4.10480
Smith, Edward Conrad, 1891- ed. 4.7795
Smith, Edwin William, 1876-1957. 1.1843
Smith, Elaine. 5.5144
Smith, Elizabeth H., 1939-. 4.4971
Smith, Elsdon Coles, 1903-. 3.305-3.306, 5.8300
Smith, Elwyn A. (Elwyn Allen), 1919-. 1.2392
Smith, Emil L., 1911- joint author. 5.4399
Smith, Esther Marian Greenwell. 2.8246
Smith, F. B., 1932-. 5.2521
Smith, F. B. (Francis Barrymore), 1932-. 4.8462
Smith, F. Graham (Francis Graham), 1923-.
    5.1783, 5.2288
Smith, Frank, 1928-. 5.7722
Smith, Frank Ellis, 1918-. 3.7683
Smith, Fred H. 4.449
Smith, Frederick. 1.3591
Smith, G. C. Moore (George Charles Moore),
    1858-1940. 2.6485
Smith, G. E. Kidder (George Everard Kidder),
    1913-. 1.5353
Smith, G. Gregory (George Gregory),
    1865-1932. ed. 2.5502
Smith, Gaddis. 3.939
Smith, Gene. 3.8937
Smith, Geoffrey, 1930-. 4.8423
Smith, Geoffrey S. 3.7772
Smith, George, 1824-1901. 3.1235
Smith, George Adam, Sir, 1856-1942. 3.3815
Smith, George David. 4.4075
Smith, George H. E. (George Howard Edward),
    1898-1962. joint author. 4.1948-4.1949,
    4.9043
Smith, Gibbs M. 4.3587

Smith, Goldwin Albert. 3.8762
Smith, Gordon R. 3.2469, 4.8611
Smith, Gordon Ross. 2.6798
Smith, Grahame. 2.7642
Smith, Grover Cleveland, 1923-. 2.8823,
    2.11640
Smith, H. Daniel, 1928-. 5.8339
Smith, H. (Harry), 1935-. 5.3744
Smith, H. Shelton (Hilrie Shelton), 1893-.
    1.2369, 1.2918
Smith, Hallett Darius, 1907- joint ed. 2.6083
Smith, Hamilton, joint author. 5.4715
Smith, Harrison, 1888-. 2.12011
Smith, Harvey Henry. 3.3769, 3.3783, 3.3924,
    3.4066, 3.4478, 3.4490
Smith, Harvey K. (Harvey Kennedy) 2.3155
Smith, Hedrick. 3.3275
Smith, Henry Clay, 1913-. 4.4936
Smith, Henry DeWitt. 4.10146
Smith, Henry Holmes. 5.6930
Smith, Henry Nash. ed. 2.10949, 2.10961
Smith, Henry Nash. 2.10610, 2.10939, 2.10962,
    3.8467
Smith, Hilda L., 1941-. 4.6109
Smith, Homer William, 1895-1962. 5.3383,
    5.4250-5.4251
Smith, Hugh, 18th cent. 4.10629
Smith, Iain R. 3.5236
Smith, Ian W. M. 5.2892
Smith, Irwin, 1892-. 2.3328
Smith, J. A. (John Alexander), 1863-1939.
    1.283
Smith, J. Beverley. ed. 4.5337
Smith, J. C. (James Cruickshanks), 1867-1946.
    ed. 2.6523
Smith, J. M. (Joseph Mauck), 1916-. 5.6821
Smith, J. M. Powis (John Merlin Powis),
    1866-1932. ed. 1.2500
Smith, Jack, 1935-. 5.6429
Smith, James A. 4.10523
Smith, James Dale. 5.4011
Smith, James Morton. 3.7057
Smith, James Morton. ed. 3.6018
Smith, James Ward, 1917-. 1.2384
Smith, Janet Adam. 2.6123
Smith, Jean Edward. 3.2455, 3.2478, 3.2503
Smith, Jeffrey Chipps, 1951-. 1.4985
Smith, John David, 1949-. 5.8390
Smith, John Edwin. 1.532, 1.558, 1.3332
Smith, John Graham, 1936- ed. 4.2734
Smith, John Harrington. 2.5908
Smith, John Maynard, 1920-. 5.3536
Smith, Joseph, 1805-1844. 1.3379-1.3381
Smith, Joseph Russell, 1874-. 4.1865
Smith, Joseph V. 5.2922
Smith, Judith E., 1948-. 3.8018
Smith, Julian, 1937-. 2.3011
Smith, Justin Harvey, 1857-1930. 3.7139
Smith, K. Wayne. joint author. 5.7265
Smith, Kenneth Carless. 5.6465
Smith, Kenneth Manley, 1892-. 5.4472
Smith, Kirby Flower, 1862-1918. 2.780
Smith, Lacey Baldwin, 1922-. 3.1403, 3.1426
Smith, Lawrence R., 1945-. 2.4894
Smith, LeRoy W. 2.7387
Smith, Lillian Eugenia, 1897-1966.
    2.12489-2.12490, 3.6692
Smith, Lloyd H. (Lloyd Holly), 1924-. 5.4754
Smith, Logan Pearsall, 1865-1946. 2.7312
Smith, M. G. (Michael Garfield) 4.5266
Smith, Margaret, 1884-. 1.2024, 2.7474
Smith, Margo L. 5.8094
Smith, Martha K., 1944-. 5.1097
Smith, Martin Ferguson. 2.676
Smith, Maxwell Austin, 1894-. 2.4273
Smith, Merrily A. 5.7647
Smith, Michael L., 1943- joint author. 5.6661
Smith, Michael Llewellyn, 1939-. 3.2702
Smith, Michael P. 4.6196, 4.9955
Smith, Michael Townsend, 1938- comp.
    2.10803, 2.10806
Smith, Morton, 1915-. 1.2737
Smith, Myron J. 5.7838, 5.7845, 5.8177,
    5.8230-5.8231, 5.8302-5.8304, 5.8324
Smith, Nancy R. 1.4654
Smith, Nicholas D. 2.10591
Smith, Norman Kemp, 1872-1958. 1.706, 1.795,
    1.886, 1.895

Smith, Norman Obed, 1914-. 5.2259
Smith, Page. 3.6905, 3.7013, 3.7049
Smith, Paul. 4.8532
Smith, Paul G. 5.5985
Smith, Paul Jordan, 1885- joint ed. 2.6437
Smith, Pauline. 2.10091-2.10092
Smith, Peter, 1935-. 5.1518
Smith, Peter H. 3.1155, 3.9003, 3.9250, 4.3697,
    4.5258
Smith, Peter R. 1.5419
Smith, Philip G. 4.10366
Smith, Philip H. 2.6278
Smith, Philip J. 5.6876
Smith, Philip L. 4.10256
Smith, Preserved, 1880-1941. 3.150
Smith, R. A. (Robert Allan), 1909-. 5.2351
Smith, R. B. (Ralph Bernard), 1939-. 3.4383,
    3.4479
Smith, R. T. (Richard Thomas), 1925-. 5.6307
Smith, Ralph Alexander. comp. 1.1364
Smith, Ralph Ely, 1944-. 4.3292
Smith, Raymond J. 2.6935
Smith, Raymond Thomas, 1925-. 4.5610
Smith, Rebecca Washington, 1894-. 2.10471
Smith, Rhonda L. joint author. 4.8962
Smith, Richard A. (Richard Allan), 1951-.
    5.6257
Smith, Richard Eugene. 2.8377
Smith, Richard Furnald. 5.664
Smith, Richard J. (Richard Joseph), 1944-.
    5.7336
Smith, Richard Michael, 1946-. 4.5789
Smith, Richard Norton, 1953-. 3.7634, 3.7748
Smith, Robert, 1916- joint author. 4.10988
Smith, Robert A., 1918-. 4.1047
Smith, Robert Freeman, 1930-. 3.9092, 4.4181
Smith, Robert Henry Tufrey. comp. 4.4122
Smith, Robert John, 1927-. 4.5450, 4.5455
Smith, Robert Leo. 5.3526
Smith, Robert Sydney. 3.5327
Smith, Roger Cletus, 1888-. 5.3294
Smith, Roger M., 1930-. 3.4450
Smith-Rosenberg, Carroll. 4.6015
Smith, Sam B., 1929-. 3.6970
Smith, Scottie Fitzgerald. 2.11725
Smith, Sharon Oh Dunlap, joint author. 1.6413
Smith, Sheila. 4.2611
Smith, Stevie, 1902-1971. 2.9344
Smith, Susan, 1956-. 4.384
Smith, Sydney, 1911-. 5.3192
Smith, Sydney Goodsir, 1915-1975. 2.9345
Smith, T. Lynn (Thomas Lynn), 1903-. 3.9188,
    4.5269
Smith, Terence A. (Terence Arthur) joint
    author. 5.3754
Smith, Theodore Clarke, 1870-1960. 3.7489,
    4.8219
Smith, Thomas Carlyle. 4.5451
Smith, Thomas M., ed. 4.1066
Smith, Thorne, 1893-. 2.12491
Smith, Timothy Lawrence, 1924-. 1.3038
Smith, Tony, 1942-. 3.2210
Smith, V. Kerry (Vincent Kerry), 1945-. 4.2075
Smith, Valene L. 4.85
Smith, Verity, 1939-. 2.5293
Smith, Vincent Arthur, 1848-1920. 3.4224,
    3.4255
Smith, Virginia Carlson, joint author. 5.8462
Smith, Vivian Brian. 2.10160
Smith, W. Eugene, 1918-. 5.6997
Smith, W. H. C. (William Herbert Cecil),
    1925-. 3.2159
Smith, W. Robertson (William Robertson),
    1846-1894. 2.1831
Smith, Walter Buckingham. 4.1915
Smith, Whitney. 3.287, 4.7529-4.7530
Smith, Wilfred Cantwell, 1916-. 1.1520, 1.1993,
    3.3666
Smith, William, 1728-1793. 3.8029
Smith, William Edgett. 3.5299
Smith, William George. 2.3809
Smith, William James, 1918-. 2.2708-2.2709
Smith, William Jay, 1918-. 2.1648, 2.3751,
    2.13945
Smith, William Raymond. 3.6393
Smith, William Stevenson. 1.4701
Smith, Wilson, joint ed. 4.10061
Smith, Woodruff D. 3.672, 4.8929

Smithells, Colin J. (Colin James) 5.6765
Smither, Howard E. 1.4252
Smithers, Don L., 1933-. 1.4175
Smithers, Janice A., 1931-. 4.5807
Smithers, Peter, Sir, 1913-. 2.6889
Smithson, Robert. 1.5142
Smithsonian Astrophysical Observatory. 5.1677,
    5.1741
Smithsonian Institution. 2.3817, 3.8562, 5.1689,
    5.1788, 5.3647
Smitten, Jeffrey R. 2.3446
Smock, Audrey C. 4.5903
Smock, Raymond. 3.6853
Smoke, Richard. 5.7279
Smolansky, Oles M. 3.3751
Smolensky, Michael H. 5.4213
Smollar, Jacqueline. 4.5760
Smollett, Tobias George. 2.7258-2.7263
Smooha, Sammy. 4.5397
Smoot, L. Douglas (Leon Douglas) 5.6876
Smorodin, Calla, joint author. 4.1871
Smorodinskiĭ, IA. A. (IAkov Abramovich) joint
    author. 5.2069
Smout, T. C. (T. Christopher) 3.1783
Smyer, Richard I., 1935-. 2.9200
Smykla, John Ortiz. 4.6906
Smyser, Jane Worthington, ed. 2.8300
Smyth, Alfred P. 3.1787, 3.1871
Smyth, Craig Hugh. 1.5814
Smyth, Henry DeWolf, 1898-. 5.2420
Smyth, Herbert Weir, 1857- tr. 2.234, 2.332
Smyth, Margaret. 4.5508
Snaith, John G. 1.2624
Snavely, Marcia K. 5.2685
Snead, Rodman E. 4.130, 4.273
Sneddon, Ian Naismith. 5.2118
Snedecor, George Waddel, 1881-. 5.1398
Snelgrove, David L. 5.1187
Snelgrove, Dudley. ed. 1.6384
Snell, John L. 3.2291
Snell, John L. ed. 3.884
Snell, Martha E. 4.10929
Snellgrove, David L. ed. 1.1808
Snellgrove, David L. ed. and tr. 1.1744
Snepp, Frank. 3.4504
Snetsinger, John. 3.6455
Snider, James G., 1928- comp. 5.400
Sniderman, Florence M., joint author. 5.8125
Snitow, Ann Barr, 1943-. 4.5506
Snodgrass, Anthony M. 3.2516, 3.2598
Snodgrass, Donald R. 4.2456
Snodgrass, Jon. 4.6885
Snodgrass, R. E. (Robert E.), 1875-1962.
    5.3849, 5.3864, 5.3886
Snodgrass, W. D. (William De Witt), 1926-.
    2.12492
Snorri Sturluson, 1178-1241. 2.13987
Snorri Sturluson, 1179?-1241. 2.13982, 2.13988
Snow, C. P. (Charles Percy), 1905-. 1.77,
    2.8235, 2.9346, 5.1028
Snow, Catherine E. 2.124
Snow, Dean R., 1940-. 3.5744
Snow, Edgar, 1905-1972. 2.2206, 3.4755, 3.4779
Snow, Helen (Foster) 1907-. 3.4812
Snow, John W. 4.4040
Snowden, Lonnie R., 1947-. 5.4703
Snowden, P. N. (P. Nicholas) 4.4149
Snowman, A. Kenneth (Abraham Kenneth),
    1919-. 1.6653
Snowman, Daniel. 3.6188
Snustad, D. Peter. 5.4470
Snyder, Allan W., 1940-. 5.5960
Snyder, C. R. 5.471
Snyder, Franklyn Bliss, 1884-1958. 2.7507
Snyder, Gary. 2.13326-2.13328
Snyder, George Sergeant. 5.1742
Snyder, Gertrude. 1.5838
Snyder, Glenn Herald. 5.7257
Snyder, James. 1.4768
Snyder, Leon A. 5.3418
Snyder, Lloyd R. 5.2667
Snyder, Lloyd R. joint author. 5.2644
Snyder, Louis Leo, 1907-. 2.3540, 3.757, 3.768,
    3.891, 3.2193, 3.2240
Snyder, Mitch. 4.6629
So, Frank S. 4.6323
So, Jenny F. 1.6672
Soane, John, Sir, 1753-1837. 1.5403

Sobel, Bernard. 2.2831
Sobel, Mechal. 1.2422
Sobel, Raoul. 2.3250
Sobel, Robert, 1931 Feb. 19-. 3.6285, 4.4617
Sobell, Linda C. joint author. 5.4962
Sobell, Mark B. 5.4962
Sober, Elliott. 1.143, 1.482
Sober, Herbert Alexander, 1918- ed. 5.4400
Soberman, Richard M. jt. author. 4.4025
Soboul, Albert. 3.2085-3.2086, 3.2101
Sobrino, Jon. 1.2871
Soby, James Thrall, 1906-. 1.5138, 1.5703,
    1.5873, 1.6145, 1.6150, 1.6199, 1.6297
Sociaal-Wetenschappelijk Informatie- en
    Documentatiecentrum (Koninklijke
    Nederlandse Akademie van Wetenschappen)
    4.6714
Social Science Federation of Canada. 4.1253
Social Science Research Council. Committee on
    Analysis of Pre-election Polls and Forecasts.
    4.7959
Social Science Research Council. Committee on
    Biological Bases of Social Behavior. 5.370
Social Science Research Council. Committee on
    Comparative Politics. 4.7752, 4.7776, 4.8365
Social Science Research Council. Committee on
    Social and Economic Aspects of Atomic
    Energy. 3.7562
Social Science Research Council. Committee on
    Socialization and Social Structure. 5.486
Social Science Research Council. Committee on
    Sociolinguistics. 2.124
Social Science Research Council. Committee on
    the Economy of China. 4.2478
Social Science Research Council of Canada.
    Committee on Biculturalism. 3.8691
Social Science Research Council. Southern
    regional committee. 3.8162
Social Science Research Council (U.S.) 2.2151,
    4.1679, 4.2460, 5.7168
Social Science Research Council (U.S.).
    Committee on Economic Growth. 4.2373,
    4.3112, 4.6384
Social Science Research Council (U.S.).
    Committee on Mass Communications and
    Political Behavior. 4.7961
Société des textes français modernes (Paris,
    France) 2.3980, 2.4218
Society for International Development. 4.5081
Society for Old Testament Study. 1.2563,
    1.2576, 3.3705
Society for Psychical Research (London,
    England) 5.662
Society for Social Responsibility in Science
    (A.C.T.). 5.6124
Society for the Anthropology of Visual
    Communication. 5.404
Society for the History of Czechoslovak Jews.
    3.3945
Society for the History of Technology. 5.6754
Society for the North American Cultural
    Survey. 4.146
Society for the Philosophical Study of
    Dialectical Materialism. 1.479
Society for the Psychological Study of Social
    Issues. 4.3162, 4.4999, 4.8992, 4.10090
Society for the Study of Human Biology. 5.4202
Society for the Study of Human Evolution.
    5.4035
Society for the Study of Welsh Labour History.
    3.1765
Society of Actuaries. 5.4629
Society of American Foresters. 5.5421
Society of Automotive Engineers. 5.5814,
    5.6241, 5.6622, 5.6636
Society of Biblical Literature. 1.2506
Society of Chemical Industry (Great Britain)
    5.6851
Society of General Physiologists. 5.3586, 5.3588
Society of Illustrators (New York, N.Y.) 1.5832
Society of Mining Engineers of AIME. 5.6725
Society of Mining Engineers of AIME. Coal
    Division. 5.6746
Society of Motion Picture and Television
    Engineers. Journal. 5.6999
Society of the Plastics Industry. 5.6911
Socolow, Robert H. 5.6157
Socolow, Susan Migden, 1941-. 4.4223, 4.5255

Soderlund, Jean R., 1947-. 3.8082
Sømme, Axel Christian Zetlitz, 1899- ed. 3.3350
Søraas, Haakon, 1887- joint author. 2.918
Sørensen, Torben. 5.5972
Soete, Luc. 4.1862
Sofaer, Abraham D. 4.9741
Soggin, J. Alberto. 1.2516, 1.2597-1.2598
Sohmen, Egon. 4.4554
Sohn, Louis B. ed. 4.9226
Soil Conservation Society of America. 5.5288
Soisson, Harold E. 5.5685
Soja, Edward W. ed. 3.5055
Sokal, Robert R. 5.3312-5.3313
Sokatch, J. R. (John Robert), 1928-. 5.4434
Sokel, Walter Herbert, 1917-. 2.13800
Sokoloff, Natalie J. 4.3291
Sokolov, E. N. (Evgeniĭ Nikolaevich), 1920-.
    5.4327
Sokolov, Sasha, 1943-. 2.1634
Sokolovskiĭ, Vasiliĭ Danilovich, 1897-. 5.7215
Sokolowski, Robert. 1.1023
Solar Energy Research Institute. 5.6329
Solaún, Mauricio. 4.8343
Solberg, Carl, 1915-. 3.7652, 4.4084
Solberg, Carl E. 4.8959
Solberg, Winton U. 1.2982
Solbrig, Otto T. 5.3266
Solé-Leris, Amadeu. 2.5140
Soliday, Gerald Lyman. 5.8379
Sollers, Philippe, 1936-. 2.4792
Sollors, Werner. 2.12875
Solmon, Lewis C. ed. 4.10731
Solmon, Lewis C. 4.10620
Solmsen, Friedrich, 1904-. 2.311
Solnit, Albert J. joint author. 4.6548, 4.9511
Solodkoff, A. von. 1.6666
Sologub, Fyodor, 1863-1927. 2.1529-2.1533
Solomon, Arthur P. 4.3490
Solomon, Barbara Bryant, 1934-. 4.6618
Solomon, Barbara Miller. 4.10840
Solomon, Cynthia. 5.1065
Solomon, Eric. 2.10987
Solomon, Ezra. 4.2007
Solomon, Fredric. 5.4680
Solomon, Maynard. 1.3805
Solomon, Michael R. 5.7094
Solomon, Peter R., 1939- joint author. 5.6517
Solomon R. Guggenheim Museum. 1.4970,
    1.4988, 1.6304
Solomon, Robert. 4.4578
Solomon, Robert C. 5.416
Solomon, Susan, 1956-. 5.2522
Solotaroff, Theodore. 2.2654
Solov'ev, Sergeĭ Mikhaĭlovich, 1820-1879.
    3.3046
Solow, Robert M. 4.1376
Soloway, R. A. 1.3306, 4.5687
Solt, Leo Frank, 1921-. 3.1486
Solt, Marilyn Leathers. 5.7721
Soltow, Lee. 4.2113
Soltow, Martha Jane. 5.8471
Solum, Nora Olava, tr. 2.14056
Solzhenitsyn, Aleksandr Isaevich, 1918-.
    2.1635-2.1636, 2.1638-2.1639, 3.3265, 4.6922
Sombart, Werner, 1863-1941. 4.1543-4.1544,
    4.7006
Somer, Elizabeth. 5.4235
Somer, John L. joint author. 2.13401
Somerlott, Robert. 2.3431
Somero, George N. 5.4205
Somers, Gerald George. ed. 4.3319
Somers, Gerald George. 4.3349
Somers, Herman Miles. 4.1975
Somervell, D. C. (David Churchill), 1885-1965.
    3.103, 3.1595
Somerville, E. Œ. (Edith Œnone), 1858-1949.
    2.9349
Somerville, Edith Anna OEnone, 1861-1949.
    2.9350
Somerville, John, 1905-. 1.479, 1.1107
Somjen, George G. 5.4362
Somkin, Fred. 3.6168
Sommerfeld, Arnold Johannes Wilhelm, 1868-.
    5.1914, 5.1970
Sommerfelt, Alf, 1892-. 2.219
Sommers, Albert T. 4.1995
Sommers, Frederic Tamler, 1923-. 1.1181
Sommers, Joseph, 1924-. 2.5329, 2.10302

Sommers, Ronald K. 5.4794
Sommerstein, Alan H. 2.424, 2.426-2.427, 2.429-2.430
Somorjai, Gabor A. 5.2900-5.2901
Songe, Alice H. joint author. 5.7605
Sonneborn, George. joint author. 5.1738
Sonneck, Oscar George Theodore, 1873-1928. 1.3563, 1.3693, 1.3797, 1.4221
Sonnenberg, Stephen M., 1940-. 5.4946
Sonnenfeld, Marion. tr. 2.13599
Sonnichsen, C. L. (Charles Leland), 1901-. 3.8468, 3.8580
Sonntag, Richard Edwin. 5.6203-5.6204
Sontag, Raymond James, 1897-1972. 3.866, 3.2262
Sontag, Susan, 1933-. 1.6681, 2.2683, 2.13330, 5.6942
Soong, T. T. 5.1546
Soper, Alexander Coburn, tr. 1.5060, 1.5075, 1.5453, 1.6315
Sopher, David Edward. 4.6193
Sopher, David Edward. joint author. 1.1588
Sophocles. 2.541-2.543, 2.545, 5.176
Sorabji, Richard. 1.297, 1.315, 1.1342
Sorauf, Frank J. (Frank Joseph), 1928-. 4.8171, 4.9723
Sorby Centennial Symposium on the History of Metallurgy (1963: Cleveland, Ohio) 5.6754
Sorby, Henry Clifton, 1826-1908. 5.6754
Sorcar, Prafulla C. 5.6340
Sorel, Albert, 1842-1906. 4.9066
Sorel, Georges, 1847-1922. 4.4886
Sorell, Walter, 1905-. 4.1114-4.1115
Sören Sörenson. 2.916
Sorensen. Gerald C., joint comp. 2.6241
Sorensen, Theodore C. 3.7870
Soria, Martin Sebastian. 1.5040
Sorin, Gerald, 1940-. 3.7261
Sorokin, Pitirim Aleksandrovich, 1889-1968. 4.4840, 4.4864, 4.4875, 4.4887-4.4888, 4.4977, 4.5050, 4.6371
Sorre, Maximilien, 1880-1962. 4.368
Sorrell, Martin. 2.4658
Sorum, Paul Clay, 1943-. 4.8927
Sosin, Jack M. 3.8372
Soskice, Juliet M. (Hueffer) tr. 2.1403
Sosna, Morton. 3.8165
Sosniak, Lauren A. 5.609
Sosnick, Stephen H. 4.2922
Součková, Milada, 1901-. 2.1655
Soucy, Robert, 1933-. 2.4387, 2.4516
Soudakoff, Stephen, joint comp. 4.796
Souders, Mott, 1904-. 5.5668, 5.5671
Soukup, James Rudolph, 1928-. 4.8196
Soule, George Henry, 1887-1970. 4.1880
Soule, James. 5.5335
Soulé, Michael E. 5.3217-5.3219
Soulié, Marguerite. ed. 2.3977
Sourkes, Theodore L. 5.4519
Sournia, Alain. 5.3778
Souter, Gavin, 1929-. 3.5657
South Asia Library Group. 5.8049
South Carolina. Dept. of Archives and History. 3.7069
South Caroliniana Society. 3.7069
South Dakota. Dakota Territory Centennial Commission. 3.8513
Southall, Aidan William. ed. 4.515
Southall, James Powell Cocke, 1871-. 5.4379
Southam, B. C. 2.7383, 2.11641
Southam, Brian Charles. 2.7366
Southeast Asia Development Advisory Group. 4.7120
Southeast Asian Studies Program (Institute of Southeast Asian Studies) 4.8729
Southern Anthropological Society. Meeting. (16th: 1981: Fort Worth, Tex.) 2.112
Southern, Eileen. 1.3537, 1.4305
Southern Illinois University (System) 1.585
Southern Methodist University. Institute for the Study of Earth and Man. 5.6744
Southern, R. W. (Richard William), 1912-. 1.2072, 1.2309, 1.3254, 3.136, 3.144
Southern, Richard. joint ed. 2.3089
Southern, Richard. 2.3159, 2.3284, 2.3293, 2.3311
Southern Sociological Society (U.S.) 4.5195
Southerne, Thomas, 1660-1746. 2.7268

Southgate, Donald. 3.1611
Southwell, Robert, Saint, 1561?-1595. 2.6520
Southwest Educational Development Laboratory. 4.10891
Southwick, Charles H. 5.3532
Southwick, Leslie H., 1950-. 3.6312
Southworth, Herbert Rutledge. 3.3470
Southworth, Herman McDowell, 1909-. 4.2891
Southworth, James Granville, 1896-. 2.6379-2.6380
Southworth, Michael. joint author. 1.5500
Southworth, Susan. 1.5500
Soviet Union. Komissiia po izdaniiu diplomaticheskikh dokumentov. 3.887
Soviet Union. Ministerstvo kul'tury. 1.6721
Sowell, Thomas, 1930-. 3.6528-3.6529, 4.10859, 4.10872
Sowers, George B. 5.5906
Sowers, George F. 5.5906
Sowerwine, Charles, 1943-. 4.7148
Soyinka, Wole. 2.2305-2.2306, 2.10111-2.10114, 4.6923
Spache, Evelyn B. 4.10462
Spache, George Daniel, 1909-. 4.10462
Spacks, Patricia Ann Meyer. ed. 2.6167
Spacks, Patricia Ann Meyer. 2.5566, 2.5568, 2.5809, 2.7038
Spady, Richard H., 1952-. 4.3989
Spae, Joseph John, 1913-. 1.1143
Spaeth, David A. 1.5427
Spaeth, Harold J. joint author. 4.9791
Spaeth, Sigmund Gottfried, 1885-1965. 1.4237
Spalding, Frances. 1.6024
Spalding, Phinizy. 3.8259
Spanfeller, James J. 5.7141
Spangler, Merlin Grant, 1894-. 5.5907
Spanier, Edwin Henry, 1921-. 5.1610
Spanier, Jerome, 1930-. 5.1456, 5.1490
Spanier, John W. 3.5031, 4.9162
Spanos, Nicholas P., joint author. 5.4900
Spanos, William V. 2.5927
Spark, Muriel. ed. 2.7448
Spark, Muriel. 2.9354-2.9364
Sparks, John. 5.4066
Sparks, Merrill, joint comp. 2.1312
Sparring, Åke. 4.8667
Sparrow, John Hanbury Angus, 1906-. 2.815
Sparrow, Walter Shaw, 1862- ed. 1.5860
Sparshott, Francis Edward, 1926-. 1.1361
Spate, O. H. K. (Oskar Hermann Khristian), 1911-. 3.4161, 3.5548, 4.94
Spater, George. 3.1575
Spaulding, J. L. (Jay L.) joint author. 3.5168
Spaulding, Robert Kilburn, 1898-. 2.888
Speaight, George. 2.2835, 4.1188
Speaight, Robert, 1904-. 2.6699, 2.6831, 2.8450
Speakman, J. Clare (James Clare), 1907- joint author. 5.2801
Spear, Allan H. 3.8426
Spear, Norman E. 5.324
Spear, Richard E., 1940-. 1.5015
Spear, Thomas George Percival. joint ed. 3.4123
Spear, Thomas George Percival. 3.4200, 3.4224-3.4226, 3.4254, 3.5276
Spearing, A. C. 2.5614, 2.5617
Spearman, R. I. C. (Richard Ian Campbell) 5.4117
Spears, Monroe Kirklyndorf. ed. 2.7206, 2.8410
Spears, Monroe Kirklyndorf. 2.8409, 2.10498
Spears, Richard A. 2.1165
Specht, R. L. (Raymond Louis), 1924-. 5.3551, 5.3565
Special Libraries Association. 4.4260
Special Libraries Association. Committee on Commercial Information Services. 4.4260
Speck, Frank Gouldsmith, 1881-1950. 3.5912
Speck, W. A. (William Arthur), 1938-. 2.5694, 3.1540, 3.1805
Speckhart, Frank H., 1940-. 5.5719
The Spectator. 2.6271
Spector, Robert Donald. ed. 2.6001
Spector, Ronald H., 1943-. 3.1006, 3.4468
Speech Association of America. 2.3534, 2.10649
Speech Communication Association. 1.3047
Speer, Albert, 1905-. 3.2414
Spehr, Paul C. 2.2932
Speidel, Hans, 1897-. 3.970
Speier, Hans. 4.5010

Speight, Charlotte F., 1919-. 1.6627
Speight, R. Marston, 1924-. 1.2049
Speir, Jerry, 1946-. 2.12159
Speirs, Ebenezer Brown, ed. and tr. 1.1546
Speirs, John. 2.5615, 2.6371
Spell, Jefferson Rea, 1886-. 2.5316
Spellman, A. B., 1935-. 1.3759
Spelman, Edward, d. 1767. 2.364
Spelman, M S. 5.4705
Spence, A. Michael (Andrew Michael) joint author. 4.2739
Spence, Alexander P., 1929-. 5.4142
Spence, Barbara Barrow, joint author. 4.3045
Spence, Clark C. 3.8545-3.8546
Spence, Donald P. 5.4914
Spence, J. E. (John Edward) 4.8411
Spence, J. Wayne. 5.1214
Spence, Janet Taylor. ed. 5.216
Spence, Janet Taylor. 5.492
Spence, John C. H. 5.3288
Spence, Jonathan D. 1.3030, 3.4706, 3.4717, 3.4720, 3.4750, 4.6150
Spence, Joseph, 1699-1768. 2.2529
Spence, Kenneth Wartenbee, 1907-1967. 5.216, 5.305
Spence, Mary Lee. 3.8473
Spencer, Albert G. 5.5796
Spencer, Antony James Merrill. 5.5707
Spencer, Bernard, 1909-. 2.9368
Spencer, D. M. (Douglas Malcolm), 1927-. 5.5402
Spencer, David Gelvin. joint ed. 5.7958
Spencer, Edgar Winston. 5.2968
Spencer, Elaine Glovka, 1939-. 4.3659
Spencer, Elizabeth. 2.12493-2.12495
Spencer, Frank. 4.449
Spencer, Hanna. 2.13609
Spencer, Harold, 1920-. 1.4677
Spencer, Hazelton, 1893-1944. 2.6227, 2.6867
Spencer, Hazleton, 1893-1944. 2.6226
Spencer, Herbert. 4.4841-4.4845, 4.7647, 4.10197-4.10198
Spencer, J. E. (Joseph Earle), 1907-. 4.371
Spencer, Joel H. joint author. 5.1285
Spencer, John H. (John Hathaway), 1907-. 3.5248
Spencer, John Richard. 1.5467, 1.6338
Spencer, John Walter. 2.192
Spencer, M. C. (Michael Clifford). 2.4438
Spencer, Margaret Beale. 3.6748
Spencer, Robert F. 3.5707, 3.5884
Spencer, Robin. 1.5984
Spencer, Samia I., 1943-. 4.5865
Spencer, T. J. B. (Terence John Bew), 1915-1978. 2.5574
Spencer, Virginia E. joint author. 3.5917
Spencer, Warren F., 1923-. 3.7392
Spencer, William G. 1.4558
Spender, Dale. 4.5869, 4.5942, 4.5977
Spender, Lynne. 4.5897
Spender, Stephen, 1909-. 2.2684-2.2685, 2.5488, 2.8996, 2.9369-2.9372, 4.9980
Spengemann, William C. 3.319
Spengler, Joseph John, 1902-. 4.1270, 4.1602-4.1603, 4.1623, 4.1677, 4.1699, 4.5796
Spengler, Oswald, 1880-1936. 3.17, 3.197
Spenser, Edmund, 1552?-1599. 2.6522-2.6525
Sperber, Dan. 5.398
Sperber, Hans, 1885-. 4.7796
Sperber, Richard. 5.4970
Sperry, Roger Wolcott, 1913-. 5.4313
Sperry, Stuart M. 2.7867
Sperry, Willard Learoyd, 1882-1954. 1.2385
Spevack, Marvin. 2.6687
Spicehandler, Ezra. 2.1784
Spicer, Edward Holland, 1906-. 3.5766, 3.8914
Spicer, Jack. 2.13331
Spiegel, Alan. 2.3514
Spiegel, Allen D. 5.4619
Spiegel, John Paul, 1911- joint author. 5.4936
Spiegel-Rösing, Ina-Susanne. 5.962
Spiegel, Steven L. 3.3757
Spiegelberg, Herbert, 1904-. 1.524
Spiegelman, Mortimer. 4.1624
Spielberg, Peter. 2.10851
Spielberger, Charles Donald, 1927- ed. 5.427-5.428
Spierenburg, Petrus Cornelis. 4.6921

Spiers, Edward M. 5.7306
Spiers, Richard Phené, 1838-1916. 1.5218, 1.5446
Spies, Werner, 1937-. 1.5041, 1.6154
Spiess, Eliot B. 5.3475
Spigelman, James Jacob, 1946- joint author. 5.2454
Spigler, Iancu. 4.2421
Spilhaus, Athelstan Frederick, jt. author. 5.2509
Spilka, Mark. ed. 2.8997
Spilka, Mark. 2.8998
Spillane, Mickey, 1918-. 2.12496
Spiller, Gene A. 5.4237
Spiller, Jürg, ed. 1.6176
Spiller, Robert, 1896-. 2.10604
Spiller, Robert Ernest, 1896-. 2.10252, 2.10257, 2.10272, 2.10422, 2.10889, 2.11017, 3.6073
Spiller, Roger J. 5.7199
Spillers, Hortense J. 2.10318
Spinden, Herbert Joseph, 1879-. 3.9047
Spindler, George Dearborn. 4.10180
Spinelli, Donald C. joint author. 5.8005
Spingarn, Joel Elias. 2.2467, 2.5503
Spinka, Matthew, 1890-1972. 1.2319, 1.3299-1.3301
Spinks, J. W. T. (John William Tranter), 1908- tr. 5.2302
Spinoza, Benedictus de, 1632-1677. 1.796, 1.1095-1.1097, 4.7416
Spinrad, Norman. 2.13332
Spiro, Herzl R., 1935-. 5.4701
Spiro, Melford E. 1.1765, 1.2110, 4.7169
Spiro, Rand J. 4.10360
Spitta, Philipp, 1841-1894. 1.3782
Spitz, David, 1916-. 4.7648, 4.7670
Spitz, Elaine, 1932-. 4.7584
Spitz, Lewis William, 1922-. 1.2328
Spitz, René A. (René Arpad), 1887-1974. 5.5105
Spitzer, Alan B. (Alan Barrie), 1925-. 3.2145, 4.7048
Spitzer, Leo, 1887-1960. 2.5553
Spitzer, Lyman, 1914-. 5.1825
Spivack, Bernard. 2.6812
Spivak, Burton. 3.7060
Spivak, Lawrence Edmund, 1900-. 2.10711
Spivak, Michael. 5.1629
Spivey, Donald. 4.10873
Spivey, W. Allen. 4.2643
Splittstoesser, Walter E. 5.5339
Spock, Benjamin, 1903-. 4.5713, 5.578, 5.5077
Spock, Leslie Erskine, 1900-. 5.3033
Spodek, Bernard. 4.10416, 4.10938
Spoel, S. van der. 5.3822
Spolin, Viola. 2.3132
Sponde, Jean de, 1557-1595. 2.4010-2.4011
Sponheim, Paul R. 1.3291
Spooner, Brian. ed. 4.1576
Spore Conference. 5.4454
Spores, Ronald. 3.8909
Sporne, K. R. 5.3699, 5.3734
Spoto, Donald, 1941-. 2.3054
Spottiswood, David J. 5.6753
Spottiswoode, Raymond, 1913-1970. 2.2944
Spotts, Merhyle Franklin, 1895-. 5.6194
Sprachman, Paul. 2.1978
Spradling, Mary Mace, 1905-. 5.7878
Sprafkin, Joyce N., 1949-. 4.5736
Sprague, Arthur Colby, 1895-. 2.6444, 2.6859, 2.6870
Sprague, Claire. comp. 2.9606
Sprague, Marshall. 3.8556
Sprague, Rosamond Kent. ed. 1.218
Sprague, Rosamond Kent. 1.246
Sprat, Thomas, 1635-1713. 2.6953
Sprenkle, Robert. 1.4554
Sprent, Janet I. 5.4456
Spretnak, Charlene, 1946-. 4.5892, 4.8612
Spriano, Paolo. 4.7080
Sprigg, C. St. John (Christopher St. John), 1907-1937. 2.9373
Sprigge, Elizabeth, 1900-. 2.12519
Sprinchorn, Evert. ed. 2.14067
Sprinchorn, Evert. 2.14082
Spring, Anita. 1.1615
Spring, Joel H. 4.9956, 4.9988, 4.10027
Springall, H. D. 5.2786
Springer, George S. 5.6048

Springer, Haskell S. 3.8525
Springer, Marlene. 2.5586, 2.7801, 3.8525
Springer, Otto, 1905- ed. 2.1190
Springhouse Corporation. 5.4995, 5.4999, 5.5209
Sproat, John G. 3.7415
Sproull, Robert F. joint author. 5.5651
Sprout, Harold Hance, 1901-. 3.6382-3.6383, 4.8987, 4.8999, 4.9038
Sprout, Margaret Tuttle, 1903-. 3.6383, 4.8987, 4.8999, 4.9038
Sprout, Margaret (Tuttle) Mrs., joint author. 3.6382
Sprowls, James T. 4.9892
Spruch, Grace Marmor. comp. 5.2431
Spruch, Larry. joint comp. 5.2431
Sprudzs, Adolf. 4.8976
Sprung, Barbara. 4.10306
Spry, Irene Mary Biss. 3.8849
Spufford, Margaret. 2.6068
Spuhler, James N., joint author. 5.370
Spulber, Nicolas. 4.2388
Spuler, Bertold, 1911- comp. 3.373, 3.3623
Spurgeon, Caroline Frances Eleanor, 1869-1942. 2.6354, 2.6849
Spurling, Hilary. 2.8536
Spurling, Laurie. 1.845
Spurr, Stephen Hopkins. 5.3785
Spykman, Nicholas John, 1893-1943. 3.6409
Squier, Charles L. 2.6128, 2.7288
Squier, E. G. (Ephraim George), 1821-1888. 3.9029
Squier, Susan Merrill. 2.5955, 2.9607
Squire, Geoffrey. 4.838
Squire, John Collings, Sir, 1884-1958. 2.8627, 2.9374
Squire, Lyn, 1946-. 4.3236
Squires, James Radcliffe, 1917-. 2.11934
Squires, Radcliffe, 1917-. 2.11759, 2.12577
Squyres, Wendy D. 5.4593
Srb, Adrian M. 5.3441
Sri Lanka. 4.9919
Srikantan, K. S., 1930-. 4.5681
Srinivas, Mysore Narasimhachar. 4.5430, 4.5434
Srinivasa Iyengar, K. R. 2.10121
Srinivasan, T. N., 1933- joint author. 4.4239
Srivastva, Suresh, 1934-. 4.2700
Srull, Thomas K. 4.4926
Ssu-ma, Ch'ien, ca. 145-ca. 86 B.C. 1.167, 3.4698, 4.2465
St. Anthony's guild, Paterson, N.J. 1.66
St. Armand, Barton Levi. 2.11009
St. Aubyn, Giles. 3.1680
St. Denis, Ruth, 1880-1968. 4.1157
St. John, Christopher Marie. 2.3355
St. John de Crèvecoeur, J. Hector, 1735-1813. 3.6023-3.6024, 3.6026
St. John, Nancy Hoyt. 4.10781
St. John, Spenser Buckingham, Sir, 1825-1910. 3.9113
St. John-Stevas, Norman. 4.8381
St. John's College (University of Cambridge) 4.5421
St. Joseph, John Kenneth Sinclair, joint author. 3.1721
St. Martin, Hardie. 2.5152
Staar, Richard Felix, 1923-. 3.2998
Stabb, Martin S. 1.659
Stableford, Brian M. 2.6054
Stableford, Tom. 2.1245
Stabler, Arthur Phillips. 2.3940
Stace, W. T. (Walter Terence), 1886-. 1.114
Stacey, C. P. 3.8734
Stacey, C. P. (Charles Perry), 1906-. 3.8700, 3.8752
Stacey, F. D. (Frank D.) 5.2490
Stacey, Judith. 4.5632
Stacey, William A. 4.5778
Stack, Carol B. 3.6774
Stack-Staikidis, William J., 1929-. 5.5681
Stackhouse, Jan. 4.3738
Stackhouse, Max L. 1.2927
Stackpole, Edouard A., 1905-. 5.5485
Stacy, R. H. (Robert H.), 1919-. 2.2509
Staddon, J. E. R. 5.4104
Stade, George. 2.2557
Stade, George. ed. 2.11541
Stade, George. 2.6048
Stadelmann, Rudolf, 1902-1949. 3.2303, 3.2319

Stadler, Quandra Prettyman, comp. 2.10816
Staël, Madame de (Anne-Louise-Germaine), 1766-1817. 2.2613, 2.4297-2.4298, 3.2241
Staff, Leopold, 1878-1957. 2.1732
Stafford, Barbara Maria, 1941-. 4.100
Stafford, Beth. 4.5991
Stafford, David. 3.1136
Stafford, Edward Peary. 5.7429
Stafford, Jean, 1915-. 2.12497-2.12500
Stafford, Pauline. 4.5861
Stafford, William, 1914-. 2.2748, 2.12501-2.12502
Stagg, J. C. A. (John Charles Anderson), 1945-. 3.7111
Stagner, Ross, 1909-. 4.8994
Stahl, Anne Vergati. joint author. 1.5052
Stahl, Barbara J. 5.3894
Stahl, Dorothy. 1.3624
Stahl, E. L. (Ernest Ludwig), 1902-. 2.13515
Stahl, Ernest Ludwig. 2.13654
Stahl, Franklin W. 5.3465
Staiger, Emil, 1908-. 2.13582
Staiger, Janet. 2.2909
Staines, David, 1946-. 2.8159
Stakgold, Ivar. 5.1534
Staley, Allen. 1.6361
Staley, Thomas F. 2.6059, 2.9281, 2.9286
Staley, Thomas F. ed. 2.8899, 2.8919
Stalick, Wayne M., joint author. 5.2757
Stalin, Joseph, 1879-1953. 3.887, 3.993, 3.3148, 3.3194, 3.3230-3.3232, 3.3557
Stalley, R. F. 4.7342
Stallings, Laurence, 1894-1968. 2.11313
Stallings, William. 5.6406
Stallman, R. W. (Robert Wooster), 1911-. 2.2444, 2.3433, 2.10988
Stallworthy, Jon. 2.1745, 2.3757, 2.8355, 2.9216, 2.9376-2.9378
Stallybrass, Oliver. ed. 2.8641
Stalvey, Lois Mark. 3.6693
Stam, Robert, 1941-. 2.2885
Stambaugh, John E. joint author. 1.1652
Stambler, Irwin. 1.3513, 1.3527
Stamm, Alicia. 1.5284
Stamm, H. Peter Paul. 1.4110
Stammen, Theo. 4.8377
Stammler, Wolfgang, 1886-, ed. 2.13450, 2.13631
Stamp, John Trevor, joint author. 5.5448
Stamp, L. Dudley (Laurence Dudley), 1898-1966. 3.5054, 4.74, 4.2251, 4.4123-4.4125
Stamp, Laurence Dudley, 1898-1966. 4.2437
Stampacchia, Guido. joint author. 5.1421
Stampfer, Friedrich, 1874-. 3.2375
Stampp, Kenneth M. (Kenneth Milton) 3.7182, 3.7196, 3.7304, 3.7473, 3.8398
Stanage, Sherman M. (Sherman Miller) 4.5077
Stanback, Thomas M. 4.3865
Standards Engineers Society. Metropolitan New York Section. 5.5755
Standish, Thomas A., 1941-. 5.1242
Stanfield, John H. 3.6604
Stanford, Ann. 2.10866-2.10867
Stanford Arms Control Group. 4.9163
Stanford, Derek. 2.7443, 2.8675, 2.9366
Stanford, Donald E., 1913- ed. 2.10875
Stanford, Jack Arthur, 1947-. 5.3567
Stanford, Quentin H. 4.152
Stanford Research Institute. Strategic Studies Center. 3.7573, 4.9016
Stanford University. 2.1264, 3.3567, 3.3616, 5.486
Stanford University. Center for Research on Women. 2.10289, 4.5595
Stanford University. Center for Russian and East European Studies. 4.8656
Stanford University. Institute for the Study of Human Problems. 4.6656, 4.10092
Stanford, William Bedell. 2.242-2.243, 2.418, 2.425
Stanford, William Bedell. ed. 2.482
Stanford, William Bedell. 1.6742, 2.235, 2.2419
Stang, Ragna Thiis. 1.5039
Stang, Richard, 1925-. 2.6017
Stang, Sondra J. 2.8639
Stange, George Robert, 1919- joint ed. 2.6177
Stangos, Nikos. joint author. 1.4826

Stangos, Nikos. 1.4577
Stanier, Roger Y. 5.4437
Stanislavsky, Konstantin, 1863-1938.
    2.3123-2.3125
Stanislawski, Michael, 1952-. 3.3995
Staniszkis, Jadwiga. 3.3348
Stanitski, Conrad L. 5.2629
Stankiewicz, W. J. 3.2017
Stanko, Elizabeth Anne, 1950-. 4.6709, 4.6780
Stanley, Daniel J. ed. 4.350
Stanley, David T. 4.6898
Stanley, Eric Gerald. ed. 2.6423
Stanley, George Francis Gilman. 3.8715,
    3.8855-3.8856
Stanley, H. Eugene (Harry Eugene), 1941-.
    5.2239
Stanley, Henry M. (Henry Morton), 1841-1904.
    3.5221
Stanley, Manfred. 5.5524
Stanley, Peter W. 3.4605
Stanley, Steven M. 5.2971, 5.3161, 5.3375
Stanley, Steven M. joint author. 5.3151
Stanley, Thomas A., 1946-. 4.7200
Stanley, Wendell Meredith, 1904-. 5.4475
Stanley, William D. 5.6356
Stannard, David E. 1.2944
Stannard, Martin, 1947-. 2.9504
Stansell, Christine. 4.5506
Stansfield, William D., 1930-. 5.3408, 5.3455
Stansky, Peter. 2.9184, 2.9201-2.9202
Stanton, Alfred H. 5.4807
Stanton, Domna C. 2.3925
Stanton, Elizabeth Cady, 1815-1902. 4.5976,
    4.5999, 4.8080, 4.8088
Stanton, G. N. 1.2854
Stanton, H. P. Martin. 5.6681
Stanton, Michael N. 5.7918
Stanton, Phoebe B. 1.5397
Stanton, Robert J. joint author. 5.3155
Stanton, Shelby L., 1948-. 3.4505, 5.7284
Stanton, Stephen Sadler, 1915-. 2.12739
Stanwood, P. G. 1.3055
Stapel, Wilhelm, 1882-1954, tr. 2.13539
Stapledon, Olaf, 1886-1950. 2.9379-2.9380
Staples, Hugh B. 2.12050
Staples Press, Ltd., London. 2.173
Staples, Robert. 3.6775-3.6777, 4.5773
Stapleton, Michael. 2.5524
Stapleton, Thomas, 1535-1598. 2.651
Star, Barbara. 4.5779
Starbuck, William H., 1934-. 4.2633
Stares, Paul B. 5.7412
Starfield, A. M. joint author. 5.1108
Starhawk. 5.673, 5.676
Stark, Henry, 1938-. 5.6357
Stark, Irwin, 1912- joint ed. 2.10680
Stark, Rodney. 4.6832
Starke, Aubrey Harrison. 2.11140, 2.11143
Starkie, Enid. 2.4200-2.4201, 2.5573
Starkie, Enid Mary. 2.4145, 2.4282
Starkie, Walter, 1894-. 2.5159, 3.3408
Starling, Ernest Henry, 1866-1927. 5.4190
Starnes, De Witt Talmage, 1888-1967. 2.1077
Starobin, Joseph Robert, 1913-. 4.8237
Starobinski, Jean. 2.3995
Staron, Stanislaw. 3.3990
Staropoli, Charles, joint comp. 4.10535
Starr, Chauncey. 5.6136
Starr, Chester G. 3.552, 3.2542, 3.2571, 3.2790,
    4.1736, 4.7361
Starr, George A. 2.6977
Starr, Harris Elwood, 1875-. 3.6288
Starr, Herbert Willmarth, 1916- ed. 2.7053,
    2.7055
Starr, John Bryan. 3.4837, 3.6425
Starr, Kevin. 3.8615
Starr, Paul, 1949-. 5.4627
Starr, Philip, 1935-. 5.8293
Starr, Roger. 4.2046, 4.3491
Starr, S. Frederick. 1.5036
Starr, Stephen Z. 3.7384
Starr, William. 5.6258
Starratt, Robert J. 4.10639
Starzhinskiĭ, V. M. (Viacheslav Mikhaĭlovich)
    joint author. 5.1517
Stastny, Charles. 4.6904
State Historical Society of Wisconsin. 3.8447,
    5.8478

State University of New York at Binghamton.
    Center for Medieval and Early Renaissance
    Studies. 2.2396
State University of New York at Binghamton.
    Center for Social Analysis. 4.1722
Statera, Gianni. 4.10109
Stathas, Thalia, ed. 2.6931
Stationers' Company (London, England) 5.7953
Statistics Canada. 4.1252-4.1253
Statius, P. Papinius (Publius Papinius) 2.695
Statman, Meir. 4.3796
Staton, Frances Maria. 5.7896
Staub, Ervin. 5.532
Staudenraus, P. J. 3.7230
Stauffer, Donald Alfred, 1902-1952. 2.6826
Stauffer, John Frederick. 5.4219
Stauffer, M. R. 5.3128
Stauffer, Robert C., 1913-. 5.3353
Stauffer, Russell G. 4.10466
Staveley, E. S. 4.7362
Staveley, L. A. K., 1914- joint author. 5.2928
Stavely, Keith W. 2.7164
Stavenhagen, Rodolfo, comp. 4.2836
Staves, Susan. 2.5905, 2.7289
Stavig, Mark. 2.6579
Stavrianos, Leften Stavros. 3.206, 3.764, 3.3520
Stavrou, Theofanis George, 1934-. 1.6721
Stead, Christina, 1902-. 2.10164-2.10173
Steadman, John M. 2.5587
Steadman, Philip, 1942-. 1.5464
Steady, Filomina Chioma. 4.6152
Steamer, Robert J. 4.9794
Steane, J. B. 1.3766, 2.6570, 2.6618
Stearn, William Thomas, 1911-. 5.3632
Stearns, Harold, 1891-1943. 2.3634, 3.6059
Stearns, Marshall Winslow. 1.4336, 2.6388
Stearns, Peter N. 1.3269, 3.706, 4.5288
Stearns, Samuel D. 5.6381-5.6382
Stebbins, Lucy Poate, b. 1886. 2.5567, 2.8236
Stebbins, Richard Poate, 1913- joint author.
    2.8236
Stebbins, Robert A., 1938-. 4.5076
Stebbins, Robert C. (Robert Cyril), 1915-.
    5.3923
Stebbins, Theodore E. 1.6378
Stebbins, Theodore E. joint author. 1.5916
Stebbins, William C., 1929-. 5.4372
Stechow, Wolfgang, 1896-1974. ed. 1.4769
Stedman, Murray Salisbury, 1917-. 4.8167
Stedman, Susan (Winter) joint author. 4.8167
Stedman, Thomas Lathrop, 1853-1938. 5.4489
Steefel, Lawrence Dinkelspiel, 1894-. 3.2161,
    3.2499
Steegmuller, Francis, ed. 2.4195-2.4196, 2.4271,
    2.4368, 2.4485
Steel, Anthony Bedford, 1900-. 3.1370
Steel, Ronald. 2.3617
Steel, Thomas B., 1929- joint author. 1.1255
Steel, William A. 1.4593
Steele, Arthur Robert. 5.3629
Steele, Colin. 5.7657
Steele, Guy. 5.1211, 5.1217
Steele, James B. 5.6007
Steele, Jonathan. comp. 3.3537
Steele, Richard, Sir, 1672-1729. 2.6270, 2.6272,
    2.6274-2.6275, 2.6887, 2.7269-2.7273
Steele, Richard W. 3.940
Steen, Charlie R. 3.2980
Steen, Edwin Benzel, 1901-. 5.3186
Steen, Harold K. 5.5438
Steen, Lynn Arthur, 1941-. 5.1031, 5.1603,
    5.8281
Steen, Sara Jayne, 1949-. 2.6560
Steen, Sheila C., joint author. 3.5947
Steenberghen, Fernand van, 1904-. 1.356, 1.359
Steensma, Robert C., 1930-. 2.6898
Steere, Douglas Van, 1901-. 1.3353
Steere, Norman V., comp. 5.2639
Steere, William Campbell, 1907- ed. 5.3671
Steers, J. A. (James Alfred), 1899-. 4.215
Stefan, Paul, 1879-1943. ed. 1.4021
Stefani, Raymond T. 5.6183
Stefansson, Vilhjalmur, 1879-1962. 4.54
Steffen, Charles E., 1952-. 4.3601
Steffen, Jerome O., 1942-. 3.8452, 3.8470
Steffens, Lincoln, 1866-1936. 2.3635
Steffl, Bernita M. 5.5005

Stegner, Wallace Earle, 1909-. 2.10539, 2.11560,
    2.12503-2.12506, 3.8861, 5.825
Stegun, Irene A. joint ed. 5.1123
Stehli, Francis Greenough. joint author. 5.2983
Stehr, Nico. 4.4879
Steichen, Edward, 1879-1973. ill. 2.12434
Steidel, Robert F., 1926-. 5.5697, 5.5746
Steig, Michael, 1936-. 2.7647
Steiglitz, Kenneth, 1939-. 5.1550
Steiman, Lionel B. (Lionel Bradley), 1941-.
    2.13871
Stein, Arnold Sidney, 1915-. 2.6467, 2.7067,
    2.7139, 2.12414
Stein, Barbara H., joint author. 4.2145
Stein, Bruno, 1930-. 4.3471
Stein, Clarence S. 1.5599
Stein, Deni W. 5.5368
Stein, Erwin, 1885-1958. ed. 1.3967
Stein, George H., 1934-. 3.972
Stein, Gertrude, 1874-1946. 2.12507-2.12516
Stein, Gordon. joint author. 5.8443
Stein, Herbert, 1916-. 4.1939, 4.4654
Stein, Howard F. 3.6530
Stein, Jack Madison. 1.4042
Stein, Janice Gross. 3.3880
Stein, Jess M. 2.1068, 2.1086
Stein, Jonathan B. 5.7280
Stein, Keith. 1.4555
Stein, Kenneth W., 1946-. 4.2860
Stein, Leo, 1872-1947. 2.12523
Stein, Leonard. ed. 1.4469
Stein, Leonard. 1.3474
Stein, Maurice Robert, 1926-. 4.6225
Stein, Peter J., 1937-. 4.5768
Stein, R. B., 1940-. 5.4289
Stein, Rolf Alfred, 1911-. 3.4856
Stein, Stanley J. 4.2145, 4.2175, 4.3855, 5.8402
Stein, Steve. 3.9308
Stein, Theodore J. 4.6567
Stein, Walter J. 4.2923
Stein, Werner. 3.369
Stein, William W. 4.5276
Steinbeck, John, 1902-1968. 2.12524-2.12535
Steinberg, Alfred, 1917-. 3.7620
Steinberg, Cobbett. 2.2849, 2.2874
Steinberg, David I. 3.4422
Steinberg, David Joel. ed. 3.4396
Steinberg, Franz U., 1913-. 5.4745
Steinberg, Ira S. 4.10361
Steinberg, Jonathan. 3.3509, 5.7467
Steinberg, Leo, 1920-. 1.4836, 1.5179
Steinberg, M. W. (Moses Wolfe), 1918-. 2.9934
Steinberg, Milton, 1903-1950. 1.1965
Steinberg, Raymond M. 4.6592
Steinberg, Ronnie, 1947-. 4.3240
Steinberg, S. H. (Sigfrid Henry), 1899-1969.
    3.370, 4.7214, 5.7545
Steinberg, Stephen. 3.6531
Steinberger, Peter J., 1948-. 4.8836
Steinbrunner, Chris. 2.71
Steiner, Bernard Christian, 1864-1926. 3.8106
Steiner, George, 1929-. 2.2594, 2.2818
Steiner, George Albert, 1912-. 4.2638, 4.4342
Steiner, Gilbert Yale, 1924-. 4.5601, 4.6568
Steiner, H. Arthur, 1905-, ed. 3.4828
Steiner, Herbert, 1892- ed. 2.13783
Steiner, Ivan Dale, 1917- ed. 4.4999
Steiner, Kurt, 1912-. 4.8573, 4.8891
Steiner, Rudolf, 1861-1925. 1.2098
Steiner, Stan. joint comp. 2.2323
Steiner, Zara S. 3.780, 4.9092
Steinert, Marlis G. 3.971
Steinfeld, Jeffrey I. 5.2642
Steinfels, Peter. 4.7317
Steingass, Francis Joseph, 1825-1903. 2.1964
Steinhaus, Hugo, 1887-1972. 5.1122, 5.1255
Steinhoff, William R. 2.9186
Steinkraus, Warren E. 1.952
Steinman, D. B. (David Barnard), 1886-1960.
    5.6077
Steinmann, Martin, 1915-. 2.8349
Steinmetz, Sol. ed. 2.1094
Steinmetz, Sol. 2.1095
Steinmetz, Suzanne K. joint author. 4.5780
Stekler, Herman O. 4.3830
Stella, Frank. 1.6447
Stellman, Jeanne Mager, 1947-. 5.5015-5.5016
Stelmach, George E. 5.255

Stelter, Benjamin Franklin. joint author. 2.7495
Stelter, Gilbert Arthur, 1933-. 4.6246
Stem, Carl H. 4.4590
Stendhal, 1783-1842. 2.4053, 2.4300-2.4307
Stenehjem, Michele Flynn. 3.941
Stenesh, J., 1927-. 5.4394
Stengers, Isabelle. 5.925
Stenius, Erik. 1.1229
Stenning, Henry James, 1889- tr. 4.1538
Stent, Gunther Siegmund, 1924-. 5.3419, 5.3468
Stenton, Doris Mary Parsons, Lady. 3.1333
Stenton, F. M. (Frank Merry), 1880-1967.
    1.6591, 3.1317, 3.1334
Stenton, Michael. 4.8470
Stepan, Alfred C. 4.8348
Stepanov, Nikolaĭ Leonidovich, 1902-. 2.1395
Stepanov, V. V. (Viacheslav Vasil'evich),
    1889-1950. 5.1506
Stepansky, Paul E. 5.425
Stephan, John J. 3.1015
Stephan, Walter G. 4.10793
Stephani, Hans. 5.2218
Stephanides, Theodore Ph. 2.605
Stephanopoulos, George. 5.6837
Stephans, Mark. 5.7050
Stephen, Frank H., 1946-. 4.3180
Stephen, Leslie, Sir, 1832-1904. 1.683, 1.721,
    1.1521, 2.5554, 2.5560, 2.5676, 2.8114-2.8115,
    3.1235
Stephens, Edward M., d. 1955. 2.8148
Stephens, James, 1882-1950. 2.6174, 2.6180,
    2.9381-2.9384
Stephens, John Calhoun, 1916-. 2.6275
Stephens, John H. (John Hall), 1925-. 5.5660
Stephens, Martha. 2.13224
Stephens, Meic. 2.831
Stephens, Otis H., 1936-. 4.9884
Stephens, R. I. (Ralph Ivan) joint author.
    5.5810
Stephens, Thomas M. 4.10928
Stephenson, Carl, 1886-. 3.137, 3.581, 4.8380
Stephenson, D. Grier. 4.9781
Stephenson, Gerald Robert, 1942- joint author.
    5.5413
Stephenson, Hugh, 1938-. 4.8556
Stephenson, Jill. 4.6121-4.6122
Stephenson, Joseph W. 5.5309
Stephenson, Ralph. 2.3002
Stephenson, Richard W., 1930-. 4.221
Stephenson, Thomas P. 5.1700
Stephenson, Wendell Holmes, 1899-1970. ed.
    3.7375
Steppe, Wolfhard. 2.8880, 2.8897
Stepto, Robert B. 2.10305, 2.10531, 2.10690
Steranko, 1938-. 1.5849
Sterba, Günther. 5.5456
Sterkx, H. E. 3.6800
Sterling, Christopher H., 1943-. 2.60,
    4.4057-4.4058
Sterling, Dorothy, 1913-. 3.6814
Sterling, George, 1869-1926. 2.12540
Sterling, Philip. 4.10045
Stern, Arthur C. 5.6041, 5.6044
Stern, Curt, 1902- ed. 5.3406
Stern, Daniel N. 5.557
Stern, Ephraim, 1934- ed. 3.3827
Stern, Fritz Richard, 1926-. 3.613, 3.2247
Stern, Harold P. 1.6481
Stern, J. P. (Joseph Peter). 1.1058
Stern, Louis W., 1935-. 4.4296
Stern, M. 3.3889-3.3890
Stern, Madeleine B., 1912-. 2.10897, 2.10902,
    2.10904, 5.7589
Stern, Milton R. 2.11739
Stern, Nanci. 4.6597
Stern, Paul C., 1944-. 4.3717
Stern, Raphael. 1.6693
Stern, Richard G., 1928-. 2.13333
Stern, Robert A. M. 1.5302, 1.5311
Stern, S. M. (Samuel Miklos), 1920-1969. ed.
    1.376
Sternbach, Richard A. joint author. 5.4307
Sternberg, David Joel. 4.10628
Sternberg, Les. 4.10925
Sternberg, Robert J. 5.355-5.356
Sternberg, Shlomo. 5.1630
Sterne, Laurence, 1713-1768. 2.7275-2.7277,
    2.7280

Sterne, Theodore E. 5.1764
Sternfeld, Frederick William, 1914-. 1.3488,
    1.3681, 2.6124
Sternlicht, Manny. 5.8295
Sternlicht, Sanford V. 2.8525
Sternlieb, George. 4.1678, 4.3488, 4.6353
Sternsher, Bernard, 1925-. 3.6222
Sternstein, Jerome L., joint author. 3.331
Sterrett, John Robert Sitlington, 1851-1914.
    2.393
Stetkevych, Jaroslav. 2.1830
Stetson, Erlene, 1949-. 2.10748
Stettinius, Edward R. (Edward Reilly),
    1900-1949. 3.885, 4.9197
Stettner, Louis, 1922-. 5.6995
Steven, Stewart, 1937-. 3.3342
Stevens, Barry, 1902- joint author. 5.4875
Stevens, Bronwyn Elizabeth. 4.8820
Stevens, Carl M. 4.3334
Stevens, Denis, 1922-. 1.3429, 1.4236, 1.4240
Stevens, Doris, 1892-. 4.8089
Stevens, Evelyn P. 4.3171
Stevens, Frank S. ed. 3.5584
Stevens, G. R. (George Roy), 1895-. 4.4015
Stevens, Gwendolyn. 5.80
Stevens, Halsey, 1908-. 1.3791
Stevens, Holly. ed. 2.12543
Stevens, Joan. 2.10201
Stevens, John E., 1921-. 1.3720, 2.2641
Stevens, Karl K., 1939-. 5.5739
Stevens, Kathleen R. 5.5156
Stevens, Mark, 1947-. 4.4390
Stevens, Michael. 2.9299
Stevens, Paul Douglas, 1938-. 5.7895
Stevens, Peter, 1927-. 3.8778, 5.7893
Stevens, Richard. 5.97
Stevens, Richard G., 1925-. 4.7817
Stevens, Robert Bocking. 4.3453, 4.9569
Stevens, Rosemary. 5.4524
Stevens, Rosemary. joint author. 4.3453
Stevens, S. S. (Stanley Smith), 1906-1973. 5.209,
    5.2226, 5.4373
Stevens, Thaddeus, 1792-1868. 3.7159
Stevens, Wallace, 1879-1955. 2.2740,
    2.12541-2.12543
Stevenson, Adlai E. (Adlai Ewing), 1900-1965.
    3.7519, 4.9241
Stevenson, Anne, 1933 Jan. 3. 2.11387
Stevenson, Burton Egbert, 1872-1962. ed.
    2.3730, 2.3808
Stevenson, Charles L. (Charles Leslie), 1908-.
    1.1410, 1.1461
Stevenson, D. (David), 1954-. 3.837
Stevenson, Elizabeth, 1919-. 2.11078, 3.6244
Stevenson, F. J. 5.5277
Stevenson, Frederick W. 5.1570
Stevenson, Garth. 4.8280, 4.9065
Stevenson, James, 1901-. 1.2286, 1.2488
Stevenson, Lionel, 1902-1973. 2.5827, 2.5948,
    2.6019, 2.6043, 2.7944, 2.8189
Stevenson, Lloyd G. 5.4519
Stevenson, Robert F. 3.5230
Stevenson, Robert Louis, 1850-1894. 2.7812,
    2.8117-2.8118, 2.8120-2.8122, 2.8127, 2.9405
Stevenson, Robert Murrell. 1.3733, 1.4242
Stevenson, Thomas B., 1945-. 4.5405
Stevenson, William, d. 1575. 2.6219
Stevick, Philip. 2.5952, 2.10575
Stevick, Robert David, 1928-. 2.6142
Stevin, Simon, 1548-1620. 5.2035
Steward, Julian Haynes, 1902-1972. 3.447,
    3.9156-3.9157, 4.421, 4.504, 4.5264
Stewart, Abigail J. 4.10825
Stewart, Anthony Terence Quincey. 3.1873
Stewart, Charles T., 1922-. 4.3139
Stewart, Donald Henderson, 1911-. 3.7024
Stewart, Estelle M. (Estelle May), 1887-1938.
    4.3149
Stewart, Garrett. 2.7672
Stewart, George Rippey, 1895-. 2.11055,
    2.12554, 3.5994, 3.8616
Stewart, Grace. 2.10600
Stewart, Ian. joint author. 5.1622
Stewart, Isabel Maitland. 5.5162
Stewart, J. I. M. (John Innes Mackintosh),
    1906-. 2.5708, 2.8575
Stewart, James Brewer. 3.7154, 3.7225
Stewart, Jeffrey C., 1950-. 1.6711

Stewart, Joan Hinde. 2.4505
Stewart, John, 1933-. 1.4092, 2.13334
Stewart, John Hall, 1904-. 3.2064
Stewart, John Lincoln, 1917-. 2.10465
Stewart, John M. 5.2218
Stewart, Kenneth Norman. 2.3600
Stewart, Mark B. 4.1398
Stewart, Mary White, 1945- joint author. 1.3051
Stewart-McDougall, Mary Lynn. 3.2149
Stewart, Randall, 1896-1964. 2.11064
Stewart, Rex William, 1907-1967. 1.4258
Stewart, Robert MacKenzie. 4.8529
Stewart, Walter. 3.8784
Stewart, Wilson N. (Wilson Nichols), 1917-.
    5.3177
Stich, Stephen P. 2.19, 5.630
Stichter, Sharon. 4.6154
Stichting Foundation Rembrandt Research
    Project. 1.6252
Stichting Ons Erfdeel. 2.1169
Stick, David, 1919-. 3.8232
Stickel, Donald A., 1953-. 5.8288
Stickney, Benjamin D. 4.10737
Stickney, Robert R. 5.5468
Stickney, Trumbull, 1874-1904. 2.12555
Stieber, Jack, 1919-. 4.3379, 4.3438
Stieglitz, Alfred, 1864-1946. 5.6961
Stiennon, Jacques. joint author. 1.5027
Stierlin, Henri. 3.8901, 3.9048, 3.9160
Stifter, Adalbert, 1805-1868. 2.13656-2.13657
Stiftsbibliothek Sankt Gallen. 1.3237
Stigler, George J. 1911-. 4.1313
Stigler, George Joseph, 1911-. 4.1502, 4.1508
Stiglitz, Joseph E. 4.4168
Stigum, Marcia L. 4.4445, 4.4607
Stikes, C. Scully, 1945-. 4.10860
Stil, André. 2.4754
Stiles, Karl Amos, 1897-1968. joint author.
    5.3798
Stilgoe, John R., 1949-. 4.3997
Still, Bayrd. 3.8451
Stillerman, Richard, joint author. 5.5640
Stilling, Roger, 1938-. 2.5879
Stillinger, Elizabeth. 1.6517
Stillinger, Jack. 2.7850
Stillman, Damie. 1.6547
Stillman, Deanne. joint author. 4.5749
Stillman, Edmund O. 3.752
Stillman, Frances. 2.1046
Stillman, John Maxson, 1852-1923. 5.2611
Stillman, Richard Joseph, 1943-. 4.7883, 4.8851
Stillwell, John. 5.1601
Stillwell, Richard, 1899-. 3.2520
Stilman, Leon. 2.1194
Stilwell, Joseph Warren, 1883-1946. 3.1139
Stimson, Allen. 5.2321
Stimson, Henry Lewis, 1867-1950. 3.911, 3.7687
Stinchcombe, Arthur L. 4.4818
Stineman, Esther, 1947-. 5.8464
Stinger, Charles L., 1944-. 3.2940
Stini, William A. joint author. 4.432
Stinton, Darrol, 1927-. 5.6669
Stipčević, Aleksandar. 3.557
Stirling, Brents, 1904-. 2.6792
Stites, Richard. 3.3188, 4.6130
Stitt, Fred A. 5.5643-5.5644
Stobaugh, Robert B. 4.3715
Stobaugh, Robert B. joint author. 4.4597
Stobaugh, Robert B. 5.5629
Stock, Brian. 2.174
Stock, Dennis. 2.2065
Stock, Guy. 1.745
Stock, Irvin, 1920-. 2.8265
Stock, Mildred. 2.3336
Stock, Molly. 5.980
Stock, Noel. ed. 2.12352
Stock, Noel. 2.12351
Stock, R. D. (Robert D.), 1941-. 2.6718
Stock, Ralph. 2.2664
Stocken, Lloyd A. 5.3489
Stockford, Richard. 4.6920
Stockholm International Peace Research
    Institute. 4.3837, 4.9164, 4.9168, 5.3580,
    5.7250
Stocking, George W., 1928-. 4.398, 4.497, 4.507
Stocking, George Ward, 1892-. 4.3012-4.3013,
    4.3786
Stocking, S. Holly. joint author. 4.6550

Stockwell, Edward G. 4.1622
Stockwin, James Arthur Ainscow. 4.8749
Stoddard, Charles Hatch, 1912-. 5.5424
Stoddard, Elizabeth, 1823-1902. 2.11227
Stoddard, Glenn M. 5.5424
Stoddard, Richard. 5.8147
Stoddard, Richard Henry, 1825-1903. 2.10915
Stoddard, Theodore L. (Theodore Lothrop), 1926-. 3.3288
Stoddard, Whitney S. 1.4958, 1.5701
Stodelle, Ernestine. 4.1144, 4.1148
Stoehr, Taylor, 1931-. 2.11073, 4.7518, 5.115
Stoessinger, John George. 4.9227, 4.9242
Stoff, Jesse A. 5.1877
Stogdill, Ralph Melvin, 1904-. 4.4954
Stöhr, Walter B. 4.6360
Stoianovich, Traian. 3.1974, 3.3513
Stoil, Michael Jon, 1950-. 2.2890
Stojanović, Svetozar. 4.7144
Stokely, James, joint author. 3.8154
Stoker, Bram, 1847-1912. 2.9387
Stoker, David S. 4.3751
Stokes, Anson Phelps, 1874-1958. 1.2393
Stokes, Brenda. 2.6097
Stokes, Carl. 3.8386
Stokes, Charles J. 4.3897
Stokes, Donald E. joint author. 4.8501
Stokes, Eric. 4.2864, 4.8698
Stokes, Francis Griffin. 2.6688
Stokes, J. (John) 2.3312
Stokes, Roy Bishop, 1915-. 5.7677
Stoll, Elmer Edgar, 1874-1959. 2.2595, 2.6657, 2.6807, 2.6818
Stolpe, Sven, 1905-. 3.1149
Stolper, Gustav, 1888-1947. 4.2340
Stolper, Wolfgang F. 4.2345
Stommel, Henry M., 1920-. 4.349
Stone, A. Harris. 4.10488
Stone, Albert E. 2.10344, 3.6026
Stone, Albert E. comp. 2.11106
Stone-Blackburn, Susan, 1941-. 2.9928
Stone, Calvin Perry, 1892-1954, ed. 5.10
Stone, Carla Sydney. 4.3722
Stone, Christopher D. 4.9521
Stone, Clarence N. (Clarence Nathan), 1935-. 4.6344
Stone, Donald. ed. 2.3938
Stone, Donald. 3.1960
Stone, Doris, 1909-. 3.9030
Stone, Else, 1912-. 1.3468
Stone, F. Gordon A. (Francis Gordon Albert), 1925-. 5.2780
Stone, George Winchester, 1907-. 2.3343
Stone, Gerald. joint author. 2.1223
Stone, Harry, 1926-. 2.7669
Stone, I. F. (Isidor F.), 1907-. 3.5022
Stone, Irving, 1903-. 2.12556
Stone, Jean. 2.12556
Stone, Jeanne C. Fawtier. 4.6396
Stone, Jim. 5.6948
Stone, Joe A. 4.10686
Stone, John, D. Phil. 4.7446
Stone, Julius, 1907-. 4.9282, 4.9320, 4.9327
Stone, Kurt. 1.3468, 1.4447
Stone, Lawrence. 1.5683, 3.83, 3.1395, 3.1432, 3.1462, 4.5621, 4.6396
Stone, Lawrence. ed. 4.9976
Stone, Merlin, 1948-. 4.4289
Stone, Michael E., 1938-. 1.1908, 1.1934
Stone, Michael H., 1933-. 5.4965
Stone, Morris, 1912-. 4.3576, 4.9556
Stone, Norman. 3.713, 3.806
Stone, Ralph A. 4.9195
Stone, Robert. 2.13335
Stone, Sue. 5.7602
Stone, Tabor R. 4.3871
Stone, Walter J. 4.7940
Stone, Wilfred Healey, 1917-. 2.8666
Stoneall, Linda. 4.4916
Stoneman, Elvyn A. joint author. 3.1156
Stopford, John M. 4.2735
Stopher, Peter R. 4.3931
Stopher, Peter Robert. 4.3911
Stopp, Frederick J. 2.9507
Stoppard, Tom. 2.9813-2.9817
Storch, Wolfgang. 1.4828
Storer, Tracy Irwin, 1889-. 5.3800
Storey, D. J. 4.3002

Storey, David, 1933-. 2.9820-2.9824
Storey, Edward. 2.7572
Storey, Graham. 2.3680, 2.6257, 2.7635
Storey, Haddon. 4.8818
Storey, John. 4.3427
Storey, Mark. comp. 2.7573
Storey, Mark. 2.7574
Storing, Herbert J., 1928-. 3.6629, 4.7208, 4.7829
Stork, David G. 5.2224
Stork, F. C. joint author. 2.12
Storm, Theodor, 1817-1888. 2.13660
Storr, Anthony. 5.165
Storr, R. C., joint author. 5.2851
Storr, Richard J. 4.10990
Storrer, William Allin. 1.5337
Storry, Richard, 1913-. 3.4964, 3.4975
Story, Norah. 2.9880
Story, Ronald. 4.5204
Stotland, Ezra, 1924-. 4.6751
Stott, D. H. (Denis Herbert), 1909-. 4.6866
Stott, Philip Anthony. 5.3667
Stott, William, 1940-. 2.72
Stotz, Elmer Henry, 1911-. 5.2791
Stouck, David, 1940-. 2.9884
Stouffer, Samuel Andrew, 1900-. 5.7167
Stout, David F. 5.6594
Stout, George H., 1932-. 5.2936
Stout, James H. 5.3014
Stout, Janis P. 2.10351
Stout, Neil R. 3.6928
Stout, Rex, 1886-1975. 2.12557
Stovall, Floyd, 1896- ed. 2.2512, 2.10373, 2.10377
Stovel, John A. 4.4178
Stover, John F. 4.3998-4.3999
Stow, John, 1525?-1605. 3.1744
Stowe, Harriet Beecher, 1811-1896. 2.11228-2.11229, 2.11231, 3.7262
Stowe, Richard S. 2.4180
Strabo. 2.393
Strachan, Hew. 5.7196
Strachan, Richard. 1.2222
Strache, Neil E., 1951-. 5.8478
Strachery, James, ed. 5.139
Strachey, James. 1.1564, 5.134, 5.141
Strachey, James. ed. and tr. 5.144
Strachey, James. ed. 5.135, 5.146
Strachey, John, 1901-1963. 4.7540
Strachey, Lytton, 1880-1932. 2.2596, 2.3831, 2.9388-2.9389, 2.9587, 3.1615, 3.1624
Strack, Hermann Leberecht, 1848-1922. 1.1939
Stradling, R. A. 3.3440
Straelen, H. J. J. M. van (Henricus Johannes Josephus Maria van), 1903-. 3.4955
Straeten, Edmund Sebastian Joseph van der, 1855-1934. 1.4162
Strahan, Jack, 1951-. 2.10705
Strahler, Alan H. 4.242-4.243
Strahler, Arthur Newell, 1918-. 4.242-4.243
Straight, Michael Whitney. 5.7352
Strain, Phillip S. 4.10280
Strait, E. N., joint author. 5.1983
Strakhovsky, Leonid Ivan, 1898-1963. 3.3021, 3.3116
Strand, Fleur L. 5.4196
Strand, K. Aage (Kaj Aage), 1907- ed. 5.1830
Strand, Paul, 1890-1976. 5.6968
Strandberg, Victor H. 2.12655
Strang, Barbara M. H. 2.975, 2.1002
Strang, Gilbert. 5.1110
Strang, Roger A. 4.4329
Strang, William Strang, Baron, 1893-. 3.1247, 4.9099
Stranges, Anthony N. (Anthony Nicholas), 1936-. 5.2838
Strasser, Hermann, 1941-. 4.4747
Strasser, Susan, 1948-. 5.7101
Strassmann, W. Paul (Wolfgang Paul), 1926-. 4.1896
Straszheim, Mahlon R., 1939-. 4.3872, 4.4080, 4.6291
Stratemeyer, Florence Barbara, 1900-. 4.10451
Stratford, Alan H. 5.5996
Strathern, Andrew. 3.349, 3.5664
Stratman, Bernard F. 1.3179
Stratman, Carl Joseph, 1917-1972. 5.7805, 5.7958, 5.8135, 5.8307

Stratton, Joanna L. 4.6075
Straub, Peter. 2.13336
Straughan, B. P., joint author. 5.2311
Straughan, B. P. 5.2309
Straughan, Roger. 4.10808
Straughen, A. joint author. 5.6509
Straus, Hal. 4.919
Straus, Murray Arnold, 1926-. 4.5780
Straus, Roger A. (Roger Austin), 1948-. 4.4869
Strauss, Anselm L. 4.6226
Strauss, Botho, 1944-. 2.13909-2.13910
Strauss, David Friedrich, 1808-1874. 1.2877-1.2878
Strauss, Emil, 1866-1960. 2.13602
Strauss, George, 1923- joint author. 4.3366
Strauss, Gerald, 1922- comp. 3.2275
Strauss, Howard J. 5.6828
Strauss, Leo. ed. 4.7264
Strauss, Leo. 4.7209, 4.7363, 4.7409, 4.7649
Strauss, Maurice Benjamin, 1904- comp. 5.4547
Strauss, Richard, 1864-1949. 1.3997-1.3998, 1.4488, 1.4516
Stravinsky, Igor, 1882-1971. 1.4001-1.4004, 1.4006-1.4007
Stravinsky, Igor' Fedorovich. 1.4005
Stravinsky, Vera. 1.4010
Strawson, P. F. 1.95, 1.887, 1.1152, 1.1194, 1.1271
Strayer, Joseph Reese, 1904-. 3.497, 3.567, 3.1992, 3.1997, 3.2226, 4.4702
Streater, R. F. 5.2160
Street, Brian V. 2.5982
Street, David. 4.6227
Street, Harry. 4.9418, 4.9420
Street, John. 3.9233
Street, Philip, 1915-. 5.4077
Streeten, Paul. 4.1822, 4.2510
Streeten, Paul. joint author. 4.4614
Streeter, Burnett Hillman, 1874-1937. 1.2676
Streetman, Ben G. 5.6499
Streicher, Jeanne, ed. 2.4060
Streit, Clarence Kirshman, 1896-. 4.9139
Streitwieser, Andrew, 1927-. 5.2724, 5.2823, 5.2858
Stremler, Ferrel G. 5.6358
Strémooukhoff, D. 1.1117
Streng, Frederick J. 1.1747
Stresemann, Erwin, 1889-1972. 5.3943
Stresemann, Gustav, 1878-1929. 3.2355
Stretton, Hugh. 4.7042
Stribling, T. S. (Thomas Sigismund), 1881-1965. 2.12558
Strickberger, Monroe W. 5.3420
Stricker, George. 5.550
Strickland, Rennard. 4.9772
Strickler, Susan E. 1.4899
Strickon, Arnold. 4.1556
Strickon, Arnold. ed. 4.5254
Strieder, Peter. 1.4989
Strier, Richard. 2.7068
Strindberg, August, 1849-1912. 2.14066-2.14077
Stritch, Thomas, joint author. 4.7592
Strittmatter, Erwin, 1912-. 2.13863
Strobel, Horst. 4.3912
Strobel, Margaret, 1946-. 4.5909
Strobl, Alice. 1.5806
Strode, Hudson, 1892-1976. 3.7324
Stroebel, Leslie D. 5.6916, 5.6935
Stroke, George W. 5.2287
Strom, Sharon Hartman. 4.5993
Stromberg, Ann. 4.3244
Stromberg, Karl Robert, 1931-. 5.1446
Strommen, Merton P. 1.3002
Strommenger, Eva. 1.4707
Stronach, David. 3.4068
Strong, B. Stephen, joint author. 4.689
Strong, Donald Emrys. 1.4729, 1.6510
Strong, Donald Stuart, 1912-. 4.8108, 4.8110
Strong, Eugénie Sellers. ed. 1.4711
Strong, Eugénie Sellers. 1.5638
Strong, George Templeton, 1820-1875. 3.7160, 3.7394
Strong, James, 1822-1894. 1.2503
Strong, John, 1948- joint author. 5.8454
Strong, John W., 1930-. 4.7139
Strong, Roy C. 1.6355
Strong, Roy C. joint author. 1.5389
Strong, Roy C. 1.5802, 1.6017, 5.5377

Strong, William S. 4.9546
Stroop, Jürgen, 1895- . 3.999
Strother, David Boyd, 1928- comp. 2.6268
Stroud, Barry. 1.536, 1.707
Stroud, Dorothy. 1.5403, 5.5378
Stroud, Parry Edmund, 1917-. 2.11373
Stroup, Herbert Hewitt, 1916-. 1.1703
Stroup, Richard. 4.1903
Strouse, Jean. 3.338
Strouse, Jean. comp. 4.5943
Strout, Cushing. 1.2386, 3.6281
Stroyan, K. D. 5.1434
Strozier, Charles B. 3.7284
Strub, A. S. (Albert S.) 5.6883
Struc, Roman, ed. 2.13655
Struik, Dirk Jan, 1894-. 4.7074, 5.797,
    5.1075-5.1076
Strum, Philippa. 4.9805
Strunk, Mildred. 3.193
Strunk, W. Oliver (William Oliver), 1901- tr.
    1.3637, 1.4235
Strunk, William, 1869-1946. 2.1036
Struthers, James, 1950-. 4.3447
Struve, Gleb. 2.1275
Stryer, Lubert. 5.4398
Stuard, Susan Mosher. 4.5859
Stuart, Alan, 1922- joint author. 5.1390
Stuart, Duane Reed, 1873-1941. 2.273
Stuart-Fox, Martin, 1939-. 3.4459
Stuart, Jesse, 1907-. 2.12559-2.12560
Stuart, John Leighton. 3.4756
Stuart, Robert C., 1938-. 4.2381, 4.2915, 4.2978
Stub, Holger Richard. 4.5802
Stubbendieck, James L. 5.5328
Stubbings, Frank H. joint ed. 2.506
Stubblebine, James H. 1.6200, 1.6395
Stubblebine, James H. comp. 1.6210
Stubbs, Frank Whitworth, 1898-1967. 5.5669
Stubbs, G. T. (Gordon Thomas), 1928- joint
    author. 2.2703
Stubbs, George, 1724-1806. 1.4956, 5.4112
Stubbs, John O., 1943-. 3.8750
Stubbs, P. C. (Peter C.), 1937-. 4.3899
Stubbs, William, 1825-1901. 4.8383-4.8384
Stuckenschmidt, Hans Heinz, 1901-. 1.3682,
    1.3970-1.3971
Stuckey, Sterling. comp. 3.7263
Stucky, Rita J. 5.471
Stucky, Steven. 1.3914
Studlar, Donley T. 4.8413
Studwell, William E. (William Emmett), 1936-.
    1.3512
Study Commission on U.S. Policy toward
    Southern Africa (U.S.) 3.6492
Study of Man's Impact on Climate, Stockholm,
    1970. 5.2566
Study of Parliament Group. 4.8471
Stueart, Robert D. 5.7620
Stueck, William Whitney, 1945-. 3.6434, 3.6471
Stuewer, Roger H. 5.1938
Stuhlmann, Gunther, ed. 2.12254
Stultz, Newell Maynard. 3.5470
Stumm, Werner, 1924-. 4.302
Stump, Eleonore, 1947-. 1.336
Stumpf, Florence Scovil. 4.933
Stumpf, Paul K. (Paul Karl), 1919-. 5.3750
Sturcken, H. Tracy. 2.5192
Sturge, John M. 5.6934
Sturgeon, Theodore. 2.13337
Sturges, Henry Cady, 1846-. 2.10915
Sturgess, Brian T. 5.5515
Sturm, Paul Jones. 2.8553
Sturm, Terry. 2.10154
Sturmthal, Adolf Fox. 4.3182, 4.3335, 4.3402
Sturrock, John. 2.3916
Stursberg, Peter. 3.8788
Sturtevant, David Reeves. 4.2867
Sturtevant, E. Lewis (Edward Lewis),
    1842-1898. 5.3657
Sturtevant, Edgar Howard, 1875-1952.
    2.142-2.143, 2.237
Sturtevant, Roger. 1.5562
Sturtevant, William C. 3.5701
Sturzo, Luigi, 1871-1959. 1.3208
Stutley, Margaret. 1.1676
Stutman, Suzanne. 2.12782
Stutzman, Warren L. 5.6496

Styan, J. L. 2.1495, 2.2791-2.2792,
    2.2813-2.2814, 2.3378
Stycos, J. Mayone. 4.1687, 4.5688
Styron, William, 1925-. 2.13338,
    2.13340-2.13344
Su, Shih, 1036-1101. 2.2218
Subak-Sharpe, Gerald E. joint author. 5.6528
Subrahmaniam, N. S. 1.1684
Subramanyam, K. 5.5503
Subramanyam, K. N., 1912- tr. 2.2277
Suchting, W. A. (Wallis Arthur) 4.6961
Suckling, C. W., joint author. 5.2867
Suckling, Colin J., 1947-. 5.2867
Suckling, John, Sir, 1609-1642. 2.7286-2.7287
Suckling, Keith E., 1947- joint author. 5.2867
Suckling, Norman. 1.3867
Suckow, Ruth, 1892-1960. 2.12562-2.12564
Suda, Zdeněk. 4.8575
Sudarshan, E. C. G. joint author. 5.2397
Suddard, Adrienne, ed. 3.4454
Sudhalter, Richard M. 1.4081
Sudman, Seymour. 4.1230-4.1231
Sudnik, Patricia E. 4.3794
Śūdraka. 2.1951-2.1952
Sue, Derald Wing. 5.470
Sue, Stanley. 5.4821
Sueno, Akira, 1913-. 4.3866
Suetonius, ca. 69-ca. 122. 2.696
Sugar, Max, 1925-. 5.620
Sugar, Peter F. 3.3521-3.3522, 4.5279
Sugarman, Stephen D., joint author. 4.10635
Sugawara no Takasue no Musume, b. 1008.
    2.2054-2.2055
Sugden, David E. 4.104, 4.261, 4.318
Sugg, Redding S. 2.11744
Suggs, Robert C. (Robert Carl), 1932-. 3.5647,
    4.5490
Sugiyama, Jirō, 1928-. 1.5763
Sugnet, Christopher L. 5.8060
Suh, Dae-sook, 1931-. 4.7126
Suhl, Benjamin. 2.4743
Suk, Miloš. 5.3069
Sukenick, Ronald. 2.13349
Sukhanov, N. N. (Nikolaĭ Nikolaevich),
    1882-1940. 3.3195
Sukhwal, B. L., 1929-. 5.8051
Sukiennik, Adelaide Weir, 1938-. 5.7724
Sulaiman, Khalid A. 2.1837
Suleiman, Ezra N., 1941-. 4.3070, 4.7715,
    4.8588
Suleiman, Susan. 2.2450
Sulentic, Jack W. 5.1852
Sulimirski, Tadeusz, 1898-. 4.736
Sullens, Zay Rusk, joint author. 2.6459
Sullerot, Evelyne. 2.3918
Sullivan, Alvin. 2.3688
Sullivan, Arthur, Sir, 1842-1900. 1.4015
Sullivan, Clara Katherine, 1916-. 4.4717
Sullivan, Eugene J. 4.10624
Sullivan, Harry Stack. 5.453, 5.4841-5.4842
Sullivan, Herbert. 1.4016
Sullivan, J. P. (John Patrick) 2.632, 2.758,
    4.5851
Sullivan, John J., 1919- joint comp. 5.72
Sullivan, Louis H., 1856-1924. 1.5329, 1.5484
Sullivan, Mark, 1874-. 3.7515
Sullivan, Michael, 1916-. 1.5061, 1.5110, 1.5758,
    1.6364-1.6365
Sullivan, Nancy. 2.6266, 2.10733, 2.10836
Sullivan, Richard Eugene, 1921-. 3.129
Sullivan, Walter. 2.10462-2.10463, 3.8120,
    5.3096
Sullivan, William C. 4.6825
Sullivan, Woodruff Turner. 5.1776-5.1777
Sullivant, Robert S., 1925-. 3.3304
Sully, Melanie A. 4.8574
Sultan Muhammad Shah, Sir, agha khan,
    1877-1957. 3.4322
Sultan, Stanley. 2.8356, 2.8898
Summer Theatre Seminar, Fordham University,
    1947. 2.3094
Summerfield, Ellen, 1949-. 2.13497
Summerfield, Henry. 2.8855, 2.9293
Summerfield, Penny. 3.1138
Summerhays, R. S. (Reginald Sherriff), 1881-.
    5.5446
Summers, Claude J. 2.6603, 2.8667, 2.8841
Summers, Harry G. 3.4506

Summers, Hollis Spurgeon, 1916- ed. 2.3440
Summers, Joseph H. (Joseph Holmes), 1920-.
    2.7069, 2.7140
Summers, Mark W. (Mark Wahlgren), 1951-.
    4.3984
Summers, Montague, 1880-1948. 2.3304, 2.5984,
    2.6899
Summers, Robert, 1922-. 4.1401
Summers, Wilford I. 5.6108
Summerscale, Peter. 3.2999
Summerson, John Newenham, Sir, 1904-.
    1.5206, 1.5366, 1.5375, 1.5391, 1.5395,
    1.5408, 1.5486
Summitt, Robert, 1935-. 5.5770
Sumner, Benedict Humphrey, 1893-. 3.689,
    3.3049, 3.3100
Sumner, William Graham, 1840-1910. 4.4774,
    4.5176
Sumner, William Leslie, 1904-1973. 1.4142
Sumption, Jonathan. 1.2310, 3.1993
Sun, E-tu Zen, 1921-. 4.4021
Sun-tzu, 6th cent. B.C. 5.7203, 5.7211
Sun, Yat-sen, 1866-1925. 3.4759-3.4760
Sund, Robert B. 4.10485
Sundberg, Richard J., 1938-. 5.2719
Sundberg, Sara Brooks, 1951-. 4.6074
Sundermeyer, Niels. 3.196
Sundkler, Bengt Gustaf Malcolm, 1909-. 1.2470,
    1.3020
Sundman, Per Olof, 1922-. 2.14099
Sundquist, Eric J. 2.10566
Sundquist, James L. 4.5155, 4.7878, 4.8017,
    4.8168
Sundquist, James L. ed. 4.2106
Sundrum, R. M. 4.2803
Sung, Ch'i. 2.2183
Sungolowsky, Joseph. 2.4063
Sunnucks, Anne, 1927-. 4.1069
Suomalaisen Kirjallisuuden Seura, Helsinki.
    2.1750
Supek, Rudi, 1913-. 4.6979
Super, Donald Edwin, 1910-. 5.365
Super, R. H. (Robert Henry), 1914-. 2.7350,
    2.8214
Supervielle, Jules, 1884-1960. 2.4755
Suppes, Patrick, 1922-. 1.1195
Supple, Barry Emanuel, jt. author. 4.3995
Supple, Barry Emanuel. 4.4227
Supreme Court Historical Society. 4.9442
Sūradāsa, 1483?-1563? 2.1880
Suran, Bernard G. 4.10910
Surer, Paul, 1905-. 2.3826
Suret-Canale, Jean. 3.5120
Surette, Leon. 2.12334
Suri, G. S. P., tr. 2.1912
Suri, Surindar. 3.4296
Surrey, Alexander Robert, 1914-. 5.2653
Surrey, Henry Howard, Earl of, 1517?-1547.
    2.6144-2.6145, 2.6150, 2.6547
Surrey, Stanley S. 4.9767
Surtees, Robert Smith, 1805-1864.
    2.8130-2.8133
Surtees, Virginia. 1.4955
Surtz, Edward L. 4.7175
Suryadinata, Leo. 3.4576
Suskind, Sigmund R. 5.3586
Suslov, S. P. (Sergeĭ Petrovich) 4.254
Suslova, Apollinariia Prokof'evna, 1840-1918.
    2.1349
Susman, Warren, 1927- comp. 3.6169
Sussman, George D., 1943-. 5.5084
Sussman, Gerald Jay. 5.1158
Sussman, Julie. 5.1158
Sussman, Les, 1944-. 4.6740
Sussman, Martin V. 5.2254
Sutch, Richard. joint author. 4.2024
Sutch, William Ball, 1904-. 4.3673
Sutcliffe, Anthony, 1942-. 4.6311, 4.6333,
    4.6350, 5.8187
Sutherland, C. H. V. (Carol Humphrey Vivian),
    1908-. 3.279
Sutherland, Donald, 1915-. 2.12520
Sutherland, Edwin Hardin, 1883-1950. 4.6684,
    4.6701, 4.6763
Sutherland, Gillian. ed. 4.8432
Sutherland, James Runcieman, 1900-. 2.5652,
    2.5930, 2.6064, 2.6980, 2.7233
Sutherland, John, 1903-. 2.6028, 2.8184

Sutherland, N. S. (Norman Stuart) 5.8
Sutherland, Sally J. 1.1693
Sutherland, Sarah P. 2.5881
Sutker, Patricia B. 5.4960
Suttles, Gerald D. 4.5210, 4.6228
Sutton, C W H. 3.2351
Sutton, Christine. 5.2464
Sutton, Denys. 1.5987-1.5988
Sutton, Edward William, 1871- ed. and tr.
    2.666
Sutton, Eric. 2.4733
Sutton, Francis Xavier. 4.1940
Sutton, George Paul. 5.6690
Sutton, Max Keith. 2.7402
Sutton, Paul K. 3.9137, 4.2151
Sutton, Peter C. 1.6249, 1.6368
Sutton, Roberta Briggs. 1.42
Sutton-Smith, Brian. joint author. 4.1061, 5.553
Sutton-Smith, Brian. 4.885
Sutton, Walter. ed. 2.12353
Sutton, Walter. 2.2513
Sutton, Walter. ed. 2.2445
Suvin, Darko, 1930-. 2.3496, 2.6030
Suvorov, Viktor. 5.7332
Suzuki, Beatrice Lane. 1.2156
Suzuki, Daisetz Teitaro, 1870-1966. 1.1631,
    1.1749-1.1750, 1.1753-1.1755, 1.1763, 1.2128
Suzuki, David T., 1936-. 5.3415
Suzuki, Michio. 5.1305
Suzuki, Shin'ichi, 1898-. 1.4437
Svaren, Jacqueline. 1.6602
Svartvik, Jan. joint author. 2.140, 2.1007
Svehla, G. 5.2654, 5.2672
Svejnar, Jan. 4.3179
Svelto, Orazio. 5.2379
Svennilson, Ingvar, 1908-. 4.2211
Svenonius, Elaine. 5.7626
Sverdrup, Harald Ulrik, 1888-1957. 4.326
Svevo, Italo, 1861-1928. 2.5065-2.5068
Swaaij, W. P. M. van. 5.6855
Swaan, Wim. 1.4756
Swadesh Bharati, 1941- ed. 2.1957
Swados, Harvey. 2.13350-2.13351
Swaim, Kathleen M. joint author. 2.7170
Swain, Donald C. 5.5302
Swain, N. (Nigel) 4.2351
Swain, William, 1821-1904. 3.8608
Swales, Erika, 1937-. 2.13659
Swales, Martin. 2.13500, 2.13505, 2.13659
Swaminathan, K. 2.2282
Swamy, Subramanian. 4.2486
Swan, Alfred Julius, 1890-. 1.3991
Swan, John Melvin. 5.2741
Swan, L. Alex (Llewelyn Alex), 1938-. 4.6855
Swan, Lester A. 5.5418
Swan, Robert O. 2.1892
Swan, Susan Burrows. 5.7095
Swanberg, W. A., 1907-. 2.3615, 2.3618, 2.3628,
    2.11606
Swanborough, Gordon. 5.6672
Swann, Brian. 2.2319, 2.10297
Swann, June. 4.856
Swann, Nancy Lee, 1881-, ed. and tr. 4.2465
Swann, Thomas Burnett. 2.12567
Swanson, Carl P. 5.3421, 5.3592, 5.3603
Swanson, Roy Arthur, 1925- tr. 2.529
Swanson, Stephanie. 4.5842
Swanton, John Reed, 1873-1958. 3.5708
Swanton, Michael James. comp. 2.6285
Swanwick, Keith. 1.4415
Swarbrick, Andrew. 2.7051
Sward, Robert, 1933-. 2.5831, 2.7837, 2.9565
Swartz, Robert J., ed. 1.1274
Swarzenski, Hanns, 1903-. 1.4751
Swatland, H. J., 1944-. 5.5443
Swayne, James Colin. 4.76
Swayze, Harold. 3.3243
Swearer, Donald K., 1934- comp. 1.1777
Swearingen, James E., 1939-. 2.7279
Swearingen, Roger G., 1944-. 2.8127
Sweat, Lynn. 4.10317
Swedenberg, H.T. 2.6985
Swedenberg, H. T. (Hugh Thomas), 1906-1978.
    comp. 2.5653
Swedenborg, Emanuel, 1688-1772. 1.3385
Swedish American Tercentenary Association.
    3.6594
Swedish Pioneer Historical Society. 3.6595

Sweeney, James Johnson, 1900-. 1.5664, 1.5914
Sweeney, James L. 4.3707
Sweeny, Allen. 4.4599
Sweet, Frederick Arnold, 1903-. 1.5924, 1.5991
Sweet, Henry, 1845-1912. 2.940, 2.948, 2.987
Sweet, James A. joint author. 4.1645
Sweet, James A. 4.1577
Sweet, John Philip McMurdo. 1.2734
Sweet, Louise Elizabeth, 1916- ed. 3.3702
Sweet, Paul Robinson, 1907-. 3.2495
Sweet, William Warren, 1881-1959. ed. 1.3334
Sweetland, Richard C., 1931-. 5.203
Sweetman, John. 5.7353
Sweets, John F., 1945-. 3.1065
Sweezy, Paul Marlor, 1910-. 2.2425, 3.9105,
    4.1518, 4.1539, 4.1545, 4.7073
Swenberg, Charles E. 5.4615
Swenson, David F. (David Ferdinand),
    1876-1940, tr. 1.2228, 1.3057
Swenson, Lillian B. (Marvin), joint tr. 1.3057
Swenson, Loyd S. 5.2272
Swenson, May. 2.12568-2.12569
Swenson, Sally S. 1.4871
Swerdlow, Joel L. joint author. 4.4072
Swern, Daniel, 1916-. 5.2756, 5.6894
Swets, John Arthur, 1928- joint author. 5.243
Swianiewicz, Stanisław. 4.3104
Swidler, Leonard J. 1.2561
Świeczkowski, Walerian. 2.954
Swierenga, Robert P. 3.6474, 4.387, 4.2830
Swift, Jonathan, 1667-1745. 2.7289-2.7292,
    2.7294, 2.7297-2.7298, 4.7422
Swift, M. J. (Michael John), 1939-. 5.3509
Swinburne, Algernon Charles, 1837-1909.
    2.8134-2.8137
Swinburne, Richard. 1.2832, 1.2842
Swinburne, Richard. comp. 1.1188
Swinden, Patrick. 2.9809
Swindler, William Finley. 4.9847
Swindler, William Finley. comp. 4.9609
Swingewood, Alan. 2.3418, 4.5093, 4.6962
Swinnerton, Frank, 1884-. 2.5734, 2.8457,
    2.9391
Swinton, George. 3.5885
Swire, Joseph, 1903-. 3.3603
Swisher, Carl Brent, 1897-1968. 3.7093, 4.9784,
    4.9811
Swisher, Earl, 1902-1975. ed. and tr. 3.6419
Switzer, Margaret, 1949-. 2.13352
Swope, Martha. 4.1168
Sybel, Heinrich von, 1817-1895. 3.2307
Syberberg, Hans Jürgen, 1935-. 2.3028
Sybesma, C. 5.3497
Sydenham, M. J. 3.2087, 3.2111
Sydnor, Charles S. (Charles Sackett), 1898-.
    3.8151, 3.8210
Sydnor, Charles W. 3.973
Sykes, Christopher, 1907-. 2.9508, 3.2415,
    3.3909
Sykes, Egerton. 1.1600
Sykes, J. B. (John Bradbury) 2.1082
Sykes, Percy Molesworth, Sir, 1867-1945.
    3.4071, 4.55
Sykes, Peter. 5.2859
Sykes, Richard E., 1932-. 4.6826
Sykes, Stephen. ed. 1.2857
Sylos Labini, Paolo. 4.2753
Sylvester, David. 1.5698
Sylvester, Edward J. 5.6868
Sylvester, Richard Standish. joint comp. 2.6159
Sylvester, Richard Standish. comp. 2.6149
Sylvester, Richard Standish. 3.1408
Sylvester, Richard Standish. ed. 3.1413
Symcox, Geoffrey. 3.2909
Symcox, Geoffrey. comp. 3.640
Syme, Ronald, Sir, 1903-. 2.769, 2.777, 3.2753,
    3.2776
Symeon, the New Theologian, Saint, 949-1022.
    1.3077
Symmes, Marilyn F. joint author. 1.6504
Symon, Keith R. 5.2032
Symonds, John Addington, 1840-1893. 2.285,
    2.8142, 3.2849
Symonds, Richard, 1918-. 3.4133, 4.5682
Symons, Arthur, 1865-1945. 2.3865, 2.7418
Symons, Julian. 2.9392-2.9393
Symons, Leslie. 3.3017
Symons, M. C. R. 5.2677

Symposium on Animal Sounds and
    Communication (1958: Indiana University)
    5.4088
Symposium on Cognition. 6th, Carnegie-Mellon
    University, 1970. 5.4105
Symposium on Future Automotive Fuels—
    Prospects, Performance, and Perspective,
    General Motors Research Laboratories, 1975.
    5.6877
Symposium on Hazards: Technology and
    Fairness (1985: Washington, D.C.) 5.5631
Symposium on Internal Migration, University of
    Alberta, 1972. 4.1654
Symposium on Light and Life (1960: Johns
    Hopkins University) 5.3626
Symposium on Literary Style, Bellagio, Italy,
    1969. 2.2541
Symposium on Man the Hunter (1966:
    University of Chicago) 4.531
Symposium on Metallography in Failure
    Analysis, Houston, Tex., 1977. 5.6769
Symposium on Principles of Sensory
    Communication, Endicott House, 1959.
    5.4363
Symposium on Taiwan Fiction (1979:
    University of Texas at Austin) 2.2253
Symposium on the Adequacy and Maintenance
    of Urban Public Facilities (1983: Airlie
    House) 4.2054
Symposium on the Frontal Granular Cortex
    and Behavior (1962: Pennsylvania State
    University) 5.4346
Symposium on the History of the ZGS (1979:
    Argonne National Laboratory) 5.2447
Symposium on the Mediterranean Sea,
    Heidelberg, 1971. 4.350
Symposium on the Problems of Korean
    Unification (1982: Washington, D.C.) 3.5012
Symposium on the Renaissance (1959:
    University of Wisconsin—Milwaukee) 3.163
Symposium on Translation, University of Texas,
    1959. 2.2543
Symposium on Unconventional Methods in
    Exploration for Petroleum and Natural Gas.
    (2nd: 1979: Dallas, Tex.) 5.6744
Symposium on Urbanization and Cultural
    Development in the Ancient Near East,
    University of Chicago, 1958. 3.123
Symposium on World Water Balance,
    University of Reading, 1970. 4.296
Synge, Hugh. 5.3645
Synge, J. M. (John Millington), 1871-1909.
    2.8144-2.8147
Synge, Patrick Millington. 5.5351
Synnott, Marcia Graham. 4.10993
Sypher, Wylie. 1.4770, 2.2686, 2.6835
Syracuse University. Dept. of Geography. 4.388
Syracuse University. Dept. of Sociology. 5.4702
Syrett, Harold Coffin, 1913- ed. 3.6220, 3.6969
Systematics Association. 5.3233
Systems Philosophy Symposium, 1st, State
    University of New York at Geneseo, 1973.
    4.4889
Syvanen, Michael. 5.3450
Szablowski, Jerzy. 1.6594
Szabó, George. 1.5810
Szabo, Stephen F. 3.1193
Szabolcsi, Bence, 1899-1973. 1.3703, 1.3792
Szarkowski, John. 1.5331, 5.6969, 5.6973
Szarmach, Paul E. 1.3095, 2.5598
Szasz, Thomas Stephen, 1920-. 4.9851, 5.4570,
    5.4801
Szczepanik, Edward Franciszek. 4.2490
Sze, Mai-mai. 1.6326
Sze, S. M., 1936-. 5.6500-5.6501
Szegö, G. P. 4.1392
Szegő, Gábor, 1895-. 5.1424, 5.1560
Szent-Györgyi, Albert, 1893-. 5.4285
Széplaki, Joseph. 3.6549
Szigeti, Joseph, 1892-1973. 1.4545
Szilard, Leo. 5.1887
Szklenar, Hans. 2.13864
Szold, Henrietta, 1860-1945. ed. 3.6561
Szonyi, David M. 5.8249
Szulc, Tad. joint author. 3.9106
Szwed, John Francis, 1936-. 5.8195
Szyliowicz, Joseph S. 5.5550

Szymborska, Wisława. 2.1743
Szyrocki, Marian. 2.2737, 2.13547

T-W-Fiennes, Richard N. (Richard Nathaniel),
   1909-. 5.4758
Taaffe, Edward James, joint comp. 4.4122
Taaffe, James G. joint author. 2.7155
Taagepera, Rein. 3.3305
Tabachnick, B. Robert. 4.10446
Tabakoff, Boris, 1942-. 5.4960
Tabanelli, M. R. 1.6499
Tabanelli, Rosalba. 1.6499
Tabātabā'ī, Muhammad Husayn. 1.2092
Tabb, David H. 3.6795
Tabb, William K. 4.6347
Taber, Clarence Wilbur, 1870-. 5.4490
Taber, Florence M. 4.10911
Taber, Michael. 3.9134
Tabor, David. 5.2185
Tachau, Frank, 1929-. 4.8772
Tacitus, Cornelius. 2.697, 2.774-2.775
Taddesse Tamrat. 1.2471
Tadgell, Christopher, 1939-. 1.5415
Tadmor, Zehev, 1937-. 5.6907
Taeuber, Conrad, 1906-. 4.1679
Taeuber, Irene Barnes, 1906-. 4.1679, 4.1707
Taeuber, Karl E. 4.1577
Taff, Charles Albert, 1916-. 4.4041
Taff, Laurence G., 1947-. 5.1754, 5.1765
Taft, Lorado, 1860-1936. 1.5656
Taft, Philip, 1902-. 4.3370, 4.3550-4.3551
Taft, Robert W. ed. 5.2858
Tafuri, Manfredo. 1.5275, 1.5478
Tafuro, Patricia. 5.4707
Tagare, Ganesh Vasudeo. 2.1933
Taggart, Robert, 1945- joint author. 4.3476
Tagliacozzo, Giorgio. 1.1093
Tagore, Rabindranath, 1861-1941.
   2.1867-2.1871, 4.7492
Tagore, Surendranath. 2.1871
Taha, Hamdy A. 5.5574, 5.5584
Tahara, Mildred M., 1941-. 2.2044
Tai, Hue-Tam Ho, 1948-. 1.2178
Taine, Hippolyte, 1828-1893. 1.4616, 2.5531,
   3.2141
Taira, Koji, 1926-. 4.3667
Tait, Bob. 2.9841
Tait, David. jt. ed. 4.604
Tait, Katharine, 1923-. 1.772
Tait, Robert C. 5.3460
Tait, W. H. 5.2444
Takahashi, Bin. 1.5074
Takaki, Ronald T., 1939-. 3.6532
Takakusu, Junjirō, tr. 1.1737
Takakusu, Junjirō. 1.2158
Takeda, Izumo, 1691-1756. 2.3400
Takekoshi, Yosaburō, 1865-1950. 4.2545
Takesaki, Masamichi, 1933-. 5.1478
Takeuchi, Hitoshi, 1921-. 5.3077
Takeuchi, Tatsuji, 1904-. 3.4918
Takhtadzhian, A. L. (Armen Leonovich) 5.3693
Taktsis, Costas, 1927-. 2.611-2.612
Talamini, John T. comp. 4.947
Talbert, Charles H. 1.2678
Talbert, Richard J. A., 1947-. 4.7370
Talbot, A. M. 4.190
Talbot, Charles W., ed. 1.6463
Talbot, Michael. 1.4033
Talbot, Nathan Bill, 1909-. 4.5710
Talbot, Ross B. 4.2888
Talbot, William John, joint author. 4.190
Talbott, John E. 3.5208
Talbott, Strobe. 4.9180
Talbott, Strobe. ed. 3.3269
Talese, Gay. 2.3665
Tallman, Irving. 4.5730
Tallman, Warren E., 1921- joint comp. 2.2729
Tallmer, Margot. 5.4588
Talmon, J. L. (Jacob Leib), 1916-. 4.7493,
   4.7607
Talocci, Mauro. 3.287
Tamarkin, Civia. 4.10156
Tamaru, Kenji, 1923-. 5.2895
Tamayo, Rufino, 1899-. 1.6006-1.6007
Tambiah, Stanley Jeyaraja, 1929-. 1.2112
Tamir, Lois M., 1954-. 4.4930
Tampion, John. 5.3662
Tan, Chester C. 3.4743

Tan, Chung, 1929-. 3.4725
Tan, Lek, joint author. 3.4487
Tanaka, Yukiko. 2.2039
Tancock, John L. 1.5712
Tandon, Prakash. 3.4323, 3.4352
Tanenbaum, Andrew S., 1944-. 5.1199, 5.6415
Tanford, Charles, 1921-. 5.2843
T'ang, Hsien-tsu, 1550-1616. 2.2225
Tang, Tong B. 5.774
Tange, Kenzō, 1913-. 1.5454
Tanizaki, Junichiro. 2.2121
Tanizaki, Jun'ichirō, 1886-1965. 2.2118-2.2120,
   2.2122
Tank, Ronald Warren. 4.9528
Tann, Jennifer, 1939-. 5.6213
Tannahill, Neal R., 1949-. 4.7028
Tannahill, Reay. 4.861
Tannehill, Bertha, ed. 1.39
Tannehill, John C. 5.1660
Tannenbaum, Edward R. 3.2831, 3.2858, 4.5289
Tannenbaum, Frank, 1893-1969. 3.8952
Tanner, Clara Lee. 3.5767-3.5768, 3.5841
Tanner, Daniel. 4.10452
Tanner, Helen Hornbeck. 3.5735
Tanner, J. M. (James Mourilyan) 4.5757, 5.5081
Tanner, J. R. (Joseph Robson), 1860-1931. ed.
   5.7463
Tanner, John, 1927- joint author. 3.285
Tanner, Joseph Robson, 1860-1931. 4.8399
Tanner, Laurel N. joint author. 4.10452
Tanner, Nancy Makepeace. 4.452
Tanner, Stephen L. 2.13113
Tanner, Tony. 2.3419, 2.10258, 2.10644,
   2.13288
Tanner, Väinö, 1881-1966. 3.3298
Tanselle, G. Thomas (George Thomas), 1934-.
   2.11148, 5.7745
Tansey, Richard G. 1.4673
Tanter, Raymond. 4.9000
Tantras. Hevajratantrarājānāma. 1.1744
Tao-chi, 1630-1707. 1.6332
Tao-Yüan, Shih. 1.1771
Taper, Bernard. 4.1130
Taper, Bernard. ed. 3.8624
Tapié, Victor Lucien, 1900-1974. 3.1877, 3.2022
Taplin, Oliver Paul. 2.305, 2.417
Tapp, Jack T., 1934-. 5.4582
Tappert, Theodore Gerhardt, 1904-. 1.3360,
   1.3363
Tapping, G. Craig. 2.8522
Tapsell, R. F., 1936-. 3.562
Tarassuk, Leonid. 5.7246
Tarbell, Ida M. (Ida Minerva), 1857-1944.
   4.1916, 4.3044
Tardieu, Jean, 1903-. 2.4756-2.4757
Tariq, Abdur-Rahman, 1915- comp. 3.4286
Tarjan, Robert E. (Robert Endre), 1948-.
   5.1243
Tarkington, Booth, 1869-1946. 2.11236-2.11241
Tarle, Evgeniĭ Viktorovich, 1874-1955. 3.2136
Tarling, D. H. (Donald Harvey) 5.3097, 5.6730
Tarling, Maureen P. joint author. 5.3097
Tarling, Nicholas. 3.4412
Tarn, Nathaniel. ed. 2.5410
Tarn, W. W. (William Woodthorpe), 1869-1957.
   3.2543, 3.2637, 3.4245
Tarn, William Woodthorpe, Sir, 1869-1957.
   3.2628, 5.7182
Tarner lectures, 1946. 5.866
Tarr, Joel Arthur. 3.7664
Tarr, Rodger L. 2.7555
Tarrant, Desmond. 2.11449
Tarrant, John J. joint author. 5.6138
Tarrow, Sidney G. 4.8630
Tarski, Alfred. 1.1223, 5.1050
Tart, Charles T., 1937-. 1.1569, 5.290
Taruc, Luis, 1913-. 3.4606
Tasso, Torquato, 1544-1595. 2.4978-2.4983
Tatarkiewicz, Władysław, 1886-. 1.447
Tatarunis, Alphonse M., joint author. 1.4409
Tate, Allen, 1899-. 2.2344, 2.2656, 2.2741,
   2.2764, 2.6185, 2.10505, 2.10712, 2.11389,
   2.11643, 2.12571-2.12574
Tate, Claudia. ed. 2.10313
Tate, Claudia. 2.10313
Tate Gallery. 1.4956, 1.6038, 1.6170
Tate, Merze, 1905-. 3.5644, 3.6449
Tate, Nahum, 1652-1715. 2.6680

Tate, Thad W. 3.7955, 3.8107, 3.8185
Tateishi, John, 1939-. 3.1025
Tatham, A. F. 5.8209
Tatler (London, England) 2.6276
Tatlock, J. S. P. 2.6344
Tatlock, John S. P. (John Strong Perry),
   1876-1948. 2.6315, 2.6353, 2.6377, 3.1303
Taton, René. ed. 5.759
Tattam, William M., 1941-. 4.3395
Tatu, Michel, 1933-. 3.3266
Tatum, Charles M. 2.10357
Tatum, Elbert Lee. 4.8181
Tatum, Georgia Lee. 3.7377
Tatum, Howard J., 1915- joint author. 4.5674
Tatum, James. 2.705, 2.760
Taub, Herbert, 1918-. 5.6359, 5.6473-5.6474,
   5.6481
Taub, Janet, joint author. 5.4699
Taubert, Sigfred. 5.7571
Taubman, Paul, 1939- ed. 4.10731
Taubman, William. 3.6494, 4.8880
Tauchert, Theodore R., 1935-. 5.5843
Taussig, F. W. (Frank William), 1859-1940.
   4.4204
Taussig, Frank William, 1859-1940. 4.4109,
   4.4201
Tavard, Georges Henri, 1922-. 1.2812
Taves, Ernest H. (Ernest Henry), 1916- joint
   author. 5.6698
Tavis, Lee A. 4.3025
Tavistock Child Development Research Unit.
   5.604
Tavistock Seminar on Mother-Infant
   Interaction. 5.604
Tavolga, William N., 1922- ed. 5.4088
Tavris, Carol. 5.426
Tawney, R. H. (Richard Henry), 1880-1962.
   1.2243, 4.1486, 4.2244, 4.2252, 4.2468, 4.4960
Tawney, Richard Henry. 4.2850
Tax, Sol, 1907-. 3.9065, 5.3363
Tayler, R. J. (Roger John) 5.1767
Taylor, A. E. (Alfred Edward), 1869-1945.
   1.267
Taylor, A. J. P. (Alan John Percivale), 1906-.
   3.673, 3.707, 3.788, 3.894, 3.1214, 3.1249,
   3.1641, 3.1654, 3.1889, 3.2292, 3.2316,
   3.2496, 4.8930
Taylor, Alan R. 3.3740
Taylor, Aline Mackenzie. 2.7177
Taylor, Anne (Dewees) 4.2948
Taylor, Antoinette Elizabeth, 1917-. 4.8090
Taylor, Archer, 1890-1973. 2.3810, 2.13464
Taylor, Arlene G., 1941-. 5.7627
Taylor, Arthur C. 5.6052
Taylor, Barbara, 1950-. 4.5944
Taylor, Bernard, 1931-. 4.4381
Taylor, Betty W. 4.9437
Taylor, Billy, 1921-. 1.4157
Taylor, Brian K. 4.7487
Taylor, C. C. W. (Christopher Charles
   Whiston), 1936-. 1.252, 1.1503
Taylor, Charles, 1935-. 4.7280
Taylor, Charles Fayette, 1894-. 5.6221
Taylor, Charles Holt, 1899-. 4.4702
Taylor, Charles Lewis. 4.5094
Taylor, Christopher, 1935-. 4.392
Taylor, D. R. F. (David Ruxton Fraser), 1937-.
   4.6360
Taylor, D. Wayne. 5.4583
Taylor, Daniel Crane, 1897-. 2.6947
Taylor, Denny, 1947-. 4.10755
Taylor, Donald Fraser. 2.9408
Taylor, Donald S., ed. 2.6933
Taylor, Dorothy. 1.4415
Taylor, E. G. R. (Eva Germaine Rimington),
   1879-. 4.66-4.67, 5.7492
Taylor, Edmond, 1908-. 3.728, 3.4186
Taylor, Edward, 1642-1729. 2.10875
Taylor, Edward S., 1943-. 5.5724
Taylor, Edwin F. joint author. 5.2130
Taylor, Edwin F. 5.1924
Taylor, Elizabeth, 1912-1975. 2.9394-2.9398
Taylor, Eric, 1918-. 4.8479
Taylor, F. M. (Fred Manville), 1855-1932.
   4.3068
Taylor, F. W. 5.1809
Taylor, Frank, 1910-. 3.1380
Taylor, Fred. 3.2384

Taylor, Frederick Winslow, 1856-1915. 5.5604
Taylor, George Rogers, 1895-. 3.6360, 4.1869, 4.1876
Taylor, George William, 1901- ed. 4.3135
Taylor, Gerald, 1923-   . 1.6660
Taylor, Gordon Rattray. 3.215, 5.4314
Taylor, Graham D., 1944-. 3.5809, 4.3794
Taylor, Harold, 1914-. 4.10551
Taylor, Harold McCarter, 1907-. 1.5363
Taylor, Henry Charles, 1873-. 4.2948
Taylor, Henry Osborn, 1856-1941. 3.60, 3.138, 3.169, 3.498-3.499
Taylor, Howard Canning, 1900-. 5.4255
Taylor, Ian R. 4.6683
Taylor, Irving A. 5.348
Taylor, Isaac, 1829-1901. 4.73
Taylor, J. Golden. comp. 2.10724
Taylor, James, Sir, 1902-. 2.913, 5.779
Taylor, Jared. 3.4894
Taylor, Jay, 1931-. 3.4409
Taylor, Jennifer. 1.5456
Taylor, Jenny, 1949-. 2.9031
Taylor, Jeremy, Bp. of Down and Connor, 1613-1667. 2.7312
Taylor, Jerome, 1918-. 2.5851
Taylor, Joan Sills, joint author. 1.5363
Taylor, Joe Gray. 3.8310, 3.8315
Taylor, John, 1925-. 2.6427
Taylor, John Gerald, 1931-. 5.1989
Taylor, John Robert, 1939-. 5.2077
Taylor, John Russell. 2.3055, 2.5920, 2.5924-2.5925
Taylor, John William Ransom. 5.6667
Taylor, Joseph H., joint author. 5.1848
Taylor, Joshua Charles, 1917-. 1.4906, 1.6186
Taylor, Kamala (Purnaiya), 1924-. 2.10126
Taylor, Keith. 4.6943
Taylor, Keith Weller. 3.4464
Taylor, L. B. 5.6704
Taylor, L. J. 5.7715
Taylor, Laurie, 1935-. 4.5078
Taylor, Lester D. joint author. 4.2059
Taylor, Lily Ross, 1886-. 3.2735
Taylor, Mary E., joint author. 5.3998
Taylor, Maxwell D. (Maxwell Davenport), 1901-1987. 5.7281
Taylor, Michael. 4.7191, 5.6667
Taylor, Nancy M., ed. 3.5590
Taylor, Norman Burke, 1885-. 5.4191
Taylor, Paul. 1.3586
Taylor, Peter Hillsman, 1917-. 2.12578-2.12581
Taylor, Peter J. (Peter James), 1944-. 4.7500-4.7501
Taylor, Philip A. M. 4.8945
Taylor, Philip Bates. 4.8351
Taylor, Philip Lester. 5.2199
Taylor, Philip M. 3.843
Taylor, Phillip. 4.9273
Taylor, R. E. (Royal Ervin), 1938-. 3.5695
Taylor, R. K. 5.6093
Taylor, R. K. S. (Richard K. S.) joint author. 4.6531
Taylor, Richard. 1.1328, 2.8364
Taylor, Robert, 1943-. 4.3410
Taylor, Robert J., 1945-. 5.4084
Taylor, Robert Joseph, 1917-. 3.6966, 3.8022
Taylor, Ronald, 1924-. 1.3985, 1.4043, 2.1182, 2.13479
Taylor, Ronald B. 4.3303, 4.3378
Taylor, Ronald Lewis, 1942-. 3.6716
Taylor, Samuel H. 4.6476
Taylor, Simon. 3.1310, 3.2376
Taylor, Simon Watson. 2.4591
Taylor Society. 4.2630
Taylor, Stan, 1948-. 4.8554
Taylor, Telford. 3.880, 3.959
Taylor, Theodore B., 1925- joint author. 4.3811
Taylor, Thomas Griffith, 1880-. 4.255
Taylor, Vincent, 1887-1968. 1.2653, 1.2894
Taylor, Walter, 1927-. 2.11702
Taylor, Walter Fuller, 1900-. 2.10583
Taylor, Wendell Hertig, 1905- joint author. 5.8172
Taylor, William Duncan. 2.6237
Taylor, William R. 3.8713
Taylor, William Robert, 1922-. 3.8125
Taylour, William, Lord, 1904-. 3.2587
Tayyeb, R. 5.7698

Tcherikover, Avigdor, 1895-. 3.3893
Tchobanoglous, George. 5.5987, 5.6018, 5.6028
Teaching of the Twelve Apostles. English. 1.2181
Teaford, Jon C. 4.8839
Teague, Peter. 5.1224
Teal, John. 5.3559
Teal, Mildred. joint author. 5.3559
Teasdale, Sara, 1884-1933. 2.12582-2.12583
Tebbel, John William, 1912-. 2.61, 2.3616, 5.7590
Teberosky, Ana. 4.10408
Techo, Robert. 5.6416
Tecker, Glenn H. 4.10677
Tedder, Arthur William Tedder, baron, 1890-. 3.1042
Tedder, John M. (John Michael) joint author. 5.2820
Tedeschi, Richard. 2.4557
Tedesco, Janis, 1950-. 2.9808
Tedford, Thomas L. 4.9710
Tedlock, Barbara. joint author. 3.5828
Tedlock, Barbara. 3.9062
Tedlock, Dennis, 1939-. 2.2331, 3.5828, 3.5965, 3.9061
Teece, David J. 4.3753
Teeuw, A. 2.2284, 3.8341
Teggart, Frederick John, 1870-1946. 3.437
Tehuacan Archaeological-Botanical Project. 3.8894
Teich, Albert H. comp. 5.5525
Teich, Mikuláš. 3.79
Teicher, Morton I. 4.6589
Teicholz, Eric. 5.7024
Teichova, Alice. 4.3061, 4.4630
Teilhard de Chardin, Pierre. 1.856, 1.1332, 1.2235
Teiwes, Frederick C. 4.8890
Teixeira de Mattos, Alexander, 1865-1921. 2.4599
Telfer, William, 1886- ed. and tr. 1.2210
Telford, W. M. (William Murray), 1917-. 5.6737
Tellenbach, Gerd, 1903-. 1.3209
Teller, Edward, 1908-. 5.856, 5.6137, 5.7386
Teller, Walter Magnes, 1910- ed. 2.11271
Telser, Lester G., 1931-. 4.2676
Telushkin, Joseph, 1948-. 3.4012
Temam, Roger. 5.1523
Temin, Peter. 4.1718, 4.1917, 4.9574
Temkin, Owsei, 1902-. 1.1321, 5.4506, 5.4788
Temkin, Samuel, 1936-. 5.2230
Temko, Philip, 1924-. 1.270
Temperley, Harold William Vazeille, 1879-1939. 3.688, 3.696
Temperley, Nicholas. 1.4250
Tempest, N. R. 4.10923
Temple, Elżbieta. 1.6407
Temple, Frédéric Jacques. 2.8372
Temple Newsam House. 1.6578
Temple, Ruth Zabriskie. joint author. 5.8334, 5.8335
Temple, Ruth Zabriskie. comp. 2.5740
Temple University. Center for the Study of Federalism. 3.8089
Temple, William, Sir, 1628-1699. 2.7313
Templeman, Donald C. 4.2357
Templeman, William Darby, ed. 2.6264, 5.7947
Ten Broek, Jacobus. 3.7265
Ten, C. L. 4.7442
Tendler, Judith. 4.1833
Tendriakov, Vladimir Fedorovich, 1923-. 2.1607
Teng, Ssu-yü, 1906-. 3.4675, 3.4722, 3.4734
Tennant, Kylie, 1912-. 3.5574
Tennant, Roger. 2.8576
Tennekes, H. 5.1666
Tenniel, John, Sir, 1820-1914. 2.7673
Tennov, Dorothy. 5.442, 5.4858
Tennyson, Alfred Tennyson, Baron, 1809-1892. 2.8153-2.8156, 2.8160-2.8161, 2.8167, 3.1613
Tennyson, Brian Douglas. 3.8701
Tennyson, Charles, Sir, 1879-. 2.8173, 2.8181, 3.1613
Tennyson, Emily Sellwood Tennyson, Baroness, 1813-1896. 2.8166, 2.8174
Tennyson, G. B. ed. 2.7545
Tennyson, G. B. 2.7548

Tennyson, Hallam Tennyson, Baron, 1852-1928. 2.8155, 2.8175
Tent, James F. 4.10742
Tentler, Leslie Woodcock. 4.3293
Tentler, Thomas N., 1932-. 1.3019
Teodori, Massimo, 1938- comp. 4.5164
TePaske, John Jay. 3.9302, 4.4666
Teplitz, Paul V. joint author. 4.1008
Terborg-Penn, Rosalyn. 3.6746
Terborgh, John, 1936-. 5.4031
Terence. 2.698, 2.703, 2.778
Terenzio, Stephanie. 1.6445
Teresa, Joseph G., 1941- joint author. 4.1228
Teresa, of Avila, Saint, 1515-1582. 1.3138
Teresi, Dick. 5.5948
Terkel, Studs, 1912-. 2.2844, 3.333, 3.7773
Terman, Frederick Emmons, 1900-. 5.6425
Ternon, Yves. 3.4044
Terrace, Herbert S., 1936-. 5.4037
Terrace, Vincent, 1948-. 2.2853
Terraine, John. 3.795, 3.1051, 3.1270, 3.1284
Terras, Victor. 2.1244, 2.1340, 2.1349
Terrell, Carroll Franklin. 2.12329
Terrell, Mary Church, 1863-1954. 3.6851
Terres, John K. 5.3957
Terrett, I. B., joint ed. 3.1724
Terrill, Ross. 4.7031
Terrill, Tom E. 4.5197
Terry, Charles Sanford, 1864-1936. 1.3783-1.3784
Terry, Ellen, Dame, 1848-1928. 2.3355
Terry, Garth M. 2.1376
Terry, Herbert A. 4.9541
Terry, John Skally, 1894-. 2.12787
Terry, Megan. 2.13353
Terry, Patricia Ann, 1929-. 2.3926, 2.3957, 2.4686
Terry, Sarah Meiklejohn, 1937-. 3.2996
Terry, Wallace. 3.4508
Terry, Walter. 4.1159, 4.1167, 4.1181
Tersine, Richard J. 5.7038
Terts, Abram, 1925-. 2.1267, 4.9918
Tertullian, ca. 160-ca. 230. 1.2186
Tertz, Abram, pseud. 2.1251
Terwiel, B. J. (Barend Jan), 1941-. 3.4524
Terzaghi, E. A. (Eric A.), 1936-. 5.3398
Terzaghi, Karl, 1883-1963. 5.5908-5.5909
Tesconi, Charles A. 4.10733
Teski, Marea. 4.5808, 4.5826
Tetel, Marcel. 2.3988, 2.3996, 2.4006
Teternikov, Fedor Kuz'mich, 1863-1927. 2.1534
Teukolsky, Saul A. (Saul Arno), 1947-. 5.1845
Teveth, Shabtai, 1925-. 3.3911
Tew, Brian. 4.4579
Texas. University at Austin. Dept. of Germanic Languages. 2.13967
Texas. University. Dept. of Germanic Languages. 2.13506
Textile Museum (Washington, D.C.) 4.635, 5.7079
Teynac, Françoise. 1.6596
Thacker, Christopher. 1.1397, 5.5375
Thacker, Ernest W. joint author. 4.8267
Thackeray, Henry St. John, 1869?-1930. 2.376
Thackeray, William Makepeace, 1811-1863. 2.6067, 2.7044, 2.8183-2.8184, 2.8186
Thackray, Arnold, 1939-. 5.693, 5.2619
Thackston, W. M. (Wheeler McIntosh), 1944-. 1.2086
Thale, Jerome. 2.7710
Thaler, Alwin, 1891-. 2.3283
Thalheim, Karl Christian. 4.2234
Thalmann, Marianne, 1888-. 2.13663
Thalmann, William G., 1947-. 2.412
Tham, Seong Chee. 2.2255
Thant, U, 1909-. 3.1151, 3.1172
Thapar, Romila. 3.4226, 3.4248
Tharp, Roland G., 1930-. 4.624
Tharpe, Jac. 2.12886, 2.13247-2.13248
Thatcher, Benjamin Bussey, 1809-1840. 3.5786
Thaw, Eugene V. 1.4902
Thaxton, Ralph, 1944-. 4.7127
Thayer, Alexander Wheelock, 1817-1897. 1.3806
Thayer, Charles Wheeler, 1910-. 4.9090
Thayer, H. S. (Horace Standish), 1923-. 1.533
Thayer, William Roscoe, 1859-1923. 3.2867
Theatre Communications Group. 2.10801

Theatre Library Association. 5.8306
Theil, Henri. 4.1459
Theis, Paul A., 1923- ed. 3.6302
Thelen, David P. (David Paul) 3.8449, 4.2037
Themba, Can, 1924-1968. 2.10094
Theobald, Robert. 4.5190
Theocritus. 2.552-2.555
Theodorson, Achilles G., joint author. 4.4736
Theodorson, George A. 4.4736
Theoharis, Athan G. 3.7540, 3.7803
Theophanes, the Confessor, d. ca. 818. 3.518
Theophilus, Presbyter. 1.5099
Theophrastus. 2.394-2.396, 2.557-2.558
Theoretical Archaeology Group (England) 3.221
Thérèse, de Lisieux, Saint, 1873-1897. 1.3261
Thernstrom, Stephan. 3.6515, 4.5191, 4.5205
Theroux, Paul. 2.10015, 2.13354-2.13357
Thesen, Arne. 5.5575
Thesing, William B. 5.7975
Theunissen, Michael. 1.459
Theurer, Charles. 5.5829
Thewlis, James. 5.1888
Thibaudet, Albert, 1874-1936. 2.3856
Thibault, Edward A., 1939-. 4.6799
Thibaut, G. (George), 1848-1914. 1.1680
Thibodeaux, Louis J. 5.2632
Thiébaux, Marcelle. 2.11783
Thieblot, Armand J. 4.9560
Thielcke, Gerhard. 5.3969
Thiele, Gary A. joint author. 5.6496
Thielicke, Helmut, 1908-. 1.2782
Thieme, Ulrich, 1865-1922. 1.4584-1.4585
Thierauf, Robert J. 5.5614
Thierry, Jean Jacques. 2.4234
Thies, Frieda Charlotte, 1880-. 2.11140
Thiher, Allen, 1941-. 2.4515
Thimann, Kenneth Vivian, 1904-. 5.3747, 5.4425
Thinès, Georges, 1923-. 5.210
Thirion, André, 1907-. 2.4758
Thirlwall, A. P. 4.4525
Thirring, Walter E., 1927-. 5.1971
Thirsk, Joan. 4.2308, 4.2847, 5.5250
Thirsk, Joan. comp. 4.2268
Thiselton, Anthony C. 1.2520
Thody, Philip Malcolm Waller, 1928-. 2.4744
Tholfsen, Trygve R. 3.657, 4.3644
Thom, Gary, 1941-. 4.7318
Thom, René, 1923-. 5.3314
Thoman, Richard S., 1919-. 4.4126
Thomas, A. D. (Alan David), 1946-. 5.1579
Thomas, Alan, 1925-. 5.6222
Thomas, Alastair H. 4.8378, 4.8670
Thomas, Alexander. 4.5709, 5.605, 5.634
Thomas, Aquinas, Saint, 1225?-1274. 1.390, 1.1275, 1.2824, 1.3139, 1.3197, 4.7379
Thomas, Benjamin Platt, 1902-1956. 3.7285, 3.7332
Thomas, Brinley, 1906-. 4.8941
Thomas, Caitlin. 2.9399
Thomas, Clara. 2.9942
Thomas, D. M. 2.1537, 2.9825
Thomas, Daniel H. 3.2971
Thomas, Daniel H. ed. 3.269
Thomas, David, 1931-. 3.1756
Thomas, David Hurst. 3.265
Thomas, David Oswald. 1.1423
Thomas, Deborah A., 1943-. 2.7664
Thomas, Donald. 3.1283
Thomas, Donald Serrell. 4.9422
Thomas, Dorothy Swaine Thomas, 1899-. 4.1656
Thomas, Dylan, 1914-1953. 2.9400-2.9413
Thomas, E. E. (Edward Eastaway) 3.1134
Thomas, E. J. (Edward Joseph), 1869-. 1.1773
Thomas, Edward, 1878-1917. 2.9423-2.9424
Thomas, Emory M., 1939-. 3.7378
Thomas, Ernest Chester, 1850-1892. 5.7671
Thomas, F. Richard. 2.10432
Thomas, Frank, 1912-. 1.5856
Thomas, Gillian. 2.7930
Thomas, Gordon L., 1914- joint comp. 2.10855
Thomas, Gwyn, 1913-. 2.840, 2.842
Thomas, Hugh, 1923-. 3.1766, 3.3469, 4.7030
Thomas, Isaiah, 1749-1831. 5.7551
Thomas, J. W. (John Wesley), 1916-. 2.13531
Thomas, James L., 1945-. 4.10292

Thomas, James P., 1827-1913. 3.7214
Thomas, James P. (James Peringer), 1932-. 5.266
Thomas, John L. 3.7249, 4.5143
Thomas, John L. ed. 4.7179
Thomas, Keith Vivian. 1.2358
Thomas, L. J. 5.6747
Thomas, Lewis, 1913-. 5.4532
Thomas, Lewis Gwynne, 1914-. 3.8838-3.8839
Thomas, Lewis Herbert, 1917-. 4.8322
Thomas, Lindon C., 1941-. 5.2268
Thomas, Merlin. ed. 2.4043
Thomas, Michael Frederic. 4.264
Thomas, Milton Halsey, 1903-. 3.7983
Thomas, Morley K. 5.2579
Thomas Nelson & Sons. 1.2502
Thomas, Norman, 1884-1968. 4.7702
Thomas, Norman C. 4.10661
Thomas, Owen Paul. ed. 2.11245
Thomas, Paul. 4.7184
Thomas, Paul R., 1953-. 5.7115
Thomas, Peter, 1939-. 2.8811
Thomas, Peter David Garner. 3.1564, 3.6859
Thomas, R. George. 2.9423
Thomas, R. George. ed. 2.6208
Thomas, R. Murray (Robert Murray) 4.10136, 4.10141
Thomas, R. S. (Ronald Stuart), 1913-. 2.9427-2.9428
Thomas, Robert David, 1939-. 4.7159
Thomas, Robert Paul. joint author. 4.2207
Thomas, the Rhymer, 1220?-1297? 2.9843
Thomas, Theodore H. 4.2450
Thomas, Tony, 1949- comp. 3.6714
Thomas, Wayne H. 4.9880
Thomas, William Isaac, 1863-1947. 4.4812, 4.4846, 4.6694
Thomas, William L., 1920-. 4.395
Thomas, William Leroy, 1920- ed. 4.2, 4.371
Thomas, William Moy, 1828-1910, tr. 2.4238
Thomas, William R. 4.9677
Thomasma, David C., 1939- joint author. 5.4557
Thomason, Richmond H. 1.1224
Thomes, Mary Margaret, joint author. 4.5637
Thomlinson, Ralph. 4.1604
Thompson, A. R. 4.10149
Thompson, Ann. 2.6713
Thompson, Bard, 1925- ed. 1.2988
Thompson, Bruce. 2.13591
Thompson, Colin J. 5.1972
Thompson, Craig R. (Craig Ringwalt), 1911-. 2.823
Thompson, D. B. (David B.) 5.3064
Thompson, Daniel C. (Daniel Calbert) 3.6778, 4.10861
Thompson, Daniel Varney, 1902-. 1.6375
Thompson, D'Arcy Wentworth, 1860-1948. 5.4212
Thompson, David, 1938- comp. 3.2712
Thompson, Dorothy, 1923-. 4.3654
Thompson, E. A. 3.2842, 3.3419
Thompson, E. P. (Edward Palmer), 1924-. 2.7971, 3.408, 4.3641, 4.9177
Thompson, Edgar Tristan, 1900- joint ed. 4.5195
Thompson, Edward John, 1886-1946. 3.4268-3.4269
Thompson, Edward Maunde, Sir, 1840-1929. 5.7534
Thompson, Ernest Trice, 1894-. 1.3391
Thompson, Esther Katherine. 5.5242
Thompson, Ewa Majewska, 1937-. 2.1704
Thompson, F. M. L. (Francis Michael Longstreth) 4.5311
Thompson, Faith, 1893-1961. 4.8390
Thompson, Flora. 3.1739
Thompson, Francis, 1859-1907. 2.2597
Thompson, G. H. B. (George Horace Brooke) 5.5955
Thompson, George, 1941-. 5.8272
Thompson, Gerald E. 5.5592
Thompson, I. A. A. 5.7354
Thompson, J. M. (James Matthew), 1878-1956. 3.655, 3.2103, 3.2130, 3.2160
Thompson, J. M. T. 5.5861
Thompson, James D. 4.2670

Thompson, James Westfall, 1869-1941. 3.153, 3.406, 3.2267
Thompson, Jerry L. 1.5769
Thompson, John, 1953-. 3.8537
Thompson, John D. 5.4706
Thompson, John Eric Sidney, Sir, 1898-1975. 3.9041-3.9042
Thompson, John M. joint author. 3.3159
Thompson, John M. 3.860, 3.3196
Thompson, John W., 1891-. 5.8481-5.8482
Thompson, Kenneth, 1923-. 4.4749
Thompson, Kenneth A. 1.855
Thompson, Kenneth W., 1921-. 3.1173, 3.1660, 4.9014, 4.9051
Thompson, Kristin, 1950-. 2.2909
Thompson, Laura, 1905-. 3.5890
Thompson, Laurence G. 5.8440-5.8441
Thompson, Lawrance Roger, 1906-1973. 2.11703, 2.11750, 2.11760-2.11762
Thompson, Lawrence Sidney, 1916-. 5.7732
Thompson, Leonard Monteath. 3.5475
Thompson, Leonard Monteath. joint author. 3.5464
Thompson, Lester. 5.6248
Thompson, Margaret. 1.855
Thompson, Margaret M. 5.8272
Thompson, Neil B., 1921-. 5.7289
Thompson, Oscar, 1887-1945. 1.3500
Thompson, Paul. 4.3428
Thompson, Paul Richard, 1935-. 1.5383, 4.5320
Thompson, Philip C. 4.2724
Thompson, Raymond H. (Raymond Henry), 1941-. 2.6049
Thompson, Richard F. 5.4339
Thompson, Robert Farris. 1.5090, 1.6727, 3.5689
Thompson, Robert Grainger Ker, Sir, 1916-. 5.7231
Thompson, Roger, 1933-. 4.5549, 4.5870
Thompson, Sharon. 4.5506
Thompson, Stith, 1885-. 2.2701, 3.5821, 4.752, 4.760, 4.805, 4.818
Thompson, Virginia McLean, 1903-. 3.4432, 3.5375, 3.5379, 3.5386-3.5387, 3.5556, 4.8808
Thompson, Wilbur Richard, 1923-. 4.6229
Thompson, William Fletcher, 1929-. 3.8442
Thomson, Dale C. 3.8790
Thomson, David, 1912-. 3.658, 3.2115
Thomson, Derick S. 2.830
Thomson, Ester Sylvia, ed. 1.6590
Thomson, F. P. (Francis Paul) ed. 1.6590
Thomson, G. P. (George Paget), Sir, 1892- joint author. 5.2382
Thomson, George Derwent. 2.407
Thomson, George H., 1924- ed. 2.8643
Thomson, Gladys Scott. 3.3105
Thomson, H. J. 2.689
Thomson, J. A. K. (James Alexander Kerr), 1879-1944. 2.5570-2.5571, 2.6830
Thomson, J. E. P. (John Edward Palmer) 5.8087
Thomson, J. J. (Joseph John), Sir, 1856-1940. 5.2382
Thomson, J. (John), 1837-1921. 3.4620
Thomson, J. Michael (John Michael), 1928-. 4.3928
Thomson, James, 1700-1748. 2.7314-2.7316, 2.7318, 2.8197
Thomson, James Oliver. 4.58
Thomson, John Hunter, joint author. 5.2288
Thomson, John M., 1937-. 4.925
Thomson, Judith Jarvis. 1.137
Thomson, Patricia. 2.6551
Thomson, Patricia. comp. 2.6552
Thomson, Peter, 1938-. 2.3306, 2.6865, 2.7438
Thomson, R. H. (Ronald Hunter) 5.2790
Thomson, Robb M. (Robb Milton), 1925- joint author. 5.2201
Thomson, Rodney M. 1.3267
Thomson, Samuel Harrison, 1895-1975. 3.1909
Thomson, Sarah Katharine, 1928-. 5.7654
Thomson, Virgil, 1896-. 1.3479
Thomson, W. G. (William George), 1865-1942. 1.6590
Thomson, Walter Gary, 1939- joint author. 5.5688
Thomson, William A.R. (William Archibald Robson), 1906-. 5.4491

Thomte, Reidar. 1.2914
Thonssen, Lester, 1904-. 2.3535, 2.10859
Thorburn, David. 2.8577, 2.13384
Thorburn, Hugh G., 1924-. 4.8300, 4.8319
Thordarson, Bruce. 3.8785
Thoreau, Henry David, 1817-1862.
  2.11245-2.11246, 3.7991, 3.8809, 5.6980
Thormann, Joan, 1945-. 4.10294
Thorn, Richard S. ed. 4.4482
Thornbrough, Emma Lou. 2.3613, 3.8393
Thornburn, Thomas Hampton, joint author.
  5.5919
Thornbury, William D. (William David), 1900-.
  4.245, 5.2998
Thorndike, Alan M., joint author. 5.2391
Thorndike, Edward L. (Edward Lee),
  1874-1949. 4.10362-4.10363, 5.120
Thorndike, Lynn, 1882-1965. 4.10108, 5.760,
  5.8224
Thorndike, Tony. 4.2157
Thorne, Barrie. 2.128, 4.5595
Thorne, Kip S. joint author. 5.2215
Thorne, Malcolm J., joint author. 5.4059
Thorner, Alice, 1917- joint author. 4.2987
Thorner, Daniel. 4.2987
Thornes, John B. 4.257, 4.738
Thornhill, Randy. 5.3861
Thornhill, William T., 1926-. 4.4405
Thornley, George, b. 1614. 2.378
Thornton, A. P. (Archibald Paton)
  4.7541-4.7542, 4.8915
Thornton, Barbara C., 1936-. 5.4481
Thornton, Earl A. (Earl Arthur), 1936-. 5.5727
Thornton, J. Mills, 1943-. 4.8266
Thornton, James. 2.7804
Thornton, John Kelly, 1949-. 3.5422
Thornton, John Leonard. 5.8285
Thornton, Peter. 1.6549
Thornton, Robert D. (Robert Donald), 1917-
  ed. 2.7499
Thornton, Thomas Perry. joint ed. 4.6976
Thornton, Weldon. 2.8150, 2.8882
Thorp, Rosemary. 4.2142
Thorp, Willard, 1899-. 2.10423
Thorpe, Francis Newton, 1857-1926. comp.
  4.9610
Thorpe, James Ernest, 1915-. 2.2365, 2.5495,
  2.7010, 2.7152
Thorpe, John A. joint author. 5.1600
Thorpe, Michael. comp. 2.7585
Thorpe, W. H. (William Homan), 1902-. 5.3968
Thorslev, Peter Larsen. 2.7538
Thorson, Gerald. 2.14059
Thouless, D. J. 5.2164
Thouless, Robert Henry, 1894-. 1.1568
Thrall, William Flint, 1880-. 2.2348
Thrasher, Frederic M. 4.6716
Threlfall, W. (William), 1888- joint author.
  5.1598
Thring, M. W. (Meredith Wooldridge), 1915-.
  5.5675
Throckmorton, Burton Hamilton, 1921- ed.
  1.2683
Throwe, Anita Narciso. 5.5210
Thrower, Norman Joseph William. 4.228
Thrupp, Sylvia Lettice, 1903-. 1.2950, 4.4232
Thrush, Paul W. 5.6720
Thucydides. 2.397, 2.559-2.560, 3.545,
  3.2607-3.2608
Thuesen, G. J., 1938-. 4.2726, 5.5702
Thuesen, H. G. (Holger George), 1898-. 5.5702
Thuillier, Jacques. 1.6103
Thumann, Albert. 5.6160
Thumboo, Edwin, 1933-. 2.10137
Thünen, Johann Heinrich von, 1783-1850.
  4.2887
Thupten Wangyal. joint author. 1.5070
Thurber, James, 1894-1961. 1.5850, 2.3631,
  2.3796, 2.12586-2.12587
Thurber, Kenneth J. 5.1154
Thurley, Geoffrey. tr. 2.1555
Thurman, Harold V. 5.3250
Thurman, Joseph E. 5.5622
Thurman, Judith, 1946-. 2.14021
Thurman, Robert A. F. 1.2136
Thurman, Wallace, 1902-1934. 2.12591-2.12592
Thurnher, Eugen. 2.13537
Thurow, Lester C. 4.1283, 4.2101, 4.4699

Thursby, Marie. joint author. 4.3682
Thurston, Frederick. 1.4556
Thurston, Herbert, 1856-1939. 1.3246
Thurstone, Louis Leon, 1887-1955. 5.56-5.57
Thursz, Daniel. 4.6589
Thwaite, Ann. 2.7749
Thwaite, Anthony. 2.9429-2.9430
Thwaites, C. J. (Colin John), 1927-. 5.6790
Thwaites, Reuben Gold, 1853-1913. 3.8477
Thyssen, Fritz, 1873-1951. 3.2423
Tibawi, Abdul Latif. 4.10147
Tiberius, Emperor of Rome, 42 B.C.-37 A.D.
  2.314
Tibullus. 2.647, 2.655, 2.780
Tice, George A. 3.8069
Tice, Terrence N. ed. 1.1536
Tice, Terrence N. 1.103
Tichi, Cecelia, 1942-. 2.10345, 2.10907
Tichy, Noel M. 4.4359
Tidwell, James Nathan. ed. 2.10670
Tidwell, Sam B. 4.10665
Tidy, Michael. 3.5091
Tieck, Ludwig, 1773-1853. 2.13663-2.13664
Tiede, David Lenz. 1.2691
Tiedemann, Rolf. 1.966
Tiedt, Iris M. joint author. 4.10836
Tiedt, Pamela L. 4.10836
Tienda, Marta. 4.3612
Tienken, Robert L., comp. 4.8139
Tiepolo, Giovanni Battista, 1696-1770. 1.5816,
  1.6491
Tiepolo, Giovanni Domenico, 1726?-1804.
  1.5816, 1.6491
Tiepolo, Lorenzo, b. 1736-1776. 1.6491
Tierney, Brian. 1.2996, 1.3211, 3.575
Tietenberg, Thomas H. 4.2052
Tietze-Conrat, Erika, 1883-. 1.5813, 1.6215
Tietze, Hans, 1880-1954. 1.5813, 1.6225
Tiffin, Joseph, 1905- joint author. 4.4352
Tifft, William G., joint author. 5.1852
Tiger, Virginia. 2.8714
Tigerstedt, Eugène Napoleon, 1907-. 3.2650
Tignor, Robert L. 3.5274, 4.2615
Tilden, Freeman, 1883-. 3.6001-3.6002
Tiles, Mary. 1.826
Tilghman, Tench Francis. joint ed. 2.2548
Till, William C. 5.6541
Tiller, William A., ed. 5.5771
Tillery, Dale. joint author. 4.10565
Tillery, Dale. 4.10561
Tilley, Steven D., 1937-. 3.7015
Tillich, Paul, 1886-1965. 1.1477, 1.1508, 1.2265,
  1.2367, 1.2758, 1.2770, 1.2783, 1.2934,
  1.3282, 1.3296
Tillinghast, Pardon E. 3.407
Tillman, David A. 4.3840, 5.6872
Tillman, Seth P. 3.855, 3.3758
Tillotson, Geoffrey. 2.5555, 2.5673, 2.5713,
  2.6089, 2.7081, 2.7204, 2.7974, 2.8195-2.8196
Tillotson, Kathleen Mary. ed. 2.7624
Tillotson, Kathleen Mary. 2.6018, 2.7649
Tilly, Charles. 4.4824, 4.5086, 4.5351, 4.5357
Tilly, Charles. ed. 4.8365
Tilly, Charles. joint author. 4.3177
Tilly, Louise. joint author. 4.5351
Tilly, Louise. 4.3299
Tilly, Richard H. joint author. 4.5351
Tillyard, E. M. W. (Eustace Mandeville
  Wetenhall), 1889-1962. 2.5556-2.5557, 2.5569,
  2.5640, 2.5962, 2.6751-2.6752, 2.6773
Tilman, Rick. 4.4776
Tilton, Timothy Alan, joint author. 4.6488
Timberlake, Charles E. 4.8975
Timberlake, Craig. 2.3245
Timberlake, Michael. 4.6349
Timberlake, Richard Henry, 1922-. 4.4530
Timbrook, Janice. 3.5859
Time-Life Books. 5.2226, 5.6937, 5.7139
Times Books (Firm) 4.116, 4.125, 4.9092
Timko, Michael, 1925-. 2.7583
Timmerhaus, Klaus D. 5.6146
Timmerman, John H. 2.2395
Timms, Noel. 4.6466
Timms, Rita. 4.6466
Timoshenko, Stephen. 5.1655, 5.1673-5.1674,
  5.5747, 5.5776, 5.5780, 5.5844
Timrod, Henry, 1828-1867. 2.11258-2.11259

Tinbergen, Jan, 1903-. 4.1284, 4.2804-4.2806,
  4.4158, 4.9036
Tinbergen, Niko, 1907-. 5.3964, 5.4067-5.4068,
  5.4093, 5.4099
Tindale, Norman Barnett, 1900-. 4.667
Tindall, George Brown. 3.8166, 4.8187
Tindall, William York, 1903-. 2.2409, 2.5735,
  2.6921, 2.8866, 2.8920-2.8922, 2.8961, 2.8999,
  2.9422
Ting, K. H. 2.2150
Ting, Ling, 1904-. 2.2235
Tingley, Donald Fred, 1922-. 5.8411
Tingsten, Herbert Lars Gustaf, 1896-. 4.7103
Tinker, Chauncey Brewster, 1876-1963. 2.5674,
  2.6280-2.6281, 2.6903, 2.7363
Tinker, Hugh. 3.4297, 4.6454
Tinker, Irene. 4.5962, 4.6181
Tinker, Miles Albert, 1893-. 4.10463
Tinker, Philip Bernard Hague. joint author.
  5.5279
Tinkham, Michael. 5.2165, 5.2354
Tinklenberg, Jared R. 5.4428
Tinling, Marion, 1904-. 3.8190-3.8192
Tinoco, Ignacio. 5.3336
Tinoco, Ignacio. joint author. 5.2795
Tinsley, Elizabeth J. 5.2957
Tinsley, Ian J., 1929-. 5.3574
Tinto, Vincent. 4.10750
Tintoretto, 1512-1594. 1.6225
Tippie, Virginia K. 4.354
Tiptree, James. 2.13358
Tirion, Wil. 5.1743
Tirpitz, Alfred von, 1849-1930. 3.2357
Tirro, Frank. 1.4337
Tischler, Barbara L., 1949-. 1.3697
Tischler, Nancy Marie Patterson. 2.10562
Tischler, Steven. 4.1021
Tisdale, Samuel L. 5.5294
Tisdall, Caroline. 1.4847, 1.4988
Titchmarsh, E. C. (Edward Charles), 1899-.
  5.1339, 5.1557
Titley, Norah M. 1.6419
Titmuss, Richard Morris, 1907-1973. 4.5321
Titon, Jeff. 1.3457, 1.4315, 1.4365
Titus, David Anson, 1934-. 4.8755
Titus, Edna Mae Brown, 1900-. 5.8319
Tiusanen, Timo. 2.13735
Tiutchev, F. I. (Fedor Ivanovich), 1803-1873.
  2.1425-2.1426
Tivy, Joy. 5.3768
Tjalsma, H. W. 2.1265
Tjepkema, Sandra L., 1953-. 1.3568
Tjoa, Hock Guan, 1943-. 1.727
Tobias, Barbara. 5.8110
Tobias, J. J. (John Jacob) 4.6788
Tobias, Marilyn, 1942-. 4.10992
Tobias, Richard Clark, 1925-. 2.12590
Tobias, Sheila. 5.1061
Tobin, Dianne. 4.10915
Tobolsky, Arthur Victor. 5.2769
Toch, Hans. 4.6695, 4.6844
Tocqueville, Alexis de, 1805-1859. 3.2088,
  3.2148, 3.6039, 4.7446, 4.7842
Tod, Marcus Niebuhr, 1878- ed. 3.2565
Todd, Carl David. 5.6521
Todd, D. J. 5.6172
Todd, David Keith, 1923-. 4.308, 4.311, 5.6015
Todd, Harry F. 4.9376
Todd, Hollis N. joint author. 5.6916
Todd, Janet M., 1942-. 2.8291-2.8292
Todd, John, 1911-. 5.1428
Todd, Loreto. 2.2338
Todd, Mabel Elsworth. 5.4272
Todd, Malcom, FSA. 3.2720
Todd, Otis Johnson, tr. 2.398
Todd, Richard. 2.9776
Todd, Ruthven, 1914- ed. 1.6013
Todd, William Mills, 1944-. 2.1264
Todorov, Tsvetan, joint author. 2.11
Todorov, Tzvetan, 1939-. 1.1310, 2.84, 2.3463,
  3.5982
Todorovich, Miro. 4.10427
Tödtling, Franz. 4.3372
Toelken, Barre. 4.756
Tønnessen, J. N. (Johan Nicolay), 1901-. 5.5486
Toeplitz, Otto, 1881-1940. joint author. 5.1260
Toesca, Pietro, 1877-1962. 1.6217
Toff, Nancy. 1.4168

Toffler, Alvin. 4.5107
Toivonen, Sulo. joint author. 5.4138
Toklas, Alice B. 2.12521, 5.7136
Toklas, Alice B.. 2.12522
Tokugawa Bijutsukan. 1.4667
Tolansky, S. (Samuel), 1907-. 5.2295
Tolbert, Emory J., 1946-. 3.6836, 3.8623
Tolchin, Martin. 4.9756
Tolchin, Susan J. 4.9756
Toledo Museum of Art. 1.6009
Toliver, Harold E. 2.2753
Tolkien, J. R. R. (John Ronald Reuel),
    1892-1973. 2.6134, 2.6414, 2.9431-2.9433
Toll, Robert C. 1.4222, 2.3201
Toll, William. 3.8639
Toller, Thomas Northcote, 1844- ed. 2.945
Tolles, Frederick Barnes, 1915-. 1.3347-1.3348,
    1.3352, 3.8077
Tollison, C. David, 1949-. 5.4953
Tollison, Robert D. 4.1514
Tolman, Edward Chace, 1886-. 5.7, 5.220
Tolman, Richard Chace, 1881-1948. 5.1925,
    5.2186
Tolson, Melvin Beaunorus. 2.12593-2.12594
Tolstoĭ, Il'ia L'vovich, graf, 1866-1933. 2.1437
Tolstoy, Aleksey Nikolayevich, 1883-1945.
    2.1608-2.1609
Tolstoy, Leo, graf, 1828-1910. 1.4617,
    2.1429-2.1432
Tolstoy, Nikolai. 3.3032
Toma, Peter A. 3.1945
Tomalin, Claire. 2.8293
Toman, Walter. 5.587
Tomasevich, Jozo, 1908-. 3.3567
Tomasi di Lampedusa, Giuseppe, 1896-1957.
    2.5072
Tomaskovic-Devey, Donald, 1957-. 4.2014
Tomassini, Luciano. 4.4726
Tomazinis, Anthony R. 5.5933
Tombaugh, Clyde William, 1906-. 5.1821
Tombs, Robert. 3.2169
Tomczak, M., 1941-. 5.3563
Tomek, Ivan. 5.1230
Tomes, G. J. 5.5449
Tomeski, Edward Alexander. 5.1128
Tomiak, J. J. 4.10135
Tomimoto, Kenkichi, 1886-1963. 5.6899
Tomita, Shigeaki, ed. 5.8398
Tomkins, Mary E. 2.12570
Tomkins, Silvan Solomon, 1911-. 5.414
Tomlin, Brian W. joint author. 3.8780
Tomlinson, Andrew, tr. 5.575
Tomlinson, Charles, 1927-. 2.1425, 2.3745,
    2.9436-2.9438, 2.12204
Tomlinson, H. M. (Henry Major), 1873-1958.
    2.9439
Tomlinson, Joan, tr. 5.575
Tomory, William M. 2.9159
Tompkins, E. Berkeley, 1935-. 3.7604
Tompkins, Eugene. 2.3218
Tompkins, J. M. S. (Joyce Marjorie Sanxter),
    1897-. 2.5998, 2.7895
Tompkins, Jane P. 2.2487, 2.10584
Tompkins, Jane P. comp. 2.11128
Tompkins, Keitha, ed. 4.7182
Tompson, Benjamin, 1642-1714. 2.10877
Tompson, Richard S. 4.10115
Toner, Amy. 5.6394
Tong, Rosemarie. 4.9865
Tonghwa Ch'ulp'ansa. 1.5081
Tönnies, Ferdinand, 1855-1936. 4.4858, 4.6963
Toole, John Kennedy, 1937-1969. 2.13359
Toole, K. Ross (Kenneth Ross), 1920-1981.
    3.8547
Tooley, Michael, 1941-. 4.5699
Tooley, R. V. (Ronald Vere), 1898-. 4.223,
    4.229
Toomer, Jean, 1894-1967. 2.12597-2.12598
Toomey, Deirdre. 1.6453
Toong, Hoo-min D. 5.1140
Tooze, John. 5.3461
Topham, J. 2.10705
Topkis, Gladys S. 5.7568
Toplin, Robert Brent, 1940-. 4.6439
Topoff, Howard R. ed. 5.3888
Tops, Guy A. J. 2.1172-2.1173
Topsfield, L. T. 2.3952
Tordoff, William. 4.8791, 4.8797

Torgerson, Warren S. 5.58
Torney-Purta, Judith, 1937-. 4.5733
Toro, Carlos E. 4.3969
Toronto Public Library. 5.7896
Torrance, Thomas Forsyth, 1913-. 1.2773,
    5.2363
Torre, Susana, 1944-. 1.5459
Torrence, Ridgely, 1875-1950. 2.12402
Torrence, Robin. 3.262
Torrence, Susan Walker. 4.8857
Torrens, Paul R. (Paul Roger), 1934-. 5.4623
Torrens, R. (Robert), 1780-1864. 4.1421
Torres, Sergio. 1.3227
Torretti, Roberto, 1930-. 5.2092
Torrey, Norman L. (Norman Lewis), 1894-
    joint ed. 2.3919
Torricelli, Evangelista, 1608-1647. 5.2035
Torrielli, Andrew Joseph, 1912-. 3.6170
Tortora, Gerard J. 5.4197
Tosh, John. 3.5267
Toss, Brion. 5.7515
Total Environmental Action, Inc. 5.6106
Toth, L. M. (Louis McKenna), 1941-. 5.6302
Tóth-Ubbens, Magdi. joint author. 1.6255
Totman, Conrad D. 3.4913, 3.4943-3.4944,
    3.4954
Tottel, Richard, d. 1594. 2.6150
Tottle, C. R. 5.6764
Toulmin, Stephen Edelston. 1.1240-1.1242,
    1.1343, 1.1411, 5.936-5.937
Toulmin, Stephen Edelston. ed. 1.88
Touloukian, Y. S. (Yeram Sarkis), 1918-. 5.3038
Toulouse-Lautrec, Henri de, 1864-1901. 1.6152,
    1.6502
Touraine, Alain. 4.3663
Touring Club Italiano. 4.117
Tourneur, Cyril, 1575?-1626. 2.6876
Tournier, Michel. 2.4793
Tourtellot, Arthur Bernon. 3.6993
Toussaint, Manuel, 1895-1955. 1.4920
Tout, Thomas Frederick, 1855-1929. 3.1366
Touval, Saadia. 3.3884
Tovell, Rosemarie L. 1.6449
Tovey, Donald Francis, Sir, 1875-1940.
    1.3480-1.3481, 1.3807, 1.4186, 1.4479, 1.4505,
    1.4532
Tovey, John. 1.4848
Tow, William T. 3.3634, 5.7335
Tower, Margene. joint author. 5.4696
Towers, T. D., 1914-. 5.6476
Towle, Charlotte. 4.6483
Towner, Lawrence W. joint author. 4.235
Townes, Charles H. 5.2316
Townsend, Charles R. 1.4063
Townsend, Colin R. 5.3514
Townsend, E. Reginald, ed. 3.5416
Townsend, Harvey Gates, 1885-1948. 1.560
Townsend, James Benjamin, 1918-. 2.7621
Townsend, James R. (James Roger) 4.8737,
    4.8742
Townsend, Peter, 1928-. 4.2309
Towsen, John H. 4.1194
Toy, Wing N., 1926- joint author. 5.6581
Toye, Francis, 1883-. 1.3961, 1.4026
Toye, Hugh. 3.4457
Toye, William. 2.9879
Toynbee, Arnold, 1889-1975. 1.2266, 4.2269
Toynbee, Arnold Joseph, 1889-1975. 1.1541,
    3.18, 3.34-3.35, 3.103, 3.207, 3.747, 3.862,
    3.2523, 3.2670, 3.2682, 3.2733, 3.4646,
    3.6171, 5.7147
Toynbee, J. M. C. (Jocelyn M. C.), d. 1985.
    1.4729-1.4730, 1.5639, 1.5787, 3.2740, 5.3809
Toynbee, Paget Jackson, 1855-1932. 2.4932,
    2.7055
Toynbee, Philip. 2.9440, 3.18
Trabasso, Tom. 2.1157
Tracey, Esther M., joint author. 1.5155
Tracey, R. J., joint author. 4.162
Tracey, William R. 4.4377
Trachtenberg, Alan. 2.10403, 2.11527, 3.6172
Trachtenberg, Marc, 1946-. 3.856
Tracor Jitco, Inc. 5.4725
Tracy, Berry B. 1.6567
Tracy, Clarence Rupert. ed. 2.7052, 2.7237
Tracy, David. 1.2759, 1.2784, 1.3169
Tracy, Honor, 1915-. 2.9826-2.9827
Trafton, Dain A. 2.4981

Trafzer, Clifford E. 3.5777
Trager, Frank N. 5.8057
Trager, Frank N. ed. 3.4408
Trager, George Leonard, 1906-. 2.144
Tragesser, Robert S., 1943-. 1.98
Trahanovsky, Walter S., 1938-. 5.2750
Traherne, Philip, d.1723. 2.7320
Traherne, Thomas, d. 1674. 1.3074, 2.7320
Traill, H. D. (Henry Duff), 1842-1900. 2.7544
Traina, Richard P. 3.6497
Trainer, James. 2.7211
Trainor, Lynn E. H., 1921-. 5.1973
Traister, John E. 5.6448
Traister, Robert J. 5.6448
Trakl, Georg, 1887-1914. 2.13864-2.13865
Tran, Van Dinh, 1923-. 2.13360
Tran, Van Tra. 3.4438
Transtroemer, Tomas, 1931-. 2.14062
Tranter, William H. joint author. 5.6360
Trapnell, Edward R., joint author. 4.3812
Trapp, Frank. 1.6096
Trask, Anne E., joint author. 4.10670
Trask, David F. 3.829, 3.7503, 5.8261
Trask, Roger R. joint author. 5.8261
Trattner, Walter I. 4.6521, 5.8360
Traube, Alex, 1946-. 3.8577
Traubel, Horace, 1858-1919. 2.11271
Traubner, Richard. 1.4231
Traugott, Elizabeth Closs. 2.1031
Traugott, Michael W. 4.8116
Traulos, Iōannēs N., 1908-. 1.5223
Trautmann, Joanne. 2.9586
Traver, Robert, 1903-. 2.13361
Travis, David, 1948-. 5.6929
Travis, Lee Edward, 1896- ed. 5.4791
Travis, Peter W. 2.5857
Trawick, Buckner B. 2.7578
Treadgold, Donald W., 1922-. 3.3068, 3.3138,
    3.3170, 4.2869
Treash, Gordon. 1.912
Treasure, G. R. R. (Geoffrey Russell Richards)
    3.2026
Trebat, Thomas J. 4.3087
Trebilcock, Clive. 4.2212
Trebilcot, Joyce. 4.5670
Tredell, Nicolas. 2.9830
Tredennick, Hugh, tr. 2.346-2.347
Treece, Henry. 2.9441-2.9443
Trefil, James S., 1938-. 5.1689, 5.1882, 5.2037,
    5.2432
Trefny, Beverly Robin, 1945-. 2.2787
Trefousse, Hans Louis. 3.1016, 3.7164, 3.7266,
    3.7450
Tregaskis, Richard, 1916-1973. 3.1018
Tregear, Mary. 1.6620
Tregear, T. R. (Thomas R.) 3.4623
Treglown, Jeremy. 2.7228, 2.7232
Tregoe, Benjamin B. joint author. 4.2665
Tregonning, K. G. 3.4582
Treharne, R. F. (Reginald Francis), 1901-1967.
    3.1361, 4.122
Treiman, Donald J. 4.3260
Treitschke, Heinrich Gotthard von, 1834-1896.
    3.2293-3.2294, 4.7453
Trejo, Arnulfo D. 5.7864
Trelawny, Edward John, 1792-1881. 2.8199
Trelease, Allen W. 3.7474
Trelease, Jim. 4.10467
Tremaine, Marie. 5.7896
Tremblay, Michel, 1943-. 2.4832
Treml, Vladimir G. 5.8016
Trend, John Brande, 1887-. 2.5117
Trendall, A. D. (Arthur Dale), 1909-. 1.5166
Trenn, Thaddeus J. 5.798
Trenner, Richard. 2.12991
Trensky, Paul I. 2.1656, 2.1660
Trent, Darrell Melvin, 1938- joint author.
    4.6712
Trent, James W. 4.10516
Trent, Judith S. 4.7737
Très riches heures du duc de Berry. 1.6428
Trescott, Paul B. 4.4523
Treseder, Neil G. 5.5352
Treseler, Kathleen Morrison. 5.5176
Treshow, Michael. 5.3748
Tressell, Robert, 1870-1911. 2.9444

Trethowan, Illtyd, 1907- tr. 1.383
Trevelyan, George Macaulay, 1876-1962.
    3.1243, 3.1371, 3.1447, 3.1513, 3.1537,
    3.1586, 3.1634, 3.2872-3.2873, 3.2935
Trevelyan, George Otto, Sir, 1838-1928. 3.6906
Trevelyan, Hannah More (Macaulay) Lady,
    1810-1873, ed. 2.7918
Trevelyan, Janet Penrose (Ward), 1879-. 3.2837
Trèves, François, 1930-. 5.1525
Treves, Marco, joint ed. and tr. 1.4643
Trevor, Elleston. 2.9445
Trevor-Roper, H. R. (Hugh Redwald), 1914-.
    3.365, 3.2383, 3.2407
Trewartha, Glenn Thomas, 1896-. 3.4882,
    4.1597, 4.1625, 5.2567-5.2568
Trewin, J. C. (John Courtenay), 1908-. 2.3313,
    2.5841, 2.6860, 2.6871
Trexler, Richard C., 1932-. 3.2924
Treybal, Robert Ewald, 1915-. 5.6845
Triandis, Harry Charalambos, 1926-. 4.622
Tribe, Laurence H. 4.9630
Trible, Phyllis. 1.2571
Tricart, Jean. 4.265, 4.285
Trice, Harrison Miller, 1920-. 4.4370
Triche, Charles W. 5.8290
Triche, Diane Samson, joint author. 5.8290
Trickett, Rachel, 1923-. 2.5654
Triebel, Walter A. 5.1227
Triffin, Robert. 4.4511, 4.4570
Trifonov, IUrii Valentinovich, 1925-.
    2.1642-2.1643
Trigault, Nicolas, 1577-1628. 1.3244
Trigg, George L. 5.1889, 5.2190
Trigg, Joseph Wilson, 1949-. 1.2212
Trigger, Bruce G. 3.235, 3.259, 3.5151, 3.5180,
    3.5730, 3.5891-3.5892
Triggs, Stanley. ed. 3.8660
Trigo, Eduardo. 5.5256
Trilateral Commission. 4.7559
Trilling, Diana. ed. 2.8960
Trilling, Lionel, 1905-1975. 2.2598, 2.7347,
    2.7355, 2.8668, 2.12600-2.12603
Trimingham, J. Spencer (John Spencer), 1904-.
    1.2006-1.2007
Trimpi, Wesley. 2.6604
Tringham, Ruth. 4.709
Trinity College (Dublin) 1.4943
Trinkaus, Charles Edward, 1911-. 3.164
Trinkaus, Erik. 4.456
Trinterud, Leonard J., 1904-. 1.3390
Tripathi, Bansi Dhar. 1.1719
Tripathi, Surya Kant, 1896-1961. 2.1893
Triplett, Jack E. 4.3147
Tripodi, Tony. 4.6465
Tripp, Edward. 1.1601
Tripp, Rhoda Thomas. 2.3731
Tripp, Richard B., joint author. 4.351
Trippensee, Reuben Edwin, 1894-. 5.5494
Triska, Jan F. 4.3629, 4.9072
Triska, Jan F. jt. author. 4.8979
Tristan. 2.3967
Trittschuh, Travis, jt. author. 4.7796
Troeller, Gary. 3.4055
Troeltsch, Ernst, 1865-1923. 4.5116, 4.7275
Trofimenkoff, Susan Mann, 1941-. 3.8816
Troide, Lars E., 1942-. 2.7332
Troili, Giulio, 1613-1685. 2.3152
Trojanowicz, Robert C., 1941-. 4.6827
Troland, Leonard Thompson, 1889-. 5.4294
Troll, Carl, 1890-. 4.131
Troll, Christian W., 1937-. 1.2021
Trollope, Anthony, 1815-1882. 2.8190,
    2.8200-2.8227, 2.8229-2.8230, 3.6048
Trollope, Frances (Milton), 1780-1863. 2.8242,
    3.6041-3.6042
Trollope, Henry Meripale, 1846-. 2.8230
Tromberg, Sheldon. 2.3019
Trompf, G. W. 3.500
Troper, Harold Martin, 1942-. 3.8796
Troppmann, Robert. joint author. 4.907
Trotman-Dickenson, A. F., ed. 5.2697
Trotsky, Leon, 1879-1940. 2.1277, 3.3149,
    3.3154, 3.3171, 3.3197, 3.3235, 3.4757, 4.6974
Trotter, James M. 1.3751
Trotter, Joe William, 1945-. 4.3609
Trotter, Robert T. 4.782
Trotter, William Finlayson, 1871- tr. 1.805
Troupe, Quincy. 2.3702

Trout, Charles H. 3.7995
Troxell, Janet Camp. 2.8006
Troy, Leo. 4.4411
Troy, Nancy J. 1.5021
Troy, Thomas F. 4.7914
Troyat, Henri, 1911-. 2.1417, 2.1438
Troyen, Carol. 1.6378
Troyer, Henry. 5.3621
Truax, Charles B. 5.4859
Trubetskoĭ, Nikolaĭ Sergeevich, kniaz',
    1890-1938. 2.178, 2.1194
Truchet, Jacques. comp. 2.3934
Trudeau, Pierre Elliott. 4.8281
Trudel, Jean, 1940- joint author. 1.6000
Trudgill, Peter. 2.212
Trueb, Linda. 5.3930
Trueblood, Kenneth N. 5.2932
Truett, Carol, 1942-. 4.10299
Truettner, William H. 1.5926
Truffaut, François, 2.2893, 2.3056
Truffaut, François. ed. 2.3063
Trullinger, James Walker. 3.4513
Truman, D. E. S. (Donald Ernest Samuel),
    1936-. 5.3618
Truman, David Bicknell, 1913-. 4.8018, 4.8037
Truman, Harry S., 1884-1972. 3.7804,
    3.7806-3.7807, 3.7813
Trumbull, John, 1750-1831. 1.5978, 2.10878
Trumbull, Robert. 3.5549
Trump, David H. joint author. 3.120
Trump, J. Lloyd, 1908-. 4.10495
Trungpa, Chogyam, 1939-. 1.2172
Trunk, Isaiah. 3.1121-3.1122
Trunz, Erich. 2.13568
Truong, Nhu Tang. 4.4470
Truscott, Alan F. ed. 4.1066
Trussler, Simon. 2.6237, 2.9215
Truxal, John G. 5.5692
Tryon, Alice F. 5.3700
Tryon, Rolla Milton, 1916-. 5.3700
Trypanis, C. A. (Constantine Athanasius),
    1909-. 2.278
Ts'ao, Che'eng-hsiu. 2.2147
Ts'ao, Hsüeh-ch'in, ca. 1717-1763. 2.2233
Tschebotarioff, Gregory Porphyriewitch, 1899-.
    5.5920
Tschichold, Jan, 1902-1974. 1.6477
Tschiževskij, Dmitrij, 1894-. 1.2457, 2.1196,
    2.1247, 2.1257, 2.1651
Tschudi-Madsen, Stephan, 1923-. 1.4929
Tschudy, Robert H. 5.3178
Tsiang, Katherine R. 1.6622
Tsiaras, Alexander. 4.869
TSK KPSS. 4.8658
Ts'o, Paul O. P. (Paul On Pong), 1929-. 5.2796
Tsou, Tang, 1918-. 3.4780, 3.4786
Tsoulfanidis, Nicholas, 1938-. 5.2487
Tsouvelli, Voula. 2.420
Tsuboi, Chūji, 1902-. 5.1760
Tsuchigane, Robert. 4.3294
Tsuchiya, Henry Mitsumara. 5.3725
Tsuji, Masatsugu, 1894-1960. 5.1499
Tsujimoto, Karen. 1.5912
Tsukamoto, Zenryū, 1898-. 1.2117
Tsunoda, Ryusaku. 3.4931
Tsunoda, Ryūsaku, ed. 3.4895
Tsurumi, E. Patricia, 1938-. 4.10140
Tsurumi, Kazuko, 1918-. 4.5452
Tsurumi, Rebecca R. joint author. 4.4194
Tsurumi, Yoshi. 4.3062, 4.4194
Tsurutani, Taketsugu. 4.8758, 5.7342
Tsushima, Yūko. 2.2135
Tsuzaki, Stanley M., ed. 2.215
TSvetaeva, Marina, 1892-1941. 2.1610-2.1611
TSytovich, N. A. (Nikolaĭ Aleksandrovich)
    5.5912
Tu, Fu, 712-770. 2.2212
Tu, Loring W. 5.1615
Tubman, William V. S., 1895-1971. 3.5416
Tucci, Giuseppe, 1894-. 1.1809, 1.1822, 3.4857
Tuchman, Barbara Wertheim. 3.615, 3.777,
    3.792, 3.7614
Tuchman, Mitch. 1.4878
Tuchmann-Duplessis, Herbert. 5.4167
Tucholsky, Kurt, 1890-1935. 2.13866
Tuck, Donald H. (Donald Henry) 5.8176
Tucker, Alan, 1943 July 6-. 5.1279, 5.1287
Tucker, Barbara M. 4.3862

Tucker, David. 4.3795
Tucker, David M., 1937-. 3.6843, 4.8867
Tucker, Gene M. 1.2567
Tucker, Gilbert Norman, 1898-1955. 4.2119
Tucker, Herbert F. 2.7494
Tucker, Martin. joint comp. 2.5740
Tucker, Martin. 2.9877
Tucker, Nancy Bernkopf. 3.6435
Tucker, Patricia, joint author. 5.491
Tucker, Robert C. 1.1042, 3.3236, 4.6947,
    4.6964, 4.7094
Tucker, Robert W. 4.9319
Tucker, Robert W. ed. 4.9296
Tuckerman, Frederick Goddard, 1821-1873.
    2.11261
Tuckey, John Sutton, 1921-. 2.10940
Tuden, Arthur, ed. 4.5464
Tudesq, André Jean. 3.2144
Tudor, Andrew, 1942-. 2.2970
Tudor, Dean. 1.3621
Tuerck, David G. joint author. 4.4199
Tuetey, Charles Greville, 1930-. 2.1839
Tuffrau, Paul, 1887-. 2.3825, 2.3827
Tufts, Eleanor. 1.5195
Tufts University. School of Medicine. 5.4708
Tugwell, Franklin, 1942- comp. 3.69
Tugwell, Rexford G. (Rexford Guy), 1891-.
    3.7749, 3.7784-3.7785, 4.7788, 4.7806
Tulasīdāsa, 1532-1623. 2.1886
Tulchin, Joseph S., 1939- ed. 3.7437
Tulchinsky, Gerald J. J., 1933-. 4.2130
Tulis, Jeffrey. 4.7930
Tull, Donald S. joint author. 4.4304
Tullock, Gordon. joint author. 4.7565
Tullock, Gordon. 4.1514, 4.7762
Tulpule, Shankar Gopal, 1914-. 2.1907
Tulving, Endel. 5.337
Tuma, Jan J. 5.2013
Tumarkin, Nina. 3.3152
Tumin, Melvin Marvin, 1919-. 4.5265, 4.6385
Tuncel, Selim. 5.1463
Tung, Chieh-yüan, fl. 1189-1208. 2.2219
Tunin, G. I. (Grigoriĭ Ivanovich) 4.8982
Tunnard, Christopher. 1.5600, 4.6230
Tunnell, Jane C., ed. 2.10905
Tunstall, Jeremy. 2.55, 2.62
Tuominen, Arvo, 1894-. 4.7095
Tupper, Allan, 1950-. 4.3086
Tupper, Charles, Sir, 1821-1915. 3.8764
Tupper, Harmon. 4.4022
Tūqān, Fawwāz. tr. 2.1844
Turabian, Kate L. 4.10619
Turbayne, Colin Murray. 1.691
Turberville, Arthur Stanley, 1888-1945. 1.2312,
    3.1533
Turgenev, Ivan Sergeevich, 1818-1883.
    2.1447-2.1461
Turiel, Isaac. 5.4670
Turk, Amos. joint author. 5.2638
Türk, Daniel Gottlob, 1750-1813. 1.4540
Turkington, Darrell A. 4.1394
Turleau, Catherine. 5.4739
Turley, C. David, joint author. 5.6049
Turnbull, Andrew. 2.11724-2.11725, 2.11740,
    2.12797
Turnbull, Ann P., 1947-. 4.6581
Turnbull, Colin M. 3.5418, 3.5421
Turnbull, Eleanor L. (Eleanor Laurelle) ed. and
    tr. 2.5154
Turnbull, Eleanor L. (Eleanor Laurelle) ed.
    2.5151
Turnbull, Grace Hill, 1880- ed. 1.340
Turnbull, H. Rutherford. 4.6581
Turnbull, Harvey. 1.4178
Turnbull, Philip. joint author. 4.10681
Turnell, Martin. 2.3887, 2.3895-2.3897, 2.4146
Turner, Arlin. 2.10921, 2.10923, 2.11065
Turner, B. L. (Billie Lee), 1925-. 5.3650
Turner, Bryan S. joint author. 4.4966
Turner, Bryan S. 1.2075, 4.4768
Turner, Bryan Stanley. 4.2427
Turner, Clarence Donnell, 1903-. 5.4248
Turner, D. H. 1.4935
Turner, Darwin T., 1931-. 2.10331, 2.10817,
    2.12598, 5.7879
Turner, Donald F. joint author. 4.3057
Turner, Dorothea, 1910-. 2.10228
Turner, Francis J. 5.3041, 5.3073, 5.3127

Turner, Francis John, 1904-. 5.3049
Turner, Francis Joseph, 1929-. 4.6475, 4.6494
Turner, Frederick Jackson, 1861-1932. 3.6326, 3.6359, 3.7083, 3.8476
Turner, Frederick W., 1937- comp. 3.5709
Turner, Henry Ashby. 3.2377, 4.3072
Turner, J. M. W. (Joseph Mallord William), 1775-1851. 1.6038, 1.6041
Turner, James, 1946-. 1.1886
Turner, Jonathan H. 4.4813, 4.5192
Turner, Julius. 4.8177
Turner, Justin G. 3.7290
Turner, Linda Lovitt, joint author. 3.7290
Turner, Lynn W. 3.7010, 3.7964
Turner, Mary, 1931-. 4.6436
Turner, Nat, 1800?-1831. 2.13339
Turner, Paul, 1917-. 2.8182
Turner, Ralph H. ed. 4.4837
Turner, Ralph V. 4.9426
Turner, Raymond, 1947-. 5.1016
Turner, Rodney J., joint author. 5.4466
Turner, Roland. 5.5664
Turner, Samuel M., 1944-. 5.4822
Turner, Thomas Reed, 1941-. 3.7297
Turner, Victor Witter. 3.5522-3.5523, 4.539, 4.559
Turner, W. Craig. 2.10652
Turner, Wayne C., 1942-. 5.6125
Turow, Joseph. 4.5013
Turow, Scott. 4.9493
Turowetz, Allan. 4.5076
Turro, Nicholas J., 1938-. 5.2917
Turtledove, Harry. 3.518
Turvey, Ralph. 4.3797
Turville-Petre, Gabriel. 2.13974, 2.13977
Turville-Petre, Thorlac. 2.955
Tusiani, Joseph, 1924- tr. 2.4983
Tuska, Jon. 2.2981, 3.8558
Tuskegee Institute. 5.4606
Tuso, Joseph F. 2.6291
Tussing, A. Dale. 4.2102
Tute, Warren. 3.962
Tuteur, Franz B., joint author. 5.6357
Tutko, Thomas A. 4.970
Tutorow, Norman E. 5.7835
Tuttle, Dean W. 4.6598
Tuttle, Frederick B. 4.10914
Tuttle, William M., 1937-. 3.8427
Tuttleton, James W. 2.10540, 2.11107
Tutuola, Amos. 2.10117-2.10118
Tuve, George Lewis. ed. 5.5666
Tuve, Rosemond, 1903-1964. 2.2657, 2.5618, 2.5793, 2.7159
Tuveson, Ernest Lee. 3.6282
Tuwim, Julian, 1894-1953. 2.1733
Tver, David F. 4.322, 5.6798
Twain, Mark, 1835-1910. 2.10935-2.10942, 2.10946-2.10949, 3.5637, 3.8301, 3.8624
Twelve southerners. 3.8121
Twentieth Century Fund. 3.6479, 4.1795, 4.1973, 4.2435, 4.3012, 4.3085, 4.4685
Twentieth Century Fund. Committee on Cartels and Monopoly. 4.3013
Twentieth Century Fund. Task Force on Federal Elementary and Secondary Education Policy. 4.10662
Twentieth Century Fund. Task Force on the Future of New York City. 4.2047
Twersky, Isadore. 1.1946
Twersky, Isadore. ed. 1.1961
Twinam, Ann, 1946-. 4.2178
Twitchett, Denis Crispin. 3.4663
Twohig, Dorothy. 3.7036
Twyman, Michael. 1.6500
Twyman, Robert W., 1919-. 3.8113
Tyack, David B. 4.10640, 4.10738, 4.10832, 4.10965
Tydeman, John. 5.6566
Tydeman, William. 2.3171, 2.6219
Tygiel, Jules. 4.1004
Tylecote, R. F. 5.6759
Tyler, Albert, 1906- joint ed. 5.3588
Tyler, Anne. 2.13362
Tyler, Gary R. 5.7801
Tyler, James. 1.4179
Tyler, John K. 5.2801
Tyler, Leona Elizabeth, 1906-. 5.59, 5.498

Tyler, Moses Coit, 1835-1900. 2.10365-2.10366
Tyler, Parker. 2.2988
Tyler, Ralph Winfred, 1902-. 4.10453
Tyler, Ronnie C., 1941-. 1.6450
Tyler, Royall, 1757-1826. 2.10880
Tyler, Stephen A., 1932-. 3.4187
Tylor, Edward Burnett, Sir, 1832-1917. 4.431, 4.522
Tymn, Marshall B., 1937-. 2.3453, 2.3485, 2.5969, 5.7971, 5.8174
Tyn Myint U. 5.1526
Tynan, Kenneth, 1927-. 2.2476
Tyree, Melvin T. 5.3683
Tyrnauer, Gabrielle. 4.6904
Tyrrell, John. 1.3906
Tyrrell, Joseph M. 3.2005
Tyrrell, R. Emmett. 4.7033
Tyrrell, Robert Yelverton, 1844-1914. ed. 2.714
Tyrrell, William Blake. 1.1665
Tyson, Alan. 1.3799, 1.3809
Tyson, Joseph B. 1.2300
Tyson, Laura D'Andrea, 1947-. 4.2423
Tyson, W. J. (William James), 1946- joint author. 4.3899
Tytell, John. 2.10430
Tzafestas, S. G., 1939-. 5.6188
Tzagoloff, Alexander, 1937-. 5.3613
Tzannes, N. S. (Nicolaos S.), 1937-. 5.6437
Tzara, Tristan, 1896-1963. 2.4759-2.4760

U.S. Atomic Energy Commission. 5.2427
U.S. Bureau of Mines. 5.6720
U.S. Civilian Production Administration. 4.1971
U.S. Commission on Obscenity and Pornography. 4.5543
U.S. Congress. Senate. Committee on Armed Services. 3.5023
U. S. Dept. of Agriculture. Agricultural History Branch. 5.5216
U.S. Dept. of State. 3.6436
U.S. Dept. of the Army. Office of Military History. 3.1021
U.S. Fish and Wildlife Service. 5.3263
U.S. National Aeronautics and Space Administration. Scientific and Technical Information Branch. 5.6648
U.S. National Commission on the Causes and Prevention of Violence. 4.5156
U.S. News Books. 5.4149
U.S. President's Commission for the Observance of Human Rights Year, 1968. 4.10008
U.S. President's Commission on an All-Volunteer Armed Force. 5.7365
U.S. President's Commission on Law Enforcement and Administration of Justice. 4.6767
U.S. Strategic Bombing Survey. 3.1007
U.S. Task Force on Demonstrations, Protests, and Group Violence. 4.5163
U.S. Treasury Dept. 4.4590
Ubbelohde, Carl. 3.8557
Uccello, Paolo di Dono, known as, 1396 or 7-1475. 1.6228
Uchino, Tatsurō, 1925-. 4.2557
Udall, Nicholas, 1505-1556. 2.6219, 2.6877
Udall, Stewart L. 5.5303
Udovitch, Abraham L. 4.2440
Udvardy, Miklos D. F., 1919-. 5.3958
Ueda, Akinari, 1734-1809. 2.2066-2.2068
Ueda, Makoto, 1931-. 2.1994, 2.2002, 2.2009
Ueda, Taizo. 4.2549
Uehling, Theodore Edward. 1.467
Uglow, Jennifer S. 3.350
Ugural, A. C. 5.5781
Uhlan, Miriam. 5.8369
Uhland, Ludwig, 1787-1862. 2.13665
Uhlendorf, Bernhard Alexander, 1893-. 5.7756
Uhlmann, D. R. (Donald Robert) joint author. 5.6900
Ujfalussy, József. 1.3793
Ujifusa, Grant, joint author. 4.7851
Ujifusa, Grant. 4.7995
Ulaby, Fawwaz T. (Fawwaz Tayssir), 1943-. 4.29
Ulak, James T. 1.5076
Ulam, Adam Bruno, 1922-. 3.3111, 3.3128, 3.3139, 3.3210, 3.3237, 3.3267, 3.3566, 3.6489, 4.6940

Ulam, Stanislaw M. 5.1099
Ulanov, Ann Belford. 1.1570, 4.5945, 5.432
Ulanov, Barry. 1.4338, 5.432
Ulanov, Barry. joint author. 1.1570
Ulich, Robert, 1890-. 4.9946, 4.9951, 4.9957
Ullathorne, William Bernard, Abp., 1806-1889. 1.3121
Ullendorff, Edward. 3.5240, 3.5247
Ullman, B. L. (Berthold Louis), 1882-1965. 5.7532
Ullman, Edward Louis, 1912-1976. 4.80, 4.3890
Ullman, Jeffrey D., 1942-. 5.1159, 5.1200, 5.1226, 5.1238, 5.1240, 5.1371
Ullman, Marsha Davis. 4.10982
Ullman, Michael, 1945-. 1.4259
Ullman, Montague. 5.656
Ullman, Richard H. (Richard Henry) joint author. 4.9000
Ullmann, John. 2.3567
Ullmann, John E. 5.5703
Ullmann, Lisa. 2.3133
Ullmann, Manfred. 5.4514
Ullmann, Stephen. 2.200-2.201, 2.1067, 2.3898
Ullmann, Walter, 1910-. 1.391, 1.3147-1.3148, 1.3155, 3.165, 4.7373
Ulloa, Antonio de, 1716-1795. 3.9152, 3.9302
Ullom, Harry Herbert,ed. 3.8324
Ullyot, Joan, 1940-. 4.1052
Ulman, Joseph N. 5.5508
Ulman, Lloyd. 4.2214, 4.3371
Ulrich, Carolyn Farquhar, 1881-. 2.3580, 5.8314
Ulrich, Celeste. 4.901
Ulrich, Gael D. 5.6836
Ulrich, Homer, 1906-. 1.4187, 1.4194
Ulysses S. Grant Association. 3.7403
Umans, Stephen D. 5.6308
Umbreit, John. 5.5092
Umbreit, Wayne William, 1913-. 5.4219
Umphlett, Wiley Lee, 1931-. 2.10543
Unamuno, Miguel de, 1864-1936. 1.1133-1.1134, 1.2261, 2.5113, 2.5182, 2.5285-2.5289
Unbegaun, Boris Ottokar, 1898-1973. 2.1226, 2.1231, 2.1237
Underdown, David. 3.1487
Underhill, Evelyn, 1875-1941. 1.2979, 1.3091
Underhill, Frank Hawkins, 1889-. 3.8677, 4.8427
Underhill, Ruth Murray, 1884-. 1.4310, 3.5935
Underhill, Stefan. 4.3064
Underwood, Benton J., 1915-. 5.211, 5.338
Underwood, Dale. 2.7013
Underwood, Geoffrey. 5.310, 5.393
Underwood, James E. 4.8263
Underwood, Jane Hainline. 4.459
Underwood, Paul Atkins. 1.5538
Undset, Sigrid. 2.14052-2.14053
Unekis, Joseph K. 4.7999
Unesco. 1.79, 1.6310, 1.6336, 1.6486-1.6487, 3.104, 3.5071, 4.36, 4.296, 4.5015, 4.9387, 4.10933, 5.955, 5.8374
Unesco. Division of Statistics on Culture and Communication. 4.4056
Unesco. International Scientific Committee for the Drafting of a General History of Africa. 3.5072
Ungar, Sanford J. 3.7910
Ungaretti, Giuseppe, 1880-1970. 2.5073-2.5076
Unger, Aryeh L. 4.8642
Unger, Debi. joint author. 4.10095
Unger, Hans-Georg, 1926-. 5.5961
Unger, Helga. 2.13639
Unger, Irwin. 4.4509, 4.10095
Unger, Jonathan. 4.5457, 4.10139
Unger, Leonard. ed. 2.10278
Unger, Leonard. 2.11644
Unger, Rhoda Kesler. 4.5832, 4.5947
Unger, Richard, 1939-. 2.13614
Unger, Roberto Mangabeira. 4.5034
Ungerer, Horst. 4.4512
Union of American Biological Societies. 5.3289
Union of Concerned Scientists. 5.6056
Union of International Associations. 4.9103
United Kingdom Atomic Energy Authority. Research Group. 5.5752
United Media Enterprises. 4.883
United Nations. 4.1832, 4.9202, 4.9205, 4.9223, 5.1786, 5.8114, 5.8268

United Nations. Bureau of Economic Affairs. 4.1780

United Nations. Bureau of Social Affairs. 4.1703

United Nations. Centre for Development Planning, Projections, and Policies. 4.1780

United Nations Conference on the Exploration and Peaceful Uses of Outer Space. (2nd: 1982: Vienna, Austria) 5.1786

United Nations Conference on the Human Environment (1972: Stockholm, Sweden) 4.374

United Nations. Conference on the Human Environment, Stockholm, 1972. 4.1850

United Nations Conference on the Law of the Sea. (3rd: 1973-1982: New York, N.Y., etc.) 4.9316

United Nations. Dept. of Economic Affairs. 4.1238

United Nations. Dept. of Economic and Social Affairs. 4.1238, 4.1578, 4.1641, 4.2429, 4.2736

United Nations. Dept. of International Economic and Social Affairs. 4.1238

United Nations. Dept. of Public Information. 4.9201-4.9202

United Nations. Dept. of Social Affairs. 4.1238

United Nations. Economic Commission for Africa. 4.2604

United Nations. Economic Commission for Asia and the Far East. 4.2429

United Nations. Economic Commission for Europe. 5.6154

United Nations Educational, Scientific and Cultural Organization. Annuaire statistique. 1.79

United Nations. General Assembly. 4.9199, 4.9205, 4.9246

United Nations Institute for Training and Research. 4.2750, 4.4157, 4.9250

United Nations. Ocean Economics and Technology Branch. 4.6359

United Nations Research Institute for Social Development. 4.2901

United Nations. Secretariat. 4.1256

United Nations. Statistical Office. 4.1237-4.1238, 4.1401, 4.4091, 4.4115, 5.6119

United Nations. Statistical Office. Dept. of Economic and Social Affairs. 4.4115

United Nations University. 4.5081

United States. 3.6929, 3.7133, 4.3458, 4.7817, 4.8974, 4.8976, 4.9587, 4.9607, 4.9610, 4.9629, 4.9771, 4.9776, 4.9906

United States. Air Force. 3.6430, 4.2483

United States. Air Force. Office of Air Force History. 5.7411

United States. Arms Control and Disarmament Agency. 4.9165, 4.9260

United States. Army Engineer Waterways Experiment Station. Environmental Laboratory. 4.339

United States. Army Service Forces. Information and Education Division. 5.7168

United States. Attorney General's National Committee to Study the Antitrust Laws. 4.9524

United States. Board on Geographic Names. 4.72

United States. Bureau of Labor Statistics. 4.3149, 4.3545, 4.4262

United States. Bureau of Land Management. 5.2996

United States. Bureau of Mines. 5.6723-5.6724

United States. Bureau of the Budget. 4.4679

United States. Bureau of the Census. 4.150, 4.1250, 4.2956, 4.3833, 4.3864, 4.3879, 4.4316-4.4317, 4.4322-4.4323, 4.8831

United States. Central Intelligence Agency. 4.81

United States Chess Federation. 4.1071

United States Coast and Geodetic Survey. 4.206

United States. Commission on Organization of the Executive Branch of the Government. 4.3885

United States. Commission on Organization of the Executive Branch of the Government (1947-1949) 4.7974

United States. Commission on Population Growth and the American Future. 4.1666

United States. Congress. 4.7991, 4.7993-4.7994, 5.7772

United States. Congress. House. 4.3368, 4.7205

United States. Congress. House. Comm. on the Judiciary. 3.7913

United States. Congress. House. Committee on Education and Labor. Select Subcommittee on Labor. 4.3238

United States. Congress. House. Committee on the Judiciary. 3.7917

United States. Congress. House. Committee on Un-American Activities. 3.7539

United States. Congress. House. Select Committee on Assassinations. 3.7882

United States. Congress. House. Select Committee on Presidential Campaign Activities. 3.7914

United States. Congress. Joint Economic Committee. 4.4697

United States. Congress. Office of Technology Assessment. 4.3321, 4.3971, 4.6595, 5.6004

United States. Congress. Senate. 4.7204

United States. Congress. Senate. (1st: 1789-1791). 4.7202-4.7203

United States. Congress. Senate. Committee on Agriculture, Nutrition, and Forestry. 4.2935

United States. Congress. Senate. Committee on Foreign Relations. 4.8974, 4.9045, 4.9228

United States. Congress. Senate. Committee on Government Operations. 4.7989

United States. Congress. Senate. Committee on Rules and Administration. 4.9732

United States. Congress. Senate. Library. 4.8139

United States. Congress. Senate. Special Committee to Investigate the Munitions Industry. 4.9046

United States. Constitutional Convention (1787). 4.7821-4.7822

United States. Continental Congress. 3.7015, 4.7201

United States. Defense Mapping Agency. Hydrographic/Topographic Center. 4.200

United States. Delegation to the United Nations Conference on International Organization, San Francisco, 1945. 4.9197

United States. Department of State. 3.881

United States. Dept. of Agriculture. 4.153, 5.5215, 5.5225

United States. Dept. of Agriculture. Centennial Committee. 5.5216

United States. Dept. of Agriculture. Library. 5.8092

United States. Dept. of Defense. 3.6501, 4.200, 5.8207

United States. Dept. of Health, Education, and Welfare. 4.3214, 4.7703, 4.9932

United States. Dept. of Labor. Manpower Administration. 4.3218, 4.3226

United States. Dept. of State. 3.849, 3.5090, 3.9019, 4.7988, 4.8972-4.8974, 4.9045, 4.9093

United States. Dept. of State. Historical Division. 4.9048

United States. Dept. of State. Historical Office. 4.9048-4.9049

United States. Dept. of State. Office of Media Services. 4.4

United States. Dept. of State. Office of the Historian. 3.6444

United States. Dept. of the Air Force. 4.78

United States. Dept. of the Army. 3.4497, 3.6365, 4.78, 5.7144

United States. Dept. of the Army. Office of Military History. 3.910, 3.1020, 3.5024

United States. Dept. of the Interior. Division of Documents. 5.7774

United States. Dept. of Transportation. 4.3931

United States. District Court. Nebraska. 4.9776

United States. Domestic Policy Council. Working Group of Federalism. 4.9649

United States. Earth Resources Observation Systems Data Center. 5.6711

United States Employment Service. 4.1664

United States. Energy Information Administration. Office of Energy Information Services. 5.8166

United States. Environmental Data and Information Service. 5.2547

United States. Environmental Data Service. 4.145, 5.2546-5.2547

United States. Environmental Protection Agency. Office of Energy, Minerals, and Industry. 5.6149

United States. Farm Security Administration. 4.5144

United States. Federal Bureau of Investigation. 4.6765

United States. Federal Power Commission. 4.3800

United States. Federal Register Division. 4.7206

United States. Flight Standards Service. 5.6659

United States. Forest Service. 4.154

United States. Geographic Names Division. 4.72

United States. Government Printing Office. 5.7564, 5.7769

United States Gymnastics Safety Association. 4.921

United States. Interdepartmental Committee on Scientific and Cultural Cooperation. 3.9157

United States. Interdepartmental Group for Africa. 4.9057

United States. Internal Revenue Service. 4.9766

United States. Joint Chiefs of Staff. 5.7172

United States Lawn Tennis Association. 4.1036

United States. Library of Congress. Subject Cataloging Division. 5.7637

United States Lutheran-Roman Catholic Dialogue (Group) 1.2901

United States. Marine Corps. 3.1024, 3.5026

United States Military Academy. Dept. of Geography and Computer Science. 4.128

United States Military Academy. Dept. of Military Art and Engineering. 4.157, 4.166

United States. Minerals Management Service. 5.2996

United States. National Advisory Committee on Oceans and Atmosphere. 4.3975

United States. National Aeronautics and Space Administration. Scientific and Technical Information Branch. 4.26, 5.1818-5.1819

United States. National Archives. 5.7741

United States. National Archives and Records Service. 3.6053, 5.7736

United States. National Bipartisan Commission on Central America. 3.9053

United States. National Bureau of Standards. 5.2532

United States. National Capital Planning Commission. 4.6329

United States. National Commission on Excellence in Education. 4.10046

United States. National Commission on the Causes and Prevention of Violence. 3.8419, 4.6774

United States. National Commission on the Causes and Prevention of Violence. Task Force on Historical and Comparative Perspectives. 4.5131

United States. National Criminal Justice Information and Statistics Service. 4.6766

United States. National Highway Traffic Safety Administration. 4.3822

United States. National Historical Publications and Records Commission. 3.270, 4.9479

United States. National Historical Publications Commission. 5.7829

United States. National Oceanic and Atmospheric Administration. 5.2575

United States. National Park Service. 5.5387

United States. National Resources Committee. 4.1944, 4.1946

United States. National Resources Planning Board. 4.1945

United States. National Wetlands Technical Council. 4.2928

United States. Naval Air Systems Command. 5.7483

United States. Naval History Division. 3.6954

United States Naval Institute. 5.7424, 5.7426

United States Naval Institute, Annapolis. 3.7325

United States Naval Observatory. Nautical Almanac Office. 5.1678

United States. Navy. 5.7424

United States. Navy Dept. 4.78

United States. Office of Business Economics. 4.2080-4.2082

United States. Office of Education. 4.10783
United States. Office of Educational Research and Improvement. Center for Education Statistics. 4.9931
United States. Office of Geography. 4.72
United States. Office of Management and Budget. 4.4129, 4.4678
United States. Office of Naval Research. 5.4454
United States. Office of Strategic Services. 3.1106
United States. Office of the Chief of Naval Operations. 4.8830, 5.7483
United States. Office of the Federal Register. 4.7206, 4.7886
United States. Permanent Committee for the Oliver Wendell Holmes Devise. 4.9783
United States Pharmacopœial Convention. 5.5150
United States. President. 4.7206
United States. President (1801-1809: Jefferson) 3.6972
United States. President. Public papers of the Presidents of the United States. 4.7207
United States. President's Commission for the Study of Ethical Problems in Medicine and Biomedical and Behavioral Research. 5.4571, 5.4579
United States. President's Commission on Campaign Costs. 4.8121
United States. President's Commission on Campus Unrest. 4.10091
United States. President's Commission on Income Maintenance Programs. 4.2103
United States. President's Commission on Registration and Voting Participation. 4.8075
United States. President's Committee on Administrative Management. 4.7887
United States. President's Committee on Mental Retardation. 4.6609, 4.9508
United States Professional Tennis Association. 4.1039
United States. Public Health Service. Division of Occupational Health. 5.5617
United States. Soil Conservation Service. 5.5284
United States Steel Corporation. 5.6787
United States Strategic Bombing Survey. 3.1043-3.1045
United States. Superintendent of Documents. 5.7766, 5.7768, 5.7770, 5.7773
United States. Supreme Court. 4.9440, 4.9446, 4.9531, 4.9581, 4.9607, 4.9716
United States. Surgeon General's Scientific Advisory Committee on Television and Social Behavior. 4.5738
United States. Task Force on Corrections. 4.6892
United States. Task Force on Organized Crime. 4.6768
United States. Technical Committee on Industrial Classification. 4.4129
United States. USAF Historical Division. 3.1054
United States. Veterans Administration. 4.4262
United States. War Dept. 3.911
United States. Warren Commission. 3.7877
United States. Weather Bureau. 5.6659
United States. Work Projects Administration. 5.2312
United Technical Publications. 5.6544
United Technologies Corporation. 1.4956
Universal Negro Improvement Association. 3.6836
Universidad del Valle. 4.1687
Università di Padova. 4.9172
Universitah ha-'Ivrit bi-Yerushalayim. 4.1340
Universitah ha-'Ivrit bi-Yerushalayim. Makhon le-Yahadut zemanenu. 3.4009
Universität Hamburg. Institut für Friedensforschung und Sicherheitspolitik. 4.9216
Universitat Hefah. Makhon le-heker ve-limud ha-Mizrah ha-tikhon. 3.3879
Universitat Tel-Aviv. Makhon le-heker Berit ha-Mo'atsot u-Mizrah Eropah. 3.3324
Universities—National Bureau Committee for Economic Research. 4.1546, 4.1636, 4.3198
University Centers for Rational Alternatives. 4.10427

University Health Policy Consortium (Mass.) 5.4678
University League for Social Reform. 3.5956
University of Akron. Dept. of Mechanical Engineering. 5.5712
University of Alberta. Dept. of English. 2.9887
University of Birmingham. 5.4285
University of California, Berkeley. 5.4085
University of California, Berkeley. Center for Chinese Studies. 1.1139, 1.1425, 3.4799, 4.5416, 4.5457
University of California, Berkeley. Center for Japanese and Korean Studies. 4.10143
University of California, Berkeley. Center for Research and Development in Higher Education. 4.10078
University of California, Berkeley. Center for South and Southeast Asia Studies. 1.1736, 3.4324, 3.4378, 4.3689, 4.5434, 4.8722
University of California, Berkeley. Institute of Industrial Relations. 4.3098, 4.6382
University of California, Berkeley. University Art Museum. 1.6304, 1.6337, 1.6369
University of California, Los Angeles. African Studies Center. 1.1844, 4.9927
University of California, Los Angeles. Center for Medieval and Renaissance Studies. 3.3429
University of California, Los Angeles. Center for Russian and East European Studies. 1.1584
University of California, Los Angeles. Latin American Center. 5.8402
University of California, San Francisco. AIDS Clinical Research Center. 5.4984
University of Cambridge. 2.6864
University of Cambridge. Centre for South Asian Studies. 4.5421
University of Cape Town. Centre for Intergroup Studies. 4.10150
University of Chicago. 1.1, 3.4218
University of Chicago. Center for Policy Study. 3.4786
University of Chicago. Committee on Southern Asian Studies. 4.6408
University of Chicago. Dept. of Anthropology. 2.92
University of Chicago. Dept. of Education. 2.929, 4.10453
University of Chicago. Divinity School. 1.1563
University of Chicago. Law School. 4.9888, 4.9904
University of Chicago. Press. 5.7563
University of Colorado, Boulder. 5.6714
University of Edinburgh. Institute for Advanced Studies in the Humanities. 2.7429
University of Exeter. Centre for Arab Gulf Studies. 3.4063, 4.2449
University of Georgia. Marine Institute. 4.338
University of Glasgow. Institute of Soviet and East European Studies. 4.2347, 4.2421
University of Hawaii at Manoa. Center for Korean Studies. 5.8071
University of Hawaii (Honolulu) 1.1141
University of Illinois at Chicago Circle. College of Business Administration. 4.8953
University of Illinois at Urbana-Champaign. Office of International Programs and Studies. 2.1737
University of Illinois (Urbana-Champaign campus) 5.4454
University of Kent at Canterbury. 1.2002
University of Liverpool. Dept. of Geology. 5.3072
University of London. Institute of Education. 4.33
University of London. Institute of Germanic Studies. 5.8013
University of London. Institute of Historical Research. 5.7983
University of London. Institute of Latin American Studies. 3.946
University of London. Institute of Psychiatry. 5.4302
University of London. School of Oriental and African Studies. 3.3626, 3.5130
University of London. School of Oriental and African Studies. Library. 5.8452
University of Michigan. 4.10542

University of Michigan. Center for Afroamerican and African Studies. 5.7865
University of Michigan. Museum of Art. 1.6447
University of Michigan. School of Dentistry. 3.5144
University of Michigan. Survey Research Center. 4.2087, 4.8115, 4.8117
University of Minnesota. 2.3430, 2.10278
University of Minnesota, Duluth. 5.2988
University of Minnesota (Minneapolis-St. Paul campus) 1.97
University of Minnesota. University Gallery. 1.6721
University of Mississippi. Dept. of History. 3.7193
University of Nebraska—Lincoln. Center for Great Plains Studies. 2.10277, 2.11473, 3.8479-3.8480, 3.8493, 3.8516
University of New Hampshire. 5.2956
University of Nottingham. Treaty Centre. 4.8966
University of Oklahoma. Science and Public Policy Program. 5.6149
University of Oregon. Museum of Art. 4.851
University of Oregon. Rehabilitation Research and Training Center in Mental Retardation. 4.10934
University of Pennsylvania. Near East Center. 4.1576
University of Pennsylvania. University Museum. 4.1576
University of Pittsburgh. 4.2159
University of Pittsburgh. Learning Research and Development Center. 5.360
University of Puerto Rico (Río Piedras Campus). Social Science Research Center. 4.5264
University of Rhode Island. Center for Ocean Management Studies. 4.354
University of Rochester. Memorial Art Gallery. 1.6538
University of Sheffield. Dept. of Archaeology and Prehistory. 3.221
University of Southampton. Dept. of Archaeology. 3.221
University of Southern California. Interdisciplinary Development Study Group. 4.2450
University of Southern Mississippi. Institute of Anglo-American Studies. 4.8413
University of Sussex. Institute of Development Studies. 4.1819
University of Texas. Art Museum. 1.4855
University of Texas at Austin. 5.3343
University of Texas at Austin. College of Fine Arts. 2.6045
University of Texas at Austin. College of Humanities. 2.6045
University of Texas at Austin. College of Liberal Arts. 5.6691
University of Texas at Austin. Institute of Latin American Studies. 4.8331, 4.8350
University of the Philippines. Asian Center. 3.4591
University of the South Pacific. Institute of Pacific Studies. 4.5676
University of Toronto. Centre for Research in Librarianship. 5.7884
University of Tulsa. Graduate Institute of Modern Letters. 2.8899
University of Victoria (B.C.). 5.7722
University of Victoria (B. C.). Faculty of Law. 4.8291
University of Victoria Symposium on Children's Response to a Literate Environment: Literacy before Schooling (1982) 5.7722
University of Virginia. 2.10979, 5.4849
University of Virginia. Bibliographical Society. 5.7753
University of Warwick. Urban Transport Research Group. 5.5929
University of Washington. Center for Contemporary Chinese and Soviet Studies. 3.4685
University of Washington. Far Eastern and Russian Institute. 3.4731
University of Washington. Graduate School of Public Affairs. 5.5474

University of Western Ontario. 4.1340
University of Wisconsin. Dept. of Economics. 4.1955
University of Wisconsin. Division of Humanities. 3.146
University of Wisconsin—Madison. 4.1773
University of Wisconsin—Madison. Center for Demography and Ecology. 4.1577
University of Wisconsin—Madison. Institute for Research on Poverty. 4.2104
University of Wisconsin. Theoretical Chemistry Laboratory. 5.2064
Unlisted Market Service Corporation. 4.4620
Unny, T. E. 5.5971
Unrue, Darlene Harbour. 2.12321
Unruh, David R. 4.5804
Unruh, Glenys G. 4.10429
Unruh, John David, 1937-1976. 3.8487
Unschuld, Paul U. (Paul Ulrich), 1943-. 5.4537-5.4538
Unterberger, Betty Miller. 3.3201
Unterecker, John Eugene, 1922-. 2.8357-2.8358, 2.11531
Untermeyer, Louis, 1885-1977. 2.6103, 2.6183, 2.10709, 2.10721, 2.10763
Unwin, Derick. 4.10321
Unwin, George, 1870-1925. 4.2252
Upanishads. English. 2.1932
Updike, Daniel Berkeley, 1860-1941. 5.7561
Updike, John. 2.13363-2.13379
Upfield, Arthur William, 1888-1964. 2.10177
Uphaus, Suzanne Henning, 1942-. 2.13386
Uphoff, Norman Thomas. comp. 4.7716
Uppal, J. S., 1927-. 4.2438, 4.2504, 4.2506, 4.2511, 4.4459
Upton, Anthony F. 3.3295, 4.8667
Upton, Leslie Francis Stokes. 3.5906
Upton, William Treat, 1870-1961, ed. 1.3563
Ural, Oktay. 5.5835
Urbach, Reinhard, 1939-. 2.13862
Urban America. 4.5165
Urban Coalition. 4.5165
Urban, Glen L. 4.4300
Urban Institute. 4.3292, 4.3919, 4.4680, 4.5596
Urban, Wayne J. 4.10685
Urban, Wilbur Marshall, 1873-. 1.1272, 2.96
Urdang, Laurence. 2.14, 2.1086, 2.1102-2.1103, 2.1106, 2.3804, 3.326
Urdang, Stephanie. 4.6162
Ure, Peter. 2.8359-2.8361
Uri, Pierre. 4.1823
Urmson, J. O. 1.460, 1.693
Urmson, J. O. ed. 1.738
Urofsky, Melvin I. 3.4022-3.4023, 3.7425, 4.9806
Urquhart, Brian. 3.1150
Urquhart, Fred, 1912-. 2.9848
Urquhart, John, 1934-. 5.475
Ursin, Holger. 5.4208
Urwick, L. F. (Lyndall Fownes), 1891- joint ed. 4.7756
Urwick, L. (Lyndall), 1891-. 5.5559
Ury, Marian. 2.2042
Ury, William. 5.473
Useem, Elizabeth L., 1943- comp. 4.10641
Useem, Michael. joint comp. 4.10641
Uselding, Paul J. 4.1726
Usha Rao, N. J. (Nandalike Jagannath) 4.6144
Usher, Dan, 1934-. 4.1854, 4.2807
Usher, Michael B., 1941-. 5.3807
Usigli, Rodolfo. 2.5356
Usry, Milton F. 4.4415
Ussher, Arland. 2.9857
Ussher, Robert Glenn, 1927- ed. 2.423, 2.557
Utechin, Sergej, 1921-. 3.3013
Utermark, Walther, 1898-. 5.2905
Utku, Senol, joint author. 5.5841
Utley, Francis Lee, 1907-. 2.11661, 3.166
Utley, Robert Marshall, 1929-. 3.5773, 3.5779, 5.7285
Uttal, William R. 5.4297, 5.4359
Utter, William Thomas, 1895-. 3.8381
Uvarov, E. B. (Eugene Boris), 1910-. 5.710
Uyeda, Seiya, 1929-. 5.3077, 5.3098
Uysal, Ahmet E., joint author. 4.801
Uzunoglu, Vasil. 5.6407

Vācaspatimiśra, fl. 976-1000. 1.204

Vacca, Jo Anne L. 4.10344
Vacca, Richard T. 4.10344
Vacha, Robert. 3.2345
Vachon, André, 1933-. 3.8709
Vaculík, Ludvík. 2.1693
Vaganova, A. IA. (Agrippina IAkovlevna), 1879-1951. 4.1180
Vaidya, Karuna Kar, 1917- comp. 2.1911
Vaihinger, Hans, 1852-1933. 1.1063
Vail, R. W. G. (Robert William Glenroie), 1890-1966. 5.7730
Vaillant, George E., 1934-. 5.4963
Vajda, Miklós, 1931-. 2.1755
Vajpeyi, Dhirendra K. 4.8712
Vakalopoulos, Apostolos E. (Apostolos Euangelou), 1909-. 3.2674, 3.2688
Vakar, Nicholas P. 3.3300
Valbuena Prat, Angel, 1900-. 2.5088
Valdés, Juan de, d. 1541. 1.2320
Valdés, Mario J. ed. 2.5288
Valdés, Nelson P. ed. 3.9093
Valdman, Albert. 2.2336
Vale, Eugene. 2.3020
Valency, Maurice Jacques, 1903-. 2.8087
Valenstein, Suzanne G. 1.6618
Valentin, Veit, 1885-1947. 3.2300
Valentine, Bettylou, 1937-. 3.6742
Valentine, James W. joint author. 5.3365
Valentine, Jeanette. 4.10941
Valéry, Paul, 1871-1945. 2.4562, 2.4761-2.4764
Valette, Jean Paul. joint author. 4.3870
Váli, Ferenc A. (Ferenc Albert), 1905-. 3.1946
Valkenier, Elizabeth Kridl. 1.6279, 4.4190
Vallance, Elizabeth, joint comp. 4.10436
Vallance, Elizabeth (Elizabeth M.) 4.5967
Valle-Inclán, Ramón del, 1870-1936. 2.5291-2.5292
Valle, Ronald S. 5.276
Vallee, Lillian. 2.3385
Vallejo, César, 1892-1938. 2.5427
Valletutti, Peter J. 5.5078
Valli, Linda, 1947-. 4.3267
Vallier, Dora. 1.6147
Vallières, Pierre. 3.8690
Vālmīki. 1.1693, 2.1938-2.1939, 2.9650
Vambe, Lawrence, 1917-. 3.5515
Vampilov, Aleksandr Valentinovich. 2.1644
Van Abbé, S. (Salomon), 1883- illus. 2.7841
Van Alstyne, Richard Warner, 1900-. 3.6361
Van Alstyne, William W. 4.9705
Van Andel, Tjeerd H. (Tjeerd Hendrik), 1923-. 5.2961
Van Buren, Martin, 1782-1862. 3.7129
Van Buren, Paul Matthews, 1924-. 1.2262, 1.2788
Van Cleve, Thomas Curtis, 1888-. 3.2272
Van Creveld, Martin L. 5.7225, 5.7319
Van Dalen, Deobold B., 1911-. 4.898
Van Dam, Andries, 1938- joint author. 5.5647
Van de Kamp, Peter, 1901-. 5.1835
Van de Velde, Th. H. 4.5508
Van Deburg, William L. 3.7197
Van den Berghe, Pierre L. 4.583, 4.4847, 4.6455, 4.10744
Van den Haag, Ernest. 4.6853
Van den Toorn, Pieter C., 1938-. 1.4011
Van der Leeden, Frits. 4.289
Van der Merwe, Hendrik W. 4.10150
Van der Poel, Jean. 3.5503
Van der Zee, Barbara. 5.5139
Van der Zee, Barbara. joint author. 3.8030
Van Deusen, Glyndon G. (Glyndon Garlock), 1897-. 3.2074, 3.7091, 3.7155, 3.7158, 3.7165
Van Donzel, E. 3.3659
Van Doren, Carl, 1885-1950. 2.12604, 3.6994, 4.7825
Van Doren, Charles Lincoln, 1926-. 2.2447, 2.3805
Van Doren, Mark, 1894-1972. 2.2599, 2.2758, 2.6754, 2.7004, 2.10736, 2.12435, 2.12605-2.12609, 4.10824
Van Druten, John, 1901-1957. 2.9446
Van Duyn, Mona. 2.12610
Van Dyke, Vernon, 1912-. 4.7234, 4.7650, 4.7671
Van Dyne, George M., 1932-. 5.3555
Van Fossen, R. W., ed. 2.6585

Van Fraassen, Bastiaan C., 1941-. 5.938
Van Ghent, Dorothy Bendon, 1907-. 2.5949, 2.7870
Van Helden, Albert. 5.1686
Van Hess, H.C. (Hendrick C.) 5.6821
Van Holde, K. E. (Kensal Edward), 1928-. 5.3498
Van Hooft, Karen S. 2.2495
Van Horne, John, ed. 2.5234
Van Horne, John C. 1.6380
Van Itallie, Jean Claude, 1935-. 2.13387
Van Kirk, Sylvia. 3.8840
Van Landingham, Hugh F., 1935-. 5.6366
Van Laun, Henri, 1820-1896. 2.4025
Van Loon, Borin. 5.3201
Van Mondfrans, Adrian P., joint author. 4.3310
Van Nostrand Reinhold Company. 5.1116, 5.7574
Van Ort, Suzanne R. 5.5183
Van Over, Raymond. 5.119
Van Rensburg, W. C. J. 4.3725-4.3726
Van Riper, Charles, 1905-. 5.4792
Van Riper, Paul P. 4.7975
Van Santvoord, George, 1891-. 2.11048
Van Seters, John. 3.3720
Van Sickle, John. 2.792
Van Sickle, Neil D. ed. 5.6657
Van Slyke, Lyman P. 3.4802
Van Tassel, David D. (David Dirck), 1928-. 3.6223
Van Tassel, Dennie, 1939-. 5.1201
Van Thal, Herbert Maurice, 1904-. 3.1239
Van Tieghem, Paul, 1871-1948. 2.2613
Van Tieghem, Philippe, 1898-. 2.3828, 2.3844, 2.3863, 2.4274
Văn, Tiên Dũng. 3.4495
Van Til, William. 4.10508
Van Tine, Warren R. 4.3373
Van Toller, C. 5.4315
Van Tyne, Claude Halstead, 1869-1930. 3.6960
Van Valkenburg, M. E. (Mac Elwyn), 1921-. 5.6281, 5.6515
Van Vechten, Carl, 1880-1964. 2.12507, 2.12611, 4.1116
Van Vlack, Lawrence H. 5.5768-5.5769, 5.5797
Van Vleet, Clarke. 5.7483
Van Vliet, Willem. 4.3481
Van Vogt, A. E. (Alfred Elton), 1912-. 2.12612
Van Wazer, John R. 5.2824
Van Witsen, Leo, 1912-. 1.4573
Van Wylen, Gordon John. 5.6204
Van Wylen, Gordon John. joint author. 5.6203
Van Young, Sayre. 5.1156
Van Zyl Slabbert, F. (Frederik) 3.5477
Vanagunas, Stanley. 4.6800
VanArsdel, Rosemary T. 2.3690, 2.7701
Vanasse, George A. 5.2307
Vanbrugh, John, Sir, 1664-1726. 2.7322-2.7324
Vance, Carole S. 4.5512
Vance, Cyrus R. (Cyrus Roberts), 1917-. 3.7934
Vance, Eugene. 2.3962
Vance, Jack, 1916-. 2.11974
Vance, James E. 4.6188
Vance, John A., 1947-. 2.7335
Vance, Lucile E. 1.5155
Vance, Rupert Bayless, 1899-. 4.2025
Vance, Stanley C. 4.3016
Vance, Vera Lindholm. 2.14022
Vande Kieft, Ruth Marguerite, 1925-. 2.12674
Vande Vegte, Jr. (John) 5.6187
Vandenberg, Arthur Hendrick, ed. 3.7805
Vandenbergh, John G. 5.4048
Vandenbosch, Amry, 1894-. 3.2988
Vandeputte, Omer. 2.1169
Vander, Arthur J., 1933-. 5.4198
Vanderbilt, Amy. 1.1518
Vanderbilt, Arthur T., 1888-1957. ed. 4.9474
Vanderbilt Institute for Public Policy Studies. 4.10816
Vanderbilt, Kermit. 2.11188
Vanderbilt Sociology Conference. 3d, Vanderbilt University, 1974. 4.5080
Vanderbilt University. 2.5113, 3.357
Vandercammen, Edmond, 1901-. 2.4770
Vandergraft, James S. 5.1429
VanderMeer, Philip R., 1947-. 3.8399
Vanderplas, James M. 5.121
Vanderstappen, Harrie A., 1921-. 5.8192

Vanderwerken, David L. 4.946
Vanderwerth, W. C., comp. 3.5822
VanderZwaag, Harold J. 4.909, 4.942, 4.948
Vandiver, Frank Everson, 1925-. 3.7327, 3.7379, 3.7390
Vandiver, Susan T. 4.6065
Vane-Wright, Richard Irwin. 5.3879
Vanek, Jaroslav. 4.3181
Vanger, Milton I. 3.9234
Vann, J. Don (Jerry Don), 1938-. 2.3690
Vannicelli, Maurizio. 4.8372
Vansina, Jan. 3.438, 3.5223
Vansittart, Peter. 2.9091
VanStone, James W. 3.5844
VanTassel-Baska, Joyce. 4.10916
Vanzetti, Bartolomeo, 1888-1927. 4.6704
Varberg, Dale E. joint author. 5.1491
Varenne, Jean. 1.206
Varèse, Louise McCutcheon, 1890-. 2.4602
Varey, Simon, 1951-. 3.1547
Varga, Eugen, 1879-1964. ed. 4.1533
Vargas Llosa, Mario, 1936-. 2.5428-2.5436
Vargyas, Lajos. 1.4343
Varley, H. Paul. 3.4904
Varley, John, 1947-. 2.13388
Varma, Arvind. 5.6853
Varnedoe, Kirk, 1946-. 1.6284
Varner, J. E. 5.3751
Varon, Bension. joint author. 4.3721
Varro, Marcus Terentius. 2.654
Vars, Gordon F., joint author. 4.10508
Vartanian, Aram, 1922-. 1.811
Varughese, P. N. 4.8706
Vàrvaro, Alberto. 2.3966
Vasak, Karel. 4.9387
Vasarely, Victor, 1908-. 1.6154
Vasari, Giorgio. 1.5009, 1.5100
Vasella, Alessandro, joint author. 1.5313
Vasil, R. K. 3.4547
Vasiliev, Alexander Alexandrovich, 1867-1953. 3.2665
Vasilikos, Vasilēs, 1934-. 2.623
Vasils, Theodora. 2.593
Vassallo, Peter. 2.7539
Vassar, Rena L. 4.10018
Vassberg, David E. (David Erland), 1936-. 4.2858
Vatcher, William H. 3.5035
Vater, Michael G., 1944-. 1.922
Vatican Council (2nd: 1962-1965). 1.3123-1.3124
Vatikiotis, P. J. (Panayiotis J.), 1928-. 3.4034, 3.5161
Vatsyayan, Sachchidanand Hiranand, 1911-. 2.1894
Vatter, Harold G. 4.1883, 4.1996
Vatuk, Sylvia. 4.5629
Vaucouleurs, Antoinette de. joint author. 5.1857
Vaucouleurs, Gérard Henri de, 1918-. 5.1857
Vaughan, Alan. joint author. 5.656
Vaughan, Alden T., 1929-. 3.5784, 3.7956-3.7957, 3.8199
Vaughan, Charles Edwyn, 1854-1922. 4.7265, 4.7432
Vaughan, David, 1924-. 4.1128
Vaughan, David J., 1946- joint author. 5.3022
Vaughan, Diane. 4.6761
Vaughan, George B. 4.10563
Vaughan, Henry, 1622-1695. 2.7325
Vaughan, Richard, 1927-. 1.3230, 3.2220-3.2221
Vaughan, Terry A. 5.3975
Vaughan, Williams. 1.4798, 1.6163, 1.6170
Vaughan Williams, Ralph, 1872-1958. 1.3482, 1.4019
Vaughan Williams, Ursula. 1.4019
Vaughn, Charles L., 1911-. 4.4319
Vaughn, Jack A., 1935-. 2.2786, 2.7008
Vaughn, William Preston. 4.10877
Vaux, Roland de, 1903-1971. 3.3822, 3.3836
Vayda, Andrew Peter. comp. 4.380
Vayda, Andrew Peter. joint ed. 5.3808
Vazov, Ivan Minchov, 1850-1921. 2.1204
Vázquez de Espinosa, Antonio, d. 1630. 3.5986
Vear, Kenneth Charles. joint author. 5.5315
Veatch, Henry Babcock. 1.1409
Veatch, Jeannette, 1910-. 4.10464
Veatch, Richard, 1926-. 4.9193

Veatch, Robert M. 5.4580
Veblen, Oswald, 1880-1960. 5.1571
Veblen, Thorstein, 1857-1929. 3.2245, 4.1271-4.1272, 4.1369, 4.1454, 4.1572, 4.1941, 4.1969, 4.4259, 4.9123
Vedder, Elihu, 1836-1923. 1.4906
Vedeler, Harold C. 3.787
Veeder, William R. 2.11129
Veen, Klaas W. van der. 4.5628
Vega, Garcilaso de la, 1539-1616. 2.5188, 3.5984, 3.9295
Vega, Lope de, 1562-1635. 2.5207
Vegetius Renatus, Flavius. 5.7204, 5.7211
Veinott, Cyril G. (Cyril George) 5.6313
Veinus, Abraham. 1.4200
Veit, Helen E. 4.9479
Velázquez de la Cadena, Mariano, 1778-1860. 2.903
Velázquez, Diego, 1599-1660. 1.6300
Veldhuis, Matthew K. 5.5342
Veldman, Ilja M. 1.5023
Velie, Alan R., 1937-. 2.2326, 2.10678
Velimirović, Miloš M. 1.4243
Véliz, Claudio. 4.8326
Vella, Dorothy B. joint author. 3.4529
Vella, Walter Francis, 1924-. 3.4527, 3.4529
Vellacott, Philip. tr. 2.558
Vellacott, Philip. 2.409, 2.472
Velz, Clarence J. 5.6033
Vemuri, V. 5.995
Venables, Peter Percy Frederick Ronald, Sir, 1904-. 5.5624
Vendler, Helen Hennessy. 2.7868, 2.8337, 2.10774, 2.12552
Vendler, Zeno. 1.468
Venkata Sitapati, Gidugu, 1885-1969. 2.2283
Venkataramani, M. S., 1925-. 3.6451
Venkataraman, B. 5.5845
Vennard, William. 1.4567
Vennewitz, Leila. 2.13683
Ventris, Michael, 1922-1956. 3.284
Ventura Castro, Jovita. 2.2293
Venturi, Franco. 3.2830, 3.3112, 4.7091
Venturi, Lionello, 1885-1961. 1.5120, 1.6075, 1.6341
Venturi, Robert. 1.5491
Ver Nooy, Winifred, 1891-1967 joint comp. 5.8129
Ver Steeg, Clarence Lester, 1922-. 3.7006
Verba, Sidney. joint author. 4.7235
Verba, Sidney. 4.4955, 4.7654, 4.8179
Verba, Sidney. joint ed. 4.7776
Verbeke, Gérard. 1.329
Verburg, JoAnn. 5.6983
Vercors, 1902-. 2.4431-2.4432
Vercoutter, Jean, 1911-. 1.5192
Verdeyen, Joseph Thomas. 5.5949
Verdi, Giuseppe, 1813-1901. 1.4021, 1.4029
Verene, Donald Phillip, 1937-. 1.977, 1.1093-1.1094, 4.7454
Verga, Giovanni, 1840-1922. 2.5012-2.5016
Vergara, Lisa, 1948-. 1.6276
Verger, Jean Baptiste Antoine de, 1762-1851. 3.6947
Vergilius Maro, Publius. 2.785
Vergo, Peter. 1.5144
Verhaeren, Emile, 1855-1916. 2.4313-2.4314
Verhave, Thom, 1929-. 5.213
Verhelst, Wilbert, 1923-. 1.5776
Verhoeven, John D., 1934-. 5.6780
Verhoogen, John, 1912-. 5.3049, 5.3078
Verlaine, Paul, 1844-1896. 2.4315-2.4318
Verleger, Philip K. 4.3755
Vermès, Géza, 1924-. 1.1906, 1.1935, 1.2872, 3.3891
Vermes, Pamela. joint author. 1.1906
Vermeule, Cornelius Clarkson, 1925-. 1.5618, 1.5620, 1.6668
Vermeule, Emily. 3.2588
Vernadsky, George, 1887-1973. 3.3002, 3.3036, 3.3047, 3.3082
Vernant, Jean Pierre. 3.2545, 3.2552-3.2553
Verne, Jules, 1828-1905. 2.4320-2.4325
Vernon, Betty. 3.1678
Vernon, R. H. (Ronald Holden) 5.3070
Vernon, Raymond, 1913-. 4.2045, 4.2048, 4.2147, 4.2720, 4.3029, 4.3058
Veronee-Verhaegen, Nicole, ed. 1.6230

Veronis, Andrew. 5.6545
Verrall, John, 1908-. 1.4481
Verrier, Anthony. 3.1046
Verrill, Glenn. 4.4433
Verschueren, Karel. 5.6006
Verwey, W. D. 4.8988
Very, Jones, 1813-1880. 2.11262
Vesilind, P. Aarne. 5.6034, 5.6038
Vesper, Karl H. 4.1555
Vetterling-Braggin, Mary. 2.129, 4.5926, 4.6046
Vey, Horst. 1.5019
Veysey, Laurence R. 4.7158, 4.10068
Via, Dan Otto, 1928-. 1.2891
Viallaneix, Paul. ed. 2.4332
Vian, Boris, 1920-1959. 2.4771
Viau, Théophile de, 1590-1626. 2.4060
Vicens Vives, Jaime. 3.3414
Vicens Vives, Jaime. ed. 3.3406
Vicente, Gil, ca. 1470-ca. 1536. 2.5211
Vicinus, Martha. 2.5718, 4.5771, 4.6098, 4.6100
Vick, Charles R. (Charles Ralph) 5.1179
Vickers, Brian. 2.294, 2.6755, 2.7099
Vickers, Michael, joint author. 4.8802
Vickers, Roy. 2.9447
Vickers, William T. 3.9161
Vickery, John B. 1.1604
Vickery, Michael. 3.4442
Vickery, Olga W. 2.11704
Vickery, Walter N., 1921-. 2.1300, 2.1418
Vico, Giambattista, 1668-1744. 1.1090
Victor, Edward, 1914-. 4.10489
Victor, Paul Emile. 4.103
Victor, Thomas. 4.1120
Victoria and Albert Museum. 1.6525, 1.6574, 1.6595, 1.6679, 5.6924
Victoria, Daizen, 1939- joint author. 1.2177
Victoria, Queen of Great Britain, 1819-1901. 3.1613
Victoria University of Manchester. Dept. of Drama. 2.3306
Vidal de La Blache, Paul Marie Joseph, 1845-1918. 4.79, 4.369
Vidal, Gore, 1925-. 2.12613-2.12624
Vidal-Naquet, Pierre, 1930- joint author. 4.1730
Vidich, Arthur J. 1.2397, 4.6373
Vidich, Charles. 4.4042
Vidler, Alexander Roper, 1899-. 1.2366
Vidor, King, 1895-1982. 2.3070
Vidyākara. comp. 2.1954
Vidyāpati Thākura, 15th cent. 2.1877
Viel Vicuña, Benjamin. 4.5683
Vierdag, Gerda. 3.5476
Viereck, Leslie A. 4.154
Viereck, Peter Robert Edwin. 2.12628, 4.7617-4.7618
Viessman, Warren. 5.5979
Viessman, Warren. joint author. 5.6014
Vieth, David M. ed. 2.7227
Viëtor, Karl, 1892-. 2.13584-2.13585
Vietor, Richard H. K., 1945-. 4.3746
Viezzer, Moema. joint author. 4.6087
Vigée-Lebrun, Louise-Elisabeth, 1755-1842. 1.6155
Vigilante, Joseph L. 4.6589
Vignelli, Massimo. joint author. 1.6559
Vigny, Alfred de, 1797-1863. 2.4332
Vikan, Gary, ed. 1.6416
Viktoria Luise, Herzogin zu Braunschweig und Lüneburg, 1892-. 3.2345
Vilar, Pierre, 1906-. 3.3415
Vile, M. J. C. 4.7720
Villanucci, Robert S., 1944-. 5.6482
Villard, de Honnecourt, 13th cent. 1.5420
Villard, François. joint author. 1.4714-1.4715
Villard, François. 1.4716
Villard, Oswald Garrison, 1872-1949. 3.7275
Villari, Luigi, 1876-. 3.2893
Villee, Claude Alvin, 1917-. 5.3802
Villehardouin, Geoffroi de, d. ca. 1212. 3.586, 3.594
Villiers, Alan John, 1903-. 5.7487
Villiers de L'Isle-Adam, Auguste, comte de, 1838-1889. 2.4336-2.4338
Villiers de L'Isle-Adam, comte de, 1838-1889. 2.4335
Villoldo, Alberto, 1949-. 5.5213

Villon, François, b. 1431. 2.3975-2.3976
Vinacke, William Edgar, 1917-. 5.394
Vinaver, Eugène, 1899-. 2.6407-2.6408
Vinay, Jean Paul. 2.871
Vince, Charles Anthony, 1855- tr. 2.361
Vince, James Herbert, 1865-. 2.359, 2.361-2.362
Vincent, Eric Reginald Pearce, 1894- ed. 4.7393
Vincent, Howard Paton, 1904- comp. 2.11151
Vincent, John Russell. 4.8553
Vincent, Julian F. V. 5.3499
Viner, Jacob, 1892-1970. 4.4110, 4.4159
Vines, Kenneth Nelson, 1924-. 4.8247
Viney, Linda L. 5.4586
Vinnicombe, Susan. 4.4345
Vinogradoff, Paul, Sir, 1854-1925. 4.2257, 4.9400
Vinsauf, Geoffrey de, fl. 1200. 2.2535
Vinson, James, 1933-. 2.2612, 2.3032, 2.5835, 2.5926, 2.6044
Vinterberg, Hermann, 1881-. 2.921
Vinton, John. 1.3508
Vinyard, Jo Ellen. 3.8436
Viola, Herman J. 3.5803, 4.99
Viollet-le-Duc, Eugène-Emmanuel, 1814-1879. 1.4980, 1.5472
Virchow, Rudolf Ludwig Karl, 1821-1902. 5.4480, 5.4736
Virgil. 2.700, 2.783-2.784, 2.786-2.790, 2.796-2.798, 2.805, 2.6469
Virginia. 4.7831
Virginia Museum of Fine Arts. 1.5921
Viśākhadatta. 2.1952, 2.1955
Viscusi, W. Kip. 4.3505
Visher, Emily B., 1918-. 4.5726
Visher, John S., 1921- joint author. 4.5726
Visscher, Charles de, 1884-. 4.9294
Vital, David. 3.4024, 4.7549
Vitek, Alexander. 2.1236
Vitek, John D. 4.146
Viti, Gorizio. 2.5002
Vitruvius Pollio. 1.5469, 2.699
Vitsaxis, Basile. 1.6471
Vitt, A. A. (Aleksandr Adol'fovich), d. 1937. joint author. 5.1659
Vittorini, Elio, 1908-1966. 2.5078
Vivante, Paolo. 2.505
Vivas, Eliseo. 2.2368, 2.2600, 2.9000
Vivas, Eliseo. ed. 1.1349
Vivelo, Frank Robert, joint comp. 2.2320
Vivelo, Jackie. joint comp. 2.2320
Viveros-Long, Anamaria, 1942- joint author. 4.5586
Vivian, Sylvanus Percival, Sir, 1880-. 2.6441
Viviani, Nancy. 3.5648
Vivien, Jean-Denis. 1.6596
Vizenor, Gerald Robert, 1934-. 3.5857
Vlach, Jiří. 5.6466
Vlach, John Michael, 1948-. 1.4917
Vlad, Roman, 1919-. 1.3845, 1.4012
Vlasov, V. Z. (Vasiliĭ Zakharovich) 5.6081
Vlasto, A. P. 1.2313
Vlastos, Gregory. comp. 1.268
Vlastos, Gregory. 1.228
Vlekke, Bernard Hubertus Maria, 1899-. 3.4565
Võ, Nguyên Giáp, 1912-. 3.4439
Voegeli, Henry E. (Henry Edward) 5.6138
Voegelin, Eric, 1901-. 4.7278, 4.7465
Voeks, Virginia. 4.10606
Voet, Léon, 1919-. 3.2979
Voge, Marietta, 1918-. 5.4760
Vogel, Amos. 2.2972
Vogel, Arthur Israel. 5.2672, 5.2730
Vogel, David, 1947-. 4.2712
Vogel, Ezra F. 4.3083, 4.5454, 4.6402
Vogel, Friedrich, 1925-. 5.3442
Vogel, James S. 5.4266
Vogel, Lise. 4.7149
Vogel, Manfred H. 1.956
Vogel, Morris J. 5.4710
Vogel, Susan Mullin. 1.5769
Vogeler, Ingolf. 4.1801
Vogely, William A. 4.3722
Voget, Fred W. 4.416
Vogler, David J. 4.8019
Vogt, Hannah. 3.2450
Vogt, Joseph, 1895-. 4.6416
Vogt, Paul, 1926-. 1.5878
Vogt, Thomas M. 5.4685

Voice of America (Organization). 2.1, 2.10656
Voigt, David Quentin. 4.1002
Voigt, Robert G. 5.1667
Voĭnovich, Vladimir, 1932-. 2.1645-2.1647
Voisin, Russell L., 1932-. 4.115
Vojta, George. 4.2671
Volbach, Wolfgang Friedrich, 1892-. 1.4741, 1.5170, 1.5172
Vold, George B. (George Bryan), 1896-1967. 4.6687
Völgyes, Iván, 1936- joint author. 3.1945
Volin, Lazar, 1896-1966. 5.5251
Volkart, Edmund Howell, 1919- ed. 4.4846
Vol'kenshteĭn, M. V. (Mikhail Vladimirovich), 1912-. 5.3505
Volkov, Solomon. 1.3987
Voll, John Obert, 1936-. 1.1998
Volland, Hans. 5.2549
Volland, Louise Henriette, known as Sophie, 1716-1784. 2.4071
Vollmer, Donald C. 5.7056
Vollmer, Hans, 1878-. 1.4584-1.4585
Vollmer, John. 1.6640
Vollmer, John E. 4.851
Volodarskiĭ, V. M. (Vsevolod Matveevich) 1.6278
Volpe, E. Peter (Erminio Peter) 5.5069
Volpe, Edmond Loris. 2.11705
Voltaire, 1694-1778. 2.4101-2.4104, 2.4106, 3.2030
Voltmer, Edward Frank. 4.905
Volwiler, Albert Tangeman. 3.8079
Volz, Wolfgang. 1.5041
Von Abele, Rudolph Radama, 1922-. 3.7333
Von Békésy, Georg, 1899-1972. 5.4360, 5.4374
Von Blum, Paul. 1.4862
Von Braun, Wernher, 1912-1977. 5.6689
Von Eckardt, Wolf. 1.5424
Von Eckartsberg, Rolf, 1932-. 5.276
Von Grunebaum, Gustave E. (Gustave Edmund), 1909-1972. 3.600, 3.3670, 3.3708
Von Hagen, Victor Wolfgang, 1908-. 3.9153, 3.9294
Von Hallberg, Robert, 1946-. 2.10645
Von Hirsch, Andrew. 4.9895
Von Kármán, Theodore, 1881-1963. 5.6656
Von Klemperer, Klemens, 1916-. 3.2378
Von Laue, Theodore H. (Theodore Hermann) 3.423, 3.3140, 4.2371
Von Mises, Ludwig, 1881-1973. 4.1471-4.1472, 4.1487, 4.7672
Von Mises, Richard, 1883-1953. 1.514, 5.6665
Von Neumann, John, 1903-1957. 5.1129, 5.1380, 5.2151
Von Ostermann, George F. (George Frederick), 1873-1952. 5.7564
Von Sauer, Franz A. 4.8335
Von Tunzelmann, G. N. 5.6214
Vondracek, Felix John, 1901-. 3.1919
Vonèche, Jacques. 5.593
Vonnegut, Kurt. 2.13389-2.13398
Voogd, J. joint author. 5.4152
Voorhies, Barbara, 1939- joint author. 4.460
Voorhis, Horace Jeremiah, 1901-. 3.7537
Vorgrimler, Herbert. 1.2222
Vose, Allan D. 4.4083
Vose, Clement E. 4.9512
Voss, Burton E. (Burton Elmer), 1927-. 5.3308
Voss, Edward G. (Edward Groesbeck), 1929-. 5.3654
Voss, Egon. joint author. 1.4036
Voss, Harwin L. joint author. 4.6871
Voss, John, 1917-. 1.81
Voss, Stuart F. 4.5609
Voss, Thomas G. 2.10916
Vossler, Karl, 1872-1949. 2.4939, 2.5107
Vovelle, Michel. 3.2079
Vowell, Faye Nell. 5.7858
Voxman, Himie. 1.3603
Voxman, William L. joint author. 5.1586
Voydanoff, Patricia. 4.3119
Voznesenskiĭ, Andreĭ, 1933-. 2.1648
Vrana, Stan A., 1939-. 5.7948
Vredevoe, Donna L. 5.4773
Vreeland, Nena, 1934-. 3.4533, 3.4552, 3.4557, 3.4587
Vries, A. B. de (Ary Bob de), 1905-. 1.6255
Vroom, Victor Harold. 4.4353

Vryonis, Speros, 1928-. 3.2661
Vuchic, Vukan R. 4.4026
Vucinich, Alexander, 1914-. 1.57, 4.2389, 5.787
Vucinich, Wayne S. 3.3567
Vucinich, Wayne S. ed. 3.3616
Vurpillot, Éliane. 5.619
Vvedenskiĭ, Aleksandr Ivanovich, 1904-1941. 2.1298
Vyāsa. 1.204-1.205
Vygotskiĭ, L. S. (Lev Semenovich), 1896-1934. 1.6687, 2.97, 5.291
Vyshinskiĭ, Andreĭ IAnuar'evich, 1883-1954. 4.8643

W., Bill. 4.6643
W.E. Upjohn Institute for Employment Research. 4.3204, 4.3582
Wace, A. J. B. (Alan John Bayard), 1879-1957. ed. 2.506
Wacher, J. S. 3.1307
Wachhorst, Wyn. 5.6253
Wachs, Martin. 4.5809
Wachtel, Howard M. 4.3191
Wachtel, Nathan. 3.9300
Wackenroder, Wilhelm Heinrich, 1773-1798. 1.6684
Wackernagel, Martin, 1881-. 1.5008
Waddams, Austen Lawrence. 5.6896
Waddell, Eric. 4.532
Waddell, Helen, 1889-1965. 1.2481, 2.814
Waddell, Jack O., 1933- comp. 3.5829
Waddell, Roberta. 1.6539
Wadden, R. A. 5.6047
Waddington, C. H. (Conrad Hal), 1905-1975. 5.939
Waddington, Conrad Hal, 1905-. 1.5874, 4.4125
Waddington, Miriam. 2.9971
Waddington, Raymond B. 2.5643
Waddy, Ruth G., 1909- joint author. 1.4915
Wade, Allan, 1881-1955. 2.3084, 2.8341
Wade, Bonnie C. 1.3739
Wade, E. C. S. (Emlyn Capel Stewart), 1895- ed. 4.9402
Wade-Gery, Henry Theodore. 3.2556
Wade, Gladys Irene, 1895- ed. 2.7320
Wade, Ira Owen, 1896-. 1.812, 2.4105
Wade, Mason. 2.11191, 3.6255, 3.6260, 3.8691-3.8693
Wade, Nicholas. 5.857, 5.4376
Wade, Richard C. joint author. 3.8412
Wade, Richard C. 3.8391
Wade, Robert Graham. 4.1073
Wädekin, Karl Eugen. 4.2970, 4.2975, 4.2979
Wadhams, Stephen. 2.9198
Wadlington, Warwick, 1938-. 2.10589
Wadsworth, Michael Edwin John. 4.6880
Wadsworth, Philip Adrian, 1913-. 4.4032
Waerden, B. L. van der (Bartel Leendert), 1903-. 5.1080, 5.1271, 5.2123
Waerden, B. L. van der (Bartel Leendert van der), 1903-. 5.1266
Wafer, Lionel, 1660?-1705? 3.9081
Wagar, W. Warren. 3.65
Wagatsuma, Hiroshi, 1927-. 4.6889
Wagaw, Teshome G., 1930-. 4.10151
Wagenaar, Alexander C. 4.4036
Wagener, Hans, 1940-. 2.13502
Wagenheim, Kal. 3.6590
Wageningen. Landbouwhoogeschool. 5.4135
Wagenknecht, Edward, 1900-. 2.3049, 2.3184, 2.10541, 2.10963
Wagg, Susan W. 1.5349
Waggoner, Diana. 2.3464
Waggoner, Hyatt Howe. 2.10476, 2.10483, 2.11030, 2.11072
Waghorne, Joanne Punzo. 1.1707
Wagley, Charles, 1913-. 3.9196, 3.9220
Wagner, Frits A. 1.5057
Wagner, Gerrit A. 4.3030
Wagner, Harvey M. 4.2629
Wagner, Helmut R. 4.4764
Wagner, Jean, 1919-. 2.10332
Wagner, Jon. 4.5786
Wagner, Joseph Frederick, 1900-1974. 1.4494
Wagner, Linda Welshimer. 2.12080, 2.12750, 2.12755
Wagner, Philip Laurence, 1921-. 4.358

Wagner, Richard, 1813-1883. 1.4035, 1.4038,
    1.4046
Wagner, Robert Léon. 2.861
Wagner, Robert P. 5.3443
Wagner, Vern. 3.6245
Wagoner, David. 2.12629
Wagoner, Robert V. 5.1880
Wagret, Paul. 4.2927
Wagstaff, J. Malcolm (John Malcolm), 1940-
    joint author. 3.3687
Wagtendonk, K. 1.2036
Wahl, Edward F. 5.6211
Wahl, John Robert, ed. 2.8017
Wahlstrom, Ernest Eugene, 1909-. 5.2929
Wahrig, Gerhard. 2.1187
Wai, Dunstan M. 3.5184
Waidson, H. M. 2.13501, 2.13551
Wain, Harry, 1907-. 5.4493
Wain, John. ed. 2.5822
Wain, John. 2.6093, 2.7089, 2.9448-2.9457
Waingrow, Marshall, joint comp. 2.6089
Waingrow, Marshall. 2.8121
Wainhouse, David Walter, 1900-. 4.9165,
    4.9259-4.9260
Wainwright, Geoffrey, 1939-. 1.2785, 1.2985
Wainwright, Mary Doreen. 3.4287
Wainwright, Nicholas B. 3.8085, 3.8371
Waismann, Friedrich. 1.1087
Waite, Peter B. 3.8735, 3.8757, 3.8763, 3.8765,
    4.8282
Waite, Robert George Leeson, 1919-. 3.2369,
    3.2408
Waite, William G. 1.3653
Waith, Eugene M. 2.5888, 2.5900, 2.6557
Wakaizumi, Kei, 1930-. 3.207
Wake, Clive. joint comp. 2.4845
Wakefield, Basil John, 1934-. 5.2785
Wakefield, Ernest Henry, 1915-. 5.6630
Wakefield, Walter Leggett. 3.1977
Wakelin, Martyn Francis. 2.1110
Wakelyn, Jon L. 2.11226, 3.7314
Wakeman, Frederic E. 3.4859, 4.5416
Wakeman, John. 2.2550
Wakoski, Diane. 2.13404-2.13405
Walbank, F. W. (Frank William), 1909-. 2.539,
    3.2634, 3.2638, 3.2746
Walberg, Herbert J., 1937- ed. 4.10963
Walcot, Peter. 2.298
Walcott, Derek. 2.10019-2.10025
Walcutt, Charles Child, 1908-. 2.2542, 2.5622,
    2.10646
Wald, Alan M., 1946-. 2.10481
Wald, Robert M. 5.2104
Waldau, Roy S. 2.3272
Waldberg, Patrick. 1.4852
Walden, Daniel, 1922- joint comp. 2.10696
Walden, David B., 1932-. 5.5325
Walden, John C. 4.10650
Walder, Andrew George. 4.3669
Walder, David. 3.4399
Waldfogel, Diana. 4.6497
Waldhorn, Arthur, 1918-. 2.11865, 5.7708
Waldman, Anne, 1945- comp. 2.10710
Waldman, Carl. 3.5710
Waldman, Diane. 1.5691
Waldman, Guido. tr. 2.4962
Waldman, Harry. 5.6167
Waldmeir, Joseph J. 2.12883
Waldo, Dwight. 4.7763
Wales, Horace Geoffrey Quaritch, 1900-. 4.8766
Wales, Nym, 1907-. 3.4812
Walett, Francis G., ed. 3.8009
Waley, Arthur. tr. 2.2020
Waley, Arthur. 1.157, 1.1775, 2.2025, 2.2213,
    3.4617, 3.4726
Waley, Arthur. tr. 2.2182, 2.2196
Waley, Arthur. ed. and tr. 1.1802
Waley, Daniel Philip. 3.2822, 3.2950
Walford, Albert John. 5.7715, 5.8331
Walford, Rex. ed. 4.43
Walgrave, J. H. 1.3276
Walicki, Andrzej. 4.5372
Walker, Alan, 1930-. 1.3838, 1.3911-1.3912,
    5.4221
Walker, Alice, 1944-. 2.2719, 2.11908,
    2.13406-2.13410
Walker and Gertrude Cisler Library. 1.2455
Walker, Andrew L. joint author. 4.6672

Walker Art Center. 1.5020, 1.5857
Walker, Cheryl, 1947-. 2.10285
Walker, Christopher J., 1942-. 3.4043
Walker, Clarence Earl. 1.3373
Walker, D. P. (Daniel Pickering) 1.2945, 1.2960
Walker, Dale L. 2.12021-2.12022
Walker, Daniel. 3.8419
Walker, David, 1923-. 3.1763, 5.3758
Walker, David Allan, 1941-. 3.6295
Walker, David Bradstreet, 1927-. 4.7867
Walker, David M. 4.9347
Walker, Donald A. (Donald Anthony), 1934-.
    4.1367
Walker, Donald Smith. 3.1190
Walker, Eric A. (Eric Anderson), 1886-. 3.1217,
    3.5466
Walker, Ernest, 1870-1949. 1.3713
Walker, Ernest P. (Ernest Pillsbury), 1891-.
    5.3976
Walker, Frank, 1907-1962. 1.4030, 1.4065
Walker, G. (Graham), 1930-. 5.6217
Walker, George E. (George Elizur), 1947-.
    3.6601
Walker, George William, 1913- joint author.
    5.3432
Walker, I. M. (Ian Malcolm) 2.11207
Walker, Imogene B., 1906-. 2.8198
Walker, J. R. (James R.), b. 1849. 3.5929
Walker, James W., 1941-. 4.4366
Walker, Janet A., 1942-. 2.2014
Walker, Jearl, 1945-. 5.2001, 5.5954
Walker, John, 1933-. 1.4664, 2.1049, 2.8715
Walker, John Albert, 1938-. 1.4580
Walker, Kenneth R. (Kenneth Richard) 4.3683
Walker, Lenore E. 4.6748
Walker, Leslie Joseph, 1877-. 4.7390
Walker, Mack. 4.6261
Walker, Mack. comp. 3.697
Walker, Margaret, 1915-. 2.12630-2.12631
Walker, Ralph Charles Sutherland. 1.902
Walker, Ralph Spence, 1904-. 2.6594
Walker, Richard D., 1931- joint author. 5.6064
Walker, Robert Harris, 1924-. 3.6269
Walker, Robert James, 1801-1869. 3.7134
Walker, Robert John, 1909-. 5.1580
Walker, Roger G. 5.3132
Walker, S. D. (Stanley D.) 5.2309
Walker, Sheila S. 1.2466
Walker, Shirley, 1927-. 2.10144
Walker, Stephen, 1944-. 4.10777
Walker, Steven F. 2.556
Walker, Susan W. 3.8249
Walker, Theodore D. joint author. 5.5381
Walker, Thomas G., joint author. 4.8157
Walker, Thomas W. 3.9074-3.9075
Walker, Warren Franklin. joint author. 5.3802
Walker, Warren Franklin. 5.4115
Walker, Warren S. 4.801, 5.8180
Walker, William, 1824-1860. 3.9072
Walker, Williston, 1860-1922. 1.2279
Walkland, S. A. 4.8471
Walkowitz, Daniel J. 4.3532
Walkowitz, Judith R. 4.5542
Wall, C. Edward. ed. 4.10327
Wall, C. Edward. 2.1107, 5.8317
Wall, C. G. (Colin G) 5.6801
Wall, Joseph Frazier. 3.8506
Wall, Patrick D. 5.4365
Wall, William Douglas. 4.10380
Wallace, Alfred Russel, 1823-1913. 3.9221,
    5.3351, 5.3816
Wallace, Anthony F. C., 1923-. 3.5947, 4.3852
Wallace, Ben J., 1937-. 4.630
Wallace, Bruce, 1920-. 5.3444, 5.3476, 5.3628
Wallace, Donald Mackenzie, Sir, 1841-1919.
    3.3012
Wallace, Edgar, 1875-1932. 2.9459
Wallace-Hadrill, J. M. (John Michael) 1.2292,
    3.1981
Wallace, Hugh N. 3.8869
Wallace, John M. (John Malcolm), 1928-.
    2.7109
Wallace, Karl Richards, 1905-1973. ed. 2.3534
Wallace, Lew, 1827-1905. 2.11263
Wallace, Malcolm William, 1873-1960. 3.1437
Wallace, Martin. 4.8569
Wallace, Michael. joint comp. 3.6341
Wallace, Phyllis Ann. 4.3297

Wallace, Robert K., 1944-. 1.4068
Wallace, Robert Strachan, 1882-, ed. 3.1368
Wallace, Stephen R. 4.6539
Wallace, Tina. 4.3632
Wallace, W. Stewart (William Stewart),
    1884-1970. ed. 3.341, 3.8654, 3.8841
Wallace, Walter L. joint author. 4.8091
Wallace, Willard Mosher, 1911-. 3.6933
Wallace, William, 1941-. 1.930, 4.2222, 4.9068
Wallace, William V. 3.1906
Wallach, Michael A. 5.579
Wallack, Stanley. 5.4678
Wallant, Edward Lewis, 1926-1962.
    2.13411-2.13412
Wallas, Graham, 1858-1932. 4.5000, 4.7779
Wallechinsky, David, 1948-. 4.976
Wallenrod, Reuben. 2.1777
Wallenstein, Barry. joint comp. 2.10850
Waller, Alfred Rayney, 1867-1922. 2.5512,
    2.6954, 2.7804
Waller, Edmund, 1606-1687. 2.7329
Waller, Robert. 4.8467
Waller, Ross Douglas. ed. 2.6612
Waller, Willard Walter, 1899-1945. 4.5648
Wallerstein, Immanuel Maurice, 1930-. 3.5095,
    4.1745, 4.2608
Wallerstein, Robert S. 5.4843
Wallerstein, Ruth Coons, 1893-. 2.5787
Wallich, Henry Christopher, 1914-. 4.2344
Wallis, Brian, 1953-. 1.6702
Wallis, Charles Glenn, tr. 1.418
Wallis, Kenneth Frank. 4.1398
Wallis, Lawrence Bergmann, 1897-. 2.6558
Wallis, Michael. 5.3658
Wallis, Roy. 1.2103, 4.462
Wallis, W. Allen (Wilson Allen), 1912-. 4.1241
Wallman, Sandra. 4.2799
Wallraff, Charles F. 1.1031
Wallston, Barbara Strudler. 4.5832
Wallwork, John Anthony, 1932-. 5.3817
Walmsley, Robert, 1905-. 3.1749
Walpole, Horace, 1717-1797. 2.7331-2.7332,
    3.1528, 3.1565
Walpole, Hugh, Sir, 1884-1941. 2.8237,
    2.9460-2.9461
Walpole, Ronald E. 5.1387
Walras, Léon, 1834-1910. 4.1466
Walser, Martin, 1927-. 2.13911-2.13919
Walsh, Annmarie Hauck. 4.3085
Walsh, Chad, 1914-. 4.7174
Walsh, Froma. 4.5646
Walsh, George. 5.6926
Walsh, George B., 1946-. 2.265
Walsh, Huber M. joint ed. 4.10482
Walsh, James, 1920-. 1.3072, 1.3085
Walsh, James J. (James Jerome), 1924-. 1.345
Walsh, Jeffrey. 2.10434
Walsh, John, 1937-. 1.5028
Walsh, John Joseph, 1942-. 5.3561
Walsh, John R. (John Richard), 1926-. 5.5002
Walsh, Kenneth. 4.3172
Walsh, Martin, d. 1977. 2.2989
Walsh, P. G. (Patrick Gerard) 2.735, 2.759
Walsh, Roger N. 5.4893
Walsh, Thomas. jt. tr. 2.5292
Walsh, Vivian Charles. 4.1405
Walsh, W. Bruce, 1936-. 4.4263, 5.59
Walsh, W. H. (William Henry) 3.501
Walsh, William, 1916-. 2.10013, 2.10190
Walsh, William Henry. 1.888
Walshe, Maurice O'C. (Maurice O'Connell)
    2.13461
Walshok, Mary Lindenstein. 4.3295
Walter, Arnold M., ed. 1.3700
Walter, Bruno, 1876-1962. 1.3917, 1.4106
Walter, Claire. 1.52
Walter, Gérard, 1896-1974. ed. 2.4066
Walter Hines Page School of International
    Relations. 3.3176, 3.6362
Walter, Ingo, 1940-. 4.1856, 4.2717, 4.4621
Walter, Ingo. joint author. 4.2732
Walter, J. Jackson, 1940-. 4.7984
Walter, Richard J. 4.8338
Walters, A. A. (Alan Arthur), 1926-. 4.4034
Walters Art Gallery. 1.4965, 5.7566
Walters, David R., 1934-. 4.6569
Walters, Everett, 1915- joint ed. 3.7508
Walters, F. P. (Francis Paul), 1888-. 4.9191

Walters, Peter, 1943-. 5.1464
Walters, Ray, 1912-. 3.6996
Walters, Ronald G. 3.7267, 4.5177
Walters, S. M. (Stuart Max) 5.3790
Walters, Sally. 5.5455
Walther, Fritz R. 5.4042
Walther, von der Vogelweide, 12th cent.
  2.13537-2.13538
Waltman, Jerold L., 1945-. 4.8413
Walton, Craig, 1934-. 1.1464
Walton, Douglas N. 5.4581, 5.4718
Walton, Evangeline. 2.13413
Walton, Gary M. joint author. 4.4216
Walton, Hanes, 1941-. 3.6842, 4.8169
Walton, Izaak, 1593-1683. 2.6455, 3.1448,
  5.5489
Walton, J. Michael, 1939-. 2.306
Walton, John Nicholas. 5.4488
Walton, Paul. joint author. 4.6683
Walton, Peter D. 5.5327
Walton, Richard J. 3.7815
Walton, William Clarence. 4.303-4.304
Waltz, Jon R. 5.4716
Waltz, Kenneth Neal, 1924-. 4.9007, 4.9052
Walvin, James. 3.1296, 4.5329
Walzer, Michael. 1.2444, 1.2559, 4.7519,
  4.7585, 4.7655
Walzer, Michael. comp. 3.2052
Walzer, Peter. 5.6633
Walzer, Pierre Olivier. 2.3869
Wamsley, Gary L. 4.7764
Wanat Bhruksasri. 4.644
Wand, David Hsin-Fu. 2.10671
Wand, Mitchell. 5.1202
Wandersee, Winifred D. 4.3248
Wandycz, Piotr Stefan. 3.3278, 3.3282, 3.6478
Wang, Chi-chên, 1899- tr. 2.2209-2.2210
Wang, Chu-Kia, 1917-. 5.5879
Wang, Ch'ung-hui, 1881-1958. tr. 3.4671
Wang, George C. 4.2477
Wang, Gungwu. 3.4548, 3.4704
Wang, Herbert. 5.5970
Wang, James C. joint author. 5.3336
Wang, Kai, fl. 1677-1705. 1.6326
Wang, Ling. 3.4642
Wang, N. T. (Nian-Tzu), 1917-. 4.4696
Wang, Pi, 226-249. 1.1799
Wang, Shih-fu, fl. 1295-1307. 2.2223
Wang, Shyh, 1925-. 5.6456
Wang, Wei, 701-761. 2.2215
Wang, Y. C. (Yi Chu), 1916-. 3.4647
Wang, Yang-ming, 1472-1529. 1.174-1.175,
  1.1140
Wangensteen, Owen Harding, 1898-. 5.5030
Wangensteen, Sarah D. joint author. 5.5030
Wangermann, Ernst. 3.1887
Wangsness, Roald K. 5.2365
Wanjohi, G. J. 4.647
Wank, Solomon. 4.9120
Wanklyn, Harriet Grace. 4.10
Wann, Kenneth D., 1915- joint author. 4.10381
Wann, T. W., ed. 5.2
Wanner, Eric. 2.120
Wannier, Gregory H. 5.2200
Wanniski, Jude, 1936-. 4.1455
Wannsee-Konferenz (1942: Berlin, Germany)
  3.1106
Wapner, Seymour, 1917-. 5.3
Warburg Institute. 3.479
Warch, Richard, 1939-. 4.10998
Ward, A. C. (Alfred Charles), 1891- ed. 2.2801
Ward, Adolphus William, Sir, 1837-1924.
  2.5512, 2.7615, 3.1250, 3.2295
Ward, Aileen. 2.7860
Ward, Alan D. 3.5612
Ward, Alan J. 3.1864
Ward, Allen Mason, 1942-. 3.2786
Ward, Barbara, 1914-. 3.101, 3.1168, 4.374,
  4.1831
Ward, Barbara McLean. 1.6658
Ward, Benedicta, 1933- tr. 1.2990
Ward, Benjamin Needham. 4.1329
Ward, C. H. (Calvin Herbert), 1933-. 5.6024
Ward, Catherine Elena, 1935- tr. 2.5391
Ward, Charles Eugene. 2.6994, 2.6999
Ward, Dederick C. 5.8217
Ward, Dennis. 2.1227
Ward, Elizabeth, 1952-. 2.2916

Ward, Gerald W. R. 1.6658
Ward, Harry M. 3.8220, 4.7810
Ward, Henry Baldwin, 1865-1945. 5.3255
Ward, Humphry, Mrs., 1851-1920. 2.8244
Ward, J. A. (Joseph Anthony), 1931-. 2.11130
Ward, J. B. (J. Barrie) 5.4451
Ward-Jackson, Peter W. 1.6574
Ward, James V. 5.3567
Ward, John M. 3.5569, 4.8916
Ward, John Manning, 1919-. 3.5555
Ward, John Powell, 1937-. 2.8328
Ward, John William, 1922-. 3.7126
Ward, Lawrence M. 5.237
Ward, Lester Frank, 1841-1913. 4.4779, 4.4848
Ward, Maisie, 1889-. 2.7566
Ward, Mary Jane, 1905-. 2.12632
Ward, Nathaniel, 1578-1652. 2.10882
Ward, Norman. 4.4665, 4.8269
Ward-Perkins, J. B. (John Bryan), 1912-.
  1.5229-1.5230, 3.2724
Ward, Philip. 2.5083
Ward, Ralph Gerard. 4.2597
Ward, Richard B. 5.2515
Ward, Robert Edward. 4.8752
Ward, Robin. 4.8967
Ward, Russel Braddock. joint author. 3.5564
Ward-Smith, A. J. (Alfred John) 5.4283
Ward, Theodora Van Wagenen, 1890-. 2.10995
Ward, W. Reginald (William Reginald) 1.2447
Wardale, Edith Elizabeth. 2.949
Warde, Alan. 4.8542
Wardell, Morris L., 1889- joint author. 3.8529
Wardell, William M. 5.5148
Warden, John, 1936-. 1.1668
Warder, Anthony Kennedy. 1.2105, 3.4215
Wardle, David. 4.10113
Wardle, Miriam Gayle. 5.5552
Wardle, Ralph Martin, 1909-. 2.7050, 2.7811
Wardman, Alan. 2.538
Wardroper, John. 1.5853
Wardropper, Bruce Wear, 1919-. 2.5132
Wards, Ian McLean. 4.192
Ware, Caroline Farrar, 1899-. 4.3851
Ware, Charles Pickard, 1840-1921, joint comp.
  1.3438
Ware, Gilbert. 4.9491, 4.9696
Ware, James Roland. tr. 1.165
Ware, Norman Joseph, 1886-. 4.3561, 4.3577
Wareing, Eustace Bernard Foley, 1890-. 4.3096
Warfield, Benjamin Breckinridge, 1851-1921.
  1.2490
Warford, Jeremy J. 4.4053
Wark, Kenneth, 1927-. 5.2255, 5.6045
Warkentin, John, 1928- ed. 3.8661, 4.2121
Warlock, Peter, 1894-1930. 1.3852
Warmbrunn, Werner. 3.2992
Warming, Wanda, 1947-. 5.7076
Warmington, E. H. (Eric Herbert), 1898-.
  2.683, 4.56, 4.59
Warnecke, Steven Joshua. 4.3070
Warner, Anne. 1.3435
Warner, Arthur George. 2.1967
Warner, Cecil Francis, 1915- joint author.
  5.6045
Warner, Deborah Jean. 5.1744
Warner, Denis Ashton, 1917-. 3.4400
Warner, Edmond. 2.1967
Warner, Edward L. 5.7329
Warner, Ezra J. 3.7315-3.7316, 4.8268
Warner, Frank. 1.3432
Warner, Garth, 1940-. 5.1539
Warner, Hoyt Landon. 3.8384
Warner, Jeff. 1.3435
Warner, Langdon, 1881-1955. 1.5761
Warner, Malcolm. 4.3317
Warner, Marina, 1946-. 1.2900, 3.2004
Warner, Peggy. joint author. 3.4400
Warner, Ralph E. 4.9577
Warner, Rex, 1905-. 2.9464-2.9468
Warner, Sam Bass, 1928-. 3.8086, 4.5206,
  4.6232
Warner, Sylvia Townsend, 1893-. 2.9469-2.9472,
  5.3213
Warner, W. Lloyd (William Lloyd), 1898-1970.
  4.5145-4.5146, 4.5198, 4.6386-4.6388
Warner, William Beatty. 2.7218
Warnicke, Retha M. 4.6099
Warnier, Jean Dominique. 5.1130-5.1131

Warnke, Frank J. joint ed. 2.6086
Warnke, Frank J. 2.2659, 2.2706, 2.6084
Warnock G.J. (Geoffrey James), 1923-. 1.737
Warnock G.J. (Geoffrey James), 1923- ed. 1.738
Warnock, Mary. 1.1421, 5.349
Warnod, Jeanine. 1.6153
Warrack, John Hamilton, 1928-. 1.3521, 1.4056
Warre Cornish, Francis, 1839-1916. tr. 2.655
Warren, Alba Houghton, 1915-. 2.2724
Warren, Andrew. joint author. 4.281
Warren, Austin, 1899-. 2.2369, 2.2601, 3.7942
Warren, Charles, 1868-1954. 4.7805, 4.9478
Warren, David B. 1.6521
Warren, Donald R., 1933-. 4.10644
Warren, Earl, 1891-1974. 4.9832
Warren, Frank A. 3.7553
Warren, Gordon H., 1944-. 3.7355
Warren, Harris Gaylord, 1906-. 3.9230
Warren, Henry Clarke, 1854-1899. ed. and tr.
  1.1740
Warren, J. Benedict. 3.8954
Warren, J. M. (John M.) ed. 5.4346
Warren, Larry. 4.1145
Warren, Mary Anne. 4.5658
Warren, Robert Penn, 1905-. 2.3426, 2.6071,
  2.10273, 2.10663, 2.10767, 2.10810, 2.11284,
  2.11607, 2.11706, 2.12319, 2.12633-2.12634,
  2.12636-2.12648
Warren, Roland Leslie, 1915-. 4.6233
Warren, Stuart G. 5.2742
Warren, Sylvia B., 1949-. 4.219
Warren, Wilfred Lewis. 3.1347, 3.1351
Warren, William E., 1941-. 4.971
Warrender, Howard. 4.7410
Warrick, Patricia S. 2.10831
Warriner, Doreen, 1904- ed. 4.2241
Warrington, Peter. 5.6699
Warshaw, Martin R. 4.4280
Warshofsky, Fred. joint author. 5.4373
Warshofsky, Fred. 5.2226
Warth, Robert D. 3.3150
Wartmann, Wilhelm, 1882-. 1.6501
Wartofsky, Marx W. 4.5901, 5.940
Warton, Thomas, 1728-1790. 2.5744, 2.6538
Warwick, Peter. 3.5506
Wasby, Stephen L., 1937-. 4.7684, 4.9691,
  4.9795
Washburn, Albert Lincoln, 1911-. 4.286
Washburn, Dorothy Koster. 3.5889
Washburn, Edward Wight, 1881-. 5.992
Washburn, S. L. (Sherwood Larned), 1911- ed.
  4.703
Washburn, Wilcomb E. comp. 3.5810
Washburn, Wilcomb E. 3.5711, 3.8200, 4.9774
Washington, Booker T., 1856-1915. 3.6853
Washington, Booker Taliaferro, 1859?-1915.
  3.6854
Washington Center of Foreign Policy Research.
  4.9165, 4.9260
Washington, D.C. Holy Name College. 1.66
Washington, D. C. Peace Research Institute.
  4.9127
Washington, George, 1732-1799. 3.7035-3.7036
Washington Institute for Values in Public
  Policy. 4.3810
Washington, John A., 1936-. 5.4445
Washington, Joseph R. 1.2423, 3.6630
Washington, Lawrence C. 5.1344
Washington, M. Bunch. 1.4890
Washington Researchers. 4.3046
Wasiolek, Edward. 2.1349, 2.1377
Wasiolek, Edward. ed. 2.1339, 2.1342
Waskow, Arthur I. 4.9127
Wasserman, Earl R. (Earl Reeves), 1913-.
  2.5768, 2.5791, 2.7192, 2.7869, 2.8111
Wasserman, George Russell, 1927-. 2.45, 2.6927
Wasserman, Jeanne L. 1.5648
Wasserman, Paul. 3.6507, 4.2065, 4.2725,
  4.9445, 5.8431
Wasserman, Steven R. 2.3265
Wasserstrom, Robert. 3.8891
Wasserstrom, William. 2.10259
Wasson, John T. 5.1824
Waswo, Richard. 2.6436
Wat, Aleksander. 2.1734
Watahomigie, Lucille J. 2.2330
Watanabe, Kazuo, 1921-. 4.183
Watanuki, Jōji, 1931-. 4.7559, 4.8759

Waten, Judah L. 2.10146
Water Information Center, Inc. 4.144, 4.289
Water Pollution Control Federation. 5.6020
Water Resources Council (U.S.) 4.2931
Waterbury, John. 4.2616
Waterhouse, Ellis Kirkham, 1905-. 1.6014,
    1.6037, 1.6185
Waterhouse, Roger. 1.1006
Waterman, Alan S. 5.499
Waterman, Arthur E., 1926-. 2.11785
Waterman, D. A. (Donald Arthur), 1936-.
    5.1246
Waterman, John T. 2.1175
Waterman, Stanley. 4.7499
Waters, Edward N. (Edward Neighbor), 1906-.
    2.10758
Waters, Kenneth H. 3.547
Waters, Kennth Harold, 1913-. 5.6741
Waterston, Elizabeth, 1922-. 2.9885
Watkin, David, 1941-. 1.5260, 1.5360, 1.5374,
    1.5386, 5.5371
Watkings, Myron Webster, joint author. 4.1967
Watkins, Alfred J. 4.6240
Watkins, Floyd C. 2.12648, 2.12798
Watkins, Frederick Mundell. 4.7651
Watkins, Gwen. 2.9476
Watkins, Jane Iandola. 1.6368
Watkins, L. H. 5.6001
Watkins, Mel. 3.5956
Watkins, Myron Webster, 1893- joint author.
    4.3012-4.3013
Watkins, Vernon Phillips, 1906-1967.
    2.9473-2.9477
Watkinson, Raymond. 1.4940
Watlington, Patricia. 3.8357
Watman, Melvyn Francis. 4.1048
Watrous, James. 1.5820, 1.6435
Watson, Bernard C. 4.10900
Watson, Burton, 1925-. 1.169, 1.171, 2.2070,
    2.2158, 2.2189, 2.2195, 2.2218, 3.4661, 3.4698
Watson, Colin. 2.5960
Watson, David Robin. 3.2183
Watson, Derek. 1.4044
Watson, Ernest Bradlee, 1879-. 2.3323
Watson, G. A. 5.1431
Watson, G. N. (George Neville), 1886- joint
    author. 5.1542
Watson, George, 1927-. 2.2508, 2.7686, 5.7937,
    5.7939-5.7940
Watson, George Ronald. 5.7184
Watson, Glegg. 4.4339
Watson, Harry L. 3.8230
Watson, Hugh J. 5.5609
Watson, J. A. L. 5.3878
Watson, J. R. (John Richard), 1934-. 2.5662
Watson, J. Wreford (James Wreford), 1915-.
    4.5147
Watson, James B. (James Bennett), 1918-.
    3.5665
Watson, James D., 1928-. 5.2763, 5.3461,
    5.3468, 5.3501
Watson, John Broadus, 1878-1958. 5.221
Watson, John Steven. 3.1559
Watson, Kenneth M. joint author. 5.2479
Watson, N. (Neil), 1939-. 5.6223
Watson, O. Michael. joint comp. 3.5829
Watson, Patty Jo, 1932-. 3.222, 4.636
Watson, Peter. 5.618, 5.7170
Watson, Philip S. (Philip Saville), 1909- tr.
    1.1496
Watson, Richard L. joint author. 3.6207
Watson, Rita. 2.117
Watson, Ritchie Devon. 2.10467
Watson, Robert Irving, 1909-. 5.76, 5.81,
    5.8414-5.8415
Watson, Rubie S. (Rubie Sharon), 1945-. 4.5461
Watson, Sara Ruth. 2.9300, 5.6077
Watson, William, 1917-. 1.5062, 1.5065, 1.5762,
    1.6619, 3.4383
Watson-Williams, Helen. 2.4717
Watt, Bernice K. (Bernice Kunerth), 1910-.
    5.7126
Watt, Donald, 1938-. 2.8824
Watt, Donald Cameron. 3.895, 4.8977
Watt, Ian P. 2.5999, 2.8578
Watt, Ian P. ed. 2.7384
Watt, Ian P. comp. 2.6022
Watt, James, 1736-1819. 5.5665, 5.6213

Watt, John A. 1.2451
Watt, John Robertson, 1934-. 4.8889
Watt, Kenneth E. F., 1929-. 4.1851
Watt, Norman F. joint author. 5.4827
Watt, Richard M. 3.804, 3.3338
Watt, Tom. 4.993
Watt, W. Montgomery (William Montgomery)
    1.2017-1.2018, 1.2058-1.2059, 1.2079, 3.105,
    3.3428, 3.3651, 3.3654, 4.7326
Watt, William Montgomery, tr. 1.373
Watteau, Antoine, 1684-1721. 1.4981
Watters, Pat. 4.8095
Watters, Pat. ed. 4.6820
Watters, Reginald Eyre. 5.7889-5.7890
Watts, Alan, 1915-1973. 1.1756
Watts, Cedric Thomas. 2.8716
Watts, Cedric Thomas. ed. 2.8552
Watts-Dunton, Theodore, 1832-1914. 2.8845
Watts, Emily Stipes. 2.10286, 2.10354
Watts, Harold Holliday, 1906-. 2.12331
Watts, Harold W. ed. 4.2084
Watts, Michael, 1918-. 5.8063
Watts, Michael R. 1.3313
Watts, Nevile, 1884- tr. 2.660
Watts, Peter Christopher. 2.1150
Watts, S. J. (Sheldon J.) 4.5290
Watts, William, 1590?-1649. 2.650
Wauchope, Robert, 1909-. 3.5696, 3.9031
Waugh, Alec. 2.9479-2.9480
Waugh, Evelyn. 2.9481-2.9501
Waugh, Hillary. 2.13414
Waugh, Linda R. joint author. 2.176
Waugh, Norah. 5.7091-5.7092
Wauthier, Claude, 1923-. 3.5077
Wawn, Brian. 4.2526
Wax, Murray Lionel, 1922-. 4.10181
Waxman, Chaim Isaac. 3.6576
Waxman, Meyer, 1884-. 2.1772
Waxman, Samuel Montefiore, b. 1885. 2.3369
Way, Douglas S. 4.266
Wayembergh, Josse. joint author. 5.5372
Wayman, Alex, tr. 1.2129
Wayman, Hideko, tr. 1.2129
Wayman, Tom, 1945-. 2.9972
Wayne, Michael, 1947-. 4.2906
Wayne, Stephen J. 4.7924, 4.7939
Weale, Magdalene Marie. 2.1115
Weales, Gerald Clifford, 1925-. 2.10525-2.10526
Weare, Walter B. 4.4641
Wearing, J. P. joint author. 5.7951
Wearing, J. P. 2.3324-2.3327
Weast, Robert C. 5.2649
Weatherall, Marie, 1897-. 2.1665
Weatherall, Robert, 1899-. 2.1665
Weatherby, Harold L., 1934-. 2.2751
Weatherford, Roy, 1943-. 1.1233
Weatherhead, Andrew Kingsley, 1923-. 2.8736
Weaver, Bennett, 1892- joint ed. 2.6171
Weaver, Carolyn L. 4.3472
Weaver, Frederick Stirton, 1939-. 4.2164
Weaver, Gordon. 2.10576, 2.13415
Weaver, Herbert, ed. 3.7071
Weaver, John, 1673-1760. 4.1088
Weaver, John E. (John Ernest), 1884-1966.
    5.3786-5.3787
Weaver, Kathleen. 2.3749
Weaver, Lynn E. 5.6606
Weaver, Muriel Porter. 3.8890
Weaver, Norman. 5.3898
Weaver, Robert, 1921-. 2.9901, 2.9903
Weaver, W. Timothy. 4.10524
Weaver, Warren, 1894-. 5.6354
Weaver, William, 1923-. 1.4027-1.4028, 2.3379,
    5.5846
Webb, Beatrice Potter, 1858-1943. 3.6054,
    4.1540, 4.3406-4.3407, 4.7034
Webb, Bernice Larson. 4.1010
Webb, Charles Richard, 1939-. 2.13416
Webb, Geoffrey. 2.5520
Webb, Geoffrey Fairbank, 1898-. 1.5364, 2.7322
Webb, Herschel. 3.4945
Webb, James H. 2.13417
Webb, John Winter. joint author. 4.82
Webb, Kempton Evans. 3.8974
Webb, Mary Gladys (Meredith) 1883-1927.
    2.9509
Webb, Maurice J. 5.5679
Webb, Michael Gordon. 4.3708

Webb, Peter, 1941-. 1.6741
Webb, R. K. (Robert Kiefer), 1922-. 2.7931
Webb, Richard Charles, 1937-. 4.1808
Webb, Robert H. 5.3575
Webb, Sidney, 1859-1947. 4.1540, 4.3406-4.3407
Webb, Stephen Saunders, 1937-. 3.8201, 4.8921
Webb, Timothy. 2.8112
Webb, Walter Prescott, 1888-1963. 3.96, 3.6266,
    3.8329, 3.8469
Webb, William H., 1935-. 5.8354
Webber, Alan, 1954-. 4.4513
Webber, Frederick Roth, 1887-1963. 1.2983
Webber, Herbert H. 5.3250
Webber, Joan. 2.6468, 2.7141
Webber, Michael John. 4.2692
Webber, Sarah K. 4.8371
Weber, Adna Ferrin, 1870-1968. 4.1662
Weber, Alfred, 1868-1958. 3.45
Weber, Arnold Robert. 4.3695
Weber, Brom, 1917-. 2.11523
Weber, Carl. 2.13906
Weber, Carl Jefferson, 1894-1966. 2.7780
Weber, David C., 1924-. 5.7615
Weber, David J. comp. 3.6584
Weber, David J. 3.8576
Weber, Eugen Joseph, 1925-. 3.97,
    3.1967-3.1968, 3.2199, 4.5353, 4.7608
Weber, Heidi. 2.1118
Weber, Henri, professeur. ed. 2.3977
Weber, Lillian. 4.10406
Weber, Marianne, 1870-1954. 4.1363
Weber, Martin E. joint author. 5.1668
Weber, Max, 1864-1920. 1.1579, 1.1792, 1.1814,
    1.2244, 1.4370, 4.1197, 4.1216-4.1217, 4.1473,
    4.1729, 4.4859-4.4860, 4.5426, 4.6300, 4.9344
Weber, Michael P. 3.8095
Weber, Nancy S. joint author. 5.3727
Weber, Nicholas Fox, 1947-. 1.5805
Weber, Olga S. 5.7708
Weber, R. David, 1941-. 5.8163
Weber, Ralph Edward. 5.7531
Weber, Robert L., 1913-. 5.1944, 5.1988
Weber, Walter J., 1934-. 5.6026
Webster, Arthur Gordon, 1863-1923. 5.1656
Webster, Bruce. 3.1785
Webster, Charles, 1936-. 5.780, 5.4533
Webster, Charles Kingsley, 1886-. 3.698,
    3.1047, 3.1599, 3.2140, 4.9091
Webster, Daniel, 1782-1852. 3.7072, 3.7094
Webster, Frederick E. 4.4290
Webster, Graham. 5.7185
Webster, Harvey Curtis, 1906-. 2.7781, 2.8772
Webster, James K. 5.5502
Webster, John, 1925-. 2.6878-2.6879, 2.6881,
    5.3723
Webster, John G., 1932-. 5.4611, 5.5036
Webster, Leslie. 1.4935
Webster, Peter L., 1940-. 5.3603
Webster, Richard A., 1928-. 4.8627
Webster, Robert. 5.3025
Webster, T. B. L. (Thomas Bertram Lonsdale),
    1905-1974. 1.5166, 1.6637, 2.283, 2.307, 2.324
Webster, William G. (William Gerald) 4.10687
Wechsler, David, 1896-. 5.367
Wechsler, Harold S., 1946-. 4.10610
Wechsler, Henry, 1932-. 5.4595
Wechsler, Howard J. 3.4703
Wechsler, James Arthur, 1915-. 4.3588
Wechsler, Judith, 1940-. 1.5854
Wecter, Dixon, 1906-1950. 3.6008, 3.6093,
    3.6299
Wedberg, Anders, 1913-1978. 1.133, 1.281
Wedde, Ian. tr. 2.1844
Wedderburn, Alexander Dundas Oligvy, 1854-.
    2.8023
Weddle, Robert S. 3.8299
Wedeen, Richard P., 1934-. 5.5000
Wedekind, Frank, 1864-1918. 2.13867
Wedell, E. G. (Eberhard George), 1927- joint
    author. 4.4062
Wedemeyer, Albert C. (Albert Coady), 1896-.
    3.912
Wedepohl, Karl Hans. 5.3106
Wedgeworth, Robert. 5.7692
Wedgwood, C. V. (Cicely Veronica), 1910-.
    2.5647, 3.366, 3.639, 3.1470, 3.1478-3.1479,
    3.2027, 3.2964
Wedlock, Bruce D., 1934-. 5.6551

Weegee, 1899-1968. 5.6995
Weekes, Richard V., 1924-. 3.3646
Weekley, Ernest, 1865-1954. 2.1062
Weeks, Albert Loren, 1929-. 4.7089
Weeks, Edward, 1898-. 2.3637
Weeks, Jeffrey, 1945-. 4.5492
Weeks, Jeffrey R., 1956-. 5.1613
Weeks, Kent R. joint author. 3.5144
Weeks, Mary Elvira, 1892-. 5.2833
Weeks, Robert Percy, 1915- ed. 2.11866
Weems, Clarence Norwood, 1907- ed. 3.4998
Weevers, Theodor, 1904-. 2.13941
Wegelin, Oscar, 1876-1970. 5.7806, 5.7815,
  5.7822
Weglyn, Michi, 1926-. 3.1027
Wegman, David H. 5.5010
Wegner, Glen. 5.4714
Wegner, Robert E. 2.11545
Wehlage, Gary. 4.10446
Wehler, Hans Ulrich. 3.2324
Wehr, Hans, 1909-. 2.1832
Weibel, Ewald R. 5.4231
Weibel, Kathryn. 4.6069
Weichert, Charles K. (Charles Kipp), 1902-.
  5.4111
Weick, Ann. 4.6065
Weick, Karl E. 4.4919
Weigand, Hermann John, 1892-. 2.2602,
  2.13542, 2.13839
Weigel, Dale R., 1938- joint author. 4.2719
Weigel, John A. 2.9831, 2.10191
Weigelt, Horst, 1928-. 5.5934
Weigert, Alfred, 1927-. 5.1682
Weigl, Bruce, 1949-. 2.12982
Weigle, Luther A. (Luther Allan), 1880-. 1.2494
Weigle, Marta. 1.3241
Weigley, Russell Frank. 3.981, 3.8085,
  5.7286-5.7287
Weik, Martin H. 5.6362
Weil, André, 1906-. 5.1333
Weil, Andrew. 5.4596
Weil, Irwin. 2.1511
Weil, Martin. 4.9096
Weil, Roman L. 4.4398
Weil, Simone, 1909-1943. 1.857-1.859, 1.3069
Weil, Thomas E. 3.9080, 3.9114, 3.9121, 3.9178,
  3.9187, 3.9228, 3.9232, 3.9237, 3.9257,
  3.9272, 3.9311
Weiland, Heribert, 1942-. 3.5476
Weilbacher, William M. 4.4429
Weiler, Lawrence D. 4.9163
Weill, Alain, 1946-. 1.5858
Weimann, Robert. 2.6757
Weimer, David R. (David Rhoads) ed. 4.6234
Weimer, Walter B. 5.292, 5.981
Weinbaum, Stanley Grauman, 1902-1935.
  2.12656
Weinberg, Albert Katz. 3.6362
Weinberg, Alvin Martin, 1915-. 4.3810
Weinberg, Arthur, 1915- comp. 4.5178
Weinberg, Bernard, 1909-1973. 2.4875
Weinberg, Bill, 1941-. 3.8177
Weinberg, Carole. 2.6384
Weinberg, Daniel H. 4.3489
Weinberg, Daniela. joint author. 5.1545
Weinberg, Daniela. 4.629
Weinberg, Edgar. 4.3582
Weinberg, Gerald M. 5.996, 5.1203, 5.1545,
  5.5576
Weinberg, Gerhard L. 3.947, 3.2451-3.2452
Weinberg, Helen. 2.10647
Weinberg, Herman G. 2.3072
Weinberg, Julius Rudolph. 1.96, 1.357
Weinberg, Lila Shaffer. joint comp. 4.5178
Weinberg, Martin S. joint author. 4.5528
Weinberg, Martin S. 4.5526
Weinberg, Meyer, 1920-. 4.10795,
  4.10901-4.10902
Weinberg, Paul. 4.3325
Weinberg, Robert S. (Robert Stephen) 4.952
Weinberg, Steven. 5.1881, 5.1926, 5.2007,
  5.2465
Weinberger, Marvin. 4.8136
Weinberger, Moses, b. 1854. 3.8053
Weinbrot, Howard D. 2.5681
Weindling, Paul. 5.736
Weiner, Alan R., 1938-. 5.8273
Weiner, Annette B., 1933-. 4.683

Weiner, H. B., tr. 1.3821
Weiner, Linda. 4.10841
Weiner, Myron. 3.4095, 4.1659, 4.7786, 4.8714
Weiner, Myron E. 4.6492
Weiner, Rex. 4.5749
Weingart, Richard E. 1.2931
Weingarten, Kathy. 4.5659
Weingarten, Roger. 2.10731
Weingartner, Charles. joint author. 4.10041
Weinmann, Alexander, 1901- ed. 1.3611
Weinreb, Lloyd L., 1936-. 4.9878
Weinreich, Uriel. 2.167
Weinryb, Bernard Dov, 1900-. 3.3988
Weinstein, Allen. comp. 3.7198
Weinstein, Arnold L. 2.3515, 2.3531
Weinstein, Brian. 3.9115, 4.8807, 4.8922
Weinstein, Edwin A., 1909-. 3.7725
Weinstein, James, 1926-. 3.7538, 4.6994
Weinstein, Leo. 1.822
Weinstein, Martin. 3.9235
Weinstein, Martin E., 1934-. 3.4380
Weinstein, Michael, 1945-. 5.1306
Weinstein, Michael A. joint author. 4.7520
Weinstein, Robert A. 5.6951
Weinstock, Herbert, 1905-. 1.3811, 1.3839,
  1.3855, 1.3962, 1.4184
Weinstock, John M., 1936-. 2.13967
Weintraub, E. Roy. 4.1285
Weintraub, Frederick J. 4.9600
Weintraub, Karl Joachim, 1924-. 3.320
Weintraub, Sidney, 1914-. 4.1803
Weintraub, Stanley, 1929- ed. 2.5552, 2.8072,
  2.8713
Weintraub, Wiktor. 2.1717
Weir, Alan J. 5.1460
Weir, J. E. (John Edward), 1935-. 2.10209
Weir, Robert F., 1943-. 5.4575, 5.5090
Weir, Robert M. 3.8243
Weir, T. H. (Thomas Hunter) ed. 1.2016
Weis, Elisabeth, 1944-. 2.3057
Weis, Lois. 4.10874
Weisband, Edward, 1939- joint author. 4.7968
Weisberg, Gabriel P. 1.4965, 1.4968
Weisberg, Sanford, 1947-. 5.1410
Weisberger, Bernard A., 1922-. 1.3039, 2.3591,
  3.758, 4.3821
Weisbrot, Robert. 1.3344
Weisenburger, Francis Phelps, 1900-.
  3.8380-3.8381
Weiser, Irwin H., comp. 5.7821
Weiskel, Thomas. 1.1398
Weismann, Elizabeth Wilder, 1908-. 1.4921,
  1.5680
Weiss, Anne. 5.7784
Weiss, Charles. 4.4584
Weiss, Edmond H. 5.5509
Weiss, Edwin. 5.1307
Weiss, Helmut H., 1937- joint author. 5.5934
Weiss, Irving, 1921-. 5.7784
Weiss, Johannes, 1863-1914. 1.2661
Weiss, Joseph, 1924-. 5.4908
Weiss, Leon. 5.4158
Weiss, Leonard W. 4.1942
Weiss, Lionel E. (Lionel Edward), 1927- joint
  author. 5.3127
Weiss, Murray. 1.5712
Weiss, Paul, 1901-. 1.652, 3.502, 4.949, 4.10182
Weiss, Peg. 1.6283
Weiss, Peter, 1916-. 2.13920
Weiss, Piero. comp. 1.3498
Weiss, Richard, 1934-. 4.5148, 5.1582
Weiss, Robert Stuart, 1925-. 4.5724
Weissbort, Daniel. 2.1315
Weisser, Michael R. 4.5387
Weisskopf, Thomas E. 4.2009
Weisskopf, Victor Frederick, 1908-. 5.840,
  5.2020, 5.2422, 5.2460
Weissman, Dick. joint author. 1.3452
Weissman, Harold H. 4.6484
Weissman, James C., 1947-. 4.6669
Weissman, Ronald F. E. 4.5366
Weissman, Stephen R. 3.6502
Weisz, Paul B., 1921-. 5.3803
Weitenkampf, Frank, 1866-1962. 3.6331
Weitz, Morris. 1.1350, 2.2379
Weitz, Raanan, 1913-. 4.5108
Weitzman, Lenore J. 4.9510
Weitzman, Martin L., 1942-. 4.3210

Weitzmann, Kurt, 1904-. 1.4694-1.4695, 1.5180,
  1.5182, 1.6401-1.6402, 1.6416
Weizenbaum, Joseph. 5.1132
Weizsäcker, Carl Friedrich, von, Freiherr.
  5.853, 5.941
Welborn, David M., 1934-. 4.7990
Welbourn, Frederick Burkewood. 1.2472
Welby, Victoria, Lady, 1837-1912. 2.82
Welch, Claude. joint author. 1.3280
Welch, Claude. 1.2760, 1.2992
Welch, Claude Emerson. 3.5319
Welch, David. 2.2995
Welch, Holmes. 1.1751-1.1752, 1.1806, 1.2119
Welch, James, 1940-. 2.13418-2.13421
Welch, Paul Smith, 1882-. 5.3257, 5.3805
Welch, Richard E. 3.6440, 3.7436, 3.7504
Welch, Stuart Cary. 1.6423
Welch, Walter Leslie, 1901- joint author. 5.7084
Welcher, Frank Johnson, 1907-. 5.2662, 5.2693
Weldon, Fay. 2.7385, 2.9516
Weldon, Thomas Dewar. 1.889, 4.7244
Welford, W. T. 5.2285, 5.6234
Welland, Dennis Sydney Reginald. 2.5715,
  2.9219
Wellek, René. ed. 2.1370
Wellek, René. 2.1654, 2.2369, 2.2456, 2.2464,
  2.5623
Wellenius, Bjorn. 4.4053
Weller, Jac. 5.7245
Weller, Patrick Moray. 4.8820
Weller, Robert C., joint author. 5.8177
Wellershoff, Dieter. ed. 2.13678
Welles, Orson, 1915-. 2.3025
Welles, Sumner, 1892-. 3.9122
Wellesley College. 5.7919
Wellesley College. Center for Research on
  Women. 4.3240
Wellesz, Egon, 1885-1974. 1.4243
Wellhausen, Julius, 1844-1918. 3.3672, 3.3886
Wellington, Harry H. 4.3513, 4.9557
Wellington, Hubert. 1.6093
Wellington, John H. 3.5433, 3.5439
Wellington, N.Z. National Library Centre.
  5.8085
Wellman, Manly Wade, 1905-. 2.12657
Wells, A. F. (Alexander Frank), 1912-. 5.2876
Wells, A. K. (Alfred Kingsley) 5.3046
Wells, Arthur James, 1912- ed. 5.7912
Wells-Barnett, Ida B., 1862-1931. 3.6816,
  4.6720
Wells, C. M. (Colin Michael) 3.2243
Wells, Christine L., 1938-. 5.5029
Wells, Deane. 5.5050
Wells, Dorothy Pearl, 1910-. 5.8363
Wells, Evelyn Kendrick. 1.4345
Wells, H. G. (Herbert George), 1866-1946.
  2.8247-2.8250, 2.8251a, 2.8252
Wells, H.G. (Herbert George), 1866-1946.
  2.8251
Wells, Henry Willis, 1895-. 2.12553, 5.7950
Wells, J. C. (John Christopher) 2.1112
Wells, John Edwin, 1875-1943. 2.5607
Wells, Joseph, 1855-1929, jt. author. 2.476
Wells, Katharine F. 5.4277
Wells, Kenneth Elmer, 1896-. 1.2113
Wells, Louis T. 4.2720
Wells, Louis T. joint author. 4.2735
Wells, Louis T. 4.3031, 5.5629
Wells, M. K. (Maurice Kingsley), 1921-. 5.3046
Wells, Peter S. 4.715
Wells, Robert V., 1943-. 4.1665
Wells, Stanley W. 2.6650, 2.6799, 5.7952
Wells, Tom Henderson. 5.7453
Wellstone, Paul David. 4.8862
Wellwarth, George E., 1932-. 2.2815, 2.3939
Welsch, Erwin K. 5.7880
Welsch, Roger L. 3.5931
Welsh Academy. 2.831
Welsh, Alexander. 2.7666, 2.8062
Welsh, Alexander. comp. 2.8191
Welsh Arts Council. 2.8811, 2.8859
Welsh, D. J. A. 5.1288
Welsh, David John. 4.10150
Welsh, David John. joint author. 3.5477
Welsh, James R., 1933-. 5.5320
Welsh, Joseph P., 1933- joint author. 5.5872
Welter, Barbara. 4.6070
Welter, Rush. 3.6043

Welton, John M. 4.7487
Welty, Claire, 1954-. 5.5979
Welty, Eudora, 1909-. 2.12658-2.12667
Welty, James R. 5.5753, 5.6197
Welwood, John, 1943-. 5.275
Wemple, Suzanne Fonay. 4.5862
Wen, Yu, 1901-. 1.5757
Wenburg, Kristine. 4.5511
Wendel, François. 1.3403
Wendel, Thomas. 3.6923
Wendell, Barrett, 1855-1921. 2.10260
Wendlandt, Wesley William. 5.2670
Wendorf, Richard. 2.6939-2.6940
Weng, Wango H. C. 1.4668
Wenger, Karl F., 1918-. 5.5421
Wenig, Steffen. 1.5163
Wenk, Arthur B. 1.3557-1.3558
Wenk, E. 4.335
Wenk, Ernst A. 4.10721
Wenkam, Robert, 1920-. 3.5619
Wenner-Gren Foundation for Anthropological
 Research. 4.515, 4.531, 4.568, 4.636, 4.703,
 4.5485, 4.6408, 4.9355
Wenner, Lettie McSpadden. 4.9570
Wennerstrom, Mary H. comp. 1.4438
Wenning, Elisabeth. 5.7717
Wensinck, Arent Jan, 1882-1939. 1.2047, 1.2060
Wentworth, Harold, 1904-. 2.1146, 2.1148
Wentworth, Michael. 1.6151
Wenzel, W. (Wolfgang), 1929-. 5.1842
Weppner, Robert S. 4.6674
Werblowsky, R. J. Zwi (Raphael Jehudah Zwi),
 1924-. 1.1896
Werden, Frieda. 3.6808
Werfel, Franz, 1890-1945. 1.4021,
 2.13869-2.13870
Werge, Thomas, joint author. 5.7795
Werhane, Patricia Hogue. 4.4274
Werkman, Chester Hamlin, 1893-. 5.4408
Werkmeister, Lucyle (Thomas). 2.3692
Werlich, David P., 1941-. 3.9306
Werlinder, Henry, 1937-. 5.4826
Wermer, John. 5.1479
Werner, Arnold, 1938-. 5.4797
Werner, Eric. 1.3643
Werner, Heinz, 1890-. 5.110, 5.399
Werner, Hugo. 2.13714
Wernham, A. G. 5.6855
Wernham, Guy, tr. 2.4170
Wernham, R. B. (Richard Bruce), 1906-.
 3.1393, 3.1427, 3.1433
Werninck, E. H. 5.6311
Wernstedt, Frederick L. 5.2529
Wert, Charles Allen. 5.2201
Wertenbaker, Thomas Jefferson. 3.6019, 3.6875,
 3.8202-3.8203
Werth, Alexander, 1901-. 3.994, 3.2207, 3.3222,
 3.3268
Wertheim, Gunther K. 5.2329
Wertheim, W. F. (Willem Frederik), 1907-.
 4.5404, 4.5440
Wertheimer, Barbara M. 4.3296
Wertheimer, Max, 1880-1943. 5.228
Wertheimer, Mildred Salz, 1896-. 3.2261
Wertsch, James V. 5.273
Wertz, Dorothy C., joint author. 1.1718
Wertz, John E., 1916-. 5.2413
Wertz, Spencer K. 4.946
Wery, Mary K., joint author. 5.8471
Weschler, Lawrence. 3.3343
Wescott, Glenway, 1901-. 2.12675-2.12678
Wesker, Arnold, 1932-. 2.9828
Weslager, C. A. (Clinton Alfred), 1909-. 3.5872,
 3.6926
Wesley, Charles, 1707-1788. 2.7336
Wesley, Charles H. (Charles Harris), 1891-1987.
 3.6633, 3.6743
Wesley, John, 1703-1791. 1.2933
Wesleyan University (Middletown, Conn.).
 Center for the Arts. 1.6443
Wess, Julius. 5.2143
Wesser, Robert F. 3.7648
Wesson, Robert G. 3.3052, 3.9169, 3.9219,
 4.7012, 4.7543
West, Anthony, 1914-. 2.2603, 2.8256
West, Anthony R. 5.2866
West, Clarence Jay, 1886-. 5.992
West, D. C. 5.3782

West, D. J. (Donald James), 1924-. 4.6887
West, David Alexander. 2.740
West, Donald M. joint author. 5.2689
West, Dorothy Herbert, 1901- ed. 5.8132
West, Elliott, 1945-. 3.6266, 3.8541
West, Felicia E. 5.8422
West, Franklin H., 1921-. 5.5353
West, Gail B., 1940- joint author. 4.10513
West, Geoffrey P. (Geoffrey Philip) 5.5460
West, Guida. 4.6528
West, Harry H., 1936-. 5.5847
West, James L. W. 2.13347
West, Jessamyn. 2.12680
West, John B. (John Burnard) 5.4191
West, John F. (John Frederick) 3.3372
West, M. L. (Martin Litchfield) 2.311, 2.478,
 2.480
West, Nathanael. 2.12682
West Publishing Company. 4.9443-4.9444
West, Ray Benedict, 1908-. 2.2457, 2.3433,
 2.10581
West, Rebecca. 2.2370, 2.9510-2.9513, 3.3561
West, Richard Sedgewick, 1902-. 3.6384
West, Robert Cooper, 1913-. 3.8963, 3.9144
West, Robert W. (Robert William), 1892-.
 2.1017
West, Ruth, 1948-. 4.10421
West, W. J. (William J.) 2.9174-2.9175
Westbrook, J. H. (Jack Hall), 1924- ed. 5.6781
Westbrook, Perry D. 2.10441-2.10442, 2.11486
Westcott, Cynthia, 1898-. 5.5400
Westcott, Edward Noyes, 1847-1898. 2.11264
Westerfield, Bradford, 1928-. 3.7607
Westerfield, H. Bradford, 1928-. 3.7774
Westergaard, John H. 4.5342
Westermann, Claus. 1.2590-1.2592, 1.2611,
 1.2613
Westermann, William Linn, 1873-1954. 4.6417
Westermarck, Edward, 1862-1939. 4.5556
Western Association of Map Libraries. 4.219
Western Canadian Studies Conference,
 University of Calgary, 1977. 3.5731
Western Electric Company. 5.5603
Western, John R. 4.8401
Western Pennsylvania Historical Survey. 3.7041,
 3.8071, 3.8093
Westernhagen, Curt von. 1.4045
Westerterp, K. R. 5.6855
Westfall, Carroll William. 1.5604
Westfall, Richard S. ed. 5.884
Westfall, Richard S. 5.1958
Westhill College. 4.10777
Westhill Sociology of Education Conference.
 (5th: 1982: Westhill College) 4.10777
Westin, Alan F. ed. 4.7696
Westin, Alan F. 4.2713, 4.7862, 4.9551, 5.4613
Westing, Arthur H. 5.3580
Westinghouse Research Laboratories. 5.2046
Westling, Louise Hutchings. 2.10601
Westman, Walter E., 1945-. 5.3528
Westmoreland, William C. (William Childs),
 1914-. 3.4511
Westoff, Charles F. joint author. 4.1669, 4.5694
Westoff, Charles F. 4.1639
Westoff, Leslie Aldridge. 4.5694
Weston, Brett. 5.6978
Weston, Corinne Comstock. 4.8441, 4.8468
Weston, Edward, 1886-1958. 5.6932, 5.6974
Weston, Jessie Laidlay, 1850-1928. 2.2639
Weston, John Charles. 2.8782
Weston-Smith, Miranda. 5.836, 5.4552
Westphal, Merold. 1.938, 1.1560
Westrup, J. A. (Jack Allan), 1904-1975. 1.3509,
 1.3952, 1.4247
Westwood, J. N. 4.3978
Wetherbe, James C. 5.5607
Wetherbee, Winthrop, 1938- ed. 2.818
Wethey, Harold E. (Harold Edwin), 1902-1984.
 1.4925, 1.6227, 1.6286, 1.6299
Wetstone, Gregory. 4.9571
Wettstein, Howard K. 1.467
Wettstone, Eugene. 4.921
Wetzel, Robert G. 5.3258
Wetzsteon, Ross. 2.10802
Wevill, David, 1935-. 2.9973
Wexler, Arnold R. 5.2532
Wexler, Elizabeth M. joint author. 4.9599
Wexler, Imanuel. 4.2213

Wexler, Victor G. joint comp. 3.358
Weyand, Norman T., ed. 2.7832
Weydt, Günther, 1906-. 2.13546
Weyl, Hermann, 1885-1955. 5.1051, 5.1095,
 5.1308, 5.1496, 5.1914
Weyl, Nathaniel, 1910-. 3.6173
Weymuller, Frederick, joint author. 4.1038
Whalen, Barbara, 1928-. 4.9681
Whalen, Carol K. 5.5113
Whalen, Charles W. 4.9681
Whaley, Lucille F., 1923-. 5.5087
Whalley, Janet, 1945-. 5.5064
Whalley, Joyce Irene. 1.6603
Whalon, Marion K. 5.8308
Wharey, James Blanton, 1872-1946. ed. 2.6918
Wharton Applied Research Center. 4.1836
Wharton, Edith Newbold Jones, 1862-1937.
 1.6550, 2.3432, 2.12689-2.12694,
 2.12696-2.12698
Wharton School. 4.4463, 4.4601
Wharton School. Industrial Research Unit.
 4.3219, 4.9560
Wharton School. Pension Research Council.
 4.3465
Wharton, William. 2.13422
Whately, Richard, 1787-1863. 4.1419
Wheale, Peter. 5.5515
Wheat, Carl I. (Carl Irving), 1892-1966. 5.7556
Wheat, James Clements. 5.8215
Wheatley, Henry Benjamin, 1838-1917. 2.6111
Wheatley, Paul. 4.182
Wheatley, Phillis. 2.10883, 2.10885
Wheatley, Ronald. 3.1031
Wheatstone, Charles, Sir, 1802-1875. 5.4376
Wheeler, Arthur Leslie, 1871-1932, tr. 2.682
Wheeler-Bennett, John Wheeler, 1902-. 3.727,
 3.830, 3.922, 3.1698, 3.1920, 3.2350, 3.2379,
 4.9166
Wheeler, Burton Kendall, 1882-. 3.7693
Wheeler, Charles Bickersteth, 1862-. 2.7044
Wheeler, Daniel. 1.4803
Wheeler, Douglas L. 3.3502, 3.3505, 3.5406
Wheeler, Geoffrey. 3.3325
Wheeler, Harvey, 1918-. 2.11434
Wheeler, John Archibald, 1911- joint author.
 5.1924, 5.2215
Wheeler, Marcus. 2.1237
Wheeler, Marjorie W. 5.8217
Wheeler, Post, 1869-. 1.1840
Wheeler, Robert Eric Mortimer, Sir, 1890-.
 3.236, 3.260, 3.2632, 3.4222, 3.4246
Wheelwright, Carolyn. 1.6390
Wheelwright, Philip Ellis, 1901-. 2.98, 2.2741
Wheen, Arthur Wesley, 1897- tr. 2.13848
Whelan, Joseph G. 3.6495
Whetten, Nathan Laselle, 1900-. 3.9060
Whewell, William, 1794-1866. 5.942
Whibley, Leonard, 1862 or 3-1941, ed. 2.7055
Whicher, George Frisbie, 1889-1954. 2.817,
 2.10274, 2.11010
Whicher, Stephen E., joint ed. 2.11025
Whicher, Stephen E. 2.11027
Whiffen, Marcus. 1.5289-1.5290, 1.5304, 1.5530,
 3.8222
Whigham, Dennis F. 5.3549
Whinney, Margaret Dickens. 1.5686
Whipple, Fred Lawrence, 1906-. 5.1801, 5.1823
Whisnant, David E., 1938-. 3.8179
Whistler, James McNeill, 1834-1903. 1.4907,
 1.6489
Whiston, William, 1667-1752. tr. 3.3896
Whitaker, Arthur Preston, 1895-. 3.8300,
 3.8340, 3.8969, 3.9021, 3.9163
Whitaker, Ben, 1934-. 4.6837
Whitaker, David. 5.5577
Whitaker, Donald P. 3.4441, 3.4458, 3.4613,
 3.4875
Whitaker, George Herbert, 1846 or 7-1930.
 2.383
Whitaker, J. Russell (Joe Russell), 1900- ed.
 3.6346
Whitaker, Jennifer Seymour, 1938-. 4.2612
Whitaker, John King. 4.1333
Whitaker, John O. 5.3986
Whitaker, Joseph, 1820-1895. 1.68
Whitaker, Reginald. 4.8308
Whitaker, Stephen. 5.2269
Whitaker, Virgil Keeble, 1908-. 2.6821

Whitbeck, Philip H. 4.2645
White, Abraham, 1908-. 5.4399
White, Alan, 1951-. 1.924
White, Alastair T. 3.9067
White, Antonia, 1899-. 2.9517-2.9518
White, Barbara Anne. 2.10820
White, Barbara Ehrlich. 1.6143
White, Beatrice, 1902-. 2.6694
White, Benjamine Franklin, 1800-1879. 1.3444
White Burkett Miller Center. 4.7930
White, C. Langdon (Charles Langdon), 1897-. 3.6060
White, Carl Milton, 1903-. 5.8354
White, Christopher. 1.5807, 1.6494
White, Dana F. 4.5196
White, David Manning. joint comp. 3.6186
White, Donald Cedric, 1939-. 1.2928
White, Dorothy Neal. 2.2705
White, E. B. (Elwyn Brooks), 1899-. 2.1036, 2.3797, 2.12702-2.12706
White, Edmund, 1940-. 2.13423
White, Emmons E. 1.3740
White, Eric Walter, 1905-. 1.4013, 1.4227
White, Estelle E. joint author. 4.10983
White, Frank M. 5.6198
White, G. Edward. 4.9800, 4.9835
White, Gilbert, 1720-1793. 5.3213, 5.3277-5.3278
White, Gilbert Fowler, 1911-. 4.247, 4.256, 4.293, 4.297, 4.319, 5.7234
White, Gordon. 5.6444
White, Guy K. (Guy Kendall) 5.2236
White, Harvey Elliott, 1902-. 5.2281, 5.2310
White, Hayden V., 1928-. 3.409
White, Helen, 1914-. 2.11744
White, Helen Constance, 1896-1967. 2.5806, 2.6085, 2.7435
White, Horace, 1834-1916. tr. 2.335
White, J. Peter (John Peter), 1937-. 4.750
White, J. Todd. 5.7833
White, John. 1.5003, 1.5822, 1.6201
White, John David, 1931-. 1.4439
White, John Warren, 1939-. 5.644
White, Joseph F., 1938-. 5.6549
White, Joseph L., 1932-. 3.6722
White, K. D. 2.401, 5.5229, 5.5296, 5.5535
White, Katharine Angell, Sergeant, joint ed. 2.3797
White, Landeg. 2.10014
White, Lawrence J. 4.3828
White, Leonard Dupee, 1891-1958. 4.7835, 4.7837, 4.7839, 4.7845, 4.7889
White, Leslie A., 1900-1975. 3.19, 3.5836, 4.501
White, Lonnie J. 3.5780
White, Lucia. joint author. 4.6190
White, Lynn Townsend, 1907-. 3.145, 5.5536
White, M. J. D. (Michael James Denham), 1910-. 5.3604, 5.3608
White, Michael. 1.5798
White, Minor. 5.6938, 5.6962, 5.6970
White, Morton Gabriel, 1917-. 1.461, 1.559, 3.440, 4.6190
White, Nathan N. 4.9061
White, Newman Ivey, 1892-1948. 2.8104-2.8105
White, Nicholas P., 1942-. 4.7351
White, P. S. 5.3577
White, Patrick. 2.10178-2.10186
White, Peter, 1947-. 2.10877
White, Ralph K. 4.4920
White, Ray Lewis. 2.12627
White, Ray Lewis. ed. 2.11317, 2.11325-2.11326, 2.11330
White, Richard E. 5.3889
White, Richard E. joint author. 5.3860
White, Richard N. 5.5831
White, Robert Lee, 1928-. 2.11390
White, Robert Winthrop. 5.191, 5.507, 5.536, 5.4827
White, Rodney. 4.31
White, Stephen, 1945-. 4.7591
White, T. H. (Terence Hanbury), 1906-1964. 2.9519
White, Theodore Harold, 1915-. 3.1139, 3.1194, 3.4772, 3.7852, 3.7892, 3.7895, 3.7915, 3.7924
White, Virginia P. 4.4450
White, Walter Francis, 1893-1955. 3.6858
White, Weeks. 5.5900
White, Welsh S., 1940-. 4.9863

White, William, 1910-. 2.11837-2.11838
White, William Allen, 1868-1944. 2.3638, 3.6313, 3.7738
White, William Hale, 1831-1913. 2.8262-2.8264
White, William Smith. 4.8044
Whitecotton, Joseph W., 1937-. 3.8915
Whitehall Palace. 1.5389
Whitehead, Alfred North, 1861-1947. 1.774-1.775, 1.778, 1.783, 1.1263, 1.1331, 1.1538, 3.27, 4.10176, 4.10235, 5.854, 5.943-5.946
Whitehead, Christine M. E. 4.2813
Whitehead, David. 3.2531, 3.2555
Whitehead, Harriet. 4.569
Whitehead, Harry. 5.6799
Whitehead, John S. 4.10761
Whitehead, Laurence. 4.2142
Whitehill, Walter Muir, 1905-. 3.6376, 3.7992
Whitehouse, H. L. K. (Harold L. K.) 5.3445
Whitehouse, John Howard, 1873-. 2.8028
Whitehouse, N. D. (Norman Dan) 5.6220
Whitehouse, Ruth. 3.219
Whitehouse, Wilfrid. 2.2045
Whitehurst, Clinton H., 1927-. 4.3976
Whitelaw, James K. 5.6240
Whitelaw, James Sydney. joint author. 3.5597
Whitelaw, William Menzies, 1890-. 3.8736
Whiteley, Paul. 4.8544
Whitelock, Dorothy. ed. 2.940, 3.1309
Whitelock, Dorothy. 2.6302, 3.1311, 3.1318
Whiteman, Roberta Hill. 2.13424
Whitesell, J. Edwin. 2.5622
Whiteside, Derek Thomas, ed. 5.1103
Whitfield, Francis J. (Francis James), 1916- ed. 2.1249
Whitfield, Jane Shaw. 2.1046
Whitfield, John Humphreys. 2.4970
Whitfield, Philip. 5.3792
Whitfield, Stephen J., 1942-. 3.6577
Whitford, Frank. 1.4651, 1.6482
Whitford, Richard, fl. 1495-1555? 1.3070
Whiting, Allen Suess, 1926-. 3.4684, 3.5032
Whiting, Bartlett Jere, 1904- joint comp. 2.3810
Whiting, Beatrice Blyth. 4.5731, 5.566
Whiting, Beatrice Blyth. ed. 4.5707
Whiting, John Robert, 1917-1963. 2.9520
Whiting, John Wesley Mayhew. 4.593, 4.5714, 4.5731
Whitlark, Frederick Louis. 4.3967
Whitley, Alvin, joint ed. 2.6166
Whitley, William Thomas, 1858-1942. 1.5977
Whitman, Cedric Hubbell. 2.435, 2.507, 2.551
Whitman, Robert V., 1928- joint author. 5.5899
Whitman, Ruth, 1922- tr. 2.1802
Whitman, Walt, 1819-1892. 2.11265-2.11271
Whitmarsh, David. 4.3699
Whitmore, Joanne Rand, 1938-. 4.10922
Whitmore, John K. 4.8695
Whitmore, T. C. (Timothy Charles) 5.3279
Whitnah, Donald Robert, 1925-. 3.1904, 4.7891
Whitney, Eleanor Noss. 5.4236, 5.4242
Whitney, Lois, joint ed. 2.6087
Whitney Museum of American Art. 1.4882, 1.4892, 1.4898, 1.4908, 1.5657, 1.5679, 1.5908, 1.5910, 1.5913, 1.5941, 1.5946, 1.5970, 1.6381, 1.6615, 1.6708
Whitney, Simon Newcomb, 1903-. 4.3059
Whitridge, Arnold, 1891-. 3.708
Whitrow, G. J. 5.1757
Whittaker, C. R. tr. 2.369
Whittaker, C. R. 4.4094
Whittaker, Cynthia H., 1941-. 2.1409
Whittaker, E. T. (Edmund Taylor), 1873-1956. 5.947, 5.1542, 5.1657, 5.2213
Whittaker, James K. 4.6482, 4.6485
Whittaker, Molly. 3.3847
Whittaker, Peter A., 1939-. 5.3757
Whittaker, Robert Harding, 1920-. 5.3529, 5.3533
Whittaker, Ruth. 2.9367
Whittaker, Thomas, 1856-1935. 1.323
Whittaker, W. G. (William Gillies), 1876-1944. 1.4520
Whittaker, William. 5.8043
Whittall, Mary. 1.4038
Whittemore, Colin Trengove. 5.5451
Whittemore, Edward P. 2.3697
Whittemore, Henry, 1833-. 3.296

Whittemore, Reed, 1919-. 2.12756
Whitten, Norman E. 3.9313, 4.5274
Whitten, Phillip. 4.408
Whittick, Arnold, 1898-. 4.6309, 4.6332
Whittier, John Greenleaf, 1807-1892. 2.11283-2.11285
Whittle, A. W. R. 4.708
Whittle, Amberys R., ed. 2.12555
Whitton, B. A. 5.3275, 5.3569
Whittow, John Byron. 4.239
Whitworth, Kernan B., joint author. 2.3908
Whorf, Benjamin Lee, 1897-1941. 2.10
Whorton, James, 1942-. 5.4649, 5.4734
Whyte, Arthur James Beresford. 3.2868-3.2869
Whyte, Iain Boyd, 1947-. 1.5429
Whyte, John Henry, 1928-. 1.2450, 1.3168
Whyte, Martin King. 4.6271
Whyte, Martin King. joint author. 4.5631
Whyte, W. S. (Walter S.) 5.5826
Whyte, William Foote, 1914-. 4.3187, 4.4367, 4.6715
Whyte, William Hollingsworth. 1.5601, 5.500
Wiberg, Kenneth B. 5.2750
Wichern, Dean W. 5.1408
Wick, T. E. 3.2607
Wickberg, Edgar. 3.4589
Wickens, G. M. 2.1974
Wickens, G. M. ed. and tr. 1.1483
Wickens, M. R. joint author. 4.1397
Wicker, Elmus R. 4.4506
Wickes, George, ed. 2.12194
Wickham, Glynne William Gladstone. 2.3136, 2.3172, 2.3285, 2.6203
Wickler, Wolfgang. 5.3582
Wickman, Peter M. 4.6750
Wickman, Stephen B., 1953-. 3.2965
Wicks, Charles E. 5.5753
Wicks, Susanne R. joint author. 5.3712
Wicksell, Knut, 1851-1926. 4.1267, 4.1477, 4.1496, 4.4490
Wicksteed, Joseph Hartley, 1870-. 2.7409
Wicksteed, Philip Henry, 1844-1927. 2.348, 4.1456, 4.1497
Widdows, Richard. 4.1018
Widdowson, J. D. A. (John David Allison) 2.1111
Widdowson, Peter. 2.8646
Wideman, John Edgar. 2.13425, 4.6700
Widenor, William C. 3.7442
Widmer, Kingsley, 1925-. 2.12688
Widrow, Bernard, 1929-. 5.6382
Wiebe, Paul D. 4.3500
Wiebe, Robert H. 3.7416
Wiebenson, Dora. 5.5376
Wiecek, William M., 1938-. 4.9624, 4.9650, 5.7263
Wiechmann, Ulrich E. 4.4298
Wieck, Friedrich, 1785-1873. 1.4417
Wieczynski, Joseph L., 1934-. 3.3029
Wiedemann, Thomas E. J. 4.6414
Wiedenbeck, M. L. (Marcellus Lee) 5.2344
Wieder, Sol. 5.2124
Wiederrecht, Ann E., joint author. 5.8462
Wiegert, Richard G. 5.3558
Wieland, Christoph Martin, 1733-1813. 2.13667
Wiemken, Helmut, ed. 2.13511
Wiener, Aaron. 4.2929
Wiener, Anthony J., joint author. 3.72
Wiener, Joel H. comp. 3.1251, 3.1518
Wiener, Jon. 1.4093
Wiener, Leo, 1862-1939. 2.1793
Wiener, Martin J. 3.1596
Wiener, Norbert, 1894-1964. 5.948-5.949, 5.1100-5.1101
Wiener, Philip P. 3.109
Wiener, Philip Paul, 1905-. 1.483, 1.630
Wienpahl, Paul. 1.1101
Wierzbiańska, Alina, joint comp. 1.1389
Wierzyński, Kazimierz, 1894-1969. 2.1735
Wiese, Benno von, 1903-. 2.13484, 2.13490, 2.13496, 2.13499, 2.13639, 2.13651
Wiese, Michael. 2.3003
Wiesenfarth, Joseph. 2.7691
Wieser, Friedrich, Freiherr von, 1851-1926. 4.1498
Wiesner, Jerome B. (Jerome Bert), 1915-. 5.799
Wiesner, Merry E. 4.5866, 5.8465
Wiet, Gaston, 1887-1971. 3.3689, 3.5182

Wigdor, Alexandra K. 4.10709
Wiget, Andrew. 2.2317-2.2318
Wiggert, James M., joint author. 5.5966
Wiggin, Gladys Anna, 1907-. 4.10739
Wiggins, Jerry S. 5.539
Wiggins, Sarah Woolfolk, 1934-. 3.8283
Wigglesworth, Vincent B. (Vincent Brian), Sir,
    1899-. 5.3868-5.3869, 5.3873
Wight, Martin. joint ed. 4.9023
Wightman, A. S. joint author. 5.2160
Wightman, W. P. D. (William Persehouse
    Delisle) 5.761
Wiginton, John C. joint author. 4.4596
Wigley, D. A. 5.5791
Wigley, Philip G. 3.1259
Wigman, Mary, 1886-1973. 4.1099, 4.1161
Wigmore, J. K. 5.2234
Wigmore, John Henry, 1863-1943. 4.9346
Wigoder, Geoffrey, 1922-. 1.1896, 3.3809
Wiig, Elisabeth H. 5.4790
Wikan, Unni, 1944-. 4.6137
Wikgren, Allen Paul, 1906-. 2.376
Wikstrom, Nelson. 4.8860
Wilber, Charles K. 4.2800
Wilber, Donald Newton. 3.4072, 3.4113, 3.4124
Wilber, Ken. 5.293
Wilbert, Johannes. 3.9180
Wilbour, Charles E. (Charles Edwin),
    1833-1896. tr. 2.4236
Wilbur, C. Martin (Clarence Martin), 1908-.
    3.4761, 3.4769
Wilbur, James Benjamin, 1856-1929, ed.
    2.10880
Wilbur, John Benson, 1905- joint author. 5.5841
Wilbur, Richard, 1921-. 2.11440,
    2.12708-2.12711
Wilcken, Ulrich. 3.2629
Wilcock, Richard Carrington. 4.3223
Wilcox, Bruce A., 1948-. 5.3217
Wilcox, Charles F., 1930- joint author. 5.2727
Wilcox, Clair, 1898-. 4.1970
Wilcox, Earl J., 1933-. 2.12023
Wilcox, Wayne Ayres. 3.3643, 3.4097, 3.4134
Wilczynski, J. (Jozef), 1922-. 4.2242-4.2243,
    4.2600, 4.3032, 4.3439, 4.4160
Wild, Alan. 5.5266
Wild, John Daniel, 1902-1972. 1.275, 1.604
Wildavsky, Aaron B. 4.1218, 4.3225, 4.3799,
    4.4684, 4.7967
Wildavsky, Aaron B. comp. 4.7933
Wildavsky, Aaron B. joint author. 4.4722
Wilde, Alan. 2.8669, 2.8842
Wilde, Oscar, 1854-1900. 2.6673, 2.8266-2.8272
Wilde, W. H. (William Henry) joint author.
    5.8081
Wildenstein, Georges. 1.6114
Wilder, Alec. 1.4293
Wilder, Amos Niven, 1895-. 1.2644, 1.2663,
    1.2681
Wilder, Raymond Louis, 1896-. 5.1077
Wilder, Thornton, 1897-1975. 2.12713-2.12719
Wilders, John. ed. 2.6925
Wildgen, John K. 5.7268
Wildhagen, Karl, 1873-1945. 2.1191
Wildiers, N. M., 1904-. 1.1333
Wilding, L. P. 5.5265
Wilding, Michael. 2.5976
Wilding-White, T. M. 5.6712
Wildy, Peter. 5.4474
Wilenski, Reginald Howard, 1887-. 1.6047
Wilensky, Harold L. 4.3374, 4.5109, 4.6522
Wilentz, Sean. 4.3620
Wiles, Cheryl B. 5.5120
Wiles, Maurice F. 1.2200
Wiles, Peter John de la Fosse. 4.4165
Wiley, Bell Irvin, 1906-. 3.7383, 3.7395, 3.8153
Wiley, David, 1935-. 3.5063
Wiley, E. O. 5.3384
Wiley, Peter. 4.2027
Wiley, Roland John. 1.3835
Wiley, William Leon. 2.3363, 3.1961
Wilf, Herbert S., 1931- joint author. 5.1276
Wilford, John Noble. 4.210
Wilgus, A. Curtis (Alva Curtis), 1897-1981.
    3.8964
Wilgus, D. K. 1.4294
Wilhelm, Hellmut, 1905-. 2.2180
Wilhelm, James J. 2.885

Wilhelm, John. 4.1835
Wilhelm, Kate. 2.13426
Wilhelm, Richard, 1873-1930. tr. 2.2181
Wilk, Christopher. 1.6569, 5.7070
Wilk, Richard R. 4.5485
Wilken, Robert Louis, 1936-. 1.2282
Wilkening, Laurel L. 5.1822
Wilkes, K. V. 5.33
Wilkes, Binnie Tate, 1933-. 5.7723
Wilkin, Robert Nugen, 1886-. 4.9399
Wilkins, A. S. (Adam S.), 1945-. 5.3398
Wilkins, Burleigh Taylor. 3.420, 3.503
Wilkins, D. A. (David Arthur). 2.37
Wilkins, Ernest Hatch, 1880-1966. 2.4880,
    2.4945, 2.4949, 2.4952
Wilkins, Mira. 4.2737
Wilkins, Robert P., 1914-. 3.8509
Wilkins, Roy, 1901-. 4.6833
Wilkins, Wynona H., joint author. 3.8509
Wilkinson, Bertie, 1898-. 5.7987
Wilkinson, Cyril Hackett, 1888-1960. ed. 2.7097
Wilkinson, Doris Yvonne. 4.6716
Wilkinson, Douglas, 1919-. 5.3272
Wilkinson, Elizabeth M. (Elizabeth Mary) ed.
    1.1372
Wilkinson, Frederick, 1922-. 4.1059
Wilkinson, Geoffrey, Sir, 1921-. 5.2698, 5.2780
Wilkinson, Henry Robert. joint author. 4.204
Wilkinson, J. Harvie, 1944-. 3.8214
Wilkinson, James D., 1943-. 3.742, 3.1060
Wilkinson, John Craven. 4.2934
Wilkinson, John P. D., joint author. 5.5856
Wilkinson, L. P. 2.648, 2.727, 2.753, 2.795
Wilkinson, Louise Cherry. 4.10312
Wilkinson, Paul. 4.7521, 4.7615
Wilkinson, Spenser, 1853-1937. 3.2295
Wilks, Ivor. 3.5334, 4.3176
Wilks, J. (John), 1922-. 5.2238
Wilks, S. S. (Samuel Stanley), 1906-1964. joint
    author. 5.5715
Willard, Beatrice E. joint author. 5.3552
Willard, Charity Cannon. 2.3974
Willard, Charles Arthur. 1.1237
Willard, Frances Elizabeth, 1839-1898. ed.
    3.354
Willard, Hobart Hurd, 1881-. 5.2669
Willard, Rudolph, 1892- joint ed. 2.6077
Willard, Stephen, 1941-. 5.1602
Willcock, Gladys Doidge, ed. 2.2719
Willcox, William Bradford, 1907- ed. 3.6967
Willems, Jane Sisk. joint author. 5.4609
Willems-Treeman, Elizabeth. 1.6238
Willett, Edward F. 4.9733
Willett, Frank. 1.5083, 1.5768
Willett, Frank. joint author. 1.5088
Willett, John. ed. and tr. 2.3083
Willett, John. 2.3377, 2.13702, 2.13704-2.13705
Willetts, R. F., 1915-. 3.2593, 3.2642
Willey, Basil, 1897-. 1.684, 1.716-1.717
Willey, Gordon Randolph, 1913-.
    3.5697-3.5698, 4.697
Willgoose, Carl E. 5.4656
William Blake Bicentenary Committee. 2.7431
William II, German Emperor, 1859-1941.
    3.2343
William, of Malmesbury, ca. 1090-1143. 3.1345
William, of Ockham, ca. 1285-ca. 1349. 1.389
William, of Tyre, Archbishop of Tyre, ca.
    1130-ca. 1190. 3.587
William Rockhill Nelson Gallery of Art and
    Mary Atkins Museum of Fine Arts. 1.6327
Williams, Alan F. 3.3351
Williams, Arthur Bernard, 1940-. 5.6525
Williams, Aubrey L. 2.6949, 2.7190
Williams, B. R. (Bridget R.) 3.5602
Williams, Basil, 1867-1950. 3.1527, 3.1541
Williams, Bernard Arthur Owen. 1.734, 1.797
Williams, Byron, 1934-. 3.9128
Williams, C. Ray. 4.10528
Williams, Cedric E. 2.13936
Williams, Charles, 1886-1945. 2.4940, 2.5759,
    2.6695, 2.9521-2.9529
Williams, Charles G. S. 2.4059
Williams, Christopher John Fards. 5.832
Williams, Clifford John. 2.7173
Williams College. Museum of Art. 1.6439
Williams, D. Dudley. 5.3568

Williams, Daniel Day, 1910-1973. 1.3003,
    1.3066
Williams, David, 1900-. 3.1770, 3.6600
Williams, David John, 1937-. 5.2770
Williams, Denys Stephen Dodsley, 1897- ed.
    5.6224
Williams, Donald T. 4.10591
Williams, Dudley. 5.2187, 5.2308
Williams, Edgar M. 5.7012
Williams, Edward Bennett. 4.9494
Williams, Edwin Bucher, 1891-1975. 2.905
Williams, Elizabeth M. (Elizabeth Marie),
    1950-. 4.3046
Williams, Emlyn. 2.9533
Williams, Eric Eustace, 1911-. 3.9089, 3.9137,
    4.2270
Williams, Ernest William, 1916-. 4.3876, 4.3892
Williams, Forrest, joint comp. 4.7135
Williams, Frederick, 1933-. 4.4049, 4.10300,
    5.4280
Williams, Frederick D. ed. 3.7402
Williams, Fredrick A. 5.4994
Williams, Gareth L. joint author. 4.10681
Williams, Gavin. 4.5467
Williams, George Christopher, 1926-. 5.3400
Williams, George Huntston, 1914-. 1.2320,
    1.2331, 1.2974, 1.3162
Williams, George Walton, 1922- ed. 2.6964
Williams, Glanmor. 3.1754, 3.1758
Williams, Gordon Willis. 2.637, 2.806
Williams, Gordon Willis. ed. 2.718
Williams, Gregory Howard. 4.9751
Williams, Gwyn. 2.834
Williams, Gwyn. comp. 2.849
Williams, Gwyn A. 3.1759, 3.1767, 3.1772,
    3.5971, 4.3653
Williams, H. P. 5.5585
Williams, Harold Herbert, Sir, 1880-1964.
    2.7291, 2.7297-2.7298
Williams, Henry, 1951-. 3.6657
Williams, Hermann Warner, jt. author. 1.5959
Williams, Howel, 1898-. 5.3041
Williams, Ifor, Sir 1881-. 2.835
Williams, Ioan M. 2.3517
Williams. Ioan M., comp. 2.6000, 2.7948
Williams, Iwan Prys. 5.1802
Williams, J. G. (James Gordon), 1938-.
    5.5805-5.5806
Williams, James D. (James De Bois), 1926-.
    3.6626
Williams, Jeffery. 3.1269
Williams, Joanna Gottfried, 1939-. 1.5540
Williams, John, 1908-. 1.6418, 3.801
Williams, John Adrian, 1935-. 3.5615
Williams, John Alden. ed. 1.2052
Williams, John Alden. comp. 1.1991
Williams, John Alfred, 1925-. 2.13427-2.13428
Williams, John Eric Charles. 5.2355
Williams, Jon L. 5.307
Williams, Joseph M. 2.976
Williams, Joyce E. 4.6741
Williams, Juanita H., 1922-. 4.5946
Williams, Judith LaVor. 5.4621
Williams, Kathleen. 2.6539
Williams, L. O. 5.6880
Williams, L. Pearce (Leslie Pearce), 1927-.
    5.766
Williams, Lawrence E. joint author. 5.3492
Williams, Lea E. 3.4398
Williams, Marilyn, 1921- joint author. 4.5214
Williams, Marjorie. ed. 2.7241
Williams, Martha E. 5.7641
Williams, Martin T. ed. 1.4339
Williams, Martin T. 1.4260-1.4261,
    1.4265-1.4266, 1.4340, 2.3817
Williams, Mary Pat. joint author. 5.959
Williams, Mary Wilhelmine, 1878-1944. 4.9040
Williams, Meg Harris, 1951-. 2.5775
Williams, Melvin D., 1933-. 1.2424
Williams, Mentor Lee, 1901- , ed. 3.5820
Williams, Miles. 4.8942
Williams, Miller. joint author. 2.10734
Williams, Miller. 2.4987, 2.12372
Williams, Neville, 1924-. 3.374-3.375
Williams, Oscar, 1900-1964. 2.6104, 2.6194,
    2.10737
Williams, Paul Frederick, 1938- joint author.
    5.3126

Williams, Penry. 4.8396
Williams, Peter F. 1.4143, 1.4530
Williams, Peter W. 1.1877
Williams, Philip L., 1949-. 4.1314
Williams, Philip Maynard. 3.1666, 3.2216, 4.8586, 4.8589
Williams, R. D. (Robert Deryck), 1917-. 2.783, 2.786, 2.788
Williams, R. Hal. 3.7493
Williams, R. J. P. (Robert Joseph Paton) joint author. 5.2696
Williams, Raymond. 2.2558, 2.5628, 2.6020, 3.1597, 3.1645, 4.7136
Williams, Raymond. comp. 2.9203
Williams, Richard Hay, 1912-. 5.626
Williams, Richard S. 5.2974
Williams, Robert B. 5.6010
Williams, Robert Chadwell, 1938-. 1.5031
Williams, Robert Hardin. 5.4989
Williams, Robin Murphy. 3.6533
Williams, Roger, 1604?-1683. 3.5911
Williams, Roger M., 1934-. 3.6817
Williams, Roger Terry, 1936- joint author. 5.2582
Williams, Sam P. 5.7664
Williams, Sherley Anne, 1944-. 2.10333, 2.13430-2.13431
Williams, Stanley Thomas, 1888-1956. 2.10340, 2.11097, 3.6024
Williams, Stephen, 1942-. 3.2810
Williams, Stephen Joseph, 1948-. 5.4623
Williams, T. David. 3.5496
Williams, T. Harry (Thomas Harry), 1909-. 3.6373, 3.7317, 3.7319, 3.7359, 3.7663
Williams, Tennessee, 1911-. 2.12723-2.12736, 2.12738
Williams, Thomas, 1926-. 2.13432
Williams, Thomas Desmond. joint ed. 3.1849
Williams, Trevor Illtyd. joint author. 5.5530
Williams, Trevor Illtyd. 5.5532, 5.5537
Williams, Victoria. 4.10300
Williams, W. D. (William David) 5.3283
Williams, Walter E. (Walter Edward), 1936-. 4.9564
Williams, Walter L. 1.3031, 3.5754, 5.7260
Williams, William Appleman. 3.6339, 3.6410, 3.6490, 3.7608, 4.1918
Williams, William Carlos, 1883-1963. 2.12740-2.12745, 2.12747-2.12750, 2.12754
Williams, William Glynn, tr. 2.668
Williams, William Henry. 2.7058
Williams, William Morgan, 1926-. 4.5331
Williamson, Craig, 1943-. 2.6307
Williamson, D. G. 3.2325, 3.2453
Williamson, Edward C., 1916-. 3.8276
Williamson, George, 1898-1968. 2.5799, 2.5935, 2.11645
Williamson, Hugh Albert Fordyce, 1918-. 5.7537
Williamson, Jack, 1908-. 2.12757-2.12758
Williamson, James Alexander, 1886-. 3.1276, 3.1428
Williamson, Jane. 2.3348, 5.8460
Williamson, Jeffrey G., 1935-. 4.4587
Williamson, Joel. 3.6694, 3.6806
Williamson, John, 1937-. 4.4580, 4.4582, 4.4727
Williamson, John B. 4.5824
Williamson, John B. joint author. 4.5816
Williamson, John B. 4.4823
Williamson, Karina. 2.7254
Williamson, Kenneth L. 5.2728
Williamson, M. H. (Mark Herbert) 5.3548
Williamson, Marilyn L., 1927-. 2.6105
Williamson, Oliver E. 4.2661
Williamson, Robert Wood, 1856-1932. 4.675
Willie, Charles Vert, 1927-. 3.6715, 3.6780, 4.10796-4.10797, 4.10855, 5.4702
Willier, Benjamin Harrison, 1890- ed. 5.4133
Willig, Robert D., 1947-. 4.2998
Willigan, J. Dennis. 4.1580
Willingham, Calder, 1922-. 2.12759
Willingham, Warren W. 4.10609
Willinsky, John, 1950-. 4.10514
Willis, Frederick Charles, 1883-. 1.4584
Willis, J. C. (John Christopher), 1868-1958. 5.3634
Willis, James F. 4.9333
Willis, Jerry. 5.458

Willis, John. 2.2867
Willis, John (John A.) 2.3206
Willis, John Ralph. 4.6447
Willis, Parker B. (Parker Brown), 1907-. 4.4535
Willis, Raymond S. (Raymond Smith), 1906- ed. 2.5201
Willis, Roy G. 3.5296
Willis-Thomas, Deborah, 1948-. 5.6927
Willmer, E. N. (Edward Nevill) 5.3593
Willmott, H. P. 3.1010, 5.7420
Willmott, J. C. (John Charles) 5.2047
Willmott, Peter. joint author. 4.3161
Willmott, William E., ed. 4.2461
Willoughby, Leonard Ashley, 1885- ed. 1.1372
Willoughby, Malcolm Francis. 3.1034
Willoughby, Westel Woodbury, 1867-1945. 3.4848
Willrich, Mason. 4.3811
Wills, A. J. (Alfred John) 3.5489
Wills, Garry, 1934-. 2.7567, 3.6929, 3.7034, 3.7883
Wills, John E. (John Elliot), 1936-. 3.4706
Willson, A. Leslie (Amos Leslie), 1923-. 2.2501
Willson, David Harris, 1901-. 3.1465
Willson, James D. 4.4595
Wilmarth, Mary Grace, 1866-1949. 5.2945
Wilmerding, John. 1.4863, 1.5951, 1.6357
Wilmes, Douglas R. 2.10364
Wilmeth, Don B. 2.2776, 2.10990, 4.1196, 5.7807, 5.8426
Wilmore, Gayraud S. 1.2425, 1.2796
Wilmore, Jack H., 1938-. 4.902
Wilmot, Chester. 3.956
Wilmot, Philip D. 5.5632
Wilmotte, Raymond Maurice, 1901- joint author. 4.4081
Wilmshurst, T. H. 5.6552
Wilshire, Bruce. 5.109
Wilshire, Howard Gordon, 1926-. 5.3575
Wilson, A. E. (Albert Edward), 1885-1949. 2.2842
Wilson, A. Jeyaratnam. 3.4101, 3.4373
Wilson, A. N., 1950-. 2.8051, 2.8451
Wilson, Albert Edward, ed. 2.7388
Wilson, Angus. 2.3516, 2.4349, 2.7896, 2.9534-2.9543
Wilson, Arthur McCandless, 1902-. 2.4073
Wilson, Brayton F. (Brayton Fuller), 1934-. 5.5427
Wilson, Bryan R. 1.1580-1.1581
Wilson, Carolyn F. 4.6710
Wilson, Cecil Leeburn. 5.2654
Wilson, Charles, 1914-. 3.631, 3.1257, 3.2991
Wilson, Clyde Norman. 3.6233, 3.7069
Wilson, Colin, 1931-. 2.9829, 3.20-3.21, 5.665
Wilson, Conrad, music critic. 1.3509
Wilson, David A. 4.8769
Wilson, David B. 5.3386
Wilson, David C. 5.6036
Wilson, David Gordon. 5.6205
Wilson, David McKenzie. 1.4937, 3.1323
Wilson, David McKenzie. joint author. 3.3360
Wilson, David Woodburn, 1917-. 5.2654
Wilson, Derek A. 4.97
Wilson, Dick, 1928-. 3.4817
Wilson, Dorothy Clarke. 3.5932
Wilson, E. Bright (Edgar Bright), 1908-. 5.2136
Wilson, Edmund, 1895-1972. 2.1263, 2.2604, 2.2687, 2.10237, 2.10381, 2.10425-2.10426, 2.11388, 2.11721, 2.12760-2.12767, 3.1186, 3.6061, 4.6941
Wilson, Edmund B. (Edmund Beecher), 1856-1939. 5.3594
Wilson, Edward Adrian, 1872-1912. 4.108
Wilson, Edward Arthur, 1886-1970. illus. 2.4322
Wilson, Edward L., 1931- joint author. 5.5725
Wilson, Edward Meryon, 1906-. 2.5127
Wilson, Edward Osborne, 1929-. 4.511, 5.3243, 5.3446, 5.4055, 5.4094
Wilson, Edward Thomas. 3.5129
Wilson, Elizabeth, 1936-. 4.6094
Wilson, Elizabeth A. M. 2.1238
Wilson, Emily Herring. 3.6803
Wilson, Ethel, 1890-. 2.9547
Wilson, Eva D. 5.4243
Wilson, F. P. 2.6641

Wilson, F. P. (Frank Percy), 1889-1963. 2.3809, 2.5635, 2.5852, 2.6448, 2.6619
Wilson, Frances. 2.1950
Wilson, Garff B. 2.3195, 2.3199
Wilson, George Buckley Laird. 4.1082
Wilson, George Earl, 1891-. 3.8716
Wilson, George M. (George M.), 1937-. 3.4967
Wilson, George Pickett, 1888-. 2.1149
Wilson, George Wilton, 1928-. 4.3933
Wilson, Harold, Sir, 1916-. 3.1718, 4.8450
Wilson, Harriet E., 1808-ca. 1870. 2.11287
Wilson, Ian, 1941-. 1.2898
Wilson, J. J., 1936- joint author. 1.4583
Wilson, J. (John), 1939-. 5.2372
Wilson, J. Tuzo (John Tuzo), 1908-. 5.3074, 5.3093
Wilson, James Grant, 1832-1914. ed. 3.6284
Wilson, James H. (James Harrison), 1920-. 2.5595
Wilson, James Q. joint author. 4.8843
Wilson, James Q. 4.6773, 4.6828, 4.8038, 4.8205
Wilson, James Q. ed. 4.6343
Wilson, Jason, 1944-. 2.5349
Wilson, John, 1924-. 3.1635
Wilson, John Albert, 1899-. 1.1591, 3.5136, 3.5143
Wilson, John Dover, 1881-1969. 2.6254, 2.6658-2.6659, 2.6678, 2.6765, 2.6813, 4.5318
Wilson, John Harold, 1900-. 2.3305, 2.5655, 2.6238, 2.6559, 2.6967
Wilson, John Steuart, 1913-. 1.4341
Wilson, John T. (John Todd), 1914-. 5.800
Wilson, Juliet, joint author. 1.6291
Wilson, Katharina M. 2.2622
Wilson, Lanford, 1937-. 2.13433-2.13435
Wilson, Larman Curtis, joint author. 3.6441, 3.9008
Wilson, Logan, 1907-. 4.10089, 4.10532-4.10533
Wilson, M. J. (Michael John), 1939-. 4.1200
Wilson, Major L. 3.7084, 3.7131
Wilson, Margaret, 1921 (Aug. 22)-. 2.5128, 2.5205
Wilson, Mona, 1872-. 2.7420
Wilson, Monica Hunter. 3.5297, 3.5464, 4.608
Wilson, Nigel Guy. joint author. 5.7521
Wilson, Peter J. 3.9177
Wilson, Phillip John. 2.10230
Wilson, R. McL. (Robert McLachlan) ed. 1.2735
Wilson, R. McL. (Robert McLachlan) 1.2971
Wilson, Richard, 1713-1782. 1.6043
Wilson, Richard Middlewood. 3.310
Wilson, Robert Charles, 1920-. 4.10573, 5.7064
Wilson, Robert E. (Robert Elliott) 5.5753
Wilson, Robert Forrest, 1883-1942. 2.11233
Wilson, Robert MacLachlan, ed. 1.2966
Wilson, Robert R., 1942-. 1.2585
Wilson, Robert W. 4.3809
Wilson, Rodney. 4.2574, 4.4547
Wilson, Sloan, 1920-. 2.12772
Wilson, Stephen, 1941-. 3.4013
Wilson, Suanna J., 1943-. 4.6503
Wilson, Theodore A., 1940-. 3.882, 3.6406
Wilson, Trevor, 1928-. 3.1691
Wilson, William Eade, 1900-. 2.5168
Wilson, William J., 1935-. 3.6631, 4.6456
Wilson, Woodrow, 1856-1924. 3.6327, 3.7713, 4.7849, 4.8020
Wilt, Fred, 1920-. 4.1050
Wilt, Judith, 1941-. 2.5985, 2.7949, 2.8061
Wilton-Ely, John. 1.5017
Wiltse, Charles Maurice, 1907-. 3.7072, 3.7089
Wiltshire, David. 4.4769
Wiltwyck School for Boys, Esopus, N.Y. 5.4880
Wimbush, S. Enders. 3.3028, 4.7152
Wimmer, Franz. 2.912
Wimsatt, William K. (William Kurtz), 1907-1975. 2.2446, 2.2458, 2.2465, 2.2725, 2.2736
Winburne, John N. (John Newton), 1911-. 5.5222
Winch, Donald. 4.7274, 4.7421
Winch, Kenneth L., ed. 5.8210
Winch, Peter. 4.1219
Winch, Robert Francis, 1911-. 4.5649
Winchester, Alice. 1.6518
Winchilsea, Anne Kingsmill Finch, Countess of, 1661-1720. 2.7058, 2.7337

Winckel, Fritz. 1.4377
Winckelmann, Johann Joachim, 1717-1768. 1.5143
Wind, Yoram. 4.4301
Windal, Floyd W. 4.4396
Windelband, W. (Wilhelm), 1848-1915. 1.131
Windfuhr, Manfred. ed. 2.13603
Windholz, George. 5.8295
Windholz, Martha. 5.5145
Windle, J. L. 4.3310
Windley, B. F. (Brian F.) 5.3099
Windley, Lathan A. 3.7226
Windmuller, John P. 4.3425
Windrow, Martin. ed. 3.958
Windschuttle, Elizabeth. 4.6165
Windsor, Alan. 1.4987
Windsor Castle. Royal Library. 1.5841
Wine, Martin L., ed. 2.6679
Winearls, Joan. 4.142
Winegarten, Ruthe. 3.6808
Wineman, David, joint author. 4.5721
Winer, Bart Keith, joint ed. 2.3782
Wines, Roger. 3.491
Winfield, Percy Henry, Sir, 1878-1953. 4.9406
Winfrey, Robley, 1899-. 5.6060
Wing, Donald Goddard, 1904-. 5.7916
Wingate, John Williams, 1899-. 4.4320
Wingert, Paul S. (Paul Stover), 1900-1974. 1.4689, 1.5766
Wingfield-Stratford, Esmé Cecil, 1882-. 3.1468
Wingren, Gustaf, 1910-. 1.2761
Wingrove, David. 2.5977
Winick, Charles, 1922-. 4.410
Winick, Myron. 5.4241
Winius, George D. (George Davison) 3.4369
Winkel, David E. 5.6587
Winkler, Helmut G. F., 1915-. 5.3071
Winkler, Johan, 1840-1916. 2.1010
Winkler, Paul W. (Paul Walter) 5.7628
Winkler, Robert L. 5.1414
Winkler, Ruthild, 1941-. 5.880
Winks, Robin W. 3.1209, 3.6363, 3.7356, 3.8678, 3.8797
Winks, Robin W. joint comp. 3.4538
Winks, Robin W. joint author. 3.6228
Winkworth, Peter S. 1.6448
Winn, James Anderson, 1947-. 1.4402
Winner, Ellen. 1.6688
Winner, Langdon. 5.5526
Winnicott, Clare. 5.5114
Winnicott, D. W. (Donald Woods), 1896-1971. 5.5104, 5.5114
Winnifrith, Tom. 2.7447
Winny, James. 2.6372, 2.6491
Winny, James. ed. 1.402
Winogrand, Garry, 1928-. 5.5442
Winpenny, Thomas R. 4.3007
Winship, George Parker, 1871-1952. ed. 3.9081
Winslow, Ola Elizabeth. 1.3341, 2.6922, 3.7984, 3.8016
Winsor, Mary P. 5.3836
Winstedt, Eric Otto, ed. and tr. 2.669
Winstedt, Richard Olof, Sir, 1878-. 2.2289
Winston, Clara. tr. 1.1062
Winston, David. 1.338
Winston, Kathryn Teich, 1946- joint author. 4.3246
Winston, Michael R. 3.6812
Winston, Patrick Henry. 5.999, 5.1003, 5.1017, 5.1218
Winston, Richard. tr. 1.1062, 3.2438
Winston, Roland. joint author. 5.6234
Winstone, H. V. F. (Harry Victor Frederick) joint author. 3.4047
Wint, Guy. 3.900, 3.3610
Winter, David G., 1939-. 4.10825
Winter, Ella, 1898-. 2.9548
Winter, George, 1907-. 5.5880
Winter, Henry James Jacques. 5.762
Winter, J. M. 4.7032
Winter, Keith John, 1935-. 3.5845
Winter, Ralph K., 1935- joint author. 4.3513
Winter, Robert, 1945-. 1.3799
Winter, Sidney G. 4.1280
Winterbottom, Michael. joint comp. 2.264
Winterkorn, Hans Friedrich, 1905-. 5.5921
Winternitz, Emanuel. 1.3492, 1.3499

Winters, Donald L. 4.2919, 5.5225
Winters, Kenneth, 1929-. 1.3538
Winters, Wendy Glasgow. 4.10704
Winters, Yvor, 1900-1968. 2.2459, 2.2514, 2.10275, 2.12409, 2.12773
Winton, Harry N. M. 5.8114, 5.8267
Winton, John. 5.7428
Wintringham, Thomas Henry, 1898-1949. 5.7176
Winwar, Frances, pseud. tr. 2.4908
Wionczek, Miguel S. 4.4726
Wipper, Audrey. 1.1855
Wireman, Peggy. 4.5220
Wirsing, Robert. 4.6174
Wirt, Frederick M. 4.10740
Wirth, Arthur G. 4.10826
Wirth, Louis, 1897-1952. 3.3900, 4.4802, 4.4849
Wirth, Niklaus. 5.1204, 5.1222
Wirths, Claudine G. 5.626
Wirtz, Willard, 1912-. 4.10835
Wirz, Albert. 3.3635
Wisconsin Center for Film and Theater Research. 2.3030
Wisconsin Institute for Medieval and Renaissance Studies. 3.146
Wisconsin Research and Development Center for Cognitive Learning. 4.10371
Wisconsin Seminar on Natural Resource Policies in Relation to Economic Development and International Cooperation (1977-1978: University of Wisconsin—Madison) 4.1773
Wisconsin. University. Dept. of Indian Studies. 3.4181
Wisdom, John. 1.1296
Wisdom, John Oulton. 1.113
Wisdom, William A., joint author. 1.1177
Wise, Arthur, 1923-. 4.1054
Wise, David. 4.7915
Wise, David A. 4.3307, 4.3468
Wise, Gene. 3.6224
Wise, James H. 4.10707
Wise, Leonard F., joint author. 3.563
Wise, Mark B., 1953- joint author. 5.1973
Wise, S. F. (Sydney F.), 1924-. 3.538, 5.7404
Wise, Stephen. 4.738
Wiseberg, Laurie S. 4.7637
Wiseman, Christopher. 2.9131
Wiseman, D. J. (Donald John) ed. 3.3705
Wiseman, Henry. 4.9256
Wiseman, Jack. joint author. 4.4688
Wisenthal, J. L. 2.14040
Wiser, Charlotte Melina (Viall) 3.4171
Wiser, William Henricks, 1890-1961. joint author. 3.4171
Wish, Harvey, 1909-. 3.6174, 3.6225
Wiskemann, Elizabeth. 3.1907
Wisman, Josette A. 2.3973
Wist, Abund Ottokar. 5.6595
Wister, Owen, 1860-1938. 2.11288
Wistrich, Robert S., 1945-. 3.346
Wiswall, Irving W. 5.8167
Wiswell, Ella Lury, 1909-. 4.98
Witcover, Jules. joint author. 3.7855
Witczak, Matthew W., joint author. 5.6069
Witemeyer, Hugh. 2.7712
Witham, W. Tasker. 2.10602
Wither, George, 1588-1667. 2.6548
Witherell, Julian W. 5.8075-5.8076
Withers, Carl. 4.4988, 4.5149
Withers, Charles C. 5.5500
Withers, Josephine. 1.5741
Witherspoon, Alexander M. (Alexander Maclaren), 1894-. 2.6084, 2.6086
Witherspoon, Gary. 3.5925-3.5926
Withey, Lynne. 3.7054, 4.6244
Withycombe, Elizabeth Gidley, 1902-. 3.304, 5.7932
Witke, Roxane. 3.4814, 4.6139
Witkiewicz, Stanisław Ignacy, 1885-1939. 2.1736-2.1738, 2.1748
Witkin, Herman A. 5.537
Witkin, Lee D. 5.6913
Witschi, Jelia C. joint author. 5.4234
Witt, Elder. 3.7918
Witt, Shirley Hill, comp. 2.2323
Witte, John F. 4.3186

Witte, Sergieĭ IUl'evich, graf., 1849-1915. 3.3158
Wittek, Paul, 1894-. 3.3578
Witter, John A. 5.5405
Wittfogel, Karl August, 1896-. 4.7557
Wittgenstein, Ludwig, 1889-1951. 1.1065-1.1068, 1.1070-1.1073, 1.1075-1.1076, 1.1078, 1.1087, 1.1225-1.1226, 5.632, 5.1035
Wittig, Kurt, 1914-. 2.9836
Wittig, Monique. 2.4795-2.4796
Wittke, Carl Frederick, 1892-1971. 2.3407, 2.3644, 3.8381, 4.8950
Wittkower, Margot. joint author. 1.4625
Wittkower, Margot. 1.5726
Wittkower, Rudolf. ed. 1.5010
Wittkower, Rudolf. joint author. 1.4932
Wittkower, Rudolf. 1.4625, 1.5006, 1.5726, 1.5777
Wittner, Lawrence S. 4.9146
Wittrock, M. C. (Merlin C.), 1931-. 4.10286
Witunski, Michael. 3.6433
Witvliet, Theo. 1.2808
Wixman, Ronald, 1947-. 3.3026
Wobschall, Darold. 5.6553
Wodarski, John S. 4.6542
Woddis, Jack. 4.1824
Wodehouse, P. G. (Pelham Grenville), 1881-1975. 2.9549-2.9553, 2.9555-2.9558, 2.9561
Wodehouse, Pelham Grenville, Sir, 1881-. 2.9554
Woelfle, Robert M. 5.5499
Woellmer, Elizabeth H. 4.10526
Woerner, Gert. 2.2352
Woese, Carl R. 5.3447
Wohl, Anthony S. 4.3498
Wohl, Martin. 4.3930
Wohl, Martin. joint author. 4.3937
Wohl, Robert. 3.84
Wohl, Stanley. 5.4641
Wohlstetter, Roberta. 3.1017
Wohlwill, Joachim F. 5.316
Woinowsky-Krieger, S., joint author. 5.1674
Woito, Robert. 5.8258
Woiwode, Larry. 2.13436
Wolanin, Thomas R., 1942-. 4.7899
Wolbarsht, Myron. joint author. 5.5953
Wolchik, Sharon L. 4.5964
Wolcott, Harry F., 1929-. 4.10671
Wolf, A. (Abraham), 1876-1948. ed. 1.1096
Wolf, Christa. 2.13922-2.13929
Wolf, Edwin, 1911-. 3.8085
Wolf, Emil. joint author. 5.2277
Wolf, Eric Robert, 1923-. 1.1519, 3.608
Wolf, John Baptist, 1907-. 3.643, 3.2038, 3.5206
Wolf, Leonard. ed. 2.9387
Wolf, Margery. 4.6139-4.6140
Wolf, Martin, 1946-. 4.4240
Wolf, Paul R. 5.5820, 5.6990
Wolf, R. Craig. 2.3155
Wolf, Stephanie Grauman. 4.5211
Wolf, Stewart, 1914- ed. 5.4935
Wolf, Walter James, 1927-. 5.7129
Wolfe, Bertram David, 1896-1977. 1.6005, 2.1512, 3.3151, 3.3238
Wolfe, Don Marion, 1902-. 2.7146, 2.7153
Wolfe, Donald M. joint author. 4.5585
Wolfe, Douglas A. joint author. 5.1411
Wolfe, Gary K., 1946-. 2.10574
Wolfe, Gene. 2.13437
Wolfe, Julia Elizabeth (Westall), 1860-1945. 2.12787
Wolfe, Peter, 1933-. 2.9270, 2.9695, 2.9777, 2.10192
Wolfe, Richard J. 1.3545, 1.3564
Wolfe, Robert, 1921-. 3.1106
Wolfe, Stephen L. 5.3605-5.3606
Wolfe, Thomas, 1900-1938. 2.12774-2.12787
Wolfe, Tom. 1.5875, 2.13438, 3.6067, 3.6175
Wolfensberger, Wolf. joint author. 4.6609
Wolfenstein, Martha, 1911-1976. joint ed. 4.5706
Wolfers, Arnold, 1892-. 3.753, 3.7609, 5.7384
Wolff, Cynthia Griffin. 2.10818, 2.12701
Wolff, Hans Walter. 1.2586, 1.2617-1.2618
Wolff, Harold G. (Harold George), 1898-. 5.4349, 5.4935
Wolff, Janet. 2.2384

Wolff, Konrad. 1.3981, 1.4073, 1.4158
Wolff, Kurt H., 1912- ed. 4.4757, 4.4857
Wolff, Leon. 3.794
Wolff, Michael, 1927-. 2.3689, 4.6254
Wolff, Philippe, 1913-. 3.139
Wolff, Robert Lee. 2.6029, 2.7541, 2.7933,
    3.3538
Wolff, Robert Paul. 1.1261, 4.7660
Wolff, Sidney C. 5.1717
Wölfflin, Heinrich. 1.4678, 1.4771, 1.4990,
    1.5004, 1.5433
Wolfgang, Charles H. 4.10701
Wolfgang, Marvin E., 1924-. 4.5043, 4.6729,
    4.6886
Wolfheim, Jaclyn H. 5.4028
Wolfinger, Raymond E. 4.8111
Wolfram, von Eschenbach, 12th cent.
    2.13539-2.13541
Wolfram, Walt, 1941-. 2.1013, 2.1128
Wolfschütz, Hans. 2.13935
Wolfson, Harry Austryn, 1887-1974. 1.301,
    1.339, 1.1102, 1.2750
Wolfson, Nicholas. 4.3084
Wolin, Sheldon S. 4.7266
Wolins, Martin. comp. 4.6575
Wolkenfeld, Jack. 2.8511
Wolko, Howard S. 5.6651
Wolkstein, Diane. 1.1785
Woll, Allen L. 2.3216
Woll, Josephine. 5.8016
Wollen, Peter. 2.2973
Wollheim, Richard, 1923-. 1.1362
Wollman, Élie L. 5.4449
Wollstonecraft, Mary, 1759-1797. 2.8291,
    4.6101
Wolman, Benjamin B. 5.16, 5.83, 5.550, 5.640,
    5.654, 5.4779
Wolman, Benjamin B. ed. 3.436
Wolman, Benjamin B. 5.4909, 5.4944
Wolman, Yecheskel, 1935-. 5.2603
Woloch, Isser, 1937-. 3.182, 5.7371
Wolpe, AnnMarie. 4.5880
Wolpe, Joseph. ed. 5.4849
Wolpert, Stanley A., 1927-. 3.4098, 3.4137,
    3.4227
Wolpin, Miles D. 4.7717
Wolseley, Roland Edgar, 1904-. 2.3650
Wolt, Irene. joint author. 2.3659
Wolter, Allan Bernard, 1913- ed. and tr. 1.384
Wolters, Clifton. tr. 1.3220
Wolters, Raymond, 1938-. 4.9593, 4.10875
Womack, James P. joint author. 4.3915
Woman's Rights Convention. (1st: 1848: Seneca
    Falls, N.Y.). 4.8078
Woman's Rights Convention. (1st: 1848: Seneca
    Falls, N.Y.) 4.8078
Woman's Rights Convention. Rochester, N.Y.,
    1848. 4.8078
Women in Transition Inc. 4.5784
Women's Action Alliance. 4.6587, 4.10306
Wong, David B. 1.1463
Wong, Donna L., 1948-. 5.5087
Wong, Glenn M. 4.9578
Wong, H. Y. 5.6199
Wong, Jeffrey Tze-Fei, 1937-. 5.4416
Wong, Jo Yung. 5.6634
Wong, John, 1939-. 4.2439
Wong, Kam W., 1940-. 5.5824
Wong, Yu Jen, 1945-. 5.6467
Wonnacott, Paul. joint author. 4.4206
Wonnacott, Paul. 4.4207
Wonnacott, Ronald J. 4.1399, 4.4206
Wonnacott, Thomas H., 1935- joint author.
    4.1399
Wood, Allen W. 1.897, 1.920, 1.1043
Wood, Beth. 4.4628
Wood, Brian J. B. 5.6888
Wood, Bryce, 1909-. 3.9022-3.9023, 3.9162
Wood, Christopher. 1.6018
Wood, Clement, 1888-1950. 2.1050
Wood, Corinne Shear. 4.467
Wood, David Norris. 5.8218
Wood, Derek, 1930-. 3.1048
Wood, Donna, 1949-. 5.5641-5.5642
Wood, E. R. (Edward Rudolf), 1907-. 2.6236
Wood, Eric F. 5.6009
Wood, Frederick Thomas, 1905-. 2.6928
Wood, Gordon S. 4.7319

Wood, Henry Harvey, 1903-. 2.6622, 2.8294
Wood, Houston, 1944- joint author. 4.4803
Wood, Karen A. 5.7771
Wood, Manfri Frederick. 3.5682
Wood, Marilynn J. 5.5186
Wood, Marion M. joint author. 4.4341
Wood, Neal. ed. 5.7202
Wood, Peter H., 1943-. 3.7219
Wood, Robert Coldwell, 1923-. 4.6235
Wood, Robert L. 3.8643
Wood, Robin, 1931-. 2.3051, 2.3058
Wood, Sally. 2.11792
Wood, Stephen B. 4.9568
Wood, Susan, 1948-1980. 2.3459
Wood, W. Raymond. 3.5738
Wood, William Alfred Rae, 1878-. 3.4525
Wood, William Burke, 1779-1861. 2.3232
Woodard, Kim. 4.3779
Woodbey, George Washington, b. 1854. 4.7140
Woodbridge, Frederick James Eugene,
    1867-1940. 1.97, 1.653, 1.671
Woodbridge, Hensley Charles, 1923-. 5.8024
Woodbridge, Linda, 1945-. 2.5642
Woodbridge, Sally Byrne. 1.5562
Woodbury, Marda. 5.8364
Woodbury, Richard Benjamin, 1917-. 4.420
Woodcock, David. 5.5415
Woodcock, Eric Charles. 2.254
Woodcock, George. 2.8831, 2.9064, 2.9204,
    2.9889, 2.9891-2.9892, 3.5791, 4.1361, 4.7185,
    4.7187, 4.7195
Woodcock, R. C. 5.1585
Wooden, John R. 4.1013
Wooden, Warren W. 2.6479
Wooden, Wayne S. 4.6752
Woodfield, Ian. 1.4160
Woodfin, Maude Howlett. 3.8192
Woodforde, James, 1740-1803. 3.1534
Woodgate, Gordon Kemble. 5.2078
Woodham Smith, Cecil Blanche Fitz Gerald,
    1896-. 3.1616, 3.1850, 5.7413
Woodham Smith, Cecil Blanche (FitzGerald)
    1896-. 3.1600
Woodhead, A. G. (Arthur Geoffrey) 2.564,
    3.282
Woodhead, Ronald W. joint author. 5.5705
Woodhouse, A. S. P. (Arthur Sutherland
    Pigott), 1895-1964. 2.7160
Woodhouse, C. M. (Christopher Montague),
    1917-. 3.2683, 3.2697-3.2698, 3.2701
Woodhouse, John Robert. 1.1512
Woodhouse, William John, 1866-1937. 3.2600
Woodhull, Victoria C. (Victoria Claflin),
    1838-1927. 4.5175
Woodman, Dorothy. 3.4236
Woodman, Harold D. 4.3685
Woodmason, Charles, ca. 1720-ca. 1776. 3.8244
Woodress, James Leslie. 2.11243, 2.11473,
    5.7816
Woodress, James Leslie. ed. 2.10373
Woodring, Carl Ray, 1919-. 2.6263
Woodroffe, John George, Sir, 1865-1936.
    1.1691-1.1692, 1.1722-1.1723
Woodrow Wilson School of Public and
    International Affairs. 4.3116
Woodrow Wilson School of Public and
    International Affairs. Center of International
    Studies. 3.3380, 3.4390, 3.4477, 3.7792,
    4.3656, 4.5044, 4.6964, 4.6976, 4.8799,
    4.8809, 4.8987, 4.9033, 4.9125, 4.9275
Woodruff, Michael F. A., Sir. 5.5033
Woodruff, Paul, 1943-. 1.257
Woods, Donald, 1933-. 3.5471
Woods, George Benjamin, 1878-1958, ed.
    2.6182
Woods, H. D. 4.3625
Woods Hole Oceanographic Institution. 4.320
Woods, James Haughton, 1864-1935, tr. 1.204
Woods, Kenneth Brady, 1905- ed. 5.6061
Woods, L. B., 1938-. 5.7599
Woods, Mary E., 1930-. 4.6498
Woods, Michael. 1.285
Woods, Richard, 1941-. 1.1632
Woods, Richard Donovon. 5.7905, 5.7908
Woodside, Arch G. 4.4310
Woodson, Carter Godwin, 1875-1950.
    3.6632-3.6633, 3.6789
Woodson, Herbert H. 5.2408

Woodson, Thomas. comp. 2.11198
Woodsworth, James Shaver, 1874-1942. 3.8795
Woodward, Anthony. 2.12330
Woodward, Bob. joint author. 3.7916
Woodward, Bob. 3.7925
Woodward, C. Vann (Comer Vann), 1908-.
    3.6695-3.6696, 3.7367-3.7368, 3.7454, 3.7483,
    3.8164, 3.8167
Woodward, David R., 1939-. 3.1694
Woodward, E. L. (Ernest Llewellyn), Sir, 1890-.
    3.666, 3.674, 3.802, 3.930, 3.1587
Woodward, Gary C. 4.7854
Woodward, George Evertson. 1.5560
Woodward, George Ratcliffe, 1848-. 2.355
Woodward, George William Otway. 1.3235
Woodward, James B. 2.1482
Woodward, Joan. 4.2662
Woodward, John B. 5.7517
Woodward, Kathleen M. 3.212
Woodward, Margaret. 5.7092
Woodward, R. B. (Robert Burns), 1917-1979.
    5.2819
Woodward, Ralph Lee. 3.9050, 5.7899
Woodworth, George Wallace. 1.3698
Woodworth, Robert Sessions, 1869-1962. 5.212
Woody, Kennerly M. 1.3119
Woody, Robert H. (Robert Hilliard), 1903-.
    3.6995
Woody, Thomas, 1891-1960, ed. 4.10188
Woodyard, George William. 2.5309
Wooldridge, Dean E. 5.4342
Wooldridge, Susan, 1940-. 4.4349
Woolery, George W., 1937-. 2.2861
Woolf, Bertram Lee, 1884-. 1.2675
Woolf, Harry. 5.1948
Woolf, Harry. ed. 1.88
Woolf, Leonard, 1880-1969. 2.9562-2.9567,
    2.9570, 2.9572, 2.9584, 4.1760, 4.2580, 4.7544
Woolf, S. J. 3.2830
Woolf, S. J. (Stuart Joseph) 3.868
Woolf, S. J. (Stuart Joseph) ed. 3.2906
Woolf, Virginia, 1882-1941. 1.5151, 2.2555,
    2.2605-2.2606, 2.3411, 2.9296, 2.9568-2.9570,
    2.9572-2.9584, 2.9586-2.9587, 2.9605
Woolf, Virginia Stephen, 1882-1941. 2.9571
Woolhouse, R. S. 1.680
Woollcott, Alexander, 1887-1943. 2.12799
Woolman, John, 1720-1772. 1.3356
Woolrych, Austin H. 3.1490
Woolsey, John M. 2.8881
Woolverton, John Frederick, 1926-. 1.3316
Wooster, Ralph A. 3.7183
Wootton, Barbara, 1897-. 4.3136
Woozley, A. D. (Anthony Douglas) 1.245
Worcester Art Museum. 1.4899
Worcester, David. 2.3790
Worcester, Donald Emmet, 1915-. 3.9204
Wordsworth, Dorothy, 1771-1855.
    2.8295-2.8296
Wordsworth, Jonathan. 2.8302-2.8303
Wordsworth, William, 1770-1850.
    2.8298-2.8304, 2.8307-2.8308, 3.1738
Work in America Institute. 4.2685, 4.3203
Work, James Aiken. 2.7277
Workshop on Estuarine and Wetland Processes
    and Water Quality Modeling (1979: New
    Orleans, La.) 4.339
Workshop on the Comparative Study of
    Communism, Center for Advanced Study in
    the Behavioral Sciences, 1968. 3.1178
World Academy of Art and Science. 4.1635
World Bank. 4.1814, 4.1822, 4.1825, 4.1828,
    4.2155, 4.2561, 4.2563, 4.2599, 4.3236,
    4.3797, 4.10970
World Bank. Development Research Center.
    4.1819
World Congress on National Parks (1982: Bali,
    Indonesia) 5.5384
World Employment Programme. 4.2876, 4.5484,
    4.6155
World Future Society. 3.66, 3.70
World Law Fund. 4.1784
World Meteorological Organization. 4.296,
    5.2537
World Order Models Project. 4.1784
World Peace Foundation. 4.8971
World Population Conference (2nd: 1965:
    Belgrade) 4.1578

World Zionist Organization. Dor Hemschech
  Institutes. 5.8236
Worldwatch Institute. 4.1793, 4.2763
Wormald, B.H.G. 3.1501
Wormald, Jenny, 1942-. 3.1792
Wormald, Patrick. 3.1314
Wormeley, Katherine Prescott, 1830-1908.
  2.4115
Wormell, Donald Ernest Wilson. 3.2644
Wörner, Karl Heinrich, 1910-1969. 1.3638,
  1.3972, 1.3996
Worringer, Wilhelm, 1881-1965. 1.4602, 1.4755
Worsley, Peter. 1.1880
Worster, Donald, 1941-. 3.8561, 4.2030,
  5.3530-5.3531
Worster, William John Alexander, 1882-1929,
  tr. 2.14044
Worswick, Clark. 3.4278, 3.4281
Wortman, Andrze J. 5.6236
Wortman, Miles L., 1944-. 4.5609
Wortman, Richard. 3.3129
Wortman, William A., 1940-. 5.8279
Wortzel, Lawrence H. 4.4309
Wouk, Herman, 1915-. 2.12800-2.12802
Wouters, Liliane. 2.4797
Woy, James B. 4.4261
Woytinsky, Emma Shadkhan, 1893-1968. joint
  author. 4.1795
Woytinsky, Wladimir S., 1885-1960. 4.1795
Wrage, Ernest J., ed. 2.10856
Wray, Harry, 1931-. 3.4957
Wrenn, Charles Leslie, 1895-. 2.932, 2.977,
  2.6289
Wrenn, John H. 2.11589
Wriggins, W. Howard (William Howard),
  1918-. 3.4131
Wright, A. D. (Anthony David) 1.2363
Wright, A. W. 4.3647
Wright, Albert Hazen, 1879-. 5.3929, 5.3931
Wright, Allen. 2.7392
Wright, Andrew H. 2.7386, 2.8512
Wright, Andrew H. joint author. 5.7928
Wright, Anna (Allen) 1882-. 5.3929, 5.3931
Wright, Arthur F., 1913-1976. 1.158, 1.2115,
  3.4699
Wright, Arthur W., 1938-. 4.2369
Wright, Austin. ed. 2.5709, 2.5714
Wright, Austin McGiffert, 1922-. 2.3434,
  2.10648
Wright, Basil. 2.3043
Wright, Benjamin Fletcher, 1900-. 4.7320,
  4.9633, 4.9652
Wright, Charles, 1935-. 2.5031
Wright, Chauncey, 1830-1875. 1.655
Wright, Christopher, 1926-. 5.750
Wright, Christopher Amyas, 1928-. 5.3843
Wright, Conrad. 1.3416
Wright, David, 1920-. 1.5475, 2.6188, 2.10054
Wright, David McCord, 1909-. 4.3330
Wright, Deil Spencer, 1930-. 4.4664
Wright, Edward Maitland, 1906- joint author.
  5.1324
Wright, Edward Reynolds. ed. 3.5009
Wright, Elizabeth Mary, 1863-. 2.952, 2.988
Wright, Elizabeth Mary (Lea) 1863- jt. author.
  2.933
Wright, Erik Olin. 4.6389
Wright, Esmond. ed. 3.6914
Wright, Esmond. 3.6907
Wright, Frances, 1795-1852. 3.6031
Wright, Frank Lloyd, 1867-1959. 1.5276,
  1.5332-1.5339, 1.5473, 1.5561, 1.5585
Wright, Frederick Adam, 1869-1946. 2.808
Wright, G. H. von (Georg Henrik), 1916-.
  1.451, 1.1067, 1.1088, 1.1153, 1.1189
Wright, G. H. von (Georg Henrik von), 1916-.
  1.1068, 1.1071, 1.1078, 1.1338, 5.1035
Wright, Gary A. 3.5771
Wright, Gavin. 4.2026
Wright, George Ernest, 1909-1974. 1.2544,
  1.2547, 1.2552
Wright, Gordon, 1912-. 3.913, 3.2009, 4.2854,
  4.6790
Wright, H. E. (Herbert Edgar), 1917-.
  5.3145-5.3146
Wright, Harold A. 5.5603
Wright, Harold Bunker, 1907- ed. 2.7206
Wright, Helen, 1914-. 5.852

Wright, Henry A. 5.3264
Wright, J. Leitch (James Leitch), 1929-. 3.5755,
  3.6869, 3.6943
Wright, Jack Mason, 1931- joint author. 5.341
Wright, James Arlington, 1927-.
  2.12804-2.12806, 2.13770
Wright, Janet. 1.5343
Wright, Janet B. 1.5563
Wright, Jay. 2.13439-2.13440
Wright, John Kirtland, 1891-1969. 4.1, 4.63,
  4.156, 5.8199
Wright, John L. 3.5201
Wright, John P. 1.708
Wright, Joseph, 1855-1930. 2.933, 2.952, 2.988,
  2.1113
Wright, Judith. 2.10193
Wright, Lawrence, 1906-. 1.5117
Wright, Louis B. (Louis Booker), 1899-. 1.4864,
  2.5636, 3.6020, 3.6870, 3.8184, 3.8190-3.8191,
  3.8204, 3.8236
Wright, Lyle H. (Lyle Henry), 1903-. 5.7819
Wright, Lyle Henry, 1903-. 5.7817-5.7818
Wright, Marcia. 4.9925
Wright, Margaret H. 5.1549
Wright, Mary (Clabaugh) ed. 3.4744
Wright, Mary (Clabaugh) 3.4740
Wright, Michael, 1941-. 5.5455
Wright, Michael A. 3.5266
Wright, Nathalia. 1.5667
Wright, Olive. 3.5595
Wright, Paul H. 5.5927, 5.6062, 5.6683
Wright, Quincy, 1890-1970. 4.9001, 4.9124,
  4.9283, 5.7148
Wright, Richard, 1908-1960. 2.12807-2.12811,
  2.12813-2.12816
Wright, Richard A. 1.1146
Wright, Richard W. ed. 4.2734
Wright, Robert K., 1946-. 5.7288
Wright, Robert L. 5.6600
Wright, Robin B., 1948-. 3.3741
Wright, Sewall, 1889-. 5.3477
Wright, Sheila, 1919-. 5.5037
Wright, Thomas, 1859-1936. 2.7421
Wright, Walter Francis, 1912-. 2.7950
Wright, Will. 2.3013
Wright, William, 1930-. 2.1831, 2.11834
Wright, William Aldis, 1834-1914, ed. 2.6429
Wright, Wilmer Cave France. 2.377, 2.386
Wrigley, E. A. (Edward Anthony), 1931-.
  4.1694
Wriston, Henry Merritt, 1889-. 4.9094
Writers Guild of America, West. 2.3074
Writers' Program (Ala.) 3.8284
Writers' Program (Arizona) 3.8578
Writers' program. Arkansas. 3.8342
Writers' Program (California) 3.8621
Writers' Program. California. 3.8627, 3.8632
Writers' program. Indiana. 3.8400
Writers' program. Louisiana. 3.8309
Writers' Program. Maryland. 3.9109
Writers' Program. Michigan. 3.8433
Writers' Program. Montana. 3.8548
Writers' program (Nevada) 3.8587
Writers' program. New York. 3.8035
Writers' Program of the Work Projects
  Administration in the State of Missouri.
  3.8364
Writers' Program of the Work Projects
  Administration in the State of Oklahoma.
  3.8532
Writers' Program of the Work Projects
  Administration in the State of Wyoming.
  3.8554
Writers' Program. Ohio. 3.8385
Writers' Program (Oregon) 3.8638
Writers' program. Pennsylvania. 3.8083
Writers' program. South Carolina. 3.8237
Writers' Program (Tex.) 3.8330
Writers' Program (Utah) 3.8581
Writers' Program. Virginia. 3.8213
Writers' Program (Wash.) 3.8642
Writers' Program. West Virginia. 3.8225
Writers' Program. Wisconsin. 3.8450
Wrobel, Paul, 1942-. 3.8440
Wrone, David R. joint author. 3.7880
Wroth, Lawrence C. (Lawrence Counselman),
  1884-1970. 5.7553
Wroth, Peter. joint author. 5.5902

Wu, Ch'eng-en, ca. 1500-ca. 1582.
  2.2226-2.2227
Wu, Ching-tzu, 1701-1754. 2.2234
Wu, Nelson Ikon, 1919-. 1.5450
Wu, Silas H. L., 1929-. 3.4719
Wu, Tung, joint author. 1.5063
Wuest, Deborah A. 4.900
Wulf, Kathleen, 1941-. 4.10454
Wulf, Maurice Marie Charles Joseph de,
  1867-1947. 1.358, 1.362
Wulf, William Allan. 5.1175
Wulff, Donna Marie, 1943-. 1.1717
Wundt, Wilhelm Max, 1832-1920. 5.111
Wuorinen, John H. (John Henry), 1897-. 3.3291
Wurman, Richard Saul, 1935-. 4.891
Wurmser, Leon. 5.445
Wuthnow, Robert. 1.1578, 1.1878, 1.2478,
  4.4871
Wyatt, Alfred John, 1858-. 2.941
Wyatt, Antony. 5.2940
Wyatt-Brown, Bertram, 1932-. 3.7264, 3.8126
Wyatt, David K. 3.4523, 5.8328
Wyatt, H. V. (Harold Vivian) joint author.
  5.3293
Wyatt, Thomas, Sir, 1503?-1542. 2.6144-2.6145,
  2.6150, 2.6549
Wybourne, Brian G. ed. 5.2074
Wycherley, R. E. (Richard Ernest) 1.5603
Wycherley, William, 1640-1716. 2.7338-2.7339
Wyckoff, Alexander. 1.4859
Wyckoff, D. Daryl. 4.3985
Wyckoff, Ralph W. G. (Ralph Walter
  Graystone), 1897-. 5.2937
Wyczynski, Paul, 1921- joint author. 2.4805
Wye, Deborah. 1.5661
Wyer, Robert S. 4.4926
Wyeth, Andrew, 1917-. 1.5990-1.5991
Wykes, David. 2.7000
Wykes-Joyce, Max. 2.9337
Wyld, Henry Cecil Kennedy, 1870-1945.
  2.978-2.979, 2.989
Wyld, Lionel D. 3.6270
Wyler, Seymour B. 1.6662
Wylie, Elinor, 1885-1928. 2.12824-2.12828
Wylie, Francis James, Sir, 1865-1952. 2.7363
Wylie, Laurence William, 1909-. 3.2227
Wylie, Philip, 1902-1971. 3.6176
Wylie, Ruth C. 5.501
Wyllie, Peter J., 1930-. 5.2962
Wyly, Thomas J. 4.4271
Wyman, David S. 3.1123
Wyman, Donald, 1903-. 5.5365
Wyman, Leland Clifton, 1897-. 3.5927
Wyman, Mark. 4.3534
Wymore, A. Wayne. 5.5693
Wynar, Anna T., 1944- joint author. 3.6534
Wynar, Bohdan S. 5.7627, 5.7711, 5.8105
Wynar, Lubomyr Roman, 1932-. 3.6534, 5.7857
Wyndham, Francis. 2.9277
Wyndham, John, 1903-1969. 2.8705
Wyngaarden, James B., 1924-. 5.4754
Wynkoop, Sally. comp. 5.7777
Wynkoop, Sally. 5.7780
Wynn, Ellen. 2.3709
Wynn, Neil A. 3.1130
Wynne, Michael James. 5.3709
Wyon, Olive, tr. 1.1481, 1.2906
Wyschogrod, Michael, 1928-. 1.1972
Wyszecki, Günter. joint author. 5.2333
Wythe, George, 1893-. 4.2173

X, Malcolm, 1925-1965. 3.6675, 3.6844
Xanthakos, Petros P. 5.5922
Xenophon. 1.241, 2.398-2.400, 3.545
Xue, Muquio, 1904-. 4.2488
Xydēs, Stephanos G., 1913-1975. 3.2704
Xydis, Dorothy Peaslee. ed. 4.9379
Xydis, Dorothy Peaslee. 4.9235
Xydis, Stephen George. 4.9235

Yaacobi, Gad, 1935-. 4.8783
Yaakov, Juliette. 5.8179
Yaalon, Dan H. 5.5269
Yabes, Leopoldo Y. 2.10135-2.10136
Yad va-shem, rashut ha-zikaron la-Sho'ah vela-
  gevurah. 3.1124, 3.3955
Yad Vashem International Historical
  Conference. (4th: 1980: Jerusalem) 3.1124

Yadin, Yigael, 1917-1984. 1.1936, 3.3812,
   3.3820-3.3821, 3.3898, 5.7177
Yager, Joseph A., 1916-. 4.3710
Yago, Glenn. 4.3914
Yahraes, Herbert C. 5.5112
Yājñika, Ramanalāla Ke., 1895-1960. 2.3394
Yaldiz, Marianne. 1.5185
Yale Center for British Art. 1.4956
Yale University. 1.4855, 3.3056
Yale University. Art Gallery. 1.4660, 1.4986,
   1.5979, 1.6161, 1.6369, 1.6382, 1.6667
Yale University. Clinic of Child Development.
   5.580
Yale University. Concilium on International
   Studies. 3.5114, 3.5119
Yale University. Institute of Human Relations.
   4.593, 4.5065, 4.10373
Yale University. Institute of International
   Studies. 3.4417, 3.9012, 4.8028, 5.7384
Yale University. Louis Stern Memorial Fund.
   1.978
Yale University. Mary Cady Tew fund. 1.432
Yale University. School of Medicine. Historical
   Library. 5.8282
Yale University. School of Music. 1.3901
Yale University. School of Nursing. 5.8292
Yale University. William McKean Brown
   Memorial Publication Fund. 2.7283
Yalman, Nur. 3.4365
Yalom, Marilyn. 2.10289, 4.5595
Yamada, Sōbin. joint author. 1.2153
Yamagiwa, Joseph K. (Joseph Koshimi), 1906-.
   2.2030
Yamaguchi, Mas. 5.5338
Yamamoto, Tsunetomo, 1659-1719. 1.1426
Yamamura, Sakae, 1918-. 5.6317
Yamanouchi, Hisaaki, 1934-. 2.2003
Yamazaki, Masakazu, 1934-. 2.2136
Yamazaki, Tomoko, 1932-. 4.6149
Yamey, Basil S. joint author. 4.2760
Yamey, Basis S. 4.4386
Yanagisawa, Eizo, 1902-. 2.2045
Yancey, William L., joint author. 3.6779
Yandle, Bruce. 4.2002
Yaney, George L. 4.2879
Yáñez, Agustín, 1904-. 2.5357
Yang, Boda. 1.4668
Yang, C. K., 1910-. 1.1793, 4.5418, 4.5627
Yang, Chen Ning, 1922-. 5.2404
Yang, Edward S. 5.6502
Yang, Gladys. 2.2211
Yang, Gladys. ed. 2.2239
Yang, Gladys. 2.2235
Yang, Hsien-i. 2.2211, 2.2235
Yang, T. Y. 5.5848
Yang, Winston L. Y. 5.8045-5.8046
Yankelovich, Daniel. 4.5166
Yannella, Donald. 2.11031
Yannopoulos, George N., 1936- joint author.
   3.2706
Yanowitch, Murray. comp. 4.5380
Yans-McLaughlin, Virginia, 1943-. 3.8060
Yar-Shater, Ehsan. 3.4065
Yarbro, Chelsea Quinn. 2.13441
Yarbrough, Tinsley E., 1941-. 4.9492
Yardley, Alice. 4.10407
Yardley, Jonathan. 2.11987
Yariv, Amnon. 5.5950, 5.6489
Yarmac, Raymond F., joint author. 5.6049
Yarmolinsky, Adam. 4.10792
Yarmolinsky, Avrahm, 1890-. 2.1316, 2.1321,
   2.1329, 2.1411, 2.1464, 3.3113, 3.3158
Yarnold, Edward. 1.2985
Yarrow, Philip John. 2.3849
Yarumaro, d. 723. 1.1840
Yarwood, Doreen. 4.827, 4.831
Yarwood, Edmund. 2.1497
Yashpal. 2.1895
Yāsīn, al-Sayyid. 4.2573
Yasser, Joseph. 1.4381
Yasuoka, Shōtarō, 1920-. 2.2137
Yates, Douglas, 1944-. 4.4959, 4.8849
Yates, Frances Amelia. 1.413, 1.6593, 2.6756,
   5.669
Yates, Frank. joint author. 5.3315
Yates, J. G. 5.6844
Yates, Norris Wilson. 2.10658
Yates, W. E. 2.13592

Yavetz, Zvi, 1925-. 3.2788
Yaws, Carl L. 5.6858
Ybarra-Frausto, Tomás, 1938-. 2.10302
Ybarra, Thomas Russell, 1880-. 3.2343
Yeager, Leland B. 4.4199
Yeager, Peter C. joint author. 4.6762
Yeager, Rodger. 3.5293
Yearbook (Central Conference of American
   Rabbis) 1.1916
Yearns, W. Buck (Wilfred Buck), 1918- joint
   author. 4.8268
Yeates, Maurice. 4.6198
Yeats, W. B. (William Butler), 1865-1939.
   2.6191, 2.8329-2.8336, 2.8338-2.8341, 2.8351,
   4.791, 5.666
Yeazell, Ruth Bernard. 3.337
Yee, Min S. 4.6915
Yeh, K. C. (K'ung-chia), 1924- joint author.
   4.2483
Yeldham, Charlotte, 1951-. 1.4966
Yellen, Samuel, 1906-. 4.3165
Yellin, Jean Fagan. 2.10361
Yelton, Donald Charles. 2.8579
Yeo, Kim Wah. 4.8727
Yepsen, Roger B. 5.5417
Yergin, Daniel. 4.3715
Yerkes, Ada (Watterson) joint author. 5.4038
Yerkes, Robert Mearns, 1876-1956. 5.4038
Yershov, Peter, 1895-. 2.1282, 2.1508
Yerushalmi, Yosef Hayim, 1932-. 3.3848,
   3.3979
Yetkin, Şerare. 1.6586
Yevtushenko, Yevgeny Aleksandrovich, 1933-.
   2.1557-2.1559
Yi, Ki-baek. 3.4999
Yinger, J. Milton (John Milton), 1916-. 4.5106,
   4.5110
Yip, George S. 4.3035
Yivo Institute for Jewish Research. 3.3983
Yoder, Eldon J. (Eldon Joseph) 5.6069
Yohalem, Alice M. 4.3243, 4.3245
Yohannan, John D. 2.1760
Yokochi, Chihiro. 5.4147
Yokoi, Yūhō, 1918-. 1.2177
Yokomitsu, Riichi, 1898-1947. 2.2123
Yolton, John W. 1.677, 1.681-1.682, 1.685
Yonge, Charlotte Mary, 1823-1901.
   2.8367-2.8368
York, Herbert Frank, comp. 4.9178
York, Neil Longley. 5.5625
Yoshida, Kenkō, 1282?-1350. 2.2058
Yoshida, Kōsaku, 1909-. 5.1475
Yoshida, Shigeru, 1878-1967. 3.4982
Yoshihara, Kunio, 1939-. 4.2539, 4.3034
Yoshihashi, Takehiko, 1912-. 3.4489
Yoshino, M. Y. (Michael Y.) 4.3063
Yoshino, Masatoshi, 1928-. 5.2524
Yost, Charles Peter, 1922- ed. 4.906
Yost, Charles Woodruff. 3.754
Youcha, Geraldine. 4.6638
Youings, Joyce A. 4.5330
Young, Al, 1939-. 1.4267, 2.13442-2.13444
Young, Alfred Fabian, 1925-. 3.6896, 4.8211
Young, Alison, 1922- joint author. 2.6442
Young, Andrew McLaren. 1.5984
Young, Arthur, 1741-1820. 3.1868, 3.1952,
   5.5226, 5.5231
Young, Arthur C. ed. 2.7742
Young, Arthur N. (Arthur Nichols), 1890-.
   3.4781, 4.4675
Young Bear, Ray A. 2.13445
Young, Bertram Alfred, 1912-. 3.5482
Young, Brian J., 1940-. 3.8742
Young-Bruehl, Elisabeth. 4.7457
Young, Charles R. 3.1335
Young, Christine Alice, 1946-. 3.8006
Young, Crawford, 1931-. 3.5099, 3.5429, 4.7718
Young, David, 1930-. 2.3717, 2.10769
Young, Dennis R., 1943-. 4.2723
Young, Diony, 1938-. 5.5071
Young, Donovan Harold, 1904-. 5.1655, 5.5747,
   5.5780, 5.5844
Young, E. H. (Emily Hilda), 1880-1949. 2.9610
Young, Edward, 1683-1765. 2.7344
Young, Edwin. joint ed. 4.3351
Young, Ernest D. 3.4768
Young, Forrest W. 5.55
Young, Frederic Harold, 1905- ed. 1.630

Young, G. M. (George Malcolm), 1882-1959.
   2.7919, 3.1612, 3.1652
Young, George, 1928-. 4.3807
Young, Gerard Mackworth, 1884-. 1.5619
Young, Heartsill, 1917-. 5.7693
Young, Hugh D. 5.1987
Young, J. Francis. joint author. 5.5799
Young, J. Z. (John Zachary) 4.448, 5.3893,
   5.3977, 5.4050
Young, James O. 2.10334
Young, James Sterling. ed. 4.7994
Young, James Sterling. 3.7085
Young, Jock. joint author. 4.6683
Young, John Frederick. 5.6174
Young, John Wesley, 1879-1932. 5.1571
Young, Karl, 1879-. 2.2805
Young, Kenneth, 1916-. 2.9073
Young, Kevin, 1945-. 4.2529
Young, Margaret Labash. 5.827
Young, Matt, 1941-. 5.2286
Young, Michael Dunlop, 1915-. 4.3161
Young, Oran R. 4.1796, 4.9125
Young, Patricia A. 5.7608
Young, Paul Thomas, 1892-. 5.112
Young, Percy M. (Percy Marshall), 1912-.
   1.3714, 1.3862, 1.3908, 1.3986, 1.4108
Young, Peter, 1915-. 4.127
Young, Philip, 1918-. 2.10542
Young, Rhett, Y. W. 1.1803
Young, Robert, 1822-1888. 1.2504
Young, Robert F. (Robert Freeman), 1940-.
   4.4437
Young, Roland Arnold, 1910-. 3.7775, 4.8021
Young, Stark, 1881-1963. 2.2793, 2.12830
Young, T. Cullen. 1.1843
Young, Thomas, 1934-. 5.6383
Young, Thomas Daniel, 1919-. 2.11554,
   2.12369, 2.12373-2.12374, 3.8127
Young, Tzay Y., 1933-. 5.6567
Young, Vernon R. (Vernon Robert), 1937-.
   5.4239
Young, Walter D. 4.8307
Young, Whitney M. 3.6697
Young, William Arthur, 1867-1955. 2.7891
Young, William Caldwell, 1899- ed. 5.4258
Young, William J. joint author. 5.3421
Young, William J. (William Jack), 1935-.
   5.6143
Younger, Calton. 3.1865
Youngs, William D. joint author. 5.5480
Youniss, James. 4.5760
Yourcenar, Marguerite. 2.4772-2.4775
Yourdon, Edward. 5.1168
Youth, Alcohol, and Social Policy Conference
   (1978: Arlington, Va.) 4.6639
Youtsey, John W. joint author. 5.4996
Yoxen, Edward. 5.6866
Yoyotte, Jean. 1.4702
Yronwode, Catherine, 1947-. 2.3813
Yu, Anthony C., 1938-. 2.2227
Yu, Beongcheon. 2.10337
Yu, David C. 5.8441
Yu, Frederick T. C., 1921-. 3.4804
Yu, George T., 1931-. 3.3640, 4.8748
Yu, Jason C. 5.5928
Yu, Pauline, 1949-. 2.2215
Yü, Tsung-hsien. 4.2457
Yüan, Chen, 779-831. 2.2223
Yuan, Luke C. L., ed. 5.2390
Yüan, Ts'ai, chin shih 1163. 1.1510
Yüan, T'ung-li, 1895-1965. 5.8192
Yudkin, Michael. 1.78
Yuen, Joseph H. 5.6719
Yukl, Gary A., 1940-. 4.4956
Yule, Henry, Sir, 1820-1889. 2.1162
Yung, Kai Kin. 1.4665
Yungblut, John R. 1.3094
Yust, Walter, 1894- ed. 1.14
Yūsuf, khāṣṣ-ḥājib, 11th cent. 2.1979

Zaanen, Adriaan Cornelis, 1913- joint author.
   5.1477
Zabalza, Antoni, 1946-. 4.10681
Zabarenko, Lucy, joint author. 5.4601
Zabarenko, Ralph N. 5.4601
Zabeeh, Farhang. comp. 1.550
Zabel, Morton Dauwen, 1901-1964. 2.2688,
   2.8542, 2.11104

Zabicky, Jacob. 5.2758
Zablocki, Benjamin David, 1941-. 1.3368, 4.5787
Zacharias, Ellis M., 1890-. 3.1174
Zacher, Hans Friedrich, 1928-. 4.3444
Zacher, Mark W. 4.9126
Zacher, Mark W. joint author. 4.9391
Zackrison, Harry B. 5.6153
Zadeh, Lotfi Asker. 5.1543
Zadig, Ernest A., 1899-. 5.7512
Zaehner, R. C. (Robert Charles), 1913-1974.
    1.1633, 1.1704, 1.1783
Zagarell, Sandra A. 2.11227
Zager, Robert. 4.3203
Zagoria, Donald S. 3.3073, 3.4414
Zagoria, Janet D., ed. 4.8660
Zagorin, Perez. 3.616, 3.1467
Zahan, Dominique. 1.1850
Zahareas, Anthony N. 2.5294
Zahlan, Rosemarie Said. 3.4060
Zahler, Helene Sara, 1911-. 3.6321
Zahniser, Marvin R. 3.7009
Zahorik, John A. 4.10444
Zahorski, Kenneth J., 1939- joint author.
    2.5969
Zaĭonchkovskiĭ, Petr Andreevich. 3.3130
Zajonc, Robert B. (Robert Boleslaw), 1923-.
    5.549
Zakythēnos, Dionysios A., 1905-. 3.2692
Zald, Mayer N. joint author. 4.7764
Zaleski, Eugène. 4.2390, 4.2396
Zaleski, Marek B. 5.4469
Zall, Paul M. 3.6986-3.6987
Zall, Paul M. ed. 2.8301, 2.10882
Zaller, John, 1949-. 4.5229
Zaltman, Gerald. 4.4890
Zambrana, Ruth E. 4.3247
Zamiatin, Evgeniĭ Ivanovich, 1884-1937.
    2.1614-2.1615
Zammattio, Carlo. 5.823
Zander, Alvin Frederick, 1913-. 4.4354, 4.4934
Zandvoort, R. W. (Reinard Willem), 1894-.
    2.1003
Zaner, Richard M. comp. 1.525
Zangrando, Robert L. 4.6722
Zangwill, Israel, 1864-1926. 2.8369
Zanotti-Bianco, Umberto. 1.4724
Zantwijk, R. A. M. van (Rudolf A. M.), 1932-.
    3.8907
Zar, Jerrold H., 1941-. 5.3537
Zarca, Albert. 3.2895, 3.2904
Zaretsky, Irving I. 2.2396
Zaretsky, Kathleen M. 4.568
Zariski, Oscar, 1899-. 5.1362
Zarlino, Gioseffo, 1517-1590. 1.4422a
Zarnecki, George. 1.4738, 1.4934, 1.5684-1.5685
Zartman, I. William. 3.5189, 4.2623, 4.5396,
    4.8810, 4.9322
Zasloff, Joseph Jermiah. 4.7120
Zasloff, Joseph Jermiah. joint author. 3.4455
Zatlin-Boring, Phyllis. 2.5278
Zauberman, Alfred. 4.1365, 4.2808
Zauderer, Erich. 5.1531
Zaustinskiy, Eugene. 5.1633
Zavarzadeh, Mas'ud, 1938-. 2.10563
Zawodny, J. K. (Janusz Kazimierz) 5.8254
Zax, Melvin. 5.595
Zbavitel, Dušan. 2.1856
Zea, Leopoldo, 1912-. 1.660, 1.662
Zebel, Sydney Henry, 1914-. 3.1653
Zebrowski, Ernest. 5.2008
Zeckhauser, Richard. 4.1251
Zee, A. 5.2484
Zee, Henri A. van der. 3.2993, 3.8030
Zegeer, David A. 5.6746
Zegger, Hrisey D. 2.9324
Zehr, Howard. 4.6793
Zeig, Jeffrey K., 1947-. 5.4898
Zeiger, Arthur, 1916-. 5.7708
Zeigler, Joseph Wesley. 2.3212
Zeigler, L. Harmon (Luther Harmon), 1936-.
    4.8260, 4.10642, 4.10663
Zeine, Zeine N. 3.3759, 3.3800
Zeisel, Hans. joint author. 4.9888
Zeisel, Hans. 4.9904
Zeitlin, Maurice. 3.9265
Zeitlin, Solomon, 1886-1976. 3.3894
Zeitlin, Steven J. 4.774

Zelan, Karen. 4.10337
Zelazny, Roger. 2.13446
Zeldin, Jesse, 1923- tr. 2.1426
Zeldin, Mary-Barbara. joint ed. 1.1103
Zeldin, Theodore, 1933-. 3.1969, 3.2157, 3.2170
Zelin, Madeleine. 4.4674
Zelinsky, Wilbur, 1921-. 4.146, 4.1606
Zelizer, Viviana A. Rotman. 4.5748
Zell, Hans M. 2.2691
Zeller, Bernhard. ed. 2.13597
Zeller, Eduard, 1814-1908. 1.320
Zellner, Arnold. 4.1303
Zelman, Patricia G. 4.6025
Zelomek, A. Wilbert, 1900-. 3.6177
Zeman, Z. A. B. 3.1900
Zeman, Z. A. B. (Zbyněk A. B.), 1928-. 3.826
Zemansky, Mark Waldo, 1900-. 5.1987, 5.2231,
    5.2237
Zenger, John Peter, 1697-1746. defendant.
    4.9456
Zen'kovskiĭ, V. V. (Vasiliĭ Vasil'evich),
    1881-1962. 1.1105, 1.1108
Zenkovsky, Betty Jean. 3.3079
Zenkovsky, Serge A. 2.1308
Zenkovsky, Serge Alexander, 1907-. 3.3079
Zenz, Carl, 1923-. 5.5011
Zernicke, Ronald F. joint author. 5.4263
Zernike, Frits, 1930-. 5.2300
Zernov, Nicolas. 1.3111
Zetterbaum, Marvin. 4.7448
Zetterberg, J. Peter. 5.3350
Zettl, Herbert. 2.2860
Zevi, Bruno, 1918-. 1.5207, 1.5465
Zevin, Jack. joint author. 4.10367
Zewde Gabre-Sellassie. 3.5244
Zeydel, Edwin H., ed. 3.1989
Zeydel, Edwin Hermann, 1893-. 2.13575
Zhukov, Georgiĭ Konstantinovich, 1896-1974.
    3.3239
Ziegler, E. N. (Edward N.) 5.5983
Ziegler, Philip. 3.1607, 5.4765
Ziekursch, Johannes, 1876-. 3.2327
Ziemer, Rodger E. 5.6360, 5.6393
Zienkiewicz, O. C. 5.5836
Zienkiewicz, O. C. ed. 5.5863
Zietz, Dorothy. 4.6551
Ziff, Larzer, 1927-. 2.10378, 2.10387
Ziff, Paul. 2.202, 5.312
Zigerell, James. 2.7175
Zigler, Edward, 1930-. 4.6573, 4.10941, 5.4977,
    5.4979
Zikmund, Joseph, joint comp. 3.8091
Zilbergeld, Bernie. 5.4869
Zilboorg, Gregory, 1890-1959. 5.4806
Zillmann, Dolf. 5.489
Zils, Michael. 5.690
Zilversmit, Arthur. 3.7227
Zim, Herbert Spencer, 1909-. 5.3956
Ziman, J. M. (John M.), 1925-. 5.950, 5.963,
    5.969, 5.2125, 5.2202, 5.2203
Zimansky, Curt Arno, ed. 2.7236, 2.7324
Zimbardo, Rose A. 2.7341
Zimen, Erik, 1941-. 5.3996
Zimet, Carl N., joint author. 5.4844
Zimmels, Hirsch Jakob. 3.1125
Zimmer, Heinrich Robert, 1890-1943. 1.190,
    1.1819, 1.5049
Zimmerli, Walther, 1907-. 1.2615
Zimmerman, Barry J. joint author. 5.298
Zimmerman, Carle Clark, 1897- joint ed. 4.6371
Zimmerman, David R. 5.5091
Zimmerman, Enid. 4.10917
Zimmerman, Franklin B. 1.3612
Zimmerman, Jan. 4.5898
Zimmerman, Joseph Francis, 1928-. 4.9750
Zimmerman, Martin B. 4.3747
Zimmerman, Mikhail. 5.711
Zimmermann, Erich W. (Erich Walter), 1888-.
    4.4127
Zimmermann, Helmut. 5.1682
Zimmermann, Martin Huldrych, 1926-. 5.3683
Zimmermann, Odo John, 1906-. 1.3256
Zimmern, Alfred Eckhard, Sir, 1879-1957.
    4.9192
Zimmern, Helen, 1846-1934, tr. 1.1045
Zimmers, Emory W. 5.7025
Zimring, Franklin E. 4.6845
Zinberg, Israel, 1873-1938. 2.1773

Zinberg, Norman Earl, 1921-. 5.257
Zindel, Paul. 2.13447
Zinkin, Maurice. 3.106
Zinn, Howard, 1922-. 3.6698, 3.7661
Zinner, Paul E. 3.1921, 3.1947
Zinoviev, Aleksandr, 1922-. 2.1649-2.1650
Ziolkowski, Theodore. 2.13508, 2.13781
Ziomek, Henryk. 2.5129
Zipes, Jack David. 2.10826, 2.13510
Zippin, Leo, joint author. 5.1303
Zirin, Harold. 5.1795
Ziring, Lawrence, 1928-. 3.3625, 3.3627, 3.3711,
    3.4102, 3.4131, 3.4135, 4.8721
Zisk, Betty H., 1930-. 4.8871
Zitkala-Ša, 1876-1938. 3.5961
Zittel, Karl Alfred, ritter von, 1839-1904.
    5.2953
Ziv, Avner. 5.437
Zizzi, Andrea. 3.5992
Zla-ba-Bsam-'grub, Kāzī, 1868-1922, tr. 1.1741
Zlobin, Vladimir. 2.1500
Zmud, Robert W., 1946-. 5.5615
Znaniecki, Florian, 1882-1958. 4.4814, 4.4850
Zneimer, John. 2.9168
Zoglin, Mary Lou, 1928-. 4.10568
Zohary, Michael, 1898-. 1.2557
Zohn, Harry. 2.13807
Zola, Emile, 1840-1902. 2.4340-2.4341,
    2.4343-2.4344, 2.4346
Zola, Irving Kenneth, 1935-. 4.6696
Zolberg, Aristide R. 3.5320
Zollar, Ann Creighton. 3.6781
Zoltai, Tibor. 5.3014
Zoltners, Andris A. 4.4299
Zonis, Marvin, 1936-. 5.5408
Zoological Society of London. 5.3806, 5.3830,
    5.4202
Zorach, Cecile. 2.985
Zorach, William, 1887-1966. 1.5678
Zorbaugh, Harvey Warren. 3.8416
Zorilla, José, 1817-1893. 2.5227
Zornow, William Frank. 3.7305, 3.8522
Zoshchenko, Mikhail, 1895-1958. 2.1617-2.1618
Zottoli, Angelandrea, ed. 2.4965
Zottoli, Robert. 5.3248
Zoubek, Charles E., 1913-. 2.1028
Zubatsky, David S., 1939-. 5.8247
Zuber, Jean Bernard. joint author. 5.2155
Zubin, Joseph, 1900-. 5.544
Zuck, Lowell H. 1.2316
Zucker, Paul, 1889-1971. 1.5588
Zucker, Seymour. 4.2006
Zuckerkandl, Victor. 1.4371
Zuckerman, Ben, 1943-. 5.1726
Zuckerman, Harriet. 5.831
Zuckerman, Solly Zuckerman, Baron, 1904-.
    5.951, 5.973, 5.4029
Zuckermann, Wolfgang, 1922-. 1.4151
Zuckmayer, Carl, 1896-1977. 2.13872
Zuesse, Evan M. 1.1851
Zukin, Sharon. 4.7104
Zukofsky, Louis, 1904-1978. 2.12831-2.12832,
    2.12834-2.12835
Zulauf, Sander W., comp. 5.7821
Zulueta Francis de, 1878- ed. 4.9400
Zuntz, Günther, 1902-. 2.456
Zunz, Olivier. 4.2044
Zupan, Jeffrey M. joint author. 4.3909
Zurcher, Arnold John, 1902-. 3.1202, 4.7795
Zürcher, Erik. 1.2118
Zurcher, Louis A. 4.5551
Zureik, Elia. 4.5398
Zuriff, G. E. (Gerald E.) 5.222
Zusne, Leonard, 1924-. 5.93, 5.649
Zussman, J. joint author. 5.3015
Zussman, J. ed. 5.3017
Zussman, J. 5.3027
Zvelebil, Kamil. 2.2271-2.2272
Zvesper, John, 1948-. 4.8152
Zwalf, W. 1.5184
Zweibel, Kenneth. 5.6329
Zweifach, Benjamin William. 5.4228
Zweig, Arnold, 1887-1968. 2.13874-2.13875
Zweig, Paul. 2.11277
Zweig, Stefan, 1881-1942. 2.13877-2.13878
Zweigenhaft, Richard L. 3.6579
Zwerdling, Alex. 2.9206

Title Index

This computer-generated index lists all main entry titles and title page titles from entries traced in the Library of Congress record and also list any variant titles and any title analytics that are traced. The following Library of Congress MARC fields were selected to compile this index: 245, 740, 212, and 222. Individual titles or many major novels and plays do not appear here because they are included in a recommended edition of collected works not analyzed. The file has been sorted according to ALA filing rules as much as possible. The file order is word by word. Any group of letters separated from another with a space are treated as a word. Acronyms and initials set without spaces or periods between letters are filed as words. Titles beginning with numbers expressed in numerals are arranged numerically before A.

¹³C NMR spectroscopy. 5.2682
I & II Kings. 1.2601
I & II Samuel. 1.2600
1 arm. 2.12731
1 Corinthians. 1.2713
1 more spring. 2.12239
1st encounter. 2.11580
1st flight. 2.11313
2 cheers for democracy. 2.8653
The 2 lives of Edith Wharton. 2.12700
2nd skin. 2.11818
The 2 X 2 game. 5.1379
3 American plays. 2.11313
3 by Irving. 2.13096
3 essays on America. 2.10264
3 guineas. 2.9577
The 3 hostages. 2.8488
3 Rossettis. 2.8006
3 soldiers. 2.11585
III tragedies: Blood wedding, Yerma, Bernarda Alba. 2.5251
The 3 voices of poetry. 2.2745
3 worlds. 2.12604
The 4 adventures of Richard Hannay. 2.8488
4 essays on Gulliver's travels. 2.7293
4 plays. 2.11347
4 tudor comedies. 2.6219
5 miscellaneous essays. 2.7313
5 New World primates. 5.4031
5 readers reading. 2.2376
The 5th amendment today. 4.9885
5th of July. 2.13433
The 5th queen. 2.8630
The 5th queen crowned. 2.8630
6 18th-century plays. 2.6238
6 Caroline plays. 2.6221
6 great poets. 2.5770
6 Tennyson essays. 2.8181
The 7 lively arts. 2.3194
7 years from somewhere. 2.13139
The 8th day. 2.12716
10 cases in engineering design. 5.5697
10 classic mystery and suspense plays of the modern theatre. 2.6199
12 Americans. 1.4876
12 modern French Canadian poets. 2.4808
12 more modern Scottish poets. 2.9847
12 original essays on great English novels. 2.5951
12 photographers of the American social landscape. 3.6063
12th century Europe. 3.147
The 12-year Reich. 3.2439
13 lectures on Fermat's last theorem. 5.1338
The 13th valley, a novel. 2.12967
14th century verse and prose. 2.6080
15 Americans. 1.4875
15 Canadian poets plus 5. 2.9900
16-bit microprocessors. 5.1227
16 studies. 1.5140
17th and 18th century art. 1.4775
18 stories. 2.13684
18th-century prose. 2.6259
18th century symphonies. 1.4198
19 century fiction. 5.7965

19th-century America: furniture and other decorative arts. 1.6522
19th century art. 1.4779
19th century literature criticism. 2.2664
19th-century sculpture. 1.5647
20 contemporary Norwegian poets. 2.14032
XXe siècle. 2.3920
The 20th century capitalist revolution. 4.3010
20th century Chinese drama. 2.2198
20th century French drama. 2.3890
20th-century French literature. 2.3869
20th century journey. 2.12468
20th century pleasures. 2.2767
The 20th-century poster. 1.5857
20th-century Richmond. 4.6328
The 20th-century Spanish-American novel. 2.5310
22 unpublished letters of Elizabeth Barrett Browning and Robert Browning. 2.7467
24 favorite one-act plays. 2.10796
The 25-year war. 3.4502
25 years of world shipping. 4.3959
27 wagons full of cotton. 2.12733
31 letters and 13 dreams. 2.11905
36 children. 4.10879
36 lectures in biology. 5.3300
39 poems. 2.11502
The 39 steps. 2.8488
39 steps. 2.8489
42nd parallel. 2.11586
50 golden years of Oscar. 2.2926
50 modern American & British poets, 1920-1970. 2.10709
50 years of American poetry. 2.10767
55 short stories from the New Yorker. 2.10845
60-minute gourmet. 5.7131
60 minutes (Television program) 3.1180
60 Minutes verbatim. 3.1180
60 years of hockey. 4.995
63, dream palace. 2.12358
$70 billion in the Black. 4.2056
87th precinct. 2.11907
98.6. 2.13349
100 billion suns. 5.1832
100 years of Negro freedom. 3.6648
101 years' entertainment. 2.3716
110 Livingston Street revisited. 4.10100
200 years of American sculpture. 1.5657
200 years of great American short stories. 2.10834
250 years of Afro-American art. 5.8190
300 years of American seating furniture. 1.6583
334. 2.12987
The 900 days. 3.995
1000 years of Greek vase painting. 1.6631
1001 questions answered about astronomy. 5.1709
1676, the end of American independence. 3.8201
1812. 3.7114
1830 in France. 3.2147
1848. 3.706
1848; chapters of German history. 3.2300
1848; the revolution of the intellectuals 3.703

1848: the romantic and democratic revolutions in Europe. 3.705
1876. 2.12614
1900, the generation before the Great War. 4.5289
1905. 3.3171
1914. 3.725
The 1932 campaign. 4.7957
1933; poems. 2.13138
1939; the making of the Second World War. 3.892
1940; the fall of France. 3.950
The 1954 Geneva Conference. 3.5034
1967 census of governments. 4.8831
The 1975 referendum. 4.2223
The 1980 census, policymaking amid turbulence. 4.1248
1982 census of agriculture. 4.2956
1982 census of manufactures. 4.3833
1982 census of retail trade. Geographic area series. 4.4322
1982 census of retail trade. Industry series. 4.4323
1982 census of service industries. 4.3864
1982 census of transportation. 4.3879
1982 census of wholesale trade. Geographic area series. 4.4316
1982 Census of wholesale trade. Industry series. Miscellaneous subjects. 4.4317
1984. 2.9185
2000 books and more. 5.8236
2000 sefer va-sefer. 5.8236
2001; a space odyssey. 2.8519
5000 years of the art of Mesopotamia. 1.4707
12,000 words. 2.1093
20000 lieues sous les mers 2.4324
20,000+ words. 2.1028
20,000 years of fashion. 4.829

'A' 2.12832
'A' 22 & 23. 2.12834
A. B. Guthrie, Jr. 2.11804
A.E. Housman, a critical biography. 2.7839
The A.F. of L. from the death of Gompers to the merger. 4.3550
The A.F. of L. in the time of Gompers. 4.3551
A.I. business. 5.999
A. K. Tolstoy. 2.1427
A.L.A. glossary of library and information science. 5.7693
A.L.A. portrait index. 1.5162
The A.L.A. yearbook. 5.7606
A la recherche du temps perdu. 2.4661
A.M.A. and US health policy since 1940. 5.4477
A. Mitchell Palmer. 3.7678
A & P. 4.3693
A. Persi Flacci et D. Iuni Iuvenalis saturae. 2.646
A. Philip Randolph. 3.6848
A Rebours. 2.4245
A.S.C.A.P. biographical dictionary. 1.3540
A.S.E.A.N. states. 4.2525
A.S.M. handbook of engineering mathematics. 5.5712

A to Z of offshore oil and gas. 5.6799
A.V. instruction. 4.10324
An A-Z of offshore oil & gas. 5.6799
AAPG bulletin; v. 67, no. 5. 5.2946
Aaron Burr. 3.6983
Aaron Copland. 1.3842
Aaron Siskind, photographer. 5.6930
Aaron's rod. 2.8962
The ABA and the politics of judicial selection. 4.8066
The abacus and the rose. 5.842
The abandonment of the Jews. 3.1123
Abba Eban. 3.3934
The abbé Grégoire, 1787-1831. 3.2067
L'Abbé Prévost. 2.4085
The Abbess of Crewe. 2.9355
Abbreviations dictionary. 2.1108
ABC for book-collectors. 5.7694
The ABC of acid-base chemistry. 5.4223
The ABC of communism. 4.7096
ABC of reading. 2.2420
The ABC of relativity. 5.1921
The ABCs of literacy. 4.10479
Abe Lincoln in Illinois. 2.12463
Abelard and the origin and early history of universities. 4.9974
Der abenteuerliche Simplicissimus. 2.13543
ABHB. 5.7538
Abhijñāna-Śakuntalā. 2.1949
Abigail Adams, an American woman. 3.7053
Ability testing. 4.10709
The Abinger edition of E. M. Forster. 2.8641
Abinger harvest. 2.8644
The abnormal personality. 5.4827
The abolition of slavery in Brazil. 4.6439
The abolition of war. 4.9140, 4.9160
Abolitionism. 3.7261
The abolitionist legacy. 3.6678
Abolitionists and working-class problems in the age of industrialization. 4.6443
Aboriginal Australians. 4.665
Aboriginal men of high degree. 4.669
Aboriginal tribes of Australia. 4.667
Abortion. 4.5700
The abortion. 2.11412
Abortion. 4.5696
Abortion, an annotated indexed bibliography. 5.8289
Abortion and infanticide. 4.5699
Abortion and the politics of motherhood. 4.5702
Abortion freedom. 4.5697
Abortion in America. 4.9864
Abortion politics. 4.5701
The abortive revolution. 3.4771
About fiction. 2.3527
About French poetry from Dada to 'Tel quel' 2.3882
About Harry Towns. 2.13017
About looking. 1.4619
About philosophy. 1.1261
Above the battle. 3.6367
ABPR cumulative, 1985-. 5.7729
Abraham Isaac Kook. 1.1894
Abraham Lincoln. 3.7285, 3.7296
Abraham Lincoln, 1809-1858. 3.7291
Abraham Lincoln and Reconstruction. 3.8312
The Abraham Lincoln encyclopedia. 3.7280
Abraham Lincoln, his speeches and writings. 3.7301
Abraham Lincoln, the man behind the myths. 3.7281
Abraham Lincoln, the prairie years. 3.7293
Absalom, Absalom! 2.11659
Absent mandate. 4.8294
Absentee ownership and business enterprise in recent times. 4.1941
Absenteeism. 4.3156
The absolute bourgeois: artists and politics in France, 1848-1851. 1.4964
The absolute weapon: atomic power and world order. 5.7384
Absolutism, 1613-1801. 3.3092
Absorption and theatricality. 1.6051
Abstract expressionism, the formative years. 1.5910
Abstract harmonic analysis. 5.1552

Abstract of an artist. 1.5114
Abstract painting. 1.5869
Abstract painting and sculpture in America. 1.5906
Abstract painting and sculpture in America, 1927-1944. 1.4883
Abstraction and empathy. 1.4602
The absurd hero in American fiction. 2.10618
Abuse of power. 3.4485
Abuse of the elderly. 4.6590
Abusing science. 5.3392
Abyss. 5.3246
The abyss. 2.4772
The abyss of time, changing conceptions of the earth's antiquity after the sixteenth century. 5.3082
Academic American encyclopedia. 1.10
Academic dress and insignia of the world. 4.10629
The academic ethic. 4.10534
Academic freedom in our time. 4.10579
The academic man. 4.10532
The academic mind and reform. 4.1371
The academic revolution. 4.10063
Academic science, higher education, and the federal government, 1950-1983. 5.800
Academic women. 4.10581
Academic women and employment discrimination. 4.10580
Academic work and educational excellence. 4.10028
Academic year abroad. 4.10622
Academies of art, past and present. 1.4647
The Academy and French painting in the Nineteenth century. 1.4650
Academy awards. 2.2929
The Acadians: creation of a people. 3.8802
Accelerated development in Sub-Saharan Africa. 4.2601
Accents of English. 2.1112
Accept me as I am. 5.7724
Acceptable risk. 4.2714
Acceptable risks. 5.4655
The acceptance world. 2.9225
The accessible city. 4.3907
Accident prevention manual for industrial operations. 5.5554
The accidental century. 3.190
An accidental man. 2.9748
Accomplices of silence. 2.2011
An account of the conquest of Guatemala in 1524. 3.9054
The accountants' guide to computer systems. 4.4406
Accounting, evaluation, and economic behavior. 4.4392
Accounting evolution to 1900. 4.4385
Accounting for genocide. 3.1089
Accounting for United States economic growth, 1929-1969. 4.1956
The accounting profession. 4.4394
The accounting professional. 4.4396
Accounting systems and practice in Europe. 4.4387
Accounting theory. 4.4397
Accredited institutions of postsecondary education. 4.9936
Accredited institutions of postsecondary education, programs, candidates. 4.9936
Acharnians. 2.426
The achievement of Robert Penn Warren. 2.12652
The achievement of Samuel Johnson. 2.7083
The achievement of Sherwood Anderson. 2.11330
The achievement of T. S. Eliot. 2.11639
The Achievement of Ted Hughes. 2.9719
The achievement of Walter Scott. 2.8055
The Achievement of William Styron. 2.13345
Achievements in residential services for persons with disabilities. 4.6611
Achievements of the left hand: essays on the prose of John Milton. 2.7150
The achieving society. 4.2794
Achilles Tatius. 2.331
Achim von Arnim. 2.13549
Acia. 2.1453
Acid-base chemistry. 5.4223

Acid deposition, atmospheric processes in eastern North America. 5.6003
Acid rain and transported air pollutants. 5.6004
Acid rain information book. 5.6005
The Acoma Indians. 3.5836
Acoustic communication in birds. 5.3967
The acoustic sense of animals. 5.4372
The acoustical foundations of music. 1.4372
Acousticks. 1.5496
Acoustics. 5.6344
The acquisition of syntax in children from 5 to 10. 4.10473
The acquisitive society. 4.1486
Acres of flint. 2.10441
Acronyms, initialisms & abbreviations dictionary. 2.205
Acronyms, initialisms, and abbreviations dictionary. 2.205
Across Spoon River. 2.12119
Across the frontiers. 5.1912
Across the river and into the trees. 2.11839
Across the wild Missouri. 3.8472
ACS directory of graduate research. 5.2620
The ACS style guide. 5.2599
Act and being. 1.2799
The act of creation. 5.344
The act of fiction in an age of inflation. 2.10639
The act of reading. 2.2448
The act of the mind. 2.12550
Act without words. 2.4406
Acting. 2.3113
Action and purpose. 1.1328
Action for mental health. 5.4832
Action française. 3.8816
Action française: royalism and reaction in twentieth-century France. 3.2199
The action of hormones in plants and invertebrates. 5.4425
Active learning. 4.10305
Activism replaces isolationism. 3.7568
Activity networks. 5.5596
The actor at work. 2.3112
The actor-managers. 2.3332
An actor prepares. 2.3124
Actors and American culture, 1880-1920. 2.3204
Actors on acting. 2.3122
Actors' television credits, 1950-1972. 2.2855
The actor's ways and means. 2.3121
Acts and other events. 1.137
Acts of implication. 2.5670
Acts of mind. 2.10508
The Acts of the Apostles. 1.2699
Acts of the Buddha. 1.2127
Actual art. 1.4804
Ad Lucilium epistulae morales. 2.693
Ada. 2.12224, 5.1209
Ada, Countess of Lovelace. 2.7533
Adalbert Stifter. 2.13658-2.13659
Adam and Hepplewhite and other neo-classical furniture. 1.6576
Adam, and, The train. 2.13695
Adam by Adam. 3.7679
Adam Elsheimer. 1.4991
Adam Smith. 4.1355, 4.1357
Adam Smith's moral and political philosophy. 1.1430
Adam Smith's politics. 4.7421
Adams family correspondence. 3.7050
Adam's haunted sons. 1.2540
The Adams-Jefferson letters. 3.7044
An adaptation model. 5.5168
Adaptation to environment. 5.3819
Adapted physical education. 4.915-4.916
Adaptive behavior and learning. 5.4104
Adaptive filters. 5.6510
Adaptive responses of native Amazonians. 3.9161
Adaptive signal processing. 5.6382
The added dimension. 2.13220
The addict and the law. 4.9575
The Addictions. 5.4955
Addison and Steele, the critical heritage. 2.5660
Addresses to the German nation. 3.2283
Adelphoe. 2.778

Adenauer and the new Germany. 3.2507
The Adenauer era. 3.2472
Adhocism. 1.6686
Ādi-Granth. English. Selections. 1.1823
Adjusting to technological change. 4.3319
Adjustment to severe physical disability.
   5.5038
Adlai Stevenson and the world. 3.7684
Adlai Stevenson of Illinois. 3.7685
Administering federalism in a democracy.
   4.7879
Administration. 4.7755
Administration and politics in a Nepalese town.
   4.8885
Administration in developing countries. 4.7759
Administration of high school athletics. 4.974
The administration of justice in the courts.
   4.9777
The administration of Normandy under Saint
   Louis. 3.2226
Administration of police organizations. 4.6800
Administrative behavior. 4.2660
The administrative behavior of federal bureau
   chiefs. 4.7982
Administrative law and government. 4.9753
Administrative law treatise. 4.9752
Administrative leadership. 4.10592
Administrative politics in British government.
   4.8433
The administrative process. 4.9757
The administrative reforms of Frederick
   William I of Prussia. 4.8616
The Administrative 'revolution' in Whitehall.
   4.8454
The administrative state. 4.7758, 4.7763
Administrative theories and politics. 4.7760
Admiral of the Fleet Earl Beatty. 3.1285
Admiral of the ocean sea. 3.5974
Admirals, generals, and American foreign
   policy, 1898-1914. 3.7561
Admirals of American empire. 3.6384
Adolescence in literature. 2.10822
The adolescent. 2.1357
The adolescent in the American novel,
   1920-1960. 2.10602
The adolescent parent. 4.5672
Adolescent relations with mothers, fathers, and
   friends. 4.5760
Adolescent socialization in cross-cultural
   perspective. 4.5730
The adolescent society. 4.5752
Adolf Loos, theory and works. 1.5411
Adolphe. 2.4155
Adrienne Rich's poetry. 2.12384
Adrift in Soho. 2.9829
Adult education and training in industrialized
   countries. 4.10973
The adult learner. 4.10976
Adultery in the novel. 2.3419
Adulthood and aging. 5.623
Adults as learners. 4.10978
The advance of American nursing. 5.5155
Advanced bacterial genetics. 5.3449
Advanced calculus. 5.1448, 5.1455
Advanced database machine architecture.
   5.1233
Advanced dynamics. 5.1655
Advanced engineering mathematics. 5.1541
An advanced geography of northern and
   western Europe. 4.2189
Advanced geological map interpretation.
   5.2979
Advanced inorganic chemistry. 5.2698
Advanced learner's dictionary of current
   English. 2.857
Advanced linear programming. 5.5590
Advanced logic for applications. 1.1210
Advanced mathematics for engineers. 5.5708
Advanced microprocessors. 5.1140
Advanced organic chemistry. 5.2719, 5.2721
An advanced organic laboratory course. 5.2729
Advanced practical inorganic chemistry.
   5.2635
Advanced propulsion systems for urban rail
   vehicles. 5.6076
Advanced strength and applied elasticity.
   5.5781
The advanced theory of statistics. 5.1390

Advanced urban transport. 5.5929
The advancement of learning. 1.668
Advances in argumentation theory and
   research. 1.1237
Advances in enzymology and related subjects.
   5.4408
Advances in inorganic chemistry and
   radiochemistry. 5.2695
Advances in learning and behavioral disabilities.
   5.5115
Advances in maritime economics. 4.3958
Advances in physical organic chemistry.
   5.2847
Advances in tall buildings. 5.6088
Advances in the social psychology of language.
   2.20
The advent of war, 1939-40. 3.951
Adventure, mystery, and romance. 2.3427
The adventure of archaeology. 3.254
Adventure playgrounds. 4.912
An adventure with a genius. 2.3626
Adventurer in archaeology. 3.261
Adventures in American diplomacy, 1896-1906.
   4.9044
Adventures in criticism. 2.2652
Adventures in the skin trade, and other stories.
   2.9404
Adventures in time and space. 2.3723
The adventures of Arabella. 2.7095
Adventures of a biographer. 2.11400
Adventures of a mathematician. 5.1099
Adventures of a young man. 2.11579
Adventures of a younger son. 2.8199
The adventures of Augie March. 2.11348
The adventures of David Simple. 2.7030
The adventures of Don Quixote. 2.5171
Adventures of Huckleberry Finn. 2.10942
Adventures of ideas. 3.27
The Adventures of Lindamira, a lady of quality.
   2.6886
The Adventures of Peregrine Pickle. 2.7262
The adventures of Roderick Random. 2.7259
The adventures of Tapiola. 2.12237
Adventures of the dialectic. 1.475
Adventures of the letter I. 2.12473
Adventures with D. W. Griffith. 2.3047
The adversaries. 3.1159
Adversary politics and electoral reform. 4.8521
The adversary within. 2.13962
Adverse effects of foods. 5.4985
Adverse reactions to foods. 5.4982
Advertisements for myself. 2.12102
Advertising and competition. 4.4421
Advertising and social change. 4.4422
The advertising controversy. 4.4435
Advertising in America; the consumer view.
   4.4429
Advertising in the broadcast and cable media.
   4.4438
Advertising the American dream. 4.4423
Advertising, the uneasy persuasion. 4.4424
Advertising's hidden effects. 4.4425
The advice and consent of the Senate. 4.8046
Advise and consent. 2.11608
Advocacy for child mental health. 5.5079
Advocates of reform, from Wyclif to Erasmus.
   1.2319
Aegean Islands, and other poems. 2.9368
Aegina, society and politics. 4.1731
Aelfric. 2.6286
Aeneas, Sicily, and Rome. 1.1664
The Aeneid. 2.796
The Aeneid of Virgil. 2.783, 2.797-2.798
Aeneidos. 2.785-2.786
Aeneidos liber primvs. 2.784
Aeneidos, liber quartus. 2.787
Aeneidos, liber quintus. 2.788
Aequanimitas. 5.4478
Aerial piracy and international law. 4.9337
Aerial piracy and international terrorism.
   4.9337
Aero-hydrodynamics of sailing. 5.7510
The aerobics program for total well-being.
   5.4693
The aerodynamic design of aircraft. 5.6663
Aerodynamics for engineers. 5.6661
Aeronomy of the middle atmosphere. 5.2522
Aeschylus. 2.332, 2.413

Aeschylus in his style. 2.418
Aeschylus' Prometheus bound. 2.411
The aesthetic and critical theories of John
   Ruskin. 2.8040
Aesthetic as science of expression and general
   linguistic. 1.1382
The aesthetic dimension. 1.1038
The aesthetic movement. 1.6534
Aesthetic paganism in German literature, from
   Winckelmann to the death of Goethe.
   2.13468
Aesthetic quality. 1.1378
The aesthetic theories of Kant, Hegel, and
   Schopenhauer. 1.907
Aesthetic theory. 1.966
Aesthetics. 1.1355, 1.4592
Aesthetics and history. 1.4606
Aesthetics and problems of education. 1.1364
Aesthetics and the theory of criticism. 1.1357
Aesthetics from classical Greece to the present.
   1.1365
Aesthetics in twentieth-century Poland. 1.1389
The aesthetics of architecture. 1.5463
Aetia, Iambi, lyric poems, Hecale, minor epic
   and elegiac poems, and other fragments.
   2.357
AF encyclopedia of textiles. 5.7077
Afanasy Fet. 2.1424
Affairs of party. 4.8199
Affairs of State. 3.7414
Affect, cognition, and personality. 5.414
Affinities. 2.9474
Affinity as a value. 4.633
Affluence and the French worker in the Fourth
   Republic. 4.3656
The affluent society. 4.1985
The Afghan connection. 3.1638
Afghanistan. 3.4108-3.4109, 3.4111-3.4112
Afghanistan in the 1970s. 3.4110
Afghanistan: its people, its society, its culture.
   3.4113
Afghanistan research materials survey. 5.8042
Afghanistan's foreign affairs to the mid-
   twentieth century: relations with the USSR,
   Germany, and Britain. 3.4114
AFL-CIO: labor united. 4.3547
Africa. 1.5082, 3.5044
Africa: a study in tropical development. 3.5054
Africa adorned. 4.852
Africa and Africans. 3.5066
Africa and Europe. 3.5065
Africa and the international economy,
   1800-1960. 4.2578
Africa and the islands. 3.5051
Africa and the Victorians. 3.5115
Africa & the West. 3.5322
Africa in economic crisis. 4.2602
Africa in history. 3.5068
Africa in social change. 4.5465
Africa in the days of exploration. 3.5050
Africa in the Iron Age, c500 B.C. to A.D.
   1400. 4.716
Africa in the United Nations. 4.9231
Africa: its peoples and their culture history.
   3.5056
Africa must unite. 3.5093
Africa on film and videotape, 1960-1981.
   3.5063
Africa since 1800. 3.5075, 3.5083
Africa South of the Sahara 1972. 3.5220
Africa: the politics of unity. 3.5095
The African-Arab conflict in the Sudan.
   3.5184
African archaeology. 4.745
An African aristocracy. 4.614
African art. 1.5083
African art & leadership. 1.5085
African art in motion. 1.6727
African authors. 2.2300
African Christian theology. 1.1849
African Christianity. 1.2466, 1.2469
African cities and towns before the European
   conquest. 4.6284
The African city. 4.6280
African civilisations in the New World. 3.5688
The African colonization movement, 1816-1865.
   3.7230
African congress. 4.6460

African debt and financing. 4.4727
The African diaspora. 4.646
African dilemma tales. 4.810
African discovery. 3.5049
The African dream. 3.6822
African economic development. 4.2576
The African experience. 3.5055
The African experience in Spanish America,
    1502 to the present day. 3.9026
An African experiment in nation building.
    3.5401
African furniture & household objects. 1.6580
African genesis. 5.3376
African history. 3.5064
African history in maps. 4.187
African ideas of God. 1.1843
The African image. 2.2303
African independence. 3.5096
African journal, 1853-1856. 3.5437
African kingdoms. 4.654
African kingships in perspective. 3.5231
African language literatures. 2.2298
African law. 4.9927
African literature in French. 2.4842
The African middle ages, 1400-1800. 3.5079
African music. 1.3747
African nationalism. 3.5113
The African past. 3.5069
African philosophy. 1.1145-1.1146
African political systems. 4.602
An African popular literature. 2.10100
The African queen. 2.8640
African religions. 1.1848
African religions & philosophy. 1.1846
The African religions of Brazil. 1.1879
African rhythm and African sensibility. 1.4348
The African slave in colonial Peru, 1524-1650.
    4.6440
The African slave trade. 3.5326
African socialism. 4.7131
African societies. 4.655
African stories. 2.9009
African survey. 3.5052
An African survey. 3.5046
African systems of kinship and marriage.
    4.582
African textiles and decorative arts. 1.6675
African traditional religion. 1.1845
African tribal images; the Katherine White
    Reswick Collection. 1.5765
The African voice in Southern Rhodesia,
    1898-1930. 3.5511
African voices. 2.3708
The African witch. 2.8493
African women. 4.6156
African women & the law. 4.9925
African women and the law. 4.9925
African women south of the Sahara. 4.6154
The African world. 3.5062
African worlds; studies in the cosmological
    ideas and social values of African peoples.
    3.5059
African writers at the microphone. 2.10042
African writers on African writing. 2.2301
African writers talking. 2.10043
African writing today. 2.2309
The Africans. 4.657
Africans abroad. 4.6411
Africans and Creeks. 3.5868
Africa's international relations. 3.5110
Afrikaner politics in South Africa, 1934-1948.
    3.5470
The Afro-American and the Second World
    War. 3.1130
The Afro-American artist. 1.4913
The Afro-American experience: a cultural
    history through emancipation. 3.6612
Afro-American fiction, 1853-1976. 5.7799
Afro-American folk art and crafts. 1.6523
Afro-American folk culture. 5.8195
Afro-American folktales. 4.781
Afro-American literature. 2.10305
The Afro-American novel since 1960. 2.10306
Afro-American poetry and drama, 1760-1975.
    5.7797
Afro-American reference. 5.7870
Afro-American religious history. 1.2417

The Afro-American tradition in decorative arts.
    1.4917
The Afro-American woman. 3.6746
Afro-American writers. 5.7879
Afro-American writing. 2.10685
The Afro-Yankees. 3.8019
Afrocommunism. 4.7129
After alienation. 2.10633
After Anzac Day. 2.10216
After Daley. 3.8417
After hegemony. 4.4145
After imperialism. 3.4402, 4.4185
After Joyce. 2.8902
After leaving Mr. Mackenzie. 2.9272
After many a summer dies the swan. 2.8815
After Mao. 2.2161
After modern architecture. 1.5277
After nine hundred years. 1.3105
After seven years. 3.7764
After slavery. 3.6806
After the Armada. 3.1433
After the banquet. 2.2114
After the fact. 3.6209
After the fall. 2.12167
After the first death there is no other. 2.13249
After the genteel tradition. 2.10400
After the Gold Rush. 3.8619
After the hunt. 1.5940
After the lost generation. 2.10611
After the new criticism. 2.2472
After the school bell rings. 4.10786
After the storm; landmarks of the modern
    Mexican novel. 2.5329
After the wake. 1.6703
After Vietnam. 3.7847
After virtue. 1.1453
After Yalta. 3.7770
Afterimages. 4.1106
Aftermath. 2.10905
The aftermath of rape. 4.6744
The aftermath of revolt: India, 1857-1870.
    3.4279
Aftermath of revolution. 3.7038
The aftermath of revolution in Latin America.
    3.9002
Afternoon. 2.4314
Afterthoughts on material civilization and
    capitalism. 4.1744
Against interpretation, and other essays.
    2.2683
Against mediocrity. 4.10816
Against method. 5.883
Against our will. 4.6732
Against racism. 3.6827
Against the Academics. 1.2185
Against the age. 2.7968
Against the American grain. 3.6135
Against the crime of silence. 4.9341
Against the current. 2.1517
Against the grain. 2.4244, 2.5515
Against the law. 4.9877
Against the state. 4.2874
Against the tyrant. 4.7616
Agamemnon. 2.410
Agape. 1.3065
Agape and Eros. 1.3064
Age and anthropological theory. 4.588
Age & anthropological theory. 4.588
L'Age d'homme. 2.4604
The age of Adam. 1.5381
The age of alignment: Chris Cook. 4.8485
The age of Balfour and Baldwin, 1902-1940.
    4.8530
The age of belief. 1.344
The age of birds. 5.3947
The age of capital, 1848-1875. 3.667
The age of Catherine de Medici. 3.2011
The age of Constantine and Julian. 3.2812
The age of Constantine the Great. 3.2813
An age of crisis. 1.809
An age of criticism: 1900-1950. 2.2516
The age of Drake. 3.1428
The age of energy. 3.6120
The age of enlightenment. 2.3919
Age of enormity. 2.2654
The age of enterprise. 4.1870
The age of equipoise. 3.1609
The age of Erasmus. 3.167

Age of excess. 3.6049
An age of fiction. 2.3909
The age of German liberation, 1795-1815.
    3.2282
The age of humanism and reformation: Europe
    in the fourteenth, fifteenth, and sixteenth
    centuries. 3.625
The age of ideas. 3.1963
The age of improvement. 3.1581
The age of Inigo Jones. 1.5390
The age of innocence. 2.12690
The age of Jackson. 3.7124
The Age of Johnson. 2.5674
The age of Kipling. 2.7894
The age of Louis XIV. 3.2030
The age of MacDiarmid. 2.8785
The age of Mackenzie King. 3.8746
The age of Metternich, 1814-1848. 3.695
The Age of Milton. 2.5643
The age of nationalism. 3.756
The age of nationalism and reform, 1850-1890.
    3.671
The age of permanent revolution. 4.6974
The age of power. 3.173
Age of reason. 1.1883
The age of reason. 2.4721
The age of reconnaissance. 4.50
The age of reform. 3.7527
The age of reform (1250-1550) 1.2315
The age of reform, 1815-1870. 3.1587
The age of reptiles. 5.3170
The age of revolution: Europe 1789-1848.
    3.654
The age of Roosevelt. 3.7771
Age of spirituality. 1.4694-1.4695
Age of surrealism. 1.1400
The age of surveillance. 4.7905
The age of suspicion. 2.3529
Age of suspicion. 2.4713
The age of the avant-garde. 1.4783
The age of the baroque, 1610-1660. 3.633
The age of the cathedrals. 1.4736
The age of the democratic revolution. 3.652
The age of the masses. 3.183
The age of the Vikings. 3.3364
The age of uncertainty. 4.1306
Agee on film. 2.2875
The agency. 4.7912
Agency-based social work. 4.6484
The ages of American law. 4.9481
Aggression. 4.5040, 5.424
Aggression: a social psychological analysis.
    5.419
Aggression and world order. 4.9320
Aggression in global perspective. 5.417
Aggression, theoretical and empirical reviews.
    5.418
The Aggressions of civilization. 3.5797
The aggressive child. 4.5721
Aging. 4.3454
The aging, a guide to public policy. 4.5822
Aging and adaptation. 3.7998
Aging and public health. 5.4665
Aging and public policy. 4.5824
Aging and retirement. 4.5811
Aging, social change. 4.5795
Aging, the ethnic factor. 4.5815
The aging worker. 4.3312
Agnes Grey. 2.7440
An agnostic's apology, and other essays.
    1.1521
Agony in New Haven. 4.9464
The agony of Christianity and Essays on faith
    1.2261
The agony of the American left. 4.5136
The agony of the Republic. 3.2152
Agrarian elites and Italian fascism. 3.2947
The Agrarian history of England and Wales.
    4.2847
The agrarian history of Western Europe, A.D.
    500-1850. 4.2969
The agrarian origins of modern Japan. 4.5451
Agrarian policies and rural poverty in Africa.
    4.2993
Agrarian policies in communist Europe.
    4.2970
The agrarian problem in the sixteenth century.
    4.2850

Agrarian problems and peasant movements in Latin America. 4.2836
The agrarian question and reformism in Latin America. 4.2962
Agrarian reform in contemporary developing countries. 4.2876
Agrarian socialism. 4.8305
The agrarian sociology of ancient civilizations. 4.1729
Agrarian structure and productivity in developing countries. 4.2893
An agricultural atlas of India. 5.5253
Agricultural botany. 5.5315
Agricultural change in tropical Africa. 5.5254
Agricultural development. 4.2889
Agricultural development and economic growth. 4.2891
Agricultural development in the Middle East. 4.2983
Agricultural development planning. 4.2894
Agricultural dictionary. 5.5221
Agricultural economics in the United States, 1840-1932. 4.2948
Agricultural exports, farm income, and the Eisenhower administration. 4.2944
Agricultural implements of the Roman world. 5.5296
Agricultural origins and dispersals. 5.5228
The Agricultural Research Service. 5.5218
The agricultural revolution, 1750-1880. 5.5247
The agricultural systems of the world. 5.5230
Agriculture and structural transformation. 4.2898
Agriculture and the Civil War. 4.1922
Agriculture in ante-bellum Mississippi. 5.5245
Agriculture in China's modern economic development. 4.2989
Agriculture in the postbellum South. 4.2959
Agriculture in the Third World. 4.2900
Agrippa d'Aubigné. 2.3979
Agrippa d'Aubigné's Les Tragiques. 2.3978
Aha! Gotcha. 5.1258
Ahasverus död. 2.14087
Ahmedabad; a study in Indian urban history. 4.2512
Ahnung und Aufbruch. 2.13525
The AI business. 5.999
AIDS. 5.4983
Aids to geographical research 5.8199
Aimé Césaire; Black between worlds. 2.4838
Aimé Césaire, the collected poetry. 2.4835
Aimé Césaire, une étude de Lilyan Kesteloot. 2.4836
Aims, methods and achievements in social anthropology. 4.474
The aims of education & other essays. 4.10235
The aims of interpretation. 2.2438
Ainsi parla l'oncle. 4.786
Ainslie's complete Hoyle. 4.1065
Ain't I a woman. 4.5984
Air and water pollution control. 4.1842
Air and water pollution control law, 1982. 4.9571
The Air Force integrates, 1945-1964. 3.6726
The air net. 4.4078
Air pollution. 5.6044
Air pollution and plant life. 5.3748
Air pollution, its origin and control. 5.6045
Air pollution: physical and chemical fundamentals. 5.6043
Air power. 5.7395
Air power and armies. 5.7405
Air power in war. 3.1042
Air Power: Key to survival. 5.7398
Air-sea interaction. 4.347
Air transportation. 4.4083
The air war, 1939-1945. 3.1041
Air war and emotional stress. 5.7396
Aircraft carriers. 5.7442
Aircraft engines and gas turbines. 5.6676
Aircraft propulsion. 5.6673
Aircraft structures for engineering students. 5.6671
Airline deregulation. 4.4082
Airline regulation in America. 4.4089
Airport access. 4.4081
Airport engineering. 5.6683
Airport operations. 5.6681

Airport systems planning. 5.6684
Airports and the environment. 5.5996
Aishah, the beloved of Mohammed. 1.2022
Aissa saved. 2.8494
Ajanta; Ajanta painting of the sacred and the secular. 1.6397
Ajanta painting of the sacred and the secular. 1.6397
Ajax. 2.543
Akbar, the Great Mogul, 1542-1605. 3.4255
Aké. 2.10114
Akhlaq-i Nasiri. 1.1483
Aksel Sandemose. 2.14051
Al filo del agua. 2.5357
al-Ghazali's Tahafut al'falasifah. 1.374
al-Kindī's Metaphysics. 1.375
Al margen de los clásicos. 2.5105
al-Mu'allaqāt. 2.1838
Al Smith: hero of the cities. 3.7681
ALA filing rules. 5.7634
The ALA glossary of library and information science. 5.7693
ALA world encyclopedia of library and information services. 5.7692
Alabama. 3.8280
Alabama, a guide to the deep South. 3.8284
Alabama bound. 4.6914
Alain Robbe-Grillet. 2.4694
Alan Paton. 2.10090
Alan Turing. 5.1098
Alanbrooke. 3.1268
Alaska, a Bicentennial history. 3.8645
The Alaska Purchase and Russian-American relations. 3.7475
Alba. 3.3444
Alban Berg. 1.3814
Alban Berg's Wozzeck. 1.4513
Albania. 3.3603
Albania and the Albanians. 3.3601
The Albanian national awakening, 1878-1912. 3.3602
Albergo Empedocle, and other writings. 2.8643
Albert Bierstadt: painter of the American West. 1.5919
Albert Camus. 2.4458
Albert Camus and the literature of revolt. 2.4457
Albert Einstein's special theory of relativity. 5.2083
Albert Gallatin. 3.6996
Albert J. Beveridge. 3.7629
Albert P. Ryder. 1.5966
Albert Schweitzer. 1.1061
Alberto Giacometti. 1.5705
Alberuni's India. 3.4192
The Albigensian Crusade. 3.1993
The Albigensian Crusades. 3.1992
Albion's fatal tree. 4.6786
Albrecht Dürer. 1.4989, 1.6388
Albrecht Dürer: master printmaker. 1.6462
Albrecht Dürer, paintings, prints, drawings. 1.4989
Album of American history. 3.6332
The Alcestiad. 2.12715
Alcestis. 2.463
Alchemy. 5.2612
Alchemy and early chemistry. 5.2611
Alcide de Gasperi. 3.2898
Alcohol and alcohol problems. 4.6647
Alcohol and the family. 4.6636
Alcohol education materials. 5.8438
Alcohol problems and alcoholism. 4.6633
Alcohol, reform, and society. 4.6649
Alcohol, use and abuse in America. 4.6653
Alcohol use and world cultures. 5.8437
Alcohol, young drivers, and traffic accidents. 4.4036
The alcoholic republic, an American tradition. 4.6648
Alcoholics Anonymous comes of age. 4.6643
Alcoholism and its treatment in industry. 4.4369
The alcoholism problems. 4.6632
Alcools. 2.4365
The Alcotts. 2.10896
Aldous Huxley. 2.8828-2.8829
Aldous Huxley; a literary study. 2.8825

Aldous Huxley: a study of the major novels. 2.8826
Aldous Huxley; satire and structure. 2.8830
Aldous Huxley, satirist and novelist. 2.8827
Aldous Huxley, the critical heritage. 2.8824
The Aldrich library of infrared spectra. 5.2679
Aldrich library of N.M.R. spectra. 5.2683
The Aldrich library of NMR spectra. 5.2683
Alejandro Casona. 2.5281
Alejo Carpentier. 2.5363
Aleksandr Blok. 2.1470
Aleksandr Blok: between image and idea. 2.1472
Aleksandr Pushkin, epigrams and satirical verse. 2.1409
Aleksandr Solzhenitsyn: critical essays and documentary materials. 2.1637
Aleksandra Kollontai. 3.3229
Alessandro Algardi. 1.5725
Alessandro Scarlatti: his life and works. 1.3965
Alesso Baldovinetti. 1.6190
Aleut and Eskimo art. 3.5881
Alex La Guma. 2.10086
Alexander Calder. 1.5664
Alexander H. Stephens. 3.7333
Alexander Hamilton. 3.6998-3.6999
Alexander I of Russia. 3.3116
Alexander I: Tsar of war and peace. 3.3115
Alexander II and the modernization of Russia. 3.3127
The Alexander memoirs, 1940-1945. 3.798
Alexander of Macedon, 356-323 B.C. 3.2625
Alexander Pope. 2.7198
Alexander Pope & the arts of Georgian England. 2.7205
Alexander Pope, the genius of sense. 2.7203
Alexander Pope: the poetry of allusion. 2.7201
Alexander Pushkin. 2.1418, 2.1420
Alexander Pushkin, complete prose fiction. 2.1408
Alexander the Great. 3.2626, 3.2628-3.2630
Alexander the Great and the Greeks. 3.2619
Alexandre Dumas (père) 2.4180
The Alexandria quartet. 2.8606
Alexandrian Christianity. 1.2209
The Alexiad of the Princess Anna Comnena. 3.2671
Alexis de Tocqueville on democracy, revolution, and society. 4.7446
Alexis, tsar of all the Russias. 3.3095
Alfalfa Bill Murray. 3.8538
Alfonso Sastre. 2.5282
Alfonso X, el Sabio. 2.5160
Alfonso X of Castile. 3.3433
Alfred de Vigny. 2.4334
Alfred Deakin. 3.5573
Alfred Döblin. 2.13730
Alfred Jarry. 2.4594
Alfred Jarry, nihilism and the theater of the absurd. 2.4595
Alfred Jarry, une étude par Jacques-Henry Levesque. 2.4593
Alfred Kroeber. 4.421
Alfred Lord Tennyson; a memoir. 2.8175
Alfred North Whitehead. 1.777, 1.780
Alfred North Whitehead: an anthology. 1.774
Alfred Schutz. 4.4764
Alfred Stieglitz and the photo-secession. 5.6955
Alfred Stieglitz, photographs & writings. 5.6961
Alfred Tennyson. 2.8168, 2.8173
Alfred Thayer Mahan. 3.6379
Alfred the Great, Asser's Life of King Alfred and other contemporary sources. 3.1320
Alfred V. Kidder. 4.420
The algae. 5.3711
Algal cultures and phytoplankton ecology. 5.3707
Algebra. 5.1267, 5.1270-5.1272
Algebraic curves. 5.1582
Algebraic curves. 5.1580
Algebraic number theory. 5.1317
The algebraic theory of quadratic forms. 5.1335
Algebraic topology. 5.1588, 5.1610
Algebraic topology, an introduction. 5.1609
Algeria, a country study. 3.5204

Algorithms. 5.1195
Algorithms + data structures=programs. 5.1204
Algorithms for graphics and image processing. 5.5652
Alice Adams. 2.11236
The Alice B. Toklas cook book. 5.7136
Alice Hamilton, a life in letters. 5.4531
Alice James, a biography. 3.338
Alice Meynell; a memoir. 2.7953
Alice's adventures in Wonderland. 2.7675-2.7676
Alien powers. 4.7243
The alien vision of Victorian poetry. 2.5825
Alien wisdom. 3.2551
The alienated 'loyal' opposition. 4.8335
Alienation. 4.5070
Alienation and charisma. 4.5787
Alienation and freedom. 4.3430
Aliens and dissenters. 3.7551
Aliens and linguists. 2.3490
Alison's house. 2.11784
Aljian's Purchasing handbook. 4.4324
All-American English. 2.1129
All American music. 1.3696
All faithful people. 1.2416
All fires the fire, and other stories. 2.5378
All God's dangers. 4.2910
All Hallow's eve. 2.9523
All in one lifetime. 3.7632
All men are brothers. 1.207
The all new complete book of bicycling. 4.1045
All our kin: strategies for survival in a Black community. 3.6774
All over. 2.12837
All passion spent. 2.9294
All possible worlds. 4.48
All quiet on the western front. 2.13848
All said and done. 2.4401
All scientists now. 5.695
All silver and no brass. 2.9862
All Stalin's men. 3.3224
All that dwell therein. 4.6631
All that fall. 2.8419
All that is native & fine. 3.8179
All that is native and fine. 3.8179
All that is solid melts into air. 3.187
All the conspirators. 2.8832
All the empty palaces. 1.4672
All the good people I've left behind. 2.13194
All the happy endings. 2.10288
All the king's men. 2.12634
All the little live things. 2.12503
All the moves. 4.1009
All the paintings of Giorgione. 1.6206
All the paintings of Masaccio. 1.6216
All the President's men. 3.7916
All the Queen's men. 3.1793
All the women are White, all the Blacks are men, but some of us are brave. 3.6747
All the world's a fair. 5.5655
All the world's aircraft. 5.6640
All the world's airships. 5.6640
All the world's fighting ships, 1860-1905. 5.7434
All the world's fighting ships 1898-. 5.7446
All the world's fighting ships, 1906-1921. 5.7435
All the world's fighting ships, 1922-1946. 5.7430
All the world's fighting ships, 1947-1982. 5.7431
All the young men. 2.11975
All things are possible. 1.3035
All things vain. 2.6062
All this, and heaven too. 2.11718
All together now. 1.3626
Allah's Commonwealth. 1.1996
Allan Nevins on history. 3.402
Allan Ramsay. 2.7210
The allegorical drama of Calderón. 2.5162
Allegorical imagery; some mediaeval books and their posterity. 2.2657
Allegory. 2.2389
The allegory of love. 2.2640
The allegory of The Faerie Queene. 2.6535

Allen and Greenough's New Latin grammar for schools and colleges, founded on comparative grammar. 2.253
Allen Ginsberg. 2.11771
Allen Tate. 2.12575
Allen Tate and his work. 2.12577
Alley life in Washington. 3.6797
Allgemeines Lexikon der bildenden Künstler des XX. Jahrhunderts. 1.4585
Allgemeines Lexikon der bildenden Künstler von der Antike bis zur Gegenwart. 1.4584
The alliance 3.1204
Alliance policy in the cold war. 3.7609
Alliance politics. 3.6447
Alliances and the third world. 4.9034
Allied intervention in Russia. 3.3200
The Allied occupation of Japan. 3.4979
The Allies and the Russian collapse, March 1917-March 1918. 3.3203
Allies, Pearl Harbor to D-Day. 3.919
The alliterative Morte Arthure. 2.6420-2.6421
The alliterative revival. 2.955
Allusions in Ulysses. 2.8882
Alma mater. 4.10843
The Almanac of American history. 3.6200
The Almanac of American politics. 4.7995
The almanac of American politics. 4.7851
The almanac of British politics. 4.8467
Almanac of business and industrial financial ratios. 4.4411
The almanac of world military power. 5.7258
Almanack..established by Joseph Whitaker. 1.68
Almost-periodic functions and functional equations. 5.1555
Almost to the Presidency. 3.7651
Alone of all her sex. 1.2900
Alone with America. 2.10492
Along the ancient silk routes. 1.5185
Along this way. 3.6838
L'alouette. 2.4359
Alpayim sefer va-sefer. 5.8236
Alpha- beta- and gamma-ray spectroscopy. 5.2415
The alphabet. 2.169
The Alphabet. 1.6599
The alphabet of economic science. 4.1497
Alphonse de Lamartine. 2.4257
Alphonse Mucha. 1.5858
The altar and the altarpiece. 1.6233
Altered harvest. 4.3681
Altered states. 2.11487
Altered states of consciousness. 5.290
Alternate states of consciousness. 5.257
Alternate worlds. 2.3488
Alternating current machines. 5.6315
The alternative. 4.6980
Alternative America. 4.5143
Alternative energy sources. 5.6116
Alternative models of elementary education. 4.10425
Alternative schools. 4.10303
Alternative social structures and ritual relations in the Balkans. 4.603
An alternative sociology. 4.4861
Alternative technologies for power production. 5.6871
An alternative to war or surrender. 3.7594
Alternative voices. 1.4205
Alternative work schedules. 4.3153
Alternatives to the internal combustion engine. 5.6626
Alternatives to the multinational enterprise. 4.3019
Altgeld's America. 3.8414
Alton Locke, tailor and poet. 2.7875
The altruistic imagination. 4.6510
Aluminum alloy structures. 5.5888
Aluminum alloys. 5.6782
Alvar Aalto and the international style. 1.5445
Álvar Núñez Cabeza de Vaca; the journey and route of the first European to cross the continent of North America, 1534-1536. 3.5983
Álvaro Obregón. 3.8947
Always merry and bright. 2.12192
The AMA and U.S. health policy since 1940. 5.4477

AMA drug evaluations. 5.5135
AMA handbook of poisonous and injurious plants. 5.4732
L'amant. 2.4518
Amante anglaise. 2.4519
Les amants de Venise. 2.4294
The amateur astronomer's handbook. 5.1735
The amateur Democrat. 4.8205
Amateurs. 2.12887
The amazing brain. 5.4339
Amazon town. 3.9220
Amazons, a study in Athenian mythmaking. 1.1665
Amazons and warrior women. 2.5891
The ambassadors. 2.11105
An ambassador's memoirs. 3.3189
The ambidextrous historian. 3.8468
The ambidextrous universe. 5.2060
Ambiguity and choice in organizations. 4.10643
Ambiguity in Greek literature. 2.242
The ambiguity of Henry James. 2.11126
Ambiguous Africa; cultures in collision. 3.5224
The ambiguous consensus. 4.8877
The ambiguous image. 2.2888
The ambiguous Iroquois empire. 3.5801
Ambitions and realities. 3.1717
Ambrose Bierce. 2.10911
Ambulatory care. 5.4621
America, a sketch of its political, social, and religious character. 1.2383
America and the Allies in Germany, 1918-1923. 3.858
America and the image of Europe. 3.6084
America and the Mediterranean world, 1776-1882. 3.3756
America and the survivors of the Holocaust. 4.8957
America and the world of our time. 3.7563
America and the world revolution and other lectures. 3.6171
America as a civilization. 3.6131
America as a world power, 1872-1945. 3.7566
America at mid-century. 3.6166
America at the polls. 4.7948
America begins. 2.10840
America by design. 5.5522
America comes of age. 3.6167
America encounters Japan. 3.6465
America goes to war. 3.7338
America, history and life. Part C, American history bibliography, books, articles and dissertations. 5.7824
America hurrah and other plays. 2.13387
America in a divided world, 1945-1972. 3.7567
America in crisis. 3.6334
America in midpassage. 3.6076
America in our time. 4.5160
America in perspective. 3.6095
America in the Gilded Age. 3.7405
America in the modern world. 3.6087
America in the sixties. 3.6080, 4.2000
America is West. 2.10725
America learns to dance. 4.1103
America moves west. 3.8466
America now. 4.5159
The America of George Ade, 1866-1944. 2.10891
The America of José Martí. 3.5683
America revised. 3.6271
America takes the stage. 2.3197
America through women's eyes. 3.6003
America votes. 4.8106
The American. 2.11107, 3.6068
The American 1890s. 2.10387
American academics. 4.10533
The American Adam. 2.10374
The American and Canadian West. 5.7854
American and English popular entertainment. 5.8426
American anthropologist. 3.4590
American apocalypse. 1.2406
The American approach to foreign policy 3.6407
American archaeology in the mideast. 3.3699
American architecture, 1607-1976. 1.5290
American architecture, and other writings. 1.5297

American architecture and urbanism. 1.5288
American architecture comes of age. 1.5293
American architecture since 1780. 1.5289
American art. 1.4863
American art directory. v. [1]- 1898-.
  1.4590
American art of our century. 1.4882
American art of the 20th century. 1.4870
American art since 1900. 1.4880-1.4881
American artists on art from 1940 to 1980.
  1.4868
American authors, 1600-1900. 2.10234
American authors and books, 1640 to the
  present day. 5.7784
The American autobiography. 2.10344
American autobiography, 1945-1980. 5.8110
The American automobile. 4.3824
The American automobile industry. 4.3825
American automobile manufacturers. 4.3826
American automobiles. 5.6621
American Ballet Theatre. 4.1162
American baseball. 4.1002
American battleships, 1886-1923. 5.7437
American bibliography. 5.7751
American bibliography, a preliminary checklist
  for 1801-1819. 5.7758
The American book of days. 4.873
American book-prices current. 5.7673
American book publishing record. 5.7729
American book trade directory. 5.7591
American book trade manual 1915-22. 5.7591
American booktrade directory 1925-49. 5.7591
American broadsides. 3.6192
American buffalo. 2.13166
American building. 1.5283
American buildings and their architects.
  1.5287
American business and public policy. 4.4171
The American business creed 4.1940
American business history. 4.4214
American business in the twentieth century.
  4.1932
The American business system. 4.1933
The American campaigns of Rochambeau's
  army, 1780, 1781, 1782, 1783. 3.6947
American capital and Canadian resources.
  4.4625
American capitalism. 4.1524
American carnival. 4.1195
The American catalogue. 5.7748
The American catalogue of books, 1861-1871.
  5.7747
The American catalogue of books, (original and
  reprints,) 5.7747
The American Catholic experience. 1.3173
American Catholic social ethics. 1.3203
American Catholicism. 1.3174
American Catholics. 1.3177
The American cause. 3.6124
The American chair. 1.6581
The American challenge. 3.1206
The American character. 3.6088
American chemical industry. 5.6811
The American children of Krsna. 1.1710
American Christianity. 1.2369
American chronicle. 2.3604
The American cinema. 2.2928
American cinematographer manual. 5.7002
American city planning since 1890. 4.6324
The American Civil War. 3.7346
American civilization. 3.6270
American civilization and the Negro. 3.6688
The American class structure. 4.5237
The American clock, 1725-1865. 1.6667
The American cockroach. 5.3875
The American college. 4.10090
The American college and the culture of
  aspiration, 1915-1940. 4.10070
The American college and university, a history.
  4.10067
The American college dictionary. 2.1089
American college fraternities 1st-5th. 4.11013
The American colonial mind and the classical
  tradition. 3.6014
American Colonial prose. 2.10839
The American Colonies in the eighteenth
  century. 3.6879

The American colonies in the seventeenth
  century. 3.6873
American commodity flow. 4.3890
The American common school. 4.10020
The American Commonwealth. 4.7848
American communism and Soviet Russia.
  4.6988
American communism in crisis, 1943-1957.
  4.8237
The American Communist Party. 4.8235
The American community college. 4.10560
American community, technical, and junior
  colleges. 4.9937
The American composer speaks. 1.3495
The American Congress. 4.8021
American conservatism in the age of enterprise.
  4.7311
The American constitutional system. 4.9632
American convictions. 3.6075
American counterpoint. 3.6695
The American counties. 3.6364
American country houses of the Gilded Age
  (Sheldon's 'Artistic country-seats') 1.5571
American county histories. 5.7851
American couples. 4.5651
The American cowboy. 3.8492
American crime. 4.6771
American criminal justice. 4.9858
An American crisis. 3.7459
An American crusade. 2.10929
American culture on the eve of the Revolution.
  3.6127
American decorative arts. 1.6541
American defense policy since 1945. 5.7856
American delinquency, its meaning and
  construction. 4.6872
American demagogues: twentieth century.
  3.7618
American democracy. 3.6128
American design ethic. 5.7013
American dialects. 2.1142
American diaries. 5.8111
The American diaries of Richard Cobden.
  3.6045
American diary, 1898. 3.6054
An American dilemma. 3.6656
The American dimension. 3.6062
American diplomacy. 3.6403
American diplomacy, 1900-1950. 3.7579
American diplomacy and the Spanish Civil
  War. 3.6497
American diplomacy during the second World
  War, 1941-1945. 3.939
American diplomacy during the world war.
  3.835
American diplomacy in the 20th century.
  3.7600
American diplomacy in the twentieth century.
  3.7600
American diplomatic history. 3.6399
American diplomatic relations with the Middle
  East, 1784-1975. 3.3753
The American doctrine of judicial supremacy.
  4.9644
American drama criticism. 5.7804
American drama from its beginnings to the
  present. 5.7802
The American drama since 1918. 2.10524
American drama since World War II. 2.10525
American drama to 1900. 5.7803
The American dream. 2.12838
An American dream. 2.12093
The American dream in the Great Depression.
  3.6118
American dreams, American nightmares.
  2.10419
American dreams, lost and found. 3.333
The American earthquake. 3.6061
American economic and business history
  information sources. 5.8409
American economic history. 4.1883, 4.1888
American economic life. 4.1889
American economic policy since 1789. 4.1892
The American economy. 4.1958, 4.2086
The American economy in transition. 4.1977
American education. 4.10021
American education, a national failure.
  4.10009

American education and vocationalism.
  4.10831
American education, the national experience,
  1783-1876. 4.10022
American educators' encyclopedia. 4.10164
The American elections of 1980. 3.7936
The American elections of 1982. 3.8113
The American encyclopedia of soccer. 4.1022
American English. 2.1126
American English grammar. 2.1132
American-English usage. 2.1139
The American environment. 5.5300
American environmental history. 4.2079
American epoch. 3.7510
The American essays 2.10266
The American establishment and other reports,
  opinions, and speculations. 3.7536
American ethics and public policy. 3.6122
The American ethos. 4.5229
The American experience. 3.6152
American export register. 4.4210
American fabrics and fashions. 5.7077
The American family. 4.5568, 4.5583
American family history. 4.5566
The American family in social-historical
  perspective. 4.5574
American farm policy, 1948-1973. 4.2955
The American farmer and the New Deal.
  4.2945
American farmers. 4.3528
The American Federation of Labor. 4.3548
American fiction. 2.10538
American fiction, 1774-1850. 5.7817
American fiction, 1851-1875. 5.7818
American fiction, 1876-1900. 5.7819
American fiction, 1900-1950. 5.7816
American fiction, 1920-1940. 2.10613
American fiction to 1900. 5.7812
American fictions, 1940-1980. 2.10629
The American film industry. 2.2906
The American Film Institute guide to college
  courses in film and television. 2.2933
An American first. 3.941
American folk art in wood, metal and stone.
  1.6516
American folk decoration. 1.6520
American folk painters of three centuries.
  1.5891
American folk poetry. 2.10756
American folklore. 4.775
American foreign policy; basic documents,
  1950-1955. 4.9049
American foreign policy current documents.
  4.9048
American foreign policy in the Congo,
  1960-1964. 3.6502
American foreign policy in the making,
  1932-1940. 3.7750
American foreign relations. 4.8971
American forum: speeches on historic issues,
  1788-1900. 2.10856
The American frontier. 3.6352
The American frontier in Hawaii. 3.5640
American furniture. 1.6562
American furniture in the Henry Francis du
  Pont Winterthur Museum. 1.6563
American furniture, the Federal period, in the
  Henry Francis du Pont Winterthur Museum.
  1.6564
American genesis. 3.8199
American geography. 4.38
American geological literature, 1669 to 1850.
  5.8219
American glass. 1.6644
American growth and the balance of payments,
  1820-1913. 4.4587
American handbook of psychiatry. 5.4796
American harvest. 2.10712
American heritage. 1.6513, 4.1885, 5.6643
The American Heritage dictionary of the
  English language. 2.1080
The American heritage history of American
  business & industry. 4.1885
The American heritage history of flight. 5.6643
American heroes. 3.6292
American heroine: the life and legend of Jane
  Addams. 4.6469
The American high school today. 4.10492

American higher education. 4.10061
The American historian. 3.6225
American historians and European immigrants, 1875-1925. 3.6219
American historical explanations. 3.6224
The American historical novel. 2.10554
American historiography. 3.6220
American history and American historians. 3.6203
American history and its geographic conditions. 3.6357
American history bibliography. 5.7824
American history in American thought: Christopher Columbus to Henry Adams. 3.6214
The American home. 1.5558
American humor. 2.10655
The American humorist. 2.10658
American hunger. 2.12815
American husbandry. 5.5231
The American idea of industrial democracy, 1865-1965. 4.3184
The American idea of mission. 3.6090
American ideals versus the New Deal. 4.1961
The American image. 3.6053
The American image of Russia, 1775-1917. 3.6482
The American image of Russia, 1917-1977. 3.6481
American immigration policy, 1924-1952. 4.8948
American imperialism. 3.7421
American impressionism. 1.5898
American imprints. 5.7750, 5.7760
The American Indian and the United States. 3.5810
American Indian fiction. 2.10295
The American Indian in urban society. 3.5829
American Indian leaders. 3.5785
American Indian literature. 2.2326
American Indian painting of the Southwest and Plains areas. 3.5813
American Indian policy in the Jacksonian era. 3.5808
American Indian prose and poetry. 2.2320
The American Indian speaks. 2.2321
American Indian stories. 3.5961
American Indian women, telling their lives. 3.5833
American Indians. 5.7736
American industry and the European immigrant, 1860-1885. 4.3604
American insects. 5.3863
American Institute of Physics handbook. 5.2011
American intellectual histories and historians. 3.6232
American interests and policies in the Middle East, 1900-1939. 3.3754
American interpretations of natural law, a study in the history of political thought. 4.7320
American intervention: 1917 and 1941. 3.7585
The American Irish. 3.6555
American jazz music. 1.4328
The American jeremiad. 2.10527
American Jewish history. 5.8245
The American Jewish woman. 4.5913
The American Jewish woman, 1654-1980. 4.5912
American Jewish year book. 3.6561
American Jewish yearbook. 3.6561
American journalism. 2.3586
American journey. 3.6028
American Judaism. 1.1927
American Judaism: adventure in modernity. 1.1930
The American judicial tradition. 4.9800
The American jury. 4.9888
American kinship. 4.5581
American labor and immigration history, 1877-1920s. 4.3611
American labor songs of the nineteenth century. 1.3443
American labor struggles. 4.3165
American labor unions and politics. 4.3598
The American language. 2.1127
American law publishing, 1860-1900. 4.9437

American lawyers in a changing society, 1776-1876. 4.9487
The American Left. 4.5231
American liberal disillusionment. 3.834
American library & book trade annual. 5.7659
American library annual. 5.7659
American library annual and book trade almanac 1959. 5.7659
American library directory. 5.7660
American library resources. 5.7682
American light. 1.6357
American literary criticism. 2.2511, 2.10242
American literary naturalism, a divided stream. 2.10646
The American literary revolution, 1783-1837. 2.10604
American literary scholarship. 2.10232
American literature. 2.10663
American literature, 1764-1789. 2.10367
American literature and the experience of Vietnam. 2.10433
American literature in nineteenth century England. 2.10338
American literature: Poe through Garland. 5.7794
American machinist. 5.7019
American magazines. 2.3639
The American magic. 3.1080
The American mail. 4.4045
The American maritime industries and public policy, 1789-1914. 5.7504
American master drawings and watercolors. 1.6378
The American Medical Association family medical guide. 5.4756
The American Medical Association's handbook of first aid and emergency care. 5.4757
American medical bibliography 1639-1783. 5.8286
American medical directory. 5.4548
American medical directory update. 5.4548
American medicine and the public interest. 5.4524
American medicine in transition 1840-1910. 5.4527
American men & women of science. 5.806
American men and women of science. 5.806
American men of science. 5.809
American mercury. 2.10711
The American mercury reader. 2.10711
American Methodist pioneer. 1.3375
American military government. 3.1057
American military history. 3.6365
American military thought. 5.7277
The American mind. 3.6096
American moderns, from rebellion to conformity. 2.10619
American monetary policy, 1928-1941. 4.4501
The American monomyth. 3.6184
An American music. 1.3697
American musical revue. 1.4215
The American musical theater. 1.4217
American musical theater. 1.4218
American musical theatre. 1.4216
The American myth of success. 4.5148
American nationalism. 3.6126
American nativism, 1830-1860. 3.7144
American naval power, The rise of. 3.6382
The American Navy, 1789-1860: a bibliography. 5.8302
The American Navy, 1865-1918. 5.8303
The American Navy, 1918-1941. 5.8304
The American Negro. 3.6782
The American Negro Academy. 3.6637
American Negro art. 1.4909
American Negro poetry. 2.10749
The American Negro reference book. 3.6610
The American Negro revolution. 3.6709
American Negro short stories. 2.10813
American Negro slave revolts. 3.7228
American Negro slavery. 3.7184, 3.7194, 3.7198
American neutrality, 1914-1917. 3.836
The American newspaperman. 2.3591
American newspapers, 1821-1936. 5.8318
The American newsreel, 1911-1967. 2.3646
American nicknames; their origin and significance. 3.6342

American nonpublic schools. 4.10727
American notes. 2.7879
American notes and Pictures from Italy. 3.6032
The American novel. 5.7810, 5.7813
The American novel and its tradition. 2.10536
The American novel: from James Fenimore Cooper to William Faulkner. 2.10539
The American novel through Henry James. 5.7811
American novelists revisited. 2.10595
American nursing. 5.5158
The American occupation of Austria. 3.1904
The American occupation of Germany. 3.2457, 3.2460
The American occupation of Japan. 3.6467
The American occupational structure. 4.3215
American opinion on world affairs in the atomic age. 3.7562
American outpost. 2.12480
The American pageant. 3.6328
American painting. 1.5888, 1.5901
American painting, history and interpretation. 1.5884
American painting in the twentieth century. 1.5903
American painting of the nineteenth century. 1.5896
American painting: the 20th century. 1.5907
American paintings in the Metropolitan Museum of Art. 1.5887
American paradox. 3.6099
The American party system. 4.8175
The American party systems. 4.8171
The American past. 3.6337
The American peace movement and social reform, 1898-1918. 4.9144
The American people. 4.1674, 4.1676
The American people and foreign policy. 3.7556
The American people in the twentieth century 3.6116
American perspectives. 3.6073
American philosophy in the twentieth century. 1.570
American photography. 5.6923
American physicians in the nineteenth century: from sects to science. 5.4523
American picturebooks from Noah's ark to the Beast within. 1.5829
American place-names. 3.5994
The American planner. 4.6316
The American playhouse in the eighteenth century. 1.5549
American plays. 2.10779
American poetry. 2.10729
American poetry and culture, 1945-1980. 2.10645
American poetry in the twentieth century. 2.10497
American poets, 1630-1930. 2.10736
American poets, from the Puritans to the present. 2.10476
The American police state. 4.7915
American policy toward Communist China, 1949-1969. 3.6421
The American political dictionary. 4.7793
American political ideas. 4.7313
American political terms. 4.7796
American political writing during the founding era, 1760-1805. 4.7813
The American politician. 3.7619
American popular music. 1.3523
American popular song. 1.4293
American practical navigator. 5.7493
American pragmatism. 1.530
American pragmatism and education, an interpretation and criticism. 4.10223
The American pragmatists. 1.528
American preservation commissions. 3.5992
The American presidency. 4.7927, 5.7846-5.7847
The American Presidency. 4.7929, 4.7932
The American president. 4.7938
American Presidents and the Presidency. 4.7918
American primitive painting. 1.5899
The American printer, 1787-1825. 5.7552

American printmaking. 1.6435
American prints and printmakers. 1.6436
American prisons. 4.6903
The American private eye. 2.10545
American pronunciation. 2.1016
American prose and criticism, 1820-1900.
  5.7823
American prose masters: Cooper, Hawthorne,
  Emerson, Poe, Lowell, Henry James.
  2.10528
American Protestantism. 1.2376
American proverbs and proverbial phrases.
  2.3810
American public address. 2.10649
American public addresses, 1740-1952. 2.10853
American public administration. 5.8357
American public school law. 4.9580
The American Puritans, their prose and poetry.
  2.10707
The American quest for a supreme fiction.
  2.10493
The American radical press, 1880-1960. 4.6924
American railroad politics, 1914-1920. 4.3996
American railroads. 4.3998
American railroads and the transformation of
  the antebellum economy. 4.3992
The American railway. 4.3990
American realism. 2.10566
American realists and magic realists. 1.4874
American reference books annual.
  5.7710-5.7711, 5.8105
American reformers, 1815-1860. 4.5177
American refugee policy. 4.6538
American regionalism. 3.6354
American religion and philosophy. 5.8442
American religious thought. 1.2372
American renaissance. 2.10375
The American renaissance, 1876-1917. 1.4866
The American Republic. 4.7847
The American revisionists. 3.7726
The American Revolution. 3.6896, 3.6906
The American Revolution, 1775-1783. 3.6895
The American revolution considered as a social
  movement. 3.6911
The American Revolution in Georgia,
  1763-1789. 3.8202
The American Revolution in its political and
  military aspects, 1763-1783. 3.6904
The American Revolution reconsidered. 3.6903
American rhetoric from Roosevelt to Reagan.
  2.10858
The American right wing. 4.7860
American romantic painting. 1.5889
American romanticism and the marketplace.
  2.10393
American-Russian relations, 1781-1947. 3.6490
An American saga. 4.5996, 5.6655
The American sailing Navy. 5.7449
American sailing ships. 5.7503
The American scene. 2.12125
American schoolbooks. 4.11015
American science in the age of Jefferson. 5.791
The American science of politics. 4.7305
American sculpture in process, 1930-1970.
  1.5659
American seashells. 5.3846
The American secretaries of state and their
  diplomacy. 3.6396
American Secretaries of the Navy. 5.7473
The American self. 3.6072
The American senator. 2.8201
American ships of the Colonial and
  Revolutionary periods. 5.7502
American short novels. 2.10808
The American short story. 2.10580
The American short story, 1900-1945. 2.10575
The American short story, 1945-1980. 2.10576
The American short story in the twenties.
  2.10648
American silent film. 2.2914
American silver, 1655-1825, in the Museum of
  Fine Arts, Boston. 1.6655
American silver, pewter, and silver plate.
  1.6657
American skyline. 4.6230
American slavery, American freedom. 3.7220
The American small businessman. 4.1981

American social attitudes data sourcebook,
  1947-1978. 4.5180
American social fiction, James to Cozzens.
  2.10638
American social reform movements. 4.5132
American society: problems of structure.
  4.5192
American sociological theory. 4.4771
American sociology. 1.2397
The American soldier. 5.7167
American song. 1.3574, 2.11646
The American South. 3.8115, 3.8128
American-Spanish euphemisms. 2.907
American speeches. 2.3781
American spiders. 5.3855
The American spirit. 3.6077
The American spirit in literature. 2.10254
The American sporting experience. 4.938
The American stage. 2.3187
The American stage to World War I. 5.7807
American State politics. 4.8246
The American steel navy. 5.7451
The American story transformed. 2.10833
American strategy in World War II. 3.904
American studies. 3.6269, 5.7830
American studies international. 3.6269
American surnames. 3.306
The American symphony orchestra. 1.3691
The American system. 4.7871
The American theatre. 2.3193
The American theatre today. 2.3180
American theatre, 1860-1985. 2.3206
The American theatre as seen by its critics,
  1752-1934. 2.3192
American third parties since the Civil War.
  5.8385
American thought. 1.555
American thought and writing. 2.10842
American thought before 1900. 1.553
American thought: Civil War to World War I.
  2.10860
American trade union democracy. 4.3359
The American tradition in literature. 2.10665
An American tragedy. 2.11591
American transcendentalism, 1830-1860. 1.564
The American transcendentalists, their prose
  and poetry. 2.10720
American transportation in prosperity and
  depression. 4.3994
American treasure and the price revolution in
  Spain, 1501-1650. 4.1506
An American triptych. 2.10477
American universities and colleges. 4.10056
The American university. 4.10057, 4.10085
American urban history. 4.6200
American usage and style, the consensus.
  2.1040
American vaudeville, its life and times. 2.2830
American violence. 3.6341
American violence and public policy. 4.6774
The American vision. 2.10582
American visionary poetry. 2.10483
An American visitor. 2.8495
The American Vitruvius. 1.5581
The American voter. 4.8117
American war literature, 1914 to Vietnam.
  2.10434
The American way of death. 4.867
The American West. 3.8459
The American West, new perspectives, new
  dimensions. 3.8452
The American West transformed. 4.2029
The American western novel. 2.10594
The American woman. 4.6038
The American woman in sport. 4.962
American women and politics. 5.8474
American women and the labor movement,
  1825-1974. 5.8471
American women artists. 1.4861
American women: fifteen hundred biographies
  with over 1,400 portraits. 3.354
American women in jazz. 1.4270
American women writers. 2.10283
The American writer and the European
  tradition. 2.10336
American writers. 2.10278
American writers before 1800. 2.10364

American writing in the twentieth century.
  2.10423
American writing since 1945. 2.10427
American writing today: its independence and
  vigor. 2.10424
American Zionism from Herzl to the holocaust.
  3.4022
The Americana annual. 1.11
The Americanization of Edward Bok. 2.3605
Americanization of the common law. 4.9900
The Americanization of the Synagogue,
  1820-1870. 1.1928
Americanizing the American Indians. 3.5805
The Americans. 3.6963
The Americans. 3.6085, 3.6322, 3.6864
Americans, 1942. 1.4877
Americans and Chinese. 3.4635
Americans from Germany. 3.6545
Americans in eastern Asia. 3.4416
Americans in transition. 4.10982
America's ascent. 3.7418
America's Black musical heritage. 1.4296
America's cities. 4.6218
America's city halls. 1.5516
America's coming-of-age. 2.10264
America's failure in China, 1941-50. 3.4780
America's favorite movies. 2.2907
America's first civilization. 3.8883
America's first Hamlet. 2.11195
America's foreign policy, 1945-1976. 3.7853
America's front page news, 1690-1970. 3.6195
America's frontier heritage. 3.6343
America's garden book. 5.5366
America's golden bough. 5.798
America's great cities. 4.160
America's heroes. 3.6113
America's hidden success. 4.7861
America's housing. 4.3488
America's housing crisis. 4.3487
America's humor. 2.10650
America's indigo blues. 5.6904
America's Jews in transition. 3.6576
America's lighthouses. 5.7495
America's longest war. 3.4500
America's military past. 5.7843
America's music, from the pilgrims to the
  present. 1.3683
America's musical stage. 1.4219
America's old masters. 1.5892
America's outward thrust; approaches to
  foreign affairs, 1865-1890. 3.7422
America's quest for the ideal self. 4.5158
America's rise to world power, 1898-1954.
  3.7565
America's road to empire. 3.7502
America's Siberian expedition, 1918-1920.
  3.3201
America's ski book. 4.997
America's sporting heritage, 1850-1950. 4.932
America's strategy in world politics. 3.6409
America's struggle against poverty, 1900-1980.
  4.5161
America's teacher quality problem. 4.10524
America's unelected government. 4.7984
America's white working-class women. 5.8467
America's working women. 4.3275
Amerigo and the New World. 3.5987
Amerika Samoa. 3.5674
Amerikanuak. 3.5687
L'Ameto. 2.4909
Amílcar Cabral. 3.5410
Amiri Baraka/LeRoi Jones. 2.12875
Amish society. 1.3367, 3.6581
Amistad (New York, N.Y.) 3.6638
Amnesty International, the human rights story.
  4.7646
Among the elephants. 5.4039
Amor and Psyche. 2.704
Amores. 2.680, 2.743
Amoskeag. 4.3544
Les amours jaunes. 2.4156
Amusing the million. 3.8061
Amy Lowell. 2.12039-2.12040
The Amy Vanderbilt complete book of
  etiquette. 1.1518
Anabaptism; a social history, 1525-1618.
  1.3303
The Anabaptist view of the church. 1.3302

Anaïs Nin. 2.12255
Anaïs Nin reader. 2.12248
Analog and digital communication systems. 5.6402
Analog-digital conversion handbook. 5.6577
Analog filter design. 5.6515
Analog integrated circuit design. 5.6530
Analog integrated circuits. 5.6524, 5.6532
The analogical imagination. 1.2784
The analogy of religion. 1.2958
Analyses of nineteenth-century music. 1.3557
Analyses of twentieth-century music, 1940-1970. 1.3558
Analysis and adjustment of survey measurements. 5.5827
Analysis and design of analog integrated circuits. 5.6529
Analysis and design of digital integrated circuits. 5.6470
Analysis and design of digital systems. 5.6407
Analysis and design of integrated electronic circuits. 5.6523
The analysis, design, and implementation of information systems. 5.6513
The analysis, design, and synthesis of electrical filters. 5.6513
Analysis II. 5.1443
The analysis of beauty. 1.4610
Analysis of coniferous forest ecosystems in the Western United States. 5.3677
Analysis of consumer policy. 4.1836
Analysis of decisions under uncertainty. 4.2727
Analysis of electric machinery. 5.6310
Analysis of electrical machines. 5.6307
Analysis of foods and beverages. 5.7122
Analysis of heat and mass transfer. 5.2263
An analysis of John Barth's Weltanschauung. 2.12884
An analysis of knowledge and valuation. 1.1294
The analysis of linear partial differential operators. 5.1530
Analysis of messy data. 5.1412
Analysis of metallurgical failures. 5.5809
The analysis of music. 1.4439
Analysis of ordinal categorical data. 5.1405
The analysis of political behaviour. 4.7210
The analysis of sensations and the relation of the physical to the psychical. 5.4361
Analysis of structures. 5.5847
The analysis of the self. 5.4912
Analysis of turbulent boundary layers. 5.1665
Analysis of vertebrate populations. 5.3338
Analysis of vertebrate structure. 5.4109
The analytic attitude. 5.4918
Analytic functions and distributions in physics and engineering. 5.1969
Analytic inequalities. 5.1419
Analytic number theory. 5.1341
Analytic philosophy and phenomenology. 1.462
The Analytical approach. 5.2659
Analytical archaeology. 3.230
Analytical chemistry. 5.2689
Analytical concordance to the Bible on an entirely new plan containing about 311,000 references, subdivided under the Hebrew and Greek originals. 1.2504
The analytical didactic of Comenius. 4.10184
Analytical foundations of Marxian economic theory. 4.1328
Analytical mechanics. 5.1646
Analytical philosophy of history. 3.464
Analytical philosophy of knowledge. 1.1278
Analyzing demand behavior. 4.3702
Analyzing Marx. 1.1039
Analyzing multivariate data. 5.1407
Analyzing teaching behavior. 4.10271
Analyzing the impact of regulatory change in public utilities. 4.3041
The anarchical society. 4.9128
Anarchism. 4.7186
Anarchism. 4.7185
Anarchism, a theoretical analysis. 4.7190
Anarchism & the Mexican working class, 1860-1931. 4.7193
Anarchism; from theory to practice. 4.7180
The anarchist prince. 4.7195

The Anarchist reader. 4.7187
The anarchists. 4.7181
The anarchists of Casas Viejas. 4.7199
Anarchy, state, and utopia. 4.7644
The anathemata. 2.8852
The anatomical and mechanical bases of human motion. 5.4276
The anatomical works of George Stubbs 5.4112
The anatomy of a business strategy. 4.4075
Anatomy of a metropolis. 4.2045
Anatomy of a murder. 2.13361
Anatomy of a park. 5.5386
The anatomy of a party. 4.8307
The anatomy of a scientific institution. 5.698
The anatomy of American popular culture, 1840-1861. 3.6083
The anatomy of bibliomania. 5.7672
The anatomy of British sea power. 5.7458
Anatomy of criticism. 2.2436
The anatomy of dependence. 5.431
The anatomy of disillusion. 1.1001
The anatomy of historical knowledge. 3.513
Anatomy of horror. 2.5983
The anatomy of influence. 4.9265
The anatomy of inquiry. 5.932
The Anatomy of loneliness. 5.438
The anatomy of love. 2.13530
The anatomy of melancholy. 2.6437
The anatomy of nonsense. 2.2514
The anatomy of nonsense. 2.10275
Anatomy of paradise. 4.662
The anatomy of peace. 4.9121
Anatomy of printing. 5.7544
Anatomy of reality. 5.929
The anatomy of revolution. 4.7612
The anatomy of satire. 2.3789
The anatomy of terror. 3.3234
Anatomy of the dicotyledons. 5.3691
Anatomy of the fourth gospel. 1.2694
Anatomy of the honey bee. 5.3886
Anatomy of the human body. 5.4141
The anatomy of the Israeli army. 5.7345
Anatomy of the law. 4.9350
Anatomy of the monocotyledons. 5.3735
Anatomy of the newborn. 5.4145
Anatomy of the orchestra. 1.4193
Anatomy of wonder. 2.3454
The anatomy of work; 4.3118
Panchatantra. English. 2.1941
The Anchor anthology of Jacobean drama. 2.6220
The Anchor anthology of seventeenth-century verse. 2.6159
The Anchor anthology of sixteenth-century verse. 2.6149
The ancien régime. 3.2041
Ancient African kingdoms. 3.5080
Ancient & mediaeval grammatical theory in Europe. 2.161
Ancient and Oriental music. 1.3639
Ancient art and ritual. 1.1369
Ancient art of the American Woodland Indians. 3.5733
Ancient arts of the Andes. 3.9158
Ancient China, art and archaeology. 1.5068
Ancient China in transition. 4.5415
Ancient China's technology and science. 5.770
The ancient city. 4.7333-4.7334
Ancient civilizations. 4.499
The ancient civilizations of Peru. 3.9287
Ancient cosmologies. 1.1329
The ancient economy. 4.1727
Ancient Egypt. 3.5151
Ancient Egyptian religion. 1.1852
The ancient Egyptians. 2.1765
Ancient environments. 5.3157
Ancient Europe from the beginnings of agriculture to classical antiquity. 3.555
The ancient explorers. 4.56
Ancient fiction. 2.269
Ancient formal logic. 1.1156
Ancient France. 4.710
Ancient furniture. 1.6557
Ancient Ghana and Mali. 3.5378
Ancient Greece. 3.2563
Ancient Greece at work. 4.3095
Ancient Greek architects at work. 1.5217

The ancient Greek historians. 3.2567
Ancient Greek literature and society. 2.274
Ancient Greek military practices. 5.7181
Ancient Greek sculpture of South Italy and Sicily. 1.5631
The ancient Greeks. 3.2534
The ancient historians. 3.2515
Ancient history. 3.2513
Ancient India 3.4240
Ancient Indonesian art 1.5056
Ancient Israel: its life and institutions. 3.3836
The ancient Khmer Empire. 3.4443
Ancient law. 4.7321, 4.9354
The ancient library of Qumrân and modern Biblical studies. 1.1905
Ancient literary criticism. 2.264
Ancient lives. 3.5141
The ancient mariners. 3.558
The ancient Maya. 3.9040
Ancient Maya civilization. 3.9037
Ancient Mesopotamia. 3.3765
The ancient Near East. 1.2573, 3.3719
The ancient Near East in pictures, relating to the Old Testament. 1.2574
Ancient Near Eastern texts relating to the Old Testament. 1.2572
Ancient Polynesian society. 3.5621
Ancient records of Assyria and Babylonia. 3.3763
Ancient records of Egypt. 3.5135
Ancient Roman religion. 1.1659
The ancient romances. 2.271
Ancient Rome at work. 4.3096
Ancient sedimentary environments and their sub-surface diagnosis. 5.3061
Ancient Siamese government and administration. 4.8766
Ancient Sicily, to the Arab conquest. 3.2943
Ancient slavery and modern ideology. 4.6413
Ancient slavery and the ideal of man. 4.6416
Ancient society. 4.564, 4.7322
Ancient Syriac documents relative to the earliest establishment of Christianity in Edessa. 1.2305
Ancient Syriac documents relative to the earliest establishment of Christianity in Edessa and the neighbouring countries, from the year after our Lord's ascension to the beginning of the fourth century. 1.2305
Ancient Tahitian society. 3.5679
Ancient tales in modern Japan. 4.808
The ancient theology. 1.2960
Ancient voyagers in Polynesia. 3.5626
Ancient wisdom revived. 1.2097
Ancient writing and its influence. 5.7532
Ancilla to classical reading. 2.262
Ancilla to The pre-Socratic philosophers. 1.219
Ancren riwle. 2.6308
The Ancrene riwle (the Corpus ms.: Ancrene wisse). 2.6308
And be a villain. 2.12557
And even now. 2.8436
And I worked at the writer's trade. 2.10401
And justice for all. 3.1025
And keep your powder dry. 3.6139
And Muhammad is his messenger. 2.1761
And not to yield. 2.9548
And quiet flows the Don. 2.1603
And the poor get children. 4.5692
And the war came. 3.7182
And then. 2.2086
And we shall shock them. 3.976
Andean culture history. 3.9282
Andersonville. 2.11942
Andō Shōeki and the anatomy of Japanese feudalism. 3.4942
Andragogy in action. 4.10974
André Breton. 2.4429-2.4430
André Breton, magus of surrealism. 2.4428
André Chénier. 4.4067
André Gide. 2.4564
André Gide par lui même. 2.4565
André Kertész. 5.6929
André Kertész: sixty years of photography, 1912-1972. 5.6971
André Malraux. 2.4622-2.4623
Andrea del Castagno. 1.6198
Andrea del Sarto. 1.6222

Andrew Bradford, colonial journalist. 2.3607
Andrew Jackson and the course of American democracy. 3.7125
Andrew Jackson and the course of American empire. 3.7125
Andrew Jackson and the course of American freedom. 3.7125
Andrew Jackson, symbol for an age. 3.7126
Andrew Johnson and Reconstruction. 3.7467
Andrew Marvell. 2.7105
Andrew Marvell. 2.7106
Andrew Marvell: poet, puritan, patriot. 2.7107
Andrew Wyeth. 1.5991
Andrey Bely, a critical study of the novels. 2.1476
Andromache. 2.4047
Anecdotes of destiny. 2.14017
Anecdotes of the late Samuel Johnson. 2.7088
Aneurin Bevan. 3.1699
Ange-Jacques Gabriel. 1.5415
An angel at my table. 2.10222
Angel City & other plays. 2.13318
Angel pavement. 2.9243
Angel with horns, and other Shakespeare lectures. 2.6748
Angela Davis 3.6821
The Angelo Herndon case and southern justice. 4.9459
Angels in marble. 4.3651
Angels of the night. 1.3764
Anger, and beyond. 2.10321
Anger, the misunderstood emotion. 5.426
Angevin kingship 4.8440
Angkor: art and civilization. 3.4445
Angle of ascent. 2.11819
Anglo-American cataloguing rules. 5.7628
Anglo-American folksong scholarship since 1898. 1.4294
Anglo-American Isthmian diplomacy, 1815-1915. 4.9040
Anglo-American relations at the Paris Peace Conference of 1919. 3.855
The Anglo-American west, New Spain and. 3.8339
Anglo-Irish literature. 2.9851, 2.9853-2.9854
The Anglo-Irish tradition. 3.1835
The Anglo-Japanese alliance. 3.4923
Anglo-Norman England, 1066-1166. 3.1340
Anglo-Norman Ireland, c1100-1318. 3.1822
Anglo-russkiĭ slovar'. 2.1234
An Anglo-Saxon and Celtic bibliography (450-1087). 5.7985
Anglo-Saxon architecture. 1.5363
Anglo-Saxon art. 1.4933, 1.4937
Anglo-Saxon attitudes. 2.9534
Anglo-Saxon charters, edited with translation and notes. 4.9409
Anglo-Saxon chronicle. 3.1308-3.1311, 3.1750
An Anglo-Saxon dictionary. 2.945
Anglo-Saxon England. 3.1317
Anglo-Saxon England and the Norman Conquest. 4.2255
Anglo-Saxon manuscripts, 900-1066. 1.6407
Anglo-Saxon military institutions on the eve of the Norman Conquest. 3.1315
Anglo-Saxon oral poetry. 2.5594
The Anglo-Saxon poetic records. 2.6277
The Anglo-Saxon poetic records. 2.6278
Anglo-Saxon prose. 2.6285
Anglo-Saxon reader in prose and verse. 2.940
The Anglo-Saxon world. 2.6279
The Anglo-Saxons. 3.1314
Anglo-Spanish rivalry in North America. 3.6869
Anglo-Welsh poetry, 1480-1980. 2.9872
Angola. 3.5405-3.5406
Angola, a country study. 3.5403
Angola under the Portuguese. 3.5407
The Angolan revolution. 3.5409
The angry theatre. 2.5924
Die Angst des Tormanns beim Elfmeter. 2.13885
Anguish. 2.5478
Angular momentum in quantum mechanics. 5.2468
Angus Wilson. 2.9546
Angus Wilson, mimic and moralist. 2.9545
Anhelli 2.1731

ANI series on aging. 5.5003
Aniara. 2.14095
Animal agents and vectors of human disease. 5.4761
Animal behavior. 5.4052, 5.4055
Animal behavior, theory and research. 5.4065
Animal behaviour. 5.4058, 5.4066
Animal camouflage. 5.3581
Animal communication by pheromones. 5.4098
Animal cytology and evolution. 5.3604
Animal diversity. 5.3405, 5.3799
Animal ecology. 5.4056, 5.4074
Animal engineering. 5.4188
Animal farm 2.9176
Animal function; principles and adaptations. 5.4189
Animal identification. 5.8480
The animal in its world. 5.4067
Animal learning. 5.4103
Animal life encyclopedia. 5.3791
Animal locomotion. 5.4275
Animal migration and navigation. 5.4077
Animal migration, orientation, and navigation. 5.4076
Animal morphogenesis. 5.4137
Animal parasites: their life cycles and ecology. 5.4082
Animal parasitism. 5.4083
Animal physiology. 5.4180, 5.4182-5.4183, 5.4185
Animal societies from the bee to the gorilla. 5.4092
Animal sounds and communication. 5.4088
Animal species and evolution. 5.3395
Animal tissue techniques. 5.4161
Animals and why they matter. 1.1455
Animals as navigators. 5.4100
Animals in art and thought to the end of the Middle Ages. 1.5164
Animals in Roman life and art. 5.3809
Animals in winter. 5.4075
Animals of the tidal marsh. 5.3818
Animals without backbones. 5.3832
The animation book. 5.7007
Ann Radcliffe, a biography. 2.7998
Ann Vickers. 2.12000
Anna Akhmatova. 2.1538-2.1539
Anna Karenina. 2.1430
Anna of the Five Towns. 2.8452
Anna Pavlova. 4.1154
Anna St Ives. 2.7076
Annalen der deutschen Literatur. 2.13454
Annales; économies, sociétés civilisations. 4.2186
Annales; économies, sociétés, civilisations. 4.5085
Annalists and historians. 3.390
Annals of Australian literature. 5.8082
Annals of English drama, 975-1700. 5.7954
Annals of English literature, 1475-1950. 5.7932
Annals of opera, 1597-1940. 1.3518
The Annals of Q. Ennius. 2.717
Annals of the French stage, from its origin to the death of Racine. 2.3362
Annals of the New York stage. 2.3230
Annals of the parish, or, The chronicle of Dalmailing during the ministry of the Rev. Micah Balwhidder, written by himself. 2.7717
Anne & Frank Warner collection. 1.3435
Anne Bradstreet, the worldly Puritan. 2.10867
Anne Brontë. 2.7442
Anne Hébert. 2.4817
Anne Sexton. 2.12459-2.12460
Anne Thackeray Ritchie. 2.8002
Année sociologique. 4.4852
The Annenbergs. 2.3602
Annette. 2.11451
The annexation of Bosnia, 1908-1909. 3.766
Annie Allen. 2.11420
Anniversaries. 2.13900
Anniversaries and holidays. 4.872
The annotated Alice. 2.7675
An annotated bibliography of American Indian and Eskimo autobiographies. 5.7733
The Annotated bibliography of Canada's major authors. 5.7887

Annotated bibliography of expository writing in the mathematical sciences. 5.8281
An annotated bibliography of French language and literature. 5.8005
An annotated bibliography of modern Anglo-Irish drama. 5.7996
An Annotated bibliography of texts on writing skills. 5.7979
The annotated Christmas carol. 2.7631
The annotated Dracula. 2.9387
The annotated Gulliver's travels. 2.7292
The annotated Huckleberry Finn. 2.10941
The annotated Jules Verne, From the earth to the moon, direct in ninety-seven hours and twenty minutes. 2.4321
The annotated Mother Goose, nursery rhymes old and new. 2.14101
The annotated Sherlock Holmes. 2.7680
The annotated Snark. 2.7677
Annotations to Finnegans wake. 2.8873
Annuaire démographique. 4.1238
Annuaire des organisations internationales. 4.9103
Annuaire FAO de la production. 4.2903
Annuaire statistique. 1.79, 4.1237
Annual A.S.T.M. standards. 5.5756
Annual American catalog. 5.7748
Annual ASTM standards. 5.5756
Annual bibliography of English language and literature. 5.7936
Annual bibliography of the history of the printed book and libraries. 5.7538
Annual book of A.S.T.M. standards. 5.5756
Annual book of ASTM standards. 5.5756
The annual register. 3.356
Annual register of grant support. 1.58
The annual register of world events. 3.356
Annual review of biochemistry. 5.4389
Annual review of information science and technology. 5.7638
Annual review of physical chemistry. 5.2586
Annual review of psychology. 5.10
Annual review of United Nations affairs, 1970-1971. 4.9198
Anomalistic psychology. 5.649
Anonymous Americans. 4.5123
Anorexia nervosa. 5.4940
Anorexia nervosa & bulimia. 5.4938
Anorexia nervosa and bulimia. 5.4938
Another chance. 3.6183
Another country. 2.12856
Another life. 2.1642, 2.10020
Another life; and, The House on the embankment. 2.1642
Another man gone. 2.10360
Another part of the twenties. 3.6092
Another secret diary of William Byrd of Westover, 1739-1741. 3.8192
Another World. 2.10710
Anrufung des Grossen Bären. 2.13673
The Anschluss movement, 1931-1938, and the great powers. 3.1902
Anselm. 1.381
Anselm and talking about God. 1.2821
Anselm's discovery. 1.2828
Answer to history. 3.4089
Answerable style: essays on Paradise lost. 2.7139
Ante-bellum Kentucky. 3.8358
The Ante-Nicene fathers. 1.2194
The antecedents of self-esteem. 5.615
Antecedents of the English novel, 1400-1600. 2.5991
The Antelope. 3.7224
Antenna engineering handbook. 5.6430
Antenna theory. 5.6491
Antenna theory and design. 5.6496
Antennas and radiowave propagation. 5.6492
Anthologie de la nouvelle poésie algérienne. 2.4846
Anthologie des écrivains français du Maghreb 2.4847
Anthologie négro-africaine. 2.3714
Anthologie poétique française, XVIIe siècle. II. 2.3930
Anthologie poétique française, XVIIIe siècle. 2.3931
Anthologies by and about women. 4.5839

An anthology. 1.3414
Anthology for musical analysis. 1.4440
An anthology of Austrian drama. 2.13938
Anthology of Chinese literature. 2.2185
Anthology of contemporary Latin American
   literature, 1960-1984. 2.5322
Anthology of critical prefaces to the nineteenth-
   century French novel. 2.3908
Anthology of Czech poetry. 2.1661
Anthology of Danish literature. 2.14001
An anthology of German poetry from Hölderlin
   to Rilke in English translation. 2.13516
An anthology of Indian literature. 2.1928
Anthology of Japanese literature, from the
   earliest era to the mid-nineteenth century.
   2.2017
An anthology of labor economics. 4.3110
Anthology of magazine verse 1980-. 2.3737
Anthology of magazine verse and yearbook of
   American poetry. 2.3737
An anthology of modern Arabic poetry.
   2.1841
An anthology of modern Yiddish literature.
   2.1825
An anthology of neo-Latin poetry. 2.816
An anthology of new music. 1.3424
An anthology of Old English poetry. 2.6282
Anthology of Poems on affairs of state. 2.6122
Anthology of romanticism. 2.6069
An anthology of Russian neo-realism. 2.1325
An anthology of Russian plays. 2.1318
Anthology of Sanskrit court poetry. 2.1954
An anthology of Scandinavian literature, from
   the Viking period to the twentieth century.
   2.13970
Anthology of Serbian poetry. 2.1218
An anthology of Spanish American literature.
   2.5320
An anthology of Spanish literature in English
   translation. 2.5149
An anthology of the New England poets from
   colonial times to the present day. 2.10721
An anthology of twentieth-century Brazilian
   poetry. 2.5467
Anthology of twentieth-century music. 1.4438
Anthology of younger American poets.
   2.10777
Anthony Burgess. 2.9648-2.9649
Anthony Caro. 1.5690-1.5691
Anthony Comstock. 4.6758
Anthony Eden. 3.1665
Anthony Powell. 2.9233
Anthony Trollope. 2.8231, 2.8233, 2.8240
Anthony Trollope. 2.8237
Anthony Trollope; a critical study. 2.8232
Anthony Trollope, his art and scope. 2.8239
Anthracite people. 4.3537
Anthropological archaeology. 3.223
Anthropological bibliographies. 5.8094
An anthropological bibliography of South Asia.
   5.8095
Anthropological glossary. 4.409
Anthropological perspectives on education.
   4.10181
An anthropologist at work. 4.397
An anthropologist looks at history. 3.9
Anthropology. 4.429, 4.431
Anthropology and anthropologists. 4.473
Anthropology and modern life. 4.433
Anthropology & the colonial encounter. 4.411
Anthropology from a pragmatic point of view.
   1.894
The anthropology of ancient Greece. 3.2550
The anthropology of art. 1.4638
Anthropology of folk religion. 4.547
The anthropology of sport. 4.541
The Anthropology of Taiwanese society. 4.642
Anthropology of the Old Testament. 1.2586
Anthropology on the Great Plains. 3.5738
Anthropology today. 4.394
Anthropology toward history. 3.7961
The Anti-aesthetic. 1.1395
Anti-apartheid. 3.5458
Anti-Dühring. 4.7065
Anti-imperialism in the United States. 3.7604
Anti-intellectualism in American life. 3.6119

The anti-lynching movement, 1883-1932.
   4.6723
The anti-man culture, bureautechnocracy and
   the schools. 4.10733
Anti-memoirs. 2.4613
The anti-Soviet Soviet Union. 2.1646
Antic hay and The Gioconda smile. 2.8816
Anticipations of The general theory? and other
   essays on Keynes. 4.1342
The antifederalists. 4.7814-4.7815
Antigonos Gonatas. 3.2637
Antioch and Rome. 1.2643
The antiphon. 2.11345
Antiques. 1.6518
The Antiques guide to decorative arts in
   America, 1600-1875. 1.6517
The antiques treasury of furniture and other
   decorative arts. 1.6518
Antiquités de Rome. 2.3998
Antiquity and the Middle Ages. 5.763
Antiquity and the middle ages. 1.133
Antisemitic propaganda. 5.8246
Antisemitism in modern France. 3.3960
Antislavery. 3.7190
The antislavery appeal. 3.7267
Antislavery reconsidered. 3.7231
The antislavery vanguard. 3.7242
The antitheatrical prejudice. 2.3102
The antitrust laws of the United States of
   America. 4.9527
The antitrust paradox. 4.9525
Antitrust policies. 4.3059
Antitrust policy. 4.3057
Antoine and the théâtre-libre. 2.3369
Antoine de Saint-Exupéry. 5.6654
Antoine Watteau. 1.6157
Antología de la poesía hispanoamericana.
   2.5321
Antologia delle opere minori volgari. 2.4902
Antología mayor. 2.5364
Anton Čechov, 1860-1960. 2.1489
Anton Chekhov's life and thought. 2.1488
Anton Chekhov's plays. 2.1485
Anton von Webern, a chronicle of his life and
   work. 1.4058
Anton Von Webern perspectives. 1.4059
Anton Webern; an introduction to his works.
   1.4057
Antonin Artaud. 2.4382-2.4383
Antonio Buero Vallejo. 2.5240
Antonio Gramsci. 3.2899, 4.7077
Antonio Gramsci and the origins of Italian
   Communism. 4.7078
Antonio Gramsci and the Party. 4.7080
Antonio Gramsci and the revolution that failed.
   4.7079
Antonio Machado. 2.5274
Antonio Vivaldi. 1.4031
Antonio's revenge. 2.6623
Antony van Leeuwenhoek and his 'Little
   animals'. 5.3208
Antwerp, the golden age. 3.2979
Anuario FAO de producción. 4.2903
Anxiety and educational achievement. 5.428
Anxiety: current trends in theory and research.
   5.427
Anxiety in elementary school children. 5.586
The anxious object. 1.4829
The anxious years: America in the nineteen
   thirties. 2.10713
Anyang. 3.4862
Anything can happen. 2.10280
Anza's California expeditions. 3.8603
AP; the story of news. 2.3581
Apache Indian baskets. 3.5841
Apachean culture history and ethnology.
   3.5837
Apaches, a history and culture portrait. 3.5840
Apartheid. 3.5449
Apartment in Athens. 2.12676
Apes, angels, and Victorians. 5.3200
The apes: the gorilla, chimpanzee, orangutan,
   and gibbon. 5.4024
Apex of power. 4.8287
Aphasia in children. 5.5094
APL programming and computer techniques.
   5.1207
Apocalypse. 1.2731, 4.9170

Apocalypse and the writings on Revelation.
   1.2729
Apocalypse delayed. 1.3377
The apocalyptic imagination. 1.2554
Apocalyptic spirituality. 1.2948
Apocryphal stories. 2.1666
Apolitical politics. 4.7312
Apollinaire, poet among the painters. 2.4368
Apollonius Rhodius, the Argonautica. 2.334
Apollo's blended dream. 2.9077
Apologia and two folk plays. 2.14068
Apologia pro vita sua. 1.3273
An apology for the life of Mrs. Shamela
   Andrews. 2.7020
Apology for the middle class. 2.6451
The apostate angel. 2.12625
Apostle of culture in a democracy. 2.11188
Apostles of culture. 5.7663
Apostles of silence. 2.2829
The Apostolic Fathers. 1.2195
The Apostolic fathers. 2.327
Apostolic fathers. English & Greek. 2.327
The apothecary's shop. 2.2570
Apotheosis in ancient portraiture. 1.5160
Appalachia on our mind. 3.8178
Apparent places of fundamental stars. 5.1679
The appeal that was never made. 3.3297
Appeal to arms. 3.6933
Appearance and reality. 1.1265
Appian's Roman history. 2.335
The apple barrel: selected poems, 1955-63.
   2.9376
The apple of the eye 2.12677
Apple staff and silver crown. 2.9958
Apples. 5.5340
Appleton's cyclopaedia of American biography.
   3.6284
Appleton's new Cuyás English-Spanish and
   Spanish-English dictionary. 2.900
Application debugging. 5.1163
Applications in artificial intelligence. 5.1002
Applications of algebraic topology. 5.1594
Applications of digital signal processing.
   5.6363
Applications of inductive logic. 1.1182
Applications of infrared, raman, and resonance
   raman spectroscopy in biochemistry. 5.4401
Applications of Lie groups to differential
   equations. 5.1521
Applications of soil physics. 5.5272
Applications of undergraduate mathematics in
   engineering. 5.5710
Applied anthropology. 4.428
Applied circuit theory. 5.6268
Applied combinatorics. 5.1279, 5.1287
Applied digital control. 5.6188
Applied economics; resource allocation in rural
   America. 4.2885
Applied electromagnetism. 5.6264
Applied fluid dynamics handbook. 5.5748
Applied geophysics. 5.6737
Applied hydraulics in engineering. 5.5966
Applied hydrogeology. 4.305
Applied linear programming for the
   socioeconomic and environmental sciences.
   5.5589
Applied linear regression. 5.1410
Applied mathematical demography. 4.1617
Applied mathematical programming. 5.1548
Applied mathematics. 5.1114
Applied medical geography. 5.4704
Applied multivariate statistical analysis. 5.1408
Applied nonlinear optics. 5.2300
Applied nonlinear programming. 5.5595
Applied optics. 5.2292
Applied plastic design in steel. 5.5884
Applied science & technology index. 5.8455
Applied social science. 4.4848
Applied sociology. 4.4825
Applied stream sanitation. 5.6033
Applied superconductivity, metallurgy, and
   physics of titanium alloys. 5.6784
Applied techniques in track & field. 4.1049
Applied techniques in track and field. 4.1049
Appointment in Samarra. 2.12266

Appraising vocational fitness by means of psychological tests. 5.365
Appreciating India's music. 1.3740
Appreciation and interest. 4.1295
The apprenticeship of Duddy Kravitz. 2.9962
An approach to Congreve. 2.6949
An approach to 'Hamlet.' 2.6655
An approach to King Lear. 2.6667
An approach to Shakespeare. 2.6753
An approach to the Indian theory of art and aesthetics. 1.1388
Approach to the purpose. 2.11635
Approaches to American economic history. 4.1869
Approaches to Asian civilizations. 3.107
Approaches to beginning reading. 4.10417
Approaches to Gravity's rainbow. 2.13279
Approaches to language. 2.99
Approaches to social archaeology. 3.224
Approaches to teaching Melville's Moby Dick. 2.11156
Approaches to the history of Spain. 3.3414
Approaches to the Oriental classics. 2.1758
Approaches to Victorian autobiography. 2.5939
Appropriate technology and social values. 5.5514
Approximate man, and other writings. 2.4759
Approximation methods for electronic filter design. 5.6511
Approximation theory and methods. 5.1315
Approximation theory and numerical methods. 5.1431
L'Après-midi d'un faune. 4.1182
Aprismo. 3.9307
Apuleius and The golden ass. 2.705
Aquaculture. 5.5466
The Aquarian conspiracy. 5.459
The Aquarium encyclopedia. 5.5456
Aquatic chemistry. 4.302
Aquatic plants. 5.3668
Aquinas. 1.2822
Aquis submersus. 2.13662
The Arab-African connection. 3.3742
Arab attitudes to Israel. 3.3868
The Arab awakening. 3.3730
The Arab balance of power. 3.3740
The Arab economy today. 4.2570
The Arab-Israeli conflict. 3.3860
The Arab-Israeli dilemma. 3.3872
The Arab-Israeli wars. 3.3856
The Arab kingdom and its fall. 3.3672
Arab nationalism. 3.3733
Arab painting. 1.5882
Arab politics. 3.3722
Arab politics in Palestine, 1917-1939. 3.3918
The Arab predicament. 3.3737
The Arab radicals. 3.3738
Arab reach. 3.3874
Arab society. 4.5462
Arab society in transition. 4.5462
The Arab States and the Arab League. 3.3647
The Arab states and the Palestine conflict. 3.3881
Arab strategies and Israel's response. 3.3867
The Arab world. 3.3663, 3.3674, 4.2574
The Arab world, 1900-1972. 4.8789
The Arab world's legacy. 3.3662
Arab-Zionist negotiations and the end of mandate. 3.3862
Arabian nights. English. Selections. 2.1842
The Arabian nights' entertainments. 2.1842
Arabic literature to the end of the Umayyad period. 2.1833
Arabic materials in English translation. 5.8039
Arabic thought and its place in history. 1.366
Arabic thought in the liberal age, 1798-1939. 4.7283
The Arabs. 3.3649, 3.3718, 3.4052
Arabs and Berbers. 3.5210
The Arabs and mediaeval Europe. 3.141
The Arabs and Zionism before World War I. 3.3875
The Arabs in history. 3.4053
Arabs in the Jewish State. 3.3841
Aragon. 2.4369
Aramco, the United States, and Saudi Arabia. 4.3787

Arapahoe politics, 1851-1978. 3.5843
ARBA guide to biographical dictionaries. 5.8105
Arbitration and collective bargaining. 4.9555
El árbol de la ciencia. 2.5232
The Arbor House treasury of great Western stories. 2.10838
Arcades, the history of a building type. 1.5542
Arcadia. 2.6508
Archaeoastronomy and the roots of science. 5.1687
Archaeological ethnography in western Iran. 4.636
Archaeological geology. 3.242
An archaeological perspective. 3.227
Archaeological researches in retrospect. 4.697
Archaeologist of morning. 2.12278
Archaeology. 3.265
Archaeology, a bibliographical guide to the basic literature. 5.8100
Archaeology and its problems. 3.234
Archaeology and the Dead Sea scrolls. 3.3822
Archaeology as human ecology. 3.250
Archaeology by experiment. 3.231
Archaeology from the earth. 3.236
Archaeology in the Holy Land. 3.3829
Archaeology in the USSR. 3.257
The archaeology of ancient China. 3.4625, 3.4687
The archaeology of ancient Turkey. 3.4038
The Archaeology of Anglo-Saxon England. 3.1323
The archaeology of Arizona. 3.5717
The archaeology of beekeeping. 5.5459
The archaeology of California. 3.8602
The Archaeology of lower Central America. 3.9030
The archaeology of Mesopotamia. 3.3762
The archaeology of New England. 3.5744
The archaeology of New York State. 3.5746
The archaeology of Roman Britain. 3.1305
Archaeology of the Bible. 1.2543
Archaeology of the boat. 5.7499
Archaeology of the central Mississippi Valley. 3.5742
Archaeology of the cinema. 2.2881
The archaeology of the Industrial Revolution. 5.5541
The archaeology of the land of Israel. 3.3828
The archaeology of weapons. 5.7244
Archaeology under water. 3.240
Archaic and Classical Greece. 3.2531
Archaic and classical Greek coins. 3.276
The archaic gravestones of Attica. 1.5788
Archaic Greece. 3.2598-3.2599
Archaic Greek art (620-480 B.C.) 1.4714
Archaic marble sculpture from the Acropolis. 1.5619
Archaic Roman religion, with an appendix on the religion of the Etruscans. 1.1660
The archaic style in Greek sculpture. 1.5627
Archduke of Sarajevo. 3.1897
Archeological explanation. 3.222
The archeology of the New Testament. 1.2645-1.2646
Archery at the dark of the moon. 2.511
Arches & light. 2.13033
Arches and light. 2.13033
Archetypal patterns in women's fiction. 2.5989
Archetypal psychology. 5.198
The archetypal world of Henry Moore. 1.5697
The Archidamian War. 3.2614
Archilochus of Paros. 2.422
The Architect. 1.5457
Architect and patron. 1.5365
Architect and sculptor in classical Greece. 1.5634
The architect of Salem. 1.5315
Architects' designs for furniture. 5.7086
Architects of illusion. 3.7796
Architects of Yiddishism at the beginning of the twentieth century. 2.1788
Architectural acoustics. 1.5493
The architectural heritage of Newport, Rhode Island. 1.5303
Architectural sculpture in Romanesque Provence. 1.5503

Architectural symbolism of imperial Rome and the Middle Ages. 1.5228
Architecture. 5.8184
Architecture, ambition, and Americans. 1.5281
Architecture and design, 1890-1939. 1.5264
Architecture and interior design. 1.5210
Architecture and its interpretation. 1.5487
Architecture and people. 1.5477
Architecture and politics in Germany, 1918-1945. 1.5423
Architecture and rural art. 1.5560
Architecture and the crisis of modern science. 1.5356
Architecture and utopia. 1.5478
Architecture as space. 1.5465
Architecture in Britain. 1.5364
Architecture in Britain, 1530 to 1830. 1.5366
Architecture in Italy, 1400 to 1600. 1.5431
Architecture in the Age of Reason. 1.5246
Architecture in wood. 5.6095
Architecture: nineteenth and twentieth centuries. 1.5258
The architecture of America. 1.5282
The architecture of ancient Greece. 1.5218
The architecture of country houses. 1.5567
The architecture of Frank Lloyd Wright. 1.5337
The architecture of H.H. Richardson and his times. 1.5324
The architecture of Ireland. 1.5376
The architecture of Japan. 1.5452
The architecture of John Wellborn Root. 1.5326
The architecture of Michelangelo: catalogue 1.5441
The architecture of Richard Neutra. 1.5321
Architecture of solitude. 1.5528
The architecture of the Anglo-Saxons. 1.5362
Architecture of the arts and crafts movement. 1.5367
The architecture of the French Enlightenment. 1.5413
Architecture of the industrial age, 1789-1914. 1.5595
Architecture of the Islamic world. 1.5234
The architecture of the Italian Renaissance. 1.5430
The architecture of the Italian renaissance. 1.5432
Architecture of the nineteenth century in Europe. 1.5357
Architecture of the picturesque in Canada. 1.5563
Architecture of the Renaissance. 1.5244
The architecture of the Roman Empire. 1.5226
Architecture of the Western World. 1.5209
The architecture of Wren. 1.5407
Architecture without architects. 1.5461
Architecture, you and me. 1.5130
Archives in the ancient world. 3.268
Archy and Mehitabel. 2.12115
Archy does his part. 2.12115
Archy's Life of Mehitabel. 2.12115
The Arco book of soccer techniques and tactics. 4.1018
Arctic and Antarctic. 4.104
Arctic bibliography. 5.8207
The Arctic coast. 5.3272
An Arctic ecosystem. 5.3268
The Arden edition of the works of William Shakespeare. 2.6646
The Arden Shakespeare. 2.6646
The ardent exile. 3.8729
The Ardis anthology of recent Russian literature. 2.1294
The Ardis anthology of Russian futurism. 2.1310
The Ardis anthology of Russian romanticism. 2.1295
Ardor, a family chronicle. 2.12224
Are quanta real? 5.2114
Area and power. 4.8833
Area handbook for Albania. 3.3600
Area handbook for Bangladesh. 3.4143
Area handbook for Bolivia. 3.9272
Area handbook for Bulgaria. 3.3545
Area handbook for Burma. 3.4421
Area handbook for Burundi. 3.5301

Area handbook for Ceylon. 3.4362
Area handbook for Chad. 3.5388
Area handbook for Costa Rica. 3.9077
Area handbook for Ecuador. 3.9311
Area handbook for El Salvador. 3.9066
Area handbook for Finland. 3.3288
Area handbook for Ghana. 3.5337
Area handbook for Guinea. 3.5380
Area handbook for Guyana. 3.9185
Area handbook for Haiti. 3.9114
Area handbook for Hungary. 3.1936
Area handbook for Ivory Coast. 3.5383
Area handbook for Jamaica. 3.9110
Area handbook for Laos. 3.4458
Area handbook for Lebanon. 3.3783
Area handbook for Liberia. 3.5411
Area handbook for Malawi. 3.5491
Area handbook for Mauritania. 3.5393
Area handbook for Mongolia. 3.4866
Area handbook for Nepal, Bhutan, and Sikkim.
    3.4375
Area handbook for North Vietnam. 3.4490
Area handbook for Pakistan. 3.4121
Area handbook for Peru. 3.9281
Area handbook for Portugal. 3.3492
Area handbook for Rwanda. 3.5304
Area handbook for Senegal. 3.5390
Area handbook for Sierra Leone. 3.5371
Area handbook for Singapore. 3.4552
Area handbook for South Korea. 2nd ed. 1975.
    3.4992
Area handbook for South Vietnam. 3.4478
Area handbook for Spain. 3.3398
Area handbook for the Dominican Republic.
    3.9121
Area handbook for the Federal Republic of
    Germany. 3.2464
Area handbook for the Khmer Republic
    (Cambodia) 3.4441
Area handbook for the Malagasy Republic.
    3.5311
Area handbook for the Persian Gulf states.
    3.4057
Area handbook for the Soviet Union. 3.3010
Area handbook for the United Republic of
    Cameroon. 3.5396
Area handbook for the Yemens. 3.4061
Area handbook for Trinidad and Tobago.
    3.9136
Area handbook for Uganda. 3.5285
Area handbook for Uruguay. 3.9232
Area handbook for Venezuela. 3.9178
Area handbook for Yugoslavia. 3.3604
Area research, theory and practice. 3.447
Arena. 2.3208
Argentina: a city and a nation. 3.9238
Argentina, a country study. 3.9237
Argentina and the failure of democracy.
    3.9250
The Argentina republic 3.9243
Argentina, the United states, and the Inter-
    American system 1880-1914. 3.9248
Argentine dictator. 3.9246
The Argentine Republic, 1516-1971. 4.2166
Argonautica. 2.334
Argonauts of the Western Pacific. 4.680
The argument of Ulysses. 2.8898
Argumentation and debate. 2.3538
Arguments and doctrines. 1.1892
Arguments for democracy. 4.8426
Arguments for socialism. 4.8543
Arid-land ecosystems. 5.3541
Arid lands. 4.282
Aridic soils and geomorphic processes. 5.5269
Ariel. 2.13255
Ariel 2.5443
Ariel; the life of Shelley. 2.8103
Ariosto. 2.13441
Ariosto e Tasso. 2.4984
Arise, arise. 2.12835
Aristocracy and people. 3.1598
Aristocracy in America. 3.6034
Aristocracy in Greek society. 4.7353
The aristocrat. 2.12388
The aristocratic ideal in ancient Greece.
    3.2546
Aristocratic society in ancient Crete. 3.2642
Aristocrats and traders. 4.5386

Aristophanes and the comic hero. 2.435
Aristophanes with the English translation of
    Benjamin Bickley Rogers. 2.336
Aristophanic comedy. 2.432
The aristos. 1.749
The Aristotelian ethics. 1.313
An Aristotelian theory of comedy. 2.2825
Aristotle. 1.298, 1.304-1.308, 2.348, 2.352
Aristotle and his philosophy. 1.303
Aristotle and logical theory. 1.316
Aristotle and Xenophon on democracy and
    oligarchy. 4.7338
Aristotle in the ancient biographical tradition.
    1.302
Aristotle in the West. 1.359
Aristotle on comedy. 2.2826
Aristotle the philosopher. 1.295
Aristotle: The poetics. 2.349
Aristotle's Art of poetry. 2.2727
Aristotle's Constitution of Athens and related
    texts. 1.286
Aristotle's criticism of Plato and the Academy.
    1.299
Aristotle's criticism of presocratic philosophy.
    1.300
Aristotle's De generatione et corruptione.
    5.832
Aristotle's De motu animalium. 5.3797
Aristotle's ethical theory. 1.312
Aristotle's Eudemian ethics, books I, II, and
    VIII. 1.285
Aristotle's Metaphysics. 1.288, 2.438
Aristotle's philosophy of action. 1.310
Aristotle's Physics. 5.833
Aristotle's Physics, books III and IV. 5.834
Aristotle's Poetics. 2.2728
Aristotle's Posterior analytics. 1.292
Aristotle's syllogistic from the standpoint of
    modern formal logic. 1.317
Aristotle's theory of the will. 1.314
Arizona. 3.8579
Arizona, the Grand Canyon State. 3.8578
Arkansas. 3.8341
Arkhitektura vychislitelnykh setei. 5.6412
The Armada. 3.1440
Armadale. 2.7605
The Armageddon rag. 2.13170
Armed forces of the world. 5.7259
Armed struggle in Palestine. 3.3877
The armed vision. 2.2471
Armenia, cradle of civilization. 3.4041
Armenia, the survival of a nation. 3.4043
The Armenians, from genocide to resistance.
    3.4044
Armies and politics in Latin America. 3.9006
Armies and societies in Europe, 1494-1789.
    5.7294
Armies in Europe. 5.7295
The armies of ignorance. 4.7904
The armies of the first French Republic and the
    rise of the marshals of Napoleon I ... 3.2092
The armies of the night. 2.12094
The armies of the streets. 3.8037
Arming the Luftwaffe. 4.3829
Arminius. 1.3319
Armor. 5.7390
Armored train 14-69. 2.1615
Armored warfare. 5.7389
The Armory show. 1.4669
Arms and men. 3.6369
Arms and oil. 5.7276
Arms and the state. 3.7586
Arms & weapons. 5.7246
Arms and weapons. 5.7246
Arms control. 4.9164, 4.9178
Arms control agreements. 4.9165
Arms, defense policy, and arms control.
    4.9167
The arms race. 4.2067
The arms trade with the Third World. 4.3837
Arms transfers and American foreign policy.
    4.3839
Arms uncontrolled. 4.9168
The Army Air Forces in World War II.
    3.1054
The army & politics in Argentina. 5.7293
The army and society, 1815-1914. 5.7306
Army ants. 5.3888

An army for empire. 3.7505
Army, industry, and labor in Germany,
    1914-1918. 4.2342
Army life in a black regiment. 3.7386
Army logistics. 5.7224
The Army of Flanders and the Spanish road,
    1567-1659. 3.2962
Army of Frederick the Great. 5.7320
The army of the future. 5.7310
Arna Bontemps-Langston Hughes letters,
    1925-1967. 2.11395
Arnold and God. 2.7356
Arnold Bennett. 2.8458-2.8459
Arnold Schoenberg. 1.3969-1.3970
Arnold Toynbee and the crisis of the West.
    3.3
Arnold Zweig. 2.13876
Around the world in eighty days. 2.4322
Around the world on the Kamchatka,
    1817-1819. 4.98
Around theatres. 2.3315
Arousal and curiosity. 5.214
Arp. 1.5703
El arpa y la sombra. 2.5359
Harper's magazine. 2.10667
Arquitectura prehispánica. 3.8898
Array signal processing. 5.6364
Arrest. 4.9879
Arrest and movement. 1.4698
Arrian. 2.353
The arrivants. 2.9985
The arrogance of humanism. 1.499
The arrogance of power. 3.7569
An arrow in the wall. 2.1648
Arrow of God. 2.10101
Arrowsmith. 2.12001
Ars amatoria. 2.678
Ars amatoria, book I. 2.744
Ars sacra, 800-1200. 1.4742
Arsenic and old lace. 2.11961
Art. 1.4914, 1.5124
Art actuel. 1.4804
Art after modernism. 1.6702
Art and aesthetics in primitive societies.
    1.4693
Art and archaeology. 1.5123
Art and architecture in Belgium, 1600 to 1800.
    1.5025
Art and architecture in France, 1500 to 1700.
    1.4959
Art and architecture in Italy, 1250 to 1400.
    1.5003
Art and architecture in Italy, 1600 to 1750.
    1.5006
Art and architecture in Spain and Portugal and
    their American dominions, 1500 to 1800.
    1.5040
The art and architecture of ancient America.
    3.5694
The art and architecture of ancient Egypt.
    1.4701
The art and architecture of China. 1.5060
The art and architecture of India. 1.5048
The art and architecture of Japan. 1.5075
The art and architecture of Russia. 1.5029
The art and architecture of the ancient Orient.
    1.4697
Art and architecture of the eighteenth century
    in France. 1.4960
Art and artefacts of the Pacific, Africa and the
    Americas. 1.4690
Art and artifice in Shakespeare. 2.6818
Art and artists. 1.4577
Art and ceremony in late antiquity. 3.2741
Art and culture. 1.6699
Art and culture in nineteenth-century Russia.
    1.6721
Art and death in a Senufo village. 3.5385
Art and education. 1.5101
Art and existence. 1.1375
Art and experience in classical Greece. 1.4719
The art and history of frames. 1.5199
The art and history of personal combat.
    4.1054
Art and human values. 1.1381
Art and illusion. 1.4609
The art and imagination of W. E. B. Du Bois.
    2.11609

Art and its objects. 1.1362
Art and its significance. 1.1352
Art and life in America. 1.4860
Art and logic in Hegel's philosophy. 1.952
The art and mind of Flannery O'Connor.
    2.13220
The art and mind of Shaw. 2.8083
Art and morality. 1.4627
Art and order. 2.8669
Art & other serious matters. 1.5141
Art and other serious matters. 1.5141
Art and philosophy. 1.4615
Art and photography. 1.4635, 5.6922
The art and practice of diplomacy. 4.9091
Art and psychoanalysis. 2.2560
Art and sexual politics. 1.5193
Art and society. 1.4639
Art and substance in George Meredith. 2.7950
Art and the aesthetic. 1.1356
Art and the computer. 1.5119
Art and the Reformation in Germany. 1.5176
Art and the stage in the 20th century. 1.4828
The art and thought of Heraclitus. 1.236
Art and time in Mexico. 1.4921
Art and visual perception. 1.4618
Art as an element of culture, especially in
    Negro-Africa. 1.4629
Art as experience. 1.4596
Art-as-politics. 1.5909
Art chronicles, 1954-1966. 1.4886
Art criticism from a laboratory. 1.6376
The art criticism of John Ruskin. 1.5135
Art, culture, and environment. 1.4646
Art deco. 1.4839
Art deco furniture. 1.6579
Art et décoration. 1.6539
Art for the millions. 1.5203
Art forms and civic life in the late Roman
    Empire. 1.4728
Art in a desacralized world. 1.1384
Art in America. 1.4657
Art in East and West. 1.5107
Art in Latin American architecture. 1.5278
Art in Paris, 1845-1862. 1.4670
Art index. 5.8183
Art is my life. 1.5678
Art, myth, and ritual. 3.4688
Art news. 1.5193
Art nouveau. 1.4794-1.4795, 1.4832, 1.4834
Art nouveau architecture. 1.5259
The Art nouveau style in jewelry, metalwork,
    glass, ceramics, textiles, architecture, and
    furniture. 1.6539
Art now. 1.4824
The art of accompanying and coaching. 1.4483
Art of Africa. 1.5087
The art of Albrecht Dürer. 1.4990
The art of Alfred Hitchcock. 2.3054
The Art of all nations, 1850-73. 1.4787
Art of ancient Egypt. 1.4699
The art of ancient India. 1.5047
The art of ancient Iran. 1.4710
The art of ancient Mesopotamia. 1.4704
The art of assemblage. 1.4833
The art of Bacchylides. 2.443
The art of bassoon playing. 1.4558
The art of Benin. 1.5089
The art of Beowulf. 2.6294
The art of Biblical narrative. 1.2568
The art of Biblical poetry. 1.2605
The art of brass playing. 1.4547
The art of Brazil. 1.4923
The art of Buddhism. 1.5183
The art of building cities. 1.5586
The art of Burma, Korea, Tibet. 1.5050
The art of Byzantium and the medieval West.
    1.4744
The art of Charlotte Brontë. 2.7455
The art of Chinese poetry. 2.2163
The art of clarinet playing. 1.4555
The art of color. 1.6352
The art of computer programming. 5.1185
The art of Constantinople. 1.4743
The art of Crete and early Greece. 1.4718
The art of describing. 1.6237
The art of digital design. 5.6587
The art of diplomacy. 4.9042
The art of Eastern India, 300-800. 1.5753

The art of editing. 2.3563
The art of electronics. 5.6449
The art of Emily Carr. 1.5997
The art of fiction. 2.3511, 2.3519
The art of French fiction. 2.3897
The art of George Eliot. 2.7708
The art of Graham Greene. 2.8769
The art of grit. 2.13112
The art of Gupta India. 1.5540
The art of Hogarth. 1.6034
The art of I. Compton-Burnett. 2.8533
Art of Indian Asia. 1.5049
The art of Indochina, including Thailand,
    Vietnam, Laos and Cambodia. 1.5054
The art of Isaac Babel. 2.1541
Art of Islam. 1.4747
The art of James Joyce: method and design in
    Ulysses and Finnegans wake. 2.8896
The arts of James Thurber. 2.12590
The art of jazz. 1.4339
The art of John Dryden. 2.7003
The art of John Webster. 2.6882
The Art of Kabuki. 2.3399
The art of La Celestina. 2.5199
Art of Latin America since independence.
    1.4855
The art of laughter. 2.3785
The art of leadership in war. 5.7474
The art of life. 2.9285
The art of literary research. 2.5489
The art of living, and other stories. 2.13027
The art of love. 2.678
The art of making dances. 4.1121
The Art of Margaret Atwood. 2.9911
The art of Mark Twain. 2.10968
Art of Mesopotamia. 1.4707
The art of modern fiction. 2.3433
The art of musical interpretation... 1.4116
Art of nineteenth-century Europe 1.4792
The art of oboe playing. 1.4554
The art of officiating sports. 4.979
The art of Oliver Goldsmith. 2.7051
The art of Oscar Wilde. 2.8287
The art of Paul Verlaine. 2.4319
The art of persuasion in Greece 2.309
The art of Philip Larkin. 2.8946
The art of piano playing. 1.4543
Art of poetry. 2.2727
The art of politics. 4.7788
The art of psychological warfare, 1914-1945.
    3.842
The art of quarterbacking. 4.1028
The art of rhetoric in the Roman world, 300
    B.C.-A.D. 300. 2.643
The art of Richard Wright. 2.12821
The art of Romare Bearden. 1.4890
The art of Rome. 1.4726
The art of Rudyard Kipling. 2.7895
The art of satire. 2.3790
The art of scientific investigation. 5.972
The art of sculpture. 1.5775
The art of Sinclair Lewis. 2.12012
The art of stage lighting. 2.3141
The art of T.S. Eliot. 2.11633
The art of Tahiti and the neighbouring Society,
    Austral and Cook Islands. 1.5096
The art of teaching. 4.10259
The art of Ted Hughes. 2.9720
The art of the Aeneid. 2.799
Art of the ancient Near East. 1.4696
Art of the Aztecs and its origins. 3.8901
The art of the Byzantine Empire, 312-1453.
    1.4746
The art of the Canterbury tales. 2.6329
The art of The compleat angler. 2.7333
The art of the Conquistadors 1.4854
The art of the dance. 4.1119
The art of the European silversmith, 1430-1830.
    1.6659
The art of the film. 2.2958
The art of the Hittites. 1.4708
Art of the Holocaust. 1.5097
Art of the Incas and its origins. 3.9160
The art of the Japanese puppet theatre. 2.2836
Art of the Maya. 3.9048
Art of the medieval world. 1.4738
The art of the Middle English lyric. 2.5621
Art of the Northwest Coast Indians. 3.5815

The art of the novel. 2.11102
Art of the October Revolution. 1.5032
The Art of the Pacific Islands. 1.5092
The art of the print: masterpieces, history,
    techniques. 1.6430
The art of the Renaissance in northern Europe.
    1.4760
The Art of the Romans. 1.4730
The art of the story-teller. 4.10320
The art of the theatre. 2.3372
The art of the West in the Middle Ages.
    1.4750
The art of Thomas Hardy. 2.7791
The art of Thomas Wolfe. 2.12790
The art of Thornton Wilder. 2.12721
Art of Tibet. 1.5069
The art of Vergil. 2.803
The art of Victorian prose. 2.5937
The Art of Walker Percy. 2.13244
The art of Walt Disney. 1.5855
The art of war. 5.7202-5.7203, 5.7209
The art of war: from the age of Napoleon to
    the present day. 5.7190
The art of war in the Middle Ages, A.D.
    378-1515. 5.7188
The art of warfare in Biblical lands in the light
    of archaeological study. 5.7177
The art of warfare in the age of Marlborough.
    5.7189
The art of warfare in the age of Napoleon.
    5.7193
The art of Wilhelm Lehmbruck. 1.5717
The art of William Blake. 1.6025
The art of William Golding. 2.8713
The art of writing. 2.3522
The art of written forms. 5.7519
Art, perception and reality. 1.4624
Art research methods and resources. 1.4645
L'art romantique. 2.3859
Art styles of the Papuan Gulf. 1.5095
The art theater. 2.3213
Art through the ages. 1.4673
Art today and its audience. 1.4829
Art treasures of the Vatican. 1.4666
The Artamonov business. 2.1504
Artaud and after. 2.4384
Artculture. 1.6704
The arte of English poesie. 2.2719
Arthropod anatomy. 5.3849
Arthropod phylogeny with special reference to
    insects. 5.3850
Arthur Erickson. 1.5347
Arthur Hugh Clough. 2.7581-2.7582
Arthur Hugh Clough, the uncommitted mind.
    2.7580
Arthur Lee, a virtuous revolutionary. 3.7003
Arthur Meighen. 3.8769
Arthur Miller. 2.12176
Arthur Miller. 2.12178, 2.12180
Arthur Miller: the burning glass. 2.12179
Arthur of Britain. 2.2636
Arthur Rex. 2.12903
Arthur Rimbaud. 2.4282
Arthur Schnitzler. 2.13862
Arthur Sullivan, a Victorian musician. 1.4014
Arthur Wing Pinero. 2.7996
Arthur Young and his times. 5.5226
An Arthurian dictionary. 2.2635
Arthurian literature and society. 2.2417
Arthurian literature in the Middle Ages.
    2.2418
The Arthurian poems of Charles Williams.
    2.9524
Arthurian triptych; mythic materials in Charles
    Williams, C. S. Lewis, and T. S. Eliot.
    2.9532
Arthur's Britain; history and archaeology, AD
    367-634. 3.1313
The Articles of confederation. 4.7820
Articles on American literature, 1900-1950.
    5.7790
Articles on American literature, 1950-1967.
    5.7791
Articles on American literature, 1968-1975.
    5.7792
Articles on Aristotle. 1.297

Articles on twentieth century literature: an annotated bibliography, 1954 to 1970. 5.8278
Articulate energy. 2.5748
Articulation disorders. 5.4794
Artie. 2.10892
Artifacts and the American past. 3.5999
'Artificial curiosities' 4.664
Artificial intelligence. 5.1017
Artificial intelligence, an MIT perspective. 5.1003
Artificial intelligence & expert systems sourcebook. 5.1000
Artificial intelligence and expert systems sourcebook. 5.1000
Artificial intelligence and natural man. 5.1005
Artificial intelligence programming. 5.1019
Artificial reality. 1.6692
Artigas and the emancipation of Uruguay. 3.9233
Artillery. 5.7382
The artillery of the press. 2.3558
The artisan republic. 3.2149
Artisans and sans-culottes. 4.3653
Artisans of the New Republic. 4.3005
The artist. 1.4623
Artist and computer. 1.5118
Artist and patron in postwar Japan. 1.6745
The artist and social reform. 1.4631
The Artist and society in Shakespeare's England. 2.5637
The artist and the book, 1860-1960. 1.5827
The artist as creator; an essay of human freedom. 1.1376
Artist beware. 5.5013
An artist in America. 1.5918
An artist in the rigging. 2.11168
Artist of 1848. 3.6077
Artistic country-seats. 1.5571
Artistic theory in Italy, 1450-1600. 1.5000
The artistic transaction and essays on theory of literature. 2.2600
Artists and traditions. 1.6312
The artist's handbook of materials and techniques. 1.6373
Artists in aprons. 1.6514
Artists on art, from the XIV to the XX century. 100 illustrations. 1.4643
Artists, portraits from four decades. 5.6987
The Arts and cognition. 1.6685
The arts and crafts movement. 1.6531
The arts and crafts movement in America, 1876-1916. 1.6532
Arts and the schools. 1.6695
The arts and their interrelations. 1.5104
The arts, cognition, and basic skills. 1.6694
The Arts in America. 1.4864
The arts of Assyria. 1.4705
Arts of China. 1.5066
The arts of China. 1.5061
The arts of design. 1.4859
The arts of Japan. 1.5074
The Arts of Korea. 1.5081
Arts of Korea. 1.5080
The arts of Nepal. 1.5053
Arts of the ancient Greeks. 1.4712
The arts of the beautiful. 1.1373
The Arts of the book in Central Asia, 14th-16th centuries. 1.6420
Arturo Toscanini. 1.4105
Artworks and packages. 1.4830
Arya dharm. 1.1729
As a man grows older. 2.5067
As equals and as sisters. 4.3273
As for me and my house. 2.9969
As he saw it. 3.7782
As her whimsy took her. 2.9308
As I crossed a bridge of dreams. 2.2055
As I lay dying. 2.11678
As I was going down Sackville Street. 2.8691
As if. 2.11499
As it is on earth. 3.194
As it was. 3.7827
As minority becomes majority. 4.3290
As once in May. 2.9517
As sociology meets history. 4.5086
As they liked it. 2.6824
As we saw them. 3.6463

Asa Gray, 1810-1888. 5.3638
Asante before the British. 3.5333
Asante in the nineteenth century. 3.5334
ASCAP biographical dictionary. 1.3540
The ascent of F6. 2.8392
The ascent of man. 5.869
The ascent of mount Fuji. 2.1620
Ascent to Omai. 2.10027
Asceticism and eroticism in the mythology of Śiva. 1.1709
ASEAN economies in perspective. 4.2439
ASEAN literatures. 2.10137
The ASEAN states. 4.2525
Ashenden. 2.9096
Ashes. 2.13136
Ashes and diamonds. 2.1698
Ashes out of hope. 2.1828
Ashikari and The story of Shunkin. 2.2118
ASHRAE handbook. 5.6099
Asia. 3.3610, 4.2437
Asia and the international system. 3.3643
Asia and the major powers. 3.3630
Asia and the road ahead. 3.3642
Asia and the West. 3.106
Asia and the western Pacific. 3.3636
Asia and U.S. foreign policy. 3.3631
Asia in the making of Europe. 3.81
Asia, reference works. 5.8034
Asia urbanizing. 4.6265
Asian-American heritage. 2.10671
Asian American literature, an introduction to the writings and their social context. 2.10293
Asian art. 1.5043
The Asian century. 3.3641
Asian drama; an inquiry into the poverty of nations. 4.2435
Asian frontiers. 3.3629
The Asian in North America. 3.6539
The Asian political dictionary. 3.3625
Asian revolutionary. 4.7123
Asian voices in Christian theology. 1.2762
Asia's lands and peoples. 3.3609
Asia's new giant. 4.2548
Asia's nuclear future. 3.3637
The Asiatics. 2.12355
Asimov's biographical encyclopedia of science and technology. 5.807
Ask me tomorrow. 2.11512
Ask your mama. 2.11890
Asking questions. 4.1230
ASM handbook of engineering mathematics. 5.5712
Aśoka 3.4247
Aśoka and the decline of the Mauryas. 3.4248
Gli Asolani. 2.4964
Aspects and impressions. 2.2645
Aspects de Racine, suivi de L'histoire littéraire d'un couple tragique. 2.4051
Aspects of Alice. 2.7674
Aspects of Altaic civilization. 3.3618
Aspects of Chinese sociolinguistics. 2.2141
Aspects of development and underdevelopment. 4.1821
Aspects of dramatic form in the English and the Irish Renaissance. 2.5871
Aspects of genre in late medieval French drama. 2.3884
Aspects of Islamic civilization, as depicted in the original texts. 1.2026
Aspects of medieval and Renaissance music. 1.3462
Aspects of music in Canada. 1.3700
Aspects of narrative. 2.3409
Aspects of palynology. 5.3178
Aspects of prehistory. 3.113
Aspects of Racinian tragedy. 2.4054
Aspects of religion in the Soviet Union, 1917-1967. 1.1673
Aspects of Schenkerian theory. 1.4423
Aspects of scientific explanation. 5.896
Aspects of social change in modern Japan. 4.5446
Aspects of the ancient world. 3.553
Aspects of the novel. 2.3421
Aspects of the presidency. 3.7799
Aspects of the theory of syntax. 2.190
Aspects of the theory of tariffs. 4.4196

Aspects of topology. 5.1586
The aspirin age, 1919-1941. 3.6130
Asquith. 3.1677
Assam, a valley divided. 3.4326
The assassination of Henry IV. 3.2020
The assassination of John F. Kennedy. 3.7880
The Assault on world poverty. 4.1828
The Assembly of the League of Nations. 4.9182
Assessing vital functions accurately. 5.5174
Assessment in special education. 4.10930
An Assessment of maritime trade and technology. 4.3971
Assessment of multihandicapped and developmentally disabled children. 5.5116
Assessment of organic intellectual impairment. 5.4789
Asset formation plans in the Western World. 4.3066
Asset markets and exchange rates. 4.4562
Asset markets, exchange rates, and economic integration. 4.4563
The assignats. 4.4519
Assignment in Utopia. 3.730
Assimilation and association in French colonial theory, 1890-1914. 4.8928
Assimilation in American life. 4.5130
Assisi and the rise of vernacular art. 1.6395
The assistant. 2.13154
Association football laws illustrated. 4.1019
Assumption and myth in physical theory. 5.2014
The assurance sciences. 5.7030
Assyrian palace reliefs in the British Museum. 1.5615
Assyrian sculpture in the British Museum. 1.5614
The astonished muse. 4.881
The Astors. 3.298
L'astragale. 2.4791
Astrodynamics. 5.6717
Astrology in the Renaissance. 5.686
Astronomers. 5.1690
The Astronomical almanac for the year ... 5.1678
The astronomical scrapbook. 5.1721
Astronomical techniques. 5.1746
Astronomy and astrophysics for the 1980's. 5.1704
Astronomy and cosmology. 5.1702
Astronomy data book. 5.1736
Astronomy from space. 5.1751
Astronomy of star positions. 5.1834
Astrophysical concepts. 5.1770
Astrophysical formulae. 5.1772
Astrophysical journal. 5.1681
Astrophysical quantities. 5.1768
Astrophysical techniques. 5.1771
Astrophysics. 5.1774
Asylum piece and other stories. 2.8615
The asymmetric society. 4.4898
Asymptotic analysis. 5.1430
At atomic phantasy, Krakatit. 2.1662
At Freddie's. 2.9679
At heaven's gate. 2.12636
At home in America. 3.8051
At odds. 4.6008
At play with Krishna. 2.1878
At Swim-Two-Birds. 2.9169
At the crossroads. 5.6722
At the end of the open road. 2.12474
At the grass roots in the Garden State. 4.8210
At the Long Sault. 2.9936
At the Moon's inn. 2.12058
At the ocean's verge. 2.9933
At the Royal Court. 2.3329
At the sign of the Reine Pédauque, and The revolt of the angels. 2.4213
At the vanishing point. 4.1104
Atala and René. 2.4150
Ataturk. 3.3596
Atatürk, founder of a modern state. 3.3595
Athapaskan adaptations: hunters and fishermen of the subarctic forests. 3.5844
Athenian black figure vases. 1.6636
The Athenian constitution. 2.338
Athenian democracy. 4.7365
The Athenian empire. 3.2605

Athenian properted families, 600-300 B.C. 3.301
Athenian red figure vases. 1.6639
The Athenian tribute lists. 3.2556
The Athens charter. 1.5578
Athens in decline, 404-86 B.C. 3.2652
Athletic training. 4.972
Athletic training and physical fitness. 4.902
Athletic training and sports medicine. 5.5025
Athleticism in the Victorian and Edwardian public school. 4.908
The Athlone history of music in Britain. 1.3710
Atlante internazionale. 4.117
The Atlantic civilization: eighteenth-century origins. 3.180
The Atlantic economy and colonial Maryland's Eastern Shore. 4.2035
Atlantic empires. 4.4221
The Atlantic Frontier. 3.6870
The Atlantic migration, 1607-1860. 4.8946
The Atlantic provinces. 3.8799
The Atlantic slave trade and British abolition, 1760-1810. 4.6449
Atlas and glossary of primary sedimentary structures. 5.3057
Atlas coeli 1950.0. 5.1737
Atlas de France (Métropole) 4.173
Atlas des formes du relief. 4.129
An atlas of African history. 4.188
Atlas of African prehistory. 4.186
Atlas of American agriculture. 4.153
An atlas of anatomy for artists. 1.5823
Atlas of antebellum southern agriculture. 4.161
Atlas of astronomy. 5.1739
The atlas of Britain and Northern Ireland. 4.169
Atlas of Canada. 4.139
An atlas of cat anatomy. 5.3998
Atlas of Central Europe. 4.174
Atlas of demographics. 4.147
Atlas of E.E.C. affairs. 4.2218
Atlas of early American history. 4.158
The atlas of early man. 3.120
Atlas of economic development. 4.134
An atlas of EEC affairs. 4.2218
Atlas of female anatomy. 5.4148
An atlas of fine structure: the cell, its organelles, and inclusions. 5.3590
An atlas of functions. 5.1490
Atlas of Great Lakes Indian history. 3.5735
An atlas of human anatomy. 5.4143
Atlas of human histology and ultrastructure. 5.4162
An atlas of Irish history. 4.172
Atlas of Japan. 4.183
Atlas of landforms. 4.128
Atlas of male anatomy. 5.4144
Atlas of man. 4.512
Atlas of maritime history. 4.137
Atlas of military strategy. 5.7212
Atlas of rock-forming minerals in thin section. 5.3028
An atlas of Russian history. 4.176
Atlas of sedimentary rocks under the microscope. 5.3050
Atlas of spectral data and physical constants for organic compounds. 5.2725
Atlas of stereochemistry. 5.2871
Atlas of the American Revolution. 4.159
Atlas of the Arab world. 3.3648
Atlas of the Arab world and the Middle East. 4.178
An atlas of the chromosome numbers in animals. 5.3615
Atlas of the classical world. 3.2518
Atlas of the early Christian world. 4.133
Atlas of the Greek and Roman world in antiquity. 4.126
Atlas of the Greek world. 3.2539
Atlas of the historical geography of the United States. 4.156
Atlas of the Islamic World since 1500. 3.3645
Atlas of the Lewis & Clark expedition. 3.8480
Atlas of the Lewis and Clark expedition. 3.8480
Atlas of the North American Indian. 3.5710
Atlas of the oceans. 4.193

Atlas of the Pacific Northwest. 4.163
Atlas of the Roman world. 3.2725
Atlas of the Second World War. 4.127
Atlas of the solar system. 5.1789
Atlas of the Union of South Africa. 4.190
Atlas of the world. 4.116
Atlas of United States trees. 4.154
Atlas of world history. 4.123, 4.125
Atlas of world population history. 4.1582
Atlas shrugged. 2.12366
Atmosphere and ocean. 4.332
Atmospheric chemistry. 5.2512
Atmospheric diffusion. 5.2521
The atom and its nucleus. 5.2045
Atomic absorption and fluorescence spectroscopy. 5.2676
Atomic and electron physics. 5.2065
Atomic and laser spectroscopy. 5.2378
Atomic and molecular collisions. 5.2482
Atomic and molecular physics of controlled thermonuclear fusion. 5.2449
Atomic and molecular structure. 5.2818
Atomic and nuclear physics. 5.2070
The atomic bomb and the end of World War II. 3.1008
Atomic diplomacy: Hiroshima and Potsdam. 3.7790
The Atomic Energy Commission. 4.3812
Atomic energy for military purposes. 5.2420
Atomic energy levels as derived from the analyses of optical spectra. 5.2436
Atomic nuclei and their particles. 5.2424
The atomic nucleus. 5.2426
The atomic papers. 5.8256
Atomic physics. 5.2047
Atomic physics and human knowledge. 5.1897
Atomic quest. 5.2416
Atomic spectra. 5.2310, 5.2313
Atomic spectra and atomic structure. 5.2302
Atomic theory and the description of nature. 5.2051
Atoms and information theory. 5.2172
Atoms for the world. 5.6597
Atoms in the family. 5.2421
Attachment and loss. 5.434
Attack at Michilimackinac. 3.8434
The attack on big business. 4.1936
The attack on leviathan. 3.6104
Attack upon 'Christendom,' 1854-1855. 1.2217
Attacking rural poverty. 4.10970
Attacks. 5.7242
The attainment of Delacroix. 1.6096
The Attalids of Pergamon. 3.4040
Attention and effort. 5.309
Attention and Memory. 5.310
Atthis. 3.2569
Attic black-figure. 1.6635
Attic black-figure vase-painters. 1.6634
The Attic orators from Antiphon to Isaeos. 2.308
Attic red-figure vase-painters. 1.6638
Attica. 4.6916
Attitudes and attitude change in special education. 4.10931
Attitudes toward English usage. 2.982
Attitudes toward history 3.462
Attribution: perceiving the causes of behavior. 4.4921
Auden, a carnival of intellect. 2.8401
Auden; a collection of critical essays. 2.8410
Auden, an introductory essay. 2.8406
The Auden generation. 2.5743
The audience of Beowulf. 2.6302
Audience ratings. 4.4063
Audiences for public television. 4.4067
The Audiencia of New Galicia in the sixteenth century. 4.8330
Audio video market place. 4.10323
Audiology. 5.5040
Audiovisual instruction. 4.10324
Auditing. 4.4404
Auditing, an integrated approach. 4.4402
Auditing methods. 4.4403
The auditory periphery. 5.4367
Audubon. 5.3795
The Audubon Society encyclopedia of North American birds. 5.3957

The Audubon Society field guide to North American birds 5.3958
The Audubon Society field guide to North American butterflies. 5.3882
The Audubon Society field guide to North American fishes, whales, and dolphins. 5.3908
The Audubon Society field guide to North American insects and spiders. 5.3862
The Audubon Society field guide to North American mammals. 5.3986
The Audubon Society field guide to North American reptiles and amphibians. 5.3921
The Audubon Society field guide to North American trees. 5.3686
The Audubon Society handbook for birders. 5.3948
The Audubon Society master guide to birding. 5.3951
Audubon water bird guide. 5.3955
Audubon western bird guide. 5.3959
Audubon's Birds of America. 5.3950
Die Auflösung der Weimarer Republik. 3.2371
Die Aufzeichnungen des Malte Laurids Brigge. 2.13852
August 1914. 2.1635
August Strindberg. 2.14079
The Augustan idea in English literature. 2.5679
The Augustan milieu. 2.5661
Augustan studies. 2.5673
The Augustan world. 3.1530
Augustan worlds. 2.5662
Augustans and Romantics, 1689-1830. 2.5520
Auguste Comte. 4.4749
Augustine of Hippo. 1.2485
Augustine on evil. 1.1486
Augustus and Nero. 3.2796
Augustus and the Greek world. 3.2795
Augustus Caesar in 'Augustan' England. 2.5681
Augustus to Constantine. 1.2295
Aunt Julia and the scriptwriter. 2.5436
The aunt's story. 2.10178
Aurélien. 2.4370
Aurora Leigh, and other poems. 2.7464
Aus dem Tagebuch einer Schnecke 2.13752
The Auschwitz album. 3.1077
Auschwitz, beginning of a new era? 1.1976
'Ausgeführte Bauten' of 1911. 1.5338
Ausgeführte Bauten und Entwürfe. 1.5336
Ausgewählte Werke. 2.13627
Austin Clarke. 2.8522
Austin Elliot. 2.7882
Australia. 3.5570, 5.8079
Australia; a study of warm environments and their effect on British settlement. 4.255
Australia and America through 200 years; 1776-1976. 3.6411
Australia and Papua New Guinea. 4.8827
Australia goes to press. 2.3700
Australia in New Guinea. 4.8828
Australia in peace and war. 3.5580
Australia in world affairs. 3.5571
Australia, New Zealand, and the Pacific Islands since the First World War. 3.5578
Australia, New Zealand, and the South Pacific. 3.5532
Australia, New Zealand and the Southwest Pacific. 3.5541
The Australian aborigines. 3.5583
The Australian colonists. 3.5576
The Australian Commonwealth. 3.5579
The Australian Council of Trade Unions. 4.3672
Australian dictionary of biography. 3.5559
Australian diplomacy and Japan, 1945-1951. 3.5572
The Australian encyclopaedia. 3.5560
Australian explorers. 3.5561
Australian fiction. 2.10143
The Australian Labor Party and federal politics. 4.8820
Australian literature. 5.8080
Australian literature from its beginnings to 1935. 5.8083
Australian literature to 1900. 5.8081
Australia's constitution. 4.8818

Australia's corner of the world. 3.5563
Australia's Great Barrier Reef. 5.3281
Austria, Germany, and the Anschluss, 1931-1938. 3.1878
Austria, Great Britain, and the Crimean War. 3.3125
Austrian banking and financial policy. 4.4543
Austrian intellectual history. 3.1875
The Austrian mind. 3.1874
Austrian poetry today. 2.13937
Austria's eastern question, 1700-1790. 3.1883
Austro-German relations in the Anschluss era. 3.1903
Austro-Marxism. 4.7043
The authentic Mark Twain. 2.10956
An author index to selected British 'little magazines,' 1930-1939. 1.27
Author-title index to Joseph Sabin's Dictionary of books relating to America. 5.7731
The authorised daily prayer book. 1.1979
The Authoritarian personality. 4.5022
Authoritarian politics in modern society. 4.7594
Authoritarianism and corporatism in Latin America. 4.8327
Authority. 4.5030, 4.7619
Authority and conflict. 3.1461
Authority and freedom in education. 4.10237
The authority and interpretation of the Bible. 1.2529
Authority and participation in industry. 4.3183
Authority and power in the free church tradition. 1.3320
Authority and resistance in the Investiture Contest. 1.3151
Authority in the Church. 1.3210
Authority in the modern state. 4.7510
The Authority of experience. 2.5585
The authority of the Bible and the rise of the modern world. 1.2528
Authority 4.2469
Authority, responsibility, and education. 4.10238
Authority revisited. 4.7249
Authors on film. 2.2937
Authorship and narrative in the cinema. 2.2959
Autism, a reappraisal of concepts and treatment. 5.5109
The autistic child. 5.5111
Auto engines of tomorrow. 5.6627
The autobiographical notes of Charles Evans Hughes. 3.7437
An autobiographical novel. 2.12380
Autobiographies. 5.3195
An autobiography. 1.748
Autobiography. 2.7040, 3.6987, 5.3190
Autobiography. 1.5693, 2.9114
An autobiography. 1.6002, 2.9127
Autobiography. 1.3261, 1.3963, 2.3263, 2.9237, 2.12481, 3.7706
An autobiography. 2.8230
Autobiography. 2.12609
Autobiography. 2.12749
An autobiography. 1.5333
Autobiography and essays. 5.846
Autobiography and letters of Mrs. Margaret Oliphant. 2.7977
Autobiography: consisting of Reveries over childhood and youth. 2.8340
Autobiography, essays theoretical and critical. 3.316
The autobiography of a curmudgeon. 3.7653
The autobiography of Alice B. Toklas. 2.12516
The autobiography of an ex-coloured man. 2.11936
The autobiography of an idea. 1.5329
The autobiography of an unknown Indian. 3.4166
The autobiography of Benjamin Franklin. 3.6985-3.6986
The autobiography of Benvenuto Cellini 1.5728
The autobiography of Bertrand Russell. 1.766
The autobiography of Carl Schurz. 3.7448
The autobiography of Colonel John Trumbull, patriot-artist, 1756-1843. 1.5978

The autobiography of Du Pont de Nemours. 3.2043
The autobiography of Eleanor Roosevelt. 3.7786
The autobiography of Emperor Haile Sellassie I. 3.5247
The autobiography of G. K. Chesterton. 2.7563
The autobiography of Harry S. Truman. 3.7806
The autobiography of John Middleton Murry. 2.9136
The autobiography of Leigh Hunt. 2.7844
The autobiography of Lincoln Steffens. 2.3635
The autobiography of Lord Alfred Douglas. 2.8600
The autobiography of Malcolm X. With the assistance of Alex Haley. 3.6844
The autobiography of Mark Rutherford, dissenting minister. 2.8262
The autobiography of Mark Twain [pseud.] 2.10947
The autobiography of Martin Van Buren. 3.7129
The autobiography of Maxim Gorky. 2.1506
The autobiography of Miss Jane Pittman. 2.13024
The autobiography of Sam Houston. 3.8324
The Autobiography of surrealism. 1.6738
Autobiography of Swami Dayanand Saraswati. 1.1730
The autobiography of W. E. B. DuBois. 3.6828
The autobiography of William Allen White. 2.3638
The autobiography of William Plomer. 2.9224
Autocracy and democracy. 4.4920
Autographs and manuscripts, a collector's manual. 5.7522
Automated people movers. 5.5935
Automatic control systems. 5.6178
Automatic testing. 5.6588
Automatic vehicle locating systems. 4.4032
Automation and work design. 5.5622
Automation, production systems, and computer-aided manufacturing. 5.7048
Automobile age Atlanta. 4.2041
The automobile and the environment. 4.3906
The automobile industry since 1945. 4.3828
Automobile workers and the American dream. 4.3521
Automotive aerodynamics. 5.6636
The automotive engine. 5.6628
Automotive suspension, steering, and brakes. 5.6637
Automotive technician's handbook. 5.6624
Autonomous technology. 5.5526
Autos, transit, and cities. 4.3917
AV instruction. 4.10324
Available light. 2.11396
The available man. 3.7736
Avalanche-diode microwave oscillators. 5.6519
Avant-garde. 1.6701
Avant-garde: the experimental theater in France. 2.3891
L'avant-garde théâtrale. 2.3936
The Avant-garde tradition in literature. 2.2669
L'Avant-scène, cinéma. 2.4380
Avcienna on theology. 1.369
L'aventure ambiguë. 2.4871
The avenue bearing the initial of Christ into the New World. 2.11963
Averroes on Plato's Republic. 4.7348
Avian biology. 5.3938
Avian ecology. 5.3942
The avian embryo. 5.4132
Aviation. 5.6645
Aviation space dictionary. 5.6666
Aviation weather, for pilots and flight operations personnel. 5.6659
Avicenna, his life and works. 1.371
The Avignon papacy, 1305-1403. 1.3154
AVMP. 4.10323
Awakened conscience. 2.9874
The awakening. 2.10931
Awakening in Bengal in early nineteenth century. 3.4327
The awakening land: I. The trees. 2.12389

The awakening of American nationalism, 1815-1828. 3.7075
The awakening of faith, attributed to Aśvaghosha. 1.1745
The awakening of Southern Italy. 4.2353
The awakening of the Greek historical spirit. 3.2571
Awakening the inner eye. 5.279
Awakening to literacy. 5.7722
The awakening to the truth; Nichiren. 1.2120
Awards, honors & prizes. 1.51
The awkward years. 3.7487
Awo. 3.5361
The ax within: Italian fascism in action. 3.2892
The axe. 2.1693
Axe handles. 2.13326
Axel. 2.4335
Axel's castle. 2.2687
The axiom of choice. 5.1351
Ayala's angel. 2.8202
The Ayodhya canto of the Ramayana. 2.2275
The Ayub Khan era. 3.4135
Azadi. 2.10128
The Azande: history and political institutions. 3.5175
Azorín (José Martínez Ruiz) 2.5275
The Aztec arrangement. 3.8907
Aztec art. 3.8906
The Aztec image in Western thought. 3.8885
The Aztecs in Western thought. 3.8885
The Aztecs, Maya, and their predecessors. 3.8890
The Aztecs; people of the sun. 3.8903
The Aztecs under Spanish rule. 3.8892
Azuela and the Mexican underdogs. 2.5335
Azumakagami. 3.4936

B.A.S.I.C. programs for land surveying. 5.5828
B.B.C. pronouncing dictionary of British names. 2.1096
B. F. Skinner. 5.102
'B' movies. 2.2924
The Bab ballads. 2.7728
Babbitt. 2.12002
Babel-17. 2.12968
The Babeuf plot. 3.2115
Babi Yar. 2.1624
Baby and child care. 5.5077
Babyhood. 5.5080
Bacchae. 2.452
Bacchylides. 2.441
Bach. 1.3771-1.3772
The Bach family. 1.3776
The Bach reader. 1.3774
Bach the borrower. 1.3773
Bachelard, science and objectivity. 1.826
The bachelors. 2.9356
Bach's orchestra. 1.3783
Back. 2.8730
Back of the yards. 4.5209
Back on the street. 4.6868
Back to nature. 3.6164
Back to the sources. 1.1937
Backfire. 3.4498
Background notes. 4.4
The background of ecology. 5.3521
The Background of English literature, classical & romantic, and other collected essays & addresses. 2.5537
The background of Napoleonic warfare. 5.7316
The background of the rebellion of An Lu-shan. 3.4701
The background of Thomson's Seasons. 2.7317
Background to danger. 2.8381
Background to revolution. 3.9092
Backgrounds of American literary thought. 2.10249
Backgrounds to medieval English literature. 2.5599
Backgrounds to Victorian literature. 2.5712
Backward areas in advanced countries. 4.2756
A backward glance. 2.12698
The Bacteria. 5.4434
Bacteria, plasmids, and phages. 5.3450
Bacterial and bacteriophage genetics. 5.3448
Bad blood. 5.4606
Bad dreams. 2.1533

Bad Nigger! 4.1055
Bādarāyana. 1.1680
The badge and the bullet. 4.6831
The badgers. 2.1570
Badger's Illustrated catalogue of cast-iron architecture. 1.5501
Baedae Opera historica. 2.651
Baghdad. 3.3689
Baghdad during the Abbasid caliphate from contemporary Arabic and Persian sources. 3.3688
Bags and purses. 4.858
The Bahá'í faith. 1.2096
Bahá'í world faith. 1.2095
Bahrain and the Gulf. 4.2450
Bail reform in America. 4.9880
Bailey's Industrial oil and fat products. 5.6894
Baillière's atlas of female anatomy. 5.4148
Baillière's atlas of male anatomy. 5.4144
Baird's manual, American college fraternities 11th-14th. 4.11013
Baird's manual of American college fraternities. 4.11013
Baker's Biographical dictionary of musicians. 1.3529
A baker's dozen. 3.6298
Bakke & the politics of equality. 4.9592
Bakke and the politics of equality. 4.9592
Bakunin on anarchy. 4.7196
Balance of intrigue. 3.5004
Balance of power: the Negro vote. 4.8180
Balanchine, a biography. 4.1130
Balanchine's Complete stories of the great ballets. 1.4508
Balancing jobs and family life. 4.5586
The balcony (Le balcon) 2.4533
The bald soprano. 2.4579
Baldesar Castiglione. 1.1512
Balfour. 3.1653
Balkan cultural studies. 2.211
Balkan federation. 3.764
The Balkan trilogy. 2.9742
Balkan village. 3.3546
The Balkans. 3.3515, 3.3517
The Balkans in our time. 3.3538
The Balkans in transition. 3.3518
The Balkans since 1453. 3.3520
The Ball red book. 5.5345
The ballad and the folk. 2.9839
The ballad and the source. 2.9005
The ballad of Peckham Rye. 2.9360
Ballad of the Mari Lwyd, and other poems. 2.9475
Ballad of the sad café. 2.12840
The ballad of the sad café. 2.12070
The ballad tree. 1.4345
Ballads and poems, 1915-1930. 2.11367
Ballet, bias and belief. 4.1175
Ballet guide. 4.1181
Ballistic missile defense. 5.7409
Ballot position and voter's choice. 4.7745
Ballots for freedom. 3.7260
Balthazar. 2.8606
Baltic literature. 2.1749
The Baltic nations. 3.3307
The Baltic States. 3.3308
The Baltic States, years of dependence, 1940-1980. 3.3305
Baltimore, the building of an American city. 4.2042
Balzac. 2.4126-2.4127
Balzac and the French Revolution. 2.4128
Balzac and The human comedy. 2.4121
Balzac's Comédie humaine. 2.4112
Balzac's comedy of words. 2.4129
Banach algebra techniques in operator theory. 5.1480
Banach algebras and several complex variables. 5.1479
Banana Bottom. 2.12082
The banana wars. 3.9148
Banāras, City of Light. 1.1697
Bancroft's works. 3.8588
Band of angels. 2.12637
A Band of prophets. 3.8120
Band scoring. 1.4494
Bandeirantes and pioneers. 3.9195
Bangla Desh. 3.4140

Bangla Desh economy: problems and prospects. 4.2521
Bangladesh. 3.4141-3.4142, 3.4144, 3.4146
Bangladesh economy. 4.2522
Bangladesh, the first decade. 3.4148
Bangwa kinship and marriage. 3.5397
Banjo. 2.12083
Bank of Canada operations and policy. 4.4539
The Bank of England. 4.4541
The Bank of England, 1891-1944. 4.4542
The Bank of Lebanon. 4.4545
Bank performance annual. 4.4526
Bankers almanac. 4.4529
Bankers and pashas. 4.4548
Bankers' diplomacy. 4.4540
Banking and finance in the Arab Middle East. 4.4547
Banking & finance in the Arab Middle East. 4.4547
Banking and monetary statistics. 4.4533
Banking deregulation and the new competition in financial services. 4.4532
Banking on death. 2.13129
Banks and politics in America, from the Revolution to the Civil War. 4.4531
The banquet years. 3.2174
Bantam-Megido milon 'Ivri ve-Angli hadash. 2.1771
Bantu, Boer, and Briton. 3.5453
Bantu prophets in South Africa. 1.2470
The Bantu-speaking tribes of South Africa. 3.5460
Baptism in the New Testament. 1.3015-1.3016
Bar-Kokhba. 3.3898
Barabbas. 2.14088
Baraka. 2.12871
The barbarian within, and other fugitive essays and studies. 2.2583
Barbarians and Romans, A.D. 418-584. 3.2817
The Barbary Coast. 3.5206
Barbary legend. 3.5196
Barbary shore. 2.12095
Barbey d'Aurevilly. 2.4132
Barbizon revisited, essay and catalogue. 1.6056
The Barbizon School and 19th century French landscape painting. 1.6059
La barca sin pescador. 2.5280
Barchester Towers. 2.8203
Bardo thödol. 1.1741
Barefoot boy with cheek. 2.12469
Barefoot in the head. 2.9612
Bargaining behavior. 4.1567
Bargaining for job safety and health. 4.3480
Bargaining for reality. 3.5216
Barlaam and Joasaph. English. 2.355
Barley. 5.5323
Barnes & Noble thesaurus of physics. 5.1892
Barnett Newman. 1.4901
The Barnhart dictionary of new English since 1963. 2.1094
Barnhart dictionary of new English since 1963. 2.1095
The baron in the trees. 2.5025
The baronial plan of reform, 1258-1263. 3.1361
Baroque. 1.4776
Baroque & rococo. 1.5245
Baroque and rococo in Latin America 1.4857
Baroque and Rococo pictorial imagery. 1.5165
Baroque architecture. 1.5247
Baroque art and architecture in central Europe: Germany, Austria, Switzerland, Hungary, Czechoslovakia, Poland. 1.4927
Baroque book illustration. 1.5828
The Baroque concerto. 1.4199
Baroque music. 1.3656
The baroque poem. 2.2765
The baroque theatre. 2.3173
Baroque times in old Mexico. 3.8876
La barraca. 2.5236-2.5237
Barranca abajo. 2.5444
Barred from school, 2 million children! 4.10936
Barren ground. 2.11772
The barrier and the javelin. 3.1010
Barriers to entry. 4.3035
Barriers to new competition. 4.1562

Barron's profiles of American colleges. Descriptions of the colleges. 4.9938
The Barrymores. 2.3233, 2.3235
The Barsukov triangle, The two-toned blonde & other stories. 2.1326
Barter in the world economy. 4.4116
A Barthes reader. 1.6681
Bartholomew fair. 2.6589
Bartleby in Manhattan. 2.11815
Bartók. 1.3788
Bartók. 1.3789
Bartók. 1.3790
Bartolomé de las Casas; a selection of his writings. 3.8991
Bartolomé Esteban Murillo, 1617-1682. 1.6298
Bartolomeo Scala, 1430-1497, Chancellor of Florence. 3.2929
Baruch. 3.7624
Base-catalyzed reactions of hydrocarbons and related compounds. 5.2757
Baseball economics and public policy. 4.1008
The Baseball encyclopedia. 4.1007
Baseball's great experiment. 4.1004
Bases of hearing science. 5.4369
Basic algebra. 5.1268
Basic anatomy. 5.4114
Basic astronomical data. 5.1830
Basic books in the mass media. 5.8120
Basic complex analysis. 5.1489
Basic concepts in population, quantitative, and evolutionary genetics. 5.3471
Basic concepts in relativity and early quantum theory. 5.2090
Basic concepts in sociology. 4.4860
Basic documents of American public administration, 1776-1950. 4.7882
Basic documents of American public administration since 1950. 4.7883
Basic documents on human rights. 4.9382
Basic ecology. 5.3522
Basic electromagnetic theory. 5.2360
The Basic experiments in parapsychology. 5.637
Basic food chemistry. 5.7114
Basic food microbiology. 5.4460
Basic forms of prophetic speech. 1.2611
Basic handbook of child psychiatry. 5.5096
Basic health planning methods. 5.4619
Basic human anatomy. 5.4142
Basic Judaism. 1.1965
The basic laws of arithmetic. 1.1208
Basic lubrication theory. 5.6244
Basic metric surveying. 5.5826
A Basic music library. 1.3546
Basic needs, poverty, and government policies in Sri Lanka. 4.2455
Basic neurology. 5.4323
Basic nuclear engineering. 5.6600
Basic numerical mathematics. 5.1428
Basic operator theory. 5.1481
Basic pathology. 5.4740
Basic pattern drafting for the theatrical costume designer. 2.3128
Basic photovoltaic principles and methods. 5.6329
Basic physics of atoms and molecules. 5.2055
Basic population genetics. 5.3476
Basic principles and calculations in chemical engineering. 5.6824
Basic principles in nucleic acid chemistry. 5.2796
Basic principles of classical ballet. 4.1180
Basic principles of curriculum and instruction 4.10453
Basic principles of organic chemistry. 5.2723
Basic principles of psychoanalysis. 5.130
The basic problems of phenomenology. 1.991
Basic processes of gaseous electronics. 5.2381
BASIC programs for land surveying. 5.5828
Basic questions in theology. 1.2791
Basic readings in neuropsychology. 5.4291
Basic research methods for librarians. 5.7644
Basic steel design. 5.5885
Basic steps in planning nursing research. 5.5186
Basic structural analysis. 5.5838
Basic studies in social psychology. 4.4992
Basic tables in business and economics. 4.4418

Basic tables in electrical engineering. 5.6261
Basic tactics. 5.7230
The basic training of Pavlo Hummel, and Sticks and bones. 2.13289
Basic verities, prose and poetry. 2.4645
The basic works of Aristotle. 1.282
Basic writings. 1.169, 1.379, 3.3154, 5.166
Basic writings, 1903-1959. 1.761
Basic writings from Being and time (1927) to The task of thinking (1964) 1.988
Basic writings in the history of psychology. 5.81
The basic writings of Sigmund Freud. 5.133
Basic writings on politics and philosophy. 4.7069
Basil Seal rides again, or, The rake's regress. 2.9483
Basin and range. 5.3000
The basin of Mexico. 3.8893
Basin Street to Harlem. 1.4269
The basis of criticism in the arts. 1.1379
The basis of motor control. 5.4265
The basis of obligation in international law, and other papers. 4.9284
The basis of religious liberty. 1.3010
The basketball man, James Naismith. 4.1010
Basque Americans. 5.7855
The Basque insurgents. 3.3481
Basque nationalism. 3.3483
The Basque phase of Spain's first Carlist war. 3.3451
Basque politics. 3.3479
A Basque shepherding community. 3.2238
The Basques. 3.3480
The Basques, the Franco years and beyond. 3.3482
The bass saxophone. 2.1681
The bassoon and contrabassoon. 1.4172
Bassoon technique. 1.4557
The bastard war. 3.812
Bastardy and its comparative history. 4.5789
The Basuto. 3.5478
Basutoland. 3.5479
La Bâtarde. 2.4600
Bateman New Zealand encyclopedia. 3.5593
The bathtub hoax and other blasts and bravos. 2.12126
Bats. 5.4011
The battered child. 4.6558
The battered woman syndrome. 4.6748
The battle cry of freedom. 3.8524
The battle for Butte. 4.3729
The battle for Italy. 3.982
The battle for public opinion. 3.7922
The battle for Stalingrad. 3.985
The battle for the Labour Party. 4.8538
The battle for the public schools. 4.10039
The battle ground. 2.11772
The battle lost and won. 2.9743
Battle maps and charts of the American Revolution. 3.6930
The battle of Downing Street. 4.3646
Battle over Britain. 3.958
The battles of Coxinga. 2.2061
Battre la campagne. 2.4676
Baudelaire. 2.4143-2.4146
Baudelaire, man of his time. 2.4142
Baudelaire on Poe. 2.11201
Baudelaire the damned. 2.4141
Bauhaus. 1.4651
The Bavarian rococo church. 1.5533
Bay area houses. 1.5562
Bayeux in the late eighteenth century. 4.2335
The Bayeux tapestry. 1.6591
Bayle. 1.785
The bayonets of the Republic. 5.7314
Bayreuth, the early years. 1.4054
BBC pronouncing dictionary of British names. 2.1096
The beach of Falesá 2.9405
Beaches and coasts. 4.271
Beachheads in space. 5.6707
The beadle. 2.10091
The Beagle record. 5.3179
Beam weapons. 5.7392
The bear. 2.11661
Bear, man, & God. 2.11661
Beardsley. 1.5842

Beardsley and his world. 1.5800
The beast must die. 2.8595
Beasts of the southern wild and other stories. 2.12907
The beat generation. 4.5765
Beating the bushes. 2.4676
Beating wife-beating. 4.6745
The Beatles forever. 1.4100
Beatrice Webb's American diary, 1898. 3.6054
Beaumarchais. 2.4063
The beautiful in music. 1.4397
Beauty and sadness. 2.2101
The beauty of doing mathematics. 5.1029
The beauty of sport. 4.945
The Beaux-arts and nineteenth-century French architecture. 1.5460
Les beaux dimanches. 2.4827
Les beaux quartiers. 2.4371
The beaux' stratagem. 2.7015
Beaverbrook. 3.1654
Because I was flesh. 2.11551
Bech. 2.13364
Bechuanaland. 3.5482
The Bechuanaland Protectorate. 3.5481
Becket. 2.4359
The Becket conflict and the schools. 3.1356
Beckett. 2.8431
Becoming a heroine. 2.5970
Becoming a Kwoma. 4.593
Becoming American. 3.6503
Becoming; basic considerations for a psychology of personality. 5.17
Becoming Browning. 2.7492
Becoming clerical workers. 4.3267
Becoming deviant. 4.5069
Becoming female. 4.5920
Becoming partners; marriage and its alternatives. 4.5655
The bedbug [a play] and selected poetry. 2.1572
Bede's ecclesiastical history of the English people. 1.2431
Beef cattle feeding and nutrition. 5.5444
Beekeeping in the Midwest. 5.5458
Beelzebub sonata. 2.1736
Been in the storm so long. 3.6635
Bees: their vision, chemical senses, and language. 5.3884
Beethoven. 1.3798, 1.3800, 1.3805, 1.3807
Beethoven and his nine symphonies. 1.4524
Beethoven as I knew him. 1.3804
Beethoven: biography of a genius. 1.3801
The Beethoven companion. 1.3803
Beethoven: impressions by his contemporaries. 1.3797
The Beethoven quartets. 1.4533
The Beethoven reader. 1.3796
The Beethoven sketchbooks. 1.3799
Beethoven studies. 1.3809
Beethoven's pianoforte sonatas discussed. 1.4531
Beethoven's sketches. 1.3802
Before and after Socrates. 1.223
Before civilization. 4.729
Before it's too late. 5.6598
Before Kampuchea. 3.4448
Before Marx. 4.7046
Before photography. 1.4789
Before Silent spring. 5.4734
Before the Armada. 3.1393
Before the best interests of the child. 4.9511
Before the deluge. 3.2501
Before the fact. 2.8586
Before the fall. 3.7908
Before the five frontiers. 3.9082
Before the ghetto; black Detroit in the nineteenth century. 3.8438
Before the Golden Age. 2.10828
Before the Industrial Revolution. 4.2190
Before the Mayflower. 3.6606
Before the Molly Maguires. 3.8084
Before the revolution. 4.5438
The beggar. 2.586
The beggar maid. 2.9952
Beginning again. 2.9565
Beginning badminton. 4.1041
The beginning of ideology. 3.1958
The beginning of the road. 3.986

The beginning of the third republic in France. 3.2171
The beginning of the U.S. Army, 1783-1812. 3.6366
Beginning values clarification. 1.1516
Beginning with O. 2.12924
Beginnings. 3.6748
The beginnings of Chinese civilization. 3.4650
The beginnings of dialectic theology. 1.2800
The beginnings of English literature to Skelton, 1509. 2.5518
The beginnings of English society. 3.1318
The beginnings of naturalism in American fiction. 2.10533
The beginnings of Nyasaland and North-eastern Rhodesia, 1859-95. 3.5490
The beginnings of Russian-American relations,1775-1815. 3.6483
The beginnings of Russian history. 3.3078
Beginnings of sisterhood. 4.6061
The Beginnings of solid state physics. 5.2189
The beginnings of the English newspaper: 1620-1660. 2.3685
The beginnings of the Hanoverian dynasty. 3.1522
The beginnings of Unitarianism in America. 1.3416
Begotten or made? 5.5048
Behavior and evolution. 5.548
Behavior and misbehavior. 4.10691
Behavior and psychological man. 5.7
Behavior and the natural environment. 5.316
Behavior modification in Black populations. 5.4822
Behavior modification: theory and practice. 5.457
The behavior of domestic animals. 5.5463
The behavior of industrial prices. 4.1508
The behavior of organisms. 5.4293
Behavior pathology. 5.189
Behavior system. 5.217
Behavior theory and conditioning. 5.305
Behavior therapy. 5.4889
Behavioral archeology. 3.249
Behavioral ecology. 5.4054
Behavioral individuality in early childhood 5.605
Behavioral mechanisms in ecology. 5.4064
Behavioral medicine. 5.4582
Behavioral objectives. 4.10309
The behavioral persuasion in politics. 4.7237
Behavioral problems in geography revisited. 4.383
Behavioral regulators of behavior in primates. 5.4014
Behavioral social work. 4.6542
A behavioral theory of the firm. 4.2664
Behavioral travel-demand models. 4.3931
Behavioral treatment of alcohol problems. 5.4962
Behaviorism. 5.221-5.222
Behaviorism and phenomenology. 5.2
Behaviorism and schooling. 4.10361
The behaviour of animals. 5.4059
Behaviour of wolves, dogs, and related canids. 5.3992
Behavioural ecology. 5.4054
Behemoth. 3.1475, 3.2421
Behind a mask. 2.10897
Behind appearance. 1.5874
Behind closed doors. 3.1174, 4.5780
Behind every successful man. 4.5669
Behind ghetto walls. 3.6772
Behind mud walls, 1930-1960. 3.4171
Behind Spanish American footlights. 2.3278
Behind the ballots. 3.7640
Behind the classroom door. 4.10004
Behind the green curtains; Figuro in the night; The moon shines on Kylenamoe. 2.9147
Behind the lines in the Southern Confederacy. 3.7375
Behind the mask. 3.4885
Behind the President. 4.7936
Behind the screen. 2.2880
Behind the veil in Arabia. 4.6137
Behold the promised land. 3.5414
Beijing street voices. 4.8741
Being and having. 1.833

Being and nothingness. 1.491
Being and some philosophers. 1.1313
Being and time. 1.994
Being female. 4.571
Being geniuses together. 2.12060
Being here. 2.12638
Being Indian in Hueyapan. 3.8910
Being, man, & death. 1.997
Being Pakeha. 3.5565
The Beirut massacre. 3.3790
Beka Lamb. 2.10026
Bel-ami. 2.4270
Béla Bartók. 1.3793
Béla Bartók, his life in pictures. 1.3792
Béla Bartók letters. 1.3787
A beleaguered city. 2.7975
Belgian foreign policy between two wars,
   1919-1940. 3.2975
Belgium. 3.2966
Belgium, a country study. 3.2965
Belgium and Europe. 3.2970
Belgium's return to neutrality. 3.2978
Belief: the Gifford lectures delivered at the
   University of Aberdeen in 1960. 1.1299
The beliefs of politicians: ideology, conflict, and
   democracy in Britain and Italy. 4.7523
The bell. 2.9749
A bell for Adano. 2.11868
The bell jar. 2.13256
La belle Hortense. 2.4790
Les belles-soeurs 2.4832
Bells and man. 3.266
Bells in winter. 2.1718
Bell's introduction to the Qur'ān. 3.3651
The bells of the Kremlin. 4.7095
Belorussia. 3.3300
The beloved returns. 2.13831
The Belton estate. 2.8204
Bemerkungen über die Farben. 5.632
Ben-Gurion. 3.3910
Ben-Gurion and the Palestinian Arabs. 3.3911
Ben-Hur, a tale of the Christ. 2.11263
Ben Jonson. 2.6587, 2.6596, 2.6603
Ben Jonson and the language of prose comedy.
   2.6605
Ben Jonson, dramatist. 2.6597
Ben Jonson of Westminster. 2.6595
Ben Jonson, public poet and private man.
   2.6601
Ben Jonson's plays and masques. 2.6588
Ben Jonson's poems. 2.6604
The bench and the ballot. 4.9728
The Benchley roundup. 2.11365
Benchmarks. 4.9451
A bend in the river. 2.10007
The bending cross. 4.6997
The bending of the bough. 2.7954
Benedetto Croce's Poetry and literature.
   2.2726
Benedict Kiely. 2.9736
Benedictine monachism. 1.3238
The benefactor. 2.13330
Beneficial insects; nature's alternatives to
   chemical insecticides: animal predation
   5.5418
Benefit-cost analyses of social regulation.
   4.2002
The benefits of environmental improvement.
   4.1843
The Benelux countries: an historical survey.
   3.2956
'Benevolent assimilation' 3.4600
Bengali literature. 2.1854, 2.1856
Bengali women. 4.6143
Benito Juárez. 3.8935
Benito Pérez Galdós. 2.5225
Benjamin Britten. 1.3824
Benjamin Constant and the making of modern
   liberalism. 4.7444
Benjamin Constant's philosophy of liberalism.
   4.7443
Benjamin Franklin. 3.6990, 3.6993-3.6994
Benjamin Franklin, an American man of letters.
   2.10869
Benjamin Franklin and a rising people. 3.6991
Benjamin Franklin and Pennsylvania politics.
   3.8074
Benjamin Franklin Tracy. 3.7452

Benjamin Franklin Wade, radical Republican
   from Ohio. 3.7164
Benjamin Franklin's autobiography. 3.6987
Benjamin Franklin's experiments. 5.2338
Benjamin Harrison. 3.7494
Benjamin Henry Latrobe. 1.5314
Benjamin Lundy and the struggle for Negro
   freedom. 3.7222
Benjamin Péret. 2.4647
Benjamin Strong, central banker. 4.4537
Benjamin Thompson, Count Rumford. 5.826
Benjamin Tompson, colonial bard. 2.10877
Benjamin West. 1.5982
Benjamin West and the taste of his times.
   1.5983
Bentham. 1.724
Bentham's handbook of political fallacies.
   4.7728
Bentham's Theory of fictions. 1.723
Beowulf. 2.6288-2.6292, 2.6295, 2.6299
Beowulf and its analogues. 2.6292
Beowulf and the appositive style. 2.6303
Beowulf and the Beowulf manuscript. 2.6298
Beowulf and The fight at Finnsburg. 2.6288
Beowulf. English. 2.6291
Beowulf. English. 2.6293
Beowulf. English. 1984. 2.6296
Beowulf. English & Anglo-Saxon. 2.6290
The Berbers; their social and political
   organisation. 3.5211
Berenike. 2.12378
La bergerie. 2.3997
Bergey's manual of determinative bacteriology.
   5.4452
Bergey's manual of systematic bacteriology.
   5.4452
Bergman on Bergman. 2.3035
Bergson and the stream of consciousness novel.
   2.3483
Bering Strait. 4.351
Bering's voyages. 4.95
Berkeley. 1.691-1.694
Berkeley physics course. 5.1976
Berkeley's Philosophical writings. 1.686
Berl. 3.4027
Berlin Alexanderplatz. 2.13729
Berlin diary. 3.1140
The Berlin memorandum. 2.9445
The Berlin novels of Theodor Fontane.
   2.13567
The Berlin Secession. 1.4983
The Berlin stories. 2.8833
Berlioz and the romantic century. 1.3817
Bernanos par lui-même. 2.4415
Bernard Berenson. 1.5150
The Bernard Berenson treasury. 1.5196
Bernard Bloch on Japanese. 2.1988
Bernard Malamud. 2.13164
Bernard Malamud and the critics. 2.13163
Bernard Mandeville. 2.7102
Bernard Maybeck. 1.5318
Bernard Shaw. 2.8080
Bernard Shaw and Mrs. Patrick Campbell.
   2.8070
Bernard Shaw and the actresses. 2.8079
Bernard Shaw and the art of drama. 2.8081
Bernard Shaw, his life, work, and friends.
   2.8075
Bernard Shaw's Marxian romance. 2.8089
Bernard Shaw's nondramatic literary criticism.
   2.5552
Bernardo O'Higgins and the independence of
   Chile. 3.9263
Bernini and the unity of the visual arts. 1.5012
Bernini's drawings. 1.5010
Beroul's Rōmance of Tristran. 2.3966
Berryman's sonnets. 2.11376
Bertolt Brecht. 2.13708
Bertolt Brecht. 2.13710
Bertolt Brecht in America. 2.13711
Bertrand Barere. 3.2065
Bertrand Russell. 1.760, 1.767, 1.769
El beso de la mujer araña. 2.5400
Bessie Graham's bookman's manual 1948-54.
   5.7707
Best American plays. 2.10793
Best American short stories and the Yearbook
   of the American short story. 2.10809

Best and Taylor's Physiological basis of medical
   practice. 5.4191
The best and the brightest. 3.7864
Best ghost stories of Algernon Blackwood.
   2.8465
Best ghost stories of J.S. Le Fanu. 2.7911
The best men. 3.7415
Best mystery and suspense plays of the modern
   theatre. 2.6198
The best of Bill Nye's humor. 2.3794
The best of Bret Harte. 2.11054
The best of C. L. Moore. 2.13180
The best of Clarence Day. 2.11555
The best of Cordwainer Smith [i.e. P. M. A.
   Linebarger] 2.12017
The best of Don Marquis. 2.12117
The best of S.J. Perelman. 2.3795
The best of times, the worst of times. 1.3266
Best one-act plays. 2.3758
Best plays. 2.3763
The Best plays of.... 2.3762
Best plays of the early American theatre.
   2.10782
Best plays of the modern American theatre.
   2.10793
Best plays of the seventies. 2.6245
Best plays of the sixties. 2.10804
Best radio plays. 2.6200
Best radio plays of ... 2.6200
Best reference books, 1981-1985. 5.7711
The Best short plays. 2.3758
Best short stories. 2.3707, 2.11590
The best short stories by Negro writers.
   2.10814
Best short stories of Jack London. 2.12020
The best short stories of Ring Lardner.
   2.11980
The best short stories of Rudyard Kipling.
   2.7890
Best stories. 2.12436
The best stories of Guy de Maupassant. 2.4269
The best stories of Paul Laurence Dunbar.
   2.11012
A bestiary for Saint Jerome. 1.6367
Betrayal from within. 3.870
The betrayal of the Negro, from Rutherford B.
   Hayes to Woodrow Wilson. 3.6676
Betrayed by Rita Hayworth. 2.5403
Betrayers of the truth. 5.857
The betrothed. 2.5004
The betrothed 'I promessi sposi' 2.5003
Betsy Sheridan's journal. 2.7249
Better gymnastics. 4.918
Better homes and gardens. 5.4690
Better patient care through nursing research.
   5.5185
Better readers for our times 1956. 4.10455
Between belief and unbelief. 5.629
Between capitalism and socialism. 4.2775
Between continents/between seas. 3.9078
Between elite and mass education. 4.10741
Between God and man. 2.2104
Between ideals and reality. 4.7144
Between money and love. 4.3291
Between ourselves. 4.5664
Between Pacific tides. 5.3823
Between past and future, six exercises in
   political thought. 3.454
Between science and values. 5.957
Between State and Nation. 4.7869
Between the acts. 2.9570
Between the guillotine and liberty. 4.6790
Between the lines. 2.8355
Between tradition and modernity. 4.8735
Between two ages. 3.7840
Between two empires. 3.4602
Between two rivers. 2.13108
Between two worlds. 2.9136, 4.10874
Between war and peace. 3.883
Beware the people weeping. 3.7297
Beyond alcoholism. 5.4958
Beyond amazement. 2.11338
Beyond bias. 4.10697
Beyond Broadway. 2.3211
Beyond busing. 4.9589
Beyond Cuba. 3.9007
Beyond culture. 2.12601, 4.5005
Beyond desegregation. 4.10893

Beyond despair. 4.5190
Beyond domination. 4.5837
Beyond equality; labor and the radical
   Republicans. 4.3599
Beyond formalism. 2.2646
Beyond freedom and dignity. 5.547
Beyond God the Father. 4.5873
Beyond good and evil: prelude to a philosophy
   of the future. 1.1048
Beyond high school. 4.10516
Beyond human scale. 4.2671
Beyond ideology. 1.1590, 4.7226
Beyond life. 2.11442
Beyond love and loyalty. 2.12783
Beyond Marx and Tito. 4.7104
Beyond modern sculpture. 1.5649
Beyond neo-Darwinism. 5.3366
Beyond Orpheus. 1.4477
Beyond positivism. 4.1384
Beyond psychiatric expertise. 4.9509
Beyond Punjab, 1937-1960. 3.4323
Beyond separate spheres. 4.5990
Beyond socialist realism. 2.1291
Beyond supply and demand. 4.1337
Beyond survival. 4.2509
Beyond the automobile; reshaping the
   transportation environment. 4.3871
Beyond the bedroom wall. 2.13436
Beyond the best interests of the child. 4.6548
Beyond the body. 5.662
Beyond the codices. 3.8881
Beyond the cold war. 4.9177
Beyond the fringe 2.9620
Beyond the glass. 2.9518
Beyond the Hiss case. 3.7540
Beyond the information given. 5.259
Beyond the ivory tower. 4.10575, 5.973
Beyond the labyrinth. 2.9131
Beyond the melting pot. 3.8045
Beyond the mountains. 2.12378
Beyond the nation-state. 4.3324
Beyond the New Deal. 3.7798
Beyond the open door. 4.10078
Beyond the pleasure principle. 5.139
Beyond the primitive. 4.545
Beyond the ruling class. 4.4952
Beyond the single vision. 2.3526
Beyond the tragic vision. 1.444
Beyond the turning point. 4.2007
Beyond the urban fringe. 4.2829
Beyond the veil. 4.5907
Beyond the waste land. 2.10640
Beyond the welfare state. 4.4152
Beyond Top Secret Ultra. 3.1081
Beyond tragedy. 1.2232
Beyond ujamaa in Tanzania. 4.2881
Beyond vision. 5.6988
Beyond words. 4.4932
Beyong the hundredth meridian. 5.825
The Bhagavad gītā. 2.1934
The Bhagavadgītā in the Mahābhārata. 1.1686
Bhagavadgītā. Sanskrit and English. 2.1934
The Bhāgavata purāna: pt. 1-2. 2.1933
Bhartrihari: poems. 2.1943
Bhutan. 3.4333
Bhutan: a kingdom in the Himalayas. 3.4334
Bias in mental testing. 5.368
The Bible and recent archaeology. 1.2545
The Bible as literature. 8.8445
Bible, church, tradition: an Eastern Orthodox
   view. 1.3101
Bible dictionary. 1.2506
Bible. English. 1951. Authorized. 1.2526
Bible. English. 1951. Revised standard. 1.2526
Bible. English. 1966. Jerusalem Bible. 1.2499
Bible. English. American Revised. 1901.
   1.2496
Bible. English. Authorized. 1963. 1.2493
Bible. English. Authorized. 1973. 1.2491
Bible. English. Layman's parallel. 1973. 1.2491
Bible. English. Living Bible. 1973. 1.2491
Bible. English. Modern language. 1973. 1.2491
Bible. English. New English. 1970. 1.2498
Bible. English. Revised standard. 1973. 1.2491,
   1.2497
Bible. English. Selections. 1972. 4.5976
Bible. English. Smith-Goodspeed. 1939. 1.2500
Bible. English. Today's English. 1979. 1.2501

The Bible in early English literature. 1.2537
The Bible in its ancient and English versions.
   1.2511
The Bible in Middle English literature. 2.5608
The Bible in Spain. 3.3400
Bible. N.T. Acts. English. 1.2699
Bible. N.T. Apocryphal books. English. 1963.
   1.2735
Bible. N. T. Apocryphal books. Epistle of
   Barnabas. English. 1948. 1.2181
Bible. N.T. Apocryphal books. Epistle of
   Barnabus. 2.327
Bible. N.T. Colossians. English. Poehlmann &
   Karris. 1971. 1.2718
Bible. N.T. Corinthians, 1st. English. Leitch-
   MacRae. 1975. 1.2713
Bible. N.T. Corinthians, 2nd. English. Furnish.
   1984. 1.2714
Bible. N.T. English. Selections. 1967. Revised
   standard. 1.2662
Bible. N.T. Ephesians. English. Barth. 1974.
   1.2717
Bible. N.T. Epistles of John. 1973. 1.2728
Bible. N.T. Epistles of John. English. Brown.
   1982. 1.2726
Bible. N.T. Galatians. English. Betz. 1979.
   1.2716
Bible. N.T. Gospels. Anglo-Saxon. Lindisfarne
   Gospels. 1.6426
Bible. N.T. Gospels. English. 1964. Revised
   standard. 1.2683
Bible. N.T. Gospels. English. Harmonies.
   American revised. 1945. 1.2682
Bible. N.T. Gospels. Latin. Lindisfarne Gospels.
   1.6426
Bible. N.T. James. English. 1976. 1.2723
Bible. N.T. James. English. Laws. 1980.
   1.2724
Bible. N.T. John. English. 1966. Brown.
   1.2727
Bible. N.T. Luke IX. English. Fitzmyer. 1981.
   1.2692
Bible. N.T. Mark. English. 1974. 1.2689
Bible. N.T. Mark. English. Today's English.
   1970. 1.2690
Bible. N.T. Matthew. 1.2685
Bible. N.T. Pastoral Epistles. English. Koester.
   1972. 1.2720
Bible. N.T. Pastoral Epistles. English. Revised
   standard. 1976. 1.2721
Bible. N.T. Philemon. English. Poehlmann &
   Karris. 1971. 1.2718
Bible. N.T. Revelation. English. American
   revised. 1977. 1.2733
Bible. N.T. Revelation. English. Caird. 1984.
   1.2732
Bible. N.T. Revelation. English. Revised
   standard. 1979. 1.2734
Bible. N.T. Romans. English. 1975. 1.2710
Bible. N.T. Romans. English. 1980. 1.2711
Bible. N.T. Thessalonians. Best. 1972. 1.2719
Bible. O.T. Amos. English. Wolff. 1977.
   1.2618
Bible. O.T. Apocrypha. 1-2 Maccabees. English.
   New English. 1973. 1.2625
Bible. O.T. Apocrypha. Ecclesiasticus. New
   English Bible. 1974. 1.2624
Bible. O.T. Apocrypha. English. 1979. 1.2501
Bible. O.T. Apocrypha. English. New English.
   Selections. 1972. 1.2620
Bible. O.T. Apocrypha. Esdras, 1st. English.
   New English. 1979. 1.2622
Bible. O.T. Apocrypha. Esdras, 2nd English.
   New English. 1979. 1.2622
Bible. O.T. Apocrypha. Wisdom of Solomon.
   1.2623
Bible. O.T. Chronicles. English. New English.
   1976. 1.2602
Bible. O.T. Deuteronomy. English. 1966.
   Revised standard. 1.2596
Bible. O.T. English. Jewish Publication Society.
   1985. 1.2562
Bible. O.T. Exodus. English. Childs. 1974.
   1.2593
Bible. O.T. Ezekiel. English. Zimmerli. 1979.
   1.2615
Bible. O.T. Ezra. English. New English. 1976.
   1.2603

Bible. O.T. Hagiographa. English. Jewish
   Publication Society. 1982. 1.2599
Bible. O.T. Hosea. English. Wolff. 1974.
   1.2617
Bible. O.T. Isaiah I-XXXIX. English. New
   English. 1973. 1.2612
Bible. O.T. Jeremiah. English. Bright. 1964.
   1.2614
Bible. O.T. Job. English. 1985. 1.2606
Bible. O.T. Joel. English. Wolff. 1977. 1.2618
Bible. O.T. Joshua. English. 1972. 1.2597
Bible. O.T. Kings. English. 1970. 1.2601
Bible. O.T. Leviticus. English. Revised
   standard. 1965. 1.2594
Bible. O.T. Micah. English. 1976. 1.2619
Bible. O.T. Nehemiah. English. New English.
   1976. 1.2603
Bible. O.T. Numbers. English. Revised
   standard. 1968. 1.2595
Bible. O.T. Pentateuch. English. 1963. Jewish
   Publication Society. 1.2588
Bible. O.T. Psalms. English. New English. 1977.
   1.2607
Bible. O.T. Samuel. English. 1964. 1.2600
The Bible, religion, and the public schools.
   4.10745
The Bible word book. 1.2494
Biblical affirmations of woman. 1.2561
Biblical archaeologist. 1.2544
The Biblical archaeologist reader. 1.2544
Biblical archaeology. 1.2546-1.2547
Bibliografia chicana. 5.7864
Bibliografia de la literatura hispánica. 5.8025
A bibliographic guide to educational research.
   5.8148
Bibliographic guide to the two world wars.
   5.8228
Bibliographic index. 5.7681
Bibliographical essays in medieval Jewish
   studies. 5.8238
A bibliographical guide to Black studies
   programs in the United States. 5.7867
A bibliographical guide to Danish literature.
   5.8020
Bibliographical guide to Iran. 5.8072
A bibliographical guide to the history of Indian-
   white relations in the United States. 5.7743
A bibliographical guide to the study of
   Southern literature. 5.7793
Bibliographical guide to the study of the
   literature of the U.S.A. 5.7787
Bibliographical series. 3.5704
Bibliographie de la littérature française,
   1930-1939. 5.8000
Bibliographie de la littérature française,
   1940-1949. 5.8001
Bibliographie der französischen
   Literaturwissenschaft. 5.8003
Bibliographie d'histoire littéraire française.
   5.8003
Bibliographie du sport. 5.8425
Bibliographie internationale de science
   économique. 5.8374
Bibliographies for African studies, 1970-1975.
   5.8073
Bibliographies in American history, 1942-1978.
   5.7825
Bibliographies of studies in Victorian literature
   for the ten years 1945-1954 2.5709
Bibliographies of studies in Victorian literature
   for the ten years 1955-1964. 5.7945
Bibliographies of studies in Victorian literature
   for the thirteen years 1932-1944. 5.7947
Bibliographies, their aims and methods. 5.7678
Bibliographisches Handbuch der deutschen
   Literaturwissenschaft, 1945-[1972] 5.8008
Bibliography and textual criticism. 2.5508
Bibliography; current state and future trends.
   5.7683
A bibliography of Afghanistan. 5.8043
Bibliography of agriculture. 5.8092
A bibliography of American county histories.
   5.7851
A bibliography of American naval history.
   5.7844
A bibliography of antislavery in America
   5.7849
Bibliography of Asian studies. 5.8030

A bibliography of astronomy, 1970-1979. 5.8101
Bibliography of bibliographies in American literature. 5.7786
Bibliography of Black music. 1.3565
Bibliography of books and pamphlets on the history of agriculture in the United States, 1607-1967. 5.8093
Bibliography of British history. 5.7989-5.7990
Bibliography of British history, 1789-1851, issued under the direction of the American Historical Association and the Royal Historical Society of Great Britain. 5.7991
Bibliography of British history, 1851-1914. 5.7992
Bibliography of British history, Stuart period, 1603-1714. 5.7988
A bibliography of Canadian folklore in English. 5.8196
A bibliography of Canadiana. 5.7896
Bibliography of comparative literature. 5.8274
A bibliography of computer music. 1.3568
Bibliography of contemporary Spanish literature. 5.8028
A bibliography of dancing. 5.8429
A bibliography of Danish literature in English translation, 1950-1980. 5.8022
Bibliography of discographies. 1.3616
A bibliography of drug abuse, including alcohol and tobacco. 5.8381
A bibliography of early secular American music, 18th century. 1.3563
A Bibliography of English history to 1485. 5.7984
Bibliography of English language and literature 1920-22. 5.7936
Bibliography of English translations from medieval sources, 1943-1967. 5.8277
Bibliography of geography. 5.8203
Bibliography of geography, Part 1: Introduction to general aids. 5.8201
Bibliography of international law. 5.8252
A bibliography of jazz. 1.3573
Bibliography of Jewish bibliographies. 5.8237
Bibliography of Jewish music. 1.3554
A bibliography of Latin American bibliographies. 5.7903
A bibliography of Latin American bibliographies published in periodicals. 5.7904
Bibliography of literary criticism. 5.8270
Bibliography of medieval drama. 5.8135
Bibliography of Mexican American history. 5.7863
A bibliography of modern history. 5.8227
A bibliography of modern prosody. 5.7974
A bibliography of North American folklore and folksong. 5.8197
Bibliography of place-name literature. 5.8299
A bibliography of publications on Old English literature to the end of 1972. 5.7942
A bibliography of studies on Hindi language and linguistics. 5.8340
Bibliography of the American theatre, excluding New York City. 5.7805
Bibliography of the continental reformation: materials available in English. 5.8447
Bibliography of the Eddas. 2.13972-2.13973
A bibliography of the English printed drama to the restoration. 5.7953
Bibliography of the history of technology. 5.8457
Bibliography of the peoples and cultures of mainland Southeast Asia. 5.8032
Bibliography of the philosophy in the Iberian colonies of America. 5.8348
A bibliography of theatre technology. 5.8146
A bibliography of United States-Latin American relations since 1810. 5.8261
Bibliography of western writings on Chinese art and archaeology. 5.8192
A bibliography of works on Canadian foreign relations. 5.8259
A bibliography on herbs, herbal medicine, 'natural' foods, and unconventional medical treatment. 5.8288
Bibliography on Holocaust literature. 5.8248

Bibliography on scheduled castes and scheduled tribes. 5.8056
Bibliotheca americana. 5.7746
Bibliotheca Americana. 5.7730
Bicycle road racing. 4.1046
Bicycle transportation. 4.4044
Bicycles and tricycles. 5.6639
Bid me to live. 2.11569
'Bid the sickness cease' 5.4546
Bid time return. 2.13171
Bidwell's guide to government ministers. 4.7722
Big band jazz. 1.4195
The big bands. 1.4271
Big business. 4.3008
Big business and the policy of competition. 4.1982
The big change: America transforms itself, 1900-1950. 3.6070
Big city boss in depression and war. 3.8415
Big-city police. 4.6819
The big clock. 2.11711
Big Cypress: a changing Seminole community. 3.5946
The Big Eight. 4.4390
Big enterprise in a competitive system. 4.1988
Big game of North America. 5.3982
The big knife. 2.12257
The big knockover. 2.11809
Big money. 2.11586
Big road blues. 1.4274
The big rock candy mountain. 2.12504
The big sea. 2.11899
The big sky. 2.11802
Big structures, large processes, huge comparisons. 4.4824
The big two. 3.6488
The Bījak of Kabir. 2.1885
Biko. 3.5471
Bilan hydrique mondial. 4.296
Bilan littéraire du XXe siècle. 2.3913
A Bilateral bicentennial. 3.6474
Bildungswesen in der Bundesrepublik Deutschland. English. 4.10741
The bilingual brain. 5.4795
Bilingual education. 4.10890
Bilingual schooling in the United States. 4.10891, 4.10895
Bilingualism and bilingual education. 2.113
Bilingualism, social issues and policy implications. 2.112
Bill Haywood's book. 4.3586
The Bill James historical baseball abstract. 4.1000
The Bill of rights. 4.9669
The Bill of Rights: a documentary history. 4.9654
The Bill of rights and what it means today. 4.9667
Bill of Rights reader. 4.9656
Billard um Halbzehn. 2.13686
Billers, banners, and bombast. 4.4441
Billiards at half-past nine. 2.13687
Billy Budd. 2.11151
Billy Budd, sailor. 2.11150
Billy Graham, a parable of American righteousness. 1.3041
Billy Graham, evangelist to the world. 1.3042
Billy Mitchell. 5.7403
Billy the Kid, a bio-bibliography. 3.8558
Bingo & The sea. 2.9622
Bio-bibliographical index of musicians in the United States of America since colonial times. 1.3542
The bio-medical fix. 5.4650
Bioacoustics, a comparative approach. 5.4366
A biobibliography of native American writers, 1772-1924. 5.7742
Biochemical adaptation. 5.4205
The biochemical basis of neuropharmacology. 5.4301
Biochemical engineering. 5.6867
Biochemical frontiers in medicine. 5.4743
Biochemistry. 5.3333, 5.3335, 5.4398, 5.4401
The biochemistry and physiology of bone. 5.4220
Biochemistry and physiology of plant hormones. 5.3746

Biochemistry and physiology of protozoa. 5.3838
Biochemistry of cell differentiation. 5.4390
The biochemistry of cytodifferentiation. 5.3618
The biochemistry of development. 5.4134
Biochemistry of exercise. 5.4266
Biochemistry of nonheme iron. 5.4402
Biochemistry of photosynthesis. 5.3760
The Biochemistry of plants. 5.3750
Biochemistry of the amino acids. 5.4424
The biochemistry of the nucleic acids. 5.4417
The biochemistry of viruses. 5.4476
Biocultural aspects of disease. 5.4683
Bioelectric phenomena. 5.4288
Bioenergetics. 5.3506
Bioethics. 5.3329
Biofeedback. 5.8416
Biogeography. 5.3237-5.3238, 5.3241, 5.3768
Biographic dictionary of Chinese communism, 1921-1965. 3.4811
The Biographic register. 4.7988
Biographical books, 1876-1980. 5.8107
Biographical dictionaries and related works. 5.8109
A biographical dictionary of actors, actresses, musicians, dancers, managers & other stage personnel in London, 1660-1800. 2.3333
Biographical dictionary of Afro-American and African musicians. 1.3537
Biographical dictionary of American science. 5.809
A biographical dictionary of British architects, 1600-1840. 1.5378
Biographical dictionary of dance. 4.1125
Biographical dictionary of Japanese history. 3.4905
Biographical dictionary of Japanese literature. 2.1997
Biographical dictionary of jazz. 1.3530
Biographical dictionary of musicians. 1.3529
Biographical dictionary of psychology. 5.93
Biographical dictionary of Republican China. 3.4810
The Biographical dictionary of scientists. Astronomers. 5.1690
The Biographical dictionary of scientists. Physicists. 5.1942
Biographical dictionary of the Confederacy. 3.7314
Biographical dictionary of World War I. 3.769
Biographical directory of American colonial and Revolutionary governors, 1607-1789. 3.6861
Biographical directory of American territorial governors. 3.6295
Biographical directory of the American Congress, 1774-1971. 4.7991
Biographical directory of the governors of the United States, 1789-1978. 3.6285
The biographical encyclopaedia & who's who of the American theatre. 2.3237
Biographical encyclopedia of science and technology. 5.807
Biographical memoirs. 5.811
Biographical register of the Confederate Congress. 4.8268
Biographical sketches of Loyalists of the American Revolution. 3.6959
Biographical truth. 2.5639
Biography. 2.11347, 3.313
Biography and genealogy master index. 5.8112
Biography index. 5.8106
Biography news. 3.327
The biography of a river town: Memphis. 3.8352
The Biography of an institution. 4.8288
A biography of philosophy. 1.132
Biography: the craft and the calling. 3.311
Biological abstracts. 5.3289
Biological and agricultural index. 5.8091
The Biological aspects of rare plant conservation. 5.3645
The biological basis of human freedom. 4.4892
The biological basis of personality. 5.546
Biological education in American secondary schools, 1890-1960. 5.3307
Biological effects of radiation. 5.3627
Biological foundations of language. 2.155
Biological foundations of psychiatry. 5.4782

Biological nomenclature. 5.3233
Biological politics. 4.5846
Biological process design for wastewater treatment. 5.6031
Biological rhythms and medicine. 5.4213
Biological spectroscopy. 5.3317
The biologist's handbook of pronunciations. 5.3184
The Biology and management of lobsters. 5.3851
Biology as inquiry. 5.3308
Biology in the nineteenth century. 5.3297
The Biology of aging. 5.4215
The biology of alcoholism. 5.4959
Biology of amphibians. 5.3930
Biology of animals. 5.3801
Biology of aphids. 5.3877
The Biology of butterflies. 5.3879
The biology of cell reproduction. 5.3614
The biology of centipedes. 5.3853
Biology of communication. 5.4096
Biology of earthworms. 5.3840
The biology of estuaries and coastal waters. 5.3253
The biology of estuarine animals. 5.3824
Biology of fertilization. 5.3484
Biology of fishes. 5.3895
The biology of free-living nematodes. 5.3842
Biology of lichenized fungi. 5.3716
The biology of lichens. 5.3714
Biology of microorganisms. 5.4435
The biology of mosses. 5.3704
The Biology of mutualism. 5.3584
The biology of nitrogen-fixing organisms. 5.4456
The biology of peace and war. 5.421
The biology of people. 5.4195
Biology of plants. 5.3642
The biology of populations. 5.4073
Biology of sewage treatment and water pollution control. 5.6032
The biology of the amphibia. 5.3933
Biology of the cell. 5.3605
Biology of the fungi, their development, regulation, and associations. 5.3722
Biology of the plant rusts. 5.5403
Biology of the reptilia. 5.3918
The biology of trematodes. 5.3844
Biology of women. 5.5047
Biology teachers' handbook. 5.3305
Biomaterials. 5.3499
Biomechanics. 5.4274
Biomechanics of women's gymnastics. 4.922
Biometrical genetics. 5.3453
Biometry. 5.3312
Bioorganic mechanisms. 5.4409
Biophysical aerodynamics and the natural environment. 5.4283
Biophysical chemistry. 5.3334
Biophysical science. 5.3492
Biostratigraphy. 5.3130
Biotechnical slope protection and erosion control. 5.5897
Biotechnology. 5.4442, 5.6865
The biotic provinces of North America. 5.3261
Biracial politics. 3.8334
Bird. 1.4085
Bird in the bush. 2.12379
A bird in the house. 2.9937
Bird migration. 5.3971
Bird navigation. 5.3970
Bird sounds. 5.3969
Bird vocalisations. 5.3968
The birds fall down. 2.9511
Birds of America. 5.3950
Birds of North America. 5.3952, 5.3956
Birds of passage. 4.3314
Birds of the ocean. 5.3936
Birds of the world. 5.3937
Birdy. 2.13422
Birth. 2.11764
The birth and death of the sun. 5.1698
The birth and development of the geological sciences. 5.2947
Birth and fortune. 4.1672
The birth and rebirth of pictorial space. 1.5822
Birth control and controlling birth. 5.5051
Birth control and foreign policy. 4.5679

Birth control and the population question in England, 1877-1930. 4.5687
The birth control book. 5.5053
Birth control technologies. 5.5054
The birth of a consumer society. 4.2295
The birth of a dilemma. 3.5507
The birth of a grandfather. 2.12442
The birth of a new Europe. 4.2198
The birth of a new physics. 5.2026
The birth of a plural society. 3.5516
The birth of China. 3.4649
The birth of civilization in the Near East. 4.740
The birth of Europe. 3.93
The birth of Indian civilization. 3.4188
The birth of mass political parties, Michigan, 1827-1861. 4.8192
The birth of modern America, 1820-1850. 3.6037
The birth of purgatory. 1.2946
The birth of Saudi Arabia. 3.4055
The birth of the Bill of Rights, 1776-1791. 4.7831
The birth of the Christian religion (La naissance du christianisme) and The origins of the New Testament. 1.2299
Birth of the Communist manifesto. 4.7074
The birth of the Irish Free State, 1921-1923. 3.1861
The birth of the Republic, 1763-89. 3.6902
The birth of the talkies. 2.2976
The birth of tragedy. 1.1047
The birth of Vietnam. 3.4464
The birth of western Canada. 3.8856
The birth of Western economy. 4.1742
The birth primer. 5.5063
The birth project. 1.4893
The birthday king. 2.8414
Bishop Heber in northern India. 3.4163
The Bishop of Broadway. 2.3245
The Bishop's bonfire. 2.9148
Bismarck. 3.2161, 3.2311, 3.2315-3.2316
Bismarck and British colonial policy. 3.5435
Bismarck and Germany, 1862-1890. 3.2325
Bismarck and the development of Germany. 3.2313-3.2314
Bismarck and the German Empire. 3.2312
Bismarck, Gladstone, and the Concert of Europe. 3.721
Bismarck; some secret pages of his history. 3.2310
Bismarcks Ringen um Deutschlands Gestaltung. 3.2309
A bit of singing and dancing. 2.9706
A bit of the map, and other stories. 2.9535
Biting off the bracelet. 5.5086
Bits of ivory. 2.7378
The Bitter air of exile. 2.1296
Bitter glory. 3.3338
Bitter herbs. 3.1118
Bitter lemons. 3.3696
Bitter sugar. 4.3103
Bitter wages: Ralph Nader's study group report on disease and injury on the job. 5.5021
The bitter woods. 3.957
The bitter years. 3.1058
Bix: man & legend. 1.4081
The Black abolitionist papers. 3.7233
Black abolitionists. 3.7258
Black access. 5.7875
The Black aesthetic. 1.6713
Black African literature in English. 5.8077
Black America. 3.6608
Black American literature. 2.10817
Black American literature essays. 2.10817
The Black American writer. 2.10310
Black American writers past and present. 5.7800
Black Americans and the evangelization of Africa, 1877-1900. 1.3031
Black Americans and the political system. 3.6662
Black Americans in autobiography. 5.7866
Black Americans in the Roosevelt era. 3.6654
Black Americans in World War II. 3.1126
Black and conservative. 2.3632
Black and white identity formation. 5.599

Black and white power subreption. 3.6630
Black and white styles in conflict. 3.6707
Black April. 2.12312
Black artists in the United States. 5.8189
Black artists of the new generation. 1.4911
Black artists on art. 1.4915
Black athletes in the United States. 5.8430
Black ballots. 4.8094
Black Bolshevik. 4.6999
Black bondage in the North. 3.7192
The Black book. 3.3996
The black book. 2.8608
Black Bostonians. 3.8000
Black bourgeoisie. 3.6667
Black boy. 2.12816
Black Britannia. 3.1295
Black British, white British. 3.1290
Black business enterprise. 3.6730
Black business in the New South. 4.4641
Black capitalism. 3.6733
Black Chicago. 3.8426
Black children. 4.10851
Black colleges in America. 4.10855
The Black composer speaks. 1.3754
Black consciousness, identity, and achievement. 4.10856
The Black Corps. 3.2428
Black crusader. 3.6857
Black culture and black consciousness. 4.771
Black dance in the United States from 1619 to 1970. 4.1107
The Black Death. 5.4765
Black death to Industrial Revolution. 4.2261
Black Detroit and the rise of the UAW. 3.8439
Black dialects & reading. 4.10854
Black drama. 2.10515
Black drama anthology. 2.10786
Black Easter; The day after judgment. 2.11391
Black education: myths and tragedies. 4.10859
Black elected officials. 3.6710, 4.8091
Black Elk speaks. 3.5789
Black empowerment. 4.6618
Black English. 2.1153, 2.1157
The black extended family. 3.6771
Black families in white America. 3.6750
The Black family and the Black woman. 5.7873
The Black family in slavery and freedom, 1750-1925. 3.6764
The Black family in the United States. 5.7868
Black feminist criticism. 2.10317
Black fiction. 2.10560
Black film as genre. 2.2997
Black fire. 2.10687
Black folk art in America, 1930-1980. 1.4916
Black foremothers. 3.6814
Black genealogy. 3.294
Black gods and kings. 1.5090
Black God's shadow. 2.13181
Black hands on a white face. 2.10843
Black heritage in social welfare, 1860-1930. 4.6617
Black history. 3.6613
Black holes and warped spacetime. 5.1843
Black holes in space. 5.1844
Black holes, quasars, and the universe. 5.1846
Black holes, white dwarfs, and neutron stars. 5.1845
The black homelands of South Africa. 4.8795
Black humor. 2.13018
The Black image in the white mind. 3.6618
Black images in the American theatre. 2.2779
Black immigration and ethnicity in the United States. 5.7865
Black into white. 3.9224
Black is the color of the cosmos. 2.10358
Black Jack Davey. 2.12300
The Black Jacobins. 3.9119
Black-Jewish relations in the United States, 1752-1984. 5.7869
Black journals of the United States. 2.3642
Black lamb and grey falcon. 3.3561
Black leaders of the twentieth century. 3.6809
Black lesbians. 4.5524
Black liberation & socialism. 3.6714
Black life in corporate America. 4.4339
Black lightning. 2.9996

Black literature and literary theory. 2.10311
Black literature in America. 2.10686
Black literature in white America. 2.10328
Black Mafia; ethnic succession in organized crime. 4.6779
Black magic. 2.12867
Black majority. 3.7219
The Black male in America. 3.6716
The Black man. 3.6640
The black man. 3.6811
The Black man in slavery and freedom in colonial Brazil. 3.9227
Black managers. 4.4527
Black Manhattan. 3.8055
Black marriage and family therapy. 3.6751
Black masculinity. 3.6775
Black mask. 2.10824
The black maskers. 2.1467
Black masks. 2.10562
Black mathematicians and their works. 5.1087
Black men. 3.6752
The black Messiah. 3.6729
Black messiahs and Uncle Toms. 3.6720
Black metropolis. 3.8423
Black migration in America. 3.6765
The Black military experience. 3.7385
Black Milwaukee. 4.3609
The Black mind: O. R. Dathorne. 2.2296
Black mischief. 2.9485
Black Moses. 3.6835
Black mother. 3.5226
Black music, four lives. 1.3759
Black music in the United States. 1.3566
The Black Muslims in America. 3.6673
Black narcissus. 2.8687
Black nationalism. 3.6666
Black New Orleans, 1860-1880. 3.8318
Black odyssey. 3.7191
Black Ohio and the color line, 1860-1915. 3.6804
Black over white. 3.6805
The Black panther. 3.6699
The Black Panther leaders speak. 3.6699
Black parties and political power. 4.8096
Black Pentecostalism. 1.3388
Black photographers, 1840-1940. 5.6927
Black poets in South Africa. 2.10052
Black poets of the United States. 2.10332
Black political development. 3.6703
Black political life in the United States. 3.6669
Black political parties. 4.8169
A Black political theology. 1.2781
Black politics in New York City. 3.8056
Black politics in Philadelphia. 3.8091
Black power. 1.2916, 3.6701
Black power in South Africa. 3.5459
Black power/white control. 4.5207
Black preaching. 1.3046
The Black presence. 1.1296
The Black presence in the era of the American Revolution, 1770-1800. 3.6813
The Black press, U.S.A. 2.3650
The black prince. 2.9750
The black prince, and other stories. 2.13054
Black protest; issues and tactics. 3.7235
Black rage. 3.6717
Black rain. 2.2097
Black reconstruction in America. 3.7462
Black religion. 1.2423
Black religion and American evangelicalism. 1.2421
Black religion and Black radicalism. 1.2425
Black religions in the new world. 1.1865
The black republic. 3.9113
Black response to the American left: 1917-1929. 3.6657
Black rhetoric. 5.7872
Black rose. 2.1914
Black Shakespearean actors. 2.6868
Black short story anthology. 2.10815
Black sister. 2.10748
Black slavery in the Americas. 5.8390
Black socialist preacher. 4.7140
Black sociologists. 4.4772
Black southerners, 1619-1869. 3.7186
Black star. 3.5343
Black street speech. 2.1156
Black struggle for freedom in America. 3.6704

Black students in higher education. 4.10860
Black studies 3.6603
Black suburbanization. 3.6787
The black swan. 2.13826
Black Tennesseans, 1900-1930. 3.6807
Black theater. 2.10788
Black theater, U.S.A.; forty-five plays by Black Americans, 1847-1974. 2.10785
Black theology. 1.2796
Black theology and black power. 1.2916
A Black theology of liberation. 1.2786, 1.2797
Black thunder. 2.11394
The black tower. 2.9721
The Black towns. 3.6649
The Black underclass. 3.6763
The black unicorn. 2.13140
The black urban condition. 3.6620
Black violence. 4.6724
Black voices. 2.10691
Black/white/green/red. 4.10894
Black-white racial attitudes. 5.7876
The Black woman. 3.6753
The Black woman cross-culturally. 4.6152
The Black woman in America: sex, marriage, and the family. 3.6776
Black women in white America. 3.6768
Black women novelists. 2.10559
Black women writers (1950-1980) 2.10312
Black women writers at work. 2.10313
The Black worker. 3.6731
Black workers and the new unions. 3.6732
Black workers in white unions. 4.9563
Black writers in French. 2.4802
Black writers of the thirties. 2.10334
The Black years of Soviet Jewry, 1939-1953. 3.3997
Blackberry winter; my earlier years. 4.424
The blacker the berry ... 2.12591
The Blackfeet; raiders on the Northwestern Plains. 3.5950
Blacking up. 1.4222
Blackness and the adventure of Western culture. 2.10324
The blacks. 2.4537
Black's agricultural dictionary. 5.5221
Blacks and criminal justice. 4.6816
Blacks and social justice. 3.6700
Blacks and the military in American history. 3.6725
Blacks and whites. 3.6734
The Blacks in Canada. 3.8797
Blacks in Gold Rush California. 3.6796
Blacks in Mexico, 1570-1650. 4.6428
Blacks in suburbs, a national perspective. 3.6784
Blacks in the American armed forces, 1776-1983. 5.7841
Blacks in the Army Air Forces during World War II. 3.1129
Blacks in the city. 3.6647
Blacks in the military. 5.7375
Blacks in the United States Armed Forces. 3.6723
Blacks in the West. 3.6794
Black's Law dictionary. 4.9443
Black's medical dictionary. 5.4491
Blacks, medical schools, and society. 5.4543
Blacks on John Brown. 3.7274
Black's veterinary dictionary. 5.5460
Blaise Cendrars. 2.4463
Blaise Pascal. 1.807
Blake in context. 1.6026
Blake, prophet against empire. 2.7425
Blake studies. 1.4948
Blake's apocalypse. 2.7424
Blake's humanism. 2.7436
Blake's Innocence and Experience. 2.7409
Blake's poetry and designs. 2.7405
Blake's visionary universe. 2.7423
Blakiston's Gould medical dictionary. 5.4484
Blam! the explosion of pop, minimalism, and performance, 1958-1964. 1.6708
Blaming the victim. 4.5188
Blanche of Castile. 3.1996
Blasons anatomiques du corps féminin. Selections. 1983. 2.3928
The Blaue Reiter almanac. 1.4811
BLC to 1975. 5.7670

Blé de semences. 2.4776
Bleak house. 2.7628
Die Blechtrommel. 2.13754
The blending of races: marginality and identity in world perspective. 4.6458
Die Blendung. 2.13717
Blenheim. 3.1537
Blessed rage for order, the new pluralism in theology. 1.2759
The blessing. 2.9116
The blessing way. 2.13087
Blessingway. 3.5927
Blind ambition. 3.7919
Blind date. 2.13119
The blind musician. 2.1514
Blind voices. 2.13292
Blindenschrift. 2.13737
Blindness. 2.8731
Blithe spirit. 2.8582
The Blithedale romance. 2.11058
The blitzkrieg era and the German General Staff, 1865-1941. 5.7317
Block diagrams and other graphic methods used in geology and geography. 4.217
Blood groups in man. 5.4225
Blood in my eye. 3.6705
Blood is their argument. 3.5660
The blood knot. 2.10065
Blood of my blood. 3.6557
Blood of Spain. 3.3465
The blood of the Bambergs. 2.9212
The blood of the lamb. 2.11561
The blood oranges. 2.13069
Blood, toil, tears and sweat. 3.927
Bloodhounds of heaven. 2.6012
The bloodless revolution. 3.1496
Bloodline. 2.13025
Bloods, an oral history of the Vietnam War. 3.4508
The bloody chamber. 2.9652
Bloody murder. 2.3475
The Bloomsbury group. 2.5733, 3.1747
Blow-up, and other stories. 2.5380
The Blue and Brown books. 1.1076
The Blue and the Gray. 3.7311
The Blue Berets. 4.9253
The blue bird; and, The betrothal. 2.4605
The blue-coated worker. 4.6836
Blue collar community. 4.3531
Blue-collar marriage. 4.5644
Blue-collar women. 4.3295
Blue-collar workers in Eastern Europe. 4.3629
Blue dragon, white tiger. 2.13360
Blue Juniata. 2.11510
The blue lantern. 2.4493
The Blue Nile. 3.5171
Blue plate special. 2.12421
Blue voyage. 2.11300
Bluegrass breakdown. 1.4272
The Bluejackets' manual. [1st]- ed.; 1902-. 5.7424
Blueprint for medical care. 5.4617
Blues. 1.4295
Blues for Mister Charlie. 2.12857
Blues, ideology, and Afro-American literature. 2.10307
Blues people. 1.4301
Blues who's who. 1.3511
The bluesmen. 1.4312
The bluest eye. 2.13183
The blush, and other stories. 2.9394
The boat of longing. 2.14057
Boatman of the Padma. 2.1858
Boccaccio. 2.4912
Bodies & soul. 1.4267
Bodily changes in pain, hunger, fear and rage. 5.4347
The Bodley Head Ford Madox Ford. 2.8629
The Bodley Head Jack London. 2.12019
The Bodley Head Leacock. 2.9946
The Bodley Head Scott Fitzgerald. 2.11720
The Body at work. 5.4262
Body consciousness. 5.494
Body movement. 5.254
The body of faith. 1.1972
Bodyguard of lies 3.1133
The Boer War. 3.5505
Boesman and Lena and other plays. 2.10064

Boethius, the consolations of music, logic, theology, and philosophy. 1.337
Boethius's De topicis differentiis. 1.336
The bog people. 4.714
Bohemia in the eighteenth century. 3.1915
The Bohemian Grove and other retreats. 4.6178
Bohemian lights. 2.5291
Bohuslav Martinů. 1.3922
Boileau and the nature of neo-classicism. 2.4013
A bold stroke for a wife. 2.6931
Bolingbroke and his circle. 3.1546
Bolívar and the political thought of the Spanish American Revolution. 3.9164
Bolívar and the war of independence. 3.9165
Bolivia. 3.9271, 3.9273
Bolivia, the evolution of a multi-ethnic society. 3.9274
Bolivia: the uncompleted revolution. 3.9278
Bolshevik feminist. 4.6128
The Bolshevik revolution, 1917-1918. 3.3175
The Bolshevik tradition. 3.3223
The Bolsheviks. 3.3139
The Bolsheviks come to power. 3.3202
The Bolshoi Ballet. 4.1167
The bomber offensive. 3.1046
Le bon usage. 2.866
The Bonanza West. 3.8457
Bonaventure. 1.3134
Bond, a study of his plays. 2.9624
Bondage of the will. 1.1497
The Bonds. 3.6817
The bonds of wickedness. 1.2477
The bonds of womanhood. 4.6007
The bone people. 2.10226
Bones for the archaeologist. 3.247
Bones of contention. 3.1183
Bonheur d'occasion. 2.4820
Bonheur d'occasion. English. 2.4821
Bonjour tristesse 2.4682
Bonsai. 5.5359
Book finder. 5.8361
The book in America. 5.7587
Book marketing handbook. 5.7575
The book named The governor. 4.7556
The book of Abigail and John. 3.7051
The book of American Negro poetry. 2.10754
Book of American Negro spirituals. 1.3439
The book of architecture. 1.5470
Book of ballads. 2.6109
The Book of calendars. 3.271
The book of Canadian poetry. 2.9899
The book of change. 1.1800
Book of changes. 1.1795, 2.2181
A book of common prayer. 2.12983
The Book of Concord. 1.3363
The book of costume. 4.832
A book of curves. 5.1573
The Book of Daniel. 1.2616, 2.12988
A book of Danish ballads. 2.14000
The book of Dede Korkut. 2.1984
Book of enlightenment. 1.1949
The book of Exodus. 1.2593
The book of fire, stories. 2.1810
The book of flags. 3.286
The book of good counsels. 2.1940
The book of government. 4.7324
The book of hours. 1.6427
The book of Irish verse. 2.9865
The book of jazz, from then till now. 1.4322
The Book of Job. 1.2606
The book of laughter and forgetting. 2.1690
Book of lieder. 2.13518
The book of Lieh-tzŭ. 1.1804
The book of life. 5.687
A book of London English, 1384-1425. 2.1115
The book of Lord Shang. 4.7330
The book of Margery Kempe. 2.6389
The Book of Mormon. 1.3379
Book of Mormon. 1.3379
The book of Negro folklore. 4.769
The book of old silver. 1.6662
The book of paradise. 2.1807
Book of poetry for children. 2.10739
The book of pottery and porcelain. 1.6610
The book of questions. 2.4585
A book of religious verse. 2.6116

The Book of Revelation. 1.2733
The Book of shooting for sport and skill. 4.1059
The book of snobs. 2.8184
The book of songs. 2.2182
A Book of South African verse. 2.10049
The book of tea. 4.865
A book of the Basques. 3.2218
The Book of the cat. 5.5455
The book of the courtier. 1.1513
Book of the dance. 4.1113
The Book of the dead. 2.1764
Book of the dead. 2.1764
The Book of the goddess, past and present. 1.1617
The Book of the piano. 1.4147
The book of the prophet Isaiah, chapters 1-39. 1.2612
The Book of the States. 4.8242
Book of the three virtues. 1.1515
The book of Troilus and Criseyde. 2.6335
The book of whales. 5.4004
The book of wisdom. 1.2086
A Book of women poets from antiquity to now. 2.3748
The book of world-famous music. 1.3550
Book publishing. 5.7568-5.7569
The book publishing annual. 5.7594
The Book review digest. 5.7763
Book review index. 5.7706
The book, the ring, & the poet. 2.7484
The book trade of the world. 5.7571
Bookbinding in America. 5.7567
Booker T. Washington. 3.6855-3.6856
The Booker T. Washington papers. 3.6853
The bookfinder. 5.8361
Booklist and subscription books bulletin. 5.7714
Booklist (Chicago, Ill.: 1969) 5.7714
Bookmaking. 5.7536
The Bookman's glossary. 5.7539
Bookman's manual 1921-41, 1958. 5.7707
Bookman's price index. 5.7674
Books. 5.7584
Books and book people in 19th-century America. 5.7589
The books at the wake. 2.8869
Books before five. 2.2705
Books for the millions. 5.7565
Books in general. 2.2651
The books in my life. 2.12187
Books in print. 5.7755-5.7757, 5.7764
Books in print (New York) 5.7756
Books in series in the United States. 5.7749
The Books of American Negro spirituals. 1.3439
The books of Ezra and Nehemiah. 1.2603
Books of the brave. 3.8995
The bookshop. 2.9677
The booster and the snitch. 4.6753
Booth Tarkington. 2.11242-2.11243
Boranes in organic chemistry. 5.2710
Borden. 3.8739
Borderline conditions and pathological narcissism. 5.4925
Borges. 2.5377
Borges, a reader. 2.5375
Boris Godunov. 3.3088
Boris Godunov, Tsar of Russia. 3.3089
Boris Pasternak, his life and art. 2.1597
Born in exile. 2.7730
Born of the people. 3.4606
Born on the Fourth of July. 3.4510
Born under Saturn. 1.4625
Born yesterday. 2.11941
Borodino and the War of 1812. 3.2137
Borromini. 1.5438
Borromini and the Roman oratory. 1.5534
Borstal boy. 2.8443
The Borzoi anthology of Latin American literature. 5.5323
The Borzoi book of modern dance. 4.1126
Bosnian chronicle. 2.1208
The boss and the machine. 4.8161
The bosses. 3.6390
The bosses. 3.7620
Bosses, machines, and urban voters. 4.8838
Boston. 2.12477, 3.7992

Boston adventure. 2.12498
Boston capitalists and western railroads. 4.3995
Boston, the Great Depression, and the New Deal. 3.7995
Boston's immigrants [1790-1880] 3.7996
The Boswellian hero. 2.6907
Boswell's column. 2.6902
Boswell's political career. 2.6905
Botanical histochemistry. 5.3752
Botanical Latin. 5.3632
Botany in the United States. 5.3636
Both ends of the avenue. 4.7970
Both your houses. 2.11312
The bottle factory outing. 2.9615
Bottled energy. 5.6325
Bottom dogs. 2.11547
Bougainville. 3.5676
The Boulanger affair. 3.2181
Boule de suif. 2.4267
Boulez on music today. 1.3667
The boundaries of eros. 4.5520
The boundaries of the Canadian Confederation. 3.8694
Boundaries, possessions, and conflicts in Central and North America and the Caribbean. 3.9055
The boundary hunters. 3.8649
Boundary layer climates. 5.2570
Boundary-making. 4.9308
The boundless resource. 4.10835
The bounds of sense. 1.887
Bounds out of bounds. 2.10487
Bourbon democracy of the Middle West, 1865-1896. 3.8305
The Bourbon kings of France. 3.1971
Les bourgeois de la compagnie du Nord-Ouest. 3.8845
The bourgeoisie in 18th century France. 4.6400
Bournonville and ballet technique. 4.1178
Les bouts de bois de Dieu: Banty Mam Yall. 2.4858
Bouvard and Pecuchet. 2.4184
Bovard of the Post-dispatch. 2.3606
The bowels of the earth. 5.3079
Bowes and Church's Food values of portions commonly used. 5.7123
The Bowker annual of library and book trade information. 5.7659
Box. 2.12841
Box and Quotations from Chairman Mao Tse-tung. 2.12841
The box man. 2.2124
Box man. 4.6702
The box of daylight. 3.5751
A box of lives. 2.1668
The Boxer catastrophe. 3.4743
The Boxer Uprising, a background study. 3.4738
The boy from Winnipeg. 3.342
Boy in darkness. 2.8705
The boy in the bush. 2.8963
Boys & girls. 4.10412
Boys and girls. 4.10412
The boys in the barracks. 5.7243
The boys of summer. 4.1006
Boys together. 4.10837
BPI v. 1-3. 5.7674
BPR cumulative 1981-1984. 5.7729
The braggart in Renaissance comedy. 2.2788
Brahmanas. Śatapathabrāhmana. English. 1.1690
The Brahmo Samaj and the shaping of the modern Indian mind. 3.4198
Brahms. 1.3822
Brahms, his life and work. 1.3821
The Brain. 5.4329
Brain biochemistry. 5.4328
Brain death. 4.718
Brain mechanisms and intelligence. 5.224
Brain systems and psychological concepts. 5.4304
The Brains Trust. 3.7749
The bramble bush. 4.9473
Brancusi. 1.5743
Brandeis. 4.9804
The Brandeis/Frankfurter connection. 4.9798

Brandung. 2.13911
The Brannan plan. 4.2939
The Brantwood diary of John Ruskin. 2.8027
Branwell Brontë. 2.7461
Branwen ferch Llŷr. 2.13413
Braque. 1.6067
The brass butterfly. 2.8693
Brass instruments. 1.4165
Brass Valley. 4.3738
Brassaï. 5.6964
The brave bulls. 2.11992
Brave new world. 2.8817
Brave new world revisited. 4.4970
Braving the elements. 2.12139
Brazil. 4.2172
Brazil, a country study. 3.9187
Brazil, a political analysis. 3.9216
Brazil, an expanding economy. 4.2173
Brazil builds. 1.5353
Brazil, from colony to world power. 3.9204
Brazil in transition. 3.9219
Brazil; people and institutions. 4.5269
Brazil: people and institutions. 3.9188
Brazil: politics in a patrimonial society. 3.9218
Brazil: the land and people. 3.9203
The Brazilian-American alliance, 1937-1945. 3.943
Brazilian cinema. 2.2885
The Brazilian corporative state and working-class politics. 4.8339
The Brazilian cotton manufacture. 4.3855
Brazilian culture. 3.9189
Brazilian literature. 2.5466
The Brazilian monarchy and the South American republics, 1822-1831. 3.9212
The Brazilian peasantry. 4.2839
Brazil's state-owned enterprises. 4.3087
Breach of faith. 3.7924
Bread & circuses. 4.5002
Bread and circuses. 4.5002
Bread and wine. 2.5071
The bread of those early years. 2.13689
Break of noon. 2.4472
The break-up of Britain. 4.8430
The break-up of the Habsburg Empire, 1914-1918. 3.1900
The break-up of the Soviet Empire in Eastern Europe. 3.3533
Breakfast at Tiffany's. 2.11463
Breakfast of champions. 2.13389
Breaking and entering. 4.6805
Breaking bread. 1.3117
Breaking new ground. 3.7443
The breaking of the circle. 2.5804
Breaking the access barriers. 4.10565
Breaking the land. 4.3686
Breaking the mould? 4.8555
The breaking wave. 3.959
Breaklight: the poetry of the Caribbean. 2.9983
Breakthrough. 2.10680
Breakthrough fictioneers. 2.3703
Breakthrough, Meister Eckhart's creation spirituality, in new translation. 1.3086
The breast of the Earth. 2.2295
Breathings. 2.4782
Brecht. 2.13706, 2.13709
Brecht on theatre. 2.3083
The Brechtian aspect of radical cinema. 2.2989
Breckinridge. 3.6982
Breeding and improvement of farm animals. 5.5441
Bret Harte, argonaut and exile. 2.11055
Brett Weston, photographs from five decades. 5.6978
Bretton Woods. 4.4462
Brett's History of psychology. 5.70
Breve historia de la literatura española. 2.5087
Breve historia de la literatura hispanoamericana. 2.5305
Brewer's Dictionary of phrase and fable. 2.2350
Brewster and Wheatstone on vision. 5.4376
Brian Moore. 2.9951
Bribery and extortion in world business. 4.6760
The bridal canopy. 2.1779
Bride of Acacias. 2.1977
The bride of Messina. 2.13647

The bride of the Innisfallen, and other stories. 2.12659
Bride of the revolution. 3.3142
Brideshead revisited: the sacred and profane memories of Captain Charles Ryder. 2.9484
The bridge and the abyss. 2.1512
Bridge complete. 4.1067
The bridge of San Luis Rey. 2.12714
The bridge on the Drina. 2.1210
A bridge too far. 3.983
Bridges and their builders. 5.6077
The bridges at Toko-ri. 2.12152
A brief guide to sources of metals information. 5.6766
A brief history of Chinese fiction. 2.2171
A brief history of student teaching. 4.10537
A brief life. 2.5439
Briefe. 2.13834
Briefe an Goethe. 2.13573
Briefe. English. 1.3795
Briefing for a descent into Hell. 2.9011
Brigham Young. 1.3384
Bright book of life. 2.10630
Bright Eyes. 3.5932
The bright lights. 2.3264
Bright particular star. 2.3252
The bright star catalogue. 5.1847
A brighter sun, a novel. 2.10016
Brighter than a thousand suns. 5.2418
Brighton rock. 2.8741
Bright's Old English grammar & reader. 2.939
Brillouin zones and electronic states in crystals. 5.2205
Bringing back the parties. 4.8164
Bringing the Left back home. 4.7318
The brink of all we hate. 2.5695
Brisingamen. 2.13238
Britain. 3.1730, 3.5235, 4.2292
Britain against itself. 4.8424
Britain, America and the sinews of war, 1914-1918. 3.839
Britain and America. 3.6188
Britain and Argentina in the nineteenth century. 3.9240
Britain and Chinese Central Asia. 3.4852
Britain and Europe in the seventeenth century. 3.1445
Britain and European resistance, 1940-1945. 3.1136
Britain and France between two wars. 3.753
Britain and Germany in Africa: imperial rivalry and colonial rule. 3.5114
Britain and her army, 1509-1970. 3.1264
Britain and Ireland 1914-23. 3.1863
Britain & Ireland 1914-23. 3.1863
Britain and Palestine, 1914-1948. 5.8251
Britain and the Arabs. 3.3745
Britain and the Cold War, 1941-1947. 3.1258
Britain and the ending of the slave trade. 4.6442
Britain and the onset of modernization in Brazil 1850-1914. 3.9194
Britain and the origins of the First World War. 3.780
Britain and the origins of the new Europe, 1914-1918. 3.827
Britain and the People's Republic of China, 1949-74. 3.1261
Britain & the war for the union. 3.7358
Britain and the Western seaways. 3.539
Britain and West Germany: changing societies and the future of foreign policy. 3.1705
Britain at the polls, 1979. 4.8492
Britain at the polls, 1983. 4.8493
Britain, Greece, and the politics of sanctions. 3.2685
Britain in agony. 4.5343
Britain in decline. 4.2289
Britain in Europe. 4.2222
Britain in Europe, 1789-1914. 3.1585
Britain in the century of total war. 3.1644
Britain in the Far East. 3.4411
Britain in the Pacific Islands. 3.5553
Britain in world affairs. 3.1247
Britain, progress and decline. 4.8422
Britain says yes. 4.2225
Britain's elusive empire in the Middle East, 1900-1921. 5.8041

Britain's imperial century, 1815-1914. 4.8913
Britain's moment in the Middle East, 1914-1971. 3.3746
Britain's theatrical periodicals, 1720-1967. 5.8307
Britain's withdrawal from the Middle East, 1947-1971. 3.3744
Britannica. 1.13
Britannica book of the year. 1.14
The Britannica encyclopedia of American art. 1.4858
Britannica world atlas international. 4.111
Britannica world language dictionary. 2.204
Britannicus. 2.4047
British admirals of the eighteenth century. 5.7427
The British agent. 2.9096
British analytical philosophy. 1.734
British and American utopian literature, 1516-1975. 5.7977
British and Irish elections, 1784-1831. 4.8480
British and Irish library resources. 5.7665
British appeasement in the 1930s. 3.1256
The British architect. 1.5359
British art and the Mediterranean. 1.4932
British art since 1900, an anthology. 1.4942
British attitudes towards Canada, 1822-1849. 3.8718
British attitudes towards India, 1784-1858. 3.4260
British authors before 1800. 2.5559
British authors of the nineteenth century. 2.5697
British autobiographies. 5.7994
British battleships. 5.7462
British battleships of World War Two. 5.7436
British books in print, 1874-. 5.7914
British Cabinet Ministers. 4.8449
British civil aircraft since 1919. 5.6649
British coal-miners in the nineteenth century. 4.3536
British colonial policy, 1754-1765. 4.8910
British Columbia, a history 3.8863
The British Commonwealth. 4.8427
British Commonwealth affairs, 1931-1952. 3.1226
The British Communist Party. 4.8528
The British constitution. 4.9403
British defence policy in a changing world. 5.7300
British democracy at the crossroads. 4.8502
The British drama. 2.5839
British drama. 2.5841
British dramatists from Dryden to Sheridan. 2.6228
British economic growth, 1688-1959. 4.2247
British economic growth, 1856-1973. 4.2282
British economic growth during the industrial revolution. 4.2263
British economy of the nineteenth century. 4.2280
British elections. 4.8506
The British Empire, 1558-1983. 3.1383
British Empire, 1763-1793. 3.1556
The British empire, 1815-1939. 3.1223
The British Empire before the American Revolution. 3.1542
The British film. 2.2896
British foreign policy, 1918-1945. 5.8260
British foreign policy 1945-1973. 3.1706
British foreign policy in the age of Walpole. 3.1539
British foreign policy in the Second World War. 3.930
British foreign policy since Versailles, 1919-1963. 3.1651
The British General Election of 1950. 4.8488
The British general election of 1951. 4.8481
The British general election of 1955. 4.8495
The British general election of 1959. 4.8498
The British general election of 1964. 4.8482
The British General Election of 1966. 4.8483
The British general election of 1970. 4.8499
The British general election of 1979. 4.8500
The British general election of 1983. 4.8494
The British general election of February, 1974. 4.8496

The British general election of October 1974.
4.8497
British gliders and sailplanes, 1922-1970.
5.6686
British government and its discontents. 4.8423
British history in the nineteenth century and
after, 1782-1919. 3.1586
British humanities index. 1.28
British immigrants in industrial America,
1790-1950. 3.6537
British imperial policy in India and Sri Lanka,
1858-1912. 3.4271
British intelligence in the Second World War.
3.1134
The British Isles. 3.1732
The British Isles: a geographic and economic
survey. 4.2251
British labor and the American Civil War.
3.7357
The British Labour Party. 4.8535
British landscape painting of the eighteenth
century. 1.6360
The British Library general catalogue of printed
books to 1975. 5.7670
British literary magazines. 2.3688
The British Marxist historians. 4.1725
British monetary policy, 1926-1931. 4.4514
The British national bibliography. 5.7912
British national bibliography cumulated subject
catalogue. 5.7913
British opinion and the American revolution.
3.6939
British Orientalism and the Bengal renaissance.
3.4329
The British overseas: exploits of a nation of
shopkeepers. 3.1218
British overseas trade, 1870-1914. 4.4229
British overseas trade from 1700 to the 1930s.
4.4230
British parliamentary parties, 1742-1832.
4.8519
British poetry of the eighteen-nineties. 2.6176
British poetry since 1960. 2.5837
British policy and Canada, 1774-1791. 4.4186
British policy and the independence of Latin
America, 1804-1828. 3.9010
British policy and the nationalist movement in
Burma, 1917-1937. 3.4427
British policy in the South Pacific, 1786-1893.
3.5555
British political facts, 1900-1967. 4.8412
British political finance, 1830-1980. 4.8515
British political parties. 4.8527
British politics and the American Revolution.
3.1569
British politics in perspective. 4.8411
British politics in the age of Anne. 4.8405
British politics in the collectivist age. 3.1647
British prehistory. 4.733
The British Prime Minister. 4.8446
British prisons. 4.6919
British propaganda during the First World
War, 1914-1918. 3.843
British public addresses, 1828-1960. 2.6267
British public finances, their structure and
development, 1880-1952. 4.4670
British rearmament in the thirties. 5.7303
The British régime in Michigan and the Old
Northwest, 1760-1796. 3.8432
The British régime in Wisconsin and the
Northwest. 3.8444
The British seaman 1200-1860. 5.7489
British short fiction in the nineteenth century.
2.6008
British slave emancipation. 4.2158
British social anthropologists and language.
2.15
British society since 1945. 4.5315
British town planning. 4.6333
British trade and the opening of China,
1800-42. 4.4231
British trade unionism. 4.3639
British trade unionism against the Trades
Union Congress. 4.3634
British tropical Africa. 3.5116
British war aims and peace diplomacy,
1914-1918. 3.779
The British West Indies. 3.9138

The British wool textile industry, 1770-1914.
4.3856
British workers and the Independent Labour
Party, 1888-1906. 4.8534
Briton Hadden. 2.3676
Broad and alien is the world. 2.5424
The Broad scope of ego function assessment.
5.4847
Broadcast/cable programming. 2.2857
Broadcast fairness. 4.9540
Broadcast regulation. 4.9536
Broadcasting and government. 4.9539
Broadcasting cablecasting yearbook. 4.4054
Broadcasting in Africa. 4.4059
Broadcasting in Asia and the Pacific. 4.4060
Broadcasting in the Arab world. 2.2843
Broadcasting in the Third World. 4.4062
Broadcasting in the United Kingsom. 4.4065
Broadcasting research methods. 2.2856
The broadside ballad. 2.5773
A broadside treasury. 2.10750
Broadway. 2.3221
Broca's brain. 5.363
Brockhaus Enzyklopädie in zwanzig Bänden.
1.18
The broken arc. 2.11526
Broken bottles, broken dreams. 4.6637
Broken code. 5.3458
The broken commandment. 2.2091
The broken compass. 2.6602
The broken covenant. 2.6079
The broken eagle. 2.13936
Broken earth. 4.5458
The broken fountain. 4.5365
Broken record. 2.10061
The broken spears. 3.8924
Broken star. 4.9186
The broken sword. 2.12850
A broken world, 1919-1939. 3.866
Brokenburn. 3.7373
Bromeliads. 5.5350
A Bromfield galaxy. 2.11416
Bronislava Nijinska 4.1153
The Brontës, the critical heritage. 2.7449
The Brontës' web of childhood. 2.7454
The bronze age in Europe. 4.713
Bronzino as draughtsman. 1.5814
Brooklyn USA. 3.8059
Brooks Adams; a biography. 3.419
Das Brot der frühen Jahre. 2.13688
Brother man. 2.9996
Brother to dragons. 2.12639
The brothers. 2.8303
Brothers and keepers. 4.6700
Brothers & sisters 4.6585
Brothers and sisters 4.6585
The brothers Ashkenazi. 2.1821
The Brothers Karamazov. 2.1352
The brothers Mann. 2.13819
Brothers of light, brothers of blood. 1.3241
Brothers under the skin. 3.6521
The brother's wife. 2.8367
Brought to bed. 5.5061
Brown heritage: essays on Philippine cultural
tradition and literature. 2.2290
Brown of the Globe. 3.8717
Browning. 2.7488
The Browning critics. 2.7485
The Browning cyclopaedia. 2.7477
A Browning handbook. 2.7482
Browning: the critical heritage. 2.7486
Browning's beginnings. 2.7494
Browning's characters. 2.7489
The Brownings' correspondence. 2.7480
Browning's later poetry, 1871-1889. 2.7493
Browning's major poetry. 2.7490
Bruce Jay Friedman. 2.13021
Bruckner. 1.3827
Bruckner and Mahler. 1.3826
Bruegel. 1.6260-1.6261
Bruno, or, On the natural and the divine
principle of things. 1.922
Bruno Taut and the architecture of activism.
1.5429
Bruno's dream. 2.9751
The brutal friendship: Mussolini, Hitler, and the
fall of Italian fascism. 3.2894
Bubbles, drops, and particles. 5.1668

The buccaneer. 2.11313
The buccaneers of America. 3.9142
Buckingham, the life and political career of
George Villiers, first Duke of Buckingham,
1592-1628. 3.1466
Buckle at the ballet. 4.1177
Buckling of bars, plates, and shells. 5.5862
Bucolici Graeci. 2.552
Buddenbrooks. 2.13827
Buddha. 2.597
The Buddhacarita. 1.2127
Buddhism. 1.2140, 1.2142
Buddhism and American thinkers. 1.214
Buddhism and society. 1.1765, 1.2110
Buddhism and the state in sixteenth-century
Japan. 1.2122
Buddhism, art and faith. 1.5184
Buddhism in America. 1.2168
Buddhism in China, a historical survey. 1.1748
Buddhism in Chinese history. 1.2115
Buddhism in the modern world. 1.2143
Buddhism in translations. 1.1740
Buddhism; its essence and development.
1.1766
Buddhism of Tibet. 1.2144
The Buddhism of Tibet and The key to the
middle way. 1.2144
Buddhism under Mao. 1.2119
Buddhist art in Siam. 1.5055
Buddhist backgrounds of the Burmese
revolution. 1.1764
The Buddhist conquest of China. 1.2118
Buddhist India. 3.4193
Buddhist logic. 1.1180
Buddhist Mahāyāna texts. 1.1737
Buddhist meditation. 1.1769
Buddhist monastic discipline. 1.2137
A Buddhist paradise. 1.6399
Buddhist philosophy. 1.2146
Buddhist philosophy in India and Ceylon.
1.215
The Buddhist philosophy of universal flux.
1.216
The Buddhist religion. 1.2141
The Buddhist revival in China 1.1752
Buddhist scriptures. 1.1738
Buddhist suttas. 1.1743
The Buddhist teaching of totality. 1.1779
Buddhist texts through the ages. 1.1739
Buddhist thought in India. 1.2107
The Buddhist tradition in India, China &
Japan. 1.2126
Buddhist wisdom books. 1.2132
Budget innovation in the States. 4.4687
Budget of the U.S. Government FY 1983-1984.
4.4678
Budget of the United States Government.
4.4678
Buenos Aires. 4.5267
Bug Jack Barron. 2.13332
Buganda in the heroic age. 3.5266
The build-up. 2.12743
Builders of the Bay colony. 3.7982
Building a character. 2.3123
Building a new American state. 4.7844
Building a sustainable society. 4.2763
Building an antislavery wall. 3.1293
Building an Austrian nation. 4.8572
Building character in the American boy.
4.6179
Building classroom discipline. 4.10694
Building ethnic collections. 5.7857
Building expert systems. 5.1246
Building feminist theory. 4.6036
The building of Renaissance Florence. 1.5435
Buildings and projects, 1921-1961. 1.5305
Buildings and society. 1.5476
Buildings for music. 1.4398
Buile Suibhne Geilt. 2.9704
Bukharin and the Bolshevik Revolution.
3.3225
Bulgakov. 2.1544
Bulgaria 1878-1918. 3.3542
Bulgaria under Communist rule. 3.3544
Bulgarian communism. 4.8685
Bulgarian economic development since World
War II. 4.2418
Bulgarian folktales. 4.802

The bull from the sea. 2.9266
Bullet Park. 2.11491
Bulletin of the Public Affairs Information
    Service. 5.8356
Bullivant and the Lambs. 2.8529
Bulozi under the Luyana kings. 3.5519
The bulwark. 2.11592
Bulwer and Macready. 2.7917
The bungalow. 1.5569
Bunraku. 2.2836
Bunyoro. 3.5284
The burden of Brown. 4.9593
The burden of Egypt. 3.5143
Burden of empire. 3.5104
The burden of guilt. 3.2450
The burden of time. 2.10465
The Bureau. 4.6825
The Bureau of Labor Statistics. 4.3546
The Bureau of Land Management. 4.2815
Bureaucracy and democracy. 4.7765
Bureaucracy and political development. 4.7752
Bureaucracy and the public. 4.7766
Bureaucracy, aristocracy, and autocracy.
    4.8615
Bureaucracy in modern society. 4.7749
Bureaucracy, the Marshall Plan, and the
    national interest. 4.2183
The bureaucratic phenomenon. 4.2663
Bureaucratic politics. 4.7893
Bureaucratic politics and foreign policy. 4.9095
Bureaucratic reform in the Ottoman Empire.
    4.8773
The bureaucratization of the world. 4.7748
Bureaucrats and politicians in western
    democracies. 4.8367
The Burger Court. 4.9838
The Burger Court and civil liberties. 4.9677
The Burgess nonsense book. 2.11435
Burghley: Tudor statesman, 1520-1598. 3.1434
The Burgundian Netherlands. 3.2958
Buridans Esel. 2.13884
Buried child, & Seduced, & Suicide in B♭.
    2.13319
The buried life. 2.8187
Burke and the nature of politics. 3.1561
Burke's presidential families of the United
    States of America. 3.297
El burlador de Sevilla y convidado de piedra.
    2.5204
The burlesque tradition in the English theatre
    after 1660. 2.2828, 2.5847
Burlington route. 4.4008
Burma. 3.4428
Burma, a country study. 3.4421
Burma, a profile. 3.4335
Burma: a selected and annotated bibliography.
    5.8057
Burma, a socialist nation of Southeast Asia.
    3.4422
The Burma delta: economic development and
    social change on an Asian rice frontier,
    1852-1941. 4.2453
The Burman. 3.4336
Burma's foreign policy. 3.4342
Burmese days. 2.9177
Burmese drama. 2.2257
Burmese economic life. 4.2452
Burmese family. 3.4424
Burmese political values. 4.8720
Burmese politics. 3.4429
The burn. 2.1622
The Burned-over District. 1.2413
Burnham of Chicago, architect and planner.
    1.5308
Burnham's celestial handbook. 5.1732
The burning brand: diaries, 1935-1950. 2.5054
The burning fountain. 2.98
The burning oracle. 2.5754
The burning plain, and other stories. 2.5352
Burnout. 5.409
Burns. 2.7508
The Burns encyclopedia. 2.7500
A Burns handbook.. 2.7501
The burnt flower-bed. 2.5024
A burnt-out case. 2.8742
Burr. 2.12615
Burrows Textbook of microbiology. 5.4439
Bury my heart at Wounded Knee. 3.5772

Bush negro art. 1.4924
Business: a profession. 4.1930
Business and capitalism. 4.4253
Business and investment almanac. 4.4248
Business and politics in India. 4.8708
Business and society. 4.4257
Business and society in Japan. 4.2549
Business atlas. 4.155
Business behavior, value and growth. 4.3009
Business civilization in decline. 4.1528
Business cycles and economic policy. 4.1789
Business enterprise in the American
    Revolutionary Era. 4.1907
Business in American life. 4.4213
Business in politics. 4.7895
Business in the public eye. 4.3030
Business in the shadow of apartheid. 4.3064
Business index [microform]. 5.8367
Business index (Quarterly). 5.8367
Business information sources. 5.8368
The Business insurance handbook. 4.4638
The business of America. 4.4254
The Business of book publishing. 5.7568
The business of criticism. 2.2453
The business of organized crime. 4.6775
The business of shipping. 4.3961
The business of show business. 2.3111
The business of the Supreme court. 4.9839
The business of the theatre. 2.3266
Business organizations, agencies, and
    publications directory. 4.4211
Business periodicals index. 5.8366
The business response to Keynes, 1929-1964.
    4.1338
Business values and social justice. 4.4269
Business week (New York) 4.1885, 4.2006
The businessman in American literature.
    2.10354
Busman's honeymoon. 2.9304
But some of us are brave. 3.6747
The Butcher. 3.1805
Butley. 2.9700
Der Butt. 2.13756
Butterfield 8. 2.12267
The Butterflies of North America. 5.3880
A buyer's market. 2.9225
By any means necessary. 3.6675
By fire and axe. 3.2705
By force of will. 2.11858
By-line. 2.11837
By little and by little. 4.5117
By love possessed. 2.11513
By reason or force. 3.9264
By the sweat of their brow. 4.3615
By the sweat of thy brow. 4.3092
Byng of Vimy. 3.1269
Byron. 2.7526, 2.7528
Byron, a poet before his public. 2.7536
Byron, a self-portrait. 2.7522
Byron and the Honourable Augusta Leigh.
    2.7531
Byron: the critical heritage. 2.7537
Byron, the Italian literary influence. 2.7539
The Byronic hero. 2.7538
Byron's letters and journals. 2.7521
Byron's poetry. 2.7527
Byzantine architecture. 1.5233
Byzantine art in the making. 1.4745
The Byzantine churches of Istanbul. 1.5536
The Byzantine commonwealth. 3.2664
Byzantine Jewry from Justinian to the Fourth
    Crusade. 3.3905
Byzantine portraits. 3.2657
The Byzantine theocracy. 1.3104
Byzantine theology. 1.3110
Byzantine wall painting in Asia Minor. 1.6396
Byzantium. 3.2655
Byzantium and Bulgaria. 3.2662
Byzantium and the decline of Rome. 3.2818
Byzantium endures. 2.9745
Byzantium: greatness and decline. 3.2659
Byzantium, the empire of New Rome. 3.2658

C3, C4. 5.3758
C.A.D./C.A.M. 5.7025
C.A.D./C.A.M. handbook. 5.7024
C.A.D., principles and applications. 5.5696
C, a reference manual. 5.1211

C.B.E. style manual. 5.3295
C. Ben Ross and the New Deal in Idaho.
    3.8550
C.E.O. 4.1867
C.L.C. Contemporary literary criticism. 2.2671
La C.N.T. [Confederación nacional del trabajo]
    en la revolución española ... 4.3665
C. P. Snow. 2.9348
C.P. Snow, the politics of conscience. 2.9347
The C programming language. 5.1212
C.R.C. handbook of lubrication. 5.6245
C.T.F.T. 2.3234
C. Wright Mills. 4.4775-4.4776
A cab at the door. 2.9254
The Cabal. 3.1497
The Cabala. 2.12714
The cabaret. 2.3185
The Cabinet. 4.8448
Cabinet government and war, 1890-1940.
    4.8444
Cabinet government in Australia. 4.8819
Cabinet reform in Britain, 1914-1963. 4.8443
The Cable/broadband communications book.
    4.4069
Cable communication. 4.4068
Cable television. 5.6445
Cabot Wright begins. 2.12356
The cacti of the United States and Canada.
    5.3694
CAD/CAM. 5.7025
CAD/CAM handbook. 5.7024
CAD, principles and applications. 5.5696
Cadenza. 1.4102
Cadiz to Cathay. 4.3948
Caesar: politician and statesman. 3.2787
Caesar. The civil wars. 2.652
Caesar's gate. 2.11612
Cahiers du cinéma. 2.2949
Cahiers du cinéma, the 1950s. 2.2949
The Caine mutiny. 2.12802
Cairo: 1001 years of the city victorious. 3.5181
Cairo, city of art and commerce. 3.5182
Cakes and ale. 2.9097
Calamity town. 2.12363
Calamus. 2.3719
Calculated kindness. 4.8955
The calculation of atomic structures. 5.2162
Calculator programming for chemistry and the
    life sciences. 5.5152
Calculus. 5.1435
The calculus of consent, logical foundations of
    constitutional democracy. 4.7565
A calculus of suffering. 5.5034
Calculus of variations. 5.1465, 5.1467
Calculus of variations and partial differential
    equations of the first order. 5.1466
The calculus of variations in the large. 5.1469
Calcutta. 3.4358
Calder. 1.5663
Calder; an autobiography with pictures. 1.5662
Calderón de la Barca. 2.5165
Calder's universe. 1.4892
Caleb Williams. 2.7747
Calendar: a quarterly review. 2.2440
Calendar of creative man. 1.6696
A calendar of Soviet treaties, 1917-1957.
    4.8979
A calendar of Soviet treaties, 1958-1973.
    4.8980
California. 3.8601, 3.8613
California and the Dust Bowl migration.
    4.2923
California archaeology. 3.5723
California conquered. 3.8605
California expeditions. 3.8603
California gold. 3.8609
The California progressives. 3.8610
California's prodigal sons. 3.8611
Caligari's cabinet and other grand illusions.
    2.3007
Caligula. 2.4448
Caligula & three other plays. 2.4443
A call in the midst of the crowd. 2.12957
The call of the wild. 2.12023
Calligrammes. 2.4366
Calligraphy & handwriting in America,
    1710-1962. 5.7528

Calligraphy and Islamic culture.   1.6608
Calvin.   1.3403
Calvin: commentaries.   1.2523
Calvin Coolidge.   3.7737
Calypso.   5.7514
Camara Laye.   2.4850
Cambio de piel.   2.5339
Cambodia.   3.4449, 4.5437
Cambodia, 1975-1982.   3.4442
Cambodia in the Southeast Asian war.   3.4487
Cambodia's foreign policy.   3.4450
Cambrian of the new world.   5.3136
The Cambridge ancient history.   3.549
The Cambridge astronomy guide.   5.1731
The Cambridge atlas of astronomy.   5.1739
The Cambridge atlas of the Middle East and
    North Africa.   3.3679
Cambridge bibliography of English literature
    600-1950.   5.7940
The Cambridge economic history of Europe.
    4.2187
The Cambridge economic history of India.
    4.2496
The Cambridge edition of the letters and works
    of D.H. Lawrence.   2.8958
The Cambridge encyclopaedia of astronomy.
    5.1699
The Cambridge encyclopedia of Africa.   3.5045
The Cambridge encyclopedia of archaeology.
    3.263
The Cambridge encyclopedia of China.   3.4612
The Cambridge encyclopedia of earth sciences.
    5.2960
The Cambridge encyclopedia of Russia and the
    Soviet Union.   3.3005
Cambridge essays, 1888-99.   1.759
The Cambridge guide to English literature.
    2.5524
The Cambridge guide to the material world.
    5.2080
The Cambridge historical encyclopedia of Great
    Britain and Ireland.   3.1244
The Cambridge history of Africa.   3.5067
Cambridge history of Africa.   3.5151
The Cambridge history of British foreign policy,
    1783-1919.   3.1250
The Cambridge history of China.   3.4663
The Cambridge history of English literature.
    2.5512, 2.5528
The Cambridge history of India.   3.4221
The Cambridge history of Iran.   3.4070
The Cambridge history of Islam.   3.3644
The Cambridge history of Judaism.   1.1899
The Cambridge history of later Greek and early
    medieval philosophy.   1.221
The Cambridge history of later medieval
    philosophy.   1.347
The Cambridge history of Latin America.
    3.8975
The Cambridge history of Poland.   3.3276
The Cambridge history of the Bible.   1.2509
The Cambridge history of the British Empire.
    3.1217
The Cambridge Italian dictionary.   2.855
Cambridge lectures.   2.5547
The Cambridge medieval history.   3.572, 3.574
Cambridge Middle English lyrics.   2.6138
The Cambridge photographic atlas of the
    planets.   5.1809
Cambridge physics in the 30's.   5.2009
Cambridge physics in the thirties.   5.2009
The Cambridge shorter history of India.
    3.4220
Camera lucida.   5.6953
Camera obscura.   2.13808
The Camera viewed.   5.6954
The Cameroon Federal Republic.   4.8811
The Cameroons, from mandate to
    independence.   3.5398
Cameroun.   3.5400
Camilla.   2.6891
Camille.   2.4181
Camille Pissaro.   1.6135
Camille Pissarro: letters to his son Lucien.
    1.6134
Camilo José Cela.   2.5244
El camino.   2.5247
Camp David.   3.3939

Campaign addresses of Governor Alfred E.
    Smith.   3.7739
Campaign finance in America.   4.8122
Campaign money.   4.8127
Campaigning for Congress.   4.8116
The campaigns of Napoleon.   3.2091
The campaigns of the Pacific war.   3.1007
Campesino.   3.9063
Campion's works.   2.6441
Camus.   2.4456
Can government go bankrupt?   4.4648
Can language be planned?   2.25
Can modern war be just?   5.7150
Can science save us?   4.4821
Can these bones live.   2.11548
Can we teach children to be good?   4.10808
Can you forgive her?   2.8205
Canada.   3.8760
Canada, 1763-1841, immigration and settlement.
    4.2832
Canada 1874-1896.   3.8765
Canada, 1896-1921; a nation transformed.
    3.8740
Canada: a geographical interpretation.   3.8661
Canada, a modern history.   3.8668
Canada; a political and social history.   3.8674
Canada, a story of challenge.   3.8669
Canada, an economic history.   4.2117
Canada and imperial defense.   5.7302
Canada and imperialism, 1896-1899.   3.8759
Canada and the age of conflict.   3.8700
Canada and the British army, 1846-1871.
    3.8734
Canada and the French-Canadian question.
    3.8682
Canada and the League of Nations.   4.9193
Canada and the new constitution.   4.8274
Canada and the Third World.   3.8775
Canada and the transition to Commonwealth.
    3.1259
Canada and the United States.   4.9058
Canada and the United States, dependence and
    divergence.   3.6413
Canada and the United States: the Civil War
    years.   3.7356
Canada and war.   3.8695
Canada as an international actor.   3.8780
Canada at the polls.   4.8296
Canada at the polls, 1979 and 1980.   4.8295
Canada before Confederation.   4.2121
Le Canada français d'aujourd'hui.   3.8680
Canada gazetteer atlas.   4.140
Canada in the North Atlantic triangle.   3.8683
Canada in the world economy.   4.4178
Canada in world affairs.   3.8696
Canada since 1867.   5.7895
Canada since 1945.   3.8774
Canada under Louis XIV, 1663-1701.   3.8702
Canada votes.   4.8298
Canada year book.   4.1252
Canada's first century, 1867-1967.   3.8743
Canada's search for new roles.   3.8776
Canada's war.   3.8768
Canadian almanac and directory.   1.67
The Canadian almanac and legal and court
    directory.   1.67
The Canadian almanac and miscellaneous
    directory.   1.67
Canadian-American relations.   3.6415
Canadian-American relations in wartime.
    3.6414
Canadian annual review.   3.8651
Canadian architecture, 1960/70.   1.5346
Canadian books in print.   5.7882
Canadian business and economics.   5.8395
The Canadian career of the Fourth Earl of
    Minto.   3.8758
The Canadian city.   4.6246
The Canadian commercial revolution,
    1845-1851.   4.2119
The Canadian corporate elite.   4.5249
Canadian dualism.   3.8691
Canadian economic history.   4.2115
Canadian economic thought.   4.1381
The Canadian economy.   4.2120
The Canadian encyclopedia.   1.20
Canadian fiction.   5.7891
Canadian forum.   3.8778

The Canadian frontier, 1534-1760.   3.8703
The Canadian identity.   3.8699
Canadian labour in politics.   4.3626
The Canadian left.   4.7008
The Canadian legislative system.   4.8290
Canadian literature.   2.9892-2.9893
Canadian men and women of the time.   3.8741
Canadian official publications.   5.7886
Canadian painting in the thirties.   1.5995
The Canadian political nationality.   4.8284
The Canadian prairie west and the ranching
    frontier, 1874-1924.   4.3698
The Canadian prairies.   3.8857
Canadian provincial politics.   4.8302
The Canadian public service.   4.8289
Canadian reference sources.   5.7885
Canadian regions.   3.8662
Canadian relations with South Africa.   3.8701
Canadian selection.   5.7884
Canadian short fiction anthology.   2.9902
Canadian short stories.   2.9903
Canadian short stories, third series.   2.9901
The Canadian who's who ...   3.8741
Canadian writers and their works.   2.9878
Canadian writing today.   2.9895
Canadiana.   3.8655, 5.7883
Canadians in the making.   3.8664
Canaletto.   1.6194-1.6195
Canals and American economic development.
    4.3944
Canarsie.   3.8042
Canary.   2.1742
The canary and other tales of martial law.
    2.1742
The Canary Islands after the conquest.   3.3484
Cancer.   5.4770
Cancer care nursing.   5.4774
Cancer, the outlaw cell.   5.4775
Cancer ward.   2.1636
Candide; or, Optimism.   2.4104
The candle in the wind.   2.9519
Candleford Green.   3.1739
Cane.   2.12597
The cankered muse.   2.6066
The cannibal.   2.11817
The cannibal galaxy.   2.13231
Cannibals all!   3.7244
Cannibals and kings.   4.503
Canon Charles Kingsley.   2.7881
Canons and decrees of the Council of Trent.
    1.3130
Canova.   1.5727
Cantar de mío Cid.   2.5185
Cantares en idioma mexicano. English & Aztec.
    2.2334
Cantares mexicanos.   2.2334
The cantatas of Johann Sebastian Bach, sacred
    and secular.   1.4520
La Cantate à trois voix.   2.4471
The Canterbury tales.   2.6316, 2.6322, 2.6328
A canticle for Leibowitz.   2.12195
Cántico.   2.5265
The cantos of Ezra Pound.   2.12326-2.12327
Canute the Great, 995 (circ)-1035.   3.3371
Il canzoniere (1900-1954)   2.5064
Capability Brown.   5.5378
A capacity to punish.   4.6913
The Capetian kings of France.   3.1990
Le capitaine Fracasse, texte complet (1863).
    2.4217
Capital.   4.1535
Capital and growth.   4.1435
Capital and interest.   4.1520
Capital and time.   4.1530
Capital cities of Arab Islam.   3.3669
Capital expansion and capacity in postwar
    manufacturing.   4.3835
Capital formation and economic growth.
    4.1546
Capital formation in Canada, 1896-1930.
    4.4626
The capital of the tycoon.   3.4879
Capital punishment.   4.6849, 4.6851
Capital theory and dynamics.   4.1522
Capitalism and a new social order.   4.7303
Capitalism and class in the Middle East.
    4.2427
Capitalism and freedom.   4.1523

Capitalism and modern social theory. 4.4740
Capitalism & slavery. 4.2270
Capitalism and the state in modern France. 4.2328
Capitalism and underdevelopment in Latin America. 4.2168
Capitalism, socialism, and democracy. 4.6983
Capitalism, socialism, and the environment. 4.7042
Capitalist democracy in Britain. 4.8425
Capitalist patriarchy and the case for socialist feminism. 4.6037
Capodistria: the founder of Greek independence. 3.2698
Captain Blackman. 2.13427
Captain Dreyfus. 3.2191
The captain from Connecticut. 5.7422
Captain James Cook and his times. 4.91
Captain Sam Grant. 3.7480
Captains & cabinets. 3.829
The captains and the kings. 2.9730
The captive and the free. 2.8496
A captive spirit. 2.1611
The captured womb. 5.5059
Caput and colonate. 4.4650
Caravaggio. 1.6197
Caravaggio studies. 1.6196
Caravan. 3.3680
Caravan cities. 3.3686
Carbohydrate biochemistry and metabolism. 5.4422
The Carbohydrates. 5.2762
Carbonate sediments and their diagenesis. 5.3062
The card index, and other plays. 2.1725
Cardano. 5.817
Cardinal principles of the national entity of Japan. 3.4883
Cardinal Richelieu and the development of absolutism. 3.2026
Cardiovascular disorders. 5.4993
The care of the sick. 5.5159
Career development. 4.4264
Career development in organizations. 4.4371
Career dynamics. 4.4378
Career management in organizations. 4.4375
Career mobility in a corporate hierarchy. 4.3213
The career of Alphonse Daudet. 2.4168
The career of philosophy. 1.423
The careers of professional women. 4.3245
Careline poets. 2.6162
Caretaker of the dead. 4.868
'Cargo' cults in Melanesia. 1.1880
Les cariatides. 2.4130
Caribbean. 3.9146
The Caribbean as Columbus saw it. 3.5975
The Caribbean islands. 3.9085
Caribbean literature. 2.2694
Caribbean migrants. 4.8958
Caribbean narrative. 2.9980
The Caribbean policy of the United States, 1890-1920. 3.9014
Caribbean transformations. 4.6430
Caribbean verse. 2.9981
Caribbean voices. 2.9982
Caribbean writers. 2.2693
Caribou and the barren-lands. 5.4045
The caricatures of George Cruikshank. 1.5853
Caring, a feminine approach to ethics & moral education. 1.1502
Caring for the burned. 5.5035
A caring society. 4.3564
Carl Becker. 3.420
Carl Fabergé. 1.6653
Carl Maria von Weber. 1.4056
Carl Nielsen, symphonist. 1.3942
Carl Orff. 1.3943
Carl Philip Emanuel Bach's autobiography. 1.3785
Carl Sandburg. 2.12433-2.12435
Carl Schurz. 3.7449
Carl Schurz, a biography. 3.7450
Carl Zuckmayer. 2.13873
Carlo Cattaneo and the politics of the Risorgimento, 1820-1860. 3.2865
Carlo Goldoni. 2.4995

Carlo Maderno and Roman architecture, 1580-1630. 1.5442
Carlos Fuentes. 2.5346
Carlos Montezuma and the changing world of American Indians. 3.5962
Carlyle. 2.7554
Carlyle and German thought: 1819-1834. 2.7556
Carlyle and the idea of the modern. 2.7557
Carlyle past and present. 2.7555
A Carlyle reader. 2.7545
The Carmen de Hastingae proelio. 2.821
Carmichael's manual of child psychology. 5.561
Carmina. 2.645
Carnacki: the ghost-finder. 2.8804
The Carnegie Council on Policy Studies in Higher Education. 4.10758
Carnival in Romans. 3.2237
A carnival of buncombe. 3.7516
Carnival of fury. 3.8316
The carnivores. 5.3991
Carnivorous plants of the United States and Canada. 5.3774
The Carolina Backcountry on the eve of the Revolution. 3.8244
Caroline Gordon as novelist and woman of letters. 2.11793
Caroling dusk. 2.10751
Carolingian and Romanesque architecture, 800 to 1200. 1.5232
The Carolingian empire. 3.1982
Carolingian painting. 1.6404
Carolingian portraits. 3.2268
The Carolingian renaissance. 1.4741
The Carolingians and the Frankish monarchy. 3.1988
Carriers of the dream wheel. 2.10743
Carrying the fire. 5.6706
Carson McCullers. 2.12078
The cart and the trumpet. 2.8087
Cartels in action. 4.3012
Cartes de visite in nineteenth century photography. 5.6985
Cartesian linguistics. 2.147
Cartesian meditations: an introduction to phenomenology. 1.1012
Cartier's Hochelaga and the Dawson Site. 3.5892
Cartographic design and production. 4.203
Cartography. 4.206
La casa verde. 2.5428
Casablanca. 2.3024
The Casablanca connection. 3.5213
Casablanca (Motion picture) 2.3024
Casals and the art of interpretation. 1.4077
The case against direct election of the President. 4.7964
The case for animal rights. 4.6630
The case for bureaucracy. 4.7890
The case for change. 5.3306
The Case for Mars. 5.6714
The case for the welfare state. 4.6488
Case management and the elderly. 4.6592
The case of Charles Dexter Ward. 2.12037
A case of conscience. 2.11392
The case of Dora and other papers. 5.137
The case of Sergeant Grischa. 2.13875
The case of the gilded fly. 2.9123
The case of the helmeted airman. 2.8403
The case of the sulky girl. 2.11766
The case of Walter Pater. 2.7984
Case studies in American industry. 4.1942
Case studies in European economic union. 4.4183
Case workbook in personality. 5.507
A Casebook of grant proposals in the humanities. 1.73
A casebook on Dylan Thomas. 2.9415
Cases in operations research. 4.2627
Cases on United Nations law. 4.9226
Casework, a psychosocial therapy. 4.6498
Casey Agonistes, and other science fiction and fantasy stories. 2.13146
Casino Royale. 2.9680
The cask. 2.8589
Caspar David Friedrich. 1.6171

Caspar David Friedrich, 1774-1840: romantic landscape painting in Dresden: [catalogue of an exhibition held at the Tate Gallery, London, 6 September-16 October, 1972. 1.6170
Cass Timberlane. 2.12003
Cassandra. 2.13923
Casse-pipe. 2.4507
Cassell's encyclopaedia of world literature. 2.2346
Cassell's French dictionary. 2.879
Cassell's French-English, English-French dictionary. 2.879
Cassell's German dictionary. 2.1189
Cassell's Italian-English, English-Italian dictionary. 2.856
Cassell's New English-Dutch, Dutch-English dictionary. 2.1171
Cassell's new Latin dictionary. 2.260
Cassell's Spanish-English, English-Spanish dictionary. 2.899
CASSI. 5.8117
Cassiodorus. 1.2486
Cast a cold eye. 2.12062
Cast iron. 5.5817
Cast-iron architecture. 1.5501
Castaway. 2.11514
Caste and class in a southern town. 3.8158
Caste and kinship in central India. 3.4177
Caste and race in India. 3.4174
Caste, class, and power. 3.4172
Caste, class, & race. 4.6378
Caste differentiation in social insects. 5.3878
Caste in India, its nature, function and origins. 3.4175
Castellani and Giuliano. 1.6661
Casting out anger. 1.1862
Casting stones. 2.12951
The castle. 2.13792
Castle Corner. 2.8497
The Castle diaries, 1964-70. 3.1713
Castle keep. 2.11620
The castle of crossed destinies. 2.5026
The Castle of Fratta. 2.5007
The castle of Otranto. 2.7331
Castle Rackrent. 2.7686
Castlereagh. 3.1577
Castlereagh and Adams. 3.7113
The castrati in opera. 1.3762
Castroism and communism in Latin America, 1959-1976. 4.7011
The cat. 2.4490
Cat anatomy. 5.3997
Cat and mouse. 2.13761
Cat owner's home veterinary handbook. 5.5464
The Catalans. 3.3485
Catalog of published concert music by American composers. 1.3559
Catalog of the public documents of the ... Congress ... 5.7768
Catalogue de reproductions en coleur de peintures. 1.6487
Catalogue de reproductions en couleurs de peintures antérieures à 1860. 1.6486
Catalogue des livres canadiens en librairie. 5.7882
Catalogue of bright stars. 5.1847
A catalogue of crime. 5.8172
Catalogue of early German and Flemish woodcuts. 1.6474
Catalogue of Greek sculptures. 1.5625
Catalogues and counters. 4.4333
Catalysis in chemistry and enzymology. 5.2882
Catalytic hydrogenation in organic synthesis. 5.2749
The catastrophe; Kerensky's own story of the Russian revolution. 3.3185
The Catastrophe of European Jewry. 3.1085
Catastrophe survived. 2.465
Catastrophe theory and its applications. 5.1622
Catch-22. 2.13080
The catcher in the rye. 2.12423
The categorical imperative. 1.910
Categories for the working mathematician. 5.1289
The Category of the person. 5.493
Catharine Beecher. 4.6000
Catharine Furze. 2.8263

The cathedral. 2.9460
The cathedral builders. 1.5519
The cathedral folk. 2.1398
La cathédrale. 2.4246
The cathedrals of England. 1.5526
Catherine de Médicis. 3.2015
Catherine Furze. 2.8263
Catherine of Aragon. 3.1404
Catherine the Great. 3.3103
Catherine the Great, and other studies. 3.3104
Catherine the Great and the expansion of Russia. 3.3105
The Catherine wheel. 2.12499
The Catholic Church and Ireland in the age of rebellion, 1859-1873. 3.1853
The Catholic Church and Nazi Germany. 1.3191
The Catholic Church in the modern world. 1.3163
Catholic Encyclopedia. 1.3131
The Catholic left. 1.3172
The Catholic periodical and literature index. 1.29
A Catholic philosophy of education. 4.10234
The Catholic rediscovery of Protestantism. 1.3207
Catholic theories of Biblical inspiration since 1810. 1.2522
The Catholic vote. 4.8077
Catholicism. 1.3199, 1.3201
Catholicism and education. 4.10810
Catholicism in America. 1.3176
Catholics in Colonial America. 1.3175
Catholics in western democracies. 1.3168
The Catilinarian conspiracy in its context. 3.2780
Cato the censor. 3.2770
Cat's cradle. 2.13390
Cats of the world. 5.3990
The cattle kings. 3.8489
The cattle on a thousand hills. 3.8614
The Catullan revolution. 2.711
Catullus. 2.706-2.707, 2.709, 2.712
Catullus and Horace. 2.710
Catullus, Tibullus, and Pervigilium Veneris. 2.655
Caucasians only. 4.9512
Caught. 2.8732
Caught in the web of words. 2.925
Causal models in panel and experimental designs. 4.4784
Causality and chance in modern physics. 5.1896
Causality and determinism. 1.1338
Causality and modern science. 1.1334
Causality, physical, The child's conception of. 5.571
Cause, experiment, and science. 5.2039
Cause for alarm. 2.8381
Causes and consequences of the American Revolution. 3.6914
Causes and consequences of World War II. 3.931
The causes and cures of neurosis. 5.4927
Causes of death: life tables for national population. 4.1649
The causes of evolution. 5.3359
Causes of international war. 4.9119
The causes of the English Revolution, 1529-1642. 3.1462
The causes of the War of 1812. 3.7108
Cavafy. 2.585
Cavafy's Alexandria. 2.584
Cavalcade. 2.10694
Cavalcade of the American novel. 2.10541
Cavalier and Yankee. 3.8125
Cavalier drama. 2.5889
The cavalier in Virginia fiction. 2.10467
Cavalier poets. 2.6155
The Cavalier spirit and its influence on the life and work of Richard Lovelace (1618-1658) 2.7098
Il Cavaliere Inesistente. 2.5030
Cavalleria rusticana. 2.5014
The cave. 2.12640
The cave and the mountain. 2.8666
The cave artists. 1.4688
Cave birds. 2.9711

The cave temples of Maichishan. 1.5758
Caveat. 3.7938
Caveats and critiques. 1.463
The Cavendish Laboratory, 1874-1974. 5.2010
The caves of steel 2.12853
Caviar and cabbage. 2.12593
Cavour. 3.2866
Cavour and Garibaldi, 1860. 3.2877
CB. 3.1635
CBE style manual. 5.3295
The ceaseless wind. 5.2517
The Čechs (Bohemians) in America. 3.6536
Cecil Textbook of medicine. 5.4754
Cecilia. 2.6892
Celebrated cases of Judge Dee = Dee goong an. 2.2229
Celebrating the Duke, and Louis, Bessie, Billie, Bird, Carmen, Miles, Dizzy, and other heroes. 1.4324
Celebration. 2.13350
A Celebration of American family folklore. 4.774
The celebration of heroes. 4.4948
Celebrations of death. 4.590
Celebrations of life. 4.434
Celestial handbook. 5.1732
Celestial mechanics. 5.1763, 5.1765
Celestial omnibus. 2.8642
La Celestina. 2.5197
Céline and his vision. 2.4514
Céline: the novel as delirium. 2.4515
The cell. 5.3603
Cell and molecular biology. 5.3602
Cell and tissue regeneration. 5.3489
The cell: biochemistry, physiology, morphology. 5.3589
Cell biology. 5.3595, 5.3599
Cell differentiation and morphogenesis. 5.4135
Cell fusion. 5.3429
Cell heredity. 5.3439
The cell in development and inheritance. 5.3594
The Cell in medical science. 5.3596
The cell, its organelles and inclusions. 5.3590
Cell movement and cell behaviour. 5.3625
Cell physiology. 5.3622
Cell ultrastructure. 5.3591
Cells and organelles. 5.3600
Cells & organelles. 5.3600
Cellular basis of behavior. 5.4310
Cellular neurophysiology and integration. 5.4297
Cellular pathology as based upon physiological and pathological histology. 5.4736
The cellular role of macromolecules. 5.3620
The cellular slime molds. 5.3729
The celluloid closet. 2.2991
The celluloid South. 2.3009
Celtic Britain. 3.1304
The Celtic churches. 1.2433
The Celtic consciousness. 3.85
Celtic craftsmanship in bronze. 1.6669
Celtic Leinster. 3.1871
A Celtic miscellany. 2.827
Celtic painting and Anglo-Saxon painting. 1.6403
The Celts. 3.556
Cement. 2.1563
Cemmîn. 2.2269
Cenote of sacrifice. 3.9045
The censor marches on. 4.9872
Censors in the classroom. 4.10708
Censorship and obscenity. 5.7597
The censorship of English drama, 1737-1824. 2.3100
Censorship of the movies. 4.9605
Censorship: the search for the obscene. 4.9875
Census of manufactures (1982) 4.3833
Census of retail trade (1982). Geographic area series. 4.4322
Census of retail trade (1982). Industry series. 4.4323
Census of service industries (1982) 4.3864
Census of transportation (1982) 4.3879
Census of wholesale trade (1982). Geographic area series. 4.4316
Census of wholesale trade (1982). Industry series. 4.4317

Cent nouvelles nouvelles. English. 2.3968
The centaur. 2.13365
The centenary edition of the works of Nathaniel Hawthorne. 2.11056
The centennial edition of the works of Sidney Lanier. 2.11140
The centennial history of Illinois. 3.8407
The centennial history of the Civil War. 3.7339
Central America. 3.9056
Central America, a nation divided. 3.9050
The Central American crisis. 3.9051
Central and local government in Scotland since 1707. 4.8561
Central Asia. 3.3321
Central Asia: Turkmenia before the Achaemenids. 4.741
Central European democracy and its background. 4.5287
The Central Middle East. 3.3702
The central motion. 2.12976
The central philosophy of Buddhism. 1.2159
Central planning in Czechoslovakia. 4.2319
Central problems in social theory. 4.4793
The central questions of philosophy. 1.742
The centralist tradition of Latin America. 4.8326
Centre-State relations. 4.8706
Centuries and styles of the American chair, 1640-1970. 1.6581
Centuries of childhood. 4.5743
Centuries, poems, and thanksgivings. 1.3074
The century after Cortés. 3.8926
Century handbook of English literature. 2.5486
Century of American printmaking, 1880-1980. 1.6435
A century of British painters. 1.6013
A century of ceramics in the United States, 1878-1978. 1.6614
A Century of chair design. 1.6582
A century of civil rights. 4.8068
A Century of commentary on the works of Washington Irving, 1860-1974. 2.11095
A century of DNA. 5.4420
A century of Dutch manuscript illumination. 1.6417
A century of French painting, 1400-1500. 1.6048
A century of Georgia agriculture, 1850-1950. 5.5243
A century of Indian National Congress, 1885-1985. 4.8717
Century of innovation. 2.3176
A century of labor-management relations at McCormick and International Harvester. 4.3701
A century of Latin-American thought. 3.8966
A century of music-making. 1.4068
A century of Negro migration. 3.6789
A century of pay. 4.3123
A Century of plays by American women. 2.10789
A century of political cartoons. 3.6331
A Century of psychology as science. 5.114
The century of revolution, 1603-1714. 3.1442
A century of Russian agriculture. 5.5251
Century of service. 5.5216
Century of struggle. 4.5983
Century of the essay. 2.2433
The century of total war. 3.746
A century of Whitman criticism. 2.11279
Century's ebb. 2.11577
CEO. 4.1867, 4.4342
Ceramic sculpture. 1.6615
Ceramics. 1.6625
The Cercle social, the Girondins, and the French Revolution. 3.2098
Ceremonies in dark old men. 2.12999
Ceremony. 2.13321
The ceremony & other stories. 2.11947
The ceremony and other stories. 2.11947
Ceremony in Lone Tree. 2.12210
CERN proton synchrotron. 5.2446
A certain measure. 2.11774
Certain people of the Book. 1.2541
A certain woman. 2.2072
Cervantes. 2.5176-2.5178
Cervantes, a biography. 2.5175

Cervantes across the centuries [essays] 2.5179
Cesar Chavez. 4.3375
César Franck. 1.3871-1.3872
César Franck and his circle. 1.3870
Cesare Beccaria and the origins of penal reform. 4.6842
Cette île qui est la nôtre. 2.4841
Ceylon. 3.4366
Ceylon. 3.4367
Ceylon. 4.2456
Ceylon. 1.6310
Ceylon's foreign policy under the Bandaranaikes (1956-65) 3.4370
Cézanne. 1.6070-1.6071, 1.6075
Cezanne; his life and art. 1.6072
Cézanne's composition: analysis of his form. 1.6073
Chaco Canyon. 3.5745
Chagall. 1.5038
Chaim Weizmann. 3.3913
Chain of being. 1.136
Chain stores in America, 1859-1962. 4.4334
The chairs. 2.4579
Chaiyo!, King Vajiravudh and the development of Thai nationalism. 3.4529
The chalcolithic and early bronze ages in the Near East and Anatolia. 4.712
The chalk garden 2.8411
The chalk giants. 2.9806
The challenge of basic Christian communities. 1.3227
The challenge of crime in a free society. 4.6767
The challenge of man's future. 4.362
The challenge of pain. 5.4365
Challenge of psychical research. 5.642
The challenge of the American dream. 3.6540
The challenge of urban growth. 4.6212
The challenge of world poverty. 4.1816
Challenge to affluence. 4.1992
The challenge to isolation. 3.7582
A Challenge to social security. 4.3460
Challenge to the Court. 3.6684
Challenge to the poles. 5.6650
Challenges and choices facing American labor. 4.3579
The challenges of drought. 4.2617
Challenging the men. 4.965
Challinor's dictionary of geology. 5.2940
Chamber music. 2.8866
Chamber music. 1.4187
Champion 4.1056
Championship track and field for women. 4.1050
Champlain, the life of fortitude. 3.8710
Chamulas in the world of the sun. 3.8913
Chan Kom. 3.9043
Chance acquaintances. 2.4494
Chance and intelligence in Thucydides. 3.2609
Chance, love, and logic. 1.625
Chance, luck and statistics. 4.1068
Chance or destiny. 3.6275
A chance to learn. 4.10901
The chancelleries of Europe. 3.670
Chandalika. 2.1870
Chandragupta Maurya and his times 3.4249
The Chaneysville incident. 2.12916
Chang Tso-lin in northeast China, 1911-1928. 3.4813
Change and continuity in seventeenth-century England 3.1453
Change and continuity in twentieth-century America. 3.7508
Change and uncertainty in a peasant economy. 4.2149
Change in agriculture. 5.5233
Change in Communist systems. 3.1178
Change in contemporary South Africa. 3.5475
Change in the contemporary South. 3.8176
The change in the European balance of power, 1938-1939. 3.877
Change in the international system. 4.9025
Change of heart. 2.4434
Change of light. 2.5379
A change of season. 2.1549
Change processes in international organizations. 4.9266

Changeable scenery, its origin and development in the British theatre. 2.3159
The changed political thought of the Negro, 1915-1940. 4.8181
The Changeling. 2.6633
The changeling. 2.6634
Changes in market structure of grocery retailing 4.3692
Changes in the land. 4.386
Changes in the location of manufacturing in the United States since 1929. 4.2069
A changing America. 3.6177
The changing anatomy of Britain. 3.1711
The Changing Bedouin. 3.3840
Changing boundaries. 4.5829
The changing British party system, 1945-1979. 4.8522
Changing childbirth. 5.5071
Changing conceptions of the American character since Turner. 3.6117
Changing concepts of art. 1.6693
Changing: essays in art criticism. 1.5146
The changing face of inequality. 4.2044
Changing ideals in modern architecture, 1750-1950 1.5242
Changing ideas about women in the United States, 1776-1825. 4.6009
The changing image. 1.6493
Changing Japanese attitudes toward modernization 3.4889
Changing Melanesia. 4.5479
Changing of the gods. 1.1610
The changing party elite in East Germany. 4.8614
Changing patterns in American civilization. 3.6093
Changing patterns in foreign trade and payments. 4.4586
Changing patterns in residential services for the mentally retarded. 4.6609
Changing patterns of military politics. 5.7255
Changing patterns of security and stability in Asia. 3.3639
The Changing politics of school finance. 4.10656
The changing politics of the South. 4.8245
The changing population of the United States. 4.1679
The changing profile of pensions in America. 4.3455
The changing role of fathers? 4.5662
Changing room. 2.9822
Changing rural society. 4.5268
The changing social structure of England and Wales, 1871-1951. 4.5304
The changing structure of international law. 4.9279
The changing television audience in America. 4.4066
Changing the curriculum. 4.10615
The changing world market for iron ore, 1950-1980. 4.3732
The channels of Mars. 5.1815
Channing, the reluctant radical. 1.3417
La chanson de Roland. 2.3959
Chanson de Roland. English. 2.3961
Chanson de Roland. English & Old French. 2.3960
La Chanson de Roland; publiée d'après le manuscrit d'Oxford et traduite par Joseph Bédier. 2.3958
Chant of saints. 2.10690
Chants de Maldoror. 2.4169
Chants democratic. 4.3620
Chaos or community. 3.6706
Chapayev. 2.1562
The Chapel of the Cardinal of Portugal, 1434-1459, at San Miniato in Florence. 1.5535
Chapel Road. 2.13957
Chaplin. 2.3249-2.3250
Chapman's Homer. 2.484
The chapter in fiction. 2.5952
Chapters in a mythology. 2.13264
Chapters in Western civilization. 3.90
Chapters on Chaucer. 2.6366
Character analysis. 5.4907
Character-analysis. 5.185

Character and characterization in Shakespeare. 2.6802
Character and opinion in the United States. 1.644
Character and society in Shakespeare. 2.6806
The character of England. 3.1288
The character of John Adams. 3.7048
The character of King Arthur in medieval literature. 2.2637
The character of physical law. 5.1997
The Character of Swift's satire. 2.7304
The character of the good ruler. 4.7808
Character problems in Shakespeare's plays. 2.6805
Characteristics. 1.695
Characteristics and identification of gifted and talented students. 4.10914
Characteristics of men, manners, opinions, times. 1.695
Characters. 2.4025, 2.6924
The characters. 2.558
Characters in the Waverley novels. 2.8045
Characters of finite groups. 5.1294
The characters of love. 2.2421
Characters of Shakespeare's plays. 2.6801
The characters of Theophrastus. 2.394
The Characters of Theophrastus. 2.557
Chardin, 1699-1779. 1.6076
Charismatic bureaucrat. 3.4947
Chariton. 2.445
Charity costumes of children, scholars, almsfolk, pensioners. 4.843
Charlemagne. 3.1985-3.1986
Charlemagne and the Carolingian Empire. 3.1983
Charles A. Beard: an appraisal. 3.6250
Charles A. Beard, an intellectual biography. 3.6252
Charles-Augustin Sainte-Beuve. 2.4284
Charles Babbage and his calculating engines. 5.1126
Charles Beard and the Constitution. 4.7824
Charles Booth's London. 4.6624
Charles Brasch. 2.10213
Charles Brockden Brown, an American tale. 2.10913
Charles Bulfinch, architect and citizen. 1.5307
Charles Churchill. 2.6935
Charles Cotesworth Pinckney, founding father. 3.7009
Charles Darwin and the problem of creation. 5.3198
Charles Darwin's natural selection. 5.3353
Charles Dickens. 2.7651, 2.7657, 2.7662
Charles Dickens, a critical introduction. 2.7636
Charles Dickens, a pictorial biography. 2.7641
Charles Dickens and his publishers. 2.7646
Charles Dickens' book of memoranda. 2.7632
Charles Dickens, David Copperfield. 2.7630
Charles Dickens, his tragedy and triumph. 2.7638
Charles Dickens, new perspectives. 2.7650
Charles Dickens' quarrel with America. 2.7665
Charles d'Orléans. 2.3970
Charles E. Wilson and controversy at the Pentagon, 1953 to 1957. 5.7282
Charles Egbert Craddock (Mary Noailles Murfree). 2.11183
Charles Eliot Norton, apostle of culture in a democracy. 2.11188
Charles Evans Hughes. 3.7647-3.7648
Charles Evans Hughes and American democratic statesmanship. 3.7646
Charles Francis Adams, 1807-1886. 3.7318
Charles Francis Adams, 1835-1915. 3.7423
Charles Grant and British rule in India. 3.4276
Charles Gravier, Comte de Vergennes. 3.2044
Charles Ives and his America. 1.3905
Charles Ives and his music. 1.3902
Charles Ives remembered. 1.3904
Charles Ives, the ideas behind the music. 1.3900
Charles James Fox. 3.1563
Charles Kemble, man of the theatre. 2.3348
Charles Lamb. 2.7903
Charles Lamb and his contemporaries. 2.7905

Charles Lamb and the theatre. 2.7908
Charles Lamb: the evolution of Elia. 2.7904
Charles M. Russell. 1.5965
Charles Macklin. 2.3351
Charles Morgan and the development of
  Southern transportation. 4.3896
Charles Peirce. 1.620
Charles Peirce's empiricism. 1.627
Charles Perrault. 2.4045
Charles Reade. 2.8000
Charles Rennie Mackintosh. 5.7072
Charles Rennie Mackintosh and the modern
  movement. 1.5394
The Charles River Bridge case. 4.9758
Charles Sanders Peirce. 1.621
Charles Sheeler. 1.5970
Charles Sheeler, artist in the American
  tradition. 1.5971
Charles Stewart Parnell. 3.1855
Charles Sumner and the coming of the Civil
  War. 3.7161
Charles Sumner and the rights of man. 3.7162
Charles the Bold. 3.2221
Charles XII of Sweden. 3.3394
Charles W. Chesnutt. 2.10928, 2.10930
Charles W. Eliot. 4.10995
Charles Williams, poet of theology. 2.9530
Charles Willson Peale. 1.5962
Charles Willson Peale and his world. 1.5961
Charley is my darling 2.8498
Charlie Chaplin. 2.3248
Charlotte Brontë. 2.7451
Charlotte Perkins Gilman. 2.11043, 4.6003
The Charlotte Perkins Gilman reader. 2.11041
Charlotte Temple. 2.11218
A charm of words. 2.1056
A charmed life. 2.12063
La Charte d'Athènes. 1.5578
Charter of the United Nations. 4.9197
The Charterhouse of Parma. 2.4303
Charting the future. 4.9793
The Chartists. 4.3654
The chasm. 4.10880
The chasm ahead. 3.214
A Chaste maid in Cheapside. 2.6633
Chateaubriand. 2.4152-2.4153
Les châteaux de France. 1.5575
The Chatham administration, 1766-1768.
  3.1567
Chaucer. 2.6355, 2.6361
Chaucer: an introduction. 2.6360
Chaucer and his poetry. 2.6364
Chaucer and medieval estates satire. 2.6320
Chaucer and the fifteenth century. 2.5600
Chaucer and the French tradition. 2.6349
Chaucer and the imagery of narrative. 2.6330
Chaucer and the Italian trecento. 2.6347
Chaucer and the making of English poetry.
  2.6362-2.6363
Chaucer and the mediaeval sciences. 2.6374
Chaucer and the Roman poets. 2.6351
A Chaucer glossary. 2.6376
A Chaucer handbook. 2.6341
Chaucer in his time. 2.6345
Chaucer, Langland, and the creative
  imagination. 2.5612
Chaucer life-records. 2.6340
Chaucer: sources and backgrounds. 2.6348
Chaucer, the critical heritage. 2.6358
Chaucer, the maker. 2.6371
Chaucer, the poet as storyteller. 2.6373
Chaucer's Boccaccio. 2.6352
Chaucer's 'Book of fame' 2.6331
Chaucer's dream-poems. 2.6372
Chaucer's knight. 2.6325
Chaucer's Troilus and Cressida. 2.6333
Chauncey Wright. 1.656
Chauncey Wright and the foundations of
  pragmatism. 1.657
Chautauqua. 4.10987
Chavez and the farm workers. 4.3378
The Chebyshev polynomials. 5.1559
A checklist of American imprints for 1820-
  5.7760
A checklist of American imprints for 1830- .
  5.7750
A checklist of Canadian literature and
  background materials, 1628-1960. 5.7889

Checklist of major U.S. Government series.
  5.7775
Checklist of the world's birds. 5.3945
Checklist of United States public documents
  1789-1909. 5.7766
Cheep theatricks! 2.13237
A cheerful nihilism. 2.10654
The cheese and the worms. 1.2456
Chekhov. 2.1486, 2.1491
Chekhov, a study of the four major plays.
  2.1493
Chekhov in performance. 2.1495
The Chekhov play. 2.1494
Chekhov, the early stories, 1883-1888. 2.1484
Chekhov's great plays. 2.1492
The Chemehuevis. 3.5848
Chemical abstracts. 5.2585
Chemical Abstracts Service source index.
  5.8117
Chemical analysis. 5.2655, 5.2688
Chemical and biochemical aspects of electron-
  spin resonance spectroscopy. 5.2677
Chemical and process technology encyclopedia.
  5.6808
Chemical applications of group theory. 5.2813
Chemical applications of Raman spectroscopy.
  5.2685
The chemical basis of life. 5.3490
The chemical bond. 5.2820
Chemical bond. 5.2837
Chemical bonding. 5.2812
Chemical bonds and bond energy. 5.2822
Chemical calculations. 5.2634
Chemical concepts in pollutant behavior.
  5.3574
Chemical dictionary. 5.2591
Chemical ecology of insects. 5.3865
The chemical economy. 5.6814
Chemical embryology. 5.4136
Chemical encyclopaedia. 5.2593
Chemical engineering. 5.6829
Chemical engineering drawing symbols. 5.6816
Chemical engineers' handbook. 5.6827
Chemical evolution. 5.3318
The chemical evolution of the atmosphere and
  oceans. 5.2513
The Chemical formulary. 5.6822
Chemical hydrogeology. 4.309
Chemical information. 5.2603
Chemical kinetics and transport. 5.2883
Chemical methods of rock analysis. 5.3042
Chemical microbiology. 5.4453
Chemical neurobiology. 5.4300
Chemical oceanography. 4.341
Chemical principles. 5.2626, 5.2629
Chemical process control. 5.6837
Chemical publications, their nature and use.
  5.2602
Chemical reaction and reactor engineering.
  5.6853
Chemical reaction engineering. 5.6854
Chemical reactor design and operation. 5.6855
Chemical research faculties. 5.2633
The chemical senses. 5.4358
Chemical synonyms and trade names. 5.6810
Chemical technicians' ready reference
  handbook. 5.2640
Chemical technology. 5.6857
Chemical technology handbook. 5.6823
Chemical thermodynamics. 5.2894
Chemicals from petroleum. 5.6896
Chemistry. 5.2631, 5.4775
The chemistry and physics of clays and allied
  ceramic materials. 5.6902
Chemistry in two dimensions. 5.2900
The chemistry of alkenes. 5.2758
Chemistry of carbon compounds. 5.2718
The Chemistry of diazonium and diazo groups.
  5.2755
The Chemistry of double-bonded functional
  groups. 5.2849
Chemistry of glasses. 5.2694
Chemistry of hazardous materials. 5.6110
The chemistry of human behavior. 5.4338
Chemistry of interfaces. 5.2897
The Chemistry of natural products. 5.2790
The chemistry of non-aqueous solvents. 5.6863

The chemistry of nucleosides and nucleotides.
  5.4426
The chemistry of organolithium compounds.
  5.2785
The chemistry of our environment. 5.2628
Chemistry of pesticides. 5.5414
The chemistry of phosphorus. 5.2711
Chemistry of specific, selective, and sensitive
  reactions. 5.2652
The Chemistry of the carbon-carbon triple
  bond. 5.2759
The chemistry of the carbon-nitrogen double
  bond. 5.2760
The chemistry of the coordination compounds.
  5.2839
Chemistry of the elements. 5.2830
Chemistry of the environment. 5.2627
Chemistry of the metal-gas interface. 5.2899
The chemistry of the thiol group. 5.2761
Chemistry through models. 5.2867
The chemists and the word. 5.2606
The chemist's companion: a handbook of
  practical data, techniques, and references.
  5.2648
Chemmeen. 2.2269
Chemodynamics, environmental movement of
  chemicals in air, water, and soil. 5.2632
Chen Duxiu, founder of the Chinese
  Communist Party. 3.4766
Chen Village. 4.5457
Chéri and The last of Chéri. 2.4491
Cherokee removal. 3.5849
Cherubim and Seraphim. 1.3327
The Chesapeake in the seventeenth century.
  3.8107
Chesapeake politics, 1781-1800. 4.8189
Chess. 4.1070
The Chester mystery plays. 2.6202
Chester plays. 2.6202
Chesterton, man and mask. 2.7567
Chevengur. 2.1602
The Cheyenne Indians. 3.5853
The Cheyennes. 3.5854
Chicago and the American literary imagination,
  1880-1920. 2.10473
Chicago breakdown. 1.4304
Chicago divided. 3.8420
Chicago: growth of a metropolis. 3.8412
The Chicago manual of style. 5.7563
The Chicago pragmatists. 1.531
Chicago renaissance. 2.10418
The Chicago renaissance in American letters.
  2.10472
The Chicago school of architecture. 1.5301
The Chicago school of sociology. 4.4822
Chicago stories. 2.10893
The Chicago Tribune. European ed. 3.2228
Chicago's White City of 1893 5.5657
La Chicana. 3.6583
Chicano families in the urban Southwest, 1848
  to the present. 3.8564
Chicano literature. 2.10301, 2.10357
Chicano voices. 2.10681
Chicanos in a changing society. 3.8631
The Chicanos: Mexican American voices.
  2.10683
Chicorel theater index to plays in anthologies,
  periodicals, discs, and tapes. 5.8126
Chidambara sanchayan. 2.1888
Chief contemporary dramatists. 2.3767
Chief contemporary dramatists, second series.
  2.3768
Chief contemporary dramatists, third series.
  2.3769
Chief plays. 2.4017
Chief pre-Shakespearean dramas. 2.6201
The chief sources of English legal history.
  4.9406
Chief works, and others. 4.7388
Chiefship and cosmology. 3.5419
Child abuse. 4.6545, 4.6560, 5.4966
Child abuse, an annotated bibliography. 5.8363
Child abuse and neglect. 4.6563
The child and his environment in Black Africa.
  4.647
The child and his family. 4.5716
The child and his welfare. 4.6555
The child and society. 4.5718, 5.563

The child and the curriculum. 4.10384
Child care and the growth of love. 4.5715
Child care, family benefits, and working parents. 4.5616
Child care in the family. 4.5746
Child development. 5.560, 5.565
Child development and education. 4.10213
Child, family, neighborhood. 4.6546
The child from five to ten. 4.5719
Child language. 4.10392, 5.8330
Child mental health in international perspective. 5.5101
Child of conflict. 3.6470
Child of fortune. 2.2135
A child of the century. 2.11825
Child of the dark. 4.5272
Child protection report. 4.6564
Child protection report's national directory of children & youth services 1979-. 4.6564
Child sexual abuse. 5.4954
The child, the parent, and the state. 4.10050
Child training and personality. 4.5714
Child welfare. 4.6547
Child welfare in Israel. 4.6571
Child welfare services. 4.6559
Child welfare: services and perspectives. 4.6551
The child who never grew. 4.6584
Childhood. 2.1505
Childhood and society. 4.5727
Childhood in contemporary cultures. 4.5706
Childhood information resources. 5.8364
Childhood psychosis in the first four years of life. 5.5118
Childhood's end. 2.8518
Children and arson. 4.6752
Children and behavior therapy. 5.5108
Children & behavior therapy. 5.5108
Children and decent people. 4.6566
Children and older people. 2.12562
Children and politics. 4.5732
Children and the environment. 5.316
Children and the language arts. 4.10477
Children and their primary schools. 4.10120
Children and work. 4.5740
Children and youth in America. 4.6553
Children are civilians too. 2.13685
Children in foster care. 4.6579
Children in jail. 4.6870
Children is all. 2.12357
The children of Aataentsic. 3.5891
Children of Abraham. 1.1903
Children of alcoholism. 4.6638
Children of bondage. 3.6755
Children of crisis. 4.2091a
The children of light and the children of darkness. 4.7580
The children of Llyr. 2.13413
The children of pride. 3.8265
The children of Sánchez, autobiography of a Mexican family. 4.5611
Children of six cultures. 4.5731
The children of the desert. 4.666
The children of the dream. 4.5745
Children of the light. 5.5487
Children of the revolution. 4.10103
'Children of the sea,' and three other unpublished plays. 2.12285
Children of the storm: black children and American child welfare. 4.6552
Children of the universe. 5.1713
Children of the yellow earth. 4.3624
Children of violence. 2.9012, 4.10688
Children, school, and society in nineteenth-century England. 4.10116
Children who hate. 4.5721
Children with handicaps. 5.5082
The children's cause. 4.6568
Children's crusade. 2.13398
Children's freedom. 4.11010
Children's friendships. 4.5711
Children's games in street and playground. 4.1063
Children's literature; a guide to reference sources. 5.7717
Children's literature in the elementary school. 4.10469
Children's minds. 4.10377

Children's plays in collections, 1975-1984. 2.2787
Children's sexual thinking. 4.5734
Children's social values. 4.10381
Children's speech. 2.156
Children's television, the first thirty-five years, 1946-1981. 2.2861
A child's Christmas in Wales. 2.9406
The child's conception of geometry. 4.10390
The Child's conception of language. 2.118
The child's conception of number. 5.610
The child's conception of physical causality. 5.571
The child's conception of space. 5.596
The child's conception of the world. 5.575
Child's garden. 4.10413
A child's mind; how children learn during the critical years from birth to age five. 4.10398
Child's play. 5.553
Child's talk. 2.117
The child's understanding of number. 5.1263
Childwold. 2.13195
Chile. 3.9258, 3.9268
Chile, a country study. 3.9257
Chile, an economy in transition. 4.2176
Chile and the United States, 1880-1962. 3.6418
Chile: land and society. 4.2841
The Chilean Communist Party and the road to socialism. 4.8341
Chilean rural society from the Spanish conquest to 1930. 4.5273
Chilly scenes of winter. 2.12899
Chimera. 2.12876
Les chimères. 2.4223
Chimes of change and hours. 4.6034
The chimpanzees of Gombe. 5.4034
Ch'in Shih-huang ling ping ma yung. 3.4694
Chin tai Chung-kuo she hui yen chiu. 5.8398
China. 3.4632, 3.6420, 3.6423
China, a country study. 3.4613
China, a geographical survey. 3.4623
China, ancient kilns and modern ceramics. 1.6621
China and Africa in the Middle Ages. 3.5128
China and America. 3.6422
China and Christianity. 3.4739
China and Inner Asia. 3.4093
China and Malaysia, 1949-1983. 3.4672
China & Russia. 3.4681
China and Southeast Asia. 3.4409
China and the brave new world. 3.4725
China and the helping hand, 1937-1945. 4.4675
China and the major powers in East Asia. 3.4679
China and the overseas Chinese. 3.4656
China and the West, 1858-1861. 3.4735
China and the world. 3.4844
China at the center. 3.4714
China crosses the Yalu. 3.5032
China facts & figures annual. 3.4841
The China hands. 4.9060
China in crisis. 3.4786
China in disintegration. 3.4749
China in maps. 4.181
China in revolution: the first phase, 1900-1913. 3.4744
China in the sixteenth century. 1.3244
China, liberation and transformation, 1942-1962. 3.4785
The China lobby in American politics. 3.6427
China on the eve of Communist takeover. 3.4774
The China quagmire. 3.4919
China, radicalism to revisionism, 1962-1979. 3.4806
China scapegoat, the diplomatic ordeal of John Carter Vincent. 3.7691
China shakes the world. 3.4775
China South Asian relations, 1947-1980. 3.4103
The China tangle. 3.6424
China, the land and its people. 3.4620
China turned rightside up. 4.7127
Chinabound. 3.4660
China's changing map. 3.4801
China's cultural legacy and communism. 3.4651

China's destiny. 3.4671
China's early industrialization. 4.2467
China's economic development. 4.2471, 4.2474
China's economic revolution. 4.2475
China's economic system. 4.2473
China's economy. 4.2479
China's economy in global perspective. 4.2487
China's entrance into the family of nations. 4.9078
China's first unifier. 3.4692
China's foreign relations in the 1980s. 3.4845
China's forty millions. 3.4652
China's gentry. 4.5413
China's imperial past. 3.4636
China's intellectuals. 3.4805
China's language reforms. 2.2145
China's management of the American barbarians. 3.6419
China's minorities. 3.4653
China's modern economy in historical perspective. 4.2460
China's new party leadership. 4.8743
China's one-child family policy. 4.5685
China's open door policy. 4.4634
China's political economy. 4.2485
China's response to the West. 3.4675
China's turbulent quest. 3.4677
China's wartime finance and inflation, 1937-1945. 3.4781
Chinese and Indian architecture. 1.5450
The Chinese and their rebellions, viewed in connection with their national philosophy, ethics, legislation, and administration. 3.4730
Chinese art of the warring states period. 1.6528
Chinese art under the Mongols. 1.5064
The Chinese bronzes of Yunnan. 1.6670
Chinese calligraphy. 1.6606-1.6607
Chinese carpets. 1.6587
The Chinese city between two worlds. 4.6266
Chinese civilization. 3.4634
Chinese civilization and bureaucracy. 3.4629
The Chinese classics. 2.2178
Chinese color prints from the Ten Bamboo Studio. 1.6477
Chinese communism and the rise of Mao. 3.4748
The Chinese Communist Army in action. 5.7337
Chinese Communist power and policy in Xinjiang, 1949-1977. 3.4861
The Chinese Communists: sketches and autobiographies of the Old Guard. 3.4812
The Chinese cookbook. 5.7138
The Chinese cultural revolution. 3.4788
Chinese defence policy. 5.7335
The Chinese economy. 4.2484
Chinese educational policy. 4.10743
Chinese-English dictionary of contemporary usage. 2.2148
The Chinese exhibition. 1.5065
Chinese family and kinship. 4.5630
The Chinese family in the communist revolution. 4.5627
Chinese fiction from Taiwan. 2.2253
Chinese figure painting. 1.6354
The Chinese garden. 5.5369
The Chinese gentry. 4.5411
The Chinese hospital. 5.4712
The Chinese in Indonesia. 3.4560
The Chinese in Philippine life, 1850-1898. 3.4589
The Chinese in Southeast Asia. 3.4389
The Chinese inflation, 1937-1949. 4.4521
Chinese intellectuals and the revolution of 1911. 3.4745
Chinese intellectuals and the West, 1872-1949. 3.4467
Chinese labor in California, 1850-1880. 4.3610
Chinese landscape painting. 1.6364
The Chinese language. 2.2143-2.2144
The Chinese literati on painting; Su Shih (1037-1101) to Tung Ch'i-ch'ang (1555-1636). 1.6321
Chinese literature for the 1980s. 1.6723
A Chinese look at literature. 2.2243
Chinese narrative. 2.2170

The Chinese novel at the turn of the century. 2.2175
The Chinese on the art of painting. 1.6318
Chinese painting. 1.6313, 1.6319
Chinese painting style. 1.6317
The Chinese People's Liberation Army. 5.7338
Chinese philosophy, 1949-1963. 5.8346
Chinese philosophy in classical times. 1.155
Chinese pictorial art. 1.6314
Chinese politics after Mao. 3.4842
The Chinese potter. 1.6617
Chinese railways and British interests, 1898-1911. 4.4021
Chinese religion in Western languages. 5.8440
Chinese religions. 1.1791
Chinese rhyme-prose. 2.2195
Chinese society in Thailand. 3.4521
Chinese theater. 2.3388
Chinese theater in the days of Kublai Khan. 2.3390
The Chinese theatre in modern times, from 1840 to the present day. 2.3389
Chinese theories of literature. 2.2496
Chinese thought and institutions. 3.4631
Chinese thought, from Confucius to Mao Tsê-tung. 1.151
Chinese traditional historiography. 3.4658
The Chinese transformation of Buddhism. 1.2114
The Chinese vernacular story. 2.2173
A Chinese village in early Communist transition. 4.5418
Chinese warlord. 3.4819
Chinoiserie. 1.5109
The chip-chip gatherers. 2.10003
The Chippewa and their neighbors. 3.5856
Chippewa music. 1.4306
Chisholm's handbook of commercial geography. 4.4123
Chit-chat in a letter to a lady in the country. 2.7271
Chivalric ideas and practices in mediaeval France. 3.292
Chivalric romances. 2.5620
The chivalrous society. 4.5084
Chivalry. 3.291
Chivalry in English literature. 2.5581
Choderlos de Laclos. 2.4077
Choice and chance. 1.1187
Choice of adjustment to floods. 4.297
A choice of Kipling's verse, made by T.S. Eliot, with an essay on Rudyard Kipling. 2.7888
Choices and echoes in Presidential elections. 4.7955
Choiseul, Vol.1: Father and son, 1719-1754. 3.2049
Choix de poèmes. 2.4313, 2.4755
Choix de poèmes [de] Leconte de Lisle. 2.4259
Cholera, 1832. 5.4762
Choosing an electoral system. 4.7739
Choosing educational software. 4.10299
Chopin. 1.3609, 1.3839
Chopin's musical style. 1.3836
Choral conducting. 1.4499
Choral conducting; a symposium. 1.4500
The chordates. 5.3890
Chosen children. 4.6577
Chosen country. 2.11578
The chosen people in America. 1.1973
The chosen place, the timeless people. 2.13169
Chōshū in the Meiji Restoration. 3.4989
Chou En-lai: China's gray eminence. 3.4816
Ch'ou pan i wu shih mo. English. Selections. 3.6419
The Chouans. 2.4116
Chrétien de Troyes. 2.3951-2.3952
Chrétien de Troyes, the man and his work. 2.3950
Christ and culture 1.2242
Christ and time. 1.2787
Christ, faith and history: Cambridge studies in Christology. 1.2857
Christ in a pluralistic age. 1.2858
Christ in Christian tradition. 1.2848
Christ in concrete. 2.11566
Christ in Eastern Christian thought. 1.2850
Christ in the light of the Christian-Jewish dialogue. 1.2873

The Christ of faith and the Jesus of history. 1.2877
Christ stopped at Eboli. 3.2946
Christ, the experience of Jesus as Lord. 1.2868
Christ, the sacrament of the encounter with God. 1.3224
Christgau's Record guide. 1.3627
A Christian America. 1.2375
Christian and Oriental philosophy of art. 1.5127
Christian attitudes toward war and peace. 1.2922
The Christian century in Japan, 1549-1650 1.2464
Christian Democracy in Venezuela. 4.8354
Christian Dietrich Grabbe. 2.13588
Christian discourses, and The lilies of the field and the birds of the air, and Three discourses at the communion on Fridays. 1.2218
Christian England. 1.2432
The Christian faith. 1.2775
Christian faith and natural science. 1.2774
The Christian faith and the Marxist criticism of religion. 1.2268
Christian history and interpretation. 1.2179
The Christian humanism of Flannery O'Connor. 2.13218
Christian influence upon the ideology of the Taiping Rebellion, 1851-1864. 3.4727
Christian-Latin poetry. 2.812
The Christian life. 1.1478
Christian martyrs of the world. 1.2475
Christian-Marxist dialogue in Eastern Europe. 4.7138
A Christian moral theology. 1.3205
Christian Morgenstern. 2.13841
Christian mysticism. 1.3092
Christian philosophy. 1.392
The Christian philosophy of Saint Augustine. 1.333
The Christian philosophy of St. Thomas Aquinas. 1.394
Christian political theory and church politics in the mid-twelfth century. 1.3152
Christian realism and political problems. 1.2253
Christian religion in the Soviet Union. 1.2458
The Christian renaissance. 2.2378
Christian rite and Christian drama in the Middle Ages. 1.3216
Christian spirituality. 1.3053
Christian theology. 1.2738, 1.2789
Christian theology and old English poetry. 2.5595
The Christian tradition. 1.2749
The Christian tradition in modern British verse drama. 2.5927
The Christian year. 2.7874
Christianity among the religions of the world. 1.2266
Christianity and classical culture. 1.2303
Christianity and history. 1.2246
Christianity and Igbo culture. 1.1858
Christianity and Japan. 1.2465
Christianity and revolution. 1.2316
Christianity and the encounter of the world religions. 1.2265
Christianity and the Shona. 1.1860
Christianity and the social crisis. 1.2926
Christianity and Western civilization. 3.92
Christianity in a revolutionary age. 1.2365
Christianity in independent Africa. 1.2467
Christianity, social tolerance, and homosexuality. 4.5532
Christianity through the ages. 1.2283
Christians and Jews in the Ottoman empire. 3.3709
Christians in the American Revolution. 3.6912
Christians in the Arab East. 1.2461
Christina Rossetti. 2.8011
Christina Rossetti, a divided life. 2.8010
Christina Rossetti, critical perspectives, 1862-1982. 2.8012
Christina Stead. 2.10174-2.10175
Christina Stead, ocean of story. 2.10171
A Christina Stead reader. 2.10164
Christine de Pizan. 2.3974
Christmas carol. 2.7631

Christmas carols. 1.3512
Christmas Eve. 2.12920
Christmas in Biafra, and other poems. 2.10102
The Christmas tree. 2.9735
Christo. 1.5742
Christo, complete editions, 1964-1982. 1.5042
Christology at the crossroads. 1.2871
Christology of the later Fathers. 1.2855
The Christology of the New Testament. 1.2846
Christoph Martin Wieland. 2.13668
Christopher and his kind, 1929-1939. 2.8840
Christopher Brennan. 2.10154
Christopher Columbus. 3.5973
Christopher Columbus, a radio play. 2.9075
Christopher Fry: an appreciation 2.8675
Christopher Gadsden and the American Revolution. 3.6995
Christopher Isherwood. 2.8841
Christopher Isherwood. 2.8842
Christopher Marlowe, a study of his thought, learning, and character. 2.6616
Christopher Marlowe, biographical and critical study. 2.6614
Christopher Smart, scholar of the university. 2.7255
Christus victor. 1.2874
Chromatographic methods. 5.2664
Chromatography. 5.2663
Chromosome botany and the origins of cultivated plants. 5.3789
The chromosomes. 5.3608
Chronic inflation in Latin America. 4.4510
The chronicle of Aethelweard. 3.1312
A chronicle of conflict. 3.2980
The chronicle of Dalmailing. 2.7717
Chronicle of Morea. 3.2672
The chronicle of the election of Hugh, Abbot of Bury St. Edmunds and later Bishop of Ely. 1.3267
The Chronicle of the Łódź ghetto, 1941-1944. 3.3989
The chronicle of Theophanes. 3.518
Chronicles. 3.564-3.565
Chronicles of conscience. 2.9191
Chronicles of Matthew Paris. 1.3230
Chronicles of the Crusades. 3.586
The chronicles of the Deryni. 2.13126
The chronicles of Thomas Covenant, the Unbeliever. 2.12993
Chronicon Aethelweardi. 3.1312
Chronique des Pasquier. 2.4517
Chronological history of United States foreign relations, 1776 to January 20, 1981. 3.6398
A chronological list of prose fiction in English printed in England and other countries, 1475-1640. 5.7969
Chronologies in New World archaeology. 3.5695
Chronologies in Old World archaeology. 3.546
Chronologisch-thematisches Verzeichnis sämtlicher Tonwerke Wolfgang Amadé Mozarts. 1.3611
A chronology and fact book of the United Nations, 1941-1976. 4.9210
The chronology of oral tradition. 3.5060
A chronology of photography. 5.6917
Chronology of the expanding world, 1492-1762. 3.374
Chronology of the modern world. 3.375
Chronology of the war at sea, 1939-1945 3.1028
Chronology of world history. 3.368
The chrysanthemum and the sword. 3.4884
Chu Hsi and his masters. 1.163
Chu Hsi, life and thought. 1.164
Ch'u tz'u. English. 2.2184
Chuck Berry. 1.4087
Chuck Berry, rock 'n' roll music. 1.4088
Chūgoku no bijutsu. 3. Kaiga. 1.6313
Chung-hua jen min kung ho kuo jen ming lu. 3.4809
Chung-hua yüan lin. 5.5370
Chung-kuo chin tai hsiao shuo. 5.8045
Chung-kuo hua chih feng ko. 1.6317
Chung-kuo ku tien hsiao shuo. 5.8046
Chung-kuo ti i jih. English. 3.4758
The church. 1.3196

The church and residential desegregation. 3.6783
Church and society. 1.3159
Church and society in England 1770-1970. 1.2430
Church and society in the last centuries of Byzantium. 3.2660
Church and state. 1.3208
Church and state in Ethiopia, 1270-1527. 1.2471
Church and state in Mexico, 1822-1857. 3.8931
Church and state in modern Ireland, 1923-1979. 1.2450
Church and state in Revolutionary Virginia, 1776-1787. 1.2414
Church and state in Russia. 1.3115
Church and state in the United States ... 1.2393
Church and state in Tonga. 1.2473
Church and state in Yugoslavia since 1945. 1.2460
The church and the age of reason, 1648-1789. 1.2364
The church and the city, 1865-1910. 1.2998
The church and the national security state. 1.2804
The church and the sacraments. 1.3223
The church and the second sex. 4.5975
Church architecture in New France. 1.5522
Church dogmatics. 1.2773
Church history in the age of science. 1.2271
A church history of Scotland. 1.2449
The church in a secularised society. 1.3158
The Church in an age of revolution. 1.2366
The church in Brazil. 1.3187
The church in medieval Ireland. 1.2451
The Church in the power of the Spirit. 1.2993
The church in the Roman Empire. 1.2304
Church life in England in the thirteenth century. 1.2440
The Church of the Covenant, 1637-1651. 1.3392
Church, politics, and society in Spain, 1750-1874. 1.3194
Church, state, and Christian society at the time of the investiture contest. 1.3209
Church, state, and education. 4.7212
Church, state, and opposition in the U.S.S.R. 1.2459
The church struggle in South Africa. 3.5450
Church symbolism. 1.2983
Church wealth in Mexico. 1.3186
Churches and politics in Latin America. 1.2426
Churches and the working classes in Victorian England. 1.2445
The churches of Mexico, 1530-1810. 1.5523
Churchill and De Gaulle. 3.926
Churchill, Roosevelt, Stalin. 3.920
Chūshingura. 2.3400
The CIA and the U.S. intelligence system. 4.7902
CIA and the United States intelligence system. 4.7902
Ciano's diary, 1939-1943. 3.2896
Ciano's diplomatic papers. 3.2897
The Ciba collection of medical illustrations. 5.4737
Cicero. 3.2782, 3.2784
Cicero and his friends. 3.2781
Cicero and the end of the Roman Republic. 3.2783
Cicero and the Roman Republic. 3.2760
Cicero. Letters to Atticus. 2.669
Cicero, the ascending years. 3.2785
Cicero's letters to Atticus 2.715
Cid. 2.4016
CID, 1985. 5.8121
The Cid and his Spain. 3.3427
The Cid; Cinna; The theatrical illusion. 2.4016
El Cid Campeador. 2.5186
Cid (Epic cycle) 2.5185
Cien años de soledad. 2.5417
CIJE. 5.8149
Cimarron. 2.11712
CINAHL 1977-. 5.8291
Cincinnatus. 3.7034

Cinderella, a folklore casebook. 4.765
Cinderella and her sisters. 5.432
Cineliteracy. 2.2952
Cinema and society. 2.3008
The cinema as art. 2.3002
Cinema beyond the Danube. 2.2890
Cinema booklist. 5.8142
The cinema of Federico Fellini. 2.3042
The cinema of Ousmane Sembene, a pioneer of African film. 2.3068
Cinema verite in America: studies in uncontrolled documentary. 2.2922
Cinq grandes odes. 2.4471
The CIO and the Democratic Party. 4.3596
The CIO challenge to the AFL. 4.3354
The circle of mountains. 3.2238
The circle of the Baal Shem Tov. 1.1988
Circling back. 2.13090
Circuit analysis with computer applications to problem solving. 5.6278
Circuit and system theory. 5.6273
Circuit design for electronic instrumentation. 5.6553
The circuit rider. 2.11015
Circuit theory. 5.6276
Circuits, signals, and systems. 5.6274
Circular letters of Congressmen to their constituents, 1789-1829. 3.7019
The circulation of the blood and other writings. 5.4226
Circumpolar peoples. 4.689
Circus. 4.1184
The Circus from Rome to Ringling. 4.1186
The circus in the attic. 2.12641
The circus of Dr. Lao. 2.11719
CIS U.S. serial set index. 5.7782
Cisalpine Gaul. 3.2714
The citadel. 2.8590
Citadel. 4.8044
Cities. 5.8394
Cities and city planning. 4.6339
Cities and planning in the ancient Near East. 1.5606
Cities & society in colonial Latin America. 4.5255
Cities and society in colonial Latin America. 4.5255
Cities and suburbs. 4.6286
The cities and the Federal system. 4.7874
Cities and years. 2.1561
Cities in evolution. 1.5579
Cities in revolt. 3.6010
Cities in the wilderness. 3.6871
Cities in world perspective. 4.6185
Cities of light and sons of the morning. 2.2380
Cities of peasants. 4.6247
Cities of the American West. 4.6242
The cities of the eastern Roman provinces. 3.2557
Cities of the interior. 2.12250
Cities of the mind. 4.6206
Cities of the Soviet Union. 4.6263
Cities, suburbs, and states. 4.8847
Cities with little crime. 4.6795
Citizen Hearst. 2.3615
The citizen in court. 4.9779
The Citizen Kane book. 2.3025
Citizen Kane (Motion picture) 2.3025
Citizens and politics. 4.8716
Citizens for decency. 4.5551
Citrus science and technology. 5.5342
La città del sole. 4.7177
The city. 4.6256, 4.6298
City. 2.12470
The city. 4.6300
City and country in America. 4.6234
City and hinterland. 4.6220
The city and man. 4.7363
The city and social theory. 4.6196
The city and the grassroots. 4.6192
The city and the pillar. 2.12616
The city and the theatre. 2.3223
The city and the veld. 2.9035
City classification handbook. 4.6302
City College and the Jewish poor. 4.10814
City development. 4.6335
The City in Communist China. 4.6267
The City in cultural context. 4.6193

The city in history: its origins, its transformations, and its prospects. 4.6187
The City in late imperial China. 4.6268
The City in Russian history. 4.6262
The City in southern history. 4.6245
The city in the American novel, 1789-1900. 2.10544
The city in the ancient world. 4.6191
City invincible. 3.123
The city is the frontier. 4.6199
City life. 2.12888
City life in Japan. 4.6273
City limits. 4.8848
The city of Dickens. 2.7666
City of God against the pagans. 1.2204
City of nature. 2.10394
City of Sokrates. 3.2651
The city of the living, and other stories. 2.12505
City of the Sun. 4.7177
The city of to-morrow and its planning. 1.5590
The city of trembling leaves. 2.11503
City of words. 2.10644
The city state, The growth of. 4.7335
City traffic. 5.5934
City trenches. 4.8870
La ciudad y los perros. 2.5430
Civic art. 1.5581
The civic culture. 4.7235
The civic world of early Renaissance Florence. 3.2922
Civil disobedience. 2.11245, 4.7511
Civil disobedience and political obligation. 1.2995
Civil engineering systems analysis and design. 5.5711
Civil engineer's reference book. 5.5667
Civil liberties. 4.7684
Civil liberties and American democracy. 4.9663
Civil liberties and Nazis. 4.7688
Civil liberties and the Vinson Court. 4.9676
Civil-military relations in Sierra Leone. 3.5374
Civil religion in Israel. 3.3835
Civil rights. 4.9653
Civil rights and liberties in the United States. 5.8377
Civil rights and the crisis of liberalism. 4.8201
The civil rights of teachers. 4.9598
The civil war. 2.6955
The Civil War and Reconstruction. 3.7347
The Civil War dictionary. 3.7337
Civil War history. 3.7398
Civil War in China. 3.4782
Civil War in Russia. 3.3184
Civil War in South Russia, 1919-1920. 3.3199
The Civil War party system. 4.8190
Civil War prisons. 3.7398
The civil wars. 2.652
A Civil War treasury of tales, legends, and folklore. 3.7401
The civil wars in Chile, or, The bourgeois revolutions that never were. 3.9265
The civilian and the military. 3.6107
Civilisation: a personal view. 3.39
La civilisation de l'Europe classique. 3.176
Civilities and civil rights. 3.8233
Civilization and capitalism, 15th-18th century. 4.1747
Civilization and its discontents. 5.143
Civilization and the Caesars. 3.2790
Civilization in the United States: an inquiry by thirty Americans. 3.6059
The civilization of ancient Crete. 3.2593
The civilization of ancient India. 3.4195
Civilization of India syllabus. 3.4181
The civilization of Rome. 3.2726
The civilization of the Old Northwest. 3.8368
The Civilization of the Renaissance. 3.153

The civilization of the Renaissance in Italy. 3.2845
Civilization on trial. 3.103
The civilizations of the East. 3.99
The civilized imagination. 2.5936
Civilizing American cities. 4.6322
The civilizing process. 3.44
Civilizing the machine. 5.5520
Cladistic biogeography. 5.3232
Cladistics and vicariance. 5.3235
The claim of reason. 1.1276
The clairvoyant eye. 2.12551
Clamor at the gates. 4.8952
Clan leaders and colonial chiefs in Lango. 3.5267
Clara Schumann, a dedicated spirit. 1.4074
Clara Schumann, the artist and the woman. 1.4075
Clare; the critical heritage. 2.7573
Clarel. 2.11152
Clarendon. 3.1501
Clarendon and the English Revolution. 3.1500
The Clarendon Dickens. 2.7624
The Clarendon edition of the novels of the Brontës. 2.7444
Claret and chips. 4.8556
Clarice Lispector. 2.5471
Clarinet. 1.4170
The clarinet. Revised, and with a repertory. 1.4171
Clarinet technique. 1.4556
Clarissa, or, The history of a young lady. 2.7214
Clarissa's ciphers. 2.7215
The clash of cultures. 3.5487
Clash of cultures. 3.611
Class. 4.5240
Class and class conflict in industrial society. 4.6379
Class and community. 4.3522
Class and ideology in the nineteenth century. 4.5341
Class and religion in the late Victorian city. 1.2448
Class and society in central Chiapas. 3.8891
Class awareness in the United States. 4.5238
Class, Bureaucracy, and schools. 4.10961
Class, caste and entrepreneurship. 4.2514
Class, codes and control. 2.24
Class conflict, slavery, and the United States Constitution. 3.6980
Class, crisis, and the state. 4.6389
Class, ethnicity, and politics in Liberia. 4.5476
Class in a capitalist society. 4.5342
Class, state, & crime. 4.6697
Class, state, and industrial structure. 4.2164
Class, status, and power. 4.6374
Class structure. 4.6377
The class structure of the advanced societies. 4.6380
The class struggle in the ancient Greek world. 3.2560
Class struggle in the first French republic. 3.2106
Classic American women writers. 2.10818
Classic Americans. 2.10246
Classic and romantic music. 1.3466
Classic art. 1.5004
Classic Australian short stories. 2.10146
Classic Buddhist sculpture. 1.5763
The classic Chinese novel. 2.2172
Classic descriptions of disease. 5.4735
Classic essays in English. 2.6269
The Classic Maya collapse. 3.9033
Classic music. 1.3660
Classic papers in genetics. 2.2616, 5.3435
The classic slum. 4.5333
The classic Southwest. 3.5759
The classic theatre. 2.4898
The classic vision. 2.10251
The classical accounts of India. 3.4162
The classical age of German literature, 1740-1815. 2.13467
Classical and Christian ideas in English Renaissance poetry. 2.5789
Classical and foreign quotations. 2.3726
Classical and modern physics. 5.1992

Classical and neoclassical theories of general equilibrium. 4.1405
Classical Arab Islam. 3.3652
Classical Arabic poetry. 2.1839
The classical background of English literature. 2.5570
Classical Chinese fiction. 5.8046
Classical Chinese tales of the supernatural and the fantastic. 2.2199
Classical conditioning. 5.304
A classical dictionary of India. 3.4154
The classical drama of France. 2.3886
The classical dynamics of particles: Galilean and Lorentz relativity. 5.1658
The classical economists. 4.1317
Classical electricity and magnetism. 5.2342
Classical electrodynamics. 5.2357
Classical Greece. 1.5633
Classical Greek art (480-330 B.C.) 1.4715
Classical handbook. 3.2509
The classical heritage and its beneficiaries. 3.88
Classical Hindu mythology. 1.1688
The classical Hollywood cinema. 2.2909
Classical influences on English prose. 2.5571
A classical introduction to modern number theory. 5.1326
A classical invitation to algebraic numbers and class fields. 5.1340
Classical Islam. 3.3670
The classical language of architecture. 1.5206
Classical Marāthī literature. 2.1907
Classical Marxism, 1850-1895. 4.7452
Classical mechanics. 5.1643
Classical, modern, and humane. 2.2154
The classical moment. 2.3887
Classical mythology in Shakespeare. 2.6827
Classical myths in English literature. 1.1642
The classical papers of A. E. Housman. 2.7838
Classical sculpture. 1.5617
The classical style: Haydn, Mozart, Beethoven. 1.3661
The classical theory of electricity and magnetism. 5.2366
The classical theory of fields. 5.2362
Classical thermodynamics for advanced students of physics. 5.2251
Classical topology and combinatorial group theory. 5.1601
The classical tradition. 2.2700
The classical tradition in poetry. 2.2761
The classical tradition in Western art. 1.4682
Classical Urdu literature from the beginning to Iqbāl. 2.1898
Classical voices; studies of Corneille, Racine, Moliére, Mme de Lafayette. 2.3848
Classics and commercials. 2.10425
The classics and English Renaissance poetry. 2.5774
The classics and Renaissance thought. 3.158
Classics in management. 4.2634
Classics in psychoanalytic technique. 5.4916
Classics in radio astronomy. 5.1777
Classics in scientific management. 4.2630
Classics in software engineering. 5.1168
Classics in the theory of public finance. 4.4643
Classics of cardiology. 5.4994
Classics of Christian missions. 1.3021
Classics of neurology (from Emerson C. Kelly's 'Medical classics'). 5.4785
Classics of organization theory. 4.2645
Classics of organizational behavior. 4.2694
The classics of science. 5.730
Classics or charity. 4.10115
Classification in mental retardation. 5.4973
Classification of wetlands and deepwater habitats of the United States. 5.3263
Classification problems in ergodic theory. 5.1463
A classified Shakespeare bibliography, 1936-1958. 2.6798
The classless profession. 4.10520
Classroom computers. 4.10295
Classroom measurement & evaluation. 4.10713
Classroom measurements and evaluations. 4.10713
Classrooms that work. 4.10908
Claude Debussy, his life and works. 1.3849
Claude Lévi-Strauss. 4.423

Claude Lorrain, 1600-1682. 1.4974
Claude Monet. 1.6125
Claude Monet, observation and reflection. 1.6124
Claude Simon. 2.4752
Claude Simon's mythic muse. 2.4751
Claudius. 2.8720
Clausewitz and the state. 3.2494
Clausewitz, philosopher of war. 5.7149
The Claverings. 2.8206
Clay and glazes for the potter. 1.6626
Clayhanger. 2.8453
The Clayhanger family. 2.8453
Clea. 2.8606
Cleanness. 2.6381
Clélie. 2.4056
Clemens Brentano. 2.13553
Clement of Alexandria. 1.2487
Clementi. 1.3840
Clergy and the American Revolution. 3.6917
A clergyman's daughter. 2.9178
A clerk of Oxenford. 2.2573
Cliché-verre, hand-drawn, light-printed. 1.6504
!Click song. 2.13428
Client-centered therapy, its current practice, implications, and theory. 5.4873
Clifford Odets. 2.12262
Clifford Odets, playwright-poet. 2.12260
Clifford Odets: the thirties and after. 2.12261
Clifford Sifton. 3.8761
Cligès. 2.3948
Climate and life. 5.2492
Climate and weather in the tropics. 5.2580
Climate Canada. 5.2579
Climate change and society. 5.2516
Climate in a small area. 5.2524
Climate in earth history. 5.2527
The climate near the ground. 5.2501
Climate: present, past and future. 5.2562
Climate through the ages. 5.2526
The climates of the continents. 5.2561
Climates of the states. 5.2575
Climatology, an introduction. 5.2564
Climatology from satellites. 5.6713
Climatology: fundamentals and applications. 5.2563
The climax of French imperial expansion, 1914-1924. 3.2194
The climax of populism. 4.8227
Climbing in North America. 4.894
Climbing Jacob's ladder. 4.8095
Climbing the ladder. 5.801
Clinical atlas of human chromosomes. 5.4739
The clinical interview of the child. 5.5106
Clinical laboratory tests. 5.5176
Clinical papers and essays on psycho-analysis. 5.4915
Clinical parasitology. 5.4759
Clinical pharmacology. 5.5136
Clinical psychology and behavioral medicine. 5.4845
Clinical social work. 4.6471, 4.6497
Clinical social work in health care. 4.6539
Clinical social work in the eco-systems perspective. 4.6493
Clinics, contraception, and communication. 4.5688
Clio and the doctors. 3.410
Clio unbound. 3.1385
Les cloches de Bâle. 2.4372
The clock. 2.1525
Clock without hands. 2.12071
The clocks of Columbus. 2.12588
A clockwork orange. 2.9639
Cloning of frogs, mice, and other animals. 5.3463
Close quarters. 2.8694
Close to Colette. 2.4502
Closely watched films. 2.2887
Closely watched trains. 2.1687
The closing of the American mind. 3.6082
Closing the frontier. 3.8537
Closing the gold window. 4.4592
Cloth and clothing in medieval Europe. 4.3850
Clothes for a summer hotel. 2.12725
The clothing of Clio. 3.415
The cloud of danger. 3.7926
The cloud of unknowing. 1.3085

Cloud of unknowing. 1.3085
Clouds. 2.424
Clouds and storms. 5.2534
Clouds of the world. 5.2533
Clouds, rain, and rainmaking. 5.2535
Clough: the critical heritage. 2.7585
The cloven viscount. 2.5030
The clown 2.13683
Clowns. 4.1194
The clubwoman as feminist. 4.6172
Clues of the Caribbees. 2.12558
Cluster analysis for social scientists. 4.1244
Cluster development. 1.5601
CO₂ metabolism and plant productivity. 5.3761
Co-ordination. 2.8642
Coaching and motivation. 4.971
Coaching, athletics, and psychology. 4.969
Coal. 2.13141, 5.6874
Coal age operating handbook of underground mining. 5.6795
Coal and modern coal processing. 5.6793
Coal combustion and gasification. 5.6876
Coal in America. 5.6797
Coal, iron, and slaves. 3.7216
Coal, its role in tomorrow's technology. 5.6794
Coal mine ground control. 5.6749
Coal myths and environmental realities. 4.3748
Coal utilisation. 5.6875
Coalition government in Western Europe. 4.8364
Coastal area management and development. 4.6359
Coastal landforms and surface features. 4.273
Coasts. 4.272
A Coat of many colors. 3.6564
Cobbler in Congress. 3.7167
Cobden and Bright: a Victorian political partnership. 3.1601
The Coblentz Society desk book of infrared spectra. 5.2319
COBOL for the 80's. 5.1214
Cocaine. 4.6660
Cochrane. 3.1283
The cockatoos. 2.10179
Cockpit. 2.13120
Cocksure. 2.9963
Cocteau, a biography. 2.4485
Code international de la nomenclature botanique. 5.3654
The code of Maimonides. 1.1945
The code of Terpsichore. 4.1087
Code of the quipu. 3.9290
The code of the Woosters. 2.9550
Codes of conduct. 4.3022
The Codex Huygens and Leonardo da Vinci's art theory. 1.4594
The Codex Nuttall. 3.8882
Codex Nuttall. 3.8882
Coding and information theory. 5.1375
Coed prison. 4.6906
Coercion. 4.5028
Coercion to speak. 2.8563
Un coeur simple. 2.4193
Coevolution. 5.3385
Coexistence and commerce. 4.4154
Coexistence of species. 5.3583
Coffee and capitalism in the Venezuelan Andes. 4.2182
Coffee and conflict in Colombia, 1886-1910. 3.9175
A coffin for Dimitrios. 2.8379, 2.8381
Cogeneration. 5.6295
Cogeneration sourcebook. 5.6293
Cogewea, the half blood. 2.12223
The cogito in Husserl's philosophy. 1.1017
Cognition. 5.286
Cognition and behavior modification. 5.455
Cognition and reality. 5.277
Cognition and the symbolic processes. 5.292
The cognition of the literary work of art. 2.2362
Cognition, stress, and aging. 5.5003
The cognitive basis of the intellect. 5.369
Cognitive development. 5.592
Cognitive learning in children. 4.10371
Cognitive orientation and behavior. 5.272

Cognitive processes of nonhuman primates. 5.4105
Cognitive psychology. 5.278
Cognitive sociology. 4.5061
The coherence of theism. 1.2842
Coherent optics and holography. 5.2287
The cohesion of Saudi Arabia. 3.4054
Cohomology of groups. 5.1307
Cointelpro. 4.6829
Coke of Norfolk. 4.2904
Colbert and a century of French mercantilism 4.1360
The cold and the dark. 5.3578
Cold Comfort Farm. 2.8685
The cold fire. 4.5072
The cold war, 1945-1972. 3.7583
The cold war and its origins, 1917-1960. 3.3060
The cold war as history. 3.1165
Cold War, cold peace. 3.758
The cold war in biology. 5.3433
Cold war theories. 3.1173
A colder eye. 2.9856
A colder fire. 2.12655
The Colditz story. 3.1076
Cole Porter. 1.3945
Coleridge. 2.7595
Coleridge on the seventeenth century. 2.5648
Coleridge, opium, and Kubla Khan. 2.7591
Coleridge, the damaged archangel. 2.7600
Coleridge, the visionary. 2.7596
Colette. 2.4501, 2.4503-2.4505
Colin Wilson. 2.9831
Collaborationism in France during the Second World War. 3.1063
Collage: personalities, concepts [and] techniques. 1.4810
The collapse of British power. 3.1642
The collapse of the Tokugawa bakufu, 1862-1868. 3.4954
Collected and new poems, 1924-1963. 2.12605
The collected books of Jack Spicer. 2.13331
The collected correspondence and London notebooks. 1.3893
Collected earlier poems. 2.12741
Collected earlier poems, 1940-1960. 2.13133
Collected early poems of Ezra Pound. 2.12323
Collected economic papers 4.1263
Collected essays. 2.2344, 2.8738, 2.8813, 2.9569
Collected essays in literary criticism. 2.2591
The collected essays, journalism, and letters of George Orwell. 2.9173
The collected essays of Christopher Hill. 3.1443
The collected essays of J. V. Cunningham. 2.11546
The collected essays of John Peale Bishop. 2.11388
The collected essays of Leslie Fiedler. 2.13014
The collected Ewart, 1933-1980. 2.9673
The collected ghost stories of M.R. James. 2.8843
Collected impressions. 2.8469
The collected later poems. 2.12742
Collected letters. 2.7594, 2.8069, 2.9217
The collected letters. 2.9412
The collected letters of D. H. Lawrence. 2.8978
The collected letters of John Millington Synge. 2.8147
The collected letters of Joseph Conrad. 2.8547
The collected letters of Katherine Mansfield. 2.9080
The collected letters of Oliver Goldsmith. 2.7049
The collected letters of Thomas and Jane Welsh Carlyle. 2.7549
The collected letters of Thomas Hardy, Vol.1: 1840-1892. 2.7772
The collected letters of William Morris. 2.7967
Collected logical works. 1.1199
The collected longer poems. 2.12377
The collected novels of Conrad Aiken. 2.11300
Collected papers. 1.606, 1.773, 4.1215, 4.5403, 5.141, 5.183, 5.1885
The collected papers of Charles Darwin. 5.3352

The collected papers of Franco Modigliani. 4.1450
Collected papers on acoustics. 1.5497
Collected papers on mathematics, logic, and philosophy. 5.1023
Collected papers on wave mechanics. 5.2147
Collected plays. 2.9619, 2.10210, 2.13703
Collected plays. 2.8521
The collected plays. 2.11830
Collected plays. 2.9093, 2.12166
Collected plays. 2.4704, 2.9144, 2.10111
The collected plays. 2.9533
Collected plays. 2.8331
The collected plays of Graham Greene. 2.8739
The collected plays of Neil Simon, volume II. 2.12472
The collected plays of Peter Shaffer. 2.9312
The collected plays of Terence Rattigan. 2.9258
Collected poems. 2.8390, 2.8462, 2.8490, 2.10209, 2.10213, 2.11301, 2.11402
Collected poems. 2.581, 2.8520, 2.8580, 2.8594, 2.10059, 2.11507
The collected poems. 2.11558
Collected poems. 2.8624, 2.8628, 2.12996
Collected poems. 2.8690, 2.8862, 2.9049, 2.9068, 2.9074, 2.9126, 2.11799, 2.11872, 2.11906, 2.11917, 2.12160, 2.12282
The collected poems. 2.13254
Collected poems 2.9223
Collected poems. 2.9257, 2.9259, 2.12410
The collected poems. 2.12418
Collected poems. 2.9289
Collected poems. 2.8120, 2.9326, 2.9338, 2.9374, 2.9381, 2.9441, 2.11258, 2.12541, 2.12773, 2.12804
Collected poems, 1909-1962. 2.11626
Collected poems, 1912-1944. 2.11568
Collected poems, 1917-1982. 2.12088
Collected poems, 1919-1976. 2.12571
Collected poems, 1923-1953. 2.11393
Collected poems, 1924-1962. 2.8790
Collected poems, 1928-1985. 2.9369
Collected poems, 1929-1959. 2.9262
Collected poems, 1930-83. 2.12157
Collected poems, 1930-1955. 2.8413
Collected poems (1930-1973). 2.12441
Collected poems, 1930-1976. 2.11622
Collected poems, 1930-1978. 2.8416
Collected poems, 1931-1974. 2.8605
Collected poems, 1936-1961. 2.8676
Collected poems 1940-1978. 2.12461
Collected poems, 1941-1975. 2.9345
Collected poems, 1942-1970. 2.10193
Collected poems, 1943-1983. 2.9325
Collected poems, 1944-1979. 2.8382
Collected poems, 1947-1980. 2.11770
Collected poems, 1948-1976. 2.8370
Collected poems, 1948-1984. 2.10019
Collected poems, 1950-1970. 2.8591
Collected poems, 1951-1971. 2.11310
Collected poems, 1958-1970. 2.9740
Collected poems, 1966. 2.8718
Collected poems, 1970-1983. 2.8592
Collected poems and plays of Rabindranath Tagore. 2.1867
Collected poems by Edwin Arlington Robinson. 2.12403
Collected poems in one volume. 2.9142
Collected poems, nineteen sixty-six. 2.8718
The collected poems of E.J. Pratt. 2.9959
The collected poems of Edward Thomas. 2.9423
Collected poems of Elinor Wylie. 2.12825
The collected poems of Frank O'Hara. 2.12263
The collected poems of George Oppen. 2.12299
The collected poems of Howard Nemerov. 2.12243
The collected poems of Irving Layton. 2.9943
The collected poems of James Agee. 2.11292
The collected poems of James Elroy Flecker. 2.8627
Collected poems of John G. Neihardt. 2.12242
The collected poems of John Peale Bishop 2.11389
The collected poems of Joseph Hall. 2.6482
Collected poems of Kenneth Fearing. 2.11709

The collected poems of Kenneth Patchen. 2.12304
Collected poems of Padraic Colum. 2.8524
The collected poems of Robert Creeley, 1945-1975. 2.11533
The collected poems of Sara Teasdale. 2.12582
The collected poems of Sterling A. Brown. 2.11426
The collected poems of Stevie Smith [i.e. F. M. Smith]. 2.9344
The collected poems of Weldon Kees. 2.11946
The collected poetry of Aldous Huxley. 2.8814
The collected poetry of Dorothy Parker. 2.12301
The collected prose. 2.11385
Collected prose. 2.11820, 2.13725
Collected prose of Elinor Wylie. 2.12826
The collected satires and poems of Osbert Sitwell. 2.9330
The collected scientific papers of Paul A. Samuelson. 4.1265
Collected short fiction, 1892-1912. 2.11471
Collected short prose. 2.1592
Collected short stories. 2.11299
Collected short stories. 2.8581, 2.8812
The collected short stories of Edith Wharton. 2.12689
Collected short stories of Julia Peterkin. 2.12310
Collected shorter plays. 2.8418
The collected shorter poems. 2.12376
The collected stories. 2.1540
Collected stories. 2.5416, 2.9156, 2.9329, 2.11657, 2.11773, 2.11990, 2.12316
The collected stories. 2.9400
Collected stories. 2.12606
Collected stories, 1939-1976. 2.12912
Collected stories, including May we borrow your husband? 2.8740
The collected stories of Caroline Gordon. 2.11786
The collected stories of Colette. 2.4488
The collected stories of Elizabeth Bowen. 2.8468
The collected stories of Hortense Calisher. 2.12942
The collected stories of Jean Stafford. 2.12497
Collected stories of Katherine Mansfield. 2.9085
The collected stories of Peter Taylor. 2.12578
Collected tales and plays. 2.1379
The collected tales of E.M. Forster. 2.8642
Collected verse plays. 2.11621
Collected works. 1.728, 2.1601, 2.7960, 2.8146, 2.11401, 3.7299, 5.9, 5.1884
Collected works. 2.7041
The collected works of Abraham Lincoln; Supplement, 1832-1865. 3.7300
The collected works of Bernard Shaw. 2.8063
The collected works of Dante Gabriel Rossetti. 2.8013
Collected works of Edgar Allan Poe. 2.11196
The collected works of G.K. Chesterton. 2.7560
The collected works of Isaac Rosenberg. 2.9288
The collected works of Leo Szilard. 5.1887
Collected works of Noël Coward. 2.8582
Collected works of Pádraic H. Pearse. 2.9221
The collected works of Paul Valéry. 2.4762
The collected works of Ralph Waldo Emerson. 2.11017
The collected works of Rudyard Kipling. 2.7886
The collected works of Samuel Taylor Coleridge. 2.7586
The collected works of Spinoza. 1.1095
The Collected works of St. John of the Cross. 1.3136
The collected works of St. Teresa of Avila. 1.3138
Collected works of V.I. Lenin. 3.3145
The collected writings. 2.7622
Collected writings. 2.11266
The collected writings of Ambrose Bierce. 2.10909
Collected writings of Edgar Allan Poe. 2.11197

The collected writings of John Maynard Keynes. 4.1441
Collection development. 5.7622
Collection development in libraries. 5.7620
The collection of Alfred Stieglitz. 5.6957
A collection of English prose, 1660-1800. 2.6261
A Collection of neutrality laws, regulations and treaties of various countries. 4.9331
A collection of tales from Uji. 2.2057
Collection, use, and care of historical photographs. 5.6951
Collective and corporate responsibility. 4.2705
Collective bargaining and the decline of the United Mine Workers. 4.3388
Collective bargaining by public employees in Canada. 4.3516
Collective bargaining, contemporary American experience. 4.3349
Collective bargaining in African countries 4.3424
Collective bargaining in public employment. 4.3511
Collective bargaining in Sweden. 4.3419
Collective bargaining in the basic steel industry. 4.3385
Collective bargaining in the Federal civil service. 4.3510
Collective behavior. 4.4998
Collective dream in art. 3.4
The collective farm in Soviet agriculture. 4.2915
Collective violence. 4.5043
The collector. 2.9682
College. 4.10075
College basketball. 4.1009
The College blue book. 4.10059
The College cost book. 4.10599
The College handbook. 4.10608
College mystery novels. 2.10546
The college novel in America. 2.10590
College professors and their impact on students. 4.10573
College zoology. 5.3798
Collegiate dictionary of zoology. 5.3794
Colley Cibber, three sentimental comedies. 2.6936
Collision theory. 5.2479
The colloquial short story in China. 2.2252
The colloquial style in America. 2.10535
La colmena. 2.5241
Colombia. 3.9171, 3.9173
Colombia, a country study. 3.9172
Colonel Jack. 2.6971
The Colonel's daughter. 2.8374
Colonial Africa. 3.5103
Colonial America. 4.5127
Colonial American poetry. 2.10761
Colonial Anglicanism in North America. 1.3316
Colonial architecture and sculpture in Peru. 1.4925
Colonial art in Mexico. 1.4920
The colonial background of the American Revolution. 3.6916
Colonial Connecticut. 3.8022
Colonial Delaware. 3.8099
Colonial development. 4.8908
The colonial empires. 4.8897
The colonial encounter. 2.6050
Colonial folkways. 3.6009
Colonial Georgia. 3.8257
The colonial heritage of Latin America. 4.2145·
Colonial Hispanic America. 3.8976
The colonial idiom. 2.10855
Colonial Lucknow, 1856-1877. 3.4359
Colonial Maryland, a history. 3.8105
Colonial Massachusetts. 3.7974
Colonial New England. 4.2019
Colonial New Hampshire. 3.7963
Colonial New Jersey. 3.8066
Colonial New York. 3.8028
Colonial North Carolina. 3.8228
Colonial Pennsylvania. 3.8076
The colonial period of American history. 3.6862
Colonial policy and practice. 3.4340
The colonial printer. 5.7553

The colonial reckoning. 3.5112
The Colonial revival in America. 1.6707
Colonial Rhode Island. 3.8013
Colonial rule and the Kamba. 3.5272
Colonial self-government. 4.8916
Colonial South Carolina. 3.8242-3.8243
The Colonial South Carolina scene. 3.8239
A colonial Southern bookshelf. 5.7690
The colonial transformation of Kenya. 3.5274
Colonial travelers in Latin America. 3.5991
Colonial urban development. 4.6337
Colonial Virginia. 3.8185, 3.8197
Colonialism, 1870-1945. 4.8898
Colonialism and Christian missions. 1.3022
Colonialism and cold war. 3.6452
Colonialism by treaty in early America. 3.5802
Colonialism in Africa, 1870-1960. 3.5105
Colonists & Canadiens, 1760-1867. 3.8720
Colonists from Scotland: emigration to North America, 1707-1783. 3.6596
Colonists in bondage. 4.3106
The colonization of Australia (1829-42) 3.5577
Colony and confederation. 2.9891
Colony and mother city in ancient Greece. 4.8895
Color. 2.11536
Color atlas of human anatomy. 5.4146
Color in business, science, and industry. 5.2333
A color notation. 1.6353
Color of darkness. 2.12358
The color purple. 2.13406
Color television picture tubes. 5.6441
Colorado. 3.8556
Colorado; a guide to the highest State. 3.8555
A Colorado history. 3.8557
A colored woman in a white world. 3.6851
Colossians and Philemon. 1.2718
The colossus & other poems. 2.13257
Colour class, and the Victorians. 3.1294
Colour encyclopedia of musical instruments. 1.3514
Colours of the stars. 5.1839
The Columbia book of Chinese poetry. 2.2189
Columbia dictionary of modern European literature. 2.2670
Columbia essays on modern writers. 2.6048
The Columbia history of the world. 3.525
Columbia human rights law review. 4.5695, 4.7681
The Columbia Lippincott gazetteer of the world. 4.69
The columnists. 2.3645
Combinatorial algorithms. 5.1277
Combinatorial algorithms for computers and calculators. 5.1276
Combinatorial enumeration. 5.1280
Combinatorial optimization. 5.1550
Combinatorial optimization for undergraduates. 5.1275
Combinatorial theory. 5.1273
Combustion. 5.2902
The combustion of organic polymers. 5.2771
Come back, Dr. Caligari. 2.12889
Come together. 1.4093
Comeback, case by case. 4.3083
Comecon, integration problems of the planned economies. 4.2232
The comedians. 2.8744
Comedians. 2.9701
La comédie humaine. 2.4110
Comedies,. 2.6945
Comedies. 2.4041
The comedies of Machiavelli. 2.4971
Comedy and America. 2.11099
Comedy and conscience after the Restoration. 2.5894
Comedy and culture. 2.5716
Comedy and society from Congreve to Fielding. 2.5917
Comedy in space, time, and the imagination. 2.2823
Comedy in the Soviet theater. 2.1282
The comedy of manners. 2.5898
The comedy of Neil Simon. 2.12471
The Comedy of wit, 1660-1710. 2.5906
Comets. 5.1822
The comforters. 2.9360

Comic art in America. 1.5847
Comic faith. 2.6010
The comic imagination in American literature. 2.10656
The comic mind. 2.2980
Comic relief. 2.10657
The comic sense of Henry James. 2.11125
The comic spirit in George Meredith. 2.7951
Comic terror. 2.13074
The comic theatre of Greece and Rome. 2.299
The comics. 2.3816
Comics; anatomy of a mass medium. 1.5844
Coming apart. 3.7842
The coming boom. 4.2013
The coming crisis of Western sociology. 4.4797
The coming fury. 3.7339
Coming into being among the Australian aborigines. 4.567
Coming into being among the Australian Aborigines. 4.670
The coming of age. 4.6588
Coming of age in America: growth and acquiescence. 4.10493
Coming of age in Mississippi. 3.6846
Coming of age in Samoa; a psychological study of primitive youth for western civilisation. 3.5671
Coming of age in Shakespeare. 2.6800
The coming of Christianity to England. 1.2434
The coming of industrial order. 4.2036
The coming of post-industrial society. 4.5101
The coming of sound to the American cinema. 2.2977
The coming of the book. 5.7518
The coming of the Civil War. 3.7074
Coming of the French Revolution, 1789. 3.2104
The coming of the Maori. 3.5611
The coming of the mass market, 1850-1914. 4.2307
The coming of the Revolution, 1763-1775. 3.6910
The coming of the Spanish Civil War. 3.3459
The coming of the war, 1914. 3.776
The coming race. 4.7178
Coming through slaughter. 2.9956
Coming to light. 2.10289
Coming to terms with the short story. 2.3435
Coming up for air. 2.9179
Comings and goings. 2.13353
Command decisions. 3.910
The command of the air. 5.7393
Command under sail. 5.7421
Comment c'est. 2.4403
Commentaries on American law. 4.9503
Commentaries on the laws of England. 4.9410
A commentary on book one of the Epigrams of Martial. 2.742
A commentary on Heidegger's Being and time. 1.995
A commentary on Herodotus 2.476
A commentary on Horace. 2.726
A commentary on Horace: Odes, book 1. 2.725
A commentary on Kant's Critique of practical reason. 1.882
A commentary on Livy, books 1-5. 2.734
A commentary on Livy, books XXXI-XXXIII. 2.732
A commentary on Livy, books XXXIV-XXXVII. 2.733
Commentary on Romans. 1.2711
A commentary on Tennyson's In memoriam. 2.8162
A commentary on The anathemata of David Jones. 2.8854
A commentary on the Apostles' Creed. 1.2189
A commentary on the Aristotelian Athenaion politeia. 4.7341
A commentary on the collected plays of W. B. Yeats. 2.8363
A commentary on the Complete Greek tragedies 2.414
A commentary on the creed of Islam. 1.2046
A commentary on the Epistle of James. 1.2724
A commentary on the First and Second Epistles to the Thessalonians. 1.2719
A commentary on the First Epistle to the Corinthians. 1.2712

A commentary on the General prologue to the Canterbury tales. 2.6319
A commentary on the Gospel according to St. John. 1.2696
Commentary on the Lao Tzu. 1.1799
A commentary on the poems of Thomas Hardy. 2.7797
A commentary on the Revelation of St. John the Divine. 1.2732
A commentary on the satires of Juvenal. 2.730
A commentary on Wordsworth's Prelude, books I-V. 2.8305
A commentary to Kant's Critique of pure reason. 1.886
The commerce of nations. 4.4195
Commerce of the prairies. 3.8575
Commercial atlas 1927-35. 4.155
Commercial atlas and marketing guide. 4.155
Commercial atlas & marketing guide. 4.155
Commercial atlas of America 1911-26. 4.155
Commercial crisis and change in England, 1600-1642. 4.4227
A commercial geography. 4.4124
Commercial information services handbook 1924. 4.4260
Commercial motor transportation. 4.4041
The commercial production of climbing plants. 5.5356
Commercial relations between Spain and Spanish America in the era of free trade, 1778-1796. 4.4236
The commercial revolution of the Middle Ages, 950-1350. 4.4095
Commissars, commanders, and civilian authority. 4.8644
Commissioner Lin and the Opium War. 3.4723
Commitment and community. 4.7156
Commitment to freedom. 2.3658
The committee and its critics. 3.7541
The Committee of One Million. 4.9059
A commodity of dreams & other stories. 2.12244
Commodity price stabilization. 4.4168
Commodity prices and the new inflation. 4.1503
Commodity year book. 4.4128
The common agricultural policy. 4.2972
The common asphodel. 2.5763
Common Cause. 4.8036
Common crisis North-South. 4.4143
Common culture and the great tradition. 3.6109
Common differences. 4.6058
A common faith. 1.1528
Common ground. 3.7997
The common heart. 2.11883
Common human needs. 4.6483
COMMON L.I.S.P. 5.1217
The common law. 4.9412
The common law of mankind. 4.9287
The common law tradition. 4.9852
The common law zone in Panama. 4.9041
Common learning. 4.10819
COMMON LISP. 5.1217
The common people, 1746-1946. 3.1517
The common pursuit. 2.5543
The common reader, first series. 2.2605
Common sense. 3.6923
The common sense of political economy, and selected papers and reviews on economic theory. 4.1456
The common sense of science. 5.870
The common Slavic element in Russian culture. 2.1194
The Commons in perspective. 4.8478
The Commons today. 4.8471
The Commonwealth and Restoration stage. 2.3299
The Commonwealth and the nations. 4.8429
The Commonwealth Caribbean. 4.2155
The Commonwealth experience. 3.1225
The commonwealth of man. 4.9111
The commonwealth of music. 1.3463
The Commonwealth of nations. 3.1224
Commonwealth to protectorate. 3.1490
The communal experience. 4.7158
Communalism. 3.4285

The communards of Paris, 1871. 3.2165
Communes in the counter culture. 4.7157
Communicating naturally in a second language. 2.36
Communicating sequential processes. 5.1181
Communicating with the patient. 5.4705
Communication and expression in hoofed mammals. 5.4042
Communication and persuasion. 2.50
Communication and radar systems. 5.6437
Communication & society series. 2.55
Communication and society series. 2.55
Communication and the aging process. 4.4930
Communication and the evolution of society. 4.4893
Communication arts in the ancient world. 2.56
Communication command and control systems. 5.6377
Communication control in computer networks. 5.6414
Communication for dental auxiliaries. 5.5120
Communication, language, and meaning. 2.52
Communication strategies for family planning. 4.5673
Communication systems. 5.6348, 5.6367
Communications policy and the political process. 4.4052
The communications revolution. 4.4049
Communications satellite systems. 5.6397
A communicative grammar of English. 2.1007
The communings with himself of Marcus Aurelius Antoninus, Emperor of Rome, together with his speeches and sayings. 2.354
Communism. 4.6971
Communism and China. 4.7112
Communism and political systems in Western Europe. 4.7027
Communism and revolution. 4.6976
Communism and the French intellectuals, 1914-1960. 4.7054
Communism and the Yugoslav national question. 4.8690
Communism in Africa. 3.5086
Communism in American unions. 4.3365
Communism in Central America and the Caribbean. 4.7012
Communism in Eastern Europe. 4.7021
Communism in Hungary. 4.7045
Communism in Indian politics. 4.7117
Communism in Indochina. 4.7120
Communism in Italy and France. 4.8630
Communism in Japan. 4.8764
Communism in Kerala. 4.7118
Communism in Korea. 4.7125
Communism in Rumania, 1944-1962. 3.3551
Communism in Scandinavia and Finland. 4.8667
Communism, national and international. 4.7018
Communist China: the early years, 1949-55. 3.4783
Communist China's economic growth and foreign trade. 4.2476
Communist China's economy, 1949-1962. 4.2472
The communist controversy in Washington: from the New Deal to McCarthy. 3.7548
Communist economic strategy. 4.2470
The Communist insurrection in Malaya, 1948-1960. 3.4546
The Communist International, 1919-1943. 4.6926
The Communist manifesto. 4.7073
Communist manifesto after 100 years. 4.7073
The Communist movement. 4.6965
The Communist movement in China. 3.4769
Communist neo-traditionalism. 4.3669
The Communist parties of Italy, France, and Spain. 4.8372
The Communist parties of Western Europe. 4.7028
The Communist Party in Canada. 4.8304
The Communist Party in Spain. 4.8682
Communist Party membership in the U.S.S.R., 1917-1967. 4.8662
The Communist Party of Bulgaria. 4.8686

Communist Party of Indonesia,1951-1963.
4.8730
The Communist Party of the Soviet Union.
4.8663
The Communist Party vs. the C.I.O. 4.3552
Communist political systems. 4.7591
Communist regimes in Eastern Europe. 3.2998
The Communist road to power in Vietnam.
3.4465
Communist ships and shipping. 4.3962
Communist strategies in Asia. 3.3638
Communist strategy and tactics in
Czechoslovakia, 1918-48. 3.1921
Communist studies and the social sciences.
4.7141
Communists in Harlem during the depression.
4.8238
The communists in Spain. 4.8683
The Communists of Poland. 4.8669
Communitas; means of livelihood and ways of
life. 1.5580
Communities and ecosystems. 5.3529
Communities in transition. 4.5202
Communities of women. 2.5986
Community. 4.4732
Community, anarchy, and liberty. 4.7191
Community and capital in conflict. 4.3206
Community and polity. 3.6567
Community & society (Gemeinschaft und
Gesellschaft) 4.4858
Community-based corrections. 4.6890
The community called church. 1.3200
Community control and the urban school.
4.10802
Community ecology. 5.3515
Community health and nursing practice.
5.5205
Community health nursing practice. 5.5207
Community in a Black Pentecostal church.
1.2424
The community in America. 4.6233
Community nursing. 5.5206
A community of character. 1.1473
The community of scholars. 4.10258
Community of strangers. 4.661
Community of the new age. 1.2686
Community organizing. 5.102
Community planning and conceptions of
change. 4.6341
Community political systems. 4.7239
Community politics and educational change.
4.10796
Community power and political theory. 4.8869
Community power structure. 4.4950
The community press in an urban setting.
2.3569
Community studies. 4.6180
Community treatment and social control.
4.6881
Community treatment of juvenile offenders.
4.6876
Commutative algebra. 5.1361-5.1362
Compact. 2.4789
Compadrinazgo. 4.684
A companion to Beethoven's pianoforte sonatas.
1.4532
A companion to California. 3.8598
Companion to Chaucer studies. 2.6370
A companion to Greek tragedy. 2.289
A companion to Homer. 2.506
A Companion to Joyce studies. 2.8905
A companion to Latin studies. 3.2728
A companion to Mozart's piano concertos.
1.4525
A companion to Plato's Republic. 4.7351
A companion to Sanskrit literature. 2.1851
Companion to Scottish literature. 2.9832
A companion to Shakespeare studies. 2.6696
A companion to 'The art of fugue' (Die Kunst
der Fuge) J.S. Bach. 1.4479
A companion to the Cantos of Ezra Pound.
2.12329
Companion to the Divine comedy. 2.4944
Companion to the pre-Socratic philosophers.
1.220
A companion to the study of St. Anselm.
1.3253

A companion to the study of St. Augustine.
1.2484
A companion to Victorian literature. 2.5707
A companion to William Carlos Williams's
Paterson. 2.12746
A companion to Wittgenstein's 'Philosophical
investigations' 1.1075
A companion to Wittgenstein's Tractatus.
1.1227
Companions of our youth. 2.10819
Companions on the trail. 2.11037
Company K. 2.11461
The company she keeps. 2.12064
Comparable worth. 4.3257
A comparative analysis of complex
organizations. 4.4900
Comparative animal behavior. 5.4063
Comparative animal physiology. 5.4181
A comparative atlas of America's great cities.
4.160
A comparative atlas of zooplankton. 5.3822
Comparative biochemistry. 5.3330
Comparative communism. 4.6966
Comparative development of India and China.
4.2504
A comparative economic history of Latin
America. 4.2134
Comparative economic systems. 4.1321
Comparative education. 4.9964, 4.9973
Comparative embryology of the vertebrates.
5.4129
Comparative endocrinology. 5.4245
Comparative guide to American colleges.
4.9939
Comparative histology. 5.4154
Comparative history of Slavic literatures.
2.1196
Comparative immunobiology. 5.4466
Comparative industrial relations. 4.3435
Comparative marketing. 4.4315
Comparative mass media systems. 4.5003
Comparative method in education. 4.9972
Comparative morphology of vascular plants.
5.3732
Comparative national balance sheets. 4.1852
Comparative pathology and experimental
biology. 5.4742
Comparative perspectives of Third World
women. 4.6167
Comparative perspectives on the development of
memory. 5.324
Comparative philosophy. 1.427
Comparative physiology. 5.4179
Comparative physiology of renal excretion.
5.4249
The comparative physiology of respiratory
mechanisms. 5.4230
The comparative politics of birth control.
4.5680
Comparative psychology of mental
development. 5.110
Comparative public policy. 4.5184
Comparative reading. 4.10338
The comparative reception of Darwinism.
5.3343
Comparative reproduction of nonhuman
primates. 5.4016
Comparative socialist systems. 4.7587
Comparative studies of how people think. 5.65
Comparative urbanization. 4.6288
Comparative women's rights and political
participation in Europe. 4.8360
Comparing adult education worldwide.
4.10975
Comparing notes. 3.18
Comparison advertising. 4.4436
Comparisons of distance, size, area, volume,
mass, weight, density, energy, temperature,
time, speed and number throughout the
universe. 5.2005
The compass flower. 2.12147
The compassionate satirist: Ben Jonson and his
imperfect world. 2.6599
Compelling belief. 4.10734
The compelling image. 1.6329
Compendium of meteorology. 5.2495
Compendium of organic synthetic methods.
5.2735

Compensation administration. 4.3125
The competent woman. 4.5919
Competing equalities. 4.9920
Competition among the few. 4.3011
Competition and coercion. 3.6736
Competition and coexistence of species. 5.3583
Competition and collective bargaining in the
needle trades, 1910-1967. 4.3381
Competition and entrepreneurship. 4.1491
Competition and monopoly in American
industry. 4.1970
Competition as a dynamic process. 4.1565
Competition, collusion, and game theory.
4.2676
Competition for empire, 1740-1763. 3.641
Competition in oil. 4.3770
Competition in the midwestern coal industry.
4.3750
Competition in the open economy. 4.2739
Competition in the pharmaceutical industry.
4.3796
Competitive advantage. 4.2674
The competitive economics of nuclear and coal
power. 4.3802
The Competitive status of the U.S. auto
industry. 4.3820
Competitive strategy. 4.2675
Compilers, principles, techniques, and tools.
5.1226
Les complaintes. 2.4251
The compleat angler. 5.5489
The Complete anti-Federalist. 4.7829
The complete Bible. 1.2500
The complete Bolivian diaries of Ché Guevara,
and other captured documents. 3.9277
Complete book of ballets. 4.1170
The complete book of boating. 5.7512
The complete book of breast care. 5.5058
The Complete book of exercises. 5.4692
The complete book of hunting. 5.5492
The complete book of running. 4.1051
The complete book of swimming. 4.989
The complete book of the Olympics. 4.976
The complete book of U.S. presidents. 3.6308
Complete book of United States presidents.
3.6308
Complete book of US presidents. 3.6308
The complete canoeist's guide. 4.983
The complete Caribbeana, 1900-1975. 5.7901
A complete catalogue of the paintings of G.B.
Tiepolo. 1.6224
A complete checklist of the birds of the world.
5.3946
The complete Claudine. 2.4492
A complete concordance or verbal index to
words, phrases, and passages in the dramatic
works of Shakespeare. 2.6683
A complete concordance to the Iliad of Homer.
2.517
A complete concordance to the Odyssey of
Homer. 2.516
The complete critical prose and letters. 2.1575
The complete directory to prime time network
TV shows, 1946-present. 2.2847
The Complete dog book. 5.5454
The complete edition of the paintings [of]
Rembrandt. 1.6251
The complete encyclopedia of arms & weapons.
5.7246
Complete encyclopedia of arms and weapons.
5.7246
Complete encyclopedia of exercises. 5.4692
The complete encyclopedia of hockey. 4.994
The complete encyclopedia of horses. 5.5445
The complete encyclopedia of popular music
and jazz, 1900-1950. 1.3524
The complete encyclopedia of television
programs, 1947-1976. 2.2853
The complete English poems. 2.7104
Complete English poems. 2.6516
The complete English poetry of John Milton.
2.7114
The complete fairy tales of the Brothers
Grimm. 2.13510
The complete field guide to North American
wildlife, Eastern edition. 5.3826
Complete field guide to North American
wildlife, Western edition. 5.3827

The complete Gilbert & Sullivan opera guide. 1.4015
Complete Gilbert and Sullivan opera guide. 1.4015
The complete graphic works of Ben Shahn. 1.6446
The complete graphic works of William Blake. 1.6453
Complete Greek tragedies. 2.414
The complete guide to furniture styles. 1.6553
The complete guide to Middle-earth. 2.9434
The complete guide to modern dance. 4.1122
A complete guide to monkeys, apes and other primates. 5.4018
The complete guide to women's health. 5.5046
The complete handbook of holistic health. 5.4555
Complete handbook of operational and management auditing. 4.4405
The complete handbook of poultry-keeping. 5.5457
Complete handbook of sports scoring and record keeping. 4.980
A complete history of Guam. 3.5646
The complete illustrated works of Lewis Carroll. 2.7673
The complete introductory lectures on psychoanalysis. 5.144
The complete journal of Townsend Harris, first American consul and minister to Japan. 3.6460
The complete Justine. 2.4096
The complete letters of Lady Mary Wortley Montagu. 3.1551
The complete letters of Sigmund Freud to Wilhelm Fliess, 1887-1904. 5.147
The complete letters of Vincent van Gogh. 1.6243
The complete major prose plays. 2.14035
A complete manual of field archaeology. 3.239
Complete multilingual dictionary of computer terminology. 5.1136
The complete narrative prose of Conrad Ferdinand Meyer. 2.13636
The Complete nonsense of Edward Lear. 2.7910
The complete notebooks of Henry James. 2.11114
The complete Odes and Epodes. 2.721
The complete plays. 2.11627
Complete plays. 2.6610
The complete plays. 2.9789
Complete plays. 2.8064
Complete plays and prose. 2.13555
The complete plays of Henry James. 2.11101
The complete plays of William Congreve. 2.6944
Complete poems. 2.442, 2.7837
The complete poems. 2.6592, 2.11924
Complete poems. 2.8956
The complete poems. 2.12457
Complete poems. 2.11261
Complete poems, 1913-1962. 2.11538
Complete poems, 1920-1976. 2.8780
The complete poems, 1927-1979. 2.11384
The complete poems and fragments. 2.9216
Complete poems and major prose. 2.7116
The complete poems and selected letters and prose of Hart Crane. 2.11523
Complete poems and selected letters of Michelangelo. 2.4966
The complete poems of Anne Brontë. 2.7439
The complete poems of Carl Sandburg. 2.12430
The complete poems of Cavafy. 2.582
The complete poems of Christina Rossetti. 2.8007
The complete poems of John Wilmot, earl of Rochester. 2.7227
Complete poems [of] Keith Douglas. 2.8601
The complete poems of Marianne Moore. 2.12199
The complete poems of Paul Laurence Dunbar. 2.11011
The complete poems of Richard Aldington. 2.8373
Complete poems of Robert Frost, 1949. 2.11747

The complete poems of Samar Sen. 2.1866
The complete poems of Thomas Gray. 2.7053
The complete poems of Walter de la Mare. 2.8596
The complete poems [of] William Blake. 2.7406
The complete poetical works. 2.7519
Complete poetical works. 2.7111, 2.9698, 2.12038
The complete poetical works of Geoffrey Chaucer, now first put into modern English. 2.6315
The complete poetical works of James Thomson. 2.7314
The complete poetical works of Oliver Goldsmith. 2.7042
The complete poetical works of Percy Bysshe Shelley. 2.8096
The complete poetical works of Thomas Hardy, volume 1. 2.7762
The Complete poetical works of Thomas Hood. 2.7818
Complete poetry. 2.6593
The complete poetry and prose of Chairil Anwar. 2.2287
The complete poetry and prose of William Blake. 2.7404
Complete poetry and selected prose. 2.11265
Complete poetry of Osip Emilevich Mandelstam. 2.1576
The complete poetry of Richard Crashaw. 2.6964
The complete poetry of Robert Herrick. 2.7071
Complete postcards from the Americas. 2.4460
The complete prefaces of Bernard Shaw. 2.8067
Complete presidential press conferences of Franklin D. Roosevelt. 3.7769
The complete printmaker. 1.6468
The complete prints of Leonard Baskin. 1.6437
The complete Professor Challenger stories. 2.7682
Complete prose works. 2.7146, 2.7350
The Complete reference guide to United Nations sales publications, 1946-1978. 5.8268
The complete Roman drama. 2.703
The complete Ronald Firbank. 2.8625
The complete Sherlock Holmes. 2.7681
Complete short stories. 2.9095
The complete short stories. 2.8200
Complete short stories & Three fat men. 2.1589
The complete short stories of H. G. Wells. 2.8248
The complete shorter fiction of Virginia Woolf. 2.9568
Complete stories. 2.11452
The complete stories. 2.13789
The complete stories. 2.13208
The complete stories of Lu Xun. 2.2240
Complete stories of the great ballets. 1.4508
The complete tales of Henry James. 2.11103
The complete tales of Nikolai Gogol. 2.1380
The complete tales of Uncle Remus. 2.11047
A complete treatise on the art of singing. 1.4568
The complete trees of North America. 5.3685
The complete Uncle Abner. 2.12322
Complete walker 3. 4.895
The complete walker III. 4.895
The complete white oxen. 2.11436
A complete word and phrase concordance to the poems and songs of Robert Burns. 2.7510
The complete work of Paolo Uccello. 1.6228
Complete works. 2.6984
The complete works. 2.6480
Complete works. 2.9791
The complete works. 2.6505
Complete works. 2.3975, 2.6878, 2.12682
The complete works in prose and verse, of Francis Quarles. 2.7208
The complete works of Anne Bradstreet. 2.10865
The complete works of Aristotle. 1.284
The complete works of Chuang Tzu. 1.1798
Complete works of Frank Norris. 2.11184

The complete works of Han Fei tzu ... 1.167
The complete works of John Lyly. 2.6490
The complete works of John M. Synge. 2.8144
The complete works of John Ruskin. 2.8023
The complete works of Kate Chopin. 2.10932
The complete works of Marcel Duchamp. 1.6101
The complete works of Montaigne. 2.3992
The complete works of O. Henry [i.e. W.S. Porter] 2.11211
Complete works of Oscar Wilde. 2.8266
The complete works of Robert Browning. 2.7471
Complete works of Saint Thomas More. 2.6495
The complete works of Saki. 2.9132
The complete works of Sir John Vanbrugh. 2.7322
The complete works of St. Thomas More. 2.6495
The complete works of the Gawain-poet. 2.6132
The complete works of Thomas Chatterton: a bicentenary edition. 2.6933
The complete works of Thomas Lodge, 1580-1623?. 2.6487
The complete works of Washington Irving. 2.11094
The complete works of William Hazlitt. 2.7804
Complete works, selected letters. 2.4278
The complete writings of Thomas Paine. 4.7423
Complex analysis. 5.1483, 5.1487
The complex fate. 2.10276
Complex organizations. 4.4911
The complex roles of the teacher. 4.10528
Complex systems. 5.995
Complexity and contradiction in architecture. 1.5491
Compliance in health care. 5.4583
Compliance with therapeutic regimens. 5.4583
The component element method in dynamics. 5.5856
The composer's advocate. 1.4497
Composers on music. 1.3496
The composer's voice. 1.3469
A composer's world, horizons and limitations. 1.4367
The compositional process of J. S. Bach. 1.3780
A comprehensible world: on modern science and its origins. 5.841
Comprehensive analytical chemistry. 5.2654
A comprehensive bibliography for the study of American minorities 5.7858
A comprehensive bibliography of American constitutional and legal history, 1896-1979. 4.9613
Comprehensive biochemistry. 5.2791
Comprehensive classroom management. 4.10699
A comprehensive dictionary of psychological and psychoanalytical terms. 5.14
A comprehensive etymological dictionary of the English language. 2.1057
A Comprehensive grammar of the English language. 2.995
Comprehensive group psychotherapy. 5.4878
A Comprehensive handbook of the United Nations. 4.9212
Comprehensive heterocyclic chemistry. 5.2775
The comprehensive high school. 4.10051
Comprehensive income taxation. 4.4712
Comprehensive index of U.S. Government publications. 5.7768
Comprehensive index to English-language little magazines, 1890-1970, series one. 5.8316
Comprehensive index to the publications of the United States government, 1881-1893. 5.7774
Comprehensive inorganic chemistry. 5.2697
A comprehensive introduction to differential geometry. 5.1629
Comprehensive Italian-English, English-Italian dictionary. 2.859
Comprehensive organic chemistry. 5.2714

Comprehensive organometallic chemistry. 5.2780

A comprehensive Persian-English dictionary. 2.1964

A comprehensive treatise on inorganic and theoretical chemistry. 5.2623

Compromise in ethics, law, and politics. 4.7255

A compromise of principle. 3.7458

Compromised compliance. 4.9727

Compton Mackenzie. 2.9073

Compulsion. 2.11999

Compulsory education and the Amish. 4.10747

Compulsory mis-education, and The community of scholars. 4.10258

Computational analysis of present-day American English. 2.1141

Computational fluid mechanics and heat transfer. 5.1660

A computational logic. 5.1231

Computational models of discourse. 5.1007

Computational physics. 5.1966

Computational spherical astronomy. 5.1754

Computational techniques in operations research. 5.5563

The Computer age. 5.1232

Computer-aided analysis of electronic circuits. 5.6459

Computer aided circuit design. 5.6460

Computer-aided design. 5.6457

Computer-aided design and manufacture. 5.5695

Computer-aided power systems analysis. 5.6289

Computer algorithms. 5.1160

The computer and the brain. 5.1129

Computer applications in operations analysis. 5.5570

Computer arithmetic. 5.6580

Computer-assisted cartography. 4.202

Computer-based information systems. 5.5609

Computer-communication network design and analysis. 5.6405

Computer communications. 5.6410

Computer controlled urban transportation. 4.3912

Computer crime, abuse, liability, and security. 5.8122

Computer crime bibliography. 5.8122

Computer dictionary. 5.1138

Computer environments for children. 5.1065

The computer from Pascal to von Neumann. 5.6571

Computer graphics. 5.5645, 5.5653

Computer graphics, computer art. 1.5821

The computer graphics glossary. 5.5649

Computer graphics programming. 5.5646

The Computer in education. 4.10291

Computer insecurity. 4.4348

Computer mathematics. 5.1248

Computer methods for circuit analysis and design. 5.6466

Computer methods for literary research. 2.2423

Computer methods in geology. 5.2992

Computer methods in operations research. 5.5575

The computer modelling of mathematical reasoning. 5.1253

Computer network architectures and protocols. 5.6411

Computer networks. 5.6415

Computer power and human reason. 5.1132

Computer programming for spatial problems. 4.201

Computer publishers & publications. 5.7577

Computer publishers and publications. 5.7577

Computer-readable data bases. 5.7641

Computer-readable databases. 5.7641

Computer simulation techniques in hydrology. 4.294

Computer software for data communications. 5.1197

Computer solution of ordinary differential equations. 5.1522

Computer structures. 5.1228

Computer system architecture. 5.1229

Computer systems performance evaluation. 5.1245

Computer technology for the handicapped in special education and rehabilitation. 4.10934

Computer vision. 5.5939

Computerized buckling analysis of shells. 5.5868

Computerized manufacturing automation. 4.3321

Computers and communications. 5.6392

Computers and human intelligence. 5.1130

Computers and intractability. 5.1176

Computers and literacy. 4.10756

Computers and thought. 5.1018

Computers at work. 5.1250

Computers, communications and society. 5.6413

Computers, health records, and citizen rights. 5.4613

Computers in manufacturing. 5.7019

Computers in science. 5.990

Computers, information processing & telecommunications. 5.1137

Computers today and tomorrow. 5.1150

Computing for engineers and scientists with Fortran 77. 5.5721

Computing in psychology. 5.61

Computing information directory. 5.8121

Comrade Chiang Ch'ing. 3.4814

Comstockery in America. 4.9873

Le comte de Monte-Cristo. 2.4172

The Comuneros of Castile. 3.3441

Conan the conqueror. 2.11885

Conceiving the self. 5.497

A concentrated course in traditional harmony with emphasis on exercises and a minimum of rules. 1.4465

Concentration camps USA: Japanese Americans and World War II. 3.1026

Concentration, mergers, and public policy. 4.3036

The concentration of economic power. 4.1966

The concept of a person. 1.743

The concept of a Riemann surface. 5.1496

The concept of anxiety. 1.2914

The concept of belief in Islamic theology. 1.2080

The concept of benevolence: aspects of eighteenth-century moral philosophy. 1.1501

The concept of consciousness. 5.271

The Concept of creativity in science and art. 1.1392

The concept of cultural systems. 4.501

The concept of empire in Western Europe from the fifth to the fourteenth century. 4.7533

The Concept of evidence. 1.1236

The concept of human rights. 4.7628

The concept of irony. 1.1394

The concept of Jacksonian democracy. 3.8031

The concept of law. 4.9366

The Concept of nature. 5.944

The concept of nature in nineteenth-century English poetry. 2.5814

The concept of representation. 4.7741

The concept of woman. 4.5844

The concept of worship. 1.2981

The conception of God. 1.2826

The conception of immortality. 1.1620

Conceptions of modern psychiatry. 5.4841

Concepts and applications of finite element analysis. 5.5850

Concepts and methods of biostratigraphy. 5.3130

Concepts and models in groundwater hydrology. 5.5969

Concepts and models of inorganic chemistry. 5.2846

Concepts and theories of human development. 5.552

Concepts in film theory. 2.2946

The concepts of calculus. 5.1447

Concepts of criticism. 2.2456

Concepts of force. 5.2021

Concepts of God in Africa. 1.1594

Concepts of leisure. 1.1505

Concepts of mass. 5.2067

Concepts of modern art. 1.4826

Concepts of oncology nursing. 5.4773

Concepts of particle physics, v. 1. 5.2460

Concepts of science. 5.861

Concepts of the hero in the Middle Ages and the Renaissance. 2.2396

The concepts of value. 1.1301

Conceptual bases of professional nursing. 5.5169

The conceptual development of quantum mechanics. 5.2113

The conceptual foundations of contemporary relativity theory. 5.1910

Conceptual foundations of scientific thought. 5.940

Conceptual models for nursing practice. 5.5194

The conceptual nervous system. 5.4309

Conceptualization and measurement in the social sciences. 4.1204

Concerning being and essence. 1.2824

Concerning the city of God against the pagans. 1.2204

Concerning the spiritual in art, and painting in particular. 1912. 1.4601

The Concert of Europe. 3.709

The concerto. 1.4200

A concise Anglo-Saxon dictionary. 2.946

A concise biographical dictionary of singers. 1.3763

The concise Cambridge bibliography of English literature, 600-1950. 5.7940

The concise Cambridge history of English literature. 2.5528

Concise Dictionary of American biography. 3.6291

Concise dictionary of American history. 3.6199

A Concise dictionary of law. 4.9405

Concise dictionary of modern Japanese history. 3.4956

Concise dictionary of proper names and notable matters in the works of Dante. 2.4932

Concise dictionary of Soviet terminology, institutions, and abbreviations. 2.1239

A concise economic history of Britain. 4.2245

A concise economic history of Britain, from 1750 to recent times. 4.2246

Concise encyclopaedia of Arabic civilization. 3.5188

A concise encyclopaedia of Russia 3.3013

A Concise encyclopaedia of the Italian Renaissance. 3.2828

The concise encyclopedia of American antiques. 1.6512

The concise encyclopedia of antiques. 1.6505

The Concise encyclopedia of archaeology. 3.218

Concise encyclopedia of astronomy. 5.1682

The concise encyclopedia of English and American poets and poetry. 2.5488

Concise encyclopedia of solid state physics. 5.2190

A concise etymological dictionary of modern English. 2.1062

A concise etymological dictionary of the English language. 2.1061

A concise glossary of geographical terms. 4.76

A concise history of Buddhist art in Siam. 1.5055

A concise history of Canadian painting. 1.5994

The concise history of costume and fashion. 4.830

A concise history of Hungarian music. 1.3703

A concise history of Italy from prehistoric times to our own day. 3.2836

A concise history of Latin American culture. 3.8968

A concise history of mathematics. 5.1075

A concise history of mining. 5.6721

A concise history of modern painting. 1.5872

A concise history of modern sculpture. 1.5654

A concise history of opera. 1.4212

A concise history of Spain. 3.3411

A concise history of the common law 4.9414

A concise history of the Middle East. 3.3716

A concise history of the Spanish Civil War. 3.3467

The Concise history of woman suffrage. 4.8080

The Concise Oxford dictionary of ballet. 4.1081

The Concise Oxford dictionary of current English. 2.1082
The concise Oxford dictionary of English place-names. 3.1734
The concise Oxford dictionary of French literature. 2.3821
The concise Oxford dictionary of opera. 1.3521
The Concise Oxford French dictionary. 2.880
The concise Oxford history of music. 1.3631
The Concise Scots dictionary. 2.1116
Concluding. 2.8733
Concluding unscientific postscript. 1.2228
Conclusive evidence. 2.12233
A concordance of the Qur'an. 1.2033
A concordance to Finnegan's wake. 2.8872
A concordance to Milton's English poetry. 2.7170
Concordance to poems and songs of Robert Burns. 2.7510
A concordance to the Anglo-Saxon poetic records. 2.6278
A concordance to the complete poetical works of Sir Thomas Wyatt. 2.6550
A concordance to the complete works of Geoffrey Chaucer, and to the Romaunt of the Rose. 2.6377
A concordance to the Divine comedy of Dante Alighieri. 2.4945
A concordance to the English poems of George Herbert. 2.7066
A concordance to the English poems of John Donne. 2.6459
A concordance to the English poems of Thomas Gray. 2.7057
A concordance to the poems of Alexander Pope. 2.7194
A concordance to the poems of Edmund Spenser. 2.6541
A concordance to the poems of John Keats. 2.7852
A concordance to the poems of Matthew Arnold. 2.7352
A concordance to the poems of Oliver Goldsmith. 2.7048
A concordance to the poems of Robert Browning. 2.7495
A concordance to the poems of Robert Herrick. 2.7073
A concordance to the poems of W. B. Yeats. 2.8354
Concordance to the poetical works of John Dryden. 2.6993
A concordance to the poetry of Samuel Taylor Coleridge. 2.7592
La concorde des deux langages. 2.3985
Concrete. 5.5799
The condemned of Altona. 2.4732
The condemned playground. 2.8537
Condensed chemical dictionary. 5.2590
The condition, elevation, emigration, and destiny of the colored people of the United States. 3.6611
The Condition of education. 4.9931
The condition of man. 3.25
Conditionality. 4.4582
Conditioned reflexes. 5.4343
Conditioned reflexes and neuron organization. 5.4326
Conditioning and learning. 5.300
The conditioning therapies. 5.4849
The conditions for economic recovery. 4.1783
The conditions of economic progress. 4.1768
Conditions of knowledge. 4.10255
Condon report on unidentified flying objects. 5.6694
The condor passes. 2.13055
The conduct of inquiry. 4.1206
The conduct of war, 1789-1961. 5.7191
Conduction heat transfer. 5.6195
Conduction of electricity through gases. 5.2382
The conduction of the nervous impulse. 5.4324
The conductor; the theory of his art. 1.4498
Conductors. 1.3767
A Coney Island of the mind, poems. 2.11715
The Confederacy. 3.7376
A confederacy of dunces. 2.13359
Confederate commanders. 3.7316

The Confederate Constitutions. 4.9906
Confederate leaders in the New South. 3.7313
The Confederate nation, 1861-1865. 3.7378
The Confederate Navy. 5.7453
The Confederate Navy in Europe. 3.7392
Confederation. 3.8722
The Confederation debates in the Province of Canada, 1865. 4.8282
The Confederation of British Industry. 4.3073
The Conference Board business fact book. 4.1866
The conference of the birds. 2.1966
Conference proceedings - International Reading Association. 4.10455
The Conferences at Malta and Yalta, 1945. 3.881
Confessing one faith. 1.3364
The confessional imagination: a reading of Wordsworth's Prelude. 2.8306
Confessions. 1.3083
Confessions and Enchiridion. 1.2203
Confessions and Fantasies. 1.6684
Confessions of a congressman. 3.7537
The confessions of a Harvard man. 2.3634
Confessions of a hooligan. 2.1555
Confessions of a mask. 2.2109
Confessions of a spent youth. 2.11397
Confessions of a young man. 2.7955
Confessions of an advertising man. 4.4419
Confessions of Felix Krull, confidence man. 2.13824
The confessions of Jean Jacques Rousseau. 2.4088
The confessions of Lady Nijō. 2.2059
The confessions of Nat Turner. 2.13338
The confessions of T. E. Lawrence. 2.9003
Confessions of 'the Old Wizard'. 3.2413
Confessions of Zeno. 2.5066
The confidante in Henry James. 2.11131
The confidence game in American literature. 2.10589
The confidence-man: his masquerade. 2.11154
The confidence man in American literature. 2.10532
The confidence man in modern fiction. 2.3420
Confidence men and painted women. 4.6403
The confident years: 1885-1915. 2.10383
The confidential agent. 2.8743
Confidentiality in social work. 4.6503
Configurations of culture growth. 3.23
Confinement and flight. 2.5689
Confirmation, an anthology of African American women. 2.10693
Confirmation, an anthology of AfricanAmerican women. 2.10693
Conflict. 3.5020, 4.4944
Conflict and accommodation. 4.3602
Conflict and cohesion in socialist Yugoslavia. 4.8689
Conflict and compromise. 4.9297
Conflict and consensus in Switzerland. 4.5389
Conflict and control in late Imperial China. 4.5416
Conflict and crisis. 3.7793
Conflict and defense. 4.4938
Conflict and political change in Venezuela. 4.8353
Conflict and violence in Lebanon. 3.3788
Conflict, arousal, and curiosity. 5.214
The conflict in education in a democratic society. 4.10232
Conflict in higher education. 4.10760
Conflict in Laos. 3.4453
Conflict in northwest Africa. 3.5218
Conflict in the classroom. 4.10948
Conflict in world society. 4.9130
The conflict of European and Eastern Algonkian cultures 1504-1700. 3.8663
The conflict of generations. 4.9977
A conflict of ideas in the late Roman Empire. 3.2816
A conflict of interest. 4.6126
The conflict of interpretations. 1.1308
The conflict of the church and the synagogue. 1.1959
Conflict, politics, and the urban scene. 4.2882
Conflict, power, and politics in the city. 4.6351

The conflict society: reaction and revolution in Latin America. 3.8989
Conflict sociology. 4.4785
Conflict within the AFL. 4.3549
Conflicting conceptions of curriculum. 4.10436
Conflicts and conspiracies: Brazil and Portugal, 1750-1808. 3.9208
Conformational analysis. 5.2868
Confrontation, conflict, and dissent. 5.8410
Confrontation in the Caribbean basin. 3.9149
Confucian China and its modern fate. 3.4638
Confucian gentlemen and barbarian envoys. 3.5003
Confucius. 1.166
Conglomerate mergers. 4.3014
Congo, background of conflict. 3.5428
Congo diary and other uncollected pieces. 2.8543
Congo, my country. 3.5427
The Congregationalists. 1.3334
Congress. 4.8023
Congress against itself. 4.8063
Congress and campaign financing. 4.8135
Congress and foreign policy. 4.8028
Congress and its members. 4.8009
Congress and money. 4.4681
Congress and national defense. 5.7268
Congress and the bureaucracy. 4.7969
Congress and the Nation. 4.9438
Congress and the politics of U.S. foreign economic policy, 1929-1976. 4.4174
Congress at the crossroads. 4.8010
Congress at work. 4.8007
Congress in change. 4.8034
Congress, keystone of the Washington establishment. 4.8025
Congress makes a law. 4.9550
The Congress of Berlin and after. 3.685
The Congress of Vienna. 3.2139
The Congress of Vienna, 1814-1815. 3.2140
The Congress Party in Rajasthan. 4.8722
Congress reconsidered. 4.8008
Congress; two decades of analysis. 4.8012
Congressional behavior. 4.8014
Congressional committee politics. 4.7999
Congressional conservatism and the New Deal. 3.7767
Congressional directory. 4.7993
Congressional district atlas of the United States. 4.150
Congressional government. 4.8020
Congressional odyssey. 4.8024
The Congressional party. 4.8018
Congressional politics in the Second World War. 3.7775
Congressional power. 4.8004
Congressional procedures and the policy process. 4.8033
The congressional process. 4.8031
Congressional quarterly. 4.7791
Congressional quarterly almanac. 4.7791
Congressional Quarterly, inc. 4.8016
Congressional Quarterly's federal regulatory directory 1979/80-. 4.9754
Congressional Quarterly's Guide to Congress. 4.7997
Congressional Quarterly's Guide to the U.S. Supreme Court. 4.8067
Congressional Quarterly's Guide to U.S. elections. 4.8107
Congressional quarterly's Washington information directory. 3.8109
Congressional realignment, 1925-1978. 4.8052
Congressional spending. 4.4685
Congressional staff directory. 4.7996
Congressional staffs. 4.8029
Congressional women. 4.8053
Congressman from Mississippi. 3.7683
Congresmen in committees 4.7998
Congreve. 2.6948
Congreve's plays on the eighteenth-century stage. 2.6950
Coningsby. 2.7393
Conjectures and refutations. 1.1307
Conjure; selected poems, 1963-1970. 2.13293
The conjure woman. 2.10926
Conjuring. 2.10318
Connecticut, a bicentennial history. 3.8020

The Connecticut wits. 2.10369
Connecting spheres. 4.5868
Connections. 5.5527
Connections between sex and aggression. 5.489
Connoisseur. 1.6524
The Connoisseur's complete period guides to the houses, decoration, furnishing and chattels of the classic periods. 1.6524
Connoisseurs of chaos. 2.10486
The conquerors. 2.4615
Conquerors and rulers. 4.5412
Conquerors and slaves. 4.6415
Conquest, coexistence, and change. 3.1760
The conquest of America. 3.5982
The conquest of happiness. 1.1504
The conquest of Mexico. 3.8925
The conquest of Michoacán. 3.8954
The conquest of nihilism. 3.45
The conquest of the Incas. 3.9296
The conquest of the material world. 4.2206
The conquest of the River Plate. 3.9241
Conquest of the skies. 4.4084
Conquest of violence. 4.5035
The conquistadors; first-person accounts of the conquest of Mexico. 3.8923
Conrad Aiken. 2.11303, 2.11305
Conrad Ferdinand Meyer. 2.13637
Conrad Grebel. 1.3304
Conrad in the nineteenth century. 2.8578
Conrad Richter. 2.12395
Conrad Richter's Ohio trilogy. 2.12394
Conrad the novelist. 2.8566
Conrad under familial eyes. 2.8559
Conrad's Eastern world. 2.8573
Conrad's later novels. 2.8565
Conrad's Polish background. 2.8550
Conrad's politics; community and anarchy in the fiction of Joseph Conrad. 2.8562
Conrad's prefaces to his works. 2.8545
Conrad's romanticism. 2.8577
Conrad's Western world. 2.8574
Conscience and convenience. 4.6519
Conscience in medieval philosophy. 1.363
Conscience in politics. 3.8410
The conscience of a Conservative. 4.7856
The conscience of the revolution: Communist opposition in Soviet Russia. 4.7085
Conscience of the twentieth century. 2.10658
The conscience of words. 2.13718
Consciencism. 4.7128
Consciousness and class experience in nineteenth-century Europe. 4.5297
Conscripts and volunteers. 4.7366
The consensual democracies? 4.8670
Consensus and beyond. 4.8542
Consensus and disunity. 3.1689
Consensus, conflict, and American historians. 3.6222
Consequences of class and color. 4.5260
The consequences of consent. 4.7517
Consequences of party reform. 4.7944
Conservation and economic efficiency. 4.4131
Conservation and evolution. 5.3219
Conservation and the gospel of efficiency. 4.1900
Conservation biology. 5.3217-5.3218
Conservation in the Soviet Union. 5.5304
Conservation in the United States. 4.1901
Conservation of library materials. 5.7645
The conservation of orbital symmetry. 5.2819
The conservationist. 2.10070
Conservatism: from John Adams to Churchill. 4.7617
Conservatism in America. 4.7803
Conservatism in early American history. 3.6865
Conservatism revisited. 4.7618
The conservative intellectual movement in America, since 1945. 3.7534
Conservative Judaism. 1.1920
Conservative minds in America. 4.7310
Conservative Party from Peel to Churchill. 4.8531
The Conservative Party from Peel to Thatcher. 4.8531
Conservative Party politics. 4.8533
Conservative politics in Western Europe. 4.8373

The conservative tradition in America. 3.6114
Conservatives in an age of change. 3.7907
Consider her ways. 2.8705
Considerations on representative government. 4.7579
Considerations on Western Marxism. 4.7015
The consolation of philosophy. 1.335
The conspiracy against Hitler in the twilight war. 3.2429
Conspiracy at Mukden. 3.4849
Conspiracy of Catilina. 3.2749
The Conspiracy of Pontiac. 3.5776
Constable, the natural painter. 1.6029
Constantin Brancusi. 1.5744
Constantine and Eusebius. 3.2811
Constantine Porphyrogenitus and his world. 3.2670
Constantine the Great. 3.2814
The constants of physics. 5.2007
Constituency service. 4.8026
The Constitution and the Court. 4.9631
The Constitution and what it means today. 4.9628
The Constitution in crisis times, 1918-1969. 4.9615
The constitution in flux. 4.8415
The constitution of liberty. 4.7665
The constitution of society. 4.4794
The Constitution of the United States of America: analysis and interpretation. 4.9607
The Constitution, the courts, and human rights. 4.9674
Constitutional amendment in Canada. 4.8276
Constitutional and administrative law. 4.9418
A constitutional and legal history of medieval England. 4.8388
Constitutional choices. 4.9630
Constitutional civil liberties. 4.9675
Constitutional conflicts between Congress and the President. 4.9636
Constitutional counterrevolution? 4.9840
Constitutional development in the USSR. 4.8642
Constitutional dictatorship. 4.7721
The Constitutional doctrines of Justice Harlan. 4.9627
The constitutional documents of the Puritan revolution 1625-1660. 3.1473
Constitutional faiths. 4.9799
Constitutional fate. 4.9641
Constitutional government and democracy. 4.7711
Constitutional government in India. 4.8702
Constitutional government in the United States. 4.7849
A constitutional history of Australia. 4.8817
The constitutional history of England. 4.8382
The constitutional history of England in its origin and development. 4.8383
The constitutional law dictionary. 4.9626
Constitutional law of the federal system. 4.9629
Constitutional politics in the progressive era. 4.9568
Constitutional problems under Lincoln. 4.7838
Constitutional relations between Britain and India. 3.4289
Constitutional theory. 4.9419
Constitutionalism. 4.9381
Constitutionalism, ancient and modern. 4.7706
Constitutionalism and resistance in the sixteenth century. 4.7552
Constitutionalism & the changing world. 4.7707
Constitutionalism and the separation of powers. 4.7720
The constitutionalist. 4.9700
Constitutions, elections, and legislatures of Poland, 1493-1977. 4.8668
Constitutions of dependencies and special sovereignties. 4.9380
Constitutions of nations. 4.9379
The constitutions of the Australian states. 4.8832
Constitutions of the countries of the world. 4.9377
Constitutions of the United States, national and state. 4.9608

Constructing quarks. 5.2456
Construction and design of cable-stayed bridges. 5.6084
Construction and design of prestressed concrete segmental bridges. 5.6082
Construction and geotechnical engineering using synthetic fabrics. 5.5872
Construction estimating. 5.6087
Construction materials. 5.5763
The construction of Christian poetry in Old English. 2.5592
The construction of Gothic cathedrals. 1.5238
Constructive analysis. 5.1433
Constructive education for children. 4.10380
The constructive revolutionary. 1.3400
Constructivism; origins and evolution. 1.4827
The consul's file. 2.13354
Consultants and consulting organizations directory. 4.2725
Consultation in social work. 4.6489
Consumer and commercial credit management. 4.4549
Consumer choice. 4.4308
Consumer demand in the United States. 4.2059
Consumer research for management decisions. 4.4311
Consumer response to income increases. 4.2060
Consumer sourcebook. 4.2065
Consumerism in the United States. 4.2063
The consumer's electric car. 5.6630
Consumers in trouble. 4.4551
Contact and conflict. 3.5718
Le conte fantastique en France de Nodier à Maupassant. 2.3907
Contemplating music. 1.4360
The contemplative life; The giants; and, Selections. 1.338
Contemporaries. 2.11945
Contemporaries of Erasmus. 2.822
Contemporary accounting theory. 4.4393
Contemporary Africa. 3.5225
Contemporary American artists. 1.4888
Contemporary American authors. 2.10420
Contemporary American composers. 1.3753
Contemporary American essays. 2.10861
Contemporary American-Jewish literature. 2.10300
Contemporary American literature, 1945-1972. 2.10413
Contemporary American novelists of the absurd. 2.10624
Contemporary American philosophy. 1.569
Contemporary American poetry. 2.10501, 2.10765, 2.10768, 2.10774
Contemporary American realism since 1960. 1.4884
Contemporary American theologies. 1.2767
Contemporary American usage. 2.1137
Contemporary approaches to psychology. 5.106
Contemporary archaeology; a guide to theory and contributions. 4.696
Contemporary architects. 1.5265
The contemporary arranger. 1.4493
Contemporary art and artists. 1.4821
Contemporary art in Latin America. 1.4856
Contemporary artists. 1.4807
Contemporary authors. 5.7785
Contemporary Bengali literature: fiction. 2.1876
Contemporary Black artists in America. 1.4908
Contemporary Black drama. 2.10787
Contemporary British novelists. 2.6047
Contemporary British philosophy. 1.735
Contemporary Canadian art. 1.4918
Contemporary Chicana poetry. 2.10303
Contemporary Chicano theatre. 2.10784
Contemporary Chinese stories. 2.2209
Contemporary civilization in the West. 3.1
Contemporary composers on contemporary music. 1.3679
A contemporary critique of historical materialism. 3.510
Contemporary cultures and societies of Latin America. 4.5252

Contemporary Danish poetry. 2.14002
Contemporary Danish prose; by Elias
  Bredsdorff] 2.14004
Contemporary developments in mathematical
  psychology. 5.40
Contemporary dramatists. 2.5926
Contemporary Europe. 3.742, 4.5291
Contemporary feminist thought. 4.6043
Contemporary France. 3.2195
Contemporary French literature, 1945 and after.
  2.3871
Contemporary French women poets. 2.3923
Contemporary games. 4.10304
The contemporary Greek cinema. 2.2899
Contemporary Indian philosophy. 1.185
Contemporary Indonesian poetry. 2.2286
Contemporary industrial relations in Japan.
  4.3668
Contemporary influences in early childhood
  education. 4.10403
Contemporary instrumental techniques. 1.4536
Contemporary Irish poetry. 2.9867
Contemporary Irish writing. 2.9859
Contemporary Israeli literature. 2.1783
Contemporary Italian literature. 2.4882
Contemporary Japanese fiction, 1926-1968.
  2.2016
Contemporary Japanese literature. 2.2029
The contemporary Jew in the Elizabethan
  drama. 2.5878
Contemporary jewelry. 5.7068
Contemporary Laos. 3.4459
Contemporary Latin American fiction. 2.5314
Contemporary literary criticism. 2.2671
Contemporary literary criticism yearbook.
  2.2671
Contemporary literary critics. 2.10239
Contemporary literary scholarship. 2.5509
Contemporary macroeconomic modelling.
  4.1400
Contemporary metropolitan America. 4.6207
The contemporary Middle East, 1948-1973.
  5.8035
Contemporary music in Europe. 1.3702
Contemporary New Zealand poetry. 2.10203
Contemporary North Africa. 3.5190
The contemporary novel. 5.7808
The Contemporary novel in German. 2.13506
Contemporary novelists. 2.6044
Contemporary optics for scientists and
  engineers. 5.2284
Contemporary painters. 1.5873
Contemporary perspectives in the philosophy of
  language. 1.467
Contemporary philosophical logic. 1.1165
Contemporary philosophy. 1.451
Contemporary photographers. 5.6926
Contemporary poetry in America. 2.10490
Contemporary poetry in America and England,
  1950-1975. 5.7820
Contemporary poets. 2.5835
Contemporary Polish poetry, 1925-1975.
  2.1697
Contemporary Portugal. 3.3501, 3.3503
Contemporary Portuguese poetry. 2.5451
Contemporary psychology of sport. 4.903
Contemporary readings in logical theory
  1.1147
Contemporary Republic of China. 3.4869
Contemporary reviews of romantic poetry.
  2.5822
Contemporary Russian drama. 2.1319
Contemporary Russian prose. 2.1322
Contemporary Scottish studies. 2.9834
Contemporary Scottish verse, 1959-1969.
  2.9846
Contemporary sculpture. 1.5650
Contemporary social problems. 4.5111
Contemporary Soviet education. 4.10133
Contemporary Spanish-American fiction.
  2.5316
The contemporary Spanish economy. 4.2414
The contemporary Spanish novel, 1939-1975.
  2.5135
Contemporary Spanish poetry. 2.5154
Contemporary Spanish poetry (1898-1963)
  2.5120

The contemporary Spanish theater (1949-1972)
  2.5131
Contemporary suburban America. 4.6355
Contemporary Swedish poetry. 2.14063
Contemporary theatre, film, and television.
  2.3234
Contemporary theories about the family.
  4.5638
Contemporary theory in international relations.
  4.9013
Contemporary tone-structures. 1.3669
Contemporary trade strategies in the
  Philippines. 4.4297
Contemporary Turkish literature. 2.1983
Contemporary women novelists. 2.5568
The Contemporary world poets. 2.3740
Contemporary Yemen. 3.4063
Contemporary Yugoslavia. 3.3567
Contempt of Congress. 4.9868
The contempt power. 4.9869
Contenders. 2.9448
Contending theories of international relations.
  4.9027
Content. 2.3679
Content addressable parallel processors. 5.1174
The content and style of an oral literature.
  3.5861
Content area reading. 4.10344
Les contes bleus du chat perché. 2.4386
Contes cruels. 2.4336
Contes du lundi. 2.4159
Contes et nouvelles. 2.4268
Contes et nouvelles de Charles Nodièr. 2.4275
Contest for the South China Sea. 4.9307
Contestable markets and the theory of industry
  structure. 4.2998
Contested terrain. 4.3429
Conteurs français du XVIe siècle. 2.3942
The context of biological education. 5.3306
Contexts of Canadian criticism. 2.9883
Contexts of criticism. 2.2579
A continent astray. 3.1200
The Continental Army. 5.7288
The Continental congress. 3.7014
Continental drift. 5.3095, 5.3097
The continental model. 2.2499
The continental novel. 5.8169
The Continental Op. 2.11811
Continental stagecraft. 2.3279
Continents adrift and continents aground.
  5.3093
Continents in motion. 5.3096
Continuance and change. 2.6056
Continuatio des abenteuerlichen Simplicissimi.
  2.13543
A continuation of Mr. Bunyan's life. 2.6915
Continued fractions. 5.1420
A continuing journey. 2.12089
Continuing the revolution. 3.4837
Continuities in psychological anthropology.
  4.621
Continuities in social research. 5.7169
Continuities in the study of social conflict.
  4.4939
Continuity and change in modern Iran. 4.5409
Continuity in history, and other essays. 4.2197
The continuity of American poetry. 2.10475
Continuous frames of reinforced concrete.
  5.5874
The continuous wave. 5.6423
The continuum of inductive methods. 1.1200
Contour in time. 2.12289
Contra Celsum. 1.2211
Contraception. 4.5684
The contract clause of the Constitution. 4.9652
Contradictions. 2.3262
Contrary music. 2.6468
The contrast. 2.10880
Contrasts in emerging societies. 4.2241
Contre Sainte-Beuve; suivi de Nouveaux
  mélanges. 2.4666
Contributions to L'Année sociologique. 4.4852
Contributions to urban sociology. 4.6182
Control mechanisms in cellular processes.
  5.3586
Control of communicable diseases in man.
  4.4672
Control of electric machines. 5.6319

The control of fluid power. 5.6237
Control of food quality and food analysis.
  5.6890
Control of Japanese foreign policy. 3.4973
Control of long-term international capital
  movements. 4.4612
The control of trusts. 4.3056
Controlled drinking. 4.6644
Controlled thermonuclear reactions. 5.2448
Controllership, the work of the managerial
  accountant. 4.4595
Controlling hospital costs. 5.4709
Controlling industrial pollution. 4.2051
Controlling nuclear weapons. 4.7597
Controlling software projects. 5.1172
Controlling the cost of social security. 4.3461
Controlling the offender in the community.
  4.6894
Controlling unlawful organizational behavior.
  4.6761
Controls from within. 4.5721
Controls of metamorphism. 5.3072
Controversial issues in psychology 5.121
The controversial Sholem Asch. 2.1801
Controversy. 5.5518
Controversy and coalition. 4.6048
Controversy in Victorian geology. 5.3137
The conurbations of Great Britain. 4.1663
Convention: a philosophical study. 1.469
Convention decisions and voting records.
  4.8141
A convergence of lives. 5.1096
Convergent evolution in Chile and California.
  5.3401
Convergent evolution in warm deserts. 5.3266
Conversación en la catedral. 2.5431
Conversation. 2.11300
Conversation in the cathedral. 2.5432
Conversation with Burman. 1.791
Conversations with architects: Philip Johnson,
  Kevin Roche, Paul Rudolph, Bertrand
  Goldberg, Morris Lapidus, Louis Kahn,
  Charles Moore, Robert Venturi & Denise
  Scott Brown. 1.5474
Conversations with economists. 4.1462
Conversations with Goethe. 2.13577
Conversations with Igor Stravinsky. 1.4003
Conversations with Katherine Anne Porter,
  refugee from Indian Creek. 2.12320
Conversations with Kennedy. 3.7872
Conversations with Klemperer. 1.4101
Conversations with Ogotemmêli. 1.1857
Conversations with Stalin. 3.3557
Conversations with Walker Percy. 2.13239
Conversion to Islam in the medieval period.
  3.3668
The convert. 2.11217
Converts, dropouts, returnees, a study of
  religious change among Catholics. 1.3179
Convex functions. 5.1491
Convicting the innocent. 4.9896
Conviction. 4.9891
Convoy. 5.7428
Conway's all the world's fighting ships,
  1860-1905. 5.7434
Conway's All the world's fighting ships,
  1906-1921. 5.7435
Conway's All the world's fighting ships,
  1922-1946. 5.7430
Conway's All the world's fighting ships,
  1947-1982. 5.7431
Coolie. 2.10124
Coöperative news gathering. 2.3588
Cooper's Creek. 3.5562
Coordination chemistry. 5.2840, 5.2844
The Copernican revolution. 5.1695
Coping with U.S.-Japanese economic conflicts.
  4.4177
Copland. 1.3841
Copland on music. 1.3483
Copper. 4.3740
Copper camp; stories of the world's greatest
  mining town. 3.8548
Copper in iron and steel. 5.5818
Cops and rebels. 3.6754
Coptic art and archaeology. 1.5084
The copyright book. 4.9546
The coral. 2.13804

The corbaccio. 2.4910
Corbin on contracts. 4.9513
Le Corbusier at work. 1.5418
Le Corbusier, elements of a synthesis. 1.5417
CORE; a study in the civil rights movement, 1942-1968. 3.6680
Corea, the hermit nation. 3.4995
Corelli: his life, his work. 1.3843
The Corfu incident of 1923. 3.2710
Cork of the colonies. 2.13291
Cork Street, next to the hatter's. 2.8846
Corn. 5.5324
Corneille, his heroes and their worlds. 2.4019
Cornelii Taciti Annalium libri I-IV. 2.774
The Cornell Wordsworth. 2.8299
Le cornet à dés. 2.4588
Le cornet à dés, II. 2.4589
De corona and De falsa legatione. 2.361
Coronación. 2.5405
The Coronado expedition, 1540-1542, Narratives of. 3.5985
The coronation of Charlemagne, 25 December 800. 3.1987
Corot. 1.6079
Corporal punishment in American education. 4.10707
Corporate 500. The Directory of corporate philanthropy. 4.6527
Corporate affiliations. 4.4605
Corporate cash management. 4.4603
Corporate crime. 4.6762
Corporate diversification. 4.3033
The Corporate finance sourcebook. 4.4604
Corporate five hundred. The Directory of corporate philanthropy. 4.6527
Corporate giving 3. 1.6746
Corporate governance and institutionalizing ethics. 4.4273
The corporate ideal in the liberal state, 1900-1918. 3.7538
Corporate information systems management. 5.5611
Corporate leadership. 4.3016
Corporate mergers. 4.3015
Corporate power and social responsibility. 4.3051
Corporate power in an African state. 4.3730
The corporate social audit. 4.2703
Corporate strategies of the automotive manufacturers. 4.3822
Corporate-strategy perspective. 4.3035
The corporation in modern society. 4.3048
The corporation income tax 4.3018
Corporations and morality. 4.2704
Corporations, classes, and capitalism. 4.1542
Corporatism and welfare. 4.5312
The Corpus Christi play of the English Middle Ages. 2.6212
A Corpus of Rembrandt paintings. 1.6252
Corpus Vitrearum. 1.6646
Correctional intervention and research. 4.6891
Correctional treatment. 4.6893
Corrections. 4.6892
Corrections and punishment. 4.6895
Corrections in the community. 4.6908
Correctness in English usage. 2.981
Correggio and his legacy. 1.5812
Correlative anatomy of the nervous system. 5.4150
The correspondence. 2.714
Correspondence. 1.6027, 2.7195, 2.7579
The correspondence and public papers of John Jay, 1763-1826. 3.6971
The correspondence between Prince A. M. Kurbsky and Tsar Ivan IV of Russia, 1564-1579. 3.3085
The correspondence of Charles Darwin. 5.3192
The correspondence of Emerson and Carlyle. 2.11023
Correspondence of James K. Polk. 3.7071
The correspondence of Jonathan Swift. 2.7297
The correspondence of Pope Gregory VII. 1.3150
The correspondence of Richard Steele. 2.7273
The correspondence of Spinoza. 1.1096
Correspondence of Thomas Gray. 2.7055
The correspondence of W. E. B. Du Bois. 3.6829

Correspondence of Wagner and Liszt. 1.4035
Corrosion and corrosion protection handbook. 5.5792
Cosa, the making of a Roman town. 3.2721
The cosmic code. 5.2139
The cosmic connection. 5.1729
The cosmic dancers. 5.839
The cosmic fragments. 1.237
The cosmic frontiers of general relativity. 5.1720
Cosmic horizons. 5.1880
Cosmic rays. 5.2326
Cosmicomics. 2.5028
The Cosmographia of Bernardus Silvestris. 2.818
The cosmological distance ladder. 5.1883
The cosmological eye. 2.12184
Cosmological letters on the arrangement of the world-edifice. 5.1697
Cosmology. 5.1879
Cosmology + 1. 5.1863
The cosmology of Giordano Bruno. 1.411
Cosmopolitan ideal in Enlightenment thought ... 1.437
The cosmopolitan ideal in Enlightenment thought, its form and function in the ideas of Franklin, Hume, and Voltaire, 1694-1790. 1.437
Cosmopolitanism and the national state. 4.8599
Cosmos and history. 1.1344
Cosmos & tragedy. 2.415
Cost accounting. 4.4412, 4.4415
Cost and choice; an inquiry in economic theory. 4.1479
Cost-benefit analysis. 4.1335
The cost of capital, estimating the rate of return for public utilities. 4.3040
The cost of discipleship. 1.2892
Costa Rica, a country study. 3.9077
The Costa Ricans. 3.9076
The costs of democracy. 4.8128
The costs of economic growth. 4.2796
The costs of higher education. 4.10597
Costume for births, marriages & deaths. 4.844
Costume of the western world. 4.831
Costumes of Mexico. 4.837
Costumes of the East. 4.850
Costuming for opera. 1.4573
Cotter's England. 2.10168
Cotton fields and skyscrapers. 4.6238
Cotton fields no more. 4.2960
The cotton kingdom. 3.8141
The Cotton Kingdom. 3.8146
Cotton Mather. 2.10874, 3.7978
Coulomb and the evolution of physics and engineering in eighteenth-century France. 5.818
Coulson's Valence. 5.2836
The Council of Constance. 1.3119
Councils of governments. 4.8860
Counseling and psychotherapy. 5.4874
Counseling men. 5.4815
Counseling the culturally different. 5.470
Counsels in contemporary Islam. 1.2053
Counsels of war. 5.7271
Count Albert de Mun, paladin of the Third Republic. 3.2187
Count Belisarius. 2.8721
Count Frontenac and New France under Louis XIV. 3.8707
Count Julian. 2.5263
The count of Monte Cristo. 2.4173
Count Witte and the Tsarist government in the 1905 revolution. 3.3159
Counter cultures. 4.4331
The counter-reformation. 1.2363
The Counter-Reformation, 1550-1600. 1.2362
The Counter Reformation, 1559-1610. 3.630
The counter-Renaissance. 3.168
The counter-revolution: doctrine and action, 1789-1804. 3.2080
Counter-statement. 2.2565
Countercultures. 4.5110
Counterexamples in analysis. 5.1441
Counterexamples in topology. 5.1603
Counterfactuals. 1.1245

The counterfeiters; with Journal of The counterfeiters. 2.4551
Counterpoint. 1.4471, 1.4473, 3.6585
Counterpoint; based on eighteenth-century practice. 1.4472
The Countess of Pembroke's Arcadia (the old Arcadia). 2.6508
Counting the ways and Listening. 2.12842
Country and court. 3.1494
The country and the city. 2.5628
Country arts in early American homes. 1.4865
Country boys and merchant princes. 4.4219
The Country doctor. 2.4120
The country girl. 2.12258
The country girls. 2.9784
The country-house ethos in English literature, 1688-1750. 2.5686
The country life book of nautical terms under sail. 5.7419
Country life, city life. 4.4916
Country life in classical times. 2.401
Country music, U.S.A. 1.4276
Country music, USA. 1.4276
Country people. 2.12563
The country waif. 2.4286
Country, western, and gospel music. 1.3685
The country wife. 2.7339
The county agent ... 5.5260
A county community in peace and war. 3.1740
The county year book. 4.8837
The coup. 2.13366
Couples. 2.13367
Courage and hesitation. 3.7898
Courage, the adventuress. 2.13545
The courage to be. 1.1508
The courage to create. 5.345
Courbet and the naturalistic movement. 1.6081
Courir les rues. 2.4676
A course in arithmetic. 5.1337
Course in general linguistics. 2.141
A course in mathematical logic. 5.1045
A course in mathematical physics. 5.1971
A course in modern linguistics. 2.135
A course in multivariate analysis. 5.1391
A course in process design. 5.6832
A course in Russian history: the seventeenth century. 3.3094
A course in thermodynamics. 5.2248
The course of American democratic thought. 3.6112
The course of American economic growth and development. 4.1886
The course of empire. 3.6348
The course of German history. 3.2292
The Course of Irish History. 3.1816
The Course of life. 5.511
The course of Mexican history. 3.8917
A course of modern analysis. 5.1542
The course of modern Jewish history. 3.3908
A course of pure mathematics. 5.1454
Course of theoretical physics. 5.1980
A course of time. 2.13961
Court and Constitution in the twentieth century. 4.9847
The court and the castle. 2.2370
The court and the country. 3.1467
Court house, a photographic document. 1.5517
Court, kirk, and community. 3.1792
The Court of Burgundy. 3.2219
The court society. 4.6390
The court wits of the Restoration. 2.5655
Courtaulds: an economic and social history. 4.3857
The courtesan of Lucknow (Umrao Jan Ada) 2.1902
The courtesan's jewel box. 2.2211
Courtier and commoner in ancient China. 3.4696
The courtly love tradition. 2.2623
The courts and the public schools. 4.9583
Courts, judges, and politics. 4.9778
Cousin Bazilio. 2.5456
Cousin Bette. 2.4118
Covenant on Civil and Political Rights. 4.9388
The covenant sealed. 1.3013
A covenant with death. 4.9616
A covenant with power. 3.7572
The Covent-Garden journal. 2.7019

Coventry Patmore. 2.7987, 2.7990
Coverdale and his Bibles. 1.2492
The covered wagon. 2.11884
The Coverley papers from the Spectator.
   2.6887
Cow country. 3.8491
The cowards. 2.1684
Cowboy songs and other frontier ballads.
   2.10758
The Cowden Clarkes. 2.7575
Cowper's poetry. 2.6963
Cows, pigs, wars & witches. 4.485
The CPR West. 4.4017
Crab antics. 3.9177
The Crab Nebula. 5.1853
Crabbe. 2.7619
Crabgrass frontier. 4.6358
A Crack in the mirror. 4.492
The crack-up. 2.11721
A crackling of thorns. 2.11876
Cradle of the middle class. 4.5605
The craft and art of Dylan Thomas. 2.9420
The craft and context of translation. 2.2543
The craft of calligraphy. 5.7527
Craft of fiction. 2.13662
The craft of fiction. 2.3428
The craft of intelligence. 5.7364
The craft of musical composition. 1.4450
The craft of old-master drawings. 1.5820
The craft of Ralph Ellison. 2.13007
The craft of teaching. 4.10263
The craftsman's handbook. 1.6339
Craftsmen in Greek and Roman society.
   4.3094
Crainquebille, Putois, Riquet et plusieurs autres
   récits profitables. 2.4204
Cranach, a family of master painters. 1.6167
Cranford. 2.7720
Crashaw and the Baroque. 2.6965
Crashworthiness of vehicles. 5.6625
Crazy Horse called them walk-a-heaps. 5.7289
CRC atlas of spectral data and physical
   constants for organic compounds. 5.2725
CRC handbook of atmospherics. 5.2549
CRC handbook of high resolution infrared
   laboratory spectra of atmospheric interest.
   5.2511
CRC handbook of laboratory safety. 5.2639
CRC handbook of lubrication. 5.6245
CRC handbook of materials science. 5.5770
CRC Handbook of Microbiology. 5.4436
CRC handbook of tables for applied engineering
   science. 5.5666
CRC handbook of tables for probability and
   statistics. 5.1401
CRC standard mathematical tables. 5.1125
The cream of the jest. 2.11443
Created equal? 3.7295
The created legend. 2.1530, 2.1534
Creating a role. 2.3125
Creating abundance. 5.6150
Creating computer programs for learning.
   4.10297
Creating jobs. 4.3217
Creating political order. 3.5320
Creating the entangling alliance. 4.9018
Creating the modern American novel. 2.10626
Creation and discovery. 2.2368
The creation of a Democratic majority,
   1928-1936. 4.8204
The creation of matter. 5.1866
The creation of modern Georgia. 3.8267
The creation of Nikolai Gogol. 2.1388
The creation of states in international law.
   4.9300
The creation of the American Republic,
   1776-1787. 4.7319
The creation of the Anglo-American alliance,
   1937-41. 3.929
The creation of the rococo decorative style.
   1.4962
The creation of the Roman frontier. 3.2716
The creation of the universe. 5.1867
Creative and mental growth. 1.4652
Creative dramatics and English teaching.
   2.3405
The creative element. 2.2685
The creative elite in America. 3.6173

Creative encounters in the classroom. 4.10367
Creative evolution. 1.828
Creative fidelity. 1.1555
Creative financing for energy conservation and
   cogeneration. 4.3801
Creative management techniques in
   interscholastic athletics. 4.907
Creative music education. 1.4414
Creative play direction. 2.3108
The creative process in the autograph musical
   documents of Hector Berlioz, c. 1818-1840.
   1.3818
Creative teachers: who wants them? 4.10494
Creative writing in New Zealand, a brief critical
   history. 2.10195
Creativity. 5.342
Creativity and intelligence. 5.597
Creativity, imagination, logic. 1.89
Credits and collections. 4.4383
Creeds, councils, and controversies. 1.2286
The Creeds of Christendom. 1.2955
Creeds of the churches. 1.2954
Crescas' critique of Aristotle. 1.301
Crestwood Heights. 4.6356
The Cretan glance. 2.602
Crete and Mycenae. 1.4723
Crick crack, monkey. 2.9999
The cricket beneath the waterfall. 2.1219
Cricket in the road. 2.9997
Cries from a wounded Madrid. 2.5156
Crime and custom in savage society. 4.611
Crime and justice. 4.6675
Crime and modernization. 4.6682
Crime and punishment. 2.1358
Crime and punishment in early Massachusetts,
   1620-1692. 4.9857
Crime and the development of modern society.
   4.6793
Crime and the law. 4.6785
Crime & the law. 4.6785
Crime as play. 4.6879
Crime commission report. 4.6767
Le Crime de Sylvestre Bonnard. 2.4205
Crime fiction, 1749-1980. 5.7963
Crime in city politics. 4.6769
Crime in England, 1550-1800. 4.6787
Crime in good company. 2.3444
Crime in society. 4.6770
Crime, law, and social science. 4.6680
Crime, madness, & politics in modern France.
   4.5359
Crime, madness, and politics in modern France.
   4.5359
Crime news and the public. 4.6778
The crime of Claudius Ptolemy. 5.1694
The crime of Galileo. 5.1692
The crime of Sylvestre Bonnard. 2.4206
Crimes of the powerful. 4.6782
Crimes of war. 4.9339
Crimes without victims. 4.6728
The criminal elite. 4.6754
Criminal justice and drugs. 4.6669
Criminal justice and the community. 4.6827
Criminal justice in colonial America, 1606-1660.
   4.9856
Criminal man. 4.6688
The criminal process in the People's Republic
   of China, 1949-1963. 4.9922
Criminal sentences; law without order. 4.9889
Criminal violence. 4.6776
Criminal violence, criminal justice. 4.6772
Criminalistics. 4.6810
The criminality of women. 4.6692
The criminological enterprise. 4.6676
Criminology. 4.6678
The crises of power. 3.7897
Crisis and catharsis. 1.2730
Crisis and change. 1.3183
Crisis and compromise. 4.8586
Crisis and conflict. 2.3570
Crisis and conflict in Han China, 104 BC to
   AD 9. 3.4695
Crisis and decline. 4.4667, 4.8595
Crisis center/hotline; a guidebook to beginning
   and operating. 5.4699
A crisis for the American press. 2.3597

Crisis government in the modern democracies.
   4.7721
Crisis in agriculture. 4.2950
Crisis in blanc and white. 3.8810
Crisis in Buganda, 1953-55. 3.5264
Crisis in command. 5.7283
The crisis in communism. 4.6977
Crisis in English poetry, 1880-1940. 2.5833
Crisis in freedom. 3.7056
Crisis in identity and contemporary Japanese
   novels. 2.2015
The Crisis in social security. 4.3462
The crisis in social security. 4.3472
Crisis in Soviet agriculture. 4.2981
Crisis in the classroom. 4.10043
Crisis in the East European economy. 4.2228
Crisis in the workplace. 4.3502
The crisis of 1830-1842 in Canadian-American
   relations. 3.8723
The crisis of Chinese consciousness. 3.4640
The crisis of church & state, 1050-1300.
   1.2996
The crisis of democracy. 4.7559
The crisis of European sciences and
   transcendental phenomenology. 1.1016
Crisis of fear: secession in South Carolina.
   3.8246
The crisis of German ideology. 3.2358
A crisis of identity. 3.3925
The crisis of Indian planning: economic
   planning in the 1960s. 4.2510
The crisis of our age. 4.4887
The crisis of Parliaments: English history
   1509-1660. 3.1391
The crisis of Quebec, 1914-18 3.8679
The crisis of Russian populism. 3.3129
The crisis of the aristocracy, 1558-1641.
   3.1432
The crisis of the constitution. 4.8400
The crisis of the early Italian Renaissance.
   3.2851
Crisis of the house divided. 3.7294
The crisis of the Negro intellectual. 3.6744
The crisis of the Roman republic. 3.2778
The crisis of Turkish democracy. 3.3597
Crisis theory. 5.5191
Criteria for the life history, with analyses of six
   notable documents. 4.4787
A critical and exegetical commentary on the
   Epistle to the Romans. 1.2710
Critical & historical essays. 2.7921
A critical anthology of Spanish verse. 2.5145
Critical approaches to American literature.
   2.10265
Critical approaches to literature. 2.2432
Critical approaches to medieval literature.
   2.2627
A Critical bibliography of French literature.
   5.7999
A critical bibliography of German literature in
   English translation, 1481-1927. 5.8011
A critical bibliography of religion in America.
   1.2384
A critical dictionary of English literature.
   5.7925
The critical difference. 2.2439
The Critical edge. 1.5298
A critical edition of Yeats's A vision (1925)
   5.666
Critical elections and the mainsprings of
   American politics. 4.8099
The critical essays. 2.365
Critical essays. 2.13736
Critical essays of the seventeenth century.
   2.5503
Critical essays on American humor. 2.10652
Critical essays on American transcendentalism.
   2.10396
Critical essays on Angus Wilson. 2.9544
Critical essays on Anne Bradstreet. 2.10866
Critical essays on Charles Brockden Brown.
   2.10914
Critical essays on Erskine Caldwell. 2.11458
Critical essays on Eugene O'Neill. 2.12291
Critical essays on F. Scott Fitzgerald's The
   great Gatsby. 2.11722
Critical essays on Flannery O'Connor. 2.13215
Critical essays on Frank Norris. 2.11185

Critical essays on George W. Cable. 2.10921
Critical essays on Harriet Beecher Stowe. 2.11234
Critical essays on Henry Adams. 2.10890
Critical essays on Joel Chandler Harris. 2.11052
Critical essays on John Barth. 2.12883
Critical essays on John Greenleaf Whittier. 2.11286
Critical essays on John Updike. 2.13380
Critical essays on Jonathan Edwards. 1.3339
Critical essays on Joseph Heller. 2.13083
Critical essays on Louisa May Alcott. 2.10902
Critical essays on Margaret Drabble. 2.9667
Critical essays on Margaret Fuller. 2.11192
Critical essays on Mark Twain, 1910-1980. 2.10954
Critical essays on Native American literature. 2.2318
Critical essays on Phillis Wheatley. 2.10884
Critical essays on Ralph Waldo Emerson. 2.11028
Critical essays on Randall Jarrell. 2.11928
Critical essays on Robert Penn Warren. 2.12651
Critical essays on the poetry of Tennyson. 2.8177
Critical essays on the western American novel. 2.10592
Critical essays on Theodore Dreiser. 2.11599
Critical essays on W.D. Howells, 1866-1920. 2.11092
Critical essays on Willa Cather. 2.11476
Critical essays on William Faulkner. 2.11690
Critical essays on William Styron. 2.13347
A critical exposition of the philosophy of Leibniz. 1.872
Critical fictions. 2.4740
The critical historians of art. 1.4655
A critical history of children's literature. 2.2704
A critical history of English literature. 2.5514
A critical history of English poetry. 2.5751
A critical history of modern Irish drama, 1891-1980. 2.9861
A critical history of Old English literature. 2.5589
The critical index. 5.8140
A critical introduction to the New Testament. 1.2630
A critical introduction to twentieth-century American drama. 2.10520
Critical issues in medical technology. 5.4633
Critical path analysis. 5.7036
Critical path methods in construction practice. 5.5705
The critical performance. 2.2507
The critical period of American history, 1783-1789. 3.7016
Critical perspectives on Amos Tutuola. 2.10119
Critical perspectives on Chinua Achebe. 2.10107
Critical perspectives on Ngugi wa Thiong'o. 2.10098
The critical phase in Tanzania, 1945-1968. 4.7132
Critical practice. 2.2428
Critical problems in the history of science. 5.737
Critical realism. 1.1283
Critical responses to Kenneth Burke, 1924-1966. 2.11437
Critical state soil mechanics. 5.5902
A critical study of Ādi Granth, being a comprehensive and scientific study of Guru Granth Sahib, the scripture of the Sikhs. 1.1824
A critical study of Beethoven's nine symphonies: by Hector Berlioz. 1.3808
A critical study of William Drummond of Hawthornden. 2.6474
Critical survey of drama. 2.5838
A critical survey of Hindi literature. 2.1882
A critical survey of studies on Malay and Bahasa Indonesia. 5.8341
The critical temper of Alain Locke. 1.6711

The critical theology of Theodore Parker. 1.3419
The critical theory of Jürgen Habermas. 1.987
Critical theory since Plato. 1.1351
Critical thinking and education. 4.10249
Critical understanding. 2.2429
The critical vision. 1.4862
The critical works of Thomas Rymer. 2.7236
Critical writings. 2.8865
The critical year. 3.7457
The critical years. 3.8731
Criticism. 2.2431, 2.2443
Criticism and fiction, and other essays. 2.3502
Criticism and ideology. 2.2478
Criticism and medieval poetry. 2.5614
Criticism and the growth of knowledge. 5.900
Criticism and the nineteenth century. 2.5713
Criticism in America. 2.10240
Criticism in the wilderness. 2.2470
Criticism: the major texts. 2.2460
Critics and criticism, ancient and modern. 2.2430
Critics & crusaders. 3.6296
The critics & the ballad. 2.10660
Critics of culture. 2.10403
Critics of empire: British Radical attitudes to colonialism in Africa 1895-1914. 4.8914
Critics on Caribbean literature. 2.9974
Critics, values, and Restoration comedy. 2.5907
Critics's choice. 2.10798
Critique of aesthetic judgement. 1.890
Critique of dialectical reason, theory of practical ensembles. 1.476
Critique of Hegel's 'Philosophy of right'. 1.931
The critique of judgement. 1.890
A critique of modern textual criticism. 2.31
Critique of practical reason. 1.881
Critique of pure reason. 1.883
A critique of revolutionary humanism. 4.7481
Critique of scientific reason. 5.898
Critique of teleological judgement. 1.890
Critique of the Gotha programme. 4.7072
A critique of the study of kinship. 4.591
A critique of welfare economics. 4.1445
Critiques and essays in criticism, 1920-1948. 2.2444
Critiques and essays on modern fiction, 1920-1951, representing the achievement of modern American and British critics. 2.3425
Critiques of God. 1.2827
Croatia: land, people, culture. 3.1932
The Croatian immigrants in America. 3.6541
The crock of gold. 2.9382
Crockett's victory garden. 5.5367
The crocodile. 2.1355
Crome yellow. 2.8819
Cromwell and the new model foreign policy. 3.1253
Cromwell, the Lord Protector. 3.1491
Cromwellian Ireland. 3.1834
Cromwell's army. 5.7305
Cromwell's generals. 3.1480
Cronache di poveri amanti. 2.5060
Crónica de una muerte anunciada. 2.5419
The crooked hinge. 2.11470
The crooked house. 2.8516
The cross and the fasces. 4.8627
The cross-country ski book. 4.999
Cross-cultural counseling and psychotherapy. 5.467
Cross-currents in 17th century English literature. 2.5645
Cross currents in English literature of the XVIIth century. 2.5645
Cross fire. 4.2952
The cross of culture. 3.8304
Crosscurrents in modern art. 1.4823
Crossing frontiers. 2.9887
Crossing the border. 2.13196
Crossings. 2.13173
A crossroads of freedom. 3.7713
Crossroads of power. 3.1523
Crossroads to Israel. 3.3909
Crow. 2.9712
The Crow Indians. 3.5870
The crowd. 4.5047

The crowd and the public, and other essays. 4.5048
The crowd in the French Revolution. 3.2100
Crowded years. 3.7665
Crowell's handbook of classical drama. 2.268
Crowell's handbook of classical literature. 2.229
Crowell's handbook of classical mythology. 1.1601
Crowell's handbook of contemporary drama. 2.2810
Crowell's handbook of Elizabethan & Stuart literature. 2.5487
Crowell's handbook of world opera. 1.3519
The crown and the establishment. 4.8442
The Crown guide to the world's great plays, from ancient Greece to modern times. 2.3775
The crown of life. 2.6738
The crowning privilege. 2.5764
The crucial decade. 3.7797
The crucible of race. 3.6694
Crucibles. 5.2617
The crucified God. 1.2865
Crucifixion by power. 4.5259
Cruel and unusual. 4.9862
Cruel habitations. 4.3496
Cruel tales. 2.4337
Cruelty and kindness. 5.422
Cruisers. 5.7438
The crumbling walls. 4.6899
Crusade against ignorance. 4.10199
Crusade against slavery. 3.7243
Crusade for justice. 3.6816
Crusade in Europe. 3.902
The crusade in the later Middle Ages. 3.595
Crusader figural sculpture in the Holy Land. 1.5746
Crusader in crinoline. 2.11233
The crusader kingdom of Valencia. 3.3488
Crusaders and compromisers. 3.7234
Crusaders as conquerors. 3.2672
Crusaders for fitness. 5.4649
The Crusaders' kingdom. 3.596
Crusading warfare (1097-1193) 3.591
The cry for justice. 4.5082
Cry, the beloved country. 2.10087
Crying for a vision. 3.5846
The crying of lot 49. 2.13277
Cryptography. 5.7530
Cryptography, a primer. 5.7529
The Crystal Night Pogrom. 3.1098
Crystal oscillator design and temperature compensation. 5.6518
The crystal spirit. 2.9204
Crystal structure analysis. 5.2932
The crystal structure of solids. 5.2924
Crystal structures. 5.2937
Crystals and crystal growing. 5.2925
Crystals and X-rays. 5.2934
Crystals, X-rays, and proteins. 5.2935
CTFT. 2.3234
Cuba, a country study. 3.9091
Cuba: anatomy of a revolution. 3.9105
Cuba and the revolutionary myth. 3.9099
Cuba between empires, 1878-1902. 3.9094
Cuba, Castro, and the United States. 3.6437
Cuba, dilemmas of a revolution. 3.9102
Cuba in the world. 3.9107
The Cuban-American experience. 3.6542
The Cuban insurrection, 1952-1959. 3.9096
The Cuban Invasion. 3.9106
The Cuban missile crisis. 3.7861
The Cuban revolution. 3.9100
Cubism. 1.6346
Cubism: a history and an analysis, 1907-1914. 1.5877
Cubism and abstract art. 1.4841
Cubism and twentieth-century art. 1.4844
Cubism/futurism. 1.4843
The Cubist epoch. 1.4842
Cubists and cubism. 1.5876
Cuentos Chicanos. 2.10812
The cult experience. 1.1872
The cult of Tārā. 1.2150
The cult of the saints. 1.3226
Cultivated broad-leaved trees & shrubs. 5.5360

Cultivated broad-leaved trees and shrubs. 5.5360
Cults in America. 1.1868
The cults of the Greek states. 1.1643
Cultural analysis. 4.4871
Cultural and historical geography of Southwest Guatemala. 4.389
Cultural and natural areas of native North America. 3.5703
Cultural atlas of Africa. 3.5057
Cultural atlas of China. 3.4630
The cultural awakening. 3.139
The cultural background of personality. 4.4895
The cultural contradictions of capitalism. 3.6178
The cultural critics. 4.4876
Cultural foundations of education. 4.10177
Cultural foundations of industrial civilization. 3.213
Cultural foundations of Iranian politics. 4.8770
Cultural geography. 4.371
Cultural heritage of Burma. 3.4423
The cultural heritage of Pakistan. 3.4123
A Cultural history of India. 3.4179
A cultural history of Spanish America, from conquest to independence. 3.8971
A cultural history of the American Revolution. 1.6706
A cultural history of the Enlightenment. 3.178
A cultural history of the modern age. 3.149
Cultural imperialism and exact sciences. 5.1940
The cultural life of the American Colonies. 3.6020
The cultural life of the American Colonies, 1607-1763. 3.6020
The cultural life of the new Nation, 1776-1830. 3.6151
The Cultural migration. 3.6098
Cultural options and the role of tradition. 2.2285
The cultural pattern in American politics. 4.8148
Cultural relativism; perspectives in cultural pluralism. 4.524
Cultural revolution in Russia, 1928-1931. 3.3211
Cultural surveys of Panama 3.9028
Cultural transformations and ethnicity in modern Ecuador. 4.5274
Culture. 4.4877
Culture against man. 4.5153
Culture and anarchy. 4.5318
Culture and art. 1.1353
Culture and behavior. 4.489
Culture and commitment. 4.4881
Culture and commitment, 1929-1945. 3.6169
Culture & communication. 4.505
Culture and conduct. 4.480
Culture and conquest. 3.8967
Culture and cultural entities. 1.90
Culture and curing. 4.462
Culture and experience. 4.399
Culture and history. 3.458
Culture and human fertility. 4.1638
Culture and political economy in western Sicily. 4.2358
Culture and practical reason. 4.494
Culture and society, 1780-1950. 3.1597
Culture and society in classical Weimar, 1775-1806. 3.2506
Culture and the crowd. 3.185
Culture and the educative process. 4.10179
Culture and value. 1.1068
Culture as praxis. 4.4870
The culture factory. 4.10098
Culture, faith, and philosophy in an English country house. 2.7924
Culture in crisis. 3.5890
Culture in the Middle West. 3.6274
Culture methods for invertebrate animals. 5.3805
The culture of a community college. 4.10564
The culture of cities. 4.6296
The culture of narcissism. 4.5186
The culture of professionalism. 4.10069
The culture of public problems. 4.4035
The culture of technology. 5.5549

The culture of the Meiji period. 3.4897
The culture of the school and the problem of change. 4.10010
Culture out of anarchy. 4.10064
Culture wars. 4.10776
Cultures and societies of Africa. 4.656
Cultures in conflict. 1.69, 4.8882
Cultures in contact. 4.619
The cultures of prehistoric Egypt. 3.5137
Cultures of the north Pacific coast 3.5749
Cumulated fiction index. 5.8168
Cumulated index to the books. 5.7765
The Cumulated index to the U.S. Department of State papers relating to the foreign relations of the United States, 1939-1945. 4.8973
The Cumulated indexes to the public papers of the Presidents of the United States. 4.7207
The Cumulative book index. 5.7765
Cumulative index to nursing & allied health literature. 5.8291
Cumulative index to the annual catalogues of Her Majesty's Stationery Office publications, 1922-1972. 5.7923
Cumulative record. 5.6
Cunning intelligence in Greek culture and society. 3.2545
Cunninghame Graham. 2.8716
The cup of Jamshid. 2.1904
A cup of news. 2.6498
Curanderismo, Mexican American folk healing. 4.782
Curate's friend. 2.8642
Curious fragments. 2.12022
Curious naturalists. 5.4068
Currency and credit. 4.4470
Current anthropology. 4.395
Current biography. 3.324
Current biography yearbook. 3.324
The current crisis in American politics. 4.8173
Current developments in anthropological genetics. 4.458
Current economic problems in China. 4.2488
Current index to journals in education. 5.8149
Current international treaties. 4.8967
Current issues in energy. 5.6136
Current issues in linguistic theory. 2.132
Current issues in natural resource policy. 4.1898
Current issues in nursing. 5.5179
Current issues in U.S. environmental policy. 4.2073
Current issues in urban economics. 4.6291
Current literary terms. 2.2359
Current national bibliographies. 5.7679
Current personality theories. 5.512
Current practice in program budgeting (PPBS) 4.4677
Current problems in sociobiology. 4.508
Current research in marijuana. 5.4427
Current studies in social psychology. 4.4999
Current trends in linguistics. 2.3
Current trends in the Soviet and East European food economy. 4.2975
Currents, contemporary directions in the visual arts. 1.4835
Currents in the contemporary Argentine novel. 2.5373
Curriculum. 4.10616
Curriculum and evaluation. 4.10433
Curriculum design. 4.10421, 4.10454
Curriculum development. 4.10432
Curriculum development: theory into practice. 4.10452
Curriculum for better schools. 4.10448
Curriculum improvement. 4.10435
Curriculum innovation. 4.10270
Curriculum inquiry. 4.10434
Curriculum planning for better teaching and learning. 4.10447
Curriculum theorizing. 4.10422
Curriculum theory. 4.10444
Currier & Ives. 1.6497
Currier and Ives. 1.6497
Curso superior de sintaxis española 2.892
A curtain of green, and other stories. 2.12658
Curves and singularities. 5.1631
Curving road. 2.13334

Custer died for your sins. 3.5799
Custer in '76. 3.5781
Custom and conflict in Africa. 4.649
The custom of the country. 2.12691
The cut of men's clothes, 1600-1900. 5.7091
The cut of women's clothes, 1600-1930. 5.7092
The cutting and polishing of electro-optic materials. 5.5957
The cyberiad; fables for the cybernetic age. 2.1708
Cybernetics. 5.948
Cybernetics and the philosophy of mind. 5.123
The cycle of American literature. 2.10257
Cycles of conquest. 3.5766
The cycles of social reform. 5.4697
Cycles of soil. 5.5277
Cyclic stress and strain. 5.5784
The cyclopaedia of India and of eastern and southern Asia. 3.4152
The Cyclopaedia of American biography. 3.6287
Cyclopedia of American agriculture. 5.5255
Cyclopedia of literary characters. 2.2353
Cyclopedia of world authors. 2.2548
Cyclopedic medical dictionary. 5.4490
Cyclopedic survey of chamber music. 1.4185
Cymru ac America. 3.6600
Cynewulf. 2.6306
The cypresses believe in God. 2.5260
Cyprian Norwid. 2.1721
Cyprus. 4.9235
Cyprus, a country study. 3.3692
Cyprus, conflict and negotiation, 1960-1980. 3.3698
The Cyprus revolt. 3.3695
Cyprus, the impact of diverse nationalism on a state. 3.3694
Cyrano de Bergerac. 2.4700, 2.9640
Cyril of Jerusalem and Nemesius of Emesa. 1.2210
Cyropaedia. 2.400
Cytogenetics. 5.3421
Cytological technique. 5.4160
Cytology and cell physiology. 5.3587
Cytology and cytogenetics. 5.3592
Cytology and evolution. 5.3593
Cytoplasmic genes and organelles. 5.3440
Czartoryski and European unity, 1770-1861. 3.3335
Czech drama since World War II. 2.1660
Czech literature. 2.1653
Czech literature since 1956. 2.1656
The Czech romantics. 2.1655
Czech writers and politics, 1945-1969. 2.1657
The Czechoslovak political trials, 1950-1954. 3.1924
The Czechoslovak reform movement. 3.1923
Czechoslovakia. 3.1906, 3.1908
Czechoslovakia, a country study. 3.1905
Czechoslovakia enslaved. 3.1927
Czechoslovakia in European history. 3.1909
Czechs & Germans. 3.1907
The Czechs under Nazi rule. 3.1922

D-day. 3.962
D. H. Lawrence. 2.8986, 2.8992, 2.8995, 2.8997, 2.9000
D. H. Lawrence, a calendar of his works. 2.8994
D. H. Lawrence & Susan his cow. 2.8999
D.H. Lawrence and the experience of Italy. 2.8987
D. H. Lawrence and the psychology of rhythm. 2.8971
D. H. Lawrence, his life and works. 2.8990
A D. H. Lawrence miscellany. 2.8989
D. H. Lawrence: novelist, poet, prophet. 2.8996
D. H. Lawrence: son of woman. 2.8993
D. H. Lawrence: the critical heritage. 2.8984
D. H. Lawrence, the man and his work; the formative years: 1885-1919. 2.8983
D. Ivnii Ivvenalis satvrae XIV. 2.728
D. J. Williams. 2.845
The D.O.'s. 5.5212
D.R.I. model of the U.S. economy. 4.2010
D. W. Griffith: his life and work. 2.3048

Da Silva da Silva's cultivated wilderness. 2.10028
Dada & Surrealism. 1.6732
Dada and surrealist art. 1.4853
Dada, Surrealism, and their heritage. 1.4831
Dædalus. 3.6071
The dæmon in the wood. 4.763
Dafydd ap Gwilym. 2.836-2.837
Dag Hammarskjöld. 3.1149
Dag Hammarskjöld revisited. 4.9200
The daguerreotype in America. 5.6949
Dahāyā al-kharītah. 2.1840
Dahomean narrative. 4.815
Dai Greatcoat. 2.8858
Daily life in ancient India. 3.4190
Daily life in ancient Rome. 3.2729
Daily life in China, on the eve of the Mongol
  invasion, 1250-1276. 3.4633
Daily life in Greece at the time of Pericles.
  3.2548
Daily life in Johnson's London. 3.1746
Daily life in Portugal in the late Middle Ages.
  3.3493
Daily life in Spain in the golden age. 3.3405
Daily life in the world of Charlemagne. 3.1956
Daily living in the twelfth century, based on the
  observations of Alexander Neckam in
  London and Paris. 4.825
The daily newspaper in America. 2.3585
Daily variety. 2.2775, 2.2971
Dakota panorama. 3.8513
Dakota Territory, 1861-1889. 3.8512
Dali and surrealism. 1.6289
La dama del alba. 2.5280
Damaged parents, an anatomy of child neglect.
  4.6554
Damaged souls. 3.6286
La dame aux camélias. 2.4182
The damnable question. 3.1862
The damnation of Theron Ware. 2.11033
The damndest Yankees. 3.6889
The Damocles syndrome. 5.4777
The Damrosch dynasty. 1.3750
Dan Jacobson. 2.10084
Dance. 4.1091, 5.8427
The dance. 4.1113
Dance and mime film and videotape catalog.
  4.1094
Dance and society in Eastern Africa, 1890-1970.
  3.5238
The dance, art, and ritual of Africa. 4.1111
The dance catalog. 4.1093
Dance directory. 4.1086
The dance encyclopedia. 4.1080
The dance experience. 4.1098
Dance film directory. 4.1097
The dance has many faces. 4.1114
Dance in elementary education. 4.1183
The dance in India. 4.1110
Dance index. v. 1-7, no. 7/8. 4.1078
The dance makers. 4.1127
Dance notation. 4.1083
The dance of death. 2.14072
The dance of legislation. 4.9736
The dance of life. 2.8621
Dance of the millions. 3.9176
Dance out the answer. 4.1146
The dance technique of Doris Humphrey and
  its creative potential. 4.1148
A dance to the music of time. 2.9226-2.9228
A dance to the music of time: A question of
  upbringing. 2.9225
Dance to the piper. 4.1131
The dance writings of Carl Van Vechten.
  4.1116
Dancers, buildings and people in the streets.
  4.1171
The dancer's image. 4.1115
Dancing. 2.13443
Dancing, a guide for the dancer you can be.
  4.1095
The dancing bears. 2.12148
The dancing master. 4.1089
The dancing Socrates. 2.1733
Dandelion wine. 2.11408
The danger tree. 2.9743
Dangerous acquaintances. 2.4075
Dangerous currents. 4.1283

The dangerous edge. 2.3472
Dangerous plants. 5.3662
Dangerous properties of industrial materials.
  5.5557
Dangerous relations. 3.3267
The dangerous summer. 2.11850
Dangling man. 2.11349
Daniel Blum's Screen world. 1949-1965.
  2.2867
Daniel Chester French, an American sculptor.
  1.5665
Daniel Defoe; a critical study. 2.6980
Daniel Defoe and middle-class gentility. 2.6979
Daniel Defoe, citizen of the modern world.
  2.6976
Daniel Martin. 2.9683
Daniel O'Connell. 3.1848
Daniel Webster. 3.7095
Daniel Webster. 3.7098
Daniel Webster and the trial of American
  nationalism, 1843-1852. 3.7097
Daniele Manin and the Venetian revolution of
  1848-49. 3.2917
The Danish Americans. 3.6591
Danish literature. 2.13999
Danish literature in English translation. 5.8021
The Danish system of labor relations. 4.3664
D'Annunzio. 2.5019
Dans le Labyrinthe. 2.4687
Dans le leurre du seuil. 2.4417
Danse macabre. 2.75
Dansk-engelsk ordbog. 2.921
Dante. 2.4930
Dante and philosophy. 2.4941
Dante commentaries. 2.4929
Dante Gabriel Rossetti. 2.8018
Dante Gabriel Rossetti and the limits of
  Victorian vision. 1.6718
Dante, poet of the desert. 2.4938
Dante, poet of the secular world. 2.4935
Dante the maker. 2.4934
Dante's Divine comedy. 2.4936
Dante's drama of the mind. 2.4942
Dante's lyric poetry. 2.4918
Dante's Paradise. 2.4928
Dante's style in his lyric poetry. 2.4943
Danton. 3.2066
Danwei. 4.4712
The 'Danzig trilogy' of Günter Grass. 2.13766
Daphnis & Chloe. 2.378
D'après tout. 2.4529
D'Arcy Cresswell. 2.10214
Dare call it treason. 3.804
The daring young man on the flying trapeze
  and other stories. 2.12438
The dark abyss of time. 3.494
Dark ancestor. 2.2696
Dark as the grave wherein my friend is laid.
  2.9055
The dark child. 3.5381
Dark cinema. 2.2981
The dark comedy. 2.2813
Dark conceit. 2.2390
The dark glass. 2.8020
Dark horse. 3.7695
The dark is light enough: Christopher Fry.
  2.8672
The dark island. 2.9442
The dark labyrinth. 2.8609
Dark lanterns. 3.7307
Dark laughter. 2.11319
A dark night's passing. 2.2089
Dark paradise. 4.6661
Dark places of the heart 2.10168
Dark salvation. 1.3372
The Dark side of families. 4.5776
The dark side of the landscape. 1.6015
The dark sun. 2.8985
Dark symphony. 2.10697
Dark Thoreau. 2.11255
The dark tower, and other radio scripts.
  2.9076
The dark window. 2.9341
The darkening glass. 2.8038
A darker shade of pale. 1.4089
Darker than you think. 2.12757

The Darker vision of the Renaissance. 3.154
The darkling plain. 2.5828
Darkness and day. 2.8527
Darkness at noon. 2.8939
Darkness casts no shadow. 2.1675
Darkness in summer. 2.2132
Darkness visible. 2.8695
Darkroom. 5.6939
Darkroom dynamics. 5.6948
Darkwater; voices from within the veil. 3.6641
Darśan, seeing the divine image in India.
  1.1705
Darstellungen aus der Sittengeschichte Roms in
  der Zeit von August bis zum Ausgang der
  Antonine. Band 1-3 English. 3.2732
Darwin and his critics. 5.3355
Darwin and his flowers. 5.3194
Darwin and the Darwinian revolution. 5.3199
Darwin and the naked lady. 2.8526
Darwin for beginners. 5.3201
Darwin, Marx, and Wagner. 3.152
Darwin on man: A psychological study of
  Scientific creativity. 5.3197
The Darwinian revolution. 5.3349
Darwin's century. 5.3344
Darwin's finches; an essay on the general
  biological theory of evolution. 5.3965
Darwin's plots. 2.6026
Darwin's universe. 5.1877
Dasa-kumara-charita. 2.1944
Data analysis for scientists and engineers.
  5.1393
Data and computer communications. 5.6406
Data base computers. 5.1234
Data bases and systems of the U.S. Geological
  Survey, 1983. 5.2996
Data books of who's who in technology today
  1982-. 5.5546
Data communications. 5.6416
Data compilations in physics. 5.8423
Data compression. 5.1239, 5.6369
Data converters. 5.6578
Data, instruments, and theory. 5.862
Data structure techniques. 5.1242
Data structures. 5.1162
Data structures and algorithms. 5.1240
Data structures and network algorithms.
  5.1243
Data structures and operating systems. 5.1194
Data structures and program design. 5.1186
Data structures in Pascal. 5.1241
Databanks in a free society. 4.7696
Database processing. 5.1237
Database systems. 5.1238
Dateline, Toronto. 2.11838
Datensammlungen in der Physik. 5.8423
Dating in archaeology. 3.244
A daughter of the middle border. 2.11038
Daughters of joy, sisters of misery. 4.5540
Daughters of the conquistadores. 4.6088
Daughters of the earth. 3.5834
Daughters of the reconquest. 4.5860
David. 1.4969
David Belasco; naturalism in the American
  theatre. 2.3244
David Crockett. 3.8348
David Garrick. 2.7032
David Garrick, a critical biography. 2.3343
David Garrick, director. 2.3341
David Glasgow Farragut. 3.7325
David Harum. 2.11264
David Jones. 2.8859-2.8860
David O. Selznick's Hollywood. 2.3067
David Smith. 1.5674
David Smith, painter, sculptor, draftsman.
  1.4905
David Smith, the sculptor and his work.
  1.5675
David to Delacroix. 1.6055
Davitt and Irish revolution, 1846-82. 3.1854
Davy. 2.13235
Dawn and the darkest hour. 2.8831
The dawn and twilight of Zoroastrianism.
  1.1783
The dawn of a new era, 1250-1453. 3.573
The dawn of animal life. 5.3166
The dawn of Bohemianism. 1.4967
The dawn of civilization. 3.116

The dawn of European civilization. 3.554
The dawn of modern geography ... 4.60
Dawn of modern science. 5.765
The dawn of tantra. 1.2172
Dawn to the West. 2.2001
The day before. 2.9439
Day by day. 2.12043
Day by day in Jewish history. 3.3844
Day care. 4.6573
A Day in the country. 1.6362
The day is born of darkness. 2.1627
The day lasts more than a hundred years.
  2.1619
Day of infamy. 3.1014
The day of the carpetbagger. 3.8288
The day of the owl; Equal danger. 2.5082
Dayānanda Sarasvatī, his life and ideas. 1.1731
Daycare. 4.6572
The days grow short. 1.4062
A day's march nearer home. 3.928
Days of 1945-1951. 2.609
The days of Henry Thoreau. 2.11249
Daytime star, the story of our sun. 5.1794
DDT. 5.3579
Los de abajo. 2.5333
De anima. 2.437
De causis plantarum, 1. 2.396
De cive. 4.7404
De diuersis artibus. 1.5099
De finibus bonorum et malorum. 2.664
De Gaulle. 3.2204-3.2205
De generatione et corruptione. 5.832
De inventione; De optimo genere oratorum;
  Topica. 2.658
De la division du travail social. English.
  4.2679
De la littérature considérée dans ses rapports
  avec les institutions sociales 2.2613
De la recherche du bien. 1.1464
De la terre à la lune. 2.4320
De l'Allemagne. 3.2241
De los siglos oscuros al de Oro. 2.5097
De miseria condicionis humane. 1.2905
De motu animalium. 5.3797
De natura deorum. 2.656
De officiis. 2.665
De oratore. 2.666
De pequeñas causas. 2.5234
De profectione Ludovici VII in orientem.
  3.593
De profundis. 2.8269
De re metallica. 5.6760
De re publica, De Legibus, with an English
  translation by Clinton Walker Keyes. 2.667
De-regulating Wall Street. 4.4621
De rerum natura. 2.676, 2.738
De senectute, De amicitia, De divinatione.
  2.657
De servo arbitrio. 1.1497
De Stijl, 1917-1931. 1.5020
The De Stijl environment. 1.5021
De topicis differentiis. 1.336
De vita Agricolae. 2.775
Dead cert. 2.9696
Dead end. 4.4038
The Dead Sea scrolls. 5.8240
The Dead Sea Scrolls. 1.1906
Dead Sea scrolls. English. 1.1935
The Dead Sea Scrolls in English. 1.1935
Dead souls. 2.1382
Deadline every minute. 2.3582
The deadlock of democracy. 3.6385
Deadly gambits. 4.9180
Deaf children. 4.6601
Dean Acheson. 3.7623
Dear and honoured lady. 3.1613
Dear comrade. 3.3259
Dear John, dear Coltrane. 2.13066
Dear Lord Rothschild. 5.3796
'Dear Master' 3.7209
'Dearest Emmie,' Thomas Hardy's letters to his
  first wife. 2.7773
Dearest friend. 3.7054
Dearest Isa. 2.7479
Death. 5.8123
Death and burial in the Roman world. 3.2740
Death and consciousness. 5.661
Death and dying. 4.5828

The death and letters of Alice James. 3.337
The death and life of great American cities.
  1.5597
The death and life of Malcolm X. 3.6845
The death and rebirth of the Seneca. 3.5947
Death and renewal. 4.7368
Death and the enlightenment. 4.5827
Death at Cross Plains. 3.8285
Death by choice. 5.4577
Death by melancholy. 2.10462
The Death camp Treblinka. 3.1078
Death, dying, and the biological revolution.
  5.4580
Death in a promised land. 3.8539
A death in Delhi. 2.1896
Death in the afternoon. 2.3596, 4.1053
A death in the family. 2.11294
Death in the woods, and other stories. 2.11318
Death of a hero. 2.8375
Death of a lake. 2.10177
Death of a simple giant, and other modern
  Yugoslav stories. 2.1202
Death of a song and other stories 2.1917
Death of a utopia. 4.10109
The death of Adam. 5.3347
The death of Ahasuerus. 2.14087
The death of Artemio Cruz. 2.5341
The death of Bessie. 2.12847
The death of Che Guevara. 2.12948
The death of Christopher Marlowe. 2.6615
The death of God. 1.2801
The death of Jim Loney. 2.13418
The death of Mr. Baltisberger. 2.1686
The death of nature. 5.802
The death of Nora Ryan. 2.11647
Death of the fox. 2.13036
The death of the gods. 2.1519
The death of the heart. 2.8470
Death of the hero. 1.6057
The death of the imperial dream. 3.1221
The death of the law. 4.9500
The death of tragedy. 2.2818
The death of white sociology. 3.6766
The death of woman Wang. 4.6150
Death on the installment plan. 2.4509
Death penalties. 4.9860
The death penalty. 4.6853
The Death penalty in America. 4.9861
The death rituals of rural Greece. 4.869
Death Row: an affirmation of life. 2.10700
Death, sleep & the traveler. 2.13070
Deathbird stories. 2.13001
Deaths and entrances. 2.9407
Death's duel. 1.3071
Death's master. 2.9738
Deathwatch. 2.4534
The debacle (1870-71) 2.4340
Debate about the earth. 5.3077
The debate on the English Revolution. 3.1476
The debate on the French Revolution,
  1789-1800. 3.1246
The debate over slavery. 3.7203
The debates and decrees of Vatican Council II.
  1.3128-1.3129
The debates and decrees of Vatican Council II,
  September 14 to December 8, 1965. 1.3126
The debates in the Federal Convention of 1787.
  4.7821
The debates in the several State conventions on
  the adoption of the Federal Constitution.
  4.7822
Debates with historians. 3.474
The debt dilemma of developing nations.
  4.4728
Debussy. 1.3847-1.3848
Debussy on music. 1.3846
The debut. 2.9630
Les débuts de l'estampe imprimée au Canada.
  1.6448
A decade later. 5.4833
A decade of American foreign policy. 4.9045
A decade of censorship in America. 5.7599
Decade of dealignment. 4.8505
Decade of disillusionment. 3.7841
A Decade of Federal antipoverty programs.
  4.2104
A decade of revolution, 1789-1799. 3.659
Decadent societies. 3.5

The Decameron. 2.4904-2.4905, 2.4907-2.4908
Il Decameron. 2.4903
Decameron. 2.4906
The decapitated chicken, and other stories.
  2.5442
The decay of capitalist civilization. 4.1540
The decay of the angel. 2.2113
Deceit, desire, and the novel. 2.3506
Decent interval. 3.4504
A decent respect to the opinions of mankind.
  4.7201
Decentralization: achieving reform. 4.10646
Deception in World War II. 3.914
Les déchets humains. 2.4872
Deciding to forego life-sustaining treatment.
  5.4579
Deciduous forests of eastern North America.
  5.3781
Deciphering the Maya script. 3.9049
The decipherment of linear B. 2.227
Decision by debate. 2.3537
Decision in Germany. 3.2454
Decision making. 5.376
Decision making at child welfare intake.
  4.6567
Decision over Schweinfurt. 3.974
Decision support systems. 4.2636-4.2637
Decision systems for inventory management and
  production planning. 4.2673
The decision to disarm Germany. 5.7301
The decision to divide Germany. 3.1145
Decisionmaking for arms limitation. 4.9157
Decisions about the teaching of English.
  4.10513
Decisions in Israel's foreign policy. 3.3857
Decisions with multiple objectives. 5.5600
Decisive battles of World War II. 3.905
The Declaration of independence. 4.7818
The Declaration of Independence and the
  Constitution of the United States of America.
  4.7817
The Declaration of Rights, 1689. 3.1512
The Declaration on the relation of the Church
  to non-Christian religions. 1.3124
The declassified Eisenhower. 3.7820
Decline and fall. 2.9486
The decline & fall of British capitalism. 4.2281
Decline and fall of Byzantium to the Ottoman
  Turks. 3.2673
The decline and fall of radical Catholicism.
  1.3178
The decline and resurgence of Congress.
  4.8017
Decline and rise of Europe. 3.1196
The decline of American gentility. 3.6156
The decline of American Liberalism. 3.6386
The decline of Bismarck's European order.
  3.3070
The decline of democracy in the Philippines.
  4.7682
The decline of hell. 1.2945
The decline of imperial Russia, 1855-1914.
  3.3131
The decline of laissez faire, 1897-1917. 4.1879
The decline of medieval Hellenism in Asia
  Minor. 3.2661
The decline of politics. 4.8309
The decline of power, 1915-1964. 3.1687
The decline of socialism in America, 1912-1925.
  4.6994
The decline of the ancient world. 3.2806
The decline of the German mandarins; the
  German academic community, 1890-1933.
  4.10129
The decline of the progressive movement in
  Wisconsin, 1890-1920. 3.8447
The decline of the Venetian nobility as a ruling
  class. 3.2913
The decline of the West. 3.197
The decline of transit. 4.3914
The decline of working-class politics. 4.3650
Decline or renewal? France since the 1930s.
  3.2197
The decline, revival, and fall of the British
  Empire. 3.1220
Declining population growth revisited. 4.1602
The declining significance of race. 3.6631
Decoding dragons. 4.851

Decoding the past. 3.444
Decolonization. 3.755, 4.8907
Decomposition in terrestrial ecosystems. 5.3509
Deconstruction, theory and practice. 2.2483
Deconstructive criticism. 2.2482
The decoration of houses. 1.6550
Decorative plasterwork in Great Britain. 1.5504
The decorative Thirties. 1.6540
The decorative Twenties. 1.4838
The decorative work of Robert Adam. 1.6547
A dedicated man, and other stories. 2.9395
Deductive logic. 1.1177
Dee goong an. 2.2229
The deed of life. 2.8991
The deeds of Frederick Barbarossa. 3.2270
The deeds of god in Rddhipur. 1.1700
The deeds of Henry the Fifth. 3.1380
The deep blue good-by. 2.13144
Deep blues. 1.4275
Deep down in the jungle ... 4.767
The deep end. 2.11424
Deep rivers. 2.5426
Deep-sea biology. 5.3247
Deep song. 4.1144
Deep song and other prose. 2.5253
Deep South. 4.5198
Deep space. 5.1878
Deep space telecommunications systems engineering. 5.6719
Deep water. 2.13086
The deeper life. 1.3093
The deeps of deliverance. 2.13951
The deer park. 2.12096
Defeated leaders. 3.2200
Defeating Communist insurgency. 5.7231
Defective medicine. 5.4594
A defence of liberty against tyrants. 4.7386
A defence of ryme. 2.6444
Defender of the race. 1.3318
Defending my enemy. 4.9709
The defense. 2.1584
The defense of Berlin. 3.2503
The defense of community in Peru's central highlands. 4.2845
Defense or delusion? 5.7266
Defensible programs for the gifted. 4.10919
Defensible space; crime prevention through urban design. 4.6698
Defensive mechanisms in social insects. 5.3870
The deferential worker. 4.2925
Defiance in Manchuria. 4.4847
Defining child abuse. 4.6570
Defining international aggression, the search for world peace. 4.9317
Definition. 1.1247
Definitions in political economy. 4.1416
The Definitive Dr. Jekyll and Mr. Hyde companion. 2.8119
Defoe and fictional time. 2.6982
Defoe & spiritual autobiography. 2.6977
Defoe's narratives; situations and structures. 2.6978
Deformation and fracture mechanics of engineering materials. 5.5789
Deformation geometry for materials scientists. 5.5783
The deformation of the earth's crust. 5.3090
Deformation processing. 5.7053
Degas. 1.6089, 1.6091, 1.6098, 1.6460
DeGaulle. 3.2217
The degradation of the academic dogma: the university in America, 1945-1970. 4.10065
The degradation of the democratic dogma. 3.453
Degree theory. 5.1608
Degrees of freedom. 2.9772
The degrees of knowledge. 1.1284
Degrés. 2.4433
The dehumanization of art. 1.1383
Dehydrated culture media and reagents for microbiology. 5.4446
The deindustrialization of America. 4.3205
Deinstitutionalization and community adjustment of mentally retarded people. 4.6613

Deinstitutionalization and the welfare state. 4.6524
Deirdre. 2.9290, 2.9383
Deities and dolphins. 3.3825
Dekaochtō lianotragouda tēs pikrēs patridas. 2.619
Del sentimiento trágico de la vida en los hombres y en los pueblos. 1.1133
Del Siglo de Oro a este siglo de siglas. 2.5093
Delacroix. 1.6095
Delaware. 3.8098
Delaware, a guide to the first state. 3.8097
The Delaware Indians. 3.5872
Delaware prehistoric archaeology. 3.5732
Delay in the court. 4.9904
A delicate balance. 2.12839, 4.10746
The 'Délie' of Maurice Scève. 2.4008
Delight. 2.9244
Delinquency. 4.6866
Delinquency and crime: a biopsychosocial approach. 4.6867
Delinquency and dropout. 4.6871
Delinquency and the juvenile justice system. 4.6875
Delinquency in a birth cohort. 4.6886
Delinquency in India. 4.6901
Delinquency, its roots, careers, and prospects. 4.6887
Delius as I knew him. 1.3851
A Delius companion. 1.3850
Deliverance. 2.12977
The deliverance. 2.11772
Deliverance to the captives. 1.3049
Delmore Schwartz. 2.12454-2.12455
DeLong's guide to bicycles & bicycling: the art & science. 5.6638
The Delphic oracle. 3.2643-3.2644
Delphine. 2.4298
Delta wedding. 2.12660
The deluge: an historical novel of Poland, Sweden and Russia. 2.1729
The deluge; British society and the First World War. 3.1693
Delusions and discoveries. 2.5972
Demagogues. 3.7618
Demand analysis and inventory control. 4.2681
The demand and supply of primary energy in mainland China. 4.3711
The demand and supply of public goods. 4.4644
The demand for durable goods. 4.2057
The Demand for primary health services in the Third World. 5.4657
The demes of Attica, 508/7-ca. 250 B.C. 3.2555
Demetrius. 2.13647
Demian. 2.13771
The demise of a rural economy. 4.2965
Democracy. 2.10888
Democracy ancient and modern. 4.7364
Democracy and classical Greece. 3.2573
Democracy and development in Turkey. 3.3576
Democracy and disobedience. 4.5039
Democracy and distrust. 4.9643
Democracy and economic change in India. 4.5429
Democracy and education. 4.10225
Democracy and elections. 4.8370
Democracy and empire. 3.1620
Democracy and social ethics. 4.5168
Democracy and the amendments to the Constitution. 4.9635
Democracy and the novel. 2.10610
Democracy and the organization of political parties. 4.7785
Democracy and the party movement in prewar Japan. 4.8761
Democracy and the public service. 4.7979
Democracy and totalitarianism. 4.7251
Democracy at gunpoint: the Greek front. 3.2708
Democracy at the polls. 4.7735
Democracy, authority, and alienation in work. 4.3186
Democracy in America. 4.7842
Democracy in Costa Rica. 3.9079

Democracy in Jonesville. 4.5145
Democracy in the United States. 4.7800
Democracy or anarchy? 4.7744
Democracy, the threshold of freedom. 4.7734
Democracy's body. 4.1166
Democracy's college. 4.10066
Democracy's railroads; public enterprise in Jacksonian Michigan. 4.4004
A Democrat looks at his party. 4.8198
The Democratic and Republican Parties in America. 4.8386
The democratic art. 1.6503
Democratic despot. 3.2158
Democratic dogma. 3.453
Democratic humanism and American literature. 2.10388
The democratic movement in Germany, 1789-1914. 3.2291
The democratic movement in Italy, 1830-1876. 3.2861
The Democratic Party and the Negro. 4.8203
The Democratic Party and the politics of sectionalism, 1941-1948. 4.8197
The democratic philosophy of education. 4.10226
Democratic promise. 3.7410
Democratic representation. 4.9731
The Democratic Republic, 1801-1815. 3.7082
The Democratic-Republican societies, 1790-1800. 3.7020
Democratic-Republican societies, 1790-1800. 3.7021
The Democratic Republicans of New York. 4.8211
The democratic revolution. 3.652
The democratic Roosevelt. 3.7784
Democratic theory. 4.7575, 4.7578, 4.7583
The democratic vista. 3.6094
The Democrats. 4.8207
Demographic analysis. 4.1620, 4.1623
Demographic and economic change in developed countries. 4.1636
Demographic dimensions of the New Republic. 4.1251
Demographic dynamics in America. 4.1669
The demographic explosion. 4.5683
Demographic statistics of Hawaii, 1778-1965. 4.1682
Demographic trends and economic reality. 4.1678
Demographic vistas. 2.2852
Demographic yearbook. 4.1238
Demography. 4.1613
Demography of the Black population in the United States. 5.7874
Demography of the Dobe !Kung. 3.5483
The demography of tropical Africa. 4.1710
The demolished man. 2.12906
A demon in my view. 2.9805
The demon in the aether. 5.1952
Demon of progress in the arts. 1.4815
The demon of the absolute. 2.2581
The demon within. 2.9238
Demos. 2.7731
Demosthenes. 3.2622
Demosthenes against Meidias, Androtion, Aristocrates, Timocrates, Aristogeiton. 2.359
Demystifying parole. 4.6897
The Dene Nation, colony within. 3.5956
Denial of justice. 4.9878
Denis Johnston's Irish theatre. 2.8850
Denishawn, the enduring influence. 4.1164
Denmark. 3.3366
The denominational society. 1.2373
Dental care for everyone. 5.5125
Dentistry. 5.5121
Departing glory; Theodore Roosevelt as ex-President. 3.7702
The Department of Agriculture. 5.5219
The Department of Dead Ends. 2.9447
Department of Defense dictionary of military and associated terms. 5.7172
The Department of Health, Education, and Welfare. 5.4616
The Department of Labor. 4.3091
Dependency and development in Latin America. 4.2136
Dependency under challenge. 4.2151

Deportation of the Jews to the east. 3.1103
Depositional sedimentary environments, with reference to terrigenous clastics. 5.3059
Depositional systems. 5.3120
Depression decade. 4.1881
Depression in the elderly. 5.4931
The depression of the nineties. 4.1911
Deprivation and delinquency. 5.5114
Deprogrammers, anti-cultists, and the new religions. 1.1875
The deputy. 2.13898
Deregulating the airlines. 4.4087
Deregulating Wall Street. 4.4621
Deregulation and the new airline entrepreneurs. 4.4086
Le dernier des Justes. 2.4746
Derniers vers. 2.4252
Deryni Checkmate. 2.13126
Deryni Rising. 2.13126
Des Minnesangs Frühling. 2.13527
Descartes. 1.792, 1.794, 1.797
Descartes against the skeptics. 1.798
Descartes' Conversation with Burman. 1.791
Descartes' philosophy interpreted according to the order of reasons. 1.793
Descartes' philosophy of science. 5.875
Descartes's Rules for the direction of the mind. 1.790
The descent from heaven. 2.2771
Descent from power. 4.9067
Descent into hell. 2.9525
Descent of Euphues. 2.6491
Descent of man. 2.12915
Deschooling society. 4.10006
A description of Patagonia, and the adjoining parts of South America. 3.9255
Description of the Indies, c. 1620. 3.5986
A descriptive catalogue of the bibliographies of 20th century British poets, novelists and dramatists. 5.7931
A descriptive catalogue of the government publications of the United States, September 5, 1774-March 4, 1881. 5.7772
A descriptive dictionary of the Indian islands & adjacent countries. 3.4553
Descriptive Italian grammar. 2.854
Descriptive linguistics. 2.1014
Descriptive physical oceanography. 4.345
Descriptive set theory. 5.1355
Desegregated schools. 4.10788
Desegregation from Brown to Alexander. 4.9691
Desegregation of the U.S. Armed Forces. 3.6724
The desert fathers. 1.2481
The desert generals. 3.1000
Desert immigrants. 3.8333
The desert of love. 2.4629
Desert trails of Atacama. 3.9269
The desert year. 5.3267
The deserted house. 2.1545
Deserted medieval villages. 3.1326
Deserts on the march. 4.385
The design and analysis of computer algorithms. 5.1159
Design and analysis of computer communication networks. 5.6408
Design and analyusis of experiments in psychology and education. 5.49
Design and applications in diesel engineering. 5.6223
Design and construction of concrete shell roofs. 5.6097
Design and form. 1.4649
Design and marketing of new products. 4.4300
Design and truth in autobiography. 3.318
Design for human ecosystems. 4.2810
Design in America. 1.4648
Design in Chaucer's Troilus. 2.6337
Design of agricultural machinery. 5.6248
Design of automatic machinery. 5.6179
Design of concrete structures. 5.5880
The design of development. 4.2804
Design of feedback control systems. 5.6183
The design of high-efficiency turbomachinery and gas turbines. 5.6205
Design of machine elements. 5.6194
Design of man-computer dialogues. 5.1157

The design of microprocessor, sensor, and control systems. 5.6593
Design of modern concrete highway bridges. 5.6079
Design of modern steel highway bridges. 5.6080
Design of prestressed concrete. 5.5883
Design of prestressed concrete structures. 5.5882
Design of testable logic circuits. 5.6475
The design of the aeroplane. 5.6669
The design of the present. 2.10350
The design of Virgil's Bucolics. 2.792
Design on the land. 5.5380
Design, planning, and development methodology. 5.5698
Design principles in resource recovery engineering. 5.6037
Design since 1945. 5.5636
Design theory of fluidic components. 5.6238
Design with nature. 4.2078
The designated heir. 2.11968
Designer's handbook of integrated circuits. 5.6525
Designing and implementing local area networks. 5.6409
Designing and space planning for libraries. 5.7616
Designing correctional organizations for youths. 4.6884
Designing curriculum. 4.10441
Designing for people. 5.7016
Designing intelligent systems. 5.1001
The designs and drawings of Antonio Gaudí. 1.5443
Desire, and the novel. 2.3506
Desk book of infared spectra. 5.2319
Desolate angel. 2.11960
Les Désordres de l'amour 2.4021
Despair. 2.1582
A desperate character. 2.1449
Desperate faith; 2.10623
Dessa Rose. 2.13431
Les dessins de Norman McLaren. 1.5798
The destination of man. 1.921
Destinations. 3.1182
Destiny his choice: the loyalism of Andrew Marvell. 2.7109
The destiny of a king. 1.1817
The destiny of Europe's Gypsies. 3.5681
The destiny of man. 1.1110
Destroyers. 5.7439
The destruction of nature in the Soviet Union. 5.5993
The destruction of the European Jews. 3.1093
Detachment and the writing of history: essays and letters of Carl L. Becker. 3.379
Detective and mystery fiction. 5.8171
Detente. 4.8975
Détente. 3.3265
Détente and confrontation. 3.6493
Determinants and consequences of maternal employment. 4.3247
The Determinants and effects of mergers. 4.3017
Determinants of fertility in developing countries. 4.1640
Determinants of infant behaviour [I-IV]. 5.604
Determination. 2.5500
The determination of ionization constants. 5.2915
Determined survivors. 4.5807
Deterrence and defense. 5.7257
Deterrence; the legal threat in crime control. 4.6845
Deterrent diplomacy. 3.4922
Deterrents and reinforcement. 5.302
Deuteronomy. 1.2596
Das deutsche Drama vom Barock bis zur Gegenwart. 2.13490
Deutsche Erzähler. 2.13523
Deutsche Geschichte 1800-1866. 3.2288
Deutsche Geschichte im neunzehnten jahrhundert, von Franz Schnabel ... 3.2290
Deutsche Literatur der Gegenwart. 2.13478
Deutsche Literatur im bürgerlichen Realismus, 1848-1898. 2.13476
Deutsche Literaturgeschichte. 2.13455

Deutsche Literaturgeschichte in Tabellen. 2.13458
Deutsche Literaturwissenschaft. 5.8008
Die deutsche Lyrik. 2.13484
Die deutsche Plastik 1350-1550. 1.5714
Das Deutsche Reich von 1918 bis heute. 3.2360
Der deutsche Roman vom Barock bis zur Gegenwart. 2.13499
Deutsche Sozial- und Wirtschaftsgeschichte. 4.2336
Die deutsche Tragödie von Lessing bis Hebbel 2.13496
Deutsches Wörterbuch. 2.1185
Deutsches Wörterbuch mit einem 'Lexikon der deutschen Sprachlehre' 2.1187
Deutschland seit 1945. 3.2458
Deutschlands Weg zur Grossmacht. 4.2337
Deutschstunde: Siegfried Lenz. 2.13811
The devastating boys and other stories. 2.9396
The developers. 4.2833
Developing a curriculum for modern living. 4.10451
Developing effective communications strategy. 4.4293
Developing language skills in the elementary schools. 4.10476
Developing open education in America. 4.10307
Developing talent in young people. 5.609
Developing the core curriculum. 4.10423
Development. 5.4123
The development and chronology of Chaucer's works. 2.6353
Development and crisis in Brazil, 1930-1983. 4.2171
Development and diffusion of the nuclear reactor. 5.6607
The development and scope of higher education in the United States. 4.10062
Development and the rural-urban divide. 4.2766
Development and underdevelopment in historical perspective. 4.2786
Development by people. 4.1829
Development economics. 4.2803
Development economics in action. 4.2585
Development from above or below? 4.6360
Development from below. 4.516
The development gap. 4.2764
Development in infancy. 5.554
The development of academic freedom in the United States. 4.9984
The development of African drama. 2.10040
The development of American citizenship, 1608-1870. 4.8073
The development of American lexicography 1798-1864. 2.1075
The development of American literary criticism. 2.2512
The development of American petroleum pipelines. 4.3789
The development of American romance. 2.10605
The Development of an African working class. 4.3670
The development of Arthurian romance. 2.2634
The development of Attic black-figure. 1.6635
Development of biochemical concepts from ancient to modern times. 5.4392
The development of capitalism in Africa. 4.2611
The development of capitalism in colonial Indochina (1870-1940) 4.2527
The development of constitutional guarantees of liberty. 4.7698
The development of Darwin's theory. 5.3202
The development of English drama in the late seventeenth century. 5.5893
The development of English humor. 2.6061
The development of Germanic verse form. 2.914
The development of Greek biography. 2.272
The Development of Indonesia society. 3.4561
The development of international law by the International Court. 4.9150

The development of Islam in West Africa. 1.2008
The development of logic. 1.1155
The development of mathematics in China and Japan 5.1082
The development of modern chemistry. 5.2607
The development of modern English. 2.973
The development of modern France, 1870-1939. 3.2172
The development of Neo-Confucian thought. 1.159
The Development of Neo-Confucian thought. 1.1796
Development of nerve cells and their connections. 5.4325
The development of North American archaeology 3.5713
The development of Plato's ethics. 1.272
The development of political attitudes in children. 4.5733
The development of political theory. 4.7415
The development of realism in the fiction of Tsubouchi Shōyō. 2.2092
The development of Samuel Beckett's fiction. 2.8432
The development of sex differences. 5.486
The development of Shakespeare as a dramatist. 2.6815
The development of Shakespeare's imagery. 2.6842
The development of Southern sectionalism, 1819-1848. 3.8151
The development of the American short story. 2.10579
The development of the British economy, 1914-1980. 4.2283
Development of the chick. 5.4128
The development of the Communist bloc. 3.3535
The development of the economies of continental Europe, 1850-1914. 4.2202
The development of the English playhouse. 1.5550
The development of the idea of history in antiquity. 3.490
The development of the Italian schools of painting. 1.6179
The development of the logical method in ancient China. 1.156
The development of the playhouse. 1.5548
The development of the Soviet economic system. 4.2372
The Development of the theatre. 2.3165
The Development of welfare states in Europe and America. 4.6468
Development theory. 4.5480
Development without dependence. 4.1823
Developmental anatomy. 5.4121
Developmental-behavioral pediatrics. 5.5075
Developmental biology of cultured nerve, muscle, and glia. 5.3488
A developmental view of the psychoanalytic process. 5.4913
Developments in mathematical psychology, information, learning, and tracking. 5.50
Developments in operational research. 5.5566
Developments in structural form. 5.6085
Developments in the avant-garde drama. 2.2815
Deviance and control. 4.5063
Deviance and society. 4.5078
Deviance in Soviet society. 4.6794
Deviant behavior. 4.5053
Deviant logic. 1.1166
Deviant science. 5.648
Deviant street networks. 4.5541
The Devil. 1.1618
The devil and Daniel Webster. 2.11369
The Devil & the Good Lord, and two other plays. 2.4723
The devil in the flesh. 2.4684
The devil, the gargoyle, and the buffoon. 2.2412
The devil theory of war. 4.9046
The devil tree. 2.13121
The devil wagon in God's country. 4.4037
The devils. 2.9520
The Devil's Bride. 2.12365

The Devil's Church and other stories. 2.5473
The devil's dictionary. 2.10910
The devils of Loudun. 5.671
The Devil's race-track. 2.10940
Devolution. 4.8435
Devotion. 2.13910
Devotions upon emergent occasions. 1.3071
Dewey decimal classification and relative index. 5.7635
Dewey, Russell, Whitehead. 4.9960
The Dewey School. 4.11004
Dhalgren. 2.12969
The Dharma bums 2.11950
The Dhimmi. 3.3657
Le Diable au corps. 2.4683
Le diable et le bon Dieu. 2.4722
Diachronic and synchronic aspects of language. 2.219
Diaghilev. 4.1132
Diagnosis and reliable design of digital systems. 5.6468
Diagnostic psychological testing. 5.4848
The diagonal line. 2.10349
Diagramming techniques for analysts and programmers. 5.5571
Dialect and language variation. 2.206
Dialect of defeat. 4.6935
The dialectic of ideology and technology. 4.7143
Dialectical approach to understanding science. 5.862
The dialectical imagination. 4.1225
Dialectical materialism. 1.472
Dialectics of Third World development. 4.1801
Dialectology. 2.207
Dialogorum libri duodecim. 2.770
The Dialogue between theology and psychology. 1.1563
A dialogue on comparable worth. 4.3258
Dialogue on John Dewey 1.591
Dialogue on poetry and literary aphorisms. 2.13655
Dialogue with an audience. 2.2744
Dialogue with Erich Fromm. 5.157
Dialogue with Erik Erikson. 5.96
Dialogues and a diary. 1.4004
Dialogues des carmélites. 2.4412
Dialogues from infancy. 5.5105
Dialogues in limbo. 1.645
Dialogues of Alfred North Whitehead. 1.775
Dialogues on metaphysics. 1.799
Dialogues on the philosophy of Marxism, from the proceedings of the Society for the Philosophical Study of Dialectical Materialism. 1.479
Dialogues with contemporary continental thinkers. 1.453
Dialogues with Leucò. 2.5051
Dialogues with Marcel Duchamp. 1.6099
Diamond's Japan business directory. 4.2541
Diamond's JB directory < 1976->. 4.2541
Diamonds of the night. 2.1676
The Dianas. 2.10172
Diane Arbus. 5.6958
Dianying. 2.2886
Diaries, 1918-1939. 2.13833
Diaries 1920-1922. 2.13705
The diaries of a Cabinet Minister. 3.1714
The diaries of Evelyn Waugh. 2.9499
The diaries of George Washington. 3.7036
The diaries of John Ruskin. 2.8028
Diary. 3.1502, 3.4616, 3.7160
Diary, 1794-1845. 3.7121
Diary and autobiography. 3.7043
The diary and letters of Kaethe Kollwitz. 1.5808
Diary by E. B. B. 2.7466
A diary in America. 2.7927
The diary of a country parson, 1758-1802. 3.1534
The diary of a country priest. 2.4413
The diary of a superfluous man. 2.1450
The diary of a writer. 2.1348
The diary of a young girl. 3.1091
The diary of Anaïs Nin. 2.12254
The diary of Beatrice Webb. 4.7034
Diary of Cotton Mather. 3.7976

The diary of Ebenezer Parkman, 1703-1782. First Part. three volumes in one, 1719-1755. 3.8009
The diary of James A. Garfield. 3.7402
The diary of Jane Somers. 2.9014
Diary of John Quincy Adams. 3.7120
Diary of King Philip's War, 1675-76. 3.5775
The diary of Richard Wagner 1865-1882. 1.4066
The diary of Samuel Pepys. 3.1503
The diary of Samuel Sewall, 1674-1729. 3.7983
Diary of the Civil War, 1860-1865. 3.7394
Diary of the Rev. Ralph Josselin 1616-1683. 1.3312
Diary of the Sinai Campaign. 3.3824
Diary of the Terra Nova Expedition to the Antarctic, 1910-1912. 4.108
The diary of Vaslav Nijinsky. 4.1151
The diary of Virginia Woolf. 2.9582
The diary of W. M. Rossetti 1870-1873. 2.8021
The (Diblos) notebook. 2.12141
Diccionario critico etimológico de la lengua castellana. 2.893
Diccionario de historia de España 3.3409
Diccionario de la lengua española. 2.896
Diccionario de sinónimos. 2.895
Diccionario de uso del español. 2.897
Diccionario etimologico español e hispánico. 2.894
Diccionario general de Americanismos ... 2.908
Diccionario general ilustrado de la langua española. 2.898
Diccionario inglés y español. 2.905
Diccionario internacional Simon and Schuster. 2.901
Diccionario multilingüe de términos técnicos cartográficos. 4.75
Diccionaro de la lengua española (Real Academia Española) 2.896
Dichter der neueren Schweiz. 2.13939
Das dichterische Werk. 2.13675
Dichtungen, Briefe, Reden. 2.13665
Dichtungen und Briefe. 2.13864
Dicionário brasileiro da lingua portuguesa. 2.910
Dick Gregory's political primer. 3.6388
Dickens. 2.7640
Dickens and charity. 2.7671
Dickens and crime. 2.7667
Dickens and education. 2.7668
Dickens & Ellen Ternan. 2.7643
Dickens and his readers. 2.7654
Dickens and mesmerism. 2.7639
Dickens and Phiz. 2.7647
Dickens and the city. 2.7648
Dickens and the invisible world. 2.7669
Dickens and the parent-child relationship. 2.7670
Dickens and the rhetoric of laughter. 2.7660
Dickens and the short story. 2.7664
Dickens and the trials of imagination. 2.7672
Dickens and the twentieth century. 2.7658
Dickens and women. 2.7644
Dickens at work. 2.7649
A Dickens companion. 2.7663
The Dickens critics. 2.7655
A Dickens dictionary. 2.7634
Dickens, money, and society. 2.7642
Dickens on America & the Americans. 2.7627
Dickens on the romantic side of familiar things. 2.7629
Dickens, the novelist. 2.7661
The Dickens theatre. 2.7656
The Dickens world. 2.7645
Dickens's apprentice years. 2.7653
Dickinson and the Romantic imagination. 2.10997
Dickinson, strategies of limitation. 2.10998
Dickinson, the modern idiom. 2.11006
Dictatorship in Spanish America. 3.8981
Dictionar român-englez. 2.850
A dictionarie of the French and English tongues. 2.878
Dictionaries. 2.203
Dictionary for accountants. 4.4391

A dictionary of acronyms and abbreviations in library and information science. 5.7698
Dictionary of African historical biography. 3.5233
Dictionary of Afro-American slang. 2.1167
Dictionary of Afro-Latin American civilization. 3.8970
A Dictionary of agricultural and allied terminology. 5.5222
Dictionary of air transport and traffic control. 5.6642
Dictionary of American biography. 3.6288-3.6291
Dictionary of American communal and utopian history. 4.7154
Dictionary of American diplomatic history. 3.6405
A dictionary of American English on historical principles. 2.1135
A dictionary of American-English usage, based on Fowler's Modern English usage. 2.1139
Dictionary of American history 3.6198
Dictionary of American history. 3.6199
Dictionary of American medical biography. 5.4529
Dictionary of American military biography. 5.7199
Dictionary of American Negro biography. 3.6812
Dictionary of American politics. 4.7795
Dictionary of American pop/rock. 1.3526
A Dictionary of American proverbs and proverbial phrases, 1820-1880. 2.3810
Dictionary of American regional English. 2.1144
Dictionary of American religious biography. 1.1587
Dictionary of American slang. 2.1148
A Dictionary of Americanisms on historical principles. 2.1136
A dictionary of anonymous and pseudonymous publications in the English language. 5.7728
Dictionary of anthropology. 4.407, 4.410
A dictionary of arbitration and its terms; labor, commercial, international. 4.9853
A dictionary of architecture. 1.5205
Dictionary of art and artists. 1.4577
A dictionary of ballet. 4.1082
A dictionary of battles. 3.534
Dictionary of battles. 3.533
Dictionary of behavioral science. 5.16
The Dictionary of Bible and religion. 1.2220
Dictionary of biochemistry. 5.4394
Dictionary of biology. 5.3186
A Dictionary of birds. 5.3935
A dictionary of books relating to America. 5.7730
A dictionary of botany. 5.3631
A dictionary of British folk-tales in the English language. 4.788
Dictionary of British sculptors, 1660-1851. 1.5689
A dictionary of British surnames. 3.310
Dictionary of Canadian biography. 3.8653
Dictionary of Canadian English. 2.1161
A Dictionary of Canadianisms on historical principles. 2.1161
Dictionary of ceramic science and engineering. 5.6898
Dictionary of ceramics: by A.E. Dodd. 5.6897
Dictionary of Chinese and Japanese art. 1.5059
Dictionary of civil engineering. 5.5658
Dictionary of classical ballet. 4.1174
Dictionary of classical mythology. 1.1639
Dictionary of comparative pathology and experimental biology. 5.4742
A Dictionary of comparative religion. 1.1523
Dictionary of computers, information processing, and telecommunications. 5.1137
Dictionary of concepts in history. 3.404
Dictionary of concepts in human geography. 4.357
Dictionary of contemporary American artists. 1.4888
A dictionary of contemporary American usage. 2.1137
Dictionary of contemporary music. 1.3508

Dictionary of contemporary photography. 5.6916
Dictionary of contemporary usage. 2.1101
Dictionary of data communications. 5.6404
Dictionary of dates. 3.372
A dictionary of drug abuse terms and terminology. 4.6658
A dictionary of early music. 1.3507
Dictionary of earth sciences. 5.2944
A dictionary of ecology, evolution, and systematics. 5.3510
Dictionary of education. 4.10166
Dictionary of electronics. 5.6446
Dictionary of energy. 5.6120
A dictionary of English costume. 4.839
Dictionary of film terms. 5.6998
Dictionary of foreign phrases and abbreviations. 2.1099
Dictionary of foreign terms. 2.1100
The dictionary of foreign terms in the English language. 2.1098
A dictionary of foreign words and phrases in current English. 2.1097
Dictionary of French literature. 2.3820
A dictionary of gastronomy. 5.7107
A dictionary of genetics. 5.3408
A dictionary of geography. 4.77
Dictionary of geology. 5.2940
Dictionary of geophysics. 5.2489
Dictionary of German history, 1806-1945. 3.2286
Dictionary of German synonyms. 2.1184
A dictionary of Hinduism. 1.1676
The Dictionary of human geography. 4.356
A dictionary of Indian history. 3.4212
A dictionary of information technology. 5.7697
A dictionary of Irish biography. 3.344
Dictionary of Irish literature. 2.9850
A dictionary of irregular Russian verb forms. 2.1229
A dictionary of Islam. 1.1994
Dictionary of Italian literature. 2.4874
A dictionary of Japanese artists. 1.5078
A dictionary of Japanese history. 3.4903
Dictionary of language and linguistics. 2.12
Dictionary of life sciences. 5.3290
Dictionary of literary biography. 2.5484
Dictionary of literary biography, English & American. 2.5482-2.5483
A dictionary of literary terms. 2.2347
A dictionary of literature in the English language from 1940-1970. 5.7927
A dictionary of literature in the English language, from Chaucer to 1940. 5.7926
Dictionary of living religions. 1.1522
Dictionary of logical terms and symbols. 5.1041
Dictionary of mapmakers. 4.223
Dictionary of medieval civilization. 3.126
A dictionary of metallurgy. 5.6755
A Dictionary of microbial taxonomy. 5.4429
Dictionary of microbiology. 5.4430
Dictionary of military and associated terms. 5.7172
Dictionary of Ming biography, 1368-1644. 3.4710
A dictionary of mining, mineral, and related terms. 5.6720
A dictionary of modern English usage 2.1090
A dictionary of modern history, 1789-1945. 3.656
A dictionary of modern Indian history, 1707-1947. 3.4213
Dictionary of modern Italian history. 3.2854
A dictionary of modern written Arabic. 2.1832
A dictionary of musical themes. 1.3569
Dictionary of mythology, folklore and symbols. 4.754
The dictionary of national biography. 3.1235
Dictionary of naval terms. 5.7416
Dictionary of new information technology acronyms. 5.1135
Dictionary of nutrition and food technology. 5.7103
Dictionary of occupational titles. 4.1664
A dictionary of official titles in Imperial China. 4.8740
A dictionary of opera and song themes. 1.3596

Dictionary of organic compounds. 5.2715
Dictionary of organometallic compounds. 5.2781
Dictionary of Oriental literatures. 2.1757
Dictionary of oriental philosophy. 1.148
A Dictionary of philosophy. 1.100
A dictionary of philosophy. 1.102
Dictionary of philosophy and psychology, including many of the principal conceptions of ethics, logic, aesthetics, philosophy of religion, mental pathology, anthropology, biology, neurology, physiology, economics, political and social philosophy, philology, physical science, and education, and giving a terminology in English, French, German, and Italian. 1.99
Dictionary of phrase and fable. 2.2350
The dictionary of phrase and fable, giving the derivation, source, or origin of common phrases, allusions, and words that have a tale to tell. 2.2351
Dictionary of physical geography. 4.239
Dictionary of physics and mathematics. 5.1891
Dictionary of place names, United States and Canada. 3.5993
Dictionary of political economy. 4.1275
A dictionary of political thought. 4.7216
A dictionary of politics. 3.734
Dictionary of popular slang. 2.1147
Dictionary of pronunciation. 2.1024
The dictionary of publishing. 5.7574
Dictionary of quotations. 2.3729
Dictionary of reading and learning disability. 4.10932
Dictionary of religions. 1.1526
Dictionary of robotics. 5.6167
Dictionary of rocks. 5.3030
Dictionary of Russian historical terms from the eleventh century to 1917. 3.3030
A dictionary of Russian verbs. 2.1230
Dictionary of science and technology. 5.707
Dictionary of scientific biography. 5.808
A dictionary of scientific units. 5.2023
A dictionary of selected synonyms in the principal Indo-European languages. 2.224
A Dictionary of sexist quotations. 4.5830
Dictionary of shipping/international trade terms and abbreviations. 4.3956
A dictionary of slang and unconventional English. 2.1164
A dictionary of social science methods. 4.1200
Dictionary of social welfare. 4.6466
A dictionary of statistical terms. 5.1400
Dictionary of subjects and symbols in art. 1.5156
Dictionary of telecommunications. 5.6361
Dictionary of the Bible. 1.2507
The dictionary of the biological sciences. 5.3182
Dictionary of the Black theatre. 2.3216
A dictionary of the characters & proper names in the works of Shakespeare. 2.6688
A dictionary of the characters and scenes in the stories and poems of Rudyard Kipling 1886-1911. 2.7891
A dictionary of the characters in the Waverley novels of Sir Walter Scott. 2.8045
Dictionary of the decorative arts. 1.6506
Dictionary of the English language. 2.1079
A dictionary of the flowering plants and ferns. 5.3634
Dictionary of the history of science. 5.724
Dictionary of the Middle Ages. 3.567
A dictionary of the Old West, 1850-1900. 2.1150
A dictionary of the older Scottish tongue. 2.1117
A dictionary of the underworld, British & American. 2.1166
Dictionary of theology. 1.2222
Dictionary of theoretical concepts in biology. 5.3292
Dictionary of twentieth-century art. 1.4822
A dictionary of Urdū, classical Hindī, and English. 2.1881
Dictionary of waste and water treatment. 5.5985

The Dictionary of Welsh biography down to 1940. 3.1751
Dictionary of women artists. 1.4588
Dictionary of word and phrase origins. 2.1058
Dictionary of world history. 3.367
Dictionary of world literary terms, forms, technique, criticism. 2.2349
A dictionary of zoology. 5.3793
A dictionary, Persian, Arabic and English. 2.1964
Dictionary Spanish and English. 2.905
Dictionary to the plays and novels of Bernard Shaw. 2.8068
Dictionnaire alphabétique et analogique de la langue française. 2.876
Dictionnaire biographique des personnages fictifs de La comédie humaine. 2.4113
Dictionnaire critique et documentaire des peintres, sculpteurs, dessinateurs et graveurs ... 1.4581
Dictionnaire critique et documentaire des peintres, sculpteurs, dessinateurs et graveurs de tous les temps et de tous les pays. 1.4581
Dictionnaire de la langue française. 2.875
Dictionnaire de litterature contemporaine. 2.3867
Dictionnaire des idées reçues. 2.4185
Dictionnaire des lettres françaises. 2.3822
Dictionnaire des littératures de langue française. 2.3819
Dictionnaire des œuvres littéraires du Québec. 2.4804
Dictionnaire des peintres, sculpteurs, dessinateurs et graveurs. 1.4581
Dictionnaire du français classique. 2.882
Dictionnaire méthodique du français actuel. 2.877
Dictionnaire multilingue de termes techniques cartographiques. 4.75
Dictionnaire pratique des auteurs québécois. 2.4805
Did monetary forces cause the Great Depression? 4.1718
Did the Devil make Darwin do it? 5.3386
The Didache, The epistle of Barnabas, The epistles and The martyrdom of St. Polycarp, The fragments of Papias, The epistle to Diognetus. 1.2181
Diderot. 1.815, 2.4072-2.4073
Diderot and Descartes. 1.811
Diderot, the embattled philosopher. 1.814
Diderot's letters to Sophie Volland. 2.4071
Die, nigger, die! 3.6819
Died in the wool. 2.9088
The Dies committee. 3.7552
Diet for a small planet. 5.7121
Diet, nutrition, and cancer. 5.4772, 5.4776
The dieter's dilemma. 5.5131
Le dieu caché. 2.3953
Les dieux ont soif. 2.4207
Diez comedias del Siglo de Oro. 2.5148
Difco manual. 5.4446
Different strokes. 3.7999
Differential algebra. 5.1345
Differential and difference equations. 5.1502
Differential diagnosis and treatment in social work. 4.6494
Differential equations. 5.1504
Differential equations and mathematical biology. 5.3311
Differential equations, dynamical systems, and linear algebra. 5.1515
Differential equations from the algebraic standpoint. 5.1509
Differential forms. 5.1535
Differential forms in algebraic topology. 5.1615
Differential geometry. 5.1629-5.1630
Differential geometry of curves and surfaces. 5.1627
Differential inclusions. 5.1500
Differential topology. 5.1616
The differentiation of cells. 5.3617
A difficult soul. 2.1500
Diffraction theory and antennas. 5.6426
Diffusion in solids, liquids, gases. 5.2220
Diffusion, mass transfer in fluid systems. 5.6840
Diffusion of innovations. 4.4885

The Diffusion of new industrial processes. 4.1861
A digest of 500 plays. 2.3774
Digging for God and country. 3.256
Digging up Jerusalem. 3.3813
Digital and analog communication systems. 5.6353
Digital bipolar integrated circuits. 5.6527
Digital circuits and microprocessors. 5.6473
Digital coding of waveforms. 5.6374
Digital communications. 5.6391
Digital communications and spread spectrum systems. 5.6393
Digital communications by satellite. 5.6390
Digital computer fundamentals. 5.6572
Digital computers in research. 5.60
Digital control of dynamic systems. 5.6182
Digital control system analysis and design. 5.6190
Digital control systems. 5.6185, 5.6189
Digital design. 5.6584
Digital filters and signal processing. 5.6514
Digital image processing for remote sensing. 4.20
Digital image processing of remotely sensed data. 5.5940
Digital integrated circuits and operational-amplifier and optoelectronic circuit design. 5.6526
Digital integrated electronics. 5.6474
Digital processing of remotely sensed images. 5.5942
Digital processing of speech signals. 5.6569
Digital signal analysis. 5.6381
Digital signal processing. 5.6378
Digital system design with LSI bit-slice logic. 5.6585
Digital systems fundamentals. 5.5691
Digital transmission systems. 5.6398
Dignity. 4.6040
The dilemma of access. 4.10889
Dilemma of American nursing, 1850-1945. 5.5157
The dilemma of democratic socialism. 4.7067
The dilemma of education in a democracy. 4.10736
The dilemma of freight transport regulation. 4.3877
The dilemma of Mexico's development. 4.2147
Dilemmas. 1.1243
The dilemmas of an upright man. 5.1962
Dilemmas of change in British politics. 4.8413
The Dilemmas of euthanasia. 5.4574
Dilemmas of government. 4.2224
Dilemmas of growth in prewar Japan. 3.4971
Dilemmas of progress in tsarist Russia. 4.7086
Dilemmas of schooling. 4.10122
Dilemmas of social reform. 4.5187
The dilemmas of the dollar. 4.4560
Dilemmas of welfare policy. 4.6526
Dimension theory. 5.1596
Dimensional analysis. 5.2004
Dimensional analysis for engineers. 5.5724
Dimensions. 1.5492, 4.589
Dimensions in urban history. 4.6214
Dimensions internationales des droits de l'homme. English. 4.9387
Dimensions of congressional voting. 4.8055
Dimensions of moral creativity. 1.1445
The Dimensions of quantitative research in history. 3.428
The dimensions of Robert Frost. 2.11753
Dimensions of the modern novel. 2.13508
The Dimensions of the past. 3.429
Dimensions of tolerance. 4.7694
Dimity convictions. 4.6070
Ding Ling's fiction. 2.2236
Diocletian and the Roman recovery. 3.2810
Dionysiac poetics and Euripides' Bacchae. 2.453
Dionysius of Halicarnassus On literary composition, being the Greek text of the De compositione verborvm, edited with introduction, translation, notes, glossary, and appendices 2.449
Dionysus and the city. 2.10498
Dionysus in Paris. 2.3888
Diophantine equations. 5.1334

Diophantine geometry. 5.1578
Dio's Roman history. 2.358
The diploma disease. 4.10623
Diplomacy. 4.9088
Diplomacy and diplomats in nineteenth century Asante. 3.5332
Diplomacy and enterprise. 3.1260
Diplomacy and its discontents. 4.9012
Diplomacy and persuasion: how Britain joined the Common Market. 4.2226
Diplomacy at the U.N. 4.9213
Diplomacy at the UN. 4.9213
Diplomacy for victory. 3.1144
Diplomacy in a changing world. 4.9087
Diplomacy in a democracy. 4.9094
Diplomacy in ancient Greece. 3.2554
Diplomacy in the nuclear age. 4.9089
The diplomacy of annexation. 3.6356
The diplomacy of ideas. 3.7766
The diplomacy of imperialism, 1890-1902. 3.719
The diplomacy of India. 4.9236
The diplomacy of Napoleon. 3.2127
Diplomacy of power. 5.7325
The diplomacy of the American Revolution. 3.6934
The diplomacy of the Balkan wars, 1912-1913. 3.3527
The diplomacy of the Quadripartite Agreement on Berlin. 4.9305
Diplomat. 4.9090
Diplomat in carpet slippers. 3.7354
A diplomat in Japan. 3.4953
Diplomatic correspondence of the United States concerning the independence of the Latin-American nations 3.9019
Diplomatic history, 1713-1933. 3.619
A diplomatic history of Europe since the Congress of Vienna. 3.678
A diplomatic history of the American people. 3.6394
A diplomatic history of the American Revolution. 3.6936
The diplomatic history of the Canadian boundary, 1749-1763. 3.8708
A diplomatic history of the First World War. 3.826
The diplomatic history of the Southern Confederacy. 4.9064
A diplomatic history of the United States. 3.6397
Diplomatic history of the United States, 1775-1921. 5.8263
Diplomatic investigations. 4.9023
Diplomatic relations between the United States and Brazil. 3.6412
The diplomats: 1919-1939. 3.873
Diplomats and bureaucrats. 4.9086
Direct energy conversion. 5.6322
Direct legislation. 4.9724
The Direct marketing handbook. 4.4327
Directing the play. 2.3109
The direction of time. 5.1920
Directions for a candidate of the ministry. 1.3045
Directions for historical linguistics. 2.148
Directions in modern theatre and drama. 2.3181
Directions in physics. 5.2018
Directions in sociolinguistics. 2.27
The Director. 4.1079
The director at work. 2.3105
Directors on directing. 2.3109
The Directory for exceptional children. 4.10924
Directory of agencies. 4.6509
Directory of American college theatre. 2.3137
Directory of American Jewish institutions. 3.6578
Directory of American preservation commissions. 3.5992
Directory of American scholars. 1.82, 4.10154
A directory of American silver, pewter, and silver plate. 1.6657
Directory of applied geographers. 4.8
Directory of archives and manuscript repositories in the United States. 3.270
Directory of automated library systems. 5.7612

Directory of British official publications. 5.7924

Directory of business and financial services. 4.4260, 4.4444

Directory of corporate affiliations. 4.4605

Directory of corporate philanthropy. 4.6527

Directory of ERIC microfiche collections. 4.10282

A directory of ethnic publishers and resource organizations. 3.6527

Directory of financial aids for women. 4.10584

Directory of food and nutrition information services and resources. 5.7109

Directory of foreign manufacturers in the United States. 4.3832

Directory of graduate research. 5.2620

Directory of historical societies and agencies in the United States and Canada. 3.6190

Directory of medical specialists. 5.4549

Directory of military aircraft. 5.6672

Directory of national and international labor unions in the United States. 4.3545

Directory of online databases. 5.7642

Directory of periodicals online. 5.7643

Directory of poetry publishers. 5.7572

Directory of private U.S. companies. 4.4606

Directory of private US companies. 4.4606

Directory of research grants. 4.10585

Directory of special libraries and information centers. 5.7609, 5.7662

The directory of special opportunities for women. 4.3252

Directory of state and local history periodicals. 5.7850

Directory of the American theater, 1894-1971. 2.3763

Directory of the film. 2.2963

Directory of the theater. 5.8305

The directory of tunes and musical themes. 1.3571

Dirksen of Illinois. 3.7635

Dirksen: portrait of a public man. 3.7857

'A dirty filthy book' 4.5677

Dirty hands. 2.4720

Dirty politics. 4.8182

Disability and work. 4.3474

The disadvantaged consumer. 4.2055

The disappearance of God. 2.5726

Disarmament and the economy. 4.1979

Disarmament: negotiations and treaties, 1946-1971. 4.9171

Disarmament without order. 4.9169

Disaster and fiction. 2.569

Disaster and the millennium. 1.2949

Disaster by decree. 4.9588

The disasters of war. 1.6495

The discarded image. 2.2625

Discerning the way. 1.2788

Le disciple. 2.4148

Discipline and punish. 4.6846

Discipline in the schools. 4.10695

The discipline of power. 3.1160

Discipline of power. 3.8783

A discipline of programming. 5.1173

The disciplined heart. 2.9777

A disciplined intelligence. 3.8665

Disclosing the past. 4.422

Discontent at the polls. 4.8167

Discopaedia of the violin, 1889-1971. 1.3623

Discourse and its presuppositions. 2.108

Discourse and political reflections on the Kingdoms of Peru, their government, special regimen of their inhabitants, and abuses which have been introduced into one and another, with special information on why they grew up and some means to avoid them. 3.9302

A discourse of the contests and dissentions between the nobles and the commons in Athens and Rome: with the consequences they had upon both those states. 4.7422

Discourse on free will. 1.2937

Discourse on universal history. 3.523

Discourse strategies. 2.65

The discourses. 4.7392

The discourses of Niccolò Machiavelli. 4.7390

Discourses on architecture. 1.5472

Discourses on art. 1.5133

The discoverers. 3.40

Discoveries. 2.6594

Discovering God within. 1.3094

Discovering music. 1.4415

Discovering past behavior. 3.5757

Discovering reality. 4.5877

Discovering relativity for yourself. 5.2089

Discovering science. 5.837

Discovering Shakespeare. 2.6852

Discovering the comic. 1.1391

Discovering the natural laws. 5.2006

Discovering the news. 2.3590

Discovery '84. 4.6596

The discovery and conquest of Mexico, 1517-1521. 3.8922

Discovery and exploration. 4.46

The Discovery of a Norse settlement in America. 3.8871

The discovery of abundance: Simon N. Patten and the transformation of social theory. 4.1375

The discovery of animal behaviour. 5.4066

Discovery of animal behaviour (Television program) 5.4066

The discovery of insulin. 5.4407

The discovery of language. 2.40

The discovery of New Zealand. 3.5594

The discovery of South America. 3.5978

The discovery of subatomic particles. 5.2465

The discovery of the child. 4.10206

The discovery of the electron. 5.2389

Discovery of the elements. 5.2833

The discovery of the great West: La Salle. 3.8713

The discovery of the Pacific Islands. 3.5537

The discovery of the sea. 4.51

The discovery of time. 1.1343

Discovery, the search for DNA's secrets. 5.3410

Discretion and lawlessness. 4.9892

Discretionary justice. 4.9755

Discrimination in international trade. 4.4153

Discrimination in labor markets. 4.3116

Discrimination in organizations. 4.5182

Discriminations. 2.13143

Discussions of the Canterbury tales. 2.6326

Discussions of the short story. 2.3440

Discussions on war and human aggression. 5.7155

Disease and history. 5.4544

Disease and its control. 5.4502

Disease change and the role of medicine. 5.4663

Disease diagnosis and control in North American marine aquaculture. 5.5472

Disease in African history. 5.4682

Disease, life, and man. 5.4480

The disease of the soul. 5.4764

Diseases and pests of ornamental plants. 5.5390

The diseases of occupations. 5.5014

The disenchanted. 2.12448

Disintegration and political action. 4.8844

Disjoined partners. 4.9070

Disloyalty in the confederacy. 3.7377

Dismantling America. 4.9756

The dismantling of the good neighbor policy. 3.9022

Dismantling the universe. 5.915

The dismemberment of Orpheus. 2.2677

Disney animation. 1.5856

Disorder in crystals. 5.2928

Disorderly conduct. 4.6015

Disorders of sexual desire and other new concepts and techniques in sex therapy. 5.4951

The disorders of war. 3.6946

Disorganized crime. 4.6718

The dispossessed. 2.13130

Dispossessing the American Indian. 3.5795

The dispute of the New World. 3.5686

Dispute resolution. 4.3580

The Disputing process. 4.9376

A disquisition on government. 4.7840

Disraeli. 3.1629

Disraeli and his world. 3.1630

Disraeli, Gladstone, and the Eastern question. 3.687

Disraeli the novelist. 2.7396

Disraelian Conservatism and social reform. 4.8532

The disruption of American democracy. 3.7176

The disruption of the solid South. 4.8187

Dissemination. 1.8

Dissension in the House of Commons. 4.8476

Dissension in the House of Commons, 1974-79. 4.8477

Dissent in American religion. 1.2394

Dissent in the Supreme Court. 4.9841

Dissent on development. 4.2758

The dissenters. 1.3313

The dissenting academy. 4.10823

The dissident press. 2.3655

The dissolution of the medieval outlook. 1.353

The dissolution of the monasteries. 1.3235

Dissolution of the Virginia Company. 3.8194

Dissonance. 5.313

Dissonant voices in Soviet literature. 2.1297

Distance and human interaction. 4.1483

Distance education. 4.10986

The distances. 2.12280

Distant dominion. 3.8593

The distant magnet. 4.8945

The distant mountains. 1.6325

A distant trumpet. 2.11881

Distant view of a minaret and other stories. 2.1848

Distinguish to unite. 1.1284

The distorted image. 3.6117

Distorting mirrors. 4.5041

Distortions of agricultural incentives. 4.2883

Distributed computing. 5.1244

Distributed telecommunications networks via satellites and packet switching. 5.6403

The distribution and abundance of animals. 5.4053

The distribution and diversity of soil fauna. 5.3817

The distribution of farm subsidies. 4.2953

The distribution of wealth. 4.1564

The distribution of wealth (1893) With an introductory essay, The foundations of Commons' economics. 4.1566

Distribution's place in the American economy since 1869. 4.4212

Distributive justice. 4.1574

The district magistrate in late imperial China. 4.8889

District of Columbia. 2.11579, 3.8111

Disturber of the peace. 2.12135

Dithyramb. 2.293

Ditte. 2.14027

Div, grad, curl, and all that. 5.1365

Divergent series. 5.1418

Diversification and integration in American industry. 4.2072

Diversity and depth in fiction. 2.3516

Diversity by design. 4.10548

Divesting nature's capital. 4.1838

The divided academy: professors and politics. 4.10081

Divided and conquered. 3.979

Divided loyalties. 4.8273

Divided we fought. 3.7348

La divina commedia. 2.4917

Divine comedies. 2.12140

The Divine comedy. 2.4915

The divine comedy. 2.4916, 2.4924

The divine comedy of Dante Alighieri. 2.4923

The Divine consort. 1.1717

Divine dancer. 4.1158

The divine feminine. 1.2539

The divine hierarchy. 1.1696

The divine imperative. 1.1481

The divine milieu. 1.2235

The divine player. 1.1712

The divine poems. 2.6453

Divine poetry and drama in sixteenth-century England. 2.5633

The divine relativity. 1.1593

The divine right of kings. 4.7554

The divine right of kings and the right of resistance. 4.7555

The divine vision. 2.7431

The divine wind. 3.1055

The diviners. 2.9938
Diving deep and surfacing. 1.1609
Division and cohesion in democracy. 3.3380
Division and reunion, 1829-1889. 3.6327
The division of labor in society. 4.2679
Divisions on a ground. 3.8666
The divorce revolution. 4.9510
Divorced in America. 4.5782
The Dixie frontier. 3.8338
Dixiecrats and Democrats. 4.8209
Dixie's forgotten people. 4.2023
Dixon-Yates. 4.3799
I dizionari Sansoni 2.858
Dizionario inglese italiano, italiano inglese.
   2.857
Djibouti, pawn of the Horn of Africa. 4.8808
Djilas, the progress of a revolutionary. 3.3607
Djinn. 2.4688
DNA and chromosomes. 5.3607
DNA replication. 5.4419
The DNA story. 5.3461
Do parties make a difference? 4.8525
Do these bones live. 2.11548
Do you hear them? 2.4714
The doctor and the devils. 2.9408
Doctor Dev. 2.1915
Doctor Fausti Weheklag. 2.13511
Doctor Faustus. 2.6611, 2.13828
Doctor Fischer of Geneva. 2.8745
Doctor Kinsey and the Institute for Sex
   Research. 4.5497
Doctor Rat. 2.13125
Doctor Sax. 2.11951
Doctor Thorne. 2.8208
The doctor tree. 5.4601
Doctor Zhivago. 2.1594
Doctors and their workshops. 5.4639
Doctors' dilemmas. 5.4567
Doctors of philosophy. 2.9357
The doctor's wife. 2.2127
Doctrine and covenants. 1.3380
The doctrine and covenants, of the Church of
   Jesus Christ of Latter-Day Saints. 1.3380
Doctrine and ethos in the Labour Party.
   4.8548
The doctrine of being in the Aristotelian
   Metaphysics. 1.290
The doctrine of correctness in English usage,
   1700-1800. 2.981
Doctrine of the law and grace unfolded.
   1.2215
The doctrine of the law and grace unfolded and
   I will pray with the Spirit. 1.2215
The doctrine of the Sūfis. 1.2078
The doctrine of the trinity. 1.2836
The doctrines of American foreign policy.
   3.6400
Doctrines of imperialism. 4.7541
Doctrines of revolution in the twentieth
   century. 4.7608
The doctrines of the great educators. 4.9953
Document catalogue. 5.7768
Documentary and educational films of the
   1930s. 2.2897
A documentary chronicle of Sino-Western
   relations, 1644-1820. 3.4715
Documentary expression and thirties America.
   2.72
Documentary film. 2.2986
A documentary history of American economic
   policy since 1789. 4.1892
A Documentary history of American industrial
   society. 4.1872
A documentary history of art. 1.4681
A documentary history of Chinese communism.
   4.7109
A documentary history of education in the
   South before 1860. 4.9991
Documentary history of Reconstruction.
   3.7464
A documentary history of religion in America,
   to the Civil War. 1.1871
Documentary history of the First Federal
   Congress, 1789-1791. 4.9479
Documentary history of the First Federal
   Congress of the United States of America,
   March 4, 1789-March 3, 1791. 4.9479

The Documentary history of the first Federal
   elections, 1788-1790. 4.7834
A documentary history of the Jews in the
   United States, 1654-1875. 3.6573
A documentary history of the Negro people in
   the United States. 3.6605
The Documentary history of the ratification of
   the Constitution. 4.9606
The documentary sources of Greek history.
   3.2530
A documentary survey of the French
   Revolution. 3.2064
The documentary tradition. 2.2985
Documentation of the threshold limit values.
   5.4726
Documentation of TLVs. 5.4726
Documents and materials relating to the eve of
   the Second World war. 3.886
Documents and speeches on British
   Commonwealth affairs, 1931-1952. 3.1226
Documents for the study of the Gospels.
   1.2679
Documents illustrating papal authority, A.D.
   96-454. 1.3144
Documents illustrating the reigns of Augustus
   & Tiberius. 2.314
Documents illustrative of the Continental
   Reformation. 1.2318
Documents illustrative of the history of the
   slave trade to America. 3.7188
Documents in early Christian thought. 1.2200
Documents in India's foreign policy, 1947-72.
   3.4295
Documents in Mycenaean Greek. 3.284
Documents of American broadcasting. 4.9538
Documents of American Catholic history.
   1.3170
Documents of American history. 3.6193
Documents of destruction. 3.1094
Documents of European economic history.
   4.2208
Documents of German history. 3.2240
The documents of Iriki, illustrative of the
   development of the feudal institutions of
   Japan. 3.4870
Documents of life. 4.4805
Documents of modern literary realism. 2.2402
Documents of Russian history, 1914-1917.
   3.3141
Documents of the American Revolution,
   1770-1783. 3.6885
Documents of the Christian Church. 1.2272
Documents of United States Indian policy.
   4.9773
The documents of Vatican II. 1.3123
Documents on American foreign relations
   1938/39-1970. 4.8971
Documents on Canadian foreign policy,
   1917-1939. 3.8772
Documents on German foreign policy,
   1918-1945, from the archives of the German
   Foreign Ministry. 4.8978
Documents on Germany, 1944-1985. 3.6444
Documents on international affairs. 1928-.
   3.748
Documents on Nazism, 1919-1945. 3.2445
Documents on the Holocaust. 3.1087
Documents on the International Court of
   Justice 4.9152
Documents on the laws of war. 4.9323
Documents on the Suez crisis, 26 July to 6
   November, 1956. 4.8977
Documents relating to the North West
   Company. 3.8841
Documents relating to the sentimental agents in
   the Volyen Empire. 2.9013
The dodgers. 2.1535
Dod's Parliamentary companion. 4.8470
Dodsworth. 2.12004
Does Canada need a new electoral system?
   4.7743
Does college matter? 4.10731
Does deconstruction make any difference?
   2.2434
Does God exist? 1.2830
Does khaki become you? 5.7162
Does socialism liberate women? 4.6089

The dog beneath the skin, or, Where is Francis?
   2.8393
Dog owner's home veterinary handbook.
   5.5465
Dog soldiers. 2.13335
Dog years. 2.13759
The dogs of March. 2.13076
Doing social life. 4.4928
Doing theology in a revolutionary situation.
   1.2805
The doll. 2.1702
The dollar in world affairs. 4.4585
The dollmaker. 2.11333
The dolphin. 2.12044
Dom Casmurro. 2.5474
Dom Pedro II. 3.9211
The dome, a study in the history of ideas.
   1.5499
The dome and the rock. 2.12544
Domenichino. 1.5015
Domenico Scarlatti. 1.3966
Domesday book. 3.1336
Domesday Book. 3.1338
Domesday book. 3.1337, 3.1339
Domesday book and beyond. 4.8391
Domesday England. 3.1722
Domesday gazetteer. 3.1733
The Domesday geography of eastern England.
   3.1723
The Domesday geography of midland England.
   3.1724
The Domesday geography of northern England.
   3.1725
The Domesday geography of south-east
   England. 3.1726
The Domesday geography of South-west
   England. 3.1727
The Domestic context of Soviet foreign policy.
   3.3248
Domestic enemies. 4.3525
Domestic manners of the Americans.
   3.6041-3.6042
Domestic monetary management in Britain,
   1919-38. 4.4516
Domestic particulars. 2.12937
Domestic transportation. 4.3894
The domestication of women. 4.6169
The dominant ideology thesis. 4.4966
Dominant mammal. 5.3325
Dominations and powers. 4.7464
The Dominican Republic: rebellion and
   repression. 3.9124
Dominion of the North. 3.8672
Don Fernando. 2.9103
Don flows home to the sea. 2.1603
Don Juan de Onate, colonizer of New Mexico,
   1595-1628. 3.8570
Don Juan Manuel. 2.5192
Don Juan Tenorio. 2.5227
Don Quijote de la Mancha. 2.5169
Don Quixote. 2.5173, 2.5181
Don Quixote de la Mancha. 2.5172
Don Segundo Sombra. 2.5389-2.5390
Doña Barbara. 2.5447
Dona Flor and her two husbands. 2.5468
Doña Perfecta. 2.5219
Donald Barthelme. 2.12895-2.12896
Donald Barthelme's fiction. 2.12897
Donald Davidson. 2.11554
The Donatist Church. 1.2964
Donizetti and his operas. 1.3854
Donizetti and the world of opera in Italy, Paris
   and Vienna in the first half of the nineteenth
   century. 1.3855
The Donne tradition. 2.5799
Donovan and the CIA. 4.7914
Don't bet on the prince. 2.10826
Don't let them scare you. 2.3612
Don't make no waves 3.8418
Don't tell Alfred. 2.9117
Don't touch that dial! 2.2846
The doomsday book; can the world survive?.
   3.215
Doomsday Cult. 1.1567
The doors of perception. 5.5140
Doors to the sacred. 1.3222
Dorian's Dictionary of science and technology.
   5.707

Doris Humphrey: an artist first. 4.1147
Doris Lessing. 2.9028, 2.9030, 2.9033
Dorland's Illustrated medical dictionary.
    5.4485
Dorothy and Red. 2.12585
Dorothy L. Sayers. 2.9309-2.9311
Dorothy Parker. 2.12302
Dorothy Richardson. 2.9284, 2.9286
Dorothy Wordsworth. 2.8297
The Dorr Rebellion. 3.8017
The Dorr War. 4.8262
DO's. 5.5212
Dos Passos. 2.11588
Dossier. 4.7697
Dostoevsky. 2.1364-2.1367, 2.1370
Dostoevsky & Gogol. 2.1372
Dostoevsky and romantic realism. 2.1373
A Dostoevsky dictionary. 2.1362
Dostoevsky: his life and work. 2.1369
Dostoevsky: the major fiction. 2.1377
Dostoevsky; works and days. 2.1371
Dostoevsky's underground man in Russian
    literature. 2.1259
Dostoyevsky, his life and work. 2.1368
The double. 2.1353
The double dream of spring. 2.11334
Double exposure. 5.4667
The double face of Janus and other essays in
    the history of medicine. 5.4506
The double helix. 5.3468
The double helix; a personal account of the
    discovery of the structure of DNA. 5.2763
The double invention of Komo. 2.13439
The double man. 2.8394
The double patriots. 3.4975
The double-purpose high school. 4.10498
Doubt and dogmatism. 1.324
Douglas Haig. 3.1270
The Douglas opinions. 4.9448
Douglas Stewart. 2.10176
Douze poètes modernes du Canada français.
    2.4808
Doves and diplomats. 4.9120
The Dow Jones averages, 1885-1980. 4.4619
The ... Dow Jones-Irwin business and
    investment almanac. 4.4248
Dow Jones Irwin business and investment
    almanac. 4.4248
Down along the Mother Volga. 2.1293
Down and out in Paris and London. 2.9180
Down & out in the Great Depression. 3.6056
Down and Out in the Great Depression.
    3.6056
Down by the riverside. 3.8251
Down from equality. 4.10878
Down from the hill. 2.9316
Down home. 2.10577
Down in the holler. 2.1149
Down the line. 3.6689
Down there (La bas). 2.4248
Down these mean streets a man must go.
    2.11480
The downfall of the anti-Semitic political parties
    in imperial Germany. 4.8603
The downfall of the Liberal Party, 1914-1935.
    3.1691
Downhill all the way. 2.9566
Downhome blues lyrics. 1.3457
Down's syndrome. 5.4980
Downstream. 2.8932, 5.3259
The Downy mildews. 5.5402
Doxographi graeci. 2.322
Doxology. 1.2785
Dr. Ambedkar. 3.4299
Dr. Bowdler's legacy. 5.7699
Dr. Cotnoir. 2.4830
Dr. E. Œ. Somerville, a biography. 2.9353
Dr. Goebbels, his life and death. 3.2385
Dr. John Arbuthnot. 2.6898
Dr. Johnson's Dictionary. 2.1078
Dr. Kinsey and the Institute for Sex Research.
    4.5497
Dr. Lavendar's people. 2.10993
Dr. Sam: Johnson, detector. 2.11556
Dr. Spock talks with mothers. 5.578
Dr. Strangelove. 2.9699
The Dr. Thorndyke omnibus. 2.8670
Dr. Wortle's school. 2.8209

A draft of shadows, and other poems. 2.5347
The drafting of the Covenant. 4.9187
The dragon can't dance. 2.10000
Dragon Country. 2.12726
A dragon defiant. 3.4471
Dragon seed. 2.11427
Dragonflight. 2.13142
The dragons of Eden. 5.364
The dragon's teeth? 5.7402
Dragon's teeth. 2.12478
Drainage of agricultural land. 5.5284
Drake's voyages: a re-assessment of their place
    in Elizabethan maritime expansion. 3.1274
Drama A to Z. 2.2786
Drama criticism. 5.7801
Drama in a world of science, and three other
    lectures. 2.3136
The drama of Chekhov, Synge, Yeats, and
    Pirandello. 2.2807
The drama of Denishawn dance. 4.1165
The drama of Euripides. 2.468
The drama of power: 2.6771
The drama of revolt. 2.13556
The drama of sensibility. 2.5913
The drama of the medieval church. 2.2805
Drama of the storm and stress. 2.13493
The drama scholars' index to plays and
    filmscripts. 5.8134
Drama, stage, and audience. 2.2791
Drama was a weapon. 2.3224
Drama with children. 2.3406
The dramas and dramatic dances of non-
    European races. 2.3169
Dramas, fields, and metaphors. 4.539
Dramas from the American theatre, 1762-1909.
    2.10780
The drama's patrons. 2.3316
Dramatic art in Aeschylus's Seven against
    Thebes. 2.412
The dramatic concepts of Antonin Artaud.
    2.4385
Dramatic criticism index. 5.8125
Dramatic design in the Chester cycle. 2.5857
The dramatic event. 2.3205
The dramatic festivals of Athens. 2.304
The dramatic genius of Verdi. 1.4024
The dramatic imagination. 2.3095
Dramatic irony in Chaucer. 2.6375
The dramatic records of Sir Henry Herbert,
    master of Revels, 1623-1673. 2.3296
Dramatic satire in the age of Walpole,
    1720-1750. 2.5916
Dramatic soundings. 2.2782
Dramatic technique. 2.2795
Dramatic theory and criticism: Greeks to
    Grotowski. 2.2780
The dramatic use of bawdy in Shakespeare.
    2.6727
Dramatic works. 2.3983, 2.6566
Dramatic works and poems. 2.6874
The dramatic works in the Beaumont and
    Fletcher canon. 2.6554
The dramatic works of Denis Johnston. 2.8849
The dramatic works of Richard Brinsley
    Sheridan. 2.7245
Dramatic works of Thomas Dekker. 2.6568
The dramatic writings of Nicholas Udall.
    2.6877
Dramatis personae. 2.3207, 2.8340
Dramatist in America. 2.11314
Dramatists in Canada. 2.9893
Dramatists in perspective. 2.5130
Dramatists in revolt. 2.5309
La dramaturgie de Beaumarchais. 2.4062
Die Dramen. 2.13675, 2.13869
Dramen. 2.13783, 2.13920
Drastic measures. 4.2111
Drawing down the Moon. 5.677
Drawing the line. 3.4415, 4.7518
Drawings and digressions. 1.5797
The drawings of Josef Albers. 1.5805
The drawings of Milton Avery. 1.5794
The drawings of Norman McLaren. 1.5798
The drawings of Pieter Bruegel the elder.
    1.5840
The drawings of Poussin. 1.5803
The drawings of Raphael. 1.5815

The drawings of the Florentine painters.
    1.5839
The drawings of the Venetian painters in the
    15th and 16th centuries. 1.5813
The drawings of Thomas Gainsborough.
    1.5801
Drawings; the complete albums. 1.5817
Drawn in color: African contrasts. 3.5446
The dream. 5.1696
Dream and reality. 1.1111
The dream and the deal. 3.6227
Dream and thought in the business community,
    1860-1900. 4.1912
Dream children. 2.13048
Dream in Shakespeare; 2.6832
The dream maker. 4.3821
The dream of a common language. 2.12385
The dream of Alcestis. 2.12222
The dream of Arcady. 2.10454
Dream of empire. 4.8933
The dream of learning. 2.6823
The dream of Lhasa. 3.4853
The dream of reason. 3.6091
The dream of the golden mountains. 2.11511
Dream of unity. 3.5319
A dream of wings. 5.6647
Dream on Monkey Mountain. 2.10021
The dream songs. 2.11377
Dream tales and prose poems. 2.1451
Dream telepathy. 5.656
The dream thought of Piers Plowman. 2.6402
A dreamer's journey. 1.581
Dreamers of decadence. 1.6700
Dreamers of dreams. 2.5722
Dreaming of heroes. 2.13227
Dreaming the dark. 5.676
Dreams, illusion, and other realities. 5.655
Dreams of empire. 3.8709
Dreams of passion. 2.5058
The dreams of reason. 5.844
Dred. 2.11228
The Dred Scott case, its significance in
    American law and politics. 4.9620
Dreiser. 2.11606
Dress and society, 1560-1970. 4.838
Dress and undress. 4.854
The Dreyfus case. 3.2190, 3.2193
The Dreyfus trials. 4.9911
DRG 1981-. 4.10585
The DRI model of the U.S. economy. 4.2010
Drift and mastery. 4.5173
Drinking. 4.6650
Drinking and crime. 4.6635
Drinking in America. 4.6652
The driver's seat. 2.9358
Droit japonais. 4.9924
Droll stories. 2.4117
Drops of blood. 2.1534
Drowned valley. 3.7966
Drug abuse. 4.6659
Drug dealers. 4.6655
Drug evaluations. 5.5135
Drug use and abuse. 5.4956
Drugs, alcohol, & sex. 5.5138
Drugs and minority oppression. 4.6671
Drugs: medical, psychological and social facts.
    4.6657
The druids. 1.1671
The Druids. 1.1672
The drum and the hoe. 4.785
Drumbeats, masks, and metaphor. 2.3214
The drummer, man. 1.4182
Drums along the Mohawk. 2.11624
The drums of Father Ned. 2.9149
The drunk in the furnace. 2.12194
A drunk man looks at the thistle. 2.8782
The Druze faith. 1.1786
The Druzes. 3.3794
Dry farming in the northern Great Plains,
    1900-1925. 5.5235
Dryden and the conservative myth. 2.6991
Dryden, the public writer, 1660-1685. 2.7006
Dryden's heroic plays. 2.7005
Dryden's poetry. 2.7001
Dryden's political poetry. 2.7007
Drylongso. 3.6757
Du mouvement et de l'immobilité de Douve.
    2.4417

Du Pont and the international chemical
   industry. 4.3794
The du Ponts. 4.3793
Dual-career couples. 4.5587
The dual heritage. 3.3843
The dual mandate in British tropical Africa.
   3.5116
La dualité canadienne. 3.8691
Dubin's lives. 2.13155
Dubious alliance. 3.8500
Dublin. 2.9871
Dublin diary. 2.8909
Dublin, the deposed capital. 4.2317
Dubliners. 2.8867
Dublin's Joyce. 2.8911
Duccio. 1.6201
Duccio di Buoninsegna and his school. 1.6200
The Duchess of Malfi. 2.6879-2.6880
Duck variations. 2.13168
Due process. 4.9699
Duel between the first ironclads. 3.7364
Dufay. 1.3857
Duke. 1.3864
The Duke's children. 2.8207
The Dukes of Norfolk. 3.1238
The Duke's province. 4.7811
The Dulanys of Maryland. 3.8104
Dulles. 3.7638
Dunbar, a critical exposition of the poems.
   2.6477
Duncan Phyfe and the English Regency,
   1795-1830. 1.6570
Dune. 2.13084
Gli duoi fratelli rivali. 2.4976
Duplessis. 3.8812
DuPont and the international chemical
   industry. 4.3794
Dura-Europos and its art. 3.3804
The durable desperadoes. 2.5956
Dürer drawings in the Albertina. 1.5806
Dürer in America: his graphic work. 1.6463
Dürer: the artist and his drawings. 1.5807
Die Dürerzeichnungen der Albertina. 1.5806
During my time. 3.5886
Durkheim and modern sociology. 4.4751
Durkheim and the law. 4.9369
Durkheim on religion. 1.1539
Durrah al-fākhirah. 1.2061
Dürrenmatt. 2.13735
Duse, a biography. 2.3379
Dusk of dawn. 3.6823
The Dust Bowl. 5.5237
Dust Bowl. 3.8561
The dust of combat. 2.7880
Dust tracks on a road. 2.11911
The dust which is God. 2.11375
Dusty answer. 2.9006
Dutch and Flemish painters. 1.6229
Dutch civilisation in the seventeenth century.
   3.2984
Dutch foreign policy since 1815. 3.2988
The Dutch in Brazil, 1624-1654. 3.9207
The Dutch in Java. 3.4580
The Dutch in the seventeenth century. 3.2959
Dutch interior. 2.13945
The Dutch language. 2.1168
The Dutch Republic and American
   independence. 3.6950
The Dutch Republic and the civilisation of the
   seventeenth century. 3.2991
The Dutch Republic and the Hispanic world,
   1606-1661. 3.2960
The Dutch revolt. 3.2963
The Dutch seaborne empire, 1600-1800. 4.8934
Dutch society. 4.5368
Dutch, the language of twenty million Dutch
   and Flemish people. 2.1169
The Dutch under German occupation,
   1940-1945. 3.2992
Dutchman and The slave, two plays. 2.12868
Duties beyond borders. 4.8991
Dutton's Navigation & piloting. 5.7494
Dutton's Navigation and piloting. 5.7494
Duty, honor, country: a history of West Point.
   5.7241
Dvořák. 1.3858-1.3859
The dwarf. 2.14089

Dwight L. Moody, American evangelist,
   1837-1899. 1.3044
The dyer's hand, and other essays. 2.8395
The Dying community. 4.4899
The dying earth. 2.11974
Dying inside. 2.13323
The dying Lion. 3.5246
Dylan Thomas. 2.9417
Dylan Thomas, his life and work. 2.9414
Dylan Thomas in America. 2.9416
Dynamic administration. 5.5559
The dynamic earth: textbook in geosciences.
   5.2962
Dynamic factors in industrial productivity.
   4.2656
Dynamic heterogeneous catalysis. 5.2895
The dynamic liquid state. 5.2036
The dynamic performance. 1.4495
Dynamic physical education for elementary
   school children. 4.914
Dynamic programming. 5.1367
Dynamic sociology. 4.4848
Dynamic systems. 5.1544
A dynamic theory of forward exchange.
   4.4559
A dynamic theory of personality. 5.524
Dynamical aspects of critical phenomena.
   5.2175
Dynamical systems in the plane. 5.1606
The dynamical theory of gases. 5.2171
A dynamical theory of the electromagnetic field.
   5.2363
Dynamics. 5.5742
Dynamics and control of continuous distillation
   units. 5.6841
Dynamics of a creole system. 2.2337
The dynamics of a labor market; 4.3221
Dynamics of academic reform. 4.10080
The dynamics of aging. 4.5813
The dynamics of architectural form. 1.5490
Dynamics of atmospheric flight. 5.6662
The dynamics of atoms in crystals. 5.2208
Dynamics of bases and foundations. 5.5915
The dynamics of behavior development. 5.478
The dynamics of bureaucracy. 4.7750
The dynamics of change. 3.196
The dynamics of Chinese politics. 3.4843
The dynamics of communism in Eastern
   Europe. 4.7016
Dynamics of faith. 1.2934
The dynamics of folklore. 4.756
The Dynamics of host defence. 5.5404
Dynamics of machinery. 5.6162
Dynamics of marine vehicles. 5.7508
Dynamics of nuclear reactors. 5.2445
The dynamics of particles and of rigid plastic,
   and fluid bodies. 5.1656
Dynamics of physical circuits and systems.
   5.6161
Dynamics of polymeric liquids. 5.5749
Dynamics of snow and ice masses. 4.317
The dynamics of spectroscopic transitions.
   5.2317
Dynamics of structures. 5.5855
The dynamics of the arms race. 4.9172
Dynamics of the party system. 4.8168
The Dynamics of Victorian business. 4.4258
The dynamics of world history. 3.466
Dynamics 5.1653
Dynamics, theory and applications. 5.5741
Dynamite. 4.3342
The dynastic arts of the Kushans. 1.4733
The dynasts. 2.7765
Dyscolus. 2.312
The dyskolos. 2.524
Dyskolos. 2.523
Dyslexia. 5.5093

E. B. White. 2.12707
E.C.A. and Africa's development, 1983-2008.
   4.2604
E. E. Cummings. 2.11542-2.11543
E.J. Brill's first encyclopaedia of Islam,
   1913-1936. 3.3660
E.J. Pratt. 2.9960
E.J. Pratt, the truant years, 1882-1927. 2.9961
E.L. Doctorow. 2.12992

E.L. Doctorow, essays and conversations.
   2.12991
E. M. Forster. 2.8657-2.8658, 2.8662
E.M. Forster. 2.8664, 2.8667
E. M. Forster. 2.8668
E. M. Forster, a human exploration. 2.8660
E.M. Forster, centenary revaluations. 2.8661
E. M. Forster's Howards End. 2.8646
E. M. Forster's India. 2.8659
Eadweard Muybridge. 5.7001
Eagle against the sun. 3.1006
Eagle forgotten. 3.8409
Eagles in cobwebs. 3.3534
Eagles' nest. 2.8614
Eakins watercolors. 1.6379
Eamon de Valera. 3.1867
Earl Grey and the Australian colonies,
   1846-1857. 3.5569
Earl Warren, a public life. 4.9835
Earl Warren, the judge who changed America.
   4.9833
Earle Birney. 2.9914-2.9915
Earlier diplomatic history, 1492-1713. 3.618
The earlier Tudors, 1485-1558. 3.1396
Earlier writings. 1.2201
Earliest Christianity. 1.2661
Earliest civilizations of the Near East. 3.115
The earliest wheeled transport. 4.728
The early Abbasid Caliphate. 3.3673
Early American architecture, from the first
   colonial settlements to the national period
   1.5292
Early American fiction, 1774-1830. 5.7815
Early American hurricanes, 1492-1870. 5.2548
Early American magazines, 1741-1789. 2.3641
Early American music engraving and printing.
   1.3545
The early American novel. 2.10603
Early American plays, 1714-1830. 5.7806
Early American poetry. 2.10762, 5.7822
Early American silver. 1.6656
Early American taverns. 4.871
Early American tornadoes, 1586-1870. 5.2498
Early American winters. 5.2499
Early and medieval Christianity. 1.2288
Early Arab-Zionist negotiation attempts,
   1913-1931. 3.3862
Early Auden. 2.8408
Early autumn. 2.11416
Early Black bibliographies, 1863-1918. 5.7871
Early Buddhist Japan. 3.4932
The early career of Alexander Pope. 2.7200
Early Caucasian carpets in Turkey. 1.6586
Early Ch'an in China and Tibet. 1.2174
Early childhood education. 4.10400
Early Chinese civilization. 3.4648
Early Chinese literature. 2.2158
Early Chinese texts on painting. 1.6372
Early Christian and Byzantine architecture.
   1.5518
Early Christian and Byzantine art. 1.5168
Early Christian art. 1.5172
Early Christian creeds. 1.2956
The early Christian doctrine of God. 1.2820
Early Christian doctrines. 1.2748
The early Christian fathers. 1.2199
Early Christian fathers. 1.2198
Early Christian Ireland: introduction to the
   sources. 3.1812
Early Christian rhetoric. 1.2644
Early Christian worship. 1.2976
Early Christianity and Greek paideia. 1.2269
The early church. 1.2293
The early church to the dawn of the
   Reformation. 1.2273
The early churches of Constantinople:
   architecture and liturgy. 1.5537
Early concert-life in America. (1731-1800)
   1.3693
Early dark. 2.13273
Early days; Sisters; and Life class. 2.9821
Early diagenesis. 5.3118
The early doors. 2.2832
Early downhome blues. 1.4315
Early Dutch painting. 1.6236
The early economic writings of Alfred
   Marshall, 1867-1890 4.1333

Early education and psychological development. 4.10401

Early embryology of the chick. 5.4130

Early English and French voyages. 3.5988

The early English carols. 2.6118

Early English stages, 1300 to 1660. 2.3285

Early experience. 5.562

The early Fidel. 3.9108

Early German philosophy. 1.861

The early Goebbels diaries, 1925-1926. 3.2381

Early Gothic manuscripts. 1.6409

Early Greece. 3.2535, 3.2541

Early Greek elegists. 2.310

Early Greek philosophy. 1.231

Early Greek science: Thales to Aristotle. 5.782

Early Greek warfare. 5.7180

The early guitar. 1.4179

The early H. G. Wells. 2.8253

The early history of the Church of Canterbury. 1.3310

The early history of the viol. 1.4160

Early India and Pakistan. 3.4246

Early Indian sculpture. 1.5748

Early Ionian historians. 3.2572

The early Irish stage. 2.3359

The early Islamic conquests. 3.3667

Early Latin America. 3.8997

Early Latin theology. 1.2197

Early Latin verse. 2.255

Early life. 5.3320

The early life and letters of Cavour, 1810-1848. 3.2868

Early life in Upper Canada 3.8826

The early life of Georges Clemenceau, 1841-1893. 3.2182

The early life of William Wordsworth, 1770-1798. 3.2181

The early love poetry of Heinrich Heine. 2.13606

Early Mādhyamika in India and China. 1.1776

Early man and the cosmos. 5.1688

The early masters of English fiction. 2.5995

Early medieval. 1.4740

Early medieval art, 300-1150. 1.4739

Early medieval art, with illustrations from the British Museum and British Library collections. 1.4737

Early medieval Germany. 3.2264

Early medieval philosophy (480-1150) 1.354

Early medieval theology. 1.2180

Early modern English. 2.980

Early modern France 1560-1715. 3.2006

The Early modern town. 4.6255

Early music discography. 1.3617

Early Muslim architecture. 1.5236

Early narratives of the Northwest, 1634-1699. 3.8370

Early Negro American writers. 2.10688

Early Negro writing, 1760-1837. 2.10699

Early Neo-Classicism in France. 1.4961

Early Netherlandish painting. 1.6230

Early Netherlandish painting, its origins and character. 1.6234

Early Netherlandish triptychs. 1.6259

The early New England cotton manufacture. 4.3851

Early opera in America. 1.4221

Early painters and engravers in Canada. 1.4919

Early Philippine literature from ancient times to 1940. 2.2292

Early poems, 1935-1955. 2.5348

Early Protestant educators. 4.10161

The early public theatre in France. 2.3363

Early puritan writers. 5.7795

Early Quaker writings, 1650-1700. 1.3346

Early Rome. 3.2718

Early Rome and the Etruscans. 3.2765

Early Rome and the Latins. 3.2759

Early schooling. 4.10415

Early Scottish poetry: Thomas the Rhymer, John Barbour, Androw of Wyntoun, Henry the minstrel. 2.9843

The early Shakespeare. 2.6839

Early South East Asia. 3.4383

The early Spanish ballad. 2.5123

The early Spanish Main. 3.9143

Early Spanish manuscript illumination. 1.6418

The early stained glass of Canterbury Cathedral, circa 1175-1220. 1.6648

The early Stuarts, 1603-1660. 3.1457

Early thematic mapping in the history of cartography. 4.227

Early theological works. 1.2346

Early travellers in New Zealand. 3.5590

The early Vasas: a history of Sweden 1523-1611. 3.3389

Early Victorian architecture in Britain. 1.5372

Early Victorian government, 1830-1870. 4.8406

Early Victorian New Zealand. 3.5601

Early Virgil. 2.790

The early window. 4.5736

The early work of Frank Lloyd Wright. 1.5338

The early works, 1882-1898. 1.585

Early writings. 3.7717

The early years of Alec Waugh. 2.9480

The Early years of radio astronomy. 5.1776

The earnest men. 3.7309

The earth. 5.2970, 5.3075

The earth. 5.2967

The earth; an introduction to physical geology. 5.3078

Earth and astronomical sciences research centres. 5.2987

Earth and life through time. 5.2971

The Earth from space. 5.1812

The earth-owl and other moon-people. 2.9713

Earth power coming. 2.10675

Earth structures engineering. 5.5913

The earth, the temple, and the gods. 1.5221

Earthbound. 4.3724

Earthly paradise. 2.4499

Earthly powers. 2.9641

Earthquakes. 5.3115-5.3116

The Earth's climate, past and future. 5.2572

The Earth's density. 5.1761

The Earth's dynamic systems. 5.2965

Earth's earliest biosphere. 5.3162

The Earth's problem climates. 5.2567

Earthworks and beyond. 1.4845

East across the Pacific. 3.6559

East Africa. 3.5258

East Africa; its peoples and resources. 4.2583

The East African coast. 3.5237

East and West. 2.9095, 3.32

East Asia. 3.4384

East Asia: a bibliography for undergraduate libraries. 5.8033

East Asia and U.S. security. 3.3632

East Asian civilization. 3.110

East-Central Europe. 3.3512, 4.2236

East Central Europe between the two World Wars. 3.2997

The East European and Soviet data handbook. 4.1255

East European economic handbook. 4.2230

East European integration and East-West trade. 4.2231

The East European predicament. 3.2999

The East European revolution. 3.3536

East German poetry. 2.13933

East German short stories. 2.13934

East Germany. 3.2475

East Los Angeles. 3.8618

East Lynne. 2.8294

East of Eden. 2.12526

East river. 2.1799

East-West in art. 1.4885

East-West parallels. 4.5404

The Eastasia edge. 4.2540

The Easter Rising. 3.1864

The Eastern Association in the English Civil War. 3.1482

Eastern Christendom. 1.3111

Eastern Europe. 4.2237

Eastern Europe between the wars, 1918-1941. 3.3530

Eastern Europe since Stalin. 3.3537

The eastern front. 3.805

The eastern front, 1914-1917. 3.806

Eastern North America. 5.5361

The Eastern Orthodox Church, its thought and life. 1.3107

The Eastern question. 3.683

The Eastern question, 1774-1923. 3.682

Eastern religions and western thought. 1.1818

Eastern science. 5.762

Eastern wisdom and Western thought. 1.430

The easy chair. 2.11559

Eating disorders. 5.4937

Eating disorders, the facts. 5.4937

Eating oil. 5.6887

Eating people is wrong. 2.9625

Eavesdropping on trial. 4.9886

The ebony tower. 2.9684

Eboué. 4.8922

ECA and Africa's development, 1983-2008. 4.2604

Eça de Queirós and European realism. 2.5457

The eccentric design. 2.10534

Ecclesiastical authority and spiritual power in the church of the first three centuries. 1.2813

The ecclesiastical history. 2.367

An Ecclesiastical history of England. 1.2428

The ecclesiastical history of Orderic Vitalis. 3.566

The Ecclesiastical sonnets. 2.8307

Ecclesiasticus, or the wisdom of Jesus son of Sirach. 1.2624

Ecclesiazusae. 2.423

The echo of the Nazi holocaust in rabbinic literature. 3.1125

The eclipse of community. 4.6225

The eclipse of Darwinism. 5.3341

Eclipse of God. 1.1543

Eclipse of reason. 1.1007

L'école romantique française. 2.3862

Ecological animal geography. 5.3814

Ecological genetics. 5.3478

Ecological perspective on human affairs. 4.8987

Ecological processes in coastal and marine systems. 5.3539

Ecological processes in coastal environments. 5.3772

Ecological psychology. 5.315

The ecological web. 5.3512

Ecology. 5.3514, 5.3525, 5.3538

Ecology and change: rural modernization in an African community. 4.5475

Ecology and field biology. 5.3526

Ecology, impact assessment, and environmental planning. 5.3528

The Ecology of a salt marsh. 5.3558

Ecology of bats. 5.4010

Ecology of coastal vegetation. 5.3780

Ecology of coastal waters. 5.3540

The ecology of early deafness. 4.6603

Ecology of European rivers. 5.3275

Ecology of exceptional children. 4.10904

The Ecology of fossils. 5.3156

Ecology of fresh water. 5.3546

Ecology of freshwater fish production. 5.3905

The ecology of freshwater phytoplankton. 5.3779

The ecology of fungi. 5.3724

The ecology of human development. 5.581

The ecology of invasions by animals and plants. 5.3516

The ecology of language. 2.28

The Ecology of natural disturbance and patch dynamics. 5.3577

The ecology of neotropical savannas. 5.3274

The ecology of North America. 5.3262

The ecology of regulated streams. 5.3567

The ecology of running waters. 5.3566

The ecology of social boundaries. 3.4588

The Ecology of the seas. 5.3540

The ecology of whales and dolphins. 5.4005

Econocide. 4.6434

Econometric methods. 4.1299

An econometric model of the United States, 1929-1952. 4.1962

Econometric models and economic forecasts. 4.1720

Econometric models and methods. 4.1292

Econometrics. 4.1399

Economic activities in the Republic of Ireland. 4.2313

The Economic almanac for 1940-. 4.1866

Economic analysis. 4.1312

Economic analysis and policy in underdeveloped countries. 4.2759
Economic analysis for highways. 5.6060
Economic analysis of law. 4.9504
The economic analysis of trade unions. 4.3331
The economic analysis of unions. 4.3357
An economic analysis of world energy problems. 4.3706
The economic and social foundations of European civilization. 3.577
The economic and social growth of early Greece, 800-500 B.C. 4.1736
Economic and social history of ancient Greece. 4.1730
Economic and social history of medieval Europe. 4.1743
Economic and social history of Quebec, 1760-1850. 4.2127
The Economic and social modernization of the Republic of Korea. 4.2560
Economic and social progress in Latin America. 4.2143
Economic and social survey of Asia and the Pacific. 4.2429
Economic anthropology. 4.530
The economic aspects of the history of the civilization of Japan. 4.2545
An economic background to Munich. 4.4630
Economic backwardness and economic growth. 4.2790
Economic bulletin for Asia and the Far East. 4.2429
Economic change. 4.1280
Economic change in precolonial Africa. 4.2581
Economic change in rural India. 4.2865
Economic change in Thailand, 1850-1970. 4.2528
Economic change in the Civil War era. 4.1920
Economic concentration and the monopoly problem. 4.3049
The Economic consequences of slowing population growth. 4.1673
Economic consequences of the size of nations. 4.2781
Economic decision analysis. 4.2726
The economic decline of empires. 4.1738
Economic democracy. 4.1287
Economic deposits and their tectonic setting. 5.6733
Economic development. 4.2793
Economic development & the labor market in Japan. 4.3667
Economic development in Communist Rumania. 4.2420
Economic development in Iran, 1900-1970. 4.2564
Economic development in South Asia. 4.2438
Economic development of a small planet. 4.1807
The economic development of Australia. 4.2596
The Economic development of Bangladesh within a socialist framework. 4.2523
Economic development of Communist China. 4.2482
The economic development of Communist China, 1949-1960. 4.2480
The economic development of continental Europe. 4.2203
The economic development of East and Southeast Asia. 4.2433
The economic development of France and Germany, 1815-1914. 4.2321
The economic development of India. 4.2498
The economic development of Japan. 4.2543
Economic development of Latin America. 4.2140
The economic development of medieval Europe. 4.2184
Economic development of Taiwan, 1860-1970. 4.2494
The economic development of the Third World since 1900. 4.1798
The economic development of the USSR. 4.2384
Economic development, peace, and international law. 4.8988

Economic development, poverty, and income distribution. 4.1802
Economic development programs for cities, counties, and towns. 4.6215
Economic diplomacy and the origins of the Second World War. 4.4234
Economic discrimination against women in the United States: measures and changes. 4.3294
The economic doctrines of Karl Marx. 4.1538
Economic dynamics. 4.1478
The economic effects of advertising. 4.4426
Economic effects of social security. 4.3459
Economic elements in the Pax Britannica. 4.4228
The economic emergence of women. 4.6031
Economic enquiry in Australia 4.1382
The economic environment of international business. 4.2720
Economic evaluation of mineral property. 5.6745
Economic exchange and social interaction in Southeast Asia. 4.640
Economic expansion and social change. 4.2259
Economic foundations of British overseas expansion, 1815-1914. 4.2272
Economic geography. 4.4117-4.4118
An economic geography of East Africa. 4.2584
An economic geography of the Philippines. 4.2537
Economic geography of the USSR. 4.2364
Economic geology and geotectonics. 5.6730
Economic growth. 4.1752
Economic growth and development in Jordan. 4.2446
Economic growth and disparities. 4.2783
Economic growth and distribution in China. 4.2481
Economic growth and neighborhood discontent. 4.6344
Economic growth and resources. 4.2782
Economic growth and social equity in developing countries. 4.2755
Economic growth in Britain and France, 1780-1914. 4.2279
Economic growth in China and India, 1952-1970. 4.2486
Economic growth in France and Britain, 1851-1950. 4.2327
Economic growth in Ireland. 4.2315
Economic growth in the Third World, 1850-1980. 4.1820
The economic growth of Brazil, a survey from colonial to modern times. 4.2169
The economic growth of Hong Kong. 4.2490
Economic growth of nations. 4.1753
The economic growth of the United States, 1790-1860. 4.1913
Economic handbook of the world. 4.1722
An economic history of Argentina in the twentieth century. 4.2167
The Economic history of Britain since 1700. 4.2265
Economic history of Canada. 5.8397
An economic history of China. 4.2466
An economic history of England. 4.2262
Economic history of Ethiopia, 1800-1935. 4.2593
Economic history of Europe, twentieth century. 4.2191
Economic history of India, 1857-1956. 4.2502
The economic history of Iran, 1800-1914. 4.2565
An economic history of Ireland since 1660. 4.2312
An economic history of Italy. 4.2352
An economic history of modern Britain ... 4.2274
An economic history of modern France. 4.2320
The economic history of modern Italy. 4.2354
An economic history of Russia. 4.2367
An economic history of Scotland in the eighteenth century. 4.2298
An economic history of Sweden. 4.2411
The economic history of the Middle East, 1800-1914. 4.2430
An economic history of the Middle East and North Africa. 4.2441

An economic history of the U.S.S.R. 4.2385
Economic history of the USSR. 4.2385
The Economic history of Turkey, 1800-1914. 4.2567
An Economic history of Ulster, 1820-1940. 4.2318
Economic history of Virginia in the seventeenth century. 3.8188
An economic history of West Africa. 4.2589
An economic history of women in America. 4.5987
The economic history of world population. 4.1761
The economic impact of the American Civil War. 4.1919
Economic imperialism. 4.1746, 4.1760
Economic integration among unequal partners. 4.2163
Economic interest, militarism, and foreign policy. 3.2256
The economic interpretation of history. 3.496
An economic interpretation of the Constitution of the United States. 4.7823
Economic issues and political conflict. 4.2138
Economic man. 4.596
Economic man in relation to his natural environment. 4.1482
Economic maturity and entrepreneurial decline. 4.3735
The economic mind in American civilization. 4.1368
Economic mineral deposits. 5.6728-5.6729
The economic novel in America. 2.10583
Economic organization in Chinese society. 4.2461
Economic origins of Jeffersonian democracy. 4.7833
Economic perspectives. 4.1436
Economic philosophy. 4.1282
Economic planning and social justice in developing countries. 4.1813
Economic policies toward less developed countries. 4.1809
Economic policy and development. 4.2550
Economic policy and industrial growth in Pakistan. 4.2517
Economic policy and projects. 4.2308
Economic redevelopment in bituminous coal. 4.3744
Economic reform in East German industry. 4.2347
Economic reform in Rumanian industry. 4.2421
Economic reform in the PRC. 4.2477
Economic reforms in Eastern Europe. 4.2239
Economic regulation of domestic air transport. 4.4088
Economic rights of women in ancient Greece. 4.5850
The economic role of Jews in Medieval Poland. 3.3986
The economic societies in the Spanish world, 1763-1821. 4.2412
Economic sociology. 4.4818
Economic stabilization in developing countries. 4.1803
An economic survey of ancient Rome. 4.1739
Economic survey of Asia and the Far East. 1947-. 4.2429
Economic theory and exhaustible resources. 4.1769
Economic theory and operations analysis. 4.1385
Economic theory and socialism. 4.1427
Economic theory and western European integration. 4.2210
Economic theory in retrospect. 4.1304
The economic theory of agricultural land tenure. 4.2917
An economic theory of democracy. 4.7753
The economic theory of fiscal policy. 4.4645
The economic theory of pollution control. 4.1855
Economic theory on technological change and employment. 4.3194
Economic thought and the Irish question, 1817-1870. 4.2311
Economic trends in Communist China. 4.2478

Economic trends in the Soviet Union. 4.2373
The Economic value of the United States merchant marine. 4.3972
Economic welfare in the Soviet Union. 4.2406
Economics. 4.1458
Economics and empire, 1830-1914. 4.8899
The economics and financing of education. 4.10658
Economics and liberalism in the Risorgimento. 3.2910
The economics and politics of East-West trade. 4.4160
The economics and politics of oil price regulation. 4.3767
The economics and politics of racial accommodation. 3.8622
Economics & the art of controversy. 4.1935
Economics and the competitive process. 4.1404
Economics and the fiction of Daniel DeFoe. 2.6981
Economics and the public purpose. 4.1998
Economics and world order from the 1970's to the 1990's. 4.1784
Economics, environmental policy, and the quality of life. 4.1837
Economics for agriculture. 4.2884
Economics in practice. 4.1777
The economics of Adam Smith. 4.1356
The economics of advertising. 4.4428
The economics of African development. 4.2577
The economics of aging. 4.3454
The economics of ancient Greece. 4.1735
Economics of change in less developed countries. 4.1800
The economics of collective action. 4.1426
The economics of collective bargaining. 4.3350
The Economics of competition in the telecommunications industry. 4.4051
The economics of competition in the transportation industries. 4.3887
The economics of control. 4.1334
The economics of David Ricardo. 4.1353
The economics of developing countries. 4.1817
The economics of discrimination. 4.3115
The economics of energy. 4.3708
Economics of environmental and natural resources policy. 4.1839
The Economics of exchange rates. 4.4552
Economics of fatigue and unrest and the efficiency of labour in English and American industry. 4.3120
The economics of feasible socialism. 4.6985
Economics of fisheries development. 4.3700
The economics of fisheries management. 5.5482
The economics of imperfect competition. 4.1494
The economics of imperialism. 4.1519
The economics of individual and population aging. 4.5796
The economics of inflation. 4.4520
The economics of international business. 4.2719
Economics of international migration. 4.8940
The economics of John Stuart Mill. 4.1412
The economics of justice. 4.7658
The economics of labor force participation. 4.3216
The economics of labor migration. 4.3212
The economics of Latin America. 4.2139
The Economics of legal minimum wages. 4.3138
Economics of marketing. 4.4279
The economics of mental retardation. 4.6608
The economics of natural environments. 4.1902
The economics of natural resources. 4.1766
The Economics of neighborhood. 4.6209
The economics of non-wage labour costs. 4.3141
Economics of overhead costs. 4.1480
The economics of political instability. 4.2626
The economics of population growth. 4.1600
The economics of poverty and discrimination. 4.2100
The economics of private pensions. 4.3456
The economics of public education. 4.10653
The Economics of public finance. 4.4655

The economics of public school finance. 4.10657
Economics of public transport. 4.3898
Economics of racism U.S.A. 3.6740
The economics of regional water quality management. 5.6022
The economics of regulation. 4.3082
Economics of regulation in shipping. 4.3964
The economics of road user charges. 4.4034
The economics of sellers' competition. 4.1492
The economics of sex differentials. 4.3284
The economics of slavery, and other studies in econometric history. 4.1756
The economics of socialism. 4.2242
The economics of Soviet oil and gas. 4.3781
The economics of Soviet planning. 4.2392
The economics of take-off into sustained growth. 4.1484
The economics of taxation. 4.4689
The Economics of taxation. 4.4690
The economics of teacher supply. 4.10681
The economics of the American theater. 2.3269
The Economics of the Caribbean Basin. 4.4700
Economics of the family. 4.5639
Economics of the Kennedy years. 4.1987
Economics of the mineral industries. 4.3722
Economics of the product markets of agriculture. 4.3680
Economics of the property tax. 4.4708
The economics of the world's mineral industries. 4.3725
The economics of trade unions. 4.3364
Economics of transportation. 4.3886
The economics of under-developed countries. 4.2760
The economics of unemployment. 4.3227
The economics of urban freight transport. 4.4043
The economics of Vilfredo Pareto. 4.1364
The economics of welfare. 4.1568
The Economics of women and work. 4.3241
The economics of women, men, and work. 4.6032
The economics of world grain trade. 4.3682
Economics selections. 5.8372
L'Économie française dans le monde. 4.2326
Economies and societies in Latin America. 4.2144
The economies of the ASEAN countries. 4.2526
The economies of the West Bank and Gaza Strip. 4.2445
The economies of West Africa. 4.2622
Economique et commerce au Canada. 5.8395
Economy and foreign policy. 4.2238
Economy and society. 4.1281, 4.4859
Economy and society in ancient Greece. 4.1732
Economy and society in early modern Europe. 4.2186
Economy, class and social revolution. 4.6945
The economy, liberty, and the state. 4.1787
The economy of Bangladesh. 4.2524
The economy of cities. 4.6346
The economy of colonial America. 4.1905
The economy of England, 1450-1750. 4.2260
Economy of Europe in an age of crisis, 1600-1750. 4.2194
The economy of Indonesia. 4.2531
The economy of Israel. 4.2444
The economy of later Renaissance Europe, 1460-1600. 4.2205
The economy of Saudi Arabia. 4.2448
The economy of Scotland in its European setting, 1550-1625. 4.2299
The economy of socialist Cuba. 4.2153
The economy of the Chinese mainland: national income and economic development, 1933-1959. 4.2483
The economy of Yugoslavia. 4.2422
Economy, society & culture in contemporary Yemen. 4.2449
Economy, society, and culture in contemporary Yemen. 4.2449
An Ecosystem approach to aquatic ecology. 5.3271

Ecosystem modeling in theory and practice. 5.3534
Écrivains français de Belgique au XIXe siécle. 2.4801
Les écrivains noirs de langue française. 2.4803
Ecstatic religion. 1.1634
Ecuador. 3.9312
Ecuador: conflicting political culture and the quest for progress. 4.8345
Ecuador: constitutions and caudillos. 4.8344
Ecuador, country of contrasts. 3.9310
L'ecume des jours. 2.4771
Ecumenical councils of the Catholic Church. 1.3118
The ecumenical revolution. 1.3098
Ed Faulkner's tennis. 4.1038
Edda. 2.13980, 2.13992
Edda Snorra Sturlusonar. English. 2.13990
Edda Snorra Sturlusonar. Prologue. 2.13992
Edgar Allan Poe. 2.11203, 2.11205, 2.11207, 2.11210
Edgar Degas. 1.6460
Edgar Hilaire Germain Degas. 1.6092
Edgard Varèse. 1.4018
The edge of an unfamiliar world. 4.333
The edge of darkness. 2.11482
The edge of objectivity. 5.729
The edge of sadness. 2.13205
The edge of the sea. 5.3245
Edifying discourses by Søren Kierkegaard ... 1.3057
Edith Sitwell, a unicorn among lions. 2.9328
Edith Sitwell: the symbolist order. 2.9327
Edith Wharton. 2.12699
Edith Wharton's New York quartet. 2.12695
Editorial practice in libraries. 2.2526
The editorial problem in Shakespeare. 2.6837
Editorials on secession. 3.7178
Editor's study. 2.11086
Edmund Burke. 3.1562, 4.7419
Edmund Burke and the revolt against the eighteenth century. 4.7290
Edmund Burke on government, politics, and society. 4.7418
Edmund Gosse. 2.7749
Edmund Kean. 2.3347
Edmund Pendleton, 1721-1803. 3.8208
Edmund Ruffin, southerner. 3.8209
Edmund Spenser and the Faerie Queene. 2.6542
Edmund Waller. 2.7330
Edmund Wilson. 2.12768, 2.12770-2.12771
Edmund Wilson's America. 2.12769
Edna O'Brien. 2.9787
Edna St. Vincent Millay. 2.12162
Eduardo Mallea. 2.5396
Educating able learners. 4.10918
Educating artistically talented students. 4.10917
Educating exceptional children. 4.10926
Educating severely and profoundly handicapped students. 4.10925
Educating the deaf. 4.6604
Education. 4.10197, 4.10872
Education and a radical humanism. 4.10248
Education and American civilization. 4.10003
Education and colonialism. 4.10887
Education and cultural process. 4.10180
Education and development in Africa. 4.10149
Education and economic productivity. 4.2754
Education and ecstasy. 4.10007
Education and equality in Japan. 4.10144
Education and freedom. 4.10001
Education and human relations. 4.10250
Education and identity. 4.10546
Education and income. 4.10011
Education and jobs. 4.10729
Education and liberty. 4.10732
Education and moral development. 5.607
Education and nationalism. 4.10739
Education and politics in India. 4.10142
Education and power. 4.10773
Education and social mobility in the Soviet Union, 1921-1934. 4.10131
Education and society in modern Europe. 4.9961
Education and sociology. 4.10767
Education and the city. 4.10959

Education and the Federal Government. 4.9584

Education and the good life. 4.10215

Education and the many faces of the disadvantaged: cultural and historical perspectives. 4.10939

Education and the modern world. 4.10216

Education and the rise of the corporate state. 4.9988

Education and the social condition. 4.10772

Education and the social order. 4.10216

Education and values. 4.10239

Education as a profession. 4.10529

Education as cultural imperialism. 4.10012

Education as history. 4.10117

Education at the crossroads 4.10204

Education between two worlds. 4.10233

Education by choice. 4.10635

Education, class, and nation. 4.10106

The Education dilemma. 4.10847

Education directory. 4.9941

The education establishment. 4.10641

Education for all American youth. 4.10052

Education for critical consciousness. 4.10768

Education for modern man. 4.10231

Education for the emerging age: newer ends and stronger means. 4.10220

Education for transformation. 4.10251

Education in a divided world. 4.9995

Education in a small democracy - New Zealand. 4.10690

Education in Africa. 4.10148

Education in American culture. 4.9981

Education in Brazil. 4.10105

Education in England and Wales. 4.10110

Education in Ethiopia. 4.10151

Education in Kenya. 4.10152

Education in Latin America. 4.10104

Education in national politics. 4.10661

Education in the 80's 4.901, 5.984

Education in the computer age. 4.10293

Education in the eighties 4.901

Education in the forming of American society. 4.9989

Education in the South. 4.9993

Education in the Soviet Union. 4.10132

Education in the technological society. 4.10826

Education in violence. 3.7334

Education, income, and human capital. 4.1955

Education index. 5.8150

Education, manpower, and economic growth. 4.3201

The education of a Christian prince. 4.7400

The education of a public man. 3.7650

The education of a WASP. 3.6693

The education of American teachers. 4.10518

The Education of Asian and Pacific Americans. 4.10883

The education of Black folk. 4.10850

The education of Black people. 4.10865

The education of Black Philadelphia. 4.10876

The education of David Stockman and other Americans. 4.2012

The education of H*y*m*a*n K*a*p*l*a*n. 2.12416

The education of Henry Adams. 3.6234

The education of historians in the United States. 3.448

The education of John Randolph. 3.7011

The education of nations. 4.9957

Education of the gifted and talented. 4.10913

Education of the senses. 5.484

Education/psychology journals. 4.10347

Education through art. 4.10214

Education today. 4.10227

Education under Mao. 4.10139

Education under six. 4.10399

Education vouchers: from theory to Alum Rock. 4.10604

Educational charters and documents 598 to 1909. 4.10111

Educational documents. 4.10112

Educational evaluation & measurement. 4.10711

Educational evaluation and measurement. 4.10711

Educational film/video locator. 4.10330

Educational film/video locator of the Consortium of University Film Centers and R.R. Bowker. 4.10330

Educational film video locator of the Consortium of University Film Centers and R.R. Bowker. 4.10330

Educational historiography. 4.9947

Educational ideologies. 4.10268

The educational imagination. 4.10437

Educational media and technology yearbook. 4.10289a

Educational organization and administration. 4.10638

Educational problems of developing societies, with case studies of Ghana, Pakistan, and Nigeria. 4.10846

Educational psychology. 4.10362

Educational roots and routes in western Europe. 4.10107

The Educational software selector. 4.10298

The educational theory of Immanuel Kant. 4.10194

The educational theory of Jean Jacques Rousseau. 4.10187

Educational thought. 4.9951

The educational thought and influence of Matthew Arnold. 4.10192

Educational views of Benjamin Franklin. 4.10188

Educational vouchers; concepts and controversies. 4.10659

Educational wastelands. 4.10218

The educational writings of John Locke. 4.10185

Educators grade guide to free teaching aids. 1.25

Educators guide to free audio and video materials. 4.10326

Educators guide to free films. 4.10329

Educators' guide to free filmstrips. 4.10328

Educators' guide to free slidefilms. 4.10328

Educators' guide to free slidefilms, 1949-1958. 4.10328

Edvard Munch. 1.5039

Edward Abbey. 2.12836

Edward Albee. 2.12848

Edward Bellamy. 2.10908

Edward Dahlberg. 2.11552

Edward Douglass White, defender of the conservative faith. 4.9836

Edward VIII. 3.1697

Edward IV. 3.1381

Edward Gibbon. 3.2745

Edward Gibbon Wakefield. 3.5607

Edward Gordon Craig. 2.3339

Edward Hopper. 1.5946

Edward Hopper, the complete prints. 1.6442

Edward Lear; the life of a wanderer. 1.6036

Edward MacDowell. 1.3915

Edward Preble. 3.7067

Edward, Prince of Wales and Aquitaine. 3.1367

Edward S. Corwin's The Constitution and what it means today. 4.9628

Edward S. Curtis in the land of the war canoes. 5.7000

Edward VII, Prince and King. 3.1680

Edward VI. 3.1417

Edward VI: the threshold of power. 3.1416

Edward II. 2.6612

Edward the Confessor. 3.1321

Edward Thomas. 2.9425

Edward Weston, his life and photographs. 5.6974

Edward Weston omnibus. 5.6932

The Edwardian theatre. 2.3313

The Edwardian turn of mind. 3.1682

The Edwardians. 2.9295, 4.5320

Edwardians and late Victorians. 2.959

Edwin Arlington Robinson. 2.12404, 2.12406-2.12407

Edwin Arlington Robinson. 2.12409

Edwin Arlington Robinson; the life of poetry. 2.12405

Edwin Forrest: first star of the American stage. 2.3255

Edwin Muir. 2.9128-2.9130

Edwin O'Connor. 2.13207

The effect of gamma rays on man-in-the-moon marigolds. 2.13447

Effective collective bargaining in public education. 4.10687

Effective FORTRAN 77. 5.1216

Effective legal research. 4.9471

Effective management information systems. 5.5614

Effective schools. 4.10281

Effective teaching and mentoring. 4.10980

Effects and functions of television. 5.8158

The effects of mass communication on political behavior. 4.7253

The effects of noise on man. 5.4688

The Effects of punishment on human behavior. 5.308

Effects of taxation. 4.3015

The Effects of television advertising on children. 4.5735

The effects of the atomic bomb on Hiroshima, Japan. 3.1044

Effects of the atomic bomb on Nagasaki, Japan. 3.1045

The effects on the atmosphere of a major nuclear exchange. 5.2531

Effi Briest. 2.13566

Efficiency of human movement. 5.4263

Efficient electricity use. 5.6151

An Efficient energy future. 5.6154

Egil's saga. 2.13982

Egils saga Skallagrímssonar. English. 2.13982

Ego and archetype. 5.195

Ego and reality in psychoanalytic theory. 5.191

The ego and the id. 5.138

Ego development. 5.199

Ego, hunger, and aggression. 5.179

Ego psychology and the problem of adaptation 5.197

Egoism and self-discovery in the Victorian novel. 2.6015

The egoist. 2.7937

The egotistical sublime. 2.8320

Egypt. 3.5155

Egypt, a country study. 3.5131

Egypt and the Fertile Crescent, 1516-1922. 3.3734

Egypt: architecture, sculpture, painting in three thousand years. 1.4703

Egypt before the pharaohs. 4.746

Egypt in search of political community. 3.5160

Egypt in the reign of Muhammad Ali. 3.5159

The Egypt of Nasser and Sadat. 4.2616

Egypt of the Pharaohs. 3.5153

Egyptian architecture as cultural expression. 1.5216

The Egyptian economy, 1952-1972. 4.2590

An Egyptian journal. 3.5132

Egyptian Nubians. 3.5178

Egyptian sculpture. 1.5613

The Egyptian way of death. 3.5145

The Egyptians. 3.5134

Egypt's agricultural development, 1800-1980. 4.2994

Egypt's liberal experiment, 1922-1936. 3.5162

Ehrengard. 2.14018

EIA data index. 5.8166

Eichmann in Jerusalem. 3.2380

Eight American authors. 2.10373, 2.10377

Eight approaches to teaching composition. 4.10474

Eight Chinese plays from the thirteenth century to the present. 2.2197

Eight dynasties of Chinese painting. 1.6327

Eight expressionist plays. 2.14070

Eight great Hebrew short novels. 2.1785

Eight hours for what we will. 4.3501

Eight men. 2.12808

Eight modern writers. 2.5708

Eight mortal ladies possessed. 2.12727

Eight philosophers of the Italian Renaissance. 1.403

Eight plays from Off-Off Broadway. 2.10803

Eight Soviet composers. 1.3752

Eight Spanish plays of the golden age. 2.5159

Eight years with Wilson's Cabinet, 1913 to 1920. 3.7715

The eighteen nineties. 2.5706

Eighteen seventy-six. 2.12614
Eighteen short songs of the bitter motherland. 2.619
Eighteen song cycles. 1.4571
Eighteen texts. 2.575
The Eighteenth century. 2.5658
The eighteenth century. 4.848
The eighteenth century background. 1.684
Eighteenth-century British logic and rhetoric. 1.1160
Eighteenth century comedy. 2.6237
The eighteenth-century commonwealthman. 4.8404
Eighteenth-century critical essays. 2.5505
Eighteenth-century England. 3.1521
Eighteenth-century English literature. 2.5659, 2.5664, 2.6089
The eighteenth-century English stage. 2.3306
The eighteenth-century enlightenment in the University of San Carlos de Guatemala. 4.11006
The eighteenth century: Europe in the age of enlightenment. 3.177
Eighteenth-century Europe, tradition and progress, 1715-1789. 3.182
The eighteenth-century French novel. 2.3905
The eighteenth-century Gothic novel. 5.7968
The eighteenth-century houses of Williamsburg. 1.5304
The eighteenth century in Russia. 3.3096
An eighteenth-century musical tour in Central Europe and the Netherlands. 1.3657
An eighteenth-century musical tour in France and Italy. 1.3658
Eighteenth-century plays. 2.6235
Eighteenth-century poetry. 2.6167
Eighteenth century poetry & prose. 2.6087
Eighteenth century prose. 2.6259
The eighteenth century renaissance. 3.1752
The eighteenth-century revolution in Spain. 3.3447
Eighteenth century tragedy. 2.6234
The eighth circle. 2.13000
The eighth day. 2.12716
The eighth day of creation. 5.4418
The eighth day of the week. 2.1705
Eighty poems of Antonio Machado. 2.5273
Eighty years and more. 4.8088
Eimi. 2.11539
Einführung in die Bücherkunde zur deutschen Literaturwissenschaft. 5.8009
Das Einhorn. 2.13912
The Einsatzgruppen or murder commandos. 3.1105
The Einstein intersection. 2.12970
Einstein's theory of relativity. 5.1899
Einstein's universe. 5.2086
Der einzig mögliche Beweisgrund. 1.912
Eisenhower. 3.7822, 3.7833
The Eisenhower administration, 1953-1961. 3.7819
The Eisenhower administration and Black civil rights. 3.6664
Eisenhower and the American crusades. 3.7829
Eisenhower and the cold war. 3.7821
Eisenhower at war, 1943-1945. 3.7836
Eisenhower: captive hero. 3.7835
The Eisenhower diaries. 3.7832
Eisenhower: the President nobody knew. 3.7838
The Eisenhower years; affairs of state. 3.7831
Eisenhower's lieutenants. 3.981
Eisenstein. 2.3040
Either/or. 2.14016
The ejido; Mexico's way out. 4.2838
El, or, The last book. 2.4585
Elastic instability phenomena. 5.5861
Elasticity, plasticity and structure of matter. 5.2221
Elasto-hydrodynamic lubrication. 5.6242
Elbeuf during the revolutionary period, history and social structure. 3.2235
Elbow room. 2.13151
Elbridge Gerry, founding father and republican statesman. 3.6997
Elckerlijc. English. 2.13943

The Elder Pliny's chapters on the history of art. 1.4711
Elderly criminals. 4.6777
Elderly people and the environment. 5.316
Elders, shades, and women. 4.554
The Elders wrote. 3.5712
Eleanor and Franklin. 3.7788
Eleanor Dark. 2.10155
Eleanor of Aquitaine and the four kings. 3.1352
Eleanor: the years alone. 3.7789
Electing Black mayors; political action in the Black community. 4.8855
Electio Hugonis. English. 1.3267
The Election of 1976. 4.7960
The Election of 1980. 4.7962
The Election of 1984. 4.7963
Elections and party management. 4.8486
Elections and political development. 4.8713
Elections and the political order. 4.8115
Elections, politics, and society in Ireland, 1832-1885. 3.1842
An electoral atlas of Europe, 1968-1981. 4.8371
Electoral change in advanced industrial democracies. 4.7773
The electoral system in Britain, since 1918. 4.8484
Electra. 2.454
Electric circuit theory. 5.6271
The electric interurban railways in America. 4.4029
Electric machinery. 5.6308
Electric machinery and transformers. 5.6309
Electric motor handbook. 5.6311
Electric motors and their applications. 5.6312
Electric networks. 5.6280
Electric power at low temperatures. 5.6290
Electric power distribution system engineering. 5.6331
Electric power transmission systems. 5.6283
Electric waves. 5.2358
Electrical distribution engineering. 5.6332
Electrical engineering handbook. 5.6263
Electrical engineers' handbook. 5.6262
Electrical engineer's reference book. 5.6254
Electrical instruments and measurements. 5.6266
Electrical interactions in molecular biophysics. 5.4396
Electrical measurements. 5.2344
Electrical measurements and their applications. 5.2343
Electrical project management. 5.6267
The electrical researches of the Honourable Henry Cavendish. 5.2339
Electrical wiring and design. 5.6258
The electrical workers. 4.3527
Electricity economics. 4.3797
Electricity for rural America. 4.3806
Electro-chemical science. 5.2912
Electrochemical methods. 5.2911
Electrodynamics of continuous media. 5.2340, 5.2359
Electroheat. 5.6342
Electromagnetic fields. 5.2364-5.2365
Electromagnetic radiation. 5.2361
Electromagnetic theory. 5.2369
Electromagnetic waves and radiating systems. 5.6256
Electromagnetism 5.2407
Electromagnetism and life. 5.4207
Electromechanical dynamics. 5.2408
Electron densities in molecules and molecular orbitals. 5.2824
Electron spin resonance. 5.2413
Electron transfer reactions. 5.2880
Electronic and radio engineering. 5.6425
Electronic cinematography. 5.7006
Electronic circuits, discrete and integrated. 5.6464
Electronic communications systems. 5.6356
Electronic components and measurements. 5.6551
Electronic components handbook. 5.6480
Electronic design of microprocessor-based instruments and control systems. 5.6595
Electronic devices and circuit theory. 5.6458

Electronic devices for rehabilitation. 5.5036
Electronic displays. 5.6564-5.6565
Electronic engineering applications of two-port networks. 5.6454
Electronic instrumentation and measurements. 5.6550
Electronic interpretation of organic chemistry. 5.2889
Electronic materials and devices. 5.6498
Electronic media. 4.4057
Electronic music synthesis. 1.4459
Electronic principles. 5.6450, 5.6497
Electronic processes in non-crystalline materials. 5.2206
Electronic publishing plus. 5.7578
Electronic speech synthesis. 5.6568
Electronic surveying and navigation. 5.5830
Electronic techniques. 5.6482
Electronics engineers' handbook. 5.6451
Electrons and phonons. 5.2202
Electrons (+ and -), protons, photons, neutrons, and cosmic rays. 5.2398
Electrons and valence. 5.2838
Electrons in metals. 5.2204
Electroplating. 5.7067
Electrostatics and its applications. 5.2346
An elegant art. 4.835
Elegiac romance. 2.3524
Elegies. 2.765, 2.9672
Elegies and Camille. 2.4065
The elegies, and The songs and sonnets. 2.6454
Elegies, I-IV. 2.764
The Elegies of Albius Tibullus. 2.780
Elegy and iambus. 2.330
Elementary aspects of peasant insurgency in colonial India. 3.4261
Elementary atomic structure. 5.2078
Elementary computer graphics. 5.5650
Elementary differential equations. 5.1507
Elementary differential equations and boundary value problems. 5.1501
Elementary electromagnetic theory. 5.2367
Elementary engineering fracture mechanics. 5.5786
Elementary excitations in solids. 5.2207
The elementary forms of the religious life. 4.543
Elementary functional analysis. 5.1474
Elementary general relativity. 5.2099
Elementary general thermodynamics. 5.2254
Elementary geometry from an advanced standpoint. 5.1565
Elementary hearing science. 4.4368
An elementary historical new English grammar. 2.988
Elementary linear algebra. 5.1356
Elementary logic. 1.1216
Elementary mathematics from an advanced standpoint: arithmetic, algebra, analysis. 5.1111
An elementary middle English grammar. 2.952
Elementary nuclear theory. 5.2049
Elementary number theory. 5.1329
Elementary particle physics. 5.2392-5.2393, 5.2397
Elementary particles. 5.2390-5.2391, 5.2404
Elementary particles and symmetries. 5.2474
Elementary particles and their currents. 5.2457
Elementary plasma physics. 5.2383
An elementary primer for gauge theory. 5.2471
Elementary principles in statistical mechanics. 5.2177
Elementary school objectives. 4.10426
The elementary school principalship. 4.10650
Elementary school science and how to teach it. 4.10490
Elementary statistical thermodynamics. 5.2259
Elementary statistics. 4.1240
Elementary structural analysis. 5.5841
The elementary structures of kinship. 4.581
Elementary surveying. 5.5820
An elementary textbook of psychoanalysis. 5.4902
Elementary training for musicians. 1.4443
Elementary wave mechanics. 5.2145
Elements of acoustics. 5.2230

Elements of advanced quantum theory. 5.2125
Elements of cartography. 4.207
Elements of chordate anatomy. 5.4111
Elements of Christian philosophy. 1.392
Elements of classical thermodynamics for advanced students of physics. 5.2251
The elements of drama. 2.2792
The elements of editing. 2.2528
Elements of engineering electromagnetics. 5.2370
Elements of episodic memory. 5.337
Elements of general linguistics. 2.138
Elements of geographical hydrology. 4.290
Elements of group theory for physicists. 5.2140
The elements of industrial relations. 4.3434
The elements of input-output analysis. 4.1279
The elements of John Updike. 2.13383
Elements of lettering. 1.6599
Elements of map projection with applications to map and chart construction 4.212
Elements of materials science and engineering. 5.5768
Elements of mathematical biology. 5.3299
The elements of mathematical logic. 1.1221
Elements of number theory. 5.1327
The elements of Old English. 2.938
Elements of ordinary differential equations. 5.1503
Elements of photogrammetry, with air photo interpretation and remote sensing. 5.6990
Elements of physical geography. 4.242
Elements of physical metallurgy. 5.6774
Elements of port operation and management. 4.3950
Elements of practical coal mining. 5.6746
The elements of programming style. 5.1183
Elements of psychophysics. 5.242
Elements of pure economics. 4.1466
The elements of real analysis. 5.1436
Elements of semiology. 2.146
Elements of social organization. 4.521
Elements of solid state theory. 5.2200
Elements of statistical mechanics. 5.2178
Elements of strength of materials. 5.5780
The elements of style. 2.1036
Elements of the theory of computation. 5.1372
Elements of the theory of functions and functional analysis. 5.1485
Elena Quiroga. 2.5278
The elephant. 2.1741
The elephant man. 2.9796
Elephants and their habitats. 5.4040
Eleusis and the Eleusinian mysteries. 3.2645
Eleven essays in the European novel. 2.3507
Eleven verse plays. 2.11311
The Eleventh amendment and sovereign immunity. 4.9520
Elgar. 1.3861
Elgar, O. M. 1.3862
Elihu Root. 3.7446
Elihu Root and the conservative tradition. 3.7447
Elijah P. Lovejoy, abolitionist editor. 3.7253
Elinor Wylie, the portrait of an unknown lady. 2.12829
Eliot and his age. 2.11637
Eliot's compound ghost. 2.11644
Elisa. 2.4230
Elisabeth Louise Vigée Le Brun, 1755-1842. 1.6155
Elite accommodation in Canadian politics. 4.8292
Elite communication in Samoa. 3.5672
Elite conflict in a plural society. 3.4330
Elite politics in an ideological state. 4.5436
Elites, ethnographic issues. 4.4820
Elites in France. 4.5358
Elites in South Asia. 4.5421
Elites in the Middle East. 4.5396
Elizabeth Barrett to Miss Mitford. 2.7469
Elizabeth Bishop. 2.11387
Elizabeth Bishop and her art. 2.11386
Elizabeth Bowen. 2.8483
Elizabeth Bowen, an estimation. 2.8484
Elizabeth Bowen, an introduction to her novels. 2.8482

Elizabeth Cady Stanton, Susan B. Anthony, correspondence, writings, speeches. 4.5999
Elizabeth Gaskell. 2.7724-2.7726
Elizabeth I and her Parliaments. 3.1431
Elizabeth Madox Roberts. 2.12400
Elizabeth Tudor. 3.1426
Elizabethan acting. 2.3119
Elizabethan and Jacobean. 2.5635
Elizabethan and Jacobean comedy. 2.6226
Elizabethan and Jacobean tragedy. 2.6227
Elizabethan and metaphysical imagery. 2.5793
The Elizabethan conquest of Ireland. 3.1830
Elizabethan critical essays;. 2.5502
Elizabethan drama. 2.5869, 2.5872, 2.5875
Elizabethan drama, 1558-1642. 2.5870
Elizabethan drama and the viewer's eye. 2.5864
Elizabethan drama; modern essays in criticism. 2.5873
Elizabethan fiction. 2.6252
Elizabethan literature. 2.5638
Elizabethan lyrics from the original texts. 2.6151
The Elizabethan madrigal. 1.4234
The Elizabethan mind in literature. 2.5634
Elizabethan minor epics. 2.6152
Elizabethan plays. 2.6224
Elizabethan plays and players. 2.5867
Elizabethan poetry in the eighteenth century. 2.5791
Elizabethan poetry; modern essays in criticism. 2.5790
Elizabethan prose fiction. 2.6253
The Elizabethan puritan movement. 3.1429
The Elizabethan Renaissance. 4.5310
Elizabethan revenge tragedy, 1587-1642. 2.5883
An Elizabethan song book. 1.3442
The Elizabethan stage. 2.3288
Elizabethan stage conditions. 2.6864
Elizabethan stage conventions and modern interpreters. 2.5863
The Elizabethan underworld. 4.6789
The Elizabethan world picture. 2.5640
The Elizabethans and America. 3.6868
Elizabeth's army. 5.7304
Elle et lui. 2.4285
Ellen Glasgow. 2.11778, 2.11781, 2.11783
Ellen Glasgow and the ironic art of fiction. 2.11779
Ellen Glasgow's American dream. 2.11782
Ellen Terry. 2.3356
Ellen Terry and Bernard Shaw. 2.3355
Ellen Wilkinson, 1891-1947. 3.1678
Elliptic functions. 5.1497
Ellis Wynne. 2.840
Elmer Gantry. 2.12005
Éloges and other poems. 2.4602
Eloquent animals. 5.4095
Elusive reform. 4.10126
The elusive revolution. 3.2213
The elusive science. 5.636
Elvis. 1.4096
Emaki, narrative scrolls from Japan. 1.6334
The emancipated. 2.7732
The emancipation of French Indochina. 3.4431
The emancipation of the Jews in Britain. 3.3951
The emancipation of the Polish peasantry. 4.2857
The emancipation of women. 4.7146
The Emancipation proclamation. 3.7276
Émaux et camées. 2.4218
Embarkation. 2.13309
Embassy at war. 3.5029
Embassy for the Christians. 1.2190
An embassy to China. 3.4619
Embattled democracy. 3.8362
The embattled mountain. 3.1072
The embattled Northeast. 3.5835
The embattled philosopher. 1.814
Embattled reason. 4.4826
The embers and the stars. 1.1337
Embezzlers. 2.1566
Emblem and expression. 1.4939
The embouchure. 1.4548
The embroidered tent. 3.355
The embryology of behavior. 5.601

The embryology of early human behavior. 5.602
Embryology of the pig. 5.4131
Emergence of a free press. 4.9717
The emergence of a national economy, 1775-1815. 4.1874
Emergence of a new nation in a multi-polar world. 3.4150
The emergence of African capitalism. 4.2605
The emergence of agricultural science. 5.5239
The emergence of Arab nationalism. 3.3759
The emergence of Bangladesh. 3.4097
The emergence of Black politics in Senegal. 3.5392
The emergence of Christian Science in American religious life. 1.3330
The emergence of Conservative Judaism. 1.1919
The emergence of German as a literary language, 1700-1775. 2.1176
The emergence of Greek democracy, 800-400 B.C. 3.2575
The emergence of humankind. 4.450
The emergence of Indian nationalism: competition and collaboration in the later nineteenth century. 3.4274
The emergence of liberal Catholicism in America. 1.3180
The emergence of Lincoln. 3.7145
The Emergence of man. 4.448
The emergence of metropolitan America, 1915-1966. 4.6216
The emergence of modern Afghanistan. 3.4116
The emergence of modern America, 1865-1878. 4.1924
The emergence of modern Lithuania. 3.3316
The emergence of modern Turkey. 3.3588
The emergence of oligopoly. 4.3687
The emergence of philosophy of religion. 1.1545
The emergence of political catholicism in Italy. 3.2889
The emergence of Richard Wright. 2.12820
The emergence of Russian Panslavism, 1856-1870. 3.691
The emergence of society. 4.700
The emergence of the American university. 4.10068
The emergence of the British two-party system, 1760-1832. 4.8517
The emergence of the great powers, 1685-1715. 3.643
The emergence of the Latin American novel. 2.5312
The emergence of the modern Middle East. 3.3721
The emergence of the new South, 1913-1945. 3.8166
The emergence of the Palestinian-Arab national movement, 1918-1929. 3.3919
Emergence of the presidential nominating convention, 1789-1832. 4.8142
The emergence of the Republic of Bolivia. 3.9275
The emergence of the Romanian national State. 3.3548
The emergence of the theory of the firm. 4.1314
Emergencies. 5.5209
The Emergent middle school. 4.10503
The emerging city. 4.6293
The emerging Constitution. 4.7806
An emerging entertainment. 2.10512
Emerging from poverty. 4.2751
The emerging Republican majority. 4.8225
Emerging Southeast Asia. 4.2431
The emerging states of French Equatorial Africa. 3.5386
Emerson: a collection of critical essays. 2.11025
Emerson as poet. 2.11030
Emerson in his journals. 2.11022
Emerson on the soul. 2.11032
Emerson's angle of vision. 2.11029
Emerson's literary criticism. 2.2341
Emerson's Nature. 2.11019
The emigrants. 2.14042
The emigrants. 2.9989, 2.14098

Emigration in a south Italian town. 3.2945
Emil Nolde. 1.4998
Émile Durkheim. 4.4853
Émile Durkheim. 4.4752-4.4753
Émile Durkheim. 4.4755
Emile Durkheim, 1858-1917. 4.4757
Emile Durkheim and his sociology. 4.4758
Émile Durkheim, contributions to L'Année
   sociologique. 4.4852
Émile Durkheim; his life and work. 4.4754
Émile for today. 4.10186
Émile Zola. 2.4347, 2.4349-2.4350
Émile Zola; principes et caractères généraux de
   son oeuvre. 2.4351
Emily Brontë. 2.7460
Emily Dickinson. 2.11000
Emily Dickinson. 2.11001
Emily Dickinson. 2.11002, 2.11005, 2.11007
Emily Dickinson and her culture. 2.11009
Emily Dickinson's poetry. 2.10996
Emily Post's Etiquette. 1.1517
The Emin Pasha Relief Expedition, 1886-1890.
   3.5236
Eminent Chinese of the Ch'ing period
   (1644-1912) 3.4657
Eminent contributors to psychology. 5.8414
Eminent Indians who was who, 1900-1980, also
   annual diary of events. 3.347
The eminent tragedian. 2.3352
Eminent Victorians. 3.1624
Emissions trading, an exercise in reforming
   pollution policy. 4.2052
Emma. 2.7446
Emma Willard, pioneer educator of American
   women. 4.10158
Emmanuel Chabrier and his circle. 1.3833
Emmeline: the orphan of the castle. 2.7256
Emmy Noether. 5.1097
Emotion and meaning in music. 1.4368
The Emotions. 5.411
Emotions, cognition, and behavior. 5.549
Emperor and nation in Japan. 3.4940
The Emperor and the Roman Army, 31 BC-
   AD 235. 3.2793
The Emperor Frederick II of Hohenstaufen,
   immutator mundi. 3.2272
The Emperor Gaius (Caligula) 3.2799
Emperor Hirohito and his chief aide-de-camp.
   3.4972
The Emperor Julian. 3.2815
Emperor Michael Palaeologus and the West,
   1258-1282. 3.2677
Emperor Nicholas I of Russia. 3.3121
Emperor of China. 3.4717
The emperor of ice-cream. 2.9949
Empire and aftermath. 3.4987
Empire & commerce in Africa. 4.2580
Empire & commonwealth. 4.8270
Empire and liberty. 3.6882
Empire and nation: Letters from a farmer in
   Pennsylvania, John Dickinson. 3.6927
Empire in Brazil. 3.9210
Empire of knowledge. 1.57
The empire of reason. 3.6022
Empire of the Columbia. 3.8596
The empire of the seas. 3.6381
The empire of the St. Lawrence. 3.8671
The empire of the steppes. 3.4851
Empire on the Pacific. 3.6349
Empire to welfare state. 3.1650
Empire's children. 3.8912
Empires in the sun. 4.2027
Empires of the sky. 4.4077
Empirical studies of psychoanalytical theories.
   5.4910
Employers associations and industrial relations.
   4.3425
Employment & equilibrium. 4.1451
Employment in developing nations. 4.3200
Employment policies in the Soviet Union and
   Eastern Europe. 4.3230
Employment policy in a developing country.
   4.3234
Employment policy in developing countries.
   4.3236
Employment security in a free economy.
   4.3203
Emptiness. 1.1747

The empty fortress. 5.5110
An empty room. 2.1732
The empty space. 2.2790
Emrys ap Iwan. 2.841
En marge des vieux livres. 2.4260
The enchaféd flood. 2.2405
The enchanted glass. 2.5634
The enchanted loom. 5.4334
The enchanted voyage. 2.12238
The enchiridion. 1.3058
Enciclopedia dantesca. 2.4931
Enciclopedia dello spettacolo. 2.2783
Enciclopedia ragionata delle armi. English.
   5.7246
Enciclopedia universale dell' arte. 1.4575
Enclosed seas. 5.3542
The encomienda in New Spain. 3.8998
An encore for reform. 3.7524
Encounter at Shimoda. 3.6459
Encounter; group processes for interpersonal
   growth. 4.4935
Encounter with emancipation. 3.6565
Encounter with mathematics. 5.1107
Encounters. 4.5066
Encounters in history. 3.411
Encounters with Verdi. 1.4023
Encouraging girls in mathematics. 5.1062
Enculturation and socialization in an Ijaw
   village. 3.5353
Encyclopaedia Britannica. 1.13-1.14
Encyclopædia Britannica. 1.3480
Encyclopaedia for horsemen. 5.5446
Encyclopædia Iranica. 3.4065
Encyclopaedia Judaica. 3.3808
The encyclopaedia of chess. 4.1069
The Encyclopaedia of educational media
   communications and technology. 4.10321
The encyclopaedia of Gandhian thoughts.
   3.4306
The Encyclopaedia of ignorance. 5.836
Encyclopaedia of Indian culture. 3.4184
Encyclopaedia of Ireland. 3.1870
The Encyclopaedia of Islam. 3.3659
Encyclopaedia of Islam. 3.3660
The Encyclopaedia of medical ignorance.
   5.4552
An encyclopaedia of metallurgy and materials.
   5.6764
An encyclopaedia of New Zealand. 3.5592
Encyclopaedia of occupational health and
   safety. 5.5012
Encyclopaedia of Papua and New Guinea.
   3.5650
Encyclopaedia of swimming. 4.988
An encyclopaedia of textiles from the earliest
   times to the beginning of the 19th century.
   1.6674
Encyclopaedia of the social sciences. 4.1199
Encyclopaedia of the Upanisads. 1.1684
An encyclopaedic dictionary of heraldry. 3.285
The Encyclopaedic dictionary of physical
   geography. 4.237
Encyclopaedic dictionary of physics. 5.1888
The Encyclopedia Americana. 1.12
Encyclopedia buying guide. 5.7709
Encyclopedia Canadiana. 3.8655
Encyclopedia of aircraft. 5.6667
Encyclopedia of American agricultural history.
   5.5241
Encyclopedia of American antiques. 1.6512
Encyclopedia of American automobiles. 5.6621
Encyclopedia of American biography. 3.331
The encyclopedia of American crime. 4.6771
Encyclopedia of American economic history.
   4.1882
The encyclopedia of American facts and dates.
   3.6201
Encyclopedia of American history. 3.6202
Encyclopedia of American political history.
   3.6387
The encyclopedia of American religions.
   1.1873
Encyclopedia of anthropology. 4.408
The Encyclopedia of applied geology. 5.2941
Encyclopedia of archaeological excavations in
   the Holy Land. 3.3827
Encyclopedia of architects. 1.5208
Encyclopedia of artificial intelligence. 5.1009

Encyclopedia of associations. 1.54
Encyclopedia of aviation. 5.6641
Encyclopedia of banking and finance. 4.4443
The Encyclopedia of beaches and coastal
   environments. 4.269
Encyclopedia of bioethics. 5.3328
Encyclopedia of birds. 5.3940
Encyclopedia of Black America. 3.6614
Encyclopedia of business information sources.
   4.4261
Encyclopedia of cartoons. 1.5845
Encyclopedia of chemical technology. 5.6809
Encyclopedia of chemistry. 5.2596
The Encyclopedia of climatology. 5.2496
Encyclopedia of computer science and
   engineering. 5.1134
Encyclopedia of computer science and
   technology. 5.5572
Encyclopedia of Continental Army units
   3.6940
Encyclopedia of crime and justice. 4.6675
The encyclopedia of drug abuse. 4.6659
Encyclopedia of ecology. 5.3518
Encyclopedia of economics. 4.1273
Encyclopedia of educational research. 4.10165
Encyclopedia of energy. 5.6131
Encyclopedia of English and American poets
   and poetry. 2.5488
Encyclopedia of entrepreneurship. 4.1555
Encyclopedia of environmental science. 5.3511
Encyclopedia of environmental science and
   engineering. 5.5983
Encyclopedia of ethology. 5.4057
Encyclopedia of evolution. 5.3150
Encyclopedia of folk, country, & western music.
   1.3513
The encyclopedia of furniture. 1.6556
The encyclopedia of geochemistry and
   environmental sciences. 5.3101
The encyclopedia of geomorphology. 4.238
Encyclopedia of golf. 4.1032
Encyclopedia of governmental advisory
   organizations, 1988-89. 4.7898
Encyclopedia of horticulture. 5.5334
The encyclopedia of human behavior. 5.15
The Encyclopedia of Indian philosophies.
   1.179
Encyclopedia of Indian philosophies. 1.195
Encyclopedia of indoor gardening. 5.5355
Encyclopedia of information systems and
   services. 5.7607
Encyclopedia of Japan. 3.4871
The encyclopedia of jazz. 1.3517
The encyclopedia of jazz in the seventies.
   1.3534
The encyclopedia of jazz in the sixties. 1.3533
Encyclopedia of Jewish history. 3.3852
Encyclopedia of Latin America. 3.8959
Encyclopedia of library and information science.
   5.7695
The Encyclopedia of mammals. 5.3972
The Encyclopedia of management. 4.2635
The encyclopedia of marine resources. 5.5473
The encyclopedia of microscopy and
   microtechnique. 5.3285
The encyclopedia of military history from 3500
   B.C. to the present. 3.532
The Encyclopedia of mineralogy. 5.3009
Encyclopedia of music in Canada. 1.3538
Encyclopedia of mystery and detection. 2.71
The Encyclopedia of natural insect & disease
   control. 5.5417
The Encyclopedia of natural insect and disease
   control. 5.5417
Encyclopedia of North American birds. 5.3957
The encyclopedia of oceanography. 4.321
The Encyclopedia of paleontology. 5.3147
The Encyclopedia of philosophy. 1.101
Encyclopedia of physical education, fitness, and
   sports. 4.926
The Encyclopedia of physics. 5.1890
Encyclopedia of physics. 5.1889, 5.1978
Encyclopedia of polymer science and
   engineering. 5.6905
Encyclopedia of polymer science and
   technology. 5.6905
Encyclopedia of pop, rock and soul. 1.3527
Encyclopedia of psychology. 5.11-5.12

The Encyclopedia of religion. 1.1525
Encyclopedia of science & technology. 5.703
Encyclopedia of science and technology. 5.703
The encyclopedia of science fiction and fantasy through 1968. 5.8176
The encyclopedia of sedimentology. 5.3054
Encyclopedia of skiing. 4.998
Encyclopedia of social work. 4.6473
The Encyclopedia of soil science. 5.5267
The Encyclopedia of Southern history. 3.8113
The encyclopedia of sports. 4.927
Encyclopedia of statistical sciences. 5.1399
The Encyclopedia of structural geology and plate tectonics. 5.3124
The encyclopedia of superheroes. 2.74
Encyclopedia of television. 2.2848
Encyclopedia of textiles. 5.7077
Encyclopedia of the American Indian. 3.5700
The encyclopedia of the biological sciences. 5.3183
The encyclopedia of the chemical elements. 5.2831
The encyclopedia of the Jewish religion. 1.1896
The encyclopedia of the New York stage, 1920-1930. 2.3225
The encyclopedia of the United Nations and international agreements. 4.9224
An encyclopedia of the violin 1.4161
Encyclopedia of the world's rivers and lakes. 4.312
Encyclopedia of track and field athletics. 4.1048
Encyclopedia of U.S. Air Force aircraft and missile systems. 5.7411
Encyclopedia of urban planning. 4.6309
Encyclopedia of US Air Force aircraft and missile systems. 5.7411
The Encyclopedia of visual art. 1.4574
Encyclopedia of wines & spirits. 5.6892
Encyclopedia of world art. 1.4575
Encyclopedia of world costume. 4.827
An encyclopedia of world history. 3.526
Encyclopedia of world literature in the 20th century. 2.2674, 2.5304
The encyclopedia of world regional geology. 5.2942
The encyclopedia of world soccer. 4.1017
The encyclopedia of world theater. 2.3087
The encyclopedia of X-rays and gamma rays. 5.2322
Encyclopedic dictionary of electronic terms. 5.6448
Encyclopedic dictionary of mathematics. 5.1026
The Encyclopedic dictionary of psychology. 5.13
Encyclopedic dictionary of the sciences of language. 2.11
Encyclopedic directory of ethnic organizations in the United States. 3.6534
The Encyclopédie. 1.16
Encyclopédie, ou Dictionnaire raisonné des sciences, des arts et des métiers. 1.15
Encyclopædia of religion and ethics. 1.1524
The end and the beginning. 3.4129
End as a man. 2.12759
The end of American innocence. 3.6138
The end of an illusion. 5.4618
The end of arcadia. 3.8345
The end of colonial rule in West Africa. 3.5329
The end of empire. 4.7540
The end of French predominance in Europe. 4.4454
The end of ideology. 4.5125
The end of intelligent writing. 2.10417
The end of kings. 4.7560
The end of liberalism. 4.5033
The end of North's ministry, 1780-1782. 3.1568
The end of obscenity. 4.9874
The end of serfdom. 4.2856
End of summer. 2.11347
The end of the absolute monarchy in Siam. 3.4530
The end of the affair. 2.8746

The end of the ancient world and the beginnings of the Middle Ages. 3.2808
End of the battle. 2.9494
The end of the Byzantine Empire. 3.2675
End of the chapter. 2.8677
The end of the notables. 3.2176
The end of the old order in rural Europe. 4.5281
The end of the Russian Empire. 3.3183
The end of the World. 2.3667
The end of the world. 5.1874
The end of the world news. 2.9642
The end of Utopia. 2.8818
An end to innocence. 3.6108
End to torment. 2.12341
Endangered and threatened plants of the United States. 5.3647
Das Ende der Parteien, 1933. 3.2420
Endeavors in psychology. 5.118
Endeavors of art. 2.5865
Enderby. 2.9644
Enderby's dark lady. 2.9643
Enderby's dark lady, or, No end to Enderby. 2.9643
Endgame. 2.4406
Endless war. 3.9057
Endocrine disorders. 5.4990
Endocrines and aging. 5.4246
Endocrinology. 5.4247
Endocrinology and human behaviour. 5.4302
Ends and means. 4.5099
Ends and means in education. 4.9963
Endurance fitness. 5.4269
The Endurance of Frankenstein. 2.8092
The enduring Federalist. 4.7826
Enemies and friends. 3.4802
Enemies of promise. 2.5730
The enemy. 2.9048
Enemy at the gates. 3.996
Enemy salvoes. 2.2649
Enemy way music. 1.4309
Energetics, kinetics, and life. 5.2886
The energies of art. 2.2563
Energy. 5.6126
Energy, a guidebook. 5.6134
Energy and ecology. 5.3576
Energy and man. 5.6123
Energy and people. 5.6124
Energy and the atmosphere. 5.2506
Energy and the earth machine. 5.6121
The energy balance in Northeast Asia. 4.3710
Energy changes in biochemical reactions. 5.2884
Energy conservation in heating, cooling, and ventilating buildings. 5.6155
Energy conservation techniques for engineers. 5.6153
Energy deskbook. 5.6139
Energy, electric power, and man. 5.6284
Energy, force, and matter. 5.1933
Energy from alcohol. 5.6878
Energy from biomass. 5.6883
Energy from heaven and earth. 5.6137
Energy from the West. 5.6149
Energy future. 4.3715
Energy handbook. 5.6140
Energy, hydrocarbon fuels and chemical resources. 5.6135
Energy in a finite world. 5.6130
Energy in electromagnetism. 5.2406
Energy in the American economy, 1850-1975. 4.3720
Energy in the United States. 4.3745
Energy in transition, 1985-2010. 5.6148
Energy information guide. 5.8163
Energy management handbook. 5.6125
Energy management principles. 5.6152
Energy methods in stress analysis. 5.5735
Energy options. 5.6129
Energy or extinction? 5.6608
Energy principles in structural mechanics. 5.5843
Energy regulation by the Federal Power Commission. 4.3714
Energy research programs. 5.6144
Energy resource recovery in arid lands. 5.6146
Energy resources. 5.6132
Energy, resources & policy. 5.6122

Energy resources and supply. 5.6114
Energy resources in an uncertain future. 5.6145
Energy risk assessment. 5.6000
Energy saving lighting systems. 5.6340
Energy statistics. 5.8162
Energy, the biomass options. 5.6881
Energy, the conservation revolution. 5.6147
Energy, the next twenty years. 4.3716
Energy transformations in living matter. 5.4200
Energy use. 4.3717
Energybook. 5.6127
L'enfant noir 2.4849
Les enfants terribles. 2.4480
Enfin Malherbe. 2.4038
The enforcement of English apprenticeship. 4.3107
Enforcing international law. 4.8983
Engaged in writing. 2.9370
Engels on Capital. 4.1537
Engelsk-dansk ordbog. 2.920
Engine emissions; pollutant formation and measurement. 5.6048
The engineer of human souls. 2.1683
Engineering and operations in the Bell System. 5.6417
Engineering anthropometry methods. 5.5688
Engineering circuit analysis. 5.6270
Engineering economy. 5.5702
Engineering electromagnetic fields and waves. 5.6255
Engineering heat transfer. 5.6197
Engineering materials. 5.5757, 5.5760
Engineering mathematics. 5.5707
Engineering mechanics. 5.5733, 5.5736, 5.5740
Engineering network analysis. 5.6279
Engineering plasticity. 5.5790
Engineering reliability. 5.7042
Engineering statistics. 5.5673
Engineering surveying. 5.5825
Engineering thermodynamics. 5.6202
Engineers & electrons. 5.6251
Engineers and electrons. 5.6251
The engineers and the price system. 4.1969
The engineer's companion. 5.5671
The engineer's conscience. 5.5675
Engineer's desk reference. 5.5670
Engines of the mind. 5.1139
England, 1868-1914. 3.1594
England, 1870-1914. 3.1619
England and Ireland since 1800. 3.1846
England and the discovery of America, 1481-1620. 3.5990
England and the Middle East. 3.3591
England and the Near East: The Crimea. 3.688
England in Shakespeare's day. 2.6081
England in the age of Hogarth. 3.1531
England in the age of the American Revolution. 3.1557
England in the age of Wycliffe. 3.1371
England in the eighteen-eighties. 4.5303
England in the late Middle Ages. 3.1298
England in the later Middle Ages. 3.1358
England in the reign of Charles II. 3.1498
England in the Restoration and early eighteenth century. 2.5653
England in the Seven Years' War. 3.1279
England made me. 2.8747, 2.8758
England, their England. 2.9070
England under George I. 3.1522
England under Queen Anne ... 3.1537
England under the Stuarts. 3.1447
England under the Tudors. 3.1388
England's Helicon, 1600, 1614. 2.6153
English. 2.1001
English ancestral names. 3.309
English and American judges as lawmakers. 4.9748
The English and Scottish popular ballads. 2.6107
English architecture. 1.5360
English art. 1.4930
English art in the modern period, 1900-1939. 1.4941
English as a world language. 2.1109
The English Auden. 2.8391

English baronies. 3.299
English baroque architecture 1.5368
The English Bible. 1.2512
English bishops' chanceries, 1100-1250. 1.2439
The English book trade. 5.7549
English books & readers, 1475 to 1557. 5.7546
English-Canadian literature to 1900. 5.7888
The English carol. 1.4239
English carols. 2.6119
English cathedral music. 1.4247
The English Catholic community, 1570-1850. 1.3189
The English church, 1000-1066. 1.2435
The English church, 1066-1154. 1.2437
The English church & the papacy, from the conquest to the reign of John. 1.2438
The English comic characters. 2.6063
English comic drama, 1700-1750. 2.5914
English comic writers. 2.5538
The English common people. 4.5326
English common reader. 5.7686
The English Constitution. 4.8385
English constitutional conflicts of the seventeenth century, 1603-1689. 4.8399
English constitutional ideas in the fifteenth century. 4.8394
English constitutional theory and the House of Lords, 1556-1832. 4.8468
The English cotton industry and the world market, 1815-1896. 4.3853
The English country house. 1.5572
English country houses. 1.5573
English country houses: Baroque, 1685-1715. 1.5574
English country houses: Caroline, 1625-1685. 1.5565
The English countryman, his life and work, A.D. 1500-1900. 5.5259
English critical essays (sixteenth, seventeenth, and eighteenth centuries). 2.5498
English critical essays, twentieth century. 2.2506, 2.5499
English critical texts, 16th century to 20th century. 2.2505
English culture and the decline of the industrial spirit, 1850-1980. 3.1596
The English curriculum under fire. 2.929
The English decorated style. 1.5361
English decoration in the 18th century. 1.6543
English democratic ideas in the seventeenth century. 4.8398
The English dialect dictionary. 2.1113
English dialects. 2.1110
The English dictionary from Cawdrey to Johnson, 1604-1755. 2.1077
English diplomatic administration, 1259-1339. 4.9098
English discovery of America to 1585. 3.5989
The English drama, 1485-1585. 2.5852
English drama, 1660-1800. 5.7955
English drama, 1900-1950. 5.7956
English drama, a critical introduction. 2.5844
English drama and theatre, 1800-1900. 5.7951
English drama, excluding Shakespeare. 5.7952
English drama in transition, 1880-1920. 2.6244
English drama to 1660, excluding Shakespeare. 5.7957
English dramatic companies, 1558-1642. 2.3292
The English dramatic critics. 2.5845
The English elegy. 2.5781
English emblem books. 2.5792
The English epic and its background. 2.5569
The English essays of Edward Gibbon. 2.7039
The English fact in Quebec. 3.8822
English farming, past and present. 5.5248
English fiction, 1660-1800. 5.7967
The English folk-play. 2.5849
English, French, German and Italian techniques of singing. 1.4565
English furniture designs of the eighteenth century. 1.6574
English furniture styles from 1500 to 1830. 1.6571
English gardens and landscapes, 1700-1750. 5.5382
An English grammar. 2.998
English grammar. 2.1000

English grammar for students of French. 2.984
English grammar for students of German. 2.985
English grammatical categories and the tradition to 1800. 2.983
English historical documents. 3.1232
English history. 3.1240
English history, 1914-1945. 3.1641
The English history play in the age of Shakespeare. 2.5877
The English house. 1.5566
The English humourists. 2.6067
The English infant school and informal education. 4.10406
The English Jacobin novel 1780-1805. 2.5994
The English Jewry under Angevin kings. 3.3949
English journey. 3.1731
The English judiciary in the age of Glanvill and Bracton, c. 1176-1239. 4.9426
English keyboard music before the nineteenth century. 1.4159
English landed society in the eighteenth century. 4.5306
English landed society in the nineteenth century. 4.5311
The English language. 2.963, 2.977
The English language in America. 2.1124
English language in modern times, since 1400. 2.974
English language notes. 5.8276
English literary criticism. 2.2503, 2.5501
English literary criticism: 17th and 18th centuries. 2.2502
English literary criticism: restoration and 18th century. 2.5506
English literary criticism: the Renascence. 2.2504
English literary history. 5.8276
English literary journals, 1900-1950. 5.7918
English literature. 2.2515
English literature, 1660-1800. 5.7935
English literature, 1789-1815. 2.5685
English literature, 1815-1832. 2.5700
English literature and society in the eighteenth century. 2.5676
English literature at the close of the middle ages 2.5611
English literature from Dryden to Burns. 2.5625
English literature in history, 1730-80. 2.5690
English literature in the earlier seventeenth century, 1600-1660. 2.5644
English literature in the early eighteenth century, 1700-1740. 2.5678
English literature in the mid-eighteenth century. 2.5657
English literature in the sixteenth century. 2.5630
English literature of the late seventeenth century. 2.5652
English local administration in the Middle Ages. 4.8873
English lordship in Ireland, 1318-1361. 3.1826
English Loyalists and the French Revolution. 3.1572
English lyrics of the XIIIth century. 2.6130
The English madrigal composers. 1.4233
English madrigal verse, 1588-1623. 2.6124
English medieval sculpture. 1.5682
The English medieval town. 4.6258
English melodrama. 2.5919
English men and manners in the eighteenth century. 3.1533
English metrists. 2.1042
The English miniature. 1.6392
English miracle plays, moralities and interludes. 2.6207
English monarchs. 3.1382
The English Moore, or, The Mock-mariage. 2.6560
English moral interludes. 2.6203
The English morality and related drama. 2.5854
The English musical renaissance. 1.3716
English mystery plays. 2.6204
The English mystical tradition. 1.3081
The English navigation laws. 4.3965

English neoclassical art. 1.4938
The English newspaper. 2.3684
English-Norwegian dictionary. 2.918
The English novel. 2.5940, 2.5947-2.5948, 5.7961
English novel, 1578-1956. 5.7959
The English novel, 1740-1850. 5.7960
English novel explication. 5.7970
The English novel, form and function. 2.5949
The English novel from Dickens to Lawrence. 2.6020
The English novel in transition, 1885-1940. 2.6036
The English ode from Milton to Keats. 2.5784
English-Old English, Old English-English dictionary. 2.947
English overseas trade statistics, 1697-1808. 4.4224
The English parish church. 1.5527
The English parliament in the Middle Ages. 4.8457
English pastoral poetry. 2.5583
English pastoral poetry, from the beginnings to Marvell. 2.6126
English peasant farming. 5.5250
The English peasantry in the later Middle Ages. 4.2849
The English people and the English revolution, 1640-1649. 3.1483
The English people on the eve of colonization, 1603-1630. 3.1454
English period furniture. 1.6573
English philosophy since 1900. 1.737
English phonetics. 2.1015
English place-names. 3.1734
English plays of the nineteenth century. 2.6239
The English poetic mind. 2.5759
English poetic theory, 1825-1865. 2.2724
English poetry. 2.5747, 2.5769
English poetry, 1660-1800. 5.7973
English poetry in a changing society, 1780-1825. 2.5811
English poetry in the sixteenth century. 2.5786
English poetry of the mid and late eighteenth century. 2.6166
English poetry of the nineteenth century. 2.6170
English political caricature. 1.5851
English political thought in the nineteenth century. 4.7289
English pronunciation 1500-1700. 2.1020
English pronunciation from the fifteenth to the eighteenth century. 2.1019
English prose and criticism, 1900-1950. 5.7975
English prose fiction. 5.7964
English prose fiction, 1558-1700. 2.5993
English prose of the Victorian era. 2.6264
English prose of the XVII century. 2.6255
English prose, prose fiction, and criticism to 1660. 5.7976
English prose style. 2.1039
English provincial society from the Reformation to the Revolution. 3.1737
The English radical tradition, 1763-1914. 3.1519
The English Reformation. 1.2355
English reformers. 1.2357
English religious drama of the Middle Ages 2.5850
The English Renaissance 1510-1688. 2.5519
The English Renaissance miniature. 1.6355
English Renaissance prose fiction, 1500-1660. 5.7962
The English revolution, 1688-1689. 3.1513
English romanesque art, 1066-1200. 1.4934
English romanesque sculpture, 1066-1140. 1.5684
The English romantic poets. 2.5818
English romantic poets. 2.5815, 2.6174
English romantic writers. 2.6090
English-Russian dictionary. 2.1234
English-Russian, Russian-English dictionary. 2.1233
English satire. 2.6064
English satires on women, 1660-1750. 2.5695
English scholars, 1660-1730. 3.1210
English schools in the Middle Ages. 4.10114
The English sermon. 1.3308

The English settlements. 3.1316
English society in the early middle ages, (1066-1307) 3.1333
English society in the eleventh century. 4.2257
English sounds and inflections. 2.1011
English sources of 'The scarlet letter.' 2.6499
English spelling and spelling reform. 2.1027
The English Spenserians. 2.6155a
English tests and reviews. 5.7978
The English theatre. 2.3281
English theatre music in the eighteenth century. 1.4229
English thought in the nineteenth century. 3.1595
English Towns in transition 1500-1700. 4.6253
English toy theatre. 2.2835
English trade in the fifteenth century. 4.4226
English Trotula. English & English (Middle English) 5.5044
English urban life, 1776-1851. 4.5329
The English utilitarians. 1.720-1.721
The English utilitarians and India. 4.8698
The English verb. 2.1029
English verse between Chaucer and Surrey. 2.6135
English versification, 1570-1980. 5.7980
English villagers of the thirteenth century. 3.1331
The English vision. 5.5371
English wayfaring life in the Middle Ages. 3.1332
English works. 2.6429
The English works of Thomas Hobbes of Malmesbury. 1.670
The Englishman. 2.6270
The Englishman and his history. 3.1207
The Englishness of English art. 1.4931
The enigma of Felix Frankfurter. 4.9815
The enigma of Soviet petroleum. 4.3783
The Enigma of time. 5.1755
The enigmatic chancellor. 3.2346
Enjoyment of laughter. 2.3784
The enjoyment of mathematics. 5.1260
The enjoyment of music. 1.4430
Enlarged business atlas and shippers' guide 1889-1910. 4.155
Enlarging the temple. 2.10506
The Enlightenment; a comprehensive anthology. 1.434
The Enlightenment, an interpretation. 1.435
The Enlightenment in America. 3.6025
The Enlightenment in national context. 3.79
The Enneads. 1.341
Ennin's travels in T'ang China. 3.4618
Enormous changes at the last minute. 2.13233
The enormous room. 3.817
Enquiries concerning human understanding and concerning the principles of morals. 1.697
The enquiries of Doctor Eszterhazy. 2.12966
Enquiry. 4.7420
Enquiry into plants and minor works on odoùrs and weather signs. 2.395
Ensayos de literatura hispánica. 2.5094
Ensayos sobre poesía española. 2.5115
Ensk-íslensk orthabók: meth alfraethilegu ívafi. 2.916
Entailment. 5.1036
Entangling alliance. 3.7026
Enter foot and horse. 4.1187
Entering industry. 5.5676
Entering space. 5.6710
Entering the maze. 3.200
Enterprise denied. 4.3982
Enterprise guidance in Eastern Europe. 4.2740
Enterprise in the nonprofit sector. 4.2722
The enterprise of Florida. 3.8273
The enterprising Americans: a business history of the United States. 4.1931
The entertainer. 2.9207
Entertaining Satan. 5.678
Enthusiasm. 1.2238
Enthusiast in wit. 2.7231
Entomology. 5.8164
The entrepreneur. 4.1558
Entrepreneur and gentleman. 4.3866
Entrepreneurs in cultural context. 4.1556
Entrepreneurship and economic development. 4.1552

Entretiens familiers avec L.-F. Céline. 2.4507
Entretiens sur la métaphysique. 1.799
The entry of the Slavs into Christendom. 1.2313
Environment and archeology. 4.699
Environment and cultural behavior. 4.380
Environment and culture. 5.316
The environment as hazard. 4.319
The Environment for entrepreneurship. 4.1557
The environment, from surplus to scarcity. 4.1849
Environment, natural systems, and development. 4.1840
Environment, North and South. 4.1818
The environment of early man in the British Isles. 4.731
Environment, planning, and the multinational corporation. 4.2738
Environmental analysis of transportation systems. 5.6002
Environmental and occupational medicine. 5.5009
Environmental awakening. 5.3224
Environmental biology. 5.3303
Environmental chemistry. 5.2630
Environmental chemistry of the elements. 5.2624
Environmental conservation. 5.5306
The environmental decade in court. 4.9570
The Environmental effects of nuclear war. 5.7234
Environmental effects of off-road vehicles. 5.3575
Environmental engineering. 5.5987
Environmental engineering and sanitation. 5.4668
Environmental engineers' handbook. 5.5986
Environmental geology. 5.2972, 5.5890
Environmental geomorphology and landscape conservation. 4.262
Environmental impact analysis. 5.5994
Environmental impact assessment. 5.5995
Environmental impact of roads and traffic. 5.6001
Environmental improvement through economic incentives. 4.1841
Environmental management planning for traffic. 4.3923
Environmental perception and behavior. 4.30
Environmental physiology. 5.4232
Environmental physiology of animals. 5.4203
Environmental policy under Reagan's executive order. 4.2075
Environmental politics and the coal coalition. 4.3746
Environmental protection. 5.5990
Environmental quality and residuals management. 4.1845
Environmental quality and water development. 5.5977
Environmental reform in American literature from the Puritans through Whitman. 2.10345
Environmental regulation and the U.S. economy. 4.2076
Environmental regulation of industrial plant siting. 4.2068
Environmental scenography. 2.3140
Environmental trends. 5.5991
Environmentalists, vanguard for a new society. 4.1847
Environments and organizations. 4.4908
Envoy extraordinary. 2.8705
The envoy from mirror city. 2.10223
Enzymatic synthesis of DNA. 5.4405
Enzyme kinetics. 5.4415
Enzyme nomenclature, 1978. 5.4414
Enzyme structure and mechanism. 5.4412
The Enzymes. 5.4411
Ephesians. 1.2717
Epic and romance. 2.2624
Epic and romance in the Argonautica of Apollonius. 2.421
The epic in the making. 2.1215
Epic mythology. 1.1687
The epic of Russian literature from its origins through Tolstoy. 2.1250
The epic strain in the English novel. 2.5962

Epics of the Philippines. 2.2293
Epictetus. 2.366
Epicurus. 1.331
Epicurus and his philosophy. 1.330
Epicurus, the extant remains. 2.451
Epidemiology. 5.4684
Epigrams. 2.677
Epiphany in the modern novel. 2.6052
The Episcopal Church in the United States, 1789-1931. 1.3314
The episcopate and the primacy. 1.3004
Epistemological problems of economics. 4.1471
The epistle of the prison of human life; with, An epistle to the Queen of France; and, Lament on the evils of the civil war. 2.3973
Epistle to Bathurst. 2.7192
Epistle to Diognetus. 2.327
The Epistle to the Romans. 1.2708
The Epistles of John. 1.2726
The epistles of St. Clement of Rome and St. Ignatius of Antioch. 1.2208
Epistolarity. 2.3477
The epistolary novel. 2.3478
Epitaph for a spy. 2.8380
Epitaph for George Dillon. 2.9208
Epitaph of a small winner. 2.5476
The epithalamions, anniversaries, and epicedes. 2.6456
Epoch and artist. 2.8851
An epoch of miracles. 2.2332
Epochs of Greek and Roman biography. 2.273
Eponymic syndromes, and diseases, and their synonyms. 5.4487
Eponyms dictionaries index. 2.1074
La epopeya castellana a través de la literatura española. 2.5122
L'Époque contemporaine. 3.189
Epstein. 1.5692
Equal educational opportunity for Blacks in U.S. higher education. 4.10857
Equal employment issues. 4.3114
Equal employment policy for women. 4.3240
The Equal Pay Act. 4.9566
Equal pay for comparable worth. 4.3259
Equal rights. 3.8684
The equal rights amendment. 4.9693
Equal rights for children. 4.5741
Equal their chances. 4.10785
Equal under law. 3.7265
Equalities. 4.4959
Equality. 4.4960, 4.7653
Equality and efficiency, the big tradeoff. 4.1322
Equality and liberty. 4.7652
Equality and liberty: theory and practice in American politics. 4.7690
Equality by statute. 4.9685
Equality in America. 4.7654, 4.7689
Equality of educational opportunity. 4.10783
Equality under the constitution. 4.9697
The equilibrist. 2.12370
Equilibrium analysis. 4.1964
Equilibrium thermodynamics. 5.2240
Equilibrium thermodynamics for engineers and scientists. 5.2260
Equitable payment. 4.3132
Equity issues in radioactive waste management. 5.6054
ERA, may a state change its vote? 4.9634
The era of Franklin D. Roosevelt. 3.7754
The era of good feelings. 3.7116
The era of Reconstruction, 1865-1877. 3.7473
The era of reform, 1830-1860. 4.5169
The era of the French revolution (1715-1815). 3.2042
The era of the muckrakers. 3.7512
Era of the oath. 3.7306
The era of Theodore Roosevelt, 1900-1912. 3.7698
The era of Trujillo, Dominican dictator. 3.9123
The erasers. 2.4690
Erasmus of Christendom. 1.414
Erec. 2.13531
Érec et Énide. 2.3945
Erewhon. 2.7512
Erewhon revisited. 2.7512
Ergodic problems of classical mechanics. 5.1654

Ergodic theory. 5.1461, 5.1605
Ergodic theory and topological dynamics.
    5.1604
Ergodic theory, randomness, and dynamical
    systems. 5.1462
Ergonomic design for people at work. 5.5616
Eric Mendelsohn. 1.5424
Eric Partridge in his own words. 2.924
Eric Voegelin's thought. 1.1064
Erich Fromm. 1.594
Erich Maria Remarque. 2.13849
Ericksonian approaches to hypnosis and
    psychotherapy. 5.4898
Erie. 3.8429
Erik Dorn. 2.11823
Erik Erikson, an introduction. 5.97
Erik Satie. 1.3964
Erin's daughters in America. 3.6551
Ernest. 2.11857
Ernest Bevin. 3.1700
Ernest Hemingway. 2.11856
Ernest Hemingway; a life story. 2.11853
Ernest Hemingway, selected letters, 1917-1961.
    2.11852
Ernst Barlach. 1.5716
Eros and civilization. 5.174
Erosion and soil productivity. 5.5291
The erotic arts. 1.6741
The erotic poems. 2.747
Erotica. 2.620
Errand into the wilderness. 3.6141
Errors and expectations. 2.1034
Ersatz in the Confederacy. 4.1925
Erskine Caldwell. 2.11459
ERTS-I. 5.2974
Eruptive rocks. 5.3048
Erzählende Schriften. 2.13809
Die Erzählungen. 2.13880
Erzählungen, Hörspiele, Aufsätze. 2.13682
The escape from Elba. 3.2138
Escape from freedom. 4.5024
Escape from the doll's house. 4.10842
Eschatology and ethics in the teaching of Jesus.
    1.2663
Esdaile's Manual of bibliography. 5.7677
ESEA; the Office of Education administers a
    law. 4.9587
Esenin. 2.1556
Eskimo art. 3.5882
Eskimo poems from Canada and Greenland.
    2.2314
Eskimos. 3.5874
Eskimos and explorers. 3.5879
Eskimos, Chicanos, Indians. 4.2094
The Eskimos of Bering Strait, 1650-1898.
    3.5883
Essai d'explication du Cimetière marin. 2.4765
Essai sur la nature du commerce en général.
    4.1406
Essais. 2.4440
An essay concerning human understanding.
    1.674
An essay in aid of a grammar of assent.
    1.2231
An essay in defence of the female sex. 4.5916
An essay on Anaxagoras. 1.235
An essay on comedy. 2.2824
An essay on economic growth and planning.
    4.2768
An essay on man. 1.978
An essay on metaphysics. 1.1266
An essay on nature. 1.653
An essay on philosophical method. 1.1305
Essay on rime. 2.12462
An essay on taste (1759) 1.4641
An essay on the distribution of wealth and on
    the sources of taxation. 4.1512
Essay on the freedom of the will 1.1498
An essay on the nature & significance of
    economic science. 1.1452
An essay on the principle of population.
    4.1587
An essay on the production of wealth. 4.1421
An essay on the psychology of invention in the
    mathematical field 5.1042
Essay on the true art of playing keyboard
    instruments. 1.4541
An essay on the Vita nuova. 2.4922

Essays. 1.665, 2.7692
Essays, 1958-1962, on atomic physics and
    human knowledge. 5.1898
Essays & addresses on the philosophy of
    religion. 1.1550
Essays and introductions. 2.8333
Essays and poems and simplicity, a comedy.
    2.7172
The essays, articles, and reviews of Evelyn
    Waugh. 2.9482
Essays by Francis Bacon. 2.6430
Essays in American historiography. 3.6220
Essays in American history dedicated to
    Frederick Jackson Turner. 3.6196
Essays in ancient and modern historiography.
    3.400
Essays in biography. 3.1685
Essays in Canadian economic history. 4.2116
Essays in conceptual analysis. 1.1148
Essays in criticism and research. 2.5555
Essays in development economics. 4.2762
Essays in economic history. 4.1723
Essays in economic thought. 4.1270
Essays in German and comparative literature.
    2.13472
Essays in Hegelian dialectic. 1.947
Essays in historical materialism. 3.516
Essays in idleness. 2.2058
Essays in imperial government. 4.8920
Essays in international economic theory.
    4.4138
Essays in Jewish thought. 1.1902
Essays in Kant's aesthetics. 1.905
Essays in linguistics 2.6
Essays in literary criticism. 2.2592
Essays in medieval culture. 2.2629
Essays in modern literary criticism. 2.2457
Essays in monetary economics. 4.4473
Essays in monetary theory. 4.4480
Essays in musical analysis. 1.4186, 1.4505
Essays in neobehaviorism. 5.216
Essays in our changing order. 4.1271
Essays in persuasion. 4.1776
Essays in philosophy. 1.596
Essays in positive economics. 4.1262
Essays in radical empiricism. 1.597
Essays in religion and morality. 1.1540
Essays in Russian literature; the conservative
    view: Leontiev, Rozanov, Shestov. 2.1261
Essays in science and philosophy. 5.945
Essays in social anthropology. 4.658
Essays in sociological theory. 4.4733
Essays in Swedish history. 3.3387
Essays in the economic and social history of
    Tudor and Stuart England, in honour of R.
    H. Tawney. 4.2266
Essays in the history of early American law.
    4.9486
Essays in the history of embryology and
    biology. 5.4120
Essays in the history of ideas. 1.608
Essays in the philosophy of science. 1.623
Essays in the public philosophy. 4.7459
Essays in the theory of economic growth.
    4.2769
Essays in the theory of society. 4.4830
Essays in Zen Buddhism, first series. 1.1754
Essays by Zen Buddhism (second series) 1.1753
Essays by Zen Buddhism (third series) 1.1749
Essays, letters, and reviews. 2.7349
Essays, literary & educational. 2.5556
Essays of E. B. White. 2.12702
The essays of Henry Timrod. 2.11259
Essays of three decades. 2.13821
Essays on accountancy. 4.4400
Essays on actions and events. 135
Essays on African population. 4.1708
Essays on American Antebellum politics,
    1840-1860. 3.7142
Essays on Aristotle's ethics. 1.287
Essays on Bentham. 4.9368
Essays on Biblical interpretation. 1.2518
Essays on career education and English, K-12.
    4.10830
Essays on Czech literature. 2.1654
Essays on developing economies. 4.1810
Essays on economic dependence in perspective.
    4.2145

Essays on economic policy. 4.2785
Essays on economic stability and growth.
    4.1439
Essays on education. 4.10175
Essays on ego psychology. 5.160
Essays on Elizabethan drama. 2.5872
Essays on English and American literature.
    2.5553
Essays on faith. 1.2261
Essays on Fielding's Miscellanies. 2.7026
Essays on Freedom and power. 4.7623
Essays on geography and economic
    development 4.4119
Essays on Goldsmith. 2.7044
Essays on government. 4.7475
Essays on Gupta culture. 3.4239
Essays on Haitian literature. 2.4834
Essays on J.S. Bach. 1.3778
Essays on literature and politics, 1932-1972.
    2.2653
Essays on literature and society in Southeast
    Asia. 2.2255
Essays on logic and language. 1.1149
Essays on medieval civilization. 3.129
Essays on Middle English literature. 2.5603
Essays on modernization of underdeveloped
    societies. 4.5481
Essays on money and inflation. 4.4489
Essays on moral development. 5.607
Essays on music. 1.3470
Essays on New Testament themes. 1.2652
Essays on New Zealand literature. 2.10196
Essays on performance theory, 1970-1976.
    2.3099
Essays on population policy. 4.1671
Essays on primitivism and related ideas in the
    Middle Ages. 3.140
Essays on Schubert. 1.3975
Essays on sex equality. 4.5893
Essays on Shakespeare and other Elizabethans.
    2.6700
Essays on sociology and social psychology.
    4.4832
Essays on the American Revolution. 3.6897
Essays on the caste system. 3.4173
Essays on the depopulation of Melanesia.
    3.5617
Essays on the eighteenth-century English stage.
    2.3306
Essays on the eighteenth-century novel. 2.6001
Essays on the law of nature. 1.673
Essays on the nature and principles of taste.
    1.4640
Essays on the Philippine novel in English.
    2.10134
Essays on the ritual of social relations. 4.523
Essays on the scientific study of politics.
    4.7208
Essays on the Semitic background of the New
    Testament. 1.2649
Essays on the sociology of knowledge. 4.4815
Essays on 'the welfare state' 4.5321
Essays on the works of Erasmus. 2.825
Essays on Troilus and Criseyde. 2.6336
Essays on value and distribution. 4.1440
Essays on Walras. 1.1367
Essays on Walter Prescott Webb. 3.6266
Essays on Wittgenstein's Tractatus. 1.1228
Essays, plays and sundry verses. 2.6954
Essays, reviews, and reports. 4.1369
Essays (selected) 2.7843
Essays, speeches & public letters. 2.11658
The essence of Bruckner. 1.3828
Essence of decision. 3.6480
The essence of Judaism. 1.1963
The essence of Plotinus. 1.340
The essence of reasons. 1.996
Essential articles for the study of Thomas
    More. 3.1408
The essential Brecht. 2.13707
The essential Comte. 1.819
The Essential Frankfurt School reader. 4.4872
The essential Gandhi. 3.4304
Essential Japanese. 2.1989
The essential Jung. 5.165
The essential Kropotkin. 4.7182
The essential Lippmann. 4.7460
The essential Montessori. 4.10209

The essential Newman. 1.3137
Essential papers on borderline disorders. 5.4965
Essential papers on depression. 5.4932
Essential papers on narcissism. 5.4947
Essential papers on object relations. 5.200
The essential Paul Elmer More. 2.11178
The essential Piaget. 5.593
Essential relativity. 5.2091
The essential Stalin. 3.3232
The essential tension. 5.909
The essential works of anarchism. 4.7183
The essential writings of Merleau-Ponty. 1.840
Essentials of accounting. 4.4401
Essentials of behavior. 5.218
The essentials of Buddhist philosophy. 1.2158
Essentials of economic theory. 4.1424
Essentials of educational research. 4.10285
Essentials of English grammar. 2.993
Essentials of fitness. 5.5024
Essentials of forestry practice. 5.5424
Essentials of genetics for nurses. 5.4752
Essentials of human embryology. 5.4163
The essentials of Indian philosophy 1.181
The essentials of Lenin. 3.3143
Essentials of materials science. 5.5761
Essentials of Padé approximants. 5.1975
The essentials of psycho-analysis. 5.140
Essentials of psychological testing. 5.202
L'essor industriel et l'impérialisme colonial (1878-1904) 3.716
The establishment of human antiquity. 4.692
The establishment of the Balkan national states, 1804-1920. 3.3525
The establishment of the European hegemony, 1415-1715. 4.8894
Esther. 2.10889
Esther Waters. 2.7956
Esthetics: lectures and essays. 1.1387
Esthetics of music. 1.4391
The esthetics of negligence. 2.4030
Estimates in art. 1.5895
Estonia. 3.3311
Estranging dawn. 2.11176
Estuaries. 4.338, 4.340
Estuaries and enclosed seas. 5.3542
Estuarine and wetland processes, with emphasis on modeling. 4.339
The estuarine ecosystem. 5.3543
The etchings of James McNeill Whistler. 1.6489
The etchings of the Tiepolos. 1.6491
L'été. 2.4445
The eternal crossroads. 2.13217
Eternal hope. 1.2941
Eternal lawyer. 4.9399
Eternal life? 1.1621
Eternal moment. 2.8642
The eternal present. 1.4692
The eternal slum. 4.3498
Ethan Frome. 2.12692
The ethereal aether. 5.2272
Etherege and the seventeenth-century comedy of manners. 2.7013
The ethic of time. 2.6835
The ethical and political works of Motse. 1.172
Ethical dilemmas and nursing practice. 5.5195
Ethical dilemmas in social service. 4.6491
The ethical foundations of Marxism. 1.1036
Ethical issues in death and dying. 5.4575
Ethical issues in sex therapy and research. 5.4838
Ethical studies. 1.1431
Ethical systems and legal ideals. 4.9360
Ethical theory. 1.1406
Ethical theory and business. 4.4268
Ethico-religious concepts in the Qur'ān. 1.2035
Ethics. 1.1479-1.1480
Ethics. 1.1407, 1.1437-1.1438, 1.1448
Ethics and language. 1.1410
Ethics and nuclear deterrence. 1.2239
The ethics and selected letters. 1.1097
Ethics and society. 1.1485
Ethics and the management of computer technology. 4.4272
Ethics and the multinational enterprise. 4.4273a

Ethics and the rule of law. 1.1415
Ethics and the urban ethos. 1.2927
Ethics at the edges of life. 5.4568
Ethics, economics, and the law. 4.9370
Ethics for bureaucrats. 4.7900
Ethics from a theocentric perspective. 1.1472
Ethics in medicine. 5.4560
Ethics in social and behavioral research. 4.1223
The ethics of ambiguity. 1.1465
The ethics of deliberate death. 5.4576
The ethics of fetal research. 5.4607
The ethics of G. E. Moore. 1.754
The ethics of war. 5.7165
Ethics of withdrawal of life-support systems. 5.4581
Ethics since 1900. 1.1421
Ethics without God. 1.1459
Ethiopia. 3.5243, 4.2618
Ethiopia, a country study. 3.5239
Ethiopia, an heretical revolution? 3.5252
Ethiopia at bay. 3.5248
Ethiopia, Great Britain, and the United States, 1941-1974. 3.5250
Ethiopia, politics, economics, and society. 3.5253
The Ethiopian revolution. 3.5251
An Ethiopian romance. 2.474
The Ethiopians. 3.5240
The ethnic almanac. 3.6504
Ethnic America. 3.6528
Ethnic American minorities. 3.6518
Ethnic and tourist arts. 1.4691
Ethnic change. 4.616
Ethnic chauvinism. 4.617
Ethnic conflict. 3.4364
The ethnic dilemma in social services. 4.6616
The ethnic dimension in American history. 3.6523
Ethnic diversity and conflict in Eastern Europe. 4.5279
The ethnic factor in family structure and mobility. 4.5592
The Ethnic frontier. 3.8421
Ethnic groups of insular Southeast Asia. 4.641
Ethnic groups of mainland Southeast Asia 3.4387
Ethnic identity. 4.618
The Ethnic image in modern American literature, 1900-1950. 2.10703
The ethnic imperative. 3.6530
Ethnic information sources of the United States. 3.6507
Ethnic leadership in America. 4.4947
The ethnic myth. 3.6531
Ethnic perspectives in American literature. 2.2690
The ethnic phenomenon. 4.6455
Ethnic plurality in India. 3.4203
Ethnic politics in Malaysia. 3.4547
The ethnic revival. 4.7491
Ethnic-sensitive social work practice. 4.6615
Ethnic soldiers. 5.7373
Ethnic stratification. 4.4896
Ethnic theatre in the United States. 2.3196
Ethnicity and family therapy. 5.4819
Ethnicity and medical care. 5.4661
Ethnicity and nationality. 5.8097
Ethnicity in the United States. 3.6510
Ethnicity on the Great Plains. 3.8493
Ethnographic atlas. 4.526
Ethnographic atlas of Ifugao. 4.185
Ethnographic bibliography of North America. 5.7740
Ethnography and qualitative design in educational research. 4.10284
An ethnography of a retirement hotel. 4.5808
An ethnography of Santa Clara Pueblo, New Mexico. 3.5953
Ethnological theory. 4.412
Ethnomusicology. 1.4361
An ethological study of children's behavior. 4.10405
Ethos and identity. 4.615
Etiquette. 1.1517-1.1518
Etruscan and early Roman architecture. 1.5224
Etruscan art. 1.4725

Etruscan cities and their culture. 3.2756
The Etruscan language. 2.228
Etruscan sculpture ... 1.5637
The Etruscans. 3.2757
The Etruscans, their art and civilization. 3.2758
Etudes sur la France des dix-septième et dix-huitième siècles. 3.2016
Études sur la France des XVIIe et XVIIIe siècles. 3.2016
An etymological dictionary of family and Christian names. 3.302
Etymological dictionary of the Russian language. 2.1232
Etymologisches Wörterbuch der deutschen Sprache. 2.1183
Etymology, with especial reference to English. 2.1012
The Eucharist and human liberation. 1.3225
Eudemian ethics. 1.285
Eudora Welty. 2.12670-2.12672, 2.12674
Eudora Welty's chronicle. 2.12669
Eugène Emmanuel Viollet-le-Duc, 1814-1879. 1.5421
Eugene Onegin. 2.1412-2.1413
Eugene O'Neill and the tragic tension. 2.12293
Eugénie Grandet. 2.4119
Eugenio Montale. 2.5040
Eugenio Montale: a critical study of his poetry, prose, and criticism. 2.5042
Eugenio Montale's poetry. 2.5041
Eulenspiegel. English. 2.13514
Eulenspiegel (Satire). 2.4157
Euphues. 2.6491
Eurhythmics, art, and education. 1.4441
Euripidean drama. 2.466
Euripides. 2.464
Euripides and his age. 2.471
Euripides and his influence. 2.470
The Euro-dollar system. 4.4555
Eurocommunism. 4.7026
Eurocurrencies and the international monetary system. 4.4590
Eurofutures. 4.2217
The Europa year book. 4.8355
The Europa year book (1959) 4.8355
Europe, 1780-1830. 3.661
Europe & China. 3.100
Europe and the decline of Spain. 3.3440
Europe and the Europeans, an international discussion. 3.1195
Europe and the French imperium, 1799-1814. 3.660
Europe and the money muddle. 4.4511
Europe and the people without history. 3.608
Europe at war 1600-1650. 3.634
Europe between revolutions, 1815-1848. 3.693
Europe divided, 1559-1598. 3.626
L'Europe et le monde à fin du XVIIIe siècle. 3.650
Europe in decay. 3.865
Europe in the age of Louis XIV. 3.174
Europe in the central Middle Ages, 962-1154. 3.602
Europe in the eighteenth century. 4.5286
Europe in the eighteenth century, 1713-1783. 3.647
Europe in the fourteenth and fifteenth centuries. 3.603
Europe in the nineteenth century. 3.675
Europe in the sixteenth century. 3.621
Europe in the twentieth century. 3.743
Europe of the invasions. 1.5170
Europe overseas: phases of imperialism. 4.7531
Europe since Napoleon. 3.658
Europe: the emergence of an idea. 3.560
Europe: the world's banker, 1870-1914. 4.4446
Europe transformed, 1878-1919. 3.713
Europe under the old regime. 4.9066
Europe without Baedeker. 3.1186
European alliances and alignments, 1871-1890. 3.718
European and American musical instruments. 1.4125
The European and the Indian. 3.5817
European armies and the conduct of war. 5.7196

European authors, 1000-1900. 2.2547
European colonial rule, 1880-1940. 3.3635
The European communities. 5.8399
The European Community and Eastern Europe. 4.2221
European decolonization, 1918-1981. 4.8902
The European demographic system, 1500-1820. 4.1690
European demography and economic growth. 4.1689
European diet from pre-industrial to modern times. 5.7118
European diplomacy between two wars, 1919-1939. 3.875
European drama criticism, 1900-1975. 5.8131
European drawings, 1375-1825. 1.5799
The European economy. 4.2195
European elections and British politics. 4.8362
The European energy challenge. 4.3712
The European family. 4.5554
European fascism. 3.868
European folk dance, its national and musical characteristics. 4.1108
The European folktale. 4.787
European freebooters in Moghul India. 3.4259
European historical statistics, 1750-1975. 4.1254
European historical statistics, seventeen fifty-nineteen seventy-five. 4.1254
European imperialism in the nineteenth and twentieth centuries. 3.672
European industrial relations. 4.3630
The European inheritance. 3.86
European labor and multinationals. 4.3325
European labour protest, 1848-1939. 4.3628
The European Left. 4.7022
European literature and the Latin Middle Ages. 2.2626
European literature in the nineteenth century. 2.2667
The European mind. 3.644
The European miracle. 4.2200
The European monetary system. 4.4512
European music in the twentieth century. 1.3671
The European nations in the West Indies, 1493-1688. 3.9087
European of yesterday. 2.13879
European paintings. 1.6009
European paintings before 1500. 1.4659
The European Parliament and the European community. 4.8363
European peasants and their markets. 4.2968
The European philosophers from Descartes to Nietzsche. 1.419
European plays on the American stage. 2.3771
European political facts, 1648-1789. 4.8356
European political facts, 1848-1918. 4.8358
European political facts, 1918-84. 4.8359
European political parties. 4.8374
The European powers and the German question, 1848-71. 3.2297
European prehistory. 4.726
The European revolution & correspondence with Gobineau. 3.2088
European social class: stability and change. 4.5280
European society in the eighteenth century. 4.5282
European society in upheaval. 4.5288
European theories of the drama. 2.2796
European thought in the eighteenth century. 1.436
European vision and the South Pacific, 1768-1850. 1.5094
European witch trials. 5.682
European women on the left. 4.7145
European writers. 2.2557
Europe's crucial years. 3.761
Europe's giant accelerator. 5.2446
Europe's inner demons. 5.681
Europe's steppe frontier, 1500-1800. 3.3524
Euroship 84. 4.3966
Eusebius as church historian. 1.2287
Eustace and Hilda. 2.8797
Eustace Chisholm and the works. 2.12359
The Eustace diamonds. 2.8210
Eutectic solidification processing. 5.6772

The euthanasia controversy, 1812-1974. 5.8290
Eva Perón. 3.9252
Eva Trout. 2.8471
Evaluation and the elementary curriculum. 4.10428
The Evangelical Alliance for the United States of America, 1847-1900. 1.3096
The evangelical faith. 1.2782
Evangelist of race. 3.2348
Evatt; politics and justice. 3.5574
Eve and the New Jerusalem. 4.5944
The eve of the revolution. 3.6918
Evelina. 2.6893
Evelyn Waugh. 2.9507-2.9508
Evelyn Waugh and his world. 2.9506
Evelyn Waugh, the critical heritage. 2.9504
Evelyn Waugh, writer. 2.9503
Even the rat was white. 5.85
An evening of Brahms. 2.13314
The Evening post. 2.3662
The evening stars. 2.3652
Evenings with the orchestra. 1.3815
The event of the Qu'rān. 1.2029
The everlasting circle. 2.6113
The everlasting man. 1.1527
The everlasting South. 3.8124
Every man in his humor. 2.6590
Every second year. 4.8059
Everybody's hockey book. 4.992
The everyday art of India. 1.6527
Everyday life in Babylon and Assyria. 3.3774
Everyday mother talk to toddlers. 4.5723
Everyman, and medieval miracle plays. 2.6205
Everyman his own historian. 3.459
Everyman's book of British ballads. 1.3441
Everyman's book of English folk tales. 4.789
Everyman's book of English verse. 2.6093
Everyman's dictionary of literary biography. 2.5482
Everyman's dictionary of literary biography, English & American. 2.5483
Everyman's dictionary of non-classical mythology. 1.1600
Everyman's dictionary of Shakespeare quotations. 2.6651
Everyman's Judaica. 3.3809
Everyone was brave. 4.7163
Everyone's United Nations. 4.9201
Everything in its path. 4.6536
Everything to live for. 2.11882
Everywhere spoken against. 2.6025
Evidence and meaning. 1.541
Evidence for authorship. 2.5492
Evidence of love. 2.10082, 2.13056
Evil and the god of love. 1.2844
The Evil eye. 4.561
Evita by Evita. 3.9251
Evolution above the species level. 5.3360
Evolution after Darwin. 5.3363
The evolution and classification of flowering plants. 5.3692
Evolution and culture. 4.528
Evolution and ecology. 4.504
Evolution and the diversity of life. 5.3373
Evolution and the founders of pragmatism. 1.483
Evolution and the genetics of populations. 5.3477
Evolution as entropy. 5.3384
Evolution by natural selection. 5.3351
Evolution from molecules to men. 5.3340
Evolution, morality, and the meaning of life. 1.1458
The evolution of American educational theory. 4.10538
The Evolution of American electoral systems. 4.8102
The evolution of American foreign policy. 3.6408
The evolution of Buddhist architecture in Japan. 1.5453
The evolution of chemistry. 5.2605
The evolution of Christian thought. 1.2744
The evolution of culture in animals. 5.4090
The evolution of designs. 1.5464

The evolution of diplomatic method, being the Chichele lectures delivered at the University of Oxford in November 1953. 4.9083
The evolution of giant firms in Britain. 4.3836
The evolution of India and Pakistan, 1858 to 1947. 3.4280
The evolution of insect mating systems. 5.3861
The evolution of medieval thought. 1.352
The evolution of modern capitalism. 4.2997
Evolution of nervous control from primitive organisms to man. 5.4290
The evolution of North America. 5.2994
The evolution of our Latin-American policy. 3.9017
The evolution of Parliament. 4.8456
The evolution of physics. 5.1932
The Evolution of Prussia. 3.2481
The evolution of scientific thought from Newton to Einstein. 5.1893
The evolution of sex. 5.3483
The Evolution of social insurance, 1881-1981. 4.3444
The evolution of society. 4.4845
The evolution of Soviet politics. 4.8641
The evolution of Soviet security strategy, 1965-1975. 3.3251
The evolution of stars: how they form, age, and die. 5.1833
The Evolution of the crystalline rocks. 5.3066
Evolution of the earth. 5.2969
The evolution of the French novel, 1641-1782. 2.3903
The evolution of the human brain. 5.4151
The evolution of the igneous rocks. 5.3044
The evolution of the international economic order. 4.4107
The evolution of the international monetary system, 1945-77. 4.4579
The evolution of the Labour Party, 1910-1924. 4.8545
Evolution of the modern presidency. 5.8407
The evolution of the Negro college. 4.10867
The evolution of the Polynesian chiefdoms. 4.673
The evolution of the Sikh community. 3.4210
The evolution of the southern backcountry. 3.8216
Evolution of the vertebrates. 5.3168
The evolution of urban society: early Mesopotamia and prehispanic Mexico. 4.598
The evolution of wage structure. 4.3124
The evolution of Walt Whitman. 2.11274
The evolution of war. 5.7152
Evolution, the history of an idea. 5.3342
Evolution versus Creationism. 5.3350
Evolutionary biology. 5.3368, 5.3374
Evolutionary biology and human social behavior. 4.509
Evolutionary ecology. 5.3524
Evolutionary ecology of marsupials. 5.4013
The evolutionary process. 5.3370
Evolutionary socialism. 4.7057
The Evolutionary synthesis. 5.3367
An evolutionary theory of economic change. 4.1280
An evolutionary view of economic growth. 4.2772
Evolutions and plants of the past. 5.3175
Evolving. 5.3365
The evolving continents. 5.3099
The evolving firm. 4.2652
The evolving self. 5.551
Evreinov, the theatre of paradox and transformation. 2.3382
The Ewings. 2.12268
Ex-prodigy. 5.1101
The exact sciences in antiquity. 5.1079
An examination of cartography in relation to culture and civilization. 4.228
An examination of Plato's doctrines. 1.260
An examination of the place of reason in ethics. 1.1411
Examining controversies in adult education. 4.10984
The example of Edward Taylor. 2.10876
The example of Melville. 2.11160
Examples and counterexamples in graph theory. 5.1283

Examples & exercises in operations research. 5.5567
Examples of groups. 5.1306
Excavating in Egypt. 3.5133
Excavation handbook. 5.5914
Excavation in Palestine. 3.3831
Excavations at Star Carr. 4.706
Excellence. 4.4958
Excellent women. 2.9799
Except the Lord. 2.8499
Exceptional language and linguistics. 2.149
Excess and restraint. 4.677
Exchange control in central Europe. 4.4556
Exchange control in Germany. 4.4593
Exchange-rate determination. 4.4558
Exchange rate theory and practice. 4.4465
Exchange rates and international macroeconomics. 4.4464
Exchange systems in prehistory. 4.719
Excise systems. 4.4716
Excited states in organic chemistry. 5.2920
Exclusion Crisis. 3.1505
Exclusiveness and tolerance. 1.1957
An excursion into creative sociology. 1.1292
Excuses. 5.471
Execution eve, and other contemporary ballads. 1.5
The executioner's song. 2.12097
Executions in America. 4.6850
The executive mind. 4.2700
The executive overseas. 4.2729
Executive privilege. 4.9639
Executive reorganization and reform in the New Deal, the genesis of administrative management, 1900-1939. 4.7978
An exemplary history of the novel. 2.3513
The exemplary middle school. 4.10499
Exercices de style. 2.4678
Exercise prescription for fitness. 4.925
Exercises in econometrics. 4.1397
Exeter book. English. Selections. 2.6307
The exhaustive concordance of the Bible: showing every word of the text of the common English version of the canonical books, and every occurrence of each word in regular order. 1.2503
The exhibition of archaeological finds of the People's Republic of China. 1.5065
Exhibitions: universal marketing tools. 5.5656
Exhortation and controls. 4.2110
Exhortation to martyrdom. 1.2188
The exhortation to the Greeks, the rich man's salvation, and the fragment of an address entitled To the newly baptized. 1.2487
Exhumations. 2.8834
Exil. 2.4603
Exile and the kingdom. 2.4447
Exiles. 2.8868
Exiles and marriages. 2.11807
Exile's return. 2.10402
Existence and faith. 1.2740
Existence and other poems. 2.1916
Existence and the existent. 1.489
The existence of God. 1.2832
Existential battles. 2.12103
Existential errands. 2.12098
Existential folktales. 2.13352
Existential Marxism in postwar France. 1.824
The existential pleasures of engineering. 5.5513
Existential psychology. 5.63
The existential sociology of Jean-Paul Sartre. 1.852
Existentialism and humanism. 1.492
Existentialism from Dostoevsky to Sartre. 1.488
The existentialists. 1.486
The existentialists and Jean-Paul Sartre. 1.850
Exodus and revolution. 1.2559
Exodusters. 3.6799
Exotica 4. 5.5347
The expanding circle. 1.1414
Expanding liberties. 4.9671
The expanding universe. 5.1865
Expansion and coexistence. 3.3210
L'expansion coloniale et les rivalités internationales de 1871 à 1914. 4.8901
The expansion of Elizabethan England. 3.1425
The expansion of England. 3.1228

Expansionism in American history. 3.6362
Expansionists of 1812. 3.7110
Expansionists of 1898. 3.7499
Expectant peoples; nationalism and development. 3.1154
The expedition of Humphrey Clinker. 2.7261
The expeditions of John Charles Frémont. 3.8473
Expelled to a friendlier place. 4.10726
An expenditure tax. 4.4709
The expense of greatness. 2.5736
Experience and art. 1.4654
Experience and education. 4.10228
Experience and enlightenment. 4.5334
Experience and judgment. 1.1013
Experience and prediction. 1.1288
The experience of defeat. 3.1477
The experience of dying. 5.4590
An experience of India. 2.9726
The experience of songs. 2.5772
An experience of women. 4.6090
Experiences in a promised land. 3.8589
Experiences in painting (T'u-hua chien-wên chih) 1.6315
Experiencing. 5.231
Experiencing architecture. 1.5479
Experiential learning. 4.10626
Experiment and theory in physics. 5.2016
Experiment in autobiography. 2.8252
The experimental analysis of behavior. 5.213
An experimental approach to projective techniques. 5.544
Experimental cinema in America, 1921-1947. 2.2918
Experimental design in psychological research. 5.45
Experimental electrochemistry for chemists. 5.2914
Experimental embryology of echinoderms. 5.4127
The experimental foundations of modern immunology. 5.4462
Experimental high-resolution electron microscopy. 5.3288
Experimental methods and instrumentation in psychology. 5.37
Experimental modelling in engineering. 5.5699
Experimental nuclear physics. 5.2075
Experimental physical chemistry. 5.2808
Experimental psychology. 5.208, 5.211
Experimental psychology. 5.212
Experimental reactor physics. 5.2441
Experimental researches in electricity. 5.2336
Experimental spectroscopy. 5.2306
Experimental stress analysis. 5.5782
Experimental techniques in low-temperature physics. 5.2236
Experimental theater from Stanislavsky to Peter Brook. 2.3183
Experimental theatre. 2.3183
Experimental theatre from Stanislavsky to Peter Brook. 2.3183
Experimentation in American religion. 1.1878
Experimentation with microprocessor applications. 5.1144
Experimenter effects in behavioral research. 5.67
Experimenting with MSI, LSI, IO, and modular memory systems. 5.6591
Experiments, design, and analysis. 5.986
Experiments in family planning. 4.5678
Experiments in hearing. 5.4374
Experiments in microbial genetics. 5.4447
Experiments in molecular genetics. 5.3456
Experiments in physical chemistry. 5.2809
Experiments in plant hybridisation. 5.3407
Explaining delinquency. 4.6860
Explaining emotions. 5.415
Explaining human behavior. 5.22
Explaining organizational behavior. 4.2698
Explaining the brain. 5.4341
An explanation of America. 2.13252
The explanation of culture change: models in prehistory. 4.690
Explication as criticism. 2.2446
Explications/interpretations. 2.13440
The Explicator. 2.5622
The Explicator cyclopedia. 2.5622

Exploding poetry. 2.3875
The exploding suns. 5.1831
The exploits of Arsène Lupin. 2.4599
Exploration and empire. 3.8456
Exploration and mining geology. 5.6732
The exploration diaries of H. M. Stanley, now first published from the original manuscripts. 3.5221
Exploration mining and geology. 5.6732
The exploration of New Zealand. 3.5600
The Exploration of North America, 1630-1776. 3.5977
The exploration of northern Canada, 500 to 1920. 3.8867
The exploration of the Colorado River. 3.8562
Exploration of the Pacific. 3.5535
Exploration of the universe. 5.1717
Explorations. 2.5649, 2.8336, 2.10029
Explorations 3. 2.5541
Explorations in African systems of thought. 4.648
Explorations in developmental biology. 5.3487
Explorations in early Southeast Asian history. 4.8695
Explorations in enterprise. 4.4249
Explorations in psychohistory. 3.430
Explorations in the life of fishes. 5.3903
The explorers. 4.88
Explorers' maps. 4.230
Explorers of Arabia from the Renaissance to the end of the Victorian Era. 3.4047
The explorers of North America, 1492-1806. 3.5966
Explorers of the body. 5.4504
Exploring India's sacred art. 1.5189
Exploring social geography. 4.384
Exploring the city. 4.514
Exploring the dangerous trades. 4.4530
Exploring the galaxies. 5.1855
Exploring the visual art of Oceania. 1.5093
Explosive volcanism. 5.3110
The Export-Import Bank. 4.4550
Export strategy, markets and competition. 4.4113
Exports and economic growth of developing countries. 4.4164
L'exposition chinoise. 1.5065
L'exposition des découvertes archéologiques de la République Populaire de Chine. 1.5065
Expositions and developments. 1.4005
Expression and meaning. 2.66
The expression of the emotions in man and animals. 5.4348
Expressionism. 1.4984, 1.5878
Expressionism in art. 1.6345
The expressive arts therapies. 5.4886
Expressive singing. 1.4566
Expropriation of U.S. investments in Cuba, Mexico, and Chile. 4.4627
The Extended family. 4.5956
The Extended family in black societies. 3.6760
The extended phenotype. 5.3402
The extension of man. 5.1929
The extensions of man. 2.51
Exterminator! 2.12933
External construction by animals. 5.4078
The external degree. 4.10625
Extinct languages. 2.226
Extinction. 5.3161
Extra-sensory perception. 5.645
Extraction metallurgy. 5.6761
The extraordinary landscape. 5.6982
The extraordinary Mr. Wilkes: his life and times. 3.1570
Extraterrestrials-where are they? 5.1726
Extreme magic, a novella and other stories. 2.12943
The Eye. 5.4377
The eye in the mandala. 2.10187
The eye of man. 1.4759
The eye of the storm. 2.9994
The eye of the storm. 2.10180
The eye of the story. 2.12661
'The eye that never sleeps' 4.6814
Eye witness to therapy. 5.4892
Eyeless in Gaza. 2.8820
Eyewitness in Greece. 3.2707
Eyewitness testimony. 4.9887

Eyewitness; the Negro in American history.
3.6653
Eyewitnesses of Shakespeare. 2.6853
Ezekiel 1. 1.2615
Ezra Pound. 2.12340, 2.12344,
2.12348-2.12349, 2.12353
Ezra Pound and Dorothy Shakespear, their
letters, 1909-1914. 2.12335
Ezra Pound and The cantos. 2.12332
Ezra Pound and The cantos. 2.12331
Ezra Pound and The Pisan cantos. 2.12330
Ezra Pound perspectives. 2.12352
Ezra Pound: poet as sculptor. 2.12339
Ezra Pound, the last rower. 2.12343
Ezra Pound, the voice of silence. 2.12347

F.B.I. and Martin Luther King, Jr. 3.6839
F. D. R. 3.7783
F.O. Matthiessen, 1902-1950. 2.2425
F. Scott Fitzgerald. 2.11728, 2.11730-2.11731,
2.11735, 2.11737
F. Scott Fitzgerald and the craft of fiction.
2.11732
F. Scott Fitzgerald, his art and his technique.
2.11734
F. Scott Fitzgerald in his own time. 2.11726
The Faber book of ballads. 2.6109
The Faber book of comic verse. 2.6123
The Faber book of modern American verse.
2.10771
The Faber book of modern verse. 2.6193
The Faber book of nonsense verse. 2.3756
The Faber book of twentieth-century verse.
2.6188
Fabian essays in socialism. 4.7038
The Fabians. 4.6925
A fable. 2.11662
Fable. 2.4652
A fable of modern art. 1.6698
The fable of the bees: or, Private vices, publick
benefits. 1.1507
Fables of aggression. 2.9045
Fables of identity. 2.5762
The fables of La Fontaine. 2.4031
The fables of Marie de France. 2.3954
Fabric of Chinese society. 4.5417
The fabric of dialogue. 2.7377
Fabric of ductile strain. 5.3128
Fabric of freedom, 1763-1800. 3.6907
The fabric of geology. 5.2977
Fabulation and metafiction. 2.3530
The fabulous life of Diego Rivera. 1.6005
Fabulous voyager. 2.8892
The façade of Saint-Gilles-du-Gard; its influence
on French sculpture. 1.5701
The face of battle. 3.536
The face of Spain. 3.3401
The face of the ancient Orient. 3.3700
The face of the deep. 4.337
Face of time. 2.11649
Faces in my time. 2.9230
Faces in the crowd. 5.635
Faces in the water. 2.10217
The faces of Eve. 2.10597
Faces of feminism. 4.5871
Faces of Jesus. 1.2861
The faces of power. 3.7560
Facies interpretation and the stratigraphic
record. 5.3133
Facies models. 5.3132
Facing East. 3.760
Facing life. 4.5756
Facing Mount Kenya. 3.5280
Facing the dictators. 3.1662
Facing total war. 4.5363
Facing two ways. 3.4900
Facing west. 3.5825
Facing zero population growth. 4.1603
Die Fackel im Ohr. 2.13720
Facsimile-atlas to the early history of
cartography. 4.118
Fact and fancy in television regulation. 4.4071
Fact and lore about Old English words. 2.944
Fact, fiction, and forecast. 1.1183
Factional politics in an Indian state. 3.4357
A factious people. 3.8027
Factoring and finance. 4.4384
Factory and manager in the USSR. 4.2743

The Factory girls. 4.3298
The factory worker and his industry. 4.3430
The facts about 'drug abuse' 4.6670
Facts about the presidents. 3.6309
Facts and artifacts of ancient Middle America.
3.8887
Facts and values, studies in ethical analysis.
1.1461
Facts in perspective. 2.3564
The Facts on File dictionary of archaeology.
3.219
The Facts on File dictionary of astronomy.
5.1680
The Facts on file dictionary of first names.
3.303
The Facts on File dictionary of religions.
1.1526
The Facts on File dictionary of
telecommunications. 5.6361
Facts on file yearbook. 3.723
Faculty bargaining. 4.10582
Fads and foibles in modern sociology and
related sciences. 4.4840
The Faerie queene. 2.6529
The faerie queene. 2.6525
Fahrenheit 451. 2.11409
Fail-safe. 2.11434
Failure of a mission. 3.925
Failure of a revolution: Germany 1918-19.
3.2416
The failure of freedom. 3.4899
The failure of the Prussian reform movement,
1807-1819. 4.8617
The failure of world monetary reform, 1971-74.
4.4580
Fair enough. 2.3625
Fair fights and foul. 4.9489
Fair Greece! Sad relic. 2.5574
The fair house. 2.10063
The fair penitent. 2.7233
Fair sex, family size and structure in Britain,
1900-39. 4.1646
A fairly honourable defeat. 2.9752
The fairytale as art form and portrait of man.
2.3465
The faith and fiction of Muriel Spark. 2.9367
Faith and fratricide. 1.1960
Faith and history. 3.515
Faith and knowledge. 1.1548
The faith and practice of al-Ghazzali. 1.373
Faith and the good thing. 2.13097
Faith and understanding. 1.2741
Faith and violence. 1.2921
Faith, hope and charity. 1.2207
Faith in fiction. 2.10570
The faith of a liberal. 1.579
The faith of our feminists. 2.10363
The faith of the Christian church. 1.2772
Faith, reason, and civilization. 1.2772
Faith, reason, and the plague in seventeenth-
century Tuscany. 5.4766
Faithful are the wounds. 2.12443
Faithful shepherd. 2.4970
The faithful shepherd. 1.2401
Falange. 3.3461
Falconer. 2.11492
The fall. 2.4444
The fall & rise of Mackenzie King: 1911-1919.
3.8749
The fall of Kruger's Republic. 3.5502
Fall of Mevar. 2.1865
The fall of Mussolini. 3.2900
The fall of Paris. 3.2163
The fall of the Byzantine Empire. 3.2678
The fall of the dynasties. 3.728
The fall of the French monarchy, 1787-1792.
3.2079
Fall of the German Empire, 1914-1918. 3.2341
The fall of the House of Habsburg. 3.1894
The fall of the house of Usher. 2.11198
Fall of the Inca empire and the Spanish rule in
Peru, 1530-1780. 3.9304
The fall of the Roman Empire. 3.2804
The fall of the royal government in Mexico
City. 3.8930
The fall of the royal government in Peru.
3.9305
The fall of the Russian monarchy. 3.3162

The fall of the Spanish American empire.
3.8986
Falling in love. 5.440
The falling sickness. 5.4788
Der falsche Nero. 2.13739
The false dawn. 4.8896
False entry. 2.12944
The false messiah. 2.13545
False promises. 4.3562
False science. 5.7328
False start in Africa. 4.2575
Fame and the founding fathers. 4.7828
La familia. 3.8564
La familia de Pascual Duarte. 2.5242
Familiar medical quotations. 5.4547
Familiar quotations. 2.3728
Families. 4.5577
Families against the city. 4.5606
Families and communities. 3.6218
Families in former times. 4.5623
Families of Black prisoners. 4.6855
The families of flowering plants. 5.3656
Families of the slums. 5.4880
Families that work. 4.5652
Families under stress. 4.5643
Families, what makes them work. 4.5589
The family. 2.2244, 4.5637
Family. 2.2245
The family. 4.5648
A family album. 4.5572
A family and a fortune, and More women than
men. 2.8528
Family and community. 3.8060
Family and community in Ireland. 4.626
Family and fortune: studies in aristocratic
finance in the sixteenth and seventeenth
centuries. 3.1395
Family and friends. 2.9631
Family and kinship in the Soviet Union. 4.628
Family and property in Sung China. 1.1510
Family and social network. 4.5636
The family and the sexual revolution. 4.5582
The family arsenal. 2.13355
The family Carnovsky. 2.1822
Family-centered social work practice. 4.6543
The family chronicle. 3.3031
Family connections. 3.8018
Family constellation. 5.587
The family encounters the depression. 4.5633
A family gathering. 2.12922
The family herds. 4.533
The family idiot: Gustave Flaubert, 1821-1857.
2.4199
The Family in business. 4.2715
The family in classical Greece. 4.5560
The Family in Imperial Russia:new lines of
historical research. 4.5625
The family in Soviet Russia. 4.5626
Family in transition. 4.5563
The family in various cultures. 4.5555
The family letters of Christina Georgina
Rossetti. 2.8009
Family letters of Robert and Elinor Frost.
2.11751
The family letters of Samuel Butler, 1841-1886.
2.7516
Family life and illicit love in earlier generations.
4.5553
Family life and school achievement. 4.10864
Family life in central Italy, 1880-1910. 4.5624
The family life of Black people. 3.6780
Family literacy. 4.10755
The family Mashber. 2.1806
Family matters. 4.5590
Family names. 3.307
The family of Max Desir. 2.13012
The family of Pascual Duarte. 2.5243
The family planning program in the
socioeconomic context. 4.5681
Family relationships in Shakespeare and the
Restoration comedy of manners. 2.5848
Family roles and interaction. 4.5641
Family sayings. 2.5034
The family secret. 4.5778
The family, sex and marriage in England,
1500-1800. 4.5621
Family, socialization and interaction process.
4.5654

Family structure in Jamaica. 4.5614
Family structure in nineteenth century
    Lancashire. 4.5619
Family therapy. 5.4881
Family therapy, concepts and methods. 5.4884
Family therapy techniques. 5.4883
Family ties. 2.5470
Family violence. 4.5777
Family, women, and socialization in the
    kibbutz. 4.7166
Family word finder. 2.1068
The family's construction of reality. 4.5647
Famous first facts. 1.22
Famous last words. 2.1123
Famous names in engineering. 5.5662
Famous pianists & their technique. 1.4156
Famous problems of elementary geometry.
    5.1568
The Fannie Farmer cookbook. 5.7133
Fanny Burney. 2.6897
Fanny Elssler in America. 4.1137
Fanny Hill. 2.6938
Fanny Kemble. 2.3349
Fanny Wright. 4.6001
Fanshen. 4.2862
Une fantaisie du Docteur Ox. 2.4323
The fantastic. 2.3463
Fantastic art, dada, surrealism. 1.4818
Fantastic films. 2.2990
The fantastic in literature. 2.2393
The fantasts. 2.5965
Fantasy and feeling in education. 4.10372
Fantasy literature. 2.5969
Fantasy, the literature of subversion. 2.3458
The fantasy tradition in American literature.
    2.10550
The fantasy worlds of Peter Beagle. 2.12898
FAO production yearbook. 4.2903
The far and the deep. 5.7429
Far country. 3.5587
The Far East and Australasia. 3.3608
The Far Eastern policy of the United States.
    3.4417
Far from Cibola. 2.11883
Far from home. 2.12923
The Far North. 3.5876
The far side of paradise. 2.11736
Far Southwest, 1846-1912. 3.8559
The Far Western frontier, 1830-1860. 3.8453
Faraday, Maxwell, and Kelvin. 5.1943
Farce. 2.2827
Farce and fantasy. 3.2229
Farces and festival plays 2.5211
Farewell in June. 2.1644
The farewell party. 2.1689
A farewell to arms. 2.11841
Farewell to European history. 3.45
Farewell to reform. 3.7522
Farewell to the bloody shirt. 3.7411
Farewell to the South. 3.8171
The farm. 2.11417
Farm and nation in modern Japan. 4.2988
The Farm Bureau and the New Deal. 4.2938
Farm crisis, 1919-1923. 4.2946
Farm policies and politics in the Truman years.
    4.2943
Farm policies of the United States, 1790-1950.
    4.2937
Farm prices, myth and reality. 4.2940
Farm structure. 4.2935
Farm women on the prairie frontier. 4.6074
Farm workers and agri-business in California,
    1947-1960. 4.3377
The farmer's age: agriculture, 1815-1860.
    4.1875
Farmers' daughters. 2.12744
Farmers' last frontier. 4.1877
The farmer's last frontier. 4.2949
The farmers of old England. 5.5249
Farmers without farms. 4.2919
Farming and democracy. 4.2812
Farming in prehistory. 4.717
The farming of fish. 5.5470
Farming the edge of the sea. 5.5469
Farms, villages, and cities. 4.715
Faroe: the emergence of a nation. 3.3372
The farther reaches of human nature. 5.528
The Fascination of statistics. 5.1396

Fascism. 4.7598
Fascism and the industrial leadership in Italy,
    1919-1940. 4.3074
Fascism, Comparison and definition. 4.7603
Fascism; doctrine and institutions. 3.2890
Fascism from above. 3.3456
Fascism in Europe. 3.868
Fascism in Ferrara, 1915-1925. 3.2949
Fascism in France. 2.4387
The Fascist challenge and the policy of
    appeasement. 3.893
The fascist dictatorship in Italy. 3.2891
The Fascist experience: Edward R.
    Tannenbaum. 3.2831
Fascist intellectual, Drieu La Rochelle. 2.4516
Fascist movements in Austria. 3.1895
The Fascist persuasion in radical politics.
    4.7600
The fashion and future of history. 3.364
Fashion production terms. 5.7088
Fast algorithms for digital signal processing.
    5.6365
Fast Fourier transform and convolution
    algorithms. 5.1554
Fast talk & flush times. 2.10588
Fast talk and flush times. 2.10588
Fasting in the Koran. 1.2036
Fat cats and Democrats. 4.8206
Fat mutton and liberty of conscience. 3.8012
The fatal environment. 3.6358
The fatal friendship: Stanley Loomis. 3.2055
The fatal history of Portuguese Ceylon. 3.4369
The fatal impact. 4.92
The fatal mirror. 2.6436
Fatal necessity. 3.5598
Fatal remedies. 4.5142
The fatal shore. 3.5575
Fate of a cockroach. 2.1845
The fate of man in the modern world. 3.186
The fateful alliance. 3.772
The Fateful choice. 3.4917
The fateful years. 3.2437
Father and son. 2.11648
Father and son: a study of two temperaments.
    2.7748
The Father Brown omnibus. 2.7561
The Father Brown stories. 2.7561
Father, child, and sex role. 5.611
Father-daughter incest. 4.5515
Father Divine. 1.3345
Father Divine and the struggle for racial
    equality. 1.3344
The father in primitive psychology. 4.566
Father Louis Hennepin's Description of
    Louisiana. 3.8298
Father of radio. 5.6424
Father of the blues. 1.3892
Fatherhood and family policy. 4.5660
Fathering behaviors. 4.5661
Fathers. 2.13049
The fathers. 2.12573
Fathers and children. 2.1458
Fathers and daughters in Roman society.
    4.5853
The fathers, and other fiction. 2.12572
The Fathers of the Church. 1.2196
The fathers of the Greek Church. 1.2482
The fathers of the Latin Church. 1.2483
Fathers work for their sons. 3.5354
Fatigue and fracture in steel bridges. 5.6083
Fatigue failure of metals. 5.5812
Faulkner. 2.11685
Faulkner; a collection of critical essays.
    2.11706
The Faulkner-Cowley file. 2.11689
Faulkner: myth and motion. 2.11684
Faulkner's heroic design. 2.11696
Faulkner's narrative. 2.11699
Faulkner's 'Negro' 2.11692
Faulkner's search for a South. 2.11702
Fault tolerant and fault testable hardware
    design. 5.6582
Fauré. 1.3867
Faust. 2.1453
Fausto and Anna. 2.5032
The fauves. 1.5879
Fauvism. 1.4846, 1.6063
Le fauvisme. 1.6063

The favorite Uncle Remus. 2.11048
The FBI and Martin Luther King, Jr. 3.6839
Fear and trembling, and The sickness unto
    death. 1.2230
Fear in battle. 5.7163
The fear of the word: censorship and sex.
    4.9704
A fearful joy. 2.8500
Fearful symmetry. 2.7426
A feast of creatures. 2.6307
A feast of snakes. 2.12959
A feast of words. 2.12701
Feasts of fear and agony. 2.13959
Feathers from the Green Crow, Sean O'Casey,
    1905-1925. 2.9150
Feature films on 8mm, 16mm, and videotape.
    2.3075
Feature films on eight millimeter, sixteen
    millimeter, and videotape. 2.3075
Features and figures of the past. 3.3161
The Fed, a history of the South Wales miners
    in the twentieth century. 4.3535
The Federal and State constitutions. 4.9610
The Federal budget in brief. 4.4679
Federal censorship. 4.9530
Federal conservation policy, 1921-1933. 5.5302
The Federal funds market. 4.4534
The Federal funds market, its origin and
    development. 4.4535
Federal furniture and decorative arts at
    Boscobel. 1.6567
Federal Government and urban problems.
    4.6325
The Federal Government service. 4.7977
The federal lands revisited. 4.2822
The Federal lands since 1956. 4.2823
The Federal machine. 4.7976
Federal narcotics enforcement. 4.6673
The Federal presence. 1.5514
Federal-provincial diplomacy. 4.8279
Federal register. 4.7886
Federal regulation of personnel and human
    resource management. 4.9561
Federal regulatory directory. 4.9754
Federal Republic of Germany. 3.2464
The Federal Republic of Germany. 3.2467
Federal Reserve monetary policy, 1917-1933.
    4.4506
The Federal Reserve System. 4.4536
The Federal revenue system: facts and
    problems, 1961. 4.4697
The federal story. 4.8815
Federal tax policy. 4.4658
Federal tax reform, the impossible dream?
    4.9765
The Federal Theatre, 1935-1939. 2.3209
Federal wheat commodity programs. 4.3684
Federalism. 4.7876
Federalism and nation-building. 4.8803
Federalism and the French Canadians. 4.8281
Federalism and the organization of political life.
    4.8272
Federalist. 4.7826
The Federalist. 4.7827
Federalist Delaware, 1775-1815. 3.8100
The Federalist era, 1789-1801. 3.7022
The Federalists. 4.7835
Fedor Dostoevsky. 2.1375
Feedback control systems. 5.6187
A feeling for the organism. 5.3412
Feininger: his graphic work. 1.6440
Felix Frankfurter and his times. 4.9816
Felix Frankfurter reminisces, recorded in talks
    with Harlan B. Phillips. 4.9814
Felix S. Cohen's Handbook of federal Indian
    law. 4.9772
Fellah and townsman in the Middle East.
    4.5394
Fellini on Fellini. 2.3041
Fellow feelings. 2.13092
The fellowship of the ring. 2.9432
Female adolescent development. 5.620
Female crime and delinquency. 4.6691
The female experience and the nature of the
    divine. 1.1612
Female experience in 18th and 19th century
    America. 4.5981

The female experience in eighteenth- and nineteenth-century America. 4.5981
The female imagination. 2.5566
The female man. 2.13308
Female of the species. 4.460
The Female offender. 4.6689
The female poets of Great Britain. 2.6105
Female power and male dominance. 4.5831
Female psychology. 4.5924
The female Quixote. 2.7095
Female revolt. 3.5842
Female soldiers 5.7374
The female world. 4.5921
Feminine consciousness in the modern British novel. 2.6058
The feminine in Jungian psychology and in Christian theology. 4.5945
The feminine mystique. 4.6018
Feminine personality and conflict. 4.5925
Feminine psychology. 4.5929
Feminine spirituality in America. 4.6067
'Femininity,' 'masculinity,' and 'androgyny' 4.5926
Feminism and art history. 1.4628
Feminism and linguistic theory. 2.126
Feminism and materialism. 4.5880
Feminism and philosophy. 4.6046
Feminism and sexual equality. 4.6044
Feminism and suffrage. 4.6026
Feminism and the Bolshevik Revolution. 3.3229
Feminism in American politics. 4.6051
Feminism in eighteenth-century England. 4.6108
Feminism in France. 4.6115
Feminism in Russia, 1900-17. 4.6132
The feminist challenge. 4.6102
Feminist criticism. 2.5585
Feminist criticism and social change. 2.10292
Feminist criticism of Shakespeare. 2.6809
Feminist critics read Emily Dickinson. 2.10999
Feminist drama. 2.10517
Feminist frameworks. 4.6057
Feminist futures 2.10552
Feminist interpretation of the Bible. 1.2560
Feminist literary criticism. 2.2493
Feminist literary studies. 2.5510
The Feminist mystic, and other essays on women and spirituality. 4.5974
The feminist papers: from Adams to de Beauvoir. 4.5894
Feminist politics and human nature. 4.5930
A feminist position on mental health. 5.4890
Feminist quotations. 4.5881
Feminist theatre. 2.5928
Feminist theorists. 4.5869
Feminist theory. 4.6047
Feminist theory from margin to center. 4.6056
The feminists. 4.5879
Feminists and bureaucrats. 4.10845
Feminists in politics. 4.5973
The feminization of American culture. 2.10291
Fénelon. 2.4023
Fenimore Cooper 2.10974
The feral classroom. 4.10153
Ferdinand de Saussure. 2.48
Ferdinand Hodler. 1.6303-1.6304
Ferdinand I of Austria. 3.1882
Fergus Lamont. 2.9725
The ferment of realism. 2.10382
Fernand Léger. 1.6115
Fernando Botero. 1.6008
Fernando Cortes, his five letters of relation to the Emperor Charles V [1519-1526] 3.8921
Fernando de Rojas. 2.5198
Ferns and allied plants. 5.3700
Ferns & fern-allies of the United States & Canada. 5.3701
Ferns and fern-allies of the United States and Canada. 5.3701
Ferrara. 3.2948
Ferromagnetodynamics. 5.2405
Fertility and scarcity in America. 4.1644
Fertility in developing countries. 4.1647
Fertilizers and soil amendments. 5.5292
Fertilizers and soil fertility. 5.5293
The fervent years. 2.3273
Festival. 2.9245

Festivals and ceremonies of the Roman Republic. 4.874
Festivals and songs of ancient China. 3.4628
Festivals of the Athenians. 3.2562
Festivals of the Jewish year. 1.1981
Feudal England. 3.1341
Feudal Germany. 3.2267
The feudal monarchy in France and England, from the tenth to the thirteenth century. 3.1991
Feudal society. 3.580
Feudalism in history. 4.7374
The Feynman lectures on physics. 5.1991
Fiasco. 2.1712
Fiber optics and lightwave communications standard dictionary. 5.6362
Ficciones. 2.5285
Fiction and the camera eye. 2.3514
Fiction and the reading public. 2.5945
Fiction as truth. 2.2342
Fiction catalog. 5.8170
Fiction index. 5.8168
The fiction of André Pieyre de Mandiargues. 2.4650
The fiction of J. D. Salinger. 2.12428
The fiction of John Fowles. 2.9694
The fiction of Katherine Mansfield. 2.9087
The fiction of Nathanael West. 2.12687
The fiction of Philip Roth and John Updike. 2.10643
Fiction of the forties. 2.10616
Fictional technique in France, 1802-1927. 2.3906
Fictions of feminine desire. 2.3902
Fictions of the self, 1550-1800. 2.3515
Fiddler crabs of the world (Ocypodidae: genus Uca). 5.3852
The fiddler's home. 2.8523
Fidel Castro's personal revolution in Cuba: 1959-1973. 3.9103
Fides quaerens intellectum. 1.381
Field & laboratory methods for general ecology. 5.3537
Field and laboratory methods for general ecology. 5.3537
Field archaeology in Britain. 3.232
Field archaeology: tools and techniques of field work for archaeologists. 3.239
Field book of animals in winter. 5.4075
Field crop diseases handbook. 5.5398
Field geology. 5.2964
The field god, and In Abraham's bosom. 2.11796
Field guide. 2.13067
A field guide to American houses. 1.5557
A field guide to American windmills. 5.6235
A field guide to animal tracks. 5.4089
A field guide to Atlantic Coast fishes of North America. 5.3906
A field guide to edible wild plants of Eastern and Central North America. 5.3659
Field guide to North American butterflies. 5.3882
Field guide to North American insects and spiders. 5.3862
Field guide to North American mammals. 5.3986
A field guide to Pacific Coast fishes of North America. 5.3907
A field guide to reptiles and amphibians of Eastern and Central North America. 5.3920
A field guide to rocks and minerals. 5.3018
A field guide to shells, of the Atlantic and gulf coasts and the West Indies. 5.3847
A field guide to shells of the Pacific Coast and Hawaii, including shells of the Gulf of California. 5.3848
Field guide to soils and the environment. 5.5268
A field guide to the atmosphere. 5.2505
A field guide to the beetles of North America. 5.3889
A field guide to the birds. 5.3954
Field guide to the birds of North America. 5.3952
A field guide to the butterflies of North America, east of the Great Plains. 5.3881

A field guide to the ferns and their related families of northeastern and central North America. 5.3702
A field guide to the insects of America north of Mexico. 5.3860
A field guide to the mammals. 5.3983
A field guide to the moths of eastern North America. 5.3883
A field guide to the stars and planets. 5.1734
A field guide to trees and shrubs. 5.3689
A field guide to western birds. 5.3960
A field guide to western reptiles and amphibians. 5.3923
A field guide to wildflowers of Northeastern and North-Central North America. 5.3676
A field guide to your own back yard. 5.3265
Field hockey. 4.1043
A field manual of the ferns & fern-allies of the United States & Canada. 5.3701
Field notes. 2.9935
The field of nonsense. 2.6065
The Field of social work. 4.6477
The field of vision. 2.12211
Field photography. 5.6991
Field studies of monkeys and apes. 5.4017
Field theory. 5.2158
Field work. 2.9703
The fields. 2.12389
Fields and particles. 5.2157
Fields of change among the Iteso of Kenya. 3.5271
Fields of fire. 2.13417
The fierce embrace. 2.10495
The fiery angel, a sixteenth century romance. 2.1473
Fieser and Fieser's Reagents for organic synthesis. 5.2732
Fiesta en noviembre, novela. 2.5394
Fiesta in Aztlan. 2.10745
Fiestas. 2.5262
Fifteen American authors before 1900. 2.10376
Fifteen Canadian poets plus five. 2.9900
Fifteen centuries of children's literature. 5.7716
Fifteen thousand hours. 4.10121
Fifteen weeks (February 21-June 5, 1947) 3.7800
The fifteenth century. 3.604
The fifteenth century, 1399-1485. 3.1375
Fifteenth century engravings of northern Europe from the National Gallery of Art, Washington, D.C. 1.6452
Fifteenth century woodcuts and metalcuts from the National Gallery of Art, Washington, D.C. 1.6472
Fifth business. 2.9922
Fifth century styles in Greek sculpture. 1.5628
The fifth column. 2.11835
The Fifth estate. 4.3410
The fifth monarchy men. 3.1489
The fifth pestilence. 2.1526
The fifth queen. 2.8630
The fifth queen crowned. 2.8630
The fifth year of the Nixon watch. 3.7906
The fifties. 3.6066
The fifties: fiction, poetry, drama. 2.10407
Fifty-eight lonely men. 4.10631
Fifty million acres: conflicts over Kansas land policy, 1854-1890. 4.2819
Fifty poems from Chidambara. 2.1888
Fifty poems of Hafiz. 2.1968
Fifty stories. 2.11403
Fifty years (and twelve) of classical scholarship. 2.261
Fifty years in China. 3.4756
Fifty years of American drama, 1900-1950. 2.10522
Fifty years of American poetry. 2.10767
Fifty years of Chinese philosophy, 1898-1948. 1.1138
Fifty years of Russian prose. 2.1327
The fight for conservation. 5.5307
The fight for the Panama route. 4.9039
Fighters and lovers. 2.13385
Fighters for independence. 5.7833
Fighting computer crime. 4.6764
Fighting liberal. 3.7675
Fighting power. 5.7319

Fighting ships. 5.7446
Fighting ships and prisons. 5.7505
The fighting ships of the Rising Sun. 5.7471
Fighting spirit. 5.7166
Fighting terms. 2.8794
Fighting two colonialisms. 4.6162
The figure in film. 2.2950
The figure of Beatrice. 2.4940
The figure of Dante. 2.4921
Figures in the foreground. 2.9391
Figures of earth. 2.11444
Figures of thought. 2.2733
Figures of transition. 2.5705
Figuro in the night. 2.9147
Fiji. 3.5633
Fiji, a short history. 3.5636
Filippo Brunelleschi. 1.5439
La fille Élise. 2.4231
Film. 2.2919, 2.2939
Film. 1967/68-   . 2.2864
The film: a psychological study. 2.2962
Film, a reference guide. 2.2868
Film acting. 2.2967
The film actor. 2.2965
Film & literature, an introduction. 2.2974
Film & radio propaganda in World War II.
  3.1131
Film and radio propaganda in World War II.
  3.1131
Film and reality. 2.2876
Film and the narrative tradition. 2.2915
Film as a subversive art. 2.2972
Film as art. 2.2934
Film as film. 2.2966
Film before Griffith. 2.2879
Film bibliography. 5.8143
The film book bibliography, 1940-1975. 5.8138
The film encyclopedia. 2.2871
Film facts. 2.2874
Film form. 2.2953
Film guide. 2.2869
Film in the aura of art. 2.2947
Film literature index. 5.8139
Film noir. 2.2916
Film noir in cultural perspective. 2.2981
Film notes. 2.3076
Film on the left. 2.2982
Film research. 5.8137
Film review annual. 2.2955
The film sense. 2.2954
Film technique, and Film acting. 2.2967
Film theory and criticism. 2.2941
Filmgoer's companion. 2.2870
The films of Akira Kurosawa. 2.3060
The films of Carl-Theodor Dreyer. 2.3038
Films of comment and persuasion of the 1930s.
  2.2898
The films of D. W. Griffith. 2.3049
Fin-de-siècle Vienna. 3.1934
The final days. 3.7925
Final dress. 2.3257
Final entries, 1945. 3.2383
A final promise. 3.5818
Final report of the scientific study of
  uniedentified flying objects. 5.6694
The final solution. 3.3954
The final solution and the German Foreign
  Office. 3.1084
The 'Final solution' in the extermination camps
  and the aftermath. 3.1107
Finance capital. 4.1531
The finance of international business. 4.4600
Finance, trade, and politics in British foreign
  policy 1815-1914. 4.4188
Financial analyst's handbook. 4.4609
Financial and managerial accounting ...
  4.10665
Financial and managerial accounting for
  elementary and secondary school systems.
  4.10665
Financial crises. 4.1715
Financial deepening in economic development.
  4.4449
The financial effects of inflation. 4.4500
Financial handbook. 4.4447
A financial history of the United States.
  4.4651
A financial history of Western Europe. 4.4453

Financial institutions and markets in Southeast
  Asia. 4.4458
Financial institutions and policies in Indonesia.
  4.4460
Financial management, theory and strategies.
  4.4596
Financial markets. 4.4610
Financial planning for libraries. 5.7618
Financial responsibilities of governing boards of
  colleges and universities. 4.10600
The financial role of multinational enterprises.
  4.4594
Financial statement analysis. 4.4408-4.4409
The financial system of Canada. 4.4452
Financial tools for the non-financial executive.
  4.4598
The financier. 2.11593
Financiers and railroads, 1869-1889. 4.3988
Financing adjustment with growth in sub-
  Saharan Africa, 1986-90. 4.2607
Financing and managing fast-growth companies.
  4.4624
Financing community colleges. 4.10558
Financing education in a climate of change.
  4.10654
Financing elections. 4.8131
Financing government in a Federal system.
  4.4661
Financing politics. 4.8124
Financing presidential campaigns. 4.8121
Financing state and local governments. 4.4659
Financing the 1980 election. 4.8125
Finding the center. 2.2331
Finding the Old Testament in the New. 1.2648
The fine art of reading and other literary
  studies. 2.5534
Fine arts. 5.8182
Fine arts market place. 1.4591
Fine clothes to the Jew. 2.11891
Fine frenzy. 2.6097
Fine points of furniture. 1.6566
The finer tone: Keats' major poems. 2.7869
Finest stories. 2.9160
Finite-dimensional vector spaces. 5.1364
Finite element analysis: fundamentals. 5.5852
The Finite element method. 5.5851
The finite element method. 5.5726
Finite element method. 5.5729
The finite element method. 5.5836
Finite element method: basic concepts and
  applications. 5.5835
The finite element method for elliptic problems.
  5.1528
The finite element method for engineers.
  5.5727
Finite element simulation in surface and
  subsurface hydrology. 4.287
Finite element structural analysis. 5.5848
Finite elements. 5.5728
Finite elements for electrical engineers. 5.6265
Finite mathematics with business applications.
  4.4417
Finite reflection groups. 5.1293
Finite simple groups. 5.1297
Finite strip method in structural analysis.
  5.5849
Finland between East and West. 3.3290
Finland in the twentieth century. 3.3294
Finland's relations with the Soviet Union,
  1944-84. 3.3293
Finley Peter Dunne. 2.11617
Finley Peter Dunne & Mr. Dooley. 2.11618
Finnegans wake. 2.8875-2.8876
Finnesburh. 2.6289
The Finnish dilemma. 4.9076
Finnish folk poetry, epic. 2.1750
Finnish neutrality. 3.3292
The Finnish political system. 4.8666
The Finnish Revolution, 1917-1918. 3.3295
Fire and ice. 2.11760
Fire and iron. 2.13984
The fire & the sun. 1.269
Fire-bell in the night. 3.6668
Fire department hydraulics. 5.5967
The fire-dwellers. 2.9939
Fire, earth, and water. 3.8900
Fire ecology, United States and southern
  Canada. 5.3264

Fire from heaven. 2.9265
Fire in America. 5.5429
Fire in the ashes: Europe in mid-century.
  3.1194
Fire in the lake. 3.4480
Fire in the minds of men. 4.5051
Fire in the morning. 2.12493
The fire next time. 3.6659
The fire of life. 5.4238
The fire of love. 1.3220
Fire protection handbook. 5.6109
The firebrand. 3.8730
Firebreak; poems. 2.9973
Fireflies. 2.10004
The fires of spring. 2.12153
Fires on the plain. 2.2116
The First amendment and the future of
  American democracy. 4.9701
The first American Revolution. 3.6017
The first Americans, 1607-1690. 3.6875
The first and second books of Esdras. 1.2622
The first and second books of the Chronicles.
  1.2602
The First and Second Books of the Maccabees.
  1.2625
The first and second discourses. 2.4090
First approaches to the Northwest coast.
  3.8594
The first Austrian Republic, 1918-1938. 3.1901
The first Bolshevik. 4.7089
The first casualty. 2.3578
The first century of English feudalism,
  1066-1166. 3.1334
The First century of experimental psychology.
  5.204
The first Chinese embassy to the West. 3.4676
The first circle. 2.1639
The first collected edition of the works of Oscar
  Wilde, 1908-1922. 2.8267
The First Council of the Vatican. 1.3122
A first course in general relativity. 5.2103
A first course in the mathematical foundations
  of thermodynamics. 5.2250
A first course in turbulence. 5.1666
The first Crusade. 3.592
The first dance of freedom. 3.5092
The first day of Friday. 2.9826
The first day on the Somme, 1 July 1916.
  3.796
The first emancipation. 3.7227
The First Emperor of China. 3.4693
First encounter. 2.11580
First encyclopaedia of Islam. 3.3660
The first European revolution, 1776-1815.
  3.662
First Federal elections, 1788-1790. 4.7834
First feminists. 2.6073
First fire. 2.2327
First five-year plan for development of the
  national economy of the People's Republic of
  China in 1953-1957. 4.2458
The first five years of life. 5.580
First flight. 2.11313
First flowers of our wilderness. 1.5893
The first four Georges. 3.1524
First freedom. 5.7598
The first freedom. 2.58
The first freedom today. 5.7598
The first French republic, 1792-1804. 3.2087
The first gentlemen of Virginia. 3.8204
The first great civilizations. 3.3704
First images of America. 3.5967
First in the field. 5.3187
The first industrial revolution. 4.2264
First International Conference on Optical Fibre
  Sensors, 26-28 April 1983. 5.5959
First introduction to the Critique of judgment.
  1.896
The First Labour Party, 1906-1914. 4.8550
The first Lady Chatterley. 2.8965
A first look at numerical functional analysis.
  5.1473
First love. 2.1454
The first magazine. 2.3693
First majority, last minority. 4.2947
First man West. 3.8844
The first modern comedies. 2.7012
The first moderns. 1.5249

The first New Deal. 3.7765
The first new Nation. 3.6132
The first of the Tudors. 3.1397
The first offensive 1942. 3.940
The first one hundred justices. 4.9782
The first one hundred years of American
   geology. 5.2955
The first partition of Poland. 3.3280
First-person America. 3.6057
First person female American. 5.8466
First person rural. 2.3608
First person singular. 2.10279
The first pregnancy. 5.5067
The first R. 4.10456
The first Romanovs, 1613-1725. 3.3093
The first Russian revolution, 1825. 3.3123
The first scientific exploration of Russian
   America and the purchase of Alaska. 3.8647
The first sentimental education. 2.4189
The first six hundred years. 1.2290
The first South. 3.8136
The first summit. 3.882
The first taint of civilization. 3.5629
First things first. 4.1822, 4.2624
The first three minutes. 5.1881
First-time. 3.9186
First trilogy: Herself surprised. 2.8501
The First Turkish Republic. 3.3594
The first two years of the Nixon watch. 3.7903
The first urban Christians. 1.2302
The first Vietnam crisis. 3.4474
The first Whigs. 3.1505
The first world disarmament conference,
   1932-1933 and why it failed. 4.9155
The First World War. 3.788
The First World War, 1914-1918. 4.1774
The First World War in fiction. 2.3499
Firsthand report. 3.7816
Fiscal and monetary policies and problems in
   developing countries. 4.4461
The fiscal crisis of the state. 4.4657
Fiscal federalism. 4.4649
The fiscal revolution in America. 4.4654
Fiscal theory and political economy. 4.1423
The Fischer-Dieskau book of lieder. 2.13518
Fischer vs. Spassky. 4.1072
Fish communities in tropical freshwaters.
   5.3910
Fish physiology. 5.3915
Fish population dynamics. 5.5475
Fisher of Kilverstone. 3.1286
Fisheries biology. 5.3904
Fisheries economics. 4.3699
Fisheries management. 5.5477
Fisheries resources of the sea and their
   management. 5.5476
Fishery management. 5.5479
Fishes. 5.3899
Fishes of the world. 5.3902
Fishke the lame. 2.1778
Fission, fusion and the energy crisis. 5.6602
Fists and flowers. 4.9978
Fitting the task to the man. 5.4264
Fitz Hugh Lane. 1.5951
Fitzgerald's Rubáiyát. 2.1971
The Fitzhenry & Whiteside book of Canadian
   facts and dates. 3.8656
Five Afro-Caribbean voices in American
   culture, 1917-1929. 3.6690
Five bodies. 4.468
The five books of Gargantua and Pantagruel in
   the modern translation of Jacques Le Clercq.
   2.4004
Five books on consideration. 1.3143
Five centuries of famous ships. 5.7496
Five centuries of Polish poetry, 1450-1970.
   2.1745
The five clocks. 2.1038
Five courtier poets of the English Renaissance.
   2.6144
Five Elizabethan tragedies. 2.6223
The five faces of Thailand. 3.4517
Five families; Mexican case studies in the
   culture of poverty. 4.5612
Five heroic plays. 2.6231
Five hundred years of Chaucer criticism and
   allusion, 1357-1900 ... 2.6354
Five hundred years of printing. 5.7545

Five Italian Renaissance comedies. 2.4897
Five kingdoms. 5.3234
Five masters. 2.3503
Five miscellaneous essays. 2.7313
Five modern nō plays. 2.2023
Five New World primates. 5.4031
Five plays. 2.12928
Five plays. 2.1404, 2.4478, 2.6574, 2.11886,
   2.12760
Five plays; comedies and tragicomedies. 2.5252
Five pre-Shakespearean comedies. 2.6215
Five restoration tragedies. 2.6232
Five stages of Greek religion. 1.1645
Five stories of Ferrara. 2.5021
Five Stuart tragedies. 2.6222
Five temperaments. 2.10509
The five ways. 1.2823
Five women who loved love. 2.2062
The fixer. 2.13156
Flags and arms across the world. 4.7529
Flags of convenience. 4.3970
Flags of the world. 3.288
Flags through the ages and across the world.
   4.7530
The Flagstad manuscript. 1.4090
Flamboyant drama. 2.5855
Flames across the border. 3.7105
Flames over Persepolis. 3.2632
The flaming heart. 2.5575
The flamingo's smile. 5.3229
A Flann O'Brien reader. 2.9171
A Flannel shirt and liberty. 4.6079
Flannery O'Connor. 2.13213, 2.13216
The Flannery O'Connor companion. 2.13221
Flannery O'Connor, the imagination of
   extremity. 2.13212
Flannery O'Connor: voice of the peacock.
   2.13219
Flannery O'Connor's dark comedies. 2.13223
Flannery O'Connor's South. 2.13214
Flash of the spirit. 3.5689
Flatland. 5.1638
Flaubert. 2.4197
Flaubert; a collection of critical essays. 2.4202
Flaubert: the making of the master. 2.4200
Flaubert: the master. 2.4201
Flawed victory. 3.7336
Flawed words and stubborn sounds. 1.3832
The fledgling province. 3.8258
Fleet Admiral King. 3.6376
Flemish art from Ensor to Permeke. 1.5026
The Flemish tapestries at Wawel castle in
   Cracow. 1.6594
Fletcher, Beaumont & company. 2.6558
Les fleurs du mal. 2.4134, 2.4136
Flexible assembly systems. 5.7047
Flexible exchange rates. 4.4554
Flexible working hours. 4.3154
Ein fliehendes Pferd. 2.13914
Flight and rebellion. 3.7221
The flight from the enchanter. 2.9753
The flight of Icarus. 2.4680
Flight of the 7th moon. 3.5864
The flight of the Eagle. 2.14099
Flight of the seventh moon. 3.5864
Flight out of time. 1.6731
Flight through the ages. 5.6646
Flight to Canada. 2.13294
Flight to Mercury. 5.6705
Flint and feather. 2.8845
FLO: A biography of Frederick Law Olmsted.
   5.5379
Floating exchange rates and national economic
   policy. 4.4557
The floating opera. 2.12877
The floating world in Japanese fiction. 2.2010
Flood tide of empire. 3.8592
Flooding and plant growth. 5.3755
Floras of the world. 5.8115-5.8116
Florence and the Medici. 3.2925
The Florence Baptistery doors. 1.5786
Florence in the forgotten centuries, 1527-1800.
   3.2918
Florence Nightingale. 5.5164
Florence Nightingale, 1820-1910. 5.7413
Florentine codex. 3.8888-3.8889
Florentine Gothic painters from Giotto to
   Masaccio. 1.6187

Florentine painting and its social background.
   1.5007
Florentine politics and society, 1343-1378.
   3.2923
Florida. 3.8272, 3.8274
Florida archaeology. 3.5734
The Florida edition of the works of Laurence
   Sterne. 2.7275
Florida frenzy. 2.12960
Florida in the American Revolution. 3.6943
The Florida of the Inca. 3.5984
Florida politics in the gilded age, 1877-1893.
   3.8276
The flounder. 2.13757
Flow-induced vibration. 5.5743
The flow of the news. 2.3572
Flow through porous media. 4.295
Flow visualization. 5.5750
The flowering of New England. 2.10436
The flowering of the Middle Ages. 3.130
Flowering plants. 5.3693
Flowers for Algernon. 2.13114
Flowers for the king. 5.3629
Flowers in salt. 4.6148
Flowers in the mirror 2.2231
Flowers of evil. 2.4135-2.4136
Flowers of fire. 2.2139
Fluctuations in American business, 1790-1860.
   4.1915
Fluid mechanics. 5.1661
Fluid mixing technology. 5.6846
Fluid signs. 3.4211
Fluidization. 5.6843
Flukes and snails. 5.3843
Fluorides and dental caries. 5.5127
Flush, a biography. 2.9571
The flute. 1.4166
The flute book. 1.4168
The flute-player. 2.9825
Fluvial processes in geomorphology 4.244
Fly and the fly-bottle. 1.664
The flying circus of physics: with answers.
   5.2001
The Focal encyclopedia of photography.
   5.6914
The focalguide to shooting animation. 5.7008
Foch versus Clemenceau. 3.857
Focus. 2.12171
Focus on change. 4.10495
Focus on The birth of a nation. 2.3023
Foetus into man. 5.5081
La foire d'empoigne. 2.4359
Fokine: memoirs of a ballet master. 4.1138
The folded leaf. 2.12121
Folded, spindled, and mutilated. 4.9468
Foliage plant production. 5.5358
Folk and traditional music of the western
   continents. 1.4285
Folk art of the Americas. 1.6511
Folk Buddhist religion. 1.2116
Folk music in the United States. 1.4292
Folk music instruments. 1.4286
Folk music of Hungary. 1.4342
The folk music source book. 1.3452
The folk of Southern fiction. 2.10459
Folk poetry of modern Greece. 2.572
Folk religion in Japan. 1.1832
Folk song style and culture. 1.4284
The folk songs of North America, in the
   English language. 1.3432
Folklore. 5.8193
Folklore and fakelore. 4.751
Folklore and folklife. 4.759
Folklore and literature in the United States.
   5.7789
The folklore of capitalism. 4.1517
The folklore of Spain in the American
   Southwest. 4.783
The folklore of Warwickshire. 4.790
Folklore: selected essays. 4.761
Folksingers and folksongs in America. 1.4288
The folktale. 2.2701
Folktales and society. 4.792
Folktales of China. 4.807
Folktales of Japan. 4.809
Folktales of Mexico. 4.784
Folktales of Norway. 4.799
Following the color line. 3.6658

Les fondements biologiques de la géographie humaine. 4.368
Les fondements de la géographie humaine. 4.368
Fontamara. 2.5070
The Fontana economic history of Europe. 4.2196
Food. 4.3676
Food and money in ancient China. 4.2465
The food crisis in prehistory. 4.721
Food for life. 5.7108
Food grain procurement and consumption in China. 4.3683
Food in Chinese culture. 4.862
Food in history. 4.861
Food in the social order. 4.864
Food, land, and manpower in Western Europe. 4.3677
The Food manufacturing industries. 4.3679
Food, nutrition, and diet therapy. 5.5130
Food, nutrition & diet therapy. 5.5130
Food, politics, and agricultural development. 4.2888
Food, population, and employment. 4.2895
Food science. 5.6885, 5.7112
Food values of portions commonly used. 5.7123
Foods and food production encyclopedia. 5.7104
Foods of the world. 5.7139
The fool and the princess. 2.9370
Fool for love. 2.11727
The fool of quality. 2.6910
Fools crow. 2.13419
'Fools say' 2.4705
Football coaching. 4.1030
The football handbook. 4.1024
The football playbook. 4.1025
Footballers and businessmen. 4.1021
For a new liberty. 4.7701
For a new novel: essays on fiction. 2.3528
For all mankind. 5.6704
For better, for worse. 4.5617
For bread with butter. 3.8092
For capital punishment. 4.6848
For colored girls who have considered suicide, when the rainbow is enuf. 2.13316
For freedom of imagination. 2.1267
For friends at home. 3.8657
For God and country. 3.6586
For her own good. 4.6042
For king, constitution, and country. 3.1572
For king, constitution & country. 3.1572
For Lizzie and Harriet. 2.12045
For Marx. 1.1032
For men and elders. 3.5297
For my people. 1.2798, 2.12630
For peace and justice. 4.9141
For Queen and country. 3.1589
For spirits and kings. 1.5769
For the ancestors. 1.4092
For the common defense. 3.6368
For the time being. 2.8396
For those who come after. 3.5787
For Weber. 4.4768
For whom the bell tolls. 2.11842
Forbidden books in American public libraries, 1876-1939. 5.7652
Force and freedom: reflections on history. 3.461
Force and statecraft. 3.749
Force de l'âge. 2.4394
La force des choses. 2.4398
Force of circumstance. 2.4399
The force of knowledge. 5.963
Force, order, and justice. 4.9319
Forced labor in the 'people's democracies.' 4.3101
Forced labour and economic development. 4.3104
Forced options. 4.4976
Forces in modern British literature, 1885-1946. 2.5735
The forces of economic growth and decline. 4.2753
The forces of nature. 5.2470
Ford Madox Ford. 2.8634-2.8636, 2.8639

A Ford, not a Lincoln. 3.7929
Forecast for Japan. 3.4981
The Forecasting accuracy of major time series methods. 4.1242
Forecasting presidential elections. 4.8138
The Foreign affairs 50-year bibliography. 5.8253
Foreign affairs, and other stories. 2.9161
Foreign affairs bibliography. 5.8255
Foreign affairs (Council on Foreign Relations) 5.8255
Foreign affairs (New York) 5.8253
Foreign clientelae, 264-70 B. C. 3.2736
Foreign dialects. 2.3130
Foreign enterprise in developing countries. 4.3023
Foreign exchange risk. 4.4463
Foreign finance in continental Europe and the United States, 1815-1870. 4.4629
Foreign influences in American life; essays and critical bibliographies. 3.6081
Foreign investment and development in the southwest Pacific, with special reference to Australia and Indonesia. 4.4633
Foreign investment and economic development in China, 1840-1937. 4.4631
Foreign investment, transnationals, and developing countries. 4.4614
Foreign maps. 4.218
The foreign ministers of Alexander I. 3.3117
The Foreign Office. 4.9099
The foreign policies of the Taft administration. 3.7711
The foreign policies of West Germany, France, and Britain. 3.2468
Foreign policy and democratic politics. 4.9052
Foreign policy and party politics. 3.7774
Foreign policy and the democratic process. 4.9010
Foreign policy by Congress. 4.7968
The foreign policy of Canning, 1822-1827. 3.696
The foreign policy of Castlereagh, 1812-1815. 3.698
The foreign policy of Czechoslovakia, 1918-1935. 3.1919
The foreign policy of Hitler's Germany. 3.2451-3.2452
The Foreign policy of modern Japan. 4.9081
The foreign policy of North Korea. 3.5042
The foreign policy of Palmerston, 1830-1841. 3.1599
The foreign policy of Senegal. 3.5391
The foreign policy of Soviet Russia, 1929-1941. 3.3057
The foreign policy of the Soviet Union. 3.3062
The foreign policy of Victorian England, 1830-1902. 3.1608
The foreign policy process in Britain. 4.9068
Foreign relations of the United States. 4.8972
Foreign trade and economic controls in development. 4.4192
Foreign trade and U.S. policy. 4.4199
Foreign trade of Japan. 4.4242
Foreign trade under central planning. 4.4235
Foreigners in their native land. 3.6584
A Foremost nation. 4.9065
Forensic science. 4.6809
Forerunners of the French novel. 2.3843
Forerunners of the Reformation. 1.2739
Foresight and understanding. 5.936
Foresight in science. 5.975
Forest and range policy, its development in the United States. 5.5433
The forest and the sea. 5.3513
Forest ecology. 5.3785
Forest entomology. 5.5405
The Forest Goddess. 2.1864
Forest hydrology. 4.299
Forest island dynamics in man-dominated landscapes. 5.3544
Forest measurements. 4.1765
Forest mensuration. 5.5431
The forest of symbols. 3.5522
The forest people. 3.5421
Forest products. 4.3840
The forest ranger. 5.5436
The Forest Service. 5.5435, 5.5437

Forest soils. 5.5425
Forest succession. 5.3782
Forestry handbook. 5.5421
Forests for whom and for what? 5.5432
Forever flowing. 2.1564
The forever fuel. 5.6879
Forevermore, nuclear waste in America. 5.6007
Forewords and afterwords. 2.2562
Forge of democracy. 4.8060
Forged from the love of liberty. 3.9137
The Forger's art. 1.5201
Forging handbook. 5.7056
The forging of a rebel. 3.3455
The forging of American socialism. 4.6993
The forging of an aristocracy. 4.5204
The forging of the cosmic race. 3.8928
Forging world order. 4.9271
Forgive and remember. 5.5032
Forgotten children. 4.5704
The forgotten farmers. 4.2908
The forgotten friendship: Israel and the Soviet Bloc, 1947-53. 3.3075
The forgotten frontier. 3.5195
The forgotten language. 5.653
Forgotten pages of American literature. 2.10676
Forgotten partnership. 3.6416
The forgotten peace, Brest-Litovsk, March 1918. 3.830
Forgotten prophet. 2.11399
The forgotten senses. 5.4357
The forgotten victim. 5.7164
Form and fable in American fiction. 2.10608
Form and function in birds. 5.3966
Form and function: remarks on art, design, and architecture. 1.5666
Form and meaning in drama. 2.290
Form and style. 4.10618
Form and thought in Herodotus. 2.477
Form and value in modern poetry. 2.5760
Form in Gothic. 1.4755
Form in modern poetry. 2.2721
Form in music. 1.4475
Form, style, tradition. 1.5072
Formal logic. 1.1154, 1.1176
Formal logic. 1.1192
Formal organizations. 4.2642
Formal penmanship and other papers. 5.7526
The formal principle in the novel. 2.3434
Formal specification of programming languages. 5.1206
Formaldehyde toxicity. 5.4731
Formalism and Marxism. 1.1363
Formalism in ethics and non-formal ethics of values. 1.1060
Formalization of logic. 1.1202
The formation of historical theology. 1.3286
The formation of Islamic art. 1.4748
The formation of men's attitudes. 4.5019
The Formation of national States in Western Europe. 4.8365
The formation of the American medical profession; the role of institutions, 1780-1860. 5.4522
The formation of the Baltic States. 3.3306
The formation of the British Liberal Party. 4.8553
The formation of the Chinese people. 3.4654
The formation of the Christian Bible. 1.2514
The formation of the great Russian state. 3.3084
The formation of the New England railroad systems. 4.4003
The formation of the Soviet Union. 3.3209
The formative era of American law. 4.9482
The formative period of Islamic thought. 1.2058
The formative years of social security 4.3457
Former secrets. 4.7916
Formeries. 2.4757
The forming of an American tradition: Leonard J. Trinterud. 1.3390
Forms and functions of twentieth-century architecture. 1.5269
Forms and substances in the arts. 1.5112
The forms of autobiography. 3.319
Forms of lyric. 2.5782

Forms of modern British fiction. 2.6045
Forms of modern fiction. 2.3430
Forms of talk. 2.63
Formulas, facts, and constants for students and professionals in engineering, chemistry, and physics. 5.2012
Formulas for natural frequency and mode shape. 5.5854
Forrestal and the Navy. 3.7641
Forsaken. 2.1722
The forsaken, or, Meir Ezofowich. 2.1722
Forster; a collection of critical essays. 2.8656
The Forsyte saga. 2.8678
Fort Gibson, terminal on the trail of tears. 3.5741
Forthcoming books. 5.7764
The forties. 2.12764
The Forties: fiction, poetry, drama. 2.10408
Fortitude. 2.9461
FORTRAN 77. 5.5720
FORTRAN 77 and numerical methods for engineers. 5.5720
Fortress. 5.7388
Fortress besieged. 2.2237
Fortunata and Jacinta. 2.5221
Fortunata y Jacinta. 2.5220
The fortunate mistress. 2.6974
Fortune. 4.2000
Fortune and Elizabethan tragedy. 2.5885
Fortune is a woman. 4.7398
Fortune's merry wheel. 4.4637
The fortunes of Falstaff. 2.6813
Forty-two lives in treatment. 5.4843
Forty years 2.3621
Forum: Canadian life and letters, 1920-70. 3.8778
The forum of Faust. 2.13569
Forward into battle. 5.7222
The forward movement of the fourteenth century. 3.166
The fossil hunters. 5.3173
Fossils and the history of life. 5.3152
Foster care of children. 4.6576
Foundation analysis and design. 5.5916
The foundation and construction of ethics compiled from his lectures on practical philosophy. 1.1466
The Foundation Center national data book. 1.59
The Foundation directory. 1.60
Foundation engineering. 5.5918-5.5919
Foundation engineering handbook. 5.5921
The Foundation grants index. 1.61
Foundation grants to individuals. 4.10583
The foundation of the Conservative Party, 1830-1867. 4.8529
The foundation of the German Empire. 3.2304
The foundation pit. 2.1600
Foundational theology. 1.2777
Foundations. 4.6506
Foundations and principles of music education. 1.4412
Foundations in sociolinguistics. 2.22
Foundations in the dust. 3.3767
The foundations of American constitutional and political thought, the powers of Congress, and the President's power of removal. 4.7798
The foundations of American constitutionalism. 4.7809
Foundations of American diplomacy, 1775-1872. 3.6404
Foundations of American independence, 1763-1815. 3.6880
The foundations of arithmetic. 5.1040
Foundations of Canadian nationhood. 3.8675
Foundations of cataloging. 5.7626
Foundations of chemical analysis. 5.2655
Foundations of Christian faith. 1.2780
Foundations of colonial America. 4.7807
The foundations of conservative thought. 4.7308
Foundations of constitutional government in modern Japan, 1868-1900. 4.8750
Foundations of differential geometry. 5.1628
Foundations of economic analysis. 4.1393
Foundations of electromagnetic theory. 5.2371

The foundations of empirical knowledge. 1.1293
Foundations of English opera. 1.4228
Foundations of ethics. 1.1440
Foundations of experimental embryology. 5.4133
Foundations of geometry. 5.1632
Foundations of historical knowledge. 3.440
Foundations of inductive logic. 1.1184
Foundations of international politics. 4.9038
Foundations of logic and mathematics. 5.1037
The foundations of mathematical genetics. 5.3452
The foundations of metaphysics in science. 1.1268
Foundations of modern analysis. 5.1439
Foundations of modern art. 1.5121
The foundations of modern political thought. 4.7263
Foundations of music history. 1.4359
The foundations of New Testament Christology. 1.2847
Foundations of nuclear physics. 5.2050
Foundations of parapsychology. 5.639
Foundations of physical education and sport. 4.900
Foundations of physics. 5.1913
The foundations of psychoanalysis. 5.159
The foundations of quantum theory. 5.2124
Foundations of reading instruction. 4.10457
The foundations of science. 5.921
The foundations of scientific inference. 5.930
Foundations of scientific method. 5.884
Foundations of solid mechanics. 5.1647
The foundations of the nineteenth century. 3.43
Foundations of Western linguistics. 2.39
Foundations: retaining and earth structures. 5.5920
Founders of British science. 5.777
The founders of geology. 5.2950
Founders of the Middle Ages. 3.135
Founding fathers. 3.7944
The Founding Fathers. 3.7023
The founding of a nation. 3.6877
The founding of the Federal Republic of Germany. 4.8607
The founding of the French Socialist Party, 1893-1905. 4.8596
The founding of the German Empire by William I. 3.2307
The founding of the Kamakura shogunate, 1180-1185. 3.4936
The founding of the Roman Empire. 3.2773
The founding of the Second British Empire, 1763-1793. 3.1556
Founding the American colonies, 1583-1660. 3.6874
Fountain of discontent. 3.7355
The fountainhead. 2.12367
The four adventures of Richard Hannay. 2.8488
Four African literatures: Xhosa, Sotho, Zulu, Amharic. 2.2299
Four American Indian literary masters. 2.10678
Four before Richardson. 2.6260
The four books of architecture. 1.5468
Four centuries of fine printing. 5.7562
Four comedies. 2.4993
Four critical years. 4.10073
Four dynamite plays. 2.12929
Four essays on Gulliver's travels. 2.7293
Four essays on liberty. 4.7663
Four farces. 2.4528
Four French Renaissance plays. 2.3940
Four French Symbolist poets. 2.3924
The four-front war. 3.1119
Four generations: population, land, and family in colonial Andover, Massachusetts. 3.8001
The four Georges. 2.6067
The four Gospels. 1.2676
The four horsemen of the Apocalypse. 2.5238
The four loves. 1.3063
Four masterworks of American Indian literature: Quetzalcoatl/The ritual of condolence/Cuceb/The night chant. 2.2324

Four modern philosophers: Carnap, Wittgenstein, Heidegger, Sartre. 1.1003
Four other gospels. 1.2736
Four-party politics in America. 3.6385
Four plays. 2.5163
The four plays of William Wycherley. 2.7342
Four plays: Romulus the Great. The marriage of Mr. Mississippi. An angel comes to Babylon. The physicist. 2.13733
Four plays: The bald soprano, The lesson, Jack. 2.4579
Four playwrights and a postscript: Brecht, Ionesco, Beckett, Genet. 2.2812
Four Renaissance tragedies. 2.3938
Four Russian plays. 2.1317
Four screenplays. 2.14083
Four stages of Renaissance style. 1.4770
Four stories 2.14052
Four tales. 2.4064
Four theories of the press: Fred S. Siebert, Theodore Peterson, Wilbur Schramm. 2.3546
Four tragedies, and Octavia. 2.771
Four Tudor comedies. 2.6219
Fourier series, a modern introduction. 5.1556
Fourier series and integrals of boundary value problems. 5.1532
The fourteenth century, 1307-1399. 3.1365
Fourteenth century verse and prose. 2.6080
The fourth branch of Government. 2.3553
The fourth dimension. 2.617
Fourth International Conference on Energy Options. 5.6129
The fourth session. 1.3126
The fourth shore. 3.5200
The fourth year of the Nixon watch. 3.7905
The fox in the attic. 2.9709
Fox Talbot and the invention of photography. 5.6931
Fra Angelico. 1.6202
The fractal geometry of nature. 5.1566
Fractals. 5.1567
Fractional and subfractional horsepower electric motors. 5.6313
The fractional calculus. 5.1456
Fracture and fatigue control in structures. 5.5785
Fracture mechanics of polymers. 5.5805
Fragile victory. 3.4962
A fragment on government. 4.7439
The fragmented forest. 5.3221
The fragmented metropolis: Los Angeles, 1850-1930. 3.8620
The fragmented state. 4.7498
Fragments, a text and translation. 1.238
Fragments from my diary. 2.1507
Fragments of a journal. 2.4580
Fragments of Attic comedy. 2.321
Fragments of empire. 3.5554
Fragments of my fleece. 3.7622
Fragonard; biographical and critical study. 1.6103
Frame by frame. 2.2999
The frame of order. 1.402
Frame of the universe. 5.1864
The framed houses of Massachusetts Bay, 1625-1725. 1.5300
Frames of mind. 5.352
The framing of the Constitution of the United States. 4.9612
The framing of the Fourteenth amendment. 4.7832
Framley Parsonage. 2.8211
France. 4.2329
France, 1848-1945. 3.2170
France and Britain in Africa: imperial rivalry and colonial rule. 3.5119
France and Europe in 1848. 3.2153
France and Latin-American independence. 3.9009
France and the Atlantic revolution of the eighteenth century, 1770-1799. 3.2059
France and the economic development of Europe, 1800-1914. 4.2188
France and the origins of the first World War. 3.2180
France and the United States from the beginnings to the present. 3.6443

La France au 17 et 18 siècles. 3.1964
France faces depopulation. 4.1699
France, fin de siècle. 3.1967
France in America. 3.5684
France in modern times: 1760 to the present.
3.2009
France in the 1980s. 4.2331
France in the age of Louis XIII and Richelieu.
3.2022
France in the classical age. 3.2008
France in the golden age. 1.6053
France in the nineteen eighties. 4.2331
France in the sixteenth century. 3.1960
France overseas: the Great War and the climax
of French imperial expansion. 3.2194
France reviews its revolutionary origins.
3.2077
France under Napoleon. 3.2121
France under the directory. 3.2113
Frances Perkins, that woman in FDR's cabinet!
4.3592
France's Rhineland diplomacy, 1914-1924.
3.2198
Frances Trollope. 2.8243
Francesco Guicciardini. 3.2833
Franchising. 4.4319
Franciabigio. 1.6204
Francis and Clare. 1.3135
Francis Bacon. 1.6022
Francis Bacon. 1.6023
Francis Bacon: his career and his thought.
1.669
Francis I. 3.2013
Francis Hutcheson. 1.1427
Francis Parkman. 3.6257-3.6258
Francis Parkman, heroic historian. 3.6260
Francis Parkman's works. 3.8705
Francis Ponge. 2.4658
Francis Poulenc. 1.3947
Francis Poulenc, the man and his songs.
1.3946
Francis Rattenbury and British Columbia.
1.5351
Francisco I. Madero. 3.8946
The Franco-Prussian War. 3.2162
The Franco-Russian Alliance, 1890-1894.
3.720
Francogallia. 4.8576
François Couperin and the French classical
tradition. 1.3844
François Hotman. 3.2012
François le Champi. 2.4289
François Mansart. 1.5419
François Mitterrand, a political odyssey.
3.2212
François Truffaut. 2.3069
Frank Capra. 2.3037
Frank Lloyd Wright. 1.5341
Frank Lloyd Wright on architecture. 1.5473
Frank Murphy. 4.9825
Frank Norris. 2.11186
Frank O'Connor. 2.9159
Frank O'Hara. 2.12265
Frank Wedekind. 2.13868
Frankenstein. 2.8091
The Frankfurt Parliament 1848-1849. 3.2301
The Frankish Church. 1.2292
Franklin and his French contemporaries.
3.6988
Franklin D. Roosevelt. 3.7781
Franklin D. Roosevelt and American foreign
policy, 1932-1945. 3.7757
Franklin D. Roosevelt & conservation,
1911-1945. 5.5301
Franklin D. Roosevelt and foreign affairs.
3.7518
Franklin D. Roosevelt and the city bosses.
4.8841
Franklin D. Roosevelt and the New Deal,
1932-1940. 3.7761
Franny and Zooey. 2.12424
Frantz Fanon. 4.7481
Franz Boas. 4.419
Franz Grillparzer. 2.13591
Franz Kafka. 2.13800
Franz Kafka: literature as corrective
punishment. 2.13797
Franz Kafka; parable and paradox. 2.13799

Franz Liszt. 1.3911-1.3912
Franz Rosenzweig. 1.1989
Franz Schubert's letters and other writings.
1.3973
Franz Werfel, the faith of an exile. 2.13871
The Fraser. 3.8864
Fraternal organizations. 4.6173
Fray Juan Crespi, missionary explorer on the
Pacific coast, 1769-1774. 3.8604
The Fred Astaire & Ginger Rogers book.
4.1129
Frédéric Chopin. 1.3608
Frederic Chopin. 1.3837
Frederic Chopin; profiles of the man and the
musician. 1.3838
Frédéric Le Play on family, work, and social
change. 4.4759
Frederic Remington: paintings, drawings, and
sculpture in the Amon Carter Museum and
the Sid W. Richardson Foundation
collections. 1.4904
Frederick Ashton and his ballets. 4.1128
Frederick Delius. 1.3852
Frederick Douglass on women's rights. 4.6041
The Frederick Douglass papers, Series 1:
Speeches, debates, and interviews. Vol.1:
1841-46. 3.7236
Frederick Jackson Turner: historian, scholar,
teacher. 3.6265
Frederick the Great. 3.2486
Frederick the Great; a historical profile.
3.2489
Frederick the Great on the art of war. 5.7207
Frederick the Second, 1194-1250. 3.2271
Free air. 2.12006
Free and faithful in Christ. 1.1471
The free and prosperous commonwealth; an
exposition of the ideas of classical liberalism.
4.7672
A free and responsible press. 2.3548
Free-born John. 3.1481
Free fall. 2.8696
Free in the forest. 3.4460
Free lunch. 4.2009
Free men all. 4.9623
The free Negro in ante-bellum Louisiana.
3.6800
Free Negroes in the District of Columbia,
1790-1846. 3.6798
Free press/free people. 2.3549
Free-radical chain reactions. 5.2726
Free soil, free labor, free men. 3.7175
The Free Soilers. 4.8220
Free speech. 4.7679, 4.9532
Free speech and its relation to self-government.
4.7677
Free speech in the church. 1.3007
Free speech in the United States. 4.7675
The free spirit. 2.5971
Free the children. 4.10302
Free trade and sailors' rights. 5.7834
Free trade between the United States and
Canada. 4.4206
Free will and predestination in early Islam.
1.2079
The free women of Petersburg. 4.6030
Freedmen, philanthropy, and fraud. 4.4538
Freedom and after. 3.5282
Freedom and beyond. 4.10246
Freedom and civilization. 4.4878
Freedom and domination. 3.46
Freedom and equality of access to information.
5.7651
Freedom and fate. 2.11027
Freedom and fate in American thought. 1.561
Freedom and fulfillment. 1.2025
Freedom and man. 1.3011
Freedom and power in the Caribbean. 3.9125
Freedom and reason. 1.1451
Freedom and resentment, and other essays.
1.95
Freedom and responsibility in the American
way of life. 4.7683
Freedom and the Court. 4.9662
Freedom and the tragic life. 2.1374
Freedom and unity: Uhuru na umoja. 3.5298
Freedom and welfare. 4.5382
Freedom at midnight. 3.4291

Freedom for the college student press. 4.9597
Freedom, grace, and destiny. 1.2226
Freedom in Fulani social life. 3.5395
Freedom in meditation. 1.1635
Freedom in the Western World, from the Dark
Ages to the rise of democracy. 3.94
Freedom, loyalty, dissent. 4.7685
Freedom of clay and brush through seven
centuries in northern China. 1.6622
Freedom of expression. 4.9702
Freedom of expression in Japan. 4.7680
The freedom of French classicism. 2.3851
Freedom of speech in the United States.
4.9710
Freedom of the mind in history. 3.60
The freedom of the poet. 2.5624
Freedom of the press. 5.8309
Freedom of the press for whom? 4.9714
Freedom of the press from Hamilton to the
Warren Court. 4.9713
Freedom of the press from Zenger to Jefferson.
4.9712
Freedom or death. 2.591
The freedom principle. 4.4257
Freedom rising. 3.5455
Freedom, the individual, and the law. 4.9420
Freedom to die. 5.4578
Freedom to learn for the 80's. 4.10359
Freedom, virtue & the first amendment. 4.7673
Freedom's fetters. 3.7057
The freeholder. 3.1538
Freeing intelligence through teaching. 4.10364
Freeing the natural voice. 2.3536
The freeman, and other poems. 2.11775
Freemasonry and American culture, 1880-1930.
4.6175
Freethought in the United States. 5.8443
Freight transport regulation. 4.3989
Freight transportation in the Soviet Union,
including comparisons with the United States
4.3876
Frémont, explorer for a restless nation. 3.7153
The French. 3.1969
French 20 bibliography. 5.8002
French absolutism: the crucial phase 1620-1629.
3.2021
French achievement in literature. 2.3830
French African verse. 2.4845
French and English science dictionary. 5.708
The French armies in the Seven Years' War.
5.7311
The French Army and politics, 1870-1970.
5.7313
French Baroque music. 1.3704
French Canada in transition. 3.8819
The French-Canadian idea of Confederation,
1864-1900. 3.8689
The French-Canadian outlook. 3.8692
French-Canadian society. 3.8688
The French Canadians; 1760-1967. 3.8693
French capitalism in the nineteenth century.
4.2324
French chivalry; chivalric ideas and practices in
mediaeval France. 3.292
French cinema. 2.2891-2.2892
French cinema of the occupation and resistance.
2.2893
French cities in the nineteenth century. 4.6260
French classical literature. 2.3847
French colonialism, 1871-1914. 4.8923
French colonialism in tropical Africa,
1900-1945. 3.5120
French comic drama, from the sixteenth to the
eighteenth century. 2.3893
The French Communists. 4.8593
The French critic, 1549-1967. 2.2497
French economic growth. 4.2333
The French economy and the state. 4.2325
The French education of Henry Adams.
3.6237
French eighteenth-century painters. 1.6052
The French encounter with Africans. 3.5121
A French-English dictionary for chemists.
5.2594
The French Enlightenment and the Jews.
3.3957
The French experience in Mexico, 1821-1861.
3.1978

French explorers in the Pacific. 3.5536
French feminism in the 19th century. 4.6117
French feminism in the nineteenth century. 4.6117
French feminist poems from the Middle Ages to the present. 2.3925
French fiction today. 2.3915
French Gothic architecture of the 12th and 13th centuries. 1.5531
French historical method. 3.1974
French Indo-China. 3.4432
French institutions: values and politics. 3.1954
French introspectives, from Montaigne to André Gide. 2.3833
The French language. 2.860
French legitimists and the politics of moral order in the early Third Republic. 3.2177
The French lieutenant's woman. 2.9685
French literature from 1795 to our era. 2.3856
French local government. 4.8878
French master drawings of the nineteenth century. 1.5843
French music, from the death of Berlioz to the death of Fauré. 1.3706
The French new criticism. 2.2498
The French new novel. 2.3916
The French novel since the War. 2.3914
French opinion on war and diplomacy during the Second Empire. 3.711
The French Pacific Islands. 3.5556
French painting. 1.6047
French painting 1774-1830. 1.6050
French painting 1774-1830, the Age of Revolution. 1.6054
French painting between the past and the present. 1.6058
French painting in the time of Jean De Berry. 1.6412
French painting in the time of Jean de Berry. 1.6413, 1.6415
The French Parliament: politics in the Fifth Republic. 4.8589
French periodical index 1973-1974. 1.43
French poets and novelists. 2.3860
French policy and the American alliance of 1778. 3.6935
The French prerevolution, 1787-1788. 3.2057
The French presence in Cochinchina and Cambodia. 3.4440
The French press. 2.3694
French public opinion and foreign affairs, 1870-1914. 3.1976
French reference grammar for schools and colleges. 2.868
The French régime in Prince Edward Island. 3.8808
The French régime in Wisconsin and the Northwest. 3.8445
The French Renaissance in England. 2.5572
The French Revolution. 3.2084, 3.2089, 3.2094, 3.2099, 3.2103
The French Revolution, 1787-1799. 3.2085
The French Revolution and the Church. 3.2095
The French Revolution and the poor. 4.6533
French Revolution documents. 3.2062
The French Revolution in Germany. 3.2500
The French Revolution in miniature. 3.2116
The French revolution of 1830. 3.2146
French revolutionary warfare from Indochina to Algeria, the analysis of a political and military doctrine. 5.7312
The French romantics. 3.1965
French rural history. 4.2852
French sculpture at the beginning of the Gothic period, 1140-1225. 1.5699
The French Second Republic. 3.2151
The French Socialist experiment. 4.7052
The French Socialist Party. 4.8594
French society, 1789-1970. 4.5347
French-speaking Africa. 3.5090
The French stage in the eighteenth century. 2.3368
The French stage in the nineteenth century. 2.3366
The French stake in Algeria, 1945-1962. 3.2210

The French theory of the nation in arms, 1866-1939. 5.7309
French tragic drama in the sixteenth and seventeenth centuries. 2.3892
The French veteran from the Revolution to the Restoration. 5.7371
French XX bibliography. 5.8002
French war aims against Germany, 1914-1919. 3.837
French West Africa. 3.5375
French women and the Age of Enlightenment. 4.5865
The French workers' movement. 4.3414
French writers and their society, 1715-1800. 2.3855
Frenchman's creek. 2.8603
Frenzy of Orlando. 2.4961
Frequency synthesis by phase lock. 5.6516
The fresh & salt water fishes of the world. 5.3898
A fresh approach to the New Testament and early Christian literature. 1.2627
Fresh-water biology. 5.3255
Fresh-water invertebrates of the United States. 5.3825
Freshwater ecology. 5.3547
Freshwater vegetation. 5.3777
Freshwater wetlands. 5.3549
Freud. 5.151
Freud and his patients. 5.153
Freud and man's soul. 5.149
Freud and modern psychology. 5.4824
Freud and the post-Freudians. 5.150
The Freud/Jung letters. 5.4911
Freud, the mind of the moralist. 5.156
Freudianism and the literary mind. 2.2375
The Friar's, Summoner's, and Pardoner's tales from the Canterbury tales. 2.6317
The Frick Collection. 1.4661
Friday's footprint. 2.10071
Frieda Lawrence. 2.9002
Friedel-Crafts chemistry. 5.2748
Friedrich der Grosse. 3.2490
Friedrich Engels. 4.7066
Friedrich Froebel. 4.10191
Friedrich Hebbel. 2.13600
Friedrich Hölderlin. 2.13614
Friedrich List, economist and visionary, 1789-1846. 4.1362
Friedrich Ratzel. 4.10
Friedrich Schiller. 2.13651-2.13653
Friedrich Schiller's drama. 2.13654
Friedrich von Holstein, politics and diplomacy in the era of Bismarck and Wilhelm II. 3.2318
Friend and foe. 3.5796
Friendly fire. 3.4509
Friendly Islands. 3.5680
Friends, for life. 5.433
Friends not masters. 3.4136
Friends of friends. 4.5058
The friends of liberty. 3.1573
Friends of libraries sourcebook. 5.7617
Friends; [play] 2.2126
Friends, you drank some darkness. 2.14062
The frightening angels. 4.2741
Fringe of leaves. 2.10181
Fritz Lang. 2.3061
The frog who dared to croak. 2.13315
The frogs. 2.425
From a logical point of view. 1.1178
From a writer's notebook. 2.11422
From affluence to praxis. 1.117
From Alexander to Cleopatra. 3.2527
From ape to angel. 4.472
From art to theatre. 2.3163
From atoms to quarks. 5.2432
From barter to slavery. 3.9205
From Baudelaire to surrealism. 2.3876
From behind the veil. 2.10531
From Bismarck to the world war. 3.2337
From black clouds to black holes. 5.1828
From Bolzano to Wittgenstein. 1.133
From Brown to Boston. 5.8152
From Byzantium to Sasanian Iran and the Islamic world. 1.5108
From chance to purpose. 5.5049
From Chekhov to the revolution. 2.1262

From classic to romantic. 1.1386
From colony to country. 3.6123
From colony to empire. 3.6410
From colony to nation. 3.9209
From Columbus to Castro. 3.9089
From community to metropolis. 3.9223
From confederation to nation. 4.9617
From conquest to collapse. 3.677
From Cortés to Castro. 3.8977
From crisis to crisis: Pakistan 1962-1969. 3.4128
From Croesus to Constantine. 1.4732
From crossbow to H-bomb. 5.7173
From cubism to surrealism in French literature. 2.3870
From Cuchulainn to Gawain. 2.6417
From death to morning. 2.12774
From Descartes to Wittgenstein. 1.425
From deserts the prophets come. 1.6729
From despotism to revolution, 1763-1789. 3.651
From Dessalines to Duvalier. 3.9118
From Domesday book to Magna Carta, 1087-1216. 3.1325
From Dreyfus to Vichy. 3.3961
From empire to nation. 4.7486
From Enlightenment to Revolution. 4.7278
From Euclid to Eddington. 5.947
From falling bodies to radio waves. 5.1936
From fiction to film: D. H. Lawrence's 'The rocking-horse winner.' 2.8972
From field to factory. 4.5431
From fish to philosopher. 5.3383
From flintlock to rifle. 5.7380
From Flushing to Calvary. 2.11549
From folk psychology to cognitive science. 5.630
From frontier to plantation in Tennessee. 3.8343
From Gautier to Eliot. 2.5573
From genesis to genocide. 4.4866
From glory to glory. 1.3089
From 'good order' to glorious revolution. 3.8006
From Gorky to Pasternak. 2.1273
From graven images. 4.1755
From group dynamics to group psychoanalysis. 5.4920
From H-bomb to star wars. 5.7280
From hand ax to laser. 5.6159
From Hayes to McKinley; national party politics, 1877-1896. 3.7404
From Hegel to Marx. 1.1034
From Hegel to Nietzsche. 1.441
From here to eternity. 2.13100
From humanism to science, 1480-1700. 3.175
From hunters to farmers. 4.744
From impotence to authority. 4.9908
From Italy to San Francisco. 3.8629
From Joseph II to the Jacobin trials. 3.1887
From kingdom to commonwealth. 4.7293
From King's College to Columbia, 1746-1800. 4.10991
From know-how to nowhere. 5.5538
From Latin to modern French, with especial consideration of Anglo-Norman. 2.863
From Lenin to Khrushchev, the history of world communism. 4.6973
From Leonardo to Lavoisier, 1450-1800. 5.717
From LeRoi Jones to Amiri Baraka. 2.12873
From Little Rock to Boston. 4.10791
From Loyalist to Founding Father. 3.7001
From Madagascar to the Malagasy Republic. 3.5314
From magic to science. 5.756
From Main Street to State Street. 4.6211
From Main Street to Stockholm. 2.12011
From Mankind to Marlowe. 2.5859
From many countries. 2.1797
From many, one. 4.9107
From Marx to Hegel. 1.473
From Max Weber. 4.1197
From medical police to social medicine. 5.4647
From Ming to Ch'ing. 3.4706
From modern to contemporary. 2.10489
From Munich to the Liberation, 1938-1944. 3.1061
From myth to the modern mind. 5.712

From Napoleon to Stalin, and other essays. 3.668

From now to zero. 4.5694

From one to zero. 5.1264

From option to opening. 2.3267

From Paris to Sèvres. 3.861

From peasant to farmer. 4.5108

From peasants to farmers. 3.8308

From physical concept to mathematical structure. 5.1973

From plan to planet: life studies. 3.6644

From plantation to ghetto. 3.6622

From poor law to welfare state. 4.6521

From prairie to corn belt. 4.2958

From prejudice to destruction. 3.4010

From private vice to public virtue. 4.5693

From protest to challenge. 3.5451

From Puritan to Yankee. 3.8021

From realignment to reform. 3.8034

From religion to philosophy. 1.232

From renaissance to renaissance. 2.1776

From resistance to revolution. 3.6921

From reverence to rape. 2.3014

From Rhodesia to Zimbabwe. 3.5515

From ritual to record. 4.955

From ritual to romance. 2.2639

From Rousseau to Lenin. 4.7142

From Sand Creek. 2.13228

From self to society, 1919-1941. 3.6097

From shadows to reality. 1.2521

From Shylock to Svengali. 2.5584

From slavery to freedom. 3.6616

From Solon to Socrates. 3.2533

From Spanish court to Italian ghetto. 3.3979

From stone age to Christianity. 1.1595

From Stonehenge to modern cosmology. 5.1869

From symbolism to Baudelaire. 2.4140

From Tennessee slave to St. Louis entrepreneur. 3.7214

From tension to tonic. 2.12849

From the American system to mass production, 1800-1932. 5.7017

From the black bar. 4.9696

From the calculus to set theory, 1630-1910. 5.1070

From the closed world to the infinite universe. 1.1330

From the Dardanelles to Oran. 5.7459

From the dark tower. 2.10319

From the deep woods to civilization. 3.5945

From the diaries of Felix Frankfurter. 4.9813

From the diary of a snail. 2.13753

From the dreadnought to Scapa Flow. 5.7460

From the easy chair. 2.10989

From the family farm to agribusiness. 4.2933

From the Gracchi to Nero. 3.2775

From the ground up. 1.5483

From the modern repertoire. 2.3760

From the Molly Maguires to the United Mine Workers. 4.3389

From the other shore, and The Russian people and socialism. 3.702

From the sketchbooks of the great artists. 1.5793

From the terrace. 2.12269

From the Wagner act to Taft-Hartley. 4.3507

From thirty to seventy. 4.5818

From tin foil to stereo. 5.7084

From Tobacco Road to Route 66. 2.10445

From tradition to Gospel. 1.2675

From trucial states to United Arab Emirates. 3.4059

From trust to terror. 3.1163

From unification to Nazism. 3.2305

From Utopia to nightmare. 4.7174

From Van Eyck to Bruegel. 1.6231

From Vietnam to America. 3.4512

From Virgil to Milton. 2.2770

From vital force to structural formulas. 5.2848

From Vulgar Latin to Old French. 2.864

From war to cold war, 1942-48. 3.917

From war to war: the Arab-Israeli confrontation, 1948-1967. 3.3882

From Wesley to Asbury. 1.3371

From wilderness to empire. 3.8600

From writer to reader. 2.2527

From x-rays to quarks. 5.1937

La Fronde. 3.2028

Front and center. 2.3258

Front-bench opposition. 4.8445

The frontal granular cortex and behavior. 5.4346

Frontenac, the courtier governor. 3.8704

The Frontenacs. 2.4630

Frontier America. 3.6347

Frontier: American literature and the American West. 2.10352

The frontier camp meeting. 1.3374

A frontier family in Minnesota. 3.8497

The frontier in American history. 3.6359

The frontier in American literature. 2.10347

The frontier in Latin American history. 3.8983

Frontier politics and the sectional conflict. 3.8595

Frontier regulars; the United States Army and the Indian, 1866-1891. 3.5779

The frontier republic. 3.8382

Frontier theatre. 2.3277

The frontier thesis: valid interpretation of American history?. 3.6344

Frontier women. 4.6076

Frontiers. 4.7502

Frontiers in comparative medicine. 5.4741

Frontiers in geographical teaching. 4.32

Frontiers of astrophysics. 5.1769

Frontiers of change. 4.1906

The frontiers of criticism. 2.2452

The frontiers of drama. 2.2781

The frontiers of international law. 4.9291

The frontiers of public administration. 4.7889

Frontiers of the Northwest. 3.8495

Frontiers of theology in Latin America. 1.2806

Frontiersmen in blue; the United States Army and the Indian, 1848-1865. 5.7285

Frost. 2.11757

Froude's Life of Carlyle. 2.7552

The fruited plain. 5.5234

Les fruits d'or. 2.4706

Fruits of propaganda in the Tyler administration. 3.7134

The fruits of the earth. 2.4554

Frustrations and aggression. 4.5065

Der Fuehrer. 3.2401

Fuel economy of the gasoline engine. 5.6222

Fuels, furnaces, and refractories. 5.6212

Fuente ovejuna. 2.5202

The Fugger news-letters. 3.620

The fugitive. 2.4810

The Fugitive group. 2.10446

Fugitive industry. 4.3208

The Fugitives. 2.10443

Fugue and invention in theory and practice. 1.4481

La fuite. 2.4760

Fulbright of Arkansas. 3.7523

Full circle. 3.1663

Full employment in a free society. 4.3229

Full fathom five. 3.1439

Fullness of life. 1.2930

Function circuits. 5.6467

The function of criticism. 2.2459, 2.2461

The function of law in the international community. 4.9288

The function of mimesis and its decline. 2.2372

The function of reason. 1.1263

Functional analysis. 5.1472, 5.1475

Functional anatomy of the newborn. 5.5088

Functional design in fishes. 5.3914

Functional programming. 5.1180

The functional theory of politics. 4.9138

The functional tradition in early industrial buildings. 1.5545

Functionalism and world politics. 4.1834

Functionalism, exchange and theoretical strategy. 4.4834

Functionalism historicized. 4.507

The Functioning of freshwater ecosystems. 5.3545

Functioning of the multinational corporation. 4.2716

Functions of painting. 1.4613

The functions of social conflict. 4.4940

The functions of the executive. 4.2641

Fund accounting. 4.4730

Fund-raising, grants, and foundations. 5.8375

Fundamental algorithms. 5.1185

Fundamental concepts of programming systems. 5.1200

Fundamental legal conceptions as applied in judicial reasoning. 4.9358

The fundamental physical constants and the frontier of measurement. 5.2025

Fundamental principles of heat transfer. 5.2269

The fundamental principles of the metaphysic of ethics. 1.878

Fundamental problems in phonetics. 2.179

Fundamental problems of philosophy; the world of action and the dialectical world. 1.1144

The fundamental questions of philosophy. 1.1257

Fundamental reference sources. 5.7712

Fundamental structures of computer science. 5.1175

Fundamental transition metal organometallic chemistry. 5.2782

Fundamentalism. 1.2793

Fundamentalism and American culture. 1.2794

Fundamentals handbook of electrical and computer engineering. 5.6260

Fundamentals of acoustics. 5.2228

Fundamentals of air pollution. 5.6041

Fundamentals of applied electrostatics. 5.2345

Fundamentals of applied entomology. 5.5407

Fundamentals of chemical reaction engineering. 5.6813

Fundamentals of classical thermodynamics. 5.6204

Fundamentals of contemporary set theory. 5.1348

The fundamentals of corrosion. 5.5816

Fundamentals of curriculum development. 4.10450

Fundamentals of cyclic stress and strain. 5.5784

Fundamentals of data structures in Pascal. 5.1241

Fundamentals of earthquake engineering. 5.5859

Fundamentals of elementary particle physics. 5.2394

Fundamentals of energy engineering. 5.6160

Fundamentals of energy production. 5.6158

Fundamentals of engineering geology. 5.5889

Fundamentals of experimental design. 5.1413

Fundamentals of flight. 5.6664

Fundamentals of fluidized-bed chemical processes. 5.6844

Fundamentals of fracture mechanics. 5.5787

Fundamentals of gas turbines. 5.6218

Fundamentals of geophysical data processing. 5.6743

Fundamentals of geotechnical analysis. 5.5896

Fundamentals of heat transfer. 5.2265, 5.2268

Fundamentals of interactive computer graphics. 5.5647

Fundamentals of language. 2.181

The fundamentals of learning. 4.10363

Fundamentals of linear algebra. 5.1312

Fundamentals of modern physics. 5.2053

Fundamentals of momentum, heat, and mass transfer. 5.5753

Fundamentals of musical acoustics. 1.4373

Fundamentals of neurology. 4.4318

Fundamentals of nuclear physics. 5.2048

Fundamentals of numerical reservoir simulation. 5.6806

Fundamentals of optics. 5.2281

Fundamentals of park technology. 5.5385

Fundamentals of personal rapid transit. 5.5936

Fundamentals of physical measurement. 5.2008

Fundamentals of physical metallurgy. 5.6780

Fundamentals of pipe flow. 5.6239

Fundamentals of plant genetics and breeding. 5.5320

Fundamentals of plant pathology. 5.5399

Fundamentals of plasma physics. 5.2387

Fundamentals of Portland cement concrete. 5.5801

Fundamentals of programming languages. 5.1205

Fundamentals of queueing theory. 5.5599
Fundamentals of semiconductor devices.
    5.6502
Fundamentals of soil behavior. 5.5901
Fundamentals of soil physics. 5.5273
Fundamentals of statistical and thermal physics.
    5.2183
Fundamentals of surveying. 5.5824
Fundamentals of temperature, pressure, and
    flow measurements. 5.2232
Fundamentals of the fungi. 5.3721
Fundamentals of transport economics. 4.3868
Fundamentals of transportation systems
    analysis. 4.3878
Funeral speech, Erotic essay 60, 61, Exordia
    and Letters. 2.447
Fungal genetics. 5.3719
Fungal nutrition and physiology. 5.3718
Funk & Wagnalls standard dictionary of
    folklore, mythology and legend. 4.753
Funk and Wagnalls standard dictionary of
    folklore, mythology, and legend. 4.753
Fur trade and empire. 3.8850
Fur trade and exploration. 4.3861
Fur trade in Canada. 3.8836
The furious passage of James Baldwin. 2.12863
Furniture. 1.6555
Furniture for the Victorian home. 1.6552
The furniture of historic Deerfield. 1.6568
The furniture of Robert Adam. 1.6575
Furniture of the 1950s. 5.7073
Furniture styles. 1.6553
Furniture treasury (mostly of American origin)
    1.6565
Further confessions of Zeno. 2.5065
Further essays in monetary economics. 4.4474
Further extracts from the note-books of Samuel
    Butler. 2.7514
Further letters of Gerard Manley Hopkins,
    including his correspondence with coventry
    Patmore. 2.7828
Fusion. 5.2450
Fusion of psychiatry and social science. 5.4842
Fusion welding and brazing of copper and
    copper alloys. 5.7058
Futile diplomacy. 3.3862
The futility of family policy. 4.5601
The future. 3.70
The future as history. 3.7576
The future as nightmare. 2.8257
Future automotive fuels. 5.6877
The future comes; a study of the New Deal.
    4.1948
Future developments in telecommunications.
    5.6350
The future for automotive technology. 5.6633
Future indefinite. 2.8585
Future issues in health care. 5.4624
The future of American politics. 3.7533
The Future of American transportation.
    4.3892
The future of an illusion. 1.1564
The future of architecture. 1.5276
The future of arid lands. 4.293
The Future of cultural minorities. 4.7487
The future of higher education: some
    speculations and suggestions. 4.10550
The future of history. 3.357
The Future of international organization.
    4.9216
The future of law in a multicultural world.
    4.9276
The future of mankind. 3.1169
The future of marriage. 4.5561
The future of nonmetropolitan America.
    4.2114
The Future of North America. 4.8275
The future of oil. 4.3761
The Future of our liberties. 4.9668
The future of political science. 4.7228
The future of public education. 4.10026
The future of Roman Catholic theology.
    1.3125
The future of social security. 4.3467
The future of socialism. 4.7037
The future of student affairs. 4.10279
The Future of the automobile. 4.3817
The future of the future. 3.75

The Future of the international legal order.
    4.9275
The Future of the international monetary
    system. 4.4566
The future of the novel. 2.3424
The Future of the printed word. 5.7570
The future of the Soviet economic planning
    system. 4.2377
The Future of the university in Southern
    Africa. 4.10150
The future of the world economy. 4.1832
The Future of US-China relations. 3.6425
Future shock. 4.5107
Future tense. 2.3006
The Future that doesn't work. 4.7033
Futurism. 1.4847, 1.6186, 2.1310
Futurist manifestos. 1.6734

G. B. Shaw; a collection of critical essays.
    2.8076
G. D. H. Cole and socialist democracy. 4.3647
G. E. Moore: essays in retrospect. 1.753
G E R. 1.19
G. Howard Ferguson. 3.8825
G-men, Hoover's F.B.I. in American popular
    culture. 4.6823
G-men, Hoover's FBI in American popular
    culture. 4.6823
Gabon. 4.8807
Gabriel Dumont. 3.5791
Gabriel Fauré, 1845-1924. 1.3866
Gabriel Fielding. 2.8415
Gabrielle Roy. 2.4825
Gaelic and Gaelicised Ireland in the Middle
    Ages. 3.1824
The Gaelic vision in Scottish culture. 2.829
Gaining ground. 4.2907
Gains and losses. 2.6029
Gainsborough. 1.6031
Gainsborough as printmaker. 1.6490
Galactic structure. 5.1840
Galatians. 1.2716
Galaxies. 5.1851
Galaxies and quasars. 5.1854
The Galaz ruin. 3.5908
Galen On the natural faculties. 2.368
Galileo. 5.1691
Galileo and the art of reasoning. 1.416
Galileo studies. 5.1693
Gallegos: Donã Bárbara. 2.5446
A gallery of Southerners. 2.10456
The Gallic war. 2.653
Gallipoli. 3.807-3.808
The Gallup poll. 4.5228
The Gallup Poll; public opinion, 1935-1971.
    4.5227
The Gallup report (Princeton, N.J.); no. 236.
    1.1866
Galois theory. 5.1292
The Galton case. 2.12158
Gambetta and the making of the Third
    Republic. 3.2184
Gambetta and the national defence. 3.2185
The gambler, with Polina Suslova's diary.
    2.1349
Gambling with history. 3.7937
Gambling with truth. 5.910
The Game. 4.1031
A game at chesse. 2.6635
Game of cards and other stories. 2.2274
A game of hide and seek. 2.9397
The game of logic. 5.1257
The game of the impossible. 2.5964
Game theory. 5.1378
Game theory in the social sciences. 4.1220
Game without rules. 2.8686
Games ancient and oriental. 4.878
The games must go on. 4.975
Games people play. 4.4923
Gametes & spores. 5.3480
Gametes and spores. 5.3480
Gammer Gurton's needle. 2.6219
Ganadevata (The temple pavilion). 2.1862
Gandhãran art in Pakistan. 1.5051
Gandhi and civil disobedience. 3.4307
Gandhi in South Africa. 3.5461
Gandhian thoughts. 3.4306
The gang. 4.6716

Gangs in Chicago. 4.6716
Gaon. 4.5433
García Lorca. 2.5259
Garcilaso de la Vega. 2.5190
The garden and the city. 2.7199
The garden and the wilderness. 4.7881
Garden cities of to-morrow. 4.6306
The garden of Adonis. 2.11787
A garden of earthly delights. 2.13197
The garden of Eden. 2.11843
The Garden of Eden. 5.3644
The garden of the Finzi-Continis. 2.5023
The gardener's directory. 5.5309
Gardening encyclopedia. 5.5365
Gardening indoors with house plants. 5.5354
The gardens of China. 5.5370
The gardens of Japan. 5.5373
The gardens of Pompeii. 3.2723
Gardner's Art through the ages. 1.4673
Gargantua and Pantagruel. 2.4004
Gargoyles. 2.11824
Garibaldi. 3.2871
Garibaldi and the making of Italy. 3.2872
Garibaldi and the Thousand. 3.2873
Garibaldi's defence of the Roman Republic,
    1848-9. 3.2935
The garland of letters. 1.1692
The Garland Shakespeare bibliographies.
    2.6796
Garrets and pretenders. 2.10281
Garrick. 2.3340
The Garrick stage. 2.3307
The Garrick year. 2.9657
Gary Snyder's vision. 2.13329
Garzanti comprehensive Italian-English,
    English-Italian dictionary. 2.859
Gas chromatography with glass capillary
    columns. 5.2665
Gas I. 2.13802
Gas II. 2.13803
Gas tables. 5.2041
The gas turbine engine. 5.6631
Gas turbine theory. 5.6219
Gascony, England's first colony, 1204-1453.
    3.2223
Gaseous electronics. 5.2381
Gases, liquids, and solids. 5.2185
Gastrointestinal disorders. 5.4998
The gate of darkness. 2.2159
The Gate of Heavenly Peace. 3.4750
Gatekeepers of black culture. 5.7585
The gates. 2.9731
The gates of horn. 2.3900
Gates report on an all-volunteer armed force.
    5.7365
The Gateway. 4.8953
Gathering evidence. 2.13881
A gathering of fugitives 2.12602
A gathering of old men. 2.13026
Gathering the tribes. 2.13015
The gaucho Martín Fierro. 2.5391
Gauchos and the vanishing frontier. 3.9254
Gaudeamus igitur. 2.1673
Gaudete. 2.9714
Gaudí. 1.5444
Gaudy night. 2.9305
Gauguin's paradise lost. 1.6107
The Gaullist phenomenon. 3.2214
Gauss. 5.1093
Gautrek's saga. 2.13981
Gavin Douglas. 2.6470
Gawain and the Grene Knight. 2.6132, 2.6134,
    2.6414
The Gawain-poet; studies in his personality and
    background. 2.6419
Gay American history. 4.5535
The gay couple in Restoration comedy. 2.5908
Gay/lesbian almanac. 4.5538
Gay men's health. 5.4768
The gay science. 1.1046
Gazetteer. 4.72
The Gazetteer of India. 3.4156
Gedichte aus dem Nachlass. 2.13701
Gedichte und Interpretationen. 2.13485
Geist der Goethezeit. 2.13466
Le Gel. 2.4797
Gelede. 3.5355

Gemini. 2.13046
Gemini G.E.L. 1.6441
Gemini GEL. 1.6441
Gemini; The transfiguration of Benno Blimpie.
  2.13095
Gems, their sources, descriptions, and
  identification. 5.3025
Gemstone & mineral data book. 5.7069
Gemstone and mineral data book. 5.7069
Gender, fantasy, and realism in American
  literature. 2.10568
Gender politics. 4.6059
Gender-related behaviors of children in abusive
  situations. 4.6562
Gender roles in development projects. 4.5833
Gendercide. 4.5658
The gene. 5.3423
The gene age. 5.6868
Gene banks and the world's food. 5.5321
The gene business. 5.6866
Gene expression. 5.3466
Genealogical guide to the early settlers of
  America. 3.296
The genera of Myxomycetes. 5.3728
General and comparative endocrinology.
  5.4244
General and comparative physiology. 5.4186
General and industrial management. 4.2648
General anthropology. 4.426
The General Assembly of the United Nations.
  4.9207
General cartography. 4.205
General catalogue of printed books to 1975.
  5.7670
General chemistry, principles and structure.
  5.2625
General competitive analysis. 4.1290
General Custer and the Battle of the Little Big
  Horn. 3.5782
General education in a free society. 4.10005
General endocrinology. 5.4248
General equilibrium systems. 4.1298
General Gage in America. 3.6890
General genetics. 5.3418, 5.3441
General George B. McClellan. 3.7329
General history of Africa. 3.5072
The General history of Africa: studies and
  documents. 3.5071
A general history of the pyrates. 4.101
A general history of the science and practice of
  music. 1.3630
General history of the things of New Spain.
  3.8888-3.8889
General Horatio Gates. 3.6891
The general method of social work practice.
  4.6462
A general model for multivariate analysis.
  5.1406
General parasitology. 5.4080
General phonetics. 2.180
General physics. 5.1979
General physiology of cell specialization.
  5.3588
General principles of criminal law. 4.9394
The general prologue to the Canterbury tales
  and the Canon's yeoman's prologue and tale.
  2.6318
General relativity. 5.2104, 5.2218
General relativity from A to B. 5.2101
General science index. 5.8418
The General Strike, 1926. 4.3174
General textbook of entomology. 5.3857
The general theory of alternating current
  machines. 5.6316
The general theory of electrical machines.
  5.6316
A general theory of magic. 5.684
General theory of population. 4.1599
General theory of relativity. 5.2102
General theory of value, its meaning and basic
  principles construed in terms of interest.
  1.1303
General topology. 5.1602
General topology and homotopy theory.
  5.1593
A general view of positivism. 1.821
General zoology. 5.3800, 5.3802
Generalization in ethics. 1.1442

Generals and admirals. 5.7233
Generals & politicians. 3.2206
Generals in blue. 3.7315
Generals in gray. 3.7316
Generals vs. presidents. 3.9005
The generalship of Alexander the Great.
  5.7200
The generation of 1914. 3.84
The Generation of 2000. 2.10773
Generation of animals. 2.341
A generation of materialism, 1871-1900. 3.712
A generation of schooling. 4.10119
Generation of vipers. 3.6176
A generation on trial: U. S. A. v. Alger Hiss.
  3.7547
Generation without farewell. 2.11404
The generations. 2.2277
A generative theory of tonal music. 1.4429
A generous man. 2.13274
Genes. 5.3416
Genes in populations. 5.3475
Genes, organisms, populations. 5.3403
Genes, radiation, and society. 5.3413
Genesis. 5.1714
Genesis 1-11. 1.2591
Genesis 12-36. 1.2592
Genesis 37-50. 1.2590
Genesis A. 2.6304
The genesis and evolution of time. 5.1756
Genesis and structure of Hegel's
  Phenomenology of spirit. 1.933
Genesis (Anglo-Saxon poem) 2.6304
Genesis of a music. 1.4204
The genesis of Bangladesh. 3.4151
The genesis of German conservatism. 3.2244
The genesis of modern British town planning.
  1.5602
The genesis of modern Chinese literary criticism
  (1917-1930) 2.2153
The genesis of Napoleonic imperialism. 3.2122
Genesis one to eleven. 1.2591
The genetic basis of evolutionary change.
  5.3473
The genetic code. 5.3447
Genetic complementation. 5.3427
Genetic counseling. 5.4750-5.4751
Genetic diversity and natural selection. 5.3404
Genetic engineering of plants. 5.5319
Genetic epistemology. 5.594
Genetic fix. 5.3457
Genetic load, its biological and conceptual
  aspects. 5.3444
Genetic maps. 5.3464
Genetic recombination. 5.3465
The genetical theory of natural selection.
  5.3357
Genetics. 5.3420
The Genetics and biology of Drosophila.
  5.3479
Genetics and conservation. 5.3220
Genetics and education. 5.357
Genetics and metabolism. 5.3443
Genetics and society. 5.3422
Genetics and the origin of species. 5.3356
Genetics experiments with bacterial viruses.
  5.4470
Genetics notes. 5.3414
The Genetics of aging. 5.3508
The genetics of bacteria and their viruses.
  5.4448
The genetics of human populations. 5.3424
Genetics: questions and problems. 5.3432
Geneva 1954. 3.4437
Geneva and the coming of the wars of religion
  in France, 1555-1563. 3.2010
Geneva and the consolidation of the French
  Protestant movement, 1564-1572. 1.3408
The 'genius' 2.11594
Genius and lust. 2.12182
Genius and the mobocracy. 1.5332
The genius of American politics. 4.7304
The genius of Italy. 3.2825
The genius of John Ruskin. 2.8026
The genius of the future. 1.5149
The genius of the German lyric. 2.13489
Genius of the Italian theater. 2.4899
The genius of Wilhelm Busch. 2.13715

Genji monogatari ekotoba. English. 1983.
  1.6335
Genocide. 4.9332
Genreflecting. 2.10565
Gentile da Fabriano. 1.6205
The Gentile Zionists. 3.3921
The gentle art of lexicography as pursued and
  experienced by an addict. 2.1076
The gentleman & cabinet-maker's director.
  1.6577
Gentleman boss: the life of Chester Alan
  Arthur. 3.7490
The gentleman from Indiana. 2.11237
The Gentleman from San Francisco, and other
  stories. 2.1477
Gentleman in a dustcoat. 2.12373
The gentleman in the parlour. 2.9103
A gentleman of Broadway. 2.12422
The gentleman of Renaissance France. 3.1961
Gentleman's agreement. 2.11875
Gentleman's progress. 3.6015
Gentlemen freeholders. 3.8210
Gentlemen of science. 5.693
Gentlemen prefer blondes. 2.12036
Gentlemen, scholars, and scoundrels. 2.10667
The gentlemen theologians. 1.2410
Gentrification, displacement, and neighborhood
  revitalization. 4.6342
The gentry. 4.6395
Geo Katalog. 5.8216
Geo Katalog (Stuttgart, Germany: 1980)
  5.8216
Geochemistry. 5.3103
Geocryology. 4.286
Geodesic math and how to use it. 5.5864
Geoffrey Chaucer. 2.6342
Geoffrey Chaucer of England. 2.6338
Geographers abroad. 4.40
The geographic background of Greek & Roman
  history. 3.2517
The geographic regions of Puerto Rico. 3.9126
A Geographical bibliography for American
  libraries. 5.8202
The geographical dictionary of ancient and
  mediaeval India. 3.4153
The geographical distribution of animals.
  5.3816
Geographical ecology. 5.3240
Geographical essays. 4.3
Geographical guide to floras of the world.
  5.8116
Geographical history in Greek lands. 3.2532
The geographical lore of the time of the
  Crusades. 4.63
Geographical perspectives in the Soviet Union.
  4.2397
Geographical regions of France. 4.252
Géographie politique. 5.8205
Géographie universelle. 4.79
Geography. 4.83
Geography and cartography. 4.6
Geography and economic development. 4.4119
Geography & ethnic pluralism. 4.4874
Geography and ethnic pluralism. 4.4874
Geography and geographers. 4.359
Geography and politics in a world divided.
  4.7495
Geography and politics in America. 4.7494
Geography and world power. 4.370
Geography as a fundamental research discipline.
  4.11
Geography as spatial interaction. 4.80
Geography in relation to the social sciences.
  4.12
Geography in the making. 4.1
Geography in the Middle Ages. 4.61
Geography in the schools of Europe. 4.12
Geography in undergraduate liberal education.
  4.39
A geography of American sport: from Cabin
  Creek to Anaheim. 4.939
Geography of Bangladesh. 3.4145
The geography of economic activity. 4.4126
A geography of Europe. 3.1187
A geography of Europe. 3.1185
The geography of evolution. 5.3815
The geography of faith. 1.3263
A geography of Ghana. 3.5336

Geography of Latin America. 3.8974
A geography of mankind. 4.82
The geography of modern Africa. 3.5053
A geography of Norden. 3.3350
Geography of population. 4.1651
The geography of Puerto Rico. 4.2161
The geography of religion in England. 1.2225
The geography of Strabo. 2.393
The geography of the Bible. 1.2550
Geography of the biosphere. 5.3239
Geography of the E.E.C. 4.2216
Geography of the EEC. 4.2216
The geography of the flowering plants. 5.3665
The geography of the Mediterranean region. 3.1189
Geography of the Soviet Union. 4.2401
A geography of the U.S.S.R. 4.2393
Geography of the U.S.S.R. 3.3015
The geography of towns. 4.6259
Geography of western civilization. 4.6188
The geography of western Europe. 4.5292
Geokartenbrief. 5.8216
GeoKatalog. 5.8216
Geologic evolution of Europe. 5.3004
Geologic field methods. 5.2990
Geologic reference sources. 5.8217
A Geologic time scale. 5.3085
Geological background to fossil man. 5.3141
The geological evolution of Australia & New Zealand. 5.3008
Geological observations on coral reefs, volcanic islands, and on South America. Part 1. 5.3117
Geological oceanography. 5.2985
Geological sciences. 5.2947
Geology and earth sciences sourcebook for elementary and secondary schools. 5.2988
Geology and the urban environment. 5.2986
Geology illustrated. 5.2959
Geology in the field. 5.2989
Geology in the nineteenth century. 5.2951
Geology of Africa. 5.3006
The geology of continental margins. 5.2981
The geology of Europe. 5.3003
The geology of ore deposits. 5.3023
Geology of the nonmetallics. 5.6792
Geology of the U.S.S.R. 5.3005
Geometric algebra. 5.1357
Geometric Greece. 3.2580
Geometric inequalities. 5.1572
Geometric theory of dynamical systems. 5.1618
Geometrical and physical optics. 5.2282
Geometrical and structural crystallography. 5.2922
Geometrical investigations. 5.1034
Geometrical methods. 5.1069
Geometrical methods in the theory of ordinary differential equations. 5.1510
Geometry and algebra in ancient civilizations. 5.1266
Geometry and the imagination. 5.1635
Geometry in ancient and medieval India. 5.1085
A geometry of international trade. 4.4114
Geometry of molecules. 5.2767
Geomorphology. 4.260-4.261
Geomorphology and time. 4.257
Geomorphology in deserts. 4.281
Geomorphology of cold environments. 4.285
Geophysical anomalies. 5.2507
Geophysical fluid dynamics. 5.2493
Geophysical methods in geology. 5.3080
Geophysical signal processing. 5.6739
Geopolitics of the Caribbean. 3.9147
Georg Büchner. 2.13557
Georg Büchner and the birth of the modern drama. 2.13558
Georg Cantor. 5.1347
Georg Kaiser. 2.13805
Georg Lukács. 1.1136
Georg Philipp Telemann. 1.4017
George Ade. 2.10894
George Ade, warmhearted satirist. 2.10895
George Bancroft. 3.6248
George Bancroft, Brahmin rebel. 3.6247
George Bancroft, the intellectual as Democrat. 3.7086

George Bellows and the ashcan school of painting. 1.5917
George Berkeley in America. 1.690
George Bernard Shaw. 2.8082
George Bernard Shaw: his life and personality. 2.8078
George Borrow, eccentric. 2.7437
George C. Marshall. 3.7612
George Caleb Bingham. 1.5920
George Canning, politician and statesman. 3.1574
George Catlin and the old frontier. 1.5925
George Colman, the elder. 2.6942
George Crabbe. 2.7618
George Croghan and the westward movement, 1741-1782. 3.8079
George Croghan, wilderness diplomat. 3.8371
George Eliot. 2.7709
George Eliot; a biography. 2.7702
George Eliot, a centenary tribute. 2.7701
George Eliot and community. 2.7713
George Eliot and her world. 2.7704
George Eliot & John Chapman. 2.7705
George Eliot & the novel of vocation. 2.7697
George Eliot and the visual arts. 2.7712
A George Eliot dictionary. 2.7714
George Eliot, her mind and her art. 2.7700
The George Eliot letters. 2.7698
George Eliot: the critical heritage. 2.7706
George Eliot's early novels. 2.7703
George-Etienne Cartier. 3.8742
George Farquhar. 2.7017
George Frideric Handel. 1.3890
George Frisbie Hoar and the half-breed Republicans. 3.7436
George Gascoigne, Elizabethan courtier, soldier, and poet. 2.6581
George Gissing. 2.7743
George Gissing, a critical biography. 2.7746
George Gissing, ideology and fiction. 2.7745
George Grosz. 1.4994
George Grosz. English. 1.4994
George Grove, 1820-1900. 1.4108
George Henry Lewes. 1.727
George Herbert. 2.7069
George Herbert and the seventeenth-century religious poets. 2.6156
George Herbert Mead: self, language, and the world. 1.616
George Herbert, the critical heritage. 2.7065
George Herbert's lyrics. 2.7067
George Howe. 1.5311
George Inness. 1.5947, 1.5949
George M. Cohan, prince of the American theater. 2.3251
George Macdonald, an anthology. 2.7922
George Mason, reluctant statesman. 3.7005
George Meredith. 2.7942
George Meredith and English comedy. 2.7947
George Meredith, his life and work. 2.7941
George Moore: the artist's vision, the storyteller's art. 2.7959
George N. Peek and the fight for farm parity. 4.2941
George Nelson on design. 1.5489
George of Bohemia, King of Heretics. 3.1913
George Orwell. 2.9188, 2.9193, 2.9195, 2.9199, 2.9203
George Orwell, a life. 2.9192
George Orwell and the origins of 1984. 2.9186
A George Orwell companion. 2.9194
George Peabody. 4.6470
George Peele. 2.6645
George Pierce Baker and the American theatre. 2.3239
George Rickey. 1.5671
George S. Counts and American civilization. 4.1201
George S. Counts, educator for a new age. 4.10243
George S. Schuyler. 2.12450
George Sand et Alfred de Musset: correspondance. 2.4292
George Sand's theatre career. 2.4295
George Sandys, poet-adventurer. 2.6504
George Seferis: collected poems, 1924-1955. 2.608

George Segal. 1.5673
George Stubbs, 1724-1806. 1.4956
George Theotokas. 2.613
George III and the historians. 3.1554
George W. Cable. 2.10920
George W. Cable, a biography. 2.10923
George W. Cable: the life and times of a Southern heretic. 2.10922
George W. Norris. 3.7676
George Washington. 3.7028-3.7030
George Washington and American independence. 3.7032
George Washington and the new nation, 1783-1793. 3.7033
George Washington Carver. 5.5223
George Washington Carver, scientist and symbol. 5.5224
George Washington Harris. 2.11046
George Washington, man and monument. 3.7027
George Washington's generals. 3.6888
George Whitefield; the life and times of the great evangelist of the eighteenth-century revival. 1.3395
Georges Bizet, his life and work. 1.3820
Georges Braque. 1.6068
Georges Clemenceau: a political biography. 3.2183
Georges Rouault. 1.6144-1.6145
Georges Seurat. 1.6148
Georgia. 3.8254
Georgia and the Union in 1850. 3.8266
Georgia O'Keeffe. 1.5960
Georgian grace. 1.4772
The Georgian literary scene, 1910-1935: by Frank Swinnerton. 2.5734
Georgian London. 1.5375
Georgian poetry, 1920-1922. 2.6187
The Georgian scene. 2.5734
Georgian scene painters and scene painting. 2.3156
The Georgian triumph, 1700-1830. 3.1535
The Georgics of Virgil. 2.795
Georgy girl. 2.9681
Geotechnical engineering. 5.5900
Geotechnical engineering investigation manual. 5.5891
Geothermal energy. 5.6208
Geothermal energy; resources, production, stimulation. 5.6294
Geothermal energy: review of research and development. 5.6291
Geothermal energy utilization. 5.6211
Geothermal reservoir engineering. 5.6209
Gerald of Wales, 1146-1223. 3.1353
Gérard de Nerval. 2.4224, 2.4226
Gérard de Nerval, the mystic's dilemma. 2.4225
Gerard Manley Hopkins. 2.7836
Gerard Manley Hopkins (1844-1889) 2.7833
Gerard Manley Hopkins meets Walt Whitman in heaven and other poems. 2.12965
Gerard Manley Hopkins, priest and poet. 2.7835
Die gerettete Zunge. 2.13721
Gerhart Hauptmann. 2.13768
Geriatric medicine. 5.5002
Géricault and his work. 1.6108
Géricault, his life and work. 1.6109
The germ of laziness. 5.4674
German aesthetic and literary criticism. Kant, Fichte, Schelling, Schopenhauer, Hegel. 1.1385
German air power in World War I. 3.823
German-American relations and German culture in America. 5.7860
The German Army and the Nazi Party, 1933-1939. 5.7318
German baroque drama. 2.13491
The German baroque novel. 2.13502
German baroque poetry, 1618-1723. 2.13486
German big business and the rise of Hitler. 4.3072
The German Bildungsroman from Wieland to Hesse. 2.13500
German books in print. 5.8007
The German catastrophe. 3.2444
The German church conflict. 1.2453

The German church struggle and the Holocaust. 1.2455
The German churches under Hitler. 1.2454
The German colonial empire. 4.8929
A German community under American occupation: Marburg, 1945-52. 3.2504
The German conception of history. 3.2248
German culture in America. 3.6160
The German Democratic Republic. 3.2476
The German Democratic Republic since 1945. 3.2477
The German dictatorship. 3.2434
The German drawings in the collection of Her Majesty the Queen at Windsor Castle. 1.5804
The German economy, 1870 to the present. 4.2340
The German element in the United States. 3.6546
The German Empire, 1871-1918. 3.2324
A German-English dictionary for chemists. 5.2595
A German-English dictionary of idioms. 2.1182
German-English science dictionary. 5.706
German expressionist drama. 2.13495
German expressionist painting. 1.6164
German expressionist poetry. 2.13488
German expressionist sculpture. 1.5715
German feminism. 4.6124
German foreign policy, 1871-1914. 3.2328
The German generals talk. 3.967
German history, 1933-45. 3.2443
German home towns: community, state, and general estate, 1648-1871. 4.6261
German humanism. 2.13465
German idea of freedom. 3.2259
The German ideology. 4.7071
The German influence in France after 1870. 3.2178
German intonation. 2.1181
The German Jew. 3.3966
German-Jewish pioneers in science, 1900-1933. 5.2618
The German language 2.1177
German language and literature. 5.8013
The German-language press in America. 2.3644
The German lesson. 2.13812
German liberalism in the nineteenth century. 3.2298
The German lied and its poetry. 1.4238
German literature. 2.13452
German literature in English translation. 5.8012
German literature in the sixteenth and seventeenth centuries: renaissance, reformation, baroque. 2.13463
German literature under National Socialism. 2.13480
The German lyric of the baroque in English translation. 2.13519
German Marxism and Russian communism. 4.7062
German masters of the nineteenth century. 1.4982
German medieval tales. 2.13526
The German naval mutinies of World War I. 3.840
The German naval officer corps. 5.7476
The German Navy in World War Two. 5.7466
The German Navy's story. 3.1029
The German novel. 2.13498
German Novelle. 2.13501
The German Novelle. 2.13505
The German officer-corps in society and state, 1650-1945. 5.7372
The German opposition to Hitler. 3.2432
German painting, from Dürer to Holbein. 1.6159
German painting from romanticism to expressionism. 1.6162
German painting of the 19th century. 1.6161
German painting; the late Middle Ages (1350-1500). 1.6158
German poetic realism. 2.13473
German poetry. 2.13483
German poetry, 1910-1975. 2.13517

German poetry in the Age of the Enlightenment. 2.13487
The German policy of Augustus. 3.2243
The German problem reconsidered. 3.2321
German pronunciation and phonology. 2.1179
German Renaissance architecture. 1.5422
The German resistance. 3.2386
The German Revolution, 1918-1919. 3.2417
German romantic criticism. 2.2501
German romantic painting. 1.6163
German rule in Russia, 1941-1945. 3.1071
German social democracy, 1905-1917. 4.8606
German sociology. 4.4760
The German Sturm und Drang. 2.13470
German theatre today. 2.3375
German theories of the corporative state. 4.7595
The German Werkbund. 1.6526
German women in the nineteenth century. 4.6125
The Germanic invasions. 3.583
The Germanic peoples. 1.4734
The Germans. 3.2463
Germans and Jews. 3.4014
Germans in the Cameroons, 1884-1914. 3.5399
Germany. 3.2242
Germany, 1815-1890. 3.2295
Germany, 1866-1945. 3.2322
Germany, 1918-1933. 3.2376
Germany after Bismarck, the Caprivi era, 1890-1894. 3.2335
Germany and Eastern Europe since 1945. 3.2466
Germany and England: background of conflict, 1848-1894. 3.2262
Germany and the approach of war in 1914. 3.2338
Germany and the Soviet Union 1939-1941. 3.947
Germany at the polls. 4.8610
Germany beyond the wall. 3.2478
Germany in our time. 3.2459
Germany in the eighteenth century. 3.2281
Germany in the High Middle Ages, c. 1050-1200. 3.2269
Germany in the later Middle Ages. 3.2273
Germany in the Thirty Years War. 3.2280
Germany tried democracy. 3.2363
Germany under the Salian and Hohenstaufen emperors. 3.2265
Germany without Bismarck. 3.2336
Germany without Jews. 3.3967
Germany's aims in the First World War. 3.778
Germany's colonial demands. 4.8932
Germany's comeback in the world market. 4.4233
Germany's drive to the west (Drang nach Westen) A study of Germany's western war aims during the First World War. 3.2339
Germany's economic preparations for war. 4.2343
Germany's first bid for colonies, 1884-1885. 4.8930
Germany's new conservatism, its history and dilemma in the twentieth century. 3.2378
Germany's underground. 3.2430
Germinal. 2.4341
Germs that won't die. 5.5134
Geronimo; a biography. 3.5839
Gerontology, a core list of significant works. 5.8382
Gerontology, a cross-national core list of significant works. 5.8382
Gershom Scholem. 1.1990
Gershwin, his life and music. 1.3874
Gertrude Stein, a biography of her work. 2.12520
Gertrude Stein, her life and work. 2.12519
Gertrude Stein in pieces. 2.12517
Gerusalemme liberata di Torquato Tasso raccontata da Alfredo Giuliani. 2.4979
Gesammelte Erzählungen 2.13810
Gesammelte Hörspiele. 2.13732
Gesammelte Schriften. 2.13769, 2.13788
Gesammelte Werke. 2.13676, 2.13678, 2.13700-2.13701, 2.13712
Gesammelte Werke. 2.13586, 2.13631, 2.13640, 2.13727, 2.13820, 2.13840, 2.13859, 2.13866

Gesammelte Werke in 5 Bänden. 2.13724
Gesammelte Werke in fünf Bänden. 2.13724
Das Gesamtwerk. 2.13698
Das Gesamtwerk des Zeichners und Dichters. 2.13714
Geschichte der arabischen Litteratur. 2.1834
Geschichte der deutschen Literatur. 2.13453
Geschichte der deutschen literatur bis zum ausgang des mittelalters. 2.13459
Geschichte der deutschen Sprache. 2.1174
Geschichte der politischen Parteien in Deutschland. 4.8602
Geschichte Friedrichs des Grossen. 3.2487
Gesta Henrici Quinti. 3.1380
Gesta Stephani. 3.1344
Gesta Stephani, Regis Anglorum. English & Latin. 3.1344
The gestalt approach & Eye witness to therapy. 5.4892
Gestalt psychology. 5.226
Gestalt therapy verbatim. 5.4866
The gestalts of war. 5.7151
El gesticulador. 2.5356
Der gestiefelte Kater. 2.13664
Die gestundete Zeit. 2.13674
Get your ass in the water and swim like me. 2.10661
Getting married. 2.14074
Getting started. 4.3305
Getting to know him. 1.4109
Getting to yes. 5.473
Getting what we ask for. 4.10962
Das Gewicht der Welt. 2.13887
Ghana. 3.5338
Ghazals of Ghalib. 2.1899
The Ghaznavids. 3.4078
The Ghent altarpiece and the art of Jan van Eyck. 1.6263
The ghetto. 3.3900
A ghetto takes shape. 3.8388
The ghost dance. 1.1533
The ghost-dance religion and Wounded Knee. 3.5827
Ghost story. 2.13336
The ghost writer. 2.13298
The ghostly lover. 2.11816
Ghosts in the mind's machine. 5.319
Ghosts of the gothic. 2.5985
Giacomo Manzù. 1.5731
Giambattista and Domenico Tiepolo. 1.5816
Giambattista Vico's science of humanity. 1.1093
Gian Lorenzo Bernini. 1.5726
Giant enterprise: Ford, General Motors, and the automobile industry. 4.3819
Giant talk. 2.3702
The giants. 4.9062
Giants in the earth. 2.14054
The giant's rival. 3.9011
Gide. 2.4563
Gideon Welles. 3.7335
Gideon's day. 2.8587
Gideon's trumpet. 4.9881
Gifford Pinchot, forester-politician. 3.7444
The gift. 2.11570, 4.866
The Gift. 2.1581
The gift of a cow. 2.1890
The gift of government. 4.7742
The gift of language. 2.95
The Gift outright. 2.10759
Gigi. 2.4494
Gilbert & Sullivan opera guide. 1.4015
Gilbert and Sullivan opera guide. 1.4015
Gilbert, his life and strife. 2.7729
Gilbert Keith Chesterton. 2.7566
Gilbert Stuart. 1.5975
Gilbert Stuart. 1.5977
Gilbert Stuart and his pupils. 1.5976
The gilded age. 3.6050
Giles and Phineas Fletcher. 2.6478
Giles Cooper award winners. 2.6200
Giles goat-boy. 2.12878
Gilgamesh. 2.1767
Gilgamesh. English. 2.1767
The Gilgamesh epic and Old Testament parallels. 2.1768
The Gill history of Ireland. 3.1817

Gimpel the fool, and other stories. 2.1819
The ginger man. 2.8599
The gingerbread age. 1.5294
The Gioconda smile. 2.8816
Giono par lui-même. 2.4567
Giordano Bruno and the Hermetic tradition. 1.413
Giordano Bruno; his life and thought. 1.412
Giorgio de Chirico. 1.6199
Giorgione. 1.6207
Giotto. 1.6208
Giotto in perspective. 1.6209
Giotto: the Arena Chapel frescoes. 1.6210
Giovanni and Lusanna. 4.5775
Giovanni Gabrieli. 1.3873
Giovanni Verga. 2.5017
Giovanni's room. 2.12858
The giraffe. 5.4046
Giraffes, black dragons, and other pianos. 1.4154
Giraudoux. 2.4572
Girl from the beach. 2.10172
A girl in winter. 2.8940
The girls. 2.4640
Girls at war, and other stories 2.10103
Girls in their married bliss. 2.9785
The girls of slender means. 2.9359
Girl's puberty ceremony. 3.5916
The Girondins. 3.2111
Gissing, the critical heritage. 2.7744
Giulio Romano. 1.6211
Giuseppe Ferrari and the Italian Revolution. 3.2870
Giuseppe Ungaretti. 2.5077
Giuseppe Verdi, his life and works. 1.4026
Give birth to brightness. 2.10333
Give us bread but give us roses. 4.3278
Give us each day. 2.11610
Given giving. 2.4781
Giving up the gun. 3.4938
Glacial and Pleistocene geology. 5.3143
Glacial and Quaternary geology. 5.3144
Glacial geomorphology. 4.277
Glacier variations and climatic fluctuations. 4.316
Glaciers and glacial erosion. 5.3119
Glaciers and landscape. 4.318
Gladstone. 3.1625, 3.1627
Gladstone and liberalism. 3.1628
Glaister's Glossary of the book. 5.7540
Glaister's medical jurisprudence and toxicology. 5.4715
The Glasgow edition of the works ... 4.1266
The Glasgow edition of the works and correspondence of Adam Smith. 1.3, 4.1420
Glass. 1.6643
The glass bead game (Magister Ludi). 2.13772
The glass house. 1.5511, 2.12413
A glass of blessings. 2.9800
The Glass Palace chronicle of the kings of Burma. 3.4426
Glass science. 5.6903
The glass village. 2.12364
A Glastonbury romance. 2.9235
The Glenn Gould reader. 1.3471
Glenway Wescott. 2.12679
A glimpse of Sion's glory. 3.7946
Glimpses of unfamiliar Japan. 2.11077
The gloaming, oh my darling. 2.13353
A global approach to national policy. 4.9028
The global debt crisis. 4.4588
Global ecology. 5.3532
Global order. 3.1181
Global reach. 4.2730
The Globe Playhouse. 2.6706
The Globe restored: a study of the Elizabethan theater. 2.6707
Glooskap's children; encounters with the Penobscot Indians of Maine. 3.5937
Gloriana. 2.9744
Glories. 5.2555
The glorious cause. 3.6900
The glorious Revolution in America. 3.6872
The glory and the dream: a narrative history of America, 1932-1972. 3.7762
Glory Road. 3.7360
Glory road. 2.11827
Glossary. 5.5984

Glossary for horticultural crops. 5.5335
Glossary of art, architecture, and design since 1945. 1.4580
Glossary of astronomy and astrophysics. 5.1681
A glossary of botanic terms. 5.3630
Glossary of chemical terms. 5.2592
Glossary of genetics and cytogenetics. 5.3409
A glossary of geographical terms. 4.74
Glossary of geology. 5.2939
Glossary of linguistic terminology. 2.13
A glossary of literary terms. 2.2356
Glossary of mapping, charting, and geodetic terms. 4.200
Glossary of meteorology. 5.2497
Glossary of Russian abbreviations and acronyms. 2.1240
Glossary of terms frequently used in weather modification 5.2540
Glossary of the book. 5.7540
Gloves. 4.857
Gluck. 1.3876
Gluck and the opera. 1.3877
Gnosis. 1.2966, 1.2971
The gnostic dialogue. 1.2970
The gnostic Gospels. 1.2969
The gnostic Paul. 1.2700
Gnosticism and early Christianity. 1.2967
Gnys at wrk. 4.10420
Go. 2.13089
Go down, Moses. 2.11663
Go East, young man: the early years. 4.9808
Go tell it on the mountain. 2.12860
The goalie's anxiety at the penalty kick. 2.13886
The goals of psychotherapy. 5.4855
The goatibex constellation. 2.1628
God and man in the Koran. 1.2034
God and other minds. 1.2831
God and philosophy. 1.2825
God and political duty. 4.7385
God and skepticism. 1.535
God and the permission of evil. 1.2845
God and the rhetoric of sexuality. 1.2571
God bless you, Mr. Rosewater, or, Pearls before swine. 2.13391
The God boy. 2.10215
God, guilt, and death. 1.1560
God, history, and historians. 1.2248
God in modern philosophy. 1.1335
God in search of man. 1.1966
God in Yoruba belief. 1.1864
God, power, and evil. 1.2843
The God that failed. 4.6982
God, the future of man. 1.2811
God the problem. 1.2829
Godard on Godard; critical writings. 2.3046
The goddess. 1.1653
Goddesses, whores, wives, and slaves. 4.5848
Gödel, Escher, Bach. 5.1056
Gödel's proof. 5.1047
Godkin lectures. 4.10555
God's altar. 2.10485
Gods and heroes of the Greeks. 2.419
Gods and rituals. 4.549
God's bits of wood. 2.4859
God's caliph. 1.2065
God's choice. 4.10811
God's Englishman. 3.1492
Gods, ghosts, and ancestors. 1.1810
Gods, graves, and scholars. 3.255
God's little acre. 2.11453
Gods of flesh/gods of stone. 1.1707
Gods of the ancient Northmen. 1.1670
God's playground. 3.3329
God's playground, a history of Poland. 3.3329
God's plot. 1.3343
God's plot & man's stories. 2.6003
God's plot and man's stories. 2.6003
God's rule and kingdon. 1.2818
The gods themselves. 2.12854
God's trombones. 2.11937
God's world; an anthology of short stories. 2.1847
Godwin's 'Political justice.' 4.1559
Goebbels and National Socialist propaganda, 1925-1945. 3.2436
The Goebbels diaries, 1939-1941. 3.2384

The Goebbels diaries, 1942-1943. 3.2382
Goethe. 2.13582, 2.13584
Goethe; a critical introduction. 2.13583
Goethe and the novel. 2.13571
Goethe edition. 2.13574
Goethe, the lyrist. 2.13575
Goethe, the poet. 2.13585
Goethe's autobiography, Poetry and truth from my own life. 2.13576
Goethes Briefe. 2.13572
Goethe's collected works. 2.13574
Goethe's major plays. 2.13570
Gogol. 2.1384, 2.1387
Gogol from the twentieth century. 2.1389
Going after Cacciato. 2.13204
Going down fast. 2.13251
Going for the rain. 2.13229
Going it alone. 4.5724
Going north, migration of Blacks and whites from the South, 1900-1950. 4.6357
Going to meet the man. 2.12859
Going to Shakespeare. 2.6860
Going to the territory. 2.13003
Going too far. 4.6063
Gold coast and slum. 3.8416
The gold diggers, and other stories. 2.11534
Gold is the cornerstone. 3.8606
The gold rushes. 5.6751
The Golden Age. 1.6238
The golden age: drama, 1492-1700. 2.5127
Golden age drama in Spain: general consideration and unusual features. 2.5126
The Golden age of Anglo-Saxon art, 966-1066. 1.4935
The golden age of Black nationalism, 1850-1925. 3.6683
The golden age of Brazil, 1695-1750. 3.9206
The Golden age of British photography, 1839-1900. 5.6924
The golden age of Chinese drama, Yüan 'tsa-chü' 2.2168
The golden age of colonial culture. 3.6019
The golden age of English manuscript painting (1200-1500) 1.6410
The golden age of Japan, 794-1192. 1.6726
The golden age of Persia. 3.4077
The golden age of science fiction. 2.10829
The golden age of Spain, 1516-1659. 3.3437
The golden age: prose and poetry. 2.5103
The golden apples. 2.12662
The golden ass. 2.649
The golden bough. 1.1603
The golden cage. 5.4939
The Golden casket. 2.2201
The golden day. 3.6146
The golden door. 3.8047
Golden fleece. 2.11374
The golden fruits. 2.4707
The Golden grove. 2.7312
The golden horns. 2.13965
The Golden labyrinth. 2.5840
Golden Latin artistry. 2.648
The golden legend. 1.3247
The Golden Lotus. 2.2228
The golden lyre. 2.288
The golden moment: the novels of F. Scott Fitzgerald. 2.11739
Golden multitudes. 5.7701
The golden notebook. 2.9016
The golden peaches of Samarkand. 4.4096
The golden road to modernity. 3.4337
The golden tradition. 2.1905, 3.3952
The golden treasury of the best songs & lyrical poems in the English language. 2.6102
Goldsworthy Lowes Dickinson. 2.8598
The Goldwater caper. 3.7644
Golf. 4.1033
Golf magazine. 4.1032
Golf magazine's encyclopedia of golf. 4.1032
Golf my way. 4.1034
The Goliard poets. 2.817
The Golovlyov family. 2.1423
The Golovlyov family. 2.1422
Les gommes. 2.4689
Goncharov. 2.1393
The Goncourt brothers. 2.4229
The Goncourt journals, 1851-1870. 2.4228
Gondal's queen. 2.7458

Gone with the wind. 2.12196
Gone with the wind letters, 1936-1949.
　2.12198
Good and evil, two interpretations. 1.1491
Good and faithful labor. 4.2909
Good and mad women. 4.6164
The good apprentice. 2.9754
Good as Gold. 2.13081
Good behaviour. 2.8928
Good-bye Dolly Gray. 3.5504
Good-bye, Mr. Chips. 2.8801
Good-bye to all that. 2.8726
The good companions. 2.9246
Good company. 4.608, 4.6628
The good earth. 2.11428
Good food book. 5.5133
The good life. 1.1436
A good man. 3.7639
Good morning, midnight. 2.9274
Good morning, revolution. 2.11892
The good news according to Mark. 1.2690
Good news Bible. 1.2501
Good night, sweet prince. 2.3241
Good reading. 5.7708
Good Samaritan, and other stories. 2.12270
The good soldier. 2.8631
The good soldier Švejk and his fortunes in the
　World War. 2.1669
The good terrorist. 2.9015
Good tidings. 3.65
A good woman. 2.11416
Goodbye, Columbus, and five short stories.
　2.13299
Goodbye, Gutenberg. 2.3575
Goodbye to Berlin. 2.8833
Goode's World atlas. 4.112
Gora. 2.1871
Gordon Allport, the man and his ideas. 5.513
Gordon Childe, revolutions in archaeology.
　3.259
Gore Vidal. 2.12626
Gore Vidal. 2.12627
Goren's Bridge complete. 4.1067
Gorgias 2.533
Gorgias. 1.247
Gorilla, my love. 2.12865
Gorillas in the mist. 5.4033
Gorky. 2.1511
Gormenghast. 2.9220
The Gormenghast trilogy. 2.9220
Gosforth. 4.5331
The Gospel according to John. 1.2727
The gospel according to Luke (I-IX) 1.2692
The Gospel according to Mark. 1.2689
The Gospel according to St. John. 1.2697
The Gospel and the land. 1.2672
Gospel hymns and social religion. 1.2991
The Gospel of peace and justice. 4.5118
The gospel of Sri Ramakhrishna. 1.210
The gospel of wealth, and other timely essays.
　4.1573
Gospel parallels. 1.2683
The Gospels, their origin and their growth.
　1.2680
Gossamer odyssey. 5.6688
The gossamer years. 2.2053
The Gotha programme. 4.7072
The Gothic. 1.5239
Gothic. 1.4754
Gothic architecture. 1.5240-1.5241
Gothic art 1140-c. 1450. 1.4753
The Gothic cathedral. 1.5520
Gothic politics in the Deep South. 3.8175
The Gothic quest. 2.5984
The Gothic revival. 1.5250
Gothic revival. 1.5377
The Gothic revival, 1745-1845. 1.5369
Gothic revival in Canadian architecture.
　1.5344
Gothic revival in Europe and Britain: sources,
　influences, and ideas. 1.5252
The gothic revival style in America, 1830-1870.
　1.6521
The Gothic romance. 2.3456
Gothic sculpture in France, 1140-1270. 1.5700
The Gothic tradition in fiction. 2.3461
The Goths in Spain. 3.3419
Gottfried Benn. 2.13679

Gottfried Kellers Leben, mit Benutzung von
　Jakob Baechtolds Biographie. 2.13621
Gotthold Ephraim Lessing. 2.13632
Die göttliche Komödie. 2.4939
Gould medical dictionary. 5.4484
The gourd dancer. 2.13175
The Gourman report. A rating of graduate and
　professional programs in American and
　international universities. 4.9933
Gourmet. 5.7140
Gourmet cook book. 5.7140
The Gourmet cookbook. 5.7140
Governance and self-government in Canada.
　4.8270
The governance of Anglo-Saxon England,
　500-1087. 4.8386
The governance of Britain. 4.8450
Governance of Federal regulatory agencies.
　4.7990
The governance of mediaeval England from the
　conquest to Magna carta. 4.8392
Governing America. 4.5157
Governing American schools. 4.10642
Governing greater Stockholm. 4.8881
Governing metropolitan areas. 4.8859
Governing our fifty States and their
　communities. 4.8243
Governing Soviet cities. 4.8880
Governing the UAW. 4.3379
Governing the ungovernable city. 4.8853
Governing the university. 4.10574
Governing under pressure. 4.8438
Governing without consensus. 4.8571
Government agencies. 4.7891
Government and administration in Western
　Europe. 4.8366
Government and community, England,
　1450-1509. 3.1377
Government and economic life. 4.1967
Government and labor in early America.
　4.3560
Government and local power in Japan, 500 to
　1700. 4.8893
Government and Parliament. 4.8434
Government and people in Hong Kong,
　1841-1962, a constitutional history. 4.8725
Government and politics in Africa. 4.8791
Government and politics in India. 4.8712
Government and politics in the Middle Ages.
　4.7373
The government and politics of China,
　1912-1949. 4.8732
The government and politics of India. 3.4294
The government and politics of Ireland. 4.8565
Government and politics of Northern Ireland.
　4.8568
Government and politics of Singapore. 4.8729
The Government and politics of the Middle
　East and North Africa. 3.3725
The government and politics of the PRC.
　3.4807
The government and politics of the Soviet
　Union. 4.8638
Government and politics of Uruguay. 4.8351
Government and society in colonial Peru.
　4.8347
Government and the networks of public policy-
　making. 4.8451
Government and the sports business. 4.934
The Government as a source of union power.
　4.3333
Government by investigation. 4.8039
Government by judiciary. 4.9745
Government by pen. 3.1800
Government coalitions in western democracies.
　4.7723
Government control of the economic order.
　4.3068
Government finance in developing countries.
　4.4676
Government in Canada. 4.8285
Government in the Soviet Union. 4.8650
Government ministers. 4.7722
The government of Canada. 4.8269
The government of Israel. 4.8783
The government of Italy. 4.8622
The Government of Manitoba. 4.8323
The government of New South Wales. 4.8821

The Government of Nova Scotia. 4.8317
The government of Prince Edward Island.
　4.8320
The government of Queensland. 4.8822
The government of republican Italy. 4.8623
A government of strangers. 4.7981
The government of the Ottoman empire in the
　time of Suleiman, the Magnificent. 3.3583
The government party. 4.8308
The government policy of Protector Somerset.
　3.1415
Government promotion of American canals and
　railroads, 1800-1890. 4.3981
Government publications and their use. 5.7781
Government reference books. 5.7777
Government research directory. 5.971
Government versus trade unionism in British
　politics since 1968. 4.3635
The governmental process. 4.8037
Governments and politics of Southeast Asia.
　4.8696
Governments and politics of the German-
　speaking countries. 4.8597
The governor. 4.7556
The Governor and the rebel. 3.8200
Governor Philip F. La Follette, the Wisconsin
　Progressives, and the New Deal. 3.8446
Governor Rockefeller in New York. 4.8263
The Governors-General. 4.8921
Goya. 1.6293
Goya and his critics. 1.6292
Goya, his complete etchings, aquatints, and
　lithographs. 1.6465
Goya: his life and work. 1.6291
Goya in perspective. 1.6294
Goya, the origins of the modern temper in art.
　1.6295
Goya's Caprichos. 1.6492
Gracchus Babeuf. 3.2114
Grace abounding to the chief of sinners.
　2.6915
Grace abounding to the chief of sinners, and,
　The pilgrim's progress from this world to
　that which is to come. 2.6916
Grace King. 2.11139
Grace King of New Orleans. 2.11138
The graduate. 2.13416
Graduate programs in physics, astronomy and
　related fields. 5.1998
Graduate study in psychology and associated
　fields. 5.69
Graham Greene. 2.8770-2.8771, 2.8775
Graham Greene. 2.8778-2.8779
Graham Greene: a collection of critical essays.
　2.8774
Graham Greene on film. 2.2956
Graham Greene; some critical considerations.
　2.8772
Graham Greene, the major novels. 2.8776
Graham report on violence in America. 4.5131
The Grail. 2.2638
Grail. Legend. 2.3947
Gramática de la lengua castellana. 2.890
Gramática do português contemporâneo. 2.909
Grammar of assent. 1.2231
The grammar of conducting. 1.4502
A Grammar of contemporary English. 2.996,
　2.1007
A grammar of motives. 1.576
A grammar of politics. 4.7472
The grammar of science. 5.919
A grammar of the Arabic language. 2.1831
A grammar of the film. 2.2944
Grammar of the Yiddish language. 2.1790
Grammatical man. 5.1022
Gramsci's politics. 4.7478
Gran enciclopedia Rialp, G E R. 1.19
Grand atlas de l'astronomie. English. 5.1739
Grand Central Terminal. 1.5544
Le Grand Cyrus. 2.4056
The grand design. 2.11579
The grand design of God. 1.2250
The grand domestic revolution. 4.6054
The Grand Duchy of Luxembourg. 3.2981
Le Grand Meaulnes. 2.4530
Grand Old Party. 4.8216
Grand Ole Opry. 1.3484
The Grand Prix, 1906 to 1972. 5.6632

The grand strategy of the Roman Empire from the first century A.D. to the third. 5.7183
The grand titration. 5.771
The grand tradition. 1.3766
The Grand Trunk Railway of Canada. 4.4019
Grand unified theories. 5.2483
La Grande encyclopédie ... 1.17
La grande nation. 3.2081
Les grandes doctrines littéraires en France de la Pléiade au surréalisme. 2.3844
Grandeur and illusion. 2.3850
The Grandissimes. 2.10918
Grandma Moses. 1.5957
The grandmothers. 2.12678
Les grands auteurs français du programme. 2.3917
The Granger movement. 4.2817
Granger's Index to poetry. 2.2709-2.2710
Granger's index to poetry. 2.2707
Granger's Index to poetry. 2.2708
Granite and rainbow. 2.3411
Granny. 2.1678
Grant. 3.7481
Grant & Hackh's chemical dictionary. 5.2591
Grant and Hackh's chemical dictionary. 5.2591
Grant & Lee, a study in personality and generalship. 3.7342
Grant moves south. 3.7477
Grant proposals that succeeded. 4.4450
Grant takes command. 3.7478
Grant Wood. 1.5989
The Grants register. 4.10586
The grapes of wrath. 2.12527
Graphic design. 1.5837
Graphic representations of the periodic system during one hundred years 5.2834
The Graphic works of the impressionists. 1.6459
Graphical enumeration. 5.1286
Graphical methods for data analysis. 5.1402
Graphs and algorithms. 5.1284
Graphs, models, and finite mathematics. 5.1113
Graphs, surfaces, and homology. 5.1607
The grass harp 2.11464
The grass is singing 2.9017
Grass on the wayside (Michikusa) 2.2085
The grass roots cookbook. 5.7132
Grass roots government. 4.8857
Grass roots history. 3.6004
Grass-roots socialism. 4.8240
Grassland ecosystems of the world. 5.3554
The grassland of North America. 3.8463
Grasslands of the Great Plains. 5.3786
Grasslands, systems analysis, and man. 5.3555
Graven images; New England stonecarving and its symbols, 1650-1815. 1.5789
Gravitation. 5.2215
Gravitation and cosmology: principles and applications of the general theory of relativity. 5.1926
Gravitation and relativity. 5.2214
Gravitation and spacetime. 5.2217
Gravitational curvature. 5.2088
Gravity. 5.1760
Gravity and grace. 1.859
Gravity, black holes and the universe. 5.2216
Gravity's rainbow. 2.13278
Gray. 2.7054
The graying of working America. 4.3313
Gray's Anatomy. 5.4141
Gray's Manual of botany. 5.3674
The Graywolf annual. 2.10835
Graziella. Raphaël. 2.4255
Great adventures and explorations from the earliest times to the present. 4.54
The great age of Chinese poetry. 2.2165
The great age of Japanese Buddhist sculpture, AD 600-1300. 1.5760
Great ages and ideas of the Jewish people 3.3838
The great air war. 3.821
The great American newspaper. 2.3666
The great American novel. 2.13300
The great American nude. 1.5159

A great and necessary measure, George Grenville and the genesis of the Stamp Act, 1763-1765. 4.4669
The Great apes. 5.4035
The great apes. 5.4038
The great Arab cities in the 16th-18th centuries. 4.6277
The great ascent. 4.2776
The great awakening and American education. 4.9987
The Great Awakening in New England. 1.2399
The great awakening in Virginia, 1740-1790. 1.2415
Great Basin Kingdom. 4.2040
The great book of Currier & Ives' America. 1.6498
Great books. 4.10821
Great books of the Western World. 1.1
The Great Bridge. 5.6078
Great Britain and Europe in the eighteenth century. 3.1252
Great Britain and the American Civil War. 3.7352
Great Britain and the War of 1914-1918. 3.802
Great Britain: foreign policy and the span of empire, 1689-1971. 3.1251
Great Britain from Adam Smith to the present day. 4.2277
Great Britain great empire. 4.8911
Great Britain: the lion at home. 3.1518
Great Britain's woodyard. 4.3842
The Great Bronze Age of China. 1.6671
The great bronze age of China. 1.6672
The great campaigns: reform and war in America, 1900-1928. 3.7525
The great chain of being. 1.136
The great chain of life. 5.4061
Great chemists. 5.2615
The great church-state fraud. 1.2391
Great circle. 2.11300
The great circle. 2.10337
Great cities and their traffic. 4.3928
Great cities of the world. 4.6299
Great classical myths. 2.402
The great coalfield war. 4.3168
The Great Columbia Plain. 3.8597
The great comic book heroes. 2.3568
The great conductors. 1.3769
The great crash, 1929. 4.1716
The great crisis in American Catholic history, 1895-1900 1.3181
Great day coming; folk music and the American left. 1.4356
Great days. 2.12890
The great days. 2.11581
The Great debates. 3.7931
The great departure. 3.7730
The Great Depression. 3.7763, 5.8406
The great depression. 4.1778
Great detectives. 2.10823
The great detective stories, 1841-1941. 2.3716
The great Devonian controversy. 5.3138
The great dialogue. 4.7358
The great divorce. 1.1487
The great education debate. 4.10737
The Great Elector. 3.2483
Great engineers and pioneers in technology. 5.5664
Great expectations. 4.5154
Great expectations for small schools. 4.10645
Great experiments in behavior modification. 5.458
The great explorers. 3.5968
The great famine. 3.1849
The great father. 3.5806
The Great Fear of 1789. 3.2105
Great foreign language writers. 2.2612
The great French Revolution, 1789-1793. 3.2083
The Great Frontier. 3.96
The great geographical atlas. 4.113
Great geological controversies. 5.2952
Great German short novels and stories. 2.13524
The great god Pan, and, The inmost light. 2.9071

The Great housing experiment. 4.3489
The great hunger: Ireland 1845-1849. 3.1850
The great illusion, 1900-1914. 3.750
The great instauration. 5.780
Great Irish short stories. 2.9870
The great Jewish plays. 2.1827
Great Lakes archaeology. 3.5736
The great lover. 2.3357
Great magazine covers of the world. 1.5831
The great meadow. 2.12396
The great medical bibliographers. 5.8282
The great merger movement in American business, 1895-1904. 4.3047
The great Moghuls. 3.4253
Great morning!. 2.9334
The great movie shorts. 2.2921
Great musicals of the American theatre. 1.3454
The Great Mutiny. 3.4277
The great North American ski book. 4.997
The great painters of China. 1.6316
The great patriotic war of the Soviet Union. 3.993
Great performers series. 1.4105
The great philosophers 1.130
The great pianists. 1.3761
The Great Plains. 3.8469
The Great Plains in transition. 3.8461
The great powers. 3.733
The great powers and Eastern Europe 3.3528
The Great Powers & Poland, 1919-1945. 3.3339
Great powers and Poland, 1919-1945. 3.3339
The great powers and the decline of the European states system, 1914-1945. 3.744
The Great powers and the end of the Ottoman Empire. 3.765
The great powers and the European states system, 1815-1914. 3.679
The great psychologists. 5.76
The great rebellion. 3.8951
The Great Reform Act. 4.8461
The great rehearsal. 4.7825
The Great Revival, 1787-1805. 1.3033
Great river. 3.8332
The great road. 3.4818
Great rock musicals. 1.3453
The great Roman-Jewish war. 3.3896
The great Russian revolution. 3.3178
Great Russian short novels 2.1323
The Great Salt Lake. 3.8584
The great school debate. 4.10033
The great school wars, New York City, 1805-1973. 4.10099
Great scientific experiments. 5.985
The great secession winter of 1860-61, and other essays. 3.6335
The great Siberian migration. 4.2869
The great singers. 1.3765
Great singers on great singing. 1.4206
The Great Sioux nation. 4.9776
Great slave narratives. 3.7208
The great society. 4.5000
The great song thesaurus. 1.3591
Great spy stories from fiction. 2.3724
The great terror. 3.3214
Great times, good times. 2.3243
The great tradition. 2.10384
The great transformation. 4.1759
Great transition. 3.188
Great treasury of Western thought. 2.3805
The Great Trek. 3.5466
A Great trial in Chinese history. 4.9923
The great Victorian boom, 1850-1873. 4.2273
The Great War. 3.781, 3.784
The Great War, 1914-1918. 3.785
The Great War and modern memory. 2.5741
The Great War at sea, 1914-1918. 3.818
Great western salt works. 1.4607
The great world. 2.1602
Greater Ethiopia. 4.5477
The greater Roman historians. 3.2743
The greater trumps. 2.9526
The greatest power on earth. 5.2452
Greatness in music. 1.4396
The greatness of Flaubert. 2.4198
The greatness of the soul [and] The teacher. 1.2182

Greece. 3.2679
Greece and Rome at war. 5.7178
Greece and the British connection, 1935-1941.
  3.2686
Greece and the Great Powers, 1944-1947.
  3.2704
Greece and Yugoslavia. 4.2348
Greece at the polls. 4.8621
Greece in the bronze age. 3.2588
Greece under military rule. 3.2706
Greece without columns. 3.2684
The Greek accounts of Eastern history. 3.3713
Greek and Latin authors, 800 B.C.-A.D. 1000.
  2.230
Greek and Latin in scientific terminology.
  5.970
The Greek and Latin literatures. 5.8334
Greek and Roman authors. 5.8333
The Greek and Roman critics. 2.263
Greek and Roman maps. 4.231
Greek and Roman sculpture. 1.5617
Greek and Roman sculpture in America.
  1.5618
Greek and Roman slavery. 4.6414
Greek and Roman technology. 5.5535
Greek and Roman voting and elections. 4.7362
The Greek anthology. 2.320, 2.325
Greek anthology. 2.325
Greek architecture. 1.5219
Greek art. 1.4713
Greek art and architecture. 1.4717
Greek art and literature, 700-530 B.C. 2.283
Greek athletes and athletics. 4.879
The Greek attitude to poetry and history.
  3.2568
Greek bronzes. 1.5640
The Greek Bucolic poets 2.554
Greek burial customs. 3.2561
The Greek city from Alexander to Justinian.
  3.2558
Greek coins. 3.274-3.275
A Greek critic: Demetrius on style. 2.446
The Greek dark ages. 3.2581
Greek drama in its theatrical and social context
  2.298
A Greek-English lexicon. 2.247
Greek, Etruscan, & Roman bronzes in the
  Museum of Fine Arts, Boston. 1.6668
Greek folk religion. 1.1646
Greek geography. 4.59
Greek geometric art. 1.4722
Greek grammar. 2.234
A Greek grammar of the New Testament and
  other early Christian literature. 2.248
The Greek historians. 3.545, 3.2566
Greek homosexuality. 4.5533
Greek literary papyri. 2.326
Greek literature. 2.275
Greek lyric poetry. 2.316
Greek lyric poetry from Aleman to Simonides.
  2.267
Greek lyrics. 2.404
Greek mathematical works. 2.329
Greek metaphor, studies in theory and practice.
  2.243
Greek metre. 2.244-2.245
Greek musical writings. 1.3644
Greek mythology. 1.1651
The Greek nation, 1453-1669. 3.2688
Greek painted pottery. 1.6632
The Greek particles. 2.239
The Greek passion. 2.589
Greek pastoral poetry. 2.555
The Greek philosophers, from Thales to
  Aristotle. 1.225
Greek philosophy. 1.222
The Greek phoenix. 3.2689
Greek poetry. 2.278
Greek political theory. 4.7354
Greek politics at a crossroads. 4.7106
Greek popular morality in the time of Plato
  and Aristotle. 1.1420
Greek prose style. 2.241
Greek religion. 1.1649
The Greek revival. 1.5370
Greek revival architecture in America. 1.5291
Greek scenic conventions in the fifth century
  B.C. 2.301

Greek science. 5.781
Greek science after Aristotle. 5.783
Greek science in antiquity. 5.716
Greek sculptors at work. 1.5622
Greek sculpture. 1.5624
Greek society. 3.2536
The Greek state. 4.7356
The Greek state at war. 5.7181
The Greek stones speak. 3.2540
The Greek struggle for independence,
  1821-1833. 3.2695
Greek temples, theatres, and shrines. 1.5220
Greek theatre practice. 2.306
Greek theatre production. 2.307
Greek tragedy. 2.292, 2.295
Greek tragedy, a literary study. 2.291
Greek tragedy in action. 2.305
The Greek tyrants. 3.2596
Greek word order. 2.240
The Greek world. 3.2680
Greek world, 479-323 B.C. 3.2604
The Greek world, 479-323 BC. 3.2604
The Greeks. 3.2544
The Greeks and the irrational. 5.667
The Greeks and their eastern neighbours.
  3.2583
The Greeks and their gods. 1.1644
The Greeks and their heritages. 3.2682
The Greeks in Bactria & India. 3.4245
The Greeks in Bactria and India. 3.4245
The Greeks in Ionia and the East. 3.2640
The Greeks in the United States. 3.6547
The Greeks on pleasure. 1.1503
The Greeks overseas. 3.2639
Green and gold. 2.1874
The green bay tree. 2.11416
Green centuries. 2.11788
The green child. 2.9260
The green fool. 2.8924
The green hat. 2.8387
The green man. 2.9443
The green millennium. 2.11997
The green pastures. 2.11509
Green pharmacy. 5.5139
A Green place. 2.3751
Green planet. 5.3766
Green politics. 4.8612
The Green Shirts and the others. 3.1944
Green with beasts. 2.12150
The greenback era. 4.4509
Greene & Greene. 1.5309
The greengage summer, a novel. 2.8688
The greening of America. 4.5162
The greening of the South. 5.5420
Greenmantle. 2.8488
Green's functions and boundary value problems.
  5.1534
The greenstone door. 2.10229
Greenwich time and the discovery of the
  longitude. 5.1758
Gregarious saints. 3.7248
Gregorian chant. 1.4244
Gregorius. 2.13532
Grenada. 4.2157
The Grenada papers. 3.9133
Grendel. 2.13028
Grettir's saga. 2.13983
Grettis saga. 2.13983
Greuze. 1.6110
La grève des Bàttu. 2.4872
Greyhounds of the sea. 5.7488
The grid for sales excellence. 4.4325
Grieg. 1.3880
Grierson on documentary. 2.2984
The Grigorenko papers. 3.3250
Grillparzer: a critical introduction. 2.13592
The Grimké sisters from South Carolina.
  3.7250
Grimm. 2.1185
La gringa and Barranca abajo. 2.5444
A Grit's triumph. 2.12961
Groot woordenboek Engels-Nederlands. 2.1172
Groot woordenboek Nederlands-Engels. 2.1173
Groping for ethics in journalism. 2.3561
Groping in the dark. 4.1790
Die grössere Hoffnung. 2.13670
Grotowski and his laboratory. 2.3385

Ground movements and their effects on
  structures. 5.6093
Ground water pollution control. 5.6023
Ground water quality. 5.6024
Ground-water resources of the United States.
  4.311
Groundwater. 4.306
Groundwater contamination. 5.6008
Groundwater contamination from hazardous
  wastes. 5.6009
Groundwater hydrology. 4.308
Groundwater resource evaluation. 4.304
Groundwater treatment technology. 5.6025
The group. 2.12067
Group 47: the reflected intellect. 2.13482
Group care for children. 4.6549
Group differences in attitudes and votes.
  4.8076
Group dynamics. 4.4934
Group marriage. 4.5785
Group portrait with lady. 2.13691
Group processes in the classroom. 4.10311
Group psychology and the analysis of the ego.
  5.145
Group representation before Congress. 4.7816
Group theory. 5.1305
Group theory and quantum mechanics. 5.2165
Group theory and symmetry in chemistry.
  5.2815
Group theory for physicists. 5.2140
Group therapy. 5.4879
Groups at work. 4.4354
Groups in harmony and tension. 4.4915
Groups, rings, modules. 5.1360
Grover Cleveland. 3.7492
The groves of academe. 2.12066
Growing. 2.9564
Growing and propagating wild flowers. 5.5364
The growing economy. 4.1449
Growing minds. 4.10157
Growing old. 4.5816
The growing tree. 5.5427
Growing up forgotten. 4.5758
Growing up in America. 4.10035
Growing up in college. 4.10723
Growing up in New Guinea. 4.681
Growing up southern. 3.8159
Growing up to be violent. 5.585
Growth. 2.11238
Growth and culture. 4.5742
Growth and fluctuations, 1870-1913. 4.1757
Growth and stagnation in the European
  economy. 4.2211
Growth and structure in the economy of
  modern Italy 4.2355
The growth and structure of Elizabethan
  comedy. 2.5876
The growth and structure of human
  populations. 4.1628
The growth and structure of the Chilean
  economy. 4.2177
Growth and structure of the English language.
  2.968
Growth and welfare in the American past.
  4.1895
Growth of a prehistoric time scale. 5.3083
The growth of American Constitutional law.
  4.9633
The growth of American English. 2.1122
The growth of American law. 4.9484
Growth of American manufacturing areas.
  4.1893
The growth of American thought. 3.6100
Growth of an American invention. 4.10556
The growth of biological thought. 5.3298
The growth of British industrial relations.
  4.3642
The growth of Canadian policies in external
  affairs 3.8697
The growth of cities in the nineteenth century.
  4.1662
Growth of industrial production in the Soviet
  Union. 4.2387
The growth of integrated oil companies.
  4.3771
The growth of logical thinking from childhood
  to adolescence. 5.567
The growth of medical thought. 5.4748

The growth of Papal government in the Middle Ages. 1.3147
The growth of parliamentary parties, 1689-1742. 4.8520
The growth of philosophic radicalism. 1.718
The growth of physical science. 5.738
The growth of political thought in the West. 4.7260
The growth of Presidential power. 4.7919
The growth of public expenditure in the United Kingdom. 4.4688
The growth of Reform Judaism. 1.1918
The growth of responsible government in Stuart England. 3.1446
The growth of scientific ideas. 5.761
The growth of Southern civilization, 1790-1860. 3.8142
The growth of Southern nationalism, 1848-1861. 3.8140
The growth of the American Republic. 3.6324
The growth of the Athenian economy. 4.1733
Growth of the bacterial cell. 5.4455
The growth of the Biblical tradition. 1.2532
The growth of the city state: lectures on Greek and Roman history. 4.7335
The growth of the law. 4.9359
Growth of the soil. 2.14044
The growth of Victorian London. 4.6334
Growth with self-management. 4.2419
Grünewald: drawings. 1.6172
Gruppenbild mit Dame. 2.13690
Grzimek's Animal life encyclopedia. 5.3791
Grzimek's Encyclopedia of ecology. 5.3518
Grzimek's Encyclopedia of ethology. 5.4057
Grzimek's Encyclopedia of evolution. 5.3150
Guadalcanal diary. 3.1018
The guarantee clause of the U.S. Constitution. 4.9650
The guarantee of Belgian independence and neutrality in European diplomacy, 1830's-1930's. 3.2971
Guard of honor. 2.11515
The Guardian. 2.6275
The guardian of Boston: William Monroe Trotter. 3.6852
Guardians of the flutes. 4.679
Guatemala. 3.9060
Guatemala, a country study. 3.9059
Les guérillères. 2.4796
Les Guérillères. 2.4795
Guernica. 1.6127
Guernica, and other plays. 2.4379
The Guernica generation. 3.3471
Guernica! Guernica! 3.3470
La guerra del fin del mundo. 2.5433
Guerrilla. 5.7229
Guerrilla communism in Malaya. 3.4540
Guerrilla warfare. 5.7227
Guerrillas. 2.10008
A guest for the night. 2.1780
The Guggenheim Museum collection. 1.4663
The guidance of exceptional children. 4.10907
The guidance of learning activities. 4.10257
Guide bibliographique des études littéraires. 5.8004
A Guide for better technical presentations. 5.5499
A guide for field workers in folklore. 4.755
Guide for planning educational facilities. 4.10719
A Guide for writing better technical papers. 5.5506
The guide of the perplexed. 1.1962
A guide through the district of the lakes in the north of England. 3.1738
Guide through the romantic movement. 2.5682
Guide to aesthetics. 1.4603
A guide to Alaska, last American frontier. 3.8648
Guide to American foreign relations since 1700. 5.8264
Guide to American graduate schools. 4.9940
The guide to American law. 4.9444
Guide to American literature and its backgrounds since 1890. 5.7788
A Guide to an effective middle school. 4.10504
Guide to Baroque Rome. 1.5434

Guide to basic information sources in engineering. 5.5501
Guide to basic information sources in English literature. 5.7929
Guide to basic information sources in the visual arts. 1.5103
Guide to bicycles & bicycling. 5.6638
Guide to Buddhist philosophy. 5.8343
Guide to Buddhist religion. 5.8454
Guide to business history. 4.1891
A guide to Chaucer's pronunciation. 2.6378
A guide to chemical engineering process design and economics. 5.6836
Guide to Chinese philosophy. 5.8347
Guide to Chinese religion. 5.8441
Guide to college courses in film and television. 2.2933
Guide to Congress. 4.7997
A guide to contemporary Italian literature, from futurism to neorealism. 2.4882
Guide to corporate giving 3. 1.6746
Guide to corporate giving in the arts 2. 1.6746
A guide to critical reviews. 5.8133
Guide to dance in film. 4.1112
Guide to dance periodicals. 5.8428
Guide to departments of geography in the United States and Canada. 4.44
Guide to diplomatic practice. 4.9084
A guide to econometrics. 4.1395
A guide to English and American literature. 5.7933
Guide to external degree programs in the United States. 4.10624
Guide to Ezra Pound's Selected cantos. 2.12333
A guide to Ezra Pound's selected poems. 2.12342
Guide to Far Eastern navies. 5.7470
A guide to foreign language grammars and dictionaries. 5.8331
Guide to fossil man. 4.453
Guide to free audio and video materials. 4.10326
Guide to government ministers. 4.7722
Guide to Hindu religion. 5.8450
A guide to historical literature. 5.8220
A guide to historical method ... 3.433
Guide to identification of marine and estuarine invertebrates. 5.3835
Guide to Islam. 5.8453
Guide to Japanese drama. 5.8069
Guide to Japanese poetry. 5.8070
Guide to Japanese prose. 5.8068
A guide to Jewish religious practice. 1.1983
A Guide to marine pollution. 5.6021
Guide to Marxist literary criticism. 5.7949
A guide to Marx's Capital. 4.1536
Guide to microforms in print. 5.7703
A Guide to nuclear power technology. 5.6601
Guide to obtaining USGS information. 5.2997
A guide to O'Casey's plays. 2.9155
A guide to Old English. 2.931
A guide to Oriental classics. 5.8337
A guide to parliamentary papers. 5.7921
A guide to psychologists and their concepts. 5.92
Guide to records in the National Archives of the United States relating to American Indians. 5.7741
Guide to reference books. 5.7713
Guide to reference material. 5.7715
Guide to reprints. 5.7675
Guide to research and reference works on Sub-Saharan Africa. 5.8074
Guide to research on North American Indians. 5.7738
A guide to serial bibliographies for modern literatures. 5.8279
Guide to social studies teaching in secondary schools. 4.1226
Guide to sources for agricultural and biological research. 5.8090
Guide to special issues and indexes of periodicals. 5.8369
Guide to standard floras of the world. 5.8115
The guide to supernatural fiction. 2.2408
A guide to the culture of science, technology, and medicine. 5.958

Guide to the diplomatic history of the United States, 1775-1921. 5.8263
The Guide to the federal budget. 4.4680
A guide to the financial markets. 4.4610
Guide to the flags of the world. 3.287
Guide to the Gothic. 2.3457
Guide to the history of cartography. 5.8212
A guide to the history of science. 5.751
Guide to the literature of art history. 5.8181
A guide to the literature of astronomy. 5.8102
Guide to the literature of the life sciences. 5.3294
A guide to the medicinal plants of the United States. 5.5146
Guide to the National electrical code. 4.9763
A guide to the official publications of the European Communities. 5.8400
Guide to the pianist's repertoire. 1.3582
A guide to the plays of Bernard Shaw. 2.8086
Guide to the research collections of the New York Public Library. 5.7664
A guide to the Slavonic languages. 2.1195
A guide to the sources of British military history. 5.7993
A Guide to the sources of United States military history. 5.7842
Guide to the study of international relations. 5.8254
A guide to the study of medieval history. 5.8224
Guide to the study of rocks. 5.3033
Guide to the study of the Soviet nationalities. 5.8017
A guide to the study of the United States of America. 5.7761
Guide to the study of United States imprints. 5.7745
Guide to the symphony. 1.4523
Guide to The tale of Genji by Murasaki Shakibu. 2.2048
Guide to the U.S. Supreme Court. 4.8067
A Guide to the United States treaties in force. 4.8976
Guide to the works of John Dewey. 4.10230
A guide to Trollope. 2.8228
A guide to tuning musical instruments. 1.4535
Guide to U.S. books about music. 1.3553
Guide to U.S. Elections. 4.8107
Guide to U.S. government directories. 5.7767
Guide to U.S. Government serials & periodicals, 1969-. 5.7776
Guide to U.S. map resources. 4.220
Guide to US government directories. 5.7767
Guide to USGS geologic and hydrologic maps. 5.8213
A guide to using CSMP 5.5719
A guide to Welsh literature. 2.832
Guide to worker productivity experiments in the United States ... 4.2685
A guide to worker productivity experiments in the United States, 1971-75. 4.2685
A guide to worker productivity experiments in the United States, 1976-81. 4.2684
A guide to writing and publishing in the social and behavioral sciences. 4.1235
A guidebook for teaching writing in content areas. 4.10478
A guidebook to nuclear reactors. 5.6613
A guided tour of the living cell. 5.3598
Guidelines for collection development. 5.7619
Guidelines for style analysis. 1.4428
Guiding growth in reading in the modern elementary school. 4.10461
Guillaume Apollinaire and the cubist life. 2.4367
Guillaume de Machaut. 1.3881
Guillén de Castro. 2.5168
Guillén on Guillén. 2.5266
Guilt and gratitude. 1.1500
Guilty pleasures. 2.12891
Guinea. 3.5382
The Guinness book of weather facts & feats. 5.2560
Guinness book of world records. 1.24
The guitar, from the Renaissance to the present day. 1.4178
The Gulag Archipelago, 1918-1956. 4.6922

The Gulf and the search for strategic stability. 5.7347
The Gulf coast refinery market, 1925-1950. 4.3770
The gulf of years. 2.8030
The Gulf Stream. 4.349
Gulf to Rockies. 4.4009
The Gulistan, or Rose garden of Sa'di. 2.1975
Gulliver's travels. 2.7292
Gulliver's troubles. 3.7577
The gull's hornbook. 2.6447
The gun in America. 4.6806
Gun in cheek. 2.10548
Gunboat frontier. 3.5719
The Gunn-Hilsum effect. 5.6517
Gunpowder justice. 3.8328
The guns of August. 3.792
Gunslinger. 2.11576
Günter Grass, the writer in a pluralist society. 2.13765
The Gupta Empire. 3.4241
Gupta sculpture. 1.5750
The Gurkhas. 5.7346
Guru Nanak and his times. 1.1825
Gurū Nānak and the Sikh religion. 1.1826
Gustav Adolf the great. 3.3391
Gustav Klimt. 1.6045
Gustav Mahler. 1.3916-1.3920, 1.4506
Gustav Mahler; memories and letters. 1.3921
Gustav Stresemann. 3.2355
Gustave Courbet. 1.6083
Gustave Courbet. 1.6080
Gustave Moreau. 1.6126
Gustavus Adolphus. 3.3392
Gustavus Adolphus and the rise of Sweden. 3.3393
Guys and dolls. 2.12421
Gylfaginning. 1982. 2.13992
Gymnastics guide. 4.919
Gymnastics safety manual. 4.921
Gymnosperms: structure and evolution. 5.3697
Gyn/ecology; the metaethics of radical feminism. 4.5874
The gypsy ballads of Federico García Lorca. 2.5254
Gzi brjid. English & Tibetan. Selections. 1.1808

H. G. Wells. 2.8255, 2.8259
H.G. Wells. 2.8256
H.G. Wells and the culminating ape. 2.8260
The H. G. Wells scrapbook. 2.8254
H. H. Richardson and his office, a centennial of his move to Boston, 1874. 1.5325
H.H. Richardson, complete architectural works. 1.5323
H.L. Mencken, a portrait from memory. 2.12132
H.L. Mencken and the American mercury adventure. 2.3673
H.L. Mencken, literary critic. 2.12136
H. L. Mencken's Smart set criticism. 2.12124
H. M. Pulham, esquire. 2.12107
Haakon 7 of Norway. 3.3383
Haakon VII of Norway. 3.3383
The habit of being. 2.13211
The habit of loving 2.9018
Habitat, economy and society. 4.595
The Habsburg Empire, 1790-1918. 3.1888
The Habsburg monarchy, 1809-1918. 3.1889
The Habsburgs: portrait of a dynasty. 3.1876
Hacia Cervantes. 2.5099
The Hadrianic school. 1.5639
Haft bab-ī Shah Sayyid Nāsir. 1.2094
The Hague School. 1.6239
A haiku journey. 2.2065
Hail and farewell. 2.7957
The hair of Harold Roux. 2.13432
Haiti. 3.9115
Haiti: its stagnant society and shackled economy. 4.2160
The Haitian economy. 4.2154
The Haitian people. 3.9116
Hal Porter. 2.10161
Half a truth is better than none. 1.6705
Half bitter, half sweet. 3.6456
The half-opened door. 4.10993
Half the world. 3.4646

The half-way covenant. 1.3399
Halfway houses for the mentally ill. 5.4981
Halldór Laxness. 2.13998
Halliday. 2.159
Halliwell's film guide. 2.2869
Halliwell's Filmgoer's companion. 2.2870
Hallucinogens and culture. 4.6662
Hallucinogens, cross-cultural perspectives. 4.553
Hamada. 1.6624
Hamamatsu chūnagon monogatari. 2.2054
Hamilton and Hardy's industrial toxicology. 5.4727
Hamilton, Boyd and Mossman's human embryology. 5.4165
Hamilton Fish. 3.7433
The hamlet. 2.11664
Hamlet. 2.6657
Hamlet and Œdipus. 2.6654
The Hamlet of Edwin Booth. 2.6873
Hamletmachine and other texts for the stage. 2.13906
Hamlin Garland. 2.11040
Hammarskjold. 3.1150
Hammer blows and other writings. 2.4870
Hammer or anvil. 4.3657
The Hammett equation. 5.2888
The Hammonds of Redcliffe. 3.8248
The Han Dynasty. 3.4697
Han social structure. 4.5410
Han tomb art of West China. 1.5757
Hand and soul. 2.8014
The hand & the glove. 2.5475
Hand-book of politics. 4.7846
Hand in hand. 2.9377
Handbook for chemical technicians. 5.6828
Handbook for effective department leadership. 4.10649
Handbook for evaluating and selecting curriculum materials. 4.10438
Handbook for geography teachers. 4.33
Handbook for measurement and evaluation in early childhood education. 4.10378
Handbook for proxemic research. 5.404
Handbook for radio engineering managers. 5.6428
Handbook for scientific photography. 5.6989
Handbook for sound engineers. 5.6558
Handbook for storytellers. 4.10316
Handbook of abnormal psychology. 5.4828
Handbook of accounting methods. 4.4399
Handbook of adolescent psychology. 5.621
Handbook of advertising management. 4.4432
Handbook of affective disorders. 5.4933
Handbook of aging and the social sciences. 4.5798
Handbook of air pollution analysis. 5.6050
Handbook of algorithms and data structures. 5.1177
Handbook of American folklore. 4.776
A handbook of American minorities. 5.7859
Handbook of American popular culture. 3.6115
Handbook of American private schools 1916-1925/26. 4.9942
The Handbook of antenna design. 5.6493-5.6494
Handbook of applicable mathematics. 5.1104
Handbook of applied chemistry. 5.6825
Handbook of applied hydrology. 4.288
Handbook of applied mathematics. 5.1114
Handbook of applied meteorology. 5.5706
Handbook of applied psycholinguistics. 2.17
The Handbook of artificial intelligence. 5.1010
Handbook of atomic data. 5.2081
Handbook of auditing methods. 4.4403
Handbook of batteries and fuel cells. 5.6323
Handbook of Biblical chronology. 1.2553
Handbook of biochemistry. 5.4400
Handbook of biochemistry and molecular biology. 5.3332
Handbook of British chronology. 3.1245
Handbook of business finance and capital sources. 4.4442
Handbook of chemical engineering calculations. 5.6818
Handbook of chemical property estimation methods. 5.2744

Handbook of chemistry. 5.2650
Handbook of chemistry and physics. 5.2649
A handbook of child welfare. 4.6557
A handbook of Chinese ceramics. 1.6618
A Handbook of Christian theologians. 1.2756
Handbook of circuit analysis languages and techniques. 5.6461
Handbook of classical drama. 2.268
Handbook of classical literature. 2.229
Handbook of classical mythology. 1.1601
Handbook of clinical social work. 4.6497
Handbook of commerical, financial and information services 1944-56. 4.4260
Handbook of common polymers: fibres, films, plastics, and rubbers. 5.6909
Handbook of community health nursing. 5.5208
Handbook of composite construction engineering. 5.5871
Handbook of composites. 5.5793
The Handbook of computers and computing. 5.1145
Handbook of concrete engineering. 5.5873
Handbook of conducting. 1.4503
A handbook of Coniferae and Ginkgoaceae. 5.3695
Handbook of contemporary developments in world ecology. 5.3519
Handbook of contemporary urban life. 4.6227
Handbook of cooperative education. 4.10301
Handbook of cost accounting methods. 4.4413
A handbook of costume. 4.828
A handbook of critical approaches to literature. 2.2437
Handbook of cross-cultural counseling and therapy. 5.469
Handbook of cross-cultural human development. 5.566
Handbook of cross-cultural psychology. 4.622
Handbook of cubik math. 5.1575
Handbook of dam engineering. 5.5980
Handbook of denominations in the United States. 1.2395
Handbook of developmental psychology. 5.550
Handbook of dietary fiber in human nutrition. 5.4237
Handbook of digital logic ... with practical applications. 5.6469
Handbook of dreams. 5.654
Handbook of early American sheet music, 1768-1889. 1.3544
Handbook of electronic safety procedures. 5.6455
Handbook of Elizabethan and Stuart literature. 2.5487
Handbook of emergency toxicology. 5.4723
The Handbook of employee benefits. 4.3142
Handbook of energy technology and economics. 5.6128
Handbook of engineering economics. 5.5701
Handbook of engineering fundamentals. 5.5668
Handbook of engineering management. 5.5703
Handbook of English costume in the eighteenth century. 4.847
Handbook of English costume in the nineteenth century. 4.849
Handbook of English costume in the seventeenth century. 4.846
Handbook of English costume in the sixteenth century. 4.840
A handbook of English grammar. 2.1003
Handbook of English mediaeval costume. 4.842
Handbook of environmental data on organic chemicals. 5.6006
Handbook of essential formulae and data on heat transfer for engineers. 5.6199
Handbook of experimental psychology. 5.209
Handbook of federal Indian law. 4.9772
Handbook of fiberglass and advanced plastics composites. 5.5793
Handbook of financial markets and institutions. 4.4447
Handbook of fluids in motion. 5.2038
Handbook of free speech and free press. 4.9715
Handbook of frogs and toads of the United States and Canada. 5.3931

Handbook of futures markets. 4.4636
Handbook of geochemistry. 5.3106
Handbook of geology in civil engineering. 5.5892
Handbook of geothermal energy. 5.6210
Handbook of gerontological nursing. 5.5005
The handbook of golf. 4.1033
A handbook of Greek art. 1.4720
A handbook of Greek constitutional history. 4.7357
A handbook of Greek literature, from Homer to the age of Lucian. 2.277
A handbook of Greek mythology. 1.1648
Handbook of health, health care, and the health professions. 5.4622
Handbook of health professions education. 5.4597
Handbook of heat and mass transfer. 5.6196
Handbook of heat transfer. 5.2267
Handbook of heavy construction. 5.5669
Handbook of high resolution infrared laboratory spectra of atmospheric interest. 5.2511
Handbook of human factors. 5.5686
Handbook of human intelligence. 5.355
Handbook of humor research. 5.436
Handbook of hydraulics for the solution of hydraulic engineering problems. 5.5965
Handbook of indoor games and contests. 4.1076
Handbook of industrial and organizational psychology. 4.4350
Handbook of industrial chemistry. 5.6815
Handbook of industrial engineering. 5.5560
Handbook of industrial robotics. 5.7049
Handbook of infant development. 5.555
Handbook of instructional resources and references for teaching the gifted. 5.8154
A handbook of integer sequences. 5.1416
Handbook of integrated circuits. 5.6534
Handbook of intercultural communication. 4.5006
Handbook of international business. 4.2717
Handbook of international financial management. 4.4599
Handbook of interpersonal psychotherapy. 5.4872
Handbook of laboratory safety. 5.2639
Handbook of laboratory unit operations for chemists and chemical engineers. 5.6856
Handbook of Latin American studies. 5.7909
A handbook of Latin literature: from the earliest times to the death of St. Augustine. 2.628
Handbook of leadership. 4.4954
Handbook of learning and cognitive processes. 5.265
Handbook of legumes of world economic importance. 5.5332
Handbook of livestock management techniques. 5.5439
Handbook of major Soviet nationalities. 3.3024
Handbook of marine mammals. 5.3979
Handbook of marketing research. 4.4303
Handbook of materials science. 5.5770
Handbook of mathematical functions. 5.1123
Handbook of mathematical psychology. 5.51
A handbook of medical hypnosis. 5.4899
Handbook of medical specialties. 5.4595
Handbook of mental deficiency. 5.4974
Handbook of mental retardation syndromes. 5.4972
Handbook of meteorology. 5.2500
A handbook of method in cultural anthropology. 4.493
Handbook of methods in nonverbal behavior research. 5.461
Handbook of Middle American Indians. 3.9031
A handbook of Middle English. 2.953
Handbook of military institutions. 5.7208
Handbook of minimal brain dysfunctions. 5.5095
Handbook of modern accounting. 4.4398
Handbook of modern electronics and electrical engineering. 5.6452
Handbook of modern marketing. 4.4283
Handbook of modern personality theory. 5.520

Handbook of modern personnel administration. 4.4357
Handbook of municipal administration and engineering. 5.5988
Handbook of natural resource and energy economics. 4.3707
A handbook of new nations. 3.1156
Handbook of noise control. 5.6051
Handbook of North American birds. 5.3953
Handbook of North American Indians. 3.5701
The Handbook of nursing. 5.5177
Handbook of nutritive value of processed food. 5.7124
Handbook of operations research. 5.5568
Handbook of optical constants of solids. 5.2209
Handbook of organizational design. 4.2633
Handbook of organizations. 4.4906
Handbook of ornament. 1.6546
Handbook of oscilloscopes. 5.6554
Handbook of package engineering. 5.7052
Handbook of parapsychology. 5.640
Handbook of pattern recognition and image processing. 5.6567
Handbook of perception and human performance. 5.266
A handbook of personal insurance terminology. 4.4639
Handbook of personality theory and research. 5.506
Handbook of photography and reprography. 5.6934
Handbook of phycological methods. 5.3708
Handbook of physical calculations. 5.2013
Handbook of physics. 5.1977
Handbook of physiology. 5.4170
Handbook of plastics and elastomers. 5.6910
Handbook of poisoning. 5.4724
Handbook of political communication. 4.7238
Handbook of political fallacies. 4.7728
Handbook of political psychology. 4.7246
Handbook of powder science and technology. 5.6847
Handbook of practical electrical design. 5.6336
Handbook of practical gear design. 5.6163
The Handbook of private schools. 4.9942
Handbook of private schools for American girls and boys 1926/27-1950/51. 4.9942
Handbook of projective techniques. 5.543
Handbook of psychobiology. 5.4306
Handbook of psychophysiology. 5.4307
Handbook of psychotherapy and behavior change. 5.4854
Handbook of public water systems. 5.6010
Handbook of rational-emotive therapy. 5.4895
Handbook of reactive chemical hazards. 5.5556
Handbook of research design and social measurement. 4.1227
Handbook of research on teaching. 4.10286
Handbook of Russian literature. 2.1244
Handbook of separation techniques for chemical engineers. 5.6850
A handbook of services for the handicapped. 4.6594
Handbook of sex therapy. 5.4948
A handbook of Slavic studies. 3.3021
Handbook of snakes of the United States and Canada. 5.3929
Handbook of snow. 5.2542
Handbook of social and cultural anthropology. 4.477
Handbook of social cognition. 4.4926
The Handbook of social psychology. 4.4986
Handbook of software engineering. 5.1179
Handbook of solid waste disposal. 5.6035
Handbook of South American geology. 5.3002
Handbook of South American Indians. 3.9157
Handbook of special education. 4.10909
Handbook of speech pathology and audiology. 5.4791
Handbook of stress. 5.447
Handbook of structural concrete. 5.5798
Handbook of studies on depression. 5.4934
Handbook of subsurface geology. 5.2973
Handbook of synfuels technology. 5.6882
Handbook of tables for applied engineering science. 5.5666

Handbook of tables for organic compound identification. 5.2754
Handbook of tables for probability and statistics. 5.1401
Handbook of technical writing. 5.5504
Handbook of the best private schools of the United States and Canada 1915. 4.9942
Handbook of the biology of aging. 5.4216
The handbook of the bond and money markets. 4.4611
Handbook of the economy of the German Democratic Republic. 4.2346
Handbook of the Indians of California. 3.5722
Handbook of the law of torts. 4.9516
Handbook of the nutritional contents of foods. 5.7126
Handbook of the psychology of aging. 5.624
Handbook of turtles. 5.3924
Handbook of United States economic and financial indicators. 4.2015
A handbook of useful facts about business, labor and government in the United States and other areas. 4.1866
Handbook of vocational psychology. 4.4263
Handbook of water quality management planning. 5.6011
Handbook of world philosophy. 1.448
A handbook of wrestling terms and holds. 4.1060
A handbook on the care of paintings. 1.6377
Handbook on undergraduate curriculum. 4.10612
A handbook to literature. 2.2348
Handbuch der deutschen Geschichte. 3.2250, 3.2253
Handbuch der Editionen. 5.8010
Handbuch der Physik. 5.1978, 5.2190
Handel. 1.3883-1.3884, 1.3887-1.3888
Handel, the man and his music. 1.3889
Handel's dramatic oratorios and masques. 1.3885
Handel's Messiah; origins, composition, sources. 1.3891
Handel's operas, 1704-1726. 1.3886
A handful of authors. 2.2568
A handful of dust. 2.9487
The handicapped child. 4.6580
The Handicapped in literature. 2.10827
Handicapped newborns. 5.5090
Handley Cross. 2.8131
A handlist to James Joyce's Ulysses. 2.8897
The handloom weavers. 4.3543
The handmaid's tale. 2.9906
Hands and hearts. 4.5774
Handwörterbuch der Naturwissenschaft und Technik. 5.707
The handyman. 2.9746
Hangsaman. 2.11919
Han'guk misul chŏnjip. 1.5081
Hankow. 4.4243
Hannah Arendt, for love of the world. 4.7457
The Hannibalic War's effects on Roman life. 3.2733
Hannibal's legacy. 3.2733
Hanoverian London, 1714-1808. 3.1745
Hans Baldung Grien, prints & drawings. 1.4986
Hans Baldung Grien, prints and drawings. 1.4986
Hans Bethe, prophet of energy. 5.1945
Hans Christian Andersen. 2.14009-2.14010
Hans Hofmann. 1.5942
The Hans legacy. 5.84
Hans Memling. 1.6269
Happiness, justice, and freedom. 1.733
Happy birthday, Wanda June. 2.13392
Happy days. 2.8420
Happy days, 1880-1892. 2.12128
A happy death. 2.4449
Happy ending. 2.11044
Happy rural seat. 2.6009
Har Dayal, Hindu revolutionary and rationalist. 3.4300
Hara Kei in the politics of compromise, 1905-1915. 3.4960
Harambee! 3.5281
Harbor and town. 4.3951
Harbottle's Dictionary of battles. 3.533

Hard and soft acids and bases. 5.2863
Hard and soft acids and bases principle in
    organic chemistry. 5.2861
The hard blue sky. 2.13057
The hard-boiled omnibus. 2.10824
Hard candy. 2.12728
Hard choices. 3.7934, 4.6019
The hard essential landscape. 2.12921
Hard facts. 2.10607
Hard hitting songs for hard-hit people. 1.3433
Hard labor. 2.5052
Hard living on Clay Street. 4.2050
Hard rock & heavy metal. 1.3528
Hard rock and heavy metal. 1.3528
Hard rock epic. 4.3534
Hard times. 3.7773
The hard-to-employ: European programs.
    4.3226
The hard way to peace. 4.9159
The harder we run. 4.3608
The hardest drug. 4.6663
The Harding era. 3.7734
Hardware and software concepts in VLSI.
    5.6531
Hardwater country. 2.12938
Hardy. 2.7788
Hardy and the sister arts. 2.7787
A Hardy companion. 2.7769
Hardy of Wessex, his life and literary career.
    2.7780
Hardy, the novelist. 2.7785
Hardy's use of allusion. 2.7801
Harlan Fiske Stone. 4.9827
Harland's half acre. 2.10158
Harlem. 3.8044
Harlem gallery. 2.12594
The Harlem Renaissance. 1.6709
Harlem renaissance. 1.6714
The Harlem Renaissance. 5.8191
The Harlem renaissance remembered. 2.10315
Harlem; the making of a ghetto. 3.8057
Harlequin in his element. 2.2841
Harlequin Sheridan, the man and the legends.
    2.7251
The Harley lyrics. 2.6136
Harmonic analysis. 5.1553
Harmonic analysis on semi-simple Lie groups.
    5.1539
Harmonic practice. 1.4470
Harmonic technique in the rock idiom. 1.4463
Harmonization of national economic policies
    under free trade. 4.4207
Harmony. 1.4456, 1.4467
The harmony of reason. 1.903
A harmony of the synoptic gospels. 1.2682
Harold Lloyd. 2.3261
Harold Macmillan. 3.1674
Harold Nicolson. 2.9141
Harold Pinter. 2.9794-2.9795
Harper & Row's Complete field guide to North
    American wildlife, Western edition. 5.3827
The Harper anthology of poetry. 2.6098
Harper dictionary of contemporary usage.
    2.1101
Harper encyclopedia of the modern world.
    3.605
Harper's Bible dictionary. 1.2506
Harper's dictionary of Hinduism. 1.1676
Harper's grammar of French. 2.867
Harper's stereotype ed. 2.7685
Harper's university. 4.10990
Harpist in the wind. 2.13147
The harpoon gun. 2.623
Harpsfield's life of More. 2.6496
Harrap's French and English business
    dictionary. 4.4102
Harrap's French and English science dictionary.
    5.708
Harrap's new standard French and English
    dictionary. 2.881
Harrap's standard French and English
    dictionary. 2.881
Harriet Beecher Stowe. 2.11232
Harriet Martineau. 2.7930-2.7931
Harriet Martineau, the woman and her work,
    1802-76. 2.7929
Harriet Martineau's autobiography. 2.7928

Harrod's Librarians' glossary of terms used in
    librarianship, documentation and the book
    crafts, and reference book. 5.7696
Harry Benson on photojournalism. 5.6994
Harry Byrd and the changing face of Virginia
    politics, 1945-1966. 3.8214
Harry Dexter White: a study in paradox.
    4.4653
Harry Emerson Fosdick. 1.3325
Harry S. Truman. 3.7808, 3.7811
Harsh and lovely land. 2.9890
Hart Crane. 2.11527
Hart Crane; an introduction to the poetry.
    2.11528
Hart Crane: the patterns of his poetry. 2.11532
Hart Crane's holy vision, White buildings.
    2.11524
Hart's Bridge. 2.11530
The Harvard book of contemporary American
    poetry. 2.10774
Harvard case histories in experimental science.
    5.719
Harvard concise dictionary of music. 1.3506
The Harvard concordance to Shakespeare.
    2.6687
Harvard encyclopedia of American ethnic
    groups. 3.6515
Harvard guide to American history. 5.7826
Harvard guide to contemporary American
    writing. 2.10412
The Harvard guide to modern psychiatry.
    5.4823
The Harvard report on reading in elementary
    schools. 4.10456
Harvest of a quiet eye. 2.6007
The harvest of Hellenism. 3.3706
The harvest of medieval theology. 1.2752
Harvests of change: American literature,
    1865-1914. 2.10385
Harvey and the Oxford physiologists. 5.4171
Has history any meaning? 3.503
Has man a future? 4.9176
The Hasidic anthology. 1.1924
Hasidic prayer. 1.1978
Hateful contraries. 2.2458
Hats. 4.855
The haunted bookshop. 2.12205
The Haunted dusk. 2.10587
The Haunted heroes of Eugene O'Neill.
    2.12292
A haunted house, and other short stories.
    2.9572
The haunted mirror. 2.12398
The haunting of Hill House. 2.11920
Havelock Ellis. 2.8623
Haven and home. 3.6570
The haven-finding art. 5.7492
Haven in a heartless world. 4.5564
Havoc. Hærværk. 2.14026
Hawaii. 2.12154, 3.5639
Hawaii pono. 4.5478
Hawaii: reciprocity or annexation. 3.5644
Hawaii under the rising sun. 3.1015
The Hawaiian Kingdom. 3.5641
The Hawaiian Republic, 1894-98, and its
    struggle to win annexation. 3.5642
The Hawaiian Revolution, 1893-94. 3.5643
Hawaiian sculpture. 1.5784
The Hawaiians. 5.8089
Hawaii's people. 4.1680
The hawk in the rain 2.9715
Hawk of May. 2.12919
Hawkes. 2.13073
Hawkins of Plymouth. 3.1276
Hawks about the dovecote. 2.11221
Hawks, doves, and owls. 5.7236
Hawksmoor. 1.5388
Hawley's condensed chemical dictionary.
    5.2590
Hawthorne. 2.11063, 2.11072
Hawthorne and the historical romance of New
    England. 2.11066
Hawthorne, Melville, and the American
    character. 2.10391
Hawthorne, Melville, and the novel. 2.11067
Hawthorne: the critical heritage. 2.11068
Hawthorne's early tales; a critical study.
    2.11069

Hawthorne's fiction. 2.11070
Hawthorne's mad scientists. 2.11073
Haydn. 1.3895
Haydn, a documentary study. 1.3894
Hayek on liberty. 4.1344
Hayti. 3.9113
Hazard assessment of chemicals: current
    developments 5.3573
Hazardous waste in America. 5.6039
Hazardous waste processing technology.
    5.6040
Hazards. 5.5631
The hazards of holiness. 2.11331
Hazlitt. 2.7811
Hazlitt and the spirit of the age. 2.7810
Hazlitt on English literature. 2.5526
Hazlitt on theatre. 2.7805
Hazor; the rediscovery of a great citadel of the
    Bible. 3.3820
The heads of religious houses, England and
    Wales, 940-1216. 1.3232
The healing hand. 5.4511
Health and behavior. 5.4585
Health and healing. 5.4596
Health and society. 5.4500
Health and the human condition. 4.464
Health and the law. 4.9573
Health and the war on poverty. 5.4651
Health assessment in clinical practice. 5.5175
Health care in big cities. 5.4620
Health care of homeless people. 5.4686
The health care survival curve. 5.4637
Health communication. 5.4481
The health economy. 5.4632
Health education in the elementary school.
    4.10491
Health, medicine, and mortality in the sixteenth
    century. 5.4533
The health of China. 5.4664
Health of the state. 5.4679
Health plan. 5.4634
Health purifiers and their enemies. 5.5214
The health revolution in Cuba. 4.1650
Health teaching in secondary schools. 5.4656
The healthiest city. 5.4660
Healthy people in unhealthy places. 4.4356
A healthy state. 5.4626
Hear us O Lord from heaven thy dwelling
    place. 2.9056
Hearing. 5.4370
Hearing in children. 5.5041
Heart and mind. 1.1456
A heart for the gods of Mexico. 2.11300
The heart grown brutal. 2.9858
The heart is a lonely hunter. 2.12072
Heart of Europe. 3.3330
Heart of oak. 5.7456
The heart of the matter. 2.8748
The heart Sutra. 1.2132
A heartbeat away. 3.7855
Heartbook. 5.4991
Hearth & home, preserving a people's culture.
    3.8102
Hearth and home preserving a people's culture.
    3.8102
Heartland of cities. 3.3766
Heart's needle. 2.12492
Heartsease, or, The brother's wife. 2.8367
Heat and dust. 2.9727
Heat and thermodynamics. 5.2231
The heat balance of the earth's surface. 5.2530
Heat exchanger design. 5.6200
The heat of the day. 2.8472
Heat transfer. 5.2262, 5.2264, 5.6198
Heat transfer in flames. 5.2261
Heathen days, 1890-1936 2.12131
The heathens, primitive man and his religions.
    4.546
Heathlands and related shrublands. 5.3551
Heaven & other poems. 2.11952
Heaven, earth, and man in The book of
    changes. 2.2180
The heavenly city of the eighteenth century
    philosophers. 1.432
Heavenly mansions, and other essays on
    architecture. 1.5486
The heavenly muse. 2.7160
The heavens and the earth. 5.6702

Heaven's my destination. 2.12717
Heavy weather. 2.9551
Hebbel's prose tragedies. 2.13601
The Hebrew Bible and its modern interpreters. 1.2567
The Hebrew goddess. 1.1953
The hedgehog and the fox. 2.1445
Hegel. 1.942, 1.946, 1.948, 1.951
Hegel, a re-examination. 1.945
Hegel and after. 1.446
Hegel on tragedy. 1.925
Hegel's concept of experience. 1.992
Hegel's development, night thoughts (Jena 1801-1806) 1.943
Hegel's development: toward the sunlight, 1770 - 1801. 1.944
Hegel's educational theory and practice. 4.10193
Hegel's idea of philosophy. 1.940
Hegel's lectures on the history of philosophy. 1.939
Hegel's Phenomenology: dialogues on the life of the mind. 1.937
Hegel's Phenomenology part I: analysis and commentary 1.934
Hegel's Philosophy of mind. 1.930
Hegel's philosophy of nature. 1.929
Hegel's political philosophy. 4.7449-4.7450
Hegel's Science of logic. 1.941
Hegel's social and political thought. 4.7454
The Heibonsha survey of Japanese art. 1.5071
Heidegger. 1.1004
Heidegger and the quest for truth. 1.999
A Heidegger critique. 1.1006
Heidegger, Kant & time. 1.901
Heidegger, the man and the thinker. 1.998
Heike monogatari. English. 2.2056
Heimatmuseum. 2.13813
Heimskringla. 2.13987
Heineman report on income maintenance. 4.2103
Heinrich Böll. 2.13697
Heinrich Heine. 2.13607-2.13609
Heinrich Pestalozzi, father of modern pedagogy. 4.10189
Heinrich Schütz; his life and work. 1.3980
Heinrich von Kleist. 2.13626
Heinrich von Treitschke. 3.2320
The heir of Redclyffe. 2.8368
Heir of sea and fire. 2.13147
Heirs and rebels. 1.4019
Helen. 2.455
Helen in Egypt. 2.11571
Helena. 2.9488
Hélène Cixous. 2.4780
The helicopter. 5.6678-5.6679
Helicopter theory. 5.6680
Hellenism. 3.2523
Hellenism and the modern world. 3.64
The Hellenism of Mary Renault. 2.9269
Hellenistic art (330-50 B.C.) 1.4716
Hellenistic Athens. 3.2654
Hellenistic civilisation. 3.2543
Hellenistic civilization and the Jews. 3.3893
Hellenistic culture. 3.2537
Hellenistic epigrams. 2.320
Hellenistic military & naval developments. 5.7182
Hellenistic philosophy. 1.325
Hellenistic queens. 3.2635
The Hellenistic world. 3.2634
The Hellenistic world and the coming of Rome. 3.2766
The Hellenistic world from Alexander to the Roman conquest. 3.2633
Helmets, poems. 2.12978
Helmholtz's treatise on physiological optics. 5.4379
Helmuth von Moltke. 3.2410
Heloise and Abelard. 1.3262
Helping exceptional students succeed in the regular classroom. 4.10906
Helping people change. 5.454
Helping relationships. 5.466
Helping the abuser. 4.5779
Hemingway. 2.11866
Hemingway, a biography. 2.11863
Hemingway and his critics. 2.11854

Hemingway and the movies. 2.11862
Hemingway, the critical heritage. 2.11861
Hemingway, the writer as artist. 2.11855
Hemlock and after. 2.9536
The hemoglobins in genetics and evolution. 5.4224
Henderson, the rain king. 2.11351
Henderson's dictionary of biological terms. 5.3291
Hengist, king of Kent, or, The mayor of Queenborough. 2.6636
Hengwrt manuscript. 2.6313, 2.6316
Henley's twentieth century book of formulas, processes and trade secrets. 5.5548
Henri Cartier Bresson, photographer. 5.6976
Henri Matisse. 1.6120
Henri Michaux. 2.4633, 2.4636-2.4637
Henri Rousseau. 1.6146-1.6147
Henri Saint-Simon (1760-1825) 4.7053
Henrici's Molds, yeasts, and actinomycetes. 5.3725
Henrik Ibsen. 2.14037
Henry Adams. 3.6241-3.6242, 3.6244
Henry Adams and Brooks Adams. 3.6238
Henry Adams and his friends. 3.6235
A Henry Adams reader. 2.10887
Henry Adams: scientific historian. 3.6239
Henry and Cato. 2.9755
Henry Cabot Lodge. 3.7441
Henry Cabot Lodge and the search for an American foreign policy. 3.7442
Henry Cantwell Wallace, as Secretary of Agriculture, 1921-1924. 5.5225
Henry Clay and the art of American politics. 3.7090
Henry Cowell's New Music, 1925-1936. 1.3695
Henry David Thoreau. 2.11251, 2.11257
Henry Fielding. 2.7028
Henry Fielding and the Augustan ideal under stress: 'Nature's dance of death' and other studies. 2.7027
Henry Fielding and the politics of mid-eighteenth-century England. 2.7029
Henry IV. 3.2019
Henry George. 4.1373
Henry George in the British Isles. 4.1430
Henry Green. 2.8735
Henry Highland Garnet. 3.7259
Henry Irving. 2.3346
Henry James. 2.11116-2.11118, 2.11129
Henry James; a collection of critical essays. 2.11120
Henry James, autobiography. 2.11113
Henry James: the critical heritage. 2.11121
Henry James, the early novels. 2.11123
Henry James, the major phase. 2.11124
Henry Lawson, poet and short story writer. 2.10152
Henry Lawson's best stories. 2.10151
Henry Mayhew. 2.7935
Henry Miller. 2.12193
Henry Miller and the critics. 2.12194
Henry Miller, expatriate. 2.12190
The Henry Miller reader. 2.12183
Henry Moore. 1.5696
Henry Moore on sculpture. 1.5695
Henry Moore, sculpture and drawings. 1.5698
Henry Purcell, 1659-1695. 1.3612
Henry Purcell and the London stage. 1.3951
Henry Saint John, Viscount Bolingbroke. 3.1547
Henry II. 3.1347
Henry Sylvester Williams and the origins of the pan-African movement, 1869-1911. 3.5109
Henry Timrod. 2.11260
Henry Vaughan. 2.7327
Henry Vaughan, the achievement of Silex scintillans. 2.7326
Henry VII in Italy. 3.2850
Henry VIII. 3.1401-3.1402
Henry VIII: the mask of royalty. 3.1403
Henry von Ofterdingen. 2.13594
Henry W. Grady, spokesman of the New South. 3.7434
Henry Wallace, Harry Truman, and the Cold War. 3.7815
Henry's fate & other poems, 1967-1972. 2.11378

Hen's teeth and horse's toes. 5.3369
The Heptameron. 2.3986
L'Heptaméron. 2.3987
Heptaplus. 1.418
Her. 2.11716
Heraclitean fire. 5.4393
The herald of spring. 2.1869
Herb Lubalin. 1.5838
Herbals, their origin and evolution. 5.3635
Herbert H. Lehman and New York's Little New Deal. 3.8033
Herbert Hoover, a public life. 3.7745
Herbert Hoover, forgotten progressive. 3.7746
Herbert Marcuse and the crisis of Marxism. 1.611
Herbert Spencer on education. 4.10198
Herbicides in war. 5.3580
The Herculean hero in Marlowe, Chapman, Shakespeare and Dryden. 2.5888
Hercules, my shipmate. 2.8722
Herder and the beginnings of comparative literature. 2.13611
Herder and the foundations of German nationalism. 3.2246
Here at the New Yorker. 2.11769
Here for good. 4.3632
Here I stand. 1.2338
Here is Einbaum. 2.12212
Here to stay. 4.5584
Heredity and society. 5.3454
Heredity, East and West. 5.3431
Here's looking at you, kid. 2.3080
Here's New England! 3.7958
Heresy, crusade, and inquisition in southern France, 1100-1250. 3.1977
Heresy in the later Middle Ages. 1.2962
The heretical imperative. 1.2754
Hereward the Wake. 2.7876
The heritage. 2.13814
The heritage of America. 3.6318
Heritage of endurance. 4.6889
The heritage of Persia. 3.4074
The heritage of Russian verse. 2.1313
Heritage of symbolism. 2.2766
The heritage of Thai sculpture. 1.5756
The heritage of the Bounty. 3.5670
The heritage of the Reformation. 1.3281
The Heritage of Vietnamese poetry. 2.2262
Herman Melville. 2.11161-2.11162, 2.11164
Herman Melville's Clarel. 2.11153
Herman Wouk, the novelist as social historian. 2.12803
Hermann Hesse. 2.13779
El hermano asno. 2.5404
Hermas. 2.327
Hermeneutic phenomenology. 1.846
Hermeneutics and social science. 1.1304
Hermetic definition. 2.11572
Hermios. 2.12378
The Hermit & The love thief. 2.1953
Hero & saint: Shakespeare and the Graeco-Roman heroic tradition. 2.6811
The hero and the blues. 2.2397
Hero, artist, sage, or saint? 5.4695
The hero in America. 3.6299
The hero in eclipse in Victorian fiction. 2.6016
The hero in history. 3.511
The Hero in Scandinavian literature. 2.13967
The hero in the earthly city. 2.6296
A hero of our time. 2.1396
The hero of the Waverley novels. 2.8062
A hero on a donkey. 2.1211
Herodian. 2.369
The Herodian period. 3.3851
Herodias. 2.4194
Hérodias. 2.4193
Herodotos, the historian. 3.547
Herodotus. 2.370, 2.475
Heroic epic and saga. 2.2392
The heroic ideal in American literature. 2.10348
Heroic love. 2.6515
Heroic poetry of the Basotho. 2.2313
The heroic temper. 2.548
Heroides and Amores. 2.680
Heroin, deviance, and morality. 4.6672
Herovit's world. 2.13165
Herpetology. 5.3919

Herr Walther von der Vogelweide. 2.13537
The herring gull's world. 5.3964
Herself surprised. 2.8501
Herzl. 3.4026
Herzog. 2.11350
Hesiod. 2.371
Hesse companion. 2.13780
The Hesse-Mann letters. 2.13778
The Hessian view of America, 1776-1783.
  3.6949
Hester Lynch Piozzi (Mrs. Thrale) 2.7185
Heterogeneous catalysis in practice. 5.6839
The Hevajra Tantra. 1.1744
Die Hexe im Landhaus. 2.13904
The heyday of American communism. 4.6992
The heyday of Sir Walter Scott. 2.8057
Heywood Broun. 2.11423
Hickory dickory death. 2.8516
The Hicksite separation. 1.3351
The Hidalgo revolt. 3.8932
The hidden crisis in American politics. 3.7843
The Hidden curriculum and moral education.
  4.10809
The hidden dimension. 5.405
The hidden face of free enterprise. 4.1980
The Hidden half. 3.5740
The hidden-hand presidency. 3.7837
Hidden hands. 2.10820
The hidden hippopotamus. 3.5520
The hidden history of the Korean War. 3.5022
The hidden order of art. 1.4621
The hidden persuaders. 4.4430
The hidden sun. 4.6145
The hidden worlds of Polynesia. 3.5647
Hideyoshi. 3.4939
Hier régnant désert. 2.4417
Hieronymus Bosch. 1.6240, 1.6242
Hieronymus of Cardia. 3.548
The High Court of Parliament and its
  supremacy. 4.8464
High Deryni. 2.13126
High energy astrophysics. 5.2327
High energy costs 4.3719
High-frequency amplifiers. 5.6485
High frequency circuit design. 5.6385
The high Middle Ages in England, 1154-1377.
  5.7987
High-performance liquid chromatography.
  5.2666
High performance liquid chromatography.
  5.2692
High resolution NMR. 5.2681
High-rise building structures. 5.6092
High school. 4.10047
High school achievement. 4.10048
High tension. 2.3603
High times and hard times. 2.11045
High Victorian design. 1.6508
The High Victorian movement in architecture,
  1850-1870. 1.5373
A high wind in Jamaica. 2.8810
High windows. 2.8941
The higher circles. 4.5150
The higher Civil Service in Britain. 4.8453
Higher cortical functions in man. 5.4344
Higher education and the American resurgence.
  4.10084
Higher education as a field of study. 4.10571
Higher-education budgeting at the state level.
  4.10603
Higher education developments. 5.5624
Higher education in tomorrow's world.
  4.10542
Higher education in transition. 4.10058
The higher education system. 4.10547
Higher education: who pays? Who benefits?
  Who should pay? 4.10598
Higher, faster, and farther. 5.6644
The 'higher law' background of American
  constitutional law. 4.9618
The higher learning in America. 4.10544
Highland peoples of New Guinea. 4.678
Highland river. 2.8791
Highlanders of Thailand. 4.644
The Highlands and isles of Scotland. 3.1810
Highway benefits. 4.3932
Highway engineering. 5.6059, 5.6062
Highway engineering handbook. 5.6061

Highway materials. 5.6064
Highway revenue and expenditure policy in the
  United States. 4.3935
Highways and our environment. 4.3940
The Hikayat Abdullah. 3.4541
Hilaire Belloc. 2.8448-2.8449, 2.8451
Hilaire Belloc, an anthology of his prose and
  verse. 2.8447
Hilbert. 5.1095
Hilbert's fourth problem. 5.1633
Hilbert's third problem. 5.1574
Hilda Doolittle (H. D.) 2.11574
Hilda Lessways. 2.8453
Hilda's letter. 2.8797
Hilgard and Marquis' Conditioning and
  learning. 5.300
Hill farms and padi fields. 3.4386
The hills beyond. 2.12775
Hills beyond a river. 1.6323
The hills of faraway. 2.3464
The hills were joyful together. 2.9996
Hillslope materials and processes. 4.268
Him with his foot in his mouth and other
  stories. 2.11352
The Himalaya borderland. 3.4343
Himalayan frontiers. 3.4236
The Himalayan kingdoms: Bhutan, Sikkim, and
  Nepal. 3.4331
A Himalayan tribe. 3.4204
Himalayan village. 3.4206
Himalayas. 3.4344
Himmler. 3.2389
Hindenburg:the wooden Titan. 3.2350
Hindi Literature from its beginnings to the
  Nineteenth century. 2.1883
Hindi literature in the twentieth century.
  2.1884
Hindu epics, myths, and legends in popular
  illustrations. 1.6471
Hindu intellectual tradition. 1.1701
Hindu manners, customs and ceremonies.
  3.4167
Hindu monastic life. 1.1718
Hindu places of pilgrimage in India. 1.1720
Hindu polytheism 1.1708
The Hindu religious tradition. 1.1702
The Hindu social system. 4.5426
Hindu society. 4.6406
Hindu society at cross roads. 4.5425
Hindu tantric and 'Sākta literature. 1.1727
The Hindu temple. 1.5539
The Hindu tradition. 1.1695
The Hindu view of life. 1.186
Hinduism. 1.1677, 1.1704, 1.1706
Hinduism and Buddhism. 1.1675
Hindus of the Himalayas. 3.4360
Hints on household taste in furniture,
  upholstery, and other details. 1.6551
Hippias major. 1.257
Hippies of the Haight. 4.5751
Hippocrates. 2.372
Hippocrates. 5.4495
Hippocratic writings. 5.4494
Hippodrama in England and France. 4.1187
Hippolyte Taine. 1.822
Hippolytos. 2.457
Hired hands. 4.2922
Hiroshima. 3.1011
Hiroshima and Nagasaki, the physical, medical,
  and social effects of the atomic bombings.
  3.1012
Hiroshima and Potsdam. 3.7790
His exits and his entrances. 2.6716
His Majesty's Opposition, 1714-1830. 3.1520
His master's voice. 2.1713
His very self and voice. 2.7534
Hispanic culture in the United States. 5.7881
The Hispanic elderly. 4.5812
Hispanic folk music of New Mexico and the
  Southwest. 1.3437
Hispanics' education and background. 4.10848
Hispanics in the U.S. economy. 4.3612
Hispanics in the United States. 2.10674
The Hispanization of the Philippines: Spanish
  aims and Filipino responses, 1565-1700.
  3.4597
Hiss the villain. 2.6240
Histoire comique. 2.4020

Histoire de Belgique. 3.2969
Histoire de France depuis les origines jusqu'à la
  révolution. 3.1975
Histoire de la Belgique et de son expansion
  coloniale. 3.2967
Histoire de la littérature française. 2.3828
Histoire de la littérature française au XVIIe
  siècle. 2.3846
Histoire de la littérature française au XXe
  siècle. 2.3872
Histoire de la litterature francaise, du
  symbolisme a nos jours. 2.3866
Histoire de l'Espagne musulmane 3.3424
Histoire de l'urbanisme. 1.5591
Histoire de ma vie. 2.4291
Histoire du chevalier Des Grieux et de Manon
  Lescaut. 2.4083
Histoire du roman français depuis 1918.
  2.3912
Histoire d'une langue. 2.862
Histoire économique de la France entre les deux
  guerres. 4.2330
Histoire économique et sociale du Québec,
  1760-1850. 4.2127
L'Histoire littéraire d'un couple tragique.
  2.4051
Une Histoire vivante de la littérature
  d'aujourd'hui. 2.3868
Histoires et d'autres histoires. 2.4659
Histological and histochemical technics. 5.4159
Histology. 5.4157-5.4158
Histology of the vertebrates. 5.4153
Historia animalium. 2.328
Historia de la lengua española. 2.887
Historia de la literatura española. 2.5084
Historia de la literatura española. 2.5088,
  2.5092
Historia de la literatura española e
  hispanoamericana. 2.5086
Historia de la literatura hispanoamericana.
  2.5296
Historia de la literatura nacional española en la
  edad de oro. 2.5104
Historia de la novela hispanoamericana. 2.5311
Historia de una escalera. 2.5239
Historia destructionis Troiae. 2.819
The Historia novella. 3.1345
Historia social y económica de España y
  América. 3.3406
Historia von Doctor Johann Fausten. English.
  2.13512
Historian and scientist. 3.405
The historian and the believer. 1.2249
The historian and the city. 4.6304
The historian as a political force in central
  Europe. 3.445
The Historian at work. 3.414
Historians against history. 3.6279
Historians and historiography in the Italian
  Renaissance. 3.2832
Historians and the American West. 3.8460
An historian's approach to religion. 1.1541
Historians at work. 3.358
The historian's craft. 3.381
A historian's creed. 3.499
Historians' fallacies. 3.431
The historian's handbook. 5.8222
Historians in the Middle Ages. 3.570
Historians of India, Pakistan and Ceylon.
  3.4214
Historians of medieval India. 3.4216
The historian's workshop. 3.427
Historic America. 1.5284
Historic architecture of the Royal Navy.
  5.7465
Historic costume for the stage. 2.3126
Historic documents of the Muslim freedom
  movement. 3.4282
Historic documents of World War I. 3.768
The historic origin of the eight hours day.
  4.3160
Historic pottery of the Pueblo Indians,
  1600-1880. 3.5941
The historic reality of Christian culture.
  1.2241
Historic towns. 4.171
An historical account of the Island of Saint
  Vincent. 3.9135

Historical and critical dictionary. 3.323
Historical and philosophical roots of perception. 5.260
Historical anthology of music. 1.3425
An Historical anthology of select British speeches. 2.3780
Historical archaeology. 3.225, 3.5295
Historical atlas. 4.124
Historical atlas, medieval and modern. 4.122
Historical atlas of Africa. 4.189
Historical atlas of Britain. 4.170
Historical atlas of Canada. 4.141
An historical atlas of China. 4.182
An Historical atlas of Islam. 4.164
Historical atlas of religion in America. 4.148
A Historical atlas of South Asia. 4.180
Historical atlas of the Muslim peoples. 4.165
Historical atlas of the religions of the world. 1.1588
The historical atlas of United States Congressional districts, 1789-1983. 4.151
The historical background of chemistry. 5.2608
A historical commentary on Arrian's History of Alexander. 3.2624
A historical commentary on Polybius. 2.539
A historical commentary on Thucydides. 2.562
Historical conceptions of psychology. 5.72
The historical-critical method. 1.2517
Historical demography. 4.1580, 4.1616
The historical development of the calculus. 5.1451
Historical dictionary of Fascist Italy. 3.2884
Historical dictionary of Oceania. 3.5531
Historical dictionary of the Spanish Civil War, 1936-1939. 3.3466
Historical essays. 3.365
Historical explanation. 3.509, 3.514
Historical foundations of the common law. 4.9413
An historical geography of Europe; 450 B.C.-A.D. 1330. 3.529
An historical geography of Europe, 1500-1840. 3.530
An historical geography of Iran. 3.4067
Historical geography of the United States. 3.6346, 5.7839
Historical German phonology and morphology. 2.1180
Historical guide to World War II. 3.891
Historical guide to World War Two. 3.891
Historical inevitability. 3.505
Historical introduction to modern psychology. 5.79
Historical knowing. 3.476
Historical knowledge. 3.480
Historical linguistics. 2.137, 2.157
Historical materialism. 4.7097
Historical memoirs of the duc de Saint-Simon. 3.2040
The historical novel. 2.3467
Historical outlines of English sounds and inflections. 2.1011
Historical perspectives on homosexuality. 4.5527
Historical plant geography. 5.3667
Historical poems of the XIVth and XVth centuries. 2.6139
Historical reason. 1.1127
Historical records of New Zealand. 3.5589
Historical recurrence in Western thought. 3.500
The historical revolution. 3.449
The historical road of Eastern Orthodoxy. 1.3103
Historical roots of contemporary psychology. 5.83
Historical scholarship in the United States, 1876-1901: as revealed in the correspondence of Herbert B. Adams. 3.6246
Historical sets, collected editions, and monuments of music. 1.3551
Historical statistics of Canada. 4.1253
Historical statistics of the United States, colonial times to 1970. 4.1250
Historical study in the west: France, Great Britain, Western Germany, the United States. 3.446

The Historical study of African religion. 1.1844
The historical study of the mother tongue. 2.978
Historical survey of pre-Christian education. 4.9959
Historical tables, 58 BC-AD 1985. 3.370
Historical times illustrated encyclopedia of the Civil War. 3.7343
Historical tradition in the Fourth Gospel. 1.2698
Historical understanding in the thought of Wilhelm Dilthey. 1.985
Historical writing in England. 3.1208
Historical writing on American science. 5.792
Historical writing on the peoples of Asia. 3.3626
Historical writings. 3.1233
Historie de la littérature française. 2.3825
The historie of the damnable life and deserved death of Doctor John Faustus. 2.13512
The histories. 2.391
The Histories. 2.697
Histories of the dividing line betwixt Virginia and North Carolina. 3.8189
Historiography. 3.382
Historiography and urbanization. 3.6197
The historiography of the British Empire-Commonwealth. 3.1209
Historisch-kritische Gesamtausgabe der Werke. 2.13603
Historism; the rise of a new historical outlook. 3.485
History. 3.387, 3.393
History. 2.5043, 2.12047, 3.502
History and American society: essays of David M. Potter. 3.6217
History and bibliography of American newspapers, 1690-1820. 5.8322
History and biography. 3.380
The history and character of Calvinism. 1.3406
History and class consciousness. 4.7044
History & criticism. 3.396
History and criticism of American public address. 2.10649
The History and culture of Iroquois diplomacy. 3.5896
The history and development of advertising. 4.4420
History & ecology. 4.387
History and ecology. 4.387
A history and encyclopedia of country, western, and gospel music. 1.3685
History and geography of the most important diseases. 5.4497
History and government of the State of Washington. 3.8640
A history and guide to Judaic bibliography. 5.8234
History and historians in the nineteenth century 3.388
The history and literature of surgery. 5.5031
The history and philosophy of the metaphysical movements in America. 1.2390
The history and politics of colonialism 1870-1914. 3.5105
The history and politics of community mental health. 5.4700
The history and present state of Virginia. 3.8184
History and psychoanalysis. 3.443
The history and remarkable life of the truly honourable Col. Jacque, commonly call'd Col. Jack ... 2.6971
History and sources of the common law: tort and contract. 4.9411
History and the dialectic of violence. 1.849
History and the Homeric Iliad. 2.502
History and the humanities. 3.360
History and theology in the Fourth Gospel. 1.2695
History and theory of early childhood education. 4.10402
The history and theory of environmental scenography. 2.3140
The history and topography of Ireland. 3.1818

History and truth in Hegel's Phenomenology. 1.938
History as a system, and other essays toward a philosophy of history. 3.488
History as a way of learning. 3.6339
History as art and as science. 3.434
History as romantic art: Bancroft, Prescott, Motley, and Parkman. 3.6231
History as the story of liberty. 3.386
History begins at Sumer. 3.3772
History, guilt, and habit. 1.4
History in a changing world 3.377
History in communist China. 3.4659
History in the United States, 1800-1860. 3.6206
History, its purpose and method. 3.492
The history makers. 3.727
The history man. 2.9626
A history of 18th century Russian literature. 2.1255
A history of 1000 years of Greek vase painting. 1.6631
History of a literary radical and other essays. 2.11398
The history of a young lady. 2.7214
A history of accounting in America. 4.4389
A history of aesthetic. 1.1366
A history of Africa. 3.5070
History of African civilization. 3.5074
A history of African exploration. 3.5048
A history of aggression in Freud. 5.425
A history of agriculture in Europe and America. 5.5227
History of agriculture in Ontario, 1613-1880. 4.2961
History of agriculture in the northern United States, 1620-1860. 5.5232
History of agriculture in the southern United States to 1860. 5.5242
History of Alaska, 1730-1885. 3.8644
History of Alexander and Indica. 2.353
The history of Alexander the Great. 3.2627
History of algebraic geometry. 5.1576
A history of American acting. 2.3199
A history of American archaeology. 3.5697
The history of American business & industry. 4.1885
The history of American church music. 1.3684
History of American costume, 1607-1870. 4.836
History of American diplomacy. 3.7567
A history of American economic life. 4.1889
The History of American electoral behavior. 4.8103
A history of American foreign policy. 3.6401
A history of American labor. 4.3559
A history of American law. 4.9483
A history of American literature, 1607-1765. 2.10365
A history of American magazines. 2.3639
A history of American pewter. 1.6673
A history of American philosophy. 1.557
History of American presidential elections, 1789-1968. 3.6392
History of American psychology. 5.89
The history of American sailing ships. 5.7503
History of American schoolbooks. 4.11015
The history of American sculpture. 1.5656
The history of American wars from 1745 to 1918. 3.6373
History of ancient geography. 4.58
The history of ancient geography among the Greeks and Romans, from the earliest ages till the fall of the Roman Empire. 4.57
The history of anti-Semitism. 3.4011
A history of Antioch in Syria. 3.3803
History of architecture. 1.5211
A history of architecture. 1.5212
A history of Argentina 3.9239
A history of Argentine political thought. 4.8337
A history of Argos to 500 B.C. 3.2589
History of Arizona and the New Mexico, 1530-1888. 3.8567
History of art. 1.4676
History of art criticism 1.5120
History of Assyria. 3.3770
History of astronomy. 5.1685

A history of astronomy from Thales to Kepler. 5.1684
A history of Australia. 3.5567
History of Australian literature. 2.10138
The history of Barbados. 3.9130
A history of Belize. 3.9058
History of Bengali literature. 2.1855
History of Black Americans. 3.7247
A history of bolshevism from Marx to the first Five years' plan. 3.3192
A history of book illustration. 1.5826
A history of book publishing in the United States. 5.7590
The history of bookbinding, 525-1950 A.D. 5.7566
A history of Brazil. 3.9202
The history of British journalism. 2.3682
A history of British music. 1.3714
A history of British trade unionism. 4.3408
The history of broadcasting in the United Kingdom. 4.4065
A history of Buganda from the foundation of the kingdom to 1900. 3.5279
A history of building types. 1.5513
A history of Bulgaria, 1393-1885. 3.3541
A history of Bulgarian literature 865-1944. 2.1203
History of Burma. 3.4339
A history of business. 4.4252
A history of Cambodia. 3.4444
A history of Canada, Dominion of the North. 3.8672
A history of Canadian external relations. 3.8698
History of cartography. 4.224
The history of Catholic Church music. 1.4241
A history of cavalry from the earliest times. 5.7381
History of Central Africa. 3.5232
The history of central Africa. 3.5489
The history of chemical technology. 5.8456
A history of chemistry. 5.2609
A history of Chicago ... 3.8413
History of children's costume. 4.853
A history of children's play. 4.885
A history of China. 3.4664
A history of Chinese drama 2.2169
A history of Chinese philosophy. 1.152
A history of Chinese political thought. 4.7282
A History of Christian doctrine. 1.2745
A history of Christian-Latin poetry from the beginnings to the close of the Middle Ages. 2.812
A history of Christian missions. 1.3024
A history of Christian missions in China. 1.3027
History of Christian philosophy in the Middle Ages. 1.124
A history of Christian theology. 1.2747
A history of Christianity. 1.2276, 1.2280
History of Christianity in the Middle Ages: from the fall of Rome to the fall of Constantinople. 1.2289
History of civilization in England. 3.33
A history of classical Malay literature. 2.2289
A history of classical scholarship. 2.231
History of classical scholarship from 1300 to 1850. 1.76
History of classical scholarship from the beginnings to the end of the Hellenistic age. 1.75
A history of clinical psychology. 5.4846
History of Colombia. 3.9174
History of comics. 1.5849
History of coöperative news-gathering in the United States. 2.3588
A history of criticism and literary taste in Europe from the earliest texts to the present day. 2.2463
A history of cynicism from Diogenes to the 6th century A. D. 1.321
A history of Cyprus. 3.3693
A history of deeds done beyond the sea. 3.587
History of Doctor Johann Faustus. 2.13513
History of dogma. 1.2743
A history of early American magazines, 1741-1789. 2.3641
A history of early Chinese Buddhism. 1.2117

A history of early Renaissance Italy: from the mid-thirteenth to the mid-fifteenth century. 3.2844
History of early Russian literature. 2.1253
History of East Africa. 3.5260
A history of East Asian civilization 3.110
History of economic analysis. 4.1312
A history of economic theories. 4.1500
A history of education in American culture. 4.9981
A history of educational thought. 4.9950
History of educational thought. 4.9951
A history of Egypt. 3.5152
The history of Egypt. 3.5161
A history of Egypt under the Ptolomaic dynasty. 3.5156
A history of Egyptian architecture. 1.5215
A history of embryology. 5.4119
A History of engineering and science in the Bell System. 5.6418
A history of engineering in classical and medieval times. 5.5659
The history of England. 3.1241
History of England from the accession of James I. to the outbreak of the civil war 1603-1642. 3.1458
History of England from the accession of James II. 3.1495
A history of English. 2.975
A history of English criminal law and its administration from 1750 4.9427
A history of English criticism. 2.5494
A history of English drama, 1660-1900. 2.5842
A history of English law. 4.9407
The history of English law before the time of Edward I. 4.9408
A history of English literature. 2.5525
A history of English literature. 2.5530
History of English literature. 2.5531
A history of English opera. 1.4227
History of English poetry. 2.5744
A History of English prose rhythm. 2.1051
A history of English prosody, from the twelfth century to the present day. 2.1045
A history of English spelling. 2.1025
A history of English syntax. 2.1031
History of English thought in the eighteenth century. 1.683
A history of engraving & etching from the 15th century to the year 1914. 1.6431
A history of esthetics. 1.1367
A history of Ethiopia. 3.5242
A history of Ethiopia, Nubia [and] Abyssinia. 3.5241
The history of ethnological theory. 4.412
A history of ethnology. 4.416
A history of Europe from 1198 to 1378. 3.559
A history of European socialism. 4.7017
A history of European thought in the nineteenth century. 1.443
A history of experimental psychology. 5.77
A history of exploration from the earliest times to the present day. 4.55
The history of Fanny Burney. 2.6896
A history of Far Eastern art. 1.5058
A history of farm buildings. 5.5299
A history of Fiji. 3.5634
A history of films. 2.2878
A history of Finland. 3.3289, 3.3291
A history of firearms, from earliest times to 1914. 5.7383
A history of fishes. 5.3900
A history of Fisk University, 1865-1946. 4.10881
The history of Florence. 3.2926
History of Florence and of the affairs of Italy, from the earliest times to the death of Lorenzo the Magnificent. 3.2920
History of Florence, from the founding of the city through the Renaissance. 3.2919
A history of formal logic. 1.1154
History of freedom movement in Bangladesh, 1943-1973. 3.4147
A history of freedom of teaching in American schools. 4.10577
A history of French Louisiana. 3.8311
The history of gardens. 5.5375

A history of geographical discovery and exploration. 4.45
History of geology and palæontology to the end of the nineteenth century. 5.2953
A history of geometrical methods. 5.1069
A history of German literature. 2.13456-2.13457
A history of Germany, 1815-1985. 3.2285
History of Germany in the nineteenth century. 3.2293
The history of Germany since 1789. 3.2287
A history of graphic design. 5.7559
History of graphic design and communication. 1.5835
A history of Greece. 3.2576
A history of Greece to 322 B.C. 3.2577
A history of Greece to the death of Alexander the Great. 3.2574
A history of Greek art. 1.4721
A history of Greek literature. 2.276
History of Greek literature. 2.281
A history of Greek philosophy 1.226
A history of Greek political thought. 4.7360
A history of Greek religion. 1.1647
A history of haiku. 2.2006
The history of haute couture, 1850-1950. 5.7090
The history of Henry Fielding. 2.7024
A history of herbal plants. 5.3660
A history of higher education in Canada, 1663-1960. 4.10101
A history of historical writing. 3.376, 3.406
The history of historical writing in America. 3.6212
A history of Hong Kong. 3.4863
The history of human marriage. 4.5556
History of Hungary 3.1938
History of Iceland. 3.3374
History of Icelandic prose writers, 1800-1940. 2.13993
A history of ideas in Brazil. 1.663
History of ideas on woman. 4.5917
The history of impressionism. 1.4796
The history of India. 3.4217
A history of India. 3.4226
The history of India, as told by its own historians. 3.4251
History of Indian and eastern architecture. 1.5446
History of Indian and Indonesian art. 1.5044
A history of Indian philosophy 1.178
A history of Indian political ideas. 4.7327
A history of industrial design. 5.7040
A history of interest rates. 4.4528
A history of Iowa. 3.8505
History of Iranian literature. 2.1963
A history of Islamic law. 1.2040
A history of Islamic philosophy. 1.365
A history of Islamic Spain. 3.3428
A history of Israel. 3.3885
The history of Israel. 3.3853
A history of Israel in Old Testament times. 1.2581
A history of Italian fascism. 3.2885
History of Italian literature. 2.4878
A history of Italian literature. 2.4879-2.4880
History of Italian Renaissance art. 1.5001
A history of Italian unity. 3.2859
The history of Italy. 3.2853
A history of Italy, 1871-1915. 3.2878
A history of Jamaica from its discovery by Christopher Columbus to the year 1872. 3.9111
The history of Japan. 3.4909
A history of Japan. 3.4910
A history of Japan. 3.4912
The history of Japanese printing and book illustration. 1.6466
The history of Java. 3.4578
The history of jazz. 1.4335
A history of jazz in America. 1.4338
A history of Jewish costume. 4.834
A history of Jewish literature. 2.1772-2.1773
A history of journalism in Canada. 2.3677
A History of Judaism. 1.1900
The history of King Lear. 2.6680
The history of king's works. 1.5358
The history of Korea. 3.4996

A history of Korea. 3.4997
History of Korea. 3.4998
A history of labor in modern Japan. 4.3422
History of labour in the United States. 4.3557
A history of late nineteenth century drama, 1850-1900. 2.5918
A history of later Latin literature from the middle of the fourth to the end of the seventeenth century. 2.808
A history of Latin America, from the beginnings to the present. 3.8984
A history of Latin literature. 2.629
A history of Latvia. 3.3313
A history of lay judges. 4.9416
A history of literary criticism in the Italian Renaissance. 2.4875
A history of literary criticism in the Renaissance. 2.2467
A history of local government in the twentieth century. 4.8876
A history of Macedonia. 3.3598
History of Macy's of New York, 1858-1919. 4.4332
A history of magic and experimental science. 5.760
A history of Malayalam literature. 2.2266
A history of Malaysia. 3.4537
History of mankind: [cultural and scientific development. 3.519
The history of manned space flight. 5.6716
The history of marketing thought. 4.4276
A history of mathematical notations. 5.1068
A history of mathematics. 5.1067
History of mathematics ... 5.1074
History of mediæval philosophy. 1.358
A history of mediæval political theory in the West. 4.7267
A history of medical education. 5.4599
A history of medical psychology. 5.4806
History of medicine. 5.4501
A history of medieval Austria. 3.1879
A history of medieval Ireland. 3.1827
A history of medieval Latin literature. 2.810
A history of medieval philosophy. 1.348
A history of medieval Spain. 3.3418
A history of mental retardation. 5.4978
A history of metallurgy. 5.6759
A history of metals. 5.6756
A history of Mexican archaeology. 3.8880
A history of Mexico. 3.8918
History of military mobilization in the United States Army. 5.7144
The history of Minoan pottery. 3.2590
A History of Missouri. 3.8360
History of modern architecture. 1.5254
History of modern art. 1.4803
The history of modern astronomy and astrophysics. 5.8103
A history of modern Brazil, 1889-1964. 3.9213
A history of modern Burma. 3.4338
A history of modern Chinese fiction. 2.2176
A history of modern colloquial English. 2.979
A history of modern criticism: 1750-1950. 2.2464
A history of modern culture. 3.150
A history of modern France. 3.2007
The history of modern furniture. 1.6558
A history of modern Germany. 3.2276
A history of modern Greek literature. 2.566
A history of modern Hebrew literature (1785-1930) 2.1775
A history of modern Indonesia, c. 1300 to the present. 3.4563
A history of modern Jewry. 3.3907
A history of modern Norway, 1814-1972. 3.3381
A history of modern philosophy. 1.426
A history of modern Sabah (North Borneo, 1881-1963) 3.4582
A history of modern Thailand, 1767-1942. 3.4524
The history of modern whaling. 5.5486
History of music. 1.3638
A history of music education in the United States. 1.4418
A history of music in England. 1.3713
The history of music in performance. 1.4116
A history of music in pictures. 1.3493

The history of musical instruments. 1.4134
A history of musical style. 1.4114
History of my heart. 2.13253
A history of narrative film. 2.2877
A history of national socialism. 3.2373
The history of nature. 5.941
A history of nautical astronomy. 5.7491
A history of naval tactical thought. 5.7425
A history of naval tactics from 1530 to 1930. 5.7426
History of Nebraska. 3.8519
A history of Negro education in the South. 4.10863
A history of New Zealand. 3.5603
A history of Niger, 1850-1960. 3.5389
History of nineteenth-century Russian literature. 2.1257
History of North Africa: Tunisia, Algeria, Morocco. 3.5194
History of North Dakota. 3.8508
A history of Northern Rhodesia. 3.5524
A history of Norwegian literature. 2.14030
A history of nursing. 5.5161
A history of nursing, from ancient to modern times. 5.5162
A history of Ohio. 3.8380
History of Oklahoma. 3.8529
The history of orchestration. 1.4122
A history of ornament ... 1.6537
A history of Orthodox theology since 1453. 1.3109
A history of Ottoman poetry. 2.1982
A history of pantomime. 2.2839
History of Parliament. 4.8475
A history of Pennsylvania. 3.8073
A history of Pentateuchal traditions. 1.2589
A history of Persia. 3.4071
The history of philosophy. 1.127
A history of philosophy. 1.122
A history of philosophy. 1.123
History of philosophy. 1.126
A history of philosophy. 1.131, 1.133
A history of philosophy in America. 1.556
The history of philosophy in Islam. 1.364
The history of photography. 5.6918-5.6919
A history of physical education and sports in the U.S.A. 4.899
History of Poland. 3.3332
A history of Poland. 3.3331
The History of Poland since 1863. 3.3337
The history of Polish literature. 2.1696
History of political philosophy. 4.7264
A history of political theory. 4.7262
A history of political thought in the sixteenth century. 4.7273
A history of popular music in America. 1.4237
History of Portugal. 3.3497
A history of Portugal. 3.3498
The history of post-war Southeast Asia. 3.4405
A history of postwar Africa. 3.5089
A history of postwar Britain, 1945-1974. 3.1704
A history of pottery. 1.6609
History of primitive Christianity. 1.2294
The history of printing in America with a biography of printers & an account of newspapers. 5.7551
A history of prophecy in Israel. 1.2582
The history of psychiatry. 5.4802
History of psychology. 5.70
The history of psychology and the behavioral sciences. 5.8415
A History of psychology in autobiography. 5.86
The History of psychotherapy. 5.4863
A history of public administration. 4.7747
The history of Rasselas, Prince of Abissinia. 2.7081
A history of recreation. 3.6005
A history of relations between the National Collegiate Athletic Association and the Amateur Athletic Union of the United States (1905-1963) 4.978
A history of religion East and West. 1.1589
A history of religious ideas. 1.1530
History of Renaissance art: painting, sculpture, architecture throughout Europe. 1.4761
A history of Rhodesia. 3.5512

History of rocketry & space travel. 5.6689
A history of Roman religion. 1.1658
The history of Rome. 3.2751
A history of Rome down to the reign of Constantine. 3.2754
A history of Rome, from its origins to 529 A.D. 3.2747
The history of Rome Hanks and kindred matters. 2.12308
A history of Rome through the fifth century. 3.2750
A history of Russia. 3.3041-3.3042
History of Russia. 3.3044, 3.3048
A history of Russia. 3.3045
History of Russia. 3.3046
A history of Russia. 3.3047
A history of Russia: medieval, modern, and contemporary. 3.3038
A history of Russian and Soviet sea power. 3.3055
A history of Russian literature. 2.1249
History of Russian literature. 2.1247
A history of Russian music. 1.3729
History of Russian music. 1.3730
History of Russian philosophy. 1.1104
A history of Russian philosophy. 1.1105
A history of Russian thought from the enlightenment to marxism. 4.5372
The history of sacerdotal celibacy in the Christian church. 1.3050
A history of Sanskrit literature. 2.1920
A history of Sanskrit literature. 2.1922
A history of Sanskrit literature, classical period. 2.1919
History of Sanskrit poetics. 2.1852
A history of Scandinavia. 3.3356
A history of Scandinavian archaeology. 3.3352
A history of Scandinavian literature, 1870-1980. 2.13968
The history of scepticism from Erasmus to Spinoza. 1.408
A history of science. 5.752
History of science. 5.759
A history of science and its relations with philosophy & religion. 5.722
History of science and medicine. 5.736
A history of science and technology. 5.727
A history of scientific & technical periodicals. 2.3573
A history of Scotland. 3.1781
History of Scottish literature. 2.9835
A history of sculpture. 1.5612
A history of secular Latin poetry in the Middle Ages. 2.811
A history of seventeenth-century Russian literature. 2.1254
A history of Siam, from the earliest times to the year A.D. 1781. 3.4525
A history of Sicily. 3.2943
A history of Sierra Leone. 3.5372
A history of Sierra Leone, 1400-1787. 3.5373
The history of Sir Charles Grandison. 2.7221
The history of slavery in Mauritius and the Seychelles, 1810-1875. 4.6445
A history of social welfare and social work in the United States. 4.6517
History of socialism. 4.6928
A history of socialist thought. 4.6931
A History of sociological analysis. 4.4743
A history of song. 1.4236
The history of South-Carolina. 3.8235
History of South Dakota. 3.8511
A history of South-East Asia. 3.4394
A history of South India from prehistoric times to the fall of Vijayanagar. 3.4219
The History of Southern literature. 2.10448
A history of Southern Rhodesia. 3.5508
A history of Soviet Russia. 3.3206
A history of Spain and Portugal. 3.3413
A history of Spanish Golden Age drama. 2.5129
A history of Spanish literature. 2.5085, 2.5090
A history of Spanish painting. 1.6286
A history of Sparta, 950-192 B.C. 3.2648
History of speech education in America. 2.3534
A history of strategic bombing. 5.7408

A history of suffrage in the United States. 4.8074

The history of surrealism. 1.1401

The history of surrealist painting 1.6348

A history of Swedish literature. 2.14061

History of Syria. 3.3795

A history of tapestry from the earliest times until the present day. 1.6590

A history of Tasmania. 3.5616

A History of technology. 5.5533

A history of technology & invention. 5.5529

History of Telugu literature. 2.2283

A history of textile art. 1.6677

The history of the adventures of Joseph Andrews, and of his friend Mr. Abraham Adams. 2.7020

A history of the African people. 3.5073

A history of the alphabet. 2.173

A history of the American bar. 4.9478

A history of the American drama, from the beginning to the civil war. 2.10513

A history of the American drama from the Civil war to the present day. 2.10514

The history of the American sailing Navy. 5.7449

History of the American theatre. 2.3193

A history of the American theatre, 1700-1950. 2.3191

History of the American theatre, and anecdotes of the principal actors. 2.3188

History of the American worker, 1920-1933. 4.3565

History of the American worker, 1933-1941. 4.3564, 4.3566

A history of the ancient world. 3.551-3.552

A history of the Arab State of Zanzibar. 3.5289

History of the Arabs from the earliest times to the present. 3.3661

History of the art of war within the framework of political history. 5.7174

History of the arts of design. 1.4859

A history of the Asians in East Africa, c.1886 to 1945. 3.5259

A history of the Balkan peoples. 3.3526

History of the Balkans. 3.3516

History of the Belgians. 3.2968

A history of the Bemba. 3.5521

The history of the Boston Theatre, 1854-1901. 2.3218

The history of the British coal industry, 1700-1830. 4.3751

The history of the British film. 2.2896

The history of the British film, 1929-1939. 2.2898

The history of the British film 1929-1939. 2.2897

History of the Byzantine Empire, 324-1453. 3.2665

History of the Byzantine state. 3.2666

The history of the calculus and its conceptual development. 5.1447

A history of the calculus of variations from the 17th through the 19th century. 5.1468

History of the Canadian National Railways. 4.4015

History of the Canadian Pacific Railway. 4.4018

A history of the Canadian west to 1870-71. 3.8838

History of the Christian church. 1.2278

A history of the Christian church. 1.2279

A history of the church. 1.2275

History of the church. 1.2281

A history of the Church in England. 1.2429

A history of the church to A.D. 461. 1.2297

A history of the cinema from its origins to 1970. 2.2884

A history of the circus. 4.1188

A history of the circus in America. 4.1189

The history of the colony and province of Massachusetts-bay. 3.7973

A history of the comic strip. 1.5846

History of the comic strip. 2.3811

History of the Commonwealth and Protectorate, 1649-1656. 3.1459

History of the Communist party of the Soviet union (bolsheviks) Short course. 4.8658

History of the Communist Party of the United States. 4.8234

History of the conquest of Peru. 3.9299

A history of the Council of Trent. 1.3120

A history of the Crusades. 3.589-3.590

A History of the Czechoslovak Republic, 1918-1948. 3.1917

The history of the decline & fall of the Roman empire. 3.2802

A history of the development of Japanese thought from A.D. 592 to 1868. 3.1917

The history of the Dominican Order. 1.3240

History of the Dvaita school of Vedānta and its literature. 1.191

A history of the early church. 1.2298

A history of the Eastern Roman Empire from the fall of Irene to the accession of Basil I, 802-867. 3.2669

A history of the ecumenical movement. 1.3099

A history of the English language. 2.967

The history of the English novel. 2.5941

The history of the English novel: Volume XI: Yesterday and after. 2.6043

A history of the English people in the nineteenth century. 3.1582

A history of the English-speaking peoples. 3.1219

The history of the English toy theatre. 2.2835

A history of the expansion of Christianity. 1.2277

History of the family and kinship. 5.8379

History of the First World War. 3.786

A history of the French Revolution. 3.2102

A history of the Gambia. 3.5335

History of the German General Staff, 1657-1945. 3.2254

A history of the German language. 2.1175

History of the German novel. 2.13497

A history of the German Novelle. 2.13501

A history of the German Republic. 3.2365

The history of the German resistance, 1933-1945. 3.2431

A history of the Gothic revival. 1.5377

History of the great American fortunes. 4.1894

History of the great civil war, 1642-1649. 3.1460

The history of the Greek and Roman theater. 2.303

A history of the Greek city states, ca. 700-338 B.C. 3.2578

A history of the greenbacks. 4.4508

A history of the Habsburg Empire, 1526-1918. 3.1881

A history of the Highland clearances. 4.2918

History of the House of Representatives. 4.8049

A history of the Hussite revolution. 3.1912

History of the idea of progress. 4.4883

A history of the Igbo people. 3.5352

A history of the Indian nationalist movement. 3.4231

History of the Indians of New Spain. 3.8886

A history of the International Council of Nurses, 1899-1964. 5.5153

History of the International Labor Organization. 4.3506

The history of the island of Dominica. 3.9131

A History of the Jewish people. 3.3850

A history of the Jewish people in the age of Jesus Christ (175 B.C. - A.D. 135) 3.3891

History of the Jews. 3.3849

A history of the Jews in Babylonia. 3.3941

A history of the Jews in Christian Spain. 3.4003

A history of the Jews in England. 3.3950

History of the Jews in Russia and Poland, from the earliest times until the present day. 3.3993

The history of the Jews of Italy. 3.3976

A history of the Kikuyu, 1500-1900. 3.5273

A history of the kingdom of Denmark. 3.3368

A history of the kingdom of Nkore in Western Uganda to 1896. 3.5286

History of the Kings of Britain 3.1302

History of the labor movement in the United States. 4.3352

A history of the Labour Party from 1914. 4.8536

History of the later Roman Empire from the Death of Theodosius I. to the Death of Justinian. 3.2801

A history of the League of Nations. 4.9191

A history of the Maghrib. 3.5193

A history of the Marranos. 3.3904

A history of the medieval Church, 590-1500. 1.2306

History of the militia and the National Guard. 5.7291

A history of the modern world. 3.609

A history of the Moghuls of central Asia. 3.3620

The history of the Mongol conquests. 3.3622

History of the Mongolian People's Republic. 3.4867

History of the Mongols. 3.3621

History of the Mongols, based on Eastern and Western accounts of the thirteenth and fourteenth centuries. 3.3623

A history of the Monroe doctrine. 4.9053

History of the national economy of Russia, to the 1917 revolution. 4.2366

A history of the National intelligencer. 2.3672

History of the Naval Weapons Center, China Lake, California. 5.7480

The history of the Nazi Party. 3.2425

The history of the new deal, 1933-1938. 3.7768

History of the Norwegian people. 3.3379

A history of the oratorio. 1.4252

The history of the organ in the United States. 1.4144

A history of the original peoples of northern Canada. 3.5725

History of the Ottoman Empire and modern Turkey. 3.3572

History of the Ottoman Turks. 3.3571

A history of the Pacific from the stone age to the present day. 3.5542

A history of the people's democracies: Eastern Europe since Stalin. 3.3532

History of the Persian Empire, Achaemenid period. 3.4076

History of the popes. 1.3145

History of the pre-romantic novel in England. 2.6004

A history of the problems of education. 4.9949

The history of the Province of New York. 3.8029

The history of the psychoanalytic movement. 5.4783

The history of the rebellion and civil wars in England begun in the year 1641. 3.1472

A history of the Reformation in Germany to 1555. 3.2277

History of the Reformation in Scotland. 1.2361

History of the reign of Ferdinand and Isabella, the Catholic. 3.3436

The history of the reign of King Henry the Seventh. 3.1398

History of the rise and progress of the arts of design in the United States. 1.4859

A history of the Roman world from 30 B.C. to A.D. 138. 3.2792

A history of the Roman world from 146 to 30 B.C. 3.2774

A history of the Roman world from 753 to 146 B.C. 3.2763

A history of the Romanian Communist Party. 4.8688

History of the Royal Navy. 5.7455

The history of the Russian Revolution. 3.3197

A history of the Scottish people, 1560-1830. 3.1783

History of the Second World War. 3.907

A history of the Sikhs. 3.4354

A history of the Southern Confederacy. 3.7372

A history of the Southern Sudan, 1839-1889. 3.5166

A history of the Spanish stage: from medieval times until the end of the seventeenth century. 2.3384

The history of the Standard oil company. 4.3044

The history of the state of Ohio. 3.8381

The history of the Sudan from the coming of Islan to the present day. 3.5167

History of the Supreme Court of the United States. 4.9783
A history of the Swedish people. 3.3386
The history of the synoptic tradition. 1.2674
History of the tantric religion. 1.1733
History of the theatre. 2.3161
A history of the theatre in America from its beginnings to the present time. 2.3190
A history of the theories of aether and electricity. 5.2213
A history of the theories of production & distribution in English political economy, from 1776 to 1848. 4.1345
History of the theory of numbers ... 5.1322
A history of the United Nations. 4.9221
A history of the United Nations Charter. 4.9196
A history of the United States. 3.6317
A history of the United States Air Force, 1907-1957. 5.7400
History of the United States Army. 5.7286
History of the United States civil service. 4.7975
History of the United States from the Compromise of 1850 to the McKinley-Bryan campaign of 1896. 3.7147
History of the United States of America during the administration of Jefferson and Madison. 3.6978
History of the United States of America, from the discovery of the continent. 3.6314
The History of the University of Oxford. 4.11009
A history of the Vikings. 3.3354
The history of the violin. 1.4162
History of the wars. 3.2667
A History of the Weimar Republic. 3.2362
A history of the West Indies. 3.9086
The history of the world. 3.550
A history of the world economy. 4.1762
History of the ZGS (Argonne, 1979) 5.2447
The History of trade unionism. 4.3406
A history of trade unionism in the United States. 4.3362
A history of transportation in the Ohio Valley, with special reference to its waterways, trade and commerce from the earliest period to the present time. 4.3968
History of transportation in the United States before 1860. 4.3882
The history of Troy in Middle English literature. 2.5610
The history of U.S. ethnic policy and its impact on European ethnics. 3.6544
History of U.S. Marine Corps operations in World War II. 3.1024
History of U.S. political parties. 4.8166
A history of Ukraine. 3.3302
A history of Ukrainian literature, from the 11th to the end of the 19th century. 2.1651
A history of underground comics. 2.3814
History of United States naval operations in World War II. 3.1032
A history of urban America 4.6210
The history of urban and regional planning. 5.8187
History of urban form. 4.6313
A history of Urdu literature. 2.1897
The history of violence in America. 4.5131
History of wages in the United States from colonial times to 1928. 4.3149
A history of Wales. 3.1762
A history of Wales, 1485-1660. 3.1766
A history of Wales, 1660-1815. 3.1764
A history of war at sea. 3.542
A history of Welsh literature. 2.833
History of West Africa. 3.5323
A history of West Africa. 3.5324
A history of Western education. 4.9948
A history of western music. 1.3634
The History of Wisconsin. 3.8442
A history of women's bodies. 5.5043
A history of world theater. 2.3167
History of Wyoming. 3.8552
A history of Yiddish literature. 2.1791
The history of Yiddish literature in the nineteenth century. 2.1793
A history of Yugoslav literature. 2.1198

History of Yugoslavia. 3.3553
A history of Zambia. 3.5525
History of Zanzibar, from the Middle Ages to 1856. 3.5287
A history of Zen Buddhism. 1.1761
A history of Zionism. 3.4021
History 3.397
History will absolve me. 3.9101
Hitch. 2.3055
Hitchcock. 2.3056
Hitchcock, the first forty-four films. 2.3053
Hitchcock's films. 2.3058
Hitler. 3.2395-3.2396, 3.2398
Hitler, a film from Germany. 2.3028
Hitler among the Germans. 3.2394
Hitler and his generals. 3.2397
Hitler and the Beer Hall Putsch. 3.2399
Hitler and the final solution. 3.1090
Hitler directs his war. 3.963
Hitler, ein Film aus Deutschland (Motion picture) 2.3028
Hitler's death camps. 3.1088
Hitler's decision to invade Russia, 1941. 3.964
Hitler's letters and notes. 3.2405
Hitler's social revolution. 3.2448
Hitler's spies. 3.1135
Hitler's war. 3.966
Hitler's war aims. 3.2447
Hitler's war and the Germans. 3.971
Hitler's war on Russia. 3.991
Hitler's youth. 3.2403
Hitopadeśa. English. 2.1940
The Hittites. 3.3760
The Hittites and their contemporaries in Asia Minor. 3.3761
Hmannān maha yazawintawkyī. English. 3.4426
Hobbes. 4.7408
Hobbes and his critics. 4.7406
Hobbes and Locke, the politics of freedom and obligation. 4.7639
Hobbes and Rousseau. 1.672
Hobbes on civil association. 4.7407
The hobbit. 2.9431
Hobson-jobson. 2.1162
Hoffa and the teamsters. 4.3394
Hofmannsthal's festival dramas. 2.13785
Hogarth. 1.4954
Hogarth and his place in European art. 1.6033
Hogarth: the complete engravings. 1.6457
Hogarth to Cruikshank. 1.5852
Hogarth's graphic works. 1.6456
Hogup Cave. 3.5769
Die Hohenzollern und ihr Werk. 3.2480
The Hohokam, desert farmers & craftsmen. 3.5716
Holbein. 1.6175
Holding the line. 3.7817
The holiness revival of the nineteenth century. 1.3357
Holinshed's Chronicle as used in Shakespeare's plays. 2.6714
Hollywood and the profession of authorship, 1928-1940. 2.3034
Hollywood directors, 1914-1940. 2.3001
Hollywood musicals. 2.2994
The Hollywood studio system. 2.2917
Hollywood, the dream factory. 2.2931
Holmes-Laski letters. 4.9820
Holmes-Pollock letters. 4.9819
Holmes Principles of physical geology. 5.2966
The Holocaust. 5.8249
The holocaust. 3.1117
The Holocaust in historical perspective. 3.1083
A Holocaust reader. 3.1095
The Holstein papers. 3.2317
The Holy Bible. 1.2493, 1.2496
The Holy Land. 2.14090
The Holy Roman empire. 3.2252
The Holy Roman Empire. 3.2251
The Holy Sinner. 2.13829
The holy teaching of Vimalakīrti. 1.2136
The holy war. 2.6917
Holy warriors. 3.7225
Holy Week. 2.4376
The holy well. 2.1567
Holy Writ or Holy Church. 1.2812

Holzman's basketball: winning strategy and tactics. 4.1012
Homage to Catalonia. 3.3472
Homage to Daniel Shays. 2.12613
Homage to Mistress Bradstreet. 2.11379
Homage to Oceania. 2.9197
Homage to Theodore Dreiser, August 27, 1871-December 28, 1945. 2.11607
The home. 4.5653
Home. 2.9822
Home and foreign investment, 1870-1913. 4.4455
Home before dark. 2.11496
The home book of quotations, classical and modern. 2.3730
Home environments. 5.316
A home for the homeless. 1.2725
The home front and beyond. 4.6020
The home hospital. 5.5178
Home, inc. 4.1997
Home life in colonial days. 3.6012
Home style. 4.8057
Home sweet home. 2.9965
Home; The changing room; and Mother's day. 2.9822
Home to Harlem. 2.12084
Homecoming. 2.2117, 2.10035
Homecoming at twilight. 2.1804
The homecoming game. 2.12245
Homelessness in America. 4.6629
A homemade world. 2.10416
Homemakers, the forgotten workers. 4.5663
Homer and Mycenae. 2.500
Homer and the heroic age. 2.498
Homer and the heroic tradition. 2.507
The Homeric hymns. 2.483
The Homeric hymns. 2.491
The Homeric imagination. 2.505
The Homeric Odyssey. 2.512
Homeric renaissance. 2.509
Homērou Ilias. 2.481
Homeward bound. 2.1803
Homo faber. 2.13741
Homo hierarchicus. 4.6405
Homo ludens. 3.55
Homo viator; introduction to a metaphysic of hope. 1.835
Homology theory. 5.1591
Homosexual behavior. 4.5531
The homosexual tradition in American poetry. 2.10478
Homosexualities. 4.5528
Homosexuality, a history. 4.5530
Homosexuality: a selective bibliography of over 3,000 items. 5.8389
The homosexualization of America. 4.5534
Homotopy theory. 5.1592
Honda Motor. 4.3818
Honduras. 3.9070
Honen, the Buddhist saint. 1.1774
'Honest enough to be bold' 3.8828
Honest John Adams. 3.7046
The honest mind. 1.1423
The honest muse. 2.5654
Honest to God. 1.2771
Honey for the bears. 2.9645
L'honneur de Dieu. 2.4359
The honor plays of Lope de Vega. 2.5210
Honorable men. 4.7903
An honorable Titan. 2.3624
The honorary consul. 2.8749
Honoré Daumier. 1.6085, 1.6501
Honoré Daumier; catalogue raisonné of the paintings, watercolours, and drawings. 1.6086
Honoré de Balzac, a biography. 2.4123
Honourable members. 4.8473
The Hoosier politician. 3.8399
The Hoosier school-master. 2.11016
The Hoover administration. 3.7741
The Hoover Commission report on organization of the Executive Branch of the Government. 4.7974
Hoover, Roosevelt, and the Brains Trust. 3.7743
Hoover, the Nation, the depression. 3.7742
Hope abandoned. 2.1579
Hope against hope. 2.1578

Hope and dignity. 3.6803
Hope and the future of man. 1.3062
The hope of progress. 5.847
Hopi kachina. 3.5889
Hopi kachina dolls. 3.5887
Hopkins. 2.7829
A Hopkins reader. 2.7826
Hopscotch. 2.5384
Hora actual de la novela española. 2.5133
Horace. 2.724
Horace & his lyric poetry. 2.727
Horace Bushnell's theory of language. 2.86
Horace Greeley. 3.7155
Horace Mann. 4.10202
Horace on poetry. 2.719
Horace Walpole; a biography. 3.1529
Horace Walpole's Miscellany, 1786-1795.
 2.7332
Horace White, nineteenth century liberal.
 3.7166
Horace's compromise. 4.10055
Horacio Quiroga Sus mejores cuentos. 2.5441
Horatio Greenough, the first American sculptor.
 1.5667
Hordubal. 2.1667
Hormone action in the whole life of plants.
 5.3747
Hormones and behavior. 5.4298
The horn; a comprehensive guide to the modern
 instrument & its music. 1.4173
Horn technique. 1.4559
Horowitz. 1.4066
Horror literature. 5.7971
The horrors of the half-known life. 4.5493
A horse of another color. 2.13230
The horse of pride. 3.2222
Horse sense in American humor, from
 Benjamin Franklin to Ogden Nash. 2.10651
Horse-shoe Robinson. 2.11136
The horse's mouth. 2.8501
Horticultural science. 5.5336
Horticulture. 5.5337
Hortus third. 5.5311
Hosea. 1.2617
The hospice alternative. 5.4589
A Hospice handbook. 5.4587
The hospital. 5.4706
Hospital costs and health insurance. 4.3451
Hospital with a heart. 5.4539
The hostage. 2.8442
Hosteen Klah, Navaho medicine man and sand
 painter. 3.5924
Hostiles and horse soldiers. 3.5780
Hosts and guests. 4.85
The hot-blooded dinosaurs. 5.3171
The hot gates, and other occasional pieces.
 2.8697
Hot jazz. 1.4331
The Hot l Baltimore. 2.13434
The hotel. 2.8474
The Hotel Baltimore. 2.13434
Hotel & travel index. 5.7143
Hotel du Lac. 2.9632
Hour of gold, hour of lead. 5.6652
Hours in a library. 2.5554
The Hours of Catherine of Cleves. 1.6429
Hours of work. 4.3152
House and home in the Victorian city. 4.3495
The house at Pooh Corner. 2.9111
House, bridge, fountain, gate. 2.11969
The House built on sand. 3.1070
The house by the Medlar-tree. 2.5015
The House Committee on Un-American
 Activities, 1945-1950. 3.7542
A house divided. 2.11429, 3.9247
A house for Mr. Biswas. 2.10009
The house in Clewe Street. 2.8947
The house in Paris. 2.8473
House made of dawn. 2.13176
House of all nations. 2.10165
The house of breath. 2.11794
A house of children. 2.8502
The House of Commons, 1604-1610. 4.8474
The House of Commons, 1754-1790. 4.8475
The House of Commons at work. 4.8479
The house of Desdemona. 2.3466
The house of fiction. 2.3520
A house of gentlefolk; a novel. 2.1456

House of incest. 2.12251
The house of Islam. 1.2048
The house of labor. 4.3356
The House of Lords and contemporary politics,
 1911-1957. 4.8469
The house of mirth. 2.12693
A house of my own. 4.5277
The house of Ptolemy. 3.5156
The House of Representatives and foreign
 affairs. 4.8051
The house of Saud. 3.4056
The house of Saulx-Tavanes. 3.300
The house of Seleucus. 3.3797
The house of the arrow. 2.9092
House of the Dead. 2.1360
The house of the seven gables. 2.11059
The house on Coliseum Street. 2.13058
The house on marshland. 2.13047
The house on the canal. 2.13948
House on the embankment. 2.1642
The house the Left built. 4.2290
House united, house divided. 4.643
The house with the green shutters. 2.7462
The house without a key. 2.11383
Houseboy. 2.4856
Household taste in furniture, upholstery, and
 other details. 1.6551
Household technology from the open hearth to
 the microwave. 5.7100
Households. 4.5485
Households, employment, and gender. 4.5588
The Houses of Parliament. 1.5515
Housewife or harlot. 4.6119
Housing and identity. 4.3482
Housing and the money market. 4.3491
Housing and urban development in the USSR.
 4.3499
Housing markets and public policy. 4.3486
Housing markets and racial discrimination.
 4.3493
Housing needs and policy approaches. 4.3481
Housing the urban poor. 4.3490
The hovering giant. 3.9013
How and how much can intelligence be
 increased. 5.356
How animals work. 5.4184
How arbitration works. 4.9558
How Boston played. 4.940
How Britain votes. 4.8503
How can I keep from singing. 1.4098
How children fail. 4.10424
How children learn. 4.10365
How children learn mathematics. 5.1262
How courts govern America. 4.9749
How democratic is the Constitution? 4.7797
How does a poem mean? 2.10734
How does the Constitution secure rights?
 4.9670
How Europe underdeveloped Africa. 4.2609
How green was my valley. 2.9052
How I became a holy mother, and other stories.
 2.9728
How I learned to stop worrying and love the
 bomb. 2.9699
How it is. 2.4404
How it was. 2.11860
How many miles to Babylon? 2.9732
How much is enough? 5.7265
How musical is man?. 1.4389
How nations behave. 4.9030
How nations negotiate. 4.9321
How nations see each other. 4.5015
How our laws are made. 4.9733
How Pol Pot came to power. 3.4447
How Russia is ruled. 4.8647
How Spanish grew. 2.888
How taxes affect economic behavior. 4.4698
How teachers taught. 4.10025
How the Greeks built cities. 1.5603
How the other half lives. 4.6621
How the rural poor got power. 4.8862
How the Soviet system works: cultural,
 psychological, and social themes. 3.3205
How the Soviet Union is governed. 4.8648
How the steel was tempered. 2.1590
How they became governor. 4.8253
How to become a musical critic. 1.3721

How to complete and survive a doctoral
 dissertation. 4.10628
How to do psychotherapy and how to evaluate
 it. 5.4861
How to do things with words. 1.739
How to encourage girls in math & science.
 5.989
How to find chemical information. 5.2601
How to find information about companies.
 4.3046
How to grow science. 5.914
How to increase reading ability. 4.10346
How to know the lichens. 5.3717
How to know the mosses and liverworts.
 5.3703
How to know the seaweeds. 5.3713
How to live to be 100. 5.4214
How to play hockey. 4.993
How to predict elections. 4.8137
How to read. 2.2449
How to read a book. 2.2447
How to read a film. 2.2942
How to read a page. 2.2451
How to read annual reports intelligently.
 4.4602
How to read Shakespeare. 2.6795
How to read the Bible as literature. 1.2535
How to solve it. 5.1059
How to succeed in organic chemistry. 5.2720
How to suppress women's writing. 2.2554
How to use an astronomical telescope. 5.1749
How to write and publish a scientific paper.
 5.5505
How to write short stories (with samples)
 2.11978
How voters decide. 4.8504
How wars end. 4.9252
How we learn. 4.10350
How we lived. 3.8048
The Howard Fast reader. 2.11656
Howard Hawks. 2.3050-2.3051
Howards End. 2.8645
The Howe brothers and the American
 Revolution. 3.6948
Howells and the age of realism. 2.11090
Howells, his life and world. 2.11089
Hsiao-hsiao-shêng. 2.2228
[Hsin Han Ying tz'u tien. 2.2150
Hua-yen Buddhism. 1.2166
Huang Hsing and the Chinese revolution.
 3.4820
Huasipungo. 2.5422
Hubert Howe Bancroft, historian of the West.
 3.6249
Hubert Humphrey. 3.7652
Hubert Walter. 1.2442
The huddled masses. 4.8944
Hudibras. 2.6925
Hudson river bracketed. 2.12694
The Hudson's Bay Company as an imperial
 factor, 1821-1869 3.8847
Hue and cry. 2.13152
Huerta; a political portrait. 3.8944
Huey Long. 3.7663
Huey Long's Louisiana: State politics,
 1920-1952. 3.8314
The huge season. 2.12213
Hugging the shore. 2.13368
Hugh Gaitskell. 3.1666
A Hugh Henry Brackenridge reader, 1770-1815.
 2.10862
Hugh Johnson's Modern encyclopedia of wine.
 5.6893
Hugh MacDiarmid. 2.8787-2.8788
The Hugh MacDiarmid anthology. 2.8781
Hugh MacDiarmid, the man and his work.
 2.8789
Hugh of Saint Victor on the sacraments of the
 Christian faith (De sacramentis) 1.3221
Hugh Walpole. 2.9462
Hugh Wynne, free Quaker. 2.11174
Hugo Black. 4.9802
Hugo Black and the Bill of Rights. 4.9658
Hugo Black and the judicial revolution. 4.9801
Hugo Riemann's Theory of harmony. 1.4113
Hugo von Hofmannsthal. 2.13784
Hugo Wolf. 1.4064-1.4065
The Huguenots in America. 3.6548

The Huk rebellion. 3.4607
The Huks: Philippine agrarian society in revolt. 3.4608
Human action. 4.1472
Human adaptability. 4.379
Human adaptation and population growth. 4.1596
Human, all too human. 1.1049
Human anatomy. 5.4140
Human anatomy & figure drawing. 1.5824
Human and ecologic effects of nuclear power plants. 5.5998
Human and mammalian cytogenetics. 5.3430
Human behavior and environment. 5.316
The human body. 5.4193
Human bondage in Southeast Asia. 4.3105
Human brain and psychological processes. 5.4336
The human brain and spinal cord. 5.4317
Human capacities. 5.367
Human capital. 4.1548, 4.10543
The human central nervous system. 5.4152
Human characteristics and school learning. 4.10349
The human comedy. 2.12439
A human comedy. 1.5854
Human communication disorders. 5.4790
The human condition. 3.41, 4.4964
Human ecology. 4.4831
Human economy. 5.8371
Human embryology. 5.4166
Human embryology; prenatal development of form and function. 5.4165
Human emotions. 5.412
The human enterprise. 1.617
Human evolution. 1.481, 4.447
The human factor. 2.8750
Human factors in engineering and design. 5.5687
Human family systems. 4.583
Human fertility and national development. 4.1641
Human food uses. 5.8098
Human genetics. 5.3442
Human geography. 4.360, 4.369, 4.5112
Human geography, an attempt at a positive classification, principles and examples. 4.363
Human geography of the South. 4.2025
The human group. 4.4987
Human growth. 5.4210
Human histology. 5.4155
The human impact. 4.381
The human imperative. 4.443
Human knowledge, its scope and limits. 1.1282
Human learning. 5.297
Human liberation in a feminist perspective 1.2939
Human memory. 5.325, 5.328, 5.332
Human memory and amnesia. 5.326
Human migration. 4.1652, 4.1655
The human mind. 5.175
The human model. 5.477
The human mosaic. 4.375
The human mystery. 5.4330
Human nature and history. 4.7627
Human nature and the social order. 4.4982
Human nature and the study of society. 4.402
Human nature in American thought. 3.6101
Human nature in politics. 4.7247, 4.7779
Human nutrition. 5.4233
Human personality and its survival of bodily death. 5.643
Human physiological work capacity. 5.4270
Human physiology. 5.4198
The human primate. 5.479
The human problems of an industrial civilization. 4.3316
The human prospect. 3.2
Human reality and the social world. 1.1130
Human reproduction. 5.4255
Human reproduction and sexual behavior. 5.4256
Human resource development in the organization. 5.8384
Human resource implications of robotics. 4.3322
Human resource planning. 4.4366, 4.4376

Human resources management and development handbook. 4.4377
Human resources management & development handbook. 4.4377
Human rights. 4.7635
Human rights and American foreign policy. 4.7636
Human rights and state sovereignty. 4.7630
Human rights and world order politics. 4.7624
Human rights and world politics. 4.7631
Human rights and world public order. 4.9383
Human rights, ethnicity, and discrimination. 4.7650
Human rights in Latin America, 1964-1980. 5.8378
Human rights in the world. 4.9385
The human rights of aliens in contemporary international law. 4.9390
Human rights, the United States, and world community. 4.7671
The human senses. 5.238
Human services and resource networks. 4.6529
Human services in industry. 4.3503
Human services management. 4.6492
Human setlements. 4.1850
Human sexual behavior. 4.5490
Human sexual inadequacy. 5.4952
Human sexual response. 4.4257
Human sexuality. 4.5504, 5.488, 5.490
Human sexuality across the life span. 5.485
Human sexuality in four perspectives. 4.5503
Human sexuality in nursing process. 5.5201
Human sexuality, new directions in American Catholic thought. 4.5513
Human sickness and health. 4.467
The human side of enterprise. 4.4361
The human skeleton. 5.4221
Human society in ethics and politics. 1.1441
Human speech. 5.4281
Human stress and cognition in organizations. 4.4355
Human types. 4.427
Human understanding. 1.1240
The human use of human beings. 5.949
Human variation and human microevolution. 4.459
Human welfare. 4.3718
Humanhood. 5.4561
Humanism. 1.407
Humanism and terror. 4.6970
Humanism and the physician. 5.4556
Humanism and the social order in Tudor England. 1.406
Humanism as a philosophy. 1.501
Humanism in Italian Renaissance musical thought. 1.3725
Humanism in personology. 5.526
Humanistic geography. 4.376
Humanistic psychology. 5.230
Humanistic psychology and the research tradition. 5.229
The humanitarian movement in eighteenth-century France. 4.5349
Humanities index. 1.30
The humanity of God. 1.2753
Humanizing schools: new directions, new decisions. 4.10034
The humanoids. 2.12758
Humboldt. 5.820
Humboldt's gift. 2.11353
Humbug. 4.1192
Hume. 1.703, 1.707
Hume and the problem of causation. 1.709
Hume's moral epistemology. 1.710
Hume's moral theory. 1.711
Hume's philosophical development. 1.705
Hume's philosophy of belief. 1.699
Hume's philosophy of common life. 1.704
Humid landforms. 4.267
Humidity and moisture. 5.2532
Humor, its origin and development. 5.598
Humor of the old Southwest. 2.10726
Humphrey Clinker. 2.7261
The hunchback of Notre Dame. 2.4237
Hundejahre. 2.13758
A hundred and fifty years of archaeology. 3.252

The hundred flowers campaign and the Chinese intellectuals. 3.4803
The hundred tales. 2.3968
The hundred thousand songs. 2.2256
Hundred-year statistics of the Japanese economy. 4.1258
A hundred years of anthropology. 4.413
A hundred years of archaeology. 4.691
A hundred years of geography. 4.68
A hundred years of international relations. 4.9015
A hundred years of metallurgy. 5.6757
A hundred years of music. 1.3662
A hundred years of philosophy. 1.736
A hundred years of war. 3.715
The Hundred Years War. 3.1998-3.2000
Hungarian ballads and the European ballad tradition. 1.4343
The Hungarian economy in the twentieth century. 4.2350
The Hungarian revolt. 3.1949
The Hungarian revolution; a white book. 3.1948
Hungarian short stories. 2.1756
The Hungarians in America, 1583-1974. 3.6549
Hungary. 3.1935, 3.1937, 4.2349
Hungary 1956. 3.1950
Hungary, a decade of economic reform. 4.2351
Hunger. 2.14047
The hunger for salt. 5.4403
The hunger winter. 3.2993
The hungered one. 2.12930
The hungry ghosts. 2.13198
Hungry Gulliver. 2.12790
Hunted heretic. 1.3420
Hunter-gatherer subsistence and settlement. 4.720
Hunters, fishers and farmers of Eastern Europe, 6000-3000 B.C. 4.709
The hunters or the hunted? 4.701
Hunting & shooting, from earliest times to the present day. 5.5490
The hunting of the snark. 2.7677
Hurd's Letters on chivalry and romance, with the third Elizabethan dialogue. 2.7077
The hurried child. 5.5099
Hurry on down. 2.9449
Husbands & wives. 4.5585
Husserl: an analysis of his phenomenology. 1.1022
Husserl and Frege. 1.1021
Husserl and the search for certitude. 1.1019
Husserl, shorter works. 1.1011
Husserlian meditations; how words present things. 1.1023
The Hussite King. 3.1914
The Hussite revolution. 3.1912
Hustlers, beats, and others. 4.5141
Hustling and other hard work. 3.6742
Hutterite society. 1.3369
Hybridization of somatic cells. 5.3426
Hybrids and hybridizers, rhododendrons and azaleas for Eastern North America. 5.5353
Hydraulics of sediment transport. 5.5968
Hydrodynamic and hydromagnetic stability. 5.1663
Hydrogen power. 5.6880
Hydrogeology. 4.310
Hydrological forecasting. 4.301
Hydrology for engineers. 4.291
Hydrothermal processes at seafloor spreading centers. 5.3100
Hymn of the universe. 1.856
Hymns for the drowning. 2.2276
Hymns of Guru Nanak. 1.1829
Hymns of the Atharva-Veda. 2.1931
The hymns of the Rgveda. 1.1678
Hymns to the night. 2.13595
Hyperactive children. 5.5113
The hypercycle, a principle of natural self-organization. 5.3387
Hypertension. 5.4995
Hypnos walking. 2.4466
Hypnosis. 5.659
Hypnosis for the seriously curious. 5.658
Hypnosis, imagination, and human potentialities. 5.4900

The hypocrisy of justice in the Belle Epoque. 4.9912

Hypothesis and evidence in psychoanalysis. 5.194

Hysterical personality. 5.4930

I am a camera. 2.9446
I am a composer. 1.3898
I am a mathematician. 5.1100
I am a memory come alive. 2.13793
I am Annie Mae. 3.6808
I and Thou. 1.970
I.B.M. and the US data processing industry. 4.3808
I can't go on, I'll go on. 2.8421
I Ching. 1.1795
I ching. 1.1795
The I ching. 2.2181
I ching. 2.2180
I ching. English. 1.1800, 2.2181
I, Claudius. 2.8723
I come as a thief. 2.11340
I. Compton-Burnett. 2.8534
I.D.A. in retrospect. 4.4568
I don't need you any more. 2.12172
I.E.E.E. standard dictionary of electrical and electronics terms. 5.6249
I give thee my daughter. 4.5628
I knew a phoenix. 2.12446
I, Lars Hård. 2.14084
I love myself when I am laughing ... and then again when I am looking mean and impressive. 2.11908
I.M.F. and stablization. 4.4581
I.M.F. conditionality. 4.4582
I.N.T.E.L.S.A.T. global satellite system. 5.6396
I never had it made. 4.1003
I/O design. 5.1236
I paid Hitler. 3.2423
I, Pierre Rivière, having slaughtered my mother, my sister, and my brother ... 4.6703
I protest. 2.3633
I promessi sposi. 2.5002
I remember! 2.9165
I remember. 2.1595
I, robot. 2.12855
I: six non-lectures. 2.11540
I speak of freedom. 3.5341
I spy blue. 4.6838
I that was born in Wales. 2.9476
I, the jury. 2.12496
I thought of Daisy. 2.12761
I too am here. 2.7542
The I. W. W. 4.3554
I will pray with the Spirit and with the understanding also. 1.2215
I wonder as I wander. 2.11900
I wouldn't have missed it. 2.12234
IAC magazine index: microform. 1.31
IAC national newspaper index. 1.44
IBM and the U.S. data processing industry. 4.3808
Ibn Khaldūn's philosophy of history. 3.571
Ibsen. 2.14038
Ibsen and the temper of Norwegian literature 2.14031
Ibsen, the man and his work. 2.14039
Ibsen's dramatic method. 2.14041
Ice. 2.8616
The ice age. 2.9658
The ice in the bedroom. 2.9552
Iceland fisherman. 2.4329
The Icelandic family saga. 2.13979
Icelandic poems and stories. 2.13994
The Icelandic saga. 2.13978
Ichthyology. 5.3896
The icon. 1.5180
Icon and idea. 1.4599
The icon and the axe. 3.3022
Iconography of Christian art. 1.5167
Iconography of the Tale of Genji. 1.6335
Iconology. 1.4766
Icons. 1.5177
Icons and their dating. 1.5181
The ICP encyclopedia of photography. 5.6915
Ida. 2.12511
IDA in retrospect. 4.4568

Ida M. Tarbell. 2.12570
Idaho. 3.8549
Idaho, a bicentennial history. 3.8551
Idanre. 2.10112
Idea and act in Elizabethan fiction. 2.5992
Idea & experience. 1.1015
The idea and practice of world government. 4.9137
Idea art. 1.6730
The idea of a party system. 4.8147
The idea of a social science and its relation to philosophy. 4.1219
The idea of a town. 4.6314
The idea of a university. 4.10545
The idea of Coleridge's criticism. 2.7599
The idea of freedom. 1.139
The idea of historical recurrence in Western thought. 3.500
The idea of history. 3.385
The idea of history in the ancient Near East. 3.467
The idea of Louis Sullivan. 1.5331
The idea of national interest. 4.9043
The idea of nationalism, a study in its origins and background. 4.7489
The idea of politics. 4.7220
The idea of poverty. 4.6623
The idea of prehistory. 4.698
The idea of progress. 3.38
The idea of progress in classical antiquity. 3.62
The idea of revelation in recent thought. 1.2839
The idea of Rome. 3.2712
The idea of social structure. 4.605
The idea of the Canterbury tales. 2.6324
The idea of the gentleman in the Victorian novel. 2.6024
The idea of the holy. 1.1535
The idea of the novel in Europe, 1600-1800. 2.3517
The ideal city, its architectural evolution. 1.5593
The ideal image. 1.5752
Ideal man in classical sociology. 4.4786
Ideal marriage. 4.5508
The ideal of the practical. 5.5623
Idealism and revolution. 4.5232
The idealist tradition: from Berkeley to Blanshard. 1.503
Ideals and realities of Islam. 1.2056
Ideals, beliefs, attitudes, and the law. 4.9514
Ideas and men. 3.89
Ideas and politics of Chilean independence 1808-1833. 3.9262
Ideas and weapons. 5.7401
Ideas, concepts, doctrine. 5.7399
Ideas; general introduction to pure phenomenology. 1.1014
Ideas in America. 2.10267
The ideas in Barotse jurisprudence. 4.612
Ideas of greatness. 2.5900
Ideas of Jewish history. 3.3846
The ideas of Le Corbusier on architecture and urban planning. 1.5482
Ideas of life and matter. 5.4172
Ideas of order in the novels of Thomas Pynchon. 2.13284
The ideas of particle physics. 5.2458
Ideas of the Restoration in English literature, 1660-71. 2.5650
The ideas of the woman suffrage movement, 1890-1920. 4.8083
Identity & reality. 1.1285
Identity and the life cycle. 5.196
The identity of Yeats. 2.8342
Ideological coalitions in Congress. 4.8005
Ideological differences and world order. 3.13
The ideological origins of Black nationalism. 3.7263
Ideologies in Quebec. 4.7279
The ideologies of the developing nations. 3.1171
The ideologies of violence. 4.7520
Ideology and classic American literature. 2.10392
Ideology and crime 4.6681
Ideology and curriculum. 4.10763
Ideology and development in Africa. 3.5099

Ideology and discontent. 4.7483
Ideology and economics. 3.6485
Ideology and experience. 3.4013
Ideology and organization in Communist China. 3.4800
Ideology and politics. 1.505
Ideology and politics in contemporary China. 3.4792
Ideology and popular protest. 4.5049
The ideology and program of the Peruvian Aprista movement. 4.8349
Ideology and revolution in modern Europe. 3.657
Ideology and social order. 4.5083
Ideology and the urban crisis. 4.8836
Ideology and utopia. 4.4802
Ideology, culture & the process of schooling. 4.10015
Ideology, culture, and the process of schooling. 4.10015
Ideology in America. 4.5200
The ideology of French imperialism, 1871-1881. 4.8924
The ides of March. 2.12718
Idi Amin Dada. 3.5265
The idiom of poetry. 2.2739
The idiom of the people. 2.6114
Idioms and phrases index. 2.1103
The idiot. 2.1354
Idiot de la famille. English. 2.4199
Idiot's delight. 2.12464
Idiots first. 2.13157
IEEE standard dictionary of electrical and electronics terms. 5.6249
IES lighting handbook. 5.6337
If all we did was to weep at home. 4.5985
If he hollers let him go. 2.11873
If it die. 2.4561
If not for profit, for what? 4.2723
If not now, when? 1.1967
If on a winter's night a traveler. 2.5029
If they come in the morning. 4.6909
Ife in the history of West African sculpture. 1.5768
Ignatius Donnelly. 3.7432
Igneous and metamorphic petrology. 5.3043, 5.3049
Igor Stravinsky, an autobiography. 1.4002
Ijeshas and Nigerians. 3.5356
Ikhwān al-Safā'. 1.367
L'île des pingouins. 2.4208
Îles de tempête. 2.4851
The Iliad. 2.373, 2.485-2.486, 2.499
The Iliad, a commentary. 2.495
The Iliad, the Odyssey, and the epic tradition. 2.493
The Illearth War. 2.12993
The ill-framed knight. 2.6412
The ill-made knight. 2.9519
I'll take my stand. 3.8121
Illegal alien workers in the United States. 4.3614
Illegal aliens in the Western Hemisphere. 4.8942
Illinois. 3.8408
Illinois; a descriptive and historical guide. 3.8405
Illinois; a history of the Prairie State. 3.8406
The Illinois Central Railroad and its colonization work. 4.4010
Illiterate America. 4.10757
Illuminated books of the Middle Ages. 1.6400
Illuminated Greek manuscripts from American collections. 1.6416
The illuminated manuscript. 1.6424
Illumination engineering for energy efficient luminous environments. 5.6338-5.6339
Illuminations. 2.2609, 2.4279
Illusion in nature and art. 5.246
The illusion of immortality. 1.2951
The illusion of neutrality. 3.7759
The illusion of peace. 3.851
The illusion of permanence. 3.4263
The illusion of power. 2.3303
The Illusion of presidential government. 4.7926
The illusion of technique. 1.450
The illusionist 2.4607

The illusions of progress. 4.4886
Illustrated catalogue of cast-iron architecture. 1.5501
The illustrated dance technique of José Limón. 4.1179
Illustrated dictionary of eponymic syndromes, and diseases, and their synonyms. 5.4487
The illustrated dictionary of microcomputers. 5.6570
Illustrated dictionary of place names, United States and Canada. 3.5993
Illustrated encyclopaedia of the classical world 3.2511
The illustrated encyclopedia of medieval civilization. 3.143
The Illustrated encyclopedia of space technology. 5.6692
Illustrated English social history. 3.1243
Illustrated flora of the Northeastern United States and adjacent Canada. 5.3673
An illustrated flora of the Pacific States. 5.3679
Illustrated handbook of vernacular architecture. 1.5564
The illustrated history of magic. 4.1077
An illustrated history of the horror films. 2.2992
Illustrated human embryology. 5.4167
Illustrated woman's almanac. 4.5840
Illustration and the novels of Thomas Hardy. 2.7767
Illustration index. 1.5155
Illustrations of Greek drama. 1.5166
Illustrations of the English stage, 1580-1642. 2.3290
Illustrations on the moral sense. 1.1428
The illustrator in America, 1880-1980. 1.5832
Illustrious immigrants. 3.6508
The Illyrians. 3.557
Ilocano rice farmers. 4.5444
The Ilocanos. 3.4591
Ilongot headhunting, 1883-1974. 3.4592
Ilya Ehrenburg. 2.1554
Im Querschnitt Volker Braun. 2.13882
I'm the king of the castle. 2.9707
Im Westen nichts Neues. 2.13847
The image. 3.6086
Image and experience. 2.5698
Image and idea. 2.2588
Image and meaning. 2.5788
Image and mind. 5.320
Image and reality in economic development. 4.2802
The image and the eye. 1.5139
Image before my eyes. 3.3983
The image men. 2.9247
Image, music, text. 2.2339
The image of God among the Sotho-Tswana. 1.1856
The image of man. 1.1318
The image of Peter the Great in Russian history and thought. 3.3101
The image of the architect. 1.5458
The Image of the Black in Western art. 1.5192
The Image of the Buddha. 1.5187
The image of the city. 1.5598
The image of the city, and other essays. 2.9521
The image of the future. 3.50, 3.68
The image of the Jew in American literature. 2.10355
Image of the people. 1.6082
The Image of the prostitute in modern literature. 2.2415
The Image of war, 1861-1865. 3.7350
Imagery. 5.318
The imagery and poetry of Lucretius. 2.740
The imagery of Euripides. 2.473
Images and ideas in seventeenth-century Spanish painting. 1.6287
Images and self-images. 4.812
Images & themes in five poems by Milton. 2.7159
Images from the floating world. 1.6484
Images in clay sculpture. 1.6627
Images of America. 1.5912
Images of Asia. 3.4637
Images of good and evil. 1.1491
Images of illness. 5.4586

Images of kingship in Paradise lost. 2.7124
Images of the American city. 4.6226
Images of the dance. 4.1096
Images of the mind. 1.6370
Images of the Negro in American literature. 2.10359
Images of the Ohio Valley. 3.8390
Images of women in literature. 2.3725
Images, stone, B. C. 3.5814
Imaginary interviews. 2.4552
Imaginary social worlds. 4.4924
The imaginary voyage in prose fiction. 2.3452
The imaginary witness. 4.1209
Imagination. 5.347, 5.349
Imagination and language. 2.3857
The Imagination as glory. 2.12982
Imagination in Coleridge. 2.7589
The imagination of Charles Dickens. 2.7652
The imagination of Jean Genet. 2.4541
Imaginative reason. 2.7357
An imagined world. 5.4468
Imagism. 2.10479
Imago Dei. 1.1565
Imamu Amiri Baraka (Leroi Jones) 2.12874
The IMF and stabilization. 4.4581
IMF conditionality. 4.4582
Imitatio Christi. English. 1.3070
The imitation of Christ. 1.3070
Imlil, a Moroccan mountain community in change. 3.5214
Immaculate & powerful. 1.1611
Immaculate and powerful. 1.1611
Immaculate deception. 5.5062
The immigrant church. 1.3182
Immigrant destinations. 4.8943
The immigrant in American history. 4.8947
Immigrant minorities and the urban working class. 4.3603
The immigrant press and its control. 2.3643
Immigrant socialists in the United States. 4.6991
Immigrant workers and class structure in Western Europe. 4.3633
Immigrants and minorities in British society. 4.8960
Immigrants and the city. 3.8402
Immigrants and unions, a case study, Italians and American labor, 1870-1920. 4.8956
Immigrants at school, New York City, 1898-1914. 4.10903
The Immigrants' influence on Wilson's peace policies. 3.7727
Immigration and ethnicity. 5.8405
Immigration and industrialization. 4.5217
Immigration and nationalism, Argentina and Chile, 1890-1914. 4.8959
Immigration as a factor in American history. 3.6512, 4.8954
The immobilized patient. 5.4745
The immoderate past. 2.10450
Immodest acts. 1.3264
An immodest agenda. 4.2011
Immoral memories. 2.3039
The immoralist. 2.4553
Immortal boy. 2.7845
Immortal diamond. 2.7832
The immortal eight. 1.5897
The immortal profession. 4.10265
Imms' General textbook of entomology. 5.3857
Immunisation. 5.4671
Immunogenetics. 5.4469
Immunology. 5.4464, 5.4467
Immunology, a synthesis. 5.4463
The impact of air power. 5.7394
The impact of American constitutionalism abroad. 4.7712
The impact of Chinese secret societies in Malaya. 3.4535
The impact of collective bargaining on management. 4.3575
The impact of college on students. 4.10060
The Impact of government manpower programs in general, and on minorities and women. 4.3219
The impact of highway investment on development. 4.3933
Impact of marine pollution on society. 4.354
The impact of Negro voting. 4.8093

The impact of plague in Tudor and Stuart England. 5.4677
The impact of science on society. 5.928
The impact of strikes, their social and ecconomic costs. 4.3164
The impact of taxes on the American economy. 4.4699
The impact of the union; eight economic theorists evaluate the labor union movement. 4.3330
Impact of uncertainty on location. 4.2692
The impasse of European communism. 4.7020
Impatient crusader. 4.5134
Impeachment. 4.9734
The impeachment and trial of Andrew Johnson. 3.7455
Impeachment in America, 1635-1805. 4.9735
Impeachment inquiry. 3.7913
Impeachment inquiry Books I-III: January 31-July 23, 1974. 3.7913
The impending crisis, 1848-1861. 3.7310
The impending crisis of the South: how to meet it. 3.7251
The imperative of freedom. 2.3542
The imperative of responsibility. 1.1495
Imperatives and their logics. 1.1244
The imperatives of nonalignment. 3.4232
The imperfect panacea. 4.9994
An imperfect union. 4.9622
The imperial achievement. 3.1215
Imperial Britain in South-East Asia. 3.4412
The imperial bureaucrat. 4.8800
Imperial Caesar. 2.9464
Imperial cities and the Reformation. 1.2330
Imperial economic policy, 1917-1939. 4.2306
The imperial factor in South Africa. 3.5467
Imperial Germany. 3.2323
Imperial Germany and the industrial revolution. 3.2245
The imperial idea and its enemies. 4.8915
The imperial image. 1.6421
The imperial intellect. 4.10196
Imperial Mughal painting. 1.6423
Imperial nomads. 3.4854
The imperial order. 4.7543
The imperial Osages. 3.5933
The imperial Presidency. 4.7921
The imperial republic. 3.7557
Imperial Russia. 3.3000
Imperial Russia in frontier America. 3.8646
The imperial self. 2.10371
Imperial Spain, 1469-1716. 3.3438
Imperial sunset. 3.1648
Imperial Texas. 3.8320
The imperial theme. 2.6785
The imperial years. 3.6402
Imperialism. 4.7535, 4.8428, 4.8904, 4.8912
Imperialism. 4.7536
Imperialism and civilization. 4.7544
Imperialism and nationalism in the Fertile Crescent. 3.3859
Imperialism and nationalism in the Sudan. 4.8814
Imperialism and social classes. 4.7539
Imperialism and world economy. 4.1521
Imperialism in the twentieth century. 4.7542
Imperialism, the highest stage of capitalism. 4.1532
The imperiled union. 3.7304
Impingement of man on the oceans. 4.355
Implementation. 4.3225
Implementing organizational innovations. 4.10636
Implementing the learning society. 4.10728
The implications of literacy. 2.174
The implied reader. 2.3509
The importance of being Constance. 2.8273
The impossible railway. 4.4016
Impressionism and post-impressionism, 1874-1904. 1.6350
The improbable era. 3.8174
Improved indexed business atlas and shippers' guide 1885-88. 4.155
The improvement of humanity. 4.10125
Improving practice in continuing education. 4.10981
Improving world energy production and productivity. 5.6118

Improvisation for the theater. 2.3132
Improvising jazz. 1.4485
The impulse of fantasy literature. 2.5966
The ... IMS directory of publications. 5.8321
In a defiant stance. 4.9901
In a different voice. 4.5927
In a free state. 2.10010
In a glamorous fashion. 5.7093
In a hundred graves; a Basque portrait. 3.3478
In a minor chord. 2.10331
In a moment of enthusiasm. 4.5471
In America. 3.6064
In and out of the ivory tower. 4.10994
In at the beginnings. 5.1954
In Black and white. 5.7878
In brief authority. 4.9490
In Catilinam I-IV. 2.659
In celebration. 2.9823
In contact with the physical world. 5.283
In country sleep, and other poems. 2.9409
In defence of Canada. 3.8767
In defence of empirical psychology. 5.64
In defence of free will. 1.1444
In defence of politics. 4.7222
In defense of academic freedom. 4.10578
In defense of industrial concentration. 4.3053
In defense of Plato. 1.264
In defense of reading. 2.5496
In defense of reason. 2.10275
In defense of the Indians. 3.8990
In defense of the national interest. 3.7587
In defiance of oligarchy. 4.8557
In dubious battle. 2.12528
In every war but one. 3.5033
In Flanders fields. 3.794
In fragments. 1.2885
In her own right. 4.6005
In her own words. 5.4540
In her prime. 4.570
In his image, but ... 1.2918
In its own image. 4.981
In labor. 5.5074
In love & trouble. 2.13407
In memoriam. 2.8160
In Memoriam. 2.8161
In memory of her. 1.2270
In ole Virginia. 2.11193
In one lifetime. 1.3994
In opposition to core curriculum. 4.10614
In our time. 2.11844
In parenthesis; seinnyessit e gledyf ym penn
    mameu. 2.8856
In Polish woods. 2.1808
In praise of America. 1.6519
In praise of Krishna. 2.1875
In praise of newspapers, and other essays on
    the margin of literature. 2.1663
In pursuit of power. 3.6791
In pursuit of relevance. 3.202
In pursuit of the English. 2.9026
In pursuit of the past. 3.262
In quest of identity. 1.659
In quest of justice. 3.3246
In recognition of William Gaddis. 2.13023
In response to aggression. 5.4969
In search of a character. 2.8766
In search of beauty in music. 1.4395
In search of Canadian liberalism. 3.8677
In search of Chaucer. 2.6357
In search of France. 3.2196
In search of heresy. 2.10397
In search of history. 3.3720
In search of mind. 5.95
In search of modern Portugal. 3.3505
In search of Omar Khayyam. 2.1973
In search of our mothers' gardens. 2.13410
In search of peace. 3.871
In search of political stability. 4.7524
In search of Roosevelt. 3.7785
In search of Schrödinger's cat. 5.2106
In search of self. 4.10382
In search of Southeast Asia. 3.4396
In search of the golden West. 3.8488
In search of the physical basis of life. 5.3623
In search of the primitive. 4.484
In search of the silent South. 3.8165
In search of theater. 2.3175
In search of York. 3.8483

In Sicily. 2.5078
In small things forgotten. 3.7943
In spite of the system. 4.10900
In St. Jürgen. 2.13662
In Stalin's time. 2.1283
In struggle. 3.6790
In suspect terrain. 5.2999
In the absence of power. 3.7933
In the active voice. 4.534
In the beginning. 1.227, 5.3397
In the belly of the beast. 4.6905
In the castle of my skin. 2.9990
In the cause of flight. 5.6651
In the cause of peace. 4.9220
In the clap shack. 2.13340
In the company of educated women. 4.10840
In the court of public opinion. 3.7546
In the dark body of metamorphosis & other
    poems. 2.5036
In the days of McKinley. 3.7496
In the eye of the storm. 3.5408
In the eyes of the law. 4.9903
In the fourth world. 2.13044
In the fullness of time. 3.7636
In the heart of the heart of the country, and
    other stories. 2.13041
In the heart's last kingdom. 2.12649
In the human interest. 4.1592
In the land of the Olmec. 3.8896
In the life of a Romany gypsy. 3.5682
In the matter of color. 4.9686
In the Miro District and other stories. 2.12579
In the money. 2.12745
In the name of the people. 3.3128
In the nature of materials, 1887-1941. 1.5340
In the People's Republic. 3.4622
In the presence of the Creator. 5.1956
In the presence of the Dragon Throne. 1.6640
In the running. 4.5971
In the shade of spring leaves. 2.2074
In the shadow of F.D.R. 3.7531
In the shadow of FDR. 3.7531
In the shadow of Florence. 4.2360
In the shadow of the poorhouse. 4.6515
In the stoneworks. 2.11500
In the stopping train & other poems. 2.8593
In the summer house. 2.11401
In the Tennessee mountains. 2.11181
In the twilight of antiquity. 3.2807
In the winter of cities. 2.12729
In the year of jubilee. 2.7733
In the year of Munich. 3.1702
In this house of Brede. 2.8689
In this most perfect paradise. 1.5604
In this our life. 2.11776
In this world and the next. 2.1809
'In vain I tried to tell you' 2.2329
In war's dark shadow. 3.3133
In watermelon sugar. 2.11413
In wildness is the preservation of the world,
    from Henry David Thoreau. 5.6980
The inaccessible earth. 5.3089
Inadmissible evidence. 2.9209
Inadvertent climate modification. 5.2566
Inanna, queen of heaven and earth. 1.1785
The Inca concept of sovereignty and the
    Spanish administration in Peru. 4.8346
The Incas. 3.9294
Incense to idols. 2.10206
Incentive. 5.303
Incentives for environmental protection. 4.1844
Incest, the last taboo. 4.5521
Incident at Vichy. 2.12173
Incidents in the life of a slave girl. 3.7211
Income. 4.1570
Income & wealth of the United States. 4.1890
Income and welfare in the United States.
    4.2087
Income distribution and economic development.
    4.1853
Income distribution and growth in the less-
    developed countries. 4.1808
Income distribution in the United States.
    4.2080
Income distribution policy in developing
    countries. 4.2563
Income distribution theory. 4.1563
Income maintenance and labor supply. 4.2084

The income of the Chinese gentry. 4.2493
Income security. 4.9569
The incomparable Max. 2.8435
The incompleat folksinger. 1.3475
The incomplete adult. 5.525
An incomplete guide to the future. 4.1719
The incorporation of America. 3.6172
Increase Mather, the foremost American
    Puritan. 3.7980
Increasing leadership effectiveness. 4.10977
The incredible Canadian. 3.8748
The incredible Eurodollar. 4.4591
The incredulity of Father Brown. 2.7561
Incunabula in American libraries. 5.7557
Indecent exposure. 4.6757
Independence and nationhood. 3.1790
Independence documents of the world. 4.9378
The independence movement in Quebec,
    1945-1980. 3.8817
The independence movements in Arab North
    Africa. 3.5197
Independent African; John Chilembwe and the
    origins. 3.5494
Independent aging. 4.5799
Independent Eastern Europe, a history. 3.3529
Independent feature film production. 2.3000
The independent filmmaker's guide. 2.3003
Independent filmmaking. 5.7003
Independent Iraq, 1932-1958. 3.3776
Independent women. 4.5771
The indeterminate world. 2.8507
Index Aristotelicus. 2.440
Index fossils of North America. 5.3164
Index-gazetteer of the world. 4.70
Index Islamicus, 1906-1955. 5.8452
Index/Journals of the Continental Congress
    1774-1789. 3.7015
Index kewensis plantarum phanerogamarum
    nomina et synonyma omnium generum et
    specierum a Linnaeo usque ad annum
    MDCCCLXXXV complectens nomine
    recepto auctore patria unicuique plantae
    subjectis. 5.3633
The Index of American Design. 1.6542
Index of American periodical verse. 5.7821
An index of early Chinese painters and
    paintings. 1.6328
Index of economic journals. 5.8373
An index of mathematical tables. 5.1124
The index of Middle English verse. 5.7941
An index of musical wind-instrument makers.
    1.3770
Index of printers. 5.7752
Index of vibrational spectra of inorganic and
    organometallic compounds. 5.2311
Index of wind-instrument makers. 1.3770
Index to 16mm educational films. 4.10331
Index to 35mm educational filmstrips. 4.10332
Index to America. 5.7828
Index to American little magazines. 1.33
Index to artistic biography. 1.4582
Index to Black American literary anthologies.
    5.7798
Index to British literary bibliography. 5.7930
Index to characters in the performing arts.
    2.2774
Index to children's plays in collections,
    1975-1984. 2.2787
Index to children's poetry. 2.2711
Index to Commonwealth little magazines. 1.32
Index to critical film reviews in British and
    American film periodicals. 5.8136
Index to current urban documents. 5.8408
An index to early music in selected anthologies.
    1.3555
Index to educational audio tapes. 4.10333
Index to educational video tapes < 1980->.
    4.10334
Index to educational videotapes. 4.10334
Index to fairy tales, myths and legends. 5.8194
Index to festschriften in Jewish studies. 5.8233
Index to illustrations of living things outside
    North America. 5.8481
Index to illustrations of the natural world.
    5.8482
Index to literary biography. 5.8269
Index to little magazines. 1.34

An index to musical festschriften and similar publications. 1.3575
An index to one-act plays. 5.8129
Index to opera, operetta, and musical comedy synopses in collections and periodicals. 1.3576
Index to plays, 1800-1926. 5.8127
Index to plays in collections. 5.8130
Index to plays in periodicals. 5.8128
Index to poetry. 2.2707-2.2710
Index to producers and distributors. 4.10322
Index to record reviews. 1.3628
Index to record reviews, 1978-1983. 1.3629
Index to reproductions of American paintings. 1.5886
Index to reproductions of European paintings. 1.5861
Index to science fiction anthologies and collections. 5.7809
An index to scientific articles on American Jewish history. 5.8241
Index to sixteen millimeter educational films. 4.10331
Index to Spanish American collective biography. 5.7910
Index to stories in thematic anthologies of science fiction. 5.8174
An index to 'The Elizabethan stage' and 'William Shakespeare'. 2.2694
Index to the first ten years, 1972-1982. 4.5991
Index to The London stage, 1660-1800. 2.3300
Index to the Wilson authors series. 2.2546
Index to thirty-five millimeter educational filmstrips. 4.10332
Index to two-dimensional art works. 1.5154
India. 3.4155, 3.4157-3.4158, 3.4169, 3.4225, 4.4239, 4.8704, 5.8053-5.8054
India, a political economy of stagnation. 4.2507
India: an anthropological perspective. 3.4187
India and Bhutan. 3.4233
India and Britain, 1947-1968. 3.4237
India and China. 4.2504
India and Pakistan. 3.4161, 3.4250
India and Pakistan; a political analysis. 3.4297
India and Sikkim, 1814-1970. 3.4356
India and the Third World. 4.4191
India and the West, the problem of understanding. 1.91
India at the polls, 1980. 4.8714
India Britannica. 3.4266
India; paintings from Ajanta caves. 1.6398
India, Pakistan, Bangladesh, and the major powers. 3.4100
India, population, economy, society. 4.1706
India, Russia, China, and Bangla Desh. 3.4096
India; the transfer of power 1942-7. 3.4289
India wins freedom. 3.4283
Indian affairs. 4.9771
Indian architecture. 1.5447
The Indian army. 5.7339
Indian art in America. 3.5812
Indian art of Mexico and Central America. 3.8899
Indian baskets of the Southwest. 3.5767
Indian biography. 3.5786
Indian Buddhism. 1.2105
The Indian caste of Peru, 1795-1940. 3.9291
The Indian civil service, 1601-1930 4.8710
Indian communism: split within a split. 4.7115
The Indian concept of values. 1.180
Indian economic planning. 4.2511
The Indian economy. 4.2503
Indian film. 2.2900
Indian foreign policy in the United Nations. 4.9236
The Indian frontier of the American West, 1846-1890. 3.5773
Indian idealism. 1.192
The Indian in America. 3.5711
Indian legends from Algic researches. 3.5820
Indian life in the Upper Great Lakes, 11,000 B.C. to A. D. 1800. 3.5737
Indian literature in English translation. 5.8338
Indian logic and atomism. 1.197
Indian mediaeval sculpture. 1.5751
Indian metaphysics and epistemology. 1.195

Indian nationalism and Hindu social reform. 4.5422
The Indian nationalist movement, 1885-1947. 4.8703
The Indian Ocean. 3.4099
Indian Ocean, five island countries. 3.4107
Indian oratory. 3.5822
Indian painting. 1.6307
Indian Parliament. 4.8711
Indian people in Natal. 3.5497
Indian philosophy. 1.176, 1.182, 1.187, 1.189, 1.1820
Indian philosophy today. 1.1137
Indian poetry today. 2.1957, 2.1961
Indian policy in the United States. 3.5807
The Indian political system. 4.8700
The Indian struggle, 1920-1942. 3.4284
Indian summer. 1.5392
The Indian theatre. 2.3394
The Indian tribes of North America. 3.5708
Indian village. 4.5432
The Indian wants the Bronx. 2.13091
Indian-white relations in the United States. 5.7744
Indian writing in English 2.10121
Indiana. 3.8397, 3.8400
The Indiana companion to traditional Chinese literature. 5.8044
Indiana in the Civil War era, 1850-1880. 3.8393
Indiana in transition. 3.8394
Indiana politics during the Civil War. 3.8398
Indiana through tradition and change. 3.8395
Indiana to 1816; the colonial period. 3.8392
The Indiana way. 3.8396
The Indianized states of Southeast Asia. 3.4393
The Indians' book. 3.5819
Indians in the fur trade. 3.5729
The Indians of Canada. 3.5727
The Indians of New Spain. 3.8886
Indians of North America. 3.5691, 5.7735
Indians of the American Southwest. 3.5758
Indians of the Northwest coast. 3.5750
Indians of the Pacific Northwest. 3.5747
India's China war. 3.4298
India's economic problems. 4.2506
India's ex-untouchables. 3.4176
India's exports. 4.4240
India's green revolution. 4.2986
India's past. 2.1923
India's political economy, 1947-1977. 4.2505
India's quest for technological independence. 5.5544
India's rural development. 4.2985
Gli indifferenti. 2.5045
Indigenization of African economies. 4.2606
The indigo bunting. 2.12165
Indira Gandhi. 3.4301-3.4302
Indira Gandhi's emergence and style. 3.4303
Indirect taxation in developing economies. 4.4695
Individual and community. 4.7361
The individual and his religion. 1.1561
The individual and his society. 4.487
The individual and the cosmos in Renaissance philosophy. 1.399
The individual and the social self. 4.4991
Individual choice behavior. 5.52
Individual freedom and governmental restraints. 4.7884
The individual in twelfth-century romance. 2.2631
The individual income tax. 4.4711
The individual psychology of Alfred Adler. 5.127
Individual rights in the corporation. 4.9551
The individual, society, and education. 4.9985
Individualism and economic order. 4.1269
Individuality. 5.498
Individuals. 1.1271
The individual's guide to grants. 1.74
The Indo-Greeks. 3.4242
Indonesia. 1.5057, 3.4556-3.4558, 3.4567
Indonesian communism under Sukarno. 4.8731
The Indonesian economy. 4.2532
The Indonesian economy during the Soeharto era. 4.2533

The Indonesian national revolution, 1945-1950. 3.4572
Indonesian Society in transition. 4.5440
The Indonesian tragedy. 3.4575
Indonesian upheaval. 3.4574
Indonesia's foreign policy. 3.4571
Indoor air pollution. 5.6047
Indoor air quality. 5.6046
Indoor air quality and human health. 5.4670
Induction. 5.375
Induction, probability, and causation. 1.746
Induction, recursion, and programming. 5.1202
The Indus civilization. 3.4222
Industrial activity and economic geography. 4.2688
Industrial air pollution handbook. 5.6042
Industrial applications of lasers. 5.5952
Industrial archaeology. 5.5542
Industrial arts index 1913-57. 5.8455
Industrial change in India. 4.2501
The industrial composition of income and product. 4.1954
Industrial conflict. 4.3162
Industrial democracy. 4.3407
Industrial design. 5.7015
The industrial development of South Wales, 1750-1850. 4.2302
Industrial electrochemical processes. 5.6869
Industrial electrochemistry. 5.6870
The industrial environment 5.5617
Industrial growth and world trade. 4.4100
Industrial growth, trade, and dynamic patterns in the Japanese economy. 4.2556
Industrial hygiene and toxicology. 5.5022
Industrial hygiene aspects of plant operations. 5.5020
Industrial innovation in the Soviet Union. 4.2408
Industrial lasers and their applications. 5.5947
Industrial lighting systems. 5.6341
Industrial lubrication. 5.6243
Industrial market structure and economic performance. 4.3054
Industrial marketing. 4.4281
Industrial marketing research. 4.4302
Industrial marketing strategy. 4.4290
Industrial mobilization for war. 4.1971
The industrial muse. 2.5718
Industrial oil and fat products. 5.6894
Industrial organization. 4.2662
Industrial organization and public policy. 4.1976
Industrial planning in France. 4.2334
Industrial policies. 4.4167
Industrial policies in Western Europe. 4.3070
Industrial politics. 4.3404
Industrial power systems handbook. 5.6330
Industrial process control systems. 5.7032
Industrial progress and human welfare. 4.3007
Industrial psychology. 4.4352
Industrial relations and manpower in construction. 4.3524
Industrial relations and the social order. 4.3433
Industrial relations in Canada. 4.3397
Industrial relations in India. 4.3666
Industrial relations in Latin America. 4.3627
Industrial relations in planned economies, market economies, and the third world. 4.3439
Industrial relations systems. 4.3436
The industrial revolution. 4.2269
The industrial revolution, 1760-1830. 4.2271
The industrial revolution in France, 1815-1848. 4.2322
The Industrial Revolution in North Wales. 4.2301
The industrial revolution in the eighteenth century. 4.2267
Industrial robots and robotics. 5.7050
Industrial safety. 4.3477
Industrial society and social welfare. 4.6522
Industrial sociology. 4.3426
Industrial source sampling. 5.6049
Industrial structure and policy in less developed countries. 4.3069

The industrial structure of American cities. 4.1928
Industrial toxicology. 5.4727
The industrial urban community. 4.6287
Industrial ventilation. 5.6100
Industrial waste disposal. 5.6053
Industrial water pollution. 5.6029
The industrial worker, 1840-1860. 4.3561
Industrialism and industrial man. 4.2632
Industrialism and industrial man reconsidered. 4.3432
Industrialism and the American worker, 1865-1920. 4.3567
Industrialization and labor. 4.3111
Industrialization and planning under Polish socialism. 4.2404
Industrialization in India. 4.4632
Industrialization in the Low Countries, 1795-1850. 4.2362
The industrialization of Egypt, 1939-1973. 4.2591
The industrialization of Russia. 4.2914
The industrialization of São Paulo, 1880-1945. 4.2174
The industrialization of the continental powers, 1780-1914. 4.2212
Industry and economic decline in seventeenth-century Venice. 4.2361
Industry and empire. 4.2248
Industry and ethos. 3.1806
Industry and government in France and England, 1540-1640. 4.3071
Industry & trade. 4.2999
Industry comes of age. 4.1878
Industry in Tudor and Stuart England. 4.2275
Industry norms and key business ratios. 4.4410
Industry series. 4.4323
Industry series, miscellaneous subjects. 4.4317
Inequalities. 5.1417, 5.1423, 5.1453
Inequality. 4.10778
Inequality among brothers. 4.5461
Inequality and social mobility in Brazil. 4.5270
The 'Inequality' controversy. 4.10784
Inequality in an age of decline. 4.4957
The inequality of states. 4.7549
Inertial confinement fusion. 5.6614
Inevitable revolutions. 3.9052
Infallible? An inquiry. 1.2994
Infancy and early childhood. 5.600
The infancy of Nazism. 3.2409
Infant and toddler programs. 4.5722
Infant baptism in the first four centuries. 1.3018
Infant development. 5.602
Infants of the spring. 2.9231, 2.12592
Infants without families. 4.5717
Inferences of patients' pain and psychological distress. 5.5196
The infernal machine, and other plays. 2.4479
The Inferno. 2.4925
Inferno, Alone, and other writings. 2.14067
Infidels and heretics. 1.1882
The infiltrators. 4.4613
Infinite Abelian groups. 5.1296, 5.1299
The infinite moment, and other essays in Robert Browning. 2.7491
Infinitesimals. 5.1434
Infinity and continuity in ancient and medieval thought. 1.1316
Infinity on the anvil. 2.7427
Inflation. 4.4485
Inflation and stabilisation in Latin America. 4.2142
Inflation, causes and effects. 4.4488
Inflation, exchange rates, and the world economy. 4.4564
Inflation, saving and growth in developing economies. 4.4525
The influence of Beaumont and Fletcher on Restoration drama. 2.6559
The influence of Islam on Medieval Europe. 3.105
The influence of Islam upon Africa. 1.2006
The influence of Milton on English poetry. 2.7156
The influence of sea power upon history, 1660-1783. 3.540

The influence of sea power upon the French Revolution and Empire, 1793-1812. 3.2093
The Influence of the United States on Canadian development: eleven case studies. 3.6417
Influences of geographic environment, on the basis of Ratzel's system of anthropo-geography. 4.367
Influencing voters. 4.8507
Information America. 5.7608
Information and behavior in a Sikh village. 3.4209
Information and control in the living organism. 5.998
The information machine. 3.7610
The information machines. 2.57
Information on music. 1.3552
Information please almanac. 1.64
Information please almanac 1947-1960. 1.64
Information please almanac, atlas and yearbook. 1.64
The information process. 2.3574
Information resource management. 4.4346
Information sources in economics. 4.1278
Information sources in engineering. 5.5500
Information sources in physics. 5.8349
Information sources in the history of science and medicine. 5.736
Information sources of political science. 5.8353
Information system specification and design road map. 5.5606
Information systems. 5.5605
Information systems in organizations. 5.5615
Information technology. 5.7697
Information theory and coding. 5.1021
Information through the printed word. 5.7581
Information transmission, modulation, and noise. 5.6352
Information U.S.S.R. 3.3006
The informed vision. 4.10174
Informing the people. 4.7987
Infrared and Raman spectra of inorganic and coordination compounds. 5.2678
Ingeld and Christ. 2.5596
The ingenious gentleman Don Quixote de la Mancha. 2.5172
Ingres. 1.6112, 1.6114
Ingres, in pursuit of perfection. 1.6111
The inheritors. 2.8698
Inigo Jones. 1.5391
Injurious to public morals. 2.2004
Injustice. 4.3658
The ink-smeared lady. 2.2026
The inland waters of tropical Africa. 5.3280
The inlander. 1.4891
The inmost leaf. 2.2577
The inmost light. 2.9071
Innate ideas. 2.19
Inner Asian frontiers of China. 3.4615
The inner Civil War. 3.7351
The inner game of soccer. 4.1020
Inner landscapes. 2.13320
The inner man. 2.13919
The inner planets. 5.1810
The innocence of Father Brown. 2.7561
The innocent eye. 2.3043
Innocent Victorian. 2.7583
L'innommable. 2.4407
Innovation and entrepreneurship. 4.3004
Innovation, competition, and government policy in the semiconductor industry. 4.3809
The innovation decision in Soviet industry. 4.2400
Innovation diffusion. 4.1860
Innovation in marketing, new perspectives for profit and growth. 4.4284
Innovations. 5.5626
Innovations in education. 4.10276
Innovative school discipline. 4.10696
Inorganic and organometallic reaction mechanisms. 5.2877
Inorganic chemistry. 5.2696, 5.2699, 5.2702
Inorganic chemistry, a modern introduction. 5.2701
Inorganic chemistry, series one. 5.2700
Inorganic reactions and structure. 5.2622
Inorganic solids. 5.2864
Inorganic syntheses. 5.2705
Input-output analysis. 4.1402

Input-output economics. 4.1990
Inputs for risk analysis in water systems. 5.5971
Inquest. 3.7879
Inquiries. 1.3141
Inquiries into the fundamentals of aesthetics. 1.1358
Inquiries into truth and interpretation. 2.104
Inquiring spirit. 2.7588
Inquiry and essays. 1.713
An inquiry concerning beauty, order, harmony, design. 1.1427
An inquiry into meaning and truth. 1.762
Inquiry into science. 5.933
An inquiry into the human prospect. 3.201
Inquiry into the military situation on the Far East and the facts surrounding the relief of General of the Army Douglas MacArthur from his assignment in that area. 3.5023
An inquiry into the nature and origin of public wealth and into the means and causes of its increase, 1804. 4.1414
An inquiry into the nature and progress of rent. 4.1513
An inquiry into the nature of peace and the terms of its perpetuation. 4.9123
An inquiry into the original of our ideas of beauty and virtue. 1.1429
The inquisition in Hollywood. 2.2912
Insanity runs in our family. 2.12902
Insatiability. 2.1737
Insect behavior. 5.3871
Insect ecology. 5.3858
Insect morphology. 5.3864
Insect physiology. 5.3867-5.3868
The insect play. 2.1664
Insects in flight. 5.3874
The insecurity of nations. 3.754
Inside be-bop. 1.4323
Inside bureaucracy. 4.7754
Inside computer understanding. 5.1020
Inside foreign aid. 4.1833
Inside India today. 4.8701
Inside international trade policy formulation. 4.3734
Inside jazz. 1.4323
Inside Lincoln's Cabinet. 3.7148
Inside rugby. 4.1023
Inside Soviet schools. 4.10134
Inside the black box. 4.1864
Inside the Company. 4.7901
Inside the earth. 5.3087
Inside the fashion business. 4.3859
Inside the great house. 4.5604
Inside the multinationals. 4.3027
Inside the Soviet army. 5.7332
Inside the Third Reich. 3.2414
Inside the Wall Street journal. 4.4618
Inside the Warren court. 4.9792
Inside U.S.A. 3.6058
Insight vs. desensitization in psychotherapy. 5.4865
The insistence of horror. 2.5809
L'insoumise. 2.4811
Inspiration and poetry. 2.2755
Inspiration in Milton and Keats. 2.5775
Instead of regulation. 4.3081
Instigations of Ezra Pound. 2.2682
Institut für Asienkunde. 3.4517
Institutes of the Christian religion. 1.3404
Institutional change and American economic growth. 4.1871
Institutional economics, its place in political economy. 4.1305
Institutional reform and economic development in the Chinese countryside. 4.2489
Les institutions de la France sous la Révolution et l'émpire. 4.8582
Institutions in agricultural development. 4.2897
Institutions of advanced societies. 4.5092
The institutions of France under the absolute monarchy, 1598-1789. 4.5350
Institutions of rural development for the poor. 4.5104
The Instituto oratoria of Quintilian. 2.690
The instructed conscience. 1.1422
Instructional design. 4.10266

Instructional media. 4.10290
Instructional media and the new technologies of instruction. 4.10290
Instructional models for course design & development. 4.10442
Instructional supervision. 4.10633
Instructions for practical living and other Neo-Confucian writing. 1.174
Instrumental methods of analysis. 5.2669
Instrumental methods of chemical analysis. 5.2668
Instrumental methods of organic functional group analysis. 5.2745
Instrumental music printed before 1600. 1.3570
Instrumental variables. 4.1394
Instrumentation for astronomy with large optical telescopes. 5.1747
Instrumentation fundamentals and applications. 5.5683
Instrumentation in industry. 5.5685
Instruments in the history of Western music. 1.4130
The instruments of America's foreign policy. 3.7607
The instruments of music. 1.4127
Instruments of the Middle Ages and Renaissance. 1.4132
Insular manuscripts, 6th to the 9th century. 1.6406
The insulted and injured. 2.1359
Insuring the nation's health. 4.3450
Insurrection or loyalty. 3.9000
Integer and mixed programming. 5.5580
Integer programming. 5.5584, 5.5591
Integral equations. 5.1561
Integrated circuit engineering. 5.6528
Integrated circuit fabrication technology. 5.6545
Integrated circuits. 5.6541
Integrated electronics: analog and digital circuits and systems. 5.6538
Integrated production control systems. 5.7034
An integrated system of classification of flowering plants. 5.3690
Integration and competition in the petroleum industry. 4.3768
Integration, enlightenment, and industrialization. 3.1802
Integration in finite terms. 5.1457
Integration of the Armed Forces, 1940-1965. 5.7376
Integration of the Indian States. 4.8718
The integrative action of the nervous system. 5.4292
Integrative activity of the brain. 5.4335
The integument. 5.4117
The intellectual adventure of ancient man. 1.1591
Intellectual America. 2.10247
An intellectual and cultural history of the Western World. 3.22
The intellectual capital of Michał Kalecki. 4.1366
The intellectual crisis in American public administration. 4.7315
The intellectual development of Karl Mannheim. 4.4762
Intellectual freedom manual. 5.7653
An intellectual freedom primer. 5.7600
Intellectual giftedness in disabled persons. 4.10922
Intellectual growth in young children. 4.10385
Intellectual hero. 2.3899
The intellectual history of Europe. 1.128
An intellectual history of Islam in India. 1.2003
Intellectual life in America. 3.6154
Intellectual life in Jefferson's Virginia, 1790-1830. 3.8206
Intellectual life in the Colonial South, 1585-1763. 3.8132
The intellectual life of colonial New England. 3.7954
The intellectual life of western Europe in the middle ages. 3.127
The intellectual migration. 3.6110
The intellectual milieu of John Dryden. 2.6995

Intellectual origins of the English revolution. 3.1449
The intellectual origins of the French enlightenment. 1.812
The intellectual origins of the Prague spring. 3.1925
The intellectual resistance in Europe. 3.1060
Intellectual trends in the Ch'ing period. 3.4639
The intellectual versus the city, from Thomas Jefferson to Frank Lloyd Wright. 4.6190
Intellectuals and decolonization in France. 4.8927
The intellectuals and McCarthy. 3.7669
Intellectuals and the state in modern China. 3.4713
Intellectuals in labor unions. 4.3374
Intelligence. 5.350
The Intelligence community. 4.7906
The intelligence controversy. 5.351
Intelligence in ape and man. 5.362
Intelligence in the modern world. 1.586
Intelligence requirements for the 1980's. 5.7363
The intelligent woman's guide to socialism, capitalism, sovietism, and fascism. 4.7041
The intelligible world. 1.1272
The INTELSAT global satellite system. 5.6396
Intending and acting. 1.134
Intensive care. 2.10218
The intent of Toynbee's History. 3.36
Intention. 1.1248
Intentionality, an essay in the philosophy of mind. 1.138
The intentions of intentionality and other new models for modalities. 1.1163
Inter-university Study of Human Resources in National Development. 4.3432
Inter-university Study of Labor Problems in Economic Development. 4.3432
Interaction process analysis. 4.5054
Interactive computer graphics. 5.5648
Interactive processes in reading. 5.397
Intercolonial aspects of American culture on the eve of the Revolution. 3.6127
Intercourse between India and the Western World. 3.4244
Los intereses creados. 2.5234
Interest and prices (Geldzins und Güterpreise) 4.4490
Interest groups in Italian politics. 4.8624
The interest of America in sea power, present and future. 5.7447
Interethnic relations. 4.620
Interfacial phenomena in metals and alloys. 5.6776
The interferon crusade. 5.4471
Interferon, or on theater. 2.1672
Intergovernmental military forces and world public order. 5.7260
Interim report on the books Jesus & Christ. 1.2870
The interior distance. 2.3858
The interior landscape. 2.2280
The interior of the earth. 5.3088
Interlibrary loan policies directory. 5.7654
The interlingual critic. 2.2164
Intermediate differential equations. 5.1508
Intermediate economic statistics. 4.1296
Intermediate quantum mechanics. 5.2126
Intermetallic compounds. 5.6781
Intermolecular forces. 5.2817
Intermountain flora. 5.3678
Internal colonialism. 3.1248
The internal-combustion engine in theory and practice. 5.6221
Internal combustion engines. 5.6220
Internal labor markets and manpower analysis. 4.3218
Internal rotation and inversion. 5.2872
International agencies. 4.9269
The international airline industry. 4.4080
International and regional politics in the Middle East and North Africa. 5.8262
International arbitration, from Athens to Locarno. 4.9116
International arid lands meetings. 4.293
International arms control. 4.9163

International art exhibition, Berlin, 1982. 1.4801
The international aspects of the South African Indian question, 1860-1971. 3.5462
International behavior. 4.8992
International bibliography of discographies. 1.3548
International bibliography of economics. 5.8374
The International Bill of Rights. 4.9388
International books in print. 5.7917
International business and Central Europe, 1918-1939. 4.3061
International business in the Pacific Basin. 4.4247
International calligraphy today. 5.7525
International claims. 4.9335
International cloud atlas. 5.2537
International code of botanical nomenclature. 5.3654
International codes and multinational business. 4.9392
International conflict in the twentieth century. 4.9024
International conflicts and collective security, 1946-1977. 4.9126
International cookbook. 5.7141
The International Court of Justice. 4.9151
International crises. 4.8996
International critical tables of numerical data, physics, chemistry and technology. 5.992
The International cyclopedia of music and musicians. 1.3500
International dental care delivery systems. 5.5124
The International dictionary of films and filmmakers. 2.3032
International dictionary of food and cooking. 5.7106
International dictionary of geophysics. 5.2489
International dictionary of medicine and biology. 5.4486
International dictionary of regional European ethnology and folklore. 4.471
The International dictionary of women's biography. 3.350
The International dimensions of human rights. 4.9387
International directory of little magazines and small presses. 5.8315
International discography of women composers. 1.3625
International diversification and the multinational enterprise. 4.4616
International economic co-operation and the World Bank. 4.4575
International economic integration. 4.4158
International economics. 4.4147, 4.4159
The international economics of development. 4.4151
International economics of pollution. 4.1856
The international economy and industrial development. 4.1799
The international economy and the undeveloped world 1865-1914. 4.1811
The international economy since 1945. 4.4156
The international encyclopedia of dogs. 5.5453
The International encyclopedia of education. 4.10167
The international encyclopedia of hard rock & heavy metal. 1.3528
The international encyclopedia of higher education. 4.10168
International encyclopedia of population. 4.1579
International encyclopedia of psychiatry, psychology, psychoanalysis & neurology. 5.4779
The International encyclopedia of sociology. 4.4735
International encyclopedia of the social sciences. 4.1198
International encyclopedia of unified science. 5.901
International encyclopedia of women composers. 1.3531
The international energy relations of China. 4.3779

International equilibrium. 4.9035
International exhibition of modern art. 1.4669
International finance and Latin America. 4.4725
International finance handbook. 4.4569
International financial management. 4.4567, 4.4576
The International foundation directory. 4.6461
International governmental organizations. 4.9270
International guide to library, archival, and information science associations. 5.7605
International handbook of education systems. 4.10169
International handbook of industrial relations. 4.3437
International handbook of universities. 4.9934
International handbook of universities and other institutions of higher education. 4.9935
International handbook on aging. 4.5800
International historical statistics. 4.1260
International history of city development. 4.6184
International Institute of African languages and cultures. 4.602
International institutions in trade and finance. 4.4149
International ISBN publishers' index. 5.7573
The international labor movement. 4.3326
The international labor movement in transition. 4.3335
International law. 4.9290, 4.9293
International law for seagoing officers. 4.9277
The international law of human rights. 4.9386
International list of geographical serials. 5.8204
International manual on collective bargaining for public employees. 4.3508
International maps and atlases in print. 5.8210
International marketing management. 4.4111
International medical who's who. 5.4510
International minerals. 5.6727
International monetary economics. 4.4553
The international monetary system, 1945-1976. 4.4578
The International monetary system under flexible exchange rates. 4.4570
The international money game. 4.4561
The international money market. 4.4589
The international money markets. 4.4448
International motion picture almanac. 2.2865
International ocean shipping. 4.3957
International organization. 4.9134
International organization and integration. 4.8969
International organization: politics & process. 4.9134
International organizations. 4.9263, 4.9267, 5.959, 5.8257
International peace observation. 4.9259
International peacekeeping at the crossroads. 4.9260
International political economics. 4.4140
International politics. 3.561
International politics and the Middle East. 3.3723
The international politics of natural resources. 4.1770
International production and the multinational enterprise. 4.3021
International proverb scholarship. 5.8412
International radio broadcasting. 4.4064
International regionalism. 4.9249
International regions and the international system. 4.9251
The international relations dictionary. 4.8981
The international relations of the Chinese Empire. 3.4678
International rivalry in the Pacific islands, 1800-1875. 3.5550
The international secretariat. 4.9188
International shipping cartels. 4.3963
International stratigraphic guide. 5.3134
The international style. 1.5270
An international survey of recent painting and sculpture. 1.4809
International television & video almanac. 5.6438

International television and video almanac. 5.6438
International terrorism bibliography. 5.8393
The international thesaurus of quotations. 2.3731
International trade. 4.4092, 4.4109
International trade and economic development. 4.4110
International trade and economic growth. 4.4106
International trade theory. 4.4103
International trade under communism. 4.4182
The international uranium market. 4.3742
An international vocabulary of technical theatre terms, in eight languages: American, Dutch, English, French, German, Italian, Spanish, Swedish. 2.3089
The International who's who. 3.328
International who's who in music and musicians' directory. 1.3539
International zoo yearbook. 5.3806
Internationaler Code der botanischen Nomenklatur. 5.3654
Internationales Bibliotheks-Handbuch. 5.7658
Internationales Verlagsadressbuch. 5.7573
Internationales Verzeichnis wissenschaftlicher Verbande und Gesellschaften. 5.690
Interneurons. 5.4287
Internships. 4.9943
Interpersonal communication. 4.5001
Interpersonal dynamics. 4.4922
Interpersonal relations in nursing. 5.5198
The interpersonal theory of psychiatry. 5.453
The interpersonal world of the infant. 5.557
The interplay of East and West. 3.101
Interpretating Mozart on the keyboard. 1.3935
Interpretation of aerial photographs. 5.6993
The interpretation of Bach's keyboard works. 1.4528
An interpretation of Christian ethics. 1.1475
The interpretation of cubism. 1.6062
The interpretation of cultures. 4.475
The interpretation of dreams. 5.652
The interpretation of early music. 1.4123
The interpretation of French song. 1.4570
The interpretation of history. 3.497
Interpretation of mass spectra of organic compounds. 5.2743
The interpretation of music. 1.4115
The Interpretation of ordinary landscapes. 4.382
The interpretation of psychological tests. 5.4844
Interpretation of schizophrenia. 5.4923
The interpretation of science. 5.943
An interpretation of the logic of Hegel. 1.953
The interpretation of the music of the XVII and XVIII centuries revealed by contemporary evidence. 1.4136
An interpretation of Whitehead's metaphysics. 1.776
Interpretations of legal history. 4.9345
Interpretations of poetry and religion. 2.2749
Interpretations of the First Amendment. 4.9705
Interpretative reporting. 2.3566
Interpretative translations of Thai poets. 2.2259
The interpreted design as a structural principle in American prose. 2.10529
The interpreters. 2.10113
The Interpreter's Bible. 1.2526
The Interpreter's dictionary of the Bible. 1.2508
Interpreter's house. 2.12979
The Interpreter's one volume commentary on the Bible. 1.2527
Interpreting American history. 3.6338
Interpreting Bach's Well-tempered clavier. 1.4529
Interpreting Blake. 2.7429
Interpreting elections. 4.7951
Interpreting mathematical economics and econometrics. 4.1389
Interpreting modern philosophy. 1.421
Interpreting the French Revolution. 3.2058
Interpretive conventions. 2.2486
Interregional and international trade. 4.4092

The interregnum of despair. 3.7744
Interrelations of cultures. 3.104
Interrelations of literature. 2.2371
An interrupted life. 3.3982
Interstate. 4.3941
The interstate commerce omission, the public interest and the ICC. 4.3891
Intervention and reflection. 5.4562
Intervention, civil war, and communism in Russia, April-December 1918. 3.3176
Interviews and conversations. 5.7948
Interviews and conversations with 20th-century authors writing in English. 5.7948
Interviews and conversations with twentieth-century authors writing in English. 5.7948
Interviews with Black writers. 2.10327
Interviews with William Carlos Williams. 2.12750
Intimate conversations. 1.2086
The intimate history of a publishing enterprise. 5.7586
Intimate intrusions. 4.6709
Intimate journals. 2.4139
The intimate journals of Paul Gauguin. 1.6104
Into the demon universe; a literary exploration of Oscar Wilde. 2.8286
Into the mainstream, conversations with Latin-American writers. 2.5302
Into the twenties. 3.7718
Into the unknown. 2.5980
The intonation of American English. 2.1134
Intra-Asian international relations. 3.3640
The intricate knot. 2.10361
Intrigue. 2.8381
Introduccion a la literatura Española del siglo de oro. 2.5107
Introducción a una historia de la novela en España en el siglo XIX. 2.5137
Introducción al teatro religioso del Siglo de Oro. 2.5132
Introducing cellular communications. 5.6433
Introducing India in liberal education. 3.4218
Introducing James Joyce. 2.8863
Introducing semiotic. 2.78
Introducing Shakespeare. 2.6697
Introducing Tom Wayman. 2.9972
Introduction à la linguistique française. 2.861
Introduction and guide to the marine bluegreen algae. 5.3712
The introduction of farm machinery in its relation to the productivity of labor in the agriculture of the United States during the nineteenth century. 5.5298
The introduction of the ironclad warship. 5.7433
An introduction to a history of woodcut. 1.6473
Introduction to adaptive filters. 5.6512
An introduction to agricultural geography. 5.5257
Introduction to algebraic K-theory. 5.1291
An introduction to American archaeology. 3.5698
Introduction to ancient history. 5.8223
An introduction to Anglo-Saxon England. 3.1319
An introduction to animal behavior. 5.4060
An introduction to applied mathematics. 5.1108
Introduction to applied mathematics. 5.1110
Introduction to applied numerical analysis. 5.1426
Introduction to applied solid state physics. 5.2192
Introduction to approximation theory. 5.1314
An introduction to artificial intelligence. 5.1004
Introduction to artificial intelligence. 5.1006
An introduction to Asian politics. 3.3627
Introduction to astronomy. 5.1718
An introduction to atmospheric physics. 5.2518
Introduction to atomic and nuclear physics. 5.2076
Introduction to atomic spectra. 5.2310
Introduction to audiology. 5.5039
Introduction to automata theory, languages, and computation. 5.1371

Introduction to automation for librarians. 5.7613

An introduction to Bayesian inference and decision. 5.1414

An introduction to Bayesian inference in econometrics. 4.1303

An introduction to behavioural ecology. 5.3393

An introduction to biophysics. 5.3497

Introduction to biostatistics. 5.3313

Introduction to Black sociology. 3.6777

An introduction to Brazil. 3.9196

Introduction to calculus and analysis. 5.1450

Introduction to cataloging and classification. 5.7627

An introduction to celestial mechanics. 5.1764

Introduction to cell biology. 5.3606

Introduction to ceramics. 5.6900

An introduction to chaotic dynamical systems. 5.1624

Introduction to chemical engineering and computer calculations. 5.6831

An introduction to chemical engineering kinetics & reactor design. 5.2887

Introduction to chemical engineering thermodynamics. 5.6821

Introduction to chemical kinetics. 5.2891

Introduction to chemical nomenclature. 5.2597

Introduction to chemical process control. 5.6833a

An introduction to Chinese literature 2.2156

An introduction to Chinese politics. 3.4790

Introduction to classical and modern optics. 5.2283

Introduction to classical real analysis. 5.1446

An introduction to climate. 5.2568

An introduction to coal technology. 5.6873

An introduction to coherent optics and holography. 5.2287

An introduction to color. 5.2332

Introduction to combinators and [lambda]-calculus. 5.1053

Introduction to combustion phenomena. 5.2903

Introduction to communication command and control systems. 5.6377

Introduction to communication science and systems. 5.6351

Introduction to communication systems. 5.6358

Introduction to community recreation. 4.886

Introduction to commutative algebra. 5.1358

Introduction to comparative philosophy. 1.429

An introduction to complex analysis in several variables. 5.1484

An introduction to composite materials. 5.5794

Introduction to computer engineering. 5.6573

Introduction to computer engineering hardware and software design. 5.6573

Introduction to computer graphics. 5.5645

Introduction to computer music. 1.4457

Introduction to computer organization. 5.1230

Introduction to computer science. 5.1146

An Introduction to computer simulation in applied science. 5.5771

Introduction to concepts and theories in physical science. 5.1994

Introduction to contemporary civilization in the West. 3.1

Introduction to contemporary Japanese literature. 2.1996

Introduction to contemporary music. 1.3675

An introduction to controlled thermonuclear fusion. 5.2451

Introduction to cosmology. 5.1875

Introduction to counseling and guidance. 4.468

An introduction to criminalistics. 4.6810

Introduction to critical theory. 4.4798

An introduction to crystallography. 5.2921

Introduction to cyclotomic fields. 5.1344

An introduction to database systems. 5.1235

An introduction to democratic theory. 4.7578

Introduction to demography. 4.1624

An introduction to descriptive linguistics. 2.1014

Introduction to designing and conducting research. 5.978

An introduction to differentiable manifolds and Riemannian geometry. 5.1620

Introduction to digital techniques. 5.6472

Introduction to dislocations. 5.2926

Introduction to Dutch. 2.1170

An introduction to dynamic meteorology. 5.2519

Introduction to dynamic programming. 5.1367

Introduction to dynamic systems. 5.1544

Introduction to dynamics. 5.1626

Introduction to educational administration. 4.10634

An introduction to eighteenth-century drama, 1700-1780. 2.5910

An introduction to eighteenth century France. 3.2048

Introduction to electric circuits. 5.6272

Introduction to electric power engineering. 5.6257

Introduction to electrodynamics. 5.2374

Introduction to electrodynamics and radiation. 5.2356

An introduction to electromagnetic theory. 5.2368

Introduction to elementary particle physics. 5.2397

Introduction to Elizabethan literature. 2.5638

Introduction to elliptic curves and modular forms. 5.1583

An introduction to embryology. 5.4122

Introduction to engineering design and graphics. 5.5694

An introduction to environmental archaeology. 3.251

Introduction to environmental physiology. 5.4204

Introduction to environmental remote sensing. 4.19

An introduction to ergodic theory. 5.1464

Introduction to existentialism. 1.487

Introduction to floriculture. 5.5346

An introduction to fluid dynamics. 5.1662

Introduction to forest resource management. 5.5422

Introduction to forestry. 5.5423

Introduction to formal language theory. 5.1373

Introduction to French local government. 4.8878

An introduction to French sixteenth century poetic theory: texts and commentary. 2.872

Introduction to freshwater vegetation. 5.3777

Introduction to fungi. 5.3723

An introduction to Gaelic poetry. 2.830

An introduction to general and comparative endocrinology. 5.4244

Introduction to general relativity. 5.2098

An introduction to general systems thinking. 5.996

An Introduction to genetic analysis. 5.3415

Introduction to geochemistry. 5.3104

Introduction to geological maps and structures. 5.2980

Introduction to geometry. 5.1564

Introduction to geophysical prospecting. 5.6738

An introduction to geotechnical engineering. 5.5898

An introduction to Greek and Latin palaeography. 5.7534

Introduction to groundwater modeling. 5.5970

An introduction to group representation theory. 5.1300

An introduction to haiku. 2.2027

An introduction to harmonic analysis. 5.1553

An introduction to health psychology. 5.4584

Introduction to health services. 5.4623

An introduction to Hegel. 1.950

Introduction to high energy physics. 5.2463

Introduction to Hilbert space and the theory of spectral multiplicity. 5.1637

An introduction to homological algebra. 5.1290

Introduction to Hp spaces, with an appendix on Wolff's proof of the corona theorem. 5.1486

An Introduction to immunology. 5.4465

An introduction to Indian historiography. 3.4215

An introduction to Indian music. 1.3735

Introduction to insect pest management. 5.5406

Introduction to integral equations with applications. 5.1562

An introduction to interferometry. 5.2295

Introduction to Islamic law. 1.2054

Introduction to Islamic theology and law. 1.2045

Introduction to Japanese law. 4.9924

An introduction to Japanese trade unionism. 4.3423

An introduction to knot theory. 5.1621

An introduction to lasers and masers. 5.6488

An introduction to legal reasoning. 4.9496

Introduction to library research in women's studies. 5.8463

An introduction to library science. 5.7601

Introduction to ligand fields. 5.2841

An introduction to linguistic science. 2.142

Introduction to linguistic structures. 2.992

An introduction to liquid helium. 5.2238

Introduction to liquid state chemistry. 5.2907

An introduction to literature in Brazil. 2.5461

Introduction to logic. 1.1191, 1.1195

An introduction to logic and scientific method. 1.1190

Introduction to logic and to the methodology of deductive sciences. 5.1050

Introduction to logic programming. 5.1182

Introduction to logical theory. 1.1194

An introduction to macromolecules. 5.2765

Introduction to map projections. 4.213

Introduction to marine biology. 5.3248

Introduction to marine micropaleontology. 5.3154

Introduction to Marxist theory. 4.7004

Introduction to material and energy balances. 5.6820

An introduction to mathematical learning theory. 4.10348

Introduction to mathematical logic. 1.1204, 5.1046

Introduction to mathematical philosophy. 5.1049

Introduction to mathematical psychology. 5.54

Introduction to mathematical statistics. 5.1388-5.1389

Introduction to mathematics for life scientists. 5.3309

Introduction to matrix methods in optics. 5.2279

An introduction to mechanical vibrations. 5.5746

Introduction to mechanics of solids. 5.5778

An introduction to medieval and Renaissance literature. 2.2625

An introduction to metallic corrosion. 5.5815

Introduction to metamathematics. 5.1044

An introduction to metaphysics. 1.1273, 1.1315

An introduction to microelectronic technology. 5.6539

An introduction to Middle English. 2.949, 2.951

Introduction to mineral processing. 5.6753

An Introduction to mining. 5.6747

An introduction to modal logic. 1.1251

Introduction to modern Bulgarian literature. 2.1205

Introduction to modern France, 1500-1640. 3.1959

Introduction to modern liquid chromatography. 5.2667

Introduction to modern optics. 5.2294

Introduction to modern Polish literature. 2.1744

Introduction to modern Spanish literature. 2.5150

Introduction to molecular biology. 5.3500

An introduction to morphology and syntax. 2.187

Introduction to multidimensional scaling. 5.55

An introduction to neo-colonialism. 4.1824

Introduction to nervous systems. 5.4316

An introduction to New Testament thought. 1.2637

Introduction to Newton's 'Principia' 5.1641

An introduction to Nigerian government and politics. 4.8801
Introduction to Nigerian literature. 2.10099
Introduction to non-linear optimization. 5.1551
An introduction to nonlinear oscillations. 5.1520
Introduction to nuclear physics. 5.2054
Introduction to nuclear reactions. 5.2481
An introduction to numerical analysis. 5.1425
Introduction to numerical computations. 5.1429
Introduction to nursing. 5.5168
An introduction to Old English. 2.934
An introduction to Old English. 2.935
An introduction to operating systems. 5.1171
Introduction to operations research. 4.2628, 5.874, 5.5569
Introduction to optical electronics. 5.5950, 5.6489
An introduction to optical waveguides. 5.5938
Introduction to optimization methods. 5.1547
Introduction to particle physics. 5.2401
Introduction to perturbation techniques. 5.1505
Introduction to phase transitions and critical phenomena. 5.2239
An introduction to philosophical logic. 1.1174
An introduction to philosophy of history. 3.501
Introduction to phosphorus chemistry. 5.2712
Introduction to photoelectron spectroscopy. 5.2684
Introduction to physical oceanography. 4.344
Introduction to planetary geology. 5.1804
Introduction to planning history in the United States. 4.6320
Introduction to plant diseases. 5.5397
Introduction to plant population ecology. 5.3770
An introduction to plant taxonomy. 5.3651
Introduction to plasma theory. 5.2386
An introduction to Plato's Laws. 4.7342
An introduction to Plato's Republic. 4.7347
An introduction to political theory. 4.7218
Introduction to polymer spectroscopy. 5.2320
An introduction to population ecology. 5.3520
An introduction to population genetics theory. 5.3425
An introduction to practical biochemistry. 5.2793
Introduction to probability theory. 5.1382
An introduction to probability theory and its applications. 5.1381
Introduction to properties of materials. 5.5766
Introduction to psychology. 5.107
Introduction to quantitative genetics. 5.3470
Introduction to quantum mechanics. 5.2136
An introduction to quantum physics. 5.2130
An introduction to reasoning. 1.1241
Introduction to reference work. 5.7649
An introduction to relativistic quantum field theory. 5.2159
Introduction to remote sensing of the environment. 4.21
An introduction to Roman legal and constitutional history. 4.9398
An introduction to Ruskin. 2.8033
Introduction to Russian art and architecture. 1.5030
An Introduction to Russian history. 3.3040
An introduction to Russian language and literature. 2.1222
Introduction to safety engineering. 5.5552
Introduction to Saint Thomas Aquinas. 1.3139
Introduction to satellite oceanography. 4.323
An introduction to Scandinavian literature, from the earliest time to our day. 2.13966
Introduction to Schenkerian analysis. 1.4427
An introduction to scholastic philosophy, medieval and modern. 1.362
Introduction to seismology. 5.3114
Introduction to semantics, and Formalization of logic. 1.1202
An introduction to semiconductors. 5.2347
An introduction to separation science. 5.2644
Introduction to sequencing and scheduling 5.7035

An introduction to seventeenth century France. 3.2018
An introduction to Shi'i Islam. 1.2091
Introduction to signal transmission. 5.6343
An introduction to social anthropology. 4.491
Introduction to social work practice. 4.6481
Introduction to soil physics. 5.5274
Introduction to solid state physics. 5.2195
An introduction to Spanish literature. 2.5091
Introduction to special relativity. 5.2105
Introduction to sport studies. 4.942
Introduction to statistical analysis. 5.1395
An introduction to statistical mechanics. 5.2174
Introduction to stellar atmospheres and interiors. 5.1838
Introduction to stereochemistry 5.2873
Introduction to stochastic processes. 5.1385
An introduction to Stuart drama. 2.5862
Introduction to superconductivity. 5.2354
Introduction to switching theory and logical design. 5.6478
Introduction to symbolic logic and its applications. 1.1201
An introduction to Tantric Buddhism. 1.2170
Introduction to telephone switching. 5.6420
An introduction to tensegrity. 5.5865
An introduction to the administrative history of mediaeval England. 4.8387
An introduction to the African novel. 2.10044
Introduction to the algae. 5.3709
An introduction to the American underground film. 2.2987
An introduction to the analysis and processing of signals. 5.6375
An introduction to the Apocrypha. 1.2621
Introduction to the arithmetic theory of automorphic functions. 5.1498
Introduction to the art of playing on the piano forte. 1.4538
An introduction to the Australian novel, 1830-1930. 2.10142
An introduction to the botany of the major crop plants. 5.5313
An introduction to the botany of tropical crops. 5.5317
Introduction to the Code of Maimonides (Mishneh Torah) 1.1946
Introduction to the constitutional history of modern Greece. 4.8619
Introduction to the Croatian and Serbian language. 2.1206
Introduction to the dance. 4.1092
Introduction to the design and analysis of algorithms. 5.1178
An introduction to the development of modern Malay language & literature. 2.2288
Introduction to the devout life. 1.3218
An introduction to the English novel. 2.5944
An introduction to the finite element method. 5.5729
An introduction to the French Caribbean novel. 2.4833
An introduction to the French poets: Villon to the present day. 2.3874
An introduction to the French theatre. 2.3364
An introduction to the Greek theatre. 2.302
An introduction to the history of Central Africa. 3.5489
An introduction to the history of medicine. 5.4501
Introduction to the history of plant pathology. 5.5395
An introduction to the history of sociology. 4.4738
Introduction to the history of the Muslim East. 5.8038
An introduction to the Indo-European languages. 2.220
Introduction to the lakes. 4.3967
An introduction to the logic of the sciences. 5.891
An Introduction to the logic of the sciences. 5.887
An introduction to the mathematical theory of finite elements. 5.1533
Introduction to the mathematics of population. 4.1632

Introduction to the mechanics of a continuous medium. 5.1649
An introduction to the mechanics of solids. 5.5734
An Introduction to the medieval mystics of Europe. 1.3095
Introduction to the New Testament. 1.2628, 1.2633, 1.2659
Introduction to the Old Testament as Scripture. 1.2565
Introduction to the Old Testament, from its origins to the closing of the Alexandrian canon. 1.2516
An introduction to the philosophy of Charles S. Peirce. 1.628
Introduction to the philosophy of history. 3.455
An introduction to the philosophy of law. 4.9365
An introduction to the philosophy of science. 5.918
An introduction to the physical properties of large molecules in solution. 5.2768
Introduction to the physics of fluids and solids. 5.2037
An introduction to the politics of tropical Africa. 4.8790
Introduction to the practice of fishery science. 5.5481
Introduction to the primates: living and fossil. 5.4026
An introduction to the principles of morals and legislation. 1.722
Introduction to the psychology of hearing. 5.251
An introduction to the psychology of religion. 1.1568
Introduction to the Qur'ān. 3.3651
Introduction to the Raj quartet. 2.9808
Introduction to the reading of Hegel. 1.935
Introduction to the representation theory of compact and locally compact groups. 5.1538
An introduction to the rock-forming minerals. 5.3015
Introduction to the science of sociology. 4.4836
Introduction to the sociology of 'developing societies' 4.5482
Introduction to the sociology of music. 1.4362
An introduction to the sociology of rural development. 4.5483
An introduction to the sonnets of Shakespeare for the use of historians and others. 2.6678
Introduction to the strong interactions. 5.2485
Introduction to the study of animal populations. 5.4070
An introduction to the study of insects. 5.3856
An introduction to the study of map projections. 4.215
An introduction to the study of Southwestern archaeology. 3.5762
Introduction to the study of the law of the Constitution. 4.9402
An introduction to the study of the New Testament. 1.2629
Introduction to the Talmud and Midrash. 1.1939
An introduction to the technology of pottery. 5.6901
An introduction to the theoretical basis of nursing. 5.5173
Introduction to the theory of Fourier integrals. 5.1557
Introduction to the theory of infinitesimals. 5.1434
Introduction to the theory of music. 1.4424
An introduction to the theory of numbers. 5.1324
Introduction to the theory of relativity. 5.2084
Introduction to the theory of solid state physics. 5.2196
Introduction to the theory of statistics. 5.1394
Introduction to the work of Melanie Klein. 5.172
Introduction to theoretical linguistics. 2.110
Introduction to thermodynamics: classical and statistical. 5.6203

Introduction to topology and modern analysis. 5.1599

An introduction to transportation engineering. 5.5923

Introduction to transportation engineering and planning. 5.5926

An introduction to Tudor drama. 2.5860

An introduction to twentieth century music. 1.3670

Introduction to United States public documents. 5.7779

An introduction to urban design. 1.5582

An introduction to variational inequalities and their applications. 5.1421

An introduction to Vietnamese literature. 2.2260

An introduction to Virgil's 'Aeneid' 2.800

Introduction to VLSI systems. 5.6536

Introduction to Wallace Stevens. 2.12553

An introduction to water quality modelling. 5.6019

An introduction to Welsh literature. 2.834

Introduction to wildland fire. 5.5428

Introduction to wildlife management. 5.5495

Introduction to wind turbine engineering. 5.6236

Introduction to world peace through world law. 4.9211

Introduction to Yugoslav literature. 2.1201

Introductory circuit analysis. 5.6269

Introductory combinatorics. 5.1274

Introductory econometrics. 4.1398

Introductory engineering statistics. 5.5715

Introductory functional analysis with applications. 5.1471

An introductory guide to The anathemata and The sleeping lord sequence of David Jones. 2.8855

Introductory laboratory animal science. 5.5452

Introductory mass spectrometry. 5.2318

Introductory modal logic. 1.1252

Introductory mycology. 5.3720

Introductory nuclear theory. 5.2425

Introductory nutrition. 5.7113

Introductory plant physiology. 5.3742

Introductory soil mechanics and foundations. 5.5906

Introductory system engineering. 5.5692

Intruder in the dust. 2.11665

Intruders on the rights of men. 4.5897

Intuition and science. 5.871

Inuit behavior and seasonal change in the Canadian Arctic. 3.5875

Invasion 1944. 3.970

The invasion of America. 3.7948

The invasion of Europe by the barbarians. 3.582

The invasion of New Zealand by people, plants and animals. 3.5596

Invented lives. 2.11733

Invented worlds. 1.6688

Inventing America. 3.6929

Inventing motherhood. 4.5667

Inventing the dream. 3.8615

The invention of printing in China and its spread westward. 5.7550

The invention of the American political parties. 4.8149

The invention of the modern hospital, Boston, 1870-1930. 5.4710

The Invention of tradition. 4.824

Inventor's handbook. 5.5639

Inventory systems. 4.2682

Invertebrate fossils. 5.3167

Invertebrate palaeontology and evolution. 5.3165

Invertebrate Spain. 3.3416

Invertebrate zoology. 5.3831, 5.3833-5.3834

Investigating linguistic acceptability. 2.140

Investigating the FBI. 4.6820

Investigation and responsibility. 4.8251

Investigations in currency & finance. 4.4472

Investigations on the theory of the Brownian movement 5.2219

The investigators. 4.6828

Investment banking in America. 4.4623

Investment in education. 4.10651

Investment in human capital. 4.1547-4.1548

Investment in learning. 4.10074

The invisible alcoholics. 4.6640

Invisible astronomy. 5.1781

Invisible barriers to invisible trade. 4.4170

Invisible cities. 2.5027

The invisible farmers. 5.5240

The invisible French. 3.8834

Invisible friends. 2.7468

Invisible immigrants. 3.6538

Invisible lives. 4.5804

Invisible man. 2.13004-2.13005

The Invisible minority. 4.5194

The invisible picture. 5.646

Invisible poets. 2.10330

The invisible presidency. 3.6294

The Invisible soldier. 3.1127

The invisible universe. 5.1700

Invitation to a beheading. 2.1583

Invitation to sociology. 4.4827

Invitation to the waltz. 2.9007

L'invitee. 2.4388

Involuntary labour since the abolition of slavery. 4.3102

Involvement in learning. 4.10083

Inward bound. 5.1985

Iolo Morganwg. 2.838

Ion 2.458

Ionesco. 2.4584

Ionian vision; Greece in Asia Minor, 1919-1922. 3.2702

The Ionians and Hellenism. 3.4039

Ions in aqueous systems. 5.2673

Iowa. 3.8503, 3.8506

Iowa interiors. 2.12564

Ioway to Iowa. 3.8504

Iphigenia. 2.12378

Iphigenia in Tauris. 2.459

Ira Aldridge. 2.3336

Iran, a country study. 3.4066

Iran between two revolutions. 3.4085

Iran, past and present. 3.4072

Iran under the Pahlavis. 3.4083

Iran under the Safavids. 3.4080

Iraq. 3.3778

Iraq, a country study. 3.3769

Iraq after the Muslim conquest. 3.3775

Iraq and Iran. 3.4073

Iraq between the two world wars. 3.3777

Iraq: its people, its society, its culture. 3.3768

Ireland. 3.1844

Ireland, a general and regional geography. 3.1869

Ireland and Scotland 1600-1850. 4.2314

Ireland and the Irish. 3.1813

Ireland before the famine, 1798-1848. 3.1847

Ireland before the Normans 3.1819

Ireland before the Vikings. 3.1821

Ireland in prehistory. 4.735

Ireland in the age of imperialism and revolution, 1760-1801. 3.1838

Ireland in the eighteenth century. 3.1837

Ireland in the Empire, 1688-1770. 3.1836

Ireland in the later Middle Ages. 3.1823

Ireland in the twentieth century. 3.1858

Ireland in the war years. 3.944

Ireland since the famine. 3.1851

Ireland under the Normans 1196-1333. 3.1825

Ireland under the Union. 3.1843

Ireland's civil war. 3.1865

Ireland's English question. 3.1832

Iris Murdoch. 2.9771, 2.9774, 2.9776

Iris Murdoch, work for the spirit. 2.9773

Iris Murdoch's comic vision. 2.9775

The Irish-American experience. 5.7861

Irish-American nationalism, 1870-1890. 3.6550

Irish Americans. 3.6552

Irish art in the early Christian period, to 800 A. D. 1.4945

The Irish countryman. 4.627

The Irish; emigration, marriage, and fertility. 4.1697

Irish fairy and folk tales. 4.791

Irish folk-history plays. 2.7753

The Irish in Ontario. 3.8830

The Irish in Philadelphia. 3.8090

Irish literature, 1800-1875. 5.7995

The Irish on the urban frontier. 3.8436

The Irish parliamentary party, 1890-1910. 4.8563

The Irish parliamentary tradition. 4.8566

The Irish question, 1840-1921. 3.1852

The Irish R. M. complete. 2.9349

The Irish renaissance. 2.9855

The Irish short story. 2.9863

The Irish short story from George Moore to Frank O'Connor. 2.9864

Irish stories and plays. 2.8492

Iron and steel in the German inflation, 1916-1923. 4.3736

The iron blast furnace. 5.6786

Iron cages. 3.6532

The iron century. 4.5285

The ironclad warship. 5.7433

The iron flood. 2.1521-2.1522

The iron heel. 2.12024

The iron triangle. 5.7270

Ironic drama. 2.472

The ironies of progress. 2.10259

The irony of American history. 3.7591

The irony of early school reform. 4.10096

The irony of Vietnam. 3.6498

The Iroquois and the New Deal. 3.5895

The Iroquois in the American Revolution. 3.5894

Irrational man. 1.484

The irreconcilables. 4.9195

Irregular serials and annuals. 5.8310

The irrelevant English teacher. 2.927

The irrepressible conflict, 1850-1865. 3.7141

The irresistible theatre. 2.3282

Irving Layton, the poet and his critics. 2.9945

Is Britain dying? 3.1716

Is Cuba socialist? 4.7014

Is God a white racist? 1.2915

Is Massa Day dead? 3.9139

Is the Mexican Revolution dead? 3.8950

Is there a text in this class? 2.2435

Isaac Backus and the American pietistic tradition. 1.3324

Isaac Israeli. 1.376

Isaac Newton. 5.1955

Isabelle. 2.4556

Isadora speaks. 4.1133

Isaiah 40-66. 1.2613

Isak Dinesen. 2.14021

Isamu Noguchi. 1.5670

Ise monogatari. English. 2.2041

The Isenheim Altarpiece. 1.6174

Ishi in two worlds. 3.5792

Ishi, the last Yahi. 3.5960

Ishiwara Kanji and Japan's confrontation with the West. 3.4966

Islam. 1.2050

Islam. 1.2051-1.2052

Islam and Muslim art. 1.4749

Islam and politics. 1.2001

Islam and revolution. 3.4087

Islam and the trade of Asia. 4.4237

Islam and the West. 1.2070

Islam and tribal art in West Africa. 1.5086

Islam, continuity and change in the modern world. 1.1998

Islam, Europe and Empire. 3.3731

Islam, from the Prophet Muhammad to the capture of Constantinople. 3.3655

Islam from within. 1.2049

Islam in a world of nation-states. 4.7325

Islam in east Africa. 1.2007

Islam in modern history. 3.3666

Islam in revolution. 1.2000

Islam in South-East Asia. 1.2002

Islam in the political process. 1.2076

Islam observed. 1.2010

Islam under the crusaders. 3.3489

Islamic and Christian Spain in the early Middle Ages. 3.3421

Islamic architecture. 1.5235

The Islamic dynasties. 1.2028

Islamic education: its traditions and modernization into the Arab national systems. 4.10147

Islamic history. 3.3671

Islamic law. 1.2040

Islamic law in the modern world. 1.2039

Islamic literatures of India. 2.1925

Islamic medicine. 5.4514
Islamic messianism. 1.2066
The Islamic Middle East, 700-1900. 4.2440
The Islamic Near East and North Africa.
  5.8036
Islamic peoples of the Soviet Union. 3.3027
Islamic philosophy and theology. 1.2059
Islamic political thought. 4.7326
Islamic pottery of the eighth to the fifteenth
  century in the Keir Collection. 1.6611
Islamic society and the West. 3.3665
Island biogeography. 5.3243
Island biogeography in the Sea of Cortéz.
  5.3273
Island biology, illustrated by the land birds of
  Jamaica. 5.3961
The island of Crimea. 2.1621
Island populations. 5.3548
Island refuge; Britain and refugees from the
  Third Reich, 1933-1939. 4.8961
The islanders. 2.1615
The islands in between: essays on West Indian
  literature. 2.9975
Islands in the stream. 2.11845
Islands in time. 5.3269
Islands of the South Pacific. 4.195
Íslenzk-ensk orthabók. 2.915
Isocrates. 2.375
Isolated state. 4.2887
Isolation and security. 3.7564
Isoperimetric inequalities in mathematical
  physics 5.1424
Israel. 3.3812, 4.5397
Israel, a country study. 3.3924
The Israel-Arab reader. 3.3871
Israel, chaos and challenge. 4.2443
Israel divided. 3.3928
Israel in the Third World. 3.3858
Israel: its politics and philosophy. 3.3930
Israel: social structure and change. 4.5401
Israel, the embattled ally. 3.3932
Israel, the Palestinians, and the West Bank.
  3.3883
Israel: years of challenge. 3.3926
The Israeli Army. 5.7344
Israeli security planning in the 1980s. 5.7343
Israeli society. 4.5400
The Israelis: founders and sons. 3.3927
The Issa Valley. 2.1719
Issue voting and party realignment. 4.8110
Issues for community college leaders in a new
  era. 4.10563
Issues in British politics since 1945. 4.5339
Issues in higher education and the professions
  in the 1980s. 4.10554
Issues in Socialist economic modernization.
  4.1327
Istihsān al-khawd fī 'ilm al-kalām. 1.2044
Istitutioni harmoniche. 1.4422a
It all would have startled Columbus. 3.6330
It began with a stone. 5.2949
It can't happen here. 2.12007
It seemed like nothing happened. 3.6179
It sure looks different from the inside. 3.7927
Italian Americans. 5.7862
Italian Americans. 3.6558
Italian art, 1400-1500. 1.5002
Italian baroque painting. 1.6185
The Italian baroque stage. 2.3152
Italian cinema. 2.2901
The Italian cinema. 2.2902
The Italian city-republics. 3.2822
Italian comedy in the Renaissance. 2.4884
The Italian Communist Party. 4.8629, 4.8632
Italian drawings in the Albertina. 1.5811
The Italian economy. 4.2357
The Italian Fascist Party in power. 4.8634
Italian folktales. 4.795
Italian foreign policy, 1870-1940. 3.2879
Italian foreign policy under Mussolini. 3.2893
The Italian girl. 2.9756
Italian Gothic sculpture. 1.5721
Italian High Renaissance and Baroque
  sculpture. 1.5723
Italian humanism. 3.2846
The Italian influence in English poetry, from
  Chaucer to Southwell. 2.5576

The Italian influence on Scottish literature.
  2.9837
Italian kitchen. 5.7137
The Italian labor movement. 4.3416
The Italian language. 2.852
The Italian language today. 2.853
The Italian madrigal. 1.4235
Italian nationalism and English letters. 3.2864
The Italian Nationalist Association and the rise
  of fascism in Italy. 3.2883
The Italian navy in World War II. 3.1036
Italian opinion on America as revealed by
  Italian travelers. 3.6170
An Italian passage. 3.8062
The Italian prefects. 4.8879
The Italian problem in European diplomacy,
  1847-1849. 3.707
The Italian Renaissance in its historical
  background. 3.2847
Italian Renaissance sculpture. 1.5722
The Italian road to socialism. 4.8631
The Italian Socialist movement. 4.7081
The Italians. 3.6556
Italians in Chicago, 1880-1930. 3.8422
Italo Svevo. 2.5069
Italy. 3.2824, 3.2835, 4.3660
Italy, a country study. 3.2821
Italy, a study in economic development.
  4.2356
Italy and Italians. 3.2826
Italy and the Allies. 3.2840
Italy and the approach of the First World War.
  3.2882
Italy and the enlightenment. 3.2830
Italy and the Vatican at war. 3.2936
Italy at the Paris Peace Conference. 3.859
Italy at the polls. 4.8626
Italy at the polls, 1979. 4.8625
Italy from liberalism to fascism, 1870-1925.
  3.2880
Italy from Napoleon to Mussolini. 3.2856
Italy in the age of the Risorgimento, 1790-1870.
  3.2834
Italy in the Giolittian era. 3.2881
Italy in the making. 3.2857
An item from the late news. 2.10153
Iterated maps on the interval as dynamical
  systems. 5.1623
Itô Jinsai. 1.1143
It's a battlefield. 2.8751
Iturbide of Mexico. 3.8933
Iunctura callidus acri. 2.755
Ivan Bunin. 2.1481-2.1482
Ivan Krylov. 2.1395
Ivan Meštrović. 1.5745
Ivan the Great of Moscow. 3.3086
Ivan the Terrible. 3.3087
Ivan Turgenev. 2.1462
Ives. 1.3903
An Ives celebration. 1.3901
Ivo Andrić. 2.1209
Ivory and slaves. 4.4245
Ivory & slaves in East Central Africa. 4.4245
Ivy Compton-Burnett. 2.8532, 2.8535
Ivy, the life of I. Compton-Burnett. 2.8536
Iwein. 2.13533

'J.B.', a play in verse. 2.12090
J. B. Fischer von Erlach. 1.5410
J. B. Priestley. 2.9251
J. B. Priestley, an informal study of his work.
  2.9252
J. D. Salinger. 2.12427, 2.12429
J. E. Spingarn and the rise of the NAACP,
  1911-1939. 3.6646
J.F.K., the presidency of John F. Kennedy.
  3.7875
J. L. Austin. 1.741
J. M. Barrie. 2.7391-2.7392
J. M. Synge, 1871-1909. 2.8148
J. M. Synge and his world. 2.8149
J. M. Synge and the Western mind. 2.8150
J.P.L. and the American space program.
  5.6660
J.R.R. Tolkien. 2.9435
J. Robert Oppenheimer. 5.1959
J. S. Bach. 1.3781

J'accuse, ou, Nice côté-ombre. 4.6791
J'accuse, the dark side of Nice. 4.6791
Jacinto Benavente. 2.5235
Jack. 2.12035
Jack Kerouac. 2.11957
Jack Kerouac, prophet of the new romanticism.
  2.11959
Jack London. 2.12032, 2.12034
Jack London, American rebel. 2.12031
Jack of shadows. 2.13446
Jack; or, The submission. 2.4579
The jack-roller, a delinquent boy's own story.
  4.6882
The Jack-Roller at seventy. 4.6885
Jacke Jugeler. 2.6219
Jack's book. 2.11958
Jackson Pollock. 1.4902
Jackson Pollock, drawing into painting. 1.4903
Jacksonian America. 3.7079
Jacksonian democracy. 3.7073, 3.8031
The Jacksonian economy. 4.1917
The Jacksonian persuasion. 3.7078
Jacksonian politics and community conflict.
  3.8230
The Jacksonians. 4.7839
The Jacksonians versus the banks. 3.7128
Jacob Jordaens. 1.6265
Jacob Lawrence. 1.6381
Jacob van Ruisdael. 1.5024
Jacobean and Caroline comedies. 2.6230
The Jacobean and Caroline stage. 2.3297
The Jacobean drama. 2.5866
Jacobean pageant. 3.1463
Jacobean tragedy. 2.5887
The Jacobin clubs in the French Revolution.
  3.2110
The Jacobin Republic, 1792-1794. 3.2078
The Jacobins. 3.2109
The Jacobite risings in Britain, 1689-1746.
  3.1804
Jacob's room. 2.9573
Jacopo della Quercia, sculptor. 1.5737
Jacques Cousteau's Calypso. 5.7514
Jacques Lipchitz. 1.5707
Jacques Lipchitz: his sculpture. 1.5708
Jacques-Louis David. 1.6087
The jade mountain. 2.2192
Jahrestage. 2.13899
Jailed for freedom. 4.8089
Jails, the ultimate ghetto. 4.6910
Jain philosophy. 1.217
Jaina Āgama. Selections. English. 1.1735
The Jaina path of purification. 1.1736
Jaina Sutras. 1.1735
Jalna. 2.9930
La jalousie. 2.4691
The Jama Mapun. 3.4594
Jamaica Inn. 2.8603
Jamaica woman. 2.9993
James. 1.2723
James A. Michener. 2.12156
James Agee. 2.11297-2.11298
James Agee, selected journalism. 2.11293
James B. McMillan. 2.964
James Baldwin. 2.12864
James Beard's theory & practice of good
  cooking. 5.7130
James Boswell. 2.6908
James Boswell, the later years, 1769-1795.
  2.6906
James Branch Cabell. 2.11448-2.11449
James Dickey. 2.12981
James Dickey, the poet as pitchman. 2.12980
James Fenimore Cooper. 2.10977
James Fenimore Cooper, a collection of critical
  essays. 2.10975
James Ford Rhodes. 3.6263
James Forrestal. 3.7642
James Gibbs. 1.5387
James Gould Cozzens. 2.11522
James Harrington. 4.7403
James Henry Hammond and the Old South.
  3.8247
James Hogg. 2.7816-2.7817
James J. Hill and the opening of the Northwest.
  4.4000
James Jones. 2.13104-2.13105
James Joyce. 2.8906

James Joyce. 2.8908
James Joyce. 2.8912
James Joyce and the making of Ulysses.
  2.8885
James Joyce, his way of interpreting the
  modern world. 2.8920
A James Joyce miscellany. 2.8913-2.8915
James Joyce today: essays on the major works,
  commemorating the twenty-fifth anniversary
  of his death. 2.8919
James Joyce: two decades of criticism. 2.8917
James Joyce's Odyssey. 2.8886
James Joyce's Ulysses. 2.8889, 2.8891
James K. Baxter. 2.10212
James K. Polk, Jacksonian, 1795-1843. 3.7170
James Lane Allen and the genteel tradition.
  2.10906
James Larkin, Irish labour leader, 1876-1947,
  by Emmet Larkin. 4.3649
James Logan and the culture of provincial
  America. 3.8077
James Madison. 3.7099-3.7100
James McNeill Whistler. 1.5987
James McNeill Whistler at the Freer Gallery of
  Art. 1.4907
James Mill and the art of revolution. 4.7514
James Monroe: the quest for national identity.
  3.7118
James Parton, the father of modern biography.
  3.6261
James Purdy. 2.12361-2.12362
James Russell Lowell. 2.11146-2.11147
James II. 3.1509
James Shepherd Pike. 3.7157
James Shirley. 2.6875
James Stephens, his work and an account of his
  life. 2.9385
A James Stephens reader. 2.9384
James Stewart, Earl of Moray. 3.1796
James T. Rapier and Reconstruction. 3.6850
James Thomson. 2.7319
James Thomson (B.V.), a critical study. 2.8198
James Thurber. 2.12589
James Tissot. 1.6151
James Weldon Johnson, Black leader, Black
  voice. 2.11938
James Wilson. 3.7013
The Jameson Raid. 3.5503
Jamestown, 1544-1699. 3.8218
Jan van Eyck. 1.6264
Jane Austen. 2.7365, 2.7371-2.7372, 2.7374,
  2.7384
Jane Austen, a study of her artistic
  development. 2.7381
Jane Austen and her art. 2.7375
Jane Austen and the drama of woman. 2.7387
A Jane Austen companion. 2.7376
Jane Austen, her life and letters. 2.7370
Jane Austen; irony as defense and discovery.
  2.7382
Jane Austen: the critical heritage. 2.7383
Jane Austen's letters to her sister Cassandra
  and others. 2.7368
Jane Austen's novels. 2.7377, 2.7386
Jane Brody's Good food book. 5.5133
Jane Mander. 2.10228
Jane Shore. 2.7233
Jane's aircraft. 5.6640
Jane's all the world's aircraft. 5.6640
Jane's dictionary of military terms. 5.7171
Jane's dictionary of naval terms. 5.7416
Jane's fighting ships. 5.7446
Jane's pocket book of space exploration.
  5.6712
Jane's spaceflight directory. 5.6709
Jane's weapon systems. 5.7210
Janet Frame. 2.10225
The Jap-ji. 1.1823
Japan. 3.4872, 3.4875, 3.4881-3.4882, 3.4892,
  3.4911, 4.8749
Japan; a historical survey. 3.4908
Japan: ancient Buddhist paintings. 1.6336
Japan and East Asia. 3.4413
Japan and her destiny. 3.4985
Japan and the decline of the West in Asia,
  1894-1943. 3.4964
Japan and the Philippines, 1868-1898. 3.4924
Japan, art and civilization. 3.4891

Japan as number one. 4.5454
Japan before Buddhism. 3.4933
Japan before Perry. 3.4913
The Japan biographical encyclopedia & who's
  who. 3.4906
Japan business directory. 4.2541
Japan, China and the modern world economy.
  4.2463
Japan erupts. 3.4965
Japan examined. 3.4957
The Japan experience. 3.4901
Japan faces China. 3.4920
Japan in the Chinese dynastic histories. 3.4931
Japan; its land, people and culture. 3.4874
Japan statistical yearbook. 4.1257
Japan, the fragile superpower. 3.4888
Japan: the government-business relationship.
  4.3076
Japan today. 3.4977
The Japanese. 3.4876
The Japanese and Sun Yat-sen. 3.4762
Japanese and the other Altaic languages.
  2.1987
Japanese architecture. 1.5451
The Japanese are coming. 4.3062
The Japanese Army in North China, July, 1937
  - December, 1941. 3.4777
Japanese Buddhism. 1.2121
Japanese Buddhist sculpture. 1.5760
The Japanese challenge. 4.2551
Japanese cinema. 2.2903
Japanese colonial education in Taiwan,
  1895-1945. 4.10140
The Japanese colonial empire, 1895-1945.
  4.8939
The Japanese Communist movement,
  1920-1966. 4.8765
The Japanese Communist Party 1922-1945.
  4.8763
Japanese costume and textile arts. 1.6678
Japanese court poetry. 2.2008
Japanese decorative style. 1.5073
Japanese economic growth. 4.2553
Japanese-English character dictionary. 2.1993
The Japanese family storehouse. 2.2063
Japanese finance. 4.4546
Japanese folk literature. 5.8067
Japanese folk-plays. 2.2026
Japanese foreign policy, 1853-1868. 3.4915
Japanese foreign policy, 1869-1942. 3.4958
Japanese gardens. 5.5372
Japanese history. 5.8066
The Japanese imperial institution in the
  Tokugawa period. 3.4945
Japanese industrial competition to 1990.
  4.2552
Japanese ink painting. 1.6391
Japanese ink paintings from American
  collections. 1.6390
The Japanese islands. 4.2555
The Japanese language. 2.1985
Japanese law. 4.9924
Japanese linked poetry. 2.2007
Japanese literature. 2.1995
Japanese Marxist. 4.7124
The Japanese mind. 3.4887
Japanese mind. 1.1141
Japanese music and musical instruments.
  1.3742
Japanese, Nazis & Jews. 3.3942
The Japanese novel of the Meiji period and the
  ideal of individualism. 2.2014
The Japanese oligarchy and the Russo-Japanese
  War. 3.4401
Japanese patterns of behavior. 3.4890
Japanese poetry, the 'uta.' 2.2020
Japanese policy and east Asian security.
  5.7342
Japanese politics: patron-client democracy.
  4.8753
The Japanese print. 1.6478
The Japanese print: its evolution and essence.
  1.6480
Japanese prints. 1.6479
Japanese prints and Western painters. 1.6482
Japanese religion in the modern century.
  1.1835
The Japanese school. 4.10145

Japanese sculpture of the Tempyo period.
  1.5761
The Japanese seizure of Korea, 1868-1910.
  3.5002
Japanese short stories. 2.2035
Japanese society. 4.5449-4.5450
Japanese theatre. 2.3396
Japanese things. 3.4886
Japanese trade policy formulation. 4.4193
Japanese trade unionism. 4.3423
Japanese-trained armies in Southeast Asia.
  5.7334
Japanese women. 4.6147
Japanese woodblock prints. 1.6483
Japanese words and their uses. 2.1992
Japan's American interlude. 3.4978
Japan's decision for war. 3.945
Japan's decision to surrender. 3.1146
Japan's economic security. 4.2546
Japan's economy in war and reconstruction.
  4.2542
Japan's emergence as a modern state. 3.4949
Japan's first modern novel: Ukigumo of
  Futabatei Shimei. 2.2073
Japan's first student radicals. 4.10146
Japan's foreign policy. 3.4984
Japan's Greater East Asia Co-prosperity Sphere
  in World War II. 3.4403
Japan's multinational enterprises. 4.3063
Japan's new Buddhism. 1.1760
Japan's new middle class; the salary man and
  his family in a Tokyo suburb. 4.6402
Japan's parliament. 4.8756
Japan's political system. 4.8752
Japan's postwar economy. 4.2557
Japan's quest for autonomy. 3.4970
Japonisme. 1.4965
Le jardin d'acclimatation. 2.4786
Jaroslav Hašek. 2.1671
Jason and Medeia. 2.13029
Jasper Johns. 1.4898, 1.6443
Jasper Johns drawings, 1954-1984. 1.5796
Java in a time of revolution. 3.4569
The Javanese family. 4.579
Javanese Gamelan. 1.4197
Jawaharlal Nehru. 3.4320
Jawaharlal Nehru, an anthology. 3.4316
Jawaharlal Nehru, an autobiography. 3.4318
The Jay treaty. 3.7040
Jayanta Bhatta's Nyāya-mañjarī. 1.196
Jayaprakash. 3.4315
Jayaprakash Narayan. 3.4314
Jay's treaty. 3.7039
Jazz. 1.4337, 1.4341
The jazz age revisited. 3.6125
The jazz book. 1.4316
Jazz composition and orchestration. 1.4454
The jazz ensemble. 1.4504
Jazz heritage. 1.4266
Jazz, hot and hybrid. 1.4334
Jazz improvisation. 1.4484, 1.4486
Jazz, its evolution and essence. 1.4329
Jazz lives. 1.4259
Jazz masters in transition, 1957-69. 1.4260
Jazz masters of the fifties. 1.3757
Jazz masters of the forties. 1.3760
Jazz masters of the thirties. 1.4258
Jazz masters of the twenties. 1.3758
Jazz, New Orleans, 1885-1963. 1.4319
Jazz; new perspectives on the history of jazz by
  twelve of the world's foremost jazz critics
  and scholars. 1.4327
Jazz on record. 1.3618
Jazz panorama. 1.4265
Jazz piano. 1.4157
A jazz retrospect. 1.4326
Jazz review. 1.4265
Jazz style in Kansas City and the Southwest.
  1.4333
Jazz styles. 1.4325
The jazz tradition. 1.4340
Jazzmen. 1.4332
JBS: the life and work of J. B. S. Haldane.
  5.3203
Jealousy. 2.4692
Jean Arp. 1.5702
Jean-Auguste-Dominique Ingres. 1.6113
Jean-Baptiste-Camille Corot. 1.6078

Jean Barois. 2.4625
Jean Bodin and the rise of absolutist theory.
  4.7384
Jean-Christophe. 2.4698
Jean-Christophe in Paris. 2.4699
Jean de la Bruyère. 2.4026
Jean Dubuffet. 1.4970
Jean-François Millet. 1.6121
Jean-Francois Millet. 1.4978
Jean Giraudoux; his life and works. 2.4573
Jean-Jacques. 2.4092
Jean-Jacques Rousseau. 1.817, 2.4093
Jean-Jacques Rousseau. 2.4094
Jean Paul Friedrich Richter. 2.13645
Jean-Paul Sartre. 2.4744
Jean-Paul Sartre: the philosopher as a literary
  critic. 2.4743
Jean-Philippe Rameau: his life and work.
  1.3955
Jean Piaget. 5.285, 5.591
Jean Racine. 2.4050
Jean Renoir. 2.3063-2.3064
Jean Rhys. 2.9273, 2.9278-2.9279
Jean Rhys, a critical study. 2.9281
Jean Rhys, the complete novels. 2.9271
Jean Rhys, woman in passage. 2.9280
Jean Santeuil. 2.4668-2.4669
Jean Sibelius. 1.3989
Jean Toomer, artist. 2.12599
Jeeves. 2.9553
Jefferson & civil liberties. 4.7693
Jefferson and his time. 3.7062
Jefferson Davis. 3.7322-3.7324
Jefferson Davis and his cabinet. 3.7374
The Jefferson image in the American mind.
  3.7065
Jeffersonian America. 3.6027
The Jeffersonian crisis. 4.9747
The Jeffersonian persuasion. 3.6979
The Jeffersonians. 4.7837
Jefferson's English crisis. 3.7060
Jelly Roll, Jabbo, and Fats. 1.4262
Jenner's smallpox vaccine. 5.4534
Jennie Gerhardt. 2.11595
Jens Peter Jacobsen. 2.14014
Jeremiah. 1.2614
Jeremias Gotthelf. 2.13551
Jeremy Bentham. 1.725
Jeremy Bentham's economic writings. 4.1408
Jerome. 1.2489
The Jerome Biblical commentary. 1.2525
Jerome Kern. 1.3907
Jerusalem. 2.14065, 3.3814-3.3815
The Jerusalem Bible. 1.2499
Jerusalem delivered. 2.4982-2.4983
Jerusalem, or, On religious power and Judaism.
  1.1968
The Jerusalem question, 1917-1968. 3.3817
Jerusalem the golden. 2.9659
Jerusalem, the torn city. 3.3818
Jerzy Kosinski. 2.13124
Jessamyn West. 2.12681
Jesse Buel, agricultural reformer. 5.5258
Jesse Stuart, Kentucky's chronicler-poet.
  2.12561
A jest of God 2.9940
Jest, satire, irony and deeper significance.
  2.13587
The Jesuit relations and allied documents.
  3.8714
The Jesuits. 1.3242
The Jesuits, a history. 1.3243
Jesuits and Jacobins. 3.1886
Jesus. 1.2859, 1.2869
Jesus and Christian origins. 1.2881
Jesus and freedom. 1.2862
Jesus and Judaism. 1.2899
Jesus and the constraints of history. 1.2882
Jesus and the spirit. 1.2236
Jesus as mother. 1.3052
Jesus Christ liberator. 1.2856
Jesus, God and man. 1.2867
Jesus in the Qur'An. 1.2071
Jesús, ni vencido ni monarca celestial. English.
  1.2861
Jesus of Nazareth. 1.2879
Jesus of Nazareth in New Testament preaching.
  1.2854

Jesus on trial. 1.2897
Jesus' parables and the war of myths. 1.2681
Jesus, Son of Man. 1.2884
Jesus the Christ. 1.2863
Jesus the Jew. 1.2872
Jesus through the centuries. 1.2852
The Jet age. 5.6675
Jet-stream meteorology. 5.2543
Le jeu du souterrain. 2.4609
Jeux et sapience du moyen âge ... 2.3943
Les jeux sont faits. 2.4725
The Jew. 2.1452
The Jew and his history. 3.3845
The Jew in American literature 2.10356
The Jew in American society. 3.6574
The Jew in the medieval world, a source book,
  315-1791. 3.3903
The Jew in the modern world. 3.3805
Jewellery of the ancient world. 1.6663
Jewelry of the ancient world. 1.6663
Jewels of the pharaohs. 1.6665
Jewish biblical exegesis. 1.2575
The Jewish community in America. 5.8244
The Jewish community in British politics.
  3.3946
The Jewish community: its history and
  structure to the American Revolution.
  3.3902
Jewish culture in Eastern Europe. 3.3839
Jewish education in the United States. 4.10813
Jewish emigration. 3.1102
Jewish emigration 1938-1940, Rublee
  negotiations, and Intergovernmental
  Committee. 3.1101
Jewish emigration from 1933 to the Evian
  conference of 1938. 3.1100
The Jewish encyclopedia. 3.3810
The Jewish experience in America. 3.6571
Jewish genealogy. 5.8247
The Jewish government and other stories.
  2.1818
Jewish history atlas. 4.120
Jewish ideas and concepts. 1.1971
Jewish law in ancient and modern Israel.
  3.3833
Jewish leadership during the Nazi era. 3.1114
Jewish life under Islam. 3.3816
A Jewish life under the tsars. 3.4001
The Jewish minority in the Soviet Union.
  3.3999
Jewish music in its historical development.
  1.4351
Jewish mystical testimonies. 1.1984
The Jewish people in the first century. 3.3890
The Jewish people in the first century. 3.3889
Jewish people, Jewish thought. 1.1901
Jewish publishing in America. 5.7588
Jewish radicals. 3.3948
Jewish reactions to German anti-Semitism,
  1870-1914. 3.3965
Jewish reference sources. 5.8235
The Jewish religion in the Soviet Union.
  1.1932
Jewish resistance in Nazi-occupied Eastern
  Europe. 3.1082
Jewish responses to Nazi persecution. 3.1121
A Jewish understanding of the New Testament.
  1.2638
The Jewish woman. 4.5911
The Jewish woman in America. 3.6569
Jewish worship. 1.1977
The Jewish writer in America. 2.10299
Jewish writings of the Second Temple period.
  1.1934
Jews and Arabs. 3.4008
Jews and Arabs, their contacts through the
  ages. 3.3854
Jews and Christians. 3.3847
Jews and intermarriage. 4.5790
Jews and Judaism in New York. 3.8053
Jews in an Arab land. 3.3980
The Jews in medieval Germany. 3.3964
The Jews in Poland. 3.3985
The Jews in Poland and Russia. 5.8242
The Jews in Soviet Russia since 1917. 3.3994
The Jews in Spain, their social, political and
  cultural life during the Middle Ages. 3.4004
Jews in the eyes of the Germans. 3.3969

Jews in the Protestant establishment. 3.6579
The Jews in the Roman world. 3.3888
Jews of ancient Rome. 3.3977
The Jews of Czechoslovakia. 3.3945
The Jews of East Central Europe between the
  world wars. 3.3953
The Jews of Europe and the Inquisition of
  Venice, 1550-1670. 3.3978
The Jews of Georgian England, 1714-1830.
  3.3947
The Jews of Ireland. 3.3974
The Jews of Islam. 1.2073
The Jews of Moslem Spain. 3.4002
The Jews of Palestine. 3.3901
The Jews of Poland. 3.3988
The Jews of Rhodes. 3.3971
Jews of the Latin American republics. 3.9027
The Jews of the United States, 1790-1840.
  3.6562
The Jews of Vienna, 1867-1914. 3.3940
The Jews of Warsaw, 1939-1943. 3.3991
The Jews: their history, culture, and religion.
  3.3806
Jews, Turks, and infidels. 3.6563
The Jews under Roman rule. 3.3892
JFK, the presidency of John F. Kennedy.
  3.7875
The Jicarilla Apaches. 3.5898
Jig Cook and the Provincetown Players.
  2.3275
Jill. 2.8942
Jim Crow's defense. 3.6685
Jim Dine prints, 1970-1977. 1.6439
Jimmy Carter, in search of the great White
  House. 3.7935
Jinnah, creator of Pakistan. 3.4312
Jinnah of Pakistan. 3.4137
Jirel of Joiry. 2.13181
Joachim Patinir. 1.6270
Joan Didion. 2.12986
Joan, Maid of Orleans. 3.2002
Joan of Arc. 3.2001, 3.2003-3.2004
Job burnout in public education. 4.10679
The job of the Federal executive. 4.7980
Job satisfaction 4.4374
Job stress and burnout. 5.407
Jobless pay and the economy. 4.3449
Jobs and gender. 4.3251
Jobs for disadvantaged workers. 4.3220
Jobs for the disabled. 4.3476
Jocelyn. 2.4256
Jock. 4.953
The Jodrell Bank telescopes. 5.1784
Joe Egg. 2.9781
Joe Tumulty and the Wilson era. 3.7690
Joel and Amos. 1.2618
Joel Chandler Harris. 2.11049-2.11050
Joel Chandler Harris, folklorist. 2.11053
Jogjakarta under Sultan Mangkubumi,
  1749-1792. 3.4581
Johann Sebastian Bach. 1.3779
Johann Sebastian Bach; his life, art, and work.
  1.3775
Johann Sebastian Bach, his work and influence
  on the music of Germany, 1685-1750.
  1.3782
Johann Sebastian Bach (Kassel, Germany).
  English. 1.3779
Johann Sebastian Bach; the culmination of an
  era. 1.3777
Johann Wolfgang Goethe. 2.13580
Johannes Bobrowski. 2.13680
Johannes Brahms. 1.3607
Johannesevangelium. 1.2697
The Johannine circle. 1.2693
The Johannine epistles. 1.2728
John A. Macdonald. 3.8756
John A. Williams. 2.13429
John Adams. 3.7049
John Adams and the diplomacy of the
  American Revolution. 3.6937
John and William Bartram's America. 5.3189
John Andrews. 1.5456
John Ashbery, an introduction to the poetry.
  2.11339
John Augustus: first probation officer. 4.6900
John Bale. 2.6431
John Barth. 2.12886

John Berryman, a critical commentary. 2.11381
John Bright. 3.1633
John Brown, 1800-1859. 3.7275
John Brown and the legend of fifty-six. 3.8523
John Brown's body. 2.11370
John Bunyan. 2.6920, 2.6922
John Bunyan, mechanick preacher. 2.6921
John C. Calhoun. 3.7089
John C. Calhoun, opportunist. 3.7088
John Cage. 1.3831
John Calvin. 1.3402
John Calvin on God and political duty. 4.7385
The John Carroll papers. 1.3265
John Cheever, the hobgoblin company of love. 2.11497
John Christian Bach. 1.3784
John Clare. 2.7569, 2.7571
John Cleland's Memoirs of a woman of pleasure. 2.6938
John Coltrane. 1.4082
John Company at work. 4.2497
John Courtney Murray. 1.3272
John Cowper Powys: novelist. 2.9239
John Crome. 1.6030
John Crowe Ransom. 2.12374
John Dalton. 5.2619
John Davidson, poet of Armageddon. 2.7621
John Dewey. 1.587, 1.592
John Dewey in perspective. 1.589
John Dewey, philosopher of science and freedom. 1.590
John Donne. 2.6464
John Donne, a life. 2.6460
John Donne, life, mind, and art. 2.6461
John Donne's lyrics. 2.6467
John Dos Passos. 2.11587
John Dos Passos. 2.11589
John Dowland; his life and works. 1.3856
John Dryden. 2.7002
John Dryden. 2.6998
John Dryden, a study of his poetry. 2.7004
John Dryden: some biographical facts and problems. 2.6996
John Edgar Hoover. 4.6796
John F. Kennedy, President. 3.7876
John Fiske. 3.6253
John Flaxman. 1.4953
The John Fletcher plays. 2.6573
John Ford. 2.6576
John Ford and the Caroline theatre. 2.6580
John Ford and the drama of his time. 2.6577
John Ford and the traditional moral order. 2.6579
John Foster Dulles. 3.7637
John Fowles. 2.9691, 2.9693
John Fowles, magus and moralist. 2.9695
John Foxe. 2.6479
John Frederick Kensett, an American master. 1.4899
John Galsworthy. 2.8682-2.8683
John Galt. 2.7718
John Gay. 2.7038
John Gay, dramatic works. 2.7035
John Gay, social critic. 2.7036
John Gower, moral philosopher and friend of Chaucer. 2.6385
John Gower's poetry. 2.6384
John Greenleaf Whittier's poetry. 2.11284
John Hawkes. 2.13075
John Hus. 1.3300
John Hus and the Czech reform. 1.3301
John Hus at the Council of Constance. 1.3299
John J. Crittenden. 3.7092
John J. Pershing, General of the Armies. 3.6370
John Keats. 2.7855
John Keats, his life and writings. 2.7856
John Keats; the making of a poet. 2.7860
John Kennedy. 3.7873
John Knox. 1.3393
John Locke. 1.678
John Locke and the way of ideas. 1.681
John Locke: problems and perspectives. 1.682
John Locke's political philosophy. 4.7401
John Loughborough Pearson. 1.5396
John Lyly. 2.6492-2.6493

John Maitland of Thirlestane and the foundation of the Stewart despotism in Scotland. 3.1798
John Marin. 1.5954
John Marshall: a life in law. 4.9821
John Marston of the Middle Temple. 2.6627
John Marston, satirist. 2.6625
John Marston's plays. 2.6628
John Marston's theatrical drama. 2.6626
John Masefield's Letters from the front, 1915-1917. 2.9091
John Maynard Keynes. 4.1350-4.1351
John Milton. 2.7152, 2.7158
John Milton and the English Revolution. 2.7163
John Milton, Englishman. 2.7149
John Muir and his legacy. 5.3226
John Oldham. 2.7175
John Ostell, architect, surveyor. 1.5350
John Ostell, architecte, arpenteur. 1.5350
John P. Hale and the politics of abolition. 3.7156
John P. Marquand. 2.12114
John Peale Bishop. 2.11390
John Philip Kemble. 2.3350
John Philip Sousa; American phenomenon. 1.3993
John Quincy Adams and the foundations of American foreign policy. 3.7122
John Quincy Adams and the Union. 3.7123
John Rawls' theory of social justice. 4.4971
John Ray, naturalist, his life and works. 5.3211
John Ruskin. 2.8034, 2.8037, 2.8039
John Ruskin, the passionate moralist. 2.8032
John Singer Sargent. 1.5968
John Singer Sargent: paintings, drawings, watercolors. 1.5967
John Singleton Copley. 1.5929-1.5930
John Skelton, the complete English poems. 2.6516
John Skelton's poetry. 2.6518
John Sloan, 1871-1951. 1.5973
John Sloan's New York scene. 1.5972
John Soane. 1.5402
John Soane, the making of an architect. 1.5401
John Steinbeck. 2.12536
John Steuart Curry's pageant of America. 1.5931
John Strachey. 4.7030
John Stuart and the Southern colonial frontier. 3.8134
John Stuart Mill. 1.731
John Stuart Mill and Harriet Taylor. 1.729
John Stuart Mill and the pursuit of virtue. 1.732
John Stuart Mill on education. 4.10195
John Thomas and Lady Jane. 2.8967
John Torrey. 5.3640
John Trumbull. 1.5979, 2.10879
John Trumbull, patriot-artist of the American Revolution. 1.5980
John Updike. 2.13384, 2.13386
John Updike's novels. 2.13381
John Von Neumann and Norbert Wiener. 5.1088
John Wain. 2.9458
John Webster. 2.6885
John Webster: a critical anthology. 2.6884
John Wesley. 1.3376
John Willis' screen world. 1966-. 2.2867
John Žižka and the Hussite revolution. 3.1911
Johnson, Grant, and the politics of Reconstruction. 3.7468
Johnson on Shakespeare. 2.6717
Johnson's Journey to the western islands of Scotland. 3.1809
The joint. 4.6917
The Joint Chiefs of Staff. 5.7358
The joke. 2.1692
The joker of Seville & O Babylon! 2.10022
Jokes and their relation to the unconscious. 2.3788
The Jonathan David dictionary of popular slang. 2.1147
Jonathan Edwards. 1.3338, 1.3340
Jonathan Edwards, 1703-1758. 1.3341
Jonathan Sewall. 3.6962

Jonathan Swift. 2.7302
Jonathan Swift and Ireland. 2.7307
Jonathan Swift, essays on his satire and other studies. 2.7305
Jonathan Swift, political writer. 2.7309
Jonathan Swift, the complete poems. 2.7290
Jonathan Wild. 2.7021
Jonson and Elizabethan comedy. 2.6598
Jonson's moral comedy. 2.6600
Jordaens. 1.6265
Jordan. 3.4030, 3.4036
Jordan, a country study. 3.4029
Jorrocks' jaunts and jollities. 2.8130
Jo's boys. 2.10898
José Donoso. 2.5407
José María de Pereda. 2.5217
José Martí, major poems. 2.5366
José Ortega y Gasset. 1.1131
Joseph and his brothers. 2.13830
Joseph and Thomas Warton. 2.7335
Joseph Beuys. 1.4988
Joseph Brant, 1743-1807, man of two worlds. 3.5893
Joseph Chamberlain, a political study. 3.1636
Joseph Conrad. 2.8548, 2.8568, 2.8571, 2.8575-2.8576
Joseph Conrad, a chronicle. 2.8572
Joseph Conrad, a critical biography. 2.8555
Joseph Conrad: a personal remembrance. 2.8564
Joseph Conrad and his circle. 2.8557
Joseph Conrad as I knew him. 2.8558
Joseph Conrad: Józef Teodor Konrad Nałęcz Korzeniowski, Poland's English genius. 2.8556
Joseph Conrad, life and letters. 2.8554
Joseph Conrad, the modern imagination. 2.8560
Joseph Conrad, the way of dispossession. 2.8561
Joseph Conrad's letters to R. B. Cunninghame Graham. 2.8552
Joseph Cornell. 1.4895
A Joseph Cornell album. 1.4894
Joseph E. Brown of Georgia. 3.7426
Joseph Fourier, 1768-1830. 5.1092
Joseph Furphy. 2.10149
Joseph Haydn. 1.3610
Joseph Howe. 3.8803
Joseph Lister, 1827-1912. 5.4535
Joseph P. Kennedy. 3.7656
Joseph Pilsudski, the memories of a Polish revolutionary and soldier. 3.3287
Joseph Priestley. 5.702
Joseph Priestley, selections from his writings. 1.2
Joseph Pulitzer and the New York World. 2.3627
Joseph Pulitzer, reminiscences of a secretary. 2.3626
Joseph Smith and the beginnings of Mormonism. 1.3383
Joseph Stella. 1.5974
Joseph II. 3.1885
Joseph von Eichendorff. 2.13562
Joseph Wright of Derby: painter of light. 1.6044
Josephus. 2.376
Josephus, the Jewish war; newly translated with extensive commentary and archaeological background illustrations. 3.3897
Joshua: a commentary. 1.2597
Joshua R. Giddings and the tactics of radical politics. 3.7154
Josiah Gregg and his vision of the early West. 3.8574
Josiah Royce. 1.641
Josiah Walls. 3.7453
Josquin des Prez. 1.3853
Journal. 3.5976
The journal. 3.7149
Journal. 2.4227, 2.9079
Journal, 1939-1942. 2.4560
The journal and major essays of John Woolman. 1.3356
Journal du Voleur. 2.4535
Journal of a residence on a Georgian plantation in 1838-1839. 3.8264

Journal of a soul. 1.3160
Journal of a tour to the Hebrides with Samuel
  Johnson, LL.D. 3.1809
The Journal of Albion Moonlight. 2.12305
The journal of Eugène Delacroix. 1.6093
Journal of family history. 5.8379
The journal of George Fox. 1.3355
The journal of Gideon Olmstead. 3.6894
Journal of researches into the geology and
  natural history of the various countries
  visited by H.M.S. Beagle. 5.3180
The journal of Samuel Curwen, loyalist.
  3.6961
The journal of Sir Simonds D'Ewes. 3.1471
The journal of Sir Walter Scott. 2.8052
Journal of The Counterfeiters. 2.4551
Journal of the House of Representatives.
  4.7205
The Journal of the Senate, including the
  Journal of the Executive proceedings of the
  Senate. 4.7204
The journal to Eliza. 2.7276
Journal to Stella. 2.7298
Journalistic freedom. 4.9533
The journals. 2.8457, 2.12909
Journals. 5.3277
Journals and journeymen. 2.3592
The journals and letters of Fanny Burney
  (Madame D'Arblay). 2.6894
Journals and miscellaneous notebooks. 2.11021
Journals and papers. 2.7823
The journals of Alfred Doten, 1849-1903.
  3.8607
The journals of André Gide. 2.4559
The journals of David E. Lilienthal. 3.7662
Journals of Dorothy Wordsworth. 2.8296
The journals of Francis Parkman 3.6255
The journals of Jean Cocteau. 2.4484
Journals of John D. Lee, 1846-47 and 1859.
  3.8582
The journals of Sylvia Plath. 2.13260
The Journals of the Lewis and Clark
  Expedition. 3.8479
Journals of the Lewis & Clark Expedition.
  3.8479
The journals of Thornton Wilder, 1939-1961.
  2.12719
Journaux intimes. 2.4138
The journey back. 2.10308
Journey from Jim Crow. 4.9683
Journey from obscurity. 2.9218
A journey from Prince of Wales's Fort in
  Hudson's Bay to the Northern Ocean, 1769,
  1770, 1771, 1772. 3.8842
A journey from St. Petersburg to Moscow.
  4.5375
Journey from the north. 2.8844
Journey into fear. 2.8381
Journey into the self. 2.12523
Journey into the whirlwind. 3.3242
The journey narrative in American literature.
  2.10351
The journey, not the arrival matters. 2.9567
The journey of Niels Klim to the world
  underground. 2.14006
Journey of Tapiola. 2.12237
A journey through Texas. 3.8327
Journey to America. 3.6039
A journey to Arzrum. 3.3585
Journey to the end of the night. 2.4512
The journey to the west. 2.2227
Journey to the western islands of Scotland.
  3.1809
Journey with genius. 2.8981
Journey without maps. 3.5412
Journeyman. 2.11454
Joy of cooking. 5.7134
The joy of running. 5.5026
The joy of sports. 4.937
Joyce. 2.8916
Joyce annotated. 2.8907
Joyce Cary. 2.8509, 2.8512
Joyce Cary and the dimensions of order.
  2.8508
Joyce Cary: the developing style. 2.8511
Joyce Cary's Africa. 2.8510
Joyce Cary's trilogies. 2.8506
The Joyce country. 2.8921

Joyce's Portrait, criticisms & critiques. 2.8879
Joyce's voices. 2.8893
The joyful community. 1.3368
Joys and sorrows. 1.4076
JPL and the American space program. 5.6660
Juan Boscán. 2.5161
Juan Meléndez Valdés. 2.5216
Juan Ramón Jiménez. 2.5269
Juan Ruiz de Alarcón. 2.5203
Juan Rulfo. 2.5355
Juan Valera. 2.5226
Jubilee. 2.12631
Judaica. 3.3809
Judaism. 1.1897
Judaism and Christian beginnings. 1.1907
Judaism and modern man. 1.1964
Judaism eternal. 1.1893
Judaism in America. 1.1926
Judaism in the beginning of Christianity.
  1.1910
Judaism in the first centuries of the Christian
  era. 1.1909
Jude the obscure. 2.7763
Judenrat. 3.1122
The Judeo-Spanish ballad chapbooks of Yacob
  Abraham Yoná. 2.906
Judge and jury in imperial Brazil, 1808-1871.
  4.9909
Judge Frank Johnson and human rights in
  Alabama. 4.9492
Judge, lawyer, victim, thief. 4.6780
Judges, a commentary. 1.2598
Judgment day. 2.11653
Judgments. 4.9614
Judgments on history and historians. 3.524
Judicial craftsmanship or fiat? 4.9837
Judicial legislation. 4.9746
Judicial power and Reconstruction politics.
  4.9790
The judicial process. 4.9375
The judicial record of Justice William O.
  Douglas. 4.9809
The Judicial system and the Jews in Nazi
  Germany. 3.1108
The Judiciary. 4.7799
Die Jugend des Königs Henri Quatre. 2.13817
The Jugurthine War. 3.2749
The Juilliard report on teaching the literature
  and materials of music. 1.4422
Jules Ferry and the renaissance of French
  imperialism. 4.8925
Jules Henry on education. 4.10245
Jules Laforgue. 2.4253
Jules Simon. 3.2142
Jules Verne, inventor of science fiction. 2.4326
Julia and the bazooka, and other stories.
  2.8617
Julian Green. 2.4577
Julian the Apostate. 2.1519
Julie. 2.4089
Julie de Carneilhan. 2.4494
Julio Cortázar. 2.5386
Julio Gonzalez. 1.5741
Julio Jurenito. 2.1548
Julius Caesar and his public image. 3.2788
Julius Caesar on stage in England and America,
  1599-1973. 2.6660
Jullien's plan for comparative education,
  1816-1817. 4.10203
July 1914. 3.767
July's people. 2.10072
Jump-rope rhymes. 2.1047
The jumping-off place; American drama in the
  1960's. 2.10526
Jung on elementary psychology. 5.169
The jungle. 2.12479
The junior college: progress and prospect.
  4.10566
The junior high school. 4.10500
Junky. 2.12934
Jurassic environments. 5.3140
Jurassic geology of the world. 5.3139
Jurgen. 2.11445
Jurisprudence and legal essays. 4.9364
The jurisprudence of John Marshall. 4.9822
Juror number four. 4.9457
Jusepe de Ribera, lo Spagnoletto, 1591-1652.
  1.6220

The just and the unjust. 2.11516
Just assassins. 2.4443
Just before the origin. 5.3212
Just Mahalia, baby. 1.4091
A just measure of pain. 4.6918
Just schools. 4.10790
Just so much honor. 2.6462
The just war in the middle ages. 1.2923
Justice. 4.7656
Justice and corrections. 4.6821
Justice at Nuremberg. 4.9334
Justice at war. 4.9769
Justice by consent. 4.9882
Justice Hugo Black and the first amendment.
  4.9711
Justice in grey. 4.9907
Justice in the U.S.S.R. 4.9916
Justice Joseph Story and the rise of the
  Supreme Court. 4.9828
Justice, morality, and education. 4.10782
The Justice motive in social behavior. 4.4972
Justice Oliver Wendell Holmes. 4.9818
Justice William O. Douglas. 4.9810
Justices and Presidents. 4.9787
Justices Black and Frankfurter. 4.9844
The justices of the United States Supreme
  Court, 1789-1969. 4.9797
Justification. 1.2932, 4.7256
The justification of induction. 1.1188
Justifying historical descriptions. 3.398
Justifying violence. 4.5245
Justine. 2.4097, 2.8606
Jutland, 1916. 3.819
Juvenal and Persius. 2.673
Juvenal the satirist. 2.731
Juvenile court laws in the United States.
  4.6867
Juvenile delinquency. 4.6863, 4.6865
Juvenile delinquency and its origins. 4.6862
Juvenile delinquency and the juvenile justice
  system. 4.6875
Juvenile delinquency in perspective. 4.6861
Juvenile justice in Britain and the United States.
  4.9396
The Juvenile justice system. 4.6874
Juvenile victimization. 4.6869
Juzgado de Capellanias. 1.3186

K.C. 3.8367
K.G.B. today. 4.6840
Kabbalah. 1.1951
Kabuki. 2.2034
The kabuki theatre. 2.3397
The kabuki theatre of Japan 2.3401
The Kabul, Kunduz and Helmand Valleys and
  the national economy of Afghanistan. 4.2451
The kachina and the white man. 3.5888
The Kafirs of the Hindu-Kush. 3.4120
Kafr el-Elow. 4.5472
Kafū the Scribbler. 2.2081
Kagi. 2.2119
Kaimokushō. 1.2120
The Kaiser and his times. 3.2344
The Kaiser's daughter. 3.2345
The Kaiser's memoirs, Wilhelm II, emperor of
  Germany, 1888-1918. 3.2343
Kak zakalialas' stal'. 2.1590
Kalahari hunter-gatherers. 3.5484
Kalambo Falls prehistoric site. 4.747
Kalami pir. 1.2094
Kaleidoscope; poems by American Negro poets.
  2.10752
The Kaleidoscopic lens. 2.2993
The Kalevala. 2.1752
Kalevala. 2.1751
Kalevala, the land of heroes. 2.1751
Kālidāsa. 2.1948
Kālidāsa's Abhijñāna-Śakuntala. 2.1949
Kalki. 2.12617
The Kami Way. 1.1838
Kandinsky, complete writings on art. 1.5144
Kandinsky in Munich. 1.6283
Kandinsky, the development of an abstract
  style. 1.6282
The kandy-kolored tangerine-flake streamline
  baby. 3.6175
K'ang-hsi and the consolidation of Ch'ing rule,
  1661-1684. 3.4718

Kangaroo. 2.8964
Kansas. 3.8521-3.8522
Kansas, a guide to the Sunflower State. 3.8526
Kant. 1.900, 1.902
Kant and the problem of metaphysics. 1.915
Kant and the transcendental object. 1.914
Kant, Fichte, Schelling, Schopenhauer, Hegel. 1.1385
Kant on history and religion. 1.919
Kant, ontology & the a priori. 1.916
Kant: the philosophy of right. 1.909
Kanthapura 2.10130
Kant's aesthetic theory. 1.904
Kant's cosmogony. 5.1871
Kant's criticism of metaphysics. 1.888
Kant's Critique of pure reason. 1.889
Kant's Dialectic. 1.906
Kant's ethical theory. 1.880
Kantś first critique. 1.884
Kant's inaugural dissertation and early writings on space. 1.895
Kant's life and thought. 1.899
Kant's metaphysic of experience. 1.885
Kant's political thought. 1.917
Kant's political writings. 4.7437
Kant's pre-critical ethics. 1.911
Kant's rational theology. 1.920
Kant's theory of mind. 1.918
The Kāpālikas and Kālāmukhas. 1.1724
The kapetanios; partisans and civil war in Greece, 1943-1949. 3.1067
Kappler report on Indian affairs. 4.9771
Karamanlis, the restorer of Greek democracy. 3.2701
A Karamazov companion. 2.1340
Karen Horney. 5.4780
Karīm Khān Zand. 3.4081
The Kariye Djami, Vol.4: Studies in the art of the Kariye Djami and its intellectual background. 1.5538
Karl Barth. 1.3284
Karl Bodmer's America. 1.6389
Karl Jaspers; an introduction to his philosophy. 1.1031
Karl Kautsky and the socialist revolution, 1880-1938. 4.7058
Karl Korsch. 4.7055
Karl Kraus. 2.13807
Karl Marx. 1.1043, 4.6945, 4.6952, 4.6955, 4.6959
Karl Marx and the anarchists. 4.7184
Karl Marx collective. 4.2916
Karl Marx, Frederick Engels. 4.6944
Karl Marx; his life and environment. 4.6949
Karl Marx, his life and teachings (Leben und Lehre) 4.6963
Karl Marx's philosophy of man. 1.1040
Karl Marx's theory of history. 3.506
Karl Radek, the last internationalist. 4.7088
Karlstadt's battle with Luther. 1.2317
The karma of words. 2.1999
Karst geomorphology. 4.279
Karst hydrogeology. 4.300
The Kashf al-mahjúb. 1.2084
The Kashmir problem. 3.4345
Kassandra. 2.13922
Kate Chopin. 2.10933-2.10934
Kate Roberts. 2.844
Käthe Kollwitz. 1.5809
Katherine Anne Porter. 2.12318-2.12319
Katherine Mansfield. 2.9083, 2.9086
Katherine Mansfield's letters to John Middleton Murry, 1913-1922. 2.9082
Katsura. 1.5454
Katz und Maus. 2.13760
The Kautilīya Arthaśāstra. 4.7328
Kautilya's Arthaśāstra. 4.7329
Kazan on Kazan. 2.3059
Kazantzakis. 2.601
Keats. 2.7862, 2.7864-2.7865
Keats and his world. 2.7858
Keats and the Victorians. 2.7861
Keats as a narrative poet. 2.7863
The Keats circle. 2.7859
Keats, skepticism, and the religion of beauty. 2.7872
Keats, the myth of the hero. 2.7870
Keats the poet. 2.7867

The keen delight. 2.2751
Keep me warm one night: early handweaving in eastern Canada. 5.7097
Keep the aspidistra flying. 2.9181
Keep tightly closed in a cool dry place. 2.13353
The keeper of antiquities. 2.1546
The keepers of light. 5.6947
Keepers of the game. 3.5728
The keepers of the house. 2.13059
Keeping graduate programs responsive to national needs. 4.10620
The Keeping of animals. 4.6367
Keeping the faith. 4.3391
Keeping track. 4.10717
Keesing's contemporary archives. 3.724, 3.2466
Kefauver: a political biography. 3.7654
Keir Hardie. 4.3648
Keith Douglas, 1920-1944. 2.8602
Kellogg-Briand pact. 4.9261
Ken Kesey. 2.13111, 2.13113
Kenkyūsha shin Ei-Wa daijiten. 2.1990
Kenkyusha's new English-Japanese dictionary. 2.1990
Kenkyusha's new Japanese-English dictionary. 2.1991
Kennedy. 3.7870
Kennedy and Roosevelt. 3.7777
The Kennedy imprisonment. 3.7883
Kennedy justice. 4.9743
The Kennedy promise. 3.7863
Kenneth Grahame, a biography. 2.7751
Kent Cooper and the Associated Press. 2.3611
Kentucky. 3.8355, 3.8359
A Kentucky cardinal & Aftermath. 2.10905
Kentucky in the new republic. 3.8356
Kenya. 3.5278
Kenya, a country study. 3.5268
Kenya: the politics of participation and control. 4.8799
Kenya's past. 3.5276
Kenyatta. 3.5277
Kenyon critics. 2.2680
Kept in the dark. 2.8212
Kerouac. 2.11956
Kethubim. 1.2599
Kett's rebellion. 3.1418
Ketuvim. 1.2599
The key. 2.2119
A key into the language of America. 3.5911
Key monuments of the history of art. 1.4679
The key of remembrance. 2.6368
Key papers in information science. 5.7640
Key sources in comparative and world literature. 5.8272
The key to the universe. 5.2434
The key to Uncle Tom's cabin. 3.7262
The key to weaving. 5.7096
Key treaties for the great powers, 1814-1914. 4.8965
Keyboard interpretation from the 14th to the 19th century. 1.4140
Keyboard music. 1.4149
The keyboard music of C. P. E. Bach, considered in relation to his musical aesthetic and the rise of the sonata principle. 1.4527
The keyboard music of John Bull. 1.3829
Keyguide to information sources in cartography. 5.8209
Keynes, Cambridge, and The general theory. 4.1340
Keynes' monetary thought. 4.1343
Keynes's 'General theory' 4.1442
KGB: the secret work of Soviet secret agents. 4.6839
KGB today. 4.6840
Khmer sculpture and the Angkor civilization. 1.5755
Khronika tekushchikh sobytiĭ. 3.3258
Khrushchev. 3.3270, 3.3272
Khrushchev and Brezhnev as leaders. 4.8653
Khrushchev and Stalin's ghost. 3.3238
Khrushchev and the Soviet leadership, 1957-1964. 3.3271

Khrushchev remembers; the last testament. 3.3269
The Kibbutz. 5.8401
The kibbutz. 4.7168
Kibbutz. 4.7169
Kibbutz Makom. 4.7167
Kick the can, and over 800 other active games and sports for all ages. 4.1062
Kicked a building lately? 1.5485
The kidney. 5.4250
Kierkegaard. 1.3289
Kierkegaard: a kind of poet. 1.1123
Kierkegaard and Christendom. 1.1125
Kierkegaard and radical discipleship. 1.3290
A Kierkegaard anthology. 1.1119
Kierkegaard on Christ and Christian coherence. 1.3291
Kierkegaard's Concluding unscientific postscript. 1.2228
Kierkegaard's Fear and trembling. 1.2229
Kierkegaard's 'Fragments' and 'Postscript' 1.1126
Kierkegaard's thought. 1.1124
Killers of the dream. 3.6692
The kiln book. 5.7099
Kin, clan, raja, and rule. 4.8707
Kinaaldá. 3.5916
Kind and usual punishment. 4.6912
The kind of motion we call heat. 5.2184
Kindai Chūgoku shakai kenkyū. 5.8398
Kinder- und Hausmärchen. English. 2.13510
Kinder- und Hausmärchen gesammelt durch die Brüder Grimm. 2.13509
Kindergarten and early schooling. 4.10411
Kindergarten chats (revised 1918) and other writings. 1.5484
The kindergarten crusade. 4.10414
Kindheitsmuster. 2.13925
Kindlers Literatur Lexikon. 2.2352
Kindly bent to ease us. 1.2162
Kindness, clarity, and insight. 1.2164
Kinesics and context. 5.460
Kinesiology. 5.4277
Kinetic theory and entropy. 5.2173
The kinetic theory of gases. 5.2182
Kinetic theory of gases, with an introduction to statistical mechanics. 5.2180
Kinetic theory of liquids. 5.2188
Kinetics and dynamics of elementary gas reactions. 5.2892
Kinetics and mechanism. 5.2890
Kinetics of enzyme mechanisms. 5.4416
King. 3.6840
King and Commons, 1660-1832. 4.8439
A king and no king. 2.6555
King Arthur and his knights. 2.6408
King Arthur's death. 2.6413
King Charles the martyr, 1643-1649. 3.1468
King Coffin. 2.11300
King cotton & his retainers. 4.3685
King Cotton diplomacy. 3.7380
King Edward the Seventh. 3.1679
King George VI, his life and reign. 3.1698
King George III. 3.1560
King George III and the politicians. 3.1558
King George the Fifth. 3.1684
King Harald's saga. 2.13988
King Henry III and the Lord Edward. 3.1360
The king in yellow. 2.10924
The king is dead. 3.3714
The King James Bible translators. 1.2495
King James VI and I. 3.1465
King John. 3.1351
King Lear. 2.6666
King Lear, the space of tragedy. 2.3029
King Leopold's Congo. 3.5424
King Leopold's legacy. 3.5425
King, lords, and peasants in medieval England. 4.6409
The king of Elfland's daughter. 2.8604
King of the mountain. 2.13037
King, Parliament, and public finance in medieval England to 1369. 4.4668
King Solomon's ring. 5.4062
King Vidor on film making. 2.3070
King William IV. 3.1607
Kingdom and community. 1.2301
The kingdom and the power. 2.3665

The kingdom in Mark. 1.2687
The kingdom of Canada. 3.8676
The kingdom of God and primitive Christianity. 1.2819
The kingdom of God in America. 1.2815
The kingdom of God in the teaching of Jesus. 1.2817
The Kingdom of Johor, 1641-1728. 3.4550
The Kingdom of Kongo. 3.5422
Kingdom of Laos. 3.4452
The kingdom of Naples under Alfonso the Magnanimous. 3.2941
The Kingdom of Quito in the seventeenth century. 3.9314
Kingdom of the seashell. 5.3845
Kingdoms of Elfin. 2.9469
Kingdoms of the savanna. 3.5223
Kingdoms of the Sudan. 3.5168
Kings and kinsmen. 3.5404
Kings and Vikings. 3.3365
The King's Arcadia 1.5389
The king's coffer. 4.4673
Kings of the Bs. 2.2920
Kings or people. 4.7550
The King's Parliament of England. 4.8458
The King's peace, 1637-1641. 3.1478
Kings, rulers, and statesmen. 3.563
The king's State. 4.8578
The king's trial. 3.2051
The King's two bodies. 4.7553
The King's war, 1641-1647. 3.1479
Kingship and community in early India. 3.4194
Kingship and law in the middle ages: I. The divine right of kings and the right of resistance in the early middle ages. 4.7555
Kingship and the gods. 1.1608
Kingship and unity. 3.1788
Kingship of God. 1.2814
Kingsley Amis. 2.8385
Kingzett's chemical encyclopaedia. 5.2593
Kino, a history of the Russian and Soviet film. 2.2905
Kinship & community in two Chinese villages. 4.5420
Kinship and marriage. 4.578
Kinship and marriage among the Nuer. 4.575
Kinship and urbanization. 4.5629
Kinship ideology and practice in Latin America. 4.5610
Kinship in an urban setting. 4.5607
Kinship in Bengali culture. 4.631
Kipling. 2.7889
Kipling and the critics. 2.7893
Kipling, Auden & Co. 2.11925
Kipling's mind and art, selected critical essays. 2.7898
Kipps. 2.8249
Kira Georgievna. 2.1588
Kirk-Othmer encyclopedia of chemical technology. 5.6809
Kiss of the spider woman. 2.5401
The kiss of the unborn, and other stories. 2.1529
Kissinger. 3.7860
The Kissinger study of Southern Africa. 4.9057
Kister's Atlas buying guide. 5.8211
The Kit Carson campaign. 3.5777
Kitāb al-Luma'. 1.2044
Kitab-i Dede Korkut. English. 2.1984
Kitchener. 3.8831
Kitchener: portrait of an imperialist. 3.1267
Kith. 2.9138
Kitty Foyle. 2.12206
Kleiner Mann, was nun? 2.13728
Klingsor's last summer. 2.13773
The Klondike fever. 3.8650
The Knapp Commission report on police corruption. 4.6835
The knight, the lady, and the priest. 4.5622
Knights. 2.427
Knight's gambit. 2.11666
Knight's Modern seamanship. 5.7490
Knock on any door. 2.13186
Knocking on the door. 2.10088
Knoll design. 1.6559
Knots and links. 5.1612

The knower and the known. 1.1280
Knowing one's enemies. 5.7360
Knowing right from wrong. 4.9428
Knowing the score. 1.4232
Knowledge and explanation in history. 3.457
Knowledge and human interests. 1.1287
Knowledge and ignorance in economics. 4.1277
Knowledge & politics. 4.5034
Knowledge and wonder, the natural world as man knows it. 5.840
Knowledge, its creation, distribution, and economic significance. 1.80
The knowledge machine. 5.1013
Knowledge of the evening. 2.12247
Knowledge of the higher worlds and its attainment. 1.2098
The known and the unknown. 2.10574
The Knox brothers. 1.3268
Knut Hamsun. 2.14049
Ko, or, A season on earth. 2.11966
Kobbé's complete opera book. 1.4509
The Kodály context. 1.4410
Kodansha encyclopedia of Japan. 3.4871
Kohler's Dictionary for accountants. 4.4391
Kojiki. 3.4929
Kojiki. English. 3.4929
Kokin wakashū. English. 2.2022
Kokinshū. 2.2022
Kokoro. 2.2083
Kokutai no hongi. 3.4883
Kolyma Tales. 2.1631
Komödien. 2.13731
Konfrontasi. 3.4566
Konjaku monogatari. English. Selections. 2.2042
Konjaku monogatari-shū. 2.2043
Konoe Fumimaro. 3.4968
Konrad Adenauer, 1876-1967. 3.2473
Konrad Lorenz. 5.99
Konrad Wallenrod and other writings of Adam Mickiewicz. 2.1714
Konstantin Batyushkov. 2.1337
Konstantin Leontev, 1831-1891. 1.1116
Koran. 1.2033
Koran. English. 1.2027
The Koran interpreted. 1.2027
Korea. 3.5036, 3.4990, 4.2561
Korea: a history. 3.4994
Korea; democracy on trial. 3.5010
Korea, the politics of the vortex. 3.5000
Korea, the untold story of the war. 3.5018
Korea today. 3.5006
Korea under new leadership. 3.5037
Korean-American relations; documents pertaining to the Far Eastern diplomacy of the United States. 3.5001
The Korean Communist movement, 1918-1948. 4.7126
Korean community in New York. 3.8054
The Korean decision, June 24-30, 1950. 3.5030
Korean development. 4.2559
The Korean diaspora. 3.6580
The Korean minority in Japan 3.4914
Korean politics in transition. 3.5009
Korean reunification. 3.5012
The Korean War. 3.5028
The Korean war: How we met the challenge: How all-out Asian war was averted: Why MacArthur was dismissed: Why today's war objectives must be limited. 3.5021
Korea's heritage. 3.4991
Korea's response to the West. 3.4993
Korea's Syngman Rhee. 3.5007
Kostis Palamas. 2.606
Kōtoku Shūsui, portrait of a Japanese radical. 3.4961
Kouroi: archaic Greek youths. 1.5636
Kraka, The lay of. 2.13991
Krakatau, 1883 5.3112
Krakatit. English. 2.1662
Krákumál. 2.13991
Krapp's last tape, and other dramatic pieces. 2.8422
The Kremlin and the Prague spring. 3.1928
The Kremlin and world politics. 3.3255
The Kremlin since Stalin. 3.3253

Krieghoff. 1.5999
Krishna, myths, rites, and attitudes. 1.1715
Krishna, the divine lover. 1.6744
Kristin Lavransdatter: The bridal wreath, The mistress of Husaby, The cross. 2.14053
Kritisches Lexikon zur deutschsprachigen Gegenwartsliteratur. 2.13449
Krylov's fables. 2.1394
The Ku Klux Klan. 5.7840
Kuan wu liang shou ching. 1965. 1.1737
K'uei hsing. 2.1759
Kuleshov on film. 2.2940
The !Kung of Nyae Nyae. 3.5434
The !Kung San. 3.5485
Kunstgeschichtliche Grundbegriffe. English. 1.4678
Kurt Schwitters. 1.4999
Kurt Vonnegut. 2.13400
Kurt Vonnegut, Jr. 2.13402
Kurt Weill, an illustrated biography. 1.4060
Kurt Weill in Europe. 1.4061
Kuruntokai. English. Selections. 2.2280
Kurusu. 4.5455
Kuwait, social change in historical perspective. 4.5407
Kwaio religion. 1.1881
Kwakiutl art. 3.5902
Kwakiutl ethnography. 3.5901

L. Annaei Senecae Dialogorum libri duodecim. 2.770
L.I.S.P. 5.1218
L. J. M. Daguerre. 5.6928
L. P. Hartley. 2.8798
Là-bas. 2.4247
La Follette and the rise of the Progressives in Wisconsin. 3.7440
La Follette's autobiography. 3.7439
La Guardia, a fighter against his times. 3.7659
La Guardia in Congress. 3.7661
La Rochefoucauld: his mind and art. 2.4035
La Verendrye, fur trader and explorer. 3.8843
Labanotation. 1.1084
Laban's principles of dance and movement notation. 4.1085
Labeling deviant behavior. 4.5073
Labeling women deviant. 4.5940
The labelling of deviance. 4.5080
Labor and immigration in industrial America. 4.3606
Labor and management. 4.3569
Labor and monopoly capital. 4.2678
Labor and the American community. 4.3346
Labor and the environment. 5.8167
Labor and the law. 4.9552
Labor and the left. 4.3358
Labor and the legal process. 4.9557
Labor and the New Deal. 4.3351
Labor and trade unionism. 4.3329
The labor arbitration process. 4.9559
Labor baron: a portrait of John L. Lewis. 4.3588
Labor commitment and social change in developing areas. 4.3112
Labor displacement and public policy. 4.3207
The labor force under changing income and employment. 4.3196
Labor in American politics. 4.3597
Labor in crisis. 4.3167
Labor in developing economies. 4.3098
Labor in the South. 4.3396
Labor in the twentieth century. 4.3100
Labor-managed firms. 4.3180
Labor-management contracts at work. 4.9556
Labor-management cooperation. 4.3582
Labor martyr: Joe Hill. 4.3587
The labor movement in the United States, 1860-1895. 4.3577
Labor of love, labor of sorrow. 4.3250
Labor organization. 4.9549
Labor relations in professional sports. 4.931
Labor-religion prophet. 4.5120
Labor supply. 4.3195
Labor union theories in America. 4.3361
Laboratory experiments in organic chemistry. 5.2727
Laboratory handbook of petrographic techniques. 5.3039

Laboratory handbook of toxic agents. 5.4722
Laboratory procedures in clinical microbiology. 5.4445
The laboratory school of the University of Chicago, 1896-1903. 4.11004
Laboratory techniques in electroanalytical chemistry. 5.2691
Laboratory tests. 5.4738
Laboring and dependent classes in colonial America, 1607-1783. 4.5239
Laboring classes and dangerous classes. 4.6792
Labor's grass roots. 4.3344
Labor's war at home. 4.3553
Labour and leisure in the Soviet Union. 4.3231
Labour and poverty in Kenya, 1900-1980. 4.3235
Labour and socialism. 4.3412
Labour at the crossroads. 4.8537
Labour disputes in Soviet Russia, 1957-1965. 4.3662
Labour Government, 1964-1970. 3.1718
The labour governments, 1945-51. 3.1708
Labour in power? 4.8546
Labour in power, 1945-1951. 3.1707
The Labour Party and the struggle for Socialism. 4.8547
The Labour Party Conference. 4.8539
The Labour Party in crisis. 4.8544
Labour policy in Canada 4.3625
Labouring life in the Victorian countryside. 4.2924
Labour's turning point, 1880-1900. 4.5302
The labyrinth. 2.10211
The Labyrinth of language. 1.537
The labyrinth of solitude: life and thought in Mexico. 3.8877
The labyrinthine ways of Graham Greene. 2.8777
Labyrinths of power. 4.5258
Lace. 1.6679
Lacrosse. 4.1035
The ladder of success in Imperial China. 4.5414
Der Laden. 2.13863
Laden choirs. 2.10192
Ladies of the leisure class. 4.6116
Lads, citizens, and ordinary kids. 4.5762
The lady & the Virgin. 4.5863
Lady and the Virgin. 4.5863
Lady Audley's secret. 2.7934
Lady Chatterley's lover. 2.8966
The lady from Dubuque. 2.12843
Lady Gregory. 2.7756-2.7757
Lady Gregory's Journals, 1916-1930. 2.7754
Lady into fox, and A man in the zoo. 2.8684
The lady laureates. 1.63
The lady of the vineyards. 2.621
Lady oracle. 2.9907
Lady Tennyson's journal. 2.8174
Lae, village and city. 3.5668
Lafayette in the age of the American Revolution. 3.6893
Lafayette in the French revolution. 3.2068
Lafcadio Hearn. 2.11078
Lafcadio's adventures. 2.4550
The Laird of Abbotsford. 2.8051
The lais of Marie de France. 2.3955
Laissez faire and the general-welfare state. 4.5128
The lake. 2.2100
The lake and the woods. 2.1523
Lakes 4.315
Lakota society. 3.5929
Lamartine. 2.4258
Lamb as critic. 2.7900
Lambert's Worldwide government directory, with inter-governmental organizations. 4.7708
Lamb's criticism. 2.5542
Lame Deer, seeker of visions. 3.5952
Lament for a maker. 2.9386
Lament for Agnes. 2.13958
Lament for the death of a bullfighter and other poems. 2.5250
The Lāmībe of Fombina. 3.5360
The lamp at noon. 2.9970
The lamp of beauty. 1.5136
Lancashire in decline. 4.3854

Lancastrian Normandy, 1415-1450. 3.1379
Lancelot. 2.13240
Lancelot, or, The knight of the cart. 2.3946
The land. 2.8523
Land above the trees. 5.3552
Land and class in Kenya. 4.2871
Land and labor in China. 4.2468
Land and labor in Europe in the twentieth century. 4.2846
Land and labour in India. 4.2987
Land and life. 4.373
Land and society in Golden Age Castile. 4.2858
The land before her. 3.6351
Land fever. 3.8448
Land hunger: David L. Payne and the Oklahoma boomers. 3.8535
The land is shrinking. 4.1702
Land, labor, and rural poverty. 4.2984
Land of savagery/land of promise. 3.8490
Land of the 500 million. 3.4621
Land of the Bible. 1.2549
Land of the living 2.9995
Land of the Tollund man; the prehistory and archaeology of Denmark. 3.3367
Land or death. 4.2843
Land policies of Upper Canada. 4.2834
The land question. 4.1433
The land question and European society since 1650. 4.5284
The land question in Palestine, 1917-1939. 4.2860
Land reform. 4.2814
Land reform in China and North Vietnam. 4.2878
The land systems of Mexico. 4.2837
Land-use and prehistory in south-east Spain. 4.738
Land utilization in China. 4.2863
Landed estates in the colonial Philippines. 4.2866
Landessprache. 2.13738
Landlocked. 2.9012
Landlords and farmers in the Hudson-Mohawk region, 1790-1850. 4.2820
Landmarks in American civil engineering. 5.5661
Landmarks in French literature. 2.3831
Landmarks of modern British drama. 2.6246
Landmarks of the American Revolution. 3.5995
Landon of Kansas 3.8527
Landowners in colonial Peru. 4.2844
Landowska on music. 1.4067
The lands between. 3.3519
The lands of partitioned Poland, 1795-1918. 3.3282
The lands of St. Peter. 3.2933
The lands of the Eastern Caliphate: Mesopotamia, Persia, and Central Asia from the Moslem conquest to the time of Timur. 3.3683
Landsat data users handbook. 5.6711
The Landsat tutorial workbook. 4.26
The landscape and the looking glass. 2.11477
Landscape as photograph. 5.6979
Landscape drawings. 1.5825
Landscape ecology. 5.3223, 5.3517
Landscape into art. 1.6356
Landscape of death. 2.622
The landscape of Thomas Hardy. 2.7800
The landscape paintings of Thomas Gainsborough. 1.6032
Landscape plants for eastern North America. 5.5361
Landscape turned red. 3.7366
Landscapes and portraits, appreciations of Japanese culture. 2.2005
The landscapes of Frederic Edwin Church. 1.5928
Landscapes of learning. 4.10178
Landslides and related phenomena. 5.3122
Un Langage-univers. Jacques Bens. 2.4771
Langdon Cheves of South Carolina. 3.7102
Langenscheidt's new Muret-Sanders encyclopedic dictionary of the English and German languages. 2.1190
Lange's Handbook of chemistry. 5.2650

Langsame Heimkehr. 2.13891
Langston Hughes. 2.11901, 2.11903
Langston Hughes, before and beyond Harlem. 2.11902
Langston Hughes in the Hispanic world and Haiti. 2.11889
The Langston Hughes reader. 2.11887
Language. 2.34, 2.94, 2.131
Language acquisition. 2.120
Language and art in the Navajo universe. 3.5925
The language and background of Homer. 2.513
Language and cinema. 2.2961
Language and cognition. 5.273
Language and deafness. 4.6605
Language & deafness. 4.6605
Language and dialect in Hawaii. 2.215
The language and imagery of the Bible. 1.2536
Language and insight. 5.4919
Language and its structure. 2.136
Language and languages. 2.144
Language and literacy. 5.396
Language and mind. 2.102
Language and myth. 2.88
Language and perception. 5.386
Language and philosophy. 1.538
Language and poetry. 2.5116
Language and reality. 2.96
Language and silence. 2.2594
Language and social identity. 2.23
Language and style in Leaves of grass. 2.11282
Language and the poet. 2.10488
Language and the world. 2.111
Language and thinking in school. 4.10480
The language and thought of the child. 4.10397
Language as gesture. 2.2738
Language as social semiotic. 2.21
Language as symbolic action. 2.2566
Language change and linguistic reconstruction. 2.150
Language crafted. 2.2427
Language development. 2.121, 2.123
Language development and language disorders. 4.10391
Language development from birth to three. 2.115
The language-experience approach to the teaching of reading. 4.10466
Language, gender, and society. 2.128
Language in America. 2.1125
Language in culture. 2.92
Language in relation to a unified theory of the structure of human behavior. 2.162
Language in the British Isles. 2.212
Language in the inner city. 2.1154
Language in the USA. 2.209
Language in thought and action. 2.1066
Language intervention with children. 4.10905
Language, its nature, development and origin. 2.93
The language lottery. 2.122
A language not to be betrayed. 2.9424
The language of 1984. 2.9190
The language of allegory. 2.5579
The language of American popular entertainment. 2.2776
The language of Canaan. 2.10439
The language of dance. 4.1099
The language of ethnic conflict. 2.1145
The Language of images. 1.6680
The language of morals. 1.1462
The language of oppression. 4.7674
The language of poetry. 2.2741
Language of politics. 4.7242
The language of post-modern architecture. 1.5271
The language of Renaissance poetry. 2.5776
The language of Shakespeare's plays. 2.6844
The language of social research. 4.1208
The language of the classical French organ. 1.4145
The language of the Gospel. 1.2644
The language of the night. 2.3459
Language reform in China. 2.2146
Language, religion and politics in North India. 4.8705

Language shift. 2.114
Language skills in elementary education.
   4.10471
Language structure and language use. 2.4
Language structure and translation. 2.8
Language, the loaded weapon. 2.101
Language, thought and culture. 2.32
Language, thought, and reality. 2.10
Language, truth and logic. 1.105
Language understanding. 2.160
Languages and literatures of modern India.
   2.1853
Languages and their status. 2.109
Languages in contact. 2.167
The languages of Africa. 2.2294
Languages of art. 1.1402
The languages of Britain. 2.214
The languages of Italy. 2.851
Languages of the British Isles past and present.
   2.213
Languages of the U.S.S.R. 2.217
The Lankavatara sutra: a Mahayana text.
   1.2128
Lao Tzu. 1.1803
Laocoön. 1.4593
Laos: buffer state or battleground. 3.4457
Laos; its people, its society, its culture. 3.4454
Laos: war and revolution. 3.4456
The Lapps. 3.3396
The Lapps. 3.3397
The lapsed. 1.2191
The Lardners. 2.13128
The large family system. 4.5635
The large international firm in developing
   countries. 4.3764
Large scale computer architecture. 5.1154
The large sutra on perfect wisdom, with the
   divisions of the Abhisamayālaṅkāra. 1.2131
The larger hope. 1.3421
The lark. 2.4354
Lark Rise to Candleford. 3.1739
Larousse encyclopedia of mythology. 1.1605
Larousse gastronomique. 5.7105
Larry McMurtry. 2.13148
Lars Gyllensten. 2.14085
Lascaux. 1.4685
Laser applications. 5.5944
Laser electronics. 5.5949
Laser-induced chemical processes. 5.2642
Laser physics. 5.2299
Laser safety handbook. 5.5951
Laser spectroscopy. 5.2315
Laser, supertool of the 1980s. 5.5948
Lasers. 5.6487
Lasers and light. 5.2271
Lasers and their applications. 5.5945
Lasers, the light fantastic. 5.5946
Last 100 years, household technology. 5.7102
The last actor-managers. 2.3335
The last Adam. 2.11517
The last alternatives. 2.12576
Last among equals. 3.5645
Last and first men, & Star maker. 2.9379
The last and greatest art. 2.7189
The last attachment. 2.7530
The last best West. 4.6081
The last cannon shot. 3.8685
The last caravan. 3.5219
The last centuries of Byzantium, 1261-1453.
   3.2676
The last chronicle of Barset. 2.8213
The last Confucian. 1.1139
The last days of Hitler. 3.2407
The last days of Pompeii. 2.7914
The last days of united Pakistan. 3.4127
Last diaries. 2.1431
The Last Empire. 3.4278
Last essays. 2.13471
Last exit to Brooklyn. 2.13313
The last exodus. 3.4000
The last feast of the Fianna. 2.9089
The last foray in Lithuania. 2.1716
The last frontier. 4.5797
The last gentleman. 2.13241
The last half-century. 4.5133
The last hundred years, household technology.
   5.7102
The last hurrah. 2.13206

Last lectures. 1.5128
The last letter home. 2.14097
The last lion, Winston Spencer Churchill.
   3.1657
The last little citadel. 4.10053
The last lords of Palenque. 3.8908
The last Mycenaeans and their successors.
   3.2582
The last of Chéri. 2.4491
The last of Mr. Norris. 2.8833
The last of the big-time bosses. 4.8213
The last of the just. 2.4745
The last of the lairds. 2.7716
The last of the provincials. 2.10620
The last of the Southern girls. 2.13182
The last of the wine. 2.9267
The last post. 2.8632
The last Puritan. 2.11219
The last Puritan? 3.7686
The last rising. 4.3175
Last seen wearing ... 2.13414
The last September. 2.8475
The last stand of Chinese conservatism; the
   T'ung-chih restoration, 1862-1874. 3.4740
The last temptation of Christ. 2.596
The last trolley ride. 2.12946
Last tsar. 3.3167
The last two years of Salvador Allende. 3.9267
Late antique and early Christian book
   illumination. 1.6401
Late antique, early Christian and mediaeval art.
   1.5171
The late Augustans. 2.6168
Late Baroque and Rococo architecture. 1.5248
Late George Apley. 2.12108
Late harvest. 2.10272
The late John Marquand. 2.12113
Late Latin writers and their Greek sources.
   2.284
The late Lord Byron. 2.7529
Late-medieval England, 1377-1485. 5.7986
Late medieval mysticism. 1.3079
The late Middle Ages. 1.4756, 1.5173
Late-Quaternary environments of the United
   States. 5.3145
Late Saxon and Viking art. 1.4936
Late Tudor and early Stuart geography,
   1583-1650. 4.66
Late Victorian plays, 1890-1914. 2.6242
The later career of Tobias Smollett. 2.7266
The later D.H. Lawrence. 2.8961
Later English Romanesque sculpture,
   1140-1210. 1.5685
The later Ghaznavids. 3.4115
The later Heidegger and theology. 1.1005
Later Islamic pottery: Persia, Syria, Egypt,
   Turkey. 1.6612
Later medieval English prose. 2.6078
Later medieval France: the polity. 4.5348
Later Mughals. 3.4258
The later paintings and drawings of John
   Constable. 1.4951
The later Parliaments of Henry VIII,
   1536-1547. 4.8460
The later Plantagenets. 3.1357
Later poems of Rabindranath Tagore. 2.1868
The later Roman Empire, 284-602. 3.2805
The later Stuarts, 1660-1714. 3.1493
Later works. 1.2202
The later works, 1925-1953. 1.584
The latest avant-garde. 1.6288
Latin. 2.251
Latin America. 3.8962, 3.9170, 5.8402
Latin America: a cultural history. 3.8965
Latin America, a guide to illustrations. 3.8964
Latin America, a guide to the historical
   literature. 5.7906
Latin America; an economic and social
   geography. 4.2137
Latin America and Caribbean contemporary
   record. 3.8957
Latin America and the enlightenment. 3.8969
Latin America and the Second World War.
   3.946
Latin America and the United States. 3.9018
Latin America and world economy. 4.4179
Latin America, countrysides and united regions.
   3.8973

Latin America: geographical perspectives.
   4.2135
Latin America in English-language reference
   books. 5.7905
Latin America in its literature. 2.5298
Latin America in the international political
   system. 4.9017
Latin American architecture since 1945.
   1.5279
Latin-American civilization, colonial period.
   3.8978
Latin American experiments in neoconservative
   economics. 4.2162
Latin American foreign policies. 3.9008
Latin American literature in English
   translation. 5.7911
Latin American literature in the 20th century.
   2.5304
Latin American media. 2.69
The Latin-American mind. 1.660
Latin American poetry. 2.5317
The Latin American policy of the United
   States. 3.9012
Latin-American political thought and ideology.
   4.7297
Latin American politics. 4.8328
The Latin American revolution. 3.9004
The Latin American short story. 2.5318
Latin American social thought. 4.4770
Latin American thought. 1.658
Latin American urbanization. 5.8403
Latin American women. 4.6082
A Latin dictionary founded on Andrews'
   edition of Freund's Latin dictionary. 2.258
Latin elegiac verse. 2.257
The Latin language 2.252
Latin literature. 2.624, 2.627
Latin literature of the fourth century. 2.634
The Latin love elegy. 2.640
The Latin love poets. 2.631
Latin metre, an introduction. 2.256
Latin squares and their applications. 5.1282
The Latin tinge. 1.4253
Latrobe's view of America, 1795-1820. 1.6380
Lattice theory. 5.1309-5.1310
Laughable loves. 2.1688
Laughing Boy. 2.11976
The laughing Savior. 1.2965
Laughing to keep from crying. 2.11893
The laughing tradition. 2.5911
Laughter, an essay on the meaning of the
   comic. 2.3786
Laughter in the dark. 2.1580
Laughter in the next room. 2.9335
Laughter in the wilderness. 2.10706
Laurel & thorn. 2.10429
Laurel and thorn. 2.10429
The laurels and limitations of historical fiction.
   2.3466
Laurence Sterne. 2.7278
Laurence Sterne, the early & middle years.
   2.7281
Laurier. 3.8754
Laurier, a study in Canadian politics. 3.8753
Lautréamont. 2.4171
Law and authority in early Massachusetts.
   4.9899
Law and business of the sports industries.
   4.9578
Law and constitution. 4.7555
The law and custom of the constitution.
   4.9401
Law and economic organization. 4.9356
Law and economic policy in America. 4.9526
Law & force in American foreign policy.
   4.9050
Law and force in American foreign policy.
   4.9050
Law and legal information directory. 4.9445
Law and letters in American culture. 2.10389
Law and minimum world public order. 4.9325
Law and obedience. 1.245
Law and opinion in England in the 20th
   century. 4.5319
Law and peace in international relations.
   4.9295
Law and politics. 4.8065

The law and politics of police discretion. 4.9751
The law and practice of the International Court. 4.9153
Law and public order in space. 4.9336
Law and revolution. 4.9349
Law and society in Puritan Massachusetts. 4.9902
Law and society in the relations of states. 4.9278
Law and society in traditional China. 4.9921
Law and the modern mind. 4.9371
Law and warfare. 4.9351
Law books for non-law libraries and laymen. 4.9436
Law, bureaucracy, and politics. 4.9688
Law dictionary. 4.9443
Law enforcement in colonial New York. 4.9905
The law in America. 4.9485
Law in American history. 4.9480
The law in classical Athens. 4.9397
Law in culture and society. 4.9355
Law in diplomacy. 4.9003
Law in economy and society. 4.9344
Law in society. 5.7597
Law in the Middle East 1.2041
Law, legislation, and liberty. 4.7666
Law, morality, and the relations of states. 4.8993
Law, morality, and war in the contemporary world. 4.9318
The law of civilization and decay. 3.504
The law of criminal correction. 4.9859
The law of higher education. 4.9603
The law of nations. 4.9285
The law of primitive man. 4.9353
The law of the Commonwealth and Chief Justice Shaw. 4.9488
The law of the sea. 4.9309
The Law of the sea. 4.9316
The law of the Soviet State. 4.8643
The law of the United Nations. 4.9219
The law of torts. 4.9515
Law of torts. 4.9516
The law of treaties. 4.9312
The Law of war. 4.9324
Law without precedent. 4.9929
Lawd today. 2.12809
The lawful revolution. 3.1941
The lawmakers. 4.8114
Lawrence Durrell [and] Henry Miller. 2.8611
Lawrence Durrell, and the Alexandria quartet. 2.8607
Laws and explanation in history. 3.507
Laws, modalities, and counterfactuals. 1.1246
The laws of Manu. 1.1685
The laws of Plato. 4.7343
Laws of the game. 5.880
Lawsuits and litigants in Castile, 1500-1700. 3.3434
A lawyer looks at the Equal rights amendment. 4.9695
Lawyers and judges. 4.8066
Lawyers before the Warren Court. 4.9476
Lawyers in early modern Europe and America. 4.9348
Lay bare the heart. 3.6832
Lay Buddhism in contemporary Japan. 1.2167
Lay culture, learned culture. 3.2239
Lay my burden down. 3.7210
The lay of the land. 2.10250
Lay people in the church. 1.3212
The layman's parallel Bible. 1.2491
A layman's view of history. 3.498
The lays of ancient Rome. 2.7920
Lazarillo de Tormes. 2.5194
Lazarillo de Tormes. English. 2.5193
Lazarus. 2.4621
The lazy South. 3.8116
The leader. 4.2687
Leadership. 4.4945
Leadership and ambiguity. 4.10589
Leadership in 19th century Africa. 3.5082
Leadership in administration. 4.2658
Leadership in Communist China. 4.8746
Leadership in organizations. 4.4956

Leading issues in economic development. 4.2795
The League committees and world order. 4.9184
The League for Social Reconstruction. 4.7007
The League of Nations. 4.9185
The League of Nations and the rule of law, 1918-1935. 4.9192
The League of nations and world order. 4.9189
League of the Ho-dé-no-sau-nee or Iroquois. 3.5897
The lean years. 4.3565
Leaping poetry. 2.3736
Lear. 2.9623
A Lear of the steppes. 2.1453
Learned Hand's Court. 4.9848
Learning. 4.10354
Learning about India. 5.8055
Learning and change in groups. 4.4937
Learning and cognition in the mentally retarded. 5.4970
Learning and memory. 5.333
Learning disabilities. 4.10952, 4.10954-4.10955
Learning-disabled/gifted children. 4.10915
Learning from clients. 4.6544
Learning from our mistakes. 4.9968
Learning how to behave. 3.6007
Learning how to mean. 2.119
Learning lessons. 4.10275
Learning sequences in music. 1.4411
The learning society. 4.9966
Learning the library. 5.7648
Learning theory and behavior. 4.10356
Learning theory and the symbolic processes. 4.10357
Learning to heal. 5.4604
Learning to read. 4.10341, 4.10345, 4.10458
Learning to rock climb. 4.897
The Learning traveler. Vol.2, Vacation study abroad. 4.10621
The Learning traveler. Vol. 1, Academic year abroad. 4.10622
Leave it to Psmith 2.9554
Leaven of malice. 2.9923
Leaves from the notebook of a tamed cynic. 1.3292
Leaves of grass: authoritative texts, prefaces, Whitman on his art, criticism. 2.11267
Leaving college. 4.10750
Lebanon in history: from the earliest times to the present. 3.3785
Lebesgue integration and measure. 5.1460
The lecherous professor. 4.10841
Lecture notes on elementary topology and geometry. 5.1600
Lectures and orations. 1.3335
Lectures in China, 1919-1920. 1.116
Lectures in projective geometry. 5.1569
Lectures on algebraic topology. 5.1588
Lectures on art. 1.4616
Lectures on differential geometry. 5.1630
Lectures on early Welsh poetry. 2.835
Lectures on economic principles. 4.1264
Lectures on elementary number theory. 5.1331
Lectures on European history, 1789-1914. 3.655
Lectures on modern history. 3.610
Lectures on modern idealism. 1.877
Lectures on nuclear theory. 5.2069
Lectures on ordinary differential equations. 5.1513, 5.1516
Lectures on philosophical theology. 1.897
Lectures on philosophy. 1.858
Lectures on physics. 5.1991
Lectures on political economy. 4.1477
Lectures on psychical research. 5.638
Lectures on revivals of religion. 1.3032
Lectures on rhetoric and belles lettres. 2.1035
Lectures on Romans. 1.2709
Lectures on the English comic writers. 2.5538
Lectures on the English poets. 2.5766
Lectures on the fine arts. 1.715
Lectures on the philosophy of religion, together with a work on the proofs of the existence of God. 1.1546
Lectures on the principles of political obligation. 4.7632

Lectures on the relation between law & public opinion in England, during the nineteenth century. 4.7724
Lectures on the theory of functions of a complex variable. 5.1488
Lectures on the whole of anatomy. 5.4139
Lectures on theoretical physics. 5.1970
Lee Krasner. 1.5950
Lee's lieutenants. 3.7363
The Left Bank. 3.2233
The Left Bank revisited. 3.2228
The left hand of darkness. 2.13131
Left hand, right hand! 2.9332
Left Handed, a Navajo autobiography. 3.5920
The left-handed woman. 2.13893
Left of center. 4.3402
The leg. 2.13960
The legacy of Egypt. 3.5138
The Legacy of Greece. 3.82
The legacy of Hegel. 1.949
The legacy of Hiroshima. 5.7386
The legacy of Islam. 3.3653
The Legacy of logical positivism. 1.513
The legacy of Malthus. 4.6452
The legacy of Persia. 3.4069
The legacy of Rosa Luxemburg. 4.7060
The legacy of Sacco and Vanzetti. 4.9855
Legacy of suppression. 4.7676
Legal and ethical issues in human research and treatment: psychopharmacologic considerations. 5.4876
Legal and political issues in special education. 4.9601
Legal aspects of geology. 4.9528
Legal controls of international conflict. 4.9327
Legal effects of United Nations resolutions. 4.9209
Legal ethics. 4.9477
Legal fictions. 4.9367
Legal foundations of capitalism. 4.1499
Legal research in a nutshell. 4.9470
Legalizing the Holocaust. 3.1096
Legalizing the Holocaust, the later phase, 1939-1943. 3.1097
The legend of Brynhild. 2.2689
The legend of John Brown. 3.7272
The legend of Sparta in classical antiquity. 3.2650
The legend of St. Julian Hospitator. 2.4194
The legend of the Founding Fathers. 3.6208
The légendary history of Britain. 3.1303
La légende de Saint Julien l'Hospitalier. 2.4193
La legende et les aventures héroïques, joyeuses et glorieuses d'Ulenspiegel et de Lamme Goedzak au pays de Flandres et ailleurs. 2.4157
Legende vom Glück ohne Ende. 2.13908
Légendes et poèmes. 2.4852
Legends of the Hasidim. 1.1923
The legends of the Jews 1.1952
The legends of the saints. 1.3250
Legged robots that balance. 5.6169
Legislative and political development. 4.8776
Legislative issues in the fifty States. 4.8257
The Legislative process in Canada. 4.8291
The legislative process in Congress. 4.8011
Legislative reference checklist. 4.9439
The legislative struggle. 4.8032
Legitimation crisis. 4.1763
Legitimation of social rights and the western welfare state. 4.5098
Leibniz. 1.866-1.867, 1.869, 1.873
Leibniz: logic and metaphysics. 1.870
Leibniz's philosophy of logic and language. 1.874
Leigh Hunt, a biography. 2.7846
Leigh Hunt and his circle. 2.7846
Leisure and class in Victorian England. 4.884
Leisure and the changing city, 1870-1914. 4.5324
Leisure leadership. 4.887
Leisure resources, its comprehensive planning. 4.890
Lélia, the life of George Sand. 2.4293
Lend-lease, loans, and the coming of the Cold War. 3.942
The length and depth of acting. 2.3116
Lenin. 3.3147, 3.3149-3.3150

Lenin and his rivals. 3.3170
Lenin and philosophy, and other essays. 1.1115
Lenin and the end of politics. 4.7100
Lenin lives! 3.3152
Leninism. 4.6968
Leninism. 4.7102
Leninism or Marxism? 3.3186
Leninism. 3.3148
Lens design fundamentals. 5.2293
Lens mechanism technology. 5.6945
Leo Rosten's treasury of Jewish quotations. 2.3735
Leo Tolstoy. 2.1435
Léon Blum. 3.2202-3.2203
Léon Blum, humanist in politics. 3.2201
Leon Trotsky. 4.7090
Leonard Cohen. 2.9920
Leonard Maltin's TV movies and video guide. 2.3077
Leonard Wood. 3.6374
Leonardo da Vinci. 1.5841, 1.6214
Leonardo the inventor. 5.5547
Leonardo the scientist. 5.823
The leopard. 2.5072
A Leopardi reader. 2.4999
Leopold II of the Belgians. 3.2974
Leopold III and the Belgian royal question. 3.2976
Leopold Ranke, the formative years. 3.423
Léopold Sédar Senghor. 2.4864
Leopold's way. 2.13088
Leoš Janáček, Káta Kabanová. 1.3906
Les Brown's Encyclopedia of television. 2.2848
Lesbian studies. 4.5522
Leslie Stephen. 2.8116
The less deceived. 2.8943
The less developed realm: a geography of its population. 4.1625
Less than angels. 2.9801
Lessing: Sein und Leistung. 2.13634
Lessing, the founder of modern German literature. 2.13633
The lesson. 2.4579
A lesson from Aloes. 2.10066
The lessons of wage and price controls, the food sector. 4.3678
Lester Frank Ward. 4.4779
Lester Horton, modern dance pioneer. 4.1145
Lester Pearson and the dream of unity. 3.8788
Let freedom come. 3.5085
Let history judge: the origins and consequences of Stalinism. 3.3219
Let it come down. 2.12913
Let me speak! 4.6087
Let my people go. 3.5472
Let no man write my epitaph. 2.13187
Let the trumpet sound. 3.6841
Let us now praise famous men. 3.8278
A letter concerning toleration. 4.7412
Letter from Peking. 2.11430
Letter to Pilgrims. 1.2722
Letteratura dell'Italia unita, 1861-1968. 2.4887
The letterbook of Eliza Lucas Pinckney, 1739-1762. 3.8241
Lettering as drawing. 1.6600
Lettering; modes of writing in western Europe from antiquity to the end of the 18th century. 1.6598
Letters. 1.3925, 1.3967, 1.6273, 2.1415, 2.6975, 2.7390, 2.8017, 2.8098, 2.8137, 2.8272, 2.8341, 2.8900, 2.9044, 2.11115, 2.11200, 2.12123, 2.12161, 2.12543, 2.12786, 2.12879, 3.7150, 3.7707
Letters, 1848-1888. 2.7353
Letters, 1907-1941. 2.12336
Letters and documents. 1.1121
Letters and documents. 2.7318
Letters and journals. 2.10973
Letters, and Panegyricus. 2.685
Letters and papers from prison. 1.3287
Letters and papers of Alfred Thayer Mahan. 3.6377
Letters and people of the Spanish Indies, sixteenth century. 3.8996
The letters and private papers of William Makepeace Thackeray. 2.8186

The letters and prose writings of William Cowper. 2.6960
The letters and writing of George Frideric Handel. 1.3882
Letters from AE. 2.9292
Letters from Africa, 1914-1931. 2.14020
Letters from America (Radio program) 3.6055
Letters from an American farmer. 3.6023
Letters from an American farmer; and, Sketches of eighteenth-century America. 3.6026
Letters from Iceland. 2.8397
Letters from Jack London. 2.12029
Letters from Jenny. 5.117
Letters from Joseph Conrad, 1895-1924. 2.8549
Letters from Mesopotamia: official business, and private letters on clay tablets from two millennia. 3.3771
Letters from my mill. 2.4161
Letters from New England. 3.7975
Letters from Ring. 2.11983
Letters from the front, 1915-1917. 2.9091
Letters from the Sandwich Islands. 3.5637
Letters from Vatican City. 1.3127
Letters from Venice, 1851-1852. 2.8031
Letters home. 2.13261
Letters of a Javanese princess. 3.4579
Letters of Aldous Huxley. 2.8823
The letters of Alfred Lord Tennyson. 2.8167
Letters of Anthony Trollope. 2.8229
Letters of Anton Chekhov. 2.1487
The letters of Arthur Henry Hallam. 2.7759
The letters of Beethoven. 1.3794
The letters of Carl Sandburg. 2.12432
The letters of Charles Dickens. 2.7635
The letters of Charles Lamb. 2.7902
Letters of composers through six centuries. 1.3498
Letters of E. B. White. 2.12706
The letters of Emily Dickinson. 2.10995
The letters of Emily Lady Tennyson. 2.8166
The letters of Evelyn Waugh. 2.9501
The letters of F. Scott Fitzgerald 2.11724
Letters of Francis Parkman. 3.6256
Letters of Fyodor Michailovitch Dostoevsky to his family and friends. 2.1363
Letters of George Gissing to Eduard Bertiz. 2.7742
Letters of George Gissing to members of his family. 2.7741
The letters of George Meredith. 2.7940
The letters of Gerard Manley Hopkins to Robert Bridges. 2.7827
Letters of Giacomo Puccini, mainly connected with the composition and production of his operas. 1.3949
Letters of Gorky and Andreev, 1899-1912. 2.1508
Letters of Grover Cleveland, 1850-1908. 3.7491
The letters of Gustave Flaubert, 1830-1857. 2.4196
Letters of Hart Crane and his family. 2.11525
Letters of Henry Adams ... 3.6236
The letters of Herman Melville. 2.11159
The letters of Hugh MacDiarmid. 2.8783
Letters of James Agee to Father Flye 2.11296
Letters of James Boswell. 2.6903
The letters of James Branch Cabell. 2.11447
Letters of James Gillespie Birney, 1831-1857. 3.7232
The letters of Jean Rhys. 2.9277
The letters of John Clare. 2.7570
The letters of John Dryden. 2.6994
The letters of John Gay. 2.7037
The letters of John Greenleaf Whittier. 2.11285
The letters of John Keats, 1814-1821. 2.7853
The letters of John Wilmot, Earl of Rochester. 2.7228
The letters of Joseph Addison. 2.6888
Letters of Joseph Conrad to Marguerite Poradowska, 1890-1920. 2.8553
The letters of Katherine Mansfield. 2.9081
Letters of King James VI & I. 3.1464
Letters of Laurence Sterne. 2.7280
Letters of Louis D. Brandeis. 3.7424

Letters of Madame de Sévigné to her daughter and her friends. 2.4057
The letters of Macaulay. 3.1211
The letters of Margaret Fuller. 2.11190
The letters of Mary W. Shelley. 2.8094
The letters of Mozart and his family. 1.3934
Letters of Nikolai Gogol. 2.1383
The letters of Philip Dormer Stanhope, 4th Earl of Chesterfield. 3.1548
The letters of Ralph Waldo Emerson ... 2.11020
The Letters of Richard Brinsley Sheridan. 2.7247
The letters of Robert Burns. 2.7502
The letters of Robert Louis Stevenson. 2.8122
The letters of Rupert Brooke. 2.8486
The letters of Sacco and Vanzetti. 4.6704
The letters of Samuel Johnson. 2.7082
Letters of Sherwood Anderson. 2.11327
Letters of Sir George Etherege. 2.7011
The letters of Sir Walter Scott. 2.8053
The letters of St. Bernard of Clairvaux. 1.3257
The letters of the Brontës. 2.7448
Letters of the Lewis and Clark Expedition. 3.8484
The letters of Thomas Babington Macaulay. 3.1211
Letters of Thomas Hood, from the Dilke papers in the British Museum. 2.7819
The letters of Tobias Smollett. 2.7263
The letters of Virginia Woolf. 2.9586
The letters of Vita Sackville-West to Virginia Woolf. 2.9296
Letters of Walter Pater. 2.7981
The letters of William Cullen Bryant. 2.10916
Letters of William Gilmore Simms. 2.11224
The letters of William James. 1.599
The letters of William Morris to his family and friends. 2.7966
The letters of William Shenstone, arranged and edited with introduction. 2.7241
Letters on dancing and ballets. 4.1101
Letters on literature and politics, 1912-1972. 2.12767
Letters on the equality of the sexes and the condition of woman, addressed to Mary S. Parker. 4.6028
Letters on wave mechanics: Schrödinger, Planck, Einstein, Lorentz. 5.2146
Letters to Alice on first reading Jane Austen. 2.7385
Letters to apprentices. 1.5334
Letters to Atticus. 2.715
Letters to Felice. 2.13795
Letters to friends, family, and editors. 2.13794
Letters to Granville Barker. 2.8071
Letters to his daughter. 2.11725
The letters to his friends. 2.668
Letters to John Middleton Murry, 1913-1922. 2.9082
Letters to Lady Cunard, 1895-1933. 2.7958
Letters to Ottla and the family. 2.13796
Letters to Russell, Keynes, and Moore. 1.1078
Letters to Thomas and Adele Seltzer. 2.8979
Letters to William Blackwood and David S. Meldrum. 2.8551
Letters: Virginia Woolf & Lytton Strachey. 2.9587
Letting go. 2.13301
Lettres. 2.4058
Lettres à Sophie Volland. 2.4070
Lettres de mon moulin. 2.4160
Lettres vivantes. 2.4799
The Levant trilogy. 2.9743
The Leveller tracts, 1647-1653. 3.1474
The Levellers and the English revolution. 3.1488
Levels of schizophrenia. 5.4926
Leviathan. 4.7405
Leviticus. 1.2594
The Levittowners. 4.5213
The Lewis acid-base concepts. 5.2862
Lewis and Clark among the Indians. 3.8485
Lewis & Clark. 3.8482
Lewis and Clark, pioneering naturalists. 3.8478
Lewis Carroll. 2.7678
Lewis Morris, 1671-1746. 3.8065
Lewis Namier: a biography. 3.421

Lewis Tappan and the evangelical war against slavery. 3.7264
Lexical borrowing in the Romance languages. 2.874
Lexicon in 8 languages. 5.5893
Lexicon of Black English. 2.1160
Lexicon of geologic names of the United States (including Alaska) 5.2945
A lexicon of the Homeric dialect. 2.515
Li Ch'ing-chao, complete poems. 2.2216
Li Po and Tu Fu. 2.2212
Li Ta-chao and the origins of Chinese Marxism. 4.7111
Liam O'Flaherty the storyteller. 2.9167
Liang Ch'i-ch'ao and modern Chinese liberalism. 3.4742
Liang Ch'i-ch'ao and the mind of modern China. 3.4821
The liar. 2.14023
The Libera me Domine. 2.4653
The liberal and technical in teacher education. 4.10517
Liberal catholicism, reform catholicism, modernism. 1.3166
Liberal democracy. 4.7572, 4.7581
Liberal education. 4.10824
Liberal England. 3.1688
The liberal imagination. 2.12603
The liberal mind, 1914-1929. 4.8409
The liberal mind in a conservative age. 3.6185
The liberal papers. 3.7598
Liberal party politics in Britain. 4.8551
Liberal politics in the age of Gladstone and Rosebery. 4.8552
Liberal reformers in the gilded age. 3.7415
The liberal theory of justice. 4.7657
The liberal tradition in America. 3.6276
Liberalism. 4.5031
Liberalism and American education in the eighteenth century. 4.9990
Liberalism and the origins of European social theory. 4.4748
Liberalism and tradition. 3.1966
Liberalism at wits' end. 4.7643
Liberalism in the South. 3.8118
Le libéralisme rhénan, 1815-1848. 3.2498
Liberals and communism. 3.7553
The Liberals in power, 1905-1914. 3.1681
Liberating education. 4.10272
Liberation and the aims of science. 3.54
The liberation of Lord Byron Jones. 2.13016
Liberation of theology. 1.2807
Liberation theology: human hope confronts Christian history and American power. 1.2938
The liberator, William Lloyd Garrison. 3.7249
Liberia. 3.5413
Liberia, a country study. 3.5411
The libertarian alternative. 4.7641
The Libertarian reader. 4.7668
The libertarians and education. 4.9955
Liberties & communities in medieval England. 3.1327
Le libertinage. 2.4373
Libertine literature in England: 1660-1745 4.5544
Liberty. 4.7662
Liberty, a better husband. 4.5770
Liberty against government. 4.7686
The Liberty and Free Soil Parties in the Northwest. 4.8219
Liberty and property. 4.7291
Liberty and slavery. 3.8138
Liberty and Union. 3.7076
Liberty in the modern state. 4.7667
The liberty line. 3.7269
Liberty; The castle of indolence, and other poems. 2.7315
Liberty's daughters. 4.6011
Librarians' glossary of terms used in librarianship, documentation and the book crafts, and reference book. 5.7696
Libraries and librarianship in the West: a brief history. 5.7656
The library. 2.333
Library and archives conservation. 5.7646
Library journal. 5.7659
Library of America. 2.10668

Library of Congress catalog. 5.7668
Library of Congress catalog; a cumulative list of works represented by Library of Congress printed cards. Books: subjects 1950-54. 5.7668
Library of Congress catalog. Books-subjects. 5.7668
Library of Congress subject headings. 5.7630
The library of Greek mythology 2.420
The Library preservation program. 5.7647
Library promotion handbook. 5.7655
Library research guide to education. 4.10287
Library research guide to history. 3.432
Library surveys. 5.7602
Libro de buen amor. 2.5201
Il libro dell'arte. 1.6339
Libros en venta en Hispanoamérica y España. 5.7907
Libros y autores clásicos. 2.5098
Libros y autores contemporáneos. 2.5109
Libya, a country study. 3.5199
Libya, a modern history. 3.5201
License for empire. 3.5802
The lichen-forming fungi. 5.3715
Lichenized fungi. 5.3716
Lichine's encyclopedia of wines & spirits. 5.6892
Lie down in darkness. 2.13341
Lie groups, Lie algebras, and some of their applications. 5.1537
The lies of art. 2.8440
Lieutenant Lee of Beale Street. 3.6843
A life. 2.5068, 2.12214
Life against death. 3.6
Life among the surrealists. 2.10415
The life and adventures of Peter Wilkins. 2.7179
The life and adventures of Sir Launcelot Greaves. 2.7260
The life and art of Albrecht Dürer. 1.6169
The life and art of Andrew Ducrow & the romantic age of the English circus. 4.1193
Life and art of Vladimir Nabokov. 2.1585
Life and death in Milpa Alta. 3.8955
The life and death of an ideal. 3.2008
The life and death of Carthage. 3.5187
The life and death of Mary Wollstonecraft. 2.8293
The life and death of Mr. Badman. 2.6915
The life and death of Sr Thomas Moore, knight, sometymes Lord high Chancellor of England. 2.6496
Life and death of the salt marsh. 5.3559
The life and death of Tom Thumb the Great. 2.7022
The life and decline of the American railroad. 4.3999
Life and disease. 5.4479
The life and extraordinary adventures of Private Ivan Chonkin. 2.1645
Life and Gabriella. 2.11772
The life and good times of William Randolph Hearst. 2.3616
Life and human habitat. 1.5554
Life and labor in the old South. 3.8122
The life and letters of Charles Darwin. 5.3191
The life and letters of Edward Thomas. 2.9426
The life and letters of James Abram Garfield. 3.7489
The life and letters of James Macpherson. 2.7101
The life and letters of Joel Chandler Harris. 2.11051
The life and letters of John Donne, dean of St. Paul's. 2.6463
The life and letters of John Keats. 2.7854
Life and letters of Sir Joseph Dalton Hooker. 5.3639
Life and letters of Sir Joseph Dalton Hooker, O.M., G.C.S.J. 5.3639
Life and letters of Sir Wilfrid Laurier. 3.8755
The life and letters of the Rt. Hon. Sir Charles Tupper, bart. K. C. M. G. 3.8764
Life and letters of Thomas Henry Huxley 5.3205
Life and literature in the Roman republic. 2.630
The life and mind of John Dewey. 1.588

Life and miracles of St. Benedict. 1.3256
The life and music of Béla Bartók. 1.3791
The life and opinions of Malachi Mailings Esq., of Auldbiggings. 2.7716
The life and opinions of Tristram Shandy, gentleman. 2.7277
Life and ritual in old Siam. 3.4520
The life and strange surprizing adventures of Robinson Crusoe of York, mariner. 2.6970
The life and symphonies of Anton Bruckner. 1.3825
Life and the dream. 2.11508
Life and thought in old Russia. 3.3018
Life and thought in the Greek and Roman world. 3.2521
The life and times of Cavour. 3.2867
The life and times of Confederation, 1864-1867. 3.8735
The life and times of Cotton Mather. 3.7979
The life and times of Coventry Patmore. 2.7989
The life and times of Emile Zola. 2.4348
The life and times of James Connolly. 3.1866
The life and times of Laurence Sterne. 2.7283
The life and times of liberal democracy. 4.7576
The life and times of Menelik II. 3.5245
The life and times of Po Chü-i, 772-846 A. D. 2.2213
The life and times of Sir Alexander Tilloch Galt. 3.8727
The life and times of Sukarno. 3.4573
The life and times of William Howard Taft. 3.7712
The life and travels of John Bartram from Lake Ontario to the River St. John. 5.3637
The life and travels of Kah-ge-ga-gah-bowh. 3.5790
Life and work in medieval Europe. 4.3097
The life and work of C. R. Cockerell. 1.5386
Life and work of Gerardus Joannes Vossius (1577-1649) 2.232
The life and work of Henry Roberts, 1803-1876. 1.5398
The life and work of John Nash, architect. 1.5395
The life and work of Sigmund Freud. 5.155
Life and work of Susan B. Anthony. 4.8086
The life and work of Thomas Eakins. 1.5934
The life and work of Thomas Hardy. 2.7770
The life and work of Winslow Homer. 1.5945
The life and works of Evgenij Zamjatin. 2.1616
The life and works of George Peele. 2.6644
The life and works of Jāhiz. 2.1843
The life and writings of Frederick Douglass. 3.7237
A life apart. 4.3637
Life, art, and letters of George Inness. 1.5948
Life before man. 2.9908
Life (Chicago) 5.4373
Life cycle. 5.196
Life cycle group work in nursing. 5.4877
The life divine. 1.1732
Life histories and psychobiography. 5.36
Life histories of North American wild fowl. 5.3963
Life in a Welsh countryside. 3.1771
Life in America. 3.6333
Life in classrooms. 4.10310
Life in inland waters. 5.3283
Life in letters of William Dean Howells. 2.11088
Life in mud and sand. 5.3564
A life in our times. 4.1372
Life in Renaissance France. 3.1957
Life in rural America. 3.6065
Life in Shakespeare's England. 2.6254
Life in the Argentine Republic in the days of the tyrants. 3.9244
Life in the balance. 4.9863
Life in the classroom and playground. 4.10765
Life in the English country house. 4.6393
The life in the fiction of Ford Madox Ford. 2.8638
Life in the iron mills, and other stories. 2.10991
A life in the theatre. 2.3345
Life in the tomb. 2.604

Life in the universe. 5.1728
Life is a dream. 2.5164
Life is like a chicken coop ladder. 4.793
Life, its nature, origin and development. 5.3322
Life library of photography. 5.6937
Life, literature, and learning in America. 3.6158
The life model of social work practice. 4.6495
Life of a man. 2.5074
The life of Aleksandr Blok. 2.1471
The life of Apollonius of Tyana. 2.385
Life of Beethoven. 1.3806
The life of Bernini. 1.5011
The life of Bertrand Russell. 1.770
The life of Billy Yank, the common soldier of the Union. 3.7383
The life of birds. 5.3939
The life of Brunelleschi. 1.5440
The life of Buddha as legend and history. 1.1773
The life of Byron. 2.7525
The life of Captain James Cook. 4.89
Life of Carlyle. 2.7552
The life of Charlemagne. 3.1989
The life of Charles Dickens. 2.7637
The life of Charles Lamb. 2.7907
The life of Charlotte Brontë. 2.7450
Life of Dante. 2.4933
The life of David Hume. 1.701
The life of Dylan Thomas. 2.9418
The life of Edward the Second. 3.1364
The life of Emily Dickinson. 2.11008
The life of Ezra Pound. 2.12351
The life of fishes. 5.3897
Life of Flavius Josephus. 3.3896
The life of Fulke Greville. 2.6435
The life of George Crabbe. 2.7616
A life of George Herbert. 2.7064
The life of Henry Brulard. 2.4307
The life of Henry Clay. 3.7091
The life of Henry George. 4.1374
The life of Hilaire Belloc. 2.8450
The life of Ibn Sina. 1.370
Life of Ibsen. 2.14036
The life of J.M.W. Turner, R.A. 1.6039
The life of Jack Wilton. 2.6643
The life of Jane Austen. 2.7373
The life of Jean Jaurès. 3.2186
The life of Jesus. 1.2875-1.2876
The life of Jesus, critically examined. 1.2878
The life of John Adams. 3.7045
The life of John Berryman. 2.11382
The life of John Bright. 3.1634
The life of John Dryden. 2.6997
The life of John Dryden. 2.6999
The life of John Marshall. 3.7004
The life of John Maynard Keynes. 4.1349
The life of John Middleton Murry. 2.9137
The life of Johnny Reb, the common soldier of the Confederacy. 3.7395
Life of Johnson. 2.7086
Life of Johnson, together with Journal of a tour to the Hebrides and Johnson's Diary of a journey into North Wales. 2.7085
The life of Jonathan Wild. 2.7021
The life of Joseph Addison. 2.6889
The life of Katherine Mansfield. 2.9084
The life of King Edward. 3.1322
The life of Lady Mary Wortley Montagu. 3.1552
The life of Lazarillo of Tormes. 2.5193
The life of Lenin. 3.3146
The life of Lope de Vega, 1562-1635. 2.5209
The life of Mahatma Gandhi. 3.4308
The life of mammals. 5.4050
The life of mammals. 5.3977
The life of man. 2.1467
A life of Matthew G. Lewis. 2.7913
The life of Michelangelo. 1.5013
The life of Miranda. 3.9182
The life of Mohammad. 1.2016
Life of Mozart. 1.3939
The life of Muhammad. 1.2013-1.2014
The life of music in north India. 1.3736
The life of Nelson. 3.1282
The life of Neville Chamberlain. 3.1701
The life of Niccolò Machiavelli. 3.2932

The life of Oscar Wilde. 2.8283
The life of Percy Bysshe Shelley. 2.8102
The life of Raymond Chandler. 2.11481
The life of reason. 1.646
The life of reptiles. 5.3917
The life of Richard Steele. 2.7274
The life of Richard Wagner ... 1.4040
The life of Robert Baldwin. 3.8716
The life of Robert Browning. 2.7483
Life of Robert Burns. 2.7506
The life of Robert Burns. 2.7507
The life of Robert Owen. 4.7162
The life of Robert Southwell, poet and martyr. 2.6521
The life of Saint Antony. 1.2183
The life of Sarmiento. 3.9245
The life of science. 5.753
Life of Sheridan. 2.7250
The life of Sir Philip Sidney. 3.1437
The life of St. Anselm, Archbishop of Canterbury. 1.3252
The life of St. Louis. 3.1994
The life of Stephen F. Austin, founder of Texas, 1793-1836. 3.8322
The life of the Admiral Christopher Columbus 3.5972
The life of the ant. 5.3887
The life of the Buddha. 1.1772, 1.2124
The Life of the Buddha, as it appears in the Pali canon, the oldest authentic record. 1.2123
The life of the green plant. 5.3741
The life of the mind. 1.83
The life of the mind in America. 3.6140
The life of Themistocles. 3.2606
The life of Thomas Hardy, 1840-1928. 2.7778
The life of Thomas Paine. 4.7424
The life of Tolstoy. 2.1434
The life of vertebrates. 5.3893
The life of Villiers de l'Isle-Adam. 2.4339
The life of Washington Irving. 2.11097
The life of Wilkie Collins. 2.7610
The life of William Blake. 2.7420
The life of William Blake. 2.7421
The life of William Ewart Gladstone. 3.1626
The life of William Morris. 2.7970
The life of William Pitt, earl of Chatham. 3.1527
Life on Earth. 5.3364
Life on the English manor. 4.2258
Life on the Mississippi. 3.8301
The life records of John Milton. 2.7148
Life science in the twentieth century. 5.3296
The life story of the fish. 5.3901
Life, the science of biology. 5.3301
The Life-threatened elderly. 5.4588
The life to come, and other short stories. 2.8647
Life with heroin. 4.6664
Life with the enemy. 3.1059
Life, work, and rebellion in the coal fields. 4.3538
Life's career 4.5801
The life-style of the people of the Caucasus. 5.4214
Lifestyles and consumer behavior of older Americans. 4.2061
Lifting, handling and helping patients. 5.5203
Ligand fields. 5.2841
Light. 5.2278, 5.2280, 5.2289
Light and darkness. 2.2084
Light and its uses. 5.5954
Light and life. 5.3626
Light and vision. 5.4381
Light, colour and vision. 5.4380
A light from Eleusis. 2.12334
Light in August. 2.11667
The light in Holland. 3.2983
The light in the forest. 2.12390
The light in the piazza. 2.12495
Light of Asia. 1.5186
The light of common day. 2.10567
The light of the mind. 1.334
Light on a dark horse. 2.10060
Light verse and satires. 2.11441
The lighter side of gravity. 5.1759
Lighting handbook. 5.6337
Lighting in the theatre. 2.3142

Lightning and its spectrum. 5.2550
Lightning, auroras, nocturnal lights, and related luminous phenomena. 5.2556
Lightning protection. 5.6107
Like a great river. 1.1703
Lilies. 5.5351
Lilith. 2.7923
Lillian Hellman. 2.11834
Lillian Roxon's Rock encyclopedia. 1.3525
Limba stories and story-telling. 4.816
The Limbourgs and their contemporaries. 1.6413
The limewood sculptors of Renaissance Germany. 1.5783
Limited-dependent and qualitative variables in econometrics. 4.1396
Limited government: a comparison. 4.7713
Limited war in the nuclear age. 5.7254
Limiting oil imports. 4.3772
The limits and divisions of European history. 3.527
The limits of corporate responsibility. 4.2707
The Limits of educational reform. 4.9998
The limits of Hitler's power. 3.2406
The limits of intervention. 3.4486
The limits of law. 4.9363
The limits of power. 3.7580
The limits of rationality. 4.4766
The limits of reform in the Enlightenment. 4.10124
The limits of science. 5.912
The limits of scientific reasoning. 5.881
The limits to capital. 4.1527
The Limits to growth. 4.1788
Limits to solar and biomass energy growth. 5.6230
Limners and likenesses. 1.5885
Limnological methods. 5.3257
Limnology. 5.3258
Limnology in North America. 5.3256
The Lin Piao affair. 3.4822
Lincoln. 2.12618
Lincoln and Black freedom. 3.7287
Lincoln and his generals. 3.7359
Lincoln and his party in the secession crisis. 3.7181
Lincoln and the Civil War in the diaries and letters of John Hay. 3.7435
Lincoln and the Negro. 3.7288
Lincoln & the party divided. 3.7305
Lincoln and the tools of war. 3.7381
Lincoln as they saw him. 3.7286
The Lincoln encyclopedia. 3.7302
The Lincoln nobody knows. 3.7279
The Lincoln reader. 3.7278
Lincoln reconsidered. 3.7298
Lincoln Steffens. 2.3636
Lincoln, the president. 3.7283
Lincoln's quest for union. 3.7284
Lincoln's war cabinet. 3.7277
Linda Tressel. 2.8216
Lindamira. 2.6886
Linden Hills. 2.13189
The Lindisfarne Gospels. 1.6426
A line of power. 3.5664
Line spectra. 5.2305
Linear algebra. 5.1311
Linear and nonlinear programming. 5.5581
Linear associative algebras. 5.1363
Linear circuits: discrete and integrated. 5.6486
Linear differential equations with periodic coefficients. 5.1517
Linear network theory. 5.6334
Linear networks and systems. 5.6275
Linear operators. 5.1482
Linear partial differential equations with constant coefficients. 5.1525
Linear programming. 5.5587-5.5588
Linear programming; an elementary introduction. 5.5592
Linear programming and economic analysis. 4.1276
Linear programming and extensions. 5.1368
Linear programming and network flows. 5.5586
Linear programming and the theory of the firm 4.2643
Linear system theory. 5.1543

Linear systems and digital signal processing. 5.6383
The lineman's and cableman's handbook. 5.6333
The lines of life. 3.314
Lingering shadow. 2.1889
The Linguistic atlas of England. 2.1111
Linguistic change. 2.143
Linguistic communication and speech acts. 2.67
Linguistic evolution. 2.153
A linguistic history of English. 2.971
Linguistic minorities, policies, and pluralism. 2.125
The linguistic moment. 2.5780
Linguistic structures. 2.992
Linguistic theory in America. 2.163
The linguistic turn. 1.547
Linguistics. 2.147
Linguistics and literature. 2.2537
Linguistics and style. 2.192
Linguistics and the teacher. 2.30
Linguistics, English, and the Language arts. 2.928
Linguistics in language teaching. 2.37
Linguistics today. 2.1
Linkage politics. 4.9033
Die linkshändige Frau. 2.13892
Linnaeus. 5.3214
Linnaeus, the man and his work. 5.3215
Le Lion. 2.4596
The lion and the fox. 2.6803
The lion and the honeycomb. 2.10263
The lion and the unicorn. 2.9182
A lion for love. 2.4308
Lion rampant. 4.8919
The lionheads. 2.12932
Lions and shadows. 2.8835
The lion's roar of Queen Śrīmālā. 1.2129
The lion's share. 2.2913, 3.1227
Lipchitz. 1.5706
Lipid biochemistry. 5.4423
Lipids in plants and microbes. 5.3764
Lippincott's pronouncing gazetteer. 4.69
The Lisle letters. 3.1414
LISP. 5.1218
List of subject headings. 5.7631
Listening. 4.10470
Listening in the dark. 5.4087
Listening with the third ear. 5.186
Liszt. 1.3910
Literacy and development in the West. 4.10751
Literacy as a human problem. 4.10753
Literacy before schooling. 4.10408
Literacy in the open-access college. 4.10617
The literary achievement of Rebecca West. 2.9515
Literary admirers of Alfred Stieglitz. 2.10432
Literary and art theories in Japan. 2.1994
Literary and educational writings. 2.823
Literary and philosophical essays. 2.2608
The Literary appreciation of Russian writers. 2.1245
The literary art of Edward Gibbon. 3.2803
The literary career of Charles W. Chesnutt. 2.10927
Literary criticism. 2.2465, 2.2510, 2.5539, 2.8301
Literary criticism and historical understanding. 2.2426
Literary criticism for New Testament critics. 1.2642
Literary criticism in the Italian Renaissance. 2.4875
Literary criticism index. 5.8273
Literary criticism of Alexander Pope. 2.7188
Literary criticism of George Henry Lewes. 2.2454
The literary criticism of John Ruskin. 2.8024
Literary criticisms. 2.2597
The literary critics. 2.2508
Literary democracy. 2.10378
Literary disruptions. 2.10634
Literary dissent in Communist China. 3.4789
Literary essays. 2.2584
Literary essays. 2.2596
The literary fallacy. 2.10405

A literary gazetteer of England. 2.5562
A literary history of America. 2.10260
Literary history of Canada. 2.9882
A literary history of England. 2.5511
The literary history of Meistergesang. 2.13464
A literary history of Persia 2.1962
A literary history of Rome, from the origins to the close of the Golden Age. 2.625
A literary history of Rome in the silver age. 2.633
The literary history of the American Revolution, 1763-1783. 2.10366
A literary history of the Arabs. 2.1836
A literary history of the Bible. 1.2513
A literary history of the English people. 2.5529
Literary history of the United States. 2.10252
The Literary humor of the urban Northeast, 1830-1890. 2.10718
The literary impact of the Authorised version. 2.9037
The literary impact of The golden bough. 1.1604
Literary influences in colonial newspapers, 1704-1750. 2.3593
The literary journal in America, 1900-1950. 5.8323
Literary loneliness in mid-eighteenth-century England. 2.5687
Literary market place. 2.2525
A literary Middle English reader. 2.6074
The literary mind. 2.2673
The literary mind and the carving of dragons. 2.2155
The literary mind of medieval & Renaissance Spain. 2.5102
Literary notebooks, 1797-1801. 2.2367
Literary opinion in America. 2.2688
Literary origins of surrealism. 2.3877
The literary relationships of Chaucer's Clerkes tale. 2.6350
Literary research guide. 5.8271
Literary reviews and essays, on American, English, and French literature. 2.11112
Literary, rhetorical, and linguistics terms index. 2.14
Literary sociology and practical criticism. 2.2490
The literary South. 2.10722
Literary studies. 2.5533
Literary style. 2.2541
Literary swordsmen and sorcerers. 2.5963
The literary symbol. 2.2409
Literary terms. 2.2357
Literary theory. 2.2468
Literary transcendentalism; style and vision in the American Renaissance. 2.10395
The literary underground of the Old Regime. 3.2046
The literary use of the psychoanalytic process. 2.2484
The literary vision of Gabrielle Roy. 2.4826
The literary vision of Liam O'Flaherty. 2.9168
Literary women. 2.2553
The literary works of Matthew Prior. 2.7206
The literary works of Ou-yang Hsiu (1007-72) 2.2217
The literate revolution in Greece and its cultural consequences. 2.238
Literatura española. 2.5142
Literatura española, siglo XX. 2.5111
Literatura hispanoamericana. 2.5319
Literature and art. 2.2385
Literature and dogma. 1.2531
Literature and politics in the age of Nero. 2.632
Literature and popular culture in eighteenth century England. 2.5693
Literature and revolution. 2.1277
Literature and revolution in Soviet Russian, 1917-1962. 2.1270
Literature and science. 2.2388
Literature and sincerity. 2.2699
Literature and society in early Virginia, 1608-1840. 2.10466
Literature and society in Germany, 1918-1945. 2.13479

Literature and society in imperial Russia, 1800-1914. 2.1264
Literature and society in Southeast Asia. 2.2255
Literature and the arts in twentieth century China. 3.4644
Literature and the delinquent. 2.3449
Literature and the image of man. 2.2381
Literature and the sixth sense. 2.2666
Literature & theology in colonial New England. 2.10370
The literature and thought of modern Africa. 3.5077
Literature as opera. 1.4405
Literature as recreation in the later Middle Ages. 2.2374
Literature in medieval Germany. 2.13460
The literature of American Jews. 2.10679
The literature of American music in books and folk music collections. 1.3560
The literature of ancient Egypt. 2.1766
The literature of East Germany. 2.13930
The literature of eighteenth-century Russia. 2.1305
The literature of fantasy. 5.7966
The literature of geography. 5.8200
The literature of jazz. 1.3572
Literature of medieval history, 1930-1975. 5.8225
The literature of memory. 2.10447
The literature of modern Israel. 2.1777
The literature of rock, 1954-1978. 1.3587
The literature of roguery. 2.3450
The literature of Spain in English translation. 2.5095
The literature of terror. 2.5626
Literature of the American Indian. 2.2322
The literature of the American people. 2.10256
The literature of the American West. 2.10724
The literature of the ancient Egyptians. 2.1763
The literature of the Anglo-Saxons. 2.5588
Literature of the early Republic. 2.10666
The literature of the English Renaissance, 1485-1660. 2.5525
Literature of the Hundred Flowers. 2.2162
Literature of the low countries. 2.13940
The literature of the middle western frontier. 2.10470
The literature of the nineteenth and early twentieth centuries, 1798 to the First World War. 2.5525
Literature of the occult; a collection of critical essays. 2.5975
Literature of the People's Republic of China. 2.2186
The literature of the piano. 1.4526
The literature of the Restoration and the eighteenth century, 1660-1798. 2.5525
Literature of the Spanish people. 2.5089
The literature of the United States. 2.10261
A literature of their own. 2.5565
The Literatures of India. 2.1921
Literatures of the world in English. 2.9875
Lithography. 1.6499
Lithography, 1800-1850. 1.6500
Lithuania 700 years. 3.3314
Lithuania in crisis. 3.3315
The litigious society. 4.9497
Litografia. English. 1.6499
Littérature française. 2.3824
La littérature française du siècle philosophique (1715-1802) 2.3854
Littérature présente. 2.3873
Littératures de langue française hors de France. 2.4798
Little, big. 2.12963
Little big man. 2.12904
Little clay cart. 2.1951
The little clay cart. 2.1952
A little commonwealth. 4.5608
The little community. 4.4913
The little disturbances of man. 2.13234
Little flower. 3.7658
The little flowers of St. Francis. 1.3259
The little girls. 2.8476
The little hotel. 2.10166
The Little Karoo. 2.10092

A Little learning. 2.9500
The little magazine. 2.3580
Little men. 2.10900
Little murders. 2.13011
The little Ottleys. 2.9036
The Little review. 2.10714
The Little review anthology. 2.10714
The Little Rock crisis. 4.9897
Little science, big science. 5.850
A little tea, a little chat. 2.10169
The little that is all. 2.11501
The little time-keeper. 2.9314
A little treasury of British poetry. 2.6104
A little treasury of modern poetry, English & American. 2.6194
Little Wilson and big God. 2.9647
Little women. 2.10899
The little world of the past. 2.4988
Liturgies of the Western church. 1.2988
Liu Shao-ch'i and the Chinese cultural revolution. 3.4823
Livable streets. 4.3924
Live and remember. 2.1629
Live cycle. 4.4930
The Lively arts information directory. 2.3265
The lively experiment. 1.2381
The lively membranes. 5.3611
Lives and letters. 3.322
The lives and times of Archy and Mehitabel. 2.12115
The lives and times of the patriots. 3.8728
Lives and works, talks with women artists. 1.4871
Lives in progress. 5.536
The lives of children; the story of the First Street School. 4.11005
The lives of Dr. John Donne, Sir Henry Wotton, Mr. Richard Hooker, Mr. George Herbert, 1670. 3.1448
Lives of eminent philosphers. 2.363
The lives of the Buddha in the art and literature of Asia. 1.6743
Lives of the English poets. 2.5807
The lives of the Greek poets. 2.282
Lives of the later Caesars. 3.2791
Lives of the modern poets. 2.10496
The lives of the noble Grecians and Romans. 3.2512
The lives of the novelists. 2.5950
The lives of the painters, sculptors, and architects. 1.5009
Lives of the poets. 2.12989
Lives of the saints. 1.3246-1.3247
The lives of the Sophists. 2.386
Lives of their own. 3.8095
The lives of William Benton. 3.7628
Lives through the years. 5.626
Livestock husbandry techniques. 5.5440
The living alphabet. 2.168
Living and dying at Murray Manor. 5.4713
The living and the dead. 2.1605, 2.10182
Living and working in the sea. 4.336
Living archaeology. 3.245
Living architecture: Chinese. 1.5449
Living by fiction. 2.3525
Living cell. 5.3598
Living China. 2.2206
The living city. 1.5585
The living heart. 5.4992
Living ideas in America. 3.6194
Living in prison. 4.6844
Living in the present. 2.9450
Living materials. 1.5778
The Living novel. 2.10627
The living of Charlotte Perkins Gilman. 2.11042
Living room. 2.13107
Living-room war. 2.2850
The living temple. 2.7062
Living the revolution. 4.5262
The living thoughts of Mazzini. 3.2874
Living together. 4.5808
The living tradition of María Martínez. 3.5944
Living under apartheid. 4.6282
Livingstone. 3.5438
Livingstone's companions; stories. 2.10073
Le livre de mon ami. 2.4210
Le livre des questions. 2.4586

Les Livres de l'année-Biblio. 5.7998
Livy. 2.674, 3.2748
Livy: his historical aims and methods. 2.735
Liza of Lambeth. 2.9098
El llano en llamas. 2.5351
Llareggub revisited; Dylan Thomas and the state of modern poetry. 2.9419
Lloyd George and the generals. 3.1694
Lloyd George, from peace to war, 1912-1916. 3.1668
Lloyd George, the people's champion, 1902-1911. 3.1669
Lo amut, ki ehyeh. 2.1787
Lo-to Hsiang Tzu. 2.2249
Loading mercury with a pitchfork. 2.11414
Lobbying for the people. 4.8035
Lobbying; interaction and influence in American state legislatures. 4.8260
Lobbying the corporation. 4.2712
Lobbyists and legislators. 4.7733
Local anaesthetic. 2.13763
Local fields. 5.1343
Local government in Britain since reorganisation. 4.8875
Local government in China under the Ch'ing. 4.8886
Local government in Japan. 4.8892
The local historians of Attica. 3.2570
Local interest politics. 4.8871
Local loads in plates and shells. 5.5870
The local service airline experiment. 4.4079
The local union. 4.3366
Location and space-economy. 4.2689
Location in space. 4.4120
Locational analysis in human geography. 4.377
Locke. 1.679-1.680
Locke and the compass of human understanding. 1.677
Locked-out Americans. 3.8424
Locked rooms and other impossible crimes. 2.3469
Locomotion of animals. 5.4261
The lodger. 2.9053
Logic. 1.1212
Logic. 1.1170, 1.1193
Logic and knowledge. 1.763
Logic and language (second series) 1.1150
The logic and limits of trust. 4.5055
Logic and philosophy. 1.1151
The logic book. 1.1198
Logic for mathematicians. 1.1222
Logic, language-games and information. 1.1169
The logic of divine love. 1.2931
The logic of explanation in psychoanalysis. 5.311
The logic of liberty. 4.5029
The logic of life. 5.3411
The logic of millennial thought. 1.2398
The logic of modern physics. 5.1900
The logic of moral discourse. 1.1435
The logic of natural language. 1.1181
The logic of perception. 5.287
The logic of questions and answers. 1.1255
The logic of scientific discovery. 5.923
The logic of society. 1.115
The logic of the humanities. 1.979
The Logic of the sciences. 5.887
The logic of tragedy. 2.409
The logic of unity. 4.2220
Logic, semantics, metamathematics. 1.1223
Logic, the theory of inquiry. 1.1161
Logic without metaphysics, and other essays in the philosophy of science. 1.1164
Logical construction of systems. 5.1131
Logical foundations of probability. 1.1230
Logical positivism. 1.507, 1.512
Logical studies. 1.1153
The logical syntax of language. 1.1203
Logics for artificial intelligence. 5.1016
Logisch-philosophische Abhandlung. 1.1225
Logistical management. 4.4312
Lolita. 2.12226
London, 800-1216. 4.2303
London, 1808-1870. 4.2304
London; a portrait of the poor at the turn of the century. 4.6624
London, city of the Romans. 3.1742
The London daily press, 1772-1792. 2.3692

The London diary, 1717-1721, and other writings. 3.8190
London English, 1384-1425. 2.1115
London in the age of Chaucer. 3.1743
London labour and the London poor. 4.6625
London life in the eighteenth century. 4.5332
London music in 1888-89 as heard by Corno di Bassetto (later known as Bernard Shaw) with some further autobiographical particulars. 1.3722
London notebooks. 1.3893
The London stage, 1660-1800. 2.2778
The London stage, 1890-1899. 2.3324
The London stage, 1900-1909. 2.3325
The London stage, 1910-1919. 2.3326
The London stage, 1920-1929. 2.3327
London, the unique city. 3.1741
The London theatre world, 1660-1800. 2.3301
London transformed. 2.5691
Lone wolf. 2.12030
The loneliest campaign. 3.7814
Loneliness. 5.439
The loneliness at the core. 2.12791
The loneliness of the long-distance runner. 2.9317
The lonely African. 3.5418
The lonely crowd. 5.628
The lonely girl. 2.9786
The lonely hunter. 2.12077
Lonely in America. 4.4925
The lonely Londoners. 2.10017
The lonely muse. 2.8095
The lonely passion of Judith Hearne. 2.9950
The lonely voice. 2.3436
A long and happy life. 2.13272
Long day's journey into night. 2.12286
A long, deep furrow. 4.2957
The long dream. 2.12810
The long encounter. 2.11165
The long fuse. 3.773
The long-haired kings, and other studies in Frankish history. 3.1981
The long march. 2.13342
The long march to power. 4.8745
Long memory. 3.6639
The long night. 2.12059
Long-range ballistic missiles. 5.7397
Long remember. 2.11943
The long revolution. 3.1645
The long road north. 4.3613
Long steel rail. 1.4289
The long struggle. 3.6769
A long time burning. 4.9422
A long time coming. 4.3376
The long valley. 2.12529
The long wave cycle. 4.1713
A long way from home. 2.12085
The long week end. 3.1643
Longer hours or more jobs? 4.3155
Longes mac nUsnig. 2.9383
The longest day: June 6, 1944. 3.961
The longest debate. 4.9681
The longest journey. 2.8648
Longfellow: his life and work. 2.11145
A longing for the light. 2.5228
'Longinus' On the sublime. 2.518
The Longman anthology of American drama. 2.10783
The Longman anthology of contemporary American poetry, 1950-1980. 2.10769
Longman dictionary of English idioms. 2.1104
Longman dictionary of geography. 4.5
Longtime Californ' 3.8626
Longus. 2.519
Look at me. 2.9633
Look back in anger. 2.9210
Look homeward, angel. 2.12776
Look how the fish live. 2.13269
Looking at the dance. 4.1172
Looking away. 2.3011
Looking backward, 2000-1887. 2.10907, 4.7179
Looking forward. 3.67
Looking on darkness. 2.13964
Looking outward. 4.9241
Lope de Vega. 2.5208
Lope de Vega and Spanish drama. 2.5125
Lorca. 2.5258
Lorca and the Spanish poetic tradition. 2.5117

Lorca's Romancero gitano. 2.5255
Lord and peasant in Russia, from the ninth to
    the nineteenth century. 4.6410
Lord Burghley and Queen Elizabeth. 3.1435
Lord Byron. 2.7523-2.7524
Lord Byron's wife. 2.7532
Lord Chatham. 3.1525
Lord Chatham and America. 3.1526
Lord Chesterfield and his world. 3.1549
Lord Darcy. 2.13040
Lord Darcy investigates. 2.13040
Lord Durham's report. 3.8726
Lord Foul's bane. 2.12993
Lord Haldane; scapegoat for liberalism. 3.1667
Lord Hervey; eighteenth-century courtier.
    3.1550
Lord John Russell. 3.1632
Lord Kelvin and the age of the earth. 5.3084
Lord Liverpool. 3.1576
Lord North. 3.1564
Lord of the flies. 2.8699
The lord of the rings. 2.9432
Lord Peter. 2.9303
Lord Randolph Churchill. 3.1637
The lords of human kind. 4.8905
Lords of life. 3.4526
Lordship and feudalism in the Middle Ages.
    4.1741
Lordship to patronage. 3.1799
The lore and language of schoolchildren. 4.817
Lore and science in ancient Pythagoreanism.
    1.239
Lorelei Two. 2.11304
Lorenzo Ghiberti. 1.5730
Lorna Doone. 2.7401
Los Angeles. 3.8621
Loser takes all. 2.8737, 2.8762
The losers. 4.6878
The losing and taking again of the town of
    Mansoul. 2.6917
Losing battles. 2.12663
Losing the peace. 4.8226
Loss distributions. 4.4640
A loss of mastery. 3.6229
Loss of the self in modern literature and art.
    2.2686
Lost America. 3.5997
Lost America: from the Mississippi to the
    Pacific. 3.5998
Lost bearings in English poetry. 2.5830
'The lost center' and other essays on Greek
    poetry. 2.567
The lost childhood, and other essays. 2.5536
The lost cities of Africa. 3.5228
Lost city of the Incas. 3.9288
The lost civilization. 3.9035
The lost colony. 2.11797
Lost copper. 2.13297
The lost crusade. 3.4484
The lost Eden. 2.5448
The lost histories of Alexander the Great.
    3.2631
The lost honor of Katharina Blum. 2.13693
Lost horizon. 2.8802
Lost in the funhouse. 2.12880
The lost land. 3.8563
A lost language, and other essays on Chaucer.
    2.6365
The lost pathfinder, Zebulon Montgomery Pike.
    3.8475
The lost sisterhood. 4.5539
The lost soul of American politics. 4.7307
The lost steps. 2.5361
The Lost tradition. 2.2414
Lost tribes & sunken continents. 3.5696
Lost victories. 3.968
A lot to ask. 2.9139
Lothair. 2.7394
Lotte in Weimar. 2.13831
Lotte in Weimar. English. 2.13831
The lottery. 2.11921
The lotus of the true law. 1.2133
The Lotus Sutra in Chinese art. 1.5067
Louis. 1.4079
Louis and Antoinette. 3.2050
Louis Blanc. 4.7047
Louis C. Tiffany, rebel in glass. 1.6645
Louis D. Brandeis. 4.9805

Louis D. Brandeis and the progressive tradition.
    4.9806
Louis D. Brandeis, Felix Frankfurter, and the
    New Deal. 4.9796
Louis 'David' Riel. 3.8854
Louis-Ferdinand Céline. 2.4513
Louis I. Kahn. 1.5313
Louis IX and the challenge of the Crusade.
    3.1995
Louis Jouvet, man of the theatre. 2.3373
Louis L. Snyder's Historical guide to World
    War II. 3.891
Louis MacNeice. 2.9078
Louis Napoleon and the Second Empire.
    3.2160
Louis Pasteur. 5.824
Louis Riel. 3.8855
Louis Simpson. 2.12476
Louis St. Laurent, Canadian. 3.8790
Louis Sullivan, prophet of modern architecture.
    1.5330
Louis Wirth on cities and social life. 4.4849
Louis XI. 3.2005
Louis XIV. 3.2038
Louis XIV and absolutism. 4.8580
Louis XIV and Europe. 3.2033
Louis XIV and the craft of kingship. 3.2037
Louis XIV and twenty million Frenchmen.
    3.2036
Louis XIV et l'Europe. 3.2032
Louis XV. 3.2047
Louisa May. 2.10903
Louisa May Alcott. 2.10904
Louise Bourgeois. 1.5661
Louise Nevelson. 1.5669
Louisiana. 3.8309
Louisiana, a bicentennial history. 3.8310
Louisiana reconstructed, 1863-1877. 3.8315
Love among the cannibals. 2.12215
Love among the ruins. 2.9489
Love and death in a hot country. 2.10005
Love and death in Renaissance tragedy. 2.5879
Love and death in the American novel.
    2.10557
Love & like. 2.13050
Love and limerence. 5.442
Love and napalm: export U.S.A. 2.9617
Love and other stories of Yokomitsu Riichi.
    2.2123
Love and salt water. 2.9547
Love & the American delinquent. 4.9894
Love and the quest for identity in the fiction of
    Henry James. 2.11132
Love and the woman question in Victorian
    literature. 2.5728
Love at second sight. 2.9036
The love command in the New Testament.
    1.2671
Love, death, and the ladies' drill team.
    2.12680
The love ethic of D. H. Lawrence. 2.8998
Love, guilt, and reparation & other works,
    1921-1945. 5.171
Love in a cold climate. 2.9118
Love in the ruins. 2.13242
Love in the Western World. 4.5507
Love in the winter. 2.12964
Love is not enough. 4.5708
Love known. 2.7068
Love medicine. 2.13008
Love, mystery, and misery. 2.6002
The love nest, and other stories. 2.11981
The love of Krishna. 2.1950
The love of learning and the desire for God.
    1.3231
Love of order. 3.8245
The love pavilion. 2.9810
Love poems. 2.13311
Love song of the dark lord. 2.1945
Love songs of Vidyāpati. 2.1877
The love that failed. 2.8665
The loved and the lost. 2.9916
The loved ones. 2.9490
A lovely Sunday for Creve Coeur. 2.12730
The lover. 2.7271
The lovers. 2.13010
Love's body. 5.193
Love's old sweet song. 2.12440

Love's shadow. 2.9036
The loving friends. 3.1748
The low countries, 1780-1940. 3.2972
The Low Countries in early modern times.
    3.2957
Low intensity operations; subversion,
    insurgency, peace-keeping. 5.7228
Low temperature laboratory techniques. 5.2235
Low temperature physics. 5.2002
Low-wage workers in an affluent society.
    4.3139
Lowell Institute lectures, 1926. 1.1538
The lower depths and other plays. 2.1503
The loyal and the disloyal. 4.7513
Loyalist literature. 5.7831
The loyalists in Revolutionary America,
    1760-1781. 3.6956
The loyalists in the American revolution.
    3.6960
The Loyalists of Revolutionary Delaware.
    3.6958
The loyalties of Robinson Jeffers. 2.11934
Loyalty in America. 4.8071
Lu Hsün's vision of reality. 2.2242
Lu Xun and his legacy. 2.2241
Luca della Robbia. 1.5738-1.5739
Lucan. 2.675, 2.736
Luce and his empire. 2.3618
Luces de Bohemia. 2.5291
Luchino Visconti. 2.3071
Lucian. 2.380
Lucian and his influence in Europe. 2.521
Lucian, satirist and artist. 2.520
Lucifer, the Devil in the Middle Ages. 1.2952
The luck of Ginger Coffey. 2.9948
Lucky Jim. 2.8383
Lucky Kristoffer. 2.14024
Lucky poet. 2.8784
Lucretia Borgia, according to original
    documents and correspondence of her day.
    3.2934
Lucretius and Epicurus. 1.332
Lucrezia Floriani. 2.4287
Lucy Church, amiably. 2.12512
Lucy Parsons. 4.3590
Lucy, the beginnings of humankind. 4.455
Ludendorff's own story, August 1914-November
    1918. 3.793
Ludus Coventriae. 2.6208, 2.6212
Ludvig Holberg. 2.14007
Ludwig van Beethoven. 1.3810
Ludwig Wittgenstein. 1.1089
Ludwig Wittgenstein, philosophy and language.
    1.1079
Luftwaffe. 3.1053
Lugard. 3.1671
Lugbara religion. 4.550
Luigi Dallapiccola. 1.3845
Luigi Pirandello. 2.5059
Luis Cernuda. 2.5246
The Lumbee problem. 3.5869
Lumumba speaks. 3.5430
Lunatics, lovers, and poets: 2.3179
Lupercal. 2.9716
The lure of Africa: American interests in
    tropical Africa, 1919-1939. 3.5127
The lure of God. 1.2810
The Lusiads. 2.5453-2.5454
The Lusitania disaster. 3.820
Luther. 1.2350
Luther, an experiment in biography. 1.2342
Luther and Erasmus: Free will and salvation.
    1.1496
Luther and the false brethren. 1.2340
Luther in mid-career, 1521-1530. 1.2344
Luther the expositor. 1.2347
Lutheran confessional theology in America,
    1840-1880. 1.3360
Lutheranism. 1.3361
The Lutherans in North America. 1.3359
Luther's last battles. 1.2345
Lutosławski and his music. 1.3914
Luv. 2.13312
Luxury and capitalism. 4.1544
Luxury fleet. 3.2258
Luxury trains from the Orient Express to the
    TGV. 5.6074
Lying. 1.1492

The lying days. 2.10074
The lynchers. 2.13425
Lyndon, an oral biography. 3.7891
Lyndon B. Johnson and the world. 3.7884
Lyndon B. Johnson; the exercise of power. 3.7888
Lyndon Johnson and the American dream. 3.7890
The Lyon uprising of 1834. 3.2230
Lyonel Feininger; a definitive catalogue of his graphic work: etchings, lithographs, woodcuts. 1.6440
The lyric age of Greece. 3.2597
The lyric genius of Catullus. 2.708
Lyric poems and ballads. 2.13605
Lyrica Graeca selecta. 2.318
The lyrical and the epic. 2.2160
Lyrical ballads. 2.8308
Le Lys rouge. 2.4211
The Lysenko affair. 4.2980
Lysias and the corpus Lysiacum. 2.522
Lysias, with an English translation by W.R.M. Lamb. 2.379
Lysistrata. 2.428
Lytton Strachey; a critical biography. 2.9390

M. and M. Karolik collection of American paintings, 1815 to 1865. 1.5883
M.I.T.I. and the Japanese miracle. 4.3075
M.I.T. wavelength tables. 5.2312
M.L.A. handbook for writers of research papers. 2.1041
Maarten van Heemskerck and Dutch humanism in the sixteenth century. 1.5023
The Mabinogion. 2.847
Mabinogion. 2.847
Macaulay and the Whig tradition. 3.1213
Macaulay: the shaping of the historian. 3.1212
The Maccabees. 3.3887
MacDiarmid. 2.8786
Macdonald. 3.8757
Macedonia. 3.3599
Machado de Assis. 2.5477
Machiavelli and Guicciardini. 3.2930
Machiavelli and the art of Renaissance history. 3.2931
Machiavelli & the Renaissance. 4.7397
The Machiavellian moment: Florentine political thought and the Atlantic republican tradition. 4.7399
Machiavelli's new modes and orders. 4.7391
Machiavellism. 4.7382
Machina carnis. 5.4284
Machina ex dea. 5.5521
The machine in the garden. 3.6136
Machine intelligence. 5.1012, 5.8104
Machine politics in transition. 4.8212
Machine stops. 2.8642
The machinery of justice in England. 4.9425
The machinery of the brain. 5.4342
The machinery question and the making of political economy, 1815-1848. 4.1316
Machines, languages, and computation. 5.1370
Machines that think. 2.10831
Machines who think. 5.1011
The machinists. 4.3387
Mackenzie King. 3.8747, 3.8750
The Mackenzie King record. 3.8751
The Mackerel plaza. 2.11562
Mackintosh architecture. 1.5393
Maclear & Co.'s Canadian almanac. 1.67
The Macmillan atlas history of Christianity. 4.132
The Macmillan atlas of the Holocaust. 4.167
The Macmillan Bible atlas. 4.179
Macmillan biographical encyclopedia of photographic artists & innovators. 5.6925
The Macmillan book of proverbs, maxims, and famous phrases. 2.3808
The Macmillan dictionary of Canadian biography. 3.341, 3.8654
Macmillan encyclopedia of architects. 1.5208
The Macmillan film bibliography. 5.8143
Macmillan illustrated animal encyclopedia. 5.3792
Macro. 5.5674
Macro-economic theory. 4.1288
Macroeconomic activity. 4.1983

Macroeconomic theory. 4.1387
Macroeconomics after Keynes. 4.1461
Macroevolution, pattern and process. 5.3375
The macroscope. 4.1213
The maculate muse. 2.300
Macy's of New York. 4.4332
Madagascar. 3.5310
Madagascar rediscovered. 3.5313
Madam Secretary, Frances Perkins. 4.3591
Madame Bovary. 2.4187
Madame Bovary and the critics. 2.4188
Madame de Lafayette. 2.4028
Madame de Sévigné. 2.4059
Madame de Staël, novelist. 2.4299
Madame de Staël on politics, literature, and national character. 2.4297
Madame Vestris and the London stage. 2.3358
Madeleine. 2.4558
Mademoiselle de Maupin. 2.4219
The madman and the nun, and other plays. 2.1738
A madman's defense. 2.14077
Madness and sexual politics in the feminist novel. 2.5990
The madness in sports. 4.950
Madoc, the making of a myth. 3.5971
Madrid and the Spanish economy, 1560-1850. 4.2416
The madwoman in the attic. 2.5563
Maestro. 1.3768
Maeve. 2.9089
The Mafia of a Sicilian village, 1860-1960. 4.6719
Mafteah ha-maftehot. 5.8237
Magazine index. 1.31
Magazines for libraries. 5.8311
Magazines in the twentieth century. 2.3640
Maggie, a girl of the streets. 2.10981
A maggot. 2.9686
The Maghreb in the modern world: Algeria, Tunisia, Morocco. 3.5191
Magic and the millennium. 1.1580
The magic barrel. 2.13158
The magic factory. 2.3022
The magic feather. 4.10912
The magic goes away. 2.13192
Magic in the web. 2.6670
The magic-maker, E. E. Cummings. 2.11544
The magic mirror. 2.3085
The magic mirror of M. C. Escher. 1.5022
The magic mountain. 2.13832
The Magic mountain. 2.13839
Magic, science, and civilization. 3.209
Magic, science and religion. 4.405
Magic shots. 5.4673
The magic striptease. 2.13038
Magic, witchcraft, and curing. 4.560
Magical medicine. 4.823
Magical realist fiction. 2.3717
The magician, the witch, and the law. 5.683
Magill's bibliography of literary criticism. 5.8270
Magill's cinema annual. 2.2866
Magill's survey of cinema 2.2872, 2.2978
The Maginot Line syndrome. 3.7850
The magistrate's tael. 4.4674
Magna Carta and the idea of liberty. 4.8393
Magna carta; its role in the making of the English Constitution, 1300-1629. 4.8390
Magna Graecia. 1.4724
Magnalia Christi Americana, Books 1 and 2. 3.7950
Magnetic recording. 5.6562
The magnificent Ambersons. 2.11238
The magnificent Ambersons. 2.11239
Magnificent microbes. 5.4443
Magnificent voyagers. 4.99
Magnolias. 5.5352
Magritte. 1.6267
The magus. 2.9687
A magyar zenetortenet Kezikonyve. English. 1.3703
The Mahābhārata. 2.1935
Mahābhārata. 2.1936-2.1937
Mahābhārata. Bhagavadgītā. English & Sanskrit. 1.1686
Mahābhārata. English. 2.1935
Mahābhārata. English. Selections. 2.1936

Mahan on sea power. 3.6378
Mahatma Gandhi. 3.4311
Mahatma Gandhi and his apostles. 3.4310
Mahayana Buddhism. 1.2154, 1.2156
Mahāyāna Buddhist meditation. 1.2155
A Mahayana text. 1.2128
Mahāyāna texts. 1.1737
The Maias. 2.5455
The Maid of Orleans. 2.13649
The maids. 2.4534
Maids, madonnas & witches. 1.5790
Maigret and the man on the bench. 2.4747
Mailer, his life and times. 2.12105
Maillol. 1.5709
A Maimonides reader. 1.1961
Main currents in American thought. 2.10253
Main currents in Caribbean thought. 3.9145
Main currents in sociological thought. 4.4737
Main currents in the history of American journalism. 2.3583
Main currents of Marxism. 4.6937
Main currents of Western thought. 3.87
Main line to oblivion. 4.4006
Main line west. 2.11883
The main of light. 2.2714
The main stalk. 3.5915
Main Street. 2.12009
Main street on the middle border. 3.8307
Main-travelled roads. 2.11035
Maine. 3.7959
Maine: a guide to the Vacation State. 3.7960
Mainland Southeast Asia. 3.4385
Mains sales. 2.4726
Mainsprings of civilization. 4.365
Mainsprings of the German revival. 4.2344
Mainstreaming outsiders. 4.10862
Mainstreaming young children. 4.10938
Mainstreams of modern art. 1.4780
Maintenance management. 5.7051
La maison de papier. 2.4610
Maistre Pierre Pathelin, reproduction en fac-similé de l'édition imprimée en 1489 par Pierre Levet. 2.3972
Les maîtres sonneurs. 2.4288
Maize breeding and genetics. 5.5325
The majesty that was Islam. 3.3654
Major British poets of the romantic period. 2.6092
Major Canadian authors. 2.9884
The major comedies of Alexander Fredro. 2.1701
The major critics. 2.5497
Major English writers of the eighteenth century. 2.6088
The major features of evolution. 5.3361
Major governments of Asia. 4.8692
The major international treaties, 1914-1973. 4.8968
Major libraries of the world. 5.7657
Major lyricists of the Northern Sung, A.D. 960-1126. 2.2167
The major ordeals of the mind, and the countless minor ones. 2.4635
Major peace treaties of modern history, 1648-1967. 4.8964
Major plays of Chikamatsu 2.2060
Major poetry. 2.6311
Major problems in contemporary European philosophy, from Dilthey to Heidegger. 1.439
The major seaports of the United Kingdom. 4.3953
The major Shakespearean tragedies. 2.6797
Major social issues. 4.5106
Major Soviet nationalities. 3.3024
Major technological risk. 4.3479
The major themes of Robert Frost. 2.11759
Major themes of the Qur'ān. 1.2032
Major trends in Jewish mysticism. 1.1985
Major trends in Mexican philosophy. 1.661
The major works of Heinrich von Kleist. 2.13625
Majority leadership in the U.S. House. 4.8062
Majority rule. 4.7584
Makar's dream, and other stories. 2.1513
Make it new. 2.2585
Make prayers to the raven. 3.5900
Maker of heaven and earth. 1.2904

Makers of American diplomacy. 3.6406
Makers of modern journalism. 2.3600
Makers of modern strategy. 5.7214
Making an issue of child abuse. 4.6565
Making babies. 5.5050
Making certain it goes on. 2.11904
Making desegregation work. 4.10787
Making federalism work. 4.7878
Making health care decisions. 5.4571
Making health decisions. 5.4685
Making it crazy. 5.4810
Making money, making movies. 2.3019
Making ocean policy. 4.334
The making of a hero. 2.1590
The making of a missile crisis, October 1962. 3.7862
The making of a musical. 1.4482
The making of a new Eastern Question. 3.1262
The making of a profession. 5.6250
The making of a scientist. 5.815
The making of a special relationship. 3.6426
The making of Americans. 2.12513
The Making of America's Soviet policy. 4.9063
The making of an American community. 4.5201
The making of an Arab nationalist. 3.3712
The making of an ethnic middle class. 3.8639
The making of an inmate. 4.6907
The making of an insurgent. 3.7657
The making of black America. 3.6623
The making of Black revolutionaries. 3.6833
The making of British colonial development policy, 1914-1940. 4.2305
The making of Citizen Kane. 2.3026
The making of colonial Lucknow, 1856-1877. 3.4359
The making of contemporary Africa. 3.5081
The making of Dutch towns. 1.5605
The making of economic society. 4.1751
The making of Elizabethan foreign policy, 1558-1603. 3.1427
The making of English towns. 4.6257
The making of Europe. 3.142
The making of foreign policy in China. 4.9077
The making of geography. 4.47
The making of geology. 5.2954
The making of George Orwell. 2.9189
The making of Homeric verse. 2.514
The making of India's foreign policy. 3.4229
The making of Italy, 1796-1870. 3.2860
The making of jazz. 1.4320
The making of Medieval Spain. 3.3423
The making of men. 4.10182
The making of mind. 5.100
The making of modern advertising. 4.4427
The making of modern British politics, 1867-1939. 3.1623
The making of modern English society, 1530-1780. 4.2254
The making of modern English society, 1750 to the present day. 4.2248
The making of modern English society from 1850. 4.5309
The making of modern Greece. 3.2692
The making of modern Holland. 3.2987
The making of modern Ireland, 1603-1923. 3.1831
The making of modern Lebanon. 3.3784
The making of modern Mexico. 3.8939
The making of modern Zionism. 3.4017
The making of new cultures. 4.500
The making of new Germany. 3.2354
The making of Pakistan. 3.4133
The making of political women. 4.5957
The making of Roman Italy. 3.2755
The making of Russian absolutism, 1613-1801. 3.3092
The making of South East Asia. 3.4420
The making of the Auden canon. 2.8400
The making of the Australian constitution. 4.8816
The making of the Constitution. 4.7805
The making of the English landscape. 3.1720
The making of the English working class. 4.3641
The making of the good neighbor policy. 3.9023

The making of the Habsburg monarchy, 1550-1700. 3.1880
The making of the labor bureaucrat: union leadership in the United States, 1870-1920. 4.3373
The Making of the mayor, Chicago, 1983. 4.8866
The Making of the Middle Ages. 3.136
The Making of the modern family. 4.5656
The Making of the modern world. 3.606
The making of the Monroe doctrine. 3.7117
The making of the National Labor Relations Board. 4.9553
The making of the President, 1960. 3.7852
The making of the President, 1964. 3.7892
The making of the President, 1968. 3.7895
The making of the President, 1972. 3.7915
The making of the representative for Planet 8. 2.9020
The making of The return of the native. 2.7764
The making of the Second Reform Bill. 4.8462
The making of urban America. 1.5596
The making of urban Europe, 1000-1950. 4.6251
The making of Victorian England. 3.1593
The making of Wordsworth's poetry, 1785-1798. 2.8322
Making sense of Marx. 4.6951
The Making, shaping, and treating of steel. 5.6787
Making the American mind; social and moral ideas in the McGuffey readers. 2.1005
Making the connections. 4.5952
Making the grade. 4.10662
Making the invisible woman visible. 4.5998
Making the most of the least. 4.1812
The Makioka sisters. 2.2120
The Malacia tapestry. 2.9613
The Malagasy and the Europeans. 3.5315
A Malamud reader. 2.13153
Malawi. 3.5495
Malawi. 3.5492-3.5493
Malawi, the politics of despair. 3.5496
The Malay world of Southeast. 5.8059
Malaya, Indonesia, Borneo, and the Philippines. 3.4555
Malayan forest primates. 5.4019
Malaysia. 3.4533, 3.4538-3.4539, 3.4548, 5.8064
Malaysia and Singapore. 3.4543
Malaysia, growth and equity in a multiracial society. 4.2529, 4.8726
Malaysian politics. 3.4544
Malcolm. 2.12844
Malcolm Lowry. 2.9059, 2.9061-2.9062
Malcolm Lowry: his art & early life. 2.9060
Malcolm Lowry: the man and his work. 2.9064
The malcontent. 2.6624
Maldoror (Les chants de Maldoror) 2.4170
Male and female. 4.5505
Male dominance and female autonomy. 4.584
The male machine. 4.5834
Malebranche. 1.801
Le malentendu. 2.4448
The malformed infant and child. 5.5076
Les malheurs de la vertu. 2.4097
The maligned states. 4.8248
Mallarmé. 2.4263, 2.4265
Mallarmé and the art of being difficult. 2.4264
Mallet du Pan (1749-1800) 3.2069
Malnutrition and poverty. 5.7117
Malone dies. 2.4410
Malone meurt. 2.4408
A Malory handbook. 2.6410
Malory's Morte d'Arthur. 2.6409
Malory's originality. 2.6411
Malraux; a collection of critical essays. 2.4624
Malraux par lui-même. 2.4611
Malthus. 4.1590
Malvina Hoffman. 1.5668
Mamba's daughters. 2.11870
Mammalian cell membranes. 5.4047
Mammalogy. 5.3975
The mammals. 5.3973
The mammals of Canada. 5.3988
Mammals of North America. 5.3984

The mammals of North America. 5.3985
Mammals of the world. 5.3976
A man. 2.5081
Man adapting. 5.4551
Man against mass society. 1.834
Man and aggression. 5.423
Man and atom. 5.6604
Man and cosmos. 5.1788
Man and crisis. 3.47
Man and culture. 4.404
Man and God in art and ritual. 1.4637
Man and his government. 4.7231
Man and his myths. 2.8157
Man and land in Chinese history. 4.1660
Man and land in Peru. 4.2842
Man and land in the Far East. 4.2861
Man and nature. 4.366
Man and nature in the Renaissance. 5.764
Man and society. 4.7277
Man and technics. 3.17
Man and technology. 1.1311
Man and the conquest of the poles. 4.103
Man and the environment. 5.8114
Man and the sea; classic accounts of marine explorations. 4.330
Man and the stars. 5.1752
Man and the state. 4.7476
A man and two women. 2.9019
Man and value. 1.1494
Man and woman. 2.5973
Man and woman among the Azande. 3.5176
The man Bilbo. 3.7630
A man called White. 3.6858
A man could stand up. 2.8632
Man, culture, and animals. 5.3808
Man, culture, and society. 4.406
The man died: prison notes of Wole Soyinka. 4.6923
A man for all seasons. 2.8466
Man for himself. 1.1412
The man from Halifax. 3.8763
The man from Main Street. 2.12008
A man from the north. 2.8454
Man: his first two million years. 4.430
The man I pretend to be. 2.5035
Man in adaptation. 5.3378
Man in nature. 5.3377
Man in revolt. 1.2906
Man in society. 4.4847
The man in the gray flannel suit. 2.12772
The man in the high castle. 2.12973
Man in the Holocene. 2.13743
The man in the iron mask. 2.4176
Man in the modern age. 3.191
Man in the Pacific Islands. 4.2597
The man in the principal's office. 4.10671
The man in the street. 3.6395
Man is not alone. 1.1547
Man is the measure. 1.104
Man is the measure of all things. 2.3096
Man-made America: chaos or control? 1.5600
The man-made object. 1.5106
The man-made sun. 5.6615
Man makes himself. 3.118
The man Mencken. 2.12134
Man, metals, and modern magic. 5.6758
The man of feeling. 2.7099
Man of fire. 1.6004
'A man of genius' 1.5916
The man of Independence. 3.7809
A man of letters. 2.9253
The man of letters in New England and the South. 2.10440
A man of letters in the nineteenth-century South. 2.11075
The man of reason. 1.1238
A man of the people. 2.10104
Man on his own. 1.1542
Man on his past. 3.383
The man on horseback. 4.7719
'Man over money' 4.8229
Man, play, and games. 3.53
Man Ray. 5.6960
Man Ray, the photographic image. 5.6977
Man, state, and society in East European history. 3.3511
Man the hunter. 4.531
Man, the state and war. 4.9007

Man through the ages. 3.29
Man, time, and fossils. 5.3381
The man to send rain clouds. 2.10811
The man Verdi. 1.4030
The man versus the state, with four essays on politics and society. 4.7647
The man who kept the secrets. 4.7909
The man who lost China. 3.4815
The man who loved children 2.10170
The man who was not with it. 2.13051
The man who would be perfect. 4.7159
Man with a bull-tongue plow. 2.12559
The man with the golden arm. 2.11307
The man within. 2.8752
A man without a mask. 2.7411
The Man without qualities. 2.13843
The managed economy. 4.1993
Management and labor in imperial Germany. 4.3659
Management and operations of American shipping. 4.3973
Management and the worker. 5.5603
Management and unions. 4.3645
Management classics. 4.2654
Management development and training handbook. 4.4381
Management information systems. 5.5608, 5.5612
The management of Britain's external relations. 4.9100
The Management of common human miseries. 5.5181
The management of information systems. 5.5607
Management of lakes and ponds. 5.5471
The management of marine fisheries. 5.5478
Management of organizational behavior. 4.2695
The management of Pakistan's economy, 1947-82. 4.2515
Management of the industrial firm in the USSR. 4.2380
Management rights and union interests. 4.3431
Management science. 4.2640
Management: tasks, responsibilities, practices. 4.2647
The Managerial and cost accountant's handbook. 4.4414
Managerial freedom and job security. 4.3576
Managerial prerogative and the question of control. 4.3427
The managerial revolution. 4.7466
Managers and subordinates. 4.4360
Managers and work reform. 4.3563
Managers and workers. 4.3006
Managers of virtue. 4.10640
Managing academic change. 4.10593
Managing an organization. 4.2644
Managing cooperative advertising. 4.4437
Managing ethnic tensions in multi-ethnic societies. 3.4372
Managing foreign exchange risk. 4.4463
Managing human assets. 4.4362
Managing international risk. 4.4601
Managing local government for improved performance. 4.8846
Managing our wildlife resources. 5.5497
Managing professional people. 4.3520
Managing the multinational enterprise. 4.2735
Managing the ocean. 4.352
The Manawaka world of Margaret Laurence. 2.9942
Manchild in the promised land. 3.6818
Mandala. 1.1821
Mandarin ducks and butterflies. 2.2177
The Mandarins. 2.4389
The mandarins. 3.4712
Mandarins, Jews, and missionaries. 3.3944
Les mandarins 2.4390
Mandate in British tropical Africa. 3.5116
Mandelstam. 2.1577
Manet. 1.6118
Manet, 1832-1883. 1.4975
Manet and his critics. 1.6116
Manet and the modern tradition. 1.6117
Manhattan transfer. 2.11582
The maniac in the cellar. 2.6031
Manias, panics, and crashes. 4.1715

Manierismus in der Literatur. 2.2619
Manifest destiny. 3.6362
Manifest destiny and mission in American history. 3.6353
Manifestations of discontent in Germany on the eve of the Reformation. 3.2275
Manifestoes of surrealism. 1.1399
Manitoba, a history. 3.8858
Mankind at the turning point. 4.1791
Mankind evolving. 5.3379
Manley and the new Jamaica. 3.9112
Der Mann ohne Eigenschaften. 2.13842
Mannerism. 1.4763
Mannerism. 1.4767
Mannerism and anti-mannerism in Italian painting, two essays. 1.6183
Mannerism and Renaissance poetry. 2.2620
The manners and customs of the modern Egyptians. 3.5149
The manners and customs of the police. 4.6815
Manometric & biochemical techniques. 5.4219
Manon Lescaut. 2.4083-2.4084
Manpower shortage and the fall of the Roman Empire in the West. 3.2809
Manpower utilization in the railroad industry. 4.3986
Man's changing mask. 2.2542
Man's conquest of the Pacific. 4.748
Man's fate. 2.4614
Man's glassy essence. 4.540
Man's hope. 2.4616
Man's most dangerous myth. 4.479
Man's place. 2.8407
Man's place in nature. 1.1320, 5.3380
A man's reach, the philosophy of Judge Jerome Frank. 4.9449
Man's role in changing the face of the earth. 4.2
Man's unconquerable mind. 2.5513
Man's Western quest. 3.15
Manservant and maidservant. 2.8529
The mansion. 2.11669
The Mansions and the shanties (Sobrados e mucambos) 3.9193
Mantegna. 1.6215
The manticore. 2.9924
Mantissa. 2.9688
The mantram handbook. 1.1625
Manual de bibliografía de la literatura española. 5.8026
Manual de gramática histórica española. 2.889
Manual de pronunciación española. 2.891
A manual for writers of term papers, theses, and dissertations. 4.10619
A manual of aquatic plants. 5.3668
Manual of bibliography. 5.7677
Manual of botany. 5.3674
Manual of classification for librarians. 5.7636
Manual of cultivated broad-leaved trees & shrubs. 5.5360
Manual of cultivated broad-leaved trees and shrubs. 5.5360
Manual of cultivated conifers. 5.5357
The manual of cultivated orchid species. 5.5349
Manual of cultivated plants most commonly grown in the continental United States and Canada. 5.3669
Manual of cultivated trees and shrubs hardy in North America exclusive of the subtropical and warmer temperate regions. 5.3687
A manual of European languages for librarians. 2.210
A manual of experimental embryology. 5.4126
Manual of foreign languages for the use of librarians, bibliographers, research workers, editors, translators, and printers. 5.7564
A manual of Greek mathematics. 5.1078
Manual of Hispanic bibliography. 5.8023
A manual of historic ornament. 1.6536
A manual of international law. 4.9292
Manual of mineralogy (after James D. Dana) 5.3021
A Manual of new mineral names, 1892-1978. 5.3010
Manual of photogrammetry. 5.5829

Manual of political economy. 4.1475
Manual of remote sensing. 4.23
Manual of soil laboratory testing. 5.5910
Manual of solid state circuit design and troubleshooting. 5.6463
Manual of the grasses of the United States. 5.3696
A manual of the theory and practice of classical theatrical dancing (méthode Cecchetti) 4.1117
Manual of the trees of North America (exclusive of Mexico) 5.3688
A manual of the writings in Middle English, 1050-1400. 2.5607
Manual of traffic engineering studies. 4.3943
Manual of traffic signal design. 5.6066
Manual of vascular plants of Northeastern United States and adjacent Canada. 5.3672
Manual of woody landscape plants. 5.3684
Manual of Zen Buddhism. 1.1755
Manual on the Federal budget process. 4.4683
Manuductio ad ministerium. 1.3045
Manuel de Falla. 1.3865
Manuel des études littéraires françaises. 2.3826
Manuel Gálvez. 2.5388
Manuel illustré d'histoire de la littérature française. 2.3827
Manufacturing, the formidable competitive weapon. 5.7023
The manuscript of Shakespeare's Hamlet and the problems of its transmission. 2.6658
Manuscript painting at the court of France. 1.6411
The many colored coat. 2.9917
Many dimensions. 2.9527
The many faces of primitive art. 1.4684
The Many facets of human settlements. 4.6181
Many Mexicos. 3.8919
Many-minded Homer. 2.497
Many tender ties. 3.8840
Many-valued logic. 1.1196
Many voices. 4.10888
A many-windowed house. 2.10379
Many worlds. 3.4313
The Manyōshū. 2.2021
Man'yōshū. 2.2021
Mao. 3.4830
Mao and the Chinese revolution. 3.4831
Mao papers. 3.4825
Mao Tse-tung. 3.4833
Mao Tsê-tung. 3.4835
Mao Tse-tung and I were beggars. 3.4832
Mao Tse-tung in opposition, 1927-1935. 3.4834
Mao Zedong, a preliminary reassessment. 3.4836
Maoism, a sourcebook. 3.4828
Maoism in India 4.7116
The Maoist educational revolution. 4.10137
The Maori. 3.5608
Maori. 3.5614
Maori poetry. 1.4350
Maori wood sculpture of New Zealand. 1.5770
The Maoris of New Zealand. 3.5609
Mao's China. 4.2462, 4.8747
Mao's China and after. 3.4796
Mao's people. 4.5459
Mao's way. 3.4799
Map collections in the United States and Canada. 4.221
Map index to topographic quadrangles of the United States, 1882-1940. 4.234
A Map of Australian verse. 2.10141
The map of knowledge. 1.747
Map projection equations. 4.214
Map sources directory. 5.7579
Map use. 4.208
The mapmakers. 4.210
Mapping the American Revolutionary War. 4.235
Mapping the Transmississippi West, 1540-1861. 5.7556
Mapping the world's vegetation. 5.3643
Maps. 4.222
Maps and charts published in America before 1800. 5.8215
Maps and diagrams. 4.204
Maps & man. 4.228
Maps and map-makers. 4.229

Maps and their makers. 4.226
The maps of Canada. 4.236
Maps of the heavens. 5.1742
Maps, topographical and statistical. 4.197
The marble threshing floor. 2.571
Marc Chagall. 1.6280-1.6281
Marcel Breuer, furniture and interiors. 1.6569
Marcel Dubé. 2.4829
Marcel Duchamp. 1.4972, 1.6100
Marcel Proust. 2.4665
Marcel Proust and deliverance from time.
  2.4663
Marcel Proust, selected letters, 1880-1903.
  2.4670
Marcella's Italian kitchen. 5.7137
The march of folly. 3.615
The march of journalism. 2.3681
The march of literature, from Confucius to
  modern times. 2.2610
The March of time, 1935-1951. 2.3647
The march to Zion. 3.6453
Marching men; a critical text. 2.11317
Marching to glory. 1.3409
Marco Polo's Asia. 3.3613
Marcus Alonzo Hanna. 3.7500
Marcus Crassus and the late Roman Republic.
  3.2786
Marcus Garvey and the vision of Africa.
  3.6834
The Marcus Garvey and Universal Negro
  Improvement Association papers. 3.6836
Marcus Porcius Cato, On agriculture. 2.654
The Marcus W. Jernegan essays in American
  historiography. 3.6254
La mare au diable. 2.4289
Margaret Atwood. 2.9912
Margaret Drabble. 2.9666, 2.9670
Margaret Drabble, existing within structures.
  2.9668-2.9669
Margaret Fuller. 2.11191
Margaret Fuller, American romantic. 2.11189
Margaret Laurence. 2.9941
Margaret Mead and Samoa. 4.685
Margaret Mitchell's Gone with the wind letters,
  1936-1949. 2.12198
Margaret Sanger. 4.5675
Margin released. 2.9250
Marginal natives. 4.488
The Marginal revolution in economics. 4.1331
Marguerite de Navarre's Heptameron: themes,
  language, and structure. 2.3988
Marguerite Duras. 2.4523
María. 2.5412
Maria Edgeworth. 2.7687-2.7689
Maria Malibran. 1.4094
Maria Montessori. 4.10210
Maria Nephele. 2.580
Maria Theresa. 3.1884
The Marian paintings of Jan van Eyck.
  1.6263a
Marianne Moore. 2.12201, 2.12203-2.12204
A Marianne Moore reader. 2.12200
Marianne Moore; the cage and the animal.
  2.12202
Mariano Azuela. 2.5336
MariChem 85. 5.6859
Marichem 85 proceedings. 5.6859
Marie Antoinette. 3.2053-3.2054
Marie de France. 2.3956
Marie Grubbe, a lady of the seventeenth
  century. 2.14012
Marie; or, Slavery in the United States. 3.7200
Marihuana, the first twelve thousand years.
  5.234
Marijuana. 4.9577
Marijuana and health hazards. 5.4428
Marijuana and social evolution. 4.6666
Marijuana use and criminal sanctions. 4.9576
Marine biology. 5.3249-5.3250
Marine botany. 5.3776
Marine ecology. 5.3562
The marine environment and structural design.
  5.5982
Marine gas turbines. 5.7517
Marine geology. 5.2982
Marine life. 5.3820
Marine mammals and fisheries. 5.3980
Marine manganese deposits. 5.3024

Marine optics. 4.346
Marine transportation in the United States.
  4.3975
Marinetti; selected writings. 1.6735
Marino Marini. 1.5732
Mario Vargas Llosa. 2.5437-2.5438
Marion Fay. 2.8214
The Maritime dimension. 4.9314
The maritime rights movement, 1919-1927.
  3.8798
The maritime story. 4.3392
Maritime trade and state development in early
  Southeast Asia. 4.4241
Maritime trade and technology. 4.3971
The Maritimes and Canada before
  confederation. 3.8736
Marius the Epicurean. 2.7980
Marivaux. 2.4080
Mark Twain. 2.10953, 2.10961-2.10962
Mark Twain; 2.10963
Mark Twain: a biography. 2.10960
Mark Twain and his world. 2.10958
Mark Twain & Huck Finn. 2.10943
Mark Twain & the South. 2.10971
Mark Twain as a literary comedian. 2.10970
Mark Twain at work. 2.10966
Mark Twain. God's fool. 2.10964
Mark Twain-Howells letters. 2.10949
Mark Twain of the Enterprise. 2.10939
The Mark Twain papers. 2.10935
Mark Twain: the critical heritage. 2.10967
Mark Twain's America. 2.10955
Mark Twain's Huckleberry Finn. 2.10944
Mark Twain's last years as a writer. 2.10965
Mark Twain's letters. 2.10948
Mark Twain's Notebooks & journals. 2.10937
Mark Twain's San Francisco. 3.8624
Market structure and innovation. 4.1863
Market structure, bargaining power, and
  resource price information. 4.3723
Marketing and development: the Thailand
  experience. 4.4292
Marketing and economics. 4.4289
The marketing channel. 4.4285
Marketing channels. 4.4296
Marketing decision models. 4.4299
The marketing environment. 4.4278
Marketing information. 4.4294
Marketing management in multinational firms.
  4.4298
Marketing research and knowledge
  development. 4.4306
Marketing/research people. 4.4305
Marketing to the changing household. 4.4309
Markets and hierarchies, analysis and antitrust
  implications. 4.2661
Markets and macroeconomics. 4.1463
Markets & macroeconomics. 4.1463
Markets and states in tropical Africa. 4.2992
Markets for power. 4.3803
Markings. 3.1148
Marko the Prince. 2.1216
Marlborough, his life and times. 3.1515
Marlowe. 2.6618
Marlowe and the early Shakespeare. 2.6619
Maroon societies. 4.6426
Marquand. 2.12112
The Marquis de Sade. 2.4100
The Marquis de Sade, a biography. 2.4099
The Marquise of O. 2.13624
La marquise sortit à cinq heures. 2.4627
The marriage. 2.1703
Marriage à la mode. 2.6990
Marriage and divorce. 4.1648
Marriage and love in England. 4.5620
Marriage and marital therapy. 5.4882
Marriage and rank in Bengali culture. 3.4328
Marriage and sexuality in Islam. 4.5565
Marriage, authority, and final causes. 4.580
Marriage, class and colour in nineteenth-
  century Cuba. 4.5613
Marriage, divorce, remarriage. 4.5571
The marriage feast. 2.14091
Marriage in tribal societies. 4.577
Marriage, morals, and sex in America. 4.5573
The marriages between zones three, four, and
  five (as narrated by the chroniclers of zone
  three) 2.9021

Married life in an African tribe. 4.565
Married to the job. 4.5668
Marry me. 2.13369
Mars. 5.1817
Marsden Hartley. 1.5941
The Marshall Plan revisited. 4.2213
Marsilius of Padua. 4.7377
Martereau. 2.4708-2.4709
Martha Graham. 4.1140, 4.1142
Martha Graham; portrait of the lady as an
  artist. 4.1141
Martha Graham, sixteen dances in photographs.
  4.1143
Martha W. Griffiths. 3.7645
The Martial metropolis. 4.6219
The martial spirit. 3.7501
A Martian Odyssey and other science fiction
  tales. 2.12656
A Martian sends a postcard home. 2.9803
Martin A. Hansen. 2.14025
Martin Buber. 1.973
Martin Buber, Jewish existentialist. 1.971
Martin Buber's life and work. 1.972,
  1.974-1.975
Martin Dies. 3.7545
Martin Dies' story. 3.7544
Martin Eden. 2.2349, 2.12025
Martin Heidegger. 1.1002
Martin Luther. 1.2339, 1.2343
Martin Luther on the bondage of the will.
  1.1497
Martin Van Buren. 3.7130
Martini. 1.5733
Martyrdom and persecution in the early church.
  1.2474
Martyrdom of Polycarp. 1.2181, 2.327
The martyred. 2.13116
Marva Collins' way. 4.10156
Marvell and the civic crown. 2.7108
Marvelous journey. 2.5462
A marvelous world. 2.4646
Marx against the Marxists. 4.7137
Marx, an introduction. 4.6961
Marx and Engels on the population bomb.
  4.1589
Marx and justice. 4.6950
Marx and modern social theory. 4.6962
Marx and the Bible. 1.2533
Marx and the Marxists. 4.6967
Marx before Marxism. 4.6956
Marx, Engels, Marxism. 4.7101
The Marx-Engels reader. 4.6947
Marx on money. 4.1324
The Marxian revolutionary idea. 4.6964
Marxian socialism in the United States. 4.6986
Marxism. 4.6938, 4.6958
Marxism after Marx. 4.6939
Marxism and art. 4.7135
Marxism and domination. 4.7586
Marxism and form. 2.2480
Marxism and imperialism. 4.6936
Marxism and literary criticism. 2.2479
Marxism and literature. 4.7136
Marxism and modernism. 1.474
Marxism and politics. 4.7589
Marxism and the human individual. 1.477
Marxism and the metropolis. 4.6347
Marxism and the oppression of women. 4.7149
Marxism and the philosophy of science. 1.478
Marxism and the reality of power, 1919-1980.
  4.6972
Marxism in modern France. 4.7050
Marxism in Southeast Asia. 3.4408
Marxism in the twentieth century. 1.471
Marxism in the U.S.S.R. 1.1106
Marxism in the USSR. 1.1106
Marxism: the unity of theory and practice.
  4.7005
Marxist historians. 4.1725
A Marxist looks at Jesus. 1.2864
Marxist thought in Latin America. 4.7010
Marx's concept of man. 4.6953
Marx's fate. 4.6960
Marx's interpretation of history. 1.1041
Marx's Paris writings. 4.6957
Mary Baker Eddy, an interpretive biography of
  the founder of Christian Science. 1.3331
Mary Barton: a tale of Manchester life. 2.7721

Mary Boykin Chesnut. 3.335
Mary Cassatt. 1.5922, 1.6438
Mary Cassatt: oils and pastels. 1.5923
Mary Chesnut's Civil War. 3.7367
Mary Ellen Chase. 2.11486
Mary in the New Testament. 1.2901
Mary Lavin. 2.8949, 2.8951
Mary Lavin, quiet rebel. 2.8950
Mary Lincoln; biography of a marriage. 3.7289
Mary Lyon and Mount Holyoke. 4.11002
Mary, Mother of the Lord. 1.2902
Mary O'Grady. 2.8948
Mary Olivier: a life. 2.9322
Mary Peters. 2.11483
Mary, Queen of Scots. 3.1794
Mary Queen of Scots. 3.1795
Mary Renault. 2.9270
Mary Shelley's journal. 2.8093
Mary Stuart. 2.13649
Mary Todd Lincoln: her life and letters.
    3.7290
The Mary Wigman book. 4.1161
Mary Wollstonecraft. 2.8292, 4.6096
Maryland. 3.8100a, 3.8101
Maryland under the commonwealth. 3.8106
Maryland's revolution of government,
    1689-1692. 3.8103
Marzubān-nāmah. English. 2.1762
Masada; Herod's fortress and the Zealot's last
    stand. 3.3821
Masaoka Shiki. 2.2076
Masculinity & femininity. 5.492
Masers and lasers. 5.6490
Mashpee, the story of Cape Cod's Indian town.
    3.8004
Mask and sword. 2.2136
The mask of Apollo. 2.9264
The mask of Keats. 2.7857
The mask of shame. 5.445
Mask or face. 2.3353
Masks and façades. 1.5404
Masks in a pageant. 3.6313
Masks, mimes and miracles. 2.2803
The masks of King Lear. 2.6665
The masks of Othello. 2.6671
Masks or faces? 2.3115
Mason on library buildings. 5.7614
The masquerade. 2.10108
Masques in Jacobean tragedy. 2.5881
Mass communication in China. 2.54
Mass culture revisited. 3.6186
The mass media. 2.60
Mass media and the Supreme Court. 4.9531
The mass media election. 4.7961
Mass media law. 4.9535
Mass-mediated culture. 4.5011
Mass persuasion in Communist China. 3.4804
Mass spectrometry for chemists and
    biochemists. 5.2680
Mass-transfer operations. 5.6845
Massachusettensis de conditoribus. 3.7982
Massachusetts. 3.7969
Massachusetts: a guide to the Pilgrim State.
    3.7990
Massachusetts Institute of Technology
    wavelength tables. 5.2312
Masses and man. 3.681
Masses in Latin America. 4.5253
The master and Margarita. 2.1543
The master builders. 1.5416
Master drawings. 1.5792
Master European realists of the nineteenth
    century. 2.2661
Master guide to birding. 5.3951
The master guide to photography. 5.6940
'Master Harold' 2.10067
Master index to the J. F. K. assassination
    investigations. 3.7881
A master list of nonstellar optical astronomical
    objects. 5.1738
The master of go. 2.2099
The Master of the Amsterdam Cabinet, or, The
    Housebook Master, ca. 1470-1500. 1.4996
Master of the battlefield. 3.1272
The Master of the Housebook. 1.6432
Master Roger Williams. 3.8016
Master Tung's Western chamber romance.
    2.2219

Masterful images. 2.5749
Mastering the art of French cooking. 5.7135
Masterman Ready. 2.7925
Masterpieces from the House of Fabergé.
    1.6666
Masterpieces of architectural drawing. 1.5488
Masterpieces of glass. 1.6642
Masterpieces of Italian drawing in the Robert
    Lehman Collection, the Metropolitan
    Museum of Art. 1.5810
Masterpieces of music before 1750. 1.3427
Masterpieces of the modern Italian theatre.
    2.4900
Masterpieces of the modern Spanish theatre.
    2.5157
Masterpieces of Western sculpture. 1.5641
Masterplots. 2.2354
Masterplots annual. 2.2355
Masters and disciples. 2.1805
The masters and the slaves. 3.9191
Masters of Chinese political thought. 4.7281
Masters of Japanese calligraphy, 8th-9th
    century. 1.6371
Masters of modern art. 1.4819
Masters of modern drama. 2.3764
The masters of past time. 1.6232
Masters of seventeenth-century Dutch genre
    painting. 1.6368
Masters of sociological thought. 4.4739
Masters of the dew. 2.4840
Masters of the drama. 2.2802
Masters of the keyboard 1.4155
Masters of the keyboard. 1.4158
Masters without slaves. 3.7470
Masterworks of the German cinema. 2.3021
The mastery of drawing. 1.5819
The mastery of movement. 2.3133
Mastro-don Gesualdo. 2.5016
The matchmaker. 2.12713
Mate-selection. 4.5649
The material basis of evolution. 5.3358
Material civilization and capitalism. 4.1744
The material culture of the Chumash
    interaction sphere. 3.5860
Material culture studies in America. 3.6137
Material requirements planning. 5.7028
Materialism in Indian thought. 1.193
The materialist conception of history. 3.482
Materials and devices for electrical engineers
    and physicists. 5.6453
The materials and methods of sculpture.
    1.5781
The materials and techniques of medieval
    painting. 1.6375
Materials handbook. 5.5759
Materials management systems. 5.7037
The materials of the artist and their use in
    painting. 1.6343
Materials science and metallurgy. 5.5765
Materials science for engineers. 5.5769
Maternal behavior in mammals. 5.4086
Maternal employment. 4.3247
Maternity policies and working women. 4.3261
Math equals. 5.1090
Mathematical analysis for economists. 4.1289
Mathematical and biological interrelations.
    5.3310
Mathematical astronomy with a pocket
    calculator. 5.1719
Mathematical biology. 5.3299
Mathematical biophysics; physico-mathematical
    foundations of biology. 5.3495
The mathematical career of Pierre de Fermat
    (1601-1665). 5.1091
Mathematical cosmology. 5.1873
Mathematical discovery. 5.1120
The mathematical experience. 5.1032
The mathematical foundations of quantum
    mechanics. 5.2163
Mathematical foundations of quantum
    mechanics. 5.2151
Mathematical foundations of statistical
    mechanics. 5.2181
Mathematical gems. 5.1325
The mathematical groundwork of economics.
    4.1291
Mathematical handbook for scientists and
    engineers. 5.1115

A mathematical introduction to logic. 5.1039
Mathematical investigations in the theory of
    value and price, 1892. 4.1295
Mathematical logic. 1.1220
Mathematical method. 5.1059
Mathematical methods in economics. 4.1391
Mathematical methods in engineering. 5.5709
Mathematical methods of statistics. 5.1386
Mathematical modeling of water quality.
    5.6017
Mathematical models for the growth of human
    populations. 4.1585
Mathematical models of arms control and
    disarmament. 4.9161
Mathematical models of economic growth
    4.1284
Mathematical neurobiology. 5.4319
Mathematical philosophy. 5.1049
Mathematical physics; an essay on the
    application of mathematics to the moral
    sciences. 4.1294
Mathematical programming. 5.5582
Mathematical programming for management
    and business. 5.5579
Mathematical psychology. 5.41, 5.54
Mathematical recreations of Lewis Carroll
    [pseud.]. 5.1257
The mathematical revolution in Soviet
    economics. 4.1365
Mathematical snapshots. 5.1255
Mathematical sociology. 4.4790
Mathematical statistical mechanics. 5.1972
Mathematical statistics. 5.1387
Mathematical theory in Soviet planning.
    4.2808
The mathematical theory of communication.
    5.6354
Mathematical theory of computation. 5.1190
The mathematical theory of relativity. 5.1906
Mathematical thought from ancient to modern
    times. 5.1071
The mathematical work of Charles Babbage.
    5.1084
The mathematical works of Isaac Newton.
    5.1103
A mathematician's apology. 5.1028
Mathematico deductive theory of rote learning.
    4.10369
Mathematics. 5.1030
Mathematics, a human endeavor. 5.1254
Mathematics and computers in archaeology
    3.233
Mathematics and plausible reasoning. 5.1048
Mathematics and the physical world. 5.1072
Mathematics as a cultural system. 5.1077
Mathematics dictionary. 5.1025
Mathematics for innumerate economists.
    4.1390
Mathematics for physical chemistry. 5.2807
Mathematics in the time of the Pharaohs.
    5.1083
Mathematics of Kalman-Bucy filtering. 5.1546
Mathematics of population. 4.1632
The mathematics of Sonya Kovalevskaya.
    5.1438
The mathematics of the ideal villa, and other
    essays. 1.5555
The mathematics of time. 5.1619
Mathematics teaching and learning. 5.1058
Mathematics tomorrow. 5.1031
The Mathers. 3.7981
Mathews' Chinese-English dictionary. 2.2149
Matinee tomorrow. 2.3229
Matisse. 1.4977
Matisse, his art and his public. 1.6119
Matisse in the collection of the Museum of
    Modern Art, including remainder-interest and
    promised gifts. 1.4976
Matrilineal kinship 4.585
Matrix analysis of framed structures. 5.5846
Matrix of man. 1.5592
The matrix of modernism. 2.10504
Matrix structural analysis. 5.5837
Matroid theory. 5.1288
Matter and light. 5.2052
Matter and memory. 1.829
Matter & method. 5.892
Matter at low temperatures. 5.2234

A matter of honour. 5.7340
A matter of life and death. 2.13953
A matter of principle. 4.9495
Matters mathematical. 5.1112
Matters of life and death. 1.1454
Matthew. 1.2684
Matthew, a commentary on his literary and
   theological art. 1.2685
Matthew Arnold. 2.7355
Matthew Arnold, a life. 2.7354
Matthew Arnold and American culture.
   2.7362
Matthew Arnold, prose writings. 2.7361
Matthew Arnold, the ethnologist. 2.7359
Matthew Arnold, the poetry: the critical
   heritage. 2.7358
Matthew Prior, poet and diplomatist. 2.7207
Matthias Erzberger and the dilemma of
   German democracy. 3.2349
Matthias Lexers mittelhochdeutsches
   Taschenwörterbuch. 2.1192
The maturing of multinational enterprise.
   4.2737
The Maugham enigma. 2.9108
The Maugham reader. 2.9094
Maule's curse. 2.10275
Maupassant. 2.4271
Maurice. 2.8649
Maurice Bishop speaks. 3.9134
Maurice Prendergast, 1859-1924. 1.5963
Maurice Scève. 2.4009
Mauritania. 3.5394
Mausoleum book. 2.8115
Mauve gloves & madmen, clutter & vine, and
   other stories, sketches, and essays. 2.13438
Max Beckmann. 1.6165-1.6166
Max Carrados. 2.9342
Max Ernst. 1.4992
Max Ernst: life and work. 1.4993
Max Havelaar, or, The coffee auctions of the
   Dutch Trading Company. 2.13950
Max Perkins, editor of genius. 2.2520
Max Rafferty on education. 4.10253
Max Reinhardt. 2.3378
Max Weber. 4.1363, 4.4765
Max Weber on law in economy and society.
   4.9344
Maxfield Parrish. 1.5833
Maxim Gorky 2.1509
Maxime Weygand and civil-military relations in
   modern France. 5.7201
Maximilian and Carlota. 3.8937
Maximilian I (1459-1519) 3.2274
Maximizing leadership effectiveness. 4.10587
Maxims. 2.4034
Maximum feasible misunderstanding. 4.2105
Maximum security ward and other poems.
   2.11805
The Maximus poems. 2.12281
Maxwell Anderson, the playwright as prophet.
   2.11315
The May fourth movement: intellectual
   revolution in modern China. 3.4752
May Sinclair. 2.9324
The Maya. 3.9034, 3.9039
Maya art and civilization. 3.9047
Maya cities: placemaking and urbanization.
   3.9046
Maya history and religion. 3.9041
Maya society under colonial rule. 3.9036
Mayakovsky. 2.1573
Mayday. 2.11668
The mayor of Casterbridge. 2.7766
The mayor of Queenborough. 2.6636
Mazo De La Roche of Jalna. 2.9932
Mazzini. 3.2876
Mazzini and the secret societies. 3.2875
McCarthy and his enemies. 3.7666
McCarthy and the Communists. 3.7670
McClane's new standard fishing encyclopedia
   and international angling guide. 5.5488
McClellan, Sherman, and Grant. 3.7317
McGraw-Hill dictionary of art. 1.4578
McGraw-Hill dictionary of earth sciences.
   5.2944
The McGraw-Hill dictionary of modern
   economics. 4.1274

McGraw-Hill dictionary of physics and
   mathematics. 5.1891
McGraw-Hill dictionary of scientific and
   technical terms. 5.709
McGraw-Hill encyclopedia of energy. 5.6131
McGraw-Hill encyclopedia of environmental
   science. 5.3511
McGraw-Hill encyclopedia of science &
   technology. 5.703
McGraw-Hill encyclopedia of science and
   technology. 5.703-5.704, 5.3511
McGraw-Hill encyclopedia of the geological
   sciences. 5.2943
McGraw-Hill encyclopedia of world drama.
   2.2785
McGraw-Hill modern men of science. 5.810
McGraw-Hill modern scientists and engineers.
   5.810
McGraw-Hill personal computer programming
   encyclopedia. 5.1191
McGraw-Hill yearbook of science and
   technology. 5.704
McKim, Mead, and White. 1.5317
McKim, Mead & White, architects. 1.5317
The McMahon Line and after. 3.4234
The McNamara strategy. 5.7247
'Me grandad 'ad an elephant!' 2.2267
Mead's other Manus. 3.5628
Meaning. 1.140-1.141
Meaning and action. 1.533
Meaning and existence. 1.508
Meaning and necessity. 1.540
The meaning and sources of marketing theory.
   4.4282
Meaning and translation. 2.195
Meaning & void. 5.631
Meaning-based translation. 2.194
Meaning in children's art. 1.4653
Meaning in history. 3.512
Meaning in texts. 1.2634
Meaning in the visual arts: papers in and on art
   history. 1.5132
Meaning in Western architecture. 1.5214
The meaning of addiction. 5.4957
The meaning of anxiety. 5.430
The meaning of Aphrodite. 1.1669
The meaning of art. 1.5105
The meaning of contemporary realism. 2.2403
The meaning of culture. 4.10725
The Meaning of death. 1.1324
The meaning of Europe. 3.1197
The meaning of fossils. 5.3148
The meaning of God in human experience.
   1.1549
The meaning of Heidegger. 1.1000
The meaning of Henry Ward Beecher. 1.3336
The meaning of history. 3.460
The meaning of Hitler. 3.2400
The meaning of independence. 3.7047
The meaning of More's Utopia. 4.7176
The meaning of relativity. 5.2087
The meaning of revelation. 1.2840
The meaning of saints. 1.3249
The meaning of Shakespeare. 2.6731
The meaning of the city. 1.2558
The meaning of the Middle Ages. 3.125
The meaning of the twentieth century. 3.188
The meaning of truth. 1.527
The meaning of Yalta. 3.884
Meaning, quantification, necessity. 1.1172
Meanings and situations. 4.5059
The Meanings of Gandhi. 3.4309
The meanings of modern art. 1.4785
Means and ends in American abolitionism.
   3.7252
Means and ends in education. 4.10261
Meany. 4.3589
Measure and category. 5.1459
Measure for measure, the law, and the convent.
   2.6669
The measure of man. 1.454
The measure of value stated and illustrated,
   with an application of it to the alterations in
   the value of the English currency since 1790.
   4.1493
Measure theory. 5.1590
The measurement and behavior of
   unemployment. 4.3198

Measurement and detection of radiation.
   5.2487
Measurement and evaluation in teaching.
   4.10712
The measurement and evaluation of library
   services. 5.7611
The measurement and prediction of judgment
   and choice. 5.38
Measurement in physical education. 4.913
The measurement of economic growth. 4.2807
The Measurement of labor cost. 4.3147
The measurement of meaning. 1.544
The measurement of values. 5.56
The measurement of work performance.
   4.4379
Measures for psychological assessment. 5.541
Measures of social psychological attitudes.
   4.4994
Measuring human behavior. 5.542
Measuring productivity. 4.2088
Measuring profitability and capital costs.
   4.1554
Measuring the benefits of clean air and water.
   4.1846
Measuring the condition of the world's poor.
   4.1815
Measuring the universe. 5.1686
Meat and poultry inspection. 5.7083
Meat science. 5.7120
Mechanical design and systems handbook.
   5.6191
Mechanical engineering design. 5.6192-5.6193
Mechanical engineers' handbook. 5.6112
The mechanical investigations of Leonardo da
   Vinci. 5.822
Mechanical measurements. 5.5682
Mechanical metallurgy. 5.5774, 5.5813
Mechanical metamorphosis. 5.5625
A mechanical people. 4.3616
Mechanical properties of materials at low
   temperatures. 5.5791
Mechanical technician's handbook. 5.5679
Mechanical vibrations. 5.5744
Mechanical working of metals. 5.7054
Mechanics. 5.1645, 5.1648, 5.2031-5.2032,
   5.5773
Mechanics and energetics of animal locomotion.
   5.4267
Mechanics and manufacturers in the early
   industrial revolution. 4.3523
Mechanics and thermodynamics of propulsion.
   5.6674
The mechanics of Baltimore. 4.3601
Mechanics of composite materials. 5.5795
Mechanics of elastic structures. 5.5842
The mechanics of frozen ground. 5.5912
Mechanics of materials. 5.5772, 5.5776-5.5777
Mechanics of solids. 5.5778
Mechanism and structure in organic chemistry.
   5.2716
Mechanism and theory in organic chemistry.
   5.2856
Mechanisms of homogeneous catalysis from
   protons to proteins. 5.2879
Mechanisms of inorganic reactions. 5.2708
The mechanization of the world picture. 5.725
Medals of the Renaissance. 3.281
Medea. 2.460
Media and the American mind. 4.5223
The media are American. 2.62
The media in America. 2.61
The media in Britain. 2.55
Media industries. 4.5013
Media power in politics. 4.5224
Media review digest. 4.10327
The mediaeval architect. 1.5231
Mediaeval craftsmen. 5.7085
Mediaeval culture. 2.4939
Mediaeval drama in Chester. 2.5856
Mediaeval feudalism. 3.581
Mediaeval Germany, 911-1250. 3.2263
Mediaeval Greece. 3.2663
Mediaeval heresy & the Inquisition. 1.2312
Mediaeval institutions. 3.137
Mediaeval Latin lyrics. 2.814
The mediaeval mind. 3.138
Mediaeval Netherlands religious literature.
   2.13944

Mediaeval Orvieto. 3.2950
Mediaeval romance in England. 2.5619
Mediaeval society. 3.134
The mediaeval stage. 2.3170
The Mediating person. 4.5008
Medical America in the nineteenth century. 5.4521
Medical and health information directory. 5.4482
Medical and social aspects of alcohol abuse. 5.4960
Medical anthropology. 4.463
A medical bibliography (Garrison and Morton) 5.8284
Medical books, libraries and collectors. 5.8285
Medical botany. 5.5151
Medical care, morbidity, and costs. 5.4642
Medical choices, medical chances. 5.4554
Medical classics. 5.4785
Medical costs, moral choices. 5.4636
Medical dictionary. 5.4485, 5.4489, 5.4491
Medical education in the United States and Canada. 5.4603
Medical ethics. 5.4565
Medical ethics and the law. 5.4566
Medical ethics in Imperial China. 5.4538
Medical experiments on Jewish inmates of concentration camps. 3.1104
Medical hubris. 5.4646
Medical hypnosis. 5.4899
The Medical implications of nuclear war. 5.4680
The medical industrial complex. 5.4641
Medical instrumentation. 5.4611
Medical jurisprudence. 5.4716
Medical jurisprudence and toxicology. 5.4715
Medical nemesis. 5.4645
The medical offenders. 5.4717
Medical parasitology. 5.4760
Medical physics. 5.4614-5.4615
Medical physiology. 5.4194
Medical problems in the classroom. 5.5078
Medical psychology. 5.4806
Medical reference works, 1679-1966. 5.8283
Medical risks. 5.4629
Medical sociology. 5.8294
Medical thinking. 5.4503
Medical writing. 5.4483
Medicine. 5.4505
Medicine and its technology. 5.4610
Medicine and society in America, 1660-1860. 5.4518
Medicine and the management of living. 5.4591
Medicine and the reign of technology. 5.4515
Medicine in China. 5.4537
Medicine in the Bible and the Talmud. 5.4512
Medicine, law, & public policy. 5.4714
Medicine, morals, and the law. 5.4564
Medicine woman. 3.5865
Medieval and early modern science. 5.720
Medieval and Renaissance moral symbols. 2.5587
Medieval and Renaissance Pistoia. 3.2952
Medieval and Renaissance studies. 3.363
The medieval Chinese oligarchy. 4.5419
Medieval chronicles and the rotation of the earth. 5.1796
Medieval cities, their origins and the revival of trade. 4.8835
Medieval colonialism. 4.2415
The medieval contribution to political thought, Thomas Aquinas, Marsilius of Padua, Richard Hooker. 4.7271
Medieval culture and society. 3.131
Medieval dream-poetry. 2.5617
The medieval economy and society. 4.2256
Medieval England. 3.1299, 3.1721, 4.5305
Medieval English drama. 2.5851
Medieval English literature. 2.5605
Medieval English lyrics. 2.6133
Medieval English poetry. 2.5615
Medieval English verse and prose in modernized versions. 2.6077
Medieval epics. 2.3754
The medieval foundations of England. 3.1300
Medieval foundations of renaissance humanism. 3.165

Medieval French miniatures. 1.6414
Medieval German literature. 2.13461
Medieval Germany and its neighbours, 900-1250. 3.2266
Medieval heresy. 1.2963
Medieval humanism. 3.144
Medieval humanism and other studies. 3.144
Medieval imagination. 2.3841
The medieval imprint. 3.576
Medieval Islam. 3.600
A medieval Italian commune. 3.2953
Medieval Italy. 3.2827
Medieval Jewry in Northern France. 3.3956
Medieval literature in translation. 2.2621
Medieval logic. 1.1158
Medieval logic and metaphysics 1.1159
The medieval lyric. 2.2642
The medieval Manichee. 1.2311
Medieval medicus. 5.4513
Medieval music. 1.3646, 1.3648-1.3649
Medieval number symbolism. 5.685
Medieval panorama. 3.1329
The medieval papacy. 1.3146
The medieval papacy, St. Thomas and beyond. 1.391
Medieval people. 3.579
Medieval philosophy. 1.355
Medieval philosophy; selected readings from Augustine to Buridan. 1.346
Medieval political philosophy. 4.7269
Medieval readers and writers, 1350-1400. 2.5609
Medieval religion and technology. 5.5536
Medieval religious houses, England and Wales. 1.3233
Medieval romance. 2.2641
Medieval romances. 2.2633
Medieval Russia. 3.3001
Medieval Russia's epics, chronicles, and tales. 2.1308
Medieval sculpture. 1.5642
Medieval Sicily, 800-1713. 3.2943
Medieval studies. 3.569
Medieval technology and social change. 3.145
The medieval theatre. 2.3172
The medieval theatre in the round. 2.3284
Medieval thought. 1.351
Medieval universities. 4.9975
The medieval vision. 3.128
Medieval Welsh society 4.5337
Medieval woman's guide to health. 5.5044
Medieval women. 4.5857-4.5858
Medieval women writers. 2.2622
The medieval world: Europe, 1100-1350. 3.601
Medieval writers and their work. 2.5602
Meditation, classic and contemporary perspectives. 5.4893
Meditations on a hobby horse, and other essays on the theory of art. 1.5131
The Mediterranean and the Mediterranean World in the age of Philip II. 3.2525
Mediterranean countrymen. 4.5295
The Mediterranean feud. 3.2687
The Mediterranean in the ancient world. 3.2528
The Mediterranean lands. 3.1190
Mediterranean poems. 2.1734
The Mediterranean Sea. 4.350
A Mediterranean society. 3.598
Mediterranean type ecosystems. 5.3572
Mediterranean-type shrublands. 5.3565
The medium, the mystic, and the physicist. 5.641
Meet me in the green glen. 2.12642
The meeting at Telgte. 2.13764
A meeting by the river. 2.8836
Meeting house and counting house. 1.3352
The meeting of East and West. 3.14
The meeting of Eastern and Western art from the sixteenth century to the present day. 1.5110
The Meeting of the ways. 5.275
The megalith builders of Western Europe. 4.725
Megalopolis. 4.6237
Megara, the political history of a Greek city-state to 336 B.C. 3.2646
The megastates of America. 3.7844

Megastructure. 1.5261
Mehmed the Conqueror and his time. 3.3581
Mehrsprachiges Wörterbuch kartographischer Fachbegriffe. 4.75
Meiji ikō hompō shuyō keizai tōkei. 4.1258
The Meiji restoration. 3.4950
Mein kampf. 3.2390
Meister Eckhart. 1.3088
Meister Eckhart, the essential sermons, commentaries, treatises, and defense. 1.3087
Meisterdramen. 2.13872
The melancholy history of Soledad Prison. 4.6915
Melanchthon and Bucer. 1.2352
Mélanges 2.4101
Melbourne. 3.1603
Melmoth the Wanderer. 2.7932
Melodrama, plots that thrilled. 2.2821
Melodrama unveiled. 2.2822
The melting of the ethnics. 4.10897
Melting point tables of organic compounds. 5.2905
Melville. 2.11163, 2.11172
Melville: a collection of critical essays. 2.11167
Melville, the critical heritage. 2.11166
Melville's later novels. 2.11169
Melville's short fiction, 1853-1856. 2.11170
Melvin B. Tolson, 1898-1966. 2.12596
Melvin B. Tolson's Harlem gallery. 2.12595
A member of the family. 3.6781
Member of the House. 4.8054
The member of the wedding. 2.12073
Membranes and their cellular functions. 5.3609
Memento mori. 2.9360
Memo from David O. Selznick. 2.3066
Memoir of a revolutionary. 3.3556
Memoir of a thinking radish. 5.4461
Memoir of Jane Austen. 2.7369
Memoir on ancient and modern Russia. 3.3081
Memoir on the motive power of heat. 5.2243
Mémoires d'Hadrien. 2.4774
Mémoires d'outre-tombe. 2.4151
Mémoires d'une jeune fille rangée. 2.4396
Mémoires improvisés. 2.4475
Memoirs. 2.4986, 3.1916, 3.2471
The memoirs. 3.2308
Memoirs. 2.8339, 2.12736, 3.731, 3.1038, 3.1942, 3.2411, 3.3228, 3.7655, 3.7747, 3.7813
Memoirs: 1921-1941. 2.1553
Memoirs and anecdotes of Dr. Johnson. 2.7088
Memoirs and opinions, 1926-1974. 2.12574
Memoirs from the House of the Dead. 2.1360
Memoirs of a cavalier or a military journal of the wars in Germany, and the wars in England; from the year 1632, to the year 1648. Written threescore years ago by an English gentleman... 2.6972
Memoirs of a Chinese revolutionary. 3.4759
Memoirs of a Dada drummer. 1.6733
Memoirs of a dutiful daughter. 2.4397
Memoirs of a midget. 2.8597
Memoirs of a physicist in the atomic age. 5.1949
The memoirs of a shy pornographer. 2.12306
Memoirs of a Social Democrat. 3.2354
Memoirs of a space traveler. 2.1710
The memoirs of a survivor. 2.9022
Memoirs of a tourist 2.4304
Memoirs of a woman of pleasure. 2.6938
The memoirs of Aga Khan. 3.4322
Memoirs of American Jews, 1775-1865. 3.6572
Memoirs of an infantry officer. 3.845
The Memoirs of Anne, Lady Halkett and Ann, Lady Fanshawe. 3.1499
Memoirs of Anthony Powell. 2.9231-2.9232
Memoirs of Carlo Goldoni. 2.4994
The memoirs of Catherine the Great. 3.3102
The memoirs of Cordell Hull. 3.7649
The memoirs of Count Witte. 3.3158
Memoirs of Dr. Johnson. 2.7088
The memoirs of Earl Warren. 4.9832
The memoirs of General Makriyannis, 1797-1864. 3.2694
Memoirs of Hadrian, and reflections on the composition of memoirs of Hadrian. 2.4775
Memoirs of Hecate County. 2.12762

The memoirs of Hector Berlioz, member of the French Institute. 1.3816
Memoirs of hope. 3.1164
The memoirs of John Addington Symonds. 2.8142
Memoirs of King Abdullah of Transjordan. 3.4035
The memoirs of Marshal Mannerheim. 3.3299
The memoirs of Marshal Zhukov. 3.3239
The memoirs of Prince Max of Baden. 3.2351
Memoirs of Prince von Bülow. 3.2347
Memoirs of Rear-Admiral Paul Jones. 3.6892
The memoirs of Richard Nixon. 3.7911
Memoirs of the crusades. 3.594
Memoirs of the extraordinary life, works, and discoveries of Martinus Scriblerus. 2.7191
Memoirs of the life and writings of the late Dr. Samuel Johnson. 2.7088
Memoirs of the life of John Constable, composed chiefly of his letters. 1.6028
Memoirs of the life of the Rt. Hon. Richard Brinsley Sheridan. 2.7250
Memoirs of the Polish Baroque. 3.3334
Memoirs of war, 1914-15. 3.844
Memoirs; sixty years on the firing line. 3.7530
Memorbook. 3.3981
The memorial. 2.8837
Memorials of Alfred Marshall. 4.1446
Memories. 1.4006, 2.9069
Memories, an autobiography. 2.3240
Memories and impressions. 2.8633
Memories and portraits. 2.1480
Memories, dreams, reflections. 5.98
Memories II. 5.3204
Memories of a Catholic girlhood. 2.12065
Memories of my life, being my personal, professional, and social recollections as woman and artist. 2.3371
Memories of the moderns. 2.2648
Memory and agony. 2.13956
Memory and attention. 5.387
Memory and awareness. 5.327
Memory and intelligence. 5.334
Memory and mind. 5.330
Memory organization and structure. 5.331
The memory palace of Matteo Ricci. 1.3030
Memos. 1.3899
Memphis since Crump. 4.8867
Men against McCarthy. 3.7667
Men and brethren. 2.11518
Men and citizens. 4.7436
Men and events. 3.365
Men and ideas. 3.361
Men and movements in American philosophy. 1.554
Men and movements in the American Episcopal Church. 1.3317
Men and politics. 3.729
Men and power, 1917-1918. 3.1692
Men and society in an age of reconstruction. 4.5090
Men and wealth in the United States, 1850-1870. 4.2113
Men and women of the corporation. 4.2696
Men and work. 3.1661
Men at arms. 2.9494
Men at midlife. 4.5794
Men at war. 2.3710
Men, cities, and transportation. 4.3895
Men from under the sky. 3.5632
Men in arms. 3.538
Men in business. 4.4215
Men in crisis. 3.708
Men in uniform. 5.7253
Men, mules, and mountains. 3.8643
The men of Cajamarca. 3.9297
Men of destiny. 3.7617
Men of good hope. 3.6283
Men of ideas. 1.457
Men of letters and the English public in the eighteenth century, 1660-1744, Dryden, Addison, Pope. 2.5656
Men of mathematics. 5.1086
Men of science in America. 5.793
The men of the First French Republic. 3.2107
The men of the old stone age (palaeolithic & mesolithic) 4.704
Men under stress. 5.4936

Men who have walked with God. 1.1626
Men who manage. 4.2646
Men who rape. 4.6733
The men who ruled India. 3.4265
Men without art. 2.2650
Men, women and dogs. 1.5850
Men, women and pianos. 1.4148
Men, women, messages, and media. 2.53
The menace of atomic energy. 5.6609
Menander, the principal fragments. 2.381
Mencius. 1.170
Mencken. 2.12133
Mendel. 5.3209
Mendelssohn. 1.3927
The Mendoza family in the Spanish Renaissance, 1350 to 1550. 3.3410
Meno. 2.534
The Menomini Indians of Wisconsin. 3.5904
The Menopause. 5.5057
Men's ideas/women's realities. 4.6062
Men's studies. 5.8380
Men's studies modified. 4.5977
Der Mensch erscheint im Holozän. 2.13742
The Mensheviks. 4.8665
Menstrual disorders and menopause. 5.5056
Mental and physical health practices of older people. 5.4666
The mental and social life of babies. 5.558
Mental deficiency. 5.4976
Mental health and going to school. 4.10278
Mental health and people of color. 5.4820
Mental health & people of color. 5.4820
Mental health consultation. 5.4834
Mental health interventions for the aging. 5.4813
The mental health of Asian Americans. 5.4821
The mental hospital. 5.4807
Mental illness. 5.4840
Mental illness and American society, 1875-1940. 5.4811
Mental imagery and human memory. 5.335
Mental images: a defence. 5.317
Mental images and their transformations. 5.321
Mental institutions in America. 5.4812
Mental maps. 4.31
The ... Mental measurements yearbook. 5.8155
Mental retardation. 4.6582, 5.4971
Mental retardation in school and society. 4.6610
Mental retardation, the developmental-difference controversy. 5.4977
The mentally retarded. 5.4975
The Mentally retarded and society. 4.6612
The mentally retarded child. 5.5117
The mentally retarded child and his family. 4.6583
The Mentally retarded citizen and the law. 4.9508
The Mentor book of major American poets. 2.10737
Menzies observed. 3.5582
Mercantilism. 4.1323
Mercenaries and Mandarins. 5.7336
Mercenaries and their masters. 3.2852
The mercenaries of the Hellenistic world. 3.2559
The merchant class of medieval London, 1300-1500. 4.4232
Merchants and manufacturers. 4.4291
Merchants and merchandise. 4.4099
Merchants, farmers & railroads. 4.4005
Merchants, landlords, magistrates. 3.345
The merchants of Buenos Aires, 1778-1810. 4.4223
Merciful disguises. 2.12610
The Merck index. 5.5145
The Merck manual of diagnosis and therapy. 5.4755
The Merck veterinary manual. 5.5462
Mere Christianity. 1.2263
Meredith. 2.7943
Meredith: a change of masks. 2.7945
Meredith now: some critical essays. 2.7946
Meredith, the critical heritage. 2.7948
Merely players. 2.3184
Meridian. 2.13408
Merit and responsibility. 1.1418

Merit, measurement, and money. 4.10677
Merleau-Ponty's philosophy. 1.844
The mermaid Madonna 2.603
Merman. 1.4095
Mersād al-'ebād men al-mabdā' elā'l-ma'ād. 1.2082
The Merthyr rising. 3.1772
Meso-scale atmospheric circulations. 5.2520
Message poétique du symbolisme. 2.3879
The messenger's motives. 2.3562
Messengers of day. 2.9232
Messiaen. 1.3929
The messianic idea in Israel, from its beginning to the completion of the Mishnah. 1.1974
The Messianic idea in Judaism and other essays on Jewish spirituality. 1.1975
The Messier album. 5.1850
Metabolic arrest and the control of biological time. 5.3507
Metahistory: the historical imagination in nineteenth-century Europe. 3.409
Metal casting of sculpture. 1.5779
Metal deposits in relation to plate tectonics. 5.6734
Metal fatigue in engineering. 5.5810
Metal forming and impact mechanics. 5.7055
Metal resources and energy. 4.3703
The metallic elements. 5.2709
Metallography in failure analysis. 5.6769
Metallurgy and heat treatment of tool steels. 5.7064
Metallurgy & plastics for engineers. 5.6762
Metallurgy of the ferrous metals 5.6785
Metallurgy of the non-ferrous metals. 5.6788
Metalogic. 1.1197
The metalogicon of John of Salisbury. 1.387
Metals handbook. 5.5807
Metals information. 5.6766
Metals joining manual. 5.7063
Metals reference book. 5.6765
Metalwork in medieval Islamic art. 1.6654
Metamorphic petrology. 5.3073
Metamorphic processes. 5.3070
Metamorphic verse. 2.5796
Metamorphism and metamorphic belts. 5.3068
Metamorphoses. 2.681
Metamorphoses in nineteenth-century sculpture. 1.5648
Metamorphoses of Ovid. 2.748
Metamorphoses of science fiction. 2.3496
Metamorphoses in Keats. 2.7871
The metamorphosis of Ajax. 2.6483
The metamorphosis of Greece since World War II. 4.5393
The metamorphosis of the gods. 1.4633
The metaphorical brain. 5.997
The Metaphors of consciousness. 5.276
Metaphors of masculinity. 4.800
Metaphors of self. 3.317
Metaphors we live by. 2.107
Metaphysical art. 1.4852
The metaphysical foundations of modern physical science. 1.120
Metaphysical foundations of natural science. 1.891
Metaphysical lyrics & poems of the seventeenth century. 2.6157
The metaphysical poets. 2.5806, 2.6146
The metaphysical poets: Donne, Herbert, Vaughan, Traherne. 2.5800
The metaphysical theory of the state. 4.7504
Metaphysics. 1.289
The Metaphysics ... 2.346
Metaphysics. 1.288, 1.1264
The metaphysics of Descartes. 1.786
The metaphysics of logical positivism. 1.509
The metaphysics of love. 2.5797
The metaphysics of St. Thomas Aquinas. 1.396
Meteor. 2.1667
Meteorites. 5.1824
Meteorologica. 2.345
Meteorological instruments. 5.2509
The meters of Greek and Latin poetry. 2.233
The method and theory of V. Gordon Childe. 3.258
Method for the easy comprehension of history. 3.426
Method in social anthropology. 4.490

The method of Descartes. 1.789
A method of lighting the stage. 2.3143
The method of realizing nirvāna knowing the mind. 1.2104
The method of sociology. 4.4814
A method to their madness. 2.3138
Methodicum chimicum. 5.2657
Methodology in the study of international relations. 4.8998
The methodology of economics. 4.1383
Methodology of the social sciences. 4.1207
The methodology of the social sciences. 4.1216
Methods and materials for secondary school physical education. 4.911
Methods and materials in microelectronic technology. 5.6533
The methods and materials of demography. 4.1622
Methods for educating the handicapped. 4.10927
Methods improvement for construction managers. 5.5704
Methods in enzymology. 5.4410
Methods of book design. 5.7537
Methods of enzymatic analysis. 5.3316
The methods of ethics. 1.1433
Methods of logic. 1.1179
Methods of mathematical physics. 5.1540
Methods of modern mathematical physics. 5.1974
Methods of numerical integration. 5.1432
Methods of regional analysis. 4.2690
Methods of rhetorical criticism. 2.3533
Methods of theoretical physics. 5.1968
Methods of thermodynamics. 5.2252
Metropol. 2.1301
Metropol', 1979 g. English. 2.1301
Metropolis, 1890-1940. 4.6350
Metropolis 1985. 4.2048
Metropolis and region. 4.6208
Metropolitan corridor. 4.3997
The Metropolitan Midwest. 4.6239
The Metropolitan Opera, 1883-1966. 1.4224
Metropolitan Opera annals. 1.4225
The Metropolitan Opera stories of the great operas. 1.4511
Metropolitan transportation planning. 4.3903
The metropolitan transportation problem. 4.3938
Metternich and his times. 3.1890
Metternich's diplomacy at its zenith, 1820-1823. 3.1892
Metternich's Europe. 3.697
Metternich's German policy. 3.1891
Mevar patan, or Fall of Mevar. 2.1865
The Mexican American experience. 3.6582
The Mexican-American War. 5.7835
Mexican architecture of the sixteenth century. 1.5352
Mexican cinema. 2.2904
Mexican folk ceramics. 1.6616
The Mexican frontier, 1821-1846. 3.8576
Mexican government in transition. 4.8332
The Mexican historical novel, 1826-1910. 2.5330
Mexican illegal alien workers in the United States. 4.3614
Mexican landscape architecture from the street and from within. 5.5383
Mexican manuscript painting of the early colonial period. 1.6405
The Mexican novel comes of age. 2.5328
Mexican painting in our time. 1.6001
Mexican politics. 4.8333
The Mexican reform, 1855-1876. 3.8936
Mexican Revolution. 3.8941
The Mexican Revolution. 5.7898
The Mexican Revolution, 1910-1914. 3.8940
The Mexican Revolution and the Catholic Church, 1910-1929. 3.8948
Mexican Revolution: the constitutionalist years. 3.8942
Mexican society during the revolution. 2.5331
The Mexican War. 3.7138
The Mexican War, 1846-1848. 3.7135
Mexicano resistance in the Southwest. 3.8565
Mexico. 3.8873, 3.8904, 3.8929, 4.2146
Mexico, 1910-1982. 3.8943

Mexico, a country study. 3.8874
Mexico and the United States, 1821-1973: conflict and coexistence. 3.6473
Mexico in its novel. 2.5326
Mexico in sculpture, 1521-1821. 1.5680, 3.8945
Mexico views manifest destiny, 1821-1846. 3.6472
Mexico's Accion Nacional. 4.8334
Mexico's agricultural dilemma. 4.2963
Mexico's way out. 4.2838
M'Fingal. 2.10878
The MGM story. 2.3078
[Mi-shire Byalik] 2.1782
Miami and the siege of Chicago; an informal history of the Republican and Democratic Conventions of 1968. 4.8221
The Miami riot of 1980. 3.8277
Miau. 2.5222-2.5223
Micah. 1.2619
Michael. 2.8303
Michael Arlen. 2.8388
Michael Bakunin. 4.7198
Michael Drayton, a critical study. 2.6472
Michael Pacher. 1.4957
Michel Butor. 2.4438
Michel Foucault. 1.830-1.831
Michel Tournier. 2.4794
Michelangelo. 1.5014
Michelangelo, the Sistine Chapel ceiling. 1.6192
Michelangelo's David. 1.6193
Michelangelo's poetry. 2.4968
Michigan. 3.8430
Michigan, a guide to the Wolverine State. 3.8433
Michigan, a history of the Wolverine State. 3.8431
Michio Ito. 4.1149
Micmacs and colonists. 3.5906
Micro-PROLOG. 5.1219
Microbe hunters. 5.4431
Microbes and men. 5.4441
Microbial cell walls and membranes. 5.4451
Microbial ecology. 5.4458
The Microbial world. 5.4437
Microbiology. 5.4438
Microbiology, including immunology and molecular genetics. 5.4440
Microbiology of fermented foods. 5.6888
The microbiology of the atmosphere. 5.4459
Microcartography, applications for archives and libraries. 4.219
Microcircuit engineering. 5.6537
Microcirculation. 5.4228
Microcomputers and exceptional children. 4.10935
Microcomputers and modern control engineering. 5.6177
Microcomputers in astronomy. 5.1724
Microcomputers in elementary education. 4.10300
Microcomputers in special education. 4.10294, 4.10911
Microcomputers in the schools. 4.10292
Microcosmos. 5.3394
Microcounseling. 4.1224
Microeconomic foundations of employment and inflation theory. 4.1510
Microeconomic theory. 4.1434
Microelectronic circuits. 5.6465
Microelectronic technology. 5.6533
Microfossils. 5.3153
Microfoundations. 4.1285
Micrographics. 5.7624
Micronesia. 3.5619
Micronesia, 1944-1974. 5.8096
Micronesia at the crossroads. 4.8829
Micronesia, trust betrayed. 4.9306
Microprocessor applications handbook. 5.6594
Microprocessor-based process control. 5.7031
Microprocessor support chips. 5.6592
Microprocessor system design concepts. 5.1141
Microprocessors. 5.6583
Microprocessors and logic design. 5.1149
Microprocessors and microcomputer development systems. 5.1251
Microprocessors and microcomputers. 5.1151

Microprocessors and programmed logic. 5.1152
Microprocessors, manpower, and society. 4.3317
Microprocessors/microcomputers. 5.1147
Micropublishing. 5.7580
Microscopic petrography. 5.3040
MicroSource. 5.1156
Microstructure and thermal analysis of solid surfaces. 5.2898
Microwave engineering and applications. 5.6548
Microwave mobile communications. 5.6432
Microwave remote sensing. 4.29
Microwave semiconductor circuit design. 5.6547
Microwave semiconductor engineering. 5.6549
Microwave spectroscopy. 5.2316
Microworlds. 2.3455
Mid-century American poets. 2.10772
Mid-century modern. 5.7073
The mid-eighteenth century. 2.5657
The mid-Tudor crisis, 1539-1563. 3.1389
Mid-twentieth century American philosophy: personal statements. 1.571
Midcentury. 2.11583
The middle age of Mrs. Eliot. 2.9537
Middle age, old age. 2.3721
The middle ages. 2.5101
The Middle Ages. 1.2307, 2.3839
Middle America, its lands and peoples. 3.9144
Middle America; its lands and peoples. 3.8963
Middle-class Blacks in a white society. 4.6176
Middle-class culture in Elizabethan England. 2.5636
Middle-class democracy and the Revolution in Massachusetts, 1691-1780. 3.7970
The Middle East. 3.3682, 3.3684, 3.3687, 3.3703, 3.3715, 3.3739, 4.639
Middle East. 1948-63. 3.3685
The Middle East, abstracts and index. 3.3675
Middle East and Islam. 5.8037
The Middle East and North Africa. 3.3685, 3.3724
The Middle East and North Africa in world politics. 3.3676
The Middle East and North Africa on film. 3.3681
The Middle East and the West. 3.3736
The Middle East city. 4.6274
The Middle East in the world economy, 1800-1914. 4.2442
The Middle East in world affairs. 3.3727
Middle East oil. 4.3786
The Middle East political dictionary. 3.3711
Middle East politics: the military dimension. 3.3726
A Middle East studies handbook. 3.3710
The Middle East today. 3.3729
Middle Eastern Muslim women speak. 4.5908
A Middle English anthology. 2.6076
Middle English dictionary. 2.957
Middle English literature. 2.5601, 2.5604
Middle English lyrics. 2.6112
Middle English prose. 2.5606
The middle ground. 2.9660
The Middle High German poem of Willehalm. 2.13541
Middle market. 4.4251
The middle of the journey. 2.12600
The middle parts of fortune. 2.10159
The middle passage. 4.6421
The middle Platonists, 80 B.C. to A.D. 220. 1.322
The middle school. 4.10502
Middle school. 4.10506
Middle West. 3.8374
The middle western farm novel in the twentieth century. 2.10551
The middle works, 1899-1924. 4.10224
The middle works, 1899-1924. 1.583
The middle years. 2.11113
Middlemarch. 2.7693, 2.7696
Middlemarch: critical approaches to the novel. 2.7695
Middlemarch from notebook to novel. 2.7694
Middleton's tragedies. 2.6639
Middletown. 4.5137

Middletown families. 4.5569
Middletown in transition. 4.5138
Mideast file. 3.3677
Midnight. 2.2248
Midnight movies. 2.2957
Midnight oil. 2.9255
Midnight on the desert. 2.9248
Midnight's children. 2.10133
The Midrash on Psalms. 1.1944
Midrash Rabbah. 1.1943
Midrash rabbah. English. 1.1943
Mies van der Rohe. 1.5425-1.5427
Mighty Casey, all-American. 2.11244
The mighty endeavor. 3.955
The Mighty Five. 1.3756
Mighty Stonewall. 3.7327
Migrants of the mountains. 3.4522
Migrants, sharecroppers, mountaineers. 4.2092
Migration and economic growth; a study of
    Great Britain and the Atlantic economy.
    4.8941
Migration in post-war Europe. 4.1658
The migration of British capital to 1875.
    4.4456
Miguel Angel Asturias. 2.5370
Miguel de Unamuno. 2.5290
Miguel Hernández. 2.5267
Miguel Mihura. 2.5277
Mike. 3.8786
Mikhail Lermontov. 2.1397
Mikhail Sholokhov and his art. 2.1604
The Milagro beanfield war. 2.13191
Milankovitch and climate. 5.2528
Miles Davis. 1.4083
Milestones in mass communication research.
    4.5007
Milestones in microbiology. 5.4444
Milestones of modern chemistry. 5.2614
Milindapañhā. 1.1742
The militant South, 1800-1861. 3.8144
Militarism. 5.7248
Militarism and social revolution in the Third
    World. 4.7717
The militarization of space. 5.7412
The military and politics in modern times.
    5.7160
The military and society in colonial Peru,
    1750-1810. 3.9301
The military and society in Latin America.
    3.8985
Military architecture. 5.7391
Military bibliography of the Civil War. 5.7836
Military customs and traditions. 5.7239
Military deterrence in history. 5.7218
Military development in Africa. 5.7348
The Military draft. 5.7367
Military expenditure limitation for arms
    control. 4.9154
A military history and atlas of the Napoleonic
    Wars. 4.166
A military history of Germany. 3.2255
A military history of modern China, 1924-1949.
    3.4670
A military history of the Western World.
    3.535
The military in contemporary Soviet politics.
    5.7329
The military in Greek politics. 3.2700
The military in the political development of
    new nations. 5.7158
The military-industrial complex. 4.2066
The military institutions of the Romans.
    5.7204
Military music and its story. 1.4201
Military music of the American Revolution.
    1.4203
Military occupation and the rule of law: Ernst
    Fraenkel. 4.9328
Military regimes in Africa. 3.5088
The military staff, its history and development.
    5.7357
Military strategy and the origins of the First
    World War. 3.775
Milking the public. 4.3690
The Milky Way. 5.1858-5.1859
Mill and town in South Carolina, 1880-1920.
    4.3846
Mill on liberty. 4.7442

The mill on the Po. 2.5020
Millais and the Ruskins. 2.8036
The millenarian piety of Roger Williams.
    1.3326
Millenarianism and peasant politics in Vietnam.
    1.2178
Millennial dreams in action. 1.2950
The miller of Old Church. 2.11772
A million and one nights. 2.2927
Million dollar directory. 4.4251
The millionaire's gospel modernised. 2.2063
Millions of strange shadows. 2.13077
The millstone. 2.9661
Milton: a biography. 2.7151
Milton and Augustine. 2.7127
Milton and his England. 2.7153
Milton and his epic tradition. 2.7141
Milton and the baroque. 2.7137
Milton and the English Revolution. 2.7162
Milton and the Puritan dilemma, 1641-1660.
    2.7165
Milton and the science of the saints. 2.7166
A Milton encyclopedia. 2.7147
Milton Friedman's monetary framework.
    4.4475
A Milton handbook. 2.7155
Milton's contemporary reputation. 2.7154
Milton's epic voice. 2.7126
Milton's Eve. 2.7134
Milton's God. 2.7167
Milton's good God. 2.7123
Milton's grand style. 2.7136
Milton's imagery and the visual arts. 2.7161
Milton's prosody. 2.7171
Milton's theatrical epic. 2.7125
Milwaukee. 3.8451
Mimbres painted pottery. 3.5909
Mimbres pottery. 3.5910
The mime book. 2.3131
Mimesis. 2.2401
Mimesis and metaphor. 2.8579
The mimic men. 2.10011
Mimicry in plants and animals. 5.3582
Mind. 5.122
The mind and art of Chaucer. 2.6344
The mind and art of Coventry Patmore.
    2.7991
The mind and art of Giovanni Battista Piranesi.
    1.5017
The mind and art of Henry Miller. 2.12191
The mind and art of Jonathan Swift. 2.7303
The Mind and art of Victorian England.
    1.6715
Mind and emotion. 5.274
Mind and its place in nature. 5.103
Mind and madness in ancient Greece. 5.4805
The mind and method of the historian. 3.1973
The mind and society. 4.4863
The mind and the art of Henry Adams. 3.6240
Mind cure in New England. 5.476
The mind in conflict. 5.410
Mind in science. 5.26
Mind in society. 5.291
Mind models: new forms of musical experience.
    1.3677
The mind of a mnemonist. 5.339
The mind of a poet. 2.8313
The mind of America, 1820-1860. 3.6043
The mind of Frederick Douglass. 3.7240
The mind of John Paul II. 1.3162
The mind of Kierkegaard. 1.1122
The mind of Napoleon. 3.2132
A mind of one piece. 3.7425
The mind of primitive man. 4.536
The mind of the founder. 3.6974
The mind of the Maker. 1.2234
The mind of the Middle Ages, A.D. 200-1500.
    3.124
The mind of the Negro as reflected in letters
    written during the crisis, 1800-1860. 3.6632
The mind of the Old South. 3.8143
The mind of the Oxford movement. 1.3307
The mind of the Qur'ān: chapters in reflection.
    1.2031
The mind of the South. 3.8117
The mind-reader. 2.12709
Mind, self & society from the standpoint of a
    social behaviorist. 4.4990

Mindful pleasures. 2.13285
Minds and mechanisms. 5.18
The mind's best work. 5.346
Minds, brains, and science. 5.124
Mindstorms. 5.1064
Mine eyes have seen the glory. 2.11083
Mineral exploration. 5.6742
Mineral facts and problems. 5.6723
Mineral names. 5.3011
Mineral nutrition of plants. 5.3753
Mineral resources and their management.
    5.6726
Mineralogy. 5.3014
Mineralogy, concepts, descriptions,
    determinations. 5.3013
Minerals yearbook. 5.6724
Miners, merchants, and farmers in colonial
    Colombia. 4.2178
Miners, millhands, and mountaineers. 4.2020
The mines of Neptune. 5.6750
The Ming dynasty, its origins and evolving
    institutions. 3.4707
The mingling of heaven and earth. 2.8350
Mini/microcomputer hardware design. 5.6581
Minima moralia. 1.967
Minimal art. 1.4849
Mining frontiers of the Far West, 1848-1880.
    3.8464
Mining geology. 5.6731
The mining industry and the developing
    countries. 3.3721
Ministers of reform. 3.7406
The minister's seal. 2.1952
Ministry in America. 1.3002
The Ministry in historical perspectives. 1.3003
The ministry of fear. 2.8753
Minna von Barnhelm. 2.4593
Minnesota. 3.8496, 3.8499, 3.8501
Minnesota farmer-laborism. 4.8239
Minnesota rag. 4.9467
The minor arts of Islam. 1.6548
Minor classics of nineteenth-century fiction.
    2.6262
Minor poets of the Caroline period ... 2.6162
Minor poets of the seventeenth century. 2.6158
Minor White. 5.6970
Minor works ... 2.339
Minorities and women. 5.8476
Minorities in American higher education.
    4.10892
Minority aging. 4.5819
Minority organizations 1978-. 3.6522
Minority organizations: a national directory.
    3.6522
Minority report. 2.12382
Minority students. 4.10902
The minute man in peace and war. 5.7290
The minutemen and their world. 3.8002
Mirabell, books of number. 2.12142
Miracle at Midway. 3.1035
Miracle of the rose. 2.4536
Miraculous stories from the Japanese Buddhist
    tradition. 1.2152
Mirage in the West. 3.6106
Mires 5.3550
Miró in America. 1.6296
The mirror and the lamp: romantic theory and
    the critical tradition. 2.2668
The mirror for magistrates. 2.6428
Mirror for man. 4.435
Mirror for the moon. 2.2051
A mirror for witches in which is reflected the
    life, machinations, and death of famous Doll
    Bilby. 2.11746
The mirror in the roadway. 2.3512
Mirror, mirror. 4.6069
The mirror of art. 1.4963
The mirror of music, 1844-1944. 1.3712
The mirror of perfection. 1.3259
The Mirror of salvation. 2.13943
Mirror of the heart. 2.12583
Mirror of the Indies. 2.13955
A mirror to Kathleen's face. 4.10123
Mirror to the Son of Heaven. 3.4703
Mirrors, messages, manifestations. 5.6962
Mirrour for magistrates. 2.6428
The Mirth of a nation. 2.10841
Mis poemas mejores. 2.5229

Miscellaneous essays and The lays of ancient Rome. 2.7920
Miscellaneous prose of Sir Philip Sidney. 2.6507
Miscellaneous subjects. 4.4317
A miscellany. 2.5535
Les misérables. 2.4236
The misfits. 2.12174
Misfits (Motion picture) 2.12174
Mishkat al-masabih. 1.2037
Mishnah. 1.1938
The Mishnah. 1.1940
Mishnah. 1.1938
Mishnah. English. 1.1940
Mishnayot. 1.1938
Mishpokhe. 3.8050
The mismeasure of man. 5.353
Misregulating television. 4.9542
Miss Herbert (the suburban wife) 2.10167
Miss Lulu Bett. 2.11765
Miss Marjoribanks. 2.7976
Miss Mary Cassatt. 1.5924
Miss May Sinclair: novelist. 2.9323
Miss Mole. 2.9610
Miss Ravenel's conversion from secession to loyalty. 2.10992
Miss Silver's past. 2.1682
Missing persons and other essays. 2.13681
The mission and expansion of Christianity in the first three centuries. 1.2296
Mission for life. 1.3323
Mission for my country. 3.4090
Mission on the Rhine. 4.10742
Mission to earth. 5.1813
Mission to Kala. 2.4869
Mission to Mars. 5.6715
The missionary enterprise in China and America. 1.3028
Missions of the college curriculum. 4.10613
Mississippi, a Bicentennial history. 3.8291
The Mississippi Chinese. 3.8294
The Mississippi question, 1795-1803. 3.8300
Mississippi: the closed society. 3.8292
Mississippi, the view from Tougaloo. 4.10882
The Mississippi Valley in British politics. 3.8297
Mississippian settlement patterns. 3.5907
Missouri. 3.8361, 3.8364
Missouri, a Bicentennial history. 3.8363
The Missouri controversy, 1819-1821. 3.7119
Mistaken convictions and their consequences. 4.9429
Mister Facey Romford's hounds. 2.8132
Mister Jelly Roll. 1.3933
Mister Johnson. 2.8503
Mister Roberts. 2.11826
Mistress Pat. 2.3337
Mistress to an age. 3.2075
The mists of Avalon. 2.12918
Misunderstanding. 2.4443
The Misuse of alcohol. 5.4961
MIT wavelength tables. 5.2312
MITI and the Japanese miracle. 4.3075
Mitochondria. 5.3613
The mitochondrion. 5.3612
Mitre and sceptre. 1.3315
Mitsou. 2.4496
Mitteleuropa in German thought and action, 1815-1945. 3.759
Mixed company. 5.7378
The Mixtecs in ancient and colonial times. 3.8909
A mixture of frailties. 2.9925
MLA handbook for writers of research papers. 2.1041
MLA international bibliography of books and articles on the modern languages and literatures. 5.8332
The MLA style manual. 2.2518
Mnemosyne: the parallel between literature and the visual arts. 2.2386
Mnogoiazychnyĭ slovarʹ tekhnicheskikh terminov kartografii. 4.75
Mo Tzu. 1.171
Mobile. 2.4436
Mobilizing women for war. 3.1137
Moby-Dick. 2.11155
Moby-Dick and Calvinism. 2.11157

Modal logic. 1.1249
Modal logics. 1.1250
Model building in mathematical programming. 5.5585
Model city charter. 4.8852
The model company town. 4.6236
The model country. 3.9234
The model ombudsman. 4.8826
Model or ally? 4.7134
Model State constitution. 4.8250
Model theory. 5.1055
Modeling and analysis. 5.1148
Modeling and simulation in chemical engineering. 5.6830
Modeling dynamic phenomena in molecular and cellular biology. 5.3504
Modeling nature. 5.3339
Modeling of complex systems. 5.995
Modeling the bipolar transistor. 5.6506
Models in archaeology. 3.229
Models in ecology. 5.3536
Models in geography. 4.199
Models in paleobiology. 5.3160
Models of achievement. 5.91
Models of madness, models of medicine. 5.4800
Models of thought. 5.391
Moderates and conservatives in Western Europe. 4.8376
Moderato cantabile. 2.4521-2.4522
The Modern age to romanticism. 1.133
Modern airmanship. 5.6657
The Modern American college. 4.10082
Modern American criticism. 2.2513
Modern American literature. 2.10404
The modern American novel. 2.10614
Modern American poetry. 2.10494
Modern American poetry. 2.10763
The modern American political novel, 1900-1960. 2.10564
Modern American sculpture. 1.5660
Modern American usage. 2.1138
The modern American vice presidency. 4.7971
Modern antenna design. 5.6495
Modern applications of linear IC's. 5.6544
The modern Arabic literary language. 2.1830
Modern architecture. 1.5243, 1.5256, 1.5273, 1.5275
Modern architecture, 1851-1945. 1.5255
Modern architecture and design. 1.5257
Modern architecture since 1900. 1.5266
Modern arms and free men. 5.7205
Modern art, 19th & 20th centuries. 1.4786
Modern art and modernism. 1.4784
Modern art and the new past 1.5138
Modern artists on art. 1.4808
Modern atomic physics. 5.2128
Modern Australian poetry, 1920-1970. 5.8084
Modern Australian prose, 1901-1975. 5.8078
Modern Austrian writing. 2.13935
Modern Belgian literature, 1830-1960. 2.4800
Modern Bhutan. 3.4332
Modern Black poets. 2.10480
Modern book design, from William Morris to the present day. 5.7547
A modern book of esthetics. 1.1347a
Modern Britain, 1885-1955. 3.1639
Modern British eloquence. 2.6268
Modern British literature. 2.5740
Modern British poetry. 2.6183
Modern building. 1.5263
Modern Canadian verse in English and French. 2.9898
Modern capitalism. 4.1792
Modern cellular automata. 5.1374
Modern chemical kinetics. 5.2881
Modern Chicano writers. 2.10302
A modern China and a new world. 3.4741
Modern Chinese economic history. 4.2457
Modern Chinese fiction. 5.8045
Modern Chinese literature in the May Fourth Era. 2.2151
Modern Chinese society. 5.8398
Modern Chinese stories and novellas, 1919-1949. 2.2204
Modern chivalry. 2.10863
A modern comedy. 2.8679
Modern Commonwealth literature. 2.9877

Modern communication circuits. 5.6429
Modern communications and spread spectrum. 5.6368
The modern conductor. 1.4501
Modern continental literary criticism. 2.2558
Modern control systems. 5.6181
The modern corporation. 4.3084
The modern corporation and private property. 4.3055
Modern county government. 4.8856
A modern course in statistical physics. 5.2169
The modern critical spectrum. 2.2469
Modern criticism. 2.2464
Modern criticism, theory and practice. 2.2445
The modern dance. 4.1118
Modern dance in America 4.1163
Modern democracies. 4.7558
Modern developments in audiology. 5.4371
Modern dictionary of electronics. 5.6447
A modern dictionary of sociology. 4.4736
The modern diesel: development and design. 5.6224
Modern digital and analog communication systems. 5.6349
Modern digital control systems. 5.6184
Modern drama. 5.8124
Modern drama and German classicism. 2.13492
Modern drama in theory and practice. 2.2814
Modern eclectic therapy. 5.4862
Modern economic growth: rate, structure, and spread. 4.2787
Modern education for the junior high school years. 4.10508
Modern electrical communications. 5.6357
The modern encyclopedia of basketball. 4.1011
The Modern encyclopedia of Russian and Soviet history. 3.3029
Modern encyclopedia of wine. 5.6893
Modern engelsk svensk och svensk engelsk ordbok. 2.923
Modern engelsk-svensk ordbok. 1984. 2.923
Modern English and its heritage. 2.962
Modern English-Canadian poetry. 5.7893
Modern English-Canadian prose. 5.7892
A modern English grammar on historical principles. 2.986
Modern English painters. 1.6021
Modern English structure. 2.1002
Modern English usage. 2.1090
Modern Englishes. 2.2338
Modern European imperialism. 5.8226
Modern European sculpture, 1918-1945. 1.5681
Modern European social history. 4.5293
Modern fantasy. 2.5967
Modern fishing gear of the world. 5.5483
Modern French criticism. 2.2500
Modern French Marxism. 4.7049
Modern French music, from Fauré to Boulez. 1.3707
Modern French philosophy. 1.823
Modern French poetry. 2.3926
Modern French theatre. 2.3889, 2.3939
Modern German drama. 2.13494, 2.13521
Modern German literature, 1870-1940. 2.13477
Modern German philosophy. 1.964
Modern Germany. 3.2289, 3.2331
Modern Greece. 3.2683, 3.2693
Modern Greek poetry. 2.570, 2.573
Modern Greek writers: Solomos, Calvos, Matesis, Palamas, Cavafy, Kazantzakis, Seferis, Elytis. 2.568
The modern harpsichord. 1.4151
Modern Hebrew literature. 2.1786
Modern Hebrew literature, from the Enlightenment to the birth of the State of Israel. 2.1774
Modern heroism; essays on D. H. Lawrence, William Empson, & J. R. R. Tolkien. 2.5551
Modern historians on British history, 1485-1945. 5.7981
The modern history of Iraq. 3.3781
The modern history of Israel. 3.3929
The modern history of Mongolia. 3.4865
The modern history of Peru. 3.9293
A modern history of Somalia. 3.5257

The modern history of Somaliland. 3.5257
The modern history of Soviet Central Asia. 3.3325
A modern history of Soviet Georgia. 3.3312
A modern history of Tanganyika. 3.5300
Modern housing prototypes. 1.5556
Modern Hungarian poetry. 2.1755
Modern India. 3.4223, 3.4272
Modern Indian poetry. 2.1958
Modern Indian poetry in English. 2.10122
Modern Indian short stories. 2.1959-2.1960
Modern India's economy; two decades of planned growth. 4.2508
Modern Indonesian literature. 2.2284
Modern industrial marketing. 4.4288
Modern introduction to classical mechanics & control. 5.1642
A modern introduction to international law. 4.9004
The modern Irish drama. 2.9860
Modern Irish drama, 1891-1980. 2.9861
Modern Irish short stories. 2.9869
Modern Islam. 3.3708
Modern Italy. 3.2858
Modern Japanese fiction 1868-1926. 2.2013
Modern Japanese fiction and its traditions. 2.2012
Modern Japanese literature. 2.2018
The Modern Japanese military system. 5.7341
Modern Japanese poetry. 2.2032
Modern Japanese poets and the nature of literature. 2.2009
Modern Japanese stories. 2.2037
Modern Japanese writers and the nature of literature. 2.2002
The modern language of architecture. 1.5207
Modern Latin America. 3.9003
Modern Latin American literature. 2.5299, 2.5301
A modern law of nations. 4.9280
Modern literary criticism. 2.2559
Modern literary criticism, 1900-1970. 2.2473
Modern literary realism. 2.2402
Modern M.O.S. technology. 5.6508
Modern man in search of a soul. 5.167
Modern manuscripts. 3.267
Modern maps and atlases. 4.232
Modern marine terminal operations and management. 4.3949
Modern materials management. 5.7038
Modern methods in the history of medicine. 5.4507
The modern metropolis. 4.6308
Modern Mexican art. 1.4922
Modern molecular photochemistry. 5.2917
Modern MOS technology. 5.6508
The modern novel in America, 1900-1950. 2.10628
Modern nutrition in health and disease. 5.4239
Modern olive production. 5.5341
Modern optics. 5.2275
Modern painting. 1.5872
Modern painting and the northern romantic tradition. 1.5867
Modern perspectives in Western art history. 1.5122
Modern petroleum technology. 5.6802
Modern philosophy, an introduction. 1.108
Modern philosophy: Descartes to Kant. 1.422
Modern philosophy of science. 5.927
Modern physical geography. 4.243
Modern physical metallurgy. 5.6779
Modern physics for scientists and engineers. 5.1983
A modern pilgrimage in New Testament christology. 1.2853
The modern poetic sequence. 2.5834
Modern poetry. 2.2746
Modern poetry and the tradition. 2.2762
Modern poetry from Africa. 2.2308
Modern political analysis. 4.7522
The modern Presidency. 4.7920
The modern prince, and other writings. 4.7083
Modern principles of athletic training. 4.972
Modern prints & drawings. 1.6470
The modern reader's Japanese-English character dictionary. 2.1993
Modern religious movements in India. 1.1811

The modern researcher. 3.378
Modern retailing management. 4.4318
Modern revivalism: Charles Grandison Finney to Billy Graham. 1.3036
The modern rhyming dictionary. 2.1048
Modern rhythmic gymnastics. 4.924
Modern rhythmic notation. 1.4445
The modern rise of population. 5.4545
The modern Russian dictionary for English speakers. 2.1238
Modern Russian historiography. 3.3034
Modern Russian history. 3.3109
Modern Russian poetry. 2.1312
The modern school movement. 4.10024
Modern science and human values. 5.961
Modern science and modern man. 5.843
Modern scientists and engineers. 5.810
Modern Scotland. 3.1775
Modern Scottish short stories. 2.9848
Modern scribes and lettering artists. 1.6605
Modern sculpture. 1.5654
Modern seamanship. 5.7490
Modern Shakespearean criticism. 2.6736
Modern Sicily, after 1713. 3.2943
Modern Slavic literatures. 2.1197
Modern social politics in Britain and Sweden. 4.5301
Modern sound reproduction. 5.6560
Modern Soviet society. 4.5373
Modern Spain, 1875-1980. 3.3453
The modern Spanish novel. 2.5134
The modern Spanish novel, 1898-1936. 2.5136
The modern Spanish stage: four plays. 2.5158
Modern Sri Lanka. 3.4361
The modern stage and other worlds. 2.3280
Modern state. 4.7510
Modern stories from Holland and Flanders. 2.13946
The modern structural theory of organic chemistry. 5.2850
Modern svensk-engelsk ordbok. 1984. 2.923
Modern Swedish-English and English-Swedish dictionary. 2.923
Modern synthetic reactions. 5.2736
The modern technique of rock blasting. 5.6748
Modern telecommunication. 5.6345
The modern temper. 1.455
Modern theatre. 2.14092
The modern theme. 1.1128
The modern theory of solids. 5.2198
Modern times. 3.738
Modern transportation economics. 4.3883
Modern transportation; selected readings. 4.3880
Modern Turkey. 3.3574
Modern verse in English, 1900-1950. 2.6185
Modern Wales. 3.1755
Modern weed control. 5.5391
Modern world drama. 2.2808
The modern world-system. 4.1745
The modern writer and his world. 2.5732
Modern Yiddish culture. 2.1789
Modern Yugoslav satire. 2.3798
The modernist idea. 2.5464
The modernist impulse in American Protestantism. 1.2792
The modernist movement in Brazil. 2.5465
The modernist Muslim movement in Indonesia, 1900-1942. 1.2005
The modernity of tradition: political development in India. 4.6407
Modernization and African labor. 4.3671
Modernization, dislocation, and Aprismo. 4.8350
Modernization in South-East Asia. 4.5406
Modernization of agriculture in developing countries. 4.2892
The modernization of French Jewry. 3.3959
The modernization of sex. 4.5496
The moderns. 2.10717
Modes of being. 1.652
Modes of imperialism. 4.7538
Modes of individualism and collectivism. 4.1211
Modes of thinking in young children. 5.579
Modes of thought. 1.783
Modest Mussorgsky, his life and works. 1.3941
La Modification. 2.4435

Modula-2. 5.1220
Modula-two. 5.1220
Modular forms and functions. 5.1336
Modular functions and Dirichlet series in number theory. 5.1318
The modularity of mind. 5.263
Module, proportion, symmetry, rhythm. 1.4642
Modules in applied mathematics. 5.1109
Mohammed. 1.2012
Mohammed and Charlemagne. 3.578
Mohammedanism. 1.1995
Moïra. 2.4576
The mole. 5.4012
Molecular beams. 5.2073, 5.2469
The molecular biology of cell membranes. 5.3610
The Molecular biology of plant cells. 5.3744
Molecular biology of the cell. 5.3601
Molecular biology of the gene. 5.3501
Molecular biophysics. 5.3496, 5.3505
Molecular cell biology. 5.3597
Molecular cloning. 5.3462
Molecular evolution. 5.3398
Molecular evolution and protobiology. 5.3321
Molecular evolution and the origin of life. 5.3319
Molecular evolutionary genetics. 5.3417
Molecular genetics. 5.3419
Molecular geometry. 5.2870
Molecular orbital theory for organic chemists. 5.2724
Molecular organization and cell function. 5.3624
Molecular physics. 5.2187
Molecular quantum mechanics. 5.2825
Molecular reality. 5.1961
Molecular spectra and molecular structure. 5.2303
Molecular structure. 5.2801, 5.2835
Molecular structure and dynamics. 5.2814
Molecular theory of gases and liquids. 5.2064
Molecules and life. 5.4391
Molière: a new criticism. 2.4044
Molière, a playwright and his audience. 2.4042
Molière: stage and study. 2.4043
Moll Flanders. 2.6973
Molloy. 2.4409
Molloy, Malone dies and The unnamable. 2.4410
Moltke und der staat. 3.2319
Moly, and My sad captains. 2.8795
The moment of creation. 5.1882
The moment of explosion. 2.7120
The moment of poetry. 2.2743
A moment of true feeling. 2.13895
Moments of being. 2.9583
Moments of vision. 5.6952
Mon frère Yves. 2.4327
The monadology and other philosophical writings. 1.862
The Monarch of wit. 2.6465
Monarchism in the Weimar Republic 3.2374
Monarchs, rulers, dynasties, and kingdoms of the world. 3.562
Monarchy and revolution. 4.8401
Monarchy in the emperor's eyes. 3.4716
The monarchy of France. 4.8579
Monasteries of Western Europe. 1.5521
Monastery and cathedral in France. 1.4958
The Monastery of Saint Catherine at Mount Sinai, the icons. 1.5182
Monastic life at Cluny, 910-1157. 1.3236
Monde. 5.835
Le monde, ou, Traité de la lumière. 5.835
Monet. 1.6123
Monetarism. 4.4484
Monetarist perspectives. 4.4493
Monetary equilibrium. 4.4476
A monetary history of the United Kingdom, 1870-1982. 4.4513
A monetary history of the United States, 1867-1960. 4.4502
Monetary policy under the international gold standard. 4.4494
Monetary statistics of the United States: estimates, sources, methods. 4.4503
Monetary theory and policy. 4.4482

Monetary trends in the United States and the United Kingdom, their relation to income, prices, and interest rates, 1867-1975. 4.4497
Monet's years at Giverny. 1.6122
Money. 4.4481
Money and banking in the Chinese Mainland. 4.4522
Money and motivation. 4.4367
Money and politics in America, 1755-1775. 4.4498
Money and politics in the United States. 4.8130
Money and power in fifteenth-century France. 4.4518
Money, banking, and the economy. 4.4507
Money, capital, and fluctuations. 4.4471
Money, credit & commerce. 4.4492
Money, financial flows, and credit in the Soviet Union. 4.4457
Money from home. 2.12421
Money in congressional elections. 4.8129
Money, in disequilibrium. 4.4467
Money, in equilibrium. 4.4468
Money in international exchange. 4.4571
Money in politics. 4.8126
Money in the bank. 2.9555
Money in the multinational enterprise. 4.4597
Money, information, and uncertainty. 4.4469
Money, interest, and prices. 4.4478
The money market. 4.4445
Money market calculations. 4.4607
Money markets. 4.4448
The money-order; with, White genesis. 2.4860
Money, sex, and power. 4.4903
The Money supply and the exchange rate. 4.4517
Mongkut, the King of Siam. 3.4528
The Mongol Empire. 3.3619
The Mongol mission. 3.3611
Mongolia's culture and society. 3.4860
The Mongols of Manchuria. 3.4846
Monitoring for health hazards at work. 5.5019
The monk. 2.7912
A monk of St. Bertin. 3.1322
Monkey. 2.2226
Monkeys, apes and other primates. 5.4018
Monmouth's rebels. 3.1508
A monograph of the works of McKim, Mead & White, 1879-1915. 1.5316
Monographic series. 5.7669
Monographic series - Library of Congress. 5.7669
Monopolists and freebooters. 3.5548
Monopoly and free enterprise. 4.3013
Monopoly capital. 4.1518
The Monroe doctrine, 1823-1826. 4.9054
The Monroe doctrine, 1826-1867. 4.9055
The Monroe doctrine, 1867-1907. 4.9056
The Monroe doctrine and American expansionism, 1843-1849. 3.7168
Monsoon Asia. 3.3614
Mont-Saint-Michel and Chartres. 3.1951
Montaigne. 2.3993, 2.3996
Montaigne en mouvement. 2.3995
Montaigne's discovery of man. 2.3994
Montaigne's Travel journal. 2.3991
Montaillou. 3.2236
Montale. 2.5040
Montana. 3.8544-3.8545
Montana, a state guide book. 3.8542
Montana, high, wide and handsome. 3.8543
Montauk. 2.13746-2.13747
Montcalm and Wolfe. 3.6881
Montesquieu. 4.7431
Montesquieu and Rousseau. 4.7429
Montesquieu's philosophy of liberalism. 4.7430
Montessori, a modern approach. 4.10211
The Montessori method. 4.10205
Monteverdi. 1.3931
Monteverdi, creator of modern music. 1.3932
A month in the country. 2.1447
A month of Sundays. 2.13370
Monthly catalog of United States Government publications. 5.7770
Monthly check-list of state publications. 5.7783
Montrose. 3.1801
Monty. 3.1271

The monument rose. 2.11767
Monumenta Serbocroatica. 2.1217
Monuments of medieval art. 1.4735
Monuments of Romanesque art. 1.4751
Monuments of the Incas. 3.9284
Moody's industrial manual. 4.4622
The moon. 5.1797
The moon and sixpence. 2.9099
The moon and the bonfires. 2.5053
A moon for the misbegotten. 2.12287
Moon of wintertime. 3.5726
The moon shines on Kylenamoe. 2.9147
Moonies in America. 1.3410
The moon's acceleration and its physical origins. 5.1798
Moons and planets. 5.1787
The Moon's dominion. 2.8980
The moons of Jupiter. 2.9953
The moonstone. 2.7606
The Moors in Spain. 3.3430
The Moors in Spain and Portugal. 3.3431
Moral and political philosophy. 1.1430
The moral and political thought of Mahatma Gandhi. 4.7482
The moral and political tradition of Rome. 3.2731
The moral art of Dickens. 2.7659
Moral aspects of health care. 5.4558
The moral basis of a backward society. 4.5364
Moral development and behavior. 1.1404
Moral development, moral education, and Kohlberg. 5.608
The moral economy of the peasant. 4.2920
Moral education. 4.10805
Moral education ... it comes with the territory. 4.10807
Moral essays. 2.692
The moral foundation of democracy. 4.7570
The moral judgement of the child. 4.10383
The moral law. 1.879
Moral man and immoral society. 4.4974
Moral philosophy. 1.1417
The moral philosophy of Josiah Royce. 1.639
The moral point of view. 1.1434
Moral relativity. 1.1463
The moral teaching of Paul. 1.2706
Moral treatment in community mental health. 5.4860
The moral Trollope. 2.8238
Moral values and political behaviour in ancient Greece. 1.1419
The moral vision of Jacobean tragedy. 2.5886
The moral vision of Oscar Wilde. 2.8290
Moralia. 2.390
Morality and architecture. 1.5260
Morality and beyond. 1.1477
Morality and foreign policy. 4.9051
Morality and population policy. 4.1627
Morality and power in a Chinese village. 1.1425
The morality of consent. 4.7512
The morality of law. 4.9361
The morality of spending. 4.2058
Morals pointed and tales adorned. 2.1974
Moravagine. 2.4462
Mordecai Richler. 2.9967-2.9968
More debits than credits. 4.4407
The More developed realm. 4.1597
More nineteenth century studies. 1.716
A more perfect Union. 4.7843
More plays from Off-Off Broadway. 2.10806
More poems, 1961. 2.8717
More power than we know. 4.5234
More prefaces to Shakespeare. 2.6732
More pricks than kicks. 2.8423
More stately mansions. 2.12288
More than a labour of love. 4.6080
More than a trial. 3.2192
More than human. 2.13337
More than meets the eye. 2.3623
More than survival. 4.10077
More women than men. 2.8528
More work for mother. 5.7100
Moreau de St. Méry's American journey < 1793-1798 >. 3.6028
Morgante. 2.4977
The Morgesons and other writings, published and unpublished. 2.11227

Mori Ōgai. 2.2080
Mori Ōgai and the modernization of Japanese culture. 2.2079
Morley Callaghan. 2.9919
Mormonism. 1.3378
Mormonism and the American experience. 1.3382
The morning after; selected essays and reviews. 2.9812
A morning at the office, a novel. 2.9121
The morning breaks. 4.9458
Morning, noon, and night. 2.11519
Morning yet on creation day. 2.10037
Moroccan Islam. 1.2011
Morocco, a country study. 3.5209
Morocco and Tunisia, a comparative history. 3.5212
Morphogenesis. 5.3485
Morphological integration. 5.4107
Morphology. 2.188
Morphology and biology of reptiles. 5.3916
Morphology and syntax. 2.187
The morphology of gymnosperms. 5.3734
The morphology of landscape. 4.240
Morphology of plants and fungi. 5.3730
The morphology of pteridophytes. 5.3699
Morphology of the angiosperms. 5.3733
Morphology of the folktale. 4.821
Morphology of vascular plants. 5.3731
Morphology, the descriptive analysis of words. 2.189
Morris Dictionary of word and phrase origins. 2.1058
Morris Graves, vision of the inner eye. 1.4897
Morris Louis, 1912-1962. 1.5952
Morris Rosenfeld. 2.1817
Morrison R. Waite. 4.9831
The Morrow anthology of younger American poets. 2.10777
Morse theory. 5.1595
Morskoĭ sbornik. 5.7469
Mort à crédit. 2.4508, 2.4511
Une mort très douce. 2.4391
Mortality and morbidity in the United States. 5.4630
Le Morte Arthur. 1974. 2.6413
Morte Arthure. 2.6420-2.6421
Morte Authure. 1974. 2.6413
Morte d'Urban. 2.13270
The mortgaged heart. 2.12074
Morvern transformed. 3.1811
MOS (metal oxide semiconductor) physics and technology. 5.6507
Mosaics, a survey of their history and techniques. 1.5505
The mosaics of Norman Sicily. 1.5507
The mosaics of Rome, from the third to the fourteenth centuries. 1.5509
The mosaics of San Marco in Venice. 1.5508
Mosby's memoirs and other stories. 2.11355
Moscow 2042. 2.1647
Moscow and Chinese Communists. 3.4683
Moscow and the West. 3.3067
Moscow two thousand forty two. 2.1647
Moscow's Muslim challenge. 3.3326
Moses and monotheism. 1.2542
Moses Mendelssohn. 1.875-1.876
Moshe Dayan. 3.3933
The Mosher survey. 4.5511
Mosquitoes. 2.11670
Mosquitoes, malaria, and man. 5.4676
Mössbauer effect. 5.2328
The Mössbauer effect. 5.2330
Mössbauer effect. 5.2329
Mosses and liverworts. 5.3703
Mosses of Eastern North America. 5.3705
The most dangerous man in America: scenes from the life of Benjamin Franklin. 3.6989
A most fortunate ship. 5.7452
The most important art. 2.2889
Most likely to succeed. 2.11584
The most of P. G. Wodehouse. 2.9549
The Most popular plays of the American theatre. 2.10799
The most probable world. 3.195
The most splendid failure. 2.11679
The most unsordid act. 3.935
Mother. 2.1501

Mother Bombie. 2.6219
Mother earth, and other stories. 2.1612
Mother Goose. 2.14101
The mother machine. 5.4254
Mother night. 2.13393
The mother of Eve 4.10396
Mother of the blues. 1.4097
Mother poem. 2.9986
Mother wit from the laughing barrel. 4.768
Mothering. 4.5670
The mothers. 4.5552
Mothers and daughters. 4.6133
Mothers and more. 4.6021
Mothers at work. 4.3246
Mother's day. 2.9822
A mother's kisses. 2.13019
Motif-index of folk-literature. 4.760
Motion and time study. 5.5620-5.5621
Motion picture almanac 1929-1935/36. 2.2865
Motion picture and television almanac 1952/53-55. 2.2865
Motion picture directors. 5.8144
Motion study. 5.5601
Motivation. 5.215
Motivation and emotion. 5.112
Motivation in education. 4.10370
Motives and mechanisms. 5.449
Motives and thought. 5.162
The motives of eloquence. 2.2466
La motocyclette 2.4648
Motor activity and the education of retardates. 4.10950
Motor control. 5.255
The motorcycle. 2.4649
The motorcycle betrayal poems. 2.13404
Les mots. 2.4736
Mottoes. 2.3804
Moulds of understanding. 5.767
The mound builders. 2.13435, 4.532
Mound builders of ancient America:the archaeology of a myth. 3.5699
Mount St. Helens, 1980. 5.3680
Mountain, field, and family. 4.2180
Mountain gloom and mountain glory. 2.5779
The mountain lion. 2.12500
Mountain monarchs. 5.4044
Mountain sheep. 5.4043
Mountain standard time. 2.11883
The Mountain States of America: people, politics, and power in the eight Rocky Mountain States. 3.8540
Mountain weather and climate. 5.2581
Mountains without handrails, reflections on the national parks. 3.6000
Mountbatten. 3.1287
Mountolive. 2.8606
The mourning bride, poems, & miscellanies. 2.6946
Mouth full of earth. 2.1214
Le Mouvement syndical sous la Troisième République. 4.3415
A moveable feast. 2.11851
The movement. 4.10095
Movement & metaphor. 4.1176
Movement education. 4.917
The Movement for Greek independence, 1770-1821. 3.2691
Movement of animals. 2.342
The movement of English prose. 2.5929
Movements and issues in American Judaism. 1.1929
Movements of political protest in Canada, 1640-1840. 3.8670
Movements of thought in the nineteenth century. 1.442
Movie journal. 2.2923
The moviegoer. 2.13243
Movies and methods. 2.2943
The movies begin. 2.2932
The moving American. 3.6159
The moving image. 2.2938
Moving in cities. 4.3910
Moving pictures. 5.8145
A moving target. 2.8700
Moving the masses. 4.3922
Moving the mountain. 4.5993
Le Moyen âge. 2.3840

The Moynihan report and the politics of controversy. 3.6779
Mozambique. 3.5305-3.5306
Mozambique: the Africanization of a European institution. 4.2872
Mozart, a documentary biography. 1.3937
The Mozart companion. 1.3940
Mozart, his character, his work. 1.3938
Mozart's operas. 1.3936
Mr. Andrews. 2.8642
Mr. Ass comes to town. 2.1903
Mr. Baruch. 3.7625
Mr. Black labor; the story of A. Philip Randolph. 3.6849
Mr. Bridge. 2.12953
Mr. Britling sees it through. 2.8250
Mr. Cibber of Drury Lane. 2.6937
Mr. Clemens and Mark Twain. 2.10959
Mr. Conservative: Barry Goldwater. 3.7643
Mr. Crump of Memphis. 3.8353
Mr. Dooley. 2.3792
Mr. Dooley remembers: edited with an introd. and commentary by Philip Dunne. 2.11616
Mr. Dooley's Chicago. 2.11619
Mr. Facey Romford's hounds. 2.8132
Mr. Fortune objects. 2.8412
Mr. Fortune's maggot. 2.9470
Mr. Hodge & Mr. Hazard. 2.12827
Mr. Jorrocks's hunt. 2.8131
Mr. Justice Black, absolutist on the Court. 4.9803
Mr. Justice Miller and the Supreme Court, 1862-1890. 4.9824
Mr. Justice Murphy. 4.9826
Mr. Lincoln's Army. 3.7361
Mr. Madison's war. 3.7111
Mr. Midshipman Easy. 2.7926
Mr. Peale's Museum. 1.48
Mr. Polk's war: American opposition and dissent, 1846-1848. 3.7140
Mr. Republican. 3.7689
Mr. Sammler's planet. 2.11354
Mr. Samuel McIntire, carver. 1.5315
Mr. Secretary Cecil and Queen Elizabeth. 3.1436
Mr. Secretary Peel. 3.1605
Mr. Secretary Walsingham and the policy of Queen Elizabeth. 3.1438
Mr. Sponge's sporting tour. 2.8133
Mr. Standfast. 2.8488
Mr. Stone and the knights companion 2.10012
Mrcchakatikā. 2.1951
MRD. 4.10327
Mrs. Bridge. 2.12952
Mrs. Dalloway. 2.9574
Mrs. Fiske and the American theatre. 2.3254
Mrs. Humphry Ward. 2.8246
Mrs. Palfrey at the Claremont. 2.9398
Mrs. Pat. 2.3337
Mrs. Thatcher's first administration. 3.1710
The muckrakers. 4.5178
Mudan ting. 2.2225
La muerte de Artemio Cruz. 2.5340
The mugging. 4.6755
Mughal rule in India. 3.4252
Muhammad. 1.2015, 1.2019
Muhammad and the Christian. 1.2069
Muhammad at Mecca. 1.2017
Muhammad at Medina. 1.2018
Muhammad's people. 3.599
Muir's historical atlas: medieval and modern. 4.122
Mukat's people. 3.5847
Mul ha-homah ha-segurah. 3.3818
The mulberry bush. 2.9538
Mules and men. 4.770
Multi-party Britain. 4.8524
The multibus design guidebook. 5.6589
Multicriterion optimization in engineering with FORTRAN programs. 5.5718
Multicultural education in a pluralistic society. 4.10481
Multicultural teaching. 4.10836
Multidimensional digital signal processing. 5.6372
Multilateral trade negotiations. 4.9393
Multilateral treaties. 4.8966

Multilingual dictionary of remote sensing and photogrammetry. 4.24
Multilingual dictionary of technical terms in cartography. Dictionnaire multilingue de termes techniques cartographiqes. 4.75
Multilingualism in the Soviet Union. 2.216
A Multimedia approach to children's literature. 5.7719
Multinational accounting. 4.4416
The multinational company. 4.2733
Multinational corporate strategy. 4.2718
Multinational corporations and U.N. politics. 4.3022
Multinational corporations in world development. 4.2736
The multinational empire. 3.1896
Multinational enterprise and economic analysis. 4.3020
Multinational managers and poverty in the Third World. 4.3025
Multinational marketing management. 4.4112
Multinational oil. 4.3760
The multinationals and East-West relations. 4.3032
Multinationals in a changing environment. 4.3065
Multinationals in Latin America. 4.3028
Multinationals under fire. 4.2732
Multinationals, unions, and labor relations in industrialized countries. 4.3438
Multiple exposure. 3.7627
Multiple-factor analysis. 5.57
Multiple man. 5.4968
The multiple plot in English Renaissance drama. 2.5882
Multiplicative number theory. 5.1321
Multiplying villanies. 2.3476
Multivariate analysis. 5.1391
Mumbo jumbo. 2.13295
Mumu. 2.1454
Munch. 1.6285
Munera pulveris. 4.1418
Munich. 3.874, 3.880
Munich 1938. 3.878
Munich: prologue to tragedy. 3.1920
Municipal administration in the Roman Empire. 4.8834
Municipal bonds. 4.4729
The municipal revolution in America. 4.8839
The Municipal year book. 4.8850
Munshi Premchand of Lamhi village. 2.1892
Munyakare: African civilization before the batuuree. 3.5229
The Muqaddimah; translated from the Arabic by Franz Rosenthal. 3.451
The Muqaddimah, an introduction to history. 3.452
The mural painters of Tuscany. 1.6394
Mural painting in ancient Peru. 3.9289
The Murals of Alchi, Western Himalayas. 1.6399
Murasaki Shikibu, her diary and poetic memoirs. 2.2050
Murder and magic. 2.13040
The murder at the vicarage. 2.8515
The murder book of J.G. Reeder. 2.9459
Murder must appetite. 2.5957
The murder mystique. 2.3473
The murder of Roger Ackroyd. 2.8514
Muriel Bradbrook on Shakespeare. 2.6722
Muriel Spark. 2.9365-2.9366
A Muriel Spark trio. 2.9360
A murky business. 2.4114
Murnau. 2.3062
Murphy. 2.8424
A muse for heroes. 2.3842
The muse's method. 2.7140
Museum of Fine Arts, Boston. 1.4658
The Museum of Modern Art, New York. 1.4662
Museums and women, and other stories. 2.13372
Museums in crisis. 1.4657
Museums of the world. 1.46
The mushroom hunter's field guide. 5.3727
Mushrooms of North America. 5.3726
Music, acoustics & architecture. 1.5494

Music and aesthetics in the eighteenth and early-nineteenth centuries. 1.4394
Music and dance research of Southwestern United States Indians. 1.4308
The music and history of the baroque trumpet before 1721. 1.4175
Music and imagination. 1.4403
Music and its instruments. 1.4128
Music and musical life in Soviet Russia. 1.3731
Music and musicians. 1.3981
Music and musicians in early America. 1.3689
Music & poetry in the Early Tudor Court. 1.3720
Music and poetry of the English Renaissance. 1.3718
Music and poetry, the nineteenth century and after. 1.4401
Music and society. 1.4357
Music and some highly musical people. 1.3751
Music and the line of most resistance. 1.4072
Music as heard. 1.4406
Music at the court of Frederick the Great. 1.3709
Music criticism. 1.3549
Music criticisms, 1846-99. 1.3472
Music cultures of the Pacific, the Near East, and Asia. 1.3734
Music education. 1.3450
Music for chameleons. 2.11465
Music for more than one piano. 1.3583
Music for patriots, politicians, and presidents. 1.4291
Music for piano and orchestra. 1.3584
Music for sight singing. 1.4569
Music for the voice. 1.3600
Music hall in Britain. 2.2833
Music-Hall sidelights. 2.4496
Music-hall sidelights. 2.4500
Music here and now. 1.3673
Music in a new found land. 1.3690
Music in America. 1.3426
Music in American society, 1776-1976. 1.3692
Music in Bali. 1.3745
Music in Britain. 1.3710
Music in Canada. 1.3701
Music in Europe and the United States. 1.3633
Music in India. 1.3739
Music in London, 1890-1894. 1.3723
Music in medieval Britain. 1.3715
Music in my time. 1.3923
Music in primitive culture. 1.4287
Music in Shakespearean tragedy. 1.3488
Music in the 20th century, from Debussy through Stravinsky. 1.3666
Music in the baroque era, from Monteverdi to Bach. 1.3655
Music in the classic period. 1.3659
Music in the culture of northern Afghanistan. 1.4347
Music in the cultured generation. 1.3694
Music in the French secular theater, 1400-1550. 1.3705
Music in the medieval world. 1.3652
Music in the middle ages. 1.3651
Music in the mind. 1.3744
Music in the modern age. 1.3681
Music in the New World. 1.3686
Music in the Renaissance. 1.3647, 1.3650
Music in the romantic era. 1.3663
Music in the United States. 1.3687
Music in western civilization. 1.3635
The Music index. 1.3556
Music industry directory. 1.3449
Music is my mistress. 1.3863
Music notation. 1.4446
Music notation in the twentieth century. 1.4447
The music of Africa. 1.3748
The Music of Alban Berg. 1.3812
The music of Benjamin Britten. 1.3823
The music of Black Americans. 1.4305
The music of Central Africa. 1.4346
The music of Gustav Holst. 1.3897
The music of Igor Stravinsky. 1.4011
The music of Schubert. 1.3974
The music of Spain. 1.3732
The music of survival. 2.12754

The music of the English church. 1.4248
The music of the English parish church. 1.4250
The music of the Jews. 1.3642
The music of the Sumerians and their immediate successors, the Babylonians & Assyrians. 1.3641
The music of William Walton. 1.4507
The music profession in Britain since the eighteenth century. 1.3711
The music school. 2.13371
Music since 1900. 1.3680
Music, sound and sensation. 1.4377
Music, the arts, and ideas. 1.4369
Music, the listener's art. 1.4434
The Music theater of Walter Felsenstein. 1.4110
Music therapy. 1.4408
Music, ways of listening. 1.4436
Musical acoustics. 1.4375
Musical allusions in the works of James Joyce. 1.3486
Musical America: annual directory issue. 1.3446
Musical analysis. 1.4186
Musical applications of microprocessors. 1.4458
Musical articles from the Encyclopaedia britannica. 1.3480
Musical autographs from Monteverdi to Hindemith. 1.3499
Musical comedy in America. 1.4220
Musical design in Aeschylean theater. 1.3645
The musical experience of composer, performer, listener. 1.3476
Musical form. 1.4478
Musical form and musical performance. 1.4476
Musical instrument collections. 1.3615
Musical instruments. 1.3515
Musical instruments and their symbolism in Western art. 1.3492
The musical instruments of the native races of South Africa. 1.4139
Musical instruments through the ages. 1.4126
Musical interludes in Boston, 1795-1830. 1.3699
The Musical quarterly. 1.3702
Musical settings of American poetry. 1.3599
Musical stages. 1.3960
Musical wind instruments. 1.4164
Musicals! 1.3451
A musician talks ... 1.3481
Musicians since 1900. 1.3532
Musicological literature. 1.3737
Musics of many cultures. 1.4363
Die Musik in Geschichte und Gegenwart. 1.3502
The Muslim and Christian calendars. 3.272
The Muslim architecture of Egypt. 1.5455
Muslim brotherhoods in nineteenth century Africa. 1.2081
Muslim cities in the later Middle Ages. 4.6276
Muslim civilization in India. 3.4196
The Muslim community of the Indo-Pakistan sub-continent, 610-1947. 3.4197
Muslim contribution to geography. 4.64
The Muslim contribution to mathematics. 5.1081
The Muslim creed. 1.2047
The Muslim creed, its genesis and historical development. 1.2060
The Muslim discovery of Europe. 3.3743
The Muslim Filipinos. 3.4593
Muslim institutions. 3.3664
Muslim neoplatonists. 1.367
Muslim peoples. 3.3646
Muslim society. 1.2074
Muslim Spain, its history and culture. 3.3432
Muslim studies. 1.1992
A Muslim theologian's response to Christianity. 1.2067
Muslim women in Mombasa, 1890-1975. 4.5909
Muslims, Christians, and Jews in the crusader kingdom of Valencia. 3.3490
The Muslims of British India. 3.4262
Muslims of the Soviet empire. 3.3028
Mussolini. 3.2901, 3.2903

Mussolini: a study in power. 3.2902
Mussolini: an intimate biography. 3.2904
Mussolini and fascism. 3.2841
Mussolini and the Jews. 3.3975
Mussolini's early diplomacy. 3.2839
Mussolini's Roman Empire. 3.2888
Must Canada fail? 3.8781
Must corporate income be taxed twice? 4.4710
Must we bus? 4.10798
Mustard Seed Garden manual of painting. 1.6326
Mutagenicity, carcinogenicity, and teratogenicity of industrial pollutants. 5.4728
Mutant. 2.11973
Mutiny on the Bounty. 2.12256
Mutmassungen über Jakob. 2.13901
Mutual accommodation. 3.6533
Mutual aid. 4.4905
The mutual flame. 2.6675
The mutual friend. 2.12939
My apprenticeships, and Music-hall sidelights. 2.4500
My autobiography. 2.3619
My brother's keeper. 2.8910
My country and my people. 3.4641
My country and the world. 3.3261
My country is the whole world. 4.9147
My days of anger. 2.11650
My diary, North and South. 3.6047
My experiences in the world war. 3.815
My Father, Bertrand Russell. 1.772
My father's son. 2.9158
My first fifty years in politics, as told to Robert J. Donovan. 3.7672
My heart's in the Highlands. 2.12440
My house; poems. 2.13045
The My Lai Massacre and its cover-up. 3.4497
My land and my people. 1.1778
My last million readers. 2.3614
My last sigh. 2.3036
My last two thousand years. 2.13052
My life. 4.7056
My life. 1.4038, 1.6046, 2.8622, 3.2352, 3.5363, 4.1134
My life and Ethiopia's progress, 1892-1937. 3.5247
My life and hard times. 2.3796
My life and loves. 2.7803
My life and music. 1.4071
My life and my films. 2.3065
My life & my views. 5.714
My life and The Times. 2.3609
My life and times. 2.12188
My life as a man. 2.13302
My life as a rebel. 4.7084
My life in pictures. 2.3247
My lifetime in letters. 2.12482
My long life. 2.7576
My Lord, what a morning. 1.4086
My many years. 1.4069
My Mark Twain: reminiscences and criticisms. 2.10957
My memoirs ... 2.4178
My memoirs. 3.2357
My mother's house. 2.4495
My music, my life. 1.3738
My Olympic years. 4.982
My other loneliness. 2.12782
My own story. 4.8511
My past and thoughts. 3.3118-3.3119
My place in the bazaar. 2.9479
My prisons. 2.5010
My quarter century of American politics. 3.7430
My Québec. 3.8818
My recollections. 1.3924
My Russian memoirs. 3.3136
My sad captains. 2.8795
My several worlds. 2.11432
My sister Eileen. 2.12086
My soul is rested. 3.6686
My theater. 2.4546
My troubles are going to have trouble with me. 4.3286
My truth. 3.2895
My uncle Dudley. 2.12216
My village, my life: portrait of an Indian village. 4.5428

My war memoirs. 3.1931
My years with Louis St. Laurent. 3.8789
My young years. 1.4070
My youth in Vienna. 2.13861
Mycenaean Greece. 3.2584
The Mycenaean origin of Greek mythology. 1.1657
The Mycenaean world. 3.2579
The Mycenaeans. 3.2587
Mycenaeans and Minoans. 3.2586
'Myne owne ground' 3.8215
Myra Breckinridge. 2.12619
Myron. 2.12620
Myself. 2.10207
Myself, the autobiography of John R. Commons. 4.1370
Mysteries. 2.14045
The mysteries of Udolpho, a romance. 2.7997
The mysterious Mr. Quin. 2.8517
The mysterious North 3.8658
The mystery of comets. 5.1823
The mystery of Dr. Fu Manchu. 2.9463
The mystery of iniquity. 2.11173
The mystery of Orcival. 2.4216
The mystery of the mind. 5.4340
The Mystery story. 2.3474
The mystery writer's art. 2.10547
Mystic art of ancient Tibet. 1.5070
The mystic art of written forms. 1.6601
The mystic north. 1.6359
Mystical Bedlam. 5.4804
The mystical design of Paradise lost. 2.7122
Mystical dimensions of Islam. 1.2085
The mystical world of Indonesia: culture & economic development in conflict. 3.4564
Mysticism. 1.1631, 1.3091
Mysticism: a study and an anthology. 1.1627
Mysticism and logic. 1.765
Mysticism and philosophical analysis. 1.1628
Mysticism and philosophy. 1.114
Mysticism and religious traditions. 1.1629
Mysticism east and west. 1.1630
The Mysticism of William Blake. 2.7435
Mysticism, sacred and profane. 1.1633
Myth and Christianity. 1.1552
Myth and literature in the American renaissance. 2.10390
Myth and method. 2.3414
Myth and society in ancient Greece. 3.2552
Myth and symbol: critical approaches and applications. 2.2561
Myth, legend, and custom in the Old Testament. 1.2548
Myth, literature, and the African world. 2.2305
The myth makers. 2.2665
The myth of Black progress. 3.6741
The myth of Christian beginnings. 1.2282
The myth of deliverance. 2.6761
The myth of educational reform. 4.10446
The myth of marginality. 4.5271
The myth of mass culture. 4.5093
The myth of 'Mau Mau' 3.5283
The myth of Sisyphus, and other essays. 2.4451
The myth of the American frontier. 3.6363
The myth of the deprived child. 4.10940
The myth of the Judeo-Christian tradition. 1.1955
Myth of the machine. 3.211
The myth of the ruling class. 4.7480
The myth of the state. 4.7458
Myth, religion, and society. 1.1656
Mythago wood. 2.9708
Le mythe de Sisyphe. 2.4450
The mythic image. 1.1607
Mythologies. 1.7, 2.8335
Mythologies of the world. 1.1599
The Mythologizing of Mark Twain. 2.10969
Mythology and humanism. 2.13835
Mythology and the Renaissance tradition in English poetry. 2.5777
Mythology and the romantic tradition in English poetry. 2.5778
The mythopoeic reality. 2.10563
Myths and realities. 3.8130
Myths and symbols in Indian art and civilization. 1.1819

Myths in education. 4.10242
The myths of cabinet government. 4.8447
Myths of coeducation. 4.10839
Myths of gender. 5.4201
Myths of information. 3.212
Myths of male dominance. 4.572
Myths of the Greeks and Romans. 1.1640
Myths of the Hindus & Buddhists. 1.1813

N.B.A.'s official encyclopedia of pro basketball. 4.1014
N.B.C. handbook of pronunciation. 2.1021
N.B.S./N.R.C. steam tables. 5.6206
N.C.L.C. 2.2664
N.F. Fedorov. 1.1114
N.I.C.E.M. index to educational audio tapes. 4.10333
N.I.C.E.M. index to educational video tapes. 4.10334
N I C E M index to producers & distributors. 4.10322
N.I.C.E.M. index to sixteen millimeter educational films. 4.10331
N.I.C.E.M. index to thirty-five millimeter filmstrips. 4.10332
N. M. Karamzin, a Russian sentimentalist. 2.1333
N. M. Karamzin: a study of his literary career, 1783-1803. 2.1332
N. Scott Momaday, the cultural and literary background. 2.13178
N. W. Rowell, Ontario nationalist. 4.9430
The NAACP crusade against lynching, 1909-1950. 4.6722
The nabobs. 3.4200
Nabokov's Ada. 2.12225
Nabokov's dozen. 2.12227
Naboth's vineyard. 3.9122
Nacha Regules. 2.5387
Nachahmung und Schöpfung im Barock. 2.13546
Nachdenken über Christa T. 2.13928
Nachricht vom Tag. 2.13671
Nada. 2.5270
The Nader report: bitter wages. 5.5021
Nadine Gordimer. 2.10079
Nadja. 2.4423
The nag. 2.1794
Nag Hammadi codices. 1.2968
The Nag Hammadi Library in English. 1.2968
Nagauta: the heart of kabuki music. 1.3743
Naive set theory. 5.1350
Naked and fiery forms. 2.10290
The naked and the dead. 2.12099
Naked angels. 2.10430
The naked ape; a zoologist's study of the human animal. 445
Naked lunch. 2.12935
Naked masks, five plays. 2.5055
Naked to mine enemies. 3.1411
The naked year. 2.1613
Name and subject index to the Presidential chronology series. 5.7827
Name into word. 2.1064
The name of the rose. 2.5079
Name reactions in organic chemistry. 5.2653
The names. 2.13177
Names and descriptions. 1.142
Names and their varieties. 2.197
The names of the lost. 2.13137
Naming-day in Eden. 2.196
Naming names. 2.2925, 5.7727
Naming the whirlwind. 1.1583
Nana. 2.4343
Napoleon. 3.2128
Napoleon and the birth of modern Spain. 3.3450
Napoleon Bonaparte. 3.2129-3.2130
Napoleon, for and against. 3.2131
Napoleon, from 18 Brumaire to Tilsit, 1799-1807. 3.2123
Napoleon; from Tilsit to Waterloo, 1807-1815. 3.2124
Napoleon III. 3.2159
Napoleon III and Mexico. 3.8934
Napoleon III and the Concert of Europe. 3.2156

Napoleon III and the rebuilding of Paris. 3.2231
The Napoleon of Notting Hill. 2.7562
Napoleon, the Jews, and the Sanhedrin. 3.3958
Napoleonic propaganda. 3.2126
Napoleon's invasion of Russia, 1812. 3.2136
Narcissus and Goldmund. 2.13774
The narc's game. 4.6812
Narrative and dramatic sources of Shakespeare. 2.6712
Narrative discourse. 2.4664
Narrative of a pilgrimage to El-Medinah and Meccah. 3.4048
The narrative of Hosea Hudson, his life as a Negro Communist in the South. 4.7000
Narrative of the expedition of an American squadron to the China Seas and Japan, performed in the years 1852, 1853, and 1854, under the command of Commodore M. C. Perry, United States Navy 3.4880
Narrative of the life and adventures of Henry Bibb. 3.7207
A narrative of the life of David Crockett of the State of Tennessee. 3.8347
Narrative of the life of Frederick Douglass. 3.7238
A narrative of travels on the Amazon and Rio Negro. 3.9221
Narrative poems. 2.12607
Narrative truth and historical truth. 5.4914
Narratives of the Coronado expedition, 1540-1542. 3.5985
The narrow margin. 3.1048
The narrow road to the Deep North, and other travel sketches. 2.2064
Nashville in the new South, 1880-1930. 3.8354
The Nasirean ethics. 1.1483
Naskapi. 3.5912
Nassau Senior and classical economics. 4.1354
Nathalie Sarraute. 2.4715
Nathalie Sarraute and the war of the words. 2.4716
Nathan the Wise. 1.4593
Nathanael West. 2.12688
Nathanael West: an interpretative study. 2.12684
Nathanael West; the art of his life. 2.12686
Nathanael West, the ironic prophet. 2.12683
Nathanael West's novels. 2.12685
Nathaniel Hawthorne. 2.11071
Nathaniel Hawthorne, a biography. 2.11064-2.11065
Nation. 1.621
Nation against nation. 4.9215
Nation and family. 4.1701
A nation at risk. 4.10046
Nation-building. 4.7381
Nation-building in Malaysia, 1946-1974. 3.4545
A Nation in arms. 5.7307
A Nation in the making. 3.4605
A nation of behavers. 1.2378
A nation prepared. 4.10527
A Nation so conceived. 3.6278
The nation state and national self-determination. 4.9302
National anthems of the world. 1.3431
The national atlas of Canada. 4.139
The national atlas of the United States of America. 4.143
National avenue. 2.11238
The National Catholic almanac. 1.66
National character and the factors in its formation. 3.77
National consciousness, history, and political culture in early-modern Europe. 3.617
National consciousness in eighteenth-century Russia. 3.3097
The national conventions and platforms of all political parties, 1789 to 1905. 4.8145
National conventions in an age of party reform. 4.8143
The National cyclopedia of American biography. 3.6297
National data book. 1.59
National defense. 5.7267
National directory of children & youth services. 4.6564

National directory of children and youth services. 4.6564
National directory of newsletters and reporting services. 5.8312
The National electrical code handbook. 5.6108
The National faculty directory. 4.9944
National formulary. 5.5149
The National Front in English politics. 4.8554
National Gallery of Art, Washington. 1.4664
National Geographic atlas of the world. 4.114
National health insurance. 4.3452
National heraldry of the world. 3.289
National housing finance systems. 4.3483
National income and its composition, 1919-1938. 4.1963
National index of American imprints through 1800. 5.7759
National interests and the multinational enterprise. 4.2731
The National newspaper index [microform]. 1.44
National newspaper index (Monthly) 1.44
National oil companies. 4.3778
The National Park Service. 5.5388
The national parks. 3.6001
National parks, conservation, and development. 5.5384
National party platforms. 4.8144
National policy and higher education. 4.9932
National Portrait Gallery. 1.4665
National power survey. 4.3800
National review (Washington, D.C.) 3.7541
The National Road. 4.3942
National romanticism in Norway. 3.3377
National security and individual freedom. 4.7692
National security and the nuclear dilemma. 5.7279
National security policy. 5.7251
National socialsim, A history of. 3.2373
National theatre conference. 2.3113
National transportation policy. 4.3885
National union catalog. 5.7666
The National union catalog of manuscript collections. 5.8280
The National union catalog, pre-1956 imprints. 5.7667
The national wealth of the United States in the postwar period. 4.2053
The national welfare rights movement. 4.6528
Nationalism. 4.7492
Nationalism and after. 4.7484
Nationalism and communism in the Balkans. 3.3534
Nationalism and imperialism in the hither East. 3.763
Nationalism and new states in Africa from about 1935 to the present. 3.5091
Nationalism and revolution in Indonesia. 3.4570
Nationalism and sexuality. 4.5491
Nationalism and social communication. 4.7485
Nationalism and the cultural crisis in Prussia, 1806-1815. 3.2479
Nationalism and the multinational enterprise. 4.2734
Nationalism in colonial Africa. 3.5107
Nationalism in Eastern Europe. 3.3522
Nationalism in Ireland. 3.1840
Nationalism in Japan. 3.4916
Nationalism in the Soviet Union. 3.3216
Nationalism in the U.S.S.R. & Eastern Europe in the era of Brezhnev & Kosygin. 4.8655
Nationalism in the U.S.S.R. and Eastern Europe in the era of Brezhnev and Kozygin. 4.8655
Nationalism in the USSR & Eastern Europe in the era of Brezhnev & Kosygin. 4.8655
Nationalism in the USSR and Eastern Europe in the era of Brezhnev and Kosygin. 4.8655
Nationalism, its meaning and history. 4.7488
The nationalist revival in France, 1905-1914. 3.1968
The nationality question in Soviet Central Asia. 3.3322
The nationalization of the Bill of Rights. 4.9672

The nationalizing of business, 1878-1898. 4.1916
Die nationalsozialistische Machtergreifung. 3.2435
Nations and states. 3.544
The nation's families, 1960-1990. 4.5593
Nations in alliance. 4.9298
Nations on record. 4.9246
Nations on record: Supplement. 4.9247
Nations on record: United Nations General Assembly roll-call votes (1946-1973) 4.9247
The Nation's water resources. 4.2931
The nations within. 3.5832
Nations without a State. 4.1198
Native administration in the British African territories. 4.8793
Native American folklore, 1879-1979. 5.7734
The native American heritage. 3.5816
Native American humor. 2.3791
Native American literature. 2.2317
Native American renaissance. 2.10296
The native Americans. 3.5707
Native Californians. 3.5724
Native peoples of South America. 3.9156
The native problem in Africa. 3.5102
Native realm: a search for self-definition. 2.1720
Native son. 2.12811
Native sons. 2.10326
Natives and newcomers. 3.5730, 4.3623
Natives of Hemsö. 2.14075
NATO in the 1960's. 5.7298
NATO, the entangling alliance. 5.7297
NATO's nuclear dilemmas. 5.7299
Natura sanat non medicus. 5.115
The natural. 2.13159
The natural and the supernatural Jew. 1.1914
The natural childbirth primer. 5.5073
The natural environment. 5.8420
Natural hazards, local, national, global. 4.247
Natural history. 2.686-2.687
The natural history of alcoholism. 5.4963
The natural history of H.G. Wells. 2.8261
A natural history of man in Britain. 4.390
Natural history of marine animals. 5.3821
A natural history of marine mammals. 5.3981
The natural history of otters. 5.4003
The natural history of religion. 1.1551
The natural history of Selborne. 5.3278
A natural history of sex. 5.3481
The natural history of the mind. 5.4314
Natural history of the West Indies. 3.9084
The natural house. 1.5561
Natural insect & disease control. 5.5417
Natural law and the theory of society, 1500 to 1800. 4.7275
The natural man observed. 1.5926
Natural monopoly. 4.3037
Natural order. 5.744
A natural passion. 2.7223
The natural philosophy of time. 5.1757
Natural products chemistry. 5.2792
Natural regions of the U.S.S.R. 4.253
Natural regions of the United States and Canada. 4.248
The natural regulation of animal numbers. 5.4072
Natural resources. 4.1903
Natural resources and public property under the Canadian Constitution. 4.9435
Natural resources measurements. 4.1765
Natural resources of the Soviet Union: their use and renewal. 4.2368
Natural right and history. 4.7649
Natural selection. 5.3353
Natural selection in human populations. 4.457
Natural shocks. 2.13333
Natural solar architecture. 1.5475
The natural superiority of women. 4.5934
Natural supernaturalism. 2.2614
Natural symbols. 1.1529
A natural theology for our time. 1.1592
Natural value. 4.1498
The natural world of the California Indians. 3.5721
Naturalism in nineteenth century English literature. 2.5723

The naturalistic tradition in Indian thought. 1.194
The nature and art of workmanship. 5.7041
Nature and culture. 1.6358
Nature and culture in the Iliad. 2.503
The nature and destiny of man. 1.2907
The nature and evolution of female sexuality. 5.4259
Nature and historical experience. 1.634
Nature and life. 5.946
The nature and logic of capitalism. 4.1529
Nature and mind. 1.97
Nature and natural science. 1.654
The nature and necessity of interest. 4.1549
The nature and properties of engineering materials. 5.5764
The nature and properties of soils. 5.5261
Nature & significance of economic science, An essay on the. 4.1452
Nature and society. 2.5812
The nature and sources of the law. 4.9502
Nature and the American. 5.3228
The nature and types of sociological theory. 4.4744
Nature, and Utility of religion. 1.1556
Nature, culture, and human history. 4.432
Nature heals. 5.115
Nature in American literature. 2.10341
Nature in Shakespearian tragedy. 2.6831
Nature into myth. 2.5587
Nature, man, and society in the twelfth century. 1.2751
The nature novel from Hardy to Lawrence. 2.5974
The nature of adolescent judgment. 5.622
The nature of African customary law. 4.9926
The nature of ball lightning. 5.2551
Nature of biography. 3.312
The nature of biological diversity. 5.3585
The nature of culture. 4.400
The nature of geography. 4.14
Nature of geography. 4.15
The nature of Greek myths. 1.1650
The nature of historical explanation. 3.509
The nature of history in ancient Greece and Rome. 3.2514
The nature of human conflicts. 5.207
The nature of human intelligence. 5.354
The nature of intelligence. 5.360
The nature of life. 5.3491
Nature of life. 5.4285
The nature of light & colour in the open air. 5.2554
The nature of literature. 2.2589
The nature of love. 1.1322
The nature of maps. 4.209
The nature of mass poverty. 4.1858
The nature of matter. 5.2058
The nature of metaphysics. 1.1270
The nature of morality. 1.1452
The nature of narrative. 2.3504
The nature of natural history. 5.3302
The nature of nature. 1.6176
The nature of necessity. 1.1254
The nature of nursing. 5.5172
The nature of perceptual adaptation. 5.250
The nature of personality. 5.502
The nature of philosophy. 1.107
The nature of physical theory. 5.1901
The nature of prejudice. 5.444
The nature of psychological explanation. 5.34
The nature of recreation. 4.891
The nature of representation. 1.4595
The nature of Roman comedy. 2.642
The nature of selection. 1.482
The nature of structural design and safety. 5.5860
The nature of the chemical bond and the structure of molecules and crystals. 5.2837
The nature of the child. 5.568
The nature of the non-Western World. 3.108
The nature of the physical universe. 5.2455
The nature of the physical world. 5.879
The nature of the stratigraphical record. 5.3129
The nature of thermodynamics. 5.2241
The nature of things. 2.739
The nature of thought. 5.380

The nature of true virtue. 1.1506
The nature of work. 4.3428
Nature's economy. 5.3530-5.3531
Nature's nation. 3.6142
Nauru, phosphate and political progress. 3.5648
Nausea. 2.4728
Nautical astronomy. 5.7491
The Navaho. 3.5919
Navaho legends. 3.5922
Navaho weaving. 3.5830
Navajo architecture. 3.5917
The Navajo blanket. 3.5918
Navajo Blessingway Singer. 3.5923
Navajo kinship and marriage. 3.5926
Navajo wars; military campaigns, slave raids, and reprisals. 3.5921
Naval & maritime history. 5.8301
Naval documents of the American Revolution. 3.6954
A naval history of England. 5.7457
A naval history of the American Revolution. 3.6952
The naval history of the civil war. 3.7391
The naval profession. 5.7475
The naval side of King William's war, 16th/26th November 1688-14th June 1690. 3.646
Naval surgeon. 5.7484
Naval tactical thought. 5.7425
The Naval war of 1812. 3.7114
The naval war of 1812. 3.7115
Navarra, the durable kingdom. 3.3487
Naven. 3.5649
Navier-Stokes equations. 5.1523
Navigation and piloting. 5.7494
The Navy, the Company, and Richard King. 3.8869
The Nayars today. 3.4207
The Nazarenes. 1.6160
The Nazi concentration camps. 3.1124
The Nazi dictatorship. 3.2441
The Nazi era, 1919-1945. 5.8014
The Nazi holocaust. 3.1125
The Nazi Olympics. 4.977
The Nazi organisation of women. 4.6121
The Nazi Party. 4.8604
The Nazi seizure of power. 3.2433
The Nazi/Skokie conflict. 4.9708
The Nazi voter. 4.8600
Nazis and workers: National Socialist appeals to German labor, 1919-1933. 3.2424
Nazis in Skokie. 4.9706
Nazism, resistance & holocaust in World War II. 5.8250
Nazism, resistance and holocaust in World War II. 5.8250
The NBA's official encyclopedia of pro basketball. 4.1014
NBC handbook of pronunciation. 2.1021
NBS/NRC steam tables. 5.6206
NCLC. 2.2664
The Neapolitan revolution of 1820-1821. 3.2942
The Near East and the foundations for civilization. 3.112
The Near East and the Great Powers. 3.3732
The Near East in history. 3.3717
Neblette's Handbook of photography and reprography. 5.6934
Nebraska. 3.8517
Nebraska, a guide to the Cornhusker State. 3.8518
The Nebraska question, 1852-1854. 3.7173
Nebulae and interstellar matter. 5.1773
The necessary angel. 2.2740
Necessary evil. 2.7543
The necessary majority. 4.6235
The necessary revolution in American education. 4.9997
The necessities of war. 3.2611
Necessity, cause, and blame. 1.315
The necessity for choice. 3.7825
Necker, reform statesman of the Ancien Régime. 4.4672
Nectar in a sieve. 2.10126
A Needle, a bobbin, a strike. 4.3265
The needle's eye, a novel. 2.9662

Negations; essays in critical theory. 1.610
Negative dialectics. 1.968
The negative imagination. 2.11127
The neglected brother. 2.7885
Negotiating peace. 4.9330
Negotiating the mainstream. 3.6625
Un nègre à Paris. 2.4853
The Negritude poets. 2.4844
The Negro almanac. 3.6626
The Negro American. 3.6650
Negro and Christianity in the United States. 1.2423
The Negro and his music. 1.4303
The Negro and organized labor. 3.6738
The Negro and the Communist Party. 3.6687
The Negro and the First amendment. 4.9692
The Negro author, his development in America to 1900. 2.10325
The Negro caravan. 2.10689
The Negro church in America. 1.2419
The Negro family in the United States. 3.6761
Negro folk music, U.S.A. 1.4297
Negro housing. 3.6786
The negro in American civilization. 3.6652
The Negro in American culture. 1.6712
The Negro in American film, 1900-1942. 2.2998
The Negro in Brazilian literature. 2.5463
The Negro in Brazilian society. 3.9226
The Negro in colonial New England. 3.7217
The Negro in our history. 3.6633
The Negro in the American Revolution. 3.6951
The Negro in the Civil War. 3.7389
The Negro in the United States. 3.6617, 5.7880
Negro labor in the United States, 1850-1925. 3.6743
Negro metropolis. 3.8044
Negro migration. 3.6789
Negro militia and Reconstruction. 3.7472
Negro musicians and their music. 1.4300
The Negro novel in America. 2.10314
Negro playwrights in the American theatre, 1925-1959. 2.10518
Negro poetry and drama. 2.10316
The Negro press in the United States. 2.3648
The Negro revolt. 3.6677
Negro sermons in verse. 2.11937
Negro slavery in Latin America. 4.6427
Negro thought in America, 1880-1915. 3.6655
Negro troops in the Union Army, 1861-1865. 3.7388
Negro youth at the crossways. 3.6651
The Negroes in America. 3.6770
Nehru. 3.4321
Nehru, the first sixty years. 3.4319
Neighborhood networks for humane mental health care. 5.4701
Neighborhoods and urban development. 4.5218
Neighborhoods, people, and community. 4.5216
Neighbors in conflict. 3.8046
Neil M. Gunn; the man and the writer. 2.8792
Neill! Neill! Orange peel! 4.11011
Neither Athens nor Sparta? 5.7240
Neither Black nor white. 3.9225
Neither conservative nor liberal. 4.9673
Neither East nor West. 3.1147
Neither slave nor free. 4.6425
Neither war nor peace. 3.1153
Nekrassov. 2.4723, 2.4729-2.4730
Nelly's version. 2.9675
Nelson Algren. 2.11309
Nelson and sea power. 3.1281
Nelson, the commander. 3.1280
Nelson's complete concordance of the Revised standard version of the Bible. 1.2502
Nemesis. 3.5027
The nemesis of power. 3.2379
Neo-classicism. 1.4778
Neo-colonialism. 4.2579
Neo-colonialism in West Africa. 4.2592
Neo-Marxism, the meanings of modern radicalism. 4.6984
The Neo-Platonists. 1.323
Neoclassical architecture in Canada. 1.5345

The neoclassical theory of production and distribution. 4.1332
Neoclassicism and romanticism, 1750-1850. 1.4777
The neoconservatives. 4.7317
The neolithic cultures of the British Isles. 4.707
Neolithic Europe. 4.708
The Neolithic of the Near East. 4.711
The neon wilderness. 2.11306
Neoplatonism in the poetry of Spenser. 2.6546
Nepal. 3.4348, 3.4377
Nepal, a cultural and physical geography. 3.4349
Nepal in perspective. 3.4376
Nepal; strategy for survival. 3.4378
Nepalese short stories. 2.1911
Nepali politics. 4.8779
Nepali visions, Nepali dreams. 2.1910
The nephew. 2.12360
Nerve and muscle. 5.4289
Nerve, muscle, and synapse. 5.4303
The nervous body. 5.4315
Nervous people, and other satires. 2.1617
The nervous system. 5.4320
A nest of simple folk. 2.9162
The nether world. 2.7735
Netherlanders in America. 3.6543
The Netherlands. 3.2982, 3.2985, 4.2363
The Netherlands in the seventeenth century. 3.2990
Netherlands India. 3.4562
Netochka Nezvanova. 2.1356
The Netsilik Eskimo. 3.5873
Network analysis. 5.6281
Network architectures for distributed computing. 5.6412
Network flow programming. 5.5597
Network optimisation practice. 5.5598
Networks and marginality. 4.5256
Networks of interdependence. 4.9268
Networks of power. 5.6288
Neue Gesamtausgabe der Werke und Schriften in vier Bänden. 2.13561
Neue internationale Atlas. 4.115
Neural mechanisms of learning and memory. 5.4351
Neurobiology. 5.4296
Neuroethology. 5.4305, 5.4308
Neurologic critical care. 5.4786
Neurologic disorders. 5.4787
Neurology. 5.4318
Neuromancer. 2.11768
The neuropsychology of Lashley. 5.206
The Neurosciences. 5.4321
Neuroses. 5.4928
The neurotic personality of our time. 5.4784
Neurotic styles. 5.4929
The neurotic trillionaire. 3.7901
The neutral theory of molecular evolution. 5.3391
The neutral Yankees of Nova Scotia. 3.8800
Neutrality for the United States. 4.9047
Neutrality laws, regulations and treaties. 4.9331
Neutron scattering in chemistry. 5.2811
Nevada. 3.8586-3.8587
Never at rest. 5.1958
Never call retreat. 3.7339
Never done. 5.7101
Never in doubt. 2.10428
Never die! 2.1787
Neveryóna. 2.12971
Neveryóna, or, The tale of signs and cities. 2.12971
The new achievers. 4.3121
New acronyms, initialisms & abbreviations. 2.205
A new age now begins. 3.6905
New alliances, 1940-41. 3.918
The new American cinema. 2.2948
The new American dilemma. 4.10789
New American Gothic. 2.10637
A new American justice. 4.4973
The new American philosophers. 1.572
New American plays. 2.10800
New American poetry. 2.10775
New American poets of the 80's. 2.10731

The New American political system. 4.8069
The new American poverty. 4.2097
The new American right. 3.7818
New American world. 3.5969
New and collected poems, 1961-1983. 2.12995
New and old voices of Wah'kon-tah. 2.10742
New and selected poems. 2.11710
New & selected poems. 2.9282
New and selected poems. 2.12456
New and selected poems. 2.12629
New & selected things taking place. 2.12569
The New Ansel Adams photography series. 5.6933
The new Appleton dictionary of the English and Portuguese languages. 2.911
A New approach to the economics of health care. 5.4638
New approaches in introductory college geography courses. 4.42
The new Arab social order. 4.2571
The new architecture and the Bauhaus. 1.5267
New Arden Shakespeare. 2.6646
The new art. 1.4805
New art from the Soviet Union. 1.5034
New art in America: fifty painters of the 20th century. 1.5900
The new astronomy. 5.1701
New atlas of relief forms. 4.129
The new atlas of the universe. 5.1716
The New authoritarianism in Latin America. 4.8329
The new avant-garde. 1.4872
The new Bantam-Megiddo Hebrew & English dictionary. 2.1771
New bearings in English poetry. 2.5831
New Beethoven letters. 1.3795
New biographical dictionary. 3.325
A new birth of freedom. 4.9684
New Black playwrights. 2.10797
The New black politics. 3.6711
New Black voices. 2.10692
The New Black vote. 3.6712
The new book of world rankings. 4.1246
The new brahmins; scientific life in America. 5.830
The new British drama. 2.5922, 2.6247
The new Britton and Brown illustrated flora of the Northeastern United States and adjacent Canada. 5.3673
New Brunswick. 3.8806
The New Cambridge bibliography of English literature. 5.7937
New Cambridge bibliography of English literature. 5.7939
The New Cambridge modern history. 3.607
The new Cambridge Shakespeare. 2.6648
A new case for the liberal arts. 4.10825
The New Cassell's French dictionary. 2.879
A New catechism: Catholic faith for adults. 1.3214
New Catholic encyclopedia. 1.3131
The New Century classical handbook. 3.2509
The New Century cyclopedia of names. 2.1081
The New Century handbook of English literature. 2.5486
The new CEO. 4.4342
New Chinese-English dictionary. 2.2150
The New Christian right. 1.2478
The new citizenship. 3.8449
The new class. 4.7105
New collected poems. 2.8719
The new college encyclopedia of music. 1.3509
New colleges for new students. 4.10079
The New Columbia encyclopedia. 1.21
A new commentary on the poems of W.B. Yeats. 2.8351
The new commonwealth, 1877-1890. 3.7408
The New Communist Third World. 4.4165
A new companion to Shakespeare studies. 2.6682
New complete book of the American musical theater. 1.4218
New concepts in wage determination. 4.3135
The New Congress. 4.8000
New conservatism - What went wrong? 4.7618
The new corporatism. 4.7592
The new covenant. 2.10556
The new cratylus. 2.2731

The new criminology: for a social theory of deviance. 4.6683
The new criticism. 2.2720
New data for V. I. Lenin's 'Imperialism, the highest stage of capitalism.' 4.1533
The New Deal. 3.7756
The new deal. 4.1957
The New Deal and American Indian tribalism. 3.5809
The New Deal and the States. 4.7877
The New Deal and the West. 4.2028
The New Deal and world affairs. 3.7589
The New Deal for artists. 1.5202
A new deal for Blacks. 3.6691
The new decade. 1.5908
The new demons. 1.1884
New designs for the elementary school curriculum. 4.10443
New dictionary of American family names. 3.305
New dictionary of American slang. 2.1146
New dictionary of modern sculpture. 1.5610
New digital troubleshooting techniques. 5.6471
New dimensions in foreign policy. 4.9069
New dimensions in popular culture. 2.10271
New dimensions of political economy. 4.1999
New diplomacy. 3.825
New directions in European historiography. 3.394
New directions in geography teaching. 4.43
New directions in New Testament study. 1.2635
New directions in prose and poetry. 2.10715
New directions in the study of language. 4.10394
A new discourse of a stale subject, called The metamorphosis of Ajax. 2.6483
New discoveries in China. 3.4626
New documents of Indian painting. 1.6422
A new economic geography of Bangladesh. 4.2520
The New economic systems of Eastern Europe. 4.2234
The new economics of growth. 4.2500
The new Eloise. 2.4089
New empire. 3.7420
The New Encyclopaedia Britannica. 1.13
New energy technology 5.6111
New England. 4.2018
New England and the sea. 4.4218
New England and the South Seas. 3.5585
The New England clergy and the American Revolution. 3.6917
New England dissent, 1630-1833. 1.3321
New England frontier. 3.7956
New England in the English nation, 1689-1713. 3.7947
New England: Indian summer. 2.10437
New England life in the 18th century. 3.7941
New England literary culture from revolution through renaissance. 2.10438
The New England mill village, 1790-1860. 4.3845
The New England mind: from colony to province. 3.7951
The New England mind: the seventeenth century. 3.7952
A New England reader. 2.10719
New England saints. 3.7942
New England State politics. 4.8185
A New England town. 3.8003
The New England town in fact and fiction. 2.10442
New England's outpost. 3.8801
The New English Bible with the Apocrypha. 1.2498
New English-Chinese dictionary. 2.2147
New English-Dutch, Dutch-English dictionary. 2.1171
New English-Japanese dictionary. 2.1990
The new English literatures. 2.9876
The new Englishes. 2.1118
New essays. 2.7046
New essays in philosophical theology. 1.2769
New essays on Dostoyevsky. 2.1376
New essays on human understanding. 1.864
New essays on Plato and Aristotle. 1.259

The new Europe, an economic geography of the EEC. 4.2219
The new Europe: today, and tomorrow. 3.1191
A new Eusebius. 1.2488
New Fabian essays. 4.7036
The new face of Buddha. 1.1770
The new family and the new property. 4.9373
The New feminist criticism. 2.2494
New feminist scholarship. 5.8460
The new film index. 5.8141
The new France. 4.2332
New France. 3.8715
New French feminisms. 4.6120
New French imperialism, 1880-1910. 3.5117
New generation. 2.7393
The new generation in Meiji Japan. 3.4898
New German film. 2.2895
The New Grove dictionary of American music. 1.3510
The New Grove dictionary of music and musicians. 1.3503
The New Grove dictionary of musical instruments. 1.3516
New Grub Street. 2.7734
A new guide to Federal cable television regulations. 4.9543
The new guide to the diplomatic archives of Western Europe. 3.269
The new guide to the federal budget. 4.4680
New Guinea. 3.5653, 3.5657
New Guinea on the threshold. 3.5651
The New Guinea villager. 3.5656
New Hampshire. 3.7962
The New Harvard dictionary of music. 1.3504
The new heavens and new earth. 1.2386
The new hermeneutic. 1.2519
A new historical geography of England. 3.1719
A New history of Australia. 3.5568
A new history of India. 3.4227
A New history of Ireland. 3.1815
A new history of Korea. 3.4999
A new history of Portugal. 3.3495
A new history of Spanish American fiction. 2.5307
A new history of the organ from the Greeks to the present day. 1.4143
The New history, the 1980s and beyond. 3.1155
New horizons in psychology. 5.5
The new humanism. 1.500
The New hunter's encyclopedia. 5.5493
New Iberian world. 3.8993
The new image of the common man. 4.7568
New images of man. 1.5157
New indexed business atlas and shipper's guide -1884. 4.155
The new industrial state. 4.1986
New information systems and services. 5.7607
The new international atlas. 4.115
New international dictionary of refrigeration. 5.6891
The New international economic order. 4.4135
A new introduction to bibliography. 5.7535
The New Italian poetry, 1945 to the present. 2.4894
New Japanese-English dictionary. 2.1991
New Jersey. 3.8063
New Jersey from Colony to State, 1609-1789. 3.8064
The new Jerusalem, planning and politics. 1.5607
New Jerusalems. 4.2284
New Korea. 3.5008
A new language for psychoanalysis. 5.190
The New Larousse encyclopedia of animal life. 5.3804
New Latin grammar for schools and colleges, founded on comparative grammar. 2.253
A new Latin syntax. 2.254
The new left. 4.5164
New left diplomatic histories and historians: the American revisionists. 3.7602
New letters. 2.7478
New letters of Abigail Adams, 1788-1801. 3.7052
The new Leviathan. 4.7471
A new life. 2.13160
A new life of Anton Chekhov. 2.1490

New light on Pope. 2.7196
New light on the most ancient East. 3.3615
The New limerick. 2.3799
New lines. 2.6186
New lives for old. 3.5627
New maps of hell. 2.5978
New masters. 4.2905
The New Mediterranean democracies. 3.3476
The new men of power. 4.3360
The new Mencken letters. 2.12130
New Mexico. 3.8568
New Mexico, a guide to the colorful State. 3.8566
The New Michaelis, illustrated dictionary. 2.912
New military politics in Latin America. 3.9169
The new movement in the theatre. 2.3154, 2.3178
New movements in the study and teaching of English. 2.960
The new music. 1.3676
The new music, 1900-1960. 1.3668
A new mythos. 2.10600
The New naked poetry. 2.10776
The New Nation. 3.7017
The new nationalism. 3.757
New nations. 3.1156
New Native American drama. 2.13043
The new Negro. 3.6745
The new Negro on campus. 4.10875
The new Negro renaissance. 2.10695
The new novel in America. 2.10647
The New organon, and related writings. 1.667
New Orleans in the gilded age. 3.8317
The New our bodies, ourselves. 5.4689
The new Oxford annotated Bible with the Apocrypha. 1.2497
The New Oxford book of American verse. 2.10732
The New Oxford book of Australian verse. 2.2692
The New Oxford book of Canadian verse in English. 2.9896
The New Oxford book of Christian verse. 2.6120
The New Oxford book of eighteenth century verse. 2.6164
The New Oxford book of English light verse. 2.6099
The new Oxford book of English verse, 1250-1950. 2.6094
The New Oxford companion to music. 1.3505
New Oxford history of music. 1.3636
The New Oxford illustrated Dickens. 2.7625
The new painting. 1.5870
The New Partisan reader, 1945-1953. 2.3706
New patterns of democracy in India. 3.4292
New patterns of management. 4.2653
The New Pelican guide to English literature. 2.5523
New periodical title abbreviations. 5.8317
The New periodicals index. 1.35
New perspectives in archeology. 3.217
New perspectives in physics. 5.2144
New perspectives on Black studies. 3.6602
New perspectives on geographic education. 4.35
New perspectives on Melville. 2.11171
New perspectives on teacher education. 4.10519
New perspectives on the House of Representatives. 4.8061
New perspectives on the Pueblos. 3.5943
The new physics. 5.1989
New plays U.S.A. 2.10801
New plays USA. 2.10801
New poems. 2.5038
The New poetry. 2.6184
The new poets. 2.10511
The new politicians of fifth-century Athens. 3.2653
The new politics of human rights. 4.7638
The new politics of science. 5.790
The New Poor Law in the nineteenth century. 4.9417
New priorities in the curriculum. 4.10269
New-product forecasting. 4.4301

A new pronouncing dictionary of the Spanish and English languages. 2.903
The New psychohistory. 3.435
New quantitative techniques for economic analysis. 4.1392
The new race for space. 5.6703
The new radicalism in America, 1889-1963. 4.5172
A new reader's guide to African literature. 2.2691
New readings vs. old plays. 2.5868
New realism. 1.4850
The new reformers. 4.8170
The New religions of Africa. 1.1847
The new religious-political right in America. 3.7932
The new Republic, or, Culture, faith, and philosophy in an English country house. 2.7924
The New Right, 1960-1968. 4.7309
New roles for youth in the school and the community. 4.5759
New rules of sociological method. 4.4741
New rules, searching for self-fulfillment in a world turned upside down. 4.5166
The new Rumania: from people's democracy to socialist republic. 3.3550
The new Russian poets, 1953-1966. 2.1314
The new rythum, and other pieces. 2.8626
The new Sabin. 5.7732
The new Schaff-Herzog encyclopedia of religious knowledge. 1.2223
The new science of management decision. 4.2728
The new science of politics, an introduction. 4.7465
The new sculpture. 1.5653, 1.5688
New selected poems. 2.1715, 2.9710
New serial titles. 5.8320
The new sex therapy. 5.4950
The new societies of tropical Africa. 4.5468
The new society. 4.2631
The New solar system. 5.1790
A new song. 4.5769
New sounds for woodwind. 1.4549
The new South creed. 3.8119
New Spain and the Anglo-American west. 3.8339
New special libraries. 5.7662
New standard fishing encyclopedia and international angling guide. 5.5488
New structures of campus power. 4.10595
New studies in the philosophy of Descartes. 1.795
The new sufferings of young W. 2.13907
New technology of pest control. 5.5409
The New Testament. 1.2636
The New Testament, an introduction. 1.2632
The New Testament and mythology and other basic writings. 1.2651
The New Testament and Rabinic Judaism. 1.2639
New Testament Apocrypha. 1.2735
The New Testament environment. 1.2660
New Testament essays. 1.2653
New Testament foundations. 1.2631
New Testament history. 1.2657
New Testament interpretation. 1.2650
New Testament interpretation through rhetorical criticism. 1.2647
New Testament theology. 1.2860
The New Testament world. 1.2640
A new theatre. 2.3219
A new theory of beauty. 1.1360
The new Thoreau handbook. 2.11250
New towns. 4.6310
The new towns. 4.6332
New towns in America. 4.6317
New trade strategy for the world economy. 4.4197
The New Trouser Press record guide. 1.3620
New Unesco source book for geography teaching. 4.36
New urban immigrants. 3.8054
A new variorum edition of Shakespeare. 2.6647
A new view of current acid-base theories. 5.2860

A new view of society and other writings. 4.7161
The new view of the Earth. 5.3098
New viewpoints in American history. 3.6280
New views on American economic development. 4.1868
New views on an old planet. 5.2961
The new vigilantes. 1.1875
The New vision, 1928. 1.5114
A new voyage and description of the Isthmus of America. 3.9081
The new Walt Whitman handbook. 2.11273
The New Washington. 3.8642
The new wave. 2.2894
A new way to pay old debts. 2.6630
New ways in psychoanalysis. 5.163
The New Wessex edition. 2.7761
The New Westminster dictionary of the Bible. 1.2505
The new Wildhagen German dictionary. 2.1191
The new woman and the Victorian novel. 2.6033
New woman, new earth. 4.5895
The New woman's survival catalog. 4.6066
The New women's movement. 4.5887
The New women's theatre. 2.10790
New world chess champion. 4.1074
New world in the Tropics. 3.9190
New world, new earth. 2.10345
The New World primates. 5.4030
New worlds for old. 2.10572
New writing from the Middle East. 2.1760
New writing in Israel. 2.1784
New writing in Japan. 2.2019
New writing in the Caribbean. 2.3701
New writing in Yugoslavia. 2.1200
New writings by Swinburne. 2.8134
New York 1900. 1.5302
New York, a Bicentennial history. 3.8025
New York Aurora. 2.11269
The New York Botanical Garden illustrated encyclopedia of horticulture. 5.5334
The New York cab driver and his fare. 4.4042
The New York City Ballet. 4.1168
New York City guide. 3.8036
The New York hotel industry. 4.3529
New York scene. 1.5972
New York, State and city. 3.8026
New York Times. 2.2777, 2.2963-2.2964, 2.3609, 3.332, 3.745, 3.6500, 3.6672, 3.7914, 4.3569, 5.8305
The New York Times 60-minute gourmet. 5.7131
The New York Times book review index 1896-1970. 1.49
The New York Times cook book. 5.7142
The New York Times directory of the film. 2.2963
The New York Times directory of the theater. 5.8305
The New York Times film reviews. 2.2964
The New York Times index. 1.45
New York Times index. 5.8108
The New York Times international cook book. 5.7141
The New York Times obituaries index. 3.332
The New York Times theater reviews, 1920-1970. 2.2777
The New York Times theater reviews, 1920-1970. 5.8305
New York 4.2047
The New Yorker (1925-) 2.10846, 3.2232
The New Yorker (New York, 1925-) 1.5848, 2.10845, 2.10847
The New Yorker twenty-fifth anniversary album, 1925-1950. 1.5848
The New Yorkers. 2.12945
New York's first theatrical center. 2.3203
New Zealand. 3.5597, 5.8086
New Zealand atlas. 4.192
The New Zealand Constitution. 4.8825
New Zealand drama. 2.10197
New Zealand encyclopedia. 3.5593
New Zealand fiction. 2.10198
New Zealand literature, a survey. 2.10194
New Zealand literature to 1977. 5.8087
New Zealand love poems. 2.10204

New Zealand national bibliography to the year 1960. 5.8085
New Zealand notables. 3.5591
The New Zealand novel, 1860-1965. 2.10201
New Zealand novels and novelists, 1861-1979. 5.8088
The New Zealand official year-book. 3.5588
The New Zealand political system. 4.8823
New Zealand short stories. 2.10199
The New Zealand wars. 3.5599
New Zealand writing since 1945. 2.10200
The New Zealander. 2.8215
Newar art. 1.5052
Newbery and Caldecott Medal and Honor books. 5.7721
Newcomb's Wildflower guide. 5.3675
Newfoundland; economic, diplomatic, and strategic studies. 4.2125
Newfoundland in the nineteenth and twentieth centuries. 3.8870
The newly industrializing countries in the world economy. 4.4163
Newman. 1.3274-1.3275
Newman the theologian. 1.3276
Newnes dictionary of dates. 3.372
The News. 2.3679
News and the human interest story. 2.3541
The news in America. 2.3587
The newsmongers; journalism in the life of the Nation, 1690-1972. 2.3589
The newspaper. 2.3547
The newspaper and the historian. 2.3545
Newspaper days, 1899-1906. 2.12129
Newspaper story. 2.3657
Newspapering in the Old West. 2.3656
Newspapers in microform: United States. 5.8326
Newspapers in microform. 5.8326
Newspapers on microfilm. 5.8326
Newton D. Baker. 3.814
Newton demands the muse. 2.5810
Newton on the Continent. 1.1957
Newtonian mechanics. 5.2030
The Newtonian revolution. 5.1931
The next 500 years. 3.73
The next America. 4.5152
The next million years. 3.71
The next nuclear gamble. 5.6057
Next week, Swan Lake. 4.1100
The Next world. 2.10746
Nexus. 2.12189
NF. 5.5149
The NFL's official encyclopedic history of professional football. 4.1029
Ngugi wa Thiong'o, an exploration of his writings. 2.10097
The Nibelungenlied. 2.13535-2.13536
Nibelungenlied. 2.13534-2.13535
Das Nibelungenlied. 2.13534
Nicaragua. 3.9071, 3.9075, 5.7899
Nicaragua in revolution. 3.9074
The Nicaragua route. 4.3947
The nice and the good. 2.9757
NICEM index to 16mm educational films <1980->. 4.10331
NICEM index to 35mm educational filmstrips 1975-. 4.10332
NICEM index to educational audio tapes 1974-. 4.10333
NICEM index to educational video tapes 1974-. 4.10334
NICEM index to producers and distributors. 4.10322
Niche. 5.3533
Nichiren. 1.1759
Nicholas and Alexandra. 3.3160
Nicholas I and official nationality in Russia, 1825-1855. 3.3122
Nicholas I, emperor and autocrat of all the Russias. 3.3120
Nicholas of Cusa and medieval political thought. 1.3277
Nicholas Rowe. 2.7235
The Nick Adams stories. 2.11846
Nickel and its alloys. 5.6791
Nickel mountain. 2.13030
Nicola Pisano and the revival of sculpture in Italy. 1.5736

Nicolas Poussin. 1.6137-1.6138
Nicomachean ethics. 2.344
Niebla. 2.5288
Niels Lyhne. 2.14013
The Nien army and their guerrilla warfare, 1851-1868. 3.4734
The Nien Rebellion. 3.4733
Nietzsche. 1.1053-1.1054, 1.1057
Nietzsche, a critical life. 1.1052
Nietzsche and philosophy. 1.1056
Nietzsche: philosopher, psychologist, antichrist. 1.1055
Nigeria. 3.5349
Nigeria, a country study. 3.5350
Nigeria and Ghana. 3.5359
Nigeria and its British invaders, 1851-1920. 3.5365
Nigeria: background to nationalism. 3.5348
Nigeria in maps. 4.191
Nigeria since 1970. 4.2625
Nigerian historical studies. 3.5357
Nigerian images. 1.5767
Nigerian perspectives. 3.5347
Nigerian political parties. 3.5367
Nigger heaven. 2.12611
The nigger of the 'Narcissus' 2.8544
Night and day. 2.9575
Night and hope. 2.1677
Night and silence, who is here? 2.8847
Night comes to the Cumberlands. 4.2032
Night creature. 1.4268
Night Flying Woman. 3.5855
The night land. 2.8805
Night light. 2.11940
The night mirror. 2.11877
A night of violence. 3.8335
Night rider. 2.12643
Night riders in Black folk history. 3.7204
Night-side. 2.13199
Night thoughts. 2.12763
Night thoughts of a classical physicist. 5.1934
Nightingale fever. 2.1278
The nightingale's burden. 2.10285
The nightmare. 5.657
Nightmare. 3.7923
The nightmare of reason. 2.13798
Nightmares and visions: Flannery O'Connor and the Catholic grotesque. 2.13222
Nights and days. 2.12143
Nights at the circus. 2.9653
Nights in the gardens of Brooklyn. 2.13351
Night's master. 2.9739
Nightwood. 2.11345
Nihon shi bunken kaidai. 5.8066
Nihon shoki. English. 3.4930
Nihon shoki. English. 1.1840
Nihongi; chronicles of Japan from the earliest times to A.D. 697. 3.4930
Nijinsky. 4.1152
Nikolai Bukharin. 3.3226
Nikolai Gogol. 2.1386
Nikolaus Lenau. 2.13629
Nikolay Gogol. 2.1385
Nikolay Karamzin. 2.1334
Nikolay Leskov. 2.1402
Nikolay Novikov, enlightener of Russia. 2.1335
The Nikonian chronicle. 3.3079
Nikonovskiĭ svod. 3.3079
Nikos Kazantzakis. 2.600
The Nile basin. 3.5172
The Nile Campaign: Nelson and Napoleon in Egypt. 3.2134
Nim. 5.4037
Nina Balatka. 2.8216
Nine brothers. 2.1816
Nine Mayan women. 4.6085
Nine modern moralists. 1.1468
Nine soviet portraits. 3.3241
Nine stories. 2.12445
The nine tailors. 2.9306
The nine ways of bon. 1.1808
The nineteen. 2.1560
Nineteen eighty-four. 2.9185
Nineteen nineteen. 2.11586
The nineteenth century. 2.5108, 5.766
The nineteenth century, 1814-80. 3.1584
The nineteenth century, 1830-1890. 2.13475

Nineteenth-century aether theories. 5.2212
Nineteenth century art. 1.4779
Nineteenth-century crime in England: prevention and punishment. 4.6788
Nineteenth-century English verse drama. 2.6241
Nineteenth century fiction. 5.7965
Nineteenth-century literature criticism. 2.2664
Nineteenth-century painters and painting. 1.5866
Nineteenth century philosophy. 1.447
Nineteenth century plays. 2.6243
Nineteenth century readers' guide to periodical literature, 1890-1899. 1.40
Nineteenth-century romanticism in music. 1.3664
Nineteenth century Russian literature. 2.1256
Nineteenth-century sculpture. 1.5647
Nineteenth-century Southern literature. 2.10455
Nineteenth century studies. 1.717
Nineteeth century literature criticism. 2.2664
Ninth new collegiate dictionary. 2.1092
The ninth state. 3.7964
Nisa, the life and words of a !Kung woman. 3.5486
Nisei. 3.6560
Nixon in the White House. 3.7899
Nixon watch. 3.7903
Njáls saga. 2.13985-2.13986
NMR & EPR. 5.2409
No boundary, Eastern and Western approaches to personal growth. 5.293
No cease fires. 4.2049
No chariot let down. 3.8252
No compromise. 2.13806
No easy walk to freedom. 3.5454
No end to Enderby. 2.9643
No exit (Huis clos). 2.4724
No-fault insurance. 4.4642
No fault of their own. 4.3447
No fist is big enough to hide the sky. 3.5432
No gods and precious few heroes. 3.1808
No haven for the oppressed. 3.1092
No high ground. 3.1013
No! in thunder. 2.2571
No laughing matter. 2.9539
No longer at ease. 2.10105
No longer human. 2.2093
No magic bullet. 5.4769
No man is an island. 1.3228
No man's land. 3.790
No mentor but myself. 2.12021
No more masks! 2.10740
No more parades. 2.8632
No more Vietnams? 3.7851
No name. 2.7607
No other gods. 5.796
No place of grace. 3.6129
No place to be somebody. 2.13053
The nō plays of Japan. 2.2025
No sense of place. 4.5009
No star is lost. 2.11651
No time for youth; growth and constraint in college students. 4.10092
Noah Webster. 2.926
Noah's Ark. 3.1062
Noam Chomsky. 2.47
Nobel lectures in molecular biology, 1933-1975. 5.3502
Nobel prize winners in chemistry, 1901-1961. 5.2616
Nobel Prize winners in medicine and physiology, 1901-1965. 5.4519
Nobel, the man and his prizes. 1.62
The nobility of failure. 3.4907
The nobility of later medieval England. 4.6394
The nobility of Toulouse in the eighteenth century. 4.6392
Noble lovers. 2.2398
The noble savage. 2.5577
The noble voice. 2.2758
Nobody knows my name. 3.6660
Noces. 2.4452
Nocturne. 1.5988
Nocturnes for the King of Naples. 2.13423
The Noh drama. 2.2024
The noh theater. 2.3402

Noise, buildings, and people. 5.6096
Noise control. 5.6052
Nomads of the nomads. 3.4050
Nomenclator litterarius. 2.2358
Nomenclator zoologicus. 5.3830
Nomination and election of the President and
   Vice President of the United States, 1984.
   4.9732
Nomination and election of the President and
   Vice President of the United States, including
   the manner of selecting delegates to national
   political conventions. 4.8139
Nomination politics. 4.7940
Nommo. 2.4843
Nomos and the beginnings of the Athenian
   democracy. 2.246
Non-aqueous solvents. 5.6861
The non-dramatic works of Thomas Dekker.
   2.6569
Non-Euclidean geometry. 5.1634
The non-objective world. 1.5871
Non-sexist education for young children.
   4.10306
Non-verbal communication. 5.465
Non-violent resistance (Satyagraha) 4.5036
Non-voting, causes and methods of control.
   4.8120
None is too many. 3.8796
None of the above. 4.10611
The nonexistent knight & The cloven viscount.
   2.5030
Nonfiction film. 2.2983
The nongraded elementary school. 4.10716
Nonlinear methods in econometrics. 4.1297
Nonlinear ordinary differential equations.
   5.1518
Nonlinear partial differential equations in
   engineering. 5.5723
Nonlinear programming. 5.5593-5.5594
Nonlinear waves in one-dimensional dispersive
   systems. 5.1669
Nonmetropolitan industrialization. 4.2071
Nonparametric statistical methods. 5.1411
Nonsense novels. 2.9947
Nonstate actors in international politics.
   4.9273
Nontariff distortions of international trade.
   4.4169
Nonvascular plants. 5.3698
Nonverbal communication. 2.85
Nonverbal communication in human
   interaction. 5.463
Nonviolence in America. 4.5038
The Nootka connection. 3.8865
Nor is it over yet; Florida in the era of
   Reconstruction, 1863-1877. 3.8275
Nordic democracy. 4.8671
The Nordic parliaments. 4.8673
Normal accidents. 5.5551
Normal aging. 5.4218
Normal aspects of speech, hearing, and
   language. 5.4280
Normal family processes. 4.5646
Normal neurosis. 5.627
Normality and pathology in childhood. 5.5100
Norman castles in Britain. 1.5576
The Norman conquerors. 3.1763
The Norman conquest and the English coinage.
   3.280
The Norman conquests. 2.9614
The Norman empire. 3.2225
Norman Lindsay. 2.10157
Norman Mailer. 2.12104, 2.12106
Norman Washington Manley and the new
   Jamaica. 3.9112
Normandy before 1066. 3.2224
Normandy under Saint Louis. 3.2226
The Normans in Scotland. 3.1789
The normative structure of sociology. 4.4747
Norms and human behavior. 4.5056
Norms & nobility. 4.10820
Norms and nobility. 4.10820
Norna-Gests saga. English. 2.13990
The Norse king sagas. 2.13987
Norse sagas translated into English. 5.8019
North. 2.4510
North Africa. 3.5198

The North Alaskan Eskimo. 3.5884
North America. 3.5690
North America. 3.6048
North America divided. 3.7136
North America from earliest discovery to first
   settlements. 3.5970
North America, its people and the resources,
   development, and prospects of the continent
   as the home of man. 4.1865
The North American city. 4.6198
The North American deserts. 5.3244
North American forest and conservation
   history. 5.8198
North American geology. 5.2995
The North American grasshoppers. 5.3876
North American horticulture, a reference guide.
   5.5333
North American housing markets into the
   twenty-first century. 4.3485
North American human rights directory.
   4.7637
North American Indian reader. 3.5709
North American Indians. 3.5702
North American Indians in historical
   perspective. 3.5705
North American prairie. 5.3787
North American range plants. 5.5328
North American stratigraphic code. 5.2946
North and South. 2.7722
North Atlantic run. 3.1037
The North Atlantic world in the seventeenth
   century. 4.8900
North Carolina. 3.8226-3.8227
North Carolina planters and their children,
   1800-1860. 4.5570
North Dakota. 3.8509
North Dakota, a guide to the northern prairie
   state. 3.8507
North from Mexico. 3.8560
North Korea. 3.5038-3.5039
North Korea in transition. 3.5040
North Korea today. 3.5041
The North Korean Communist leadership,
   1945-1965. 3.5043
North of Jamaica. 2.12475
North of slavery. 3.6788
The North reports the Civil War. 3.7396
North Sea oil and gas. 4.3780
North-South, a programme for survival.
   4.4142
The north-south dialogue. 4.4144
The North, the South, and the powers,
   1861-1865. 3.7353
North Vietnam and the Pathet Lao. 3.4455
The North Wales quarrymen, 1874-1922.
   4.3441
The North West Company. 3.8835
Northeast Asian security after Vietnam. 3.4380
Northern editorials on secession. 3.7180
Northern Ireland: 50 years of self-government.
   4.8569
Northern light. 1.6284
The northern magus. 3.8792
Northern mists. 4.52
Northern painting from Pucelle to Bruegel:
   fourteenth, fifteenth, and sixteenth centuries.
   1.6010
Northern plainsmen. 3.8860
Northern Renaissance art. 1.4768
Northern Renaissance art, 1400-1600. 1.4769
Northern sphinx. 3.3375
The northerners. 3.1349
Northernizing the South. 3.8129
Northrop Frye in modern criticism. 2.2424
Northwest passage. 2.12401
The Norton anthology of American literature.
   2.10669
Norton anthology of English literature. 2.6072
The Norton anthology of English literature.
   The major authors. 2.6072
The Norton anthology of literature by women.
   2.10701
The Norton anthology of modern poetry.
   2.10766
The Norton anthology of poetry. 2.6095
The Norton anthology of short fiction. 2.3776
Norton anthology of western music. 1.3423

The Norton anthology of world masterpieces.
   2.3704
The Norton introduction to poetry. 2.3744
The Norton scores. 1.3422
Norton's star atlas and reference handbook
   (Epoch 1950.0) 5.1740
Norway. 3.3376
The Norwegian economy, 1920-1980. 4.2410
Norwegian English dictionary. 2.919
The Norwegian language in America. 2.917
Norwegian migration to America, 1825-1860.
   3.6592
Norwegian resistance, 1940-1945. 3.1069
Not as far as you think. 4.3287
Not by bread alone. 2.1547
Not by strange gods. 2.12399
Not-God. 4.6645
Not guilty. 4.9453
Not honour more. 2.8504
'Not I, but the wind ...' 2.9001
Not in our genes. 5.314
Not quite posthumous letter to my daughter.
   2.9399
Not slaves, not citizens. 4.668
A not-so-still life. 1.5936
Not without laughter. 2.11894
Notable American women. 3.353
Notable American women, 1607-1950. 3.352
Notable family networks in Latin America.
   4.5609
Notation in new music. 1.4444
The notation of medieval music. 1.4118
The notation of polyphenic music, 900-1600.
   1.4117
The notation of Western music. 1.4119
Notations in elementary mathematics. 5.1068
Notebook. 2.12042
The notebook of William Blake. 2.7407
Notebooks. 1.6176, 2.4455, 2.7513, 2.7593
Notebooks, 1914-1916. 1.1070
Notebooks and some letters from Julia Augusta
   Martin. 2.7771
The notebooks for A raw youth. 2.1343
The notebooks for Crime and punishment.
   2.1344
The notebooks for the Brothers Karamazov.
   2.1341
The notebooks for The idiot. 2.1342
The notebooks for The possessed. 2.1339
Notebooks, memoirs, archives. 2.9031
The notebooks of Leonardo da Vinci. 1.6212
The notebooks of Malte Laurids Brigge.
   2.13853
The notebooks of Thomas Wolfe. 2.12784
Notes and comments on Vertebrate
   paleontology. 5.3169
Notes and counter notes. 2.4581
Notes and index to Sir Herbert Grierson's
   edition of the letters of Sir Walter Scott.
   2.8054
Notes and projects for the Large Glass. 1.6102
Notes for Joyce; an annotation of James Joyce's
   Ulysses. 2.8888
Notes from a child of paradise. 2.12958
Notes from the land of the dead, and other
   poems. 2.8933
Notes from underground. 2.1361
Notes of a native son. 3.6661
Notes of a pianist. 1.3878
Notes of a son and brother. 2.11113
Notes on a cowardly lion; the biography of Bert
   Lahr. 2.3260
Notes on Central America. 3.9029
Notes on Haiti, made during a residence in that
   republic. 3.9117
Notes on novelists. 2.3521
Notes on nursing. 5.5165
Notes on political economy. 4.1409
Notes on the methodology of scientific research.
   5.981
Notes on the State of Virginia. 3.8207
Notes towards the definition of culture. 3.8
Notes without music. 1.3930
Nothing but freedom. 4.6424
Nothing happens in Carmincross. 2.8930
Nothing like the sun. 2.9638
The notorious triangle. 3.7218
Notre Dame de Paris. English. 2.4237

Nottingham, nobles, and the North. 3.1510
Les nouveaux contes d'Amadou Koumba. 4.811
Nouveaux mélanges. 2.4666
Nouvel atlas des formes du relief. 4.129
Nouvel atlas international. 4.115
La nouvelle Héloïse. 2.4089
Nouvelles découvertes en Chine. English. 3.4626
Nouvelles pièces noires. 2.4356
Nouvelles récréations et joyeux devis. 2.3980
Nova Scotia and Confederation, 1864-74. 3.8804
Nova Scotia's Massachusetts. 3.8805
Novalis. 2.13596
Novel and reader. 2.3518
The novel and revolution. 2.3418
Novel and romance, 1700-1800. 2.6000
The novel and the modern world. 2.6035
The novel in antiquity. 2.270
The novel in England, 1850-1870. 2.6017
The novel in English. 2.5946
The novel in France. 2.3895
The novel in motion. 2.10641
The novel in seventeenth-century China. 2.2174
The novel of adultery. 2.3468
The novel of manners in America. 2.10540
The novel of violence in America. 2.10617
The novel of worldliness. 2.3904
Novel to romance: a study of Cervantes's Novelas ejemplares. 2.5170
La novela española contemporánea. 2.5138
Novela/Nivola. 2.5289
Novelas completas. 2.5423
The novelist as philosopher. 2.3910
The novelist at the crossroads. 2.6046
The novelistic vision of Doris Lessing. 2.9032
Novelists on the novel. 2.3408
Novels. 2.6450, 2.7364
Novels. 2.11810, 2.13641
Novels and novelists. 2.6041
The novels and related works of Charles Brockden Brown. 2.10912
The novels and stories of Willa Cather ... 2.11472
Novels and stories. 2.8118
The novels and tales of Henry James. 2.11100
The novels and tales of Mrs. Gaskell. 2.7719
The novels of A. C. Swinburne. 2.8136
The novels of Anthony Powell. 2.9234
The novels of August Strindberg. 2.14080
The novels of Ayi Kwei Armah. 2.10095
The novels of Charles Williams. 2.9531
The novels of Claude Simon. 2.4753
The novels of Colin Wilson. 2.9830
The novels of Doris Lessing. 2.9034
The novels of Frank Norris. 2.11187
The novels of George Eliot. 2.7707, 2.7710
The novels of George Lamming. 2.9992
The novels of Harriet Beecher Stowe. 2.11235
The novels of Hermann Hesse. 2.13781
The novels of Jane Austen. 2.7380
The novels of John Steinbeck. 2.12537, 2.12539
The novels of Margaret Drabble. 2.9671
The novels of Max Frisch. 2.13748
The novels of Nathalie Sarraute, towards an aesthetic. 2.4717
The novels of Robbe-Grillet. 2.4695
The novels of Samuel Beckett. 2.8429
The novels of Samuel Richardson. 2.7212
The novels of Saul Bellow. 2.11362
Novels of the eighteen-forties. 2.6018
The novels of the German romantics. 2.13503
The novels of the Harlem renaissance. 2.10561
The novels of Tobias Smollett. 2.7264
The novels of Virginia Woolf. 2.9598-2.9599
The novels of William Faulkner. 2.11704
The novels of William Golding. 2.8708
The novels of Wright Morris. 2.12219
November 22, 1963. 3.7878
Nôvo atlas internacional. 4.115
Nôvo Michaelis, dicionário ilustrado ... 2.912
Now and then. 2.12644
Now it can be told. 5.2417
Now we are six. 2.9113
Les noyers de l'Altenburg. 2.4617

NP-completeness. 5.1176
Nubia. 3.5185
Nubia under the pharaohs. 3.5180
Nubian ceremonial life. 3.5186
Nubians in Egypt. 3.5179
Nuclear America. 5.7263
Nuclear and particle physics. 5.2459
Nuclear arms control. 4.9174
The nuclear barons. 5.2454
Nuclear chemical engineering. 5.6617
Nuclear chemistry. 5.2916
The Nuclear connection. 4.3810
The nuclear delusion. 4.9075
Nuclear energy. 5.6605
Nuclear energy conversion. 5.6612
Nuclear energy: its physics and its social challenge. 5.2453
Nuclear energy technology. 5.6603
Nuclear exchange. 5.2531
Nuclear fission reactors. 5.6611
Nuclear fuel management. 5.6618
Nuclear magnetic resonance. 5.2411-5.2412
The nuclear many-body problem. 5.2142
Nuclear physics. 5.2062, 5.2068, 5.2071, 5.2423, 5.2429
Nuclear power. 5.6296, 5.6599, 5.6610
Nuclear power and its environmental effects. 5.5997
Nuclear power and nuclear weapons proliferation. 4.9179
Nuclear power and social planning. 4.3814
Nuclear power safety. 5.6606
Nuclear radiation detection. 5.2443
Nuclear radiation physics. 5.2430
Nuclear reactions. 5.2480
Nuclear safeguards analysis. 5.6619
Nuclear structure theory. 5.2066
Nuclear theft: risks and safeguards. 4.3811
Nuclear waste management abstracts. 5.6055
Nuclear winter. 5.7235
Nuclei and particles. 5.2403
Nucleic acids research. 5.4421
Nucleotide sequences 1984. 5.4421
Nude. 1.5158
Nudes, 1945-1980. 5.6984
The Nuer. 3.5177
Nuer religion. 1.1861
Nueva antología poética. 2.5371
Nuevo atlas internacional. 4.115
Nuffield Workshop on 'The Very Early Universe' (1982: Cambridge, Cambridgeshire) 5.1862
Les nuits de Paris. 2.4086
Numa Roumestan: moeurs parisiennes. 2.4162
Number and nightmare, forms of fantasy in contemporary fiction. 2.10632
Number one. 2.11579
Number our days. 3.8633
Number theory. 5.1319, 5.1333
Number theory in digital signal processing. 5.6376
Number theory in science and communication. 5.1332
Number words and number symbols. 5.1265
Numbers: a commentary. 1.2595
Numerical analysis. 5.1427
Numerical control. 5.6247
Numerical initial value problems in ordinary differential equations. 5.1512
Numerical lists and schedule of volumes of the reports and documents of Congress. 5.7769
Numerical methods for engineering application. 5.5714
Numerical methods for partial differential equations. 5.1524
Numerical methods in finite element analysis. 5.5725
Numerical prediction and dynamic meteorology. 5.2582
Numerical solution of ordinary differential equations. 5.1519
Nunaga. 3.5880
Nuncle, and other stories. 2.9451
Nuns and soldiers. 2.9758
Nuremberg, a Renaissance city, 1500-1618. 1.4985
The Nuremberg Party rallies: 1923-39. 3.2426
The Nürnberg case. 3.1074

The nursery rhyme murders. 2.8516
Nurses, a political force. 5.5199
The Nurse's almanac. 5.5171
The nurse's guide to diet therapy. 5.5129
The nurse's role in community mental health centers. 5.4696
Nursing. 5.5193
Nursing & allied health (CINAHL) 1986-. 5.8291
Nursing and allied health index 1977- <78>. 5.8291
Nursing and nursing education. 5.5184
Nursing and thanatology. 5.5202
Nursing and the aged. 5.5006
Nursing care of infants and children. 5.5087
Nursing care of victims of family violence. 5.4967
Nursing care planning. 5.5166, 5.5170
Nursing critically ill patients confidently. 5.5211
Nursing for the future. 5.5182
Nursing in society. 5.5160
The Nursing profession. 5.5190
Nursing research. 5.5188
Nursing studies index. 5.8292
Nursing theories. 5.5192
Nusantara, a history of Indonesia. 3.4565
Nutrition. 5.4234
Nutrition, an integrated approach. 5.4240
Nutrition and anthropology in action. 4.529
Nutrition and environmental health. 5.4669
Nutrition, concepts and controversies. 5.4236
The Nutrition debate. 5.7115
The nutrition desk reference. 5.4235
Nutrition in adolescence. 5.5085
Nutrition in the 20th century. 5.4241
Nutrition in the middle and later years. 5.5004
Nutrition reviews. 5.7110
Nutrition reviews' present knowledge in nutrition. 5.7110
Nutritional strategies and agricultural change in a Mexican community. 5.7119
Nutritional toxicology. 5.4986
Nyāya-mañjari. 1.196
The nymph of Fiesole. 2.4911

O-gi-maw-kwe mit-i-gwa-ki. 3.5794
O. Henry (William Sydney Porter) 2.11212
O Jerusalem. 3.3935
O.P.E.C. behavior and world oil prices. 4.3753
O.P.E.C. in a changing world economy. 4.3757
O.P.E.C's investments and the international financial system. 4.4615
O.R. on the microcomputer. 5.5577
O genteel lady! 2.11745
O rare Don Marquis. 2.12116
O strange new world. 3.6121
O the chimneys. 2.13857
The oasis. 2.12068
The oaten flute. 2.2772
Obedience to authority. 4.5027
Oberman. 2.4296
The Obie winners. 2.10802
Obituaries from the Times, 1961-1970, including an index to all obituaries and tributes appearing in the Times during the years 1961-1970. 3.329
Object relations in psychoanalytic theory. 5.158
Object-relations theory and clinical psychoanalysis. 5.4904
An objective psychology of music. 1.4385
The obligation of contracts clause of the United States Constitution. 4.9651
Obligations. 4.7519
Obligations of society in the XII and XIII centuries. 4.8389
Oblomov. 2.1390
Oblomov and his creator. 2.1392
The oboe. 1.4169
Oboe. 1.4553
Obra completa. 2.5350
Obra gruesa. 2.5411
Obras completas. 2.5189, 2.5214, 2.5218, 2.5248, 2.5279, 2.5332, 2.5374, 2.5393, 2.5440, 2.5445
Obras completas del Inca Garcilaso de la Vega. 2.5188

Obscenities. 2.12950
Obscenity and freedom of expression. 4.9870
Obscenity and pornography. 4.9876
Obscenity and public morality. 4.9871
El obsceno pájaro de la noche. 2.5406
Obscure religious cults. 2.1857
Observation and interpretation. 5.2108
Observation and reflection, Claude Monet. 1.6124
Observation in modern astronomy. 5.1733
Observations, anecdotes, and characters of books and men. 2.2529
Observations on life, literature, and learning in America. 3.6158
Observations on some of Aristotle's lost works. 1.294
Observations on the Fairy queen of Spenser. 2.6538
Observations on the feeling of the beautiful and sublime. 1.1371
Observatories of the world. 5.1745
Observer's directory of military aircraft. 5.6672
Observers observed. 4.497
The obsession. 5.5132
Obsessive images. 2.10482
Obsolete Communism; the Left-Wing alternative. 3.2215
The obstacle race. 1.5859
Occasion for loving. 2.10075
Occasional form. 2.7025
Occasional papers of T.R. Malthus on Ireland, population, and political economy, from contemporary journals, written anonymously and hitherto uncollected. 4.1415
Occasional verse. 2.7270
The occult; a history. 5.665
The occult philosophy in the Elizabethan age. 5.669
The occult sciences in the Renaissance. 5.668
Occupation and resistance. 3.1068
Occupation, Israel over Palestine. 3.3823
Occupation: writer. 2.8724
Occupational health. 5.5010
Occupational health nursing. 5.5017
Occupational medicine. 5.5011
Occupational outlook handbook. 4.4262
Occupational safety management and engineering. 5.5553
Occupational therapy strategies and adaptations for independent daily living. 5.5142
Ocean and marine dictionary. 4.322
The ocean basins and margins. 5.2983
The ocean of air. 5.2504
Ocean of destiny. 3.4397
Ocean of story. 2.10171
Ocean wave energy conversion. 5.6300
The ocean world. 5.3251
Oceania, a regional study. 3.5533
Oceania and beyond. 3.5551
Oceanic sculpture: sculpture of Melanesia. 1.5771
Oceanography. 4.331
Oceanography, a view of the earth. 4.327
Oceanography, the present and future. 4.320
The oceans, their physics, chemistry, and general biology. 4.326
Ocherki polstorii russkoĭ kul'tury. 3.3020
Ochikubo monogatari. 2.2045
Ochikubo monogatari. English. 2.2045
The ochre robe. 1.1699
Ockham, Descartes, and Hume. 1.96
Octavio Paz. 2.5349
The Octavius of Marcus Minucius Felix. 1.2193
October 1917. 3.3181
October fifteenth; a history of modern Hungary, 1929-1945. 3.1943
October light. 2.13031
The October Revolution. 3.3187
The October revolution. 3.3194
Odd destiny, the life of Alexander Hamilton. 3.7000
The odd women. 2.7736
Odes funambulesques. 2.4131
The Odes of Horace. 2.723
The odes of John Keats. 2.7868

The odes of Pindar. 2.387, 2.526
Odilon Redon. 1.6139-1.6140
Odilon Redon, Gustave Moreau [and] Rodolphe Bresdin. 1.6141
Odious commerce. 4.6431
Odysseus Elytis, selected poems. 2.578
The Odyssey. 2.374, 2.490, 2.592
The Odyssey of an American composer. 1.3913
The Odyssey of Homer. 2.482, 2.489
The odyssey of style in Ulysses. 2.8895
The odyssey of the American right. 4.7314
Oedipus, a folklore casebook. 4.766
Oedipus and Theseus. 2.4555
Oedipus at Thebes. 2.544
Oedipus: myth and complex. 5.176
L'oeuvre de Stendhal: histoire de ses livres te de sa pensée. 2.4312
Œuvres. 2.3977
Oeuvres. 2.4014
Œuvres. 2.4154, 2.4486
Oeuvres. 2.4068
Œuvres. 2.4022
Oeuvres. 2.4203
Œuvres. 2.4598
Oeuvres. 2.3976, 2.4221, 2.4283, 2.4685, 2.4703, 2.4761
Oeuvres choisies. 2.4422
Œuvres complètes. 2.4012, 2.4464
Œuvres complètes. 2.4066
Œuvres complètes. 2.4015
Œuvres complètes ... 2.4524
Œuvres complètes. 2.4183
Œuvres complètes. 2.4024, 2.4532, 2.4590
Œuvres complètes. 2.4029
Œuvres complètes. 2.4033
Œuvres complètes. 2.4074, 2.4169
Œuvres complètes. 1.802, 2.3989-2.3990, 2.4039, 2.4081, 2.4261, 2.4274
Œuvres complètes. 2.4003
Œuvres complètes. 2.3999, 2.4046, 2.4277
Œuvres complètes. 2.4095
Œuvres complètes. 2.4332
Œuvres complètes d'Albert Camus. 2.4439
Œuvres complètes [de] Baudelaire ... 2.4133
Œuvres complètes [de] Charles Cros [et] Tristan Corbière. 2.4158
Œuvres complètes de Marcel Pagnol. 2.4643
Œuvres complètes. 2.4087
Oeuvres en prose complètes. 2.4315
Oeuvres intimes de Stendhal pseud. 2.4300
Œuvres littéraires, suivies d'Écrits apologétiques avec des Juvénilia. 2.4011
Oeuvres poétiques. 2.4363
Œuvres poétiques. 2.3928, 2.4037, 2.4254
Œuvres poétiques. 2.4060
Oeuvres poétiques complètes. 2.4317, 2.4644
Œuvres poétiques de Louise Labé. 2.3981
Œuvres romanesques. 2.4069, 2.4718
Œuvres romanesques complètes. 2.4566
Œuvres romanesques et théâtrales complètes. 2.4628
Œuvres romanesques et voyages ... 2.4149
Oeuvres romanesques, suivies de Dialogues des carmélites. 2.4412
Of divers arts. 1.5129
Of dramatic poesy, and other critical essays. 2.6992
Of foxes and hen houses. 5.4628
Of grammatology. 2.89
Of human bondage. 2.9100
Of human freedom. 3.51
Of human potential. 4.9970
Of islands and men. 3.5547
Of law and life & other things that matter. 4.9450
Of learned ignorance. 1.388
Of mice and magic. 2.3031
Of mind and other matters. 1.87
Of music and music-making. 4.4106
Of Plymouth Plantation, 1620-1647. 3.7987
Of the just shaping of letters, from the Applied geometry of Albrecht Dürer, book III. 1.6604
Of the standard of taste and other essays. 1.698
Of time and the river. 2.12777
Of time and widowhood. 4.5792

Of woman born. 4.5671
Off-Broadway. 2.3226
The off-Broadway experience. 2.3222
The off-shore petroleum resources of South-east Asia. 4.3785
Offense and defense in the international system. 4.9009
The office of Governor in the United States. 4.8252
The Office of Management and Budget and the Presidency, 1921-1979. 4.7888
The Office of the Prime Minister in India. 4.8709
Office without power. 3.732
Office work can be dangerous to your health. 5.5016
Officers and gentlemen. 2.9494
Official chess handbook. 4.1071
Official congressional directory. 4.7993
The official encyclopedia of bridge. 4.1066
Official encyclopedia of tennis. 4.1036
The Official guide to U.S. law schools. 4.9475
Official histories; essays and bibliographies from around the world. 5.8296
The official history of the Royal Canadian Air Force. 5.7404
The Official museum directory. 1.47
Official papers. 4.1447
The official papers of William V. S. Tubman, President of the Republic of Liberia. 3.5416
Official publications in Britain. 5.7922
Official publications of Western Europe. 5.7583
Official table of distances. 4.78
Offshore. 2.9678
Offshore geography of northwestern Europe. 4.9311
Offshore petroleum engineering. 5.8329
Oficio de tinieblas. 2.5338
Ogilvy on advertising. 4.4434
Oglethorpe in America. 3.8259
Ognennyĭ angel. 2.1473
The ogre. 2.4793
Oh, Dad, poor Dad, Mama's hung you in the closet and I'm feelin' so sad. 2.13118
Oh! Pascal! 5.1221
The O'Hara concern. 2.12276
Ohio. 3.8379
Ohio canal era. 4.3945
The Ohio guide. 3.8385
Oil and the congressional process. 4.3774
Oil and turmoil. 4.3776
Oil and world power. 4.3762
Oil in the Middle East. 4.3784
Oil markets in turmoil. 4.3755
Oil prices, energy security, and import policy. 4.3773
The oil sketches of Peter Paul Rubens. 1.6272
Ōkagami. English. 3.4934
Okagami, the Great mirror. 3.4934
Oklahoma. 3.8530-3.8532, 3.8534
Oklahoma politics. 3.8533
Old age in a changing society. 4.5814
Old age in the new land. 4.5810
Old and Middle English literature. 5.7944
Old and Middle English literature from the beginnings to 1485. 2.5525
Old as the hills. 1.4311
Old boys 4.9565
Old Brick, Charles Chauncy of Boston, 1705-1787. 1.3337
Old Bullion Benton, Senator from the new West: Thomas Hart Benton, 1782-1858. 3.7087
The old country. 2.1813
The old country school. 4.10971
Old Creole days. 2.10919
Old Dartmouth on trial. 4.10992
The old dog barks backwards. 2.12235
The Old Dominion and the new nation, 1788-1801. 3.8205
The Old Dominion in the seventeenth century. 3.8186
Old Drury of Philadelphia. 2.3232
Old English; an introduction. 2.937
Old English and medieval literature. 2.6075
Old English and Middle English poetry. 2.5593, 2.5756
The old English baron. 2.7211

An Old English grammar. 2.932
Old English grammar. 2.933
Old English grammar & reader. 2.936
The Old English homily and its backgrounds.
  2.5598
Old English instruments of music. 1.4138
Old English language and literature. 2.930
Old English literature in context. 2.5590
Old English plays. 2.6218
Old Europe. 3.80
Old farm tools and machinery. 5.5295
Old friends. 2.8444
Old gentlemen's convention. 3.7179
The Old Glory. 2.12048
Old hatreds and young hopes. 3.2145
Old High German literature. 2.13462
Old Icelandic poetry. 2.13976
The old jest. 2.9733
Old Jules. 3.8520
The old man. 2.1643
The old man and the medal. 2.4642
The old man and the sea. 2.11847
The old man in the corner. 2.9172
The old manor house. 2.7257
The old men at the zoo. 2.9540
Old mistresses. 1.5194
Old New York. 2.12696
Old Norse-Icelandic literature. 2.13975
The Old Northwest. 3.8369, 3.8373
The Old Northwest as the keystone of the arch
  of American federal union. 3.8375
Old people and the things that pass. 2.13949
Old Possum's book of practical cats. 2.11628
The old province of Quebec. 3.8719
The old religion in the brave new world.
  1.2382
The Old Republicans. 3.7080
The old revolutionaries. 3.6981
Old, sick, and helpless. 5.5008
The old social classes and the revolutionary
  movements of Iraq. 4.8774
Old societies and new States. 4.7548
The Old South. 5.7853
The Old Testament. 1.2564
The Old Testament and modern study. 1.2563
Old Testament theology. 1.2579
Old Testament theology: basic issues in the
  current debate. 1.2578
Old textbooks. 4.11016
Old Thad Stevens. 3.7159
Old times in the Faulkner country. 2.11691
The old ways. 2.13327
The old wives' tale. 2.8455
The Old woman, the wife, and the archer.
  2.2036
The old world and the new 1492-1650. 3.172
The Old yellow book. 2.7476
The older Middle West, 1840-1880. 3.8374
The older Sophists. 1.218
The Oldest revolutionary. 2.10870
Oldtown folks. 2.11229
Ole Rølvaag, artist and cultural leader.
  2.14059
Oligopoly theory. 4.3038
Olive and Mary Anne. 2.11652
The olive and the sword. 2.6740
Olive Schreiner. 2.10056
Oliver Goldsmith. 2.7050
Oliver Wendell Holmes. 2.11081
Olivier Messiaen and the music of time. 1.3928
Olmsted South, old South critic, new South
  planner. 4.5196
Olódùmarè; God in Yoruba belief. 1.1864
-ologies & -isms. 2.1102
-ologies and -isms. 2.1102
Olson's new deal for California. 3.8612
Olympia: the sculptures of the temple of Zeus.
  1.5632
The Olympian and Pythian odes. 2.313
Olympio. 2.4240
Olynthiacs. 2.362
Omaha tribal myths and trickster tales. 3.5931
Oman in the twentieth century. 3.4058
Omensetter's luck. 2.13042
The omni-Americans. 3.6624
An omnibus of short stories. 2.11655
On 1984. 2.9184
On a Chinese screen. 2.9103

On a darkling plain. 2.7781
On a field azure. 2.1527
On active service in peace and war. 3.7687
On active service in war and peace. 3.6226
On actors and the art of acting. 2.3174
On adolescence, a psychoanalytic interpretation.
  4.5750
On architecture. 2.699
On art and artists. 1.5134
On art and connoisseurship 1.5102
On art and literature, 1896-1919. 2.4667
On art and socialism. 2.7965
On art, religion, philosophy. 1.927
On beauty, wisdom, and the arts. 1.270
On becoming a person. 5.4868
On becoming an educated person. 4.10606
On becoming human. 4.452
On being a Christian. 1.2959
On being a Jewish feminist. 1.1987
On being a mother. 4.5665
On being a teacher. 4.10038
On being and the one. 1.418
On being black. 2.10696
On being creative. 2.2360
On being human. 4.4894
On Bentham and Coleridge. 1.726
On boxing. 4.1057
On Calderón. 2.5167
On Canadian literature , 1806-1960. 5.7890
On Capitol Hill. 4.8002
On certainty. 1.1071
On character and libido development. 5.192
On Christian doctrine. 1.2205
On Christianity; early theological writings.
  1.928
On cities and social life. 4.4849
On civilized stars. 5.1725
On community, family, and delinquency.
  4.4828
On competence. 4.10828
On cultural freedom. 3.3344
On culture and social change. 4.4884
On death and dying. 5.633
On deconstruction. 2.2481
On design. 1.5489
On development. 5.3486
On directing. 2.3107
On domestic architecture. 1.5553
On early English pronunciation, with especial
  reference to Shakspere and Chaucer. 2.1010
On economic theory and socialism. 4.1427
On editing Shakespeare. 2.6836
On education. 4.10245
On English poetry: being an irregular approach
  to the psychology of this art, from evidence
  mainly subjective. 2.5750
On English prose. 2.5930
On equality of educational opportunity.
  4.10898
On escalation: metaphors and scenarios.
  5.7256
On every front. 3.7595
On evolution. 5.3372
On extended wings. 2.12552
On fighting poverty. 4.2106
On first philosophy. 1.375
On Forsyte 'change. 2.8680
On free choice of the will. 1.2206
On God and society. 1.119
On growth and form. 5.4212
On heroes and tombs. 2.5398
On heroes, hero-worship and the heroic in
  history. 2.7546
On higher education. 4.10086
On historians. 3.412
On historical materialism. 1.515
On history. 1.913, 3.359
On human communication. 2.49
On human conduct. 1.1511
On human finery. 4.833
On human nature. 4.511
On Jews and Judaism in crisis. 3.3970
On Keynesian economics and the economics of
  Keynes. 4.1341
On knots. 5.1611
On learning to read. 4.10337
On liberty. 4.7670

On liberty; Representative government; The
  subjection of women. 4.7669
On library buildings. 5.7614
On lies, secrets, and silence. 2.12386
On literacy. 4.10754
On literature. 2.1266
On love and loving. 5.441
On lynchings. 4.6720
On modern art. 1.4813
On modern literature. 2.5540
On modern physics. 5.2019
On monsters and marvels. 5.4168
On morality and society. 4.4750
On motion, and On mechanics. 5.2027
On music and musicians. 1.3981
On native grounds. 2.10631
On Neoclassicism. 1.4773
On Nineteen eighty-four. 2.9184
On Noam Chomsky. 2.46
On numbers and games. 5.1320
On our law and its study. 4.9473
On our own. 5.4694
On painting. 1.6338
On painting and On sculpture. 1.5098
On perception, event structure, and
  psychological environment. 5.161
On photography. 5.6942
On playing the flute. 1.4552
On power, its nature and the history of its
  growth. 4.7505
On prison education. 4.6854
On problem-solving. 5.383
On Racine. 2.4052
On reading French verse. 2.873
On religion. 1.1536, 1.1890
On religious power and Judaism. 1.1968
On rereading Chaucer. 2.6367
On revolution. 4.7611
On revolution; selected writings, 1920-66.
  3.4489
On revolutions and progress in economic
  knowledge. 4.1307
On Russian music. 1.3727
On schizophrenia, phobias depression,
  psychotherapy, and the farther shores of
  psychiatry. 5.4839
On science and surgery. 5.5033
On science, necessity, and the love of God.
  1.857
On sculpture. 1.5098
On social control and collective behavior.
  4.4837
On social evolution. 4.4841
On social organization and social personality.
  4.4812
On social psychology. 1.615
On socialist democracy. 4.8637
On socialist realism. 2.1251
On sophistical refutations [and] On coming-to-
  be and passing away. 2.340
On Soviet dissent. 3.3254
On Stalin and Stalinism. 3.3220
On stories, and other essays on literature.
  2.9038
On strategy. 3.4506
On teaching. 4.10267
On the accuracy of economic observations.
  4.1302
On the aesthetic education of man, in a series
  of letters. 1.1372
On the art of the theatre. 2.3090
On the basis of morality. 1.959
On the boundary. 1.3296
On the continuity of English prose from Alfred
  to More and his school. 2.5931
On the correct handling of contradictions
  among the people. 3.4795
On the design of stable systems. 5.1545
On the dignity of man. 1.418
On the economic theory of socialism. 4.3068
On the edge of destruction. 3.3984
On the edge of reason. 2.1220
On the eternal in man. 1.1559
On the freedom of the will. 1.1498
On the frontier. 2.8398
On the frontier of change Mto Wa Mbu,
  Tanzania. 3.5302
On the game of politics in France. 4.8584

On the heavens. 2.343
On the history and method of economics.
   4.1309
On the Kabbalah and its symbolism. 1.1950
On the limits of poetry, selected essays:
   1928-1948. 2.2656
On the manners and customs of the ancient
   Irish. 3.1820
On the margins of discourse. 2.2387
On the margins of the good earth. 4.2996
On the modes. 1.4422a
On the motive power of heat. 5.2243
On the natural and the divine principle of
   things. 1.922
On the nature of organizations. 4.4897
On the origin of species. 5.3354
On the philosophy of higher education.
   4.10552
On the philosophy of history. 3.481
On the place of Gilbert Chesterton in English
   letters. 2.7564
On the poems of Henry Vaughan. 2.7328
On the poet and his craft. 2.2747
On the poetry of Keats . 2.7866
On the poetry of Pope. 2.7204
On the psychology of women. 4.5941
On the razzle. 2.9813
On the road. 2.11953
On the sacraments of the Christian faith.
   1.3221
On the sensations of tone as a physiological
   basis for the theory of music. 1.4382
On the silence of the Declaration of
   independence. 4.7819
On the social contract. 4.7434
On the social contract, with Geneva manuscript
   and Political economy. 4.7434
On the soul. 2.337
On the study of Indian art. 1.5046
On the sublime. 2.518
On the syllogism, and other logical writings.
   1.1206
On the theology of death. 1.2943
On the theory of economic policy 4.2805
On the theory of social change: how economic
   growth begins. 4.2773
On the way to language. 2.106
On theater. 2.1672
On theatre. 2.3083
On thermonuclear war. 5.7385
On these I stand. 2.11535
On thinking. 5.390
On thrones of gold. 2.2838
On Thucydides. 2.450
On translating Homer. 2.510
On translation. 2.2544
On trial. 4.9918
On understanding Islam. 1.1993
On understanding poverty. 4.2098
On understanding science. 5.983
On understanding women. 4.5845
On war. 3.1158, 5.7206
On weaving. 5.7080
On what is learned in school. 4.10766
On wings of song. 1.3926
On with the show! 2.3201
On women & Judaism. 1.1986
On Zion. 1.2556
Onabe, Teruhiko, 1908- Nijisseiki. 3.3264
The once and future king. 2.9519
A once charitable enterprise. 5.4711
Once upon a time. 2.1978
One act plays. 5.8129
One act; short plays of the modern theatre.
   2.3772
One and inseparable. 3.7096
One arm, and other stories. 2.12731
The one best system. 4.10965
One century later. 3.5731
One country or two? 3.8686
One day in China, May 21, 1936. 3.4758
One day in the life of Ivan Denisovich. 2.1638
One day in the 'New Life' 2.1535
One dimensional man. 4.4880
One flew over the cuckoo's nest. 2.13109
The one-gallused rebellion. 3.8281
One greater man. 2.7129
One half of Robertson Davies. 2.9926

One hundred billion suns. 5.1832
One hundred favorite folktales. 4.752
One hundred Middle English lyrics. 2.6142
One hundred more poems from the Japanese.
   2.2033
One hundred pages for the future. 3.76
One hundred problems in elementary
   mathematics. 5.1122
One hundred ten Livingston Street revisited.
   4.10100
One hundred years of solitude. 2.5418
One kind of freedom. 4.2024
One L. 4.9493
One man's America. 3.6055
One man's freedom. 4.9494
One man's meat. 2.12704
One man's stand for freedom: Mr. Justice Black
   and the Bill of rights. 4.9446
One million dead. 2.5261
One million men. 3.7382
One more spring. 2.12239
One more unfortunate. 2.9065
One nation indivisible. 4.7866
One nation, so many governments. 4.7868
One possible basis for a demonstration of the
   existence of God. 1.912
One third of a nation. 4.1959
One thousand souls. 2.1406
One to one. 4.4929
One, two, three ... infinity. 5.838
One union in wood. 4.3395
One way pendulum. 2.9320
One writer's beginnings. 2.12667
One year later. 4.5165
Oneida Community. 4.7160
O'Neill. 2.12295
O'Neill, a collection of critical essays. 2.12294
O'Neill and his plays, four decades of criticism.
   2.12290
O'Neill: son and artist. 2.12297
O'Neill, son and playwright. 2.12298
Ongka. 3.349
The onion, memory. 2.9804
Online searching. 5.7639
Only a miner. 1.4353
An only child. 2.9157
Only connect. 2.2703
Only halfway to paradise. 4.6094
The only land they knew. 3.5755
Only one earth. 4.374
The only teller. 2.3445
The only way to cross. 4.3955
Only yesterday. 3.7506
Ontario's history in maps. 4.142
Ontogeny and phylogeny. 5.3389
The Ontogeny of vertebrate behavior. 5.4106
Ontological relativity. 1.545
OPEC behavior and world oil prices. 4.3753
OPEC in a changing world economy. 4.3757
OPEC's investments and the international
   financial system. 4.4615
The open-air churches of sixteenth-century
   Mexico. 1.5524
The open and closed mind. 5.340
The open door at home. 4.1949
The open door college. 4.11001
Open education: the informal classroom.
   4.10118
An open elite? 4.6396
The open fields. 4.2848
The open heaven. 1.2555
The open mind. 5.2435
Open-mindedness and education. 4.10173
Open poetry. 2.3741
Open prisons. 4.6920
The open sea, and other poems. 2.12137
The open society and its enemies. 1.118
Open veins of Latin America. 4.2141
The opening of an era: 1848. 3.701
The opening of the field. 2.11613
Opera. 1.4207
The opera. 1.4208
Opera. 1.3577
Opera & ideas. 1.4226
Opera and ideas. 1.4226
Opera as drama. 1.4404
Opera companion to 20th-century opera.
   1.4510

The opera companion to twentieth-century
   opera. 1.4510
Opera et dies. 2.311
Opera in the twentieth century. 1.4214
The opera industry in Italy from Cimarosa to
   Verdi. 1.4230
Opera production. 1.4572
Operant behavior. 5.301
Operant learning. 5.307
The operas of Alban Berg. 1.3813
The operas of Benjamin Britten. 1.3455
The operas of Mozart. 1.4514
The operas of Puccini. 1.4515
The operas of Verdi. 1.4022
The Operating Engineers. 4.3382
Operating experience with nuclear power
   stations in member states in 1975. 5.6298
Operating system concepts. 5.1193
Operating system elements. 5.1166
Operating system principles. 5.1142
Operating systems. 5.1188
Operating systems theory. 5.1169
Operation Menace. 3.1003
Operation Sea Lion. 3.1031
Operation Sunrise. 3.921
Operational calculus and generalized functions.
   5.1563
Operational philosophy. 1.497
Operations management. 4.2659
Operations research. 5.5574
Operations research in production planning,
   scheduling, and inventory control. 5.7020
Operations research support methodology.
   5.5572
Opere. 2.4901, 2.4955, 2.4972, 2.4985, 2.4989,
   2.5001, 2.5005-2.5006, 2.5008
Opere ... 2.5009
Opere. 2.5012
Opere de Giacomo Leopardi. 2.4997
Opere minori. 2.4959
Opere: teatro e polemiche teatrali. 2.4996
Operetta. 1.4231
Operette morali. 2.5000
The Operon. 5.3467
The Ophiuchi hotline. 2.13388
The opium-eater, a life of Thomas De Quincey.
   2.7623
The Opium War, 1840-1842. 3.4724
The Opium War through Chinese eyes. 3.4726
The Oppenheimer hearing. 5.1960
Opportunities and uses of the ocean. 4.353
The opposing self. 2.2598
The opposition press of the Federalist period.
   3.7024
Optical communication systems. 5.6388
Optical communications. 5.6387
Optical crystallography. 5.2929
Optical fiber transmission systems. 5.6389
Optical fibre sensors. 5.5959
Optical information processing and holography.
   5.5937
Optical mineralogy. 5.3019
Optical oceanography. 4.346
The optical papers of Isaac Newton. 5.2273
Optical production technology. 5.7065
Optical shop testing. 5.2291
Optical waveguide theory. 5.5960
Opticks. 5.2274
Optics. 5.2285, 5.2288
Optics and lasers. 5.2286
The optics of nonimaging concentrators.
   5.6234
Optimal control. 5.6176
The optimal personality. 5.510
Optimisation in economic analysis. 4.1403
Optimism. 2.4104
The optimist's daughter. 2.12664
Optimization in economic theory. 4.1388
Optimization in industry. 5.5583
Optimization-theory and applications. 5.1470
The optimum quantity of money. 4.4504
Optimum structural design. 5.5863
Optoelectronics. 5.5958
Optoelectronics, an introduction. 5.2372
Opus majus. 1.382
Opus posthumous 2.12542
OR on the micro. 5.5577
Oral-formulaic theory and research. 4.757

Oral historiography. 3.442
Oral history. 5.8221
Oral history for the local historical society. 3.425
Oral literature in Africa. 2.2297
The oral tales of India. 4.805
Oral tradition. 3.438
Oral traditional literature. 4.762
Orality and literacy. 2.16
Orang Asli. 4.638
Orang-utan behavior. 5.4036
The oranging of America, and other stories. 2.12852
The orators. 2.8399
Orators & philosophers. 4.10822
Orators and philosophers. 4.10822
The oratory of Negro leaders, 1900-1968. 3.6810
Orbital and electron density diagrams. 5.2823
Orbiting the sun. 5.1801
Orchesography. 4.1088, 4.1090
Orchestra. 2.6445
The orchestra from Beethoven to Berlioz. 1.4137
Orchestral music. 1.3578
Orchestral music in print. 1.3579
Orchestral percussion technique. 1.4561
Orchestration. 1.4490
The ordeal. 2.1626
Ordeal by fire. 3.7344
Ordeal by hunger. 3.8616
Ordeal by slander. 3.7549
The ordeal of assimilation: a documentary history of the white working class. 4.3605
The ordeal of consciousness in Henry James. 2.11122
The ordeal of desegregation. 4.10871
The ordeal of George Meredith. 2.7944
Ordeal of Gilbert Pinfold. 2.9491
The ordeal of Mark Twain. 2.10950-2.10951
The ordeal of power. 3.7823
Ordeal of the Union. 3.7146
The ordeal of Thomas Hutchinson. 3.7972
The ordeal of total war, 1939-1945. 3.913
The ordeal of Woodrow Wilson. 3.7722
Ordeal therapy. 5.4853
Order and dispute. 4.9357
Order and progress. 3.9192
Order and reason in politics. 4.7551
Order and rebellion in tribal Africa. 4.650
Order, empiricism, and politics. 4.7292
Order of battle, U.S. Army, World War II. 5.7284
Order of battle, US Army, World War II. 5.7284
Order of battle WW 2. 5.7284
Order of battle WW II. 5.7284
Order of battle WW Two. 5.7284
The Order of the Death's Head. 3.2427
The order of things. 1.70
Order out of chaos. 5.925
Ordered to care. 5.5157
Orders and families of recent mammals of the world. 5.3974
Ordinary differential equations. 5.1511
Ordinary differential equations in the complex domain. 5.1514
An ordinary life. 2.1667
Ordinary people and everyday life. 4.5167
The ordination of women. 1.3006
Ore deposit geology and its influence on mineral exploration. 5.6736
Ore deposits. 5.3023
Ore microscopy and ore petrography. 5.3022
Oregon. 3.8636
Oregon, end of the trail. 3.8638
The Oregon question. 3.8637
The Oregon trail. 3.8635
The Oregon Trail. 3.8474
Oreo. 3.6715
The Oresteia. 2.408
The Oresteia of Aeschylus. 2.407
Organ building and design. 1.4141
The organ; its evolution, principles of construction and use. 1.4142
Organ literature. 1.4146
Organ music in print. 1.3580-1.3581
The organ music of J.S. Bach. 1.4530

Organic analytical reagents. 5.2662
Organic chemical process encyclopedia, 1969. 5.6895
Organic chemistry. 5.2722
The Organic chemistry of iron. 5.2784
The organic chemistry of nitrogen. 5.2786
Organic chemistry of sulfur. 5.2788
The organic chemist's book of orbitals. 5.2816
Organic experiments. 5.2728
Organic peroxides. 5.2756
Organic phosphorus compounds. 5.2787
Organic plant protection. 5.5417
Organic reactions. 5.2717
Organic reactions and orbital symmetry. 5.2851
Organic structure determination. 5.2857
Organic syntheses. Collective volume. 5.2738-5.2739
Organic syntheses via boranes. 5.2783
Organic synthesis, the disconnection approach. 5.2742
The organisation of thought, educational and scientific. 4.10176
Organismic theories of the state. 4.7526
The Organization and administration of physical education. 4.905
The organization and efficiency of solid waste collection. 4.3089
Organization and environment. 4.2666
Organization and management. 4.2651
Organization and pathology of thought. 5.4901
The organization and personnel of the Shakespearean company. 2.6862
Organization and representation in perception. 5.280
Organization development. 4.2701
The organization man. 5.500
The organization of behavior. 5.205
The Organization of knowledge in modern America, 1860-1920. 1.81
Organization of the middle grades. 4.10501
Organization theory. 4.2657
Organizational analysis. 4.4912
Organizational culture and leadership. 4.2699
Organizational environments. 4.4907
Organizations. 4.2655, 4.4914
Organizations and their members. 4.2667
Organizations in action. 4.2670
Organiz'd innocence. 2.7432
Organized crime. 4.6768
Organized democracy. 4.8676
Organized for prohibition. 4.6646
Organized labor and the Black worker, 1619-1973. 4.3340
Organized labor and the Negro. 3.6739
Organized labor in American history. 4.3370
Organized labor in Latin America. 4.3398
Organized labor in Mexico. 4.3399
Organized labour and pressure politics. 4.3624
Organized medicine in the progressive era. 5.4526
Organized miracles. 1.3051
Organizing, a guide for grassroots leaders. 4.4951
Organizing China. 4.8738
Organizing crime. 4.6686
Organizing for change: new priorities for community colleges. 4.10559
Organizing for defense. 5.7351
Organizing for national security. 4.7989
Organizing for peace. 4.9214
Organizing the executive branch. 4.7885
Organizing women office workers. 4.3266
Organometallic chemistry reviews. 5.2789
Organometallics in organic synthesis. 5.2741
The Organon. 2.347
The Organon, or Logical treatises, of Aristotle. 1.291
L'Orient et la Grèce antique. 3.117
The oriental carpet. 1.6585
Oriental despotism. 4.7557
Oriental Jones. 2.1849
Oriental philosophies. 1.147
Oriental renaissance. 3.111
Oriental rugs and carpets. 1.6584
Orientalism. 3.3617
Orientation and form. 5.253
Origen. 1.2212

The origin. 2.12556
The origin and development of psychoanalysis. 5.142
The origin and development of the state cult of Confucius. 1.1797
Origin and distribution of the elements. 5.3105
The origin and goal of history. 3.395
The origin and meaning of Hasidism. 1.1922
Origin and significance of the Frankfurt School. 4.4810
The origin of Christology. 1.2851
The origin of consciousness in the breakdown of the bicameral mind. 5.269
Origin of cultivated plants. 5.5314
The origin of genetics. 5.3406
The origin of landscapes. 4.258
The origin of Manchu rule in China. 3.4709
The origin of medical terms. 5.4492
The origin of modern capitalism and eastern Asia. 4.2434
Origin of sedimentary rocks. 5.3051
The origin of the chemical elements. 5.1767
The origin of the communist autocracy. 3.3212
The origin of the family, private property, and the state, in the light of the researches of Lewis H. Morgan. 4.5557
The origin of the idea of chance in children. 5.588
The origin of the idea of crusade. 3.588
Origin of the land tenure system in the United States. 4.2816
The origin of the planets. 5.1802
The origin of the solar system. 5.1791
The origin of the theater. 2.2804
The origin of the West German Republic. 4.8609
Original essays. 2.7807
Original journals of the Lewis and Clark Expedition, 1804-1806. 3.8477
The original statutes of Cambridge University. 4.11007
Original teachings of Ch'an Buddhism, selected from The transmission of the lamp. 1.1771
The original water-color paintings. 5.3944
The originality of the avant-garde and other modernist myths. 1.4814
The originals. 2.2413
Originals. 1.4873
Les Origines intellectuelles de la Révolution française, 1715-1787. 3.2060
Origins. 2.1060
The origins and development of labor economics. 4.3109
The origins and development of the English language. 2.972
Origins and early development of Shi'a Islam. 1.2088
The origins and international economics of space exploration. 5.6708
The origins and prehistory of language. 2.154
Origins and rise of the Filipino novel. 2.2291
Origins of agriculture. 4.718
The origins of American intervention in the First World War. 3.831
The origins of Ancrene wisse. 2.6309
The origins of anti-semitism. 1.1956
The origins of Cauchy's rigorous calculus. 5.1452
The origins of central banking in the United States. 4.4530
The origins of certainty. 1.803
The origins of chemistry. 5.2613
The Origins of Chinese civilization. 3.4689
The origins of Christian art. 1.5169
Origins of class struggle in Louisiana. 3.8313
The origins of contemporary France. 3.2141
Origins of crime. 4.6696
The origins of culture. 4.522
The origins of English words. 2.1052
The origins of evil in Hindu mythology. 1.1489
The origins of Faulkner's art. 2.11701
The origins of feedback control. 5.6180
The origins of France. 3.1980
The origins of Greek civilization, 1100-650 B.C. 3.2542
The origins of Greek thought. 3.2553
Origins of Icelandic literature. 2.13974

The origins of intelligence in children. 5.573
The origins of international rivalry in Samoa, 1845-1884. 3.5673
The origins of life: molecules and natural selection. 5.3323
The origins of Malay nationalism. 3.4542
Origins of Marvel Comics. 2.3815
The origins of modern African thought. 3.5317
The origins of modern Germany. 3.2249
The Origins of modern humans. 4.449
The origins of modern musical criticism. 1.4407
The origins of modern science: 1300-1800. 5.715
Origins of modern sculpture: pioneers and premises. 1.5646
The origins of modern town planning. 1.5583
The origins of Muhammadan jurisprudence. 1.2042
Origins of papal infallibility, 1150-1350. 1.3211
The origins of political stability, England, 1675-1725. 4.8403
Origins of Pre-Columbian art. 3.5693
The origins of Prussia. 3.2482
The origins of psycho-analysis. 5.136
The origins of Russia. 3.3082
The origins of science. 5.899
The origins of scientific thought. 5.723
Origins of sex. 5.3482
The origins of socialism. 4.6942
Origins of Southeast Asian statecraft. 4.8695
The origins of Spain and Portugal. 3.3417
The origins of strategic bombing. 3.822
The origins of the American party system. 3.7018
The origins of the British colonial system, 1578-1660. 4.8909
Origins of the Chinese revolution, 1915-1949. 3.4751
The origins of the civil rights movement. 3.6682
The origins of the cold war in the Near East. 3.3735
The origins of the cultural revolution. 3.4808
The origins of the English Civil War. 3.1485
Origins of the English language, a social and linguistic history. 2.976
Origins of the French revolution. 3.2076
The origins of the great schism. 1.3155
Origins of the Greek nation. 3.2674
Origins of the Japanese language. 2.1986
The origins of the Korean War. 3.5014
The origins of the Labour Party, 1880-1900. 4.8540
The origins of the Maori wars. 3.5604
Origins of the mind. 5.4332
The origins of the modern Jew: Jewish identity and European culture in Germany. 1.1931
Origins of the new South, 1877-1913. 3.8167
Origins of the New Testament. 1.2299
The origins of the Peloponnesian War. 3.2612
The origins of the popular press in England, 1855-1914. 2.3687
The Origins of the Scottish enlightenment. 1.696
The origins of the Second Republic in Spain. 3.3457
The origins of the Second World War. 3.894, 3.7593
Origins of the state. 4.610
Origins of the state and civilization. 4.607
The origins of the turbojet revolution. 5.6677
The origins of the United Arab Emirates. 3.4060
Origins of the urban school. 4.10097
The origins of the war of 1914. 3.770
The origins of the World War. 3.771
The origins of theoretical population genetics. 5.3437
The origins of totalitarian democracy. 4.7607
The origins of totalitarianism. 4.7593
The origins of trade union power. 4.3411
Oriomo Papuans. 3.5661
Orkneyinga saga. 2.13989
Orkneyinga saga. English. 2.13989
Orlando. 2.9576
Orlando furioso. 2.4960-2.4961
Orlando Furioso. 2.4962

Orlando furioso. 2.4958
Orlando Gibbons and his family. 1.3875
Orley farm. 2.8217
Ormolu: the work of Matthew Boulton. 5.7014
Ornamental horticulture. 5.5343
Ornamental ironwork. 1.5500
Ornithology from Aristotle to the present. 5.3943
Oroonoko. 2.7268
Orozco!, 1883-1949. 1.6003
The orphan. 2.7177
The orphan angel. 2.12828
Orphan Street. 2.4831
Orpheus and Greek religion. 1.1667
Orpheus in America. 3.6051
Orpheus in the New World. 1.4196
Orpheus, the metamorphoses of a myth. 1.1668
Orphic songs. 2.5031
Ortega as phenomenologist. 1.1132
Ortega y Gasset. 1.1129
The Orthodox Church. 1.3102
The Orthodox Church. 1.3106
The Orthodox churches and the secular state. 1.3112
Orthodox consensus and radical alternative. 4.4781
Orthodoxy. 1.2259
Orthodoxy and heresy in earliest Christianity. 1.2961
Orthogonal polynomials. 5.1560
Orthopaedic biomechanics. 5.4273
Ortho's complete guide to successful gardening. 5.5368
Örtlich betäubt; Roman. 2.13762
Orwell and the Left. 2.9206
The Orwell reader. 2.9187
Orwell, the lost writings. 2.9174
Orwell, the transformation. 2.9201
Orwell, the war commentaries. 2.9175
Os Lusiadas. 2.5452
Oscar Niemeyer. 1.5354
Oscar Wilde. 2.8275-2.8278, 2.8280-2.8282, 2.8285, 2.8288
Oscar Wilde; a collection of critical essays. 2.8284
Oscar Wilde, a summing up. 2.8274
Oscar Wilde, his life and wit. 2.8283
Osteology of the reptiles. 5.3934
Österreichische Lyrik heute. 2.13937
Osteuropas Nahrungswirtschaft Gestern und Morgen. 4.2975
Ōsugi Sakae, anarchist in Taishō Japan. 4.7200
Oswald Mosley. 3.1686
The other. 1.459
The other America. 4.6513
The other Arab-Israeli conflict. 3.3757
The other battleground. 3.801
The other Bostonians. 4.5205
The other civil war. 4.5980
Other criteria: confrontations with twentieth-century art. 1.4836
Other cultures; aims, methods and achievements in social anthropology. 4.474
Other days, other eyes. 2.9811
Other exiles. 2.9987
The other government. 2.3554
The other John Updike. 2.13382
Other kingdom. 2.8642
The other man. 2.8765
Other Mexicos. 3.8938
Other minds. 1.1296
The other one. 2.4497, 2.4575
Other people's money. 4.6756
The Other persuasion. 2.3718
The other Pushkin. 2.1421
The other side. 4.6467
Other side of the Hedge. 2.8642
The other side of the hill. 3.967
The other side of the medal. 3.4268
The other South: Southern dissenters in the nineteenth century. 3.7371
The other State Department: the United States Mission to the United Nations. 4.9237
The other Texas frontier. 3.8321
Other voices, other rooms. 2.11466
The other Western Europe. 3.1199

Other worlds: Cyrano de Bergerac. 2.4020
Other worlds. 2.2395
Other worlds, other gods. 2.10832
Otherwise. 2.5039
El otoño del patriarca. 2.5420
Ottawa Waterway. 3.8820
Ottemiller's Index to plays in collections. 5.8130
Otto Kleppner's Advertising procedure. 4.4433
Otto Rank, a rediscovered legacy. 5.182
Otto Wagner 1841-1918. 1.5412
Ottoline. 3.1676
The Ottoman centuries. 3.3580
The Ottoman Empire. 3.684, 3.3579
Ottoman Empire and Islamic tradition. 3.3575
The Ottoman Empire and its successors. 3.3728
The Ottoman Empire and its successors, 1801-1927. 3.3584
Otway and Lee. 2.7178
Ou-Yang Hsiu, an eleventh-century Neo-Confucianist. 1.173
Our American music. 1.3688
Our American sisters. 4.6022
Our Appalachia. 3.8177
Our Bible and the ancient manuscripts. 1.2510
Our bodies, ourselves. 5.4689
Our business civilization. 3.6069
Our changing order. 4.1271
Our crowded islands. 4.5676
Our crowded planet. 4.1583
Our Cuban colony. 3.6439
Our dramatic heritage. 2.3759
Our earliest colonial settlements, their diversities of origin and later characteristics. 3.6863
Our endangered rights. 4.9659
Our experience of language. 2.965
Our father who art in hell. 1.2102
Our forgotten past. 4.6366
Our friend James Joyce. 2.8904
Our great spring victory. 3.4495
Our hearts were young and gay. 2.12486
Our hidden heritage: five centuries of women artists. 1.5195
Our huckleberry friend. 1.3458
Our Irish theatre. 2.3360
Our knowledge of the external world. 1.764
Our lady of darkness. 2.11996
Our Lady of the Flowers. 2.4538
Our lives for ourselves. 4.5772
Our living tradition. 3.8652
Our man in Havana. 2.8754
Our Mark Twain. 2.10952
Our more perfect union. 4.7801
Our naked frailties. 2.6668
Our national park policy. 5.5389
Our Nig, or, Sketches from the life of a free Black, in a two-story white house, north, showing that slavery's shadows fall even there. 2.11287
Our right to choose. 4.5698
Our rising empire, 1763-1803. 3.6964
Our sexuality. 4.5499
Our times, 1900-1925. 3.7515
Our town. 2.12713
Our two lives. 1.4103
Our Vichy gamble. 3.936
Our way. 3.8440
Our wildlife legacy. 5.5496
Our world from the air. 4.372
Ours once more. 4.794
Ourselves to know. 2.12271
Out cry. 2.12734
Out of Africa. 3.5269
Out of balance. 4.7875
Out of bounds. 2.9378
Out of China's earth. 3.4627
Out of my later years. 5.1946
Out of my system. 2.2399
Out of our lives. 2.10816
Out of our past. 3.6319
Out-of-the-body travel. 2.13266
Out of the darkness, the planet Pluto. 5.1821
Out of the past of Greece & Rome. 3.122
Out of the shadows. 3.1019
Out of the silent planet. 2.9039
Out of uniform and into trouble. 5.4696

Out to work. 4.3282
The outbreak of the Peloponnesian War.
  3.2613
Outbreaks, the sociology of collective behavior.
  4.4995
Outcaste. 3.3973
Outdoor recreation in America. 4.892
Outer space. 4.9338
Outgrowing democracy. 3.6133
The outlawed party. 4.8605
The outlaws. 3.2412
Outlaws of the marsh. 2.2224
An outline history of Spanish American
  literature. 2.5303
Outline of comparative literature from Dante
  Alighieri to Eugene O'Neill. 2.2698
An outline of English phonetics. 2.1015
An outline of European architecture. 1.5355
An outline of Middle English grammar. 2.950
An outline of psycho-analysis. 5.135
The outline of sanity. 2.7565
Outline of stratificational grammar. 2.152
An outline of structural geology. 5.3126
An outline of the religious literature of India.
  1.1812
An outline of the science of political economy.
  4.1419
An outline of the theology of the New
  Testament. 1.2655
Outline of world cultures. 4.527
Outlines of a philosophy of the history of man.
  3.478
Outlines of a theory of the light sense. 5.4383
Outlines of biochemistry. 5.4395
Outlines of psychology. 5.111
Outlines of Russian culture. 3.3020
Outlines of structural geology. 5.3125
Outlines of the history of ethics for English
  readers. 1.1416
Outposts of monopoly capitalism. 4.4635
Output, employment, and productivity in the
  United States after 1800. 4.1952
Outrageous fortune. 3.2977
An outside chance. 2.13145
The outsider. 2.12813, 3.20
Outsider art. 1.4626
The outsiders. 3.4267
Outsiders in a hearing world. 4.6602
Outsiders in urban societies. 4.4943
Outsiders on the inside. 4.3288
Outsiders; studies in the sociology of deviance.
  4.6668
Over here. 3.816
Over to Candleford. 3.1739
The Overburian characters, to which is added,
  A wife. 2.6500
Overcoming math anxiety. 5.1061
The overeducated American. 4.3308
Overeducation in the U.S. labor market.
  4.3309
Overexposure. 5.6946
Overhead costs. 4.1480
Overland from Canada to British Columbia.
  3.8848
The overland mail, 1849-1869. 4.4046
The Overlook illustrated dictionary of nautical
  terms. 5.7415
The overproduction trap in U.S. agriculture.
  4.2954
The overreacher. 2.6617
Ovid. 2.749-2.750
Ovid and his influence. 2.752
Ovid as an epic poet. 2.751
Ovid recalled. 2.753
Ovid with an English translation: Tristia, Ex
  Ponto. 2.682
Ovid's Amores, Book 1. 2.743
Ovid's Fasti. 2.679
Ovid's Heroides. 2.745
Ovid's Metamorphoses. 2.746
Owen Wister. 2.11289
Owen Wister, chronicler of the West, gentleman
  of the East. 2.11290
The owl and the nightingale. 2.6423
The owl in the tree, poems. 2.9429
The owl of Minerva. 1.106
Owls do cry. 2.10219
The Ox-Bow incident. 2.11504

The Ox on the Roof. 1.3708
Oxford addresses on poetry. 2.5765
Oxford American dictionary. 2.1140
The Oxford anthology of Australian literature.
  2.10145
The Oxford anthology of English literature.
  2.6070
Oxford Bible atlas. 1.2551
The Oxford book of American light verse.
  2.10735
The Oxford book of American verse. 2.10730
The Oxford book of aphorisms. 2.3803
The Oxford book of ballads. 2.6110
The Oxford book of Canadian verse, in English
  and French. 2.9897
The Oxford book of children's verse in
  America. 2.10738
The Oxford book of contemporary New
  Zealand poetry. 2.10203
The Oxford book of contemporary verse,
  1945-1980. 2.6190
The Oxford book of death. 2.3715
The Oxford book of eighteenth century verse.
  2.6165
The Oxford book of English mystical verse.
  2.6117
The Oxford book of English prose. 2.6250
The Oxford book of English verse, 1250-1918.
  2.6100
The Oxford book of English verse of the
  Romantic period, 1798-1837. 2.6173
The Oxford book of food plants. 5.3658
The Oxford book of French verse, XIIIth
  century-XXth century. 2.3922
The Oxford book of German verse. 2.13515
The Oxford book of Greek verse. 2.317
The Oxford book of Greek verse in translation.
  2.403
The Oxford book of Italian verse. 2.4888
The Oxford book of late medieval verse and
  prose. 2.6079
The Oxford book of light verse. 2.6101
The Oxford book of medieval English verse.
  2.6141
The Oxford book of medieval Latin verse.
  2.813
The Oxford book of modern verse, 1892-1935.
  2.6191
The Oxford book of narrative verse. 2.6125
The Oxford book of New Zealand writing since
  1945. 2.10200
The Oxford book of nineteenth-century English
  verse. 2.6172
The Oxford book of Portuguese verse. 2.5450
Oxford book of regency verse. 2.6173
Oxford book of romantic verse. 2.6173
The Oxford book of Russian verse. 2.1309
The Oxford book of satirical verse. 2.6127
The Oxford book of Scottish verse. 2.9842
The Oxford book of seventeenth century verse.
  2.6160
The Oxford book of short stories. 2.6265
The Oxford book of sixteenth century verse.
  2.6148
The Oxford book of twentieth-century English
  verse. 2.6189
The Oxford book of verse in English
  translation. 2.3745
The Oxford book of Victorian verse. 2.6179
The Oxford book of war poetry. 2.3757
The Oxford Chekhov. 2.1483
The Oxford classical dictionary. 3.2510
The Oxford companion to American literature.
  2.10233
The Oxford companion to American theatre.
  2.3186
The Oxford companion to art. 1.4579
The Oxford companion to Canadian history and
  literature. 2.9880
The Oxford companion to Canadian literature.
  2.9879
The Oxford companion to children's literature.
  2.2702
The Oxford companion to classical literature.
  3.2508
The Oxford companion to English literature.
  2.5485
The Oxford companion to film. 2.2873

The Oxford companion to French literature.
  2.3823
The Oxford companion to German literature.
  2.13448
The Oxford companion to law. 4.9347
The Oxford companion to medicine. 5.4488
The Oxford companion to ships & the sea.
  5.7418
The Oxford companion to Spanish literature.
  2.5083
The Oxford companion to the decorative arts.
  1.6507
The Oxford companion to the literature of
  Wales. 2.831
The Oxford companion to the theatre. 2.3088
The Oxford companion to twentieth-century art.
  1.4820
Oxford dictionary of current idiomatic English.
  2.1105
The Oxford dictionary of English Christian
  names. 3.304
The Oxford dictionary of English etymology.
  2.1059
The Oxford dictionary of English proverbs.
  2.3809
The Oxford dictionary of modern Greek
  (Greek-English) 2.250
The Oxford dictionary of music. 1.3501
The Oxford dictionary of natural history.
  5.3185
The Oxford dictionary of nursery rhymes.
  2.14102
The Oxford dictionary of quotations. 2.3727
The Oxford dictionary of the Christian Church.
  1.2221
Oxford-Duden Bildwörterbuch. 2.1188
Oxford economic atlas of the world. 4.135
The Oxford encyclopedia of trees of the world.
  5.3682
The Oxford English dictionary. 2.1084
Oxford English dictionary. 2.1082-2.1083,
  2.1085
The Oxford English-Russian dictionary. 2.1235
The Oxford history of Australian literature.
  2.10138
The Oxford history of English art. 1.4930
The Oxford history of Hungarian literature
  from the earliest times to the present.
  2.1754
The Oxford history of India. 3.4224
Oxford history of music. 1.3636
The Oxford history of New Zealand. 3.5602
The Oxford history of South Africa. 3.5464
The Oxford history of the American people.
  3.6325
The Oxford history of the classical world.
  3.2519
The Oxford Ibsen. 2.14034
The Oxford illustrated literary guide to Great
  Britain and Ireland. 2.5561
The Oxford illustrated literary guide to the
  United States. 2.10282
Oxford Latin dictionary. 2.259
The Oxford Russian-English dictionary. 2.1237
The Oxford Shakespeare. 2.6841
The Oxford Shakespeare. 2.6650
Oxford University British commonwealth
  group. 4.8932
Das Oxforder Buch deutscher Prosa von Luther
  bis Rilke. 2.13522
Oxherding tale. 2.13098
Oxidation in organic chemistry. 5.2750
The Oyo Empire, c.1600-c.1836. 3.5346
Ozark baptizings, hangings, and other
  diversions. 3.8365
Ozark folksongs. 1.3436

P.A.C. directory. 4.8136
P.A.C. handbook. 4.7896
P.A.C.s. 4.8134
P.A.C.'s Americana. 4.8133
p-adic numbers and their functions. 5.1330
p-adic numbers, p-adic analysis, and zeta-
  functions. 5.1328
P.C.M. and digital transmission systems.
  5.6401
P. G. T. Beauregard. 3.7319
P.G. Wodehouse. 2.9559

P. H. Newby. 2.9140
P. H. Pearse. 2.9222
P.L.O. and Palestine. 3.3906
P.O.W. 4.9329
P. Vergili Maronis Aeneidos, liber quintus.
 2.788
P. Vergili Maronis Aeneidos, liber sextus.
 2.789
Pa Chin and his writings. 2.2246
Pablo Picasso, a retrospective. 1.4979
The Pabst Brewing Company. 4.3694
The PAC directory. 4.8136
The PAC handbook. 4.7896
Pacem in maribus. 4.9313
Pacific 1860. 2.8582
The Pacific basin. 3.5540
Pacific estrangement; Japanese and American
 expansion, 1897-1911. 3.6461
The Pacific islanders. 4.663
The Pacific islands. 3.5534
Pacific Islands portraits. 3.5543
Pacific islands year book. 3.5530
Pacific railways and nationalism in the
 Canadian-American Northwest, 1845-1873.
 4.4014
The Pacific salmon fisheries. 5.5484
The Pacific slope. 3.8591
The Pacific States of America. 3.8590
Pacifism in Europe to 1914. 4.9108
Pacifism in the United States. 4.9112
Pacifist's progress. 4.7002
Pacifying the plains. 3.5871
Package engineering. 5.7052
Packaging the presidency. 4.7950
PACs. 4.8134
PACs Americana. 4.8133
Paddy Chayefsky. 2.11489
Pagan. 3.4425
Pageant-master of the Republic. 1.6088
Pages. 2.4147
Pages choisies. 2.4276
Páginas escogidas. 2.5367
Paideia. 3.2538
Paideia problems and possibilities. 4.10815
The Paideia program. 4.10829
The Paideia proposal. 4.10002
Pain. 5.5200
Pain, a nursing approach to assessment and
 analysis. 5.4744
Pain, pleasure, and American childbirth.
 5.5072
Pain sensations and reactions. 5.4349
Paine. 4.7425
The painful prescription. 5.4708
The Pains of imprisonment. 4.6695
The painted bird. 2.13122
The painted veil. 2.9101
The painted word. 1.5875
The painter and the photograph. 1.4634
The Painterly print. 1.6496
The painter's choice. 1.5864
The painter's craft. 1.6374
Painters in a new land. 1.6383
Painters of the humble truth. 1.6366
Painters of the Victorian scene. 1.6020
Painters painting. 1.4878
Painters painting (Motion picture) 1.4878
Painting and experience in fifteenth century
 Italy. 1.6180
Painting and painters. 1.6341
Painting and reality. 1.6342
Painting and sculpture in Europe, 1780 to 1880.
 1.4926
Painting and sculpture in Europe, 1880-1940.
 1.4928
Painting and sculpture in Germany and the
 Netherlands, 1500 to 1600. 1.5019
Painting in America, from 1502 to the present.
 1.5890
Painting in Britain, 1530 to 1790. 1.6014
Painting in Britain: the Middle Ages. 1.6012
Painting in Canada. 1.5993
Painting in eighteenth-century France. 1.6049
Painting in eighteenth-century Venice. 1.6189
Painting in Europe, 800 to 1200. 1.5862
Painting in Florence and Siena after the Black
 Death. 1.6188
Painting in Italy, 1500 to 1600. 1.6181

Painting in the twentieth century. 1.5868
Painting of India. 1.6308
The painting of modern life. 1.6064
Painting of the high Renaissance in Rome and
 Florence. 1.6182
Painting, photography, film. 5.6966
Paintings. 1.6173
The paintings and drawings of Dante Gabriel
 Rossetti (1828-1882) 1.4955
The paintings and drawings of William Blake.
 1.4947
The paintings of Eugène Delacroix. 1.6094
The paintings of J.M.W. Turner. 1.6038
The paintings of James McNeill Whistler.
 1.5984
The paintings of Lucas Cranach. 1.6168
The paintings of Quinten Massys with catalogue
 raisonné. 1.6268
The paintings of Titian: v. II; the portraits.
 1.6227
Los paisanos. 3.8571
Pakistan. 3.4122, 3.4131, 3.4134, 4.8721,
 5.8052
Pakistan, a country study. 3.4121
Pakistan: failure in national integration. 3.4130
Pakistan, its people, its society, its culture.
 3.4124
Pakistan, the roots of dictatorship. 4.2518
Pakistan under Bhutto, 1971-1977. 3.4126
Pakistan's development, social goals and private
 incentives. 4.2519
Pakistan's foreign policy. 3.4125
Pal Joey. 2.12272
Palace and politics in prewar Japan. 4.8755
A palace for a king. 3.3445
The Palace Museum, Peking. 1.4668
The palace of honor. 2.6469
The Palace of Minos. 3.2591
Palace of the peacock. 2.10030
The palaces of Crete. 1.5222
Palaeoethnobotany. 4.722
Palauan social structure. 4.676
Pale fire. 2.12228
Paleobotany and the evolution of plants.
 5.3177
Paleocurrents and basin analysis. 5.3065
Paleoecology, concepts and applications.
 5.3155
Paleogeologic maps. 5.2978
Palestine and modern Arab poetry. 2.1837
Palestine and the Great Powers, 1945-1948.
 3.3922
Palestine in perspective. 3.3878
Palestine papers, 1917-1922. 3.3917
The Palestinian Arab national movement.
 3.3920
The Palestinian covenant and its meaning.
 3.3889
Palestinian leadership on the West Bank.
 4.8780
The Palestinian Liberation Organisation.
 3.3863
The Palestinian problem and United States
 policy. 3.3873
The Palestinian refugees in Jordan 1948-1957.
 3.4032
A Palestinian state. 3.3870
The Palestinians. 3.3864
The Palestinians and the Middle East conflict.
 3.3879
Palestrina. 1.3944
Palgrave's Dictionary of political economy.
 4.1275
The palice of honour. 2.6469
Palladian style in Canadian architecture.
 1.5342
The Palliser expedition. 3.8849
Palm Sunday. 2.13394
The palm tree of Deborah. 1.1482
The palm-wine drinkard and his dead palm-
 wine tapster in the Dead's Town. 2.10117
Palmerston, the early years, 1784-1841. 3.1604
Pamela, or, Virtue rewarded. 2.7219
Pamela-Shamela. 2.7220
The Pampangans. 4.5445
Pamphlets of the American Revolution,
 1750-1776. 3.6883
Pan. 2.14046

The pan-African movement. 3.5106
Pan-Africanism and nationalism in West Africa,
 1900-1945. 3.5331
Pan-Africanism or communism. 3.5111
Pan-Arabism and labor. 4.3420
The Pan-German League, 1890-1914. 3.2261
Pan Michael; an historical novel of Poland, the
 Ukraine, and Turkey. 2.1728
Pan-Slavism: its history and ideology. 3.690
Pan Tadeusz. 2.1716
Panama. 3.9080
Panamanian politics. 4.8336
Pañcagrama. 2.1863
Panchagram (Five villages). 2.1863
The Panchatantra. 2.1941-2.1942
Panchatantra. English. 2.1942
The panda's thumb. 5.3346
Pandosto. 2.6491
Panegyricus. 2.685
Panic on Wall Street. 4.4617
Panmunjom. 3.5035
Pannonia and Upper Moesia. 3.2717
Panofsky and the foundations of art history.
 1.5152
Panorama du théâtre nouveau. 2.3935
A panorama of pure mathematics, as seen by
 N. Bourbaki. 5.1106
A panorama of Russian literature. 2.1248
A panorama of the world's legal systems.
 4.9346
Pantomime. 2.2840
Panzer battles. 3.969
Panzer leader. 3.965
Papa. 2.11859
The Papacy in the modern world, 1914-1978.
 1.3164
The papacy today. 1.3165
Papago woman. 3.5935
Papal authority. 1.3144
The papal encyclicals in their historical context.
 1.3132
Papal envoys to the great khans. 4.96
Papal provisions. 1.3213
Paper and light. 5.6950
Paper basics. 5.7075
The paper economy. 4.1978
The paper men. 2.8701
Paperbound books in print. 5.7705
Papermaking. 5.7074
Papers. 3.6973, 3.7070, 4.402
The papers & the papers. 3.7910
The papers of Adlai E. Stevenson. 3.7519
The papers of Alexander Hamilton. 3.6969
The papers of Andrew Jackson. 3.6970
The papers of Benjamin Franklin. 3.6967
The papers of Daniel Webster. 3.7072
The papers of Dwight David Eisenhower.
 3.7517
The papers of General Lucius D. Clay:
 Germany, 1945-1949. 3.2455
The papers of General Nathanael Greene.
 3.6968
The papers of George Mason, 1725-1792.
 3.6976
The papers of James Madison. 3.6975
The papers of Jefferson Davis. 3.7321
Papers of John Adams. 3.6966
Papers on John C. Calhoun. 3.7069
The papers of Joseph Henry. 5.701
The papers of Robert Morris, 1781-1784.
 3.6977
The papers of Ulysses S. Grant. 3.7403
The papers of William Penn. 3.8081
Papers on acting. 2.3120
Papers on China. 3.4611
Papers on playmaking. 2.2798
Papers on public credit, commerce and finance.
 4.1909
Papers on the science of Administration.
 4.7756
Papers relating to political economy. 4.1261
Papists and Puritans under Elizabeth I. 3.1430
Papua New Guinea. 3.5666
Para-transit. 4.3919
Parables and instructions in the Gospels.
 1.2936
Parables and paradoxes, in German and
 English. 2.13790

The parables of Jesus. 1.2888, 1.2890
The parables of the kingdom. 1.2887
The parables; their literary and existential dimension. 1.2891
The Parade of heroes. 4.777
Parades and politics at Vichy. 3.2208
Parade's end. 2.8632
The parade's gone by. 2.2910
Paradigms and revolutions. 5.954
Les paradis artificiels. 2.4137
Le paradis des femmes. 4.6118
Paradise. 2.4928
Paradise, Incorporated 4.6654
Paradise lost. 2.7118-2.7119, 2.7130
Paradise lost as 'myth.'. 2.7133
Paradise of dissent; South Australia 1829-1857. 3.5586
Paradise on earth. 3.98
The Paradiso. 2.4927
Paradiso. 2.5365
The paradox of acting. 2.3115
The paradox of cause and other essays. 1.92
The paradox of helping: introduction to the philosophy of scientific practice. 4.6486
The paradox of progressive thought. 3.6150
The paradox of Scottish culture. 3.1803
Paradoxes and problems. 2.6458
The paradoxes of freedom. 4.7634
Paraguay. 3.9229-3.9230
Paraguay, a country study. 3.9228
Paralanguage and kinesics. 5.462
Parallel lives. 4.5618
Parallel of the orders of architecture, Greek, Roman, and Renaissance. 1.5498
Parameters of popular culture. 3.6181
The paranoid style in American politics. 3.7528
Parapsychology. 5.647
The parasite. 2.1795
Parasitology. 5.4081
Pardon and amnesty under Lincoln and Johnson. 3.7461
Parental care in mammals. 5.4051
Parenting in an unresponsive society. 4.5725
A parent's guide to children's reading. 4.10409
Parents in contemporary America. 4.5578
Parents speak out. 4.6581
Les parents terribles. 2.4481
Pariahs stand up! 4.6114
Paris. 4.6330
Paris and London in the eighteenth century. 4.5355
Paris and the arts, 1851-1896. 1.6720
The Paris Commune. 3.2167
The Paris Commune, 1871. 3.2166
Paris herald. 2.3661
Paris in the Third Reich. 3.1066
Paris journal. 3.2232
The Paris lectures. 1.1008
The Paris review. 2.3707
The Parisian sans-culottes and the French Revolution, 1793-4. 3.2101
Park Row. 2.3660
The Parkman reader. 3.8706
Parkman's history. 3.6259
Parks for America. 5.5387
The Parliament of Sweden. 4.8678
Parliament. 4.8585
Parliamentary reform 1640-1832. 4.8459
The parliamentary representation of the English boroughs during the Middle Ages. 4.8466
The parliamentary system of Israel. 4.8784
Parliaments of the world. 4.7727
Parmenides. 1.248
Parnasse et symbolisme. 2.3864
Parnassus on wheels. 2.12207
Parnell and his party, 1880-90. 3.1856
Parodies. 2.3800
Paroles. 2.4660
Parseghian and Notre Dame football. 4.1027
Parsival. 2.13179
A part of speech. 2.1625
Le parti pris des choses. 2.4657
Partial differential equations. 5.1527, 5.1529
Partial differential equations of applied mathematics. 5.1531
Partial differential equations of mathematical physics. 5.1526

Partial magic. 2.3416
Partial portraits. 2.2663
Partially ordered algebraic systems. 5.1295
Participation and democracy in Norway. 4.8677
Participation in America. 4.8179
Participation in politics. 4.7774
Participatory and self-managed firms. 4.3179
Particle accelerators. 5.2439
The particle connection. 2.2464
Particle physics. 5.2461-5.2462
The particle play. 5.2072
Particles and fields. 5.2467
Particles and fields. 5.2396
The parties. 4.8154
Parties and party systems. 4.7787
Parties and political change in Bolivia, 1880-1952. 3.9276
Parties and politics in America. 3.6391
Parties and politics in contemporary Japan. 4.8762
Parties and their environments. 4.8155
Parties, elections, and representation in the state of New York. 4.8193
Parties out of power in Japan, 1931-1941. 4.8760
Parting at the shore. 1.6324
The parting of the way. 1.1806
The partisan imperative. 3.7081
The Partisan reader. 2.3705
Partisan review. 2.3705
Partisan review (Periodical). 2.3706
The Partisan spirit. 3.8357
The Partition of India. 3.4287
The partition of Turkey. 3.3590
Partners in freedom and true Muslims. 4.7295
Partners in furs. 4.3860
Partners in science. 5.5665
Parts of animals. 2.342
Parts of speech and accidence. 2.991
Party and constituency. 4.8177
Party and factional division in Texas. 4.8196
Party and parish pump. 4.8564
Party and politics in Israel. 4.8785
Party, constituency, and congressional voting. 4.8056
Party government. 4.8176
Party government and political culture in Western Germany. 4.8611
Party government in the House of Representatives. 4.8050
Party ideology and popular politics at the accession of George III. 3.1566
Party loyalty among congressmen. 4.8003
The party of Eros. 4.5235
Party organizations and American politics. 4.8162
Party politics. 4.8516
Party politics in Canada. 4.8300
Party politics in republican China. 4.8748
Party politics in the age of Caesar. 3.2735
Party politics in the Golden State. 4.8188
Party rivalry and political change in Taishō Japan. 3.4969
The party's choice. 4.7943
Parva naturalia. 2.439
Parzival. 2.13539-2.13540
Les pas perdus. 2.4424
Pasargadae. 3.4068
Pascal, adversary and advocate. 1.808
Pascal; the emergence of genius. 1.806
Pascal user manual and report. 5.1222
Pasolini. 2.5049
Los pasos perdidos. 2.5360
Passacaglia. 2.4654
Passage through Armageddon. 3.3164
Passage through the garden. 3.8481
A passage to India. 2.8650
Passage to power. 3.4719
Passages in modern sculpture. 1.5652
Passenger and immigration lists bibliography, 1538-1900. 5.8113, 5.8376
The Passenger car power plant of the future. 5.6623
Passing. 2.11988
The passing of the great reform bill. 4.8407
Passing of the mill village. 4.5199

The Passing of the New England Theology. 1.2764
The passing of the Whigs, 1832-1886. 3.1611
Passing through transitions. 5.4870
Passing time & A change of heart. 2.4434
La passion d'Émile. 2.4641
A passion for excellence. 4.2748
The Passion in Mark. 1.2688
Passion lends them power. 2.6790
The passion narrative of St. Luke. 1.2894
The passion of al-Hallāj. 1.2023
The passion of Claude McKay. 2.12081
Passion play. 2.9782
A Passion to know. 5.813
Passionate liberator. 3.7268
The passionate shepherdess. 2.6900
Passionate virtuosity. 2.12885
The passions. 5.416
Passive resistance in South Africa. 3.5452
Passive solar design handbook. 5.6106
Passive solar heating design. 5.6105
Passive voices. 3.4293
Passwords. 2.9263
The Past and future of Presidential debates. 4.7956
The past and future people. 3.5667
Past and present. 4.5317
The past and the present. 3.83
The past in the present. 3.5312
Past master. 2.13127
Past, present and future. 1.1218
The past recaptured. 3.417
The past that poets make. 2.2753
The past through tomorrow. 2.11829
Pasternak. 2.1598
Pastmasters. 3.6228
The Paston letters. 3.1374
The Pastons. 3.343
The Pastons and their England: studies in an age of transition. 3.1373
Il pastor fido. 2.4970
Pastoral care. 1.2184
The pastoral elegy. 2.3753
The Pastoral epistles. 1.2720
The pastoral Epistles. 1.2721
Pastoral poetry & pastoral drama. 2.5785
The pastoral symphony. 2.4556
Pastors and masters. 2.8530
The Pastures of heaven. 2.12530
Pataphysical poems. 2.4676
Patch dynamics. 5.3577
Patents for chemists. 5.5638
Paternal deprivation. 5.612
Paternalism in early Victorian England. 4.5307
Paterson. 3.8069
The path between the seas. 3.9083
Path breaking. 4.8081
The path I trod. 4.3593
The path of God's bondsmen from origin to return. 1.2082
The path of purification. 1.2138
The path of the Buddha. 1.2145
The path to the double helix. 5.3503
Pather panchali. Song of the road. 2.1861
Pathetic fallacy in the nineteenth century. 2.5719
The pathogenesis of infectious disease. 5.4749
The Pathology and psychology of cognition. 5.282
Pathos of power. 4.5181
Paths in Utopia. 4.6930
The paths of culture. 3.49
Paths of resistance. 4.2037
The pathway for oxygen. 5.4231
Pathways to madness. 4.5642
Pathways to Parliament. 4.8465
Pathways to tax reform. 4.9767
Patience and fortitude. 3.7660
Patience and power. 4.6159
Patience (Middle English Poem) 2.6132
The patience of Maigret. 2.4748
The patient as person. 5.4569
Patient education. 5.4593
Patient in the womb. 5.5069
Patient teaching in nursing practice. 5.5204
Patriarchy and socialist revolution in China. 4.5632
Patrician and plebeian in Virginia. 3.8202

Patrick Henry Bruce, American modernist. 1.5921
Patrick Kavanagh. 2.8927
Patrick Moore's History of astronomy. 5.1685
Patrick White. 2.10188, 2.10191
Patrick White's fiction. 2.10190
Patrimonialism and political change in the Congo. 4.8813
Patriotic gore. 2.10381
Patriotism limited, 1862-1865. 5.7368
Patriotism on parade. 3.6191
Patronage in the Renaissance. 3.161
Patrons and musicians of the English Renaissance. 1.3719
Patrons and painters. 1.5005, 1.5198
Patten's Human embryology. 5.4166
Pattern and growth in personality. 5.503
Pattern & meaning in history. 3.468
Pattern and process in a forested ecosystem. 5.3270
Pattern design. 1.6545
A pattern language. 1.5462
The pattern of Chinese history: cycles, development, or stagnation? 3.4662
The pattern of expectation, 1644-2001. 3.74
The pattern of Hardy's poetry. 2.7790
The pattern of the Chinese past. 3.4665
The pattern of tragicomedy in Beaumont and Fletcher. 2.6557
Patterns and principles of animal development. 5.4124
Patterns from the sod. 3.8404
Patterns in criminal homicide. 4.6729
Patterns in crystals. 5.2927
Patterns in human geography. 4.361
Patterns in the dust. 3.6435
Patterns of child rearing. 4.5712
Patterns of childhood. 2.13926
Patterns of culture. 4.518
Patterns of decay. 2.6766
Patterns of discovery. 5.889
Patterns of emotions. 5.429
Patterns of evolution as illustrated by the fossil record. 5.3159
Patterns of industrial bureaucracy. 4.2649
Patterns of kingship and authority in traditional Asia. 4.8693
Patterns of mammalian reproduction. 5.4252
Patterns of political participation in Italy. 4.8628
Patterns of politics and political systems in Latin America. 4.7714
Patterns of poverty in the Third World. 4.2582
Patterns of primate behavior. 5.4015
Patterns of race in the Americas. 3.9024
Patterns of reality. 2.8481
Patterns of reformation. 1.2335
Patterns of sexual behavior. 4.5501
Patterns of shock. 5.4746
Patterns of technological innovation. 5.5627
Patterns of urbanization. 4.6195
Patterns on the earth. 4.84
Patterson's American education. 4.9945
The Patton papers. 3.7613
Patty's Industrial hygiene and toxicology. 5.5022
Paul. 1.2664, 1.2715
Paul and his letters. 1.2704
Paul and Palestinian Judaism. 1.1912
Paul and the anatomy of apostolic authority. 1.2705
Paul & the Gnostics. 1.2701
Paul and the salvation of mankind. 1.2665
Paul, apostle of liberty. 1.2667
Paul, apostle to the Gentiles. 1.2668
Paul Bunyan, last of the frontier demigods. 2.10659
Paul Celan. 2.13726
Paul Cézanne. 1.6074
Paul Cézanne, letters. 1.6069
Paul Cuffe. 3.6820
Paul Elmer More. 2.11179-2.11180
Paul Eluard. 2.4526
Paul-Émile Borduas, 1905-1960. 1.5996
Paul Gauguin. 1.6105
Paul Kane's frontier. 1.5998
Paul Klee. 1.6177
Paul Klee and cubism. 1.4995

Paul Laurence Dunbar. 2.11013-2.11014
Paul Marc Joseph Chenavard, artist of 1848. 1.6077
Paul, Paulus. 1.2666
Paul Samuelson and modern economic theory. 4.1376
Paul Scott, images of India. 2.9809
Paul Strand: a retrospective monograph. 5.6968
Paul the apostle. 1.2703
Paul, the law, and the Jewish people. 1.2707
Paul Tillich, his life & thought. 1.3298
Paul Valéry. 2.4767
Paul Valéry, an anthology. 2.4763
Paul Valéry and the poetry of voice. 2.4766
Paula Modersohn-Becker, her life and work. 1.4997
Pauline Smith. 2.10093
Paul's letters from prison. 1.2702
Pausanias Description of Greece. 2.382
Pavement management systems. 5.6068
Pavements and surfacings for highways and airports. 5.6067
Pavlov. 5.4175
Pavlova. 4.1155
The pawnbroker. 2.13411
The Pawnee Indians. 3.5936
Pax Romana. 3.2794
Pay and pensions for federal workers. 4.7986
Paycocks and others. 2.9152
Payment systems. 4.3140
Le paysan de Paris. 2.4374
Les Paysans du Nord pendant la Révolution française. 4.2853
PCM and digital transmission systems. 5.6401
PCT, spin and statistics, and all that. 5.2160
PDR for nonprescription drugs 1980-. 5.5141
Peace. 2.429
Peace and war. 4.9020
The peace brokers. 3.3884
Peace by revolution. 3.8952
The Peace Conference of 1919, organization and procedure. 3.854
The peace conspiracy. 3.4839
'Peace in our time.' 2.8582
A peace in southern Africa. 3.5513
Peace in their time. 4.9261
Peace in war. 2.5286
Peace-making and the settlement with Japan. 3.1141
Peace-making in the Middle East. 3.3880
The Peace of Nicias and the Sicilian Expedition. 3.2615
Peace or war. 4.9142
The peace reform in American history. 4.9143
Peace soldiers. 4.9255
The peace tactics of Napoleon, 1806-1808. 3.2135
Peace without victory. 3.828
Peaceable kingdom. 3.1583
Peaceful conquest. 4.2209
Peacekeeping, appraisals & proposals. 4.9256
Peacekeeping, appraisals and proposals. 4.9256
The peacemakers. 3.6938
Peacemaking, 1919. 3.852
The peach blossom fan. 2.2230
Peacock displayed. 2.7993
The peacock poems. 2.13430
Peake's commentary on the Bible. 1.2524
Pearl. 2.6424-2.6425
The Pearl. 2.12533
The pearl; an interpretation. 2.6426
Pearl; [and], Cleanness; [and], Patience; [and], Sir Gawain and the Green Knight. 2.6137
Pearl Harbor as history: Japanese-American relations, 1931-1941. 3.6457
Pearl Harbor, the continuing controversy. 3.1016
Pearl Harbor; warning and decision. 3.1017
Pearl (Middle English poem) 2.6132, 2.6424-2.6425
Pearl (Middle English poem). 1975. 2.6134
The pearl of great price. 1.3381
Pearl S. Buck. 2.11433
Pearls before swine. 2.13391
Pearson, his life and world. 3.8787
The peasant and the Raj. 4.2864

The peasant economy and social change in North China. 4.2868
Peasant life in China. 4.2492
Peasant life in India. 3.4201
The peasant marketing system of Oaxaca, Mexico. 4.4335
Peasant nationalism and communist power. 3.4776
Peasant rebellion and Communist revolution in Asia. 4.7107
Peasant revolts in China, 1840-1949. 3.4669
Peasant society and culture. 4.875
Peasant society in Koṅku. 4.5435
Peasant uprisings in seventeenth-century France, Russia, and China. 3.636
Peasant wisdom. 4.629
The peasants ... 2.1723
Peasants against politics. 4.2913
Peasants and proletarians. 4.3674
Peasants and strangers. 3.8387
Peasants in Socialist transition. 4.5345
Peasants in the Pacific. 3.5635
Peasants into Frenchmen. 4.5353
The peasants of Languedoc. 4.2855
The peasants of the Montes. 4.5387
The peasants of the Tonkin Delta. 3.4492
Peasants, rebels, and outcastes. 4.5448
Peasants, subsistence ecology, and development in the highlands of Papua New Guinea. 4.2926
Peatlands. 4.284
Pêcheur d'Islande. 2.4328
The peculiar institution. 3.7196
The peculiar war. 3.5019
The peculiarities of German history. 3.2296
Pedagogical sketchbook. 1.5818
Pedagogy of the oppressed. 4.10236
Peder Victorious. 2.14056
A pedestrian approach to quantum field theory. 5.2154
The pedlar. 2.8302
Pedogenesis and soil taxonomy. 5.5265
Pedro de Valdivia, conqueror of Chile. 3.9261
Pedro Páramo. 2.5353-2.5354
The Peelites, 1846-1857. 3.1610
Peirce and pragmatism. 1.629
Peirce's philosophy of science. 5.926
Peking diary. 3.4784
Pelagius; inquiries and reappraisals. 1.2973
Pelle the conqueror. 2.14028
The Peloponnesian War. 3.2607
Pelts, plumes, and hides. 4.3862
The Pendergast machine. 3.8366
The PENDEX. 5.7726
Penetrating Wagner's Ring. 1.4052
Penetration of Africa. 3.5047
The Penguin book of American folk songs. 1.3434
The Penguin book of contemporary American essays. 2.10861
The Penguin book of contemporary British poetry. 2.6192
The Penguin book of English madrigals. 1.3429
The Penguin book of homosexual verse. 2.3755
The Penguin book of Irish verse. 2.9866
The Penguin book of Italian verse. 2.4896
The Penguin book of Latin American verse. 2.5324
The Penguin book of Lieder. 1.3460
The Penguin book of New Zealand verse. 2.10202
The Penguin book of South African verse. 2.10050
The Penguin book of Spanish verse. 2.5144
The Penguin book of Welsh short stories. 2.9873
The Penguin book of Welsh verse. 2.848
The Penguin book of women poets. 2.3749
The Penguin dictionary of art and artists. 1.4576
The Penguin dictionary of biology. 5.3181
The Penguin dictionary of physical geography. 4.239
The Penguin dictionary of science. 5.710
The Penguin dictionary of surnames. 3.308
The Penguin dictionary of twentieth-century history. 3.735

Penguin island. 2.4209
Penhally. 2.11789
Peninsular Malaysia. 3.4534
The Peninsular War, 1807-1814. 3.2125
Penmanship of the XVI, XVII & XVIIIth
  centuries. 5.7524
Pennsylvania. 3.8072
Pennsylvania politics, 1746-1770. 3.8075
Penny capitalism. 3.9065
Penrod. 2.11240
Penrod and Sam. 2.11240
Penrod Jashber. 2.11240
The pen's excellencie. 1.6603
El pensamiento de Cervantes. 2.5180
La Pensée française au XVIIIe siècle. 2.3853
Pensées. 1.804-1.805
Pensieri. 2.4998
Pensions, economics, and public policy. 4.3465
Pensions, labor, and individual choice. 4.3468
The Pentagon papers. 3.6501
The Pentagon papers as published by the New
  York times. 3.6500
Pentagon Papers. Negotiating volumes. 3.4494
The Pentagon propaganda machine. 5.7269
The Pentecostal movement. 1.3389
Pentecostalism. 1.3387
The Pentecostals. 1.3386
Pentimento. 2.11831
The peony pavilion. 2.2225
People. 5.6986
A People and a proletariat. 3.1765
People and land in Africa south of the Sahara.
  4.2870
People and life, 1891-1921. 2.1551
People and places in Colonial Venezuela.
  4.1688
People and plans. 4.6319
The people and the court. 4.9640
The people and the party system. 4.7726
The people called Shakers. 1.3412
A people in revolution. 3.6944
The people named the Chippewa. 3.5857
The people of Africa. 4.652
The people of Alor. 4.632
The people of ancient Israel. 1.2566
The people of Aristophanes. 2.433
People of Coal Town. 4.5135
People of Nepal. 3.4350
People of paradox. 3.6016
People of plenty. 3.6161
The people of Puerto Rico. 4.5264
People of the city. 2.10110
People of the high country. 3.5771
People of the Nile. 3.5142
The people of the plain. 4.5385
The people of the Sierra. 3.3491
People of the totem. 3.5748
People on the move. 4.1654
People-oriented computer systems. 5.1128
People populating. 4.1608
People, positions, and power. 4.7983
People, princes, and paramount power. 3.4273
People, science, and technology. 5.5515
People walk on their heads. 3.8053
People without a country. 3.3690
A peopled landscape. 2.9437
Peoplepower. 4.3211
The peoples and cultures of ancient Peru.
  3.9286
Peoples and cultures of native South America.
  3.9155
Peoples and cultures of the Middle East.
  3.3701
Peoples and places of the past. 3.121
People's China. 3.4787
The people's choice: how the voter makes up
  his mind in a presidential campaign. 4.7953
The People's Democratic Republic of Yemen.
  4.8788
People's history of the American Revolution.
  3.6905
Peoples of Africa. 3.5058
Peoples of Central Asia. 3.3323
The peoples of Malaysia. 3.4554
Peoples of Old Testament times. 3.3705
The Peoples of Philadelphia. 3.8089
The peoples of the Eastern Habsburg lands,
  1526-1918. 3.2994

The peoples of the hills. 3.4042
The peoples of the Soviet Far East. 3.3320
Peoples of the U.S.S.R. 3.3026
The peoples of the USSR. 3.3026
The People's Republic of China. 3.4614
The People's Republic of China, 1949-1979.
  3.4798
The people's voice. 2.3532
The people's war; Britain, 1939-1945. 3.1703
People's war, People's Army. 3.4439
The peopling of Hawaii. 4.1681
Peppercanister poems, 1972-1978. 2.8934
Pepys. 2.7180
Pepys' Memoires of the Royal Navy,
  1679-1688. 5.7463
Perceived quality. 4.4307
Perceiving. 1.1277
Perceiving, behaving, becoming. 4.10632
Perceiving, sensing, and knowing. 1.1274
Perceiving women. 4.5891
Perception. 1.1295, 5.268
Perception and change. 1.1326
Perception and communication. 5.19
Perception and discovery. 5.890
Perception and misperception in international
  politics. 4.8997
Perception and the conditioned reflex. 5.4327
Perception and the senses. 5.4356
Perception and understanding in young
  children. 5.590
The perception of brightness and darkness.
  5.4384
The Perception of causality. 5.401
Perception, opportunity, and profit. 4.1330
Perception, sensation and verification. 5.288
Perceptions and evocations. 1.4906
Perceptions of development. 4.2799
Perceptions of the past in Southeast Asia.
  3.4418
Perceval (Romances, etc.) 2.3947
Percussion. 1.4181
Percussion instruments and their history.
  1.4180
Percy Erskine Nobbs. 1.5349
Percy Grainger. 1.3879
The Percy letters. 2.7181
The Percys of Mississippi. 3.334
Percy's reliques. 2.6111
Père Goriot, and Eugénie Grandet. 2.4119
Peregrine Pickle. 2.7262
Perelandra. 2.9040
Perelman's home companion. 2.12309
The perennial scope of philosophy. 1.1027
The perfect Wagnerite. 1.4519
The perfection of wisdom in eight thousand
  lines & its verse summary. 2.2130
Perfectionist persuasion. 1.3358
The performance of American Government:
  checks and minuses. 4.7859
The Performance of labor-managed firms.
  4.3180
The performing arts in contemporary China.
  2.3391
Performing arts research. 5.8308
Performing arts resources. 5.8306
The performing self. 2.10421
Pericles and Athens. 3.2603
Periglacial geomorphology. 4.278
The perils and prospects of Southern Black
  leadership. 3.8219
The perils of prosperity, 1914-32. 4.1965
Periodical literature on United States cities.
  5.8186
Periodical title abbreviations. 5.8317
Periodicals directory 1932-38. 5.8314
Periodicals online. 5.7643
Permanence & change. 1.577
The permanence of Yeats. 2.8349
Permanency planning for children. 4.6561
The Permanent Court of International Justice,
  1920-1942. 4.9148
Permanent errors. 2.13275
Permanent-magnet and brushless DC motors.
  5.6314
The permanent majority. 4.8006
The permanent purge. 3.3213
Permanent revolution; totalitarianism in the age
  of international civil war. 4.7602

The permanent war economy. 4.1991
Permanents. 5.1313
Permit me voyage. 2.11295
Perón, a biography. 3.9253
The perpendicular style, 1330-1485. 1.5529
Perpetual dilemma. 1.1933
The perpetual dream. 4.10071
Perpetual peace. 4.9115
Perpetuum mobile. 2.4437
Perry's Chemical engineers' handbook. 5.6827
Persia and the Greeks. 3.2601
Persian art, Parthian and Sassanian dynasties,
  249 B.C.-A.D. 651. 1.4709
The Persian boy. 2.9268
The Persian Empire. 3.4075
Persian-English dictionary. 2.1964
The Persian Gulf and United States policy.
  3.4092
Persian Gulf states. 3.4057
Persian letters. 2.4082
Persian miniature painting and its influence on
  the art of Turkey and India. 1.6419
Persian painting. 1.6306
A Persian stronghold of Zoroastrianism.
  1.1781
Persistent poverty. 4.1826
The persistent problems of psychology. 5.73
Persius. 2.756
Persius and the programmatic satire. 2.754
Person/planet. 4.5097
Person to person: the problem of being human.
  5.4875
A personal approach to teaching. 4.10262
Personal being. 5.495
Personal character and cultural milieu. 4.393
Personal destinies. 1.1499
Personal financial management. 4.4451
A personal history. 3.1214
Personal identification. 4.6808
Personal income 4.2082
Personal income during business cycles. 4.2083
Personal income taxation. 4.4713
Personal knowledge. 5.922
A personal matter. 2.2133
Personal memoirs. 3.7476
Personal name index to 'The New York times
  index,' 1851-1974. 5.8108
Personal names. 5.8300
Personal names and naming. 5.8298
Personal narrative of travels to the equinoctial
  regions of America, during the years
  1799-1804. 3.9150
Personal networks in town and city. 4.6183
Personal politics. 4.6045
Personal rapid transit. 4.3905
Personal rapid transit II. 4.3902
A personal record. 3.1718
Personal religion among the Greeks. 1.1654
Personal rule in Black Africa. 3.5097
Personal selling. 4.4328
Personal values and consumer psychology.
  4.4310
Personalism. 1.1312
Personalities and powers. 3.612
Personality. 5.504, 5.530, 5.532, 5.538
Personality and individual differences. 5.514
Personality and interpersonal behavior. 4.4933
Personality and organization. 4.2693
Personality and persuasibility. 5.474
Personality and prediction. 5.539
Personality and sense of humor. 5.437
Personality and social encounter. 5.505
The personality of Britain, its influence on
  inhabitant and invader ... 4.391
The personality of Jonathan Swift. 2.7299
Personality, power, and authority. 4.4946
Personality tests and reviews. 5.540
Personality theories. 5.527
Personalizing education. 4.10806
Das persönliche Regiment Wilhelm II. 3.2333
Personnel administration. 4.4365
Personnel administration in education. 4.10668
Personnel and industrial relations. 4.4363
Personnel/human resource management.
  4.4364
Personnel interviewing, theory and practice.
  4.4373

Personnel policies in large nonunion companies. 4.4368
Perspective in perspective. 1.5117
A perspective of wages and prices. 4.3442
Perspective on the nature of geography. 4.15
Perspectives. 4.10507
Perspectives and irony in American slavery. 3.7193
Perspectives in American history. 3.6110
Perspectives in biology and medicine. 5.4479
Perspectives in creativity. 5.348
Perspectives in psychological theory. 5.3
Perspectives in running water ecology. 5.3568
Perspectives in state school support programs. 4.10664
Perspectives of the Black press, 1974. 2.3649
Perspectives on 19th and 20th century Protestant theology. 1.2758
Perspectives on abortion. 4.5703
Perspectives on black English. 2.1155
Perspectives on cross-cultural psychology. 4.624
Perspectives on deviance. 4.6467
Perspectives on energy. 5.6133
Perspectives on environment. 5.3523
Perspectives on Federal transportation policy. 4.3893
Perspectives on history. 3.469
Perspectives on Latin America. 3.8960
Perspectives on modern literature. 2.5738
Perspectives on Peirce. 1.626
Perspectives on plant population ecology. 5.3769
Perspectives on power. 4.6157
Perspectives on presidential selection. 4.7966
Perspectives on revolution and evolution. 3.6157
Perspectives on Schoenberg and Stravinsky. 1.3461
Perspectives on social group work practice. 4.6504
Perspectives on the development of memory and cognition. 5.606
Perspectives on urban infrastructure. 4.2054
Persuasion and healing. 5.4851
Perturbed spirit. 2.7597
Peru. 3.9283, 3.9292, 3.9306
Peru, a country study. 3.9281
Peru before the Incas. 3.9285
Peruvian contexts of change. 4.5276
The Peruvian experiment reconsidered. 3.9309
Pesikta rabbati; discourses for feasts, fasts, and special Sabbaths. 1.1942
Pesikta rabbati. English. 1.1942
Pestalozzi & education. 4.10190
Pesticides. 5.5412
Pesticides studied in man. 5.4733
Pétain; a biography of Marshal Philippe Pétain of Vichy. 3.2188
Pétain, hero or traitor. 3.2189
Peter Abelard's Ethics. 1.378
Peter and Alexis. 2.1518
Peter Behrens, architect and designer. 1.4987
Peter Camenzind. 2.13775
Peter; disciple, apostle, martyr. 1.2669
Peter Handke and the postmodern transformation. 2.13896
Peter Harrison, first American architect. 1.5310
Peter in the New Testament. 1.2670
Peter Norbeck: prairie statesman. 3.8515
Peter the First. 2.1609
Peter the Great. 3.3098
Peter the Great and the emergence of Russia. 3.3100
Peter the Great, his life and world. 3.3099
Peter Weiss: a search for affinities. 2.13921
Peter Wilkins. 2.7179
The Peterborough chronicle, 1070-1154. 3.1750
Peterloo: the case reopened. 3.1749
Petersburg. 2.1474
Peterson's Who offers part-time degree programs? 4.10627
Le Petit chose ... 2.4163
Petit Larousse illustré 1985. 1.23
Petit Robert un. 2.876
La petite Fadette. 2.4290
La Petite Poule d'Eau. 2.4822

The petitioners. 4.9689
Petra. 3.3826, 3.4037
Petrarch. 2.4953-2.4954
Petrarch and his world. 2.4951
Petrarch's lyric poems. 2.4948
The petrified forest. 2.12465
Petrogenesis of metamorphic rocks. 5.3071
Petrography. 5.3041
The petroleum dictionary. 5.6798
Petroleum engineering. 5.6801
Petroleum geology. 5.6803
Petroleum in Venezuela. 4.3758, 4.3777
Petroleum reservoir engineering. 5.6800
Petrologic phase equilibria. 5.3036
Petrology. 5.3035
Petrology of igneous and metamorphic rocks. 5.3047
Petrology of metamorphic rocks. 5.3069
Petrology of the igneous rocks. 5.3046
Petrology of the metamorphic rocks. 5.3067
Petronius. 2.683
Pets and the elderly. 5.5144
The petty demon. 2.1531-2.1532
Peuples et civilisations. 3.520
Peuples et civilisations, histoire générale. 3.520
The peyote cult. 3.5826
Phaedo. 1.250
Phaedra. 2.4047-2.4048, 2.12378
Phaedra and Figaro: Racine's Phèdre. 2.4049
Phaedra and Figaro: Racine's Phèdre. 2.4049
Phaidon dictionary of twentieth-century art. 1.4822
Phaidon guide to glass. 1.6641
Phantasmion. 2.7604
Phantastes. 2.7923
Phantom lady. 2.11880
Pharaoh's people. 3.5139
The Pharmacological basis of therapeutics. 5.5128
The Pharmacopoeia of the United States of America. 5.5150
Pharos and Pharillon. 2.8651
Phase-locked loops. 5.6520
Phase transitions and critical phenomena. 5.2239
Phases of capitalist development. 4.1754
Phèdre. 2.4048
Phenomenological criticism. 2.7279
The Phenomenological Movement. 1.524
Phenomenology and analytical philosophy. 1.521
Phenomenology and existentialism. 1.525
Phenomenology and logic. 1.98
Phenomenology and natural existence. 1.522
Phenomenology and the crisis of philosophy: Philosophy as rigorous science, and Philosophy and the crisis of European man. 1.1010
Phenomenology and the return to beginnings. 1.523
Phenomenology and the science of behaviour. 5.210
Phenomenology and the social sciences. 1.520
Phenomenology and the social world. 1.845
The phenomenology of aesthetic experience. 1.1393
The phenomenology of internal time-consciousness. 1.1009
The phenomenology of Merleau-Ponty. 1.838
Phenomenology of perception. 1.519
Phenomenology of spirit. 1.932
The phenomenology of the social world. 4.4856
The phenomenon of life: toward a philosophical biology;. 1.1319
The phenomenon of man. 1.1332
The phenomenon of religion. 1.1537
Pheromones and reproduction in mammals. 5.4048
Philadelphia. 3.8085, 4.5215
Philadelphia and the China trade, 1682-1846. 4.4220
Philadelphia, here I come! 2.9697
The Philadelphia story. 2.11346
The Philadelphia theatre in the eighteenth century. 2.3231
Philanthropy and Jim Crow in American social science. 3.6604
Philaster. 2.6556

Philebus. 1.251
The Philhellenes. 3.2697
Philip Evergood. 1.5937
Philip Freneau. 2.10873
Philip Freneau and the cosmic enigma. 2.10871
Philip Freneau, champion of democracy. 2.10872
Philip II. 3.3442
Philip II and Macedonian imperialism. 3.2621
Philip II of Spain. 3.3443
Philip Larkin. 2.8945
Philip Massinger, the man and the playwright. 2.6631
Philip of Macedon. 3.2620, 3.2623
Philip Roth. 2.13305-2.13307
Philip V of Macedon. 3.2638
Philippe Bunau-Varilla, the man behind the Panama Canal. 5.5981
Philippics. 2.662
The Philippine atlas. 4.184
The Philippine economy and the United States. 4.2538
Philippine ethnography: a critically annotated and selected bibliography. 5.8065
Philippine industrialization. 4.2539
Philippine short stories, 1925-1940. 2.10135
Philippine short stories, 1941-1955. 2.10136
Philippine social history. 4.5443
Philippine studies. 3.4596
The Philippines. 3.4604, 3.4609, 4.2534-4.2535
Philippines, a country study. 3.4587
The Philippines: public policy and national economic development. 4.2536
The Philippines to the end of the commission government. 3.4601
The Philistines and their material culture. 3.3791
Phillis Wheatley and her writings. 2.10885
Phillis Wheatley in the Black American beginnings. 2.10886
Philo. 1.339, 2.383
Philobiblon. 5.7671
Philological quarterly. 5.8276
Philosopher at large. 1.574
A philosopher looks at science. 5.907
Philosophers and kings. 4.4953
The philosopher's guide to sources, research tools, professional life, and related fields. 5.8342
The philosopher's pupil. 2.9759
The Philosophes and post-revolutionary France. 4.7287
Philosophiae naturalis principia mathematica. 5.1640
Philosophic foundations of quantum mechanics. 5.2120
The philosophic mind. 2.8324
Philosophical analysis. 1.464
Philosophical analysis and history. 3.471
Philosophical analysis; its development between the two World Wars. 1.460
Philosophical and political history of the settlements and trade of the Europeans in the East and West Indies. 3.531
A philosophical basis of medical practice. 5.4557
A philosophical enquiry into the origin of our ideas of the sublime and beautiful. 1.1370
Philosophical explanations. 1.110
Philosophical faith and revelation. 1.1298
Philosophical forum. 4.5901
The philosophical foundations of Marxism. 1.1033
Philosophical foundations of probability theory. 1.1233
Philosophical fragments, Johannes Climacus. 1.1553
Philosophical grammar. 1.1072
Philosophical ideas in the United States. 1.560
Philosophical investigations. 1.1073
Philosophical logic. 1.1152
The philosophical movement in the thirteenth century. 1.356
Philosophical papers. 1.738
Philosophical papers. 1.750
Philosophical papers and letters. 1.863
Philosophical-political profiles. 1.986

Philosophical problems of psychology. 5.62
Philosophical problems of space and time. 1.1340
Philosophical reasoning. 1.1239
Philosophical sketches. 1.605
Philosophical studies. 1.751
Philosophical texts. 1.390
Philosophical theories. 1.109
The Philosophical theory of the state. 4.7440
The philosophical traditions of India. 1.188
Philosophical writings. 1.384, 1.389, 1.655
Philosophical writings of Peirce. 1.622
Philosophie contemporaine. 1.451
La philosophie dans le boudoir. 2.4098
Philosophies of art and beauty. 1.1346
Philosophies of beauty from Socrates to Robert Bridges. 1.1345
Philosophies of education in cultural perspective. 4.10221
Philosophies of India. 1.190
Philosophies of music history. 1.4366
Philosophy. 1.1026
Philosophy after Darwin. 1.445
Philosophy and archaeology. 3.220
Philosophy and education. 4.10163
Philosophy and educational development. 4.10160
Philosophy & history. 3.479
Philosophy and history. 3.487
Philosophy and its place in our culture. 1.113
Philosophy and journalism. 2.3543
Philosophy and linguistics. 1.542
Philosophy and logical syntax. 1.511
Philosophy and myth in Karl Marx. 1.1042
Philosophy and ordinary language. 2.198
Philosophy and psychology in the Abhidharma. 1.2147
Philosophy and the historical understanding. 3.472
Philosophy and the mirror of nature. 1.112
Philosophy and the modern world. 1.440
Philosophy and the nature of language. 1.466
Philosophy and the new physics. 5.1919
Philosophy and the state in France. 4.7285
Philosophy and the world. 1.1024
Philosophy as social expression. 1.125
Philosophy born of struggle. 3.6627
Philosophy East/philosophy West. 1.428
Philosophy for education. 4.9969
Philosophy, history and politics. 3.495
Philosophy in France today. 1.93
Philosophy in Germany, 1831-1933. 1.965
Philosophy in literature. 2.2379
Philosophy in the 20th century. 1.449
Philosophy in the bedroom. 2.4096
Philosophy in the Middle Ages. 1.345
Philosophy in the twentieth century. 1.449
Philosophy looks at the arts. 1.1347
The philosophy of action. 1.1114
The philosophy of Alfred North Whitehead. 1.784
The philosophy of art history. 1.5148
The philosophy of 'As if' 1.1063
The philosophy of Bertrand Russell. 1.771
Philosophy of biological science. 5.3326
The Philosophy of Brand Blanshard. 1.575
The Philosophy of C. I. Lewis. 1.607
The philosophy of civilization. 3.16
The philosophy of David Hume. 1.706
Philosophy of Edmund Burke. 4.7417
Philosophy of education. 4.10162
The philosophy of Ernst Cassirer. 1.981
Philosophy of existence. 1.1025
The philosophy of existence. 1.490
The Philosophy of F.H. Bradley. 1.745
A philosophy of free expression and its constitutional applications. 4.9703
The philosophy of G. E. Moore. 1.756
The Philosophy of Gabriel Marcel. 1.836
The philosophy of Gandhi. 1.208
Philosophy of geohistory, 1785-1970. 5.2948
The philosophy of George Santayana. 1.651
The Philosophy of grammar. 2.165
The philosophy of Hegel. 1.926
Philosophy of history. 3.470
The philosophy of history. 3.477
The philosophy of human nature. 1.162
A Philosophy of ideals. 1.502

The philosophy of J.S. Mill. 1.730
The philosophy of Jean-Paul Sartre. 1.848
The philosophy of John Dewey. 1.593
The philosophy of Jonathan Edwards from his private notebooks. 1.562
The philosophy of Josiah Royce. 1.636
The philosophy of Karl Jaspers. 1.1030
The Philosophy of Karl Popper. 1.758
The philosophy of language. 1.548
The philosophy of Leibniz. 1.871
The philosophy of literary form. 2.2567
Philosophy of logic. 1.1167-1.1168
Philosophy of logics. 1.1175
The philosophy of loyalty. 1.1509
The philosophy of Marsilio Ficino. 1.415
The Philosophy of Martin Buber. 1.976
The philosophy of mathematics. 5.1043
Philosophy of mathematics and natural science. 5.1051
The philosophy of medicine. 5.4516
The philosophy of modern art. 1.4825
The philosophy of moral development. 5.607
The philosophy of Nietzsche ... 1.1045
The Philosophy of open education. 4.10308
Philosophy of painting by Shih-T'ao. 1.6332
The philosophy of physical science. 5.1905
The philosophy of physics. 5.1918
Philosophy of Plato and Aristotle. 1.372
The philosophy of Plotinus. 1.342
The philosophy of Popper. 1.757
The philosophy of quantum mechanics. 5.2107
Philosophy of recreation and leisure. 4.877
The philosophy of rhetoric. 2.2532
Philosophy of right. 4.9362
The philosophy of Robert Grosseteste. 1.385
The philosophy of Rousseau. 1.818
The philosophy of Rudolf Carnap. 1.578
The philosophy of Santayana. 1.643
The philosophy of Sarvepalli Radhakrishnan. 1.209
The philosophy of Schopenhauer. 1.963
Philosophy of science. 5.864, 5.885, 5.918
The philosophy of science. 5.937
A philosophy of science for personality theory. 5.533
Philosophy of science today. 5.913
The philosophy of space & time. 1.1341
The philosophy of Spinoza. 1.1102
The philosophy of St. Bonaventure. 1.383
The philosophy of St. Thomas Aquinas. 1.393
The philosophy of symbolic forms. 1.980
The philosophy of the act. 1.613
The philosophy of the Church fathers. 1.2750
The Philosophy of the curriculum. 4.10427
The philosophy of the enlightenment. 1.433
The philosophy of the inductive sciences, founded upon their history. 5.942
The philosophy of the present. 1.614
The philosophy of the sixteenth and seventeenth centuries. 1.398
The philosophy of Upanishads. 1.177
The philosophy of W.V. Quine. 1.633
The philosophy of Wang Yang-ming. 1.175
The philosophy of wealth. 4.1425
The philosophy of Wilhelm Dilthey. 1.984
The philosophy of Wittgenstein. 1.1085
Philosophy of woman. 4.5938
Philosophy, politics and society. 4.7213, 4.7254
Philosophy, politics, and society, fifth series. 4.7230
Philosophy, politics and society, fourth series. 4.7227
Philosophy, politics, and society, third series. 4.7276
Philosophy, science and the sociology of knowledge. 1.1291
Philostratus, Imagines. 2.384
Phineas Finn. 2.8218
Phineas redux. 2.8219
Phoenix. 2.8952
The phoenix and the spider. 2.1260
Phonemics. 2.184
Phonetics. 2.183, 2.185, 2.1017
The phonetics of Russian. 2.1227
Phonics in proper perspective. 4.10465
Phonological analysis. 2.1013
Phonology. 2.175
Photo-lab index. 5.6941

Photo-secession. 5.6965
Photochemistry. 5.2919
The Photochemistry of atmospheres. 5.2514
Photodiscovery. 5.6967
The photograph collector's guide. 5.6913
The photographer's eye. 5.6969
Photographic anatomy of the human body. 5.4147
Photographic image. 5.6977
Photographic materials and processes. 5.6935
Photographic sketch book of the Civil War. 3.7349
A Photographic vision. 5.6956
Photographs of a lifetime. 5.6972
Photography, essays & images. 5.6943
Photography, essays and images. 5.6943
Photometry and radiometry for engineers. 5.2321
Photoreceptors. 5.4385
Photosynthesis. 5.3759, 5.3762
Photosynthetic systems. 5.3757
Photovoltaic energy systems. 5.6326
The phrasal verb in English. 2.1030
Phrasing and articulation. 1.4496
Phycology. 5.3710
Phyllis McGinley. 2.12080
Physical acoustics. 5.2227
Physical and applied acoustics. 5.2229
Physical and sexual abuse of children. 4.6569
Physical biochemistry. 5.3331, 5.3498
Physical causality, The child's conception of. 5.571
Physical ceramics for engineers. 5.5797
Physical chemistry. 5.2797-5.2798, 5.2800, 5.2802-5.2805, 5.3336
Physical chemistry for the life sciences. 5.2799
Physical chemistry of macromolecules. 5.2843
Physical chemistry of nucleic acids. 5.2795
Physical chemistry of surfaces. 5.2896
Physical climatology. 5.2565
The physical conditions of the Elizabethan public playhouse. 2.3291
Physical cosmology. 5.1876
Physical design of electronic systems. 5.6479
The physical dimensions of consciousness. 5.258
Physical disabilities and health impairments. 5.5092
The Physical environment at work. 5.5618
Physical geography. 4.241
Physical geography of Asiatic Russia. 4.254
The physical geography of the sea. 4.324
Physical geology. 5.2968
Physical hydrogeology. 4.307
Physical metallurgy. 5.6770, 5.6777
The physical metallurgy of steels. 5.6783
Physical metallurgy principles. 5.6778
Physical meteorology. 5.2503
Physical methods in determinative mineralogy. 5.3017
Physical methods in modern chemical analysis. 5.2658
Physical oceanography of coastal waters. 4.343
Physical organic chemistry. 5.2847, 5.2852
Physical organic chemistry. 5.2853, 5.2858
The physical principles of the quantum theory. 5.2112
Physical properties. 5.6858
Physical properties of chemical compounds. 5.2810
The physical properties of glass. 5.5802
Physical properties of polymers. 5.5804
Physical properties of rocks and minerals. 5.3038
Physical quality of life index. 4.1815
Physical science for biologists. 5.1981
Physical science in the Middle Ages. 5.731
Physical theory. 5.1901
Physical thought from the Presocratics to the quantum physicists. 5.1935
The physical treatises of Pascal. 5.2035
The physical universe. 5.1706
The physical world, The nature of. 5.879
Physicalism. 5.33
The physically handicapped. 5.8293
Physically handicapped children. 5.5083
The physician and sexuality in Victorian America. 4.5225

Physicians' desk reference for nonprescription drugs. 5.5141
Physicians, law, and ethics. 5.4559
Physicists. 5.1942
The physicist's conception of nature. 5.894
Physicochemical processes for water quality control. 6.6026
Physics. 5.833
Physics and archaeology. 3.226
Physics and beyond. 5.2063
The physics and chemistry of color. 5.2334
The physics and circuit properties of transistors. 5.6503
Physics and geology. 5.3074
Physics and its fifth dimension: society. 5.754
Physics and philosophy. 5.1911
Physics and politics. 4.7438
The physics and technology of xerographic processes. 5.7012
Physics for biology and medicine. 5.1986
Physics for poets. 5.1984
Physics for the inquiring mind. 5.1995
Physics in biology and medicine. 5.3493
Physics in my generation. 5.2015
Physics in the twentieth century: selected essays. 5.2020
The physics of blown sand and desert dunes. 5.3121
The physics of clouds. 5.2536
The physics of cosmic x-ray, gamma-ray, and particle sources. 5.2494
The physics of dance. 5.4282
The physics of metals. 5.5808
The physics of nuclear reactions. 5.2478
Physics of nuclei and particles. 5.2428
The Physics of pulsars. 5.1779
The physics of semiconductor devices. 5.2348
Physics of semiconductor devices. 5.6500
Physics of semiconductor laser devices. 5.5955
Physics of semiconductors. 5.2352
Physics of solids. 5.2201
The physics of sound. 5.2224
The physics of speech. 5.4279
The physics of stars. 5.1827
The physics of stellar interiors. 5.1836
Physics of the air. 5.2502
Physics of the earth. 5.2490
The physics of the stratosphere. 5.2510
The physics of time asymmetry. 5.2094
The physics of vibration. 5.2034
The Physics of welding. 5.7062
Physics. Part Two. 5.1982
Physics, principles with applications. 5.1993
Physics through the 1990's. 5.1941
Physiography of eastern United States. 4.249
Physiography of western United States. 4.250
Physiological and biochemical methods. 5.3708
Physiological anthropology. 4.441
Physiological approach to the lower animals. 5.4178
Physiological basis of medical practice. 5.4191
Physiological ecology of North American plant communities. 5.3670
Physiological plant ecology. 5.3767
Physiological, psychological, and social effects of noise. 6.6648
Physiological psychology. 5.4295
Physiology. 5.4196
Physiology and biochemistry of exercise. 5.4271
The Physiology and biochemistry of plant respiration. 5.3763
Physiology of annelids. 5.3841
The physiology of diving in man and other animals. 5.5023
Physiology of exercise. 5.4268
The physiology of fishes. 5.3913
Physiology of fitness. 5.5028
The physiology of human survival. 5.4202
The physiology of insect metamorphosis. 5.3873
The physiology of insect senses. 5.3866
The physiology of nerve cells. 5.4286
Physiology of parasites. 5.4079
Physiology of the nervous system. 5.4322
Phytoplankton manual. 5.3778
Piaget and education. 5.589
The pianist's guide to pedaling. 1.4542

The pianist's problems. 1.4537
The piano. 1.4153
Piano and song. 1.4417
The piano in chamber ensemble. 1.3567
The piano teacher's source book. 1.3585
Piano technique consisting of the two complete books The shortest way to pianistic perfection and Rhythmics, dynamics, pedal and other problems of piano playing. 1.4539
The piano works of Claude Debussy. 1.4534
Pianos and their makers. 1.4152
Piazzetta. 1.5016
Picasso. 1.6130-1.6131
Picasso, birth of a genius. 1.6128
Picasso in perspective. 1.6132
Picasso, in retrospect. 1.6133
Picasso on art. 1.5145
Picasso: the blue and rose periods. 1.6129
Picasso's Guernica. 1.6127
Picked-up pieces. 2.13373
Pictorial anatomy of the cat. 5.3999
Pictorial astronomy. 5.1711
Pictorial dictionary of ancient Athens. 1.5223
Pictorial dictionary of ancient Rome. 1.5227
Pictorial guide to the planets. 5.1799
A pictorial history of Chinese architecture. 1.5448
A pictorial history of jazz. 1.4330
A pictorial history of music. 1.3494
A pictorial history of the American carnival. 4.1195
A pictorial history of the American theatre, 1860-1985. 2.3206
The pictorial history of the Russian theatre. 2.3380
A pictorial history of vaudeville. 2.2831
A pictorial life of Jack London. 2.12033
The picture history of photography. 5.6920
The picture of Dorian Gray. 2.8270
Pictures from an institution. 2.11926
Pictures from Italy. 3.2823, 3.6032
Pictures of Fidelman. 2.13161
Picturesque expressions. 2.1106
The picturesque garden in France. 5.5376
Picturesque in architecture, landscape, and garden design. 5.5371
The picturesque prison. 2.9505
Picturing. 2.6011
Pidgin and creole linguistics. 2.2336
A piece of my mind. 2.9783
A piece of the pie. 3.6519
Pieces and pontifications. 2.12100
Pièces brillantes: L'invitation au château, Colombe, La répétition ou L'amour puni [et] Cécile, ou L'école des pères. 2.4358
Pièces costumés. 2.4359
Pièces noires. 2.4360
Pièces roses. 2.4357
Piero della Francesca. 1.6203
Pierre Auguste Renoir. 1.6142
Pierre Bonnard. 1.6066
Pierre Corneille. 2.4018
Pierre écrite. 2.4417-2.4418
Pierre Joseph Proudhon. 4.1361
Pierre-Joseph Proudhon, his revolutionary life, mind, and works. 4.7051
Pierre Loti. 2.4331
Pierre Mendès France. 3.2211
Pierre S. Du Pont and the making of the modern corporation. 4.3792
Piers Plainness. 2.6491
Piers plowman. 2.6399
Piers Plowman. 2.6390, 2.6394, 2.6396, 2.6403-2.6404
Piers Plowman and the scheme of salvation. 2.6400
Piers Plowman as a fourteenth-century apocalypse. 2.6397
Piers Plowman, the A version. 2.6395
Piers Plowman, the evidence for authorship. 2.6401
Piers the ploughman. 2.6393
Piers the Plowman: literary relations of the A and B texts. 2.6405
Pietas et societas. 1.2326
Pieter de Hooch. 1.6249
Piety versus moralism. 1.2764
Pig production. 5.5451

Pigeon feathers, and other stories. 2.13374
Pigs for the ancestors. 3.5655
Pigs, pearlshells, and women. 4.860
Pilgrim at sea. 2.14093
Pilgrim colony. 3.7989
The pilgrim hawk. 2.12675
Pilgrimage. 1.2310, 2.9283
Pilgrimage and storytelling in the Canterbury tales. 2.6327
Pilgrimage in the Hindu tradition. 1.1721
Pilgrimage to China in search of the law. 3.4616
The Pilgrims. 3.7988
Pilgrims in their own land. 1.2379
The Pilgrim's progress. 2.6919
The pilgrim's progress from this world to that which is to come. 2.6918
Pilgrims through space and time. 2.3486
The pill versus the Springhill mine disaster. 2.11413
The pillars of society. 3.2986
Pillars of the republic. 4.10023
The pillow book of Sei Shōnagon. 2.2052
Pills, petticoats, and plows. 3.8156
Piloting, seamanship and small boat handling. 5.7511
The Piltdown men. 4.454
A Pima past. 3.5938
Pinckney's treaty. 3.7037
Pindar. 2.531
Pindar's odes. 2.529
Pindar's Olympian one. 2.525
Pindar's Victory songs. 2.527
Pink Marsh. 2.10892
Pinnacles of India'a past. 1.1679
Pinter. 2.9792-2.9793
Pío Baroja. 2.5233
Pioneer. 4.10997
The pioneer fringe. 4.378
A pioneer gentlewoman in British Columbia. 3.8866
Pioneer Jews. 3.8494
Pioneer urbanites. 3.8630
Pioneer women. 4.6075
Pioneering the Union Pacific. 4.4012
Pioneers and profits: land speculation on the Iowa frontier. 4.2830
Pioneers in criminology. 4.6679
Pioneers in development. 4.2749
Pioneers of modern art in America. 1.5904
Pioneers of modern design, from William Morris to Walter Gropius. 1.4791
Pioneers of modern economics in Britain. 4.1347
Pioneers of prefabrication. 5.6094
Pioneers of science. 5.1944
Pious and secular America. 3.6149
The pipe dream of peace. 4.9166
The piper & the bard. 2.7428
Pisa in the early Renaissance. 3.2951
Pissarro, his life and work. 1.6136
Pissing in the snow and other Ozark folktales. 4.779
The pistol. 2.13101
The pit. 2.1515
Pitchfork Ben Tillman, South Carolinian. 3.7451
Pitfalls of analysis. 4.1236
Pittsburgh. 3.8094
Pittsburgh: the story of a city, 1750-1865. 3.8093
Pittsburgh's Post-gazette. 2.3668
The pity of it all. 4.6453
PL94-142. 4.9599
A place called school. 4.10032
A place in the sun. 1.2808
A place in time. 3.8217
The Place of Bonhoeffer. 1.3365
The place of business in America's future. 4.4255
The place of science in modern civilisation, and other essays. 4.1272
The place of the lion. 2.9528
The place of the reign of Edward 2 in English history. 3.1366
The place of value in a world of facts. 1.1302
A place on the corner. 4.4931
A place to come to. 2.12645

A place to feel at home. 1.2472
A place to grow old. 4.5825
Placebos and the philosophy of medicine.
    5.4550
Places for learning, places for joy. 4.10044
The plague. 2.4453
A plague of corn. 5.4987
The plague of the Spanish lady. 5.4763
The plague pamphlets of Thomas Dekker.
    2.6448
Plague, population, and the English economy,
    1348-1530. 4.1693
Plagued by the nightingale. 2.11405
Plagues and peoples. 5.4681
A plain account of Christian perfection. 1.2933
A plain and easy introduction to practical
    music. 1.4433
A plain & easy introduction to the harpsichord.
    1.4544
Plain & fancy. 5.7095
Plain folk of the Old South. 3.8148
The plain man. 2.9392
The plain people of Boston, 1830-1860. 4.1683
The plain people of the Confederacy. 3.8153
Plain pleasures. 2.11401
Plain speaking. 3.7812
Plain tales from the Raj. 3.4199
The plains across. 3.8487
Plains country towns. 4.6243
Plains woman. 3.8525
Plainville fifteen years later. 4.5129
Plainville, U. S. A. 4.5149
Plan and market. 4.2227
Plan and market in Yugoslav economic
    thought. 4.2425
The Plan of St. Gall. 1.3237
Planar optical waveguides and fibres. 5.5961
The Planetarium. 2.4711
Le planétarium. 2.4710
Planetary geology. 5.1805
Planetary interiors. 5.1806
Planets and planetarians. 5.1800
The planiverse. 5.1639
Planned behavior change. 4.6487
The planned economies of Eastern Europe.
    4.2240
Planning a tragedy. 3.4499
Planning academic and research library
    buildings. 5.7615
Planning and design of airports. 5.6685
Planning and design of ports and marine
    terminals. 5.5972
Planning and estimating underground
    construction. 5.5911
Planning and politics. 4.2294
Planning and problem solving in marketing.
    4.4275
Planning and producing instructional media.
    4.10325
Planning for agricultural development. 4.2899
Planning for economic growth in the Soviet
    Union, 1918-1932. 4.2390
Planning for rare events. 5.6299
Planning fundamentals of thermal power plants.
    5.6292
Planning Jerusalem. 1.5608
Planning of experiments. 5.877
Planning production, inventories, and work
    force. 4.2650
Planning, profit and incentives in the U. S.
    R. 4.2745
Planning reforms in the Soviet Union,
    1962-1966. 4.2396
Plans and the structure of behavior. 5.35
Plans for world peace through six centuries.
    4.9109
Plant anatomy. 5.3738
Plant biochemistry. 5.3751
Plant biosystematics. 5.3653
Plant chemosystematics. 5.3650
Plant classification. 5.3655
Plant closings and economic dislocation.
    4.3204
Plant disease handbook. 5.5400
Plant extinction. 5.3646
Plant geography. 5.3663, 5.3666
Plant growth and development. 5.3745
Plant growth regulators. 5.5322

The plant hunters. 5.5344
The plant kingdom. 5.3641
Plant layout and material handling. 5.7018
Plant life through the ages. 5.3176
Plant location, layout, and maintenance.
    5.7022
Plant mineral nutrition. 5.3754
Plant pathology and plant pathogens. 5.5396
Plant physiology. 5.3740, 5.3743
Plant propagation. 5.5318
Plant protection. 5.5410
The plant protection discipline. 5.5411
Plant sociology. 5.3765
Plant speciation. 5.3382
Plant systematics. 5.3652
Plant taxonomy: methods and principles.
    5.3649
Plant variation and evolution. 5.3790
Plant viruses. 5.4472
Plantation agriculture. 4.2875
The plantation mistress. 4.6073
The plantation of Ulster. 4.2851
Plantation slavery in Barbados. 4.6437
Plantation slavery on the east coast of Africa.
    4.6450
Planters and the making of a 'new South'
    4.2038
Planters of colonial Virginia. 3.8203
Planting Corn Belt culture. 3.8376
The planting of Christianity in Africa. 1.2468
The planting of civilization in western
    Pennsylvania. 3.8071
Plants and civilization. 5.5312
Plants in the landscape. 5.5381
Plants of the Bible. 1.2557
Plants that merit attention. 5.5362
Plasma physics. 5.2380
Plasma physics via computer simulation.
    5.2385, 5.2388
Plasmas, laboratory and cosmic. 5.2384
Plasmids. 5.4450
Plastic art and pure plastic art, 1937, and other
    essays, 1941-1943. 1.4817
The plastic deformation of metals. 5.5811
Plastics. 5.6908
Plastics as sculpture. 1.5785
Plastics engineering handbook of the Society of
    the Plastics Industry, inc. 5.6911
Plate tectonics and geomagnetic reversals.
    5.3091
Platero y yo. 2.5268
Plato. 1.261-1.262, 1.267, 2.388, 4.7350
Plato: a collection of critical essays. 1.268
Plato and education. 4.10183
Plato and Parmenides. 1.248
Plato on beauty, wisdom, and the arts. 1.270
Plato on punishment. 1.274
Platonism. 1.258
Platonism and the spiritual life. 1.649
Plato's analytic method. 1.271
Plato's cosmology. 1.255
Plato's doctrines. 1.260
Plato's earlier dialectic. 1.280
Plato's epistles. 1.256
Plato's Euthyphro, Apology of Socrates and
    Crito. 2.532
Plato's modern enemies and the theory of
    natural law. 1.275
Plato's moral theory. 1.273
Plato's Parmenides. 1.249
Plato's philosophy of mathematics. 1.281
Plato's theory of ideas. 1.277
Plato's theory of knowledge. 1.253, 1.278
Plato's theory of understanding. 1.279
Plato's thought. 1.263
Plato's thought in the making. 1.265
Plato's universe. 1.228
Plato's use of fallacy. 1.246
Plautus. 2.684
Plautus and Terence. 2.761
Plautus in performance. 2.763
Plautus, the darker comedies. 2.760
The play, a critical anthology. 2.3761
Play and playthings. 4.5728
Play as exploratory learning. 4.10388
The play called Corpus Christi. 2.5853
Play directing. 2.3110

Play, dreams, and imitation in childhood.
    5.572
Play index. 5.8132
Play it as it lays. 2.12984
Play-making. 2.2794
Play of double senses: Spenser's Faerie queene.
    2.6530
The play of the gods. 1.1716
Play parade. 2.8582
The play, The ballad of the sad café. 2.12840
Play therapy. 4.10387
Player piano. 2.13395
Players' scepters. 2.5905
Playful fictions and fictional players. 2.10585
Playing God in the nursery. 5.5089
Playing the game. 2.10555
The playmakers. 2.3227
Plays. 2.1467
... Plays. 2.4353
Plays. 2.4568, 2.7438, 2.7847, 2.9621, 2.9654,
    2.10990, 2.13623
Plays ... 2.12283
... Plays. 2.4651
Plays. 2.4773, 2.9242, 2.13648
The plays and novels of Peter Handke.
    2.13897
Plays & players. 2.3320
Plays & poems. 2.7246
The plays and poems of J. M. Synge. 2.8145
The plays and poems of Philip Massinger.
    2.6629
The plays & poems of Robert Greene. 2.6582
Plays and stories. 2.13860
Plays by Alexander Ostrovsky ... 2.1405
Plays by American women. 2.10791
Plays by American women, 1900-1930.
    2.10791
Plays by David Garrick and George Colman
    the elder. 2.6236
Plays by W.S. Gilbert. 2.7727
Plays for England. 2.9212
Plays from black Africa. 2.10047
Plays from the cynical life. 2.14069
Plays in one volume. 2.7388
The plays of Arnold Wesker. 2.9828
Plays of confession and therapy. 2.14073
The plays of David Garrick. 2.7031
The plays of Eugene O'Neill. 2.12296
The plays of Frances Sheridan. 2.7243
The plays of George Lillo. 2.7096
The plays of Hrotswitha of Gandersheim.
    2.820
The plays of Ivan S. Turgenev. 2.1448
The plays of John Marston. 2.6622
The plays of John Osborne. 2.9215
The plays of Max Frisch. 2.13749
The plays of Oscar Wilde. 2.8289
Plays of our time. 2.10794
The plays of Richard Brinsley Sheridan.
    2.7244
The plays of Richard Steele. 2.7269
The plays of Sir George Etherege. 2.7009
The plays of Susanna Centlivre. 2.6930
The plays of Thornton Wilder. 2.12722
Plays of W.B. Yeats. 2.8364
The plays of William Wycherley. 2.7338
Plays, one. 2.9780
The playwright as magician. 2.6829
The playwright as thinker. 2.2806
Playwrights for tomorrow. 2.10792
Playwrights of the new American theater.
    2.10521
Playwrights on playwriting. 2.2797
The pleasant comedy of young fortunatus.
    2.11512
The pleasant memoirs of the Marquis de
    Bradomín. 2.5292
A pleasant vintage of Till Eulenspiegel, born in
    the country of Brunswick. 2.13514
Pleasurable instruction. 2.5933
Pleasure and danger. 4.5512
Pleistocene mammals of North America.
    5.3172
Plekhanov. 4.7087
Plexus. 2.12189
The PLO and Palestine. 3.3906
Plot summary index. 5.8275
Plotinus. 1.343, 2.389

The plough and the stars. 2.2282
Ploughshares. 2.10848
The Ploughshares reader. 2.10848
The Plumed Serpent, Quetzalcoatl. 2.8969
Plunkitt of Tammany Hall. 4.8215
The plural society in the British West Indies. 4.5266
Pluralism and political geography. 4.7499
Pluralist democracy in the United States: conflict and consent. 4.7306
A pluralistic universe. 1.452
Plutarch and his times. 2.536
Plutarch and Rome. 2.537
Plutarch's Lives. 2.538
Plutarch's Moralia. 2.390
The plutonium business and the spread of the bomb. 5.6620
Pnin. 2.12229
Pobedonostsev, his life and thought. 3.3132
A pocket full of rye. 2.8516
The pocket mirror. 2.10220
Poe. 2.11204, 2.11206
Poe, a biography. 2.11202
Poe Poe Poe Poe Poe Poe Poe. 2.11208
The poem of the Cid. 2.5184, 2.5186-2.5187
Poema de mio Cid. 2.5185
Poèmes. 2.4417, 2.4425
Poèmes. 2.4863
Poèmes, 1916-1955. 2.4476
Poèmes choisis, 1931-1959. 2.4770
Poems. 2.6433, 2.6909, 2.7346
The poems. 1.2214
Poems. 2.1706, 2.4262, 2.6562, 2.6621, 2.6941, 2.6951-2.6952, 2.6988, 2.7010, 2.7093, 2.7113, 2.7498, 2.7615, 2.7848, 2.8806, 2.9090, 2.9689, 2.13770
Poems. 2.5048, 2.6547, 2.7174, 2.7187, 2.7226, 2.7291, 2.8016, 2.8156, 2.9125, 2.9373, 2.10163, 2.10875, 2.10883, 2.11216, 2.13638
The poems. 2.8330
Poems 3. 2.12997
Poems 4. 2.12998
Poems, 1645, together with poems from Bodleian MS Don d 55. 2.7329
Poems, 1906 to 1926. 2.13851
Poems, 1913-1956. 2.13704
Poems, 1922-1961. 2.11553
Poems, 1934-1969. 2.11914
Poems, 1957-1967. 2.12975
Poems, 1960-1967. 2.13134
Poems, 1965-1975. 2.9702
Poems 1968-1972. 2.13135
Poems, a selection. 2.11291
Poems, and A defence of ryme. 2.6444
Poems and contradictions. 2.9465
Poems and dramas of Fulke Greville first lord Brooke. 2.6434
Poems and essays. 2.9904
Poems and fragments. 2.13613
The poems and letters of Andrew Marvell. 2.7103
The poems and plays of William Vaughn Moody. 2.11175
Poems & political letters of F. I. Tyutchev. 2.1426
Poems and sketches of E.B. White. 2.12703
Poems and some letters. 2.8197
The poems and songs of Robert Burns. 2.7497
Poems & texts; an anthology of French poems. 2.3932
Poems & translations. 2.8935
Poems & translations, 1850-1870. 2.8014
Poems, ballads and sonnets; selections from the posthumous poems and from his translations; Hand and soul. 2.8015
Poems by Faiz. 2.1900
The Poems, English & Latin, of Edward, Lord Herbert of Cherbury. 2.6485
Poems from East Africa. 2.10046
Poems from Hesperides and Noble numbers. 2.7072
Poems from Iqbal. 2.1901
Poems from Korea. 2.2140
Poems from the Old English. 2.6284
Poems in persons. 2.2400
Poems of Alexander Lawrence Posey, Creek Indian bard. 2.11213

The poems of Algernon Charles Swinburne. 2.8135
The poems of Ambrose Philips. 2.7182
Poems of André Breton. 2.4421
The poems of Archibald Lampman (including At the Long Sault). 2.9936
The poems of Arthur Hugh Clough. 2.7577
Poems of Arthur O'Shaughnessy. 2.7978
Poems of Black Africa. 2.2306
The poems of Charles Kingsley. 2.7877
The poems of Charles of Orleans. 2.3969
The poems of Charlotte Brontë. 2.7445, 2.7447
The poems [of] Christopher Marlowe. 2.6609
The poems of Coventry Patmore. 2.7986
The poems of Cynewulf. 2.6305
The poems of Dylan Thomas. 2.9401
The poems of Emily Dickinson. 2.10994
The poems of George Herbert. 2.7060
The poems of George Meredith. 2.7939
The poems of Gerard Manley Hopkins. 2.7825
The poems of John Davidson. 2.7620
The poems of John Donne. 2.6452
The poems of John Keats. 2.7850
The poems of John Milton. 2.7112
The poems of Longfellow. 2.11144
The poems of Ossian. 2.7100
The poems of Patrick Cary. 2.6929
Poems of René Char. 2.4465
The poems of Richard Lovelace. 2.7097
The poems of Richard Wilbur. 2.12708
The poems of Robert Henryson. 2.6386
The poems of Robert Southwell, S.J. 2.6520
The poems of Samuel Johnson. 2.7080
The poems of Samuel Taylor Coleridge. 2.7587
The poems of Sir Philip Sidney. 2.6506
The poems of Sir Walter Raleigh. 2.6501
The poems of Stanley Kunitz, 1928-1978. 2.11972
The poems of T. Sturge Moore. 2.9124
The poems of Tennyson. 2.8153
Poems of the late T'ang. 2.2190
Poems of the past and the present. 2.7762
The poems of Thomas Carew. 2.6443
The poems of Thomas Hardy. 2.7793
The poems of Trumbull Stickney. 2.12555
Poems of William Carlos Williams. 2.12755
The poems of William Cowper. 2.6957
The poems of William Dunbar. 2.6475
The poems of William Habington. 2.7059
Poems of wisdom and learning in Old English. 2.6283
Poems on affairs of State. 2.6121
The poems, prose and plays by Alexander Pushkin. 2.1411
Poems retrieved. 2.12264
Poems: selected and new, 1950-1974. 2.12383
Poems to the child-god. 2.1879
Poe's tales. 2.11209
Poesía completa. 2.5427
Poesia del Novecento. 2.4895
Poesía española del siglo veinte. 2.5147
Poesías completas. 2.5272, 2.5372, 2.5415
Poésie. 2.4235
Poesie ... 2.5047
Poesie. 2.4978, 2.5011
Poésie du Québec. 2.4806
Poesie, teatro, prose. 2.5018
Poesies. 2.4249
Poésies de Théodore de Banville. 2.4130-2.4131
The poet and her book. 2.12163
The poet as citizen, and other papers. 2.2587
The poet Chaucer. 2.6339
Poet in New York. 2.5256
The poet Lucan. 2.737
Poet of exile. 2.7157
Poetae melici Graeci. 2.319
Poetarum Lesbiorum fragmenta ediderunt Edgar Lobel et Denys Page. 2.315
Poetas espanoles contemporánes. 2.5119
Poètes du Québec, 1860-1968. 2.4807
Poètes du XVIe siècle. 2.3929
Poètes et romanciers du moyen âge. 2.3944
Poeti del Duecento. 2.4889-2.4892
The poetic achievement of Ezra Pound. 2.12337
The poetic art of Robert Lowell. 2.12054
Poetic artifice. 2.10491

Poetic closure. 2.2735
Poetic creation. 2.2760
Poetic diction. 2.2713
Poetic discourse. 2.2718
The poetic image. 2.2742
The poetic themes of Robert Lowell. 2.12052
Poetic unreason. 2.2716
The poetic vision of Muriel Rukeyser. 2.12419
The Poetic world of Boris Pasternak. 2.1596
The poetic world of William Carlos Williams. 2.12753
The poetical and dramatic works of Sir Charles Sedley. 2.7238
Poetical works. 2.6934, 2.7351, 2.7518
The poetical works. 2.6983
Poetical works. 2.7070, 2.7237, 2.7849, 2.8042
The poetical works. 2.7240
Poetical works, including the plays. 2.8154
The poetical works of Alain Chartier. 2.3971
The poetical works of Alexander McLachlan. 2.9905
The poetical works of Christina Georgina Rossetti. 2.8008
The poetical works of Christopher Smart. 2.7254
The poetical works of Edmund Spenser. 2.6523
The poetical works of Edward Young. 2.7344
The poetical works of George Crabbe. 2.7614
Poetical works of Goldsmith. 2.7042
Poetical works of Henry Lawson. 2.10150
The poetical works of John Gay. 2.7034
The Poetical works of Leigh Hunt. 2.7842
The poetical works of Mark Akenside. 2.6890
The poetical works of Robert Browning. 2.7474
The poetical works of Rupert Brooke. 2.8485
The poetical works of Thomas Traherne. 2.7320
The poetical works of Whittier. 2.11283
The poetical works of William Cowper. 2.6958
The poetical works of William Cullen Bryant. 2.10915
The poetical works of William Drummond of Hawthornden. 2.6473
The poetical works of William Wordsworth. 2.8298
Poetics and interpretation of biblical narrative. 1.2534
Poetics of change. 2.5315
The poetics of manhood. 4.5835
Poetics of music in the form of six lessons. 1.4001
The poetics of Paul Valéry. 2.4768
The poetics of space. 1.825
Poetics of the holy. 2.7132
Poetics of the new American poetry. 2.2729
The poetics of Yves Bonnefoy. 2.4420
Poetics today. 2.33
Poetik des Barock. 2.2737
Poetische Werke. 2.13602
Poetries and sciences. 2.2722
Poetry. 2.2723, 2.6314
Poetry and anarchism. 4.7189
Poetry and change. 2.5755
Poetry and civilization. 2.10274
Poetry and crisis in the age of Chaucer. 2.5616
Poetry and criticism. 2.2462
Poetry and criticism of Matthew Arnold. 2.7348
Poetry and criticism of the romantic movement. 2.6171
The poetry and poetics of Amiri Baraka. 2.12872
Poetry and poets. 2.10500
Poetry & prose. 2.6953
Poetry and prose. 2.6455, 2.13604
Poetry & prose. 2.7909
The poetry and prose of E. E. Cummings. 2.11545
Poetry and prose of John Gay. 2.7033
Poetry and the age. 2.2769
Poetry and the modern world. 2.5836
Poetry and truth in Robert Browning's The ring and the book. 2.7475
The Poetry anthology, 1912-1977. 2.10770
Poetry (Chicago) 2.10770
Poetry explication. 5.7972

Poetry in East Germany. 2.13931
Poetry in English. 2.5745
Poetry in our time. 2.5829
Poetry into drama. 2.297
Poetry, language, thought. 2.2717
The poetry of Adam Mickiewicz. 2.1717
The poetry of American women from 1632 to
    1945. 2.10286
The poetry of architecture. 1.5480
The poetry of Black America. 2.10747
The poetry of Boris Pasternak, 1917-1959.
    2.1593
The poetry of Chaucer. 2.6369
The poetry of Clough. 2.7584
The poetry of commitment in South Africa.
    2.10048
The poetry of Crabbe. 2.7617
The poetry of Dada and sur-realism: Aragon,
    Breton, Tzara, Eluard & Desnos. 2.3883
The Poetry of Dannie Abse. 2.8371
The poetry of Dante. 2.4937
The poetry of Dorothy Wordsworth. 2.8295
The poetry of Dylan Thomas. 2.9421
The poetry of Edmund Spenser. 2.6545
The poetry of Ernest Dowson. 2.7679
The poetry of experience. 2.5783
The poetry of Ezra Pound. 2.12345
A poetry of force and darkness. 2.13072
The poetry of France. 2.3921
The poetry of George Wither. 2.6548
The poetry of Greek tragedy. 2.323
The poetry of Hart Crane. 2.11529
The poetry of history. 3.401
The poetry of Homer. 2.492
The poetry of John Clare. 2.7574
The poetry of John Crowe Ransom. 2.12372
The poetry of John Crowe Ransom. 2.12371
The poetry of Léopold Sédar Senghor. 2.4865
The poetry of Luis Cernuda. 2.5245
The poetry of Matthew Arnold. 2.7363
The poetry of meditation. 2.5805
The poetry of Michelangelo. 2.4969
The poetry of Richard Aldington. 2.8376
The poetry of Robert Browning. 2.7472
The poetry of Robert Frost. 2.11748, 2.11752
The poetry of Robert Graves. 2.8728
Poetry of Shakespeare's plays. 2.6850
The Poetry of Singapore. 2.10137
The poetry of Sir Philip Sidney. 2.6514
The poetry of Stephen Crane. 2.10985
The poetry of Tennyson. 2.8176
The poetry of the Aeneid. 2.804
The poetry of the early T'ang. 2.2166
The poetry of the Faerie queene. 2.6526
The poetry of the Negro, 1746-1970. 2.3747
Poetry of the Netherlands in its European
    context, 1170-1930. 2.13941
The poetry of the Old Testament. 1.2604
Poetry of the Romantic period. 2.5758
Poetry of the Spanish Civil War. 2.2752
Poetry of the Victorian period. 2.6182
The poetry of Thomas Hardy. 2.7774
The poetry of Thomas Kinsella. 2.8936
The poetry of Vachel Lindsay. 2.12015
The poetry of W. B. Yeats. 2.8353
The poetry of W. H. Auden. 2.8409
The poetry of Wang Wei. 2.2215
Poetry, prose and plays. 2.6987
The poetry reviews of Allen Tate, 1924-1944.
    2.10505
A poet's alphabet. 2.2644
Poets and critics. 2.9892
Poets and playwrights: Shakespeare, Jonson,
    Spenser, Milton. 2.2595
Poets in South Africa. 2.10051
Poets in their youth. 2.13325
The poets laureate. 2.5771
Poet's love. 1.3983
The poet's manual and rhyming dictionary.
    2.1046
A poet's notebook. 2.6702
The poets of Prague. 2.1658
Poets of reality. 2.5832
The poets of Russia, 1890-1930. 2.1279
Poets of the English language. 2.3739
Poets of the Tamil anthologies. 2.2281
Poets on Fortune's Hill. 2.5794
Poets on poetry. 2.10502

Poiesis. 2.279
Point counter point. 2.8821
The point of Christology. 1.2866
Point of it. 2.8642
Point of no return. 2.12110
The point of view for my work as an author.
    1.3288
Points of view; five essays. 2.2580
Poison in the pot. 5.5000
Poisoning. 5.4724
Poisonous and venomous marine animals of the
    world. 5.3811
Poisonous plants of the United States and
    Canada. 5.5394
Poland 1981. 3.3347
Poland, a country study. 3.3328
Poland & Czechoslovakia. 3.1910
Poland and the Western powers 1938-1939.
    3.3285
Poland, genesis of a revolution. 3.3345
Poland in the twentieth century. 3.3336
Poland's politics: idealism vs. realism. 3.3277
Poland's self-limiting revolution. 3.3348
The Polaris system development. 5.7445
Polarized light. 5.2296-5.2297
Polaroid Land photography. 5.6944
Polderlands. 4.2927
The Poles. 3.3342
The police and the community. 4.6802
Police and the elderly. 4.6813
The police and the ghetto. 4.6817
The police in society. 4.6837
Police in urban America, 1860-1920. 4.6822
Police interrogation and confessions. 4.9883
Police reform in the United States. 4.6797
Police riots; collective violence and law
    enforcement. 4.6832
Policing, a social behaviorist perspective.
    4.6826
Policraticus. 4.7375
Policy alternatives for a new international
    economic order. 4.4155
Policy analysis and management. 5.8352
Policy and government in Northern Ireland.
    4.8570
Policy and management in special education.
    4.10937
Policy and police. 3.1399
Policy and politics in Britain. 4.8452
Policy and politics in Japan. 4.2554
Policy conflicts in post-Mao China. 4.8734
Policy for the West. 3.1168
Policy making and effective leadership.
    4.10596
The policy-making process. 4.7857
Policy styles in Western Europe. 4.8368
Policymaking for social security. 4.3463
Polish Americans. 3.6587
The Polish August. 3.3341
The Polish brethren. 1.2974
The Polish complex. 1.1707
The Polish drama, 1980-1982. 3.3346
Polish-Jewish relations during the Second
    World War. 3.3987
Polish logic, 1920-1939. 1.1215
Polish plays in translation. 5.8018
Polish politics and the Revolution of November
    1830. 3.3283
Polish postwar economy. 4.2403
Polish romantic drama. 2.1747
The Polish shades and ghosts of Joseph Conrad.
    2.8570
Polish society under German occupation.
    3.3340
Polite essays. 2.2586
Political and civil rights in the United States.
    4.9655
Political and comic characters of Shakespeare.
    2.6804
Political and constitutional ideas of the court
    Whigs. 4.8558
The political and economic development of
    modern Turkey. 4.2568
The political and historical works of Louis
    Napoleon Bonaparte, President of the French
    Republic. 3.2154
Political and legal obligation. 4.7516

Political and social change in modern Egypt:
    historical studies from the Ottoman conquest
    to the United Arab Republic. 3.5130
Political and social thought in the
    contemporary Middle East. 4.7298-4.7299
The political and social thought of Charles A.
    Beard. 3.6251
Political and social upheaval, 1832-1852. 3.699
Political anthropology. 4.609
Political authority and bureaucratic power.
    4.7768
Political awakening in the Belgian Congo.
    3.5426
The political awakening of Africa. 3.5087
The political background of Aeschylean
    tragedy. 2.416
Political campaign communication. 4.7737
Political change in Britain. 4.8501
Political change in France under Richelieu and
    Mazarin, 1624-1661. 4.8577
Political change in Japan. 4.8758
Political change in Latin America. 4.8325
Political change in South Asia. 3.4095
Political change in the metropolis. 4.8858
Political clubs in New York. 4.8195
The political clubs of New York City. 4.8194
The political collapse of Europe. 3.741
Political communication in America. 4.7854
The political community. 4.7503
Political community and the North Atlantic
    area. 4.9131
Political community at the international level.
    4.7546
Political conflict in Thailand. 4.8768
Political control of literature in the USSR,
    1946-1959. 3.3243
The political crisis of the 1850s. 3.7143
Political culture and political change in
    Communist States. 4.7590
Political culture and political development.
    4.7776
The political culture of Japan. 4.8757
The political culture of the American Whigs.
    4.8218
The political development in Nepal, 1950-70.
    4.8777
Political dictionary. 4.7794
Political economics. 4.1286
A political economy of Africa. 4.2603
The Political economy of African foreign
    policy. 3.5098
The political economy of aging. 4.5820
The political economy of agrarian change.
    4.2896
The political economy of bureaucracy. 4.2672
The Political economy of Cameroon. 4.8810
Political economy of contemporary Africa.
    4.2608
The political economy of development. 4.7716
The Political economy of development and
    underdevelopment. 4.2800
The political economy of European trade.
    4.4184
The political economy of Germany in the
    twentieth century. 4.2341
The political economy of global energy. 4.3763
The political economy of growth. 4.2757
The Political economy of income distribution in
    Nigeria. 4.2588
The political economy of Ivory Coast. 4.2623
The political economy of Marx. 4.1326
The Political economy of new and old industrial
    countries. 4.2801
The political economy of prosperity. 4.2001
The political economy of public organizations.
    4.7764
The political economy of regionalism in Africa.
    4.2621
The political economy of slavery. 3.7199
The political economy of socialism. 4.1325
The political economy of soil erosion in
    developing countries. 4.2873
The political economy of the cotton South.
    4.2026
The political economy of the urban ghetto.
    3.6735
The political economy of the welfare state.
    4.2287

The political economy of underdevelopment. 4.1797
Political economy of urban areas. 4.6348
A political economy of Uruguay since 1870. 4.2181
The political element in the development of economic theory. 4.1310
The political elite of Iran. 4.5408
Political elites in Arab North Africa. 3.5189
Political essay on the kingdom of New Spain. 3.8879
Political fictions. 2.5976
Political forces in Spain, Greece, and Portugal. 4.8681
The political foundations of international law. 4.9281
Political freedom. 4.7678
Political geography. 4.7501
A political geography of Africa. 3.5101
A political geography of Community Europe. 4.8361
The political geography of the oceans. 4.9310
Political handbook of the world. 4.7709
The political history of China, 1840-1928. 3.4722
The Political history of England. 3.1242
A political history of Ghana. 3.5340
A political history of Italy. 3.2908
A political history of Japanese capitalism. 4.2547
The political ideas of the utopian socialists. 4.6943
Political ideology: why the American common man believes what he does. 4.5026
Political institutions and social change in continental Europe in the nineteenth century. 4.8357
Political integration and disintegration in the British Isles. 4.8421
The political integration of women. 4.5961
The political involvement of adolescents. 4.5763
Political justice. 4.7250
Political leadership & nihilism. 4.7629
Political leadership and nihilism. 4.7629
Political liberty. 4.7664
The political life and letters of Cavour, 1848-1861. 3.2869
Political life: why people get involved in politics. 4.7241
Political man. 4.7574
Political marketing. 4.7790
Political Messianism. 4.7493
Political money. 4.8123
The political novel. 2.3479
The political novels of Joseph Conrad. 2.8567
Political opposition and local politics in Japan. 4.8891
Political order in changing societies. 4.7219
Political organizations. 4.8038
Political origins of the new diplomacy, 1917-1918. 3.825
Political participation in Communist China. 4.8742
Political participation in the USSR. 4.8654
Political parties. 4.7778
Political parties and civic action groups. 4.8150
Political parties and elections in Austria. 4.8574
Political parties and elections in the French Fifth Republic. 4.8592
Political parties and political development. 4.7786
Political parties and the Canadian social structure. 4.8299
Political parties before the Constitution. 4.8255
Political parties in American history. 4.8153
Political parties in Europe. 4.8377
Political parties in French-speaking West Africa. 3.5377
Political parties in revolutionary Massachusetts. 4.7812
Political parties in the eighties. 4.8163
Political parties in the European Community. 4.8374
Political parties in the Republic of Ireland. 4.8567

Political parties in the West Bank under the Jordanian regime, 1949-1967. 4.8775
Political parties in Western democracies. 4.7780, 4.7783
Political parties, interest groups, and public policy. 4.8157
Political parties of Asia and the Pacific. 4.8694
Political parties of Europe. 4.7775
Political parties of the Americas. 4.8301
Political parties of the world. 4.7781
Political parties, their organization and activity in the modern state. 4.7782
The political philosophies of Plato and Hegel. 4.7349
Political philosophy. 4.7264-4.7265
Political philosophy and rhetoric. 4.8152
The political philosophy of Bakunin. 4.7197
The political philosophy of Hobbes, his theory of obligation. 4.7410
The political philosophy of Hobbes, its basis and its genesis. 4.7409
The political philosophy of Martin Luther King, Jr. 3.6842
Political pilgrims. 4.4967
The political plays of Euripides. 2.456
Political power. 4.7462
Political power and personal freedom. 4.7571
Political power and social classes. 4.7456
Political power and the press. 2.3555
Political power in Birmingham, 1871-1921. 4.8864
Political power in Ecuador. 4.5275
Political power in the ancient world. 3.2526
Political prairie fire. 4.2912
Political pressure and economic policy. 4.2291
Political primer. 3.6388
The political process and foreign policy. 3.7792
Political profiles. 3.7854
Political purpose in trade unions. 4.3652
Political reconstruction in Tennessee. 3.8344
Political representation and elections in Britain. 4.8491
Political risks in international business. 4.3026
The political role of international trades unions. 4.3323
A political romance. 2.7276
Political science. 4.7234
The political South in the twentieth century. 3.8155
The political stage: American drama and theater of the great depression. 2.10516
The political status of the Negro in the age of FDR. 3.6663
Political structure in a changing Sinhalese village. 4.8884
Political studies from spatial perspectives. 4.7500
Political support in Canada. 4.8277
The political system. 4.7224
The political system of Chile. 4.8340
The political system of Napoleon III. 3.2157
The political systems of empires. 4.7225
Political terrorism. 4.6714
Political terrorism. 4.7615
Political theories of the Middle Age. 4.7268
Political theory. 4.7221
Political theory and international relations. 4.8985
Political theory and practice. 4.7223
The political theory of Montesquieu. 4.7427
The political theory of the Federalist. 4.7830
Political thought in early Meiji Japan, 1868-1889. 4.8751
Political thought in England 1848 to 1914. 4.7288
Political thought in England from Locke to Bentham. 4.7294
Political thought in medieval Islam. 4.7272
Political thought in medieval times. 4.7270
The political thought of Mao Tse-tung. 3.4829
The political thought of Martin Luther. 4.7387
The political thought of Pierre-Joseph Proudhon. 4.7445
The Political thought of Plato and Aristotle. 4.7355
The political thought of Sallust. 2.768

The political thought of Thomas Aquinas. 4.7380
The political thought of William of Ockham. 4.7378
The political tradition of the West. 4.7651
The political transformation of Spain after Franco. 4.8680
Political unification, a comparative study of leaders and forces. 4.9248
The political uses of ideology. 1.506
Political woman. 4.5970, 4.6092
Political women in Japan. 4.5958
The political works. 4.7416
The political world of American Zionism. 3.4020
Political writings. 3.680, 4.7232
The political writings of Jean Jacques Rousseau. 4.7432
Political writings: representative selections. 4.7402
The politician. 3.7887
The politicos, 1865-1896. 3.7413
The politics. 4.7340
Politics. 2.350, 4.7233, 4.7453
Politics among nations. 4.9014
Politics and administration. 4.8178
Politics and beef in Argentina; patterns of conflict and change. 4.3697
Politics and change in Spain. 3.3477
Politics and culture in international history. 4.9002
Politics and culture in wartime Japan. 4.8754
Politics and diplomacy of peacemaking. 3.847
Politics and economics of external debt crisis. 4.4726
The politics and economics of public spending. 4.4686
Politics and geographic relationships. 4.7497
Politics & government in California. 4.8267
Politics and government in Malaysia. 4.8728
Politics and government in the Federal Republic of Germany. 4.9914
Politics and grass. 4.2827
Politics and health care organization. 5.4643
Politics and history. 3.456
Politics and history in band societies. 4.513
The politics and management of Canadian economic policy. 4.2123
Politics and markets. 4.2792
Politics and nationhood. 3.3506
The politics and philosophy of economics. 4.1308
Politics and policies in divided Korea. 3.5013
Politics and policies of the Truman Administration. 3.7802
Politics and policy. 4.5155
Politics and power. 4.8040
Politics and power in a slave society. 4.8266
Politics and process in the specialized agencies of the United Nations. 4.9262
Politics and public policy in Kenya and Tanzania. 4.8798
Politics & religion in seventeenth-century France. 3.2017
Politics & remembrance. 4.7562
Politics and remembrance. 4.7562
Politics and social conflict in South India. 3.4324
Politics and society in de Gaulle's republic. 3.2216
Politics and society in India. 3.4296
Politics and statecraft in the kingdom of Greece. 3.2699
Politics and technology in the Soviet Union. 4.2409
Politics and territory. 4.8278
Politics and the arts, letter to M. d'Alembert on the theatre. 2.3104
Politics and the churches in Great Britain, 1832-1868. 1.2446
Politics and the Constitution in the history of the United States. 4.9611
Politics and the military in Israel 1967-1977. 3.3931
Politics and the military in Jordan. 3.4034
Politics and the military in modern Spain. 5.7333
Politics and the novel. 2.3480

Politics and the restraint of science. 5.968
Politics and vision. 4.7266
Politics and world oil economics. 4.3759
Politics, culture, and class in the French Revolution. 3.2097
Politics economics and society in Argentina in the revolutionary period. 3.9242
Politics in America. 4.7850, 4.7992
Politics in Argentina, 1890-1930. 3.9249
Politics in Austria. 4.8573
Politics in Brazil, 1930-1964. 3.9215
Politics in Britain. 4.8414
Politics in China. 4.8737
Politics in Denmark. 4.8674
Politics in England. 4.8417
Politics in France. 4.8587
Politics in Ghana, 1946-1960. 3.5339
Politics in Hungary. 3.1945
Politics in independent Poland 1921-1939. 3.3286
Politics in India. 4.8699
Politics in industrial society. 4.3643
Politics in modern Greece. 4.8620
Politics in New Brunswick. 4.8319
Politics in New Guinea. 4.599
Politics in New Zealand. 4.8824
Politics in Pakistan. 3.4132
Politics in postwar Japanese society. 4.8759
Politics in Renaissance Venice. 3.2914
Politics in Sri Lanka, 1947-1973. 3.4373
Politics in states and communities. 4.8244
Politics in Thailand. 4.8769
Politics in the age of Peel. 4.8408
Politics in the American states. 4.8247
Politics in the ancient world. 4.7332
Politics in the Congo. 3.5429
Politics in the Tokugawa bakufu, 1600-1843. 3.4943
Politics in the United Nations. 4.9240
Politics in the USSR. 4.8646
Politics in Zambia. 4.8797
Politics is adjourned. 3.7731
Politics, law and ritual in tribal society. 4.9352
Politics of a colonial career. 4.9910
The politics of a literary man: William Gilmore Simms. 2.11226
The politics of Afghanistan. 3.4118
The politics of Africa's economic stagnation. 4.2610
The politics of agriculture. 5.5290
The politics of alternative technology. 5.5519
Politics of Aristotle. 4.7339
The politics of backwardness in Hungary, 1825-1945. 3.1939
The politics of basic needs. 4.2614
Politics of Belgium. 4.8635
The politics of Belleville. 4.8863
The politics of broadcast regulation. 4.9541
The politics of bureaucracy. 4.7762
The politics of Canadian foreign policy. 4.9097
The Politics of Canadian public policy. 4.8283
The politics of Ceylon (Sri Lanka) 4.8723
The politics of chaos. 3.8771
The politics of civil liberties. 4.9664
The politics of command. 3.7369
Politics of compromise. 4.8343
The politics of compromise. 4.8679
The politics of Congo-Brazzaville. 3.5387
The politics of Congress. 4.8019
Politics of conscience. 2.9347
The politics of contraception. 5.5052
The politics of cultural despair. 3.2247
The politics of cultural pluralism. 4.7718
The politics of decentralization. 4.8727
The politics of deference. 4.8487
The politics of democracy. 4.8174
The politics of development. 4.2126
The politics of deviance. 4.5074
The politics of disarmament. 4.9162
The politics of domesticity. 4.6027
The politics of drama in Augustan England. 2.5915
The politics of economic reform in the Soviet Union. 4.2399
The politics of education. 4.10752
The politics of education in the States. 4.10663
The Politics of Eurocommunism. 4.7025
The politics of fear. 3.7668

The politics of federalism. 4.8271
The politics of finance. 4.8064
The politics of force. 4.9125
The politics of friendship. 3.2779
The politics of genocide. 3.3972
The politics of history. 3.6913
Politics of hysteria. 3.752
The politics of ideas in the U.S.S.R. 3.3273
The politics of identity. 4.7245
The politics of Indian removal. 3.5867
The politics of inequality. 3.5469
The politics of inertia. 3.7482
The politics of international air transport. 4.4076
The politics of Irish literature. 3.1841
The politics of John W. Dafoe and the Free press. 3.8744
The politics of Korean nationalism. 3.5005
The politics of location. 4.1481
The politics of mass society. 4.7601
The politics of Milton's prose style. 2.7164
The politics of nationalism and devolution. 4.8436
The politics of neglect. 4.6318
The politics of Nepal. 4.8778
The politics of normalcy: governmental theory and practice in the Harding-Coolidge era. 3.7735
The politics of nuclear proliferation. 4.9175
Politics of nursing. 5.5154
The politics of oil. 4.3769
The politics of pollution. 4.2074
The politics of prejudice. 3.8634
The politics of privacy, computers, and criminal justice records. 4.6803
The politics of protest. 4.5163
The politics of provincialism. 4.8200
The politics of public utility regulation. 4.3042
The politics of race in Britain. 3.1292
The politics of race in New York. 3.6801
The politics of reality. 4.5882
The politics of reapportionment. 4.8259
The politics of reproduction. 4.5935
The politics of resistance in France, 1940-1944. 3.1065
The politics of revenue sharing. 4.4662
The politics of rights. 4.9499
The politics of riot commissions, 1917-1970. 4.6726
The politics of schools. 4.10666
The politics of shared power. 4.7864
Politics of Sino-Indian confrontation. 3.4235
The politics of social change in the Middle East and North Africa. 4.5402
The politics of survival. 4.8310
Politics of T.V. violence. 2.2858
Politics of television violence. 2.2858
The politics of the American Civil Liberties Union. 4.7687
The politics of the budgetary process. 4.4684
The politics of the Caribbean community, 1961-79. 4.2156
The politics of the equal rights amendment. 4.6033
The politics of the family, and other essays. 4.5645
The politics of the judiciary. 4.9423
The Politics of the Labour Party. 4.8549
Politics of the New Zealand Maori. 3.5615
The politics of the ocean. 4.335
The politics of the powerless. 3.1289
The politics of the Prussian Army 1640-1945. 3.2326
The Politics of the second electorate. 4.5959
The politics of the solar age. 4.1786
The politics of totalitarianism. 4.8659
The politics of TV violence. 2.2858
The politics of unreason. 3.6389
The politics of urban education. 4.10960
The politics of urban renewal. 4.6345
The politics of violence. 4.7613
The politics of war. 3.7581
The politics of wilderness preservation. 5.3225
The politics of women's liberation. 4.6050
The politics of women's spirituality. 4.5892
Politics 4.7784
Politics, position, and power. 4.7894

Politics, power, and bureaucracy in France. 4.8588
Politics, presidents, and coattails. 4.8118
Politics, pressures and the tariff. 4.4203
Politics, prices, and petroleum. 4.3788
Politics, reform and expansion, 1890-1900. 3.7407
Politics, the Constitution, and the Warren Court. 4.9842
La politique des états et leur géographie. 4.7496
La politique des partis sous la IIIe republique. 4.8591
Politische Geschichte des neuen deutschen Kaiserreiches. 3.2327
Polk. 3.7169
Pollock and after. 1.4879
Polls, television, and the new politics. 4.7858
Pollution, politics, and international law. 4.9391
Pollution, prices, and public policy. 4.2077
Pollution, property and prices. 4.2132
Polpop. 3.6180
Poltergeists. 5.670
Polyarchy; participation and opposition. 4.7731
Polybius. 3.2746
Polymer chemistry. 5.2751
Polymer conversion. 5.6906
Polymer degradation. 5.2772
Polymer handbook. 5.2773
Polymer science and engineering. 5.2770
Polymer science and materials. 5.2769
Polymer syntheses. 5.2752
Polymers. 5.2766
Polynesian navigation. 3.5622
The Polynesians. 4.672
Pompeii A.D. 79. 3.2724
The Ponder heart. 2.12665
Ponds and lakes. 5.3553
The Pooh perplex. 2.9112
Poole's index to periodical literature. 1.36
'Poor Carolina' 4.2039
The poor Christ of Bomba. 2.4868
The poor cousin. 4.10985
Poor folk. 2.1350
A poor gentleman. 2.1447
Poor law to poverty program. 4.6530
Poor Miss Finch. 2.7608
The poor mouth. 2.9170
Poor murderer. 2.1674
The poor of eighteenth-century France 1750-1789. 4.6626
Poor people's movements. 4.3600
Poor white. 2.11320
The poorhouse fair. 2.13375
Pope and bishops. 1.3153
Pope and his contemporaries, essays presented to George Sherburn. 2.5665
The Pope, his banker, and Venice. 3.2916
Pope John 23rd, shepherd of the modern world. 1.3161
Pope John XXIII, shepherd of the modern world. 1.3161
Popery and politics in England 1660-1688. 3.1507
The Popes and European revolution. 1.3156
The popes and the papacy in the early Middle Ages, 476-752. 1.3149
Pope's Dunciad. 2.7190
The Popish Plot. 3.1506
Popol vuh. 3.9061
Popol vuh. English. 3.9061
The popular book. 5.7687
Popular Chinese literature and performing arts in the People's Republic of China, 1949-1979. 1.6724
Popular culture and high culture; an analysis and evaluation of taste. 3.6182
Popular culture in early modern Europe. 3.78
Popular fiction before Richardson. 2.5996
Popular government. 4.7577
A popular guide to government publications. 5.7778
Popular Hinduism and Hindu mythology. 5.8451
Popular music, an annotated guide to recordings. 1.3621

Popular music since 1955. 1.3586
Popular names of U.S. Government reports. 5.7771
The popular novel in England, 1770-1800. 2.5998
Popular opinion and political dissent in the Third Reich, Bavaria 1933-1945. 4.5362
Popular periodical index. 1.37
Popular recreations in English society, 1700-1850. 3.1532
Popular religion in America. 1.1877
Popular science (New York, N.Y.) 4.6062
Popular song index. 1.3590
Popular uprisings in the Philippines, 1840-1940. 4.2867
Population. 4.1586, 4.1615
Population. 4.1584
Population abstract of the United States. 4.1249
Population and agricultural development. 4.1594
Population and America's future. 4.1677
Population and development in Kenya. 4.1711
Population and family planning, manpower and training. 4.5674
Population and political systems in tropical Africa. 3.5230
Population and society in twentieth century France. 4.1698
Population and technological change. 4.1591
Population and the American future. 4.1666
Population and world politics. 4.1612
Population biology of plants. 5.3773
The population bomb. 4.1607
Population, capital, and growth. 4.2788
Population control and economic development. 4.1619
The population crisis. 4.1635
Population dilemma in Latin America. 4.1687
Population dispersal. 4.1657
Population dynamics. 4.1604
Population ecology. 5.3337
Population estimates. 4.1581
A population geography. 4.1653
Population growth. 4.1576
Population growth and manpower in the Philippines. 4.1256
Population growth and socio-economic change in West Africa. 4.1712
The population history of England, 1541-1871. 4.1694
Population history of New York City. 4.1684
Population, immigration, and the Australian economy. 4.8962
Population in history. 4.1614
Population information in nineteenth century census volumes. 5.8370
Population Malthus, his life and times. 4.1588
Population, migration, and urbanization in Africa. 4.1709
Population, modernization, and social structure. 4.1631
Population movements in modern European history. 4.1692
The population of Asia and the Far East, 1950-1980. 4.1703
The population of central Mexico in the sixteenth century. 4.1686
The population of Ireland, 1750-1845. 4.1696
The population of Japan. 4.1707
The population of Latin America. 4.1685
The population of the British colonies in America before 1776. 4.1665
The population of the California Indians, 1769-1970. 3.5720
The population of the Soviet Union. 4.1700
The population of the United States. 4.1668
Population policy. 4.1626
Population policy in western Europe. 4.1691
Population policymaking in the American States. 4.1675
Population, prosperity, and poverty. 3.5351
Population redistribution and economic growth: United States, 1870-1950. 4.1656
Population, resources, environment. 4.1593
Population studies of birds. 5.3949
Population theories and the economic interpretation. 4.1629

Populations, species, and evolution. 5.3396
Populism in Peru. 3.9308
Populism, progressivism, and the transformation of Nebraska politics, 1885-1915. 3.8516
Populism to progressivism in Alabama. 3.8279
The Populist response to industrial America. 4.8230
The Populist revolt. 4.8228
Populist vanguard. 4.2911
Porcelain. 1.6629
Porgy. 2.11871
Pornography. 4.5545
Pornography and sexual aggression. 4.5547
Pornography and sexual deviance. 4.5546
Pornography, the conflict over sexually explicit materials in the United States. 5.8387
The Porphyrins. 5.2777
Port engineering. 5.5973
The port of New York. 4.4007
Portable 20th century Russian reader. 2.1303
The portable Charles Lamb. 2.7901
The portable Conrad. 2.8542
The portable D. H. Lawrence. 2.8960
The portable Dorothy Parker. 2.12303
The portable Graham Greene. 2.8755
The portable Hawthorne. 2.11057
The portable Henry James. 2.11104
The portable James Joyce. 2.8864
The portable Jung. 5.168
The portable Machiavelli. 4.7389
The portable Mark Twain. 2.10938
The portable Matthew Arnold. 2.7347
The portable Nietzsche. 1.1044
The portable North American Indian reader. 3.5709
The portable Oscar Wilde. 2.8268
The portable Ring Lardner. 2.11979
The portable Steinbeck. 2.12524
The portable Stephen Crane. 2.10980
The portable Thomas Jefferson. 3.6972
The Portable twentieth century Russian reader. 2.1303
The portable Veblen. 4.1454
The portable Victorian reader. 2.6249
The portable Voltaire. 4.102
The portable Woollcott. 2.12799
The portfolios of Ansel Adams. 5.6975
Portnoy's complaint. 2.13303
Portrait du joueur. 2.4792
Portrait in brownstone. 2.11341
Portrait of a decade. 3.6672, 5.6996
Portrait of a decision. 3.850
Portrait of a Greek mountain village. 4.5390
The portrait of a lady. 2.11109
Portrait of a marriage. 2.9298
Portrait of a period. 3.8660
Portrait of a President. 3.7874
The portrait of a tortoise. 5.3213
Portrait of America. 3.6052
Portrait of Elgar. 1.3860
Portrait of India. 3.4159
Portrait of Jennie. 2.12240
Portrait of Karl Barth. 1.3285
A Portrait of marginality. 4.5972
Portrait of Max. 2.8439
Portrait of my family. 2.7989
Portrait of my family, 1783-1896. 2.7988
Portrait of Shelley. 2.8105
Portrait of the artist as a young dog. 2.9413
A portrait of the artist as a young man. 2.8877
A portrait of the artist as a young woman. 2.10598
Portrait of the artist as an American. 1.5969
Portraits. 2.5675
Portraits by Degas. 1.6090
Portraits from life. 2.5737
Portraits of Chinese women in revolution. 4.6138
Portraits of linguists. 2.42
Portraits of Russian personalities between reform and Revolution. 4.5369
Portraits of the artist in exile. 2.8918
The portraits of the Greeks. 1.5161
Portraits of 'The Whiteman'. 3.5838
Portraying the President. 4.7935
Portugal. 3.3496, 3.3499-3.3500, 3.3504
Portugal and Africa, 1815-1910. 3.5125

Portugal and the quest for the Indies. 4.93
Portugal in Africa. 3.5123, 3.5126
Portugal, revolutionary change in an open economy. 4.8684
Portuguese Africa. 3.5122
Portuguese Brazil. 4.2170
Portuguese colonialism in Africa. 3.5124
A Portuguese-English dictionary. 2.913
Portuguese literature. 2.5449
A Portuguese rural society. 4.5388
The Portuguese seaborne empire, 1415-1825. 3.3494
Portuguese settlement on the Zambesi. 3.5308
Posada's Mexico. 1.6450
Posada's popular Mexican prints. 1.6451
The position of the laborer in a system of nationalism. 4.3108
The positive hero in Russian literature. 2.1252
The positive philosophy. 1.820
The positive thinkers. 5.88
Positivism. 1.514
Positivism and sociology. 4.4742
Positivism in Mexico. 1.662
The possessed. 2.1351, 2.4454
The possessed. 2.1339
Possibilities: essays on the state of the novel. 2.5942
The possible and the actual. 5.3390
The post-civil war Spanish social poets. 2.5121
Post-impressionism: From Van Gogh to Gauguin. 1.6351
Post-industrial America. 4.6353
Post-industrial society. 4.5105
The post-modern aura. 2.10639
Post office. 2.1870
The post-physician era. 5.4553
Post report. 4.9093
Post-scarcity anarchism. 4.7188
Post-Victorian Britain: 1902-1951. 3.1640
Post-war Britain. 3.1709
Post-war Europe. 4.2185
Post-war Japanese poetry. 2.2031
Post-war years, 1945-1954. 2.1552
Posterior analytics. 1.292
The posthumous papers of the late Sir H. M. Elliot, K.C.B. 3.4251
The postman always rings twice. 2.11450
The Postmoderns. 2.10778
Postscript to The name of the rose. 2.5080
Postwar British fiction. 2.6037
Postwar fertility trends and differentials in the United States. 4.1645
Postwar German literature. 2.13481
Postwar Polish poetry. 2.1746
Postwar productivity trends in the United States, 1948-1969. 4.2091
Postwar, the dawn of today's Europe. 3.1192
The Potawatomis, keepers of the fire. 3.5939
Potential theory in modern function theory. 5.1499
Potentials of childhood. 5.584
The potentiometer handbook. 5.6521
The Potsdam führer. 3.2484
Potter and patron in classical Athens. 1.6637
Pottery and porcelain, 1700-1914. 1.6613
Pottery technology. 3.248
Poultry-keeping. 5.5457
The Pound era. 2.12346
Pounding the pavements. 2.4676
Pounding the pavements; Beating the bushes; and other pataphysical poems. 2.4676
Pound's Cantos declassified. 2.12328
Poverty amid plenty. 4.2099
Poverty amid plenty, the American paradox. 4.2103
Poverty and discrimination. 4.2101
Poverty and policy in American history. 4.6516
Poverty and politics. 4.2951
Poverty and progress. 4.5191
Poverty and welfare in Habsburg Spain. 4.6534
The poverty curtain. 4.1804
Poverty in a dual economy. 4.2102
Poverty in America. 4.2096, 4.6520
Poverty in New York, 1783-1825. 4.6620
Poverty in the United Kingdom. 4.2309
Poverty, inequality, and development. 4.2771

The poverty of abundance; Hoover, the Nation, the depression. 3.7742
The poverty of historicism. 3.489
The poverty of philosophy. 4.1422
The poverty of power. 4.3704
The Poverty of progress. 4.5081
Povest'vremennykh let. English. 3.3080
POW. 4.9329
Power, a new social analysis. 4.7474
Power and authority in law enforcement. 4.6798
Power and choice. 4.1667
Power and class in Africa. 3.5108
Power and diplomacy in Northern Nigeria, 1804-1906. 3.5369
Power and equilibrium in the 1970s. 4.9021
Power and ideology in education. 4.10771
Power and imagination. 3.2838
Power and influence. 5.5156
Power and interdependence. 4.9032
Power and international relations. 4.9026
Power and morality. 4.4977
Power and pawn. 4.5906
Power and personality. 5.472
Power and policy in the U.S.S.R. 3.3247
Power and politics in Africa. 4.8792
Power and politics in the community college. 4.10568
Power and powerlessness. 4.2021
Power and privilege. 4.6381
Power and privilege at an African university. 4.10744
Power and responsibility. 3.7703
Power and responsibility in the American business system. 4.4270
Power and society. 3.8038
The power and the glory. 2.8756
Power and the party. 4.8375
Power and the profession of obstetrics. 5.5065
Power and the pursuit of peace. 4.9113
Power and the Soviet elite. 4.8660
Power and wealth. 4.4166
The power broker: Robert Moses and the fall of New York. 1.5589
Power control electronics. 5.6556
Power electronics. 5.6557
Power electronics and ac drives. 5.6555
The power elite. 3.6144
Power from the North. 4.3798
The power game. 4.8419
Power generation. 5.6285
Power in and around organizations. 4.2668
Power in the Kremlin: from Krushchev to Kosygin. 3.3266
Power in the Pacific. 4.9158
Power in the Senate. 4.8043
Power, morals, and the Founding Fathers. 3.6277
The power of ideals in American history. 3.6272
The power of nations. 4.4146
The power of sound. 1.4392
The power of steam. 5.6207
The power of the center. 1.5111
The power of the modern Presidency. 4.7925
The power of the poor in history. 4.5119
The power of the purse. 4.8027
Power politics. 4.9006
Power, politics, and people. 4.4882
Power, property, and history. 4.7426
Power, racism, and privilege. 4.6456
Power relations within the Chinese communist movement, 1930-1934. 4.7110
Power semiconductor circuits. 5.6509
Power structure research. 5.5241
Power system analysis. 5.6287
Power system control and stability. 5.6286
Power system protection and switchgear. 5.6321
Power systems analysis. 5.6282
The Power that Preserves. 2.12993
The power to change geography. 2.13226
Power unlimited. 4.3363
Power volleyball. 4.1042
Power without property. 4.1929
Power without responsibility. 2.3683
Powers of Congress. 4.8015
Powers of desire. 4.5506

Powers of mind 5.105
The powers that be. 2.3651
The Powys brothers. 2.9240
Prabhupāda. 1.1734
A practical approach to content area reading. 4.10515
Practical aspects of groundwater modeling. 4.303
The practical bibliographer. 5.7685
Practical coal mine management. 5.6796
Practical controllership. 4.4382
Practical counseling in the schools. 4.10277
Practical electron microscopy in materials science. 5.2923
Practical ethics. 1.1460
A practical guide to airplane performance and design. 5.6668
A practical guide to Canadian political economy. 5.8396
A practical guide to computer methods for engineers. 5.5722
A Practical guide to counseling the gifted in a school setting. 4.10916
A practical guide to graduate research. 5.980
Practical handbook of warehousing. 4.4336
A practical introduction to electronic circuits. 5.6462
Practical modern basketball. 4.1013
The practical negotiator. 4.9322
Practical NMR spectroscopy. 5.2410
Practical optimization. 5.1549
Practical organic chemistry, including qualitative organic analysis. 5.2730
Practical PL/I. 5.1224
Practical research. 5.979
Practical solid-state DC power supplies. 5.6476
Practical statistics for chemical research. 5.6819
Practice and theory of Tibetan Buddhism. 1.2165
The practice of Chinese Buddhism. 1.1751
The practice of community-oriented primary health care. 5.4654
The Practice of local government planning. 4.6323
The practice of management. 4.2747
The Practice of mental health consultation. 5.4834
The practice of philosophy. 1.1309
The practice of piety. 1.3054
The practice of social work in public welfare. 4.6512
The practice of social work in schools. 4.10704
The practice of solidarity. 4.3383
The practice-oriented medical record. 5.4612
The practicing scientist's handbook. 5.2082
Praeterita. 2.8029
Pragmatic Federalism. 4.7870
Pragmatic illusions. 3.7866
Pragmatic naturalism. 1.573
Pragmatic psychotherapy. 5.4850
The pragmatic revolt in American history. 3.6281
Pragmatism. 1.526
Prague's 200 days. 3.1930
The prairie and the making of middle America. 3.8295
Prairie liberalism. 4.8318
The prairie school; Frank Lloyd Wright and his midwest contemporaries. 1.5299
Prairie settlement, the geographical setting. 3.8837
The Prairie west to 1905. 3.8839
Prairie women. 2.10469
Praise. 2.13068
Praise the bridge that carries you over. 3.8108
Praisers of folly. 2.824
Prajnaparamitas. Astasāhasrikā. English. 1.2130
Prajnaparamitas. Sancayagatha English. 1.2130
Prajnaparamitas. Vajracchedika. English. 1.2132
Prajnaparamits. 1965. 1.1737
Prater Violet. 2.8838
Praxis and method. 4.4799
Prayer. 1.2188, 1.2989
Prayer for a town & a friend. 2.1685
Prayer in the public schools. 4.9596

The prayers and meditations of St. Anselm. 1.2990
Pre-capitalist economic formations. 4.1534
Pre-Colonial African Trade: essays on trade in Central and Eastern Africa before 1900. 4.4244
Pre-Columbian architecture of Mesoamerica. 3.8897
Pre-Columbian art. 3.5692
Pre-Columbian art of South America. 3.9159
Pre-Columbian literatures of Mexico. 2.2333
The Pre-Confederation premiers. 3.8823
The pre-conquest church in England. 1.2436
The pre-election polls of 1948. 4.7959
Pre-industrial England. 4.2249
Pre-Ottoman Turkey. 3.3577
Pre-Raphaelite art and design. 1.4940
The Pre-Raphaelite landscape. 1.6361
The Pre-Raphaelite poets. 2.5827
The Pre-Raphaelites. 2.6169
The Pre-Raphaelites in literature and art. 2.5715
Pre-Raphaelitism. 1.6717
Pre-Raphaelitism and the pre-Raphaelite brotherhood. 1.6016
Pre-Socratic philosophers. 1.219
The pre-Socratic philosophers. 1.220
The Pre-Socratics. 1.234
The preachers of culture. 4.10511
Preaching to the converted. 2.9797
The precarious balance. 4.9008
The precarious balance: English government and society, 1450-1640. 3.1392
The precarious republic. 3.3787
The precarious vision. 1.1572
Precedence networks for project planning and control. 5.5561
Precious bane. 2.9509
The precious garland and The song of the four mindfulnesses. 1.2139
Precious garland of tenets. 1.2165
The precious pearl. 1.2061
Precipitation-frequency atlas of the Western United States. 4.162
A precocious autobiography. 2.1558
Precolonial Africa. 4.653
Precolumbian art of Costa Rica. 3.9078
Predation. 5.4084
The predicament of democratic man. 4.7566
The predicament of homecoming. 3.3842
Predicament of the university. 4.10072
Preface to a twenty volume suicide note. 2.12869
A preface to democratic theory. 4.7567
A preface to Dryden. 2.7000
A preface to economic geography. 4.4121
A preface to Forster. 2.8663
A preface to morals. 1.1413
A preface to Paradise lost. 2.7131
A preface to politics. 4.5174
A preface to Pope. 2.7197
A preface to Restoration drama. 2.3305
A preface to Sartre. 1.853
A preface to Shelley. 2.8101
A preface to Spenser. 2.6544
A preface to The faerie queene. 2.6533
A preface to urban economics. 4.6229
A preface to Wordsworth. 2.8315
A preface to Yeats. 2.8345
Prefaces and essays. 2.2655
Prefaces to Shakespeare. 2.6733
Pregnancy as a disease. 5.5055
Pregnancy, childbirth, and the newborn. 5.5064
Prehistoric art in Europe. 1.4687
Prehistoric Britain and Ireland. 4.732
Prehistoric Crete. 3.2592
Prehistoric Europe. 4.594
The prehistoric foundations of Europe to the Mycenean age. 3.114
Prehistoric hunters of the High Plains. 3.5739
Prehistoric India to 1000 B. C. 3.4243
The prehistoric peoples of Scotland. 4.734
Prehistoric Russia: an outline. 4.736
Prehistoric textiles of the Southwest. 3.5761
The prehistory of Africa. 4.705
The prehistory of Australia. 4.749

A prehistory of Australia, New Guinea, and Sahul. 4.750
The prehistory of Denmark. 4.737
The prehistory of Europe. 4.727
Prehistory of Japan. 4.742
Prehistory of North America. 3.5714
The Prehistory of Polynesia. 4.674
Prehistory of the eastern Arctic. 3.5878
Prehistory of the Southwest. 3.5756
The prehistory of the Tehuacan Valley. 3.8894
Prehistory of western Siberia. 4.743
The preindustrial city, past and present. 4.6189
Prejudice and your child. 5.614
Prejudice in children. 5.613
Prejudices. 2.12127
Prelates and people. 1.3306
Preliminaries to linguistic phonetics. 2.182
Preliminary studies for the 'Philosophical investigations' 1.1076
A prelude; landscapes, characters and conversations from the earlier years of my life. 2.12765
Prelude to Civil War. 3.7127
A prelude to genetics. 5.3438
Prelude to greatness. 3.7292
Prelude to independence. 2.3595
Prelude to invasion. 3.911
Prelude to literacy. 5.7718
Prelude to modern Europe, 1815-1914. 3.674
Prelude to science. 5.664
Prelude to silence. 3.2361
Prelude to the partition of West Africa. 3.5316
Prelude to world power: American diplomatic history, 1860-1900. 3.7419
Prelude to World War II. 3.879
Premarital sexual standards in America. 4.5495
Premchand, his life and work. 2.1891
Los premios. 2.5381
Le Prénom de Dieu. 2.4778
The Prentice-Hall standard glossary of computer terminology. 5.1133
The preparation of teachers. 4.10522
Preparative inorganic reactions. 5.2707
Preparing for the next war. 5.7278
Preparing instructional objectives. 4.10296
Preparing music manuscript. 1.4442
Prepositions. 2.12831
Presbyterians in the South. 1.3391
Prescription for justice. 4.9890
The presence of grace. 2.13268
The presence of René Char. 2.4467
The presence of Śiva. 1.5754
The presence of Stoicism in medieval thought. 1.329
Presence, power, praise. 1.2480
The present age after 1920. 2.5522
The present age, and Of the difference between a genius and an apostle. 1.2219
The present age from 1914. 2.5522
The present age in British literature. 2.5731
Present at the creation. 3.7554
Present indicative. 2.8584
Present knowledge in nutrition. 5.7110
The present of things future. 5.402
The present past. 3.246
Present past, past present. 2.4583
Present philosophical tendencies. 1.458
The Present situation and trends of research in the field of special education, four studies: Sweden and other Scandinavian countries, Union of Soviet Socialist Republics, United States of America, Uruguay. 4.10933
The present state of music in Germany, The Netherlands, and United Provinces. English. 1.3657
The presentation of self in everyday life. 4.5067
Presentation piece. 2.13063
Presenting Saunders Lewis. 2.842
The Presidencies of James A. Garfield & Chester A. Arthur. 3.7486
The presidency. 5.7848
The Presidency. 4.7933
The Presidency in the constitutional order. 4.7930
The Presidency of Andrew Johnson. 3.7456

The Presidency of Dwight D. Eisenhower. 3.7830
The presidency of Harry S. Truman. 3.7811
The presidency of Herbert C. Hoover. 3.7740
The Presidency of John Adams. 3.7042
The presidency of Martin Van Buren. 3.7131
The Presidency of Rutherford B. Hayes. 3.7485
The Presidency of Thomas Jefferson. 3.7059
The Presidency of William Howard Taft. 3.7710
The Presidency of William McKinley. 3.7495
The presidency of Yuan Shih-k'ai. 3.4768
The President. 4.9738
President and Congress. 4.7922
President James Buchanan. 3.7177
The president makers. 3.7529
President Roosevelt and the coming of the war, 1941. 3.7751
Presidential advisory commissions. 4.7899
Presidential agency: OWMR, the Office of War Mobilization and Reconversion. 4.1975
Presidential also-rans and running mates, 1788-1980. 3.6312
Presidential campaign funds. 4.8132
The Presidential character. 4.7917
The Presidential-Congressional political dictionary. 4.7792
The presidential Constitution of Nigeria. 4.9928
Presidential decision making. 4.2004
Presidential economics. 4.1939
The Presidential election game. 4.7965
Presidential elections. 4.7967
Presidential families of the United States of America. 3.297
Presidential greatness. 3.6306
Presidential impeachment. 4.9742
Presidential leadership. 4.7924
Presidential management of science and technology. 5.795
The presidential papers. 3.7865
Presidential politics and science policy. 5.794
Presidential popularity and the economy. 4.7954
Presidential power. 4.7928
Presidential primaries. 4.7945
Presidential primaries and nominations. 4.7942
The presidential quest. 4.7949
Presidential Reconstruction in Mississippi. 3.8289
Presidential seizure in labor disputes. 4.3163
Presidential selection. 4.7947
Presidential spending power. 4.4656
Presidential transitions. 3.7526
The Presidents. 3.6311
The president's agenda. 4.7937
Presidents and prime ministers. 4.7715
The Presidents and the press. 3.6310
President's Cabinet. 4.7973
The President's economic advisors. 4.7897
The Presidents' men. 3.7615
Presidents, professors, and trustees. 4.10591
Presidents' secret wars. 4.7910
The Presocratic philosophers. 1.230
The presocratic philosophers. 1.233
Presocratic philosophy. 1.300
The press. 2.3577
The press and America. 2.3584
The press and foreign policy. 2.3557
Press and politics in Nigeria, 1880-1937. 2.3699
The Press & the American Revolution. 2.3594
The press as guardian of the first amendment. 4.9718
Press control around the world. 2.3551
The press in India. 2.3559
The press in Japan today. 2.3697
The press in the French Revolution. 3.2063
Press law in modern democracies. 4.9389
The press of Africa. 2.3698
Press 3.7845
The press, politics, and patronage. 2.3556
Pressure groups in Britain: a reader. 4.8437
The presumption of atheism ... 1.2216
The presumption of atheism and other philosophical essays on God, freedom, and immortality. 1.2216

Presuppositions of India's philosophies. 1.184
Pretend the world is funny and forever. 2.3134
Pretenders to the throne. 4.2064
Pretexts. 2.4547
Pretoria's praetorians. 5.7349
A pretty good club. 4.9096
The prevalence of people. 4.1609
Preventing students from dropping out. 4.10748
Prevention of alcohol abuse. 4.6634
The prevention of juvenile delinquency. 4.6864
Preventive medicine in the United States, 1900-1975. 5.4658
Price controls and the natural gas shortage. 4.3790
Price formation in natural gas fields. 4.3791
The price mechanism and the meaning of national income statistics. 4.1854
The price of glory. 3.797
The price of gold. 2.9971
The price of loyalty. 3.6957
The price of power. 3.7555
The price of stone & earlier poems. 2.9778
Price of stone and earlier poems. 2.9778
The price of the ticket. 2.12861
Price theory. 4.1457
Price Warung (William Astley) 2.10147
Prices and production. 4.4487
Prices and quantities. 4.1464
Prices and wages in England from the twelfth to the nineteenth century. 4.1505
Pricing decisions and marketing policy. 4.4287
Pricing in big business. 4.4313
Pricing power & the public interest. 4.4286
Pricing strategies. 4.4314
Pricing the priceless child. 4.5748
Prick up your ears. 2.9790
Pride against prejudice. 4.3607
Pride and passion, Robert Burns, 1759-1796. 2.7504
Pride and prejudice. 2.7367
Pride's Purge. 3.1487
Priest and revolutionary. 1.3269
The primacy of perception. 1.839
Primal dream and primal crime. 2.9200
The primal screen. 2.2968
The primary battery. 5.6324
Primary elections in the South. 4.8140
Primary embryonic induction. 5.4138
Primary health care of the older adult. 5.5007
The primary language of poetry in the 1640's. 2.5802
Primary productivity in the sea. 5.3252
The primary structures of fabrics. 5.7079
Primate behavior. 5.4017, 5.4021
Primate bio-social development. 5.4022
Primate evolution and human origins. 5.4023
Primate socialization. 5.4020
Primates in nature. 5.4025
Primates of the world. 5.4028
The Prime Minister. 2.8220
The Prime Minister of Kenya's speeches, 1963-1964. 3.5281
The Prime Ministers. 3.1239
Prime ministers and diplomats. 3.5581
Prime movers. 4.1124
The prime of life. 2.4395
The prime of Miss Jean Brodie. 2.9361
Prime time. 2.3622
Prime time network TV shows, 1946-present. 2.2847
A primer for film-making. 5.7004
A primer for the gradual understanding of Gertrude Stein. 2.12509
A primer of behavioral pharmacology. 5.232
A primer of Dutch seventeenth century overseas trade. 4.4097
A primer of Freudian psychology. 5.154
A primer of libertarian education. 4.9956
A primer of operant conditioning. 5.306
A primer of population biology. 5.3446
A primer of statistics for political scientists. 4.7240
A primer on Riemann surfaces. 5.1494
Primera memoria. 2.5276
Primitive, archaic, and modern economies. 4.1311
Primitive art. 1.4683, 1.4689

Primitive Christian symbols. 1.2984
Primitive Christianity in its contemporary
    setting. 1.2267
Primitive classification. 4.601
Primitive culture. 4.522
Primitive government. 4.660
Primitive mentality. 4.538
Primitive psychology. 4.566
Primitive religion. 4.548
Primitive religion: its nature and origin. 4.552
Primitive society. 4.592
The primitive world and its transformations.
    3.59
Primitivism and decadence. 2.10275
Primitivism and related ideas in antiquity. 3.24
'Primitivism' in 20th century art. 1.4851
'Primitivism' in twentieth century art. 1.4851
The prince. 4.7394-4.7396
The prince and The discourses. 4.7393
Prince Henry of Prussia, brother of Frederick
    the Great. 3.2485
Prince of Darkness. 2.13271
A prince of our disorder. 3.811
Prince of players: Edwin Booth. 2.3246
Prince Saionji and the 1930 London treaty
    issue. 3.4962
Princely India. 3.4281
Princes and parliaments in Germany, from the
    fifteenth to the eighteenth century. 4.8598
Princes and peasants. 5.4767
The princes of India in the twilight of Empire.
    3.4288
The Princess of Cleves. 2.4027
A princess of Mars. 2.11438
The Princeton companion to classical Japanese
    literature. 2.1998
The Princeton encyclopedia of classical sites.
    3.2520
Princeton encyclopedia of poetry and poetics.
    2.2706
The principal Upanishads. 1.1682
The principalship. 4.10672
Principia ethica. 1.1408
Principium sapientiae. 1.224
Principle and practicality. 1.161
The principle of relativity. 5.1914
The principle of water. 2.9315
Principles and applications of electrochemistry.
    5.2913
Principles and applications of organotransition
    metal chemistry. 5.2779
Principles and applications of room acoustics.
    1.5495
Principles and persuasions. 2.2603
Principles and practice of English grammar.
    2.990
Principles and practice of laser-Doppler
    anemometry. 5.6240
The Principles and practice of medicine.
    5.4753
Principles and practice of nursing. 5.5167
Principles and practice of urban planning.
    4.6323
Principles and practices of dryland farming.
    5.5316
Principles and practices of teaching reading.
    4.10460
Principles and problems of music education.
    1.4435
Principles and techniques of histochemistry.
    5.3621
Principles for electric power policy. 4.3804
Principles of adsorption and adsorption
    processes. 5.6838
The principles of aesthetics. 1.1377
Principles of algebraic geometry. 5.1577
The Principles of art. 1.4608
Principles of art appreciation. 1.5147
Principles of art history. 1.4678
Principles of artificial intelligence. 5.1014
Principles of behavior. 5.219
Principles of behavior modification. 5.4888
Principles of bibliographical description.
    5.7676
Principles of biochemistry. 5.4399
Principles of Christian theology. 1.2779
Principles of combustion. 5.2904
Principles of communication systems. 5.6359

Principles of communications. 5.6360
Principles of communism. 4.7073
Principles of comparative respiratory
    physiology. 5.4229
Principles of dance and movement notation.
    4.1085
Principles of database systems. 5.1238
Principles of demography. 4.1610
The principles of Descartes' philosophy. 1.796
Principles of development and differentiation.
    5.4125
Principles of economics. 4.1448, 4.1468
Principles of Egyptian art. 1.4700
Principles of emendation in Shakespeare.
    2.6838
Principles of engineering economy. 5.5700
Principles of fishery science. 5.5480
Principles of food science. 5.7111
Principles of foundation engineering. 5.5917
Principles of gene manipulation. 5.3459
Principles of general thermodynamics. 5.2246
Principles of geomorphology. 4.245
Principles of geotechnical engineering. 5.5895
Principles of gestalt psychology. 5.227
Principles of government and politics in the
    Middle Ages. 4.7373
Principles of heat transfer. 5.2266
Principles of human anatomy. 5.4197
The principles of human biochemical genetics.
    5.3428
Principles of human geography. 4.369
Principles of human physiology. 5.4190
Principles of industrial chemistry. 5.6812
Principles of insect morphology. 5.3864
The principles of insect physiology. 5.3869
Principles of intensive psychotherapy. 5.4852
Principles of interactive computer graphics.
    5.5651
Principles of international law. 4.9296
Principles of isotope geology. 5.3081
Principles of lasers. 5.2379
Principles of learning and memory. 5.294,
    5.324a
Principles of literary criticism. 2.2441
The principles of logic. 1.1171
Principles of mammalian aging. 5.4217
Principles of management information systems.
    5.5613
Principles of marketing channel management.
    4.4295
Principles of mathematical analysis. 5.1444
Principles of mathematical logic. 1.1211
Principles of model building. 5.5573
Principles of modern heterocyclic chemistry.
    5.2776
Principles of modern physics. 5.2057
Principles of Mössbauer spectroscopy. 5.2331
Principles of nutrition. 5.4243
Principles of operations research. 4.2629
Principles of optics. 5.2277
Principles of orchestration. 1.4492
Principles of organic synthesis. 5.2737
Principles of paleontology. 5.3151
Principles of particle accelerators. 5.2440
Principles of pavement design. 5.6069
Principles of perceptual learning and
    development. 5.264
Principles of personnel testing. 4.4372
Principles of philosophy. 1.787
Principles of phonology. 2.178
Principles of physical geology. 5.2966
Principles of physics. 5.1990
Principles of political economy. 4.1410
Principles of political obligation. 4.7632
The principles of politics. 4.7470
Principles of polymer chemistry. 5.2751
Principles of polymer processing. 5.6907
Principles of population genetics. 5.3472
The principles of power. 3.508
Principles of protein structure. 5.4406
Principles of psychoanalytic psychotherapy.
    5.4905
The principles of psychology. 5.108
The principles of psychophysiology. 5.4294
Principles of public international law. 4.9286
The principles of quantum mechanics. 5.2150
Principles of quantum mechanics. 5.2137
Principles of radar. 5.6360

Principles of relativity physics. 5.1895
Principles of renal physiology. 5.4251
The principles of science. 5.903
The principles of scientific management.
    5.5604
Principles of sedimentary basin analysis.
    5.3056
Principles of sedimentology. 5.3055
The principles of semantics. 2.200
Principles of Shakespearian production with
    especial reference to the tragedies. 2.6856
Principles of social & political theory. 4.7468
Principles of social science (1858-1859). 4.1411
Principles of sociology. 4.4844
Principles of soil mechanics. 5.5904
Principles of solar engineering. 5.6227
The principles of statistical mechanics. 5.2186
Principles of stratigraphy. 5.2958, 5.3131
Principles of surface chemistry. 5.2901
Principles of surveying. 5.5821
Principles of systematic zoology. 5.3829
Principles of textual criticism. 2.5495
The principles of the International Phonetic
    Association. 2.186
Principles of the philosophy of the future.
    1.956
Principles of the theory of solids. 5.2203
Principles of urban transport systems planning.
    4.3901
Principles of warmwater aquaculture. 5.5468
Principles of water resources planning. 5.5974
The Print Council index to oeuvre-catalogues of
    prints by European and American artists.
    5.8188
The print in Germany, 1880-1933. 1.6461
Printed art. 1.6434
Printed propaganda under Louis XIV. 3.2035
Printing and the mind of man. 5.7541
The printing press as an agent of change.
    5.7542
Printing presses; history and development from
    the fifteenth century to modern times.
    5.7560
The printing revolution in early modern
    Europe. 5.7543
Printing types, their history, forms, and use.
    5.7561
Printmaking. 1.6469
Printmaking in Canada. 1.6448
Printmaking in the age of Rembrandt. 1.6464
Printmaking today. 1.6467
The prints of Frank Stella. 1.6447
The prints of Reginald Marsh. 1.6444
The prints of Robert Motherwell. 1.6445
Prints of the twentieth century. 1.6433
Prior and posterior analytics. 2.436
Priorities for action. 4.10076
Prisma's Modern Swedish-English and English-
    Swedish dictionary. 2.923
Prisms; studies in modern literature. 2.2672
The prison and the factory. 4.6888
The prison and the labyrinth. 2.5166
The prison-house of language. 2.151
Prison life and human worth. 4.6911
Prison notebooks. 4.7076
Prison victimization. 4.6859
Prisoner of grace. 2.8505
Prisoner subcultures. 4.6843
Prisoners among us. 4.6898
Prisoners at the bar. 4.9454
Privacy. 4.7699
Privacy in a free society. 4.9517
Privacy, law, and public policy. 4.9518
Private Black colleges at the crossroads.
    4.10861
The private capital. 3.8832
The private city. 3.8086
The private diaries of Stendhal (Marie-Henri
    Beyle) 2.4306
Private enterprise in Eastern Europe. 4.3003
Private foreign investment in development.
    4.4608
The private Franklin. 3.6992
The private future: causes and consequences of
    community collapse in the West. 3.204
The private government of public money.
    4.4722
Private investigations. 2.11812

Private law sources and analogies of international law. 4.8984
Private life of an Indian prince. 2.10125
The private lives and professional identity of medical students. 5.4598
Private management and public policy. 4.2706
The private Mary Chesnut. 3.7368
The private memoirs and confessions of a justified sinner. 2.7815
Private orations. 2.360
The private papers of Henry Ryecroft. 2.7737
The private papers of Senator Vandenberg. 3.7805
Private pleasure, public plight. 4.6352
Private power for the public good. 4.9930
The private press. 5.7554
Private presses and their books. 5.7548
Private pressure on public law. 4.9823
The private reader. 2.2599
Private schools <1975->. 4.9942
The private sector in Soviet agriculture. 4.2979
Private U.S. companies. 4.4606
Private view. 2.2569
Private wants and public needs. 4.4652
The private world. 2.5287
Privilege and creative destruction. 4.9758
Privilege in the Soviet Union. 4.5378
Privileged ones. 4.2095
Privy seal. 2.8630
Prize stories. 2.10849
The Pro/Am guide to U.S. books about music. 1.3553
Pro basketball encyclopedia. 4.1014
Pro Flacco. 2.659
Pro Murena. 2.659
Pro Sulla. 2.659
Proactive police management. 4.6799
Probabilistic methods in structural engineering. 5.5833
Probabilistic models in engineering sciences. 5.5716
Probability and certainty in 17th-century England. 3.1455
Probability and certainty in seventeenth-century England. 3.1455
Probability and evidence. 5.897
Probability and inductive logic. 1.1185
Probability and literary form. 2.5504
Probability and statistical inference. 5.1383
Probability and statistics for business decisions. 4.2669
Probability, time, and space in eighteenth-century literature. 2.5671
Probable fictions. 2.9955
Probing our past. 3.6102
Problem comedies. 2.6761
The problem of historical knowledge. 3.480
The problem of John Ford. 2.6578
The problem of knowledge. 1.1286
The problem of party government. 4.8526
The problem of political obligation. 4.7515
The problem of slavery in Western culture. 4.6419
The problem of style. 2.2540
The problem of unbelief in the sixteenth century, the religion of Rabelais. 2.4007
The problem of universals. 1.146
The problem of values in educational thought. 4.10256
The problem plays of Shakespeare. 2.6661
Problem-solving through problems. 5.1119
Problems. 2.351
Problems and solutions for students. 5.2000
Problems for inorganic chemistry. 5.2703
Problems from Locke. 1.676
Problems in aesthetics. 1.1350
Problems in quantum mechanics. 5.2222
The problems of aesthetics. 1.1349
Problems of analysis. 1.465
The Problems of Arab economic development and integration. 4.2572
Problems of art. 1.4612
Problems of communism. 3.3257
Problems of economic unions. 4.4150
Problems of economics. 4.2745

Problems of economics and sociology (Untersuchungen über die Methode der Socialwissenschaften und der politischen Oekonomie insbesondere) 4.1469
Problems of metaphysics and psychology. 5.20
Problems of mind. 5.27
Problems of modern music. 1.3674
Problems of parents. 4.5713
The problems of philosophy. 1.1260
Problems of philosophy and psychology. 5.21
The problems of plenty. 4.3765
Problems of scientific revolution. 5.768
Problems of stability and progress in international relations. 4.9124
Problems of the Baltic. 3.3309
Problems of the Chinese revolution. 3.4757
The procedure of the UN Security Council. 4.9204
Procedures in sedimentary petrology. 5.3053
Proceedings. 4.1578
Proceedings and debates of the British Parliaments respecting North America, 1754-1783. 3.6859
Proceedings of the Black State conventions, 1840-1865. 3.6601
Process analysis and design for chemical engineers. 5.6834
Process and reality. 1.1331
Process instruments and controls handbook. 5.7033
Process modeling, simulation, and control for chemical engineers. 5.6833
The process of change. 5.4885
The process of education. 4.10240
The process of government. 4.7217
The process of government under Jefferson. 4.7836
The process of reading. 4.10342
The process of stratification. 4.5242
Process synthesis. 5.6835
Process theology. 1.2809
Processes and phenomena of social change. 4.4890
Processing the news. 4.5016
Processional pour saluer le siècle nouveau. 2.4471
Proconsul in politics. 3.1675
Procopius. 2.392
Procopius and the sixth century. 3.2656
A prodigal child. 2.9824
The prodigal son. 2.8937
Producers on producing. 2.3236
Producible interpretation. 2.5897
Producing the play. 2.3092
Producing your own power. 5.6113
Product design and process engineering. 5.7039
Product safety management and engineering. 5.7044
The Production and application of new industrial technology. 4.2108
Production and distribution theories, 1870 to 1895. 4.1313
Production and inventory control handbook. 5.7021
Production and inventory management. 5.7027
Production and management of cultivated forages. 5.5327
Production ecology of British moors and montane grasslands. 5.3276
Production-inventory systems. 5.7026
The production of medieval church music-drama. 1.3654
Production problems in Handel's operas. 1.4572
Production processes. 5.7045
Productive thinking. 5.228
Productivity and technical change. 4.2686
Productivity and the social system. 4.2407
Productivity, efficiency, and quality in urban transportation systems. 5.5933
Productivity growth and U.S. competitiveness. 4.2089
Productivity growth and United States competitiveness. 4.2089
Productivity handbook. 5.7045
Productivity measurement and improvement. 5.5619

Productivity prospects for growth. 4.2090
The profession of dramatist in Shakespeare's time, 1590-1642. 2.2521
The profession of government. 4.7751
The profession of player in Shakespeare's time, 1590-1642. 2.3287
The professional altruist. 4.6518
The professional arranger composer. 1.4449
Professional dissent. 5.8365
Professional engineers' examination questions and answers. 5.5681
Professional engineer's license guide. 5.5677
Professional ethics and civic morals. 4.4968
The professional fence. 4.6705
Professional forestry in the United States. 5.5419
The professional resume and job search guide. 4.4266
Professional secrets. 2.4483
The professional soldier. 5.7355
The professional stranger. 4.496
The professional thief. 4.6701
The professions: roles and rules. 4.6399
The professor. 2.7446
The professor. 2.9466
The professor of desire. 2.13304
The professor, the institute, and DNA. 5.4432
The professors. 4.10531
Professors as teachers. 4.10572
Profile of Horace. 2.722
Profile of the community college. 4.10567
A profile of the Negro American. 3.6721
Profiles and critiques in social theory. 4.4795
Profiles in belief. 1.1874
Profiles in courage. 3.6293
Profit and responsibility. 4.4274
Profit, risk, and incentives under Socialist economic planning. 4.2243
Profit sharing, employee stock ownership, savings, and asset formation plans in the Western World. 4.3066
The profits of religion. 1.1891
Profits, progress, and poverty. 4.3060
A program for monetary stability. 4.4505
Program style, design, efficiency, debugging, and testing. 5.1201
A programmed review of engineering fundamentals. 5.5680
Programming in Prolog. 5.1225
Programs and promising practices. 4.10918
Progress and its problems. 5.741
Progress and poverty. 4.1431
Progress and power. 3.61
Progress, coexistence, and intellectual freedom. 3.198
Progress in behavior modification. 5.456
Progress in physical organic chemistry. 5.2858
Progress into the past. 3.2585
The progress of a crime. 2.9393
The progress of Afro-American women. 5.7877
The progress of dulness. 2.10878
The progress of international government. 4.9289
The progress of the human mind. 3.7
The progress of underdeveloped areas. 4.1830
The progress of world-wide missions. 1.3023
Progression of animals. 2.342
Progressive education at the crossroads. 4.10219
The progressive era in Minnesota, 1899-1918. 3.8498
The progressive historians: Turner, Beard, Parrington. 3.6230
The progressive movement. 4.7855
The Progressive movement. 4.8233
Progressive Oklahoma. 3.8536
The Progressive Party in Canada. 3.8770
The progressive Presidents: Roosevelt, Wilson, Roosevelt, Johnson. 3.7520
Progressive reform. 5.7837
The progressives and the slums. 4.3492
Progressivism. 3.7532
Progressivism and muckraking. 5.8391
Progressivism in American education. 4.9992
Progressivism in Ohio, 1897-1917. 3.8384
Project appraisal and planning for developing countries. 4.2677
Project Focus. 4.10562

Project Head Start. 4.10941
Project management with CPM and PERT. 5.5562
The project method. 4.10274
Projective geometry. 5.1569, 5.1571
Projective planes. 5.1570
Projective techniques with children. 5.576
Prokofiev. 1.3948
Prolegomena for the Oxford Shakespeare. 2.6841
Prolegomena to a theory of language. 2.91
Prolegomena to any future metaphysics that will be able to present itself as a science. 1.893
Prolegomena to ethics. 1.1432
Prolegomena to the history of ancient Israel. 3.3886
Proletarianisation in the Third World. 4.3675
Proletarianization and family history. 4.3638
Prologue to conflict. 3.7172
Prologue to democracy. 3.8149
Prologue to Nuremberg. 4.9333
A prologue to population geography. 4.1606
Prologue to war. 3.7109
The prologues and epilogues of John Dryden. 2.6986
Prometheus. 2.4125
Prominent Indians of Victorian age. 3.4275
Prominent scientists. 5.814
The promise and pitfalls of revolution. 4.6969
The promise and the performance. 3.7867
The promise of America. 3.6593
The promise of American life. 4.5170
Promise of Eden. 3.8853
The promise of Eurocommunism. 4.7023
The promise of power. 4.9898
The promise of Reinhold Niebuhr. 1.3293
The promise of the coming dark age. 3.206
The promised city. 3.8052
The promised end. 2.2576
The promised land. 3.6189
Promiseland, a century of life in a Negro community. 3.8253
Promises of power. 3.8386
Promoting competence in clients. 4.6472
Promoting innovation and change in organizations and communities. 4.1228
The promotional planning process. 4.4329
Promotional strategy. 4.4280
La prononciation du français contemporain. 2.869
Pronouncing dictionary of American English. 2.1023
The pronunciation of American English. 2.1018
The pronunciation of English. 2.1022
The pronunciation of English in the Atlantic States. 2.1121
The pronunciation of Greek and Latin. 2.237
The pronunciation of standard English in America. 2.1133
Proof of the apostolic preaching. 1.2187
Proofs and refutations. 5.1033
Propaganda. 4.5019
Propaganda and aesthetics. 2.10323
Propaganda and aryanization, 1938-1944. 3.1099
Propaganda and communication in world history. 4.5010
Propaganda and the American revolution, 1763-1783. 3.6919
Propaganda and the German cinema, 1933-1945. 2.2995
Propaganda in war, 1939-1945. 3.1132
The Propaganda Movement, 1880-1895. 3.4598
The proper lady and the woman writer. 2.5729
The proper study of mankind. 4.1234
Properties and management of forest soils. 5.5426
Properties and management of soils in the tropics. 5.5282
Properties of concrete. 5.5800
The properties of gases and liquids. 5.6860
Properties of liquids and solutions. 5.2908
Properties of matter. 5.2056
The properties of nuclei. 5.2473
Propertius. 2.766
Propertius; with an English translation. 2.688

Property. 4.7705
Property and political theory. 4.1561
Property, kin, and community on Truk. 3.5630
Property, paternalism, and power. 4.2973
Property rights. 4.9374
Property taxes, housing and the cities. 4.4705
Property values and race. 3.6785
Prophecy and history in Luke-Acts. 1.2691
Prophecy and progress. 4.5105
Prophecy and society in ancient Israel. 1.2585
Prophecy in Islam. 1.2063
The prophet armed: Trotsky, 1879-1921. 3.3155
The prophet Harris. 1.3043
A prophet in politics. 3.8773
The prophet of the Great Smoky Mountains. 2.11182
The prophet outcast: Trotsky, 1929-1940. 3.3156
The prophet unarmed: Trotsky, 1921-1929. 3.3157
The prophetic imagination. 1.2583
Prophetism in Ghana. 1.1854
The Prophets. 1.2610
The prophets. 1.2584
Prophets and patrons: the French university and the emergence of the social sciences. 4.1232
Prophets and peoples. 4.7490
Prophets of extremity. 1.1396
The prophets of Paris. 1.810
Prophets of the revolution, profiles of Latin American leaders. 3.8961
Prophets of yesterday. 3.184
Prophets on the right. 3.7596
Prophets without honour. 3.3968
Proprietary capitalism. 4.3847
Propulsion systems. 5.6216
Propyläen Weltgeschichte. 3.522
Prosa, Dramen, Verse. 2.13867
Die Prosa I. 2.13675
Die Prosa II. 2.13675
Prose. 2.4947, 2.4980
Prose and poetry. 2.7919, 2.7952
Prose and poetry of the continental Renaissance in translation. 2.3711
Prose and poetry. 2.7974
Prose e rime. 2.4963
Prose observations. 2.6926
The prose of John Clare. 2.7568
Prose of Osip Mandelstam. 2.1574
Prose of the romantic period. 2.6263
Prose pieces. 2.11439
Prose selections. 2.7144
The prose works of Jonathan Swift. 2.7289
The prose works of William Wordsworth. 2.8300
Prose works other than science and health, with key to the scriptures. 1.3328
The prose writings of Robert Louis Stevenson. 2.8127
The prosodic theory of Gerard Manley Hopkins. 2.7831
The prosody of Chaucer and his followers. 2.6379
A prospect of the sea. 2.9410
Prospects for Soviet agriculture in the 1980s. 4.2977
The prospects of international adjudication. 4.9149
Prosper Mérimée. 2.4273
Prosperity decade. 4.1880
Prosperity without progress. 4.3689
Prostitution and Victorian society. 4.5542
Protagoras. 1.252
Protean poetic. 2.13262
Protecting children from abuse and neglect. 4.6550
Protection or free trade. 4.4202
Protective groups in organic synthesis. 5.2734
The protective tariff in Canada's development. 4.4205
Protein crystallography. 5.2930
Proteins. 5.4404
The proteins. 5.2794
Protest and power in black Africa. 3.5234
Protest and prejudice. 3.6708
Protest and punishment. 4.6856

Protest and response in Mexico. 4.3171
Protest at Selma. 4.8092
Protest is not enough. 3.6795
Protest movements in rural Java. 4.5441
Protestant, Catholic, Jew. 1.1867
Protestant Christianity interpreted through its development. 1.3280
Protestant church music. 1.4245
The Protestant Crusade, 1800-1860. 1.3171
The Protestant era. 1.3282
The Protestant establishment: aristocracy & caste in America. 4.5124
The Protestant ethic and the spirit of capitalism. 1.2244
The Protestant Reformation, 1517-1559. 1.2328
The Protestant temperament. 1.2374
Protestant theology in the nineteenth century. 1.2763
Protestant thought in the nineteenth century. 1.2760
Protestantism in the United States. 1.2380
Protestants and pioneers. 1.2412
Protestants in a Catholic state. 4.5344
Protestants in an age of science. 1.1596
Prothalamium, a cycle of the Holy Graal. 2.9440
Proto-Indo-European syntax. 2.222
The proton in chemistry. 5.2878
Prototractatus. 1.1226
Protozoology. 5.3837
The proud knowledge. 2.5753
Proust. 2.4671-2.4672, 2.4674
Proustian space. 2.4675
Proverbs, a new approach. 1.2609
Proverbes. Proverbes. Sprichwörter. Proverbi. Proverbios. Poslovitsy (romanized form) 2.3807
Providence. 2.9634
The providence of wit. 2.5677
Providing continuing education by media and technology. 4.10979
The Province of East New Jersey, 1609-1702. 3.8067
The province of piety. 2.11074
The Provincetown. 2.3274
A provincial lady. 2.1447
The provincial letters. 1.805
Provincial magistrates and revolutionary politics in France, 1789-1795. 4.9913
Provincial party personnel in mainland China, 1956-1966. 4.8890
Provincial politics in Canada. 4.8312
Provincial society, 1690-1763. 3.6876
The provincial universities of Mexico. 4.10102
The provincials. 3.8180
A Provision of human nature. 2.5672
Provisions. 2.10821
Provo, pioneer Mormon city. 3.8585
The provoked husband. 2.7323
The provoked wife. 2.3338
La prudencia en la mujer. 2.5204
Prudent practices for handling hazardous chemicals in laboratories. 5.2637
Prudentius. 2.689
Prussian military reforms, 1786-1813. 5.7321
The Prussian reform movement. 4.8617
Psalms. 1.2607
Psyche and demos. 4.1634
Psychiatric dictionary. 5.4798
Psychiatric disorder and the urban environment. 5.4835
A psychiatric glossary. 5.4797
The psychiatric halfway house. 5.4809
Psychiatric justice. 4.9851
The psychiatrist, and other stories. 2.5472
Psychiatry and military manpower policy, a reappraisal of the experience in World War II. 5.7414
Psychic exploration. 5.644
The psycho-analysis of children. 5.5107
The psycho-analytical treatment of children. 5.4917
Psychoanalysis. 5.132
Psychoanalysis & American literary criticism. 2.10242
Psychoanalysis and faith. 5.148
Psychoanalysis and infant research. 5.556

Psychoanalysis and women. 4.5933
Psychoanalysis as science. 5.181
Psychoanalysis of children. 5.5107
Psychoanalysis: scientific method and
    philosophy. 5.178
Psychoanalytic concepts and the structural
    theory. 5.129
Psychoanalytic explorations in art. 1.4611
Psychoanalytic interpretation in Rorschach
    testing. 5.188
The Psychoanalytic interpretation of history.
    3.436
The psychoanalytic process. 5.4908
Psychoanalytic psychology. 5.4903
Psychoanalytic studies of the sighted and the
    blind. 5.5098
Psychoanalytic techniques. 5.4909
Psychoanalytic theory. 5.170
Psychoanalytic theory of art. 1.4636
Psychoanalytical terms. 5.14
The psychobiology of sensory coding. 5.4359
Psychobiology of stress. 5.4208
Psychodiagnostics; a diagnostic test based on
    perception. 5.187
Psychodrama: theory and therapy. 5.4894
Psychoeducational foundations of learning
    disabilities. 4.10951
A psychohistory of Zionism. 3.4019
Psycholinguistics. 2.18, 5.381
Psychological abstracts. 5.1
Psychological and psychoanalytical terms. 5.14
Psychological anthropology. 4.442
Psychological aspects of international conflict.
    4.8994
Psychological aspects of learning disabilities &
    reading disorders. 4.10956
Psychological aspects of obesity. 5.4944
Psychological behavior in sport. 4.943
The psychological birth of the human infant.
    5.603
Psychological development in children. 5.577
Psychological disorders of children. 5.5103
Psychological explanation. 5.24
Psychological factors in poverty. 4.1857
Psychological foundations of sport. 4.952
The psychological frontiers of society. 4.4988
Psychological needs and political behavior.
    4.7248
Psychological processes and advertising effects.
    4.4431
Psychological processes in pattern recognition.
    5.389
Psychological reality in phonology. 2.177
The psychological society. 5.4799
Psychological testing. 5.201
Psychological tests and personnel decisions.
    5.44
Psychological thought from Pythagoras to
    Freud. 5.74
The psychological world of Natsume Sōseki.
    2.2087
Psychologie de l'art. 1.4614
Psychologist at large. 5.94
The psychologists. 5.90
Psychology. 5.104
Psychology: a study of a science. 5.31
Psychology and anthropology. 4.623
Psychology and Arthur Miller. 2.12177
Psychology and extrasensory perception. 5.119
Psychology and religion. 1.1566
Psychology and the new consciousness. 5.270
Psychology for nurses and health visitors.
    5.5197
Psychology in contemporary sport. 4.968
Psychology in Utopia. 5.87
Psychology misdirected. 5.32
The psychology of aggression. 5.420
Psychology of aging. 5.624
The psychology of animal learning. 5.4102
The psychology of art. 1.4614, 1.6687
The psychology of Black language. 2.1159
The psychology of Blacks. 3.6722
Psychology of coaching. 4.970
The psychology of cognition. 5.261
The psychology of communication. 5.464
The psychology of computer programming.
    5.1203
The psychology of consciousness. 5.281

The psychology of control. 5.450
The psychology of deductive reasoning. 5.384
The Psychology of discipline. 5.595
The psychology of ego-involvements. 5.535
The Psychology of fashion. 5.7094
The psychology of individualism. 5.499
The psychology of intelligence. 5.361
The psychology of interpersonal relations.
    5.452
The psychology of invention in the
    mathematical field. 5.1042
Psychology of judgement and choice. 5.377
The psychology of learning and memory.
    5.296
The psychology of learning applied to teaching.
    4.10352
The psychology of management. 5.5602
The psychology of mathematics for instruction.
    5.1060
The psychology of memory. 5.322
The psychology of moral development. 5.607
The Psychology of music. 1.4387
The psychology of music. 1.4383, 1.4386
Psychology of music. 1.4388
The psychology of musical ability. 1.4390
The psychology of personal constructs. 5.522
A psychology of picture perception. 5.249
Psychology of problem solving: theory and
    practice. 5.374
The psychology of radio. 5.6431
The Psychology of reading. 5.395
Psychology of sex. 4.5500
The psychology of sex differences. 5.487
The psychology of sleep. 5.651
The psychology of social classes. 4.6376
The psychology of social movements. 4.5060
The psychology of the Afro-American. 3.6718
The psychology of the child. 5.574
The psychology of thinking. 5.394
The psychology of time. 5.403
The psychology of visual perception. 5.247
The Psychology of women. 4.5838
Psychology of women. 4.5918
The psychology of women. 4.5923
Psychology of women. 4.5946
Psychology versus metapsychology. 5.180
Psychometric methods. 5.47
Psychopathia sexualis. 4.5516
The psychopathic god. 3.2408
Psychopathology and politics. 5.173
Psychopathology of aging. 5.4814
The psychopathology of everyday life. 5.146
Psychopathy. 5.4826
Psychophysical thresholds. 5.235
Psychophysiology. 5.4312
Psychosocial nursing care of the emergency
    patient. 5.5210
Psychosomatic families. 5.4941
Psychotherapy. 5.4858
The psychotic process. 5.4922
Ptolemaic Alexandria. 3.5150
Public administration. 4.7757, 4.7761
Public administration and the public interest.
    4.7892
The public administration dictionary. 4.7215
Public & private goverment. 4.7467
Public and private high schools. 4.10049
The public buildings of Williamsburg, colonial
    capital of Virginia. 3.8222
The public burning. 2.12954
Public choice. 4.7736
Public corporations and public policy in
    Canada. 4.3086
Public debt and future generations. 4.4724
Public education. 4.10013
Public education in the United States. 4.9983
Public employee relations in West Germany.
    4.3517
Public employee trade unionism in the United
    Kingdom: the legal framework. 4.3518
Public employee unionism in Belgium. 4.3515
Public employee unionism in Israel. 4.3519
Public employment compulsory arbitration in
    Australia. 4.3514
Public entrepreneurship. 4.7767
Public expenditure. 4.4720
Public finance in a democratic society. 4.4646
Public financial institutions in India. 4.4459

Public health and the medical profession in the
    Renaissance. 5.4652
The public image. 2.9362
The public image of big business in America,
    1880-1940. 4.3045
The public interest. 4.7620-4.7621
The public interest in government labor
    relations. 4.3512
The public lands. 4.2821
Public lands politics. 4.2825
Public life in Renaissance Florence. 3.2924
The public life of Thomas Cooper, 1783-1839.
    3.6984
Public man, private woman. 4.5955
Public opinion. 4.5017
Public opinion, 1935-1946. 3.193
Public opinion and Canadian identity. 3.8782
Public opinion and foreign policy. 3.6428
Public opinion in American politics. 4.5226
The public order of the oceans. 4.9315
Public papers of the Presidents of the United
    States. 4.7207
Public papers of the Presidents of the United
    States. 4.7206
Public personnel systems. 4.7985
The public philosophy. 4.7459
Public policy analysis. 4.1205
Public policy and federalism. 4.7873
Public policy & federalism. 4.7873
Public policy and the aging. 4.5817
Public policy toward disabled workers. 4.3475
The public presidency. 4.7934
Public principles of public debt. 4.4723
The public purse. 4.4665
The public readings. 2.7626
The public role in the dairy economy. 4.3691
The public school and the private vision.
    4.10016
Public school law. 4.9585
Public schools in hard times. 4.10738
Public schools of choice. 4.10031
Public sorrows and private pleasures. 1.504
The public stake in union power. 4.3347
Public transportation. 4.3908
Public transportation and land use policy.
    4.3909
Public utility economics. 4.3039
Public works history in the United States.
    5.8388
Publicans and sinners. 4.1737
Publication manual. 5.68
Publication manual of the American
    Psychological Association. 5.68
Publications of the United Nations system.
    5.8267
The public's business. 4.3085
The public's right to know. 4.9764
The publish-it-yourself handbook. 5.7576
Publishers directory. 5.7592
Publishers, distributors, and wholesalers of the
    U.S. 5.7593
Publishers international directory. 5.7573
The Publishers' trade list annual. 5.7755
Publishers' trade list annual. 5.7756-5.7757
Publishers' weekly. 5.7748
Publishers weekly. 5.7594
Publishing in the Third World. 5.7582
Puccini. 1.3950
Pudd'nhead Wilson and Those extraordinary
    twins. 2.10946
Pueblo Indian textiles. 3.5942
The Pueblo potter. 3.5940
Puer aeternus. 5.518
Puerto Rican Americans. 3.6589
The Puerto Rican community and its children
    on the mainland. 4.10849
The Puerto Rican experience. 3.6588
Puerto Rico, a colonial experiment. 3.6479
Puerto Rico: a socio-historic interpretation.
    3.9129
Puerto Rico and the Puerto Ricans. 3.9127
Puerto Rico: commonwealth, state or nation?
    3.9128
Puerto Rico; freedom and power in the
    Caribbean. 3.9125
Pugin. 1.5397
Pul Eliya, a village in Ceylon. 4.597
Pulitzer. 2.3628

Pulitzer's Post-dispatch, 1878-1883. 2.3669
Pulitzer's prize editor. 2.3610
The Pullman strike. 4.3170
Pulsars. 5.1848
Pulse and Fourier transform NMR. 5.2314
Pulse, digital, and switching waveforms. 5.6481
The pump house gang. 3.6067
The pumpkin eater. 2.9747
Punctuated equilibria. 5.3388
Punishing the perpetrators of the Holocaust. 3.1112-3.1113
The Punjab crisis. 3.4353
Punjabi century, 1857-1947. 3.4352
The puppet theatre in America. 2.2837
Puppets in America since 1948. 2.2837
The puppets' tale. 2.1859
Puranas. Bhāgavatapurāna. English. 2.1933
Puranas. English. Selections. 1.1688
Purānic encyclopaedia. 1.1689
Purcell. 1.3952
Purchasing handbook. 4.4324
Pure cultures of algae, their preparation & maintenance. 5.3706
Pure economics. 4.1474
Pure gold. 2.14058
Pure lust. 4.5875
Pure politics and impure science. 5.4675
The pure theory of domestic values. 4.4108
The pure theory of foreign trade. 4.4108
The Purgatorio. 2.4926
Purgatorio. 2.4923
The purge of Japanese leaders under the occupation. 3.4976
Purification of laboratory chemicals. 5.6848
The Puritan dilemma. 3.7986
The Puritan ethic and woman suffrage. 4.8082
The puritan experiment. 3.7945
The Puritan family. 3.7953
A Puritan in Babylon. 3.7738
Puritan influences in American literature. 2.10343
The Puritan mind. 1.3396
The Puritan moment. 3.1736
The puritan pleasures of the detective story. 2.5959
The Puritan tradition in America, 1620-1730. 3.7957
Puritan village. 3.8008
The Puritan way of death. 1.2944
Puritanism and democracy. 3.6155
Puritanism and revolution. 3.1450
Puritanism and theatre. 2.6640
Puritanism in old and New England. 1.3397
The Puritans. 2.10708
Puritans among the Indians. 3.5784
Puritans and Yankees. 3.7985
Purity and danger. 4.613
Purity in print. 4.9719
Purity (Middle English poem) 2.6132, 2.6381
Purity of diction in English verse. 2.5808
The purple cow and other nonsense. 2.11435
The purple land. 2.8809
Purpose and thought. 1.532
The purpose of American politics. 3.7588
Purposes of art. 1.4680
Purposive behaviour in animals and men. 5.220
The purposive brain. 5.4333
Purposive explanation in psychology. 5.481
Pursuing justice for the child. 4.9893
The pursuit of a dream. 3.8293
The pursuit of equality in American history. 4.9698
The pursuit of loneliness. 3.6187
The pursuit of love. 2.9119
Pursuit of power. 3.622
The pursuit of salvation. 2.8773
The pursuit of signs 2.2488
The pursuit of simplicity. 5.856
Pursuit of the ancient Maya. 3.9032
The pursuit of the millennium. 1.2314
Pushbutton fantasies. 5.6400
The Pushcart prize. 2.10662
Pushkin. 2.1416-2.1417, 2.1419
Pushkin threefold; narrative, lyric, polemic, and ribald verse. 2.1407
Puss-in-Boots. 2.13664

Put out more flags. 2.9492
Put out the light. 2.4432
La putain, respectueuse. 2.4731
Putois. 2.4204
Puttin' on ole massa. 3.7212
The puzzle palace. 5.7361
The puzzleheaded girl. 2.10172
Puzzles and epiphanies. 2.5739
Puzzles, problems and enigmas. 5.969
Pygmalion grows up. 4.10375
Pygmalion in the classroom. 4.10386
Pylon. 2.11671
Pynchon. 2.13280, 2.13286
Pynchon, the voice of ambiguity. 2.13287
The pyramid. 2.8702
The pyramids. 3.5147
The pyramids of Egypt. 3.5146
Pyroclastic rocks. 5.3045
Python. 4.822

Qian Zhongshu. 2.2238
Quadrille. 2.8582
The Quaker family in colonial America. 1.3349
The Quaker influence in American literature. 2.10342
Quaker spirituality. 1.3353
Quakers and politics; Pennsylvania, 1681-1726. 3.8078
Quakers and the Atlantic culture. 1.3348
The Quakers as pioneers in social work. 1.3354
The qualified student. 4.10610
Qualitative and quantitative social research. 4.4806
Qualitative inorganic analysis. 5.2672
Qualitative theory of differential equations. 5.1506
Qualitative variables in econometrics. 4.1396
Qualities of community life. 4.6301
Quality circles. 4.2724
Quality control and industrial statistics. 5.7029
The quality of federal policymaking. 4.3494
The quality of frozen foods. 5.6889
Quangos in Britain. 4.8451
Quantitative analytical chemistry. 5.2687
Quantitative chemical techniques of histo- and cytochemistry. 5.3619
Quantitative economic research: trends and problems. 4.1233
Quantitative ethology. 5.4069
Quantitative methods in politics. 4.8070
Quantitative methods in psychology. 5.48
Quantitative techniques in geography. 4.18
Quantum and statistical aspects of light. 5.2290
A quantum approach to the solid state. 5.2199
Quantum chemistry. 5.2826-5.2828
Quantum electrodynamics. 5.2373
Quantum field theory. 5.2155-5.2156
Quantum fields. 5.2153
Quantum mechanics. 5.2116-5.2117, 5.2121, 5.2129, 5.2134
Quantum mechanics for applied physics and engineering. 5.2131
Quantum mechanics in simple matrix form. 5.2133
The quantum mechanics of many-body systems. 5.2164
The quantum physicists and an introduction to their physics. 5.2111
Quantum reality. 5.2132
Quantum states of atoms, molecules, and solids. 5.2135
Quantum theory. 5.2110
Quantum theory of matter. 5.2122
Quantum theory of molecules and solids. 5.2138
The quantum theory of radiation. 5.2375
Quantum theory of solids. 5.2115, 5.2119
The quare fellow, and The hostage. 2.8442
Quarks. 5.2475
Quarks and leptons. 5.2476
Quarks, leptons & gauge fields. 5.2477
Quarks, leptons and gauge fields. 5.2477
Quarrels that have shaped the Constitution. 4.9785
Quartet in autumn. 2.9802

Quasars. 5.1861
Quasi-stellar objects. 5.1860
The quasi-war. 3.7055
The Quaternary era. 5.3142
Quaternary extinctions. 5.3163
The Quaternary of the United States. 5.3146
Quaternary paleoclimatology. 5.2525
Quaternary structure and beyond. 5.4413
Quebec. 4.5250, 4.8314
Quebec 70. 3.8815
The Quebec act. 3.8724
Quebec and the Constitution, 1960-1978. 4.8286
Quebec nationalism in crisis. 3.8811
Quebec: the revolutionary age, 1760-1791. 3.8732
The Queen. 3.1712
The Queen and the rebels. 2.5024
Queen Anne. 3.1536
Queen Elizabeth and the making of policy, 1572-1588. 3.1422
Queen Elizabeth and the revolt of the Netherlands. 3.1257
Queen Elizabeth I. 3.1424
The queen of air and darkness. 2.9519
Queen of the Woods. 3.5794
Queen Ortruda. 2.1534
The Queen v Louis Riel. 4.9431
Queen Victoria. 3.1615
Queen Victoria: born to succeed. 3.1614
Queen Victoria, from her birth to the death of the Prince Consort. 3.1616
Queens, concubines, and dowagers. 4.5861
Queen's quorum. 5.8173
Quelqu'un. English. 2.4655
Querelle. 2.4540
Queremos tanto a Glenda y otros relatos. 2.5382
Quesnay's Tableau économique. 4.1407
Quest. 5.1951
The quest for a just world order. 4.9135
Quest for America, 1810-1824. 3.6038
Quest for an American sociology. 4.4777
The quest for being, and other studies in naturalism and humanism. 1.595
The quest for certainty. 1.1279
The quest for Christa T. 2.13929
A quest for common learning. 4.10818
The quest for economic stability. 4.1968
The Quest for economic stabilization. 4.4583
The quest for excellence. 4.10252
The Quest for imagination. 1.1380
The quest for national efficiency: a study in British politics and political thought, 1899-1914. 3.1683
Quest for past and future. 1.1970
The quest for permanence. 2.8325
The quest for security, 1715-1740. 3.649
The quest for security in New Zealand, 1840 to 1966. 4.3673
The quest for Shakespeare's Globe. 2.6709
Quest for the necessary. 2.8405
Quest for the new moral world. 4.7163
The quest for Ulysses. 1.6742
The quest for world order. 3.1157
The quest of the historical Jesus. 1.2880
Quest (Washington, D.C.) 4.6036
The question concerning technology, and other essays. 1.993
The question of animal awareness. 5.4101
The question of being. 1.989
The question of class struggle. 4.3655
The question of Flannery O'Connor. 2.13224
The question of Hamlet. 2.6656
The question of Jean-Jacques Rousseau. 1.816
A question of judgment. 4.9812
The question of Palestine, 1914-1918. 3.3914
The question of parole. 4.9895
A question of power. 2.10080
A question of upbringing. 2.9225
Questioni e correnti di storia letteraria, a cura di U. Bosco [et. al.] 2.4873
The questionnaire, or, Prayer for a town & a friend. 2.1685
Questions about music. 1.3477
Questions and answers in attitude surveys. 4.1229
The questions of King Milinda. 1.1742

Questions of religious truth. 1.1520
Quests for a promised land. 2.14029
Quetzalcóatl and Guadalupe. 3.8875
Queuing and waiting. 4.4868
Quevedo. 2.5196
Quick springs of sense. 2.5663
Quicksand. 2.11989
Quicksilver. 4.1156
The quiet American. 2.8757
The Quiet conquest. 1.6305
The quiet crisis. 5.5303
A quiet life. 2.9616
Quiet revolution. 4.8208
The quiet therapies. 5.4867
The quiet warrior. 5.7423
The Quiller memorandum. 2.9445
The quintessence of capitalism. 4.1543
Quintet. 4.1120
Quintilian. 2.767
A quire of seven. 2.13997
Quisling: the career and political ideas of
    Vidkun Quisling, 1887-1945. 3.3382
Quit India. 3.6451
Quite early one morning. 2.9403
Quo vadis. 2.1730
The Quotable woman, 1800-1975. 2.3733
The Quotable woman, from Eve to 1799.
    2.3734
Quotations from Chairman Mao Tse-tung.
    2.12841, 3.4824
Quotations in black. 2.3732
The Qur'an and its interpreters, volume 1.
    1.2030

R.C.N. in retrospect, 1910-1968. 5.7454
R. D. Blackmore. 2.7402
R. D. Laing, the man and his ideas. 5.4781
R. Delaunay. 1.6097
R. E. Lee. 3.7328
R. E. Olds, auto industry pioneer. 4.3823
R. H. Tawney and his times. 4.7031
R. I. C. laboratory handbook of toxic agents.
    5.4722
R.U.R. and The insect play. 2.1664
A rabbinic anthology. 1.1941
Rabbit is rich. 2.13376
Rabbit redux. 2.13377
Rabbit, run. 2.13378
Rabelais. 2.4005-2.4006
Rābi'a the mystic & her fellow-saints in Islām.
    1.2024
Rābi'a the mystic and her fellow-saints in
    Islām. 1.2024
Rabindranath Tagore: Krishna Kripalani.
    2.1872
Rabota aktera nad roliu. 2.3125
Race. 3.6509
Race against time. 3.5270
Race and colour in Caribbean literature.
    2.2695
Race and economics. 3.6529
Race and ethnic relations in Latin America and
    the Caribbean. 3.9025
Race and law in Great Britain. 4.9421
Race and nationality in American life. 3.6513
Race & politics. 3.7174
Race and politics in North Carolina, 1872-1901.
    3.6802
Race and schooling in the city. 4.10792
Race and the American romantics. 2.10837
Race, class, and education. 4.10777
Race, class, and politics in colonial Mexico,
    1610-1670. 3.8927
Race, colonialism and the city. 4.6459
Race, conflict, and the international order.
    4.6454
Race conflict in New Zealand, 1814-1865.
    3.5613
Race differences in intelligence. 5.370
Race, intelligence and education. 5.372
Race, IQ, and Jensen. 5.373
Race, jobs & politics. 4.3117
Race, language and culture. 4.403
Race, marriage and the law. 4.9680
Race, reform and rebellion. 3.6679
Race relations. 3.6702
Race relations and the New York City
    Commission on Human Rights. 4.7704

Race relations in British North America,
    1607-1783. 3.6524
Race relations in the Portuguese colonial
    empire, 1415-1825. 4.8937
Race relations in the urban South, 1865-1890.
    3.6636
Race, religion, and the continuing American
    dilemma. 3.6674
Race riot. 3.8427
Race, social class, and individual differences in
    I.Q. 5.371
Races and cultures of India. 3.4202
Races, types, and ethnic groups. 4.440
Rachel Ray. 2.8221
Racial and ethnic relations in America. 3.6520
Racial equality in America. 3.6615
Racial exclusionism and the city. 3.1715
Racial myth in English history. 3.1301
Racial oppression in America. 3.6505
Racine and Shakespeare. 2.4053
Racine, or, The triumph of relevance. 2.4055
Racing with Cornelius Shields and the masters.
    4.986
Racism and American education. 4.10008
Racism and Empire. 4.8917
Racism and mental health. 5.4702
Racism and sexism in corporate life. 4.4340
Racism in American education. 4.10709
Racism: the Australian experience. 3.5584
Radar detection and tracking systems. 5.6435
Radar observation of the atmosphere. 5.2553
Radar technology. 5.6434
The Radetzky march. 2.13855
Radetzkymarsch. 2.13856
The radiance of Chartres. 1.6650
The radiant future. 2.1650
Radiation and human health. 5.4729
Radiation detection. 5.2444
Radiation detection and measurement. 5.2442
Radiation, genes, and man. 5.3628
Radiations from radioactive substances. 5.2402
Radical Christianity and its sources. 1.2755
Radical dissent in contemporary Israeli politics.
    4.8787
The radical empiricism of William James.
    1.604
The Radical Enlightenment. 3.179
The radical future of liberal feminism. 4.5878
The radical immigrant. 4.5236
Radical innocence, studies in the contemporary
    American novel. 2.10625
The radical kingdom. 1.2929
Radical nationalism in Cameroun. 4.8812
Radical nationalist in Japan. 3.4967
The radical novel in the United States,
    1900-1954: some interrelations of literature
    and society. 2.10642
Radical paradoxes. 4.5233
Radical politics in South Asia. 4.8715
Radical politics in West Bengal. 4.7119
Radical principles. 4.7585
Radical reflection and the origin of the human
    sciences. 1.1327
The Radical Reformation. 1.2331
The radical Republicans. 3.7266
Radical school reform. 4.10172
Radical sects of revolutionary New England.
    1.2404
The radical Spinoza. 1.1101
Radical theology and the death of God. 1.2801
Radical Tories. 4.7280
The radical tradition. 4.7092
Radical visions and American dreams. 3.6153
Radio and television broadcasting in Eastern
    Europe. 4.4061
Radio astronomy. 5.1778, 5.1783
Radio astrophysics. 5.1775
The radio universe. 5.1782
Radio wave propagation. 5.6427
Radioactive decay data tables. 5.2488
Radioactive waste. 5.6056
Radioisotope laboratory techniques. 5.2918
Radioisotope techniques. 5.2437
Radwaste. 5.6058
Raffles, the amateur cracksman. 2.8807
The raft. 2.10108
Rage for order. 2.2601
A rage to live. 2.12273

The ragged trousered philanthropists. 2.9444
Ragnars saga Lothrókar ok sona hans. 2.13991
Ragtime. 1.4277-1.4278, 2.12990
Rahel Varnhagen. 2.13666
A Rahner handbook. 1.3278
A Rahner reader. 1.3140
Railroad engineering. 5.6072
Railroad labor disputes. 4.3169
Railroad management. 4.3985
Railroad maps of North America. 4.138
Railroad mergers and abandonments. 4.4001
Railroad track. 5.6073
Railroad transportation and public policy.
    4.3983
The railroads. 4.3991
Railroads. 5.6071
Railroads and American economic growth.
    4.3993
Railroads and rifles. 3.2257
Railroads and the Granger laws. 4.9529
Railroads, freight, and public policy. 4.4002
Railroads, reconstruction, and the gospel of
    prosperity. 4.3984
Rails, mines, and progress. 4.4020
Railway economy. 4.3980
The railway police. 2.12946
Railways. 5.6070
Railways at war. 4.3978
Rain from heaven. 2.11347
Rain upon Godshill. 2.9249
The rainbow and the kings. 3.5420
The rainbow. 2.8970
A rainbow for the Christian West. 2.4839
Rainbow in the rock. 4.5392
Rainbows, halos, and glories. 5.2555
Raise high the roof beam, carpenters. 2.12426
A raisin in the sun. 2.11813
Raising children in modern America. 4.5710
The Raj quartet. 2.9807
Raj quartet. 2.9808
The rake's regress. 2.9483
The rakish stage. 2.5912
Raleigh's lost colony. 3.8231
Ralph Ellison. 2.13006
Ralph Nader study group report on the
    Interstate Commerce Commission and
    transportation. 4.3891
Ralph the heir. 2.8222
Ralph Waldo Emerson. 2.11031
The Ramadan war, 1973. 3.3937
The Ramakien: the Thai epic. 2.9650
The Ramayan of Valmiki. 2.1938
The Ramayana. 2.2275
The Ramayana and the Mahabharata. 2.1937
The Ramayana of Goswami Tulsidas. 2.1886
The Rāmāyana of Vālmīki. 1.1693
The Ramayana of Valmiki. 2.1939
The Ramayana tradition in Asia. 1.1694
Rambam. 1.377
Ramillies and the union with Scotland. 3.1537
Rāmmakīan. English. 2.9650
Ramón de la Cruz. 2.5215
Ramón del Valle-Inclán. 2.5293-2.5294
Ramon Guthrie's Maximum security ward.
    2.11806
Ramón J. Sender. 2.5284
Ramsay MacDonald. 3.1672
Ramsey theory. 5.1285
Ramuntcho. 2.4330
The Rand McNally atlas of the oceans. 4.193
Rand McNally atlas of world history. 4.123
Rand McNally Goode's World atlas. 4.112
Rand McNally, the new international atlas.
    4.115
The Rand McNally world atlas of exploration.
    4.49
Random harvest. 2.8803
The Random House book of poetry for
    children. 2.10739
The Random House book of twentieth-century
    French poetry. 2.3927
The Random House college dictionary. 2.1087
The Random House dictionary of the English
    language. 2.1086
The Random House thesaurus. 2.1068
Random notes on Red China (1936-1945).
    3.4779
The range of human capacities. 5.367

Ranke. 3.422
Ransoms to time. 2.615
Raoul Dufy. 1.4973
Rape and inequality. 4.6739
Rape and sexual assault. 4.6737
Rape and the limits of law reform. 4.9866
The Rape crisis intervention handbook. 4.6735
Rape in marriage. 4.6738
The rape of Clarissa. 2.7216
The rape of the lock and its illustrations, 1714-1896. 2.7193
Raphael. 1.5018, 1.6219
Raphaël. 2.4255
The rapist file. 4.6740
Rappin' and stylin' out. 3.6719
Rare books, 1983-84. 5.7700
Rare halos, mirages, anomalous rainbows, and related electromagnetic phenomena. 5.2557
Rashomon. 2.2071
The rat. 5.4041
Rates of exchange. 2.9627
The ratification of the Fourteenth Amendment. 4.9687
A rating of graduate programs. 4.10087
The rational and social foundations of music. 1.4370
Rational belief systems. 1.1297
Rational decision. 4.4979
Rational expectations. 4.1465
The rational expectations revolution in macroeconomics. 4.1460
Rational man. 1.1409
The rational manager. 4.2665
The rational peasant. 4.2921
A rational public policy for medical education and its financing. 5.4605
Rationale of the dirty joke. 2.3801
Rationalism in politics, and other essays. 4.7229
Rationes dictandi. English. 1971. 2.2535
Rattlesnakes: their habits, life histories, and influence on mankind. 5.3926
Ravel. 1.3956-1.3958
The raven. 3.8325
Raven. 1.2101
The raven and the whale. 2.10238
Ravenna mosaics. 1.5506
Ravenshoe. 2.7884
The raw and the cooked. 3.9200
The Raymond Chandler omnibus. 2.11479
Raymond of the Times. 2.3630
Rayuela. 2.5383
The razor's edge. 2.9102
The RCN in retrospect, 1910-1968. 5.7454
The re-discovery of America. 3.6111
The re-ordering of the stones. 2.9313
Re-working the work ethic. 4.3122
Reaching judgment at Nuremberg. 3.1075
Reaching the aged. 4.6589
Reaching the underserved. 5.4703
The reaction against experiment in the English novel, 1950-1960. 2.6042
Reaction and reconstruction in English politics, 1832-1852. 3.1617
Reaction and revolution, 1814-1832. 3.692
Reactionary essays on poetry and ideas. 2.2764
Reactionary modernism. 3.2367
Reactions to the English Civil War, 1642-1649. 3.1484
Reactive intermediates in organic chemistry. 5.2855
The read-aloud handbook. 4.10467
A readable Beowulf. 2.6293
The readable people of George Meredith. 2.7949
The reader. 2.7271
The reader and the writer. 2.13927
Reader in bureaucracy. 4.7746
A reader in nineteenth century historical Indo-European linguistics. 2.218
The reader in the text. 2.2450
Reader-response criticism. 2.2487
The reader, the text, the poem. 2.2366
The Reader's adviser. 5.7707
Reader's adviser and bookman's manual 1960. 5.7707
The reader's encyclopedia. 2.2345

The reader's encyclopedia of Shakespeare. 2.6684
The Reader's encyclopedia of the American West. 3.8465
The reader's encyclopedia of world drama. 2.2784
A Reader's guide to Canadian history. 5.7895
A reader's guide to Dylan Thomas. 2.9422
A reader's guide to Ernest Hemingway. 2.11865
A reader's guide to fifty modern British plays. 2.5923
A reader's guide to fifty modern European poets. 2.3746
A reader's guide to Gerard Manley Hopkins. 2.7834
A readers guide to great twentieth-century English novels. 2.6040
A reader's guide to James Joyce. 2.8922
A reader's guide to Joseph Conrad. 2.8569
A reader's guide to Marcel Proust. 2.4673
Readers' guide to periodical literature. 1.39
Readers' guide to periodical literature,1890-1899. 1.40
A reader's guide to Shakespeare's plays. 2.6794
A reader's guide to T. S. Eliot. 2.11645
A reader's guide to the contemporary English novel. 2.6039
A reader's guide to the great religions. 5.8449
A reader's guide to the nineteenth century English novel. 2.6006
A reader's guide to the plays of W.B. Yeats. 2.8364
A reader's guide to W. H. Auden. 2.8404
A reader's guide to William Butler Yeats. 2.8357
A reader's guide to William Faulkner. 2.11705
Reading and understanding. 4.10343
Reading Beowulf. 2.6300
Reading 'Capital' 4.1515
Reading Clarissa. 2.7218
Reading Coleridge. 2.7603
Reading for the plot. 2.3443
Reading, how to. 4.10340
Reading in the elementary school. 4.10462, 4.10464
The reading interests of young people. 5.7689
Reading Nabokov. 2.12232
Reading Nozick. 4.7645
A reading of Beowulf. 2.6297
A reading of Hegel's Phenomenology of spirit. 1.936
A reading of Henry Green. 2.8736
A reading of Jane Austen. 2.7379
Reading Paradise lost. 2.7121
Reading Rawls. 4.7661
Reading research and librarianship. 5.7688
Reading, 'riting, and reconstruction. 4.10870
Reading Spenser. 2.6537
Reading the fire. 2.2315
Reading: the patterning of complex behaviour. 4.10418
Reading the Rāmayāna. 5.8339
Reading the romance. 5.7725
Reading the Song of Roland. 2.3962
Reading the Victorian novel. 2.6023
Readings for nursing research. 5.5189
Readings for social studies in elementary education. 4.10482
Readings in American art since 1900. 1.4881
Readings in applied English linguistics. 2.2
Readings in art history. 1.4677
Readings in contemporary ethical theory. 1.1405
Readings in cultural geography. 4.358
Readings in early anthropology. 4.414
Readings in economic geography. 4.4122
Readings in industrial organization and public policy. 4.1976
Readings in international economics. 4.4136
Readings in labor economics and industrial relations. 4.3113
Readings in managerial psychology. 4.4351
Readings in mathematical psychology. 5.53
Readings in Philippine church history. 1.3195
Readings in price theory. 4.1502
Readings in Russian civilization. 3.3003

Readings in Russian poetics. 2.1242
Readings in semantics. 1.550
Readings in the economics of taxation. 4.4689
Readings in the history of American agriculture. 5.5238
Readings in the history of education. 4.9952
Readings in the history of music in performance. 1.4124
Readings in the philosophy of Moses Maimonides. 1.377
Readings in the philosophy of science. 5.882
Readings in the physical sciences. 5.852
Readings in the theory of international trade. 4.4104
Readings in urban transportation. 4.3889
Readings on public employment services. 4.3238
Readings on taxation in developing countries. 4.4694
The reaffirmation of Republicanism. 4.8224
Reagan. 3.7940
Reagan and the world. 3.7939
Reagent chemicals. 5.2661
Reagents for organic synthesis. 5.2732
Real analysis. 5.1492
Real and complex analysis. 5.1445
Real & complex analysis. 5.1445
The real Charlotte. 2.9350
The Real estate handbook. 4.2828
The real F. Scott Fitzgerald thirty-five years later. 2.11729
The real Inspector Hound. 2.9814
The real Isadora. 4.1135
The real life of Sebastian Knight. 2.12230
Real losses, imaginary gains. 2.12217
The real Matilda. 4.6163
The real menstrual cycle. 5.4260
Real solids and radiation. 5.2194
The Real teachers. 4.10045
The real thing. 2.9815
The Real Tripitaka. 1.1775
Real wages in manufacturing, 1890-1914. 4.3148
Real wages in Soviet Russia since 1928. 4.3443
Real wages in the United States, 1890-1926. 4.3143
Real wicked, guy. 3.1291
The real world of liberalism. 4.7648
The real world of the public schools. 4.10030
Realism. 1.4797
Realism and nationalism, 1852-1871. 3.710
Realism and naturalism in nineteenth-century American literature. 2.10386, 2.10609
Realism and reality. 2.13504
Realism and the aim of science. 5.924
Realism and the background of phenomenology. 1.534
Realism and tradition in art, 1848-1900. 1.4790
Realist fiction. 2.3717
A realist philosophy of science. 1.552
The realist tradition. 1.4968
The realistic imagination. 2.6013
The realities behind diplomacy. 3.1622
Realities of American foreign policy. 3.7824
Reality and empathy. 1.1267
Reality and rhetoric. 4.2761
Reality and the poet in Spanish poetry. 2.5118
The reality of ethnomethodology. 4.4803
The reality of faith. 1.2935
The reality of God, and other essays. 1.2790
The reality of the church. 1.2992
The reality of the historical past. 3.493
Realizations. 1.6716
Reallexikon der deutschen Literaturgeschichte. 2.13450
The really interesting question, and other papers. 2.9389
The Realm of science. 5.699
Realms of being. 1.647
The realms of gold. 2.9663
The realms of healing. 5.5213
The reappearing characters in Balzac's Comédie humaine. 2.4111
Reappraisals in British imperial history. 3.1222
Reappraisals in history. 3.392
Reason and analysis. 1.510
Reason and Existenz. 1.1028

Reason and human good in Aristotle. 1.311
Reason and morality. 1.1450
Reason and nature. 1.580
Reason and religion. 1.1558
Reason and revelation in the middle ages.
  1.350
Reason and revolution. 4.4761
Reason and rhetoric. 4.9954
Reason and romanticism. 2.2590
Reason and teaching. 4.9971
Reason and the imagination. 3.181
Reason and violence. 4.5077
Reason in ethics. 1.1411
Reason in the age of science. 1.85
Reason, the only oracle of man, or, A
  compendious system of natural religion.
  1.1889
The reason why. 3.1600
The reasonableness of Christianity. 1.2257
Reason's disciples. 4.6109
Rebecca. 2.8603
The Rebecca Riots. 3.1770
Rebecca West. 2.9514, 2.9516
Rebecca West, a celebration. 2.9510
The rebel. 4.5042
Rebel at large. 3.7633
Rebel brass. 3.7390
Rebel for rights, Abigail Scott Duniway.
  4.6002
Rebellion and democracy in Meiji Japan.
  3.4959
Rebellion and its enemies in late imperial
  China. 3.4721
Rebellion in the backlands (Os sertões) 3.9214
Rebellion or revolution?. 3.6609
The rebellious century, 1830-1930. 4.5351
Rebellious prophet. 1.1112
The rebels. 3.1162
Rebels against war. 4.9146
Rebels and ancestors. 2.10621
Rebels and gentleman. 3.8087
Rebels and revolutionaries in north China,
  1845-1945. 3.4674
Rebels and rulers, 1500-1660. 3.616
Rebels and victims. 2.10612
Rebels and whips. 4.8523
Rebels under sail. 3.6953
Rebirth of a nation. 3.1768
Rebirth of feminism. 4.6055
The rebirth of Italy, 1943-50. 3.2906
Rebuilding America. 4.2008
The rebuilding of Italy. 3.2905
Recapitalizing America. 4.2014
The recapitulated fall. 2.2630
Recasting. 2.12197
Recasting bourgeois Europe. 3.876
Recent American philosophy. 1.563
Recent developments in psychoanalysis. 5.131
Recent discoveries in Bible lands. 1.2504
Recent Japanese philosophical thought,
  1862-1962. 1.1142
Recent philosophy. 1.438
Recent poetry of Spain. 2.5153
Recent research in reading. 5.8156
Recent research on Anglo-Irish writers. 2.9854
The Reception of unconventional science.
  5.747
Reception theory. 2.13451
Recherches sur la formation de la grande
  entreprise capitaliste (1815-1848). 4.2323
Reckoners. 5.1143
The reckoning. 3.1664
Reckoning with slavery. 3.7246
Recognition in international law. 4.9301
Recognition of health hazards in industry.
  5.5018
The recognitions. 2.13022
Recognizable patterns of human malformation.
  5.4169, 5.5070
Recognizing Islam. 1.1999
Recollections. 3.2148
Recollections and experiences of an abolitionist,
  from 1855 to 1865. 3.7271
Recollections and reflections. 1.3997
Recollections of a forest life. 3.5790
The recollections of Geoffry Hamlyn. 2.7883
Recollections of Rubens. 1.6274
Recollections of Socrates. 1.241

Recollections of the table-talk of Samuel
  Rogers. 2.8005
Recombinant D.N.A. techniques. 5.3460
Recombinant DNA techniques. 5.3460
Recommended dietary allowances. 5.7125
The reconquest of Spain. 3.3425
Reconsiderations on the Revolutionary War.
  3.6887
Reconstructing American literary history.
  2.10262
Reconstructing Aphra. 2.6901
Reconstructing educational psychology.
  4.10705
Reconstructing the Union. 3.7308
Reconstruction: after the Civil War. 3.7465
The reconstruction of a Spanish Golden Age
  playhouse. 1.5552
The reconstruction of American history.
  3.6210
The reconstruction of western Europe, 1945-51.
  4.2204
Reconstruction, political & economic,
  1865-1877. 3.7463
Record guide. 1.3627
A record of the Boston stage. 2.3217
Record of the Buddhistic kingdoms. 3.3612
The recorder and its music. 1.4167
Recorder technique. 1.4551
Recording America's past. 3.6223
Records, computers, and the rights of citizens.
  4.7703
Records of the grand historian of China.
  3.4698
Recovering the word. 2.10297
Recovery of belief. 1.2227
The recovery of Germany. 3.863
Recreating the past. 1.6017
Recreation planning and management. 4.889
Recreational leadership. 4.888
Recreational sports programming. 4.973
Recreational use of wild lands. 4.893
The recruiting officer. 2.7016
The rector of Justin. 2.11342
Recursion via Pascal. 5.1223
Red and black. 2.4305
The red and the green. 2.9760
The red and the white: report from a French
  village. 4.5356
The Red Army: the Red Army, 1918 to 1945.
  5.7331
The red badge of courage. 2.10978
The red/bluecoats. 3.5774
Red brotherhood at war. 3.4434
Red Cloud and the Sioux problem. 3.5928
The red commissar. 2.1670
Red Crow, warrior chief. 3.5951
Red Emma speaks. 4.7192
The Red executive. 4.2744
Red flag over Afghanistan. 3.4119
Red giants and white dwarfs. 5.1715
Red gold. 3.9198
Red gold of Africa. 4.651
Red harvest. 4.7151
Red land, black land. 3.5140
Red man's land/white man's law. 4.9774
The red notebook of Charles Darwin. 5.3193
Red October. 3.3179
Red over Black. 3.5850
Red phoenix. 3.1056
The Red River Valley, 1811-1849. 3.8859
The Red room. 2.4608
Red scare. 3.7550
The red scare in the Midwest, 1945-1955.
  3.8306
Red star in orbit. 5.6701
Red star on the Nile. 3.3749
Red star over China. 3.4755
Red star rising at sea. 5.7469
Red virgin soil. 2.1272
Red, white, and black: the peoples of early
  America. 3.6866
Redating the New Testament. 1.2626
Redeem the time. 1.2982
Redeemer nation. 3.6282
Redeeming Shakespeare's words. 2.6846
Redesigning rural development. 4.2890
Rediscoveries in art. 1.4671
Rediscovering the teaching of Jesus. 1.2662

The rediscovery of Black nationalism. 3.6665
The rediscovery of the frontier. 2.10346
Redistribution of population in Africa. 4.1661
Redistribution with growth. 4.1819
The reduction of working time. 4.3151
Reductions in organic chemistry. 5.2753
The reef. 2.12697
Reference and generality. 1.1173
Reference and modality. 1.1253
Reference and online services handbook.
  5.7650
Reference and subscription books reviews.
  5.7714
Reference encyclopedia of the American Indian.
  3.5700
A reference grammar of modern French. 2.865
Reference grammar of the German language.
  2.1178
Reference groups; exploration into conformity
  and deviation of adolescents. 4.5761
A reference guide to English, American and
  Canadian literature. 5.7934
Reference guide to fantastic films. 2.2990
A Reference guide to modern fantasy for
  children. 2.5968
A reference guide to the literature of travel.
  5.8208
The Reference handbook of the armed forces of
  the world. 1971-. 5.7259
Reference handbook on the deserts of North
  America. 4.283
Reference materials on Latin America in
  English, the humanities. 5.7908
Reference point. 2.3094
Reference sources in English and American
  literature. 5.7938
Reference sources in library and information
  services. 5.7603
Referendums. 4.7725
Reflection seismology. 5.6741
Reflections in a golden eye. 2.12075
Reflections in a quiet pool. 1.6449
Reflections of a Jacobite. 2.3505
Reflections of a nonpolitical man. 2.13825
Reflections of reality in Japanese art. 1.5076
Reflections of women in antiquity. 4.5849
Reflections on American institutions. 3.6089
Reflections on art. 1.4644
Reflections on espionage. 2.11878
Reflections on gender and science. 5.906
Reflections on learning. 4.10247
Reflections on modern history. 3.362
Reflections on photography. 5.6953
Reflections on the cold war. 3.7597
Reflections on the Constitution. 4.8472
Reflections on the motive power of fire. 5.2243
Reflections on the revolution in France. 3.2090
Reflections on the theatre. 2.3370
Reflections on things at hand. 1.150
Reflective faith. 1.2768
Reflective thinking. 4.10366
Reflexivity in Tristram Shandy. 2.7279
The reform and abolition of the traditional
  Chinese examination system. 4.8739
Reform and insurrection in Russian Poland,
  1856-1865. 3.3284
Reform and politics in Bourbon Chile,
  1755-1796. 3.9259
Reform and rebellion in Afghanistan,
  1919-1929. 3.4117
Reform and Reformation 3.1400
Reform and regulation. 3.7696
Reform and renewal. 3.1407
Reform and revolution in Asia. 3.4407
Reform in Sung China. 4.8733
Reform in the Ottoman Empire, 1856-1876.
  3.3586
Reform Judaism: a historical perspective.
  1.1916
Reform Judaism today. 1.1917
The reform movement in China, 1898-1912.
  3.4736
The reform of FBI intelligence operations.
  4.6818
The reform of Parliament. 4.8463
Reform rule in Czechoslovakia. 3.1929
The Reformation. 1.2321, 1.2324
Reformation and revolution, 1558-1660. 3.1420

Reformation and society in sixteenth-century Europe. 1.2322
Reformation and utopia. 1.2329
The Reformation era, 1500-1650. 1.2323
Reformation Europe. 1.2327
Reformation Europe, 1517-1559. 3.627
The Reformation in England, to the accession of Elizabeth I. 1.2356
The Reformation in medieval perspective. 1.2333
The reformation of American Quakerism, 1748-1783. 1.3350
Reformation to Industrial Revolution. 4.2254
The Reformation to the present day. 1.2274
The reformed local government system. 4.8874
Reformer without a church. 1.3305
The reformers. 4.6858
Reformers in profile. 1.2334
Reformers, rebels, and revolutionaries. 4.7009
Reforming corrections for juvenile offenders. 4.6883
Reforming Federal regulation. 4.9522
Reforming medicine. 5.4625
Reforming school finance. 4.10652
Reforming the long-term-care system. 5.4678
Reforming the reforms. 4.7941
Refugee scholars in America. 3.6566
Refugees and world politics. 4.6537
Refugees in the United States. 3.6525
Refusal to conform. 2.8938
Regency. 1.5374
Regency to empire. 1.6458
La regenta. 2.5213
Regicide and revolution. 3.2052
Regimes and oppositions. 4.7732
La región más transparente. 2.5342
Region, race, and Reconstruction. 3.8164
Regional analysis. 4.6362
Regional development in Western Europe. 4.6364
Regional development strategy in southeast Europe. 4.2417
Regional diversity. 4.2005
Regional factors in national planning and development. 4.1945
A regional geography for advanced and scholarship courses. 4.4125
Regional geography of Anglo-America. 3.6060
A regional geography of Iceland. 3.3373
A regional geography of Western Europe. 3.1188
Regional geomorphology of the United States. 5.2998
The regional imperative. 3.4105
Regional industrial analysis and development. 4.6361
Regional organization and order in South-East Asia. 4.6363
Regional statistics. 5.8433
Regional theatre. 2.3212
The regional vocabulary of Texas. 2.1152
Regionalism and national unity in Nepal. 3.4379
Regionalism and nationalism in the United States. 3.6104
Regionalism and the United Nations. 4.9250
Regionalism in American politics. 4.8249
Registry of toxic effects -1980. 5.4725
Registry of toxic effects of chemical substances. 5.4725
Les regrets, suivis des Antiquités de Rome. 2.3998
Regular complex polytopes. 5.1636
Regular figures. 5.1584
Regular solutions. 5.2906
Regulating birth. 4.9545
Regulating business by independent commission. 4.3079
Regulating safety. 4.3504
Regulating the automobile. 4.3827
Regulating the poor. 4.6525
Regulating U.S. intelligence operations. 4.7908
Regulating US intelligence operations. 4.7908
Regulation and drug development. 5.5148
Regulation and its reform. 4.3080
Regulation and policies of American shipping. 4.3974
Regulation and the courts. 4.9572

Regulation in perspective. 4.3078
The regulation of American federalism. 4.5219
Regulation of entry and pricing in truck transportation. 4.4040
Regulation of transport innovation. 4.3987
Rehabilitations and other essays. 2.5544
Rehearsal for disaster. 4.1960
Rehearsal for Reconstruction. 3.8250
The Reich Marshal. 2.2387
Die reichsgründung. 3.2284
The Reichswehr and politics: 1918-1933. 3.2366
The Reichswehr and the German Republic, 1919-1926. 3.2372
The Reign of Charlemagne. 3.1984
The reign of chivalry. 3.290
The reign of Elizabeth, 1558-1603. 3.1421
The reign of error. 4.9850
The reign of ETS. 4.10714
The reign of George III, 1760-1815. 3.1559
The reign of King John. 3.1350
The reign of King Pym. 3.1469
The reign of Mary Tudor. 3.1419
The reign of Philip the Fair. 3.1997
The Reign of Richard II: essays in honour of May McKisack. 3.1369
The reign of the ayatollahs. 3.4091
The reign of Tiberius. 3.2798
The reign of wonder, naivety and reality in American literature. 2.10258
Reincarnation. 1.1619
The Reindustrialization of America. 4.2006
Reinforced concrete design. 5.5879
Reinforced concrete engineering. 5.5875
Reinforced concrete fundamentals. 5.5876
Reinforced concrete structures. 5.5877
Reinhold Niebuhr: his religious, social, and political thought. 1.3294
Reinhold Niebuhr on politics. 4.7211
El reino de este mundo. 2.5362
The reinterpretation of American economic history. 4.1884
The reinterpretation of American history and culture. 3.6207
The reinterpretation of American literature. 2.10248
The reinterpretation of early American history. 3.6205
Reinventing womanhood. 4.5928
The reivers. 2.11672
The relapse. 2.7324
Relation of the discovery and conquest of the kingdoms of Peru. 3.9298
A relation of the imprisonment of Mr. John Bunyan. 2.6915
Relations in public. 4.4901
Relations of literary study. 2.2365
Relative creatures. 2.6032
Relative values. 2.8582
Relativistic mechanics. 5.1650
Relativistic point dynamics. 5.1927
Relativistic quantum field theory. 5.2159
Relativistic quantum fields. 5.2152
Relativistic quantum mechanics. 5.2109
Relativity. 5.1908
Relativity and cosmology. 5.1872
Relativity and geometry. 5.2092
Relativity reexamined. 5.1903
Relativity, thermodynamics and cosmology. 5.1925
Relativity visualized. 5.2093
Relatos. 2.5385
The relevance of Canadian history. 3.8678
The relevance of education. 4.10351
The relevance of science. 5.853
The relevance of Whitehead. 1.778
Reliability engineering and risk assessment. 5.7043
Reliable knowledge. 5.950
Relief and rescue of Jews from Nazi oppression, 1943-1945. 3.1109
Relief in Hungary and the failure of the Joel Brand mission. 3.1110
Religio medici, and other works. 2.6912
Religion. 1.960
Religion, altered states of consciousness, and social change. 1.1562

Religion and atheism in the U.S.S.R. and Eastern Europe. 4.7139
Religion and culture. 1.1571, 4.542
Religion and empire. 3.8905
Religion and healing in Mandari. 1.1859
Religion and legitimation of power in Sri Lanka. 1.2109
Religion and legitimation of power in Thailand, Laos, and Burma. 1.2111
Religion and nationalism in Soviet and East European politics. 1.1584
The religion and philosophy of the Veda and Upanishads. 1.1698
Religion and political modernization. 1.1586
Religion and politics in Latin America. 1.3188
Religion and politics in Sri Lanka. 3.4368
Religion and politics in the age of the counterreformation. 3.2279
Religion and revolution. 1.1585
Religion and science. 1.1598
Religion and sexism; images of woman in the Jewish and Christian traditions. 1.2999
Religion and society in England, 1790-1850. 1.2447
Religion and society in industrial England. 1.2443
Religion and society in North America. 5.8448
Religion and society in the age of Saint Augustine. 1.1574
Religion and state in Iran, 1785-1906. 3.4082
Religion and the American mind, from the Great Awakening to the Revolution. 1.2402
Religion and the decline of magic. 1.2358
Religion and the people of Western Europe, 1789-1970. 1.1638
Religion and the rebel. 3.21
Religion and the rise of capitalism. 1.2243
Religion and the rise of Western culture. 1.2240
Religion and the unconscious. 1.1570
Religion in 20th century America. 1.2408
Religion in America. 1.1866, 1.2371, 1.2377, 1.2385, 1.2409, 4.148
Religion in American life. 1.2384
Religion in Chinese society. 1.1793
Religion in Communist China. 1.1788
Religion in contemporary society. 1.1870
Religion in Greece and Rome. 1.1641
Religion in Japanese history. 1.1833
Religion in primitive culture. 4.522
Religion in society. 1.1575
Religion in sociological perspective. 1.1581
Religion in the making. 1.1538
Religion in the Middle East. 1.1784
Religion in the old South. 1.2411
Religion in The secular city. 1.2776
Religion in West European politics. 1.2254
Religion, language and nationality in Wales. 3.1754
The religion of China. 1.1792
The religion of Dostoevsky. 2.1378
The religion of India. 1.1814
The religion of Israel, from its beginnings to the Babylonian exile. 1.1898
The religion of Java. 1.1831
The religion of the Chinese people. 1.1787
The religion of the Ifugaos. 3.4590
Religion, power, and protest in local communities. 1.1519
Religion, revolution, and the Russian intelligentsia, 1900-1912. 1.1674
The religion, spirituality, and thought of traditional Africa. 1.1850
Religion, state, and the Burger Court. 4.9720
Religion within the limits of reason alone. 1.892
Religion without revelation. 1.1532
Religions. 1.1526
Religions of ancient India. 1.1815
The religions of the Roman Empire. 1.1661
The religions of Tibet. 1.1809, 2.160
Religious and spiritual groups in modern America. 1.2099
Religious art in France, the thirteenth century. 1.5175
Religious art in France, the twelfth century. 1.5174
The religious aspect of philosophy. 1.642

Religious aspects of the conquest of Mexico. 3.8920

The religious attitude and life in Islam. 1.2055

Religious development in Morocco and Indonesia. 1.2010

The Religious dimension. 1.1578

The religious dimension in Hegel's thought. 1.954

The religious drop-outs. 1.3060

Religious enthusiasm in the New World. 1.2403

The religious factor. 1.1576

A religious history of the American people. 1.2370

The religious investigations of William James. 1.601

Religious liberty: an inquiry. 1.3009

Religious liberty in the United States. 1.2392

The religious life of man. 5.8439

Religious lyrics of the XIVth century. 2.6131

Religious lyrics of the XVth century. 2.6115

Religious movements in contemporary America. 1.2396

The religious orders in England. 1.3234

Religious perspectives in American culture. 1.2384

The religious philosophy of Josiah Royce. 1.635

Religious poverty and the profit economy in medieval Europe. 1.3068

The Religious Right and Christian faith. 1.2766

The religious situation. 1.2367

Religious television. 1.3001

Religious trends in modern China. 1.1789

Reliques of ancient English poetry. 2.6111

The reluctant belligerent. 3.932

Reluctant empire; British policy on the South African frontier, 1834-1854. 3.5463

Reluctant feminists in German Social Democracy, 1885-1917. 4.6127

Reluctant reformers. 4.5122

Remaking American values. 4.2708

Remaking Ibieca. 4.2880

Remarkable providences, 1600-1760. 3.6011

Remarks on colour. 5.632

Remarks on the foundations of mathematics. 5.1035

Remarriage, a study of marriage. 4.5634

Rembrandt. 1.6253

Rembrandt and his critics, 1630-1730. 1.6254

Rembrandt as an etcher. 1.6494

Rembrandt in the Mauritshuis. 1.6255

Rembrandt, the Nightwatch. 1.6250

Remember the house. 2.10132

The Remembered earth. 2.10677

The remembered gate. 4.6006

The remembered village. 4.5434

Remembering. 5.323

Remembering Orwell. 2.9198

Remembrance & Pantomime. 2.10023

Remembrance of things past. 2.4662

Remembrance rock. 2.12431

Remington's practice of pharmacy. 5.5147

Reminiscences, 1819-1899. 2.11082

Reminiscences of the Cuban Revolutionary War. 3.9098

Reminiscences of the English Lake poets. 2.5817

Reminiscences on the army for National Salvation. 3.4469

Remote control. 4.4072

Remote sensing. 4.13, 4.25

Remote sensing and image interpretation. 4.22

Remote sensing in geology. 5.2976

Remote sensing in meteorology, oceanography, and hydrology. 5.2508

Remote sensing of earth resources. 5.8206

Remote sensing, optics and optical systems. 4.27

Le rempart des béguines. 2.4606

The renaissance. 3.155, 3.160

The Renaissance. 1.6697, 3.163, 3.2829

Renaissance and baroque. 1.5433

Renaissance and Baroque lyrics. 2.3738

Renaissance and Baroque music. 1.3632

Renaissance and baroque poetry of Spain. 2.5146

The renaissance and English humanism. 1.405

Renaissance and renascences in Western art. 1.4765

Renaissance and revolution. 3.159

Renaissance architecture in Venice 1450-1540. 1.5436

The Renaissance city. 1.5594

Renaissance diplomacy. 4.9085

Renaissance England. 2.6083

Renaissance Europe: individual and society, 1480-1520. 3.629

Renaissance Florence. 3.2921

Renaissance France, 1470-1589. 2.3845

The Renaissance garden in England. 5.5377

The Renaissance Hamlet. 2.6653

Renaissance humanism, 1300-1550. 5.8344

The Renaissance idea of wisdom. 1.410

The Renaissance in historical thought. 3.156

Renaissance in Italy. 3.2849

The Renaissance in Rome. 3.2940

Renaissance in the South. 2.10444

Renaissance Latin verse. 2.815

Renaissance letters. 3.162

Renaissance man and creative thinking. 1.400

The Renaissance of the twelfth century. 2.809

Renaissance philosophy. 1.397

The Renaissance philosophy of man. 1.409

Renaissance Rome, 1500-1559. 3.2939

The renaissance stage. 2.3158

Renaissance thought. 1.401

A Renaissance treasury. 2.3712

Renaissance Venice. 3.2915

Renal and urologic disorders. 5.4999

Renal physiology. 5.4251

Renard the Fox. 2.3957

Renascent Africa. 3.5100

Render unto Caesar. 4.9595

Rendezvous with destiny. 3.7409

René. 2.4150

René A. Spitz, dialogues from infancy. 5.5105

René Char. 2.4468

Renegade in power. 3.8766

Renewable energy resources and rural applications in the developing world. 5.6115

A renewable resource economy. 4.1899

Renewing the American community college. 4.10561

Renoir, his life, art, and letters. 1.6143

Rent control, myths & realities. 4.3484

Rent control, myths and realities. 4.3484

Rent-seeking society. 4.1514

Reparation in world politics. 3.856

Repertoire for the solo voice. 1.3589

Report. 4.2124, 4.3977

The report. 4.5543

Report. 4.9524

Report from a Chinese village. 3.4797

Report from part one. 2.11421

Report of the Committee. 4.7887

Report of the National Bipartisan Commission on Central America. 3.9053

The report of the President's Commission on an All-Volunteer Armed Force. 5.7365

The report of the President's Commission on Campus Unrest. 4.10091

Report of the President's Commission on Registration and Voting Participation. 4.8075

Report of the Royal Commission on the Economic Union and Development Prospects for Canada. 4.2124

Report of the Select Committee on Assassinations, U.S. House of Representatives, Ninety-fifth Congress, second session. 3.7882

Report of the Warren Commission on the Assassination of President Kennedy. 3.7877

Report on higher education, March 1971. 4.9932

Report on registration and voting participation. 4.8075

Report to Greco. 2.599

The reporter and the law. 4.9534

The Reporter's handbook. 2.3567

Reporting. 2.3565

Reporting the wars. 2.3579

Reports. 3.9270

Reports of the Cambridge anthropological expedition to Torres Straits. 4.688

Le repos du guerrier. 2.4697

Representation. 4.7738, 4.7740

Representation and Presidential primaries. 4.7946

Representation and redistricting issues. 4.9730

The Representation of women in fiction. 2.3448

Representative American speeches. 2.10859

Representative and responsible government. 4.8410

Representative democracy. 4.8254

Representative democracy in the Canadian provinces. 4.8313

Representative government. 4.7669

Representative government in early modern France. 4.8581

Representative government in Greek and Roman history. 4.7359

Representative man. 2.11026

Representative plays. 2.8681

Representative plays by American dramatists. 2.10781

Representative selections. 2.11080

Representative South African speeches. 3.5456

Representative verse of Charles Wesley. 2.7336

Representing and intervening. 5.888

Representing Shakespeare. 2.6745

The repressible conflict, 1830-1861. 3.7399

The reprieve. 2.4733

Reproduction in domestic animals. 5.4253

Reproduction in mammals. 5.4049

Reproduction of eukaryotic cells. 5.3616

The reproduction of mothering. 4.5666

Reproductive decisions. 5.4032

Reproductive rituals. 4.859

Reptiles and amphibians of North America. 5.3922

The Republic. 2.535, 4.7345-4.7346

The Republic and the Civil War in Spain. 3.3460

The republic and the school. 4.10201

The Republic in peril: 1812. 3.7107

The Republic of Armenia. 3.4045

The Republic of Korea. 3.5015

The Republic of Lebanon. 3.3782

A Republic of nobles. 3.3333

The Republic of the Sudan. 3.5174

Republican ascendancy, 1921-1933. 3.7733

The Republican era, 1869-1901. 3.7845

The Republican experiment, 1848-1852. 3.2150

Republican foreign policy, 1921-1933. 3.7732

Republican 'Iraq. 3.3779

A Republican looks at his party. 3.7826

The Republican Party, 1854-1966. 4.8222

The Republican Party and Wendell Willkie. 3.7694

Republican Portugal. 3.3502

The Republican Right since 1945. 4.8223

Republican Rome, the army, and the allies. 3.2772

The Republican Roosevelt. 3.7700

Republicans face the Southern question. 4.8186

Republicans of the Civil War Senate. 3.7309

Requiem for a nun. 2.11673

Requiem for a Spanish peasant. 2.5283

A requiem for the renascence. 2.10463

Requiem por un campesino español. 2.5283

Required writing. 2.8944

Requirements for certification of teachers and administrators, 1939-1948/49. 4.10526

Requirements for certification of teachers, counselors, and administrators, 1940/50. 4.10526

Requirements for certification of teachers, counselors, librarians, administrators. 4.10526

Requirements for certification of teachers, counselors, librarians, administrators for elementary schools, secondary schools, junior colleges. 4.10526

Requirements for teaching certificates, 1935-1938. 4.10526

Rerum familiarium libri, XVII-XXIV: v. 3: Letters on Familiar. 2.4950

Res cogitans. 1.468

Rescue to Switzerland. 3.1111
Research and reference guide to French studies. 5.8006
Research centers directory. 1.55
The Research craft. 4.4823
Research for marketing decisions. 4.4304
Research guide for psychology. 5.8413
Research guide to philosophy. 1.103
A research guide to science fiction studies. 2.3485
Research guide to The May fourth movement. 3.4753
Research in chemistry at private undergraduate colleges. 5.2636
Research in chemistry at undergraduate institutions. 5.2636
Research in economic history. 4.1726
Research in music behavior: modifying music behavior in the classroom. 1.4413
Research in psychotherapy. 5.4856
Research in ritual studies. 5.8099
Research methods in librarianship. 5.7604
Research on agricultural development in sub-Saharan Africa. 4.2990
Research on deviance. 4.5071
Research on human subjects. 5.4608
Research on suicide. 5.8434
Research opportunities in American cultural history. 3.6215
Research periodicals of colonial India, 1780-1947. 2.3696
The research process in nursing. 5.5187
The researcher's guide to American genealogy. 3.295
Researches into the mathematical principles of the theory of wealth, 1838. 4.1293
Researches on the I Ching. 2.2179
Reshaping confederation. 4.9433
The reshaping of plantation society. 4.2906
Reshaping of the National Labor Relations Board. 4.9553
Reshaping the German right. 3.2332
Reshaping the international order: Jan Tinbergen, coordinator. 4.9036
Residential segregation, the state, and constitutional conflict in American urban areas. 4.9761
The residual years. 2.11332
Resistance at Christiana. 3.7270
Resistance in Vichy France. 3.1064
Resistance, rebellion, and death. 2.4441
Resistible theatres. 2.3312
The resisting reader. 2.10596
The resolution of conflict. 4.4941
Resolutions and decisions of the Communist Party of the Soviet Union. 4.8661
Resolving social conflicts. 4.4989
A resounding tinkle. 2.9321
Resource and environmental economics. 4.1785
Resource conservation. 4.1897
Resource management and the oceans. 4.3728
Resource regimes. 4.1796
Resources and development. 4.1773
Resources for an uncertain future. 4.1772
Resources for native peoples studies. 5.7737
Resources for the Future. 4.3719
Resources in America's future. 4.1994
Resources in education. 5.8151
Resources mondiales en énergie no. 1-2; 1929-50 5.6119
Resources of American music history. 1.3562
Resources, regimes, and world order. 4.9132
Respect for acting. 2.3118
Respect for life in medicine, philosophy, and the law. 1.1321
Respectable folly. 1.2452
A respectable minority. 4.8202
The respectful prostitute. 2.4720
Respiration and circulation. 5.4227
Respiratory emergencies. 5.4997
Respiratory patient care. 5.4996
Response effects in surveys. 4.1231
Response to imperialism. 3.7504
The response to industrialism, 1885-1914. 4.1910
Response to revolution. 3.6440
Responses. 2.12710

Responses of plants to environmental stresses. 5.3749
The responsibilities of the critic. 2.10270
The responsibilities of the novelist. 2.3410
The Responsibility of power. 3.613
The responsible electorate. 4.7952
The responsible self. 1.1476
The responsive chord. 4.5012
Responsive curriculum development. 4.10429
Ressources sur les études autochtones. 5.7737
La Restauration. 3.2143
Restitution, the land claims of the Mashpee, Passamaquoddy, and Penobscot Indians of New England. 4.9775
The restless atom. 5.2419
Restless spirit. 2.12164
The restless universe. 5.2044
The restless years. 3.5564
Restoration and early eighteenth-century English literature, 1660-1740. 5.7943
Restoration and eighteenth-century comedy. 2.6197
Restoration and eighteenth-century poetry, 1660-1780. 2.5757
Restoration and eighteenth century theatre research. 5.7958
Restoration and reaction, 1815-1848. 3.2144
Restoration carnival. 2.6163
Restoration comedy. 2.6196
Restoration comedy, 1660-1720. 2.5892
The Restoration comedy of wit. 2.5906
Restoration drama; modern essays in criticism. 2.5901
Restoration dramatists. 2.5902
Restoration literature; critical approaches. 2.5651
The restoration mode from Milton to Dryden. 2.5798
The restoration of the self. 5.496
Restoration plays. 2.6233
Restoration prose fiction, 1666-1700. 2.6256
Restoration, revolution, reaction. 4.2338
Restoration serious drama. 2.5896
Restoration stage. 2.3299
The Restoration stage. 2.3302
Restoration theatre. 2.5903
The restoration theatre. 2.3304
Restoration theatre production. 2.5899
Restoration tragedy, 1660-1720. 2.5909
Restraints on war. 4.9326
The restructuring of social and political theory. 4.1203
Resurrection. 1.2673
The resurrection of the dead. 1.2190
Retable; [La rêverie] 2.4777
Retail merchandise management. 4.4320
The Retail revolution. 4.4330
Rethinking anthropology. 4.401
Rethinking archaeology. 3.241
Rethinking crime and deviance theory. 4.5064
Rethinking federalism. 4.4660
Rethinking symbolism. 5.398
Rethinking systems analysis and design. 5.5576
Rethinking the family. 4.5595
Rethinking the Soviet experience. 3.3204
Rethinking urban education. 4.10963
Rethinking urban policy. 4.6222
Retirement and economic behavior. 4.5806
Retreat from Reconstruction, 1869-1879. 3.7466
Retreat from sanity. 5.4921
The retreat of American power. 3.7896
The retrieval system. 2.11970
Retrieving democracy. 4.7569
Retrofitting of commercial, institutional, and industrial buildings for energy conservation. 5.6156
Retrospections on social psychology. 4.4993
A Retrospective on the classical gold standard, 1821-1931. 4.4495
The return from Avalon. 2.6049
The return of Philip Latinovicz. 2.1221
The return of the king. 2.9432
The return of the soldier. 2.9512
The return of the vanishing American. 2.10593
The return to gold, 1925. 4.4515
Return to Goli. 3.5448
Return to Ithaca. 2.14086

Reunion and reaction. 3.7483
Reunion; Dark pony. 2.13167
Reunion without compromise. 3.7469
Reuters; the story of a century of news-gathering. 2.3680
Reuther. 4.3594
Revaluation. 2.5767
Reveille in Washington, 1860-1865. 3.7387
Revelation. 1.2734
Revelation and divination in Ndembu ritual. 3.5523
Revelation and reason in Islam. 1.2064
Revelation and theology. 1.2841
The Revels history of drama in English. 2.5843
Revenue sharing. 4.4663
Reverence for life. 1.1062, 1.3048
The reveries of the solitary walker. 2.4091
Reveries over childhood and youth. 2.8340
Reverse acronyms, initialisms & abbreviations dictionary. 2.205
Reverse discrimination. 4.7700
The reverse discrimination controversy. 4.9562
Review of child development research. 5.4966
Review of research. 4.3310
Review of research in education. 4.10288
Review of the United Nations Charter. 4.9228
A reviewer's ABC. 2.5532
The revised Canadian Constitution. 4.9434
The revised new general catalogue of nonstellar astronomical objects. 5.1852
A revision of demand theory. 4.1490
Revisionists. 3.7726
The revisionists revised. 4.10017
Revisor. 2.3106
Revival and reaction. 4.7316
Revivalism and separatism in New England, 1740-1800. 1.2400
Revivalism and social reform. 1.3038
Revivals, awakenings, and reform. 1.3037
La revocation de l'edit de Nantes. 2.4597
The revolt. 3.3915
Revolt against chivalry. 4.6721
The revolt against dualism. 1.480
Revolt in Athens. 3.2703
Revolt in Japan. 3.4974
Revolt in the Netherlands. 3.2973
The revolt of French Canada, 1800-1835. 3.8813
The revolt of the angels. 2.4213
The revolt of the black athlete. 4.882
The revolt of the Catalans. 3.3486
The revolt of the engineers. 5.5678
The revolt of the judges. 3.2029
The revolt of the masses. 3.48
Revolt of the moderates. 3.7828
The revolt of the Netherlands (1555-1609) 3.2989
Revolt of the rednecks. 3.8290
La revolución cubana. 3.9100
Revolution. 4.7610
Révolution à l'Ouest. 4.1984
Revolution administered: Agrarianism and communism in Bulgaria. 3.3543
Revolution and counterrevolution. 3.5307
Revolution and economic development in Cuba. 4.2966
Revolution and improvement. 3.648
Revolution and intervention in Grenada. 3.9132
Revolution and nationalism in the Sudan. 3.5169
Revolution and Papacy, 1769-1846. 1.3157
Revolution and politics in Russia. 3.3137
Revolution and reaction in Cuba, 1933-1960. 3.9097
Revolution and survival. 3.3180
Revolution and tradition in modern American art. 1.4869
Revolution and tradition in people's Poland. 4.10673
Revolution and urban politics in Provincial France. 3.2120
Revolution and war in Spain, 1931-1939. 3.3463
Revolution as tragedy. 2.5725
Revolution at Querétaro. 4.8331
Revolution from 1789 to 1906. 3.665

Revolution in American drama. 2.10523
Revolution in El Salvador. 3.9069
A revolution in European poetry, 1660-1900.
  2.2757
The revolution in German theatre, 1900-1933.
  2.3376
Revolution in Hungary. 3.1947
Revolution in nineteenth-century thought.
  1.441
Revolution in science. 5.718
The revolution in science, 1500-1750. 5.732
Revolution in Spain. 3.3449
Revolution in Tanner's Lane. 2.8264
The revolution in Tanner's Lane; Miriam's
  schooling. 2.8264
A revolution in the earth sciences. 5.3092
Revolution in the theatre. 2.2789
Revolution in time. 5.7066
The Revolution is now begun. 3.8088
The Revolution of 1525. 3.2278
The Revolution of 1688 in England. 3.1511
The revolution of American conservatism.
  3.7058
Revolution of being. 4.9136
The revolution of nihilism. 3.2422
The revolution of the intellectuals. 3.703
The revolution of the saints. 1.2444
Revolution on the Pampas. 5.5252
Revolution principles. 4.8518
The revolution that never was. 3.9217
Revolutionaries. 4.6933
Revolutionaries without revolution. 2.4758
Revolutionary America, 1763-1789. 5.7832
Revolutionary breakthroughs and national
  development. 4.8687
The revolutionary career of Maximilien
  Robespierre. 3.2071
Revolutionary change. 4.5046
Revolutionary change in Cuba. 4.2159
The revolutionary college. 4.10812
The revolutionary committees in the
  departments of France, 1793-1794. 3.2112
Revolutionary Cuba, the challenge of economic
  growth with equity. 4.2152
Revolutionary empire. 3.1216
Revolutionary Europe, 1783-1815. 3.664
The revolutionary generation, 1763-1790.
  3.6965
The Revolutionary histories. 3.6909
The revolutionary imagination. 2.10481
Revolutionary immortality. 3.4794
Revolutionary Iran. 3.3747
Revolutionary law and order. 4.9917
Revolutionary literature in China. 2.2187
The revolutionary origins of modern Japan.
  3.4988
Revolutionary path. 3.5342
A revolutionary people at war. 3.6941
Revolutionary petunias & other poems.
  2.13409
Revolutionary politics in Massachusetts.
  3.7993
Revolutionary prose of the English Civil War.
  2.6257
Revolutionary Russia. 3.3173
Revolutionary Russia, 1917. 3.3196
Revolutionary struggle, 1947-1958. 3.9093
The revolutionary theories of Louis Auguste
  Blanqui. 4.7048
Revolutionary women. 4.7147
Revolutionary writers. 2.10368
Revolutions and dictatorships. 3.864
Revolutions and reconstructions in the
  philosophy of science. 5.895
Revolutions in physics. 5.2029
Revolutions of 1848. 3.704
The revolutions of 1848-49. 3.700
Le revolver à cheveux blancs. 2.4426
Revue. 1.4223
Rewriting Russian history. 3.3033
Reynard the Fox and other mediaeval
  Netherlands secular literature. 2.13942
Reynard the Fox. English. 2.3957
Reynolds. 1.6037
Reynolds Price. 2.13276
RFD, the changing face of rural America.
  4.4047

Rh: the intimate history of a disease and its
  conquest. 5.5091
Rhetoric and philosophy in conflict. 2.2533
Rhetoric in Shakespeare's time. 2.6845
Rhetoric in the Middle Ages. 2.2531
The rhetoric of American politics. 3.6393
The Rhetoric of Aristotle. 2.2530
The rhetoric of fiction. 2.3501
A rhetoric of motives. 1.539
The rhetoric of religion. 1.1582
The rhetoric of Western thought. 2.2534
Rhetorical analyses of literary works. 2.5481
The Rhetorical tradition and modern writing.
  2.1033
Rheumatic diseases. 5.5001
Rhinoceros, and other plays. 2.4582
The rhizome and the flower. 2.8365
Rhode Island. 3.8011
Rhode Island and the African slave trade,
  1700-1807. 3.7218
Rhodes, the Tswana, and the British. 3.5480
Rhyme and revolution in Germany. 3.2302
Rhyming dictionary. 2.1050
The rhyming dictionary of the English
  language. 2.1049
Rhythm-a-ning. 1.4263
Rhythm and blues in New Orleans. 1.4273
Rhythm and tempo. 1.4120
Rhythm in the novel. 2.3447
The rhythm of twelfth-century polyphony.
  1.3653
Rhythmic activity in animal physiology and
  behaviour. 5.4211
The rhythmic structure of music. 1.4461
Rhythmics, dynamics, pedal and other problems
  of piano playing. 1.4539
The rhythms of English poetry. 2.1043
Ribbin', jivin', and playin' the dozens. 4.10969
Ribbin', jivin' & playin' the dozens. 4.10969
Ricardian economics. 4.1352
Ricardian poetry. 2.5613
Rice 5.5326
Riceyman Steps. 2.8456
Rich and poor states in the Middle East.
  4.2573
Rich country interests and Third World
  development. 4.4162
The rich get richer and the poor get prison.
  4.6824
Rich lands and poor. 4.2797
The Rich man's salvation. 1.2487
The rich nations and the poor nations. 4.1831
Richard Aldington. 2.8372, 2.8377
Richard Beer-Hofmann, his life and work.
  2.13677
Richard Brautigan. 2.11415
Richard Crashaw. 2.6966
Richard Eberhart; the progress of an American
  poet. 2.11623
Richard Estes. 1.5936a
Richard Hakluyt and the English voyages. 4.9
Richard Hughes. 2.8811
Richard Mather of Dorchester. 1.3342
Richard Meier, architect, 1964/1984. 1.5319
Richard Morris Hunt. 1.5312
Richard Murphy. 2.9779
Richard Neutra and the search for modern
  architecture. 1.5322
Richard Norman Shaw. 1.5399
Richard II. 3.1370
Richard II, 1398-1400 and Henry V. 3.1368
Richard Steele's periodical journalism, 1714-16.
  2.7271
Richard Strauss. 1.4516
Richard Strauss; a critical commentary on his
  life and works. 1.3999
Richard the Lionheart. 3.1348
Richard III. 3.1382
Richard Wagner. 1.4037, 1.4043-1.4044
Richard Wagner & the synthesis of the arts.
  1.4042
Richard Wagner's music dramas. 1.4047
Richard Wilbur. 2.12712
Richard Wilson. 1.6043
Richard Wright. 2.12819, 2.12823
Richard Wright, a collection of critical essays.
  2.12822
Richard Wright reader. 2.12807

Richard Wright's hero. 2.12818
Richelieu and reason of state. 3.2024
Richelieu and the councillors of Louis XIII.
  3.2023
Richelieu and the French monarchy. 3.2027
Richer by Asia. 3.4186
Riches, class, and power before the Civil War.
  4.2112
Richmond during the Revolution, 1775-83.
  3.8220
Rickshaw. 2.2249
The riddle-master of Hed. 2.13147
The riddle of gravitation. 5.2085
The riddle of history. 3.483
The riddle of Roman Catholicism. 1.3206
The riddle of Shakespeare's sonnets. 2.6673
Riddle of stars. 2.13147
The riddle of the early Academy. 1.276
The riddle of the pyramids. 3.5148
The riddle of the sands. 2.8513
The riddle of violence. 4.5474
Riders in the chariot. 2.10183
Riders of the purple sage. 2.11800
Riding on a blue note. 1.4264
Riding the Earthboy 40. 2.13420
Riding the midnight river. 2.10129
Riegel's Handbook of industrial chemistry.
  5.6815
Riemann surfaces. 5.1493, 5.1495
Riemann's zeta function. 5.1323
Rienzi, the last of the Roman tribunes. 2.7915
Riesz spaces. 5.1477
Rift and revolt in Hungary. 3.1946
The rigger's apprentice. 5.7515
Right & left. 4.551
The right and the good. 1.1490
The right and the power. 4.9469
Right and wrong. 1.1449, 1.1491
The right hand of power. 3.7858
The right of nations to self-determination.
  4.9304
The right of the people. 4.9666
Right on. 1.4299
Right to challenge. 4.3384
A right to song. 2.7572
The right to vote. 4.9729
Right-wing authoritarianism. 4.5020
Right you are. 2.5057
The rightangled creek. 2.10172
A righteous cause. 3.7427
Rights and regulation. 4.9523
Rights in conflict. 3.8419
The Rights of Americans. 4.9660
The rights of candidates and voters. 4.9725
The rights of doctors, nurses, and allied health
  professionals. 4.9544
The Rights of gay people. 4.9679
The rights of man and natural law. 4.7642
The rights of man in America, 1606-1861.
  4.7802
The rights of man today. 4.7633
Rights of passage. 2.9988
The rights of youth. 4.10094
Rights on trial. 4.9854
The rights we have. 4.9678
Rilke. 2.13854
RILM abstracts. 1.3445
RILM abstracts of music literature 1967-.
  1.3445
Rim of Christendom. 3.8572
Rimbaud. 2.4280
Rimbaud's poetic practice. 2.4281
Rime. 2.4919, 2.4975
Le rime, a cura di Guido Favati. 2.4913
Rime, trionfi, e poesie latine. 2.4946
Rimsky-Korsakov. 1.3959
Rinascimento. English. 3.2829
Ring. 2.11987
Ring around the moon. 2.4355
Ring Lardner. 2.11984, 2.11986
Ring Lardner and the portrait of folly.
  2.11985
A ring of bells. 2.8463
The ring of words. 1.3459
The Ring ... record book and boxing
  encyclopedia. 4.1058
Ring systems hand book. 5.2774
Ring systems handbook. 5.2774

Rings. 5.1808
Rings and ideals. 5.1342
Rings of continuous functions. 5.1587
RIO: reshaping the international order. 4.9036
Los ríos profundos. 2.5425
Riotous Victorians. 4.6727
The Ripe harvest. 4.10972
Ripe was the drowsy hour. 2.5702
Ripening seed. 2.4489
A ripple from the storm. 2.9012
Riquet. 2.4204
The rise and decline of Fidel Castro. 3.9104
The rise and decline of nations. 4.2798
The rise and demise of Democratic Kampuchea.
3.4446
The rise & development of military music.
1.4201
Rise and fall. 3.3606
The rise and fall and rise of modern dance.
4.1123
The rise and fall of an American army. 3.4505
The rise and fall of British India. 4.7532
The rise and fall of Chilean Christian
democracy. 4.8342
The rise and fall of civilization. 3.208
The rise and fall of Maya civilization. 3.9042
The Rise and fall of national test scores.
4.10715
The rise and fall of New York City. 4.2046
The rise and fall of states according to Greek
authors. 4.7337
The rise and fall of T. D. Lysenko. 5.3434
The rise and fall of the Choctaw Republic.
3.5858
The rise and fall of the Confederate
Government. 3.7370
The rise and fall of the Cyprus Republic.
3.3697
The rise and fall of the Habsburg monarchy.
3.1877
The rise and fall of the Judaean state. 3.3894
The rise and fall of the League of Nations.
4.9190
The rise and fall of the man of letters. 2.5493
The rise and fall of the people's century: Henry
A. Wallace and American liberalism,
1941-1948. 3.7692
The rise and fall of the Third Reich. 3.2449
The rise and fall of the well-made play. 2.5920
Rise and fulfilment of British rule in India.
3.4269
The rise and growth of economic nationalism in
India. 4.2499
The rise and splendour of the Chinese Empire.
3.4668
The Rise of Adventism. 1.2407
The rise of American civilization. 3.6078,
3.6315
The rise of American naval power, 1776-1918.
3.6382
The Rise of an American architecture. 1.5296
The rise of anthropological theory. 4.486
The rise of Brandenburg-Prussia to 1786.
3.2497
The rise of Chinese military power, 1895-1912.
3.4737
The rise of Chingis Khan and his conquest of
North China. 3.3624
The rise of Christianity. 1.2291
The rise of civilization. 3.3707
The rise of civilization in India and Pakistan.
3.4189
The rise of cubism. 1.6349
The rise of English literary history. 2.5623
The rise of English literary prose. 2.5932
The rise of European liberalism. 4.5032
The rise of fascism. 3.867
The rise of free trade imperialism. 4.4208
The rise of German industrial power,
1834-1914. 4.2339
The rise of guardian democracy. 4.9726
The rise of market culture. 4.3849
The rise of modern China. 3.4711
The rise of modern urban planning, 1800-1914.
4.6311
The rise of music in the ancient world, East
and West. 1.3640

The rise of nationalism in Vietnam, 1900-1941.
3.4466
The rise of New York port, 1815-1860. 4.3952
The rise of opera. 1.4209
The rise of political anti-Semitism in Germany
and Austria. 3.4015
The rise of political consultants. 4.8183
The rise of Reform Judaism. 1.1918
The rise of Robert Millikan. 5.1953
The rise of romantic opera. 1.4213
The rise of Rome to 264 B.C. 3.2762
The Rise of scientific philosophy. 1.111
The rise of social democracy in Russia. 4.8664
The rise of surgery. 5.5030
The rise of the American film, a critical history.
2.2918
The rise of the American novel. 2.10537
The rise of the Anglo-German antagonism,
1860-1914. 3.1255
The rise of the Atlantic economies. 4.2192
The rise of the Baltic question. 3.3357
The rise of the Chinese Communist Party.
4.8744
The rise of the city, 1878-1898. 4.6224
The rise of the city manager. 4.8851
The rise of the common man, 1830-1850.
3.6033
The rise of the Dutch republic. 3.2961
Rise of the fighter aircraft, 1914-18. 5.7410
The rise of the French novel. 2.3896
The rise of the great powers, 1648-1815. 3.645
The rise of the Greek epic. 2.287
The rise of the house of Duveen. 1.5200
The rise of the international organisation.
4.9264
The rise of the Latin American labor
movement. 4.3400
The rise of the Medici. 3.2927
The rise of the monophysite movement. 1.2972
The rise of the national trade union. 4.3371
The rise of the new physics. 5.2043
Rise of the new West, 1819-1829. 3.8476
The Rise of the novel. 2.5999
The rise of the Ottoman Empire. 3.3578
The rise of the Parti québécois 1967-76. 4.8315
The rise of the Pelhams. 3.1543
The rise of the Polish monarchy. 3.3279
Rise of the Russian consumer. 4.2394
The rise of the Russian novel. 2.1284
The rise of the schooled society. 4.10113
The rise of the Spanish American empire.
3.8987
The rise of the Spanish Empire in the Old
World and in the New. 3.3412
The Rise of the Sunbelt cities. 4.6240
The rise of the Victorian actor. 2.3101
The rise of the West. 3.31
The rise of the West, 1754-1830. 3.6355
The rise of the Western world. 4.2207
The rise of Theodore Roosevelt. 3.7704
Rise up, women! 4.8513
The rising American empire. 3.6361
Rising from the plains. 5.3001
The rising in western upper Canada, 1837-8.
3.8733
The rising moon. 3.4549
Risk and technological innovation. 4.1896
Risk by choice. 4.3505
Risk evaluation and management. 5.5635
Risk, uncertainty and profit. 4.1553
Risk watch. 5.475
Rite and man. 1.3215
The rites of passage. 4.557
The rites of passage in a student culture.
4.11014
Rites of passages. 2.8703
Ritsos in parentheses. 2.618
Ritual and religion among Muslims in India.
1.2004
Ritual brotherhood in Renaissance Florence.
4.5366
Ritual cosmos. 1.1851
Ritual in family living. 4.5567
Ritual in industrial society. 1.1622
Ritual irony. 2.467
Ritual, myth, and magic in early modern
Europe. 1.2427
The ritual of battle. 1.1711

The ritual of social relations. 4.523
Ritual, play, and performance. 2.3103
The ritual process. 4.559
Ritualized homosexuality in Melanesia. 4.671
Rituals. 2.13954
Rituals and power. 3.2742
Rituals of manhood. 4.682
Rituals of the Kandyan state. 1.2151
The Ritz and other plays. 2.13150
Le rivage des Syrtes. 2.4574
The rivals. 2.3984, 3.6489
The river and the gauntlet. 3.5025
The river barons. 4.2130
River ecology. 5.3569
River of wealth, river of sorrow. 4.4246
The river to Pickle Beach. 2.12908
Rivers. 4.313
Rivers, form and process in alluvial channels.
4.314
Rivers of empire. 4.2030
The Riverside Chaucer. 2.6312
The Riverside Shakespeare. 2.6649
The rivet in Grandfather's neck. 2.11446
RLS. 2.8121
RN. 3.7911
Road and bridge construction handbook.
5.6063
The road and the car in American life. 4.3939
The road from Babylon. 3.4005
Road from Colonus. 2.8642
The road to Berlin. 3.987
Road to Calvary. 2.1608
The road to Cíbola. 3.8573
The road to Confederation. 3.8725
The road to confrontation. 3.6471
Road to exile. 3.4568
The road to independence. 3.6945
The road to Khartoum. 3.1266
The road to medical enlightenment, 1650-1695.
5.4517
The road to Pearl Harbor. 3.933
The road to power. 4.7068
The road to Ramadan. 3.5163
The road to redemption. 3.8169
Road to revolution. 3.3113
The road to Sarajevo. 3.1898
The road to secession. 3.7185
The road to serfdom. 4.2774
The road to Stalingrad. 3.988
The road to total freedom. 1.2103
The road to Tryermaine. 2.7590
The road to Xanadu. 2.7601
Road traffic control. 4.3934
The road we are traveling, 1914-1942. 4.1973
Roads, rails & waterways. 5.7387
Roadside empires. 4.4321
Roanoke Island, the beginnings of English
America. 3.8232
Roanoke, the abandoned colony. 3.8196
The roar of the twenties. 3.8851
The robber bridegroom. 2.12666
Robe and sword. 3.1962
Robert Adam and his circle in Edinburgh and
Rome. 1.5380
Robert and James Adam. 1.5382
Robert Anderson. 2.11316
Robert Benchley. 2.11366
Robert Bly, an introduction to the poetry.
2.12911
Robert Browning. 2.7481
Robert Browning, a portrait. 2.7487
Robert Browning's poetry. 2.7473
Robert Bruce and the community of the realm
of Scotland. 3.1791
Robert Burns. 2.7503, 2.7505, 2.7509
Robert Burton. 2.6440
Robert Carter of Nomini Hall. 3.8193
Robert Coover. 2.12956
Robert D. FitzGerald. 2.10156
Robert Delavignette on the French Empire.
4.8926
Robert E. Park. 4.4778
Robert Elsmere. 2.8244
Robert Feke, colonial portrait painter. 1.5938
Robert Frost. 2.11754, 2.11756, 2.11758,
2.11761
Robert Frost, a biography. 2.11762

Robert Fulton, pioneer of undersea warfare. 5.7506
Robert Graves, his life and work. 2.8729
Robert Greene. 2.6583
Robert Hayden. 2.11821
Robert Henryson. 2.6387
Robert Henryson. 2.6388
Robert Herrick, 1591-1674. 2.7074
Robert J. Flaherty, a biography. 2.3044
Robert Laird Borden. 3.8738
Robert Louis Stevenson. 2.8126, 2.8128
Robert Louis Stevenson and his world. 2.8123
Robert Louis Stevenson and romantic tradition. 2.8124
Robert Louis Stevenson, the critical heritage. 2.8129
Robert Lowell. 2.12049-2.12051, 2.12053
Robert Lowell, the poet and his critics. 2.12055
Robert M. La Follette, June 14, 1855-June 18, 1925. 3.7438
Le Robert méthodique. 2.877
Robert Mills, architect of the Washington Monument, 1781-1855. 1.5320
Robert Morris: revolutionary financier. 3.7006
Robert Motherwell. 1.5958
Robert Musil and the crisis of European culture, 1880-1942. 2.13846
Robert Penn Warren. 2.12650, 2.12653
Robert Penn Warren, a collection of critical essays. 2.12654
Robert Penn Warren talking. 2.12648
Robert Schumann, his life and work. 1.3985
Robert Smithson. 1.5676
Robert Smythson & the Elizabethan country house. 1.5400
Robert Smythson and the Elizabethan country house. 1.5400
Robert Torrens and the evolution of classical economics. 4.1359
Robert's Rules of order newly revised. 4.7730
Robertson Davies, playwright. 2.9928
Robespierre. 3.2072
Robespierre; the force of circumstance. 3.2070
Robinson. 2.9363
Robinson Jeffers. 2.11931
Robinson Jeffers, a study in inhumanism. 2.11932
Robinson Jeffers: the man & his work. 2.11933
Robot motion. 5.6170
Robot vision. 5.1015, 5.6175
Robotics. 5.6174
Robotics and intelligent machines in agriculture. 5.5297
Robotics for engineers. 5.6168
Robotics research. 5.6165-5.6166, 5.6171
Robots in manufacturing. 4.3834
Robots, men, and minds. 5.113
Rochester's poetry. 2.7229
Rock archives. 1.4280
The rock art of the North American Indians. 3.5823
Rock encyclopedia. 1.3525
Rock-forming minerals. 5.3026-5.3027
The Rock Garden. 2.590
Rock gardening. 5.5374
Rock hardware. 1.4133
A rock in a weary land. 1.3373
The rock music source book. 1.4279
Rock 'n' roll is here to pay. 1.4354
Rock on. 1.3536
The rock pool. 2.8538
Rock record. 1.3622
Rockdale. 4.3852
Rockefeller medicine men. 5.4525
Rockefeller of New York. 4.8264
The Rockefellers. 3.7616
Rocket propulsion elements. 5.6690
The Rocking-horse winner. [Motion picture] 2.8972
Rockne, the coach, the man, the legend. 4.1015
Rocks and rock minerals. 5.3034
The Rocky Mountain bench. 4.9780
Rococo. 1.6525
Rococo to Revolution; major trends in eighteenth-century painting. 1.5865

Rodale's encyclopedia of indoor gardening. 5.5355
Rodd's Chemistry of carbon compounds. 5.2718
Roger B. Taney. 3.7093
Roger Baldwin, founder of the American Civil Liberties Union. 4.7691
Roger Fry. 1.5151
Roger of Salisbury, viceroy of England. 3.1346
Roger Sessions on music. 1.3478
Roger Williams. 3.8015
Roger Williams: his contribution to the American tradition. 3.8014
Roget's international thesaurus. 2.1071
Roget's Thesaurus of English words and phrases. 2.1070
Rogier van der Weyden. 1.6277
Rogue moon. 2.12927
Rogues, rebels, and reformers. 4.6711
Roister Doister. 2.6219
Roland Barthes. 2.43, 2.45
Roland Barthes, structuralism and after. 2.44
Role conflict and the teacher. 4.10678
Role of alternatives in the world energy scene. 5.6129
The role of computers in manufacturing processes. 5.7046
Role of fats in food and nutrition. 5.7128
The role of India in the emergence of Bangladesh. 3.4238
The Role of international law in the elimination of war. 4.9283
Role of materialism in Indian thought. 1.193
The role of mathematics in the rise of science. 5.1066
The role of politics in social change. 4.7463
Role of science in civilization. 3.58
The rôle of scientific societies in the seventeenth century. 5.746
The Role of terrestrial and aquatic organisms in decomposition processes. 5.3771
The Role of the legislature in Western democracies. 4.7729
The role of the military in underdeveloped countries. 5.7159
The role of the reader. 2.79
The role of transportation in regional economic development. 4.3870
The role of water in development. 4.2929
Roll, Jordan, roll. 3.7205
Rolling stone. 1.4282, 3.1182
The Rolling Stone illustrated history of rock & roll. 1.4282
Rölvaag: his life and art. 2.14060
The Roman antiquities of Dionysius of Halicarnassus. 2.364
Roman Arabia. 3.4033
Roman architecture. 1.5225, 1.5229
Roman art. 1.4729
Roman Britain. 3.1306
The Roman Catholic Church in colonial Latin America. 1.3184
The Roman citizenship. 4.7369
Roman civilization. 3.2711
Roman coins. 3.279
Roman coins from the earliest times to the fall of the Western Empire. 3.278
Roman crafts. 1.6510
Le Roman de la Rose. 2.3963
Le roman de Perceval. 2.3947
Roman de Renart. English. 2.3957
Le roman de Tristan et Iseut, renouvelé par Joseph Bédier ... 2.3967
The Roman economy. 4.1740
Roman farming. 5.5229
Roman Gaul. 3.1979
Roman government's response to crisis, A.D. 235-337. 3.2800
Roman historical portraits. 1.5787
Roman history from coins. 3.277
Roman imperial architecture. 1.5230
Roman Imperial Army. 5.7185
The Roman Imperial Army of the first and second centuries A.D. 5.7185
Roman imperial civilisation. 3.2727
Roman imperialism. 3.2734
Roman imperialism in the late republic. 3.2777
Roman laughter. 2.762

Roman law in medieval Europe. 4.9400
Roman legal and constitutional history. 4.9398
Roman life and manners under the early empire ... 3.2732
Roman literature. 2.626
The Roman middle class in the Republican period. 3.2738
The Roman mind. 1.318
Roman myths. 1.1662
The Roman nobility. 3.2737
The Roman novel. 2.759
Roman Ostia. 3.2722
Roman papers. 3.2753
The Roman poets of the Augustan age. 2.636
The Roman poets of the republic. 2.635
Roman political institutions. 4.7367
Roman politics, 220-150 B.C. 3.2769
The Roman Republic. 3.2761
The Roman revolution. 3.2776
Roman roads. 3.2713
Roman satire. 2.638-2.639, 2.644
Roman sculpture from Augustus to Constantine. 1.5638
Roman society from Nero to Marcus Aurelius. 3.2730
The Roman soldier. 5.7184
The Roman spring of Mrs. Stone. 2.12732
The Roman stage. 2.641
Roman Stoicism. 1.326
Roman tales. 2.5046
Roman women. 3.2739
The Roman world of Dio Chrysostom. 2.448
Romance. 2.8546
The Romance literatures. 5.8335
Romance of a plain man. 2.11772
The romance of American Communism. 4.6990
The romance of Leonardo da Vinci. 2.1520
The Romance of the rose. 2.3964
Romance of the sea. 5.7485
Romance of the three kingdoms. 2.2221
The romance of the western chamber. 2.2223
The romance of Tristan. 2.3965
The romance of William Morris. 2.7973
The romances of John Fowles. 2.9692
Romances sans paroles. 2.4318
Romanciers du XVIIe siècle. 2.3901
Romanciers du XVIIIe siècle. 2.3894
Romanesque architecture. 1.5237
Romanesque art. 1.5644
Romanesque Bible illumination. 1.6425
Romanesque manuscripts, 1066-1190. 1.6408
Romanesque mural painting. 1.6393
Romanesque sculpture. 1.5643
Romanesque sculpture in Italy. 1.5720
Romania, a country study. 3.3547
Romania in the 1980s. 3.3552
Romans. 2.4233, 2.4612
Romans and barbarians. 3.2842
Romans et contes. 2.4103
Romans et nouvelles. 2.4272
Romans et nouvelles [de] Stendhal [pseud.] 2.4301
Romans et oeuvres de fiction non théatrales. 2.4638
Romans, récits et soties. 2.4548
Romans, suivis de Récits, contes & nouvelles, extraits des essais et des journaux. 2.4078
The romantic agony. 2.2660
Romantic art. 1.4798
The romantic assertion. 2.5813
The romantic ballet as seen by Théophile Gautier, being his notices of all the principal performances fo ballet given at Paris during the years 1837-1848. 4.1173
Romantic bards and British reviewers. 2.5819
The romantic comedians. 2.11772
The romantic generation of modern Chinese writers. 2.2157
The romantic hero and his heirs in French literature. 2.3861
The romantic iconography of the sea. 2.2405
Romantic image. 2.2756
Romantic imagery in the novels of Charlotte Brontë. 2.7456
The Romantic movement bibliography, 1936-1970. 5.8276
Romantic music. 1.3665

Romantic narrative art. 2.5821
The romantic novel in England. 2.6005
The romantic poets. 2.5820
The romantic prison. 2.3834
The romantic quest. 2.5699
The romantic rebellion. 1.6736
The romantic sublime. 1.1398
The Romantic ventriloquists: Wordsworth,
   Coleridge, Keats, Shelley, Byron. 2.5816
Romanticism. 1.6737
Romanticism and nationalism in the Old South.
   3.8147
Romanticism in perspective. 2.2618
Romanticism; points of view. 2.5578
Romanticism reconsidered. 2.2617
Die Romantik. 2.13474
Le romantisme; l'histoire, la doctrine, les
   oeuvres. 2.3863
Rome. 3.2752
Rome against Carthage. 3.2767
Rome and the Mediterranean. 3.2768
Rome before Avignon. 3.2937
Rome haul. 2.11625
Rome in the Augustan age . 3.2797
Rome, profile of a city, 312-1308. 3.2938
Rome, the center of power. 1.4727
Rome, the late Empire. 1.4731
The Rommel papers. 3.1001
Rómulo Betancourt and the transformation of
   Venezuela. 3.9184
Romulus. 2.12621
Ronsard. 2.4000
Ronsard, sa vie et son oeuvre. 2.4002
Ronsard the poet. 2.4001
Roof slates and other poems of Pierre Reverdy.
   2.4686
Rookwood. 2.7345
Room at the top. 2.9629
A room of one's own. 2.2555
A room with a view. 2.8652
Roosevelt. 3.7778
Roosevelt and Batista. 3.6438
Roosevelt and Churchill. 3.7776
Roosevelt and Churchill, 1939-1941. 3.937
Roosevelt & the isolationists, 1932-45. 3.7755
Roosevelt and the isolationists, 1932-45.
   3.7755
Roosevelt and the Russians. 3.885
Roosevelt and World War II. 3.7780
Roosevelt: the soldier of freedom. 3.7779
The root of all evil. 2.13346
Root of bitterness. 4.5982
The root of life. 5.3231
Roots. 3.6837, 5.3661
Roots and branches. 2.11614
Roots and wings. 2.5152
Roots, family histories of familiar words.
   2.1053
The roots of American bureaucracy, 1830-1900.
   4.7841
The roots of American communism. 4.6989
The roots of American culture and other essays.
   3.6162
The roots of American economic growth,
   1607-1861. 4.1748
The roots of American loyalty. 3.6103
The roots of American order. 4.7259
The roots of ancient India. 3.4164
The roots of anti-Semitism in the age of
   Renaissance and Reformation. 1.1958
The roots of appeasement. 3.1254
The roots of Black poverty. 3.6792
Roots of caring, sharing, and helping. 4.5729
Roots of confrontation in South Asia. 3.4098
The roots of consciousness. 5.116
Roots of contemporary American architecture.
   1.5295
Roots of delinquency. 4.6880
The roots of failure. 3.1184
The roots of French imperialism in Eastern
   Asia. 3.4410
The roots of fundamentalism. 1.2795
Roots of language. 2.116
The roots of lo mexicano. 3.8878
The roots of phonics. 2.1008
The roots of psychology. 5.71
Roots of revolution. 3.3112, 3.4084, 4.7091

The Roots of rural poverty in central and
   southern Africa. 4.5463
The roots of southern populism. 3.8262
The roots of Southern writing. 2.10451
Roots of strategy. 5.7211
Roots of the American working class. 4.3621
Roots of the earth. 3.5663
The roots of the modern American empire.
   4.1918
The roots of urban discontent. 4.6223
Roots of war. 3.7558
Rope of gold. 2.11867
A rope of sand. 3.6878
Ropes of sand. 3.3755
Rosa Bonheur. 1.6065
Rosa Luxemburg. 4.7061
Rosalind Franklin and DNA. 5.4173
Rosamond Lehmann. 2.9008
Roscher and Knies. 4.1217
Roscoe Conkling of New York: voice in the
   Senate. 3.7431
Rose garden. 2.1975
Rose of Dutcher's Coolly. 2.11036
Rose, where did you get that red? 2.10672
Rosebery. 3.1631
The Rosenberg file. 4.9461
Rosencrantz & Guildenstern are dead. 2.9816
Roses and thorns. 2.2205
Ross and the New Yorker. 2.3675
Ross Macdonald. 2.12159
Rossini. 1.3961-1.3962
A roster of civilizations and culture. 3.30
The rosy crucifixion. 2.12189
La rôtisserie de la reine Pédauque. 2.4212
Roubles in words, kopeks in figures, and other
   stories. 2.1633
Les Rougon-Macquart. 2.4344
Rousseau and romanticism. 2.2615
Rousseau's Social contract. 4.7435
La route des Flandres. 2.4750
Route surveying and design. 5.6065
Rowlandson; watercolours and drawings.
   1.6387
Roxana, the fortunate mistress. 2.6974
Roy Campbell. 2.10062
Royal Air Force, 1939-1945. 3.1050
Royal cities of the Old Testament. 3.3830
Royal commentaries of the Incas, and general
   history of Peru. 3.9295
Royal Commission on Newspapers. 2.3678
The royal forests of medieval England. 3.1335
The royal governors of Georgia, 1754-1755.
   3.8256
The Royal guest, and other classical Danish
   narrative. 2.14005
The Royal Institution. 5.694
The Royal Navy in America, 1760-1775.
   3.6928
The Royal Shakespeare Company. 2.3331
The Royal Society and its fellows, 1660-1700.
   5.696
The Royal Society: concept and creation.
   5.697
The royal touch. 5.4778
The royal treasuries of the Spanish Empire in
   America. 4.4666
The royal way. 2.4620
Royall Tyler. 2.10881
Royce's metaphysics. 1.640
RS-232 made easy. 5.6576
RTECS 1981/82-. 5.4725
Ruanda-Urundi, 1884-1919. 3.5303
Rubáiyát. 2.1971
Rubáiyát of Omar Khayyám. 2.1972
Rubens. 1.6275
Rubens and his circle. 1.5028
Rubens and the poetics of landscape. 1.6276
Rudin. 2.1459-2.1460
Rudyard Kipling, his life and work. 2.7892
Rudyard Kipling: realist and fabulist. 2.7897
Rudyard Kipling's verse. 2.7887
Rue des boutiques obscures. 2.4785
Rufino Tamayo. 1.6006-1.6007
Rufus King. 3.7002
The ruined cottage. 2.8303
Rule-based expert systems. 5.1247
Rule Britannia. 5.7461
The rule of Saint Benedict. 1.3239

Rulers and governments of the world. 3.373
The rulers of Belgian Africa, 1884-1914.
   3.5423
Rulers of empire: the French colonial service in
   Africa. 4.8804
Rules and meanings. 1.1290
Rules and representations. 2.103
Rules for Kings. 4.7324
Rules for radicals. 4.5179
Rules for the direction of the mind. 1.788
Rules of order newly revised. 4.7730
Rules of procedure. 4.9199
The rules of sociological method. 4.4788
The rules of the game. 4.4565
The ruling class (Elementi di scienze politica)
   4.7479
Rumania: political problems of an agrarian
   state. 4.2859
The Rumanian national movement in
   Transylvania, 1780-1849. 3.1933
Rūmī, poet and mystic. 2.1970
Rūmī, poet and mystic, 1207-1273. 2.1969
Rumours. 2.9656
Run River. 2.12985
Run-through. 2.3259
Runaway horse. 2.13915
Runaway horses. 2.2108
Runaway slave advertisements. 3.7226
Runaways and non-runaways in an American
   suburb. 4.5764
The runner. 5.5027
Runnin' down some lines. 2.1158
Running city hall. 4.8845
The running fence project. 1.5041
Running scared. 3.6264
Rupert Brooke. 2.8487
Rural Asia. 4.2982
Rural China; imperial control in the nineteenth
   century. 4.8736
Rural China today. 4.5460
Rural Cuba. 4.5261
Rural development and women in Africa.
   4.6155
Rural development, employment, and incomes
   in Kenya. 4.2995
Rural economy and country life in the medieval
   West. 4.2967
Rural geography. 4.5313
Rural health organization. 5.4687
Rural life in Victorian England. 4.5327
Rural policy for the E.E.C.? 4.2971
A rural policy for the EEC? 4.2971
Rural problems in the Alpine region. 4.5294
Rural rebels. 1.1855
Rural revolution in France. 4.2854
Rural rides. 3.1729
Rural Russia under the old régime. 3.3169
Rural settlement and land use. 4.2811
Rural settlement in an urban world. 4.6372
Rural society. 4.6370
Rural sociology: its origin and growth in the
   United States. 4.6365
The Rural sociology of the advanced societies.
   4.6369
Rural versus urban political power. 4.8119
The rush hour of the gods. 1.1834
Rush to the Alps. 4.86
Ruskin on architecture: his thought and
   influence. 1.5251
Ruskin, the critical heritage. 1.5153
Ruskin, the great Victorian. 2.8035
Ruskin today. 2.8025
Ruskin's letters from Venice, 1851-1852.
   2.8031
Ruslan and Liudmila. 2.1414
Russell and Moore. 1.768
Russell's soil conditions and plant growth.
   5.5266
Russia. 3.3012, 3.3014, 3.3016, 3.3039
Russia, 1917. 3.3198
Russia and Asia. 3.3616
Russia and Black Africa before World War II.
   3.5129
Russia and its crisis. 3.3166
Russia and the Balkans 1870-1880. 3.689
Russia and the Golden Horde. 3.3083
Russia and the origins of the First World War.
   3.3163

Russia and the roots of the Chinese revolution, 1896-1911. 3.4746
Russia and the Soviet Union. 3.3005
Russia and the West under Lenin and Stalin. 3.3061
Russia & world order. 3.1170
Russia at the crossroads. 4.8657
Russia at war, 1941-1945. 3.994
Russia: between reform and Revolution. 3.3168
Russia, Bolshevism, and the Versailles peace. 3.860
Russia discovered. 2.1287
Russia in flux. 3.3165
Russia in the age of Catherine the Great. 3.3106
Russia in the age of modernisation and revolution, 1881-1917. 3.3134
Russia in world history. 3.3004
Russia, the atom and the West. 3.1152
Russia; the post-war years. 3.3222
Russia, the roots of confrontation. 3.3037
Russia, the Soviet Union, and the United States. 3.6484
Russia under Khrushchev. 3.3257, 3.3268
Russia under the old regime. 3.3043
Russian and Polish women's fiction. 2.1324
Russian and the Slavonic languages. 2.1193
Russian Army under Nicholas I. 3.3054
Russian art and American money, 1900-1940. 1.5031
Russian art of the avant-garde. 1.5035
The Russian autocracy in crisis, 1878-1882. 3.3130
Russian avant-garde art. 1.5036
The Russian church and the Soviet regime, 1917-1982. 1.3116
The Russian church under the Soviet regime, 1917-1982. 1.3116
Russian constructivism. 1.5037
Russian critical essays: XXth century. 2.1241
A Russian cultural revival. 2.1302
Russian culture. 3.3020
The Russian dilemma. 3.3052
Russian dramatic theory from Pushkin to the Symbolists. 2.2800
[Russian economic development from Peter the Great to] Stalin. 4.2365
Russian economic history. 5.8404
The Russian empire, 1801-1917. 3.3110
Russian-English chemical and polytechnical dictionary. 5.2589
Russian-English dictionary of the mathematical sciences. 5.1027
Russian-English idiom dictionary. 2.1236
Russian-English translators' dictionary. 5.711
Russian expansion on the Pacific, 1641-1850. 3.3318
The Russian experiment in art, 1863-1922. 1.5033
Russian factory women. 4.3262
Russian fairy tales. 2.1292
Russian folklore. 4.798
Russian foreign policy. 3.3056
Russian formalism. 2.1276
Russian futurism. 2.1280, 2.1310
Russian grammar. 2.1226
Russian heroic poetry. 2.1311
Russian historians and the Soviet State. 3.450
Russian historical grammar. 2.1224
Russian historiography. 3.3036
Russian history atlas. 4.177
The Russian idea. 3.3114
Russian intellectual history. 1.2457, 3.3023
The Russian Jew under tsars and Soviets. 3.3992
Russian land, Soviet people. 3.3007
The Russian landed gentry and the peasant emancipation of 1861. 4.6391
The Russian language since the revolution. 2.1223
Russian liberalism, from gentry to intelligentsia. 4.8636
Russian literary criticism. 2.2509
Russian literature since the Revolution. 2.1269, 2.1304
Russian literature triquarterly. 2.1306

Russian literature under Lenin and Stalin, 1917-1953. 2.1275
The Russian Marxists & the origins of bolshevism. 4.7093
The Russian menace to Europe. 3.3065
Russian Modernism. 2.1265
Russian music from the beginning of the nineteenth century. 1.3728
The Russian novel. 2.1285
The Russian novel from Pushkin to Pasternak. 2.1289
The Russian people and socialism. 3.702
A Russian philosopher, Alexander Radishchev, 1749-1802. 2.1336
Russian philosophy. 1.1103
Russian poetry, the modern period. 2.1315
Russian political thought. 4.7300
The Russian primary chronicle. 3.3080
Russian pronunciation. 2.1228
The Russian push toward Japan. 3.4925
Russian realist art. 1.6279
Russian rebels, 1600-1800. 3.3050
The Russian religious mind. 1.3114
The Russian Revolution. 3.3182, 3.3188
The Russian Revolution, 1917. 3.3195
The Russian revolution, 1917-1921. 3.3177
The Russian Revolution, and Leninism or Marxism? 3.3186
The Russian Revolution and the Soviet State, 1917-1921. 3.3174
The Russian revolutions of 1917. 3.3193
Russian romantic fiction. 2.1288
Russian romanticism. 2.1295
Russian satiric comedy. 2.1320
Russian sea power. 5.7468
Russian short story. 2.1286
The Russian struggle for power, 1914-1917. 3.3172
Russian theater, from the Empire to the Soviets. 2.3381
Russian thinkers and Europe. 1.1108
The Russian tradition in education. 4.10130
Russian versification. 2.1231
The Russian war, 1941-1945. 3.989
The Russian worker. 4.3661
Russian writers and society, 1825-1904. 2.1258
Russian writers and Soviet society, 1917-1978. 2.1271
The Russians. 3.3275
The Russians & their favorite books. 5.7691
Russians and their favorite books. 5.7691
Russians as people. 3.3274
Russia's failed revolutions. 3.3111
Russia's lost literature of the absurd: a literary discovery. 2.1298
Russia's military way to the West. 3.3053
Russia's other writers. 2.1328
Russia's protectorates in Central Asia: Bukhara and Khiva, 1865-1924. 3.3327
The Russo-German War, 1941-45. 3.992
Ruth Benedict. 4.417
Ruth Benedict, patterns of a life. 4.418
Ruth Prawer Jhabvala. 2.9729
Ruth St. Denis. 4.1157
Ruth Suckow. 2.12565-2.12566
Rutherford and physics at the turn of the century. 5.1939
Rutherford and the nature of the atom. 5.1963
Rutherford B. Hayes and his America. 3.7484
The Rwala Bedouin today. 3.4051
Rymes of Robyn Hood. 2.6427
Ryōkan, Zen monk-poet of Japan. 2.2070

S.A.E. handbook. 5.6622
S.I.P.R.I. yearbook. 5.7250
's Levens felheid. English. 1.4996
S-matrix theory of strong interactions. 5.2149
S.O.E. in the Far East. 3.1005
S. S. San Pedro. 2.11521
S/Z. 2.76
Sabbatai Sevi. 1.1925
The sabbath. 1.1980
Sabbatical. 2.12881
Saber-tooth curriculum, including other lectures in the history of paleolithic education. 4.9958
The Sabine women. 2.1467
The sable arm. 3.7388

Sacagawea of the Lewis and Clark expedition. 3.8486
The sacraments. 1.3012
Sacred and profane beauty. 1.4632
The sacred and profane love machine. 2.9761
The sacred and the profane. 1.1531
The sacred books of Confucius. 1.1794
The sacred bridge. 1.3643
The sacred canopy. 1.1573
Sacred choral music in print. 1.3598
The sacred dance. 1.1624
Sacred groves and ravaged gardens. 2.10601
The sacred harp. 1.3444, 1.4246
Sacred journeys. 1.2100
Sacred narrative, readings in the theory of myth. 1.1602
Sacred, profane, Godot. 1.4214
Sacred rage. 3.3741
Sacred sands. 3.8401
The Sacred scriptures of the Japanese. 1.1840
Sacrifice. 2.1870
The sad geraniums, and other stories. 2.13699
A sad heart at the supermarket. 2.11927
Sad swashbuckler. 3.9073
Sad toys. 2.2075
The saddest story; a biography of Ford Madox Ford. 2.8637
The Saddharma-pundarīka. 1.2133
A saddle-trip on the southwestern frontier. 3.8327
Sadhus of India. 1.1719
Sadness. 2.12892
Safe skin and scuba diving. 4.991
Safed spirituality. 1.1948
Safety in working with chemicals. 5.2638
Safety management. 4.3478
The safety of medicines, evaluation and prediction. 5.5137
Safety systems reliability. 5.6297
Safety with lasers and other optical sources. 5.5953
Safire's political dictionary. 4.7794
The saga of American society. 3.6008
The saga of Dazai Osamu. 2.2095
Saga of Ragnar Lodbrok. 2.13991
The saga of the Volsungs. 2.13991
The Saga of the Völsungs, together with excerpts from the Nornageststháttr and three chapters from the Prose Edda. 2.13990
The sage of Baltimore. 2.12135
Sahara. 3.5217
Sailing and small craft down the ages. 5.7509
The sailing-ship. 5.7497
Sailing to an island. 2.9135
Sailor-diplomat. 3.7101
Saint Anselm and his biographer. 1.3254
St. Augustine's Confessions. 2.650
Saint Basil. 2.356
Saint Benedict and the sixth century. 1.3255
St. Denis, a French-Canadian parish. 3.8821
Saint Erkenwald (Middle English poem) 2.6382
Saint Francis. 2.594
St. Francis of Assisi. 1.3258
Saint Genet. 2.4542
Saint Genet, comédien et martyr. 2.4532
Saint Jack. 2.13356
St. John Damascene Barlaam and Ioasaph, with an English translation. 2.355
St. John de Crèvecoeur. 2.10868
St John of the Cross. 1.3260
Saint-Just, apostle of the terror. 3.2073
St. Lawrence blues. 2.4812
The St. Lawrence Seaway. 4.3969
St. Patrick and the coming of Christianity. 1.3190
St. Petersburg and Moscow: tsarist and Soviet foreign policy, 1814-1974. 3.3064
Saint Peter relates an incident. 2.11935
St. Thomas Aquinas. 1.395
St. Urbain's horseman. 2.9964
The saints. 1.3248
Saints & revolutionaries. 3.7955
Saints and revolutionaries. 3.7955
Saints and scholars. 1.2441
Saints and sectaries. 3.7971
Saints in arms. 3.1486
Saints of the Atlas. 3.5192

Saints, scholars, and schizophrenics. 5.4836
Saionji-Harada memoirs. 3.4962
Saishin Kan-Ei jiten. 2.1993
Une saison dans la vie d'Emmanuel. 2.4813
Śaivism in philosophical perspective. 1.1726
Sakamoto Ryōma and the Meiji Restoration. 3.4952
Sakharov speaks. 3.3262
Saki, a life of Hector Hugh Munro. 2.9134
Śakti and Śākta. 1.1722
Śakuntalā. 2.1949
Sala'ilua, a Samoan mystery. 4.686
Salammbo. 2.4190
Salem's Lot. 2.13115
Sales taxation. 4.4719
Salesman in Beijing. 2.12169
Salesmanship and sales force management. 4.4326
Sallust. 2.691
Sallust. 2.769
Sally Bowles. 2.8839
The salmon. 5.3911
Salome. 2.8271
The saloon. 4.6641
The saloon on the Rocky Mountain mining frontier. 3.8541
Salt marshes and salt deserts of the world. 5.3788
Salt seller. 1.4971
El Salvador. 3.9067
Salvador Dali. 1.6290
El Salvador in transition. 3.9068
Salvation. 2.1800
Salvation and liberation. 1.2803
Salvation from despair. 1.1100
Salvation in history. 1.2247
The Salzburg tales. 2.10173
Sam Shepard, Arthur Kopit, and the Off Broadway theater. 2.10519
The same old story. 2.1391
The Samizdat register. 3.3263
The Samizdat register 2. 3.3264
Samoa mo Samoa. 3.5675
The Samoan tangle. 3.6446
Sample design in business research. 4.1245
Sampling techniques. 5.1404
Samson Agonistes. 2.7142
Sämtliche Romane und Erzählungen. 2.13548
Sämtliche Werke. 2.13560, 2.13589, 2.13612, 2.13639, 2.13646, 2.13723, 2.13767, 2.13782, 2.13850
Sämtliche Werke in 6 Bänden. 2.13615
Sämtliche Werke in fünf Einzelbänden. 2.13657
Sämtliche Werke in sechs Bänden. 2.13615
Sämtliche Werke und ausgewählte Briefe. 2.13619
Sämtliche Werke und Briefe. 2.13554
Samtliche Werke und Briefe. 2.13622
Sämtliche Werke und Briefe in zwei Bänden. 2.13628
Samuel Barber. 1.3786
Samuel Beckett. 2.8426-2.8428
Samuel Beckett, a critical study. 2.8430
Samuel Beckett now. 2.8433
A Samuel Beckett reader. 2.8417
Samuel Beckett, the critical heritage. 2.8434
Samuel Butler, 1835-1902. 2.7517
Samuel Daniel, a critical and biographical study. 2.6565
Samuel Davies; apostle of dissent in colonial Virginia. 1.3394
Samuel de Champlain, Father of New France. 3.8712
Samuel F. B. Morse and American democratic art. 1.5956
Samuel Gompers, a biography. 4.3585
Samuel 'Hudibras' Butler. 2.6927
Samuel Johnson. 2.7079, 2.7084, 2.7089-2.7090
Samuel Johnson and neoclassical dramatic theory. 2.6718
Samuel Johnson, biographer. 2.7092
Samuel Johnson, editor of Shakespeare. 2.7091
Samuel Jones Tilden. 3.7163
Samuel Richardson. 2.7222
Samuel Richardson; dramatic novelist. 2.7224
Samuel Richardson, printer and novelist. 2.7225

Samuel Sewall of Boston. 3.7984
Samuel Slater and the origins of the American textile industry, 1790-1860. 4.3848
The samurai. 2.2131
The samurai films of Akira Kurosawa. 2.3004
San Antonio Rose. 1.4063
San Francisco, 1846-1856. 3.8625
The San Francisco mime troupe. 2.3276
San Francisco, the bay and its cities. 3.8627
San Martín, knight of the Andes. 3.9168
Sanapia, Comanche medicine woman. 3.5863
Sanatorium under the sign of the hourglass. 2.1727
Sanctuary. 2.11675
Sand and sandstone. 5.3063
A Sand County almanac, and Sketches here and there. 5.3230
The sandbox. 2.12847
The sandcastle. 2.9762
Sandro Botticelli. 1.6191
The sane society. 4.5025
Le sang des autres. 2.4392
Sanity and survival in the nuclear age. 4.8989
Sanity in bedlam. 2.6438
The Sanskrit drama in its origin, development, theory and practice 2.1927
Sanskrit drama in performance. 2.3393
The Sansoni dictionaries: English-Italian, Italian-English. 2.858
Santa Barbara. 3.8632
Santa Clara pottery today. 3.5954
Santa Teresa de Avila. 2.5206
The Santals. 3.4208
Santayana; the later years. 1.650
Santé rationnée? English. 5.4618
The Sanusi of Cyrenaica. 3.5202
Sanyen collections. 2.2252
Sapho; moeurs parisiennes. 2.4164
Sappho and Alcaeus. 2.540
Sara Teasdale, woman & poet. 2.12584
Sarah Orne Jewett. 2.11134
Sarah Orne Jewett. 2.11135
Sarah Siddons. 2.3354
Sarah Winnemucca of the Northern Paiutes. 3.5934
Sarajevo. 3.1899
Sartor called resartus. 2.7548
Sartor resartus. 2.7547
Sartoris. 2.11674
Sartre. 2.4742
Sartre and Marxism. 1.851
Sartre as biographer. 2.4738
Sartre, life and works. 1.855
Sartre on theater. 2.4734
Sartre par lui-même. 1.854, 2.4741
The Saskatchewan. 3.8862
Satan. 1.2953
Satan in Goray. 2.1820
The Satan trap. 5.663
The Śatapatha-brāhmana. 1.1690
Satchmo. 1.4078
Satellite communications. 5.6395
Satellites of Jupiter. 5.1766
Satellites today. 5.6394
The satin slipper. 2.4473
The satire of Jonathan Swift. 2.7306
A satire of the three estates. 2.6608
Satires against man. 2.7230
Satires and miscellaneous poetry and prose. 2.6923
The satires, epigrams and verse letters. 2.6457
Satires, Epistles and Ars poetica. 2.672
The 'Satires' of Horace. 2.720
The satires of Horace and Persius. 2.702
The satiric art of Evelyn Waugh. 2.9502
Satiric poems. 2.10878
Satirical stories. 2.1399
Satow's Guide to diplomatic practice. 4.9084
Saturday night and Sunday morning. 2.9318
The Saturday night special. 4.6807
Saturn. 5.1820
The Satyricon. 2.757
The Satyricon of Petronius. 2.758
Saudi Arabia, a country study. 3.4046
The Saudi Arabian economy. 4.2447
Saudis in transition. 4.3233
Saul Bellow. 2.11358, 2.11360
Saul Bellow, vision and revision. 2.11361

Saul Bellow's enigmatic laughter. 2.11359
Saunders Lewis. 2.843
The savage and the innocent. 3.9197
The savage in literature. 2.5982
The savage mind. 4.537
The savage pilgrimage. 2.8982
A savage war of peace. 3.5207
Savagism and civility. 3.5770
Savagism and civilization. 3.5804
Saving energy in the home. 5.6157
Saving water in a desert city. 4.3088
Saxo Grammaticus and the life of Hamlet. 2.6652
Sayers' Manual of classification for librarians. 5.7636
The sayings of Confucius. 1.165
The sayings of Jesus in the churches of Paul. 1.2886
Sayyid Ahmad Khan. 1.2021
Sayyid Jamãl ad-Dīn 'al-Afghānī' 1.2020
The scalawag in Alabama politics, 1865-1881. 3.8283
Scaldic poetry. 2.13977
Scales for the measurement of attitudes. 5.341
Scaling, why is animal size so important? 5.4108
Scandalize my name. 1.4254
Scandinavia. 3.3349, 3.3351
Scandinavia at the polls. 4.8672
Scandinavia during the Second World War. 3.948
Scandinavian archaeology. 3.3353
Scandinavian loan-words in Middle English. 2.956
Scandinavian modern design, 1880-1980. 1.6544
Scandinavian plays of the twentieth century. 2.13971
The Scandinavian theatre. 2.13969
Scarcity and growth. 4.1767
The scarlet boy. 2.8491
The scarlet letter. 2.11060
The scarlet letter. 2.11061
Scarlet sister Mary. 2.12311
The scarlet tree. 2.9333
Scarlett, Rhett, and a cast of thousands. 2.3027
Scattering theory. 5.2077
Scattering theory of waves and particles. 5.2400
Scene design and stage lighting. 2.3155
A scene of adornment. 1.6538
Scenery for the theatre. 2.3146
Scenes and machines on the English stage during the renaissance, a classical revival. 2.3294
Scenes from the bathhouse. 2.1618
The scenic art: Henry James. 2.3084
Scenic form in Shakespeare. 2.6820
Scented gardens for the blind. 2.10221
The sceptical chymist. 5.2621
The sceptical feminist. 4.6104
The sceptical realism of David Hume. 1.708
Scepticism and animal faith. 1.648
Scepticism and historical knowledge. 3.484
Schaum's outline of theory and problems of genetics. 5.3455
[Schedules] 5.7637
Schedules of reinforcement. 5.299
Scheinbare Örter der Fundamentalsterne <,1985->. 5.1679
Schelling. 1.924
Schilderboeck. 1.6229
Schiller. 2.13650
Schindler. 1.5327
Schizophrenia. 5.4924
The schizophrenic child. 5.5119
Schleiermacher on Christ and religion. 1.3295
Schleiermacher's soliloquies. 1.957
The Schleswig-Holstein question. 3.2499
Schoenberg. 1.3971
Schoenberg: a critical biography. 1.3968
Schoenberg and his school. 1.3755
Schoenberg's 'Moses and Aaron;' 1.3972
The scholar adventurers. 2.5490
Scholar painters of Japan. 1.6337
Scholarly reprint publishing in the United States. 5.7596

The scholars. 2.2234
Scholars, dollars, and bureaucrats. 4.10601
Scholar's guide to intelligence literature. 5.8297
Scholastic journalism. 4.10724
A scholastic miscellany: Anselm to Ockham. 1.360
Scholasticism. 1.361
Scholasticism and politics. 4.7477
The school and society. 4.10229
School class size. 4.10702
School crime and disruption. 4.10721
School days, rule days. 4.9582
School desegregation. 4.10781, 4.10793
School desegregation and defended neighborhoods. 4.10800
School desegregation in the Carolinas. 4.10718
School discipline. 4.10692
School, family, and neighborhood. 4.10801
School finance policies and practices. 4.10660
A school for fools. 2.1634
The school in American culture. 4.10770
School is dead: alternatives in education. 4.10042
School law in changing times. 4.10630
The school music administrator and supervisor. 1.4419
School of clavier playing, or, Instructions in playing the clavier for teachers & students. 1.4540
The school of night. 2.6502
School of the prophets: Yale College, 1701-1740. 4.10998
School power. 4.10967
School prayer and other religious issues in American public education. 5.8159
The school prayer decisions from court policy to local practice. 4.9594
The school principal. 2.1976
The School psychologist. 4.10706
The school superintendent. 4.10669
School vandalism. 4.10720
School violence. 4.10703
Schooldays in Imperial Japan. 4.10143
Schooled to order. 4.10040
Schooling and the acquisition of knowledge. 4.10360
Schooling and work in the democratic state. 4.10834
Schooling for a global age. 4.10449
Schooling for the new slavery. 4.10873
Schooling in a corporate society. 4.10764
Schooling in capitalist America. 4.10730
Schooling in East Asia. 4.10141
Schooling in the ASEAN region. 4.10136
The schoolmaster. 2.10001
Schools for all. 4.10877
Schools for strategy. 5.7275
Schools in cities. 4.10964
Schools in conflict. 4.10740
Schools of linguistics. 2.41
Schools of psychoanalytic thought. 5.177
The schools, the courts, and the public interest. 4.9590
The schools we deserve. 4.10000
Schools where children learn. 4.10431
Schoolteacher. 4.10530
Schriften. 2.13593
Schubert. 1.3976-1.3977
The Schubert reader. 1.3978
The Schubert song companion. 1.3979
Schubert songs. 1.4521
Schubert; thematic catalogue of all his works in chronological order. 1.3614
Schumann. 1.3982
Schumann as critic. 1.3984
Schumpeter, social scientist. 4.1378
The Schumpeterian system. 4.1377
Schumpeter's vision. 4.1541
Das Schwanenhaus. 2.13916
Science. 4.3676, 5.743, 5.4771
Science and civilisation in China. 3.4642
Science and common sense. 5.876
Science and engineering literature. 5.8419
The science and engineering of materials. 5.5758
Science and ethical values. 5.886
Science and gender. 5.4192

Science and health with key to the Scriptures. 1.3329
Science and human values. 5.842
Science and hypothesis. 5.953
Science and imagination. 2.5546
Science and information theory. 5.867
The science and method of politics. 4.7469
Science and moral priority. 5.4313
Science & music. 1.4374
Science and patterns of child care. 4.5705
Science and philosophy in the Soviet Union. 5.786
Science and policy in France at the end of the old regime. 5.775
Science and politics in Canada. 5.769
Science and politics in the ancient world. 5.726
The science and politics of I.Q. 5.358
The science and practice of welding. 5.7057
Science & secularity. 5.5511
Science and sensibility. 5.745
Science and sentiment in America. 1.559
Science and sexual oppression. 4.5489
Science and society in restoration England. 5.778
Science and subjectivity. 1.1300
Science and technology. 5.993
Science and technology in art today. 1.4806
Science and technology in China. 5.774
Science and technology in the Middle East. 5.785
Science and the common understanding. 5.848
Science and the course of history. 5.905
Science and the Enlightenment. 5.734
Science and the future of arid lands. 4.256
Science and the goals of man. 1.498
Science and the making of the modern world. 5.742
Science and the modern world. 5.854
Science and the paranormal. 5.650
Science and the U.F.O.s. 5.6699
Science and the UFOs. 5.6699
Science and utopias. 5.844
Science as intellectual property. 5.977
Science awakening. 5.1080
Science education in nineteen countries. 5.982
Science, faith and society. 5.849
Science fiction. 2.3491-2.3493, 2.5979
Science fiction, an illustrated history. 2.3489
Science fiction and fantasy literature. 2.3484
Science fiction art. 1.5830
The science fiction encyclopedia. 2.3494
Science fiction in America, 1870s-1930s. 5.7814
Science fiction in the cinema. 2.3005
The Science fiction novel. 2.3495
The science fiction of H. G. Wells. 2.8258
The Science fiction reference book. 2.3453
Science fiction story index, 1950-1979. 5.8175
Science fiction, today and tomorrow. 2.3487
Science fiction writers. 2.10573
Science for society. 5.8422
Science for the elementary school. 4.10489
Science in America, a documentary history, 1900-1939. 5.755
Science in American society. 5.789
Science in archaeology. 3.228
Science in civilization. 5.739
Science in contemporary China. 5.974
Science in culture. 5.776
Science in history. 3.52
Science in Russian culture. 5.787
Science in the Middle Ages. 5.713
Science in traditional China. 5.772
Science instruction in the middle and secondary schools. 5.987
Science, its history and development among the world's cultures. 5.749
Science: men, methods, goals. 5.868
Science, myth, reality. 3.6759
Science observed. 5.952, 5.960
The science of color. 5.2335
The science of conflict. 4.4942
The science of culture. 3.19
Science of education and the psychology of the child. 4.10212
The science of geography. 4.34
The science of musical sounds. 1.4378

The science of political economy. 4.1428
The Science of speleology. 4.280
The science of the mind. 5.23
The science of zoology. 5.3803
Science, perception, and reality. 1.94
Science policies of industrial nations. 5.750
Science, politics, and controversy. 4.3813
Science reorganized. 5.689
Science, revolution, and discontinuity. 5.860
Science since Babylon. 5.851
Science, technology, and American foreign policy. 3.7603
Science, technology, and development in the Muslim world. 5.784
Science, technology, and economic development. 5.855
Science, technology, and national policy. 5.5539
Science, technology, and society. 5.962
Science textbook controversies and the politics of equal time. 5.988
Science: the glorious entertainment. 3.151
The sciences of the artificial. 5.934
The scientific adventure. 5.878
Scientific American. 4.9178, 5.1856, 5.1863, 5.2271, 5.2467, 5.3093, 5.3490, 5.4055, 5.4188, 5.4329, 5.4467, 5.5523, 5.5954, 5.6126
Scientific American medicine. 4.4496
The scientific analysis of personality and motivation. 5.509
Scientific and technical information resources. 5.5503
Scientific and technical information sources. 5.8417
Scientific and technical organizations and agencies directory. 5.827
Scientific and technical societies of the United States and Canada. 1.53
Scientific and technical, spatial, and bibliographic data bases and systems of the U.S. Geological Survey, 1983. 5.2996
The scientific attitude. 5.939
The Scientific basis of health and safety regulation. 5.4659
The scientific basis of the art of teaching. 4.10264
The scientific community. 5.779
The scientific credibility of Freud's theories and therapy. 5.152
Scientific culture. 5.744
Scientific development in the U. S. Department of agriculture. 5.5217
Scientific elite. 5.831
Scientific encyclopedia. 5.705
Scientific explanation. 5.866
Scientific explanation and the causal structure of the world. 5.931
Scientific foundations of vacuum technique. 5.2042
Scientific ideas to 1900. 5.757
The scientific image. 5.938
Scientific inference. 5.902
Scientific instruments of the seventeenth and eighteenth centuries. 5.991
Scientific inventory management. 4.2680
Scientific man vs. power politics. 4.7257
Scientific management and the unions, 1900-1932. 4.3572
Scientific method: optimizing applied research decisions. 5.863
Scientific papers. 5.700
Scientific papers of Arthur Holly Compton. 5.2017
The scientific renaissance, 1450-1630. 5.733
Scientific romance in Britain, 1890-1950. 2.6054
Scientific Russian. 2.1225
The scientific study of foreign policy. 4.9037
The scientific study of personality. 5.516
Scientific study of unidentified flying objects. 5.6694
Scientific technology and social change. 5.5523
Scientific temperaments. 5.1964
A scientific theory of culture. 4.437
Scientific thought 1900-1960. 5.893
The scientific use of factor analysis in behavioral and life sciences. 5.39
Scientist extraordinary. 5.3206

Scientists against time. 5.788
Scientists and war. 5.951
Scientists and world order. 5.959
Scientists, engineers, and organizations. 5.829
The scientist's role in society. 5.828
Scipio Aemilianus. 3.2771
Scobie & Balfour's Canadian almanac, and repository of useful knowledge. 1.67
Scobie's Canadian almanac. 1.67
Scoop. 2.9495
The scope and authority of the Bible. 1.2538
The scope of Renaissance humanism. 3.164
Scope of total architecture. 1.5268
Scorched earth. 2.9674
Scores. 1.3424
The scorpion god. 2.8704
The Scotch-Irish. 3.6597
Scotland. 3.1778
Scotland: 1689 to the present. 3.1780
Scotland and its first American colony, 1683-1765. 3.8070
Scotland and nationalism. 3.1782
Scotland from the earliest times to 1603. 3.1786
Scotland from the eleventh century to 1603. 3.1785
Scotland, James V to James VII. 3.1779
Scotland since 1707. 4.2296
Scotland, the making of the kingdom. 3.1777
Scotland under Morton, 1572-80. 3.1797
The Scots overseas. 3.1784
A Scots quair. 2.9115
Scott. 2.8056
Scott Fitzgerald. 2.11725, 2.11740
The Scott, Foresman Robert's Rules of order newly revised. 4.7730
Scott-King's modern Europe. 2.9493
Scott: the critical heritage. 2.8058
A Scottish ballad book. 2.6106
The Scottish book. 5.1121
Scottish democracy. 4.5323
Scottish historical documents. 3.1774
The Scottish literary revival. 2.9844
Scottish literature and the Scottish people, 1680-1830. 2.9833
Scottish literature in English and Scots. 5.7997
Scottish nationalism. 3.1807
The Scottish novel. 2.9840
Scottish poetry. 2.9838
The Scottish political system. 4.8562
Scottish population history. 4.1695
The Scottish Reformation. 1.2359
The Scottish Reformation. 1.2360
Scottish short stories. 2.9849
The Scottish sketches of R.B. Cunninghame Graham. 2.8715
The Scottish tradition in literature. 2.9836
Scott's last voyage, through the Antarctic camera of Herbert Ponting. 4.107
Scottsboro; a tragedy of the American South. 4.9463
Scoundrel time. 2.11832
The scramble for southern Africa, 1877-1895. 3.5441
A scrapbook of complex curve theory. 5.1581
Scratch. 2.12091
Screen world. 2.2867
The screens. 2.4539
The Screwtape letters. 1.2264
Scriabin. 1.3991
Scribes and scholars. 5.7521
The Scribner companion to the Brontës. 2.7452
Scripta minora. 2.399
Scriptores historiae Augustae. 3.2791
Scripts for the pageant. 2.12144
Scripts, plans, goals, and understanding. 5.289
Scripture of the blind. 2.616
Scripture of the lotus blossom of the fine dharma. 1.2134
Scriptures, sects, and visions. 1.1908
Scrutiny. 2.5500
The sculptural idea. 1.5651
The sculptural programs of Chartres Cathedral: Adolf Katzenellenbogen. 1.5532
Sculpture. 1.5777
Sculpture and drawings. 1.5698
Sculpture and enlivened space. 1.5772

The sculpture and sculptors of the Greeks. 1.5626
Sculpture in America. 1.5655
Sculpture in Britain. 1.5683
Sculpture in Britain, 1530-1830. 1.5686
Sculpture in ceramic. 1.5774
Sculpture in Italy, 1400-1500. 1.5724
Sculpture in stone. 1.5620
Sculpture in the Netherlands, Germany, France, and Spain: 1400 to 1500. 1.5645
Sculpture index. 1.5609
Sculpture inside and out. 1.5773
The sculpture of Africa. 1.5764
Sculpture of Auguste Rodin. 1.5712
The sculpture of Barbara Hepworth, 1960-69. 1.5694
The sculpture of Donatello. 1.5729
The sculpture of Edgar Degas. 1.5704
The sculpture of Henri Matisse. 1.5710
The sculpture of India, 3000 B.C.-1300 A.D. 1.5749
The sculpture of Japan. 1.5762
The sculpture of Michelangelo. 1.5734
The sculpture of Negro Africa. 1.5766
The sculpture of Picasso. 1.5711
Sculpture of the Eskimo. 3.5885
The sculpture of the Hellenistic Age. 1.5621
The sculpture of Verrocchio. 1.5740
Sculpture: tools, materials, and techniques. 1.5776
The sculptures of Michelangelo ... 1.5735
The sculptures of the Parthenon. 1.5630
Scutum. 2.311
SDS. 4.10722
The sea and prisons. 2.4459
The sea and the ice. 5.3284
The sea and the mirror. 2.8396
The sea around us. 4.328
Sea fiction guide. 5.8177
The sea floor. 5.2984
Sea grapes. 2.10024
The Sea, ideas and observations on progress in the study of the seas. 4.325
The sea lady. 2.8251
Sea life in Nelson's time. 4.102
The sea of grass. 2.12391
The sea people of Sulu. 3.4595
The sea peoples. 3.2524
Sea power. 3.543
Sea power and British North America, 1783-1820. 4.4187
Sea power in its relations to the War of 1812. 3.7104
Sea routes to Polynesia. 3.5623
The sea, the sea. 2.9763
Sea warfare. 5.7420
The sea-wolf. 2.12026
Seabirds, an identification guide. 5.3941
'The sealed angel' and other stories. 2.1400
Seamus Heaney. 2.9705
Sean O'Casey and his world. 2.9154
The Sean O'Casey reader. 2.9146
Sean O'Casey, the man I knew. 2.9153
Seance. 2.9741
The search after truth. 1.800
Search and destroy; a report. 4.6833
Search & seizure. 4.9395
Search and seizure. 4.9395
The search for a black nationality. 3.7229
Search for a method. 1.495
Search for alternatives: public policy and the study of the future. 3.69
The search for authenticity in modern Japanese literature. 2.2003
The search for Beulah Land. 3.1767
A search for civilization. 3.12
The Search for English-Canadian literature. 2.9886
A search for environmental ethics. 5.8421
A search for equality. 3.6681
The search for equity in school finance. 4.10655
The search for form. 2.11130
The search for gravity waves. 5.1762
The search for identity: Canada, 1945-1967. 3.8777
The search for JFK. 3.7871
The search for life in the universe. 5.1727

The search for order, 1877-1920. 3.7416
The search for organic reaction pathways. 5.2859
The search for quality integrated education. 4.10795
Search for relevance. 4.10088
The search for speed under sail, 1700-1855. 5.7507
The search for St. Truth. 2.6398
Searching between the stars. 5.1825
Searching for Caleb. 2.13362
Searching for your ancestors. 3.293
Searchings. 1.832
Sears list of subject headings. 5.7631
Seas, maps, and men. 4.329
A season for unnatural causes. 2.13225
A season of dreams. 2.12668
A season of inquiry. 4.7907
Season of youth. 2.5954
A season on earth. 2.11966
A season on the earth. 2.1893
Season songs. 2.9717
Seasonal variations of the Eskimo. 3.5877
The seasons. 2.7316
Seasons and months. 2.5618
The Seasons of a man's life. 5.625
A seat at the circus. 4.1185
Seat of empire. 3.8221
Seaweeds. 5.3713
The secession conventions of the South. 3.7183
The second American party system. 4.8159
The second American revolution. 3.6672
The second assault. 4.6741
The Second Athenian League. 3.2617
The Second Barnhart dictionary of new English. 2.1095
Second best. 4.10569
Second book of Negro spirituals. 1.3439
The second British Empire. 4.8918
Second chance. 3.7760
The second chance, and other stories. 2.9319
The second Chinese revolution. 3.4793
The second Common reader. 2.2606
Second Corinthians. 1.2714
The Second Empire revisited. 3.2155
Second empire style in Canadian architecture. 1.5343
A second flowering. 2.10615
Second front. 3.915
The second generation. 2.12314
Second handbook of research on teaching. 4.10286
The second industrial divide. 4.3000
The Second International, 1889-1914. 4.6927
The Second law of thermodynamics. 5.2256
The second life of art. 1.6683
The second maiden's tragedy. 2.6553
Second maiden's tragedy. 2.6553
The second man. 2.11347
The second Mrs. Hardy. 2.7760
The Second Newman report. 4.9932
Second part of the life of Lazarillo of Tormes. 2.5193
The second partition of Poland. 3.3281
Second reference catalogue of bright galaxies. 5.1857
The Second Republic. 3.1918
The second session. 1.3128
The second sex. 4.5950
Second skin. 2.11818
A second treasury of the world's great letters. 2.3782
The second treatise of government. 4.7413
The second tree from the corner. 2.12705
Second view. 5.6983
A second visit to the United States of North America. 3.6035
The second wave. 2.5925
The Second World War. 3.901
The Second World War. 3.908
The Second World War, 1939-45. 3.903
The Second World War in fiction. 2.3500
Second year of the Nixon watch. 3.7903
Secondary schools at the turn of the century. 4.10497
The secret army. 3.1857
Secret conversations, 1941-1944. 3.2392

Secret diary of William Byrd of Westover.
3.8192

The secret diary of William Byrd of Westover,
1709-1712. 3.8191

The secret diplomacy of the Vietnam War.
3.4494

The Secret Gospel. 1.2737

The secret ladder. 2.10031

Secret leaves. 2.8061

The secret of childhood. 4.10207

The secret of Father Brown. 2.7561

The secret of world history. 3.491

The secretarial ghetto. 4.4344

The Secretariat of the United Nations. 4.9244

Secretaries, management, and organizations.
4.4345

Secretaries of state. 3.6396

The Secretary-General of the United Nations.
4.9225

Secrets. 1.1493

Secrets and surprises. 2.12900

Secrets of the lotus; studies in Buddhist
meditation. 1.1777

Sectional stress and party strength. 4.8047

Sectionalism and American political
development, 1880-1980. 4.8048

Secular choral music in print. 1982 supplement.
1.3602

Secular Latin poetry in the Middle Ages.
2.811

Secular lyrics of the XIVth and XVth centuries.
2.6140

The secular meaning of the gospel, based on an
analysis of its language. 1.2262

Secular music in America, 1801-1825. 1.3564

The secular pilgrims of Victorian fiction.
2.6027

Secular ritual. 4.558

The secular scripture. 2.2404

The secularization of the European mind in the
nineteenth century. 1.1887

Securing the revolution. 4.8146

Security, accuracy, and privacy in computer
systems. 4.4347

The Security gamble. 5.7219

Security standards for data processing. 4.4349

Sedimentary environments and facies. 5.3060

Sedimentary petrology. 5.3052

Sedimentary rocks. 5.3058

Sedimentary structures. 5.3064

Seduction and betrayal. 2.2552

See so that we may see. 4.813

Seed biology. 5.3737

Seeds. 5.3736

Seeds of contemplation. 1.3229

Seeds of destruction. 1.2917, 3.4773, 5.4771

Seeds of famine. 4.2595

Seeds of Italian nationalism, 1700-1815. 3.2855

Seeds of liberty. 3.6163

Seeds of plenty, seeds of want. 4.2901

Seeds of repression. 3.7803

Seeds of separatism. 4.10689

Seeds of Southern change. 3.8154

Seeds of tomorrow. 4.7153

Seedtime. 2.4783

Seedtime of the Republic. 4.7804

Seedtime on the Cumberland. 3.8351

Seeing and knowing. 1.5126

Seeing is believing. 2.9438

Seeing is deceiving. 5.4387

Seeing through clothes. 1.5190

The seeker, and other poems. 2.13858

Seeking world order. 4.9117

Der Seekrieg. 3.1029

Seelenarbeit. 2.13918

Segmented work, divided workers. 4.3558

Segmenting the industrial market. 4.4277

Seifert and Threlfall, A textbook of topology.
5.1598

The seigneurial system in early Canada. 4.2831

Seismic stratigraphy. 5.6740

Seize the day. 2.11356

The seizure of power. 3.2887

Sĕjarah Melayu, or, Malay annals. 4.806

A select bibliography on students, politics, and
higher education. 5.8157

Select British speeches. 2.3780

A select collection of old English plays. 2.6218

Select documents in Australian history. 3.5557

Select documents in Canadian economic history,
1497-1783. 4.2118

Select documents in Canadian economic history,
1783-1885. 4.2122

Select documents on India's foreign policy and
relations, 1947-1972. 3.4295

Select documents on Japanese foreign policy,
1853-1868. 3.4915

Select documents on the constitutional history
of the British Empire and Commonwealth.
4.9424

Select letters. 2.4106

Select translations from Old English poetry.
2.6280

Select translations from Old English prose.
2.6281

A Selected annotated bibliography of
professional ethics and social responsibility in
engineering. 5.8161

A selected bibliography of American
constitutional history. 4.9625

Selected criticism, 1916-1957. 2.2582

Selected criticism, prose, poetry. 2.2564

A selected discography of solo song. 1.3624

Selected drawings from the collection of Her
Majesty the Queen at Windsor Castle.
1.5841

Selected drawings from Windsor Castle. 1.5841

A selected edition of W. D. Howells. 2.11084

Selected essays. 2.8445, 2.8620

Selected essays. 2.10273, 2.12740

Selected essays of Fredrik Barth. 4.470

Selected film criticism. 2.2969

Selected historical essays. 3.1234

Selected letters. 2.5257, 2.11371, 2.11750,
2.12411

Selected letters of André Gide and Dorothy
Bussy. 2.4557

Selected letters [of] Aretino. 2.4957

The selected letters of Bernard Berenson.
1.5197

Selected letters of Conrad Aiken. 2.11302

Selected letters of Cotton Mather. 3.7977

Selected letters of E. E. Cummings. 2.11541

Selected letters of E.M. Forster. 2.8655

Selected letters of Edward Wilmot Blyden.
3.5415

Selected letters of Edwin Arlington Robinson.
2.12402

The selected letters of Gustave Flaubert.
2.4195

Selected letters of Horace Walpole. 3.1565

Selected letters of James Joyce. 2.8901

Selected letters of John Crowe Ransom.
2.12369

Selected letters of John O'Hara. 2.12275

The selected letters of Robinson Jeffers,
1897-1962. 2.11930

Selected letters of Samuel Richardson. 2.7213

Selected literary criticism. 2.2647, 2.8955

Selected military writings. 3.4826

Selected non-dramatic writings. 2.8065

Selected odes. 2.528

Selected operas and plays of Gertrude Stein.
2.12508

Selected organic syntheses. 5.2733

Selected paintings and sculpture from the Yale
University Art Gallery. 1.4660

Selected papers, 1952-59. 2.5

Selected papers from the English Institute.
2.5480

The selected papers of Boulton & Watt. 5.6213

Selected papers of Edward Shils. 1.6

Selected papers of Karl Abraham, M.D. 5.126

The selected papers of Margaret S. Mahler,
M.D. 5.5102

Selected papers on economic theory. 4.1267

Selected papers on psycho-analysis. 5.126

Selected papers on quantum electrodynamics.
5.2377

Selected philosophical essays. 1.1059, 1.1113

Selected philosophical, social, and political
essays. 1.9

Selected philosophical works. 1.1109

Selected philosophical writings. 1.813

Selected plays. 2.7752, 2.8671

Selected plays of Kuan Han-ching. 2.2220

Selected plays of Sean O'Casey. 2.9145

Selected poems. 2.1536

Selected poems. 2.583, 2.607, 2.610, 2.1469,
2.1740, 2.1844, 2.1913, 2.5230, 2.5249,
2.5410, 2.6481, 2.7938, 2.8043, 2.8957,
2.9287, 2.11418, 2.11440, 2.11498, 2.11567,
2.11575, 2.11611, 2.11742, 2.11888, 2.11939,
2.11962, 2.12041, 2.12138, 2.12324, 2.12368

Selected Poems 2.9339

Selected poems. 2.4316, 2.5076, 2.11262,
2.12540, 2.13865

Selected poems. 2.1735, 2.9473

Selected poems, 1923-1975. 2.12633

Selected poems, 1946-1968. 2.9428

Selected poems, 1950-1975. 2.8793

Selected poems, 1951-1974. 2.9436

Selected poems, 1955-1980. 2.8588

Selected poems and letters. 2.7851

Selected poems and letters, chosen and edited
by A. Norman Jeffares. 2.6959

Selected poems and prose. 2.5271

Selected poems by Fernando Pessoa. 2.5458

Selected poems: in five sets. 2.11918

Selected poems of Agyeya. 2.1894

Selected poems of Anne Finch, Countess of
Winchilsea. 2.7337

Selected poems of Eugenio Montale. 2.5037

Selected poems of G. Sankara Kurup. 2.2268

Selected poems of Gabriela Mistral. 2.5408

Selected poems of Giuseppe Ungaretti. 2.5075

The selected poems of Jacob Glatstein. 2.1802

Selected poems [of] James Hogg. 2.7814

Selected poems of Léopold Sédar Senghor.
2.4862

Selected poems of Malcolm Lowry. 2.9054

Selected poems [of] Marina Tsvetayeva. 2.1610

Selected poems, old and new. 2.9331

Selected poetry. 2.6384

Selected poetry and critical prose. 2.8003

Selected poetry and prose. 2.7499

Selected poetry and prose of John Dryden.
2.6989

The selected poetry of Jaroslav Seifert. 2.1680

The selected poetry of Robinson Jeffers.
2.11929

The selected poetry of Vicente Huidobro.
2.5409

Selected political writings. 4.7379

Selected political writings of Rosa Luxemburg.
4.7059

Selected prose. 2.1331, 2.1524, 2.7145, 2.8066,
2.9427, 2.11749

Selected prose, 1909-1965. 2.12325

Selected prose and poetry. 2.11018

Selected prose & poetry. 2.1516

Selected prose works. 2.7578

Selected short stories. 2.1502

Selected short stories. 2.8861, 2.12277

Selected short stories [of] Honore de Balzac.
2.3818

Selected short stories of Padraic Colum.
2.8525

Selected stories. 2.9561

Selected stories of Mary E. Wilkins Freeman.
2.11034

Selected tales. 2.1401

Selected translations, 1948-1968. 2.3742

Selected works. 2.4591, 2.7043

Selected works. 2.5050, 2.7979, 2.9340, 3.4827

Selected works of Jawaharlal Nehru. Second
series. 3.4317

Selected works [of] Karl Marx and Frederick
Engels. 4.7070

Selected works of Stephen Vincent Benét.
2.11368

Selected works [of] V. I. Lenin. 3.3144

Selected works of Zinaida Hippius. 2.1498

Selected works: Spillway. 2.11345

Selected writings. 1.612, 1.666, 1.744, 1.982,
2.4222, 2.4381, 2.4461, 2.4525, 2.4764,
2.6642, 2.7806, 2.9402, 2.9522, 2.11076,
2.12151, 3.3231, 4.4756, 4.6946

Selected writings, 12 July 1849 to 20 December
1919. 5.4536

Selected writings and designs. 2.7961

Selected writings; compiled by Vincente Lecuna.
3.9166

Selected writings from a connectionist's psychology. 5.120

Selected writings in language, culture and personality. 2.9

Selected writings in sociology & social philosophy. 4.4855

The selected writings of A. R. Luria. 5.569

Selected writings of Alexandra Kollontai. 4.6129

Selected writings of Charles Olson. 2.12279

Selected writings of E. T. A. Hoffmann. 2.13616

Selected writings of Florence Nightingale. 5.5180

Selected writings of Gertrude Stein. 2.12507

Selected writings of Guillaume Apollinaire. 2.4364

Selected writings of Herman Melville: complete short stories, Typee [and] Billy Budd, foretopman. 2.11149

Selected writings of John Marin. 1.5953

Selected writings of Mahatma Gandhi. 3.4305

Selected writings of T. C. Schneirla. 5.480

Selected writings of William Dean Howells. 2.11085

Selected writings on anarchism and revolution. 4.7194

Selected writings: The space within. 2.4634

Selecting instructional media. 5.8160

Selecting materials for libraries. 5.7621

Selecting thermoplastics for engineering applications. 5.5803

A selection of English carols. 2.6119

A selection of Greek historical inscriptions. 3.2565

A selection of Greek historical inscriptions to the end of the fifth century B.C. 3.283

Selection of library materials in the humanities, social sciences, and sciences. 5.7623

The selection of national party leaders in Canada. 4.8303

Selections. 1.671, 1.3333

Selections from Canadian poets. 2.9894

Selections from Gavin Douglas. 2.6469

Selections from George Eliot's letters. 2.7699

Selections from John Gower. 2.6383

Selections from Layamon's Brut. 2.6406

Selections from Les amours jaunes. 2.4156

Selections from political writings (1921-1926) 4.7075

Selections from the correspondence of Theodore Roosevelt and Henry Cabot Lodge, 1884-1918 ... 3.7708

Selections from the critical writings of Edgar Allan Poe. 2.11199

Selections from the Edward L. Elliott family and John B. Elliott collections of Chinese calligraphy and painting at the Art Museum, Princeton University. 1.6370

Selections from the prison notebooks of Antonio Gramsci. 4.7076

Selections from the Spectator. 2.6271

Selections illustrating the history of Greek mathematics. 2.329

Selective admissions in higher education. 4.10609

Selective bibliography for the study of English and American literature. 5.7928

A selective bibliography of bibliographies of Hispanic American literature. 5.7902

Selective nontreatment of handicapped newborns. 5.5090

A selective survey of axiom-sensitive results in general topology. 5.1585

Self-analysis. 5.164

Self and experience in the writings of Herman Melville. 2.11165

Self and sensibility in contemporary American poetry. 2.10507

Self and society in Ming thought. 3.4645

The self and the dramas of history. 1.2908

The self-apparent word. 2.10635

Self-assertion for women. 4.5922

The self-concept. 5.501

Self-consistency. 5.523

Self-consuming artifacts. 2.2658

Self-determination revisited in the era of decolonization. 4.9303

Self-disclosure. 5.521

Self-esteem and adjusting with blindness. 4.6598

Self-governing socialism. 4.6979

Self-help. 4.6177

Self-help groups for coping with crisis. 4.6535

Self-help in the 1890s depression. 4.1908

Self-management. 4.3181, 4.3189

Self-management and efficiency. 4.3190

Self-portrait in a convex mirror. 2.11335

Self-portraits, the Gide/Valéry letters, 1890-1942. 2.4562

The selfish gene. 5.3451

Selling mothers' milk. 5.5084

The selling of the President, 1968. 3.7894

The selling of the South. 4.2022

Selling water by the river. 1.2176

Selma, 1965. 3.8286

La semaine sainte. 2.4375

Semantic analysis. 2.202

Semantic differential technique; a sourcebook. 5.400

Semantics. 2.199, 2.201

Semantics and necessary truth. 1.1281

Semantics: studies in the science of meaning. 2.223

Sembazuru. 2.2103

The semblance of peace. 3.922

Semi-empirical self-consistent-field molecular orbital theory of molecules. 5.2821

Semiconductor devices, physics and technology. 5.6501

Semiconductor physics. 5.2349

Semiconductors. 5.2351

Semimicro qualitative organic analysis. 5.2686

Seminumerical algorithms. 5.1185

Semiotic and significs. 2.82

Semiotics and interpretation. 2.2489

Semiotics and language. 2.81

Semper fidelis. 5.7479

Señas de indentidad. 2.5264

The Senate establishment. 4.8045

Senate executive journal and related documents. 4.7203

Senate legislative journal. 4.7202

The Senate nobody knows. 4.8041

The Senate of Imperial Rome. 4.7370

Senator Gerald P. Nye and American foreign relations. 4.7677

Senator Joe McCarthy. 3.7671

Send these to me. 3.6516

Seneca. 2.772, 4.7371

The Senecan amble. 2.5935

Seneca's drama. 2.773

Seneca's tragedies. 2.694

Senegalese literature. 2.4848

El señor presidente. 2.5368

El señor presidente. 2.5369

Sensation and perception. 5.237

Sensation & perception. 5.237

Sensation and perception in the history of experimental psychology. 5.236

Sensational designs. 2.10584

Sensational Victorian. 2.7933

Sense and non-sense. 1.841

Sense and sensibility in modern poetry. 2.10503

The sense of an ending. 2.2363

The sense of beauty, being the outlines of aesthetic theory. 1.4600

The sense of form in art: a comparative psychological study. 1.4771

The sense of history: secular and sacred. 3.465

The sense of movement. 2.8796

The sense of power. 3.8737

The sense of Shakespeare's sonnets. 2.6674

The sense of the past. 3.366

The senses considered as perceptual systems. 5.239

Sensing the world. 5.241

Sensitivity training. 4.4936

Sensor and analyzer handbook. 5.5684

Sensory coding in the mammalian nervous system. 5.4362

Sensory communication, contributions. 5.4363

Sensory inhibition. 5.4360

Sensory processes. 5.244

Sensory psychology. 5.252

The sensuous immortals. 1.5747

The sentence and its parts. 2.994

Sentences undecidable in formalized arithmetic. 1.1217

Sentido y forma del Quijote, 1605-1615. 2.5183

Sentience. 1.516

Sentimental education. 2.4186

A sentimental journey through France and Italy. 2.7276

The sentimental novel in America, 1789-1860. 2.10606

A separate peace. 2.11965

The separate problem. 4.10869

Separate spheres. 4.8509

Separated and divorced women. 4.5783

Separation and spectrophotometric determination of elements. 5.2690

Separation methods in biochemistry. 5.2645

Separation methods in chemical analysis. 5.2643

The separation of church and state in Italian thought from Cavour to Mussolini. 3.3192

The separation of college and state. 4.10761

Separation of powers 4.7865

Separations. 2.13064

The Sephardi heritage. 3.4006

The Sephardic Jews of Bordeaux. 3.3963

Sepik River societies. 3.5659

Septem quae supersunt tragoediae [sic] 2.406

Sequence in layered rocks. 5.3037

The sequence of English medieval art. 1.6011

Serengeti, dynamics of an ecosystem. 5.3828

The Serengeti lion. 5.4001

Sergei Nechaev. 3.3126

Sergei Rachmaninoff. 1.3953

Sergei Rachmaninov. 1.3954

Sergei Witte and the industrialization of Russia. 4.2371

Serial bibliographies in the humanities and social sciences. 5.7684

Serial composition and atonality. 1.4451

Serial publications, their place and treatment in libraries. 5.7625

A serious call to a devout and holy life; The spirit of love. 1.3055

Serious entertainments. 3.1297

A serious proposal to the ladies. 1.1514

Serjeant Musgrave's dance. 2.8386

Sermons. 1.3309

Sermons and devotional writings. 2.7824

Sermons and discourses. 1.3204

Sermons in American history. 1.3047

Serpent and lily. 2.593

The serpent and the rope. 2.10131

Servant of peace. 4.9218

Servants and masters in eighteenth-century France. 4.3526

The service economy. 4.3863

Services, the new economy. 4.3865

Serving personal and community needs through adult education. 4.10983

Serving women. 4.3264

Set fair for Roanoke. 3.8198

Set theory. 5.1349, 5.1352-5.1353

Set this house on fire. 2.13343

Setting conditions for creative teaching in the elementary school. 4.10523

The setting for Black business development. 3.6737

Setting national priorities. 4.4682

The setting of American foreign policy. 3.7577

The setting of the Sermon on the Mount. 1.2893

The setting sun. 2.2094

The settlers. 2.11998

Settling disputes in Soviet society. 4.8651

Seurat. 1.6149

Seven American utopias. 4.7155

The seven caves. 4.702

Seven days a week. 4.3263

Seven decades, 1895-1965. 1.4823

Seven Gothic tales. 2.14019

Seven interpretive essays on Peruvian reality. 3.9280

Seven Japanese tales. 2.2121

The seven lamps of architecture. 1.5481

Seven medieval historians. 3.568

Seven miracle plays. 2.6206

The seven mountains of Thomas Merton. 1.3271
The seven odes. 2.1838
Seven pillars of wisdom. 3.809
Seven plays. 2.4544
Seven plays. 2.12381, 2.13317
Seven plays of the modern theatre. 2.3773
Seven psychologies. 5.78
Seven science fiction novels. 2.8247
Seven states of matter. 5.2046
Seven stones. 1.5348
The seven storey mountain. 1.3270
The seven that were hanged, and other stories. 2.1468
Seven troubadours. 2.885
Seven types of ambiguity. 2.2715
Seven voices; seven Latin American writers talk to Rita Guibert. 2.5308
Seven winters. 2.8480
Seventeen. 2.11241
Seventeen black artists. 1.4912
Seventeen Danish poets. 2.14003
Seventeen modern German poets. 2.13520
The seventeenth century. 3.171
The seventeenth century, 1600-1715. 2.3849
Seventeenth-century America. 3.6018
Seventeenth-century American poetry. 2.10760, 5.7796
Seventeenth-century economic documents. 4.2268
Seventeenth-century English literature. 2.5646-2.5647
Seventeenth-century French drama. 2.3365
Seventeenth-century interior decoration in England, France, and Holland. 1.6549
Seventeenth century lyrics from the original texts. 2.6154
Seventeenth-century metaphysics. 1.431
Seventeenth-century prose. 2.5934
Seventeenth-century prose and poetry. 2.6084, 2.6086
The Seventeenth-century resolve. 1.3073
Seventeenth-century verse and prose. 2.6085
The seventh sense. 1.712
Seventy years. 2.7755
Seventy years of life and labor. 4.3583-4.3584
Severe and unusual weather. 5.2544
Severe mental retardation. 4.10949
The severe style in Greek sculpture. 1.5629
A severed head. 2.9764
Severely handicapped students. 4.10944
Sewall Wright and evolutionary biology. 5.3348
Sex and advantage. 4.5498
Sex and behavior. 5.4085
Sex & birth control. 4.5514
Sex and class in Latin America. 4.6083
Sex and Enlightenment. 2.7217
Sex and evolution. 5.3400
Sex and internal secretions. 5.4258
Sex and marriage in utopian communities. 4.5579
Sex and repression in savage society. 4.5558
Sex and sensibility. 2.5629
Sex and society in Shakespeare's age. 2.6705
Sex and temperament in three primitive societies. 3.5654
Sex bias in the schools. 4.10780
Sex, class, and culture. 4.6068
Sex, discrimination, and the division of labor. 4.3285
The sex factor and the management of schools. 4.10670
The sex game. 5.483
The sex life of flowers. 5.3775
Sex literature and censorship. 2.8973
Sex, politics, and society. 4.5492
Sex roles in contemporary American communes. 4.5786
Sex roles in the state house. 4.5969
Sex roles, life styles, and childbearing. 4.5599
Sex segregation in the workplace. 4.3256
Sex, sin, and grace. 1.2911
Sex, violence, and the media. 4.5338
Sexism and God-talk. 1.2912
Sexism and the war system. 4.9105
Sexism in school and society. 4.10838
Sexism, racism, and oppression. 4.5872

Sexist language. 2.129
Sexual abuse of children. 4.5519
Sexual and reproductive aspects of women's health care. 5.5045
Sexual bargaining: power politics in the American marriage. 4.5600
The sexual barrier. 4.9694
Sexual behavior in the human female. 4.5510
Sexual behavior in the human male. 4.5494
Sexual disorders. 5.4953
The sexual division of work. 4.3277
Sexual experience between men and boys. 4.5536
Sexual exploitation. 4.6742
Sexual harassment. 5.8469
Sexual harassment of working women. 4.9567
The sexual life of savages in north-western Melanesia. 4.5559
Sexual meanings, the cultural construction of gender and sexuality. 4.569
Sexual perversity in Chicago and The duck variations. 2.13168
Sexual politics. 4.5885
Sexual politics, sexual communities. 4.5537
Sexual practices & the medieval church. 4.5488
Sexual practices and the medieval church. 4.5488
Sexual preference, its development in men and women. 4.5526
Sexual signatures. 5.491
Sexual stigma. 4.5517
Sexual stratification. 4.573
Sexual variance in society and history. 4.5486
Sexuality and the genetics of bacteria. 5.4449
Sexuality in Islam. 1.2087
The sexuality of Christ in Renaissance art and in modern oblivion. 1.5179
Sexually abused children and their families. 4.5518
Sexus. 2.12189
Seymour, an introduction. 2.12426
Shades of Brown. 4.10794
Shadow and act. 2.10320
The shadow box. 2.12962
The shadow of eternity. 2.5803
The shadow of God and the Hidden Imam. 3.4079
The shadow of Keynes. 4.1339
Shadow of light. 5.6963
The shadow of Pearl Harbor. 3.898
The shadow of the torturer. 2.13437
The shadow of the winter palace. 3.3107
Shadow train. 2.11336
Shadows move among them. 2.9122
Shadows of the Rising Sun. 3.4894
Shadows on our skin. 2.9734
Shadows on the land. 4.2537
Shaftesbury, Rousseau, and Kant. 1.908
The Shah. 3.4088
Shah of shahs. 3.4086
Shaka Zulu. 3.5500
Shaker furniture. 1.6560
The Shaker spiritual. 1.4251
The Shakers and the world's people. 1.3411
Shakespeare. 2.6691-2.6692, 2.6725, 2.6754-2.6755, 2.6775, 2.6783, 2.6793
Shakespeare and Christian doctrine. 2.6828
Shakespeare and Elizabethan poetry. 2.6723
Shakespeare & Jonson. 2.6715
Shakespeare and the actors. 2.6859
Shakespeare and the allegory of evil. 2.6812
Shakespeare and the awareness of the audience. 2.6720
Shakespeare and the classics. 2.6830
Shakespeare and the film. 2.6861
Shakespeare and the idea of the play. 2.6719
Shakespeare and the mystery of God's judgments. 2.6784
Shakespeare and the nature of women. 2.6808
Shakespeare and the popular dramatic tradition. 2.6721
Shakespeare and the popular tradition in the theater. 2.6757
Shakespeare and the romance tradition. 2.6763
Shakespeare as a dramatic artist. 2.6816
Shakespeare at the Globe, 1599-1609. 2.6863
Shakespeare at work, 1592-1603. 2.6704

The Shakespeare companion. 2.6729
Shakespeare criticism, 1919-35. 2.6746
Shakespeare criticism, 1935-60. 2.6747
Shakespeare Factory 1. 2.13905
Shakespeare Factory eins. 2.13905
Shakespeare: from Betterton to Irving. 2.6858
Shakespeare from Richard II to Henry V. 2.6774
A Shakespeare glossary. 2.6685
Shakespeare Head Brontë. 2.7447
The Shakespeare Head edition of the novels and selected writings of Daniel Defoe. 2.6969
Shakespeare improved. 2.6867
Shakespeare in sable. 2.6868
Shakespeare in the theatre, 1701-1800. 2.6866
Shakespeare; modern essays in criticism. 2.6728
Shakespeare of London. 2.6703
Shakespeare on the American stage. 2.6869
Shakespeare on the English stage, 1900-1964. 2.6871
Shakespeare plain. 2.6742
Shakespeare: select bibliographical guides; edited by Stanley Wells. 2.6799
Shakespeare survey. 2.6681
Shakespeare survey; an annual survey of Shakespearian study and production. 2.6681
Shakespeare the dramatist. 2.6701
Shakespeare, the Globe & the world. 2.6710
Shakespeare: the last phase. 2.6764
Shakespeare, the man and his achievement. 2.6699
Shakespearean company. 2.6862
Shakespearean criticism. 2.6726
Shakespearean meanings. 2.6724
Shakespearean playhouses. 2.3286
The Shakespearean stage, 1574-1642. 2.3298
Shakespearean staging, 1599-1642. 2.3295
Shakespearean tragedy. 2.6776
Shakespearean tragedy: Hamlet, Othello, King Lear, Macbeth. 2.6777
Shakespeare's audience. 2.6854
Shakespeare's bawdy. 2.6686
Shakespeare's Blackfriars Playhouse. 2.3328
Shakespeare's Chaucer. 2.6713
Shakespeare's comedies. 2.6760
Shakespeare's comic sequence. 2.6762
Shakespeare's craft. 2.6749
Shakespeare's doctrine of nature. 2.6663
Shakespeare's dramatic challenge. 2.6786
Shakespeare's dramatic language. 2.6843
Shakespeare's English kings. 2.6772
Shakespeare's festive comedy. 2.6758
Shakespeare's happy comedies. 2.6765
Shakespeare's 'Histories' 2.6767
Shakespeare's history. 2.6769
Shakespeare's history plays. 2.6773
Shakespeare's imagery, and what it tells us. 2.6849
Shakespeare's last plays. 2.6751, 2.6756
Shakespeare's military world. 2.6834
Shakespeare's motley. 2.6810
Shakespeare's names. 2.6847
Shakespeare's philosophical patterns. 2.6822
Shakespeare's problem plays. 2.6752
Shakespeare's pronunciation. 2.6848
Shakespeare's prose. 2.6851
Shakespeare's Roman plays. 2.6768
Shakespeare's Roman plays and their background. 2.6770
Shakespeare's satire. 2.6814
Shakespeare's Second Globe. 1.5551
Shakespeare's sisters. 2.10484
Shakespeare's sonnets. 2.6677
Shakespeare's Sonnets. 2.6672
Shakespeare's sonnets. 2.6678
Shakespeare's stage. 2.6857
Shakespeare's theatre. 2.6865
Shakespeare's tragedies. 2.6791
Shakespeare's tragedies, and other studies in seventeenth century drama. 2.5846
Shakespeare's tragic frontier. 2.6781
Shakespeare's tragic heroes, slaves of passion. 2.6778
Shakespeare's tragic justice. 2.6825
Shakespeare's tragic perspective. 2.6779
Shakespeare's tragicomic vision. 2.6735
Shakespeare's use of learning. 2.6821

Shakespeare's wooden O. 2.6708
Shakespeare's wordplay. 2.6819
Shakespeare's workmanship. 2.6817
Shakespeare's world of images. 2.6826
Shakespeare's young lovers. 2.6807
Shakespearian comedy. 2.6759
Shakespearian players and performances. 2.6870
The Shakespearian tempest. 2.6737
Shakespearian tragedy. 2.6780
Shaking the pumpkin. 2.2325
Shakspere to Sheridan. 2.3283
Shakuntala and other writings. 2.1947
Shamanism: archaic techniques of ecstasy. 1.1842
The Shambaa kingdom. 3.5294
Shana Alexander's State-by-State guide to women's legal rights. 4.9506
The Shánámá of Firdausi. 2.1967
Shananditti. 3.5845
Shang civilization. 3.4690
Shanghai, key to modern China. 4.2491
The Shanidar Neandertals. 4.456
Shanks' mare. 2.2069
The shape of content. 1.5137
The shape of death. 1.2940
The shape of European history. 3.528
The shape of space. 5.1613
The shape of the liturgy. 1.2986
The shape of time. 1.4597
Shape-up and hiring hall. 4.3533
The shapes of time. 3.486
Shaping men and women. 2.2593
The shaping of America. 3.6323
The shaping of American anthropology, 1883-1911. 4.398
The shaping of American religion. 1.2384
The shaping of Black America. 3.6607
The shaping of Chinese foreign policy. 4.9079
The shaping of peace. 3.8779
The shaping of Somali society. 3.5256
The Shaping of South African society, 1652-1820. 3.5447
The shaping of Southern politics. 4.8098
The shaping of the American high school. 4.10054
The shaping of the American tradition. 3.6321
The shaping of the Elizabethan regime. 3.1423
Shaping the future. 3.7559, 4.6614
Shaping the new social work. 4.6514
Shaping the world economy. 4.2806
Shaping tomorrow's family. 4.5598
The shaping vision of Gerard Manley Hopkins. 2.7830
The share economy. 4.3210
Sharing the same bowl? 4.6161
The sharks of North American waters. 5.3912
The shattered self. 2.13618
The shattered synthesis. 3.7949
Shaw. 2.8077
Shaw; an autobiography. 2.8072
Shaw and Ibsen. 2.14040
Shaw and the nineteenth-century theater. 2.8085
Shaw in his time. 2.8073
Shaw on education. 4.10217
Shaw on music. 1.3724
Shaw on Shakespeare. 2.6750
Shaw on theatre. 2.3086, 2.8088
Shaw the villager and human being. 2.8074
Shawnee! 3.5948
Shaw's dramatic criticism (1895-98) 2.3321
Shaw's plays in review. 2.8084
She stoops to conquer. 2.7047
The she-wolf. 2.5013
The shearers and the shorn. 4.5325
Sheep and wool science. 5.5447
Sheep breeding. 5.5449
Sheep husbandry and diseases. 5.5448
The Shehus of Kukawa. 3.5368
Shelby Foote. 2.11744
The shell game. 4.985
Shelley. 2.8099, 2.8104
Shelley: a critical reading. 2.8111
Shelley and translation. 2.8112
Shelley: his thought and work. 2.8110
Shelley: the golden years. 2.8100
Shelley's annus mirabilis. 2.8109

Shelley's major poetry. 2.8107
Shelley's mythmaking. 2.8108
Shelley's Poetry and prose. 2.8097
Shelley's style. 2.8113
Shelter, sign & symbol. 4.826
The sheltered life. 2.11772
Shen Pu-hai. 4.7331
Shen Ts'ung-wen. 2.2247
Shenfan. 4.2877
Shepherds historical atlas. [1st]- ed.; 1911-. 4.124
Sheraton furniture. 1.6572
Sheridan. 2.7248
Sheridan and the drama of Georgian England. 2.7253
Sheridan to Robertson. 2.3323
Sheridan's comedies, their contexts and achievements. 2.7252
The Sherlock Holmes companion. 2.7683
Sherman, fighting prophet. 3.7330
The Sherpas of Nepal, Buddhist highlanders. 3.4347
Sherpas through their rituals. 1.1830
Sherwood Anderson. 2.11328
Sherwood Anderson. 2.11329
Sherwood Anderson's memoirs. 2.11326
Shield of Herakles. 2.479
The Shiga hero. 2.2090
Shigaraki, potters' valley. 1.6623
Shih ching. English. 2.2182
Shih yung Han Ying tz'u tien. 2.2150
Shi'ism and social protest. 1.2089
A Shi'ite creed. 1.2090
Shi'ite Islam. 1.2092
Shikasta. 2.9024
Shiloh, a novel. 2.11743
Shin Ei-Wa daijiten. 2.1990
The shingle style. 1.5559
Shining trumpets. 1.4317
Shinran's gospel of pure grace. 1.2169
Shintô; at the fountain-head of Japan. 1.1837
Shinto, the Kami Way. 1.1838
The ship of fools. 2.13528
Ship of fools. 2.12317
The ship of Ishtar. 2.12145
The ship of the line. 5.7432
Shipping, maritime trade, and the economic development of colonial North America. 4.4216
Ships and fleets of the ancient Mediterranean. 5.7486
Ships and seamanship in the ancient world. 5.7498
Ships and the sea. 5.7500
The shipwrecked. 2.8758
Shirley Ann Grau. 2.13060
Shivaji and facets of Maratha culture. 3.4346
Shoal of time. 3.5638
Shock, a nursing guide. 5.4747
Shock and vibration handbook. 5.5745
The shock of peace. 5.7350
The shock of recognition. 2.10237
The shock of the new. 1.4781-1.4782
Shock waves & man. 5.5754
The shoemaker's holiday. 2.6570-2.6571
Shoes. 4.856
The Shogun age exhibition. 1.4667
Sholom Aleichem. 2.1814
The Shona & Zimbabwe, 900-1850. 3.5510
Shona and Zimbabwe, 900-1850. 3.5510
The shooting party. 2.9655
Shop stewards in action. 4.3341
A shopkeeper's millennium. 1.3040
Shopping bag ladies. 4.6586
The shopping mall high school. 4.10509
Shore of pearls. 3.4858
Shore processes and shoreline development. 4.270
Shoreline for the public. 4.9760
The shores of light. 2.10426
Short course in biochemistry. 5.4397
A short course in general relativity. 5.2100
The short fiction of Charles W. Chesnutt. 2.10925
Short fiction of the seventeenth century. 2.6258
A short historical English grammar. 2.987
A short history of Africa. 3.5076

Short history of Anglo-Irish literature from its origins to the present day. 2.9852
A short history of archaeology. 3.253
A short history of Aurangzib. 3.4257
A short history of botany in the United States. 5.3636
A short history of Bulgaria. 3.3540
A short history of chemistry. 5.2604, 5.2610
A short history of Chinese philosophy. 1.153
A short history of Christian doctrine. 1.2746
A short history of Christianity. 1.2284
A short history of classical Arabic literature. 2.1835
A short history of costume and armor. 4.841
A short history of Denmark. 3.3369
A short history of electoral systems in Western Europe. 4.8369
A short history of English. 2.989
A short history of English literature. 2.5527
A short history of French literature. 2.3829
A short history of Greek literature. 2.280
A short history of India. 3.4160
A short history of international organization. 4.9110
A short history of Ireland. 3.1814
A short history of linguistics. 2.38
A short history of medicine. 5.4498
A short history of medieval philosophy. 1.357
A short history of modern Greece. 3.2681
A short history of Nigeria. 3.5358
A short history of Norway. 3.3378
A short history of opera. 1.4210
A short history of Russia. 3.3049
A short history of scene design in Great Britain. 2.3157
A short history of scientific ideas to 1900. 5.757
A short history of Switzerland. 3.3510
A short history of technology from the earliest times to A.D. 1900. 5.5530
A short history of the Catholic Church. 1.3142
A short history of the Chinese people. 3.4667
A short history of the French Revolution, 1789-1799. 3.2086
A short history of the Italian people, from the barbarian invasions to the present day. 3.2837
Short history of the Labour Party. 4.8541
A short history of the Middle East. 3.3628
A short history of the movies. 2.2882
A short history of the New Deal. 4.1957
A short history of the Papacy in the Middle Ages. 1.3148
A short history of the Swedish language. 2.922
A short history of the West Indies. 3.9088
A short history of the Yugoslav peoples. 3.3605
A short history of Tibet. 3.4855
A short history of twentieth-century technology c. 1900-c. 1950. 5.5537
A short history of Western philosophy. 1.129
A short introduction to archaeology. 3.264
A short introduction to English grammar. 2.999
A short introduction to English usage. 2.997
A Short introduction to the study of comparative grammar (Indo-European) 2.221
Short letter, long farewell. 2.13889
A short life of Shakespeare: abridged by Charles Williams from Sir Edmund Chambers's William Shakespeare: a study of facts and problems. 2.6695
Short novels. 2.4487
Short novels. 2.8953
Short novels and other writings. 2.13564
The short novels of Balzac. 2.4115
The short novels of Dosetoevsky. 2.1346
Short novels: Tortilla Flat, The red pony, Of mice and men, The moon is down, Cannery Row, The pearl. 2.12525
Short poems. 2.11380
The short reign of Pippin IV. 2.12531
The short season between two silences. 2.9602
Short shorts. 2.3777
Short stories. 2.5056, 2.9934, 2.11840
Short stories, 1921-1946. 2.13702

Short stories from Southern Africa. 2.10053
Short stories from the New Yorker. 2.10846
The short stories of Dostoevsky. 2.1347
The short stories of Ernest Hemingway. 2.11864
The Short stories of F. Scott Fitzgerald. 2.11738
The short stories of Sake (H.H. Munro) 2.9133
Short stories of Yashpal. 2.1895
The short story. 2.3437
The Short story, 25 masterpieces. 2.3709
The short story, a critical introduction. 2.3438
The short story in America. 2.10581
Short story index. 5.8178-5.8179
Short story index, collections indexed 1900-1978. 5.8179
Short story theories. 2.3439
Short-term psychotherapy and emotional crisis. 5.4857
A short-title catalogue of books printed in England, Scotland, & Ireland and of English books printed abroad, 1475-1640. 5.7915
Short-title catalogue of books printed in England, Scotland, Ireland, Wales, and British America, and of English books printed in other countries, 1641-1700. 5.7916
The short-title Evans. 5.7759
The short victorious war. 3.4399
A short view of Elizabethan drama, together with some account of its principal playwrights and the conditions under which it was produced. 2.5869
The shorter books of the Apocrypha: Tobit, Judith, Rest of Esther, Baruch, Letter of Jeremiah, additions to Daniel and Prayer of Manasseh. 1.2620
The shorter Cambridge medieval history. 3.574
Shorter encyclopaedia of Islam. 3.3658
A shorter Finnegans wake. 2.8875
Shorter hours. 4.3157
Shorter hours, shorter weeks. 4.3158
The Shorter new Cambridge bibliography of English literature. 5.7939
Shorter novels ... 2.6248
The shorter novels of Stendhal ... 2.4302
The shorter Oxford English dictionary on historical principles. 2.1083
The shorter Pepys. 3.1504
The shorter Science and civilisation in China. 3.4643
The shorter Strachey. 2.9388
Shostakovich. 1.3988
Should the federal government significantly curtail the powers of labor unions in the United States? 4.3368
The shouting signpainters. 3.8814
Show boat. 2.11713
Show music on record. 1.3619
A show of justice. 3.5612
Showboats. 2.3270
A shower of summer days. 2.12444
Showings. 1.3072
The showman of Vanity Fair. 2.8189
The shows of London. 5.5654
The Shrewsbury edition of the works of Samuel Butler. 2.7511
The shrimp and the anemone. 2.8797
The shrine of party. 4.8151
The shrinking of America. 5.4869
Shriven selves. 2.10569
Shroud for a nightingale. 2.9722
The Shroud of Turin. 1.2898
The Shtetl. 2.1829
Shui hu chuan. English. 2.2224
SI chemical data. 5.2646
Une si longue lettre. 2.4866
Siam in transition. 3.4531
Siam under Rama III, 1824-1851. 3.4527
Sibelius. 1.3990
Siberia and the exile system. 3.3319
Siberia today and tomorrow. 4.2566
Sibley's Harvard graduates. 3.7941
The sibling bond. 5.616
The sibyl. 2.14094
The Sicilian Vespers. 3.2944
The 'sick heart' of modern Europe. 3.3523

The sickle under the hammer. 3.3190
The sickled cell. 5.4988
Sickness and society. 5.4644
The sickness unto death. 1.2230
Sicuanga Runa. 3.9313
Siddhartha. 2.13776
Sideshow. 3.4496
Sidgwick's ethics and Victorian moral philosophy. 1.1424
Sidney Lanier. 2.11141-2.11143
Sidney's poetry: contexts and interpretations. 2.6511
Sido. 2.4495
Le siècle de Bruegel. 1.6257
Le siècle de Louis XV. 3.2045
The siege of Leningrad. 3.990
The siege of Paris, 1870-1871. 3.2164
Siegfried et le Limousin. 2.4570
Siegfried Lenz. 2.13816
Siena. 3.2955
Siena, a city and its history. 3.2954
The Sierra Club wilderness handbook. 5.5498
Sieyes: his life and his nationalism. 3.2074
Sifrut yisraelit bat zemanenu. 2.1783
Sight and mind. 5.248
Sights and spectacles. 2.3228
The sigla of Finnegans wake. 2.8874
Sign, image, symbol. 1.5113
The sign in Sidney Brustein's window. 2.11814
The sign of the fish. 2.9256
Sign, symbol, and script. 2.172
The signal. 2.1496
Signal analysis. 5.6379
Signal detection theory and psychophysics. 5.243
Signal processor chips. 5.6380
Signal recovery from noise in electronic instrumentation. 5.6552
Signals and information. 5.6373
Signals and linear systems. 5.6277
Signals, systems, and transforms. 5.6366
The significance of philosophical scepticism. 1.536
The significance of sections in American history. 3.6326
Significant accounting essays. 4.4395
Signing. 4.6606
Signs. 1.842
Signs and meaning in the cinema. 2.2973
Signs & wonders upon Pharaoh. 3.5136
Signs in contemporary culture. 2.77
Signs, language, and behavior. 1.543
The Sikhs. 1.1827
The Sikhs in relation to Hindus, Moslems, Christians, and Ahmadiyyas. 1.1828
Sikkim and Bhutan. 3.4355
Silas Crockett. 2.11484
Silence. 2.2129
Le silence de la mer. 2.4431
Silence in the snowy fields. 2.12910
Silence; lectures and writings. 1.3467
The silence of Jesus. 1.2889
The silence of the sea. 2.4432
The silenced theatre. 2.1659
Silent China; selected writings of Lu Xun. 2.2239
The silent clowns. 2.2979
The silent dictatorship. 3.2340
The silent Don. 2.1603
The silent majority. 2.6053
Silent music. 1.1636
The silent scream. 2.3057
Silent spring. 5.5416
Silent victory. 3.1040
Silent voices; poems. 2.10096
The silent world of doctor and patient. 5.4592
The Silmarillion. 2.9433
Silver. 1.6660, 4.4496
The Silver age of Russian culture. 2.1306
The silver dove. 2.1475
Silver in American life. 1.6658
Silver mines and silver miners in colonial Peru, 1776-1824. 5.6752
Silver mining and society in colonial Mexico: Zacatecas, 1546-1700. 4.3737
Silver poets of the seventeenth century. 2.6161
Silver poets of the sixteenth century. 2.6145
Simenon. 2.4749

Similarities in physics. 5.1988
The Simon and Schuster book of the opera. 1.3520
Simon & Schuster book of the opera. 1.3520
The Simon and Schuster encyclopedia of World War II. 3.890
Simon and Schuster's Guide to rocks and minerals. 5.3016
Simon and Schuster's international dictionary. 2.901
Simon Bolivar. 3.9167
Simon de Montfort. 3.1362
Simone de Beauvoir. 2.4402
Simone Weil. 1.860
The simple cobler of Aggawam in America. 2.10882
A simple heart. 2.4194
A simple honorable man. 2.12392
Simple justice. 4.9591
The simple life. 3.6165
Simple speaks his mind. 2.11895
Simple's Uncle Sam. 2.11896
The simplest game. 4.1016
Simplicity. 1.143
Simplicius simplicissimus. 2.13544
Simplified design of reinforced concrete. 5.5878
Simplified design of structural steel. 5.5886
Simultaneous and successive cognitive processes. 5.262
Sin and confession on the eve of the Reformation. 1.3019
The Sin of the book. 2.4587
Sin querer. 2.5234
Sinai and the Monastery of St. Catherine. 1.5541
Since Cézanne. 1.5125
Since Debussy. 1.3672
Since yesterday. 3.7507
Sincerely, Willis Wayde. 2.12109
Sinclair Lewis. 2.12013-2.12014
Sindh and the races that inhabit the Valley of the Indus. 3.4139
Sindhi literature. 2.1918
Sinews of empire. 4.6441
The Sinews of independence. 3.6942
The sinews of peace, post-war speeches. 3.1161
The sinews of war: Army logistics, 1775-1953. 5.7224
Sinful tunes and spirituals. 1.4298
Singapore. 4.5439
Singapore development policies and trends. 4.2530
The singer and his art. 1.4564
The singer and the voice. 1.4563
Singers of daybreak. 2.10309
Singer's repertoire. 1.3597
Singing for power. 1.4310
The singing game. 4.1064
Singing, the mechanism and the technic. 1.4567
Single. 4.5768
Single-chip micro-computers. 5.1153
Single-chip microcomputers. 5.1153
Single lens. 5.3286
The singularity of Shakespeare, and other essays. 2.6744
Singularity theory and an introduction to catastrophe theory. 5.1617
Sinister street. 2.9072
The sinner. 2.1823
Sinning with Annie. 2.13357
Sino-American normalization and its policy implications. 3.6433
Sino-American relations, 1949-1971. 3.6429
The Sino-Japanese controversy and the League of Nations. 3.4848
The Sino-Soviet conflict. 3.4685
The Sino-Soviet Conflict, 1956-1961. 3.3073
The Sino-Soviet rivalry and Chinese security debate. 3.6430
The sins of the fathers: Hawthorne's psychological themes. 2.11062
SIPRI yearbook. 5.7250
Sir Arthur Sullivan, his life, letters & diaries. 1.4016
Sir Banister Fletcher's A history of architecture. 1.5211

Sir Charles Eastlake and the Victorian art world. 1.4952
Sir Charles Grandison. 2.7221
Sir Christopher Wren. 1.5408
Sir Francis Drake. 3.1275
Sir Gawain and the Green Knight. 2.6414, 2.6416
Sir Gawain and the Green Knight, Pearl, and Sir Orfeo. 2.6134
Sir Jeffry Wyatville: architect to the king. 1.5409
Sir John Beverley Robinson. 4.9432
Sir John Davies. 2.6446
Sir John Harington. 2.6484
Sir John Soane, architect. 1.5403
Sir John Suckling. 2.7288
Sir John Suckling's poems and letters from manuscript. 2.7287
Sir Leslie Stephen's Mausoleum book. 2.8115
Sir Orfeo (Middle English poem). 1975. 2.6134
Sir Philip Sidney and the English Renaissance. 2.6510
Sir Philip Sidney as a literary craftsman. 2.6513
Sir Robert Peel. 3.1606
Sir Robert Walpole. 3.1553
Sir Samuel Ferguson. 2.7715
Sir Thomas Browne. 2.6914
Sir Thomas Browne's Pseudodoxia epidemica. 2.6913
Sir Thomas Lawrence. 1.6035
Sir Thomas Overbury's vision (1616) 2.6499
Sir Thomas Wyatt and his background. 2.6551
Sir Thomas Wyatt, The complete poems. 2.6549
Sir Walter Ralegh. 3.1277
Sir Walter Raleigh. 2.6503, 3.1278
Sir Walter Scott. 2.8046, 2.8050
Sir Walter Scott, bart. 2.8047
Sir Walter Scott, his life and personality. 2.8049
Sir Walter Scott; the great unknown. 2.8048
Sir William Chambers, Knight of the Polar Star. 1.5384
Sir William Davenant, poet venturer, 1606-1668. 2.6567
Sir William Rowan Hamilton. 5.1094
Sīrat rasūl Allāh. 1.2014
The sirens of Titan. 2.13397
The sirens' song. 2.2340
The Sirian experiments. 2.9023
The sister arts. 2.5680
Sister Carrie. 2.11596
Sister Kenny. 5.5163
Sisterhood is global. 4.5896
Sisterhood is powerful. 4.6064
Sisters of liberty. 3.2168
Sisters or citizens? 4.7148
Sit-down: the General Motors strike of 1936-1937. 4.3166
Site investigation. 5.6086
Sitting in darkness. 3.4599
Sitting pretty. 2.13444
Six American plays for today. 2.10795
The six bookes of a commonweale. 4.7383
Six Caroline plays. 2.6221
Six centuries of work and wages. 4.3640
Six contemporaneous revolutions. 3.635
Six contemporary British novelists. 2.6048
Six crises. 3.7674
Six cultures; studies of child rearing. 4.5707
Six eighteenth-century plays. 2.6238
Six Elizabethan plays (1585-1635) 2.6217
Six existentialist thinkers. 1.485
Six great poets. 2.5770
Six guns and society. 2.3013
Six justices on civil rights. 4.9661
Six lectures on economic growth. 4.2789
Six modern American plays. 2.10805
Six plays. 2.8004
Six plays by Kaufman and Hart. 2.11944
Six plays of Clifford Odets. 2.12259
Six poets of modern Greece. 2.574
Six problems for Don Isidro Parodi. 2.5376
Six Tennyson essays. 2.8181
Six thousand years of bread. 3.56
Sixteen-bit microprocessors. 5.1227
Sixteen famous European plays. 2.3765

Sixteen modern American authors. 2.10406
The sixteen satires. 2.729
Sixteen short novels. 2.3778
Sixteenth-century England. 4.5330
Sixteenth-century English literature. 2.5632
Sixteenth century English poetry. 2.6147
Sixteenth-century Europe. 3.624
Sixteenth century nationalism. 3.632
Sixteenth century North America. 3.5979
The sixth heaven. 2.8797
Sixth International Conference on Computers and the Humanities. 1.72
Sixty poems of Martial, in translation. 2.741
Sixty-three, dream palace. 2.12358
The size, composition, and growth of the population of mainland China. 4.1704
Size, structure, and future of farms. 4.2936
Sizwe Bansi is dead and The island. 2.10068
The skeleton. 5.4149
A skeleton key to Finnegans wake. 2.8870
Skelton and satire. 2.6519
Skelton, the life and times of an early Tudor poet. 2.6517
Sketch for a historical picture of the progress of the human mind. 3.7
The sketchbook of Villard de Honnecourt. 1.5420
Sketches from life. 3.339
Sketches here and there. 5.3230
Sketches of eighteenth century America. 3.6024
Ski magazine. 4.998
Ski magazine's encyclopedia of skiing. 4.998
Skiing right. 4.996
The skills of helping. 4.6464
The skin of our teeth. 2.12713
The skin senses. 5.4364
Skolnick report on violent aspects of protest and confrontation. 4.5163
Sky. 5.1833
The Sky. 5.1841
Sky & telescope. 5.1710, 5.1723, 5.1750, 5.1791, 5.1833, 5.1841
Sky atlas 2000.0. 5.1743
Sky catalogue 2000.0. 5.1676
The sky clears. 2.10741
The sky explored. 5.1744
The sky suspended. 3.1052
Skywatchers of ancient Mexico. 3.8902
Slan. 2.12612
Slang and euphemism. 2.1165
Slang to-day and yesterday. 2.1163
Slapstick. 2.13396
Slaughterhouse-five. 2.13398
The slave. 2.12868
Slave and citizen. 3.7239
Slave and freeman, the autobiography of George L. Knox. 3.8403
The slave community. 3.7201
The slave girl. 2.10109
Slave population and economy in Jamaica, 1807-1834. 4.6435
The slave power conspiracy and the paranoid style. 3.7187
Slave religion. 1.2420
Slave society in the British Leeward Islands at the end of the eighteenth century. 4.6438
Slave songs of the Georgia Sea islands. 1.3440
Slave songs of the United States. 1.3438
The slave systems of Greek and Roman antiquity. 4.6417
Slave testimony. 3.7213
Slavery. 3.7202
Slavery and freedom. 3.7195
Slavery and freedom on the middle ground. 3.7215
Slavery and human progress. 4.6412
Slavery & race in American popular culture. 3.7197
Slavery and race in American popular culture. 3.7197
Slavery and serfdom in the Middle Ages. 4.6418
Slavery and social death. 4.6420
Slavery and the annexation of Texas. 3.8326
Slavery and the evolution of Cherokee society, 1540-1866. 3.5851
Slavery defended. 3.7254

Slavery in Africa. 4.6451
Slavery in Russia, 1450-1725. 4.6444
Slavery, law, and politics. 4.9621
The slavery of sex. 4.6029
Slaves and missionaries. 4.6436
Slaves and slavery in Muslim Africa. 4.6447
Slaves, free men, citizens. 4.6429
Slaves in red coats. 4.6433
Slaves of love and other Norwegian short stories. 2.14033
Slaves of the white God. 4.6428
Slaves without masters. 3.6634
The Slavic literatures. 5.8336
Slavonic and Romantic music. 1.3464
The Slavs. 3.3514
The Slavs in European history and civilization. 3.585
Sleep and wakefulness. 5.4355
Sleep has his house. 2.8619
Sleep research; a critical review. 5.4354
The sleep walkers. 1.1597
Sleepers awake. 2.12307
Sleepers, wake! 4.3320
The sleeping lord, and other fragments. 2.8857
Sleeping on the wing. 2.2732
The sleepwalkers, a trilogy. 2.13713
Slide rule. 5.6653
Slim Buttes, 1876. 3.5783
Slim, the standardbearer. 3.1273
Slinger. 2.11576
Slipping through the cracks. 4.6024
A slot machine, a broken test tube. 5.4433
Slovo o polku Igoreve. English. 2.1330
Slow coming dark. 4.6852
Slow dance on the killing ground. 2.13065
Slow fade to Black. 2.2998
Slow homecoming. 2.13890
Slow learner. 2.13281
The slum and the ghetto. 3.8425
Slurry walls. 5.5922
Small airport management handbook. 5.6682
Small and mini hydropower systems. 5.6098
Small books and pleasant histories. 2.6068
A small boy and others. 2.11113
The Small firm. 4.3002
The small group. 4.4902
Small groups and political behavior. 4.4955
The small house at Allington. 2.8223
Small is beautiful. 4.1453
Small moments. 2.13232
A small personal voice. 2.9027
Small press record of books in print. 5.7702
The small room. 2.12445
Small-state security in the Balkans. 3.3531
The Small television studio, equipment and facilities. 5.6440
Small town Chicago. 2.10653
Small town in mass society. 4.6373
Smart set criticism. 2.12124
SME mining engineering handbook. 5.6725
The smell of hay. 2.5022
Smetana. 1.3992
The smile of Murugan on Tamil literature of South India. 2.2271
Al Smith and his America. 3.7680
Smithells metals reference book. 5.6765
Smith's Guide to the literature of the life sciences. 5.3294
Smithsonian Astrophysical Observatory star atlas of reference stars and nonstellar objects. 5.1741
The Smithsonian collection of newspaper comics. 2.3817
The Smithsonian Institution. 5.692
The Smithsonian octopus on the Mall. 5.691
Smoke. 2.1455
Smoke and ashes. 2.1534
Smoke's way. 2.12501
Smoking and politics. 4.4440
Smolensk under Soviet rule. 4.5377
Smollett studies. 2.7265
Smooth dynamical systems. 5.1625
Smoothing, forecasting and prediction of discrete time series. 5.5689
Smoothing the ground. 2.2319
Smudging. 2.13405
Smuts. 3.5473

Smyth report on military uses of atomic energy. 5.2420
The snake pit. 2.12632
Snakes. 2.13442, 5.3928
SNCC. 3.6698
Sneaky people. 2.12905
Snobbery with violence: crime stories and their audience. 2.5960
Snow country, and Thousand cranes. 2.2103
Snow in May. 2.1753
Snow White. 2.12893
Snowball berry red & other stories. 2.1632
So be it. 2.4549
So-Big. 2.11714
The so-called historical Jesus and the historic biblical Christ. 1.2883
So human an animal. 4.4963
So little time and Point of no return. 2.12110
So long a letter. 2.4867
So red the rose. 2.12830
So spoke the uncle. 4.786
Soaring. 4.1160
Sobre héroes y tumbas. 2.5397
Soccer techniques and tactics. 4.1018
Social actions. 4.4850
Social and cultural dynamics. 4.4875
Social and cultural issues of the new international economic order. 4.4157
Social and cultural mobility. 4.4864
Social and cultural perspectives in nutrition. 5.7116
A social and economic history of Britain, 1760-1980. 4.5300
A social and economic history of medieval Europe. 4.2199
The social & economic history of the Hellenistic world. 3.2636
A social and economic history of the Near East in the Middle Ages. 4.2426
The social and economic history of the Roman Empire. 3.2789
The social and educational thought of Harold Rugg. 4.10254
Social and industrial conditions in the North during the Civil War. 4.1921
The social and political conflict in Prussia, 1858-1864. 4.8618
The social and political ideas of the muckrakers. 3.7521
The social and political philosophy of Jacques Maritain. 1.837
The social and political systems of central Polynesia. 4.675
Social and political thought in Byzantium, from Justinian I to the last Palaeologus. 4.7372
The social and political thought of Herbert Spencer. 4.4769
The social and political thought of Karl Marx. 4.6948
A social and religious history of the Jews. 3.3832
The social animal. 4.4980
Social anthropology. 4.481, 4.491, 4.519-4.520, 4.658
Social anthropology and development policy. 4.517
Social anthropology and medicine. 4.466
Social anthropology in Melanesia. 3.5618
Social anthropology in perspective. 4.482
Social anthropology in Polynesia. 3.5624
Social archeology. 3.237
The social areas of Los Angeles. 4.5214
The social basis of scientific discoveries. 5.956
Social behavior. 4.5068
Social behavior and personality. 4.4846
The social behavior of the bees. 5.3885
Social behavior of the mentally retarded. 5.8295
Social behaviour in animals with special reference to vertebrates. 5.4093
The social behaviour of monkeys. 5.4027
Social casework. 4.6500, 4.6502
Social change and stratification in Eastern Europe. 4.5381
Social change and the individual. 4.5452
Social change in a Yemeni highlands town. 4.5405
Social change in modern India. 4.5430

Social change: sources, patterns, and consequences. 4.4873
Social choice and individual values. 4.5021
Social class and mental illness. 5.4831
Social class and social change in Puerto Rico. 4.5265
Social class in America. 4.6386
Social conflict and the city. 4.6186
Social conflict in ancient Greece. 3.2549
The social consequences of long life. 4.5802
Social conservatism and the middle classes in Germany, 1914-1933. 3.2368
The social construction of communities. 4.6228
The social construction of reality. 1.1289
The social content of education, 1808-1870. 4.10957
The social context of dentistry. 5.5126
The Social context of instruction. 4.10312
Social contract. 4.7525
The social contract, a critical study of its development. 4.7527
The social contract and Discourses. 4.7433
Social control in slave plantation societies. 4.6432
The social control of technology. 5.5517
The Social costs of power production. 5.5999
Social Darwinism. 4.4774, 4.4891
Social Darwinism in American thought. 4.4773
Social democracy & industrial militancy. 4.2310
Social democratic parties in Europe. 4.7024
Social democratic parties in Western Europe. 4.8378
The Social Democrats in Imperial Germany. 4.7063
Social demography. 4.1577, 4.1630
The social development of Canada. 4.5246
Social diagnosis. 4.6480
Social dimension of trade unionism in India. 4.3421
Social economy. 4.1467
The social economy of the Tlingit Indians. 3.5958
Social engineering in the Philippines. 3.4603
Social evolution. 4.693
Social exchange, dramaturgy, and ethnomethodology. 4.4867
Social exchange theory. 4.4789
Social existence. 4.4807
Social experimentation and economic policy. 4.2003
Social fabric and spatial structure in colonial Latin America. 4.388
The social foundations of German unification, 1858-1871. 3.2306
The social foundations of wage policy. 4.3136
Social geography of British elections, 1885-1910. 4.8490
A social geography of Europe. 4.5283
Social geography of the United States. 4.5147
The social gospel. 1.2928
The Social Gospel in America, 1870-1920. 1.2925
Social groups of monkeys, apes, and men. 5.4091
Social historians in contemporary France. 4.5085
Social history of American education. 4.10018
The social history of an Indonesian town. 4.5442
The social history of art. 1.4630
A social history of English. 2.969
A social history of English music. 1.3717
A social history of Germany, 1648-1914. 4.5361
A social history of housing, 1815-1970. 4.3497
A social history of music, from the Middle Ages to Beethoven. 1.4358
A social history of the American family from colonial times to the present. 4.5568
A social history of the bicycle. 4.1047
A social history of the fool. 4.870
A social history of the French Revolution. 3.2082
Social history of the United States. 5.8411
A social history of Western Europe, 1450-1720. 4.5290
The Social impact of the telephone. 4.4074

The Social implications of the scientific and technological revolution. 5.955
Social inequality. 4.568
Social institutions in an era of world upheaval. 4.5087
Social interaction process and products. 4.4997
The social interpretation of the French Revolution. 3.2096
Social intervention. 4.5142
Social judgment. 4.5018
Social justice and the city. 4.6294
Social justice in the liberal state. 4.7622
Social learning and cognition. 5.298
Social learning and imitation. 4.10373
Social learning theory. 4.10374
Social life in an Indian slum. 4.3500
Social life in early England. 3.1330
The social life of a modern community. 4.6387
Social life of early man. 4.703
The social life of monkeys and apes. 5.4029
Social limits to growth. 4.2777
The social meanings of suicide. 4.6730
Social mobility and class structure in modern Britain. 4.5340
Social mobility in Britain. 4.5299
Social mobility in industrial society. 4.6382
The social mode of restoration comedy. 2.5895
Social movements. 4.5089
Social movements and social change. 4.5100
Social movements and the legal system. 4.9501
The social novel in England, 1830-1850: Dickens, Disraeli, Mrs. Gaskell, Kingsley. 2.6014
The social order of a frontier community. 3.8428
The social order of the slum. 4.5210
Social organization. 4.4983
The social organization of gay males. 4.5529
The social organization of leisure in human society. 4.876
Social origins of dictatorship and democracy. 4.5091
The social origins of the modern Middle East. 4.5395
Social patterns in Australian literature. 2.10139
Social patterns in normal aging. 4.5821
The social philosophers: community and conflict in Western thought. 4.7261
The social philosophy of John Taylor of Caroline. 3.7012
The social plays of Arthur Wing Pinero. 2.7994
Social politics in the United States. 4.8156
The social prelude to Stalinism. 4.5371
Social pressures in informal groups. 4.4985
Social problems. 4.1429, 4.5183, 4.6467
The social progress of nations. 4.5103
Social psychology. 4.4996
Social psychology and physical activity. 4.904
Social psychology in athletics. 4.951
Social psychology of education. 4.10762
The social psychology of music. 1.4384
The social psychology of organizations. 4.4904
The social psychology of organizing. 4.4919
Social psychology, the second edition. 4.4981
Social reform and reaction in America. 5.8392
The social relations of science. 5.721
The social responsibilities of business, company, and community, 1900-1960. 4.2711
Social responsibilities of business corporations. 4.2710
Social responsibilities of the businessman. 4.2702
Social science and political theory. 4.1214
Social science reference sources. 5.8350
Social science research handbook. 5.8351
Social sciences and humanities index. 1.38
Social sciences & humanities index. 1.38
Social sciences index. 1.41
Social scientists and farm politics in the age of Roosevelt. 4.2942
Social security. 4.3464, 4.3469
Social security and pensions in transition. 4.3471
Social security financing. 4.3470
Social security in international perspective. 4.3446

Social security in Latin America. 4.3473
Social security in the United States. 4.3458
Social service organizations. 4.6507
Social service organizations and agencies
   directory. 4.6508
Social services for the elderly. 4.6591
Social services in the United States. 4.6523
The Social setting of mental health. 5.4837
The social sources of denominationalism.
   1.2255
Social statics. 4.4842
Social strategy and corporate structure. 4.2709
Social stratification. 4.6375, 4.6385
Social stratification and mobility in the USSR.
   4.5380
Social stratification in Africa. 4.5464
Social stratification in Polynesia. 3.5625
Social stratification in science. 5.967
The social stratification of English in New York
   City. 2.1151
Social structure. 4.438
Social structure and mobility in economic
   development. 4.6384
Social structure and personality. 5.531
Social structure in Southeast Asia. 3.4388
The social structure of Islam. 4.5121
The social structure of modern Britain. 4.5314
The social structure of revolutionary America.
   4.5139
Social studies for children. 4.10484
Social studies in elementary education. 4.10483
Social support networks. 4.6482
The social system. 4.4838
The social system of the Zulus. 3.5498
The social teaching of the Christian churches.
   4.5116
Social theories of fertility and the Malthusian
   debate. 4.1637
Social theories of Jacksonian democracy.
   3.7073
Social theories of the Middle Ages 1200-1500.
   3.132
Social theory and social structure. 4.4833
The social transformation of American
   medicine. 5.4627
Social treatment. 4.6485
The social uses of social science. 4.402
Social values. 4.6532
Social welfare in America. 5.8360
Social work. 4.6531
The social work interview. 4.6499
Social work issues in health care. 4.6541
Social work practice. 4.6479
Social work practice: a unitary approach.
   4.6478
Social work practice in health care. 4.6540
Social work practice in sexist society. 4.6065
Social work processes. 4.6474
Social work research. 4.6463
Social work treatment. 4.6475
Social work year book 1929-60. 4.6473
The social world of the Florentine humanists,
   1390-1460. 3.2928
Socialism. 4.6929
Socialism. 4.6932
Socialism and abundance. 4.8675
Socialism and communism in India. 4.7114
Socialism and democracy in Czechoslovakia,
   1945-1948. 3.1926
Socialism and the challenge of war. 4.7032
Socialism in America: from the Shakers to the
   Third International. 4.7003
Socialism in southern Asia. 4.7108
Socialism in sub-Saharan Africa. 4.7130
Socialism in the new society. 4.7040
Socialism, politics, and equality. 4.5296
Socialism, Utopian and scientific. 4.7064
The socialist challenge. 4.7039
The Socialist city. 4.6264
Socialist economic development and reforms.
   4.2600
Socialist economic policy. 4.2229
Socialist economics: selected readings. 4.2235
The Socialist economies of the Soviet Union
   and Europe. 4.2233
The socialist economy. 4.1329
The socialist industrial state. 4.7588
Socialist Iraq. 3.3780

Socialist Korea. 4.2562
The Socialist Party of America. 4.8241
The Socialist Party of Argentina, 1890-1930.
   4.8338
Socialist planning. 4.2770
Socialist realism. 2.1251
Socialist society and free enterprise politics.
   4.6174
Socialization for achievement. 4.5453
The socialized agriculture of the USSR. 4.2976
Societal directions and alternatives. 5.8119
Society and civilization in Greece and Rome.
   3.2547
Society and culture in America, 1830-1860.
   3.6046
Society and culture in early modern France.
   3.1953
Society and democracy in Germany. 4.5360
Society and drugs. 4.6656
Society and economy in colonial Connecticut.
   4.2031
Society and education. 4.10769, 4.10775
Society and literature in England 1700-60.
   2.5694
Society and politics in medieval Italy. 3.2843
Society and politics in revolutionary Bordeaux.
   3.2117
Society and Puritanism in pre-Revolutionary
   England. 3.1451
Society and the holy in late antiquity. 1.1663
Society and thought in America. 3.6174
Society, culture, and personality. 4.4888
Society in America. 3.6036
Society in crisis. 3.2014
Society in India. 4.5427
Society in transition. 4.5088
Society, manners, and politics in the United
   States. 3.6029
Society under siege. 4.5316
Socinianism in Poland. 1.2975
Socio-economic status of Indian women.
   4.6142
Sociobiology. 5.4094
A socioeconomic history of Argentina,
   1776-1860. 4.2165
Sociolinguistic patterns. 2.29
Sociological ambivalence and other essays.
   4.4804
The sociological imagination. 4.1210
Sociological theory. 4.4733, 4.4829
Sociological theory and modern society. 4.4839
The sociological tradition. 4.4745
Sociological writings. 4.4862
Sociology. 4.4808
The sociology and anthropology of mental
   illness. 5.8287
Sociology and estrangement: three sociologists
   of Imperial Germany. 4.4763
Sociology and philosophy. 4.4854
The sociology and politics of Congress. 4.8058
Sociology and pragmatism. 4.4817
Sociology and socialism. 4.4783
Sociology and the military establishment.
   5.7273
Sociology and the study of religion. 1.1577
Sociology and the twilight of man. 4.4801
Sociology as an art form. 4.4746
Sociology, ethnomethodology, and experience.
   4.4809
The sociology of aging. 5.8383
The sociology of art. 1.6690
The sociology of colonies. 4.8906
The sociology of deviance. 4.5076
Sociology of deviant behavior. 4.5062
The Sociology of food and eating. 4.863
The sociology of Georg Simmel. 4.4857
The sociology of housework. 4.6103
The Sociology of literature. 2.2383-2.2384
The sociology of Max Weber. 4.4767
A sociology of old Attic comedy. 2.433
Sociology of poverty in the United States.
   5.8359
The sociology of religion. 1.1579
The sociology of revolution. 4.5050
The sociology of secularisation. 1.1885
A sociology of sociology. 4.4791
Sociology of sport. 4.944
Sociology of the Black experience. 3.6778

The Sociology of the Palestinians. 4.5398
The sociology of the professions. 4.6398
The sociology of the Third World. 4.5096
The sociology of urban education. 4.10797
The sociology of work. 4.4965
Sociology, phenomenology and Marxian
   analysis. 4.4811
Socrates and legal obligation. 1.244
Socrates and the state. 4.7352
Socrates, philosophy in Plato's early dialogues.
   1.242
The sod-house frontier, 1854-1890. 3.8455
SOE in the Far East. 3.1005
Søren Kierkegaard's journals and papers.
   1.1118
Soft soap. 2.13960
The soft voice of the serpent, and other stories.
   2.10076
Software design. 5.1192
Software engineering. 5.1179, 5.1187, 5.1252
Software engineering economics. 5.1165
The software handbook. 5.1167
A software law primer. 4.9547
Software psychology. 5.1196
Software system testing and quality assurance.
   5.1161
Sogo shosha. 4.3034
Sogoshosha. 4.4194
Sohar, culture and society in an Omani town.
   3.4064
SoHo. 1.4887
Soil chemistry. 5.5275
Soil components. 5.5276
Soil conditions and plant growth. 5.5266
Soil conservation. 5.5286
The Soil Conservation Service. 5.5285
Soil engineering. 5.5907
Soil engineering in theory and practice. 5.5905
Soil erosion. 5.5287, 5.5289
Soil erosion and conservation. 5.5288
Soil exhaustion as a factor in the agricultural
   history of Virginia and Maryland, 1606-1860.
   5.5246
Soil fertility and fertilizers. 5.5294
Soil genesis and classification. 5.5262
Soil geography and land use. 5.5263
Soil landscape analysis. 5.5264
Soil mechanics in engineering practice. 5.5908
Soil mechanics, SI version. 5.5899
Soil nutrient bioavailability. 5.5278
Soil organic matter. 5.5281
Soil organic matter and its role in crop
   production. 5.5280
Soil physical properties and crop production in
   the tropics. 5.5283
The soil resource. 5.5271
Soils and geomorphology. 5.5270
Soils in construction. 5.5903
Soixante-quatre coquelicots. 2.4754
A sojourn in Neutralia. 2.9493
Sojourn in the Old Dominion. 2.11137
Sol Lewitt. 1.4900
Solar and wind energy. 5.6226
The solar atmosphere. 5.1795
Solar cells. 5.6328
Solar energy. 5.6231
The Solar energy directory. 5.6232
Solar energy experiments for high school and
   college students. 5.6229
Solar energy handbook. 5.6233
Solar heating and cooling. 5.6104
Solar heating design. 5.6102
The solar home book. 5.6101
Solaris. 2.1709
Solders and soldering. 5.7087
The soldier and social change. 5.7157
The soldier and the state. 5.7272
Soldier groups and Negro soldiers. 3.6727
A soldier reports. 3.4511
Soldiers and governments. 5.7249
A soldier's embrace. 2.10077
Soldiers in politics. 4.7772
Soldiers of destruction. 3.973
Soldiers of fortune. 3.5157
Soldiers of light and love. 4.10868
Soldiers of the sea. 5.7478
Soldiers' pay. 2.11677

Soldiers, statesmen, and cold war crises. 5.7261
A soldier's story. 3.952
Soldiers without politics. 5.7379
Solid-liquid separation. 5.6851
The solid state. 5.2197
Solid state chemistry and its applications. 5.2866
Solid-state DC motor drives. 5.6320
Solid state electronic devices. 5.6499
Solid-state electronics. 5.6456
Solid-state high-frequency power. 5.6504
Solid state laser engineering. 5.5956
Solid state physics. 5.2191, 5.2193
Solid state theory. 5.2200
Solidarité. English. 4.3663
Solidarity. 4.3663
Solidarity, Poland in the season of its passion. 3.3343
Solidification processing. 5.6773
Solitaria. 2.1528
The solitary singer. 2.11272
Solitons. 5.1670, 5.2148
The solitudes of Luis de Góngora. 2.5191
The solo song, 1580-1730. 1.3430
A Solomon Island society. 3.5677
Solon the liberator. 3.2600
Solubilities: inorganic and metal-organic compounds. 5.2651
Solubility of nonelectrolytes. 5.2909
Solute movement in the soil-root system. 5.5279
Solution equilibria. 5.2893
Solution of large networks by matrix methods. 5.6335
Solutions, minerals, and equilibria. 5.3102
Solutions to ethical and legal problems in social research. 4.9604
Solvents. 5.6862
Solvents guide. 5.6864
Solving discipline problems. 4.10701
Solving problems in secondary school administration. 4.10648
Solzhenitsyn. 2.1640
Solzhenitsyn in exile. 2.1641
Somalia, a country study. 3.5255
Somatic cell hybridization. 5.3469
El sombrero de tres picos. 2.5212
Some architectural writers of the nineteenth century. 1.5204
Some aspects of the tariff question. 4.4204
Some Cambridge controversies in the theory of capital. 4.1526
Some came running. 2.13102
Some champions. 2.11982
Some contemporary poets. 2.6195
Some contemporary poets of Britain and Ireland. 2.6195
Some do not. 2.8632
Some early impressions. 2.8114
Some facets of King Lear. 2.6662
Some forerunners of the newspaper in England, 1476-1622. 2.3686
Some historians of modern Europe. 3.418
Some kind of paradise. 2.10571
Some main problems of philosophy. 1.752
Some materials towards memoirs of the reign of King George II. 3.1545
Some must watch while some must sleep. 5.4353
Some mythical elements in English literature. 2.5557
Some new light on Chaucer. 2.6343
Some novel interpretations of the man and his life. 1.293
Some other country. 2.10205
Some persistent questions on beginning reading. 4.10410
Some prefer nettles. 2.2122
Some principles of fiction. 2.3422
Some reminiscences. 2.8022
Some Shakespearean themes. 2.6741
Some strangeness in the proportion. 5.1948
Some T'ang and pre-T'ang texts on Chinese painting. 1.6320
Some thoughts on Beethoven's Choral symphony. 1.3482
Someone. 2.4655

Somerset Maugham, a writer for all seasons. 2.9107
Somerville and Ross. 2.9351
Somerville & Ross. 2.9352
Something about the author. 2.2549
Something happened. 2.13082
Something I've been meaning to tell you... 2.9954
Something to do with books. 2.13696
Something wicked this way comes. 2.11410
Sometime, never. 2.8705
Sometimes a great notion. 2.13110
Somewhere is such a kingdom. 2.8800
Somnium. 5.1696
The son of a servant. 2.14076
The Son of God. 1.2849
Son of heaven. 3.4700
Son of Old Man Hat. 3.5793
Son of Oscar Wilde. 2.8279
The son of perdition. 2.11520
Son of Tecún Umán. 3.9064
A son of the forest. 3.5788
A son of the middle border. 2.11039
Son of the morning. 2.13200
Son of woman. 2.8993
Sonata forms. 1.4191
The sonata in the Baroque era. 1.4188
The sonata in the classic era. 1.4189
The sonata since Beethoven. 1.4190
Song and action. 2.530
Song ceramics. 1.6620
Song for an equinox. 2.4601
Song from the earth. 1.5992
Song in a weary throat. 3.6847
Song index. 1.3593
Song of a goat. 2.10108
The song of Bernadette. 2.13870
The song of deeds. 2.8853
The song of Igor's campaign: Slovo o polku Igoreve. 2.1330
Song of Lawino. 2.2311
Song of Lawino; &, Song of Ocol. 2.2310
Song of Ocol. 2.2310
The song of Roland. 2.3961
The Song of Roland. 2.3960
Song of Solomon. 2.13184
The Song of songs: Commentary and Homilies. 1.2192
Song of the road. 2.1861
Songs and sayings. 2.13538
Songs and symphonies of life and death. 1.3918
Songs from this Earth on turtle's back. 2.10744
Songs in collections. 1.3588
Songs of flying dragons. 2.2138
The songs of Homer. 2.496
The songs of Hugo Wolf. 1.4522
Songs of the Aztecs. 2.2334
The songs of the south. 2.2184
Songs of the theater. 1.3592
The songs of Thomas D'Urfey. 1.3485
Songs to Krishna. 2.2279
Sonic design. 1.4425
The Sonnet. 2.6128
The sonnet. 2.2773
Sonnets. 2.3982
Sonnets and poems of Anthero de Quental. 2.5459
Sonnets of Giuseppe Belli. 2.4987
The sonnets of Michelangelo. 2.4967
Sonnets of the English Renaissance. 2.6129
Sonnets on love and death. 2.4010
Sons. 2.11431
Sons and lovers. 2.8974-2.8975
Sons of Abraham: Jews, Christians, and Moslems. 1.2068
Sons of my skin. 2.9261
Sons of the fathers. 3.6908
Sons of the mountains. 3.4461
Sons of the soil. 4.1659
Soon, one morning. 2.10698
Sooner or later. 4.5659
Sophie's choice. 2.13344
The sophistic movement. 1.240
A sophisticate's primer of relativity. 5.1902
Sophocles. 2.542, 2.545, 2.551
Sophocles, dramatist & philosopher. 2.547

Sophoclis Fabvlae, recognovit breviqve adnotatione critica instrvxit A. C. Pearson ... 2.541
The Sorby Centennial Symposium on the History of Metallurgy, Cleveland, Ohio, October 22-23, 1963. 5.6754
Sorcerers of Dobu. 3.5631
Sorekara. 2.2086
The sorrow of the lonely and the burning of the dancers. 3.5662
Sorrow of the snows. 2.1887
A sort of life. 2.8767
Sorting and searching. 5.1185
The sorting machine. 4.10027
The sot-weed factor. 2.12882
A soul for sale. 2.8925
Soul-force: African heritage in Afro-American religion. 3.6728
Soul friend. 1.3078
The soul of a new machine. 5.6574
The souls of black folk. 3.6642
Sound and hearing. 5.2226, 5.4373
Sound and poetry. 2.958
Sound and semblance. 1.4393
Sound and sense. 2.2734
Sound and sentiment. 3.5658
Sound and sources of sound. 5.2225
Sound and symbol. 1.4371
Sound and symbol in Chinese. 2.2142
The sound and the fury; &, As I lay dying. 2.11678
Sound in the theatre. 5.6563
The sound of Greek. 2.235
The sound of the mountain. 2.2102
The sound of waves. 2.2111
The sound pattern of English. 2.1009
Sound recording practice. 5.6561
The sound shape of language. 2.176
Soundings. 3.736
Soundings in modern South Asian history. 3.4264
Sounds, feelings, thoughts. 2.1743
Source and meaning in Spenser's allegory. 2.6532
A Source book for Russian history from early times to 1917. 3.3002
Source book in astronomy, 1900-1950. 5.1675
A Source book in astronomy and astrophysics, 1900-1975. 5.1722
A source book in chemistry, 1400-1900. 5.2587
Source book in chemistry, 1900-1950. 5.2588
A source book in Chinese philosophy. 1.149
A source book in classical analysis. 5.1437
A Source book in geography. 4.53
Source book in geology, 1900-1950. 5.2938
A Source book in Indian philosophy. 1.176
A source book in mathematics, 1200-1800. 5.1076
A source book in physics. 5.1886
A source book in theatrical history. 2.3164
A source book of Advaita Vedānta. 1.199
Source book of food enzymology. 5.7127
A source book of Gestalt psychology. 5.225
A source book of medical history. 5.4499
Source book of Scottish economic and social history. 4.2297
A source book of Scottish history. 3.1773
Source book on Soviet Jewry. 5.8243
A source of embarrassment. 2.12068
Source readings in music history. 1.3637
A sourcebook for Hispanic literature and language. 5.8029
A sourcebook for the biological sciences. 5.3216
A sourcebook in Indian philosophy. 1.176
Sourcebook of criminal justice statistics, 1984. 4.6766
Sourcebook of Hispanic culture in the United States. 5.7881
Sourcebook on aging. 4.5823
Sourcebook on atomic energy. 5.2427
Sourcebook on death and dying. 4.5828
Sourcebook on the environment. 5.8165
Sources and analogues of Chaucer's Canterbury tales. 2.634
Sources and analogues of Old English poetry. 2.701

Sources and analogues of old English poetry II. 2.5591

Sources and documents illustrating the American Revolution, 1764-1788. 3.6886

Sources and documents of United States constitutions. 4.9609

The sources and literature of English history from the earliest times to about 1485. 5.7982

Sources and methods of historical demography. 4.1580

Sources for a biography of Shakespeare. 2.6689

Sources for ancient history. 3.2516

Sources for Greek history between the Persian and Peloponnesian wars. 3.2564

Sources for the history of science, 1660-1914. 5.740

Sources for the study of Greek religion. 1.1652

The sources of antislavery constitutionalism in America, 1760-1848. 4.9624

Sources of art nouveau. 1.4929

Sources of Australian history. 3.5558

Sources of Chinese tradition. 3.4610

Sources of culture in the Middle West. 3.6274

Sources of democracy. 4.7561

The sources of economic growth in the United States and the alternatives before us. 4.1934

Sources of English constitutional history. 4.8380

Sources of Indian tradition. 3.4180

Sources of information in the social sciences. 5.8354

The sources of invention. 5.5640

Sources of quantum mechanics. 5.2123

Sources of serials. 5.8313

The sources of Shakespeare's plays. 2.6711

Sources of Shang history. 3.4691

Sources of the African past. 3.5084

Sources of the Japanese tradition. 3.4895

South Africa. 3.5440, 3.6492, 4.8794

South Africa, a country study. 3.5445

South Africa and the United States. 3.6491

South Africa in southern Africa. 3.5443

South Africa, the prospects of peaceful change. 3.5476

The South African economy. 4.2620

South African explorers. 3.5436

South African stories. 2.10054

The South African War. 3.5506

South African writing today. 2.10041

South Africa's foreign policy, 1945-1970. 3.5465

South Africa's options. 3.5477

South America. 3.9154

South America and the world economy from Independence to 1930. 4.4180

South America called them. 3.9153

The South American handbook. 3.8958

The South and the concurrent majority. 3.8163

The South and the politics of slavery, 1828-1856. 3.8139

The South and the sectional conflict. 3.8152

The South and the southerner. 3.8161

South Asia. 5.8050-5.8051

South Asia and United States policy. 3.4094

South Asian bibliography. 5.8049

South Asian civilizations. 5.8048

South Asian crisis: India, Pakistan, and Bangla Desh. 3.4138

South Asian history, 1750-1950. 5.8047

South Carolina. 3.8236

The South Carolina Regulators. 3.8238

The South corner of time. 2.2328

South Dakota. 3.8510

South Dakota, a guide to the State. 3.8514

South-east Asia. 3.4382

South-East Asia. 3.4395

South-East Asia from colonialism to independence. 3.4404

South-eastern Europe. 3.751

South from the Spanish main. 3.9151

The South goes North. 4.2093

The South in American literature, 1607-1900. 2.10452

The South in architecture. 1.5285

The South in continuity and change. 4.5195

The South in the new nation. 3.8135

The South in the Revolution, 1763-1789. 3.8137

South Indian paintings. 1.6309

South Korea. 4.2558

South Korea, a country study. 3.4992

South: modern Southern literature in its cultural setting. 2.10457

The South Pole. 4.106

The South reports the Civil War. 3.7397

The South returns to Congress. 4.1926

The South Seas in the modern world. 3.5539

South Street. 2.12917

South to a very old place. 3.8173

South Wales and the rising of 1839. 4.3176

South West Africa and its human issues. 3.5433

South West Africa and the United Nations. 4.9082

The South West Africa/Namibia dispute. 4.9232

South-west Asia. 3.3678

Southeast Asia. 3.4381, 3.4398, 3.4419

Southeast Asia in international politics, 1941-1956. 3.4406

Southeast Asia: its historical development. 3.4392

Southeast Asian literatures in translation. 5.8058

Southeast Asian periodicals. 5.8328

Southeast Asian tribes, minorities, and nations. 3.4390

The Southeast Asian world. 3.4391

Southeast Asia's economy: development policies in the 1970s. 4.2432

Southeast Asia's economy in the 1970s. 4.2436

Southeast Asia's economy in the 1970's. 4.2432

Southeastern Europe under Ottoman rule, 1354-1804. 3.3521

The Southeastern Indians. 3.5753

Southeastern Indians since the Removal Era. 3.5754

Southern Africa. 3.5439, 3.5442, 3.5444

Southern African literature. 2.10045

Southern businessmen and desegregation. 3.6793

The southern colonial frontier, 1607-1763. 3.8133

The southern colonies in the seventeenth century, 1607-1689. 3.8131

Southern editorials on secession. 3.7178

The southern expansion of the Chinese people. 3.4686

Southern exposure. 3.8159

The southern frontier, 1670-1732. 3.8240

A Southern harvest. 2.10810

Southern honor. 3.8126

Southern justice. 4.9682

The Southern lady: from pedestal to politics, 1830-1930. 4.6012

Southern light. 2.13310

Southern literary study. 2.10460

The Southern mandarins. 2.11792

Southern music, American music. 1.4256

A southern odyssey. 3.8145

Southern politics and the second reconstruction. 4.8097

Southern politics in state and nation. 3.8160

The southern poor-white from Lubberland to Tobacco road. 2.10362

Southern primaries and elections, 1920-1949. 4.8108

Southern progressivism. 3.8168

Southern regions of the United States. 3.8162

A Southern Renaissance. 2.10453

Southern renascence. 2.10458

Southern writers. 2.10461

The southerner as American. 3.8123

A southerner discovers the South. 3.8157

Southwest. 2.10728

Southwest heritage. 2.10471

Southwest Indian painting. 3.5768

Southwest Pacific. 3.5538

The Southwest Pacific since 1900. 3.5544

The Southwest Pacific to 1900. 3.5545

Southwest, towards the twenty-first century. 2.10825

Southwestern archaeology. 3.5762-3.5763

Southwestern Indian ritual drama. 3.5765

Sovereign flower. 2.6739

The sovereign prerogative. 4.9845

Sovereign reason, and other studies in the philosophy of science. 5.916

The Sovereign States, 1775-1783. 3.6899

The sovereign sun. 2.577

The sovereign wayfarer. 2.13246

Sovereignty. 4.7508

Sovereignty and society in colonial Brazil. 4.8938

Sovereignty at bay; the multinational spread of U.S. enterprises. 4.3058

Sovereignty for sale. 4.3970

Sovereignty in dispute. 3.9256

The sovereignty of good. 1.1457

The Soviet Air Force. 5.7406

Soviet-American relations, 1917-1920. 3.6486

Soviet and American society. 4.5185

Soviet and Chinese influence in the Third World. 3.3260

Soviet and East European agriculture. 4.2974

Soviet-Asian relations in the 1970s and beyond. 4.9073

Soviet attitudes toward American writing. 2.10339

Soviet aviation and air power. 5.7407

The Soviet bloc, unity and conflict. 3.1177

The Soviet colossus. 3.3135

Soviet decision making in practice. 3.3076

The Soviet design for a world state. 4.7545

Soviet diplomacy and negotiating behavior. 3.6495

Soviet dissent. 4.5376

Soviet dissident literature, a critical guide. 5.8016

Soviet documents on foreign policy. 4.9071

Soviet economic development since 1917. 4.2376

Soviet economic institutions. 4.2389

Soviet economic power. 4.2374

Soviet economic structure and performance. 4.2381

The Soviet economic system. 4.2386

The Soviet economy. 4.2395, 4.2402

Soviet economy and society. 4.2391

The Soviet economy: myth and reality. 4.2379

Soviet education. 4.10133

Soviet education in the 1980s. 4.10135

The Soviet energy system. 5.6142

Soviet energy technologies. 5.6141

The Soviet estimate. 4.7911

Soviet foreign policy, 1917-1941. 3.3059

Soviet foreign policy, 1928-1934. 3.3058

Soviet foreign policy since World War II. 3.3221, 3.3249

Soviet foreign policy toward Western Europe. 4.9074

The Soviet government and the Jews, 1948-1967. 3.3998

The Soviet high command. 5.7330

The Soviet history of World War II. 3.3244

Soviet images of America. 3.7573

Soviet industrialization, 1928-1952. 4.2382

The Soviet industrialization debate, 1924-1928. 4.2378

Soviet influence in Eastern Europe. 3.2995

Soviet leadership in transition. 3.3252

Soviet literary theories, 1917-1934. 2.1246

Soviet Marxism. 4.6981

Soviet Marxism and natural science, 1917-1932. 5.904

The Soviet military and the Communist Party. 5.7326

Soviet military doctrine. 5.7197

Soviet military strategy. 5.7215

Soviet national income and product, 1940-48. 4.2405

Soviet nationalities in strategic perspective. 4.7152

Soviet nationalities policy in practice, edited by Robert Conquest. 4.8645

Soviet nationality problems. 3.3025

Soviet natural resources in the world economy. 4.2369

The Soviet novel. 2.1290

Soviet perceptions of U.S. foreign policy. 3.7849

Soviet perceptions of United States foreign policy. 3.7849
Soviet perceptions of US foreign policy. 3.7849
Soviet philosophy. 1.1107
Soviet planning. 4.2375
Soviet policies in China, 1917-1924. 3.4684
Soviet policy and the Chinese Communists, 1931-1946. 3.3072
Soviet policy in East Asia. 3.4414
Soviet policy in Eastern Europe. 3.2996
Soviet policy toward India. 3.3074
Soviet policy toward the Middle East since 1970. 3.3748
Soviet policy toward Turkey, Iran, and Afghanistan. 3.3077
Soviet-Polish relations, 1917-1921. 3.3278
Soviet political and military conduct in the Middle East. 3.3750
Soviet political indoctrination. 4.5379
The Soviet political process. 4.8639
The Soviet political system. 4.8649
Soviet politics and the Ukraine, 1917-1957. 3.3304
Soviet politics, political science, and reform. 4.7301
The Soviet polity. 4.8640
Soviet power. 4.3752
The Soviet quest for economic efficiency: issues, controversies, and reforms. 4.2398
Soviet resource management and the environment. 5.5305
The Soviet rural community. 4.5374
The Soviet rural economy. 4.2978
Soviet Russia and the East, 1920-1927. 3.3071
Soviet Russia and the West, 1920-1927. 3.3066
Soviet Russian dialectical materialism (Diamat) 1.470
Soviet Russian literature. 2.1274
Soviet Russian literature since Stalin. 2.1268
Soviet Russian nationalism. 3.3240
Soviet short stories. 2.1321
Soviet sociology of science. 5.966
Soviet South Asian relations, 1947-1978. 3.4104
Soviet sport background to the Olympics. 4.941
Soviet strategic forces. 5.7322
Soviet strategy for economic growth. 4.2388
Soviet strategy in Europe. 4.9016
Soviet strategy toward Western Europe. 3.1203
Soviet taxation. 4.4703
Soviet trade unions and labor relations. 4.3418
Soviet transportation policy. 4.3900
The Soviet Union, a systematic geography. 3.3017
The Soviet Union and disarmament. 4.9156
The Soviet Union and Eastern Europe. 3.3008, 5.8015
The Soviet Union & international oil politics. 4.3782
The Soviet Union and its geographical problems. 4.2383
The Soviet Union and the Arab East under Khrushchev. 3.3751
The Soviet Union and the arms race. 5.7324
The Soviet Union and the failure of collective security, 1934-1938. 3.3215
The Soviet Union and the Palestine Liberation Organization. 3.3866
The Soviet Union and the Third World. 4.4190
The Soviet Union in Asia. 3.3317
The Soviet Union in the Middle East. 3.3752
The Soviet Union since 1917. 3.3208
The Soviet Union since Stalin. 3.3009
Soviet wages: changes in structure and administration since 1956. 4.3150
The Soviets in international organizations. 4.9272
Sowing. 2.9563
Soybean physiology, agronomy, and utilization. 5.5329
Soybeans as a food source. 5.7129
Soziale und politische Geschichte der Revolution von 1848. 3.2303
Space adrift. 4.6340
Space and society. 5.6691
Space and time in special relativity. 5.1916

Space and time in the modern universe. 5.2095
Space commerce. 4.3831
Space into light. 1.5428
The space merchants. 2.13267
The space of literature. 2.2361
Space physics and space astronomy. 5.1785
Space science and astronomy. 5.1723
Space technology. 5.6692
Space through the ages. 5.1073
Space, time, and architecture. 1.5213
Space, time, and deity. 1.1339
Space, time, and freedom. 3.7084
Space, time, and gravitation. 5.1907
Space, time, and motion. 5.2096
Space, time, and spacetime. 5.2097
Space, time, infinity. 5.1689
Space-time structure. 5.1922
Space within. 2.4634
Spaceflight directory. 5.6709
Spacetime physics. 5.1924
Spain. 3.3399, 3.3404, 3.3415
Spain, 1469-1714. 3.3435
Spain, 1808-1939. 3.3448
Spain and Portugal in the New World, 1492-1700. 3.5980
Spain & Portugal in the New World, 1492-1700. 3.5980
Spain and the Empire, 1519-1643. 3.623
Spain & the loss of America. 3.8999
Spain and the loss of America. 3.8999
Spain and the Western tradition. 2.5100
Spain, dictatorship to democracy. 3.3473
Spain in America. 3.5685
Spain in crisis. 3.3474
Spain in the later seventeenth century, 1665-1700. 3.3446
Spain in the Middle Ages. 3.3426
Spain in the twentieth-century world. 3.3454
The Spain of Fernando de Rojas; the intellectual and social landscape of La Celestina. 2.5200
Spain under the Habsburgs. 3.3439
Spain's new wave novelists, 1950-1974. 2.5139
The Spaniard and the seven deadly sins. 3.3407
The Spaniards. 3.3403
The Spaniards in their history. 3.3408
The Spanish-American frontier, 1783-1795. 3.8340
Spanish-American literature. 2.5297
Spanish American literature since Independence. 2.5300
The Spanish American novel. 2.5313
The Spanish American revolutions, 1808-1826. 3.9001
Spanish American writing since 1941. 2.5306
Spanish and Spanish-American literature. 5.8024
The Spanish background of American literature. 2.10340
The Spanish ballad in English. 2.5155
The Spanish Brabanter. 2.13947
Spanish cathedral music in the Golden Age. 1.4242
Spanish catholicism. 1.3193
Spanish Central America. 4.2150
The Spanish character. 3.3402
Spanish character and other essays. 2.11343
The Spanish Civil War. 3.3468
Spanish Civil War. 3.3467
The Spanish Civil War. 3.3469
The Spanish cockpit. 3.3464
Spanish colonial administration, 1782-1810. 4.8324
The Spanish conquistadores. 3.8994
The Spanish-Cuban-American war and the birth of American imperialism, 1895-1902. 3.9095
Spanish drama of the golden age. 2.5128
The Spanish economy in the twentieth century. 4.2413
The Spanish empire in America. 3.8982
Spanish exploration in the Southwest, 1542-1706. 3.8569
Spanish explorers in the southern United States, 1528-1543. 3.5981
Spanish golden age poetry and drama. 2.5106
The Spanish kingdoms, 1250-1516. 3.3422
The Spanish labyrinth. 3.3452

The Spanish lake. 4.94
The Spanish language, together with Portuguese, Catalan and Basque. 2.886
Spanish literature, 1500-1700. 5.8027
Spanish music in the age of Columbus. 1.3733
Spanish mystics. 1.3082
The Spanish pastoral novel. 2.5140
The Spanish pastoral romances. 2.5124
Spanish Peru, 1532-1560. 3.9303
The Spanish picaresque novel. 2.5141
The Spanish plays of neoclassical England. 2.5904
Spanish poetry, from its beginnings through the nineteenth century. 2.5143
Spanish policy in colonial Chile. 3.9260
The Spanish Republic and the Civil War, 1931-1939. 3.3458
The Spanish rules in Peru: 1530-1780. 3.9304
The Spanish Revolution. 3.3462
The Spanish seaborne empire. 3.8988
The Spanish stage in the time of Lope de Vega. 2.3383
The Spanish struggle for justice in the conquest of America. 3.8992
The Spanish theory of empire in the sixteenth century. 4.8935
Spanish thought and letters in the twentieth century. 2.5113
The Spanish tradition in America. 3.8979
The Spanish tragedy. 2.6607
Sparta. 3.2649
Sparta and Lakonia. 3.2647
The Spartan tradition in European thought. 3.95
Sparta's bitter victories. 3.2618
Spatial analysis. 4.196
Spatial analysis, industry, and the industrial environment. 4.2691
Spatial archaeology. 3.238
Spatial cognition. 5.406
The spatial dynamics of U.S. urban-industrial growth, 1800-1914. 4.1914
Spatial form in narrative. 2.3446
Speak for yourself, Daniel. 3.7094
Speak, memory. 2.12233
Speaking frankly. 3.1143
Speaking in parables. 1.2252
Speaking of Siva. 2.2264
Speaking of standards. 5.5755
Speaking of writing. 2.9542
The speaking tree. 3.4183
Speaking truth to power. 4.1218
The special branch. 2.6055
Special children. 4.10910
Special education in America. 4.9600
Special education law. 4.9602
Special envoy to Churchill and Stalin, 1941-1946. 3.934
The special relationship between West Germany and Israel. 3.2462
Special relativity. 5.1909, 5.1923
Special relativity theory. 5.1894
The special theory of relativity. 5.1917
A species of eternity. 5.3188
Specimen days. 2.11270
Specimens of English dramatic criticism, XVII-XX centuries. 2.2801
The specious past: historians and others. 3.407
The spectacle of suffering. 4.6921
Spectacular theatre. 2.3308
The Spectator. v. 1-5. 2.6272
Spectral emanations. 2.11879
Spectral multiplicity. 5.1637
Spectrometric identification of organic compounds. 5.2747
Spectrometric techniques. 5.2307
Spectroscopic techniques for organic chemists. 5.2746
Spectroscopy. 5.2304, 5.2309
Spectroscopy, Part A. 5.2308
The spectrum in chemistry. 5.2674
Speculations about Jakob. 2.13902
The speculator, Bernard M. Baruch in Washington, 1917-1965. 3.7626
Speculum mentis. 1.747
Speech. 2.90
Speech acts: an essay in the philosophy of language. 1.549

Speech and brain-mechanisms. 5.4345
Speech and hearing in communication. 5.4278
Speech and law in a free society. 4.9707
Speech and phenomena, and other essays on
  Husserl's theory of signs. 1.1018
Speech communication in the 20th century.
  2.64
Speech communication in the twentieth century.
  2.64
Speech correction. 5.4792
Speech criticism. 2.3535
Speech education in America. 2.3534
Speech index. 1.42
Speech pathology and audiology. 5.4791
The speeches. 2.660
Speeches. 2.661, 2.7633
Speeches & documents on Indian policy,
  1750-1921. 3.4228
Speeches and documents on the British
  dominions, 1918-1931. 3.1230
Speeches and statements of Iqbal. 3.4286
Speeches by Black Americans. 2.10857
The speeches in Vergil's Aeneid. 2.801
The speeches of Adolf Hitler, April
  1922-August 1939. 3.2393
The speeches of Thucydides. 3.2608
Spellbound in darkness. 2.2883
Spelling the word. 2.7063
A Spenser handbook. 2.6543
Spenser, Marvell, and Renaissance pastoral.
  2.6540
Spenser's allegory. 2.6534
Spenser's allegory of justice in book five of the
  Faerie queene. 2.6528
Spenser's art. 2.6536
Spenser's Faerie queene. 2.6527
Spenser's minor poems. 2.6524
Spenser's world of glass. 2.6539
Spheres of justice. 4.7655
Spherical and practical astronomy. 5.1753
Spices. 5.5331
The spider book. 5.3854
Spillway. 2.11345
Spinoza. 1.1099
Spinster. 2.10208
The spinster and her enemies. 4.6106
The spiral dance. 5.673
The spire. 2.8706
The spirit and forms of Protestantism. 1.3251
The spirit and the forms of love. 1.3066
Spirit in the world. 1.2233
Spirit mountain. 2.2330
Spirit of '76 (New York) 3.296
The spirit of American philosophy. 1.558
The spirit of Catholicism. 1.3198
The spirit of Chinese philosophy. 1.154
A spirit of dissension: economics, politics, and
  the Revolution in Maryland. 4.2033
The spirit of Islam. 1.2043
The spirit of liberty. 4.9452
The spirit of man in Asian art. 1.5043
The spirit of mediæval philosophy. 1.349
The spirit of modern philosophy. 1.424
The spirit of reform. 2.5724
The spirit of Russia. 3.3019
The spirit of 'seventy-six. 3.6884
The spirit of system. 5.3207
The spirit of the common law. 4.9404
The spirit of the laws. 4.7428
Spirit of wit. 2.7232
The spirit of Zen. 1.1756
A spirit rises. 2.9471
Spirits and demons at work. 4.4370
Spiritual and Anabaptist writers. 1.2320
The spiritual conquest of Mexico. 1.3185
The spiritual crisis of the gilded age. 1.2405
The spiritual exercises of St. Ignatius. 1.3219
Spiritual problems in contemporary literature.
  2.2377
The spiritual Quixote, or The summer's ramble
  of Mr. Geoffrey Wildgoose. 2.7052
The spiritual regulation of Peter the Great.
  4.9915
Spirituals in the southern uplands. 1.4290
Splash of colors. 4.4090
The spleen. 2.7058
The splendid art of opera. 1.4211
The splendid century. 3.2034

Splendid isolation. 3.1621, 5.3989
Splendid symbols. 4.635
Splendor in the grass. 2.11916
Spline functions. 5.1316
Split seconds. 4.1139
The spoken word and the work of
  interpretation. 3.5965
Sponges. 5.3839
Spontaneous activity in education. 4.10208
Spontaneous apprentices. 4.10395
Spoon River anthology. 2.12118
Spores. 5.4454
Sport, a cultural history. 4.957
Sport; a philosophic inquiry. 4.949
Sport, a prison of measured time. 4.954
Sport and American mentality, 1880-1910.
  4.936
Sport and American society. 4.958
Sport and higher education. 4.910
Sport and social systems. 4.956
Sport and society. 4.947
Sport and the spirit of play in American fiction.
  2.10586
Sport bibliography. 5.8425
Sport, culture, and society. 4.960
Sport in Greece and Rome. 4.930
Sport inside out. 4.946
Sport management in schools and colleges.
  4.909
The sporting myth and the American
  experience. 2.10543
The sporting woman. 4.964
Sports and physical education. 5.8424
Sports and social values. 4.959
Sports dictionary. 4.928
The Sports fan's ultimate book of sports
  comparisons. 4.961
Sports for the handicapped. 4.967
Sports illustrated baseball. 4.1005
Sports in America. 4.935
Sports in American life. 4.933
Sports in the Western world. 4.929
Sports safety. 4.906
A sportsman's sketches. 2.1461
The spot. 4.7789
Spot tests in inorganic analysis. 5.2671
The spotted hyena. 5.4002
Spray drying handbook. 5.6884
The spread of Islam. 3.3656
Spread spectrum systems. 5.6371
Spreading the American dream. 3.7599
Spreading the word. 2.100
Spreading time. 2.9913
Sprightly running. 2.9457
The spring. 2.1549
Spring snow. 2.2107
Springs of scientific creativity. 5.1938
Spunk. 2.11909
Sputnik, scientists, and Eisenhower. 5.821
Spy/counterspy. 5.7359
The spy who came in from the cold. 2.9737
The square root of wonderful. 2.12076
Squire, 'most generous of men'. 2.9375
Sri Lanka. 4.1259, 4.8724, 4.9919
Sri Lanka: a survey. 3.4363
Sri Lanka from dominion to republic. 3.4371
Sri Lanka in change and crisis. 3.4374
Sri Lanka, land, people, and economy. 4.2454
Sri Lanka, the ethnic conflict. 3.4364
Śrīmālāsūtra. English. 1.2129
The SS, alibi of a nation, 1922-1945. 3.2446
Ssu-ma Ch'ien, grand historian of China.
  3.4661
Stability and strife. 3.1540
Stability of microstructure in metallic systems.
  5.6775
Stability, security, and continuity. 4.9789
Stable peace. 4.9104
Stage costume handbook. 2.3127
Stage design throughout the world, 1970-75.
  2.3148
Stage design throughout the world since 1935.
  2.3150
Stage design throughout the world since 1950.
  2.3151
Stage design throughout the world since 1960.
  2.3149
Stage directions. 2.3344

A stage for poets; studies in the theatre of
  Hugo & Musset. 2.4242
The stage is set. 2.3093
Stage lighting. 2.3144
Stage makeup. 2.3129
The stage of Aristophanes. 2.431
Stage scenery, its construction and rigging.
  2.3147
Stage scenery, machinery, and lighting. 5.8147
The stagecraft in Euripides. 2.469
The stagecraft of Aeschylus. 2.417
Staged cascades in chemical processing. 5.6849
The stages of economic growth. 4.1485
The stages of human development before birth.
  5.4164
Stages on life's way. 1.1120
Stagflation. 4.3209
The staging of plays before Shakespeare.
  2.3293
Stained glass in thirteenth-century Burgundy.
  1.6649
The stained glass of Saint-Père de Chartres.
  1.6651
The stained glass of William Morris and his
  circle. 1.6647
Stakeholders of the organizational mind.
  4.2697
The stakes of the warrior. 1.1637
Stalin. 3.3233, 3.3235
Stalin and his generals. 3.984
Stalin as revolutionary, 1879-1929. 3.3236
Stalin; the man and his era. 3.3237
Stalinism. 4.7094
The Stalinist terror in the thirties. 3.3218
Stalin's American policy. 3.6494
Stalin's correspondence with Churchill, Attlee,
  Roosevelt, and Truman: 1941-45. 3.887
Stalin's failure in China, 1924-1927. 3.4680
Stalin's foreign policy reappraised. 3.3063
Stalin's successors. 4.8652
Stamboul train. 2.8759
The Stamp Act Congress. 3.6926
The stamp act crisis. 3.6925
The stamp of Whistler. 1.6488
Stampede City. 4.2129
Stand on Zanzibar. 2.9635
Stand Watie and the agony of the Cherokee
  Nation. 3.5852
Standard catalog for public libraries: fiction
  section 1923-31. 5.8170
The standard cyclopedia of horticulture.
  5.5310
The standard edition of the complete
  psychological works of Sigmund Freud.
  5.134
Standard encyclopedia of the world's
  mountains. 4.275
Standard encyclopedia of the world's oceans
  and islands. 4.274
Standard encyclopedia of the world's rivers and
  lakes. 4.312
Standard floras of the world. 5.8115
Standard glossary of computer terminology.
  5.1133
Standard handbook for civil engineers. 5.5672
Standard handbook for electrical engineers.
  5.6259
Standard handbook for secretaries. 4.4343
Standard handbook of engineering calculations.
  5.5713
Standard industrial classification manual.
  4.4129
Standard mathematical tables. 5.1125
Standard methods for the examination of water
  and wastewater. 5.6020
Standard methods of chemical analysis. 5.2693
The Standard periodical directory. 5.8325
Standards. 2.2679
Standards for educational and psychological
  testing. 4.10710
Standing room only. 4.1621
Stanislavski on opera. 1.4112
Stanley. 3.5222
Stanley Baldwin. 3.1652
Stanton. 3.7332
The stanze of Angelo Poliziano. 2.4974
Stanze per la giostra, Orfeo-Rime [con
  un'appendice di prose volgari] 2.4973

The staple food economies of western tropical Africa. 4.2991
Star acting. 2.2945
The star-apple kingdom. 2.10025
Star atlas and reference handbook (Epoch 1950.0) 5.1740
Star atlas of reference stars and nonstellar objects. 5.1741
A star called the sun. 5.1792
Star catalog: Smithsonian Astrophysical Observatory. 5.1677
The star diaries. 2.1711
Star maker. 2.9379
The star of redemption. 1.1969
Star quilt. 2.13424
Starfish, jellyfish, and the order of life. 5.3836
Stargazer. 2.3073
Starlight. 5.1829
Stars and clouds of the Milky Way. 5.1841
Stars and clusters. 5.1826
Stars which see, stars which do not see. 2.12901
Starting out in the thirties. 2.10235
The state against Blacks. 4.9564
The State and civil society. 4.7451
The state and economic enterprise in Japan. 4.2544
State and government in medieval Islam. 4.7323
State and local government. 4.8842
State and national voting in Federal elections, 1910-1970. 4.8100
State and revolution. 4.7099
The state and social transformation in Tunisia and Libya, 1830-1980. 4.5470
State and society. 4.7252
The state and society. 4.8348
State and society in Roman Galilee, A.D. 132-212. 3.3819
State atlases. 5.8214, 5.8358
The State, France, and the sixteenth century. 4.7286
The state in capitalist society. 4.7473
The state in Northern Ireland, 1921-72. 3.1872
A state in the making. 3.5296
State income taxation. 4.4715
The state; its history and development viewed sociologically. 4.7528
The State legislature. 4.8258
State legislatures: an evaluation of their effectiveness. 4.8256
State-local relations. 4.9750
State mental hospitals, what happens when they close. 5.4808
The state of academic science. 4.10553
The State of American history. 3.6221
The state of economic science. 4.1443
The State of food and agriculture. 5.5220
The state of Ireland. 2.8931
State of siege. 2.4443
State of the art. 5.6522
The state of the art of traffic safety. 4.4033
State-of-the-art surveys on finite element technology. 5.5730
State of the environment. 5.5992
The state of the nation and the agenda for higher education. 4.10576
The state of the Presidency. 4.7923
The State of the universe. 5.1707
State of the world. 4.1793
The state of war. 4.9031
The State parks. 3.6002
State politics in contemporary India. 4.8719
State, power, socialism. 4.7455
State, private enterprise, and economic change in Egypt, 1918-1952. 4.2615
State publications. 5.7783
State, society, and university in Germany, 1700-1914. 4.10128
The state tradition in Turkey. 4.8771
The state tradition in Western Europe. 4.7284
The state, war and peace. 4.7302
Statemaking and social movements. 4.7507
Statement on race. 4.444
Statements. 2.10069, 2.10852
Statements 2. 2.10851
The States and higher education. 4.10759
States and social revolutions. 4.5052

The States and subversion. 4.9721
States of Ireland. 3.1859
States of mind. 3.1845, 5.125
The States of South Asia. 3.4101
Statesman. 4.7344
Statesman and saint. 3.1405
The statesman's book of John of Salisbury. 4.7376
The Statesman's year-book. 4.7214
Statesmen at war. 3.2133
Statesmen in disguise. 4.8455
Statics. 5.1651, 5.5738
Statics and strength of materials. 5.5737, 5.5739
Statics and strength of structures. 5.5853
Statism in Plymouth Colony. 4.7810
Statistical analysis in psychology and education. 5.1397
The statistical analysis of spatial pattern. 5.1409
Statistical and inductive probabilities. 1.1232
Statistical fluid mechanics. 5.1664
Statistical graphics. 5.1403
A statistical history of the American presidential elections. 4.8109
Statistical inference. 5.1392
A statistical manual for chemists. 5.2647
Statistical mapping and the presentation of statistics. 4.211
Statistical mechanics. 5.2167-5.2168, 5.2178-5.2179
Statistical mechanics and its chemical applications. 5.2806
Statistical methods. 5.1398
Statistical methods and the geographer. 4.41
Statistical methods for engineers. 5.5717
Statistical methods in geology for field and lab decisions. 5.2975
Statistical methods in hydrology. 4.276
Statistical methods of econometrics. 4.1301
Statistical physics. 5.2166
Statistical physics and the atomic theory of matter. 5.2079
Statistical physics and thermodynamics. 5.2247
Statistical survey techniques. 4.1243
Statistical tables for biological, agricultural, and medical research. 5.3315
Statistical theories of mental test scores. 5.359
Statistical thermodynamics. 5.2176, 5.2253, 5.2258
Statistical Yearbook. 1.79
Statistical yearbook. 4.1237
Statistics, a new approach. 4.1241
Statistics America. 5.8432
Statistics and data analysis in geology. 5.2991
Statistics and society. 4.1239
Statistics for analytical chemistry. 5.2660
Statistics on radio and television. 4.4056
Statistics sources. 5.8431
Statius. 2.695
The stature of Theodore Dreiser. 2.11601
The status of federalism in America. 4.9649
The status seekers. 4.6383
The status system of a modern community. 4.6388
Stay tuned. 4.4058
Staying on alone. 2.12521
Steady-state economics. 4.2765
Stealing the language. 2.10284
Steam at sea. 5.7516
The steam engine of Thomas Newcomen. 5.6215
Steam power and British industrialization to 1860. 5.6214
Stedman's Medical dictionary. 5.4489
Steel structures. 5.5887
Steelworkers in America. 4.3530
Steering the polity. 4.8781
Stefansson and the Canadian Arctic. 3.8868
Stein. 3.2492
Stein and the era of reform in Prussia, 1807-1815. 3.2491
Stellar atmospheres. 5.1837
Stellar paths. 5.1835
Stendhal. 2.4309-2.4311
Step by step, 1936-1939. 3.872
Step right up. 4.1190
Stepfamilies. 4.5726

Stephen A. Douglas. 3.7151-3.7152
Stephen Crane. 2.10982-2.10984, 2.10988
Stephen Crane and literary impressionism. 2.10986
Stephen Crane, from parody to realism. 2.10987
Stephen Foster, America's troubadour. 1.3869
Stephen hero. 2.8878
Stephen J. Field, craftsman of the law. 4.9811
Stephen King's Danse macabre. 2.75
Stephen Széchenyi and the awakening of Hungarian nationalism, 1791-1841. 3.1940
Stephen Vincent Benét. 2.11372-2.11373
Steppenwolf. 2.13777
Steppin' out. 3.8039
Stepping-stones. 3.5366
Stepping stones to women's liberty. 4.8508
Stepping westward. 2.9628
Steps. 2.13123
The steps of humility. 1.3067
Steps to Parnassus. 1.4448
The Steranko history of comics. 1.5849
Stereochemistry. 5.2874
Stereochemistry of carbon compounds. 5.2869
Stern. 2.13020
Sterne, the critical heritage. 2.7285
A sterner plan for Italian unity. 3.2863
Sterne's comedy of moral sentiments. 2.7282
Steroids. 5.2778
Stettinius report on the Charter of the United Nations. 4.9197
Stevenage. 4.5335
Sticks and stones. 1.5286
Still close to the island. 2.9921
Still digging. 3.260
A Still moment. 2.12673
Stillborn revolution. 3.2418
Stiller. 2.13744
A stillness at Appomattox. 3.7362
Stilwell and the American experience in China, 1911-45. 3.7614
The Stilwell papers. 3.1139
Stirling-cycle machines. 5.6217
Stitches in time. 3.8791
STOAD. 5.827
Stochastic models for social processes. 4.1202
Stock photographs. 5.5442
Stockhausen; life and work. 1.3996
Stogdill's handbook of leadership. 4.4954
The stoic. 2.11597
The Stoic and Epicurean philosophers. 1.319
Stoic logic. 1.1157
The Stoics. 1.328
The stoics. 1.327
The Stoics, Epicureans, and Sceptics. 1.320
Stomping the blues. 1.4314
A stone, a leaf, a door. 2.12778
The stone bridal bed. 2.13952
The stone circles of the British Isles. 4.730
Stone spaces. 5.1057
The stones of Assyria. 1.5616
The stones of emptiness. 2.9430
The stones of the house. 2.12221
Stopped rocking and other screenplays. 2.12724
A stopping place. 2.13174
Stopping rape. 4.6736
Storia della età barocca in Italia. 2.4881
Storia della letteratura italiana. 2.4877
Storia della lingua italiana. English. 2.852
Storia letteraria delle regioni d'Italia. 2.4876
Stories. 2.9010, 2.9166, 2.13620
Stories and tales. 2.11133
Stories by contemporary Japanese women writers. 2.2038
Stories, essays, and poems. 2.8446, 2.8959
Stories, fables & other diversions. 2.12246
Stories, fables, and other diversions. 2.12246
Stories from a Ming collection. 2.2200
Stories from the New Yorker, 1950-1960. 2.10847
Stories from the sixties. 2.10844
Stories in prose, stories in verse, shorter poems, lectures and essays. 2.7962
Stories of a lifetime. 2.13822
The stories of John Cheever. 2.11490
The stories of Muriel Spark. 2.9364
The stories of Ray Bradbury. 2.11407

Stories of the great operas. 1.4511
Stories of the streets and of the town. 2.10893
Stories of three decades. 2.13823
The stories of William Sansom. 2.9301
Stories that could be true. 2.12502
Storm. 2.12554
Storm data. 5.2546-5.2547
Storm data for the United States, 1970-1974. 5.2546
Storm data for the United States, 1975-1979. 5.2547
Storm over the multinationals. 4.3029
Storms brewed in other men's worlds. 3.5760
Stormy Ben Butler. 3.7320
Stormy petrel. 2.1510
Stormy weather. 1.3490
The story behind the word. 5.4493
Story of a life. 2.1599
The story of a novel. 2.12785
Story of a panic. 2.8642
The story of a Tlingit community. 3.5957
The story of a wonder man. 2.3793
The story of agricultural economics in the United States, 1840-1932. 4.2948
The story of alchemy and early chemistry (The story of early chemistry) 5.2611
The story of American Methodism. 1.3370
The story of an African farm. 2.10055
The story of art. 1.4674
The story of Calcutta theatres, 1753-1980. 2.3395
The story of Canada. 3.8673
The story of craft. 1.6509
The story of Ernie Pyle. 2.3629
The story of Fabian socialism. 4.7029
The story of GostaBerling. 2.14064
The story of handwriting. 5.7520
The story of jazz. 1.4336
The story of language. 2.139
The story of maps. 4.225
The story of Marie Powell. 2.8725
The story of modern art. 1.4816
The story of pantomime. 2.2842
The story of punishment. 4.6841
The story of rock. 1.4283
The story of Sadler's Wells, 1683-1977. 2.3330
The story of Shunkin. 2.2118
The story of the Abbey Theatre, from its origins in 1899 to the present. 2.3361
The story of the Armory show. 1.4669
The story of the Bible. 1.2515
The story of the eight-year study. 4.10607
The story of the Iliad. 2.501
The story of the integration of the Indian States. 4.8718
The story of the New York times, 1851-1951. 2.3663
The story of the night, studies in Shakespeare's major tragedies. 2.6782
The story of the Olympic games. 4.880
The story of the Rhodesias and Nyasaland. 3.5488
Story of the siren. 2.8642
The story of the stone. 2.2233
The story of Toronto. 3.8833
The story of Utopias. 4.7173
The story of writing. 5.7533
The story of Yamada Waka. 4.6149
Story patterns in Greek tragedy. 2.296
A story teller's story. 2.11324
The story vine. 4.10317
Storyteller. 2.13322, 4.10318
The storyteller's sourcebook. 4.764
Storytelling and mythmaking. 2.2975
Strafford, 1593-1641. 3.1470
The straight and narrow path. 2.9827
A strange attachment and other stories. 2.1860
The strange career of Jim Crow. 3.6696
The strange career of marihuana. 4.6665
The strange case of Alfred Hitchcock. 2.3052
The strange children. 2.11790
The strange death of Liberal England. 3.1688
Strange defeat. 3.977
Strange empire. 3.8852
Strange fruit. 2.12489
Strange gods. 1.1869
The strange neutrality. 3.4926
The strange ride of Rudyard Kipling. 2.7896

Strange stories from a Chinese studio. 2.2232
A strange story. 2.7916
Strange wine. 2.13002
The stranger. 2.4446
The stranger at the gate. 3.2522
Stranger in a strange land. 2.11828
The strangers all are gone. 2.9229
Strangers and brothers. 2.9346
Strangers and journeys. 2.10231
Strangers at the gate. 3.4859
Strangers devour the land. 3.5866
Strangers in the land. 3.6517
Strangers to this ground. 2.10411
Strangers within our gates. 3.8795
Strangers within the Gate City. 3.8271
Strasbourg in transition, 1648-1789. 3.2505
The strategic air offensive against Germany. 3.1047
Strategic command and control. 5.7356
Strategic human resource management. 4.4359
The strategic illusion. 5.7464
Strategic intelligence and national decisions. 4.7769
Strategic intelligence for American world policy. 4.7770
The Strategic management handbook. 4.2639
Strategic military deception. 5.7221
Strategic minerals. 4.3726
Strategic planning. 4.2638
Strategic stalemate. 5.7274
Strategic styles. 3.8005
Strategic survey. 5.7216
Strategic thought in the nuclear age. 5.7217
Strategies for African development. 4.2612
Strategies for change. 4.8072
Strategies for effective desegregation. 4.10799
Strategies for joint venture success. 4.2721
Strategies for managing behavior problems in the classroom. 4.10700
Strategies for teaching retarded and special needs learners. 4.10945
Strategies for teaching the mentally retarded. 4.10945
Strategies for the displaced worker. 4.3695
Strategies of containment. 3.7570
Strategies of curriculum development. 4.10439
Strategies of information processing. 5.393
Strategies of political emancipation. 4.7625
Strategy. 3.537
Strategy and choice in congressional elections. 4.8022
Strategy and collective bargaining negotiation. 4.3334
Strategy and compromise. 3.909
Strategy and market structure. 4.1569
Strategy and politics. 5.7213
Strategy and structure. 4.2746
Strategy for a living revolution. 4.5037
Strategy for labor. 4.3099
A strategy for rural change. 4.6368
Strategy in the missile age. 5.7252
The strategy of economic development. 4.2778
The strategy of economic planning. 4.2516
The strategy of Japanese business. 4.4176
The strategy of overthrow, 1798-1799. 3.2133
The strategy of social protest. 4.5171
The strategy of the Italian Communist Party. 4.8633
The strategy of world order. 4.9029
Stratigraphy and sedimentation. 5.3135
Stratospheric ozone and man. 5.2515
Stravinsky. 1.4008, 1.4012
The Stravinsky festival of the New York City Ballet. 1.4009
Stravinsky in pictures and documents. 1.4010
Stravinsky, the composer and his works. 1.4013
Straw sandals; Chinese short stories, 1918-1933. 2.2203
Stream of consciousness. 2.3482
Stream of consciousness in the modern novel. 2.3442
Streamers. 2.13290
Streams, lakes, ponds. 5.3254
The street. 2.1815, 2.9966, 2.12313
Street corner society. 4.6715
Street ethnography. 4.6674
The street I know. 2.3634

A street in Marrakech. 3.5215
Street-level bureaucracy. 4.6490
Street of riches. 2.4823
Street without joy. 3.4435
Streetcar suburbs. 4.5206
Streets for people. 1.5587
Der Streit um den Sergeanten Grischa. 2.13874
Strength and fracture of engineering solids. 5.5775
The strength of government. 4.7853
Strength of materials. 5.5779
Strength to love. 1.3322
Stresemann and the politics of the Weimar Republic. 3.2377
Stresemann and the rearmament of Germany. 3.2356
Stress analysis of polymers. 5.5806
Stress and disease. 5.4935
Stress and human health. 5.4209
Stress and the family. 4.5657
Stress, attitudes, and decisions. 5.448
The stress check. 5.446
Stress in childhood. 5.617
The stress of life. 5.4299
Stresses in shells. 5.5869
Strictly personal and confidential. 3.7807
Strife on the waterfront. 4.3386
Strike the father dead. 2.9452
Strikes in Europe and the United States. 4.3172
Strikes in France, 1830-1968. 4.3177
Strikes in post-war Britain. 4.3173
Striking a balance. 4.2752
Strindberg as dramatist. 2.14082
Strindberg in inferno. 2.14078
Strindberg's one-act plays. 2.14071
String music in print. 1.3594-1.3595
The string quartet. 1.4192
Stroheim. 2.3072
Strong democracy. 4.7564
Strong opinions. 2.12231
Strong poison. 2.9307
The Stroop report. 3.999
Structural analysis. 5.5840-5.5841
Structural analysis of metamorphic tectonites. 5.3127
Structural analysis of shells. 5.5866
Structural anthropology. 4.506
Structural aspects of language change. 2.145
Structural biomaterials. 5.3499
Structural changes and colonial dependency. 4.8806
Structural chemistry of silicates. 5.2713
Structural design guide to the ACI building code. 5.5881
Structural design in architecture. 5.6090
Structural design of tall concrete and masonry buildings. 5.6089
Structural dynamics. 5.5857
Structural engineering. 5.5831
Structural engineering handbook. 5.5832
Structural fabulation. 2.5981
Structural functions of harmony. 1.4469
Structural geology. 5.3076, 5.3123
Structural geology of North America. 5.2993
Structural geomorphology. 4.265
Structural hearing; tonal coherence in music. 1.4455
A structural history of English. 2.970
Structural inorganic chemistry. 5.2876
Structural linguistics. 2.134
Structural mechanics with introductions to elasticity and plasticity. 5.5845
Structural stability and morphogenesis. 5.3314
Structuralism. 1.551
Structuralism & semiotics. 2.158
Structuralism in literature. 2.2492
Structuralist poetics. 2.2491
Structure and change in Indian society. 4.6408
Structure and conflict in Nigeria, 1960-1966. 4.8802
Structure and development of meat animals. 5.5443
Structure and direction in thinking. 5.379
The structure and distribution of coral reefs. 5.3117

Structure and function in primitive society, essays and addresses. 4.606
Structure and function in the nervous systems of invertebrates. 5.4116
Structure and interpretation of computer programs. 5.1158
Structure and mechanism in organic chemistry. 5.2854
Structure and mobility. 4.5354
The structure and performance of the aerospace industry. 4.3830
Structure and process in Latin America. 4.5254
Structure and process in modern societies. 4.4910
Structure and properties of engineering materials. 5.5762
Structure determination by X-ray crystallography. 5.2933
Structure in early learning. 4.10407
The structure of allegory in the Faerie queene. 2.6531
The structure of American economy, 1919-1939. 4.1964
The structure of American English. 2.1131
The structure of American industry. 4.1927
The Structure of American industry. 4.2017
The structure of American medical practice, 1875-1941. 5.4528
The structure of appearance. 1.517
The structure of art. 1.4620
The structure of atonal music. 1.4380
The structure of Beowulf. 2.6301
The structure of Byron's major poems. 2.7535
The structure of complex words. 2.1065
The structure of English. 2.1032
The structure of freedom. 4.7626
The structure of Freudian thought. 5.517
The structure of human memory. 5.336
The structure of human personality. 5.515
The structure of labor markets. 4.3133
The structure of language. 2.133
The structure of line spectra. 5.2305
The structure of locally compact abelian groups. 5.1536
The structure of matter. 5.2061, 5.2074
The structure of nations and empires. 4.7506
The structure of organizations. 4.3239
The structure of personality in its environment. 5.508
The structure of politics at the accession of George III. 4.8402
The structure of power in North China during the five dynasties. 3.4704
The structure of psychoanalytic theory. 5.184
The structure of school improvement. 4.10273
The structure of science. 5.917
The structure of scientific revolutions. 5.908
The structure of scientific thought. 5.911
The structure of social action. 4.4865
The structure of sociological theory. 4.4813
The structure of the American economy. 4.1946
The structure of the Canterbury tales. 2.6323
The structure of the East German economy. 4.2345
The structure of the metropolitan community. 4.6203
The structure of the novel. 2.3423
The structure of the retina. 5.4118
The structure of the Terror. 3.2118
Structure of the United Nations General Assembly ... 4.9203
The structure of the United Nations General Assembly, its committees, commissions, and other organisms, 1946-1973. 4.9203
The structure of verse. 2.2730
The structure of world energy demand. 4.3754
Structure, stability and fluctuations. 5.2244
Structure, style, and interpretation in the Russian short story. 2.1286
Structured analysis and system specification. 5.5565
Structured COBOL programming. 5.1213
Structured computer organization. 5.1199
Structured concurrent programming with operating systems applications. 5.1198
The structured crowd. 4.5328

Structured learning therapy: toward a psychotherapy for the poor. 5.4829
Structured programming. 5.1170
Structures. 5.5839
Structures of domination and peasant movements in Latin America. 4.2835
The structures of the elements. 5.2829
Structures of thinking. 4.4879
Structures, symbols, and systems. 4.4909
Struggle for a birthright. 4.8794
The struggle for Arab independence. 3.3800
The struggle for Asia, 1828-1914. 3.686
Struggle for democracy. 3.4838
The struggle for equality. 3.7255
The struggle for Europe. 3.956
The Struggle for Indochina. 3.4436
The struggle for mastery in Europe, 1848-1918. 3.673
The struggle for neutrality. 3.6442
The struggle for Palestine. 3.3916
The struggle for power in Syria. 3.3801
The struggle for responsible government in the Northwest Territories, 1870-97. 4.8322
The struggle for social security, 1900-1935. 4.3466
The struggle for South Africa, 1875-1899. 3.5468
The struggle for supremacy in Germany, 1859-1866. 3.2496
The struggle for survival. 4.1974
Struggle for synthesis. 1.868
The struggle for Syria. 3.3802
The struggle for the American curriculum, 1893-1958. 4.10440
Struggle for the gulf borderlands. 3.7106
Struggle in the countryside; politics and rural labor in Chile, 1919-1973. 4.2840
The struggle of the modern. 2.2684
The struggle over Eritrea, 1962-1978. 3.5254
The struggle that must be. 3.6831
The struggle to unite Europe, 1940-1958; an historical account of the development of the contemporary European Movement from its origin in the Pan-European Union to the drafting of the treaties for Euratom and the European Common Market. 3.1202
The strumpet muse. 2.6359
Struve, liberal on the left. 3.3153
The Stuart age. 3.1441
Stuart and Cromwellian foreign policy. 3.1444
Stuart and Georgian churches. 1.5530
Stuart Davis. 1.5932
Stuart masques and the Renaissance stage. 2.5880
Stuart plays. 2.6225
Stubborn hope. 2.9637
Stubborn weeds. 2.2188
Stucco and decorative plasterwork in Europe. 1.5502
Stucke. 2.13740
Stücke, Erzählungen, Aufsätze, Gedichte. 2.13801
Student activism and protest. 4.9979
The student anthropologist's handbook. 4.439
Student expenses at postsecondary institutions. 4.10599
Student nationalism in China, 1927-1937. 3.4673
Student teaching, classroom management, and professionalism. 4.10535
The student's dictionary of Anglo-Saxon. 2.948
A student's guide to the Selected poems of Ezra Pound. 2.12338
A student's guide to the Selected poems of T. S. Eliot. 2.11641
Students. 4.10688
Students, scholars and saints. 3.3837
Students, society, and politics in imperial Germany. 4.10127
Students without teachers. 4.10551
Studies and executed buildings. 1.5336
Studies and notes supplementary to Stubbs' Constitutional history. 4.8384
Studies in African music. 1.4349
Studies in American Indian literature. 2.10298
Studies in area linguistics. 2.1143
Studies in Aristotle. 1.309
Studies in art, architecture, and design. 1.4758

Studies in Beaumont, Fletcher, and Massinger. 2.5874
Studies in behavior pathology. 5.189
Studies in British overseas trade, 1870-1914. 4.4229
Studies in British politics. 4.8420
Studies in business-cycle theory. 4.1714
Studies in child development. 4.5720
Studies in Chinese literary genres. 2.2152
Studies in Chinese thought. 1.158
Studies in class structure. 4.6377
Studies in classic American literature. 2.10269
Studies in classical and Byzantine manuscript illumination. 1.6402
Studies in comparative aesthetics. 1.1368
Studies in connoisseurship. 1.6330
Studies in diplomacy and statecraft. 3.717
Studies in early French taxation. 4.4702
Studies in early impressionism. 1.6060
Studies in early Persian Ismailism. 1.2093
Studies in Eastern chant. 1.4243
Studies in economic history. 4.2252
Studies in Elizabethan drama. 2.5875
Studies in English trade in the fifteenth century. 4.4226
Studies in ethnomethodology. 4.4792
Studies in German colonial history. 4.8931
Studies in Henry James. 2.11119
Studies in historiography. 3.399
Studies in human time. 2.3835
Studies in iconology. 1.4766
Studies in income and wealth. 4.1950
Studies in inductive logic and probability. 5.1384
Studies in intellectual breakthrough. 5.343
Studies in Japanese Buddhism. 1.1758
Studies in Jewish demography survey for 1972-1980. 3.4009
Studies in Judaism. 1.1904
Studies in labor markets. 4.3090
Studies in later Greek comedy. 2.324
Studies in leadership. 4.4949
Studies in literature. 2.5548-2.5549
Studies in literature, third series. 2.5550
Studies in maritime economics. 4.3960
Studies in medieval and Renaissance literature. 2.2628
Studies in metaphilosophy. 1.1269
Studies in monetary economics. 4.4479
Studies in New England transcendentalism. 1.566
Studies in optics. 5.2276
Studies in paleobotany. 5.3174
Studies in personnel and industrial psychology. 4.4358
Studies in pessimism. 1.961
Studies in phenomenology and psychology. 1.518
Studies in Philippine church history. 1.2463
Studies in Rāmānuja Vedānta. 1.211
Studies in Renaissance thought and letters. 3.157
Studies in Richard Hooker. 1.3311
Studies in Robertson Davies' Deptford trilogy. 2.9929
Studies in Russian music. 1.3726
Studies in secret diplomacy during the first World War. 3.824
Studies in seicento art and theory. 1.6184
Studies in self-interest: from Descartes to La Bruyère. 2.3852
Studies in seventeenth-century poetic. 2.5787
Studies in Shintō and shrines. 1.1839
Studies in Sidney and Spenser. 2.6515
Studies in social and political theory. 4.4796
Studies in social anthropology. 4.469
Studies in social psychology in World War II ... 5.7168
Studies in Spanish renaissance thought. 1.404
Studies in speculative philosophy. 1.582
Studies in symbolic action. 2.2567
Studies in taxation under John and Henry III. 4.4701
Studies in Tertullian and Augustine. 1.2490
Studies in the colonial history of Spanish America. 3.8980
Studies in the development of capitalism. 4.1749

Studies in the economics of overhead costs. 4.1480

Studies in the eighteenth century. 2.5667

Studies in the eighteenth century; II. 2.5668

Studies in the eighteenth century, III. 2.5669

Studies in the eighteenth century, IV. 2.5666

Studies in the Elizabethan theatre. 2.3318

Studies in the growth of nineteenth-century government. 4.8432

Studies in the history and methods of science. 5.758

Studies in the history of accounting. 4.4386

Studies in the history of political philosophy before and after Rousseau. 4.7265

Studies in the industrial revolution, presented to T. S. Ashton. 4.2250

Studies in the institutional history of early modern Japan. 3.4941

Studies in the intellectual history of Tokugawa Japan. 4.7296

Studies in the life and works of Petrarch. 2.4952

Studies in the origins of Buddhism. 1.2106

Studies in the philosophy of Charles Sanders Peirce. 1.630

Studies in the philosophy of David Hume. 1.702

Studies in the philosophy of G. E. Moore. 1.755

Studies in the philosophy of Paul Ricoeur. 1.847

Studies in the problem of sovereignty. 4.7509

Studies in the psychology of sex. 4.5500

Studies in the quantity theory of money. 4.4466

Studies in the recent Australian novel. 2.10140

Studies in the Russian economy before 1914. 4.2370

Studies in the scope and method of 'The Authoritarian personality.' 4.5023

Studies in the social history of modern Egypt. 4.5469

Studies in the structure of the American economy. 4.1937

Studies in the theory of economic expansion. 4.1476

Studies in war and peace. 3.676

Studies in world public order. 4.8986

Studies of a biographer. 2.5560

Studies of Congress. 4.8016

Studies of Israeli society. 4.5399

Studies of the Greek poets. 2.285

Studies of the Spanish mystics. 1.3082

Studies of the third wave. 3.6575

Studies on a just world order. 4.8963

Studies on Korea, a scholar's guide. 5.8071

Studies on Marx and Hegel. 1.1035

Studies on the civilization of Islam. 3.597

Studies on the iconography of cosmic kingship in the ancient world. 1.5191

Studies on the interior of Russia. 3.3011

Studies on the population of China, 1368-1953. 4.1705

Studies on the structure and development of vertebrates. 5.3892

Studies on twentieth-century Spanish and Spanish American literature. 2.5112

Studs Lonigan. 2.11653

The study and criticism of Italian art. 1.6178

The Study and teaching of geography. 4.37

A study in Austrian intellectual history. 3.1875

A study in Balkan civilization. 3.3513

A study in boss politics. 3.7664

A study in tyranny. 3.2395

The study of American folklore. 4.772

The study of American history. 3.6336

The Study of ancient Judaism. 1.1913

A study of bolshevism. 3.3217

A study of Cassius Dio. 2.444

The study of Chinese society. 4.5456

The study of counterpoint. 1.4448

A study of Delphic myth and its origins. 4.822

The study of dialect. 2.208

A study of early Christianity. 1.2300

A study of English romanticism. 2.5684

The study of ethnomusicology. 1.4364

The study of folklore. 4.758

A study of future worlds. 4.9133

The study of games. 4.1061

A study of Gawain and the Green Knight. 2.6418

A study of George Orwell. 2.9196

A study of Goethe. 2.13581

The study of good letters. 2.2572

The study of Greek inscriptions. 3.282

A study of history. 3.34-3.35

The study of instinct. 5.4099

The study of international relations. 4.9001

The Study of Judaism. 5.8239

The study of landforms. 4.259

The Study of liturgy. 2.985

A study of Maya art. 3.9047

A study of Nietzsche. 1.1058

The study of orchestration. 1.4487

The study of organizations. 4.4917

The study of population. 4.1595

The study of prehistoric change. 3.5764

The study of rocks in thin section. 5.3032

The study of Russian folklore. 4.796

The study of social dialects in American English. 2.1128

The study of sociology. 4.4843

A study of Sophoclean drama. 2.546

A study of Spinoza's Ethics. 1.1098

Study of St. Anselm. 1.3253

The study of the Bible in the Middle Ages. 1.2530

A study of the construction and enforcement of the federal anti-trust laws. 4.1947

The study of the future. 3.66

A study of the principles of politics. 4.7470

A study of the prose works of John Donne. 2.6466

A study of the short story. 2.3441

A study of thinking. 5.382

A Study of Thomas Mann's novel, Der Zauberberg. 2.13839

The study of trace fossils. 5.3158

The study of urbanization. 4.6194

A study of war. 5.7148

A study of writing. 2.171

Studying law. 4.9474

Studying the Presidency. 4.7939

Stuff of sleep and dreams. 2.5627

Die Stunde der wahren Empfindung. 2.13894

Stunt; the story of the great movie stunt men. 2.3010

Sturm und Drang. 2.13469

Sturtevant's edible plants of the world. 5.3657

Stuttering, the disorder of many theories. 5.4793

Style. 2.2539

Style and civilizations. 3.10

Style and idea. 1.3474

Style and idea. 1.3473

Style and substance. 4.10588

Style and temper. 2.3911

Style and tradition in Catullus. 2.713

Style guide for chemists. 5.2598

Style in French prose. 2.870

Style in ornament. 1.6535

Style in the arts of China. 1.5062

Style in the French novel. 2.3898

The style of Don Juan. 2.7520

The style of the century, 1900-1980. 1.6691

The Stylistic development of Keats. 2.7873

Stylistique comparée du français et de l'anglais. 2.871

Su Tung-p'o: selections from a Sung dynasty poet. 2.2218

Sub-Saharan Africa. 4.5467

The Subcontinent in world politics. 3.4102

The subject approach to information. 5.7629

Subject collections. 5.7661

Subject directory of special libraries. 5.7609

Subject directory of special libraries and information centers. 5.7609

Subject guide to books in print. 5.7755, 5.7757

Subject guide to microforms in print. 5.7704

Subject guide to U.S. government reference sources. 5.7780

A subject of scandal and concern. 2.9213

The subject of semiotics. 2.83

Subject women. 4.5888

The subjection of women. 4.7669

Subjective criticism. 2.35

Subjectivism in theology. 1.2935

Subjects and sovereigns. 4.8441

Submarine boats. 5.7440

Submarine design and development. 5.7513

Submission of recorded Presidential conversations to the Committee on the Judiciary of the House of Representatives. 3.7917

Subordinating the poor. 4.6511

Substance under pressure. 2.9029

Substitute teaching. 4.10682

Subsurface exploration and sampling of soils for civil engineering purposes. 5.5894

Subsurface geology. 5.2973, 5.6807

The subterraneans. 2.11954

'Subtle is the Lord 5.1947

The Subtle revolution. 4.3292

The subtler language. 2.5768

A subtreasury of American humor. 2.3797

Success and the fear of success in women. 5.4942

Success and understanding. 5.284

Success or failure? 4.5686

Success story. 2.3620

Successful gardening. 5.5368

Successful group care: explorations in the powerful environment. 4.6575

Successful love, and other stories. 2.12451

Successful schools and competent students. 4.10014

Successful schools for young adolescents. 4.10505

Successful student teaching. 4.10536

The Successor generation. 3.1193

The successors of Genghis Khan. 3.517

Such a pretty face. 5.4943

Such as us. 4.5197

Such darling dodos, and other stories. 2.9541

Such holy song. 2.7434

Such is life, being certain extracts from the diary of Tom Collins. 2.10148

Such waltzing was not easy. 2.13415

Sudan, a country study. 3.5170

The Sudan in Anglo-Egyptian relations. 3.5165

Suetonius. 2.696

Suffer and be still. 4.6098

Suffering and evil in the plays of Christopher Marlowe. 2.6620

The suffering god. 2.598

The sufferings of young Werther. 2.13578

The suffragette. 4.8512

Suffragists and Democrats. 4.8084

Suffragists and Liberals. 4.8510

Sufism. 1.2083

Sugar and slaves. 3.9141

The sugar cane. 5.5330

Sugar Creek. 3.8411

Sugar plantations in the formation of Brazilian society. 4.3688

Sugar without slaves. 4.2179

The Sui dynasty. 3.4699

Suicide: a selective bibliography of over 2,200 items. 5.8435

Suicide, a study in sociology. 4.6731

Suicide, the philosophical issues. 1.1325

Suiting everyone: the democratization of clothing in America. 5.7089

Suiting up for space. 5.6718

Suitors and suppliants. 3.853

Sukhāvatī Ivyūha. 1965. 1.1737

Sula. 2.13185

Suleiman the Magnificent, 1520-1566. 3.3582

The sum of history. 3.42

The sum of things. 2.9743

Sumatra, its history and people. 3.4577

Sumer. 1.4706

Sumerian mythology. 2.1769

Sumerian proverbs. 2.1770

The Sumerians: their history, culture, and character. 3.3773

Summa theologiae. 1.3197

The summer before the dark. 2.9025

A summer bird-cage. 2.9664

Summer brave, and eleven short plays. 2.11915

Summer knowledge; new and selected poems, 1938-1958. 2.12452

Summer lightning. 2.9556

Summer moonshine. 2.9557
Summerhays' encyclopaedia for horsemen.
5.5446
Summerhill. 4.11012
The summer's ramble of Mr. Geoffrey
Wildgoose. 2.7052
Summertime. 2.5024
Summit at Teheran. 3.923
Summoned by bells. 2.8464
A summoning of stones. 2.13078
The sun. 5.1793
The sun also rises. 2.11848
Sun and shadow, the philosophy of an architect.
1.5306
Sun & steel. 2.2112
Sun/Earth. 5.6225
Sun power. 5.6228
The sun shines over the Sanggan River. 2.2235
Sun Yat-sen and communism. 3.4763
Sun Yat-sen, frustrated patriot. 3.4761
Sun Yat-sen; his life and its meaning. 3.4765
Sun Yat-sen, reluctant revolutionary. 3.4764
Sunbelt cities. 4.6241
The Sunday of life. 2.4677
Sundown. 2.12120
Sunflower splendor. 2.2194
Sung biographies. 3.4705
The sunlight dialogues. 2.13032
Suns, myths, and men. 5.1708
The sunspace primer. 5.6103
The super 8 book. 5.7005
Super chief, Earl Warren and his Supreme
Court. 4.9834
Superalloys. 5.5819
Superconductivity. 5.2350
Superconductivity and its applications. 5.2355
Superfiction. 2.10833
Superforce. 5.1904
Superhighway 4.3936
Superiority and social interest. 5.128
Supernatural fiction writers. 2.3462
Supernatural horror in literature. 2.3460
The supernatural in fiction. 2.5953
Supernovae. 5.1849
Supersonic flight. 5.6658
Supersymmetry and supergravity. 5.2143
Supervision. 4.10639
Supervision for staff development, ideas and
application. 4.10525
Supervision of instruction. 4.10647
Supplement to Charles Evans' American
bibliography. 5.7753
A Supplement to the Oxford English dictionary.
2.1085
Supplemental appendix to the survey on
Equality of educational opportunity. 4.10783
Supply-side economics: a critical appraisal.
4.1319
The supply-side revolution. 4.2016
Supplying war. 5.7225
The suppression of the African slave-trade to
the United States of America, 1638-1870.
3.7189
Supramolecular enzyme organization. 5.4413
The Supreme Command, 1914-1918. 3.799
The Supreme Commander. 3.7834
The Supreme Court. 4.9788
Supreme Court activism and restraint. 4.9786
The Supreme Court and confessions of guilt.
4.9884
The Supreme Court and Congress. 4.9846
The Supreme Court and constitutional
democracy. 4.9744
The Supreme Court and education. 4.9581
The Supreme Court and individual rights.
4.9657
The Supreme Court and judicial review.
4.9642
The Supreme Court and libel. 4.9519
The Supreme Court and social science. 4.9498
The Supreme Court and the American
Republic. 4.9781
The Supreme Court and the Commander in
Chief. 4.9768
The Supreme Court and the Constitution.
4.9645
The Supreme Court and the quest for law.
4.9845

The Supreme Court and the second Bill of
Rights. 4.9665
The Supreme Court as final arbiter in Federal-
State relations, 1789-1957. 4.9648
Supreme Court decision making. 4.9791
The Supreme Court from Taft to Burger.
4.9843
The Supreme Court in crisis. 4.9794
The Supreme Court in the Federal judicial
system. 4.9795
A Supreme Court Justice is appointed. 4.9807
Supreme Court Justice Joseph Story. 4.9829
Supreme Court of the United States, 1789-1980.
4.9442
The Supreme Court on freedom of the press.
4.9716
The Supreme Court's impact on public
education. 4.9586
Sūr Dās. 2.1880
'Surely you're joking, Mr. Feynman!' 5.1950
Surface and symbol. 2.8884
Surface modification and alloying by laser, ion,
and electron beams. 5.6768
The surface of Mars. 5.1816
Surface physics. 5.2210
Surfacing. 2.9909
Surpassing the love of men. 4.5523
Surprise attack. 5.7220
The surprise of excellence: modern essays on
Max Beerbohm. 2.8441
Surprised by joy. 1.3075
Surprised by sin. 2.7128
Surrealism. 1.6739
Surrealism and painting. 1.5880
Surrealism and Spain, 1920-1936. 2.5114
Surrealism; the road to the absolute. 2.3881
Surrealist painting. 1.6348
The surrealist voice of Robert Desnos. 2.4506
Surrealists on art. 1.6740
The surrounded. 2.12092
Surveillance, dataveillance, and personal
freedoms. 4.7681
The surveillant science. 4.28
Survey; a short history of Canadian literature.
2.9885
A survey of binary systems. 5.1369
Survey of British commonwealth affairs.
3.1229
Survey of British Commonwealth affairs.
3.1231
Survey of cinema 2.2978
Survey of contemporary literature. 2.2355
Survey of current business. 4.2081-4.2082
Survey of economic theory on technological
change and employment. 4.3194
Survey of English dialects. 2.1114
A survey of English literature, 1780-1830.
2.5683
A survey of English literature, 1830-1880.
2.5696
A survey of general equilibrium systems.
4.1298
Survey of international affairs, 1920-23 3.747
Survey of London. 3.1744
A survey of Malayalam literature. 2.2265
A survey of modern fantasy literature. 2.2394
A survey of modernist poetry. 2.2768
Survey of organic syntheses. 5.2731
A survey of Persian art from prehistoric times
to the present. 1.5045
A survey of Puerto Ricans on the U.S.
mainland in the 1970s. 3.6590
A survey of recent Christian ethics. 1.1467
A survey of symbolic logic. 1.1213
Survey of the Sino-Soviet dispute. 3.4682
A survey of United States-Latin American
relations. 3.9020
A survey of verb forms in the eastern United
States. 2.1119
Survey research. 4.5014
Surveying. 5.5822
Surveying and charting of the seas. 4.233
Surveying fundamentals. 5.5823
Surveys and soundings in European literature.
2.2602
Surveys of economic theory. 4.1268
Surveys, polls, and samples. 4.5115
Survival. 2.9881

Survival 2001. 5.6138
Survival is not enough. 3.3256
The Survival of a counterculture. 4.5788
The survival of Charles Darwin. 5.3196
The survival of the Chinese Jews. 3.3943
Survival themes in fiction for children and
young people. 5.7723
Survival through design. 1.4598
The survival years. 2.10716
Surviving the eighties. 4.10594
Surviving the future. 3.207
The survivor and other poems. 2.1726
Survivors of Eldorado. 3.9180
Survivors, victims, and perpetrators. 3.1120
Susan B. Anthony. 4.8087
Susan B. Anthony, the woman who changed
the mind of a nation. 4.8085
Susan Glaspell. 2.11785
Susan Lenox, her fall and rise. 2.12315
Susanna Centlivre. 2.6932
'Susanna,' 'Jeanie,' and 'the old folks at home'
1.3868
The suspension of Henry Adams. 3.6245
The Sutherland papers. 4.6684
Suttapitaka. English. Selections. 1.1743
Suye mura, a Japanese village. 4.637
Suzanne Valadon. 1.6153
The Suzuki concept. 1.4437
The Swahili coast. 3.5262
Swallow barn. 2.11137
Swallow barn, or, A sojourn in the Old
Dominion. 2.11137
Swami. 1.1816
The Swan Villa. 2.13917
The Swazi. 3.5528
Swaziland. 3.5527, 4.8796
Sweated industries and sweated labor. 4.3858
The sweated trades. 4.3001
Sweatshops in the sun; child labor on the farm.
4.3303
Sweden. 3.3385, 4.3077
Sweden as a great power, 1611-1697. 3.3384
Sweden: the nation's history. 3.3388
Sweden, the welfare state. 4.5383
Sweden's 'right to be human' sex role equality.
4.5384
Swedes in America. 3.6594
Swedish exodus. 3.6595
Swedish foreign policy during the Second
World War. 3.3395
The Swedish imperial experience, 1560-1718.
3.3390
The Swedish social democrats; their ideological.
development. 4.7103
Sweeney astray. 2.9704
A sweet and alien land. 3.8030
Sweet Eros, Next, and other plays. 2.13149
Sweet promised land. 3.6535
Sweet Thursday. 2.12532
Sweetness and light. 1.5253
Sweet's Anglo-Saxon reader in prose and verse.
15th ed. 2.940
Swift. 2.7300
Swift and Anglican rationalism. 2.7295
Swift and the Church of Ireland. 2.7301
Swifter than reason. 2.8727
Swift's landscape. 2.7311
Swift's poetic worlds. 2.7308
Swift's tory politics. 2.7310
Swimming and diving. 4.987
Swimming faster. 4.990
Swinburne. 2.8138, 2.8140-2.8141
Swinburne's theory of poetry. 2.8139
Swine production. 5.5450
A swinger of birches. 2.11755
The Swiss and their mountains. 3.3508
Swiss painting. 1.6302
Switched capacitor circuits. 5.6477
Switchgear and control handbook. 5.6318
Switzerland. 3.3507
Switzerland: an international banking and
finance center. 4.4544
Switzerland, from earliest times to the Roman
conquest. 4.739
The sword. 2.13995
The sword and the distaff. 2.11221
The sword and the flute. 1.1713
The sword and the scepter. 3.2260

The sword in the stone. 2.9519
Sword of honour. 2.9494
The sword of the Republic. 3.6371
The sword of truth. 3.5370
The swordbearers; supreme command in the
    First World War. 3.791
Swords into plowshares. 4.9129
Sybil. 2.7395
Sybil. 5.4949
Syllabus for Education 360. 4.10453
A syllabus of Indian civilization. 3.4182
A syllabus of Japanese civilization. 3.4904
Sylvia Plath. 2.13263
Sylvia Plath and Ted Hughes. 2.13265
Symbiosis in cell evolution. 5.3371
Symbol formation. 5.399
Symbol, myth, and culture. 1.977
Symbol, status, and personality. 1.496
Symbolic action in the plays of the Wakefield
    Master. 2.5858
Symbolic communities. 4.5208
Symbolic crusade. 4.6651
Symbolic images. 1.4762
Symbolic interactionism. 4.5057
Symbolic logic. 1.1205, 5.1257
Symbolic logic. 1.1207
Symbolic logic. 1.1214, 1.1224
Symbolic logic and mechanical theorem
    proving. 5.1038
The symbolic meaning. 2.10268
Symbolism. 1.4800
Symbolism and fiction. 2.3510
Symbolism and interpretation. 1.1310
Symbolism and some implications of the
    symbolic approach. 2.8366
The symbolism of evil. 1.2913
The symbolist movement. 2.3878
The symbolist movement in literature. 2.3865
The symbolists. 1.6719
Symbolists and symbolism. 1.4799
Symbols of democracy. 4.7582
Symbols of eternity. 1.6365
Symbols: public and private. 1.1623
Symeon the New Theologian. 1.3077
The symmetrical family. 4.3161
Symmetry and sense. 2.6512
Symmetry and structure. 5.2842
Symmetry discovered. 5.858
A symmetry primer for scientists. 5.859
The sympathetic response. 2.7711
Sympathy and science. 5.4542
Symphonic music, its evolution since the
    Renaissance. 1.4194
The symphonies of Joseph Haydn. 1.3896
Symposium. 2.595
Symposium on J. L. Austin. 1.740
A Symposium on Light and Life. 5.3626
Synchromism and American color abstraction,
    1910-1925. 1.5913
The syndicalist tradition and Italian fascism.
    4.3417
Synge. 2.8151
Synge and Anglo-Irish drama. 2.8152
Synopsis and classification of living organisms.
    5.3236
Syntactic structures. 2.191
Synthese. 1.632
The synthesis and characterization of inorganic
    compounds. 5.2706
Synthesis and technique in inorganic chemistry.
    5.2704
Synthetic food. 5.6886
Synthetic membrane processes. 5.6027
Synthetic reagents. 5.2740
Synthetic rubbers. 5.7082
Syntony and spark. 5.6422
Syria. 3.3793
Syria, a country study. 3.3792
Syria and Lebanon, a political essay. 3.3798
Syria and the French mandate. 3.3799
Syria under Islam. 3.3796
Syrian Christians in Muslim society. 1.2462
System and function in language. 2.159
System and process in international politics.
    4.9005
System design with Ada. 5.1208
System modeling and response. 5.5690
System modelling and control. 5.6186

The system of Dante's Hell. 2.12870
The system of English grammar. 2.1000
A system of logic, ratiocinative and inductive,
    being a connected view of the principles of
    evidence and the methods of scientific
    investigation. 1.1186
The system of mineralogy of James Dwight
    Dana and Edward Salisbury Dana, Yale
    University, 1837-1892. 5.3012
System of positive polity. 4.4851
A system of social science papers relating to
    Adam Smith. 4.1358
System of transcendental idealism (1800) 1.923
System performance evaluation methodology.
    5.1148
The system-wide approach to microeconomics.
    4.1459
Systematic embryology of the angiosperms.
    5.3739
Systematic instruction of persons with severe
    handicaps. 4.10929
Systematic instruction of the moderately and
    severely handicapped. 4.10929
A systematic source book in rural sociology.
    4.6371
Systematic theology. 1.2778
Systematic theology. 1.2783
Systematics and biogeography. 5.3235
Systematics in prehistory. 3.243
Systemic fungicides. 5.5415
Systems analysis in geography. 4.16
A systems analysis of political life. 4.7236
Systems and theories in psychology. 5.28
Systems drafting. 5.5644
Systems ecology. 5.3535
Systems engineering methodology for
    interdisciplinary teams. 5.5693
Systems graphics. 5.5643
Systems of order and inquiry in later
    eighteenth-century fiction. 2.5997
Systems simulation. 5.5578
Systems, states, diplomacy and rules. 4.9022
Szigeti on the violin. 1.4545

T.A.T., C.A.T., and S.A.T. in clinical use.
    5.545
T.C.G. new play U.S.A. 2.10801
'T.E.Lawrence' in Arabia and after. 3.810
T.E.S.S. 4.10298
T.E.T., teacher effectiveness training. 4.10698
The T. L. Yuan bibliography of western
    writings on Chinese art and archaeology.
    5.8192
T.S. Eliot. 2.11632
T. S. Eliot. 2.11636, 2.11643
T. S. Eliot & education. 2.11630
T.S. Eliot, the critical heritage. 2.11642
T.S. Eliot's Four quartets. 2.11631
T.S. Eliot's intellectual and poetic development,
    1909-1922. 2.11634
T. S. Eliot's social criticism. 2.11638
T. Thomas Fortune. 2.3613
T.V. genres. 2.2854
Taber's Cyclopedic medical dictionary. 5.4490
Table of isotopes. 5.2832
Table talk, 1941-1944. 3.2392
Table talk, or, Original essays. 2.7807
Tableau économique. 4.1407
Tableau politique de la France de l'Ouest sous
    la Troisième République. 4.8583
Tables of and annotated index to the
    congressional series of United States public
    documents. 5.7773
Tables of integrals and other mathematical
    data. 5.1458
Tacitus. 2.776
Tacitus. 2.777
Tactical exercise. 2.9496
A Tagore reader. 2.1870
Tahafut al-tahafut. 1.368
Tahiti Nui. 3.5678
The Taiheiki. 3.4937
Taiheiki. 3.4937
Taiheiyō Sensō e no michi. 3.4919, 3.4965
The Taiping ideology. 3.4732
The Taiping Rebellion. 3.4731
The Taiping revolutionary movement. 3.4728
Tairora culture. 3.5665

The Taiwan experience, 1950-1980. 3.4869
Taiwan-ilha formosa. 3.4868
Take back the night. 4.5548
Taking chances. 4.5690
Taking Darwin seriously. 5.3399
Taking sides. 2.9944
Taking your medicine. 4.9574
A tale of a tub, to which is added The battle of
    the books, and the Mechanical operation of
    the spirit. 2.7294
A tale of eleventh century Japan. 2.2054
The tale of Genji. 2.2047-2.2049
A tale of millions. 3.4149
The tale of terror. 2.3456
The tale of the Heike. 2.2056
The tale of the Lady Ochikubo. 2.2045
A tale of two agencies. 4.4731
Talent and society. 5.366
A talent to annoy. 2.9120
Talents and geniuses. 2.2574
Tales. 2.12866
Tales alive in Turkey. 4.801
Tales and novels. 2.7685
Tales and stories. 2.14008
Tales form Angria. 2.7446
Tales from eternity. 4.820
Tales from modern India. 2.1956
Tales from southern Africa. 2.10085
Tales my father taught me. 2.9336
Tales of adventure. 2.12027
Tales of ancient India. 4.803
The tales of D. H. Lawrence. 2.8954
Tales of Ise. 2.2041
Tales of Known Space. 2.13193
The tales of Marzuban. 2.1762
Tales of moonlight and rain. 2.2067-2.2068
Tales of my people. 2.1798
Tales of nevèrÿon. 2.12972
Tales of Potosí. 3.9279
Tales of the Hasidim. 1.1921
Tales of the Little Quarter. 2.1679
Tales of the North American Indians. 3.5821
Tales of the South Pacific. 2.12155
Tales of the spring rain. 2.2066
Tales of times now past. 2.2042
Tales of Yamato. 2.2044
Talk: conversations with William Golding.
    2.8709
Talking computers and telecommunications.
    5.6419
Talking pictures. 2.3033
Talking to children. 2.124
Talking to myself. 2.2844
Talking to the sun. 2.3752
The talking trees, and other stories. 2.9163
Talks to teachers on psychology, and to
    students on some of life's ideals. 4.10355
The tall building artistically reconsidered.
    1.5543
Tall tales of the Southwest. 2.10727
Taman indera: a royal pleasure ground. 1.6722
Tambo and bones. 2.3407
Tamerlane. 2.7233
Tamil literature. 2.2272
Tamil temple myths. 1.1725
The taming of the troops. 5.7161
Tammany; the evolution of a political machine,
    1789-1865. 4.8214
Tanaka Giichi and Japan's China policy.
    3.4921
[Tanakh] 1.2562
The Taney period, 1836-64. 4.9784
Tang and Liao ceramics. 1.6619
Tangi. 2.10227
The tangled chain. 2.6439
The tanks. 5.7308
Tantra of the great liberation (Mahānirvāna
    Tantra) 1.1691
Tantras. Mahānirvānatantra. 1.1691
The Tantric mysticism of Tibet. 1.1757
The Tantric tradition. 1.1780
Tanzania. 4.2619
Tanzania, a country study. 3.5292
Tanzania, an African experiment. 3.5293
Tanzania; party transformation and economic
    development. 4.8809
The tao of painting. 1.6326
Taoism. 1.1805

Taoism. 1.1806
Taoism and Chinese religion. 1.1790
Tape music composition. 1.4460
Tapestry, the mirror of civilization. 1.6588
Tapiola's brave regiment. 2.12237
Taps for a Jim Crow army. 3.1128
Taps for Private Tussie. 2.12560
Tar: a Midwest childhood. 2.11325
The Tarahumar of Mexico: their environment
    and material culture. 3.8911
Tarascan Kingdom in Western Mexico,
    1521-1530. 3.8954
The target. 2.614
Targeting economic incentives for
    environmental protection. 4.1848
The tariff history of the United States. 4.4201
Tarikh. 3.5082
The tarnished dream. 3.4016
Tarr. 2.9043
Tarry Flynn. 2.8926
Tartarin de Tarascon. 2.4165
Tartarin of Tarascon. 2.4167
Tartarin on the Alps. 2.4167
Tartarin sur les Alpes. 2.4166
Tartuffe, and other plays. 2.4040
The task-centered system. 4.6501
Task Force report: corrections. 4.6892
Task Force report; organized crime. 4.6768
Tasks and masks. 2.2304
Tasso's dialogues. 2.4981
A taste for death. 2.9724
The tastemakers. 3.6134
TAT, CAT, and SAT in clinical use. 5.545
The Tatler. 2.6273-2.6274, 2.6276
Tau zero. 2.12851
The tax on value added. 4.4717
Taxation and development. 4.4696
Taxation for development. 4.4691
The Taxation of income from capital. 4.4706
The taxicab. 4.4039
Taxing agricultural land in developing
    countries. 4.4707
Taxonomy of educational objectives. 4.10170
Ta'ziyeh, ritual and drama in Iran. 2.1965
TCG new plays USA. 2.10801
Tchaikovsky. 1.3834
Tchaikovsky's ballets. 1.3835
Te Ao Hurihuri. 3.5610
Te Maori. 1.5091
Teach us to outgrow our madness. 2.2134
Teach yourself Turkish. 2.1981
Teacher. 4.10886
The teacher. 1.2182
Teacher as stranger. 4.10244
Teacher competence. 4.10676
Teacher effectiveness training. 4.10698
Teacher in America. 4.10570
The teacher of teachers. 4.10521
The teacher rebellion. 4.10684
Teacher-student relationships: causes and
    consequences. 4.10313
Teacher unions in schools. 4.10683
Teachers and learners. 4.10314
Teachers and machines. 4.10289
Teachers and texts. 4.10774
Teachers of young children. 4.10404
Teachers talk. 4.10968
The teacher's voice. 4.10155
Teaching abroad. 4.10540
Teaching adolescents in secondary schools.
    4.10496
Teaching and learning strategies for physically
    handicapped students. 4.10943
Teaching as a subversive activity. 4.10041
Teaching children science. 4.10488
Teaching clever children, 7-11. 4.10923
Teaching creative music in secondary schools.
    1.4420
Teaching creativity through metaphor. 4.10368
Teaching elementary reading. 4.10463
Teaching English. 4.10475
Teaching English as a second language. 2.1006
Teaching ethnic awareness. 4.10896
Teaching general music. 1.4421
Teaching gifted children. 4.10921
Teaching gymnastics and body control. 4.920
Teaching in collegiate schools of nursing.
    5.5183

Teaching in the early years. 4.10416
Teaching mainstreamed students. 4.10928
Teaching mathematics. 5.1261
Teaching modern languages. 2.826
Teaching music in the 20th century. 1.4416
Teaching music in the twentieth century.
    1.4416
Teaching music in today's secondary schools.
    1.4409
The teaching of Artur Schnabel. 1.4073
The teaching of English usage. 2.961
The teaching of high school English. 4.10510
The teaching of reverence for life. 1.1062
The teaching of the church regarding baptism.
    1.3017
Teaching of the twelve apostles. 2.327
Teaching reading. 4.10339
Teaching reading to the mildly retarded child.
    4.10946
Teaching reading, writing, and study strategies.
    4.10512
Teaching retarded learners. 4.10947
Teaching science through discovery. 4.10485
Teaching science to children. 4.10486
Teaching science to children: the inquiry
    approach applied. 4.10487
Teaching singing. 1.4562
Teaching spelling. 4.10468
Teaching students with learning and behavior
    problems. 4.10953
Teaching study skills. 4.10336
Teaching styles and pupil progress. 4.10260
Teaching the bilingual. 4.10899
Teaching the gifted child. 4.10680, 4.10920
Teaching young children to read. 4.10419
Teachings from the American earth. 3.5828
Teachings of Lord Caitanya. 1.1728
The teachings of Taoist Master Chuang.
    1.1807
The Teamsters Union, a study of its economic
    impact. 4.3393
Teatro. 2.5337
Technical aspects of data communication.
    5.6399
Technical change and social conflict in
    agriculture. 5.5256
Technical choice innovation and economic
    growth. 4.2107
Technical manual and dictionary of classical
    ballet. 4.1174
Technical reporting. 5.5508
Technical terms, symbols, and definitions in
    English, French, German, Italian, Portuguese,
    Russian, Spanish and Swedish used in soil
    mechanics and foundation engineering.
    5.5893
Technique and ideas in the Aeneid. 2.806
Technique & personality. 1.4686
The Technique and spirit of fugue. 1.4121
Technique in fiction. 2.3429
The technique of early Greek sculpture. 1.5623
The technique of film editing. 2.3017
The technique of kinetic art. 1.4848
The technique of lighting for television and
    motion pictures. 5.7009
The technique of my musical language. 1.4432
The technique of orchestration. 1.4489
The technique of screenplay writing. 2.3020
The technique of sculpture. 1.5780
The technique of television production. 2.2859
The technique of the sound studio. 5.6559
The technique of Thomas Hardy. 2.7783
Techniques and applications of path integration.
    5.2141
Techniques for image processing and
    classification in remote sensing. 5.5943
Techniques in nuclear structure physics.
    5.2438
Techniques in operational research. 5.5564
Techniques of attitude scale construction. 5.46
Techniques of chemistry. 5.2641
The techniques of painted Attic pottery.
    1.6633
Techniques of safety management. 5.5555
Techniques of transport planning. 4.3872
Techno stress. 5.1249
Technological change and labor in the railroad
    industry. 4.3540

The technological conscience. 5.5524
Technological frontiers and foreign relations.
    5.5540
A technological history of motion pictures and
    television. 5.6999
The Technological level of Soviet industry.
    5.5543
Technological progress and industrial
    leadership. 4.3733
The technological society. 5.5512
The technological system. 4.4978
The Technological woman. 4.5898
Technology and American economic growth.
    4.2109
Technology and culture. 5.5531
Technology and decisions in airport access.
    4.4081
Technology and economic development. 4.1827
Technology and handicapped people. 4.6595
Technology and international affairs. 5.5550
Technology and international relations. 4.8990
Technology and man's future. 5.5525
Technology and rural women. 4.6170
Technology and science in the People's
    Republic of China. 5.773
Technology and social shock. 5.5634
Technology and the changing family. 4.5580
Technology and the pastoral ideal in America.
    3.6136
Technology and values in American civilization.
    5.8118
Technology assessment. 5.5633
Technology assessment and the oceans. 5.5632
Technology crossing borders. 5.5629
Technology, finance, and development. 4.4584
Technology in the policy process. 5.5630
Technology in Western civilization. 5.5534
Technology of inorganic compounds. 5.6826
The technology of urban transportation.
    4.4024
Technology transfer, innovation, and
    international competitiveness. 5.5628
Technometry. 1.2256
Technostress. 5.1249
Tectonics and landforms. 4.263
Tectonics of Africa. 5.3007
Tecumseh and the quest for Indian leadership.
    3.5949
Ted Shawn, father of American dance. 4.1159
Teeth, teeth, teeth. 5.5123
The Tejano community, 1836-1900. 3.8336
Tektites. 5.3029
Telecom report. 5.6387
Telecommunication system engineering. 5.6384
Telecommunication transmission handbook.
    5.6347
Telecommunications. 4.4048
Telecommunications America. 4.9537
Telecommunications, an interdisciplinary
    survey. 4.4048
Telecommunications and economic
    development. 4.4053
Telecommunications in the information age.
    5.6355
The telecommunications industry. 4.4050
Telecommunications switching principles.
    5.6386
Telephony. 5.6346
Telescope. 5.1833
The Telescope. 5.1841
The telescope handbook and star atlas. 5.1730
Telescopes. 5.1748
Telescopes; how to make them and use them.
    5.1750
Teletext and videotex in the United States.
    5.6566
Television. 4.4070
Television, a guide to the literature. 5.8436
Television and behavior. 4.5738
Television and human behavior. 4.4073
Television & video almanac. 5.6438
Television and video almanac. 5.6438
Television comedy series. 2.2862
Television drama series programming. 2.2851
Television engineering handbook. 5.6439
Television, imagination, and aggression. 4.5737
Television marketing. 4.4439
Television production handbook. 2.2860

Tell about the South. 2.10449
Tell freedom; memories of Africa. 2.10057
Tell me how long the train's been gone.
  2.12862
Tellers of tales. 2.14100
Telling lives, the biographer's art. 3.315
Temperament and development. 5.634
Temperature. 5.2233
The temperature of history. 5.1930
Temperatures very low and very high. 5.2237
The temple of dawn. 2.2106
The temple of the golden pavilion. 2.2110
The Temple scroll. 1.1936
Tempo and mode in evolution. 5.3362
Temporal codes for memories. 5.338
The temptation of Saint Antony. 2.4192
The temptation of the West. 3.102
Ten books on architecture. 1.5466
Ten centuries of Spanish poetry. 2.5151
Ten days that shook the world. 3.3191
Ten faces of the universe. 5.1870
Ten great economists, from Marx to Keynes.
  4.1318
Ten Irish poets. 2.9868
Ten 'lost' plays. 2.12284
Ten master historians. 3.416
Ten miracle plays. 2.6208
Ten modern Scottish novels. 2.9841
Ten North Frederick. 2.12274
The ten princes. 2.1944
Ten twentieth-century Indian poets. 2.10123
Ten years and twenty days. 3.1038
Ten years in Japan. 3.4927
The tenant of Wildfell Hall. 2.7441
The tenants. 2.13162
The tenants of Moonbloom. 2.13412
Tender buttons: objects, food, rooms. 2.12514
Tender mercies. 2.12925
The tender tyrant. 1.4107
Tengu child. 2.2098
Tennessee. 3.8349-3.8350
Tennessee, a short history. 3.8346
Tennessee folk culture. 4.780
Tennessee Williams. 2.12739
Tennessee Williams. 2.12737
Tennis, a professional guide. 4.1039
The tennis court oath. 2.11337
Tennis: game of motion. 4.1037
Tennyson. 2.8158, 2.8169, 2.8172, 2.8179,
  2.8182
Tennyson and The princess. 2.8164
Tennyson and the reviewers. 2.8180
A Tennyson companion. 2.8171
A Tennyson dictionary. 2.8165
A Tennyson handbook. 2.8178
Tennyson, the unquiet heart. 2.8170
Tennyson's Camelot. 2.8159
Tennyson's Maud. 2.8163
Tensile architecture. 1.5512
La tentation de saint Antoine. 2.4191
Tenterhooks. 2.9036
The tenth man. 2.8760, 2.11488
The tenth muse. 2.2455, 2.10474
The tents of wickedness. 2.11563
Teoria e storia della storiografia. 3.387
The Teotihuacán map. 3.8895
Tepoztlan, a Mexican village. 3.8956
A tercentenary history of the Boston Public
  Latin School, 1635-1935. 4.11003
Terence. 2.698, 2.779
Terra-cotta warriors and horses at the tomb of
  Qin Shi Huang. 3.4694
Terra-cotta warriors & horses at the tomb of
  Qin Shi Huang. 3.4694
Terra nostra. 2.5344-2.5345
Terrain analysis. 4.266
Terre et poésie. 2.4470
The terrible secret. 3.1116
Terrible swift sword. 3.7339
The territorial dimension in government.
  4.8431
Territorial enterprise and Virginia City news.
  2.10939
Territorial government in Canada. 4.8321
Territorial politics and government in Montana,
  1864-89. 3.8546
The territory of the historian. 3.1972

Terror and decorum: poems, 1940-1948.
  2.12628
Terror and progress USSR: some sources of
  change and stability in the Soviet
  dictatorship. 3.3245
Terror and repression in revolutionary
  Marseilles. 3.2119
Terror out of Zion. 3.3861
Terrorism. 4.6712-4.6713
Terrorism and the liberal state. 4.7521
The terrors of ideological politics. 3.6216
Tertullian. 1.2213
TESS: the educational software selector.
  4.10298
Test case. 3.5249
The test of freedom. 4.7702
Test-tube women. 5.5066
A testament. 1.5335
The testament of Adolf Hitler. 3.2391
Testament of my childhood. 2.4818
Testimony. 1.3987
The testimony of the spade. 4.723
Testing monetarism. 4.4484
Testing the Roosevelt coalition. 3.8024
Tests. 5.203
Tests and measurements. 5.59
Tests and measurements in child development.
  5.582-5.583
Tests in print. 5.8153
Teton Sioux music. 1.4307
Tetum ghosts and Kin. 3.4559
Tevye's daughters. 2.1811
The Tewa world. 3.5955
Texas. 3.8319, 3.8330
Texas in the middle eighteenth century. 3.8323
The Texas Panhandle frontier. 3.8331
The Texas Rangers. 3.8329
Text and texture. 1.2569
Text-atlas of cat anatomy. 2.10757, 5.3997
A textbook of arthropod anatomy. 5.3849
Textbook of comparative histology. 5.4154
Textbook of endocrinology. 5.4989
Textbook of endocrinology (Philadelphia, Pa.)
  5.4989
A textbook of entomology. 5.3859
A textbook of European musical instruments.
  1.4129
A textbook of histology. 5.4156-5.4157
Textbook of medical physiology. 5.4194
Textbook of medicine. 5.4754
Textbook of microbiology. 5.4439
A textbook of mineralogy. 5.3020
Textbook of polymer science. 5.2764
Textbook of topology. 5.1598
A textbook on geomony. 5.2963
Textile handbook. 5.7078
Textiles in America, 1650-1870. 5.7081
Texts & pretexts. 2.2575
Textual power. 2.2474
Textual strategies. 2.2475
Thackeray. 2.8188, 2.8190
Thackeray; a collection of critical essays.
  2.8191
A Thackeray dictionary. 2.8185
Thackeray: the critical heritage. 2.8196
Thackeray, the novelist. 2.8195
Thackeray's canvass of humanity. 2.8192
Thackeray's novels. 2.8194
Thai Buddhism, its rites and activities. 1.2113
The Thai bureaucracy. 4.8767
Thai painting. 1.6311
Thai peasant social structure. 4.645
Thailand. 3.4518-3.4519, 3.4523, 5.8063
Thailand, society and politics. 3.4532
Thailand's monetary experience. 4.4523
Thaïs. 2.4214
Thaïs. 2.4215
The Thames and Hudson dictionary of art and
  artists. 1.4577
The Thames and Hudson encyclopaedia of the
  arts. 1.4577
That awful mess on Via Merulana. 2.5033
That championship season. 2.13172
That hideous strength. 2.9041
That most distressful nation. 3.6553
That myriad-minded man. 2.9293
That noble science of politics. 4.7274
That shining place. 2.12608

That summer in Paris. 2.9918
That uncertain feeling. 2.8384
That was the Life. 2.3674
That wilder image. 1.5894
The Thatcher government. 4.2293
The thaw. 2.1549
Theaetetus. 1.254
The theater and its double. 2.3082
Theater design. 1.5547
The theater essays of Arthur Miller. 2.12175
Theater in America. 2.3198
Theater in the planned society. 2.13932
Theater index to plays an anthologies,
  periodicals, discs, and tapes. 5.8126
The theater of Augustin Daly. 2.3253
The Theater of Black Americans. 2.3215
The theater of Fernando Arrabal. 2.5231
Theater of memory. 2.1946
The theater of Nikolay Gogol. 2.1381
The theater of protest and paradox. 2.2815
Théâtre. 2.4061, 2.4352, 2.4411, 2.4469
The theatre. 2.3162
Théâtre. 2.4474, 2.4477
Théâtre. 2.4543, 2.4545, 2.4569, 2.4578,
  2.4639, 2.4719
Theatre. 2.3081
The theatre advancing. 2.3091
Theatre and anti-theatre. 2.3182
Theatre and crisis, 1632-1642. 2.5890
The Theatre book of the year... 2.3210
Theatre chronicles, 1937-1962. 2.3228
Théâtre complet. 2.4079, 2.4234, 2.4527
Théâtre de chambre. 2.4756
Théâtre du XVIIe [i.e. dix-septième] siècle.
  2.3933
Théâtre du XVIIIe siècle. 2.3934
Le théâtre en France au XVIe siècle. 2.3885
Theatre for Shakespeare. 2.6855
The Theatre Guild. 2.3271
Theatre in a tent. 4.1191
The theatre in Asia. 2.3387
Theatre in India. 2.3392
Theatre in Southeast Asia. 2.3386
Theatre in the age of Garrick. 2.3342
Theatre in the age of Irving. 2.3309
Theatre in the East. 4.1109
The theatre in the Middle Ages. 2.3171
Theatre-in-the-round. 2.3139
Theatre (International Theatre Institute of the
  United States) 2.3081
Theatre lighting in the age of gas. 2.3145
Theatre management in America. 2.3268
The theatre of Aristophanes. 2.434
The theatre of Donald Oenslager. 2.3160
The theatre of Erwin Piscator. 2.3377
The theatre of Jean-Louis Barrault. 2.3367
The theatre of revolt. 2.3177
The theatre of Tennessee Williams. 2.12723
The theatre of the absurd. 2.2811
The theatre of the London fairs in the 18th
  century. 2.3319
The theatre of the Stuart Court. 1.5802
Théâtre, récits, nouvelles. 2.4442
Theatre Street. 4.1150
Theatre, the rediscovery of style. 2.3374
Theatre through the ages. 2.3168
Theatre U.S.A., 1668 to 1957. 2.3189
Theatre world. 2.3220
Theatres and auditoriums. 1.5546
The theatres of London. 2.3317
Theatres, spaces, environments. 2.3153
Theatrical companion to Shaw. 2.8090
The theatrical event. 2.3098
The Theban hegemony, 371-362 BC. 3.2616
Theft, law, and society. 4.9867
Their eyes were watching God. 2.11910
Their fathers' God. 2.14055
Their sisters' keepers. 4.6902
Their tattered flags. 3.7379
Them. 2.13201
The thematic apperception test, the children's
  apperception test, and the senior apperception
  technique in clinical use. 5.545
Thematic catalogues in music, an annotated
  bibliography. 1.3547
Thematic origins of scientific thought; Kepler to
  Einstein. 5.735
The thematic process in music. 1.4453

Thematisch-systematisches Verzeichnis der musikalischen Werke von Johann Sebastian Bach. 1.3605
Theme and structure in Swift's Tale of a tub. 2.7296
The theme is Blackness. 2.12931
Themes and conventions of Elizabethan tragedy. 2.5884
Themes and episodes. 1.4007
Themes and variations in Shakespeare's sonnets. 2.6676
Themes in fundamental moral theology. 1.1470
Themes in geographic thought. 4.17
Themes of Islamic civilization. 1.1991
Themes of work and love in adulthood. 4.5803
Themis. 1.1655
Then came each actor. 2.6872
Theocritus. 2.553, 2.556
Theodicy, abridged. 1.865
Theodicy in Islamic thought. 1.2062
Theodor Storm. 2.13661
Theodor Storm's craft of fiction. 2.13662
Theodora, Empress of Byzantium. 3.2668
Theodore Dreiser. 2.11603, 2.11605
Theodore Dreiser, apostle of nature. 2.11600
Theodore Dreiser: his world and his novels. 2.11602
Theodore Parker. 1.3418
Theodore Roethke. 2.12414
Theodore Roethke: an introduction to the poetry. 2.12412
Theodore Roosevelt. 3.7705
Theodore Roosevelt and the politics of power. 3.7701
Theodore Roosevelt and the rise of America to world power. 3.7699
Theodore Roosevelt and the rise of the modern Navy. 3.6380
Theodosian empresses. 3.2820
Theogonia. Opera et dies. Scvtvm. 2.311
Theogony. 2.478-2.479
The theologian and his universe. 1.1333
Theological and religious reference materials. 5.8444
A theological anthropology. 1.2245
Theological dictionary of the New Testament. 2.249
Theological investigations. 1.3202
A theological position. 2.12955
Theological treatises. 1.3405
Theology and the kingdom of God. 1.2816
Theology as anthropology. 1.1554
Theology in a new key. 1.2251
Theology in America. 1.2765
Theology in conflict. 1.2761
The theology of al-Ash'arī. 1.2044
The theology of Calvin. 1.3401
Theology of culture. 1.2770
Theology of hope. 1.2942
A theology of liberation: history, politics, and salvation. 1.2924
The theology of medicine. 5.4570
The theology of Paul Tillich. 1.3297
A theology of Q. 1.2677
Theology of the New Testament. 1.2654
A theology of the New Testament. 1.2656
Theology of the Old Testament. 1.2577
The Theology of unity. 1.2057
Théophile Gautier, his life & times. 2.4220
The Theophrastan character in England to 1642. 2.5580
Theoretical approaches to turbulence. 5.1667
Theoretical basis of nursing. 5.5173
Theoretical concepts in physics. 5.1967
Theoretical criminology. 4.6687
Theoretical dimensions of educational administration. 4.10637
Theoretical ecology. 5.3527
Theoretical elasticity. 5.1672
Theoretical geography. 4.198
Theoretical inorganic chemistry. 5.2845
Theoretical issues in international economics. 4.4139
Theoretical logic in sociology. 4.4780
Theoretical nuclear physics. 5.2414, 5.2422
Theoretical perspectives on deviance. 4.5075
Theoretical petrology. 5.3031
Theoretical physics. 5.1965

The theoretical side of calculus. 5.1449
Theoretical soil mechanics. 5.5909
Theoretical welfare economics. 4.1432
Theories and things. 1.121
Theories in contemporary psychology. 5.4
Theories in social psychology. 4.4984
Theories of chemical reaction rates. 5.2885
Theories of child development. 5.559
Theories of economic growth. 4.2780
Theories of ethics. 1.1403
Theories of evolution. 4.446
Theories of history. 3.473
Theories of illness. 4.465
Theories of imperialism. 4.7537
Theories of inflation. 4.4486
Theories of learning. 4.10353, 5.295
Theories of man and culture. 4.476
Theories of mass communication. 4.5004
Theories of modern art. 1.4788
Theories of perception and the concept of structure. 5.256
Theories of personality. 5.519, 5.534
Theories of primitive religion. 4.544
Theories of psychology. 5.30
Theories of scientific method. 5.865
Theories of social work with groups. 4.6505
Theories of society. 4.4734
Theories of surplus value. 4.1501
Theories of the arts in China. 1.6725
Theories of the political system. 4.7258
Theories of the symbol. 2.84
Theories of the theatre. 2.3097
Theories of women's studies. 4.5915
Theory and application of infinite series. 5.1422
Theory and applications of ultraviolet spectroscopy. 5.2675
Theory and design in the first machine age. 1.5262
Theory and design of modern pressure vessels. 5.6616
The theory and empirical analysis of production. 4.1953
Theory and explanation in archaeology. 3.221
Theory and history of folklore. 4.797
Theory and history of historiography. 3.387
The theory and measurement of demand. 4.1495
Theory and methods of scaling. 5.58
Theory and policy in international relations. 4.9000
The theory and practice of communism. 4.6934
Theory and practice of community social work. 4.6476
Theory and practice of feminist literary criticism. 2.2495
Theory and practice of good cooking. 5.7130
The theory and practice of hell. 3.2442
The theory and practice of history. 3.403
The theory and practice of human rights. 4.7640
The Theory and practice of infection control. 5.4707
Theory and practice of lubrication for engineers. 5.6246
Theory and practice of modern government. 4.7710
The theory & practice of peacekeeping. 4.9257
Theory and practice of peacekeeping. 4.9257
The theory and practice of public health. 5.4653
Theory and practice of social case work. 4.6496
The theory and practice of the Mandala. 1.1822
The theory and practice of war. 5.7145
Theory and processes of history. 3.437
Theory and reality in public international law. 4.9294
Theory in anthropology. 4.396
The theory, law, and policy of Soviet treaties. 4.9072
The theory of American literature. 2.10236
The theory of atomic collisions. 5.2399
Theory of atomic nucleus energy-sources. 5.2059

The theory of atomic spectra. 5.2313
The theory of Brillouin zones and electronic states in crystals. 5.2205
The theory of business enterprise. 4.4259
The theory of capitalist development. 4.1539
Theory of climate. 5.2569
A theory of cognitive dissonance. 5.313
Theory of collective behavior. 4.4998
The theory of commodity price stabilization. 4.4168
The theory of customs unions. 4.4209
A theory of data. 5.42
The theory of democratic elitism. 4.7563
A theory of economic-demographic development. 4.1633
The theory of economic development. 4.1470
Theory of economic dynamics. 4.1300
The theory of economic growth. 4.2791
A theory of economic history. 4.1724
The theory of economic integration. 4.4132
A theory of education. 4.10358
Theory of elasticity. 5.1671, 5.1673
The Theory of electrons and its applications to the phenomena of light and radiant heat. 5.2395
The theory of equilibrium growth. 4.2767
The theory of error correcting codes. 5.1376
A theory of evolving tonality. 1.4381
Theory of fiction. 2.3413
Theory of film. 2.2939
Theory of flight. 5.6665
The theory of functions of a complex variable. 5.1488
Theory of games and economic behavior. 5.1380
Theory of games and statistical decisions. 5.1377
The theory of general economic equilibrium. 4.1444
The theory of good and evil. 1.1439
A theory of good city form. 4.6312
Theory of ground vehicles. 5.6634
The theory of groups. 5.1298, 5.1301, 5.1304
The theory of groups and quantum mechanics. 5.1308
Theory of harmony. 1.4468
A theory of history. 3.391
The theory of interest. 4.1551
The theory of interest as determined by impatience to spend income and opportunity to invest it. 4.1550
Theory of international law. 4.8982
The theory of international values. 4.1489
The theory of intuition in Husserl's phenomenology. 1.1020
The theory of island biogeography. 5.3243
A theory of justice. 4.7659
Theory of linear induction motors. 5.6317
A theory of literary production. 2.2364
Theory of literature. 2.2369
The theory of logical types. 1.1256
The theory of matrices. 5.1366
Theory of molecular spectra. 5.2301
The theory of money. 4.4477
The theory of monopolistic competition. 4.1488
The theory of morality. 1.1446
Theory of motivation. 5.482
The theory of natural monopoly. 4.3037
Theory of operator algebras I. 5.1478
Theory of oscillators. 5.1659
The theory of partitions. 5.1281
The theory of photons and electrons. 5.2376
Theory of planetary atmospheres. 5.1803
Theory of plates and shells. 5.1674
The theory of play and recreation. 4.10389
The theory of political economy. 4.1438
Theory of population genetics and evolutionary ecology. 5.3474
The theory of prismatic society. 4.7759
Theory of prosody in eighteenth-century England. 2.1044
Theory of psychoanalytic technique. 5.4906
A theory of psychological scaling. 5.43
The theory of public finance. 4.4647
Theory of recursive functions and effective computability. 5.1054
A theory of semiotics. 2.80

The theory of social and economic organization. 4.1473
The theory of social economy. 4.1467
The theory of sound. 5.2223
Theory of spectroscopy. 5.2304
Theory of structures. 5.5844
Theory of superconductivity. 5.2353
Theory of syntax. 2.190
The theory of the arts. 1.1361
Theory of the avant-garde. 1.1390
The theory of the avant-garde. 1.6701
A theory of the consumption function. 4.1571
Theory of the film. 2.2935
A theory of the good and the right. 1.1443
A theory of the labor movement. 4.3093
The theory of the leisure class. 1899. 4.1572
The theory of the mixed constitution in antiquity. 4.7366
The theory of the novel in England, 1850-1870. 2.6017
The theory of the potential. 5.1652
The theory of the Riemann zeta-function. 5.1339
The theory of the scattering matrix for the interactions of fundamental particles. 5.2161
The theory of unemployment. 4.3197
Theory of union bargaining goals. 4.3328
Theory of value. 4.1504
The theory of wage determination. 4.3131
The theory of wages. 4.3128
The theory of wages. 4.3130, 4.3134
Theory of wages and employment. 4.3126
Theory Z. 4.2742
Thera, Pompeii of the ancient Aegean. 3.2594
Therapeutic consultations in child psychiatry. 5.5104
Therapeutic recreation service. 5.5143
The therapeutic state. 5.4801
There are alternatives! 4.9173
There is a river. 3.6704
There is confusion. 2.11708
There shall be no night. 2.12466
There we sat down: Talmudic Judaism in the making. 1.1911
Thereby hangs a tale. 2.1054
There's a trick with a knife I'm learning to do. 2.9957
Thérèse. 2.4632
Therese Raquin. 2.4346
Thermal analysis. 5.2670
Thermal computations for electronic equipment. 5.6484
Thermal conduction in solids. 5.2211
Thermal physics. 5.2257
Thermal radiation heat transfer. 5.2270
The thermal theory of cyclones. 5.2545
Thermodynamic properties of nonelectrolyte solutions. 5.2910
Thermodynamic theory of structure, stability and fluctuations. 5.2244
Thermodynamics. 5.2242, 5.2245, 5.2255, 5.6201
Thesaurus of English words and phrases. 2.1069-2.1070
Thesaurus of ERIC descriptors. 5.7632
Thesaurus of orchestral devices. 1.4491
Thesaurus of physics. 5.1892
Thesaurus of psychological index terms. 5.7633
These also believe. 1.2389
These Twain. 2.8453
Theseus. 2.4555
They all played ragtime. 1.4318
They called them greasers. 3.8337
They came for sandalwood. 4.3843
They came in chains. 3.6628
They came like swallows. 2.12122
They came to Japan. 3.4878
They chose Minnesota. 3.8502
They gathered at the river. 1.3039
They have no rights. 4.9619
They saw it happen. 3.1516
They saw it happen. 3.1384
They shoot horses, don't they? 2.12069
They sought a country. 1.3366
They stooped to folly. 2.11772
They studied man. 4.525
They taught themselves. 1.5905

They wrote on clay. 3.3764
The Thibaults. 2.4626
The thief. 2.1571
The thief of love. 4.804
The thief's journal. 2.4535
Thin film solar cells. 5.6327
The thin red line. 2.13103
Thin shell concrete structures. 5.5867
Thin-walled elastic beams. 5.6081
Things and ideals. 1.618
Things fall apart. 2.10106
Things maps don't tell us. 4.246
Things that I do in the dark. 2.13106
Thinking. 5.378
Thinking about crime. 4.6773
Thinking about development. 4.2809
Thinking about national security. 5.7262
Thinking about the unthinkable in the 1980s. 5.7237
Thinking about women. 2.2406
Thinking big. 2.3659
The thinking body. 5.4272
The thinking computer. 5.1127
The thinking eye. 1.6176
Thinking FORTH. 5.1215
Thinking: from association to Gestalt. 5.385
Thinking: its nature and development. 5.388
The thinking machine. 2.11763
Thinking matter. 1.685
Thinking photography. 5.6936
Thinking physics is gedanken physics. 5.1999
The third Arab-Israeli war. 3.3936
The third book of criticism. 2.11923
The third book of Horace's 'Odes' 2.718
Third census of Finnegans wake. 2.8871
The third child. 4.1639
The third electoral system 1853-1892. 4.8104
The third force in Canada. 4.8306
The third generation. 2.11874
The Third Indochina conflict. 3.4451
The third man; Loser takes all. 2.8762
The third option. 5.7232
Third parties in America. 4.8165
Third parties in presidential elections. 4.8160
The third Portuguese empire, 1825-1975. 4.8936
The third reformation. 1.3362
The Third Reich. 3.2453
The Third Republic of France. 3.2173
The third rose. 2.12518
The third session. 1.3129
The third voice. 2.5921
The third wedding. 2.611-2.612
The Third World and press freedom. 2.3552
Third World multinationals. 4.3031
The Third World reassessed. 4.1806
Third world urbanization. 4.6338
Third world women. 4.5889
Third World women speak out. 4.6168
The third year of the Nixon watch. 3.7904
A thirsty evil. 2.12622
The thirteen books of Euclid's Elements. 5.1102
Thirteen days. 3.6487
The thirteen pragmatisms, and other essays. 1.529
The thirteen principal Upanishads. 1.1683
The thirteenth century, 1216-1307. 3.1359
Thirteenth valley. 2.12967
The thirties. 2.10409, 2.12766
The thirties and after. 2.9371
Thirty acres. 2.4819
Thirty famous one act plays. 2.3766
The thirty-nine steps. 2.8488-2.8489
Thirty years. 4.1169
Thirty years of treason. 3.7539
Thirty years of Yugoslav literature, 1945-1975. 2.1199
The thirty years war. 3.638-3.639
The Thirty Years War, 1618-1648. 3.637
This affair of Louisiana. 3.7066
This body the earth. 2.11798
This bridge called my back. 2.10702
This business of living. 2.5054
This business of music. 1.4355
This country, Japan. 3.4877
This great stage. 2.6664
This gun for hire. 2.8761

This hallowed ground. 3.7340
This handful of dust. 2.10120
This I remember. 3.7787
This island Earth. 5.1814
This kind of war. 3.5017
This kind of woman. 2.2039
This land was theirs. 3.5706
This mighty dream. 4.5230
This New World. 3.8972
This real night. 2.9513
This remarkable continent. 4.146
This sacred trust. 3.6147
This scene of man. 4.6188
This species of property. 3.7206
This sporting life. 2.9820
This was a poet. 2.11010
This was America. 3.6006
This was Harlem. 3.8043
This way for the gas, ladies and gentlemen. 2.1699
This wild abyss. 5.1683
Thomas Alva Edison, an American myth. 5.6253
Thomas B. Reed. 3.7445
Thomas Bewick. 1.4946
Thomas Campion. 2.6442
Thomas Carlyle. 2.7551, 2.7553
Thomas Carlyle; a history of the first forty years of his life, 1795-1835. 2.7550
Thomas Carlyle: the critical heritage. 2.7558
Thomas Chippendale. 1.6578
Thomas Couture and the eclectic vision. 1.6084
Thomas Cranmer. 3.1394
Thomas Cromwell, Tudor minister. 3.1406
Thomas Dekker. 2.6572
Thomas E. Dewey and his times. 3.7634
Thomas Eakins. 1.4896
Thomas Eakins. 1.5935
Thomas Gray. 2.7056
Thomas Hardy. 2.7782
Thomas Hardy. 2.7777, 2.7784, 2.7789, 2.7796, 2.7800
Thomas Hardy, a biography. 2.7779
Thomas Hardy, art and thought. 2.7798
A Thomas Hardy dictionary. 2.7794
Thomas Hardy, distance and desire. 2.7794
Thomas Hardy from serial to novel. 2.7786
Thomas Hardy: his career as a novelist. 2.7795
Thomas Hardy: the forms of tragedy. 2.7792
Thomas Hardy, the writer and his background. 2.7799
Thomas Hardy's English. 2.7802
Thomas Hardy's later years. 2.7775
Thomas Harriot, a biography. 5.819
Thomas Heywood. 2.6586
Thomas Hill Green and the development of liberal-democratic thought. 4.7441
Thomas Hill Green & the development of liberal-democratic thought. 4.7441
Thomas Hood. 2.7820, 2.7822
Thomas Hood: his life and times. 2.7821
Thomas Jefferson. 3.7061
Thomas Jefferson and the development of American public education. 4.10200
Thomas Jefferson and the new nation. 3.7063
Thomas Jefferson & the Stony Mountains. 3.7064
Thomas Jefferson's views on public education. 4.10735
Thomas L. McKenney. 3.5803
Thomas l'imposteur, histoire. 2.4482
Thomas Lodge and other Elizabethans. 2.6489
Thomas Lodge; the history of an Elizabethan. 2.6488
Thomas Mann, a chronicle of his life. 2.13836
Thomas Mann; the uses of tradition. 2.13838
A Thomas Merton reader. 2.12146
Thomas Middleton. 2.6637
Thomas Middleton & the new comedy tradition. 2.6638
Thomas Middleton: three plays. 2.6633
Thomas Moran. 1.6382
Thomas More. 3.1409-3.1410
Thomas More and his Utopia. 1.417
Thomas Muskerry. 2.8523
Thomas Nashe; a critical introduction. 2.6497
Thomas Nelson Page. 2.11194

Thomas Nuttall, naturalist. 5.3210
Thomas Paine's Common sense. 3.6923
Thomas Pynchon. 2.13283, 2.13288
Thomas R.R. Cobb (1823-1862) 3.8261
Thomas register of American manufacturers. 5.5510
Thomas Reid's Inquiry. 1.714
Thomas Reid's inquiry and essays. 1.713
Thomas Reid's Lectures on the fine arts. 1.715
Thomas the obscure. 2.4416
Thomas Traherne. 2.7321
Thomas Wolfe. 2.12789, 2.12793-2.12796
Thomas Wolfe. 2.12797
Thomas Wolfe, three decades of criticism. 2.12788
Thomas Wolfe's characters. 2.12798
Thomas Wolfe's letters to his mother, Julia Elizabeth Wolfe. 2.12787
Thonet. 5.7070
Thor, with angels. 2.8673
Thoreau. 2.11254
Thoreau's redemptive imagination. 2.11256
Thoreau's seasons. 2.11252
Thorns & thistles. 4.6877
Thornton Wilder. 2.12720
A Thornton Wilder trio. 2.12714
Thoroughbass method; with excerpts from the theoretical works of Praetorius [and others] and numerous examples from the literature of the 17th and 18th centuries. 1.4462
Thor's hammer. 2.13035
Thorstein Veblen, a critical interpretation. 4.1380
Thorstein Veblen and his America. 4.1379
Those of the street. 3.4007
Those were the nights. 2.3314
Those who perish. 2.11550
Those who stayed behind. 4.5193
Thought, action, and passion. 1.609
Thought and behavior in modern Japanese politics. 3.4980
The thought and character of William James. 1.603
Thought and expression in the sixteenth century. 3.169
Thought and language. 2.97
Thought and letters in western Europe, A. D. 500 to 900. 3.133
Thought in the nineteenth century. 1.442
Thought reform and the psychology of totalism. 5.451
Thoughts on death and immortality. 1.955
Thoughts on design. 1.5834
Thousand cranes. 2.2103
A thousand days. 3.7869
A thousand years of Vietnamese poetry. 2.2263
The Thracians. 3.3539
The Thrales of Streatham Park. 2.7184
Thraliana. 2.7183
Threat to development. 4.4148
Three adventure novels of H. Rider Haggard. 2.7758
Three against the Third Republic: Sorel, Barrès, and Maurras. 3.2175
The three ages of the Italian Renaissance. 3.2848
Three American literatures. 2.10304
Three American modernist painters. 1.5914
Three American painters, Kenneth Noland, Jules Olitski, Frank Stella. 1.5902
Three American plays. 2.11313
Three archaic poets. 2.286
The three arrows and The servants and the snow. 2.9765
Three bags full. 2.10542
Three Catholic writers of the modern South. 2.10294
Three centuries and the island. 3.8807
Three centuries of American antiques. 1.6513
Three centuries of American furniture. 1.6561
Three centuries of English and American plays, a checklist. 5.7950
Three centuries of harpsichord making. 1.4150
Three centuries of Harvard, 1636-1936. 4.10996
Three Christian capitals. 3.2719
Three classics in the aesthetic of music. 1.3497

The three clerks. 2.8224
Three comedies. 2.4992
Three comic poems. 2.1410
Three days. 3.3923
Three dialogues between Hylas and Philonous. 1.688
Three different worlds. 4.2148
The three Edwards. 3.1363
Three essays on America. 2.10264, 2.10398
Three essays on religion. 1.1557
Three essays on the state of economic science. 4.1443
Three essays on the theory of sexuality. 4.5502
The three estates in medieval and Renaissance literature. 2.2382
Three exemplary novels. 2.5174
Three faces of fascism. 3.869
Three faces of Marxism. 4.6978
Three famous plays. 2.1447
Three-fifths of a man. 3.6621
Three great Irishmen. 2.9857
Three guineas. 2.9577
The three hostages. 2.8488
Three hours for lunch. 2.12209
Three human rights in the Constitution of 1787. 4.9505
Three hundred poems of the T'ang dynasty. 2.2192
Three hundred years of American drama and theatre. 2.3195
Three hundred years of psychiatry, 1535-1860. 5.4803
Three intellectuals in politics. 3.726
Three Japanese plays from the traditional theatre. 2.2028
Three kingdoms. 2.2222
Three lectures on the rate of wages. 4.1511
Three lives. 2.12515
Three Märchen of E. T. A. Hoffmann. 2.13617
The three Marias. 2.5460
Three medieval rhetorical arts. 2.2535
Three men. 5.223
Three Mile Island. 5.6301
The Three Mile Island accident. 5.6302
Three modernists. 1.3167
The three musketeers. 2.4175
Three novels. 2.10006, 2.13960
Three novels: Hordubal, An ordinary life [and] Meteor. 1.667
The three novels of Roger Mais. 2.9996
Three on the tower. 2.12350
The three orders. 4.5346
Three painters of America: Charles Demuth. 1.5915
Three philosophers. 1.296
Three philosophical poets: Lucretius, Dante, and Goethe. 2.2750
The three pillars of Zen. 1.2175
Three plays. 2.1873, 2.4571, 2.4696, 2.4720, 2.5024, 2.7233, 2.7995, 2.8523, 2.12440, 2.13599, 2.13745
Three plays of Racine. 2.4047
Three plays: Our town, The skin of our teeth, The matchmaker. 2.12713
Three plays: Song of a goat, The masquerade, The raft. 2.10108
Three romantic novels of Cornwall. 2.8603
Three Rossettis. 2.8006
Three Sanskrit plays. 2.1955
Three, seven, ace & other stories. 2.1607
Three soldiers. 2.11585
The three stigmata of Palmer Eldritch. 2.12974
Three stories & ten poems. 2.11836
Three studies in European conservatism: Meternich, Guizot, the Catholic church in the nineteenth century. 3.666
Three studies in the Renaissance. 2.6509
Three styles in the study of kinship. 4.574
Three tales. 2.4194
Three tenant families. 3.8278
Three theories of child development. 5.570
Three thousand futures. 4.10749
Three thousand years of educational wisdom. 4.9946
Three treatises. 1.2348
The three twins. 2.2273
Three Virginia frontiers. 3.8183

The Three voices of poetry. 2.2745
Three ways of thought in ancient China. 1.157
Three who dared. 4.10866
Three who made a revolution. 3.3151
Three works: A dream of John Ball; The pilgrims of hope; News from nowhere. 2.7963
Three worlds. 2.12604
The three worlds of Bali. 3.4586
Three worlds of development. 4.2779
The Threefold refuge in the Theravāda Buddhist tradition. 1.2148
Threshold limit values. 5.4726
The threshold of Anglo-Saxon. 2.941
Throne and mandarins: China's search for a policy during the Sino-French controversy, 1880-1885. 3.4433
The Throne of Wisdom; wood sculptures of the madonna in Romanesque France. 1.5782
Through 'Poverty's Vale'. 3.8032
Through Russian eyes. 3.6432
Through the eyes of a child. 5.7720
Through the flower. 1.5927
Through the looking-glass. 2.7676
Through the looking glass. 2.7675
Thrown to the Woolfs. 2.9004
Thucydides. 2.561
Thucydides. 2.397, 3.2610
Thucydides and Athenian imperialism. 2.563
Thucydides, Book VI. 2.559
Thucydides, Book VII. 2.560
Thucydides on the nature of power. 2.564
Thunder at Hampton Roads. 3.7365
Thunder on the left. 2.12208
Thunder out of China. 3.4772
Thunderstorm in human affairs. 5.2552
Thunderstorms 5.2552
The Thurber album. 2.12586
The Thurber carnival. 2.12587
Thurber's men, women and dogs. 1.5850
Thurlow Weed, wizard of the lobby. 3.7165
La tía Julia y el escribidor. 2.5435
The Tibetan book of the dead. 1.1741, 1.2149
The Tibetan book of the great liberation. 1.2104
Tibetan civilization. 3.4856
Tibetan paintings. 1.6331
Tibetan sacred art. 1.5188
Tibulli aliorumque carminum libri tres. 2.647
Tibullus. 2.782
Tibullus, a Hellenistic poet at Rome. 2.781
A ticket to the stars. 2.1623
Tidal energy. 5.5963
Tidal power. 5.5964
The tide at sunrise. 3.4400
A Tide of discontent. 4.8112
Tide of empires. 3.541
Tides of fortune, 1945-1955. 3.1673
The tides of history. 3.521
The tides of the planet earth. 5.2491
Tides of war. 2.3571
Tidewater towns. 4.6326
The tidings brought to Mary. 2.4472
Tiempo de silencio. 2.5295
Tiffany windows. 1.6652
The tiger and the horse. 2.8467
The tiger in the Senate. 3.7673
The tiger in the smoke. 2.8378
Till we have faces. 2.9042
Tilmann Riemenschneider, his life and work. 1.5718
Timarion. 2.576
Timarion. English. 2.576
The timber economy of Puritan New England. 4.3841
Timber; or, Discoveries. 2.6594
Time after time. 2.8929
Time and mind in Wordsworth's poetry. 2.8327
Time and modality. 1.1219
Time and the highland Maya. 3.9062
Time and the novel. 2.3498
Time and the space-traveller. 5.1915
Time and traditions. 3.235
Time, creation, and the continuum. 1.1342
A time for angels. 4.9181
A time for courage. 3.1051
Time, forward. 2.1568

Time frames. 5.3388
Time in Greek tragedy. 2.266
Time in literature. 2.2410
A time in Rome. 2.8477
Time in stratigraphy. 5.3149
Time Inc. 5.7586
Time longer than rope. 3.5457
Time must have a stop. 2.8822
A time of changes. 2.13324
A time of death. 2.1212
A time of harvest, American literature,
    1910-1960. 2.10422
The time of illusion. 3.7909
The time of indifference. 2.5045
The time of man. 2.12397
The time of the angels. 2.9766
The time of the hero. 2.5429
Time of transition. 4.5596
The time of troubles. 3.3090
The time of your life. 2.12440
Time on the cross. 3.7245
Time series analysis. 5.1415
Time, space and things. 5.1996
A time to speak. 2.12087
Time to speak. 5.5190
Time's arrow and evolution. 5.3324
Time's arrow, time's cycle. 5.3086
The Times atlas of the oceans. 4.194
The Times atlas of the world. 4.116
The Times atlas of world history. 4.125
The Times in review. 3.745
The times I've seen. 2.8692
Time's laughingstocks. 2.7762
Times (London, England) 3.329, 4.70
Times (London, England) Literary supplement.
    2.10424
The times of Melville and Whitman. 2.10372
The times of my life. 3.7930
The Times survey of foreign ministries of the
    world. 4.9092
Times three. 2.12079
The timetables of history. 3.369
Timothy Pickering and the American Republic.
    3.7008
Tin and its alloys and compounds. 5.6790
The tin drum. 2.13755
The tin flute. 2.4821
Tin-glaze pottery in Europe and the Islamic
    world. 1.6628
Tin roofs and palm trees. 3.5549
Tina. 2.14011
Tintern Abbey. 2.8302
Tintoretto: the paintings and drawings. 1.6225
Tiny Alice. 2.12845
Tirso de Molina. 2.5205
'Tis pity she's a whore. 2.6575
'Tis sixty years since. 2.8044
Tissues and organs. 5.4113
Tit-Coq, pièce en trois actes. 2.4814
The Titan. 2.11598
The Titans; a three-generation biography of the
    Dumas. 2.4179
Titans of the seas. 3.1004
Titian. 1.6226
Titian and the Venetian woodcut. 1.6475
Titles in series. 1.26
Tito. 3.3558-3.3559
Tito, Mihailović, and the Allies, 1941-1945.
    3.949
Titoism and the Cominform. 3.3566
Tito's separate road. 3.3563
Titus alone. 2.9220
Titus Groan. 2.9220
Tiwi wives. 4.586
To a blossoming pear tree. 2.12805
To a God unknown. 2.12533
To acquire wisdom. 1.1140
To advance knowledge. 5.976
To ascend from a floating base. 5.7481
[Tō axion esti] 2.579
To be a Jew. 1.1982
To be a pilgrim. 2.8501
To be equal. 3.6697
To be, or not ... to BOP. 1.4084
To be preserved forever. 4.6857
To Byzantium. 2.13013
To criticize the critic, and other writings.
    2.11629

To die for the people. 3.6713
To do no harm. 5.4730
'To double business bound' 2.2373
To dwell among friends. 4.6183
To enact a law: Congress and campaign
    financing. 4.8135
To end war. 5.8258
To enforce education. 4.10644
To establish justice, to insure domestic
    tranquility. 4.5156
To give and to have, and other poems. 2.5061
To have and have not. 2.11849
To Homer through Pope. 2.487
To Katanga and back. 3.5431
To keep art alive. 1.5955
To kill a messenger. 2.3653
To kill a mockingbird. 2.11995
To live on this earth. 3.5811
To live the orange. 2.4779
To lose a battle; France 1940. 3.980
To make a poet black. 2.10329
To make democracy safe for America. 5.7369
To mix with time, new and selected poems.
    2.12568
To move a nation. 3.7848
To purge this land with blood. 3.7273
To reclaim a legacy. 4.10827
To save a nation. 3.7772
To serve the people. 4.8026
To set the law in motion. 4.9690
To set the record straight. 4.9466
To the actor. 2.3114
To the Arctic by canoe, 1819-1821. 4.105
To the bitter end. 3.2438
To the director and playwright. 2.3106
To the end of time. 2.9380
To the Farewell address. 3.7025
To the Finland station. 4.6941
To the golden door. 3.6554
To the Golden Shore. 1.3026
To the great ocean. 4.4022
To the halls of the Montezumas. 3.7137
To the Hartford Convention: the Federalists
    and the origins of party politics in
    Massachusetts, 1789-1815. 3.7112
To the is-land. 2.10224
To the lighthouse. 2.9578
To the newly baptized. 1.2487
To the north. 2.8478
To the pure ... 4.6759
To the Webster-Ashburton treaty. 3.7133
To win a war. 3.795
To work and to wed. 4.3289
To you, Simonides. 2.405
Toad of Toad Hall. 2.9110
Tobacco colony. 4.2034
Tobacco culture. 3.8187
Tobacco road. 2.11457
Tobias Smollett; bicentennial essays presented to
    Lewis M. Knapp. 2.7267
Tocqueville and England. 4.7447
Tocqueville and the old regime. 3.2061
Tocqueville and the problem of democracy.
    4.7448
Tocqueville in America. 3.6040
Todo verdor perecerá. 2.5395
Todos los cuentos de Gabriel García Márquez
    (1947-1972). 2.5421
'Together' Black women. 3.6773
Toilers of the sea. 2.4238
Tojo and the coming of the war. 3.4986
The token economy. 5.4887
Tokugawa Ieyasu, shogun. 3.4944
Tokugawa religion. 1.1836
Told in letters. 2.5943
The tolerant Populists. 4.8232
Toleration and the Reformation. 1.2476
The toll of independence. 3.6931
Tolstoi in the 60s. 2.1444
Tolstoi in the Seventies. 2.1442
Tolstoi in the sixties. 2.1444
Tolstoy. 2.1433, 2.1436, 2.1438-2.1440, 2.1446
Tolstoy: a critical introduction. 2.1441
Tolstoy, my father. 2.1437
Tolstoy's letters. 2.1432
The Tolstoys, twenty-four generations of
    Russian history, 1353-1983. 3.3032
Tolstoy's 'War and peace' 2.1428

The Toltecs, until the fall of Tula. 3.8884
Tom Brown at Oxford. 2.7840
Tom Brown's schooldays. 2.7841
Tom Jones. 2.7023
Tom Stoppard. 2.9818-2.9819
Tom Thumb. 2.7022
Tom Watson, agrarian rebel. 3.7454
A tomb for Boris Davidovich. 2.1213
The tomb of Tutankhamen. 3.5154
Tombee. 3.8249
Tomol. 3.5859
Tomorrow is another day. 2.10599
Tomorrow's Eve. 2.4338
Tomorrow's math; unsolved problems for the
    amateur. 5.1259
Tomorrow's teachers. 4.10539
Tomorrow's tomorrow. 3.6767
Toms, coons, mulattoes, mammies, and bucks.
    2.2996
Ton und Wort. 1.4000
Tonal harmony in concept and practice.
    1.4464
The tongue set free. 2.13722
Tongues of conscience. 5.748
The tongues of men, and Speech. 2.90
Tonight at 8:30. 2.8583
Tono-Bungay. 2.8251a
Too late the phalarope. 2.10089
Too many magicians. 2.13040
Too serious a business. 3.895
Tooley's Dictionary of mapmakers. 4.223
The tools of empire. 4.7534
Tools of radio astronomy. 5.1780
Top-down structured programming techniques.
    5.1189
Topics in algebra. 5.1269
Topics in American art since 1945. 1.4867
Topics in classical biophysics. 5.3494
Topics in metallurgical thermodynamics.
    5.6771
Topics in non-ferrous extractive metallurgy.
    5.6789
Topics in stereochemistry. 5.2875
Topographia Hiberniae. English. 3.1818
Topographic mapping of the Americas,
    Australia, and New Zealand. 4.216
Topological dynamics. 5.1589
Topological groups. 5.1597
Topological transformation groups. 5.1303
Topological vector spaces. 5.1476
Topper. 2.12491
The Torah, [Torah (romanized form)] the five
    books of Moses. 1.2588
The torch in my ear. 2.13719
The torch of certainty. 1.2161
Tormented loyalty. 3.2415
Tornados, dark days, anomalous precipitation,
    and related weather phenomena. 5.2507
Toronto daily star. 2.11838
Toronto star weekly. 2.11838
Le torrent. 2.4815
The torrent; novellas and short stories. 2.4816
The torrents of spring. 2.1454
The Tory syndrome. 4.8311
The Tosa diary. 2.2046
Tossing and turning. 2.13363
Total war. 3.900
Totalitarian dictatorship and autocracy. 4.7599
The totalitarian temptation. 4.7604
Totalitarianism. 4.7596, 4.7605
Totems and teachers. 4.415
Tottel's miscellany (1557-1587) 2.6150
A touch of innocence. 4.1136
Touched with fire. 3.7393
Touching base. 4.1001
Touchstone for ethics, 1893-1943. 1.1484
Tough guy writers of the thirties. 2.10636
Tough, sweet & stuffy. 2.1037
Toulouse-Lautrec. 1.6152, 1.6502
Le tour du monde en 80 jours. 2.4323
A tour in Ireland, with general observations on
    the present state of that kingdom made in the
    years 1776, 1777 and 1778. 3.1868
A tour through England and Wales. 3.1728
Tous les hommes sont mortels. 2.4393
Tout compte fait. 2.4400
Toward a Christian moral theology. 1.3205
Toward a functioning federalism. 4.7867

Toward a general science of viable systems. 5.994
Toward a general theory of action. 4.4961
Toward a general theory of social control. 4.5079
Toward a history of Ukrainian literature. 2.1652
Toward a just correctional system. 4.6896
Toward a just social order. 4.4975
Toward a manpower policy. 4.3222
Toward a modern Japanese theatre. 2.2105
Toward a more natural science. 5.4563
Toward a more responsible two-party system. 4.8172
Toward a national health policy. 5.4640
Toward a new Christianity. 1.2802
Toward a new earth. 2.10549
Toward a new music. 1.4184
Toward a new order of sea power. 3.6383
Toward a new world outlook. 4.10138
Toward a patriarchal Republic. 3.8263
Toward a philosophy of sport. 4.948
Toward a politics of the planet earth. 4.8999
Toward a psychology of art. 1.4604
Toward a psychology of being. 5.529
Toward a rational society. 4.10549
Toward a recognition of androgyny. 2.2407
Toward a reconstructed philosophy of education. 4.10222
Toward a science of comparative education. 4.9967
Toward a science of human nature. 5.82
Toward a social history of American English. 2.1130
Toward a theory of instruction. 4.10241
Toward a theory of the rent-seeking society. 4.1514
Toward a warless world. 4.9145
Toward an aesthetic of reception. 2.2485
Toward an anthropology of women. 4.461
Toward an urban vision. 4.6202
Toward Balzac. 2.4124
Toward benevolent neutrality. 4.9722
Toward effective counseling and psychotherapy: training and practice. 5.4859
Toward excellence. 4.6611
Toward explaining human culture. 4.495
Toward Lexington. 3.6922
Toward loving. 2.8734
Toward new towns for America. 1.5599
Toward rational technology in medicine. 5.4609
Toward restoration. 3.4951
Toward reunion in philosophy. 1.461
Toward Samson Agonistes. 2.7143
Toward science in aesthetics. 1.1359
Toward sustained development in sub-Saharan Africa. 4.2613
Toward the end. 2.10578
Toward the scientific study of history. 3.6268
Toward the truth. 1.1746
Toward the year 2000; work in progress. 3.6071
Toward understanding women. 4.5937
Toward Vatican III. 1.3169
Toward world peace. 3.1172
Towards a liberatory biology. 5.3327
Towards a mythology. 2.8361
Towards a new architecture. 1.5471
Towards a new cold war. 3.7846
Towards a new international economic order. 4.4137
Towards a new past. 3.6204
Towards a normative theory of international relations. 4.8995
Towards a poor theatre. 2.3117
Towards a sociology of the novel. 2.3417
Towards a visual culture. 4.10335
Towards an American army. 5.7287
Towards an understanding of the mechanism of heredity. 5.3445
Towards Greek tragedy. 2.294
Towards standards. 2.10241
Towards standards of criticism. 2.2440
Towards the managed economy. 4.2285
Towards understanding relationships. 4.4927
The tower and the bridge. 5.5834
Towers, bridges, and other structures. 5.5660

The towers of Trebizond. 2.9066
The town. 2.11680, 2.12389
Town and country in Brazil. 3.9222
Town and county. 4.8840
Town and square, from the agora to the village green. 1.5588
Town into city. 3.8007
Town-talk in a letter to a lady in the country. 2.7271
Towneley plays. 2.6209-2.6210
The towns of Roman Britain. 3.1307
Toxic substances sourcebook. 5.5558
Toxicity testing. 5.4719
Toxicology. 5.4720
Toxicology of drugs and chemicals. 5.4721
Trabelin' on. 1.2422
Trace elements in the atmosphere. 5.2523
Tracers in the sea. 4.342
Traces of the brush. 1.6369
Traces on the Rhodian shore. 4.364
The track of the cat. 2.11505
Tractatus Coislinianus. 2.2825
Tractatus logico-philosophicus. 1.1225-1.1226
Tracts and other papers relating principally to the origin, settlement, and progress of the colonies in North America from the discovery of the country to the year 1776. 3.6860
Tracts and pamphlets. 2.7272
The trade and administration of China. 4.2464
Trade and aid. 4.4173
Trade and conflict in Angola. 3.5402
Trade and diplomacy on the China coast. 4.4238
Trade and dominion. 4.8903
Trade and employment in developing countries. 4.3237
Trade and industry in classical Greece. 4.1734
Trade and market in the early empires. 4.1728
Trade and politics in ancient Greece. 4.4093
Trade and politics in the Niger Delta, 1830-1885. 4.2587
Trade, balance of payments and growth. 4.4134
Trade in the ancient economy. 4.4094
Trade names dictionary. 5.5641
Trade names dictionary: company index. 5.5642
Trade, plunder, and settlement. 4.4225
Trade preferences for developing countries. 4.4200
Trade prospects for developing countries. 4.4133
Trade strategy for rich and poor nations. 4.4198
Trade, tariffs and growth. 4.4105
Trade union democracy in Western Europe. 4.3401
Trade union government and administration in Great Britain. 4.3409
The trade union rank and file. 4.3403
Trade union wage policy. 4.3332
Trade unions and national economic policy. 4.3631
Trade unions and pressure group politics. 4.3405
Trade unions and society. 4.3327
Trade unions in the developed economies. 4.3336
Trademarks. 4.9548
The trading world of Asia and the English East India Company, 1660-1760. 4.4098
Tradition. 1.144, 4.824
Tradition and change in a Turkish town. 3.3691
Tradition and change in education. 4.9962
Tradition and contract. 4.600
Tradition and crisis. 3.3834
Tradition and design in the Iliad. 2.508
Tradition and experiment in English poetry. 2.5752
Tradition and experiment in Wordsworth's lyrical ballads (1798) 2.8309
Tradition and folk life. 3.1753
Tradition and innovation in Chaucer. 2.6356
Tradition and interpretation. 1.2576
Tradition and modernization in Japanese culture. 3.4896

Tradition and originality in Roman poetry. 2.637
Tradition and politics. 4.8786
Tradition and reality. 1.1915
Tradition and reform in the teaching of English. 4.10472
Tradition and revolution in Vietnam. 3.4516
Tradition and the modern world. 1.3407
The tradition of constructivism. 1.4840
The tradition of resistance in Mozambique. 3.5309
The tradition of the new. 2.12415
The tradition of Western music. 1.3465
Traditional American folk songs from the Anne & Frank Warner collection. 1.3435
The Traditional artist in African societies. 1.6728
Traditional Balinese culture. 3.4585
The traditional Chinese state in Ming times (1368-1644). 3.4708
Traditional Chinese stories. 2.2207
Traditional Chinese tales. 2.2210
Traditional cultures, and the impact of technological change. 3.210
The traditional history of the Jie of Uganda. 3.5263
Traditional India: structure and change. 3.4185
Traditional literatures of the American Indian. 2.2316
The traditional music of Japan. 1.3741
The traditional music of Thailand. 1.3746
The traditional theater of Japan. 2.3398
The traditional tunes of the Child ballads. 1.4344
Traditionalism, conservatism and British political culture. 4.8418
Traditions of American education. 4.9982
Traditions of civility. 3.37
The traditions of Islam. 1.2038
Traditions of Japanese art. 1.5077
Trafalgar. 3.1284
Traffic flow theory and control. 4.3925
Traffic planning and engineering. 4.3926
Traffic system analysis. 4.3930
La tragédie du roi Christophe. 2.4837
The tragedies. 2.6561
The tragedies of Ennius. 2.716
The tragedies of George Chapman. 2.6563
Tragedy. 2.2816
Tragedy and civilization. 2.550
Tragedy in Dedham. 4.9462
A tragedy in two acts. 2.8392
Tragedy is not enough. 1.1029
Tragedy, modern essays in criticism. 2.2817
The tragedy of American diplomacy. 3.7608
The tragedy of Arthur. 2.6422
The tragedy of Chile. 3.9266
The tragedy of Jane Shore. 2.7234
The tragedy of Lyndon Johnson. 3.7889
The tragedy of Master Arden of Faversham. 2.6679
The tragedy of Philotas. 2.6564
The tragedy of Sir John French. 3.803
The tragedy of the Chinese revolution. 3.4747
The tragedy of tragedies, or, The life and death of Tom Thumb the Great. 2.7022
The tragic actor. 2.3334
The tragic comedians: seven modern British novelists. 2.6038
The tragic conflict. 3.7312
The tragic finale. 1.494
Tragic ground. 2.11455
Tragic magic. 2.12926
Tragic muse. 1.3986
The tragic satire of John Webster. 2.6883
The tragic sense in Shakespeare. 2.6788
The Tragic sense of life in men and nations. 1.1134
A tragic vision. 2.10189
The tragical history of the life and death of Doctor Faustus. 2.6611
The tragicall history of Christopher Marlowe. 2.6613
Tragicomedy, its origin and development in Italy, France and England. 2.2819
La traición de Rita Hayworth. 2.5402
The trail of tears. 3.5800

Train. 2.13695
The train. 2.1591
Train whistle guitar. 2.13188
Training and development handbook. 4.4380
Training for the theatre. 2.3135
Traits and stories of the Irish peasantry.
    2.7540
Tramways and trolleys. 4.4023
Trance in Bali. 4.535
The trans-Appalachian frontier. 3.8377
Transactional analysis after Eric Berne. 5.4897
Transatlantic industrial revolution. 4.3844
Transatlantic revivalism. 1.3034
The transatlantic slave trade. 4.6422
The transcendence of the ego. 1.493
The transcendental masque; an essay on
    Milton's Comus. 2.7117
Transcendental number theory. 5.1346
Transcendentalism as a social movement,
    1830-1850. 1.568
Transcendentalism in New England. 1.565
The Transcendentalists. 5.8345
The transcendentalists. 1.567
Transcribing and editing oral history. 3.441
Transcultural health care. 5.4662
The transfer of care. 5.4698
The Transfer of power 1942-7. 3.4289
The Transfer of power in Africa. 3.5094
The transfer of power in India. 4.8697
The transfiguration of the commonplace.
    1.1354
Transfigurations. 1.5863
Transform methods. 5.5731
Transformation in metal. 5.6767
The transformation of American foreign
    relations, 1865-1900. 3.7417
The transformation of Europe, 1558-1648.
    3.631
The transformation of intellectual life in
    Victorian England. 3.1590
The transformation of political culture. 4.8191
The transformation of reform. 3.8435
The transformation of Russian society. 4.5370
The transformation of southern politics. 3.8170
The transformation of Spain. 3.3475
The transformation of the American economy,
    1865-1914. 4.1923
The transformation of the school. 4.9992
The transformation of Virginia, 1740-1790.
    3.8195
Transformation scene. 3.5652
Transformational syntax. 2.164
Transformations in late eighteenth century art.
    1.4774
Transformations in slavery. 4.6446
The transformations of man. 3.26
Transformations of the American party system.
    4.8158
Transforming traditional agriculture. 4.2886
Transhimalaya. 3.4857
Transistor circuit techniques. 5.6505
The transit of civilization from England to
    America in the seventeenth century. 3.6013
Transit systems theory. 5.5930
Transition and revolution. 1.2332
The transition from feudalism to capitalism.
    4.1545
Transitions. 4.556
Translated documents of Greece and Rome.
    3.2529
Translating literature. 2.2545
Translation. 2.5641
Translation & translators. 2.193
Translations. 2.3713
Translations from early Japanese literature.
    2.2030
Translations from the Chinese. 2.2196
Translations from the night. 2.4857
Translations from the philosophical writings of
    Gottlob Frege. 1.1209
Translations of Ezra Pound. 2.3713
Transmission electron microscopy of silicon
    VLSI circuits and structures. 5.6535
Transmission lines for communications. 5.6370
Transparent designs. 2.6060
Transparent minds. 2.3481
Transpersonal psychologies. 1.1569
Transplant. 5.4222

The transplanted. 3.6506
Transport and communication in early medieval
    Europe, A.D. 500-1100. 4.3874
Transport economics. 4.3899
Transport engineering economics. 5.5924
Transport investment and economic
    development. 4.3875
The transport of love. 2.1948
Transport processes and unit operations.
    5.6852
Transportation and behavior. 5.316
Transportation and economic development in
    Latin America. 4.3897
Transportation and town planning. 4.3927
Transportation and traffic engineering
    handbook. 4.3929
Transportation demand analysis. 4.3873
Transportation economic analysis. 4.3869
Transportation: economics and public policy.
    4.3888
Transportation energy and the future. 5.5925
Transportation engineering. 5.5927-5.5928
Transportation for cities. 4.3918
Transportation for the elderly. 4.5809
Transportation in America. 4.3881
The transportation revolution, 1815-1860.
    4.1876
Transportation through the ages. 4.3867
Transportation to the seaboard. 4.3884
Trauma and its wake. 5.4945
The Trauma of war. 5.4946
The travail of religious liberty. 1.3008
Travel and discovery in the Renaissance,
    1420-1620. 4.65
Travel and travellers of the Middle Ages. 4.62
The travel books. 2.9103
Travel in Asia. 5.8031
Travel index 1938-. 5.7143
Travel journal. 2.3991
Travel literature and the evolution of the novel.
    2.3451
The traveler in black. 2.9636
The Traveling salesman problem. 5.1278
A travelling woman. 2.9453
Travels and adventures in Canada and the
    Indian territories between the years 1760 and
    1764. 3.8434
The travels and adventures of Benjamin the
    Third. 2.1796
Travels between the Hudson & the Mississippi,
    1851-1852. 3.6044
Travels in Arabia Deserta. 3.4049
Travels in France during the years 1787, 1788
    & 1789. 3.1952
Travels in North America, 1822-1824. 3.8302
Travels in North-America [in the years 1780,
    1781, and 1782. 3.6021
Travels in the Mogul empire, A. D. 1656-1668.
    3.4256
Travels in the Old South, selected from
    periodicals of the times. 3.8150
The travels of an alchemist. 3.4617
The travels of Fa-hsien (399-414 A. D.).
    3.3612
Travels through the northwestern regions of the
    United States. 3.8378
Travels with my aunt. 2.8764
La traversée du pont des Arts. 2.4701
Travesties. 2.9817
Travesty. 2.13071
Trawthe and treason. 2.6415
Treacherous river. 3.4536
Treasure of the city of ladies. 1.1515
The treasure of the city of ladies, or, The book
    of the three virtues. 1.1515
Treasures among men. 3.4946
Treasures of ancient Nigeria. 1.5088
The treasures of darkness. 1.1841
Treasures of early Irish art, 1500 B.C. to 1500
    A.D. 1.4943
Treasures of Ireland. 1.4944
Treasures of Korean art. 1.6529
Treasures of the pharaohs. 1.4702
Treasures on the Tibetan middle way. 1.2171
Treasury control. 4.4671
Treasury of American design. 1.6515
A treasury of American folk humor. 2.10670
Treasury of American poetry. 2.10733

The Treasury of American short stories.
    2.10836
A treasury of Ben Hecht. 2.11822
Treasury of big game animals. 5.5491
A treasury of Damon Runyon. 2.12420
A treasury of early music. 1.3428
The Treasury of English poetry. 2.6096
The treasury of English short stories. 2.6266
A treasury of great American speeches.
    2.10854
A treasury of great poems, English and
    American. 2.6103
A treasury of great reporting. 2.3540
A treasury of great Russian short stories,
    Pushkin to Gorky. 2.1329
A treasury of Jewish letters. 3.3855
Treasury of Jewish quotations. 2.3735
A treasury of responsa. 1.1947
A treasury of Romanesque art. 1.5027
A treasury of Russian literature. 2.1299
A treasury of the theatre. 2.3770
Treasury of the world's great letters. 2.3782
A treasury of the world's great letters from
    ancient days to our own time. 2.3783
A treasury of Yiddish poetry. 2.1826
A treasury of Yiddish stories. 2.1824
Treat it gentle. 1.4080
Treaties and alliances of the world. 4.9299
Treaties, conventions, international acts,
    protocols and agreements between the United
    States of America and other powers ...
    4.8974
A treatise concerning the principles of human
    knowledge. 1.689
Treatise of civil government and A letter
    concerning toleration. 4.7412
A treatise of human nature. 1.700
Treatise of man. 5.4177
A treatise on advanced calculus. 5.1440
Treatise on analysis. 5.1439
Treatise on analytical chemistry. 5.2656
Treatise on architecture. 1.5414, 1.5467
A treatise on dinitrogen fixation, Section 3:
    Biology. 5.4457
A treatise on electricity and magnetism.
    5.2341
A treatise on induction and probability. 1.1189
Treatise on instrumentation, enl. and rev.
    1.4488
A treatise on limnology. 5.3260
Treatise on materials science and technology.
    5.5767
Treatise on painting. 1.6340
Treatise on physiological optics. 5.4379
A treatise on probability. 1.1231
Treatise on solid state chemistry. 5.2865
A treatise on the analytical dynamics of
    particles and rigid bodies. 5.1657
A treatise on the constitutional limitations.
    4.9646
Treatise on the dental art founded on actual
    experience. 5.5122
Treatise on the fugue. 1.4480
A treatise on the fundamental principles of
    violin playing. 1.4546
Treatise on the gods. 1.1534
Treatise on the love of God. 1.3217
A treatise on the novel. 2.3415
Treatises on marriage and remarriage: To his
    wife, An exhortation to chastity, Monogamy.
    1.2186
Treatment and disposal of wastewater sludges.
    5.6034
Treatment in crisis situations. 5.4871
Treatment of Palestinians in Israeli-occupied
    West Bank and Gaza. 3.3876
The treatment of Shakespeare's text by his
    earlier editors, 1709-1768. 2.6840
The Treaty of Versailles and after. 3.849
The Treaty of Washington, 1871. 3.8762
The tree. 2.9690
The tree climber. 2.1846
A tree grows in Brooklyn. 2.12487
The tree of culture. 4.436
The tree of man. 2.10184
A tree of night. 2.11467
The tree of the sun. 2.10032
The trees. 2.12389

Trees. 5.3683
Trees of North America. 5.3685
Trees of the world. 5.3681
Trees on the mountain. 2.2183
Treitschke's history of Germany in the nineteenth century. 3.2294
The trembling of the veil. 2.8340
A tremor in the blood. 4.6811
Trench warfare, 1914-1918. 3.789
Trends and structure in contemporary Thai poetry. 2.2258
Trends and variations in fertility in the United States. 4.1643
Trends in British society since 1900. 4.5322
Trends in financial indicators of colleges and universities. 4.10602
Trends in genetic analysis. 5.3436
Trends in Indonesia, II. 3.4576
Trends in modern American society. 3.6145
Trends in natural resource commodities. 4.4130
Trends in the American economy in the nineteenth century. 4.1951
Trent's case book [comprising] Trent's last case, Trent's own case. 2.8461
Trent's last case. 2.8460
Tres comedias: Sin querer, De pequeñas causas, Los intereses creados. 2.5234
Très riches heures du duc de Berry. 1.6428
The Très riches heures of Jean, Duke of Berry. 1.6428
Tres tristes tigres. 2.5358
The Tretyakov Gallery, Moscow. 1.6278
Tri-quarterly. 2.1296
The triad of genius. 2.9337
The trial. 2.13791
The trial begins. 2.1606
Trial by television. 5.7352
The trial of Callista Blake. 2.13236
The trial of Dr. Spock. 4.9465
The trial of Jesus of Nazareth. 1.2896
The trial of Lady Chatterley. 2.8968
The trial of Peter Zenger. 4.9456
Trial of the major war criminals before the International Military Tribunal, Nuremberg, 14 November 1945-1 October 1946. 3.1073
Trials of the word. 2.10243
Le triangle noir. 2.4076
Tribalism in crisis. 3.5798
Tribe, caste, and nation. 3.4351
Tribes of India. 4.634
The tribes of Yahweh. 1.2587
Tribes without rulers. 4.604
The trickster. 3.5959
Trigonometric series. 5.1558
Trilby. 2.7684
Trillion year spree. 2.5977
Trilogy. 2.11573
The Trinitarian controversy. 1.2835
The Trinity and the kingdom. 1.2838
Tripitaka. Sūtrapiṭaka. Laṅkāvatārasūtra. 1.2128
Tripitaka. Sūtrapiṭaka. Prajñāpāramitā. Pañcaviṃśatisāhasrikā. 1.2131
Tripitaka. Sūtrapiṭaka. Prajñāpāramitā. Vajracchedikā. English. 1965. 1.1737
Tripitaka. Sūtrapiṭaka. Saddharmapuṇḍarīkasūtra. 1.2133
Tripitaka. Sūtrapiṭaka. Saddharmapuṇḍarīkasūtra. English. 1.2134
Tripitaka. Vinayapiṭaka. Pratimokṣasūtra. English. 1.2137
Triple alliance and triple entente. 3.722
The triple demism of Sun Yat-sen. 3.4760
Triple pursuit. 2.8763
The triple stream. 2.2611
Triptych. 2.1694
Tristan und Isold. 2.13529
Tristes tropiques. 3.9201
Tristia. 2.682
Tristram Shandy. 2.7277
Triumph in the west. 3.899
The triumph of American capitalism. 4.1887
The triumph of American painting. 1.5911
The Triumph of art for the public. 1.4793
The triumph of conservatism. 4.1938
Triumph of freedom, 1775-1783. 3.6901

The triumph of grace in the theology of Karl Barth. 1.3283
The triumph of relevance. 2.4055
The triumph of science and reason, 1660-1685. 3.642
The triumph of sectionalism. 3.8383
The triumph of the egg. 2.11321
The triumph of the English language. 2.966
Triumph of the intelligent. 4.451
The triumph of the middle classes. 4.1758
The triumph of the novel. 2.3508
The triumph of the spider monkey. 2.13202
The triumphs of Petrarch. 2.4949
The Triune God. 1.2833
The triune identity. 1.2837
Troades. 2.462
Troilus and Cressida. 2.6333
Troilus and Criseyde. 2.6332, 2.6335
Troilus and Criseyde and selected short poems. 2.6334
Trois contes. 2.4193
Les trois mousquetaires. 2.4174
The troll garden. 2.11473
Trollope. 2.8234
Trollope, his life and art. 2.8235
Trollope: the critical heritage. 2.8241
The Trollopes. 2.8236
The trombone. 1.4176
Trope and allegory. 2.6730
Les trophées. 2.4232
Tropic of Cancer. 2.12185
Tropic of Capricorn. 2.12186
Tropica. 5.5348
Tropical Africa. 3.5227
Tropical geomorphology. 4.264
The tropical rain forest. 5.3784
Tropical rain forest ecosystems. 5.3557
Tropical rain forests of the Far East. 5.3279
Tropical savannas. 5.3556
The tropical world. 4.110
The tropics. 5.3242
The tropics and economic development. 4.2599
Tropisms. 2.4712
Tropisms, and The age of suspicion. 2.4713
Trotula. 5.5044
Troubadour. 2.11967
The troubadours. 2.883
Trouble in July. 2.11456
The trouble makers. 3.1249
The Trouble with technology. 5.5637
Troubled children/troubled systems. 4.10942
The troubled crusade. 4.9999
The troubled encounter: the United States and Japan. 3.6464
The troubled farmer, 1850-1900. 5.5236
The troubled giant. 3.1690
Troubled journey. 3.7514
The troubled partnership. 3.1176
Troubled sleep. 2.4735
Troubleshooting electronic equipment without service data. 5.6483
The troublesome helpmate. 2.2411
Trouser Press guide to new wave records. 1.3620
Trout fishing in America. 2.11413
Troy and the Trojans. 3.2595
The truants. 3.8041
Truants from life. 5.5097
Trudeau. 3.8793
Trudeau and foreign policy. 3.8785
Trudeau in power. 3.8784
True BASIC reference manual. 5.1210
The true believer. 4.5045
True Christianity. 1.3056
The true confessions of an albino terrorist. 2.13963
True love and perfect union. 4.6014
The Truman administration. 3.7791
The Truman administration, its principles and practice. 3.7804
Truman, American Jewry, and Israel, 1945-1948. 3.4018
Truman and Taft-Hartley. 4.3570
Truman and the steel seizure case. 4.9740
Truman Capote. 2.11469
The Truman Doctrine and the origins of McCarthyism. 3.7795

The Truman-MacArthur controversy and the Korean War. 3.5031
The Truman Presidency. 3.7801
The Truman scandals and the politics of morality. 3.7810
Truman, the Jewish vote, and the creation of Israel. 3.6455
The trumpet and trombone. 1.4174
The trumpet shall sound. 1.1880
The trumpet soundeth. 3.7429
Trumpet technique. 1.4560
'Trust to good verses' 2.7075
The truth about the trusts. 4.3050
Truth and art. 1.1374
Truth and consequence in mediaeval logic. 1.1235
Truth and method. 1.1306
Truth and other enigmas. 1.84
Truth and vision in Katherine Anne Porter's fiction. 2.12321
Truth, freedom, and evil. 1.380
Truth, probability and paradox. 1.1234
Truth; translated from the definitive Leonine text. 1.1275
The truthful lens. 5.7011
Truthfulness and tragedy. 1.1474
Ts'ao Yin and the K'ang-hsi Emperor. 3.4720
Tsar Nicholas I and the Jews. 3.3995
Tsarist Russia and Balkan nationalism. 3.3069
The Tsungli yamen. 4.9102
Tu Fu, China's greatest poet. 2.2214
The Tuareg. 3.5205
The tuba family. 1.4177
Tucson, the life and times of an American city. 3.8580
Tudor and Stuart Ireland. 3.1829
Tudor church music. 1.4240
The Tudor constitution. 4.8395
Tudor Cornwall. 3.1735
Tudor dynastic problems, 1460-1571. 3.1390
Tudor economic documents. 4.2244
Tudor England. 3.1386
Tudor foreign policy. 3.1387
Tudor geography, 1485-1583. 4.67
The Tudor interlude. 2.3289
Tudor Ireland. 3.1828
Tudor plays. 2.6216
Tudor poetry and prose. 2.6082
The Tudor regime. 4.8396
The Tudor revolution in government. 4.8397
Tudor to Augustan English. 2.942
Tudor women. 4.6097
Tuition tax credits for private education. 4.4714
Tulapai to Tokay. 5.7739
Tulsa race riot of 1921. 3.8539
Tumultuous years. 3.7794
Tundra ecosystems. 5.3570
Tune in yesterday. 2.2845
El tunel. 2.5399
The túngara frog. 5.3932
Tuning and temperament. 1.4379
The tuning of the world. 1.4376
Tunisia. 3.5203
The tunnel of love. 2.11564
The turbulent era. 4.6725
Turbulent flows in engineering. 5.5751
Turbulent years. 4.3566
Turgenev. 2.1464-2.1465
Turgenev, his life and times. 2.1463
Turgot and the ancien régime in France. 3.2056
Turkey, a country study. 3.3569
Turkey: an introductory geography. 3.3568
Turkey in Europe. 3.3573
Turkey in the world capitalist system. 4.2569
Turkey, the great powers, and the Bagdad railway. 3.762
Turkey, the politics of authority, democracy, and development. 4.8772
Turkey's political crisis. 3.3593
The Turkish experiment in democracy, 1950-1975. 3.3592
Turkish grammar. 2.1980
Turkish nationalism and Western civilization. 3.3570
Turkmenia before the Achaemenids. 4.741
The turmoil. 2.11238

Turmoil and tradition. 3.7688
Turn again Tiger. 2.10018
The turn of the screw. 2.11110
The turn of the tide. 3.975
Turner. 1.6041-1.6042
Turner and Beard. 3.6273
Turner and the sociology of the frontier. 3.6350
Turner: Rain, steam, and speed. 1.6040
The Turner thesis concerning the role of the frontier in American history. 3.6360
The turning point. 3.924, 5.872
Turning point in China. 3.4791
Turning points in American electrical history. 5.6252
Turning points of the Civil War. 3.7400
Turtle Island. 2.13328
Turtles of the United States. 5.3925
Tuscans and their families. 4.2359
Tusculan disputations. 2.670
Tutira. 5.3282
Tutorial. 5.6543
Tutorial, computer graphics. 5.5653
Tutorial essays in psychology. 5.8
Tutorial on robotics. 5.6173
Tutorial supercomputers. 5.1155, 5.6542
Tutte le commedie. 2.4956
Tutte le opere. 2.4914
Tutte le opere di Carlo Goldoni. 2.4991
Tutte le opere di Matteo M. Boiardo. 2.4965
Tutte le poesie. 2.5062
TV facts. 2.2849
TV genres. 2.2854
TV movies and video guide. 2.3077
TVA. 5.6303
TVA and the grass roots. 4.3805
Twelfth-century Europe and the foundations of modern society. 3.146
Twelve African writers. 2.2302
Twelve against empire. 3.7498
The twelve chairs. 2.1565
Twelve contemporary economists. 4.1320
Twelve doors to Japan. 3.4873
Twelve famous plays of the restoration and eighteenth century. 2.6229
Twelve modern French Canadian poets. 2.4808
Twelve modern Scottish poets. 2.9845
Twelve more modern Scottish poets. 2.9847
Twelve original essays on great English novels. 2.5951
The twelve patriarchs; The mystical ark; Book three of The Trinity. 1.3090
Twelve photographers of the American social landscape. 3.6063
Twelve thousand words. 2.1093
Twelve to sixteen. 4.5757
Twelve-tone tonality. 1.4452
Twelve who ruled. 3.2108
The twelve words of the Gypsy. 2.605
The twenties. 2.10410
The twenties; American writing in the postwar decade. 2.10414
The twentieth century. 2.5110, 3.192, 3.199
Twentieth-century American foreign policy. 3.7605
Twentieth-century American historians. 3.6233
Twentieth century American literary naturalism. 2.10558
Twentieth century American nicknames. 3.326
Twentieth-century architecture. 1.5274
Twentieth century authors. 2.2681
The Twentieth century biographical dictionary of notable Americans. 3.6287
Twentieth century British jewellery, 1900-1980. 1.6664
The twentieth century, c. 1900 to c. 1950. 5.5532
Twentieth-century Chinese drama. 2.2198
Twentieth century Chinese poetry. 2.2191
Twentieth century Chinese stories. 2.2202
Twentieth century church music. 1.4249
Twentieth-century crime and mystery writers. 2.6051
Twentieth century encyclopedia of religious knowledge. 1.2223
Twentieth-century French drama. 2.3937
Twentieth-century French literature. 2.3869
Twentieth-century French poetry. 2.3927

Twentieth-century Germany: from Bismarck to Brandt. 3.2359
Twentieth-century harmony. 1.4466
Twentieth century interpretations of 1984. 2.9183
Twentieth century interpretations of All the king's men. 2.12635
Twentieth century interpretations of Billy Budd. 2.11151
Twentieth century interpretations of Crime and punishment. 2.1345
Twentieth century interpretations of Death of a salesman. 2.12170
Twentieth century interpretations of Invisible man. 2.13005
Twentieth century interpretations of Moby-Dick. 2.11158
Twentieth century interpretations of Native son. 2.12812
Twentieth century interpretations of Poe's tales. 2.11209
Twentieth century interpretations of Sanctuary. 2.11676
Twentieth century interpretations of The ambassadors. 2.11106
Twentieth century interpretations of The crucible. 2.12168
Twentieth century interpretations of The fall of the house of Usher. 2.11198
Twentieth century interpretations of The portrait of a lady. 2.11108
Twentieth century interpretations of The scarlet letter. 2.11061
Twentieth century interpretations of The turn of the screw, and other tales. 2.11128
Twentieth century interpretations of Walden. 2.11247
Twentieth-century Italian poetry. 2.4893
Twentieth-century literary criticism. 2.2676
Twentieth century literature. 5.8278
Twentieth-century Montana. 3.8547
Twentieth century music. 1.3678
Twentieth century music. 1.3682
Twentieth-century music idioms. 1.4431
The twentieth century novel. 2.3523
Twentieth-century pacifism. 4.9118
Twentieth-century pessimism and the American dream. 3.6143
Twentieth-century Pittsburgh. 4.6327
Twentieth century pleasures. 2.2767
Twentieth-century Polish avant-garde drama. 2.1748
Twentieth-century poster. 1.5857
Twentieth-century religious thought. 1.456
Twentieth-century Richmond. 4.6328
Twentieth century Rumania. 3.3549
Twentieth century Russia. 3.3138
Twentieth-century Russian drama. 2.1281
Twentieth-century Russian literary criticism. 2.1243
Twentieth-century short story explication. 5.8180
Twentieth-century women novelists. 2.6059
Twenty best European plays on the American stage. 2.3771
Twenty best plays of the modern American theatre. 2.10793
Twenty contemporary Norwegian poets. 2.14032
The Twenty-fifth Congress of the CPSU. 4.8656
Twenty-five-year war. 3.4502
Twenty-five years of economic development, 1950 to 1975. 4.1814
Twenty-five years of world shipping. 4.3959
Twenty-one stories. 2.1781
Twenty thousand leagues under the sea. 2.4325
Twenty thousand plus words. 2.1028
Twenty-two unpublished letters of Elizabeth Barrett Browning and Robert Browning. 2.7467
Twenty years after. 2.4177
Twenty years at Hull-house. 4.6627
The twenty years' crisis, 1919-1939. 4.9011, 4.9274
Twenty years later. 4.5744
The twice-born. 3.4165

The Twickenham edition of the poems of Alexander Pope. 2.7186
Twilight in Delhi. 2.1906
The twilight of capitalism. 4.6954
The twilight of federalism. 3.7077
The twilight of France, 1933-1940. 3.2207
Twilight of the gods. 1.4099
Twilight of the Mughuls. 3.4254
The twilight of the Presidency. 4.7931
The twilight years. 2.2128
Twins. 5.618
The twisted dream: capitalist development in the United States since 1776. 4.1873
Two adolescents. 2.5044
Two African statesmen. 3.5526
Two ages. 2.14015
Two-bit culture. 5.7595
Two blades of grass. 5.5217
Two-block fox. 5.7444
Two captains. 2.1569
The two-career family. 4.5575
Two centuries of American medicine, 1776-1976. 5.4520
Two centuries of Black American art. 1.4910
Two centuries of Russian verse. 2.1316
Two cheers for capitalism. 4.3052
Two cheers for democracy. 2.8653
Two citizens. 2.12806
Two comedies. 2.7008
Two Crows denies it. 3.5930
Two cultures? 1.78
The two cultures; and, A second look. 1.77
Two cultures of policing. 4.6834
The two deaths of Christopher Martin. 2.8707
Two-dimensional world. 5.1639
Two dramas. 2.4472
Two Dreisers. 2.11604
Two early Tudor lives. 3.1413
The two faces of chemistry. 5.6817
Two faces of Eve. 2.1912
The two faces of TASS. 2.3695
Two French moralists. 2.4036
The two horizons. 1.2520
Two hundred fifty years of Afro-American art. 5.8190
Two hundred years of American educational thought. 4.9986
Two hundred years of geology in America. 5.2956
Two Jamaicas. 4.5263
Two Japanese novelists. 2.2088
The Two Koreas in East Asian affairs. 3.5011
The two lives of Edith Wharton. 2.12700
Two minutes of silence. 2.14022
Two nations, many cultures. 3.8794
Two nations over time. 3.6496
Two new sciences, including centers of gravity & force of percussion. 5.2028
The two ocean war. 3.1033
Two of the Saxon chronicles parallel. 3.1311
Two-part inventions. 2.13093
Two-part prelude. 2.8302
The two-party South. 3.8172
Two paychecks. 4.5602
Two-phase flow and heat transfer. 5.5752
Two-phase flows in chemical engineering. 5.6842
Two plays. 2.587
Two plays of ancient India. 2.1952
The two revolutions. 4.7082
The two rival brothers. 2.4976
Two roads to Sumter. 3.7303
The two Rosetos. 3.8096
Two serious ladies. 2.11401
The two sources of morality and religion. 1.827
Two Spanish masterpieces. 2.5202
Two symphonies. 2.4556
Two Tahitian villages. 4.687
Two thousand books and more. 5.8236
The two towers. 2.9432
Two tracts on civil liberty, the war with America, the debts and finances of the kingdom. 3.6924
Two treatises of government. 4.7411
Two types of faith. 1.1954
The two Viet-Nams. 3.4473
Two villages on stilts. 4.5473

Two virgins. 2.10127
The two wheels of dhamma. 1.2108
Two worlds and their ways. 2.8531
Two worlds of Andrew Wyeth. 1.5990
The two worlds of William March. 2.11462
Two writers and the cultural revolution.
  2.2250
The two-year college. 4.10557
The two Yemens. 3.4062
The Twyborn affair. 2.10185
Tynan right & left. 2.2476
Types of modern theology. 1.2757
Types of philosophy. 1.1258
Types of religious philosophy. 1.1544
The types of the folktale. 4.818
The tyranny of distance. 3.5566
Tzintzuntzan. 4.5257

U.B. Phillips, a southern mind. 3.6262
U-boats against Canada. 3.1039
U-boats under the Swastika. 5.7441
U.D.I.; the international politics of the
  Rhodesian rebellion. 3.5514
U.F.O.s. 5.6699
U.N.I.X. for people. 5.1164
U.N.I.X. programming environment. 5.1184
U.N.O. and war crimes. 4.9342
U Nu of Burma. 3.4341
U. S. A. 2.11586
U.S. aircraft carriers. 5.7443
The U.S. airline industry. 4.4085
U.S. Army in Vietnam. 3.4468
The U.S. coal industry. 4.3747
The U. S. Coast Guard in World War II.
  3.1034
The U.S. crusade in China, 1938-1945. 3.6431
U.S. defense policy. 5.7264
U.S. economic policy toward the Association of
  Southeast Asian Nations. 4.4175
The U.S. economy demystified. 4.1995
The U.S. economy in the 1950's. 4.1996
U.S. energy policy. 4.3713
U.S. foreign assistance. 4.1835
U. S. foreign policy. 3.7584
U.S. foreign policy and Asian-Pacific security.
  3.3634
U.S. foreign policy and multilateral
  development banks. 4.4577
U.S. foreign relations. 5.8265
The U.S. Forest Service. 5.5438
U.S. Government serials & periodicals. 5.7776
U.S. Grant and the American military tradition.
  3.7479
U. S. iana, 1650-1950: compiled by Wright
  Howes. 5.7754
U.S. immigration and refugee policy. 4.8949
U.S. income and output. 4.2081
U.S. intelligence and the Soviet strategic threat.
  5.7362
The U.S. intelligence community. 4.7913
U.S. international monetary policy. 4.4574
U.S. Marine operations in Korea, 1950-1953.
  3.5026
The U.S. merchant marine. 4.3976
The U.S. Navy. 5.7448
U.S. occupation in Europe after World War II.
  3.2456
U.S. policy toward Japan and Korea. 3.6462
U.S. policy toward Korea. 4.9061
U.S. power and the multinational corporation.
  4.4172
U.S.S.R. and the Muslim world. 3.3324
The U.S.S.R. in maps. 4.175
U.S.S.R. in Third World conflicts. 5.7327
U.S. Senators and their world. 4.8042
U.S. television network news. 5.8324
U.S., the U.N., and the management of global
  change. 4.9229
UBC 85. 4.9762
Über die Linie. English. 1.989
Über Gewissheit. 1.1071
The ubiquitous atom. 5.2431
The Ubu plays. 2.4592
The UFO controversy in America. 5.6696
The UFO enigma. 5.6698
The UFO experience. 5.6695
UFOs. 5.6697
UFO's 5.6693

Ugetsu monogatari. 2.2068
The ugly American. 2.11994
Uhuru na umoja. 3.5298
Uhuru's fire. 2.10036
The Uighur Empire according to the T'ang
  dynastic histories. 3.4655
Ujamaa 4.7133
Uji shūi monogatari. English. 1970. 2.2057
Ukiyo-e painting. 1.6481
The Ukraine. 3.3301
Ukrainian nationalism. 3.3303
Ulrich's international periodicals directory.
  5.8314
Ulrich's periodicals directory 1943-62. 5.8314
The Ulster crisis. 3.1873
The ultimate foundation of economic science.
  4.1487
The ultimate resource. 4.1601
Ultime lettere di Jacopo Ortis. 2.4990
Ultra in the West. 3.960
Ultramarine. 2.9057
Ultrasonic communication by animals. 5.4097
Ultrasonic transducers for nondestructive
  testing. 5.5788
Ultraviolet spectroscopy. 5.2675
Ulysses. 2.8880-2.8881, 2.8894
Ulysses: fifty years. 2.8899
Ulysses in progress. 2.8890
Ulysses on the Liffey. 2.8887
The Ulysses theme. 2.2419
The UN Secretary-General and the maintenance
  of peace. 4.9245
Unabridged rhyming dictionary. 2.1050
An unabridged translation of Simplicius
  simplicissimus. 2.13544
Unaccountable accounting. 4.4388
The unadjusted girl. 4.6694
Unamuno. 1.1135
Unarmed victory. 3.1175
Unassigned frequencies. 2.10510
The Unavoidable issue. 4.8951
The unbearable lightness of being. 2.1691
Unbought and unbossed. 3.7856
The unbound Prometheus. 4.2201
The Unbroken chain. 2.2208
Uncensored Russia: protest and dissent in the
  Soviet Union. 3.3258
Uncertain futures. 4.1221
Uncertain greatness. 3.7902
Uncertain mandate; politics of the U.N. Congo
  operation. 4.9234
An uncertain tradition. 3.7575
The uncertain trumpet. 5.7281
Uncertainties and other poems. 2.9241
Uncertainty and structure as psychological
  concepts. 5.25
The unchaste. 2.2270
The uncivil wars. 3.1860
The unclassed. 2.7738
Uncle Fred in the springtime. 2.9558
Uncle Sam's acres. 4.2824
Uncle Sam's farmers. 4.2818
Uncle Tom's cabin. 2.11231
Uncle Tom's cabin and American culture.
  2.11230
Uncle Tom's campus. 4.10858
Uncle Tom's children. 2.12814
An uncommon man. 3.7748
The uncompleted past. 2.13507
Unconditional surrender. 3.1142
Unconventional methods in exploration for
  petroleum and natural gas II. 5.6744
The undecided college student. 4.10605
Under a colored cap: articles merry and
  mournful with comments and a song. 2.9151
Under a glass bell. 2.12252
Under milk wood. 2.9411
Under plain cover. 2.9212
Under siege. 2.5742
Under the bo tree. 3.4365
Under the ivi tree. 4.2598
Under the microscope. 5.3287
Under the mountain wall. 3.5669
Under the net. 2.9767
Under the sidewalks of New York. 5.6075
Under the sun of Satan. 2.4414
Under the volcano. 2.9058
Under the yoke. 2.1204

The underachieving school. 4.10036
The underclass. 4.6619
Underdeveloped Europe. 4.2215
Underdevelopment in Kenya. 4.2586
The underdogs. 2.5334
Undergraduate analysis. 5.1442
The undergraduate curriculum. 4.10590
Underground film. 2.2988
The underground press in America. 2.3654
The underground woman. 2.11406
Understanding abusive families. 4.6556
Understanding African poetry. 2.10039
Understanding aircraft structures. 5.6670
Understanding arguments. 1.1162
Understanding culture. 4.478
Understanding digital electronics. 5.6586
Understanding education. 4.10283
Understanding Europe. 3.91
Understanding fiction. 2.3426
Understanding gliding. 5.6687
Understanding group behavior of boys and
  girls. 4.10376
Understanding history. 3.389
Understanding human sexuality. 4.5487
Understanding imperial Russia. 3.3091
Understanding intergovernmental relations.
  4.4664
Understanding Locke. 1.675
Understanding media. 2.51
Understanding mental retardation. 5.4979
Understanding mysticism. 1.1632
Understanding nutrition. 5.4242
The understanding of the brain. 5.4331
Understanding poetry. 2.6071
Understanding productivity. 4.2683
Understanding psychological research. 5.66
Understanding Rawls. 4.7660
Understanding school boards. 4.10667
Understanding social anthropology. 4.483
Understanding social life. 4.1212
Understanding the atom. 5.2431
Understanding the environment. 4.1851
Understanding the Greek Orthodox church.
  1.3108
Understanding the new Black poetry. 2.10753
Understanding the new religions. 1.1876
Understanding the New Testament. 1.2658
Understanding the Old Testament. 1.2580
Understanding the primary curriculum.
  4.10430
Understanding the rape victim. 4.6734
Understanding the Scottish economy. 4.2300
Understanding Toscanini. 1.4104
Understanding understanding. 5.312
Understanding Whitehead. 1.781
Understanding women. 5.4891
Underwater minerals. 5.6735
The undiscovered continent. 2.11003
Unearthing China's past. 1.5063
The uneasy case for progressive taxation.
  4.4693
The uneasy chair. 2.11560
Uneasy partnership. 4.4217
The uneasy state. 3.7509
Unelected representatives. 4.8030
Unemployment. 4.3192
Unemployment and technical innovation.
  4.1862
Unemployment in history. 4.3193
Unemployment in the UK. 4.3228
Unemployment in Western countries. 4.3202
Unemployment insurance in the American
  economy. 4.3448
Unequal development. 4.1516
Unesco annuaire statistique. 1.79
Unesco statistical yearbook. 1.79
Unfair arguments with existence. 2.11717
Unfinished business. 5.4817
The unfinished quest of Richard Wright.
  2.12817
Unfinished rebellions. 4.10988
The unfinished revolution. 4.6940
An unfinished woman. 2.11833
Unfit for modest ears. 4.5549
The unfolding of Neo-Confucianism. 1.160
The unfortunate traveller. 2.6643
The unfulfill'd queen. 2.9744
Unfulfilled union. 4.8280

Das ungezwungne Leben Kasts. 2.13883
The ungovernable city. 4.8849
Unhappy families. 4.5781
The unhappy medium. 5.660
The UNIA and Black Los Angeles. 3.8623
The unicorn. 2.9769
The Unicorn. 2.13913
The unicorn tapestries. 1.6592
The unification of Greece, 1770-1923. 3.2690
A unified introduction to mathematical economics. 4.1386
Unified numbering system for metals and alloys. 5.5814
Uniform building code. 4.9762
Uniform crime reports for the United States. 4.6765
The uniform of colour. 3.5529
Uniform system of citation. 4.9472
The unimpressible race. 4.10884
The union and the coal industry. 4.3390
The Union cavalry in the Civil War. 3.7384
The union challenge to management control. 4.3178
Union list of newspapers. 5.8318
Union list of serials in libraries of the United States and Canada. 5.8319
Union-management cooperation. 4.3338
The Union nationale. 3.8687, 4.8316
Union now. 4.9139
Union of South Africa. 4.190
The union of the Canadas; the growth of Canadian Institutions, 1841-1857. 3.8721
Union organizing. 4.3339
Union Pacific country. 4.4011
The Union Pacific Railroad. 4.4013
Union policies and industrial management. 4.3369
Union policy and the older worker. 4.3311
Union power and public policy. 4.9554
Union printers and controlled automation. 5.7558
Union Square. 2.3203
Union violence. 4.9560
Unionism and relative wages in the United States. 4.3144
Unions and economic crisis. 4.3413
Unions and public schools. 4.10686
The unions and the cities. 4.3513
Unions and union leadership: their human meaning. 4.3345
Unions in crisis and beyond. 4.3372
Unions, management, and the public. 4.3343
Unions, wages, and inflation. 4.3146
The uniqueness of the individual. 5.3304
Unit operations in resource recovery engineering. 5.6038
Unit planning: a model for curriculum development. 4.10445
Unit processes of extractive metallurgy. 5.6763
The Unitarians and the universalists. 1.3415
Unitary group representations in physics, probability, and number theory. 5.1302
Unitary symmetry and elementary particles. 5.2472
United Artists. 2.3079
The United Brotherhood of Carpenters. 4.3380
United Europe; challenge and opportunity. 3.1201
United Kingdom facts. 4.8416
The United Media Enterprises report on leisure in America. 4.883
The United Nations. 4.9206
The United Nations and promotion of the general welfare. 4.9205
The United Nations and the control of international violence. 4.9222
The United Nations and the population question, 1945-1970. 4.5682
The United Nations & the superpowers. 4.9242
The United Nations and the superpowers. 4.9227
The United Nations as a political institution. 4.9223
United Nations Convention on the Law of the Sea (1982). 1983. 4.9316
The United Nations Emergency Force. 4.9258

The United Nations in a changing world. 4.9217
The United Nations in Bangladesh. 4.9233
United Nations International Comparison Project. 4.1401
United Nations law. 4.9226
United Nations peacekeeping, 1946-1967. 4.9254
United Nations yearbook. 4.9202
The United States. 3.6329
The United States, 1830-1850. 3.7083
The United States and Africa. 5.8075
The United States and Britain. 3.6448
The United States and Canada. 4.152
The United States and China. 3.4666
The United States and Germany. 3.6445
The United States and India. 3.6450
The United States and India, Pakistan, Bangladesh. 3.4290
The United States and Israel. 3.6454
The United States and Italy. 3.2907
The United States and Japan. 3.6466
The United States and Latin America. 3.9015
The United States and Latin American wars, 1932-1942. 3.9162
The United States and Mexico. 3.8916
United States and N.A.T.O. 4.9019
United States and NATO. 4.9019
The United States and Pakistan. 3.6475
The United States and Poland. 3.6478
The United States and revolutionary nationalism in Mexico, 1916-1932. 4.4181
The United States and sub-Saharan Africa. 5.8076
The United States and the Berlin Blockade, 1948-1949. 3.2502
The United States and the Far Eastern crisis of 1933-1938. 3.4850
The United States and the Greek War for Independence, 1821-1828. 3.2696
The United States and the Hawaiian Kingdom. 3.6449
The United States and the independence of Latin America, 1800-1830. 3.9021
The United States and the League of Nations, 1918-1920. 4.9183
The United States and the origins of the cold war, 1941-1947. 3.7571
The United States and the Philippines. 3.6477
The United States and the Republic of Korea. 3.6469
The United States and the Second Hague Peace Conference. 4.9106
The United States and the southern cone. 3.9163
The United States and the Southwest Pacific. 3.5552
The United States and the Trujillo regime. 3.6441
The United States and the unity of Europe. 3.1205
The United States and world organization, 1920-1933. 4.9194
The United States and World War II. 3.1022
The United States Army and Reconstruction, 1865-1877. 3.7471
United States Army in the Korean War 3.5024
United States Army in Vietnam. Advice and support. 3.4468
United States Army in World War II. 3.1020
United States Army in World War II. Master index. 3.1021
The United States as seen by Spanish American writers, 1776-1890. 3.9016
The United States catalog. 5.7762
United States catalogue; books in print. Supplement. 5.7765
United States-Comanche relations. 3.5862
The United States Congress. 4.8013
The United States Congressional Directories, 1789-1840. 4.7994
United States congressional districts, 1788-1841. 4.149
United States diplomatic codes and ciphers, 1775-1938. 5.7531
United States economy demystified. 4.1995
The United States energy atlas. 5.6143

United States foreign oil policy, 1919-1948. 4.3775
United States foreign policy and Asian-Pacific security. 3.3634
United States foreign policy and multilateral development banks. 4.4577
The United States government manual. 4.7886
The United States government manual (Washington, D.C.: 1973) 4.7886
United States in a chaotic world. 3.7590
The United States in the Middle East, interests and obstacles. 3.3758
The United States in the world arena. 3.7513
The United States in world affairs. 4.152
The United States in World War I. 5.8229
United States Japan Expedition. 3.4880
United States-Japanese political relations: the critical issues affecting Asia's future. 3.6468
United States-Japanese relations, the 1970's. 3.6458
United States-Latin American relations. 3.9020
United States law and the Armed Forces. 4.9770
United States local histories in the Library of Congress. 5.7852
The United States Marines, 1775-1975. 5.7477
United States merchant marine. 4.3976
United States/Middle East diplomatic relations, 1784-1978. 5.8040
United States music. 1.3561
United States naval administration of the Trust Territory of the Pacific Islands. 4.8830
United States naval aviation, 1910-1980. 5.7483
The United States Navy and Coast Guard, 1946-1983. 5.7845
The United States Navy and defense unification, 1947-1953. 5.7450
The United States Navy and the Vietnam conflict. 3.4507
The United States Navy in the Pacific, 1897-1909. 3.6375
The United States occupation of Haiti, 1915-1934. 3.9120
The United States of America, a syllabus of American studies. 3.6105
The United States of America v. one book entitled Ulysses by James Joyce. 4.9460
United States relations with China. 3.6436
The United States since 1865. 3.6320
The United States Strategic Bombing Survey. 3.1043
United States Supreme Court decisions. 4.9441
United States Supreme Court reports. 4.9440
United States Supreme Court reports. Lawyers' edition. 4.9440
The United States, the United Nations, and human rights. 4.9384
United States v. Nixon. 4.9638
Units of measurement. 5.2022
Unity in diversity. 5.8355
Unity in Shakespearian tragedy. 2.6792
Unity of forces in the universe. 5.2484
The unity of Homer. 2.504
The unity of mankind in Greek thought. 1.229
The unity of Plato's thought. 1.266
The unity of the Catholic Church. 1.2191
Unity of the churches 1.3100
The unity of the senses. 5.240
Unity of the stream. 2.9477
Universal algebra. 5.1359
Universal fascism. 3.2886
Universal higher education: costs, benefits, options. 4.10089
The universal human and Soul-body interaction. 1.3385
The Universal Jewish encyclopedia. 3.3811
Universal joint and driveshaft design manual. 5.6241
The universal penman. 5.7523
The universal self. 2.4769
Universality in chaos. 5.2170
Universals and scientific realism. 1.145
The universe. 5.1712
Universe. 5.1703
The Universe of galaxies. 5.1856
The universe within. 5.267
Universities in the urban crisis. 4.10804

The universities of Europe in the Middle Ages. 4.9975
University astronomy. 5.1705
University drama in the Tudor Age. 2.5861
The University in society. 4.9976
The University of Cambridge. 4.11008
The University of Chicago Spanish dictionary. 2.902
The university of Utopia. 4.9996
The University of Virginia edition of the works of Stephen Crane. 2.10979
University physics. 5.1987
University records and life in the Middle Ages. 4.10108
University science and engineering libraries. 5.7610
UNIX for people. 5.1164
The UNIX programming environment. 5.1184
The unknown country. 3.8659
The Unknown dimension. 4.7019
The unknown light. 2.5195
The unknown Orwell. 2.9202
The unknown soldiers. 3.841
The unknown war. 3.805, 3.4778
Unlikely heroes. 4.9849
The Unlisted market guide. 4.4620
The unmaking of a president. 3.4503
Unmastered lute. 2.1894
The unmediated vision. 2.2662
The unnatural scene. 2.6789
An unofficial rose. 2.9768
Unplanned careers. 4.3249
Unprofessional essays. 2.5545
The unpublished opinions of Mr. Justice Brandeis. 4.9447
Unquestioning obedience to the President. 4.9739
Unquiet eagle; memory and desire in the idea of American freedom, 1815-1860. 3.6168
The unquiet grave. 2.8539
Unquiet soul. 2.7453
Unrepentant radical. 4.7001
Unsafe at any speed. 5.6635
An unsettled people. 4.5126
Unsolved problems in number theory. 5.1118
Unspeakable practices, unnatural acts. 2.12894
The unspeakable Skipton. 2.8848
Unspoken worlds. 1.1613
An unsuitable job for a woman. 2.9723
Unsung. 1.3489
Unsuspected eloquence. 1.4402
Untended gates. 2.3598
Der Untertan. 2.13818
Unterweisung im Tonsatz. 1.4450
Untimely meditations. 1.1051
Untitled subjects. 2.13094
Unto a good land. 2.14096
An Untouchable community in South India, structure and consensus. 3.4325
The Untouchables in contemporary India. 3.4178
The untuning of the sky. 1.4399
The unvanquished. 2.11681
Unwanted workers; permanent layoffs and long-term unemployment. 4.3223
Unwelcome muse. 2.2254
The unwritten alliance. 3.1655
The unwritten war. 2.10244
Up against apartheid. 2.3560
Up before daylight. 3.8282
Up country. 2.11971
Up from communism. 4.6987
Up from liberalism. 4.7852
Up from Nigger. 2.3256
Up from slavery. 3.6854
Up from the footnote. 2.3601
Up from the pedestal. 4.5986
Up front. 3.916
Up ship! 5.7482
Up the walls of the world. 2.13358
Up to now. 3.7682
Upanishads. 1.1682
The Upanishads. 2.1932
Upanishads. Darśanopaniṣad. English. Selections. 1.206
Upanishads. English. 1.1682, 1.1684
Upanishads. English. Selections. 1.1683

Updated Unsafe at any speed. 5.6635
The upper Amazon. 3.9199
Upper Canada. 3.8824
The Upper Canada trade, 1834-1872. 4.4222
Uprising in the Warsaw ghetto. 3.998
The uprooted. 3.6514
Uprooted children. 4.6578
The upstart crow. 2.6743
The upstart earl. 3.1833
Upton Sinclair. 2.12483
Upton Sinclair, American rebel. 2.12484
Upwelling ecosystems. 5.3563
Urban anthropology. 4.515, 4.6336
Urban blues. 1.4302
Urban Canada. 4.8872
Urban change and planning. 4.6331
Urban change in China. 3.4864
The urban climate. 5.2571
Urban commune experiments in Communist China. 4.8888
The urban community: housing and planning in the progressive era. 4.6321
The urban crucible. 3.6867
Urban decline and the future of American cities. 4.6205
Urban deprivation and government initiative. 4.6622
Urban design as public policy. 4.6307
Urban dynamics in black Africa. 4.6283
Urban dynamics in Black Africa. 4.6279
Urban economic development. 4.6213
The urban economies, 1985. 4.2070
Urban education. 4.10958
Urban entomology, interdisciplinary perspectives. 5.5408
Urban ethnicity. 4.625
Urban Europe. 4.6315
The urban experience. 4.6221, 4.6292
The Urban explosion in Latin America. 4.6249
Urban forestry. 5.5363
The urban frontier. 3.8391
Urban growth in colonial Rhode Island. 4.6244
The urban guerrilla. 4.7614
Urban history. 5.8185
Urban hydrology. 5.5976
The urban impact on American Protestantism 1865-1900. 1.2997
Urban land policy, issues and opportunities. 4.2813
Urban life in contemporary China. 4.6271
Urban life in Mediterranean Europe. 4.6252
Urban mass transit planning. 4.4030
Urban mass transportation. 4.3921
Urban masses and moral order in America, 1820-1920. 4.6204
The urban nation, 1920-1960. 3.7511
Urban neighborhoods, networks, and families. 4.5220
Urban networks in Ch'ing China and Tokugawa Japan. 4.6270
Urban planning and design criteria. 1.5584
Urban policy and political conflict in Africa. 4.8805
Urban policy and the exterior city. 4.5189
Urban policymaking and metropolitan dynamics. 4.6231
Urban politics in India. 4.8883
Urban politics in the suburban era. 4.8861
An urban profile of the Middle East. 4.6275
Urban public transportation. 4.4026
The urban question. 4.6290
Urban rail transit. 4.4025
Urban renegades. 3.5905
Urban renewal. 4.6343
The urban school: a factory for failure. 4.10853
Urban social space. 4.6303
Urban social structure. 4.6289
Urban society. 4.6295
The urban threshold. 4.5212
Urban transit. 4.4027
Urban transport appraisal. 4.3916
Urban transport economics. 4.3913
Urban transportation and public policy. 4.4028
Urban transportation modeling and planning. 4.3911
Urban transportation planning. 4.3904, 5.5931

Urban transportation policy and management. 4.3920
The urban transportation problem. 4.3937
The urban transportation system. 4.3915
Urban transportation technology. 5.5932
Urban utopias in the twentieth century. 4.6305
Urban village. 4.5211
The urban villagers. 4.5203
The urban wilderness. 4.6232
The urban world. 4.6297
Urbanism and the changing Canadian society. 4.5247
Urbanization and settlement systems. 4.6197
Urbanization and social change in West Africa. 4.6285
Urbanization in China. 4.6269
Urbanization in contemporary Latin America. 4.6248
Urbanization in Israel. 4.6272
Urbanization in Nigeria. 4.6281
Urbanization in the world-economy. 4.6349
Urbanization, national development, and regional planning in Africa. 4.6278
The urbanization of America, 1860-1915. 4.6217
The urge to mobilize. 4.2879
The urge to the sea. 3.3051
Uruguay. 3.9231, 3.9235
Uruguay in transition. 3.9236
US airline industry. 4.4085
US economy demystified. 4.1995
US foreign assistance. 4.1835
US foreign policy and Asian-Pacific security. 3.3634
US foreign policy and multilateral development banks. 4.4577
US international monetary policy. 4.4574
US merchant marine. 4.3976
US-South Asian relations, 1947-1982. 3.4106
The US, the UN, and the management of global change. 4.9229
Use and abuse of history. 3.475
The Use and abuse of medicine. 5.4648
The use and significance of pesticides in the environment. 5.5413
The use of biological literature. 5.3293
Use of chemical literature. 5.2600
Use of earth sciences literature. 5.8218
Use of economics literature. 4.1278
Use of engineering literature. 5.5500
Use of mathematical literature. 5.1117
Use of physics literature. 5.8349
The use of poetry and the use of criticism. 2.5761
The use of technology in the care of the elderly and the disabled. 5.5037
The use of the Bible in Milton's prose. 2.7169
The useful arts and the liberal tradition. 4.10833
A user's guide to computer peripherals. 5.6575
User's guide to spectral sequences. 5.1614
A user's handbook of D/A and A/D converters. 5.6579
Uses & abuses of social research in social work. 4.6465
The uses of a liberal education and other talks to students. 4.10817
The uses of argument. 1.1242
The uses of enchantment. 4.819
The uses of power. 4.7862
Uses of the future. 3.203
The uses of the past. 3.28
Uses of the past in the novels of William Faulkner. 2.11700
The uses of the university. 4.10555
USGS geologic and hydrologic maps. 5.8213
Using sociology. 4.4869
The USSR and the Muslim world. 3.3324
The USSR in Third World conflicts. 5.7327
The 'uta.' 2.2020
Utage no Ato. 2.2114
Utah. 3.8581, 3.8583
The Utah UFO display. 5.6700
Utamaro. 1.6485
Utilitarianism. 1.719
Utility of religion. 1.1556
The Utilization of classroom peers as behavior change agents. 4.10280

Utopia. 4.7175
Utopia and its enemies. 4.7171
Utopia in power. 3.3207
Utopian communism in France. 4.7164
Utopian craftsmen. 1.6530
Utopian fantasy. 2.6057
The Utopian vision of Charles Fourier. 4.7165
Utopias and Utopian thought. 4.7172
Utopias of the classical world. 4.7170
Uwe Johnson. 2.13903

V., a novel. 2.13282
V.L.S.I. system design. 5.6540
The V.N.R. dictionary of publishing. 5.7574
V.S. Naipaul. 3.4168
V. S. Naipaul. 2.10013-2.10015
V. Sackville-West. 2.9299-2.9300
V was for victory. 3.7752
Vachel Lindsay; a poet in America. 2.12016
The vagabond. 2.4498
Vagabond stars. 2.3404
Vagaries and varieties in constitutional
    interpretation. 4.9647
Vale and other poems. 2.9291
Valency and molecular structure. 5.2835
Valiant friend. 4.6004
Valley of darkness. 3.1009
Valley of democracy. 3.8389
The valley of the lower Thames, 1640 to 1850.
    3.8829
Vālmīki. 2.1937
Valois Burgundy. 3.2220
The Valois tapestries. 1.6593
Valour fore & aft ... 3.6955
Valour fore & aft, being the adventures of the
    continental sloop Providence, 1775-1779,
    formerly flagship Katy of Rhode Island's
    Navy. 3.6955
Valuation of wildland resource benefits. 4.2826
The Value-added tax. 4.4718
Value and capital. 4.1437
Value, capital and rent. 4.1496
Value conflicts in health care delivery. 5.4572
Value for money in health services. 5.4631
The value of the individual. 3.320
Value, price and profit. 4.1509
Values and ideals of American youth. 4.5747
Values and teaching. 4.10315
Values in a universe of chance. 1.624
Valuing environmental goods. 4.1575
Van Dale groot woordenboek Engels-
    Nederlands. 2.1172
Van Dale groot woordenboek Nederlands-
    Engels. 2.1173
Van Gogh, a documentary biography. 1.6244
Van Gogh, Gauguin, and the Impressionist
    circle. 1.6061
Van Nostrand Reinhold encyclopedia of
    chemistry. 5.2596
Van Nostrand's scientific encyclopedia. 5.705
Vanbrugh. 1.5405
Vance and Nettie Palmer. 2.10160
Vanessa Bell. 1.6024
Vanguard of nazism. 3.2369
Vanished supremacies. 3.669
The vanishing adolescent. 4.5753
Vanishing Georgia. 3.8255
The vanishing hitchhiker. 4.773
The vanishing peasant. 4.5352
The vantage point. 3.7885
Variable plants and herbivores in natural and
    managed systems. 5.3872
Variable stars. 5.1842
Variation and change in language. 2.130
The variational principles of mechanics. 5.1644
Variations in human physiology. 5.4206
The varied sociology of Paul F. Lazarsfeld.
    4.4800
The varieties of enchantment. 2.265
Varieties of fascism. 4.7608
Varieties of monetary experience. 4.4483
The varieties of psychedelic experience. 5.233
Varieties of psychohistory. 3.439
The varieties of religious experience. 1.2237
Varieties of sexual experience. 4.587
Varieties of southern evangelicalism. 1.2479
Varieties of unbelief. 1.1888
Varieties of visual experience. 1.4622

Variety entertainment and outdoor amusements.
    4.1196
Variety film reviews, 1907-1980. 2.2971
Variety international showbusiness reference.
    2.2775
Variety music cavalcade, 1620-1969. 1.3601
A Variorum commentary on the poems of John
    Milton. 2.7168
A variorum edition of Elizabeth Barrett
    Browning's Sonnets from the Portuguese.
    2.7465
The variorum edition of the plays of W. B.
    Yeats. 2.8332
The variorum edition of the poems of W. B.
    Yeats. 2.8329
A variorum edition of the works of Geoffrey
    Chaucer. 2.6313
The various arts. 1.5099
Vasarely. 1.6154
Vasari on technique. 1.5100
Vascular plants. 5.3731
Vascular plants of Northeastern United States
    and adjacent Canada. 5.3672
Les vases communicants. 2.4427
Vasilika. 4.5391
Vasily Zhukovsky. 2.1466
Vassouras, a Brazilian coffee county, 1850-1900.
    4.2175
The vast majority. 4.1805
Vathek. 2.7397
The Vatican Council, 1869-1870, based on
    Bishop Ullathorne's letters. 1.3121
Vatican III. 1.3169
Vaudeville U.S.A. 2.2834
Vaulting ambition. 4.510
Vector mechanics for engineers. 5.5732
Vedanta and the West. 1.201
Vedanta for modern man. 1.201
The Vedānta Sūtras of Bādarāyaṇa. 1.1680
Vedantic approaches to God. 1.200
Vedas. Atharvaveda. English. 2.1931
Vedas. Rgveda. English. 1.1678
Vedas. Rgveda. English. Selections. 1.1679,
    2.1930
Vedic hymns. 2.1930
Vedic literature. 1.1681
A Vedic reader for students. 2.1850
Vega and other poems. 2.8610
Las Vegas, New Mexico. 3.8577
The vegetable. 2.11723
Vegetable growing handbook. 5.5339
Vegetation and soils. 5.3664
Vehicle engines. 5.6629
Veiled countries; Lives. 2.4809
Vein of iron. 2.11772
Velázquez. 1.6300
Velazquez, Goya and the dehumanization of
    art. 1.6301
The velvet chancellors. 3.2465
The velvet horn. 2.12057
Velvet on iron. 3.7697
Ven Yash iz gekumen. 2.1804
Venceremos! 4.7013
The Vendee. 4.5357
Venetian architecture of the early Renaissance.
    1.5437
The venetian glass nephew. 2.12824
The Venetian vespers. 2.13079
Venezuela. 3.9181
Venezuela, a century of change. 3.9183
Venezuela, politics in a petroleum republic.
    4.8352
Venezuelan archaeology. 3.9179
Venice. 3.2911
Venice, a maritime republic. 3.2912
Venomous animals of the world. 5.3810
Venomous reptiles. 5.3927
Venture capital in high-tech companies. 4.3807
The venture of Islam. 3.3650
Venus, an errant twin. 5.1811
Venus observed. 2.8674
Venustiano Carranza's nationalist struggle,
    1893-1920. 3.8949
Verbal art, verbal sign, verbal time. 2.33
Verbal behavior. 5.392
The verbal icon. 2.2725

Verdi. 1.4027
The Verdi companion. 1.4028
Verdi; his music, life and times. 1.4025
Verdi, the man in his letters. 1.4021
Verdict of twelve. 2.9798
Verdi's Aida. 1.4029
Vergil in the Middle Ages. 2.807
Die verlorene Ehre der Katharina Blum.
    2.13692
Vermeer of Delft. 1.6256
The vermilion bird. 3.4702
Vermilion sands. 2.9618
Vermont. 3.7968
Vermont, a Bicentennial history. 3.7967
Vernon Watkins and the spring of vision.
    2.9478
The Verrine orations. 2.663
The versatile Defoe. 2.6968
Verschenkter Rat. 2.13672
Verses of cadence. 2.6379-2.6380
Versification: major language types. 2.2736
The versification of Robert Browning. 2.7496
Versions from Fyodor Tyutchev, 1803-1873.
    2.1425
Versions of baroque. 2.2659
Versions of the past. 2.10553
The vertebrate body. 5.4110
Vertebrate dissection. 5.4115
Vertebrate history: problems in evolution.
    5.3894
Vertebrate paleontology. 5.3169
Vertebrates of the United States. 5.3891
Vertical integration in the oil industry. 4.3766
The vertical mosaic. 4.5248
Die Verwirrungen des Zöglings Törless.
    2.13844
Verwoerd. 3.5474
A very double life. 3.8752
The Very early universe. 5.1862
Verzeichnis lieferbarer Bücher. 5.8007
Veterinary dictionary. 5.5460
Veterinary medicine and human health. 5.5461
Vexed and troubled Englishmen, 1590-1642.
    3.1456
Viability theory. 5.1500
Vibration problems in engineering. 5.5747
Vibrations and waves in physics. 5.2033
The vicar of Bullhampton. 2.8225
The vicar of Wakefield, and other writings.
    2.7045
Vice Chamberlain Coke's theatrical papers,
    1706-1715. 2.3322
Vice-presidential power. 4.7972
The viceroys. 2.5063
Vichy France and the Jews. 3.3962
Vichy France: old guard and new order,
    1940-1944. 3.2209
Vicious circles. 4.6717
Vicky: Princess Royal of England and German
    Empress. 3.2330
Vico. 1.1090-1.1091
Vico and Herder. 1.1092
Vico's science of imagination. 1.1094
The victim. 2.11357
The victim as criminal and artist. 2.10335
Victim compensation. 4.6847
Victims of a map. 2.1840
Victims of change. 4.6873
Victims of groupthink. 3.7578
Victims of justice. 4.9455
Victims of personal crime. 4.6707
Victims of progress. 4.502
Victims of the system. 4.6706
Victor Amadeus II. 3.2909
The Victor book of the opera. 1.4512
Victor Emanuel, Cavour and the Risorgimento.
    3.2862
Victor Hugo. 2.4239, 2.4241
Victor Hugo and the visionary novel. 2.4243
The Victoria Woodhull reader. 4.5175
The Victorian age in literature. 2.5703
A Victorian album. 2.5567
Victorian and later English poets. 2.6180
Victorian architecture. 1.5371
Victorian architecture and rural art. 1.5560
The Victorian city. 4.6254
Victorian conventions. 2.5720
The Victorian country house. 1.5568

Victorian critics of democracy: Carlyle, Ruskin, Arnold, Stephen, Maine, Lecky. 4.7573
Victorian dramatic criticism. 2.2799
The Victorian economy. 4.2276
Victorian England. 3.1612
The Victorian experience, the poets. 2.5826
Victorian fantasy. 2.5717
Victorian fiction. 2.6019
The Victorian frame of mind, 1830-1870. 3.1592
Victorian heretic. 2.8245
The Victorian imagination. 2.5710
Victorian literary critics. 2.5507
Victorian literature; modern essays in criticism. 2.5714
Victorian minds. 3.1591
Victorian noon. 2.5704
The Victorian novel. 2.6022
Victorian novelists. 2.6021
Victorian novelists and publishers. 2.6028
Victorian origins of the British welfare state. 4.5308
Victorian panorama. 1.6018
Victorian people. 3.1618
Victorian people and ideas. 3.1588
The Victorian periodical press. 2.3689
Victorian periodicals. 2.3690
Victorian poetry. 2.6175, 2.6178, 2.6181
Victorian poetry and poetics. 2.6177
The Victorian poets, a guide to research. 2.5824
Victorian poets and prose writers. 5.7946
Victorian prose. 2.5938
Victorian reader. 2.6249
A Victorian romantic. 2.8019
The Victorian sage. 2.5711
Victorian science and Victorian values. 5.965
Victorian science fiction in the UK. 2.6030
Victorian scrutinies: reviews of poetry, 1830-1870. 2.5823
Victorian sculpture. 1.5687
Victorian spectacular theatre, 1850-1910. 2.3308
The Victorian temper. 2.5701
The Victorian theatre. 2.3311
The Victorian theatre, 1792-1914. 2.3310
Victorian women's fiction. 2.6034
The Victorians and after, 1830-1914. 2.5521
The victors. 2.4720
Victors and vanquished. 5.7315
Victors divided. 3.858
Victors' justice. 4.9343
Victory garden. 5.5367
Victory in the West. 3.953
Victory over violence, Jesus and the revolutionists. 1.2920
La vida. 3.8058
Vida de Don Quijote y Sancho según Miguel de Cervantes Saavedra. 2.5182
Vida y obra de Galdós, 1843-1920. 2.5224
Video production handbook. 5.6442
Video recording; record and replay systems. 5.6444
The Video source book. 2.2863
Videodisc and optical memory systems. 5.6590
The videotape book. 5.6443
Vie de Balzac ... 2.4122
Une vie de boy. 2.4854
Vie de Mallarmé. Édition complète en un volume. 2.4266
La vie littéraire. 2.3832
La vie, mode d'emploi. 2.4787
La vie quotidienne sous Louis XIV. 3.2031
Vienamese literature. 2.2261
Vienna and the young Hitler. 3.2402
The Viennese Revolution of 1848. 3.1893
Die vierzehn Jahre der ersten deutschen Republik. 3.2375
Viet Cong. 3.4482
Viet Cong memoir. 3.4470
Viet-Nam and the West. 3.4479
Viet Nam; the origins of revolution. 3.4477
Viet rock, Comings and goings, Keep tightly closed in a cool dry place, The gloaming, oh my darling. 2.13353
A Vietcong memoir. 3.4470
Vietnam. 3.4462-3.4463, 3.4481
Vietnam, a guide to reference sources. 5.8062

Vietnam, a history. 3.4501
Vietnam; a political history. 3.4472
Vietnam, a television history (Television program) 3.4501
Vietnam, history of the bulwark B2 theatre. 3.4438
Vietnam literature anthology, a balanced perspective. 2.10705
Vietnam since the fall of Saigon. 3.4514
The Vietnam trauma in American foreign policy, 1945-75. 3.6499
Vietnam veterans. 5.7370
The Vietnam war and international law. 4.9080
Vietnam War bibliography. 5.8060
Vietnamese communism, 1925-1945. 4.7122
The Vietnamese revolution. 4.7121
Vietnamese tradition on trial, 1920-1945. 3.4467
Vietnam's will to live. 3.4476
Vieux carré. 2.12735
Le vieux nègre et la médaille. 2.4855
A view by the sea. 2.2137
View from another shore. 2.3722
A view from Black Mesa. 3.5715
The View from Goffman. 4.4816
The view from language. 2.7
The view from the barrio. 4.5278
A view from the spire. 2.8710
View from the UN. 3.1151
A viewer's guide to film theory and criticism. 2.2951
Views and reviews in American literature, history and fiction: first series. 2.11223
Views of society and manners in America. 3.6031
Vigil of Venus. 2.655
Vigilantes in gold rush San Francisco. 3.8628
Vigny, l'homme et l'oeuvre. 2.4333
The Viking achievement. 3.3360
The Viking age in Denmark. 3.3370
The Viking book of aphorisms. 2.3802
The Viking book of folk ballads of the English-speaking world. 2.6108
Viking civilization. 3.3355
The Viking legacy. 2.1063
The Viking road to Byzantium. 3.3359
The Viking ships; their ancestry and evolution. 5.7501
The Vikings. 3.3358
The Vikings in Britain. 3.1324
The Vikings in history. 3.3363
Vikings of the sunrise. 3.5620
Vile bodies. 2.9497
The Villa d'Este at Tivoli. 1.5570
The villa in the life of Renaissance Rome. 1.5577
The village. 2.1478
Village and bureaucracy in Southern Sung China. 4.8887
Village and family in contemporary China. 4.5631
Village and farmstead. 4.392
Village at war. 3.4513
Village in August. 2.2251
The village in the jungle. 2.9562
Village in the Vaucluse. 3.2227
Village in Vietnam. 3.4475
Village India; studies in the little community. 4.5424
The village Indians of the upper Missouri. 3.5903
Village Japan. 4.5447
Village life in insular Southeast Asia. 4.630
Village life in northern India. 4.5423
Village notables in nineteenth-century France. 4.6401
The village of Ben Suc. 3.4488
Village on the Seine. 3.2234
Village school downtown. 4.10966
A village that chose progress. 3.9044
The Vimalakīrti nirdeśa sūtra. 1.2135
Vimalakīrtinirdeśa. English. 1.2135-1.2136
Vince Lombardi on football. 4.1026
Vincent van Gogh. 1.6245
Vincenzo Bellini. 1.3811
A vindication of the rights of woman. 4.6101
The vindication of tradition. 1.71

The vineyard of liberty. 3.6316
Vingt ans après. 2.4174
Vingt mille lieues sous les mers. 2.4324
XXe siècle. 2.3920
Vintage years of the Theatre Guild, 1928-1939. 2.3272
Violence. 1.2919
Violence against wives. 4.6746
Violence against women. 4.6710
Violence and civil disorder in Italian cities, 1200-1500. 4.5367
Violence and crime in cross-national perspective. 4.6685
Violence and reform in American history. 4.5244
Violence and thought. 4.5466
Violence as protest. 4.5243
Violence in America. 4.5131
Violence in the family. 5.8362
The violence of pity in Euripides' Medea. 2.461
Violence, values, and justice in the schools. 4.10693
The violent bear it away. 2.13209
The violent home. 4.5591
The violent land. 2.5469
The violet in the crucible. 2.8112
Viollet-le-Duc. 1.4980, 1.5421
Vipers' tangle. 2.4631
Virgil. 2.700
Virgil, a study in civilized poetry. 2.802
A Virgil Thomson reader. 1.3479
Virgil's Aeneid; a critical description. 2.805
Virgil's Georgics. 2.793
Virgil's pastoral art. 2.791
Virgil's poem of the earth. 2.794
The virgin. 1.2903
The virgin and the gipsy. 2.8976
Virgin land. 3.8467
Virgin soil. 2.1457
Virginia. 2.11772, 3.8182
Virginia: Bourbonism to Byrd, 1870-1925. 3.8212
The Virginia conservatives, 1867-1879. 3.8211
A Virginia profile, 1960-2000. 4.8265
Virginia, the new dominion. 3.8181
Virginia Woolf. 2.9591-2.9592, 2.9594-2.9595, 2.9600, 2.9608
Virginia Woolf; a biography. 2.9590
Virginia Woolf; a collection of critical essays. 2.9606
Virginia Woolf, a study of her novels. 2.9588
Virginia Woolf, a writer's life. 2.9596
Virginia Woolf and her works. 2.9597
Virginia Woolf and London. 2.9607
Virginia Woolf and the androgynous vision. 2.9589
Virginia Woolf, her art as a novelist. 2.9585
Virginia Woolf, new critical essays. 2.9609
Virginia Woolf's London. 2.9593
Virginia Woolf's reading notebooks. 2.9605
The Virginian. 2.11288
Virginians at home. 3.8223
Virgins and viragos. 4.6112
Virgins & viragos. 4.6112
The virtues. 1.3061
Virtues and vices and other essays in moral philosophy. 1.1447
The virtuoso. 2.7239
The virus. 5.4473
The viruses. 5.4475
Viruses of vertebrates. 5.4474
Visage premier. 2.4470
Visage premier; Suivi de, Terre et poésie. 2.4470
Il Visconte Dimezzato. 2.5030
The visible and the invisible. 1.843
The visible hand. 4.4256
Visible man. 4.6743
Visible saints. 1.3398
Visible words. 1.3014
Visigothic Spain. 3.3420
A vision. 2.8338
Vision. 5.666
Vision and re-vision in Alexander Pope. 2.7202
Vision and refuge. 2.10277
Vision and response in modern fiction. 2.3531

Vision and revision. 2.7602
Vision and stagecraft in Sophocles. 2.549
Vision and virtue. 1.1469
Vision and visual perception. 5.4378
Vision: human and electronic. 5.6596
Vision in man and machine. 5.5941
Vision in motion. 1.5115
Vision in spring. 2.11682
Vision in vertebrates. 5.4375
The vision of Piers Plowman. 2.6391
The vision of self in early Vedānta. 1.198
The vision of the vanquished. 3.9300
A Vision shared. 4.5144
Visionary and dreamer. 1.6019
The visionary eye. 1.6682
The Visionary hand. 1.4949
Visionary novels. 2.7923
Visions from Piers Plowman. 2.6392
Visions of Cody. 2.11955
Visions of history. 3.408
Visions of Kerouac. 2.12994
Visions of the end. 1.2947
Visions of world order. 4.9282
The visit. 2.13734
Visit to a small planet, and other television plays. 2.12623
Visits to Bedlam: madness and literature in the eighteenth century. 2.5692
Visual anthropology. 4.498
The visual arts. 1.4675
The Visual arts and medical education. 5.4600
The visual arts today. 1.4812
The Visual encyclopedia of nautical terms under sail. 5.7419
Visual handicaps and learning. 4.6599
Visual handicaps & learning. 4.6599
A visual history of costume. 4.845
A visual history of twentieth-century architecture. 1.5274
Visual illusions. 5.4388
Visual perception. 5.245, 5.4382
Visual puns in design. 1.5836
Visual space perception. 5.4386
Visual thinking. 1.4605
The visual world of the child. 5.619
The visually handicapped child in school. 4.6600
Vita. 2.9297
Vita d'un uomo. 2.5073
Vita nuova. 2.4920
Vita sexualis. 2.2078
Vitae Patrum. 1.2481
The vital balance. 5.4825
The vital center. 4.7606
Vital statistics on Congress. 4.8001
Vitruvius. 1.5469
Vitruvius Britannicus; or. 1.5359
Viva la muerte. 2.4380
Vivaldi. 1.4033
Vivaldi, genius of the baroque. 1.4032
Vive moi! 2.9164
Vivre l'orange. 2.4779
Vladimir Nabokov. 2.1586
Vladimir Soloviev and his messianic work. 1.1117
VLB 1971/72-. 5.8007
VLSI handbook. 5.6546
VLSI system design. 5.6540
VLSI testing & validation techniques. 5.6542
VN, the life and art of Vladimir Nabokov. 2.1585
The VNR concise encyclopedia of mathematics. 5.1116
The VNR dictionary of ships & the seas. 5.7417
The vocabulary of politics. 4.7244
The vocal songs in the plays of Shakespeare. 1.3487
The vocation of man. 1.921
Vogel's qualitative inorganic analysis. 5.2672
Vogel's Textbook of practical organic chemistry, including qualitative organic analysis. 5.2730
Voice and the actor. 2.3539
The voice at the back door. 2.12494
The voice of Bharati. 2.2278
The voice of experience. 5.413
The voice of the people. 2.11772
The voice of the poet. 2.11004

The voice of things. 2.4656
The voice that is great within us. 2.10764
Voiceless India. 3.4170
Voices at play. 2.9354
Voices for the future. 2.3497
Voices from an empire. 2.5479
Voices from the corner. 3.8437
Voices from the Harlem renaissance. 2.10704
Voices in stone. 2.225
Voices of a people. 1.4352
Voices of America. 3.6340
Voices of Aztlan. 2.10682
Voices of change in the Spanish American theater. 2.5325
Voices of Jacob, hands of Esau. 3.6577
The voices of Matthew Arnold. 2.7360
Voices of melancholy. 2.5631
Voices of protest. 3.7753
Voices of resurgent Islam. 1.1997
Voices of the Black theatre. 2.3238
Voices, visions, and a new reality. 2.5327
La voie royale. 2.4619
Volcanic hazards. 5.3107
Volcanoes. 5.3111
Volcanoes as landscape forms. 5.3109
Volcanoes of the Earth. 5.3108
Voles, mice and lemmings. 5.4071
Volpone. 2.6591
Völsunga saga. 2.13991
Völsunga saga. English. 2.13990
Voltaire. 2.4108-2.4109
Voltaire; a collection of critical essays. 2.4107
Voltaire and Candide. 2.4105
Voltaire, historian. 3.424
Volts to Hertz 5.2337
Volume the second. 2.7366
Voluntary associations. 4.4918
The Von Hassell diaries, 1938-1944. 3.2388
Vonnegut. 2.13399
Vonnegut in America. 2.13403
The Vonnegut statement. 2.13401
La vorágine. 2.5413
Voraussetzungen einer Erzählung, Kassandra. 2.13924
Das Vorbild. 2.13815
The vortex. 2.5414
Voss. 2.10186
Voting. 4.7958
Voting in revolutionary America. 4.8101
Voting in the Security Council. 4.9208
Voting Rights Act. 4.9727
Vox. 2.898
Vox Graeca: a guide to the pronunciation of classical Greek. 2.236
Vox new college Spanish and English dictionary. 2.904
Voyage au bout de la nuit, suivi de Mort à crédit. 2.4511
The Voyage in. 2.5987
Voyage in the dark. 2.9275
Voyage into substance. 4.100
The voyage of the Astrolabe, 1840. 3.5595
The voyage out. 2.9959
The voyage that never ends. 2.9063
A voyage to Arcturus. 2.9050
Voyage to Jupiter. 5.1818
A voyage to Pagany. 2.12747
A voyage to South America. 3.9152
Voyage to windward. 2.8125
Voyager. 2.11531
Voyages of Peter Esprit Radisson, being an account of his travels and experiences among the North American Indians, from 1652 to 1684. 3.8846
Voyages of Samuel de Champlain 1604-1618. 3.8711
Voyages to Saturn. 5.1819
Les voyageurs de l'Impériale. 2.4377
Le voyeur. 2.4693
Vremia, vpered. 2.1568
Vsevolod Garshin. 2.1497
Vtoraia kniga. 2.1579
Vuillard. 1.6156

W. 2.4788
W. A. P. Martin, pioneer of progress in China. 1.3029
W. B. Yeats. 2.8362

W. B. Yeats, man and poet. 2.8344
W. B. Yeats, the tragic phase. 2.8352
W. D. Howells as critic. 2.11087
W.E.B. Du Bois. 3.6830
W. E. B. Du Bois on sociology and the Black community. 3.6758
A W. E. B. Du Bois reader. 3.6825
W. E. B. Du Bois speaks. 3.6643
W. Eugene Smith, master of the photographic essay. 5.6997
W.H. Auden, a biography. 2.8402
W. I. Thomas on social organization and social personality. 4.4812
W.P.A. guide to New York City. 3.8036
W. Somerset Maugham. 2.9105
W. Somerset Maugham and the quest for freedom. 2.9106
Wade Hampton and the Negro. 3.7326
The Waffen SS. 3.972
Wage determination under trade unions. 4.3129
Wage-earning women. 4.3293
Wage-labour and capital. 4.1509
Wage politics in Britain, 1945-1967. 4.3636
The wage-price issue. 4.4499
The wage rate under collective bargaining. 4.3137
Wage restraint. 4.2214
Wages. 4.3127
Wages and earnings in the United States, 1860-1890. 4.3145
Wagner. 1.4036, 1.4039, 1.4045
Wagner and Aeschylus. 1.4051
Wagner and Nietzsche. 1.4053
Wagner and the romantic disaster. 1.4034
Wagner as a man & artist. 1.4041
Wagner at Bayreuth: experiment and tradition. 1.4055
The Wagner companion. 1.4048
The Wagner operas. 1.4517
Wagner, the wehr-wolf. 2.8001
Wagner's Rienzi. 1.4049
Wagner's 'Ring' and its symbols. 1.4050
The Wahhabiyya. 1.2009
Waiting for a 'Pearl Harbor' 3.4983
Waiting for God. 1.3069
Waiting for Godot. 2.4405
The waiting years. 2.2096, 2.10322
The Wakefield mystery plays. 2.6210
Wakefield pageants in the Towneley cycle. 2.6209
Waking. 2.9676
The waking brain. 5.4337
Waking their neighbors up. 3.8127
Walden, and Civil disobedience. 2.11245
Walden Two. 2.12485
Waldo Emerson. 2.11024
Waldo Williams. 2.846
Wales. 3.1756
Wales and America. 3.6600
Wales in the early Middle Ages. 3.1761
Wales through the ages. 3.1757
Walford's guide to reference material. 5.7715
Walk in beauty. 3.5913
A walk in the sun. 2.11425
A walk on the wild side. 2.11308
Walker Evans. 5.6959
Walker Percy. 2.13247
Walker Percy, an American search. 2.13245
Walker Percy, art and ethics. 2.13248
Walker report on the violent confrontation of demonstrators and police in the parks and streets of Chicago. 3.8419
Walker's Mammals of the world. 5.3976
Walker's rhyming dictionary of the English language. 2.1049
Walking machines. 5.6172
Walking softly in the wilderness. 4.896
Walking to sleep. 2.12711
The wall. 2.11869
The Wall. 2.4727
The wall of separation. 4.9723
Wallace Stevens. 2.12546
Wallace Stevens. 2.12547
Wallace Stevens; a collection of critical essays. 2.12545
Wallace Stevens; an approach to his poetry and thought. 2.12549

Wallace Stevens: poetry as life. 2.12548
The wallet of Kai Lung. 2.9343
Wallpaper, a history. 1.6596
Wallpaper in America. 1.6597
Wallpapers. 1.6595
The walls came tumbling down. 3.6645
The walls of Rome. 3.2720
The walnut trees of Altenburg. 2.4618
Walpole and the wits. 2.5688
Walt Whitman. 2.11277
Walt Whitman, a life. 2.11276
Walt Whitman of the New York Aurora; editor
    at twenty-two. 2.11269
Walt Whitman reconsidered. 2.11275
Walt Whitman, the critical heritage. 2.11278,
    2.11281
Walt Whitman's Camden conversations.
    2.11271
Walter Bagehot. 4.8381
Walter Lippmann and the American century.
    2.3617
Walter Nash. 3.5605
Walter Pater. 2.7982
Walter Pater, the critical heritage. 2.7985
Walter Pater, the scholar-artist. 2.7983
Walter Prescott Webb. 3.6267
Walter Scott. 2.8060
Walther Rathenau; his life and work. 3.2353
The waltz of the toreadors. 2.4361
The wanderer. 2.14048
The wanderer (Le grand Meaulnes) 2.4531
Wanderers in the sky. 5.1710
Wandering continents and spreading sea floors
    on an expanding earth. 5.3094
The waning of the Middle Ages. 3.1955
The Wannsee Protocol and a 1944 Report on
    Auschwitz by the Office of Strategic Services.
    3.1106
Wanted. 3.3912
The wanting seed. 2.9646
The Wapshot chronicle. 2.11493
The Wapshot scandal. 2.11494
War. 2.4784
The war, 1941-45. 2.1550
The war against East Timor. 3.4584
The war against Paris, 1871. 3.2169
War against pro-slavery religion. 3.7256
The war against proslavery religion. 3.7256
The war against the Amazons. 4.5855
The war against the Jews, 1933-1945. 3.1086
War aims and strategic policy in the Great
    War, 1914-1918. 3.774
War and administration. 5.7353
War and aftermath, 1914-1929. 3.739
War and children. 4.5739
War and civilization. 5.7147
War and diplomacy in the French Republic.
    3.2179
War and diplomacy in the Japanese empire.
    3.4918
The war and German society. 3.2342
War and government in Habsburg Spain,
    1560-1620. 5.7354
War and human progress. 3.216
War and imperialism in Republican Rome,
    327-70 B.C. 3.2764
War and industrial society. 4.1781
War and justice. 5.7153
War and peace in the law of Islam. 1.2077
War and prices in Spain, 1651-1800. 4.1507
War and remembrance. 2.12800
War and society. 4.5140
War and society in Europe, 1870-1970. 3.714
War and society in Renaissance Europe,
    1450-1620. 5.7194
War and society in revolutionary Europe,
    1770-1870. 3.653
War and society in the seventeenth century.
    3.170
War and the liberal conscience. 4.9114
War and the Soviet Union. 5.7323
War as an instrument of national policy and its
    renunciation in the Pact of Paris. 4.9122
War as I knew it. 3.897
The war behind the war, 1914-1918. 3.782
War comes to Long An. 3.4491
War commentaries. 2.9175

War criminals, their prosecution & punishment.
    4.9340
War, diplomacy, and imperialism, 1618-1763.
    3.640
War, economy, and society, 1939-1945. 4.1779
The war for America, 1775-1783. 3.6898
The War for Independence. 3.6932
The war for Lebanon, 1970-1985. 3.3789
The War for the Union. 3.7345
War for the world. 3.1023
War, foreign affairs, and constitutional power.
    4.9741
War in European history. 5.7195
The war in France and Flanders, 1939-1940.
    3.954
The war in heaven. 2.7135
War in heaven. 2.9529
War in medieval English society. 3.1328
War in modern society. 4.4819
The war in Nicaragua. 3.9072
War in peacetime. 3.5016
The war in the air. 3.1049
War in the ancient world. 5.7179
War in the desert. 3.1002
War in the Middle Ages. 5.7187
War in the modern world. 5.7192
War in the shadows. 5.7226
The War Industries Board. 4.1943
War, its causes and correlates. 5.7154
The War lords. 5.7198
The war lords of Washington. 4.1972
War memoirs. 3.978
War memoirs of David Lloyd George ... 3.800
War memoirs of Robert Lansing, Secretary of
    State. 3.832
The war ministry of Winston Churchill.
    3.1659
War music. 2.488
The War of 1812. 3.7103
The war of American independence. 3.6920
The War of Atonement, October, 1973. 3.3938
The war of dreams. 2.9651
War of illusions. 3.2334
The war of the doomed. 3.1115
The war of the end of the world. 2.5434
War on the mind. 5.7170
The war over the family. 4.5650
War, peace, and the Viet Cong. 3.4483
War powers of the President and Congress.
    4.7880
War speeches. 3.896
War, strategy, and maritime power. 5.7156
The war, the West, and the wilderness. 2.2911
War through the ages. 5.7175
The war to end all wars. 3.813
The war with Mexico. 3.7139
The war with Spain in 1898. 3.7503
War with the newts. 2.1665
The war without a name. 3.5208
War without victory. 3.1579
A warbler's song in the dusk. 2.2040
The warden. 2.8226
Ward's directory of ... private U.S. companies.
    4.4606
Ward's directory of ... private US companies.
    4.4606
Warehouse operations, a handbook. 4.4337
Warehousing. 4.4336
Warfare and diplomacy in pre-colonial West
    Africa. 3.5327
Warfare in England, 1066-1189. 3.1263
Warfare in feudal Europe, 730-1200. 5.7186
Warfare in the enemy's rear. 5.7223
Warlord politics. 3.4754
Warlord politics in China, 1916-1928. 3.4770
Warlord: Yen Hsi-shan in Shansi Province,
    1911-1949. 3.4840
Warlords and holy men. 3.1787
The warped vision. 3.1696
The Warrant Chiefs: indirect rule in
    southeastern Nigeria, 1891-1929. 3.5364
Warren Hastings and British India. 3.4270
The warrior and the priest. 3.6307
Warrior government in early medieval Japan.
    3.4935
The warrior merchants. 3.4205
The Warrior tradition in modern Africa.
    3.5078

Warrior women. 2.5891
Warriors and politicians in modern Greece.
    3.2709
Warriors at Suez. 3.5164
The warriors; reflections on men in battle.
    5.7146
Wars and revolutions. 3.1555
Wars and welfare. 3.1649
The wars in Vietnam, Cambodia, and Laos,
    1945-1982. 5.8061
The Wars of the Roses. 3.1376, 3.1378
A Warsaw diary. 2.1700
The Warsaw diary of Adam Czerniakow.
    3.3990
The Warsaw pact. 3.1179
The Warsaw Rising of 1944. 3.997
Warships of the Imperial Japanese Navy,
    1869-1945. 5.7472
Wartime women. 4.6016
Was war necessary? 3.6372
The washing of the spears; a history of the rise
    of the Zulu nation under Shaka and its fall in
    the Zulu War of 1879. 3.5499
Washington. 3.8110
Washington, a bicentennial history. 3.8641
Washington and the Revolution. 3.7031
Washington, city and capital. 3.8112
The Washington community 1800-1828. 3.7085
The Washington correspondents. 2.3670
Washington information directory. 3.8109
Washington Irving. 2.11096, 2.11098
Washington journal. 3.7920
The Washington post. 2.3671
Wasps. 2.430
Waste management. 5.6036
Wastewater engineering. 5.6028
Wastewater treatment technology. 5.6030
The watcher on the cast-iron balcony: Hal
    Porter. 2.10162
Watching the dance go by. 4.1105
Water; a primer. 4.298
Water and tribal settlement in South-east
    Arabia. 4.2934
Water and wastewater control engineering.
    5.5984
Water at the surface of the earth. 4.292
Water atlas of the United States. 4.144
Water-colour painting in Britain. 1.6384
Water-colours illustrating the poems of Thomas
    Gray. 1.6386
Water crisis. 4.2932
Water deficits and plant growth. 5.3756
The water encyclopedia. 5.6015
Water in environmental planning. 5.5989
Water management. 5.5979
Water quality. 5.6018
Water quality criteria for freshwater fish.
    5.3909
Water quality management. 5.6016
Water resources. 5.5975
Water-resources engineering. 5.5962
Water resources of the world. 4.289
Water resources planning. 5.5978
Water rights. 4.9759
Water supply. 4.2930
Water supply and pollution control. 5.6014
Water supply engineering design. 5.6013
Water with berries. 2.9991
The waterfall. 2.9665
The waterfowl of the world. 5.3962
Watergate. 3.7912, 3.7918, 5.7838
Watergate and the Constitution. 4.9637
The Watergate hearings: break-in and cover-up.
    3.7914
The waters of Kronos. 2.12393
The waters of Siloe. 1.3245
The watershed of two eras. 3.614
Watership Down. 2.9611
Watt. 2.8425
Watteau, 1684-1721. 1.4981
Watteau's shepherds. 2.5958
Wave mechanics and its applications. 5.2118
Wavelength tables. 5.2312
Waverley. 2.8044
The Waverley novels. 2.8041
The Waverley novels and their critics. 2.8059
The waves. 2.9580

Waves and beaches. 4.348
Waves and photons. 5.2298
Waves in fluids. 5.2040
The way; an anthology of American Indian
    literature. 2.4323
The way and its power. 1.1802
The Way of a pilgrim and The pilgrim
    continues his way. 1.3113
The way of a ship. 5.7487
The way of all flesh. 2.7515
Way of all the Earth. 2.1537
The way of duty. 3.336
The way of Lao Tzu (Tao-tê ching) 1.1801
The way of the animal powers. 1.1606
The way of the masks. 3.5752
The way of the samurai. 1.1426
The way of the storyteller. 4.10319
Way of truth. 1.248
The way the world works. 4.1455
The way to Christ. 1.3084
The way to Nicea. 1.2834
The way to rainy mountain. 3.5899
The way we live now. 2.8227
The way we think; a collection of essays from
    the Yiddish. 3.3807
The way west. 2.11803
The wayfarer. 2.2082
Wayfarers. 2.14043
Ways of escape and A fuller life. 2.8768
The ways of paradox, and other essays. 1.631
Ways of seeing. 1.5116
The ways of the poem. 2.3743
Ways of thinking of Eastern peoples. 3.109
The ways of white folks. 2.11897
Ways of worldmaking. 1.1314
Ways with words. 4.10393
The wayward and the seeking. 2.12598
The wayward bus. 2.12534
The wayward pressman. 2.3599
Wayward technology. 5.5516
We. 2.1614, 4.576
We always lie to strangers. 2.10723
We always treat women too well. 2.4679
We are Chicanos. 2.10684
We are one! 3.4023
We Barrymores. 2.3242
We can't breathe. 2.13009
We eat the mines and the mines eat us. 4.3539
We have always lived in the castle. 2.11922
We have eaten the forest. 3.4430
We have taken a city. 3.8234
We love Glenda so much and A change of
    light. 2.5379
We love Glenda so much and other tales.
    2.5379
We must run while they walk. 3.5299
We shall be all; a history of the Industrial
    Workers of the World. 4.3555
'We the people' and others. 3.6526
We were there. 4.3296
We who built America. 4.8950
Weak interactions of leptons and quarks.
    5.2486
The weaker vessel. 4.6093
Wealth against commonwealth. 4.3043
Wealth and poverty. 4.1525
Wealth and power in America. 4.2085
Wealth and virtue. 4.1346
Wealth of a nation to be. 4.1904
The wealth of England from 1496-1760.
    4.2253
A wealth of wild species. 5.3222
Wealthy Corinth. 3.2641
The weapons acquisition process. 4.3838
Weapons and hope. 5.7238
Weapons and tactics. 5.7176, 5.7245
Weapons of criticism. 2.2643
The weary blues. 2.11898
Weather. 5.2559
The Weather almanac. 5.2576
Weather and climate modification. 5.2539
Weather and life. 5.3571
Weather atlas of the United States. 4.145
Weather facts and feats. 5.2560
The weather for poetry. 2.11808
The weather handbook. 5.2574
Weather in the West. 5.2578
Weather lore. 5.2584

The weather machine. 5.2573
Weather modification by cloud seeding. 5.2538
Weather of U.S. cities. 5.2577
Weather of US cities. 5.2577
Weather on the planets. 5.1807
Weather prediction by numerical process.
    5.2583
Weaver's study course, ideas and techniques.
    5.7098
Weaving arts of the North American Indian.
    3.5831
The web and the rock. 2.12779
The web of government. 4.7461
Web of group-affiliations. 4.4944
The web of interdependence. 4.9239
Weber and Islam. 1.2075
Webs of power. 4.3024
Webster's collegiate thesaurus. 2.1072
Webster's new biographical dictionary. 3.325
Webster's new collegiate dictionary. 2.1092
Webster's new dictionary of synonyms. 2.1073
Webster's new geographical dictionary. 4.71
Webster's New World dictionary of the
    American language. 2.1091
Webster's ninth new collegiate dictionary.
    2.1092
Webster's sports dictionary. 4.928
Webster's third new international dictionary of
    the English language, unabridged. 2.1088,
    2.1093
The wedding. 2.12056
Wedding man is nicer than cats, Miss. 4.10885
The Wedemeyer mission. 3.6434
Wedemeyer reports!. 3.912
Weeds. 2.11949, 5.5393
Weegee. 5.6995
A week on the Concord and Merrimack Rivers.
    3.7991
Weep before God. 2.9454
Der Weg zurück. 2.13847
The weight of the world. 2.13888
Weimar. 3.2370
The Weimar in crisis. 3.2419
Weimar Republic. 3.2362
The Weimar Republic. 3.2364
Welcome to our city. 2.12780
Welding and other joining processes. 5.7060
Welding process technology. 5.7059
Welding processes. 5.7061
Weldon Kees. 2.11948
Welfare and competition. 4.1336
Welfare medicine in America. 4.3453
Welfare policy and industrialization in Europe,
    America, and Russia. 4.3445
The welfare state. 4.2288
The welfare state and Canadian federalism.
    4.2131
The welfare state and equality. 4.5109
The well at the world's end. 2.7964
The well of days. 2.1479
The well of the unicorn. 2.12354
Well-tempered clavier. 1.4529
The well-tempered critic. 2.2538
The well-tempered tongue. 4.10514
The well-tun'd word. 1.4400
Well-weighed syllables. 2.5795
The well wrought urn. 2.5746
The Wellesley index to Victorian periodicals,
    1824-1900. 5.7919
Wellington. 3.1265
Wells Coates, a monograph. 1.5385
The Welsh in America. 3.6599
The Welsh in the United States. 3.6598
The Welsh in their history. 3.1759
The Welsh Nationalist Party, 1925-1945.
    4.8560
Welsh poems, sixth century to 1600. 2.849
The Welsh question. 3.1769
Welsh rural communities. 4.5336
Welsh society and nationhood. 3.1758
Welsh verse. 2.848
Die Welt als Labyrinth: Gustav René Hocke.
    1.4764
Die Welt von Gestern. 2.13877
Weltkarten zur Klimakunde. 4.131
Wendell Phillips, Brahmin radical. 3.7257
We're in the money: Depression America and
    its films. 2.2908

The werewolf. 2.14050
Das Werk Beethovens. 1.3606
Werke. 2.13552, 2.13568, 2.13597-2.13598,
    2.13660, 2.13663, 2.13667, 2.13750,
    2.13786-2.13787
Werke in 10 Bänden. 2.13610
Werke in einem Band. 2.13547
Werke in sechs Bänden. 2.13590
[Werke in vierzehn Bänden.] 2.13550
Werke in zehn Bänden. 2.13610
Werke in zwei Bänden. 2.13559, 2.13635
Werke, Schriften und Briefe. 2.13563
Werke und Briefe. 2.13656
Werke und Briefe in 12 Bänden. 2.13630
Werke und Briefe in zwölf Bänden. 2.13630
Werke [von] Jean Paul. 2.13644
The Wesleyan edition of the works of Henry
    Fielding. 2.7018
Wessex poems. 2.7762
West Africa. 3.5321, 3.5325
West Africa. 3.5376
West Africa partitioned. 3.5330
West Africa under colonial rule. 3.5328
West African religion. 1.1853
West Africa's Council of the Entente. 3.5379
West Bank/East Bank. 3.4031
The west European city. 4.6250
The West German model. 3.2469
The West German Social Democrats,
    1969-1982. 4.8613
West Germany. 3.2461
West Germany, a European and global power.
    4.4189
West Germany, politics and society. 4.8608
The west-going heart. 2.12016a
The West in Russia and China. 3.3068
West Indian literature. 2.9976, 5.7900
The West Indian novel. 2.9978
The West Indian novel and its background.
    2.9979
West Indian poetry. 2.9977
West Indian societies. 3.9090
West Indian stories. 2.9984
The West Indies before and since slave
    emancipation. 3.9140
West of Suez. 2.9214
West of Wichita. 3.8528
The West Point atlas of American Wars. 4.157
West Virginia. 3.8224
Westcott's Plant disease handbook. 5.5400
The Westering experience in American
    literature. 2.10353
Westering women and the frontier experience,
    1800-1915. 4.5988
Western America. 3.8458
Western Apache raiding and warfare. 3.5842
Western approaches to eastern philosophy.
    1.183
Western aristocracies and imperial court, A.D.
    364-425. 3.2819
Western art. 1.4658
Western asceticism; selected translations.
    1.3076
Western attitudes toward death: from the
    Middle Ages to the present. 1.1323
Western Canada since 1870. 5.7897
Western chamber. 2.2223
Western chamber romance. 2.2219
The Western church in the later Middle Ages.
    1.2308
Western economists and Eastern societies.
    4.2495
Western enterprise in Far Eastern economic
    development, China and Japan. 4.2459
Western Europe. 4.168
Western Europe & Japan between the
    superpowers. 5.7296
Western Europe and Japan between the
    superpowers. 5.7296
Western Europe in the Middle Ages, 300-1475.
    3.575
Western European party systems. 4.8379
The Western films of John Ford. 2.3045
The Western, from silents to cinerama. 2.3012
The western Greeks. 3.2715
The Western intellectual tradition, from
    Leonardo to Hegel. 1.420

Western lands and the American Revolution. 3.6915
Western Marxism. 4.6975
The western Mediterranean world. 4.251
Western mysticism. 1.3080, 5.8446
Western Ontario and the American frontier. 3.8827
Western psychology. 5.75
Western reports on the Taiping. 3.4729
Western reptiles and amphibians. 5.3923
Western sculpture. 1.5611
The western slave coast and its rulers: European trade and administration among the Yoruba and Adja-speaking peoples of South-western Nigeria, southern Dahomey and Togo. 3.5318
Western society and the Church in the Middle Ages. 1.2309
The Western tradition. 3.97
Western transition. 4.2128
Western views of Islam in the Middle Ages. 1.2072
Western women in colonial Africa. 4.6153
The Western World and Japan. 3.4893
Western writing. 2.10468
Western Yorubaland under European rule, 1889-1945. 3.5344
The Westerners. 3.8454
The westernization of Asia. 4.8691
The Westminster Chronicle, 1381-1394. 3.1372
The Westminster dictionary of Christian theology. 1.2224
The Westminster historical atlas to the Bible. 1.2552
Westward expansion. 3.6345
Westward ho! 2.7878
Westward to Vinland. 3.3361
Wet coastal ecosystems. 5.3560
Wetland functions and values. 4.2928
Whales & destiny. 5.5485
Whales, dolphins, and porpoises. 5.4006
Whales, dolphins, and porpoises. 5.4007
What a kingdom it was. 2.11964
What about murder? 2.3470
What Coleridge thought. 2.7598
What color is your parachute? 4.4265
What computers can't do. 5.1008
What country have I? 3.6629
What crucified Jesus? 1.2895
What did Luther understand by religion? 1.2351
What difference could a revolution make? 4.2964
What do unions do? 4.3353
What do you say after you say hello? 5.4896
What does Judaism say about? 1.1895
What every engineer should know about engineering information resources. 5.5502
What happened in history. 3.119
What happens in Hamlet. 2.6659
What I do not believe. 1.88
What is a Gospel? 1.2678
What is a law of nature? 1.1336
What is a thing? 1.990
What is an editor? 2.2519
What is art? 1.1348, 1.4617
What is art history? 1.4656
What is Buddhism? An introduction to the teachings of Lord Buddha with reference to the belief in and the practice of those teachings and their realization. 1.1767
What is Christianity? 1.2260
What is cinema? 2.2936
What is feminism? 4.5899
What is history?. 3.463
What is life? 5.845
What is literature? 2.2607
What is mathematical logic? 5.1052
What is mathematics? 5.1105
What is philosophy? 1.1262
What is political philosophy? 4.7209
What is property? 4.1560
What is remembered. 2.12522
What is structural exegesis? 1.2641
What is symbolism? 2.3880
What is the world made of? 5.2466
What is this thing called science? 5.873
What is to be done? 2.1338, 4.7098

What makes Sammy run? 2.12449
What manner of woman. 2.5586
What Marx really meant. 4.7035
What price economic growth? 4.1989
What price glory. 2.11313
What real progress has metaphysics made in Germany since the time of Leibniz and Wolff? 1.898
What schools are for. 4.10171
What social classes owe to each other. 4.5176
What the Buddha taught. 1.1768
What the Negro can do about crime. 4.6781
What time is this place? 3.63
What to do about AIDS. 5.4984
What to listen for in music. 1.4426
What's to become of the boy?, or, Something to do with books. 2.13696
The wheel of fire. 2.6787
The wheel of life. 1.2125
The wheel of love. 2.13203
When and where I enter. 3.6762
When biology became destiny. 4.6123
When consumers complain. 4.2062
When dreams and heroes died. 4.10093
When fathers ruled. 4.6787
When governments come to Washington: Governors, mayors, and intergovernmental lobbying. 4.7872
When Harlem was in vogue. 1.6710
When honour's at the stake. 2.6833
When Jerusalem burned. 3.3895
When LaGuardia was mayor. 3.8040
When Navajos had too many sheep. 3.5914
When prophecy fails. 5.688
When rain clouds gather. 2.10081
When the going was good. 2.9498
When the mind hears. 4.6607
When the music mattered. 1.4281
When the shooting stops ... the cutting begins. 5.7010
When the spider danced. 3.5384
When the war was over. 3.7460
When unions merge. 4.3337
When we were very young. 2.9113
When workers fight. 4.3573
Whence the power? 2.11363
Where angels fear to tread. 2.8654
Where angels sell eggs and other stories. 2.1909
Where do we go from here. 3.6706
Where does the time go? 4.883
Where have all the wildflowers gone? 5.3648
Where is Francis? 2.8393
Where is science going? 5.920
Where late the sweet birds sang. 2.13426
Where nests the water hen. 2.4824
Where science and politics meet. 5.799
Where the air is clear. 2.5343
Where the law ends. 4.9521
Where the light falls. 2.12408
Where the wasteland ends. 3.205
Where the waves fall. 3.5546
Where we agree. 4.3749
Where winter never comes. 4.109
Where's the melody? 1.4261
Which ones are the enemy? 2.13039
Which side were you on? 4.8236
A Whig embattled. 3.7132
The whig interpretation of history. 3.384
The Whig Party in the South. 4.8217
The Whig supremacy, 1714-1760. 3.1541
The Whigs in opposition, 1815-1830. 4.8559
While England slept. 3.1695
While Messiah tarried. 4.3315
The Whilton dispute, 1264-1380. 4.9415
The whirligig of politics. 3.7412
The whirlpool. 2.7739
Whiskey rebels. 3.7041
The whispered meanings. 2.2578
Whistle blowing. 4.2713
Whistle-blowing. 4.2713
Whistler. 1.5986
Whitaker's almanack. 1.68
Whitaker's cumulative book list. 5.7920
White City of 1893. 5.5657
White collar. 4.6404
White-collar and economic crime. 4.6750
White-collar crime. 4.6749, 4.6751

White collar crime. 4.6763
The white death: the epic of the Soviet-Finnish Winter War. 3.3296
The white devil. 2.6881
White ensign. 3.1030
White Fang. 2.12028
The white guard. 2.1542
White holes. 5.1868
White House watch. 3.7928
White House witness, 1942-1945. 3.7758
White House years. 3.7900
White land, black labor. 3.8268
White-maa's saga. 2.9051
White male monopolies. 4.4973
The white man's burden. 3.7223
The white man's Indian. 3.5824
White mule. 2.12745, 2.12748
White niggers of America. 3.8690
The White Nile. 3.5173
White over black: American attitudes toward the Negro, 1550-1812. 3.6619
The white oxen. 2.11436
White papers for white Americans. 3.6670
The white pony. 2.2193
The white rajahs. 3.4583
White rat. 2.13099
White sociology. 3.6766
White spirituals in the southern uplands. 1.4290
White teacher. 4.10852
White terror. 3.7474
The white tribe of Africa. 3.5501
Whitehall and the wilderness. 3.8372
A Whiteheadian aesthetic. 1.782
Whitehead's metaphysics. 1.779
Whiteoaks of Jalna. 2.9931
Whitewater canoeing. 4.984
Whitman, a collection of critical essays. 2.11280
Whitman's manuscripts. 2.11268
Who are you! 2.8618
Who blowed up the church house? 4.778
Who can be happy and free in Russia. 2.1403
Who commits crimes. 4.6784
Who controls our schools? 4.10037
Who fears the devil? 2.12657
Who goes there? Seven tales of science-fiction. 2.12947
Who governs? 4.8868
Who is she? 2.10144
Who knows. 2.59
Who lived where. 3.5996
Who makes British foreign policy? 3.1646
Who makes the laws? 4.9737
Who offers part-time degree programs? 4.10627
Who owns the media? 2.73
Who paid the taxes, 1966-85? 4.4692
Who pays for clean water? 5.6012
Who pays the property tax? 4.4704
Who pushed Humpty Dumpty? 4.10029
Who rules America? 4.5151
Who rules America now? 4.5221
Who rules Israel? 4.8782
Who rules the joint? 4.6904
Who shall live? Health, economics, and social choice. 5.4635
Who should decide? 5.4573
Who speaks for the child. 4.9507
Who voted? 4.8105
Who voted for Hitler? 4.8601
Who votes? 4.8111
Who was who. 3.1237
Who was who, 1900-1980. 3.347
Who was who in America. 3.6300
Who was who in World War II. 3.889
Who were the Fascists. 4.7609
Who wrote the movie and what else did he write? 2.3074
Whodunit? 2.5961
Whole days in the trees. 2.4520
The Whole film sourcebook. 2.2930
The whole truth. 3.7921
The whole world is watching. 2.70
Wholeness and the implicate order. 5.2127
Who's afraid of Virginia Woolf? 2.12846
Who's he when he's at home. 2.8903
Who's new wave in music. 1.3447

Who's running America? 4.5222
Who's who. 3.1236
Who's who in Africa South of the Sahara.
  3.5220
Who's who in America. 3.6301
Who's who in American art. 1.4889
Who's who in American history. 3.6300-3.6301
Who's who in American Jewry. 3.6578
Who's who in American Jewry (Los Angeles)
  3.6578
Who's who in American music. Classical.
  1.3543
Who's who in American politics. 3.6302
Who's who in Canadian literature 1983-1984.
  2.9888
Who's who in colored America. 3.6815
Who's who in engineering. 5.5663
Who's who in European institutions,
  organizations and enterprises. 1.56
Who's who in German politics. 3.2470
Who's who in graphic art. 1.5791
Who's who in Nazi Germany. 3.346
Who's who in opera. 1.3522
Who's who in Scottish history. 3.1776
Who's who in technology today. 5.5546
Who's who in the Central States 1947. 3.7621
Who's who in the East. 3.6303
Who's who in the East and Eastern Canada.
  3.6303
Who's who in the Midwest. 3.7621
Who's who in the Midwest and Central Canada
  [1965-66]-[1967-68] 3.7621
Who's who in the Pacific Coast. 3.6305
Who's who in the People's Republic of China.
  3.4809
Who's who in the South and Southwest.
  3.6304
Who's who in the United Nations and related
  agencies. 4.9230
Who's who in the West and Western Canada.
  3.6305
Who's who in the world. 3.330
Who's who of British members of Parliament.
  4.8470
Who's who of Indian writers. 2.1924
Who's who of Indian writers, 1983. 2.1926
Who's who of jazz! 1.3541
Whose land? A history of the peoples of
  Palestine. 3.3899
Why are we in Vietnam? 2.12101
Why buildings stand up. 5.6091
Why can't they be like us? America's white
  ethnic groups. 3.6511
Why do the Jews need a land of their own?
  2.1812
Why does language matter to philosophy?
  2.105
Why growth rates differ. 4.2193
Why I am a separatist. 3.8681
Why Ireland starved. 4.2316
Why is there no socialism in the United States?
  4.7006
Why isn't Johnny crying. 5.5112
Why Johnny can't add. 5.1063
Why Johnny still can't read. 4.10459
Why Lenin? Why Stalin? A reappraisal of the
  Russian Revolution. 3.3140
Why marry her? 4.563
Why men rebel. 4.5044
Why nations realign. 3.1167
Why not victory? 3.7574
Why people go to psychiatrists. 5.4864
Why poor people stay poor. 4.1859
Why Switzerland? 3.3509
Why teachers organized. 4.10685
Why the Crimean War? 3.3124
Why the Jews? 3.4012
Why the Lyrical ballads? 2.8310
Why the North won the Civil War. 3.7341
Why we can't wait. 3.6671
Why we lost the ERA. 4.5966
Why we never danced the Charleston. 2.13061
The whys of a philosophical scrivener. 1.86
Wickedness. 1.1488
Wickford Point. 2.12111
The wide net, and other stories. 2.12658
Wide Sargasso Sea. 2.9276
The wide world of John Steinbeck. 2.12538

The widening gulf. 3.3633
The widening gyre. 2.2675
A Widening sphere. 4.6100
Die Widmung. 2.13909
Widow. 5.435
The widow Barnaby. 2.8242
Widowhood in an American city. 4.5793
The widows of Thornton. 2.12580
The widsom of the heart. 2.12181
Wieland. 2.13669
A wife. 2.6500
Wife battering, a systems theory approach.
  4.6747
The wife of Bath's prologue and tale and the
  Clerk's prologue and tale from the
  Canterbury tales. 2.6321
Wife to Mr. Milton. 2.8725
Wilberforce. 3.1580
Wild and woolly. 3.8462
Wild Bapu of Garambi. 2.1908
The 'wild beasts' 1.4846
Wild berries. 2.1557
The wild canids. 5.3993
Wild cats of the world. 5.4000
Wild flowers of the United States. 5.3671
The wild garden = or, Speaking of writing.
  2.9542
The wild geese. 2.2077
The wild goose chase. 2.9467
Wild mammals of North America. 5.3987
The wild man from Sugar Creek. 3.8269
The wild man within. 2.2416
Wild oats. 2.7173
The wild palms. 2.11683
Wild sanctuaries. 5.5308
The wild shore. 2.13296
Wild thyme, winter lightning. 2.8799
Wilderness. 2.12646
Wilderness and the American mind. 3.6148
Wilderness handbook. 5.5498
Wilderness manhunt. 3.8299
Wildflower guide. 5.3675
Wildlife conservation evaluation. 5.3807
Wildlife management. 5.5494
Wildly successful plants. 5.5392
The wildness pleases. 1.1397
The Wiley engineer's desk reference. 5.5670
Wilfred Grenfell, his life and work. 3.8872
Wilfred Owen; a critical study. 2.9219
Wilhelm Busch. 2.13716
Wilhelm Dilthey. 1.983
Wilhelm Lehmbruck. 1.5719
Wilhelm Meister, apprenticeship and travels.
  2.13579
Wilhelm Raabe. 2.13642-2.13643
Wilhelm Tell. 2.13647
Wilhelm von Humboldt. 3.2495
The Wilhelmstrasse. 4.9101
Wilkes and liberty. 3.1571
Wilkie Collins. 2.7611, 2.7613
Wilkie Collins, a biography. 2.7612
Will and spirit. 5.29
Will-o'-the-wisp. 2.13960
The will of heaven. 3.4515
The will to believe and other essays in popular
  philosophy. 1.598
The will to change. 2.12387
The will to die. 2.10094
The will to power. 1.1050
Will you please be quiet, please? 2.12949
Will you still need me, will you still feed me,
  when I'm 84? 4.6593
Willa Cather. 2.11475, 2.11478
Willa Cather's gift of sympathy. 2.11474
Willehalm. 2.13541
Willem de Kooning. 1.5933
Willem de Kooning drawings. 1.5795
William and John Linnell, eighteenth century
  London furniture makers. 5.7071
William Barnes. 2.7791
William Beckford. 2.7398
William Belden Noble lectures. 1.3098
William Billings of Boston: eighteenth-century
  composer. 1.3819
William Blake. 2.7415, 2.7419
William Blake and the moderns. 1.6454,
  2.7433

William Blake, his philosophy and symbols.
  2.7412
William Blake, printmaker. 1.6455
William Blake, the politics of vision. 2.7417
William Blake's illustrations to the poetry of
  Milton. 1.6385
William Blake's Jerusalem. 2.7408
William Blake's writings. 2.7403
William Burges and the High Victorian dream.
  1.4950
William Butterfield. 1.5383
William Byrd. 1.3830
William Carleton, Irish peasant novelist.
  2.7541
William Carlos Williams. 2.12751
William Carlos Williams; a collection of critical
  essays. 2.12752
William Carlos Williams, poet from Jersey.
  2.12756
William Caxton. 5.7555
William Clark. 3.8470
William Cobbett, the poor man's friend.
  3.1575
William Collins and eighteenth-century English
  poetry. 2.6940
William Congreve. 2.6947
William Cowper. 2.6961
William Cowper of the Inner Temple, Esq.
  2.6962
William Cullen Bryant. 2.10917
William Dean Howells. 2.11091, 2.11093
William Dunbar. 2.6476
William Ernest Henley; a study in the 'counter-
  decadence' of the 'nineties. 2.7813
William Faulkner. 2.11686-2.11688, 2.11707
William Faulkner. 2.11693-2.11694, 2.11703
William Faulkner, his life and work. 2.11697
William Faulkner, the Yoknapatawpha world
  and black being. 2.11698
William Faulkner's As I lay dying. 2.11660
William Faulkner's Yoknapatawpha. 2.11695
William Gilmore Simms. 2.11225
William Glackens and the Ashcan group.
  1.5939
William Golding. 2.8711, 2.8714
William Golding: a critical study. 2.8712
William Goyen. 2.11795
William Hale White (Mark Rutherford) 2.8265
William Harvey and his age. 5.4174
William Hastie. 4.9491
William Hazlitt. 2.7808
William Hazlitt, critic of power. 2.7809
William Henry Seward. 3.7158
William Hickling Prescott. 2.11214-2.11215
William Howard Taft: a conservative's
  conception of the Presidency. 3.7709
William Howard Taft, Chief Justice. 4.9830
William Jaffé's Essays on Walras. 4.1367
William James. 1.600
William James. 1.602
William James and other essays on the
  philosophy of life. 1.637
William James and phenomenology. 5.109
William Jennings Bryan. 3.7428
William Lyon Mackenzie King. 3.8745
William Makepeace Thackeray. 2.8193
A William March omnibus. 2.11460
William Marshal. 3.1354
William Marshal, knight-errant, baron, and
  regent of England. 3.1355
William McKinley and his America. 3.7497
William Morris. 2.7971-2.7972
William Morris and W.B. Yeats. 2.7969
William Morris textiles. 1.6676
William of Auvergne and Robert Grosseteste.
  1.386
William Paterson, lawyer and statesman,
  1745-1806. 3.7007
William Pember Reeves, New Zealand Fabian.
  3.5606
William Penn and early Quakerism. 3.8080
William Penn and the founding of
  Pennsylvania, 1680-1684. 3.8082
William Penn, politics and conscience. 4.7414
William Plumer of New Hampshire, 1759-1850.
  3.7010
William Rufus. 3.1343
William S. Burroughs. 2.12936

William Sansom. 2.9302
The William Saroyan reader. 2.12437
William Satchell. 2.10230
William Shakespeare. 2.6690, 2.6693, 2.6698
William Shakespeare, a reader's guide. 2.6734
William Shenstone. 2.7242
William Sidney Mount, 1807-1868. 1.5959
The William Stanley Braithwaite reader. 2.11411
William Strickland, architect and engineer, 1788-1854. 1.5328
William Styron. 2.13348
William Styron's Nat Turner. 2.13339
William Sylvis, pioneer of American labor. 4.3595
William Tecumseh Sherman. 3.7331
William the Conqueror. 3.1342
William the Silent, William of Nassau, prince of Orange, 1533-1584. 3.2964
William III and the defense of European liberty, 1650-1702. 3.1514
William Vaughn Moody. 2.11177
William Warburton. 2.7334
William Wetmore Story and his friends. 1.5677
William Wilberforce. 4.6423
William Wilkins, 1778-1839. 1.5406
William Wordsworth. 2.8304, 2.8311
William Wordsworth, a biography. 2.8314
William Wordsworth, his life, works, and influence. 2.8312
William Wycherley. 2.7340, 2.7343
William Zorach. 1.5679
Williams Pantycelyn. 2.839
Williwaw. 2.12624
Will's visions of Piers Plowman and Do-well. 2.6395
Willy Brandt; portrait of a statesman. 3.2474
Wilson. 3.7723
Wilson and the peacemakers. 3.846
Wilson and Wilson's Comprehensive analytical chemistry. 5.2654
Wilson Harris. 2.10033
The wind. 2.12447
The wind and beyond. 5.6656
Wind and windspinners. 5.6304
The wind band, its literature and technique. 1.4202
Wind effects on structures. 5.5858
Wind energy systems. 5.6306
The wind in the willows. 2.7750
Wind over Wisconsin. 2.11557
Wind, sand, and stars. 2.4702
The winding passage. 4.4782
The window of memory. 2.12792
A window on Russia, for the use of foreign readers. 2.1263
Windows on the mind. 5.4352
Windows on the world. 2.3576
Windpower. 5.6305
Winds of doctrine, and Platonism and the spiritual life. 1.649
The winds of war, a novel. 2.12801
The wind's twelve quarters. 2.13132
Windswept. 2.11485
Windthorst. 3.2299
Windy McPherson's son. 2.11322
The wine of astonishment. 2.10002
Winesburg, Ohio. 2.11323
The wings of the dove. 2.11111
The winner names the age. 2.12490
Winners and losers in East-West trade. 4.4141
Winners, the blue ribbon encyclopedia of awards. 1.52
Winnie the Pooh. 2.9111
Winning elections: a handbook in participatory politics. 4.8184
Winning hearts and minds. 2.10755
The winning of the Midwest: social and political conflict, 1888-1896. 3.8303
The winning of the West. 3.8296
Winning squash racquets. 4.1040
Winning the games scientists play. 5.935
The winning ticket. 4.8865
Winning volleyball: fundamentals, tactics and strategy. 4.1044

Winning ways, for your mathematical plays. 5.1256
The winning weapon. 3.1166
Winnipeg. 4.5251
Winslow Homer. 1.5944
Winslow Homer, American artist: his world and his work. 1.5943
Winston Churchill. 3.1658
Winston Churchill and the second front, 1940-1943. 3.915
Winston Churchill, the wilderness years. 3.1656
Winston Churchill's world view. 3.1660
Winter in April. 2.12241
Winter in the air and other stories. 2.9472
Winter in the blood. 2.13421
A winter in the hills. 2.9455
Winter of artifice. 2.12253
The winter of our discontent. 2.12535
Winter of the salamander. 2.13445
Winter trees. 2.13258-2.13259
The winter war: Finland against Russia, 1939-1940. 3.3298
Winter wheat in the golden belt of Kansas. 5.5244
A Winterthur guide to Chinese export porcelain. 1.6630
Winthrop's Boston. 3.7994
Wisconsin. 2.3030, 3.8441, 3.8443
Wisconsin, a guide to the Badger State. 3.8450
Wisdom in Israel. 1.2608
The wisdom of Catholicism. 1.3133
The wisdom of China and India. 2.1929
The wisdom of Father Brown. 2.7561
The Wisdom of many. 2.3806
Wisdom of royal glory. 2.1979
The Wisdom of Solomon. 1.2623
The wisdom of the body. 5.4187
The wisdom of the outlaw. 2.828
Wise and foolish kings. 3.1970
Wise blood. 2.13210
The wise men of foreign affairs. 3.7601
Wishes, lies and dreams. 2.10673
Wit and its relation to the unconscious. 2.3787
The wit of love: Donne, Carew, Crashaw, Marvell. 2.5801
The witch-herbalist of the remote town. 2.10118
Witch hunting, magic, and the new philosophy. 5.964
Witchcraft and sorcery. 5.672
Witchcraft in France and Switzerland. 5.680
Witchcraft in the Middle Ages. 5.674
Witchcraft, oracles, and magic among the Azande. 3.5183
Witchcraft, oracles and magic among the Azande. 4.562
Witchcraft today. 5.675
Witches & historians. 5.679
The witches of Eastwick. 2.13379
With a daughter's eye. 4.425
With Captain James Cook in the Antarctic and Pacific. 4.90
With Japan's leaders. 3.4928
With Kennedy. 3.7868
With love somehow, poems. 2.8540
With malice toward none. 3.7282
With mortal voice. 2.7138
With the power of each breath. 4.6597
With these hands. 4.6013
Within the whirlwind. 3.3227
Without a stitch in time. 2.11565
Without fear or favor. 3.3664
Without God, without creed. 1.1886
Without honor. 3.4493
Without my cloak. 2.9143
Without shelter. 2.11780
Without stopping. 2.12914
Without wheels. 4.4031
Witkacy. 2.1739
Witness. 3.7543
The witness of poetry. 2.2754
The witness of William Penn. 1.3347
Witness to history, 1929-1969. 3.7631
Witnesses to a vanishing America. 5.3227
Witnessing slavery. 2.10530
Witold Gombrowicz. 2.1704
Wittgenstein. 1.1080-1.1082, 1.1088

Wittgenstein and scientific knowledge. 1.1084
Wittgenstein and the Vienna Circle. 1.1087
Wittgenstein on rules and private language. 1.1083
Wittgenstein: the Philosophical Investigations. 1.1086
Wittgenstein, understanding and meaning. 1.1074
Wittgenstein's doctrine of the tyranny of language. 1.1069
Wittgenstein's Lectures, Cambridge, 1930-1932. 1.1066
Wittgenstein's Lectures, Cambridge, 1932-1935. 1.1065
Wittgenstein's Tractatus. 1.1077, 1.1229
Wives and daughters. 2.7723
Wives for cattle. 4.659
The wizard war. 3.1079
Wladyslaw Stanislaw Reymont. 2.1724
Wm. Osler: the continuing education. 5.4602
Wo warst du, Adam? und Erzählungen. 2.13694
Wodehouse. 2.9560
The woeful Victorian. 2.8143
Wole Soyinka. 2.10116
The wolf. 5.3994
The wolf, a species in danger. 5.3996
Wolf Solent. 2.9236
Wolf willow. 3.8861
Wolfram's Parzival. 2.13542
Wolfwinter. 2.12567
A Wollstonecraft anthology. 2.8291
Wolsey. 3.1412
Wolves for the blue soldiers. 3.5778
Wolves of the world. 5.3995
Woman. 4.5931
Woman and nature. 2.13062
Woman and temperance. 4.6642
Woman and the demon. 2.5727
Woman as force in history. 4.5841
Woman as image in medieval literature from the twelfth century to Dante. 2.2632
The woman citizen. 4.6060
Woman, culture, and society. 4.5939
Woman, dependent or independent variable? 4.5947
The woman from Sarajevo. 2.1207
The woman in Egyptian art. 1.5163
Woman in sexist society. 4.5883
Woman in the crested kimono. 3.348
The woman in the dunes. 2.2125
Woman in the Muslim unconscious. 4.5509
Woman in the nineteenth century. 4.5890
Woman in Western thought. 4.5843
The woman in white. 2.7609
A woman killed with kindness. 2.6585
Woman, new dimensions. 4.5900
The woman of Andros. 2.12714
Woman of letters. 2.9604
A woman of means. 2.12581
Woman on the edge of time. 2.13250
The Woman question. 4.5948
The woman runner. 4.963
A woman speaks. 2.12249
Woman suffrage and politics. 4.8079
The woman suffrage movement in Canada. 4.8293
The woman suffrage movement in Tennessee. 4.8090
The woman taken in adultery and The Poggenpuhl family. 2.13565
The woman within. 2.11777
Womanguides. 1.1614
Woman's almanac. 4.5840
The woman's Bible. 4.5976
Woman's body, woman's right. 4.5689
Woman's estate. 4.5886
Woman's fiction. 2.10287
Woman's health and medical guide. 5.4690
A woman's life in the court of the Sun King. 3.2039
Woman's nature. 4.5949
The Woman's part. 2.6809
Woman's place. 4.3279
Woman's place is at the typewriter. 4.3276
Woman's Rights Conventions, Seneca Falls & Rochester, 1848. 4.8078

Woman's role in economic development. 4.3302
A woman's touch. 1.6533
Woman's transformations. 1.2910
Woman's 'true' profession. 4.10675
Womanspirit rising. 1.1616
Women. 4.5903, 4.6071
Women, a bibliography of bibliographies. 5.8458
Women against censorship. 4.5550
Women and American socialism, 1780-1920. 4.6035
Women & analysis. 4.5943
Women & art. 1.4587
Women and change in Latin America. 4.6084
Women and child care in China. 4.6574
Women and crime. 4.6783
Women and development. 4.5484
Women and economics. 4.6053
Women and equality. 4.6039
Women and film. 2.3015
Women and health in America. 5.4691
Women and madness. 5.4816
Women and male violence. 4.6708
Women & men midwives. 5.5060
Women and men on the overland trail. 4.5603
Women and men speaking. 2.127
Women and minorities in science. 5.804
Women and philosophy. 4.5901
Women and politics. 4.5954, 4.5960
Women and politics in Western Europe. 4.5965
Women and property in Morocco. 4.6160
Women and property, women as property. 4.9372
Women and psychotherapy. 5.4818
Women and public policies. 4.6052
Women and religion. 1.2909
Women and religion in America. 1.2387
Women and revolution. 4.7150
Women and Russia. 4.6135
Women and sexuality in America. 5.8475
Women and slavery in Africa. 4.6448
Women and spirituality. 1.3059
Women and the American labor movement. 4.3270-4.3271
Women and the American left. 5.8472
Women and the cinema. 2.3016
Women and the comics. 2.3813
Women and the English Renaissance. 2.5642
Women and the family in rural Taiwan. 4.6140
Women and the family in the Middle East. 4.6151
Women and trade unions in eleven industrialized countries. 4.3269
Women and utopia. 2.10591
Women and women's issues. 4.5914
Women and work in preindustrial Europe. 4.3253
Women and worship. 1.2987
Women & worship. 1.2987
Women artists. 1.4583
Women artists, 1550-1950. 1.4757
Women artists in history. 1.4589
Women artists in nineteenth-century France and England. 1.4966
Women as candidates in American politics. 4.5968
Women as interpreters of the visual arts, 1820-1979. 1.4586
Women as mythmakers. 1.6689
Women as widows. 4.5791
Women at work. 4.3268, 4.3280
Women beware women. 2.6633
Women, class, and history. 4.6165
Women confined. 5.5068
Women, crime, and criminology. 4.6693
Women cross-culturally. 4.5836
Women, gender, and social psychology. 4.5832
Women have always worked. 4.3283
Women helping women. 4.6587
Women, history & theory. 4.5884
Women-identified women. 4.5525
Women in a developing society. 4.6144
Women in Africa. 4.6158
Women in American architecture. 1.5459
Women in American music. 1.3604

Women in American religion. 1.2388
Women in American society. 4.6023
Women in American theatre. 2.3200
Women in changing Japan. 4.6146
Women in Chinese society. 4.6139
Women in college. 4.10844
Women in Cuba, twenty years later. 4.6086
Women in culture and politics. 4.5951
Women in development. 4.5904
Women in England, 1870-1950. 4.6107
Women in English society, 1500-1800. 4.6110
Women in graduate and professional school education. 4.10842
Women in Hellenistic Egypt. 4.5854
Women in Iberian expansion overseas, 1415-1815. 4.5867
Women in industry; a study in American economic history. 4.3274
Women in Irish society. 4.6113
Women in law enforcement. 4.6804
Women in love. 2.8977
Women in management. 4.4341, 5.8468
Women in mathematics. 5.1089
Women in medicine. 5.4541
Women in medieval society. 4.5859
Women in music. 1.3491
Women in Nazi society. 4.6122
Women in particular. 4.5997
Women in perspective. 5.8461
Women in popular culture. 4.6049
Women in print. 2.3691
Women in ritual and symbolic roles. 1.1615
Women in Roman law & society. 4.5852
Women in Roman law and society. 4.5852
Women in science. 5.812
Women in scientific and engineering professions. 5.805
Women in social and political thought. 4.5955
Women in Soviet society. 4.6134
Women in Stuart England and America. 4.5870
Women in the ancient world. 4.5851
Women in the House. 4.5967
Women in the labour movement. 4.6105
Women in the Middle Ages. 4.5856, 4.5864
Women in the military. 5.7377
Women in the Muslim world. 4.5910
Women in the sixteenth century. 5.8465
Women in the wall. 2.9788
Women in the workplace. 4.3297
Women in the world. 4.5902
Women in Third World development. 4.6166
Women in transition. 4.5784
Women in Washington. 4.5962
Women in Western political thought. 4.5936
Women look at biology looking at women. 5.4199
Women managers. 4.4338
The women novelists. 2.5564
Women novelists in Spain and Spanish America. 2.5096
Women of action in Tudor England. 4.6095
Women of America. 4.5992
Women of 'Amran. 4.6136
The women of Brewster Place. 2.13190
Women of crisis. 4.5994
Women of crisis II. 4.5995
The Women of England. 4.6111
Women of ideas and what men have done to them. 4.5942
Women of iron and velvet. 2.3838
Women of notes. 1.3535
The women of psychology. 5.80
Women of spirit. 1.3000
Women of the Depression. 4.6078
Women of the English Renaissance and Reformation. 4.6099
Women of the medieval world. 4.5862
Women of the Reformation in France and England. 1.2336
Women of the Reformation in Germany and Italy. 1.2337
Women of the Republic. 4.6010
Women of value, men of renown. 4.683
Women of wisdom. 1.2163
Women on film. 2.2960
Women on heroin. 5.4964
Women on love. 2.3918

The women on the porch. 2.11791
The women on the wall. 2.12506
Women on top. 4.4267
Women painters of the world. 1.5860
Women, philosophy, and sport. 4.966
Women poets of the world. 2.3750
Women, power, and change. 4.6065
Women, power, and economic change. 3.5275
Women, power, and policy. 4.6072
Women, power, and subversion. 2.5988
Women priests: yes or no? 1.3005
Women, race, & class. 3.6756
Women, reason, and nature. 4.5932
Women returning to work. 4.3243
Women scientists in America. 5.803
Women, sex, and the law. 4.9865
Women, sport & performance. 5.5029
Women, state, and party in Eastern Europe. 4.5964
Women teachers on the frontier. 4.10674
Women, the family, and freedom. 4.6091
The women troubadours. 2.884
Women united, women divided. 4.5905
Women, war, and revolution. 4.5963
Women, war, and work. 4.3281
Women who kill. 4.6690
Women, wives, mothers. 4.6017
Women, work, and family. 4.3299
Women, work, and family in the Soviet Union. 4.6131
Women, work, and national policy. 4.6025
Women, work, and protest. 4.3272
Women, work, and wages. 4.3260
Women workers in the Second World War. 3.1138
Women working. 4.3244
Women writers and the city. 2.5955
Women writers in Black Africa. 2.10034
Women writers in France: variations on a theme. 2.3837
Women writers in Russian modernism. 2.1307
Women writers of the contemporary South. 2.10464
Women writers of the Middle Ages. 2.2551
Women-writers of the nineteenth century. 2.5721
Women's activism and social change. 4.6077
The Women's annual, ... the year in review. 4.5978
Women's autobiography. 3.321
The Women's book of world records and achievements. 3.351
Women's consciousness, women's conscience. 4.5953
Women's gymnastics. 4.923
The women's health movement. 5.5042
Women's history sources. 5.8477
The women's liberation movement in Russia. 4.6130
Women's life in Greece and Rome. 4.5847
The women's movement in the seventies. 5.8462
The women's movement, political, socioeconomic, and psychological issues. 4.5876
Women's organizations. 4.6171
Women's periodicals and newspapers from the 18th century to 1981. 5.8478
Women's poetry index. 2.2712
Women's quest for power. 4.6141
Women's rights almanac. 4.5979
Women's rights at work. 4.3254
The women's rights movement in the United States, 1848-1970. 5.8473
Women's running. 4.1052
The Women's sharp revenge. 2.6251
Women's studies. 5.8459, 5.8464, 5.8479
Women's Studies International. 4.5991
Women's Studies Newsletter. 4.5991
Women's Studies Quarterly. 4.5991
Women's suffrage and party politics in Britain, 1866-1914. 4.8514
Women's suffrage and social politics in the French Third Republic. 4.8590
Women's two roles: home and work. 4.3242
Women's work and family values, 1920-1940. 4.3248

Women's work and wages in the Soviet Union. 4.3300
Women's work in Britain and America. 5.8470
The wonder of snow. 5.2541
The wonder that was India. 3.4191
The wonderful country. 2.11993
Wonderful fool. 2.2130
Wood and wood products. 5.5796
Wood as an energy resource. 5.6872
Wood, brick, and stone. 1.5280
Wood, brick, & stone. 1.5280
Wood engraving. 1.6476
Wood structure and identification. 5.5430
Woodcraft, or, Hawks about the dovecote; a story of the South at the close of the Revolution. 2.11221
The wooden churches of Eastern Europe. 1.5525
The wooden shepherdess. 2.9709a
The Wooden Star. 2.13117
Wooden titan. 3.2350
Woodland ecology. 5.3783
Woodrow Wilson. 3.7721, 3.7724, 3.7729
Woodrow Wilson, a medical and psychological biography. 3.7725
Woodrow Wilson and the balance of power. 3.7714
Woodrow Wilson and the great betrayal. 3.846
Woodrow Wilson and the lost peace. 3.846
Woodrow Wilson and the politics of morality. 3.7720
Woodrow Wilson and the progressive era, 1910-1917. 3.7716
Woodrow Wilson and world politics. 3.7728
Woodrow Wilson; life and letters. 3.7719
Woodrow Wilson, Revolutionary Germany, and peacemaking, 1918-1919. 3.848
Wood's Unabridged rhyming dictionary. 2.1050
Woods-working women. 5.5434
Woodstock census. 4.5749
Woodward's architecture and rural art. 1.5560
Woodward's Victorian architecture and rural art. 1.5560
Woodwind instruments and their history. 1.4163
Woodwind music guide. 1.3603
Woodwinds. 1.4550
Woody Guthrie. 1.4111
The wool-hat boys. 4.8231
Word and faith. 1.2742
Word and object. 1.546
The word and verbal art. 2.2343
Word-by-word translations of song and arias. 1.3456
A word carved on a sill. 2.9456
A word child. 2.9770
A word geography of the eastern United states. 2.1120
Word-hoard. 2.943
Word index to James Joyce's Ulysses. 2.8883
A word index to Plato. 1.243
The word is here. 2.2307
The word of God and the word of man. 1.2258
Word order patterning in Middle English. 2.954
Word play; what happens when people talk. 2.26
Word plays. 2.10807
Wordplays. 2.10807
The words. 2.4737
Words and deeds. 2.68
Words and objections. 1.632
Words and phrases index. 2.1107
Words and pictures. 1.5178
Words and places: illustrations of history, ethnology & geography. 4.73
Words and their use. 2.1067
Words and their ways in English speech. 2.1055
Words and things. 2.87
Words for Dr. Y. 2.12458
Words in stone. 2.4418
Words into type. 2.2524
Words on words. 2.1004
Words that won the war. 3.838

Wordsworth: a collection of critical essays. 2.8318
Wordsworth and Coleridge, 1795-1834. 2.8317
Wordsworth and the human heart. 2.8323
Wordsworthian criticism. 2.8321
Wordsworth's language of men. 2.8328
Wordsworth's 'natural Methodism'. 2.8326
Wordsworth's poetry, 1787-1814. 2.8319
Work. 2.10901
Work and authority in industry. 4.6397
Work and equality in Soviet society. 4.3232
Work & family. 4.3119
Work and family. 4.3119
Work and family in the United States. 4.5576
Work and human behavior. 5.408
Work and motivation. 4.4353
Work, culture, and society in industrializing America. 4.3568
The work ethic in business. 4.4271
The work ethic in industrial America, 1850-1920. 4.3574
Work in America. 4.3214
Work in progress. 2.8923
Work is dangerous to your health. 5.5015
Work of art. 2.12010
The work of Atget. 5.6973
The work of Augustus Saint-Gaudens. 1.5672
The work of living art. 2.3096
The work of the gods in Tikopia. 4.555
Work performance. 4.4379
Work, society, and politics. 4.2278
Work, technology, and education. 4.10019
Work transformed. 4.3318
Work, youth, and schooling. 4.10832
Worker and community. 4.3617
The worker and the job: coping with change. 4.3578
Worker city, company town. 4.3532
Worker cooperatives in America. 4.3067
Worker in the cane. 4.3542
Worker militancy and its consequences, 1965-75. 4.3440
Worker participation and American unions. 4.3185
Worker participation and ownership. 4.3187
The worker views his union. 4.3367
Workers and Utopia. 4.3355
Workers and wages in an urban labor market. 4.3224
Workers' control in America. 4.3571
Workers' control under plan and market. 4.3188
Workers councils. 4.3182
Workers, factories, and social change in India. 4.2513
Workers in industrial America. 4.3348
Workers in the dawn. 2.7740
Workers' management and workers' wages in Yugoslavia. 4.3191
Workers on the edge. 4.2043
Workers' rights. 4.3581
The working brain. 5.4311
Working-class community in industrial America. 4.3619
Working class Conservatives in urban England. 4.3651
Working class radicalism in mid-Victorian England. 4.3644
Working-class suburb. 4.6354
The working-class Tories. 4.8489
Working for the railroad. 4.3541
Working for the sovereign. 4.3509
Working friendship. 1.3998
Working hours in British industry. 4.3159
Working papers in the theory of action. 4.4962
Working papers on Canadian politics. 4.8297
A working peace system. 4.7547
Working people of Philadelphia, 1800-1850. 4.3622
Working the street. 4.6801
Working wives, working husbands. 4.5594
Working women in Japan. 4.3301
Working women in Renaissance Germany. 4.5866
Working women in socialist countries. 4.1642
Working your way to the bottom. 4.3255
Workingmen's democracy. 4.3556

Works. 1.2347, 2.6310, 2.6471, 2.6876, 2.6911, 2.7094, 2.7325, 2.7470, 2.11772, 3.3230
Works and correspondence. 4.1417
The works and days. 2.479
Works & days. 2.480
Works, and miscellaneous short poems. 2.6584
The works in architecture of Robert & James Adam. 1.5379
The works in verse and prose of Nicholas Breton. 2.6432
Works issued by the Hakluyt Society. 4.87
The works of Allan Ramsay. 2.7209
The works of Anne Bradstreet. 2.10864
The Works of Aphra Behn. 2.6899
The works of Aristotle translated into English ... 1.283
The works of Arnold Schoenberg. 1.3613
The works of Charles and Mary Lamb. 2.7899
The works of Charles Reade. 2.7999
The works of Colonel John Trumbull. 1.5981
The works of Congreve: Comedies: Incognita: Poems. 2.6943
The works of Edmund Spenser. 2.6522
The works of George Farquhar. 2.7014
The works of George Herbert. 2.7061
The works of George Meredith. 2.7936
The works of Hsüntze. 1.168
The Works of Hubert Howe Bancroft. 3.8588
The works of Israel Zangwill. 2.8369
The works of J. M. Barrie. 2.7389
The works of James McNeill Whistler. 1.5985
The works of John Dryden. 2.6985
The works of John Milton. 2.7110
The works of John Ruskin. 2.8023
The works of Jonathan Edwards. 1.3332
The Works of Joseph Conrad. 2.8541
The works of Joseph Légaré, 1795-1855. 1.6000
The works of Karlheinz Stockhausen. 1.3995
The works of Leo Tolstoy ... 2.1429
The works of Lord Macaulay, complete. 2.7918
Works [of] Malory. 2.6407
Works of man. 5.5528
The works of Mark Twain. 2.10936
The works of Oliver Wendell Holmes. 2.11079
The works of Ralph Vaughan Williams. 1.4020
The works of Robert Louis Stevenson. 2.8117
The works of Schopenhauer, abridged. 1.958
The works of Sir David Lindsay of the Mount, 1490-1555. 2.6486
The works of Sir John Suckling. 2.7286
The works of Stefan George. 2.13751
The works of Tennyson. 2.8155
The works of the Emperor Julian. 2.377
The works of the Gawain-poet. 2.6143
The works of Thomas Carlyle. 2.7544
The works of Thomas Deloney. 2.6449
The works of Thomas Kyd. 2.6606
The works of Thomas Love Peacock. 2.7992
The works of Thomas Lovell Beddoes. 2.7399
The works of Thomas Middleton. 2.6632
The works of Thomas Nashe. 2.6641
The works of Thomas Otway; plays, poems, and love letters. 2.7176
The works of Tobias Smollett. 2.7258
The works of W. E. Henley. 2.7812
The works of William Collins. 2.6939
The works of William E. Channing. 1.3413
The Works of William Makepeace Thackeray. 2.8183
Works on English orthography and pronunciation. 2.1026
Works on vision. 1.687
Works translated into English under the editorship of W. D. Ross. 1.283
World. 5.835
World accumulation, 1492-1789. 4.1750
The world after the Peace conference. 3.862
The World almanac and book of facts. 1.65
The world and the individual. 1.638
The world and the west. 3.103
World armaments and disarmament. 5.7250
The world as power. 1.1723
The world as will and idea. 1.962
World Atlas. 4.112
World atlas of agriculture. 4.136

World atlas of exploration. 4.49
World atlas of geomorphic features. 4.130
A world atlas of military history, 1861-1945. 4.119
A world atlas of military history, 1945-1984. 4.121
World authors, 1950-1970. 2.2550
The world automotive industry. 4.3816
The World Bank since Bretton Woods. 4.4572
The world between the wars, 1919-39. 4.1775
A world bibliography of bibliographies. 5.7680
World bibliography of international documentation. 5.8266
World broadcasting systems. 4.4055
A world by itself. 2.10976
World canals. 4.3946
The world chess championship. 4.1073, 4.1075
World Christian encyclopedia. 1.2285
World chronology series. 3.371
World climatic data. 5.2529
World coin encyclopedia. 3.273
World conqueror and world renouncer. 1.2112
The world copper industry. 4.3739
The World Council of Churches. 1.3097
The world crisis. 3.783
The world crisis and American responsibility. 3.7592
The world crisis in education. 4.9965
World crop statistics: area, production and yield, 1948-64. 4.2902
A world destroyed. 3.938
World development report. 4.1825
World drama. 2.2785
World drama from Æschylus to Anouilh. 2.3166
World economic development. 4.2784
World economic report. 4.1780
World economic survey. 4.1780
A world elsewhere. 2.10255
The world encompassed. 4.97
The World encyclopedia of cartoons. 1.5845
The World encyclopedia of comics. 2.3812
World encyclopedia of political systems & parties. 4.7777
World energy outlook. 4.3709
World energy production and productivity. 5.6117
World energy supplies. 5.6119
World enough and time. 2.12647
The world factbook. 4.81
World factbook (Washington, D.C.) 4.81
World fish farming. 5.5467
World fisheries policy. 5.5474
The world from Brown's Lounge. 3.6749
World furniture. 1.6554
World geography of petroleum. 5.6804
World guide to libraries. 5.7658
World guide to scientific associations. 5.690
World guide to scientific associations and learned societies. 5.690
World handbook of political and social indicators. 4.5094
The world health market. 4.3795
A world history of photography. 5.6921
A world history of physical education: cultural, philosophical, comparative. 4.898
World history of the dance. 4.1102
A world history of the twentieth century. 3.737
A world I never made. 2.11654
The world in depression, 1929-1939. 4.1717
The World in figures. 4.1247
The World in space. 5.1786
The world in the attic. 2.12218
The world in the crucible, 1914-1919. 3.787
World index of economic forecasts. 4.1721
World industrial archaeology. 5.5545
World inflation and the developing countries. 4.4524
The world is a wedding. 2.12453
World labour report. 4.3199
World light (Heimslxjós) 2.13996
A world list of mammalian species. 5.3978
World maps of climatology. 4.131
World military and social expenditures. 4.4721
World mineral trends and U.S. supply problems. 4.3727
World minorities. 4.6457

A world more attractive. 2.2678
World motor vehicle data. 4.3815
World moves on. 3.5610
The world my wilderness. 2.9067
World (New York, 1966-) 2.10710
The World of abstract art. 1.4802
The world of apples. 2.11495
The world of baroque & classical musical instruments. 1.4135
The world of Bede. 2.6287
The world of Bemelmans. 2.11364
The world of Black singles. 4.5773
The World of Buddhism. 1.2142
The world of business. 4.4250
The world of Canadian writing. 2.9889
The world of Christopher Robin. 2.9113
The world of Count Basie. 1.3749
The world of Evelyn Waugh. 2.9481
World of fiction. 2.3412
The world of George Jean Nathan. 2.12236
The World of George Orwell. 2.9205
A World of grace. 1.3279
The world of Gwendolyn Brooks. 2.11419
The world of Harlequin. 2.4886
The world of humanism, 1453-1517. 3.628
The world of Indonesian textiles. 5.7076
The world of Japanese ceramics. 5.6899
The world of Jean Anouilh. 2.4362
The world of John Lardner. 2.11977
The world of law. 2.3720
The world of Lawrence. 2.8988
The world of Lawrence Durrell. 2.8612
The World of learning. 1.50
World of learning. 1.50
A world of love. 2.8479
The world of mathematics. 5.1024
The world of measurements. 5.2024
The world of Medieval & Renaissance musical instruments. 1.4131
The world of melodrama. 2.2820
The world of mission. 1.3020
The world of music. 1.3698
The world of nations. 4.5095
The world of Odysseus. 2.494
A world of order and light. 2.13034
World of our fathers. 3.8049
The world of Paul Slickey. 2.9212
World of percussion. 1.4183
The World of poetry. 2.2759
The World of Pooh. 2.9111
A world of scarcities. 4.1771
A world of secrets. 4.7771
The world of Somerset Maugham. 2.9109
The world of stereographs. 5.6992
A world of strangers. 2.10078
The world of swing. 1.4321
The world of Tennessee Williams. 2.12738
The world of the ancient Maya. 3.9038
The world of the burglar. 4.6699
The world of the family. 4.5562
The world of the Florentine Renaissance artist. 1.5008
The world of the French Revolution. 3.663
The world of the Huns. 3.584
The world of the older woman. 4.5805
The world of the past. 4.694
The world of the Phoenicians. 3.3786
The world of the Reformation. 1.2325
The world of the shining prince. 3.4902
The world of the thriller. 2.3471
The world of the urban working class. 4.3618
The world of the Vikings. 3.3362
The world of Time Inc. 5.7586
The world of Washington Irving. 2.10380
World of wonders. 2.9927
The world of yesterday. 2.13878
A world on paper. 5.1928
World outlook and state of food and agriculture. 5.5220
World over. 2.9095
World peace through world law. 4.9211
The world petroleum market. 4.3756
World petroleum resources and reserves. 5.6805
World politics and international economics. 4.4161
World politics in the General Assembly. 4.9243

World population. 4.1618
World population and development. 4.1605
World population and production. 4.1795
World population and resources. 4.1598
World population control. 4.5695
World population crisis. 4.5691
World population, past growth and present trends. 4.1611
World prehistory. 4.695
World press encyclopedia. 2.3550
World product and income. 4.1401
World radio TV handbook. 5.6421
The world railway system. 4.3979
World resources. 4.1764
World resources and industries. 4.4127
A world restored. 3.694
World revolution and family patterns. 4.5640
The world rushed in. 3.8608
World shipping. 4.3954
World steel in the 1980s. 4.3731
World survey of climatology. 5.2558
The world system: models, norms, applications. 4.4889
World tables. 4.1794
World tapestry, from its origins to the present. 1.6589
The world, the text, and the critic. 2.2442
The world theatre of Wagner. 1.4518
The world their household. 1.3025
The world tin market. 4.3741
World trade annual. 4.4091
World treaty index. 4.8970
The world turned upside down. 3.1452
World vegetables. 5.5338
World War 2 from an American perspective. 5.8232
World War 2, the European and Mediterranean theaters. 5.8231
The World War and American isolation, 1914-1917. 3.833
World War I and the American novel. 2.10399
World War I and the origin of civil liberties in the United States. 4.7695
World War II and its origins. 3.740
World War II at sea. 5.8230
World War II from an American perspective. 5.8232
World War II, policy and strategy. 3.888
World War II, the European and Mediterranean theaters. 5.8231
World War Two from an American perspective. 5.8232
World water balance. 4.296
The world we have lost. 4.5298
World who's who in science. 5.816
World within walls. 2.2000
World within world. 2.9372
The world without a self. 2.9603
World without borders. 4.1782
The World yearbook of robotics research and development. 5.6164
The world zinc industry. 4.3743
The worldly philosophers. 4.1315
Worldmark encyclopedia of the nations. 4.7
Worlds apart. 4.2750, 4.10803
The world's beef business. 4.3696
World's birds. 5.3945
The world's body. 2.2763
The world's great dailies. 2.3544
The world's great speeches. 2.3779
Worlds in consciousness; mythopoetic thought in the novels of Virginia Woolf. 2.9601
Worlds in regression. 2.1587
The world's legal systems. 4.9346
The world's living languages: basic facts of their structure, kinship, location, and number of speakers. 2.166
The world's money. 4.4573
The Worlds of Alfonso the Learned and James the Conqueror. 3.3429
The worlds of Maurice Samuel. 3.4028
Worlds of music. 1.4365
Worlds of pain. 4.5597
The worlds of Robert E. Sherwood. 2.12467
The worlds of Truman Capote. 2.11468
The world's whales. 5.4008
Worlds within worlds. 5.2433

Worldwide directory of national earth-science agencies and related international organizations. 5.2957
Worldwide government directory, with inter-governmental organizations. 4.7708
Worldwide inflation. 4.4491
The Worm Ouroboros. 2.8613
The worried man's guide to world peace. 4.9127
Worship. 1.2979
Worship in the early church. 1.2978
Worship; its theology and practice. 1.2980
The worship of the early church. 1.2977
Wörterbuch der deutschen Umgangssprache. 2.1186
Worthy of the nation. 4.6329
The wound and the bow. 2.2604
Wozzeck. 1.4513
The WPA guide to New York City. 3.8036
A wreath for Udomo. 2.10058
Wrestlin' Jacob. 1.2418
Wrestling terms and holds. 4.1060
The wretched of Canada. 4.2133
The wretched of the earth. 3.5118
Wright Morris. 2.12220
Writer and public in France. 2.3836
The writer and the absolute. 2.2522
The writer and the screen. 2.3018
Writers and friends. 2.3637
Writers & society in contemporary Italy. 2.4883
Writers and society in contemporary Italy. 2.4883
A writer's Britain. 2.5582
A writer's diary. 2.9584
A writer's guide to book publishing. 2.2523
Writers in crisis; the American novel, 1925-1940. 2.10622
Writer's life. 2.9596
A writer's notebook. 2.9104
A writer's notebook, 1854-1879, and uncollected writings. 2.7691
Writers on the left, episodes in American literary communism. 2.10431
Writers on writing. 2.2517
Writing. 2.170
Writing American history. 3.6211
Writing & designing operator manuals. 5.5507
Writing and designing operator manuals. 5.5507
Writing and sexual difference. 2.2556
Writing beyond the ending. 2.10435
Writing book reviews. 2.2477
Writing degree zero. 2.2536
Writing in content areas. 4.10478
Writing in society. 2.5558
Writing 'independent' history. 3.5061
Writing nature. 2.11248
The writing of American history. 3.6213
The writing of Canadian history. 3.8667
The Writing of East and Central Africa. 2.10038
The writing of fiction. 2.3432
The Writing of history. 3.413
The writing of history in nineteenth-century Egypt. 3.5158
The writing of history in the Soviet Union. 3.3035
The writing of modern fiction. 2.3431
The writing of Past and present. 2.7559
The writing of Wole Soyinka. 2.10115
The Writing on the wall. 2.1695
The writing on the wall. 2.12061
Writing southern history. 3.8114
The writing system for engineers and scientists. 5.5509
Writing the Australian crawl. 2.2748
Writing Tom Sawyer. 2.10945
The Writings. 1.2599
Writings. 1.969, 1.5272
The writings. 2.11148
Writings and buildings. 1.5339
Writings and speeches of Eugene V. Debs. 4.6995
Writings by W.E.B. Du Bois in non-periodical literature edited by others. 3.6824
Writings by W.E.B. Du Bois in periodicals edited by others. 3.6826

Writings in periodical literature. 3.6826
The writings of a savage. 1.6106
The writings of Anna Freud. 5.564
Writings of Charles S. Peirce. 1.619
The writings of Eduardo Mallea. 2.5392
The writings of Elliott Carter. 1.3468
The writings of George Eliot. 2.7690
The writings of George Washington from the original manuscript sources 1745-1799. 3.7035
The writings of Henry D. Thoreau. 2.11246
The writings of James Fenimore Cooper. 2.10972
The writings of Jean-Paul Sartre. 2.4739
Writings of John Quincy Adams. 3.7068
The writings of Robert Smithson. 1.5142
The writings of William Gilmore Simms. 2.11220
Writings on American History. 5.7829
Writings on art. 1.5143
Writings on British history. 5.7983
Writings on Canadian English, 1792-1975. 5.7894
Writings on economics. 4.1413
Written letters. 1.6602
The Wrong set and other stories. 2.9543
Wrongful imprisonment. 4.9429
Wrought iron in architecture ... 1.5510
Wu tse t'ien ssu ta ch'i an. English. Selections. 2.2229
Wuthering Heights, revised. 2.7459
WW II. 3.906
Wyatt, the critical heritage. 2.6552
Wycherley's drama. 2.7341
Wyman's Gardening encyclopedia. 5.5365
Wyndham Lewis. 2.9046
Wyndham Lewis, the novelist. 2.9047
Wyoming. 3.8553-3.8554

X. 2.12940
X-ray analysis and the structure of organic molecules. 5.2931
X-ray crystallography. 5.2323
X-ray spectroscopy. 5.2325
X-ray structure determination. 5.2936
X-ray studies of materials. 5.2324
X-raying the pharaohs. 3.5144
Xala. 2.4861
Xenophon. 2.398, 2.565
Xerxes' invasion of Greece. 3.2602
The Xhosa Ntsomi. 4.814

Yad Washem studies on the European Jewish catastrophe and resistance. 3.3955
Yale. 4.11000
Yale College. 4.10999
The Yale edition of Horace Walpole's correspondence. 3.11528
Yale edition of the complete works of St. Thomas More. 2.6495
The Yale edition of the private papers of James Boswell. 2.6904
The Yale edition of the works of Samuel Johnson. 2.7078
The Yale Gertrude Stein. 2.12510
Yama: <The pit> a novel in three parts. 2.1515
Yamagata Aritomo in the rise of modern Japan, 1838-1922. 3.4963
Yankee City. 4.5146
Yankee from Olympus. 4.9817
Yankee from the West. 3.7693
A Yankee in Canada. 3.8809
Yankee politics in rural Vermont. 4.8261
Yankee science in the making. 5.797
Yankee stonecutters. 1.5658
Yankee theatre. 2.3202
Yanqui politics and the Isthmian Canal. 3.6476
Yaqui deer songs. 2.2335
The Yaquis. 3.8914
Yardsticks of the universe. 5.2003
The yawning heights. 2.1649
The Year 1200. 1.4752, 3.148
The year 2000. 3.72
A year from Monday. 2.12941
The year in San Fernando. 2.9998
The year of decision, 1846. 3.8471

Year of decisions. 3.7813
The year of liberty. 3.1839
The year of protest, 1956. 2.1300
Year of the 3 kaisers. 3.2329
The year of the monkey. 4.10989
The year of the people. 3.7893
The year of the three kaisers. 3.2329
The year of the whale. 5.4009
The year of the young rebels. 4.9980
Yearbook. 4.2428, 4.9202
Yearbook - National Council for the Social Studies. 4.1222
Yearbook of agriculture. 5.5215
Yearbook of American and Canadian churches. 1.2368
Yearbook of anthropology. 4.395
Yearbook of comparative and general literature. 2.2697
Yearbook of higher education. 4.10541
Yearbook of international organisations. 4.9103
Yearbook of international organizations. 4.9103
Yearbook of international trade statistics. 4.4115
Yearbook of robotics research and development. 5.6164
The Yearbook of school law. 4.9579
Yearbook of science and technology. 5.704
Yearbook of the American short story. 2.10809
Yearbook of the Encyclopedia Americana. 1.11
Yearbook of the National Society for the Study of Education. 4.10159
The yearling. 2.12375
Yearning for yesterday. 5.443
The years. 2.9581
The years as catches. 2.11615
Years of decision. 3.7493
Years of infamy. 3.1027
The years of Lyndon Johnson. 3.7886
The years of MacArthur. 3.7611
Years of protest. 2.10850
Years of recovery. 4.2286
Years of the golden cockerel: the last Romanov tsars, 1814-1917. 3.3108
The years of triumph? 3.2440
Years of upheaval. 3.7859
A year's residence in the United States of America. 3.6030
The years with Ross. 2.3631
Yeats. 2.8346-2.8347, 2.8358
Yeats & American poetry. 2.10499
Yeats and American poetry. 2.10499
Yeats and Anglo-Irish literature. 2.8359
Yeats at his last. 2.8356
Yeats, the man and the masks. 2.8343
Yeats: the nineteenth century matrix. 2.8348
Yeats, the playwright. 2.8360
Yeats's Vision and the later plays. 2.8337
Yeki bud, yeki nabud. 2.1978
The Yellow book. 2.6091
Yellow book. 2.6091
Yellow wallpaper, and other fiction. 2.11041
The Yemassee. 2.11222
The Yemens. 3.4061
The Yenan Way in revolutionary China. 4.7113
The Yeshiva. 2.1805
Yesterday and today. 3.7839
Yesterdays. 1.4255
Yesterday's children. 4.10379
Yesterday's deterrent. 5.7467
Yesterday's soldiers. 5.7292
Yet again. 2.8437
Les Yeux d'Elsa. 2.4378
Yevtushenko's reader. 2.1559
Yiddish literature. 2.1792
The Yiddish theatre in America. 2.3403
[Ying Hua ta tz'u tien] 2.2147
Yoga and the Hindu tradition. 1.206
Yoga as philosophy and religion. 1.202
Yoga; immortality and freedom. 1.203
Yoga philosophy of Patañjali. 1.205
The Yoga-system of Patañjali. 1.204
Yogavāsistharāmāya.na. 5.655
Yohannes IV of Ethiopia. 3.5244

The Yoknapatawpha country. 2.11686
Yoknapatawpha world and black being.
2.11698
Yongbi ŏch'ŏn'ga. English. 1975. 2.2138
Yorck and the era of the Prussian reform,
1807-1815. 3.2493
Yorick and the critics. 2.7284
The York cycle of mystery plays. 2.6211
York mystery plays. 2.6214
York plays. 2.6211
The York plays. 2.6213
York plays. 2.6213
York plays. Selections. 2.6214
Yoruba beliefs and sacrificial rites. 1.1863
The Yoruba today. 3.5345
Yosemite and the range of light. 5.6981
Yosemite and the Sierra Nevada. 3.8617
Yoshe Kalb. 2.1823
The Yoshida memoirs. 3.4982
Yoshida Shōin, forerunner of the Meiji
restoration. 3.4955
You and your leaders. 3.7535
You are happy. 2.9910
You are not alone. 5.4830
You can't go home again. 2.12781
You live and love and other stories. 2.1630
You shall be as gods. 1.2570
The young Caesar. 2.9468
Young Charles Lamb, 1775-1802. 2.7906
Young Edward Gibbon, gentleman of letters.
3.2744
Young endeavour. 5.728
The Young Fanny Burney. 2.6895
Young Frederick Douglass. 3.7241
Young Germany. 4.5114
The young Hegelians and Karl Marx. 1.1037
The young Henry Adams. 3.6243
The young Hitler I knew. 3.2404
Young India. 3.4230
Young Japan. 3.4948
Young La Fontaine. 2.4032
The young Lloyd George. 3.1670
Young Lonigan. 2.11653
Young man Luther. 1.2341
Young man Thoreau. 2.11253
Young man with a horn. 2.11344
The young manhood of Studs Lonigan.
2.11653
Young radicals. 4.5766
The young rebel in American literature.
2.10245
The young Richelieu. 3.2025
Young Sam Johnson. 2.7087
The young Shelley. 2.8106
Young Thomas Hardy. 2.7776
The young Tolstoi. 2.1443
Young Törless. 2.13845
The Young Turks. 3.3587, 3.3589
The young visiters. 2.8389
The young voter's manual. 4.7863
The younger Pitt. 3.1578

The youngest science. 5.4532
Your child is a person. 4.5709
Your Federal income tax for individuals.
4.9766
Your man at the UN. 4.9238
Your memory, a user's guide. 5.4350
Your voice at city hall. 4.8854
Youth. 4.5754
Youth, alcohol, and social policy. 4.6639
Youth and dissent. 4.5767
Youth and history. 4.5755
Youth and the labor market. 4.3306
Youth drug abuse. 4.6667
The youth labor force, 1945-1995. 4.3304
The Youth labor market problem. 4.3307
The youth of Frederick the Great. 3.2488
The youth revolution. 4.5113
Yuan Shih-k'ai. 3.4767
The Yugoslav economic system and its
performance in the 1970s. 4.2423
Yugoslav literature, 1945-1975. 2.1199
Yugoslavia. 3.3554, 3.3560
Yugoslavia, a country study. 3.3604
Yugoslavia and the new communism. 3.3565
Yugoslavia and the nonaligned world. 3.3562
Yugoslavia and the Soviet Union, 1939-1973.
3.3555
Yugoslavia; patterns of economic activity.
4.2424
The Yugoslavs. 3.3564
Yukiguni. 2.2103
Yün-kang shih k'u. 1.5759
Yunkang caves. 1.5759
Yves Bonnefoy. 2.4419
Yves Tanguy. 1.6150
Ywain. 2.3949

Zachary Taylor. 3.7171
Zadkine. 1.5713
Zaïre, a country study. 3.5417
Zaire, the political economy of
underdevelopment. 4.2594
Zakhor, Jewish history and Jewish memory.
3.3848
Zamani. 3.5261
Zambia. 3.5517
Zambia, a country study. 3.5518
Zane Grey. 2.11801
Zanzibar. 3.5288, 3.5291
Zanzibar, its society and its politics. 3.5288
The Zanzibar, revolution and its aftermath.
3.5290
Zapata. 3.8953
The Zapotecs. 3.8915
Der Zauberer. 2.13837
Zazie dans le metro. 2.4681
Zealots and rebels. 4.8575
Zeit-Geist. 1.4801
Zeitgeist. 1.4801
Zelda. 2.11741
Zen and Japanese culture. 1.1763

Zen and Shinto. 1.212
Zen and the art of motorcycle maintenance.
3.340
Zen at Daitoku-ji. 1.2153
Zen Buddhism. 1.1755
Zen Buddhism, selected writings. 1.1750
Zen enlightenment. 1.2173
Zen Master Dōgen. 1.2177
The Zen Master Hakuin: selected writings.
1.1762
Zen painting & calligraphy. 1.5881
Zermelo's axiom of choice. 5.1354
Zero. 1.4837
Zero gradient synchrotron. 5.2447
Zero population growth 4.1670
Zeta-functions. 5.1579
Zettel. 1.1067
Zeus. 1.1666
Zhou Enlai. 3.4817
Zik. 3.5362
Zimbabwe, a country study. 3.5509
Zimbabwe: prose and poetry. 2.2312
The Zimmermann telegram. 3.777
Zimmermann's World resources and industries.
4.4127
Zinaida Hippius. 2.1499
Zion in America. 3.6568
Zionism and the Palestinians. 3.3865
Zionism at the UN. 3.4025
Zionism, the formative years. 3.4024
'Znanie' School of Maxim Gorky. 2.1325
Zohar. English. Selections. 1.1949
Zohar, the book of enlightenment. 1.1949
Zola's Germinal. 2.4342
Zola's Son Excellence Eugène Rougon. 2.4345
Zoltán Kodály. 1.3909
Zoltán Kodály, a Hungarian musician. 1.3908
Zone of emptiness. 2.2115
Zone, pièce en trois actes. 2.4828
Zone system manual: previsualization, exposure,
development, printing. 5.6938
The zoo story. 2.12847
Zoogeography. 5.3813
Zoogeography of the land and inland waters.
5.3812
Zoonomia. 5.4176
Zoonoses and the origins and ecology of human
disease. 5.4758
Zoosporic plant pathogens. 5.5401
Zora Neale Hurston. 2.11912-2.11913
Zorba the Greek. 2.588
Zoroastrianism. 1.1782
Zothique. 2.12488
Zukofsky's 'A' 2.12833
Zuleika Dobson. 2.8438
The Zulu and the zeide. 2.10083
Zuñi. 3.5964
The Zunis of Cubola. 3.5963
Zwingli. 1.2353
Zwingli and Bullinger. 1.2354

Subject Index

Unlike the computer-produced Author and Title indexes, with specific references to each book listed in BCL3, this subject index is a limited guide to LC classification. It points to class numbers where some books on selected topics may be found. Most index entries indicate clusters of three or more books on a given subject classed at the same (or adjacent) numbers. Some class number references, however, especially within a string of several, may point to just one or two books.

There are no personal names, but books about people may often be found with books by them noted in the author index, and personal names begin many entries in the Title Index. In addition, Title Index entries starting with key subject words will lead to books on topics not included as entry terms in this index.

LC subject headings (or sometimes "see" references) are used as entry terms. The few bracketed items are BCL ad-ditions. Many specific and narrow entry terms are used. Natural word order is preferred. Broadterms are not often repeated with subdivisions that echo the classified arrangement of the main class number. Rather, subdivisions point to aspects of the topic classified elsewhere. For further outline-style breakdown of broad topics within their main class numbers, the Contents pages in each volume may be helpful.

To aid interdisciplinary area studies, multiple references after region and country names include, as appropriate, history (D–F), atlases (G), general economic history (HC), trade union and labor history (HD), social history (HN), politics and law (HX, JK–JQ, KD–KQ), and bibliography (Z). Added entry lines locate area groupings in philosophy and religion (B–BX), art (N–NX), language and literature (P–PT), and bibliography (Z). Bibliography references are also given for many other entries.

AIDS (disease), RC607
Abbreviations, P365, PE1693
Ability, BF431
Abortion, HQ767, Z6671.2
Academic dissertations. See LB2369, LB2386
Academic freedom, LA205.H55, LB2332, LC72.2
Accounting, HF5601-5689
Acid rain, TD196
[Acid-base theory], QD477
Acoustics. See ML3805-3817, NA2800, QC223-243
Acronyms, P365, PE1693
Acting, PN2055-2078
Actors, PN2205, PN2285-2287, PN2597-2598
Adaptation (Biology, Physiology), QP82
Administrative law—U.S., KF5401-5425
Adolescence, BF724, HQ793-799
Adult education, LC5201-6691
Advertising, HF5801-6191
Aerodynamics, TL570
Aeronautics, HE9761-9900, TL500-777, UG630-670
Aerospace industries, HD9711
Aesthetics, BH, N61-79
Afghanistan, DS350-375, HC416-420
Africa, DT, G2446-2695, GN643-661, HC501-591, HC800-1085, HD961-1030, HD2117-2118, HD6857, HD8776-8809, HN771-839, HT148, HX437-457, JQ1870-3981, KR, Z3501-3999
Africa—Religion, BL2400-2490, BR1360-1470
Africa, South. See South Africa
African art. See N7380-7399, NB1080-1099
African languages, PL8005
African literature, PL8000-8844, PQ3980-3989, PQ9900-9948, PR9340-9387, Z3508
African philosophy. See B5305
Afrikaans literature, PT6500-6592
Afro-American art, N6538, NX511-512.3, Z5956.A47
Afro-American authors, PS153.N5, PS374.N4, PS508.N3, PS647.N35, Z1229.N39
Afro-American music, M1670, ML128.B45, ML3556. See also: Jazz
Afro-American press, PN4888.N4
Afro-American theater, PN2270.A35
Afro-Americans, E184.5-185.97, F128.9.N3, F548.9.N3, F2659, JK1923-1929, KF4756-4757, KF4764, LC2701-2913, Z1361.N39
Afro-Americans—Folklore, GR103

Afro-Americans—Religion, BR563.N4, BT82.7, BT734.2
Afro-Americans in literature, PS173.N4
Age and employment, HD6279-6280. See also: Youth—Employment
Aggregates, QA248
Aggression (International law), JX4471
Aggressiveness (Psychology), BF575.A3
Aging, BF724.5-724.8, HQ1060-1064, HV1451-1493, QH529, QP86, RC952-954, Z7164.O4
Agricultural industries, HD9000-9490
Agricultural machinery, S671-751
Agriculture and state—U.S., HD1761-1765
Agriculture—Economic aspects, HD1405-2210
Agriculture, Prehistoric, GN799.A4
Agriculture, S, Z5071-5076
Air—Pollution, HC110.A4, KF3812, RA575.5, TD881-890
Air transportation, HE9761-9900
Air warfare, D600-607, D785-792, UG
Aircraft carriers, V874
Alaska, F901-951
Albania, DR701.S5
Alchemy, QD13
Alcoholism, HV5001-5720, RC565, Z7721
Algae, QK565-580
Algebra, QA150-297
Algeria, DT271-299
Allegiance, JC328
Allegory, PN56.A5
Allergy, RC581-596
Alliances, JX4005
Almanacs, AY, QB8
Alphabet, P211
America, E-F, HC95-239, HD6501-6651, HD8051-8370, HN51-370, HX81-235, JK-JL, KF-KH, Z1201-1945
American art. See N6505-6538, NA705-738, NB205-237, ND205-237, NE507-539
American literature, PS, Z1201-1231
American philosophy. See B850-945
Americanisms, PE2801-3101
Amino acids, QP801
Analysis (Mathematics). See QA300-433; see also: Calculus, QA300-316; Functions, QA331-355; and Harmonic analysis, QA403-404
Analysis (Philosophy), B808.5
Analytic mechanics. See QA803-931
Analytical chemistry. See QD71-131
Anarchism and anarchists, HX821-999

Anatomy, Artistic, NC760-776
Anatomy, Comparative, QL799-949. See also: Botany—Anatomy, QK641-693
Anatomy, Human, QM
Ancient history. See CB311, D51-95. See also individual countries
Anglo-Saxon art. See N6763, NA963
Anglo-Saxon language, PE100-408
Anglo-Saxon literature, PR171-236, PR1490-1799
Anglo-Saxons, DA150-155
Angola, DT611
Animal behavior, QL750-785
Animals, QL
Animals, Domestic. See SF
Animals, Treatment of, HV4708-4711
Anonyms and pseudonyms, Z1041-1065
Antarctic regions, G850-890
Antennas, TK7871.6
Anthropo-geography, GF
Anthropology, GN1-673, Z5111-5119
Anthropology, Philosophical. See BD450
Anthropology, Prehistoric, GN700-875
Antisemitism, BM535, DS145-146
Anxiety, BF575.A6
Apes, QL737.P9
Aphasia, RC425
Aphorisms and apothegems, PN6271
Apportionment (Election law)—U.S., JK2493, KF4905
Arab countries (General), DS35.3-40, DS56-63, HC498, HN766, JQ1850. See also individual countries
Arab-Jewish relations. See DS119
Arabia. See DS201-244
Arabic language, PJ6001-7144
Arabic literature, PJ7501-8518
Arabic philosophy. See B741-753
Arachnida, QL451-459
Arbitration, International, JX1901-1991
Arbitration and award, KF9085
Archaeology, CC, Z5131. See also: Classical antiquities, and other regions and countries, D-F, e.g. E61-74
Archaeology, Industrial. See T26, T37
Archaeology, Prehistoric, GN700-875
Architecture, NA, Z5941
Archives, CD931-4279
Arctic regions, G575-890, GB641, GN673
Argentina, F2801-3021, HC175, JL2011-2098
Argentine literature, PQ7600-7799
Arid regions, GB611-612, GB665.A55

Arithmetic, QA101-145, QA248
Armaments, UA10
Armed forces, UA15
Armenia, DS175-195.5
Arms and armor, HD9743, U800-815
Arms control, JX1974-1974.76
Art, N-NX, Z5931-5961
Art, African, etc. See under national, period,
    regional or religious adjectives, e.g. Greek art,
    Renaissance art, African art, Islamic art, etc.
Art nouveau, N6465.A7
Arthropoda, QL434-581
Artificial intelligence, Q335-336
Artificial satellites, TL796-798
Asceticism, BV5017
Asia, DS, HC410-498, HN651-770, HX381-417,
    JQ1-1825, Z3001-3500
Associations, institutions, etc., AS, HS
Assyria, DS68, DS71
Assyro-Babylonian art. See N5370, NB80
Astrology, BF1676-1680
Astronautics, TL787-873
Astronomy, QB, Z5151-5154
Astronomy, Nautical. See VK549-555
Astrophysics, QB461-462, Z5154
Athletics. See Sports
Atlantic States, F106-205
Atlases, G1001-2799
Atmosphere, QC879.6-883
Atomic bomb, D767.25, D785, QC773
Atomic power. See HD9698, TK9001-9401
Atomic warfare. See U263, UA11, UF
Audio-visual education, LB1042.5-1044.9
Auditing, HF5667-5668.25
Australia, DU80-398, DU450-470, HC603,
    HD2152-2177, HD8842, JQ4000-4711, JS10.3,
    Z4001-4024
Australian aborigines, GN665-666
Australian literature, PN849.A9, PR9600-9619,
    Z4011-4024
Austria, DB30-99.1, JN1601-2030
Austrian literature, PT3810-3826
Authoritarianism, HM271
Authorship, PN101-249. See also: Dissertations,
    Academic; Report writing; Technical writing
Autism, RJ506.A9
Autobiography, CT. See also: Biography
Autographs, Z41
Automatic machinery. See TJ213
Automation, HD6331
Automobile industry and trade, HD9710
Automobiles, TL1-275
Automotive transportation. See HE5601-5720
Aviation. See HE9761-9803, JX5775, TL500-777
Aztecs, F1219

Babylonia, DS67-75
Backpacking, GV199.6. See also: Camping,
    SK601
Bacteriology, QR
Bahai Faith, BP300-395
Balance of payments, HG3883
Balance of power, JX1318
Balance of trade, HF1014
Bali Island (Indonesia), DS647.B2
Balkan Peninsula, DR1-48.5, HC401-407,
    JN9600-9799. See also: Eastern question
    (Balkan), D371-378, D461-472, and individual
    countries
Ballet, GV1787-1790, MT95
Baltic literature, PH302
Baltic States, DK511
Bands (Music), ML1300-1311
Bangladesh, DS393-395, HC440.8
Banks and banking, HG1501-3540
Baptists, BX6201-6495
Baseball, GV862-881
Basketball, GV882-888
Basques, DP302.B
Bassoon, ML950, MT400
Basuto (African people). See DT782
Bees, QL568.A6, SF523-524
Behavior modification, BF637.B4
Behavior therapy, RC489.B4
Behaviorism (Psychology), BF199
Belgian literature (French). See PQ3810-3858
Belgium, DH401-811, JN6165
Belief and doubt, BD215, BF773

Belize, F1441-1457
Bengali literature, PK1700-1799
Best sellers [Books], Z1033.B3
Bible, BS
Bibliography [General], Z1001-1121
Bibliography, National, Z1201-5000
Bibliography, [Subject]. See Z5051-7999
Bicycles, GV1040-1059, HE5736, TL400-410
Bilingualism, P115
Bill of Rights (U.S. Constitution). See
    KF4741-4750
Biochemistry. See QD415-433, QH345,
    QP501-801
Bioclimatology, QH543
Bioenergetics, QD501, QH511
Biography, CT, Z5301-5305. See also: for literary
    figures, the author index; major political
    figures, their period in the history of their
    country; others, the subject field of their
    activity
Biography (as a literary form), CT21, CT31
Biological chemistry, QD415-433, QH345,
    QP501-801
Biological physics. See QH505, QP6, QP31
Biology, QH
[Biomechanics], QP303
Biometry, QH323.5
Biophysics, QH505, QP6, QP31
Bird-song, QL698.5
Birds, QL672-699, SF487
Birth control, HQ763-766
Black English, PE3102.N4
Blacks. See Afro-Americans
Black holes (Astronomy), QB843, QC178
Blood, QP93-106
Boats and boating, VM331-341
Boer War, 1899-1902. See DT930
Bolivia, F3301-3359
Bone, QP88.2
Book industries and trade, Z116-550
Bookbinding, Z266-275
Books—Conservation and restoration, Z700-701
Books and reading, Z1003
Botanical chemistry, QK861-870
Botany, QK, Z5351-5358
Botany, Fossil. See QE901-993
Botswana, DT791
Boundaries, JC323, JX4111
Boxing, GV1115-1137
Brahmanism, BL11-15
Brain, QM455, QP376-425
Brainwashing, BF633
Brazil, F2501-2659, HC187, HN283-290, JL2415
Brazilian literature, PQ9500-9699
Bridge (Game). See: GV1282.3
Bridges, TG
Britain. See Great Britain
British art. See N6761-6797, NA961-997,
    NB461-497, ND461-497, NE642
[British Empire.] See DA16-18, JV1001-1061.
    See also individual countries
British philosophy. See B1111-1674
Broadcasting, HE8689-8700, KF2763-2849,
    PN1990-1992
Bronzes, NK7907-7983
Bryophytes, QK533-541
Buddhism, B162, BL1400-1495, BQ
Buddhist art and symbolism, N8190-8195,
    NB1021-1053
Budget—U.S., HJ2051
Building, TH
Bulgaria, DR51-98, JN9609
Bulgarian literature, PG801-1158
Bullfights, GV1107
Bureaucracy, JF1321-1501
Burma, DS527.4-530, DS485.B8-.B892, HC422,
    JQ442
Burmese drama, PL3971
Burundi, DT449.B8
Business, HF5000-6191, Z7164.C8
Business cycles, HB3711-3840
Business ethics, HF5387
Business law, KF1416, KF1600-2940
Business mathematics, HF5695-5699
Byzantine art. See N6250
Byzantine empire, DF501-649

Cabinet officers—U.S., JK611

Cabinet system—Great Britain, JN401
Calculus, QA303-316
Calculus of differences. See QA431
Calendars, CE
Calligraphy, ND1457, NK3600-3640, Z40-43
Cambodia. See DS554, HN700.C3
Cameroon, DT564-576, JQ3521-3529
Campaign funds, JK1991, JN1039
Camping, SK601. See also: Backpacking,
    GV199.6
Canada, F1001-1140, G1115-1116, HC111-120,
    HD311-320, HD1785-1790, HD6524,
    HD8106-8108, HN101-110, HX101-109,
    JL1-500, KE, Z1365-1401, Z7165.C2
Canadian art. See N6545-6548, NA740-749,
    ND240-249
Canadian literature, PR9180-9199, Z1375-1377.
    See also: French-Canadian literature
Canals, HE395-537
Cancer, RC261-281
Cape Verde, DT671
Capital, HB501
Capital punishment, HV8694-8699, KF9227
Capitalism, HB501
Carbon compounds, QD245-433
Caribbean area, F1601-2183, HC151-160. See
    also individual countries
Caribbean literature, PN849.C3, PR9210-9272.9
Caricatures and cartoons, NC1300-1763
Carthage (Ancient city), DT168
Cartography, GA, Z6021-6028
Cartoons. See NC1300-1763
Caste, DS422.C3, HT720
Cataloging, Z693-695
Catholic Church, BX801-4795
Cats, QL737.C23, SF442
Cattle, SF203
Cavalry, UE
Celestial mechanics. See QB351
Cells, QH573-652
Celtic literatures, PB1001-3029
Censorship, KD4114, KF4775, KF9444,
    Z657-659, Z711.4. See also: Freedom of the
    press; Moving pictures—Censorship, KF4300
Central America, F1421-1577. See also
    individual countries
Ceramics, NK3700-4695, TP785-810, TT924
Ceylon. See Sri Lanka
Chad, DT546.4
Chain of being (Philosophy), B105.C5
Chamber music, ML1100-1165
Chants (Plain, Gregorian, etc.), ML3082
Chemical bonds, QD461
Chemical elements, QD466
Chemical engineering, TP155-161
Chemical evolution, QH325
Chemical industry, HD9651, TP200-248
Chemical laboratory safety, QD51
Chemical literature, QD8.5
Chemical reactions, QD73, QD501-502
Chemical technology. See TN-TP, Z7914.C4
Chemistry, QD, Z5523
Chemistry, Technical, TP
Chess, GV1313-1458
Child development, HQ767.8-792, LB1101-1139,
    RJ131
Child psychology, BF719-723
Child welfare, HV701-1416, Z7164.C5
Childbirth, RG518-960
Children—Care and hygiene, RJ
Children—Language, LB1139.L3
Children as artists, N350
Children's literature, PN1009, PN6109.97,
    PS586.3, PZ8.3, Z1037
Chile, F3051-3285, HC192, HD505, HN293,
    JL2615-2698
Chilean literature, PQ7900-8099
China, DS701-796, G2305-2306, HC426-430,
    HD866-868, HN671-680, HN731-740,
    HT147.C48, HX387, HX417, JQ1500-1519,
    JS7352-7354, JX1570, KQK, UA835-839,
    Z3101-3109
China—Religion, BL1800-1975
Chinese art. See N7340-7349, NA1540-1543,
    NB1043-1047, ND1040-1049, NK4165-4166,
    NX583
Chinese language, PL1001-2245
Chinese literature, PL250-3208, Z3108

Chinese philosophy. See B125-128, B5231-5234
Chivalry, CR4501-4595. See also: Feudalism
Christian art and symbolism, BV150-155, N7790-8199, NA4590-5870
Christian ethics, BJ1190-1278
Christian Science, BX6901-6996
Christianity, BR-BX, G1046.E4-.E42
Christology, BT198-590
Chromosomes, QH600-605
Chronology, Historical, D11
Church and education, LC111, LC473-580
Church and race relations, BT734-734.2
Church and social problems, HN30-39
Church and state, BR516, BV630, JK361, KF4865-4869
Church architecture, NA4590-6113
Church history, BR, BX
Church music, ML2900-3275
Cinematography, TR847-899
Ciphers, Z103
Circus, GV1800-1828
Cities and towns, HT101-384, JS, Z5942, Z7164.U7
Cities and towns—U.S., HC108, HN80, JS. See also: F1-970
City planning, HT161-169, NA9000-9284, Z5942
Civil disobedience. See JC328.3
Civil engineering, TA-TH
Civil rights, JC571-599, KF4741-4788, Z7164.L6. See also: Human rights
Civil service—U.S., HD8005-8008, JK631-901
Civilization, CB, HM101, Z5579. See also regions and countries
Clarinet, ML945, MT380
Classical antiquities, DE, DF1-289, DG1-365, G1033
Classical art. See N5603-5896, NA210-340, NB69-169
Classical languages, PA1-1179, PA2001-2995
Classical literature, PA3000-4500, PA6000-6971
Classical mythology. See BL700-820
Classification—Books, Z696
Classroom management, LB3011-3012
Climatology, QC980-993
Clinical psychology, RC467
Cloning, QH442-442.2
Clothing and dress, GT500-2370, TT490-507
Clothing trade, HD6515.C5, HD9940
Cloud physics, QC921-922
Clouds, QC921-922
Coaching (Athletics), GV711
Coal mines and mining, HD6515.M, HD8039.M, HD9540-9559
Coasts, GB451-460
Cognition, BF311, BF723.C5
Coins, CJ
Cold war. See D843
Collective bargaining, HD6483, HD8008-8013
Collective settlements, HX626-795. See also: Utopias, HX806-811
College costs, LB2342
College teachers, LB1778-1779, LB2331-2335
Colleges. See Universities and colleges
Colombia, F2251-2299, JL2831
Colombian literature, PQ8160-8180
Colonies, JV1-5299
Color, ND1280, QC495
Colorimetry, QD113
Combinatorial analysis, QA164
Combustion, QD516
Comedy, PN1920-1929
Comic books, strips, etc., PN6700-6790, NC1300-1429
Commedia dell'arte, PQ4155
Commerce, HF1-4040
Commercial law, KF1416, KF1600-2940
Commercial policy, HF1401-1650
Common law, KD671
Common Market. See European Economic Community
[Commonwealth literature (General)]. See PR9080
Commonwealth of Nations, DA16-18, JN248-276. See also individual countries
Communal settlements. See HQ971-971.5, HX626-795. See also: Utopias, HX806-811
Communicable diseases, RA643-644, RC112-201
Communication, HM258, P87-99. See also: Mass media

Communication and traffic, HE
Communism, HX1-550
Communist countries [General], D847. See also individual countries
Communist state, JC474
Community and school, LC215-238
Community colleges, LB2328-2329
Community mental health services, RA790
Comparative education, LA132-133
Comparative government, JF
Competition, HB771, HD41
Composers, ML390, ML410
Composition (Art), N7430
Composition (Music), ML430-455, MT40-67
Computer-assisted instruction, LB1028.5
Computer crimes, HV6773, Z5703.4.C63
Computer graphics, T385
Computer music, ML128.E4, MT41
Computer vision, TA1632
Computers, QA75.5-76.95, TK7885-7895, Z5640. See also: Electronic data processing
Concerto, ML1263
Concrete, TA439
Conditioned response, BF319, QP372
Conducting, MT85-86
Conductors (Music), ML402, ML422
Confederate States of America, E482-489, JK9663, JX1429, KFZ
Confucianism, BL1830-1870
Congo. See Zaire
Congo (Brazzaville), DT546.2
Congregational churches, BX7101-7260
Congress. See: G1201.F7-.F9, JK1000-1447, KF4930-5005
Consciousness, BF311
Conservation of natural resources, S900-972, Z5322.E2
Conservatism, JA84.U5, JC501
Consolidation and merger of corporations, HD2741-2746.5
Constitutional history, JK-JQ
Constitutional law, KD-KQ
Construction. See Architecture, NA; Building, TH. See also: Bridges, Roads, etc.
Consumers, HC110.C6, HF5415.3
Consumption (Economics), HB801-843, HC110.C63
Contempt of legislative bodies—U.S., KF9405-9415
Continental drift, QE501, QE511.4-511.7
Continuing education, LC5219-5251
Continuity, B105.C5
Contract bridge, GV1282.3
Contracts—U.S., KF801
Controllership, HF5550
Cookery, TX651-840
Coordination compounds, QD471-474
Copyright, KF2986-3086
Coral reefs and islands, QE565
Corporations, HD2709-2930, HG4001-4495
Corporations—Corrupt practices, HV6768-6769
Corrections, HV9261-9430
Corrosion, TA462
Cosmic rays, QC485
Cosmogony, QB981
Cosmology, BD493-708, QB981-991
Cost accounting, HF5686.C8
Costa Rica, F1541-1557
Costume, GT500-2370, PN2067
Counseling, BF637.C6. See also: LB1027.5
Counterfactuals (Logic), BC199.C66
Counterpoint, MT55
Counter-Reformation, BR430, D228
Courts—U.S., KF8700-9075
Creation, BT695
Creation (Literary, artistic, etc.), BF408
Credit, HG3751-3756
Creole dialects, PM7801-7895
Crete, DF221.C8, DF261.C8
Crime and criminals, HV6001-9920
Criminal law, K5018, KF9201-9760
Criticism, BH39-41, PN75-99
Croatian literature, PG1600-1696
Crowds, DC158.8, HM281
Crusades, D151-173
Crustacea, QL444
Cryogenics. See QC33, QC278; see also: Refrigeration and refrigerating machinery, TP490

Cryptograms, QK505-635
Cryptography, Z103
Crystallography, QD905-951
Cuba, F1751-1849, HC152.5, HC157.C9, HN203
Cuban literature, PQ7370-7390
Cubism, N6494.C8, ND196.C8, ND1265
Culture, CB, GN357-367, HM101
Curriculum planning, LB1570-1571, LB2361-2365, Z5814.C9
Customs, Social. See GT
Cybernetics, Q175.W, Q310
Cycling, GV1040-1059, HE5736, TL400-410
Cyprus, DS54-54.9
Cytogenetics, QH427, QH430-431, QH581
Cytology, QH573-651
Czech literature, PG5000-5198
Czechoslovakia, DB191-217, HC267, JN2229

DNA. See QD431-433, QP551
Dadaism, NX600.D3
Dams, TC540
Dancing, GV1580-1799, Z7514.D2
Dancing—Religious aspects, BL605
Danish language, PD3640
Danish literature, PT7601-8260, Z2571-2574
Data processing. See HF5548.2-.5, QA76
Day care centers, HV851-861
Dead Sea scrolls, BM175, BM487-488
Deaf, HV2390-2395. See also: Hearing disorders
Death, BD444, BF789.D4, BT825, GT3203, HQ1073, R726-726.8, Z5725
Debates and debating, PN4181
Debts, Public, HJ8003-8897
Decision-making, HD38, HD69.D4
Decoration and ornament, NA3310-4050, NK1160-1590
Decorative arts, NK
Definition (Logic), BC199.D4
Deformations (Mechanics), TS213
Degrees, Academic, LB2381-2391
Democracy, JC421-458
Demography, JB881-3700, Z7164.D3
Denmark, DL101-291, HD8546, JN7161-7365
Dentistry, RK
Deoxyribonucleic acid, QD431, QP551
Department stores, HF5461-5467
Depressions, HB3716-3717
Deserts, GB611-612
Design, NC997-998
Design, Decorative, NK1160-1590
Design, Industrial, T180, TS23, TS140-149, TS171
Detective and mystery stories, PN3448.D4, PR830.D4, PS374.D4, Z5917.D5
Developing countries—Economic conditions, HC59.7-60, HD72-89, HN980. See also individual regions and countries
Developmental psychology, BF713-719
Deviant behavior, HM291
Dialectical materialism, B809.8
Dialectical theology, BT83
Dialectology, P367
[Dictionaries]. See languages, e.g. English language; see also: Lexicography
Diet, RM216-237. See also: Nutrition, QP141, TX349-558; Reducing diets, RM237
Difference equations, QA431
Differential equations, QA371-377
Digital control systems, TJ216-223
Digital electronics, TK7868
Dilemma, BC185
Diplomacy, JX1621-1894
Disarmament, JX1974-1974.6, UA10
Disarmament—Economic aspects, HC110.D4. See also: Defense contracts, HD9743
[Discographies]. See ML156
Discoveries (in geography), G80-89, G161-420. See also individual regions, e.g., DT3, DU19, DU97-102, DU410, E101-135
Discrimination in education, KF4154-4155, LA210.R3, LC212-214. See also: Afro-Americans—Education, LC2701-2913
Discrimination in employment, E185.8, HD4903, HD6060, HF5500.3, KF3464-3467, Z7963
Discrimination in housing, E185.89.H6, HD7288.72, HD7304.S2, KF662
Diseases—Causes and theories of causation, RB151-153

Dissertations, Academic, LB2369, LB2386
Diving, Submarine, RC1015
Divorce, HQ811-960, KF535
Dogs, QL737.C22, SF422-426
Dolphins, QL737.C4
Domestic animals, SF
[Domestic servants]. See HD6072, HD8039.D52
Dominican Republic, F1931-1941
Draft [Military], UB340-353
Drama, PN1600-1988, Z5781-5785. See also
  national literatures, e.g., American drama,
  PS330-351, Z1231.D7
Drama—Collections, PN6111-6120. See also
  national literatures, e.g., American drama,
  PS623-635
Drawing, NC
Dreams, BF1074-1099
Dress. See GT500-2730, TT490-507
Dressmaking, TT494-504
Drug abuse, HV5800-5840, Z7164.N17
Drugs, QP917-981, RM, RS
Drugs—Law and legislation—U.S., KF3885-3894
Drugs—Physiological effect, QP917-981
Druids and Druidism, BL910
Dutch art. See N6925-6973, ND625-653
Dutch language, PF1-979
Dutch literature, PT5001-5980
Dynamics, QA845-871

Earth sciences, QE. See also: Geography,
  Meteorology, Oceanography
Earthquakes, QE534
Earthworms, QL391
East and West, CB251
East Asia [General], DS501-519, HC411, JQ1-39,
  Z3001. See also individual countries.
East-West trade. See International economic
  relations
Easter Island, F3169
Eastern Europe [General]. See D847, DJK,
  HC244. See also individual countries.
Eastern question (Balkan), D371-378, D461-472
Ecology, QH104-104.5, QH130, QH135, QH137,
  QH540-548, Z5322. See also: Botany—Ecology,
  QK101, QK901-938; Zoology—Ecology,
  QL751-752
Ecology, Human. See GF, Z5322
Econometrics, HB74.M3, HB131-145
Economic anthropology, GN420-448, GN489,
  GN799
Economic assistance, HC59.7-60
Economic assistance, Domestic—U.S.,
  HC110.P63
Economic development, HC59.7-60, HD72-89,
  HN980
Economic forecasting, HB3730
Economic geography. See HF1021-1027
Economic geology, TN260-263
Economic history, HC
Economics, HB-HJ, Z7164.E2
Economics, Medical, R728, RA714-715. See
  also: Health insurance
Ecuador, F3701-3799, HN317-320, JL3011-3031
Ecumenical movement, BX6.5-8.2
Edible plants, QK98.5
Education, L-LT, Z5811-5819. See also: Medical
  education
Education, Bilingual, LC3719, LC3731, P115
Education and religion. See LC111, LC473-743
Education and state, LC71-120, LC173
Educational anthropology, LB45
Educational exchange, LB2283, LB2375-2376
Educational law and legislation, KF4101-4258,
  LB2523-2527
Educational psychology, LB1051-1091
Educational sociology, LC189-191
Educational tests and measurements, LB3051,
  Z5814.E9
Egypt, DT43-107, DT133-154, HC535, HC830,
  HD2123, HN783, HN786-790
Egyptian art. See N5350-5351
Egyptian literature, PJ1481-1989
Eighteenth century, CB411, D284-309
El Salvador. See F1481-1537
Elasticity, QA931, TA645
Elections, JF1001-1191
Elections—U.S., JK524-528, JK1951-2246,
  KF4885-4921

Electric engineering, TK9-8304
Electric filters, TK7872
Electric utilities, HD9685-9688
Electricity, QC503-711
Electrochemistry, QD553-561
Electromagnetism, QC661-670
Electronic data processing, HF5548.2. See also:
  Computers
Electronic digital computers, circuits, TK7888.3
Electronic industries, HD9696
Electronic music, ML128.E4, MT41
Electronics, TK7800-8304
Electrophysiology, QP331-341
Elementary education. See LB1555-1601
Embryology, QL951-971
Embryology, Human, QM601-602
Emigration and immigration, JV6000-9500
Emotions, BF531-575, QP401
Employee participation in management. See
  HD5650-5660
Employer-employee relations. See HD6961-6971,
  HF5549-5549.5
Employment discrimination. See E185.8,
  HD4903, HD6060, HF5500.3, KF3464-3467,
  Z7963
Encyclopedias and dictionaries, AE, AG, Z1035
Endocrinology, QP187, RC648-649
Endowments, AS911, HV7, LB2336, Z7164.F5
Energy industries, HD9502-9505
Engineering, T-TP
Engineering mathematics, QA401
England. See Great Britain
English art. See British art
English language, PE
English literature, PR, Z2001-2014. See also
  regions and countries outside England
English philosophy. See B111-1674
Engraving, NE
Enlightenment, B802, B1925.E5, CB411
Entomology, QL463-581, Z5856
Entrepreneurship, HB615
Environmental policy, HC79.E5, HC110.E5,
  Z5861-5863, Z7405.N38
Environmental pollution. See HC79.P55,
  TD170-196. See also: Air—Pollution; Marine
  pollution; Noise; Water—Pollution
Environmental psychology, BF373
Enzymes, QD501, QP601
Epidemics, RA643-651
Epigraphy. See CN
Epilepsy, RC372
Episcopal Church, BX5800-5995
Epistemology. See BD140-241
Equality, HM146, JC575
Erosion, QE576, S622-624
Eschatology, BT819-821.2
Eskimos, E99.E7
Espionage, UB250-270. See also: Intelligence
  service
Estonia, DK511
Etching, NE
Ether (of space), QC177
Ethics, BJ
Ethics, Business. See HF5387
Ethics, Medical. See R724-725
Ethiopia, DT371-398, HC591.A3, HC845.Z9,
  HN840.E82
Ethnic groups. See Ethnicity; Minorities; Race
  relations
Ethnicity, GN495.6-496, Z5118.E84
Ethnological jurisprudence, K190
Ethnology, GN301-686, Z5111-5118
Ethnomethodology, HM24
Ethnomusicology, ML3797-3798
Ethnopsychology, GN270-273, GN451, GN502,
  HM107
Etiquette, BH1853
Etruscans, DG223, DG233
Europe [General], D, G1801, G1880,
  HC240-244, HD1917-1920, HD6656-6657,
  HD8371-8378, HN371-380, HT131,
  HX236-239, JN1-97. See also individual
  countries
Europe, Eastern [General], DJK, HC244. See
  also individual countries
European Economic Community, HC241.2,
  HD1920.5, HF1531-1532, Z7165.E8
European War, 1914-1918, D501-680, Z6207

Euthanasia, R726
Evangelists, BV3775-3785
Evolution, B818, HM106, QH359-425
Exceptional children—Education, LC3950-3990
Executive power—U.S., JK511-609
Executives, HF5500. See also: Government
  executives
Exercise, GV461-481, QP301, RA781
Existentialism, B819
Explorers, G200-420. See also: Discoveries (in
  geography)
Export marketing, HF1009.5
Expressionism (Art), N6868.5, ND568.5
Extinct languages, P901-1078
Eye, QL949, QP475-495

Family, HQ503-734, Z7164.M2. See also:
  Kinship
Family law. See K644, K670, KF535, KF547
Family violence, HQ809, HV713-742, HV6626
Fantastic fiction, PN3435, PR830.F3
Far East [General]. See DS501-519, HC411,
  JQ1-39, Z3001. See also individual countries
Farm life, HT421, S521
Fascism, JC481
Fashion, GT500-2370, TT490-507
Father and child, BF723.P25, HQ756
Federal government—U.S., JK310-339, KF4600
Fellowships. See LB2336-2338
Feminism, HQ1101-2030.7
Ferns, QK521-525
Fertility, Human, HB891-1108
Feudalism, D131, JC109-116
Fiction, PN3311-3503, Z5916-5918. See also
  national literatures, e.g. American fiction,
  PS371-379, PS643-659, Z1231.F4
Fiji, DU600, HC687
Files and filing (Documents). See Z695.95
Finance, HG
Finance, Public, HJ
Financial statements, HF5681
Finite-element method, T347, TA640.2-646
Finland, DK445-465, JN6700-6719
Finnish literature, PH300-498
First aid in illness and injury, RC86
Fiscal policy—U.S., HJ257
Fisheries, HD9450.5, SH201-400
Fishes, QL615-639
Fishing, SH135-433
Flags, CR101-115, JC345
Flemish art. See N6925-6973, ND661-673
Flemish literature, PT6000-6471
Flood control, GB665, TC423
Flowers, QK, SB405
Fluid dynamics, QA911-930. See also:
  Aerodynamics, TL570
[Fluid flow], TP156
Fluid mechanics, QA901-930, QC143-157,
  TA357
Fluids, QC143-157
Flute, ML935, MT342
Flying saucers. See TL789-789.3
Folk art, NK801-1094
Folk music, M1629-1678, ML3545-3780
Folklore, GR, PN1001, Z5984
Food, GN799.F6, GT2850-2910, TX341-641
Food habits, GT2853, Z5118.F58
Food industry and trade, HD9000-9490,
  TP368-659
Fools and jesters, GT3670
Football, GV937-959
Forecasting, CB158-161
[Foreign aid]. See HC59.7-60
Foreign exchange, HG205, HG3810-4000
Foreign trade regulation, K3943, K4603
Forensic medicine. See KF2905, RA1001-1171
Forensic psychiatry, KD7897, KF480, KF8922,
  KF8965
Forest ecology, QH105, QH541.5
Forest products, HD9750-9769
Forests and forestry, SB436, SD, Z5991. See
  also: Trees
Formosa. See Taiwan
[Fossil humans]. See GN282-283, QH368
Fossil plants. See QE901-996
Fossils. See QE701-996
Foster home care, HV875-881
Foundations. See Endowments

Foundations [(Engineering)], TA710-775
Fourth dimension, QA691-699
France, DC, G1840, HC271-280, HD643-649, HD6684, HN421-440, HX261-270, JN2301-3007, JS4881-4883, JV1800-1899, KJ, UA700-709, Z2161-2189
France—Church history, BR845, BX9454
France—History—Revolution, D308, DC139-195
Franchises (Retail trade), HF5429, HF5429.235
Fraternities. See LJ
Free radical reactions, QD258
Free trade and protection, HF1701-2701
Free will and determinism, BJ1460-1468
Freedom. See B105.L45, HM271, JC571, JC585-599
Freedom of information, Z711.4
Freedom of religion, BV740-741, KF4783, KF4865-4869
Freedom of speech, JC591, KF4770-4772
Freedom of the press, K3255, KF4774-4775, PN4735, Z657, Z6940
French art. See N6841-6853, NA1041-1053, NB541-553, ND541-553, NE647-650
French-Canadian literature, PQ3900-3919
French-Canadians, F1027, F1053
French language, PC2001-3761
French literature, PQ1-3999, Z2171-2175
French philosophy. See B1801-2430
Fresh-water biology, QH96-98
Freshwater fauna, QL141, QL633-637
Frogs, QL667-669
Frontier and pioneer life, E179.5, F596-597
Frontiers, JC323, JX4111
Fruit growing, SB363-369
Fugue, ML448, MT59
Functions [Mathematics], QA331-343
Fundamentalism, BT82.2
Funeral rites and ceremonies, GN486, GT3203, GT3251
Fungi, QK583-635
Fur trade, HD9944
Furniture, NK2200-2750, TS810-889, TT196
[Future]. See Forecasting, CB158-161
Futurism (Art), N6494.F8, NX600.F8

Gabon, JQ3407
Galaxies, QB851-857
Gambia, DT509
Game theory, QA269
Games, GV1200-1511. See also: Play
Games, Educational. See LB1029.G3
Gangs, HV6439
Gardening, SB450.9-467
Gas chromatography, QD79
Gases, Ionization of. See Ionization of gases, QC711-718
Gases, Kinetic theory of, QC175
Genealogy, CS, Z5301-5319
General semantics, B820
Genetic counseling, RB155
Genetic engineering, SB123
Genetic psychology, BF699-711
Genetics, QH361, QH427-499
Genetics, Medical. See RB155
Geochemistry, QE515
Geography, G-GF, Z6001-6028
Geography, Economic, HF1021-1027
Geography, Mathematical, GA
Geography [of individual countries], D-F
Geology, QE, Z6031-6040. See also: Physical geography.
Geology, Economic, TN260-271
Geology, Structural, QE601-606. See also: Geomorphology
Geometry, QA445-699
Geomorphology, GB400-648. See also: Structural geology
Geophysics, QC801-809, QE501
Geopolitics, JC319
Geriatrics, RC952-954. See also Aging
German art. See N6861-6888, NA1061-1088, NB561-588, ND561-588
German language, PF3001-5999
German literature, PT1-4899, Z2231-2235
German philosophy. See B2521-3396
Germanic languages, PD-PF
Germany, DD, HC281-290, HD8450-8459, HN441-460, HX271-280, JN3201-4979, JV2000-2099, KK, UA710-719, Z2221-2249

Germany (Democratic Republic), DD261, HC287.A2, HC290.78
Germany—Church history, BR850-859
Gerontology. See BF724.5-.8, HQ1060-1064, HV1451-1493, QH529, QP86, RC952-954
Gestalt psychology, BF203
Ghana, DT510-512, HC517.G6, JQ3028
Gifted children—Education, LC3991-4000
Glacial epoch, QE696
Glaciers, GB2401-2403.2, QE576
Glass (Chemistry), QD139.G5
Glass painting and staining, NK5308-5398
Glassware, NK5100-5440
Gnosticism, BT1390
God [Christianity], BT98-180
Golf, GV961-987
Good and evil, BJ1400-1408
Gorillas, QL737.P9
Gothic art. See N6310-6320, NA440-480
Gothic revival (Architecture), NA610
Gothic revival (Literature), PN3435
Government, Resistance to, JC328
Government and the press, PN4738
Government employees. See HD8001-8013
Government executives—U.S., JK723. See also: Presidents—U.S.
Government publications. See: [U.S.], Z1223
Grail, PN686.G7
Grammar, Comparative and general, P151-295. See also individual languages
Graph theory, QA166
Graphic arts, NC, NE. See also: Printing
Grasses, QK495
Gravity, QB331-341
Great Britain, DA, G1810-1814, HC251-260, HD593-594, HD6664-6668, HD8381-8399, HF3501-3540, HN381-400, HT133, HX241-250, JN101-1371, JS3041-3111, JV1000-1099, JX1543, KD, UA647-688, VA454-460, Z2001-2027
Great Britain—Church history, BR740-789, BX5003-5203
Greece [Ancient], DE-DF289, G1033, HC37, HD4844, HF375, JC51, JC71-79
Greece [Ancient]—Religion, BL700-793
Greece [Modern], DF701-951, HN650, JN5001-5185
Greek art. See N5630-5720, NA270-280, NB85-140, NK4645-4649
Greek language, PA201-1179
Greek letter societies, LJ
Greek literature, PA3050-4500, PA5000-5665
Greek philosophy. See B165-491
Grenada, F2056.6-.83
Group psychotherapy, RC488
Group relations training, HM133
Group theory, QD461, QD471
Groups, Theory of, QA171, QC174.17
Growth (Plants), QK731
Guam, DU647
Guatemala, F1461-1477, HN143.5
Guerrilla warfare, U240
Guidance, Student. See LB1027.5, LB2243. See also: Vocational guidance
Guinea, DT543
Guinea-Bissau, DT613, DT671
Guitar, ML1015.C9
Guyana, F2351-2471
Gymnastics, GV460-464
Gynecology, RG
Gypsies, DX

Haiku, PL729, PL768.H3
Haiti, F1900-1930, HC153, HC157.H2
Handicapped, GV445, GV709.3, HD7255-7256, HV1551-3024
Handicapped children, HV888-907, KF4210, LC4001-4803
Harbors, HE551-560
Harmony, MT50
Harpsichord, ML650-651
Hawaii, DU620-629, HN933
Health insurance. See HD7101-7104
Hearing, BF251, QP306, QP461
Hearing disorders, HV2390-2395, RF290-291
Heart, RC666-681
Heat, QC254-331
Heating, TH7011-7414

Hebrew literature, PJ5001-5060
Hellenism, DE71, DF77
Heraldry, CR
Heredity, BF341, QH431
Heresy, BT1313-1490
Hermeneutics, BD241
Heterocyclic compounds, QD400
High schools, LA222, LB1603-1695
Higher education. See L900-901, LA173-186, LA225-229, LB2300-2411, LC173, LC1752-1756, LC2781
Highway engineering, TE
Hindi literature, PK1931-2142
Hinduism, B130-133, BL1100-1295, Z7835.B8
Histochemistry, QH611-613
Histology, QM551-557
Historic buildings—U.S., E159. See also: Literary landmarks
Historical fiction, PN3441
Historical geology, QE28.3, QE651-696
Historiography, D13-15, DA1-3, DF211, E175
History, C-F, G1030-1038, Z6201-6209
History, Ancient, CB311-325, D51-95. See also individual regions and countries
History, Medieval. See CB351-355, D111-203. See also individual regions and countries
Hittites, DS66, N5385
Hockey, GV847
Holidays, GT3930, GT4803
Holland. See Netherlands
Holocaust, Jewish, D810.J4, G1797.21
Holy Roman Empire, DD125-198.7
Home economics, TX
Homosexuality, HQ75-76.8, Z7164.S42
Honduras, F1501-1517
Hong Kong, DS796.H7, HN55.2, JQ673
Hormones, QP187, QP356, QP801.H7
Horn (Musical instrument), ML955, MT420
Horses, SF277-278, UE
Horticulture, SB
Hospice care, R726.8
Hospitals, RA967-997
Hotels, taverns, etc., GT3803, TX907
Hours of labor, HD5106-5250
Housing, HD7285-7390
Huguenots, BX9454.2, DC116.5
Human anatomy. See QM
Human ecology, GF, Z5322.E2
Human embryology. See QM601-691
Human engineering, T59.7
Human evolution, GN281-289, QH368
Human genetics, QH431
Human influence on nature, GF31, GF75, QC981.8, GH541
Human mechanics, QP301-303
[Human origins], QH368
Human population genetics, GN289
Human rights, K3240-3240.6, Z7164.L3. See also: Civil rights
Humanism, B778, B821
Humanistic education. See LC1001-1021
Humanistic psychology, BF204
Humanities, AZ
[Humans, Prehistoric]. See CB301, GN700-875, QH368
Humor. See Wit and humor
Hundred Years' War, 1339-1453, DC96-105
Hungarian literature, PH3001-3445
Hungary, DB901-975, HC300.2, HN420.5
Hunting, SK21-33
Hunting and gathering societies, GN388, GN422
Hydraulic engineering, TC145-774
Hydrodynamics, QA911
Hydrogen-ion concentration, QD561
Hydrology, GB651-2398
Hyperspace, QA691
Hypnotism, BF1141, RC490-495

Ice, GB2401-2403
Iceland, DL301-398
Icelandic language, PD243
Icelandic literature, PT7351-7550. See also: Old Norse literature
Icons, N8187-8189
Idealism, B823
Ideology, B823.3
Identity, BF697
Illegitimacy, HQ998-999

Illumination of books and manuscripts, ND2890-3416
Illustration of books, NC960-996
Image processing, TA1632
Imagery (Psychology), BF367
Immigrants—U.S., E184
Immigration. See JV6000-9500
Immortality, BT921
Immunology, QR181-184
Imperialism, JC359, JV1-5299
Impressionism (Art), N6465.I4, ND1265
Improvisation (Music), MT68
Incas, F3429-3430.1, F3442
Income—U.S., HC110.I5
Income tax, HJ4621-4824, KF6369
Incunabula, Z240
Independent regulatory commissions—U.S., JK901, KF5406
India, DS401-488, HC431-440, HD874-879, HD2072, HD8686, HN681-690, HX392-395, JQ200-459, JS7025-7065, Z3201-3208
India—Religion, BL2000-2030
Indian literature—North America, PM, PS153.I5, PS508.I5, PS591.I5
Indians [of America], E51-99, F1219-1221, F1435-1435.3
Indians of Central America, F1434-1435
Indians of Mexico, F1219-1221
Indians of North America, E76-99, KF8201-8228, Z1209-1209.2
Indians of North America—Music, ML3557
Indians of South America, F2229-2230.2, F2519-2520.1, F3429-3430.1, F3442
Indic art. See N7300-7310, NA1460-1501, NB1001-1015
Indic literature (English), PR9490-9499
Indic literatures, PK
Indic philosophy. See B130-133
Individuality, BF697
Indo-European languages, P511-765
[Indo-Iranian literatures], PK
Indochina, French (to 1954), DS531-553
Indonesia, DS611-649, HC447, HN703-710, JQ779
Indonesian literature, PL5080-5089
[Indoor air pollution], TD883.1
Induction (Logic), BC91
Industrial archaeology, T26, T37
Industrial chemistry. See TP
Industrial design. See TS23, TS140-149, TS171
Industrial engineering, T55.4-60.8
Industrial hygiene, HD7651-7654
Industrial management, HD21-70, TS155-161
Industrial organization, HD21-70, HD2321-4730
Industrial relations, HD6961-6971. See also: Personnel management
Industrial safety, HD7262-7269, QD51, T54-55.3
Industrial sociology, HD6951-6961
Industrial toxicology, RA1199-1229
Industry, HD
Industry—Location, HC110.D5, HD58, HF1025
Industry—Social aspects, HD59-60.5
Industry and education, LC1085
Industry and state, HD3611-4730. See also: Trade regulation
Infantry, UD
Inflation (Finance), HG229
Information science, Z662-718
Information theory, Q350
Inorganic chemistry. See QD151-181
Insanity—Jurisprudence, KD7897, KF480, KF8922, KF8965
Inscriptions, CN
Insects, QL463-581
Insects, Injurious and beneficial, SB951
Insects as carriers of disease, RA644
Instinct, QL781
Instrumentation and orchestration, ML455, MT70-74
Insurance, HG8011-9970
Insurance, Health, HD7101-7104
Insurance, Social. See HD7090-7250.7, KF3643
Intellect, BF431-433
Intelligence service, JF1525.I6, JK468.I6, UB250-270
Intelligence tests, BF431-433. See also: Educational tests and measurements
Intention (Logic), BC199.I5

Interest, HB 531-549, HG1621
Intergovernmental fiscal relations, HJ275, JK310-325
Interior decoration, NK1700-3505
International business enterprises, HD62.4, HD69.I7, HD2755.5, HF1009.5, HG4026-4027.5
International economic relations, HF1401-1650
International finance, HG3881
International law, JX, Z6461
International organization, JC361-363, JX1901-1981, JX1995
International relations, JX1305-1598, Z6461-6485. See also individual countries, D-F
Interpersonal relations, BF636, HM132
Inventions, T15, T211-212
Inventories, HD55
Invertebrates, QL362-581
Investments, HG4501-5990
Ionization of gases, QC711-718
Iran, DS251-318, HC475, HN670.2, JQ1785
Iranian art. See N5390, N7280
Iranian literature, PK6001-6996
Iraq, DS67-79.9, JQ1825.I7
Ireland, DA900-995, G1831, HC260.I5, JN1401-1571
Ireland—Church history, BR793-794
Ireland, Northern. See DA990.U45-.U46, JN1572
Irish art. See N6782-6784, NA982
Irish literature, PR8700-8897, Z2037-2039
Iron age, GN780
Iron industry and trade, HD8039.I52, HD9510-9529
Islam, BP1-295, D198-199, JC49, Z7835.M5-.M6
Islamic art. See N6260, NA380-381, ND198, NK1674
Islamic countries, DS35.3-40, G1786, G2205. See also individual countries
Islamic philosophy, B741-753
Island ecology, QH105-107, QH541.5
Islands of the Pacific, DU, Z4001-4021
Israel, DS126.5-128, HC415.25, HN660, HX742.2, JQ1825.P3, UA853.I8
Italian art. See N6911-6923, NA1111-1123, NB611-623, ND611-623
Italian language, PC1001-1977
Italy, DG, HC301-310, HD6709, HD8478, HN471-490, HX286-295, JN5201-5660
Italy—Church history, BR870-879
Ivory Coast, DT545, HC1025, JQ3386

Jainism, B162.5, BL1300-1365
Jamaica, F1861-1896, HN223
Japan, DS801-897, G2355, HC461-465, HD2092, HD6832, HD8724-8726, HN721-730, HX412, JQ1600-1699, JS7372-7384, JV5260, JX1577, KQP, UA845, Z3301-3309
Japan—Religion, BL2200-2222, BR1305
Japanese art. See N7350-7359, NA1550-1557, NB1053, ND1050-1059, NE1310-1325
Japanese language, PL501-699
Japanese literature, PL700-888, Z3306-3308
Japanese philosophy. See B135-138, B5241-5244
Jazz music, ML128.J3, ML3506-3508, ML3561.J3
Jazz musicians, ML105-106, ML394-395, ML419
Jet stream, QC935
Jewelry, NK7307-7398, TS740
Jewish-Arab relations, DS119
Jewish philosophy, B759. See also: Judaism
Jews, D810.J4, DS101-151, G1030, G1797.21, Z6366-6373
Jews in the United States, E184.J5
Jordan, DS153-154, HC415.26, JQ1825.J
Journalism, PN4700-5650
Judaism, BM, Z6366-6373
Judicial error, KF9756
Judicial power—U.S., KF5130
Judicial review—U.S., KF4575
Judiciary. See Courts
Junior colleges, LB2327-2329
Jurisprudence, K201-487, KF380-385
Jury—U.S., KF9680
Just war doctrine, U21.2
Justice, HM216, JC575-578

Juvenile courts, KF9709
Juvenile delinquency, HV9051-9230

Kampuchea, DS554
Karma, BL2015.K3
Kashmir, DS485.K2
Kenya, DT433.5-434, HC517.K4, JQ2947
Keynesian economics, HB99.7, HB103.K47
Kidneys, QP211
Kindergarten, LB1141-1499
Kinesiology, QP303
Kinetic theory of gases, QC175
Kinship, GN480, GN487. See also: Family
Knots and splices, VM533
Knowledge, Sociology of, BD175
Knowledge, Theory of, BD140-241
Knowledge, Theory of (Religion), BL51
Koran, BP100-130
Korea, DS901-935, HC466-470, HX415.5, Z3316
Korean art. See N7360-7363
Korean literature, PL901-988
Korean War, 1950-51953, DS918-921.7

Labor and laboring classes, HD4801-8943
Labor laws and legislation, KF3301-3580
Labor productivity, HC110.L3, HD57
Labor relations. See Industrial relations
Labor supply, HD5701-5852
Labor-unions. See HD6350-6940.7
Laboratory animals, SF406
Lamaism. See Tibet—Religion
Land. See HD101-1395. See also: Cities and towns—Planning; Regional planning
Landforms, GB400-648. See also: Geology, Structural
Landscape painting, ND1340-1367
Landslides, QE599
Language and languages, P1-409, Z7004. See also names of particular languages or groups of cognate languages
Language arts, LB1575-1576, LB1631
Languages—Philosophy, P105-106. See also: Semantics
Languages—Psychology. See Psycholinguistics
Laos, DS555
Lapland, DL971.L2
Lasers, QC446.2, TK7871.3-7871.4
Latin America, F1201-3799, HC121-239, HD320.5-580, HD1790-1900, HD6530.5-6597, HN110.5-370, HT127-129, HX110-235, JL950-3899, KG-KH, Z1411-1945, Z7165.L3
Latin America—Religion, BR600. See also: Liberation theology
Latin American art. See N6502, N6553-6739, NA702, NA753-859, ND250-439
Latin American literature, PQ7801-8550, PQ9500-9699
Latin American philosophy. See B1001-1084
Latin language, PA2001-2995
Latin literature, PA6000-6961, PA8001-8595
Latvia, DK511
Law, K-KR
Law, International. See JX
Law, Islamic. See BP144, BP163
Law enforcement, HV7551-8280
Leadership, BF637.L4, HM141
League of Nations, JX1975-1975.5
Learned institutions and societies, AS
Learning, Psychology of, BF318, LB1051-1091
Learning and scholarship, AZ
Learning disabilities, LC4704
Lebanon, DS80-89, JQ1825.L4
Legal medicine. See KF2905, RA1001-1171
Legal research, KF240-246
Leisure, BJ1498, GV14, GV45, GV53
Leisure class, HB831
Leptons, QC793.5
Lesotho, DT781-782
Lettering, NK3600-3640
Letters, PN6131
Lexicography, P327. See also individual languages
Libel and slander—U.S., KF1266
Liberal education. See LC1001-1021
Liberalism, HM276, JC571
Liberation theology, BT83.57
Liberia, DT621-637
Liberty, HM271, JC571, JC585-599

Library science, Z662-1006
Libya, DT211-239
Lichens, QK583-587
Life (Biology), QH325, QP81-82
Light, QC350-495
Light—Physiological effect, QH651
Limericks, PN6231.L5
Limnology, QH96-98
Linear programming, QA265, T57.74
Linguistics, P31-85, P121-146
Literacy, LC149-151
Literary landmarks, PR109, PS141
Literature [General], PN, Z6511-6525,
   Z7006-7049. See also individual literatures,
   e.g. American literature, PS; Classical
   literature, PA
Literature and music. See ML80, ML3849
Lithography, NE2425-2505
Lithuania, DK511
Liverworts, QK533
Livestock, SF65-140
Lobbying, JF529, JK1118, JK2498
Local finance, HJ9145
Local government, JS
Logic, BC
Logic, Symbolic and mathematical, BA131-135,
   QA9-10.3
Logical positivism, B824.6
Logistics, U168
Love, BD436, BF575.L8
Love—Religious aspects, BV4639
Low temperatures, QC33, QC278. See also:
   Refrigeration and refrigerating machinery
Lumber trade, HD9750-9769
Lutheran Church, BX8001-8080
Luxembourg, DH908
Lynching, HV6457-6459

Machinery, TJ1059-1480
Machinery in industry, HD6331
Macroeconomics, HB172.5
Madagascar, DT469.M
Madrigal, ML2631-2633
Magazines. See PN4700-5650, Z6940-6962
Magic, BF1585-1623, GN475. See also: GV1543
Magnetism, QC507-762
Make-up, Theatrical, PN2068
Malagasy Republic. See DT469.M
Malawi, DT858-862
Malay literature, PL5130
Malayalam literature, PL4711-4723
Malaysia, DS591-599, HC445.5, JQ713-745
Mammals, QL703-739
Man, BD431
Man (Theology), BT700-701. See also: Woman
   (Theology)
Man—Influence of environment, BF353, GF31,
   GF51, HM206, QP82
Man—Influence on nature, GF31, GF75,
   QC981.8, QH541
Man—Origin, QH368
Man, Prehistoric, CB301, GN700-875, QH368
Management, HD21-70, HF5500-5549,
   TS155-161
Mandala, BL2015.M3
Mannerism (Art), N6370
Manners. See BJ1853
Manners and customs, GT
Manufactures, HD9720-9940, TS
Manuscripts, Z6620. See also: Illumination of
   books and manuscripts; Paleography
Many-body problem, QC174.17-.5
Maoris, DU423
Maps, GA, Z6021-6028. See also: Atlases,
   G1001-2799
Marathi literature, PK2351-2458
Marine biology, QH91-95.9
Marine fauna, QL114-139. See also: Fishes,
   QL615-639; Marine mammals, QL713.2
Marine pollution, GC1080-1085
Marine resources, GC1000-1025. See also:
   Fisheries
Maritime law, HE582-587, JX4408-4421
Marketing, HF5410-5417.5
Marriage, HQ503-1058
Marshes, Tide, QK938.S27
Marxian economics, HB97.5, HB501.M3-.M5
Marxism, B3305.M74, HX39.5

Mass media, HE7601-8700, HM258, P92-96,
   PN4700-5650, Z5630
Materialism, B825
Mathematical analysis, QA300-432. See also:
   Algebras, Linear, QA251
Mathematical economics. See HB74.M3,
   HB135-145
Mathematical logic. See BC131-135, QA9-10.3
Mathematical physics, QA401, QC20
Mathematical recreations, QA93-95
Mathematical sets. See QA248
Mathematical statistics, QA276-280
Mathematics, QA, Z6651
Matrices, QA263
Matrix mechanics, QC174.3
Mauritania, DT553
Mayas, F1435-1435.3
Measures. See QC82-88
Meat industry, HD94
Mechanical engineering, TJ
Mechanics, QA803-931, QC122-166
Mechanics, Analytical, QA803-931
Mechanics, Applied, TA350
Mechanics, Celestial, QB351
Medical anthropology, GN296
Medical botany, QK99
Medical economics, R728, RA714-715. See also:
   Health insurance
Medical ethics, R724-725.5
Medical jurisprudence, KF2905, RA1001-1171
Medical parasitology, RC119
Medical physics, R895
Medical social work, HV687
Medicine, R-RZ, Z6658-6676
Medicine, Veterinary. See SF600-998
Medieval art. See N5940-6311. See also: sections
   for individual countries, N6501-7413, and
   both general and country sequences for types
   of art, e.g. Painting, ND140-146 and
   ND201-1113
Medieval history. See Middle Ages
Medieval philosophy. See B720-765
Meditation, BL627
Mediterranean region, D972-973, DE
Melanesia, BL2620, BL2630, DU490-500,
   HN935
Melodrama, PN1910-1919
Melting points, QD518
Memory, BF370-385
Men, HQ1090
Mennonites, BX8101-8143
Mental health, RA790
Mental illness, RC334-576
Mental retardation, RC569.7-571
Mental tests. See BF176, BF431-433, LB3051,
   Z5814.E9
Mentally handicapped, HV3004-3006,
   RC569.7-571
Mentally handicapped children, HV891-897,
   LC4601-4700, RJ506.M4
Merchant marine, HE731-953, VK
Mergers, Corporate. See HD2741-2746.5
Mesopotamia. See Iraq
Metal industry, HD9506-9539
Metal-work, Art. See NK6400-8450
Metallurgy, TN605-799
Metals, QD171, TA459-480
Metaphysics, BD100-131
Meteorites, QB852-998
Meteorology, QC852-998
Meteors, QB755
Methodist Church, BX8201-8495
Methodology, BD240-241
Metropolitan areas, HT330-334
Mexican-American literature, PS153.M4,
   PS508.M4
Mexican Americans, E184.M5, Z1361.M4
Mexican literature, PQ7100-7300
Mexico, F1201-1392, HC131-140, HD325,
   HD1792, HN120, JL1200-1299
Microbiology, QR
Microforms, Z1033.M5
Micronesia, DU500, JQ6451
Microscope and microscopy, QH203-212
Middle Ages, CB351-355, D111-203, JC101-126,
   Z6203. See also individual regions and
   countries
Middle classes, HT680-690

Middle East, DS41-326, HC410.7, HC415,
   HN656-670, HN766, HT147.N4, JQ1825,
   Z3013-3045
Middle schools, LB1623
Middle West, F351-355, F476-705
Migration, Internal, HB195-2121
Military art and science, U-V
Military history, D25-27, U27-55, Z6724. See
   also individual countries, D-F, and particular
   wars
Military music, ML1300-1311
Milk trade, HD9282
Milky Way, QB819, QB857.7
Millennialism, BT82.2, BT876-891
Mimicry (Biology), QH546
Mind and body, BF161
Mineral industries, HD9506-9585, TN
Mineralogy, QE355-399
Miners, HD6515.M, HD8039.M
Mines and mineral resources, HD9506-9585, TN
Mining engineering, TN
Minorities—Canada, F1027, F1035, F1053
Minorities—U.S., E184-185, LC2667-3743,
   Z1361.E4
Missions [Christian], BV2000-3705
Modality (Logic), BC199.M6
Modern art. See N6447-6494
Modern dance, GV1783
Mohammedanism. See Islam
Molds (Botany), QK604
Molecular biology, QH505-506, QH611
Molecular theory, QD461
Mollusks, QL403-417
Monarchy, JC374-393
Monasticism and religious orders, BX2410-4560
Monetary policy, HG221-1496
Money, HG201-1496
Mongolia, DS798
Mongolism (Disease). See RC571
Mongols, DS19-23
Monopolies, HD2709-2930
Moon, QB581
Moral education, BF723.M54, LC251-311
Mormon Church, BX8601-8695
Morocco, DT301-330
Morphogenesis, QH491, QL963
Morphology (Animals), QL799-805
Morphology (Plants). See QK641-693
Mosaics, NA3750-3850
Mössbauer effect, QC490-491
Mosses, QK533-541
Mother and child, HQ759
Motion study, T60.4-.7
Motivation (Psychology), BF683
Motivation research (Marketing), HF5415.2-.3.
   See also: HF5822
Motor ability, BF295
Mountaineering, GB501, GV199.44
Mountains, GB501
Movement, Psychology of, BF295
Moving picture music, ML2075
Moving pictures, PN1993-1999, Z5784.M9. See
   also: Cinematography
Moving pictures—Censorship—U.S., KF4300
Mozambique, DT453-465
Municipal government, JS
Munitions, HD9743
Mural painting and decoration, ND2550-2888
Muscles, QP301, QP321
Museums, AM, N400-3990
Mushrooms, QK583-617
Music, M-MT
Music therapy, ML3920
Musical revue, comedy, etc., ML128.M78,
   ML1711, MT67
Mysticism, BL625, BM723, BP189,
   BV5070-5095
Mythology, BL300-325, BL700-910

[NATO]. See D845, JX1393.N6, UA646
NMR spectroscopy, QD96
Names, Geographical, E155, E179, G103-108,
   Z6824
Names, Personal, CS2300-3090, Z6824
Narcotic laws—U.S., KF3885-3894
Narcotics, HV5800-5840, RC563-568,
   Z7164.N17
National parks and reserves, E160, SB481-482

Nationalism, JC311-323. See also:
　Self-determination, National, JX4054
Natural history, QH
Natural resources, HC55, HC103.7, Z5322.E2.
　See also: Conservation of natural resources;
　Environmental policy; Land; Marine
　resources; Mines and mineral resources; Power
　resources; Wildlife conservation
Natural selection, QH365-366, QH375, QH401
Nauru, DU715
Naval art and science, V, Z6831-6836
Naval history, D27, V-VM. See also individual
　countries, D-F, and particular wars
Navigation, VK
Near East. See Middle East
Negotiation, BF637.N4
Negroes. See Afro-Americans
Neo-Confucianism, B127
Neoclassicism (Art), N6425
Neoplatonism, B517
Nepal, DS485.N4, DS493.4-495, JQ1825.N4
Nepali literature, PK2595-2599
Nervous system, QL925, QM451-455,
　QP352-425
Netherlands, DH1-207, DJ1-411, HC310.5-330,
　HN513.5, JV2511
Neurology, QP352, QP361, RC334-386
Neutrality, JX5355
New England, F1-105
New Guinea. See DU740-746
New Jerusalem Church, BX8712
New Zealand, DU400-430, HD8866,
　JQ5800-5829, Z4101-4114
New Zealand literature, PR9620-9639
Newspapers, PN4700-5650, Z6940-6962
Nicaragua, F1521-1537
Niger, DT547
Nigeria, DT513-515.9, HC517.N48, HC1055,
　HN800, JQ3082-3086
Nigerian literature, PR9387
Nile River, DT115-117
Nineteenth century, CB415-417, D351-400
Nobel prizes, AS911.N
Noise, RA772.N7, TD892. See also: Sound,
　QC223-243
Nongraded schools, LB3061
Nonprofit corporations. See HD62.6
Nonverbal communication, BF637.C45
Nonviolence, HM278
North America, E. See also individual countries
North Atlantic Treaty Organization, D845,
　JX1393.N6, UA646
North Korea. See Korea
North Vietnam. See Vietnam
Northern Ireland, DA990.U45-.U46, JN1572
Norway, DL401-596, HC365, JN7461-7621
Norwegian language, PD2571-2699
Norwegian literature, PT8301-9155
Nuclear arms control, JX1974-1974.76,
　Z6464.D6
Nuclear engineering, TK9006-9360
Nuclear industry, HD9698
Nuclear magnetic resonance, QC454, QC762,
　QD96
Nuclear physics, QC173, QC721, QC771-795.8
Nuclear warfare, U263, UA11, UF, Z6464.D6
Nucleic acids, QP551, QP801, QD341
Numbers, Theory of, QA241
Numeration, QA141
Numerical analysis, QA297-299.82
Numismatics, CJ
Nursery rhymes, PZ8.3
Nursery schools, LB1140.2
Nursing, RA790.5, RC954, RC966, RT,
　Z6675.N7
Nursing—Law and legislation, KF2905
Nutrition, QP141, RM216, TX349-558
Nyasaland. See DT853.5-862

Oboe, ML940, MT360
Obscenity (Law), KF224.R33, KF4775, KF9444
Occultism, BF1405-1999
[Occupational health], R154, RC963-967,
　T54-55.3
Occupations, HB2595, HF5381, HM211. See
　also: Professions
Ocean engineering, TC1645
Oceania, DU, Z4001-4021. See also individual
　countries and islands

Oceanography, G2800, GC
Office practice, HF5546-5547
Oil. See TN860-879, TP670-699
Oil industries. See HD9560-9581
Old age. See BF724.5, HQ1060-1064,
　HV1451-1493, QH529, QP86, RC952-954,
　Z7164.O4
Old age pensions, HD7105-7250
Old Norse literature, PT7101-7338
Olefins, QD305
Olympic Games, GV23, GV721-722, GV742.42
Oman, DS247.O68, DS248
On-line bibliographic searching, Z699
Ontology, BD300-444
Open plan schools, LB1029.O6
Opera, ML102.O6, ML128.O4, ML1700-2100,
　ML3858, MT95-110, MT955
Operations research, HD20.5, T57.6
Optical illusions, QP495
Optics, QC351-495
Optics, Physiological, QP475-495
Oral communication, P95
Oral-formulaic analysis, GR44, GR72, GR74.4
Oral history, D16, D16.14
Orchestral music, ML128.O5, ML1200-1270,
　MT125-130
Orchestration. See ML455, MT70-74
Ores, QE390
Organ, ML550-649
Organic chemistry. See QD245-433
Organization, HD31, HM131
Organizational behavior, HD58.7-58.8,
　HF5548.8
Organized crime, HV6446
Organometallic compounds, QD411-412
Organonitrogen compounds, QAD305, QD401,
　QD412
Oriental art. See Chinese art, Indic art, etc.
Oriental civilization. See CB253
Oriental literature [General], PJ1-995, Z7046.
　See also individual literatures
Oriental philosophy [General]. See B121. See
　also: Chinese philosophy, etc.
Ornithology, QL672-699
Orthodox Eastern Church, BX200-750
Outdoor recreation, GV191.2-200.5, SK601

Pacific area, DU
[Pacific islands art]. See N7410-7411
Pacific States [U.S.], F851-951
Pacifism, JX1944, JX1961-1963
Pain, QP401, RB127
Painting, ND
Pakistan, DS376-392, HC440.5, HN690.5,
　JQ556, Z3196
Pakistan, East. See Bangladesh
Paleobotany, QE901-996
Paleography, Z105-115
Paleontology, QE701-996
Palestine, DS101-151
Palestinian Arabs, DS119, DS126
Panama, F1561-1577, JL1648
Panama Canal, JX1398
Pangermanism, D447, DD119
Panjabi literature, PK2630-2659
Panslavism, D377.3-.5
Pantomime, PN1985-1988
Papacy, BX950-1389
Paper, TS1090-1105
Paperback books. See Z479, Z1033.P3
Papua New Guinea, DU740, DU850,
　GN671.N5, JQ6311
Paraguay, F2661-2699
Parapsychology. See BF1001-1389
Parasites, QL757
Parks, E160, SB481-485
Parliamentary practice, JF515, JK1096, JN688
Parodies, PN6231.P3
Parole, HV9304
[Particle physics], QC721, QC793-793.5
Particles (Nuclear physics), QC721, QC793-793.5
Passive resistance, HM278
Patents, T211-212
Pathology, RB
Patriotism, JC328
Pavements, TE250-251
Peace, JX1901-1989, Z6464.Z9
Peasantry, GT5650, HD594-951, HD1513,
　HD1537

Pediatrics, RJ
Penology. See HV8301-9920
Pentecostal churches, BX8762-8795
Perception, BF311
Percussion instruments, ML1030, MT655
Performing arts, PN1560-1590, Z6935,
　Z7511.W53. See also: Dancing, GV1580-1799;
　Music, M-MT; Theater, PN1600-3299
Periodicals, PN4700-5650, Z692.S5, Z6940-6962
Periodicals—Indexes, AI
Persia. See Iran
Persian Gulf States, DS247.A13, DS326
Persian literature, PK6001-6996
Personality, BF698
Personnel management, HF5549-5549.5
Personnel service in education, LB1027.5,
　LB2343
Persuasion (Psychology), BF637.P4
Peru, F3401-3619, HD553-559, HN343-344,
　JL3400-3498
Peruvian literature, PQ8300-8499
Pesticides, SB951-959
[Pesticides—Environmental aspects], QH545
Petroleum, TN865-871.15, TP690-692, Z6972
Petroleum—Industry and trade, HD9560-9581
Petrology, QE423-475
Pets, SF422-456.5, SF756-991
Peyote, E98.R3, RM666.P48
Pharmaceutical industry, HD9666
Pharmacology, QP917-981, RM
Pharmacy, RS
Phenomenology, B829.5
Philippine literature, PL5533-5544, PR9550
Philippines, DS651-689, G2391, GN671.P5,
　HC455, HD904-905, HN713-720, Z3296
Philology, P
Philosophical anthropology, BD450
Philosophy, B-BD, BH-BJ, Q175, T14,
　Z7125-7129
Philosophy, American, etc. See under national,
　regional and period adjectives, e.g. American
　philosophy, African philosophy, Medieval
　philosophy, etc.
Philosophy of religion. See BL51
Philosophy of [topics]. See the topic
Phoenicians, DS81
Phonetics, P221-240. See also individual
　languages
Phonorecords. See ML155.5-157
Phosphorus, QD181
Photochemistry, QD601-715
Photogrammetry, TA593, TR693, TR810
Photography, TR
Photography, Aerial, TR810
Photosynthesis, QK882
Physical anthropology, GN49-294
Physical chemistry. See QD450-715
Physical education and training, GV201-555. See
　also: Physical fitness
Physical fitness, GV481-567, RC1210-1235
Physical geography, GB. See also: Geology, QE
Physical measurements, QC39
Physics, QC, Z7141
Physiology, QP. See also: Plant physiology,
　QK711-898
Physiology, Pathological, RB121
Phytogeography, QK101
Phytoplankton, QK933-935
Pianists, ML397, ML417
Piano, ML650-749, MT220-224
Piano music, ML128.P3, ML700
Picaresque literature, PN3428-3430
Pitcairn Island, DU800
Planets, QB601-701
Planning, City. See HT161-169, NA9000-9284
[Planning, Economic]. See Economic
　development; see also individual countries,
　HC101-1085
Planning, Regional. See HT390-395
Plant anatomy. See QK641-693
Plant chemistry. See QK861-898
Plant diseases, SB731-761
Plant ecology, QK901-938
[Plant morphology]. See QK641-693
Plant physiology, QK711-898
Plants, QK, RS81
Plants, Cultivated, SB
Plants, Edible, QK98.5

Plasma (Ionized gases), QC711-718
Plasticity, TA418.14, TA645
Plastics, TP1087-1130
Play, BF717, CB151, LB1137
Plays—Collections. See PN6111-6120. See also:
    Drama, PN1600-3299, and national literatures,
    e.g. American
Poetry, PN1010-1551. See also national
    literatures, e.g. American poetry, PS301-326,
    Z1231.P7
Poetry—Collections, PN6099-6110. See also
    national literatures, e.g. American poetry,
    PS580-619
Poisonous animals, QL100, QL666
Poisonous plants, QK100, SB617
Poisons, RA1195-1270
Poland, DK400-443, DK4010-4800, HC337.P7,
    HD8537, JN6750-6769
Polar regions, G575-890, GN673
Police, HV7551-8280
Polish literature, PG7001-7498
Political anthropology, GN490, GN492
Political conventions—U.S., JK2255
Political parties, JF2011-2111. See also
    individual countries, JK-JQ, e.g. U.S.,
    JK2251-2391, Z7164.P8
Political psychology, JA74
Political science, J-JX, Z7161-7165
Political sociology, JA76
Politics in literature, PN3448.P6
Pollution, HC79.P55, TD170-196. See also: Air—
    Pollution; Marine pollution; Noise; Water—
    Pollution
Polymers and polymerization, QD281,
    QD381-388, TP1087
Polynesia, DU510, GN670
Popular music, ML102.P66, ML3475-3547
Population, HB849-3700, Z7164.D3
Population policy, HQ766
Porcelain, NK3700-4695
Pornography, HQ450-471, Z7164.P84. See also:
    Obscenity (Law)
Porpoises, QL737.C4
Portugal, DP501-776, HN593.5, JN8502,
    JV4211-4266
Portuguese language, PC5001-5498
Portuguese literature, PQ9001-9999
Positivism, B2223-2228
Positivism, Logical. See B824.6
Post-impressionism (Art), ND1265
Postal service, HE6000-7500
Posters, NC1800-1850
Pottery, NK3700-4695, TP785-810, TT904,
    TT924
Poultry, SF487
Poverty, HC79.P6, HC110.P6, HV4023-4505,
    Z7164.C4
Power resources, HD9502-9505, HD9545-9581,
    TJ153-163.25, Z5853.P83
Pragmatism, B832
Prairies, QK938.P7
Precious stones, TS752
Prediction. See CB158-161
Prehistoric antiquities. See CC, GN700-875. See
    also earliest period subdivisions for individual
    countries, regions, etc., D-F
[Prehistoric humans]. See CB301, GN700-875,
    QH368
Prejudices, BF575.P9, BF723.P75
Preraphaelitism, N6767.5, ND467, NX543
Presbyterian Church, BX8901-9225
Preschool education. See LB1140
Presidents—U.S., E176.1, E311-879, JK511-609,
    KF5050-5125, Z1249.P7
Press, PN4700-5650. See also: Freedom of the
    press
Pressure groups, JF529, JK1118, JK2498
Price policy, HF5416.5-5417
Prices, HB221-236, HG229
Primates, QL737.P9, QL785.5.P7
Primitive art. See N5310-5311. See also names
    of peoples and regions
Primitive religion. See GN470-474
Primitive society. See GN400-499
Printing, Z116-265
Prints, NE
Prisons, HV8301-9920
Privacy, Right of, JC597, JC599.U5P75, KF1262

Private schools, L901.H3, LC49
Probabilities, BC91, BC141, QA273
Problem of many bodies. See QC174.17-174.5
Production engineering, TS155-195
Professions, HT687
Profit, HB601
Program budgeting, HJ2031, HJ2052-2053
Programmed instruction, LB1028.5
Programming (Electronic computers),
    QA76.6-76.8
Progress, CB67, CB155, HM101
Propaganda, D632, D639.P6-.P7, D810.P6-.P7,
    HM263
Property, HB701
Prophecies, CB158-161
Proportional representation, JF1071
Prospecting, QE33, TN265-271
Prostitution, HQ101-440
Proteins, QD431, QP551
Protestantism, BX4800-9999
Protozoa, QL366-369
Proverbs, PN6400-6525, Z7191
Pseudonyms, English. See Z1041-1065
Psychiatry, RC435-473
Psychical research, BF1001-1045
Psychoanalysis, BF173, RC500-509
Psychohistory, D16, D16.16
Psycholinguistics, BF455, P37, P105-106
Psychology, BF, Z7201-7205
Psychology, Industrial, HF5548.8
Psychology, Military, U22
Psychology, Pathological, RC454
Psychology, Physiological, QP355-356
Psychology, Political, JA74
Psychology, Religious, BL53
[Psychology of art]. See N70-71
[Psychology of music]. See ML3830-3838
Psychotherapy, RC475-489
Public administration, JF1321-1501. See also
    individual countries, JK-JQ; local government,
    JS
Public finance. See HJ
Public health, RA421-772
Public opinion, HM261, HN29, HN90.P8
Public utilities, HD2763, HD2766. See also:
    Electric utilities, Water-supply
Public welfare, HV1-699, Z7164.C4
Publishers and publishing, Z278-550
Puerto Ricans in the U.S., E184.P85, F128.9.P8
Puerto Rico, F1951-1983, HN233-240
Punic wars, DG242
Punishment, HV8497-8699
Punjab, DS485.P
Puppets and puppet-plays, PN1970-1982
Puritans, BX9301-9359, F7, F67

Quakers. See Society of Friends
Qualitative analysis. See QD81-98
Quantitative analysis. See QD101-139
Quantum field theory, QC174.45
Quantum theory, QC173.98-174.13
Quarks, QC793.5
Quasars, QB857-860
Quotations, PN6080-6095
Qur'an. See BP100-130

Race relations [General], HT1521-1523
Race relations—Religious aspects, BT734-734.2
Radar, TK6575
Radar meteorology, QC973.5
Radiation, QC475-495. See also: Radioactivity,
    QC795
Radiation chemistry, QD601-604
Radiation—Physiological effect, QH652
Radicalism, HN90.R3
Radicals (Chemistry), QD258
Radio, HE8689-8699, PN1991, TK6540-6571
Radio astronomy, QB462.5-479
Radioactive waste disposal, TD898
Radioactivity, QC795
Radiobiology, QH652
Railroad engineering, TF
Railroads, HD8039.R, HE1001-3560
Rain and rainfall, QC921-928
Rain forests, QK938
Rape, HV6558-6568
Rare plants, QK86
Rational expectations (Economic theory),
    HB172.5

Rationalism, BL2700-2790
Reading, BF456.R2, LB1050, LB1140.5, LB1525,
    LB1573, LB1631-1632, PN83, Z1003,
    Z5814.R25
Realism, B835
Reasoning, BC177
Recombinant DNA, QH442
Recorder, ML935, MT340
Recreation, GV
Recreation, Outdoor. See GV191.2-200.5, SK601
Recycling (waste, etc.), TD791-794.5
Reducing diets, RM237
Reference books, Z1035-1035.1
Reform, Social. See HN, Z7164.S66
Reformation, BR300-420, D228
Reformed Church, BX9400-9595
Refrigeration and refrigerating machinery,
    TP490
Regeneration (Biology), QH499
Regional planning, HT390-395
Regulation. See Industry and state; Trade
    regulation
Reinforcement (Psychology), BF319
Relativity (Physics), QC6-7
Religion, BL-BX, Z7751-7860
Religion, Primitive, GN470-474
Religion and education. See LC111, LC473-743
Religion and social problems. See HN30-40
Religious art. See Buddhist art; Christian art and
    symbolism; Church architecture; Islamic art
Religious psychology. See BL53
Religious sociology. See BL60
Remote sensing, G70.4, QC871, QE33.2,
    Z6004.R38
Renaissance, CB359-369
Renaissance art. See N6370-6375. See also
    sections for individual countries, N6501-7413,
    and both general and country sequences for
    types of art
Renaissance philosophy. See B770-785
Rent (Economic theory), HB401
Report writing, LB2369, PE1478, T11
Representative government and representation,
    JF1051
Reproduction, QP251-263
Reptiles, QL640-669
Research, Q180-180.55. See also particular
    subjects, e.g. Educational research, LB1028
Resistance to government. See JC328
Respiration, QP121
Resumés (Employment), HF5383
Retail trade, HF5429
Retirement, HQ1062-1063
Réunion, DT468
Revelation, BT127
Revivals, BV3750-3799
Revolutions, HM281-283, JC491-495
Rhetoric, PN173-185
Rhodesia. See DT853.5-858, DT946-963
Right to counsel—U.S., KF9646
Riots, HV6477
Rites and ceremonies, GN473, Z5118.R5
Rivers, GB1203-1205
Roads, HE355-373, TE
Robotics, TJ210.3
Rock climbing, GV199.44, GV200.21
Rockets (Aeronautics), TL781-782
Rocks, QE423-475
Roman art, N5740-5849, NA300-310
Roman law, KBD
Romance languages, PC
Romance literatures, PQ
Romances [Medieval literature], PN682-688,
    PQ1411-1545, PR2040-2125, PT1375-1695
Romanesque art. See N6280, NA390, NB175
Romania, DR201-298, HC407.R8, HD833,
    JN9623-9639
Romanian language, PC779
Romanticism, PN603, PR447
Romanticism in art, N6465.R6, NX600.R6
Rome [Ancient], DE, DG11-365, G1033, HC39,
    JC81-89
Rome [Ancient]—Religion, BL800-820
Rugs, NK2775-2883
Rumania. See Romania
Rural education. See LC5146-5148
Rural sociology. See HT401-485
Russia. See Soviet Union

Russian art. See N6976-6999, ND681-699
Russian language, PG2001-2850
Russian literature, PG2900-3698, Z2491-2505
Russian philosophy. See B4201-4279
Russo-Japanese war, DS517
Rwanda, DT449.R9

Sacred music. See ML2900-3275
Sagas, PT7101-7338
Sahara, DT331-346
Sailing ships, VK18, VK23, VM15-23, VM144
Saints, BX4654-4662, BX4700
Salesmen and salesmanship, HF5438-5440
Salvation Army, BX9716
Samoan Islands, DU813-819
Sanitary engineering, TD
Sanskrit literature, PK414, PK871, PK2901-4485
Saudi Arabia, DS201-244
Scandinavia, DL, HC341-380, HN540-580,
    JN7001-7995, Z2551-2650
Scandinavian literature, PT7001-7099
Schizophrenia, RC514
Scholarship and learning. See AZ
Scholarships, LB2336-2338
Scholasticism, B734
School boards, LB2831
School buildings, LB3205
School discipline, LB3011-3095
School finance, LB2824-2830
School law. See KF4101-4258, LB2523-2525
School management and organization,
    LB2801-2997. See also: Classroom
    management
School music, MT1-3
School sports, GV346
Science, Q-QR, Z7401-7409. See also:
    Technology, T-TX; Medicine, R-RZ
Science—Philosophy, Q175
Science—Study and teaching (Elementary),
    LB1585
Science and civilization, CB151, Q125. See also:
    Technology and civilization
Science and religion, See BL239-265
Science and state—U.S., Q127
Science and the humanities, AZ361
Science fiction, PN3448.S45, PR830.S35,
    PS374.S35, PS648.S3, Z5917.S36
Scientific research. See Q180-180.55
Scotland, DA750-890, HC257.S4, HN398.A2,
    HN398.S3, JN1187-1371, Z2057
Scottish literature, PB1607, PR8500-8697, Z2057
Scottish philosophy. See B1401-1559
Sculpture, NB
Seashore biology, QH91-95.9
Secretaries, HF5547
Secularism, BL2747-2765
Sedimentation and deposition, QE581
Segregation in education, KF4154-4155,
    LA210.R3, LC210-214. See also:
    Afro-Americans—Education, LC2701-2913
Seismology, QE534.2
Self-determination, National, JX4054. See also:
    Nationalism, JC311-323
Self-incrimination, KF9668
Selling, HF5438
Semantics, P325, PE1585
Semantics (Philosophy), B840
Semantics, General. See B820
Semiconductors, QC611-612, TK7871.85-7872
Semiotics, P99
Senegal, DT549, JQ3396
Senses and sensation, BF231-299, QP431-499
Sentences (Criminal procedure), KF9685
Separation (Technology), QD63
Separation of powers, JF229, JK305,
    KF4565-4570
Serbo-Croatian literature, PG1201-1798
Serial publications. See Periodicals
Service industries, HD9980-9999
Set theory, QA248
Seventeenth century, CB401, D242-283
Sewage purification, TD755
Sex, BF692, HQ12-471, QH471-485, QL761,
    QP251-285
Sex (Biology), QH471-481
Sex role, HQ1075
Sexism in language, P120.S48
Sexual disorders, RC555-556

Shakers, BX9751-9793
Sheep, SF375-376
Shells (Engineering), TA660
Shiah, BP192-193
Shinto, BL2220-2222
Shipbuilding, VM
Shipping, HE381-971
Ships, VK-VM
Shore-lines, GB451-460
Short stories, PN6014-6071, PZ1, Z5917.S5. See
    also national literatures, e.g. French fiction,
    PQ1261-1279
Short story, PN3373-3375. See also national
    literatures, e.g. French fiction, PQ631-671
Shrubs, QK475-495, SB435-435.5
Siam. See Thailand
Sickle cell anemia, RC641.7
Sierra Leone, DT516
Signal processing, TK5102.5
Sikhism, BL2017-2018
Silverwork, NK7112-7230
Singapore, DS598.S7
Singers, ML400, ML420
Singing, MT820-892
Single people, HQ800
Sixteenth century, CB367-401, D220-234
Skepticism, B837
Skis and skiing, GV854-855
Slavery, HT851-1445
Slavery in the U.S., E441-453, KF4545.S5,
    Z7164.S6
Slavic languages, PG
Slavic literatures, PG500-9198
Slavs, D147. See also: Panslavism, D377.3-.5
Sleep, BF1071, QP425
Small groups, HM133
Smithsonian Institution, Q11
Snakes, QL666
Snow, QC929.S7
Soccer, GV943-944
[Social aspects of industry]. See HD59-60.5
Social case work, HV43
Social change, HM101
Social classes, HN90.S6, HT601-1445
Social conflict, HM136
Social ethics, HM216
Social groups, HM131-133, HQ-HT
Social history, HN
Social insurance. See HD7090-7250.7, KF3643
Social interaction, HM291
Social medicine, RA418
Social problems, HN, HV
Social psychology, HM251-291
Social reform. See HN, Z7164.S66
Social sciences [General], H, Z7161-7165
Social sciences—Study and teaching
    (Elementary), LB1584
Social security, HD7091, HD7124-7250, KF3643
Social service, HV1-699, Z7164.C4
Social surveys, HN29
Social work. See HV1-699, Z7164.C4
Socialism, HX1-550
Societies, AS, HS
Society of Friends, BX7601-7795
Sociobiology, GN365.9, QL775
Sociolinguistics, P40-41, P381
Sociology, HM-HV, Z7161-7165
Sociology, Military, U21.5
Sociology and religion. See BL60
Soil conservation, S622-624
Soil mechanics, TA710-775
Soils, S591-621
Solar energy, TJ810
Solar system, QB501-701
[Solid-state physics], QC176-176.8
Solids, QC176.8
Solitons, QA927, QC174.26
Solomon Islands, DU850
Solubility, QD66, QD541-544.5
Solution (Chemistry), QD541-544.5
Somalia, DT401-420
Sonata, ML1156
Songs. See Vocal music
Sound, QC223-243. See also: Hearing, QP461;
    Noise, RA772.N7, TD892
Sound recordings, ML155.5-157
South Africa, DT751-995, HC905, JQ1988-1999
South African literature (English),
    PR9350-9369.3. See also: Afrikaans literature

South African war, 1899-1902, DT930
South America, F2201-3799. See also: Latin
    America
South Asia, DS335-499, Z3185
Southeast Asia. See DS501-689, HC412,
    HC441-455, HN691-720, JQ96, Z3221-3299
Southern states, F206-475
Sovereignty, JC327
Soviet Union, DK1-276, G2110-2111,
    HC331-340, HD1992-1993, HD6732, HD8526,
    HN521-539, HT145.R9, HX311-315.7,
    JN6500-6625, JX1555, KM, UA770-779,
    Z2483-2537
Soviet Union—Religion, BL980, BR932-933,
    BX485-492
Space and time, BD621-638, BF469, QC6
Space flight, TL787-3025
Space law, JX5760-5810
Space perception, QP491
Space sciences, QB500, TL787-3025
Spain, DP1-402, HC381-390, HD779, HD2025,
    HN590, JN8101-8395, JV4062, Z2681-2709
Spanish America. See Latin America
Spanish-American literature, PQ7081-8929
Spanish art. See N7101-7113, NA1313,
    ND801-813
Spanish language, PC4001-4977
Spanish literature, PQ6001-8929, Z2691-2695
Sparta, DF261.S8
Species, QH371
Spectroscopy. See QC451-491, QD95-96
Spectrum analysis, QC451-463, QD95-96
Speech, QP306
Speech, Disorders of, RC423-425, RJ496
Speech acts (Linguistics), P95.5
Speeches, addresses, etc., PN6121-6122,
    PR1321-1322, PS662-668
Spermatophyta. See QK475-495
Spiders, QL457-458.4
Sports, GV561-1195, Z7511
Sports medicine, RC1210-1235
Sri Lanka, DS488-490, HC424, JQ653-659
Stage lighting, PN2091.E4
Stage-setting. See PN2091.S8, Z5784.S8
Stained glass. See NK5308-5398
Stars, QB801-855
The State, JC
State and church. See BR516, BV630, JK361,
    KF4865-4869
State and education. See LC71-120, LC173
State and industry. See HD3611-4730. See also:
    Trade regulation
State governments, JK2403-9600, KF4530. See
    also individual states, F1-970
Statistical mechanics, QC175
Statistical thermodynamics, QC311.5
Statistics, HA, Z7551-7556
Statistics, Mathematical. See QA276-280
Steam engines, TJ275-485
Steel industry and trade, HD8039.I52,
    HD9510-9529
Stereochemistry, QD481
Steroids, QD405
Stochastic processes, QA274
Stocks, HG4910-4930
Stoics, B528
Stone age, GN768-776
Storms, QC941-968
Storytelling, LB1042
Strategy, U161-162, UA11
Stratigraphic geology. See QE651-696
Stream ecology, QH541.5
Stream of consciousness fiction, PN3448.P8
Strength of materials, TA405-409
Stress (Physiology), QP82-82.2, QP356
Stress (Psychology), BF575.S75
Strikes and lockouts, HD5306-5450
Structures, Theory of, TA642-646
Student movements, LA186, LA229, Z5814.S86
Student teaching, LB2157
Style, Literary, PN203
Submarine boats, V210, V857-859, VM365
Submarine geology, QE39
Sub-Saharan Africa [General]. See DT351-364,
    HN773.5, HN777, JQ1872
Suburbs, HT351-384
Sudan, DT108, DT154.1-159, JQ3981
Suffrage, JF831, JK1846-1936

Suicide, HV6545, Z7615
Sumerian literature, PJ4001-4091
Sumerians, DS72
Sun, QB501-542
Superconductivity, QC612
Supreme Court—U.S. See JK1571, KF8741-8748
Surgery, RD
Surrealism, BH301.S75, N6494.S8, NX600.S9
Surveying, TA545-595
Swaziland, DT971
Sweden, DL601-876, HC373, HD3616, HD6757, HN571-580, JN7721-7995
Swedish language, PD5075, PD5640
Swedish literature, PT9201-9999
Swimming, GV837
Swine, SF395
Swiss art, ND844-853
Swiss literature (German), PT3868
Switzerland, DQ, G155, GN585.S9, HG3204, HN603
Symbiosis, QH548
Symbolism, BF458, BH301.S8, BL600
Symbolism (Art movement), N6465.S9
Symbolism in literature, PN56.S9
Synonyms and antonyms. See PE1591
Syntax. See P291-295, PE1361
Syria, DS92-99
System analysis, QA402
System theory, Q295

Tahiti, DU870
Tailoring, TT504
Taiwan, DS895.F7, GN635.T28, HC430.5
Tales, GR, PN1001
Tall buildings, TH845
Talmud, BM500-509
Tamil literature, PL4751-4763
Tank warfare, UG446.5
Tanzania, DT435-446, HC885, HN814, HX448-457, JQ3519
Taoism, BL1900-1940
Tapestry, NK2975-3296
Tariff, HF1701-2701
Taxation, HJ2240-7395, KF6271-6795
Teachers, LA2301-2317, LB1705-2278, LB2331-2335, LB2832-2844
Teachers—Certification, LB1771
Teachers, Rating of, LB2838
Teachers, Training of, LB1705-2278
Teaching, LB1025-1050. See also: Classroom management, LB3011-3012
Technical assistance, HC60
Technical literature, T10.5-10.7
Technical writing, T11
Technological innovations, HC79.T4, HC110.T4, T173-174
Technology, T-TX, Z7913-7914
Technology—Social aspects, T14-14.5
Technology and civilization, CB478, HM221, Z5579. See also: Science and civilization; Technology—Social aspects
Telecommunication, HE7601-9715, TK5101-6720
Telephone, HE8701-9715, TK6023
Telescope, QB88
Television, HE8689-8700, PN1992, TK6630-6720, Z7711
Television—Law and legislation, KF2761-2849
Television and children, HQ784.T4
Television in education, LB1044.7
Tempo (Music), ML437
Tennis, GV990-1005
Territorial waters, JX4131-4135
Territoriality (Zoology), QL775
Terrorism, HV6431, Z7164.T3
Tests, Mental. See BF176, BF431-433, LB3051, Z5814.E9
Textbooks, LB3047, LT
Textile industry, HD8039.T42, HD9850-9869, NK8800-9499, TP930, TS1300-1865
Thai poetry, PL4202-4206
Thailand, DS563-589, GN635.T4, HC445, JQ1742-1745
Theater, PN1600-1988, PN2000-3299, Z5781-5785. See also national literatures
Theaters—Construction, NA6821-6840
Thematic catalogs (Music). See ML128.I65, ML128.V7, ML134

Theology [Christian], BT-BV
Therapeutics, RM
Thermal analysis, QD79
Thermochemistry, QD516-518
Thermodynamics, QC254, QC311-318, QD501, TJ265, TP149
Thermometers and thermometry, QC271
Theses. See LB2369, LB2386
Third World. See Developing countries
Thirty Years' War, 1618-1648, D258
Thought and thinking, BF455
Tibet, DS785-786
Tibet—Religion, BL1485-1489, BL1943-1945
Tibetan literature, PL3748
Time, BD638, BF468, QB209-223
Time study, T60.4-.7
Tonga, DU880
Topology, QA611-613.64
Tortoises. See QH31.W58. See also: Turtles, QL666.C5
Torts—U.S., KF1250
Totalitarianism, JC481
Tourist trade, G155
Toxicology, RA1195-1270
Track-athletics, GV1060.5-1097
Trade regulation, K3943, K4603, KF1600-2940. See also: Industry and state
Trade-unions, HD6350-6940.7
Trade unions—Teachers. See LB2844.53-.59
Traffic engineering, HE331-373, TE
Tragedy, PN1890-1899
Transactional analysis, RC489.T7
Transcendentalism (New England), B905
Transistors, TK7871.85-7872
Translating and interpreting, P306, PN241
Transplantation of organs, tissues, etc., QP89
Transportation, HE, TA1145-1207. See also means of transportation
Transportation, Automotive, HE5601-5720
Travel. See Tourist trade; Voyages and travels
Treaties, JX120-191, JX235-236, JX756-757, JX4165
Trees, QK475-482, SB428-436. See also: Forests and forestry, SD
Trials—U.S., KF220-228
Trinidad and Tobago, F2119-2122
Tropics, G905, QH84.5
Troy (Ancient city), DF221.T8
Trucial states. See United Arab Emirates
Trumpet, ML960, MT440
Trusts, Industrial, HD2731, HD2766-2795, KF1649
Truth, BC171
Tundra ecology, QH105, QH541.5
Tunisia, DT241-269, HD8809
Turkey, DR401-593, HC491-495, JQ1802-1806
Turkish literature, PL55-248
Turtles, QL666.C5
Twentieth century, CB425-428, D401-847
Twenty-first century—Forecasts, CB161
Typography. See Printing

Uganda, DT434.U2
Ukraine, DK508.5-508.8
Ukranian literature, PG3900-3998
Ulster (Northern Ireland). See DA990.U45-.U46, JN1572
Underdeveloped areas. See HC59.7-60, HD72-89. See also individual regions and countries
Unemployment, HD5701-5856
Unidentified flying objects, TL789-789.3
Unification Church, BX9750
Unitarianism, BT1480, BX9801-9869
United Arab Emirates, DS247.T
United Nations, JX1976-1977.8, JX1981, Z6481-6485
United States, E151-F970, HC101-110, HD6501-6509, HD8051-8085, HN51-90, Z1201-1363, Z7165.U5
U.S.—Constitutional history, JK11-371, KF4541-4651, KF8741-8748
U.S.—Foreign population, E184, JV6403-7127
U.S.—Foreign relations, E183.7-183.8, JX1405-1428
U.S.—Government publications—Bibliography, Z1223
U.S.—History, Military, E181, U

U.S.—History, Naval, E182, V
U.S.—Politics and government, HX81-92, JK, JS300-1565
U.S.—Religion, BL2500-2530, BR513-569
U.S. Air Force, UG633
U.S. Army, UA25
U.S. Congress, G1201.F7-.F9, JK1000-1447, KF4930-5005
U.S. Declaration of Independence, JK128
U.S. Marine Corps, VE
U.S. National Guard, UA42
U.S. Navy, VA49-395
U.S. Supreme Court, JK1571, KF8741-8748
Universalist Church of America, BX9933
Universities and colleges, L900-901, LA173-183, LA225-228, LB2300-2411, LC1752-1756, LC2781, LD-LF
Universities and colleges—Directories, L900-901, LA226, LB2351
Unmarried mothers, HQ999
Upanishads, BL1120-1124, PK3505
Urban anthropology, GN395
Urban economics, HT321
Urban education. See LC5101-5143
Urban renewal, HT170-178
Urban sociology. See HT101-384
Urban transportation, HE300-311, HE3601-5260, TA1205
Urdu literature, PK2151-2200
Uruguay, F2701-2799, JL3611
Uruguayan literature, PQ8510-8519
Utopias, HX806-811. See also: Collective settlements, HX626-795

Vacuum, QC166
Valence (Theoretical chemistry), QD469
Value, HB201-205
Values, BD232
[Vandalism, School]. See LB3249
Vatican Council, BX830
Vaudeville, PN1967-1969
Vector analysis, QA261
Vedanta, B132.V3
Vedas, BL1112-1115
Vedic literature, PK3000-3581
Vegetable gardening, SB320-321
Venereal diseases, RC200-201
Venezuela, F2301-2349, JL3881-3898
Venezuelan literature, PQ8530-8550
Ventilation, TH7011-7392
Vertebrates, QL605-739
Veterans, UB356-359
Veterinary medicine, SF609-991
Vibration, QC136, TA355
Vice-presidents—U.S., JK609.5
Vietnam, DS556-560, HN700.V5, HX400, JX1573
Vietnamese Conflict, DS557-559, E183.8.V5, JX1573, Z3226-3228
Vietnamese literature, PL4371-4833
Vikings, DL65
Violence, HN90.V5, HQ809, HV6250.4
Violin, ML800, MT260-262
Viruses, QR351
Vision, QP475-495
Visual perception, BF241, N71
Vocal music, M1495-2199, ML128.S3, ML128.V7, ML1400-3275, MT820-892
Vocational education, LC1045
Vocational guidance, HF5381-5383, HF5549.5.M3
Volcanoes, QE522-523
Volleyball, GV1015, GV1017.V6
Voting, JF825-1091, JK1965-1967. See also: Elections
Voyages and travels, G80-89, G149-890, Z6011. See also individual countries, regions, etc., D-F

Wages, HB301, HD4906-5100, HD7023, HD7035
Wales, DA700-745, HC257.W3, HN398.W26, JN1159
Walking, GV199.6
Wallpaper, NK3375-3496
War, CB481, U, V. See also particular wars
War and society, HM36.5
War crimes, D804, JX6731

War (International law), JX4505-5326
Warehouses, HF5485
Warships, V765-874
Water, GB651-2398
Water—Pollution, TD223-426
Water resources development, HD1691-1741,
    TC
Water sports, GV770.3-840, VM331-341
Water-supply, TD201-500
Water transportation. See HE381-971
Watercolor painting, ND1700-2495
Watergate Affair, 1972-1974, E859-860,
    KF224.W33, KF228.U5J3
Wave mechanics, QC174.2
Wealth, HB771, HB835, HC110.W4. See also:
    Income
Weather, QC852-998
Weather control, QC928
Weathering, QE571
Weaving, TS1475, TT848
Weeds, SB611-612
Weights and measures, QC82-88
Welfare economics, HB99.3
Welfare work. See HV1-699, Z7164.C4
Welsh literature, PB2202-2369, PR8900-8997
West Indian literature (English), PR9210-9272.9
West Indies, F1601-2151, HC157, HN192-245
West (U.S.), F591-900
Wetland ecology, QH104, QH541.5
Whales, QL737.C4
White collar crimes, HV6635
Wholesale trade, HF5419-5422
Widows, HQ1058
Wild flowers, QK118
Wildlife conservation, QL82, S962

Wildlife management, SK353-361
Wind instruments, ML930-970, MT339-440
Wines and wine making, TP546-548
Wit and humor, BF575.L3, PN6147-6231,
    PR931-933, PS430-438
Witchcraft, BF1563-1583, GN475
Woman (Theology), BT704
Women, CT3200-3830, D810.W7, GN294,
    GN479.7, GV464, GV709, HQ1101-2030,
    HV1445, HV6046, HV6250.4, HV6558-6626,
    HV8023, HX546, RG, UB416, UB418.W65,
    Z7961-7965
Women—Education, LC1401-2571
Women—Employment, HD6050-6223, Z7963.E7
Women—Legal status, laws, etc., K644, KF478,
    KF4758, KF9315-9329, KFN5124
Women—Suffrage, JK1880-1991, JN976-979
Women and religion, BL458, BM729, BT704,
    BV639.W7, BV676
Women artists, N8354, ND38
Women authors, PN471, PN6109.9, PR115-116,
    PS147-152, PS647.W6
Women in literature, PN469.W65, PR830.W6,
    PR878.W6, PS374.W6
Women in science, Q130
Women musicians, ML82, ML105, ML156.4.W6
Wood, S536, TA419
Wood-engraving, NE1000-1325
Work, BF481, HD4904-4905
World government. See International
    organization
World history, D17-21.3
World War, 1914-1918, D501-680, E768-780,
    Z6207
World War, 1939-1945, D731-838, G1038,
    Z6207

[Worms], QL391
Worship [Christian], BV5-10.2
Worth. See BD232
Wrestling, GV1195
Writing, P211, Z40-115
Writing (Authorship). See PN101-249. See also:
    Report writing; Technical writing

X-Rays, QC481-482

Yearbooks, AY
Yeast, QK604
Yemen, DS247.Y4, HN664, JQ1825.Y5
Yiddish literature, PJ5111-5192
Yoga, B132.Y6
Youth, BF724-724.3, HQ793-799
Youth—Employment, HD6270-6273
Yugoslav literature, PG551-584
Yugoslavia, DR301-396, DR1202-2285, HC407,
    HX365.5

Zaire, DT644-665, JQ3603
Zambia, DT963, HN803
Zanzibar, DT435
Zen Buddhism, BL1432.Z4, BQ9262-9449
Zimbabwe, DT853.5, DT946-963
Zionism, DS149-151
Zoo animals, QL76
Zoogeography, QL101
Zoology, QL, Z7991-7999
Zoology—Ecology, QL751-785.5
Zoonoses, RC112
Zoroastrianism, BL1500-1590
Zulus, DT878.Z9